ENCYCLOPEDIA
of
U.S. CATHOLIC
HISTORY

OUR SUNDAY VISITOR'S
ENCYCLOPEDIA
of
U.S. CATHOLIC
HISTORY

Our Sunday Visitor Publishing Division
Our Sunday Visitor, Inc.
Huntington, Indiana 46750

Copyright © 2013 by Our Sunday Visitor. Published 2013.

18 17 16 15 14 13   1 2 3 4 5 6 7 8 9

All rights reserved. With the exception of short excerpts for critical reviews, no part of this work may be reproduced or transmitted in any form or by any means whatsoever without permission in writing from the publisher. Contact: Our Sunday Visitor Publishing Division, Our Sunday Visitor, Inc., 200 Noll Plaza, Huntington, IN 46750; 1-800-348-2440; bookpermissions@osv.com.

ISBN: 978-1-59276-686-4 (Inventory No. T965)
LCCN: 2012949299

Cover design: Lindsey Reisen
Cover art: Archbishop Fulton Sheen, cathedral, OSV archive images;
Pope Benedict XVI, Pope John Paul II, Catholic News Service;
Christopher Columbus, Bridgeman Art Library;
John F. Kennedy, St. Elizabeth Ann Seton, The Granger Collection;
Archbishop John Carroll
Interior design: Sherri L. Hoffman
Interior art: Margaret Bunson

PRINTED IN THE UNITED STATES OF AMERICA

CONTENTS

DEDICATION

This book is dedicated to the countless women and men who gave their lives to building the Catholic Church in the New World and especially the United States over the last five centuries.

I would also like to dedicate this book to the memory of Margaret R. Bunson, my mother, who passed away in May 2012 not long after the text for this book was finished.

FOREWORD

For many years the dean of American Catholic history was the late Monsignor John Tracy Ellis, professor of Church history at The Catholic University of America. He was also my mentor and a close personal friend. Monsignor Ellis was not only an outstanding scholar but a devout and dedicated priest. On many occasions I heard him say that, next to the grace of God, it was his knowledge of Church history that strengthened his faith and steadied his nerves during times of crisis in the Church.

For that reason Monsignor Ellis made every effort to promote knowledge of Church history not only among professional historians, but also among the general public. He was convinced that familiarity with this history would enable Catholics to see that God's guiding hand had led the Church through far worse crises in the past than any that they were likely to experience in their own lifetime. At the same time, Monsignor Ellis insisted that Church history should always be honest history and that the Church should not be afraid to confront the dark chapters in its own past. He liked to quote Pope Leo XIII's endorsement of Cicero's standard that "the first duty of a historian is not to tell a lie, and the second duty is not to be afraid to tell the truth."

Like Monsignor Ellis, I welcome this opportunity to urge my fellow American Catholics to take a deeper interest in their own history. It is a magnificent and inspiring story that deserves greater recognition and appreciation, especially on the part of American Catholics. Our history gives us a unique understanding of our roots, an informed perspective from which to view the present, and a well-grounded hope and guidance for the future. It is essentially our story, but, if we American Catholics do not take an interest in our own history, why should we expect anyone else to do so?

Readers of this one-volume popular encyclopedia of U.S. Catholic history will find a rewarding collection of articles on the Catholic Church on all fifty states, the history of every American diocese, a survey of many of the ethnic groups that compose the American Catholic community, and the role of the principal figures — lay, religious, and clerical — who have made invaluable contributions to the shaping of U.S. Catholicism over the past five centuries. There is also a detailed chronology of American Catholic history, and four appendices that list the missionaries to the Americas, saints of the Americas, Catholics in the Statuary Hall of the U.S. Capitol, and the most significant cathedrals, basilicas and shrines in the United States.

I hope that this encyclopedia will receive a wide readership and encourage our fellow citizens, Catholic and non-Catholic alike, to explore further the rich heritage of American Catholicism.

✠ Timothy Michael Cardinal Dolan
Archbishop of New York
December 5, 2012

INTRODUCTION

In America, Christian faith has found expression in an impressive array of witnesses and achievements. We must recall with gratitude the inspiring work of education carried out in countless families, schools and universities, and all the healing and consolation imparted in hospitals and hospices and shelters. We must give thanks for the practical living out of God's call in devoted service to others, in commitment to social justice, in responsible involvement in political life, in a wide variety of charitable and social organizations, and in the growth of ecumenical and interreligious understanding and cooperation. In a more global context, we should thank God for the great generosity of American Catholics whose support of the foreign missions has greatly contributed to the spiritual and material well-being of their brothers and sisters in other lands. The Church in the United States has sent brave missionary men and women out to the nations, and not a few of them have borne the ultimate witness to the ancient truth that the blood of martyrs is the seed of Christianity.

So proclaimed Pope John Paul II during Mass at Oriole Park at Camden Yards, Baltimore, during his visit to the United States in 1995. The history of the Catholic Church in the United States truly has been a long, profound, and poignant journey of faith against often-difficult circumstances and ideologies. From the first missionaries who braved the wilderness and persecutions, to the immigrant Catholics who sought freedom in the teeming cities, to the modern Catholics confronted with a materialist and increasingly hostile secular society, the Church in America has demonstrated resiliency, courage, and zeal that have emerged at the darkest moments to advance the Gospel in new situations and with new eloquence.

The extraordinary story of American Catholicism serves as the foundation of Our Sunday Visitor's Encyclopedia of U.S. Catholic History, covering the whole of the Catholic story in the United States, from the earliest travels of the Spanish and French missionaries to the Church in the new millennium. This encyclopedia offers to the average reader a valuable and unique reference guide. Geared toward the general Catholic layperson, but researched in an exhaustive and scholarly fashion, this encyclopedia is intended to be a handy, accessible, affordable, and unbiased reference to American Catholicism. It also strives to be the most modern and up-to-date encyclopedia on Catholic history in the United States ever attempted, representing developments in the American Church in the first years of a new century.

The entries in the A to Z section strive to encompass virtually every aspect of American Catholic history. There are thus biographies on people (major and minor Catholics, Native Americans, Irish immigrants, African-Americans, Hispanics, and more), places (New York, Boys Town, the Rendezvous of the Mountain Men), every state, all past and present dioceses and archdioceses, writings (both Catholic and anti-Catholic), events (the Great Depression, the world wars, and the many faceted flourishing of the Church throughout America), organizations (Knights of Columbus, Cursillo, Opus Dei, the Knights of Labor, and Catholic Youth organizations), and, of course, a major section on Anti-Catholicism, and many other topics (Vatican-U.S. relations, capital punishment, abortion, etc.). Further, there are significant entries on the popes who have played a role in shaping the Catholic faith in the United States, from Alexander VI (1492–1503) to Benedict XVI (2005–).

For someone unfamiliar with the wide patterns of U.S. Catholic history, this book might at first seem very daunting. The best way to start out, then, is by reading through the Chronology of American Catholic History at the very start. This will provide a useful introduction to the wide sweep of events and names. You might proceed from there to the individual states and the biographies of the key leaders in American Catholicism (e.g., Archbishop John Carroll, Cardinal James Gibbons, and others) who appear in the chronology. From there, you might read the individual dioceses and archdioceses, starting with the largest, such as Baltimore (the first), New York, Philadelphia, and Los Angeles. Next, you could move on to the different ethnic groups who have all contributed so much to the vibrant historical life of the Church in the United States, including the Irish, Germans, Italians, Hispanics, and African-Americans. Finally, you can turn to the different events covered with individual entries, such as the American Revolution, the Civil War, the Great Depression, the Vietnam War, the Sex Abuse Crisis, and the development of Catholic schools.

One of the most immediate features is the coverage of every diocese and archdiocese (present and historical) and the Catholic history in every state. Every effort has been made to ensure that the histories of the dioceses and archdioceses and each state are as comprehensive as possible within the obvious limits of space for a single-volume reference book. Dates, events, and personalities have been included wherever possible, and readers should come away with a general sense of the patterns of history. The life of American Catholicism — as is true with the whole Church — is an ongoing one, and by the time this book reaches the shelves of bookstores and libraries, it is inevitable that changes will have occurred in many places, with new bishops and archbishops appointed to many sees and new and surprising events taking place.

ACKNOWLEDGMENTS

There are many individuals to whom a special debt is owed for their kind assistance in bringing this large project to completion. First, special thanks go to Greg Erlandson, president of Our Sunday Visitor, for his enduring patience over the years as this book slowly came together. Likewise, I am grateful to Jackie Lindsey, acquisitions editor, and York Young, managing editor, both of Our Sunday Visitor, as well as Jane Cavolina, the copy editor, for her many hours of work with the manuscript.

Thanks are owed also to Robert Lockwood, former president of Our Sunday Visitor, for his many suggestions and improvements of the manuscript, Mike Aquilina, the late Ann Ball, and Russell Shaw.

Finally, I am extremely grateful to His Eminence Timothy Cardinal Dolan, Archbishop of New York, for his foreword to the encyclopedia and also his support and encouragement over the last years.

CHRONOLOGY OF
UNITED STATES CATHOLIC HISTORY

The following are key dates in U.S. Catholic history, including those prior to the signing of the Declaration of Independence. Reprinted from *Our Sunday Visitor's Encyclopedia of American Catholic History*.

1492 Christopher Columbus sailed to the New World and reached San Salvador (probably Watlings Island in the Bahamas). He subsequently made three voyages and established a Spanish presence on Santo Domingo (Hispaniola).

1497 John Cabot, a Genoese sailing under the English flag, reached the coasts of Labrador and Newfoundland.

1499 Alonso de Ojeda and Amerigo Vespucci reached Venezuela and explored the South American coast.

1500 Pedro Cabral reached Brazil.

1511 Diocese of Puerto Rico established as suffragan of Seville, Spain. Bishop Alonso Manso, sailing from Spain in 1512, became first bishop to take up residence in the New World.

1513 Juan Ponce de León reached Florida and sailed as far north as the Carolinas.

1519 Hernando Cortés began the conquest of Mexico; by the next year, the Aztec Empire had been conquered and the Spanish rule over Mexico was established.

1521 Missionaries accompanying Ponce de León and other explorers probably said first Masses within present limits of the United States.

1526 Lucas Vázquez de Ayllón attempted to establish a colony in South Carolina; it later failed.

1534–36 Jacques Cartier explored the Newfoundland area and sailed up the St. Lawrence River.

1539 Hernando de Soto journeyed through Florida and as far north as Arkansas.

1540 Francisco Vázquez de Coronado set out to find the Seven Cities of Gold, journeying through Texas, Kansas, and New Mexico. Franciscans Juan de Padilla and Marcos de Niza accompanied Coronado's expedition through the territory. They celebrated the first Mass within the territory of the thirteen original colonies.

c. 1540 Juan de Padilla, the first martyr of the United States, was murdered on the plains of Kansas by local Indians.

1565 The city of St. Augustine, the oldest in the United States, founded by Pedro Menéndez de Avilés, who was accompanied by four secular priests. America's oldest mission, Nombre de Dios, was established. Father Francisco Lopez de Mendoza Grajales became the first parish priest of St. Augustine, where the first parish in the United States was established.

1602 Carmelite Anthony of the Ascension offered the first recorded Mass in California on the shore of San Diego Bay.

1606 Bishop Juan de las Cabeyas de Altamirano, O.P., conducted the first episcopal visitation in the United States.

1608 Samuel de Champlain established the first permanent French colony at Québec.

1609 Henry Hudson entered New York Bay and sailed up the Hudson River. Santa Fe was established as a mission in New Mexico; it later served as a headquarters for missionary efforts in the American Southwest.

1611 Pierre Biard, S.J., and Enemond Masse, S.J., began missionary labors among the Indians of Maine.

1612 First Franciscan province in the United States erected under the title of Santa Elena; it included Georgia, South Carolina, and Florida.

1613 Four Jesuits attempted to establish permanent French settlement near mouth of the Kennebec River in Maine.

1619 French Franciscans began work among settlers and Indians. They were driven out by the English in 1628.

1620 The Mayflower Compact drawn up by the Pilgrims. The chapel of Nombre de Dios was dedicated to *Nuestra Senora de la Leche y Buen Parto* (Our Nursing Mother of the Happy Delivery) in Florida; it is the oldest shrine to the Blessed Mother in the United States.

1622 Pope Gregory XV established the Congregation de Propaganda Fide to oversee all mission territories. The Catholics of America remained under its jurisdiction until 1908.

1630 New England was made a prefecture apostolic in charge of French Capuchins.

1634 The ships *Ark* and *Dove* reached Maryland with the first settlers. Maryland established by Lord Calvert; two Jesuits were among first colonists. First Mass offered on St. Clement's Island in the Lower Potomac by Jesuit Father Andrew White.

1638 Jean Nicolet discovered the water route to the Mississippi.

1642 Jesuits Isaac Jogues and René Goupil were mutilated by Mohawks; Goupil was killed shortly afterward. Dutch Calvinists rescued Father Jogues. The colony of Virginia outlawed priests and disenfranchised Catholics.

1646 Jesuit Isaac Jogues and Jean de Lalande were martyred by Iroquois at Ossernenon, now Auriesville, New York.

1647 Massachusetts Bay Company enacted an anti-priest law.

1649 The General Assembly of Maryland passed an act of religious toleration for the colony.

1653 Jesuits opened a school at Newton Manor, the first school in the American English colonies.

1654 Following the English Civil War and the deposition of King Charles I, the installed Puritan regime in Maryland repealed the Toleration Act in Maryland.

1656 Church of St. Mary erected on Onondaga Lake, in the first French settlement in New York. St. Kateri Tekakwitha, the "Lily of the Mohawks," was born at Ossernenon, now Auriesville. She was canonized in 2012.

1660 Jesuit René Menard opened the first regular mission in Lake Superior region.

1668 Jesuit Father Jacques Marquette founded Sainte Marie Mission at Sault Ste. Marie.

1671 Simon de Saint-Lusson and Claude Allouez, S.J., arrived at Mackinac Island and claimed possession of the western country in the name of France.

1673 Louis Joliet and Jacques Marquette, S.J., began their expedition down the Mississippi River.

1674 Father Marquette set up a cabin for saying Mass in what later became the city of Chicago.

1675 Father Marquette established the Mission of the Immaculate Conception among Kaskaskia Indians, near present site of Utica, New York; transferred to Kaskaskia in 1703.

1678 Franciscan Recollect Louis Hennepin, the first white man to describe Niagara Falls, celebrated Mass there.

1680 Louis Hennepin followed the Mississippi to its source. The missions of New Mexico destroyed by a local Indian uprising.

1682 Mission Corpus Christi de Isleta (Ysleta) founded by Franciscans near El Paso, the first mission in present-day Texas.

1682 Religious toleration extended to members of all faiths in Pennsylvania.

1683 New York Colony passed the Charter of Liberties providing for religious freedom for believers in Christ.

1687 Eusebius Kino, S.J., launched the missions in Arizona at Pimería Alta.

1688 Maryland became a royal colony as a result of the so-called Glorious Revolution in England; the Anglican Church became the official religion in 1692. Catholics were disenfranchised and persecuted until 1776. Ann Glover, an elderly Irish-Catholic widow who refused to renounce her Catholic religion, was hanged.

1689 Jesuit Claude Allouez died after thirty-two years of missionary activity among the Indians of the Midwest; he had evangelized Indians of twenty different tribes. Jesuit Jacques Gravier succeeded Allouez as vicar general of Illinois.

1690 Mission San Francisco de los Tejas founded in east Texas.

1692 The Church of England officially established

in Maryland. New Mexico resubjugated by the Spanish and the missions reopened.

1697 Religious liberty granted in South Carolina to all except "papists."

1700 Jesuit Eusebius Kino established Mission San Xavier del Bac, near Tucson, Arizona. In 1783, under Franciscan administration, construction of the Mission San Xavier del Bac was begun near the site of the original mission; it is still in use as a parish church. Although the New York Assembly had enacted a bill calling for religious toleration for all Christians in 1683, other penal laws were now enforced against Catholics; all priests were ordered out of the province.

1701 Tolerance granted in New Jersey to all except "papists."

1703 Mission San Francisco de Solano founded on the Rio Grande River; it was rebuilt in 1718 as San Antonio de Valero, or the Alamo.

1704 Destruction of Florida's northern missions by English and Indian troops led by Governor James Moore of South Carolina. Franciscans Juan de Parga, Dominic Criodo, Tiburcio de Osorio, Augustine Ponze de León, Marcos Delgado, and two Indians — Anthony Enixa and Amador Cuipa Feliciano — were slain by the invaders.

1709 French Jesuit missionaries obliged to give up their central New York missions.

1716 Venerable Antonio Margil de Jesús, O.F.M., began his missionary labors in Texas.

1718 Catholics in Maryland officially disenfranchised. New Orleans founded by Jean-Baptiste Le Moyne, Sieur de Bienville.

1727 Ursuline nuns founded convent in New Orleans, the oldest convent in what is now the United States; they conducted a school, hospital, and orphan asylum.

1735 Bishop Francis Martinez de Tejadu Diaz de Velasco, auxiliary of Santiago, was the first bishop to take up residence in the United States, at St. Augustine.

1740s The First Great Awakening among Protestants.

1741 Because of an alleged popish plot to burn the city of New York, four whites were hanged and eleven blacks burned at the stake.

1744 Mission Church of the Alamo built in San Antonio.

1751 First Catholic settlement founded among Huron Indians near Sandusky, Ohio, by Jesuit Father de la Richardie.

1754–63 The French and Indian War (the Seven Years' War in Europe), the first world war; the conflict ended with the defeat of France and the loss of their American colonies.

1755 Fifty-six Catholics of Acadia expelled to the American colonies; those landing in Boston were denied the services of a Catholic priest.

1763 The Jesuits were banished from the territories of Louisiana and Illinois. Spain ceded Florida to England. The English also gained control of all French territories east of the Mississippi River following the cessation of the French and Indian War.

1765 The Quartering Act imposed on the colonies by the British as a means of paying the cost of colonial defense. It was followed by the Stamp Act, sparking the rise of the Sons of Liberty and the convening of the Stamp Act Congress.

1767 Jesuits expelled from Spanish territory. The Spanish crown confiscated their property, including the Pious Fund of the Californias. The Upper California missions were entrusted to Franciscans.

1769 Franciscan Junípero Serra, missionary in Mexico for twenty years, began establishment of the Franciscan missions in California, in present-day San Diego. He was beatified in 1988.

1770 The Boston Massacre resulted in the deaths of five colonists in Boston.

1773 The Tea Act sparked the Boston Tea Party. The British responded with the Intolerable Acts in 1774. Catholic Charles Carroll of Carrollton published the "First Citizen" letter in defense of the Church and Catholics against Daniel Dulany and the royal colonial government in Maryland.

1774 Elizabeth Ann Bayley Seton, foundress of the American Sisters of Charity, was born in New York City on August 28. She was canonized in 1975. The British Parliament passed the Québec Act granting the French in the region the right to their own religion, language, and customs. The first Continental Congress was convened.

1775–81 The American Revolution, in which Catholics played a major role. In 1790 newly elected President George Washington wrote to American Catholics to thank them for their instrumental role in the war for American freedom.

1775 The Continental Congress denounced the rampant anti-Catholicism in the colonies to King George III. General Washington discouraged a Guy Fawkes Day procession, in which the pope was carried in effigy.

1776 Charles Carroll received an appointment, with Samuel Chase and Benjamin Franklin, to a commission of the Continental Congress seeking aid from Canada; Father John Carroll accompanied them on their mission. Virginia became the first state to vote for full religious freedom in the new state's bill of rights. Similar provisions were passed by Maryland and Pennsylvania. The birth of United States historically recognized as the Continental Congress passed the Declaration of Independence (Charles Carroll was the longest surviving signer). The New Jersey State Constitution tacitly excluded Catholics from office.

1777 The New York State Constitution gave religious liberty, but the naturalization law, the Test Oath, required an oath to renounce allegiance to any foreign ruler, ecclesiastical or civil.

1778 Father Pierre Gibault aided George Rogers Clark in the campaign against the British in the conquest of the Northwest Territory.

1780 The Massachusetts State Constitution granted religious liberty, but required a religious test to hold public office and provided for a tax to support Protestant teachers of piety, religion, and morality.

1781 Expedition from San Gabriel Mission founded Pueblo "de Nuestra Senora de los Angeles," the present-day city of Los Angeles. British General Cornwallis surrendered at Yorktown, effectively ending the American Revolution.

1783 The Treaty of Paris officially ended the American Revolution; Great Britain recognized the independence of the United States.

1784 The Vatican appointed Father John Carroll to the post of superior of the American Catholic missions. The New Hampshire State Constitution included a religious test that barred Catholics from public office; local support was provided for public Protestant teachers of religion.

1787 Catholics Daniel Carroll of Maryland and Thomas Fitzsimons of Pennsylvania signed the Constitution of the United States.

1788 First public Mass said in Boston on November 2 by Father Claude Florent Bouchard de la Poterie, first resident priest.

1789 Pope Pius VI erected the first U.S. diocese, Baltimore; John Carroll named the first bishop.

1790 Catholics given right to vote in South Carolina.

1791 French Sulpicians opened the first seminary in the United States, St. Mary's in Baltimore. Georgetown Academy was established and began holding classes. Bishop Carroll convoked the first synod of the clergy of the diocese. The Bill of Rights was ratified by Congress. Pierre Charles L'Enfant designed the Federal City of Washington. His plans were not fully implemented until the early 1900s.

1792 James Hoban designed the White House.

1793 Reverend Stephen T. Badin became the first priest ordained by Bishop Carroll; he soon began missionary work in Kentucky.

1799 Prince Demetrius Gallitzin (Father Augustine Smith) arrived in the Allegheny Mountains. He labored there for the next forty years and established the Church in western Pennsylvania, at Loretto.

1800 Jesuit Leonard Neale became the first bishop consecrated in the present limits of the United States.

1801 Start of the Second Great Awakening among Protestants.

1802 The first mayor of Washington, appointed by President Thomas Jefferson, was Catholic Judge Robert Brent.

1803 The Louisiana Purchase resulted in the

acquisition by the United States of all French lands from the Mississippi River to the Rocky Mountains, for $15 million.

1804–06 President Thomas Jefferson sponsored the expedition of Lewis and Clark into the Louisiana Territory.

1806 New York anti-Catholic 1777 Test Oath for naturalization repealed.

1808 Pope Pius VII declared Baltimore the first metropolitan see of the United States, erecting at the same time the new dioceses of Bardstown (Kentucky), Boston, New York, and Philadelphia as suffragans.

1809 Mother Elizabeth Ann Seton established the first Native American congregation of sisters, at Emmitsburg, Maryland.

1810 The United States annexed west Florida under the pretext that it was included in the Louisiana Purchase.

1811 Catholic Canadian trappers and traders with John Jacob Astor expedition founded first American settlement in Oregon, at Astoria. Reverend Guy Chabrat became first priest ordained west of the Allegheny Mountains.

1812 The War of 1812; ended by the signing of the Treaty of Ghent in 1814.

1814 St. Joseph's Orphanage, Philadelphia, opened, the first Catholic asylum for children in the United States.

1818 Religious freedom established by a new constitution in Connecticut, although the Congregational Church remained, in practice, the state church. Bishop Louis William Dubourg arrived at St. Louis, with Vincentians Joseph Rosati and Felix de Andreis. Rose Philippine Duchesne arrived at St. Charles, where she founded the first American convent of the Society of the Sacred Heart. She was beatified in 1940 and canonized in 1988.

1822 Bishop John England founded the *United States Catholic Miscellany*, the country's first Catholic newspaper of a strictly religious nature. The Society for the Propagation of the Faith was founded in France; it sent missionaries throughout the world. Vicariate Apostolic of Mississippi and Alabama was established.

1823 President James Monroe proposed the Monroe Doctrine of foreign policy. Father Gabriel Richard elected delegate to Congress from Michigan territory; he was the first priest elected to the House of Representatives.

1828 The New York State Legislature enacted a law upholding the sanctity of the seal of confession. The first hospital opened west of the Mississippi in St. Louis, staffed by the Sisters of Charity from Emmitsburg, Maryland.

1829 The First Provincial Council of Baltimore convoked. The Oblate Sisters of Providence, the first African-American congregation of women religious in the United States, was established in Baltimore.

1831 Xavier University founded.

1833 Father Irenaeus Frederick Baraga celebrated the first Mass in present-day Grand Rapids, Michigan.

1834 The first native New Yorker to become a secular priest, Reverend John McCloskey, was ordained. Indian missions in the Northwest entrusted to Jesuits by the Holy See. A mob of Nativists attacked and burned down the Ursuline Convent at Charlestown, Massachusetts.

1835 Samuel F. B. Morse published *The Foreign Conspiracy Against the Liberties of the United States*.

1836 Texans under Stephen F. Austin declared their independence from Mexico; the Battle of the Alamo in San Antonio resulted in the deaths of 188 Texans, including the commander William B. Travis and perhaps Davy Crockett. Texas soon won its independence and was annexed in 1845. A future bishop, St. John Nepomucene Neumann arrived in the United States from Bohemia and was ordained in Old St. Patrick's Cathedral in New York City. The infamous work, Maria Monk's *Awful Disclosures of Maria Monk, or, The Hidden Secrets of a Nun's Life in a Convent Exposed*, detailing supposed scandals among Catholic religious, was published. President Andrew Jackson nominated the Catholic Roger Brooke Taney as chief justice of the Supreme Court.

1838 Fathers Francis Norbert Blanchet and Modeste Demers, "Apostles of the Northwest," sent to the territory by the archbishop of Québec.

1839 Pope Gregory XVI condemned the slave trade in his decree *In Supremo Apostolatus*.

1840 St. Theodore Guérin founded the Sisters of Providence of St. Mary-of-the-Woods in Indiana.

1842 Father Augustin Ravoux began ministrations to French and Indians at Fort Pierre, Vermilion, and Prairie du Chien, Wisconsin; he printed a devotional book in the Sioux language the following year. Henriette De-Lille and Juliette Gaudin began the Sisters of the Holy Family in New Orleans, the second African-American community of women religious. University of Notre Dame founded by Holy Cross Father Edward Sorin and Brothers of St. Joseph on land given to the Diocese of Vincennes by Father Stephen T. Badin.

1844 Thirteen people were killed and two churches and a school burned in Know-Nothing riots in Philadelphia. Orestes A. Brownson was received into the Church; he subsequently founded *Brownson's Quarterly Review*.

1845 Nativists opposed to Catholics and Irish immigration established the Native American Party. Issac Thomas Hecker was received into the Church. The potato famine began in Ireland, causing in part the mass migration of Irish to the United States. The St. Vincent de Paul Society was founded in the United States.

1846–48 The Mexican-American War was caused by a border dispute between the United States and Mexico. Catholic chaplains were appointed to the army to minister to Mexican Catholics.

1846 Peter H. Burnett, who became the first governor of California in 1849, was received into the Catholic Church. The First Benedictine Abbey in the United States was founded near Latrobe, Pennsylvania, by Father Boniface Wimmer.

1847 The bishops of the United States requested Pope Pius IX to name the Immaculate Conception the patron of the United States.

1848 The first permanent American Trappist foundation was established, in Kentucky. Jacob L. Martin was named the first American representative to the Vatican.

1852 The First Plenary Council of Baltimore was held. Redemptorist St. John Nepomucene Neumann became the fourth bishop of Philadelphia. He was beatified in 1963 and canonized in 1977.

1853 Calling for the exclusion of Catholics and foreigners from office and a twenty-one-year residence requirement, the American Party, known also as the Know-Nothing Party, was founded.

1854 Members of the Benedictine Swiss-American congregation established a community at St. Meinrad in southern Indiana.

1855 The German Catholic Central Verein founded. The "Bloody Monday" Riots in Louisville, Kentucky, left twenty dead.

1857 The Supreme Court issued the Dred Scott Decision; Chief Justice Roger B. Taney stated that Congress could not exclude slavery from the territories since, according to the Constitution, slaves were property and could be transported anywhere. The American College at Louvain opened.

1858 Jesuit Father Pierre-Jean De Smet accompanied General William Selby Harney as chaplain on an expedition sent to settle troubles between Mormons and the U.S. government. The Paulists, the first native religious community for men, was established. The cornerstone of second (present) St. Patrick's Cathedral, New York City, was laid; the cathedral was completed in 1879.

1859 The North American College was founded in Rome as a training center for American seminarians.

1860 South Carolina seceded from the Union.

1861–65 The American Civil War. Catholics participated in large numbers on both sides. There were approximately 40 Catholic chaplains in the Union Army and 28 in the Confederate army. More than 500 Catholic nuns ministered to the sick and wounded. Over 20 generals in the Union Army and 11 generals in the Confederate Army were Catholics.

1861 The Confederacy was formed after eleven

states seceded from the Union. Jefferson Davis was elected president of the Confederacy.

1865 *Catholic World* was founded. A Test Oath law (called the Drake Convention) was passed by the state legislature to crush Catholicism in Missouri. The law was declared unconstitutional by the Supreme Court in 1866. Reverend H. H. Spalding, a Protestant missionary, published the "Whitman Myth" to hinder the work of Catholic missionaries in Oregon. President Abraham Lincoln was assassinated. The murder sparked anti-Catholicism, including charges that Jesuits orchestrated his death. Congress passed the Thirteenth Amendment, abolishing slavery.

1866 The Second Plenary Council of Baltimore was held.

1867 Reconstruction was launched in the South; the presence of federal troops did not end until 1877. The Ku Klux Klan was founded to defeat Reconstruction, oppose Catholicism, and establish white supremacy in the postwar South. The United States purchased Alaska for $7.2 million; organized by Secretary of State William Seward, the purchase was called "Seward's Folly."

1869–70 The First Vatican Council was convoked. Most of the bishops of the United States took part in the deliberations of the council.

1869 The Transcontinental Railroad completed, with the two tracks meeting at Promontory, near Ogden, Utah. The Knights of Labor was founded.

1870 The Holy Name Society was organized.

1873 St. Damien de Veuster of the Sacred Hearts Fathers arrived in Molokai, Hawaii, and spent the remainder of his life working among lepers. He was canonized in 2009.

1875 James Augustine Healy, the first African-American bishop consecrated in the United States, became the second bishop of Portland, Maine. Archbishop John McCloskey of New York became the first American prelate to be elevated to the College of Cardinals.

1876 Lieutenant Colonel George Armstrong Custer was killed at the Battle of the Little Bighorn (in the Second Sioux War) in Montana. *The American Catholic Quarterly Review* wass established. James Gibbons published *Faith of Our Fathers*.

1878 The Franciscan Sisters of Allegany became first Native American community to send members to foreign missions.

1880 William Russell Grace became the first Catholic mayor of New York City.

1882 Knights of Columbus founded by Father Michael J. McGivney.

1884 The Third Plenary Council of Baltimore was held. John Gilmary Shea began the United States Catholic Historical Society.

1886 Archbishop Charles J. Seghers, "Apostle of Alaska," was murdered by a guide; he had surveyed southern and northwest Alaska in 1873 and 1877. Archbishop James Gibbons of Baltimore named the second American cardinal. Augustus Tolton ordained the first African-American priest in the United States. The Knights of St. John was established.

1887 The American Protective Association (APA) established to resist the growth of immigration. The Dawes Act was passed, dissolving all Indian tribes and distributing their lands among their former members, who were not permitted to dispose of their property for twenty-five years.

1889 The Catholic University of America opened. The first African-American Lay Congress was held in Washington, D.C.; subsequent congresses were held in Cincinnati (1890), Philadelphia (1892), Chicago (1893), and Baltimore (1894). Mother Frances Xavier Cabrini arrived in New York City to begin work among Italian immigrants. She was canonized in 1946. *American Ecclesiastical Review* was begun.

1890 Archbishop John Ireland delivered an address on public and private schools at the gathering of the National Education Association in St. Paul, Minnesota.

1891 Vicariate Apostolic of Oklahoma and Indian Territory was established. Katharine Drexel founded the Sisters of the Blessed Sacrament for Indians and Colored People. She was canonized in 2000. The Rosary Society was organized.

1893   The apostolic delegation under Archbishop Francesco Satolli was established in Washington, D.C.; it became an apostolic nunciature in 1984 with the establishment of full diplomatic relations between the United States and the Holy See. The first Catholic college for women in the United States, the College of Notre Dame of Maryland, was established. *St. Anthony Messenger* was launched.

1898   Puerto Rico was ceded to the United States (and became a self-governing commonwealth in 1952); its inhabitants were granted U.S. citizenship in 1917. The United States annexed Hawaii; the monarchy had been overthrown in 1897.

1898   The Spanish-American War.

1899   Pope Leo XIII issued *Testem Benevolentiae.*

1901   President William McKinley assassinated.

1904   The National Catholic Educational Association founded. First publication of the *Catholic Almanac.*

1905   The Catholic Church Extension Society for home missions was established.

1907   The first volume of the *Catholic Encyclopedia* was published by The Catholic University of America.

1908   Pope St. Pius X published *Pascendi Domini Gregis,* against modernism. Pope Pius issued the bull *Sapienti Consilio,* by which the Church in the United States was removed from mission status and from the jurisdiction of the Congregation de Propaganda Fide. The first American Missionary Congress was held in Chicago.

1909   The Holy Name Society was established. *America* magazine was founded by the Jesuits.

1911   The Catholic Foreign Mission Society of America (Maryknoll) was founded.

1912   *Our Sunday Visitor* was founded.

1914–18 World War I.

1917   The United States entered World War I. The National Catholic War Council founded. Over one million Catholics served in the Armed Forces (over 20 percent of the total U.S. military).

1919   The bishops' *Program of Social Reconstruction* was published. The National Catholic Welfare Council founded. Peter Guilday began the American Catholic Historical Association.

1920   The National Catholic News Service (now the Catholic News Service) was established.

1924   The Federated Colored Catholics of the United States established. *Commonweal* magazine was founded by Michael Williams.

1925   The Supreme Court declares the Oregon School Law unconstitutional. The Scopes Trial, also called the Dayton Monkey Trial, took place in Dayton, Ohio.

1926   The Twenty-eighth International Eucharistic Congress was held in Chicago.

1928   Alfred E. Smith of New York was nominated for president by the Democratic Party; he was the first Catholic ever chosen to head a major party national ticket. He was defeated by Herbert Hoover, in part because of his faith and his opposition to Prohibition.

1929   The stock-market crash signaled the start of the Great Depression. The Catholic Church devoted enormous resources to alleviating the suffering of those afflicted by the global depression.

1932   Franklin Delano Roosevelt was elected president, launching the New Deal period (1933–45).

1933   The Catholic Worker Movement was established by Dorothy Day and Peter Maurin.

1934   John LaFarge, S.J., began the first Catholic Interracial Council in New York.

1937   The Association of Catholic Trade Unionists was established.

1939   Myron C. Taylor named personal representative of President Roosevelt to Pope Pius XII.

1939–45 World War II.

1941   Pearl Harbor attacked by Japan; the United States entered World War II. Catholics comprised over 25 percent of the Armed Forces.

1945   World War II ended. Delegates from fifty nations established the Charter of the United Nations.

1947   The Christian Family Movement was begun by Pat and Patty Crowley. The Supreme Court issued the decision *Everson v. Board of Education,* approving the use of public school buses to carry Catholic students to parochial schools.

1948 Protestants and Other Americans for the Separation of Church and State was founded.

1951 President Harry S. Truman nominates General Mark Clark as ambassador to Vatican City. The nomination was later withdrawn in the face of anti-Catholic protests.

1954 The Sisters Formation Conference was founded. The Supreme Court decided *Brown v. Board of Education of Topeka*, which declared that segregation in public schools was unconstitutional.

1955 John Tracy Ellis published *American Catholics and the Intellectual Life*.

1956 Conference of Major Superiors of Men was founded.

1958 Christopher Dawson named the first holder of the Chauney Stillman Chair of Roman Catholic Studies at Harvard Divinity School.

1959 Pope John XXIII announced his intention to convoke the Second Vatican Council.

1960 John F. Kennedy elected president of the United States, the first Catholic president.

1962–65 The Second Vatican Council.

1962 Gustave Weigel, S.J., was appointed by the Vatican to be one of the five Catholic observers at the third general assembly of the World Council of Churches at New Delhi. Archbishop Joseph Francis Rummel of New Orleans announced the integration of archdiocesan Catholic schools.

1963 The Catholic University of America prohibited Hans Küng, John Courtney Murray, S.J., Gustave Weigel, S.J., and Godfrey Diekmann, O.S.B., from speaking at the school. Elizabeth Ann Seton became the first American to be beatified. President Kennedy assassinated in Dallas.

1964 The Civil Rights Act was passed.

1965 Pope Paul VI visited the United Nations, the first pope to visit the United States. Gommar A. De Pauw organized the Catholic Traditionalist movement.

1966 The National Conference of Catholic Bishops and the United States Catholic Conference were organized. Harold Perry, S.V.D., became the second African-American to be named a bishop.

1967 The Land O' Lakes Statement was issued.

The Catholic Charismatic Movement began. The Catholic Committee on Urban Ministry was established.

1968 Pope Paul VI issued *Humanae Vitae*. The National Black Catholic Clergy Caucus, the National Black Sisters' Conference, the National Black Catholic Seminarians Association, and the National Federation of Priests' Councils were formed. Catholics United for the Faith was established.

1969 The Organization of Priests Associated for Religious, Educational, and Social Rights (PADRES) and the Campaign for Human Development were established.

1970 Patricio Fernández Flores, the first modern Latino bishop, was ordained.

1971 The Leadership Conference of Women Religious was established.

1972 The Religious Brothers Conference established.

1973 *Roe v. Wade* decision handed down by the Supreme Court, legalizing abortion.

1975 Pope Paul VI canonized the first American saint, Elizabeth Ann Seton.

1976 The United States celebrated the Bicentennial.

1977 The Fellowship of Catholic Scholars was established.

1979 Pope Blessed John Paul II visited the United States.

1983 The National Conference of Catholic Bishops issued the *Challenge of Peace*.

1986 The National Conference of Catholic Bishops issued *Economic Justice for All*. The Vatican and The Catholic University of America removed Father Charles Curran from teaching theology at the university.

1987 Blessed John Paul II visited the United States for the second time. The National Black Catholic Congress was convoked in Washington, D.C.

1991 The United States played a major role in the Gulf War.

1992 The Council of Major Superiors of Women Religious was founded.

1993 World Youth Day was held in Denver.

1995 Blessed John Paul II visited the United Nations, Baltimore, and New York.

1997 U.S. bishops took part in a special assembly

of the Synod of Bishops on the Church in the Americas.

1999 Pope Blessed John Paul II visited St. Louis.

2001 The United States was attacked on September 11. The National Conference of Catholic Bishops and United States Catholic Conference merged to form the United States Conference of Catholic Bishops; Bishop Wilton Gregory of Belleville, Illinois, was elected the first black president of the USCCB.

2002 The pedophilia crisis erupted across the country; the United States Conference of Catholic Bishops passed a series of protective norms.

2003 The United States launched the Iraq War to topple Saddam Hussein.

2004 President George W. Bush was reelected president. The Democratic nominee, Senator John Kerry, a Catholic, caused considerable controversy because of his pro-abortion position. The issue sparked a national debate over the issue of Catholic politicians and abortion.

2008 Pope Benedict XVI visited Washington, D.C., and New York, his first apostolic voyage to the United States as pope. Senator Barack Obama was elected the first African-American president; his running mate, Senator Joseph Biden of Delaware, became the first Catholic vice president.

2011 The Archdiocese of Philadelphia suspended twenty-one priests facing sexual abuse accusations; the largest suspension since the start of the sexual abuse crisis.

A

Abbelen, Peter M. (August 8, 1843–August 24, 1917)

A priest and patron of German-American Catholics, Peter M. Abbelen was a consultor for Church affairs. He was born in Germany and educated in scholastic institutions there. Migrating to America as a young man, he entered St. Francis Seminary in Milwaukee, Wisconsin, having received the grace of a priestly vocation, and there completed his studies and was ordained on January 2, 1868.

Father Abbelen then held pastoral assignments at Chippewa Falls, La Crosse, and Prairie du Chien in the state, working always to preserve German traditions, devotions, and language in the local parishes at a time when nationalist tendencies were matters of debate in the American Church.

He served as a consultor for the Third Plenary Council in Baltimore in 1884 and advocated German national parishes, making every effort to have Church authorities in the United States maintain the German traditions embraced by the immigrants from his homeland. Father Abbelen understood the various problems that beset the new German Catholic Americans. He wanted to maintain German Catholic traditions because he believed that the various attempts being made to "Americanize" the new generations of immigrants would not assist the Germans in transition or bolster their faith. Upon his return to Milwaukee from the council, despite the opposition he had received at that gathering of prelates, Father Abbelen became the vicar general of the archdiocese.

Opposed even more ardently by several members of the American hierarchy as the immigrant question took on national ramifications, Father Abbelen wrote *The Memorial of the German Question* in 1886. This document provided a rationale for halting the assimilation and integration processes that were being implemented in some regions of the country as a defense against the rabid anti-Catholic groups of the era. Designed to persuade Americans and Vatican officials of the needs of German-American Catholics, the document was addressed to the Sacred Congregation of the Propaganda of the Faith in Rome. Father Abbelen hoped to receive consideration from that congregation and approval of his efforts. The congregation, however, rejected his proposals, and he was forced to continue his efforts to protect Germanic customs without official sanction. He was made a monsignor in 1907 and labored for many more years before retiring and dying in Milwaukee.

Abbey. *See* Belmont Abbey, Benedictines, Carmelites, Cistercians, Gethsemani Abbey, *and* Trappists

Abell, Robert (November 25, 1792–June 28, 1873)

A dedicated missionary, Robert Abell was a priest educator in the young United States. He was born in Louisville, Kentucky, one of ten children in a devout Catholic family. His father served in the first Kentucky State Legislature and was the only Catholic in the state's Constitutional Convention in 1799, as Protestant bigotry kept Catholics from any public office in many communities.

Father Abell was educated at St. Thomas Seminary in Bardstown, Kentucky, and ordained in 1818 by the celebrated missionary Bishop Benedict Joseph Flaget. After ordination he began his ministry as a companion of the famous horseback priest, Father Charles Nerinckx. They labored in a parish that covered some eight hundred square miles and were constantly visiting the far-flung communities within their pastoral jurisdiction. Father Abell was six foot four inches tall and an imposing figure in the towns and byways of the areas he served.

In 1820 he started a boarding school to provide educational opportunities for the Catholic children of the region, and he invited the Sisters of Charity of Nazareth to open Mount Carmel convent and school to further the much-needed educational programs. Four years later he was assigned to Louisville, and there he also started parishes and built churches for the growing populace. In 1840 Father Abell became the vice president of St. Joseph's College in Bardstown. He served the faithful in this capacity for two decades and then retired in 1860, at which time the faith was firmly established in Kentucky because of his efforts and those of his companions. (*See also* Bardstown, Diocese of; Flaget, Benedict Joseph; and Nerinckx, Charles.)

Abolition Movement

The activities that opposed slavery in the United States were labeled the abolition movement and were the result of a slowly evolving commitment among Americans. The abhorrence of slavery was evident to some extent in the colonies in 1619, as colonials were shocked when the first slaves arrived to be sold within the various settlements. Most of the colonists did not approve of the practice. There was no public opposition, however, except for occasional demonstrations by Mennonites and Quakers, and these were limited to their colonial designations and largely ignored by political forces.

The first organized opposition to slavery did not surface, in fact, until after the Revolutionary War. Thomas Jefferson, Patrick Henry, and other American leaders expressed their opposition to slavery at that time, and many Americans manumitted their slaves as an act of charity in a new beginning. Some freed their slaves soon after the war, while others provided for the freedom of their slaves in their last wills and testaments. In 1817 the American Colonization Society sent freed slaves back to their homelands in Africa, and the nation of Liberia was founded.

The declining economy in many states aided the abolition cause, as Americans believed that slaves were not only victims of immoral practices but were unprofitable and uneconomical because of the costs involved in their daily upkeep. As early as 1810 Northerners were quite vocal in their antislavery views, and abolition groups were forming. In the South, however, the invention of the cotton gin once again reinforced the need for slave labor in the vast fields used for the crop. The use of slaves was increased as new methods of harvesting cotton were called into play on plantations, proving economical. As a result, the original antislavery groups in the South were silenced while opposition was renewed with vigor in the North. By 1830 organizations that openly opposed slavery and denounced the immorality of the practice flourished and gained political power.

William Lord Garrison became one of the nation's leading antislavery spokesmen in 1831, when he published the weekly *Liberator*. Garrison and his followers demanded the immediate abolition of slavery in the United States, prompting other groups to begin their own activities. The New England Anti-Slavery Society was established, along with the American Anti-Slavery Society of Philadelphia, adding to the debate. Arthur and Lewis Tappan were active in New York, and Reverend Charles Grandison Finney, an evangelist preacher, took up the crusade and spoke everywhere about the slavery issue. Other speakers included the Grimké sisters, who were members of a slaveholding family in South Carolina. They added lurid details and their own grim memories to the growing furor. Harriet Beecher Stowe's book *Uncle Tom's Cabin* appeared and provided more dramatic images that enflamed the movement and raised it to the level of a national crisis. Petitions for the enactment of national abolition laws appeared everywhere as the battle raged on, and thousands of Americans signed the petitions to signify their concern.

In 1840 the abolition movement assumed actual political aspirations. The Liberty Party, an abolitionist society, entered the political arena, and the party's candidate, James G. Birney, gained votes in a presidential election in 1844. By 1848 the Free Soil Party was active nationally, and the Republican Party came into existence in 1854, surviving both the era and the issue to become a major political factor in the nation.

The abolitionists, however, did not confine themselves to demonstrations, meetings, or political protests. Throughout the decades, individuals and groups worked to move runaway slaves from the plantations of the South to northern havens. The Underground Railroad, a series of safe houses and escape routes for runaway slaves, was in operation, and in 1849 Harriet Tubman went north and began her great apostolate to free other slaves. By 1850 Fugitive Slave Laws were enacted, and the nation faced a critical divide that set the stage for the Civil War.

The Catholic response to the abolition issue was mixed, as bishops and religious orders were among the slaveholders. Some Catholics viewed slavery as a political rather than a moral issue, despite the fact that Pope Gregory XVI had issued an apostolic letter condemning the slave trade and the very institution of slavery. Two bishops were vocal in their opposition to slavery. Archbishop John Baptist Purcell of Cincinnati and Bishop Josue Moody Young of Erie called for an end to slavery. Catholics had just been freed from the many decades of the dreadful penal period laws, legislation that called for the execution or imprisonment of Catholic priests in many areas of the colonies, and the Church was not yet able to take a leading role in social or political issues. A series of confrontations, debates, and consultations concerning rights as defined by the new state constitutions had provided American Catholics with long overdue recognition as citizens and had ended the harsh anti-Catholic laws that had been in operation. Catholics, however, were still facing particularly menacing groups who singled out the Irish and opposed the general growth of the Church as a threat to America. In 1860 American Catholic theologians condemned slavery as unjust on moral grounds, following the lead of the pope and Vatican officials. Catholics did not have sufficient influence in social or legislative circles, however, and many in the American Church recommended a moderate approach to abolition, one that would not rupture the Union. (*See also* African-American Catholics; Civil War; American.)

Abortion

Abortion is the act of terminating the life of an unborn child by separating it from its mother's womb before it is capable of living outside of that womb. The state in which an unborn child can survive removal from the womb is called viability. Abortion can be spontaneous or indirect, induced or direct. Spontaneous abortion, also called miscarriage, is a natural physical process involving no guilt on the part of the parents. Indirect abortion is the result of medical procedures or an act performed for some other medical purpose and involves no guilt. Induced abortion, performed by various medical procedures, including live-birth abortion, is morally evil. Direct abortion, another term for induced abortion, is the deliberate taking of the life of a child. It is condemned on both moral and humanitarian grounds.

The Catholic position, as presented by Pope Paul VI in *Humanae Vitae* (1968), remains unchanged, despite the legalization of abortion in countries around the world. Pope Paul VI, in the *Declaration on Procured Abortion,* was quite specific: "Respect for human life is called for from the time that the process of generation begins, from the time that the ovum is fertilized, which is neither that of the father nor of the mother. It is rather the life of a new human being with its own growth. It would never be made human life if it were not human already."

Pope Blessed John Paul II was particularly active around the world in speaking out on abortion, birth control, and sterilization, perceiving their inevitable effect upon all people and the eroding of the value of all human life. Under his leadership, the Church had been, and remains today, ever vigilant in studying the latest trends in this area. The Pontifical Commission for the Authentic Interpretation of the Code of Canon Law extended the official definition of abortion to include the deliberate eradication of an immature fetus, a step approved by the pope on May 23, 1988.

The pope made the issue of abortion one of the central themes of his encyclicals *Veritatis Splendor* (1993) and *Evangelium Vitae* (1995). In the latter, the pope wrote: "The moral gravity of procured abortion is apparent in all its truth if we consider the specific elements involved. The one eliminated is a human being at the very beginning of life. No one more absolutely innocent could be imagined." He added, "In the case of an intrinsically unjust law, such as a law permitting abortion or euthanasia, it is . . . never licit to obey it, or to 'take part in a propaganda campaign in favor of such a law or vote for it.'"

Abortion was found in America at an early time, just as it was found in virtually every culture in the world, and it was considered a grave crime. Those who performed abortions or committed infanticide were liable to receive severe punishment, and abortion was viewed uniformly as a negative action that brought severe consequences for society as a whole. Various British colonies adopted laws drawn from English common law; such a legal approach made abortion prior to "quickening" (the capacity to feel movement) a misdemeanor, and after "quickening" a felony.

By the nineteenth century, the legal foundation for the outlawing of abortion was expressed in a British law of 1869, the Offenses Against the Persons Act, which imposed a felony upon anyone who performed an abortion as early as fertilization, as it was recognized that life begins at that point. In the United States at the same time, every state passed some kind of law against abortion.

The twentieth century proved a time of fertile growth for the culture of death that climaxed in the United States with the *Roe v. Wade* decision of 1973. The origins of the abortion movement in the United States can be traced to such figures as the nineteenth-century philosopher Thomas Malthus and Margaret Sanger, founder of Planned Parenthood, and to such ideologies as Nazism, which regularly practiced abortion as part of its program of genocide. Malthus proposed theories on population growth and economic stability that essentially mandated the extermination of excess children for the greater good of the wider human population. Margaret Sanger supported the policies of sterilization, abortion, and euthanasia found in Nazi Germany, and advocated contraception and abortion as a means of removing the "human weeds" and "genetically inferior races" from modern civilization.

After the founding of the Planned Parenthood Federation of America in 1916, support for legalized abortion — in conjunction with the promotion of promiscuity, contraception, and the sexual revolution advocated by Alfred Kinsey — grew steadily in the form of various radical organizations such as the National Association for the Repeal of Abortion Laws (NARAL) and the Population Council. Political lobbying by pro-abortion groups pursued a pattern of watering down legal restrictions on abortion in the late 1960s and early 1970s, so that by April 1970 one-fifth of the states had approved measures allowing abortion in various circumstances. Several states (New York, California, Hawaii, and Alaska) were even more aggressive in removing restrictions.

The long-term objective of the pro-abortion movement was to secure a Supreme Court decision in favor of abortion. The key case originated in Texas in March 1970 with *Roe v. Wade*. The woman at the heart of the case, Norma McCorvey ("Jane Roe"), challenged Texas's abortion law. McCorvey has since publicly disavowed her association with the case, declares that she was used by political opportunists who sought to advance the cause of abortion, and now works to overturn the original decision.

The case reached the U.S. Supreme Court (*Jane Roe v. Dallas District Attorney Henry Wade*), and on January 22, 1973, the Supreme Court rendered a decision that made abortion legal throughout the land. The vote was 7–2. The majority opinion was written by Justice Harry Blackmun, a Catholic, and in it the court declared that the Fourteenth Amendment guarantees a woman's "right of privacy," held that the fetus is not a person, and asserted that the decision to abort should be left up to a woman and her doctor. The decision denied "personhood" to the unborn, as an earlier Supreme Court had denied that status to black slaves, and regulated abortions in the states. One of the foundations for the decision was the 1965 case *Griswold v. Connecticut*, in which the Supreme Court had recognized a "right of privacy" that extends from the "penumbra" of assorted provisions of the Bill of Rights. The *Griswold* ruling recognized constitutional protections for birth control, and subsequently this right was extended in 1972's *Eisenstadt v. Baird*.

In the decades following the Supreme Court decision, the issue has remained bitterly divisive, socially and politically. Moreover, claims that legalizing abortions would make them rare have been utterly disproved. Approximately fifty million abortions have been performed since 1972. Original restrictions, including limitations on abortions in the second and third trimesters, were systematically set aside, and one out of every three children conceived in the United States since 1972 has been aborted, demonstrating that abortion is now used as merely one more form of contraception. The embrace of abortifacients such as RU-486 will only increase the number of abortions.

Recent years have seen efforts to restrict unfettered access to abortion, with particular attention paid to the gruesome procedure called partial-birth abortion, in which a live fetus is withdrawn almost completely out of the womb and the child has its brains extracted from its skull using a sharp

Roe v. Wade's Dissenting Opinions

Associate Justices Byron R. White and William H. Rehnquist wrote determined dissenting opinions in the case of *Roe v. Wade* in 1973. The following are excerpts from the opinions:

Justice Byron R. White

"I find nothing in the language or history of the Constitution to support the Court's judgment. . . . The Court simply fashions and announces a new constitutional right for pregnant mothers and, with scarcely any reason or authority for its action, invests that right with sufficient substance to override most existing state abortion statutes. The upshot is that the people and the legislatures of the 50 States are constitutionally disentitled to weigh the relative importance of the continued existence and development of the fetus, on the one hand, against a spectrum of possible impacts on the mother, on the other hand. As an exercise of raw judicial power, the Court perhaps has authority to do what it does today; but, in my view, its judgment is an improvident and extravagant exercise of the power of judicial review that the Constitution extends to this Court.

"The Court apparently values the convenience of the pregnant mother more than the continued existence and development of the life or potential life that she carries. Regardless of whether I might agree with that marshaling of values, I can in no event join the Court's judgment because I find no constitutional warrant for imposing such an order of priorities on the people and legislatures of the States. In a sensitive area such as this, involving as it does issues over which reasonable men may easily and heatedly differ, I cannot accept the Court's exercise of its clear power of choice by interposing a constitutional barrier to state efforts to protect human life and by investing mothers and doctors with the constitutionally protected right to exterminate it. This issue, for the most part, should be left with the people and to the political processes the people have devised to govern their affairs."

Justice William H. Rehnquist

"The Court's opinion decides that a State may impose virtually no restriction on the performance of abortions during the first trimester of pregnancy. . . . The Court uses her complaint against the Texas statute as a fulcrum for deciding that States may impose virtually no restrictions on medical abortions performed during the first trimester of pregnancy. In deciding such a hypothetical lawsuit, the Court departs from the long-standing admonition that it should never formulate a rule of constitutional law broader than is required by the precise facts to which it is to be applied. . . . The Court's sweeping invalidation of any restrictions on abortion during the first trimester is impossible to justify under that standard, and the conscious weighing of competing factors that the Court's opinion apparently substitutes for the established test is far more appropriate to a legislative judgment than to a judicial one.

"To reach its result the Court necessarily has had to find within the scope of the Fourteenth Amendment a right that was apparently completely unknown to the drafters of the amendment. As early as 1821 the first state law dealing directly with abortion was enacted by the Connecticut Legislature. Conn. Stat., Tit. 22, §§ 14, 16. By the time of the adoption of the Fourteenth Amendment in 1868, there were at least 36 laws enacted by state or territorial legislatures limiting abortion. While many States have amended or updated their laws, 21 of the laws on the books in 1868 remain in effect today. Indeed, the Texas statute struck down today was, as the majority notes, first enacted in 1857 and 'has remained substantially unchanged to the present time.'

"There apparently was no question concerning the validity of this provision or of any of the other state statutes when the Fourteenth Amendment was adopted. The only conclusion possible from this history is that the drafters did not intend to have the Fourteenth Amendment withdraw from the States the power to legislate with respect to this matter."

instrument and a vacuum. In the 1970s, Congress passed the Hyde Amendment, which barred federal funding for abortion, and abortions have been prohibited under various administrations in overseas military hospitals and the United States is restricted from assisting international family planning organizations that advocate abortions. Although the Supreme Court struck down various state efforts to restrict abortions, it has upheld restrictions on funding, including the Hyde Amendment.

On November 5, 2003, President George W. Bush signed into law the Partial-Birth Abortion Ban Act, climaxing years of legislative efforts to bring an end to the medical procedure he termed "an abhorrent practice." The U.S. Senate passed the bill by a 64–34 margin on October 21, 2003; three weeks earlier the House of Representatives passed the same measure on a 281–142 vote. The law was subsequently challenged in several jurisdictions as unconstitutional by Planned Parenthood, and it came as little surprise that on June 1, 2004, a federal judge in the Northern District of California declared the Partial-Birth Abortion Ban Act in violation of *Roe v. Wade*. Other legal challenges were pending in federal courts in New York and Nebraska. Cathy Cleaver Ruse, Esq., spokesperson for the United States Conference of Catholic Bishops' Secretariat for Pro-Life Activities, stated: "Once again a federal judge has declared that *Roe v. Wade* stands for the right to kill a child in the process of being born." She added, "The American Medical Association says this procedure is never medically necessary. . . . To say that it is a fundamental constitutional right makes a mockery of the Constitution."

The 2004 presidential election also raised significant questions regarding the issue of abortion and American politics. The candidacy of Senator John F. Kerry as the nominee of the Democratic Party led to an open debate about whether a Catholic politician who supports legalized abortion, as well as Catholic voters who vote for pro-choice candidates, should be permitted to receive Communion?

Various answers were provided by different bishops around the country, and a formal statement was finally issued by the bishops after a closed-door special assembly in Denver in June 2004. By a vote of 183–6, the bishops adopted a short statement

called *Catholics in Political Life*. Dated June 18, the statement reiterated the Church's doctrine that abortion is intrinsically evil and said that the bishops would tell Catholic public officials that "their acting consistently to support abortion on demand risks making them cooperators in evil in a public manner." Regarding the issue of denying Communion, the statement said: "Given the wide range of circumstances involved in arriving at a prudential judgment on a matter of this seriousness, we recognize that such decisions rest with the individual bishop in accord with the established canonical and pastoral principles. Bishops can legitimately make different judgments on the most prudent course of pastoral action. Nevertheless we all share an unequivocal commitment to protect human life and dignity . . . Respect for the Holy Eucharist . . . demands that it be received worthily."

On February 24, 2006, the South Dakota State Legislature passed a bill that was signed into law by Governor Mike Rounds declaring all abortions to be subject to a felony, including those for pregnancies resulting from rape or incest. The bill does not include exceptions for a woman's health, but it does include an exception for the life of the mother; doctors performing abortions for health or life reasons will not be prosecuted. The sponsors of the bill clearly hope that a court challenge of the law will bring the case to the Supreme Court. The pro-life movement was encouraged by the appointments of Chief Justice John G. Roberts and Associate Justice Samuel Alito.

The 2008 political season brought new focus on the issue of abortion because of the presence of Senator Joe Biden, a pro-abortion Catholic, on the Democratic ticket, with then-candidate Senator Barack Obama. The subsequent Obama administration was noted for the presence of Catholics who were publicly supportive of abortion.

The Catholic Church throughout the world has never stopped its protest and admonitions against abortions and the inevitable disrespect for life that has ensued. This has brought powerful forces against the Church, as the constant pro-life activities conducted by Catholics and their Protestant allies have challenged the modern feminist and liberal philosophies in vogue and have exposed the act of abortion, especially partial-birth terminations, as acts of evil, morally unjustified, and unacceptable.

An obvious shift in public opinion concerning abortion has been slow but steady, as more and more Americans view the procedure with repugnance and seek a better legal framework for such medical procedures. State legislatures are beginning to curb abortionists with new restrictions, some of which have been struck down in the courts, particularly those that involve minors and the lack of parental notification, and more and more groups are supporting the annual protest marches and related legislative proposals concerning the procedure.

Acadians

The Acadians were the people who settled on the present peninsula of Nova Scotia and in the colony of Maine, where they practiced the Catholic faith and maintained their own ethnic traditions. The French established the first Acadian colony on the Bay of Fundy in 1610. Port Royale, Grand Pré, and Beaubassin were also settled, and the Acadians emerged as a solid Catholic force in that area of the New World. King Henri IV of France had granted the territory, called *La Cadie,* to Sieur de Monts on November 8, 1603, and he sold it to the Marquise de Guercheville, who believed the region extended far beyond its actual borders.

Monts and Samuel de Champlain went to Acadia to investigate the territories provided in the grant, actually landing on the coast of Maine, and began a settlement on an island they named Sainte-Croix. They also entered Port Royal, now Annapolis. Soon after, the Jesuit missionaries Fathers Pierre Baird and Enemond Masse entered the area and established the colony of St. Sauveur on the modern site of Bar Harbor, Maine, hoping to use the site as an outpost for further missionary endeavors. In 1610 the Acadian settlements on the Bay of Fundy, and Port Royal, Grand Pré, and Beaubassin were solidified and then expanded. In 1613 however, the pirate Argal, of the British colony of Virginia, attacked St. Sauveur and took the Jesuit priests as prisoners. The mission was destroyed, and all trace of the faith was erased. The British had temporary ownership of the region because of a European treaty then in effect, and Sir William Alexander occupied Acadia and called it

Nova Scotia. Because of their allegiance to France and their loyalty to the Holy See, the Acadians endured terrible ordeals at the hands of the British authorities.

In 1632 France once again owned Acadia because of political conditions in Europe, and Isaac de Razilly was installed as the French governor, bringing stability and peace to the region. At his death in 1636, his lieutenants fought one another for control of the colony, inspiring the British to invade once again because of the obvious signs of disarray and weakness. Acadia changed hands officially in 1667 through the Treaty of Breda, and the British had to withdraw, leaving France once again the master of the colony.

By 1687 there were 800 residents in Acadia, and in 1747 the population had risen to 12,500. Acadians suffered constant assaults by the British in 1710 and were invaded in 1713. The political contests conducted in Europe impacted on American regions once again, making the Acadians suspect because they maintained their Catholic religion and their political neutrality. Wanting to migrate to British-controlled Canadian areas, an opportunity available because of a ruling made by Queen Anne, the Acadians tried to leave their homes, but the local authorities would not honor the queen's pledge. A series of governors abused the local Acadians because of the constant French threats in the region and because the Acadians remained neutral in all political and military contests between England and France. In 1730 a "qualified oath" of allegiance to the British crown was attempted so that the Acadians could maintain their neutrality and their Catholicism, but the local British authorities were not satisfied.

In 1755 Governor Charles Lawrence gave orders to deport the Acadians to southern regions so that British supporters could be placed in this critical political area. It was thought that the Acadians could be assimilated into the populations and "cured" of their Catholic leanings. An estimated nine thousand or more Acadian men, women, and children were put on ships and sent into exile. Some died on the way to the ships, and others died during the voyages. Their farms, homes, cattle, and personal possessions were confiscated, and the British authorities deliberately broke up Acadian families. Children were taken from their parents and put ashore alone, and the elderly were placed in anti-Catholic colonies.

The colony of Virginia, displaying a resolute anti-Catholicism, refused to accept any of the resettled Acadians, and other colonies complained about having to absorb the refugees. As a result, some Acadians were taken to England, where they were held in shocking conditions as prisoners of war until 1763. In South Carolina and Georgia, Acadians were made indentured servants. Other colonies accepted them but then forced them out of their holdings because of their faithfulness to Catholicism. Some Acadians managed to return home in due course, and a good many went to Louisiana. They reached Louisiana by 1758, starting the communities of Les Attakapas on the Bayou Teche, Poste de Opelousas south of Baton Rouge, and another settlement on Bayou Lafourche. Other communities followed, and the "Cajun" traditions remain evident in the region today. The poem "Evangeline," written by Henry Wadsworth Longfellow, depicts the suffering of the Acadians.

Politically, the forced migration of Acadians and the sufferings inflicted upon them were damaging to the British government in America. The colonists, having little love for Catholicism, still watched the injustice and cruelty and began to recognize the fact that others would become victims of British manipulations in time if Americans did not band together and work to secure their own destinies in the New World. (See also Louisiana.)

African-American Catholics

Brought into the New World as slaves, African-American Catholics responded to events and individuals in their eras with faith and a steadfastness that enabled them to form cohesive communities in bondage or as freed individuals. Africans were part of America as early as 1565, as parish records in St. Augustine, Florida, attest. The Spanish had founded St. Augustine as a Catholic domain and had assumed a vast mission apostolate among the tribes in Florida and Georgia. Instruction in the faith was readily available to everyone in the region.

The arrival of English colonists in the northern areas on the Atlantic coast of America brought European political realities into play, however, and the Spanish missions were endangered. The Spanish welcomed slaves from English colonies, and these individuals were afforded a measure of freedom and safety. The Spanish had adopted a code, *Las Siete Partidas*, that was based on old Roman law. As a result of this enlightened treatment, untold numbers of such slaves made their way out of English territories. In turn, African-Americans formed militias and served as forces of protection for the missions and settlements. In education, there was no discrimination, as school records indicate that black youths were taught beside Spanish youths in school classrooms. Eventually, however, separate records were maintained for black families in the missions.

The assaults on Spanish territories that were conducted by the English of Georgia and other colonies led to the withdrawal of the Spanish in 1763, actually the result of the Seven Years' War. In the melees that resulted, many blacks were killed or taken to British colonies to be sold again as slaves. Despite an obvious resistance on the part of many colonists in America, slaves were in use throughout the region and were taken to the interior settlements when pioneering individuals or groups developed communities in uncharted geographical regions. Records from the great Missions of Cahokia and Kaskaskia, as well as parish logs, list the baptisms of the accompanying slaves.

A new class of African-Americans emerged around the time of the Revolutionary War. These were "freedmen," slaves who had gained their liberty either by manumission or by their own labors. One of the first settlers in the area of present-day Chicago, Illinois, was just such a freedman, Jean Baptiste Pointe du Sable. He had married into the Potawatomi tribe and was a prosperous trader, well respected by the growing community. The children of freedmen were called "free people of color," and they worked together to form their own communities and their own destinies.

The Gulf coastal area had a large settlement of free people of color, who integrated French culture into their lives and developed uniquely. The African-Americans in Maryland were also successful as free people of color, joined in time by Haitian refugees fleeing the chaos and violence of that Caribbean island.

In New York, a remarkable individual, Venerable Pierre Toussaint, epitomized the faith and the energies of the free people of color throughout the young nation. He had been born in St. Domingue (Haiti) in 1766 and was a slave of Jean Bérard. Venerable Pierre was allowed the freedom of his owner's library and learned to read and speak French fluently. He accompanied the Bérard family when it fled to New York in 1787 to escape the violence of the revolution in Haiti. Jean Bérard returned to Haiti the following year to try to regain his lands, and he died there. His wife, Mary Elizabeth, was left penniless and alone in a new land. Venerable Pierre, however, had already learned the hairdressing profession and had a salon that provided funds for him and the widow. Venerable Pierre supported the widow until she remarried, and she and her new husband freed him on July 2, 1807, just weeks before she died. He continued to aid slaves and bought his own sister and others out of bondage, all the while displaying heroic faith.

African-American Catholics in this and other eras of the nation's history were extremely devout and active. They organized confraternities and lay organizations, even as the debate about slavery deepened in the United States. Catholics had to face their own involvement in slavery, and for many this was a painful experience. Bishops and religious orders owned slaves, and they depended upon their labors throughout their missions. Some viewed slavery as a political rather than a moral issue, while others noted that Pope Gregory XVI had written an apostolic letter condemning not only the slave trade but the institution itself. Some Southern bishops, hoping to make the Church appear more in tune with their contemporaries, defended slavery on several grounds. The Northern bishops sided with the abolitionists, and two of them, Archbishop John Baptist Purcell of Cincinnati and Bishop Josue Moody Young of Erie, called for an end to slavery.

When the Civil War began, African-American Catholics in the South enlisted in Union regiments that were being formed. These units were a scandal to the inhabitants of New Orleans and other Southern cities, and the soldiers were outcasts, even in death. Father Claude Pascal Maistre, seeing the need for priestly work among the regiments, labored for the black population and was suspended by Archbishop John M. Odin.

At the Baltimore Council of 1866, following the Civil War, the American bishops demonstrated little eagerness to be involved in new apostolates for African-Americans. Archbishop Martin J. Spalding of Baltimore tried to propose a national Catholic apostolate to the blacks, but the idea met with fierce opposition and was dropped. A partial solution to the lack of such an apostolate came in 1871, when the Mill Hill Missionaries of England arrived in Baltimore. The American branch of the Mill Hill Congregation separated from the English foundation and became the Society of St. Joseph of the Sacred Heart. These religious priests conducted missions and ministries among African-Americans. In 1906 the Society of the Divine Word arrived in the United States from Germany and began a successful black apostolate. St. Katharine Drexel used part of her vast fortune to build educational and religious facilities for African-Americans, founding the Sisters of the Blessed Sacrament.

Elizabeth Lange (d. 1882), a former Haitian, and Henriette DeLille (d. 1862), the daughter of a former slave, both started religious communities for African-American Catholic women. The Oblate Sisters of Providence, founded by Lange and Sulpician Father James Hector Nicholas Joubert, served Baltimore. One of the original members of this community, Theresa Duchemin, was part of the founding of the Sisters, Servants of the Immaculate Heart of Mary (I.H.M.) in Monroe, Michigan. The Sisters of the Holy Family was started by DeLille, whose cause for canonization has been opened. This congregation served in New Orleans. In Savannah, Georgia, Mother Theodore Williams started a third black religious community of women, moving to Harlem, New York, where the congregation still serves as the Franciscan Handmaids of Mary.

Priestly vocations rose slowly at the same time, as seminaries for African-Americans were part of the Divine Word apostolate. Some African-American priests held positions of prominence in their own eras. The second bishop of Portland, Maine, for example, was the son of an Irish slaveholder and a slave. James Augustine Healy was the first African-American bishop in the nation. His brothers and sisters entered the religious life and the priesthood.

African-American laypeople managed to stay active and vital throughout the various eras as well, despite setbacks and a lack of cohesive planning by American Church officials. In 1889 the first Black Catholic Congress was held in Washington, D.C., and other congresses followed. The laypeople participating called upon the Church to aid the African-American community, and the Holy See offered encouragement for such leadership. The congresses did not last, however, replaced in time by the Federated Colored Catholics, an organization started by Thomas W. Turner in 1924.

In 1968 the National Black Catholic Clergy Caucus was formed, followed by the National Black Sisters' Conference and the National Black Seminarians' Association. Two years later the National Office of Black Catholics was opened, replaced in 1988 by the Secretariat for African-American Catholics for the National Conference of Catholic Bishops. In 1979 the American bishops had issued a pastoral letter, "Brothers and Sisters to Us," that defined racism as a sin. In 1984 the black bishops of America wrote "What We Have Seen and Heard," calling upon African-American Catholics to evangelize themselves and the Church. In 1992 the Black Catholic Congresses were renewed, and these congresses are still promoting the African-American Catholic cause.

There are presently approximately 2.3 million African-American Catholics in the United States. They are served by 1,300 parishes and 75 African-American pastors. There are approximately 250 African-American priests, 300 African-American sisters, and 380 African-American deacons.

Since the episcopal ordination of Bishop Healy, there have been many African-American bishops. Those in the past have included: Joseph A. Francis, S.V.D. (1923–1997), Eugene A. Marino, S.S.J. (1934–2000), Raymond Rodly Caeser, S.V.D. (1932–1987), James Lyke, O.F.M. (1939–1992), Carl A. Fisher, S.S.J. (1945–1993), Emerson J. Moore (1938–1995), and Harold R. Perry, S.V.D. (1916–1991).

There were sixteen (ten active) black bishops as of September 1, 2011. Six were heads of dioceses: Archbishop Wilton D. Gregory (Atlanta, president of the USCCB, 2000–2004), and Bishops Curtis J. Guillory, S.V.D. (Beaumont), George V. Murry, S.J. (Youngstown), John H. Ricard, S.S.J. (Pensacola-Tallahassee), Edward K. Braxton (Belleville), and J. Terry Steib, S.V.D. (Memphis). Four were auxiliary

bishops: Guy A. Sansaricq (Brooklyn), Shelton J. Fabre (New Orleans), Joseph N. Perry (Chicago), and Martin D. Holley (Washington). Elliott G. Thomas, of St. Thomas, Virgin Islands (ret., June 30, 1999), Joseph L. Howze of Biloxi (ret., May 15, 2001), Moses Anderson, S.S.E., of Detroit (ret., October 24, 2003), Leonard J. Olivier, S.V.D., of Washington (ret., May 18, 2004), and Dominic Carmon, S.V.D., of New Orleans (ret., Dec. 13, 2006), are retired. Bishop Gordon D. Bennett was named bishop of Mandeville on July 6, 2004; he retired on August 8, 2006.

Alabama

The twenty-second state of the Union is called the Heart of Dixie and is located in the southern part of the nation, bordered on the north by Tennessee, on the east by Georgia, on the south by Florida, and on the west by Mississippi. The state is composed of five natural land divisions: the Appalachian Valley, the Interior Low, Cumberland, the Piedmont Plateaus, and the East Gulf Coast. Alabama entered the Union on December 4, 1819. The Native American tribes of the Alibamu, Cherokee, Chickasaw, Choctaw, and Creeks were the original inhabitants of the Alabama area.

The Catholic history of Alabama begins with the first expeditions of the Spanish, who came into contact with native populations as they explored the region. The first identified European in the state was Alonso Alvarez de Pineda, who sailed into Mobile Bay in 1512. In 1540 Hernando de Soto arrived and conducted an expedition into the interior of Alabama with a large force of men. He was accompanied by Catholic priests. On October 18 of that year, de Soto fought the local Native American tribes at Mauvila, considered by many to be the bloodiest Indian battle ever conducted on the continent.

Twenty years later, other Spaniards arrived and started a colony at Nanipacna, possibly in Wilcox County, but the settlement did not survive long because of local native hostilities. In 1682 René-Robert Chevalier, Sieur de La Salle, claimed the area for the French, calling it Louisiana, and in 1699, Pierre Le Moyne, Sieur d'Iberville, and Jean-Baptiste Le Moyne, Sieur de Bienville, settled at Old Biloxi, near modern Ocean Springs, Mississippi. The Jesuit priests Father Anastase Douay and Father Antoine Davion were with this French expedition and conducted services for their companions.

In January 1702 the settlement was moved from Old Biloxi to 27-Mile Bluff on the Mobile River, where it was renamed Fort Louis de la Mobile. Father Henri Rolleaux de los Vente was the first pastor. The first Catholic Church was erected soon after, served by Jesuits, Capuchin Franciscans, and Carmelites, and three years later, French farmers were on Dauphin Island.

In 1711 Fort Louis was moved to the present site of Mobile, and another outpost, Fort Toulouse, was established at the confluence of the Coosa and Tallapoosa Rivers. The first slaves were brought into Mobile ten years later to serve the settlement. A third site occupied was Fort Tombeckbé, erected in 1736 on the Tombigbee River. The French remained in the area until February 18, 1763, when, as a result of the European Seven Years' War, France ceded the territory to the British.

In 1775 however, Spanish colonists reentered Alabama, encouraged by the Revolutionary War, but they gave up their settlements eventually. In 1798 Alabama became part of the Mississippi Territory, enacted by Congress on April 7. General Andrew Jackson defeated the Creeks in the area in 1814, in order to pacify the Native Americans who resented losing their traditional homelands.

Three years later, Alabama became a separate United States territory by act of Congress and entered the Union as the twenty-second state. In 1825 Father Michael Portier was made vicar apostolic of Alabama and the Floridas, and four years later, on May 15, 1829, the Diocese of Mobile was erected with Bishop Portier having episcopal jurisdiction.

The following year, Spring Hill College opened in Mobile and was entrusted to the Jesuits in 1847. The political upheavals of the abolition question, however, led to the Civil War, and in 1861 Alabama seceded from the Union, with the city of Montgomery becoming the "Cradle of the Confederacy." In 1864 the Battle of Mobile Bay included the famous proclamation of Admiral David Glasgow Farragut, who ordered, "Damn the torpedoes, full steam ahead."

The Reconstruction period that followed the war affected many in Alabama as "carpetbaggers," opportunists from the North, allied with corrupt Southern politicians and punished the people of the state for their efforts during the war. In 1881 Booker T. Washington, the black educator, founded Tuskegee Institute. Alabama's manufacturing prospered as iron, steel, and textile industries developed, but the state's agricultural sectors suffered. Bishop Jeremiah O'Sullivan of Mobile opened St. Bernard Abbey and College at Cullman in 1892.

During World War I, Mobile became a shipbuilding center, which aided the local economy. The Great Depression following the war brought tragic consequences to the people, as it affected communities nationwide. In the 1930s, however, the Tennessee Valley Authority revitalized the area slowly. World War II again brought about shipbuilding and increased demands for steel products, and Huntsville emerged as a modern technology center. The first successful space satellite, the Explorer, was developed at Redstone Arsenal.

In 1954 the Diocese of Mobile was redesignated as the Diocese of Mobile-Birmingham. Birmingham became a center of protest in 1963, as civil rights groups united against segregation. The University of Alabama was integrated in 1963 as Governor George C. Wallace protested and President John F. Kennedy called out the National Guard to enforce the integration. Governor Wallace also tried to stop integration in Birmingham and Tuskegee. Catholic parochial schools in Alabama were integrated in 1964. On June 22, 1969, the Diocese of Mobile was redesignated once again, becoming an archdiocese on November 16, 1980, with Archbishop Oscar H. Lipscomb its first shepherd. In 2011 there were 157,000 Catholics, served by 244 priests, 233 women religious, and 130 parishes.

Alaska

The largest state in the Union, and called the Last Frontier, Alaska is located in the northwestern part of North America. Alaska is bounded on the north by the Arctic Ocean, on the east by the Yukon and British Columbia, and on the south by the Pacific Ocean, the Bering Sea, and the Arctic Ocean. There are five geographical divisions in the state: the Arctic Slope in the north, the Central Uplands, the Alaska Range, the Pacific Mountains, and the Aleutian Islands. Mount McKinley, rising over 20,300 feet, is the highest peak in North America. The original inhabitants of the state were the Aleuts, Eskimos, Athapaskan, Haida, Tlingit, and Tsimishian Indian tribes.

The Catholic history of Alaska was late in starting because of the remoteness of the area and the political realities in historical eras. In 1728 and in 1741 Captain Vitus Bering, a Danish navigator in the employ of the Russian government, visited Alaska, claiming the territory for the tsars. Other explorers from England, France, and Spain were also in the area. On May 13, 1779, Father Juan Riobo, a Spanish Franciscan, celebrated a Mass at Porto Santa Cruz on lower Bucareli Bay. In 1785 there were Russian settlements at Three Saints Bay. Catholic missionaries arrived in the region, but Russian Orthodox missions were already in operation. In 1799 the Russian-American Company conducted fur trade at Sitka, which was the center of Russian activities. The United States received trade rights in 1824.

Bishop Modeste Demers was appointed administrator and first bishop of Vancouver Island (Victoria) in 1847. Soon after, Oblate Father Jean Seguin was at Fort Yukon. In 1870 another Oblate, Father Emile Petitot, was also serving the needs of Catholics at the fort. Oblate Bishop Isidore Clut and Father Auguste Lecarré were in Yukon and at St. Michael's in 1872 and 1873. Father Joseph Mandart served in the state's Panhandle area.

Alaska had become an American asset while these first Catholic missionaries were opening various territories to the faith. In 1867 Secretary of State William H. Seward purchased Alaska from the Russians for $7,200,000. In 1873 Bishop Charles J. Seghers of Vancouver Island, honored as the "Apostle of Alaska," made the first of five trips to Alaska to open missions and to strengthen the ones in operation. Bishop Seghers had been given jurisdiction over the area in 1868. Father Joseph Mandart accompanied him on one of these trips, and they stayed in Nulato for a year. In 1879 Bishop Seghers founded a mission at Sitka, and visited Kodiak and Unalaska, leaving Father William Heynen at the mission as pastor. He also founded a

mission at Wrangall. Father John Althoff became a resident missionary in 1879.

Having received the rank of archbishop, Seghers took Jesuit Fathers Paschal Tosi and Aloysius Robaut on another mission tour in 1886. Leaving the Jesuits established at a site on the Yukon River, Archbishop Seghers started a trip to Nulato with a guide, Francis Fuller, who was apparently suffering a mental collapse. The guide killed the archbishop on the trail on November 27. Father Tosi, hearing of the murder, went to the Jesuit superior, Father Joseph M. Cataldo, asking him for permission to assume the Alaskan missions. Father Tosi also went to Rome to discuss the matter with Pope Leo XIII, who encouraged him in the apostolate. In 1894 Alaska became a Prefecture Apostolic, with Father Tosi as administrator and Jesuit superior.

Two years later the Gold Rush started in the Klondike, bringing new settlers, and in 1912 Alaska became a U.S. Territory. Alaska was made a vicariate apostolic in 1916, administered by Bishop Joseph R. Crimont, another Jesuit. By 1923 the Alaska Railroad was in operation, and in 1942 the Alaska Highway was completed. During World War II, the military forces of Japan briefly occupied a part of Alaska.

The Diocese of Juneau was erected in 1951, with Bishop Dermot O'Flanagan establishing the administrative agencies and protocols. Alaska became the forty-ninth state in 1959. In 1962 the

Mission of Alaska, Yukon

Diocese of Fairbanks was erected, headed by Bishop Francis Gleeson. The Archdiocese of Anchorage was established on February 9, 1966. In 2011 there were 50,000 Catholics, served by 64 priests and 78 parishes.

Albany, Diocese of

Established on April 23, 1847, by Pope Blessed Pius IX, the Diocese of Albany serves counties in eastern New York. Albany is the capital of the state of New York and a port of entry and eastern terminal of the Canal System. The French reportedly had a small fort on the island of Westerlo by 1540, visited by Henry Hudson in 1609. Fort Nassau was established on the island by the United Netherlands Company in 1614, and Walloon families erected Fort Orange on the site of present-day Albany in 1624. The settlement changed ownership and names until 1664, when the British took control and named it Albany in honor of the future James II of England, then Duke of Albany. The Diocese of Albany is a suffragan see of the Archdiocese of New York.

The Catholic history of Albany dates to 1642, when Cardinal Richelieu of France was assigning various religious orders to the missions and the Jesuits accepted the Canadian apostolate. By August of that year, expansive missionary efforts were underway, and the Jesuit martyrs St. Isaac Jogues and St. René Goupil were captured by the Mohawk Indians, along with a company of valiant Christian Indians, and taken to Ossernenon (Auriesville). St. René was slain, as were the Christian Indians, and St. Isaac was tortured hideously before being released. His ordeals did not deter him from his missions, however, and he returned to Ossernenon to negotiate a treaty. The Mohawks were no longer interested in such dealings with the whites and took the priest captive. He was martyred there on October 18, 1646, with St. Jean de Lalande.

Other Jesuits labored in the area despite the threats, including Jesuit Fathers Joseph Poncet, Simon Le Moyne, John Pierron, Francis Boniface, and Jacques de Lamberville. Father de Lamberville baptized St. Kateri Tekakwitha on Easter Sunday 1676, at the site of the martyrdom of the earlier missionaries. The Jesuit missions flourished for a time, but then were halted abruptly by command of the English.

The term of British Governor Thomas Dongan, from 1682 to 1686, however, provided Catholics with renewed opportunities, as he was a Catholic and allowed the priests to carry on their ministries. He even brought Jesuits with him when he arrived in the colony: Fathers Thomas Harding, Henry Harrison, and Charles Gage, as well as two lay brothers of the Society. The Calvinists in the colony started an armed rebellion against Catholic participation, and Dongan was replaced, having to flee for his life. Catholic priests were once again expelled from the area.

The Catholic faith continued to prosper, however, despite adversities, as daring missionaries served the laypeople by moving from place to place in disguises. The young colonies were also prospering and entertaining the first desires for freedom. In 1754 Albany hosted Benjamin Franklin's "Plan of Union," a conference that led to the Congress of 1765 and to the Continental Congress of 1774, and ultimately to the Revolutionary War.

In 1790 Jesuit Father John Carroll was given authority over the Catholic Church in the newly independent United States. Bishop Carroll directed Albany's affairs as he directed the day-to-day Catholic business for the entire nation from Baltimore. Seven years later, St. Mary's Church was erected in Albany, serving as the only Catholic Church between St. Peter's in New York City and the newly built parish in Detroit.

In 1808 New York City was established as a diocese, and Albany's faithful saw the completion of new parishes: St. Peter's in Troy in 1827; St. John the Baptist in Schnectady and St. Mary's in Hudson Falls in 1830; as well as St. Mary's in Amsterdam in 1838. In 1847 the Diocese of Albany was established, and Bishop John McCloskey (later to serve as America's first cardinal) was transferred to Albany on May 21 of that year, having served as coadjutor bishop of New York. He began establishing agencies and ministries for diocesan administration and laid the cornerstone for the Cathedral of the Immaculate Conception on July 2, 1848. Bishop McCloskey also built French and German parishes, and increased the numbers of religious institutions and priests. He was promoted to the

Archdiocese of New York on May 6, 1864, and was made a cardinal in 1875.

During this period, the diocese witnessed a considerable increase in immigrants of Irish, German, French, Italian, Polish, Lithuanian, Slovak, and Ukrainian descent, prompting the need for additional pastoral outreach to the new arrivals. The Religious of the Sacred Heart, the Sisters of Mercy, and the Sisters of St. Joseph of Carondelet arrived to aid the educational system, and the Christian Brothers conducted their ministry. The Daughters of Charity, who directed an orphanage for girls in Albany and a hospital, also responded to the needs of the area. The Society of Jesus, the Augustinians, and the Franciscans of the Order of Minor Conventual also answered the call to aid the growing Catholic population.

On October 15, 1865, Bishop John J. Conroy, the second bishop of the diocese, was consecrated for the episcopacy and began his administration in Albany. Over the years he added twenty new parishes to the diocese to accommodate its growing needs. Bishop Conroy had been the pastor of St. Joseph's parish in Albany and had aided in the founding of St. Peter's Hospital, an orphanage and industrial school, and homes for the aged. He retired on October 16, 1877.

His successor, Bishop Francis McNierny, who had served as coadjutor to Bishop Conroy since 1871, acceded to the see on October 16, 1877. He opened Polish and Italian churches and completed the imposing Cathedral of the Immaculate Conception. Bishop McNierny also invited religious communities into the diocese and established apostolates for the immigrants arriving in the area. He died on January 2, 1894.

The fourth bishop of the diocese was Thomas M. A. Burke, who was consecrated on July 1, 1894. He opened fifteen new parishes, including one in the Maronite rite, and established a diocesan school system. Bishop Burke also faced increased numbers of immigrants and expanding demands on the Church's services. The new arrivals in Albany at that time were from Southern and Eastern Europe, and Bishop Burke labored to provide them with spiritual care. He died on January 20, 1915.

The first wartime bishop of the diocese was Thomas F. Cusack, who had been an auxiliary bishop of the Archdiocese of New York since 1904. He was transferred to Albany on July 5, 1915. There he encouraged the diocesan priests to become military chaplains, placed the diocesan facilities at the disposal of the federal government, and founded the Catholic Women's Service League. He died on July 12, 1918.

Bishop Edmund F. Gibbons, the sixth bishop of the diocese, was consecrated on March 25, 1919, and conducted a vast expansion program to aid parishes and schools. Bishop Gibbons instituted a "Mission Aid" program, a collection held annually, and invited religious congregations to Albany to staff the expanded schools. Mater Christi Seminary was opened, and a diocesan newspaper was founded. The bishop's long tenure included the grim eras of the Great Depression and World War II. Bishop Gibbons retired on November 10, 1954. When he died in 1964, he was the oldest bishop in the United States.

Bishop William A. Scully, the seventh bishop, was appointed coadjutor to Bishop Gibbons in 1945 and acceded to the see on November 10, 1954. He handled the needs posed by the increase in immigrants into the diocese and expanded agencies and facilities to maintain diocesan services in an era of growth. Bishop Scully died on January 5, 1969.

Bishop Edwin B. Broderick, the eighth bishop, was a former auxiliary bishop of the Archdiocese of New York. He was transferred to Albany on March 19, 1969, and there continued the expansion programs of his predecessor until 1976, when he resigned on June 2 to become the executive director of Catholic Relief Services.

Bishop Howard J. Hubbard, the ninth bishop, was appointed to the diocese on February 1, 1977, and installed on March 27. Throughout his long tenure, Bishop Hubbard has remained faithful to the two pastoral letters he issued soon after his arrival, promising collaboration, collegiality, and shared responsibility. He has promoted the laity into positions of leadership in parishes and diocesan departments. He has also promoted ecumenical dialogue, including a very fruitful relationship with the Albany Episcopal Diocese and the local Jewish community. In 2011 there were 334,000 Catholics in the diocese, served by 285 priests, more than 650 women religious, and 129 parishes.

Alemany, Joseph Sadoc (July 13, 1814–April 14, 1888)

The first archbishop of San Francisco from 1853 to 1884, Joseph Sadoc Alemany was a Dominican missionary to America who was superbly educated and a devoted admirer of the ideals of the United States. He was born in Vich, Spain, and entered the Dominicans at an early age, being ordained at Viterbo, Italy, in March 1837. Father Alemany was assigned as a missionary soon after his ordination and spent a decade serving Catholic communities in Ohio, Tennessee, and Kentucky in the Dominican outposts of the faith in those regions.

He learned to converse easily in English and developed a profound affection for the people and the democratic vision of the United States while working in the various parish areas. He was also a man of deep humility and simplicity, and was quite able to deal with Americans from all walks of life and all faiths. These attributes led to his appointment as the bishop of Monterey, California.

Bishop Alemany was consecrated in Rome on June 30, 1850. Three years later he was appointed archbishop of San Francisco, taking that see on July 29, 1853. Archbishop Alemany became an American citizen, not only because he was stationed in the United States for such a long period, but also because he had been drawn to this country by its democratic traditions, especially those of human freedom.

In his era, the Mexican government, still in possession of California, secularized the missions of that territory and ousted the Franciscans who had served as pioneers of the region, leaving behind them a royal road of missions and parishes all forcibly abandoned. Archbishop Alemany was astonished by the harshness of the Mexicans and realized that the needs of the Catholic people of California, both in the white and in the native populations, demanded action. He secured priests and nuns to serve the California population by inviting congregations and orders to enter the archdiocese.

His problems were aggravated by the Gold Rush, which had begun a few years before he took the see. Thousands of people, lured by the prospect of finding gold in the California hills, arrived in the region, stretching the resources of the archdiocese and local government agencies. There were only twenty-one missions in the entire California area at the time, and fewer than a dozen priests were present to minister to the thousands who sought aid and spiritual comfort. The archbishop also was forced to defend Church properties from trespassers and squatters, as hundreds of displaced families, oblivious to the history of the Catholic missions and the unique status of Church properties, moved into missions and claimed them as their own.

The Mexican government added to his difficulties by withholding payment of the Pious Fund of the Californias, a benefice instituted in Mexico in earlier decades to support Catholic efforts. Archbishop Alemany, in desperation, went to court to obtain the funds. With the assistance of the State Department of the United States, the archbishop forced Mexico to pay the amounts owed as well as the interest on all monies that had been withheld. He also set in motion the decision made at the International Board of Arbitration in the Hague in 1902 that Mexico was liable for payments to the Church in California.

Archbishop Alemany worked tirelessly until he was almost seventy. He then asked for and received a coadjutor, Archbishop P. W. Riordan. He traveled all the way to Ogden, Utah, to meet his coadjutor and to escort him to San Francisco so that the new prelate would feel welcomed and would have an introduction to the unique conditions in the archdiocese. In December 1884, Archbishop Alemany resigned from the see and was made titular archbishop of Pelusium. He set sail for Spain soon after, wanting to see his homeland again. During his many decades of service, Archbishop Alemany aided in the processes by which California was divided into three dioceses, serving some 300,000 Catholics and operating charitable and educational institutions. He died in Spain. (*See also* Pious Fund of the Californias; San Francisco, Archdiocese of.)

Alexandria, Diocese of

Established as the Diocese of Natchitoches by Pope Blessed Pius IX on July 29, 1853, this episcopal jurisdiction was transferred to Alexandria, Louisiana, on August 6, 1910. The diocese was designated as the Diocese of Alexandria-Shreveport in 1977 and redesignated as the Diocese of Alexandria in 1986, when Shreveport was made a diocese. The

Diocese of Alexandria serves northern counties of Louisiana and is a suffragan see of the Archdiocese of New Orleans.

Part of the vast Louisiana missions, Alexandria was visited by the expedition of Hernando de Soto in 1541 and then by the French expedition of René-Robert Chevalier, Sieur de La Salle, in 1682. The Franciscan Recollect, Father Zenobius Membré, later martyred, was in the expeditionary force and started missionary work in the area. In 1699 Pierre Le Moyne, Sieur d'Iberville, and Jean-Baptiste Le Moyne, Sieur de Bienville, were opening French settlements in the region. French priests from the Québec Seminary of the Foreign Missions entered the region also. Father François Jolliet de Montigny founded a chapel as he labored in the area, visiting Native Americans. The missionary priest Father Jean-François Buisson de Saint-Cosmé served in the region and was killed in 1706 by hostile Native Americans in the area.

The Venerable Antonio Margil de Jesús, a Spanish Franciscan pioneer in Louisiana and Texas, was serving the faithful in Sabine Parish in 1717. He founded San Miguel de Aguayo Mission, the first such site in northern Louisiana. Another chapel was erected at Presidio Nuestra Senora del Pilar on the site of modern Rabeline. Venerable Antonio Margil also founded St. Jean Baptiste in Natchitoches in 1714.

The Jesuits who had served faithfully in the Louisiana missions were expelled in 1763. In 1764 Capuchin Franciscan Father Stanislaus established the chapel of St. Luis de Appalaches in Pineville, Louisiana. New Orleans was established as a diocese in 1793, followed by the opening of Our Lady of Mount Carmel in Avoyelles. In 1800 Father Luis de Quintanilla, another Spanish Capuchin Franciscan, founded a chapel in Miro (Monroe).

The First Plenary Council of Baltimore, meeting in 1852, took note of the growing numbers of devout Catholics in Louisiana and recommended that another diocese be established in the area. Pope Pius IX thus erected the Diocese of Natchitoches, naming Augustus M. Martin as the first bishop of the diocese. When he arrived in the new diocese he found that he had jurisdiction over three-fifths of the state with only five priests, six parish churches, one school, and twenty thousand Catholics. Bishop Martin recruited priests and invited religious into the diocese and led the faithful during the terrible period of the Civil War and through outbreaks of yellow fever. One such epidemic claimed five of his priests in 1873. He also attended the First Vatican Council with Archbishop John M. Odin and was the author of interesting historical documents. Bishop Martin died on September 29, 1875.

The second bishop of Natchitoches, Bishop Francis Xavier Leray, was consecrated on April 22, 1877. Two years later he was appointed coadjutor bishop of New Orleans but remained the administrator of Natchitoches until 1883. He aided the Church in the recovery period and restored facilities and services. Although French-born, Bishop Leray promoted the use of English in the diocese.

Bishop Leray was promoted to the see of New Orleans in 1883. Two years later, Bishop Anthony Durier became the third bishop of Natchitoches; he was consecrated for the episcopacy on March 19, 1885. He expanded diocesan parishes and facilities and coped with the political and social tensions of that era of Reconstruction. Of particular note was his first pastoral letter, in which he ordered the creation of a Catholic school adjacent to every Catholic church in the diocese. Bishop Durier died on February 28, 1904.

Bishop Cornelius Van de Ven, who was consecrated for Natchitoches on November 30, 1904, requested that Pope St. Pius X transfer the see to Alexandria. This city, on the south bank of the Red River, had been named after Alexander Fulton, who owned the land upon which the first settlement in the region had been established in 1785. The diocese was thus transferred in August 1910. Bishop Van de Ven was appointed an Assistant at the Pontifical Throne on November 12, 1929. Renowned for his tireless efforts as bishop, he was credited with founding the first Catholic hospital in northern Louisiana. He died on May 8, 1932.

Bishop Daniel Francis Desmond succeeded to the diocese and was consecrated on January 5, 1933. On February 15, 1933, he was installed at St. Francis Xavier Cathedral. He served the diocese during the Great Depression, developing programs to alleviate the suffering of the people in the area, and he led the faithful through World War II, aiding the military efforts and adapting diocesan facilities to the needs of the crisis. He also continued the expansion and building programs, adding twenty-nine new parishes and thirty-five new churches to the diocese. Bishop Desmond died on September 11, 1945, after suffering two strokes.

His successor, Bishop Charles B. Greco, was consecrated on February 25, 1946. His nearly three decades as bishop were marked by a time of phenomenal growth: 33 new parishes, 125 churches and chapels, 100 rectories and convents, some 50 schools, a seminary, and an office for Catholic Charities. He also instituted programs and facilities for the needy, including Don Bosco's Home at Cottonport and St. Ann's Maternity Home, as well as two homes for children with special needs. Bishop Greco also founded the Maryhill Minor Seminary near Pineville and implemented the reforms of the Second Vatican Council. He retired on May 22, 1973.

Bishop Lawrence P. Graves became his successor and was installed in Alexandria on September 18, 1973. He focused diocesan efforts on continuing education for priests, offices for religious education and youth ministry, development plans, and permanent diaconate programs, as well as efforts at Catholic social communications through modern media. His Bishop's Stewardship Appeal proved vital in providing a firm financial footing for the diocesan programs. Bishop Graves retired on July 14, 1982.

On January 12, 1977, the title of the see was changed to the Diocese of Alexandria-Shreveport, and St. John Berchmans became the co-cathedral. Bishop William B. Friend was installed as the bishop of Alexandria-Shreveport on January 11, 1983. In 1986 Pope Blessed John Paul II established the Diocese of Shreveport from portions of the Diocese of Alexandria-Shreveport. Bishop William Friend became the bishop of this new diocese.

In that same year, Bishop John C. Favalora was consecrated bishop of the Diocese of Alexandria but was transferred to the Diocese of St. Petersburg on May 16, 1989, then promoted to the Archdiocese of Miami in 1992.

On August 24, 1989, Bishop Samuel G. Jacobs was installed. He continued the work of his predecessors and added facilities to meet the growing needs of the Catholics in the area. Bishop Jacobs was particularly renowned for his support of the Charismatic Movement. He was transferred to the Diocese of Houma-Thibodaux on August 10, 2003.

Bishop Ronald Herzog was appointed the bishop of Alexandria on October 27, 2004, and was installed in the diocese on November 5, 2004. In 2011 the diocese had over 48,000 Catholics, served by 75 priests, more than 60 men and women religious, and 48 parishes.

Alito Jr., Samuel A. (April 1, 1950–)

An associate justice of the United States Supreme Court and the eleventh Catholic to serve on the high court, Samuel Anthony Alito, Jr., was born in Trenton, New Jersey, and was raised a Catholic. He graduated from Princeton University's Woodrow Wilson School of Public and International Affairs in 1972, and in 1975 earned a law degree from the Yale Law School, where he served as editor of the *Yale Law Journal*. After graduating from law school, he served on active duty in the Armed Forces from September to December 1975 while attending the Officer Basic Course for Signal Corps officers at Fort Gordon, Georgia. He spent his remaining time in the army in the inactive reserves and had the rank of captain when he received an honorable discharge in 1980.

From 1976 to 1977 Alito worked as a law clerk for Leonard I. Garth of the Third Circuit Court of Appeals and from 1977 to 1981 as Assistant United States Attorney for the District of New Jersey. He subsequently served as deputy assistant to Attorney General Edwin Meese in the Reagan administration and United States Attorney for the District of New Jersey. From 1990 to 2006 he was a judge on the United States Court of Appeals for the Third Circuit. He was also adjunct professor of law at Seton Hall University School of Law in Newark, New Jersey, from 1999 to 2004. In 1995 Judge Alito was presented with that law school's St. Thomas More Medal.

Alito was nominated by President George W. Bush on October 31, 2005, as a replacement for nominee Harriet Miers to replace Justice Sandra Day O'Connor on the Supreme Court. Miers had withdrawn herself from consieration after encountering widespread opposition from many in the conservative movement and the Republican Party.

Charged with being an extremist conservative, Alito was opposed by most of the Democrats in the Senate. Major opposition was never mounted, and despite what proved partisan and at times unpleasant questioning by some Democrats on the Judiciary Committee, Alito was confirmed by a vote of 58–42. No serious effort was undertaken to filibuster the nomination, but the close vote was an indication of the severely polarized political state of affairs in the Senate and the country at large.

Allegheny, Diocese of

Among American dioceses, the Diocese of Allegheny in Pennsylvania has a curious history, having been in existence from 1876 to 1877 and then subsequently suppressed by the Holy See. The origins of the diocese are traced to the rapid expansion of the Church in western Pennsylvania throughout the 1860s and the effects of the Civil War on industries in the region. The railroad, coal, and steel industries all required skilled laborers, and many Catholics moved to the area around Pittsburgh for employment in the emerging industries. Between 1860 and 1875 the Pittsburgh diocese witnessed an increase in population from fifty thousand to two hundred thousand. The prosperity, however, could not last, and the postwar economic collapse brought massive unemployment among former soldiers and workers. The crisis only deepened during the 1873 financial scare.

The Pittsburgh diocese responded as best it could, but the pastoral needs of the Catholics convinced Bishop Joseph Domenec that a new diocese was needed for western Pennsylvania. He journeyed to a meeting of bishops in Baltimore and proposed the division of his diocese. The suggestion was approved unanimously, and Bishop Domenec then traveled to Rome to present the petition to the Vatican authorities.

On January 11, 1876, Pope Blessed Pius IX announced the creation of the Diocese of Allegh-

Bishop Domenec, Diocese of Allegheny

eny, with Bishop Domenec appointed as the first bishop of the new diocese on January 16. The division of the Pittsburgh diocese, however, did not follow natural geographical lines, but followed the east-west division of the railroad lines, with the diocesan center at Allegheny City, across the river from Pittsburgh. The new ordinary of Pittsburgh was Bishop John Tuigg. Both Bishop Domenec and Bishop Tuigg were installed on the same day, March 19, 1876.

From the very beginning of the diocese, there was a torrent of criticism over the distribution of the Pittsburgh diocese's resources. The majority of parishes facing the most difficult financial hardships were left in Pittsburgh, while growing parishes, such as those in the railroad center of Altoona, were given to the new diocese. As complaints and financial difficulties continued to mount in Pittsburgh, Bishop Tuigg appealed to Rome to reconsider the division of the diocese.

On July 29, 1877, Bishop Domenec resigned as bishop at the behest of the Congregation for the Propagation of the Faith. The Diocese of Allegheny was subsequently reunited with Pittsburgh and the Diocese of Allegheny was eventually suppressed in 1889. In 1901, after more careful planning, a new diocese for western Pennsylvania was established in Altoona. (*See also* Altoona-Johnstown, Diocese of; Pittsburgh, Diocese of.)

Allen, Frances (November 13, 1784–September or December 10, 1819)

The daughter of Ethan Allen, the American patriot and Revolutionary War hero, Frances Allen was a convert to Catholicism and a religious in Canada. She was born in Sunderland, Vermont, and was raised in a totally atheistic household. Her father, active in the new United States, had married his third wife, Frances Montressor, in 1784, and Frances was their daughter.

The Catholic faith was still under severe penal restrictions, despite the courageous service provided by Catholics in the war, and Ethan Allen did not concern himself about such matters, having declared his atheism years before. He also held the popular prejudices against Catholicism, a bias that impeded the Church and would have to be eliminated state by state in the adoption of new constitutions over a period of time. Ethan Allen died in 1789, and his widow married Dr. Jabez Penniman five years later.

The nonreligious atmosphere of the family continued, but Frances began to study Catholicism on her own because she felt drawn to the Church. She asked to be allowed to go to Montréal to continue her education in French. She was twenty-one, but in that era a young woman needed parental approval to make such a prolonged journey. The purpose of her trip was ostensibly the one that she stated, but Frances hoped to reside as a guest in a convent in order to learn more about the faith.

Her mother and stepfather agreed to the journey, but they insisted upon one stipulation in connection with her departure. Before she left the United States, Frances was baptized in the Protestant faith by the Reverend Daniel Barber, a minister in Claremont, New Hampshire. Barber would convert to the Catholic Church later, but at that time he was a staunch Protestant.

Frances went to Montréal, where she became a pupil of the Sisters of the Congregation of Notre Dame, and there received the grace of faith. She was baptized again and made her first Communion, knowing as well that she had received the grace of a religious vocation. When her parents received word of this, they recalled her and started a series of social events in order to entice her back into familiar routines. Frances promised to spend an entire year with her family before making a final decision about her religious vocation. At the end of the year, despite the galas and the tours, Frances returned to Montréal and entered Hôtel Dieu. She made her religious profession in 1810, and served in the convent until she died of a lung disease.

Allen, Fred (May 31, 1894–March 17, 1956)

One of the most talented comedians in the United States, Fred Allen was the creator of *The Texaco Star Theater* and *Allen's Alley*. He was born John Florence Sullivan in Cambridge, Massachusetts, and

showed early signs of humor and performing abilities. Allen started developing his comic routines on tours and circuits, even going to Oceania in 1916. Returning to America, he adopted the name Fred Allen and began his career in earnest, achieving starring roles in revues and shows in New York. In 1927 Fred married Portland Hoffa and continued his theater performances, entering radio in 1932. The CBS network featured Fred and Portland in *Town Hall Tonight,* which ran from 1934 through 1939. The show then became *The Fred Allen Show,* and Fred wrote most of the material used.

In 1940 he began his most popular series, *The Texaco Star Theater,* featuring a zany lineup of comedic characters that epitomized his sardonic wit. He appeared in movies and wrote two autobiographical works. Fred Allen died in New York.

Allen, George (December 17, 1808–May 28, 1876)

A noted educator, George Allen converted to the faith. He was born in Milton, Vermont, and was trained in the Episcopalian religion by his family. Allen graduated from the University of Vermont in 1827 and was admitted to the bar in 1831. He also studied theology and became the rector of St. Alban's Episcopal parish in Vermont from 1834 to 1837. He then became a professor of ancient languages at Delaware College in Newark, Delaware. By 1845 he had assumed the same position at the University of Pennsylvania at Philadelphia and then became a professor of Greek.

Dr. Allen converted to the Catholic Church in 1847, having recognized the historical authority of the Holy See. His reception into the Church stunned his Protestant friends and caused a furor in some circles. He remained a loyal defender of the faith until his death.

Allen, Gracie (July 26, 1905–August 2, 1964)

A popular comedienne, Gracie Allen was celebrated for her hilarious and bizarre routines with her husband, George Burns. She was born in San Francisco and was raised in the entertainment world, as her father, Edward, fostered her career. She was educated at Star of the Sea Convent and then embarked on a tour with her father and three sisters. She also performed with other comedic groups before meeting George Burns in 1922. The team of Burns and Allen started with this meeting, and the couple married four years later.

Appearing first in vaudeville, Burns and Allen took their routines to radio in 1930, introduced by Eddie Cantor. *The George Burns and Gracie Allen Show* was started soon after, and the team achieved popularity across America. They also starred in movies and in 1950 produced a television series. Gracie retired in 1950. She died in Los Angeles.

Allen, Steve (December 26, 1921–October 30, 2000)

A famous and popular entertainer, Steve Allen was also a noted writer and musician. He was born in Encino, California, but spent his early youth on the road as his parents were a vaudeville comedy team. His father, straight man Billy Allen, died when Steve was only eighteen months old, and his mother carried on in order to survive financially. Steve then grew up with his family and friends in Chicago, attending Catholic and public schools.

Allen became involved in radio and proved a natural for television, hosting his first variety show on CBS by Christmas 1950. This was the first major achievement in a fifty-year career that included television, radio, music, and books. In 1954 Allen was named the host of *The Tonight Show* on NBC, remaining with the program for forty months. He eventually hosted four prime-time comedy-variety series that bore his name and aired on NBC, CBS, and ABC in the 1950s, 1960s, and 1980s. He also hosted CBS's famous game show *What's My Line?* and both the network and syndicated versions of *I've Got a Secret*. He won considerable notoriety for playing the title role in the 1955 film biography *The Benny Goodman Story*. His clever talk show *Steve Allen's Meeting of Minds*, in which great figures of history gathered to discuss various topics, won him an Emmy in 1979.

Allen divorced his first wife, with whom he had three sons, and married actress Jayne Meadows in 1954. He and Meadows had one son, and she became a close collaborator in his work. In his last years, he was an advocate of restoring a sense of decency to television, serving as honorary chairman of the Parents Television Council. Honored as a modern Renaissance man, he wrote fifty-three books and wrote 7,900 songs, including "This Could Be the Start of Something Big." Steve Allen died in Encino.

Allentown, Diocese of

Established on January 28, 1961, by Pope Blessed John XXIII, the Diocese of Allentown serves counties in the east-central part of Pennsylvania. The city is an agricultural and industrial center with rich natural resources. It was founded in 1735 by William Allen, a mayor of Philadelphia and a chief justice of Pennsylvania. Munitions for the Americans during the Revolutionary War were produced in Allentown, and citizens of the area took part in the Civil War. Allentown is a center for the marketing of local mineral and agricultural products. At one time, the Zion Reformed Church of Allentown housed the Liberty Bell. The Diocese of Allentown is a suffragan see of the Archdiocese of Philadelphia and has a profound Catholic heritage.

As far back as the early 1670s, Jesuits, Sulpicians, and Recollect Franciscans were conducting mission apostolates to the Indian tribes in Pennsylvania. William Penn, the founder of the state under a charter issued in 1681 by the English King Charles II, was moderately tolerant of all faiths and allowed priests to conduct their ministries discreetly. The influx of immigrants from France, Germany, and Ireland also aided the Catholic cause in the colonies but brought about Protestant bias at the same time. Penn, therefore, asked that Catholics use care in promoting the faith in order to avoid confrontations within the colony.

In 1741 Jesuit Theodore Schneider was in the area, caring for German Catholics. Two years later, Father Schneider founded a Catholic school and St. Paul's Chapel in Goshenhoppen, near Reading. In 1752 St. Peter's parish opened in Reading. Catholics in the state were under the jurisdiction of the Diocese of Baltimore until 1808, when Philadelphia was erected as a diocese. Allentown was part of that ecclesiastical designation and prospered. Catholic participation in the Revolutionary War had earned the respect of Protestants, and new state constitutions granted Catholics the civil rights they had been denied for so many decades.

In the new era of religious freedom, building programs were continued in Catholic communities, and the Church of the Blessed Sacrament was established in 1827, containing the original St. Paul's within its walls. In 1837 Father Augustin Bally, a Jesuit, was working in the area, and Goshenhoppen was renamed Bally in his honor.

During the Civil War, a militia unit called the "First Defenders" went from Allentown in response to President Abraham Lincoln's call for volunteers. The industrial progress promoted by the war aided general growth at the war's end. The city took part in the military efforts of World War I and suffered the problems of the Great Depression and World War II.

In 1961 Allentown was established as a diocese. Bishop Joseph McShea, who had served as auxiliary bishop of the Archdiocese of Philadelphia since 1952, was installed on April 11, 1961. The Cathedral of St. Catherine of Siena, which dates originally to 1919, became the seat of the new bishop, and he set about instituting the offices and agencies for diocesan administration. He also focused on the educational system of the diocese, expanding parishes and schools to meet the growing population demands in the area, and he instituted the reforms of the Second Vatican Council. Bishop McShea retired on February 8, 1983.

The second bishop of Allentown was Bishop Thomas J. Welsh, who had served as an auxiliary bishop of the Archdiocese of Philadelphia and as the founding bishop of the Diocese of Arlington since 1974. Bishop Welsh was installed in Allentown on March 21, 1983. He continued building the diocesan programs and managed to maintain services and ministries despite the declining numbers of priests and religious. Bishop Welsh resigned on December 16, 1997.

Bishop Edward Peter Cullen, who had served as auxiliary bishop of the Archdiocese of Philadelphia since 1994, was installed as the third bishop of Allentown on February 9, 1998. Bishop Cullen launched Renew 2000, a diocesan evangelization program, and started a $28 million capital campaign to continue the expansion of facilities and charitable endeavors. He retired on May 27, 2009.

Bishop John Barres was appointed the fourth bishop of Allentown on May 27, 2009, and ordained a bishop on July 30, 2009. Barres had been a priest of the Wilmington Diocese until the time of his appointment. In 2011 the diocese had 273,000 Catholics served by 272 priests, 320 women religious, and 104 parishes.

Allouez, Claude (June 6, 1622–August 27, 1689)

Called the "Founder of Catholicity in the West," Claude Allouez, a Jesuit missionary, was the first regional vicar general of the Society of Jesus in the United States. He was born in St. Didier, Haute Loire, France, and became a Jesuit in 1639. In 1655 Father Allouez was ordained and was appointed to the Canadian missions three years later.

He began his labors in the St. Lawrence River area and then at Three Rivers, where he served as superior. In 1663, recognized for his leadership, fervor, and tireless efforts, Father Allouez was appointed the vicar general of the entire Northwest Territory, including the Great Lakes and the region between the Ohio and Mississippi rivers. He had charge of all Indian missions in the area, as well as the French trappers and settlers within his jurisdiction.

Father Allouez started touring the western missions in 1865, going in October of that year to Chequamegon Bay on Lake Superior in present-day Wisconsin. He founded La Pointe du Saint Esprit on Madeline Island as well. In 1667 he went to Nipigon, and in 1669 he was at Green Bay. One year later he went to Lake Winnebago and founded a mission at Sault Ste. Marie in 1671. There he met many Indian tribes and held conferences. The explorer Simon de Saint-Lusson aided Father Allouez at the tribal meeting.

In that same year, Father Allouez was at De Pere, near Green Bay, and there he spent time with the famous Jesuit Father Jacques Marquette. They became good friends and coworkers in the mission field. Father Marquette could advise Father Allouez on the tribal and geographical realities of the region, having explored the territory. When Father Marquette died, Father Allouez took over Kaskaskia Mission in Illinois. He remained there until he died, using that mission as an operational base. He died on a visit to a Miami village on the St. Joseph's River in southern Michigan. Father Allouez served the Chippewa, Illinois, Miami, Ottawa, Outgami, Potawatomi, Sauk, and Wyandot Christians. He preached to as many as a hundred thousand Indians of various tribes and personally baptized ten thousand converts. A cross made of granite was erected on the reported site of his grave.

Alpha Sigma Nu

A national honor society established in 1915, Alpha Sigma Nu is currently active in Jesuit institutions of higher education in the United States, with a chapter at Sogany University in Korea. Originally for men, members were traditionally chosen on the basis of scholarship, loyalty, and service. In 1973 Gamma Pi Epsilon (a similar society for women founded in 1925) merged with Alpha Sigma Nu to form a society for men and women.

Alphonsa, Mother (Hawthorne). See Hawthorne, Mother Alphonsa

Alter, Karl J. (August 18, 1885–August 23, 1977)

The archbishop of Cincinnati from 1950 to 1969, Karl J. Alter was an active participant in the Second Vatican Council. Alter was born in Toledo, Ohio, the son of John and Elizabeth Kaltner Alter. After studying at St. John's University in Toledo, he attended St. Mary's Seminary in Cleveland. Ordained to the priesthood on June 4, 1910, Father Alter was the first priest ordained for the newly formed Diocese of Toledo.

He was assigned to pastoral ministries in the area and then became the director of Catholic Charities in 1914. In 1929 he became the director of the National Catholic School of Social Service, a position he held until 1931. On April 17 of that year, he was consecrated as the bishop of the Diocese of Toledo. He started an extensive building program in his new diocese, including the completion of the Cathedral of the Blessed Virgin Mary of the Rosary.

Promoted to the Archdiocese of Cincinnati on June 21, 1950, Archbishop Alter restored the Cathedral of St. Peter in Chains, rededicating it in 1957, and founded St. Gregory's Preparatory Seminary. New convents, schools, and institutions, and recodified new diocesan laws and social structures were the result of his energetic programs.

At the Second Vatican Council, Archbishop Alter served on the Central Preparatory Commission and took part on other committees and served as chairman of the administrative board of the National Catholic Welfare Conference. He retired on July 23, 1969, and died in Cincinnati.

Altham, John (1589–1640)

The companion of Father Andrew White, John Altham was a Jesuit priest who served in the colony of Maryland. He was born in Warwickshire, England, and his family name was Grosvenor or Gravenor. The name John Altham was an alias assumed during the anti-Catholic reign of Queen Elizabeth I, when Catholic priests were imprisoned and martyred for spreading the faith. As a priest, John Altham labored in the areas of London and Devonshire, despite the dangers.

In 1633 he was assigned as a chaplain to the settlers of the new Maryland colony, a haven for Catholics in British-held American territories, and he accompanied Jesuit Father White and Brother Thomas Gervase to their new mission. They were smuggled aboard an American-bound ship at the Isle of Wight so they would not have to take the anti-Catholic oaths required by all Englishmen leaving the country. The ship sailed across the Atlantic and anchored in Chesapeake Bay on March 25, 1634. There a small mission, called St. Mary's, was opened and served as the capital of the colony until 1694.

Father Altham labored among the colonial settlers of Maryland; in 1637, he contracted yellow fever but recovered. He started a mission on Kent Island, near modern Annapolis, where he remained until 1640, when he was stricken again with yellow fever. Father Altham was placed on board a ship bound for St. Mary's, but he died on the way.

Alton, Diocese of. See Springfield in Illinois, Diocese of

Altoona-Johnstown, Diocese of

Established as the Diocese of Altoona on May 27, 1901, by Pope Leo XIII and redesignated on October 9, 1957, as the Diocese of Altoona-Johnstown by Pope Pius XII, this ecclesiastical jurisdiction serves counties in western Pennsylvania, an agricultural, farming, and manufacturing area. Altoona, a commercial center, was founded in 1849 by the Pennsylvania Railroad as a base for railroad building over the Alleghenies. The city was named for Altoon in Schleswig-Holstein in Germany, and the area was originally settled in the 1760s to provide a center for communications. Fort Roberdau was founded in 1778 as a base for the protection of lead deposits during the Revolutionary War. Johnstown was founded as Connemaugh by John Jones in 1800 and renamed thirty-four years later. It was the western terminus of the Allegheny Portage Railroad and pioneered iron and steel production. Johnstown was devastated on May 31, 1889, when the South Fork Dam collapsed and flooded the area, causing the deaths of more than two thousand people. The Diocese of Altoona-Johnstown is a suffragan see of the Archdiocese of Philadelphia and has a unique Catholic heritage.

The history of the Diocese of Altoona-Johnstown began with the arrival of small groups of Catholics in the Allegheny Mountains, most notably the family of a Revolutionary War veteran, Captain Michael McGuire, who established McGuire's Settlement in 1785, near the present-day Catholic center of Loretto. The settlement attracted other Catholics and became a small enclave of the faith, with occasional visits from priests from the Maryland Mission at Conewego.

The most prominent individual in the establishment of the Church in this region of western Pennsylvania was a Russian prince and convert, Father Demetrius Gallitzin, today revered as the "Apostle of the Alleghenies." Prince Gallitzin arrived at McGuire's Settlement in 1795 to baptize a dying woman. Four years later, he was named pastor of McGuire's Settlement by Bishop John Carroll of Baltimore. He built the first church in the area, St. Michael's, now a basilica, and celebrated Christmas Mass there in 1799.

The next year, he established the community of Loretto, in honor of the Shrine of Our Lady in Loreto, Italy. Father Gallitzin spent a

total of forty years in continuous ministry in the Alleghenies, most of them without the companionship of fellow priests. By the time of his death in 1840, the Church was solidly established in the region.

The founding of Altoona in 1849 for an engine house and a few shop buildings for the maintenance of trains brought an influx of workers and their families. The large numbers of mostly immigrant Catholic Irish and Germans needed priests to provide for their spiritual welfare. The priests of the surrounding parishes assisted whenever possible. The first pastor in the area, Father (later Bishop) John Tuigg, was named by Bishop Michael O'Connor of Pittsburgh in 1853. The Diocese of Pittsburgh was the episcopal jurisdiction for the region at the time.

The peculiar mountain geography of the region created three large Catholic enclaves in the mountains, at Loretto, Altoona, and Johnstown. All three were supported by leading churches (St. Michael's in Loretto, St. John Gualbert in Johnstown, and St. John's in Altoona) and were thus important parishes in the newly created but short-lived Diocese of Allegheny in 1876. In the years following the sup-

St. Michael's, Loretto

pression of the diocese in 1877, each community was viewed as a likely choice for a new diocese.

In 1901, when Pope Leo XIII established a new diocese for the region, the choice was made in favor of Altoona, and the first bishop of the Diocese of Altoona was Eugene Garvey. Bishop Garvey was consecrated on September 8, 1901, and instituted the agencies and offices for diocesan administration and began providing facilities for the faithful. At the time of his passing, there were 100,000 Catholics in the diocese, with 90 parishes, 141 priests, a seminary, and 42 parochial schools. Bishop Garvey died on October 22, 1920.

His successor was Bishop John McCort, who had served as an auxiliary bishop of the Archdiocese of Philadelphia and was named coadjutor bishop with right of succession to the bishop of Altoona on January 27, 1920. He acceded to the throne on October 22 and quickly earned the nickname "the Builder" for his ambitious program of diocesan expansion, in particular his initial construction of Blessed Sacrament Cathedral, a structure destined to be one of the largest in the country. Completion of the cathedral was subsequently delayed by the onset of the Great Depression, an economic collapse that hit the region with particular severity because of the financial problems in the rail, steel, and coal industries. Bishop McCort was appointed assistant at the pontifical throne on October 5, 1933. He died on April 21, 1936.

Bishop Richard Guilfoyle was the third bishop of Altoona, consecrated on November 30, 1936. He inherited the dire economic conditions of the Depression but was able to provide the diocese with a remarkable financial recovery. This renewed economic stability proved so effective that his successors completed the cathedral and launched another massive building program. Bishop Guilfoyle died on June 10, 1957.

His successor was Bishop Howard J. Carroll, who had served as the general secretary of the National Catholic Welfare Conference. The Holy See decreed the redesignation of the Diocese of Altoona as the Diocese of Altoona-Johnstown on October 9, 1957, and Bishop Carroll was consecrated on January 2, 1958, as the first bishop. St. John Gualbert's Church in Johnstown was established as the co-cathedral of the diocese. Bishop Carroll continued the building programs and served until his death on March 21, 1960.

His successor, Bishop J. Carroll McCormick, was appointed on June 25, 1960, and he started an expansion program of the diocesan parochial schools. Bishop McCormick was not destined to remain in Altoona-Johnstown. He was transferred to the Diocese of Scranton on March 4, 1966.

Bishop James J. Hogan, who had served as an auxiliary bishop of the Diocese of Trenton, was appointed as Bishop McCormick's successor on May 23, 1966. He presided over the diocese through the troubled period following the Second Vatican Council. He retired on October 17, 1986.

His successor, Bishop Joseph V. Adamec, was the first bishop of the diocese not a native of Pennsylvania and the fourth bishop of the American hierarchy of Slovak descent. He was installed in the diocese on May 20, 1987, and undertook a thorough liturgical renewal. Bishop Adamec also presided over the celebration of the 100th anniversary of the diocese in 2001. His tenure was marked by a large number of lawsuits stemming from sex abuse cases (most of which predated his arrival), but Bishop Adamec was able to avoid bankruptcy for the diocese. In addition, he established the annual Prince Gallitzin Cross Award for service to the Church in the region and received permission from the Congregation for the Causes of Saints to initiate the cause of canonization of Father Gallitzin. Bishop Adamec retired on January 14, 2011.

He was succeeded on January 14, 2011, by Bishop Mark L. Bartchak, who was ordained a bishop on April 19, 2011. In 2011 the diocese had 91,000 Catholics served by 181 priests, more than 80 men and women religious, and 88 parishes.

Amadeus of the Heart of Jesus, Mother (Dunne)
(July 2, 1846–November 10, 1920)

An Ursuline religious, Mother Amadeus of the Heart of Jesus Dunne served as a missionary to the Cheyenne. Born Sarah Theresa Dunne in Akron, Ohio, she was the daughter of the O'Dunnes of Iregan, Ireland, who migrated to California in 1856. Sarah, only ten years old at the time, and her sister, Mary, were enrolled in the Ursuline Convent in Cleveland, Ohio, by their father and did not accompany him on his further journey. Sarah was attracted to the Ursuline life and entered the order, taking her vows in Toledo on August 23, 1864.

Ten years later she was elected superior and built a new novitiate. In 1883 Bishop Richard Gilmour of Cleveland sent Mother Amadeus to Montana. He had received a message from Bishop John Baptist Brondel, the vicar apostolic of Montana, asking for religious women to open schools and other charitable institutions in the vast mission fields there. Bishop Gilmour sent word that he was assigning six Ursulines to Montana, led by Mother Amadeus, whom he called the "Flower of My Flock."

The Ursulines arrived in Miles City, Montana, in 1884 and promptly founded a convent. Mother Amadeus then led some of the nuns to the Tongue River Reservation of the Cheyenne. The Cheyenne chiefs appreciated her energetic dedication and remained loyal to her even when there was a disturbance on the reservation. The priests of the mission withdrew in the face of opposition by tribal members, but Mother Amadeus remained unmolested. She even extended her labors to other tribes, founding twelve Ursuline missions for the Native Americans.

In 1900 she received a summons from Pope Leo XIII to attend the First General Chapter of the Ursulines in Rome. At this meeting Mother Amadeus was appointed the provincial superior of the Ursulines in the United States. Her activities and spirit drew praise from Pope Leo XIII, and she was later encouraged by Pope St. Pius X and Pope Benedict XV.

In 1905 Mother Amadeus went to the Yukon delta to open a mission, and founded another one in Valdez, in modern Alaska, a year later. She administered the large network of Ursuline missions until 1918, when she was injured while traveling to Alaska. Taken to Seattle, Mother Amadeus died. As she requested, her remains were buried in the Alaskan Mission of St. Ignatius.

Amarillo, Diocese of

Established on August 25, 1926, by Pope Pius XI, the Diocese of Amarillo serves counties in northwestern Texas and is part of the region called the Panhandle. Amarillo is an industrial and commercial center in an area dedicated to agriculture and the development of natural gas and petroleum resources. The city began in 1887 as a railroad con-

struction camp and developed when the cultivation of wheat and ranching in the region became prosperous. Amarillo is now involved in atomic research and in other munitions and scientific industries. The diocese is a suffragan see of the Archdiocese of San Antonio and has a profound Catholic heritage that dates back to the earliest period of exploration in North America.

Francisco Vázquez de Coronado conducted an expedition into the area in 1541, accompanied by Franciscans, including Father Juan de Padilla, the protomartyr of the United States, who was slain circa 1542. Other expeditions and settlements followed, and the Spanish controlled the region until 1821, when Mexico won its independence and claimed all of Spain's previous territories. In 1848 the United States defeated Mexico in a revolt to free Texas and assumed these lands. In 1875 the Indian tribes in the Amarillo area were removed to reservations, and settlers began to enter the region.

St. Mary's, the first Catholic Church, was opened in Clarendon in 1892. In 1899 the Sisters of Charity of the Incarnate Word established St. Mary's Academy in Clarendon, moving that institution to Amarillo in 1913. The Catholics of the region supported the nation's military efforts in World War I and welcomed migrants to the area. The Diocese of Amarillo was designated by the Holy See in 1926.

The first bishop of Amarillo was Rudolph A. Gerken, who was installed on April 28, 1927. He organized the diocesan agencies and offices for administration and opened fourteen new parishes and missions to serve the growing Catholic population. On June 2, 1933, Bishop Gerken was promoted to the Archdiocese of Santa Fe in New Mexico.

His successor was Bishop Robert Emmet Lucey, who was installed in Amarillo on May 16, 1934. Bishop Lucey initiated Catholic Action programs to alleviate the dire needs of the people as a result of the Great Depression. He also started a diocesan newspaper, organized the Catholic Welfare Bureau, and opened a mission for black Catholics in the diocese. On January 22, 1941, Bishop Lucey was promoted to the Archdiocese of San Antonio.

Bishop Laurence J. FitzSimon was appointed the third bishop of Amarillo, and he was installed in Amarillo on November 5, 1941. Bishop Fitz-

Simon led the diocese through World War II and expanded Catholic programs to aid the military effort. He opened twenty parishes and missions and a children's home. Bishop FitzSimon died on July 2, 1958, after successfully leading the faithful through the recovery period that followed the war.

Bishop John L. Morkovsky became his successor, having served as auxiliary bishop of the diocese from 1955, and was installed in Amarillo on August 18, 1958. Bishop Morkovsky had to expand the diocesan facilities to accommodate the growing population. He founded a minor seminary and opened thirty new parishes and a home for the aged. On April 16, 1963, Bishop Morkovsky was transferred to the Diocese of Galveston-Houston as coadjutor bishop.

The fifth bishop was Bishop Lawrence M. De Falco, who was installed on June 13, 1963. Bishop De Falco continued the expansion programs for parishes and diocesan agencies while introducing the reforms of the Second Vatican Council. A program for refugees was also instituted. He died on September 22, 1979.

His successor was Bishop Leroy T. Matthiesen, who was appointed on March 25, 1980, and consecrated on May 30. Bishop Matthiesen built a retreat center and the seminary of the Missionaries of Christ the Priest. He also erected the Museum and Archives Center

The seventh bishop of Amarillo was John W. Yanta, who had served as an auxiliary bishop of the Archdiocese of San Antonio. He was appointed on January 21, 1997, and installed in the diocese on March 17, 1997. In 2005 Bishop Yanta also gave his permission for the founding of a pro-life community dedicated to the formation and training of priests, deacons, brothers, and seminarians who would devote themselves fully to the proclamation of the gospel of life. Aside from his dedicated pastoral care of the diocese, Bishop Yanta published a widely read 2006 pastoral letter, "Modesty Starts with

Purification of the Heart." Bishop Yanta retired on January 3, 2008.

The eighth bishop of the diocese, Patrick J. Zurek, was appointed on January 3, 2008. He had served as an auxiliary bishop of San Antonio since 1998. In 2011 there were 41,000 Catholics in the diocese, served by 50 priests and 38 parishes.

Amat, Thaddeus (December 31, 1810–May 12, 1878)

Pioneering bishop Thaddeus Amat was a tireless missionary who suffered intense physical disabilities but persevered in his labors. He was born in Barcelona, Spain, and became a Vincentian (Congregation of the Missions) and was ordained in Paris in 1838. In that same year, Father Amat was sent to the missions in Louisiana.

Administratively capable and a devout religious, he became the master of Vincentian novices in Missouri and in Philadelphia from 1841 to 1847. He was then named the successor of Bishop Joseph Sadoc Alemany in the Diocese of Monterey-Los Angeles, and was consecrated to his episcopal office on March 12, 1854.

When Bishop Amat arrived in his diocese, he had fewer than twenty priests. A large and diverse population was part of the diocesan challenges, and the Gold Rush had attracted white settlers from the eastern part of the United States, which complicated parish and mission matters. In order to provide adequate spiritual care for the faithful of Monterey-Los Angeles, Bishop Amat returned to Europe to obtain additional priests and religious. Vincentian priests and Vincentian Sisters of Charity responded to his call and traveled to California to take up the new mission duties there.

In 1859 Bishop Amat moved his see to Los Angeles, with the approval of the Holy See. There he opened St. Vincent's College and welcomed Franciscan Sisters into the diocesan parochial schools. The Sisters of the Immaculate Heart of Mary also entered the educational

Bishop Thaddeus Amat

programs there. Throughout this period of expansion and evangelization, Bishop Amat suffered from a severe spinal affliction that was painful and debilitating. In time he had to ask for a coadjutor bishop in order to continue the vast programs he had introduced into the area. Bishop Francis Mora, who had served as vicar general of the diocese, was consecrated on August 3, 1873, as coadjutor.

With this assistant prelate, Bishop Amat continued his labors, including the completion of the cathedral of Los Angeles, St. Vibiana. He died in his see, five years after Bishop Mora was consecrated. Bishop Amat had increased the number of priests to fifty-one, parishes to thirty-two, and the diocese had fifteen chapels, six academies, schools, and various asylums.

America

A Jesuit-run weekly journal that was established on April 17, 1909, by John Wynne, S.J., *America* offered Catholics a comprehensive view of the life of the faithful. Father Wynne first promoted the idea of the *Catholic Encyclopedia* (which was published by the Catholic University of America in 1907), aware of the need for historical materials for the Catholic market. Wynne had served from 1892 as the editor of the monthly devotional magazine *The Messenger of the Sacred Heart,* the chief publication of the Apostleship of Prayer. In 1902, however, in an effort to widen his readership, Wynne launched an offshoot simply called *The Messenger,* which was of more general interest. The transformation was completed with the founding of *America,* which was subtitled "Catholic Review of the Week." Wynne served as editor of the new periodical for only a few months.

Throughout its history, *America* has been very much a Jesuit publication, its editorial content reflecting the call for social justice and civil and human rights. In the 1960s, for example, the magazine supported the civil rights movement. The weekly was also a strong supporter of the Second Vatican Council and the subsequent reforms promulgated by the council. Among its notable editors have been John LaFarge, S.J., and Benjamin Masse, S.J.

American Catholic Historical Association

A society dedicated to the promotion of historical awareness among the United States faithful, the American Catholic Historical Association was founded in 1919 in Cleveland, Ohio. The association was affiliated with the American Historical Association.

The first officers were laymen, as clerics were not allowed to hold such positions until 1966. A permanent secretariat and executive offices are located at the Catholic University of America in Washington, D.C. Annual meetings, sessions with the American Historical Association, and a spring gathering provide the group with consultative and social events.

The *Catholic Historical Review* serves as the ACHA journal. The review has been published since 1915 by The Catholic University of America Press. The ACHA has also published annual papers and documents, edited by Leo Francis Stock, concerning United States–Vatican relations. Two book prizes are offered by ACHA: the John Gilmary Shea Prize, awarded since 1946, and a prize honoring the memory of Howard R. Mararro of Columbia University. Since 1995 the ACHA has also sponsored the John Tracy Ellis Memorial Fund to aid doctoral students with research.

The ACHA welcomes Americans, Canadians, and other foreign members and is also open to students and amateur historians. Permanent corresponding fellows from European nations provide reports on activities in their locale.

American Catholic Quarterly Review

A journal published from 1876 to 1924 in Philadelphia, the *American Catholic Quarterly Review* was founded by Monsignor James A. Corcoran. The periodical offered articles on aspects of theology, philosophy, apologetics, and history, and included significant early contributors such as James Cardinal Gibbons, Bishop John Lancaster Spalding, John Gilmary Shea, and Orestes A. Brownson. The journal was an excellent source for intellectual discussion among scholars on pertinent issues of the day, as well as a place where various professors of The Catholic University of America and elsewhere could express their opinions. Owing to a sharp decline in circulation and competition from other periodicals, the review ceased publication in 1923.

American College of Louvain. *See* Louvain, American College of

American College in Rome. *See* **North American College**

American Ecclesiastical Review

A journal published from 1889 to 1975, the *American Ecclesiastical Review* was intended for priests and seminarians. It was established by Reverend Herman J. Heuser, a German-born member of the faculty of St. Charles Borromeo Seminary in Philadelphia and an associate of Monsignor James A. Corcoran, founder of the *American Catholic Quarterly Review*. Father Heuser's objective was to assist priests and seminarians in their pastoral ministry and promote ongoing pastoral formation. Adopting the motto "For the Upbuilding of the Church" (from 1 Corinthians 14:5), the journal included articles, book reviews, and various official documents. In 1901 it was renamed the *Ecclesiastical Review*, owing to unfulfilled plans to merge with the *Irish Ecclesiastical Review*, and in 1927 the publication was signed over to The Catholic University of America. Heuser resigned at the same time and handed editorial control to Monsignor William Kerby. In 1943 the name *American Ecclesiastical Review* was reinstated, and the magazine continued publication until 1975.

American Federation of Catholic Societies

The national organization for the numerous Catholic fraternal and benevolent societies in the United States, the American Federation of Catholic Societies was established in 1900 and was eventually replaced by the National Council of Catholic Men around 1920. The AFCS began on Thanksgiving Day at a gathering in New York City of various Catholic societies, with the aim of establishing a national federation. Among the societies represented were the Ancient Order of Hibernians, the Catholic Total Abstinence Union of America, and the Catholic Benevolent Union. The Knights of Columbus, the largest Catholic society in the United States, did not send representatives. The following year, delegates at a convention in New Jersey approved a temporary constitution and endorsed the name American Federation of Catholic Societies; later that year, the first formal convention was held, attended by 250 delegates.

The federation deliberately chose to stress its lay membership and so did not seek ecclesiastical approval; neither were members of the clergy encouraged to serve on the executive board. Nevertheless, the federation sought to promote Catholic life and teachings in American society and culture. Despite some initial problems establishing a common sense of identity and a unified set of objectives, the federation grew rapidly over the next several years. By 1904 members included ten national organizations (but still not the Knights of Columbus), eleven state federations, and over three hundred county federations.

In 1908 the AFCS altered its constitution to permit diocesan and parish organizations to join. That same year, the first steps were taken to increase ecclesiastical control over the federation, a process that ended in 1917; the name was changed at this time to the Catholic Federation of the United States. By 1920 the federation was superseded by the National Council of Catholic Men, which had been launched by the Department of Lay Organizations of the National Catholic Welfare Council.

American Protective Association

One of the most virulent and dangerous organizations dedicated to the destruction of the Catholic Church in America, the American Protective Association caused considerable damage and injury to the faithful until it was exposed as a hate group. The presence of outstanding Catholic leaders and the realities of increased immigration from Catholic countries in the late 1800s prompted Protestant displays of anti-Catholicism all across the nation. The American Protective Association was a symbol of increased hatred of the Catholic Church among Protestants and offered an extreme form of religious bigotry to the foes of the Church.

The American Protective Association was founded in 1887 by Henry F. Bowers, a lawyer who saw Catholic and particularly Jesuit conspiracies in all levels of American life. Bowers also incorporated Masonic rituals, oaths, and secrecy into the association to add an exotic tone and focused his attacks on Irish politicians and the Catholic parochial school systems that were emerging at the time. A national convention of the APA in Chicago blamed America's Catholics for financial crises and for the problems workers faced. William J. Traynor, president of the APA, instituted a membership drive at the convention, demanding that Catholics be excluded from public office, as they had been during the dreaded penal period in the colonies. He also insisted that the government close parochial schools, which he saw as instruments of Catholic ambition. In the South, however, the association endorsed the Republican Party, a political error that cost it much needed support in the staunchly Democratic region.

In 1893 the American Protective Association published a so-called papal bull, which demanded the extermination of non-Catholics in the United States. The Republicans were horrified by this obviously false document and by other outrageous excesses, and they disavowed allegiance to the APA. The seventy weekly newspapers published by the association had the support of some U.S. congressmen, but Reverend Washington Gladden, a Congregational minister, exposed the APA tactics and took other Protestants to task for not opposing such lies and hatred. Others joined Gladden in his denunciations, and the APA weakened rapidly. It was unable to stop the election of President William McKinley in 1896, despite its charges that he had pro-Catholic leanings. By 1900 the American Protective Association was revealed as a hate organization and disappeared from the political scene. (*See also* Anti-Catholicism; Know-Nothing Movement.)

American Revolution. *See* War of Independence

Americanism

A philosophical approach of some Church leaders in the United States in the latter decades of the nineteenth century, Americanism divided the faithful to some extent and brought about a papal response from Pope Leo XIII. Americanism proposed that Catholicism should be adapted as much as externally possible to the modern cultural ideas and values of America, even though such cultural traditions were at times contrary to Church teachings. This philosophical approach stressed receptivity to the social movements of various national eras as well as the sociopolitical virtues of the country, such as democracy, humanitarian works, and the separation of church and state. Also proposed was a relaxation of the stringent requirements for

the acceptance of converts, in order to make the Church less singular in its dealing with the numerous faiths of America.

Americanism had the support of several prelates, including Archbishop John Ireland of St. Paul, Bishop John Joseph Keane of Richmond, and Monsignor Dennis J. O'Connell, the rector of the North American College in Rome. Other bishops of the period opposed such accommodation of prevailing attitudes and sought ways to preserve the faith and to defend it against the social trends.

Although few lay Catholics were aware of the controversy and the opinions of both sides, an incident sparked recognition of Americanism in Europe. An American archbishop lectured on the subject in Paris, setting off a rather harsh confrontation. France at the time was involved in a struggle to revitalize the faith, and two opposing groups had emerged: the monarchists, who believed that the monarchy and aristocracy could undo the damage caused by the French Revolution, and that democracies were pagan institutions that were hostile to the faith; and the progressives, who taught that the anti-Catholic horrors unleashed by the Revolution were alien to democratic ideals. The progressives sought to bolster their claims of the beneficial relations possible between church and state in a democracy, and they invited Archbishop John Ireland to Paris in 1892. He lectured on "The Church in the New World," providing an ardent picture of the democratic processes and pluralism in church-state relations. The monarchists were incensed by the archbishop's fervor.

A war of pamphlets began as a result of the lecture and erupted in 1898. Abbé Felix Klein printed *La Vie du Pere Hecker* ("The Life of Father Hecker"), which extolled the virtues of the founder of the Paulists, Isaac Thomas Hecker. In response to this popular biography, French Abbé Charles Maignen published his own biography of Father Hecker, seemingly a malicious portrayal that condemned the man and the democratic processes of the United States. Father Hecker was depicted as a misguided individual who compromised the basic doctrines of the faith in order to further his apostolate among the Americans. The alleged errors recounted in this biography were labeled Americanism, sparking debates on both sides of the issue.

Catholics in Italy and France became so embroiled in the bitter dispute that the Holy See felt obligated to mediate the matter. Pope Leo XIII, who initially had been responsive to the movement, appointed a commission of cardinals to study the situation. Upon receipt of the commission's report, he issued the apostolic letter *Testem Benevolentiae* on January 22, 1899, addressed to James Cardinal Gibbons of Baltimore.

In the letter, the pope condemned the false teachings attributed to Father Hecker by his detractors. If practiced in the United States, the pope stated, such teachings needed immediate remedy. He did not declare that such errors were in use but cautioned against them. Cardinal Gibbons responded that the American bishops welcomed the papal comments, but made it clear that such practices were "extravagant and absurd" and not evident in the American Church. The Paulist Superior, Father George Deshom, defended Father Hecker as well. The affair eventually ended with this exchange of letters.

Ammen, Daniel (May 15, 1820–July 11, 1898)

A naval officer and author, Daniel Ammen was recognized for his military inventions. He was born in Brown County, Ohio, as his family had migrated to that region from Virginia, part of the great westward movement of that period. Daniel was appointed to the United States Military Academy at West Point on July 7, 1834. He then served at sea and was sent to the Naval School near Philadelphia, becoming a lieutenant on November 4, 1849.

Committed to a naval career, Daniel rose through the ranks and was made a rear admiral on December 11, 1877. He served in Civil War campaigns, blockading the Confederate fleet under the command of Admiral Samuel Francis Du Pont. From 1869 to 1871, Daniel was chief of the Bureau of Yards and Docks, then the chief of the Bureau of Navigation from 1871 to 1878. He was acclaimed especially for inventing the "Ammen Balsa," a life raft, and other naval weapons.

Anchorage, Archdiocese of

Established on January 22, 1966, by Pope Paul VI, the Archdiocese of Anchorage serves the area from the Canadian border of the Yukon Territory in the east to the tip of the Atlantic chain in the west.

Anchorage is a port at the head of Cook Inlet, a bay of the Pacific Ocean, and was founded in 1914 as the headquarters of the Alaska Railroad. The city is now involved in the development of natural resources, defense activities, and tourism. The original inhabitants of the region were the Aleuts, Athabascans, Copper River Indians, Eskimos, and Kenai. The Russians arrived in the area in 1784; Captain Vitus Bering, a Danish navigator in the employ of Russia, had claimed the region for the tsar during his voyages of 1728 and 1741.

Catholic missionaries were not on the scene until the middle 1800s. In 1867 Alaska was bought from the Russians for $7.2 million. Archbishop Charles J. Seghers pioneered the missions of Alaska at the time, and other missionaries joined him in establishing parishes. Anchorage was deemed a safe harbor area for shippers supplying the camp involved in the gold-mining operations of that period, resulting in a steady population growth.

The city suffered a severe earthquake on March 27, 1964, and the entire downtown area was leveled in the disaster. Nearby Valdez was destroyed, and Cordova was damaged. Two years later, Anchorage was erected as an archdiocese, and Archbishop Joseph T. Ryan was installed on April 14, 1966. He began organizing the agencies and offices of a metropolitan see. On December 13, 1975, however, Archbishop Ryan was named coadjutor military vicar of the United States Armed Forces and then became the first archbishop of the Archdiocese for the Military Services of the United States.

His successor was Archbishop Francis T. Hurley, who had served as an auxiliary bishop of the Diocese of Juneau since 1970. He was installed in Anchorage on July 8, 1976, and began his ministries to his far-flung parishes, flying his own plane on parish visitations. He also expanded the archdiocesan apostolates. Archbishop Hurley retired on March 3, 2001.

The present archbishop of Anchorage is Roger Lawrence Schwietz, O.M.I. He had served as bishop of the Diocese of Duluth since 1990 and was promoted to the archdiocese as coadjutor to Archbishop Hurley on January 18, 2000. Archbishop Schwietz celebrated the fortieth anniversary of the archdiocese in 2006 and launched a ten-year Pastoral Plan, to culminate in the Golden

Jubilee Year in 2016. The Pastoral Plan will assist the archdiocese in its long-term strategic programs for evangelization and pastoral ministry. In 2011 the archdiocese had 32,000 Catholics, 29 priests, 35 men and women religious, and 23 parishes.

Ancient Order of Hibernians. *See* Hibernians, Ancient Order of

Anderson, Henry James (February 6, 1799– October 19, 1875)

A convert, scientist, and educator, Henry James Anderson directed the St. Vincent de Paul Society in New York, the city of his birth. He studied at Columbia College and at the College of Physicians and Surgeons in New York, and after receiving his medical degree, became a professor of mathematics and astronomy at Columbia. In 1848 Dr. Anderson went on a Dead Sea exploration and as a result of his studies became a zealous Catholic. In 1860 he became president of the Particular Council of the St. Vincent de Paul Society and went on to organize the Catholic Union in New York. Anderson was also made a Knight Commander of the Order of St. Gregory by Pope Blessed Pius IX. On a trip to Lourdes, Rome, Australia, and India in 1875, Dr. Anderson died in Lahore, Pakistan. His remains were returned to New York and buried in a vault in the Church of the Madonna in Fort Lee, New Jersey. Cardinal John McCloskey presided at his funeral.

Anderson, Mary Antoinette (July 28, 1859–May 29, 1940)

A famous Catholic actress, Mary Antoinette Anderson was born in Sacramento, California, the daughter of Marie Antoinette Leugers and Charles Henry Anderson. After the death of her father, she and her mother moved to Louisville, Kentucky. There, Marie remarried, and Mary's stepfather encouraged her interest in music and acting. At the age of sixteen, she debuted in Louisville and was working in New York within two years. Her career soon blossomed, and by the 1880s she was one of the country's most famous actresses.

In 1885 Mary performed Shakespeare in Stratford-upon-Avon, a remarkable honor for an American. She retired in 1889 and married the wealthy American Antonio de Navarro. She died in England.

André, Louis (1631–1714)

One of the most gifted missionaries in the languages of the Native American tribes, Louis André was a dedicated Jesuit pioneer in evangelizing the Midwestern regions of the present United States. He was born in France and entered the Society of Jesus. After his ordination, Father André was assigned to the Canadian mission territories. He labored for a time with Father Gabriel Druillettes at Sault Ste. Marie Mission in northern Michigan, learning the various languages of the tribes in the area.

When the Ottawa Indians were forced to abandon their original homeland because of migrating eastern tribes, Father André elected to accompany them westward. Seeing them safely settled in their new area, he went to the Algonquin missions located on the shores of the Great Lakes, eager to reach these isolated peoples. He established his base of operations at the Mission of St. Francis Xavier at Green Bay, Wisconsin, in 1871.

He was already fluent in the Ottawa and Algonquin languages and was able to master regional idioms and dialects with ease. Father André compiled dictionaries and catechisms for these tribes, and labored for more than ten years in the Great Lakes region, traveling on foot or by canoe and becoming a familiar figure in Native American enclaves. He also served the Chicoutimi and Seven Isles (Sept-Iles) tribes. Recalled to Québec after so many years in the missions, Father André died there in 1714.

Andreis, Felix de (December 13, 1778–October 15, 1820)

The first superior of the Congregation of Missions, the Vincentians, in the United States, Felix de Andreis was a pioneer in the Louisiana missions. He was born in Demonte, Piedmont, Italy, entered the Vincentians in 1797, and was ordained in 1801. In 1806 he was assigned to Montecitorio in Rome to recover his health after a serious illness. There Father de Andreis gave clergy missions and retreats from 1810 to 1815, becoming famous for his holiness and oratory.

In 1815 Bishop Louis Dubourg, the apostolic administrator of Louisiana, arrived in Rome and asked the Vincentians to send Father de Andreis to the Louisiana missions. When the superior of the congregation refused, declaring that the congregation could not part with him, Bishop Dubourg went to Pope Pius VII and received papal approval of the appointment.

Father de Andreis arrived in Baltimore, Maryland, on July 26, 1816. He stayed at St. Mary's Seminary there for several months with his Vincentian companions, including Father Simon William Gabriel Bruté de Rémur, who would become a bishop. The Vincentians then traveled to Bardstown, Kentucky, where they were the guests of Bishop Benedict Joseph Flaget at the seminary.

Father de Andreis founded the first Vincentian establishment in St. Louis in 1818. He started a seminary at "The Barrens," a colony some eighty miles south of St. Louis, serving as master of novices until 1818, and also built a school. Father de Andreis's academic apostolate has been noted as a direct aid to the growth of the Church in Arkansas, Illinois, Missouri, and Texas. Owing to his ceaseless labors, Father de Andreis died at the age of forty-two in St. Louis. The process of his canonization was launched in St. Louis in 1900, and he was granted the title of Venerable. His marble tomb rests below the National Shrine of Our Lady of the Miraculous Medal in St. Louis.

Angelica, Mother. *See* EWTN

Anti-Catholicism

A form of religious bigotry, anti-Catholicism is commonly defined as opposition to the Catholic Church in various forms, including intolerance, persecution, denial of civil rights, bigotry, slander, and propaganda. Anti-Catholicism has been an ongoing element in American society since the earliest periods of the nation's history. Sometimes subtle, at other times virulent and violent, anti-Catholicism in the United States had roots in European political events, in age-old rivalries, and in religious disputes that date to the Reformation.

The first Catholic missionaries in America were French or Spanish, as these European nations pioneered the exploration and colonization of the New World after its discovery. In Florida, a vast mission system emerged as part of the founding of St. Augustine, the oldest city in the present-day United States. English troops from the Colony of Georgia, as a New World response to the European Queen Anne's War from 1702 to 1713 (known in Europe as the War of the Spanish Succession), attacked Florida in 1702 and destroyed St. Augustine in October 1703, slaying priests and taking Catholic Native Americans as slaves. Florida was ceded to the English in 1763; the Spanish remained in the southwestern territories of the nation until Mexico revolted against Spanish occupation. The Spanish returned to Florida in 1783, remaining only until 1821.

The French Jesuits in the New England region did not fare better. Many were exiled or slain by English forces or their Indian allies, including Father Sebastian Râle, a Jesuit who was killed at Norridgewock on August 23, 1724. His translations and dictionaries of Native American tongues became the prized possession of Harvard College. Catholic priests were banned in other New England colonies as early as 1647.

The Colony of Maryland, founded by the second Lord Baltimore, Cecil Calvert, fared better as far as freedom of religion was concerned until Congregationalists overthrew the government and passed a law against Catholicism in 1649. Four decades later harsher laws were passed in the colony, depriving Catholics of all rights and penalizing them for allegiance to the faith. The actual penal period, the era in which Catholics were punished for their loyalty to the Church, continued for decades, despite the contributions made to the colonies by the victims of this discrimination.

European wars, carried on endlessly and culminating in the colonies in the French and Indian War, fostered an English response to France's New World empire. The English established the Church of England as the official religion in many colonies and tolerated no "popery," as they termed the Catholic faith. If Catholics did not publicly revile the pope, they lost the right to vote and to hold public office.

Even in the colonies in which freedom of religion was allowed, the "papists" were always exempt from privileges and denied the right to hold public office. This did not deter American Catholics from joining others in the dream of becoming a united, free nation, as the quest for independence from England took hold. The American response to the Québec Act dimmed the hopes of Catholics but did not stop them from joining in the rebellion. The Québec Act of 1774 established the Roman Catholic Church as a recognized entity. It followed England's seizure of Canada from France through the French and Indian War. In the northeastern coastal region, the French Catholic Acadians were severely punished for their faith and for their steadfast neutrality in Anglo-French rivalries. Over nine thousand Acadians, men, women, and children, were forcibly removed from their homes and taken on ships to colonies in the south, where they were abused.

To assist the governance of Canada, however, the English passed the Québec Act, in part to give recognition to the Catholic majority in the region and permit their participation in citizenship and public office.

Anti-Catholic Americans were horrified by the legislation and reacted loudly. The Constitutional Congress, which had been formed to put an end to British tyranny in the colonies, passed a resolution condemning the act as one of the five Intolerable Acts. The fact that residents of Québec were entitled to enjoy the free exercise of "the religion of Rome" was viewed with horror and outrage by the Americans. They vilified King George III of England as "a disguised Jesuit" because he was aiding Catholicism, "America's greatest enemy." The act in its own way thus hastened the drive to independence, even though Catholics went on to play vital roles in securing the American victory over England in the War of Independence. The act nevertheless helped to ensure the existence of a unique French-Canadian people who were the hallmark of eastern Canada.

After the demonstrations and protests, the Constitutional Congress sent a delegation to Québec to ask the Catholics there to join in the rebellion against the English. The Canadian Catholics naturally declined the invitation to join Protestants who ruthlessly persecuted their religion in the colonies. American Catholics, nevertheless offered total support for the rebellion.

Charles Carroll of Carrollton, who had conducted a series of apologetic defenses of the Catholic faith in public newspapers, writing as "First Citizen," was a fervent backer of the coming war. He signed the Declaration of Independence and became the longest-lived signer of that historic document. He was a cousin of John Carroll, the first Catholic bishop of the United States. Commodore John Barry, the true "Father of the United States Navy," and many other Catholics also earned the respect and affection of their fellow countrymen as the colonies united to fight for independence.

One tradition of the colonies had to be corrected, however, in order to appease the Catholics in the American military forces. The celebration of Pope Day, long popular in the colonies, had to be halted. Every year, Protestants in the American colonies had built effigies of the pope and marched through cities and towns, assaulting the effigies and burning Catholic symbols. General George Washington, realizing that such gross demonstrations of religious intolerance were luxuries the Americans could no longer afford, halted the celebrations. He stated that he was surprised that "there could be officers and soldiers in the army so devoid of common sense as not to see the impropriety of such a step at this juncture."

The arrival of French military officers and other trained European soldiers aided the Catholic cause during the Revolutionary War. French nobles such as the Marquis de Lafayette, the Comte de Rochambeau, the Comte de Grasse, and Count Casimir Pulaski displayed elegance, learning, and pride in their Catholicism. They were experts in war on land and sea, and their valiant aid brought about the defeat of the British forces, setting Americans free to follow their own destiny.

Following the success of the war, as the United States was formed and colonies entered the Union, state constitutions were drawn up, and in most cases Catholics were assured of their freedom to worship in peace. Some states delayed granting full civil rights to Catholics. In 1788, for example, the New York legislature, under the influence of John Jay, required officeholders to renounce foreign authorities "in all matters ecclesiastical as well as civil." Eventually, such states had to change their constitutions to bring them into line with national ideals.

In 1803 the Louisiana Purchase provided the young nation with vast tracts of land beyond the original colonies, doubling the size of the United States and bringing countless numbers of Catholics into the Union. By 1820, in fact, there were an estimated two hundred thousand Catholics in the land. Ten years later, some three hundred thousand reportedly converted to the faith, bringing about a flurry of anti-Catholic responses.

The Kensington Riots of 1844 demonstrate the violence unleashed against American Catholics in this period, especially those of Irish descent. Mobs of Protestants destroyed convents and churches, and thirteen were killed in Philadelphia. When the mobs headed to New York to carry on the rampage, Bishop John Hughes armed his Catholic New Yorkers and posted them at every Catholic facility. The mayor of New York, fearing the worst, protested the armed guards, but Bishop Hughes told him that there would be blood in the streets if the mobs attacked any Catholic property. He advised the mayor to caution the Protestants against "riling" the Irish. No assaults were recorded in the Diocese of New York.

The publicity surrounding the outrages prompted Abraham Lincoln to state on June 12, 1844: "The guarantee of the rights of conscience as found in our Constitution is most sacred and inviolable, and one that belongs no less to the Catholic than to the Protestant." His words soothed the situation, but the ongoing Protestant tirades against the Church brought about other disastrous events.

Anti-Catholic writings were a common feature of the early nineteenth century. Rebecca Reed's incendiary *Six Months in a Convent* sold two hundred thousand copies within a month of its publication in 1835. In the work, she claimed to have been held as a virtual slave as a member of the Ursuline convent near Boston; the truth was that Reed had been an employee of the convent and had been fired. Spurred on by the lies, an angry mob marched on the convent and burned it to the ground. The next year, Maria Monk's *Awful Disclosures of Maria Monk, or, The Hidden Secrets of a Nun's Life in a Convent Exposed,* by far the most infamous work in American anti-Catholic literature, was published in New York. The book, with its lurid claims of sexual crimes and abuse, became one of the most widely read tracts in the United States.

In 1853 Archbishop Gaetano Bedini was in the United States, planning a tour. A Protestant organization, the Order of the Star Spangled Banner, which became the American or Know-Nothing Party, protested the visit of the archbishop with riots in several cities. Archbishop Bedini had to be taken on a government vessel to safely board his ocean liner for the return trip to Europe.

A year later, in Old Town (Panawaniska), Maine, the Jesuit missionary Father John Bapst was taken captive by Protestants and tarred and feathered. Some in the group urged that he be slain, but cooler heads prevailed. This ghastly attack, of course, horrified the nation and halted demonstrations for a time.

The American Party taught that "Americans must rule America." Catholics, who recognized the pope as the head of the Church, were considered ineligible because of their loyalty to a foreign head of state. Millard Filmore ran for president as the candidate of the American Party. He lost the election, which hampered the American Party and led to its downfall.

In 1858 a new assault on the Church took place, but this involved the government, not angry mobs

Charlestown Ursuline Convent

or demonstrations. President Ulysses S. Grant appointed a commission to reallocate Indian missions, stripping Catholics of their traditional sites and giving them to Protestants. The Catholic Indian tribes suffered as a result, because the Protestants tried to force them into attending their services. Archbishop James Roosevelt Bayley of Baltimore countered the government's injustice by founding the Bureau of Catholic Indian Missions with Father Jean Baptiste Abraham Brouillet. Negotiations led to some remedial efforts, and in 1902 a remarkable lawyer named Charles Joseph Bonaparte, the grandnephew of the Emperor Napoleon, joined the Church's efforts. In time, Cardinal James Gibbons became a member of the government commission and was able to influence his Protestant counterparts.

On the social and political fronts, another organization, the American Protective Association, was started in 1857 by Henry F. Bower. This Protestant group blamed Catholics for all the ills of the era and demanded that they be barred from public office, and that the government close all parochial schools in the United States. In order to bolster their claims of Catholic evils, the American Protective Association published a "papal bull," which they claimed was authentic. This document supposedly called on American Catholics to kill all the Protestants in the nation. Obviously a crude forgery, the document sealed the fate of the organization, as Americans recoiled from such tactics against a major religious body. By 1900 the American Protective Association was out of power, but the group's basic tenets flourished in new associations.

Catholics in America continued to prosper, despite such opposition, consolidating facilities in the various dioceses and opening new Native American missions with the aid of St. Katharine Drexel. Some regions remained openly hostile to Catholics, and new attempts were made to curb Catholic activities. In 1912 the state of Michigan outlawed the wearing of religious garb in public schools. Ten years later, the people of Oregon passed a law making attendance in public schools mandatory; every child in Oregon was required to enter a public school by September 1, 1926. The Church in Oregon quickly moved to overturn the law and was aided by the American Civil Liberties Union and civil rights association across the nation. People of all faiths recognized the inherent danger in allowing such bias to remain unchallenged. The Church and its allies engaged in a series of legal battles that ended up in the United States Supreme Court, and on June 1, 1925, the court nullified the Oregon Compulsory Education Act.

The twentieth century witnessed the proliferation of anti-Catholic newspapers and books. With the rise of the Ku Klux Klan in the 1920s, many of the tired charges against the Church were given renewed currency, and a 1914 study by the Knights of Columbus reported that there were over sixty national anti-Catholic weekly newspapers in the United States, with a readership in the millions. In 1949 Paul Blanshard published *American Freedom and Catholic Power,* which declared the Catholic Church to be an enemy of democracy and hostile to American ideals of freedom of speech and religion. The argument was an old one, rooted in the image of Catholics as adherents of an *imperium in imperio,* a society within society, with its loyalties first to the pope before the civil government and hence essentially disloyal and untrustworthy. Catholics responded to the attacks with aggressive apologetics, such as Catholic Truth societies. Of particular note in the refutation of anti-Catholicism was the work of Archbishop John F. Noll, founder of *Our Sunday Visitor.*

World War II eased tensions among the religious denominations as the entire nation supported America's military efforts. At the close of the war, however, President Harry S. Truman tried to establish an American office of ambassador to the Vatican, and a firestorm broke out across the land. An organization called "Protestants and Other Americans for the Separation of Church and State," the forerunner of several modern groups, was founded by Paul Blanshard. He announced that Catholics were ineligible to take part in American affairs because the Church taught that there is a source of truth beyond the expressed views of secular humanists, scientists, and the majority of the country. Pope Pius XII, understanding what forces had been unleashed in America and in Europe, issued *Evangelii Praecones,* urging Catholics to recognize old philosophies in new garb.

The presidential campaign of 1960 brought

renewed anti-Catholic hostility into the open once more. The Ku Klux Klan, white supremacists, and anti-Catholic Protestants openly questioned John F. Kennedy's qualifications as an American, suggesting that he might be beholden first to the Vatican before his own country. Kennedy answered the question forcefully and narrowly won the White House.

In the wake of the Second Vatican Council, reforms and changes in Church institutions brought the unexpected loss of priests and religious, harming the educational and evangelical missions of the various dioceses. The rise of the laity aided the faith in many ways, but certain signs of discord appeared as well. The anti-Catholic forces began to celebrate the divisons that appeared in the American Church, and media events focused on the evident controversy. The Supreme Court decision concerning abortion in 1973 added new weight to anti-Catholic forces and became a hallmark of opposition to the Church. The Church made efforts to bolster its defense of life and truth, and organizations moved to bring about public recognition of the assaults being made on Catholic leaders and institutions. Father Virgil C. Blum, S.J., aware of the growing array of enemies, started the Catholic League for Religious and Civil Rights in 1973. The Catholic League defended the Church against the virulent attacks being made and continues to expose the bias evident in many facets of American society.

In recent years, anti-Catholicism has become a virtual staple of modern cultural struggles over a host of issues, from abortion and homosexuality to the disastrous sex abuse scandal. The Church is commonly lampooned by comedians and in films and on television. *The Da Vinci Code*, the bestselling novel by Dan Brown, presents the Church as having been engaged for centuries in a criminal and murderous cover-up of Jesus's true lineage and portrays the Personal Prelature of Opus Dei as filled with ultrafanatical Catholics who use assassins to silence enemies and the truth. Films such as *Dogma, Sin City, Quills, The Magdalene Laundries, King Arthur*, and many others depict Catholics as intolerant, deceitful, deranged, and corrupt. On television, pedophile priests, corrupt bishops, and insane pro-life advocates are a staple of crime dramas.

In contemporary America, anti-Catholicism is especially the realm of secularized cultural elites who see the Church as an enemy of social and scientific progress and enlightenment. Church officials and orthodox Catholics are caricatured as obscurantist, medieval in their approaches, and so unyielding in areas such as sexual liberation, euthanasia, and biomedical ethics that they pose a genuine danger to long-term human progress.

Traditional anti-Catholicism is found in many parts of the country, rooted in intolerant Protestantism and in extreme forms of evangelical Protestantism. The Church in that milieu remains the "whore of Babylon" and Catholics are pagans who oppose the true Christian faith of the Bible. The old eighteenth- and nineteenth-century images of Catholics as dangers to the state are still prevalent.

One of the chief havens for severe anti-Catholic rhetoric is the Internet. Literally thousands of anti-Catholic Web sites populate the dark corners of the Web, created by secularist enemies of the Church, more traditional Protestant bigots of the faith, and also the growing numbers of social and sexual anarchists who oppose all forms of religious expression and see the Church as one of the greatest symbols of the social order.

The sex abuse crisis over the last years has proven a powerful springboard for every manifestation of anti-Catholicism to launch attacks and seek to damage the reputation of the Church and its leaders. Unquestionably, the scandal has caused massive difficulties for the institutional Church, but the excessive media coverage, including the relentless attacks on the Church in the editorial pages of some of America's leading newspapers, points to the use that anti-Catholics are willing to put the scandal for the advancement of their own agendas.

Antonio of the Ascension (early seventeenth century)

A Discalced Carmelite monk and missionary, Antonio of the Ascension accompanied the expedition of Sebastian Vizcaino to California in 1602, with Father Andrew of the Assumption and Thomas of Aquinas, also Carmelites. The Discalced Carmelites were in Mexico in 1588, with more arriving in the mission to labor in present-day New Mexico. As the Franciscans had already been assigned to that territory, Antonio and his companions joined

Vizcaino, who was a merchant given a royal commission to explore the Pacific coastal region of present-day California. Father Andrew of the Assumption celebrated Mass on the coast at San Diego, at the time called San Miguel.

The expedition moved north, mapping the coast and charting the waters; they reached the area of Monterey, naming it Carmelo. The Carmelites wanted to return to the area, and when they were back in Mexico they urged the authorities to send missionaries north to the tribes living there. Father Antonio of the Ascension continued to describe the Carmelo region until his death. The Carmel Mission was later named in honor of their explorations.

Anunciación, Fray Domingo de la (1510–1591)

The Dominican missionary who accompanied Tristán de Luna's expedition to Florida, Fray Domingo de la Anunciación was part of an ill-fated adventure to explore and map the southeastern region of modern America. Born Juan de Ecija in Fuenteo-Ovejuna, Spain, Fray Domingo migrated to Mexico around 1523, and entered the Dominicans there in 1531 or 1532. He distinguished himself as an apostle of charity during an epidemic in Mexico in 1545 and was a faithful missionary to the local peoples.

Luis Aponte Martinez

In 1559 he set off with Tristán de Luna's expedition, along with four other Dominican companions. The expeditionary force was shipwrecked, but though Fray Domingo endured many perils and hardships he survived the disaster. He returned to Mexico and served in Dominican monasteries and councils until becoming blind in 1585. He died in Mexico, greatly esteemed by the native populations.

Aponte Martinez, Luis (August 4, 1922–April 10, 2012)

The archbishop of the Archdiocese of San Juan from 1964 to 1999, Luis Aponte Martinez was created a cardinal in 1973. He was born in Lajas, Puerto Rico, the son of Santiago Evangelista Aponte and Rosa Martinez. He studied for the priesthood at San Ildefonso Seminary at Ponce and then at St. John's Seminary in Boston, being ordained on April 10, 1950. He then began his ministry by serving in parishes at Patillas and Santa Isabel in Puerto Rico.

In 1955 Father Aponte Martinez was made secretary to the bishop and was then appointed vice chancellor and superintendent of schools. In 1960 he became chaplain of the National Guard of Puerto Rico. He was consecrated as the titular bishop of Lares and auxiliary bishop of Ponce on October 12, 1960, becoming the bishop of Ponce in 1963. He developed the Catholic University at Ponce, a distinguished educational institution on the island. On November 4, 1964, he was promoted to the Archdiocese of San Juan and began implementing the reforms of the Second Vatican Council. He was made a cardinal priest on March, 5, 1973, the first from the island to hold that rank. His titular church was St. Mary Mother of Providence in Monte Verde. Cardinal Aponte Martinez also served on the Conference of Latin American Bishops and as chairman of the Episcopal Conference of Puerto Rico. He retired from his see in 1999.

Apostleship of Prayer

A worldwide pious association of Catholics and other Christians committed to offering themselves and their labors each day in union with Christ's sacrifice in the Mass, the Apostleship of Prayer was formed in 1844 among a group of Jesuit seminarians at Vals, France, under Francis X. Gautrelet. The movement was first made popular through the efforts of Reverend Henry Ramière, S.J., who in 1861 designed its organization for parishes and various Catholic institutions and wrote the work *The Apostleship of Prayer*. In 1879 Pope Blessed Pius IX approved the first statutes, followed by a revision in 1896 approved by Pope Leo XIII. The organization eventually spread to other countries, with the general of the Society of Jesus serving as the moderator general of the association. It reached the United States in 1861 and found a wide following in American dioceses.

The statutes took as their objective the promotion of the practice of prayer for the mutual intentions of the members in union with the intercession of Christ in heaven. Three degrees of membership were established, with three practices: a daily offering of one's prayers, good works, and sufferings; daily recitation of a decade of the Rosary for the special intentions of the Holy Father; and the reception of holy Communion, monthly or weekly. Currently, the Apostleship of Prayer promotes devotion to the Sacred Heart of Jesus and the Immaculate Heart of Mary.

Apostleship of the Sea (*Apostolatus Maris*)

An international Catholic organization for the welfare of seafarers and those involved in the maritime industry, the Apostleship of the Sea was founded in 1920 in Glasgow, Scotland, by Reverend Donald Macintosh, Arthur Gannon, and Peter Anson, to assist evangelization among those engaged in a life at sea. Two years later they received the blessing of Pope Pius XI, who encouraged the Apostleship of the Sea to extend its mission to all the seas and oceans of the world. The organization was established in the United States in 1947. In 1952 Pope Pius XII approved the formal institution of the apostleship by the Holy See through the apostolic constitution *Exul Familia*. Eventually, the apostleship came under the overall direction of Pontifical Council for Migrants and Itinerant Peoples, and its norms were updated by Pope Blessed John Paul II in a 1997 *motu proprio*. A World Congress is held every five years.

The organization of the apostleship in individual countries relies upon an episcopal promoter who assists and oversees the work of a national director. The national director coordinates the efforts of individual chaplains and promotes their ministries. The national director's office also provides media outreach and produces a newsletter, *Catholic Maritime News* (in the United States). The U.S. office is an affiliate of the United States Conference of Catholic Bishops and provides port chaplains in sixty-three American ports.

Affiliated with the Apostleship of the Sea in the United States is the Apostleship of the Sea of the United States of America, formerly known as the National Catholic Conference for Seafarers. Inspired by Pope Blessed John Paul II's apostolic letter *Stella Maris*, the organization seeks to organize chaplains, clergy, religious, laity, and mariners in all matters concerning seafarers and maritime matters.

Apostolic Delegate. *See* Holy See-U.S. Relations

Apostolic Nuncio. *See* Holy See-U.S. Relations

Arbez, Edward Philip (May 16, 1881–December 27, 1967)

A biblical scholar, Edward Philip Arbez promoted reform in biblical studies. He was born in Paris, France, and migrated to the United States in 1901, entering the Sulpicians. He was ordained in 1904 after studies at The Catholic University of America. Father Arbez subsequently taught biblical studies at St. Patrick's Seminary, Menlo Park, California, and at The Catholic University of America, where, in 1943, he was named head of the department of Semitic Languages. To promote biblical studies, he supported the foundation of the Catholic Biblical Association in 1936 and the wide implementation of Pope Pius XII's encyclical *Divino Afflante Spiritu* (1943), which opened the way for much of contemporary biblical scholarship in the Church. Arbez was also instrumental in the publication of *The New American Bible*.

Argüello, Luis Antonio (1784–1830)

The governor of California from 1822 to 1825, Luis Antonio Argüello was the first native son to hold that office. He was born in San Francisco, the son of a former governor, Don José Darío Argüello. Entering military service at a young age, he served with distinction. As governor, he represented both the Mexican Empire and the provisional government leading to the Mexican Republic. In 1821 he is reported to have led an expedition to Colombia. Argüello was known as an honest and capable governor, showing compassion for people of all social levels. He died in San Francisco.

Arizona

Called the Grand Canyon State, Arizona is located in the southwestern part of the country. It is bounded on the north by Utah, on the east by New Mexico, on the south by Mexico, and on the west by Nevada and California. There are two geographical regions in the state: the Colorado Plateau in the north, and the Basin and Range in the south. The Native Americans who resided in Arizona originally were Apache, Hopi, Mohave, Navajo, Papago and Pima. Arizona entered the Union in 1912 as the forty-eighth state.

The Catholic history of Arizona began with the expedition of Marcos de Niza, who wandered in the region circa 1539, looking for Cibola, the legendary Seven Cities of Gold. De Niza brought a Moor into the region, a man named Estevan; there were also Franciscan priests traveling with the expedition. Francisco Vázquez de Coronado was in Arizona circa 1540; Franciscans Father Juan de Padilla and Father Juan de la Cruz were with Coronado's group. Father Juan de Padilla was later slain, becoming the protomartyr of the United States, the first to die for the faith.

By 1600 Franciscan priests and brothers had established missions along the Rio Grande. Jesuits arrived in the area by 1690, and the outstanding "horseback missionary" priest, Father Eusebius Francisco Kino, founded the Mission San Xavier del Bac and other outposts of the faith at Guevavi and Tumacacuri.

King Charles II of Spain sent other Jesuits into the area in 1767, and the Franciscans continued their missions. A European settlement opened in Arizona in 1776.

As a result of winning independence from Spain, Mexico assumed control of Arizona in 1821. Six years later Catholic priests, all Spanish, were expelled from the area. The missions stood mainly empty until 1846, when the Treaty of Guadalupe-Hidalgo ended the Mexican-American War, and Arizona lands north of the Gila River were ceded to the United States. The Gadsden Purchase of 1854 gained the southern Arizona territories from Mexico as well.

Bishop Jean Baptiste Lamy, the vicar apostolic of New Mexico, served the Catholics of the area as Arizona communities were attached to New Mexico in ecclesiastical matters at that time. In 1854 the first copper mines opened at Ajo, developed by Charles Debrille Poston, called the "Father of Arizona." Father J. P. Machebeuf, recognizing the number of the faithful in the area, started his apostolate in Tucson in 1859.

In 1863 the U.S. Congress created the Arizona Territory, and Mission San Xavier del Bac was revived as Catholics became more active in their communities. Five years later, Bishop John Baptist Salpointe was made vicar apostolic of Arizona. The region was still unsettled, but the faith grew, even as Geronimo, the famed Apache chief, was defeated in 1886 by U.S. troops under the command of General Nelson Miles.

In 1897 the Diocese of Tucson was erected, with Bishop Peter Bourgarde establishing agencies and offices for diocesan administration. Schools were opened for the Native Americans in the area, and Theodore Roosevelt Dam aided the economy of the region when it opened in 1911. One year later, Arizona entered the Union, and when World War I began, there were more volunteers for military duty in Arizona than in any other state.

Mission Tumacacori, Arizona

Other great dams, the Coolidge and Hoover, were built in the 1930s, easing the effects of the Great Depression. The start of World War II also spurred Arizona industry as the people supported the nation's military efforts. In 1955 Bishop Daniel J. Gerske opened Regina Cleri Seminary in Tucson. Arizona continued to prosper from its mining, farming, livestock, and tourism industries, and the Diocese of Phoenix, another Catholic stronghold in the state, was established in 1969 and has continued to expand ministries and services to the Catholics of the region.

The last decades have brought steady increases in the population of Hispanic Catholics, and the Church in the state has committed resources to their care. In 2011 there were more than one million Catholics, 397 priests, approximately 400 men and women religious, and 168 parishes.

San Xavier del Bac Mission, Arizona

Arkansas

Called the Land of Opportunity, Arkansas is located in the south-central part of the nation, bounded on the north by Missouri, on the east by the Mississippi River, on the south by Louisiana, and on the west by Texas and Oklahoma. Two geographical regions dominate Arkansas: the Lowlands in the eastern and southern sections, and the Highlands in the west and north. In the Highlands are the Ozark Plateau, the Quachita Mountains, and the Arkansas Valley. The original Native American inhabitants of the state were the Quapaws, or Ozarks, also called the Arkansas or Illinois, and the Algonquins. Arkansas entered the Union in 1836 as the twenty-fifth state.

The Catholic history of the state began in the 1540s, when Hernando de Soto led an expedition into the area. He had priests accompanying his forces. In 1673 the Jesuit Father Jacques Marquette and Louis Joliet visited Arkansas during their exploration of the Mississippi River. In 1682 René-Robert Chevalier, Sieur de La Salle, claimed Arkansas for France. Four years later, Henri de Tonti, who had served with La Salle, founded a settlement at present-day Arkansas Post. Soon after, Father Nicolas Foucault was living among the Quapaws.

There were few white settlers in the region until 1717, when a Scottish financier organized a group called the Mississippi Company, backed by France. The group was supposed to exploit the area's natural resources but failed in 1720, costing France a considerable fortune. Little progress was made toward settlement until 1763, when France ceded Arkansas and other regions to Spain. Emperor Napoleon won back Arkansas and other French holdings from Spain in 1800, then sold them to the United States as part of the Louisiana Purchase of 1803.

In 1824 Bishop Louis DuBourg administered Catholic affairs in Arkansas, while Bishop Joseph Rosati had ecclesiastical jurisdiction over the area. The U.S. Congress had designated the region as the Arkansas Territory in 1819, and in 1836 Arkansas entered the Union. Two years later, Father Richard Bole founded St. Mary's Mission in Pine Bluff, where the Sisters of Loretto opened a school. The Diocese of Little Rock was established in 1843, with Bishop Andrew Byrne opening offices and institutions for administration.

During the Civil War, Arkansas was part of the Confederacy, although the state was openly divided on the slavery issue. In 1863 Union troops occupied Little Rock, and Arkansas was the site of the Battle of Chickamauga. The state was readmitted to the Union in 1868. Two years earlier, Bishop Edward M. Fitzgerald had been appointed to Little Rock.

The diocese prospered, and parishes and institutions served the faithful. In 1878 the Benedictines founded New Subiaco Abbey, and in 1894, Bishop Fitzgerald dedicated the first black Catholic parish. Under the leadership of Bishop John B. Morris, Little Rock University opened, and a weekly Catholic newspaper was introduced.

Arkansas supported the efforts of the United States in World Wars I and II and suffered with their fellow Americans through the Great Depression. The state also faced the racial crises of the 1950s. In 1957 Little Rock was shaken when a high school was integrated and Governor Orval Faubus blocked the process. President Dwight D. Eisenhower federalized the National Guard and maintained troops in the city. In 1958 Governor Faubus closed all the high schools, but they were reopened in 1959. In 2011 there were 131,000 Catholics served by 111 priests, 178 women religious, and 89 parishes in the state.

Arlington, Diocese of

Established on August 13, 1974, by Pope Paul VI, the Diocese of Arlington serves counties in northern Virginia. Arlington, which is located near the District of Columbia, is the site of Arlington National Cemetery. The diocese is a suffragan see of the Archdiocese of Baltimore.

The Catholic history of Arlington as part of the colony of Virginia started with the presence of the Spanish, who began a colony in 1526 at the site of the later Jamestown Colony. The Dominican Father Antonio de Montesinos celebrated the first Mass with this expeditionary group. By 1607, however, Virginia was a British territory with severe restrictions against Catholics and even stricter regulations concerning priests.

The Revolutionary War ended the anti-Catholicism of the penal period across the state as a new constitution guaranteed religious liberties, and in 1789 Virginia came under the administration of the Diocese of Baltimore in Catholic affairs. However, St. Mary's Church, established by the Jesuits in 1795, served the Catholics in Arlington. Father Francis Neale erected churches there also. In 1820 the Diocese of Richmond was established; the Catholic faithful in Arlington were under this new ecclesiastical jurisdiction as the Catholic population in the area continued to expand.

The Civil War and the Reconstruction Period were severe trials for the people of Virginia, but parishes opened in the area that would become Arlington diocese. In 1858 St. Mary's of Sorrows was beginning at Fairfax Station. St. Mary's at Fredericksburg had been established twenty years earlier. Sacred Heart of Jesus Parish prospered in Winchester in 1870, and St. John the Evangelist was opened in Warrenton in 1874. The Cathedral of St. Thomas More was completed in 1938, during harsh economic times.

During World War I, the Great Depression, and World War II, Arlington endured the trials of their fellow Americans. More and more families settled in the area, and parishes and schools were erected to accommodate the growing Catholic population. The Catholic progress in Arlington was recognized in 1974, when the diocese was established.

The first bishop of the Diocese of Arlington was Thomas J. Welsh, who had served as auxiliary bishop of the Archdiocese of Philadelphia since 1970. He was installed on August 13, 1974, and instituted the agencies and offices for administration of a diocese. Bishop Welsh maintained facilities and expanded the Catholic presence in the area until he was transferred to Allentown on February 8, 1983.

The second bishop of Arlington was John R. Keating, who was consecrated and installed on August 4, 1983. He continued the expansion programs throughout the diocese until his death on March 22, 1998.

The third bishop of Arlington, Paul S. Loverde, was installed in the Cathedral of St. Thomas More on March 25, 1999. Bishop Loverde had served as an auxiliary bishop for the Archdiocese of Hartford and as the bishop of Ogdensburg before being appointed to Arlington. He served also as chairman of the U.S. Bishops' Committee on Vocations from 1995 to 1998.

At the time of his appointment, Bishop Loverde

was already noted for his labors to promote vocations and the pro-life movement, and as bishop of Arlington he has remained committed to both causes. He also presided over a highly successful $115 million diocesan capital campaign "Rooted in Faith — Forward in Hope" and the opening of five new parishes, one new mission, and the acquisition of land for further parish expansion; he has also opened an elementary school, has plans for two new high schools, a shelter for families in crisis, and a retirement home for priests. In 2011 the diocese had 413,000 Catholics, 225 priests, 185 men and women religious, and 68 parishes.

Arnoudt (Arnold), Peter Joseph (May 17, 1811– July 29, 1865)

A Jesuit writer and poet, Peter Joseph Arnoudt specialized in Greek epics. He was born in Moere, Belgium, and entered the Society of Jesus in 1831, after migrating to the United States. Professed as a Jesuit and ordained to the priesthood, Father Arnoudt taught in the colleges of the Society and vowed to promote devotion to the Sacred Heart. Many of his literary works were published during his lifetime, all received enthusiastically and translated into many languages. He also left manuscripts at his death in Cincinnati, including a Greek epic poem, Greek odes, and spiritual works.

Arvide, Martín de (c. 1586–1632)

A Franciscan missionary, Martín de Arvide was called the "Apostle of the Picuris" and was one of the early priest martyrs of the area that would become the United States. He was born in Puerto de San Sebastian, Spain, and was educated and ordained a Franciscan, having attended the order's schools as a young man.

In 1612 Father Arvide was sent with twenty companions to the missions of the modern New Mexico territory, as the apostolate in that region was expanding. There he established San Lorenzo Mission at Picuris and worked in the area until 1628. Then word came that the local Jeméz Indians had fled into the mountains to escape assaults by the neighboring Navajos. The Jeméz, reduced to the status of refugees in a harsh climate, asked Father Arvide to serve as their chaplain. He joined the Jeméz in the mountains and stayed with them for four years, aiding the tribe in obtaining food and maintaining their morale in the face of danger.

In 1632 he was asked to open a new mission for the Zipias Indians of the region of Sonora. On his way to the Zipias, Father Arvide encountered a group of Zuñis and was killed by them. A monument was erected to Father Arvide at San Lorenzo, commemorating his dedicated service and devotion.

Ashton, John (1742–1814 or 1815)

A Jesuit missionary, John Ashton founded the first recorded parish in Baltimore and demonstrated initiative and courage in a time of severe persecution. He was born in Ireland and was ordained in the Society of Jesus, becoming one of the first priests to serve the Catholic colonials in Baltimore and laboring in that city from 1776 to 1784. Father Ashton used a brick building owned by an Irishman as his base of operations, a site located near Battle Monument. He cleared out the abandoned site, including chasing hogs out of their quarters on the ground floor. Acadian refugees lived in the upper floor of the structure, and Father Ashton allowed them to stay in their haven. He transformed the lower portion into a church to meet the needs of the Catholics in the area.

Having conducted a considerable number of business transactions while serving as a missionary in England, Father Ashton served as the procurator-general of the Jesuits in the region. He also served as the superintendent for the construction of Georgetown College in 1788. He died in Maryland.

Atlanta, Archdiocese of

Announced on July 2, 1956, and canonically erected on November 8, 1956, as the Diocese of Atlanta by Pope Pius XII, and established as an archdiocese on February 21, 1962, by Pope Blessed John XXIII, the Archdiocese of Atlanta serves counties in northern George and has suffragan sees. Atlanta is the capital of Georgia and the state's largest city. It was founded in 1837 as a terminus of a railroad and was called Terminus and then Marthasville. In 1845 the city was incorporated and renamed Atlanta.

The archdiocese has a profound Catholic history as part of the early missionary efforts of the Church in the New World. Georgia was visited by Hernando de Soto in 1540, and Catholic priests were with his expedition. A group of Spanish Dominicans entered the area circa 1560, and they established missions on Georgia's southeastern coast. In time the Jesuits took over these missions, giving them to the Franciscans in later eras. Jesuit Father Pedro Martinez was slain by members of a local tribe on Cumberland Island in 1566. He is the protomartyr of the Society of Jesus in the United States.

By the early 1700s, Georgia was controlled by the British, and in 1732 Governor James Edward Oglethorpe and John Viscount Percival received a grant from King George II to found a colony. Oglethorpe and some one hundred settlers entered the Savannah area, naming the colony Georgia in honor of the king. Catholics were denied freedom of religion in the colony, although the restrictions were eased slightly when Georgia became a royal colony in 1754.

During the Revolutionary War, the Polish hero Count Casimir Pulaski was killed during the siege of Savannah. Georgia became the fourth colony to ratify the U. S. Constitution, entering the Union in 1788. Catholics were given freedom when the new state constitution was ratified.

In 1850 Pope Blessed Pius IX reorganized the Church in the far southeastern United States, and Catholics in Georgia and parts of Florida were placed under the care of a new Diocese of Savannah. The Catholic population in Georgia remained relatively small, and by the start of the Civil War in 1861 there were four thousand Catholics in the state, with parishes in Atlanta, Savannah, Macon, Columbus, and Locust Grove.

During the Civil War, Atlanta became a prime target for the Union forces under General William Tecumseh Sherman. When Sherman moved out of Atlanta on November 15, 1864, on his "March to the Sea," the city was in flames. Father Thomas O'Reilly, pastor of Immaculate Conception Church, asked Union officers not to set fires on the blocks where churches were located. The Union officers agreed to his request, and a plaque was erected in Atlanta to commemorate this event.

In 1886 the Sisters of Mercy came to the city, followed by other congregations and the Marist Fathers, who founded Marist College and Sacred Heart Parish. A Catholic newspaper was introduced, and Atlanta recovered from the Civil War disasters.

The faithful endured the difficulties of the Great Depression, as well as World War II, and the growing importance of the city was recognized by the Holy See. In 1936 Pope Pius XI founded the Diocese of Savannah-Atlanta, with its Cathedral of Christ the King. Bishop Gerald O'Hara was appointed the bishop of Savannah in 1935, the last ordinary to serve as shepherd of the entire state of Georgia.

The Diocese of Atlanta was established in 1956 when Pope Pius XII removed the northern seventy-one counties of Georgia from the Diocese of Savannah to form a new ecclesiastical territory. The number was subsequently reduced to sixty-nine with the return of two counties to the Savannah diocese. At its founding, the Diocese of Atlanta covered 23,000 square miles, with 23,600 Catholics in 23 parishes and 12 missions.

The first bishop of the Diocese of Atlanta was Francis D. Hyland, who had served as auxiliary bishop of the Diocese of Savannah-Atlanta since 1949. Bishop Hyland was installed in Atlanta on November 8, 1956. He instituted the agencies and personnel necessary for diocesan administration and added high schools and expanded diocesan facilities to meet the growing needs of the Catholics in the area. When his health failed, Bishop Hyland retired in 1961.

His successor, Bishop Paul J. Hallinan, was the former bishop of Charleston, having served there since 1958. He was promoted to the rank of archbishop on February 21, 1962, and installed as the first archbishop of Atlanta on March 29, 1962. Atlanta was henceforth the center of an ecclesiastical province that included the states of Georgia, North Carolina, South Carolina, and Florida. (Florida was removed in 1969 to become the Province of Miami.) At the time of its elevation to the rank of archdiocese, the Catholic population numbered 32,000 out of a total population of over two million. Archbishop Hallinan was dedicated to civil rights and also implemented the reforms of the Second Vatican Council in the archdiocese. He died on March 27, 1968, of hepatitis.

Bishop Thomas Andrew Donnellan was appointed as the second archbishop of the archdiocese on May 29, 1968, and was installed on July 16. He had served as the bishop of Ogdensburg since 1964. Archbishop Donnellan labored to meet the growing needs of the archdiocese, establishing over thirty parishes and expanding social and spiritual ministries. He suffered a stroke and died on October 15, 1987.

His successor was the first African-American archbishop of the United States, Eugene A. Marino, S.S.J. He had served as the auxiliary bishop of Washington, D.C., until his appointment on March 14, 1988. Archbishop Marino was installed on May 5, 1988. He resigned on July 10, 1990.

Bishop James P. Lyke, O.F.M., was his successor. He had served as the auxiliary bishop of Cleveland since 1979. He was named apostolic administrator of Atlanta on July 10, 1990, and acceded as archbishop on April 30, 1991. On December 27, 1992, Archbishop Lyke died of cancer.

His successor, Archbishop John Francis Donoghue, was named the fifth archbishop of Atlanta on June 22, 1993, having served before that as bishop of Charlotte. He was installed on August 18 of that year, leading the archdiocese into the millennium and into the complex modern era. Coping with a loss of priests and religious, Archbishop Donoghue continued expanding diocesan services and maintaining administrative apostolates. He retired on December 9, 2004, and was succeeded on the same day by Bishop Wilton D. Gregory, who had been bishop of Belleville since 1993. Archbishop Gregory was also president of the United States Conference of Catholic Bishops 2001–04. The primary focus of Archbishop Gregory's time as archbishop has been shepherding the phenomenal growth of the archdiocese. The population of the archdiocese is expected to reach one million within a decade, and it is also increasingly diverse. In 2011 the Catholic population of the archdiocese was over 900,000, served by 270 priests and 87 parishes.

Augustinian Order of the Hermit Friars of St. Augustine

This religious order developed from the widely separated communities of hermits existing across the world during the Middle Ages, all of whom adhered to the Rule of St. Augustine. In 1256 Pope Alexander IV brought the separate communities together, with the Dominican order serving as the model for unification. The monks thus became preachers and active religious in cities and towns, and eventually spread throughout Western Europe. Noted for their spiritual traditions and devotion, the Augustinians subsequently survived the Reformation era (Martin Luther had been a member of the order) and became important missionary leaders in the New World.

In the late 1600s, Augustinian monks arrived in the area that became the United States to serve as missionaries. Father Henri de la Motte was stationed in present-day Maine, and Father John Skerret served in Virginia around 1680. The establishment of St. Augustine's Church in Philadelphia in 1796, however, marks the true beginning of the Augustinian presence in the United States. Fathers Matthew Carr and John Rosseter founded the parish, receiving donations from George Washington and other prominent Americans who respected the academic excellence of the priests and their fervor. Fathers Carr and Rosseter also accepted other priestly obligations, serving as pastors of St. Mary's Church in Philadelphia as well. Bishop John Carroll of Baltimore, America's first bishop, appointed Father Carr vicar general for eastern Pennsylvania, Delaware, New Jersey, and New York.

The Augustinian Province of Our Lady of Good Counsel was established on August 27, 1796. For a time, however, there was only one Augustinian in the United States. Father Michael Hurley served alone for years until two other Augustinians came from Ireland in 1828. In 1841 the Augustinians purchased the two-hundred-acre Belle Air farm near Philadelphia, and Villanova University was founded as a college on the site.

The anti-Catholic riots in Philadelphia in May 1844 resulted in the loss of St. Augustine's Church and a vast theological library assembled by the original Augustinians in the American missions. A new church was dedicated on November 5, 1848, as the Augustinians simply set about rebuilding. Between 1848 and 1880, the Augustinians opened parishes, expanded Villanova, and became an official province of the Augustinians under the name of St. Thomas of Villanova, a status documented on August 25, 1874. The Augustinians also started missions in Puerto Rico and Cuba in 1899, and new provinces of the order slowly formed across America.

In the modern era, the Augustinians aided the U.S. efforts in World War I, and in World War II, when twenty-five Augustinians served as chaplains in the armed forces. In 1952 the Augustinians of the United States were given papal permission to establish a mission in Nagasaki, Japan. They also went to Peru. The Augustinian Sisters of Contemplative Life opened a convent in Holland, Michigan, in 1968. Expansion continued throughout the 1960s, with houses and schools established in Florida, California, and Massachusetts. Currently, the Augustinians are organized into several U.S. provinces, including the Province of Our Mother of Good Counsel and the Province of St. Augustine.

Austin, Diocese of

Established by Pope Pius XII in 1948, the Diocese of Austin serves counties in the central part of Texas. Austin is the capital of Texas and a cultural and commercial center. Founded as a riverside village called Waterloo, the city was erected as the state seat in 1839. The city was then renamed in honor of Stephen F. Austin and incorporated in 1840. When the capitol was moved to Houston in 1842 because of a Mexican threat, the people of Austin staged the "Archives War," retaining government records to force a return of state officials to the city. The Diocese of Austin is a suffragan see of the Archdiocese of San Antonio.

Catholic missionaries were in the Austin area by 1748. In December of that year, Franciscans started missions on the San Gabriel River in Williamson County. The sites were abandoned in 1755, but they were marked as historical sites. In 1836 St. Peter and St. Paul Church was founded in Frelsberg. In 1847 the Diocese of Galveston (now the Archdiocese of Galveston-Houston) was established, with authority over the entire state. In 1874 the Diocese of San Antonio was erected.

Austin's Catholics took part in the historical events of their own eras — the Civil War, World War I, World War II, and the Great Depression, supporting the military efforts of the nation and enduring the trials of economic hard times. The vitality of the faith was noted in 1947, when Austin was created as a diocese for that part of the state.

Louis J. Reicher was named the first bishop of the Diocese of Austin on November 29, 1947. He was consecrated on April 14, 1948, and installed in St. Mary's Cathedral. Bishop Reicher started the agencies and offices for diocesan affairs and also began an immense building program, supervising the construction of more than 150 buildings and institutions. He also took part in the Second Vatican Council and implemented the reforms mandated by the council. He died on February 23, 1984.

His successor was Bishop Vincent M. Harris, who had served as the bishop of Beaumont since 1966. He was transferred to Austin on April 21, 1971, and acceded to the see on November 16, 1971. Bishop Harris continued expanding diocesan facilities to accommodate the growth of the Catholic population and introduced catechetical programs. He retired on February 25, 1986.

Bishop John E. McCarthy became the third bishop of Austin after serving as the auxiliary bishop of Galveston-Houston since 1979. He was transferred to the Diocese of Austin on December 24, 1985. Bishop McCarthy led the faithful of Austin into the millennium, continuing the updating of diocesan facilities and adapting to the stresses of the modern era. He resigned on January 2, 2001.

The fourth bishop of the diocese, Gregory M. Aymond, had served as an auxiliary bishop of the Archdiocese of New Orleans since 1996. He was appointed coadjutor bishop of Austin in 2000 and acceded to the see on January 2, 2001. Bishop Aymond was appointed archbishop of New Orleans and was succeeded as bishop by Joe Steve Vásquez, who had been an auxiliary bishop in the Archdiocese of Galveston-Houston from 2001 to the time of his appointment on January 26, 2010. In 2011 the diocese had more than 500,000 Catholics, served by 200 priests and 101 parishes.

Avery, Martha (April 6, 1851–August 8, 1929)

A Catholic writer and lecturer, Martha Gallisone Moore Avery was a convert to the Church. She was born in Steuben, Maine, and raised as a Unitarian. At an early age she grew concerned for the plight of workers in the Industrial Revolution and joined the then-nascent Socialist movement in the United States. Her activism brought her into contact with the Socialist Labor Party and fellow socialist David Goldstein in the 1890s, and together they formed the Karl Marx Class (renamed the Boston School of Political Economy in 1901) to promote various Socialist causes and to serve as a forum for lectures, propaganda, and discussions.

By 1902 Avery and Goldstein had grown severely disillusioned with the Socialist cause, in particular its relentless attacks on religion in general and Christianity in particular, its advocacy of free love, and its corrosive effects on the family. Two years later, Avery entered the Catholic Church and henceforth was a dedicated opponent of Socialism who advocated authentic Catholic teachings on labor and the rights of workers. She thus promoted the 1891 encyclical *Rerum Novarum* of Pope Leo XIII and in 1917 was a co-founder, with Goldstein, of the Catholic Truth Guild. The guild had its origins the year before in Avery's enthusiastic preaching on street corners in Boston, with the full approval of Cardinal William O'Connell. She also served as president of the Catholic lay organization Common Cause Society from 1922 to 1929. (*See also* Catholic Evidence Guild.)

Ayeta, Francis de (1600s–unknown)

A prominent Franciscan friar of Mexico, Francis de Ayeta predicted the revolt of the Santa Fe Indians in their missions and then went to the aid of surviving Christians. Father de Ayeta was born in Spain and was assigned to the New World missions, becoming a superior of the Province of the Holy Evangel in New Mexico. He held other titles as well and was a noted apologist for the Franciscans in America.

In 1678 Father de Ayeta visited the Franciscans at Santa Fe, New Mexico. He was horrified at the conditions there, which included gross abuse of the Pueblo Indians of the region by Spanish settlers and some missionaries. Father de Ayeta called for reformations and stiffer garrisons, predicting to his religious superiors that the Pueblo Indians would rise up to rid themselves of the Spanish in the area, including the Franciscans, who had a share in the guilt of the white residents.

Two years later, the Pueblo revolted on August 10, slaying their abusers and forcing some two thousand Spanish and Native Americans to flee into the wilderness. Father de Ayeta was waiting for the survivors in El Paso, Texas, having brought food, clothing, and medical supplies to care for them, as he knew they would journey to that haven. Father de Ayeta was noted by his contemporaries as a man of great intellect and a realist with unending vitality.

Ayllón, Lucas Vásquez de (c. 1475–October 18, 1526)

A Spanish explorer, Lucas Vásquez de Ayllón founded an early colony in North Carolina. He was born in Toledo, Spain, and showed an interest in the explorations being made by his fellow countrymen in the New World. Ayllón discovered the Chesapeake Bay and founded a settlement near the site where Jamestown, the English colonial site, would be founded some eighty years later. He was a member of the Spanish Supreme Council and a judge in their stronghold in Santo Domingo, modern Hispaniola, and was totally dedicated to discovering a northwest passage to Asia.

In 1524 he sailed north and explored Chesapeake Bay and the James River. Two years later, Lucas Vázquez de Ayllón founded the settlement of San Miguel de Guandape on the coast of North Carolina, having received a grant from King Charles V of Spain. This grant demonstrates the attitude of the Spanish monarchs toward new explorations and colonies, and the treatment of the Native Americans: The chief motive of the explorers and colonizers was the apostolate of bringing the faith to the Native Americans.

When Ayllón built his settlement, African slaves aided in the construction, the first recorded use of African slaves in the territory of the United States. The settlement was doomed from the start, as the local Native Americans guarded their lands with vigor. Ayllón died of ship fever on the return voyage to Santo Domingo, and only 150 survivors of the original 500 of the settlement made their way safely to the south.

B

Bachelot, Alexis Jean Augustine (February 22, 1796–December 5, 1837)

A Sacred Hearts (Picpus) priest, Alexis Jean Augustine Bachelot pioneered the Catholic faith in the Sandwich Islands, the modern state of Hawaii. He was born in Grand Beauchet St. Cyr (Orne), France. At the age of ten, he entered the Sacred Hearts Seminary in Paris and began his preparatory studies. He was ordained in 1820 and was then made rector of the Irish College in Paris. Four years later he became the superior of the congregation seminary at Tours.

In 1825 the Sacred Hearts Fathers were given the missions of the Sandwich Islands. Father Bachelot was appointed the first prefect apostolic on October 29, 1825, and set sail from France with two Sacred Hearts companions, Fathers Abraham Armand and Patrick Short. A lay brother of the congregation was also in the party.

The group landed at Honolulu on July 7, 1827, and there they discovered that American Protestant missionaries had campaigned against their presence in the islands. The

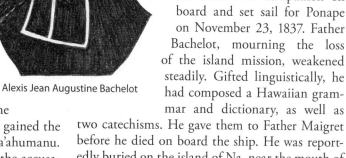

Alexis Jean Augustine Bachelot

Protestants had arrived earlier and had gained the confidence of the royal regent, Queen Ka'ahumanu. She banished the priests, relying upon the accusations made by the Americans.

Father Armand sailed to a nearby Sacred Hearts mission in the Pacific. Fathers Bachelot and Short were required to stand trial at the Fort of Honolulu. On December 24, 1831, the priests were declared a menace to island society and put on board the brig *Waverly*, bound for California. Upon reaching the coastline of California after a voyage in which they experienced considerable abuse, the priests were forced into a small boat and abandoned on a rocky beach at San Pedro Bay on January 21, 1832. The Spanish authorities of California intercepted the ship when the abandonment was discovered and tried the captain for abuse and endangerment.

Fathers Bachelot and Short went to San Gabriel Mission and labored there for a time. Father Short reportedly founded a college at Monterey. The two priests left California in 1837, however, having received news that they would be allowed to work in Honolulu. On the return, they were again abused by the Hawaiian authorities. Father Short sailed away, but Father Bachelot was too ill to accompany him. He remained bedridden in Honolulu until the Sacred Hearts priest Louis Désiré Maigret arrived. Father Maigret would become the Catholic leader of the islands in time and would inspire St. Damien de Veuster in his apostolate to the lepers on Molokai.

Discovering Father Bachelot in serious distress, Father Maigret purchased a vessel, naming it the *Notre Dame de Pais*. He carried his companion on board and set sail for Ponape on November 23, 1837. Father Bachelot, mourning the loss of the island mission, weakened steadily. Gifted linguistically, he had composed a Hawaiian grammar and dictionary, as well as two catechisms. He gave them to Father Maigret before he died on board the ship. He was reportedly buried on the island of Na, near the mouth of Metalanim Harbor. (*See also* Damien de Veuster, St.; Hawaii; and Honolulu, Diocese of.)

Bacon, William (September 15, 1813–November 15, 1874)

The first bishop of Portland, Maine, from 1855 to 1874, William Bacon served the Church in troubled times. He was born in New York City and raised in a devout family. Educated at the Sulpician College in Montréal, Canada, he entered Mount St. Mary's College in Maryland. He was ordained on December 13, 1838.

Father Bacon established a parish in Brooklyn and labored there until 1855, when he was appointed the bishop of the Portland diocese. He was consecrated on April 22 of that year. Bishop Bacon assumed his episcopal duties and established diocesan offices and agencies during a critical era in American history. Anti-Catholic organizations caused damage and took human lives in many areas of the nation, and the Civil War added other tensions and tragedy.

On July 4, 1866, a fire destroyed most of Portland, bringing suffering and homelessness to countless families. Bishop Bacon cared for the survivors and then started to rebuild the parishes and institutions of the diocese. In 1874 he sailed to Rome to make a report to the Holy See, but took ill and was carried back to New York, where he died. Archbishop John McCloskey, who would become the first cardinal of the Church in America, was the traveling companion of Bishop Bacon on that ill-fated voyage. He erected a bronze altar at St. Patrick's Church in New York to honor Portland's courageous bishop.

Badin, Stephen Theodore (July 17, 1768–April 21, 1853)

A pioneering missionary in Kentucky, Ohio, and Michigan, Stephen Theodore Badin was the first priest ordained in United States, and the donator of the land that serves as the site of the University of Notre Dame. He was born in Orléans, France, and studied at Montaigu College in Paris before entering the Sulpician Seminary in Orléans in 1789. That same year, the eruption of the French Revolution led to the closing of the seminary. He was thus forced to complete his studies for the priesthood elsewhere, and in 1791 he sailed from Bordeaux to the United States with two future bishops, Father Benedict Joseph Flaget, S.S., and Father John B. David, S.S. Reaching Philadelphia in March 1792, they traveled on to Baltimore, where they met Bishop (later Archbishop) John Carroll.

Given permission to complete

Stephen Theodore Badin

his theological studies in Baltimore, Badin was ordained by Bishop Carroll on May 25, 1793. After spending several months at Georgetown to improve his English, Father Badin was sent to the missions of Kentucky in September 1793. Journeying by foot and by flatboat, he reached Lexington, Kentucky, and celebrated his first Mass in the region on the first Sunday of Advent, in the home of Denis McCarthy.

Father Badin spent the next fifteen years serving the pastoral needs of the Catholics in Kentucky and providing important leadership. He rode on horseback extensively to reach the distant missions and Catholic communities, traveling perhaps over one hundred thousand miles, largely alone in his labors. Finally, in July 1806, he received permanent assistance in the form of the future famed missionary Reverend Charles Nerinckx. With Father Nerinckx, he lived at St. Stephen's, on Pottinger's Creek, which became the local center for the Church until 1811, when Father Flaget was appointed the first bishop of Bardstown, a diocese that covered many regions.

Almost immediately, however, the longtime cooperative friendship between Father Badin and Bishop Flaget was tested by a disagreement over deeds to Church property. To settle the matter, both went to Baltimore in 1812 to seek the counsel of Archbishop Carroll. The dispute was still not settled, however, even though Father Badin and Bishop Flaget continued to work together for the good of the Kentucky Catholics. Finally, in the spring of 1819, Father Badin left for France for the good of diocesan unity. In 1820 he accepted a post in the parish of Millaney and Marreilly-en-Gault, near Orléans, while assuring Bishop Flaget of his personal esteem and loyalty.

In 1822 Father Badin published in Paris a "Statement of the Missions in Kentucky," reiterating his own position and attesting to his goodwill toward the bishop. By 1828 he had returned to America. After some time in Michigan and

Kentucky, he offered his services to Bishop Edward D. Fenwick of Cincinnati in 1830. The bishop accepted and sent Father Badin to work among the Potawatomi Indians at St. Joseph's River. He left in 1836 and returned to Cincinnati. The next year, he went to Bardstown, where he was appointed vicar general. In 1841 he moved to Louisville (where the Bardstown diocese had relocated), donating at the same time several tracts of land he had acquired, including a parcel in northern Indiana. The farm was given to the Very Reverend Edward Sorin, who used it as the site for the founding of the future University of Notre Dame. Over the next years, Father Badin held a variety of posts, including pastor of the French settlement at Bourbonnais Grove, Illinois. In late 1848, he went back to Kentucky and in 1850 journeyed to Cincinnati as the guest of Archbishop John Baptist Purcell. Father Badin died in the archbishop's residence. He was placed in the cathedral crypt, although in 1904 his remains were transferred to the University of Notre Dame. He was honored for his essays, articles, and poetry.

Baegert, John Jacob (December 23, 1717–September or December 1777)

A Jesuit missionary, John Jacob Baegert was a noted ethnographer. He was born in Schlettstadt, Alsace, France, and entered the Society of Jesus in 1736. He was assigned to the American missions in 1749. Father Baegert founded San Ignacio Mission in Lower California and labored in that area until 1767, when the Jesuits were expelled from the missions.

Returning to Europe, he settled in Neustadt-am-Haardt in the Rhenish Palatinate, modern Germany, and started writing a detailed account of the California missions. This account included the physical characteristics of the region, the languages in use, the local traditions, and the customs of the Indian nations of California. Father Baegert's records and observations were highly revered by his contemporaries and historians. He died at Neustadt-am-Haardt.

Bailloquet, Peter (1612–June 7, 1692)

A fearless Jesuit missionary, Peter Bailloquet labored for forty-five years in the American territories. He was born in Saintes, France, and entered

the Society of Jesus in 1631. After ordination, Bailloquet was assigned to Canada as a missionary to the tribes in the Québec jurisdiction. In 1647 he began his ministry, traveling across a good part of the wilderness of the North American continent, going from Acadia on the eastern coast to Indian settlements in Illinois. The severe hardships he endured only strengthened his resolve and earned him the respect of many Native American tribes.

He served the Ottawa nation and other Native Americans, enduring threats and the ravages of the seasons in order to continue his mission tasks. Following the usual Jesuit approach to mission labors, Father Bailloquet traveled with the tribes each year as they made their way to hunting grounds, carrying his sacramental gear on his back. His labors were endless, and he fought his natural aversion to the harsh conditions under which he had to function among the tribes. Father Bailloquet was still at his mission post at the age of eighty, but was so ill throughout that year that he had to drag himself on his rounds of the villages. He died in the Ottawa nation territory, mourned by the people.

Baker, Diocese of

Established on June 19, 1903, by Pope Leo XIII, the Diocese of Baker, originally called Baker City, serves counties in the eastern part of Oregon. Settled during the Oregon Gold Rush in 1861–62, the city was laid out in 1865 and named for U.S. Senator Edward D. Baker. Baker has developed dairy, lumber, and tourist industries and is a trade hub for cattle and mining interests. The Diocese of Baker is a suffragan see of the Archdiocese of Portland in Oregon.

The Catholic history of the region dates officially to 1838, when Father Francis Norbert Blanchet and Father Modeste Demers arrived in Oregon as missionaries. The Lewis and Clark expedition had visited the area in 1804 and the American Fur Company, started by John Jacob Astor, began operations there in 1811. Father Blanchet is called the "Apostle of Oregon." In 1843 he was consecrated a bishop and vicar apostolic of Oregon. Three years later, the Archdiocese of Oregon City (now the Archdiocese of Portland in Oregon) was established on July 24, 1846, led by Archbishop Blanchet. The people of Oregon joined their fellow citizens in supporting the expansion of settlements and the westward movement, despite their remoteness. Catholics also worked to establish the presence of the Church, and wilderness areas were settled by the unending parade of immigrants and those looking for a new start in life.

In 1903, when the Diocese of Baker was erected in recognition of the labors and loyalty of the faithful in the area, the first bishop was Charles J. O'Reilly, who was consecrated on August 25, 1903. Upon assuming the see, Bishop O'Reilly discovered that he had one church and thirteen priests. The Umatilla Indian Reservation with five hundred Catholic Native Americans was part of the diocese and was served by Jesuit and Franciscan priests and by the Christian Brothers. St. Andrew's Indian Mission at Pendleton had also been founded in 1847. Bishop O'Reilly made St. Francis de Sales Church in Baker City the diocesan cathedral. The parish had been opened in 1871. He was aided by the Catholic Church Extension Society in this and other diocesan efforts, including the building of thirty-eight churches and two hospitals. On March 20, 1918, Bishop O'Reilly was transferred to the Diocese of Lincoln.

The second bishop of Baker was Joseph F. McGrath, who was consecrated on March 25, 1919. He built six new parishes and twenty-five churches. Hospitals and schools were constructed and diocesan agencies strengthened.

In 1922 anti-Catholic forces in Oregon promoted legislation that called for the closing of all private schools in the state. Aimed at the growing Catholic parochial school system, the legislation was approved in a referendum vote. Catholics responded with a series of court appeals, aided by leaders of all faiths across America and by civil rights organizations. Three years later, on June 1, 1925, the United States Supreme Court, in a unanimous decision, declared the Oregon School Law unconstitutional.

Bishop McGrath, having led the faithful of the diocese through the Great Depression, continued expanding diocesan facilities, and a religious vocation school was started in 1935. The Confraternity of Christian Doctrine was introduced into parishes at the same time. The Baker diocese supported the efforts of the nation in World War II and took part in the expansion and rebuilding programs that followed the end of the war. Bishop McGrath died on April 12, 1950.

Bishop Leo F. Fahey was appointed coadjutor to Bishop McGrath, with right of succession, in 1948, but he did not survive Bishop McGrath, dying on March 31, 1950.

The third bishop of Baker was Francis P. Leipzig, who was appointed on July 18, 1950, and consecrated on September 12. Bishop Leipzig built new churches, rectories, convents, and schools, and guided the faithful during the turbulent 1950s and 1960s. He took part in the Second Vatican Council and implemented the reforms mandated by the council. Bishop Leipzig retired on May 4, 1971.

Bishop Thomas J. Connolly was appointed as his successor in Baker and was consecrated on June 30, 1971. He continued the programs of his predecessors, maintaining ministries despite the growing decline of priests and religious in the diocese. Bishop Connolly retired on November 19, 1999.

The fifth bishop of Baker, Robert Francis Vasa, was consecrated in the Cathedral of St. Francis de Sales and installed on January 26, 2000. On January 24, 2011, Bishop Vasa was appointed coadjutor bishop of Santa Rosa. In 2011 there were 35,000 Catholics served by 51 priests and 31 parishes in the diocese.

Baker, Francis Asbury (March 30, 1820–April 4, 1865)

A convert, Francis Asbury Baker was one of the founders of the Paulist Institute. He was born in Baltimore, Maryland, the son of Dr. Samuel Baker, a noted physician. Graduating from Princeton College in 1839 and a member of the Episcopal Church, he was ordained in 1846. Father Baker served as an assistant at St. Paul's Episcopal Church and then became rector of St. Luke's in Baltimore.

He began studying Catholicism as part of his interest in the Oxford Movement, which was popular at the time. His studies led him to enter the Catholic Church in April 1853, and he made his profession of faith. Father Baker entered the Redemptorists and was ordained on September 21, 1856, in the Cathedral of Baltimore. His conversion was costly in the loss of affection and friendship among his former ties, but he was sincere and grateful for the grace of receiving the faith.

Father Baker joined the Redemptorist missionary band, an apostolic group that included the famed Fathers Isaac Thomas Hecker, Clarence A. Walworth, Francis A. Baker, and George Deshon, all converts. He proved himself a saintly and powerful preacher who gave missions to Catholics across America. He also joined the other members of the band in leaving the Redemptorists and founding the Paulists. Father Baker established the tradition of ceremonial exactitude and splendor that characterized the new congregation. He died during a typhoid epidemic, aiding victims of the disease.

Baker, Josephine (c. June 3, 1906–April 12, 1975)

An African-American dancer and singer, Josephine Baker became a French citizen and distinguished herself during World War II. Baker was born in St. Louis, Missouri, in a poverty-stricken family. By the age of sixteen, however, she was dancing professionally and building a career. By 1923 Baker was performing in New York theaters; two years later, seeking acceptance and opportunities not available in the United States, she went to France.

There she introduced a new jazz style to audiences and became a sensation. In 1926 she had her own club, Chez Josephine, and soon after began making movies. She became a French citizen in 1937 and worked with the French Resistance in World War II. Her services to the Red Cross and her tireless entertainment of troops earned her the *Croix de Guerre* and the Legion of Honor from the French government.

Baker had been married to Jean Lyon, but that union was annulled in 1940. She wed Jo Bouillos in 1947 and adopted infants of several races and nationalities. Retiring to her estate in southwestern France in 1956, she had a starring role in a film in 1959. Josephine also appeared on the New York stage in 1973 and took part in civil rights programs. She returned to Paris, where she died.

Balboa, Vasco de (1475–1517)

A Spanish explorer, Vasco de Balboa was the discoverer of the Pacific Ocean. He was born in Jerez de los Caballeros, Spain. In 1501 he joined an expedition to America led by Rodrigo de Bastidas and then settled in Hispaniola, modern-day Haiti and the Dominican Republic. In 1510 having failed in

business, Balboa stowed away on a ship bound for Colombia. There he discovered that the previous Spanish settlers had abandoned the area, but Balboa aided in establishing a new colony and took command.

In 1513 he set out with a small army and went overland, crossing to the southern shore of the Isthmus of Panama. On September 25, 1513, Balboa discovered the Pacific Ocean, naming it the South Sea and claiming it for the king of Spain. When word of his actions reached Spain, the king made him governor of Panama and an admiral of the South Seas. Soon after, he made plans for the invasion of the Incan empire in Peru. Pedrarias Dávila, who had been sent by Spain to replace Balboa in his Colombian office, favored him at first, giving him his daughter in marriage. Pedarias then charged him with treason and beheaded Balboa in Acla, Colombia.

Baltimore, Archdiocese of

The primatial see of the United States, the first diocese established in the nation, and now an archdiocese, Baltimore was erected on November 6, 1789, by Pope Pius VI. The diocese comprised the entire existing United States at that time, from the Atlantic Ocean to the Mississippi River, excluding Florida, parts of Michigan, and the territory known as Louisiana until April 8, 1808, when Baltimore became an archdiocese with four suffragan sees: Boston, Bardstown, New York, and Philadelphia. The archdiocese now comprises the city of Baltimore and counties in northern and central Maryland.

Baltimore was part of the colony of Maryland, founded in 1634 as a Catholic haven by the first Lord Baltimore and by Cecil Calvert, the second Lord Baltimore of England. The Jesuit Fathers Andrew White and John Altham came to the colony to aid the Catholic cause, traveling also with a Jesuit lay brother, Thomas Gervase. They started missions at St. Mary's, Port Tobacco, St. Inigoes, and Doncaster. Franciscan and diocesan priests arrived soon after, making it possible for the local Native American tribes to be served as well.

In 1654 the Puritans who had been allowed to settle in Maryland repealed the Toleration Act of 1649 and outlawed all Catholic services and activities, making missionary efforts impossible. The Calvert family was able to regain control of Maryland in 1658, however, and religious liberty was restored. The Catholics in the colony in that historical period were under the jurisdiction of a vicar apostolic who was based in London. There were an estimated two thousand Catholics in Maryland at this time.

In 1689 William of Orange was on the English throne, and he made Maryland a royal province, designating the Anglican Church as the official religion of the colony, supported by public taxes. Harsh penal laws were instituted against all other faiths. In 1702 all residents of the colony were granted religious freedom except Catholics. In 1704 Catholic parents were forbidden to teach the faith to their children. In this same year, however, Queen Anne of England allowed Catholics Masses to be celebrated in private chapels on Catholic estates.

Leonard Calvert, another Lord Baltimore, became a Protestant in 1713, and when the Calvert family regained control of Maryland two years later, Catholics were forbidden to send their children out of the colony for education. Priests were not allowed to evangelize or care for the faithful in Maryland, and Catholics could lose their children if they violated the colonial regulations against the faith. In 1718 Catholics were even denied the right to take part in public life, a restriction that prompted Charles Carroll, the father of Charles Carroll of Carrollton and an uncle of John Carroll, to try to purchase land in Arkansas, where he hoped to establish a Catholic colony. He was not allowed to complete the transaction.

The city of Baltimore was founded in 1729 and attracted immigrants. The wealth and culture of the leading Catholic families in Maryland blunted somewhat the harsh penal laws, and priests risked their lives to come into the colony to administer the sacraments. By 1747 the pioneering Jesuit Father Benedict Neale had a mission at Priest's Ford, and eight years later the displaced Catholic Acadians entered Maryland. A Catholic woman, Mary Ann March, tried to open a Catholic school in 1757, but was refused permission. In 1764 the Jesuit Father George Hunter purchased land from Charles Carroll of Annapolis at Charles and Saratoga Streets.

Six years later, a group raised funds to erect St. Peter's Church, which opened in 1775. The church was enlarged and served as the cathedral until 1821. It was also the residence of Bishop John Carroll after the diocese was erected.

In 1776 the Catholics of Maryland were given a Declaration of Rights, allowing them total freedom. The Treaty of Paris in 1783 ended the Revolutionary War and recognized the United States of America. One year later, Father John Carroll was appointed prefect apostolic of the new nation. In that same year, Jesuit Father Charles Sewell became the resident pastor of St. Peter's.

In 1788 the Catholic priests of the area met at Whitemarsh, Maryland, and drafted a memorial to Pope Pius VI, asking him to provide them with a bishop. Reportedly, the priests also petitioned for a special dispensation in this memorial, asking to be allowed to elect their own bishop; the pope granted them the privilege. Father John Carroll was elected and confirmed by the Holy See, with Benjamin Franklin taking credit for the appointment in his personal diary. Bishop Carroll was consecrated in England on August 15, 1790. There were an estimated thirty-five thousand Catholics in the young nation at the time.

Bishop Carroll welcomed the French Catholics who came to the United States after fleeing from the French Revolution. He also brought in the Discalced Carmelite Nuns at Port Tobacco and started the agencies and protocols of a diocese. On December 7, 1800, Father Leonard Neale was made coadjutor bishop of Baltimore to aid Bishop Carroll. By 1803 the diocese extended to the Rocky Mountains as a result of the Louisiana Purchase. Two years later, to settle a schism started by Father Caesar Reuter, a German priest, Bishop Carroll sued him in court. The court defined Bishop Carroll as having jurisdiction over Catholics of all nationalities throughout the country. Despite his many problems with the young American Church, Bishop Carroll was able to start construction on the Cathedral of the Assumption of the Blessed Virgin Mary in Baltimore.

Now honored as the Basilica of the National Shrine of the Assumption of the Blessed Virgin Mary, it was the first Roman Catholic cathedral in the United States and one of the great landmarks of

American Catholic history. Designed by the noted architect Benjamin Henry Latrobe, the first professional architect to practice in the young republic as well as the architect of the U.S. Capitol, the cathedral was built in two major efforts, from 1806 to 1810 and 1817 to 1821.

On April 8, 1808, Pope Pius VII divided parts of the United States into the four dioceses of Bardstown (now the Archdiocese of Louisville), Boston, New York, and Philadelphia. Bishop Carroll was elevated to the rank of archbishop at the same time. When he died on December 3, 1815, the Church was well established in America and expanding its frontiers with missions and settlements as political changes opened new territories.

Archbishop Neale, who was seventy years old when Bishop Carroll died, had served faithfully for fifteen years as coadjutor. He acceded to the see and continued Archbishop Carroll's programs. However, he died on June 18, 1817, after only two years as head of the archdiocese, and was buried at the Visitation Convent in Philadelphia.

On December 14, 1817, Sulpician Father Ambrose Maréchal succeeded to the see as the third archbishop of Baltimore. Three years later, at the request of Archbishop Maréchal, who understood the rapid growth patterns of the nation, the Diocese of Richmond was created, detaching Virginia and West Virginia from the archdiocese. The Diocese of Charleston was also established. Archbishop Maréchal dedicated the Cathedral of the Assumption on May 31, 1821, and went to Rome, where he submitted the historic first official report of the Archdiocese of Baltimore to the Holy See. He also had to settle schisms in Charleston, South Carolina, and in Norfolk, Virginia. He died on January 29, 1828, mourned by Catholics across the land.

The fourth archbishop was James Whitfield, who was appointed to Baltimore and consecrated on May 25, 1828. A year later, Archbishop Whitfield called the bishops of the United States to the First Provincial Council of Baltimore to unify their efforts and to develop a collegial spirit. He also used his own funds to build St. James's Church in Baltimore. St. John Nepomucene Neumann, the Redemptorist who would become the bishop of Philadelphia, served at St. James's for a time. When Archbishop Whitfield died on October 19, 1834,

having expanded the Catholic presence in Baltimore and in the wilderness areas of the continent, Catholics in the archdiocese numbered approximately eighty-seven thousand.

Archbishop Samuel Eccleston became the next archbishop on October 19, 1834. A convert to Catholicism and a Sulpician, he set up a series of expansion programs, erecting needed parishes and schools. Religious congregations answered his invitations and came to aid in the educational ministries. He also directed the Sulpicians in establishing St. Charles Minor Seminary. In 1846 Archbishop Eccleston witnessed the establishment of the second archdiocese in the nation, Oregon City (now the Archdiocese of Portland in Oregon). He died on April 22, 1851.

His successor, Archbishop Francis P. Kenrick, had served as coadjutor of Philadelphia since 1830 and was promoted to Baltimore on August 19, 1851. He convened the First Plenary Council of Baltimore on May 9, 1852, attended by forty-one American archbishops and bishops. On July 19 1858, Pope Blessed Pius IX conferred the "Prerogative of Place" on the Archdiocese of Baltimore. The decree stated that the archbishop of Baltimore takes precedence over all the archbishops of the United States (not cardinals) in councils, gatherings, and meetings of whatever kind in the American hierarchy, regardless of the seniority of the other archbishops in promotion or ordination. Archbishop Kenrick expanded the facilities of the archdiocese, including Loyola College in 1852, and established a hospital and an infant asylum. He was also active in the ongoing mission efforts throughout the land, and many missionaries looked to him as a champion of their apostolates. Archbishop Kenrick also supported the Rome-based institution that would become the North American College. When he died on July 8, 1863, the Catholic population of the archdiocese was 150,000.

Almost one year later, the seventh archbishop of Baltimore, Martin John Spalding, was appointed. He had served as the coadjutor bishop of Louisville since 1848 and was promoted to Baltimore on May 6, 1864. The Civil War impacted Americans as he started his labors in the archdiocese, building parishes, charitable institutions, and services for the needy. Archbishop Spalding presided over the

Second Plenary Council in 1866. Two years later, nine counties on Maryland's eastern shore, the peninsula between the Atlantic Ocean and Chesapeake Bay, were separated from the archdiocese and made part of the Diocese of Wilmington. In 1871 the archdiocese celebrated the anniversary of the coronation of Pope Blessed Pius IX with a citywide gala. Parades, concerts, and religious ceremonies were held. Archbishop Spalding died on February 7, 1872.

Archbishop James Roosevelt Bayley, the bishop of Newark since 1853, was promoted to Baltimore as the eighth archbishop on July 30, 1872. A convert to the faith and a nephew of St. Elizabeth Ann Seton, Archbishop Bayley heavily expanded the facilities of the archdiocese, adding 120 churches and promoting the lay apostolate. He also aided the Indian missions by establishing the Catholic Bureau of Indian Missions to protect the Church's apostolate to the Native Americans from encroachments by the Protestants in federal programs. Archbishop Bayley consecrated the Cathedral of the Assumption on May 25, 1876. This cathedral (now the Basilica of the National Shrine of the Assumption of the Blessed Virgin Mary) dates originally to the era of Archbishop Carroll in Baltimore. The ceremony of consecration had been delayed until the building debt was liquidated, and it would be one of the archbishop's last public appearances. He had always suffered from ill health and had requested a coadjutor to aid him. In 1877 Bishop James Gibbons was appointed as Archbishop Bayley's coadjutor. Five months later, on October 3, Archbishop Bayley died.

Archbishop James Gibbons was one of the most revered and popular prelates in Catholic American history. He had served as the vicar apostolic of North Carolina and then as the bishop of Richmond since 1872. He initiated an even larger expansion program

after acceding to the see upon the death of Archbishop Bayley, erecting twenty-four churches in Baltimore alone. In 1884 he presided over the Third Plenary Council of Baltimore. Two years later, in June 1886, he was created a cardinal priest with the titular church of Santa Maria in Trastavere, the second American to receive the honor of the cardinalate. In 1887 he became the chancellor ex officio of the new Catholic University of America.

Baltimore celebrated the 100th anniversary of its founding in 1889. Ceremonies were presided over by the cardinal, who was a highly respected figure in American religious and political circles. Cardinal Gibbons's presence in many government and social affairs discouraged outbreaks of anti-Catholic activities. He also aided the military efforts of the nation in World War I. Cardinal Gibbons died on March 24, 1921, and Americans of all faiths mourned his passing. His wartime services were also honored.

Cardinal Gibbons's successor was Archbishop Michael J. Curley, who had served as the bishop of St. Augustine since 1914. He was promoted to Baltimore on August 10, 1921. Archbishop Curley continued the building programs of his predecessor and founded Catholic Charities, which would continue to serve the archdiocese. He also aided the American bishops in establishing an episcopal conference for peacetime activities. In 1937 the Holy See conferred the rank of minor basilica upon

Cathedral of the Assumption in Baltimore

Baltimore's Assumption Cathedral. World War II demanded efforts and agencies to care for military personnel and refugees. Archbishop Curley supported the U.S. forces and labored to consolidate archdiocesan programs in wartime. He promoted an Office of Education, Catholic Charities, the Propagation of the Faith, the Knights of Columbus, the Holy Name Society, and other groups. In 1939 Washington, D.C., was established as an archdiocese, and separated from Baltimore on November 15, 1947. Archbishop Curley died on May 16, 1947.

In that same year, Francis P. Keough became the eleventh archbishop of Baltimore. He had served as the bishop of Providence since 1934. Archbishop Keough was promoted to Baltimore on November 29. He helped to found Villa Julie Junior College in Stevenson, Maryland, and on October 10, 1954, broke ground for a new metropolitan cathedral. Five years later, the cathedral dedicated to Mary Our Queen was consecrated, with the Cathedral of the Assumption designated as a co-cathedral. He also promoted the Confraternity of Christian Doctrine and the Catholic Youth Organization. Archbishop Keough died on December 8, 1961.

The twelfth archbishop was Lawrence J. Shehan. He had served as an auxiliary bishop of Baltimore and then as coadjutor archbishop, appointed on July 10, 1961, and acceded to the see on December 8, 1961. A successful fundraiser, he was able to renovate many archdiocesan facilities and implemented the changes brought about by the Second Vatican Council. He visited every parish in the archdiocese. Archbishop Shehan was created a cardinal priest with the titular church of San Clemente on February 22, 1965. He developed a pastoral council and had to maintain authority in the dispute over Pope Paul VI's encyclical *Humanae Vitae.* Cardinal Shehan retired on March 25, 1974.

The thirteenth archbishop of Baltimore was William D. Borders. He had served as the bishop of Orlando since 1968 and was promoted to Baltimore on March 25, 1974, and installed in the archdiocese on June 26, 1974. He began programs of social outreach and charity, started study groups and charismatic programs, and upgraded and expanded facilities. Archbishop Borders also maintained levels of service despite the loss of priests and religious. He retired on April 6, 1989.

The fourteenth archbishop of Baltimore was Cardinal William H. Keeler. He had served as the bishop of Harrisburg from 1983 and was promoted to Baltimore on April 6, 1989. On November 26, 1994, he was given the rank of cardinal priest with the titular church of San Clemente. He served as president of the National Conference of Catholic Bishops and continued the work of renovating and expanding archdiocesan facilities in order to serve the growing Catholic population. In 1995 Pope Blessed John Paul II visited Baltimore and met with agency personnel and the laity. In July 2000, Cardinal Keeler hosted a session of the Joint International Commission for theological Dialogue between the Roman Catholic Church and the Orthodox Church. He had also presided over the extensive renovation of the Basilica of the National Shrine of the Assumption of the Blessed Virgin Mary. Cardinal Keeler retired on July 12, 2007.

On July 12, 2007, Archbishop Edwin F. O'Brien was named his successor. Archbishop O'Brien had previously served as rector of the North American College in Rome and as an auxiliary bishop of New York from 1996 to 1997. In 1997 he was named coadjutor archbishop of the Military Archdiocese on April 7, 1997, and acceded to the see on August 12, 1997, serving until his transfer to Baltimore. On August 29, 2011, Archbishop O'Brien was appointed Grand Master of the Equestrian Order of the Holy Sepulchre of Jerusalem and was named a cardinal in 2012. On March 20, 2012, Bishop William Lori of Bridgeport was appointed to the see; he was installed on May 16, 2012. In 2011 there were 500,000 Catholics served by 488 priests, more than 1,000 men and women religious, and 153 parishes in the archdiocese.

Baltimore Catechism

The famous book series that was intended to serve as an instrument of standardizing catechetical instruction for the whole of the U.S. Church, the *Baltimore Catechism* was designed as a method of introducing the children of recent immigrants to the devotional practices and prayer forms that were then commonplace in American Catholicism. Although the *Baltimore Catechism* gradually won wide acceptance as a chief source of catechetical instruction in many dioceses, it also acquired the status of cultural icon among several generations of Catholics who grew up memorizing its several hundred questions and answers. At the same time, however, the catechism was criticized from the start as inadequate to the needs of catechesis and religious education and was subject to various revisions that sought to secure its universal acceptance as a national text.

The creation of the *Baltimore Catechism* is traced to November 7, 1884, when the Third Plenary Council of Baltimore began its first session of deliberations on the issues most pressing to the Catholic Church in the United States. One of the matters taken up was that of uniformity of religious instruction amid the diverse number of catechisms then in use. Termed "the vexed question of a uniform catechism in English" by the First Plenary Council of Baltimore in 1852, the issue of a standard catechism was again taken up in earnest by the council of 1884.

A number of bishops favored the standing preference of the earlier councils — namely, adapting an already existing catechism to the needs of the U.S. Church. The text that was immediately proposed was a revised edition of *Butler's Catechism*. Not surprisingly, the majority of bishops opposed the idea; they favored instead the creation of a brand-new catechism. Although judged theologically sound, *Butler's Catechism* was seen as antiquated and ill-suited to the specific needs and cultural requirements of American Catholics. Additionally, the bishops wanted to inculcate the new catechism with a theology they considered more in keeping with the Church of 1884, especially post–First Vatican Council ecclesiology.

In the end, preconciliar deliberations led to the decision on the part of Cardinal James Gibbons of Baltimore before the start of the council that a committee should examine the various options available to the bishops. As the council carried forward with its other business, the committee set to work on the proposed catechism. The result was a parallel track of labor that permitted a rough draft of the catechism to be presented to the bishops just prior to their departure from Baltimore in December. The main duty of drafting the new catechism had been given to Monsignor Januarius de Concilio, a pastor from Jersey City who attended the council

as the theologian for Bishop James O'Connor of Nebraska.

The draft that was presented to the bishops adopted the traditional question-and-answer method that characterized most catechisms of the time. It derived the questions from the *Carroll Catechism*, the *Butler-Maynooth Catechism*, and two works originating in the United States. The first was the 1825 catechism of Bishop Jean-Baptiste David. The second was a twenty-eight-page catechism by Bishop Jean-Pierre Augustin Verot of Georgia (and later Florida). He had already placed himself on record as a supporter of a universal catechism, having debated the issue robustly at the First Vatican Council.

The bishops were instructed upon their departure from the council that they should send suggestions and emendations to the committee through its head, Bishop John L. Spalding of Peoria, Illinois. Spalding conducted the process of finalizing the catechism from New York, receiving principal assistance from Monsignor de Concilio. By the end of February 1885, Spalding and de Concilio had finished their revisions and declared to Cardinal John McCloskey — who had been actively engaged in the entire process — that the catechism was completed. It was given the title *A Catechism of Christian Doctrine, Prepared and Enjoined by the Order of the Third Plenary Council of Baltimore*. Cardinal McCloskey gave his imprimatur on April 6, followed by the formal acceptance of the catechism by Archbishop Gibbons in his capacity as apostolic delegate to the United States for the Holy See.

Significantly, the bishops of the United States were not offered an opportunity to review the final draft of the catechism prior to its publication. Further, it was soon pointed out — in a harbinger of the reception of the catechism — that the title was not appropriate, given the fact that its publication had taken place prior to the *recognitio* of the council's decrees by the Congregation for the Propaganda Fide.

The first edition of the *Baltimore Catechism* was 97 pages long, with 37 chapters and 421 questions and answers. The chief concerns were the Apostles' Creed, the seven sacraments, and the Ten Commandments.

This first edition was followed almost immediately by an abridged version approximately half the length of the original. Bishop Spalding again supervised the production, and the short version was given the designation of Baltimore No. 1. None of the small changes satisfied the critics, and the nearly ceaseless complaints and calls for emendations from various quarters sparked constant minor changes that finally coalesced into the formal revision of the catechism in 1941.

The process of revising the original *Baltimore Catechism* was begun in 1935, under the direction of the Episcopal Committee for the Confraternity of Christian Doctrine of the National Catholic Welfare Conference (the predecessor of the present-day United States Conference of Catholic Bishops). As with the original catechism, supervision was given to a committee of bishops consisting of Archbishop John McNicholas, O.P., of Cincinnati, Archbishop John Murray of St. Paul, and Bishop Edwin Vincent O'Hara of Kansas City. They were assisted by more than two hundred theologians, priests, brothers, sisters, and trained laypeople. The chief figure in the revision, however, was Reverend Francis J. Connell, C.SS.R., professor of moral theology at The Catholic University of America. After further revisions, the catechism was published on July 18, 1941.

The new edition of the *Baltimore Catechism* was given the practical designation of Baltimore No. 2. It was 144 pages long, with 38 lessons and 499 questions and answers, with an appendix of sixteen questions that provided a short course in apologetics, under the title "Why I Am a Catholic." The anticipated readers of Baltimore No. 2 were students in grades of six, seven, and eight. Baltimore No. 2 was then used as the starting point for three other targeted catechisms: one for first Communicants, one for students in elementary grades, and a final one for high school students. The new editions of the *Baltimore Catechism* remained in general use until the very eve of the Second Vatican Council.

Baltimore, Councils of

A series of ecclesiastical councils held throughout the nineteenth century, the Councils of Baltimore served as opportunities for the American bishops to discuss and deal with the many pastoral questions facing the Church in the United States. There were seven provincial councils (1829, 1833, 1837, 1840, 1843, 1846, and 1849), and three plenary councils (1852, 1866, and 1884). The prelate presiding over the councils was the archbishop of Baltimore, the primatial see, but true inspiration and leadership were provided by Bishop John England of Charleston, South Carolina, who proclaimed the need for unity and harmony among the hierarchy of the Church in America.

For the early part of American history, the ecclesiastical province of Baltimore comprised the whole territory of the American republic, meaning that the provincial councils held in that city in fact gathered together the entire American hierarchy. Over time, however, several additional ecclesiastical provinces were established as the needs of the Catholic population warranted. Once these new provinces were formed, plenary councils were necessary if all the bishops in the country were to assemble.

Reflecting the changed circumstances of ecclesiastical life, the members of the Seventh Provincial Council of Baltimore requested that the Holy See grant permission to convene a plenary synod. In reply, Pope Blessed Pius IX appointed Archbishop Francis Kenrick of Baltimore as apostolic delegate to convene and preside over the council.

The Provincial Councils of Baltimore

Archbishop John Carroll had hoped to convoke the bishops of the province as early as 1812 to give direction to the Church in the United States, but the eruption of the War of 1812 ended his aspirations. As it was, no council was called during his time as archbishop, and his immediate successor, Archbishop Leonard Neale, did not proceed with plans for the council, in part because of his own poor health. Archbishop Neale's successor, Archbishop Ambrose Maréchal, S.S., the third archbishop of Baltimore from 1817 to 1828, was also unwilling to organize a council, despite the urging of Bishop John England of Charleston, as Maréchal saw little reason to do so. Once held, however, the provincial councils established important precedents in ecclesiastical organization and discipline and so helped shape the later development of the Church in the United States.

At the conclusion of the Seventh Provincial

Council, the bishops in attendance petitioned the Holy See to make Baltimore the primatial see for the United States. The request was granted in 1858, but only insofar as it granted the archbishop a primacy of honor, with precedence in processions, meetings, and assemblies.

The First Provincial Council (October 3–18, 1829): The first of the provincial councils was finally convened by Archbishop James Whitfield, who had succeeded Archbishop Maréchal in 1828. The council met in Baltimore Cathedral in thirteen private, thirteen public, and three solemn sessions. On the day the council started, Archbishop Whitfield received the pallium in the cathedral. In attendance were six bishops and the apostolic administrator of Philadelphia; three bishops did not take part, and Bishop Henry Conwell of Philadelphia was not permitted to vote. The decrees of the council declared:

- Trusteeism should be resisted by ensuring that any new churches are established in the bishop's name.
- Priests should remain in the dioceses to which they were assigned, and the system of co-pastors should be abolished.
- The use of the Douay-Reims version of the Bible should be made uniform.
- The use of the Roman ritual should be made uniform; however, vernacular translations were to be permitted in administering the sacraments after the Latin had been read.
- Accurate registers of baptisms, confirmations, marriages, and burials should be maintained.
- Mass should be said only in churches and stations approved by the bishops.
- A uniform catechism and catechism classes should be instituted in all churches.
- Catholic schools should be established to teach the faith to all Catholic children.

The decrees were approved by Pope Pius VIII in 1830 and promulgated in 1831.

The Second Provincial Council (October 20–27, 1833): Convened by Archbishop Whitfield, the second council was held in the Baltimore Cathedral; in attendance were the archbishop and nine bishops. The main decrees were:

- There should be a geographical delineation of the American dioceses.
- The method of selecting bishops should be kept in the hands of the hierarchy (this was modified by the Seventh Provincial Council).
- Seminaries should be established in keeping with the decrees of the Council of Trent.
- The use of textbooks in Catholic schools and colleges should be made uniform, and their publication should be supervised by the presidents of St. Mary's Seminary, Baltimore, Mount St. Mary's College, and Georgetown College.
- The Jesuits should be entrusted with supervision over the Indian missions in the West, and also the missions among former American slaves, repatriated in Liberia, Africa.
- The bishops also rescinded their decision of 1810 that granted faculties to priests to officiate in neighboring dioceses.

The Third Provincial Council (April 16–23, 1837): Convened by Archbishop Samuel Eccleston, S.S., the council was attended by the archbishop and eight bishops. Its decrees included:

- The faithful have an obligation to support their parishes.
- Ecclesiastical property should be secured in accordance with civil law.
- Priests should not bring ecclesiastical cases before civil tribunals.
- Priests are prohibited from soliciting money outside their own parishes.
- Pastors should not use unsuitable music in their liturgies.
- The fast on Wednesdays and Fridays of Advent should be abolished.
- Provision should be made for the care of aged and infirm priests.

The pastoral letter issued after the council lamented the harsh anti-Catholic persecutions then being conducted and reiterated the patriotism of Catholics in the country.

The Fourth Provincial Council (May 17–24, 1840): Convened by Archbishop Eccleston, the council was attended by the archbishop and twelve bishops; notably, this was the last council attended by Bishop John England, who died in 1842. Also admitted with the right to vote was Bishop Charles de Forbin-Janson of Nancy and Toul, France. The decrees of the council included:

- In the case of mixed marriages, care should be taken that the children of the union should receive baptism and a proper Catholic education.
- Temperance societies should be recommended to the faithful.
- Pastors should make every effort to ensure that children attending public school do not use the Protestant version of the Bible or take part in Protestant services.
- Bishops should control ecclesiastical property and not permit priests to hold it in their own name.
- Membership in secret societies was forbidden.

Pope Gregory XVI's apostolic letter condemning the slave trade, *In Supremo Apostolatus*, was read during the proceedings. The pastoral letter of 1840 reiterated the various decrees for the faithful, especially those on marriage, temperance, and civil rights belonging to Catholics in the face of Protestant hostility.

The Fifth Provincial Council (May 14–21, 1843): Convened by Archbishop Eccleston, the council was attended by the archbishop and sixteen bishops, including the vicar apostolic of the Republic of Texas, Bishop Claude Dubuis. The council's decrees included:

- Consecrated churches should not be used for public meetings, and laymen should not deliver orations in churches.
- Any Catholic who attempts marriage after civil divorce is automatically excommunicated.
- Priests may not incur debts in the rebuilding or repair of their churches without written permission of the bishop.
- Priests should use only Latin in all services, although prayers in English might be added.

- Confessionals should be installed in all churches.
- Catholic printing houses should be encouraged.

The Sixth Provincial Council (May 10–17, 1846): Convened by Archbishop Eccleston, the council was attended by the archbishop and twenty-three bishops. Its four decrees were:

- The feast of the Immaculate Conception was chosen as the patronal feast for the Church in the United States.
- Secular priests were prohibited from entering a religious order without permission of their ordinaries.
- The proclamation of the banns of matrimony was reiterated.

The Sixth Council was significant in its decision to choose Our Lady as the patroness of the country, under the title of the Immaculate Conception. The action came even before the definition of the Immaculate Conception in 1854.

The Seventh Provincial Council (May 6–13, 1849): Convened by Archbishop Eccleston, the council was attended by two archbishops (Samuel Eccleston and Francis P. Kenrick of St. Louis) and twenty-three bishops; the archbishop of Oregon City (established as a metropolitan see in 1846) and his suffragans did not attend. Despite the presence of two archbishops, the council was not a plenary one. The main decrees were:

- The council declared that the time was opportune to define as a dogma the Immaculate Conception of the Blessed Virgin Mary.
- A change in the election of bishops was introduced; in nominating candidates for the episcopacy, names of priests were to be sent to the other archbishops, who should inform the Holy See of their judgment of the candidates.
- All property donated to the diocese should belong to the bishop of the diocese unless the document itself stipulates that it should be given to a religious order.
- Priests were forbidden to preside at the marriage of any couples who already had a ceremony performed by a Protestant minister,

or who intended to have such a ceremony performed.

- A national council should be held in Baltimore in 1850, with the authority of the Holy See.

The council also petitioned the Holy See to raise New Orleans, Cincinnati, and New York to metropolitan dignity and to make necessary adjustments in the boundaries of the Provinces of Baltimore and St. Louis. The pastoral letter issued after the council focused on the office of the papacy and the Immaculate Conception. Three additional provincial councils were held in 1855, 1858, and 1869.

Plenary Councils of Baltimore

By 1852 the growth of the Catholic Church in the United States was marked by the presence of five other archdioceses in addition to Baltimore. It was thus necessary that any gathering after the seventh provincial council should be plenary, meaning a truly national gathering that included the archdioceses of Baltimore, St. Louis, New York, Cincinnati, Oregon, and New Orleans. As a gathering was judged expedient, the Holy See issued an apostolic letter on August 19, 1851, that called for its preparation.

First Plenary Council (May 9–20, 1852): Convened by Archbishop Kenrick, the council was attended by six archbishops and thirty-five suffragan bishops; the bishop of Monterey, California, also participated, although technically the diocese was not yet attached to the provinces of the United States. The bishop of Toronto also attended.

The council was called by Archbishop Kenrick in a letter released on November 21, 1851. Concerns were centered on two chief issues — confronting the problems of growth in the American Church and devising effective strategies for leading the Church in a predominately Protestant country. A preparatory session in Baltimore was held on May 8, 1852, where it was decided to divide the labors of the council among five major areas, with a committee of bishops assigned to each. The committees focused on canon law, administration of Church property, norms for Christian education, regularization of sacred rites and ceremonies, and settling issues of diocesan boundaries. In the end,

the council issued twenty-five decrees. Among the most significant were:

- A declaration by the council that the pope is the successor of St. Peter, Vicar of Christ, and head of the whole Church.
- Declaration that all legislation issued by the seven provincial councils of Baltimore extended to all the dioceses of the United States.
- The urging of bishops to establish chancery offices and appoint consultors who should meet periodically.
- A call for at least one major seminary in each province.
- Christian burial should be denied to any Catholic who expressed a desire to be buried in a non-Catholic cemetery.
- European priests should have letters of testimony from their bishops and approval of the bishops under whom they were to serve.
- Parish lines were to be established by the bishops.
- A parochial school with teachers paid from parish funds should exist in every parish.
- Laypeople should not be placed in charge of ecclesiastical affairs unless appointed by the bishop.
- Encouragement should be given to the Society for the Propagation of the Faith.
- Efforts should be made to prevent Catholic servicemen in the army and navy from being forced to attend non-Catholic services.

Second Plenary Council (October 7–21, 1866): Convened under Archbishop Martin J. Spalding, the council was attended by seven archbishops, thirty-eight bishops, and three abbots; additionally, 120 theologians took part, as did thousands of laypeople and onlookers. The council was the largest gathering of Catholic leaders in American history. The significance of the meeting was also underscored by the cable from Pope Pius IX that was read at the very beginning of deliberations. The essential motivation for the council on the part of Archbishop Spalding, acting as apostolic delegate, was the end the previous year of the Civil War, which had caused such suffering and division. Spalding expressed the hope that "the Catholic Church might present to the country and the world a striking proof of the strong bond of unity with which her members are knit together."

Beyond the immense task of guiding the Catholic faithful during the painful period of Reconstruction, the council also faced ongoing pressures from immigration. New Catholics required pastoral care, additional priests, churches, schools, and religious. The growth was also attended by increases in anti-Catholicism. Riots against Catholics occurred in New York and Philadelphia.

In the face of these issues, Archbishop Kenrick, in close consultation with the Congregation for the Propaganda Fide, sought to have the council reiterate Catholic teaching, issue warnings about the religious errors then being propagated, and express in clear fashion important aspects of Church discipline and law. Further, to assist pastoral care, the council urged the creation of new dioceses and suggested a special ministry among the recently emancipated slaves. Notably, the council named the Blessed Virgin Mary, under the title of the Immaculate Conception, as special patroness of the United States. President Andrew Johnson attended the final solemn session of the council. The chief decrees of the council were:

- Indifferentism, Unitarianism, universalism, spiritism, pantheism, and transcendentalism were condemned.
- A provincial council should be summoned every three years.
- Diocesan synods and clergy conferences should be held as needed.
- Care should be taken to ensure uniformity in the administration of the sacraments; there should also be uniformity in the regulation of fasts, feasts, and dispensations.
- Every parish should have a parochial school; every child in public schools should be given courses in religion.
- Industrial and reform schools under Catholic leadership should be established.
- Secret societies, including the Freemasons, Odd Fellows, and Sons of Temperance were condemned, although labor unions were not.

The conciliar decrees were not formally approved until 1868, owing to complaints by some bishops, including Kenrick and Archbishop John Baptist Purcell, that they had not received enough time during the deliberations to discuss thoroughly all the relevant matters.

Third Plenary Council (November 9–December 7, 1884): Convened by Archbishop John Gibbons, the council was attended by seventy-two bishops and marked a moment of enormous importance in American Catholic history. The council was clearly needed to assist the organizational and pastoral care of the Catholic population, swiftly growing through immigration. To give encouragement to the council, archbishops of the United States were summoned to Rome to meet with Holy See officials in 1883, in particular the Congregation for the Propaganda Fide. At the time, it was decided that Archbishop Gibbons of Baltimore should convoke the council, instead of the ailing Cardinal John McCloskey of New York; the idea had been proposed briefly that an apostolic delegate be sent to convene the gathering.

Three major issues made the council imperative. First, the increase in population required the active engagement of the entire ecclesiastical structure in the country to provide a cohesive response and proper pastoral solutions. Second, the maturing of the American Church needed to be assessed. Finally, in the period between the plenary councils, the First Vatican Council had been held and a new pope, Leo XIII, had been elected as successor to the long-reigning Pius IX. It was desired, then, that the plenary council reflect fully the new atmosphere and the changes that had resulted from it.

The council thus began with a thorough discussion of the work of Vatican I, followed by a pledge of loyalty to Pope Leo XIII. Attention then turned to the major crisis of the day — the stunning population growth in the Catholic community. Of special note was the need to provide instruction to the myriad groups of immigrants in their native languages. Similarly, it was agreed to ask the Holy See to standardize six days of obligation for the entire country in order to end the varied holy days then followed by different ethnic groups. Finally, the council urged continuing development in education, including approval of the drafting of the *Baltimore Catechism* and of standards for seminaries. Above all, an administrative board was created to found and direct The Catholic University of America. The chief decrees of the council included:

- Provision should be made for diocesan consultors, pastors, and examiners.
- Feast and fasts, and six holy days of obligation should be established for the United States.
- Regulations should be followed in the use of sacred music, and secular music should be forbidden in the liturgy.
- Catholics married by a Protestant minister should be excommunicated.
- Seminaries, both major and minor, should be established according to proper norms.
- A catechism should be prepared and its use considered mandatory.
- All pastors should build parochial schools for their parishes.
- Catholic parents should send their children to Catholic schools.
- Immigrants should receive instruction in their own languages.
- Ministry and evangelization should be undertaken among the recently emancipated slaves.
- A Catholic university should be established in Washington, D.C., under a board of directors.

This council provided lasting direction for the Church in the United States for decades to come. Its decrees provided the principal legislation that governed ecclesiastical life until the promulgation of the Code of Canon Law in 1917 by Pope Benedict XV, but its influence endured well into the twentieth century. Its emphasis on education, for example, pointed the way toward the enormously successful institution of Catholic education in the United States. Finally, following this council, the archbishops of the country began to meet annually to consider questions of Church policy, forecasting the later creation of the bishops' conference.

Bapst, John (December 17, 1815–November 2, 1887)

A Jesuit missionary and educator, John Bapst suffered severe abuse at the hands of rioting Protestants, who tarred and feathered him in Maine in 1854. He was born at La Roche, Fribourg, Switzerland, and started seminary training at the age of twelve, entered the Society of Jesus in 1835, and was ordained on December 31, 1846. After his ordination, Father Bapst was assigned to the American missions.

He arrived in New York in 1849, and went to Old Town, Maine, the famed Abenaki Indian settlement. Popular and effective with the Abenaki, whom he respected, he remained with them until 1850, when he was assigned to Eastport. There, Father Bapst again proved to be a popular pastor among Maine Catholics, which made him a target of the Know-Nothing Protestants, an extremist anti-Catholic group of that era. When he went to Ellsworth to open another mission, Father Bapst was cruelly attacked by these Protestants on June 5, 1854, tarred and feathered, ridden out of town, and told to flee the area. Some in the crowd wanted to kill Father Bapst, but cooler heads prevailed.

The furor that resulted from this act of bigotry and violence shamed the perpetrators, and anti-Catholicism was exposed as a vicious cancer in American society. Prominent leaders across the nation assailed the individuals involved. Father Bapst recovered and continued his labors, founding a parish at Bangor. In 1859 he was sent to Boston as rector of the Jesuit College there and became superior of all the Society's houses in Canada and New York. By 1879 Father Bapst's mind began to fail. He died at Mount Hope, Maryland, and was buried at Woodstock, Maryland. (*See also* Boston College.)

Baraga, Irenaeus Frederick (June 29, 1797–January 19, 1868)

The "Apostle to the Chippewas," Irenaeus Frederick Baraga was the first bishop of Marquette, Michigan. He was born at Malavas in the Austrian dukedom of Carniolia. The son of nobles, he was orphaned in 1812 and was raised by a university professor at Laibach. He entered the University of Vienna in 1816, earning a law degree and becoming fluent in English, French, Italian, and Spanish. Receiving the grace of a religious vocation, he entered the seminary and was ordained on September 21, 1823.

Attracted to the missionary efforts in the United States, Father Baraga left his homeland and went to America, where he was welcomed by Bishop Edward D. Fenwick of Cincinnati in 1831. He labored in the diocese until the following spring, when he started his ministry in Michigan. Between 1831 and 1835, Father Baraga founded missions in Arbre Croche (Harbor Springs) and Grand Rapids. In July 1835, he opened a mission for the Chippewas at La Pointe, Wisconsin, and another at L'Anse, Michigan, in 1843.

The only priest in Upper Michigan for many years, Father Baraga cared for white congregations as well as the Native Americans in the area. He founded churches and schools, going to Europe in 1836 and 1853 to gather funds and mission personnel. In his missions, Father Baraga denounced the liquor traders and others who tried to exploit the Indians.

On July 29, 1853, the Northern Peninsula of Michigan was detached from the Diocese of Detroit and made a vicariate apostolic. Father Baraga was appointed the first bishop, consecrated in the Cathedral of Cincinnati. He issued two episcopal letters soon after, one in English and the second in Chippewa. His jurisdiction extended not only to the whole northern peninsula of Michigan, but to a large part of the lower peninsula in northern Wisconsin, and the northern shore of Lake Superior. On October 23, 1864, by apostolic authority, he transferred his see from Sault Ste. Marie to Marquette, where he labored throughout the area for another fifteen years. When he was too exhausted by his ministries to ride his faithful horse, he used a sleigh that was pulled by a sturdy dog.

Bishop Baraga composed the first recorded Chippewa grammar and the first Chippewa dictionary. Both works took hours of research and study. Prayer books and catechisms were also compiled by Bishop Baraga, as well as *Dusna Tasa*, a Slovenian-language prayer book. He wrote many other literary and spiritual works as well, including

Bishop Irenaeus Frederick Baraga

an Ottawa prayer book, *Animie Misinasaigan*, and instructions and sermons.

While attending the Second Plenary Council in Baltimore, Bishop Baraga suffered a stroke. He refused prolonged medical care in Baltimore, having taken a vow to die among his beloved Indians. Carried back to Marquette, he died there. Bishop Baraga was beloved in his mission territory and in his native land. His biography was a bestseller in Europe. He is honored as the "Father of Indian Literature" in America. The cause for canonization of Bishop Baraga has been opened.

Barbelin, Felix-Joseph (May 30, 1808–June 8, 1869)

The "Apostle of Philadelphia," Felix-Joseph Barbelin was a Jesuit missionary to America and was beloved by people of all faiths during his ministry in that city. He was born in Lunéville, Lorraine, France, the oldest of six children, and he studied at a local seminary before entering the Society of Jesus on January 7, 1834, after migrating to Maryland. Ordained to the priesthood, Father Barbelin served at Georgetown as pastor of Holy Trinity Parish and then was assigned to Philadelphia in 1838.

For over thirty years he was a fervent and tireless missionary in the city, spending most of those years as pastor of Old St. Joseph's Parish at Willing's Abbey. Father Barbelin founded St. Joseph's Hospital and started parish sodalities. In 1852 he became the first president of St. Joseph's College. Father Barbelin's personal piety, kindness, and zeal won many admirers in the city, and people of all faiths applauded and supported his programs. When he died, he was mourned by all in Philadelphia.

Barber, Daniel (October 2, 1756–1834)

A soldier of the American Revolution, Daniel Barber and his family, converts to the faith, impacted all of New England in a critical formative period in American history. He was born in Simsbury, Connecticut, and was raised in a family of "Congregational Dissenters of strict Puritan rule." Barber, however, joined the Episcopal Church when he was twenty-seven. He had served as a soldier in the Continental Army and was ready to assume a position of service.

Ordained as an Episcopal minister in Schenectady, New York, he had married Chloe Case in 1787, and his family moved to Claremont, New Hampshire, where he served for three decades. In 1807 Reverend Barber baptized Frances Allen, the daughter of Ethan Allen. She, however, converted to Catholicism in Canada, and became a nun in Hôtel Dieu, Montréal. Barber visited her there and returned troubled in his own mind. He also knew Bishop Jean-Louis Lefebvre de Cheverus, the French missionary of Boston, who would become a cardinal, and the books he received from this revered prelate further called the Anglican faith into question.

Virgil Barber, Daniel's son, converted to Catholicism in 1817, as did his daughter-in-law, Jerusha. They visited Reverend Barber, bringing a missionary, the Dominican Father Charles Ffrench, and within a week the entire household became Catholic, including Chloe Barber, her children, Mrs. Noah Tyler, the sister of Daniel, and her daughter. The first bishop of Hartford, Connecticut, William Tyler, was the son of Mrs. Noah Tyler. Daniel and six other relatives converted soon after, and some of these newly baptized Catholics became Sisters of Charity.

Chloe Barber died in February 1825. Daniel spent his years as a widower living near his son. He died at the Jesuit house in St. Inigoes, Maryland. He wrote *A History on My Own Times* and other Catholic pamphlets that explained the faith to his Protestant contemporaries.

Barber, Jerusha (July 20, 1789–January 1, 1860)

A remarkable Catholic convert and religious, Jerusha Barber was a member of the well-known Barber family of New England. She was married to Virgil, son of Daniel and Chloe Barber. Jerusha converted with her husband and their five children. She received the grace of a religious vocation as a result of her conversion, as did Virgil, and under the guidance of Jesuit Father Benedict Joseph Fenwick, who became the second bishop of Boston,

they entered religious life. Jerusha and three of her daughters became Visitation nuns, while Virgil and their son, Samuel, entered the Society of Jesus. The mother of Bishop Fenwick raised the youngest child, Josephine. On July 26, 1817, Jerusha became Sister Mary Augustine. Her novitiate was difficult because of her love for her family, but she took vows in Georgetown in 1820. Sister Mary Augustine served at Georgetown, and then in the great Mission of Kaskaskia, in the Illinois territory. She also served as a mission educator in St. Louis and Mobile, Alabama.

Barber, Virgil (May 1782–March 25, 1847)

One of the remarkable members of the Barber family of New England who converted to the Catholic faith, Virgil Barber was ordained in the Society of Jesus. He was born in Claremont, New Hampshire, the son of Daniel and Chloe Barber. He was raised in the Episcopal Church but observed his father's concerns about the validity of Anglican sacraments and orders.

Virgil was ordained in the Episcopal Church and served as the principal of the Episcopal Academy at Fairfield, New York. There he came across a booklet, *A Novena to St. Francis Xavier*, which was owned by an Irish maidservant in his household. Doubts fostered by this booklet led Virgil to visit Jesuit Father Benedict Joseph Fenwick, the second bishop of Boston. As a result of further study, Virgil resigned his position and converted to Catholicism with his wife, Jerusha, and their five children.

In June 1817, Jerusha and three of their daughters became Visitation Sisters, and Virgil and their son, Samuel, entered the Society of Jesus. Virgil then was taken to Rome by Father John Grassi, the superior of Georgetown. Returning to Georgetown a year later, he continued his studies and was ordained in December 1822. He started an academy parish in Claremont, New Hampshire, but was removed in 1827. He then labored among the Abenaki in Maine. Virgil retired to Georgetown, where he remained until his death.

Barbera, Joseph (March 24, 1911–December 18, 2006)

Noted animator and cartoon artist who was best known for his long partnership with William

Hanna in Hanna-Barbera cartoons, Joseph Barbera was born in Little Italy, in New York City, and displayed a talent for drawing from early childhood. He held various jobs until 1932, when he was given a position at Van Beuren Studios, then Terrytoons in 1936. The following year, he moved to California, where he began working for MGM (Metro-Goldwyn-Mayer) and soon met William Hanna. The two formed the partnership that began with the famed Tom and Jerry cartoons.

When MGM disbanded its animation department in 1957, the two formed Hanna-Barbera, an animation studio that created some of the most beloved programs in television history, including *The Flintstones, Scooby-Doo, Yogi Bear, The Smurfs,* and *The Jetsons.* Hanna–Barbera was sold to Taft Broadcasting for $12 million in 1967, although the two men remained heads of the company until 1991. Together, they won seven Academy Awards and eight Emmy Awards. A devout Catholic, Barbera helped to bring to life animated Bible stories that were called *The Greatest Adventure: Stories of the Bible.*

Bardstown, Diocese of

Established on April 8, 1808, by Pope Pius VII, the Diocese of Bardstown, in Kentucky, was one of the oldest and largest ecclesiastical jurisdictions in the United States. It was responsible for all the territories from the Great Lakes in the north to the 35th parallel in the south, and from the Allegheny Mountains in the east to the Mississippi River in the west. The Diocese of Bardstown was transferred to Louisville in 1841. Eventually the territories served by the diocese required the establishment of thirty-five new dioceses in eleven states.

Bardstown was steeped in Catholicism from an early time in the nation's history. In 1678 the Jesuit Father Jacques Marquette was in the area on his expeditions. Nearly a century passed, however, before a settlement was opened in 1774. James Harrod founded Harrodsburg in central Kentucky. In 1785 some twenty-five Catholic families settled at Pottinger's Creek, with a second group arriving soon after. Two years later, Father Charles Whelan was sent as a missionary to the area. In 1791 Father William de Rohan built the first Catholic chapel in Kentucky.

Earlier, in 1767, Daniel Boone, a Catholic, made his way into Kentucky through the Cumberland Gap. He tried to start a settlement but was forced back by Indian attacks; his son was tortured and murdered by the Cherokees. In 1775, after blazing a second trail into Kentucky, Boone brought his wife, Rebecca, and his daughter to a site called Boonesborough.

In 1793 Father Stephen T. Badin was working in the region with Father John Thayer. Kentucky became a state in 1792, spurring settlements, and in 1795 some three hundred Catholic families arrived in the territory. In 1805 the Trappist monks made a monastic foundation in Kentucky, relocating in Missouri in 1808. Also on the scene were Father Charles Nerinckx and the Dominican missionary Edward D. Fenwick.

In 1806 St. Rose Dominican Priory opened near Springfield. The Diocese of Bardstown was established two years later. On November 4, 1810, the Sulpician Father Benedict Joseph Flaget was consecrated as the first bishop of Bardstown. The diocese had six thousand Catholics in Kentucky, served by six priests and eleven churches. In 1812 Bishop Flaget presided over a diocesan synod and then journeyed to St. Louis, Missouri, and Vincennes, Indiana, the northern outposts of the diocese. In 1817 the Sulpician Father John B. David was appointed coadjutor to Bishop Flaget.

The tours of the diocese took up considerable time and energy, but Bishop Flaget visited Ohio, Detroit, and Canada, and then, in 1819, consecrated St. Joseph's Cathedral in Bardstown, now a federally mandated national monument. In 1821 the Diocese of Cincinnati was established (now an archdiocese). Cincinnati assumed responsibility for a large part of Bardstown's original territory. In 1834 the Diocese of Vincennes (now the Archdiocese of Indianapolis) was erected as well.

Bishop Flaget resigned in 1832, intending to retire, but the Holy See responded to the countless petitions received from the Catholics in the area and reinstated him in 1834. He went to Rome soon after to make his first *ad limina* visit and spent five years on papal missions. Bardstown diocese was redesignated as Louisville on February 13, 1841. Bishop Flaget served there until his death on February 11, 1850. (*See also* Louisville, Archdiocese of.)

Cathedral of St. Joseph in Bardstown

Barr, William P. *See* **Cabinets, Catholics in Presidential**

Barron, Edward (1801–September 12, 1854)

A missionary bishop, Edward Barron was a model of charity for America and Africa. He was born in County Waterford, Ireland, to a prominent family, was educated at Trinity College, Dublin, and earned a law degree. In 1825 however, he began seminary studies and was ordained in Rome in 1829. As a priest, Father Barron returned to Ireland to teach at St. John's College, Waterford.

The American Bishop Francis P. Kenrick asked Father Barron to come to the United States to serve as the rector of the seminary in Philadelphia. Father Barron accepted the invitation and became president of St. Charles Borromeo Theological Seminary and vicar general of the diocese. In 1840 however, Father Barron joined Father John Kelly of New York in an effort to aid the Catholic missions in Africa. Father Barron left Baltimore on December 21, 1841, sailing to Cape Mesurado, where he began his ministry.

He was named prefect apostolic for Upper Guinea and went to Rome, where he was consecrated on January 22, 1842. Bishop Barron and his companions endured terrible ordeals, and he returned to America after two years. He was offered the post of auxiliary in two dioceses of the United States but was ill with pulmonary tuberculosis and went to Florida. When a yellow fever epidemic struck Georgia, Bishop Barron traveled to the stricken area and died while caring for the victims of the sickness.

Barry, Catherine (March 11, 1881–November 20, 1961)

A religious of the Adrian Dominicans, Catherine Barry was a noted educator. Born in Inagh, County Clare, Ireland, she migrated to the United States in her youth and in 1913 entered the Congregation of the Most Holy Rosary of the Dominican Sisters in Adrian, Michigan. She distinguished herself quickly as a very able teacher and in 1914 was appointed a principal and in 1921 mistress of novices. In 1933 she was elected prioress general and presided over the continued expansion of the Dominican community over the next thirty years. During her tenure, the Adrian Dominicans founded a host of schools for all grades, from college to elementary. In 1952 she was the first chairperson of the National Congress of Religious in the United States and was a key figure in the establishment of the Conference of Major Superiors of Women's Religious Institutes.

Barry, Colman James (May 21, 1921–January 7, 1994)

A Benedictine historian, Colman James Barry was president of the American Catholic Historical Association. He was born in Lake City, Minnesota, and entered St. John's University at Collegeville in 1938. Becoming a Benedictine monk in 1943, he was ordained four years later. He then earned his doctorate at The Catholic University of America and returned to St. John's to assume educational and administrative posts. During this period he wrote historical works and served as president of St. John's from 1964 to 1971.

He served as a visiting professor of Church history at Yale Divinity School as well, and in March 1973 he became the first dean of Catholic University's School of Religious Studies. As the president of the American Catholic Historical Association, he chaired the bicentennial celebrations of the group in Washington in 1976. He was honored with the *Pro Ecclesia et Pontificio* medal at Catholic University in 1977. Father Colman continued his historical writings until his death at St. John's Abbey.

Barry, John (1745–September 13, 1803)

A popular naval commander of the Revolutionary War, John Barry was one of the crucial figures in the founding of the United States Navy. Barry was born at Tacumshane, County Wexford, Ireland, and went to sea as a lad. When he was fifteen, he landed in Philadelphia and declared that he had found his home. Working his way as a seaman, he was captain of his own ship, the *Black Prince*, at age twenty-one. When the American Revolution began, Barry volunteered his experience and abilities. He started his war service as commander of the brig *Lexington*, and captured the British tender *Edward*, the first such naval prize won by an American. Barry took part in the campaigns at Trenton and Princeton in 1776 and 1777. He was then chosen to outfit a frigate but was forced to scuttle the ship in the Delaware River when the British overran American defenses. His commission, dated December 7, 1775, was the first one issued.

On another vessel, Barry led two ships into Delaware Bay and captured other enemy naval units and then encountered two British warships near Boston in September 1778. Outgunned, Barry fought for two days and ran his frigate *Raleigh* aground on the coast of Maine. The vessel was captured before it could be burned, but Barry and his crew escaped. An investigation into the incident cleared Barry; his lieutenant, assigned to fire on the ship, had failed to do so. Barry then used a privateer, the *Delaware*, to capture more enemy vessels.

In the fall of 1780, Barry was given command of a 36-gun privateer, the *Alliance*, taking the American commissioner, John Lourends, to France. On the return voyage, Barry engaged in another severe naval battle and was badly wounded. In September 1782, he captured nine enemy vessels, and in March 1783 fought the last battle of the war, accompanied by a French ship.

With the war over, Barry sailed to China and then supervised the building of the frigate *United States* and set about putting an end to French privateer activities. On February 22, 1797, Barry received the commodore rank from George Washington, and became the first to hold that rank in the United States Navy.

An ardent Catholic, he was married twice, and both of his wives became converts. His first wife died in 1771. His second wife, Sarah, died in 1831. Commodore John Barry died in Philadelphia and was buried in the cemetery of St. Mary's Church, Philadelphia, both wives beside him.

Barry's rank and honors have been obscured by the popularity of John Paul Jones. Barry, however, was and remains the "Father of the American Navy." He was also revered by his contemporaries, who sang: "There are gallant hearts whose glory Columbia loves to name, whose deeds shall live in story and everlasting fame. But never yet one man braver our starry banner bore, than saucy old Jack Barry, the Irish Commodore."

Barry, John (1799–1859)

The Irish-born bishop of Savannah from 1857 to 1859, John Barry was a veteran of the Seminole War and a model of charity for the young nation of the United States. He was born in Oylegate, County Wexford, Ireland, in 1799 and migrated to the United States to enter the seminary in Charleston, South Carolina. There he was trained by Bishop John England, who ordained him on September 24, 1825.

In 1836 the Irish Volunteers of Charleston, a militia unit, joined the forces engaged in the Seminole War in Florida. Father Barry became chaplain of this unit, returning to his pastoral ministry at the close of the military campaign. He was a rector in Augusta, Georgia, when an epidemic of yellow fever ravaged

Commodore John Barry

the city, and he turned his rectory into a hospital and asked the Sisters of Our Lady of Mercy to aid the victims.

In 1854 he was appointed administrator of Savannah and was consecrated a bishop when the diocese was erected in August 1857. Two years later, while visiting Europe, Bishop Barry became ill and died in Paris. His remains were interred in the crypt of St. Patrick's Church in Augusta.

Barry, Leonora Marie (August 13, 1849–July 15, 1930)

A leader of the Knights of Labor, Leonora Marie Barry was an active member of the Women's Suffrage Movement and the founder of the Women's Temperance Union. She was born at Kearney, County Cork, Ireland, but her family migrated to the United States, and she was raised in Pierrepont, New York. In 1871 she married William E. Barry, an Irish painter and musician, and they had three children, one of whom died at the age of eight.

Leonora, who worked in a garment factory in Amsterdam, New York, joined the Knights of Labor in 1884, becoming an active leader. She is credited with bringing about the Pennsylvania Wool Cloth Factories Act of 1889.

In 1890 Leonora married Obadiah Reed Lake, a telegraph editor, and became part of the Women's Suffrage Movement. She gave an address to the Congress of Women at the Columbian Exposition in Chicago in 1893. In addition to founding the Women's Temperance Union, she was also a leader of the Catholic Total Abstinence Union of America. She died in Minooka, Illinois.

Barrymore, Ethel (1879–June 18, 1959)

One of the great stars of American theater, Ethel Barrymore was a member of a family of celebrated actors. She was born in Philadelphia and educated by the Sisters of Notre Dame de Namur. She began her acting career in a leading role of *His Excellency, the Governor,* a play produced by Charles Frohman. A series of other roles in successful plays assured

Ethel Barrymore

her a place in the American theater. In 1909 she married Russell Griswald Colt and had three children. When the couple divorced in 1923, she never remarried. She continued acting and saw the Shubert's Ethel Barrymore Theater open in 1928. She also performed in television and film, receiving the Academy Award in 1944 for her portrayal of Cary Grant's mother in *None But the Lonely Heart.* Between 1946 and 1957, she appeared in twenty films and was popular in television dramas and variety shows. Ethel Barrymore died in Hollywood, California.

Barzynski, Vincent Michael (September 20, 1838–May 2, 1899)

A missionary and pastor, Vincent Michael Barzynski was a leader of the Polish Catholic community in the United States. Born at Sulislawice, Sandomir, Russian Poland, the son of Joseph and Mary (Sroczynska) Barzynski, he was given a private education owing to poor health as a child. In 1856, however, he entered the diocesan seminary at Lublin and was ordained on October 28, 1861. After recovering from another illness, he was named an associate pastor at Horodlo and later assistant at Tomaszew. While at Tomaszew, he became heavily involved in the uprising of 1863 against the Russians. As the uprising failed, he fled to Kraków and was given refuge by the Franciscans in that city. In 1865 he was deported to Paris and there became associated with various Polish émigrés. Attracted to the recently established Congregation of the Resurrection, he went to Rome and made his vows in 1866. The next day, he sailed for America with several other priests bound for ministry in Texas.

After pastoral work in San Antonio, he was appointed pastor of St. Stanislaus Kostka parish, Chicago, in 1874. There he remained for the rest of his life, overseeing the expansion of the parish and emerging as one of the key organizers of Polish Catholics in the United States. He was the driving force behind the first meeting of the Polish Roman Catholic Union in Chicago in 1874, and the following year he helped to found the Association of Polish Roman Catholic Priests in the United States. He also introduced the Sisters of the Holy Family of Nazareth to America, organized dozens of confraternities and sodalities, and was invaluable to the archdiocese in the establishment of Polish parishes. He founded the first Polish Catholic paper, the *Gazeta Katolicka*, and the first Polish daily Catholic paper in America, the *Dziennik Chicagoski,* which aimed to combat the pervasive influences of the liberal media, the Masons, and the socialists. Before his death, he was named the first provincial superior of the Resurrectionists in the United States.

Basilica of the National Shrine of the Immaculate Conception. *See* National Shrine of the Immaculate Conception

Baton Rouge, Diocese of

Established on July 20, 1961, by Pope Blessed John XXIII, the Diocese of Baton Rouge is situated on the banks of the Mississippi River, northwest of New Orleans, and comprises several counties in Louisiana. The third largest city in Louisiana, Baton Rouge is the state's capital. The French named the site after a red tree that served as a boundary marker between local Indian tribes. In 1719 a fort was garrisoned there to quell local uprisings, but the French and Indian War brought about British control of the region. Baton Rouge was sold to the United States in 1803 as part of the Louisiana Purchase, but the Spanish maintained a claim to the area, along with Florida. The Battle of Baton Rouge resulted in the United States gaining possession. The Diocese of Baton Rouge is a suffragan see of the Archdiocese of New Orleans.

The Catholic history of Baton Rouge, which was part of the vast Louisiana missions, started with the arrival of René-Robert Chevalier, Sieur de La Salle, who came into the area to lay claim to the territory for France circa 1682. Franciscan Father Zenobius Membré was with La Salle's expedition and was martyred later. Also prominent in the area were Pierre Le Moyne, Sieur d'Iberville, and Jean-Baptiste Le Moyne, Sieur de Bienville.

Around 1700 the Franciscan Father Anastase Douay and the Jesuit Father Paul du Ru were also in the region. Father du Ru reportedly erected a chapel at Bayou Goula. Six years later, Father Jean-François Buisson de Saint-Cosmé was killed near Donaldsville. He had baptized some two hundred local Native Americans before he was slain.

In 1722 Father Pierre Charlevoix celebrated Mass in Baton Rouge. Chapels and parishes were established after this Mass took place. In 1728 St. Francis Chapel was erected at Pointe Coupée; St. James Parish was founded circa 1757; St. Gabriel's in 1769; and a parish at Donaldson was formed in 1772. A Catholic Church was established in Baton Rouge in 1792, and one was erected in Plattenville the following year.

In 1793 the Diocese of New Orleans, now an archdiocese, was created. The area became a United States possession in 1803, and in the following year was designated the Territory of Orleans by an act of Congress. In 1812 Louisiana entered the Union as the eighteenth state. New Orleans was made an archdiocese in 1850, and the Diocese of Natchitoches, now Alexandria, was established.

The Civil War brought Union troops into New Orleans in 1862, an occupation that impacted Baton Rouge and other areas. Louisiana was readmitted into the Union in 1868, but the Reconstruction Era and its evils lasted until 1877. The Catholics of Baton Rouge experienced the revitalization of America and the eras of expansion before World War I, which was supported by the state. The Diocese of Lafayette was established in 1918. Xavier University had been founded three years earlier, and Notre Dame Seminary was opened in New Orleans in 1923.

Louisiana's economy had been devastated by the Great Depression but revived because of the demands of World War II. Area industries produced chemicals, aircraft engines, and other materials.

The Catholics of the area were recognized by the Holy See when the Diocese of Baton Rouge was established in 1961. Bishop Robert E. Tracy was appointed to the diocese on August 10 of that year. He instituted the agencies and protocols for diocesan affairs and started the Foundation Fund Drive for new high schools, a chancery, a seminary, and other diocesan institutions. He also cared for the historical parishes, hospitals, and convents of Baton Rouge, some having survived for two centuries. Bishop Tracy took part in the Second Vatican

Council and implemented the reforms mandated by the council, including liturgical renewal. He retired on March 21, 1974.

The second bishop of Baton Rouge was Joseph V. Sullivan, who was appointed on August 5, 1974. He had served as an auxiliary bishop of Kansas City-St. Joseph since 1967. He began his ministry in the diocese by continuing the expansion and renovation programs. He also served as a leader in the pro-life movement across the nation and promoted other moral and social issues of the time. Bishop Sullivan died on September 4, 1982.

His successor, Bishop Stanley Ott, an auxiliary bishop of the Archdiocese of New Orleans since 1976, was promoted to the Diocese of Baton Rouge on January 18, 1983. Evangelization and spiritual renewal were the hallmarks of his leadership, and he was active in the ecumenical apostolate until he was diagnosed with inoperable cancer of the liver. His grace-filled death on November 28, 1992, inspired the people of Baton Rouge.

Bishop Alfred C. Hughes, the fourth bishop of Baton Rouge, had served as an auxiliary bishop of the Archdiocese of Boston since 1981 and was installed in the diocese on November 4, 1993. He reorganized diocesan programs and raised funds for future expansion while maintaining the traditional projects of his predecessors. He was promoted to the Archdiocese of New Orleans as coadjutor on February 16, 2001, acceding to the see on January 3, 2002.

The fifth bishop of Baton Rouge, Bishop Robert W. Muench, had served as an auxiliary bishop of New Orleans since 1990. He was installed in Baton Rouge on March 14, 2002. The focus of his episcopal programs has been ministry to the young people in the Catholic high schools of Baton Rouge, and he has promoted lay apostolates and the presbyteral council. He also provided vital leadership to the region during the severe suffering caused by Hurricane Katrina in 2005. In 2011 there were 200,000 Catholics served by 105 priests, more than 100 men and women religious, and 68 parishes in the diocese.

Baudoin, Michel (March 8, 1692–c. 1768)

A remarkable Jesuit missionary, Michel Baudoin is revered as the "Apostle to the Choctaws." He was born in Québec, Canada, and entered the Society of Jesus in France in 1713. Ordained to the priesthood, Father Baudoin arrived in New Orleans, Louisiana, in 1728. The Louisiana mission to the Choctaw nations was vast at the time, and Father Baudoin was sent to their settlements as their pastor. He remained with the Choctaw for eighteen years.

In 1746 his Jesuit superiors recalled Father Baudoin from the Choctaw Mission because of the presence of often corrupt and indifferent British agents in the region. In 1749 he became superior general of the Louisiana missions, holding that office until the Jesuits were expelled from American missions in 1763.

Father Baudoin was not forced to leave Louisiana with his fellow Jesuits; he was given a small house on a local plantation and a pension. Revered and honored for his lifetime of service, Father Baudoin died in New Orleans.

Baum, William Wakefield (November 21, 1926–)

The archbishop of Washington from 1973 to 1980, William Wakefield Baum was created a cardinal in 1976, and served as prefect of the Congregation for Catholic Education from 1980 to 1990, and major penitentiary of the Apostolic Penitentiary from 1990 to 2001. He was born in Dallas, Texas, but grew up in Kansas City, Missouri, where he received his primary education; in 1939, at age thirteen, he entered St. John's Minor Seminary in Kansas City and then continued his preparations for the priesthood at Kenrick Seminary in St. Louis. Ordained a priest on May 12, 1951, he served as curate at the Parish of St. Aloysius in Kansas City and taught theology and Church history at the College of St. Theresa.

In 1956 he was sent to Rome, where he earned a doctorate in theology from the Pontifical University of St. Thomas, the Angelicum in 1958. He returned to the United States and held pastoral posts and was also notary of the Ecclesiastical Tribunal and vice-chancellor of the curia. During the Second Vatican Council, he was a *peritus* (or theological expert) and spoke on the important topic of Christian unity. He was also one of the Catholic delegates at several sessions of the Geneva-based World Council of Churches and executive secretary of the Committee for Ecumenical Affairs of the National Conference of Catholic Bishops from 1964 to 1967.

On February 18, 1970, Pope Paul VI appointed him as the bishop of Springfield-Cape Girardeau, and he was consecrated on April 6, 1970. Three years later, on March 5, 1973, he was named archbishop of Washington, and on May 24, 1976, Pope Paul also appointed him to the College of Cardinals, with the titular church of Holy Cross in Via Flaminia.

After four years in Washington, Cardinal Baum was named prefect of the Congregation for Catholic Education by Pope Blessed John Paul II on January 15, 1980, a post he held until April 1990. That same year, he was transferred to the post of major penitentiary of the Apostolic Penitentiary, where he remained until 2001, when he retired.

Cardinal William Baum

Bayer, Adele (July 4, 1814–January 23, 1892)

Called the "Guardian of Seamen," Adele Bayer was the eldest daughter of Andrew Parmentier, the famed horticulturalist. She was born in Belgium and migrated to America in 1824. Her family originally planned to make their home in the West Indies but were persuaded by friends to settle in New York. Andrew developed a horticultural park near Brooklyn, and he quickly became a landscape expert. A devout Catholic, he served as one of the founders of St. James, the first parish in Brooklyn. Andrew died on November 16, 1830.

Adele and her mother, Sylvia, maintained Andrew's gardens until 1832, when they were sold. Wealthy women, Adele and her mother supported many charitable works and provided the famous missionary, Jesuit Father Pierre De Smet, with large donations for his vast mission apostolate to the Native Americans.

Adele married Edward Bayer, a German Catholic merchant, in 1841. She adopted the sailors at the Brooklyn Navy Yard during the Civil War, seeing to their needs and offering spiritual encouragement. Her steadfast faithfulnewss to this charitable program earned her the epithet of the "Guardian of Seamen." Adele died in Brooklyn, a decade after her mother.

Bayley, James Roosevelt (August 23, 1814–October 3, 1877)

A nephew of St. Elizabeth Ann Seton, James Roosevelt Bayley was the first bishop of the Diocese of Newark, from 1853 to 1872, and the eighth archbishop of the Archdiocese of Baltimore, from 1872 to 1877.

He was born in Rye, New York, the son of Dr. Richard Bayley of Columbia College. His grandfather, a wealthy man, had planned to leave his fortune to James Roosevelt Bayley, until he converted to Catholicism and was ordained. The grandfather disinherited him because he was led to believe that Catholic priests did not need money.

James Roosevelt Bayley became a Catholic after studying at Amherst College and Trinity College and being ordained to the Episcopal ministry. He was the rector of St. Peter's Church in Harlem, New York, in 1835, but resigned in 1841 because of his doubts and his recognition of the authenticity of the Roman Catholic faith. He went to Rome, where he was baptized, and was educated at Saint-Sulpice in Paris. Returning to New York, he was ordained to the Catholic priesthood by Bishop John Hughes on March 2, 1844. He then became a professor and vice president of Fordham Seminary.

When the Diocese of Newark was established, Father Bayley was appointed as the first bishop and was consecrated at St. Patrick's Cathedral, New York, by the apostolic nuncio to Brazil, Archbishop Cajetano Bedini, on October 30, 1853. Bishop Bayley labored tirelessly to establish the new diocese, finding funds and personnel for Catholic institutions. He founded a college and aided St. Elizabeth Ann Seton's congregation.

On July 30, 1872, he was promoted to the Archdiocese of Baltimore and embarked on a series of programs to benefit American Catholics. He received aid from the Society for the Propagation of the Faith in Lyons, France, and from the

Leopoldine Society of Vienna. Many religious orders and congregations responded to his invitation to labor in the archdiocese. Archbishop Bayley wrote two histories and encouraged the work of the historian John Gilmary Shea.

At the request of Archbishop Francis Norbert Blanchet of Oregon, Archbishop Bayley instituted the Bureau of Catholic Indian Missions with Father Jean Baptiste Abraham Brouillet. He also presided over the elevation of Archbishop John McCloskey in 1875, the first cardinal in the United States. Archbishop Bayley convened a provincial synod in August 1875, and in the following year dedicated the Cathedral of Baltimore.

In May 1877, Bishop (later Cardinal) James Gibbons of Richmond was made coadjutor to Archbishop Bayley, allowing him to seek a cure for his serious illness abroad. In August 1877, however, he returned to his former residence in Newark and died there. Archbishop Bayley was buried in Emmitsburg, Maryland, beside St. Elizabeth Ann Seton, as he had requested. He was mourned by thousands, as he had defended Catholics during

Archbishop James R. Bayley

several critical eras and had exemplified the dignity and grace of his office in a unique manner.

Bayma, Joseph (November 9, 1816–February 7, 1892)

A Jesuit mathematician, Joseph Bayma was an honored teacher and scientist. Born in Piedmont, Italy, he entered the Society of Jesus in 1832 and was soon respected as a brilliant student of mathematics and physics. By 1860 he was rector of the episcopal seminary of Bertinoro, but owing to the problems that attended the Risorgimento (the unification of Italy under King Victor Emmanuel II), he was compelled to seek refuge in England, where he taught philosophy for seven years. In 1868 he made his way to California, where he was named rector of St. Ignatius College, in San Francisco. Three years later, he took up a post teaching in Santa Clara. He was the author of numerous books on physics, spirituality, and mathematics.

Beaumont, Diocese of

Established on September 29, 1966, by Pope Paul VI, the Diocese of Beaumont is in the Sabine area of Texas and serves thirteen complete counties and portions of two other counties. The city of Beaumont is one of the state's major ports and is also an oil-refining center. In 1825 Noah Tevis founded a settlement near present-day Beaumont and sold property ten years later to Henry Millard, who started a town he named after his brother-in-law, Jefferson Beaumont.

The site was strategically located, and by 1890 railroads were coming through it. The discovery of the Spindletop oil well in 1901 prompted a booming economy, and the completion of a deep-river canal in 1916 spurred further growth. Beaumont has a diversified manufacturing and industrial base. The diocese is a suffragan see of the Archdiocese of San Antonio.

The Catholic history of Beaumont and Texas serves as a memorial to the missionaries who entered uncharted lands to evangelize the local tribes of American Indians. The Spanish were in Texas as early as 1682, and Franciscan priests and others entered the area on mission assignments. By 1794 there were thirty-six such missions in the region, and Venerable Antonio Margil de Jesús and Father Damian Massanet were laboring in the area. The Church prospered in the state until 1794, when the Mexican authorities, having overthrown Spanish control, expelled the Spanish priests and decreed that the lands surrounding the missions were to be divided among the local tribes.

Texas rebelled against Mexico and became an independent republic in 1836. At that time, Texas was under the ecclesiastical jurisdiction of the Diocese of Monterey, Mexico. Recognizing the problems that would result from this situation, the Holy See erected a apostolic prefecture for Texas. In 1842 Bishop John M. Odin, a Vincentian who had served as apostolic prefect, was consecrated as vicar apostolic. Five years later he was appointed bishop of the Diocese of Galveston.

Bishop Odin reopened the abandoned Catholic missions, while creating new parishes and providing services and facilities for the vast number of immigrants of the faith.

In 1874 the Diocese of San Antonio (now the Archdiocese of San Antonio) was erected, and other dioceses followed. The Catholics of Texas shared in the turmoil of the Civil War and then welcomed countless new settlements in the Lone Star State.

World War I was supported in Texas, and the state suffered with other Americans in the Great Depression. Beaumont served the military efforts of the nation, as industries functioned on a wartime basis during World War II. After the war, new settlements developed throughout the state. The Archdiocese of San Antonio was established in 1926, and new dioceses aided the growth of the Church.

The Diocese of Beaumont was erected in 1966, and Vincent M. Harris was appointed as the first bishop of Beaumont. He had served as auxiliary bishop of Lafayette since 1962. Bishop Harris was consecrated on September 28, 1966, and was installed the next day in St. Anthony Cathedral. He instituted the agencies and protocols necessary for diocesan administration and began lay ministries and social services, implementing the reforms of the Second Vatican Council. On April 21, 1971, Bishop Harris was appointed coadjutor of the Diocese of Austin.

His successor was Bishop Warren L. Boudreaux, who had served as the auxiliary bishop of Lafayette from 1962. He was installed on August 25, 1971, in Beaumont. He also aided a large number of Vietnamese refugees in the diocese, providing programs to assist in their resettlement. On March 2, 1977, Bishop Boudreaux was appointed the first bishop of the Diocese of Houma-Thibodaux.

Bishop Bernard J. Ganter became the third bishop of Beaumont and was installed on December 13, 1977, having served as the bishop of Tulsa since 1973. Expansion programs and charitable institutions, including a Catholic Charities office, were promoted during Bishop Ganter's administration. In December 1986 lands were taken from Beaumont diocese to become part of the Diocese of Tyler. In that same year, the diocese also gained parts of counties previously separated. Bishop Ganter died on October 9, 1993, from brain cancer.

Bishop Joseph A. Galante was appointed Bishop Ganter's successor. He had served as auxiliary bishop of the Archdiocese of San Antonio since 1992. He was installed on May 9, 1994. In that same year the Department of Catholic Education was formed. In 1996 Bishop Galante opened a diocesan synod. Three years later, on November 23, 1999, he became the coadjutor bishop of the Diocese of Dallas.

The fifth bishop of the diocese, Curtis John Guillory, a member of the Society of the Divine Word, was installed in Beaumont on July 28, 2000. He had served as auxiliary bishop of Galveston-Houston since 1987. Bishop Guillory is the first African-American bishop in Texas and is the first bishop of Beaumont to be a member of a religious community. In 2011 there were more than 74,000 Catholics, served by 71 priests and 44 parishes.

Beauregard, Pierre Gustave Toutant (May 28, 1818–February 20, 1893)

A Civil War general, Pierre Gustave Toutant Beauregard is famed for having started the conflict by firing on Fort Sumter. He was born near New Orleans and was appointed to the United States Military Academy at West Point in 1838. Assigned to an artillery regiment, during the war with Mexico he was wounded at the close of a series of major battles. He was made Captain of Engineers in 1853.

In 1861 Beauregard was named superintendent of the United States Military Academy at West Point but resigned when the Civil War seemed imminent, going to the aid of the Southern Confederacy. He was in command of Charleston, South Carolina, when he opened the war by firing on Fort Sumter. In command of the Confederate forces at Bull Run, he was made a general. For a year and a half he repelled the Union siege of Charleston, and he joined Robert E. Lee in Virginia in May 1864. Other campaigns followed, but the Southern forces surrendered in April 1865.

After the war, Beauregard served as president of the New Orleans, Jackson & Mississippi Railroad and as adjutant-general of Louisiana. General Beauregard declined offers to become the commander of the army of the Khedive of Egypt and the military forces of Romania. He died in New Orleans.

Bedford, Gunning S. (1806–September 5, 1870)

A medical writer and educator, Gunning S. Bedford founded a hospital in New York. He was born in Baltimore, Maryland, and was a nephew and namesake of Gunning Bedford, one of the framers of the Constitution and the first attorney-general of Delaware. Bedford studied at Mount St. Mary's College, Emmitsburg, Maryland, and graduated in 1825; he then earned a degree in medicine from Rutgers College in New York. He devoted the next two years to studying abroad and in 1833 was named professor of obstetrics at Charleston Medical College. He went on to a professorship at Albany Medical College and in 1840 founded the University Medical College in New York City.

Through Bedford's influence, a clinic was established for poor women who needed obstetric care, the first such facility anywhere in the country. His funeral included a eulogy preached by Archbishop John McCloskey of New York, who had been a fellow student at Mount St. Mary's many years before.

Pierre Beauregard

Bedini, Cajetano (May 15, 1806–September 6, 1864)

A papal envoy to the United States in a troubled era, Cajetano Bedini was made a cardinal in Rome. He was born in Sinigalia, Italy. After studying for the priesthood, he was ordained and entered into Vatican service at a young age. In 1848 he was appointed by Pope Blessed Pius IX as Commissary Extraordinary to Bologna, where the people were revolting against occupation by Austrian military forces as well as their status as a papal state. He retired from his position in 1852 and was made the titular archbishop of Thebes.

In 1853 Archbishop Bedini was named apostolic nuncio to Brazil and was commissioned by the pope to visit the United States. He arrived in New York in June of that year and made a courtesy call on President Franklin Pierce in Washington, being courteously received.

His arrival, however, sparked anti-Catholic groups, and vicious demonstrations marred the archbishop's tour of America. There were even plots to assassinate him. Undaunted, the archbishop visited Pittsburgh, Louisville, and Cincinnati. Another assassination plot was foiled in Cincinnati, resulting in riots. Bedini remained in the United States until February 3, 1854, when he had to be covertly taken to his ocean liner by a tugboat.

In Rome, he served as secretary of the Congregation for the Propaganda Fide, and in September 1861 was created a cardinal with the titular church of Santa Maria sopra Minerva. Cardinal Bedini died in Viterbo.

Belleville, Diocese of

Established on January 7, 1887, by Pope Leo XIII, the Diocese of Belleville, in Illinois, was once part of the former Diocese of Alton (Quincy) and served two of the nation's major historic missions. Belleville diocese comprises counties in the southern part of the state. Founded in 1814, the city was called "Beautiful Town" in French. Originally an agricultural center, Belleville diversified its industries in the mid 1850s. The National Shrine of Our Lady of the Snows is near Belleville. The diocese is a suffragan see of the Archdiocese of Chicago.

Catholic missionaries were active in the Belleville region in the early eras of America. Jesuit

Cardinal Cajetano Bedini

Father Jacques Marquette was in the area with Louis Joliet in 1673, and he started the great Mission of Kaskaskia in 1675. Cahokia Mission was erected in 1699 as part of the Louisiana missions. In 1680 René-Robert Chevalier, Sieur de La Salle, built a French fort near Kaskaskia, and some of the most dedicated missionaries came to labor in the region, including the Franciscan Father Louis Hennepin, Father Zenobius Membré, later martyred, and Father Gabriel de la Ribourde, who was slain near modern Seneca. The Jesuit Fathers Claude Allouez and Jacques Gravier served the Native Americans in the area, and Father Gravier was badly wounded in an attack.

Kaskaskia was moved in 1680 to the eastern bank of the Mississippi River, across from St. Louis. In 1720 Father Gabriel Richard was at Prairie du Rocher, and in 1768, Father Pierre Gibault was pastor of Kaskaskia and vicar general of Illinois. The mission served as the capital of the Illinois Territory for a time and as the base of countless ministries until the Mississippi River changed its course during a devastating earthquake and demolished the site in 1881.

In 1843 the Diocese of Chicago was established, and in 1859 the Shawneetown Parish was erected on the Ohio River. Six years before, the Diocese

of Quincy, which became the Diocese of Alton, had been created. The Holy See redesignated the Diocese of Alton as the Diocese of Springfield in Illinois.

The Diocese of Belleville was established in 1887. Bishop John Janssen was appointed the first bishop of Belleville and consecrated on April 25, 1888. He started the agencies and offices necessary for diocesan administration and also founded the diocesan newspaper and built new parishes, an orphanage, and high schools. The diocese received a firm foundation from his leadership. Bishop Janssen died on July 2, 1913.

His successor was Bishop Henry J. Althoff, who was consecrated on February 24, 1914. He led the faithful of the diocese through World Wars I and II and the Great Depression. Bishop Althoff established more parishes and schools to meet the needs of the growing Catholic population and opened St. Henry's Preparatory Seminary. He also revitalized the school system by instituting an office of superintendent. He died on July 3, 1947.

Bishop Albert R. Zuroweste was appointed the third bishop of the Diocese of Belleville on November 29, 1947, and consecrated on January 29, 1948. He presided over the 250th anniversary of the founding of the great Mission of Cahokia in May of that year. He also undertook as many as one hundred individual projects of expansion and construction, renovating the Cathedral of St. Peter and restoring Cahokia. Bishop Zuroweste implemented the reforms of the Second Vatican Council and promoted new apostolates. He retired on September 3, 1976.

His successor was Bishop William M. Cosgrove, who had served as auxiliary bishop of the Diocese of Cleveland since 1968. Bishop Cosgrove was installed as the bishop of Belleville on October 28, 1976. He continued the building and expansion programs until his retirement on May 19, 1981.

Bishop John M. Wurm, who had served as the auxiliary bishop of the Archdiocese of St. Louis since 1976, was appointed the fifth bishop of the Diocese of Belleville and was installed on November 4, 1981. He served the diocese for less than three years, dying on April 27, 1984.

Bishop Wurm was succeeded by James P. Keleher, a priest of the Archdiocese of Chicago. He was appointed Bishop of Belleville on October 20, 1984, and consecrated a bishop on December 11, 1984. He served throughout the rest of the 1980s and was appointed the archbishop of Kansas City, Kansas, on June 28, 1993, and was installed on September 8, 1993.

On February 10, 1994, Bishop Wilton D. Gregory, who had served as auxiliary bishop of the Archdiocese of Chicago since 1983, was installed as the seventh bishop of the Diocese of Belleville. He was also the president of the National Conference of Catholic Bishops from 2001–04. On December 9, 2004, Bishop Gregory was promoted to the rank of archbishop of Atlanta.

The eighth bishop of the Diocese of Belleville, Edward K. Braxton, had served as auxiliary bishop of the Archdiocese of St. Louis since 1995. He was promoted to the Diocese of Lake Charles in 2000 and transferred to Belleville on March 15, 2005. In 2011 there were 91,000 Catholics, served by 149 priests and 119 parishes in the diocese.

Belmont Abbey

A Benedictine monastery, Belmont Abbey was erected in 1876 and dedicated to Mary, Help of Christians. The monastery is known as Belmont Abbey because of its location in Belmont, Gaston County, North Carolina. The abbey began as a dependent priory on land donated by the vicar apostolic of North Carolina, Bishop James Gibbons, who became a cardinal.

The Benedictine Father Hermann Wolfe took possession of the property and also started St. Mary's, which would be known as Belmont Abbey College. In 1884 Belmont Abbey became an independent priory. Father Leo Haid was the first abbot. He built the abbey church and opened a seminary. Three years later, Abbot Haid was made vicar apostolic of North Carolina. He established priories in Savannah in 1902 and Richmond in 1911. On June 8, 1910, Belmont was given a unique status by receiving the rank of *abbey nullius*. As an *abbey nullius*, Belmont Abbey was exempt from diocesan authority and was directly responsible to the Holy See. The abbot had sole jurisdiction over the religious and laity within the boundaries of the abbey. Gaston and seven other counties were separated from the Vicariate of North Carolina and placed under the jurisdiction of the abbey.

Abbot Haid died in 1924, and his successor was Abbot Vincent Taylor. Abbot Taylor governed only the abbey and its *territory nullius,* as the Diocese of Raleigh had been established, replacing the vicariate.

Belmont Abbey College became a junior college and preparatory school in 1929 and assumed the status of a senior college in 1952. On January 8, 1944, the *territory nullius* of the abbey was reduced to Gaston County. Father Walter Coggin was elected as the third Benedictine abbot in 1956. Four years later, the *territory nullius* was restricted to only the Benedictine monastic holdings in Gaston County.

Its *abbey nullius* status was suppressed on January 1, 1977, and the Benedictines became incorporated into the Diocese of Charlotte.

Holy Trinity in Belleville

Benedict XV, Pope (November 21, 1854–January 22, 1922)

The Supreme Pontiff from 1914 to 1922, Benedict XV faced the dark events of World War I. Born Giacomo Giambattista della Chiesa in Genoa, Italy, he was the sixth child of the Marchesa della Chiesa. Educated at the Instituto Danovero e Guisso in Genoa, he received a law degree from the University of Genoa in 1873. As a boy, he had expressed a desire to study for the priesthood, but his father had insisted that he earn a law degree first. That accomplished, he entered the seminary in Genoa, going on to the College Capranica in Rome in 1875 and then to the Pontifical Gregorian University. He was ordained on December 21, 1878, in the Lateran Basilica. He earned a doctorate in canon law two years later.

Father della Chiesa was appointed to the Chair of Diplomatic Style at the Academy of Noble Ecclesiastics in Rome, a preparatory institute for diplomatic service in the Church. In 1882 Archbishop Mariano Rampolla del Tindaro, the prefect of the Sacred Congregation of Extraordinary Ecclesiastical Affairs, requested Father della Chiesa's services as secretary. He accompanied the archbishop to Madrid in 1883, when the prelate was made papal nuncio to Spain. Four years later, the archbishop was given the rank of cardinal and appointed secretary of state to Pope Leo XIII. Father della Chiesa was made an undersecretary of state.

In 1907 Pope St. Pius X consecrated him in the Sistine Chapel as the archbishop of Bologna. Archbishop della Chiesa visited every parish in that vast archdiocese over a four-year period. In 1914 he was given the rank of cardinal and on September 3 of that year was elected pope, taking the name Benedict XV. He was crowned on September 6, 1914, in the Sistine Chapel.

Called the "Good Samaritan of Humanity," Pope Benedict XV found the Church embroiled in World War I. He issued *Ad Beatissimus Principus* as a guide for peace and offered a peace plan to the combatants, working to maintain neutrality while finding a way to end the slaughter on the battlefields. The pope also issued an appeal to all involved on January 22, 1915, and other appeals on July 28 of that year and on August 1, 1917. His efforts were ridiculed, but President Woodrow Wilson incorpo-

Pope Benedict XV

rated seven parts of the papal peace plan into his own proposal. Benedict XV was not invited to the peace conference at the end of the war. Pope Benedict XV issued the encyclical *Pacem dei Munus Pulcherium* ("The Beautiful Gift That Is the Peace of God") on May 23, 1920. The encyclical reminded diplomats involved in the peace negotiations that in a league founded on Christian ideals, no one was better qualified than the Catholic Church.

He promulgated a new code of Canon Law on Pentecost Sunday 1917, established the Sacred Congregation for the Oriental Church, and stressed the importance of the Scriptures in his encyclicals. In the Church in the United States, he erected the Vicariate Apostolic of Alaska in 1916, established the Diocese of Lafayette in 1918, and promoted

Archbishop Dennis J. Dougherty of Philadelphia to the cardinalate.

A statue of Pope Benedict XV was erected in Constantinople, now Istanbul, Turkey, while he was alive, because of his unbounded charities. When he died in Rome, the government of Egypt sent a letter of condolence to the Vatican, expressing sympathy "for the distressing loss."

Benedict XVI, Pope (April 16, 1927–)

Supreme Pontiff from 2005 and the successor to Pope Blessed John Paul II, Joseph Aloysius Ratzinger of Germany was, at the time of his election, the most respected Church leader in the world and one of the great theologians in the Church over the last fifty years. Joseph Ratzinger was born in the little village of Marktl am Inn, in eastern Bavaria. His family moved several times in his early years owing to his father's opposition to the Nazis, and young Joseph was forced to join the Hitler Youth. He was adamantly opposed to the Nazis and made every effort to leave the Youth at the first opportunity.

In 1939 Joseph entered the minor seminary in Traunstein, his first step toward the priesthood. World War II forced a postponement of his studies until 1945, when he reentered the seminary with his brother, Georg. In 1947 he entered the Herzogliches Georgianum, a theological institute associated with the University of Munich. Finally, on June 29, 1951, both Joseph and his brother were ordained by Cardinal Faulhaber in the Freising Cathedral, on the feast of Sts. Peter and Paul.

Continuing his theological studies at the University of Munich, he received his doctorate in theology in July 1953, with a thesis entitled *Volk und Haus Gottes in Augustins Lehre von der Kirche* ("The People and House of God in Augustine's Doctrine of the Church"). He fulfilled a requirement for teaching at the university level by completing a book-length treatise, "The Theology of History in St. Bonaventure." On April 15, 1959, he began lectures as a full professor of fundamental theology at the University of Bonn. From 1962 to 1965, he was present during all four sessions of the Second Vatican Council as a *peritus* (or theological expert) to Cardinal Josef Frings of Köln (Cologne), Germany.

In 1963 he began teaching at the University of Münster, taking, in 1966, a second chair in Dogmatic Theology at the University of Tübingen. A wave of student uprisings swept across Europe in 1968, and Marxism quickly became the dominant intellectual system at Tübingen. He found the radicalized environment to be unacceptable, so in 1969 he moved back to Bavaria and took a teaching position at the University of Regensburg. While there, he eventually would become dean and vice president. He was also a member of the International Theological Commission of the Holy See from 1969 until 1980.

In 1972, together with Hans Urs von Balthasar, Henri de Lubac, S.J, and others, he launched the Catholic theological journal *Communio*, a quarterly review of theology and culture. It has been said that this was done in response to the misinterpretation of the Second Vatican Council by various theologians, as represented by the theological journal *Concilium*.

On March 24, 1977, Father Ratzinger was appointed archbishop of Munich and Freising by Pope Paul VI. He was ordained a bishop on May 28, 1977, taking as his episcopal motto a phrase from 3 John 8, *Cooperatores Veritatis* ("Fellow Worker in the Truth"). On June 27, 1977, he was elevated to cardinal by Pope Paul VI, with the titular church of St. Mary of Consolation in Tiburtina. In 1980 he was named by Pope Blessed John Paul II to chair the special Synod on the Laity. Shortly after that, the pope asked him to head the Congregation for Catholic Education. Cardinal Ratzinger declined, feeling he should not leave his post in Munich too soon.

On November 25, 1981, Caridnal Ratzinger accepted the post of the Prefect for the Congregation for the Doctrine of the Faith, becoming at the same time ex officio the president of the Pontifical Biblical Commission and the International Theological Commission.

Cardinal Ratzinger was president of the Commission for the Preparation of the *Catechism of the Catholic Church*, and after six years of work (1986–92) he presented the new catechism to the Holy Father. On April 5, 1993, he was transferred to the order of cardinal bishops, with the suburbicarian see of Velletri-Signi. On November 9, 1998, his election as vice-dean of the Sacred College of Cardinals was approved by Pope John Paul II, and the Holy Father approved his election as dean of the College of Cardinals on November 30, 2002, with the title of the suburbicarian see of Ostia added to that of Velletri-Segni.

Besides his prefecture at the Congregation for the Doctrine of the Faith, his curial memberships includes: the Second Section of the Secretariat of State; the Congregation of Bishops, of Divine Worship and the Discipline of the Sacraments, of Catholic Education, of Evangelization of Peoples, for the Oriental Churches; and the Pontifical Councils for Christian Unity, and for Culture; as well as the Commissions *Ecclesia Dei* and for Latin America.

As dean of the college he was a key figure during the *sede vacante* after the death of Pope Blessed John Paul II on April 2, 2005, and delivered the funeral homily for the deceased pontiff. In the conclave that followed, he was elected Bishop of Rome and the 264th successor of St. Peter as Supreme Pastor of the Universal Church on April 19, 2005, after four ballots over two days. He chose the name Benedict in honor of Pope Benedict XV, an advocate of peace, and St. Benedict of Nursia, who helped to resurrect civilization in Europe during the Dark Ages. Pope Benedict XVI was invested with the pallium, the symbol of his office, on April 24, 2005, in ceremonies attended by more than half a million people in St. Peter's Square.

As Pope Benedict XVI, the pontiff has demonstrated a genuine warmth, humility, and commitment to the ideals of peace and dialogue. He has labored to promote dialogue with the Orthodox Churches and to continue the legacy of Pope Blessed John Paul II in implementing faithfully the decrees of the Second Vatican Council. While his early pontificate was not accompanied by the whirlwind travels that were a hallmark of his successor, Pope Benedict did enjoy a phenomenally successful trip to Cologne, Germany, for World Youth Day, where he was greeted with enthusiasm by hundreds of thousands of Catholic youths and made a memorable visit to the Synagogue of Cologne.

The pontiff surprised observers with his first encyclical, *Deus Caritas Est* ("God Is Love"), promulgated on January 25, 2006. In the encyclical, the Holy Father stressed the centrality of God's love to the Christian life and the importance to connect *eros* with *agape*. The pope also appointed fifteen

new members of the Sacred College of Cardinals and began a thorough reform of the Roman Curia, the central government of the Church.

As a cardinal, Joseph Ratzinger had traveled repeatedly to the United States and was well known and deeply respected in American intellectual circles. On January 27, 1988, for example, he delivered the Erasmus Lecture for that year in New York City, sponsored by the Rockford Institute Center on Religion and Society, entitled "Biblical Interpretation in Crisis: On the Question of the Foundations and Approaches of Exegesis Today." The speech was perhaps the greatest modern critique of modern approaches to biblical criticism, focusing especially on the application of philosophical hermeneutics in biblical exegesis. The cardinals was thus very familiar with the great spiritual crises facing the United States, especially the extensive problems of materialism, intolerance to Christian principles in many quarters of the culture, and the ongoing question of Catholics in political life declining to follow authentic Church teachings in such key areas as abortion.

As Prefect of the Congregation for the Doctrine of the Faith, then Cardinal Ratzinger had been closely involved in preparing the Vatican's response to the sex abuse crisis in the United States that erupted like a hurricane on the American Church in early 2002. He was one of the crucial voices in the Vatican meeting in April 2002 that brought the American cardinals and the leadership of the United States Conference of Catholic Bishops together with Curia officials to discuss the steps being taken to implement long-term solutions to the problem of the sexual abuse of minors by a small percentage of priests in the United States. The cardinal was praised both for his sensitivity to the victims of the horrendous activities of sex abuse and also for his obvious determination that full justice be achieved.

Pope Benedict made a very memorable visit to the United States in April 2008. The apostolic journey was his first to the United States since his election. He was given a formal welcome to the White House by President George W. Bush (who also celebrated the pontiff's birthday). The pope's stay in Washington included an address to representatives of Catholic universities, a meeting with leaders of other world religions, and vespers with the U.S. bishops at the National Shrine of the Immaculate Conception. In that speech, he discussed the sex abuse crisis in the United States in frank terms. He also celebrated Mass at the Washington Nationals' ballpark with fifty thousand people, and had a private session with victims of sexual abuse by priests at the apostolic nunciature. The pope next went to New York, where he addressed the United Nations General Assembly. He also celebrated Mass at St. Patrick's Cathedral, met with disabled children and their families, and had a moving encounter with more than twenty-five thousand Catholic youths. He then paid a visit to the site of the former World Trade Center and celebrated Mass at Yankee Stadium.

Pope Benedict's pontificate will also have a direct hand in shaping the future of the Church in the United States by his many appointments of the Church's leaders, several significant. Archbishop William J. Levada, former archbishop of Portland and San Francisco and the Holy Father's successor as Prefect of the Congregation for the Doctrine of the Faith, was elevated to the College of Cardinals on March 24, 2006. On the same day, the pope elevated Archbishop Sean P. O'Malley, archbishop of Boston, to the College of Cardinals. On May 16, 2006, Pope Benedict accepted the resignation of Cardinal Theodore E. McCarrick as archbishop of Washington and named Bishop Donald W. Wuerl, bishop of Pittsburgh, as his successor. Archbishop Wuerl was named a cardinal in the consistory of November 2010. Archbishop Timothy M. Dolan of Milwaukee was appointed archbishop of New York on February 23, 2009, and was named a cardinal in the consistory of February 2012. On April 6, 2010, Archbishop José Gomez was named coadjutor archbishop of Los Angeles. Archbishop Gomez succeeded Cardinal Roger M. Mahony on March 1, 2011; he is the first Hispanic archbishop of Los Angeles. On July 19, 2011, Archbishop Charles J. Chaput, O.F.M. Cap., of Denver was appointed archbishop of Philadelphia.

Benedictines (O.S.B.)

The oldest form of monastic life in the Western Church, the Order of St. Benedict was founded in the sixth century. St. Benedict of Nursia established the first monastery as a "school of the Lord's service." The order became involved in active ministries after 580, when Monte Cassino, a pioneering Benedictine monastery, was destroyed by the invading Lombards. Taking refuge in Rome, the Benedictines were recognized for their spiritual and intellectual abilities and asked to assume ministries throughout the world. Pope St. Gregory I the Great, a Benedictine, sent the monks on missions to evangelize the northern Germanic tribes, and the Benedictines were henceforth in the forefront of the Christianization of Europe. The order was one of the pillars of early medieval civilization.

Benedictines first arrived in North America through various missionary efforts of the order, but the first serious presence of the monks in the United States was undertaken under Abbot Boniface Wimmer. In 1846 Abbot Wimmer established a group of Benedictines from the Bavarian Metten Abbey in Latrobe, Pennsylvania, where they began St. Vincent Abbey (modern-day St. Vincent's Archabbey), which received approval in 1855. Other foundations followed, and Abbot Wimmer organized the Benedictine American-Cassinese congregation.

St. John's Abbey was founded in Collegeville, Minnesota, having received a donation from King Ludwig I of Bavaria. In 1857 St. Benedict's Abbey also opened in Atkinson, Kansas. This Benedictine monastery was renowned for its beautiful church, designed in the Rhenish architectural style. St. Mary's Abbey was started in Newark, New Jersey, in that same year.

In 1854 Swiss Benedictines from Eisiedeln and Engelberg, Switzerland, arrived in the United States and settled in St. Meinrad, Indiana. Benedictine Sisters from Maria Rickenbach, Melchtal, and Sarnen also came to serve American Catholics. Benedictine Martin Marty, one of the pioneering vicars and bishops in the United States, was at St. Meinrad in 1860. The Benedictines established a college and a seminary and took charge of the Dakota Territory. A Benedictine monastery was erected in Subiaco, Arkansas, in 1878, and another one in Gessen, Louisiana, in 1890. In 1872 Conception Abbey in Missouri was founded, followed by Mount Angel in Oregon. Benedictine Sisters were serving in the Dakota Territory and in Oregon.

Benedictine Isidore Robot served as the prefect apostolic of the Indian Territory in 1876. The Benedictines adjusted to the needs of the nation and to the demands of the eras. In 1950 another abbey was erected in South Dakota, named after Chief Blue Cloud.

There are currently some eight thousand Benedictines worldwide. The American Benedictines are organized into a number of congregations and communities, including: the American-Cassinese (1855), Swiss-American (1870), Congregation of St. Ottilien for Foreign Missions, Congregation of the Annunciation, English Benedictine Congregation, Camaldolese Hermits of America, Olivetans, Subiaco Congregation, and Sylvestrines.

The Benedictine nuns (Benedictine Sisters of Pontifical Jurisdiction, O.S.B.), were founded in 529 by Benedict's sister, St. Scholastica. Benedictine nuns were first brought to the United States in 1852 through the efforts of Abbot Wimmer, when three nuns from Eichstätt, Bavaria, under the leadership of Mother Benedicta Riepp, reached St. Mary's, Pennsylvania. The early years were marked by severe difficulties owing

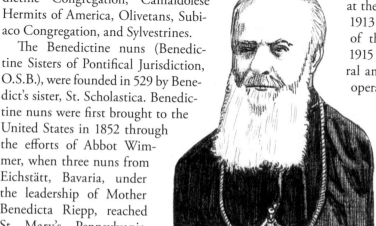

Benedictine Abbot Wimmer

to the efforts of Wimmer to exercise control over the fledgling community. From this beginning, the sisters started communities in Erie in 1852, Johnstown in 1870, and Carrolltown in 1870, as well as institutions in Minnesota, New Jersey, Kentucky, Kansas, Indiana, Virginia, Illinois, Florida, Maryland, and Alabama. They taught in schools but also assumed other needed ministries, such as catechetical work. The sisters finally received recognition from Rome in 1922 as the Congregation of St. Scholastica.

Currently, there are approximately eight thousand Benedictine nuns worldwide. In the United States, they were organized into several federations and congregations, including the Federation of St. Scholastica in 1922, the Federation of St. Gertrude the Great in 1937, and the Federation of St. Benedict in 1947.

Bennett, William J. *See* **Cabinets, Catholics in Presidential**

Benson, William (September 21, 1891–May 20, 1857)

An admiral, William Benson served as the first president of the National Council of Catholic Men. Born in Bibb County, Georgia, he converted to Catholicism as a young man and remained a devout Catholic for the rest of his life. Admitted to the U.S. Naval Academy at Annapolis, he graduated in 1877 and held a variety of posts over the next years, including instructor at the academy from 1890 to 1893. In 1913 he was appointed commandant of the Philadelphia Navy Yard; in 1915 he was promoted to rear admiral and named the first chief of naval operations for the U.S. Navy; in 1916 he became an admiral. After the end of World War I, Benson served as naval adviser to the U.S. delegation to the Paris peace talks.

While in the service, Benson was an active supporter of Church causes and was given the Laetare Medal by the University of Notre Dame in 1917. Following his retirement, he was elected the first head of the National Council of Catholic Men and served in the post from 1921 to 1925.

Bentivoglio, Anna Maria Maddalena (July 29, 1834–August 18, 1905)

A Poor Clare nun, Anna Maria Maddalena Bentivoglio was also a religious founder. Born in Rome, she entered the Poor Clare community of San Lorenzo in Panisperna, Rome, in 1864, following in the footsteps of two of her sisters, and she was given the name Maria Maddalena of the Sacred Heart in the religious life. In 1874 she accepted the invitation from Mother Ignatius Hayes, a member of the Third Order Regular of St. Francis, who was hoping to establish a convent of Poor Clares of the Primitive Observance in Minnesota. Sister Maddalena and her sister, Costanza, were received by Pope Blessed Pius IX, who gave them encouragement in their planned endeavor.

The nuns arrived in New York City in October 1875 and received word that the Minnesota convent had become impractical. This was the first of a series of setbacks over the next year, as they faced little support in finding a suitable place to begin the convent. Finally, they were invited to New Orleans by Archbishop Napoleon Perché. They arrived in New Orleans in March 1877, but in July of the same year were compelled to move to Cleveland owing to the complaints of a Franciscan visitor to the convent. They were admitted to the Poor Clare Colettines in Cleveland, but Mother Maddalena soon recognized that this Poor Clare community would not be a suitable place for the Poor Clares of the Primitive Observance. They thus departed in February 1878 and went back to New York.

In September 1878 they received a new invitation, from Bishop James O'Connor of Omaha, Nebraska. Here, the sisters at last founded a stable convent. Over the next years, several new communities were established in New Orleans and Evansville, Indiana. Mother Maddalena died in the Evansville house. Her cause for canonization was introduced in 1969 owing to her reputation for heroic virtue.

Bernardin, Joseph Louis (April 2, 1928–November 14, 1996)

The archbishop of Chicago from 1982 to 1996, and cardinal from 1983, who was falsely accused of sexual misconduct and pilloried by the media but served as a guide for the terminally ill in his last days, inspiring thousands with his spirit of forgiveness and hope. Joseph Louis Bernardin was born in Columbia, South Carolina, and studied for the priesthood at St. Mary's College, Kentucky; at St. Mary's Seminary, Maryland; and at The Catholic University of America. Ordained to the priesthood on April 26, 1952, he was assigned to pastoral ministries in South Carolina and

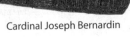
Cardinal Joseph Bernardin

then served as vice-chancellor and chancellor of Charleston, and was also appointed vicar general. He also served as a *peritus* (or theological expert) at the Second Vatican Council.

On March 4, 1966, he was appointed auxiliary bishop of the Archdiocese of Atlanta and served as the general secretary of the National Conference of Catholic Bishops and the United States Catholic Conference in Washington, D.C., from 1968 to 1972. He was elevated to archbishop of Cincinnati and was installed on December 19, 1972. Archbishop Bernardin also served as the president of the NCCB and USCC from 1974 to 1977.

On July 10, 1982, he was appointed archbishop of Chicago and revitalized the agencies and facilities of the archdiocese. He also developed a "consistent ethic of life" in Chicago. He was created a cardinal priest on February 2, 1983, with the titular church of Jesus the Divine Worker. In that same year he received the Albert Einstein Peace Award. Serving as the NCCB representative in Rome, he also was a member of the Council of the Secretariat of the Synod.

In November 1993 a young layman falsely charged the cardinal with sexual abuse. The U.S. media conducted a massive campaign against him until the young man recanted and refuted the charges. In June 1995 the cardinal was diagnosed with pancreatic cancer, a condition that spread to his liver. He also suffered from severe spinal pain. He announced his terminal illness on September 9, 1996, earning the respect of his countrymen for his courage, stability, and Christian charity. Cardinal Bernardin's patient endurance while suffering the false accusations and the campaign of the media, and his demeanor while in the last stages of cancer, earned him the Medal of Freedom, which was given to him by President Bill Clinton at a ceremony at the White House just before he died.

Beschefer, Theodore (May 25, 1630–February 4, 1711)

A Jesuit missionary, Theodore Beschefer served as a superior in the Canadian missions. He was born at Châlons-sur-marne, France, and entered the Society of Jesus at Nancy in 1647, devoting the next years to studies at Pont-a-Mousson. Father Beschefer then taught for several years in French colleges before setting sail for North America in 1665. After reaching Québec and spending three years in preparation for the hard life of the missions, he embarked on a journey to Mohawk territory and a mission to the Dutch at Albany. Father Beschefer did not reach his destinations because of unsettled situations with the Indians, however, and returned to Québec. From 1670 to 1671 he was finally in the field among the Iroquois, and in 1680 he was named superior of the Canadian missions. Resigning the post in 1687, he taught for two years and then went to France to serve as procurator of the missions. He died at Reims.

Bevilacqua, Anthony Joseph
(June 17, 1923–January 31, 2012)

The bishop of Pittsburgh from 1983 to 1988, Anthony Joseph Bevilacqua became the archbishop of Philadelphia from 1988 to 2003, and cardinal from 1991. He was born in Brooklyn, New York, to Italian immigrants Luigi Bevilacqua and Maria Giuseppina Codella. They were married in 1909 and migrated to the United States the following year. Anthony Bevilacqua was one of eleven children. He entered into studies for the priesthood at Cathedral College in Brooklyn and then the Seminary of the Immaculate Conception in Huntington, New York. He was ordained on June 11, 1949, at the Cathedral of St. James, in Brooklyn.

After pastoral assignments and a teaching post at Cathedral High School, Father Bevilacqua was sent to Rome to study canon law. He earned a doctorate in canon law in 1956 from the Pontifical Gregorian University and was assigned upon his return to the United States to the diocesan tribunal of Brooklyn. He then earned a master's degree in political science from Columbia University in 1962 and a Doctor of Laws degree from the faculty of St. John's University in Queens, New York, in 1975.

Cardinal Anthony Bevilaqua

From 1965 to 1980, he held a variety of posts in the diocese, including vice-chancellor of the diocese, instructor of canon law at the Immaculate Conception Seminary, chancellor, and professor of immigration law as adjunct professor on the law faculty of St. John's University. In 1971 he founded the Brooklyn Catholic Office for migrants and refugees. In 1976 he was named a Prelate of Honor of His Holiness.

On October 4, 1980, Monsignor Bevilacqua was appointed titular bishop of Acqualbe of Bizacena and auxiliary bishop of Brooklyn, and was consecrated on November 24, 1980. Three years later, on October 10, 1983, he was appointed bishop of Pittsburgh. On February 11, 1988, he was promoted to the Archdiocese of Philadelphia and, on June 28, 1991, was created a cardinal priest by Pope Blessed John Paul II and given the titular church of Most Holy Redeemer and St. Alphonsus on Via Merulana.

As archbishop, Bevilacqua was known for his concern for migrant workers. Aware from his own family's experiences of the challenges facing news arrivals in the United States, he brought unique abilities to his care of migrant workers. He was also a champion of the unborn, the aged, and the infirm. From 1983 to 1984, he was president of the Migration Committee of the United States Conference of Catholic Bishops and visited the refugee camps of southeast Asia and Africa. To assist pastoral care, he divided the archdiocese into six vicariates and reorganized the central administration into six secretariats. In 1990 he consolidated the schools and parishes of the archdiocese.

He retired on July 15, 2003. In the years after his retirement, his name was raised in relation to the sexual abuse scandal in the Archdiocese of Philadelphia, and the cardinal was accused of participating in coverups in various cases of abuse.

Biard, Pierre (1567–November 17, 1632)

A Jesuit missionary, Pierre Biard was taken prisoner by British forces in the northeastern region of the early United States. He was born in Grenoble, France. After entering the Society of Jesus and being ordained, Father Biard served as a professor of Scholastic Theology and Hebrew at Lyons. He was assigned to the Jesuit mission at Acadia in 1608 and joined Father Enemond Masse in sailing to the colonies in 1611. They arrived on May 22 at Port Royal.

The Protestant proprietor of the area at the time ordered the two priests out of Port Royal, and they were forced to go to Bar Harbor, where Father Biard founded in 1613 the famed mission for the Abenaki that would be revered as Saint-Sauveur. Within months, Protestants, led by Samuel Argall of Virginia, arrived at the mission and took the Jesuits and two other colonists to Jamestown. Another military expedition was outfitted, and Fathers Biard and Masse had to accompany the troops and witness the destruction of Saint-Sauveur.

Eventually, the Jesuits, after a series of maritime misadventures, returned to France. There Father Biard tried to resume his academic career but was charged as a conspirator in the destruction of Saint-Sauveur. Samuel de Champlain, the noted explorer of Canada and the settler of Québec, Canada, testified on behalf of Father Biard, recounting the British assaults and clearing the priest's name. Father Biard gained fame in his later years as a missionary in the south of France and also served as a military chaplain.

Bienville, Jean-Baptiste Le Moyne, Sieur de
(February 24, 1680–March 7, 1767)

A famous French explorer, Jean-Baptiste Le Moyne, Sieur de Bienville, was the founder of the city of New Orleans. He was born in Montréal, Canada; his father, Charles Le Moyne de Bienville, had settled there in 1645. Jean-Baptiste had three brothers — Iberville, Serigny, and Chateauguay — who were active in Louisiana in the early periods of settlement. In 1698 Jean-Baptiste accompanied Pierre Le Moyne, Sieur d'Iberville, on an expedition to the Mississippi River. They founded a colony at Biloxi, and when Pierre died in 1706, Jean-Baptiste became governor of the settlement. In 1712 La Mothe Cadillac took over the administration of Biloxi, but maintained Jean-Baptiste as his assistant. In 1715, Cadillac died, and Jean-Baptiste

again assumed control of Biloxi. An expedition to Fort Rosalie, the garrison originally started by Pierre, took place in 1716. In 1717 Jean-Baptiste was removed as governor but received a royal decoration, the Order of the Cross of Saint Louis.

By 1718 Jean-Baptiste was again governor, and he moved the seat of the colony to the site now known as New Orleans. During the following year, Jean-Baptiste had to repel Spanish troops and twice attacked Pensacola, Florida. He administrated the rapidly expanding city until 1726, when he retired, but he was returned to the city by order of the king of France. There his expeditions against the Chickasaw Indians brought royal censure. Having died in Paris, Jean-Baptiste was buried with full military honors in Montmartre.

Biloxi, Diocese of

Erected on March 1, 1977, by Pope Paul VI, the Diocese of Biloxi serves counties in southern Mississippi. The city of Biloxi was founded as a French possession by Pierre Le Moyne, Sieur d'Iberville, in 1600. The original site was Old Biloxi, now Ocean Springs. The settlement was the first capital of the Louisiana Territory. The name was taken from the Biloxi Indians and means "first people." Since its founding, Biloxi has been under many flags, including Spanish, French, English, West Florida Republic, and the Confederacy. The Diocese of Biloxi is a suffragan see of the Archdiocese of Mobile.

In 1682 René-Robert Chevalier, Sieur de La Salle, was in the area, accompanied by Father Zenobius Membré, who celebrated Mass near the present Fort Adams. In 1698 Jean-Baptiste Le Moyne, Sieur de Bienville, with Pierre Le Moyne, Sieur d'Iberville, founded Old Biloxi, now Ocean Springs. Fort Maurepan was the first capital of the Louisiana Territory, from 1699 to 1702. Fort Louis, the present Biloxi, was founded in 1719. Bienville abandoned Old Biloxi and moved the seat of the colony to New Orleans in 1718.

Catholic chapels and parishes were opened soon after at Natchez, Coles Creek, and Nogales, modern-day Vicksburg. In 1796 Bishop Luis Ignacio Peñalver y Cárdenas, the ranking bishop of the Gulf and Caribbean area, arrived in Biloxi for confirmation of Native Americans and whites. The bishop toured the area missions and forts.

The entire Mississippi territory was ceded to the United States in 1798. In that same year, the U.S. Congress established the Mississippi Territory, which was enlarged in 1804 and 1813. On December 10, 1817, Mississippi became the twentieth state.

Biloxi had already started to grow, with maritime industries dominating. Visiting Catholic missionaries were numerous, especially after 1822, when the Vicariate Apostolic of Mississippi and Alabama was established. In 1837 the Diocese of Natchez was erected, and Biloxi became part of a new ecclesiastical jurisdiction.

The Civil War and the Reconstruction Period brought suffering to Biloxi and to other southern regions. The area was also hit by a severe yellow fever plague in 1870. The Catholic population endured, however, and opened new parishes to accommodate their numbers. The Cathedral of the Nativity of the Blessed Virgin Mary in Biloxi dates to 1843. St. Paul's (Dedeaux) in Pass Christian and Our Lady of the Gulf in Bay St. Louis were started in 1847. Our Lady of Victories Church in Pascagoula dates to 1855, and St. Alphonsus in Ocean Springs was built in 1860. Other parishes were developing at this time as well.

World War I brought new commitments to the military defense of the nation, and the Great Depression following the war impacted on the area. Parishes were still opened, however, and religious education programs instituted. World War II again taxed the resources of the area, and Biloxi later adapted to the reforms of the Second Vatican Council.

When the Diocese of Biloxi was established in 1977, it was a tribute to the ongoing maturing of the Catholic faith in the region. The first bishop was Joseph Lawson Howze, who was installed in Biloxi on June 6, 1977. He had served as auxiliary bishop of Natchez-Jackson (now the Diocese of Jackson) from 1972. Bishop Howze instituted the offices and agencies for diocesan administration and expanded Catholic charitable and communication apostolates. He retired on May 15, 2001.

The second bishop of Biloxi was Thomas J. Rodi. He was appointed on May 15, 2001, and consecrated and installed on July 2, 2001. The chief event in the life of the diocese during his tenure was the severe destruction caused in August 2005 by Hurricane Katrina. Ten churches suffered damage or were inundated by the hurricane and the subsequent flooding. The diocese assisted the tens of thousands of people who were affected, including those recovering from the devastation that destroyed or damaged almost 90 percent of the houses in the area.

Bishop Rodi was appointed archbishop of Mobile on April 2, 2008. His successor, Bishop Roger Paul Morin, was named on March 2, 2009. Bishop Morin had served as an auxiliary bishop of New Orleans since 2003. In 2011 there were 60,000 Catholics served by 75 priests and 42 parishes in the diocese.

Birmingham, Diocese of

Established on July 9, 1954, as the Diocese of Mobile-Birmingham by Pope Pius XII and reestablished on June 28, 1969, as the Diocese of Birmingham by Pope Paul VI, Birmingham serves counties in northern Alabama. The largest city in the state, Birmingham was founded on a site in the Jones Valley. The city was named after Birmingham, England. Local coal deposits and vast resources of metals, ores, and stone provided the area with industrial growth. The Diocese of Birmingham is a suffragan see of the Archdiocese of Mobile.

Birmingham has a historic Catholic legacy, starting in 1540, when the Spanish explorer Hernando de Soto entered the area with a large military force and chaplains. The Battle of Mauvila took place on October 18, 1540, considered by many historians to be the bloodiest Indian confrontation on the continent. About twenty years later, the Spanish settled at a site called Nanipacna, but that outpost closed within a short time.

In 1682 René-Robert Chevalier, Sieur de La Salle, opened Fort Louisiana, claiming the area for France. In 1699 Pierre Le Moyne, Sieur d'Iberville, and Jean-Baptiste Le Moyne, Sieur de Bienville, were at Old Biloxi. Jesuit Fathers Anastase Douay and Antoine Davion were ministering there. Fort Louis de la Mobile replaced the original Old Biloxi settlement in 1702, and two years later a Catholic chapel was opened there, served by Capuchin Franciscans, Carmelites, and Jesuits.

In 1711 Fort Louis was moved to Mobile, and

two other outposts were opened: Fort Toulouse and Fort Tombeckbé on the Tombigbee River. Mission work continued in the area and in the northern regions of Alabama until 1763, when the territory was ceded to the British.

In 1798 Alabama was designated a part of the Mississippi Territory. The city of Birmingham was settled soon after, and Alabama entered the Union as the twenty-second state. The Vicariate Apostolic of Alabama and Florida was established in 1825, with Bishop Michael Portier as vicar apostolic. Four years later, the Diocese of Mobile (now the Archdiocese of Mobile), was erected.

Alabama seceded from the Union in 1861, and the Civil War and the Reconstruction period took their toll on the area, but Birmingham became a city in 1871. The Catholic population expanded, and St. Paul's Cathedral dates to the founding of Birmingham. Our Lady of the Shoals was serving Catholics in Tuscumbia as early as 1869, and Florence maintained parishes from 1873. St. Ann's opened in Decatur in 1870, and Sacred Heart was ministering to Catholics in Cullman by 1877. Our Lady of Sorrows and Holy Rosary were opened in Birmingham soon after.

World War I and the Great Depression impacted upon Birmingham, and World War II added stresses, but Birmingham's Catholic apostolate continued. Recognizing the city as a Catholic stronghold, the Holy See established the Diocese of Birmingham on June 28, 1969.

Bishop Joseph G. Vath was the first bishop of the Diocese of Birmingham. He had served as the auxiliary bishop of Mobile-Birmingham from 1966 and was transferred to the new diocese on December 9, 1969. He established the diocesan offices and agencies for diocesan administration and began expanding facilities to meet the growing Catholic needs. Parishes and schools were opened, and charitable agencies staffed. Bishop Vath died on July 14, 1987.

His successor was Bishop Raymond J. Boland, who was consecrated on March 25, 1988. Bishop Boland continued the expansion and renovation programs, promoting lay ministries and social services until he was transferred to the Diocese of Kansas City-St. Joseph on September 9, 1993.

The third bishop of the Diocese of Birmingham was David E. Foley. Serving as an auxiliary bishop

of Richmond since 1986, he was promoted to the Diocese of Birmingham and installed on May 10, 1994. He retired on May 10, 2005.

His successor was Bishop Robert Baker, who was appointed on August 14, 2007. He had served as bishop of Charleston since 1999. In 2011 there were 90,000 Catholics served by 112 priests, 122 women religious, and 54 parishes in the diocese.

Bishop, William Howard (December 19, 1885–July 11, 1953)

The founder of the Glenmary Home Missioners, William Howard Bishop promoted rural development of the Church. Born in Washington, D.C., he was educated at Harvard and then entered St. Mary's Seminary in Maryland and was ordained in 1915.

Father Bishop had been raised in a patrician Southern family but became increasingly aware of the rural areas of the country, where priests and religious were not available to meet the growing needs of Catholics. In order to bolster the apostolate of rural missions, he founded the Glenmary Home Missioners with the support of Archbishop John McNicholas, O.P., of Cincinnati. The apostolate was founded in Glendale, Ohio, in 1937, and Father Bishop enlisted priests for the ministry. A congregation of women religious was founded two years later.

He was fifty-two years old when he began this missionary effort. In addition, he opened a seminary and monastic house and started publishing *Challenge* magazine in 1938. Father Bishop administered seven rural American missions before he died. At the time of his death in Norton, Virginia, the congregation had 21 priests, 11 brothers, 51 seminarians, 16 women religious, and 26 novices.

Bishops' Meetings. *See* United States Conference of Catholic Bishops

Bismarck, Diocese of

Established on December 31, 1909, by Pope St. Pius X, the Diocese of Bismarck serves the western counties of North Dakota. Bismarck is the state capital and a center for agricultural, petroleum, and mining industries. Native American reservations are also part of the diocesan ministerial programs.

The city was originally started as Camp Hancock in 1872, a military fort designed to protect railroad crews. Named after German Chancellor Otto Von Bismarck a year later, the city became the capital of the Dakota Territory in 1883. Bismarck is a major distribution point for grain and livestock. The Diocese of Bismarck is a suffragan see of the Archdiocese of St. Paul and Minneapolis.

Missionaries were in the Dakotas early in American history, but their apostolates were not recorded until around 1818. At that time, priests were in the region serving the local Native Americans, fur trappers, and mountain men. In 1840 one of the nation's most revered Jesuit missionaries, Father Pierre-Jean De Smet, was in the Dakotas. A friend of Chief Sitting Bull and countless Indian nations, Father De Smet worked with Jesuit Father Christian Hoecken to alleviate the suffering of the Native Americans in that historical period.

In 1880 the Dakota Territory became a vicariate apostolic, with the respected Benedictine abbot Martin Marty consecrated as the vicar. A tireless missionary, he welcomed the vast numbers of settlers coming into the area. St. Peter's at Standing Rock Indian Reservation had opened two years earlier, and other Native American missions were also active. St. Patrick's in Dickinson, St. Joseph's in Mandan, and St. Mary's in Bismarck date to this era, as well as St. Vincent's at Crown Butte and Sacred Heart of Jesus parish at Glen Ullin. North Dakota entered the Union in 1889, the same year that the Diocese of Jamestown (now the Diocese of Fargo) was erected.

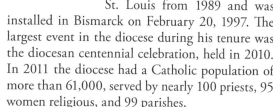

Bishop Vincent de Paul Wehrle

In 1909 the Diocese of Bismarck was established, and Benedictine Abbot Vincent de Paul Wehrle was consecrated as the first bishop on May 19, 1910. He built churches, schools, and hospitals, and instituted the offices and agencies for diocesan administration. He also led the Catholics of the area through the trials of World War I and the Great Depression. Bishop Wehrle served faithfully until he retired on December 11, 1939.

His successor, Bishop Vincent J. Ryan, was consecrated on May 28, 1940. World War II and the demands of military-defense programs impacted the area, but he continued expanding diocesan facilities, building the Cathedral of the Holy Spirit in Bismarck. He also had to address a 1948 law that prohibited the wearing of religious garb in public schools. Bishop Ryan aided the area's farmers, founded a diocesan newspaper, and introduced the Confraternity of Christian Doctrine to parishes. He died on November 10, 1951.

Bishop Lambert A. Hoch, the third bishop of Bismarck, was consecrated on March 25, 1952. He continued expanding diocesan services and facilities until his transfer to the Diocese of Sioux Falls on December 5, 1956.

His successor, Bishop Hilary B. Hacker, was appointed to Bismarck on December 29, 1956. He participated in the Second Vatican Council and implemented the reforms mandated by that council. Bishop Hacker also established educational and charitable agendas. He retired on June 28, 1982.

Bishop John F. Kinney, the fifth bishop of the Diocese of Bismarck, was installed on August 23, 1982. He maintained diocesan agencies and ministries while facing a shortage of priests and religious. He was transferred to the Diocese of St. Cloud on July 6, 1995.

The sixth bishop of the Diocese of Bismarck, is Paul A. Zipfel, had served as auxiliary bishop of the Archdiocese of St. Louis from 1989 and was installed in Bismarck on February 20, 1997. The largest event in the diocese during his tenure was the diocesan centennial celebration, held in 2010. In 2011 the diocese had a Catholic population of more than 61,000, served by nearly 100 priests, 95 women religious, and 99 parishes.

Black Catholic Caucuses

There are three black Catholic caucuses in the United States: the National Black Catholic Sisters' Conference, the National Black Catholic Clergy Caucus, and the National Black Catholic Lay Caucus. These organizations are composed of Catholic

African-Americans who have a slate of concerns and apostolates.

The caucuses review the position of black Catholics in the American Church and the position of the Church as it functions in black communities nationwide. They also study the efforts of the Church in ending racism and inequalities in the United States. The National Black Catholic Sisters' Conference focuses on elements of the educational apostolate in black communities. The National Black Catholic Clergy Caucus focuses on vocations, aspects of liturgical worship, and education. The National Black Catholic Lay Caucus is concerned with leadership training, community organizations, and social-action programs.

Black Catholic Congresses

The Black Catholic Congresses date to 1889, when a delegation of black Catholic leaders met in Washington, D.C., on January 1–4. Cardinal James Gibbons of the Archdiocese of Baltimore, a respected prelate of the era, had encouraged the formation of such a gathering in order to strengthen the black Catholic community. Another Catholic leader offering encouragement was Archbishop Henry Elder of the Archdiocese of Cincinnati.

Father Augustus Tolten, an African-American priest, celebrated Mass at the opening ceremony. The sermon was given by Cardinal Gibbons, who urged delegates to pursue unity and purpose but also to proceed with caution and prudence because of the cultural racism of that era. President Grover Cleveland reportedly provided a White House reception for two hundred of the delegates to the event.

The Black Catholic Congresses continued for a time and convened in Cincinnati in June 1890; in Philadelphia in January 1892; in Chicago in September 1893, and in Baltimore in October 1894.

The members also labored in their own areas and faced segregation and discrimination in Catholic schools. A later congress, the St. Peter Claver Catholic Union, was started but was not able to sustain an adequate membership. Black Catholics, however, kept the ideals of the congress alive over the decades. A National Black Catholic Congress met in May 1987 in Washington, D.C., and the organization was revitalized.

Black Elk (1866–1950)

An Oglala Sioux, Black Elk was called a holy man and revered by his own people and by various authors who introduced his words of wisdom to modern generations. Black Elk was a survivor of the Wounded Knee epoch. Black Elk was in Montana in 1876 when Lieutenant Colonel George Armstrong Custer died at Little Bighorn. He was part of the Ghost Dance revival among the Sioux and saw the end of the tradition in the Wounded Knee Massacre in South Dakota in 1890.

While honored by modern Americans as one of the last of the Sioux wilderness ascetics, Black Elk was actually a Catholic catechist, having converted to the faith in 1904, receiving the name Nicholas. Devout and dedicated to the faith, Black Elk prepared many Oglala Sioux for baptism, led prayer services, and remained faithful until his death.

Blackfriars Guild

A Catholic theater group, the Blackfriars Guild was founded in 1931 by Dominican Fathers Urban Nagle and Thomas Carey. The guild was designed "to spiritualize the drama and to dramatize the spiritual." The group started producing Catholic plays in New York City in 1940. The guild purchased its own theater and provided opportunities for unknown playwrights and actors. It also established the Blackfriar Institute of Dramatic Arts at The Catholic University of America in Washington, D.C., which evolved into the University's Department of Speech and Drama.

In England, the Dominicans were called the Blackfriars, and the guild commemorates the Blackfriars Priory in London that was confiscated by King Henry VIII. The lives of many saints were dramatized by Blackfriar productions, and the guild also staged a controversial anti-communist play, *Shake Hands with the Devil*. The works of Robert Anderson and Clare Boothe Luce were presented by the Blackfriars, and stage luminaries such as Geraldine Page participated in their productions.

Blanc, Antoine (1792–June 20, 1860)

The first archbishop of New Orleans, Antoine Blanc spent the last years of his life in severe pain. He was born in Sury, France, and entered a local seminary.

Bishop Louis Dubourg, the bishop of Louisiana, visited the seminary and ordained him in July 1816. Father Blanc accompanied Bishop Dubourg to Louisiana the following year and was assigned to the mission at Vincennes, Indiana. He labored there until 1820, when he was sent to Louisiana and was joined by his brother, Father Jean Baptiste Blanc.

In 1835 Father Antoine Blanc was appointed bishop of New Orleans and became archbishop in 1850. The population of the city tripled during his period of service, and he had to establish eighteen parishes for Catholics of Creole, German, Irish, and English descent. He also had charge of the entire mission areas of Texas and Mississippi. Trusteeism, plagues, and open Protestant bigotry troubled him as a bishop, but he handled each difficulty victoriously. Bishop Blanc attended the First Plenary Council of Baltimore. The yellow fever outbreak in New Orleans in 1858 took a toll, as Archbishop Blanc fell while caring for the afflicted and fractured his leg. His leg did not heal properly, and he was in severe pain until his death. He died in New Orleans a few hours after celebrating Mass.

Blanchet, Augustin Magloire (August 22, 1797–February 25, 1887)

A Canadian missionary, Augustin Magliore Blanchet is revered as the "Apostle of Washington." He was born in Saint-Pierre, Riviére du Sud, Canada, and was sent at an early age to Québec with his brother, Francis Norbert Blanchet. Ordained on June 3, 1821, he was assigned to St. Gervaise, Isles de la Madeleine, and Cape Breton Island as an associate pastor. He then was recalled to Montréal, where he served as pastor until 1846.

In that year, he was consecrated on September 27 as the bishop of Walla Walla, Washington, a newly erected diocese. In the following spring, Bishop Blanchet traveled to Washington with Father Jean Baptiste Abraham Brouillet. They were joined by members of the Oblates of Mary Immaculate at St. Louis and reached Fort Walla Walla in September 1847.

Bishop Antoine Blanc

Bishop Blanchet made an area called The Dalles his base of operations. The deaths of Protestant missionaries at the hands of the Cayuse, called the Whitman Massacre, threatened Bishop Blanchet's labors, but he and Father Brouillet countered false charges made against the Church and maintained their efforts.

In 1850 the see of Walla Walla was suppressed, and the Diocese of Nesqually was erected (now the Archdiocese of Seattle). Bishop Blanchet was stationed at Fort Vancouver. There he built a log cathedral and instituted diocesan institutions and parishes. In 1879 Bishop Blanchet resigned. He died in Washington and is revered as the founder of the Church in that state.

Blanchet, Francis Norbert (September 30, 1795–June 18, 1883)

The first archbishop of the Northwest, Francis Norbert Blanchet is honored as the "Apostle of Oregon." He was born at Saint-Pierre, Riviére du Sud, Canada. With his brother, Augustine Magloire, Francis was sent to a Québec seminary at an early age. He was ordained on July 18, 1819, and was assigned to the cathedral. A year later, Father Blanchet went to Rochibucto, New Brunswick, serving Micmacs and Acadian settlers for seven years.

In 1827, recalled to Montréal, he was appointed pastor of St. Joseph de Soulanges. When a cholera epidemic caused havoc and death in 1832, Father Blanchet labored so tirelessly that the local Protestants presented him with a testimonial. In 1832 he was named the vicar general of the Oregon missions, and he set out for that distant region with Father Modeste Demers. Traveling five thousand miles, they crossed the American continent by horseback, barge, canoe, and on foot, reaching Fort Vancouver on November 24. The Oregon missions covered approximately 375,000 square miles. In 1845 Father Blacnhet was consecrated a bishop in Montréal, named vicar apostolate of the area.

After his consecration, Bishop Blanchet visited Europe to gather missionary personnel. In 1846 he was appointed archbishop of Oregon City (now the Archdiocese of Portland in Oregon), and Father Demers was named bishop of Vancouver Island. Two years later, Archbishop Blanchet summoned his first provincial council, attended the First Plenary Council in Baltimore, and traveled extensively to recruit necessary priests and religious for Oregon.

Archbishop Blanchet also rallied American Catholics for aid in defeating the efforts to limit the Church's Indian missions, sending Father Jean Baptiste Abraham Brouillet to Washington. Archbishop James Roosevelt Bayley of Baltimore aided the cause, and assisted Father Brouillet in founding the Bureau of Catholic Indian Missions.

Archbishop Francis Norbert Blanchet

Archbishop Blanchet also met with Father Pierre-Jean De Smet, the revered Jesuit missionary, and worked with him in forming mission activities. Archbishop Blanchet retired to the hospital of the Sisters of Providence, much revered for his courageous defense of the Church and his tireless labors. He died in Portland.

Blenkinsop, Peter (April 19, 1818–November 5, 1896)

A Jesuit educator, Peter Blenkinsop was the son of a distinguished Catholic publisher. He was born in Dublin, and after migrating to the United States he studied at Georgetown College and entered the Jesuits in 1834. He was ordained on July 26, 1846. Father Blenkinsop served as president of the College of the Holy Cross in Worcester, Massachusetts, from 1854 to 1857, rebuilding the college after a disastrous fire. He then served as pastor in various Jesuit parishes and as a professor in Worcester, Georgetown, and Philadelphia.

Father Blenkinsop had a distinguished brother, William, and a sister, Catherine. William was a priest serving in the Archdiocese of Boston and a missionary in Natchez. Catherine became a Sister of Charity, taking the religious name of Euphemia. During the Civil War, she directed the activities of

her congregation in the South, becoming a visitatrix in 1866.

Blue Army, The

The Blue Army of Our Lady of Fátima is an organization that promotes the message of Our Lady of Fátima. The origins of the Blue Army in the United States are traced to the work of Father Harold Colgan, pastor of a parish church in Plainfield, New Jersey, in 1947. Aware that the message of Our Lady of Fátima was barely known in America, Father Colgan began an apostolate to spread knowledge of the events at Fátima and the powerful message of Our Lady. The newly established Blue Army became instantly popular, and membership spread across the globe. It evolved into an international apostolate with millions of members and centers in a large number of countries.

The Blue Army in the United States went on to establish a National Center and Shrine to the Immaculate Heart of Mary in Washington, New Jersey, and funded the construction of a pilgrim center for English-speaking pilgrims to Fátima, the Domus Pacis (House of Peace). The Blue Army continues to promote the message of Fátima through its active membership and its publications, including *Soul* magazine.

Boggs, Corinne Lindy. *See* Vatican-U.S. Relations

Bohachevsky, Constantine (June 17, 1884–January 6, 1961)

An archbishop, Constantine Bohachevsky was the first Metropolitan of the Byzantine Rite Archeparchy of Philadelphia. Born in Galicia, which was then under Austrian control, he studied for the priesthood at Lviv in the Ukraine and at Innsbruck, Austria, receiving ordination to the priesthood in January 1909. After ordination, he returned to Innsbruck for additional studies that led to a doctorate in sacred theology in 1910. He then devoted the next years to teaching and pastoral work, and served as vicar general of the Przemysl diocese and as a chaplain for the Austrian Army during World War I.

Events took a sudden turn in his life in 1924, when the Holy See made the decision to divide the Byzantine exarchate in the United States to provide better care for the Ruthenians and Ukrainians. Father Bohachevsky was chosen to become exarch for the Ukrainians and titular bishop of Amisus. Consecrated in Rome in May 1924, he reached New York in August of that year. He immediately faced a variety of challenges, including the need for vocations and an improved education system for his flock. He opened St. Basil's Preparatory Seminary in 1933 and St. Basil's College Seminary in 1939, both in Stamford, Connecticut. He also brought into the exarchate the Sisters Servants of Mary Immaculate in 1935 to assist with schools and founded the Missionary Sisters of the Mother of God in 1944. In 1940 he launched a diocesan journal, *The Way* (*Shlakh*), and worked to introduce several religious communities of men, including the Basilians, Byzantine Franciscans, and Redemptorists.

As a result of these many labors, in 1954 Bishop Bohachevsky was named titular archbishop of Beroe. In 1958 he was named the new Metropolitan archbishop of Philadelphia for the Ukrainians. He served as archbishop until his death and was responsible for much of the progress of Ukrainian Catholics in the twentieth century.

Boise, Diocese of

Established on August 26, 1893, by Pope Leo XIII, the Diocese of Boise serves the entire state of Idaho. Boise is the capital of the state and is named after the Boise River. French fur trappers provided that name, which means "wooded." The 1862 gold rush to Boise Basin prompted the erection of Fort Boise on the present-day government island. A community developed to provide supplies to the nearby mines. The location of the city at the crossroads of the Oregon Trail and a primary mining route ensured its growth. Boise became the center of diversified industries and pioneered commercial aviation. The Diocese of Boise is a suffragan see of the Archdiocese of Portland in Oregon.

French trappers were in the Idaho region early on, and circa 1812 some Iroquois visited the area,

led by two Native Americans, Old Ignace and Young Ignace La Mousse. The French explained the Catholic faith and urged the Flathead and Nez Perce to bring "Black Robes," or Jesuits, into the territory. For almost a quarter of a century these tribes journeyed again and again to St. Louis to ask for a missionary priest. Finally, in February 1840, Jesuit Father Pierre-Jean De Smet arrived in Idaho to begin his famed mission work. He celebrated a Mass on July 22, 1840, at Henry's Lake, the first Mass celebrated in Idaho. He also erected a mission near Coeur d'Alene Lake and visited local Indian enclaves.

Other priests, following Father De Smet, entered Idaho for mission labors, and in 1843 the Cataldo Mission was opened. Dedicated to the Sacred Heart, the mission was named for Father Joseph M. Cataldo, a pioneering local priest. Jesuit Father Nicholas Point erected the mission, which was moved and relocated to the banks of the Couer d'Alene River in 1853. It is the oldest building in Idaho.

In the Idaho Territory, which had been established by Congress, Catholics were under the ecclesiastical jurisdiction of Archbishop Francis Norbert Blanchet of Oregon until 1868, along with Montana and most of Wyoming. On March 3, 1868, Pope Blessed Pius IX erected the Vicariate Apostolic of Idaho, with Bishop Louis Aloysius Lootens serving as vicar. He attended the First Vatican Council in Rome in 1870 and then submitted his resignation. Father Joseph Cataldo was still laboring in the area, joined by a Father G. Gazzoli, who was medically trained and devoted to the local Indians.

The Nez Perce wars impacted on the missions, but in 1879 Archbishop Charles J. Seghers of Oregon City visited the region, returning each year until 1883. Two years later a new vicar apostolic was appointed, Bishop Alphonsus Joseph Glorieux. On August 26, 1893, he became the first bishop of the Diocese of Boise. The Cathedral of St. John the Evangelist was started, and Bishop Glorieux began to establish the agencies and offices for diocesan administration. He also started building programs to meet the growing needs of the Catholic population and used railroad car chapels provided by the Catholic Church Extension Society to provide services to remote areas. Bishop Glorieux died on August 25, 1917.

The second bishop of Boise was Daniel Mary Gorman, who was consecrated on May 1, 1918. He faced the troubled era of World War I but doubled the number of parishes and schools and started evangelization programs for older students. Bishop Gorman also completed the cathedral before he died on June 9, 1927.

The third bishop of Boise was Edward Joseph Kelly, who was consecrated on March 6, 1928. He was the first native of the Pacific Northwest raised to the episcopacy. Bishop Kelly led the diocese through the Great Depression and World War II, supporting the economic recovery and the military efforts of the United States. He introduced the Confraternity of Christian Doctrine into the diocese and instituted summer institutes and catechetical correspondence courses. He died on April 21, 1956.

His successor was Bishop James Joseph Byrne, who had served as auxiliary bishop of the Archdiocese of St. Paul and Minneapolis since 1947. He was promoted to the Diocese of Boise on June 16, 1956. Bishop Byrne started training programs for lay catechists and founded the diocesan newspaper. On March 19, 1962, he was promoted to the Archdiocese of Dubuque.

The fifth bishop of Boise was Sylvester William Treinen, who was consecrated on July 25, 1962. He attended the Second Vatican Council and implemented the reforms mandated by the council in the diocese. Bishop Treinen also opened an office for Catholic education and provided retreats for the faithful and student centers for the local educational institutions. He served until his retirement on August 17, 1988.

His successor was Bishop Tod David Brown, who was installed in Boise on April 3, 1989. He continued the catechetical and expansion programs and promoted lay apostolates and ministries. On July 30, 1998, he was appointed the bishop of Orange.

The seventh bishop of Boise, Michael Driscoll, had served as auxiliary bishop of Orange from 1989 and was

installed in Boise on March 18, 1999. His labors as bishop have been complicated by the rapid growth of the diocese, especially through the arrival of immigrants from Mexico and Southeast Asia. Both of these groups are now significant parts of the Catholic community. In 2011 the Catholic population in the diocese numbered around 167,000, with nearly 100 priests, 86 women religious, and 51 parishes.

Bonaparte, Charles Joseph (June 9, 1851–June 28, 1921)

A grandnephew of Napoleon Bonaparte, Charles Joseph Bonaparte was a staunch defender of Catholicism in America. Charles was born in Baltimore, Maryland, and was the grandson of Jerome, the youngest brother of Emperor Napoleon and the king of Westphalia. Charles belonged to a branch of the Bonaparte family that recognized America as the land of opportunity and transferred their assets to the United States. The Bonapartes of Baltimore conducted themselves in a manner that gained them the respect of Americans of other religious faiths, as well as of Catholics.

A graduate of Harvard and a lawyer, Charles was also a close friend of Theodore Roosevelt and considered a legal authority on Church-state relations. He was appointed by President Roosevelt to the Protestant-dominated Board of Indian Commissioners, a move that impacted the Catholic Indian missions across the land, and he was well received. His intellect, social assets, and family ties allowed Charles to explain Catholic positions concerning the Indian apostolate. His skill and legal awareness put an end to the ongoing efforts to limit the Church's rights and activities in caring for the Native Americans, and Catholic missions were protected.

In 1905, as a dedicated supporter of President Roosevelt's naval policies, Charles was appointed Secretary of the Navy. He was later named attorney general of the United States and served from 1906 to 1909. Charles was also a founder and president of the National Municipal

Charles Bonaparte

League, a reform group that was highly regarded by Americans of the time. Before his death at Belle Vista, his Maryland estate, Charles was honored by the Church for his tireless labors on behalf of the faith. He received testimonials and the Laetare Medal from the University of Notre Dame.

Bonzano, Giovanni (September 27, 1867–November 26, 1927)

The fourth apostolic delegate to the United States, Giovanni Bonzano also served as a representative of popes. He was born in Castelletto Scozzoso, Alessandria, Italy, and entered the local seminary of Vigevano. He then studied at the College Mastai of Sts. Peter and Paul for the Chinese missions in Rome in 1889, completing his education at the Urban College of the Propaganda in Rome.

Ordained on May 21, 1890, Father Bonzano volunteered for the Chinese missions in Chen-Si Province in 1891, but was forced to return to Italy after six years because of ill health. He recuperated for three years and was appointed vicar general of Vigevano in 1899, becoming chancellor in 1900. Father Bonzano also served as a member of the faculty of the Urban College of the Propaganda and became rector in 1904. Four years later, Pope St. Pius X sent Monsignor Bonzano (made a Domestic Prelate in 1904) to Messina to console the survivors of a devastating earthquake.

In 1912 he was made a titular archbishop of the see of Melitene and appointed apostolic delegate to the United States. In 1915 Archbishop Bonzano also assumed the administration of the apostolic delegation to Mexico. He remained active in America until 1922, when he was recalled to Rome. There he was created a cardinal priest with the titular church of San Pancrazio on December 14, 1922.

Pope Pius XI sent Cardinal Bonzano to the Twenty-eighth International Eucharistic Congress in Chicago, Illinois, June 20–24, 1926. Cardinal Bonzano also presided at the consecration of St. Louis Cathedral in St. Louis, Missouri, in the same month. He served in various congregations in the Vatican and died at the age of sixty in Rome.

Borrano, Francis Xavier (1901–April 16, 1993)

A Pauline pioneer in America, Francis Xavier Borrano was a founder of Alba House, the Catholic

Cardinal Giovanni Bonzano

publishing firm. He was born in San Damiano d' Asli, Italy. He was one of the members of the Society of St. Paul founded by Father James Alberione, and was ordained in 1923. In 1931 Father Borrano arrived in New York to expand the Pauline ministry and edit a magazine for Italian immigrants, also assuming two parishes on Staten Island. He worked tirelessly and was elected supervisor of the first American province in 1956. He spent his remaining years aiding the Pauline pastoral ministry and developing Alba House, located on Staten Island. Father Borrano also supervised Alba Communications in Canfield, Ohio, and established Pauline houses in Australia and Cuba. He died in Canfield, mourned by members of the congregation and by many in the Catholic publishing world.

Boston, Archdiocese of

Established as a diocese on April 8, 1808, by Pope Pius VII and as a metropolitan archdiocese on February 12, 1875, by Pope Blessed Pius IX, Boston served all of New England when originally erected as a diocese. The city is the cultural, commercial, and industrial center of New England and a major port. The Archdiocese of Boston now serves counties in eastern Massachusetts and has suffragan sees.

Boston was always a vital port in the early colonies and then in the United States. The Catholic communities there date to the seventeenth century, as French missionaries served certain parts of the area. Most of New England, however, imposed the long penal period, the era in which Catholics could not practice their faith and priests could not enter colonial boundaries. In the most dire years of this discrimination, Catholics could not vote or take part in public life. The Revolutionary War and the formation of new state constitutions provided Catholics with rights as citizens.

In 1788 Father Claude Florent Bouchard de la Poterie arrived in Boston and gathered about one hundred Catholics, forming a community. A year later, Father Louis Rousselet carried on the work and also labored among the Native Americans of Maine. Father Rousselet was joined in 1790 by Father John Thayer, a Bostonian convert to the Church. Father Francis A. Matignon arrived in Boston, joined in 1796 by one of his former students, Father Jean-Louis Lefebvre de Cheverus, who would become a cardinal of France.

Fathers de Cheverus and Matignon lived austerely and soon won the admiration of the city residents and the Indians in Maine. They also served small communities scattered throughout six states. Hailed as the "Apostles of New England," the priests saved many lives during the yellow fever epidemic of 1798. Father de Cheverus particularly won non-Catholic admirers because of his noble bearing, his obvious intelligence, and his kindness. He and Father Matignon established the Athenaeum, the first large library in Boston.

When Boston was established as a diocese in 1808, Father de Cheverus was appointed as the first bishop and consecrated on November 1, 1810. He and Father Matignon had founded the Church of the Holy Cross earlier as the first Catholic church in Boston. President John Adams and other prominent Americans donated to the building fund. Bishop de Cheverus and Father Matignon continued their labors, bringing the Ursuline Sisters to the diocese, ordaining priests, and opening parishes. Bishop de Cheverus suffered from poor health, and on January 15, 1823, resigned and was transferred to France. King Louis XVIII of France had demanded his return, despite protests

from people of all faiths in America. Americans, including Daniel Webster, petitioned the French king to allow him to remain in Boston, claiming that Americans could not prosper without him. The French monarch would not be persuaded, however. Bishop de Cheverus was created a cardinal in his native land after more distinguished service and became a Peer of France.

The second bishop of Boston was Benedict Joseph Fenwick, a Jesuit who was appointed on May 10, 1825. Father William Taylor had served as administrator in the interim. Bishop Fenwick's first concern was the lack of priests in the diocese, and he started a seminary in his own residence, training four seminarians at a time. When Father James Fitton gave Mount St. James Academy in Worcester to the diocese, the College of the Holy Cross was founded in 1843. Bishop Fenwick opened a weekly Catholic newspaper in 1829 to promote the Church in the face of Protestant antipathy. In 1834 Protestants resorted to anti-Catholic violence, burning down the local Ursuline convent. Three years later, an Irish neighborhood, Broad Street, became the target of the bigotry, with severe losses of Catholic lives and property. In 1844 Bishop Fenwick received a coadjutor bishop, John Bernard Fitzpatrick, to aid him in his defense of the faithful.

Boston was serving Connecticut Catholics and the Abenaki in Maine. Vermont and Rhode Island were also under the jurisdiction of the diocese. Bishop Fenwick, serving as an early inspiration to American Catholics throughout his episcopacy, died on August 11, 1846.

Bishop Fitzpatrick, acceding to the see upon the death of Bishop Fenwick, faced new assaults by the enemies of the Church. In 1854 a church in Dorchester was destroyed by a Protestant mob. Catholics continued to prosper, however, as more and more Irish came to Boston as a result of the Great Famine in Ireland. The Irish of Boston formed military units during the Civil War, including the "Fighting Ninth," and won the respect of their fellow countrymen. Their support for the Union quieted Protestant rage. Bishop Fitzpatrick even received an honorary degree from Harvard. He died on February 13, 1866, having led the faithful through perilous times.

His successor was Bishop John J. Williams, who

had served as his coadjutor. On February 12, 1875, he became an archbishop, as Pope Blessed Pius IX raised the diocese to the status of a metropolitan provincial see, an archdiocese with suffragan sees of Springfield and Providence. Archbishop Williams promoted expansion and the renewal of properties and facilities. He opened the new Cathedral of the Holy Cross and founded St. John's Seminary in Brighton. In 1906 he received the assistance of a coadjutor archbishop and died on August 30, 1907.

The second archbishop was William H. O'Connell, who had served as coadjutor archbishop with right of succession. He acceded to the see upon the death of Archbishop Williams. Prior to his appointment to Boston, he had served as the bishop of Portland. On November 27, 1911, he received the rank of cardinal priest of San Clemente by Pope St. Pius X. Archbishop O'Connell continued the needed expansion programs to provide archdiocesan services and put the finances of Boston on a firm footing. Catholic Charities and other social agencies were introduced as well. Cardinal O'Connell guided the faithful during World War I, the Great Depression, and World War II. He died on April 22, 1944.

His successor was one of America's most popular Catholic leaders, Cardinal Richard James Cushing. He had served as an auxiliary bishop of Boston since 1939 and was appointed as Cardinal O'Connell's successor on September 25, 1944. He received the rank of cardinal on December 15, 1958, with the titular church of Santa Susanna in Rome. In that same year he founded the St. James Society to send American priests to foreign missions. Cardinal Cushing attended the Second Vatican Council and implemented the reforms mandated by that council in the archdiocese. He also headed charities and took disabled children to Lourdes, seeing to their personal needs himself. He served as a papal legate for Pope Blessed John XXIII and was honored by foreign governments for his services and ministries. Cardinal Cushing's friendship with the Kennedy family and his care and counsel at the funeral ceremonies for

President John F. Kennedy following his assassination endeared him to Americans. He resigned on September 8, 1970, and died on November 2, 1970.

The fourth archbishop of Boston was Humberto S. Medeiros, who was appointed on September 8, 1970. He had previously served as bishop of Brownsville. On August 15, 1972, Archbishop Medeiros issued a pastoral, "Man's Cities and God's Poor." He was made a cardinal on March 5, 1973, by Pope Paul VI and was given the titular church of Santa Susanna in Rome. Cardinal Medeiros faced many problems in the archdiocese in the turbulent period after the Second Vatican Council and used his auxiliary bishops as regional authorities to aid in local ministries. He also paid off the debts of the archdiocese, and on October 1, 1979, welcomed Pope Blessed John Paul II to Boston. He underwent a triple bypass operation and died on September 17, 1983.

The fifth archbishop of Boston was Bernard Francis Law, who had served as the bishop of Springfield-Cape Giradeau since 1973. He was appointed as Cardinal Medeiros' successor on March 23, 1984. A year later, on May 25, 1985,

Cathedral of the Holy Cross in Boston

he was elevated to the College of Cardinals, with the titular church Santa Susanna. As archbishop, Cardinal Law became one of the most influential of the American members of the Sacred College and a determined reformer of archdiocesan administration. Most innovative was his establishment of a cabinet structure for administrative affairs, to provide greater bureaucratic cohesion. He also took the unusual step of appointing a layman to the post of archdiocesan chancellor and a woman religious as a judge on the archdiocesan marriage tribunal. Cardinal Law confronted the need to close older churches, but he established new ones in the suburbs as well to meet the changing demographic realities facing the archdiocese. He also erected new churches in Boston-area urban districts to provide better pastoral care for Catholics of Asian, Haitian, and Latin American backgrounds.

Cardinal Law's final years as archbishop were marked by the eruption of the sex abuse scandal that rocked the archdiocese and created the greatest crisis in its history. Facing accusations of having moved pedophile priests from one assignment to another, he resigned on December 13, 2002. He was eventually appointed archpriest of the Patriarchal Basilica of Santa Maria Maggiore, Rome, in May 2004.

Cardinal Law's successor, Bishop Seán Patrick O'Malley, O.F.M. Cap., had previously served as bishop of St. Thomas in the Virgin Islands, as bishop of Fall River, and as bishop of Palm Beach, and had already demonstrated his ability to serve as a shepherd in troubled dioceses, having dealt with the pastoral crisis in Palm Beach after the resignation of its bishop.

As archbishop of Boston from July 1, 2003, Archbishop O'Malley embarked immediately upon healing the severe spiritual and financial crises that had been caused by the sex abuse scandal. He was created a member of the College of Cardinals on March 24, 2006, by Pope Benedict XVI with the titular church of Santa Maria Della Vittoria. The archdiocese was further troubled by finances and the need to close large numbers of Catholic schools and parishes.

In 2011 there were 1.7 million Catholics served by 1,200 priests, 1,870 women religious, and 291 parishes in the archdiocese.

Boston College

A Jesuit university in Chestnut Hill, Massachusetts, between Newton and Boston, Boston College was established by the noted U.S. Army chaplain and Jesuit Father John McElroy in March 1863. Although the Jesuits had purchased land in Boston for the purpose of building the school, anti-Catholics filed a petition to block the building of a church, and the Jesuits were forced to settle in the South End, despite the efforts of Edward Everett, president of Harvard and former governor of Massachusetts. The college began its first academic semester in September 1864. The school's first president, Father John Bapst, S.J., overcame lingering and sometimes severe anti-Catholic sentiments in New England to give welcome to six Jesuit faculty members and twenty-two students, all from Boston.

From the start, Boston College attracted the sons of Irish immigrants and was a major training ground for future priests, especially as the archdiocese had no preparatory seminary of its own. It was thus useful to send students to Boston College for a strong foundation in philosophy and the classics. Within a short time, enrollment had outstripped the facilities, and it was necessary to find a new location. The search for a site began in 1907 with the appointment of Thomas I. Gasson, S.J., as the school's thirteenth president. He decided on Chestnut Hill and chose the architect Charles Donagh Maginnis to design the campus. The college moved to its present location in 1913, on a campus replete with Neo-Gothic buildings.

After World War I, the college introduced graduate and professional programs, including law, nursing, and education. This growth anticipated the continued progress after World War II, when enrollment exploded thanks to the returning veterans and the G.I. Bill. By 1948 there were over five thousand students, and expansion was launched under President Father Michael P. Walsh, S.J.

In 1970 Boston College became coeducational. Under Father J. Donald Monan, S.J., the twenty-fourth and longest serving president of the school, the university continued to grow in enrollment, faculty size, and administration. In the 1980s, the Jesuits at the university undertook a multimillion-dollar foundation effort to provide for the Jesuit Institute, a research center for Catholic theology, culture, and thought. Currently, Boston College has an enrollment of over fourteen thousand.

Boulet, John Baptist (1834–August 4, 1919)

A missionary, John Baptist Boulet was an innovative printer. He was born in Québec, Canada, and educated at Saint-Hyacinthe. Drawn to the priesthood, he went to Vermont and Holyoke, Massachusetts, to complete his studies. He also met Napoleon St. Onge, a seminarian who had volunteered to serve Bishop Augustin Magloire Blanchet in the Washington missions. Joining St. Onge at Holy Angels College in Vancouver, he was ordained on July 19, 1874.

Father Boulet was assigned to the tribal missions in Clark, Skamania, and Lewis counties in Washington, and he also conducted services on the Northwest coast. He then set out to begin an apostolate with the printed word and founded the St. James Press. When he moved his apostolate to Tulalip, he renamed the press in the honor of St. Anne. Father Boulet printed pamphlets, tracts, and magazines. He was made a monsignor in 1911 and then retired. He died in Bellingham.

Boys Town

A famed institution for troubled youths, Boys Town was established on December 10, 1917, in Omaha, Nebraska, by Father Edward Flanagan. Boys Town originated in Father Flanagan's hopes to provide young men with a chance to grow up in a caring environment that might shape their future lives. He began the home with ninety dollars he had borrowed and five boys, three from a juvenile court and two homeless newsboys. The first establishment was a Victorian house in the downtown district.

From this beginning, Flanagan soon found it necessary to find better housing for the growing number of boys who were arriving to live under his care. He thus purchased a farm just outside of Omaha and settled the boys there in October 1921. The farm developed into a genuine town and received incorporation in 1936 as the Village of Boys Town, complete with a mayor, four councilmen, and twenty-five commissioners, all boys elected by their fellow residents. The boys lived in dormitories until 1974, when smaller cottage-like facilities were established.

Through Father Flanagan's vision, Boys Town became a model both for the care of young juveniles and for methods of education. He promoted alternative forms of education and stressed vocational programs and a host of extracurricular activities, including sports, music, radio, television, and theater. Father Flanagan was also innovative in granting admission to any creed and race, requiring only that the boys attend services in their faith at least three days a week. In 1979 girls were accepted for the first time.

Following Father Flanagan's death in 1948, Monsignor Nicholas H. Wegner was appointed the director of Boys Town and held the post for the next twenty-five years. He was succeeded by Monsignor Robert P. Hupp, director from 1973 to 1985. The current director is Father Valentine J. Peter. Under Father Peter's leadership, the organization expanded its services to eighteen sites in fifteen states, including Washington, D.C. Boys & Girls Town also provides direct care to tens of thousands of children and offers various other programs that incorporate modern communications techniques. Boys & Girls Town assists over a million children each year.

Brady, Nicholas (October 25, 1878–March 27, 1930)

An immensely wealthy financier and philanthropist, Nicholas Brady was the first American recipient of the Supreme Order of Christ. Born in Albany, New York, he was the son of a self-made millionaire, Anthony Nicholas Brady, and Marcia Myers Brady. His father was a baptized Catholic but did not remain active in the faith, and his children were raised as Episcopalians. Nicholas was educated at the Albany Academy and Yale University, and after graduation he embarked on a highly successful Wall Street career. By the age of thirty-four, he was head of the New York Edison Company and was eventually one of the most influential corporate leaders in the United States.

In 1906 Brady married Genevieve Garvan, a devout Catholic, and entered the Church just before the marriage. He was a dedicated Catholic for the rest of his life and was especially devoted to the Mass and the holy Eucharist. He asked for and received permission from the apostolic delegate to have Mass celebrated in his private rail car while he vacationed in Florida. He was also extremely generous to the Church, donating over twelve million dollars to aid programs. In recognition of his contributions and his devotion to the faith, he was named a papal chamberlain and a papal duke. The Supreme Order of Christ was given to him in 1929 by Pope Pius XI; this rank is normally reserved for heads of state.

Brébeuf, St. John de (March 25, 1593–March 16, 1642)

The Jesuit missionary called Echon, "the Strong One," by the Hurons, St. John de Brébeuf was also remembered as "the Huron among the Hurons." He was born in Condé-sur-Vire, Normandy, France, and developed a religious vocation while still young. In 1617 he entered the Society of Jesus and began his studies, but at twenty-eight suffered a physical collapse and curtailed his academic schedule to receive the necessary training for ordination while recuperating.

On June 19, 1625, St. John arrived in Québec, accompanied by Father Joseph de la Roche d'Aillon, and he restored the reputation of the Jesuits among the colonists there. He went directly to the wilderness missions of the Hurons and journeyed with them to Lake Huron. With Father de Noüe he established a mission at Ikonatira, near Georgian Bay, serving alone when Father de Noüe was assigned elsewhere.

In 1629, when the colony became part of the British Empire, St. John returned to France with other missionaries. He set sail for Canada, however, when France again ruled there, and in May 1633 tried to return to Lake Huron. He made his way to his mission, and for sixteen years he labored among the Hurons without rest.

In the 1640s St. John spent time in Québec and among the Neutres, a tribe residing north of Lake Erie. St. Isaac Jogues and Father Francis Bressani had been captured by the local Native Americans, and St. John tried to reach the tribes. He traveled with another Jesuit,

reaching St. Mary's on the Wye. This mission was eventually destroyed.

In March 1649, the Iroquois, the enemy of the Huron, attacked St. Louis Mission, and St. John de Brébeuf and St. Gabriel Lallemant were taken prisoner. They were marched to St. Ignace, an Iroquois-held village. The two missionaries were beaten and tied to stakes, and St. John was seen kissing his stake, which would be the instrument of his martyrdom. The Jesuits were scalded with boiling water, slashed, and burned. Before St. John died, a red hot iron was thrust down his throat. Throughout the ordeals, he did not utter a sound.

St. John de Brébeuf and his companion were canonized in 1930. It is estimated that St. John converted as many as seven thousand Native Americans before being martyred. He also composed a dictionary and catechism in the Huron language. His feast day is October 19.

Brennan, Francis (May 7, 1894–July 2, 1968)

Prefect of the Sacred Congregation of the Sacraments in Rome in 1968, Francis Brennan was created a cardinal in 1967. He was born in Shenandoah, Pennsylvania, was educated locally, then entered St. Charles Seminary in Overlook, Philadelphia. He also studied at the Pontifical Roman Seminary at the Athenaeum S. Apollinare in Rome and was ordained on April 3, 1920.

Returning to the United States, he served in the Archdiocese of Philadelphia for the next twenty years as a pastoral minister and as a high school and seminary instructor. He also served as the officialis of the matrimonial tribunal and mediator of ecclesiastical conferences. In 1940 he became the first American to become a judge, or auditor, of the Sacred Roman Rota in Rome. He was in the Vatican during World War II, serving on various commissions and congregational offices.

In 1959 Pope John XXIII appointed him as chief judge of the Sacred Roman Rota. Other appointments and services followed, and on May 29,

Cardinal Francis Brennan

1967, he was given the rank of cardinal deacon by Pope Paul VI. Appointed Prefect of the Sacred Congregation for Discipline of the Sacraments on January 15, 1968, Cardinal Brennan served only one year, one month, and three days as a Prince of the Church. He died of cancer on July 2, 1968, at Rome's Misericordia Hospital.

Brent, Margaret (1601–c. 1671)

The first woman in Maryland to own land, Margaret Brent was a loyal supporter of the Calverts. Born in England, Margaret was one of thirteen children of Richard, Lord of Admington and Larkstoke, and his wife, Elizabeth Reed. Along with several brothers and her sister Mary, Margaret migrated to St. Mary's, Maryland, in 1638. They brought with them letters of introduction from Lord Baltimore as well as instructions to Governor Leonard Calvert to grant them the same amount of land as that provided to the earliest settlers of the colony. Margaret was able to extend the family's land, and in so doing she distinguished herself as the first woman in Maryland to hold land in her own right.

As a property holder of some note, she enjoyed considerable influence in Maryland and supported the Calverts during Claiborne's Rebellion, when she organized a troop of volunteer soldiers. Owing to her loyalty and personal qualities, she was named executrix of Governor Calvert and his representative in various proprietary interests. In her capacity as executrix and attorney she defended the estate's interests with great vigor and served in a similar capacity to her brother Giles when he resettled in Virginia in 1646. She later joined her brother and left her estate affairs to George Manners.

Brouillet, Jean Baptiste Abraham (December 11, 1813–February 5, 1884)

A founder of the Bureau of Catholic Indian Missions with Archbishop James Roosevelt Bayley of Baltimore, Jean Baptiste Abraham Brouillet was the first director of the apostolate. He was born at St. Jean Baptiste de Rouville, Québec, Canada.

The son of a farmer, he studied at St. Hyacinthe and was ordained on August 27, 1837. For the next decade he taught and served in pastoral ministries, but in 1847 he received permission to accompany Bishop Augustin Magloire Blanchet to Walla Walla (Nesqually), Washington. They traveled across the United States and arrived at Fort Walla Walla in October 1847.

Father Brouillet opened St. Anne's Mission on the Umatilla River at the request of the Cayuse tribe. He then discovered the bodies of Dr. Marcus Whitman and other Protestants, all slain by the Cayuse. Father Brouillet learned that the Cayuse blamed Dr. Whitman for the measles and smallpox that arrived in the area. He also heard threats against another Protestant, Henry Spalding, and risked the wrath of the Cayuse to warn him and save his life. Spalding spread stories that the Catholics had fomented the massacre, and the Church faced dire opposition. The Blanchet brothers, Bishop Augustin Magloire and Bishop Francis Norbert, had to rebuild the entire mission.

Becoming the vicar general of Nesqually, Father Brouillet was sent to Washington, D.C., to confer with officials over the harsh discrimination against Catholics by the Ulysses Grant administration concerning the Catholic missions to the Native Americans.

He then worked with Archbishop James Roosevelt Bayley to establish countermeasures to President Grant's policies, and on January 2, 1874, the Bureau of Catholic Indian Missions became a reality. He handled the intense political institutions and the anti-Catholic bias of the era and began to regularize and support the Indian missions.

In his capacity as director, he visited a school at Devil's Lake in the Dakota Territory. Intending to journey onward to Fargo, he was caught in a blizzard and was confined to an abandoned cabin for a week. He lost sight in his left eye as a result of snow blindness, but was finally able to reach civilization and recovered, although his physical reserves were impaired. He also began to have a series of illnesses

Jean Baptiste Brouillet

that led to his death. (*See also* Native American Catholics.)

Broun, Heywood (December 7, 1688–December 18, 1939)

A popular and respected American newspaper journalist, Heywood Broun was a convert to the Church. He was born in Brooklyn, New York, and educated in New York and at Harvard University. He did not graduate from Harvard but left to pursue a career in journalism, taking a position at the *Morning Telegraph* in New York. In 1912 he began his association with the *New York Tribune,* covering the French theater in World War I.

Broun then started his daily column, "It Seems to Me," at the *New York World* newspaper. His style was fearless and investigative, and he continued his column until 1928, when he was fired from the *World.* His column was picked up by the Scripps-Howard syndicate, however, and he became famous across the United States. He ran unsuccessfully for U.S. Congress in 1930 and organized the American Newspaper Guild in 1933. Broun wrote columns for *The New Republic* and wrote several popular books, including an autobiography in novel form. He continued his newspaper work until his death.

He had married Ruth Hale, and when she died in 1934, Broun wed Connie Madison. On May 23, 1939, he was baptized by Monsignor (later Archbishop) Fulton J. Sheen. Broun died in Stamford, Connecticut.

Brown, Father Raymond, S.S. (May 22, 1928– August 8, 1998)

A Sulpician priest, Raymond Brown was a noted Scripture scholar. Born in New York, New York, he began a long and distinguished academic career with studies at The Catholic University of America, where he earned both a bachelor's and a master's degree in 1948 and 1949, respectively, and at St. Mary's Seminary and University, where he earned a bachelors in sacred theology, after entering the Society of St. Sulpice. Ordained a priest for the Diocese of St. Augustine, in 1953, he embarked on advanced studies at Johns Hopkins University and then earned a doctorate in sacred theology from St. Mary's Seminary in 1955; his dissertation was titled *The "Sensus Plenior" of Sacred Scripture.*

He completed a doctorate in 1958 under the direction of famed biblical scholar William Foxwell Albright. Brown was then awarded a fellowship for 1958 and 1959 at the American School of Oriental Research in Jerusalem to study texts from the Qumran Caves. In 1959 and 1963 he earned additional degrees in Sacred Scripture from the Pontifical Biblical Commission.

In 1959 Brown was appointed to the faculty of St. Mary's Seminary, where he taught until 1971. He went on to teach at the Union Theological Seminary in New York in 1967 and 1968 as a visiting professor, from 1971 as professor of biblical studies, and from 1981 as Auburn Professor of Biblical Studies. Brown was also a member of the reorganized Pontifical Biblical Commission from 1972 to 1978. During his long time as a professor, he was a major advocate of the historical-critical methods then gaining popularity in academic circles, a position that brought criticism within the field. Nevertheless, Brown saw the use of such methods as part of the implementation of the wishes of Pope Pius XII in his encyclical *Divino Afflante Spiritu* (1943).

Brown was also a participant in ecumenical dialogues with the Lutherans from 1965 to 1973, the Joint Commission of the World Council of Churches and the Roman Catholic Church from 1967 to 1968, and the Faith and Order Commission of the WCC from 1968 to 1993. He was additionally a consultor to the Vatican Secretariat for Promoting Christian Unity from 1968 to 1973. He continued to write after his retirement in 1990 to St. Patrick's Seminary in Menlo Park, California.

Brown left a vast body of writings, including over thirty books. Among his most famous titles were: *The Gospel According to John* (1966, 1970), *Jesus: God and Man* (1967), *Priest and Bishop: Biblical Reflections* (1970), *The Virginal Conception and Bodily Resurrection of Jesus* (1973), *The Birth of the Messiah* (1977), *Mary in the New Testament* (1978), *The Critical Meaning of the Bible* (1981), *The Epistles of John* (1982), *Biblical Exegesis and Church Doctrine* (1985), *The Birth of the Messiah* (1993), *The Death of the Messiah* (two volumes, 1994), and *An Introduction to the New Testament* (1997). He was also editor of *Peter in the New Testament: A Collaborative Assessment by Protestant and Roman Catholic Scholars* (1973), and one of the editors of *The New*

Jerome Biblical Commentary (1990). His last book, *A Retreat with John the Evangelist* (1998), was published just before his death.

Browne, Charles Farrar (Artemus Ward) (April 26, 1834–March 6, 1867)

A popular American writer and lecturer, and a convert to the Church, Charles Farrar Browne was known to his readers as Artemus Ward. He was born in Waterford, Oxford County, Maine, where he was educated. At the age of fourteen, he was apprenticed to the *Skowhegan Clarion*, a newspaper. Browne then moved to the *Carpet-Bag* in Boston, the journal that featured his first humorous article. In 1858 he served as a reporter for the *Cleveland Plain Dealer*, under the name Artemus Ward. His writings and column poked fun at sports, séances, and political meetings. Two years later Browne was with *Vanity Fair* and gave lectures, including his famous "Sixty Minutes in Africa."

In 1866 Browne went to England, where he was enthusiastically welcomed. He wrote for the magazine *Punch* and was accepted into the Literary Club of London. He was becoming increasingly ill, however, and when confined to his bed asked to see a Catholic priest. He died unexpectedly in Southampton, England, and his remains were transferred to the family plot in Waterford, Maine.

Brownson, Orestes Augustus (September 16, 1803–April 17, 1876)

One of the most popular writers in America, Orestes Augustus Brownson was a convert to Catholicism. He was born in Stockbridge, Vermont. Raised in a Congregationalist family, he read a great deal and became a Presbyterian. He then rebelled against the theological doctrines of that denomination and became a Universalist and was ordained as a member in that church.

His writing career started early, and he demonstrated his sympathy for the working classes of the nation. He became a Unitarian minister and served as pastor in Walpole, New Hampshire, in 1832, then became a Congregationalist pastor in 1838. Orestes started the *Boston Quarterly Review*, which attracted outstanding authors. His political essays were popular and made Brownson famous. He was at odds with Christianity as he knew it and disliked capitalism and democratic concepts. In 1842 the *Boston Quarterly Review* merged with the *U.S. Democratic Review,* and was restructured as *Brownson's Quarterly Review* in January 1844. The publication continued until October 1875.

Researching continually for his essays, Orestes began studying Catholicism. His essays on "The Mediatorial Life of Jesus," published in Boston in 1842, clearly delineated a Catholic view of life and Christian objectives. Two years later, Brownson met with Bishop John Bernard Fitzpatrick and was received into the Church. As a Catholic, he set out to put an end to the severe persecution of the Church in America. He continually countered Protestant attacks, and he received a letter of praise from the Plenary Council of Bishops in April 1854.

In October 1855, he moved to New York, where he remained until 1875. His novel, *The Spirit Rapper* (1854), and his work *The Convert; or Leaves from My Experience* (1857) clearly display his spiritual journeys and were popular. He died in Detroit, Michigan, mourned as one of America's original philosophers and scholars, an individual capable of enduring great rejection in his lifelong search for truth and justice.

Brownsville, Diocese of

Established on July 10, 1965, by Pope Paul VI, the Diocese of Brownsville serves counties in southern Texas. On March 28, 1846, General Zachary Taylor erected the American flag at Fort Brown, the site of the present-day city, and Americans defended

Orestes Augustus Brownson

the area from Mexican assaults. In May 1846 the battles of Palo Alto and Resaca de la Palma were fought within the modern city's limits. Brownsville was involved in battles in the Civil War as well.

Modern Brownsville began with the arrival of the new railroad in 1904. A deep-water port, the city is part of the Gulf international waterway and serves as an oceanic shipping port as well as a center for agriculture, ranching, and the petroleum industry. The Diocese of Brownsville is a suffragan see of the Archdiocese of San Antonio.

The area has a profound Catholic heritage, having been visited by outstanding missionaries over the centuries. Brownsville and other Texas regions were part of the vast mission system that was introduced by the Franciscans, including Venerable Antonio Margil de Jesús. Texas was a province of Mexico until 1836. Pope Gregory XVI made the area a vicariate apostolic, and Bishop John M. Odin served as vicar apostolic, ministering to the region with only four priests.

When Pope Blessed Pius IX established the Diocese of San Antonio, now a metropolitan archdiocese, in 1874, Brownsville was incorporated into another vicariate apostolic, administered by Bishop Dominic Manucy, who was appointed on December 8 of that same year. He brought religious congregations to the area and moved his residence to Corpus Christi. On March 9, 1884, Bishop Manucy was appointed to the Diocese of Mobile, but asked to remain in Texas and was not moved. The Holy See approved his reappointment in February 1885, but Bishop Manucy died on December 4 of that year.

His successor as vicar apostolic was Bishop Peter Verdaguer, who was consecrated on November 9, 1890. He moved from Corpus Christi to Laredo two years later. Bishop Verdaguer established parishes and hospitals throughout the vicariate, laboring to evangelize the vast territory and to provide facilities for the faithful. He died on October 26, 1911.

In March 1912 the vicariate became a diocese, located in Corpus Christi. The Dominican Bishop Claude Jaillet administered Brownsville from 1911 to 1913. The area came under the episcopal jurisdiction of the bishops of Corpus Christ after that, as Americans faced World War I, the Great Depres-

sion, and World War II. In 1965 Brownsville was recognized as a Catholic center and established as a diocese.

The first bishop of the Diocese of Brownsville was Adolph Marx, who had served as auxiliary bishop of Corpus Christi and administrator of that diocese until his appointment to Brownsville on July 19, 1965. He instituted the diocesan offices and agencies and attended an ecumenical council in Rome. Bishop Marx died in Cologne, Germany, on November 1, 1965.

His successor was Bishop Humberto S. Medeiros, who would become an American cardinal. Bishop Medeiros was installed in Brownsville on June 29, 1966. He began his episcopacy by ministering to the quarter of a million migrant workers in the region and was called by many the "Champion of the Poor." On December 8, 1970, he was promoted to the Archdiocese of Boston. He was made a cardinal in 1973.

The third bishop of the diocese was John J. Fitzpatrick, who had served as auxiliary bishop of Miami since 1968. Bishop Fitzpatrick was installed in Brownsville on May 27, 1971. He began expansion programs and continued the migrant-worker ministry, as shortages of priests and religious became evident throughout the nation. Parish programs for renewal and lay ministries were supported by Bishop Fitzpatrick until he retired on November 30, 1991.

The fourth bishop was Bishop Enrique San Pedro, a Jesuit who had served as the auxiliary bishop of Galveston-Houston before his appointment to the diocese. He was appointed coadjutor bishop of Brownsville with right of succession on August 13, 1991. He acceded to the see upon the retirement of Bishop Fitzpatrick. Hispanic apostolates, youth ministries, and charitable programs were all major aspects of Bishop San Pedro's episcopacy until his death on July 17, 1994.

The fifth bishop, Raymundo J. Peña, had served as an auxiliary bishop of San Antonio and as the bishop of El Paso. He was appointed to Brownsville on May 23, 1995, and installed in Immaculate Conception Cathedral on August 6, 1995. Bishop Peña took as one of his most important programs the increase of vocations to the priesthood and religious life. He established the Casa San José del

Valle in 1997 to provide a regional house of studies in the diocese. He also encouraged lay formation, the charismatic movement, and traditional apostolic movements such as the Legion of Mary, Guadalupanas, and Cursillo. To coordinate all these activities, Bishop Peña launched the Vicar Episcopal's Office for Evangelization to oversee efforts of the parishes and ministries of the diocese. Bishop Peña retired on December 9, 2009.

He was succeeded by Bishop Daniel E. Flores on the same day. Bishop Flores had been an auxiliary bishop of Detroit since 2006. He was installed as bishop of Brownsville on February 2, 2010. In 2011 there were one million Catholics, served by 115 priests and 111 parishes in the diocese.

Brumidi, Constantino (1805–February 19, 1880)

An immigrant to the United States and a noted artist, Constantino Brumidi is best remembered for his magnificent fresco work in the capital in Washington, D.C, and for his religious artistry. He was

Cathedral of the Immaculate Conception in Brownsville

born in Rome and started his career by painting several local palaces and working on projects in the Vatican. There he served Pope Gregory XVI. When the French occupied Rome in 1849, Constantino sailed to America and became a citizen in 1852. He resided in New York and received many commissions in America and Mexico.

Visiting Washington, D.C., Constantino offered his services to the quartermaster general and was commissioned as a cavalry captain. His first assigned artistic endeavor was in the House Committee on Agriculture. Jefferson Davis, the secretary of war, applauded Constantino's labors and gave him a raise in pay from eight to ten dollars a day. Constantino continued his work, particularly in the Capital Rotunda. He died in Washington, honored as a unique artist.

Brunner, Francis de Sales (January 10, 1795–December 29, 1859)

The founder of the American Congregation of the Precious Blood, Francis de Sales Brunner built the congregation and recruited members. He was born in Muemliswil, Switzerland, entered the Benedictine monastery in 1812, and was ordained in 1819. Ten years later he entered the Trappists, but that monastery was suppressed and he offered his services to Pope Gregory XVI and was appointed to the missions in China.

Recalled from China, Father Brunner started a home for young boys and entered the Archconfraternity of the Most Precious Blood. His mother, who was a pious woman, then started the Sisters of the Most Precious Blood, serving as superior until her death in 1836. Her successor, Sister Clara, brought the community to America.

In 1838 Father Brunner entered the Congregation of the Most Precious Blood in Albano, Italy, and six years later, accompanied by eight priests, arrived in America. Archbishop John Baptist Purcell of Cincinnati had extended an invitation to Father Brunner, and his group served the predominantly German population near Newark, Ohio. He erected convents, schools, and parishes. Father Brunner also made several trips to Europe to raise funds and to recruit more religious. He died in the convent of Schellenberg, in the Duchy of Liechtenstein, during one of these journeys.

Bruté de Rémur, Simon William Gabriel (March 20, 1779–June 6, 1839)

A Sulpician missionary to the United States, called the "Angel of the Mount," Simon William Gabriel Bruté de Rémur was the first bishop of the Diocese of Vincennes (now the Archdiocese of Indianapolis). He was a nobleman, born in Rennes, France, where his father served as Superintendent of the Royal Domain in Brittany. The family fortune was based on middle-class businesses, however, and when the Reign of Terror of the French Revolution took place, they survived.

Young Simon visited prisons and found ways to bring letters to the priests and nobles held in them. He also brought the Eucharist to the priests. His family was not aware of his heroic adventures, but he recorded them in a diary. In 1796, when the chaos had ended, Simon studied medicine, earning his degree in 1803. He did not take up the practice of medicine, however, as he entered the Seminary of Saint-Sulpice in Paris. He was ordained on June 11, 1808, and then taught for two years before receiving an invitation to the frontiers of the young United States.

In 1810 Father Bruté de Rémur sailed to America with another outstanding missionary, Bishop Benedict Joseph Flaget, who was recruiting for the Diocese of Bardstown, Kentucky. It was reported that he brought five thousand books with him on his journey to America. Noted as a brilliant scholar, he taught at St. Mary's Seminary in Baltimore and was transferred to Mount St. Mary's College in Emmitsburg, Maryland. There he was revered as the "Angel of the Mount," laboring as the spiritual director of St. Elizabeth Ann Seton.

He was the president of St. Mary's College, Baltimore, and continued his services at the Mount. He apparently left the Sulpicians at this point, but labored among them until 1834. In that year, Father Bruté de Rémur was appointed the bishop of Vincennes, Indiana, having refused the honor earlier. He arrived in his diocese and took possession of St. Francis Xavier Cathedral on November 5, 1834. Bishop Bruté de Rémur worked alone in the region, serving some six hundred Catholics in nearby Fort Wayne.

Building parishes and making daily rounds over his vast territory, Bishop Bruté de Rémur also made a trip to Europe to collect needed funds. By 1837 his health was deteriorating, and while attending the Third Provincial Council of Baltimore he caught a cold. His lungs were badly infected, but upon returning home, Bishop Bruté de Rémur undertook a diocesan visitation of more than 1,450 miles. He was desperately ill but continued his visitation, covering the modern area of the state of Indiana and eastern Illinois. He died in Vincennes, mourned by the people of all faiths. His cause for canonization was opened in 2005 in the archdiocese of Indianapolis.

Bishop Simon Bruté de Rémur

Buckley, William F., Jr. (November 24, 1925–February 27, 2008)

Conservative writer and intellectual, best known for founding the political magazine *National Review* in 1955 and as host of the television show *Firing Line* from 1966 until 1999, William F. Buckley was also famed for his command of the English language as one of the leading figures in the conservative movement in the United States.

Born in New York City to a prominent family, he was raised with his nine brothers and sisters learning multiple languages. Drafted into the army in 1944, he went to work for the Central Intelligence Agency in 1946 and spent some time in Mexico on agency work. Returning to the United States, Buckley studied at Yale University, where he earned a bachelor's degree in 1950. He then wrote *God and Man at Yale*, a withering critique of Yale's liberal culture. After working as an editor at *The American Mercury*, he founded the conservative *National Review* to give a conservative voice in the media world. It was soon one of the most influential publications in the country.

In 1965 Buckley ran unsuccessfully for mayor of New York on the Conservative Party ticket. The next year, Buckley began hosting the political talk show *Firing Line*. He remained its host for the next three decades and was renowned for his interviews and the wide-ranging number of prominent guests. Buckley was also the author of a series of novels about fictional CIA spy Blackford Oakes.

Buffalo, Diocese of

Established on April 23, 1847, by Pope Blessed Pius IX, the Diocese of Buffalo serves counties in western New York State. A Great Lakes port and industrial center, Buffalo was laid out in 1803 for the Holland Land Company. The city was officially called New Amsterdam but was popularly called Buffalo. In 1818 the first steamboat on the Great Lakes, *Walking the Water*, was built at Buffalo. Burned by the British in 1813, the city was rebuilt and officially given its present name. The Diocese of Buffalo is a suffragan see of the Archdiocese of New York.

The area has a profound Catholic legacy that dates to early American eras. In 1678 Recollect Franciscan Father Louis Hennepin is believed to have celebrated Mass in the area of modern-day Buffalo while accompanying an expedition of René-Robert Chevalier, Sieur de La Salle, on the ship *Griffon*. Earlier, Jesuit missionaries had been in the region, and a mission, St. Mary's, had been established. Father Jacques Fremin, a noted Jesuit missionary, was there, celebrating probably the first Mass in the area on November 3, 1668. Father James Pierron, another Jesuit, was at St. James on Boughton Hill, and the Cayuga American Indians were being served at St. Joseph's at Great Gully Brook. Another mission, Immaculate Conception, served Iroquois settlements. Fort Niagara, at the mouth of the Niagara River, also had a Catholic chaplain.

The missions continued for almost a century until the British took control of the area and began to penalize Catholics, exiling the missionaries. The Catholic support of the Revolutionary War, however, brought an end to institutionalized persecution of the Church, and the establishment of the Diocese of Baltimore (now the Archdiocese of Baltimore) in 1789 aided the faithful. In 1808 the Diocese of New York (now the Archdiocese of New York) was erected, and the Buffalo area became part of that episcopal jurisdiction.

In 1820 a large number of Alsatian French settled in Erie County, and a year later Father Patrick Kelly arrived on the scene. The famous missionary, Father Stephen T. Badin, spent six weeks in the territory. A church was erected in 1828, founded by Louis Le Couteulx and other laypeople. Father John Mertz arrived a year after the founding of the church to become the first resident pastor of Buffalo. Bishop John Dubois of New York also spent time in the region. He celebrated a solemn High Mass at the courthouse and then processed through the streets.

On July 8, 1831, the cornerstone was laid for the Lamb of God Church on Main and Edward streets in Buffalo. Parishes were soon serving the faithful at East Eden, Lancaster, Lockport, North Tonawanda, Williamsville, and elsewhere. One of the priests who served these emerging parishes was St. John Nepomucene Neumann, who was in Buffalo from 1836 to 1840 and later became a bishop. He served at Kenmore, Lancaster, and Williamsville. Father Thomas McEvoy was at Java. In 1837 another parish was opened at Elicott and Batavia Streets in Buffalo.

The Diocese of Buffalo was established in 1847, and the Vincentian missionary John Timon was consecrated as the first bishop on October 17 of that year. He began a series of programs that brought converts and lapsed Catholics to the faith. He also built parishes and schools and invited religious congregations and orders to serve in the diocese. Bishop Timon founded the Brothers of the Holy Infancy to care for homeless boys and opened a diocesan newspaper. The Cathedral of St. Joseph, designed by Aristedes Leonori of Rome, was dedicated in 1855, and one year later a seminary was opened. Bishop Timon died on April 10, 1896, mourned by all the people of Buffalo for his generosity and leadership.

His successor was another Vincentian, Stephen Vincent Ryan, who was consecrated on November 8, 1868. A learned and pious bishop, he expanded diocesan facilities and apostolates. Canisius College opened in 1870, and more religious congregations accepted invitations to the diocese. Bishop Ryan died on April 10, 1896.

The third bishop of Buffalo was James Edward Quigley, who was consecrated on February 24,

1897. A trade-union supporter, he was known nationally as a foe of the socialists. In 1899 he successfully mediated a dock strike. On February 19, 1903, Bishop Quigley was promoted to the Archdiocese of Chicago.

His successor was Bishop Charles Henry Colton, who was consecrated on August 24, 1903. He continued the expansion programs and led the diocese through the troubled days preceding World War I. Bishop Colton died on May 9, 1915.

Bishop Dennis J. Dougherty was the successor of Bishop Colton. He had served the Holy See in the Philippines since 1903 and was transferred to Buffalo on December 6, 1915. He continued the expansion programs and aided the faithful with charitable and social programs. On May 1, 1918, he was promoted to the Archdiocese of Philadelphia and was created a cardinal in 1921.

The sixth bishop of Buffalo was William Turner, who was consecrated on March 30, 1919. A learned scholar and professor, Bishop Turner opened Catholic Charities in Buffalo in 1924. He built thirty new parishes and guided the diocese through the dark times of the Great Depression. Bishop Turner died on July 10, 1936.

Bishop John Aloysius Duffy was Bishop Turner's successor, transferred to the Diocese of Buffalo on April 14, 1937, from Syracuse, where he had served since 1933. He merged the two diocesan Catholic newspapers and founded a mission apostolate and the Diocesan Fund for the Faith. Bishop Duffy also instituted the Confraternity of Christian Doctrine in the diocese. He led the faithful of Buffalo through the critical years of World War II and died on September 27, 1944.

A second prelate destined to be created a cardinal was Bishop Duffy's successor, John Francis O'Hara, C.S.C., who had served as Military Delegate of the Armed Forces in World War II and as president of the University of Notre Dame. He was installed in the diocese on May 8, 1945. The focus of his labors was education, and he built high schools and elementary schools. He was also known as a profound foe of communism. Bishop O'Hara was promoted to the

Archdiocese of Philadelphia on November 23, 1951, and was created a cardinal in 1958.

His successor was Bishop Joseph A. Burke, who had served as auxiliary bishop of Buffalo since 1943. He was promoted to the see on February 9, 1952, and continued the diocesan expansion programs. He also promoted Hispanic and migration ministries. St. John Vianney Seminary in East Aurora was part of Bishop Burke's program. Having attended the Second Vatican Council, Bishop Burke died in Rome on October 16, 1962.

The tenth bishop of the Diocese of Buffalo was James A. McNulty, who was transferred from the Diocese of Patterson on February 12, 1963, where he had served since 1953. He had also served as auxiliary bishop of Newark. Bishop McNulty revolutionized the media apostolate of the diocese, starting a television ministry promoting religious vocations and lay apostolates. In addition, he implemented the reforms mandated by the Second Vatican Council. Bishop McNulty died on September 4, 1972.

His successor was Bishop Edward D. Head, who had served as an auxiliary bishop of New York. He was installed in Buffalo on March 19, 1973. Bishop Head instituted charitable and administrative offices in the diocese and consolidated activi-

St. Joseph's Cathedral in Buffalo

ties in a Catholic Center. The Outreach Ministry and vital educational and communications agencies were promoted during his episcopacy. Bishop Head retired on June 12, 1995.

He was succeeded by Henry J. Mansell, who had served as an auxiliary bishop of New York. He was transferred to the Diocese of Buffalo on April 18, 1995, and installed in the diocese on June 12. In 1997 Bishop Mansell presided over the diocese's sesquicentennial celebration. On October 20, 2003, Bishop Mansell was promoted to the Archdiocese of Hartford.

The thirteenth bishop of Buffalo, Edward U. Kmiec, acceded to the see on August 12, 2004. Bishop Kmiec had served previously as auxiliary bishop of the Archdiocese of St. Paul and Minneapolis from 1977 to 1982 and as bishop of the Diocese of Bismarck from 1982 to 2004. Bishop Kmiec was installed in the diocese on October 28, 2004. In 2011 there were 633,000 Catholics served by 436 priests, approximately 1,000 men and women religious, and 169 parishes in the diocese.

Bureau of Catholic Indian Missions. *See* Native American Catholics

Burke, John Joseph (June 6, 1875–October 30, 1936)

A Paulist editor, John Joseph Burke was the general secretary of the National Catholic Welfare Conference. He was born in New York City and educated locally. In 1896 he entered the Missionary Society of St. Paul the Apostle and was ordained on June 9, 1899. Four years later, Father Burke became an assistant editor of the Paulist magazine *Catholic World*. Within a year, he was in charge of all Paulist publications.

During his editorial and publishing years, Father Burke recognized the profound relationship between the principles of the American republic and the principles of the Catholic faith. He also promoted the doctrine of the Mystical Body of Christ, translating Abbé Anger's profound work on the subject in 1931.

In 1911 Father Burke formed the Catholic Press Association, as well as the National Catholic War Council after America's entry into World War I. In 1919, having distinguished himself in the areas

of Catholic social and civic leadership, he was appointed general secretary of the newly formed NCWC. In 1927 the Vatican conferred on him an honorary doctorate in sacred theology in recognition of his tireless labors.

Father Burke translated other works on the Mystical Body and in 1934 wrote *Christ in Us*. He took a vital role in mediating the conflict caused by the persecution of the Church in Mexico and continued to monitor the situation, serving as a liaison to American government officials. Father Burke died suddenly in Washington, D.C., from a heart attack, one month after being made a domestic prelate, or monsignor.

Burke, Raymond L. (June 30, 1948–)

An American cardinal and the Prefect of the Apostolic Signatura, the highest ranking court in the Church, Raymond Leo Burke is also honored as one of the greatest living experts on canon (or Church) law in the entire world.

He was born in Richland Center, in the Diocese of La Crosse, Wisconsin, and entered Holy Cross Seminary in La Crosse in 1966. He studied at The Catholic University of America in Washington, D.C., where he obtained a bachelor's degree in philosophy in 1970 and a master's degree in philosophy in 1971. He was then sent to study at the Pontifical Gregorian University in Rome, where he obtained a bachelor's degree in sacred theology in 1974 and a master's degree in theology in 1975.

Ordained on June 29, 1975, in St. Peter's Basilica by Pope Paul VI, he returned to the United States and served as associate rector of the Cathedral of St. Joseph the Workman in La Crosse. In 1982 he was again sent to the Pontifical Gregorian University to study canon law and earned a licentiate in canon law in 1982, a diploma in Latin letters in 1983, and a doctorate in canon law with specialization in jurisprudence in 1984.

After returning to the United States, Father Burke held several posts in the Diocese of La Crosse, but he was also subsequently a visiting professor of Canonical Jurisprudence at the Pontifical Gregorian University from 1985 to 1994 and a member of the College of Judges of the Supreme Tribunal of the Apostolic Signatura in 1989. He became the first American to hold the position of

Defender of the Bond of the Supreme Tribunal of the Apostolic Signatura.

On December 10, 1994, Burke was appointed the bishop of La Crosse and was consecrated a bishop on January 6, 1995, in St. Peter's Basilica by Pope John Paul II. He was then promoted to the metropolitan provincial see of St. Louis on December 2, 2003, and served as archbishop for five years, until June 27, 2008, when he was named by Pope Benedict XVI as Prefect of the Supreme Tribunal of the Apostolic Signatura in Rome.

Pope Benedict created him a cardinal deacon in the consistory of November 20, 2010; he received the deaconry of St. Agatha of the Goths. Cardinal Burke is the author of many scholarly works on canon law and theology.

Burlington, Diocese of

Established on July 29, 1853, by Pope Blessed Pius IX, the Diocese of Burlington serves the entire state of Vermont. Burlington is the state's largest city and is a port of entry. Governor Benning Wentworth of New Hampshire chartered the city in 1763 and named it after the Burling family, veteran pioneer landowners of the area. During the War of 1812, Battery Park in the city and British warships exchanged volleys. The city is a center for manufactured wares, including electronic machines, furniture, business machines, structural steel, lumber products, and maple syrup. The Diocese of Burlington is a suffragan see of the Archdiocese of Boston.

The Catholic history of the diocese opens in 1609 with the discovery of the lake that bears his name by Samuel de Champlain. In 1642 Sts. Isaac Jogues and René Goupil may have been at Isle La Motte for a time as Mohawk captives. In 1666 Fort Ste. Anne was opened on Isle La Motte, including a chapel. Father John Baptist Du Bois des Prinzeles, a chaplain, celebrated Mass there on July 26 of that year. Father Francis Dollier de Casson was also at the fort.

Two years later, Bishop Blessed François de Montmorency Laval came from Québec to confirm American Indian converts. Jesuit and Recollect Franciscans were serving missions in the region. Famed Jesuit Fathers Jacques Fremin, Jean Pierron, and Jacques Bruyas also labored at Isle La Motte in 1667. In 1682 Jesuits ministered to the Abenaki

in Swanston. The missions were closed when the British took control of Canada in 1760. Severe anti-Catholic laws were put in place, remaining until Catholics proved themselves during the Revolutionary War. The penal laws against Catholics were repealed in 1793.

In 1808 the Diocese of Boston (now the Archdiocese of Boston) was established, and Vermont Catholics were under the jurisdiction of this new episcopal designation. In 1818 Father Peter M. Mignault visited Vermont, and in 1830, the "Apostle of Vermont," Father Jeremiah O'Callaghan, became the first resident priest. He built a church that was burned to the ground by local Protestants. Father O'Callaghan immediately rebuilt the church and added a school. The Cathedral of the Immaculate Conception dates to this era, as the Catholic population of Burlington continued to increase and stood firm in the faith. In 1840 a large Irish immigration added to the Catholic strength.

The Diocese of Burlington was erected in 1853, and Bishop Louis de Goesbriand was consecrated for the see on October 30 of that year. He visited the entire state of Vermont to assess needs and areas of growth. There were only five priests, ten churches, and one school in operation when he started the agencies and offices for diocesan administration. In 1855 he went to France to recruit priests and funding, as well as to Brittany and Canada for personnel. Within a decade Bishop de Goesbriand had sixty-two priests, seventy-nine churches, and seventeen schools. He attended the First Vatican Council and the Councils of Baltimore, laboring to expand facilities and to institute reforms and liturgical practices. In 1892 he received a coadjutor bishop, John S. Michaud. Bishop de Goesbriand died on November 3, 1899.

Bishop Michaud acceded to the see on that day, and he immediately set about adding diocesan institutions and services. He built the Fanny Allen Hospital, in honor of Frances Allen, the daughter of the American patriot Ethan Allen. She had converted to the Catholic Church and become an Ursuline nun in Canada. Bishop Michaud also aided the founding of St. Michael's College and instituted a Knights of Columbus Council and an immigrant program. He died on December 22, 1908.

The third bishop of Burlington was Joseph J.

Rice, who was consecrated on April 14, 1910. Bishop Rice sponsored catechetical and educational programs in the diocese. He erected parish schools and a Catholic high school. He also led the faithful of the diocese through the turmoil of World War I and the Great Depression, and he faced extreme Protestant bigotry and violence as well, as the Ku Klux Klan was active in the area. Bishop Rice died on April 1, 1938.

Bishop Matthew Francis Brady succeeded Bishop Rice. A former U.S. Army chaplain, he was consecrated on October 26, 1938. Bishop Brady instituted Catholic Charities and other social service programs and founded a diocesan school office. He also took part in forming the National Council of Catholic Women in the state. World War II's military efforts were firmly supported by Bishop Brady, who was transferred to the Diocese of Manchester on November 11, 1944.

The fifth bishop of the Diocese of Burlington was Edward F. Ryan, who was consecrated on January 3, 1945. Bishop Ryan built two protective institutions for youths and introduced the Boy Scouts, the Catholic Youth Organization, and the Holy Name Society to the diocese. Many religious congregations and orders entered the diocese during Bishop Ryan's episcopacy, including the Carthusians and Benedictines. He also established new parishes, including Blessed Sacrament at Stowe, and founded a diocesan newspaper. He sponsored summer camps for children as well. Bishop Ryan died on November 3, 1956.

Bishop Ryan's successor was Robert F. Joyce, who had served as an auxiliary bishop of the diocese and acceded to the see on February 26, 1957. Bishop Joyce attended the Second Vatican Council and implemented the reforms of that council. He promoted religious education, counseling, and health and educational programs. He retired on January 24, 1972.

His successor was Bishop John A. Marshall, who was consecrated and installed on January 25, 1972. Bishop Marshall faced a critical loss of priests and religious, but he promoted charitable programs

Bishop Goesbriand

and lay ministries. He was transferred to the Diocese of Springfield on December 27, 1991.

The eighth bishop was Kenneth A. Angell, who had served as auxiliary bishop of the Diocese of Providence since 1974. Bishop Angell was installed in Burlington on November 9, 1992. He was dedicated to the pro-life cause and spoke out on a host of issues related to the culture of life, including abortion, assisted suicide, euthanasia, capital punishment, medical and genetic ethics, and care for the elderly. He testified before committees and members of the Vermont Legislature on several occasions against proposed assisted suicide and euthanasia bills, against partial-birth abortion, against the death penalty, for the preservation of traditional marriage, in support of mandatory reporting for clergy, for fair wages, and for other right-to-life issues. In addition, in 1993 he launched the Respect Life Phone Tree to galvanize lobbying efforts on key issues, and in 2002 started the diocesan Respect Life Advisory Commission. The bishop also established a House of Discernment at the University of Vermont Catholic Center to promote vocations to the priesthood, and initiated an Institute for Lay Ministry and a Commission on Women to assist the needs of women in the Church.

Bishop Angell suffered a terrible loss on September 11, 2001, when his brother, the noted television producer David Angell, and his sister-in-law, Lynn, were murdered when their plane, American Flight 11, was flown into the World Trade Center. The bishop became nationally known for his grace in the face of tragedy and for being a model of forgiveness. He retired on November 9, 2005.

Bishop Salvatore R. Matano became the ninth bishop of the diocese, having been consecrated as coadjutor bishop of Burlington as of April 19, 2005, and acceding to the see of Burlington upon Bishop Angell's retirement. Bishop Matano grappled with cases stemming from the sex abuse crisis and also with promoting vocations in the face of an aging priestly population. He likewise sought to foster a renewed zeal in the Catholic faithful in the areas of sacramental life and education. In 2011 there were 118,000 Catholics served by 137 priests, 102 women religious, and 77 parishes in the diocese.

Burnett, Peter Hardeman (November 15, 1807–May 16, 1895)

The first American governor of California, Peter Hardeman Burnett was a convert to Catholicism. He was born in Nashville, Tennessee, but was taken at a young age to Missouri. He returned to Tennessee at nineteen, married Harriet W. Rogers, studied law, and was admitted to the bar in 1839. Burnett also edited and published local newspapers. In 1843 he moved his family to Oregon, where he was a member of the territorial legislature from 1844 to 1848. Having become a Cambellite, a member of the Church of the Disciples, Burnett discovered a copy of the published debate between Alexander Campbell and Bishop John Baptist Purcell of Cincinnati. The stunning clarity of Bishop Purcell's writings led Burnett into an investigation of the Catholic faith, and he was received into the Church in June 1846.

In 1848 the family moved again, this time to California, and Burnett was elected to the legislative assembly and then aided in the drafting of the California Constitution. In 1849 he was elected governor, but in 1851 he resigned and became a Justice of the California Supreme Court. He wrote a popular book, *The Path Which Led a Protestant Lawyer to the Catholic Church,* in 1860, and other works on government and on his own pioneering and spiritual labors. He died in San Francisco.

Burtsell, Richard (April 14, 1840–February 5, 1912)

A Sulpician priest, Richard Burtsell was a noted canonist. Born in New York City, he attended Catholic schools in New York and entered the Sulpician Seminary in Montréal, Canada, at the age of eleven. In 1857 he was sent to the Propaganda College in Rome and there obtained doctorates in philosophy and theology. He was ordained on August 10, 1862, and for the next years held a variety of pastoral assignments and was responsible for establishing Epiphany Parish in 1867 and St. Benedict the Moor Parish in 1883, the first in the Archdiocese of New York to serve African-Americans. Although not a formally trained canonist, he was noted for his knowledge of canon law and was asked for assistance in Church law by fellow priests.

In 1887 Burtsell assumed the role of canonical adviser and advocate for his friend, Reverend Edward McGlynn, in his dispute with Archbishop Michael A. Corrigan of New York. Partly because of his involvement in the affair, Burtsell was removed as pastor in 1889 and lost his appeal to Rome the following year. He was named pastor of St. Mary's in Kingston, New York, where he dedicated himself until his death.

Aside from his reputation as a pastor, Burtsell was one of the country's foremost canonists and was a contributor to the old *Catholic Encyclopedia.* He was named papal chamberlain, or monsignor, in 1905 by Archbishop John Murphy Farley and in 1911 was appointed a domestic prelate by Pope St. Pius X.

Butin, Romain François (December 3, 1871–December 8, 1937)

A Marist priest, Romain François Butin was a Scripture scholar. Born at Saint-Romain d'Urfé, France, he studied at the Petit Séminaire de Saint-Jodard and then went to the United States at the age of nineteen. In America, he entered the Society of Mary (the Marists) and prepared for the priesthood at Dodon, Maryland. He was ordained a Marist in 1897 and went on to earn a doctorate in Semitic languages and literature at The Catholic University of America, where he taught from 1912 until his death.

In 1926 Father Butin was named the annual professor and acting director of the American School of Oriental Research in Jerusalem. He was also a member of the 1930 Harvard-Catholic University expedition to Sinai. He earned considerable notoriety for his work examining the origins of the alphabet and his efforts to establish the Catholic Biblical Association of America. He was the author of three books, thirty-eight articles, and twenty-one book reviews.

Butler, Pierce (March 17, 1866–November 16, 1939)

An Associate Justice of the United States Supreme Court from 1923 to 1939, Pierce Butler was a member of the judicial group called the "Four

Horsemen." He was born on St. Patrick's Day in a log cabin in Dakota County, Minnesota, to Irish immigrants from County Wicklow, Ireland, who had escaped the potato famine of 1848. In 1883 Butler was admitted to Carleton College in Northfield, Minnesota, and paid for his education by working in a local dairy. He graduated in 1887 with two bachelor's degrees and proceeded to the study of law at the firm of Pinch and Twohy in St. Paul. He passed the Minnesota bar in 1888 and established a law practice with Stan Donnelly.

In 1891 he became assistant to the county attorney for Ramsey County, and in 1893 and 1895 he was elected county attorney as a Democrat. Butler married Annie Cronin in 1891; the couple had eight children. As county attorney, he was responsible for more criminal convictions than any county attorney before him. On the basis of this work, he ran for the state senate in 1906, but narrowly lost his bid. In 1908 he was elected president of the Minnesota State Bar Association.

In 1893 Butler helped to launch a St. Paul law firm that was later named Butler, Mitchell, and Doherty, and became one of the most prominent firms in the region and boasted several powerful railroad companies as clients. During his various railroad cases, he met and became a friend of President William Howard Taft, who served on the Supreme Court as chief justice from 1921 to 1930 and later was instrumental in arranging Butler's nomination to the Supreme Court. That nomination came on November 23, 1922, when President Warren Harding chose him to succeed retiring Justice William Day. Although a Democrat, Butler was approved handily by the Republicans owing to his conservative tendencies, confirmed on December 13, 1922, and appointed by the Senate on January 2, 1923, by a vote of 61–8.

As justice, Butler wrote over 300 majority opinions and 140 dissenting opinions. He remained true to his conservative principles and became part of a block of conservative justices, with James McReynolds, George Sutherland, and Willis Van Devanter, called the "Four Horsemen." Justice Oliver Wendell Holmes called him a "monolith." As an advocate of *laissez-faire* government policy, he voted to limit the power of government, opposed state inheritance tax as unconstitutional, and was

an opponent of the efforts by the government to regulate prices. He was a dedicated opponent of the New Deal initiated by President Franklin Delano Roosevelt after his election in 1932, to the point that he was a specific target of Roosevelt's effort in 1937 to pack the Supreme Court. Over the next years, Butler was frustrated by the court's clear lurch to the left, lamenting in the decision *United States v. Rock Royal Co-op*: "Whimseys may displace deliberate action by chosen representatives and become rules of conduct. To us the outcome seems wholly incompatible with the system under which we are supposed to live."

Byrne, Patrick James (October 26, 1888–November 25, 1950)

A Maryknoll bishop and apostolic delegate, Patrick James Byrne died at the hands of the North Koreans. Born in Washington, D.C., he was the seventh child of Irish-born parents who lived on Capital Hill, on the site of the present-day Supreme Court building. Patrick lived for a time with his aunt in Auburn, New York, and upon returning to Washington witnessed the tragic drowning of younger brother Edgar in 1908.

He entered St. Charles College in Ellicott City, near Baltimore, and then St. Mary's Seminary. There he heard lectures by Father James A. Walsh and Father Thomas F. Price, the future founder of Maryknoll. When he was ordained on June 23, 1915, Father Byrne applied to Maryknoll and went to the headquarters of the new congregation, the Catholic Foreign Mission Society of America, near Ossining, New York. He served in many capacities there until 1922, when he was appointed superior of the new Maryknoll Mission in Korea.

When he arrived in Korea, there were over ninety thousand Catholics in the country. His mission field covered the northwestern province of Pyongyang, and his fellow priests worked with Maryknoll brothers and sisters to evangelize the area. In 1927 the Pyongyang Mission was made a prefecture apostolic, and Father Byrne was made prefect. In 1929, however, he returned to the United States to attend the first General Chapter of Maryknoll and was elected vicar general. This position kept him in Maryknoll until 1934, when he opened a new mission in Kyoto, Japan. The approaching war, however, brought difficulties. Following the attack on Pearl Harbor, Father Byrne was kept isolated and under house arrest in Japan. In 1945 he was asked to make a radio address to the Japanese people, and he calmed them and assured them that the approaching American troops would aid Japan in rebuilding. He also served as consultor for General Douglas MacArthur, the Supreme Allied Commander.

Two years later, Rome appointed Father Byrne apostolic visitor to Korea, and he was consecrated a bishop in Seoul on June 14, 1949. He labored there until June 1950, when the communist North Koreans invaded the south. Bishop Byrne and Father William Booth, who had volunteered to remain at his side when all other Catholic priests and religious were ordered south, tried to aid the Catholics in Seoul. They were arrested on July 17, 1950. Within a week they were transferred to Pyongyang and then to Manpo and Kosan.

Bishop Byrne and his fellow prisoners were forced on a death march by the infamous Korean commandant called "the Tiger." Blizzards, rough terrain, and cruel treatment took many lives, but the party reached Chunjen-jin, where they were forced to stand in the snow. Bishop Byrne developed pneumonia and was transferred to Ha Chang Ri, where he was put in a shack. He died on November 25. He was buried in a shallow grave in a cassock given to him by a fellow prisoner, Monsignor Quentin of the Columban Fathers.

Byrne, Richard (1832–June 10, 1864)

A brigadier general in the United States Army, Richard Byrne saw active duty in the Civil War. Born in County Cavan, Ireland, he migrated from his native country to New York in 1844. In 1849 he entered the army and joined the Second Cavalry regiment. He soon took part in several campaigns against Native Americans in Florida and Oregon, and at the start of the Civil War he was commis-

sioned a first lieutenant in the Fifth Cavalry. After distinguishing himself in the campaigns of 1861 and 1862, he was named colonel of the 28th Massachusetts Volunteers, an Irish regiment, in October 1862. He subsequently headed the regiment throughout 1863 and so participated in the bloody battles of Chancellorsville and Gettysburg. After a brief recruitment tour, he assumed command of the famed Irish Brigade. A mere two weeks later, however, he was mortally wounded on June 3, 1864, at Cold Harbor.

Byrne, William (1780–June 5, 1833)

One of the missionaries active in the early Diocese of Bardstown (now the Archdiocese of Louisville), William Byrne died caring for victims of an epidemic. He was born in County Wicklow, Ireland. The persecution of Catholics by the English occupiers of Ireland gave him a great zeal for the faith and led to his migration to the United States. In America, he applied to the Jesuits but realized that he would better serve the faith as a missionary in the wilderness areas.

Having discussed his vocation with Archbishop John Carroll of Baltimore, William was sent to Mount St. Mary's College in Emmitsburg, Maryland. He was nearly thirty years old when he began seminary studies; he was ordained in Bardstown in 1819. That year, Father Byrne started riding on horseback to the far-flung missions of the diocese. His maturity and faithfulness made him popular among people of all religious faiths in the region.

In 1821 Father Byrne opened St. Mary's College near Bardstown and welcomed fifty young men. St. Mary's burned, but Father Byrne rebuilt it and taught hundreds of young men about the faith. A cholera epidemic struck the area in 1833, and Father Byrne brought the last rites and comfort to dying victims of the plague, himself succumbing to the disease.

C

Cabeza de Vaca, Alvar Nuñez (unknown–c. 1557)
A Spanish explorer, called the "Columbus of the Continent," Alvar Nuñez Cabeza de Vaca is famous for his expeditions into Arizona, New Mexico, and Texas. He was born in Jerez de la Fontera, Spain. His family, called literally "cow's head," used the symbol of the animal as a point of honor that reflected past glories. Cabeza de Vaca entered the Spanish army in 1511 and served in campaigns against France in Naples and Ravenna, Italy, as well as in Navarre. In 1520 he took part in the extirpation of the *Comuneros*, the citizen uprising against King Charles I of Spain.

Cabeza de Vaca was appointed treasurer of Pánfilo de Narváez's expedition to Florida in 1527. The Florida territory had been discovered some fourteen years before by Ponce de León. Cabeza de Vaca commanded one of the vessels outfitted for the journey. After reaching Florida, the ships set sail for the Gulf of Mexico, where a storm broke apart the small flotilla and sank most of the vessels. The ship under the command of Cabeza de Vaca, however, managed to land west of the Mississippi. There he and his surviving crew were taken captive by the local tribe and subjected to harsh treatment, finally escaping and making their way through the wilderness.

After eight years of slavery and wandering along the Texas and Louisiana coasts, Cabeza de Vaca and three survivors reached Mexico City in 1536. The exact extent of his journeys is unclear, but his extensive account inspired the Franciscan missionary Marcos de Niza and the Spanish explorer Francisco Vázquez de Coronado and established Cabeza de Vaca and his companions as the first European explorers to travel across the mainland of North America.

Cabeza de Vaca returned to Spain in April 1537 and sought to secure support from the crown for another expedition to Florida. His hopes were soon dashed, however, as the excitement created by the conquest of the Incan empire by Francisco Pizarro prompted the crown to favor the more aggressive and politically well positioned Hernando de Soto as leader of the new effort. De Soto asked Cabeza de Vaca to join the campaign, but he refused.

In 1540 Cabeza de Vaca accepted the offer of the governorship of the province of Rio de la Plata, encompassing a large part of Spanish South America, with its capital at Asunción (modern Paraguay). As governor, he explored as far as Bolivia, but troubles with his troops and the colonial population led to his arrest and return to Spain in 1544. Exiled to Africa by the Council of the Indies for various offenses, he was pardoned in 1552 and brought back into royal favor.

Alvar Nuñez Cabeza de Vaca held the post of judge in the Supreme Court in Seville until his death there sometime around 1557.

Cabinets, Catholics in Presidential
Despite the persistent anti-Catholic atmosphere in the United States, a large number of Catholics have served in the cabinets of American presidents. The first was Roger Brooke Taney (later named first Catholic Supreme Court Justice), who was appointed in 1831 by Andrew Jackson. From 1789 to 1940, nine Catholics were appointed to cabinet posts by six of thirty-two presidents. That number increased from the time of Franklin Delano Roosevelt. The full list is given in chronological order:

Andrew Jackson: Roger B. Taney, Attorney General, 1831–33, Secretary of Treasury, 1833–34.

Franklin Pierce: James Campbell, Postmaster General, 1853–57.

James Buchanan: John B. Floyd, Secretary of War, 1857–61.

William McKinley: Joseph McKenna, Attorney General, 1897–98.

Theodore Roosevelt: Robert J. Wynne, Postmaster General, 1904–05; Charles Bonaparte, Secretary of the Navy, 1905–06, Attorney General, 1906–09.

Franklin Delano Roosevelt: James A. Farley, Postmaster General, 1933–40; Frank Murphy, Attorney General, 1939–40; Frank C. Walker, Postmaster General, 1940–45.

Harry S. Truman: Robert E. Hannegan, Postmaster General, 1945–47; J. Howard McGrath, Attorney General, 1949–52; Maurice J. Tobin, Secretary of Labor, 1948–53; James P. McGranery, Attorney General, 1952–53.

Dwight D. Eisenhower: Martin P. Durkin, Secretary of Labor, 1953; James P. Mitchell, Secretary of Labor, 1953–61.

John F. Kennedy: Robert F. Kennedy, Attorney General, 1961–63; Anthony Celebrezze, Secretary of Health, Education, and Welfare, 1962–63; John S. Gronouski, Postmaster General, 1963.

Lyndon Baines Johnson: Robert F. Kennedy, 1963–64, Anthony Celebrezze, 1963–65, and John S. Gronouski, 1963–65, reappointed to posts held in the Kennedy cabinet; John T. Connor, Secretary of Commerce, 1965–67; Lawrence O'Brien, Postmaster General, 1965–68.

Richard M. Nixon: Walter J. Hickel, Secretary of Interior, 1969–71; John A. Volpe, Secretary of Transportation, 1969–72; Maurice H. Stans, Secretary of Commerce, 1969–72; Peter J. Brennan, Secretary of Labor, 1973–74; William E. Simon, Secretary of Treasury, 1974.

Gerald R. Ford: Peter J. Brennan, 1974–75, and William E. Simon, 1974–76, reappointed to posts held in Nixon cabinet.

Jimmy Carter: Joseph Califano, Jr., Secretary of Health, Education, and Welfare, 1977–79; Benjamin Civiletti, Attorney General, 1979–81; Moon Landrieu, Secretary of Housing and Urban Development, 1979–81; Edmund S. Muskie, Secretary of State, 1980–81.

Ronald Reagan: Alexander M. Haig, Secretary of State, 1981–82; Raymond J. Donovan, Secretary of Labor, 1981–84; Margaret M. Heckler, Secretary of Health and Human Services, 1983–85; William J. Bennett, Secretary of Education, 1985–88; Ann Dore McLaughlin, Secretary of Labor, 1988–89; Lauro F. Cavazos, Secretary of Education, 1988–89; Nicholas F. Brady, Secretary of Treasury, 1988–89.

George Bush: Lauro F. Cavazos, reappointed Secretary of Education, 1989–90; Nicholas F. Brady, reappointed Secretary of Treasury, 1989–93; James D. Watkins, Secretary of Energy, 1989–93; Manuel Lujan, Jr., Secretary of the Interior, 1989–93; Edward J. Derwinski, Secretary of Veterans Affairs, 1989–92; Lynn Martin, Secretary of Labor, 1990–93; Edward Madigan, Secretary of Agriculture, 1991–93; William P. Barr, Attorney General, 1991–93.

Bill Clinton: Henry G. Cisneros, Secretary of Housing and Urban Development, 1993–97; Federico F. Peña, Secretary of Transportation, 1993–97; Donna Shalala, Secretary of Health and Human Services, 1993–2001; William M. Daley, Secretary of Commerce, 1997–2000; Andrew Cuomo, Secretary of Housing and Urban Development, 1997–2001; Alexis H. Herman, Secretary of Labor, 1997–2001.

George W. Bush: Paul O'Neill, Secretary of the Treasury, 2001–03; Tommy Thompson, Secretary of Health and Human Services, 2001–05; Mel Martinez, Secretary of Housing and Urban Development, 2001–05; Anthony Principi, Secretary of Veterans Affairs, 2001–05; Jim Nicholson, Secretary of Veterans Affairs, 2005–07; Alberto Gonzalez, Attorney General, 2005–07; Carlos Gutierrez, Commerce Secretary, 2005–08.

Barack H. Obama: Ken Salazar, Secretary of the Interior; Tom Vilsack, Secretary of Agriculture; Kathleen Sebelius, Secretary of Health and Human Services; Hilda Solis, Secretary of Labor; Ray Lahood, Secretary of Transportation; Shaun Donovan, Secretary of Housing and Urban Development; Janet Napolitano, Secretary of Homeland Security; all appointed in 2009.

There were also cabinet members who became Catholics after leaving their posts in presidential administrations. They were: Thomas Ewing, Secretary of Treasury under William H. Harrison and Secretary of Interior under Zachary Taylor; Luke E. Wright, Secretary of War under Theodore Roosevelt; Albert B. Fall, Secretary of the Interior under Warren G. Harding.

Cabot, John (Giovanni Caboto) (c. 1450–1498)

An explorer of the New World, John Cabot represented England in his New World expeditions. He was born in Genoa, Italy, but later settled in Venice (c. 1461) and acquired Venetian citizenship in 1476. He worked for a Venetian mercantile firm and traveled throughout the Mediterranean. Notably, Cabot visited Mecca, then a leading trade center. On the basis of these experiences, he became convinced that it was possible to find a water route to the East Indies, a conclusion that he reached apparently without being aware of the plans of Christopher Columbus.

His efforts to garner royal patronage brought him to England in 1484. His exact activities over the next years are unclear, but it is considered probable that he spent his time seeking royal support in Spain and Portugal. In 1496, however, he won the support of King Henry VII of England, who issued him a patent to embark upon a voyage of discovery and to enjoy a monopoly over the trade that might be established there. After an abortive attempt in 1496, Cabot set sail in May 1497 in the small ship *Matthew*, five years after Columbus's voyage.

His expedition reached Newfoundland or possibly Cape Breton on June 24, 1497. After unfurling the English and Venetian flags, he sailed along the coast from approximately Nova Scotia to Newfoundland, naming various islands and locations. He then returned to England, convinced that he had, in fact, reached the Orient.

Cabot set out again with five ships the following year, in search of Japan, after receiving a royal gift of ten pounds and a royal pension of twenty pounds, as well as a royal patent for a second expedition. Reaching North America, he sailed along the eastern coast. His voyage brought him perhaps as far south as the Chesapeake Bay. Cabot returned to England and was intending to set out on another voyage, but he died, apparently in late 1498. It is possible, on the basis of at least one contemporary record, that he died at sea. His second son, Sebastian, accompanied his father on both of his trips and later headed his own expedition. Through the efforts of John Cabot, England was able to make a claim to much of North America.

John Cabot's son, Sebastian Cabot

Cabrillo, Estévan (unknown–January 3, 1543)

A Portugese explorer, Estévan Cabrillo is best known for his voyage along the California and Oregon coasts. Cabrillo's early life is not well documented. In 1542, however, he was in the ser-

vice of Spain and was named the commander of several ships dispatched by the Viceroy Mendoza to explore the coast of western Mexico. Cabrillo sailed from Navidad and discovered the island of Santa Catalina, the Santa Barbara channel, Monterey, Cape Mendocino, and the Oregon coast. He reached as far north as latitude 43° before turning back, owing to an outbreak of scurvy among the crew. Cabrillo was noted for his kind treatment of Native Americans. He died on the island of San Bernardo. Although few details of his life are extant, he is ranked as one of the most significant explorers of the western coast of North America.

Cabrini, St. Frances Xavier (July 15, 1850–December 22, 1917)

The first American citizen to be canonized, St. Frances Xavier Cabrini was born in San Angelo, Lombardy, Italy, the youngest of thirteen children and frail at birth. Hearing a missionary's sermon about China when she was thirteen, she began to long for such a vocation. St. Frances Cabrini was educated as a teacher by the Daughters of the Sacred Heart at Arluno and taught in a village school, taking care of the area poor.

For six years she worked in the House of the Providence and was then asked by the bishop of Lodi to consider founding a religious congregation. She opened the Missionary Sisters of the Sacred Heart, taking the name Frances Xavier. Using an abandoned Franciscan monastery, St. Frances Cabrini began to accept young women to the new congregation. She was also inspired to open a house in Rome. Cardinal Lucido Parocchi received her in Rome and gave her not only permission for one foundation but a mandate for a second house.

In 1889 St. Frances Cabrini was asked to visit Pope Leo XIII, who had been watching her and her sisters, and the Holy Father asked her to become a missionary to America. Despite her dread of water, she set sail with foundation companions in March

1889, landing in New York on the last day of the month. Nothing that had been promised in New York was available, and the archbishop informed her that the original project, an orphanage, had been abandoned.

St. Frances Cabrini stayed only three months, but in that short time she opened the planned orphanage and a school. She returned to Italy for personnel and funding and began her American apostolate. In her labors she made foundations in eight American cities and opened houses in Central and South America as well. She became

St. Frances Cabrini

a naturalized American citizen in 1909. Her focus was on the sprawling slums of the United States, and she started clinics, schools, hospitals, and care institutions wherever they were needed. She labored in Illinois, California, Colorado, Louisiana, Mississippi, New Jersey, Pennsylvania, and Washington. At her death she had sixty-seven communities and convents, as well as foundations in Chile, Argentina, and Nicaragua. She also aided victims of yellow fever epidemics.

St. Frances Cabrini died in Columbus Hospital in Chicago, mourned by thousands of Americans, and her cause was opened about a decade later. She was beatified in 1938 and canonized on June 7, 1946. Pope Pius XII declared St. Frances Cabrini the "Patroness of the Immigrants" in 1950.

Cacciavillan, Agostino (August 14, 1926–)

The second papal nuncio to the United States, serving from 1991 to 1998, Agostino Cacciavillan was created a cardinal in 2001. He was born in Novale de Valdagno, Vicenza, Italy. He studied for the priesthood at the seminary of Vicenza and was ordained on June 26, 1949. After pastoral assignments, Father Cacciavillan was sent to graduate institutions and earned a licentiate in social sciences from the Pontifical Gregorian University in Rome, a doctorate in jurisprudence from the State University of Rome, and a doctorate in canon law from the Pontifical Lateran University in Rome. He then attended the course at the Pontifical Ecclesiastical

Academy, the school for training Vatican diplomats.

He worked for several months at the Secretariat of State in Rome and held a variety of posts in nunciatures in the Philippines (1960–64), Spain (1964–68), and Portugal (1968). From 1969 to 1974, he worked again in the Secretariat of State and was named a prelate of honor in 1973.

On January 17, 1976, then Monsignor Cacciavillan was appointed titular archbishop of Amiterno, pro-nuncio in Kenya, and apostolic delegate in the Seychelles. He was then named nuncio in India in 1981 and the first pro-nuncio in Nepal in 1985.

On June 13, 1990, Archbishop Cacciavillan was appointed pro-nuncio to the United States, a permanent observer before the Organization of American States, and the representative of the Holy See before the World Association of Jurists. As the nuncio to the United States, the archbishop presided over the relationship between the Holy See and the administrations of Presidents George H. W. Bush and Bill Clinton. He also served as the representative of the Holy See in the appointment of bishops across the United States and thus helped to shape the episcopate for years to come.

On November 5, 1998, Archbishop Cacciavillan was named president of the Administration of the Patrimony of the Apostolic See. In that capacity, he attended the Special Assembly for Europe of the World Synod of Bishops at Vatican City in October 1999. On February 21, 2001, he was elevated to the College of Cardinals as a cardinal deacon, with the titular church of Santi Angeli Custodi a Città Giardino. Cardinal Cacciavillan resigned the presidency of the patrimony on October 1, 2002, but continued to hold a variety of consultative posts in the Roman Curia.

Cadillac, Antoine (March 5, 1658–October 16, 1730)

A French explorer, Antoine Cadillac was the founder of the city of Detroit. He was born in Toulouse, France, the son of a member of the French Parliament and a minor nobleman. Entering the military at the age of sixteen, Cadillac was sent to Acadia as a lieutenant in 1683 for service in the Port Royal garrison, Nova Scotia. He participated in the unsuccessful Caffinière expedition and subsequently lost his own land holdings in Maine. His return to France in 1687 was thus under a financial cloud.

In 1691, however, the king sent him back to Canada, where he made himself indispensable to the Comte de Frontenac, the governor of New France. The governor named him commandant of Mackinac in 1694, and Cadillac proved adroit in his relations with the local tribes of Native Americans. He also attempted to profit from the illegal trade in goods and brandy and found himself in a disagreement with the Jesuits, who resisted his activities.

Returning to Québec in 1697, he wrote a suggestion to the crown that a fort be constructed at the head of Lake Erie to secure the line of fortifications that extended along the western line of New France and to circumvent the expansion of English fur trading. Receiving a favorable reply from the royal court, Cadillac erected Pont Chartrain in June 1701, thereby founding the city of Detroit. He built a church on the site, encouraged colonists, and invited the Franciscan Recollects (rather than the Jesuits) to minister to the local community and to support evangelization among the native tribes.

Cadillac had long-term plans to establish Detroit as a marquisat (or noble holding) for his family, and the receipt of a trade monopoly only expanded his potential wealth, as he had virtually absolute control over the growing city. The merchants of Montréal defeated Cadillac's ambitions, however, and he faced the objections of the governor, who feared the expansion of Cadillac's power at the expense of his own.

Recalled to France in 1710, Cadillac was removed from Detroit and named governor of Louisiana, assuming his duties in 1712. As governor, he once again sought to profit from local trade and was removed in 1716 and sentenced to the Bastille. Released in 1718, he eventually settled in Provence, France. Acknowledged as a significant figure in the formation of Detroit, he emerged as a potentially powerful figure in New France but was undermined by his own ambitious schemes.

Cagney, James (July 17, 1899–March 30, 1986)

An immensely popular American actor, James Cagney was ranked with Clark Gable, Gary Cooper, and Spencer Tracy as one of Hollywood's leading men. He was born in Yonkers, New York, and grew up in a Jewish neighborhood, where he was raised speaking Yiddish. His first job in the entertainment business was as a female dancer in a chorus line. He went on from there, however, to star in a host of films in a career that spanned sixty years. After retirement, Cagney came back to the studio to star in the 1981 screen adaptation of E. L. Doctorow's novel *Ragtime*. He was most famous for his tough-guy roles, including performances as gangsters in the 1930s and 1940s. Cagney earned his only Academy Award for his role as George M. Cohan in the film *Yankee Doodle Dandy*. In 1974 he was awarded the American Film Institute Life Achievement Award and was pictured on a thirty-three-cent U.S. commemorative postage stamp in the Legends of Hollywood series. He married Frances Vernon in 1922 and remained with her until his death; their marriage was a legend in Hollywood.

Cahensly, Simon Peter (October 28, 1838– December 25, 1923)

German businessman and social reformer Simon Cahensly became one of the most well-known leaders of German immigrants in the United States. Born in Limburg, Germany, he became highly successful through the grocery business he inherited. In 1861, however, he visited Le Havre, France, and was stunned by the deplorable conditions facing emigrants setting out for the United States. They were regularly mistreated by hotel owners, innkeepers, unscrupulous agents, and officials, and robbed of the money they would desperately need in America.

Convinced that he had to do something to assist them, Cahensly worked from 1872 with Father Lambert Rothmann to found the St. Raphael's Society for the Protection of Immigrants. The society's primary goals were to assist emigrants in the period just before they set sail from Europe, care for them during the often arduous voyage, and help once they arrived in the United States and other foreign lands that were at times most unwelcoming.

Cahensly traveled to the United States in 1883 to start the American branch of the St. Raphael's Society. He claimed that perhaps as many as five million Catholics had been lost to the Catholic faith because of the neglect of Catholics in the United States. He felt especially that clergy there were not doing enough to care for German Catholics. To correct this perceived deficiency, the board of directors of the European St. Raphael's Society gathered in 1890 at Lucerne, Switzerland, and endorsed a memorial that was presented to Pope Leo XIII in April 1891. The Lucerne Memorial, as it was named, implored the Holy See to appoint bishops who would better represent the peoples of differing national origins and languages in the United States. Moreover, it requested that national churches be established and staffed by priests who spoke the language of immigrant peoples and had a greater sensitivity to their pastoral needs. The campaign to implement this set of reforms became known as Cahenslyism.

The Lucerne Memorial was resisted strongly by many in the United States, especially among the hierarchy. Cardinal James Gibbons and Archbishop John Ireland declared it a European attempt to meddle in the life of the Church in America and to "Germanize" the Catholic Church in the United States. Pope Leo XIII declined to act upon the recommendations of the Lucerne Memorial, although the call for this reform remained for many years a source of tension among the various ethnic nationalities. It was likewise a factor in the controversy surrounding assimilation and "Americanization." (*See also* German Catholics.)

Cahill, T. Joe (August 7, 1877– August 18, 1964)

A generous Catholic philanthropist, T. Joe Cahill was made a Knight of St. Gregory. He was born in a supply depot in the Wyoming Territory and grew up in Cheyenne. He was raised Catholic and spent years serving as an altar boy in the first church in the area, St. John the Baptist. After a rugged early life that included work as a horse wrangler and sheriff, Cahill became dedicated to building the Church in Wyoming and assisting St. Joseph's Orphanage in Torrington. In 1946 Pope Pius XII recognized his many philanthropic efforts by naming him a Knight of St. Gregory.

Calasanctus Vives y Tuto, Felix James Joseph Francis (February 15, 1854–September 17, 1913)

A cardinal and Franciscan Capuchin, Calasanctus Vives Y Tuto served in the American missions. He was born in Lleyancas, Spain, and was educated there. In 1869 he joined a group of young men and sailed to Guatemala, where he was accepted into the Capuchin order. He made his first vows in 1870 and soon had to leave Guatemala when the order was expelled. Santa Clara Mission in California welcomed the Capuchins, and there he made his perpetual profession in 1872, and was then transferred to Milwaukee. In that same year, he sailed to Europe and continued his priestly studies, and he was ordained in Toulouse, France, on May 26, 1877.

He did not return to the United States. He was assigned to Capuchin roles in Europe and then elected definitor general of the Capuchin order in 1896. Three years later Pope Leo XIII created him a cardinal deacon. In 1908 he became prefect of the Sacred Congregation of Religious, serving Pope St. Pius X. He was also St. Pius X's confessor. Cardinal Calasanctus Vives y Tuto was buried in Rome.

Califano, Joseph. *See* Cabinets, Catholics in Presidential

California

Called the Golden State, California entered the Union in 1850 as the thirty-first state. It is located on the western shore of the United States, bounded on the north by Oregon, on the east by Nevada and Arizona, on the south by Mexico, and on the west by the Pacific Ocean. The third largest

Cardinal Felix Calasanctus Vives y Tuto

state in the Union, California has many principal land areas: the Cascade Range and the Klamath Mountains in the north, the Sierra Nevada Mountains and the Central Valley in the central region, the Los Angeles Ranges in the southwest, the Great Basin in the east, the Coast Ranges in the west, and Lassen Peak in the Cascades. California also has an active volcano. The original inhabitants of the state were the Hupa, Maida, Modoc, Mohave, Pomo, and Yuma tribes.

The history of the state is profoundly steeped in the Catholic faith, and the state was an area of active exploration in the early eras. In 1542 Juan Rodriguez Cabrillo explored the coast of California, entering San Diego Bay. Sir Francis Drake claimed the entire California territory for England in 1579, calling it New Albion, but the Spanish, eager to mount their own exploratory ventures, ignored Drake's claims.

In 1602 Sebastian Vizcaino led such an expedition, accompanied by the Carmelite priests Fathers Antonio of the Ascension, Andrew of the Assumption, and Thomas of Aquinas. Mass was celebrated in San Diego, then called San Miguel, and the expedition went north to Monterey, which they named Carmelo.

Eighty years later, Jesuit Father Eusebius Kino, the revered "Horseback Missionary" of the Southwest, charted Lower California. Jesuits founded missions in the area, but were exiled in 1760, when the Society of Jesus was suppressed. The Franciscans of Mexico assumed the mission territory with extraordinary vigor as a result. By 1769 a fort was erected in San Diego by Gaspar de Portolá.

Blessed Junípero Serra and countless Franciscans established a chain of missions on the "Camino Real," or Royal Road, in California. These missions flourished as economic and social changes took place in the region. In 1821 Mexico gained its independence from Spain and claimed California. As a result, Russian fur traders who had pioneered their industry in the area withdrew from the scene. In 1833 the Mexican government secularized the missions and banished the priests. Mexican President Antonio López de Santa Anna also took control of the Pious Fund of the Californias, a historical monetary base for mission efforts.

There were Americans in Stockton, however,

and they began a military and legal campaign to rid California of Mexican control. By May 1846 the campaign had evolved into the Mexican-American War. Two years later, the Treaty of Guadalupe-Hidalgo assigned California to the United States. In that same year, gold was found at Sutter's Mill, and Americans came to the area using every means of transportation available. California entered the Union in 1850.

The Diocese of the Two Californias, both Baja and Alta regions, had been established ten years earlier, on April 27, 1840, by Pope Gregory XVI. Francisco Garcia Diego y Moreno, a Franciscan, was consecrated for the diocese on October 4, 1840. He established his diocesan headquarters at Santa Barbara, opening a seminary there in 1846, the year he died. The seminary was later moved to Santa Ines. The Treaty of Guadalupe-Hidalgo made this diocese impractical, and the influx of Americans and events spurred development in other areas of the state. Pope Blessed Pius IX created the Diocese of Monterey-Los Angeles in 1850, and Dominican Joseph Sadoc Alemany was consecrated as the new bishop. Arriving in San Francisco in December 1850, he labored both in San Francisco and Monterey for three years but was then appointed to the newly created Archdiocese of San Francisco by the Holy See on July 29, 1853.

The Diocese of Monterey-Los Angeles extended south from Gilroy to the Mexican border, and the Vincentian Thaddeus Amat was consecrated bishop for that episcopal jurisdiction. In 1859 the Holy See allowed Bishop Amat to move his residence to Los Angeles. The Sacramento diocese was created in 1886, followed by the arrival of new waves of settlers, who rode on the transcontinental railroads.

The terrible earthquake of 1906 destroyed vast sections of San Francisco, but the people rebuilt structures, services, and facilities. Los Angeles was separated from the Monterey diocese and was becoming a vast metropolis in 1922. Thus two metropolitan sees emerged in California. The Province of San Francisco would include the dioceses of Oakland, Sacramento, San Jose, Santa Rosa, and Stockton as suffragan sees. The Province of Los Angeles would include the suffragan sees of Fresno, Monterey, Orange, San Bernadino, and San Diego.

World War I, followed by the Great Depression,

impacted on California, as new settlers migrated from drought-stricken parts of the nation to the coastal state. With the start of World War II, Californians lived with the possibility of Japanese attacks on their shores. San Diego became a major naval base, and aerospace industries opened. Between 1941 and 1961, the population of California more than doubled.

For Catholics, a parochial school system was a major priority, and dioceses all across the state had to erect parishes and charitable agencies. Los Angeles and San Francisco witnessed a surge in vocations, and their seminaries were full. Educational facilities in the dioceses were also at peak attendance, the result of the GI Bill following World War II.

After the Second Vatican Council, the Church in California, as elsewhere in the United States, suffered losses in vocations to the priesthood and the religious life. California dioceses also had significant lay ministry programs and evangelical apostolates.

The new dioceses, the erection of Mission Dolores in San Francisco, and the rank of cardinal bestowed upon Archbishop James F. McIntyre in Los Angeles were clear signs of the vitality of the Church in the Golden State. Catholics in California were also of diverse backgrounds and heritages, with a heavy Latino population and a growing population of Pacific Islanders and Asians. California has the largest Vietnamese population outside of Vietnam. There are also enclaves of Koreans and Filipinos. The Latino presence in California's Catholic dioceses is one of the most significant in the United States, and the bishops of the state have focused many pastoral initiatives for their care and education. In 2011 Archbishop José H. Gomez became the first Latino archbishop of Los Angeles.

The California dioceses were especially hard hit by the sexual abuse crisis and the legal settlements that stemmed from literally hundreds of lawsuits. From settlements dating to 2005 and beyond, several dioceses collectively paid out approximately $1 billion, most notably the Archdiocese of Los Angeles. In 2006 the archdiocese paid $60 million to settle 60 cases and in 2007 $660 million to settle more than 500 cases. That same year, the Diocese of San Diego paid $198 million to settle 144 cases;

the diocese was forced to file for Chapter 11 bankruptcy protection soon after. In 2011 there were 11.3 million Catholics, served by 3,600 priests, more than 4,700 men and women religious, and 1,075 parishes in the state.

California Missions

The great chain of California missions that stand today on the "Camino Real," or Royal Road, that stretches from north to south, are relics of unprecedented Catholic devotion and dedication to service in that part of the nation. The history of these repositories of faith opens in 1602, when the Carmelite Father Antonio of the Ascension celebrated Mass in San Diego while accompanying an exploratory expedition. San Diego was called San Miguel by the Spanish during this period.

Two years later, Jesuit Father Hyacinth Cortés was visiting Native Americans in the area, but no recorded settlement was established. The Jesuits did start a mission in San Dionisio Bay in October 1697. Jesuit Father Juan Maria Salvatierra founded a community of faith, and Jesuit Father Wenceslaus Link was exploring the region, using maps drawn by the famed missionary Jesuit Father Eusebius Kino.

Jesuit Fathers Victorian Arnes and Juan José Diez founded Nuestra Senora de Loreto (Our Lady of Loreto) around 1699. This small haven of the faith faced north and was the beginning of a great evangelizing effort. Others followed: San Francisco Xavier (1699), San Juan de Ligné (1705), Santa Rosalia de Malegé (1705), San José de Comundú (1708), La Purisima Concepción de Cadegomó (1718), Nuestra Senora del Pilar (1720), Nuestra Senora de Guadalupe (1720), Santiago de las Coras (1721), San Ignacio (1728), San José del Cabo (1730), Santa Rosa or Todos Los Santos (1733), San Luis Gonzaga (1737), Santa Gertrudis (1757), San Francisco de Borja (1759), and Santa Maria de los Angeles (1766).

The Jesuits, who had sacrificed so much in establishing their outposts of the Church were not able to continue their labors. In 1768 King Carlos III of Spain, who had long been an enemy of the Society of Jesus, recalled the Jesuits. They were chained, beaten, and taken back to Spain without recourse or mercy.

The Holy See then asked the Franciscans of the Apostolic College of San Fernando in Mexico City to assume the mission apostolate in California. In 1769 Blessed Junípero Serra led a group into the area, and within a short time about 145 Franciscans were laboring in the missions. The Franciscans established Mission San Diego (1769); Missions San Carlos, Monterey, and Carmel (1770); Missions San Antonio and San Gabriel (1771); Mission San Luis Obispo (1772); Missions San Francisco and San Juan Capistrano (1776); Mission Santa Clara (1777); Mission San Buenaventura (1782);

San Luis Rey Mission

Mission Santa Barbara (1786); Mission Purisima Concepción (1787); Missions Santa Cruz, Soledad (1791); Missions San José, San Juan Bautista, San Miguel, and San Fernando (1797); Mission San Luis Rey (1798); Mission Santa Inés (1804); Mission San Rafael (1817); and Mission San Francisco Solano (1823).

These vast spiritual communities operated under the complex system called *Bajo la Campana*, "under the bell," the mission arrangements also used in Texas. Blessed Junípero Serra and his priest companions knew that the Spanish authorities, military and civil officers, and wealthy landowners no longer followed the mandates given by Pope Paul III and Emperor Charles V of Spain concerning the Native Americans. The Spanish had a long and dark history of abusing Native Americans after their conquests, and the Franciscans had no intention of allowing such practices to be maintained within their jurisdictions. The missions were built therefore to provide a protective shield that kept the military, civil, and wealthy Spanish at bay. The terrible Pueblo uprising in New Mexico was not forgotten.

At the same time, the Franciscans were products of their own era, and they were not able to comprehend or appreciate fully the Native American traditions and values. The missions were designed as schools of civilization, in the hope that by educating the American Indians in European ways the priests could provide them with advantages for the future. The missions were secularized by the Mexican government in 1833, and the Pious Fund for the californias that had sustained many of the enclaves was taken away. In 1833 the northern missions were administered by the Franciscans of the Apostolic College of Our Lady of Guadalupe at Zacatecas. Bishop Francisco Garcia Diego y Moreno, O.F.M., was the first bishop of California. Others, such as Archbishop Joseph Sadoc

San Gabriel Mission

Alemany, would arrive on the scene and regularize the missions and the Pious Fund.

Callan, Charles J. (December 5, 1877–February 26, 1962)

A Dominican priest and noted theologian and biblical scholar, Charles Jerome Callan is best known for his literary labors with his long-time friend, colleague, and fellow Dominican Father John McHugh. Father Callan was born in Lockport, New York, and entered the Dominican novitiate in 1899. During his formation, he met and quickly became a friend of John McHugh. Both were ordained in 1905, and Father Callan was sent to Fribourg, Switzerland, for additional studies; there he earned an advanced degree in sacred theology in 1907.

Returning to the United States, he was assigned in 1909 to the faculty of the Dominican house of studies in Washington, D.C., the same school at which Father McHugh was teaching. Both priests were assigned to the parish of the Holy Rosary in Hawthorne, New York, in 1915, exchanging the title of pastor over the next years. They both also took up teaching posts at the Maryknoll seminary and began their long and remarkably prolific careers in writing.

In 1916 they assumed the post of joint editors of the *Homiletic and Pastoral Review*. They went on to collaborate on over thirty books, and both received the prestigious titles of master of sacred theology. Their most famous works included the four-volume *Parochial Course of Doctrinal Instruction* (1920), the two-volume *Moral Theology* (1930), a new translation of *The Catholic Missal* (1936), and a host of devotional and liturgical works. Noted biblical scholars, they completed the editing of Father Francis Spencer's translation of the New Testament from Greek and took part in the translation of the Vulgate into English that had been authorized by the American bishops in 1935. Callan was appointed in 1940 as a consultor to the Pontifical Biblical Commission by Pope Pius XII; he was the first native-born American to receive this prestigious honor.

After Father McHugh's passing in 1950, Father Callan continued on as editor of the *Homiletic and Pastoral Review* for another seven years. He retired from teaching in 1954 and stepped down as editor in 1957 because of health problems. He died at Milford, Connecticut, but at his request he was buried, like Father McHugh, at Maryknoll.

Calvert Family

One of the most prominent Catholic families during the British Colonial period in America, serving in the seventeenth and eighteenth centuries, the Calverts founded the colony of Maryland and oversaw its progress despite political and religious turmoil. Mostly Catholic, the Calverts pioneered freedom of religion in a period in which Catholics were abused and punished for the faith both in England and in the New World. The members of the Calvert family were:

Calvert, Cecilius (1606–1675). The second Lord Baltimore and the founder of Maryland, he was born in England as the heir of George Calvert, the first Lord Baltimore. He was educated at Trinity College, Oxford, and in 1629 married Anne Arundell of Wardour. When George Calvert died in 1632, the charter of Maryland was given to Cecilius, who became Absolute Lord of Maryland and Avalon (an earlier plantation owned by his father).

Unable to go to Maryland, Cecilius sent his brothers, Leonard and George, there to represent him. Despite Protestant protests, the Calverts set sail in November 1633, intent on establishing religious toleration. Cecilius spent forty thousand pounds outfitting this expedition, which included twenty gentlemen colonists and three hundred laborers. Cecilius never sailed to Maryland, but his battles against Protestant influences secured religious freedom for his colony. When the Virginia Company overthrew his control, Cecilius had it restored.

His disputes with the Society of Jesus were unfortunate, as Jesuits were in the first expedition to Maryland. Refusing to yield to Jesuit demands for exemption of their personnel from taxa-

Cecilius Calvert

tion and military service, Cecilius appealed to the Propaganda in Rome and received Dom Rosetti, titular archbishop of Tarsus, and two secular priests to serve Maryland. Cecilius ruled the colony in Maryland for over four decades from afar, dying in England.

Calvert, Charles (1629–February 20, 1715). The third Lord Baltimore and the second Proprietary Governor of Maryland was born in London, the son of Cecilius. Charles served as Proprietary Governor from 1661 to 1684 and as Lord Proprietor from 1675 to 1691. He married Jane Sewell of Maryland.

Charles survived many land and religious disputes with his Protestant neighbors but maintained religious freedom in the colony. He lived in Maryland but visited England from 1676 to 1680. The accession of William and Mary to the throne of England deprived Charles of all rights in 1691, and he left the colony. He died in Epsom, Surrey, England.

Calvert, George (1580–April 15, 1632). The first Lord Baltimore, a colonial visionary, was born in Kipling, Yorkshire, England. Educated at Oxford, he married and entered the service of the secretary of state, Lord Robert Cecil. Charles also held various provisional posts and was elected to Parliament, becoming a trusted favorite of King James I. In 1617 he received knighthood, and he

Charles Calvert

became a Catholic in 1624. The king did not punish him for this but elevated him to the Irish peerage as Baron Baltimore of Baltimore in County Longford.

Calvert purchased a plantation called Avalon, in 1620, in Newfoundland. In 1627 he and his family sailed to Newfoundland. A year later, he requested a grant of land in a warmer region and received it from King Charles. This grant brought him

into conflict with Virginia Company Protestants, so he sought another grant in the modern-day area of Maryland. He died in London before receiving this charter.

Lord Baltimore served as a conciliator and representative of the monarchs of England, but he was staunchly faithful to the Church after his conversion. The monarchs, respecting him, put aside the usual oaths against the Church in order to maintain his services. His vision of a colony in America where all citizens might worship freely would impact greatly upon Catholics and provide the cradle of Catholicism in the United States.

George Calvert

Calvert, Leonard (1607–June 9, 1647). The Proprietary Governor of Maryland and the second son of George Calvert, the first Lord Baltimore, Leonard was born in England. In 1629 he led an expedition to Newfoundland to aid the colony of Avalon. In 1633 Leonard was sent to Maryland, landing in America in February 1634.

On March 27, Leonard had his settlers land their two vessels, the *Ark* and the *Dove*, on St. Mary's, an island inhabited by welcoming Indians. In 1643 he returned to England, but again sailing to Maryland found himself driven out of his possessions by Protestants. Three years later, Leonard reclaimed St. Mary's and then Kent Island. He died in Maryland, and in 1890 the state of Maryland erected a monument to Leonard and his wife at St. Mary's. Leonard reportedly was a convert to Protestantism.

Calvert, Philip (1626–December 22, 1682) Proprietary Governor of Maryland, 1660 to 1661, Philip was the son of George Calvert, first Lord Baltimore, and his second wife, Arabella. He came to Maryland on the first expedition under Leonard Calvert. In 1656 he was made secretary of the province and one of its consultants. After the treason and overthrow of Governor Fendall, Calvert became governor in 1660, and displayed clemency in pardoning Fendall. In 1661 Charles Calvert was made governor, and Philip was appointed deputy-lieutenant and councilor of the province. He later negotiated a treaty with the Dutch in which they agreed to abandon disputed territory on the Delaware River. He was one of a committee that negotiated a treaty with the Indians and part of a commission that settled a boundary line between Maryland and Virginia with the Virginia authorities.

Campbell, James (September 1, 1812–January 27, 1893)

Postmaster General from 1853 to 1857, James Campbell was an active Catholic judicial figure in Pennsylvania. He was born in Philadelphia to Irish parents. After becoming a lawyer in 1833, he held various posts in the city, including being a member of the Board of Education, judge of the Court of Common Pleas, and other judicial appointments. Nominated to the State Supreme Court, he was defeated in the attempt owing to the hostile reaction of Pennsylvania anti-Catholics and supporters of the Know-Nothings. Governor William Bigler then appointed him Attorney General of Pennsylvania. He served until 1853, when he was nominated to President Franklin Pierce's cabinet as Postmaster General, serving until March 1857.

In 1861 Campbell ran against Charles R. Buckalew for the United States Senate but was defeated by a single vote. In 1873 he was elected a member of the Constitutional Convention of Pennsylvania, but declined to serve for reasons of poor health. In addition to his political and judicial activities, Campbell was vice president of St. Joseph's Orphan Asylum, the oldest Catholic asylum in the United States, chartered in 1807. He served in this capacity for forty-five years.

Cambray-Digny, Louis Antoine Jean Baptiste (1751–1822)

A lieutenant in the Continental Army of the American Revolution, Louis Antoine Jean Baptiste Cambray-Digny arrived in the colonies in 1778 to assist the cause as part of the French military forces allied with the Americans. Stationed at Monmouth, New Jersey, Cambray-Digny assisted the Corps of Engineers there until October 20, 1778, when he was

assigned to Charleston and then Pittsburgh. There he directed the construction of Fort McIntosh as an adviser. In February 1779, Congress sent him to Baltimore and then to Edenton, North Carolina. Cambray-Digny was captured on this campaign on May 12, 1780, but he was exchanged for a British prisoner. He took leave to France but returned to the American forces in 1784, where he was breveted a colonel. At the war's end, he returned to France, bearing the gratitude of the American people.

Camden, Diocese of

Established on December 9, 1937, by Pope Pius XI, the Diocese of Camden serves the southernmost counties of the state of New Jersey. In 1681 present-day Camden was the site of a homestead built by William Cooper and called Pyne Point. In 1773 James Cooper laid out the town, naming it after Charles Pratt, the first Earl of Camden. During the Revolutionary War, Camden was often occupied by the British. After the war, it prospered from increased ferry routes and then the railroads. Various industries, including the Campbell Soup Company and the Victor Talking Machine Company, developed there over the decades, and Walt Whitman was an honored resident. The Diocese of Camden is a suffragan see of the Archdiocese of Newark and shares in the profound Catholic history of the region.

Early missionaries from Canada ministered to the American Indian settlements in the region, and even when the British claimed the area and outlawed Catholicism, Jesuit priests entered the colony of New Jersey to visit Catholic families. "Father Farmer," Ferdinand Steinmeyer, a Jesuit who is called the "Apostle of New Jersey," continued his missions throughout the state, despite the personal perils involved. He began laboring among the faithful in New Jersey in 1764.

The Catholics who served in the Revolutionary War displayed such courage and fortitude that New Jersey and other colonies provided them with long-denied civil rights under new state constitutions. As a result, parishes opened and began to flourish. Catholics in New Jersey were originally under the episcopal jurisdiction of the Diocese of Baltimore and then under the jurisdiction of New York. In 1853 the Holy See erected the Diocese of Newark (now the Archdiocese of Newark). The Cathedral of the Immaculate Conception in Camden dates as a parish to this era. Other parishes, such as St. Nicholas of Tolentine in Atlantic City, were established early in the area's history. Catholics continued to grow in population and to expand the Church's presence. The faithful joined the nation in the military efforts of World War I and endured the trials of the Great Depression

When the Diocese of Camden was established in 1937, Bartholomew Eustace was consecrated as the first bishop on March 25, 1938. He dedicated the diocese to the Blessed Virgin Mary. Bishop Eustace had to deal with anti-Catholic prejudice, diocesan debts, and a shortage of priests. He established thirty-one parishes and twenty-five missions to serve the increasing Catholic population, building churches, rectories, convents, high schools, elementary schools, and medical facilities, and also stabilizing the diocesan financial situation and recruiting priests and seminarians. He led the faithful through World War II, supporting the nation's military efforts. Bishop Eustace died on December 11, 1956.

The second bishop of Camden was Julian J. McCarthy, who had served as auxiliary bishop of the Archdiocese of Newark since 1954. Bishop McCarthy was appointed to Camden on January 27, 1957. He served the diocese just a few years, dying on December 26, 1959. During that time he worked tirelessly to institute educational programs and to expand diocesan facilities. He also established a Puerto Rican apostolate to assist the immigrant population of Camden.

The third bishop of Camden, Celestine J. Damiano, had served as the apostolic delegate to South Africa since 1953 and was appointed to the diocese on January 24, 1960. The Holy See conferred the personal rank of archbishop on him when he was appointed to Camden. Archbishop Damiano continued the programs of his predecessors and instituted the House of Charity, an outreach program. He attended the Second Vatican Council and implemented the reforms mandated by that council. Archbishop Damiano died on October 2, 1967.

His successor was Bishop George H. Guilfoyle, who had served as auxiliary bishop of New York since 1964. Bishop Guilfoyle was installed in Cam-

den on March 4, 1968. He continued to implement the reforms of the Second Vatican Council and instituted care services and a retreat program. He retired on May 22, 1989.

The fifth bishop of Camden was James T. McHugh, who had served the diocese as auxiliary bishop since 1987. Bishop McHugh reorganized the administrative offices of the diocese and established a Catholic Education Endowment Fund to aid schools and religious education programs. Opening a retirement home for priests, Bishop McHugh also started a fund for parishes. On December 7, 1998, he was appointed coadjutor bishop of Rockville Centre, acceding to the see in 2000 and dying on December 10 of that year.

The successor to Bishop McHugh was Nicholas A. DiMarzio, who had served as auxiliary bishop of Newark since 1996. Bishop DiMarzio was installed in Camden on July 22, 1999. Bishop DiMarzio confronted a variety of challenges faced by the diocese, starting with the swift growth of the Catholic population in South Jersey. He founded new parishes, and to assist the pastoral needs of the increasingly diverse Catholic population, he began several parishes for Hispanics and missions and apostolates for Korean, Vietnamese, Haitian, Filipino, and Polish Catholics.

Bishop DiMarzio also developed a pastoral plan for the care of the more than one hundred thousand Hispanics in the region. To improve Catholic education, the bishop established a scholarship fund for low-income families and started new elementary schools. Bishop DiMarzio also established the Vicariate for Human Services to coordinate diocesan activities. On August 1, 2003, Bishop DiMarzio was transferred to the Diocese of Brooklyn.

The seventh bishop of Camden, Joseph A. Galante, had served as coadjutor bishop of Dallas since 1999. Bishop Galante was appointed to Camden on March 23, 2004, and was installed on April 30, 2004. To nurture the pastoral life of the diocese, Bishop Galante began a series of "Speak Up Sessions" that involved an open consultation process with parishioners and the clergy and religious of the diocese. This then permitted an analysis of pastoral priorities for the coming years. In 2011 there were 500,000 Catholics, served by 297 priests, 295 women religious, and 113 parishes in the diocese.

Cana Conference Movement

An organization established in 1943, the Cana Conference is designed to educate couples on the sacramental vocation of marriage. The movement started as a series of "Family Renewal Days" conducted by Jesuit Father Edward John Delaney in New York. Jesuit Father Edward Dowling introduced the movement to St. Louis in 1944, and he coined the phrase "Cana Conference." This is a reference to Cana, the site of a marriage and Christ's first miracle (John 2:1–12). The organization functions as a resource for married couples, nurturing spiritual growth and maturity. Couples must attend sessions together, where they meet other families and are counseled by a priest-counselor. The conferences are held once or twice a year. Other social and spiritual events continue throughout the years to inspire married partners to higher levels of holiness. Benediction of the Blessed Sacrament, renewal of marriage vows, and devotions are part of Cana Conference gatherings. Pre-Cana Conferences have also been initiated to serve engaged couples. All are part of the Christian Family Movement.

Canada, Church in

Canada, called New France in the early eras, provided the United States with decades of Catholic missions, heroic evangelizers, and spiritual guides. Canada itself has a profound Catholic heritage. The history of the Church in Canada traditionally dates to July 7, 1534, when a priest in the exploration force under Jacques Cartier said Mass on the Gaspé Peninsula. From this humble beginning, there followed some sixty years of relative inactivity, with no formal colonization commencing until 1603, when Samuel de Champlain sailed up the St. Lawrence River and established the first French settlement in North America at Port Royal in Nova Scotia. In 1608 Québec

was begun and henceforth two objectives were the focus of the French: the fur trade and the planting of the Catholic faith among the native inhabitants. The first missionaries, Franciscan Recollects who had accompanied Champlain, arrived in 1615. They were succeeded in 1625 by the Jesuits, launching a period of genuinely heroic missionary activity as these priests, called the Black Robes by the Indians, set out for the interior and preached among such tribes as the Huron, Algonquins, and Iroquois.

The city of Montréal was established in 1642. The first two Jesuits, Sts. John de Brébeuf and Gabriel Lalemant, were both martyred; they were joined in death by others. Eight missionaries put to death in the period were canonized in 1930 as the North Amerian Martyrs. Sulpician priests, who arrived in Canada in 1657, played a part in the great missionary period that ended about 1700. One of the greatest treasures of this period of evangelization was Kateri Tekakwitha, the "Lily of the Mohawks," who was baptized in 1676 and died in 1680. She was declared blessed on June 22, 1980, by Pope John Paul II and was canonized on October 21, 2012, by Pope Benedict XVI.

As the value of Canada to France increased, Cardinal Richelieu encouraged more missionaries, including more Jesuits. The communities of women religious kept pace with the priestly efforts, as heroic nuns served in the cities and in outposts. The oldest communities of religious women in Canada are the Canonesses of St. Augustine and the Ursulines, who began their missions in 1639; and the Hospitallers of St. Joseph, who have served since 1642. Communities of religious women of Canadian origin are the Congregation of Notre Dame, founded by St. Marguerite Bourgeoys in 1658, and the Grey Nuns, formed by St. Marie Marguerite d'Youville in 1737. Mother Marie (Guyard) of the Incarnation, an Ursuline nun, was one of the first three women missionaries to New France and is called the "Mother of the Church in Canada." She was declared blessed on June 22, 1980. Formal ecclesiastical organi-

Blessed Francois de Montmorency Laval

zation of Catholic affairs began with the appointment in 1658 of Blessed François de Montmorency Laval, the "Father of the Church in Canada." Appointed vicar apostolic of New France, he was the first bishop of Québec from 1674 to 1688, with jurisdiction over all French-claimed territory in North America. Bishop Laval was declared blessed on June 22, 1980, by Pope Blessed John Paul II. Under his leadership and especially that of the Jesuits, New France became a strong Catholic colony, and its treatment of the natives was in sharp contrast to the English colonies and especially the Spanish possessions in Central and South America.

In 1713 the French Canadian population numbered eighteen thousand. In the same year, the Treaty of Utrecht ceded Acadia, Newfoundland, and the Hudson Bay Territory to England. The Acadians, maintaining neutrality in the rivalries between France and England, and steadfast in the Catholic faith, were exiled by English authorities and scattered among the American colonies in 1755. French Canada survived repeated attacks by the British, but the colony finally fell in 1759 with the capture of Québec in the Seven Years' War. By the terms of the Treaty of Paris in 1763, New France was ceded to Britain. The English thus acquired possession of Canada and its seventy thousand French-speaking inhabitants.

Catholics in the former French colony were understandably concerned about the British, who had already forcibly deported the French Catholic Acadians from Nova Scotia in 1755. By the Québec Act of 1774, however, Catholics were allowed to practice their religion, although the hierarchy was not recognized and in that year the Jesuits and Recollects were dispossessed. Additional pressures were brought to bear with the establishment of the Church

Count Louis de Buade Frontenac, Governor General of New France

of England, followed by Protestant denominations. In 1793 priests who had been exiled from France during the French Revolution were allowed into the country. This influx improved the state of Catholic affairs, and by the early 1800s the Church was again on the move.

In 1819 the British government permitted Bishop Octave Plessis to become archbishop of Québec. The first Council of Québec was held in 1851. The established Catholic school system enjoyed a period of growth, and Laval University was inaugurated in 1854 and canonically established in 1876. Other sees followed and, under Lord Elgin, governor-general from 1847 to 1854, the Acts of 1851 confirmed religious freedom and opened the way for new religious communities. The see of Montréal was begun in 1836, Toronto in 1841, and Ottawa in 1847. In western Canada, the vicariate apostolic was created in 1844. Three years later, Modeste Demers became bishop of Vancouver Island. The Confederation of Canada was born in 1867 with the British North American Act.

The fifteen years following the passage in 1840 of the Act of Union, which joined upper and lower Canada, were significant. New communities of men and women religious joined those already in the country. The Oblates of Mary Immaculate, missionaries par excellence in Canada, advanced the penetration of the West, which had been started in 1818 by Abbé Provencher. Archbishop Elzear-Alexandre Taschereau of Québec was named Canada's first cardinal in 1886. The apostolic delegation to Canada was set up in 1899, becoming a nunciature on October 16, 1969, with the establishment of diplomatic relations with the Vatican.

Early in this century, Canada had eight ecclesiastical provinces, 23 dioceses, three vicariates apostolic, 3,500 priests, 2 million

Catholics, about 30 communities of men religious, and 70 or more communities of women religious. The Church in Canada was removed from the status of a mission and from the jurisdiction of the Congregation for the Propagation of the Faith in 1908.

Currently, the greatest concentration of Catholics is in the eastern portion of the country. In the northern and western sections of the country, outside of the metropolitan centers, there are some of the most difficult parish and mission areas in the world, and missionary bishops have resorted to aerial forms of transportation to reach these remote regions.

Bilingual (English-French) differences in the general population are reflected in the Church as well; for example, in the parallel structures of the Canadian Conference of Catholic Bishops, which was established in 1943. Québec is the center of French cultural influence. Many language groups are represented among Catholics, who include more than 257,000 members of Eastern rites in one metropolitan see, seven eparchies, and an apostolic exarchate.

The education of children, which had long been a source of friction between the Catholic Church and the Canadian government, is now administered by the civil provinces in a variety of arrangements authorized by the Canadian Constitution. Thus denominational schools have tax support provided in one fashion in Québec and Newfoundland, and in another way in Alberta, Ontario, and Saskatchewan. Several provinces provide tax support only for public schools, making private financing necessary for separate church-related schools.

Currently there are nearly thirteen million Catholics in eighteen metropolitan sees (archdioceses), forty-five suffragan sees, eight Oriental-rite dioceses, one archdiocese, and three eparchies immediately subject to the Holy See, and the Military Ordinariate. Overall, Catholics comprise approximately 45 percent of the population.

The Church in Canada faces a variety of modern challenges, including declining vocations and Mass attendance, and an increasingly secular culture. The Canadian government also permits abortion on demand and recently passed a law permitting homosexual marriage as recognized by law. Pope Benedict XVI, in May 2006, urged the Catholic bishops of Canada to renew their efforts to promote family life.

Cáncer de Barbastro, Luis (c. 1510–June 26, 1547)

A Spanish Dominican missionary, Luis Cáncer de Barbastro is the protomartyr of Florida. He was born in Barbastro, Spain, although virtually nothing is known about his family or his upbringing. After entering the Dominican order, he was sent to the missions of the New World and soon found himself at severe odds with the Spanish colonial policy of enslaving the native Indians. He labored on the islands of Hispaniola (modern-day Haiti and Dominican Republic) and Puerto Rico and served in the monastery of Santiago in Guatemala. While at the monastery, he became a supporter of the effort of the Dominican Superior Father Bartolomé de las Casas to improve the plight of the Indians under Spanish control. With Father Las Casas, Father Cáncer de Barbastro believed that true evangelization was possible only by authentic charity and preaching rather than slavery.

To demonstrate his point, Father Cáncer de Barbastro set out in 1537 to the Guatemalan territory of Tuzulutlan, where local tribes had been resisting the Spanish colonial government so fiercely that the region had been renamed the "Land of War." Fathers Las Casas and Cáncer de Barbastro proposed to the local governor a rule to permit only Dominican missionaries into the territory for a period of five years. Through patience and zeal, Father Cáncer de Barbastro converted the chief of the local tribe and succeeded in having a church built. So successful was the experiment that the region was given a new name: *Vera Paz,* or "True Peace."

In 1546 Father Cáncer de Barbastro traveled to Mexico to assist Father Las Casas in appealing to the colonial government to change its harsh policy concerning the native peoples. Eager to demonstrate that the policy adopted by the Dominicans in *Vera Paz* could be applied throughout the New World, Father Cáncer de Barbastro journeyed to Spain and proposed to authorities that he be allowed to work toward the conversion of the Indian tribes of Florida.

Soon after his return to Mexico in 1549, he sailed for Florida with two other Dominicans and an interpreter, a native woman and convert named Magdalen. Once they reached the Florida shore near modern Tampa, however, Magdalen turned on the Dominicans and lured them to shore. Native tribesmen martyred Father Cáncer de Barbastro and his companions on June 26, 1549, the feast of Corpus Christi.

Canon Law Society of America

A professional association dedicated to promoting the study and application of canon law in the Church, the Canon Law Society of America was established in 1939 by a group of experts in canon law in Washington, D.C. The original purpose of the society was to create a professional association for fellow canonists, with activities focused on areas of concern to canonists, relevant to both the Latin and the Eastern Catholic Churches.

Since the Second Vatican Council, the society has been instrumental in the revitalization and proper application of ecclesiastical law. On February 13, 1981, it was incorporated as a nonprofit corporation in the District of Columbia. Of particular importance is the society's work in assisting canon lawyers in the wake of the promulgation of the *Code of Canon Law* in 1983 and the *Code of Canons of the Eastern Churches* in 1990. Approximately 1,500 men and women around the world are currently members.

Among its various significant publications have been the approved English translations of the *Code of Canon Law* (1983, revised 1999) and the *Code of Canons of the Eastern Churches* (1990), both with the permission of the Holy See, and the *New Commentary on the Code of Canon Law* (2000). The society also published *Canon Law Digest, CLSA Proceedings*, and *Roman Replies and CLSA Advisory Opinions*.

Cantwell, John J. (December 1, 1874–October 30, 1947)

The first archbishop of the Archdiocese of Los Angeles, John J. Cantwell had jurisdiction over a 90,000-square-mile diocese. He was born in Limerick, Ireland, to Patrick and Ellen O'Donnell, the first of fifteen children. He entered the seminary in 1892 with the intention of serving in the United States, specifically in the Archdiocese of

San Francisco. Ordained in 1899, Father Cantwell received a posting as curate in Berkeley, California. Aside from his regular duties as a young priest, he founded a Newman Club for the University of California and was appointed in 1904 to the position of secretary to Archbishop Patrick William Riordan. In 1914 he was named vicar general for the archdiocese.

Three years later, Pope Benedict XV appointed him the bishop of Monterey-Los Angeles. He was consecrated on December 5, 1917. Bishop Cantwell inherited from his predecessor, Bishop Thomas James Conaty, a sprawling diocese that encompassed virtually the whole of the southland in California. Facing a mounting administrative task, Bishop Cantwell petitioned the Holy See to divide the diocese.

In 1922 Pope Pius XI created the Diocese of Los Angeles-San Diego, an ecclesiastical territory that covered all the southland counties from Los Angeles to the Mexican border. In further recognition of the growth of the Los Angeles diocese and Southern California, on July 11, 1936, Pope Pius XI elevated the diocese to the status of an archdiocese, creating the second metropolitan district in California. Bishop Cantwell thus became the first archbishop of the Archdiocese of Los Angeles and subsequently served as shepherd for thirty years, the longest term of any bishop in the history of California. Among his many achievements were the creation of a minor and major seminary, more than two hundred churches, thirty-four high schools, forty-three elementary schools, and sixteen hospitals and clinics. By the time of his passing, the diocese had grown in its Catholic population from 178,000 in 1917 to over 600,000, despite the changes in ecclesiastical structure that had taken place during that time.

Another notable development was the commitment of Archbishop Cantwell to the needs, spiritual and material, of the expanding non-English-speaking population in Southern California. He was especially dedicated to the welfare of Spanish-speaking Catholics, establishing more than fifty parishes and missions for the Latino population. The archbishop also founded the Catholic Motion Picture Actors Guild in 1923, the basis for the later Legion of Decency.

Capital Punishment

The subject of state executions for certain criminal acts has long been a source of debate in the world, and this present age is no exception, as various attitudes and considerations have complicated the matter. The modern world organization, the United Nations, and various religious leaders have pronounced opinions and positions on capital punishment. One of the most powerful documents, the UN's Universal Declaration of Human Rights (1948), set forth general attitudes in the matter, echoing, in fact, the words of Pope John XXIII's *Pacem in Terris* (1963). Other pontiffs have added their own concerns to the debate, particularly Pope John Paul II, who called for recognition of human dignity under God throughout his pontificate.

In the United States, capital punishment has undergone considerable debate and has been the subject of legislation and court decisions. In 1972 the U.S. Supreme Court issued a ruling that called a halt to the death penalty because of obvious inequities in imposing sentences over the decades, particularly where racial discrimination was involved. A number of states and the federal government, defending their constitutional right to impose such measures, enacted legislation to enable them to restore capital punishment, and Catholic scholars and authorities began to state positions on the matter. In November 1974 the National Conference of Catholic Bishops stated their opposition to the death penalty. Two years later, they issued another pronouncement that cited the sovereignty of God over all human life and the obligation to provide rehabilitative measures to criminals. The pronouncement also clarified that human errors could lead to miscarriages of justice and spoke about the need for true reconciliation as a vital force in society.

The bishops declared themselves against capital punishment and urged Catholics to join in the debate and to support a ban on executions to be consistent with the Church's opposition to abortion and euthanasia. This American episcopal position was mirrored in March 1976 by a pronouncement from the Catholic Bishops of Canada, who passed a resolution favoring the abolition of the death penalty. The Canadian bishops also urged prison reform and critical analysis of the entire justice system of their nation.

Pope John Paul II's stand on the death penalty was even more lucid and persuasive. The Holy Father addressed the debate as "the problem of the death penalty" and made clear his concerns in his encyclical *Evangelium Vitae* (1995). The pope stated that he joined in the growing call for the end of death sentences, but he reminded the world that adequate punishment for crimes was necessary for social justice. At the same instant, he reminded the world, criminals needed help in rehabilitating themselves and experiencing personal changes. The penal systems in many nations thus required study, evaluation, and conformity to the ideals of rehabilitation and justice.

The *Catechism of the Catholic Church* quotes *Evangelium Vitae* verbatim, but it adds yet another dimension of penal justice, stating, "The traditional teaching of the Church does not exclude recourse to the death penalty, if this is the only possible way of effectively defending human lives against the unjust aggressor" (No. 2267).

In November 2000 the U.S. Conference of Catholic Bishops included in a statement on crime and criminal justice an appeal for all Americans to "join us in rethinking the difficult issue [of capital punishment] and committing ourselves to pursuing justice without vengeance. With our Holy Father we seek to build a society so committed to human life that it will not sanction the killing of any human person."

Capra, Frank (May 18, 1897–September 3, 1991)

An Academy Award–winning film director, Frank Capra provided Americans with warm, wholesome films that have become classics. He was born in Bisacquino, Sicily, Italy, the son of a fruit picker, and came to the United States at the age of six, traveling in steerage. After graduating from the California Institute of Technology with an engineering degree and after a period of service in the military, he journeyed to Hollywood and began his career as a gag writer for Hal Roach and Mack Sennett. He then worked as a writer and director for comedian Harry Langdon. After several years, he was hired by Columbia Studios and embarked upon his legendary work as a director. His early films included *The Younger Generation* (1929), *The Miracle Woman* (1931), *The Bitter Tea of General Yen*, and *American Madness* (both 1932).

Capra became one of the top directors with his comedy *Lady for a Day* (1933), followed by the immensely successful *It Happened One Night* (1934), which became the first film ever to win all five top Academy Awards, including Best Picture. He won two more Oscars over the next four years for *Mr. Deeds Goes to Town* (1936), and *You Can't Take It with You* (1938), his second Best Picture winner.

Capra's reputation as a filmmaker benefited from his own inimitable style, in particular his recurring theme of the "little guy" against the system. After his impressive film adaptation of *Lost Horizon* (1937), Capra made one of his most beloved masterpieces, *Mr. Smith Goes to Washington* (1939). He then departed Columbia for Warner Brothers. The new collaboration proved less successful than his time with Columbia, although his first two films were notable: *Meet John Doe* (1941) and *Arsenic and Old Lace* (made in 1941, but not released until 1944).

With the start of World War II, Capra volunteered his services to the government, making the celebrated documentary series *Why We Fight*. After the war, Capra founded Liberty Pictures with George Stevens and William Wyler. While its first film, *It's a Wonderful Life* (1946), eventually became one of the most popular films of all time, it was not well received in its initial release, and *State of the Union* (1948) suffered the same fate. The film company dissolved, and Capra never recaptured his previous success.

In 1971 Capra wrote his autobiography, *The Name Above the Title*, a delightful albeit rather inaccurate account of the movie industry. He also endured the anguish of knowing that *It's a Wonderful Life* had become a traditional Christmas favorite for television but had passed into the public domain, thus providing no royalties to the retired director. In 1982 he was awarded the American Film

Cardinal John Carberry

Institute Life Achievement Award. Two of his most famous maxims (of many) were: "Behind every successful man there stands an astonished woman" and "My advice to young film-makers is this: Don't follow trends. Start them!"

Capuchins. *See* **Franciscans**

Carberry, John Joseph (July 31, 1904–June 17, 1998)

The archbishop of St. Louis from 1968 to 1979, John Joseph Carberry was honored as the "Pastor of Pastors" and became a cardinal. He was born in Brooklyn, New York, the son of James and Mary Carberry, and began preparations for the priesthood at the Cathedral College of the Immaculate Conception, then studied in Rome at the North American College. His studies in Rome culminated in doctorates in philosophy and theology. He was ordained on July 28, 1929.

Father Carberry returned to the Diocese of Brooklyn, where he was assigned to pastoral work and served on the marriage tribunal. He was then sent to The Catholic University of America for additional studies, earning a doctorate in canon law in 1934. From 1935 to 1940, he served as assistant chancellor of the Diocese of Trenton and as secretary to the bishop. Over the next years he held a variety of positions, including director of the radio and television apostolate and president of the Canon Law Society of America from 1955 to 1956. He was named a monsignor in 1948.

On May 3, 1956, he was appointed coadjutor bishop of Lafayette in Indiana, and in November 1957 he acceded to the see upon the passing of Bishop John George Bennett. While bishop of Lafayette, Bishop Carberry attended the four sessions of the Second Vatican Council; he served during the first three sessions as secretary for the American Bishops' Committee. Bishop Carberry was transferred to the Diocese of Columbus on January 16, 1965, and in November 1965, at a gathering of the American bishops in Rome, he was elected chairman of the Bishops' Committee on Ecumenism and Interreligious Affairs.

In January 1968, he received the "Pastor of Pastors" Award from the Ohio Council of Churches in recognition of his ecumenical work. A few months later, on March 25, 1968, he was transferred once more, this time to St. Louis as archbishop, succeeding Cardinal Joseph E. Ritter. A year after his arrival in St. Louis, Archbishop Carberry was created a cardinal priest with the titular church of San Giovanni Battista de Rossi (Via Latina) by Pope Paul VI on April 28, 1969.

As the archbishop of St. Louis, Cardinal Carberry distinguished himself for his commitment to a steady application of the Second Vatican Council and a dedication to Catholic education, to improving conditions for African-Americans, and to resisting the calamitous effects of the decision on January 22, 1973, by the U.S. Supreme Court legalizing abortion. In February 1973 Cardinal Carberry issued a pastoral letter on the rights of the unborn, and a month later he established an Archdiocesan Pro-Life Committee, the first such office to be established in an American diocese. On January 29, 1977, the cardinal became the first head of the St. Louis Archdiocese to ordain permanent deacons. The permanent diaconate subsequently became a mainstay of ministry in the archdiocese.

During Cardinal Carberry's time as archbishop, St. Louis struggled with demographic and sociological changes that included not only social upheaval but a flight from the city to the surrounding counties. This departure was apparent in the steady decline of population, from 622,000 in 1970 to a little under 400,000 in 1990. While six new parishes were established in this period, Cardinal Carberry was forced by circumstances to consolidate several parishes in the city. The Catholic population of the archdiocese dropped from approximately 530,000 in 1970 to approximately 516,000 in 1979.

In 1974 Cardinal Carberry was elected to a term as vice president of the U.S. Conference of Catholic Bishops. In 1971, 1974, and 1977 he attended the ordinary assemblies of the World Synod of Bishops. In 1978 he participated in both of the conclaves that elected Popes John Paul I and John Paul II. The following year, he submitted his resignation to Pope John Paul II, having turned seventy-five.

After retirement, he remained in the archdiocese until his death at the age of ninety-three.

Cardinals of the United States

The rank denoting the greatest dignity that can be bestowed upon a Caholic churchman, second only to the pope, the appointment to the cardinalate is made by the Holy Father upon individuals deemed worthy. When bestowed upon an American churchman, the rank of cardinal honors both the individual and the nation. It also serves as a token of membership in the College of Cardinals, the body that serves as principal aides and advisers to the pope and is also charged with the election of succeeding pontiffs. The first American appointee to the College of Cardinals was Archbishop John McCloskey, archbishop of New York, in 1875. The event marked a change of status for the American Church and was welcomed as a sign of papal recognition of the maturity of the faith in the United States.

As of 2012, the following cardinals were serving the American Church, according to their years of elevation:

1976: William W. Baum, major penitentiary emeritus.

1985: Bernard F. Law, archbishop emeritus of Boston.

1988: Edmund C. Szoka, governor of the Vatican City State.

1991: Roger M. Mahony, archbishop emeritus of Los Angeles; Anthony M. Bevilacqua, archbishop emeritus of Philadelphia.

1994: William H. Keeler, archbishop emeritus of Baltimore; Adam Joseph Maida, archbishop emeritus of Detroit.

1998: Francis George, O.M.I., archbishop of Chicago; James Francis Stafford, major penitentiary emeritus.

2001: Edward M. Egan, archbishop emeritus of New York; Theodore E. McCarrick, archbishop emeritus of Washington.

2003: Justin F. Rigali, archbishop emeritus of Philadelphia.

2006: William J. Levada, prefect of the Congregation for the Doctrine of the Faith; Seán

P. O'Malley, O.F.M. Cap., archbishop of Boston.

2007: Daniel N. DiNardo, archbishop of Galveston-Houston.

2010: Raymond L. Burke, prefect of the Apostolic Signatura; Donald W. Wuerl, archbishop of Washington, D.C.

2012: Timothy M. Dolan, archbishop of New York; Edwin F. O'Brien, Grand Master of the Knights of the Holy Sepulchre; Cardinal Lubomyr Husar, M.S.U., major archbishop emeritus of Lviv of the Ukrainians, an American citizen.

Americans of the past who received the rank of cardinal were:

1875: John McCloskey, archbishop of New York.

1886: James Gibbons, archbishop of Baltimore.

1911: John Murphy Farley, archbishop of New York; William O'Connell, archbishop of Boston.

1921: Dennis J. Dougherty, archbishop of Philadelphia.

1924: Patrick Joseph Hayes, archbishop of New York; George Mundelein, archbishop of Chicago.

1946: John Glennon, archbishop of St. Louis; Edward Mooney, archbishop of Detroit; Francis Spellman, archbishop of New York; Samuel Alphonsus Stritch, archbishop of Chicago.

1953: James F. McIntyre, archbishop of Los Angeles.

1958: John Francis O'Hara, C.S.C., archbishop of Philadelphia; Richard James Cushing, archbishop of Boston.

1959: Albert G. Meyer, archbishop of Chicago; Aloysius Muench, archbishop of San Bernardo alle Terme.

1961: Joseph E. Ritter, archbishop of St. Louis.

1965: Lawrence J. Shehan, archbishop of Baltimore.

1967: Francis Brennan, prefect of the Sacred Congregation of the Sacraments; John Patrick Cody, archbishop of Chicago; Patrick A. O'Boyle, archbishop of Washington; John Joseph Krol, archbishop of Philadelphia.

1969: John J. Wright, prefect of the Congregation for the Clergy; Terence J. Cooke, archbishop of New York; John F. Dearden, archbishop of Detroit; John Joseph Carberry, archbishop of St. Louis.

1973: Humberto S. Medeiros, archbishop of Boston; Timothy Manning, archbishop of Los Angeles.

1983: Joseph Louis Bernardin, archbishop of Chicago.

1985: John J. O'Connor, archbishop of New York.

1988: James A. Hickey, archbishop of Washington.

2001: Avery Dulles, theologian.

2007: John P. Foley, Grand Master of the Knights of the Holy Sepulchre; Myroslav Lubachivsky, major archbishop of Lviv of the Ukrainians, was made a cardinal in 1985. He was a citizen of the United States and metropolitan of the Philadelphia Ukrainian Rite Archeparchy from 1979 to 1981.

Prelates who became cardinals after returning to their native countries:

Jean-Louis Lefebvre de Chevrus, first bishop of Boston (1808–23) and apostolic administrator of New York (1810–15), elevated to the cardinalate, 1836, in France; Ignatius Persico, O.F.M. Cap., bishop of Savannah (1870–72), elevated to the cardinalate, 1893, in Italy; Diomede Falconio, O.F.M., a priest in Buffalo, New York, missionary in the United States, apostolic delegate to the United States (1902–11), elevated to the cardinalate, 1911, in Italy.

Carey, Mathew (January 28, 1760–September 15, 1839)

An American publisher and banker, Mathew Carey was also the co-founder of *Columbian Magazine* in 1786 and *American Museum* in 1787. He was born in Dublin, Ireland, and, eschewing his father's wishes, he embarked at the age of fifteen on a career in selling and printing books, the result in part of his longtime interest in languages and literary works. After working as an apprentice printer, he wrote his first article in 1777 in the *Hibernian Journal*, followed two years later by the controversial pamphlet "Urgent Necessity of an Immediate Repeal of the Whole Penal Code against Roman Catholics." The pamphlet was declared seditious by the British government, and Carey was forced to flee to France, where he remained for a year. While in France, he met the Marquis de Lafayette and held a position in the printing office set up in Paris by Benjamin Franklin.

After his return to Ireland, Carey published the *Freeman's Journal* and the *Volunteer's Journal*. The latter was an appeal for the political rights of Ireland in the face of the British occupation and caused his arrest in 1784. Tried before Parliament, he was sent to Newgate Prison, but was released when Parliament was dissolved. He then fled to America and arrived in Philadelphia on November 1, 1784.

With the financial assistance of Lafayette (who visited Philadelphia and gave him four hundred dollars), Carey established the *Pennsylvania Evening Herald*. He accumulated a large circulation by publishing the debates of the House of Assembly, using notes he took during the sessions. In 1786 he launched *Columbian Magazine* and in 1787 started *American Museum*, remaining with the magazine until December 1792. During this period, he became active in bookselling and printing, crafting his business into one of the largest in the United States. The following year, he married Bridget Flahavan, with whom he had nine children.

Carey's publishing firm released a large number of titles, including devotional works, starting with a reprint of *True Principles of a Catholic*, attributed to Rochard Challoner. In 1790 he published the first edition of the Douay Bible printed in America. In 1794 he released a sixty-four-page catalog of his more than 2,500 titles. He was the first publisher in the United States to publish the works of Sir Walter Scott and Charles Dickens; he also published James Fenimore Cooper, Noah Webster, Washington Irving, and Philip Freneau. In 1814 he published his best-known writing, *The Olive Branch*, calling for national union and an end to the political struggle between the Federalists and Republicans in the face of the War of 1812. He also wrote *Vindiciae Hibernicae* (1818), a defense of the Irish against the accusation that they had been responsible for an infamous massacre during the rebellion against Oliver Cromwell in 1641.

After assisting the city of Philadelphia in quelling an outbreak of yellow fever in 1793, Carey helped to establish the Hibernian Society for the Relief of Immigrants from Ireland. He also devoted many years to the most important political and social events of the time. In 1811 he supported the rechartering of the national bank; he was so instrumental in promoting the bank that he was subsequently named to the board of directors. He next campaigned for a tariff that would assist the development of American industries and helped to start the Philadelphia Society for the Promotion of National Industry. In 1822 he published *Essays on Political Economy*, a collection of fifty-nine essays and economic theories that he had penned to resist the free-trade policies being advocated by the economist Adam Smith.

A dedicated Catholic, Carey entered into the trusteeship controversy surrounding St. Mary's Church in Philadelphia during the 1820s. He tried to bring about a settlement between the two sides and then labored to refute the propaganda being spread by anti-Catholics concerning the internal struggle. He retired from publishing in 1824 to devote himself to charitable works. He wrote his autobiography for *New England Magazine*; it was published throughout 1833–34. He died in Philadelphia from injuries received in a carriage accident.

Mathew Carey

Carey, Thomas (June 14, 1904–May 8, 1972)

An outstanding theatrical producer, Thomas Carey was co-founder of the Blackfriars Guild, a Catholic production company, with Father Conrad Nagle. He was born in Chicago and educated at

Providence College. He was ordained in 1932 and earned a doctorate from The Catholic University of America in 1935. Father Carey remained on the faculty of the university.

In 1937 Father Carey founded the Blackfriar Institute of Dramatic Arts at The Catholic University of America, and in 1941, with Father Nagle, he opened the Blackfriars Guild Theater in New York City. He also served as the first secretary of the Holy Name Society. The Blackfriars Guild Theater closed before he died in New York.

Carheil, Etienne (November 1633–July 27, 1726)

A scholar, Etienne Carheil spent thirty tears as a resident missionary to the Huron and Iroquois Indian nations. He was born in Carentair, France, and entered the Society of Jesus on August 30, 1652, studying at Amiens, La Fleche, and Bourges. He also taught at Rouen and Tours.

After his ordination to the priesthood in 1666, Father Carheil was assigned to the Canadian missions and also to those chapels erected in the lands that would become part of the United States. He was in Cayuga until 1684 and then was assigned to Mackinac Mission. Father Carheil had a profound knowledge of Native American languages and was able to preach and converse with ease. He continued his labors until 1703, when he was recalled to Québec and assigned to local missions.

Carmelites

The Order of the Brothers of the Most Blessed Virgin of Mount Carmel, the Calced Carmelites or White Friars, and their counterparts, the Order of the Discalced Brothers of the Most Blessed Virgin Mary of Mount Carmel, have made significant contributions to the Catholic Church in America. The original Carmelites were crusader knights and pilgrims who retired to the "holy" mountain of Mount Carmel in the Holy Land (now in Israel). These recluses became devoted hermits, linked spiritually to the prophet Elias (Elijah), and their first settlement was built beside the traditional fountain of the prophet.

Around 1154 Sts. Berthold and Brocard gathered these eremites and formed a religious community. St. Albert, Patriarch of Jerusalem, wrote the rule for the order. About 1291, however, the Carmelites had to leave Mount Carmel because of the Muslim Saracens, who martyred many for the faith. Meanwhile, in England, St. Simon Stock, the father general of the order, had a vision of the Blessed Virgin Mary, in which he received the design for the Carmelite scapular, still a popular devotion. St. Simon had also convened a general chapter of the order in 1247, a gathering in which it was decided that the Carmelites would become a mendicant order. Carmelite monasteries and convents flourished through Europe as a result. In 1562 St. Teresa of Avila, seeking to reform the Carmelites, worked with St. John of the Cross and started the Discalced Carmelites, undertaking a stricter observance of the original rule.

In 1573 a monastery of Calced Carmelites was recorded as active in the area of present-day Santa Fe, New Mexico. Three Carmelites were with the expedition of Sebastian Vizcaino on the coast of California in 1602. Father Antonio of the Ascension and two religious companions celebrated Mass at San Diego, at that time called San Miguel. There are also records of Carmelites serving in early French missions in the northeastern part of the United States. In 1720 other Carmelites were in the vast Louisiana missions. Father John Matthew of St. Anne was at Biloxi and Mobile, and Father Charles of St. Alexis was at St. Louis Cathedral in New Orleans.

In 1790 Discalced Carmelite nuns founded a cloister at Port Tobacco, Maryland. The Port Tobacco cloister opened daughter houses in St. Louis, Boston, Brooklyn, Philadelphia, and Santa Clara. Carmelite priests also served with American troops during the Revolutionary War, while others were in Pennsylvania missions.

In 1864 Calced Carmelites from Straubing, Bavaria, made a foundation at Leavenworth, Kansas, and a new province, the Most Pure Heart of Mary, was approved and headquartered in Chicago. The Carmelites of Ireland responded to the invitation of Archbishop Michael A. Corrigan and opened a foundation in New York in 1889. All the Carmelite founders established scholarly centers and lay programs that imbued the Catholics of America with Marian devotions. The order sponsored shrines and spiritual organizations, and priests served as missionaries in Texas and New

Mexico. Dutch Carmelites were with the Choctaws in 1899. A year later the Shrine of the Little Flower opened in Chicago, and Whitefriars Hall was started in Washington, D.C., in 1926.

Spanish Discalced Carmelites were in Arizona in 1912, and then established parishes in Arkansas, Oklahoma, and Texas. In 1924 Irish Discalced Carmelites erected a foundation in Alhambra, California, and another group opened a cloister in Pennsylvania in 1927. A Spiritual Life Center was established in Miami, and parishes were assumed in 1949. Cloistered Discalced Carmelite nuns were in San Antonio as early as 1934, and in 1958 founded a cloister in Houston. In 1966 Malaysian Carmelite nuns began a cloister on Guam, and in 1973 Carmelite nuns from Hong Kong opened a cloister in Hawaii.

Third Order Carmelite congregations have also aided the American Catholic Church. These congregations staff schools, hospitals, and care facilities. There are currently worldwide over 4,000 Discalced Carmelites and over 2,000 Carmelites; there are also over 12,000 Calced Carmelite nuns and over 750 Discalced Carmelite nuns.

Carney, Andrew (May 12, 1794–April 3, 1864)

An outstanding Catholic corporate giant, Andrew Carney became an insurance director. He was born in Ballanagh, County Cavan, Ireland, and migrated to the United States in 1816. He then organized the firm of Carney and Sleeper, also becoming a director of the John Hancock Insurance Company. Carney was a devout Catholic who served Bishop John Fitzpatrick of Boston and supported the growing temperance movement. He also assisted the Jesuits in founding Boston College. Carney donated twenty thousand dollars in matching funds for the Church of the Immaculate Conception in Boston and aided many charities. He died in Boston.

Carr, Thomas Matthew (1755–September 29, 1820)

The founder of the Augustinian order in the United States, Thomas Matthew Carr received aid from President George Washington. He was born in Dublin and raised devoutly in the faith in a turbulent historical period. He entered the Augustinians and was ordained in Toulouse, France, in 1778. He then responded to the plea made by Bishop John Carroll of the United States and arrived in Philadelphia in 1796. For the remainder of his life, the focus of his ministry would be mission work and the founding of an American province of Augustinians.

Washington and other prominent American citizens aided Father Carr in establishing St. Augustine's Parish in Philadelphia. He also became vicar general of Philadelphia, Delaware, New Jersey, and New York, aiding the Church in the area with his knowledge of administrative and canonical matters. Father Carr attracted young seminarians to establish the Augustinians in the United States. Father John Rosseter, another Augustinian, aided him in this foundation, and Father Carr legally incorporated the Order of Hermits of St. Augustine in Philadelphia in 1804.

The American province of the Augustinians was established on August 27, 1796, under the name of Our Lady of Good Counsel. Father Carr published a devotional book, *Spiritual Mirror*, just before his death in Philadelphia.

Carroll, Mother Austin (February 23, 1835–November 29, 1909)

A Sister of Mercy, Mother Austin Carroll was hailed as the "Caretaker of the Poor." She was born Margaret Anne Carroll in Clonmel, County Tipperary, Ireland, one of nine children. At the age of eighteen, she entered the Sisters of Mercy in Cork, inspired by the example of Mother Catherine McAuley and taking the religious name Mary Austin. Sent to the United States in 1856 to teach the poor in Providence, Rhode Island, Mother Austin assisted her congregation in developing additional houses across the Northeast and Midwest. In 1869 she was sent to New Orleans, where she opened the first community there for the congregation and launched programs for the sick, for prison visitations, and for food for the poor. She also established shelters and homes for orphans, elderly women, and young girls in need of a place to stay when they found themselves out of work. Of particular note was her commitment to the care of victims of yellow fever outbreaks in New Orleans, honoring the sisters who gave their lives during the epidemics.

By the time of her death, she was responsible

for the establishment of sixty-five schools in the South, as well as fourteen convents, thirty-eight libraries, and various orphanages and facilities for the elderly. An accomplished writer, she wrote over forty books, including a biography of the Sisters of Mercy, school plays, and translations from the French and Spanish of spiritual writings.

Carroll, Charles, of Carrollton (September 19, 1737–November 4, 1834)

A signer of the Declaration of Independence, Charles Carroll of Carrollton was born in Annapolis, Maryland, on the vast estate of his family. He was named after his grandfather, who had served as attorney general for Lord Baltimore of Maryland. Because of the past services of the family and the wealth of the Carrolls, Charles grew up in a world somewhat removed from the Protestant majority.

He was educated at Bohemia Manor, operated by the Jesuits, and then set sail for Europe with his cousin, John, who would become America's first Catholic bishop. The Maryland Catholics who could afford European educations sent their sons abroad, not only for academic experiences but for Catholic training as well. Charles and John attended St. Omer College at Reims, and then Charles went to College Louis le Grand in Paris. He completed his law degree in London, and returned to America in 1768. His mother, Elizabeth Brooke Carroll, had died in his absence, but the family accepted the loss in faith.

Charles's father gave him a ten thousand-acre estate in Frederick County, Maryland, in 1765, and Charles would sign his name with that of the estate ever after. Many in the colonies welcomed his return, as they recognized his allegiance to their growing cause and his European training and experiences. He renewed old friendships, and married Mary Darnall in 1768, siring seven children.

In 1773 Charles Carroll of Carrollton accepted a public debate in the *Maryland Gazette* with a Protestant named Daniel Dulaney. The debate

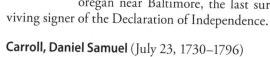

Charles Carroll of Carrollton

concerned taxes and a state-supported Church, and Charles, who called himself "First Citizen," became famous among the Americans planning a revolution against Britain. He held many public offices and finally went to the Continental Congress to ratify the Declaration of Independence as a representative of Maryland. His appearance at the Continental Congress irritated some Protestants, but his wealth — estimated at about $2 million — won the argument because the average American recognized that Charles was risking more than most in order to see America free.

In February 1776 Charles accompanied his cousin, Father John Carroll, Benjamin Franklin, and Samuel Chase to seek a Canadian alliance in the coming revolt. On August 2, 1776, he signed the Declaration of Independence as "Charles Carroll of Carrolton." He explained that he signed himself in that fashion "so that King George would know which Carroll to hunt down for treason."

Charles served as a congressman and as a U.S. senator in 1789. He retired in 1800, and his last public act was the laying of the cornerstone of the Baltimore and Ohio Railroad on July 4, 1828. He died in Doughoregan near Baltimore, the last surviving signer of the Declaration of Independence.

Carroll, Daniel Samuel (July 23, 1730–1796)

The brother of Bishop John Carroll, Daniel Samuel Carroll was a cousin of Charles Carroll of Carrollton. Daniel was born on a family estate in Upper Marlboro, Maryland. He was educated in Europe and settled into the life of a wealthy country gentleman, marrying a distant cousin, Eleanor Darnall. The plans being made for a revolution against British tyranny, however, earned Daniel's allegiance, and he became an active participant in the American cause.

He served as a member of the Continental Congress and helped frame the Constitution in 1787. President George Washington asked Daniel to develop the nation's capital, and he worked with two others to fashion a suitable site. Daniel owned a piece of land, and he knew that Daniel Carroll of Duddingston, a relative, owned an additional piece. Other gentlemen who owned adjoining tracts of land were contacted, and in the company of Daniel they met with Washington at Sutter's Tavern in Georgetown on March 27, 1791. With David Stuart, Daniel laid the cornerstone of America's capital on April 15.

He retired soon after and died five years later at his Rock Creek mansion, where Bishop Carroll had his first chapel. This chapel has been called the "Bethlehem of the American Church as truly as Baltimore is its Jerusalem."

Carroll, John (January 8, 1735– December 3, 1815)

The first Catholic bishop of the United States, John Carroll was a Jesuit priest destined to take upon his fragile shoulders the task of building the Catholic Church in America. He was born in Upper Marlborough, Maryland, on January 8, 1735, the third of seven children of Daniel and Eleanor (Darnall) Carroll. Jackey Carroll, as he was called at home and at Bohemia College, was a child of wealth and influence, and close to his brother, Daniel. The Carrolls were a distinguished family, both at Marlborough and at Annapolis. Descended from Keane Carroll of Ireland, the family was also associated with the American Darnalls, a dynasty founded by Colonel Henry Darnall, the brother-in-law of Lord Baltimore. Others related to the Carrolls were the Digges, Lees, and Horseys of Maryland, and the Carters and Brents of Virginia.

He was also a first cousin of Charles Carroll of Carrollton, a signer of the Declaration of Independence. The two young men were at school together for a time and then together again on the famed trip to Canada to seek an alliance in the coming revolt. There is evidence, however, that they were not close in the intervals, perhaps because Charles Carroll of Carrollton, although a courageous defender of the Church in the new country, was not a man given to many pious practices until later in his life.

John Carroll attended school at Bohemia Manor, recorded as the "mother" of all Catholic

young men in Maryland. The penal laws and the pervading atmosphere of the colonies were such that Catholics chose home studies or Bohemia Manor for academic training for their sons.

Bohemia Manor was allowed to prosper for only a short time, however, as the laws were strict against Catholic education and Catholic educators.

In 1748 John Carroll and his cousin were sent to St. Omer College at Reims. St. Omer had a venerable history, having been founded by the English Jesuit Father Robert Persons, a companion of the English martyr Edmund Campion. It was one of several schools for the Catholics of England. These schools dated back to 1559, when Catholic students in England's leading universities sought refuge in exiled Catholic institutions of learning. Lisbon had five; Madrid, three; Paris, eight; Douai, five; Belgium, thirteen; France, outside of Paris, seven; Rome, two.

When he graduated from St. Omer, he said goodbye to Charles and to the world. He "went up the hill," as they put it then, to Watten Jesuit Novitiate, seven miles from the college. He began his spiritual journey, a monumental career in the Church, which was to change the destiny of America in many ways. The novitiate was harsh and yet all that he required at that time in his life.

He was ordained in the Jesuit order, and he made his profession in 1771. The Jesuit order was suppressed two years later, leaving young priests like Father Carroll abandoned. When Austrian officials invaded the Jesuit College where he was staying, he was arrested. He had come to the college with 140 students, having been exiled from Flanders when the local population turned against the Jesuits. The intervention of Lord Arundell of Wardour Castle, however, saved Father Carroll. He was released and allowed to go to Wardour, where he served as chaplain to the family, in the spring of 1774. Father Carroll, caught up in the upheaval of his own society's suppression, barely escaped with his life in the turmoil of Europe.

He returned to America in 1774, arriving in June at Rock Creek, his mother's home, a cultured

Daniel Carroll

and polished man. American Catholics were few at the time. Harper's *Atlas of American History* gives the total population of the colonies in 1770 as 2,505,000. Historians estimate that the Catholic population was about 22,000. There could be no public worship in Maryland at the time, so he began the quiet life of a missionary among the people of Maryland and Virginia. He built a small chapel on his mother's estate and celebrated Mass there on Sundays. During the week he celebrated Mass in the estate mansion.

Out of the confines of this small chapel, out of the priestly dimensions of John Carroll's own life, came the foundation of the Church in America. Despite the long and arduous trip to visit Catholic families in Maryland and Virginia, he had time to renew his studies of ancient languages and to turn his attention to the state of things in America as the colonies began their journey toward freedom. The Québec Act had allowed Canadian Catholics to have religious freedom, but had brought about hatred of Catholics. General George Washington demanded that Americans put aside bigotry. His command of November 5, 1775, banning the celebration of the annual Pope Day demonstrations, brought a new era of tolerance for Catholics.

Archbishop John Carroll

Then in 1776, a committee composed of Benjamin Franklin, Samuel Chase, and Charles Carroll of Carrollton was about to be sent by the Continental Congress to ask the Canadians to remain neutral or to come to the aid of America against England. In a special resolution dated February 15, 1776, Charles Carroll was requested "to prevail upon Mr. John Carroll to accompany the committee to assist them in such matters as they think useful."

Both of the Carroll cousins had misgivings about the assignment. They had been asked to go to Canada because of their Catholic backgrounds, but they understood that it was too late to ask Canada to discuss union with the rebels or even neutrality in a war that would devastate the British colonial holdings. The reception they received from Bishop Joseph Briand in Canada confirmed their worst suspicions. Father Carroll was given no courtesy and was allowed to say Mass in the home of a Jesuit friend only.

Actually, Bishop Briand cannot be blamed for his attitude toward the colonies. European hatreds had spilled over into Canada and North America for so long that he inherited a legacy of persecution. The Québec Act changed that suddenly for all Catholics in Canada, and its coming was heralded by anger in America. The British were allowing Catholics to practice their religion unhindered and to be citizens of a nation. Bishop Briand saw no reason to put such a situation in jeopardy, especially in defense of Protestant bigots.

One thing that developed out of the trip was a friendship between Benjamin Franklin and Father Carroll. Franklin became ill during the expedition, and Father Carroll cared for his needs and was kind enough to see him back to Philadelphia. As Franklin explained it, "As to myself, I find I grow more feeble, and I think I could not have got so far but for Mr. Carroll's friendly assistance and tender care of me." The two men enjoyed sharing their cultural backgrounds and exchanged ideas and comments. Their friendship would have a demonstrable effect on the Church in America in time.

The friendship of men like Franklin was important to Father Carroll and his ministry. When he moved among Protestant Americans he was not doing it for vain reasons; he knew that they had to discover that Catholics were not the monsters of the pamphleteers, as Catholics had long remained mysterious enigmas among the colonists, bringing back memories of the Spanish Inquisition and the dread dungeons. Protestants at the time of the Revolution still trafficked in such propaganda.

During the war, Father Carroll helped where he could and supported the American cause. Many Catholics were involved in the war, especially with the vast numbers of French and other Europeans coming to the aid of the new nation — militarily trained, cultured, and intellectual nobles. Father Carroll was able to meet with many of these European allies in the midst of the chaos, and he nurtured his own people even as he recognized the small group of priests available to the Church.

When the war ended successfully, Father Carroll and five of these priests met at Whitemarsh, Maryland, on June 27, 1783, to discuss new approaches to mission work and the safety of their properties. A second meeting and then a third were held, during which the priests drafted regulations binding on all Maryland Catholic priests. These regulations stated that every priest was to be maintained on thirty pounds a year and each priest agreed to say ten Masses for every priest who died in the missions.

Father Carroll was selected as superior of the missions in the United States of America, with the power to give confirmation. The pope, responding to the request of the group, confirmed the appointment of Father Carroll on June 9, 1784, and he was asked to send a report on Catholicism in the United States. Attacks on the Church appeared as he assumed leadership, and he responded vigorously in "An Address to the Roman Catholics of the United States of North America," an article published in an Annapolis paper. He continued this public defense for decades.

In the meantime, America did need an episcopal leader, and in 1788 Rome decided to create the first diocese in the United States. On November 6, 1789, Pope Pius VI ordered the bull prepared naming John Carroll the bishop of Baltimore, thereby confirming the choice of the clergy, and also following the advice of a man named Benjamin Franklin. This old friend of Father Carroll took open credit for the appointment. He recorded in his Paris diary: "1784, July 1. The Pope's Nuncio called and acquainted me that the Pope had on my recommendation, appointed Mr. John Carroll, Superior of the Catholic clergy in America, with many powers of a Bishop, and that probably, he would be made a Bishop *in partibus* before the end of the year."

Bishop Carroll went to England, to Lulworth Chapel on the estate of Thomas Weld, in Dorset, to be ordained by Bishop Walmesley, with Father Charles Plowden preaching the ceremony. The hierarchical line of all American bishops, with the exception of a few, has come from this act of consecration, as Bishop Carroll consecrated new American bishops who established definite lines of authority and continuity across the entire American continent.

A census taken the year in which Bishop Carroll assumed office showed that the United States had a white population of 3,200,000 with approximately 30,000 Catholics. There were at the time only thirty priests serving those Catholics. Bishop Carroll had a tremendous task ahead of him, and he combined his own spiritual insight with his diplomatic and ecumenical spirit to the advantage of the Church. In "An Address of the Roman Catholics to George Washington," sent in December 1789, Bishop Carroll had stated his hopes for the Catholic future. Washington responded with his own views, stating, "To the Roman Catholics of the United States, I presume that your fellow citizens will not forget the patriotic part which you took in the accomplishment of their Revolution and the establishment of the important assistance which they received from a nation in which the Roman Catholic faith is professed."

To continue a close working relationship with government officials, something that Bishop Carroll had established over the years, he went about his duties with a cordial view of both the Church and the state. In 1791, at his first synod, he asked for the prayers of the faithful for the president and the government, initiating the present custom. He also influenced President Washington to ask Congress for an appropriation to support the work of two priests among the Indians of the Northwest Territory. His relationship with Washington had remained close, and when the first president retired, Bishop Carroll visited him at Mount Vernon. He also preached Washington's eulogy in St. Peter's Church, Baltimore, on February 22, 1800.

When Thomas Jefferson became president, Bishop Carroll worked with him also. The Louisiana Purchase of 1803 involved the Church, and Bishop Carroll secured Jefferson's protection for the Ursuline nuns and their properties in Louisiana. As a return gesture, Bishop Carroll appointed priests in the Louisiana territories who were loyal to American ideals.

Secular duties also made Bishop Carroll's position a pivotal point for Church-state relations. He was invited to lay the cornerstone for the Washington Monument, although he had to decline because of illness. From its founding until his death he remained president of the Baltimore Library Company and started its printed catalog.

Bishop Carroll also started Catholic colleges. Georgetown was begun in 1788, Baltimore (St. Mary's) was founded in 1799, and Mount St. Mary's College in Emmitsburg was founded in 1808. Academies for girls were established in Georgetown (Visitation, 1799), Emmitsburg (St. Joseph's, 1809), and Bardstown, Kentucky (Nazareth, 1814).

His conviction of the need for expanding education in America led Bishop Carroll to become a patron of secular schools as well. In 1784 he became a member of the board of directors of St. John's College, Annapolis, and was elected president of the board four years later. In 1785 both Washington and Bishop Carroll received honorary degrees from Washington College in Chesterton, Maryland.

The Church benefited most from his ecclesiastical administration. The first American bishop possessed a genius for organization, and the expansion and status of the Church in America is owing entirely to Bishop Carroll's principles and foundations. Bishop Carroll had to lay down regulations for the sacraments and had to begin the great foundation of the clergy in the mission territories of the wilderness.

He was appointed archbishop of Baltimore, as Rome recognized the phenomenal growth and vitality of the Church throughout the United States. Under his administration, the dioceses of Philadelphia, Bardstown, Boston, and New York were erected, and his recommendations for episcopal selections were adopted by Rome.

At the same time, Archbishop Carroll was eager to have religious serving in the urban areas and outposts of the country. He opened a Carmelite Monastery in Port Tobacco in 1790, and he invited the Poor Clares to settle in Fredericksburg, Maryland. The Sisters of Loretto of the Foot of the Cross were founded in 1812, at Hardin's Creek, Kentucky, and the Sisters of Charity of Nazareth were also founded in Kentucky that same year.

His work continued steadily until his death in 1815 after a brief illness. At the time there were two hundred thousand Catholics in America. This eighty-one-year-old prelate, who had guided the Church in America from the earliest days, had seen phenomenal results from his labors.

Carroll, John Patrick (February 22, 1864–November 4, 1925)

The second bishop of Helena, Montana, John Patrick Carroll was a pioneering prelate. He was born in Dubuque, Iowa, and attended St. Joseph's College (now Loras College). Entering the seminary for studies for the priesthood, he earned a Doctor of Divinity degree at the Grand Séminaire in Montréal, Canada, and was ordained in 1889. He subsequently returned to St. Joseph's College, where he served as president from 1894 to 1904 and also taught.

In 1904 Father Carroll was named the second bishop of Helena and was consecrated on December 21. As a bishop, he devoted his efforts to Catholic education, expanding the number of Catholic elementary and secondary schools in the diocese and establishing Mount St. Charles College (now Carroll College) with the aim of improving higher education in Montana as well as providing a training place for local vocations. Father Carroll's aspirations were fulfilled, and most of the secular priests serving in the Diocese of Helena (including those presently in ministry) are graduates of Carroll College.

Bishop Carroll also invited several religious orders and congregations into the diocese to operate schools and hospitals, including the Irish Christian Brothers and the Premonstratensian Fathers. He started the Cathedral of St. Helena in 1908 (consecrating the house of worship in 1924), established thirty parishes and fifty churches, and increased the number of clergy.

Carson, Christopher "Kit" (December 24, 1809–May 23, 1868)

A famous trapper, guide, and frontiersman, Christopher "Kit" Carson was a convert to Catholicism. He was born in Madison County, Kentucky, to a Revolutionary War veteran, Lindsay Carson, and his second wife, Rebecca. His father was killed in an accident in 1818 after the family moved to Howard County, Missouri, and Christopher was apprenticed to a local saddler. At the age of fifteen, he ran away from home and joined a group of traders headed to Santa Fe, New Mexico.

While traveling, he began to learn the way of the frontier, including fur trapping and trading, and he pursued the life of the frontier for some years. Eventually he made his way to Taos, where, in 1843, under the influence of Padre Antonio José Martinez, he was baptized into the Catholic faith, in part to permit his marriage to Josefa Jaramillo, the daughter of a prominent family.

Carson had met John C. Fremont in 1842 and had served as a guide to Fremont's expeditions across the West, a role he would continue to play over the next several years. Carson subsequently fought as a soldier in California against the Mexican army in 1846–47, taking part in several campaigns after being pressed into service by General Steven W. Kearny, who was in charge of the U.S. effort to claim California. Carson also served as a dispatch rider for Kearny, traveling several times to Washington, D.C., where he acquired both a reputation for bravery and skill and friends among the Washington elite.

Following the end of the war, Carson served as Indian agent to the Utes and helped negotiate peace with the Cheyenne, Arapaho, and Navajo. In 1861, however, at the start of the Civil War, he volunteered for the Union cause. Given the rank of colonel, he served in the Southwest as commander of the 1st New Mexico Volunteers. He fought several battles, including the one at Adobe Walls, Texas, on November 25, 1864. Carson had been given a commission as a brigadier general and command of Fort Garland, Colorado. Suffering from a tracheal tumor, he resigned and retired from active duty in the following year. In 1868 he was named superintendent of Indian Affairs for the Colorado Territory. He held this post until his death that same year. Kit Carson maintained respect for the various Native American tribes and received their esteem

Kit Carson

in return. He remained illiterate all his life and had to dictate his memoirs in 1856.

Carthusians

A religious order founded in France in 1084 by St. Bruno, the Order of Carthusians received its name from the Grande Chartreuse, a valley near Grenoble. The first Carthusians did not have a formal rule, and its members adhered in spirit and by custom to the example of their founder. A rule was established by Gigues de Chatel (or Guigo), the fifth prior of Grande Chartreuse, in 1127, and was given approval in 1133 by Pope Innocent II. A new edition was issued in 1258, called the *Statuta Antiqua*; the *Statuta Nova* appeared in 1368. A collection of the various ordinances of the chapter and a synopsis of the statutes was issued under the title *Tertia Compilatio* in 1509. The next year the rule was printed for the first time at Basel by Johann Amorbach, and the *Nova Collectio Statutorum* was published in 1581.

The Carthusian order has always been one of the strictest and most contemplative in the Church. Its monks pursue a life removed from the world; the initial regulations established by Bruno included silence, personal isolation, and many hours of prayer. Carthusian nuns were established in 1245 but were never numerous. The Carthusians were established in the United States in 1951 and currently are centered in the Charterhouse of the Transfiguration, Carthusian Monastery, in Vermont.

Cartier, Jacques (1491–September 1, 1557)

French mariner and explorer Jacques Cartier's expeditions on the North American coast and the St. Lawrence River served as the basis of France's claim to Canada. He was born in Saint-Malo, Brittany, and although his early life is not well documented, it is known that in 1534, on the basis of his reputation as a gifted sailor and cartographer, he received permission from King Francis I of France to set out on a voyage of exploration. He hoped to discover a passage to the East. His two ships, carrying sixty men each, set sail on April 20, 1534, from Saint-Malo, reaching Cape Bonavista, Newfoundland, after a few weeks. Cartier continued his explorations northwards, reaching the coast of Labrador as far as Brest; he then followed the western coast of Newfoundland as far as Cape St. John. From there, he visited other sites, finally reaching the estuary of the St. Lawrence before sailing back to France.

Upon reaching home, Cartier made a report of his travels and amazed his countrymen by introducing two Native Americans. On the basis of his success, the king granted him a commission to continue the explorations, and on May 26, 1535, Cartier set sail with three ships, carrying 110 men. This second voyage was in the St. Lawrence River area again, and he spent the winter at Stadacona (modern Québec). Cartier and his men were desperately ill at the time, and the local Indian residents gave them tea made from white spruce leaves and young branches, resulting in a cure. Cartier then took one small vessel to a large settlement he named Mont Royal, modern-day Montréal. An outbreak of scurvy that resulted in the deaths of twenty-five of his men convinced Cartier to return home in early May 1536.

A third voyage was taken in 1541, with five ships, this time with the intention of bringing settlers and missionaries under the leadership of Jean-François de la Rocque, Sieur de Roberval. Cartier spent the winter at the entrance of the River Cap-Rouge, naming the resulting fort Charlesbourg-Royal. There he awaited the anticipated arrival of Roberval, who had been delayed in setting out from France. After exploring the area around Montréal, Cartier returned to the fort and found his men in conflict with the local Indian tribes. As Roberval still had not appeared, he decided to evacuate the fort and return to France. Reaching Newfoundland, he met Roberval, who demanded that Cartier return to Canada. Cartier disregarded his instructions and sailed for France with what he claimed were treasures. Roberval's expedition met with disaster, and it is uncertain whether Cartier returned in 1543 or 1544 to rescue him.

Cartier retired to his manor of Limoilou at Saint-Malo and wrote an account of his explorations in 1545. The work was translated into English in 1600 by Richard Hakluyt. As for France's commitment to the New World, the disenchantment with Cartier's journeys coupled with Cartier's own dour descriptions of Canada discouraged any serious commitment to exploration and colonization for the next half century. He died at Saint-Malo.

Casey, Venerable Bernard Solanus (November 25, 1870–July 31, 1957)

A Capuchin friar, Venerable Bernard Solanus Casey was also a thaumaturgist. He was born near Prescott, Wisconsin, one of six children in an Irish immigrant family. Raised on the family farm, he worked at various occupations until he went to Superior, Wisconsin, where he was employed as a streetcar conductor. There he received the grace of a priestly vocation, despite having no high school education.

Venerable Solanus was sent to St. Francis de Sales Seminary in Milwaukee and his academic disabilities resulted in his being dismissed. Faculty members, however, urged him to enter a religious community, and he sought admittance to the Capuchin Franciscans. He received the habit in Detroit in January 1897 and was given the name Solanus in the order. In 1898 Venerable Solanus reentered the seminary, assigned to the Capuchin house of studies in Milwaukee.

Once again his inability to learn foreign languages proved a difficulty. He was ordained as a priest simplex, limited to the celebration of Mass and having no faculties to preach or hear confessions. Ordained on July 24, 1904, in Milwaukee, he was assigned as a sacristan and porter at Our Lady of Sorrows Friary in Manhattan. Three years later, he was moved to Our Lady of the Angels Friary in Harlem.

There he became well known for favors of grace that were bestowed upon visitors. He was also reported to have prophetic abilities. Venerable Solanus functioned most of the time as an enroller for the Seraphic Mass Association, conducted by the Capuchins. As his fame spread, his superior asked him to keep a record of favors received through the association.

In August 1924 he was assigned to St. Bonaventure Friary in Detroit, and more favors were received by the faithful of that city. He was given the responsibility of blessing the sick on Wednesday afternoons and was provided with a relic of the True Cross. His growing holiness, centered on the Eucharist and his devotion to the Blessed Virgin Mary inspired all who met him. In 1945 Venerable Solanus was sent to St. Michael's Friary in Brooklyn, followed by a stay in St. Felix Friary, in Huntington, Indiana. In May 1956 he returned to Detroit because of his medical needs. He celebrated his sixtieth anniversary as a Capuchin on January 14, 1957, and died in Detroit.

On June 19, 1982, Pope Blessed John Paul II approved the cause of Venerable Solanus. His body was taken from its original grave and reinterred in St. Bonaventure Friary.

Castañeda, Carlos (November 11, 1896–April 27, 1998)

A noted historian and educator, Carlos Castañeda was also a president of the Catholic Historical Association. He was born in Carmago, Mexico, but entered the United States in 1908. Castañeda received a doctorate from the University of Texas in 1936 and began an esteemed teaching career at The Catholic University of America. He also served other major universities and colleges.

Castañeda's most revered work was the seven-volume *Our Catholic Heritage in Texas, 1519–1950*. He wrote this historical series from 1938 to 1956. The author of other books, articles, and pamphlets, Castañeda served as the president of Catholic Historical Association from 1939 to 1940. Pope Pius XII made him a Knight of the Equestrian Order of the Holy Sepulchre of Jerusalem and a Knight Commander of the Order of Isabella the Catholic of Spain. Castañeda also represented the United States at various historical and philosophical congresses in the Americas. He died in Texas.

Catala, Magin (January 29, 1761–November 22, 1830)

A Spanish Franciscan called the "Holy Man of Santa Clara," Magin Catala labored there for thirty-six years. He was born in Montblanch, Spain, and entered the Franciscan order in 1777, was ordained in 1785, and soon volunteered for service in the missions of Mexico and California. Father Catala reached Mexico in 1786 and devoted the next six years to studies in missiology and native languages at the Apostolic College of San Fernando in Mexico City in order to be prepared adequately for the challenges of the missions. After finishing his studies in 1793, he was sent by his Franciscan superiors to northern California and to the mission in Monterey. He also served as a chaplain on board a Spanish vessel exploring the area around modern Vancouver Island in Canada and was then reassigned to Santa Clara Mission in 1794.

Father Catala spent the rest of his life in service at the mission, earning the well-deserved title of "Holy Man of Santa Clara." Plagued by severe rheumatism and other health problems, Father Catala concentrated his limited resources on the spiritual welfare of the mission and the surrounding indigenous peoples. The success of his efforts at evangelization over three decades was documented in the records of the mission; Father Catala personally performed over three thousand baptisms and nearly two thousand marriages. Aside from his abilities as a preacher and missionary, he was also known for his gifts of prophecy. One of these prophecies concerned Yerba Buena; Father Catala predicted that it would become a great city and that it would endure both fire and earthquake. All three took place as Yerba Buena grew into the city of San Francisco, enduring a fire and an earthquake in 1906 (another major earthquake struck in 1989). Father Catala was buried in the sanctuary of the Santa Clara Mission.

Cataldo, Joseph M. (1837–1928)

A Jesuit missionary in the Pacific Northwest, Joseph M. Cataldo is best known for his labors among the Coeur d'Alene, Spokan, and Nez Perce Indian tribes, where he was called the "Dried Salmon" by his Native American parishioners. A native of Sicily, he entered the Jesuits at the age of fifteen, going to Rome to study for the priesthood. He completed his preparations for the priesthood in Rome and in Louvain, Belgium, where he was ordained.

He was sent by the Jesuits to the United States to assist the missions, fulfilling his personal hopes to evangelize in America. Further studies were necessary in Boston to master English, and the harsh winter of the Northeast caused him physical problems. Father Cataldo was diagnosed with tuberculosis and was sent to Santa Clara in 1863. While at

Santa Clara College, Father Cataldo devoted his time to further studies of the Indian cultures of the Rocky Mountains and Pacific Northwest. Father Gregory Mengarini, S.J., a friend and collaborator of the famed Jesuit missionary Father Pierre-Jean De Smet, trained the young missionary. By 1865 Father Cataldo had recovered sufficiently to embark upon mission work in the West, and he set out for the Rocky Mountain missions and was soon engaged in evangelization and pastoral work among the Couer d'Alene and especially the Nez Perce. He earned the respect and trust of the tribes, receiving his nickname because of his appearance and his deceptively slender build. By the time of his death, he spoke ten different Indian languages and was known across the entire Northwest. He was also responsible for the building of boarding schools on various reservations and founding Gonzaga College for Native American boys.

Catechism, Baltimore. *See* Baltimore Catechism

Cathedrals, United States

The term cathedral comes from the Latin *cathedra*, or seat. Cathedrals are the "seats" of bishops in dioceses across the nation; as well as the actual thronelike chairs reserved only for the ordinary, the bishop appointed to the diocese. From these seats the bishop presides over episcopal ceremonies. The diocesan cathedral is the normal stage for the celebration of the sacraments of holy orders, the consecration of bishops, and diocesan synod rites. Confirmations may be conducted in cathedrals or in parishes.

Definitive architectural styles for cathedrals evolved over the centuries, and the diocesan cathedrals in the United States reflect the evolution of such designs. These cathedrals also illustrate the historical periods in which they were erected, because the architectural styles were elements of each era of Catholic worship or revivals of earlier designs. The Romanesque-style cathedrals in Europe date mostly to the tenth century. The design is rooted in the Roman style, blending classical elements with artistic innovations of the period. In America two profound Romanesque cathedrals were erected to depict the ideals and aspirations of that style: St. Mary Cathedral in Trenton, New Jersey (dating

originally to 1868), and the Cathedral of the Incarnation in Nashville, Tennessee, erected in 1909.

The Gothic cathedrals of Europe are elaborate structures that took decades to construct and demonstrated remarkable artistic skill and elaborate additions. The slimness of form, bay buttresses, large window areas, pointed arches, and great naves are said to reflect "Christ in Majesty," and evoke reverence and awe. The great example of this architectural form is Notre Dame in Paris. In the United States, the cathedrals of St. John in Cleveland; St. Paul in Pittsburgh; St. Helena in Helena, Montana; St. Mary in Covington, Kentucky; Queen of the Most Holy Rosary in Toledo, Ohio; Cathedral of Mary Our Queen in Baltimore; Immaculate Conception in Albany, New York; St. Patrick in New York; Sacred Heart in Rochester, New York; St. Agnes in Rockville Centre, New York; Immaculate Conception in Syracuse, New York; St. Peter in Belleville, Illinois; Holy Name in Chicago; St. Mary in Peoria, Illinois; Holy Cross in Boston; St. Paul in Worcester, Massachusetts; Immaculate Conception in Burlington, Vermont; St. John the Baptist in Charleston, South Carolina; Immaculate Conception in Denver; St. Raphael in Dubuque, Iowa; St. Joseph in La Crosse, Wisconsin; St. John the Evangelist in Lafayette, Indiana; Assumption in Louisville, Kentucky; and the Madeleine in Salt Lake City all reflect "Christ in Majesty."

The Renaissance style of architecture in European cathedrals used the classical modes of refined lines but added innovative points of interest that reflected the rebirth of the arts in that period of history. Cathedrals erected in the United States in the Renaissance style are St. Cecilia in Omaha, Nebraska; St. Matthew in Washington, D.C.; St. Paul in St. Paul, Minnesota; St. John in Milwaukee; St. Louis in New Orleans; St. Vibiana in Los Angeles; and St. James in Seattle.

Cathedrals in the Greek Revivalist style imitated the classical clarity of design of the ancient Hellenic world, using innovations to facilitate worship and yet retaining the lucid elegance of the past. The Cathedral of St. Peter in Chains in Cincinnati and the Cathedral of the Immaculate Conception in Springfield, Illinois, were designed as Greek Revivalist edifices.

The Neo-Byzantine architectural style cathedrals, associated with the ancient empire and reflecting rich and colorful designs with magnificent tiling and domes, were popular in some parts of Europe and were also used in the United States. St. Louis Cathedral in St. Louis and the National Shrine of the Immaculate Conception in Washington, D.C., incorporate the lush architectural splendors of this style.

Contemporary designs are also evident in the nation, mirroring sleek elements and near-industrial elegance. The Cathedral of the Holy Spirit in Bismarck, North Dakota; the Cathedral of the Sacred Heart in Salina, Kansas; and St. John Cathedral in Hartford, Connecticut, were built in this style. Of particular note is Our Lady of the Angels Cathedral, the cathedral church for the Archdiocese of Los Angeles. Built to replace St. Vibiana, the new cathedral was dedicated on September 2, 2002. It is eleven stories tall, built using an asymmetrical design with the stress upon lighting and an absence of right angles. It is 58,000 square feet, only 1,000 feet smaller than Notre Dame in Paris, but one foot longer than St. Patrick in New York. The cathedral took six years to build and cost $190 million.

Catholic Almanac

An annual reference book dedicated to documenting the activities of the Catholic Church in the United States and around the world, the *Catholic Almanac* originated in a publication known as *St. Antony's Almanac*, a 64-page annual with a calendar, feature articles, and an emphasis on devotion and prayer. Its chief purpose was to foster knowledge, and a devotion to St. Antony of Padua. *St. Antony's Almanac* was published by the Franciscans of Holy Name province from 1904 to 1929 under that name, save for 1911, when the title *Franciscan Almanac* was adopted. No edition was published in 1930, but recognizing a genuine need in Catholic social communications, the editors of *The Franciscan Magazine* received permission to start up the almanac once more with a revised organization and mission. The new version was published under the title *The Franciscan Almanac* and was 320 pages with an organization that would be vaguely recognizable to readers today. The early years of the Great Depression prevented continuous publication, so there were no editions in 1934 and 1935.

In 1936, however, the St. Anthony's Guild renewed the life of the almanac, establishing a relationship with the volume that lasted until 1971. It grew in size and scope steadily over the next years, reaching a massive length of 808 pages by the 1940s. Content was by now well established, with a stress upon the liturgical calendar and events pertaining to each year. The *Almanac* also eventually included over 100 pages of useful secular information, including data on the United States government, the Constitution, census information, postal regulations, the United Nations, and a chart on governments and rulers around the globe.

The title *The National Catholic Almanac* was used for the editions from 1940 to 1968; in 1969, the present title, *Catholic Almanac*, was adopted. In a statement of the influence of the Church in the United States, an agreement was made in 1959 to have the volume distributed each year by the New York publisher Doubleday. The arrangement was in effect until 1971, with several editions sometimes being printed throughout the year when events warranted. In 1951, meanwhile, a general editor was named to oversee the complex process of research and production, Father Felician Foy, O.F.M. His tenure as general editor endured from 1952 to 1998, over 45 years of service. Throughout most of that period, he was assisted by Rose Avato (1927–97).

In 1971 Our Sunday Visitor acquired the publishing rights to the *Catholic Almanac*, and the first edition was launched in 1972. OSV has since remained the book's publisher. Father Foy stepped down officially as general editor starting with the 2000 edition, although he remained actively involved with the *Catholic Almanac* until his death on February 21, 2002, from complications of heart surgery. He was succeeded as editor by Matthew Bunson in 1998. In 2004 the *Catholic Almanac* celebrated its 100th anniversary.

Catholic Charities

The name for agencies and offices used in most dioceses in the United States that provide basic care services and facilitate the charitable and social apostolates, the National Conference of Catholic Charities was founded in 1910 by Bishop Thomas J. Shahan and Monsignor William J. Kerby, in cooperation with lay leaders of the Society of St. Vincent de Paul. The organization was designed to advance and promote the charitable programs and activities of the Catholic community and social service agencies in the United States.

Catholic Charities emerged as the central and national organization for basic care services and eventually encompassed a network of more than 1,400 agencies and institutions. It provided consultation, information, and assistance in planning and evaluating social service programs under Catholic auspices. Especially notable are the diocesan member agencies that provide shelter, food, counseling, services to children, teen parents, and the elderly, and a variety of other services to people in need — without regard to religion, gender, age, or national origin. Estimates are that each year several million people are assisted by Catholic Charities.

Catholic Charities USA serves members through national and regional meetings, training programs, literature, and social policy advocacy on the national level. It is charged by the U.S. bishops with responding to disasters in this country. Catholic Charities USA's president also represents North America before *Caritas Internationalis*, the international conference of Catholic Charities, and thus maintains contact with the Catholic Charities movement throughout the world. Relevant publications include *Charities USA*, a quarterly membership magazine, and a directory of U.S. Catholic Charities agencies and institutions.

Catholic Daughters of America

An organization first established in 1903 with the aim of advancing the religious, charitable, and educational apostolates of the Church, the Catholic Daughters of America was founded in Utica, New York, in 1903 by John E. Carberry, along with several other members of the Knights of Columbus, as a charitable, benevolent, and patriotic sorority for Catholic women. Originally named the National Order of Daughters of Isabella, the group took as its motto "Unity and Charity" to express its ideals and objectives. Carberry served as the first Supreme Regent and oversaw the initial expansion of the organization. By 1908 membership had grown from fewer than one hundred to more than ten thousand, distributed across sixty-nine cities

in eighteen states. In March 1913, the Daughters of Isabella acquired a building in Utica that had belonged to the Knights of Columbus and adopted it as their official headquarters.

The Daughters were especially active during World War I (1914–18), providing assistance as nurses and fundraisers, along with a host of sewing services and clerical support. They also helped the Knights of Columbus raise millions of dollars for recreational activities for enlisted soldiers. After the war, the Daughters helped rebuild the severely damaged University of Louvain's library. In 1921 the Daughters of Isabella changed its name to the Catholic Daughters of America. Four years later, a court (or branch) was launched in Cuba.

In 1926 the national headquarters was moved to New York City, and by 1928 membership reached 170,000 in forty-five states, Panama, Puerto Rico, Cuba, and Canada. During World War II, the Catholic Daughters again sprang into action to assist the war effort. Members purchased millions in war bonds, raised funds, and were especially active in sewing, donating blood, and making bandages.

An especially significant moment came in 1952 when Bishop Fulton J. Sheen addressed the 24th Biennial Convention. He issued a challenge to the Catholic Daughters, stating, "You are the Catholic Daughters of America; I would like you to become Catholic Daughters of the World." The members took up his call, and by 1954 the title Catholic Daughters of the Americas was embraced to reflect its international membership and activities. There were 115,000 Catholic Daughters throughout the United States, Mexico, the Dominican Republic, Puerto Rico, Saipan, Guam, and the Virgin Islands.

In 1976 CDA made a gift of $750,000 to The Catholic University of America to establish a Chair in American Catholic History and has been particularly generous in donations to promote seminary training programs for priests studying at the North American College in Rome and at the American College in Louvain in Belgium.

Such was the success of the Catholic Daughters in fundraising that in 1990 the United States Conference of Catholic Bishops asked the organization to take a leading role in supporting the Papal Foundation. In a short time, the Catholic Daughters were able to present a gift of $500,000 for use by Catholic churches in the Third World. The CDA also supported SOAR! (Support Our Aging Religious!) in 1986, and has been instrumental in assisting Habitat for Humanity International and the Alzheimer's Association of America. Currently, the Catholic Daughters of the America has nearly 95,000 members across the United States, Puerto Rico, Mexico, the Dominican Republic, Guam, Saipan, and the Virgin Islands.

Catholic Evidence Guild

A unique ministry founded in England in 1917, the Catholic Evidence Guild served to defend the Catholic Church from attacks by other denominations and to educate Catholics about the dimensions of their faith. Martha M. Moore and David Goldstein, both converts, founded the guild, knowing that there was a need to coordinate defensive and apologetic activities. They started preaching in Hyde Park in London, where people gathered to hear various opinions and beliefs. The pair attracted many followers, and by 1918 there were a number of preachers in public places refuting the false charges laid against the Church.

The American Catholic Evidence Guild was started in New York in 1931, and communications from this group were varied and delivered in the emerging forms of media. Lectures were given over the radio and newspaper articles and magazine articles were distributed, as well as pamphlets concerning each new charge. In 1936 the guild held a public gathering in New York and was operating in Boston, Detroit, Pittsburgh, and elsewhere. Standard operating procedures, especially for public appearances, were adopted.

The guild members normally gave public talks, lecturing from ten to twenty minutes and then answering questions. Members had to study the faith and had to have certain oratory abilities. The guilds followed the directives of most diocesan bishops. Pope Pius XII encouraged the Catholic Evidence Guild.

Catholic Church Extension Society

An organization established on October 18, 1905, by Father Francis Clement, the Catholic Church Extension Society was founded to assist the Church in rural and isolated areas. Father Clement later became a bishop, but as a priest he recognized the needs of American home missions and established the society as a resource. The charter meeting of the Extension Society took place on December 12, 1905, and was attended by bishops, clergy, religious, and laypeople. It played an important role in developing territories and dioceses, bringing innovative ideas to the ministerial apostolate. In some dioceses, for example, the society provided chapel train cars, units adapted for the celebration of Mass and for catechetical instruction. These unique cars were attached to local railroads, thus providing transportation to and facilities for remote outposts.

Today, the society functions with papal approval and assists parishes and missions through the collection and disbursement of funds for home mission work. Since the time of the founding of the society, more than $300 million has been received and distributed. The society publishes *Extension Magazine*. In 1961 the Extension Lay Volunteers was founded. These dedicated individuals teach in home missions, performing nursing, social, and secretarial duties. A support unit, the Order of Martha, provides vestments, altar linens, and other liturgical supplies. A board supervises the work of the society.

Catholic Directory

The oldest and the only official publication on the Catholic Church in the United States, the *Catholic Directory* was established in 1817 as *Field's Laity's Directory to the Church Service* and was published by Matthew Field in New York. It evolved into *The United States Catholic Almanac or Laity's Directory for the Year 1833*, issued by James Myres in Baltimore. Publication of the directory passed in 1912 to P. J. Kenedy & Sons in New York, where it has remained ever since. From 1912 until 1956, the directory was edited by Louis Kenedy and then by Thomas B. Kenedy.

The *Catholic Directory*, printed annually, presents the official statistics for the Catholic Church, including every archdiocese and diocese, as well as membership data for the clergy and hierarchy. Additionally, it includes comprehensive listings of parishes, organizations, and houses of men and women religious. The official status of the *Catholic*

Directory is recognized by the United States Treasury Department in that all institutions and activities listed in its pages are considered tax exempt.

Catholic Foreign Mission Society of America.
See **Maryknoll**

Catholic League for Religious and Civil Rights.
See **Anti-Catholicism**

Catholic Near East Welfare Association

A papal charitable organization founded on March 11, 1926, in response to a decree by Pope Pius XI to provide aid to the Near and Middle East, the Catholic Near East Welfare Association was the result of the pontiff's desire to unite on a permanent basis all the American associations working to provide assistance to Russia and other parts of the Near East, especially in advancing and assisting the Sacred Congregation for the Oriental Churches and the Pontifical Commission for Russia.

Initial direction was placed under the archbishop of New York, who was instructed to organize a governing body chosen from the American hierarchy. The two groups most directly impacted by the papal decree were the Catholic Near East Welfare Association and the Catholic Union begun in 1925 as a branch of the *Catholica Unio* that assisted the Catholic communities in Ukraine, Romania, and Bulgaria.

In September 1926 the bishops of the United States gave their full support and decreed at their annual meeting that the new Catholic Near East Welfare Association would be the sole organization officially authorized to solicit funds for Catholic interests in Russia and the Near East. A collection taken in January 1927 proved so successful that Pope Pius XI wrote to express his pleasure and gratitude. A few years later, on August 20, 1931, Pope Pius decreed that funds should be used in mission areas entrusted to the Sacred Congregation for the Oriental Churches, and that a percentage of the monies gathered on Mission Sunday were to be allocated to the association. American cardinals were also appointed as chairmen of the group. The Catholic Near East Welfare Association was also entrusted with the Pontifical Mission for Palestine in 1949.

Pope Paul VI broadened the Pontifical Mission for Palestine to include care for people of all religions, and new programs of aid were developed to meet growing needs. Other nations also started agencies that worked in conjunction with CNEWA. The association now serves the churches and peoples of the Middle East, India, and Eastern Europe, and maintains offices in New York, Vatican City, Addis Ababa, Amman, Jerusalem, and Beirut.

Catholic Relief Services

The official overseas aid and development arm of the United States Catholic Church, Catholic Relief Services is a separately incorporated organization of the United States Conference of Catholic Bishops. Known originally as the War Relief Services, the agency was established originally by Father (later Bishop) Aloysius J. Wycislo of Chicago in 1943 and provided relief for Polish women, children, and elderly men. On June 28, 1943, the agency was incorporated in Washington, D.C., and a constitution and bylaws were established. War Relief Services functioned as part of the Bishops' War Emergency and Relief Committee, supported by a collection on Laetare Sunday. The agency then became part of the National War Fund.

In the following year, the War Relief Services managed relief programs for Poles in twenty-two cities and towns in the Holy Land. The agency also provided the largest food program in its history, following the advancing units of the Allies and distributing food, clothing, and medicines to the thousands of refugees and displaced persons left behind at the scenes of battle.

When the National War Fund was discontinued in 1947, the American Catholic bishops broadened their appeal to provide assistance overseas. The bishops renamed the agency Catholic Relief Services in July 1955, placing it within the jurisdiction of the National Catholic Welfare Conference. In 1967, when the NCWC became the U.S. Catholic Conference, Catholic Relief Services became part of that new entity.

Currently, Catholic Relief Services is the official overseas aid and development agency of U.S. Catholics and a separately incorporated organization of the U.S. Conference of Catholic Bishops.

Administrative funding for CRS comes largely from the American Bishops Overseas Appeal, while major support is derived from private, individual donors and through programs such as Operation Rice Bowl and the new Global Village Project.

Catholic Rural Life Movement

A movement that seeks to assist the pastoral needs of the Church in the rural regions of the United States, the Catholic Rural Life Movement is an apostolate that assumed greater urgency in the twentieth century owing to the relentless pace of urbanization. It owes its foundation to the labors of Father (later Bishop) Edwin Vincent O'Hara, who, after serving as a chaplain in World War I, returned to the United States and in 1920 proposed the creation of a Rural Life Bureau to assist dioceses in their pastoral outreach and care for those living in rural communities. In 1922 he published *A Program of Catholic Rural Action* and in 1927 *The Church and the Country Community.* Through his efforts, in November 1923 the National Catholic Rural Life Conference was founded. Its purpose was to develop and strengthen the Church in rural areas through various programs and correspondence courses for those engaged in ministry.

From this beginning, the NCRLC expanded its concerns to international rural life, starting with the arrival in 1940 of Monsignor Luigi Ligutti as general secretary. The Catholic Rural Life Movement then pushed for massive aid for regions directly impacted by World War II. The NCRLC was subsequently engaged in advocacy programs for family farming and major farm organizations and also such issues as soil preservation, strip mining, and environmental protection.

Catholic University of America, The

A national pontifical university, The Catholic University of America was chartered by Pope Leo XIII on March 7, 1889, in the apostolic letter *Magni Nobis Gaudii* and was the first Catholic institution of its kind to be established in the United States. The Catholic University of America was incorporated in 1887 under the laws of the District of Columbia and canonically erected.

At the Third Plenary Council of Baltimore in 1884, Bishop John Lancaster Spalding of Peoria had successfully introduced an appeal for the establishment of a national Catholic university. His proposal gained force when the council learned that Mary Gwendolyn Caldwell had offered $300,000 as a founding endowment. The bishops authorized Cardinal James Gibbons to appoint a committee to initiate the project. During the next years, the name and location were determined, and Bishop John Joseph Keane was appointed as the first rector. In 1885 Pope Leo XIII sent his private approval of the project and in 1887 gave his endorsement. On April 19, 1887, U.S. Congress incorporated the university. On March 7, 1889, in the apostolic letter *Magni Nobis Gaudii,* the pope formally approved the statutes and accorded the institution pontifical status. The university was formally opened on November 13, 1889, with President Benjamin Harrison attending.

The Catholic University of America had opened as a graduate school of theology for the clergy. It became increasingly evident, however, that a larger student body, including laymen, would enhance the standing and the fiscal base of the institution. Additional academic disciplines were also determined to be necessary, and in October 1895 the School of Philosophy and the School of Social Sciences were opened to qualified male applicants.

The original plan to depend on gifts, student fees, and a small investment income quickly became inadequate. Bishop Denis J. O'Connell, the third rector of the university, suggested a new collection to provide adequate funding. Bishop O'Connell's recommendation, strongly supported by Cardinal Gibbons as chancellor, resulted in Pope St. Pius X's authorizing an annual collection to be taken up throughout the dioceses of the United States. At the same time, the university started accepting undergraduate lay students in the fall of 1905.

Bishop Spalding had also proposed an advanced teachers' college, and in 1911 the Catholic Sisters College was founded, becoming a separate corporation in 1914. It was located apart from the main campus, but the university conferred the degrees until 1964, when it was incorporated into the university administratively. In 1968 it was discontinued.

America's entrance into World War II impacted on the university in profound ways. Europe, caught up in hostilities by 1939, was no longer a safe haven for priests and seminarians, and they chose Washington as their academic haven. The GI Bill added to the enrollment after the war, as veterans took advantage of the educational grants, and the university faced problems in providing for the increased number of applicants. In 1964 Catholic University joined with four other universities in the District of Columbia (American, George Washington, Georgetown, and Howard) to form the Washington Consortium of Universities.

In the spring of 1967 the Board of Trustees voted to terminate the services of the Reverend Charles E. Curran, an assistant professor in the School of Theology, chiefly on the basis of his contention that the Church should change its teaching regarding artificial contraception. The faculty and students protested and voiced their objections to the media, virtually bringing the daily functions of the university to a complete halt. Under enormous public pressure, Father Curran was reinstated and emerged as a noted figure in some theological circles in the United States. In the wake of Pope Paul VI's encyclical *Humanae Vitae*, Curran drafted a statement to the effect that it was possible for Catholics to dissent from such noninfallible teachings. It was signed by over six hundred various individuals involved in theology. By 1984 Curran had been investigated by the Congregation for the Doctrine of the Faith in Rome and was named specifically, among others, by the Holy See as a theologian who was advocating positions that were creating confusion and dissent from the Church's magisterium.

The affair reached a final crisis point in 1986 with the withdrawal of Father Curran's *missio canonica* by Cardinal James A. Hickey of Washington, D.C., an act that was confirmed by the Board of Trustees in April 1989. Curran sued the university in 1989, but lost the case owing to the refusal of the courts to interfere in what was seen to be possible involvement in the affairs of the Catholic Church. Curran went on to accept a professorship at Southern Methodist University in 1991. The episode, however, embodied the great upheaval in Catholic education that characterized the immediate postconciliar period. As the chief center for theological training in the United States, Catholic University was inevitably touched by this turmoil.

The Catholic University of America was mandated to promote the Catholic intellectual tradition in dialogue with American academia and to provide the faithful of the nation with educational standards and opportunities. Functioning under the governing authority of the U.S. bishops, the university's board of trustees is composed of cardinals, archbishops, priests, and laity. It is an accredited coeducational institution with scholastic divisions designed to provide the nation with a true center of Catholic culture.

Theology, law, canon law, arts, science, engineering, architecture, social services. and nursing programs were integrated into the academic levels over the decades, and professional training is also available in other fields. The university operates its own publishing house.

Catholic Worker Movement

A lay apostolate founded in 1933 by Peter Maurin and Dorothy Day, the Catholic Worker Movement promotes the practice of the works of mercy, nonviolence, personalism, and voluntary poverty. The movement is known especially for its Houses of Hospitality in over sixty U.S. cities, which provide assistance to those in need, and several communal farms in various parts of the country. The houses and centers are entirely expressions of charity and are staffed by unpaid volunteers. Members of the movement strive to emulate the activities and spirit of the founders and are hence active in care for the poor, various social justice initiatives, and social activism, including protests against racism, war, and unfair labor practices.

The chief organ of the movement is *The Catholic Worker*, although there are various publications distributed by local Catholic Worker branches. *The Catholic Worker* was established in 1933, and Day served as its editor until her death. Its editorial thrust has never changed from advancing in print the foundational ideals of the movement, and its celebrity contributors have ranged from Jacques Maritain to Thomas Merton. (*See also* Day, Dorothy.)

Catholic Youth Organization

A nationwide and popular program, the Catholic Youth Organization, or CYO, was founded in

1931 by Bishop Bernard Sheil, an auxiliary bishop of the Archdiocese of Chicago, as an athletic program that would provide young men with recreational and inspirational activities. The program was so successful that it was introduced in dioceses throughout the United States.

The CYO was originally centered on athletics, with particular emphasis on boxing programs. Basketball, football, baseball, and other sports were added in time. The CYO opened a national office in Washington, D.C., in 1940, at the request of the apostolic delegate, Archbishop (later Cardinal) Amleto Giovanni Cicognani. It became the largest single youth organization in the nation, serving some eight million young men.

The spiritual objectives of the Catholic Youth Organization remain primary, alongside efforts to provide leisure-time activities. A fivefold program of spiritual, apostolic, cultural, physical, and social activities was developed on the parish level in each diocese. Catholic Youth Week was also introduced as a national observance.

Central Verein (Catholic Central Union of America)

The central organization coordinating the German Catholic benevolent societies in the nation, the Central Verein was founded in 1854 and approved by Bishop John Timon of Buffalo, New York. It is known in German as *Deutscher romisch-katholischer Centraly Verein von Nordamerika*. The organization followed the Mainz Central Verein, and seventeen German benevolent societies banded together to make the union a success.

On April 15, 1855, the Central Verein was officially organized in St. Alphonsus Hall in Baltimore. It was deemed a powerful weapon in the defense of the Church and in opposing the tactics of Freemasonry and secret societies in general. Membership was restricted to Catholic benevolent societies whose official language was German.

The organization grew rapidly and had a membership of sixty-two societies by 1865 and 548 societies by 1895. A decline started after 1895, however, and in 1901 a reorganization movement was considered necessary. Local societies were no longer affiliated, replaced by the formation of state organizations, the *Staatsverbande*, which were then

incorporated as a whole. This plan proved a complete success. In 1907 sixteen state organizations and fifty-two local societies from states in which no *Staatsverbande* existed formed a total paid membership of 99,291.

The Holy See approved the work of the Central Verein in a reply to a letter of allegiance sent to Pope Blessed Pius IX by the eleventh general convention, held at Buffalo in 1866. Pope Blessed Pius IX praised the spirit of Catholic unity prevailing among the members and wished them every success. He also expressed his appreciation for the contributions the Central Verein had gathered for the support of the Holy See, as the society contributed about $12,000 to the Peter's Pence collection.

Concern for immigrants became a primary program of the Central Verein, which in time was affiliated with the St. Raphael's Society for the Protection of Immigrants. The result of the combined efforts was the establishment of Leo House in New York, a haven in Galveston, Texas, and a significant role in the founding of the Teachers' Seminary at St. Francis, Wisconsin.

Annual conventions, called *Katholikentage*, are conducted over four or five days, including solemn church festivities, parades, addresses, business meetings, and social gatherings, which reflect the spirit of the members.

Chabanel, St. Noel (February 2, 1613–December 8, 1649)

A Jesuit martyr, St. Noel Chabanel was slain by a Huron warrior. He was born in southern France and entered the Jesuit novitiate at Toulouse at age seventeen. After ordination, Father Chabanel was recognized as a learned scholar and taught in Jesuit institutions until he was sent to the Canadian missions in 1643. His assignment was to the Hurons, and he studied the Algonquin language and became fluent in the tongue. Father Chabanel was a companion of Father Charles Garnier, the revered veteran missionary of that era.

Father Chabanel was personally repulsed by the Huron way of life and the environment in which they lived. Fearing he would lose control and abandon his work, he made a private vow never to leave the mission, a vow he kept until his death. (*See also* North American Martyrs.)

Chabrat, Guy (December 28, 1787–November 21, 1868)

The first Catholic priest to be ordained west of the Alleghenies, Guy Chabrat was a coadjutor bishop before he was forced to retire from his labors in the young United States. He was born in Chambres, France, and entered the seminary at St. Fleur. There he met the American missionary Bishop Benedict Joseph Flaget of Bardstown, Kentucky, in 1810. Bishop Flaget was traveling in France to recruit volunteers for service in the United States missions. Seminarian Chabrat answered Bishop Flaget's call with enthusiasm and went to America. On December 21, 1811, he was ordained by the bishop in his new diocese.

Father Chabrat's first assignment was to the missions that had been in the hands of Father (later Bishop) John B. David. Father David found Chabrat's zeal admirable, although he commented in a letter that he hoped he would moderate his energies, even as he praised his hard work and willingness to endure heat and cold. His long years of subsequent ministry took place within the massive Diocese of Bardstown, a jurisdiction that encompassed the regions of Kentucky, Tennessee, and the old Northwest.

In 1834 Bishop Flaget removed Father Chabrat from the wide-ranging pastoral ministry to serve as his coadjutor bishop. The choice was opposed with some vigor by the other priests of the diocese, who complained that he was too young, was insufficiently experienced, and had spent too much time in the wilderness. Nevertheless, Bishop Flaget consecrated his friend the titular bishop of Bolina on July 20, 1834. Bishop Flaget then sailed home to France, leaving the new young bishop in charge of the diocese.

For the next thirteen years, Bishop Chabrat proved an able administrator whose relations with the priests of the diocese were sound. In 1847 failing eyesight forced him to resign, and he returned to France, where he died in Mauriac. (*See also* Bardstown, Diocese of.)

Champlain, Samuel de (c. 1567–December 25, 1635)

A French explorer and governor, Samuel de Champlain established a fort at Québec and explored Lakes Huron and Ontario, earning him the title of "Father of New France." He was born in Brouage, France, near La Rochelle, and devoted his early life to soldiering, serving in the armies of King Henry IV in the wars between the Catholics and Huguenots (1568–70) and the Spanish navy in the West Indies. In 1603 his reputation earned him royal patronage for an expedition to Canada to search for a possible route to China, to build on the earlier journeys of Jacques Cartier, and to develop the potentially lucrative fur trade. Champlain explored down the St. Lawrence River to the present site of Montréal.

In 1604 he returned to Canada with Pierre du Gast, exploring the area of Nova Scotia, New Brunswick, and parts of New England. A colony was founded on Dochet Island, New Brunswick (later moved to what became Port Royal, Nova Scotia). After a return to France, Champlain was back on the St. Lawrence, and in 1608 he founded Québec as a permanent base of operations for the fur trade and for further exploration into the wilderness of the region. The cordial relations established with the Algonquin Indians of the St. Lawrence River area required the French to assist them in their war with

Samuel de Champlain

the Iroquois in what became northern New York. While cooperating with a war party, Champlain discovered the lake in northern New York that eventually bore his name; two years later, he established a post at Montréal. For his efforts, he was appointed lieutenant governor of New France. In the fighting with the Iroquois, Champlain shot and killed a chief, an act that was neither forgotten nor ever forgiven by the Iroquois. He also tried with little success to prevent the cruel treatment of the Iroquois captives by the Huron.

After further participation with the Hurons against the Iroquois tribe of the Onondagas, Champlain pushed westward to Lake Huron and spent time on Georgian Bay. In 1615 he invited the Franciscan Recollects to Québec, the first missionaries to serve in New France. Champlain supported the Franciscans while concentrating his efforts on the fur trade, chiefly because it supported the colony financially. Nurturing Québec, he promoted agriculture and attempted to improve its defenses, but his concentration on the fur trade inhibited a more vigorous colonial expansion, a shortsighted policy that ultimately proved fatal to French interests in the New World. The defenses became important in the war with England (1626–30), although the city fell to the Kirke brothers, privateers hired by England in 1629. Champlain was captured and taken to England. He was released at the end of the hostilities and returned to New France as governor of Québec. He held the post until his death. Although the French colonies in Canada were doomed to fall in the eighteenth century, Champlain played a crucial role in their creation. He also was instrumental in planting in eastern Canada the Catholic faith, which remains strong today.

Chanath, Nicephor (1855–December 31, 1898)

A Ruthenian Catholic priest, Nicephor Chanath labored to improve the ecclesial position of Ruthenian Catholics in the United States. He was born in Uzhorod, Russia (modern-day Ukraine), and prepared for the priesthood in Uzhorod, Presov, and Budapest, returning to Uzhorod to marry shortly before his ordination in 1881. His wife died a year later.

After distinguishing himself in his early pastoral assignments in his homeland, Father Chanath was assigned to the Ruthenian community in the United States. He arrived in the country in 1891 and was assigned to a parish in Passaic, New Jersey. Ruthenians in America at the time were burdened because of their immigration status and because they were often held in suspicion by Latin Catholics, in particular members of the hierarchy who questioned both their Eastern European origin and especially the married state of their priests. The tensions and misunderstandings that characterized some dealings had already caused a number of Ruthenians to renounce the Catholic Church and enroll in the Russian Orthodox Church. To assist

the position of the Ruthenian Catholics, Father Chanath was named to a three-member group that had been formed to prevent further defections and to work with the American hierarchy to improve the lot of Ruthenian clergy. His efforts were in vain for years, but in 1897 the bishops of the United States endorsed his call for a Ruthenian vicar general. Father Chanath died the following year. (*See also* Ruthenians *under* Eastern Churches, Catholic.)

Chanche, John Mary Joseph (1795–July 22, 1852)

The first bishop of the Diocese of Natchez (now the Jackson diocese), John Mary Joseph Chanche declined several previous offers of sees out of humility. He was born in Baltimore and studied for the priesthood at St. Mary's College and St. Mary's Seminary there. Ordained in June 1819, he entered the Sulpicians the following month and spent the next years working at his two alma maters, including serving as president of St. Mary's College from 1834 to 1840.

Owing to his many intellectual talents and his reputation as a model priest, he was appointed on December 15, 1840, as the first bishop of the Diocese of Natchez, Mississippi. He had been offered the opportunity to become coadjutor of Baltimore, Boston, and New York, but had declined. After being consecrated in Baltimore on March 14, 1841, Bishop Chanche set out for his new diocese and established the agencies and offices for diocesan administration. His eleven years in the episcopacy were focused on developing the resources of the vast, understaffed diocese. He had discovered upon his arrival that there were only two priests serving an area of over 46,000 square miles. There were no standing Catholic institutions, and the Catholic population was widely scattered across Mississippi.

To meet the diverse pastoral needs of Catholics while building up administrative and financial foundations for the diocese, Bishop Chanche appealed for funds across the United States and in Europe. He promoted vocations and was active in recruiting personnel from outside the region. At the same time, he was energetic in building needed parishes, churches, missions, schools, and orphanages. His greatest endeavor, however, was the cathedral in Natchez. He erected a large Gothic edifice that clearly demonstrated a profound Catholic presence. Throughout his years of ceaseless labor, Bishop Chanche remained dedicated to the needs of his people, was a respected preacher, and was noted for his frugality and simple lifestyle. He died in Frederick City, Maryland, from overwork and exhaustion.

Chapelle, Placide Louis (August 28, 1842–August 9, 1905)

An archbishop of New Orleans, Placide Louis Chapelle was a noted diplomat. He was born in Runes, France, and studied in France and Belgium before migrating to the United States at the age of seventeen. Once in Baltimore, he entered St. Mary's Seminary and began studies for the priesthood. During his days as a seminarian, he taught at St. Charles College in Catonsville, Maryland. Ordained in June 1865, he was assigned to several pastoral positions in Baltimore and Washington, D.C. In 1891 he was named titular bishop of Arabissus and coadjutor archbishop with right of succession to Archbishop J. B. Salpointe of Santa Fe, New Mexico.

Archbishop Chapelle served there for only three years. On December 1, 1897, he was transferred to the Archdiocese of New Orleans. The following year, he was named apostolic delegate to Puerto Rico and Cuba and chargé d'affaires of the Philippine Islands. His diplomatic duties brought him to the Caribbean and to the Philippines, where he worked to secure a settlement of various property disputes and ecclesiastical disagreements. Pope Leo XIII praised Archbishop Chapelle's labors in a pontifical brief, and the archbishop was honored with the titles of Assistant at the Pontifical Throne and Count of the Roman Court.

Although traveling frequently, Archbishop Chapelle remained committed to his archdiocese and his pastoral duties. He thus encouraged growth by opening new parishes and founding St. Louis Theological Seminary in Faubourg Bouligny, a suburb of New Orleans. He also invited the Dominicans to open a community in New Orleans. Above all, he focused on improving the finances of the archdiocese, and through a series of effective measures he solved the severe debt problems that had long plagued the archdiocese. Concerned with ensuring the proper pastoral care of his flock, Arch-

bishop Chapelle began a series of parish visitations in 1905 but was forced to return to New Orleans upon learning of an outbreak of yellow fever. He displayed great concern for the stricken, serving them personally, and died from the disease.

Chaput, Charles J., O.F.M. Cap. (September 26, 1944–)

The second Native American bishop in the United States, Charles J. Chaput is also the first Native American to serve as an archbishop; he is a member of the Capuchin Franciscans.

Born in Concordia, Kansas, he is the son of Joseph and Marian DeMarais Chaput and a member of the Prairie Band Potawatomi. He grew up in Concordia and joined the Order of Friars Minor Capuchin, St. Augustine Province, in 1965. He studied at St. Fidelis College Seminary in Herman, Pennsylvania, where he earned a bachelor's degree in philosophy in 1967 and went on to earn a master's degree in religious education from Capuchin College in Washington, D.C., in 1970. He was ordained on August 29, 1970. The next year, he received a master's degree in theology from the University of San Francisco.

Father Chaput taught theology and was a spiritual director at St. Fidelis from 1971 to 1974 and executive secretary and director of communications for the Capuchin Province of St. Augustine in Pittsburgh from 1974 to 1977.

In 1977 he was named pastor of Holy Cross Parish in Thornton, Colorado, and vicar provincial for the Capuchin Province of Mid-America. Three years later, he was appointed secretary and treasurer for the province and became chief executive and provincial minister three years later.

On April 11, 1988, Pope Blessed John Paul II appointed him bishop of Rapid City, South Dakota, making him the second Native American to become a bishop (after Donald Pelotte, who had been named coadjutor bishop of Gallup, New Mexico, in 1986). On July 26, 1988, Chaput was ordained a bishop. On February 18, 1997, he was transferred to Denver as its archbishop, succeeding Archbishop James Francis Stafford. He was installed on April 7, 1997.

As the shepherd of Denver for the next fourteen years, Archbishop Chaput promoted virtually every area of Catholic life in Colorado and was especially concerned about vocations. He founded St. John Vianney Theological Seminary, an affiliate of the Pontifical Lateran University, and in his time as archbishop ordained seventy-one men for service in the Denver archdiocese. He also supported the start of the Augustine Institute, an independent graduate school for laity, and was instrumental in the Church's outreach to Hispanics through the Centro San Juan Diego and other initiatives, such as the national Catholic Association of Latino Leaders (CALL). In 2005 Archbishop Chaput was appointed a member of the official U.S. delegation to Cordoba, Spain, for the Conference on Anti-Semitism and Other Forms of Intolerance, which had been launched by the Organization for Security and Cooperation in Europe (OSCE). For his efforts on behalf of religious freedom, he was awarded the Canterbury Medal in 2009 by the Becket Fund for Religious Liberty.

Archbishop Chaput served as an apostolic visitor for the Holy See in several important investigations. The first was the examination of U.S. seminaries from 2005 to 2006, in the wake of the sexual abuse crisis; the second was an examination of the controversial statements by Bishop William Morris of Toowoomba, Australia, in 2007; and the third was an examination of the Legionaries of Christ for Canada and the United States, in 2009–10, in the aftermath of the scandal surrounding its founder, Father Maciel Delgado. Chaput also served on the board of directors for The Catholic University of America from 1994 to 2009, and the National Catholic Bioethics Center from 1993 to 2006, and has been active on the board of directors for Eternal Word Television Network in Birmingham, Alabama, since 1996.

As a member of the Prairie Band Potawatomi, Chaput has been active in the pastoral care of Native Americans, and serves as Chair of the Subcommittee on Native American Catholics. He was also instrumental in promoting the cause of canonization for St. Kateri Tekakwitha.

Chaput is the author of two books: *Living the Catholic Faith: Rediscovering the Basics* (2001) and *Render Unto Caesar: Serving the Nation by Living Our Catholic Beliefs in Political Life* (2008). The latter was on *The New York Times* bestseller list.

On June 19, 2011, Pope Benedict XVI appointed Chaput the archbishop of Philadelphia as successor to Cardinal Justin Rigali. He was installed as the thirteenth bishop and ninth archbishop of Philadelphia on September 8, 2011.

Chardon, Jean Baptiste (1672–1743)

One of the most gifted linguists serving as an American Jesuit missionary, Jean Baptiste Chardon labored for a time as the only priest west of Lake Michigan. He was born in Bordeaux, France, and entered the Society of Jesus. By 1700 Father Chardon was an ordained priest serving the Ottawa missions of America. In 1701 he went to Green Bay, Wisconsin, working there with Jesuit Father Henri Nouvel, who had been at the mission for over four decades.

Father Chardon learned the languages of the various Indian tribes with remarkable ease and respected their traditions with courtesy and enthusiasm, a trait that endeared him to the tribes. He also ministered to the Illinois Indians on the St. Joseph River, going there in 1711 and returning to Green Bay in 1728, where he spent the rest of his missionary apostolate. He retired to Québec and died there.

Charismatic Renewal

The movement for Charismatic Renewal is an international program in the Church, evolving from the Second Vatican Council. The programs offered by the movement give guidelines for personal and social conversion to Christ and openness to the charisms of the Holy Spirit. Catholic Charismatic Renewal originated in the United States and has been received in other nations of the world, where covenant communities and prayer groups have been formed and recognized by the Holy See. French communities, such as the Community of the Beatitude and the Emmanuel Community, like the American Mother of God Community in Maryland, have served as ideal groups and have fostered vocations to the priesthood. Some of these priests have undertaken pastoral ministries and now serve in America and Canada.

The Catholic Charismatic Renewal programs promote the reawakening of the faithful to the Scriptures, the sacraments, Marian devotion, and

Eucharistic adoration. At the same time, covenant communities engage in social welfare and transformation activities. The covenant community in Columbia has assumed ministries that serve the homeless and the poor. ECCLA, the Latin American umbrella organization for the renewal, coordinates activities in twenty countries and is involved in the formation of a renewed Christian culture.

The International Catholic Charismatic Renewal Services in Rome was granted ecclesiastical status with a juridical personality in September 1993. The organization conducted a retreat that same month, with a thousand delegates from ninety countries attending, including ecumenical representatives from various Protestant, Anglican, and Orthodox churches.

Additional impetus was provided in 1991 when scholarly literary works were published concerning Charismatic experiences. The movement is currently assessing the gains of the past twenty-five years and studying the ecumenical and sharing aspects of the programs.

Charleston, Diocese of

Established on July 11, 1820, by Pope Pius VII, the Diocese of Charleston serves the entire state of South Carolina. Charleston is a major Atlantic seaport and a commercial and industrial center. It was founded in 1670 as Charles Towne, for England's King Charles II, and the city was embroiled in the colonial wars against the Spanish and French in Florida and Louisiana. In 1722 the name was changed to Charles City and Port and then, in 1783, incorporated as Charleston. The Diocese of Charleston is a suffragan see of the Archdiocese of Atlanta.

The Catholic history of the diocese started around 1540, when Hernando de Soto, the Spanish explorer, led an expedition into the region. Priests accompanied the expedition, and Masses and other religious services were held, but no missions were established. Around 1586 the Spanish were once again in the area, founding a colony near modern-day Georgetown, South Carolina. The site was eventually abandoned, but Franciscans and Jesuits ministered to the tribal enclaves surrounding the former colony.

In 1670 an English colony was settled at Albemarle Point and remained an active center. In 1697 the colony was granted religious freedom, but Catholics were not included in the proclamation, as "popery," as the faith was called, was not welcomed in any English settlement. Priests entering the colony were arrested, and Catholics were punished in varying degrees for not supporting prevailing Protestant dogmas.

When the Revolutionary War started, however, Catholics in all the colonies responded vigorously and valiantly. The commitment of the American Catholics, as well as the example of the French military experts and nobles who arrived in the colonies to engage the British as American allies, brought honor and recognition to the Church. Catholics were provided with religious freedom and civil rights when the new constitution of the state of South Carolina was drawn up following the war's successful end.

In 1788 a traveling missionary celebrated Mass in Charleston, and in that same year Bishop John Carroll of Baltimore sent Father Matthew Ryan to the city. He began celebrating Catholic services in a local unused Protestant church, purchasing it the following year and naming it St. Mary's. Father Simon F. Gallagher served at St. Mary's in 1793, and he became a well-known academic leader in the city. He and the trustees of St. Mary's were involved in several disputes with Bishop John Carroll, causing scandal.

Adding to the complexity of the situation, French Catholics arrived in Charleston, having fled from the slave rebellion in Haiti. The French were accompanied by priests, and yet another group of French priests arrived in Charleston, survivors of the terrors of the French Revolution. The parishioners and trustees of St. Mary's continued to make demands about their administrative rights, and the episode became known as the Charleston Schism, lasting from 1812 until 1819. In 1817 Archbishop Leonard Neale of Baltimore, Bishop Carroll's successor, placed St. Mary's under an interdict.

Charleston was created a diocese in 1820, and one of the leading Catholic intellectuals of America was appointed to the new see. Bishop John England was consecrated on September 21, 1820, and given jurisdiction over North and South Carolina's

Catholic affairs, as well as the faithful in Georgia. Bishop England instituted the agencies and offices necessary for diocesan administration and built the Cathedral of St. John the Baptist. He also founded the first Catholic diocesan newspaper. Establishing a college, he invited religious congregations into the area and ended trusteeism and its practices. Bishop England also promoted participation of laymen and women in Church activities. With his sister, Joanna Monica England, he started the Sisters of Charity of Our Lady of Mercy. Schools for slaves and free blacks were also opened. Bishop England died on April 11, 1842.

The second bishop of Charleston was Ignatius A. Reynolds, who was consecrated on March 19, 1844. Bishop William Clancy had been appointed coadjutor bishop to Bishop England, but he was transferred to the Vicariate Apostolic of British Guiana in April 1837. Bishop Reynolds is credited in some records with laying the cornerstone of a new cathedral. He paid off diocesan debts and took part in the erection of the Diocese of Savannah in 1850, which reduced the size of Charleston. Bishop Reynolds died on March 6, 1855.

The third bishop of Charleston was Patrick Lynch, who was consecrated on March 14, 1858. He led the diocese when the Civil War began, and watched the cathedral be destroyed by fire. The entire diocese suffered during the war, and Bishop Lynch dedicated his efforts to rebuilding parishes and other properties. He went to Rome to acquaint Pope Blessed Pius IX with the Confederate cause, and prior to his return trip to America, he had to take an oath of allegiance to the United States in Paris on October 14, 1865, in order to be allowed to reenter the country. Bishop Lynch also received a pardon from President Andrew Jackson, when Archbishop (later Cardinal) John McCloskey and Archbishop Martin J. Spalding intervened. Safely returned to Charleston, he rebuilt the damaged facilities and instituted a system of parochial schools in the Charleston diocese. He died on February 26, 1882.

On January 27, 1883, Bishop Henry P. Northrop, the vicar apostolic of North Carolina, was transferred to Charleston as its fourth bishop. Three years later, a severe earthquake damaged the entire region, and Bishop Northrop led vast renova-

tion and repair programs. He established a Catholic high school, a hospital, and fifteen parishes. He also welcomed Maronite Catholics into the diocese, conducted a synod, and introduced the Knights of Columbus and the Holy Name apostolates to the faithful. He died on June 17, 1916.

The fifth bishop of Charleston, William T. Russell, was consecrated on March 15, 1917. World War I impacted on the diocese, and Bishop Russell aided the military efforts of the nation. He was also one of the organizers of the National Catholic War Council, established as a Catholic response to America's needs. In Charleston he built parishes and promoted educational programs and facilities. Bishop Russell died on March 18, 1927.

His successor was Bishop Emmet M. Walsh, who was consecrated the diocese's sixth bishop on September 8, 1927. He expanded diocesan facilities and services and built Catholic hospitals while leading the diocese through the Great Depression and World War II. Bishop Walsh also welcomed the Oratorians of St. Philip Neri and the Trappists of Our Lady of Mepkin Abbey. On September 8, 1949, Bishop Walsh was transferred to the Diocese of Youngstown as coadjutor bishop.

Bishop John J. Russell succeeded Bishop Walsh as the seventh bishop of Charleston, consecrated on March 14, 1950. He founded the diocesan newspaper, built parishes, and welcomed the Poor Clares into the diocese. He also instituted the Confraternity of Christian Doctrine. Bishop Russell was transferred to the Diocese of Richmond on July 10, 1958.

His successor was Bishop Paul J. Hallinan, who was consecrated the eighth bishop on October 28, 1958. He faced school desegregation issues and the anti-Catholicism rampant during the 1960 presidential election. On February 21, 1962, Bishop Hallinan was promoted to the Archdiocese of Atlanta.

Bishop Francis F. Reh was his successor for a brief period. He was consecrated on June 29, 1962, and continued the work of expanding facilities and diocesan services and defending Catholic rights until September 5, 1964, when he was transferred to the North American College in Rome.

The tenth bishop of Charleston was Ernest L. Unterkoefler, who had served as auxiliary bishop of Richmond since 1962. He was appointed to Charleston on December 12, 1964. Bishop Unterkoefler implemented the reforms mandated by the Second Vatican Council and introduced new agencies and programs to foster lay participation and implement liturgical reforms. He served on national committees of bishops and in September 1987 hosted Pope Blessed John Paul II during the Holy Father's visit. Bishop Unterkoefler retired on February 22, 1990, after decades of faithful service.

His successor was Bishop David B. Thompson, who had served as coadjutor bishop of the diocese since 1989. The eleventh bishop of Charleston, Thompson presided over the celebration of the 175th anniversary of the Diocese of Charleston and convened a synod. He retired on July 13, 1999.

The twelfth bishop of Charleston, Robert J. Baker, was appointed to the see on July 13, 1999, and consecrated as Bishop Thompson's successor on September 29, 1999. On August 14, 2007, Bishop Baker was transferred to the Diocese of Baker. On January 24, 2009, Father Robert E. Guglielmone was appointed the thirteenth bishop of Charleston. He was ordained bishop on March 25, 2009. In 2011 there were 174,000 Catholics served by 160 priests, 123 women religious, and 73 parishes in the diocese.

Charlotte, Diocese of

Established on January 12, 1972, by Pope Paul VI, the Diocese of Charlotte serves counties in western North Carolina. Charlotte is a diversified industrial city that serves as a center for agriculture and manufacturing. The city was incorporated in 1768, named for Princess Charlotte Sophia of Mecklenburg-Strelitz, later the queen of King George III of England. Charlotte was the center for gold production in the United States until the California Gold Rush in 1849. The Diocese of Charlotte is a suffragan see of the Archdiocese of Atlanta.

Charlotte has a historic Catholic legacy that began in 1524, when Giovanni da Verrazano, an Italian, explored the area while in the service of France. In 1526 the Spanish expedition of Lucas Vásquez de Ayllón settled on the southwestern coast of North Carolina, but left soon afterward. Hernando de Soto, another Spaniard, explored the western region of the state around 1540.

Forty-five years later, Sir Walter Raleigh attempted a settlement for the English but that lasted only a year. A second group of settlers arrived in 1584. By 1590 the larger, original group had vanished. Not until 1650 did the English start any new settlements. In 1663 King Charles II granted eight lord proprietors the right to govern North Carolina. In 1677, however, colonists led by John Culpepper established a self-rule that was crushed by English military forces.

The cradle of Catholicism in the region was at New Bern in the early 1700s, where French settlers had congregated. From 1711 to 1713, the Tuscarora Indians fought against occupation of their lands, but in 1729, King George II established royal governors in the area, individuals who managed to alienate colonists and prompt discussions about independence. North Carolina sent delegates to the First Continental Congress in 1774 and, when revolution was decided upon, became the first colony to declare independence from England.

American Catholics and the European nobles, mainly French, who arrived to aid the American cause in the Revolutionary War earned the respect of Protestants because of their bravery and commitment to the fight for liberty. As a result, North Carolina, along with other new states, provided civil rights and religious freedom to Catholics. A test oath that demanded that every citizen support the Protestant religion kept Catholics out of public office, with some notable exceptions, but this oath was eliminated in 1836.

Charlotte and other communities in North and South Carolina, and in parts of Georgia, were in the episcopal jurisdiction of the Diocese of Charleston after 1820. Bishop John England served in Charleston and was an energetic leader of the faith. By 1842, however, there were still only four churches for the faithful in North Carolina, at Fayetteville, New Bern, Raleigh, and Washington. Catholics were still targeted by bigoted Protestant groups, and some areas sustained violent attacks by mobs. In 1852 Dr. Levi Silliman Ives, an Episcopalian bishop in North Carolina, became a convert to the Catholic Church, an event that horrified his family and friends and led to further antagonisms.

The Catholics of the state took part in the Civil War, but North Carolina was among the last to secede from the Union and was readmitted in 1868. The state was occupied by federal troops until 1877, when the Reconstruction period ended. On March 3, 1868, Pope Blessed Pius IX established the Vicariate Apostolic of North Carolina, recognizing the vigor of the faithful in the face of abuse and suffering.

Bishop James Gibbons, who would become a cardinal, served as vicar apostolic of North Carolina until 1872, when he became the bishop of Richmond. He still administered the vicariate. In 1878 Bishop John Joseph Keane became vicar apostolic and bishop of Richmond. He was followed in 1882 by Bishop Henry P. Northrop. Bishop Leo B. Haid, the first Benedictine Abbot of Mary-help Abbey at Belmont, also served the vicariate.

Charlotte's first bishop, Michael J. Begley

The Catholics of North Carolina supported the military efforts of the nation during World War I and then faced the Great Depression. World War II followed, bringing more sacrifices and economic recovery to the area. The Diocese of Raleigh had been erected in 1924, and the Church was moving forward in the area as the reforms and years later programs mandated by the Second Vatican Council were implemented and laypeople became involved in evangelization.

In January 1972, the Diocese of Charlotte was established, and Bishop Michael J. Begley was consecrated as the first bishop on January 12. He instituted the offices and agencies necessary for diocesan administration and designated St. Patrick's Church as the cathedral. Bishop Begley faced a rapidly growing Catholic population and the arrival of Central American workers. Special programs to assist the Latino faithful were developed. Bishop Begley retired in 1984.

His successor was Bishop John F. Donaghue, who was consecrated as the second bishop of Charlotte on December 18, 1984. Bishop Donaghue expanded diocesan facilities and programs and erected new parishes to meet the demands of the growing Catholic population. On June 22, 1993, he was promoted to the Archdiocese of Atlanta.

Bishop William G. Curlin became the third bishop of Charlotte and was installed on April 13, 1994. He had served as auxiliary bishop of Washington since 1988. Bishop Curlin started the "Decade of Evangelization" to reach the vast numbers of "unchurched" in the diocese. He retired on September 10, 2002.

The fourth bishop of Charlotte, Peter Joseph Jugis, was appointed on August 1, 2003. He was consecrated on October 24, 2003. Bishop Jugis spent much of his first year — like other bishops in the country — dealing with the sex abuse crisis. He also devoted himself to visits to the diocesan parishes and schools. In March 2005 he issued liturgical norms for the diocese in keeping with the *General Instruction of the Roman Missal,* which was approved in an English translation in 2003, and the Holy See instruction on the Eucharist, *Redemptionis Sacramentum,* issued in 2004.

Two of the great challenges facing the diocese remain the large numbers of unchurched and the rapid growth of the population in the area. The Catholic population has grown at an equally steady pace with the general population, so that the diocese found it necessary to embrace pastoral programs. In 2011 there were 195,000 Catholics, served by 130 priests and 91 parishes in the diocese.

Chastellux, François-Jean de Beauvoir, Chevalier (1734–1788)

A noble of France, François-Jean de Beauvoir Chastellux became an ally of the Americans in the Revolutionary War. He had entered France's army at age thirteen and held the rank of second lieutenant. He was a colonel by twenty-one, and became famous in May 1755, when he became the first Frenchman to be inoculated for smallpox. He was also a writer who achieved considerable popularity. When the American Revolution started, Chastellux was designated a major general and assigned to the Comte de Rochambeau's French force, which aided the revolutionary cause.

Chastellux arrived in America in July 1780. While on duty with the American military, he wrote a series on *Travels in North America in the Years 1780, 1782 and 1792*. He served as Rochambeau's diplomatic liaison to the Americans during that period, as he was able to converse with the social elite and with common Americans easily. When the war ended, Chastellux returned to France and was made a marquis and inspector general. He also served as the military governor of Gongwy.

Chaumonot, Pierre-Joseph (1611–February 21, 1693)

A Jesuit missionary to the Hurons, Pierre-Joseph Chaumonot was an assistant to St. John de Brébeuf. He was born in a village near Châtillon-sur-Seine, France. Some records state that his family name was Calvonotti. He entered the Society of Jesus in Rome, where he completed his seminary studies. Ordained to the priesthood, Father Chaumonot was assigned to the Canadian missions.

Stationed at Lake Huron, Father Chaumonot served as an assistant to St. John de Brébeuf. When the Iroquois martyred St. John, Father Chaumonot led four hundred Catholic Hurons to Québec, where they were given haven on the Isle of Orleans, opposite the city. The Huron settlements were still targets of Iroquois raids, however. He was then assigned to assist Father Claude Daillon in the Onondaga missions in New York, founded by Father Simon Le Moyne. He stayed there for two years but had to abandon the site in 1657. The Iroquois were causing unrest, and some fifty colonists were forced to flee northward with the Jesuits. In Canada, Father Chaumonot worked with the Hurons, establishing Lorette settlement. He also founded the Congregation of the Holy Family, active in Canada. He died in Québec.

Chavez, Cesar (March 31, 1927–April 23, 1993)

The famed leader of migrant farmworkers, Cesar Chavez was the founder of the United Farm Workers. He was born near Yuma, Arizona, on a family farm. In 1939, however, the family had to give up their lands because of unpaid taxes. They entered the vast numbers of migrant workers as a result, and Chavez labored as an itinerant until 1944, when he joined the U.S. Navy.

In 1946 he went to Delano, California, where he married Helena Tabela. They had eight children and moved to San Jose. There, Chavez met Father Donald McDonnell and Fred Ross, two individuals who educated him in Catholic social doctrine and worker organization. Ross was introducing the Community Service Organization in California and enlisted Chavez's aid. In 1958 Chavez served as executive director of CSO in California and established the National Farm Workers Association in 1962. He built his membership and in 1965 joined the Agricultural Organizing Committee in a strike against grape growers in Delano.

Chavez used Catholic social teachings during the prolonged strike and introduced nonviolence, "The Cause" (*La Causa*). He and his fellow workers faced many problems and the intervention of other union groups. Chavez used marches to gather media notice and in 1968 a major grower in Sacramento signed a contract with Chavez and UFW. Economic boycotts were also used against lettuce growers in 1972. In 1975 Chavez witnessed the signing of the Agricultural Labor Relations Act to stop unfair practices against migratory workers.

Chavez was a daily communicant toward the end of his life. Membership in UFW dwindled and a boycott called by Chavez in 1984 did not prove viable. He died in Yuma, Arizona, knowing that he had translated Catholic teachings into the struggle of the invisible migrant workers of America.

Chavez, Dennis (April 8, 1888–November 18, 1962)

A United States senator born in Los Chavez, New Mexico, Dennis Chavez had only an eighth-grade education. The family moved to Albuquerque, and there he married Ismelda Espinosa in 1911. Five years later, he served in the campaign of Senator Andribus A. Jones and took a position as a U.S. Senate clerk.

Chavez took a special examination and was admitted to Georgetown University, where he received an a Bachelor of Laws in 1920. The family then returned to New Mexico, where he became involved in politics. He served as a U.S. representative from 1930 to 1936. He also served as a U.S. senator from 1936 to 1962. Chavez died in Washington, D.C. In 1976 the federal building in Albuquerque was named the Senator Dennis Chavez Federal Center.

Cheverus, Jean-Louis-Anne-Madeleine Lefebvre de (1768–July 19, 1836)

One of the most honored and beloved Catholic missionaries in early America, Jean-Louis Lefebvre de Cheverus served as the bishop of Boston and then as a cardinal of France. He was born in Notre Dame de Mayenne, France, and was well educated and cultured. Studying at Saint-Magloire with the Oratorians, he was ordained on December 18, 1790, becoming a pastor and vicar general of Mayenne. Two years later, as the horrors of the French Revolution began to take a toll on the French nobility and Catholic leaders, he refused to recognize the "Civil Constitution of the Clergy" and had to leave France.

Father de Cheverus served in England for four years, becoming a celebrated preacher and founding Tottenham Chapel, then he sailed to America, arriving in Boston on October, 3, 1796. He aided Father François Matignon in parish work and also served the Abenaki and other Indian groups in Maine. With Father Matignon, Cheverus dedicated Holy Cross Church in Boston in 1803, receiving support from George Washington and other prominent Americans.

On April, 8, 1808, he was named the first bishop of Boston by Pope Pius VII, and he was consecrated on November 1, 1810. He earned the respect of Protestants, who were impressed with his culture, refinement, and education. His fame spread throughout New England, and when he wrote literary defenses of Catholicism he earned even more respect. At one event he was given a place of honor at a banquet table, second only to President John Adams.

In 1823 King Louis XVIII summoned Bishop de Cheverus to France. This notice of recall brought a storm of protest from Americans of all faiths. A petition was sent to the French monarch and read in part: "We all hold him to be a blessing and a treasure in our social community which we cannot part with." Daniel Webster was one of the signers of that petition. Bishop de Cheverus returned to France, as King Louis would not be persuaded otherwise, and was named the bishop of Montaubon, a Huguenot stronghold. Within a few months word was sent from Montaubon, declaring: "There are no longer any Protestants at Montaubon; we are all the bishop's people."

On July 30, 1826, he was made the archbishop of Bordeaux, created a peer of France, and given honors. In the chapel of the Tuileries in Paris, he received the red hat of the cardinalate in 1836. The French king had beseeched Pope Gregory XVI for the privilege of bestowing the rank personally. Cardinal de Cheverus died in Mayenne, mourned by the French and by Americans.

Cardinal Jean Cheverus

Cheyenne, Diocese of

Established on August 2, 1887, by Pope Leo XIII, the Diocese of Cheyenne serves the state of Wyoming and Yellowstone National Park. The capital of the state, Cheyenne is also an industrial and livestock center. The first whites arrived in the area in 1867 and named the settlement after the Cheyenne Indian nation. By 1870 the town served as a center for outfitting the gold miners of the Black Hills and as a shipping point for cattle. Cheyenne was a wild frontier outpost and was called "Hell on Wheels" until vigilante groups and law officers ended the war between the cattlemen and the sheepherders. The city now has diversified manufacturing and marketing. The diocese is a suffragan see of the Archdiocese of Denver.

The Catholic heritage of Wyoming began officially with the arrival of the famous Jesuit missionary Father Pierre-Jean De Smet, who was laboring in the region around Daniel. He celebrated Mass at the Rendezvous on the Green River on July 5, 1840. The Flatheads of Wyoming, hearing about the Mass, attended with the Shoshone and Nez Perce, sitting beside American mountain men and

French trappers. The Flatheads, having been visited by Young Ignace La Mousse, an Iroquois Catholic, had sent delegations to St. Louis, requesting a "Black Robe" to minister to them, and Father De Smet was the first priest made available. A trading post had also been erected at Fort Laramie in 1834, although French trappers and hunters were in the area long before.

The present state of Wyoming was partly included in the Vicariate Apostolic of the Indian Territory, erected by the Holy See in 1850. The Vicariate Apostolic of the Rocky Mountains that was erected a year later also included Wyoming territories. Bishop Jean Baptiste Miège, another Jesuit, was vicar apostolic and established his residence in Leavenworth, Kansas. Wyoming then became part of the Vicariate Apostolic of Nebraska in 1857. Bishop James Miles O'Gorman, a Trappist, served as the vicar apostolic.

A decade later, Father William Kelly started a parish in Wyoming, and Bishop O'Gorman rode on the newly completed Union Pacific Railroad to visit the area. Father Eugene Cusson established a parish in Laramie, and in 1877 the second vicar apostolic, Bishop James O'Connor, spent three months in Wyoming. The Jesuits founded St. Stephen's Mission on the Wind River reservation in 1884 for the Shoshone and Northern Arapahoes. The Sisters of Charity of Leavenworth arrived soon after to operate the mission school, replaced by the Sisters of St. Joseph and then by Franciscan Sisters. St. Katharine Drexel founded these evangelical efforts.

On August 2, 1887, the Diocese of Cheyenne was erected as a suffragan see of the Archdiocese of St. Louis. The diocese included Yellowstone National Park, which had been so designated in 1872. Bishop Maurice Francis Burke was consecrated on October 28, 1887, as the first bishop of Cheyenne, assuming the new see. He instituted offices and agencies for diocesan administration and had to defend the faithful from Protestant uprisings that included threats from the local Know-Nothings. Bishop Burke discovered that his new diocese was about the size of Great Britain and was threatened by severe anti-Catholicism. He traveled in every possible manner to acquaint himself with the faithful and then started recruit-

ing religious and priests. Bishop Burke apparently suggested that the Holy See suppress the diocese, but no such action was taken. He was transferred on June 19, 1893, to the Diocese of St. Joseph (now the Diocese of Kansas City-St. Joseph), and Cheyenne became part of the province of Dubuque. A pastor from Laramie, Father Hugh Cummiskey, became administrator, serving in that capacity for four years.

The second bishop of Cheyenne was Thomas Mathias Lenihan, who was consecrated on February 24, 1897. He also faced anti-Catholic demonstrations and legislation, but he continued to expand diocesan facilities and opened new parishes. Bishop Lenihan suffered severe health problems and had to return to Iowa, where he died on December 15, 1901.

The third bishop of Cheyenne, James John Joseph Keane, was consecrated on October 28, 1902. He quickly grasped the mission status of the diocese and began vast expansion programs. He also incorporated the diocese to protect it legally, incorporated parishes as well, and started a cathedral on July 7, 1907. The Catholic Church Extension Society funded Bishop Keane's programs. On August 11, 1911, Bishop Keane was promoted to the Archdiocese of Dubuque.

Bishop Patrick Aloysius McGovern became the fourth bishop of Cheyenne when he was consecrated on April 11, 1912, and installed in the see. Stricken with a severe illness, Bishop McGovern underwent surgery, but returned to his labors. He convened two diocesan synods and led programs to care for orphans and abandoned children. Care institutions and schools were established throughout the diocese. Bishop McGovern collapsed and was hospitalized but returned once again to his work. He led the diocese through World War I, the Great Depression, and World War II, all the time aiding the Native Americans in the diocese and writing a history of Cheyenne. The Holy See appointed him an Assistant at the Pontifical Throne, and a coadjutor was named for the diocese. Bishop McGovern died on November 8, 1951.

Bishop Hubert Michael Newell had been consecrated as the coadjutor bishop of Cheyenne with right of succession on September 24, 1947. The fifth bishop of Cheyenne, he acceded to the see when

Bishop McGovern died and continued the vast expansion programs in the diocese. He also founded a diocesan newspaper and promoted the Catholic Youth Organization. Bishop Newell attended the Second Vatican Council and upon his return to the diocese implemented the reforms mandated by that council and promoted lay participation. He retired on January 3, 1978, but remained administrator until June.

His successor, Bishop Hubert Joseph Hart, was installed as the sixth bishop of Cheyenne on June 12, 1978. He had been auxiliary bishop since 1976. Bishop Hart opened a spiritual renewal program in the diocese, welcomed the Benedictine Nuns of Perpetual Adoration to Wyoming, and established parish councils and a diaconate program. Bishop Hart retired on September 26, 2001.

Before his retirement, Bishop Hart requested a coadjutor bishop from the Holy See, and on January 6, 2000, Pope Blessed John Paul II consecrated David Lauren Ricken. The seventh bishop, David Laurin Ricken, was appointed coadjutor bishop on December 14, 1999, and acceded to the see upon the retirement of Bishop Hart on September 26, 2001. Bishop Ricken was transferred to the Diocese of Green Bay on July 9, 2008, and Father Paul D. Etienne was named his successor on October 19, 2009; he was consecrated eighth bishop of Cheyenne on December 9, 2009. In 2011 there were 53,000 Catholics served by 63 priests and 34 parishes in the diocese.

Chicago, Archdiocese of

Established as a diocese on November 28, 1843, by Pope Gregory XVI and as an archdiocese on September 10, 1880, by Pope Leo XIII, the Archdiocese of Chicago is a metropolitan see with suffragan sees and serves northeastern Illinois. Chicago is a major American city on the shore of Lake Michigan, and a rail hub, airline center, and major port. The archdiocese is one of the largest and most financially important in the Catholic Church.

The Catholic heritage of the archdiocese dates to 1673, when Jesuit Father Jacques Marquette and the French explorer Louis Joliet entered the area in May of that year. A year later, Father Marquette returned to the area with two companions. He offered Masses and served the local Indian tribes until March 30, 1675, when he traveled to Kaskaskia.

One year later, Jesuit Father Claude Allouez, another esteemed missionary pioneer, labored in the region. In 1688 René-Robert Chevalier, Sieur de La Salle, conducted an expedition in the area, accompanied by the Franciscan Recollect Father Zenobius Membré, who would be martyred later. In 1696 Jesuit Father François Pinet established the Indian Mission of the Guardian Angel for the Miami. Jesuit Father Jean Mermet labored there until 1702, and the Jesuit priests Fathers Sebastian L. Meurin and Pierre Gibault were also serving the Native tribes in the region.

The wars between the Fox and the Iroquois against the French halted the missions for a time, and in 1763 the Illinois Territory was ceded to England. Under the terms of the Treaty of Paris, the Illinois Territory became part of the United States in 1783. In 1797 the local tribes relinquished Chicago to the United States as well.

Fort Dearborn, erected in Chicago in 1804, was abandoned in the War of 1812, but reopened in 1816. Two years later, Illinois entered the Union. Father Gabriel Richard, a Sulpician, visited Fort Dearborn, and the Catholics in Chicago appealed to the Diocese of St. Louis (now the Archdiocese of St. Louis) for priests and religious.

Father Jean Marie Irenaeus St. Cyr, who had

First Bishop of Chicago, William Quarter

been ordained only days before, was sent to Chicago on April 17, 1833. There he founded St. Mary's Church. One year later, the Diocese of Vincennes (now the Archdiocese of Indianapolis) was erected. Fathers Bernard Schaeffer and Timothy O'Meara arrived in Chicago, as the Erie Canal was transporting settlers to Chicago. The city was designated as a diocese in 1843.

The first bishop of the Diocese of Chicago was William J. Quarter. He was consecrated on March 10, 1844, and reportedly found eight priests and eighteen churches in the city, as well as a large debt on St. Mary's. He paid off debts and erected three new parishes and eight missions. Bishop Quarter also established St. Mary of the Lake and organized the agencies and offices necessary for diocesan administration. In 1847 he presided over a diocesan synod. Bishop Quarter died on April 10, 1848.

His successor was Bishop James Oliver Van de Velde, who was consecrated second bishop of Chicago on February 11, 1849. Bishop Van de Velde built schools and parishes and invited the Mercy Sisters to the diocese in 1851. He also founded a diocesan newspaper and took part in the establishment of the Diocese of Quincy (now the Diocese of Springfield in Illinois) in 1853. On July 29 of that year, Bishop Van de Velde was transferred to the Diocese of Natchez (now the Diocese of Jackson).

Bishop Anthony O'Regan was his successor, being consecrated third bishop of Chicago on July 25, 1894. Bishop O'Regan was a profound scholar and academic. He invited the Society of Jesus to come to Chicago, welcoming Jesuit Father Arnold Damen, a remarkable missionary whose apostolate covered a wide area. Bishop O'Regan retired on May 3, 1858, and went to live in London.

The fourth bishop of Chicago was James Duggan, who had served as coadjutor bishop of the Archdiocese of St. Louis since 1857. On January 21, 1859, he was transferred to Chicago, where he promoted the parochial school system and established parishes for the growing Catholic population. In 1862 Bishop Duggan attended the canonization of the Martyrs of Japan and four years later took part in the Second Plenary Council of Baltimore. On April 14, 1869, Bishop Duggan was hospitalized for a mental illness. He died on March 27, 1899.

Bishop Thomas Foley, who was appointed administrator of the diocese, was consecrated as the coadjutor of Chicago on February 27, 1870. In 1871 the city of Chicago was ravaged by fire. St. Mary's Cathedral, seven churches, schools, and thirteen thousand buildings were consumed. There were one hundred thousand homeless in the city. Bishop Foley sent priests of the diocese across the United States to beg for funds, and he started to rebuild immediately. The Franciscans, Servites, Viatorians, and other religious responded to his invitations and arrived to labor in the city. Holy Name Cathedral was dedicated on November 23, 1875. Five years earlier, Loyola University had been opened. The Diocese of Peoria was also erected in 1877, easing the burdens of Bishop Foley. He died on February 19, 1879.

The "Apostle of the Schools" was Bishop Foley's successor, Archbishop Patrick Augustine Feehan. He had served as the bishop of Nashville since 1865 and was promoted to Chicago on September 10, 1880, when Chicago was created an archdiocese. His focus was on the parochial school system of the archdiocese and on higher education, and during his term he promoted both effectively, doubling the number of elementary schools and instituting academies and colleges. Archbishop Feehan convened the first archdiocesan synod in 1887. Archbishop Feehan died on July 12, 1902.

James Edward Quigley, the second archbishop of Chicago, succeeded Archbishop Feehan, and he provided the archdiocese with a profound sense of maturity. He had served as the bishop of Buffalo since 1897 and was promoted to Chicago on January 8, 1903. He strengthened archdiocesan agencies and services and participated in the founding of the Catholic Church Extension Society. Homes for children and other facilities providing care for immigrants and the working class were added to the archdiocesan ministries. Archbishop Quigley also presided over an archdiocesan synod. He died on July 10, 1915, after suffering a stroke.

The third archbishop of Chicago was George Mundelein. The former auxiliary bishop of Brooklyn, he was promoted to the Archdiocese of Chicago on December 9, 1915, and installed on February 9, 1916. Supporting the military efforts of the nation during World War I, he also founded Quigley Preparatory Seminary and St. Mary of the Lake Seminary. He updated and renewed diocesan agencies as well, working with St. Frances Xavier Cabrini, who died in Chicago in 1917. On March 24, 1924, he was created a cardinal priest with the titular church of Santa Maria del Popolo. When Cardinal Mundelein returned from Rome he was greeted by a massive celebration, at which he received a check for $1 million for the seminary.

Cardinal Mundelein was a friend of President Franklin Delano Roosevelt and Pope Pius XI. He operated the largest school system in the United States and instituted a diocesan bank to aid poor parishes during the Great Depression. In 1926 he presided over the 28th International Eucharistic Congress. Cardinal Mundelein died on October 2, 1939.

His successor was Cardinal Samuel Alphonsus Stritch, who had served as the bishop of Toledo and as the archbishop of Milwaukee. He was appointed to Chicago and installed on March 7, 1940. During World War II, he conducted Holy Hours at Soldier Field, presiding over two hundred thousand of the faithful in these devotions. On February 18, 1946, he was created a cardinal priest, with the titular church of Santa Agnes fueri le Mura. Cardinal Stritch reorganized the archdiocesan communications programs, established the Council of Catholic Women, and assisted the Holy Name Society. He also presided over integration programs in the parishes and parochial schools. On March 1, 1958, Cardinal Stritch was promoted as Prefect of the Sacred Congregation for the Propagation of the Faith in Rome, the first American to be given that honor. He died in Rome on May 27, 1958.

Cardinal Albert G. Meyer was his successor, who had previously served as the bishop of Superior and as the archbishop of Milwaukee. He was installed in Chicago on November 16, 1959. He was created a cardinal priest on December 14, 1959, with the titular church of Santa Cecilia. Cardinal Meyer continued the integration of the parochial schools and aided the faithful during the tragedy at Our Lady of the Angels school, when a fire killed ninety-two children and three nuns. He attended the Second Vatican Council and hosted a national conference on race and religion. Cardinal Meyer also aided the Woodlawn Organization and other neighborhood groups in easing racial tensions. In

February 1965 it was announced that Cardinal Meyer suffered from a malignant brain tumor. He died on April 9, 1965.

His successor was Cardinal John Patrick Cody, who had served as auxiliary bishop of St. Louis, bishop of Kansas City-St. Joseph, and archbishop of New Orleans. He was installed in Chicago on August 24, 1965, and was created a cardinal priest, with the titular church of Santa Cecilia, on June 25, 1967. He introduced a centralization program and was opposed by an association of archdiocesan priests. Cardinal Cody also implemented the reforms mandated by the Second Vatican Council and continued the expansion programs in education and charitable ministries. He died on April 25, 1982.

The seventh archbishop of Chicago, Cardinal Joseph Louis Bernardin, was the successor to Cardinal Cody. He had served as auxiliary bishop of Atlanta and as archbishop of Cincinnati. He was installed in the Archdiocese of Chicago on August 25, 1982, and was created a cardinal priest, with the titular church of Jesus the Divine Worker, on February 2, 1983. He also served as president of the National Conference of Catholic Bishops and the United States Catholic Conference. Cardinal Bernardin developed and promoted a "consistent ethic of life" and represented the American hierarchy in Rome. He raised $62 million in ten years for Catholic inner-city schools and expanded the charitable ministries of the archdiocese.

In 1993 a young layman falsely accused Cardinal Bernardin of sexual abuse, and the media conducted a massive campaign against the cardinal. The young man recanted and refuted the charges he had made, but some in the media continued to level them vehemently without apologizing for their error. In June 1995, the cardinal was diagnosed with pancreatic cancer. Until his death on November 14, 1996, he inspired millions with his courage and dignity, receiving the Presidential Medal of Freedom, which was bestowed upon him by President Bill Clinton at the White House.

The eighth archbishop of Chicago, Cardinal Francis George, an Oblate of Mary Immaculate, had served as the bishop of Yakima until 1996, and then as archbishop of Portland in Oregon. He was appointed to the Archdiocese of Chicago on

April 8, 1997, and installed on May 7 of that year. On February 21, 1998, he was created a cardinal priest with the titular church of St. Bartholomew on Tiber Island. Cardinal George served during the tumultuous period of the sex abuse scandal in the American Church and coped with the demands of Chicago's economic and social troubles. In 2011 there were 2.3 million Catholics in the archdiocese, served by 1,580 priests, 270 men religious, nearly 2,000 women religious, and 357 parishes.

Chirouse, Eugene Casimir (1821–May 28, 1892)

Honored as the "Apostle of Puget Sound," Father Eugene Casimir Chirouse, a tireless Oblate missionary, served the American Northwest Territories and was a trusted friend of many Native American tribes. He was born in France and entered the Oblates of Mary Immaculate, and was sent to America in the midst of his seminary studies. Walking, riding, and traveling by boat across the continent, he reached Walla Walla (Nesqually), Washington, where he was ordained on January 2, 1848.

Following his ordination, Father Chirouse was assigned to the St. Rose Mission in Yakima, where he studied Indian traditions and languages. In 1852 he reopened the Cayuse Mission on the Umatilla River, which was the scene of the Whitman Massacre. He renamed the mission St. Anne's and labored to build a solid parish there. Four years later he went to Olympia, at the time called Priest's Point, on Puget Sound. For over three decades he labored in that region, building a chapel, residence, and school at Tulalip.

Father Chirouse offered not only spiritual ceremonies and the sacraments to the Native Americans of the Swinomish, Lummi, and Muckleshoot tribes, but clothed and fed them in times of crisis. He also served as a reservation agent for the Federal Bureau of Indian Affairs. He died in British Columbia, having started a new ministry there in 1878.

Christian Brothers, Congregation of

The Congregation of Christian Brothers, also known as the Christian Brothers Institute (C.F.C.) or the Irish Christian Brothers, is a teaching congregation founded in 1802 in Waterford, Ireland.

St. Edmund Ignatius Rice established the congregation to aid in the education of Irish children. The religious persecution of the Church by the English had impacted tragically upon Catholics, reducing them to poverty. St. Edmund, seeing the conditions under which young Irish lads tried to find a decent education, gave up his prosperous business and in 1802 began to instruct the neglected youth of Waterford.

In August 1808, with six companions, St. Edmund made religious vows, and he received the name Brother Ignatius. Papal approval was granted in 1820, and St. Edmund was elected the first superior general. As word of the congregation spread throughout the Catholic world, the Irish Christian Brothers were asked to aid dioceses in educating young people. Four brothers were sent to Australia in 1868, and six years later brothers were sent to Newfoundland, Canada. The British colony of Gibraltar received the congregation in 1877, and in 1886, at the request of the Holy See, schools were opened in India. In 1906 the Brothers were asked to open a school at All Saints Parish in New York City. This was the cradle of the North American province.

Christian Schools, Brothers of the

The Institute of the Brothers of the Christian Schools, also known as Christian Brothers, or de La Salle Christian Brothers, is a congregation founded by St. John Baptist de La Salle about 1680 in Reims, France. St. John Baptist de La Salle was born in 1651 to a prosperous family in Reims. Appointed canon of the cathedral at Reims at age sixteen, he was ordained on April 9, 1678. Serving in the cathedral, he became aware of the educational needs of the urban poor. He resigned his position as canon and gave his fortune to the poor in order to begin a new ministry.

In 1682 he began living with a group of educators, and by 1686 St. John had formed the teachers into a community that became known as the Brothers of the Christian Schools. The brothers with St. John took private vows of obedience renewable annually. These brothers elected him as superior, and on January 26, 1725, Pope Benedict XIII gave approval to the congregation as an institute of pontifical right in a bull of approbation.

Following the Second Vatican Council, the Brothers of the Christian Schools introduced changes in the rule to provide for new ministries and practices. Authority over the whole institute is entrusted to a superior general. The motherhouse, located originally in France, then in Belgium, has been in Rome since 1936.

The institute has faced serious crises over the centuries and has been blessed by martyrs in its ranks. In the twentieth century, the institute expanded, and by the end of the Second Vatican Council in 1965 there were more than 16,000 brothers conducting schools in eighty countries. As of October 2000, there were 6,522 brothers, 2,692 of them active in the educational ministry on all six continents.

The first de La Salle Brothers to come to the United States taught in the parish school at St. Geneviève, Missouri, from 1819 to 1822. The first permanent institution in the United States was Calvert Hall School, established in the cathedral parish in Baltimore in 1845 and staffed by two American brothers who had made their novitiate in Montréal. In 1848 four brothers were sent from France to New York to open a parish school on Canal Street. In that same year Brother Facile Rabut was appointed visitor of North America to supervise the five communities and fifty-six brothers in Canada and the United States. In 1862 a novitiate and in 1864 a provincialate were opened in New York to serve as a center for the spread of the institute to the West and South. By 1873 five districts had been created, seventy-six communities had been opened, and nine hundred brothers were teaching in more than one hundred schools. Christian Brothers College in St. Louis was chartered in 1853, followed by colleges in New York, Philadelphia, Ellicott City, New Orleans, San Francisco, Memphis, Santa Fe, and Washington, D.C. Today the Christian Brothers remain active across the United States through two provinces and are active in thirty states.

St. John Baptist de La Salle was canonized in 1900, and other Brothers have been formally canonized and beatified also. The canonized Brothers are: Benilde Romancon, in 1967; Miguel Febres-Cordero, in 1984; Mutien-Marie Wiaux, in 1989; Martyred Brothers in Spain, in 1999; Jaime Barbal, in 1999; and eight brothers with their Passionist chaplain at Turon. Beatified are Brothers Arnold Rèche, in 1987; Scubilion Rousseau, in 1989; the seven brothers martyred at Almería in Spain, in 1993; and in 2001 the five brothers martyred at Valencia.

Christophers, The

The Christophers was founded in 1945 by Father James Keller of Maryknoll to provide communication skills in print and electronic media. The Christophers are "Christ-bearers" and are dedicated to fostering Catholic values in the mainstream of American current affairs. The Christopher movement is particularly involved in applying the Catholic faith to the creative arts, education, government, and labor management. The Chrisotphers use the media to spread a message of hope and understanding to people of all faiths and of no particular faith.

Using the motto "Better to light one candle than to curse the darkness," the Christophers developed various apostolates of the media in programs over the decades. The Christophers' weekly television series, *Christopher Closeup*, begun in 1952, has promoted a universal message of encouragement and inspiration longer than any other program. *Christopher Closeup* appears weekly, on commercial TV and numerous cable outlets, and is seen in 166 foreign countries through the Armed Forces Network. Over 400 stations carry *Christopher Minutes*, the Christophers' daily radio program, across America and in many foreign countries in English as well as in Spanish. All programming is provided free of charge to program managers who ask for it.

The Christopher News Notes, published ten times a year, is mailed all over the world to millions of people and is also free of charge for those who request it. It covers topics from family life to spiritual values to social issues. Newspaper columns are also made available. The Christophers receive thousands of pieces of mail each week from people of all creeds. Some ask for guidance and help, and staff members of the Christophers answer each letter individually. The Christophers provide inspirational books and videos to young and old alike at a nominal fee.

The Christopher Awards are given each year to the creators of films, television programs, and books that "affirm the highest values of the human spirit," which are honored at a ceremony in New York City. Special Awards extol unique, widely effective achievements.

Church and State, Separation of. *See* **Separation of Church and State**

Cicognani, Amleto Giovanni (February 24, 1883–December 17, 1973)

The sixth apostolic delegate to the United States, serving from 1933 to 1958, Amleto Giovanni Cicognani was created a cardinal in 1958. He was born in Brisighella, Faenza, Romagna, Italy. His brother, Gaetano, was also a cardinal. Educated at Faenza and at the Athenaeum, he was ordained on September 23, 1905, and appointed as an official of the Sacred Congregation of the Sacraments five years later. He went on to a steady series of Vatican posts and served as a professor of canon law at the Pontifical Roman Athenaeum S. Apolinnaire in Rome. In 1924 and 1931 he undertook special missions to the United States, culminating on March 17, 1933, with his appointment by Pope Pius XI as the apostolic delegate to the United States, with the rank of titular archbishop of Ladice in Phrygia.

Apostolic Delegate Cardinal Amleto Cicognani

Archbishop Cicognani arrived in the United States on May 22, 1933. His tenure was accompanied by the immense efforts of the Catholic Church in the United States to assist the millions impacted by the Great Depression, the involvement of the United States in World War II, and the colossal expansion of the Church throughout the 1940s and 1950s. During his time, he consecrated some sixty bishops, had a hand in the creation of thirty-one new dioceses and the increase of archdioceses from fifteen to twenty-six, and was delighted to report that the Catholic population nearly doubled in size, from twenty million to thirty-six million. He also enjoyed a very favorable relationship with President Franklin Delano Roosevelt that facilitated the work of the Church to ameliorate the suffering of millions during the war. Ultimately, Archbishop Cicognani represented three popes — Pius XI, Pius XII, and Blessed John XXIII — with humor, charm, and distinction.

Pope Blessed John XXIII created him a cardinal priest of San Clemente on December 15, 1958. As a cardinal, he served on many commissions and as a member of sacred congregations. He was made secretary of state in 1961 and served as a cardinal bishop (as titular of the suburbicarian see of Frascati) in 1962. The next year, the newly elected Pope Paul VI reappointed him as a secretary of state, a post he retained until April 1969. Cardinal Cicognani died in Rome.

Cincinnati, Archdiocese of

Established on June 19, 1821, by Pope Pius VII as the Diocese of Cincinnati, and later as the Archdiocese of Cincinnati on July 19, 1850, by Pope Blessed Pius IX, this episcopal jurisdiction serves counties in southern Ohio and has suffragan sees. Cincinnati is an industrial center and a major port. In 1787 John Cleves Symmes visited the Miami Valley and soon after purchased one million acres of that land from the government. Two settlements, Columbia and Losantiville, were founded, and Fort Washington was erected in 1789. In the following year, the Losantyi Settlement was renamed Cincinnati after the Cincinnati Society of Revolutionary War Officers. The Battle of Fallen Timbers in 1794 ended Native American opposition to white settlements, and the area began to grow. The Miami and Erie Canal aided the process, and Cincinnati assumed a leadership position in the area.

Cincinnati has a historic Catholic legacy as well, as missionaries were serving Ohio in 1749. French trappers and explorers were in the region much earlier but left few records of their sojourns. In 1749 Father Joseph de Bonnecamp and Father John Potier accompanied the expedition of the French explorer Pierre Joseph Céloron de Blainville and visited the Sandusky and Vermilion regions in the Ohio Valley. In 1751 the famous missionary Jesuit Father Armand de Richardie founded a mission at Sandusky for the Hurons. The first permanent settlement in Ohio was established at Marietta in 1788. In 1795 Father Edmund Burke was serving the American Indian settlements on the Maumee at Fort Miège. A French colony had been founded earlier at Gallipolis, and Benedictine Father Peter Joseph Didier had established a small church there.

Ohio had been administered by the Diocese of Québec and then by the Diocese of Baltimore in 1789. When the Diocese of Bardstown (now the Archdiocese of Louisville) was erected in 1808, Ohio was part of that vast ecclesiastical jurisdiction. Bishop Benedict Joseph Flaget toured the region with Father Stephen T. Badin. They met with Catholics at Somerset, a colony founded in 1802, and Bishop Flaget sent the "Apostle of Ohio," Father Edward D. Fenwick, to serve the faithful of the area. A Dominican, Father Fenwick founded St. Joseph's Priory and a chapel at Somerset. In 1811 a group of Catholics in Cincinnati met to propose starting a parish, but the city had an ordinance that forbade the construction of a Catholic Church within its limits. In 1814, when Bishop Flaget celebrated the

Archbishop Purcell

first Mass in Cincinnati, he did start a parish, but he had to build it some distance from town because of the anti-Catholic ordinance.

In 1821 Cincinnati was established as a diocese, and the first bishop appointed was Edward Fenwick. He was consecrated on January 13, 1822. One of his original diocesan projects was the founding of the Cathedral of St. Peter in Chains in the city. The ordinance forbidding such a Catholic structure was no longer in effect. He then sailed to Europe for funds and religious personnel, receiving support from Pope Leo XII for his campaign. The bishop also founded the Athenaeum in 1829, as well as St. Aloysius Seminary and one of the nation's oldest diocesan newspapers. He continued to expand diocesan facilities until a cholera epidemic struck the area. Bishop Fenwick died on a charitable mission to Wooster, Ohio, on September 26, 1832.

The second bishop was John Baptist Purcell,

who would become Cincinnati's first archbishop. He was consecrated on October 13, 1833, and went immediately to the Second Provincial Council of Baltimore. In 1845 Bishop Purcell reopened the seminary, which had been closed, and three years later founded Mount St. Mary's of the West, which was transferred later to Cedar Point. He was also aware of national events and the needs of immigrants in Cincinnati. He raised funds for social and charitable programs and recruited trained personnel. In 1836 Alexander Campbell, a Protestant minister who had started the Disciples of Christ, challenged Bishop Purcell to defend the Catholic faith. The two debated publicly for seven days, and at the end of the gatherings, which were widely attended, anti-Catholicism waned and numerous converts entered the Church.

The Archdiocese of Cincinnati was erected in 1850, and Bishop Purcell became the first archbishop. Three years later, he hosted Archbishop Cajetan Bedini, the apostolic nuncio to Brazil, who was the target of lunatic anti-Catholic assaults. A Protestant mob attacked Archbishop Purcell's residence on Christmas, and police had to mount a defense of the property. Five years later, another Protestant mob attacked German Catholics and had to be dispersed by military troops using cannons.

Archbishop Purcell supported the Civil War and served as an elegant spokesman for the northern cause. Pope Blessed Pius IX honored him for his labors. The last months of his ministry, however, were marred by the financial blunders of his brother, Father Edward Purcell, whom he had trusted with vast sums of money. Archbishop Purcell retired to the Ursuline Convent of St. Martin with his brother and suffered a series of strokes. He died on July 4, 1883.

The successor to Archbishop Purcell was William Henry Elder, who had served as the bishop of Natchez and then as Archbishop Purcell's coadjutor with right of succession. Archbishop Elder acceded to the see upon the death of Archbishop Purcell, and he quickly set about restoring the financial stability of the archdiocese. In 1887 Archbishop Elder reopened Mount St. Mary's of the West, which had been closed for several years. He also founded St. Gregory's Preparatory Seminary. A saintly man, Archbishop Elder heard confessions even in his old age. He presided over provincial councils in 1883 and 1888, and died on October 31, 1904.

Archbishop Henry K. Moeller was his successor, having served as the bishop of Columbus and then as coadjutor archbishop of Cincinnati with right of succession since 1903. He acceded to the see upon the death of Archbishop Elder and started vast parish expansion programs. He also erected a new Mount St. Mary's Seminary, established a Bureau of Catholic Charities, and founded hospitals, colleges, and charitable institutions. He aided the founding of the American Board of Foreign Missions and supported the Catholic Students' Mission Crusade. Archbishop Moeller guided the faithful of Cincinnati through World War I. He died on January 5, 1923.

His successor was Archbishop John Timothy McNichols, who had served as the bishop of Duluth since 1918, having received the honors of Assistant at the Pontifical Throne while in that diocese. He was promoted to the Archdiocese of Cincinnati on July 8, 1925. Archbishop McNichols led the archdiocese through the grim times of the Great Depression but established fifty parishes and started a college. He also aided the military efforts of the nation in World War II. Lay retreats and an African-American apostolate were two of his major ministries. He died on April 22, 1950.

The sixth archbishop of Cincinnati was Karl J. Alter, who had served as the bishop of Toledo since 1931. He was appointed an Assistant at the Pontifical Throne on May 30, 1950, and promoted to the Archdiocese of Cincinnati on June 21 of that year. Archbishop Alter completed the $60 million construction projects in the archdiocese, including the restoration of the Cathedral of St. Peter in Chains and St. Gregory's Preparatory Seminary. He opened convents and schools and recodified diocesan laws. Attending the Second Vatican Council, he took part in several commissions and also served as chairman of the administrative board of the National Catholic Welfare Conference. Archbishop Alter retired on July 23, 1969, and died on August 23, 1977.

His successor was Archbishop Paul F. Leibold, who had served as auxiliary bishop of Cincinnati and then as bishop of Evansville since 1966. He was promoted to the Archdiocese of Cincinnati on July 23, 1969, and installed on October 2. Continuing the restoration and expansion programs of his predecessors, Archbishop Leibold died on June 1, 1972.

Archbishop Joseph Louis Bernardin, who would be made a cardinal in 1983, was his successor. He had served as auxiliary bishop of Atlanta since 1966 and was promoted to the Archdiocese of Cincinnati on November 21, 1972. Expanding diocesan facilities and services to meet the needs of the growing Catholic population, Archbishop Bernardin also served as president of the National Conference of Catholic Bishops and the United States Catholic Conference from 1974 to 1977. On July 10, 1982, he was transferred to the Archdiocese of Chicago and was created a cardinal priest with the titular church of Jesus the Divine Worker on February 2, 1983.

The eighth archbishop of Cincinnati, Daniel E. Pilarczyk, had served as auxiliary bishop of the archdiocese since 1974. He was promoted to the rank of archbishop on November 2, 1982, and installed in Cincinnati on December 20, 1982. Long honored as one of the most intelligent bishops in the United States, Archbishop Pilarczyk took among his priorities improving vocations to the priesthood, Catholic education, stewardship ,and evangelization. To promote vocations and better pastoral care, the archbishop launched the "Futures Project" at the start of the new millennium to assist those discerning vocations and to study the best ways to provide ongoing pastoral care as the current priestly population begins to retire in coming years. His time was also marked by the problems caused by the sexual abuse crisis. Archbishop Pilarczyk retired on December 21, 2009.

He was succeeded by Bishop Dennis Schnurr, who had been bishop of Duluth since 2001 and had been named coadjutor archbishop of Cincinnati on October 17, 2008. In 2011 there were 475,000 Catholics served by 500 priests, 900 women religious, and 214 parishes in the archdiocese.

Cisneros, Henry G. *See* **Cabinets, Catholics in Presidential**

Cistercians

The Order of Cistercians (O.Cist.), a monastic order established upon the Rule of St. Benedict in 1098 by St. Robert of Molesme, was named after its motherhouse at Cîteaux, in Burgundy. The order was born out of St. Robert's unhappiness with the lax attitude that pervaded his own monastery at Molesme. He departed the community with a group of like-minded monks and established himself at Cîteaux, where he instituted a far more austere program of life, in keeping with traditional Benedictine ideals.

St. Robert was succeeded as abbot by St. Alberic and then by the truly remarkable St. Stephen Harding, who served as abbot from 1109 to 1133. Called the second founder of the Cistercians, St. Stephen wrote the Charter of Love in 1119, the constitution of the order (approved by Pope Callistus II), which called for manual labor, a simplified liturgy, and strict asceticism. During St. Stephen's time as abbot, there arrived in 1112 the foremost member of the Cistercians, St. Bernard of Clairvaux. He founded the Abbey of Clairvaux, and through the fame and brilliance of his work, the order spread across Europe. The monks adhered to a rigorous life of work and prayer, prizing labor and distinguishing themselves by their advances in agriculture and stockbreeding. According to the order's laws, each house was to be plain and primitive, with control over its own affairs, although it was to adhere faithfully to the regulations passed by the annual general chapter, an important gathering that helped the monks to maintain discipline and introduce new or needed reforms and innovations.

The Cistercians enjoyed wide prominence during the 1100s and 1200s, deeply influencing the monasticism of the times. The White Monks, as they were called, had over five hundred abbeys at the start of the thirteenth century, including houses in Scotland and Scandinavia, and the famed house of Rievaulx. The order gradually lost its preeminence from that time and subsequently suffered from the vicissitudes of the late Middle Ages, Renaissance, and Reformation. A reform movement began in the 1600s that called for the return to a more precise adherence to the rule. The members, known as the Strict Observance, found support among many in the French houses, so that a division grew in France between those of the Strict Observance and the Common Observance. The French Revolution had a terrible impact upon the Common Observance, but the order recovered.

Meanwhile, the Cistercians of the Strict Observance became centered in the monastery of La Trappe in France, whose members were expelled by the Revolution but returned in 1817. Under their abbot, Augustine Lestrange, their austere rule was revitalized and found appeal among the houses that were reestablished throughout the country. They took their work into other countries and the name Trappists became popularly used for those of the Strict Observance. When, in 1898, Cîteaux was restored to the order, its community chose to join the Strict Observance. Its abbot is the general of the Cistercians of the Strict Observance (O.C.S.O.), which is today a separate body from the Order of Cistercians (O.Cist.). The name Trappists is still used for the monks of the Strict Observance. Trappists wear a white habit with a black scapular. There are currently over 2,500 Trappists worldwide and nearly 1,500 Cistercians.

The first Cistercian house in the United States was established in 1928 in Okauchee, Wisconsin, by a group of monks from Austria. The community was given the name Our Lady of Spring Bank. In 1935 the same foundation established Our Lady of Gerowvall, in Paulding, Mississippi. Twenty years later, Cistercians refugees from Hungary began Our Lady of Dallas Monastery just outside of Dallas, Texas. Members of the community teach at the University of Dallas. In the last century, the best known Trappist was Thomas Merton. There are also Cistercian Nuns (O.Cist.) and the Order of Cistercian Nuns of the Strict Observance (O.C.S.O.).

Ciszek, Walter (1904–December 8, 1984)

A Jesuit priest, Walter Ciszek spent twenty-three years in the prisons and gulags of the Soviet Union for preaching the Gospel among the Russian people. He was born in Shenandoah, Pennsylvania, the son of Polish immigrants. He entered the seminary and decided that he had a vocation to the Society of Jesus. Soon after entering the Jesuit novitiate, he volunteered for the dangerous ministry in the Soviet Union. To give him preparation, Ciszek was sent to Rome for studies at the Russian College and was ordained on June 24, 1937.

His superiors sent Father Ciszek to Poland, where he taught Jesuit seminarians until the start of World War II in September 1939. Both Germany and Russia invaded the country. Father Ciszek, still intent on his mission, made his way in secret across war-torn Poland and into Russia in 1940, working as a common laborer while preaching the Gospel. Within a short time, his true identity was discovered by the Russian secret police and he was arrested as a spy. Tortured and brutally interrogated, Father Ciszek was convicted by Soviet authorities for spying on the basis of a coerced confession. His cruel imprisonment included time in the dreaded Lubjanka Prison in Moscow and then terrible years of hard labor in the gulags of Siberia. Only in 1955 did the world even learn that he was still alive, and in 1963 he was freed through a prisoner exchange.

Throughout his long ordeal, Father Ciszek never ceased praying, celebrating Mass, hearing confessions, offering spiritual retreats, and performing parish and pastoral work. After his death on December 8, 1984, a Prayer League to promote his cause was launched, and in 1989, Bishop Michael J. Dudick of the Eparchy of Passaic began the official process for his canonization.

Civiletti, Benjamin. *See* Cabinets, Catholics in Presidential

Civil War, American

The bloodiest conflict ever waged on American soil, the American Civil War, from 1861 to 1865, claimed over one million casualties, with more than 600,000 dead (over 359,000 Union and 258,000 Confederate). In its aftermath not only was the pernicious and evil institution of slavery brought to an end forever in the United States, but change swept the country. The rights of states were subordinated to the broader rights of the federal system, the economic and political power of the South were shattered in favor of the Northern industrial complex, the nation moved aggressively away from an agrarian culture to a business- and factory-based urban society, and a host of attendant social problems became the inheritance of generations of Americans.

The Catholic population was as divided on the issues of slavery and states' rights as the rest of the country, with the result that Catholics held prominent positions in both the Union and the Confederacy, and Catholics in large numbers fought and died for both causes. Once the war began, however, the Catholic hierarchy and clergy and religious continued to provide their essential functions without regard to the political climate. Priests and nuns, as well as their bishops, labored in hospitals, prisons, and military camps in both the Union and the Confederacy, dispensing humanitarian and spiritual aid and comfort. The Church helped to feed, clothe, and care for orphans, widows, and crippled soldiers and civilians in the North and South. Having remained faithful not to political concerns but to the welfare of souls, the Catholic Church was able to emerge from the war in a state of unity that stood in contrast to virtually all other institutions in the country.

Nevertheless, there were many in the Church in the North who saw little incentive in supporting the Union cause, in giving their lives for a system that had for so long treated them as second-class citizens and denigrated the Catholic faith. Many Northern Catholic periodicals were vehemently opposed to the war, such as *Freeman's Journal* in New York City. James A. McMaster, editor of the journal, was jailed for his opposition to government policy, and the newspaper was denied the use of the mails. Against this position was that of the *Katholische Kirchenzeitung*, edited by Father Edward Purcell, which was ardent in its support of the Union cause.

With very few exceptions, the American hierarchy was split along political lines, such that bishops tended to support the governments that were in control of their state, even though none of the bishops in the South were native to that region. One notable exception was Bishop James Whelan of Nashville, Tennessee, who refused to give his allegiance to the Confederacy and resigned his see. Similarly, in 1864 Bishop William Elder of Natchez refused to obey the order of federal troops to have prayers for the president of the United States and Union military leaders recited publicly in all churches. Arrested for his refusal, he was tried and convicted and sent into exile in Vidalia, Louisiana, but the military court's judgment was reversed by officials in Washington.

Archbishop John Hughes of New York was especially noted for his support of the war effort in the North, seeing it in part as a means of demonstrating the patriotism of Catholics in general and Irish immigrants in particular. He flew the American flag from the cathedral roof, called upon Catholics to be loyal to the Constitution, and went so far as to journey to France and England on behalf of the American government to keep them from recognizing the Confederacy. The Union also received the assistance of Bishop Michael Domenec of Pittsburgh, who traveled to Spain, and Bishop John Fitzpatrick of Boston, who went to Belgium. Bishop Patrick N. Lynch of Charleston, South Carolina, sailed to the Papal States to plead for the Confederate cause, but he received little from Pope Pius IX, and his efforts in Ireland likewise failed to generate much sympathy for the South.

Bishops also served in hospitals as well as on the battlefield, and Archbishop John Baptist Purcell of Cincinnati and Bishop James Whelan actually ministered to the fallen while under fire. Bishop Jean-Pierre Augustin Verot of Savannah, Georgia, made pastoral visits to Andersonville prison and alleviated as much as possible the horrific suffering of the Union prisoners there.

Priests continued to assist their flocks in their respective parishes, providing pastoral care to families who had lost loved ones or whose homes and livelihoods had been destroyed in the widespread devastation that befell the Confederate states. Priests also served as chaplains in both armies. There were approximately forty Catholic chaplains in the Union Army and twenty-eight in the Confederate forces. These were supplemented by the presence of over fifty priests who provided pastoral assistance without rank as auxiliary chaplains. Without question, the tiny number of chaplains was wholly inadequate in meeting the needs of the soldiers. At the Battle of Gettysburg in 1863, there was only one Catholic chaplain for the entire Union Army, Father William Corby of the Holy Cross Fathers.

Catholic nuns also served with immense distinc-

tion throughout the war and were especially crucial in the care of the sick and wounded in the South, as sisters were the only women with any kind of formal training as nurses and hospital administrators. More than five hundred members of twenty congregations cared for the fallen of both armies, with over two hundred belonging to the Sisters of Charity; others were members of the Sisters of Mercy, and the Holy Cross Sisters of South Bend, Indiana. The nuns earned justifiable fame for their efforts, and the example they provided — along with that of the bishops and priests — helped encourage hundreds of soldiers on both sides to convert to the Catholic faith.

For the average Catholic, the war brought the same difficult choices facing other Americans. They fought and died in both armies in large numbers, and a special place of honor belonged to the Irish and German Catholics. Over 150,000 Irish Catholics and 175,000 German Catholics served in the Union Army alone.

The Irish formed several famed units, including the Irish Brigade, which suffered catastrophic losses in the fighting, as well as such regiments as the legendary 20th Maine, which proved decisive in the Union victory at Gettysburg in 1863, and the 69th New York Irish Volunteers. The Irish Brigade began the war with over five thousand soldiers; by the end of the Battle of Chancellorsville in 1863, the unit could field barely five hundred soldiers after the stunning casualties it had endured, such as at the Battle of Fredericksburg in early 1863 and the heroic but tactically suicidal charge up Marye's Heights into the full fire of Robert E. Lee's entrenched Army of Northern Virginia. Irish Catholics also fought in the Confederate Army, which commonly organized its troops according to their ethnic backgrounds.

Such was the reputation of Irish soldiers that the Union tried aggressively to recruit and draft them into service. Draft efforts in 1863, after Gettysburg, caused Irish Catholics to riot in protest, as poor Irish immigrants were most often targeted for the draft. Over 120 people were killed before the riots were suppressed by the New York police. Irish also labored in factories in the North, and some eight hundred thousand made their way to the United States to fight for the Union, thanks in large part to the Homestead Act of 1862 and the promise of a better future as American citizens.

Catholics also held key roles in both armies as generals and naval commanders. The Union Army benefited from the presence of such Catholic generals as William Rosecrans (his brother, Sylvester, became the first bishop of Columbus, Ohio), Philip Sheridan, William Tecumseh Sherman, George L. Meade, and James Shields. The Confederacy claimed such officers as General Pierre G. T. Beauregard (who began the war by firing on Fort Sumter in Charleston Harbor in 1861), Raphael Semmes, captain of the *Alabama*, and Stephen R. Mallory, Confederate secretary of the navy. In all, there were twenty-four Catholic major generals and ten brigadier generals in the Union Army and eleven Catholic generals in the Confederate Army.

The dioceses and parishes in the Confederacy suffered catastrophic destruction in the war, owing in part to the bitter struggle that characterized the conflict's last days. By the time of the surrender of Robert E. Lee at Appomattox Courthouse, Virginia, on April 9, 1865, Catholic churches, convents, schools, rectories, orphanages, and cemeteries lay in utter ruins, along with the homes and property of thousands of Catholic laypeople. The task of rebuilding was an enormous one, but the Church emerged from the war united and prepared to rebuild.

Even before the war was over, though, Catholics who had demonstrated their loyalty to the Union and had died in vast numbers on the battlefields of Pennsylvania, Maryland, Virginia, Tennessee, Georgia, and elsewhere were once again called unpatriotic because of the assassination of President Abraham Lincoln. In the investigation into the assassination, Catholics were implicated when the Surrat family was accused of aiding the plot.

Direction for the postwar Church was provided by the Second Plenary Council of Baltimore in October 1866. Convened under Archbishop Martin J. Spalding, the council had as its chief purpose to bring together the leaders of the Church after the war to work for the common purpose of repairing the damage caused by the war. Spalding expressed the hope that "the Catholic Church might present to the country and the world a striking proof of the strong bond of unity with which her members are knit together." (*See also* African-American Catholics; Slavery.)

Claretians

The Missionary Sons of the Immaculate Heart of Mary, a religious congregation, was founded in 1849 by St. Anthony Mary Claret in Vich, Spain. The Claretians were established in the wake of the severe anticlericalism that struck Spain in 1835 and that included the expulsion of religious orders and the suppression of most monasteries and religious communities, including the Dominicans and Franciscans. In response to this development, several diocesan clergy in Catalonia, Spain, under the direction of St. Anthony Mary Claret, assumed the duties of the missing orders, including catechetics, education, and preaching. From this beginning was born the Claretian order on July 16, 1849, at the diocesan seminary of Vich. St. Anthony was appointed the archbishop of Santiago, Cuba, in 1850, leaving the community without immediate direction. He was then asked in 1857 by José Xifré, later the second superior general from 1857 to 1899, to provide a rule. St. Anthony drafted a constitution with fifteen chapters that became the guiding regimen of the Claretians. Currently, there are over three thousand Claretians worldwide.

The Claretians first arrived in the United States from Mexico after receiving an invitation in 1902 to preach among the Spanish-speaking Catholics of Brownsville, Texas. As this proved immensely successful, they were invited into the Dioceses of San Antonio and Los Angeles. The first years of Claretian activity were focused chiefly on the Spanish-speaking communities in Texas, Arizona, and California, but the expansion of their apostolate was made possible starting in 1922, when the Claretians in the United States were established as a separate province from Mexico.

In 1925 the Claretians founded the National Shrine of St. Jude in Chicago. Four years later, they began the League of St. Jude to promote devotion to the beloved saint. In 1932 the Claretians began a branch of the league to provide pastoral care for the Chicago Police Department, under the special invocation of St. Jude. As this effort proved very popular, the police in Milwaukee, Indianapolis, and Grand Rapids, Michigan, all adopted St.

Jude as their special patron, although they are not affiliated with the League of St. Jude. In 1954 the American province of the Claretians was divided into two provinces, the Eastern and Western. The Claretian Missionary Sisters (Religious of Mary Immaculate) were founded in 1855, in Cuba, and established in the United States in 1956.

Clarke, Mother Mary Frances (March 2, c. 1803– December 4, 1887)

The founder of the Sisters of Charity of the Blessed Virgin Mary, Mother Mary Frances Clarke was a pioneering religious educator. She was born in Ireland and early dedicated her life to the young and poor. In 1832 she and four companions started Miss Clarke's Seminary, a school for poor girls unable to attend the local convent educational facilities. One year later, she accepted an invitation from a U.S. missionary and moved to Philadelphia to educate Irish immigrants to America.

Father Terence Donahoe became an adviser to the group and recommended that they organize as a religious congregation. Mother Mary Frances led the way, and the first members became the Sisters of Charity of the Blessed Virgin Mary, known as the B.V.M.s. In 1843 she also responded to an invitation from Bishop Mathias Loras of Dubuque, Iowa, and started a program to educate local children of Native Americans and farmers. Five sisters were sent to Dubuque to open a school in the Iowa Territory. Soon after, the entire congregation, along with Father Donahoe, moved to Dubuque.

There Mother Mary Frances recruited more than four hundred young women to become part of the B.V.M. apostolate. She opened schools in developing areas and kept in constant touch with each new foundation to encourage her religious. She opened a school in San Francisco just before she died. Mother Mary Frances was inducted into the Iowa Women's Hall of Fame on August 27, 1984, honored for her role in providing education and spiritual opportunities for the frontier areas of America.

Cleveland, Diocese of

Established on April 23, 1847, by Pope Blessed Pius IX, the Diocese of Cleveland serves counties in Ohio. The city is a major port on the southern shore of Lake Erie and part of the St. Lawrence Seaway, and it is an industrial and manufacturing center. Plans for the city were developed in 1796 and designate the site as Cleaveland. The name was changed to Cleveland in 1832. The establishment of canals and railroads aided the growth of the area, especially the Soo Canal (St. Mary's Falls Canal). The Diocese of Cleveland is a suffragan see of the Archdiocese of Cincinnati.

The Catholic history of the area began in 1749, when the Jesuit missionaries Father John Potier and Joseph de Bonnechamps visited the Vermilion and Sandusky settlements with the expedition of Celeron de Blainville. In 1751 Jesuit Father Armand de La Richardie erected a chapel for the Hurons on the present site of Sandusky. Missionary efforts in other parts of the Ohio River Valley were continuous but lacked necessary personnel, even as the settlement at Marietta was founded in 1788. In 1795, however, Father Edmund Burke built a mission at Fort Miège at present-day Maumee.

The Catholics of Ohio, at the time under the episcopal jurisdiction of the vast Diocese of Bardstown (now the Archdiocese of Louisville), asked Bishop Benedict Joseph Flaget for missionaries. Bishop Flaget and Father Stephen T. Badin toured Ohio in response to this request. The "Apostle of Ohio," Dominican Father Edward D. Fenwick, arrived soon after and built a chapel at Somerset to serve the growing number of Catholics in the area. In 1821 the Diocese of Cincinnati (now the Archdiocese of Cincinnati) was erected, and Father Fenwick was appointed the first bishop. Cleveland and other Ohio regions expanded their populations and settlements, and parishes were erected throughout. St. Joseph Parish in Cuyahoga Falls dates to 1831, Holy Trinity in Cleveland dates to 1835, and St. Vincent's in Akron was opened in 1837. St. Mary's in Elyria was founded in 1845, two years before Cleveland was erected as a diocese. Other parishes followed.

The first bishop of Cleveland was Louis Amadeus Rappe, and he was consecrated on October 10, 1847. A Frenchman, Bishop Rappe began to organize the agencies and offices necessary for diocesan administration and began St. John the Evangelist Cathedral. He also set about aiding the various national groups in the area and dialogued with lay groups intent on preserving their cultural traditions. He then went to France to collect priests and funds for the diocese, and upon his return began his extraordinary building program that resulted in 114 parishes, schools, colleges, and seminaries. A group of local Irish priests, irate over the number of German parishes, sent a false accusation about Bishop Rappe to Rome. He resigned from the diocese on July 29, 1870, and went to Vermont as a missionary. Cleared of all charges, Bishop Rappe was offered another diocese, but he refused, remaining in his mission post. He died on September 8, 1877, and was buried in the cathedral in Cleveland.

His successor was Bishop Richard Gilmour, a convert from Scotland, who was consecrated on April 14, 1872. Bishop Gilmour convoked a diocesan synod and established a diocesan newspaper. He revitalized many charitable and educational agencies and wrote the *Illustrated Bible History* and the *National Catholic Series of Readers,* which became standard parochial school texts. His mind failed, however, and he went to St. Augustine, Florida, where he died on April 13, 1891.

The third bishop of Cleveland was Ignatius Horstmann, who was consecrated on February 25, 1892. A scholarly prelate, Bishop Horstmann served as president of the American Catholic Historical Society. He founded a high school and a diocesan band of missionaries. He also requested the Holy See to provide him with an auxiliary bishop to serve the Slavic Catholics in the diocese. Bishop Joseph M. Kondelka was consecrated as the auxiliary bishop in 1907. Bishop Horstmann died suddenly of heart disease on May 13, 1908.

His successor was Bishop John Patrick Farrelly, who was consecrated on May 1, 1909. A convert also, Bishop Farrelly brought renewed stability and peace to the diocese, maintaining growth and

renovation even in the troubled days of World War I. He died on February 12, 1921.

The fifth bishop of Cleveland, Joseph Schrembs, had served as the first bishop of Toledo since 1911. He was installed in Cleveland on September 8, 1921, and began to reorganize the tribunal and chancery of the diocese. He also led expansion programs and became a noted public figure, praised as an orator. Bishop Schrembs testified in Rome on behalf of National Catholic Welfare Conference. He also led Cleveland's Catholics through the Great Depression and World War II. On March 25, 1939, the Holy See bestowed the personal rank of archbishop upon him. Bishop Schrembs died on November 2, 1945.

His successor was Bishop Edward F. Hoban, who had become the coadjutor bishop of Cleve-

Cathedral of St. John the Evangelist in Cleveland

land with right of succession in 1942. He acceded to the see upon the death of Bishop Schrembs. Bishop Hoban faced an increase in the Catholic population of Cleveland and erected sixty-one new parishes and forty-seven new schools. In 1946 he rebuilt the cathedral. Pope Pius XII bestowed the personal rank of archbishop upon him on July 23, 1951. Continuing his educational programs, Bishop Hoban instituted the Newman Apostolate and founded St. Charles Borromeo Seminary. He died on September 22, 1966.

The seventh bishop of Cleveland was Clarence G. Issenmann, who had served as coadjutor bishop of Cleveland with right of succession since 1964. He acceded to the see upon Bishop Hoban's death. Bishop Issenmann maintained the expansion programs and implemented the reforms of the Second Vatican Council. He retired on June 5, 1974.

His successor was Bishop James A. Hickey, who would become a cardinal. Bishop Hickey had served as auxiliary bishop of Saginaw and as rector of the North American College in Rome. He was installed in Cleveland on July 16, 1974. Continuing the expansion and renovation programs of his predecessors, Bishop Hickey was promoted on June 17, 1980, to the Archdiocese of Washington, D.C. Pope Blessed John Paul II created him a cardinal priest on June 28, 1988.

The ninth bishop of Cleveland was Anthony M. Pilla, who was appointed as auxiliary bishop of Cleveland and titular bishop of Scardona on August 1, 1979. He became apostolic administrator of Cleveland in 1980 at the time the future Cardinal Hickey was named archbishop of Washington. Bishop Pilla was appointed bishop of Cleveland on November 13, 1980. He was installed in the cathedral on January 6, 1981. Bishop Pilla was elected president of the National Conference of Catholic Bishops and the United States Catholic Conference from 1995 to 1998. He celebrated his twenty-fifth anniversary as bishop in January 2006 and retired on April 4, 2006.

Bishop Pilla's time as bishop was marked by his patient leadership of the diocese during a time of great social and economic change in Ohio, through the difficult period of the sex abuse crisis in the American Church, and, more happily, during the celebration of the Great Jubilee of 2000.

Bishop Richard G. Lennon, who had been auxiliary bishop of Boston since 2001, was named the ninth bishop of Cleveland on April 4, 2006. Bishop Lennon had also served as apostolic administrator of Boston from 2002 to 2003 following the resignation of Cardinal Bernard F. Law, archbishop of Boston, in the wake of the sex abuse scandal. Bishop Lennon and the diocese have faced the continuing economic travails of the greater Cleveland area and the need for pastoral care programs in the wake of these economic hardships. In 2011 there were 710,000 Catholics, served by 500 priests, more than 1,000 women religious, and 174 parishes in the diocese.

Clorivière, Joseph Pierre Picot de (November 4, 1768–September 29, 1826)

A soldier and priest, Joseph Pierre Picot de Clorivière was revered as the second founder of the Visitation Convent. He was born in Brittany, France, the son of Michel Alain Picot and Renée Jeanne Roche. For many years he was called simply Joseph Picot de Limoëlan.

He studied at the College of Rennes and the Royal Military School in Paris. Assigned to the Régiment d'Angoulême, he resigned his commission early in 1791. Chhanging sides and participating in the abortive plot to assassinate Napoleon Bonaparte on December 24, 1800, he was forced to flee France.

He crossed the Atlantic and landed in Savannah, Georgia, and became known as Joseph Picot de Clorivière. In 1808 he entered St. Mary's Seminary in Baltimore and was ordained on August 1, 1812. Father Clorivière was then assigned to Charleston, South Carolina, to care for the French refugees from Santo Domingo.

In 1814, returning from a brief visit to France, Father Clorivière discovered that he had been replaced as associate pastor by the trustees of the church. A serious scandal developed, and Father Clorivière was appointed chaplain at the Visitation Convent in Georgetown, Washington, D.C., in order to alleviate the situation. He also helped in founding St. Joseph's School in the District of Columbia. He was generous to the Visitation Convent and is considered its second founder. Father Clorivière died in Washington.

Cody, John Patrick (December 24, 1907–April 25, 1982)

The archbishop of Chicago from 1965 to 1982, John Patrick Cody was an American cardinal. He was born in St. Louis, Missouri, and educated locally and then at the North American College in Rome. While there from 1926 to 1932, he earned doctorates in philosophy and theology, and then later a third doctorate, in canon law. On December 8, 1931, he was ordained for St. Louis. In 1933 he was appointed to the staff of the Vatican Secretariat of State and was named to the staff of Cardinal Eugenio Pacelli (later Pope Pius XII) and also Giovanni Battista Montini (later Pope Paul VI). He remained at the Secretariat of State until 1938 when he was recalled to St. Louis as secretary to Archbishop (later Cardinal) John Glennon. Two years later, he was appointed chancellor and in 1947 an auxiliary bishop of St. Louis. Consecrated bishop on July 2, 1947, he remained as auxiliary to Archbishop Joseph E. Ritter until 1954, when he became coadjutor bishop of St. Joseph, Missouri. He acceded to the see the next year but was transferred in 1956 to the newly united Diocese of Kansas City-St. Joseph as coadjutor to Archbishop Edwin Vincent O'Hara. With O'Hara's passing that same year, he became archbishop.

Five years later, he became the coadjutor archbishop of New Orleans, acceding in 1964 upon the death of Archbishop Joseph Francis Rummel. Archbishop Cody's most memorable action as archbishop was to implement with considerable vigor the decree of his predecessor that instructed all Catholic schools in the archdiocese to desegregate. He remained firm in the decision against the pressure of segregationists. For his efforts, Archbishop Cody won justifiable fame and pointed the way to other Church leaders throughout the South.

He attended the Second Vatican Council, and on June 14, 1965, he was appointed to the Archdiocese of Chicago after the death of Cardinal Albert G. Meyer. Two years later, on June 26, 1967, Pope Paul VI created him a cardinal priest with the

Cardinal John Cody

titular church of Santa Cecilia. Cardinal Cody devoted his first years as archbishop in Chicago to the implementation of the decrees of the Second Vatican Council and to postconciliar documents. In the spirit of the council, he gave his blessing in 1966 to the founding of the independent Association of Chicago Priests. Relations with the association soon deteriorated and reached a nadir when the clergy voted narrowly to censure the cardinal and auxiliary bishops for failing to state their positions at the meeting of the National Conference of Catholic Bishops meeting in Detroit in 1971. Similar rocky relations plagued Cardinal Cody's dealings with the recently established Presbyteral Senate, which was intended to be a useful advisory body.

Despite these problems, he pushed ahead with an ambitious program, called Renewal, that included massive fundraising to refurbish and improve the archdiocese's many parishes and schools. He also launched the structural reform of the archdiocese, which included the division of administration into seven vicariates, and was responsible for the revitalization of the Cathedral of the Holy Name. His closure of several inner-city schools, however, provoked a firestorm of protest that was exacerbated by the hostility of the Association of Chicago Priests. The acrimonious environment only darkened in his last years and hastened his death from a heart attack.

Colorado

Called the Centennial State, Colorado entered the Union in 1876. It is located in the west-central part of the United States and is bounded on the north by Wyoming and Nebraska, on the east by Nebraska and Kansas, on the south by Oklahoma and New Mexico, and on the west by Utah. The original Native American residents of Colorado were the Apache, Arapaho, Cheyenne, Comanche, Kiowa, Navajo, Pawnee, and Utes.

The Catholic history of the state opened around 1540, when Francisco Vázquez de Coronado led a lengthy expedition into the region. In 1682 René-

Robert Chevalier, Sieur de La Salle, led another expedition into the area, claiming the territory for France. Almost a century later, France ceded the region to Spain. In 1776 Silvestre Velez de Escalante led a Spanish force into Colorado to study the terrain and residents. The Spanish ceded the area back to France, however, and Napoleon Bonaparte sold it to the United States as part of the Louisiana Purchase in 1803. Three years later, the American explorer Zebulon Pike was in Colorado, and in the 1840s Kit Carson, Stephen Long, and John C. Fremont traveled through the region. Colorado's southwestern section became a Mexican possession in 1821, but was ceded to the United States in the Treaty of Guadalupe-Hidalgo in 1848.

In the 1850s, Catholic settlements developed in the San Luis Valley, including San Luis de la Culebra, the oldest reported permanent settlement in the state. Other missions and communities followed, as at Conejos, where Bishop Jean Baptiste Lamy of Santa Fe founded Our Lady of Guadalupe Church. The Sisters of Loretto entered the area to promote education, and Jesuit Father Salvador Person pioneered area missions.

In 1861 the United States Congress established the Colorado Territory. The vicar apostolic of the Indian Territory, Bishop Jean Baptiste Miège, visited the goldfields of Colorado, which had flourished since the discovery of gold in the Rocky Mountains near Denver in 1858. Unable to protect Native American lands or to provide needed missionaries, Bishop Jean Baptiste Miège advised the Holy See to attach Colorado to the Diocese of Santa Fe. As a result, Fathers Joseph P. Machebeuf and Jean Raverdy arrived in Denver as representatives of Bishop Jean Baptiste Lamy. Father Machebeuf, a veteran missionary of over two decades, started establishing missions at Arapaho City, Golden, and Central City. He traveled in a buggy that served as his residence and chapel.

In 1868 he was appointed vicar apostolic of Colorado and ordained a bishop. Bishop Machebeuf toured the eastern United States and Europe, bringing five priests and funds to the area. By 1870 there were fourteen parishes in Colorado. A year later, the Jesuits entered into service in the vicariate and progress continued. The Diocese of Denver (now the Archdiocese of Denver) was erected,

and Bishop Machebeuf served as the first ordinary. Bishop Nicholas C. Matz was his coadjutor bishop.

The diocese prospered after the deaths of these pioneers, and Colorado supported the military efforts of World War I and then faced the grim period of the Great Depression. Hospitals, schools, a diocesan newspaper, and a vast Catholic population were present in the state. St. Frances Xavier Cabrini aided in the growth personally in 1912, and local Catholic agencies expanded their charitable and educational programs, even as Bishop John Henry Tilden defended the Church against the Ku Klux Klan and other anti-Catholic efforts in Colorado. In 1941 as America was about to enter World War II, Denver was designated a metropolitan archdiocesan province with suffragan sees. Archbishop Urban J. Vehr led the faithful and aided the establishment of the Diocese of Pueblo.

Colorado became a vital part of the nation's defense program in North American Aerospace Defense Command (NORAD) and other military establishments, and growth continued. In the archdiocese and throughout the state the reforms mandated by the Second Vatican Council were implemented. New lay apostolates and social agencies were opened. The archdiocese continued to expand facilities, despite the loss of personnel. Archbishop James V. Casey served from 1967 to 1986, succeeded by Archbishop James Francis Stafford, who was appointed president of the Pontifical Council for the Laity and created a cardinal in Rome. In 1984 the Diocese of Colorado Springs was created as a suffragan see of Denver. One of the most memorable events in the history of contemporary Catholic history was the celebration in Denver of World Youth Day in 1993, including a visit from Pope John Paul II. In 1997 the first Native American archbishop, Charles J. Chaput, O.F.M. Cap., was installed in Denver. He was appointed archbishop of Philadelphia on July 19, 2011.

The Church in Colorado has faced steady increases in the Catholic population as part of the wider movement away from the East, the demographic flight from California, and the large expansion of the Latino population. These changes place strains on the Catholic resources in the state but also present great opportunities for evangelization. In 2011 there were 700,000 Catholics, served by

416 priests, 425 women religious, and 213 parishes in the state.

Colorado Springs, Diocese of

Established on January 30, 1984, by Pope John Paul II, the Diocese of Colorado Springs serves counties in central Colorado. The city is located on a mesa near the eastern base of Pike's Peak and boasts scenic treasures and strategic military installations. Founded in 1871 by General William J. Palmer, the site was called Fountain Colony. The diocese is a suffragan see of the Archdiocese of Denver and shares in the Catholic legacy of the region.

In 1540 Francisco Vázquez de Coronado and a Spanish expedition explored the area but then moved on. René-Robert Chevalier, Sieur de La Salle, also visited the region, claiming the lands for France, but Spain gained control less than a century later. Expeditions into present-day Colorado continued, however, including one by Zebulon Pike, an American, who entered the area three years after the Louisiana Purchase of 1803.

Stephen Long, John C. Fremont, and Kit Carson were also mapping the region within the modern boundaries of the Diocese of Colorado Springs. The Treaty of Guadalupe-Hidalgo provided the United States with portions of Colorado ceded by Mexico. The U.S. Congress created the Colorado Territory in 1861, prompted by the influx of settlers that resulted from the local gold strikes. Colorado entered the Union in 1876 as the Centennial State.

Bishop Joseph P. Machebeuf, who had served as vicar apostolic previously, had erected a parish in Denver in 1860, and when the Diocese of Denver (now the Archdiocese of Denver) was established in 1887, he became the first ordinary. Colorado Springs was already thriving as Fountain Colony, established by General William J. Palmer. St. Mary's Church was serving the faithful there. Annunciation Parish was opened in Leadville in 1879, and St. Rose of Lima was built in Buena Vista in 1880. The Gold Rush of 1890 and the promotion of the area as a health resort spurred development.

In 1917, as America entered World War I, the town of Colorado Springs, renamed for the nearby Manitou Springs, consolidated with Colorado City (originally El Dorado City, founded in 1859). The new city experienced the grim realities of the Great Depression, but even during the difficult economic times other churches were opened, and the faithful in the area turned to the production of munitions, developing mining operations for the military efforts of World War II. The North American Aerospace Defense Command (NORAD) was installed in the region in 1942, becoming an integral part of the national alertness in the Cold War era following the war. Fort Carson, home of the 5th U.S. Infantry Division, is also in Colorado Springs, and in 1954 the United States Air Force Academy was established there.

Denver was elevated to the status of an archdiocese in 1941, and the Diocese of Pueblo was erected. The Diocese of Colorado Springs was established in on January 30, 1984, and Bishop Richard C. Hanifen was installed in the diocese on that day. He had served as auxiliary bishop of the Archdiocese of Denver since 1974. Bishop Hanifen instituted the offices and agencies necessary for diocesan administration and expanded facilities to accommodate the growing Catholic population, which included immigrants. He retired on January 30, 2003, having provided the new diocese with a firm foundation and facilities and spiritual programs for the Catholics of the area.

The second bishop of Colorado Springs, Michael J. Sheridan, had served as auxiliary bishop of the Archdiocese of St. Louis and then as coadjutor bishop of Colorado Springs from 2001. Bishop Sheridan acceded to the see on January 30, 2003. The chief priority for the diocese has been dealing with the rapid increase in population, and a pastoral plan for the diocese was issued in 2010 to assess the needs of the Catholic community. In 2011 there were 77,000 Catholics served by 52 priests and 41 parishes in the diocese.

Colum, Padraic (December 8, 1881–January 11, 1972)

A poet of renown, Padraic Colum was also famed as a dramatist. He was born in Longford, Ireland, and started working early. In 1896 he moved with his family to Sandy Cave, where his father served as a stationmaster. While he was in the service of the railway, Colum started writing and earned immediate attention.

The Irish National Theater Society produced one

of his plays in 1903, and the Abbey Theater produced a second drama. In 1907 Colum published a book of poetry, *Wild Earth.* In 1912 he married Mary (Molly) Maguire, and two years later they journeyed to Pittsburgh, where an aunt resided. The Colums then went to New York, and there Padraic wrote a children's book for the Hawaiian government, *Legends of Hawaii,* and then wrote for the *New York Sunday Tribune.* After a brief reunion with James Joyce in Paris in 1930, the Colums returned to New York, and both taught at Columbia University until Molly's death in 1958.

Colum, continuing his work and lecturing, served as president of the Poetry Society of America from 1938 to 1939. He also received honorary degrees from Irish and American universities. The Catholic Library Association awarded him the Regina Medal in 1961, and two years later he was elected to the American Academy of Arts and Letters.

Columbian Squires. *See* **Knights of Columbus**

Columbus, Christopher (1451–May 20 or 21, 1506)

The explorer who discovered America, Christopher Columbus was born probably in Genoa, Italy, but sailed to the New World in the service of Queen Isabella and King Ferdinand of Spain. He set out on trading voyages as early as 1470, as he and his brother were raised on tales of sea adventures. Columbus served René d'Anjou, the king of Naples, and also Genoese traders, the Centurioni. In this last employment he carried supplies to Chios in the Aegean Sea.

In 1477 Columbus went to Portugal and visited Porto Santo in the Madeiras, and married Felipa Moñiz de Perestrello. He approached King John II of Portugal to sponsor an expedition, but the monarch did not agree to the proposed venture. Columbus left Lisbon with his son, Diego, and went to Spain. In 1484 he took refuge at the monastery of La Rabida, befriended by the Franciscans there. He was introduced to the court of Queen Isabella through the auspices of

one of the monks. Columbus begged the Spanish monarchs to sponsor a fleet of ships on a voyage to Asia, which would follow a westward route. They held debates, conferences, and studies, but came to no decision until 1492. Then Columbus received command of three ships, the *Santa Maria,* the *Niña,* and the *Pinta.* On August 3, 1492, this small fleet set sail. On October 12, his crew spotted land, which Columbus named San Salvador. He then sailed to Hispaniola, Haiti, the Dominican Republic, and Cuba. He settled in Santo Domingo and built a fort and then returned to Spain, where he was given the titles of Viceroy and Admiral of the Ocean Sea.

On September 25, 1493, Columbus began his second voyage, during which he discovered the West Indian islands and Puerto Rico. He also visited the island of Jamaica. Recalled in 1496, after enemies pressed charges of mismanagement against him, Columbus was well received and given eight more ships. He set sail in May 1498, reaching Trinidad and the coast of Venezuela. However, during his absence, troubles had arisen in Hispaniola, and Columbus again faced charges. In May 1502 Columbus sailed to Cuba and to the coast of Central America, but he was shipwrecked in Jamaica and not rescued for a year. Returning to Spain, he found he had lost royal favor as a result of his enemies' campaigns. Stricken at the time with arthritis, Columbus withdrew from court life and died in obscurity.

Columbus, Diocese of

Established on March 3, 1868, by Pope Blessed Pius IX, the Diocese of Columbus serves counties in central and south-central Ohio. The capital of the state, Columbus is a leading industrial and mining center. The city was planned as a political center by the Ohio General Assembly in 1812, and the arrival of the railroads and canals added to its prosperity. The Diocese of Columbus is a suffragan see of the Archdiocese of Cincinnati.

Columbus shares in a Catholic heritage that opened in the 1600s. René-Robert Chevalier, Sieur de

Christopher Columbus

La Salle, is reported to have been in the area as early as 1680, while exploring Lake Ontario for France. The region, however, remained isolated from European influences until 1749, when Jesuit missionaries labored among the Catholic Huron. Father Joseph de Bonnechamps was in the region with the expedition of Pierre Joseph Céloron de Blainville. In 1751 the revered Jesuit Father Armand de La Richardie founded a settlement at modern Sandusky. Ohio entered the Union as the seventeenth state in 1803, but settlements were sparse in the region.

No other Catholic missions are documented until the early 1800s, when Dominican Father Edward D. Fenwick, the "Apostle of Ohio," founded St. Joseph's, a log chapel, at Somerset. Bishop Benedict Jospeh Flaget of the Diocese of Bardstown (now the Archdiocese of Louisville) visited the area with Father Stephen T. Badin. When the Diocese of Cincinnati, now an archdiocese, was erected in 1821, Father Fenwick was appointed as the first bishop.

A year later, a chapel was erected in modern-day Danville, in Knox County, at that time called Sapp's Settlement. Dominican priests served the Catholics there. Immigrants and others arrived in Ohio about that time, and by 1868 there were some forty thousand Catholics in the central and south-central part of the state. The Diocese of Columbus was erected to serve the growing number of faithful in the area.

The first bishop of Columbus was Sylvester Harden Rosecrans, a convert and a member of a distinguished family. His brother was Civil War General William Rosecrans. Bishop Rosecrans had served as an auxiliary bishop of Cincinnati since 1862 and was transferred to Columbus on March 3, 1868. He instituted the agencies and offices necessary for diocesan administration and began building parishes. He started St. Joseph's Cathedral and St. Vincent's Orphanage. Bishop Rosecrans also founded St. Aloysius Seminary. He died on October 21, 1878.

His successor was Bishop John Ambrose Watterson, who continued to expand diocesan facilities and programs. He was consecrated on August 8, 1880. Bishop Watterson was able to pay off some of the diocesan debts caused by the need for constant expansion and building. He also aided in the build-

ing of the Pontifical College Josephinum. Bishop Watterson died on April 17, 1899.

The third bishop, Henry Moeller, was consecrated for the diocese on August 25, 1900. His first priority was the reduction of the debt of $200,000 still facing the diocese, and he managed to settle all accounts within two and a half years. On April 27, 1903, Bishop Moeller was promoted as coadjutor archbishop of Cincinnati, with right of succession.

The fourth bishop of Columbus was James Joseph Hartley, who was consecrated on February 25, 1904. Bishop Hartley would lead the Catholics of Columbus for four decades, facing some of the most critical eras in American history. He continued building parishes and fostering educational facilities, and the College of St. Mary of the Springs was started in 1911.

World War I demanded sacrifices and support, and Bishop Hartley aided the cause of national defense. When the Great Depression gripped the country after the war, he tried to provide charitable resources and services and then led the diocese in the terrible years of World War II, following the attack on Pearl Harbor on December 7, 1941. Bishop Hartley died on January 12, 1944.

His successor was Bishop Michael Joseph Ready, who was consecrated the fifth bishop on December 14, 1944. Bishop Ready introduced the Catholic Welfare Bureau to the diocese and opened new schools. He also founded the diocesan newspaper and erected many new parishes throughout the diocese. Bishop Ready died on May 2, 1957.

The sixth bishop of Columbus, Clarence G. Issenmann, had served as auxiliary bishop of Cincinnati since 1954. He was transferred to Columbus on December 5, 1957, and continued the expansion of diocesan facilities and services. Bishop Issenmann took part in the Second Vatican Council. On October 7, 1964, he was promoted to the Archdiocese of Cincinnati as apostolic administrator with right of succession.

Bishop John Joseph Carberry, who would become a cardinal in 1969, was the seventh bishop of Columbus. He had served as the coadjutor bishop and then as bishop of Lafayette in Indiana since 1956, acceding to the see in 1957. He was transferred to Columbus on January 20, 1965. Three years later, on March 24, 1968, he was promoted to the Archdiocese of St. Louis and was created a cardinal priest on April 28, 1969.

His successor was Bishop Clarence E. Elwell, who had served as auxiliary bishop of Cleveland since 1962. He was transferred to Columbus on May 29, 1968. He continued renovating and expanding diocesan programs and began initiating the faithful in the reforms mandated by the Second Vatican Council. Bishop Elwell died on February 16, 1973.

The ninth bishop of Columbus, Edward J. Hermann, had served as auxiliary bishop of Washington since 1966. He was appointed to the Diocese of Columbus on June 26, 1973. Bishop Hermann implemented the new apostolates for evangelization, continued building projects, and added parishes and schools. He also faced the arduous task of guiding the diocese during the tumultuous period after the Second Vatican Council. He retired on September 8, 1989, and served as apostolic administrator until April 1983. He died on December 22, 1999.

Bishop James A. Griffin, who had served as auxiliary bishop of Cleveland since 1979, was Bishop Hermann's successor. He was installed as the tenth bishop of Columbus on April 25, 1983. Bishop Griffin, who holds degrees in canon law and civil law, launched a variety of initiatives, including the Foundation of the Catholic Diocese of Columbus (1985), the Legacy of Catholic Learning (1989), and Challenge in Changing Times (2000). He also helped start the faith-based task force "Breaking the Silence," to reduce family violence. He retired on October 14, 2004.

The eleventh bishop of Columbus, Frederick F. Campbell, had served as auxiliary bishop of the Archdiocese of St. Paul and Minneapolis. Bishop Campbell was installed in the see on January 13, 2005. In 2011 there were 262,000 Catholics, served by 188 priests, 245 women religious, and 106 parishes in the diocese.

Commonweal

The oldest lay Catholic journal in the United States, *Commonweal* was launched in 1924 as *The*

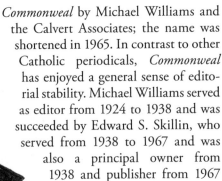

Bishop Clarence Elwell

Commonweal by Michael Williams and the Calvert Associates; the name was shortened in 1965. In contrast to other Catholic periodicals, *Commonweal* has enjoyed a general sense of editorial stability. Michael Williams served as editor from 1924 to 1938 and was succeeded by Edward S. Skillin, who served from 1938 to 1967 and was also a principal owner from 1938 and publisher from 1967 to 1999. James O'Gara became editor in 1967. He was followed by Peter Steinfels, who served from 1984 to 1988. The current editor is Paul Baumann.

From its inception, the magazine was intended to provide the average Catholic reader with coverage of the week's news and events and to offer a variety of opinions. *Commonweal* has traditionally embraced controversial editorial positions, including its condemnation of the firebombing of Dresden and the use of the atomic bomb on Hiroshima and Nagasaki, its criticism of Father Charles Coughlin and Senator Joseph McCarthy, and its active opposition to the war in Vietnam. The magazine also was outspoken in its call for an end to racism and for civil rights for African-Americans in the 1950s and 1960s. In 1968 it declared objections to Pope Paul VI's encyclical *Humanae Vitae*. The magazine remains one of the principal voices of liberal American Catholicism in the United States.

Como, Perry (May 18, 1912–May 12, 2001)

One of America's beloved television stars, Perry Como was known for his laid-back renditions and song styling. Born in the steel town of Canonsburg, Pennsylvania, he was one of thirteen children of an Italian family and got his first job in a barbershop. He began singing with the big bands in the 1930s and soon acquired fame and was especially popular on the radio and on the jukebox. In 1945 Como enjoyed his first million-selling hit song, "Till the End of Time," the first of many chart toppers. Como also was a major pioneer in television variety shows and Christmas specials during the 1950s and remained a television presence for the next twenty years. In all, he had fourteen number-one singles and more than twenty gold records, and sold more than one hundred million albums. In 1958 he won a Grammy Award as best male singer for the hit "Catch a Falling Star."

Concanen, Richard Luke (December 27, 1747–January 19, 1810)

A remarkable scholar and diplomat who was consecrated as the first bishop of the Diocese of New York, Bishop Richard Luke Concanen, O.P., never set foot on American soil. He was born in Kilbegnet, County Roscommon, Ireland, and entered the Dominican order at age seventeen. Ordained to the priesthood at the Pontifical Lateran University in Rome, Father Concanen was quickly recognized for his intellectual brilliance and holiness.

He served as novice master and master of studies in Dominican houses and was fluent in five languages. As he was stationed in Rome, Father Concanen served as an agent for the growing American Church, aiding Bishop John Carroll, the first American prelate. Father Concanen was also appointed to various dioceses as a bishop in Ireland but refused the honors in 1798 and 1802. On April 24, 1808, he was consecrated as the first bishop of New York. As there was no safe passage to the United States at the time, Bishop Concanen gathered missionary priests and funds for the new diocese from European sources. In March 1810 he obtained a French passport and went to Naples to embark on a ship. He was denied passage and had to remain in Naples, where he was sickened with a fever and died. On July 9, 1978, Cardinal Terence J. Cooke of New York dedicated a memorial in Naples, identifying the tomb of Bishop Concanen as the resting place of the first bishop of the present-day archdiocese.

Confraternity of Christian Doctrine (CCD)

The Confraternity of Christian Doctrine, a program dedicated to Catholic religious education, is the modern version of sixteenth-century Italian groups of catechists, priests, and laity involved in the instruction of youth. In Rome, a Society of Christian Doctrine (*Compagnia della Dottrina Cristiana*) was established around 1560 and received the approval of Pope St. Pius V in 1571. St. Charles Borromeo, the archbishop of Milan, was also promoting the Sodality of Christian Doctrine and established the programs in every parish.

In 1607 Pope Paul V established the Society of Christian Doctrine as an archconfraternity in the apostolic brief *Ex Credito Nobis*. The headquarters of the society were established in St. Peter's Basilica. Pope St. Pius X, honoring the earlier efforts, wrote an encyclical letter, *Acerbo Nimis,* in 1905, and ordered that the confraternity be established in every parish of the Church. The 1917 Code of Canon Law (c. 711.2) included the directive, providing the guideline that parish units be established by formal decree of the local ordinary and affiliated with the archconfraternity in Rome. Pope Pius XI and the Catechetical Office of the Holy See further decreed in *Provido Sane* in 1935 that diocesan and national offices be established to promote, support, and coordinate the work of the confraternity at local levels.

Individual parishes in the United States started their own units of the confraternity after Pope St. Pius X's encyclical letter was issued, and it slowly became a national movement. The program proved successful in New York and Pittsburgh, and in 1922 the confraternity was organized in the Diocese of Los Angeles under the auspices of the Office of Catholic Charities to reach out to immigrant families from Mexico who were moving into the area. The diocesan and parochial structure of the Los Angeles CCD became the model for other dioceses.

In the early 1930s, Bishop Edwin Vincent O'Hara of the Diocese of Great Falls, Montana, gained permission from the Holy See to establish a national office to coordinate its activities, and in 1934 an episcopal committee was established, chaired by Bishop O'Hara. A national center for the CCD was established under the auspices of the National Catholic Welfare Conference in 1935. Bishop O'Hara guided the programs, aided by Miss Miriam Marks, who served as executive secretary from 1935 to 1960.

Parish units of the CCD were firmly structured from the beginning, with the priest-director, the pastor or his delegate, functioning with a lay executive board consisting of the officers and the chairs of each of six departments: teachers, fishers, helpers, parent-educators, discussion clubs, and the Apostolate of Good Will for those who were not members of the Church. After the Second Vatican Council, the diocesan directors of the confraternity formed a national council that evolved into the National Conference of Catechetical Leadership.

The national CCD center offered many support services and from 1935 to World War II organized national congresses, the first held at Rochester, New York. After the war, national congresses were held every five years, the last in 1971 in Miami. The CCD eventually focused not only on immigrants but on the religious instruction of children who were not attending Catholic schools. The programs instituted Sunday schools, released time projects, and summer vacation schools. Preschool children and their parents were targeted for instruction, as well as adults in general, and non-Catholics. In 1975 the National Center of Religious Education, the CCD, was suppressed and the United States Catholic Conference, Department of Education was mandated to assume the educational programs and concerns.

Connecticut

Known as the Constitution State, Connecticut entered the Union in 1788 and ratified the U.S. Constitution in 1789. The state is located in the northeastern part of the nation and is bounded on the north by Massachusetts, on the east by Rhode Island, on the south by Long Island Sound, and on the west by New York. Connecticut has two major land divisions: the eastern New England Uplands and the western New England Uplands. The original Native American tribes in Connecticut were the Mohawk, Mohican, Nipmuck, Pequot, Podunk, Sequin, and the Wappinger Confederacy.

Adrian Black, a Dutch seaman, entered the area and claimed the region for the Netherlands in 1614. In 1633 a Dutch fort was erected on the present site of Hartford but was abandoned in 1654. At the same time, English colonists from Plymouth settled at Windsor. Thomas Hooker, a Congregational minister, also founded a settlement at Hartford in 1636.

One year later, the Pequot attacked the settlements, and the Great Swamp Fight took place over the intrusion of the whites into sacred Indian lands. The Pequot were defeated and mercilessly slain. Other Puritans migrated to the region as a result, and in 1638 New Haven was founded, with a colony formed near Hartford, Wethersfield, and Windsor following in 1639. The colony adopted the Puritan Fundamental Orders.

In 1651 Jesuit Father Gabriel Druillettes visited New Haven as the representative of the governor of Canada, at that time New France. The Canadians were seeking a unified effort against the sustained and powerful attacks by the Iroquois. Father Druillettes, an educated and diplomatic priest, was courteously received in New Haven as the representative of the Canadian government.

In 1663 King Charles II granted a colony patent to the English, and the area prospered, receiving new settlers. Yale University was founded in 1701. No Catholic missionary efforts are recorded in the state until 1776, when Abbé Claude Robin, a chaplain with the French fleet, celebrated Mass at Hartford. The French naval forces were allies of the Americans in the Revolutionary War. The Connecticut regiments serving under George Washington at Morristown, New Jersey, mutinied in 1780 but were quelled by troops from Pennsylvania. In 1787 the Connecticut Compromise broke a deadlock at the Constitutional Convention in Philadelphia. A year later, Connecticut became the fifth state to join the Union. Soon after, in 1791, Father John Thayer traveled throughout the area, beginning a Catholic foundation.

Industrial inventions and advances promoted the growth of the state, and immigrants entered the area steadily. The Catholics, deprived of religious freedom by the Congregationalists from the earliest eras of the settlements, received civil rights and religious freedom in a state constitution drawn up in 1818. Father Bernard O'Cavanaugh, the state's first resident priest, arrived in Hartford in 1828, assigned by Bishop Jean-Louis Lefebvre de Cheverus of Boston, later a cardinal of France. Bishop de Cheverus visited Catholics in Connecticut as well. Father O'Cavanaugh started the first Catholic newspaper in the region, and bought an abandoned Episcopalian facility and opened Holy Trinity Church.

In 1843 the Diocese of Hartford was erected (now the Archdiocese of Hartford), and the first bishop of Hartford was William Tyler, a convert to the faith. He established the offices and agencies for diocesan administration and expanded parishes and facilities, even though he resided in Providence, Rhode Island. Bishop Bernard O'Reilly, his successor, carried on the building programs until he was lost at sea in 1856.

The Catholics of Connecticut served in the Civil War with distinction, including Lawrence Stephen McMahon, who became the bishop of Hartford in 1879. The faithful, despite their service records, faced bigotry and attacks in this era. Father Michael J. McGivney, seeing the anti-Catholic assaults, founded the Knights of Columbus in 1882 to defend the Church. The support of Bishop Francis Patrick McFarland for the restored Union eased the tensions between Catholics and Protestants, and the Church prospered. Successive bishops opened a Catholic newspaper, increased parishes and diocesan facilities, and promoted educational intitiatives. World War I multiplied Connecticut's industries, but they suffered during the Great Depression following the war. During World War II, the state once again provided munitions, particularly submarines, for the nation's military efforts. In 1954 the *Nautilus*, the first atomic submarine, was launched at Groton.

One year earlier, the Diocese of Hartford was elevated to the status of a metropolitan archdiocese, and Archbishop Henry J. O'Brien opened a Hispanic ministry for newly arriving immigrants. The Second Vatican Council also provided Connecticut laypeople with new apostolates and ministries. Archbishop John F. Whealon, who served from 1969 to 1991, established the permanent diaconate and other programs. Archbishop Daniel A. Cronin, his successor, promoted evangelization and social justice. Archbishop Henry J. Mansell, the present archbishop of Hartford, was installed on December 18, 2003. In 2011 there were 1.2 million Catholics, served by 854 priests, more than 1,100 women religious, and 376 parishes in the state.

Connell, Francis (January 29, 1888–May 12, 1967)

A Redemptorist theologian, Father Francis Connell appeared on radio and television and pioneered catechetical and moral education throughout the nation. He was born in Boston and graduated from Boston Latin School with honors. He then attended Boston College for two years. He entered the Redemptorists in 1907 and was ordained in 1913. After parish ministries, he was appointed professor of dogmatic theology at Mount St. Alphonsus Seminary in 1915. Studying at the Pontifical University of St. Thomas, the Angelicum, in Rome from 1921 to 1923, he received the degree of doctor of sacred theology and then taught at Esopus from 1923 to 1940, The Catholic University of America from 1940 to 1958, and St. John's University in Brooklyn from 1958 to 1962.

Father Connell also served as rector of Holy Redeemer College in Washington from 1945 to 1950, as dean of the School of Sacred Theology at Catholic University from 1949 to 1957, and as dean for religious communities at Catholic University from 1958 to 1967. He wrote *De Sacramentis Ecclesiae, Morals in Politics and Professions, Outlines of Moral Theology, Spiritual and Pastoral Conferences for Priests,* and *Father Connell's Confraternity Edition of the New Baltimore Catechism.*

A pioneer on the national *Catholic Hour* radio program, he was a charter member and first president of the Catholic Theological Society of America. He received from Pope Pius XII the Pro Ecclesia et Pontifice award and an appointment as consultor to the Congregation of Seminaries and Universities in Rome. He was designated a *peritus* (or theological expert) for the Second Vatican Council by Pope Blessed John XXIII and served as a member of the briefing panel for English-speaking reporters. Father Connell died in Washington, D.C.

Connelly, Venerable Cornelia (January 15, 1809–1879)

The Venerable Cornelia Connelly, founder of the Society of the Holy Child Jesus, endured many hardships. She was born in Philadelphia, Pennsylvania, as Cornelia Augusta Peacock. Well educated in a wealthy family, she married an Episcopal minister, Pierce Connelly, in 1832 and moved to Natchez, Mississippi, and had two children. On September 6, 1835, Pierce announced to his congregation that he intended to become a Roman Catholic. Cornelia was also drawn to the faith, and she converted while Pierce decided to wait until he had visited Rome.

The Connellys were welcomed in Rome, and

Pierce made many friends. The family had to return to America in 1838 as they were facing financial problems, and Pierce taught at St. Charles College in Louisiana. Cornelia also had a teaching position. The couple suffered the loss of one child and the birth of two more during this period. Pierce also announced his plans to become a priest, an act that would require Cornelia's agreement to enter religious life.

In 1845 the Connellys went to England and then Rome, where Pierce was ordained in July. Cornelia and her children went to the Roman convent of the Society of the Sacred Heart. She received an

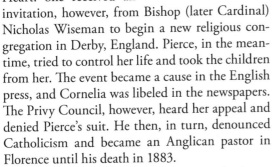

Mother Cornelia Connelly

invitation, however, from Bishop (later Cardinal) Nicholas Wiseman to begin a new religious congregation in Derby, England. Pierce, in the meantime, tried to control her life and took the children from her. The event became a cause in the English press, and Cornelia was libeled in the newspapers. The Privy Council, however, heard her appeal and denied Pierce's suit. He then, in turn, denounced Catholicism and became an Anglican pastor in Florence until his death in 1883.

Cornelia moved her congregation to St. Leonard's and faced problems with Cardinal Wiseman. He opposed her rule, which was approved in 1893. Mother Cornelia Connelly was declared venerable in 1992.

Connolly, John (1750–February 6, 1825)

A Dominican and the second bishop of New York, John Connolly was a pioneering American prelate. He was born in Slane, County Meath, Ireland, and was sent to Rome, where he held many posts of honor after his ordination. Popes Pius VI and Pius VII held him in high esteem. When the French invaded the area, Father Connolly saved Irish, Scotch, and English colleges from being ransacked and preserved other institutions through his personal intervention.

In 1814 Father Connolly was consecrated a bishop to serve the Diocese of New York, but the War of 1812 delayed his arrival in the United States until November 24, 1815. New York was poverty-stricken, he discovered. He had only four priests and three parishes to serve the Catholics in the area covering modern-day New York and New Jersey.

Despite his advanced age and the problems facing him, Bishop Connolly erected thirteen churches, founded an orphan asylum, and introduced the Sisters of Charity to the diocese. He also visited the entire region and advocated the erection of Catholic dioceses in every state in the union in order to promote the faith. He died in New York and was buried in old St. Patrick's Cathedral.

Conrardy, Louis Lambert (1841–August 24, 1914)

One of the most unique missionaries to visit the United States, Louis Lambert Conrardy was esteemed as a hero among Catholics. He was born in Liege, Belgium, and entered his local seminary while he was in his teens. He was ordained on June 15, 1866, and became a missionary to India, serving in the Pondicherry district from 1871 to 1874. Father Conrardy then returned to Belgium and studied at the American College in Louvain. He answered the call for missionaries in America and arrived in Oregon to begin his labors at the Indian mission outposts. By 1875 he was resident priest on the Umatilla Reservation, welcoming both Indians and the local whites.

In 1888, having been hailed a hero for his work by American Church leaders, Father Conrardy sailed to the island of Molokai, Hawaii, and was at the deathbed of St. Damien de Veuster, the Sacred Heart missionary to the lepers. He remained on Molokai for eight years, then enrolled at the medical school of the University of Oregon at Portland.

Earning his medical degree in 1900, Father Conrardy went to Shek Lung, near Canton, China. There he started a leper colony and won the respect and assistance of the Chinese authorities. He died of pneumonia in Hong Kong and, at his request, was buried with two lepers, wrapped in a simple mat, in the Hong Kong cemetery.

Considine, John J. (October 9, 1897–May 4, 1982)

A Maryknoll missionary and diplomat for the Vatican, John J. Considine promoted the missions throughout his priesthood. He was born in New Bedford, Massachusetts, and in 1917 entered the newly established Society of Maryknoll Missionaries. Educated at The Catholic University of America, he was ordained in 1923. From 1924 to 1934 he served as the procurator-general of the Society in Rome and was a member of the Society's general council in Maryknoll, New York, from 1934 to 1946.

Father Considine focused on establishing and coordinating projects that brought attention and support for the missions. In 1925 he directed a permanent mission exhibit on Vatican grounds and later wrote *The Vatican Missionary Exposition: A Window on the World*. He also headed the founding of the Fides News Service in 1927 and served as director for seven years. Father Considine labored as secretary on behalf of the Vatican on a diplomatic mission to Ethiopia in 1929 and then undertook an expedition to the missions, chronicling his findings in *Across a World*.

In 1934 Father Considine returned to Maryknoll headquarters in New York to serve as a member of the general council and was later elected vicar general, a post held until 1946. He aided Bishop Fulton J. Sheen and Father Fred McGuire, C.M., in establishing mission secretariat meetings in Washington, D.C. He returned to Maryknoll headquarters when advanced in years but kept working until his death.

Conway, Katherine (1852–January 2, 1927)

A journalist and editor, Katherine Conway was esteemed as a poet. She was born in Rochester, New York, the daughter of Irish Catholic immigrants, and was educated in Catholic girls' schools. She graduated from the Sacred Heart Academy in

New York City and spent a brief period as a schoolteacher. Conway soon departed from the classroom to become an assistant editor at the Buffalo *Catholic Union and Times* and went on from there to serve as the editor of the *Catholic Union*, *The Pilot*, and the *Republic*.

Conway also taught at St. Mary's College for Women in Indiana and acquired a wide following through her poetry and nonfiction. She was especially beloved as a writer for young Catholic women, especially through the five books in *The Family Sitting-room Series*. While she remained single, she was also a promoter of traditional Catholic marriage and the role of women. Her writings included *On the Sunrise Slope* (1881), *The Good Shepherd in Boston* (1892), *A Dream of Lilies* (1893), *Questions of Honor in Christian Life* (1896), *A Story of Our Set* (1900), *The Woman Who Never Did Wrong, and Other Stories* (1909), and *Fifty Years with Christ: The Good Shepherd* (1925). For her writings and work as a journalist, her years as editor, as well as her poetry, she was awarded in 1907 the Laetare Medal by the University of Notre Dame and in 1912 the Pro Ecclesia et Pontifice award by Pope St. Pius X.

Cardinal Terence Cooke

Cooke, Terence James (March 1, 1921–October 6, 1983)

Cardinal from 1969 and archbishop of New York from 1968, Terence James Cooke earned considerable fame for the courage he displayed in facing terminal cancer. He was born in New York City to immigrants from Ireland, the youngest of three children. When he was five, his family moved to the Bronx, and he attended parochial school there. He entered Cathedral College, the minor seminary, and in 1940 he entered St. Joseph's Seminary, Dunwoodie. Ordained on December 1, 1945, Father Cooke was sent to the University of Chicago and then the National Catholic School of Social Service at the Catholic University of America, where he earned a master's degree.

From 1949 to 1954 he served Catholic Charities and then became procurator of St. Joseph's Seminary. In 1959 Cardinal Francis Spellman appointed Father Cooke as his secretary. Cooke then became vice chancellor, chancellor, vicar general, and auxiliary bishop of the Archdiocese of New York, consecrated on December 13, 1965.

When Cardinal Spellman died in 1967, Bishop Cooke was not considered a likely candidate to succeed him, so there was genuine surprise when on March 8, 1968, he was named the new archbishop of New York. On the very day of his installation, April 4, 1968, Martin Luther King, Jr., was assassinated in Memphis, Tennessee, an event that was emblematic of the tumultuous time of social and political upheaval. The new archbishop visited a parish in Harlem on the same evening to make an appeal for peace. That year he became the Military Vicar of the United States Armed Forces. He was created a cardinal priest, with the titular church of Sts. John and Paul on April 28, 1969.

Cardinal Cooke was very active as Military Vicar and visited the American military overseas installations annually. His time as archbishop was marked by the challenges of the post-Second Vatican Council period, with its attendant declines in vocations and stresses upon Catholic education. To ensure the future of archdiocesan schools, Cardinal Cooke established a commission to study the needs of education. He then followed its recommendations and was thus able to stave off financial problems and school closures. He also established an annual fundraising campaign in 1979, promoted Catholic Charities, and was noted especially for his outreach to the African-American and Hispanic communities. He founded the Office of Black Catholics, gave encouragement to the Northeast Center for Hispanics, and ensured the appointment of the first African-American and Hispanic auxiliary bishops for the archdiocese.

In August 1983 Cardinal Cooke announced that he suffered from terminal cancer. When he died, thousands filed past his remains and hundreds of priests attended the funeral. He was buried in St. Patrick's Cathedral. His cause for canonization was opened in 1992, and the investigation moved to Rome in 2003.

Cope, St. Marianne (January 23, 1838–August 9, 1918)

A pioneer in Catholic affairs in Hawaii, St. Marianne Cope led a group of sister-nurses to the islands and founded the Franciscan mission there. She was born in Germany and baptized Barbara. Her family migrated to Utica, New York, when she was two, and she was raised in the United States. At age twenty-four, she entered the Sisters of St. Francis of Syracuse, receiving the religious name of Marianne.

St. Marianne Cope

St. Marianne served in educational roles for her congregation for ten years and helped to found hospitals, including St. Joseph's in Syracuse, New York, where she served as superior from 1870 to 1877. In 1883, however, St. Marianne began her special ministry when her community responded to a plea from Hawaiian leaders to labor among the lepers on the island of Oahu.

The Franciscan Sisters, led by St. Marianne, began their labors at Kakaako Hospital. They rid the property of rats and filth and then brought order and medical standards to the care of the leper patients. There were seven sister-nurses, and they assumed new roles in 1884, when St. Marianne started a hospital for the general populace on the island of Maui.

On Molokai, where most of the leper patients were housed, St. Damien de Veuster was suffering from leprosy himself. In November 1888 St. Marianne and some companions accepted an assignment at Kalaupapa, where St. Damien carried out his ministry. She took charge of a home for leprous women and young girls, and upon the death of St. Damien also took charge of the home for men and boys in the settlement. When she died, all the islands mourned her passing. The Sisters of St. Francis of Syracuse labor today in Hawaii and New York.

St. Marianne's cause for sainthood was opened

in 1983, and she was declared venerable in 1995. In early 2005, approval was given for her beatification, on the basis of a confirmed miracle. She was beatified in Rome on May 14, 2005, and canonized in Rome on October 21, 2012, by Pope Benedict XVI. Her feast day is January 23.

Coronado, Francisco Vázquez de (1500–1553)

An explorer of the American southwest, Francisco Vázquez de Coronado was the commander who led Franciscan Father Juan de Padilla, the protomartyr of the United States, into Kansas. Coronado was born in Salamanca, Spain. He went to Mexico sometime before 1538 and became a trusted aide of the local viceroy, who appointed him to positions of rank.

In 1539 Coronado was given a command to lead an expedition of three Spaniards and one thousand Indians northwest into modern New Mexico. He battled the Zunis and Pueblo Indians, but in victory he showed them courtesy and human concern and won their respect. He then moved north, visiting modern Arkansas and southern Nebraska, returning to New Mexico after six months. In April 1542 not having much to show for his efforts, Coronado started the march to Mexico. He had suffered a fall from a horse and sustained a severe head injury. Father Juan de Padilla, Father Luis, and a Portuguese soldier named Docampo remained behind, having established a mission in the region.

Coronado had been seeking Cibola, the legendary Seven Cities of Gold. Returning to his superiors without treasure, he fell into disgrace and died in Mexico, leaving a widow and eight children. His reports, however, provided valuable geographic and ethnographic details for later scholars.

Corpa, Pedro de, and Companion Martyrs (d. 1597)

Franciscan priest martyrs, these missionaries were part of the vast Florida missions. Father de Corpa was from Villabilla, Spain, and he was the first victim in the massacre on Cumberland and Parris islands in Georgia. The Franciscans had arrived there in 1584 and started their mission labors among the local Indian tribes. However, Juanita, a local chief, resented the growing influence of the missionaries and started a revolt, instigating the

murders of the priests and their helpers. Father de Corpa was clubbed to death on September 13 or 14, 1597. Father Blas de Rodriguez, a Franciscan from Cocerres, Spain, was slain on September 16; Father Miguel de Añondied with Brother Antonio de Badajóz on September 17 on St. Catherine's Island, in the Mission Santa Catalina de Guale. Father Francisco de Veráscola, another Franciscan, was away during the initial assaults but was ambushed upon his return and also martyred.

Corpus Christi, Diocese of

Established on March 23, 1912, by Pope St. Pius X, the Diocese of Corpus Christi serves counties in southern Texas. The second largest port in the state, Corpus Christi is a center for agriculture, industry, chemical manufacturing, and petroleum refining. The name was derived from the visit by Alonso Alvarez de Pineda, who sailed into the region in 1519 on the feast of Corpus Christi. The city was founded in 1838 by Colonel Henry Lawrence Kinney as a trading post. Corpus Christi developed as the railroads arrived and the deepwater port was utilized; the discovery of the Saxtet oil field in 1939 laid the foundation for a modern metropolis. The Diocese of Corpus Christi is a suffragan see of the Archdiocese of San Antonio.

Franciscans arrived in the area in the late 1600s and pioneered Catholic settlements, constructing a chain of missions throughout present-day Texas. Three distinct mission groups prospered. In 1749 missions for the Karankawa Indians were established, and in 1766 the mission and Presidio of Bahia were moved to Goliad. The bay originally named San Miguel Arcángel became Corpus Christi.

In 1838 Pope Gregory XVI transferred Texas from the jurisdiction of Mexico City to the Diocese of New Orleans. Bishop John Timon took over the administration of the area two years later, and Bishop John M. Odin at Lavaca Bay soon after. A Vincentian, Bishop Odin resided in Galveston (now the Archdiocese of Galveston-Houston), and revitalized the faith throughout the region. In 1847 the Diocese of San Antonio (now the Archdiocese of San Antonio) was erected, along with the Vicariate Apostolic of Brownsville.

Bishop Dominic Manucy was appointed vicar

apostolic on December 8, 1874, and was transferred to the Diocese of Mobile on March 9, 1884. He was reappointed vicar apostolic of Brownsville on February 1, 1885, and died on December 4 of that year. Corpus Christi became the headquarters for the vicariate activities, and religious communities entered the area to assist in evangelization programs.

Bishop Manucy's successor was Peter Verdaguer, who was consecrated on November 9, 1890. He maintained mission circuits, visiting remote parishes and encouraging the Catholics in the area. Bishop Verdaguer was on a confirmation tour when he died on October 26, 1911.

On March 23, 1912, the Holy See officially recognized the Catholic presence in Corpus Christi when the city was designated as a diocese. Paul Joseph Nussbaum was appointed the first bishop of the Diocese of Corpus Christi and was consecrated on May 20, 1913. A Passionist, Bishop Nussbaum labored for seven years in the new diocese, erecting the offices and agencies for diocesan administration. He also received a great number of priests and religious who were seeking a haven from the persecution unleashed against the Church in Mexico. Bishop Nussbaum led the faithful during World War I, supporting the military efforts of the nation. He retired on March 26, 1920, and two years later was appointed as the bishop of Marquette.

The second bishop of Corpus Christi was Emmanuel B. Ledvina, who was consecrated on June 14, 1921. A former administrator of the Catholic Church Extension Society, he labored to provide charitable aid during the Great Depression and led the faithful of the diocese through World War II. Pope Pius XI bestowed upon Bishop Ledvina the rank of Assistant at the Pontifical Throne on May 30, 1931. Bishop Ledvina retired on March 15, 1949.

Bishop Mariano S. Garriga, who had served as coadjutor bishop to Bishop Ledvina since 1936, acceded to the see of Corpus Christi upon the death of his predecessor. Three years later, Bishop Garriga also received the rank of Assistant at the Pontifical Throne from the Holy See. The first native-born Texan to be consecrated a bishop, he conducted a vast building and expansion program, founding a Benedictine Abbey, a minor seminary, and the Shrine of Our Lady of San Juan de Valle. Bishop Garriga attended the Second Vatican Council and began implementing the reforms mandated by that council. He died on February 21, 1965.

The fourth bishop, Thomas A. Drury, had served as the bishop of San Angelo since 1961. He was installed in Corpus Christi on September 1, 1965, and carried out the reforms of the Second Vatican Council. A diocesan pastoral council and other lay-oriented programs were introduced, as well as charitable programs. Bishop Drury retired on May 19, 1983.

Bishop Rene H. Gracida succeeded Bishop Drury, having served as auxiliary bishop of Miami and then as bishop of Pensacola-Tallahassee. He was installed in Corpus Christi on July 11, 1983. Bishop Gracida established the Western Vicariate of Corpus Christi, opened radio and television apostolates, and augmented the facilities and ministries of Laredo. He retired on April 1, 1997.

His successor was Bishop Roberto O. Gonzalez, who had been appointed coadjutor bishop of Corpus Christi on April 1, 1997. He served only two years, being promoted on March 26, 1999, to the Archdiocese of San Juan, Puerto Rico, but during that period he remedied the financial condition of the diocese and started preparations for the Great Jubilee of 2000.

The seventh bishop of Corpus Christi, Edmond Carmody, succeeded Bishop Gonzalez and was installed on March 17, 2000. He had previously served as the auxiliary bishop of San Antonio, as a missionary in Ecuador, and as the bishop of Tyler. Bishop Carmody took as his objectives for the diocese the seven goals established by the 1988 diocesan synod: evangelization, catechesis, worship, vocations, family life, youth, and stewardship. He supported education and helped to have a charter school opened in the city. He also worked with the Diabetes Association to expand public awareness of the disease. In October 2003 he helped to open the Mother Teresa Day Shelter for the homeless. Bishop Carmody retired on January 18, 2010, and was succeeded by Father William M. Mulvey, who was consecrated a bishop on March 25, 2010. In 2011 there were 396,000 Catholics served by 142 priests, 147 women religious, and 68 parishes in the diocese.

Corrigan, Michael Augustine (August 13, 1839–May 5, 1902)

The third archbishop of the Archdiocese of New York from 1885 to 1902, Michael Augustine Corrigan served the American Church in a difficult era. He was born in Newark, New Jersey, and studied at St. Mary's College in Wilmington, Delaware, and at Mount St. Mary's College in Emmitsburg, Maryland. In 1859 Bishop James Roosevelt Bayley of Newark (now the Archdiocese of Newark) sent him to the North American College in Rome as one of the institution's first twelve students. He was ordained in Rome in 1863, earning his doctorate and returning to America the following year.

Archbishop Michael Corrigan

Father Corrigan taught at Seton Hall College and Seminary and became vicar general of the diocese in 1868. When Bishop Bayley was appointed archbishop of Baltimore, Bishop Corrigan succeeded him in Newark and was consecrated on May 4, 1873. Seven years later he was named coadjutor and successor to Cardinal John McCloskey of New York. In that position, Bishop Corrigan represented American interests when the Italian government took over the North American College in 1884. President Chester Arthur helped the situation by stating that he was concerned that the Italians were violating the rights of American citizens by seizing the property.

The death of Cardinal McCloskey in 1885 brought about the installation of Archbishop Corrigan in St. Patrick's Cathedral on May 4, 1886. He held a synod soon after and revised the administration of the archdiocese. As a result, Father Edward McGlynn began to oppose the archbishop publicly. Father McGlynn was removed from his parish and summoned to Rome. Excommunicated because he refused to obey the summons, the priest assailed Archbishop Corrigan again and again and the matter became a national scandal. Father McGlynn was reconciled to the Church in 1893.

Even under such assaults, Archbishop Corrigan continued his labors, developing organizations to promote the faith and to support charitable proj-

ects, doubling the number of schools and churches, and bringing twenty-four religious communities to New York. He built St. Joseph's Seminary in Dunwoodie and refurbished St. Patrick's Cathedral. His body was interred in the crypt beneath the cathedral in which he died. His funeral was an event of genuine mourning for New Yorkers.

Coughlin, Charles Edward (1891–October 27, 1979)

An outspoken and popular political activist called the "radio priest," Charles Edward Coughlin was also the pastor of a Detroit parish. He was born in Hamilton, Ontario, Canada, and at the age of thirteen entered St. Michael's College in Toronto and graduated in 1911. He joined the Congregation of St. Basil and was ordained in 1916. Part of his pastoral duties included serving in parishes of the Diocese of Detroit. In February 1923, Father Coughlin left the Basilians and was incardinated into the Detroit diocese.

Father Coughlin built a parish in 1926 called "The Little Flower" and served the Catholics in Royal Oak, a suburb of Detroit. On October 17, 1926, he started a radio program on a local station to raise funds for his parish. The show was an instant success, as he addressed social and political issues, and CBS picked up the broadcasts in 1930. Father Coughlin had an estimated forty million listeners. The show was called *The Golden Hour of the Little Flower* and used Catholic doctrines and the papal encyclicals.

Believing in the policies of Franklin Delano Roosevelt, Father Coughlin supported his candidacy in the 1932 election but was alienated soon after. He attacked Roosevelt's administration in his shows and in popular lectures in Madison Square Garden and other arenas. Two years later, Father Coughlin founded the National Union for Social Justice and published an organizational newspaper supporting the candidacy of Congressmen William Lemke of North Dakota in a bid for the White House. When Lemke was soundly defeated, Father

Coughlin withdrew from his radio shows and lectures.

Bishop Michael James Gallagher of Detroit, who had been tolerant of Father Coughlin's activities, died in 1937. Without such episcopal support, the priest was vulnerable to critics who resented his attacks on Roosevelt. Archbishop Edward Mooney, the ordinary of the newly erected Archdiocese of Detroit, was not enthusiastic, therefore, when Father Coughlin decided to return to public life in 1938.

Father Coughlin's new political activism demonstrated a certain attitude of anti-Semitism. He spoke about a Jewish attempt to take over the world, and he viewed the rise of Hitler as a blow to communism. Such views alienated whole segments of the population and brought about retaliations. In 1942 the mailing privileges of his newspaper, *Social Justice*, was revoked, and Father Coughlin was informed through Archbishop Mooney that he had to cease his attacks, or at least curtail them, or he would be indicted under the Espionage Act. America was at war with Germany. Father Coughlin refrained from political activities immediately and remained the pastor of the Shrine of the Little Flower until his retirement in 1966. He died in Birmingham, Michigan.

Covington, Diocese of

Established on July 29, 1853, by Pope Blessed Pius IX, the Diocese of Covington serves the eastern sectors of Kentucky. Covington is a commercial and industrial center. A report indicates that the site was originally given to George Muse in return for military duty, but he traded it in 1780 for a keg of whiskey. The city was laid out in 1815 and was named for General Leonard Covington, who had died in the War of 1812. The diocese is a suffragan see of the Archdiocese of Louisville.

The Catholic heritage of the diocese is historically documented, and many outstanding missionaries and prelates served the region of Covington. In 1787 Jesuit Father John Carroll, who would become the first archbishop of Baltimore, was the prefect apostolic of the United States, and he sent missionaries into Kentucky. Catholics, such as the Boone family, had settled in the region, and the faith was prospering there. Five years later, Kentucky entered the Union, and Catholic settlements increased. In 1808, when Archbishop Carroll asked the Holy See to establish dioceses in the United States, Bardstown (now the Archdiocese of Louisville) was erected and headed by Bishop Benedict Joseph Flaget, a pioneering prelate.

Bardstown was established in Kentucky and administered Catholic affairs from the Allegheny Mountains to the Mississippi River. By 1837 the Diocese of Bardstown served only Kentucky, and in 1841 was transferred to Louisville, now an archdiocese. Some of America's outstanding mission priests served the vast Diocese of Bardstown, including Fathers Stephen T. Badin and Charles Nerinckx.

In 1853, when Covington was erected as a diocese, Bishop George Aloysius Carroll, a Jesuit, was consecrated on November 1 and installed in the diocese. He started increasing the presence of Catholics in the area and providing facilities and parishes for the faithful. Anti-Catholicism was rampant at the time; Catholics had been attacked in Louisville in the Protestant riot called "Bloody Monday" in an earlier decade, and the sentiment added tensions to the promotion of the Church. Bishop Carroll, however, transformed the local Catholic ministries and tripled the population of the faithful. When he died on September 25, 1868, Covington was a vital center of Catholicism.

The diocese was administered locally after the death of Bishop Carroll until January 9, 1870, when Bishop Augustus Maria Toebbe was consecrated as the second bishop of Covington. German-born, Bishop Toebbe was energetic and innovative in finding ways to support the growing Catholic ministries. He built parishes and established charitable organizations, and he died on May 2, 1884.

His successor was Bishop Camillus Paul Maes, who had studied at the American College in Louvain. He was consecrated for the Diocese of Covington on January 25, 1885, and continued the building of parishes and other facilities for the more than sixty thousand Catholics in the diocese at the time. Bishop Maes also dedicated the diocesan cathedral, the Basilica of the Assumption. He died on May 11, 1915.

Bishop Ferdinand Brossart was the fourth bishop of Covington and was consecrated for the diocese on January 25, 1916. He continued the expansion program while supporting the military efforts of the nation in World War I. In 1921 Villa Madonna College was opened in Covington. Bishop Brossart retired on March 14, 1923.

The fifth bishop of Covington was Francis William Howard, who was consecrated on July 15, 1923. Bishop Howard continued the ministries of the diocese and aided the people suffering during the Great Depression. He also led the faithful of Covington through the grim days of World War II, starting a diocesan newspaper and opening new media projects. Bishop Howard died on January 18, 1944.

Bishop William Theodore Mulloy succeeded Bishop Howard and was consecrated on January 10, 1945. He founded the diocesan seminary and expanded parish ministries throughout the region. Bishop Mulloy died on June 1, 1959.

The seventh bishop of Covington, Richard Henry Ackerman, C.S.Sp., had served as the auxiliary bishop of San Diego since 1956 and was transferred to Covington on April 6, 1960. Bishop Ackerman took part in the Second Vatican Council and implemented the reforms mandated by that council, introducing lay ministries and charitable programs. He retired on November 28, 1976.

The successor to Bishop Ackerman was Bishop William Anthony Hughes, who had served as the auxiliary bishop of Youngstown since 1974. He was appointed to Covington on April 13, 1979, and began expansion programs and measures to alleviate personnel shortages. He promoted lay ministries and diocesan lay organizations. Bishop Hughes retired on July 4, 1995.

Bishop Robert W. Muench, the ninth bishop of Covington, had served as the auxiliary bishop of New Orleans since 1990. He was transferred to Covington on January 5, 1996, and installed in the cathedral of the diocese on March 19, 1996. On December 15, 2001, Bishop Muench was transferred to the Diocese of Baton Rouge.

The tenth bishop of Covington, Roger J. Foys, was appointed to the diocese on May 30, 2002. He was consecrated and installed on July 15, 2002. Bishop Foys celebrated the sesquicentennial of the diocese in 2003 and convoked a diocesan synod to formulate a long-term plan for the life of the diocese in the new millennium. In 2011 there were 91,000 Catholics served by 101 parishes, 313 women religious, and 47 parishes in the diocese.

Creighton, Edward (August 31, 1820–November 5, 1874)

A noted philanthropist, Edward Creighton was the brother of John A. Creighton. He was born near Barnesville, Belmont County, Ohio, to Irish immigrants. With his brother, Edward embarked on various mining endeavors and then became involved in the transcontinental telegraph system, which was completed in 1861. He owned an interest in the Pacific Telegraph Company and surveyed much of the territory across which the telegraph line was established, from Omaha to Utah. Soon after, Pacific Telegraph was acquired by Western Union, a transaction that made Edward immensely wealthy. He used much of that fortune for a variety of charitable causes, especially Catholic charities. He also left provision for the financing of Creighton College (now Creighton University), in Omaha.

Creighton, John A. (October 15, 1831–February 7, 1907)

The brother of Edward Creighton, John A. Creighton was a noted philanthropist. He was born in Licking County, Ohio, to Irish immigrant parents. With his brother, he embarked on various business enterprises, including mining and the expansion of the telegraph system. Upon Edward's death in 1874, John assumed direction of their varied business dealings as well as overseeing a large number of estates, and continued the family's generosity to Creighton College (now Creighton University). In recognition for his efforts, John was named a Knight of St. Gregory and a papal count in 1895 by Pope Leo XIII.

Crétin, Joseph (1799–February 22, 1857)

A missionary bishop, Joseph Crétin was a friend of St. John Vianney. He was born in Monttuel, Ain, France, and entered the seminary at a young age to study for the priesthood. He was educated at the University of Paris with St. John Vianney, the Curé of Ars, and also attended other seminaries, including Saint-Sulpice in Paris. Ordained on December 20, 1823, Father Crétin started a school for boys in Ferney.

In 1838 he responded to the plea by Bishop Pierre Jean Matthias Loras and volunteered for mission duties in Dubuque, Iowa. He arrived in April 1839 and set about his mission duties. Father Crétin served the Winnebago Indians in the area and was made vicar general of the diocese because of his dedication and abilities. In 1850 he was appointed the first bishop of the Diocese of St. Paul (now the Archdiocese of St. Paul and Minneapolis), and was consecrated on January 26, 1851. His diocese served thirty thousand Native Americans. Bishop Crétin served the Diocese of St. Paul for six years, revitalizing the Indian missions in the area and demonstrating pastoral concern for the physical as well as the spiritual welfare of the local tribes. He also brought trained missionary religious congregations into the diocese. He died in St. Paul.

Crimmins, John Daniel (May 18, 1844–November 9, 1917)

An innovative contractor who renovated Broadway in New York, John Daniel Crimmins served the Church faithfully. He was born in New York City and educated at the Jesuit College of St. Francis Xavier. He joined his father's building and contracting firm and in 1873 became the president of the company. Crimmins renovated Broadway, changing street railways to electric railways and adding modern amenities.

He married Lily Louise Lalor in 1868 and had five sons and five daughters. From 1883 to 1888, he served as the Commissioner of Parks for New York City and was a member of the New York Constitutional Convention in 1894. A philanthropist, Crimmins funded colleges, schools, and hospitals and was a respected patron of the arts. He also served as a trustee of The Catholic University of America and of St. Patrick's Cathedral. He belonged to the Friendly Sons of St. Patrick and the American Irish Historical Society. Pope Leo XIII appointed him a Knight Commander of the Order of St. Gregory in 1901. He died in New York City.

Croix, Charles de la (1792–August 20, 1869)

A missionary to the Osage Indians of the Missouri plains, Charles de la Croix was a pioneer in Missouri and a friend of the Native Americans there. He was born in Hoorleke-St.-Cornceilles, Belgium.

and studied at the seminary of Ghent. When the French forces of Napoleon Bonaparte took over his country, he was imprisoned in Wesel Fortress, where his brother died as a result of the horrors of the incarceration. The fall of Napoleon Bonaparte brought about his release, and he was ordained to the priesthood. Father de la Croix then asked for permission to accompany Bishop Louis Dubourg of the Diocese of New Orleans (now the Archdiocese of New Orleans) to the United States. Bishop Dubourg had been touring Europe to find priests and religious for the missions of Louisiana.

In America, Father de la Croix was assigned to Borrens, Missouri, in 1818, and there he supervised the building of a seminary. He then went to Florissant, Missouri, where the Religious of the Sacred Heart were working among the local tribes and the white settlers. Father de la Croix was a pioneer in Florissant, called St. Ferdinand's at the time. In 1828 he served St. Michael's in the Lower Louisiana parish, completing the church there in 1832. In the following year he returned to Belgium and served as canon of Ghent Cathedral until his death.

Crookston, Diocese of

Established on December 31, 1909, by Pope St. Pius X, the Diocese of Crookston serves the northeastern areas of Minnesota. The center of a vast agricultural region, Crookston was settled in 1872, at that time called "the Crossing." The city now serves as a distributor and processor of farm crops. The Diocese of Crookston is a suffragan see of the Archdiocese of St. Paul and Minneapolis.

Franciscan Recollect Father Louis Hennepin, the missionary explorer, visited the Crookston area in 1680. Other missionaries had been in the region as early as 1655, but no permanent settlement had been established. In 1721 Jesuit Father Michael Guignon celebrated Mass near Crookston, and in 1732 Jesuit Father Charles Mesaiger arrived at the French fort of St. Charles near the Lake of the Woods. Father Mesaiger served the local Indian settlements, which were also visited by Jesuit Father Jean Pierre Aulneau. Father Aulneau was slain by Sioux warriors.

In 1803, as part of the Louisiana Purchase, the French ceded Minnesota to the United States, and settlers began making claims to the land. There were Catholics among the settlers, but the faith genuinely took hold in 1839, when Swiss Catholics migrated to the area from Canada. Fathers Francis Pierz and Augustin Ravoux were on hand to serve them, and Father Lucien Galtier established a mission at modern-day St. Paul in 1841. In 1850 the Diocese of St. Paul (now the Archdiocese of St. Paul and Minneapolis), was established, and Bishop Joseph Crétin began his heroic ministries.

Eight years later, Minnesota entered the Union. Benedictine priests and sisters opened Indian missions and schools at White Earth on Red Lake, funded by St. Katharine Drexel. In 1895 the Vicariate Apostolic of Northern Minnesota was established, and in 1889 the Diocese of Duluth was erected.

The Diocese of Crookston was established in 1909, and the first bishop of the diocese, Timothy Corbett, was consecrated on May 19, 1910. He erected fifty churches and twelve schools, while guiding the Catholics of the area through the grim era of World War I. He also provided aid and comfort to the people during the Great Depression, an economic disaster that brought hardships to the nation. Bishop Corbett retired on August 6, 1938.

The second bishop, John H. Peschges, was consecrated on November 9, 1938. Bishop Peschges was one of the founders of the National Catholic Rural Life Conference, to alleviate the suffering in the agricultural sectors of America. He instituted the Confraternity of Christian Doctrine in the parishes of Crookston and conducted migrant worker programs. Supporting the military efforts of the nation during World War II, Bishop Peschges died on October 30, 1944.

His successor was Bishop Francis J. Schenk, who was consecrated on May 24, 1945. He initiated charitable programs throughout the diocese, opening hospitals, homes for the aged, and other services. Bishop Schenk also built parishes and opened a diocesan newspaper. He was transferred to the Diocese of Duluth on January 27, 1960.

The fourth bishop of Crookston was Laurence A. Glenn, who was appointed on February 3, 1960. He had served as auxiliary bishop of Duluth since 1956. Bishop Glenn participated in the Second Vatican Council and implemented the reforms mandated by that council. He promoted lay ministries and social programs. Bishop Glenn retired

on July 28, 1970. Bishop Kenneth J. Povish was his successor, consecrated on September 29, 1970. Bishop Povish continued the expansion of parochial schools and charitable diocesan facilities and promoted lay ministries. On October 21, 1975, Bishop Povish was transferred to the Diocese of Lansing.

The sixth bishop of Crookston, Victor H. Balke, was appointed to the diocese on July 7, 1976. He was consecrated on September 2, 1976. The bishop took as his immediate task upon his appointment the full and effective implementation of the Second Vatican Council. He promoted a variety of societies and movements, such as Teens Encounter Christ, Cursillo, Koinonia, and Marriage Encounter, and has worked to provide a retirement program for elderly clergy. Bishop Balke was succeeded as bishop on September 28, 2007, by Father Michael J. Hoeppner, who was consecrated a bishop on November 30, 2007. In 2011 there were 35,000 Catholics, served by 50 priests and 66 parishes in the diocese.

Croquet, Adrian (1818–August 15, 1902)

A missionary from Belgium, Father Adrian Croquet spent many years in the American northwest, honored by local tribes for his constancy and courtesy for over four decades. He was born in Braine-L'Allend, Belgium, attended Malines Seminary, and was ordained in 1844. He then studied at the American College in Louvain. In 1858 Father Croquet volunteered for the American missions. After another period of study at the American College in Louvain, he sailed to the United States and started his missionary labors at the Grande Ronde Reservation in 1860. He served at the Siletz Reservation also and in the Williamette Valley of Oregon for forty years. Father Croquet brought a profound courtesy and a deep respect for the Native American culture to his missionary efforts. These attitudes resulted in tribal esteem for him and his word. In 1898, worn out by his labors, Father Croquet retired to Belgium and died in his native town.

Crosby, Harry Lillis ("Bing") (May 2, 1903–October 14, 1977)

A popular American singer, "Bing" (Harry Lillis) Crosby was also a movie star. He was born in

Tacoma, Washington, and was given the nickname Bing because of his affection for a cartoon character of that era. Crosby and his family moved to Spokane, Washington, when he was a teenager, and he attended Gonzaga High School and Gonzaga University.

While at Gonzaga, he played the drums for a band, and in 1925 he left the university with a friend, Al Rinker, seeking a show-business career in Los Angeles. After a brief stint with the Paul Whiteman Band, Bing and Al joined Harris Barris in the Rhythm Boys. This threesome was successful, and Crosby recorded "I Surrender Dear." That recording made him a national star, and he was offered stage, radio, and motion-picture opportunities.

He starred in some seventy films, including the popular series with Bob Hope, the "Road" movies, produced from 1940 to 1952. In 1944 Crosby appeared as Father O'Malley in *Going My Way* and won an Academy Award. He also made television specials. His recordings of "White Christmas" and "Silent Night" became two of his best known. Crosby, despite other successes, remained the American "crooner." He died of a heart attack in Madrid, Spain.

Curran Controversy. *See* **Catholic University of America, The; Education, Catholic**

Curran, John (June 20, 1859–November 7, 1936)
Dedicated to his priesthood and to the betterment of working conditions, Father John Curran was a friend of the leading politicians of his time. He was born in Hawley, Pennsylvania, and his family soon moved to Avaca, near Wilkes-Barre. There he worked in the mines during the days and attended school at night. Entering the Wyoming Seminary, he graduated and enrolled at St. Vincent's in Latrobe, Pennsylvania, where he received his degree in 1882. He then attended Grand Seminaries at Montréal and completed his priestly education. Father Curran was ordained for the Diocese of Scranton on August 23, 1887.

During his ministry at Carbondale and other mining communities, Father Curran became involved in the strike carried out by the United Mine Workers in May 1902. He spoke briefly on behalf of the miners and became a trusted adviser to President Theodore Roosevelt. His ability to span religious, social, and ethnic divides enabled Father Curran to take part in other labor crises, and he was valued as a just, moderate individual. He also served as an officer of the Anti-Saloon League of America and the Catholic Total Abstinence Union of America. His experiences in the mines educated him to the perils of liquor among his fellow citizens.

In 1930 Father Curran was made a domestic prelate by Pope Pius XI, and continued to advise United States presidents and industrial leaders. He maintained his friendships and allegiances until his death.

Cursillo

The Cursillo Movement is a lay organization that provides inspiration and training in evangelism and spiritual growth. The *Cursillo de Cristianidad*, or "Little Course in Christianity," is a three-day period of spiritual renewal and an intensive experience in Christian community living. The programs include talks by laymen and priests, discussions, and the celebration of the liturgy. These programs are followed up by small weekly reunions of three to five people and larger group reunions, called *ultreyas*.

Bishop Juan Hervas of Ciudad Real, Spain, is credited with developing the Cursillo Movement, but the prelate advises that the cursillos were produced by a team of clergy and laymen working under the encouragement and direction of the bishop. The Cursillo seems to have been in use in its present form in Spain in about 1949. It first made its appearance in the United States among the Spanish-speaking people of the Southwest, particularly Texas. Cursillos in Spanish spread from this area to all parts of the nation.

The movement operates within the framework of diocesan and parish pastoral plans, and functions autonomously in each diocese under the direction of the bishop, and by 1977 it was operating in 857 dioceses. There are two and a half million *cursillistas*, of whom nearly half a million are in the United States. In 1963 Pope Paul VI named St. Paul the patron of the movement.

In the United States, the Cursillo Movement

is directed by a national board of twenty-four priests and laypeople, and Bishop Joseph Green of Adrian, Michigan, is national episcopal adviser to the movement and the liaison with the United States Conference of Catholic Bishops. The national center is located in Dallas, Texas, and provides the local movements with Cursillo literature and educational material, including a monthly magazine, *Ultreya*.

Cushing, Richard James
(August 24, 1895–November 2, 1970)

Archbishop of Boston from 1944 to 1970 and a cardinal from 1958, Richard James Cushing was one of the best-known cardinals of the

Cardinal Richard Cushing

American Church and an outstanding religious and moral leader. He was born in South Boston, Massachusetts, and studied at Boston College and at St. John's Seminary, Brighton. Ordained to the priesthood on May, 26, 1921, he was assigned to the diocesan chancery and served the Society of the Propagation of the Faith. Fundraising efforts were part of his ministry, and he brought a profound respect for the foreign missions to his labors. He became director of the office in 1928.

In 1939 Cushing was named an auxiliary bishop of Boston. Five years later, he was elected apostolic administrator after the passing of Cardinal William O'Connell, and on September, 25, 1944, Pope Pius XII named him archbishop of Boston. Pope Blessed John XXIII appointed him a cardinal priest, with the titular church of Santa Susanna on December 15, 1958.

Cardinal Cushing's long term as archbishop stretched over the tumultuous period of the Second Vatican Council and its aftermath. He soon earned the reputation as one of the most approachable, affable, and outgoing members of the American hierarchy and was a leading figure in the use of radio and television for the advancement of nascent modern Catholic social communications. He enjoyed wide influence in the political life of Massachusetts and New England and was able to defeat a proposed referendum in Massachusetts to loosen restrictions on birth control. He also enjoyed a close relationship with the powerful Kennedy family. He delivered the invocation at John F. Kennedy's presidential inauguration in 1961 and then presided at his tragic funeral in 1963. As archbishop and one of the most prominent American Church leaders, he was an outspoken supporter of American policy against communism during the 1950s and the effort against communist expansion around the world.

Cardinal Cushing presided with other leaders of the Church in the United States over the explosive growth of Catholic dioceses and institutions in the period between the end of the Second World War and the Second Vatican Council. He led a burgeoning Catholic population filled with postwar optimism and was able to increase the number of parishes, hospitals, and schools. In the post-conciliar period, he implemented the documents of the council, but his determination to maintain the stability of ecclesiastical life in the turbulent era of the 1960s left archdiocesan finances with a considerable debt. Another project he undertook with vigor was the care of crippled and handicapped children. He led some hundred young patients to Lourdes, France, and cared for their needs personally.

D

Dablon, Claude (c. 1618–May 3, 1697)

An outstanding superior of the early Jesuit missions in present-day America, Claude Dablon was a scholar and a companion of Father Jacques Marquette. He made elaborate maps and accounts of their perilous journeys in the American wilderness and helped establish Sault Ste. Marie Mission. He was born in Dieppe, France, and entered the Society of Jesus at twenty-one. Following his ordination to the priesthood, Father Dablon was assigned to the American missions.

In 1655 he was laboring among the Onondaga, learning their language and traditions, and with Jesuit Father Pierre-Joseph Chaumonot he helped establish a mission among the Iroquois at Lake Ganentaa (modern-day Syracuse, New York). In 1661 he served with the Jesuit missionary, Father Gabriel Druillettes, on a journey to Hudson Bay. He was with Father Marquette and the Jesuit Father Claude Allouez on Lake Superior in 1688. He helped to found Sault Ste. Marie Mission in Michigan and sent companions on their celebrated explorations of the Mississippi River.

Father Dablon was superior general of the Jesuit missions of New France (modern-day Canada, which also included present-day sites in the United States) from 1671 to 1680 and again from 1686 to 1693. He was also editor of *Relations* from 1672 to 1679, and published the journeys of Fathers Jacques Marquette and Charles Abanel in Hudson Bay. Father Dablon died in Québec.

Dabrowski, Joseph (January 7, 1842–February 15, 1903)

A Polish-born priest and educator, Joseph Dabrowski was the founder of the Sts. Cyril and Methodius Seminary in Detroit, Michigan. He was born in Zoltańce, Poland, and studied at the University of Warsaw. Taking part in the 1863 Polish uprising against the Russians, he was forced to flee Poland and spent time in Saxony, Switzerland, and the Papal States. While in Rome, he was one of the first students admitted to the new Pontificio Collegio Polacco established by Pope Blessed Pius IX in 1866, and he was ordained on August 8, 1869.

Father Leopold Moczygemba, O.F.M. Conv., counseled Father Dabrowski to travel to the United States after his ordination in order to serve Polish Catholics in Wisconsin. Father Dabrowski built extensively in Wisconsin and brought the Felician Sisters to the United States in 1874. In 1882 Father Dabrowski started pastoral work in the Diocese of Detroit (now the Archdiocese of Detroit), helping to establish Sts. Cyril and Methodius Seminary in 1885 for Polish-American seminarians.

Daley, Richard (1902–December 20, 1976)

The mayor of the city of Chicago from 1955 until his death in office, Richard Daley ran one of the most efficient political machines in American politics. Born into an Irish-Catholic neighborhood in South Chicago, he went to Catholic schools, including a Catholic technical school where he learned secretarial skills. His political career started with various assignments and then a position as personal secretary to an alderman at City Hall. At the same time, he studied law at DePaul University School of Law and earned his law degree in 1934. Daley never had the chance to practice as an attorney, however, as he was elected soon after to the Illinois Legislature. First elected mayor of Chicago in April 1955, he became the first mayor of the city to be elected for a consecutive fourth four-year term and presided over a machine notorious for its hard, old-style city politics.

Daley campaigned vigorously for John F. Kennedy and proved essential to his victory in 1960. He likewise publicly supported President Lyndon Johnson's actions in Vietnam, although he personally opposed the war, and presided over the city during the tumultuous 1968 Democratic National Convention. To maintain order, he supplemented the 12,000-strong Chicago police force with 7,500 U.S. Army troops and 6,000 national guardsmen. The convention subsequently proved a violent episode in American history. Daley was also subpoenaed by the defense to testify in the Chicago

Seven trial. Judge Julius Hoffman denied the defense motion to classify Daley as a hostile witness, remarking famously: "The court finds there is nothing in the testimony of the witness that has indicated his hostility. His manner has been that of a gentleman." Daley attended daily Mass throughout his life. His son, William M. Daley, served as commerce secretary during the Clinton administration and followed in his father's footsteps as mayor of Chicago.

Dallas, Diocese of

Established as a diocese on July 15, 1890, by Pope Leo XIII and redesignated as the Diocese of Dallas-Fort Worth on October 20, 1953, by Pope Pius XII, the Diocese of Dallas was designated again on August 27, 1969, by Pope Paul VI. The diocese serves counties in the north-central areas of Texas, on the Trinity River. In 1841 John Neely Bryan erected a cabin on the Trinity, and the settlement that developed there was named for George Mifflin Dallas, the vice president of the United States. Swiss and French artisans joined the locals, bringing a unique style to the area. Merchants and wholesalers opened markets, and the Dallas Cotton Exchange began in 1907, serving as another base for the growth of a modern city. The city of Dallas is an industrial and cultural center with a profound Catholic heritage shared by all of Texas. The Diocese of Dallas is a suffragan see of the Archdiocese of San Antonio.

In 1685 René-Robert Chevalier, Sieur de La Salle, was in the area on an expedition to claim New World lands for France. Five years later, Franciscans from Mexico started missions for the Native Americans on the Trinity River. Other explorers followed La Salle into the region, and the missions were expanded. These outposts of the faith endured, as saintly individuals such as Venerable Antonio Margil de Jesús built chains of small enclaves across the wilderness. The missions lasted through the American Revolution, when the United States was formed and new territories were claimed. The Mexican government, independent of Spain, secularized the missions of Texas in the late 1700s, banishing priests and brothers.

In 1836 Texas rebelled against Mexican rule and fought for independence. First becoming a republic, Texas then entered the Union as a state in 1845. Four years before, Dallas had been established on the Trinity River. The administration of Catholic affairs could no longer be conducted by Mexico City, so Pope Gregory XVI transferred the jurisdiction to the Diocese of New Orleans. It was then decided to establish a prefecture apostolic, headed by the Vincentian Father John Timon. Father John M. Odin, another famous Vincentian, labored with him until 1847, when Pope Blessed Pius IX erected the Diocese of Galveston (now the Archdiocese of Galveston-Houston). Bishop Odin was installed in Galveston and had jurisdiction over the entire state. In 1874, however, the Diocese of San Antonio (now the Archdiocese of San Antonio), was established.

The growing vitality of the Church in Dallas prompted the erection of the Diocese of Dallas in 1890, and the first bishop of Dallas was Thomas Francis Brennan, who was consecrated on April 5, 1891. Bishop Brennan established the first agencies and offices for diocesan administration but resigned on November 17, 1892, and was transferred to Newfoundland and then to Rome. He died on March 21, 1916.

Bishop Edward Joseph Dunne, the successor of Bishop Brennan, was consecrated on November 30, 1893. He reorganized diocesan facilities and opened St. Paul's Hospital and Holy Trinity College (now the University of Dallas). He also established the diocesan cathedral, Sacred Heart, and now the Cathedral-Santuario de Guadalupe. The original structure dates to 1869. Bishop Dunne also provided a diocesan spiritual center. He died on August 5, 1910, while visiting Wisconsin.

The third bishop of Dallas was Joseph Patrick Lynch, who was consecrated on July 12, 1911. He was destined to lead the faithful of Dallas through World War I, the Great Depression, and World War II, serving the diocese for decades. Bishop Lynch opened more than one hundred churches and conducted charitable programs while supporting the military activities of the nation. In 1914 the Diocese of El Paso was established, and the Dioceses of Amarillo and Austin followed. On May 13, 1936, Pope Pius XI appointed Bishop Lynch an Assistant at the Pontifical Throne. Bishop Lynch died on August 19, 1954.

Bishop Thomas K. Gorman was Bishop Lynch's

successor, having served as coadjutor bishop of Dallas since 1952. He had also served as the bishop of Reno. Acceding to the see on August 19, 1954, Bishop Gorman began new programs, particularly in the area of social communications, including the revival of the diocesan newspaper. He also opened parochial schools and high schools, as well as new parishes. Bishop Gorman attended the Second Vatican Council, and implemented the reforms mandated by the council in the diocese. He also founded Holy Trinity Seminary and participated in the development of Catholic Conferences in the United States. On May 4, 1942, he was made an Assistant at the Pontifical Throne. Bishop Gorman retired on August 27, 1969, the day the Diocese of Fort Worth was erected.

His successor was Bishop Thomas Tschoepe, who had been serving as the bishop of San Angelo since 1966. Bishop Tschoepe was installed as the fifth bishop of Dallas on October 29, 1969. Humble in his lifestyle, he continued the expansion programs and opened new ministries in the diocese. He also administered the changes necessary when the Diocese of Tyler was erected in 1987. Bishop Tschoepe retired on July 14, 1990.

Bishop Charles V. Grahmann, the sixth bishop of Dallas, had served as an auxiliary bishop of the Archdiocese of San Antonio and then as the first bishop of Victoria since 1982. On December 18, 1989, Bishop Grahmann was appointed coadjutor bishop of Dallas and acceded to the see on July 14, 1990. As bishop, he promoted lay leadership in various positions in the diocese and was active in ecumenical affairs, including Catholic-Lutheran dialogue. The diocese was one of the first in the United States to be impacted sharply by the sex abuse scandal, with lawsuits stemming from cases leading a jury to award victims $120 million, part of the settlements related to the infamous activities of Father Rudolf Kos, who was subsequently laicized.

Bishop Grahmann was succeeded on March 6, 2007, by Bishop Kevin Farrell, who had served as an auxiliary bishop of Washington, D.C., since 2001.

Bishop Farrell was installed on May 1, 2007. In 2011 there were 1.1 million Catholics served by 168 priests and 69 parishes in the diocese.

Daly, John Augustin (July 20, 1838–June 7, 1899)

One of the most influential theater managers in the United States, John Augustin Daly was also a writer and playwright. He was born in Plymouth, North Carolina, but was raised in New York City after his family moved there in 1849. Daly became a drama critic for the *New York Sunday Courier* and wrote for a number of other newspapers in the city. He also wrote over ninety plays, including *Leah* in 1863 and *Under the Gaslight* in 1867, as well as essays and articles.

In 1869 he became the manager of the Fifth Avenue Theater shortly after his marriage to Mary Duff. His productions were always financial and critical successes, and Daly inspired the entire theater community. He was honored with the Laetare Medal from the University of Notre Dame in 1894. Daly died while in Paris.

Damien de Veuster, St. (January 3, 1840–April 15, 1889)

The "Hero of Molokai," St. Damien de Veuster, SS.CC., is honored as the "Apostle to the Lepers." He was born in Tremeloo, Belgium, the son of a grain merchant, and baptized Joseph. He revered his brother, Auguste Pamphile, and followed him into the Fathers of the Sacred Heart of Jesus and Mary (Picpus Fathers) in January 1859. There he had to be tutored by his brother. On October 7, 1860, he made his profession and received the name Damien.

While studying for the priesthood, St. Damien heard that his brother had been assigned to the Hawaiian Islands but was prevented from sailing by a bout of typhoid fever. St. Damien volunteered to take his brother's place. On October 29, 1863, he sailed to the Pacific, where he was ordained in the Cathedral of Our Lady of Peace on May 21, 1864.

He was then stationed on the island of Hawaii, called the Big

St. Damien de Veuster

Island. He saw many of his parishioners taken away to the island of Molokai, where a leper settlement had been opened by the Hawaiian Board of Health. During a meeting with Bishop Louis Désiré Maigret, SS.CC., St. Damien volunteered to go to Kalaupapa, an isolated beach site that served as a home for the lepers.

He arrived with Bishop Maigret at Kalaupapa on May 10, 1873. There he established order among the six hundred victims of Hansen's disease, as it is called today, who had been taken from their homes and abandoned. He cared for each victim of the disease, made their coffins, and buried them in the area called the Garden of the Dead. St. Damien then built churches, orphanages, aqueducts, homes, and clinics. In 1885 he knew that he had contracted leprosy but continued his work, joined by priests, lay brothers, and St. Marianne Cope, who brought the Franciscan Sisters from Syracuse, New York, to the apostolate.

St. Damien died at Kalaupapa and was buried there. In 1936 his body was taken to Belgium, at the request of that nation, and buried in Louvain. He represents the state of Hawaii in Statuary Hall in the U.S. Capitol. Pope Blessed John Paul II beatified Damien on June 4, 1995, and Pope Benedict XVI canonized him on October 11, 2009. His feast day is May 10.

Daniel, Anthony, St. (May 27, 1601–July 4, 1648) A Jesuit missionary, St. Anthony Daniel was slain by the Iroquois. He was born in Dieppe, Normandy, and entered the Society of Jesus in Rome on October 1, 1621. Sent to Canada two years later, St. Anthony joined his brother, Captain Daniel, who had established a fort at Cape Breton. In July 1634 he was sent to Thonatiria to the Huron Mission there, and he would remain among the Hurons until his martyrdom. The Iroquois attacked the mission while the Huron warriors were absent, and St. Anthony sheltered the old, the women, and the children in the chapel. Knowing they were doomed, he gave each Huron general absolution and then waited for the final assault. The Iroquois were startled to discover him in the chapel, but they recovered and shot him with a volley of arrows. St. Anthony and the Hurons were burned in the chapel. He was the second to receive the martyr's crown

among the Jesuits in New France, or modern-day Canada. (*See also* North American Martyrs.)

Da Ponte, Lorenzo (1749–August 17, 1838) Italian-born poet and convert, Lorenzo Da Ponte wrote some of Mozart's librettos. Born at Cenada, Italy, into a Jewish family, he was given the name Emmanuel Conegliano. When he was fourteen years old, he and his family were baptized, and the bishop, Lorenzo Da Ponte, gave young Emmanuel his name and provided him with an education in the diocesan seminary. After studies, he taught at the University of Treviso. He subsequently journeyed to Vienna, where he met the renowned composer Wolfgang Amadeus Mozart. Da Ponte composed the librettos of several of Mozart's most famous operas, *Le nozze di Figaro*, *Don Giovanni*, and *Cosi fan tutte*. He then went to London and to New York. His varied careers in New York included an effort to launch opera in the city. He took up a post as an Italian teacher associated with Columbia College and earned a reputation as a poet. Da Ponte was the first teacher in the United States to lecture on Dante's *Divine Comedy*.

Daughters of Charity of St. Vincent de Paul. *See* **St. Vincent de Paul, Society of**

Davenport, Diocese of
Established on May 8, 1881, by Pope Leo XIII, the Diocese of Davenport serves southeastern counties in Iowa. The city of Davenport is a manufacturing and trade center, founded by Colonel George Davenport, who operated a fur company. The first railroad bridge to span the Mississippi River was opened in Davenport in 1856. The Diocese of Davenport is a suffragan see of the Archdiocese of Dubuque.

In 1673 the Jesuit missionary Father Jacques Marquette and his companion, Louis Joliet, became the first white men in Iowa. They visited the area briefly but continued their explorations elsewhere. In 1788 Julien Dubuque, a French Canadian, erected a fort near modern-day Dubuque. The local Native American tribes remained hostile, however, but were visited by Jesuit Father Charles Van Quickenborne at Keokuk in 1832. In that same year, settlers began to arrive in large numbers. A Mass was offered in the area a year later by Father C. P. Fitzmorris, but no permanent chapel was erected.

The great Dominican missionary Venerable Samuel Mazzuchelli established the first Catholic church in Iowa. St. Raphael's was started in Dubuque in 1833. Four years later, the Diocese of Dubuque (now the Archdiocese of Dubuque) was erected and headed by the revered Bishop Mathias Loras. Jesuit Fathers Joseph Crétin and John A. Pelamourgues served the area, and Father Pelamourgues became the first resident pastor.

The vitality of the faith in the region was recognized in 1881 when Davenport was erected as a diocese. Bishop John M. McMullen was the first bishop of Davenport, consecrated on July 25, 1881. He provided the diocese with the offices and agencies for administration and started parishes in developing areas. Bishop McMullen also founded a diocesan newspaper and opened St. Ambrose College. He died on July 4, 1883.

His successor was Bishop Henry Cosgrove, who was consecrated on September 14, 1884. He established over seventy parishes and started charitable services and facilities. Bishop Cosgrove was the first American-born bishop west of the Mississippi River. He died on December 22, 1906.

The third bishop of Davenport was James Davis, who succeeded Bishop Cosgrove. He took part in the establishment of the Diocese of Des Moines in 1911, as the new episcopal jurisdiction assumed western counties originally administered by Davenport. Bishop Davis also supported the military efforts of the nation in World War I. He died on December 2, 1926.

His successor was Bishop Henry P. Rohlman, who was consecrated on July 25, 1927. Bishop Rohlman continued the expansion programs, despite the economic sufferings caused by the Great Depression, and promoted the establishment of Marycrest College in 1939. World War II brought new sacrifices and alarms, and Bishop Rohlman continued to lead the faithful. On June 15, 1944, he was promoted to the Archdiocese of Dubuque as coadjutor archbishop.

The fifth bishop of Davenport was Ralph Leo Hayes, who had served as the bishop of Helena and then as rector of the North American College in Rome. He was appointed to the diocese on November 16, 1944. Bishop Hayes was made an Assistant at the Pontifical Throne on April 30, 1958. He attended the Second Vatican Council and implemented the reforms mandated by that council. He also established high schools and elementary schools throughout the diocese. Bishop Hayes retired on October 20, 1966.

His successor was Bishop Gerald Francis O'Keefe, who had served as auxiliary bishop of the Archdiocese of St. Paul and Minneapolis. He was transferred to the Diocese of Davenport on October 20, 1966, and installed on January 4, 1967. Bishop O'Keefe promoted the new ministries and programs initiated by the Second Vatican Council and instituted charitable apostolates during his decades of leadership in the diocese. He retired on November 12, 1993.

The seventh bishop of Davenport, William E. Franklin, succeeded Bishop O'Keefe. Bishop Franklin had served as auxiliary bishop of the Archdiocese of Dubuque and was transferred to Davenport on November 12, 1993. He was installed in the diocese on January 20, 1994. Bishop Franklin was deeply committed to diocesan pastoral life, including several diocesan convocations: "Total Change of Mind and Heart," "Walking Together in Faith," and "Hearing the Voice of the Faithful." In 2006 he also embarked on a Parish Life Study, a detailed and annotated report by each parish of its sacramental, liturgical, financial, and demographic life. Confronted with dozens of lawsuits stemming from the sex abuse crisis, in October 2006 the diocese filed for bankruptcy protection.

That same year, on October 12, Bishop Martin Amos was appointed the new bishop of Davenport. He had served as an auxiliary bishop of Cleveland. Under his leadership, a settlement of $37 million was reached in 2008 with the victims of sexual abuse. The bishop also established a parish planning commission to help the diocese look to the pastoral needs of the future. In 2011 there were 99,000 Catholics served by 105 priests and 80 parishes in the diocese.

David, Jean Baptiste Marie (1761–1841)

A bishop of Kentucky, Jean Baptiste Marie David was the founder of the Sisters of Charity of Nazareth. He was born in France, suffering exile when the horrors of the French Revolution came upon his homeland. In November 1791 Bishop John Carroll, the first bishop of America, sent out a call for European priests to aid the United States missions, and Father David responded. He arrived in Maryland in March 1792 and was sent to the southern part of the state to serve the parishes there.

From 1803 to 1804, Father David taught at Georgetown and then was assigned to St. Mary's Seminary in Baltimore. There he also served as a chaplain to Charles Carroll of Carrollton, a signer of the Declaration of Independence. Father David was spiritual director as well of the newly founded Sisters of Charity at Emmitsburg.

In 1811 he was sent to Kentucky, where he served as a professor at St. Thomas Seminary in the Diocese of Bardstown. The following year he founded the Sisters of Charity of Nazareth. He was appointed coadjutor bishop to Bishop Benedict Joseph Flaget of Bardstown in 1819 and became the second bishop of that diocese in 1832, when Bishop Flaget retired. The Holy See, however, restored Bishop Flaget to the see. Bishop David happily resigned his office and served the people of Kentucky until his death.

Davis, Mary Anne (1680–1748)

The first American woman to become a Catholic religious, Mary Anne Davis was the daughter of Protestants in Salem, Massachusetts. At the age of six, Mary Anne was taken captive by the Abenaki Indians and remained with them until the age of seventeen. Then Father Sebastian Râle, the famed Jesuit missionary to the Abenaki, ransomed her and took her to Québec. Introduced to the Ursuline nuns, Mary Anne, who had become a Catholic while living with the Abenaki, entered the convent in 1698, receiving the name Mother Mary Benedict. She eventually became an Ursuline superior and served for more than half a century as a religious.

Day, Dorothy (November 8, 1897– November 27, 1980)

Social activist and founder of the Catholic Worker Movement, Dorothy Day was a convert to the Catholic faith. She was born in Brooklyn, New York, but her family moved to San Francisco and survived the 1906 earthquake before settling in Chicago. While there, Day first encountered Catholicism. She dropped out of the University of Illinois and moved to New York, where she worked as a reporter for *The Call*, the city's only socialist daily. She subsequently worked for *The Masses* and went to jail in 1917 for protesting in front of the White House for the right to vote, part of her lifelong commitment to various activist causes. In 1919 she became involved with a journalist, Lionel Moise, and became pregnant by him. At his urging, she had an abortion, an event of enormous importance for her life and spiritual development.

Around 1925 she purchased a small beach cottage on the western shore of Staten Island and took up residence with an amateur marine biologist, Forster Batterham. In March 1926, she gave birth to a daughter, Tamar Theresa. Continuing to search spiritually, she made her way gradually to the Catholic faith, seeing it as "the church of immigrants, the church of the poor." Finally baptized a Catholic in 1928 in the Catholic church at Tottenville, Staten Island, she ever after grounded her decades of activism in Catholic social teaching.

In 1932 Day met Peter Maurin, a French peasant and activist, with whom she founded *The Catholic Worker* in 1933 and the Catholic Worker Movement. The movement spread across the United States in the 1930s, and in 1935 she created the first of many houses of hospitality in New York.

Dorothy Day

She was a vocal opponent of the U.S. involvement in World War II, Korea, and Vietnam. Day also supported the civil rights movement and was jailed repeatedly for her positions against war and injustice. She was arrested in 1973 with Cesar Chavez during a farmworkers' demonstration. She once declared, "If I have achieved anything in my life, it is because I have not been embarrassed to talk about God."

Demanding of herself and especially of her friends, she was a strong voice for the human conscience and for raising voices in defense of the poor and the help-less. Her spirituality and commitment to social justice made her one of the most influential lay Catholics of the twentieth century. Her cause for canonization was opened in 2000. (*See also* Maurin, Aristode Pierre.*)

de Andreis, Felix. *See* Andreis, Felix de

Dearden, John F. (October 15, 1907–August 1, 1988)

The second archbishop of Detroit, from 1958 to 1980, and an American cardinal, John F. Dearden served as the president of the National Conference of Catholic Bishops. He was born in Valley Falls, Rhode Island, the first of five children of John S. and Agnes Dearden. After studies at the Cathedral Latin School in Cleveland, Ohio, he entered St. Mary's Seminary in 1925 and was then sent to study at the North American College in Rome. There he was ordained on December 8, 1932.

In 1934 Father Dearden earned a doctorate in theology from the Pontifical Gregorian University. He was subsequently named by Archbishop Joseph Schrembs to the faculty of St. Mary's Seminary, where he served from 1937 to 1944, and was rector in 1944. His firm administrative techniques as rector earned him the nickname "Iron John."

In 1948 he was named titular bishop of Sarepta and coadjutor bishop of Pittsburgh with the right of succession, and was ordained a bishop on May 14, 1948. He acceded to the see in 1950 as successor to Bishop Hugh C. Boyle. In Pittsburgh, Bishop Dearden focused on the reorganization of the diocese, overseeing its rapid expansion to meet the needs of the new postwar decades. Under his administration, twenty-eight new churches and twenty-three schools were built, and numerous organizations were promoted, including the Cana Movement, the Thomas More Society, and the Diocesan Council for Catholic Women.

On December 18, 1958, Bishop Dearden was promoted to the Archdiocese of Detroit and was

Cardinal John Dearden

installed by Cardinal O'Hara of Philadelphia on January 29, 1959. Archbishop Dearden took part in all the sessions of the Second Vatican Council and served as a member of the Secretariat for Promoting Christian Unity and the Doctrinal Commission for Faith and Morals (theological commission) from 1962 through 1965. He thus had a role in shaping the development of the chapter of *Lumen Gentium* (Dogmatic Constitution on the Church) that was concerned with the people of God and also in shaping the sections of *Gaudium et Spes* (Constitution on the Church in the Modern World) that focused on the family. Returning home from the council, he undertook the implementation of the council's documents. He had already focused especially on Catholic education, founding the Pius XII Center to train catechists in 1959. He also convened a diocesan synod in 1966, launched the Institute for Continuing Education, and issued the archdiocesan program "Church, World, and Kingdom."

In 1966 Archbishop Dearden was elected the first president of the reorganized National Conference of Catholic Bishops. As president until 1971, he promoted procedural innovations as well as the Campaign for Human Development. His fellow bishops elected him to the 1967, 1969, 1971, 1974, and 1977 Synods of Bishops; Pope Blessed John Paul II named him to the 1985 synod.

To assist pastoral ministry and the effectiveness of all archdiocesan administration, Archbishop Dearden inaugurated a diocesan pastoral council, parish councils, and vicariates. To further the contributions of laity, he started the Michigan Catholic Conference.

In the area of social justice, the archbishop began Project Commitment to assist Catholics in understanding Catholic social doctrine and was outspoken in promoting authentic justice following the 1967 Detroit race riots.

Archbishop Dearden was created a cardinal on April 18, 1969, by Pope Paul VI, with the titular church of San Pio X alla Balduina, and named to the Sacred Congregations for the Discipline of the Sacraments and for Divine Worship and to the Secretariat for Non-Christians. He was to take part in the 1977 bishops' synod but was prevented from traveling to Rome by a heart attack. He did attend the two conclaves of 1978 that elected Popes John Paul I and Blessed John Paul II. In 1980 owing to declining health, Cardinal Dearden submitted his resignation to Pope Blessed John Paul II and was succeeded by Archbishop (later Cardinal) Edmund Szoka. In 1982 he was awarded the Laetare Medal by the University of Notre Dame and in 1983 received an honorary doctorate from The Catholic University of America.

de Arvide, Martín. *See* **Arvide, Martín de**

de Cheverus, John L. *See* **Cheverus, Jean-Louis-Anne-Madeleine Lefebvre de**

de Corpa, Pedro and Four Companions. *See* **Georgia, Martyrs of**

DeBusschere, Dave (October 16, 1940–May 14, 2003)

A famous professional basketball player, Dave DeBusschere is a member of the National Basketball Hall of Fame. He was born in Detroit, Michigan, where he began his basketball career. In high school he took his team from Austin Catholic High School to a state championship in 1958. In college, he played basketball and baseball at the University of Detroit, leading the school's basketball team to the National Invitational Tournament in 1960 and 1961 and to an NCAA bid in 1962. In 1977 he was inducted into the college's Athletic Hall of Fame and had his jersey number, 22, retired.

After also earning All-American honors in baseball, DeBusschere signed with the Chicago White Sox in Major League Baseball in 1962, but was also drafted by the NBA's Detroit Pistons, and played for that team until 1968. In 1964 he was named player-coach, the youngest NBA coach in history, a post he held until 1967. His greatest pro success came after he was traded to the New York Knicks in 1968; he was a key figure in the 1970 and 1973 championships. His career included election eight times to the NBA All-Star team and six times to the All-Defensive first team. Inducted into the Basketball Hall of Fame in 1983, he was named in 1996 one of the fifty greatest players of all time in the National Basketball Association; he also served as commissioner of the now defunct American Basketball Association during the league's final season in 1975.

Deferrari, Roy Joseph (June 1, 1890–August 24, 1969)

A classics scholar, Roy Joseph Deferrari devoted almost his entire academic career to teaching at The Catholic University of America. Born in Stoneham, Massachusetts, he was the son of Italian immigrants. He studied at Dartmouth and then Princeton, earning a doctorate in 1915 in classics. After graduation, he received a position on the faculty at Princeton; three years later, he joined the faculty of Catholic University as head of the Department of Greek and Latin. He remained at the university until his retirement in 1960.

Deferrari was largely responsible for the development of Catholic University's expertise in patristics and indexes on the *Summa Theologiae* of St. Thomas Aquinas and a variety of ancient Latin sources. He was also the editor of the series *The Fathers of the Church: A New Translation* in 1947 and was responsible for several Latin textbooks. Deferrari served in a variety of administrative posts at the university, including dean of the Graduate School of Arts and Sciences. He also was a supporter of the university's decision to permit the admission of women into the undergraduate program and later the integration of the study body. In 1945 he was appointed by President Harry S. Truman to the commission of education leaders sent to Japan to provide advice to General Douglas MacArthur on the reorganization of Japan's educational system. He was named a Knight of St. Sylvester by Pope John XXIII and received numerous honorary degrees.

de Grasse, François-Joseph-Paul, Comte (September 13, 1722–January 11, 1788)

A French war hero of the American Revolution, François-Joseph-Paul, Comte de Grasse earned the respect and gratitude of the American people but suffered misfortune in his own land. He was born in Bar, France, and at the age of eleven entered the naval services of the Knights of Malta. In 1740 he entered the French Navy and was captured by the

British in an engagement and kept as a prisoner of rank for two years.

By 1779, having resumed his naval career, the Comte de Grasse held the rank of rear admiral. He came to America to aid the cause of the Revolution, and on his voyage he encountered English ships on their way to relieve General Charles Cornwallis in his battles against the Americans. De Grasse damaged the English so severely that they had to withdraw to New York instead of aiding Cornwallis. The French ships went into Chesapeake Bay, where they joined the fleet under the command of Admiral de Barras. This naval force halted all possibility of relief for Cornwallis, who surrendered.

In 1781 de Grasse sailed to the West Indies to harass British trade. During the next year he was attacked and taken prisoner, spending time in English hands in Jamaica and then in England. When he was released and returned to France, he was court-martialed for losing his flagship and for being taken captive. He was not fully condemned, but he was not actually cleared of the charges, and he asked for a new trial. King Louis XVI, however, had lost interest in him, so de Grasse resigned his commission in 1784, still honored by grateful Americans.

Compte de Grasse

Delaware

Called the Diamond State, Delaware is located on the Atlantic seaboard in the eastern part of the United States. It is bounded on the north by Pennsylvania, on the east by the Atlantic Ocean and Delaware Bay, and on the south and west by Maryland. Delaware entered the Union in 1787 as one of the original thirteen states. Two major land regions compose the geological formation of the state: the Piedmont in the north and the Atlantic Coastal Plain. The original Native Americans in the state were all of Lenni-Lenape (Delaware) heritage and included the Munsee, Una, Unalachtigo, and Unami nations.

Delaware was visited in 1609 by the explorer Henry Hudson, who was in the employ of the Dutch. The colonial and state name was chosen to honor the governor of Virginia, Thomas West, Lord De La Warr. In 1632 the Dutch West India Company attempted a colony at present-day Lewes, and six years later, the Swedes established a settlement at Christianaham, modern-day Wilmington. The Dutch regained their colony in 1655, settling at present-day New Castle. Peter Stuyvessant administered Delaware for the Dutch. The British, however, assumed control of the region in 1664, ousting the Dutch and attaching the colony to New York. Charles II of England gave the area to William Penn in 1682 as part of the Pennsylvania grant.

Catholics had settled in Delaware, and in the early 1750s Jesuit missionaries opened mission chapels and served the faithful. The Jesuits were at Appoquinimink in 1740 and then at Willow Grove and Cuba Rock. In 1772 the missionaries purchased land at White Clay Creek, and in 1788 erected St. Mary of the Assumption. Two years later, the Augustinian priests Fathers John Rosseter and Matthew Carr served Catholics in Wilmington. The Capuchin Franciscan Father Charles Whelan was also in the area.

Delaware played an important role in the American Revolution. Caesar Rodney had ridden from Dover to Philadelphia in order to cast the deciding vote for independence on July 2, 1776. Delaware was also the first state to ratify the United States Constitution on December 7, 1787. The Catholic population in the area grew rapidly after the War for Independence. In 1804 Father Patrick Kenny, who would serve the faithful in Delaware for thirty-six years, was at Coffee Run in Mill Creek Hundred. The state became part of the episcopal jurisdiction of Philadelphia, and facilities were expanded steadily. In 1816 Father Kenny started the church that would become the Cathedral of St. Peter in Wilmington; Father Matthew Sittensperger was another pioneering missionary. Others joined them in their labors, including Father George Carroll and the Daughters of Charity from Emmitsburg, Maryland. A school opened in Wilmington in 1834 by Father Patrick Reilly would become St. Mary's College. Other churches followed, as area Catholics solidified their communities.

On March 3, 1868, Pope Blessed Pius IX established the Diocese of Wilmington, having jurisdiction over Delaware and some Maryland counties. The state was prosperous, as E. I. du Pont de Nemours and Company, a leader in the chemical industry, had been serving the local economic base since 1802. The du Pont family was involved also in local and national politics.

World War I impacted on Delaware as the state supplied munitions for the American military. The Great Depression that followed the war brought distress and need, and Bishop Edmund John FitzMaurice of Wilmington expanded charitable ministries and gave aid wherever possible. World War II was another era of demand and support for the military and defense programs, and Delaware responded.

Following World War II, the state experienced a profound population growth from 1950 to 1960. Bishop Michael W. Hyle of Wilmington supported the civil rights movement and took part in sessions of the Second Vatican Council. His successors implemented the mandates and reforms of that council. The shift in population to suburban areas and the loss of priests and religious added new stresses to the Catholic role in Delaware, but new facilities were opened and social and charitable programs maintained. In 2011 there were 235,000 Catholics served by 197 priests, 224 women religious, and 57 parishes in the state.

de León, Juan Ponce (c. 1460–1521)

A Spanish explorer and seaman, Ponce de León searched for the legendary Fountain of Youth and named the modern-day state of Florida. He was born at San Servas, Spain, a member of a noble family. De León served as a page to Pedro Nuñez de Guzmán, the tutor of the brother of Emperor Charles V, the Infante Don Fernando. In 1493, however, de León took part in Christopher Columbus's second voyage to Hispaniola and subsequently proved a gifted commander in Nicolás Ovando's campaign to suppress the revolt of the local tribes in Hispaniola.

As a reward for his skills and faithful service, de León was appointed Ovando's lieutenant. During this time, he was told by local tribe members that there was vast wealth in the neighboring island of Buriquien (modern-day Puerto Rico). His expedition found considerable wealth, and using this success as leverage, he secured an appointment as governor of Boriquien. His harsh treatment of the natives, however, caused him to be removed from office.

While governor, de León heard rumors of a renowned spring that might restore youth and vitality, a version of the fabled *fons juventutis* ("fountain of youth"), which was supposedly located to the north of Hispaniola. Using his influence at the court, de León secured permission from King Charles V in 1512 to explore the island of Bimini. He set out from Puerto Rico in March 1513 and eventually reached the coast of Florida on March 27, Easter Sunday. In honor of the day (*Pascua de Flores*), he gave the name Florida to the area, especially owing to its lush vegetation. On April 2 he landed to the north of St. Augustine, claiming the territory in the name of the Spanish crown. He finally returned to Puerto Rico after several encounters with the native tribes and gained a second grant, this time for the territory of Florida. He went back to Florida in 1521 and intended to build settlements. The local tribes, however, proved hostile, and the violence compelled him to withdraw. De León suffered wounds from the attacks and died soon after reaching Cuba.

DeLille, Henriette (1812–November 16, 1862)

The founder of the Sisters of the Holy Family, Henriette DeLille was the first American-born African-American whose cause for canonization has been approved. A native of New Orleans, she was the youngest of three children born to a white Creole and a free woman of color, Jean-Baptiste DeLille-Sarpy and Marie Joseph Dias, respectively; Henriette was thus born free.

At the age of eleven, Henriette met a French nun of the Dames Hospitalières, who had established a school for free girls of color in New Orleans in 1823. Influenced deeply by this encounter, she dedicated her life to the poor, even refusing her mother's suggestion to enter a convent in France, in order to devote her energies to those in need in her city. By

1836 she had inspired a small group of white and Creole women to band together to assist the sick and dying and to catechize among her own people of color. The group eventually disbanded, however, owing to opposition from the civil government and a lack of support from Catholic authorities.

Undaunted, Henriette reestablished her community and finally received permission from Bishop Antoine Blanc, the first archbishop of New Orleans, to form the religious community of the Sisters of the Holy Family to care for the sick and forgotten. Official recognition for the Sisters came in 1842. By 1851 Henriette had purchased a home where she and her fellow sisters could live in community and advance their ministry. During the frequent outbreaks of yellow fever, cholera, and malaria, Henriette and her sisters were always to be seen assisting the afflicted.

At Henriette's death, there were twelve members of the community. Initially limited only to accepting young free women of color, the Sisters of the Holy Family were finally permitted after the Civil War to accept former black slaves and bondswomen. Only in 1872, however, were they permitted to wear habits. Henriette's foundation today is active in various ministries across the country, with its members found in the Archdioceses of New Orleans, Washington, Galveston-Houston, and Los Angeles, and in the Diocese of Lafayette. The sisters are also found in Belize and Nigeria. The cause for Henriette's canonization was opened in 1988 and given unanimous approval by the U.S. bishops in 1997.

Demers, Modeste (October 11, 1809–July 21, 1871)

The "Apostle of the Pacific Coast" of North America, Modeste Demers was the first Catholic missionary among the Native American tribes of Oregon, Washington, and British Columbia. He was born in St. Nicholas, Québec, and studied for the priesthood privately before entering the seminary there. He was ordained on February 7, 1836.

Father Demers met the future Bishop Francis Norbert Blanchet soon after his ordination and volunteered to accompany him to Oregon. They set out for Walla Walla and arrived there on November 18, 1838. He started his mission immediately,

learning the languages of the local tribes, visiting their homes, and teaching their children. Within weeks he was able to translate hymns and prayers into the tribal tongues. He traveled also, exploring the coast of British Columbia. In 1842 he went inland as far north as Stuart Lake.

On November 30, 1847, he was consecrated a bishop and appointed to Victoria on Vancouver Island. He accepted this honor with considerable reluctance, but he labored with enthusiasm and tirelessness. Bishop Demers continued his missions among the Native Americans but also had to provide facilities and personnel for the growing number of white settlers. In 1858 he brought in the Sisters of St. Anne to establish schools in the diocese and welcomed the Oblates of Mary Immaculate, who continued the Indian missions and started a college in Victoria.

In 1869 Bishop Demers traveled to the First Vatican Council. He was in a train accident while in France and suffered a compound leg fracture. Returning to Victoria, he suffered a stroke. He died at Victoria and was buried in St. Andrew's Cathedral.

Demjanovich, Miriam Teresa (March 26, 1901– May 8, 1927)

A member of the Sisters of Charity of St. Elizabeth in Convent Station, New Jersey, Miriam Teresa Demjanovich was noted for her remarkable spiritual maturity. She was born in Bayonne, New Jersey, the daughter of immigrants from Slovakia, and grew up as a member of the Byzantine Ruthenians. Although called to the religious life, her entry into the convent was delayed owing to the needs of her family. She nevertheless was able to study at the College of St. Elizabeth, operated by the Sisters of Charity. Finally, in 1926, after the death of her father, she entered the Sisters of Charity and took the religious name Miriam Teresa.

Sister Miriam Teresa taught at the convent's academy, but she was known especially for her remarkable development in the spiritual life. Known throughout her life for her holiness, she was asked by her spiritual director to author a series of conferences and instructions for her fellow sisters. These were published posthumously under the title *Greater Perfection*. In late 1926 she became ill and, as her death was seen to be approaching, was permitted to make her final profession in April 1927. Her cause was opened in 1945.

Denman, William (March 17, 1784–September 12, 1870)

A Scottish-born publisher, William Denman opened the first Catholic newspaper in New York. He was born in Edinburgh, Scotland, the son of a German father and an Alsatian mother, although he reportedly served in the English army for a time. In 1824 he moved to New York and within a year launched with George Pardow the *Truth Teller*, the first Catholic paper issued in New York. The weekly paper enjoyed some prominence for a time, but its advocacy of trusteeism cost it support from many in the Church. By 1855 Denman was forced to sell the paper to the owners of *The Irish American*.

Denver, Archdiocese of

Established as a diocese on August 16, 1887, by Pope Leo XIII, and as an archdiocese on November 15, 1941, by Pope Pius XII, the Archdiocese of Denver serves northern Colorado and has suffragan sees. The Catholic history of the archdiocese dates to early eras and involves some of America's most dedicated missionaries and builders. Denver, called the "Mile High City," was an early destination for Native Americans, trappers, and traders. The actual settlement of the site, however, dates to the gold rush period of 1859. The city was named after James W. Denver, the territorial governor in 1858. Denver survived both fire and flood to become an industrial, commercial, and transportation center.

As early as 1540, Francisco Vázquez de Coronado, the Spanish explorer, was in the area. In 1604 another Spanish expedition, including Franciscan chaplains, surveyed the area. The names of local rivers, peaks, and communities attest to a Spanish presence. In 1682 René-Robert Chevalier, Sieur de La Salle, was also in Colorado, claiming the region for France. Silvestre Velez de Escalante, a Franciscan, led another expedition into the region in 1776.

In 1803 the eastern sectors of Colorado were given to the United States as part of the Louisiana Purchase. Three years later, the American explorer Zebulon Pike traveled in the area, followed some decades later by Kit Carson and John C. Fremont, who mapped routes throughout the region for the oncoming settlers. In 1848, under the terms of the Treaty of Guadalupe-Hidalgo, Mexico surrendered the western part of Colorado to the United States. Gold was discovered in the area in 1858, bringing miners, prospectors, and families into the area, and the Colorado Territory was formed by an act of the U.S. Congress in 1861. Colorado entered the Union in 1876.

Catholics prospered during the period of formation in Colorado. Spanish Franciscans had established missions earlier, and when they were exiled from the region by the Mexican government because they were Spaniards, other priests continued to serve the needs of the faithful. In 1848 the southern Colorado missions were served by priests from New Mexico. San Luis de la Culebra was founded in 1851, followed by San Acacio, San

Immaculate Conception Cathedral in Denver

Pedro, and Conejos. In 1857 Bishop Jean Baptiste Lamy of Santa Fe established Our Lady of Guadalupe Church in Conejos.

In May 1860 Bishop Jean Baptiste Miège, the vicar apostolic of the Indian Territory, visited Colorado and then asked the Holy See to create a separate ecclesiastical jurisdiction for the region. On March 16, 1868, Father Joseph P. Machebeuf, the "Apostle of Colorado," was appointed vicar apostolic for Colorado and Utah. He became the first bishop of Denver on August 16, 1887; Utah had been transferred to the jurisdiction of San Francisco in 1871.

Bishop Machebeuf journeyed endlessly through the 104,247 square miles of his diocese establishing parishes and schools. The Jesuits arrived in the area to assume pastoral duties, and Sister Blandina Segale, a remarkable nun, also built a school and other facilities in Trinidad, having Billy the Kid as her patron. Bishop Machebeuf built hospitals, orphanages, and charitable agencies, working tirelessly. He died from exhaustion on July 20, 1889.

Bishop Nicholas C. Matz was his successor; he had been appointed coadjutor bishop with right of succession on October 28, 1887. He acceded to the see upon Bishop Machebeuf's death. Bishop Matz opened a seminary in Denver and invited religious congregations to labor in the diocese. He also instituted programs for the vast numbers of immigrants arriving in Colorado. St. Frances Xavier Cabrini aided him in this ministry, starting an orphanage in 1912. Bishop Matz visited every parish in the diocese, and his health suffered as a result of this constant travel. He died on August 9, 1917.

Bishop J. Henry Tihen, who had served as bishop of Lincoln since 1911, was transferred to Denver as Bishop Matz's successor on September 2, 1917. He arrived in the area as Americans found themselves engulfed in World War I. Bishop Tihen consecrated the Cathedral of the Immaculate Conception on October 23, 1921. He developed St. Thomas Seminary and the Catholic Charities of Denver as the Ku Klux Klan and other anti-Catholic groups attacked the faithful. He also started the Register System of diocesan newspapers, and expanded parishes and schools. Bishop Tihen retired on January 6, 1931.

On April 17, 1931, Bishop Urban J. Vehr became the fourth bishop of Denver, and in time he would become the first archbishop of Denver. The nation was in the grip of the Great Depression at the time, and he developed charitable ministries while concentrating on educational programs. Bishop Vehr raised funds for all aspects of the diocesan educational programs, including adult study classes.

On November 15, 1941, the Diocese of Denver was elevated to the status of a metropolitan see, an archdiocese, and given suffragan sees. Bishop Vehr was promoted as well, and he administered the Diocese of Pueblo until the first bishop of that jurisdiction was installed. Archbishop Vehr led the faithful of Denver through the grim days of World War II. He attended the Second Vatican Council and implemented the reforms mandated by that council. He retired after more than three decades of service on February 22, 1967.

His successor was Archbishop James V. Casey, who had served as auxiliary bishop of Lincoln since 1957. Archbishop Casey was promoted to Denver on February 22, 1967. He continued implementing the reforms of the Second Vatican Council and created agencies and offices to carry out the new lay programs instituted in the archdiocese. His special concern, however, was for the poor and the disadvantaged in the archdiocese. Archbishop Casey also founded the Catholic Pastoral Center. He died on March 14, 1986.

Archbishop James Francis Stafford, who would become a cardinal, was the successor to Archbishop Casey. Having served as the auxiliary bishop of Baltimore and as the bishop of Memphis, he was installed in the Archdiocese of Denver on July 31, 1986. During World Youth Day in 1993, Archbishop Stafford welcomed Pope Blessed John Paul II to Denver. In August 1996 he was appointed president of the Pontifical Council for the Laity in Rome, and on February 21, 1998, was created a cardinal.

Archbishop Charles J. Chaput, O.F.M. Cap., succeeded Cardinal Stafford. Archbishop Chaput, the first Native American appointed to that rank, had served as the bishop of Rapid City and was promoted to Denver on February 18, 1997. Archbishop Chaput was installed in Denver on April 7, 1997, at the age of fifty-two. His priorities included Catholic education and vocations, and his pastoral letters focused on the priesthood, marriage, penance, evangelization, and youth. On July 19, 2011, Archbishop Chaput was appointed archbishop of Philadelphia. In 2011 there were more than 540,000 Catholics served by 290 priests, 270 women religious, and 119 parishes in the Archdiocese of Denver.

de Oñate, Juan (c. 1549–1626)

A Spanish explorer, Juan de Oñate was instrumental in the founding of the Spanish colony of New Mexico. The son of a well-connected Spanish family of New Spain, de Oñate received permission from the crown in 1595 to explore and colonize the regions north of Mexico. He was able to set out on his expedition only in 1598 but swiftly established a Spanish presence near what became Santa Fe at San Juan de los Caballeros. An uprising by the Pueblos was met with brute force, and the colony itself over the next years grew disenchanted with de Oñate's style of governing, especially his long periods of exploration in Kansas and California.

A new governor was appointed in 1609, and in 1614 de Oñate was tried for his harsh treatment of both the colonists and the native people. Convicted, he was banished from New Mexico and Mexico. His remaining years were devoted to attempts at recovering his official position with the Spanish crown. Although a failure as governor, he nevertheless earned fame for his key role in forging Spanish colonies — and hence the presence of the Church — in what became the state of New Mexico.

de Padilla, Juan (c. 1500–c. 1542)

A Franciscan missionary to Native Americans, Juan de Padilla is the protomartyr of the United States. He was born in Andalusia, Spain, and spent part of his youth as a soldier before joining the Franciscans in Spain and dedicating his life to the missions. He journeyed to Mexico in 1528 and there joined the expedition of Pedro Nuñez de Guzmán in 1529 and 1530; he then traveled to Tehuantepec in 1533 to take part in the planned military expedition of Hernando Cortés to the East Indies. As this never took place, Father de Padilla entered into service in the missions of Poncitlan and Tuchpán and then established several Franciscan houses in Mexico.

In 1540 Father de Padilla set out on Francisco Vázquez de Coronado's expedition to New Mexico. He proved an active participant in the explorations, including the scouting of the Hopi pueblos and the Rio Grande pueblos. Thus, when Coronado returned to Mexico in 1542, Father de Padilla remained with the Indians. In 1542 he set out for Quivira, in the company of two Indian assistants, a Portuguese named Andrés do Campo, several servants, and a group of Indians from Quivira. While preaching among the Quivirans, however, he was killed by a group of unknown tribesmen, possibly Zuñis. Do Campo and two Indian assistants managed to survive and reach Mexico. Father de Padilla is commemorated as the first priest to be martyred in what is now the United States.

Depression, Great

Arguably the greatest economic crisis in the history of the United States, the Great Depression was a worldwide economic collapse that began in 1929 and was ended only in the late 1930s and early 1940s as the globe entered into the era of the Second World War.

The Depression began, famously, with the stock market crash in October 1929, but its roots began before, when a postwar recession led to a massive boom in the economy in the 1920s. It was fueled by the increase in American industrial output, especially the automobile industry, as well as road and highway construction and an enormous housing industry. The actual crash stemmed in part from the false prosperity of the times — corporations taking excessive profits; massive speculation in the stock market; the poorly organized and largely unsecured investment, banking, and financial sectors; severe imbalance in American loans for the payment of exports; and the mistaken belief that the prosperity could never end.

As it was, the economic good times lasted just long enough to help seal Governor Al Smith's defeat in 1928 (helped by anti-Catholicism). The Crash struck during Herbert Hoover's term, and once it hit, confidence fell, along with industrial output and deflation. The economic collapse had a domino effect around global markets, and soon the entire world was engulfed in financial and economic crises. The Depression destroyed much of

American prosperity and guaranteed the sweeping election of Franklin Delano Roosevelt as president in 1932.

By the time he was sworn into office with the promise of "a new deal for the American people," ten million Americans were unemployed, millions had lost their savings through an epidemic of bank failings, and hundreds of thousands of families lost their homes to foreclosures.

Catholics proved crucial to Roosevelt's sweeping agenda, both because of the staunch Catholic membership in the Democratic Party and also because of the growing prestige and influence of American Catholic leaders. Catholic social thought helped inform many pieces of the New Deal, so that nearly all the proposals made by the bishops in 1919 were ultimately passed into law under Roosevelt. A number of prelates, such as Cardinal William H. O'Connell of Boston and Cardinal George Mundelein considered Roosevelt a political ally and the friendliest occupant of the White House in many years.

Not every Catholic in America supported Roosevelt and the New Deal, of course. The most vocal of his opponents was Father Charles Coughlin. Known as the "radio priest," Coughlin acquired national prominence for his social commentary and was eventually heard by an estimated forty million listeners. Believing in the policies of Roosevelt, Coughlin supported his candidacy in the 1932 election but was alienated soon after. He attacked Roosevelt's administration in his shows and in popular lectures in Madison Square Garden and other arenas. Owing to his continued opposition to the New Deal, his growing political involvement, and accusations of anti-Semitism, Coughlin lost mailing privileges for his newspaper, *Social Justice*, in 1942 and was told through Archbishop Edward Mooney of Detroit that he had to cease his attacks, or at least curtail them, or he would be indicted under the Espionage Act.

The Depression also occasioned advances in Catholic teaching on social issues, as well as a greater consciousness of the need for authentic Church teaching in the areas of social justice. Much as Pope Leo XIII gave direction to Catholics facing the impact of the Industrial Revolution with his 1891 encyclical *Rerum Novarum*, so too did Pope Pius XI build on papal social teachings through his encyclical *Quadragesimo Anno* in 1931, which laid a blueprint for a social order built on justice and moral principles.

Catholic dioceses and archdioceses all across the country helped Americans with soup kitchens and shelters, but there also occurred a stunning burst of Catholic activity in the areas of social justice and labor. Catholics were important players in the formation of the CIO, the Committee for Industrial Organization, in 1935 (it became the Congress of Industrial Organizations in 1938); Catholics were more than 30 percent of the membership and 40 percent of the leadership. Catholics also founded the Association of Catholic Trade Unionists in 1937.

Similarly, Catholics founded a number of movements to deal with key social issues of the time. Among the most notable was the Catholic Worker Movement founded in 1933 by Peter Maurin and Dorothy Day (the cause for Day's canonization was opened in 2000 in the Archdiocese of New York) and devoted to the practice of the works of mercy, nonviolence, personalism, and voluntary poverty. Others in the same period were the Christian Family Movement, the Catholic Youth Organization, Cana Conferences, and the Grail Movement.

de Rémur, Simon William Gabriel Bruté *See* **Bruté de Remur, Simon William Gabriel**

Derwinski, Edward J. *See* **Cabinets, Catholics in Presidential**

Deshon, George (January 30, 1823–December 30, 1903)

A Redemptorist priest, George Deshon was one of the founders of the Congregation of St. Paul the Apostle. He was born at New London, Connecticut, and graduated from the United States Military Academy at West Point in 1843. Deshon was a classmate and roommate of General (later President) Ulysses S. Grant. Second in his class at West Point, he was quickly appointed an instructor in mathematics and ethics at the academy and subsequently promoted to the rank of captain.

In 1851, however, he resigned his commission and entered the Church, and then the Redemptorist order. Ordained in 1855, Father Deshon was soon associated with the labors of Father Isaac Thomas Hecker. In 1858 Father Deshon received permission from his Redemptorist superiors to be actively engaged in the formation of the new Paulist Institute. The first house was opened in New York City in 1859, and Father Deshon served there for his remaining years as novice master and later assistant superior. He was instrumental in opening the Chicago house of the congregation in 1903, with the permission of Archbishop Quigley. Father Deshon was also a noted homilist and writer; he compiled a book of his sermons in 1901. He died unexpectedly of heart failure. (*See also* Paulists.)

de Roaldes, Arthur Washington (January 25, 1849–June 12, 1918)

A valiant medical specialist, Arthur Washington de Roaldes was a Catholic leader in charitable missions throughout the world. He was born in Opedlousas, Louisiana, and educated at Jesuit schools in France. He graduated from the University in France in 1865, and obtained graduate degrees, including doctorates in medicine, from the University of Paris and the University of Louvain.

During the Franco-Prussian War, Dr. de Roaldes served as an assistant surgeon in the International Ambulance Corps. He received the Cross of the Legion of Honor for his meritorious acts. In 1872 de Roaldes returned to the United States and settled in New Orleans as the administrator of Charity Hospital. He also founded the Eye, Ear, Nose, and Throat Hospital and conducted charitable programs in other countries. In 1905 he received awards from France, Germany, Italy, Russia, and Spain for caring for the poor of those nations. A year later he was made a Commander of the Legion of Honor in France.

Devoutly Catholic and supportive of the Church's charitable works, he was made a Knight Commander of the Order of St. Gregory by Pope St. Pius X. The King of Italy made him a Knight of the Order of Saints Maurice and Lazarus. De

Roaldes exhausted himself by continuing to operate and conduct health missions. He lost his vision as a result of his rigorous charitable schedule. He died in New Orleans.

De Smet, Pierre-Jean (January 30, 1801–May 23, 1873)

The most revered Catholic missionary of the Native Americans west of the Mississippi River in the mid-nineteenth century, Pierre-Jean De Smet was a friend of Sitting Bull and a staunch defender of the Sioux. He was born in Termonde, Belgium, and became interested in a missionary vocation. Coming to America in 1821, he entered the Jesuit novitiate at Whitemarsh, Maryland, and completed his studies at Florissant, Missouri, where the Jesuits had established a new seminary and the Missouri Province of the Society of Jesus. He was ordained in 1827 and set out on his first mission labors. In 1833, however, he suffered a series of illnesses and went to Belgium to recover his health.

In 1838 Father De Smet returned to St. Louis and began working with the Potawatomi near Council Bluffs, Iowa. His no-nonsense missionary style was demonstrated at this stage of his apostolate. His mission, St. Joseph's, was endangered by the nearby Sioux, who threatened attacks. Father De Smet walked into the Sioux camp, introduced himself, and asked the Sioux to leave the Potawatomi and the mission in peace. The astonished Sioux heard his pleas and agreed to refrain from any such assaults.

In 1840 Father De Smet responded to a call for a "Black Robe" and went to the Rocky Mountains, where the Jesuits were establishing a missionary province. The Flatheads and Pend d'Oreilles welcomed him, and he went among the Crows, Gros Ventres, and others on a journey of 4,814 miles. In 1841 Father De Smet founded St. Mary's Mission on the Bitterroot River, thirty miles north of Missoula, Montana. Recognizing the vast numbers of local tribes and their receptive acceptance of the faith, Father De Smet went to Europe to recruit six Sisters of Notre Dame de Namur and

Pierre-Jean De Smet

other workers as well as funds. On his return to his mission area, he went by canoe to the residence of Bishop Francis Norbert Blanchet, at Fort Vancouver. The two men spent time planning the missions in the region. Father De Smet, who attended the Rendezvous of the mountain men and fur trappers, came to this planning session with great experience. He even spent time with Brigham Young in Utah, welcomed there because of his knowledge of the district and the tribes.

The hallmarks of Father De Smet's missionary work were manifold. He was a hardy traveler who endured hardship without complaint. He respected the traditions and values of the Native Americans and never took sides in debates. Because he spoke only the truth, he served as a mediator in tribal conflicts, such as the Blackfoot and Flathead confrontation in 1846. Father De Smet also served as a mediator at Fort Laramie in 1851, in the Mormon Wars in 1858, and in other regional disputes.

Founding the Kalispel St. Ignatius Mission as part of the overall mission strategy for the territory, he accompanied the Blackfoot Indians into the Yellowstone Valley in 1846. He and the tribe then went to Fort Lewis, and there the Blackfoot adopted peaceful relations with their neighbors. He addressed the ten thousand Indians holding council in Horse Creek Valley near Fort Laramie, urging peace. The United States military forces also asked him to intercede in events that threatened disaster.

Father De Smet's most unforgettable feat took place in 1868 as a result of the federal government's request for his assistance. Sitting Bull and the Sioux threatened war as a result of white treachery concerning their lands, and a federal peace commission was formed to avoid such a conflict. Father De Smet joined the commission on the way to the Sioux enclave but soon left the whites, whom he recognized as bureaucrats and politicians with their own agendas, and went his own way. He walked unarmed into a camp of five thousand Sioux warriors and asked to see Sitting Bull. Warmly received, Father De Smet and the great chief talked alone for a long period. The Jesuit missionary left the Sioux camp with a pledge of peace.

Father De Smet was honored by Native Americans and white alike as "the truest friend the Indians ever had." One reported incident details Father De Smet's concerns. A Sioux warrior confided to Father De Smet that there were deposits of gold in the Black Hills, an area considered sacred by the Sioux nation. Father De Smet warned the warrior never to speak of such matters again because the white men would enter the Black Hills if they knew that gold was available there. Father De Smet also discussed the matter with Sitting Bull, and the Sioux nation adopted severe laws against confiding word about the gold to any outsider. Father De Smet never told anyone either, and the presence of gold was not made known for decades as a result of his caution.

He logged nearly 261,000 miles through the wilderness to serve various tribes, speaking with candor and showing respect and honor in his dealings with all the Native Americans. His views were evident in his writings and reports. He died in St. Louis, Missouri, mourned by the tribes and other Americans.

Des Moines, Diocese of

Established on August 12, 1911, by Pope St. Pius X, the Diocese of Des Moines serves counties in southwestern Iowa. The capital of the state, Des Moines is Iowa's largest city and a major agricultural, printing, and insurance center. Fort Des Moines was erected in 1843 to protect the rights of the Sauk and Fox Indian tribes. Two years later, however, white settlers were allowed in the area, and East Des Moines amalgamated with Fort Des Moines. Coal fields and the designation of the city as the state capital assured its growth. The diocese is a suffragan see of the Archdiocese of Dubuque and has a profound Catholic heritage.

In 1673 the famous Jesuit explorer and missionary, Father Jacques Marquette, traveled in the area with Louis Joliet. Six years later, the Franciscan Recollect Father Louis Hennepin was also in the region. In 1788 Julien Dubuque started his settlement near present-day Dubuque. The Jesuit Father Charles Van Quickenborn served Catholics in Keokuk, Iowa, in 1832. In the following months, Iowa experienced a surge of settlers, who came into the area to claim land. The Venerable Samuel Mazzuchelli, a Dominican missionary, opened the first Catholic church in Dubuque. The Sisters of Charity of the Blessed Virgin Mary and the Trappists also came into the region.

Dubuque had been established as a diocese in 1837, and the Diocese of Davenport was erected in 1881. Des Moines was given the same ecclesiastical jurisdiction in 1911, with Bishop Daniel Austin Dowling being consecrated on April 25, 1912, as the first bishop of the diocese. He founded St. Gabriel's Seminary and opened the offices and agencies necessary for diocesan administration. On February 1, 1919, Bishop Dowling was promoted to the Archdiocese of St. Paul and Minneapolis.

His successor was Bishop Thomas W. Drumm, who was consecrated on May 21, 1919. He began expanding parishes, schools, and charitable ministries as the nation recovered from World War I. The Catholic population in the diocese continued to grow, and he built facilities and services to accommodate increased demands. Bishop Drumm also provided charitable programs to aid the needy during the first terrible months of the Great Depression. He died on October 24, 1933.

The third bishop of Des Moines was Bishop Gerald T. Bergan, who was installed on June 21, 1934. He opened more charitable programs as the suffering from the economic collapse continued. He also started a diocesan newspaper and then led the faithful of Des Moines through the grim days of World War II. On February 9, 1948, Bishop Bergan was promoted to the Archdiocese of Omaha.

His successor was Bishop Edward C. Daly, a Dominican, who was consecrated on May 13, 1948. Bishop Daly continued the diocesan expansion programs, opening new parishes and schools. On May 23, 1958, the Holy See made him an Assistant at the Pontifical Throne. Bishop Daly attended the Second Vatican Council and was killed in a plane crash in Rome on November 23, 1964, shortly after the close of the third session of the council.

The fifth bishop of Des Moines was George J. Biskup, who had served as auxiliary bishop of the Archdiocese of Dubuque since 1957 and was transferred to Des Moines on February 3, 1965. He served only two years in the diocese and was promoted to the Archdiocese of Indianapolis as coadjutor archbishop with right of succession on July 26, 1967.

His successor in the diocese was Bishop Maurice J. Dingman, who was installed on July 7, 1968. He implemented the reforms of the Second Vatican Council and continued to expand diocesan resources and commitments despite the loss of priests and religious. Bishop Dingman retired on October 14, 1986.

The seventh bishop of Des Moines was William H. Bullock, who had served as the auxiliary bishop of the Archdiocese of St. Paul and Minneapolis. Bishop Bullock was installed in Des Moines on April 2, 1987. He promoted education and the lay apostolate until he was transferred to the Diocese of Madison on April 13, 1993.

The eighth bishop of the Diocese of Des Moines, Joseph L. Charron, C.PP.S., had served as the auxiliary bishop of the Archdiocese of St. Paul and Minneapolis since 1990. He was transferred to the Diocese of Des Moines on November 12, 1993. As shepherd of the diocese, Bishop Charron concentrated on the pastoral needs of the growing Hispanic population, promoting adult faith formation, and providing the diocese with a solid financial foundation through a $20 million capital campaign, "Today's Gift . . . Tomorrow's Hope." Bishop Charron retired on April 10, 2007.

He was succeeded on April 10, 2008, by Bishop Richard E. Pates, who had been an auxiliary bishop of St. Paul and Minneapolis since 2000. He took as his immediate goals the continuatioin of the pastoral care of newcomers to the diocese, especially Hispanics, evangelization, and the promotion of vocations. In 2011 there were 90,000 Catholics served by 94 priests and 82 parishes in the diocese.

de Soto, Hernando (c. 1496 to 1500–June 1542)

A Spanish explorer, Hernando de Soto charted six southern states in present-day America and left vivid accounts of the details and descriptions of major Indian nations of the region. He was born in Villanueva de la Serena, Badajoz, Spain. In 1516 de Soto took part in the conquest of South America, but the ferocity and cruelty displayed by his fellow countrymen, especially in Peru, led him to return to Spain in 1536. He did, however, have a considerable treasury of gold.

Settling in Seville, de Soto married Inez (Isabella) de Bobadilla, the daughter of his former patron. De Soto had heard stories about Cabeza de Vaca's adventures in Florida, and he was inspired to undertake another expedition. King Charles V of Spain granted de Soto the titles of Adelantado of Florida and Governor of Cuba. He also held the rank of marquis, with land holdings to be chosen after he had conquered the southern region of North America. With these royal patents in hand, de Soto set out with a squadron of ten ships under his command on April 6, 1538.

Arriving in Cuba, he had to repel a French attack and rebuild Havana before he could set sail northward on May 18, 1539. His ship cast anchor in modern-day Tampa Bay one week later. The rest of the journey, lasting nearly three years, was on land. De Soto was seeking treasure, and his military troops brutalized the tribes they encountered, thus creating a constant state of war as word of their viciousness spread quickly to the other tribes located on their line of march. Sending his lieutenants to explore Florida and to report to Havana, de Soto moved into northern Georgia in 1540. Circling to the southwest, he met an Indian force near present-day Mobile, Alabama. Some seventy Spaniards and eleven thousand Native Americans died in this battle, which is considered by some to be the deadliest conflict ever to take place between Native Americans and Europeans.

Supply ships were anchored nearby, but exhaustion and a threat of mutiny in his ranks led de Soto to move inland to secure his position. One night in December 1540, the Spaniards lost forty men and fifty horses, and they suffered nightly attacks from that day on.

In April 1541 the Spaniards tried to storm an Indian fortress, and this effort resulted in many dead and an appalling number of wounded. De Soto cared for his troops and then marched to the Mississippi River. The winter of 1541–42 was spent on the Washita River in Arkansas. There, stricken with a fever, de Soto died. His remains were placed in a hollowed tree trunk and sunk in the river. De Soto explored Alabama, Arkansas, Florida, Georgia, Mississippi, and South Carolina. His reports provided the first descriptions of the Appalachians, Cherokees, Choctaws, Creeks, Seminoles, and other Native American tribes.

Hernando de Soto

d'Estaing, Jean-Baptiste-Charles-Henri-Hector, Comte, Marquis de Saillans (November 28, 1729–April 28, 1794)

A renowned French admiral Comte Jean-Baptiste-Charles-Henri-Hector d'Estaing, the Marquis de Saillans, took part in the struggle of the Continental Army against England during the Revolutionary War. Born at the Chateau de Ravel in Auvergne, France, he was a member of a distinguished French noble family and entered into the French army as a colonel. In 1757 he went to the East Indies as a brigadier general and took part in a campaign that ended with his capture by English colonial forces during the siege of Madras in 1759. Freed on parole, he accepted a position with the French East Indian Company. Using his military skill, he took command of ships and destroyed the British factories in Sumatra and the Persian Gulf. Captured again in 1760, he was sent to Plymouth, England, but was released a second time.

When d'Estaing returned home, he was swiftly appointed lieutenant general of the navy in 1763 and vice admiral in 1777. The next year, he set sail from Toulon harbor with a fleet of twelve battleships and fourteen frigates under orders to render such assistance as might be possible to the precariously positioned American colonies in their rebellion against Great Britain.

Eager to engage the British fleet under Admiral Richard Howe, he was prevented from battle by poor weather and so turned his attentions to the West Indies, where he mauled the British fleet under Admiral John Byron in July 1779 and captured St. Vincent and Grenada. Setting sail for the colonies, he took part in the effort to recapture Savannah, Georgia, during which he was wounded.

At the onset of the French Revolution in 1789, d'Estaing was a supporter of the new ideas of the time and was a member of the Assembly of Notables. Favored initially by the Revolutionary government, he was named commandant of the National Guard at Versailles in 1789 and admiral in 1792. This position deteriorated, however, owing to his continued effort to defend Marie Antoinette at her trial in 1793. The next year, he was arrested and sent to the guillotine.

Detroit, Archdiocese of

Established as a diocese on March 8, 1833, by Pope Gregory XVI and redesignated as a metropolitan provincial see on August 3, 1937, by Pope Pius XI, the Archdiocese of Detroit serves counties in Michigan and has suffragan sees. Detroit is the largest city in the state and is located on the Detroit River. The city is an industrial and automotive center, and a major port on the St. Lawrence Seaway.

The Catholic history of the archdiocese begins with the arrival of the earliest Catholic missionaries from Canada and involves some of the outstanding priests and prelates of the United States. In 1641 St. Isaac Jogues and Father Charles Raymbaut, both Jesuits, served the Chippewas in the present-day Sault Ste. Marie. Recollect Franciscan priests also served in Michigan, and in 1660 Jesuit Father René Menard started an Ottawa mission near the lake region. He disappeared while on a journey the following year, and he is presumed to have been slain by hostile Indians. The revered Jesuit mission superior Father Claude Allouez served at Sault Ste. Marie, joined by the Jesuit Fathers Jacques Marquette, Gabriel Druillettes, and others. René-Robert Chevalier, Sieur de La Salle, and Franciscan Recollect Father Louis Hennepin were on the St. Joseph River and Lake Michigan in 1679.

On July 24, 1701, Antoine Cadillac founded the city of Detroit, which was then called Fort Ponchartrain. One year later, St. Anne's was opened in the fort. Jesuits, including Father Armand de la Richardie, served the local Native Americans, and Franciscans ministered to the growing settlement of whites. In 1722 Recollect Franciscan Father Benedict Leonard was pastor of St. Anne's, followed by Father Simplicius Bouquet. The Hurons near Detroit were served by Fathers Armand de La Richardie and Pierre Potier.

Around 1763 the Michigan region was taken by the British as a result of the French and Indian War. The British brought Protestant missionaries to the area, as the priests were forced to return to Canada. The Revolutionary War brought Michigan under the control of the United States, but the British did not relinquish the area immediately. It was not until July 11, 1796, that the American flag flew over Detroit.

In that same year, Sulpician Father Michael Levadoux became the pastor of St. Anne's at the fort. Two years later, Sulpician Father Gabriel Richard arrived in Detroit to begin his ministries. He opened schools and seminaries and aided the founding of a university. St. Anne's was destroyed by fire in 1805 but was rebuilt.

When the Diocese of Bardstown (now the Archdiocese of Louisville) was established in 1808, Michigan was placed under that ecclesiastical jurisdiction. Bishop Benedict Joseph Flaget appointed Father Richard as vicar general for the region and visited Detroit on one of his endless pastoral journeys. In 1821 Michigan was attached to the Diocese of Cincinnati. Bishop Edward D. Fenwick of Cincinnati proposed that Detroit be elevated to the status of a diocese, and on March 4, 1827, Pope Leo XII so decreed. The actual establishment of the diocese was delayed, however, and was not announced until March 8, 1833, by Pope Gregory XVI. Father Gabriel Richard was appointed as the first bishop, but he died while caring for victims of a cholera epidemic in 1832.

The first bishop of the Diocese of Detroit was therefore Frederick Résé, who was consecrated on October 6, 1833. He began instituting the offices and agencies for diocesan administration and established educational academies and other Catholic facilities. He was summoned to Rome, however, to explain reports of his growing instability. After he had returned to Detroit, Bishop Résé's behavior brought about his being banned from residing in the United States. He left Detroit on August 19, 1840, and went to Europe, where he was treated for his illness. He remained a bishop and died on December 30, 1871.

His successor was Bishop Peter Paul Lefevere, who was consecrated coadjutor bishop of Detroit and apostolic administrator on November 20, 1841. Bishop Lefevere faced trusteeism and heavy debts in the diocese, but he set a new pace for Detroit. In 1845 the Sister Servants of the Immaculate Heart of Mary was founded as a congregation, and educational facilities were opened. Bishop Lefevere restored financial stability, started a diocesan newspaper, organized the Seminary of St. Thomas, and brought in other religious congregations. Bishop Lefevere also aided the founding of the American College in Louvain. He opened the Cathedral of Sts. Peter and Paul and erected two other seminaries. Bishop Lefevere died on March 4, 1869.

His successor was Caspar Henry Borgess, who was consecrated as coadjutor bishop and apostolic administrator on April 24, 1870. Upon the death of Bishop Résé in Europe, he became the bishop of Detroit. The ethnic rivalries in the diocese caused problems for Bishop Borgess from the first days of his episcopacy. He also faced severe fiscal problems because of the growing need for more diocesan facilities and services. He called a series of diocesan synods in order to consolidate and strengthen local programs. Schools were one of his many priorities. The Detroit College (now the University of Detroit) was founded in 1877, and other institutions flourished. A rather complex situation developed into what has been called the Polish Schism. (*See also* Polish Catholics.) Bishop Borgess retired on April 16, 1887.

The fourth bishop of Detroit was John Samuel Foley, who was consecrated on November 4, 1888, and installed on November 25. The automobile industry was stirring in the area, and Catholics started arriving in the diocese to be part of that growing labor field. In 1910 St. Mary's College was opened in Monroe, Michigan, destined to become Marygrove College. Bishop Foley supported this and other educational advances and established a reported thirty-four parishes. He died on January 5, 1918, as World War I brought sacrifices to Americans.

His successor was Bishop Michael James Gallagher, who had served as bishop of Grand Rapids since 1916. He was transferred to Detroit on July 18, 1918. When he arrived in the city, a procession of fifty thousand Catholics escorted him to his residence, cheered on by a hundred thousand participants in the streets. Bishop Gallagher opened a fundraising campaign, hoping to bring in $3 million to endow Sacred

Cardinal Dearden,
NCCB President

Heart Preparatory Seminary. Within three months he had collected $9 million. He also defeated an anti-parochial school bill in the Michigan legislature and erected 105 new parishes. The Great Depression brought suffering to the faithful of the diocese, and Bishop Gallagher opened charitable programs for the needy. He doubled the number of Catholic schools and built a new chancery office. Bishop Gallagher died on January 20, 1937.

Archbishop Edward Mooney, who would become an American cardinal, was Bishop Gallagher's successor. He was installed on August 3, 1937, the day that Detroit was elevated to the rank of metropolitan provincial see. Before coming to Detroit, Archbishop Mooney had served as the apostolic delegate to India, apostolic delegate to Japan, and the bishop of Rochester. Archbishop Mooney faced a debt of $22 million in Detroit, which he was able to eliminate by 1945. He began the economic recovery by developing a central bank for loans and deposits and an Archdiocesan Development Fund. Diocesan synods were convened in 1944–54. He also led the faithful of Detroit through the grim era of World War II. On February 18, 1946, he was created a cardinal priest with the titular church of Santa Susanna. Cardinal Mooney continued his labors, administering educational facilities and institutions. He also had to silence Father Charles Coughlin, who was causing uproar nationally with his political views. Cardinal Mooney died at the North American College in Rome on October 25, 1958, when he was about to enter the conclave that elected Pope John XXIII.

His successor in the archdiocese was Archbishop John F. Dearden, who was created a cardinal in 1969. Archbishop Dearden had served as the coadjutor bishop of Pittsburgh and was promoted to the Archdiocese of Detroit on December 18, 1958, and installed on January 29, 1959. He attended the Second Vatican Council and convened a diocesan synod in 1969. On April 28, 1969, he was created a cardinal priest with the titular church of San Pio X alla Balduina. Cardinal Dearden also served as president of the National Conference of Catholic Bishops. In Detroit, he founded Project Equality and Catholic Charities, and implemented liturgical changes and reforms. Cardinal Dearden retired on July 15, 1980.

The third archbishop of Detroit was Edmund C. Szoka, who had served as the bishop of Gaylord since 1971. On September 18, 1987, Cardinal Szoka welcomed Pope Blessed John Paul II to Detroit. He was created a cardinal priest on June 28, 1988, with the titular church of Sts. Andrew and Gregory at Monte Celio. Cardinal Szoka served as president of the Pontifical Commission for Vatican City State and on other commissions in Rome. In Detroit, he promoted Catholic social communications. Urban parishes were united to maintain facilities, and the archdiocesan tribunal was reformed. Cardinal Szoka was appointed president of the Prefecture of Economic Affairs of the Holy See on June 25, 1990.

The fourth archbishop of Detroit, Cardinal Adam Joseph Maida, was installed on June 12, 1990. He had served as the bishop of Green Bay since 1983. He was created a cardinal priest on November 26, 1994, with the titular church of Sts. Vitalis, Valeria, Gervase, and Protase. Cardinal Maida's time as archbishop was marked by wide-ranging programs, events, and initiatives. He reorganized archdiocesan administration, developed the Hispanic Pastoral Plan for the archdiocese in 1992, opened the St. John Center for Youth and Family in 1995, celebrated the 300th anniversary of the city and the Roman Catholic Church of Detroit in 2001, and was the driving force behind the Pope Blessed John Paul II Cultural Center in Washington, D.C. Cardinal Maida also issued a number of pastoral letters on subjects, including youths and assisted suicide. He confronted the economic collapse of Detroit and the sharp demographic shift out of the urban center and to the suburbs and surrounding communities. This necessitated shifting archdiocesan resources but also entailed a commitment by both Cardinal Maida and his immediate successor, Bishop Allen H. Vigneron, not to abandon the city and its people. Cardinal Maida retired on January 5, 2009, and was succeeded as archbishop by Bishop Vigneron, who had served as bishop of Oakland since 2003. In 2011 there were 1.4 million Catholics served by 587 priests,

1,200 women religious, and 271 parishes in the archdiocese.

Diego y Moreno, Francisco Garcia, O.F.M.
(September 17, 1785–April 30, 1846)

The first bishop of California, Francisco Garcia Diego y Moreno faced almost insurmountable odds in his ministry. He was born in Lagos, in the state of Jalisco, Mexico, and entered the Franciscans in 1801, making his vows the following year. He was ordained at Monterey, Nuevo Leon, in November 1808 and devoted himself chiefly over the next years to the Franciscan missions. Father Diego y Moreno also wrote a small guidebook for preaching, *Metodo de Misionar*, to assist his fellow priests.

After serving as a novice master from 1816 to 1819, he was named in 1832 to the post of superior of the missionary college of Guadalupe. That same year, he was sent with eleven fellow Mexican Franciscans to California, and Father Diego y Moreno assumed direction of Mission Santa Clara. Three years later, he returned to Mexico to ask the government's assistance in petitioning the Holy See for a diocese to be created in California to serve the needs of Catholics there. Despite its frequent hostility toward the Church, the government agreed, offering as well to pay $6,000 a year to maintain a bishop until the diocese was financially stable. After consultation with Rome, the government recommended Father Diego y Moreno to be the bishop.

On April 27, 1840, Pope Gregory XVI named Father Diego y Moreno the first bishop of Upper and Lower California, with the see at San Diego, and he was consecrated on October 4, 1840. He was soon forced to move the episcopal residence to Santa Barbara, owing to the terrible conditions in San Diego at the time. At the time of his arrival, there were only seventeen Franciscan priests for the entire diocese and a mere six towns. In February 1842 the situation became even worse when President Antonio López de Santa Anna confiscated the Pious Fund that had been allotted to the bishop, and he was forced to rely upon contributions from the few Caucasian settlers in the diocese. He managed to open a seminary at the Mission Santa Inez, in order to prepare for the future. Bishop Diego's death was hastened by the harsh conditions of his service and by his ceaseless labors. He was buried in the old Mission Santa Barbara.

Dietz, Peter (July 10, 1878–October 11, 1947)

A famous labor priest and editor, Peter Dietz based his social doctrines on the principles enunciated by Pope Leo XIII. He was born in New York City, the son of German parents. In 1900 he entered the novitiate of the Society of the Divine Word in Moedling, Germany, and was ordained by Cardinal James Gibbons on December 17, 1904. Father Dietz was concerned almost from the start of his priestly life with Catholic social doctrine, in particular the principles enunciated by Pope Leo XIII's influential encyclical *Rerum Novarum* in 1893. He subsequently became associated with other leaders in the early social justice movement, including Fathers John Ryan and William J. Kerby. With them, he encouraged the U.S. bishops to become more active in labor issues, lobbied the government for labor legislation, and called for a reorganization of Catholic social agencies to make them more responsive to the needs of the poor and workers.

From 1909 to 1910, Father Dietz served as editor of *Central-Blatt and Social Justice*, a German Catholic newspaper of the German Catholic Central Verein. He also held the post of secretary to the Social Service Commission of the American Federation of Catholic Societies from 1911 to 1918 and founded the American Academy for Christian Democracy for Women in 1915. A defender of trade unionism, he formed the Militia of Christ for Social Service, an organization of Catholic trade unionists, to promote Catholic teachings and to confront socialism. He addressed the American Federation of Labor on several occasions between 1909 and 1922, but he also earned the opposition of Catholic members of the Chamber of Commerce who complained to Archbishop J. T. McNicholas, O.P., in 1923 that he was hostile to their needs. Father Dietz spent his remaining years at St. Monica's Parish in Milwaukee, where he died.

DiMaggio, Joe (November 25, 1914–March 8, 1999)

Legendary Hall of Fame baseball player Joe DiMaggio was called "Joltin' Joe" and the "Yankee Clipper." He was born in Martinez, California, the eighth of nine children of Giuseppe and Rosalie DiMaggio, a Sicilian couple. At sixteen, DiMaggio dropped out of Galileo High and took a job at an orange-juice bottling plant. He was interested only in baseball, however, and in 1932, when his older brother Vince made the roster of a minor league team, the San Francisco Seals, he was signed to play shortstop.

DiMaggio proved so gifted in the sport that in 1934 he was sold to the New York Yankees for $25,000 and five players; the one condition was that the nineteen-year-old center fielder would be allowed to spend the 1935 season playing again with San Francisco. DiMaggio's entire career (1936–51) was with the Yankees, and he set a major league record in 1941 by hitting safely in fifty-six straight games.

In 1939 DiMaggio married actress Dorothy Arnold, at a ceremony attended by more than twenty thousand fans at the Cathedral of San Francisco. The couple was divorced in 1944. The year before, DiMaggio enlisted in the U.S. Army and served until 1945. In 1949 he signed baseball's first $100,000-a-year contract. He retired in 1951 at the age of thirty-seven. Three years later, he married Marilyn Monroe. Their union proved a brief one, lasting only eight months.

DiMaggio entered the Baseball Hall of Fame in 1955 and in 1969 was picked by fans and sportswriters as baseball's "Greatest Living Player." In 1986 he attended a state dinner at the White House and brought with him a baseball, in the hope that both President Ronald Reagan and Soviet leader Mikhail Gorbachev would sign it. The following day, Reagan appeared on television, and both he and Gorbachev signed the ball. Before his death from lung cancer, this American sports hero raised millions for the Joe DiMaggio Children's Hospital.

DiNardo, Daniel (May 23, 1949–)

Archbishop of Galveston-Houston and a cardinal, Daniel DiNardo is also a noted scholar and expert in patristics.

Born in Steubenville, Ohio, he grew up in the Diocese of Pittsburgh and began preparations for the priesthood at St. Paul Seminary, Pittsburgh. He earned a master's degree in philosophy from The Catholic University of America in Washington, D.C., and was sent to Rome for further studies.

He earned a licentiate in sacred theology from the Pontifical Gregorian University in Rome and studied patrology (the Church Fathers) at the Patristic Institute Augustinianum.

Ordained on July 16, 1977, for the Diocese of Pittsburgh, he served in the diocese and was a vice-pastor and adjunct episcopal chancellor. He worked for seven years at the Congregation for Bishops in the Roman Curia from 1984 to 1991; at the same time, he served as the director of the Villa Stritch, the house for Americans serving in the Roman Curia, and was adjunct professor at the North American College.

After returning to Pittsburgh, he was named adjunct diocesan director for education and a parish pastor as well as a member of the diocesan theological commission and of the presbyteral council.

On August 19, 1997, he was appointed coadjutor bishop of Sioux City and was ordained a bishop on October 7, 1997. He succeeded to the see of Sioux City on November 28, 1998. Six years later, he was appointed the coadjutor of Galveston-Houston on January 16, 2004, by Pope John Paul II. That same year, on December 29, 2004, he was promoted to the rank of archbishop at the same time that Galveston-Houston was elevated to the rank of a metropolitan archdiocese. He acceded to the see of Galveston-Houston February 28, 2006, and became its second archbishop.

The next year, on November 24, 2007, Archbishop DiNardo received the red biretta and the titular church of Sant'Eusebio from Pope Benedict XVI. As a cardinal, he took part in the Twelfth Ordinary General Assembly of the Synod of Bishops in Vatican City in October 2008, on "The Word of God in the Life and Mission of the Church."

As archbishop of Galveston-Houston, Cardinal DiNardo presides over one of the fastest growing and most diverse archdioceses in the United States. With more than one million Catholic faithful under his care, he has promoted vocations, pastoral care for migrants, and ways to develop Catholic education in a difficult financial period for the Church.

Divine Providence, Sisters of

A congregation of women religious founded in 1851 by Bishop Wilhelm Emmanuel von Ketteler of Mainz, Germany, the Sisters of Divine Providence are devoted to education and nursing. The sisters arrived in the United States in 1876 as a result of the political situation in Germany. The harsh *Kulturkampf* was being conducted in Germany under the direction of Prime Minister Otto von Bismarck. The programs imposed harsh conditions on the Church and impeded Catholic activities. The Sisters of Divine Providence settled in Pittsburgh, Pennsylvania, and devoted themselves to the needs of children in schools and to nursing. Currently, they are organized into three provinces in the United States: St. Peter's in 1876, St. Louis in 1930, and Our Lady of Divine Providence in 1957.

Divine Word, Society of the (S.V.D.)

A religious congregation, the Society of the Divine Word was founded in 1875 at Steyl, Holland, by St. Arnold Janssen. A priest of the Diocese of Muenster, St. Arnold envisioned secular priests laboring in foreign missions, and in time lay brothers were included. The congregation followed the rule of Dominican tertiaries until the first general chapter in 1884. At that time the group was formed into a religious congregation with public vows; it was approved by the Holy See in 1905. The congregation then numbered two thousand members and students and was established on five continents and the island of New Guinea. At the time of St. Arnold's death in 1909, the Society had been entrusted with mission territories containing fourteen million people.

The basic mission of the Society is the organization and maintenance of schools, with special emphasis placed on the training of a native clergy. The Society has also excelled in various fields, including science and the apostolate of the press. Members maintain printing plants to provide Catholic magazines and pamphlets.

The first Divine Word missionaries to the United States were two lay brothers who were sent to America to solicit subscriptions for the Society's publications. Seeing the need for the Society's labors, others joined them in 1897 and a community was formed on a farm north of Chicago. The Society of the Divine Word opened St. Joseph's Technical School (Techny), which on February 2, 1909, became the first Catholic foreign mission seminary in the United States. St. Joseph's also served as the headquarters of the Catholic Students' Mission Crusade, founded in 1918 by Clifford King, S.V.D. There are three provinces in the United States: Chicago (headquartered in Techny, Illinois), Southern (headquartered in St. Louis), and Western (headquartered in Los Angeles).

Dodge City, Diocese of

Established on May 19, 1951, by Pope Pius XII, the Diocese of Dodge City serves counties in southwestern Kansas. Dodge City is a commercial center in a region involved in agriculture, livestock, and petroleum production. The city was established in 1864 and named after Colonel Henry I. Dodge. Located on the Arkansas River, Dodge City was once a notorious frontier town on the Santa Fe Trail. The Diocese of Dodge City is a suffragan see of the Archdiocese of Kansas City in Kansas and has a profound Catholic heritage.

The protomartyr of the United States, the Franciscan Friar Juan de Padilla, was slain at Council Grove in 1542. He had entered the region with the expedition of Francisco Vázquez de Coronado and had remained in the area to evangelize the local Native Americans. No permanent missions are on record in the region until the 1700s, although missionaries served in Kansas as part of their tours and evangelizing efforts. The Spanish were still active in explorations in the 1700s, and French trappers from Canada entered the area.

Jesuit missions opened in the northeastern part of the state around 1820. Jesuit Father Charles de la Croix was with the Osage in 1822, and Jesuit Father Charles Van Quickenborne was also with the Osage in 1827, ministering as well to the Peorias, Piankishaws, and Wea. Fort St. Francis Xavier Mission opened near Leavenworth in 1836. Three years later, Jesuit Father Christian Hoecken established a mission for the Potawatomi at Sugar Creek. This trusted companion of the revered Jesuit Father Pierre-Jean De Smet had opened the mission to receive the Potawatomi, who had been forced to march to Kansas by the U.S. Army. St. Rose Philippine Duchesne, called "the Woman Who Always Prays" by the local tribes, was also in the region in 1841. In 1847 St. Mary's Mission opened in Topeka to serve the Potawatomi. The Jesuit Fathers

John Schoenmakers and John Bax founded St. Paul Osage Mission, and the Sisters of Loretto established St. Ann's Academy.

On July 19, 1850, Pope Blessed Pius IX erected the Vicariate Apostolic of Territory East of the Rocky Mountains to Missouri. Bishop Jean Baptiste Miège established Leavenworth as his see in Kansas in 1857. Religious congregations responded to his call and came to serve the faithful of the area. The Santa Fe Railroad also brought new settlers into the territory. In 1877 the Diocese of Leavenworth (now the Archdiocese of Kansas City in Kansas), was erected, and Benedictine Louis M. Fink, the first bishop, sent mission priests to Dodge City. The Diocese of Wichita was also established in 1877, and the Congregation of the Immaculate Conception of Dominican Sisters was at Great Bend. World War I, the Great Depression, and World War II impacted upon the lives of the Catholics in the Dodge City area, but their presence increased. In recognition of the dedication of these Catholics, the Diocese of Dodge City was established in 1951.

Bishop John Baptist Franz was the first bishop of Dodge City, consecrated on August 29, 1951. Bishop Franz organized the offices and agencies for diocesan administration and convened a diocesan synod in 1957. St. Mary of the Plains College was opened in 1952. On August 8, 1959, Bishop Franz was transferred to the Diocese of Peoria.

His successor was Bishop Marion F. Forst, who was consecrated on March 24, 1960. Bishop Forst expanded diocesan facilities, providing care for the Hispanic Catholics in the area and welcoming several religious congregations that accepted his invitation to serve in the diocese. He also implemented the reforms mandated by the Second Vatican Council. On October 16, 1976, Bishop Forst was transferred to the Archdiocese of Kansas City in Kansas as an auxiliary bishop.

Eugene J. Gerber was appointed the third bishop of Dodge City and was consecrated on December 14, 1976. Bishop Gerber continued consolidating parochial facilities while promoting charitable apostolates and lay ministries, such as the permanent diaconate program. On November 23, 1982, Bishop Gerber was transferred to the Diocese of Wichita.

His successor was Bishop Stanley G. Schlarman, who had served as an auxiliary bishop of Belleville since 1979. He was installed in the diocese on May 4, 1983. Bishop Schlarman continued the charitable ministries of the diocese while trying to maintain the older parishes and schools despite a shortage of priests and religious. He also aided Hispanic Catholics in the diocese and sought ways to serve migrants. Bishop Schlarman retired on May 12, 1998.

The fifth bishop of Dodge City, Ronald M. Gilmore, was installed on July 16, 1998. He recruited priests and religious for the diocese and promoted a pro-life campaign. He retired on December 15, 2010, and was succeeded by Father John B. Brungardt, a priest of the Diocese of Wichita. Bishop Brungardt was ordained a bishop on February 2, 2011. In 2011 there were 44,000 Catholics served by 35 priests and 48 parishes in the diocese.

Doherty, Catherine de Hueck (August 15, 1896–December 14, 1985)

A social activist and spiritual writer, Catherine de Hueck Doherty was the founder of Friendship House. She was born in Nijni-Novgorod (modern-day Gorky), Russia, and grew up in the Russian Orthodox Church. She was educated in several Catholic schools run by the Sisters of Sion in Alexandria, Egypt, and Paris, France. She married Boris de Hueck in 1912, and the couple spent World War I at the Russian front lines. She served as a nurse, earning several decorations for bravery.

The de Huecks fled Russia at the start of the Russian Revolution, narrowly escaping death at the hands of the communists. De Hueck pledged her life to God should she survive. After reaching England, she entered the Catholic Church, and in 1921 the couple migrated to Toronto, Canada. There she gave birth to a son, George, in July. De Hueck devoted the next years to lecturing on her experiences, but her private life was in turmoil as she and Boris grew apart. Their marriage was subsequently annulled. Remembering her promise to God, she opened Friendship House, a

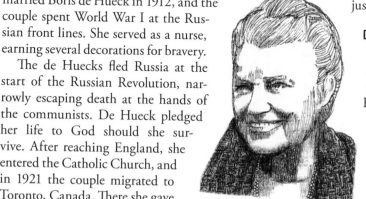

Catherine de Hueck Doherty

residence in the poorest part of Toronto, where she and several friends began a ministry to the poor and promoted Catholic social teaching. Owing to misunderstandings that led to accusations of so-called communist tendencies, she settled in the United States and, at the urging of Father John LaFarge, S.J., in 1938 she started Friendship House in Harlem, New York. In 1943 she married Eddie Doherty, a noted journalist.

Once more, problems developed in Friendship House, this time over issues of internal organization and pastoral priorities, and de Hueck left in 1947 to launch Madonna House just outside of Ontario. The new institution was a profound expression of Catherine's aspirations to make manifest in practical pastoral and spiritual activities the teachings of the Church in social justice and social doctrine. At the time of her death, Madonna House boasted a community of 150 Catholic laypeople and clergy, and additional houses were opened in England, France, Africa, and especially North America.

De Hueck was also a renowned spiritual writer and was awarded the pontifical medal *Pro Ecclesia et Pontifice* and the Order of Canada, the country's highest civilian honor, for her contributions to humanity and the Church. Her influence is still felt in many areas of Catholic social thought, and she directly influenced several generations of Catholics concerned with issues of social justice.

Dolan, Timothy M. (February 6, 1950–)

Archbishop of New York since 2009 and a cardinal since 2011, Timothy Dolan has also been president of the United States Conference of Catholic Bishops since 2010.

Timothy Michael Dolan was born in St. Louis, Missouri, to Robert Dolan and Shirley Radcliffe Dolan and was the oldest of five children. As he would later write, he felt called to the priesthood at a very early age and even pretended to say Mass when he was a child.

Dolan entered St. Louis Preparatory Seminary South in Shrewsbury, Missouri, in 1964, and earned a bachelor's degree in philosophy from Cardinal Glennon College. Having completed his preparatory studies for the priesthood, he was sent by Cardinal John Joseph Carberry for studies in Rome at the North American College and the Pontifical University of St. Thomas, the Angelicum. He earned a bachelor's degree in sacred theology and a licentiate in sacred theology. He was ordained on June 19, 1976, and then served as associate pastor at Immacolata Parish in Richmond Heights, Missouri, until 1979, when he began studies for a doctorate in American Catholic history atThe Catholic University of America. His dissertation was on the late Archbishop Edwin Vincent O'Hara, and his doctoral work included studies under the famed scholar of American Catholic history, John Tracy Ellis.

On his return to St. Louis, he served in parish ministry from 1983 to 1987, but he was also a liaison for the late Archbishop John L. May in his efforts to reorganize the educational aspects of the archdiocesan seminary system. In 1987 then Father Dolan was appointed to a five-year term as secretary to the apostolic nunciature in Washington, D.C., where he assisted Archbishop Pio Laghi, the first papal nuncio to the United States.

When Dolan returned to St. Louis in 1992, he was appointed vice rector of Kenrick-Glennon Seminary, holding as well the posts of director of spiritual formation and professor of Church history. He was also an adjunct professor of theology at St. Louis University.

Two years later, he was named rector of the North American College in Rome, where he served until June 2001. During his tenure in Rome, he also served as a visiting professor of Church history at the Pontifical Gregorian University and as a faculty member in the Department of Ecumenical Theology at the Pontifical University of St. Thomas Aquinas.

On June 19, 2001, the 25th anniversary of his ordination to the priesthood, Father Dolan was named the auxiliary bishop of St. Louis and titular bishop of Natchez. He was consecrated a bishop on August 15, 2001, and took as his episcopal motto the profession of faith of St. Peter from John 6:68: *Ad Quem Ibimus*, "Lord, to whom shall we go?"

On June 25, 2002, Bishop Dolan was named archbishop of Milwaukee and was installed on August 28, 2002. He inherited the archdiocese during a difficult ordeal that had engulfed even the retired archbishop, Rembert G. Weakland, O.S.B.

Pope Benedict XVI appointed him archbishop of New York on February 23, 2009, and he was installed on April 15, 2009, and received the pallium from Pope Benedict on June 29, 2009, at St. Peter's Basilica. On November 16, 2010, he was elected president of the United States Conference of Catholic Bishops. He succeeded Cardinal Francis George of Chicago.

On February 18, 2011, he was elevated to the College of Cardinals, with the titular church of SS. Giovanni e Paolo. One of the most popular cardinals in the United States, Cardinal Dolan is the author of several notable books, including *Priests for the Third Millennium* (2001), a collection of rector talks given to the seminarians and priests at the North American College in Rome; *Called to be Holy* (2005); and *To Whom Shall We Go?* (2009). He has been a vocal leader about the need for the Church to work for the protection of children and respond effectively to the sexual abuse crisis. He also opposed the proposed law in New York legalizing homosexual marriage and is considered one of the most articulate representatives of Catholicism in American culture.

Domenec, Michael (December 27, 1816–January 7, 1878)

The second bishop of the Diocese of Pittsburgh, from 1860 to 1876, Michael Domenec was also the first (and only) bishop of the Diocese of Allegheny. A native of Ruez, Tarragona, Spain, he began his studies in Madrid, but he was soon forced to resettle in Paris owing to the political instability of the period. While in France, he studied at the College of Montolieu in Adus and then entered the Congregation of the Missions, the Vincentians. While still engaged in preparations for ordination, he was encouraged in 1837 to journey to the United States by Father John Timon, C.M. Accepting eagerly, Domenec was ordained at the Vincentian seminary in Barrens, Missouri, in June 1839 and was assigned to the seminary faculty. He was then the youngest priest in the United States.

In 1845 Father Domenec was sent to Philadelphia to take up a teaching post at the diocesan seminary of St. Charles. At the same time, he served as a pastor in Nicetown and then established St. Vincent's Parish in Germantown. On the basis of his learning, his pastoral zeal, and his talents as a preacher, he was appointed the second bishop of the Diocese of Pittsburgh on September 23, 1860, and consecrated on December 9, 1860.

Bishop Domenec was confronted immediately by the onset of the Civil War in 1861. An ardent Unionist, he prayed for the preservation of the Union, ordered the American flag flown at the cathedral, and preached in favor of civic obligations. He also provided timely diplomatic service to the Union by traveling to Spain to intercede on behalf of the Union with the government. In this endeavor, he earned the respect and gratitude of Archbishop John Hughes of New York, who called him the most successful of the Union's ecclesiastic ambassadors during the war. Indeed, through his efforts, Spain remained neutral throughout the hostilities.

Bishop Domenec faced not only the financial hardships caused by the war but the sudden increase in the Catholic population; the number of Catholics grew sharply, from fifty thousand to two hundred thousand. In response to the growing needs, he oversaw a massive building program that included the creation of some sixty churches and several orphanages. To promote pastoral care, he encouraged the Oblate Fathers, Capuchin Franciscans, and Holy Ghost Fathers, as well as the Sisters of St. Francis, Ursulines, Carmelites, Little Sisters of the Poor, Sisters of the Good Shepherd, Sisters of St. Joseph, and Sisters of Charity to establish communities in the diocese.

His term of episcopacy in Pittsburgh was also marked by conflicts with his clergy. He attended the First Vatican Council and originally voted *non placet* on the question of papal infallibility. However, he soon changed his vote.

In 1876 Bishop Domenec requested that the growing diocese be split. His request was granted, and on January 11, 1876, he became the first bishop of the Diocese of Allegheny. The split ultimately aggravated the financial problems facing the Diocese of Pittsburgh, and the Diocese of Allegheny was suppressed in 1889 and reunited with Pittsburgh. The crisis left Bishop Domenec in poor health, and he resigned on July 27, 1877. He died in Spain.

Dominicans

St. Dominic de Guzman founded the Order of Friars Preachers, also called the Black Friars, the Order of Preachers, or the Dominicans, in 1215. He was a priest of the Diocese of Osma in Castile, Spain, who aided his local bishop in confronting the Albigensians with considerable success. Young men of the area came to study with St. Dominic, and he began founding monasteries under the Augustinian rule, receiving the first approval by Pope Innocent III in 1215. Pope Honorius III gave the Order of Preachers official sanction.

A mendicant order, the Dominicans brought a new approach to the religious life, maintaining the liturgical and monastic traditions of the past but providing opportunities for scholarly pursuits and dedicating its members to preaching and evangelization. The Dominicans were also revitalized as an army of priests under a single master general, ready and willing to accept assignments anywhere. The order drew the brightest as a result, including St. Albert the Great and St. Thomas Aquinas. The order also encouraged knowledge and awareness of the world, translating historical texts from ancient Greece and other classical works in order to enlighten new ages and to provide substantive scholarship. When the Spanish and Portuguese began exploring the New World, the Dominicans supported their efforts.

In 1539 a famous Dominican missionary, Luis Cáncer de Barbastro, was slain in Florida. Dominicans were available to the Spanish mission fields throughout the colonial period, and when the Church evolved in the young United States, other Dominicans were on hand to participate in the growth of dioceses and the promotion of Catholic teaching. One of these early Dominicans was Venerable Samuel Mazzuchelli, who pioneered the faith endlessly in the newly opened areas of America. Bishop Edward D. Fenwick, a Dominican, started his priestly vocation by serving in the missions of the Diocese of Bardstown. Having brought Dominican companions from Europe, Bishop Fenwick established the Province of St. Joseph for the Dominican order in 1828. He was appointed to the Diocese of Cincinnati and personally aided the growth of the Church in the Midwest. Other Dominican provinces followed: the Province of the Holy Name of Jesus started in 1912, the Province of St. Albert the Great in 1939, and the Province of St. Martin de Porres in 1979. The Dominicans served in New Orleans from 1903 to 1939 and in south Texas from 1925 to the present. The Order of Preachers also contributed to the American Church in Florida, Portland, Maine, and Massachusetts. The Dominicans accepted pastoral ministries, taught at universities and colleges, and provided missions and retreats for the Catholic faithful in all dioceses.

The American Dominicans also staffed foreign missions in Bolivia, Kenya, Mexico, Nigeria, and Pakistan. The order established institutions to educate and form members of the Dominicans, each province having its own *studia generalis*, which provides bases for Dominican ministries.

In response to the Second Vatican Council, the Dominicans in the United States held a general chapter to return the order to its original founding purpose, preaching and evangelizing the nation. Terms of office and voting procedures were also modernized. In 1979 the new Province of St. Martin de Porres was established in the South. A new increase in membership followed the declined experienced after the Second Vatican Council, and the Dominicans are now working with the Dominican sisters' congregations through the offices of the Dominican Leadership Conference and the Parable Conference of Dominican Life and Mission, which sponsors retreats, pilgrimages, and conferences featuring teams of friars and sisters and Dominican laity. There are currently over 6,000 Dominicans and nearly 3,500 Dominican nuns worldwide.

Donahoe, Patrick (March 17, 1811–March 18, 1901)

An Irish-born publisher, Patrick Donahoe pioneered Catholic newspapers and defended the faith in times of open prejudice in America. A native of Munnery, County Cavan, Ireland, Donahoe moved with his parents to Boston at the age of ten. At fourteen, he was apprenticed to a printer and then earned a position on the *Jesuit*, a Catholic newspaper launched by Bishop Benedict Joseph Fenwick of Boston in 1832. After Bishop Fenwick gave up the directorship, Donahoe and H. L. Devereaux continued on with the publication under the title *The Literary and Catholic Sentinel*.

In 1836 Donahoe began publication of *The Pilot*, a weekly paper intended for Irish-American Catholics. Through his efforts, the paper emerged as a leading voice for Catholics in New England and was the springboard for Donahoe's other publishing interests, including book publishing. Having amassed considerable wealth, he eventually lost it owing to catastrophic fires that burned down his printing press and loans to friends that were ill-advised. He avoided bankruptcy by selling *The Pilot* to Archbishop John J. Williams of Boston to pay off creditors. Through monies earned by various new ventures, he bought back the newspaper in 1881. In 1893 he received the Laetare Medal from the University of Notre Dame for his services to the American Church.

Dongan, Thomas, Earl of Limerick (1632–1715)

The Catholic governor of New York from 1683 to 1688, Thomas Dongan, Earl of Limerick, faced prejudice and persecution for instituting religious freedom in the colony. Dongan was born in Kildrought, County Kildare, Ireland. By 1683, as a servant of the Catholic Stuart monarchs of England, he arrived in New York colony to replace Governor Edmund Andros. Father Thomas Harvey, an English Jesuit, accompanied Dongan, joined by two other priests and Jesuit lay brothers. The religious established a school in the colony soon after arriving there.

Dongan displayed exceptional administrative skills, instituting the election of aldermen and other minor officials to bring individual colonists into the government. Reforming taxes and land grants, Dongan also managed to extend his authority over

Thomas Dongan

the Iroquois Indians. In the process he extended the influence of New York to Lake Ontario and south to modern-day Pennsylvania.

Being an Irish Catholic, Dongan faced considerable opposition, especially when he instituted religious freedom for the Church. His rule, however, ended abruptly when King James II was exiled. William of Orange, the successor to James II, was a Protestant. Dongan and other officials of James II were hunted down, and the Church of England was reestablished as the official faith in New York. Recalled to England in 1691, Dongan succeeded his brother as Earl of Limerick. There were no family estates or properties for him to inherit, however, as they had been confiscated. Dongan died in poverty in London.

Dooley, Thomas (January 17, 1927–January 18, 1961)

A physician and humanitarian, Thomas Dooley was the founder of Medico, an international health organization. He was born in St. Louis, Missouri, and studied at the University of Notre Dame. After serving two years as a Navy medical corpsman, Dooley went to the Sorbonne in Paris, and then studied medicine at St. Louis University, receiving his degree in 1953. When the Vietnam War started, Dooley volunteered as a medical officer on a naval ship for refugees. At Haiphong, he built camps and cared for over six hundred thousand refugees, as described in his book *Deliver Us from Evil* (1955).

In 1955 Dr. Dooley started a mobile medical unit in Laos, using the royalties from his books to finance the work and receiving aid from humanitarian groups. He wrote *The Edge of Tomorrow* (1958) and *The Night They Burned Down the Mountain* (1960). He also personally raised $850,000 for refugees and the needy. In 1959 Dr. Dooley was diagnosed with cancer and underwent an operation that enabled him to continue his work for a time. He returned to America and died soon after.

Dornin, Bernard (1761–1836)

The first American publisher of distinctly Catholic books, Bernard Dornin migrated to America because of political turmoil in his native land, Ireland. In 1803 he arrived in New York and began publishing books. In 1805 he published a New Testament, and in 1807 Pastorini's *History of the Church.* Serving as the leading publisher in the United States, Dornin conducted his business in Philadelphia and was highly esteemed. He closed his publishing company in the early 1830s, retiring to Ohio, where he died. Dornin spent the last days of his life with his daughters. His son, Thomas Aloysius, became a naval officer who distinguished himself by fighting the slave trade and serving in the Civil War, attaining the rank of commodore on the 1862 retirement list.

Dorsey, Anne Harmon (1815–December 26, 1896)

A convert, Anne Harmon Dorsey was a popular Catholic novelist who received honors from the Church. She was born in Georgetown, the daughter of a naval chaplain, and was well educated. In 1837 she was married to Lorenzo Dorsey and converted to Catholicism three years later. She was a pioneer in light Catholic literature, writing popular books for the young. Her son was killed in the Civil War, and she had three daughters. Pope Leo XIII sent her his benediction on two occasions, and the University of Notre Dame awarded her the Laetare Medal. Her works included *Guy the Leper, The Old Gray Rosary,* and *Cocaina, the Rose of the Algonquins.* She died in Washington, D.C.

Dorsey, John (1874–1926)

A Catholic missionary, John Dorsey was the first African-American Josephite priest ordained in the United States. He was born in Baltimore and was determined to be a priest. He studied at St. Joseph Seminary and St. Mary's Seminary and was ordained in 1902. After ordination, Father Dorsey was a strong supporter of Catholic missions among African-Americans in the South. He held a number of pastoral assignments in Tennessee and Arkansas and taught at St. Joseph's College for Negro Catechists in Montgomery, Alabama.

In 1909 he established the Knights of St. Peter Claver, a Catholic fraternal organization and mutual aid society that continues its work today. Father Dorsey served as its national chaplain until 1923. From 1918 to 1924, he was pastor of St. Monica's Church in Baltimore. In 1924 however, he was assaulted and left paralyzed for the remainder of his life. Father Dorsey also endured humiliations, persecutions, and violence for the Catholic faith in the South and for his race, including false charges of sexual misconduct.

Dougherty, Dennis J. (August 16, 1865–May 30, 1951)

The first archbishop of Philadelphia to become a cardinal, Cardinal Dennis J. Dougherty also served as a bishop in the Philippines. He was born in Holmesville, Pennsylvania, and received the grace of a priestly vocation. He attended a public elementary school and learned to defend the faith at a young age. He then studied at St. Mary's College in Montréal, at St. Charles Seminary in Overton, Pennsylvania, and then at the North American College in Rome. Ordained on May 31, 1890, he returned to St. Charles Seminary as a teacher.

On June 14, 1903, he was consecrated as the bishop of Nueva Segovia in the Philippines, the first American to administer that diocese. The Spanish-American War and a local schism complicated his early labors, but he restored the diocese and was appointed bishop of Jaro on Panoy. He made rounds on horseback to his diocesan parishes and was able to bring aid from the United States.

In 1915 Bishop Dougherty was appointed to the Diocese of Buffalo, New York, where he liquidated a debt of almost a million dollars and settled nationalism disputes. Three years later he became the archbishop of Philadelphia, and on March 20, 1921, was made a cardinal priest by Pope Benedict XV, with the titular church of SS. Nereus and Achilleus.

Cardinal Dougherty established ninety-two parishes in his first decade in Philadelphia, as well as eighty-nine new schools, three diocesan high schools, a women's college, and a preparatory seminary. He also brought thirty-five religious orders and congregations into the archdiocese. The cardinal fostered expansions in health care and in geriatric care. He was a devoted supporter of St. Katharine Drexel.

As chairman of the building committee of the National Shrine of the Immaculate Conception in Washington, D.C., and in other national roles, Cardinal Dougherty played an important part in the American political scene. He also led massive demonstrations against atheistic communism, a rising force in the world.

Cardinal Dennis Joseph Dougherty

Dougherty, John J. (September 16, 1907–March 26, 1986)

A biblical scholar, John J. Dougherty also served as an auxiliary bishop of Newark from 1962 to 1982. He was born in Jersey City, New Jersey, and studied at St. Peter's Preparatory School, Seton Hall College, and Immaculate Conception Seminary, all in New Jersey. In 1930 he was sent to the North American College in Rome for further preparation and was ordained in July 1933. The following year he earned a licentiate in sacred theology from the Pontifical Gregorian University and pursued additional postgraduate work in Rome at the Pontifical Biblical Institute, including research in Jerusalem. At that time, he was one of the few individuals in the United States to have earned a doctorate from the Institute. He also earned a licentiate and then a doctorate in Sacred Scripture in 1948.

In 1937 he was appointed a professor in Scripture at Immaculate Conception Seminary. He remained in the post until 1959, when he was named president of Seton Hall University. Three years later, on November 17, 1963, he was named titular bishop of Cotenna and auxiliary bishop of Newark.

Bishop Dougherty attended the last sessions of the Second Vatican Council and went on to hold a variety of committee positions in the National Conference of Catholic Bishops, while remaining as president of Seton Hall until 1969. In addition to his scholarly activities, he was an advocate of international peace and justice, including membership on the Vatican Committee for Peace, and he openly stated his opposition to the Vietnam War. He retired in 1982.

Doutreleau, Stephen (October 11, 1693–date uncertain)

A French missionary of the Society of Jesus, Stephen Doutreleau was wounded by a Natchez war party but was able to continue his labors in the Mississippi Valley for two decades. He was born in France, and in 1727, then a Jesuit novice, he migrated to Louisiana with the Ursuline nuns and assumed various mission assignments. He served at Port Vincennes in 1728 and two years later started a journey to New Orleans.

Father Doutreleau and a small company of travelers did not know that two Jesuits had been slain by the Natchez in a local uprising that included the Yazoo. When Father Doutreleau landed at the Yazoo River, his party was attacked. One of his French companions was slain, and the missionary was wounded in his arm. He and two companions reached their canoe and fled down the Mississippi River. They stopped at Tonica Bay, where Father Doutreleau's wound was dressed, and then continued to New Orleans.

He then served as a chaplain to the French troops in Louisiana and as a hospital chaplain. Father Doutreleau was sent back to the Illinois Indians at his own request. He labored among them until 1747, when he returned to France.

Dowling, Daniel Austin (April 6, 1868–October 31, 1930)

The first bishop of Des Moines, from 1912 to 1919, and the second archbishop of St. Paul, from 1919 to 1930, Daniel Austin Dowling was a pioneering prelate during difficult times. He was born in New York City to an Irish immigrant family and was raised in Newport, Rhode Island, where he attended the Academy of the Sisters of Charity. In 1887 he graduated with honors from Manhattan College in New York City and entered St. John's Seminary in Brighton, Massachusetts. In 1890 he was sent to The Catholic University of America in Washington, D.C., to finish his studies. He was ordained for the Diocese of Providence, on June 24, 1891, and subsequently earned a licentiate in theology from Catholic University. After a brief period in parish work, Father Dowling was named to the faculty of St. John's Seminary. In 1896 he became editor of the *Providence Visitor,* the dioce-

san newspaper, and in 1905 he was named rector of the Cathedral of Sts. Peter and Paul, in Providence.

In 1911 Father Dowling was appointed the first bishop of the newly created Diocese of Des Moines, and was consecrated in Providence on April 25, 1912. As bishop, he concentrated his efforts on establishing the offices and agencies for diocesan administration, especially ensuring proper pastoral care for the faithful and organizing a fully functioning Catholic school system. In 1919 he was promoted to succeed Archbishop John Ireland as the archbishop of St. Paul and Minneapolis. He was installed on March 25, 1919, and received the pallium on May 27. Archbishop Dowling reorganized the archdiocesan charities and encouraged a fund drive for the Archbishop Ireland Educational Fund, using the proceeds to build needed schools and a new diocesan preparatory seminary. He also played a significant role in organizing the National Catholic Welfare Conference, the antecedent of the National Conference of Catholic Bishops. Archbishop Dowling held several positions in that body, including treasurer and chairman of the department of education.

Doyle, Michael F. (July 12, 1877–March 20, 1960)

A diplomat and lawyer, Michael F. Doyle also served as president of the American Electoral College. He was born in Philadelphia, Pennsylvania, and later studied at the University of Pennsylvania. Doyle then earned a law degree and entered the U.S. State Department, where he demonstrated his abilities in a variety of posts, including counsel to the embassies in Switzerland, Belgium, and Ireland. During his period in Ireland, he assisted in the drafting of the constitution for the Irish Free State and was an adviser to Irish revolutionary and political leader Eamon de Valera.

Doyle was subsequently used by the State Department throughout the world on sensitive or challenging diplomatic missions, including counsel to Haiti and Santa Domingo in 1922, head of the American Committee to the League of Nations from 1929 to 1939, and special counsel to the president of the Philippines in 1945. Doyle was president of the American Electoral College from 1937 to 1945. In addition, he played a role in the creation of the National Conference of Catholic Charities and the Catholic Near East Welfare Association. In recognition of his role in promoting the faith, he was named a papal chamberlain by Pope Blessed John XXIII in 1960 and was granted a host of other Catholic honors.

Drexel, St. Katharine Marie

(November 26, 1858–March 3, 1955)

Called "the Million Dollar Nun," St. Katharine Marie Drexel served as the sponsor of untold Native American and black educational programs and missions. She was born in Philadelphia, the second daughter of Francis A. and Hannah Drexel; Hannah died one month later. Francis married Emma M. Bouvier, who was Catholic and raised Katharine and her sister in the faith. St. Katharine made her debut in Philadelphia society in 1879, but was inclined toward the religious life. Her stepmother died that same year, and St. Katharine's father died in 1901. As a result, St. Katharine and her sister each received an inheritance amounting to one thousand dollars a day.

In 1886 St. Katharine became ill and went to Germany to recover at a spa. While there, she recruited priests and nuns for the American Indian missions and recommended the establishment of a Catholic bureau for such endeavors. When she had an audience with Pope Leo XIII, St. Katharine was told to become a missionary. The following year she built schools in the Dakotas, Wyoming, Montana, California, Oregon, and New Mexico.

In 1889 St. Katharine entered the Sisters of Mercy novitiate, receiving her habit on November 7 from Archbishop Patrick John Ryan of Philadelphia. In 1891 she professed her vows as the first member of the Sisters of the Blessed Sacrament for Indians and Colored People. She opened a novitiate at Cornwall Heights near Philadelphia, and by the end of the year there were twenty-one in the congregation. The first mission was St. Catherine's in Santa Fe, New Mexico. Other schools followed, including Xavier University in New Orleans. Pope St. Pius X gave preliminary approval of the con-

St. Katherine Drexel

gregation in 1907. St. Katharine also instituted a fourth vow in the congregation; besides poverty, chastity, and obedience, she vowed "to be the mother and servant of the Indians and Negro races, according to the rule of the Sisters of the Blessed Sacrament, and not to undertake any work which would lead to the neglect or abandonment of Indian and Colored races." She was provided with prudent counsel on such religious matters from a contemporary holy woman, St. Frances Xavier Cabrini.

Elected superior general, St. Katharine continued to expand the scope of her congregation's labors. In 1912, while in New Mexico, she contracted typhoid fever and was forced to spend time recuperating. She recovered and in 1915 founded Xavier University in New Orleans, the first such U.S. Catholic academic institution for blacks. St. Katharine did not stop her many projects or the dispensing of her millions of inherited dollars until 1935, when a heart attack forced her to retire as superior. She went to the convent infirmary to pray and to mature in the contemplative life. She died in Cornwall Heights. Pope Blessed John Paul II beatified St. Katharine on November 20, 1988, and she was canonized on October 1, 2000.

Druillettes, Gabriel (1610–April 8, 1681)

A far-ranging Jesuit missionary, Gabriel Druillettes also served as a Canadian legate. He was born in France, where he entered the Society of Jesus. Ordained to the priesthood, Father Druillettes was assigned to the American missions and arrived in Canada around 1633. He served in New England and around the Great Lakes for four decades. In 1636 Father Druillettes labored among the Abenaki Indians of Maine at the mission on the Kennebec River and stayed in the area until 1652.

He then labored in the Canadian missions and served in an official capacity for the governor of New France. The Canadian governor wanted to arrange a treaty with the Protestants of the New England colonies in order to build a solid defense against continuing assaults by the Iroquois Confederacy and sent Father Druillettes to attend meetings with their leaders. These sessions proved futile, but Father Druillettes, a recognized authority on the American Indians, was treated with kindness and respect. He was a very holy man, and miraculous events were associated with his name in many Native American mission regions.

In 1670 Father Druillettes was in Sault Ste. Marie and other Michigan missions. He had labored as well in Green Bay, Wisconsin, twelve years earlier. Exhausted by his labors, Father Druillettes returned to Québec, where he died.

Drumgoole, John (August 15, 1816–March 28, 1888)

The founder of the largest child-care program in New York, Monsignor John Drumgoole was a popular reformer of U.S. charitable programs. He was born in Longford, Ireland, and migrated to America at the age of eight. He worked in various fields and then studied for the priesthood. He was ordained on May 24, 1869, at the age of fifty-two.

In 1870 Father Drumgoole became the chaplain of St. Vincent's Home for Children, a newly established residence, and he immediately launched plans for the Mission of the Immaculate Virgin, a project approved by Cardinal John McCloskey of New York. Catholics across the United States and the world responded to his appeals, including St. John Bosco, St. Damien de Veuster, and Pope Leo XIII.

The Mission of the Immaculate Virgin, a ten-story building, opened in December 1881. Drumgoole then erected Mount Loretto, a residence on Staten Island that housed six hundred children. He was returning from a visit to Mount Loretto when he was caught in a terrible blizzard, developed pneumonia, and died.

Dubois, John, S.S. (August 24, 1764–December 20, 1842)

The third bishop of the Diocese of New York, from 1826 to 1842, John Dubois, a Sulpician, held firm in a troubled era. Born in Paris, France, he studied at the Collège Louis-le-Grand, and then entered the Oratorian Seminary of Saint-

Magloire. He was ordained in September 1787 and was appointed to pastoral ministries in Saint-Sulpice and served as a chaplain to the Sisters of Charity at the Hospice des Petites Maisons. Owing to the dangers posed by the French Revolution that had begun in 1789 (ironically, a fellow student at the Collège had been Robespierre), Dubois fled France in disguise and made his way to the United States.

He arrived at Norfolk, Virginia, in August 1791 with a letter of introduction from the Marquis de Lafayette to James Monroe and other notables in American political life. Father Dubois was given a warm welcome and was even permitted to celebrate Mass in the Richmond State House. After serving in local parishes for a number of years, he entered the Society of Saint-Sulpice in 1808 and was instrumental in establishing Mount St. Mary's College in Emmitsburg, Maryland. He was also a friend and spiritual adviser to St. Elizabeth Ann Seton from 1809.

Following the death of Bishop John Connolly, the second bishop of the Diocese of New York, on February 6, 1825, Father Dubois was named his successor. Archbishop Ambrose Maréchal consecrated him in Baltimore on October 29, 1826. Bishop Dubois's diocese extended across the entire state of New York and much of New Jersey. To care for some 150,000 Catholics, he was assisted by eighteen priests serving twelve churches. Bishop Dubois traveled to France and Rome in 1829 to petition support from the Society for the Propagation of the Faith and also the Congregation of the Propaganda Fide in Rome. He then tried several times to found a seminary, but his efforts were set back by circumstances.

He faced as well a chronic problem in the pervasive practice of trusteeism. Then, on one occasion, the trustees of the cathedral threatened to withhold his salary, Bishop Dubois replied famously: "I am an old man, and do not need much. I can live in a basement or in a garret. But whether I

John Dubois

come up from the basement or down from the garret, I shall still be your bishop."

In 1837, at the request of Bishop Dubois, Father John Hughes of Philadelphia was appointed titular bishop of Basilinopolis and coadjutor bishop of New York, acceding to the see in 1839. By the time he retired, Bishop Dubois left a diocese with thirty-eight churches, twelve mission stations, and forty priests. Bishop Dubois died in New York, and his remains were placed in the crypt of the old St. Patrick's Cathedral.

Dubourg, Louis-Guillaume-Valentin (February 16, 1766–December 12, 1833)

The second bishop of Louisiana and the Two Floridas, a brief designation for a diocese including the modern-day state of Florida, Louis-Guillaume-Valentin Dubourg served the American Church in a time of political turmoil and then became an archbishop in France. He was born in Cap François, Santa Domingo, and entered the Company of Saint-Sulpice. Educated for the priesthood in Paris, he was ordained in 1788. Because of the French Revolution, Father Dubourg migrated to the United States in 1794 and was welcomed by Bishop John Carroll. Father Dubourg served as president of Georgetown College from 1796 to 1799. He then became the first superior of St. Mary's College in Baltimore.

On August 18, 1812, Dubourg was named the apostolic administrator of the Diocese of Louisiana and the Two Floridas. His appointment was an important one, as it involved Spanish, French, and American interests. Bishop Dubourg overcame the opposition and was consecrated a bishop in Rome on September 24, 1815. Two years later, he was in St. Louis, where he founded the parent institution of St. Louis University. Eventually he moved to New Orleans, but in November 1826 he retired, believing an American could better serve the diocese.

In 1826 he was transferred to the Diocese of Montaubon, France, and in 1833 became the archbishop of Besan-

Bishop Louis Dubourg

çon. He was one of the first patrons of the Society for the Propagation of the Faith. Archbishop Dubourg died in Besançon.

Dubuque, Archdiocese of

Established as a diocese on July 28, 1837, by Pope Gregory XVI, and as an archdiocese on June 15, 1893, by Pope Leo XIII, the Archdiocese of Dubuque serves northern Iowa. Dubuque, founded on the Mississippi River, is a manufacturing center serving an area supporting the agriculture, dairy, and livestock industries. The city was named for Julien Dubuque, who made a treaty with the Fox Indians for lead-mining rights. Lead mining and sawmilling served as the basis for Dubuque's expansion, aided by river and rail transportation. The archdiocese has suffragan sees and a complex Catholic history.

In 1673 the Jesuit missionary explorer Father Jacques Marquette traveled through the area with Louis Joliet, followed by the Recollect Franciscan Father Louis Hennepin. In 1776 a French Canadian involved in mining, Jean Marie Cardinal, settled in the Dubuque area with his Indian wife. They had eight children and traveled all the way to St. Louis to have each one baptized in the faith. Julien Dubuque, another French Canadian, arrived in the region in 1788. He made his treaties with the Fox Indians and negotiated as well with the Spanish authorities of the region, gaining control of the local lead mines at the age of twenty-eight.

Dubuque at the time was under the ecclesiastical jurisdiction of both the French Canadians and the Spanish. In 1803 the Louisiana Purchase ceded the territory to the United States, and the area came under the jurisdiction of the Diocese of Baltimore. In 1826 the Diocese of St. Louis was established, and Iowa came under that episcopal jurisdiction. In the year 1833, Jesuit Father Charles Van Quickenborne met with Dubuque Catholics and petitioned St. Louis to erect a Catholic church to serve the faithful. Father Charles F. Fitzmaurice started the church but died in the following year.

Other priests took up the work, including Venerable Samuel Mazzuchelli, the Dominican missionary. He built St. Raphael's Church (now the cathedral) as well as St. Anthony's in Davenport and St. Paul's in Burlington.

In 1837 the Diocese of Dubuque was erected, originally having jurisdiction from the Mississippi River on the east to the Missouri River, and from Canada to the northern border of Missouri. The first bishop of Dubuque was the energetic Mathias Loras, who was consecrated on December 10, 1837. He set sail to Europe to find priests and funds and returned with six ordained missionaries and financing from the Society for the Propagation of the Faith in Lyon, France, the Leopoldine Society of Vienna, and the Ludwig-Missionsverein of Munich. In 1839 Bishop Loras took a steamboat to Minnesota and returned to Dubuque by canoe, using whatever transportation was available to make the rounds of his diocese. He founded Loras College and saw Clarke College for Women open in 1843. Iowa entered the Union in 1846 as the twenty-ninth state, as Bishop Loras visited the Winnebago settlements and the remnants of other tribes in the process of losing their lands to the whites. He went to Europe again in 1849 and brought back five seminarians for the diocese. Opening national parishes and a cathedral, Bishop Loras asked for a coadjutor bishop because his health was failing. On February 19, 1858, he died, having provided the faithful of the diocese with forty-six priests and fifty churches. There were an estimated 54,000 Catholics in the diocese at the time.

His successor was the Trappist Clement Smith, who had served as coadjutor bishop of Dubuque since 1857. Bishop Smith suffered the loss of many French priests when he was installed, but he brought in Irish missionaries and pastors to provide services and administration. He acceded to the see upon the death of Bishop Loras and maintained diocesan growth throughout an era of turmoil. Bishop Smith died on September 22, 1865.

The third bishop and the first archbishop of Dubuque was John Hennessy, who succeeded

Bishop Mathias Loras

Bishop Smith and was consecrated on September 30, 1866. He raised missions and stations to the status of parishes and served an ever-increasing population. Bishop Hennessy also accommodated the arrival of the Northwestern and Illinois Railroads. When the Diocese of Dubuque was elevated to the rank of a metropolitan provincial see in 1893, he became Archbishop John Hennessy. He also started St. Joseph's College and a theological seminary, as well as 118 parishes throughout the diocese. Archbishop Hennessy died on March 4, 1900.

The second archbishop of Dubuque was John Joseph Keane, who had served as the bishop of Richmond and then as the rector of The Catholic University of America. He was promoted to the rank of titular archbishop on January 29, 1897, and transferred to the Archdiocese of Dubuque on July 24, 1900. He convened diocesan synods and welcomed religious congregations into the archdiocese. Archbishop Keane retired on April 3, 1911.

Archbishop James John Keane was the third archbishop of Dubuque, having served as the bishop of the Diocese of Cheyenne. He was promoted to the archdiocese on August 11, 1911. Archbishop Keane led the faithful through World War I and the Great Depression. He expanded parishes and schools and promoted charitable programs to alleviate the suffering caused by the economic crisis. He retired on August 2, 1929.

Archbishop Francis J. L. Beckman was the fourth archbishop of Dubuque. He had served as the bishop of the Diocese of Lincoln and as the apostolic administrator of Omaha and was promoted to the Archdiocese of Dubuque on January 17, 1930. Archbishop Beckman was designated an Assistant at the Pontifical Throne on April 21, 1928. He established Catholic Charities in the archdiocese and helped to organize the Catholic Students' Mission Crusade. Outspoken on political affairs, Archbishop Beckman expanded facilities in the archdiocese while supporting the military efforts of the nation during World War II. He retired on November 11, 1946.

Archbishop Henry P. Rohlman, who was quite elderly, was the fifth bishop of Dubuque and successor of Archbishop Beckman. He had served as the bishop of Davenport since 1927 and on June 15, 1944, was appointed coadjutor archbishop of Dubuque with right of succession and apostolic administrator. Archbishop Rohlman acceded to the see when Archbishop Beckman retired. He was made an Assistant at the Pontifical Throne on September 2, 1950. Archbishop Rohlman founded a seminary and continued expansion programs for the growing Catholic population. He retired on December 2, 1954.

His successor was Archbishop Leo Binz, who had served as coadjutor bishop and apostolic administrator of the Diocese of Winona. On October 15, 1949, he was appointed coadjutor archbishop of Dubuque with right of succession. On June 11, 1954, he was made an Assistant at the Pontifical Throne. Upon the retirement of Archbishop Beckman, he acceded to the see, and the pallium was given to him on June 12, 1958. On December 16, 1961, Archbishop Binz was transferred to the Archdiocese of St. Paul and Minneapolis.

Archbishop James J. Byrne, who had served as auxiliary bishop of the Archdiocese of St. Paul and Minneapolis and as the bishop of Boise, succeeded Archbishop Binz on March 19, 1962. Archbishop Byrne promoted secondary education facilities, establishing central high schools. He also took part in the Second Vatican Council and implemented the reforms of the council. In July 1979 he welcomed Pope Blessed John Paul II to the archdiocese, where 350,000 attended an outdoor Mass. Archbishop Byrne retired on August 23, 1983.

The eighth bishop of Dubuque was Archbishop Daniel W. Kucera, O.S.B., who had served as auxiliary bishop of Joliet and as bishop of Salina. On December 20, 1983, he was promoted to the Archdiocese of Dubuque and installed on February 23, 1984. He continued to implement the reforms of the Second Vatican Council and to promote lay ministries and educational programs. Archbishop Kucera retired on October 16, 1995.

The ninth archbishop of Dubuque, Jerome Hanus, O.S.B., had served as the bishop of St. Cloud and was promoted as coadjutor archbishop of Dubuque on August 23, 1994. He acceded to the see on October 16, 1995. The archdiocese celebrated the Great Jubilee of 2000 and has grappled with problems of population growth and the challenge of Catholic education. There were various cases of sexual abuse as well, and the diocese reached a number of settlements. In 2011 there were 206,000 Catholics served by 224 priests, 700 women religious, and 175 parishes in the archdiocese.

Dubuyson des Hayes, Charles François, Vicomte (1752–1786)

A French nobleman, Charles François Vicomte Dubuyson des Hayes, became an artillery officer and in 1776 accompanied the Marquis de Lafayette to America to aid the rebel cause. The ragtag American army, composed of volunteers who did not follow discipline, fascinated him, especially when they were successful against the British military units in the field. Dubuyson des Hayes wrote a picturesque account of his journey from Charleston to Philadelphia and his contact with the American fighters.

On October 4, 1777, Dubuyson des Hayes became a major in the Continental Army, assigned as an aide-de-camp to Baron Johann de Kalb. Promoted to the rank of lieutenant colonel, he was wounded in the Battle of Camden, suffering broken arms and a severe chest laceration. He never regained his health and returned to France in 1781. North Carolina, honoring Dubuyson des Hayes's abilities and sacrifices, made him a brigadier general of the state's militia. He died in France.

Duchesne, St. Rose Philippine (August 29, 1769– November 18, 1852)

The founder of the Society of the Sacred Heart in America, St. Rose Philippine Duchesne was revered by Native Americans, who called her "the Woman Who Always Prays." She was born in Grenoble, France, the daughter of a prominent lawyer, and was educated by the Visitation nuns. She entered the convent just as the French Revolution closed the religious houses of her nation. When the revolution ended, St. Rose tried to revive the Visitation Convent and asked St. Madeleine Sophie Barat to assume the house. St. Madeleine declined that offer but welcomed St. Rose into the Society of the Sacred Heart. She took her vows on December 31, 1804.

Fourteen years later, when St. Rose was forty-nine, the Society of the Sacred Heart responded to an invitation by Bishop Louis Dubourg of New Orleans. She was assigned to lead four companions to Louisiana. She did not speak English, but opened the first school in St. Charles, Missouri, and then founded Indian schools, orphanages, and an American novitiate for the congregation. She spent time with the Potawatomi at Sugar Creek Mission but was recalled to St. Louis, Missouri, the following year,

St. Rose Philippine Duchesne

where she died on November 18 1852, at the age of eighty-three. She is honored as a pioneer in the Hall of Fame of the state of Missouri. Pope Blessed John Paul II canonized her on July 3, 1988.

Du Coudray, Philippe-Charles-Jean-Baptiste-Tronson (September 8, 1738–September 11, 1777)

One of the trained military experts who came to America as part of the French force aiding the revolution, Philippe-Charles-Jean-Baptiste-Tronson Du Coudray lost his life in the service of American freedom.

Du Coudray was born at Reims, France, and was educated as a military man with experience as an engineer. He was adjutant general of artillery and revered in France when he volunteered to be part of the French force. Benjamin Franklin offered him a commission as a major general with command of artillery.

He arrived in May 1777, and Du Coudray's rank caused such a stir among other French officers that he was given command of the works along the Delaware and made an inspector general. On September 11, 1777,

Du Coudray was drowned while crossing the Schuylkill River at Philadelphia. His horse had become startled and plunged him to his death. A Requiem Mass was celebrated on September 18, 1777, in St. Mary's Church, and attended by Congress. Du Coudray was buried in St. Mary's churchyard.

Ducrue, Francis Bennon (June 10, 1721–March 30, 1779)

The Jesuit superior of the California missions, Francis Bennon Ducrue was also an author. He was born in Munich, Bavaria, of French parents and entered the Society of Jesus in 1738. Ten years later, he was sent to the California missions. Father Ducrue labored in those missions until 1767, when the Jesuits were expelled. He also aided the royal commission enforcing the expulsion and led his fellow Jesuits out of California. The Society of Jesus had served in the area for seventy years. When they left, they took only their personal possessions. Returning to Munich, Father Ducrue wrote *A Journey from California in the Year 1767*. He also wrote an account of the Jesuit expulsion from Mexico and California. He died in Munich.

Dudzik, Venerable Mary Theresa (August 30, 1860–September 20, 1918)

Foundress of the Franciscan Sisters of Blessed Kunegunda (now the Franciscan Sisters of Chicago), Venerable Mary Theresa Dudzik, born Josephine, was a native of Plocicz, Poland. There she learned to sew as a means of assisting her family, a profession that she continued after she and her family moved to the United States in 1881 and settled in Chicago. Active among the Third Order Franciscans, she also distinguished herself through her care and concern for the poor and suffering in the city, especially during the harsh economic conditions of the late 1880s.

In 1889, after the death of her father, Josephine opened her home to several poor women, and from this beginning she established a community of women who shared her concern for the poor. With the support of her pastor and local Church authorities, she began the Franciscan Sisters of Blessed Kunegunda. She was elected the first superior and took the name Mary Theresa. The new community soon outgrew its modest home, and Mary Theresa was able to find support to purchase a new home in Avondale, Illinois, for a convent, hospice, and shelter. The sisters moved into the new facilities in March 1898. That same year, the community's spiritual director, the pastor of St. Stanislaus parish, removed Mary Theresa as superior. She was reinstalled in 1909. In the community elections of 1910, however, she was not reelected and spent her remaining years in charge of the convent gardens. Her cause for canonization was opened in 1979, and in 1994 she received the title venerable.

Duffy, Francis Patrick (May 2, 1871–June 26, 1932)

One of America's most distinguished military chaplains during World War I, Francis Patrick Duffy was part of the nation's "Fighting 69th." He was born in Cobourg, Ontario, Canada, the third of eleven children. After studies at St. Michael's College in Toronto and St. Francis Xavier College in New York City, he entered St. Joseph's Seminary at Troy, New York, in 1894 and was ordained two years later. He continued studies at The Catholic University of America in Washington, D.C., and was then named an instructor in philosophy at the new archdiocesan seminary at Dunwoodie.

From 1905 to 1908, he served as editor of the *New York Review* and was the author of numerous articles. After parish work in the Bronx, he joined the 69th Regiment of the New York National Guard in 1914 and embarked on military chaplain duties that included service on the Mexican border in 1916–17.

Father Francis P. Duffy

When the United States entered World War I, Father Duffy went to France with the troops of the 69th. There his ministry and courage made him the best-known chaplain of the war. For his achievements, he was honored with numerous decorations, including the Distinguished Service Cross, the Distinguished Service Medal, the *Croix de Guerre*, and the Legion of Honor.

After the war, he served as president of the Catholic Summer School in Cliff Haven, New York, and then as pastor of Holy Cross Church in Manhattan from 1920 to 1932. Duffy was especially useful in 1928 to presidential candidate Governor Alfred E. Smith in answering the scurrilous accusations of Charles Marshall concerning the patriotism of Catholics. A statue was erected in his honor by the city of New York.

du Lhut (Duluth), Daniel Greysolon, Sieur (c. 1640–February 26, 1710)

One of the premier frontiersmen of his age, Daniel Greysolon, Sieur du Lhut, was the person for whom the city of Duluth, Minnesota, was named. He was born in Saint-Germain-en-Laye, France. Drawn to the military life, he served in the French army, becoming a gendarme of the King's Guard by 1664. In 1674 Du Lhut arrived in Montréal, Canada, where his cousins, the Tontys, were settled. By 1678 he was on his way west, accompanied by his brother, La Tourette, and six soldiers. In 1679 he took control of the Sioux territory for France. He also explored Lake Superior and erected a fort at Kaministiquia (Fort William) and a second post on Lake Nepigon.

Du Lhut rescued Father Louis Hennepin from his Indian captors. He was a proven warrior who could deal with the tribes, having earned their respect. In 1686 Du Lhut founded the post of Detroit and ten years later commanded Fort Frontenac. He died in Montréal after three decades of French control of the area west of the Great Lakes. Various plans and accounts written by this intrepid pioneer have survived.

Dulles, Avery (August 28, 1918–December 12, 2008)

A Jesuit priest, theologian, and cardinal, Avery Dulles is considered the foremost theologian in the United States in the second half of the twentieth century. Born in Auburn, New York, he was the son of John Foster Dulles, United States secretary of state from 1953 to 1959, and Janet Avery. Raised a Protestant, he studied classical and modern philosophers at Harvard University, and while in Boston underwent a profound conversion. In 1940 he graduated from Harvard and was baptized into the Church. In the following year, he entered Harvard

Law School and then spent the years of World War II as an officer in the U.S. Navy, serving from 1942 to 1946. While in the service, he received the *Croix de Guerre.*

After leaving the Navy, he entered the Society of Jesus on August 14, 1946. He subsequently earned a licentiate in philosophy at Woodstock College in 1951 and taught for two years at Fordham University. He then returned to Woodstock to study theology; his professors included famed theologians Gustave Weigel and John Courtney Murray. Ordained on June 16, 1956, he continued studies and earned a licentiate in theology in 1957. He then went to Munich and Rome, earning a doctorate in sacred theology from the Pontifical Gregorian University. His dissertation was entitled "Vestigia Ecclesiae: Outside the True Church." He returned to the United States and resumed teaching at Woodstock.

After the Jesuits closed Woodstock in 1974, Father Dulles was offered and accepted a professorship in systematic theology at The Catholic University of America. He remained on the faculty until 1988, when he reached retirement age. The same year he began at Catholic University, he published his immensely influential *Models of the Church,* a study of ecclesiology from the perspective of several different models. The text remains one of the most widely read in modern ecclesiological studies. In 1983 Father Dulles published *Models of Revelation,* following the basic methodology of *Models of the Church,* to examine divine revelation.

Upon retiring from Catholic University, Father Dulles was named the Laurence J. McGinley Professor of Religion and Society at Fordham University. He continued to write on theology, including *The Craft of Theology* in 1992, *The Assurance of Things Hoped For* in 1994, and *A Testimonial to Grace* in 1996. In all, he wrote over 20 books and 650 articles. He also served as president of both the Catholic Theological Society of America from 1975 to 1976 and the American Theological Society from 1978 to 1979, and was a consultant to the Papal Secretariat for Dialogue with Non-Believers from 1966 to 1973, the International Theological Commission, and the U.S. Lutheran/Roman Catholic Dialogue.

In recognition of his immense contributions to the Church, Pope Blessed John Paul II created Father Dulles a cardinal deacon on February 21, 2001. His titular church was the Most Holy Names of Jesus and Mary in Via Lata.

Duluth, Diocese of

Established on October 3, 1889, by Pope Leo XIII, the Diocese of Duluth serves counties in northeastern Minnesota. Duluth is a large port city located on Lake Superior and is an industrial center with iron and steel processing mills, manufacturing, tourism, and a military air-defense installation. The city was laid out in 1856 and incorporated in 1870. Duluth was named after Daniel Greysolon, Sieur du Lhut, a famous French voyageur who was respected by the local Native American tribes. The Diocese of Duluth is a suffragan see of the Archdiocese of St. Paul and Minneapolis. The Catholic history of the diocesan area dates to the earliest mission periods and involves some of America's finest missionaries.

In 1655 Dakota Indian settlements were visited by Catholic priests, and in 1680, the Recollect Franciscan Father Louis Hennepin was in the region, discovering and naming the Falls of St. Anthony in the Minneapolis area. Taken prisoner by local Sioux, Father Hennepin was rescued by Sieur du Lhut, who had settled tribal disputes in the region. In 1721 Jesuit Father Michael Guignas celebrated Mass at Fort Beauharnais, a French outpost, and six years later French Jesuits founded St. Michael the Archangel near Frontenac. Father Irenaeus Frederick Baraga, who would become a pioneering bishop, and other missionaries were in the area, but no recorded missions were opened until 1838, when Bishop Mathias Loras of Dubuque served at Fort Snelling.

In 1839 Father Lucien Galtier, another revered missionary, was at St. Paul, which became a diocese in 1850, with jurisdiction over all of Minnesota. In 1864 Monsignor Joseph Francis Buh built a concrete mission at Belle Prairie, with four other outposts established as well. Northern Minnesota, receiving so many Catholic immigrants, was made a vicariate apostolic in 1875. In 1889 the Holy See erected two new dioceses in Minnesota, St. Cloud and Duluth.

The first bishop of Duluth was James McGolrick,

who was consecrated on December 27, 1889. He designated the first church established in Duluth by Father John Chebul as the cathedral, but it was destroyed by fire in 1892 and had to be rebuilt. Bishop McGolrick also founded parishes, hospitals, and care programs for children and the infirm. In 1912 the College of St. Scholastica was opened. Bishop McGolrick died on January 23, 1918.

His successor was Bishop John T. McNicholas, O.P., who was consecrated on September 8, 1918. He labored to build schools and parishes and established Carmel Heights, a home for girls. He also supported the military efforts of the nation in World War I. On July 8, 1925, Bishop McNicholas was promoted to the Archdiocese of Cincinnati.

The third bishop of Duluth was Thomas A. Welch, who was consecrated on February 2, 1926. He led the diocese through the grim days of the Great Depression and World War II. In 1957 he also dedicated the Cathedral of Our Lady of the Rosary and expanded diocesan programs to meet the growing needs of the faithful. Bishop Welch died on September 9, 1959.

His successor was Bishop Francis J. Schenk, who was appointed to Duluth on January 19, 1960. Bishop Schenk had served as the bishop of Crookston since 1945. He attended the Second Vatican Council and implemented in the diocese the reforms mandated by that council. Bishop Schenk retired on April 30, 1969.

The fifth bishop of Duluth was Paul F. Anderson, who had been appointed coadjutor bishop with right of succession on October 17, 1968. He acceded to the see upon the retirement of Bishop Schenk. Bishop Anderson continued implementing the reforms of the Second Vatican Council and promoting apostolates. He resigned on August 7, 1982 and was appointed auxiliary bishop of Sioux Falls on March 25, 1983.

His successor was Bishop Robert H. Brom, who was consecrated on May 23, 1983. Bishop Brom continued the programs of his predecessors, but he served only six years in the diocese. On May 9, 1989, he was appointed coadjutor bishop of the Diocese of San Diego.

The seventh bishop of Duluth was Roger Schwietz, O.M.I., who was consecrated on February 2, 1990. He promoted lay ministries and evangeliza-tion programs until January 18, 2000, when he was promoted to the Archdiocese of Anchorage as coadjutor archbishop.

The eighth bishop of the Diocese of Duluth, Dennis M. Schnurr, was appointed on January 18, 2000. He was consecrated on April 2, 2001. Bishop Schnurr was appointed coadjutor archbishop of Cincinnati on October 17, 2008. He was succeeded by Father Paul D. Serba, a priest of the Archdiocese of St. Paul and Minneapolis, on October 15, 2009. Bishop Serba was ordained a bishop on December 14, 2009. In 2011 there were 206,000 Catholics served by 224 priests, 700 women religious, and 175 parishes in the diocese.

Duran, Narcisco (December 16, 1776–June 1, 1846)

One of the most revered Franciscan missionaries of California, Narcisco Duran saved churches and missions during eras of turmoil. He was born in Castellon de Ampurian, Catalonia, Spain. Entering the Franciscans in 1792, he volunteered for the Indian missions and became a "Fernandino," a member of the Franciscan Missionary College of San Fernando, Mexico City, Mexico. In 1806 he arrived in California, laboring in the area until 1833, when he retired to Mission Santa Barbara.

Throughout his priestly career he held many offices, and when the missions were secularized by Mexico he saved various churches from looters and vandals. The Mexican government did not expel Father Duran, allowing him to remain at Santa Barbara. He had been appointed vicar general and administrator of California just before the move by Mexico to secularize the missions. He died at Mission Santa Barbara and was buried under the sanctuary of the church.

Durante, Jimmy (February 10, 1893–January 29, 1980)

One of America's most popular comedians, Jimmy Durante was also a composer, actor, singer, and songwriter. Born and raised in New York City, Durante began his career as a Coney Island pianist and organized a five-piece band in 1916. He then opened the Club Durante with Eddie Jackson and Lou Clayton and worked with both in vaudeville and television. Having established himself in the public eye, he appeared in a number of Broadway musicals. He starred on the stage at the Palladium in London in 1936 and subsequently enjoyed popularity in radio, film, and television productions. He was also respected as a composer.

Durante's first wife, Jeanne, died in 1943, and he married Marjorie Little after a sixteen-year courtship. His famous sign-off on radio, "Goodnight, Mrs. Calabash, wherever you are," became his trademark.

Durbin, Elisha John (February 1, 1800–1887)

Called the "Apostle of Western Kentucky" and the "Patriarch-Priest of Kentucky," Elisha John Durbin defended the faith in a troubled era. He was born in Madison County, Kentucky, the son of a pioneer family. In 1816 Durbin entered St. Thomas Seminary and then St. Joseph's in Bardstown. He was ordained on September 21, 1822. Four years later, Father Durbin began his labors, serving the western and southwestern areas of Kentucky, a region of over 11,000 square miles. He had his base of operations in Union County, and for more than six decades traveled endlessly to establish parishes, stations, and congregations. He also defended Catholicism in the press, responding eloquently to attacks by Protestants.

In 1884, exhausted and elderly, Father Durbin was assigned to a small mission in Princeton, Kentucky. A year later, he suffered a stroke and became chaplain at Shelbyville, Kentucky, where he died.

Durkin, Martin P. *See* Cabinets, Catholics in Presidential

Dutton, Joseph Ira (April 27, 1843–March 26, 1931)

A companion of St. Damien de Veuster at Kalaupapa, Molokai, in the Hawaiian Islands, Joseph Ira Dutton was a pen pal of kings and presidents. He was born in Stowe, Vermont, but his family moved to Janesville, Wisconsin, and there he was educated at home because of a series of illnesses. He did attend high school and upon graduation entered the Union Army in the Quartermaster Corps, serving during the Civil War with distinction. His wife died while he was in the service, and when he was discharged he worked with the government in

establishing national cemeteries. He also became a heavy drinker but at age forty vowed never to touch liquor again. Dutton became interested in the Catholic faith as a result of studies and converted, taking the name Joseph when he was baptized.

He tried the Trappist vocation soon after his conversion, spending almost two years at Gethsemane Abbey in Kentucky, but realized he was being called to another apostolate. Leaving the monastery, he went to New Orleans, where he learned about the work of St. Damien de Veuster on Molokai.

After giving away everything he owned and sailing to Hawaii, Dutton arrived on Molokai in July 1886. St. Damien greeted him warmly, calling him "Brother Joseph." Dutton aided St. Damien in building homes for leper children and was named manager of the residence for boys.

He remained on Molokai for forty-four years, and he became well known internationally, corresponding with presidents and kings. President Theodore Roosevelt, wanting to give Dutton a special treat, redirected the Great White Fleet on its way to Japan to provide a spectacular sight for the islanders. Dutton had written the president, explaining that he wished that the lepers could see the splendors of that great armada. On July 16, 1908, the entire fleet, composed of four destroyers and sixteen battleships, sailed into the Molokai Strait, passing Dutton and the patients of the settlement in review.

Ira Joseph Dutton became ill in 1903 and was

Joseph Ira Dutton

moved to Honolulu, where he died. A government ship transferred his remains to Molokai, where he was buried beside the original grave of St. Damien.

D'Youville, Marie Marguerite, St. (October 15, 1701–December 23, 1771)

The founder of the Sisters of Charity (the Grey Nuns), Marie Marguerite d'Youville was the first Canadian to be proclaimed a saint. Pope Blessed John XXIII called her the "Mother of Universal Charity."

Born Marie Marguerite Dufrost de Lajemmerais in Montréal, she was the daughter of Christopher and Renée de Varennes Dufrost de Lajemmerais. Her brother was Pierre Gaultier de Varennes, Sieur de La Vérendrye, the famed explorer who discovered the Rocky Mountains. St. Marguerite was educated by the Ursuline Nuns in Québec, but at the age of twelve she returned home to assist her widowed mother. In 1722 she married François d'Youville and bore him six children, four of whom died young. François was engaged in the illegal liquor trade and was a wastrel. He treated Marie Marguerite rather indifferently, but when he fell ill, she cared for him for two years until he died in 1730. St. Marguerite was forced by circumstances to take up a small trade in order to support her children and pay off her dead husband's debts. At the same time, however, she devoted her meager resources to caring for the poor.

While working and raising her remaining sons, both of whom became priests, St. Marguerite supported the Confraternity of the Holy Family in Québec. She was also able to save a local hospital, originally founded in 1694. She took over as administrator of the hospital and gathered companions to form a new congregation designed to offer the people of Québec medical care united with Christian charity. The women lived in a small house and in June 1753 received permission to incorporate their activities. The rule of these Sisters of Charity was subsequently approved, and on August 25, 1755, St. Marguerite and her companions received a gray habit; they were henceforth called the Gray Nuns.

In 1747 St. Marguerite was given charge of the General Hospital in Montréal. Under her leadership the hospital cared for disabled soldiers, epileptics, the aged, the insane, the incurables, and lepers, providing as well a haven for orphans and abandoned children. Hôtel Dieu, as it was called, became renowned as a center for care and charity. The sisters made clothing for military troops in order to maintain themselves and their patients. During the French and Indian War, as the Seven Years' War was called in North America, St. Marguerite cared for English prisoners captured by French forces. She also defended the institution against various government officials who sought to limit her charity. When the hospital was destroyed by fire in 1766, St. Marguerite knelt in the ashes to sing the *Te Deum*, accepting the terrible loss with religious calm. She died in Montréal.

Declared venerable in 1890 by Pope Leo XIII, she was beatified in 1959 by Pope Blessed John XXIII and canonized by Pope Blessed John Paul II on December 9, 1990. Her feast day is December 23.

E

Eastern Catholic Churches

The term Eastern Catholic Churches is used for those Christian Churches whose members follow the Eastern rite and are in communion with Rome. The Eastern Catholic Churches, like their Orthodox counterparts, trace their origins to the four great patriarchates in the East: Alexandria, Antioch, Jerusalem, and Constantinople. The fifth, and supreme, patriarchate was, of course, Rome, in the West. These so-called Mother Churches were the bases of the various rites to which the Eastern Christians belong: the Alexandrian, Antiochene, Armenian, Byzantine, and Chaldean. They differ from each other in their liturgies, traditions, histories, theology, hierarchy, and language. Eastern Catholic Churches are distinguished from the Orthodox Churches by their acceptance of the Supreme Pontiff; most, at one time, were not in communion with Rome.

The jurisdictions of these Churches are as follows: Antiochene — Syrian, Malankar, and Maronite; Armenian; Chaldean — Chaldean and Malabar (or Syro-Malabar); and Byzantine — Albanian, Belorussian, Bulgarian, Croatian, Greek, Hungarian, Italo-Albanian, Melkite, Romanian, Russian, Carpatho-Russian (or Ruthenian), Slovak, and Ukrainian.

Also called the Galician-Ruthenian, the Ukrainian Catholic Church has recently experienced an explosion in membership in the Ukraine owing to the establishment of freedom of worship, the high degree of respect Ukrainian Catholic clergy earned during the long years of Soviet oppression, and the widespread disaffection with the Orthodox Church because of its ties to the discredited communist regime.

As in other parts of Eastern Europe, the newfound freedoms enjoyed by the Catholic Church have created friction with the Orthodox communities over such matters as property, jurisdiction, and the right to proselytize. These are part of ongoing negotiations between the Holy See and the Orthodox hierarchy.

The Second Vatican Council made special mention of the rich and important heritage and contributions of the Eastern Catholics, proclaiming their vital role in the life of the entire Church in the Decree on Eastern Catholic Churches, *Orientalium Ecclesiarum*. The decree stated, among other things:

"The Catholic Church holds in high esteem the institutions of the Eastern Churches, their liturgical rites, ecclesiastical traditions, and Christian way of life. For, distinguished as they are by their venerable antiquity, they are bright with that tradition which was handed down from the Apostles through the Fathers, and which forms part of the divinely revealed and undivided heritage of the universal Church [No. 1]. . . . Such individual Churches, whether of the East or of the West, although they differ somewhat among themselves in what are called rites (that is, in liturgy, ecclesiastical discipline, and spiritual heritage) are, nevertheless, equally entrusted to the pastoral guidance of the Roman Pontiff, the divinely appointed successor of St. Peter in supreme government over the universal Church. They are consequently of equal dignity, so that none of them is superior to the others by reason of rite [No. 3]."

The Eastern Catholic Churches are all found in the United States and are respected members of the Catholic Church in the country. Currently, Eastern Catholics number over 550,000, with approximately 680 priests, 300 women religious, 35 men religious, and 567 parishes. There are seventeen ecclesiastical jurisdictions of Eastern Catholics in the United States, including the Ukrainian metropolitan see of Philadelphia, the Ruthenian metropolitan see of Pittsburgh, thirteen eparchies, and the Armenian apostolic exarchate for Canada and the United States; other Eastern Catholics are under the jurisdiction of local Latin bishops.

The following are the principal Eastern Catholic communities represented in the United States, with their histories.

Armenians

The liturgical tradition of the Armenian Apostolic and Catholic Churches, the Armenian rite contains elements of the Syriac, Jerusalem, and

Byzantine rites. From the fifth to the seventh centuries there was strong influence from Syria and Jerusalem. More Byzantine usages were adopted later, and in the Middle Ages elements of the Latin tradition were added. The rite is found any place where Armenian faithful fled or were exiled. There are currently jurisdictions in Iraq, Egypt, Syria, Romania, Lebanon, Argentina, Mexico, France, Greece, and the United States.

The primary impetus for the immigration of Armenian Catholics to the United States was the severe massacres perpetrated by the Ottoman Turks in 1894 and 1896 and the horrendous treatment of the Armenians under Ottoman rule. To provide pastoral care for the Armenians who were settling in America, the Armenian Catholic patriarch of Cilicia, Stephen X, in 1898 granted permission for Armenian priests to serve in the Archdioceses of Boston and New York. The first Armenian priest to arrive in the United States was Father Madiros Mighirian, who reached New York in 1899 and served in New York City, Boston, and Worcester, Massachusetts.

In 1906 Father Manuel Basieganian began ministry among the Armenians in New Jersey and Pennsylvania. Over the next years, several more priests expanded service to Armenians in Cleveland, Ohio, Boston, and elsewhere in Massachusetts. By 1960, however, there were still only six priests providing ministry to over three thousand Armenians. On July 3, 1981, an apostolic exarchate for Canada and the United States was established to provide better pastoral care. The twenty-five thousand Armenian Catholics are served currently by eleven priests and eleven women religious.

Chaldeans

Also called Chaldaean rite, the broad term Chaldeans designates those Catholics who are members of the Chaldean rite as listed by the Congregation for the Oriental Churches. The Chaldeans are descendants of the ancient Nestorian Churches. These communities, long separated from Rome and existing in Turkey and Persia, were first contacted by missionaries and representatives of the Roman Church in the 1200s. The process of reunification soon began, culminating in 1692 with the return of the Chaldeans into communion with Rome

under Pope Innocent XII. The rite is derived from the Antiochene rite and is divided into two main groups, the Chaldean and the Syro-Malabar. The Chaldean rite is found in Turkey, Syria, Lebanon, Egypt, Iraq, Iran, and the United States. They are under the patriarch of Babylon of the Chaldeans, with nineteen archdioceses and dioceses, and use Syriac and Arabic for the liturgical languages.

The first Chaldean Catholic priest to arrive in the United States was Father Abdul Messih Andraos from Turkey in 1905, to provide pastoral care to Chaldean immigrants in the area around Yonkers, New York. He was followed by Father Joseph Ghariba from Syria, and Father Gabriel Oussani in 1910, who took up the post of professor of Church history, patristics, and Oriental languages at St. Joseph's Seminary in 1910.

The population of Chaldean Catholics, always comparatively small, grew significantly in the first decades of the twentieth century owing to the severe and brutal persecutions and massacres perpetrated during World War I by the Ottoman Turks and then also by the Kurds and Arabs in the aftermath of the war. The number of Chaldean immigrants was such by 1935 that the Chaldean patriarch Joseph Emanuel Thomas named Father Francis Thomay to serve the Chaldeans in the Chicago area. Father Thomay arrived that year, and by 1944 requested a separate church for the use of Chaldean Catholics. That church, St. Ephrem's, was the first Chaldean church in the Western hemisphere. Four years later, a Chaldean church was built in Detroit, followed by churches in Turlock, California, and elsewhere.

Today, there are about 115,000 Chaldean Catholics in two eparchies, served by twenty-four priests. The eparchies are St. Thomas the Apostle of Detroit (established as an exarchate in 1982 and an eparchy in 1986) and the Eparchy of St. Peter the Apostle of San Diego (established on May 21, 2002). Chaldean Catholics live throughout the country, but especially in Detroit, San Diego, Los Angeles, Chicago, Turlock, San Jose, and Arizona.

Copts

The small Coptic Catholic presence in the United States is centered in a Catholic chapel in Brooklyn, New York, and St. Mary's Coptic Catholic parish in Los Angeles, California.

Maronites

The Maronite rite is found in Lebanon, Syria, Egypt, Cyprus, the United States, Brazil, and parts of the British Commonwealth. According to Maronite historians, the Maronites date to the time of St. Maron, from whom the Church derives its name. St. Maron's followers founded a monastery on the Orontes River in Syria. Other historians, however, argue that the Maronites date to the seventh century when the monks of St. Maron's monastery adopted a fiercely independent stand in the face of the Monophysite heresy then afflicting much of the Eastern Church. The Monophysite response was reportedly severe, as over three hundred monks were massacred for remaining loyal to the decrees of the Council of Chalcedon of 451. During this period they were in contact with the Holy See.

The date customarily given for the birth of the Maronite Church is 681, the year the Council of Constantinople was held. As loyal supporters of the Byzantine emperors, the Maronites possibly adopted the heretical tenets of Monothelitism under the influence of Emperor Heraclius. In 681, however, the council condemned the heresy. The Maronites contend that they renounced Monothelitism and remained orthodox; other scholars differ on this, citing, among various sources, St. John Damascene, who called them heretics. Regardless of the specific circumstances that led up to it, by 685 the monks and bishops of the area elected their own patriarch, although the first known patriarch is said to date to 1121. Around this time, they moved from Syria to the mountainous territories of Lebanon, where they existed as an independent church under their patriarch.

The twelfth century brought to the Levant the Crusader armies and with them came representatives of the Western Church from which the Maronites had essentially been cut off for centuries. After the crusaders established good relations with them, they made the decision in 1182 to enter virtually en masse (some forty thousand) into communion with Rome. They have remained so ever since, especially from the time of the Lateran Council in 1215, during which the patriarch Jeremias al Amshiti visited Pope Innocent III and received the pallium. Pope Gregory XIII bestowed the pallium upon Patriarch Michael and in 1584 founded the Maronite College in Rome, where many distinguished scholars studied, including the Assemani, a family of noted Maronite Orientalists (Joseph Simonius, Stephen Evodius, Joseph Aloysius, and Simon) of the eighteenth and nineteenth centuries.

Owing to persecution in Lebanon and Syria by the Ottoman Turks, many thousands of Maronites were forced to flee their homeland. Many arrived in the United States as refugees, starting in 1876. Sadly, they were entirely without a priest for three years until some pastoral care was provided briefly through the arrival of Father Joseph Mokarzel and Very Reverend Louis Kazen. In 1890 Father Butrosz Korkemas was assigned on a more permanent basis. He opened a small chapel in a store in New York City, after overcoming considerable opposition and misunderstanding. His nephew, Joseph Yasbek, however, was ordained by Archbishop Michael A. Corrigan and founded the Maronite Mission in Boston. Father Yasbek went on to serve as chorespiscopus (a bishop) and the head of the Maronite community in the United States.

From this beginning, Maronite churches were established in New York, Philadelphia, Brooklyn, and elsewhere. By 1965 there were 44 Maronite churches in the country serving over 40,000 Maronites. Today, there are some 73,000 Maronites in two jurisdictions in the United States: the Eparchy of St. Maron, Brooklyn (established at Detroit as an exarchate in 1966 and an eparchy in 1972, and transferred to Brooklyn in 1977) and the Eparchy of Our Lady of Lebanon of Los Angeles (resident in St. Louis and established on March 1, 1994). Maronites are served by over 110 priests.

Melkites

Also called Melchite rite, the name Melkite is given to those Christians who adhere to the Byzantine rite but are in communion with Rome. The Melkites originated in the fifth century among the Christians of Syria and Egypt who refused to accept Monophysitism, embracing instead the decrees of the Council of Chalcedon of 451, which condemned the heresy. They were subsequently called Melkites by the Monophysites, a term from the Syriac meaning "emperor's men"; used at first for Orthodox Egyptian Christians, the name spread to all adherents of Chalcedon before becoming synonymous with the members of a particular sect. As they were united with the patriarch of Constantinople, the Melkites joined in the schism between the Eastern and Western Churches that began in 1054. Many Melkites came to promote reunion with Rome, however, and over time a separate hierarchy was developed. Finally, in 1724, a formal union was made with Rome under Cyril VI, patriarch of Antioch. Another patriarch was elected for the Orthodox Melkites. The Melkites are headed by the patriarch of Antioch, with patriarchal vicariates in Egypt, Jerusalem, Sudan, Iraq, and Kuwait. They are also in Europe, Asia, America, and Australia. The liturgy is in Arabic with readings in Greek.

Melkite Catholics began arriving in the United States in large numbers from throughout the Middle East, in particular the lands under the control of the Ottoman Turks. Many Melkite young men sought to escape the requirement of paying a bounty or tax to avoid military service in the Turkish army. The redemption from service was essential for Christians as only Muslims were permitted into the Turkish forces. To avoid severe penalties, Christians had to pay a fee. Rather than face that severe financial burden, Melkites left the Ottoman Empire for other countries.

The first Melkites arrived in New York and soon spread across Eastern and Midwestern regions of the country, including New York City, Massachusetts, Ohio, Michigan, and Wisconsin. They settled in the country and found virtually no pastoral care. To assist them, Patriarch Gregory II Yusof dispatched several priests. Of particular note was the Archimandrite Abraham Bechewaty who in 1890 began to say Mass in the basement church of St. Peter's in downtown New York City. From this beginning, the Melkites were able to secure a church and rectory over the next years. Other significant priests were Father Nicholas Cannam, who arrived in Boston in 1910, and Father Nicholas Araktingi, who went to Brooklyn in 1909.

The Melkite population was difficult to estimate for parts of the twentieth century owing to its dispersion across the country. There were approximately 25,000 Melkites in the United States around 1960. Currently there are over 29,000 under the jurisdiction of the Melkite Eparchy of Newton,

Massachusetts (established as an exarchate in 1965 and an eparchy in 1976), assisted by 62 priests.

Romanians

The Romanian Greek Catholic Church traces its modern history to around 1700, when the Romanian Orthodox in Transylvania formally entered into union with Rome. During the long period of the Ottoman Empire, some progress was made in organizing a reunion of many Romanian Christians with the Catholic Church, thanks in large measure to the missionary efforts of the Jesuits. In 1697 the Orthodox metropolitan of Alba Julia, in Translyvania, Theophilus Szeremy, summoned a synod to effect formal reunion; he died that same year, but his successor, Athanasius Anghel, accepted the reunion soon after. By 1700 there were two hundred thousand Catholic Romanians, although they were severely persecuted by both the Orthodox Church and Calvinists.

The Catholic population increased throughout the early part of the twentieth century, in particular between the two World Wars. Progress ended abruptly in 1947 with the communist takeover and the expulsion of the ruling family. On December 1, 1948, the Romanian Catholic Church was suppressed; all churches and properties were confiscated and handed to the Orthodox Church. Catholic religious were arrested and imprisoned, and many Catholic laypeople, one of the largest groups of Eastern Catholics, were ruthlessly oppressed. Conditions only worsened with the denunciation of the concordat that had been signed in 1929 and the promulgation of a Soviet-influenced constitution. Five of the six Latin-rite bishops were dispersed by the government, and the last was sentenced to eighteen years' imprisonment in 1951. Religious orders had been suppressed entirely in 1949.

Some reforms were introduced in the summer of 1964, with greater freedoms offered to Catholics. Many severe restrictions remained in effect, a situation that continued until the final collapse of the communist regime in 1990. The Eastern Catholic Church at last regained freedom, and the hierarchy was restored following the reestablishment of diplomatic relations with the Holy See.

Romanian Catholics began settling in the

United States in 1900, most from the region of Transylvania. A large number of Romanians reached Cleveland, and Bishop Ignatius Horstmann (bishop from 1892 to 1908) requested that the Holy Father send priests to provide pastoral care to the Romanians. In 1904 the first priest, Father Epaminondas Lucaciu, arrived, and two years later the Church of St. Helena in Cleveland was dedicated, the first church for Romanian Catholics in the United States. Various other churches were opened in succeeding years, but by 1910 there were still only six Romanian priests for the entire United States.

Today, there are five thousand Romanian Catholics in fifteen Romanian Catholic Byzantine-rite parishes in the United States, under the jurisdiction of the Romanian Eparchy of St. George Martyr in Canton, Ohio (established as an exarchate in 1982 and as an eparchy in 1987), assisted by eighteen priests.

Russians

The population of Russian Catholics in the United States has always been comparatively small. The first major event involving ministry to them was in 1935 when Archbishop John J. Cantwell of Los Angeles asked Father Michael Nedtochin to open a Russian Catholic mission in the city. On the other coast, Russian Catholics were served first by Father Andrew Rogosh, who used a chapel in old St. Patrick's Cathedral to offer Mass to Russians in New York City. Today there are parishes in New York City (St. Michael's) and in El Segundo in the Los Angeles area (St. Andrew's). They are under the jurisdiction of local Latin bishops.

Ruthenians

The Ruthenian Catholic Church is the name given from the sixteenth century for those Slavic Catholics who live under the Byzantine rite in parts of Russia, Poland, Hungary, and the regions around the Carpathian Mountains. Because of the geographic orientation around the Carpathian Mountains, the Ruthenians have been termed Carpatho-Russians and Carpatho-Ukrainians, as well as Greek Catholics. The Ruthenian Catholic Church began in 1646. When various Hungarian nobles who ruled over the Carpathian territories became Calvinists, sixty-three Orthodox priests chose to join the Catholic Church at the Union of Uzhhorod in order to protect their flock from the dangers of the Protestant heresies.

In 1651, when their Orthodox bishop died, the priests gathered and elected a Catholic Basilian priest as his successor, Father P. Petrovich. Consecrated by an Orthodox bishop of Transylvania, he was granted recognition nevertheless by Pope Alexander VII, who embraced as well the reunion of the diocese with Rome.

The Ruthenians suffered severely under Soviet oppression from 1945 and the annexation of Carpatho-Russia by the Soviet Union. Systematically, the communists exterminated the institutional structures of the Catholic Church in the region. Bishops, priests, men and women religious, and laypeople were thrown into prison for resisting. In 1950 a tiny group of five priests (out of 357 diocesan priests) declared the Eparchy of Presov to be no longer in communion with Rome; its bishop, Paul Gojdic, died in prison in 1960.

The first Carpatho-Russian immigrants to the United States were part of the migrations from Eastern Europe, in particular from around 1876, and from the Austro-Hungarian Empire. The immigrants settled chiefly in northeastern Pennsylvania and worked arduous and dangerous jobs as miners in the anthracite coal mines. From the start, the Ruthenian Catholics worked to organize their own churches and soon asked for priests to be sent from Europe to provide for their spiritual needs.

The first priest to serve the Greek Catholics was Father John Volansky, a Greek Catholic priest from Galicia who arrived in 1884. That same year he established the first Greek Catholic parish in the United States in Shenandoah, Pennsylvania. From this beginning, several other churches were founded, in Freeland, Pennsylvania (1886), Hazleton, Pennsylvania (1887), Kingston, Pennsylvania (1888), Wilkes-Barre, Pennsylvania (1888), Olyphant, Pennsylvania (1888), Jersey City, New Jersey (1889), Minneapolis, Minnesota (1889), Whiting, Indiana (1889), and Passaic, New Jersey (1890). Additional clergy reached the United States over the next years, so that by 1894 there were thirty Greek Catholic parishes serving more than one hundred thousand Greek Catholics.

As more and more immigrants arrived in the

country, Carpatho-Russian Catholics settled in other parts of coal country and around the steel mills in western Pennsylvania and eastern Ohio. Additional parishes were started to meet their needs, but the pastoral situation was complicated by the tensions that developed between the Eastern Catholics in such large numbers and the Latin Catholics who had difficulty understanding that these seemingly strange and different Christians — with their own rites, language, and traditions — could be just as faithful to the Catholic Church. Moreover, there was a sense in some ecclesiastical circles that these "ethnic" churches were creating problems for the assimilation of Catholics into mainstream American society. As a result, Ruthenians (and other Eastern Catholics) faced intolerance and ignorance for long years. Some bishops refused to provide assistance to priests of the Greek Catholic community because of the lack of celibacy as a possible source of scandal. Equally, priests were refused permission to conduct Greek Catholic services in Latin churches. The bishops discussed the issue of the Eastern Catholics at their annual meetings, but they also asked Rome to send only celibate priests, who were to be placed under the jurisdiction of the local Latin bishop before serving Greek Catholics.

For their part, Ruthenians resented the treatment and were, not surprisingly, combative. They resisted being placed under Latin jurisdiction, and some Greek Catholic parishes placed their properties under the heading of nonprofit corporations, meaning that they were under the control of a lay board of trustees instead of the local bishop, a reemergence of the earlier danger of trusteeism.

Finally, on October 1, 1890, the Holy See issued a decree regarding the status of Greek Catholics in the United States. The decree stipulated that the newly arrived Greek Catholic priests should be required to obtain jurisdiction from the local Latin bishop and should be under his authority. Further, the decree required that all Greek Catholic priests should be celibate and that married priests should be recalled to Europe.

The decree did nothing to solve the crisis, for the Greek Catholic clergy protested the decision and many Greek Catholics left to join the Orthodox jurisdictions. In 1891 Greek Catholic clergy protested the decree and petitioned the Holy See to name a vicar general to administer the affairs of the Ruthenians in the United States. The following year, dissatisfied with progress in the petition, the clergy elected Father Nicephor Chanat as their vicar general. His principal task was to improve relations with the American bishops. Sadly, Father Chanat resigned in 1896 owing to a lack of progress.

Finally, on March 4, 1907, the Holy See appointed Father Stephen Soter Ortynsky, a Basilian monk from Galicia, as the bishop for the Greek Catholic Church in the United States. Ortynsky's appointment, unfortunately, did not immediately end the internal problems with the Greek Catholic community, for he tended to favor the Ukrainian Catholics and so alienated Ruthenians. Equally, Ortynsky wielded only limited authority and was hard-pressed to enforce discipline. On May 13, 1913, Rome established an apostolic exarchate "for all the clergy and the people of the Ruthenian rite in the United States of America" and granted full episcopal jurisdiction to Bishop Ortynsky. The final settlement of the internal issues proved short in duration, for Bishop Ortynsky died suddenly of pneumonia on March 24, 1916, and with his passing the Greek Catholics were divided into Ukrainian and Ruthenian branches with priests serving as vicar generals. The Ruthenian Catholics continued nevertheless to grow in numbers and organization. In 1921, for example, sisters of the Order of St. Basil the Great founded their first convent at Holy Ghost Parish in Cleveland.

On March 8, 1924, Pope Pius XI made the surprise announcement that two exarchates for Greek Catholics in the United States were to be created. With the declaration, the Holy See appointed Father Basil Takach to be the bishop of all Greek Catholics in the United States who were of Ruthenian, Hungarian, Slovak, and Croatian descent; Father Constantine Bohachevsky was named bishop of all Greek Catholics of Ukrainian descent. Bishop Takach placed his residence in Pittsburgh.

The exarchate of Pittsburgh survived several years of upheaval and difficulty to flourish over the next decades. In 1950 a new seminary was opened in Pittsburgh, and in 1963 the Pittsburgh exarchate was divided into two formal eparchies, with Bishop Nicholas Elko in Pittsburgh and Bishop Stephen

Kocisko in Passaic, New Jersey. In 1969 a Byzantine metropolitan province was established with the Archeparchy of Munhall; Bishop Kocisko was installed as first metropolitan archbishop. At the same time, Bishop Emil J. Mihalik was named the first ordinary of Parma. In 1982 the Eparchy of Van Nuys was established, and Bishop Thomas Dolinay was installed as its first ordinary. Today, there are some 100,000 Ruthenian Catholics in the United States, served by about 230 priests and 120 women religious.

Syrians

The Syrian Catholic Church was established through Catholic missionary labors among the Syrian Orthodox starting in the seventeenth century. While warm relations had been established between the Crusader states and the Syrian Orthodox bishops, little progress was made toward reception into the Catholic Church until the fifteenth century. A decree of union between Syrian Orthodox and Rome was achieved at the Council of Florence in 1444, but this proved as fleeting as the reunion with the Greek Orthodox of the Byzantine Empire.

Jesuit and Capuchin missionaries began to work among the Syrian Orthodox in Aleppo. Slow progress was made over the next century, but the growing Catholic population faced persecution by the Ottoman Turks to the point that Syrian Catholics lived as an essentially underground community.

In 1782 the Syrian Orthodox Holy Synod elected Metropolitan Michael Jarweh of Aleppo as patriarch, and soon after he declared that he had become a Catholic. Forced to flee to Lebanon, he established the monastery of Our Lady at Sharfeh and so began an unbroken line of Syrian Catholic patriarchs. The Turkish government granted legal recognition to the Syrian Catholic Church in 1829, and the patriarch took up residence at Aleppo in 1831. Owing to persecution, the patriarchate was moved to Mardin (in modern-day southern Turkey) in 1850. More savage repression during World War I prompted the patriarch to move his residence to Beirut.

Syrian Catholics began arriving in the United States during the early part of the twentieth century. They came mainly from Aleppo and were served by Father Paul Kassar from 1910 to 1944. Never numerous, Syrian Catholics were spread across the country and are found in New York City, Paterson, New Jersey, Columbus, Ohio, Detroit, Michigan, and elsewhere. To provide better pastoral care for the Syrian Catholics, the Eparchy of Our Lady of the Deliverance of Newark was established in 1995 for Syrian Catholics in the United States and Canada. There are currently some 13,000 faithful in the eparchy.

Syro-Malabarese (Malabar)

Properly called the Syro-Malabar rite, this is one of the rites considered distinct by the Congregation for the Oriental Churches and listed under the broader Chaldean rite. The Malabar Christians of the rite are also St. Thomas Christians and reside in India. They claim their Church was first founded by St. Thomas the Apostle. He was believed to have been martyred near modern-day Madras, but there is little evidence to indicate that a Christian community had been established before the sixth century. Cosmas Indicopleustes, a sixth-century geographer, mentions in his writings that there were Christians in the country prior to 550. The Portuguese discoverers and merchants who first encountered the so-called Syrian Christians found them using Syriac in their liturgy. The Christians in India gave their allegiance to the papacy at the Synod of Diamper in 1599, although a separation occurred in 1653, largely resolved in 1662.

The Malabar rite uses the Syriac and Malayalam languages in its liturgy, although a number of Roman customs have been adopted, most notably Communion under one species. Currently, there are over three million members of the rite, found mostly in India, although there is also a jurisdiction for members in Chicago and a number of mission churches.

The Syro-Malabar rite is located in India, in twenty-three dioceses; the Diocese of Ernakulam-Angamaly was raised to major archepiscopal status in 1993. Malabar Christians have long faced dangers as Catholics in a region populated with a vast Hindu majority.

The key date in the recent history of the Syro-Malabar rite is September 8, 1978, when Archbishop Mar Anthony Padiyara of Changnacherry was appointed by Pope John Paul I to be an apostolic visitor to study the problems faced by the Syro-Malabar Catholics outside the traditional confines of the ecclesiastical territory of Kerala. The archbishop investigated the challenges faced by Syro-Malabar Catholics who had settled in major cities in India and who were finding it difficult to practice their faith in their own rite. Archbishop Padiyara reported to Pope Blessed John Paul II in 1980 and urged that at least one bishop from the Syro-Malabar rite should be appointed with necessary jurisdiction for the pastoral care of emigrants of the Syro-Malabar rite who were found in large numbers in the various Latin dioceses of India outside of Kerala. From this recommendation came the eventual creation of the St. Thomas Syro-Malabar Diocese of Chicago, the first such jurisdiction outside of India.

Members of the Syro-Malabar rite began arriving in large numbers in the United States and Canada in the 1960s. Many were students who came to America to study in universities and to pursue graduate degrees. The Syro-Malabar population increased over the next decades, with the need for the establishment of missions and churches in various parts of the country. The overall jurisdiction for the missions fell to the bishop designated by the Syro-Malabar Synod for the migrants. In 1996 Bishop Gregory Karotemeprel, in charge of the Syro-Malabar migrants, visited the United States and Canada in 1996 and gave a report to the Syro-Malabar Synod as well as to authorities in Rome.

Determining that the time was right, Pope Blessed John Paul II established the Syro-Malabar Eparchy of St. Thomas the Apostle of Chicago in 2001 and appointed Bishop Jacob Angadiath as its first bishop. Currently, the diocese has seven parishes and twenty-nine missions with an estimated number of one hundred thousand faithful.

Syro-Malankarese

The Syro-Malankar Church began in 1930 when two bishops, a priest, a deacon, and a layman of the Malankara Orthodox Church were received into full communion with Rome. Today the community, situated chiefly in India, claims five eparchies with some 403,000 members. The growth of the Syro-Malankar Church was recognized by the Holy See in 2005 when the see of Trivandrum was

raised to the rank of a major archdiocese. The Syro-Malankar presence in the United States comprises twelve mission parishes under the direction of the apostolic visitor for Europe and North America for the Syro-Malankars.

Ukrainians

Ukrainian Catholics are the members of the broad Byzantine rite and are found chiefly in Ukraine, in the western part of the country, where they currently comprise approximately 10 percent of the population. The origins of the Ukrainian Catholic Church date to 1595–96 when the Union of Brest brought the Ukrainian Byzantine-rite community back into communion with Rome. In 1595 Archbishop Michael Ragoza, metropolitan of Kiev, and five other bishops met at Brest Litovsk and petitioned for union with Rome. A century later, they were joined by the bishops of Lvov and Przymysl. In Catholic usage, the Ukrainians were termed Ruthenians, although the Orthodox Church derisively termed them Uniates. Despite ceaseless tensions and hostility with the Orthodox, the majority of Ukrainians remained in communion with Rome.

The Eastern Catholic Church was officially suppressed by order of Joseph Stalin, marking a period of bloody and remorseless Soviet oppression of the Church. The Catholic Church went underground in the region from the late 1940s, especially after the long years of World War II. All of Ukraine's bishops were killed or imprisoned and its property seized by the government and given to the Orthodox Church. Some Catholic priests continued to minister clandestinely under communist rule, facing threat of imprisonment and death should they be caught.

The long era of oppression ended only in the early 1990s through perestroika under Mikhail Gorbachev. The Eastern Church regained its legal status, creating almost immediate tensions with the Orthodox Church over ownership of property and the allegiance of priests and laypeople. Latin-rite dioceses were reestablished in 1991.

Ukrainian Catholics began to settle in the United States toward the end of the nineteenth century. Like their Ruthenian counterparts, they found jobs in the Eastern states in ports and especially in the coal mines of Pennsylvania. As with the Ruthenians, the Ukrainians long endured an absence of any pastoral care, but in 1884 Father John Volansky arrived to provide badly needed ministry. As with the Ruthenians, the Ukrainians faced severe hardships owing to misunderstandings on the part of Latin-rite Catholics, who looked with suspicion on their married clergy and the different liturgies and liturgical languages.

In 1907 Bishop Stephen Soter Ortynsky was appointed the bishop for Greek Catholics in the United States, although he struggled from the start to secure appropriate jurisdiction as he was compelled to serve as a vicar general under the Latin ordinary of each community in which his faithful lived. In 1913 Bishop Ortynsky was accorded full ordinary jurisdiction and independence from the Latin ordinaries. Unfortunately, Bishop Ortynsky died unexpectedly on March 24, 1916.

Rather than appoint a new bishop for Greek Catholics, the Holy See instead instructed the apostolic delegate to assign two priests to serve as temporary administrators, one for the Ukrainians and another for the Ruthenians. The separation of administration propelled the division of the Greek Catholics, a status that was made permanent in 1924 when bishop ordinaries were appointed for each group. Bishop Constantine Bohachevsky was appointed on May 20, 1924, in Philadelphia for the Ukrainians.

On July 20, 1956, Pope Pius XII created the Apostolic Exarchy of Stamford, Connecticut, with jurisdiction over the parishes of New York and New England; Bishop Ambrose Senyshyn, previously auxiliary in Philadelphia, was named the first exarch. Two years later, Pope Pius created on July 12, 1958, the Ecclesiastical Province of Philadelphia, consisting of the Archeparchy of Philadelphia of the Ukrainians, and the Eparchy of Stamford.

Further development followed on July 14, 1961, when Pope Blessed John XXIII separated the western part of the Archeparchy of Philadelphia and founded the Eparchy of St. Nicholas of Chicago for the Ukrainians to serve Ukrainian Catholics in the west. Bishop Jaroslav Gabro was installed as its first bishop. On December 5, 1983, Pope Blessed John Paul II created the Eparchy of St. Josaphat in Parma, Ohio, comprising the states of Ohio, Ken-

tucky, Tennessee, Mississippi, Alabama, Georgia, Florida, North Carolina, South Carolina, West Virginia, and western Pennsylvania. Bishop Robert M. Moskal was installed as its first bishop. Currently, there are over 100,000 Ukrainian Catholics in the United States, served by some 180 priests and 120 women religious in 200 parishes.

Eccleston, Samuel (June 27, 1801–April 22, 1851)

The fifth archbishop of Baltimore from 1834 to 1851, Samuel Eccleston was a convert to the faith. He was born near Chestertown, Maryland, the son of an Episcopalian, who died young. When his mother remarried after the death of her husband, she wed a Catholic named Stenson. Young Samuel was raised under the influence of the faith and was later sent to St. Mary's College in Baltimore, where he entered the Church. In 1819 he entered St. Mary's Seminary and was ordained in April 1825. He was then sent to Issy, France, for additional studies. Upon his return in 1827, he was named vice president of St. Mary's College and two years later became president.

On September 14, 1834, Father Eccleston was ordained titular bishop of Thermia and coadjutor archbishop, with right of succession, for the Archdiocese of Baltimore. On October 19, 1834, with the passing of Archbishop James Whitfield, Archbishop Eccleston acceded to the see. He was concerned with providing diocesan facilities for the rapidly growing population, including the cathedral, for which he contributed large amounts of his own money. In 1841 he also invited the Redemptorists from Austria to assist in the pastoral care of German Catholics. Archbishop Eccleston helped establish the Brothers of the Christian Schools in the United States in 1846 and the Brothers of St. Patrick that same year. In 1849 he presided over the opening of St. Charles College and over five provincial councils of Baltimore. (*See also* Baltimore, Councils of.) He died at Georgetown.

Edes, Ella B. (December 7, 1832–February 27, 1916)

A convert to the Church, Ella B. Edes became one of the most influential Americans in Rome. She was born in Charlestown, Massachusetts, the daughter of Captain Robert E. Edes and Henrietta Birkhead Phelps Edes, and was their only child to survive infancy. She lost both her parents early; her father drowned in 1836, and her mother died in 1856. In 1852 she converted to the Catholic faith and, soon after inheriting her family's fortune, moved to Rome in 1860.

Once settled in Italy, she took a position as secretary to Cardinal Alessandro Barnabò, then Prefect of the Sacred Congregation for the Propagation of the Faith. Aside from her famous and ardent support of the Ultramontane cause during the pontificates of Popes Blessed Pius IX and Leo XIII, Edes served as a journalist for a variety of publications, including the *New York Herald*, the *New York World*, *L'Osservatore Romano*, *The Tablet*, *Dublin Review*, and *Ave Maria*. She left Rome in 1900 and moved to Piscina in semiretirement. For many years, she was one of the most influential Americans in Rome and cultivated a wide social circle of friends among the highest leaders of the Church.

Education, Catholic

The story of American Catholic education is one of immense success over the last two centuries, even as Catholic schools in the United States today face a host of crises and challenges. It can be said that Catholic education in the country remains one of the greatest achievement of Catholicism in North America.

Much as evangelization arrived in North America from three directions — the Spanish, French, and then the English colonies — so also did Catholic education in the New World receive its foundation. In Florida, by the end of the sixteenth century, Franciscan friars had started schools as part of their missionary labors. In 1606 they began a school at St. Augustine. This was followed by other schools in the missions for both Indians and Spanish colonists in the Southwest, including Arizona, New Mexico, and Texas. In California (Lower California), the Spanish missionaries operated schools, especially under the leadership of Blessed Junípero Serra. In Maine, French Capuchins opened schools for the Native Americans there before 1640. Jesuits and Franciscans developed schools in Detroit in 1703 soon after it was founded, and they continued to start new schools over the next decades, including in Kaskaskia, Illinois, and Mackinaw, Michi-

gan. By the end of the century, there were French schools at Vincennes, Indiana, and St. Louis. These were eventually united to the school systems that were pushing from the East and the one-time English colonies.

Catholic schools in the colonies of England trace themselves to March 25, 1634, when the ships the *Ark* and the *Dove* landed at St. Clement's Island in southern Maryland. On board were the colony's first settlers, led by Leonard Calvert, Cecil Calvert's younger brother. The group consisted of seventeen gentlemen, their wives, and their households. Most of the servants were Protestants. The first Catholic Mass in the colonies was then said by the Jesuit Father Andrew White; other Jesuits serving at the time were Father John Altham and Brother Thomas Gervase. The Jesuits existed in the colony much like the gentlemen, meaning that they assumed the position of landowners. They began the first formal Catholic religious base in the colonies at the newly founded town of St. Mary's and then devoted themselves to the conversion of the Native Americans.

One of the earliest permanent Catholic establishments in the English colonies was St. Francis Xavier Mission at Old Bohemia in northern Maryland, founded by the Jesuits in 1704 to serve Catholics in Delaware, Maryland, and southeastern Pennsylvania. They established a grammar school in 1640, a college at Newton in 1677, and in the 1740s the famed Bohemia Manor that was attended by sons of prominent Catholic families in the area. The so-called mother of Catholic schools in America was started by Jesuits in Philadelphia in 1782 at St. Mary's.

Catholics were always a tiny island in a colonial sea of Protestantism, and within the cultural, political, and social limitations Catholics managed to forge for themselves clear patterns of life and worship. They were served by a shockingly small group of priests, and for most of the eighteenth century Catholics in the colonies relied heavily upon each other for the security of the faith and the proper raising of Catholic children. Throughout the seventeenth and most of the eighteenth century, Catholics worshiped out of sight of other colonists. Religion was oriented in the home, built around the family, and performed with austerity. Children were baptized in the home, often by parents or mid-wives if a priest was not available.

Religious education was crucial in the colonies, just as it was in England. There was only one Catholic school in Maryland, Bohemia Manor, but it was used almost exclusively by the upper-class Catholics in the colony. Not surprisingly, priests placed great importance on education, but the primary place of instruction was in the home.

With the appointment in 1784 of Father John Carroll — the first American bishop and first archbishop of Baltimore — encouragement was given to the arrival of religious communities and institutions of Catholic education.

The Sisters of Loretto of the Foot of the Cross was founded in 1812 at Hardin's Creek, Kentucky, and the Sisters of Charity of Nazareth was founded in Kentucky in 1812. There were also the Ursuline nuns in Louisiana from 1727 and the Visitation nuns at Georgetown in the 1790s. The first community of American origin was the Sisters of Charity of St. Joseph, founded in 1808 at Emmitsburg, Maryland, by St. Elizabeth Ann Seton. The Religious of the Sacred Heart was founded by St. Rose Philippine Duchesne, who arrived in New Orleans in 1818 and later went to St. Charles, Missouri. In 1846 the Sisters of Charity started a school in Chicago. These institutes of women religious and many others were largely responsible for the development of educational and charitable institutions in America, and the legacy of these extraordinary women religious and the many who followed is still felt today. Similar contributions were made by the orders and congregations of men religious, including the Brothers of the Christian Schools, Xaverian Brothers, Brothers of the Holy Cross, Marianists, Dominicans, Jesuits, and Franciscans.

In 1788 Father Carroll founded what became the country's oldest Catholic university, "the Academy of Georgetown, Patowmack River, Maryland." In 1805 the school was given into the care of the Jesuits, who had been granted a partial restoration by Pope Pius VII after the suppression in 1773. At the same time, Carroll helped start academies for girls in Georgetown (the Visitation School in 1799), Emmitsburg (St. Joseph's in 1809, started by Mother Seton), and Bardstown, Kentucky (Nazareth in 1814). His conviction of the need for

expanding education in America led Father Carroll to be a patron of secular schools as well. In 1784 he became a member of the board of directors of St. John's College, Annapolis, and was elected president of the board four years later. In 1785 both George Washington and Bishop Carroll received honorary degrees from Washington College, Chesterton, Maryland.

Carroll was also much concerned with starting seminaries and met with French Sulpician priests to discuss a proposal to establish a seminary for the Diocese of Baltimore. The Sulpicians arrived in Baltimore in 1791 to start St. Mary's Seminary, the first school in America for the training of priests. The Sulpicians then began St. Mary's College in Baltimore in 1799. By 1815 St. Mary's Seminary had thirty ordained alumni. Two additional seminaries, Mount St. Mary's College in Emmitsburg, Maryland, and St. Thomas at Bardstown, Kentucky, were established in 1809 and 1811, respectively. These and similar institutions later played key roles in the development and growth of the American clergy.

By the time of Archbishop John Carroll's death in 1815, there were two hundred thousand Catholics in the country. Immigrants were coming in growing numbers, and the staggering task of caring for so many souls in search of a new life in America was profoundly apparent to Carroll and all of his successor bishops in the growing Church in the United States.

The four great waves of immigrants brought a massive explosion in both the Catholic and the general population of the country. Between 1800 and 1850, the U.S. population rose from 5.2 million to 23 million. From 1850 to 1920, the population rose to 106 million. Between 1800 and 1850 it is estimated that a total of 1,071,000 Catholic immigrants landed in the United States, a figure that far outran the natural increase of the native-born Catholics. By 1920 there were almost 20 million American Catholics, and the Church included Irish, Germans, French-Canadians, Poles, Hungarians, Czechs, Italians, Austrians, African-Americans, and Spanish-speaking Catholics in the Southwest and Texas.

Concurrent with the impact of immigration was the fact that the bishops of the United States felt responsible for the religious training of both native and immigrant Catholic children, and earlier efforts to strike an accommodation with the public school system had failed when Catholics found the schools had a Protestant atmosphere. The bishops' only recourse was to establish parochial schools despite the hostile opinions of other Americans.

As early as 1829, the bishops in the First Provincial Council of Baltimore had called for schools to be set up in each parish. The sense of urgency only increased when it grew more apparent that no religious instruction would take place in public schools and that textbooks were increasingly anti-Catholic in tone. Naturally, Catholic educators considered the possibility of state and federal aid to assist parochial schools as part of the "ask-in" approach by which Catholics requested their fair share of public tax money for education. In 1840 New York Governor William H. Seward suggested that Catholics schools were entitled to tax money to fund parochial schools because of their "equal civil rights, religious tolerance, and liberty of conscience." It was also a practical need. Some twenty thousand Irish and German immigrants needed to be educated, and the eight small Catholic schools in New York were inadequate to the task. Newly arrived Catholics were unwilling to send their children to schools administered by the Public School Society as the private organization gave to the schools a clear Protestant orientation and an openly hostile anti-"Romish" attitude. The idea was supported by then Bishop Hughes of New York and was adopted for a time in parts of New York. But the violent reaction by the Protestants brought the imposition of severe disabilities on parents who sent their children to such state-funded Catholic schools.

Governor Seward

Still, several similar plans were tried, such as the one in Poughkeepsie, New York, in 1873 that provided for the state to pay the salaries of nuns. The program was ended in 1898 when it was outlawed by the state superintendent of education. By that time, of course, there had emerged harsh opposition to the idea of the state supporting Catholic schools. In 1875, for example, President Ulysses S. Grant secured the support of Congressman James G. Blaine from Maine to introduce a constitutional amendment that would have forbidden all public aid for Catholic schools. The amendment failed to muster enough support in the Senate, but it was a clear warning to Catholics and anticipated the remarkably intolerant piece of legislation that was passed in 1922 in Oregon. The Oregon School Law had the sole intent of eliminating parochial schools in Oregon. Joined by countless leaders and civil rights organizations, Catholics led by Archbishop Alexander Christie sued, and in 1925 the Supreme Court declared the Oregon School Law unconstitutional.

Among the American bishops, there was considerable disagreement in the late nineteenth century on the issue of public funding. The most controversial figure in the period was Archbishop John Ireland of St. Paul as a result of his so-called Faribault-Stillwater Plan of the 1890s, so named because it was inaugurated in the Minnesota cities of Faribault and Stillwater. The plan established the process by which parochial schools were rented to the local public school board for use during the school day but continued providing religious instruction before and after public school hours. Archbishop Ireland was attacked from two directions. Some charged him with violating the principle of separation of church and state, while Catholics, including many bishops, feared that the plan diluted Catholic education. Although the archbishop was supported by the influential Cardinal James Gibbons, the opposition compelled him to go to Rome. With Gibbons's help, he convinced Roman officials that as the plan was already in operation in ten American dioceses, it could be tolerated. Nevertheless, legal problems and anti-Catholic resistance doomed the plan.

In the end, trying to reach accommodation with

public schools failed to provide a lasting solution. The way of the future was for the Church to create an independent Catholic school system. This meant schools run by dioceses in parishes, with instruction in the hands of women and men religious. The chief obstacle, of course, was the immense burden that creating Catholic schools imposed on a diocese. But the bishops understood that the future of the Church in America rested in large measure on providing that Catholic children were raised solidly in the faith.

In 1875 the Holy See issued an instruction that stressed that Catholic parents had an obligation to send their children to parochial schools and called for the building of Catholic schools. Bishops in the United States took up the challenge and devoted available resources to doing so. By 1884, however, only 40 percent of the parishes in the United States had schools. At the Third Plenary Council of Baltimore the bishops mandated the creation of a parochial school system.

In 1840 there had been some two hundred parochial schools in operation. At the start of the twentieth century, there were 3,800 Catholic elementary schools with some 900,000 students. By 1940 there were 7,597 schools and more than 2,000,000 students. By 1960 there were 10,372 schools and more than 4,200,000 students. In 1900 there were 260 high schools and 35,000 students; by 1940, there were 2,361 schools and 480,483 students; by 1960, there were 2,433 schools and 844,299 students. Catholics in 1915 could count only 19 colleges, but by 1960 they numbered more than 250, with more than 300,000 students. From its quite humble beginnings, Catholic education in the United States became the largest private educational system in the entire world.

As noted, the concern for higher education on the part of the Church in the United States was given its start under Bishop John Carroll and the founding of what became Georgetown University in 1791. As Bishop Carroll said of Georgetown, "On this academy is built all my hope of permanency and success to our holy religion in the United States." The bishops who followed never lost his enthusiasm or recognition that such colleges and seminaries were vital to the Church's future. Hence, colleges and seminaries were often founded as one entity, both for the practical reason of supplying potential priests from the student body of young men as well as paying for the cost of the seminary through those students not destined for holy orders. New colleges and universities were added throughout the 1800s, and by 1900 there were sixty-three Catholic colleges and universities.

The education of young Catholic women took place in the women's academy. Young women were given educational opportunities through schools begun to provide them with a proper religious and moral education to help them prepare for the task of keeping the home and raising children. The first female academy was opened in 1727 in New Orleans. It was followed in 1790 by the Visitation at Georgetown.

The Catholic community witnessed the flowering of more such schools in the first half of the nineteenth century, including those founded by St. Elizabeth Ann Seton and the Sisters of Charity. There were ten academies in 1820 and one hundred by 1852. Such schools, of course, could not have flourished without the extraordinary zeal of women religious.

The creation of the Catholic education system was owed to the constant and patient efforts of the hierarchy and countless laypeople, but particular distinction should be given to the religious orders for their immense contributions to Catholic schools, colleges, universities, and seminaries throughout the history of the American Catholic Church. Jesuits, Dominicans, Franciscans, Marists, Capuchins, Sulpicians, and others were the most prominent among the orders for men while the teaching orders and congregations of nuns included Ursulines, Poor Clares, Dominicans, Franciscans, and Sisters of the Immaculate Heart of Mary. Among the leading universities was The Catholic University of America, the University of Notre Dame, Villanova, the University of San Francisco, and Georgetown.

The first Catholic college to grant academic degrees to women was Notre Dame in 1899.

There remained the desire for a national Catholic university. Papal charters had been granted to St. Mary's Seminary in 1822 and Georgetown in 1833, but neither became the kind of theological center that was needed. The bishops at the Third

Plenary Council of Baltimore called for such a school, and the project became the work of several bishops, including John Lancaster Spalding of Peoria and John Joseph Keane of Richmond. The task became easier when the twenty-one-year-old heiress Mary Caldwell donated $300,000. Approval from Pope Leo XIII was granted on Easter Sunday, April 10, 1887, and The Catholic University of America opened in 1889 as a graduate school of theology for priests. Its early history was marked by severe financial challenges.

A truly great instrument of Catholic education ordered by the Council of Baltimore was the legendary text of the *Baltimore Catechism*. Intended to serve as an instrument of standardizing catechetical instruction for the whole of the U.S. Church, the *Baltimore Catechism* was a method of introducing the children of recent immigrants to the devotional practices and prayer forms that were then commonplace in American Catholicism.

The creation of the *Baltimore Catechism* is traced to November 7, 1884, when the Third Plenary Council of Baltimore began its first session of deliberations on the issues most pressing to the Catholic Church in the United States. One of the matters taken up was that of uniformity for religious instruction amid the number of diverse catechisms then in use. Termed "the vexed question of a uniform catechism in English" by the First Plenary Council of Baltimore in 1852, the issue of a standard catechism was again taken up in earnest by the council of 1884.

The resulting first edition of the *Baltimore Catechism* was 97 pages long and remained firmly committed to the traditional question-and-answer structure. It contained 37 chapters and 421 questions and answers. The chief concerns were the Apostles' Creed, the seven sacraments, and the Ten Commandments.

This first edition was followed almost immediately by an abridged version approximately half the size of the original and given the designation of Baltimore No. 1. None of the small changes ever satisfied the critics, and the nearly ceaseless complaints and calls for emendations from various quarters sparked constant minor changes that finally coalesced into the formal revision of the catechism in 1941. The new editions of the *Baltimore Catechism* remained in general use until the very eve of the Second Vatican Council.

In June 1944 President Franklin Delano Roosevelt signed the Serviceman's Readjustment Act, known more popularly as the GI Bill of Rights. The GI Bill had a lasting influence on American Catholics as it allowed veterans returning from the war to take advantage of previously unavailable educational opportunities. By 1952 more than 7.6 million World War II veterans — half of all of those eligible — received either vocational training or a college education. Catholics took part in unprecedented numbers.

The new students pouring into Catholic colleges and universities forced wholesale changes in those institutions. Suddenly, even small colleges were expected to expand their facilities, increase their faculties, and widen their course offerings and degree programs. In effect, in return for government subsidies as part of the GI Bill, Catholic higher education lost many elements that had made it distinctively Catholic. The long-term effect of this was to risk the very real danger of secularization in Catholic colleges and universities to keep pace with modern trends in public education. The full impact was felt in the 1960s and 1970s, when a revolution against the Church's rightful authority gripped a host of Catholic schools across the nation.

In the decades that followed the Second Vatican Council, Catholic education in the United States was confronted by crises in declining vocations to the religious life for men and women, rising costs for education, demographic shifts away from the cities to the suburbs — with the attendant need to provide new schools for the suburbs while still meeting the education demands of the city schools, the closing and consolidation of parishes that meant the closing as well of many parochial schools, and the loss of Catholic identity in many schools, especially in Catholic colleges and universities.

The numbers reveal the scope of the decline in Catholic education. In 1965, considered the zenith of Catholic schools, there were nearly 11,000 elementary schools teaching 4.5 million students, 2,400 high schools teaching more than 1 million students, and 30 colleges and universities teaching 384,000 students. By 1990 there were 7,549 elementary schools teaching 1,970,000 students, 1,364 high schools teaching 661,000 students, and 232 colleges and universities teaching 571,000 students. In 2011 the *National Catholic Directory* reported 5,858 elementary schools teaching 1,517,708 students, 1,340 high schools teaching 630,587 students, and 235 colleges and universities teaching 804,826 students.

Even as the number of elementary and high schools has declined, Catholic identity in colleges and universities has also faced significant obstacles. These stemmed in large measure from the upheaval in education at large in the 1960s, when authority was questioned and traditional structures and methods of education were rejected. The wider turmoil in American society found its way into Catholic schools, above all colleges and universities.

The era of dissent in Catholic schools reached a decisive turning point toward crisis in Catholic culture in 1968 with the encyclical *Humanae Vitae*, in which Pope Paul VI courageously reiterated the Church's teaching on marriage and morality. The encyclical was met with a shocking decision by some theologians — who received praise and adulation by many in the press for their "heroism" — to dissent openly against the papal teaching.

Within a mere two days of the encyclical's release, Charles Curran, a theologian at the Catholic University of America, led a group of dissident theologians in a statement that Catholics were permitted to decide in their own consciences whether to adhere to the requirements of the encyclical. In many dioceses and archdioceses, and in Catholic colleges and universities, priests, nuns, and professors joined the dissent. In the Archdiocese of Washington, fifty priests openly dissented and were suspended by Cardinal Patrick A. O'Boyle.

The response of dissenting theologians was to some degree anticipated in the year before *Humanae Vitae*, in July 1967, when a group of twenty-six Catholic educators and college administrators, most of them American, gathered for a conference in Land O' Lakes, Wisconsin, to discuss the activities of Catholic higher education in light of the Second Vatican Council. As a result of their deliberations, the group issued a 1,500-word statement on the role and identity of Catholic universities that focused on the question of academic freedom

and the role of the Magisterium. The statement declared:

"To perform its teaching and research functions effectively the Catholic university must have a true autonomy and academic freedom in the face of authority of whatever kind, lay or clerical, external to the academic community itself. To say this is simply to assert that institutional autonomy and academic freedom are essential conditions of life and growth and indeed of survival for Catholic universities as for all universities."

The statement nevertheless went to some pains to stress that Catholic higher education should be distinctively and unmistakably Catholic by adding: "The Catholic university adds to the basic idea of a modern university distinctive characteristics that round out and fulfill that idea. Distinctively, then, the Catholic university must be an institution, a community of learners or a community of scholars, in which Catholicism is perceptibly present and effectively operative."

Supporters of the statement argued that it was a long overdue clarification of academic freedom from the Catholic standpoint. Others, however, saw in it what historian Philip Gleason termed a "declaration of independence from the hierarchy." In the end, whether it was intended as such or not, the Land O' Lakes Statement was a clarion call for many Catholic universities to separate themselves from adherence to obedience to the Magisterium.

The Curran Affair raised other critical questions regarding the identity and mission of Catholic colleges and universities. The central element in subsequent discussions was on Pope John Paul II's 1990 apostolic constitution *Ex Corde Ecclesiae*, on the pope's vision of what a Catholic university should be. On November 17, 1999, the Catholic bishops of the Unites States approved *The Application of Ex Corde Ecclesiae for the United States*, implementing the apostolic constitution. This action received the *recognitio* from the Congregation for Bishops on May 3, 2000. The implementation, including the requirement of the *mandatum*, sparked opposition in some circles to what was perceived as a discouragement of academic freedom, but it also served to remind theologians of their role in the Church.

The need for *Ex Corde Ecclesiae* — not to mention its lamentably inconsistent application — is seen in Catholic colleges and universities on a nearly daily basis and can be studied in the context of the ongoing toxic impact of the Land O' Lakes Statement. From invitations to anti-Catholic and pro-abortion leaders to staging seminars in favor of homosexuality to granting permission for production of *The Vagina Monologues* on campus grounds, Catholics are often horrified at the lack of Catholic identity and fidelity to Church teachings that plague even nationally prominent schools.

As sobering as these sad realities in Catholic education remain, there are efforts in the United States to bring the reform and renewal desired by both Popes Blessed John Paul II and Benedict XVI. The renewal is occurring from two directions. First, there is an effort to reinvigorate Catholic culture and spiritual life both on secular campuses and also in the sometimes sadly arid environments of Catholic schools. One of the chief means of accomplishing this has been the Cardinal Newman Society, founded in 1993 and dedicated to rebuilding and strengthening of Catholic identity at America's Catholic colleges and universities. The Newman Society joins the work of thousands of orthodox professors and administrators on faculties across the country in promoting true Catholic teachings and a vibrant Catholic life for students and their teachers.

Second, the last decades have witnessed a flowering of new colleges and universities determined to disprove the modern notion that it is not possible to be faithful to the Magisterium and strive for academic excellence at the same time.

Pope Benedict XVI addressed the demands of Catholic education in America when he spoke to Catholic leaders in education during his visit to the United States in April 2008. The Holy Father declared:

"A university or school's Catholic identity is not simply a question of the number of Catholic students. It is a question of conviction — do we really believe that only in the mystery of the Word made flesh does the mystery of man truly become clear (cf. *Gaudium et Spes*, 22)? Are we ready to commit our entire self — intellect and will, mind, and heart — to God? Do we accept the truth Christ reveals? Is the faith tangible in our universities and schools? Is it given fervent expression liturgically,

sacramentally, through prayer, acts of charity, a concern for justice, and respect for God's creation? Only in this way do we really bear witness to the meaning of who we are and what we uphold. From this perspective one can recognize that the contemporary 'crisis of truth' is rooted in a 'crisis of faith.' Only through faith can we freely give our assent to God's testimony and acknowledge him as the transcendent guarantor of the truth he reveals. Again, we see why fostering personal intimacy with Jesus Christ and communal witness to his loving truth is indispensable in Catholic institutions of learning."

Egan, Edward M. (April 2, 1932–)

The archbishop of New York from 2000 to 2009, and then a cardinal, Edward M. Egan guided the faithful of the archdiocese through the terrible days following the terrorist attack on September 11, 2001. He was born in Oak Park, Illinois, the son of Thomas J. and Genevieve Costello Egan. Answering a call to the priesthood, he studied at St. Mary of the Lake Seminary in Mundelein, Illinois, where he earned a bachelor's degree in philosophy in preparation for theological studies. Sent to Rome to complete his education, he attended the North American College and was ordained on December 15, 1957. The following year, he received a licentiate in sacred theology from the Pontifical Gregorian University and then returned to the United States, where he served as a curate at Holy Name Cathedral Parish. He was soon named assistant chancellor of the Archdiocese of Chicago and secretary to Cardinal Albert G. Meyer, archbishop of Chicago.

In 1960 Father Egan was appointed assistant vice rector and a teacher of moral theology and canon law at the North American College. At the same time, he studied canon law at the Pontifical Gregorian University; in 1964 he earned a doctorate in canon law. Returning to Chicago, he served as secretary to Cardinal John Patrick Cody, archbishop of Chicago, and then as co-chancellor of the archdiocese. He was also the secretary of the Archdiocesan Commissions on Ecumenism and Human Relations and served on various boards and commissions promoting interfaith and ecumenical relations. His ecumenical activities included participation in the Anglican-Roman Catholic Dialogue of the United States Conference of Catholic Bish-

Cardinal Egan

ops and Protestant Episcopal Church of America, the North American Academy of Ecumenists, and the Chicago Ecumenical Dialogue.

In 1971 Father Egan was called to Rome to serve as a judge of the Tribunal of the Sacred Roman Rota, a position he held until 1985. At the same time, he held a variety of posts in Rome and in the Roman Curia, including professor of canon law at the Pontifical Gregorian University; professor of civil and criminal procedure at the Studium Rotale, the law school of the Rota; a commissioner of the Congregation for the Sacraments and Divine Worship; a consultor of the Congregation for the Clergy; and in 1982 one of six canonists who reviewed the new Code of Canon Law prior to its promulgation in 1983.

On May 22, 1985, he was consecrated titular bishop of Allegheny and was named auxiliary bishop and vicar for education of the Archdiocese of New York. Three years later, on November 8, 1988, Pope Blessed John Paul II appointed him bishop of Bridgeport. He was installed on December 14, 1988. As bishop of Bridgeport, he was concerned especially with diocesan education programs, including the reorganization of diocesan elementary schools and founding of the St. John Fisher Seminary Residence for prospective seminarians and the Inner-City Foundation for Charity and Education. To assist diocesan health care, he launched the St. Catherine School for Children with Special Needs in Bridgeport, Connecticut,

and the Catherine Dennis Keefe Queen of the Clergy Residence for Retired Priests in Stamford, Connecticut. He also promoted Hispanic and Haitian apostolates and proved especially capable in restoring the finances of the diocese.

On May 11, 2000, Pope Blessed John Paul II appointed him archbishop of New York, eight days after the passing of Cardinal John J. O'Connor. He was installed at St. Patrick's Cathedral on June 19, 2000. On February 21, 2001, he was elevated to the College of Cardinals as a cardinal priest with the titular church of the Basilica of Sts. John and Paul.

The most important event as a cardinal archbishop was the terrible day of September 11, 2001, when terrorists flew two hijacked commercial airliners into the World Trade Center, killing approximately three thousand people and bringing colossal destruction and misery.

Cardinal Egan proved a tireless shepherd during the days and weeks that followed, helping the people of New York City cope with the tragedy, especially among the parishioners who had suffered the loss of family and friends. Cardinal Egan was also confronted by a serious financial situation. Much as he did in Bridgeport, he dedicated himself to restoring archdiocesan finances by cutting debt (he reduced the debt by some $20 million over a two-year period) and reducing expenditures. This fiscal policy entailed difficult decisions, including shutting down economically troubled schools, trimming administration, and reducing the weekly diocesan newspaper to a monthly. In addition to his duties as archbishop, Cardinal Egan also held a variety of positions in the Roman Curia, including membership in the Prefecture for the Economic Affairs of the Holy See. He retired on February 23, 2009.

Egan, Michael F. (1761–July 22, 1814)

The first bishop of Philadelphia from 1808 to 1814, Michael F. Egan confronted one of the most divisive elements of the early American Church, trusteeism. A native of Ireland, he joined the Franciscans while still in his native country. Owing to his obvious gifts and energy, he was given a variety of assignments in Ireland and Rome and volunteered for service in Pennsylvania. Bishop John Carroll (later Archbishop) of Baltimore appointed him pastor of St. Mary's Church in Philadelphia in 1803, despite the fact that Father Egan was suffering from poor health.

Five years later, in the ecclesiastical reorganization of the Church in the United States, Pope Pius VII established several new sees and named Bishop Carroll the first archbishop of Baltimore. One of the new suffragan sees was Philadelphia, and Father Egan was appointed its first bishop. His consecration did not take place until October 28, 1810, owing to the severe difficulties faced by the pope in the face of the Napoleonic Wars. Finally, the formal bulls arrived, and he was consecrated in St. Peter's Church in Baltimore.

Bishop Egan's years of episcopal service were marred by turmoil. He confronted the pernicious problem of lay trustees at St. Mary's, the very church that he had chosen for his cathedral. The trustees tried to claim the right to appoint and remove their pastors, and Bishop Egan was forced also to deal with several troublesome priests. Exhausted from these constant problems, he suffered from continuing poor health and died, weighed down by the demands of his office.

Egloffstein, Frederick W. von (May 18, 1824–1885)

An engraver of worldwide reputation, Frederick W. von Egloffstein was also a military officer of note. He was born at Aldorf, near Nuremberg, Bavaria, and was a veteran of the Prussian Army before he migrated to the United States. Once established, von Egloffstein established himself as a noted engraver. This business venture, however, was interrupted by the start of the Civil War. Owing to his previous military experience, he was commissioned a colonel in the Union Army as a volunteer from New York. In April 1862 he was wounded during a skirmish in North Carolina and, given the severity of his wounds, was retired with the brevet rank of brigadier general.

After recovering, he returned to his engraving business, this time with the support of Archbishop John McCloskey of New York (the first American cardinal). Von Egloffstein's work in engraving earned him the title the "Father of Half-tone Engraving." His methods of preventing counterfeiting in currency were proposed to the United

States government, but authorities declined his suggestions.

Elder, George (August 11, 1793–September 28, 1838)

A priest and educator, George Elder served in the vast Diocese of Bardstown in the early eras of the American Catholic Church. He was born in Kentucky and entered Mount St. Mary's College in Emmitsburg, Maryland, at the age of sixteen. He went on to study theology at St. Mary's Seminary in Baltimore and was ordained in September 1819. Father Elder served as an assistant pastor in Bardstown and was then assigned the task of establishing a small college. The first days were spent teaching in the basement of the diocesan seminary, but from this beginning Father Elder was able to create a prosperous school, especially after a large number of students from the South arrived in 1825. Despite a brief period in which he was replaced as president, Elder remained in charge of the school until his death. He also served as an editor of the *Catholic Advocate*, a Louisville newspaper begun in 1836.

Elder, William Henry (March 22, 1819–October 31, 1904)

The third bishop of Natchez, from 1857 to 1880, William Henry Elder was also appointed the second archbishop of Cincinnati, from 1880 to 1904. He was born in Baltimore, Maryland, and embarked on studies for the priesthood in 1831 when he entered Mount St. Mary's College in Emmitsburg, Maryland. To complete his theological preparation, he was sent to Rome in 1842 and to the College of the Propaganda. There he earned a doctorate of divinity and was ordained in Rome in March 1846.

After returning to Maryland, Father Elder served as professor at the Emmitsburg seminary; he was still on the faculty in 1857 when he was appointed bishop of Natchez. Consecrated by Archbishop Francis P. Kenrick on May 3, 1857, he dedicated the next years to the pastoral care of the diocese, and earned considerable notoriety in 1864 when he refused to obey the direct order of Union troops to have prayers recited publicly in all churches for the president of the United States and other northern dignitaries. Arrested for his refusal, he was tried and convicted and sent into exile in Louisiana, but officials in Washington, including President Lincoln, reversed the military court's judgment and returned Bishop Elder to his see. The Union forces had caused terrible damages in Natchez, and Bishop Elder set about restoring and rebuilding.

In 1878 Bishop Elder received renewed fame for the courageous leadership he displayed in caring for victims of yellow fever during an epidemic. Two years later, he was appointed titular bishop of Avara and coadjutor archbishop of Cincinnati with right of succession to Archbishop John Baptist Purcell. He acceded to the see on July 4, 1883, when Archbishop Purcell retired to a local convent. Archbishop Elder faced a severe financial crisis brought about by Archbishop Purcell's brother, Father Edward Purcell, but he served the people of Cincinnati with the same intellectual honesty and courage that he had displayed in Natchez and soon calmed the faithful while working through the intricacies of the financial disaster that had gripped the archdiocese. Archbishop Elder aided missionary efforts among the African-Americans and reopened the seminary of

Bishop William Henry Elder

Mount St. Mary's of the West and established St. Gregory's Preparatory Seminary. He maintained calm and resolve until his death in Cincinnati.

Ellard, Gerald (October 8, 1894–April 1, 1963)

A Jesuit priest and noted liturgist, Gerald Ellard pioneered the historical study of the liturgy. He was born in Commonwealth, Wisconsin, one of four children, all of whom entered the religious life. Ellard entered the Society of Jesus in 1912 and received ordination in June 1926. He subsequently undertook graduate studies in liturgics and studied at the University of Munich. His famed doctoral dissertation, "Ordination Anointings in the Western Church before 1000 A.D." (1933), was noted as the first such work in liturgical studies by an American. Father Ellard went on to write a number of respected works, including *Christian*

Life and Worship (1933), *Men at Work and Worship* (1940), *Mass of the Future* (1948), and *Master Alcuin, Liturgist* (1956). He was one of the founding editors of *Orate Fratres* (later, *Worship*). Father Elder also served as professor of liturgy and Church history at St. Mary's College in St. Mary's, Kansas, from 1932 to 1963 and was a dedicated supporter of liturgical reform in the years leading up to the Second Vatican Council.

Elliott, Walter (January 6, 1842–April 18, 1928)

A priest, missionary, and editor, Walter Elliott was one of the early supporters of Father Isaac Thomas Hecker. Born in Detroit, Elliott studied at St. Anne's School in Detroit and the University of Notre Dame and then proceeded to a law degree at Cincinnati. With the start of the Civil War in 1861, he enlisted in the 5th Ohio Infantry and took part in several notable campaigns, including Chancellorsville and Gettysburg in 1863. After the war, he returned and completed his law studies. He then opened a law office in Detroit.

In 1868 he attended a lecture given by Father Isaac Thomas Hecker and was so moved that he entered the Paulists. Ordained in 1872, he devoted the next years to missionary work and was a promoter of the temperance movement and active in the Catholic Total Abstinence Union of America. In 1886 he took a leave from active missionary work to assist Father Hecker, whose health was failing. Part of Father Elliott's ministry included carefully noting his conversations with Father Hecker as well as the priest's reminiscences. These provided the basis for his biography of Father Hecker, which first appeared in serial form in the *Catholic World* in 1890–91; it was then published as a book in 1891 under the title *The Life of Father Hecker*. The French translation by Abbé Felix Klein, *La Vie du Père*, caused a major uproar in 1898 because of the Abbé's interpretations of Hecker's work and was a devastating element in the Americanist controversy.

In 1893 Father Elliott was the guiding force in the effort to evangelize non-Catholics throughout the United States. He organized various mission bands and launched, with Father Alexander P. Doyle, C.S.P., the Catholic Missionary Union and *Missionary* magazine. He also established the Apostolic Mission House to train missionaries and devoted most of his remaining years to serving as rector there. Aside from his life of Isaac Hecker, Father Elliott's writings include *Missions to Non-Catholics* (1893), *The Life of Christ* (1902), *Jesus Crucified* (1906), *Manual of Missions* (1922), *A Retreat for Priests* (1924), *A Retreat for Nuns* (1925), and *Mission Sermons* (1926).

Ellis, John Tracy (July 30, 1905–October 16, 1992)

Historian, priest, and educator, John Tracy Ellis was for many years the dean of Catholic Church historians in the United States. He was born at Seneca, Illinois, the elder of two sons of Elmer Ellis and Ida Cecilia Murphy Ellis. His father was a Methodist and his mother a Catholic. After graduating magna cum laude from St. Viator College with a bacherlor's degree in English literature in 1927, he decided to pursue graduate studies at The Catholic University of America through a Knights of Columbus Fellowship, where he had the privilege of studying under famed historian Peter Guilday. He earned a master's degree and expanded his thesis, "Anti-Papal Legislation in Medieval England 1066–1377," into his doctoral dissertation, which was published as his first book in 1930. After completing his doctorate, he taught at St. Viator College and then at the College of St. Teresa in Winona, Minnesota.

While at Winona, Ellis felt the call to a priestly vocation and returned to Washington, D.C., to study for the priesthood at the Sulpician Seminary (now theological college). He also began teaching history at The Catholic University of America and so opened a career at the university that lasted from 1935 to 1964. Ordained a priest on June 5, 1938, at the College of St. Teresa in Winona, Father Ellis went back to Washington, D.C., and lived from 1938 to 1941 in the residence of then Monsignor (later Archbishop) Fulton J. Sheen, for whom he had worked earlier as a part-time personal secretary.

Incardinated a priest in the Archdiocese of Washington in 1947, he was appointed a domestic prelate of Pope Pius XII in 1955. He was asked by Robert E. Tracy, bishop of Baton Rouge, to serve as *peritus* (or theological expert) at the Second Vatican Council but declined. In 1988 Pope Blessed John Paul II named him an honorary protonotary apostolic.

From 1964 to 1976, Monsignor Ellis served as professor of Church history at the University of San Francisco. He returned to Catholic University and was also lecturer in Church history from 1976 to 1989. He taught and lectured as well at the University of Chicago (1955), the North American College in Rome (1967, 1974–76), Brown University (1967), the University of Notre Dame (1970), the Graduate Theological Union, Berkeley (1970–71), the Pontifical Gregorian University (1974–75), the Pontifical University of St. Thomas, the Angelicum (1976), and The Catholic University of America (1976). Monsignor Ellis also assisted the National Conference of Catholic Bishops as chairman of the Subcommittee on History of the Committee on Priestly Life and Ministry from 1967 to 1971 and as a member of the Subcommittee on History for the Observance of the Bicentennial from 1973 to 1976. He continued teaching at Catholic University until just before his death and received a host of awards and twenty honorary doctorates, as well as the Laetare Medal from the University of Notre Dame.

Monsignor Ellis was the author of a vast body of writings, including over 150 books, articles, pamphlets, and book reviews. Among his most famous books were *Anti-Papal Legislation in Medieval England, 1066–1377* (1930); *Cardinal Consalvi and Anglo-Papal Relations, 1814–1824* (1942); *The Formative Years of the Catholic University of America* (1946); *John Lancaster Spalding: First Bishop of Peoria, American Educator* (1961); *Perspectives in American Catholicism* (1963), a collection of essays; and *Documents of American Catholic History* (1956, revised in 1962, and published in multiple volumes in 1967 and 1987). His *American Catholicism* (1956, revised in 1969) proved an invaluable textbook for students. Of particular note was his two-volume masterpiece, *The Life of James Cardinal Gibbons: Archbishop of Baltimore, 1834–1921* (1952, reprinted in 1987). *Catholics in Colonial America* (1965) was the first volume in what proved an unrealized multipart history of American Catholicism. In 1947 he collected *A Select Bibliography of the History of the Catholic Church in the United States*, which was revised as *A Guide to American Catholic History* in 1959 and revised with Robert Trisco in 1982. He also contributed articles to the *New Catholic Encyclopedia* (1967). Beyond his writings, Ellis left a major mark on the field of Church history through his teaching and direction of numerous doctoral students at The Catholic University of America, many of whom went on to prestigious careers. Ellis's funeral Mass was presided over by Cardinal James A. Hickey, archbishop of Washington. He was buried in Seneca.

El Paso, Diocese of

Established on March 3, 1914, by Pope St. Pius X, the Diocese of El Paso serves counties in Texas and originally had jurisdiction in parts of New Mexico. The largest of the U.S.-Mexican border cities, El Paso was named in 1598 by Juan de Oñate, the Spanish colonizer of New Mexico. He called the site *El Paso de Norte*, "the Pass of the North." There were people on the site and a mission begun in 1659, and survivors of the Pueblo Revolt of 1680 to 1692 took refuge there. The town of El Paso was laid out in 1859 and now serves as a commercial and financial center for a myriad of industries and resources of the region. The Diocese of El Paso is a suffragan see of the Archdiocese of San Antonio.

The city has a profound Catholic heritage, beginning in 1536, when Alvar Nuñez Cabeza de Vaca conducted an expedition into the area. In 1581 Franciscan Father Agustin Rodriguez visited the Rio Grande region, and the Franciscans started a series of missions there. In 1678 Franciscan Father Francis de Ayeta visited the Spanish mission and settlements in Santa Fe that had been started earlier in Pueblo territory. Father de Ayeta was alarmed at the abuse and unkindness being shown by the Spanish in the area and returned to his superiors in Mexico, predicting an inevitable disaster. On August 10, 1680, the Pueblos revolted and killed their tormentors. The Spanish and Christian Indian survivors of the uprising fled across the wilderness to El Paso. Father de Ayeta, having discerned that the survivors would follow that route, was already there, waiting for them with emergency supplies.

The community of Ysleta was formed in El Paso at that time. The missions in New Mexico were restored when Diego de Vargas led a retaliatory military force into the area.

El Paso grew slowly and endured the closing of the missions by the Mexican government, who expelled all the Spanish priests after winning independence from Spain. The Texans, however, rejected Mexican rule, and the Republic of Texas was formed. Texas entered the Union in 1845, followed three years later by New Mexico. In 1859, when El Paso was laid out as a city, four railroads converged there, bringing prosperity. At the time, El Paso was part of a vicariate apostolic and then was joined to the Diocese of Dallas in 1891. In 1914 the city was erected as a diocese, a sign of recognition by the Holy See of the number of Catholics there and the vitality of the faith. A Jesuit priest, John J. Brown, was appointed as the bishop of El Paso on January 22, 1915, but he was never consecrated, resigning on June 16 of that year.

Another Jesuit was appointed as his replacement, Anthony J. Schuler, who was consecrated on October 28, 1915. He established the offices and agencies for diocesan administration and supported the military efforts of the United States in World War I. Dedicating the Cathedral of St. Patrick in El Paso, Bishop Schuler established parishes throughout the diocese. He also led the faithful through the grim era of the Great Depression, laboring to ease the sufferings of the people resulting from the economic collapse. In 1941 he received a coadjutor bishop, Sidney M. Metzger, and led the diocese during World War II. Bishop Schuler died on June 3, 1944, having served the El Paso diocese for decades, establishing a foundation of faith among the Catholics of the area.

The third bishop of El Paso was Sidney M. Metzger, who acceded to the see upon the death of Bishop Schuler and began expansion programs to provide needed parishes and schools. He also started a diocesan newspaper and St. Charles Borromeo Seminary. Attending the Second Vatican Council, Bishop Metzger implemented the reforms mandated by that council. He retired on May 29, 1978.

His successor was Patricio Fernández Flores, the first Mexican-American bishop in the United States. Bishop Flores was installed in El Paso on

May 29, 1978. On August 28, 1979, however, he was promoted to the Archdiocese of San Antonio.

Raymundo J. Peña succeeded Bishop Flores, having served as auxiliary bishop of San Antonio since 1976. He was installed in the diocese on August 28, 1979. Bishop Peña continued the expansion programs and introduced new facilities and ministries for the growing needs of the diocese. On May 23, 1995, he was appointed the bishop of Brownsville.

The sixth bishop of El Paso, Armando X. Ochoa, had served as auxiliary bishop of the Archdiocese of Los Angeles since 1986. He was installed on June 26, 1996, and was active in the pressing question of immigration and worked diligently to promote vocations in the diocese. In December 2011, he was appointed bishop of Fresno. In 2011 there were 650,000 Catholics served by 115 priests and 57 parishes in the diocese.

Elsensohn, Alfreda (1897–1989)

A Benedictine religious, Alfreda Elsensohn also served as an educator and natural scientist. Born in Grengeville, Idaho, she entered the Benedictines in Cottonwood, Idaho, in 1915 and subsequently earned several degrees in science. From 1931, she taught sciences at St. Gertrude's Academy and assembled a collection of the flora of the prairie and other specimens that later were preserved at the Historical Museum at St. Gertrude's. She was a member of the American Association of Museums, the Idaho Writer's League, the Idaho Academy of Science, the Northwest Scientific Association, and the American Benedictine Academy, and was the author of a number of books, including *Pioneer Days in Idaho County* (1947–51), *Idaho Chinese Lore* (1970), and *Idaho County's Most Romantic Character: Polly Bemis* (1980). She received the Idaho Writer of the Year Award in 1969 and the Governor's Award of Arts and Humanities in 1970.

Emmet, Thomas Addis (May 29, 1828–March 1, 1919)

A surgeon and writer, Thomas Addis Emmet was a convert to the Church and honored by the Holy See. He was born near Charlottesville, Virginia, and graduated from Jefferson Medical College in Philadelphia in 1851. In 1855 he was named to the Woman's Hospital in New York City, where he remained for the next forty-five years; he was named chief surgeon in 1861. A brilliant surgeon, he wrote *Principles and Practices of Gynecology* in 1879; it became the standard text on that medical field for many years. A convert to the Catholic faith in 1897, he received the Laetare Medal from the University of Notre Dame in 1898 and was named a Knight Commander of the Order of St. Gregory by Pope St. Pius X in 1906.

Engelhardt, Zephyrin (November 13, 1851–April 27, 1934)

A missionary to the Native Americans, Zephyrin Engelhardt was a linguist who preserved Indian languages. He was born in Bilshausen, Germany, and migrated to the United States with his family as a one-year-old. His parents settled in Covington, Kentucky, and he was raised there. In 1873 he entered the Franciscans in Illinois and was ordained in St. Louis in June 1878.

Assigned to the Indian missions in the Midwest, Father Engelhardt served from 1880 to 1900 among the Menominee at Kenosha, Wisconsin, and in Superior. He also served the Ottawa. To assist in catechizing the tribes, and to aid in the preservation of the native languages, Father Engelhardt published *Kachkenohamatwon Kesekoch* (*Guide to Heaven*) in 1882, a translation of Chippewa into Menominee, and *Kateshim* (*Catechism*) in 1884, also in Menominee. He also started the journal *Anishinabe Enamaid* (*Praying Indian*) in 1896, composed in the language of the Ottawa.

In 1900 Father Engelhardt was sent to California and focused on the famed history of the California missions. Building on his earlier histories, *The Franciscans in California* (1897) and *The Franciscans in Arizona* (1899), he wrote *Missions and Missionaries of California* (four volumes from 1908 to 1915) and studies of various missions, as well as the life of Father Fra Magín Catalá. Father Engelhardt also served as vice postulator for Catalá's cause for canonization. He died at Santa Barbara, California, where his archives are stored.

England, John (September 23, 1786–April 11, 1842)

The first bishop of the Diocese of Charleston, from 1820 to 1842, John England was one of the American Church's most influential early prelates.

Born in Cork, Ireland, he studied at St. Patrick's College in Carlow in anticipation of the priesthood. In 1805 he was active in providing catechetical instruction to the soldiers of the Cork garrison and soon after founded a female reformatory that eventually became the Presentation Convent. He was ordained in October 1808 after receiving a dispensation because he was younger than normally permitted.

Father England soon distinguished himself as a gifted preacher and pastor, serving as a lecturer at the cathedral, as chaplain to the North Presentation Convent, to the Magdalen Asylum, and the city prison, and finally as president at St. Mary's College from 1812 to 1817. From 1817 to 1820 he served as a parish priest and was then surprisingly appointed in August 1820 as the first bishop of Charleston.

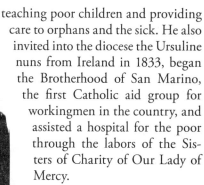

Bishop John England

Bishop England was consecrated in St. Finbar's Church in Cork in September 1820 and reached Charleston in December 1820 to assume the direction of his new diocese and its five thousand Catholics, spread out over North Carolina, South Carolina, and Georgia. Almost immediately upon assuming his duties, he issued a pastoral letter to the people of the diocese; it was the first such letter ever promulgated in the history of the American Church. He then embarked upon a visitation of the parishes and missions to familiarize himself with the pastoral needs of his people.

In 1822 Bishop England established the first Catholic newspaper in the United States, the *United States Catholic Miscellany,* with the purpose of combating the then-common anti-Catholicism in the press and society. The newspaper was published until 1861. Bishop England was also personally responsible for much of its content.

In 1922 Bishop England began the Philosophical and Classical Seminary of Charleston to provide a preparatory school for future seminarians. Three years later he opened St. John the Baptist Seminary. In 1829 he established a diocesan community of women religious, the Sisters of Charity of Our Lady of Mercy, with the apostolate of teaching poor children and providing care to orphans and the sick. He also invited into the diocese the Ursuline nuns from Ireland in 1833, began the Brotherhood of San Marino, the first Catholic aid group for workingmen in the country, and assisted a hospital for the poor through the labors of the Sisters of Charity of Our Lady of Mercy.

In 1833 Bishop England was appointed apostolic delegate to Haiti with the intent of assisting the needs of Catholics on the island, making him the first American prelate to be so honored by the Holy See. Although the mission from 1833 to 1837 did not prove a successful one, Pope Gregory XVI recognized Bishop England with the rank of Assistant at the Pontifical Throne. He was also serving at the time as vicar general of East Florida.

In the area of ecclesiastical life in the United States, Bishop England became convinced early in his episcopate of the need for a council among the hierarchy of the country. Toward that end, he became the principal voice among the bishops for the convening of the Councils of Baltimore, gatherings of bishops that provided direction in the legal and organizational future of the American Church. Archbishop James Whitfield of Baltimore convened the First Provincial Council in Baltimore in 1829.

In order to assist the financial and material needs of his diocese, Bishop England traveled across the country, and in Europe asked the Leopoldine Society for funds. Because of his fame as an orator, Bishop England was invited to address the U.S. Congress on January 8, 1826, the first Catholic ecclesiastic to be given that privilege. Before Congress he defended the Catholic Church from an attack made by President John Quincy Adams.

Bishop England placed the Diocese of Charleston on firm footing, with fourteen churches, twenty priests, and a Catholic population that had doubled during his time as bishop. His tours of Europe and his searches for priests and funds endangered his health. Bishop England became ill, but preached and conducted diocesan affairs until his death.

Erie, Diocese of

Erected on April 29, 1853, by Pope Blessed Pius IX, the Diocese of Erie serves counties in northwestern Pennsylvania. The city serves as a United States port of entry on Lake Erie and was built on the site of Fort Presque Isle, built by the French in 1753. In 1795 another Fort Presque Isle was built by the Americans, and the first settlement was laid out by General Andrew Ellicott, U.S. surveyor general, and General William Irvine. A shipyard in the city built the fleet of Commodore Oliver Hazard Perry that defeated the British in the Battle of Lake Erie in 1813. Erie is now a major shipping point. The Diocese of Erie is a suffragan see of the Archdiocese of Philadelphia.

René-Robert Chevalier, Sieur de La Salle, visited Erie early in his expeditions, and William Penn made the area part of his colony in 1681. From 1753 to 1758, the bishop of Québec administered the Catholic affairs in the region. From 1758 to 1783, a vicar apostolic in London provided guidance. Then the Diocese of Baltimore, established in 1789, placed the Catholics of Erie under the jurisdiction of America's first bishop, John Carroll. Pennsylvania had entered the Union two years earlier, the second state of the United States. In 1808 the Diocese of Philadelphia was erected, and Erie came under that ecclesiastical jurisdiction.

The Diocese of Pittsburgh was created in 1843 because of the growth of the Catholic population. The Diocese of Erie followed a decade later, and the bishop of Pittsburgh, Michael O'Connor, was transferred to Erie to begin establishing the agencies and offices necessary for diocesan administration. He assumed the see on July 29, 1853, but within seven months was returned to Pittsburgh because of a storm of protest from the clergy and laity there.

His successor was Josue Moody (Maria) Young, who was consecrated on April 23, 1854. A convert to Catholicism and baptized by the famous Dominican missionary Father Charles D. Ffrench, he took the name Maria instead of Moody. Bishop Young faced difficult problems in the diocese. There were only two parishes in Erie, St. Mary's and St. Patrick's. Outside of the city there were some twenty-eight reported parishes. Priests were not available readily, and some priests of the diocese went with Bishop O'Connor to Pittsburgh. Bishop Young, however, labored unceasingly to serve the Catholics of the area, adding new churches and recruiting priests whenever possible. In 1859 petroleum was discovered at Oil Creek, bringing more settlers into the region and industrializing some areas. In order to accommodate the spiraling Catholic population, Bishop Young maintained travel schedules and meetings throughout the diocese. He died suddenly on September 18, 1866.

Tobias Mullen was appointed as the third bishop of Erie, and he was consecrated on August 2, 1868. A graduate of Maynooth in Ireland, he had volunteered for the American missions. A new era of expansion began during his episcopacy. He replaced wooden churches with brick and stone and recruited clergy for the parishes. Tireless in his efforts, Bishop Mullen founded a Catholic weekly newspaper and completed the Cathedral of St. Peter in Erie. In May 1897 he suffered a stroke and resigned on August 10, 1899, dying the following year.

His successor was John E. FitzMaurice, who had served as coadjutor bishop of Erie since February 24, 1898. He acceded to the see upon the resignation of Bishop Mullen. Bishop FitzMaurice brought many religious congregations to the diocese and built churches to accommodate the growing demands. During World War I, he supported national defense operations and aided the troops. He also added a rectory to the cathedral and erected homes for boys. Bishop FitzMaurice died on June 18, 1920.

The fifth bishop of Erie was John Mark Gannon, who was appointed the personal title of archbishop on November 25, 1953. Bishop Gannon had served as auxiliary bishop of Erie since 1918 and was installed in Erie on December 16, 1920, as Bishop FitzMaurice's successor. He founded Gannon College in 1933 and led the diocese through the grim days of the Great Depression and World War II. On November 4, 1944, he was appointed an Assistant at the Pontifical Throne. Archbishop Gannon retired on September 21, 1966.

The successor to Archbishop Gannon was John F. Whealon, who had served as auxiliary bishop of Cleveland since 1961. He was transferred to Erie on December 14, 1966. Bishop Whealon implemented the reforms mandated by the Second Vatican

Council and expanded the facilities and programs of the diocese. On December 28, 1968, he was promoted to the Archdiocese of Hartford.

The auxiliary bishop of Erie since 1965, Alfred M. Watson succeeded Bishop Whealon in the see on March 19, 1969, as the seventh bishop of Erie. He led the diocese through the changes in personnel and practices in that era. He also faced a critical shortage of priests and religious and ordained eighty-eight young men to the priesthood. In 1975 the Diocese of Erie adopted the Diocese of Merida, Mexico, and provided a grant for programs in the Yucatan region of that nation. Bishop Watson retired on July 16, 1982.

Michael J. Murphy, who had served as auxiliary bishop of Cleveland since 1976 and as coadjutor bishop of Erie since 1978, acceded to the see upon the retirement of Bishop Watson. He inaugurated the Emmaus programs for priests and implemented pastoral projects. He was also active in national Catholic programs and in 1984 received an award for his service to seminaries. He retired on July 16, 1990.

The ninth bishop of Erie, Donald W. Trautman, had served as auxiliary bishop of Buffalo since 1985. He was installed in Erie on July 16, 1990, and immediately embarked on a tour of diocesan facilities. Bishop Trautman reorganized diocesan agencies and offices and solidified finances. He holds posts in the National Conference of Catholic Bishops and is one of the country's leading experts in liturgy and Scripture. The bishop has received numerous awards, including the Michael Mathis Award from the University of Notre Dame Center for Liturgy, its highest honor bestowed for outstanding contributions to liturgy. The Federation of Diocesan Liturgical Commissions' annual Monsignor Frederick R. McManus Award was presented to him in 2003. In 2011 there were 221,000 Catholics served by 199 priests, 326 women religious, and 117 parishes in the diocese.

Escalante, Silvestre Velez de (c. 1750–1780)

A Spanish Franciscan explorer and missionary, Father Silvestre Velez de Escalante left Santa Fe, in present-day New Mexico, with his superior, Father Francisco Atanasio Domínguez on July 29, 1776, to find a route to Monterey, California. The priests

explored what is now western Colorado and entered Utah, seeing Utah Lake and spending time with the Laguna Indians. On September 25, 1776, they crossed the Grand Canyon.

Father Escalante charted the entire expedition, detailing rivers, mountains, Indian settlements, and botanical finds. His historical accounts are highly respected. The Franciscans returned to Santa Fe, having found a way to California.

Espejo, Antonio (d. after 1583)

A Spanish explorer best known for his travels throughout New Mexico and Arizona, Antonio Espejo went in search of missing missionaries in the American Southwest. Born in Cordoba, Spain, he traveled to Mexico and made his fortune in mining. In 1582 he volunteered to fund an expedition to New Mexico to learn the fate of the protomartyr of the United States, Franciscan Juan de Padilla, who had been rumored to have been martyred. Father Espejo set out on November 10, 1582, from San Bartolomí, Chihuahua, Mexico, with fourteen soldiers and a group of Christian Indians. He learned soon after reaching the territory of the Indian tribes of Puara that the Franciscan had, indeed, been martyred at the hands of Zuñis.

Part of the expedition returned to Mexico, and Espejo then set out to explore the northern territories. He reached modern Arizona and encountered Hopi Christian Indians who had been part of Francisco Vázquez de Coronado's expedition years earlier. They treated Espejo kindly. He then explored around modern-day Prescott, where he recovered silver ore. He ended his expeditions and set out for home, bringing with him the samples of silver ore and noting the presence of various mines. His later hopes of returning to establish himself in mining in the area proved unsuccessful, as the local viceroy, jealous of his accomplishments, refused him permission.

Eucharistic Congresses

The international gatherings of Catholic faithful to promote and foster devotion to the Blessed Sacrament of the Altar, Eucharistic congresses are a recent development in the Church, originating through the effort of Marie-Marthe Tamisier of Tours, France, to organize Eucharistic pilgrimages in her native country. The first such pilgrimage, a forerunner of the formal Eucharistic congress, was held in 1874.

The first actual Eucharistic congress was organized in 1881, largely by Monsignor Louis Gaston de Ségur, and held at Lille, France. Pope Leo XIII announced papal approval for the gathering, and over four thousand people from ten countries took part in the final procession. Following the conclusion of the congress, the committee first established in 1879 to facilitate the 1881 gathering was made permanent. The 1905 Eucharistic Congress was held in Rome and presided over by Pope St. Pius X.

The custom was established soon after of having a cardinal legate appointed to serve as the direct representative of the pope for each gathering outside of Rome. The presence of the cardinal legate assumed unexpected importance in 1908 at the congress held in London. The arrival of the legate, Cardinal Vincenzo Vannutelli, marked the first entrance of such an official of the Holy See in England since the Reformation. With him were six other cardinals, fourteen archbishops, seventy bishops, and a host of priests, one of the largest gatherings of clergy outside of Rome in recent history. During the formal sessions in September 1908, over fifteen thousand Catholics gathered at Albert Hall, a significant milestone in the renewal of the Church in the British Isles.

In his 1947 encyclical *Mediator Dei*, Pope Pius XII described Eucharistic congresses (and similar devotions) as flowing from and leading to the central acts of the Church's worship, the Mass, sacraments, and prayers. Currently, international Eucharistic congresses are organized through the Pontifical Committee for International Eucharistic Congresses in Rome, the descendant of the permanent committee. Pope Blessed John Paul II made it a pontifical committee with new statutes in 1986.

There have been forty-seven Eucharistic congresses since 1881, taking place across the globe. Two have been held in the United States, in Chicago in 1926 and in Philadelphia in 1976.

Evansville, Diocese of

Established on November 11, 1944, by Pope Pius XII, the Diocese of Evansville serves counties in southwestern Indiana. A port of entry on the Ohio River, Evansville has coal deposits and oil fields in a rich agricultural area. The city was named after Robert M. Evans, a colonel of the militia and a legislator. The Diocese of Evansville is a suffragan see of the Archdiocese of Indianapolis.

Some of the earliest mission activities in America took place in and around Indiana. Jesuit Father Jacques Marquette was in the area in 1675, and René-Robert Chevalier, Sieur de La Salle, claimed the region for France in 1679, while traveling with Recollect Franciscan Father Louis Hennepin. Famous Jesuit pioneers, such as Father Claude Allouez, made their headquarters in the area. Indiana was part of the Diocese of Québec during the early mission era.

A Mass was celebrated in the area in 1702, and thirty years later, in 1732, Fort Vincennes was opened on the Wabash River. St. Francis Xavier Church was also opened on the site, and Father Pierre Gibault became the resident pastor in 1769, earning the respect and affection of all Americans because of his support in the Revolutionary War and his courage in facing the British. When the Diocese of Baltimore (now the Archdiocese of Baltimore) was established in 1789, Vincennes and other regional communities came under the jurisdiction of America's first bishop, John Carroll. In 1808 Indiana became part of the vast Diocese of Bardstown (now the Archdiocese of Louisville). Bishop Benedict Joseph Flaget, the honored missionary prelate, was in Vincennes in 1814 to administer confirmation. Two years later, Indiana entered the Union.

In 1834 one of the great missionary pioneers of America, Father Simon William Gabriel Bruté de Rémur, was consecrated as the bishop of Vincennes on October 28. Bishop Bruté de Rémur traveled endlessly throughout the diocese on horseback, building parishes and aiding Catholic communities. He died in 1839. Evansville remained a part of Vincennes as Fort Wayne was erected as a diocese in 1857. On March 28, 1898, the Diocese of Vincennes was transferred to Indianapolis, now an archdiocese, and Evansville remained a part of that ecclesiastical jurisdiction during World War I, the Great Depression, and the first years of World War II. The Diocese of Evansville was established in 1944.

The first bishop of Evansville was Henry Joseph Grimmelsman, who was consecrated on December

21, 1944. He opened the offices and agencies necessary to diocesan administration and then started a vast expansion program to meet the demands of the Catholic population. Bishop Grimmelsman established fourteen new parishes, four high schools, and a diocesan newspaper. He attended the Second Vatican Council and designated a cathedral for the diocese. After two decades of faithful service, Bishop Grimmelsman retired on October 20, 1965.

His successor was Paul F. Liebold, who had served as auxiliary bishop of Cincinnati since 1958 and was appointed to Evansville on April 6, 1966. He continued the expansion programs of the diocese and convened a diocesan synod. On July 23, 1969, Bishop Liebold was promoted to the Archdiocese of Cincinnati.

The third bishop of Evansville was Francis R. Shea, who was appointed on December 10, 1969. Bishop Shea consolidated diocesan offices and maintained facilities and ministries despite the lack of priests and religious. He promoted the ordination of permanent deacons and implemented the reforms and lay participation mandated by the Second Vatican Council. Bishop Shea retired on April 11, 1989.

The fourth bishop of Evansville, Gerald Andrew Gettelfinger, was consecrated and installed in Evansville on April 11, 1989. Aside from his dedicated care of the diocese, Bishop Gettelfinger held the fourth diocesan synod in 1993, presided over the dedication of St. Benedict Church as the diocesan cathedral in 1999, and opened the Center for Hispanic Ministry, the Guadalupe Center, in 2001. He retired on April 26, 2011, and was succeeded by Father Charles C. Thompson, who was ordained a bishop on June 29, 2011. In 2011 there were 83,000 Catholics served by 78 priests, 254 women religious, and 69 parishes in the diocese.

Ewing, Thomas (December 28, 1789–October 26, 1871)

A United States senator, Thomas Ewing also served as Secretary of the Treasury, first Secretary of the Interior, and governor of Ohio. Born in West Liberty, Virginia (modern-day West Virginia), Ewing grew up in a frontier setting and was taught how to read by his sister, Sarah. From this rudimentary education, he went on to work his way through college and earned a degree from Ohio University at Athens in 1815. He then studied law at Lancaster, Ohio, and was admitted to the bar in 1816. Soon after, he began the law firm of Beecher & Ewing, followed by a partnership with his own son, Philemon, after Beecher's death. He gained considerable prominence in the field of law and was elected in 1831 to the U.S. Senate from Ohio.

In 1841 the short-lived President William Henry Harrison appointed Ewing to the post of Secretary of the Treasury. In this capacity, he became involved in the controversy regarding the rechartering of the Bank of the United States; upon its veto by President John Tyler, he resigned from the cabinet. In March 1849 he was appointed by President Zachary Taylor to be the first Secretary of the Interior and devoted his energies to organizing the new department and giving encouragement to Congress to promote the advance of the railroads.

In 1860 he was asked by the governor of Ohio to serve on the Peace Conference that was then trying to prevent the secession of the Southern States. In the ensuing Civil War, Ewing served as an adviser to President Abraham Lincoln, and his advice was crucial in smoothing relations between England and the United States and preventing a rupture that might have risked the entire American position in the war. Following the war, Ewing opposed the radical Reconstruction. He was then nominated in February 1868 to be Secretary of War, but the nomination was not confirmed.

A member of a Presbyterian family, Ewing was not raised in any denomination. He married the Irish Catholic Maria Wills Boyle in 1820, and all their children were raised Catholic. In October 1869, Ewing suffered a stroke while arguing before the Supreme Court. He was baptized a Catholic in the courtroom.

Eternal Word Television Network (EWTN)

The Eternal Word Television Network is an American cable television and radio global Catholic network based in Irondale, Alabama, and established in 1980 by Mother Mary Angelica of the Annunciation, a Poor Clare nun. Launched officially on August 15, 1981, EWTN grew from humble beginnings into the largest religious media network in the world and is seen in 144 countries.

Mother Angelica was born Rita Antoinette Rizzo on April 20, 1923, in Canton, Ohio. She entered the Poor Clares of Perpetual Adoration in 1944 and made her solemn profession on January 2, 1953. On May 20, 1962, she officially established, with four other sisters, Our Lady of the Angels Monastery in Irondale, Alabama. Committed to evangelization, she began writing booklets on the faith and eventually secured a printing press to keep pace with the demand. Mother Angelica grew in popularity as a speaker and started a video series of her talks. To accomplish this, the nuns used a local television station in Birmingham and then constructed their own studio in a garage on the monastery grounds.

Mother Angelica perceived the need for a television station devoted to authentic Catholic programming, and in 1981 the Eternal World Television Network was launched. At first, EWTN broadcast four hours of programming each day; in 1987 it began broadcasting twenty-fours a day. In 1992 the shortwave radio station WEWN was acquired, and, in 1996 EWTN began broadcasting on AM/FM radio. In January 2011 EWTN acquired the *National Catholic Register*, a national newspaper first begun in 1924.

EWTN's programming eventually included a highly respected news division, including *The World Over Live*, covering current events and hosted by journalist Raymond Arroyo, and live broadcasts of major events, such as papal liturgies and World Youth Days. In 2005 the network provided complete coverage of the funeral and obsequies of Pope Blessed John Paul II and the succeeding conclave that elected Pope Benedict XVI. Other notable programs have featured such Catholic figures as Father Benedict Groeschel, Marcus Grodi, Cardinal Timothy Dolan, and Scott Hahn.

In 2000 Mother Angelica stepped down and handed control of EWTN to a lay board. The following year, she suffered a stroke. In 2009 she and Deacon Bill Steltemeier, the chairman of EWTN's board of governors, received the *Pro Ecclesia et Pontifice* medal from Pope Benedict XVI in recognition of their work on behalf of the Church.

Extension Society. *See* **Catholic Church Extension Society**

F

Fairbanks, Diocese of

Established on August 8, 1962, by Pope Blessed John XXIII, the Diocese of Fairbanks serves all of Alaska north of the old Territorial Third Judicial Division. Fairbanks is a large city, founded in 1902 during a gold strike. The site was named after Senator Charles Warren Fairbanks, who became vice president of the United States. A terminal for the Alaska Highway and other routes, the city serves as a center for various industries and has military installations. The Diocese of Fairbanks is a suffragan see of the Archdiocese of Anchorage.

Alaska was a mission territory since the late 1700s, and Alaskan records state that a Franciscan celebrated Mass on May 13, 1779, near present-day Craig. Alaska was part of the Diocese of Vancouver Island, headed by the famed missionary Bishop Modeste Demers. The Prefecture Apostolic of Alaska was erected on July 27, 1894, and was elevated to the rank of vicariate apostolic by Pope Benedict XV on December 22, 1916.

The earliest Catholic missions within the present diocese were founded along the Yukon River. In 1867 Bishop Charles J. Seghers of Vancouver Island had jurisdiction over the area. Women religious were also on the scene in 1898, and parishes were in operation. Our Lady of the Snows is recorded in Nulato, dating to 1877. St. Aloysius in Tanana (1887), Holy Family at Holy Cross (1888), and St. Joseph at Tununak (1889) were also serving the faithful. Immaculate Conception is recorded as opening in Fairbanks in 1904, and in 1901, St. Joseph Parish was operating in Nome.

Bishop Joseph Raphael Cremont, S.J., was appointed prefect apostolic of Alaska on March 28, 1904, and was appointed vicar apostolic of Alaska on February 15, 1917. Bishop Cremont served far-flung communities of the faithful through World War I, the Great Depression, and World War II. After decades of mission labors, he died on May 20, 1945.

His successor was Bishop Walter J. Fitzgerald, S.J., who had been appointed coadjutor vicar apostolic in 1938 and acceded to the see upon the death of Bishop Cremont. Bishop Fitzgerald continued the mission and expansion programs but died on July 19, 1947.

Bishop Francis D. Gleeson, S.J., succeeded Bishop Fitzgerald, and was consecrated on April 5, 1948, as vicar apostolic of Alaska. On August 8, 1962, he became the first bishop of Fairbanks. Bishop George T. Boileau, S.J., was consecrated on July 31, 1964, as coadjutor bishop of Fairbanks with right of succession. He died, however, on February 25, 1965, before acceding to the see. Bishop Gleeson instituted the agencies and offices for diocesan administration. He also attended the Second Vatican Council, implemented the reforms mandated by the council, and opened Sacred Heart Cathedral in 1968. On February 3, 1969, Pope Paul VI made Bishop Gleeson an Assistant at the Pontifical Throne. Bishop Gleeson retired on November 30, 1968.

The second bishop of Fairbanks was Robert Louis Whelan, S.J., who had served as coadjutor bishop with right of succession since 1967. He acceded to the see upon Bishop Gleeson's retirement. Bishop Whelan continued to implement the reforms of the Second Vatican Council and expanded lay ministries to provide spiritual care for the entire diocese. He retired on July 28, 1985.

Bishop Michael J. Kaniecki, S.J., was Bishop Whelan's successor, having served as coadjutor bishop with right of succession since 1984. He acceded to the see upon Bishop Whelan's retirement and built new parishes and introduced charitable programs. He also promoted Native American ministries. Bishop Kaniecki died unexpectedly of a heart attack on August 6, 2000, while visiting Emmonak Eskimo Village.

The fourth bishop of Fairbanks, Donald J. Kettler, was appointed to the Diocese of Fairbanks on June 7, 2002, and installed on August 22, 2002. The diocese remains the only missionary Catholic diocese in the United States, as it exists under the authority of the Congregation for the Evangelization of Peoples. It is challenged by the severe poverty of the region, with most of its parishes requiring outside assistance to ensure the pastoral care of the people. In 2011 there were 13,500 Catholics served by 24 priests and 46 parishes in the diocese.

Faith of Our Fathers

A popular book written by Cardinal James Gibbons to explain the Catholic faith to the non-Catholic people of the United States, *Faith of Our Fathers* was published in 1876 in Richmond, Virginia. Cardinal Gibbons was serving as the bishop of Richmond at the time. The book went on to sell over two million copies as the future cardinal had used his experiences as vicar apostolic in North Carolina from 1868 to 1872 to craft a narrative that provided the basics of Catholic teachings in a style that could be readily understood by the average person who possessed little or no knowledge of the faith.

The future Cardinal Gibbons hoped to use the book as a teaching tool, especially to refute frequent charges that Catholics could not be good Americans. The work proved immensely successful and was soon translated into German, French, and other languages. The Japanese edition appeared in 1892.

Faith of Our Fathers began with the Holy Trinity and the Incarnation, as Cardinal Gibbons was concerned first and foremost with those elements of Catholic teaching that were attacked by Protestants. He then devoted eleven chapters to the Church's understanding of Scripture, papal infallibility, and the temporal authority of the pope. He then turned to the saints, veneration of images, and the special place given to the Blessed Virgin Mary, followed by prayers and purgatory, and civil and religious liberties. The last chapters were spent on the sacraments and celibacy for priests.

Falconio, Diomede (September 20, 1842–February 7, 1911)

A member of the Franciscan order, Diomede Falconio was created a cardinal in 1911, and served as apostolic delegate to the United States from 1902 to 1911. Born Angelo Raffaele Gennaro Falconio in Pescocostanza, Italy, he entered the Order of the Friars Minor in September 1860 and was professed in October 1864, taking the name Diomede of Pescocostanzo in religious life. He traveled to the United States in the fall of 1865 and was ordained on January 3, 1866, in Buffalo, New York.

From 1865 to 1868, he served as a professor of philosophy at St. Bonaventure College and Seminary in Allegany, New York, and was appointed president of the school in 1868. He also served as secretary of the American Franciscan province of the Immaculate Conception in 1867. From 1871 to 1882, he was administrator, chancellor, and vicar general of Diocese of Harbor Grace, Newfoundland (modern Grand Fall), in Canada. He was a likely candidate to become bishop there, but the Irish Benevolent Society, a group that did not want an Italian bishop for the diocese, blocked his appointment. Returning to the United States, he undertook missionary work in New York and Connecticut from 1882 to 1883 and then sailed to Italy in 1883. There he became provincial of the Franciscans in the province of San Bernardino in Abruzzi, Italy, from 1884 to 1889, procurator general of the order in 1889, and visitor general to the provinces of Naples, Italy, and Pouilles, France, from 1889 to 1892.

On July 11, 1892, he was appointed bishop of Lacedonia, Italy, and consecrated on July 17, 1892. Promoted to the metropolitan see of Acerenza e Matera on November 29, 1895, he was appointed four years later to the post of apostolic delegate to Canada and transferred to the titular see of Larissa on September 30, 1899. He was named apostolic delegate to the United States on September 30, 1902. In that office, Archbishop Falconio played a part in the major decisions of the Holy See throughout the pontificate of Pope St. Pius X. He was thus posted to the United States in 1908, when the pontiff issued the apostolic constitution *Sapienti Consilio,* by which the dioceses of

Cardinal Diomede Falconio

the United States were removed from the authority of the Sacred Congregation of the Propaganda. Henceforth, the dioceses were under the common law of the Church, subject to the other congregations and offices of the Holy See. Archbishop Falconio also took part in the creation of the Dioceses of Fall River and Great Falls in 1904, Oklahoma City and Superior in 1905, Rockford in 1908, Bismarck and Crookston in 1909, Toledo in 1910, and Des Moines in 1911.

Created a cardinal priest on November 27, 1911, he was officially elevated to the College of Cardinals with the titular church of Santa Maria in Aracoeli on November 30, 1911. On May 25, 1914, he was promoted to the order of cardinal bishop and the suburbicarian see of Velletri. He took part in the conclave of 1914 that elected Pope Benedict XV and served briefly as prefect of the Congregation for Religious. He died in Rome.

Fall River, Diocese of

Established on March 12, 1904, the first such ecclesiastical jurisdiction declared by Pope St. Pius X, the Diocese of Fall River serves counties in southeastern Massachusetts. The site of modern Fall River, located on the eastern shore of Mount Hope Bay, was included in Freeman's Purchase, a tract of land bought from the local Indians in 1659 and settled in 1686. The town was incorporated as Fallriver in 1803, renamed Troy, but then called Fall River in 1831. The city is a center for industries, including textiles and clothing. The diocese is a suffragan see of the Archdiocese of Boston.

In 1650 the Canadian government sent Jesuit Father Gabriel Druillettes to Boston, despite the fact that Catholic priests were forbidden to enter the Massachusetts Colony. He was there to negotiate a treaty forming a mutual defense against attacks by the Iroquois nations. Father Druillettes, an educated and cultured individual, was courteously received, although no treaty was forthcoming. Other priests were kept out of the colony until 1732, when local Catholics formed groups to protect the faith. It was reported that a priest visited such groups secretly, celebrating Masses in the area.

The courage and patriotic valor of the Catholics in the Revolutionary War prompted repeals of the severe anti-Catholic laws in the colonies, and new state constitutions began to provide equality and religious civil rights. The right to hold public office in Massachusetts, however, was denied to Catholics until 1821.

In 1788 a French priest, Father Claude Florent Bouchard de la Poterie, became the first resident priest of Boston, and an Augustinian, Father Philip Lariscy, established a parish in New Bedford in 1821. Father Jean-Louis Lefebvre de Cheverus, the beloved missionary who would become a cardinal of France, was reportedly connected to the New Bedford parish. In 1808 the Diocese of Boston, now an archdiocese, was headed by Bishop de Cheverus. Other dioceses followed after decades. The Diocese of Providence was erected in 1872, and Fall River became part of that episcopal jurisdiction.

In 1904 the Diocese of Fall River was established in recognition of the devoted and active Catholics in the city. The first bishop of Fall River was William Stang, who was consecrated on May 1, 1904. Bishop Stang had served as the vice rector of the American College in Louvain and was a recognized scholar. He erected parishes, built a hospital, convened a diocesan synod, and issued three pastoral

St. Mary's Cathedral in Fall River

letters in three years. Bishop Stang died suddenly on February 2, 1907.

The second bishop of Fall River was Daniel Francis Feehan, who was consecrated on September 19, 1907. He continued the expansion programs, opening thirty-six parishes, including one for the Maronite rite. Bishop Feehan also labored to promote charitable facilities, especially for children, as he led the faithful through World War I and the Great Depression. He died on July 19, 1934.

The successor to Bishop Feehan was James E. Cassidy, who had served as auxiliary bishop since 1930. Bishop Cassidy introduced the annual Catholic Charities appeal and founded the Rose Hawthorne Lathrop Home. He developed residences for the elderly and took part in various social movements. He also led the faithful of the diocese through World War II, supporting the military efforts of the nation. Bishop Cassidy died on May 17, 1951.

The fourth bishop of Fall River was James L. Connolly, who had served as coadjutor bishop with right of succession since 1945. He acceded to the see upon the death of Bishop Cassidy. Bishop Connolly established facilities for the chronically ill and the aged and built schools for disabled children. He also built youth centers and regional high schools and started a diocesan newspaper. Taking part in the Second Vatican Council, Bishop Connolly implemented the reforms mandated by that council. He retired on October 30, 1970.

Bishop Daniel A. Cronin was the successor of Bishop Connolly, having served in various capacities in the Vatican and as a representative of the Holy See in Ethiopia. He had also served as auxiliary bishop of Boston from 1968. Bishop Cronin was installed in Fall River on December 16, 1970, and started implementing lay ministries, liturgical reforms, and educational programs. Catholic charities and social apostolates were also promoted. On December 9, 1991, Bishop Cronin was promoted to the Archdiocese of Hartford.

The sixth bishop of Fall River was Seán O'Malley, O.F.M. Cap., who had served as the bishop of St. Thomas, Virgin Islands, since 1985. He was installed in Fall River on August 11, 1992, and promoted Catholic education. Bishop O'Malley also handled a serious case of clerical

sexual abuse and promoted programs for AIDS victims and migrant communities as well as other social services. On September 3, 2002, he was transferred to the Diocese of Palm Beach. He was appointed archbishop of Boston in 2003 and created a cardinal on March 24, 2006.

The seventh bishop of Fall River, George William Coleman, was appointed on April 30, 2003, and consecrated on July 22, 2003. Bishop Coleman carried forward the extensive programs for child protection in the diocese and the full implementation of the Essential Norms regarding the prevention of the problem of sexual abuse. In 2011 there were 311,000 Catholics served by 250 priests and 90 parishes in the diocese.

Fargo, Diocese of

Established originally as the Diocese of Jamestown on November 12, 1889, by Pope Leo XIII, and transferred to Fargo on April 6, 1897, the Diocese of Fargo serves counties in North Dakota. Fargo is the largest city in North Dakota, founded in 1871 by the Northern Pacific Railway and named for William George Fargo of Wells, Fargo and Company. The city serves as a transportation, marketing, and distribution center in an agricultural region. The Diocese of Fargo is a suffragan see of the Archdiocese of St. Paul and Minneapolis.

The Catholic history of the area opened with the arrival of the expedition of Pierre Gaultier de Varennes, Sieur de La Vérendrye, in 1738. In 1818 Father Sévére Dumoulin served the fort at Pembina. He and Father Joseph Norbert Provencher also served at Fort Douglas, at St. Boniface. Father George A. Belcourt and Jesuit Father Pierre-Jean De Smet, the revered missionary, ministered to the local tribes in the area.

Part of the Vicariate Apostolic of North Dakota, established in 1879, Fargo was administered by Bishop Martin Marty, the pioneering Benedictine abbot and missionary. The Jesuits who had labored in the vicariate for decades moved with the American Indian tribes as they lost their original lands. Bishop Marty and other priests had established churches, schools, and a hospital, all of which served the diocese when it was erected.

Bishop John Shanley was the first bishop of the Diocese of Jamestown, consecrated on December 27, 1889. He labored among Native Americans as well as white settlers, and in 1897 asked the Holy See to transfer the diocese to Fargo. Bishop Shanley was a young man when consecrated, and he used the economic growth in the region to expand the diocesan facilities and services. When he died on July 16, 1909, the diocese reportedly had 215 churches, parochial schools, hospitals, academies, a college, and an orphanage.

His successor was James O'Reilly, who was installed as bishop on June 1, 1910. The Diocese of Bismarck was detached from Fargo in 1909. Bishop O'Reilly was an energetic builder who led the faithful during World War I, the drought, and the Great Depression. He established a recorded thirty-four new parishes and continued to extend the ministries of the diocese until his death on December 19, 1934.

The third bishop of Fargo was Aloisius Joseph Muench, who would become a cardinal in 1959. He was installed in Fargo on November 6, 1935, and began the Catholic Church Extension Fund to save parishes on the verge of bankruptcy and instituted the Confraternity of Christian Doctrine in the diocese. Bishop Muench also promoted the Catholic Rural Life Movement and the Priests Mutual Aid Fund. World War II and the last years of the Great Depression had an impact on Fargo, but Bishop Muench invited teaching congregations into Fargo and started a diocesan newspaper. On July 8, 1946, he was appointed the apostolic visitor to Germany by Pope Pius XII and given the personal rank of archbishop. In 1951 he was appointed papal nuncio to Germany, and on December 14, 1959, he was created a cardinal priest and elevated to the Curia in Rome.

Bishop Leo F. Dworschak succeeded Archbishop Muench in Fargo, having served as coadjutor bishop of Rapid City from 1946 and as auxiliary bishop of Fargo from 1947. He succeeded to the see on May 10, 1960. Bishop Dworschak attended the Second Vatican Council and continued the diocesan expansion programs. He also established

Bishop John Shanley

accredited schools of religion in Grand Forks and at the North Dakota Agricultural College in Fargo. Bishop Dworschak retired on September 8, 1970.

The fifth bishop of Fargo was Justin A. Driscoll, who was consecrated and installed in the diocese on October 28, 1970. Bishop Driscoll promoted the ministries and reforms mandated by the Second Vatican Council and maintained the Indian Missions of Turtle Mountain Reservation and Fort Totten Reservation. He died on November 19, 1984.

His successor was Bishop James S. Sullivan, who had served as auxiliary bishop of Lansing since 1972 and was appointed to Fargo on April 2, 1985. He was installed in the diocese on May 30. Bishop Sullivan promoted the permanent diaconate, communications programs, and charitable ministries, while expanding diocesan facilities to meet the growing demands of the Catholic population. He retired on May 18, 2002.

The seventh bishop of Fargo, Samuel J. Aquila, had served as the rector of St. John Vianney Seminary in Denver and then as coadjutor bishop of Fargo, appointed in 2001. He acceded to the see on March 18, 2002. In 2011 there were 83,000 Catholics served by 141 priests and 132 parishes in the diocese.

Faribault, Jean-Baptiste (October 19, 1774– August 20, 1860)

A fur trapper and early settler in present-day Minnesota and Wisconsin, Jean-Baptiste Faribault defied the British during the War of 1812. He was born in Berthier, Canada, the son of a Paris lawyer who had migrated to Canada. Faribault was highly educated and sought employment with the North West Fur Company, as he preferred life in the wilderness. In 1798 he was assigned to the company outpost at Michilimackinac (modern-day Mackinac) and began trading with the Potawatomi at Kankakee and with the Dakota Sioux at Redwood. There he met a woman of Native American ancestry, Pelagia Hanse, and they were married in 1805.

Four years later, they settled at Prairie du Chien, Wisconsin, where Faribault developed relations with the Fox, Sioux, and Winnebago. When the War of 1812 engulfed the region, Faribault refused to enlist in the British army and was imprisoned and deprived of all his property. In 1815, after the British were defeated, Faribault became a citizen of the United States and resumed trading at Prairie du Chien. Four years later, he moved to Pike Island and then to St. Peter, Mendota, Minnesota.

He was respected and trusted by the American Indians, and his fellow Americans considered him a hero after 1812. A devout Catholic, Faribault built a house for Father Lucien Galtier, the first resident priest in the area. He died at Faribault.

Faribault-Stillwater Plan. *See* **Education, Catholic**

Farley, James (May 30, 1888–June 9, 1976)

The postmaster general of the United States from 1933 to 1940, James Farley was a leading figure in the Democratic Party. He was born in Grassy Point, New York, graduated from Packard Commercial School in New York City, and then took a position in 1906 with the Universal Gypsum Company. Farley embarked on his political career by serving from 1912 to 1919 as town clerk in Stony Point, New York, before returning to New York City to hold a swift succession of offices, including port warden of the Port of New York and a member of the New York State Assembly. In 1926 Farley began a building-materials company that eventually merged with several other companies and resulted in Farley becoming president of the General Builders Supply Corporation.

In 1928 he was appointed secretary of the New York State Democratic Committee and thus was a key player in the campaign of Franklin Delano Roosevelt for governor of New York. In 1930 he became chairperson of the state party and in 1932 was head of the Democratic National Committee and chief organizer of Roosevelt's presidential campaign. In recognition of Farley's role in the campaign, Roosevelt named him postmaster general.

Farley again was active in Roosevelt's 1936 campaign, but he resigned in 1940 after disagreeing with the president on the matter of seeking a third term. He served again as state Democratic chair but

again opposed Roosevelt in seeking a fourth term in 1944. Roosevelt's victory effectively ended Farley's career. He retired from public life and received the Laetare Medal from the University of Notre Dame in 1974. Farley died in New York City.

Farley, John Murphy (April 20, 1842–September 17, 1918)

The archbishop of New York from 1902 to 1918 and a cardinal from 1911, John Murphy Farley was a mediator and peacemaker in a troubled era. He was born in County Armagh, Ireland, the fourth and youngest child of Philip and Catherine Murphy Farrelly; both parents died in his youth. After studying at local schools and at St. Macartan's College in Monaghan, he migrated to New York in 1864, where he lived with his uncle, who had arrived in New York in 1830.

He entered Fordham College (later Fordham University) and then St. Joseph's Seminary in Troy, New York, to prepare for the priesthood. Deemed a promising seminarian, he was sent to the North American College in Rome in 1866 and was ordained in Rome for the Archdiocese of New York in June 1870.

Returning to New York, Father Farley served as a curate at St. Peter's Parish on Staten Island for two years, whereupon he was named secretary to Cardinal John McCloskey. Around the same time, he changed the spelling of his name from Farrelly to Farley. In 1884 he was named pastor of St. Gabriel's in Manhattan, and from 1891 to 1902 he was vicar general of the archdiocese. On December 21, 1895, he was consecrated titular bishop of Zeugma and auxiliary bishop of New York, serving Archbishop Michael A. Corrigan. He then succeeded Archbishop Corrigan on September 25, 1902, as the fourth archbishop of the Archdiocese of New York. On November 27, 1911, Pope St. Pius X created him a cardinal priest with the titular church of Santa Maria sopra Minerva.

Upon assuming the immense duties of his office and rank, Cardinal Farley was confronted first and foremost with the task of healing the bitter divisions caused by the McGlynn Affair. With patience and a spirit of reconciliation, he was able to bring healing and demonstrated early on the cautious and peace-seeking tendencies that were the hallmarks of his episcopal service. He brought about genuine reconciliation by distributing papal honors among the clergy. The chief concerns of the period were the continuing need for pastoral care among the immigrants in the archdiocese and education at all levels. Given the influx of Italian immigrants into the archdiocese, Cardinal Farley increased the number of Italian parishes. He also opened fifty new parochial schools, supported The Catholic University of America, and encouraged the foundation of three women's colleges (the College of New Rochelle, the College of Mount St. Vincent, and Manhattanville College of the Sacred Heart). He opened a preparatory seminary in 1903, Cathedral College, and had an abiding interest in St. Joseph's Seminary at Dunwoodie, the major seminary of the archdiocese.

In literary matters, Cardinal Farley was a patron of the old *Catholic Encyclopedia* and the *New York Review*,

Cardinal John Farley

a journal that eventually ceased publication in 1908 owing to suspicions of modernism. He also wrote two books, *The History of St. Patrick's Cathedral* in 1908 and *The Life of John Cardinal McCloskey* in 1918, although the latter was reportedly largely written by the noted Catholic historian Peter Guilday. Cardinal Farley died of pneumonia and was buried in St. Patrick's Cathedral, beneath the high altar. He left the archdiocese united in a way that it had not been at the time of his accession, mostly so among the archdiocesan clergy.

Farmer, Ferdinand. *See* Steinmeyer, Ferdinand

Farrell, Walter (July 21, 1902–November 23, 1951)

A Dominican theologian and writer, Walter Farrell promoted Thomistic studies. He was born in Chicago and grew up in the city, studying at Quigley Preparatory Seminary before entering the Dominican order at St. Joseph's Priory, in Somerset, Ohio, in September 1920. He initially studied philosophy at St. Rose of Lima Priory in Springfield, Kentucky. He was ordained on June 9, 1927, and earned a

licentiate in sacred theology in 1928 and doctorate of sacred theology from the University of Fribourg, Switzerland, in 1930.

After his return to the United States, Father Farrell taught at St. Joseph's Priory until 1933, when he was sent to the Dominican house of studies in Washington, D.C. In 1939 he was named regent of studies of the Province of St. Joseph, New York, in 1939. The next year, he went to Rome and earned a master's degree in sacred theology, the highest degree possible in theology from the Dominicans. Immediately after, he was appointed president of the pontifical faculty of theology at the Dominican House of Studies. During World War II, Father Farrell served as a chaplain in the U.S. Navy and put in a year at sea on the carrier USS *Yorktown*. After the war, he was assigned to the Dominican house of studies in River Forest, Illinois, in the Province of St. Albert the Great.

A gifted lecturer and preacher, Father Farrell was also one of the most active supporters of Thomism, the vast body of theological thought established by St. Thomas Aquinas. He gave lectures for the Thomist Association with the aim of making Aquinas better understood by the laity. He helped establish the *Thomist,* a quarterly speculative review, in 1939 and was a leading contributor to its pages. He also wrote the famous four-volume compendium *A Companion to the Summa.* Father Farrell's last book, a life of Christ that he left unfinished, was published posthumously under the title *Only Son* in 1953.

Faust, Mathias (December 30, 1879–July 27, 1956)

A Franciscan friar, Mathias Faust served the American Church and promoted higher education. He was born in Oberbimbach, Germany, and was baptized Constantine. After studies at Fulda and Hereveld, Holland, he migrated to the United States in 1896 and entered the novitiate of the Friars Minor at Paterson, New Jersey. Ordained in 1906, he held several posts over the next years, including provincial minister and assistant provincial. Father Faust also was engaged in pastoral work and was chiefly responsible for the restoration of the Franciscan mission on Thirty-first Street in Manhattan, New York City.

Appointed delegate of the Franciscan Minister General for North and Central America, he exercised leadership over ten Franciscan provinces and eight commissariats and promoted higher education, including the famed Franciscan Institute at St. Bonaventure University. Father Faust also assisted the secular Third Order of St. Francis and the foundation of the St. Anthony Guild in Paterson as a means of promoting the Catholic faith through publishing endeavors. In 1945 he established the Academy of American Franciscan History in Washington, D.C. From 1946 to 1951 he was procurator general in Rome. Returning to the United States, Father Faust served in the post of delegate general for the Franciscan commissariats in North America. He died in New York and was honored by his fellow Franciscans for his enormous contributions to the order.

Feehan, Patrick Augustine (August 29, 1829–July 12, 1902)

The bishop of Nashville from 1865 to 1880 and the first archbishop of the Archdiocese of Chicago from 1880 to 1892, Patrick Augustine Feehan was a pioneering prelate of the American Church. He was born in County Tipperary, Ireland, and embarked upon studies for the priesthood at Maynooth, in County Kildare, Ireland, in 1847. He then studied at the Dunboyne Establishment in Maynooth.

In 1850 his family made the decision to leave Ireland for the United States, and he joined them. He continued studies in St. Louis and was ordained by Archbishop Peter R. Kenrick on November 1, 1852. Father Feehan was assigned immediately to teach at the Carondelet Seminary in Missouri and a mere two years later became president of the seminary. In 1858 he was appointed pastor of St. Michael's Church and then Immaculate Conception Parish.

Father Feehan remained active in pastoral ministry throughout the Civil War and earned a reputation for his remarkable care of the wounded and the many innocent victims of the fighting. Thus

when Bishop James Whelan resigned as bishop of Nashville in 1864, Father Feehan was named his successor. He declined the see initially owing to the poor health of his frail mother, but upon her passing in 1865 he accepted and was consecrated by Archbishop Kenrick in St. Louis on November 1, 1865.

Bishop Feehan assumed a diocese with only three diocesan priests and so embarked upon endless labors to increase the number of clergy and the Catholic presence in the war-ravaged state of Tennessee. He established new parishes, encouraged religious orders to settle in the diocese, and built orphanages for the poor children throughout the region. He also attended the First Vatican Council.

On September 10, 1880, Bishop Feehan was appointed the first archbishop of the Archdiocese of Chicago. Installed on November 25, he inherited an archdiocese that had experienced stunning growth in the previous years. With patience and fortitude, Archbishop Feehan devoted the next twenty-two years of his life to directing the Church's response to the needs created by the burgeoning population. Indeed, during his time, the Catholic population grew from around 230,000 to over 800,000. He increased the number of churches from 194 to 298, more than doubled the number of clergy to over 500, and doubled the number of schools to over 160. While such growth was expensive, his fiscal conservatism ensured that the archdiocese remained on a firm financial footing.

He also convoked the first archdiocesan synod in 1887 to advance the decrees of the Third Plenary Council of Baltimore in 1884 and founded the *New World* in 1892, the official Catholic newspaper for the archdiocese. Sadly, Archbishop Feehan's last years were marked by two ethnic controversies. The first involved a group of Polish Catholics belonging to St. Hedwig's Parish. They insisted on the right to name their own pastor, an act vehemently opposed by Archbishop Feehan, who reluctantly excommunicated Father Anthony Kozlowski, the associate pastor who had been the principal agitator in the case. The second incident was between the Irish-born clergy and the American-born Irish clergy over the selection of an auxiliary bishop for Chicago. The first designate, Alexander J. McGavick, was consecrated in May 1899, but he soon fell ill and was followed by Peter James Muldoon, who was named titular bishop of Tamassus and consecrated on July 25, 1901. Muldoon's appointment caused uproar among some of the Irish-born local clergy, who were opposed to an auxiliary bishop chosen from among American-born Irish. Several priests sent a letter to Archbishop Sebastiano Martinelli, the apostolic delegate, concerning their feelings on the matter. In the end, their objections were found to be baseless and their leader, Father Jeremiah Crowley, pastor of St. Mary's Church in Oregon, Illinois, was excommunicated. The second controversy appears to have hastened Archbishop Feehan's death, as he suffered a stroke.

Feeney, Leonard (February 15, 1897–January 30, 1978)

A Jesuit priest and writer, Leonard Feeney was a controversial figure because of his position on salvation outside the Church. Born in Lynn, Massachusetts, he entered the Society of Jesus in 1914 and went on to graduate work at Oxford University. Ordained at Weston College, England, in 1928, he soon established himself as a writer and poet, starting with his 1927 book of poetry, *In Towns and Little Towns*. Among his most popular books were *Fish on Friday* (1934); *Boundaries* (1935); *Riddle and Reverie* (1936); *Song for a Listener* (1936); *An American Woman* (1938, a biography of St. Elizabeth Ann Seton); *You'd Better Come Quietly* (1939); *The Ark and the Alphabet* (1939); *Survival Till Seventeen* (1941); *The Leonard Feeney Omnibus* (1943); and *Your Second Childhood* (1945). He was also editor of *America* magazine from 1936 to 1940 and president of the Catholic Poetry Society of America and was honored as one of the foremost writers in the United States by Webster College in Missouri.

In 1940 Father Feeney was assigned to a teaching position at Boston College and there encountered a student group that had been organized by Catherine Goddard Clarke, Christopher Huntington, and Avery Dulles (the future theologian and cardinal). The group founded the St. Benedict Center for students at Harvard and Radcliffe, and in 1943 Father Feeney became their chaplain. Dulles and Huntington eventually departed to embark on seminary studies and so had no role in the controversy that occurred later. Father Feeney became

an immensely popular lecturer and was known by many important leaders in New England, including Archbishop (later Cardinal) Richard James Cushing, then congressional candidate (and future president) John F. Kennedy. Clare Boothe Luce and Robert Kennedy also attended his lectures.

Father Feeney held a very rigid view on the doctrine *extra ecclesiam nulla salus* ("outside the Church there is no salvation"), and his supporters, including several students at the St. Benedict Center, argued his equally unbending position as well. What became known as the Boston Heresy case led to Father Feeney's ecclesiastical censure and to his supporters as well, and in 1949 he was dismissed from the Jesuits and summoned to Rome for clarification of his position. He declined to go, however, and was excommunicated for grave disobedience to Church authorities; Pope Pius XII confirmed the decree.

With Catherine Goddard Clarke's help, Father Feeney established a religious community of men and women, the Slaves of the Immaculate Heart of Mary. He served as spiritual director, and she served as superior of the community. In 1957–58 the group moved to a farm in Still River, Massachusetts, to pursue a monastic life. In 1972, largely through the efforts of Bishop Bernard J. Flanagan of Worcester, Cardinal Humberto S. Medeiros of Boston, and Cardinal John J. Wright of the Congregation for the Clergy, the Church removed without publicity the excommunication against Father Feeney. His followers were also restored to the Church.

Fenian Society

An Irish-American Society that was dedicated to the overthrow of English rule in Ireland, the Fenian Society was also known as the Fenian Brotherhood. The society emerged out of the various Irish revolutionary associations that flourished in New York City after Irish revolutionaries reached New York following the failure of the revolt of 1848 and in the years prior to the Civil War. These Irish rebels launched the Silent Friends to organize resistance from America, but disbanded in 1853 owing to internal disputes.

Efforts to establish a new group failed until 1858, when James Stephens, the Irish rebel leader, empowered John O'Mahony as his representative in the United States with full power to raise money for anti-English activities in Ireland. The result was the Fenian Society, named after the ancient militia of Ireland.

Progress was slow owing to internal divisions, the poverty of Irish-Americans in the wake of the depression of 1857, and above all the Civil War that brought about the deaths of thousands of Irish Catholics who served with valor on both sides. In 1863 a convention in Chicago voted to declare the American Fenians independent of the Irish leadership, with O'Mahony as their leader. As the Irish Fenians were placed under pressure by British authorities, the American Fenians split into two groups and executed ill-fated attacks in Maine and Canada in 1866 with the objective of separating Canada from the English. A final attack in Canada in 1870 was defeated easily after plans were revealed to the Canadian government.

On January 12, 1870, the Catholic Church condemned the Fenians. Church authorities had never supported the movement's intentions to bring about the violent overthrow of English rule in Ireland. Fenianism, however, continued until 1868 but declined sharply after 1870, because of the opposition of Church leaders. Nevertheless, it influenced an entire generation of Irish leaders working against English rule in Ireland and kept alive the basic principles of Irish nationalism and patriotism. It also influenced the subsequent development of Sinn Fein and so was a precursor to the successful movement for Irish independence.

Fenton, Joseph Clifford (January 16, 1906–July 7, 1969)

A theologian, priest, and supporter of neo-Scholasticism, Joseph Clifford Fenton was a professor and dean of theology at The Catholic University of America. Born in Springfield, Massachusetts, he studied at Holy Cross College and the University of Montréal, and went on to complete doctoral studies at the Pontifical University of St. Thomas, the Angelicum, in Rome in 1931. Ordained a priest in June 1930, Father Fenton held several pastoral positions in the Springfield diocese and taught philosophy at St. Ambrose College in Davenport, Iowa, from 1934 to 1935 and theology at St. Bernard's Seminary in Rochester, New York, from 1936 to 1938.

In 1938 he was appointed to the faculty of the School of Religious Education at The Catholic University of America. The following year, he was moved to the faculty for Sacred Theology and taught fundamental and dogmatic theology until his retirement in 1963. He was appointed a papal chamberlain in 1951, a domestic prelate in 1954, and a protonotary apostolic in 1963. He received the papal honor of the Pro Ecclesia et Pontifice medal in 1954, was a member of the Pontifical Roman Theological Academy, a consultor to the Sacred Congregation of Seminaries and Universities from 1950 to 1967, and a *peritus* (or theological expert) at the Second Vatican Council.

Monsignor Fenton was a charter member of the Catholic Theological Society of America and served as its first secretary from 1946 to 1947; he received the society's Cardinal Spellman Award for Theology in 1958 and was a co-founder of the Mariological Society in 1949. Monsignor Fenton was also a noted opponent of the theological approach of John Courtney Murray, S.J., regarding religious freedom and the relationship between church and state. He was editor of the *American Ecclesiastical Review* from 1944 to 1963, and wrote a number of books, including *The Theology of Prayer* (1939), *The Concept of Sacred Theology* (1941), *We Stand with Christ* (1943), *The Calling of a Diocesan Priest* (1944), *The Concept of the Diocesan Priesthood* (1951), and *The Catholic Church and Salvation* (1958), and over 150 articles. In the years just before his death, he served as a parish priest in Chicopee Falls, Massachusetts.

Fenwick, Benedict Joseph (September 3, 1782–August 11, 1846)

The second bishop of Boston from 1825 to 1846, Benedict Joseph Fenwick served as a pioneering prelate during an era of anti-Catholic assaults throughout the nation. Born near Leonardtown, Maryland, to a family noted for aiding Lord Baltimore in founding the original colony, he studied at Georgetown College (later Georgetown University) with his brother Enoch soon after its founding by Bishop John Carroll. In 1806 he joined the Society of Jesus after its novitiate was reestablished.

After studies at St. Mary's Seminary in Baltimore, he was ordained on March 12, 1808, and assigned as an assistant pastor in New York City. In 1817 he was sent back to Washington, D.C., to take up duties as president of Georgetown College. The following year, however, he was dispatched to Charleston, South Carolina, where he helped restore relations between several local Church factions and served briefly as vicar general to Bishop John England. He returned to Georgetown in 1822.

On May 10, 1825, Father Fenwick was appointed the second bishop of the Diocese of Boston and was consecrated on November 1, 1825. He assumed authority over a diocese that at the time had only three priests and a Catholic population under ten thousand, spread out across most of New England. His first priority was thus promoting vocations and increasing the number of priests and religious. He started a seminary in his own residence, training four students at a time, and aided the opening of the College of the Holy Cross in 1843.

In 1829 Bishop Fenwick started a weekly Catholic newspaper, *Jesuit* (later *The Pilot*), to promote the Church in the face of rising Protestant hatred and violence. In 1834 a Protestant mob burned down the Ursuline convent in Charlestown, and other attacks were planned against Catholic facilities, including the Broad Street Riots that targeted Irish Catholics. The anti-Catholic feeling remained severe because of the labors of several Protestant groups that

Bishop Edward Fenwick

preached against the Church throughout his episcopate. One of Bishop Fenwick's most effective measures to aid the faith was the founding in 1834 of the Irish Catholic colony of Benedicta in Maine, which was then under his jurisdiction, along with Vermont, Connecticut, and Rhode Island. He provided the Abenaki Indians with clergy and expanded the Catholic presence throughout New England with the help of the Society for the Propagation of the Faith and with funds from the Leopoldine Society of Vienna. To promote the priestly life, he convened in 1842 the first retreat for priests

and the first diocesan synod. Through all these efforts, Bishop Fenwick did much to give the Boston Diocese a firm foundation, and he became an inspiration to Catholics all over the country. He died in Boston, leaving a diocese with over fifty churches, priests, educational institutions, and charitable ministries. Bishop Fenwick welcomed the Irish coming to America because of the Great Famine and nurtured regions that in time would emerge as dioceses in other states.

Fenwick, Edward D. (August 19, 1768–September 26, 1832)

The first bishop of Cincinnati from 1822 to 1832, Edward D. Fenwick was a pioneering Dominican. Born in St. Mary's County, Maryland, he studied at first on his family's estate and then under the English Dominicans at Holy Cross College at Bornheim, Belgium. After graduating in 1788, he entered the Dominicans and was professed on March 26, 1790, and ordained in February 1793. The next year, the English Dominicans fled to England because of the dangers of the French Revolution. Father Fenwick was left in charge of the college in the mistaken belief that his American citizenship would deter the French from seizing him. Promptly arrested, he was released and sailed to England where he rejoined his fellow Dominicans.

Father Fenwick returned to the United States in 1804 and secured the support of Bishop John Carroll in founding a Dominican house. He established the Dominican province of St. Joseph in July 1806 and so made possible the establishment of St. Rose Church and Priory and the College of St. Thomas of Aquinas near Springfield, Kentucky. From 1807 to 1822 Father Fenwick was engaged actively in missionary work. With Father Nicholas D. Young in 1818, he began the first church in Ohio, near Somerset, which he used as his base for the evangelization throughout the future state.

Owing to his exemplary labors, Father Fenwick was named the first bishop of Cincinnati and received consecration at St. Rose Church on January 13, 1822. He assumed direction of his new diocese in March 1822 and, with other Dominican priests, reached Cincinnati as quickly as possible. He wasted little time in expanding the number of clergy for service by appealing to Rome to establish a Dominican province in Ohio, although the community was not finalized until 1828. Bishop Fenwick also traveled to Europe to encourage new priests to accept mission assignments and to raise money for building churches and other necessary diocesan institutions.

In 1825 he began construction of St. Peter in Chains Cathedral in Cincinnati, and in 1829 he opened St. Francis Xavier Seminary. In 1831 Bishop Fenwick launched the first newspaper in the diocese, the *Catholic Telegraph-Register*. His efforts at education and missions also prompted a Protestant counterreaction, including Lyman Beecher's *Plea for the West*. His death occurred suddenly during a cholera epidemic. By the time of his passing, however, the diocese was on a firm footing, with some twenty-four priests and twenty-two churches.

Fermi, Enrico (September 29, 1901–November 28, 1954)

An atomic physicist and Nobel Prize winner, Enrico Fermi is considered one of the chief architects of the nuclear age. He was born in Rome and graduated from the University of Pisa in 1922 and then did graduate work at the University of Gottingen and at institutions in Rome and Leyden. In 1924 he lectured at the University of Florence and two years later became a professor at the University of Rome. In 1938 Fermi received the Nobel Prize, and in the following year he migrated to the United States, becoming a citizen in 1944. He became a professor of physics at Columbia University, remaining there until 1945. He then became a professor at the University of Chicago, where his experiments in artificial radioactivity led to the discovery of uranium fission.

On December 2, 1942, Fermi set the first atomic furnace into action, beginning the atomic age. He also worked on the Manhattan Project, the secret program that developed the atomic bomb, and was at Los Alamos, New Mexico, for the preparation of nuclear weapons. Fermi proved the existence of the neutrino and discovered neptunium (element 93) and developed the theory of beta ray emission in radioactivity. He wrote *Thermodynamics* in 1937 and *Elementary Particles* in 1951.

Fichter, Joseph H. (June 10, 1908–February 23, 1994)

A Jesuit sociologist, Joseph H. Fichter promoted desegregation and labor unions. Born in Union City, New Jersey, he entered the Jesuits at New Orleans in 1930 and subsequently earned degrees from St. Louis University and a doctorate in sociology from Harvard University in 1947. Ordained a priest in 1942, he was appointed to the faculty of sociology at Loyola University in New Orleans and went on to hold a variety of other teaching posts at the University of Muenster, Germany (1953–54), the University of Notre Dame (1955–56), Catholic University of Chile (1960–61), the University of Chicago (1964–65), Harvard University (1965–70), the State University of New York at Albany (1971–72), and Tulane University (1973–74).

Aside from his active sociological studies, Father Fichter was engaged in social justice programs, such as the promotion of organized labor, the desegregation of Catholic schools, and the rights of Mexican migrant workers. He served as president of the Society for the Scientific Study of Religion and of the Southern Sociological Society and was a member of the executive council of the American Sociological Association.

Father Fichter was the author of some thirty books and over two hundred articles, including *Southern Parish* (1951), *Social Relations in the Urban Parish* (1954), *Parochial School* (1958), *Priest and People* (1965), *America's Forgotten Priests* (1968), *Rehabilitation of Clergy Alcoholics* (1982), *The Pastoral Provisions: Married Catholic Priests* (1989); and a two-volume autobiography, *One Man Research* (1973) and *The Sociology of Good Works* (1993).

Fink, Michael (July 12, 1834–March 17, 1904)

The first bishop of Leavenworth (now the Archdiocese of Kansas City in Kansas), from 1877 to 1904, Michael Fink was a member of the Benedictines. Born in Triftersberg, Bavaria, he migrated to the United States in 1850 and served as a member of the community that had been established at St.

Vincent Archabbey in Latrobe, Pennsylvania, by Archabbot Boniface Wimmer. He took his vows in January 1854 and was ordained in May 1857.

He was assigned to several parishes and then appointed prior of St. Benedict's Priory in Atchison, Kansas, in 1868. Three years later, he was named coadjutor bishop to John B. Miège, S.J., vicar apostolic of Kansas and of the Indian Territory. Consecrated on June 11, 1871, he acceded to the see in late 1874. On May 22, 1877, Pope Blessed Pius IX established the Diocese of Leavenworth, the first in Kansas, and appointed Bishop Fink to lead the new ecclesiastical jurisdiction.

Bishop Fink assumed the role of spiritual leadership over a rugged frontier diocese and made excellent use of mission stations to provide the pastoral and sacramental needs of the many Catholics who were migrating to the territory. He was also instrumental in organizing assistance to farmers who had their crops destroyed in a massive grasshopper invasion in 1874. Deeply concerned with the needs of farmers, he supported the Farmers' Alliance and issued pastoral letters urging the spiritual development of agrarian people. He moved his residence to Kansas City after the diocese was divided in 1887 with the creation of the Salina diocese.

Finotti, Joseph M. (September 21, 1817–January 10, 1879)

A priest and editor, Joseph M. Finotti was a Jesuit when he arrived in the United States. Born in Ferrara, Italy, he entered the Society of Jesus in Rome in 1833 and held several teaching posts in Italy until volunteering for service in the American Church. After being ordained at Georgetown, Father Finotti was named pastor of St. Mary's Church in Alexandria, Virginia, and served in various missions in Maryland and Virginia. In 1852 he left the Jesuits and was incardinated in the Boston diocese. He was for many years the literary editor of *The Pilot*, the diocesan newspaper, while serving in Brookline and later in Arlington, Massachusetts.

Father Finotti was also a writer and expert in American Catholic literary history. His works included *Month of Mary* (1853), *Life of Blessed Paul of the Cross* (1860), *Diary of a Soldier* (1861), *The French Zouave* (1863), and his most famous effort, the *Bibliographica Catholica Americana*, a catalog of all Catholic books published in the United States. The first part was published in 1872, listing publications to 1820; the second included books from 1821 to 1875. His final years were spent as a pastor in Central City, Colorado, where he died.

Fisher, Philip (Thomas Copley) (c. 1595–1652)

An English Jesuit missionary in Maryland, Philip Fisher was born Thomas Copley in Madrid, Spain, to an English Catholic family living in exile from Elizabethan England. He entered the Society of Jesus and apparently volunteered for service in the English colonies. Father Fisher reached Maryland in 1637 and administered the mission there until his arrest by English authorities in 1645. His companion was the famous missionary Father Andrew White, the founder of the English mission in America. Released after a period of incarceration, Father Fisher sailed back to Maryland in 1648 and once again undertook the pastoral care of the Catholic faithful in the colony. He then extended his ministry to Virginia, but little was recorded of his mission there. Father Fisher was much respected among his peers in the Society of Jesus.

Fitton, James (April 10, 1805–September 15, 1881)

A missionary priest and author, James Fitton was the founder of Holy Cross College. He was born in Boston and studied at local schools there before embarking upon preparations for the priesthood. Ordained a priest on December 23, 1827, by Bishop Benedict Joseph Fenwick, Father Fitton was assigned to various pastoral posts in Connecticut, Massachusetts, and Rhode Island, and soon distinguished himself as a missionary to the Passamaquoddy in Maine and as a major promoter of Catholic education in New England.

He was especially praised for founding Mount St. James' Seminary in Worcester, Massachusetts, later the College of the Holy Cross. Father Fitton also served as editor of the Hartford *Catholic Press* and was the author of *The Youth's Companion* (1833), *The Triumph of Religion* (1833), *St. Joseph's Manual* (1877), and the highly popular *Sketches of the Establishment of the Church in New England* (1872).

In 1855 Father Fitton was appointed pastor of

Most Holy Redeemer Parish in East Boston, and he would serve there for over a quarter of a century. He also helped establish four other parishes before celebrating the Golden Jubilee of his ordination. He died in Boston.

Fitzgerald, Edward M. (October 28, 1833–February 21, 1907)

The bishop of the Diocese of Little Rock from 1867 to 1907, Edward M. Fitzgerald was a pioneer in Catholic affairs in Arkansas. He was born in Limerick, Ireland, and migrated to the United States with his family in 1849. He entered studies for the priesthood at the Barrens in Missouri and then at Mount St. Mary's Seminary of the West in Cincinnati and Mount St. Mary's College and Seminary in Emmitsburg, Maryland. Ordained a priest for the Diocese of Cincinnati in August 1857, he was appointed pastor of St. Patrick's in Columbus, Ohio. At the time, the parish was under interdict owing to the severe dispute that had erupted between the trustees and Archbishop John Baptist Purcell. Father Fitzgerald proved eminently successful in resolving the crisis and went on to serve as pastor for almost a decade.

On February 3, 1867, he was consecrated bishop of the Diocese of Little Rock, a diocese that had been without a bishop since 1862 owing to the problems caused by the Civil War. The Catholic population numbered fewer than two thousand, assisted by five priests and four parishes, as well as several communities of the Sisters of Mercy. To assist in the development of the diocese, Bishop Fitzgerald invited Benedictine priests and nuns, the Holy Ghost Fathers, the Sisters of Charity, and the Sisters of Mercy to take up ministries in the area.

In 1870 Bishop Fitzgerald traveled to Rome and attended the First Vatican Council. He was not in favor of the definition of papal infallibility and voted *non placet* in July 1870; he was only one of seven bishops to do so. Once the definition was approved, however, he immediately accepted the dogma and was thereafter a supporter. He also took part in the Third Plenary Council of Baltimore in 1884. Owing to reasons of health complicated by a stroke, he asked for a coadjutor bishop in 1906. Under his guidance, the diocese had grown rapidly to a Catholic population of 20,000 served by 60 priests, nearly 300 women religious, and 41 churches.

Fitzgerald, John (1739–1799)

An American patriot, John Fitzgerald was born in Ireland and arrived in Alexandria, Virginia, in 1769, where he started an import-export business. He went into partnership with Valentine Piers, and the business prospered as the political climate of the colonies prompted vigorous debates about freedom. Fitzgerald married Jane Digges of Warburton Manor and began to take an interest in the growing movement toward American independence.

He was a friend of George Washington, and when the Revolutionary War was begun, he became a captain in the 3rd Virginia Infantry. Within a year, Fitzgerald was also acting major of the 9th Virginia Infantry. In November 1776 he served as aide-de-camp to General George Washington and was then wounded in the Battle of Monmouth. Fitzgerald returned to Alexandria when the war ended and continued his business affairs. He also aided Catholic causes and missions, collecting funds for Georgetown College and for St. Mary's Church in Alexandria. He died in his family home there.

Fitzgibbon, Mary Irene (May 11, 1823–August 14, 1896)

A Sister of Charity, Mary Irene Fitzgibbon aided the women and children of New York City as a foundress of care institutions. She was born in Kensington, England, and sailed to America at the age of nine with her family. The Fitzgibbon family had settled in Brooklyn, New York. After surviving a severe bout of cholera in 1849, Mary entered the recently established Sisters of Charity in 1850 and was assigned to teach at St. Peter's Academy in New York City.

In 1858 she was appointed superior of St. Peter's Convent and was soon aware of the severe crisis of abandoned and forgotten children in the city and was asked by Archbishop John McCloskey to assume direction over programs to assist the young. From humble beginnings, Sister Mary Irene eventually opened the New York Foundling Asylum (later the New York Foundling Hospital) in October 1869 and the Foundling Asylum Society, a laywomen's auxiliary, that same year to provide permanent funding. She was also instrumental in establishing St. Ann's Maternity Hospital in 1880, the Hospital of St. John for Children in 1881, and Nazareth Hospital for convalescent children in 1881, and she was a key figure in promoting care for unwed mothers and adoption plans for the children in her care.

Fitzpatrick, John Bernard (November 15, 1812–February 13, 1866)

The third bishop of the Diocese of Boston (now the Archdiocese of Boston), from 1846 to 1866, John Bernard Fitzpatrick served the American Church in a troubled era. He was born in Boston, the son of an Irish immigrant, Bernard, and a native Bostonian named Eleanor. After completing studies at the Boston Latin School, he was sent to prepare for the priesthood by Bishop Benedict Joseph Fenwick at the minor seminary of Saint-Sulpice in Montréal and then at the major seminary of Saint-Sulpice in Paris. Ordained to the priesthood in June 1840, Father Fitzpatrick served only three years before receiving appointment as the coadjutor bishop of the Diocese of Boston. He was consecrated a bishop in the chapel of the Visitation nuns at Georgetown and proved a great assistant to Bishop Fenwick. Bishop Fitzpatrick was also immediately popular with the Bostonians, who approved of a Bostonian succeeding Bishop Fenwick in 1846.

Bishop Fitzpatrick's time as bishop was dominated by two major events. The first was the Irish Potato Famine that sparked a massive influx of Irish-Catholic immigrants during the 1840s and early 1850s; the second was the Civil War. The migration of so many Irish Catholics caused a severe backlash against Catholics who were native Bostonians and the Nativist organizations that formed the American Party (known as the Know-Nothing Party) in 1854 to protect America from the supposed danger to democracy of the Catholic Irish and from their drain on resources. In the face of these assaults, Bishop Fitzpatrick was careful to prevent public violence, but he was also firm in demanding full legal rights for Catholics as American citizens.

He organized relief drives for the famine victims in Ireland; his appeal among the people of Boston netted over $150,000. To provide needed pastoral care to Irish immigrants, he established St. Vincent's Orphan Asylum and the House of the Angel Guardian to care for forgotten children, and a hospital that eventually bore his name. He also promoted education and had the pleasure of seeing the founding of Boston College by the Jesuits in 1863.

Bishop Fitzpatrick encouraged the Irish in the diocese to support the Union during the Civil War, and the courage of the Irish troops at a host of battles earned the admiration of the people of Massachusetts. Particularly notable were the 9th and 28th Regiments, made up almost entirely of Irish Catholics. Catholic chaplains also served with distinction with Bishop Fitzpatrick's support. Nevertheless, the losses endured by Irish Catholics in Boston were at times staggering, mostly so after the Battles at Antietam in 1862, Gettysburg in 1863, and the Wilderness in 1864.

Bishop Fitzpatrick was the first ordinary of Boston to make the *ad limina* visit to Rome, in 1854, a trip he used to promote the development of Catholic education in Boston. He was also responsible for appointing Father James Augustine Healy as his chancellor and secretary, a notable appointment as Healy was an African-American priest (and later bishop of the Diocese of Portland). Through his efforts, there were a number of prominent conversions, including Paul Revere's grandson, the daughter of Nathaniel Hawthorne, and the niece of Henry Wadsworth Longfellow.

FitzSimons, Thomas (1741–August 26, 1811)

An American merchant and trader, Thomas FitzSimons, also listed in some records as Fitzsimmons, was one of the framers of the Constitution of the United States. Born in Ireland, he settled sometime before 1758 in Philadelphia. In 1763 he married Catherine Meade, sister of George Meade, who worked as his partner as a merchant until 1784. FitzSimons was an early supporter of the movement that led to the American Revolution and was a deputy at the conference in Carpenters' Hall, Philadelphia, a gathering that led to the Continental Congress of 1774, in which he also served.

Elected one of the provincial deputies in July 1774, he thus held the distinction of being the first Catholic chosen for public office in Pennsylvania.

Once the Revolution began, he signed up with the militia and fought in the Trenton campaign in New Jersey. FitzSimons later assisted the Revolutionary Army by raising funds and organizing supplies through his fellow merchants.

After the end of the war, FitzSimons was elected in November 1782 as a member of the Congress of the old Confederacy and served as a member of the Continental Convention that gathered in Philadelphia in May 1787. He was, with Daniel Carroll of Maryland, one of two Catholics to hold the distinction of being a framer of the Constitution. He was then elected a member of the first House of Representatives, serving on the Committee on Ways and Means, and as a Federalist he supported enthusiastically the financial policies of Alexander Hamilton. Reelected twice, FitzSimons was defeated in 1794 and retired from public life. At the time of President George Washington's inauguration as the first president of the United States, FitzSimons was one of the four Catholic laymen (with Charles and Daniel Carroll of Maryland, and Dominic Lynch of New York) to sign the letter of congratulation sent by the Catholics of America.

FitzSimons was a founder and trustee of the National Bank of America, president of the Insurance Company of North America, and president of the Philadelphia Chamber of Commerce. A noted philanthropist, he contributed extensively to the building of churches in Pennsylvania, helped fund Georgetown College, and even donated money to the synagogue Mikvah Israel. Unfortunately, his last years brought financial decline, and he died alone and childless in Philadelphia.

Flaget, Benedict Joseph (November 7, 1763–February 11, 1850)

The first bishop of the Diocese of Bardstown (now the Archdiocese of Louisville), from 1810 to 1850, Benedict Joseph Flaget administered one of the largest dioceses in the history of the United States. He was born in Contournat, France, and was orphaned at the age of two. He and his brothers were given over to the care of various family members, including

an uncle, the Canon Benoît Flaget, at Billom. At the age of seventeen, he entered studies for the priesthood at the Sulpician Seminary at Clermont, France, and in 1783 entered the Society of Saint-Sulpice.

After his ordination at Issy around 1787, Flaget taught theology at Nantes until the French Revolution brought about the closing of seminaries in the country, which compelled him to leave for the United States in 1792 with Father John Baptist David, S.S., and a seminarian, Stephen T. Badin, who went on to become the first priest ordained in the United States.

Bishop John Carroll welcomed Father Flaget and sent him out to the missions at Fort Vincennes, Indiana. There he served with distinction for two years before being recalled by his superiors. He was then given assignments as a professor at Georgetown College in Washington, D.C., and as the unsuccessful founder of a college in Havana, Cuba, whereupon he returned to Baltimore to teach at the seminary for the next eight years.

In 1808 Father Flaget was shocked to learn of his appointment as the first bishop of the Diocese of Bardstown in Kentucky, a position he neither sought nor wanted. He was so adamant in not wanting the office that he traveled to France to seek the help of the Sulpicians in refusing the appointment. When, however, he was informed that Pope Pius VII desired his acceptance, he relented and used the opportunity while in Europe to recruit priests for the diocese. His recruits were a stellar bunch, including the future bishops Simon William Gabriel Bruté de Rémur and Guy Chabrat. Bishop Flaget was consecrated by Bishop Carroll in St. Patrick's Church in Baltimore on November 4, 1810, and was installed in Bardstown in Father Badin's cabin in June 1811. He was the sixth bishop consecrated in the United States.

Bishop Flaget's new diocese extended across Kentucky and Tennessee as well as most of the West, so that his territory actually comprised an area that later became thirty-five states. Undertaking the task of administering so vast

Bishop Benedict Joseph Flaget

a diocese with enormous energy, he visited every Catholic settlement in Kentucky and worked to establish cordial relations with political leaders and important public figures, including Senator Henry Clay of Kentucky. He also made journeys to the Catholic communities in Detroit and St. Louis. In December 1811 he ordained Guy Chabrat, the first priest to be ordained in Kentucky.

During that same winter, Bishop Flaget founded St. Thomas Seminary. He was pleased by the arrival of the Sisters of Loretto and the Sisters of Charity of Nazareth. By 1815 he reported to Rome that his diocese had a Catholic population of ten thousand, served by ten priests, nineteen churches or chapels, one monastery, and two convents. He soon added an impressive cathedral (St. Joseph's, which is now a national monument), three colleges, and several schools for girls, and promoted the arrival of additional women religious.

On August 10, 1819, Bishop Flaget consecrated John Baptist David as his first coadjutor. In 1832, however, he attempted to resign, citing his advancing age and various infirmities. Such was the uproar of the people of the diocese that Flaget resumed his episcopal duties. He consecrated Chabrat as his second coadjutor in 1834, and in 1848 consecrated Martin J. Spalding as his third coadjutor. In 1835 Bishop Flaget made his first *ad limina* visit to Rome and then spent two years visiting the diocese and archdioceses of France, at the request of Pope Gregory XVI, to promote the propagation of the faith. Upon his return home in 1839, he transferred his see to Louisville and erected the Cathedral of the Assumption. He retired in 1848 and spent his last two years in quiet rest.

Bishop Flaget served with enormous distinction and was one of the most important of the early bishops in the United States. Through his labors, the Catholic Church was given a firm footing throughout Kentucky, Tennessee, and as far as Missouri and Michigan. When he died in Louisville and was buried under the altar of the cathedral, he had witnessed eleven new dioceses erected in the territory of the original Bardstown. His vast experience and reputation for personal holiness made him an immensely influential figure at the councils of the Church in the United States, in France, and even in Rome.

Flanagan, Edward (July 13, 1886–May 15, 1948)

The founder of Father Flanagan's Boys Town in Nebraska, Edward Flanagan was a recognized authority on youths, advising U.S. officials after World War II. He was born in Roscommon, Ireland, and arrived in the United States in 1904, studying for the priesthood at Mount St. Mary's College in Emmitsburg, Maryland, and then at St. Joseph's Seminary in Dunwoodie, New York, and the Pontifical Gregorian University in Rome. Owing to poor health, he was forced to return to America, but he later studied theology at Innsbruck, Austria, and was ordained for the Archdiocese of Omaha on July 26, 1912.

Two years after his ordination, Father Flanagan decided to establish some kind of pastoral care for men out of work. He opened the Workingmen's Hotel in Omaha in 1914, but he soon recognized that the solution to the problem rested in providing better futures for young people. He thus closed the hotel and opened a building to care for abandoned and delinquent boys. In 1922 he purchased property just outside of Omaha and so began the famed Boys Town.

Guiding his ministry at Boys Town was Flanagan's desire to provide these disadvantaged children with proper educational, vocational, and social opportunities, and he created a system in which the youths lived in a caring environment that the children governed and administered, under proper direction. Boys Town was established without the intention of proselytizing, and children were accepted regardless of their religion, color, or ethnic identity. Nevertheless, students were required to attend some kind of religious service, considered fundamental to the proper development of a person.

Father Flanagan presided over the rapid growth of Boys Town and became internationally famous through the 1938 film *Boys Town*, starring Spencer Tracy. In 1946 he was named to a national panel studying the problem of juvenile delinquency and in the next year was named to the Naval Civilian Committee. He set out on a tour of Japan and Korea in 1947 to study child-welfare problems at the request of General Douglas MacArthur, and the resulting report so impressed President Harry S. Truman that he asked Father Flanagan to undertake a similar study in occupied Austria and Germany. Father Flanagan died suddenly while in Germany. (*See also* Boys Town.)

Fleming, Francis Antoninus (1749–October 1793)

A Dominican and missionary, Francis Antoninus Fleming served with distinction as vicar general to Bishop John Carroll for the northern district of the Diocese of Baltimore. He was born in Ireland and entered the Dominicans in 1765 at Holy Cross College in Louvain, Belgium. He was then assigned to the Dominican House in Lisbon, Portugal, and earned a sparkling reputation as a preacher. In 1789 he sailed to the United States for service in the slowly growing Catholic community. Assigned by John Carroll, then the superior of the American missions, to the parish of St. Mary's in Philadelphia with two other priests, Father Fleming again earned considerable respect for his preaching and his pastoral dedication.

The following year, John Carroll was named the first bishop in the United States and appointed Father Fleming as vicar general for the northern district, with authority over the vast region from New York to Maine. Father Fleming participated in the first diocesan synod in 1791 and was a vocal supporter of Bishop Carroll when he was accused of discriminating against German Catholics and showing excessive favoritism to his fellow former members of the Society of Jesus (suppressed in 1774 by Pope Clement XIV). As happened to several other priests of the period, Father Fleming died while caring for victims of yellow fever during an outbreak in Philadelphia.

Floersh, John (October 5, 1886–June 11, 1968)

The first archbishop of the Archdiocese of Louisville, from 1937 to 1967, John Floersh served throughout the immensely challenging period of World War II and the period of the Second Vatican Council. He was born in Nashville, Tennessee, and received ordination on June 10, 1911, following studies in Rome. After a brief assignment in Nashville, he was named a secretary to the apostolic delegation in Washington, D.C., and subsequently distinguished himself as a priest of considerable piety and talent. On February 6, 1923, he was appointed coadjutor bishop of Louisville to Bishop

Denis O'Donaghue and was consecrated in Rome on April 8, 1923. He acceded to the see on July 26, 1924.

Archbishop Floersh devoted his first years to assisting the Catholic faithful and the wider population of Louisville to survive the effects of the Great Depression. He promoted social care for the poor and hungry and provided spiritual comfort during a difficult time in American history. On December 10, 1937, Pope Pius XI elevated the diocese to the rank of metropolitan archdiocese, and Bishop Floersh became its first archbishop. The new title accompanied his leadership of the archdiocese during World War II, and in its aftermath he presided over a colossal building program that was a testament both to his dedication and to his skills in matters of finance and administration. He founded both the Catholic School Board and the Office of Catholic Charities and opened new high schools and Bellarmine College. He also invited the Carmelite nuns to Louisville.

Archbishop Floersh attended only the first session of the Second Vatican Council in 1962 owing to his poor health. He sent as his representative to the other sessions his auxiliary bishop, Charles Garrett Maloney. He retired on March 1, 1967, and was succeeded by Archbishop Thomas J. McDonough.

Florida

Called the Peninsular or Everglade State, Florida entered the Union in 1845 and is the most southern state in the continental United States. Juan Ponce de León, who arrived there at Eastertide in 1513, bestowed the name of the state. *Pascua florida* means the "Easter of Flowers." Florida is bounded on the north by Alabama and Georgia, on the east by the Atlantic Ocean, on the south by the Straits of Florida and the Gulf of Mexico, and on the west by the Gulf of Mexico and the Perdido River.

There are three principal land regions in Florida: the Atlantic Coastal Plain in the east, the Florida Highlands in the south-central part of the state, and the Gulf Coastal Plain in the northwest. The Everglades, a wet grassland, takes up a large part of the southern region. The original inhabitants of Florida were the Apalachee, Calusa, Seminoles, Tequestas, and Timucuans.

The Catholic heritage of Florida dates to April

3, 1513, when Ponce de León set up a stone cross in the area. He returned to Florida in 1521 to begin a colony but died of wounds inflicted by hostile local Indians. Other Spanish explorers, Francisco Fernandez de Cordova, Alonso Alvarez de Pineda, and Lucas Vázquez de Ayllón followed de Leon in 1517, 1519, and 1520. Pánfilo de Narváez, Hernando de Soto, and Tristán de Luna also explored the region. In 1549 the famed missionary Dominican Luis Cáncer de Barbastro and his companions were slain at Tampa Bay. French colonies, some started by Huguenots, were in Florida by 1562, but the Spanish closed the settlements. The colonies originated at Port Royal and Fort Caroline on the St. John's River.

On September 8, 1565, Pedro Menéndez de Avilés, a Spanish admiral, officially founded St. Augustine, the oldest city in the United States. Father Martin Francisco Lopez de Mendoza Grajales celebrated Mass on the site. Nombre de Dios Mission was established soon after. One year later, Jesuit missionaries, including Fathers Pedro Martinez, Juan Rogel, and Francisco Villareal started missions that were threatened by hostile tribes. Jesuit priests were martyred on the St. John's River, at Charlotte Harbor and at Miami. In 1573 Franciscan missions were operating in northeastern Florida.

In 1586 Sir Francis Drake attacked St. Augustine, and the Franciscans who had settled there helped defend the site. They began missions throughout the area, and on the coast of Georgia, with some losses to Indian attacks. In 1606 Bishop Juan de las Cabezas de Altamirano sailed from Havana, Cuba, to tour Florida and to confirm hundreds of converts. The Franciscans extended their missions in the following year to Gainesville, Palatka, and Tallahassee. The region became the Province of Santa Elena de las Florida in 1612.

By 1675 Bishop Diaz Vara Calderón was able to visit Florida to confirm over thirteen thousand people and to ordain seven men to the priesthood. There were reportedly seventy-five Franciscans in thirty-eight missions. Three years later, slaves from colonies on the east coast fled to Florida, seeking sanctuary at St. Augustine and receiving their freedom. From 1702 to 1708, Queen Anne's War involved the American colonies, and Governor James Moore of the British Colony of Carolina

attacked the missions, destroying them. From ten thousand to twelve thousand Catholic Indians were taken captive and sold as slaves in South Carolina. Some three thousand were slain.

In 1709 Florida had a resident bishop, Dionisio Resino, who was an auxiliary of Santiago de Cuba. Bishop Francisco de San Buenaventura y Tejada was in residence in St. Augustine from 1735 to 1745. Governor James Edward Oglethorpe of Georgia attacked St. Augustine as part of the British assault on the Spanish. He tortured and killed priests and converts and destroyed the libraries and institutions of the city and its missions. In 1763 Spain ceded Florida to the English, and the area was divided into east Florida and west Florida. Five years later, New Smyrna Plantation, a Catholic settlement, opened with a chaplain in residence. St. Augustine reopened soon after. In 1783 Florida was returned to Spain and became part of the Diocese of San Cristobal in Cuba. Catholic priests worked in the region, and Florida became part of the Diocese of Louisiana and the Two Floridas in 1793. Ten years later, Bishop John Carroll had ecclesiastical jurisdiction over the area from his diocese in Baltimore.

In December 1817 General Andrew Jackson fought the Seminoles and then took Pensacola and other parts of Florida. Two years later, Spain sold the region to the United States for $5 million. Florida was formally transferred to the United States in 1821 and made a territory by Act of Congress the following year. When the government tried to move the Seminoles out of Florida, the Seminole War started. The Vicariate Apostolic of Alabama and the Floridas, located at Mobile, administered Catholic matters in Florida at the time.

Attracting settlers, Florida grew rapidly and entered the Union in 1845 as the twenty-seventh state. In 1857 a vicariate apostolic was established for eastern Florida, administered by Bishop Jean-Pierre Augustin Verot. Florida seceded from the Union in January 1861. There was a major battle on Florida land during the Civil War, but Tallahassee was the only Confederate capital not taken by Union troops. Florida was readmitted into the Union in 1861, but was punished during the period following the war. The state was developing agricultural areas and mining processes and survived.

In 1870 Pope Blessed Pius IX erected the Diocese of St. Augustine. The state flourished economically during World War I and experienced a population growth and increased sales of real estate in the 1920s. The Great Depression caused hardship, but the military efforts of the United States aided Florida economically in World War II. Miami became a diocese in 1958 and an archdiocese in 1968, when St. Petersburg and Orlando were erected as dioceses. The space industry became part of Florida's modern economic base, and tourism brought thousands of visitors into the area. Cuban migration also added to the state's diversity. In 1975 the Diocese of Pensacola-Tallahassee was erected, and Venice became a diocese in 1984. In recent decades, the Catholic community has continued to grow both in population and diversity with the arrival of Catholics from all over the world, especially Hispanics and immigrants from the Caribbean. The Haitian and Cuban communities are especially significant. In 2011 there were 2.2 million Catholics in the state, served by 1,200 priests, 900 women religious, and 463 parishes.

Floyd, John B. *See* **Cabinets, Catholics in Presidential**

Flynn, Raymond. *See* **Holy See-U.S. Relations**

Foley, John P. (November 11, 1935–December 11, 2011)

The longtime president of the Pontifical Council for Social Communications and Grand Master of the Equestrian Order of the Holy Sepulchre of Jerusalem, John Patrick Foley was also a cardinal and one of the foremost figures in Catholic social communications.

Born in Darby, Pennsylvania, he began his studies for the priesthood in the state, at St. Joseph's Preparatory School, St. Joseph's College, where he earned a bachelor's degree in history in 1957, and at St. Charles Borromeo Seminary in Wynnewood, where he earned a bachelor's degree in philosophy in 1958.

Cardinal John Foley

Ordained a priest on May 19, 1962, he served as an assistant pastor in the Archdiocese of Philadelphia until his appointment in 1963 as assistant editor of the *Catholic Standard and Times,* the archdiocesan newspaper. He was soon assigned to graduate studies in Rome, where he was also the newspaper's Rome correspondent from 1963 until 1965. He was in Rome during the second and third sessions of the Second Vatican Council and studied at the Pontifical University of St. Thomas, the Angelicum, where he earned a doctorate in philosophy with the dissertation "Natural Law, Natural Right and the Warren Court."

Returning to the United States, he studied at Columbia University's School of Journalism and earned a master of science in journalism in 1966. He was named an assistant pastor and taught at Cardinal Dougherty High School. He returned in 1967 as an assistant editor of the *Catholic Standard and Times* and took up a post as professor of philosophy at St. Charles Borromeo Seminary. Two years later, he became news secretary for the meetings of the National Conference of Catholic Bishops in the United States from 1969 and served in the post until 1984. He was also the English-language press liaison for the visit of Pope Blessed John Paul II to Ireland and the United States in 1979 and for the Synod of Bishops held at the Vatican in 1980. In addition, from 1970 to 1984 he was editor of the archdiocese's newspaper.

On April 5, 1984, Foley was named titular bishop of Neapoli di Proconsolare and appointed president of the Pontifical Commission for Social Communications, the department in the Roman Curia with responsibility over the Church's media outreach. Four years later, the commission was promoted to the rank of a pontifical council. In his capacity as council president, Archbishop Foley was also president of the council of administration of the Vatican Television Center from August 1984 until December 1989; he was also responsible for the Vatican Film Library.

In the succeeding decades, Archbishop Foley became one of the key voices for the Holy See on the global communications stage. He was given a host of awards and honors, including the St. Francis de Sales Award from the Catholic Press Association in 1984 and the Journalism Alumni Award of Columbia University in 1985; he was awarded honorary degrees by St. Joseph's University in Philadelphia in 1985; The Catholic University of America in 1996; and the University of Portland in 2007. He also received appointments as Knight Commander with Grand Cross, Order of the Northern Star, for the Kingdom of Sweden in 1991; Knight Commander with Star of the Equestrian Order of the Holy Sepulchre of Jerusalem in 1991; Commander with Grand Cross in the Order of Bernardo O'Higgins of the Republic of Chile in 1996; Commander with Grand Cross in the Order of Libertador General San Martin of the Republic of Argentina in 2003; and Chaplain with Grand Cross of the Sovereign Military Order of Malta.

On June 27, 2007, Archbishop Foley stepped down as president of the Pontifical Council of Social Communications and was named Pro-Grand Master of the Equestrian Order of the Holy Sepulchre of Jerusalem. On November 24, 2007, he was made a member of the College of Cardinals by the hand of Pope Benedict XVI and given the deaconry of San Sebastiano al Palatino. He submitted his letter of resignation on February 8, 2011, owing to declining health.

Ford, Francis Xavier (January 11, 1892–February 21, 1952)

A Maryknoll missionary and bishop, Francis Xavier Ford was the first American to be killed by communist China. He was born in Brooklyn, New York, the son of Austin B. Ford, a noted publisher of the *Irish World,* the New York *Freeman's Journal,* and the *Monitor;* his mother, Elizabeth Rellihan Ford, was a teacher. He studied at St. Francis Preparatory School in Brooklyn and Cathedral College in New York City, and in 1912 was the first student to enter the new seminary of the Catholic Foreign Mission Society in Hawthorne, New York.

Ordained in 1917, he was named one of the first Maryknoll Missioners to set sail for Asia in 1918. In 1921 he was appointed superior of the Maryknoll Mission in Yeoungkong, China, and quickly

opened the first Maryknoll seminary for Chinese students that same year. The following year, he was delighted to welcome the first group of Maryknoll Sisters.

In 1925 Father Ford was named the prefect apostolic for evangelization in the newly established mission territory in Meihsien (Meixian), Kwangtung, or Kaying. The prefecture was elevated to a vicariate apostolic in 1935, and he was named titular bishop of Etenne. He was consecrated by Maryknoll's cofounder, Bishop James A. Walsh, on September 21, 1935. Bishop Ford erected hostels for students and started seminary training programs. By 1950 he had ordained nineteen Chinese priests. He also led the faithful during the Sino-Japanese War, starting in 1937. During World War II, his area was cut off from the rest of China, and thousands of refugees arrived in Meihsien. He managed to provide food and shelter for them. Bishop Ford served with such energy that a diocese was established in 1946.

After the war, Bishop Ford faced a new challenge when the communist Chinese sparked a brutal civil war with the Nationalist forces of Chiang Kai-shek. In December 1950 Bishop Ford was arrested and publicly humiliated on charges of "anti-Communist, counterrevolutionary, and espionage activities." Transferred to a prison in Canton in April 1951, he was subjected to further beatings and torture at each stop along the way. The continued mistreatment and cruelties inflicted on him by Chinese authorities hastened his death in prison. His passing, however, was not revealed until August 16, 1952, when Maryknoll Sister Joan Marie, who had also been arrested, was shown pictures of the bishop and was taken to his grave. (*See also* Maryknoll.)

Ford, Jeremiah (July 2, 1873–November 14, 1958)

A scholar and professor at Harvard University, Jeremiah Ford was one of the world's leading experts in Spanish and Portuguese literature. Born in Cambridge, Massachusetts, the son of Irish immigrants, Ford spent part of his youth in Ireland. He entered Harvard and earned a doctorate in 1897, by which time he was already teaching Romance languages. He remained at Harvard until 1940 and taught

French and Spanish and served as chair of the Romance Languages and Literature Department.

Known internationally for his work in Spanish and Portuguese literature, Ford wrote a number of famed books, including *Old Spanish Sibilants* in 1900, *Old Spanish Reading* in 1911, and *Main Currents of Spanish Literature* in 1919. He also served as president of the American Academy of Arts and Sciences from 1932 to 1933 and the American Catholic Historical Association in 1935. He was awarded the Laetare Medal by the University of Notre Dame in 1937 and was appointed to the French Academy in 1945.

Ford, John (February 1, 1895–August 31, 1973)

A motion-picture director and anti-communist, John Ford was the director of some 130 films and won five Academy Awards for Best Director and six in all. Born Sean Aloysius O'Fearna (or O'Feeney) in Cape Elizabeth, Maine, Ford studied at the University of Maine and first became associated with the movie industry in 1914 when he joined his brother, Francis, who was working as a silent-movie director. John had several bit parts (including playing a Klansmen in D. W. Griffith's *The Birth of a Nation* in 1915) and then began directing.

He first gained acclaim for his 1924 silent film *The Iron Horse* and won his first Academy Award in 1935 for *The Informer*, by which time he had largely perfected his distinctive directorial style. He went on to direct such legendary films as *Stagecoach* (1939), *Young Mr. Lincoln* (1939), *Drums along the Mohawk* (1939), *The Grapes of Wrath* (1940), and *How Green Was My Valley* (1941), a film that won the Best Picture Oscar. During World War II, Ford assisted the war effort by directing documentaries such as *The Battle of Midway* (1942) and by serving in the U.S. Navy as head of its photographic unit. He left the service with the rank of admiral in the Naval Reserve.

In the years after the war, Ford returned to his favorite genre, the Western. He directed another spate of famed films: *My Darling Clementine* (1946), *Fort Apache* (1948), *She Wore A Yellow Ribbon* (1949), and *Rio Grande* (1950). His later Westerns were more nostalgic, such as *The Man Who Shot Liberty Valance* (1962) and *Cheyenne Autumn* (1964). Particularly notable was *The Quiet Man*

(1952), his homage to Ireland; while cliché ridden, the film provided a lasting set of affectionate images of Ireland and the Irish people.

Noted for his gruff personality, he was nevertheless a beloved director and worked with some of the greatest talent in Hollywood, including Henry Fonda, Jimmy Stewart, and, above all, John Wayne, whose remarkable career was effectively built around his performances in Ford's films. Ford was voted the third greatest director of all time by *Entertainment Weekly* and helped shape a host of directors who followed, including Steven Spielberg, Akira Kurosawa, Sergio Leone, Clint Eastwood, and François Truffaut. Ford received the Presidential Medal of Freedom from Richard M. Nixon in 1977 and the first Life Achievement Award in 1973 from the American Film Institute.

Fordham University

The oldest Catholic institution of higher learning in the northeastern part of the United States, Fordham University opened its doors on June 24, 1841. The institution was erected at Rose Hill, New York, through the efforts of Bishop John Hughes, coadjutor bishop of New York, under the name St. John's College. The first group of six students attended a school that shared its faculty and facilities with the already established St. Joseph's Seminary. From the start, the school was plagued by financial difficulties and lacked stability in its leadership. To find a permanent solution, Bishop Hughes reached an agreement in 1845 with Father Clément Boulanger, S.J., visitor of the French Province of the Jesuits, for the Society of Jesus to assume direction of both the school and seminary.

Formal permission was granted for the college to grant degrees on April 10, 1846, by the state of New York, and the Jesuits assumed official control over the Rose Hill complex in July of that year. The first Jesuit president of the combined college and seminary was Father Augustus Thébaud. This arrangement proved ultimately unsatisfactory to Bishop Hughes, who reclaimed the seminary in 1855 only to close it in 1860 and sell the land to the Jesuits. The Society of Jesus made excellent use of the land and the college, developing a novitiate and scholasticate. Progress, while slow, was nevertheless discernible throughout the rest of the nineteenth century. By 1905 the college offered graduate programs, including a medical school (closed in 1921), followed by a law school. On the basis of these changes, St. John's College was officially renamed in 1907 as Fordham University. Over the next years, new programs were added, such as the College of Pharmacy (1911), Graduate School of Arts and Sciences (1916), and the School of Business (1920). Enrollment kept pace with these developments, so that by 1920 the student body numbered around six thousand.

Currently, Fordham University has an enrollment of over twenty thousand attending three campuses in Manhattan, the Bronx, and Tarrytown, New York. It has four undergraduate schools (Fordham College at Rose Hill, Fordham College at Lincoln Center, the College of Business Administration, and Ignatius College) and six graduate and professional schools.

Foreign Mission Society. *See* Maryknoll

Fort Wayne-South Bend, Diocese of

Established on September 22, 1857, by Pope Blessed Pius IX as the Diocese of Fort Wayne and redesignated on July 22, 1960, by Pope Blessed John XXIII as the Diocese of Fort Wayne-South Bend, this ecclesiastical jurisdiction serves counties in the northeast and north-central areas of Indiana. Fort Wayne was originally founded as a French fort erected on the site of Kekionga, the chief settlement of the Miami Indians. The fort was attacked and occupied by the English in 1760 and then by Pontiac in 1763. The Battle of Fallen Timbers in 1794, conducted by General "Mad Anthony" Wayne, subdued the Indians, and Fort Wayne was dedicated to his memory. The Wabash and Erie Canals and the railroads contributed to the economic growth of Fort Wayne as an agricultural and manufacturing center. The University of Notre Dame at South Bend is known worldwide. The Diocese of Fort Wayne-South Bend is a suffragan see of the Archdiocese of Indianapolis and has a profound Catholic heritage, having been served by some of the most outstanding missionaries in American history.

In the 1600s, Indiana territories were part of the French empire in the New World, and Jesuit missionaries came into the region from Québec. Jesuit Father Claude Allouez and others served the local American Indian nations there. Father Allouez also founded a mission on the St. Joseph River within the present diocesan limits. At the time, Indiana lands were under the jurisdiction of the bishop of Québec. When the Diocese of Baltimore (now the Archdiocese of Baltimore) was established in 1789, the area of Indiana was administered by Bishop John Carroll, and in 1808, jurisdiction moved to the Diocese of Bardstown (now the Archdiocese of Louisville). Bishop Benedict Joseph Flaget, the revered missionary prelate who headed Bardstown, traveled thousands of miles to visit the vast outreaches of the diocese. In 1816 Indiana entered the Union, and in 1834 the Diocese of Vincennes (now the Archdiocese of Indianapolis) was established with jurisdiction over all of Indiana and part of Illinois. In 1857 the Diocese of Fort Wayne was erected.

The first bishop of the Diocese of Fort Wayne was Joseph Henry Luers, who was consecrated on January 10, 1858. He founded over twenty-five parishes with about twenty priests laboring in the area, and he established the agencies and offices necessary for diocesan administration. The Cathedral of the Immaculate Conception in Fort Wayne dates to 1836. Bishop Luers expanded parishes and erected facilities to serve the needs of the growing Catholic population. He died suddenly, however, on June 29, 1871.

His successor was Bishop Joseph Dwenger, C.PP.S., who was consecrated on April 14, 1872. Bishop Dwenger established parochial schools in almost every parish and promoted the founding of St. Joseph's College at Rensselaer. He also led the first American pilgrimage to Rome and attended the Third Plenary Conference in Baltimore. He died on January 27, 1893, after visiting the North American College in Rome.

The third bishop of Fort Wayne was Joseph Rademacher, who had served as bishop of Nashville from 1883 and was transferred to Fort Wayne on July 14, 1893. He continued the building and educational programs of the diocese and renovated the cathedral in 1896. He also established parishes and charitable services. Bishop Rademacher became very ill in 1898 and died on January 12, 1900.

His successor was Bishop Herman Joseph Aldering, who was consecrated on November 30, 1900. He began new expansion programs, convened a diocesan synod, and aided facilities in the industrial areas of the diocese, from South Bend to Gary. Bishop Aldering supported the military efforts of the nation during World War I. He also wrote histories of Fort Wayne and South Bend. He died on December 6, 1924, after almost a quarter of a century of dedicated service.

The fifth bishop of Fort Wayne was John Francis Noll, who was consecrated on June 30, 1925. One year later he established the diocesan edition of *Our Sunday Visitor*, which he had founded as a priest in 1912. Bishop Noll was also prominent in opposing the Ku Klux Klan and anti-Catholicism. He led the faithful through the grim era of the Great Depression and World War II, promoting the military efforts of the United States. He established the Confraternity of Christian Doctrine in the diocese and opened Catholic Youth Organization facilities. In 1944 the Diocese of Lafayette in Indiana was established, reducing the Diocese of Fort Worth by more than half. On September 2, 1953, Pope Pius XII bestowed the rank of personal archbishop upon Bishop Noll. He died on July 31, 1956.

The successor to Bishop Noll was Leo A. Pursley, who had been consecrated on September 19, 1950, as auxiliary bishop of Fort Wayne. He succeeded to the see and was installed on February 26, 1957. In the following year, the Diocese of Gary was erected, taking more areas from Fort Wayne. In 1960, in recognition of the Catholic vitality in South Bend, the diocese was designated as Fort Wayne-South Bend. St. Matthew's in South Bend was designated as a co-cathedral. Bishop Pursley also established new schools and parishes and attended the Second Vatican Council. He retired on October 19, 1976.

The seventh bishop of Fort Wayne-South Bend was William E. McManus, who had served as auxiliary bishop of Chicago from 1967. He was installed in Fort Wayne on October 19, 1976. Bishop McManus implemented the reforms of the Second Vatican Council and continued to increase diocesan facilities and programs to meet the demands of the growing Catholic population. He retired on February 25, 1985.

The eighth bishop of Fort Wayne-South Bend, John Michael D'Arcy, succeeded Bishop McMa-

nus, having served as auxiliary bishop of the Archdiocese of Boston since 1974. Bishop D'Arcy was installed in Fort Wayne on May 1, 1985. His time as bishop was marked by the promotion of vocations and the continued institutional development of the diocese.

Bishop D'Arcy retired on November 14, 2009, and was succeeded by Bishop Kevin C. Rhoades, who had been bishop of Harrisburg since 2004. Bishop Rhoades was installed on January 13, 2010. He brought with him the same commitment to vocations that had been a hallmark of his time in Harrisburg, began long-term planning for Catholic education in the diocese, and stressed immediately the importance of the New Evangelization. In 2011 there were 159,000 Catholics served by 209 priests, more than 500 men and women religious, and 80 parishes in the diocese.

Fort Worth, Diocese of

Established on August 22, 1969, by Pope Paul VI, the Diocese of Fort Worth serves counties in north-central Texas. Originally, Pope Pius XII designated Fort Worth as part of the Diocese of Dallas-Fort Worth on October 20, 1953. Fort Worth was founded as a frontier outpost in 1849 and named for the commander of troops in Texas, Major General William J. Worth. The city served in the early 1870s as a stopover for cattle drives on the Chisholm Trail, and cattle shipping became primary when the railroads arrived. Fort Worth is now a diversified center for industry and oil production and is a transportation center. The Diocese of Fort Worth is a suffragan see of the Archdiocese of San Antonio.

Fort Worth also has a long-standing Catholic heritage, beginning in 1685, when René-Robert Chevalier, Sieur de La Salle, was in the region, claiming lands for France. In 1689 Franciscans from Mexico started missions on the Trinity River. Other explorers followed de La Salle into the region, and the missions expanded. Saintly missionary priests, such as the Venerable Antonio Margil de Jesús, built networks of Catholic settlements throughout Texas until the Mexican government, independent of Spain, closed the missions and exiled the priests.

Texas rebelled against the Mexican government

and won independence. Becoming a republic, Texas then entered the Union as a state in 1845. Four years later, Fort Worth was established as a U.S. Army outpost. Fort Worth Catholics were then under the jurisdiction of the Diocese of Galveston (now the Archdiocese of Galveston-Houston), which had jurisdiction over the entire state. In 1874 the Diocese of San Antonio (now the Archdiocese of San Antonio) was erected.

In Fort Worth, the Catholic population was expanding and becoming organized. St. Patrick's Church and St. Stanislaus, which stood until 1907, were serving the faithful. Other parishes, such as St. John the Baptist in Bridgeport, St. Joseph's in Cleburne, St. Mary's in Gainesville, St. Mary's in Henrietta, Our Lady of Mercy in Hillsboro, and Holy Family in Vernon were opened in the early eras. Parochial schools were also pioneered in the region.

Pope Leo XIII established the Diocese of Dallas in 1890, and Fort Worth was part of that ecclesiastical jurisdiction through the grim years of World War I, the Great Depression, and World War II. The Catholic population continued to expand, and Pope Pius XII recognized Fort Worth as he designated the Diocese of Dallas-Fort Worth. St. Patrick's Church was elevated to the status of a co-cathedral.

In August 1969, Pope Paul VI separated twenty-eight counties of north-central Texas and established the Diocese of Fort Worth. The first bishop of Fort Worth was John J. Cassata, who had served as auxiliary bishop of the Diocese of Dallas-Fort Worth from 1968. He was appointed on August 22, 1969. Bishop Cassata instituted the agencies and offices for diocesan administration and established new parishes and schools. He also implemented the reforms of the Second Vatican Council in the diocese. Bishop Cassata retired on September 16, 1980.

The second bishop of Fort Worth was Joseph P. Delaney. He was appointed to Fort Worth on July 10, 1981, and consecrated on September 13, 1981. Under Bishop Delaney's long term of service, the diocese dedicated itself to fostering Catholic education. Bishop Delaney also supported ecumenical efforts and succeeded in establishing a new Catholic Center to house the pastoral and administrative offices of the diocese. He valiantly battled cancer in his last years and passed away on July 12, 2005. The third bishop of Fort Worth, Kevin W.

Vann, was ordained and installed in Fort Worth on July 13, 2005, at the Daniel-Meyer Coliseum of Texas Christian University. He organized a very successful "All Things Possible" capital campaign to provide for the long-term financial well-being of the diocese. In 2011 there were 586,000 Catholics served by 123 priests and 89 parishes in the diocese.

Foster, John G. (May 27, 1823–September 2, 1874)

A Civil War officer and convert, John G. Foster distinguished himself throughout the war and later worked as a noted engineer. Born in Whitfield, New Hampshire, he graduated from the the United States Military Academy at West Point in 1846 and was appointed to the Army Corps of Engineers. He served as a lieutenant during the Mexican-American War and was wounded during the fighting. After the war, he taught engineering at West Point from 1855 to 1857. By 1861 and the start of the Civil War, Foster was in command of the forts in Charleston Harbor. He was thus in a position to be a prominent officer for the Union Army at the famed start of the war, when Confederate forces bombarded Fort Sumter.

Reassigned after the war's commencement, Foster held a variety of assignments over the next years, including commander of several departments, among them Virginia, North Carolina, and then Ohio from 1862 to 1863. Going into the field, Foster served in the campaign of General William Tecumseh Sherman in the deep South and at the sieges of Charleston and Savannah. By the end of the war, Foster held the rank of brigadier general in the Regular Army. After the war, he provided his engineering skills to massive projects in Boston and Portsmouth harbors. Foster converted to the Catholic faith in 1861 while on campaign in North Carolina.

Fournier, Mother St. John (November 13, 1814–October 15, 1875)

A member of the Sisters of St. Joseph, Mother St. John Fournier was also the founder of the Congregation of Chestnut Hill in Philadelphia. Born Julie Alexise Fournier in Arbois, France, she entered the Order of the Immaculate Conception in 1828 and made her vows in 1832. In 1836 she transferred to the Sisters of St. Joseph of Lyons in order to serve in the congregation's missions in St. Louis. In preparation, she learned how to teach the deaf. Sister St. John arrived in St. Louis in September 1837 and remained in the city until 1847. In 1845 she was appointed superior of St. Joseph's School for the Colored, but the institution had to be closed owing to the hostile attacks by racists in the city.

In 1847 she and three other sisters journeyed to Philadelphia at the invitation of Bishop Francis P. Kenrick to assume direction of St. John's Orphanage in Philadelphia. The community was the first for the congregation organized outside of St. Louis, and Mother St. John wasted no time in continuing that expansion. In 1848 she opened St. Patrick's parochial school in Pottsville, Pennsylvania, followed by over two dozen houses in Pennsylvania, Maryland, New Jersey, Delaware, and Minnesota. In 1858 Bishop (later St.) John Henry Neumann assisted Mother St. John in establishing a permanent motherhouse, Mount St. Joseph, at Chestnut Hill. Her sisters served as nurses during the Civil War, and after the cessation of hostilities she was especially concerned about the welfare of the war's many orphans. In 1860, at the advice of Bishop James F. Wood, she chose not to incorporate with the Generalate of the Sisters of St. Joseph of Carondolet. Her congregation was responsible for the establishment of the congregations of Toronto in 1851 and Brooklyn in 1856 and influenced the development of others. Papal approval was received for the rule in 1896.

Franciscan Friars of the Atonement (S.A.). *See* Graymoor

Franciscan Missions of California. *See* California Missions

Franciscans

A religious order of the Church founded in the early thirteenth century by St. Francis of Assisi, the Franciscans are divided into three independent branches: the Friars Minor (O.F.M.), the Friars Minor Conventual (O.F.M. Conv.) and the Friars Minor Capuchin (O.F.M. Cap.). In 1209 St. Francis received approval from Pope Innocent III to conduct his life of penance, preaching, and total

poverty with his disciples. Within ten years, the followers of St. Francis numbered five thousand. The original rule, however, was revised to promote prosperity and growth in the order. Pope Honorius III approved the revised rule.

St. Bonaventure, who served as minister general of the order from 1257 to 1274, is considered the second founder of the Franciscans. He maintained unity as the friars spread across Europe and into Syria and Africa. A group called the Spirituals, or Zealots, maintained that absolute poverty was the key to the order's character, while the Conventuals argued that the order needed a more moderate monastic life adapted to study and preaching. The Spirituals declined in power and were no longer a viable part of the order by 1325. Another group, called the Observants, supported by St. Bernardine of Siena and St. John of Capistrano, spread across Europe in the latter part of the fourteenth century, and in 1517 there was a division in the Franciscans. In time, the Observants were replaced by the Capuchins and became a branch of the Franciscans in 1517. Pope Leo XIII approved a new constitution and named the order the Friars Minor of the Observance.

The Franciscans were pioneering missionaries in America, arriving in 1493 and sending almost 8,500 members of the order to labor in the lands that would become the United States. Franciscans were in Florida by 1573, establishing the oldest city in the United States and a chain of missions that endured Indian uprisings and attacks by the English colonies. As early as 1528, Franciscans were with the expedition of Pánfilo de Narváez, and all were slain on the northwest coast of Florida. In 1536 Franciscan Friar Juan de Torres was with Hernando de Soto's expedition and was slain with his companions. The protomartyr of the United States, Friar Juan de Padilla, having entered the area with the expedition of Francisco Vázquez de Coronado, was martyred in Kansas in 1540.

The Friars Minor also served in New Mexico as early as 1581, expanding missions and supporting the Spanish colonials in the region. They were in Texas, Arizona, and California, and records indicate that they served as missionaries in the northeastern parts of present-day America and in French territories. Franciscans and Sulpicians were with the expedition of René-Robert Chevalier, Sieur de La Salle, in 1685 in Texas. Four years later the revered Franciscan missionary Damien Mazanet was in San Antonio and San Saba. Venerable Antonio Margil de Jesús pioneered missions in Texas, and an estimated twelve members of the mission band died in the service of the faith. The Franciscans were in the area of the St. Lawrence River and the Great Lakes in 1615 and in Louisiana from 1722.

Capuchin Franciscans were also in the American missions, reportedly serving the Acadians at Port Royal (Annapolis) in 1632. The Puritans destroyed the missions in 1655, and the Capuchins started new ones with the Micmacs. French Capuchins were in the vast Louisiana missions by 1714 and were serving in New Orleans, St. Louis, Galveston, Mobile, Pensacola, Natchez, Natchitoches, and San Antonio.

When the United States was formed after the Revolutionary War ended the British occupation, the Franciscans came into the country with European immigrants, revitalizing their presence in America. American Catholics learned about the Nativity scene (the crèche) from the Franciscans, and the friars also popularized the Stations of the Cross and the Angelus. These Franciscans were in Cincinnati in 1844, in Texas in 1852, and in Wisconsin in 1857. Many Franciscans undertook the ministries of parishes and schools, and the Friars Minor were organized into six provinces. The Capuchins had five provinces and the Conventuals four. In 2000 the Friars Minor had 1,800 members in the United States, the Capuchins numbered 730, and the Conventuals numbered 620. New groups, such as the Franciscan Friars of the Immaculate and the Franciscan Friars of the Renewal, are prospering in the United States.

Freeman's Journal and Catholic Register

One of the most popular and influential Catholic newspapers in the United States during the nineteenth century, the *Freeman's Journal and Catholic Register* was founded around 1841 by John E. White and his brother James W. White under the original name, the *New York Freeman's Journal*. The newspaper was intended to provide a voice for Irish-Americans, and the scope was widened to encompass Irish Catholics when the Whites received formal approval to merge with William E. Fitzgibbon's *New York Catholic Register*. The name was thus changed to the *Freeman's Journal and Catholic Register*. The overarching objective of the newspaper was to give useful information to Irish Catholics on events in Ireland and the Church throughout the world.

Over the next years, the paper changed hands several times. In 1842 it was sold to Thomas Walsh and Louis Ende and in 1846 passed to Bishop John Hughes of New York. Bishop Hughes appointed Reverend (later archbishop of Baltimore) James Roosevelt Bayley as its editor and declared the newspaper in 1854 to be the official organ of the Catholic community of New York. The newspaper was thus at the forefront of the effort to defend the Church against the scurrilous attacks of the press of the times.

In the meantime, James McMaster purchased the newspaper in 1848 and served as its editor. His editorial positions regarding Ireland and other issues of the day eventually cost the paper its official standing with the archdiocese in 1857, although it continued to promote the Catholic position. Nevertheless, the paper was closed during the Civil War by federal forces in 1861 to 1862 owing to McMaster's editorial positions against the war and on states' rights. The paper recovered its prominence later in the 1860s, but decline set in during the 1870s, and it was sold in 1888 to Austin E. and Robert L. Ford, the owners of the *Irish World*. The end came during World War I when the paper adopted a staunch antiwar position. With the entry of the United States into war, government authorities seized various issues so that on July 4, 1918, the paper announced that all publishing had been suspended until the right to speak freely had been restored. As it turned out, the newspaper never resumed publication.

Fremin, Jacques (March 12, 1628–July 2, 1691)

A Jesuit missionary to the American Indians, Jacques Fremin was responsible for the conversion of thousands of Native Americans. He was born at Reims, France, and entered the Society of Jesus in 1646. In 1655 he was sent to the Canadian missions. Over the next years, his labors brought him into the lands of the Cayuga, Mohawk, Huron, and Seneca, although his evangelization was frequently complicated by wars and the hostility of some of the tribes. He nevertheless became so respected among the Native Americans that in 1670 he was placed in charge of La Prairie, the mission for Christian Indians near Montréal. He devoted his remaining years to the care of Indian converts and died in Montréal.

French Catholics

The first French Catholics reached North America in the sixteenth and seventeenth centuries as part of the gradual process of discovery and settlement of the New World by France. The first Catholics of French descent were thus explorers, fur traders, and missionaries. They were joined in time by other French settlers, by the Huguenots — French Protestants fleeing persecution — and by French soldiers who were sent by the crown to establish a permanent presence in North America.

Fur-trading posts were set up along the St. Lawrence River in the Great Lakes region and around the basin of the Mississippi River, and gradual settlements were begun along the northeastern border of the English colonies to create what became known as New France, centered in the great city of Québec. By 1760 there were some seventy thousand French colonials spread out across the vast stretches of the northern regions of the continent.

Of note were the Acadians, those settlers who chose to live in the relative isolation of Nova Scotia. Driven from the region in 1755 by the English, many Acadians were forced to form a colony in Louisiana, to the west of New Orleans. They retained their own language, cultures, and traditions, and long considered French their chief tongue. Other Acadians went to Québec, some returned to France, and many hundreds died when their ships sank on the way back to Europe. (*See also* Acadians.)

From its earliest days, the French in North America were supported by an active and dedicated Church presence. First to arrive were missionaries such as the Recollects, Jesuits, Franciscans, Ursulines, and Sulpicians, who were remarkable for their labors among the Native Americans. Church structure soon followed, especially under Blessed

François de Montmorency Laval, the "Father of the Church in Canada," and the first bishop of Québec. (*See also* Canada, Church in.)

Despite the colonial effort, the French presence along the St. Lawrence River was smaller than that of the English, who naturally saw French possessions as a great threat to the long-term strategic and commercial interests of England. The inevitable conflict between the English and French colonies reflected the ongoing hostility between England and France in Europe. British colonists fought against the French colonies in Queen Anne's War from 1701 to 1713 and King George's War from 1743 to 1748. They also competed bitterly for control of the Ohio Valley, and in the French and Indian War, which climaxed with the defeat of the French and the fall of Québec in 1759. By the terms of the Treaty of Paris of 1763, England assumed control of Québec and hence political authority over the French-speaking Catholic population.

Catholics in Canada found themselves facing a potentially difficult situation under the British, especially as the Church was deeply supported by the people of the former colony and found a close identification between French-Canadian culture and the Catholic faith. By the Québec Act of 1774, Catholics were permitted to practice their religion, although the hierarchy was not recognized, and in 1774 the Jesuits and Recollects were dispossessed. Additional pressures followed as the government established the Church of England, followed by Protestant denominations. In 1793, however, French priests who had been exiled during the French Revolution were allowed into the country, and émigrés swelled the general population as Royalists and persecuted French looked for safety from the violence engulfing their country.

French Catholics who settled in Canada made their way into the eastern cities of the United States, especially New England, helping to forge a bond between France and the United States. French Catholics moved south in part because of economic opportunities. Additional incentive was given by the unsuccessful rebellion against Britain in 1837. Immigration increased considerably in the second half of the nineteenth century, with most settling in New England and upstate New York.

Another significant event in the history of

French Catholics in the United States came in 1803 with the Louisiana Purchase, in which the United States purchased the enormous territory of Louisiana from Napoleon. Founded in 1699 and named in honor of King Louis XIV, the Louisiana Territory was one of the principal homes of French Catholics, including the Acadians, refugees from France, and a number of other colonists, among them Spaniards and Germans. The French population, however, was increased substantially by the Creoles who migrated to the region from the West Indies, and so enjoyed numerical superiority. By acquiring the Louisiana Territory, the United States was enriched greatly by the addition of French culture, mostly in the two centers of French life at New Orleans, founded in 1718, and St. Louis, founded in 1764.

French Catholics in the United States were never of a size to exercise the same kind of influence as the blocs of German Catholics or Irish Catholics. Nevertheless, they were determined to preserve the faith, as well as their language and customs. Of great note was the abiding love of French Catholics for parish life, and French-speaking schools and parishes were established.

As was true with other Catholic immigrants, French Catholics in the United States often found themselves a small minority in chiefly Protestant states and persecuted by the anti-Catholic movements of the nineteenth century. The Know-Nothings were especially active in New England. Nevertheless, French Catholics rose to prominent positions in the social and political life of New England and elsewhere. At the same time, their commitment to traditional French culture caused friction with many bishops and clergy, who urged them to assimilate into mainstream American culture. Conflicts flared with Irish Catholics when French Catholics insisted on retaining their native language and close-knit parish structures. When, therefore, Irish bishops asserted their rights and tried to impose English-speaking or Irish priests on their parishes, French Catholics resisted. Crises flared several times between the 1880s and 1920s, including the bitter Sentinellist Affair in Rhode Island that ended with the excommunication of sixty French Catholics in 1928.

Although French Catholics did not assume the cultural power of other groups such as the Irish and Germans, they have still made lasting contributions to American Catholic life. The stress placed upon the central role of the parish within the Catholic community is a cherished tradition that is a model for Catholics in other parts of the country. Equally, French Catholics have long nurtured Catholic cultural devotions, such as Eucharistic adoration and to the Blessed Virgin Mary. The custom of Mardi Gras in French Catholic areas — while having lost much of its original meaning in New Orleans because of commercialization and the devastation of Hurricane Katrina — is still one of America's beloved annual events.

Fresno, Diocese of

Established as the Diocese of Monterey-Fresno by Pope Benedict XV in 1922 and designated as the Diocese of Fresno on December 15, 1967, by Pope Paul VI, the Diocese of Fresno serves counties in central California in the San Joaquin Valley. Fresno was settled in 1872 as a station of the Central (later Southern) Pacific Railroad, and the name is Spanish for "ash tree." The city is a processing and marketing center for raisins, other fruits, grains, cotton, and dairy products. The city is also a gateway to the Sierra Nevada Mountains. The Diocese of Fresno is a suffragan see of the Archdiocese of Los Angeles.

California was an early mission territory, explored by Spanish expeditions and by Jesuit priests. In 1770 Franciscans from Mexico took up the missions abandoned by the exiled Jesuits, and Blessed Junípero Serra and his companions built a chain of churches on the Camino Real. In 1834 the Diocese of the Californias was established, with the see at Santa Barbara. Upper California became part of the United States soon after, and in 1849 the Diocese of Monterey was established. Bishop Joseph Sadoc Alemany was the first bishop of the diocese and was then promoted to the Archdiocese of San Francisco. His successor in Monterey was Bishop Thaddeus Amat, who petitioned the Holy See to designate the episcopal jurisdiction as the Diocese of Monterey and Los Angeles. In 1859 Bishop Amat moved the see to Los Angeles.

The Catholic population of California continued to expand, and churches were opened in the area that would become Fresno. St. John's, destined to become the cathedral, was serving the faithful in 1882.

World War I impacted on the area as Catholics aided the military efforts of the nation. After the war, the Diocese of Monterey-Fresno was erected by the Holy See, and Bishop John B. MacGinley, who had served as the bishop of Nueva Caceres since 1910, was transferred to the new diocese on July 31, 1924. He established the offices and agencies for diocesan administration and began expansion programs to meet the growing needs of the faithful. Because of ill health, Bishop McGinley retired on September 30, 1932.

His successor was Bishop Philip G. Scher, who was consecrated on June 29, 1933. The Great Depression brought need and sacrifice to Catholics in Monterey and Fresno as Americans suffered all across the nation. Bishop Scher promoted social and relief services to provide aid and also led the diocese through the grim days of World War II. He died on January 3, 1953.

The third bishop of Monterey-Fresno was Aloysius J. Willinger, C.SS.R., who had served as the bishop of the Diocese of Ponce since 1929 and then as coadjutor bishop of the Diocese of Monterey-Fresno with right of succession since 1946. He acceded to the see on January 3, 1953, and continued the diocesan building programs. Bishop Willinger developed parishes, missions, schools, and hospitals. He retired on October 25, 1967.

His successor was Bishop Harry Anselm Clinch, who had served as auxiliary bishop of the diocese since 1956. On December 14, 1967, Bishop Clinch was transferred to the newly erected Diocese of Monterey.

The first bishop of the Diocese of Fresno was Timothy Manning, who would become an American cardinal in 1973. Bishop Manning had served as an auxiliary bishop of Los Angeles since 1946. He was installed in the Diocese of Fresno on December 15, 1967, and started the offices and agencies for diocesan administration. On May 26, 1969, Bishop Manning was promoted to coadjutor archbishop of the Archdiocese of Los Angeles with right of succession. He was created a cardinal priest on March 5, 1973.

His successor in the Diocese of Fresno was Bishop Hugh A. Donohoe, who had served as an auxiliary bishop of San Francisco and as bishop of Stockton from 1962. He was transferred to Fresno on August 28, 1969. Bishop Donohoe implemented the reforms mandated by the Second Vatican Council. He also expanded diocesan facilities and promoted lay ministries. He retired on July 1, 1980.

The third bishop of Fresno, Joseph J. Madera, M.Sp.S., had served as coadjutor bishop of the diocese with right of succession since March 4, 1980. He acceded to the see upon the retirement of Bishop Donohoe. Bishop Madera continued the diocesan expansion programs, providing parish and charitable facilities and services. He also faced a shortage of priests and religious. On May 28, 1991, Bishop Madera was transferred to the Archdiocese for Military Services in Washington, D.C.

The fourth bishop of Fresno, John T. Steinbock, had served as auxiliary bishop of the Diocese of Orange from 1984 and then as bishop of Santa Rosa since 1987. Bishop Steinbock was installed in Fresno on November 24, 1991. He led the diocese throughout the difficult years of the sex abuse crisis and was committed to preventing child abuse by the clergy. He died on December 5, 2010, after a long struggle with cancer.

On December 1, 2011, Bishop Armando X. Ochoa, bishop of El Paso since 1996, was appointed bishop of Fresno. In 2011 there were one million Catholics served by 162 priests and 89 parishes in the diocese.

Friess, Mother Caroline (August 21, 1824–October 1, 1892)

Mother Superior of the School Sisters of Notre Dame, Mother Caroline Friess served as head of the congregation in America from 1850 to 1892. Born Josefa Friess near Paris, she entered the congregation in 1840. In 1847 she was sent to the United States with the first members of the congregation, and in 1850, at the age of twenty-six, she became the superior for North America with the full confidence of the founder of the congregation, Blessed Mother Mary Theresa of Jesus Gerhardinger.

Under her direction, the first motherhouse for the School Sisters was opened in Milwaukee, and Mother Caroline presided over a remarkable period of expansion for the sisters. By 1892 her sisters had founded 265 parochial schools in 16 states and taught over 70,000 pupils, including African-American and Native American children. She also proved immensely successful in attracting vocations to the religious life; several thousand young women entered the congregation, and Mother Caroline Friess divided the Sisters in North America into two provinces.

Fumasoni-Biondi, Pietro (September 4, 1872–July 12, 1960)

The apostolic delegate to the United States from 1922 to 1933 and cardinal from 1933, Pietro Fumasoni-Biondi was the representative of the Holy See to America during the onset of the Great Depression. Born in Rome, Italy, to the noble Roman family of Fumasoni-Biondi, he studied for the priesthood at the Roman Seminary, although he served a stint in the Italian Army prior to his ordination, as required by Italian law. Ordained a priest on April 17, 1897, he was given a brief pastoral assignment and was then named secretary to Cardinal Agostino Ciasca, an adviser to Pope Leo XIII. He also served as a faculty member of the Pontifical Urbanian Athenueum de Propaganda Fide in Rome.

Over the next years, he held a variety of posts in the Roman Curia, until 1916, when he was named titular archbishop of Dioclea and appointed apostolic delegate to India. Consecrated on December 10, 1916, he reached India the following year. In 1919 he was named apostolic delegate to Japan and Korea and proved highly successful in forging improved relations between the Holy See and the Imperial Government of Japan. After a brief period in Rome, he was appointed by Pope Pius XI as apostolic delegate to the United States on December 14, 1922.

Reaching America in March 1923, he assumed his position in the midst of a period of rapid growth and development in the Church in the United States. His time was thus taken up in assisting that progress, although his last years were marked by demonstrations of concern for the plight of Americans

as a result of the sudden occurrence of the Great Depression. At the same time, he served as apostolic delegate to Mexico and was responsible for helping to negotiate the working relationship between the revolutionary government and the Church.

In 1933 Archbishop Fumasoni-Biondi was summoned back to Rome and appointed the cardinal priest of Santa Croce in Gerusalemme; he was elevated to the College of Cardinals on March 17, 1933. The day before, he had been named Prefect of the Congregation of the Propaganda Fide. In 1958, owing to his declining health and eyesight, a pro-prefect was named to assist his work. The prelate chosen for the post was Cardinal Samuel Alphonsus Stritch, archbishop of Chicago. When Cardinal Stritch died soon after arriving in Rome, he was replaced by the famed Cardinal Gregory Peter Agagianian. Cardinal Fumasoni-Biondi died two years later.

Furdek, Stephen (September 2, 1855–January 18, 1915)

A Slovak priest who labored on behalf of Slovak Catholics in the United States, Stephen Furdek was also the founder of the famous journal *Jednota*. Born in Trsztena, Slovakia (then a province in the Austrian Empire), he entered studies for the priesthood in Nitra and Prague but volunteered for service in the United States. He thus completed his seminary preparation at St. Mary's Seminary in Cleveland and was ordained on July 1, 1882.

Father Furdek was assigned to several parishes devoted to the pastoral care of Slovak and Czech immigrants and focused his ministry on the specific needs of Slovak workers. From this first outreach emerged the first Slovak parish, St. Ladislas Church, in Cleveland. He remained committed to his Slovak flock even as he dedicated himself to the Czech parishioners of Our Lady of Lourdes in Cleveland.

In 1890 Father Furdek presided over a gathering in Cleveland of various leaders from Slovak Fraternal Cath-

Archbishop Pietro Fumasoni-Biondi

olic organizations. He convinced them of the great value of merging their disparate efforts into one united organization that would work for the benefit of Slovak Catholics in the United States. The result was the foundation of the First Catholic Slovak Union. Two years later, the First Catholic Slovak Ladies' Association was also founded. Furdek also established the noted journal *Jednota* and served as its editor for some years.

Furfey, Paul Hanly (June 30, 1896–June 8, 1992)

A priest, sociologist, and social justice reformer, Paul Hanly Furfey was born in Cambridge, Massachusetts, and graduated from Boston College in 1917. He then entered St. Mary's Seminary in Baltimore to study for the priesthood, and was ordained on May 25, 1922. He went on to graduate studies at The Catholic University of America in Washington, D.C., and earned a doctorate in sociology in 1926. He also undertook postgraduate studies in Berlin and Frankfurt from 1931 to 1932. In 1934 he became a professor of sociology at Catholic Uni-

versity and became dean of the Sociology Department in 1940. He remained on the faculty until his retirement in 1966. He also taught at Catholic University from 1973 to 1975 as a visiting professor.

Father Furfey wrote his first book, *The Gang Age*, in 1926, followed by a large body of writings that ranged across the spectrum of sociological concerns, including *Social Problems of Childhood* (1930), *Fire on Earth* (1936), *The Morality Gap* (1969), *The History of Social Thought* (1942), *The Scope and Method of Sociology* (1953), *The Subculture of the Washington Ghetto* (1972), and his last book, *Love and the Urban Ghetto* (1978).

Committed to social justice issues, Father Furfey served as director of the Juvenile Delinquency Evaluation Project from 1956 to 1961 and helped establish *Il Poverello* and *Fides House*, two communities dedicated to fostering interracial relations. He was also a supporter of the Catholic Worker Movement and an antiwar activist during Vietnam. In 1982 Catholic University established the Paul Hanly Furfey Lecture in Sociology.

G

Galitzin, Princess Elizabeth (February 22, 1797–December 8, 1843)

A Russian aristocrat and religious, Princess Elizabeth Galitzin was a relative of Prince Demetrius Augustine Gallitzin and a convert to the Catholic faith. She was born in St. Petersburg, Russia, the daughter of Prince Alexis Andrevitch Galitzin, and raised as a Russian Orthodox. Her mother, Countess Protasof, converted to Catholicism, an act that was punishable by exile or death under Russian law. Princess Elizabeth was enraged by her mother's conversion, but the constancy and prayer life of the countess won her widespread admiration and brought many to the Catholic faith. Princess Elizabeth entered the Catholic Church four years after her mother.

Her spiritual director watched as the grace of a religious vocation changed the princess, and when she shared her desire to enter "an austere order devoted to education," he recommended the Society of the Sacred Heart, recently founded by St. Madeleine Sophie Barat. Princess Elizabeth entered the Society and received the habit at Metz in 1826. Her first vows were made in Rome in 1828, and her final vows in Paris in 1832.

Two years later, Mother Elizabeth was appointed secretary-general to St. Madeleine, a position she filled brilliantly. In 1839 she was elected assistant general of the Society and visitor general of the convents of the Sacred Heart in the United States. Mother Elizabeth toured the young nation and proved to be a strict observer of the Society's constitution, even pressing for sterner regulations. This attitude evolved from her aristocratic upbringing and kept her from fully embodying the spirit of the Society while on her travels, and when she realized her error, she was filled with remorse.

She asked to be sent back to the United States to undo whatever damage she may have caused with her strict interpretation of the religious life of the Society. Mother Elizabeth sailed to America and went to Louisiana to begin to restore the true vision of the Society in the convent there. A yellow fever epidemic struck, however, and she heroically cared for the many victims before she succumbed to yellow fever and died.

Gallitzin, Prince Demetrius Augustine (December 22, 1770–May 6, 1840)

The "Apostle of the Alleghenies," now designated as a Servant of God, Demetrius Augustine Gallitzin devoted forty years of his life to establishing the Church in western Pennsylvania. Born in the Hague, Holland, he was the son of the Russian Prince Demetrius Gallitzin and Countess Amalia Gallitzin, daughter of a Prussian field marshal. Amalia had been baptized a Roman Catholic, but she had ceased to practice the faith after her marriage, as her husband had introduced her to the most powerful circles of the Enlightenment philosophy that encouraged religious indifference and hostility to Christianity. Upon the arrival of their son, the couple nevertheless had him baptized in the Orthodox Church; Empress Catherine the Great of Russia was his godmother.

Amalia returned to the Catholic Church in 1786 and introduced her son to Catholicism. He entered the Catholic Church the next year. His father soon arranged for his son to have an excellent education and a posting as an aide-de-camp to the Austrian General Franz Freiherr von Lillien. It was expected that Prince Demetrius would then embark on the usual grand tour of Europe. Instead, he set sail for the United States.

By this time, he had responded to a call to the priesthood and arrived at Baltimore on October 28, 1792, and presented himself to Bishop John Carroll with the request that he be permitted to enter the seminary. After studies at St. Mary's Seminary, Demetrius Gallitzin was ordained on March 18, 1795. He was the first priest to receive all his preparation for the priesthood training and orders in the United States. (*See also* Badin, Stephen Theodore.)

After holding several pastoral positions at Port Tobacco, Maryland; Conewago, Pennsylvania; and among German Catholics in Baltimore, he was asked to make an emergency visit to the Allegheny Mountains in 1796 to deliver the last rites to a Catholic in Captain Michael McGuire's settlement in Cambria County, Pennsylvania. The visit proved a significant one, for Father Gallitzin recognized the immense pastoral opportunities and needs of the region and went so far as to buy land there with the long-range objective of founding a true Catholic community in the mountains. After several years of petitioning Bishop Carroll, Father Gallitzin was at last granted permission to serve as pastor in western Pennsylvania. Using thousands of dollars of his own money, Father Gallitzin built a church at what came to be known as Loretto and celebrated his first Mass there on Christmas Day in 1799.

For the next forty years, he served with great distinction as pastor over virtually the whole of western Pennsylvania. He encouraged the development of the Catholic community at Loretto, although his relations with his flock were at times stormy, owing in part to the rugged independent character of frontier Catholics. Nevertheless, Father Gallitzin declined several episcopal appointments to continue caring for his people; he was still appointed vicar general for western Pennsylvania. He also became one of the most widely read Catholic apologists of the period for his vigorous and often elegant

Gallitzin Memorial

defense of the Catholic faith against the Protestant polemics then being published. His decades of service left him exhausted, and he spent his last years in constant pain from an injury he incurred falling from his horse, which never healed properly. He also lost rights to his father's vast estate owing to his conversion to Catholicism. Father Gallitzin died at Loretto. His cause was for canonization was opened in 2005.

Gallup, Diocese of

Established on December 16, 1939, by Pope Pius XII, the Diocese of Gallup serves counties in northwestern New Mexico and in Arizona. Gallup, located on the Puerco River, was established in 1880 as a Westward Overland Stagecoach stop. The site was then developed as a construction headquarters for the Atlantic and Pacific Railroad and was named for David L. Gallup, the railroad paymaster. In 1895 Gallup became a railroad divisional terminal. The city is situated between Navajo and Zuñi Indian reservations, serving as a center for shipping of local products, light industry, and tourism. No other diocese in the nation serves as many Native Americans. The Diocese of Gallup is a suffragan see of the Archdiocese of Santa Fe.

The Catholic history of Gallup dates to 1539, when Franciscan Father Marcos de Niza entered the region, intent on proclaiming it the "New Kingdom of St. Francis." He had a Moor slave as a companion, and together they were seeking Cibola, the legendary Seven Cities of Gold. Soon after, the Spaniard Francisco Vázquez de Coronado was on a similar adventure and stayed in New Mexico for a time. Franciscan Father Juan de la Cruz was slain on this expedition, becoming New Mexico's first martyr. A Franciscan brother, Luis de Escalona, was also listed as a martyr in 1542 as part of the same expedition.

Despite the deaths and continued hostilities, Spanish colonies soon started, and the Franciscans began opening missions. In 1581 Franciscans Juan de Santa Maria and Francisco López were killed at Puarray, and later another Franciscan priest, Agustin Rodriguez, died. The Spanish explorer Antonio de Espejo led a small army into the area of modern-day New Mexico to ascertain their fate.

In 1598 Juan de Oñate settled a large group of

Spanish colonists at the new outpost called San Juan de los Caballeros. Two years later, the colony moved to San Gabriel. Pedro de Peralta, who built a new capital, La Villa Real de la Santa Fe de San Francisco de Asis, replaced de Oñate as governor in 1608. Franciscan missionaries started Santo Domingo Pueblo in 1610. The mission expanded and the settlements prospered.

In 1678, however, Franciscan Francis de Ayeta visited all the missions in the area and declared them potential disasters because of the suffering of the Pueblo Indians. He reported to his superiors and then took vast amounts of supplies to El Paso, now in modern-day Texas, believing that possible survivors of the impending disaster would make their way there. On August 10, 1680, the Pueblo Indians rose against their Spanish masters, including the Franciscans. Priests and brothers were killed. Some twenty-one friars died, along with four hundred Spanish settlers. On August 21, a stream of survivors made their way to El Paso, where Father de Ayeta was waiting for them. In 1692 Diego de Vargas started a *reconquista* of New Mexico, and he entered Santa Fe on December 16, 1693. Missions were reopened, and the Franciscans were joined by Jesuits in time, as evangelization continued. The missions remained active until 1821, when the Mexican government expelled all Spanish clerics. The churches and missions were abandoned, and no native New Mexican priests could conduct their ministries.

This state of affairs continued until 1848, when under the Treaty of Guadalupe-Hidalgo New Mexico became a part of the United States. Two years later, Pope Blessed Pius IX established the Vicariate Apostolic of New Mexico in Santa Fe. Bishop Jean Baptiste Lamy, the revered missionary pioneer, was appointed vicar apostolic. Santa Fe became a diocese in 1853 and an archdiocese in 1875.

America expanded, and the completion of the railroad lines brought new settlers into the area. Fathers Juan B. Brun and George Julliard labored in the region. Father Julliard erected the first Catholic Church in Gallup in 1899, and the cathedral stands on the site of that venerable house of worship. St. Katharine Drexel aided the Native American missions and founded St. Michael's. The people of Gallup, along with their fellow citizens,

faced the grim years of World War I and the Great Depression. In 1936 Cardinal Eugenio Pacelli, who would become Pope Pius XII, took an aerial tour of Gallup, and when he became the Supreme Pontiff he pursued the idea of establishing a diocese that would serve the region in which so many American Indians resided.

The Diocese of Gallup was erected in 1939, establishing an ecclesiastical jurisdiction that had a reported seventeen parishes and fifty-six mission churches. A Franciscan, Bernard T. Espelage, was appointed the first bishop of the Diocese of Gallup on July 20, 1940. He assumed the see as the first clouds of war threatened the nation. Bishop Espelage established the offices and agencies necessary for diocesan administration and led the faithful through the sacrifices of World War II. He also aided in the establishment of the Diocese of Phoenix for the non-Indian population of Arizona in 1969. Bishop Espelage retired on September 3 of that year, after guiding an infant diocese through harrowing times.

His successor was Bishop Jerome J. Hastrich, who had served as auxiliary bishop of the Diocese of Madison since 1963. He was transferred to Gallup on September 3, 1969, and installed on December 3. Bishop Hastrich implemented the reforms of the Second Vatican Council and expanded facilities and services in New Mexico and Arizona, aiding the Native American programs. He retired on March 20, 1990.

The third bishop of Gallup, Donald E. Pelotte, S.S.S., was a member of the Abenaki nation and a distinguished author and scholar. He had served as coadjutor bishop of Gallup since February 24, 1986, and acceded to the see when Bishop Hastrich retired. Bishop Pelotte resigned on February 5, 2009, owing to severe health issues, and died on January 7, 2010.

Father James S. Wall, a priest of the Phoenix diocese, was appointed bishop on February 5, 2009; he was ordained a bishop on April 23, 2009. In 2011 there were 62,000 Catholics served by 56 priests and 52 parishes in the diocese.

Galveston-Houston, Archdiocese of

Established as the Diocese of Galveston on May 4, 1847, by Pope Blessed Pius IX, and designated as the

Diocese of Galveston-Houston on July 25, 1959, by Pope Blessed John XXIII and as the Archdiocese of Galveston-Houston on December 29, 2004, by Pope John Paul II, this ecclesiastical jurisdiction serves east-central Texas. The original Diocese of Galveston was the first such ecclesiastical establishment in the state of Texas, with jurisdiction over the entire state, except for El Paso County. A deepwater port, Galveston was once the home of the famous Jean Lafitte, a pirate who aided the American cause in the War of 1812. The city was named after Don Bernardo de Gálvez, the governor of Louisiana and later viceroy of Mexico. Galveston is a major industrial and maritime center.

The Catholic heritage of Galveston and Houston opens with the arrival of René-Robert Chevalier, Sieur de La Salle, in 1686. He claimed all the lands in the area for France and discovered Galveston Island, naming it after King Louis. Three years later, Franciscan missionaries began evangelizing in the region and opening missions.

Father Damian Massanet founded San Francisco de los Tejas on the Trinity River, the first of many enclaves of faith. Missions were also erected at Matagorda Bay and at San Antonio de Bexar, today the Archdiocese of San Antonio. Such outposts flourished until the Mexican government disbanded them. Texas, however, became a republic, free of Mexican rule, and soon after Pope Gregory XVI designated the entire territory as an apostolic vicariate. Vincentian Father John M. Odin, the pioneering mission prelate, was appointed apostolic vicar. He was consecrated a bishop on March 6, 1842. Father John Timon, another Vincentian pioneer in the region, also served the area as prefect apostolic.

Texas joined the Union in 1845, and the establishment of the diocese followed two years later. Bishop Odin, the first bishop of the Diocese of Galveston, had jurisdiction over most counties in the state, and he invited religious communities to serve the faithful. Many congregations accepted his invitation and established parishes and educational institutions. Bishop Odin reportedly opened some fifty churches and St. Mary's Cathedral, now a basilica, which dates to 1847. In 1861 he was promoted to the Archdiocese of New Orleans.

His successor was Bishop Claude Marie Dubuis, who was consecrated on November 23, 1862. He led the faithful of the diocese through the Civil War and in 1866 established the Congregation of the Sisters of Charity of the Incarnated Word. In 1874 the Diocese of San Antonio (now the Archdiocese of San Antonio) was erected, as well as the Vicariate Apostolic of Brownsville, reducing the ecclesiastical jurisdiction of Galveston.

Bishop Dubuis resigned in 1881 and returned to his native land, France. He retained the title of bishop of Galveston, however, and his successor, Bishop Nicholas A. Gallagher, served as administrator of the diocese until 1892. Bishop P. Dufal, C.S.C., the former vicar apostolic of Eastern Bengal, had been appointed coadjutor bishop of Galveston in 1878, with right of succession, but he resigned in 1880.

During his period of diocesan administration, Bishop Gallagher took part in the establishment of the Diocese of Dallas (later the Diocese of Dallas-Fort Worth). The terrible storm that struck Galveston in 1900, often called the worst storm in United States history, caused untold damage and claimed thousands of lives. Many heroic acts were seen during this disaster. In 1901 the Basilian Fathers opened the seminary of St. Mary's at La Porte, and the bishop continued expanding other diocesan facilities. He also led the faithful into the trying times of World War I. Bishop Gallagher died on January 21, 1918.

The third bishop of the Diocese of Galveston was Christopher E. Byrne, who was consecrated on November 10, 1918. Bishop Byrne promoted educational programs and led the Catholics of the area through the Great Depression and World War II. He also took part in the erection of the Diocese of Austin. The city of Houston was expanding rapidly at this time, and St. Thomas University and Sacred Heart Dominican College were founded. On May 8, 1941, Bishop Byrne was appointed an Assistant at the Pontifical Throne. Having served for decades, Bishop Byrne died on April 1, 1950.

Bishop Wendelin J. Nold, a native Texan and the fourth bishop of the diocese, was consecrated on February 25, 1948. He built Catholic high schools and reestablished St. Mary's Seminary. In 1959 the diocese was designated as the Diocese of Galveston-Houston, and Sacred Heart Church in

Houston became the co-cathedral. A new chancery was built in Houston. Bishop Nold was suffering from progressive blindness, and was succeeded by his coadjutor bishop on April 22, 1975.

Bishop John L. Morkovsky, who had served as the bishop of Amarillo since 1958 and as apostolic administrator and coadjutor bishop of the Diocese of Galveston-Houston since 1963, acceded to the see. He took part in the establishment of the Dioceses of Beaumont, Tyler, and Victoria. Bishop Morkovsky also added diocesan facilities and ministries, and implemented the reforms of the Second Vatican Council. He retired on August 16, 1984.

The first archbishop of Galveston-Houston was Joseph A. Fiorenza, a native of the diocese who had served as the bishop of San Angelo since 1979. He was installed as the bishop of Galveston-Houston on February 18, 1985, and was promoted to archbishop in 2004. Galveston-Houston, becoming a metropolitan province, was given the suffragan sees of Austin, Beaumont, Brownsville, Corpus Christi, Tyler, and Victoria.

Archbishop Fiorenza presided over the diocese and then the archdiocese during a period of phenomenal growth and diversity. In 1985 the Catholic population in the diocese was around half a million. By the time of his retirement, the Catholic population was over one million. In addition, Galveston-Houston had become home to a remarkably diverse population that included Latinos, African-Americans, and African and Asian immigrants. The archdiocese was also instrumental in assisting the victims of Hurricane Katrina, who had been forced to relocate to Texas from Louisiana, in 2005. Archbishop Fiorenza retired on February 28, 2006.

The second archbishop, Daniel N. DiNardo, had served as the bishop of Sioux City since 1997. He was transferred on January 16, 2004, and installed on March 26, 2004, as coadjutor archbishop, acceding to the see upon the retirement of Archbishop Fiorenza. In 2007 Archbishop DiNardo was appointed to the College of Cardinals by Pope Benedict XVI. He continued the archdiocese's pastoral care of the growing Catholic community. In 2011 there were 1.2 million Catholics in the archdioces, served by 406 priests, 449 women religious, and 146 parishes.

Gannon, Robert Ignatius (April 20, 1893–March 12, 1978)

A Jesuit author and educator, Robert Ignatius Gannon also served as a Jesuit superior. He was born in St. George, Staten Island, New York, and was educated at Georgetown University and at Woodstock College. From 1919 to 1923, he taught at Fordham University, and in 1926 he was ordained in the Society of Jesus. He was then sent to the Pontifical Gregorian University in Rome, where he earned a doctorate in theology. Father Gannon also earned a degree at Christ's College, Cambridge.

He was assigned as dean of St. Peter's College in New Jersey and served from 1930 to 1936, then served as president both of Fordham and of the Association of Universities and Colleges of the State of New York. In 1949 Father Gannon became the director of the Manresa Retreat House on Staten Island, then served as pastor of St. Ignatius Parish and rector of Loyola School and Regis High School in New York City. He became the superior of the Jesuit Mission House, staying there until 1967, when he became retreat master at St. Ignatius Retreat House on Long Island.

Father Gannon wrote a biography of Cardinal Francis Spellman and *The Technique of the One Act Play* (1925), *After Black Coffee* (1947), *The Poor Old Liberal Arts* (1962), and *Up to Now: The Story of Fordham* (1967). Several universities and colleges honored him before he died in New York City.

Garaconthié (Garakontié) (unknown–1675)

The chief of the Onondaga Indians, Garaconthié aided the Catholic Church and became a living testament of the faith after a dramatic conversion. He was an Iroquois, born in Onondaga (in present-day New York), a nephew of the revered Tododho. Garaconthié took part in the French and Indian War and protected the missionaries, the "Black Robes," and converts.

In 1669 he was invited to Québec to confer with Bishop Blessed François de Montmorency Laval, who was a beloved figure in the region. Garaconthié and the other chiefs were encouraged to express their visions for the faith and their needs. He listened to the other chiefs in silence and then announced that he desired baptism in the Church. The other Indian chiefs were astonished, but when

Blessed Bishop Laval administered the Sacrament of Baptism in the cathedral personally, they joined Garaconthié in conversion.

He took the name Daniel, and his life became exemplary. Garaconthié walked two miles to attend Mass with his wife, sure in the faith. Others said that he "never committed a willing fault." On Christmas Eve, he took cold at Mass and became seriously ill. Receiving the last rites, Daniel Garaconthié announced, *"Onne onage che ca,"* "Behold! I die."

Garin, André (May 7, 1822–February 16, 1895)

An Oblate of Mary Immaculate, André Garin was a missionary superior and preacher of note. He was born in Côte-Saint-André, Isère, France, studying initially at the seminary in his hometown and then entering the Oblates in 1842. As he was too young to be ordained at the time, he was sent to Canada to complete his studies and was ordained on April 25, 1845. Father Garin soon set out for the Indian missions throughout eastern Canada. His mission territory extended across Hudson Bay and Labrador and brought him into forbidding territory in harsh conditions. After twelve immensely successful years, he was named superior at Plattsburg and at Buffalo.

In 1866 he preached a mission to the French-Canadian Catholics in Boston and so impressed local Church officials that Bishop (later Archbishop) John J. Williams invited Father Garin and the Oblates to head a parish and mission for the French Canadians at Lowell, Massachusetts. He remained in the area for nearly three decades and was responsible for establishing St. Joseph's Church as well as several other churches in the area. Such was the esteem of his parishioners that they erected a statue in his honor after his death.

Garnier, Charles, St. (1606–December 7, 1649)

A Jesuit missionary, St. Charles Garnier was martyred in an attack on his mission village. He was born in Paris and studied at the Jesuit College of Claremont, entering the Society of Jesus in 1634. Two years later he was sent to Canada and assigned to a Huron mission, where he labored for fourteen years. His tender care, especially of the sick and dying, earned him the nickname of the "Lamb"

among the Native Americans. The Tobacco nation then requested his presence, and St. Charles went to live among them. The Iroquois had almost decimated the Hurons, and turned their attention to the Tobacco villages. They attacked St. Joseph's village, where St. Charles went about consoling his Christians and binding their wounds. He remained calm when struck mortally, then dragged himself to the side of a dying Indian and was struck one last time while offering aid. (*See also* North American Martyrs.)

Garnier, Julien (January 6, 1643–1730)

A French Jesuit missionary, Julien Garnier was revered as the "Apostle to the Seneca" and respected by Chief Garaconthié of the Onondagas. He was born at Connerai, France, and entered the Society of Jesus in 1660. In October 1662 he sailed to Canada for service in the missions and held the distinction of being the first Jesuit to be ordained in Canada, in 1668. After ordination, he devoted time to proper preparation for the Indian missions and then embarked upon his labors among the Oneida and the Onondaga Mission. Garaconthié especially respected Father Garnier, and the priest's mission proved so successful that he was able to leave the pastoral care of the Onondaga to other missionaries in 1671 to evangelize among the Seneca with Father Jacques Frémin.

He remained among the Seneca for the next twelve years and faced hardships and dangers as he preached and baptized. In 1683, however, his labors were interrupted by the hostilities between the French colonial forces and the Seneca. Only in 1701 was he able to return to the field after peace was restored through an agreement reached at Montréal. Father Garnier was welcomed back by the Seneca and spent the next eight years with them. Owing to renewed outbreaks of violence and conflict, he was again forced to abandon his mission and spent his last years serving in the communities along the St. Lawrence. He retired in 1728.

Gary, Diocese of

Established on December 17, 1956, by Pope Pius XII, the Diocese of Gary serves counties in northwestern Indiana. Gary is a major steel center, founded in 1906 and named for Judge Elbert

H. Gary, the chairman of the board of the United States Steel Corporation. The first blast furnace was fired in December 1908, and steel production began the following year. Other cities within the diocesan jurisdiction have oil refineries and industrial complexes. The Diocese of Gary is a suffragan see of the Archdiocese of Indianapolis.

The region was served by some of America's outstanding missionaries, and French Jesuits were in the area in the late 1600s. Father Claude Allouez, the pioneering Jesuit mission superior, established a chapel on the St. Joseph River, and others labored in nearby missions. Vincennes was founded in 1732, and chapels were opened on the Wabash River at the same time. In 1769 Father Pierre Gibault arrived in the area and used Vincennes as his mission base. In 1789 Indiana became part of the Diocese of Baltimore (now the Archdiocese of Baltimore), and in 1808 became attached to the Diocese of Bardstown (now the Archdiocese of Louisville). In 1834 the entire region became part of the Diocese of Vincennes (now the Archdiocese of Indianapolis). Indiana had entered the Union in 1816, and the Holy Cross Fathers established their institutions in the northern part of the state in 1841.

Settlements increased as industrial centers developed in the region, and in 1857 the Diocese of Fort Wayne (now the Diocese of Fort Wayne-South Bend) was established. The Civil War erupted across the land in that era, and it was followed by an intense development of both the city of Gary and steel production. The industry prospered and aided the military defense of the nation in World War I. A large number of African-Americans were attracted to the city because of its industries during the war.

The Great Depression brought suffering to the people of Gary, as well as to other Americans. The Indiana University Northwest campus, however, opened in the city at this time. World War II put new demands on Gary's steel industry, and the Catholic authorities recognized the growth of the faithful in the area. The Diocese of Lafayette in Indiana was erected in 1944, and in that same year

Bishop Andrew G. Grutka

the Diocese of Indianapolis was designated as an archdiocese.

In 1956 the Diocese of Gary was established, and Holy Angels Church, which had opened in 1907, became the cathedral. Bishop Andrew Gregory Grutka was consecrated as the first bishop of the diocese on February 25, 1957. He instituted the offices and agencies for diocesan administration and began erecting needed parishes and schools. Inviting religious communities into the diocese, Bishop Grutka revitalized the Catholic ministries. He attended the Second Vatican Council and implemented the reforms mandated by that council. Bishop Grutka retired on July 9, 1984.

The second bishop of Gary was Norbert F. Gaughan, who had served as auxiliary bishop of Greensburg since 1975. Bishop Gaughan was transferred to Gary on July 9, 1984, and continued the diocesan expansion programs. He also sponsored charitable and lay ministries. Bishop Gaughan retired on June 1, 1996.

The third bishop, Dale J. Melczek, who had served as auxiliary bishop of Detroit from 1983, was appointed apostolic administrator of the Diocese of Gary on August 19, 1992, and then as coadjutor bishop on October 20, 1995. He acceded to the see on June 1, 1996. As shepherd of the diocese, Bishop Melczek focused on meeting the pastoral needs of the Catholic community and also on the issue of racism. He issued pastoral letters on diversity and the sin of racism. In 2011 there were 184,000 Catholics served by 145 priests and 69 parishes in the diocese.

Gaston, William (September 19, 1778–January 23, 1844)

A prominent Catholic leader in North Carolina, William Gaston was the first Catholic to serve in the North Carolina State Legislature and Supreme Court. He was also an abolitionist. Born in New Bern, North Carolina, he was the son of a physician killed by Tories in 1781 during the final days of the American Revolution. Determined to receive a sound education, William entered Georgetown

College in Washington, D.C., as its first student, but was forced to leave after two years because of poor health. He returned to school after recovering, graduated from Princeton in 1796, and went on to study law.

At the age of twenty-two, he was elected to the North Carolina Senate, the first Catholic in the state legislature, and it marked the start of a political career that included four terms in the state Senate and seven in the state House of Commons. He was also the trustee of the University of North Carolina for forty-two years. In 1813 Gaston was elected to the U.S. House of Representatives and won reelection in 1815. During his time in Congress, he enjoyed a position of some prominence among the Federalists.

In 1833 Gaston was approved by the legislature of North Carolina to the state supreme court, despite the fact that, as a Catholic, his appointment went against the state law that prohibited the nomination of anyone who was not a Protestant. In 1835 he was elected to the state constitutional convention and was instrumental in securing a change to the constitution that replaced the word Protestant with Christian.

Although a slaveholder, Gaston was opposed to slavery. He spoke out against it in 1832 at a commencement address at the University of North Carolina at Chapel Hill, and from the bench supported the rights of slaves against harsh treatment in *State v. Negro Will* and citizenship for slaves in *State v. William Manuel*. Gaston was awarded honorary doctorates by Harvard and Princeton Universities and the University of Pennsylvania. He also assisted Bishop John England of Charleston as a key legal adviser.

Gaylord, Diocese of

Established on July 20, 1971, by Pope Paul VI, the Diocese of Gaylord serves counties in the northern part of the Lower Peninsula of Michigan. Gaylord is the smallest Catholic cathedral city on the United States mainland and is a center for an agricultural and rural region. Sharing the Catholic legacy of older dioceses in Michigan, the Diocese of Gaylord is a suffragan see of the Archdiocese of Detroit.

The Catholic history of the region opens with the arrival of Etienne Brulé in 1620. He was a

Canadian explorer who was seeking a new passage to China. In 1641 Jesuit St. Isaac Jogues and Father Charles Raymbaut were in Sault Ste. Marie with the Chippewa. The great Sault Ste. Marie Mission evolved, as Jesuit Fathers Claude Allouez, Jacques Marquette, and Gabriel Druillettes were serving in the Straits of Mackinac. René-Robert Chevalier, Sieur de La Salle, and the Franciscan Recollect Father Louis Hennepin explored the St. Joseph River in 1679. La Salle claimed lands for France during his expeditions.

In 1701 Detroit became a settlement when Antoine Cadillac arrived there from Montréal and built Fort Ponchartrain and St. Anne's. To the north, Bishop Irenaeus Frederick Baraga pioneered missions to the Ottawa. Bishop John Carroll, the first American bishop, administered the region in 1789, and as a result of the Revolutionary War the American flag had flown over Detroit since 1796.

In 1818 public lands in Michigan were offered to settlers by the United States, and Irish and German families arrived in the area. Three years later, the faithful of Michigan were under the jurisdiction of the Diocese (now Archdiocese) of Cincinnati. When the Diocese (now Archdiocese) of Detroit was erected in 1833, Gaylord and other Michigan communities were placed under its jurisdiction. The Diocese of Grand Rapids, founded in 1882, and the Diocese of Marquette, erected in 1857, flourished.

With their fellow citizens, the Catholics of Gaylord shared in the sacrifices of World War I and in the tragedies of the Great Depression. Detroit was elevated to the status of an archdiocese as the perils of World War II loomed on the nation's horizon. The peace that followed the war brought growth to the state, and the faithful of Gaylord participated in the reforms of the Second Vatican Council.

In 1971 the Diocese of Gaylord was erected and a distinguished Catholic prelate was appointed as the first bishop. Bishop Edmund C. Szoka, who later became an American cardinal, was installed in St. Mary's Cathedral on July 20, 1971. He erected the agencies and offices for diocesan administration and organized charitable and outreach programs for the faithful. After a decade of organization and expansion of diocesan facilities, Bishop Szoka was promoted to the Archdiocese of Detroit. He was created a cardinal priest in 1988 and was appointed to the Vatican Curia in 1990.

The second bishop of Gaylord was Robert J. Rose, who was appointed to the diocese on October 13, 1981. Bishop Rose was installed in Gaylord on December 6, 1981. He continued the expansion programs and the promotion of ministries and educational programs until July 11, 1989, when he was transferred to the Diocese of Grand Rapids.

The third bishop of Gaylord, Patrick R. Cooney, had served as auxiliary bishop of the Archdiocese of Detroit since 1982. Bishop Cooney was appointed to the Diocese of Gaylord on November 21, 1989, and installed in the diocese on January 28, 1990. He retired on October 7, 2009. On that same day, Father Bernard A. Hebda, a priest of the Diocese of Pittsburgh, was named his successor. He was ordained a bishop on December 1, 2009. In 2011 there were 59,000 Catholics served by 70 priests and 80 parishes in the diocese.

George, Francis Eugene (January 16, 1937–)

The eighth archbishop of the Archdiocese of Chicago, Cardinal Francis Eugene George is a scholar and missionary of the Oblates of Mary Immaculate. He was born in Chicago, the son of Francis J. and Julia R. McCarthy, and at thirteen suffered a bout of polio that left him with permanent damage to his legs. He is the first native Chicagoan to serve as archbishop of Chicago, attending St. Pascal Grade School and St. Henry Preparatory Seminary in Belleville, Illinois. He entered the Missionary Oblates of Mary Immaculate on August 14, 1957, studied theology at the University of Ottawa, and was ordained on December 21, 1963.

Father George earned a master's degree in philosophy at The Catholic University of America in Washington, D.C., in 1965 and a doctorate in American philosophy at Tulane University in New Orleans in 1970. In 1971 he also received a master's degree in theology from the University of Ottawa. During those years, he taught philosophy at the Oblate Seminary in Pass Christian, Mississippi, from 1964 to 1969, at Tulane University in 1968, and at Creighton University in Nebraska from 1969 to 1973. From 1973 to 1974 he was provincial superior of the Midwestern Province of the Oblates in St. Paul, Minnesota. He was then elected vicar

general and served in Rome from 1974 to 1986. Father George returned to the United States and became coordinator of the Circle of Fellows for the Cambridge Center for the Study of Faith and Culture in Cambridge, Massachusetts, from 1987 to 1990. During that time, he obtained a doctorate in sacred theology in ecclesiology from the Pontifical Urban University in Rome.

Pope Blessed John Paul II appointed him bishop of Yakima on July 10, 1990, and he was installed as the fifth bishop of the Diocese of Yakima on September 21, 1990. Bishop George served there for five and a half years before being promoted to the Archdiocese of Portland in Oregon on April 30, 1996. He was installed on May 27, 1996. Less than a year later, on April 8, 1997, Pope Blessed John Paul II named him the eighth archbishop of the Archdiocese of Chicago. His installation took place at Holy Name Cathedral on May 7, 1997.

On January 18, 1998, Pope Blessed John Paul II created him a cardinal priest with the titular church of St. Bartholomew on Tiber Island. Cardinal George was also appointed a member of the Congregation for Divine Worship and the Discipline of the Sacraments, the Congregation for Institutes of Consecrated Life and for Societies of Apostolic Life, and the Pontifical Council Cor Unum. Subsequently, Cardinal George was also appointed to the Congregation for the Evangelization of Peoples, the Pontifical Commission for the Cultural Heritage of the Church, the Congregation for Oriental Churches, and the Pontifical Council for Culture.

He represented the Holy See at the 1994 World Synod of Bishops on Consecrated Life and served as a delegate and one of two special secretaries at the Synod of Bishops for America in 1997. He was also a delegate of the U.S. Conference of Catholic Bishops to the 2001 World Synod of Bishops, and was elected to the council for that synod. Cardinal George was vice president of the United States Conference of Catholic Bishops, Chairman of the USCCB Committee on Liturgy, and a member of the USCCB ad hoc Committee on Shrines and the Subcommittee on Campus Ministry. He was elected president of the USCCB for the 2007–10 term. In July 2006 he underwent successful surgery for bladder cancer.

Cardinal George is Conventual Chaplain ad

honorem of the Federal Association of the Sovereign Military Order of Malta, and Grand Prior of the North Central Lieutenancy of the United States for the Equestrian Order of the Holy Sepulchre of Jerusalem.

In the archdiocese, he is publisher of the *Catholic New World* and *Chicago Catolico*, the official newspapers of the Archdiocese of Chicago. He writes a column frequently in the *Catholic New World*. He has issued two pastoral letters, on evangelization, "Becoming an Evangelizing People" on November 21, 1997, and on racism, "Dwell in My Love" on April 4, 2001. He is the author of *The Difference God Makes: A Catholic Vision of Faith, Communion, and Culture* (2009) and *God in Action: How Faith in God Can Address the Challenges of the World* (2011).

Georgetown University

Georgetown University, founded by Bishop John Carroll, is the oldest Catholic institution of higher learning in the United States. Bishop Carroll purchased the land for the university in 1789 and opened the institution in 1792. The first faculty was composed of Sulpician priests who had fled from the horrors of the French Revolution. When the Holy See restored the Society of Jesus in 1805, Bishop Carroll, a former Jesuit, turned Georgetown over to them. These pioneering European Jesuits provided leadership in the sciences and maintained a pluralism of students of all faiths.

In 1815 Georgetown was granted a federal charter and expanded programs and the number of students enrolled from around the world. The medical school was opened in 1849. During the Civil War, Georgetown was occupied by federal troops and part of the campus became a hospital where surgeons of the army were trained. After the Civil War, new departments were added to the college, and by 1914 the law school had become one of the largest in the United States.

World War I altered the campus, as military recruitment activities were held on the grounds and training programs were instituted. The university prospered and grew during the 1920s and suffered student losses during the Great Depression. The Graduate School, however, continued to evolve, and in 1944 women were welcomed to the programs. The GI Bill for veterans of World War II

aided in recruiting, and Georgetown became a new symbol in the modern world of higher education. In the 1970s and 1980s, Georgetown continued to add facilities, centers, and specialized faculty members who were recognized in their fields. Today the university adds new dimensions to the American Catholic culture and provides leadership in the nation's capital.

Georgia

Called the Empire State of the South, Georgia is located on the southeastern seaboard of the United States. It is bounded on the north by Tennessee and North Carolina, on the east by South Carolina and the Atlantic Ocean, on the south by Florida, and on the west by Alabama. There are five natural land regions in Georgia: the Blue Ridge Mountains in the northeast, the Appalachian Valley in the northwest, the Piedmont in the central zone, the Atlantic Coastal Plain in the southeast, and the Gulf Coastal Plain in the southwest. The original inhabitants of Georgia were the Cherokee, Choctaw, Creek, Muskogee, and Seminoles.

The Catholic history of the state began in 1540, when the Spanish explorer Hernando de Soto entered the area. He was accompanied by priests and reportedly a Mass was celebrated. Two decades later, the Dominicans were on the coast of Georgia, and in 1566 Father Pedro Martinez, the Jesuit protomartyr, was killed on Cumberland Island. Father Martinez, a nobleman of Spain, had received blessings from Pope St. Pius V and St. Francis Borgia when he departed from his homeland for the American missions.

By 1598 there were several Catholic missions on the Georgia coast, and the area was visited by Bishop Juan de las Cabezas de Altamirano of Cuba. He reportedly confirmed 1,500 Native Americans while on a tour of the missions. The Catholic evangelization, however, came to a halt in Georgia during Queen Anne's War (known in Europe as the War of the Spanish Succession) from 1702 to 1713, when the British destroyed fourteen missions in the area. The Anglo-Spanish War, from 1727 to 1728, added other complications as European rivalries were fought out in the New World. In 1732 General James Edward Oglethorpe and John Viscount Percival received a charter from King George II for a colony. Georgia became a royal colony in 1754, and harsh penal laws were passed to keep Catholics out of the settlements and to halt the activities of Catholic priests.

When the American Revolution started, Georgia was stalwart in its support of the war and the striving for independence from England. British military forces captured Savannah, and Count Casimir Pulaski, the European nobleman who had come to aid the American cause, died during the siege of the city. Georgia was the fourth state to ratify the Constitution, in 1778. Five years later, the state underwent economic changes as Eli Whitney invented the cotton gin.

In 1789 the new Georgia State Constitution removed the last discriminations and legal prohibitions against Catholics. Augustinian priests were laboring in Savannah at the time. The northeastern part of Georgia, called "the cradle of Catholicity" in the state, was being heavily settled by the faithful. The Diocese of Savannah, erected in 1850, enabled the Church to serve the growing Catholic population.

In 1861 Georgia seceded from the Union as the Civil War divided America. Atlanta was burned by federal troops in 1864, and Georgia suffered as General William Tecumseh Sherman made his "March to the Sea." The Reconstruction period following the surrender of the South was also a time of suffering. A populist anti-Catholic uprising started after the war, and there were increased raids on Catholic properties by the Ku Klux Klan. The Catholic Laymen's Association of Georgia tried to combat the prejudice, and American bishops labored to defend the faith all across the nation.

World War I and the Great Depression had economic and social impacts on Georgia, and full recovery came only with the military buildup during World War II. The Diocese of Savannah-Atlanta was designated in 1937 to offer greater Catholic presence. In 1956, because of the growing Catholic populations, the diocese was divided, and in 1962 Atlanta was created as a metropolitan see, with dioceses in Georgia, North Carolina, and South Carolina.

Archbishop Paul J. Hallinan assumed leadership of this new episcopal jurisdiction. Catholics continued to prosper in Georgia, and suffragan sees were erected in Charlotte, Raleigh, and Charleston. In the late twentieth century, Georgia witnessed a significant increase in its population, thanks in large measure to the influx of residents from the Northeast. This has posed considerable pastoral challenges to the diocese of the state, especially the Archdiocese of Atlanta. In 2011 there were almost one million Catholics served by 367 priests and 142 parishes in the state.

Georgia, Martyrs of (d. 1597)

The Georgia Martyrs — Franciscan Friars Pedro de Corpa, Miguel de Añon, Antonio de Badajóz, Blas de Rodriguez, and Francisco de Veráscola — were slain in 1597 in the territory of the present-day Diocese of Savannah, which was then part of the vast Florida missions. Although the territory was then called La Florida, to distinguish these missionaries from others martyred in the territory that is now part of the state of Florida, the term "of Georgia" is used to identify them. Father de Corpa, from Villabilla, Spain, was the first victim in the massacre on Cumberland and Parris Islands in Georgia.

The Franciscans had arrived there in 1584 and had started their mission labors among the local Indian tribes. However, Juanita, a local chief, resented the growing influence of the missionaries and started a revolt, instigating the murders of the priests and their helpers. Father de Corpa was clubbed to death on September 13 or 14, 1597. Father Blas de Rodriguez, a Franciscan from Cocerres, Spain, was slain on September 16. Father Miguel de Añon, from Badejóz, Spain, died with Brother Antonio de Badajóz on September 17 on St. Catherine's Island, in the Mission Santa Catalina de Guale. Father Francisco de Veráscola, another Franciscan, was away during the initial assaults but was ambushed upon his return and also martyred. All are listed in the North American Martyrology, and their cause for canonization was formally opened in the Diocese of Savannah in 1983.

German Catholics

Catholics from Germany have long represented one of the largest and most significant segments of Catholicism in the United States. German Catholics stand with Irish Catholics and Italian Catholics as one of the largest and most influential nationalities in the development of Catholic culture and in wider contributions to American life.

The exact number of Germans and German-speaking people who migrated to the United States from the seventeenth century until the middle of the twentieth century is difficult to document with precision. It is estimated that by 1950 over 6.5 million Germans had settled in the country. The peak periods of migration were from 1840 to 1900, when nearly 5 million Germans arrived in the country; over 1.9 million migrated from 1881 to 1900 alone.

The number of Catholic German immigrants is also difficult to estimate with certainty. The famous 1925 study *Has the Immigrant Kept the Faith?*, by Gerald Shaughnessy, estimated that from 1820 one-third of all German-speaking immigrants were Catholic. According to Shaughnessy, whose absolute accuracy is doubted by some scholars, German Catholic immigrants comprised 13 percent, or 1.3 million of all European Catholic immigration in the century from 1820 to 1920.

German immigration to the United States began as early as 1683 when Francis Daniel Pastorius led thirteen families from Germany to Pennsylvania, where they settled in the area around modern-day Philadelphia. They sailed for the colony at the encouragement of William Penn, who promised them religious liberty. Pastorius established Germantown and so began an enduring German community. German settlers pushed into Maryland and then down into Virginia and South Carolina. They were joined by direct German settlers in Maryland and elsewhere. In New York, German settlers arrived from England, where they had gone in 1710 to escape the political strife in their own country. They found homes along the Mohawk and Schoharie Rivers.

Catholics were not a large group among the first Germans in America. In Pennsylvania, the first immigrants were chiefly Moravians and Mennonites, followed in much larger numbers by the Lutherans and members of the German Reformed Church. Catholic emigration was discouraged by the British government and by the severe restrictions on Catholics imposed by some of the anti-Catholic colonial governments. Nevertheless, Catholics took part in the general migration of Germans to America, and the small Catholic population required pastoral care. In 1741 two priests from Germany arrived, followed by others over the next years. By the middle of the eighteenth century, German Catholics in Pennsylvania formed the majority of Catholics in the colony. Generally, the Germans worked as farmers and were noted for their determination to retain their own language and customs. The linguistic and cultural isolation preferred by many Germans caused some tensions with English-speaking colonists, in particular the Scots-Irish.

By 1775 there were a hundred thousand Germans in Pennsylvania alone, almost one-third of the total population of the colony. The cultural uniformity was soon shattered, however, by the political strife of the War of Independence. Germans in the colonies were divided over the question of rebellion. Many Germans in the South chose to remain loyal to the British crown, while in New York sympathies were squarely with the rebels. The Germans of Pennsylvania were divided as well. In the period after the war, Bishop Carroll encountered firsthand the problems relating to German efforts to keep their own language and customs. In Baltimore and Philadelphia, German Catholics demanded their own churches and priests. This situation changed gradually over the next decades as younger German Catholics lost much of their cultural insularity and requested English-speaking priests.

Catholics were an increasing part of the migration of Germans to the young United States in the period after the start of the French Revolution and throughout the long and destructive Napoleonic Wars (1789–1815). Napoleon's wars in Germany, especially in Bavaria, brought severe carnage and suffering, and many Germans fled from Europe to find safety. The policies of the French Emperor against the Church likewise encouraged flight from Germany. In the decades that followed the end of the Napoleonic Wars and the rise of the Prussian state under famed statesman Otto von Bismarck, chief minister of Prussia from 1862 to 1890, the Church fell under increasing state pressure and enforced secularization. The climax of this process was Bismarck's policy of *Kulturkampf*. Eager to root out and destroy any element in German life that might pose a threat to the unity of the empire, he looked upon the Church as a foreign intruder that demanded loyalty to the distant authority of the Holy See, only recently bolstered by the First Vatican Council. In 1871 he launched his sweeping program, which curtailed the powers of the Church in German lands and took over the seminaries. When confronted with opposition to this repression from the clergy and the German people, he imprisoned several prelates, most notably Cardinal Mieczyslaw von Ledochowski of Posen. Many Catholics responded to this repression by leaving German lands affected by the secularization.

There were other, more positive influences at work among German Catholics that encouraged migration. There was the call to young men and women to enter the religious life and set out to assist the Catholic missions in the wilderness of North America. Providing great support and impetus to the call were the missionary organizations of the era: the Society for the Propagation of the Faith, founded in 1822 in Paris; the Leopoldinen-Stiftung, founded in Vienna, Austria, in 1829 at the urging of the Hanoverian priest (and later bishop of Detroit) Friedrich Résé; and the Ludwig Missionsverein, founded at Munich, Bavaria, on December 12, 1838, by King Ludwig I to provide financial assistance to the Catholic missions of Asia and America. The societies gave money in the millions to aid the American missions, as well as vital promotions and literature about the need for missionaries in America. German-speaking Catholics responded with great enthusiasm.

The great tide of German immigrants began after 1840. Included among them were refugees of the Revolution of 1848, who were generally well-educated and came to wield influence in newspapers, politics, and universities. As most of them were anticlerical, they provided impetus to some of the anti-Catholic atmosphere of the period. Following the patterns of migration by Germans in general, Catholic Germans made their way west and settled in western Pennsylvania and across the Midwest. By the end of the century, there were over 2,200 parishes oriented to German Catholics. German Catholics were found in very large numbers in Missouri, Ohio, Wisconsin, Minnesota, and Illinois, with the highest concentrations in such cities as Milwaukee, Chicago, Cincinnati, and St. Louis, as well as in such far-flung locations as New Orleans and Oregon. While found in many cities, German Catholics, like their Protestant counterparts, tended to settle in rural areas where they were able to retain their German language and culture and avoid the Nativist and anti-Catholic sentiments often found in the cities.

The establishment and flourishing of German Catholic communities across the Midwest were heavily dependent upon the labors and determination of the German Catholics who had arrived eager to start a new life in America. Great missionary figures also provided leadership and direction through their selfless service and years of toil, especially Father Demetrius Augustine Gallitzin, the "Apostle of the Alleghenies," who devoted forty years to establishing the Church in western Pennsylvania; John M. Henni, the first bishop and first archbishop of Milwaukee, from 1844 to 1881; Mathias Loras, the first bishop of Dubuque, from 1837 to 1858; and Joseph Crétin, the first bishop of St. Paul, from 1851 to 1857.

There was a chronic priest shortage in America during the first half of the nineteenth century, and efforts were begun to provide a steady stream of new vocations. Toward that end, Bishop Henni in Milwaukee founded a bilingual seminary in 1856. Significant contributions were made to remedying this shortage by the religious orders and congregations, which proved a crucial source of priests to serve German-speaking communities. Bishops requested and eagerly sought European religious communities to establish houses in the United States: Redemptorists and Norbertines from Austria, Franciscans and Capuchins from Switzerland, and especially the Benedictines from Bavaria. From its foundation at St. Vincent's in Pennsylvania in 1846, the Benedictines forged new monastic institutions across the country, including the immense achievement of St. John's Abbey in Minnesota in 1856. The Swiss Benedictines likewise began such famed monasteries in Indiana at St. Meinrad's in 1853 and in Missouri at Conception Abbey in 1873. Through the religious communities the number of German-speaking priests increased significantly, from barely fifty in the early 1840s to well over a thousand by the late 1860s.

Likewise, vocations to orders and congregations of women religious proved immensely helpful to the development of the Church in the United States. Like the effort to increase the presence of German-speaking priests, bishops also encouraged German-speaking nuns to run schools and hospitals and so directly shape generations of future Catholics and care for those in need. Meanwhile, a number of religious communities were started from among the German-speaking immigrants: the Sisters of the Third Order of St. Francis of Assisi were begun by Bishop Henni in 1849; the Franciscan Sisters were started by Bishop St. John Nepomucene Neumann in Philadelphia; and the Sisters of St. Agnes were founded in 1858 in Wisconsin.

The German Catholic press began in a formal sense in the 1830s when Bishop Henni launched in Cincinnati the first German-language Catholic weekly, *Der Wahrheitsfreund* (*The Friend of Truth*). This was followed by German publications across the East and Midwest. In all, there were over sixty active German-language Catholic publications in the nineteenth century. Such newspapers and periodicals also served as mechanisms for the growth of German Catholic societies and organizations. The first of the prominent organizations was the *Deutsche Römisch-Katholische Central-Verein von Nord-America* (the German Roman Catholic Central Association of North America, called commonly the Central Verein), which promoted parish mutual benefit societies. It also became involved in many of the social and educational concerns of the German Catholic population. New organizations over the next years included the *Priester-Verein*, an association for German-speaking priests in the country, and the *Katholikentag*, a gathering of representatives of the many smaller German-American Catholic organizations and societies. (*See also* Central Verein.)

Later, support for their effort to remain culturally apart was found in the work of Peter Cahensly, the German businessman and reformer who helped found the St. Raphael's Society for the benefit and care of immigrants; an American branch of the society was started in 1883. Cahensly gave his name to Cahenslyism — the movement to have German-speaking bishops appointed and for German-language churches to be established. Members of the American hierarchy, above all Cardinal James Gibbons and Archbishop John Ireland, resisted such a campaign on the grounds that it represented unacceptable meddling in American ecclesiastical life by Europeans and that there was a real danger of a national German church sprouting up in the United States. (*See also* Cahensly, Simon Peter.)

The stability of German lands in the late nineteenth century and early twentieth century, combined with the swift pace of industrialization in Prussia, led to a sharp decline in German immigration. This had the effect in the United States of weakening the traditionally united cultural bloc of German immigrants. In addition, second generation German-Americans were clearly more assimilated into American culture, and the dominance of German language and culture among German-Americans proved harder to maintain. This was manifested in the swift decline of German-language publications and organizations, and the gradual disappearance of the distinctly German parishes. *Der Wahrheitsfreund* ended its long run in 1907 owing to dwindling readership. By the late 1930s there were only a handful of German-language publications left in the country. The same fate befell many of the German organizations, such as the *Katholikentag* and the *Priester-Verein*.

World War I posed new and even more difficult challenges for Germans in the United States, who were often looked upon with suspicion, especially after the entry of the United States into the war in 1917. Anti-German hysteria and war fever placed severe pressures on German-Americans to assimilate. The years after the war gave Germans an opportunity to recapture the esteem of Americans at large, but new tensions were born from the shocking rise of Adolf Hitler and Nazi Germany. Unlike during World War I, however, German-Americans did not face suspicions regarding their loyalties, and Germans in very large numbers entered the armed forces and fought courageously in both the African-European campaigns against Germany and Italy and the Pacific campaigns against Japan. The years after the global conflict witnessed the continuing assimilation of German-Americans. Assimilation of German Catholics was exemplified by the decrease in German parishes.

The first decades of the twentieth century saw a slowing of new parishes and the movement in Catholic parochial schools away from the extensive or exclusive use of German and toward bilingualism or outright use of English. The change reflected in part assimilation, but it also stemmed from the deliberate policy of the bishops to end the various ethnic forms of Catholic communities in favor of Catholic social unity and centralized administration.

Gethsemani Abbey

The American monastery of the Cistercians of the Strict Observance, the Trappists, Gethsemani Abbey is well known across the nation. French Trappists from Melleray Abbey in Brittany founded the abbey in 1845. These monks accepted the invitation of the pioneering Bishop Benedict Joseph Flaget of the Diocese of Bardstown in Kentucky (now the Archdiocese of Louisville). Dom Eutropius Proust led the group of fifty-five Trappist monks to Kentucky and founded the monastic community. He also served as abbot from the opening of Gethsemani until 1860. The Trappists conducted a boys' school in the early decades of their founding, but the school burned in 1913.

Dom Frederick Dunne was the first American-born choir monk at the abbey, and he became abbot in 1905. Another American Trappist at Gethsemani aided in spreading word of the abbey. He was Thomas Merton, who became Father Louis when he entered the community in December 1941. His autobiography, *The Seven Storey Mountain,* was an international bestseller when published in 1948.

In 1945 the Trappists of Gethsemani opened the Monastery of the Holy Spirit in Conyers, Georgia. Two years later, Holy Trinity Abbey was founded in Huntsville, Utah, and other monasteries followed at Mepkin in Moncks Corner, South Carolina; Genesee in Pifford, New York; and New Clairvaux in Sacramento Valley, California. The Trappists welcome visitors and provide retreats for men and women.

Gibault, Pierre (1737–August 15, 1802)

Called the "Patriot Priest" by Americans, Pierre Gibault served the territory comprising modern-

day Illinois and Indiana alone. He was born in Montréal, Canada, the oldest of five children of Pierre and Marie Madeleine Brunet Gibault. He was educated for the priesthood in Québec and was ordained at age twenty-five. His first mission assignment was in present-day Illinois, where he served as vicar general of the region. Father Gibault scouted the entire mission territory, even as far north as Michilimackinac, modern-day Mackinaw, and he established his headquarters at the Mission of Kaskaskia. From there he was able to serve the Native Americans and white Catholics in Vincennes, Ste. Genevieve, Cahokia, St. Louis, Peoria, St. Joseph, and Michilimackinac.

Father Gibault spent years as the only Catholic priest in the region comprising modern-day Illinois and Indiana, and he greeted the hundreds of new settlers who arrived in the region as wagon trains were arriving every week.

On July 4, 1778, General George Rogers Clark and his troops arrived in the area to persuade the local people to aid the American cause. Father Gibault was in a difficult position, as Bishop Joseph Briand of Québec had explicitly forbidden the clergy and laity of the diocese to help the revolutionaries and had decreed suspension for priests and denial of the sacraments for the laity. Father Gibault, however, sided with the Americans, demonstrating awareness of the situation and becoming openly pro-Americans. Actually, General Clark could not have campaigned successfully without Father Gibault's aid. He talked to his parishioners and persuaded them to stand firm against the British. Cahokia and Vincennes heeded his advice and joined the revolutionaries.

Pierre Gibault

After the war, Father Gibault left Kaskaskia, which had been overrun by a new lawless element, and made his headquarters at Ste. Genevieve. The British and Canadians, of course, were outraged by his alliance with the revolution and threatened all kinds of dire punishments.

When Bishop John Carroll assumed ecclesiastical jurisdiction over the region in 1789, Father Gibault felt obliged to leave the area because he did not have proper faculties. He was an outcast from the Canadians, and he reportedly did not receive much encouragement from Bishop Carroll. Father Gibault went to New Madrid, Missouri, a Spanish-held territory, and in 1792 became the pastor of the area. He served there until his death.

Gibbons, James (July 23, 1834–March 24, 1921)

The archbishop of Baltimore from 1877 to 1921, James Gibbons was an American cardinal and one of the most esteemed Catholic prelates of the country. He was born in Baltimore, the son of immigrant Irish parents, Thomas and Bridget, and was taken to Ireland at the age of three, as his father was ailing. His father died in 1847, and his family returned to the United States in 1853, settling in New Orleans. After working as a clerk for a time, he entered St. Charles College in Ellicott City, Maryland, and then attended St. Mary's Seminary in Baltimore. He was ordained on June 30, 1861, by Archbishop Francis P. Kenrick.

Cardinal James Gibbons

He was assigned to St. Patrick's Church in Baltimore and then as pastor of St. Bridget's Church in Canton, as well as St. Lawrence O'Toole Mission. Father Gibbons served as a volunteer chaplain to the troops at Fort McHenry and at Fort Marshall. In 1865, however, he was appointed secretary to Archbishop Martin J. Spalding, and a year later became an assistant chancellor of the archdiocese and given charge of the preparations for the Second Plenary Council of October 1866. When the Vicariate Apostolic of North Carolina was established as a result of the recommendations of that council, he was consecrated as a bishop and made the vicar apostolic on August 16, 1868. One year later, Bishop Gibbons attended the First Vatican Council in Rome, returning in 1870 to find the vicariate suffering under carpetbaggers as a result of the Civil War.

In 1872 Bishop Gibbons was made apostolic administrator of the Diocese of Richmond when Bishop John McGill died. He acceded to the see the following July but maintained the vicariate of North Carolina. It was during this period that

Bishop Gibbons wrote *Faith of Our Fathers*, a simple guide to Catholic doctrine that was published in 1876 and gained instant popularity throughout America.

In 1877 Bishop Gibbons was appointed coadjutor archbishop of Baltimore with right of succession at the request of Archbishop James Roosevelt Bayley, the noted prelate who aided the Catholic missions to Native Americans and was a nephew of St. Elizabeth Ann Seton. Archbishop Bayley died on October 3, 1877, and Archbishop Gibbons became ordinary of America's primal see.

As the archbishop of Baltimore, he presided over the Third Plenary Council of 1884 as apostolic delegate. The establishment of The Catholic University of America was one of the main topics of this council, and once the location of the university was decided, Archbishop Gibbons took a leadership role in the preparatory plans and then became first chancellor.

On June 7, 1886, Pope Leo XIII created him a cardinal priest with the titular church of Santa Maria in Trastevere. He was elevated to the cardinalate at a critical time in America, and he displayed considerable awareness of the factors involved. Anti-Catholicism and Catholic participation in American secret societies were two of the difficult concerns that faced the American bishops at the time, and Cardinal Gibbons demonstrated a confident grasp of both issues when they arose.

When Catholic membership in organizations such as the Freemasons reached dangerous levels, many in the Church opted to condemn the organizations. Cardinal Gibbons preferred to withhold such condemnation until the anti-Catholic nature of such groups was exposed. He also defended the Knights of Labor when others condemned the organization in 1886. The disobedience of Father Edward McGlynn in New York was another scandal that had to be faced, and the priest was suspended and then excommunicated. Cardinal Gibbons presented his views on the issues to the Congregation for the Propagation of the Faith in February 1887, and the Holy See accepted them.

The cardinal responded with the same acute

awareness of pluralistic tendencies in America when facing the problems of national churches and rivalries between immigrant groups. He was also able to calm Protestant fears about the growing parochial school system and put an end to the charges of Americanism that resulted from the dispute over the ministry of Father Isaac Thomas Hecker and the Paulists.

Cardinal Gibbons's personality and his unabashed patriotism won over friends and foes alike. His 50th anniversary of priestly ordination celebration attracted some twenty thousand of his fellow citizens, including Presidents Theodore Roosevelt and William Howard Taft. As dean of the American hierarchy, he represented the Catholic Church to millions of his fellow citizens, and he aided the founding of the National Catholic War Council, the forerunner of the National Catholic Welfare Conference, and the Catholic Foreign Mission Society of America, Maryknoll. He died in Baltimore, and was mourned by the nation.

Gillespie, Mary of St. Angela (February 21, 1824– March 4, 1887)

The founder of the Congregation of Sisters of the Holy Cross, Mary of St. Angela Gillespie was a pioneering religious in turbulent times. She was born in Brownsville, Pennsylvania, the daughter of John and Mary Miers Gillespie and was baptized Eliza Maria. Her father died while she was young, and she moved to Lancaster, Ohio, with her widowed mother, her sister, and her brother, Neal, who became a priest. She was also the niece of Senator Thomas Ewing, who helped her take an active part in the society of Washington, D.C. While continuing her education, she opened a Sunday school for African-Americans and conducted other ministries.

In 1853 she entered the community of Holy Cross Sisters at Bertrand, Michigan, receiving the religious name Angela. Her novitiate was made in Caen, France. After taking her vows, she returned to Bertrand to direct the academy, which in 1855 was transferred to St. Mary's at Notre Dame in Indiana. There

Mother Angela Gillespie

she introduced advanced courses and developed a rounded curriculum. In April 1860 she started the *Metropolitan Readers,* which were continued as the *Excelsior Series.* Mother Angela also served as unofficial editor of *Ave Maria* after 1866, presenting such authors as Charles de Montalembert, François Chateaubriand, Louis Veuillot, Antoine-Frédéric Ozanam, Orestes A. Brownson, and Isaac Thomas Hecker to American readers.

During the Civil War, Mother Angela established eight military hospitals, staffed two hospital ships, and provided for the direction of eighty sister-nurses. She was appointed provincial superior in 1869, and she founded St. Catherine's Institute, a teacher-training institution in Baltimore in 1874, staffing it with religious and lay teachers from St. Mary's and elsewhere. During the period from 1855 to 1882, Mother Angela made forty-five foundations from New York to California and from Michigan to Texas. She died at Notre Dame.

Gillis, James Martin (November 12, 1876–March 14, 1957)

A Catholic editor and author, James Martin Gillis was a Paulist priest who carried on the work of his congregation. He was born in Boston, the son of James and Catharine Roche Gillis. After attending Boston Latin School, he went on to St. Charles College in Baltimore and St. John's Seminary in Brighton, Massachusetts. In 1900 he joined the Paulists and was ordained the following year. Father Gillis was then sent to The Catholic University of America in Washington, D.C., where he earned a licentiate in theology in 1903. He taught at St. Paul's College in Washington, D.C., until 1910, when he assumed ministerial duties.

In 1922 Father Gillis was appointed editor of the *Catholic World,* a Paulist publication. He stayed in this role until 1948 and maintained the standards and reputation of the publication with conservative political views. His newspaper column, "*Sursum Corda*: What's Right with the World," was syndicated in fifty diocesan papers. He also served as a speaker on the *Catho-*

lic Hour, the radio show produced by the National Broadcasting Company.

Father Gillis wrote popular books as well: *False Prophets* in (1925), *The Catholic Church and the Home* (1928), *The Ten Commandments* (1931), *Christianity and Civilization* (1932), *The Paulists* (1932), *This Our Day* (two volumes in 1933 and 1949), *So Near Is God* (1953), *On Almost Everything* (1955), *This Mysterious Human Nature* (1956), and *My Last Book* (1957). He was a contributor to the *Catholic Encyclopedia* and the *Encyclopedia Americana.* He was also an academy member of the Gallery of Living Catholic Authors and received many honorary degrees from American Catholic colleges.

Illness forced Father Gillis to retire in 1948, but he continued to serve as contributing editor of the *Catholic World* until his death. He was buried in the Crypt Church at St. Paul the Apostle in New York City.

Gilmour, Richard (September 28 1824–April 13, 1891)

The second bishop of the Diocese of Cleveland, from 1872 until his death, Richard Gilmour was a convert and an outstanding apologist for the faith in a time of persecution in America. Born in Scotland, he came with his family to Cumbola, Pennsylvania, when he was thirteen. Attending a temperance rally conducted by Father Theobald Mathew, he became interested in the Catholic Church and was baptized in 1842. He began studies for the priesthood, completing them at Mount St. Mary's in Emmitsburg, Maryland, and receiving ordination on August 30, 1852, by Archbishop John Baptist Purcell in Cincinnati.

Father Gilmour began his ministry on the Ohio River, erecting churches at Portsmouth and Ironton, Ohio, and visiting Catholic settlements in Kentucky and Virginia. He also served parishes in Cincinnati and Dayton, Ohio, inspiring Catholics with his knowledge and fervor. On April 14, 1872, he was consecrated bishop of the Diocese of Cleveland, where the growing anti-Catholic prejudice of the nation's Protestants was evident.

With his usual blunt announcement of the truth, Bishop Gilmour wrote his first pastoral letter the year after his consecration and challenged Catholics to refuse to be merely tolerated in their own communities. In 1874 he started the *Catholic Universe* to educate the faithful and the Catholic Central Association to aid the needy and announce the Catholic presence in the area. Bishop Gilmour suffered ill health soon after and took a two-year leave, but he returned in 1876 to lead the diocese again. He increased the number of churches in his jurisdiction from 160 to 233 and added schools and four new hospitals. Many religious congregations accepted his invitation to serve in the diocese, including Dominicans, Felicians, and Jesuits, as well as Sisters of St. Joseph, Notre Dame, and Charity of Cincinnati. Bishop Gilmour also joined his fellow bishops in calling for funds for parochial schools, a subject being debated at the time. At this time, the question of public funds for private schools was being bitterly debated in the United States. Aware of the fact that Americans would never agree to fund parochial schools, Bishop Gilmour began to build a number of Catholic schools. He successfully fought attempts by locals to tax Catholic school property in *Gilmour v. Pelton* in 1883 and wrote popular textbooks known as *Gilmour Readers* and the *Gilmour Bible History,* published by Benziger Brothers.

Bishop Gilmour taught that truth and unity would keep Catholics safe in America. He provided immigrant Catholics with churches and priests of their own language, but he demanded that they become American Catholics, knowing that nationalism would splinter the Church. He also required the Ancient Order of Hibernians in the diocese to break with the Ireland-based Fenians. When Bishop Gilmour died in 1891, the faithful of Cleveland mourned the loss and honored his memory.

Giorda, Joseph (1821–August 4, 1882)

Called *Mil'Kokan,* the "Round Head," by the Coeur d'Alene Indians, Joseph Giorda was a Jesuit missionary and superior who spent his life in the wilds of America. He was born in Italy and was of noble blood. Entering the Society of Jesus at age twenty-two, he was so brilliant that he was asked to teach in his own seminary after ordination to the priesthood. Father Giorda, however, volunteered to serve the Indian missions in 1861 and was assigned to the Sacred Heart Mission for the Coeur d'Alene nation.

After a time, Father Giorda was sent to St. Peter's Mission in eastern Montana, where he earned the respect and trust of several tribes. He was so popular in the region that he was appointed the first chaplain of the Montana Territorial Legislature at Virginia City.

When the Jesuits were reassigned to the missions of California, Father Giorda, then Jesuit superior of the Rocky Mountains missions, went to California and brought back eight priests for his abandoned region. He retired in 1866, with eight missions operating, six of which he had started personally. From 1869 until 1877, Father Giorda again served as the regional superior. He died among his beloved Coeur d'Alenes.

Glenmary Home Missioners

The Home Missioners of America is popularly known as the Glenmary Home Missioners, and is a unique organization designed to serve areas of Catholic settlement without pastors. The society was established by Father William Howard Bishop, who recognized the need for providing resident pastors in many rural areas of the United States. The Glenmary Home Missioners is composed of secular priests living in community, under oath to their superior general, and serving as pastors to communities. There are also Glenmary Brothers, who assist as catechists, parish administrators, counselors, pastoral associates, and youth directors.

Father Bishop recognized that there were more than a thousand counties in the United States without resident priests, located largely in the southeastern states. With the support and approval of Archbishop John T. McNicholas, O.P., of the Archdiocese of Cincinnati, Father Bishop began publishing *Glenmary's Challenge,* to interest qualified individuals to undertake this unusual service. In 1939 Father Bishop was able to institute his society formally when Reverend Raphael Sourd and seminarians joined him.

A diocesan congregation was canonically established in Cincinnati in 1952. The sisters who were incorporated into the society were asked to perform social work, nursing, and religious education. The first two women candidates joined Father Bishop in 1941. Archbishop Karl J. Alter officially established the community in Cincinnati. In 1953 Mother Mary Catherine Rumschlag was appointed superior general, and she received the vows of fourteen new members. In 1955 the community of forty-one professed sisters elected Mother Mary Catherine at their first general chapter. The congregation follows the Rule of St. Augustine and constitutions adapted from those of the Dominican Sisters of Adrian, Michigan, under whom the first sisters were trained. The motherhouse is in Owensboro, Kentucky.

The Glenmary Home Missioners provide resources and care for the physical and spiritual needs of the faithful, and when the congregation is strong enough to support a resident priest, the parish is returned to the diocese. The society has served in Georgia, Kentucky, North Carolina, Oklahoma, Virginia, and West Virginia, and the national headquarters is in Cincinnati.

Glennon, John Joseph (June 14, 1862–March 9, 1946)

The archbishop of St. Louis and an American cardinal, John Joseph Glennon is known as the "Cathedral Builder." He was born in Kinnegard, Westmeath, Ireland, and was educated at St. Mary's College in Mullingar, All Hallows College and Seminary in Dublin, and the University of Bonn. In 1883 he migrated to the United States and was ordained on December 20, 1884, in the Diocese of Kansas City in Missouri (now the Diocese of Kansas City–St. Joseph).

Cardinal John Joseph Glennon

For twelve years, Father Glennon served in the Diocese of Kansas City, appointed the vicar general in 1892 and the apostolic administrator in 1894. On March 14, 1896, he was appointed coadjutor bishop of Kansas City with right of succession and on April 27, 1903, was promoted to apostolic administrator and coadjutor archbishop of St. Louis, acceding to the see on October 13, 1903.

Archbishop Glennon scheduled two diocesan synods and began building care facilities for children and the disabled. Expanding the diocesan facilities to meet the needs of the growing population, Archbishop Glennon built churches, schools, hospitals, and a seminary, while earning fame as a gifted orator and speaking at gatherings across the country. In 1908 he started the Cathedral of St. Louis, now a basilica. He also invited colonists from various European countries to come to St. Louis, providing settlements and cultural assistance for them. On June 28, 1921, he was appointed an Assistant at the Pontifical Throne. Just three years before, he had opened his hundredth parish and had provided social services and charitable programs for countless faithful while supporting the military efforts of the nation in World War I.

Archbishop Glennon led the Catholics of Missouri through the grim days of the Great Depression and World War II. In recognition of his unfailing services, Pope Pius XII created him a cardinal priest on February 18, 1946. Archbishop Glennon died just nineteen days later, while visiting Dublin on his return from Rome. He was buried in the Cathedral Basilica of St. Louis.

Glorieux, Alphonsus Joseph (February 1, 1844–August 25, 1917)

The first bishop of the Diocese of Boise, Alphonsus Joseph Glorieux was a pioneering missionary of Idaho, serving the Catholics there in a critical era of American history. He was born in Dottignies, West Flanders, Belgium, and entered the seminary at Courtrai. Interested in the American missions, he studied at the American College in Louvain and was ordained on August 17, 1867.

Father Glorieux started his mission labors in Oregon but was named vicar apostolic of Idaho on October 7, 1884, and was consecrated a bishop. He chose Boise as his headquarters and began serving nineteen parishes and missions in the region. On August 26, 1893, Bishop Glorieux became the head of the new Diocese of Boise and labored to provide diocesan facilities and personnel for the Catholic population. When he died, Bishop Glorieux was credited with dedicating over ninety parish and mission churches, adding schools and hospitals, care agencies and homes, and a cathedral. Many religious communities entered the diocese to aid him in his labors.

Goesbriand, Louis de (August 4, 1816–November 3, 1899)

The first bishop of the Diocese of Burlington, from 1853 until his death, Louis de Goesbriand was a popular author in his era. He was born in St. Urbain, France, the son of Marquis Henri de Goesbriand and Emilie de Bergean. Educated at the seminaries of Quimper and Saint-Sulpice in Paris, he was ordained on July 13, 1840. Father de Goesbriand, who always had an interest in the American missions, came to the United States to aid the growing Church.

He served in the area of Cincinnati from 1840 to 1847. When the Diocese of Cleveland was erected in 1847, Father Goesbriand was appointed vicar general. He served Cleveland until July 29, 1953, when he was appointed as the first bishop of the Diocese of Burlington. He was consecrated on October 30, 1853, in New York City, and arrived in Burlington on November 5. At that time there were only twenty thousand Catholics and five priests in the state of Vermont. With the exception of eight churches and a small parochial school taught by lay teachers, there were no institutions of any kind. Between 1853 and 1891 the number of priests increased to fifty-two and the number of churches to seventy-eight; eight academies and sixteen parochial schools were established; and seven congregations of nuns were brought into the diocese to teach.

In addition to his labors in the diocese, Bishop de Goesbriand also wrote or translated a number of books and pamphlets, among them *Catholic Memoirs of Vermont and New Hampshire* (1886), *Christ on the Altar* (1890), *History of Confession* (1889), and *St. Peter's Life* (1893).

Goldstein, David (July 27, 1870–June 30, 1958)

A convert from Judaism, David Goldstein was cofounder of the Catholic Truth Guild. He was born in London, England, the son of Dutch Jewish parents who migrated to New York City in 1871. Goldstein received a fine Jewish education but had to start work at the age of eleven as a cigar maker. In 1888 the family moved to Boston, where

Goldstein joined the Socialist Labor Party and was extremely active. He met another prominent socialist, Martha Moore Avery, who educated him in the Catholic principles concerning marriage, divorce, labor, and other human fields of activity. Goldstein started looking into the Catholic faith as a result and converted. He was baptized in Immaculate Conception Church in Boston in 1905.

Two years earlier he had left the Socialist Party and in 1906 he and Avery founded the first modern lay apostolate designed to influence the average person. The organization was called the Catholic Truth Guild when it was formed and then became the Catholic Campaigners for Christ in 1935. Goldstein lectured for more than twenty-five years, defending the Church from attacks. His labors did not go unrecognized, and he received many honors, including honorary degrees, the Franciscan Distinguished Service Medal, and Knighthood in the Order of St. Gregory in 1955.

Gomez, José H. (December 26, 1951–)

The fifth archbishop of Los Angeles and the first Latino to serve as the shepherd of the archdiocese, José Horacio Gomez was born in Monterrey, Mexico, the son of Dr. José H. Gomez and Esperanza Velasco. He studied at the Monterrey Institute of Technology prior to entering the National University of Mexico, where he earned a Bachelor of Science degree in accounting and a Bachelor of Arts degree in philosophy in 1975. During his college years, he became a member of Opus Dei, and in 1978 departed Mexico to study at the Rome campus of the University of Navarre. He earned a bachelor's in theology and was ordained on August 15, 1978, in Spain. He then earned a doctorate in theology in Pamplona, Spain, in 1980.

As a priest for the Personal Prelature of Opus Dei, Father Gomez assisted lay members and served from 1987 to 1999 in San Antonio in a local parish. He also assisted in pastoral duties in the then Diocese of Galveston-Houston in Katy, Texas. He was well known among Hispanic priests in the United States and was active in the National Association of Hispanic Priests, serving as its president in 1995. He was also on the board of directors of the National Catholic Council of Hispanic Ministry and was on the steering committee for Encuentro

2000, an important gathering of Hispanic Catholics in Los Angeles for the Great Jubilee.

On January 23, 2001, he was appointed the titular bishop of Belali and auxiliary bishop of Denver. He was ordained a bishop on March 26, 2001. Four years later, he was named archbishop of San Antonio on February 15, 2005. That same year, he was named one of *Time* magazine's "25 Most Influential Hispanics" in the United States. In 2006 Archbishop Gomez launched the Catholic Community Foundation for the Roman Catholic Church of the Archdiocese of San Antonio, and Hope for the Future, a tuition assistance program for Catholic schools in the archdiocese. In 2007 he helped organize the Catholic Association of Latino Leaders to help nurture the role and contributions of Hispanics in the Church.

The following year, Archbishop Gomez was appointed by Pope Benedict XVI as a consultant to the Pontifical Commission for Latin America. He was also the first chairman of the new Committee on Cultural Diversity in the Church of the United States Conference of Catholic Bishops. On April 6, 2010, Archbishop Gomez was named coadjutor archbishop of Los Angeles. He acceded to the see on March 1, 2011, upon the retirement of Cardinal Roger M. Mahony.

Goupil, René, St. (1607–September 23, 1642)

The first of the American Jesuit martyrs, St. René Goupil was a companion of St. Isaac Jogues and a missionary to the Iroquois. He was born in Anjou, France, and was already a surgeon when he entered the Jesuit novitiate in Paris in 1631. Partially deaf, St. René served in Canada for two years as a surgeon in the hospitals of Québec and then started out for the Huron Mission with St. Isaac Jogues, whose constant companion and disciple he remained until death. The mission group was captured by the Iroquois near Lake St. Peter and taken to Ossernenon, present-day Auriesville, New York.

St. René resignedly accepted his fate. Like the other captives, he was beaten, his nails torn out, and his fingers bitten off. On the thirteen days' journey to the Iroquois country, he suffered from heat, hunger, and blows, his wounds festering and swarming with worms. Meeting halfway a band of two hundred warriors, he was forced to march between their double ranks and was clubbed almost to death.

At Ossernenon, St. René was greeted with more threats and punishments, jeers and blows, and he survived the fresh tortures inflicted on him at Andagaron, a neighboring village. Unable to instruct his captors in the faith, he made the sign of the cross over an Indian child and was marked for death. St. René was struck by a hatchet blow from an Indian, and died praising the name of Jesus. He was the first of the order in the Canadian missions to suffer martyrdom. St. Isaac Jogues wrote that St. René was "an angel of innocence and a martyr of Jesus Christ."

Grace, William Russell (May 10, 1832–March 21, 1904)

The first Irish Catholic mayor of New York City, William Russell Grace was a philanthropist and daily communicant. He was born at Cork, Ireland, a descendant of the famous Irish warrior Raymond Le Gros, on his father's side. His mother, a Russell from Tipperary, was a convert to the Catholic faith. Grace, in time, became a partner with the firm of John Bryce at Callao, Peru. This firm became Grace Brothers & Co. and W. R. Grace & Co., with offices in New York, San Francisco, and every city of importance on the west coast of South America. Grace also established the New York and Pacific Steamship Co. in New York, and other financial enterprises. In 1859 he married Lillian Gilchrist of Thomaston, Maine.

In 1878 Grace was residing in New York, and there he supported the efforts to alleviate the famine of 1878 and 1879 in Ireland. This and other acts of charity made him so popular that he was nominated for mayor of New York City and was elected in 1880, despite Protestant efforts to stop his campaign. He was the first Catholic to hold that office and was reelected in 1884. Many urged him to run for a third term, but he declined.

Grace was a daily communicant, attending Mass in St. Agnes on his way to the mayoral offices. In May 1897 he founded the Grace Institute, which he dedicated to the memory of his parents, providing young women with educations in bookkeeping, dressmaking, stenography, typing, and other skills. The Sisters of Charity operated the foundation's educational programs. William Russell Grace died in New York.

Grand Island, Diocese of

Established on March 8, 1912, by Pope St. Pius X as the Diocese of Kearney and designated as Grand Island on April 11, 1917, the diocese serves counties in central and western Nebraska. French trappers in the earliest eras of exploration in the present-day United States named the site after an island in the Platte River, which they called *Le Grande Ile*. Travelers on the road west used the area as a landmark. Grand Island is a processing and shipping center for the diverse agricultural and cattle industries of the region. A German settlement was there by 1857, but the town expanded in 1866 when the Union Pacific Railroad entered the area. The Diocese of Grand Island is a suffragan see of the Archdiocese of Omaha.

The Catholic heritage of Grand Island opens with the expeditions of Pedro de Villasur in 1720. Franciscan Father Juan Mingues was with this expedition and died in a Pawnee attack with other members of the party. In 1739 Pierre and Paul Mallet entered the area for fur trapping. No permanent settlements were reported at the time, however. The Louisiana Purchase of 1803, followed by the Lewis and Clark expedition, opened trading posts and aided the missions to the local Native American tribes.

In 1815 Nebraska was under the ecclesiastical jurisdiction of the Archdiocese of New Orleans, and transferred to St. Louis in 1827. In that year, the revered Jesuit Father Pierre-Jean De Smet, accompanied by Father Felix Verrydt, founded St. Joseph's in Council Bluffs, Iowa, for the Potawatomi. In 1838 Father De Smet visited Bellevue, Nebraska, to baptize Oto children.

Pope Blessed Pius IX in 1850 established the Vicariate Apostolic of Indian Territory East of the Rocky Mountains (Indian Territory), and present-day Nebraska was included in that jurisdiction. Bishop Jean Baptiste Miège, a Jesuit pioneer, served as vicar apostolic. One year later, in 1851, Father De Smet attended the Great Plains Council near Fort Laramie and addressed ten thousand American Indians. He also celebrated the first documented Mass in Nebraska in September of that year.

In 1854 a Catholic settlement was established in Dakota County, followed by another settlement in Holt County. Catholics from the Holt County community soon after entered into areas of present-day Grand Island. The needs of these Catholics were served by the Vicariate Apostolic of Nebraska, which was erected in 1857, and ten years later Nebraska entered the Union. The Dioceses of Omaha (now the Archdiocese of Omaha), Cheyenne, and Lincoln were erected as the Catholic presence grew in the region.

In 1912 the Diocese of Kearney was established, and Bishop James A. Duffy was consecrated as the first bishop of the see on April 16, 1913. He instituted the offices and agencies for diocesan administration and asked for additional territories for the diocese. Bishop Duffy also recognized that Kearney would not be able to sustain the infrastructures needed for the diocese and requested that the episcopal seat be transferred to Grand Island. The Holy See authorized the transfer on April 11, 1917. Bishop Duffy led the faithful of the diocese during World War I and the start of the Great Depression. He also aided Mexican laborers in the region, building Our Lady of Guadalupe Church in Scotts Bluff. The Nativity of the Blessed Virgin Mary Church, erected in 1864, was designated as the cathedral. Bishop Duffy retired on May 7, 1931.

His successor was Bishop Stanislaus V. Bona, who was consecrated on February 25, 1932. Bishop Bona continued the expansion programs in progress and started charitable ministries to aid the faithful in the remaining years of the Great Depression. He also supported the military efforts of the nation in World War II. On December 2, 1944, Bishop Bona was appointed coadjutor bishop of the Diocese of Green Bay.

The third bishop of Grand Island was Edward J. Hunkeler, who was appointed to the diocese on March 10, 1945, and consecrated on May 1. Bishop Hunkeler labored during the postwar period to provide diocesan facilities for the growing Catholic population and to maintain ministries and educational programs. On March 31, 1951, however, he was transferred to the Diocese of Kansas City in Kansas, where he was promoted to archbishop when the diocese was elevated to the status of a metropolitan see.

His successor in Grand Island was Bishop John L. Paschang, who was consecrated on October 9, 1951. Bishop Paschang promoted education in the diocese. He attended the Second Vatican Council and implemented the reforms mandated by the council until his retirement on July 25, 1972. When he died on March 21, 1999, at the age of 103, he was the world's oldest Catholic bishop.

The fifth bishop of Grand Island was John J. Sullivan, who was consecrated on September 19, 1972. He labored to maintain diocesan ministries and services while facing the loss of priests and religious. On August 17, 1977, Bishop Sullivan was transferred to the Diocese of Kansas City-St. Joseph.

His successor was Bishop Lawrence J. McNamara, who was installed in the diocese on March 28, 1978. Bishop McNamara joined Archbishop Elden Francis Curtiss of Omaha and Bishop Fabian W. Bruskewitz of Lincoln in supporting a "Defense of Marriage" referendum in Nebraska. He also joined in maintaining the feast of the Ascension on Thursday, its traditional day of celebration. He retired on October 14, 2004.

Bishop McNamara was succeeded as bishop by Bishop William J. Dendinger, who had served for thirty-one years as a chaplain in the United States Air Force and had retired in 2001 as a two-star general. Bishop Dendinger was consecrated as the seventh bishop on December 13, 2004, at the Cathedral of the Nativity of the Blessed Virgin Mary in Grand Island. In 2011 there were 50,000 Catholics served by 69 priests and 36 parishes in the diocese.

Grand Rapids, Diocese of

Established on May 19, 1882, by Pope Leo XIII, the Diocese of Grand Rapids serves counties in western Michigan. The city was founded in 1826 by a Frenchman, Louis Campau, on the site of converging Ottawa Indian trails at the rapids of the Grand River. The manufacture of furniture became a leading economic base in Grand Rapids, which is now an industrial center serving agricultural and manufacturing interests. The Diocese of Grand Rapids is a suffragan see of the Archdiocese of Detroit.

The diocese has a profound Catholic history beginning in 1640, when French priests reportedly celebrated a Mass in the area while accompanying an expedition into the region. In 1641 St. Isaac Jogues was with the Chippewa Indians in the north. Other Jesuits followed, and Sault Ste. Marie and Mackinac were opened in 1668 and 1671. Jesuit Fathers Jacques Marquette, Claude Allouez, Philip Pierson, and Louis André labored in the area, and in 1679 René-Robert Chevalier, Sieur de La Salle, was on the St. Joseph River with Franciscan Recollect Father Louis Hennepin. Detroit was founded by Antoine Cadillac in 1701 as Fort Ponchartrain, but settlers were not in the region in great numbers until after the American Revolution.

In 1831 Father Irenaeus Frederick Baraga, the revered nobleman from Europe who would become a bishop, established a mission at Arbre Croche, present-day Harbor Springs. Two years later he opened a school and parish in Grand Rapids. Father Ignatius Mrak, who also became a bishop, aided Father Baraga when he was appointed as the first bishop of the Diocese of Marquette. When these pioneering missionaries left Grand Rapids, Father Andrew Viszosky remained as the first resident pastor of the area.

In 1882 the Diocese of Grand Rapids was erected, comprising the northern half of the Lower Peninsula of Michigan. The first bishop of the Diocese of Grand Rapids was Henry Joseph Richter, who was consecrated on April 22, 1883. A careful administrator, he began the offices and agencies necessary for diocesan administration. The Catholic population tripled during his years of service, and he built parishes and schools. In 1903 Bishop Richter convened a diocesan synod. He also welcomed priests and religious to Grand Rapids and founded St. Joseph Seminary. Bishop Richter died on December 26, 1916.

The second bishop was Michael James Gallagher, who had been appointed coadjutor bishop of Grand Rapids with right of succession in 1915. He acceded to the see upon the death of Bishop Richter and continued the expansion programs. Bishop Gallagher also supported the military efforts of the nation. On July 18, 1918, he was transferred to the Diocese (now Archdiocese) of Detroit.

His successor was Bishop Edward D. Kelly, who had served as auxiliary bishop of Detroit since 1911 and was appointed to the Diocese of Grand Rapids on January 16, 1919. Bishop Kelly conducted an energetic building program while aiding the military personnel of the nation in World War I and its aftermath. He also defended the Church against anti-parochial school legislation proposed in Michigan. He founded a preparatory seminary, a college, schools, and a diocesan newspaper. Bishop Kelly died on March 26, 1926.

The fourth bishop of Grand Rapids was Joseph G. Pinten, who had been serving as the bishop of Superior since 1922. He was transferred to Grand Rapids on June 25, 1926. Bishop Pinten began his labors by paying off the debts of the diocese and by preparing for worsening economic times. The Diocese of Detroit was elevated to the rank of metropolitan province, an archdiocese, in 1937, and the Diocese of Superior was established. Bishop Pinten led the faithful through the grim era of the Great Depression, even as his health was failing. On November 1, 1940, the state of his health forced him to seek retirement.

His successor was Bishop Joseph Casimir Plagens, who had served as auxiliary bishop of Detroit from 1924 and as the bishop of Marquette from 1935. He was installed in Grand Rapids on February 18, 1941. World War II began soon after, and he supported the military efforts of the nation. He also promoted youth programs and had to refurbish the cathedral after a devastating fire. Bishop Plagens suffered a series of heart attacks as a result of his dedicated labors and died on March 31, 1943.

The sixth bishop of Grand Rapids was Francis Haas, who was consecrated and installed in the cathedral on November 18, 1943. Bishop Haas was a nationally acclaimed labor mediator, serving Presidents Franklin Delano Roosevelt and Harry S. Truman. He convened a diocesan synod in 1948 and started a new diocesan newspaper. Bishop Haas died on August 29, 1953.

His successor was Bishop Allen J. Babcock, who had served as an auxiliary bishop of the Archdiocese of Detroit since 1947. He was appointed to Grand Rapids on March 23, 1954. Bishop Babcock continued the expansion and building programs of the diocese and took part in the Second Vatican Council, implementing the reforms mandated by that council. Bishop Babcock died on June 27, 1969.

The eighth bishop of Grand Rapids was Bishop Joseph M. Breitenbeck, who had served as auxiliary bishop of the Archdiocese of Detroit since 1965. He was appointed to the Diocese of Grand Rapids on October 15, 1969. Bishop Breitenbeck promoted educational programs in the diocese and instituted charitable ministries while facing a shortage of personnel. He retired on August 3, 1989, after two decades of faithful service.

His successor was Bishop Robert J. Rose, who had served as the bishop of Gaylord since 1981. Bishop Rose was installed in Grand Rapids on August 30, 1989. He instituted lay ministries and evangelization programs to care for the growing Catholic population while consolidating facilities and maintaining services to the faithful. Bishop Rose retired on October 13, 2003.

The tenth bishop of Grand Rapids was Kevin M. Britt, who had served as auxiliary bishop of the Archdiocese of Detroit since 1993 and as coadjutor bishop of Grand Rapids since December 10, 2002. Bishop Britt acceded to the see upon the retirement of Bishop Rose. He made a trip to Rome and shortly after his return on May 16, 2004, was found dead in his residence.

Bishop Britt was succeeded by Bishop Walter A. Hurley on June 21, 2005. Bishop Hurley was installed in the diocese on August 4, 2005. He had served as an auxiliary bishop of the Archdiocese of Detroit since 2003. In 2011 there were 178,000 Catholics, served by 119 priests, 322 women religious, and 91 parishes in the diocese.

Grässel, Lorenz (August 18, 1753–October 1793)

The coadjutor-elect of the Diocese of Baltimore, Lorenz Grässel was a former Jesuit missionary in the young United States. He was born in Ruemannsfelden, Bavaria, Germany, and was a novice in the Society of Jesus when that order was suppressed. Ordained a priest, Father Grässel was invited by Father Ferdinand Steinmeyer to serve in the city of Philadelphia. In March 1787 he arrived in Philadelphia to assume the pastorate of St. Mary's. Father Grässel spent six years there and was revered for his intelligence and holiness. When it was decided that Bishop John Carroll, America's first bishop, needed assistance, Father Grässel was nominated for the office of coadjutor bishop, and a petition for his formal appointment was sent to the Holy See on September 24, 1793. The appointment was approved by Rome, but Father Grässel did not live long enough to receive the office. A plague of yellow fever struck Philadelphia in 1793, and Father Grässel went into the homes of the faithful to care for victims of the disease. He succumbed to yellow fever in the service of others.

Grasso, Ella T. (May 10, 1919–February 5, 1981)

The first woman to become an American governor in her own right, Ella T. Grasso was an ardent figure in the pro-life movement. She was born in Windsor Locks, Connecticut, and attended Chaffee School and Mount Holyoke College. In 1942 she married Thomas A. Grasso and worked as part of the Federal Manpower Commission. She was elected to the Connecticut House of Representatives in 1952 and 1954. Four years later she was elected secretary of state, serving until 1970. In 1972 she was elected to the United States House of Representatives and helped pass the Emergency Employment Act and the Higher Education Act.

In 1974 Grasso made a successful bid for the governorship of Connecticut and worked to stabilize the state's economy during the recession of the era. Reelected in 1978, she publicly announced that she was suffering from cancer, a condition that forced her to resign in 1980. She died in Hartford.

Gravier, Jacques (1651–1708)

An honored Jesuit missionary of the American Church, Jacques Gravier suffered an arrow wound that could not be aided surgically and caused his slow and painful death. He was born in Loulins, France, where he joined the Society of Jesus in 1670, studying theology at the Collège Louis-le-Grand in Paris. Ordained a priest, he was sent to the Canadian missions in 1685. He served first at Michilimackinac, modern-day Mackinac, and then succeeded the famous Father Claude Allouez in Illinois, gathering the Kaskaskia and Peoria Indians into the Kaskaskia Mission. Records indicate that he celebrated a Mass in Arkansas on November 1, 1700. A year before, he had become vicar general of the area around Mackinac.

In 1708, returning to the Illinois area, Father Gravier was caught up in a Peoria war and received an arrow wound. The arrow could not be extracted from his arm, and infection set in. Father Gravier became so ill that he was sent to Paris for medical care. Surgeons were unable to remove the arrow, and Father Gravier returned to the missions with his wound, going to the vast Louisiana region, where he died of his infection. A brilliant linguist and scholar, he had given a decade of his life to the Kaskaskian and Peoria nations and had written a grammar for the Illinois.

Graymoor

The Society of the Atonement, popularly known as the Graymoor or Atonement Friars, is a branch of the Third Order Regular of St. Francis. Lewis Thomas Wattson, a convert to the faith who became known as Father Paul Francis, founded the Society in 1898. The Graymoor Friars were involved in social, pastoral, and ecumenical activities and spread throughout the United States, Canada, England, Italy, and Japan. Father Paul Francis had been an Episcopalian clergyman who knew the value of a Society dedicated to atonement and to the Franciscan ideal of poverty. He met Mary Lurana White, and she started the Franciscan Sisters of the Atonement. Graymoor was established as a result, with the first friars' building erected on the Mount of the Atonement in 1900.

On October 30, 1909, Father Paul, Mother Lurana, and fifteen companions were received into the Catholic Church through permission granted by Pope St. Pius X. Soon after, the group was received into the Franciscan order. Father Paul was ordained on July 16, 1910, and spent the next decades working for Christian unity.

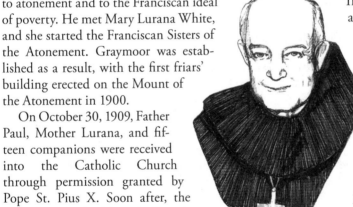

Father Paul Francis

Father Paul had started the Chair of Unity Octave, a prayer crusade for religious unity in 1908, and it was approved by the Holy See in 1909. Pope Benedict XV extended the practice to the universal Church in 1916, and Pope Pius XII and successive pontiffs endorsed the program. Overseas missions followed, and the Atonement Friars produced the *Ave Maria Hour* on radio between 1935 and 1969.

Friars today serve in parishes throughout the United States, Canada, and England, as well as in ecumenical ministry in the United States, Canada, England, Japan, and Italy. The Franciscan Sisters of the Atonement serve as a missionary congregation of women engaged in a multitude of ministries, including religious education, social welfare, health care, pastoral work, hospital and prison ministries, home visitation, adult day care, child day care and kindergartens, youth ministry, justice and peace work, and retreat house ministries.

Great Falls-Billings, Diocese of

Established on May 18, 1904, by Pope St. Pius X, the Diocese of Great Falls was designated as the Diocese of Great Falls-Billings in 1980 by Pope Blessed John Paul II. The diocese serves the eastern counties of the state of Montana. Great Falls is named for a natural wonder, and Lewis and Clark observed the Great Springs nearby in 1805. Both Great Falls and Billings have large Catholic populations, and both serve as commercial and industrial centers in a chiefly rural area.

The Diocese of Great Falls-Billings is a suffragan see of the Archdiocese of Portland in Oregon.

The Catholic history of the region began on July 26, 1840, when the revered Jesuit missionary Father Pierre-Jean De Smet celebrated the first Mass within the borders of the present state of Montana. The area had been visited earlier by the Lewis and Clark expedition in 1804, and was a popular trapping territory. Father De Smet came into Montana as a result of requests by the Flatheads to have a "Black Robe" in their settlements. Iroquois Catholics, including Young Ignace La Mousse, had made their way from New York to Montana and had spread word of the faith. Father De Smet celebrated the first Mass near present-day Three Forks for the Flatheads. Within decades, Jesuit missionaries started four missions in Montana.

In 1864, by an act of Congress, the Montana Territory was established. The Vicariate Apostolic of Montana, once part of the Vicariate Apostolic of Utah, was erected in 1883. The Diocese of Helena was established in 1884, and Bishop John Baptist Brondel, who had served as vicar apostolic, was appointed the first bishop of Helena.

In 1904 the Diocese of Great Falls was erected, assuming jurisdiction over the eastern two-thirds of Montana. Bishop Mathias Clement Lenihan was appointed to this new ecclesiastical jurisdiction, and he was consecrated on September 21, 1904. Bishop Lenihan was installed in Great Falls and set about instituting the offices and agencies for diocesan administration. He invited religious orders into the diocese and recruited priests while supporting the nation's military efforts in World War I. Bishop Lenihan built parishes, missions, schools, a hospital, and academies, supporting at the same time the Native American apostolate. St. Ann's Cathedral was reportedly dedicated in December 1907. Bishop Lenihan retired on January 18, 1930, after decades of faithful service in founding diocesan services and facilities.

His successor was Bishop Edwin Vincent O'Hara, who was consecrated on October 28, 1930, for Great Falls diocese. He was already recognized as a national Catholic leader, having spearheaded the organization of the Confraternity of Christian Doctrine and having led the Catholic opposition to the anti–parochial school bill in Oregon. He was also involved in the founding of the National Catholic Rural Life Conference. Bishop O'Hara was made an Assistant at the Pontifical Throne on January 5, 1949, and was given the personal title of archbishop in 1954. He continued the expansion and development programs in Great Falls, despite the problems of the Great Depression, until April 15, 1939, when he was transferred to the Diocese of Kansas City (now the Diocese of Kansas City-St. Joseph).

The third bishop of Great Falls was William Joseph Condon, who was consecrated on October 18, 1939. He continued to strengthen diocesan services and to expand facilities, and on December 9, 1963, was made an Assistant at the Pontifical Throne. Bishop Condon promoted education and labored to provide parishes for the growing Catholic population, building over thirty churches. He led the faithful of the diocese during World War II and was part of the Second Vatican Council. Bishop Condon died on August 17, 1967.

His successor was Bishop Eldon Bernard Schuster, who had served as auxiliary bishop of Great Falls since 1967. Bishop Schuster was installed in the diocese on January 23, 1968. He promulgated the reforms mandated by the Second Vatican Council and promoted social services and care programs for the area. He retired on December 27, 1977.

The fifth bishop of the Diocese of Great Falls was Thomas Joseph Murphy, who was installed in the diocese on August 21, 1978. He also took part in the designation of the diocese as Great Falls-Billings. St. Patrick's in Billings was established as a co-cathedral. Bishop Murphy consolidated parishes and schools and promoted the Priests' Senate. On May 26, 1987, he was promoted to coadjutor archbishop of Seattle.

His successor, Bishop Anthony Michael Milone, had served as auxiliary bishop of the Archdiocese of Omaha since 1981. He was installed in the Diocese of Great Falls-Billings on February 23, 1988, and supported lay movements and programs for young people. He retired on July 12, 2006, and was succeeded on November 20, 2007, by Bishop Michael W. Warfel, who had been bishop of Juneau since 1996. In 2011 there were 44,000 Catholics served by 77 priests and 55 parishes in the diocese.

Green Bay, Diocese of

Established on March 3, 1868, by Pope Blessed Pius IX, the Diocese of Green Bay serves counties in northeastern Wisconsin. Jean Nicolet established a trading post at Green Bay in 1634, and the French built a fort in the area in 1717. At the time, Green Bay was called La Baye. The present city was laid out in 1829. A port of entry, Green Bay is a county seat, located where the Fox River empties into the bay, which is an inlet of Lake Michigan, and it is a commercial and distribution center. The Diocese of Green Bay is a suffragan see of the Archdiocese of Milwaukee.

The Catholic heritage of the diocese starts also with Jean Nicolet's trading post. Pierre Radisson and Medard Chouart de Groseilliers followed Nicolet and opened fur trading in present-day Wisconsin. In 1669 Jesuit Father Claude Allouez founded St. Francis Xavier Mission and served Bayfield and De Pere. René-Robert Chevalier, Sieur de La Salle, also conducted an expedition in the region, and

Jesuit Father Jacques Marquette and Louis Joliet explored throughout the area. The Jesuit Father René Menard was reportedly slain near Green Bay in 1661. Within a short time, the Jesuits established over twenty missions for the Native Americans. Wars of European origin overtook events on the American continent, however, and in 1712 there was a campaign over the Fox and Wisconsin rivers, and Fort Francis, now a part of the Diocese of Green Bay, was destroyed.

In 1754 the French and Indian War dealt a blow to the missions, as the victorious British took over the entire region. Itinerant priests continued to visit American Indian settlements in the early 1800s, and they benefited from the outcome of the War of 1812, as the defeated British forces had to withdraw from Wisconsin. The Hudson Bay Company had dominated the region but was forced to retire into Canada. In 1816 Fort Howard was erected, and Father Gabriel Richard, the noted Sulpician, was active in the area, alongside Venerable Samuel Mazzuchelli, a Dominican missionary. Father Edward D. Fenwick, who would become a pioneering American bishop, was also active in Wisconsin.

The Black Hawk War took a toll on settlements in 1832, but four years later the Wisconsin Territory was erected by an act of Congress. Milwaukee was established as a diocese (now the Archdiocese of Milwaukee) in 1843, and Wisconsin entered the Union in 1848. The Civil War brought about sacrifices in the region, but the Catholic presence expanded as the Church consolidated its membership and ministries.

The Diocese of Green Bay was established in 1868, and the first bishop was appointed. Joseph Melcher was consecrated on July 12, 1868, and began instituting the offices and agencies for diocesan administration. He discovered a burgeoning Catholic population in Green Bay and recruited priests and expanded the diocesan parishes to accommodate growing demands. Bishop Melcher attended the First Vatican Council and invited religious congregations to serve the faithful in Green Bay. He died on December 20, 1873.

His successor was Bishop Francis Xavier Krautbauer, who was consecrated on September 21, 1886. He erected St. Francis Xavier Cathedral and established schools and parishes. Bishop Krautbauer instituted programs to provide for veteran priests of the diocese and established social and evangelizing programs. After less than a decade of faithful service, he died on December 17, 1885.

The third bishop of Green Bay was Frederick Xavier Katzer, who was consecrated on September 21, 1886. Dedicated to enhancing Catholic education and serving children, Bishop Katzer opposed the Bennett Law of 1889 that made English compulsory in Wisconsin schools. The law was repealed in 1890. On January 30, 1891, Bishop Katzer was promoted to the Archdiocese of Milwaukee.

Bishop Sebastian Gebhard Messmer was the successor to Bishop Katzer, and was consecrated on March 27, 1892. He invited the Norbertines to establish a college in De Pere and erected parishes throughout the diocese. He also instituted social and care services and promoted education. Bishop Katzer was promoted to the Archdiocese of Milwaukee on November 28, 1903.

The fifth bishop of Green Bay was Joseph John Fox, who was a native son and was consecrated on July 25, 1904. Bishop Fox promoted charitable ministries, establishing an orphanage and other services. He strengthened the parochial schools in the diocese and continued laboring, despite ill health. After ten years, Bishop Fox retired because of his health on December 4, 1914.

His successor was Bishop Paul Peter Rhode, who had served as auxiliary bishop of Chicago since 1908. He was promoted to Green Bay on July 5, 1915. He founded new parishes in the diocese and established Catholic Charities and a diocesan education department. Centralizing the diocesan offices, Bishop Rhode promoted social services and lay participation in sodalities and other Catholic organizations. The Vatican honored Bishop Rhode for his decades of service, having led the faithful of Green Bay through World War I, the Great Depression, and World War II. He died on March 3, 1945.

The seventh bishop of Green Bay was Stanislaus V. Bona. He had served as the bishop of Grand Island since 1931 and then as coadjutor bishop of Green Bay with right of succession. He acceded to the see upon the death of Bishop Rhode. Bishop Bona promoted education, erecting over sixty elementary schools, high schools, and a college. He also founded Sacred Heart Seminary and a diocesan newspaper. He introduced Newman Clubs and the National Catholic Rural Life Conference to the diocese and took part in the Second Vatican Council. He died on December 1, 1967.

His successor was Bishop Aloysius J. Wycislo, who had served as auxiliary bishop of the Archdiocese of Chicago since 1960. He was promoted to Green Bay on March 8, 1968. Bishop Wycislo implemented the reforms mandated by the Second Vatican Council and formed a permanent diaconate program in the diocese. Lay associations, ministries to migrants and young people, and an urban apostolate were established as well. Bishop Wycislo retired on May 10, 1983.

The ninth bishop of Green Bay was Adam Joseph Maida, who would become an American cardinal in 1994. Bishop Maida was the successor to Bishop Wycislo, and was consecrated on January 25, 1984. He continued lay leadership programs and implemented catechetical projects throughout the diocese. A diocesan synod was convened in 1988, and Bishop Maida raised millions of dollars to further ministries. On June 12, 1990, he was promoted to the Archdiocese of Detroit and in 1994 was created a cardinal.

His successor was Bishop Robert Joseph Banks, who had served as the auxiliary bishop of Boston since 1985. He was appointed to Green Bay on October 16, 1990. Bishop Banks continued promoting lay leadership and established a diocesan advisory council. He also conducted ecumenical programs with Protestant churches in the area and served as chairman for the Bishops' Committee on Education and the National Catholic Educational Association. Bishop Banks retired on December 12, 2003.

The eleventh bishop of Green Bay, Bishop David A. Zubik, had served as auxiliary bishop of the Diocese of Pittsburgh from 1997. He was installed in the Diocese of Green Bay on December 12, 2003, and was appointed bishop of Pittsburgh on July 18, 2007. He was succeeded on July 9, 2008, by Bishop David Laurin Ricken, who had been bishop of Cheyenne since 2001. He was installed on August 28, 2008. He issued several pastoral letters, including "A New Moment for Catechesis in the Diocese of Green Bay" in 2009 and "Pastoral Statement on Living Justice in the Diocese of Green Bay" in 2011. He also issued the "Decree on the Authenticity of the Apparitions of 1859 at the Shrine of Our Lady of Good Help" in Champion, Wisconsin, to Adele Brise in December 2010, making him the first diocesan bishop in the United States to give approval to a Marian apparition. In 2011 there were 324,000 Catholics served by 278 priests, 469 women religious, and 157 parishes in the diocese.

Greensburg, Diocese of

Established on March 10, 1951, by Pope Pius XII, the Diocese of Greensburg serves counties in southwestern Pennsylvania. Named for Revolutionary War hero General Nathanael Greene, the city was founded in 1782. The railroad and rich local deposits aided the local economy and Greensburg became a county seat. The Diocese of Greensburg is a suffragan see of the Archdiocese of Philadelphia.

William Penn, who received a charter from the English crown in 1681, founded Pennsylvania and made toleration a hallmark of the settlement. Diverse traditions and faiths were not persecuted by Penn, and as a result Jesuit missionaries moved freely in the colony. In 1673 Father John Pierron was there, and others labored until 1693, when Protestants demanded that Pennsylvania require a Test Oath, making citizens express allegiance to the Protestant cause or face severe discrimination. The Test Oath was in use until 1775, keeping Catholics from public office.

In 1787 Catholic settlements were flourishing in Pennsylvania, and Blessed Sacrament Cathedral of the Diocese of Greensburg sits on land purchased in 1789. A Recollect Franciscan, Father John B. Causey, and Father Theodore Brouwers were at Sportsman Hall, near modern-day Latrobe. Father Demetrius Augustine Gallitzin, the "Apostle of the Alleghenies," established missions and parishes in the area. In 1808 the Diocese of Philadelphia (now the Archdiocese of Philadelphia) was established.

In 1846 Father Boniface Wimmer, the Benedictine pioneer, established St. Vincent's at Latrobe. At the same time, St. John Nepomucene Neumann served in present-day Greensburg, which was prospering and benefiting from the local steel mills. The Catholic population grew over the decades, as more dioceses were established in the United States and the faithful saw parishes and schools erected to serve their needs. America was involved in World War I, suffered during the Great Depression, and put forth a total effort to defeat the enemies of the nation in World War II. The Catholic presence in southwestern Pennsylvania continued to expand, responding to the needs of the times, and in 1951 the Diocese of Greensburg was erected in recognition of the population and the enthusiasm of Catholics in the area.

Bishop Hugh L. Lamb was appointed as the first bishop of Greensburg. He had served as the auxiliary bishop of the Archdiocese of Philadelphia

Blessed Sacrament Cathedral of the Diocese of Greensburg

since 1935. He was installed in Greensburg on January 16, 1952. Bishop Lamb instituted the agencies and offices for diocesan administration and led the young diocese in a period of phenomenal growth. He built parishes, schools and other facilities and promoted the construction of a hospital. The diocese received a firm foundation under his leadership. Bishop Lamb retired on December 8, 1959.

The second bishop of Greensburg was William G. Connare, who was consecrated and installed on May 4, 1960. Bishop Connare started a fund drive for diocesan programs, convened a diocesan synod, and started a Catholic newspaper. He also took part in the Second Vatican Council and implemented the reforms of that council in the diocese. Properties damaged by fires and floods were renovated and restored, and lay ministries were promoted. Bishop Connare retired on January 20, 1987.

His successor was Bishop Anthony G. Bosco, who had served as auxiliary bishop of the Diocese of Pittsburgh since 1970. He was promoted to the Diocese of Greensburg on April 14, 1987, and was installed on June 30. Bishop Bosco continued the reforms mandated by the Second Vatican Council and supported lay ministries and programs. He also maintained the diocesan facilities and services in the face of dwindling numbers of priests and religious. He retired on January 2, 2004.

The fourth bishop of Greensburg, Lawrence B. Brandt, a former member of the Vatican Diplomatic Corps, was appointed to the diocese on January 2, 2004, and was installed in the diocese of March 4, 2004. The new bishop embarked immediately upon plans for the diocese. He announced in August 2004 a new vocations initiative; issued a pastoral letter, "Integrity and the Political Arena," to reiterate the Church's teachings on life issues; and in early 2005 launched a diocesan planning committee for the future of the Catholic community in the area. In 2011 there were 156,000 Catholics served by 175 priests, 196 women religious, and 85 parishes in the diocese.

Gregory XVI, Pope (September 8, 1765–June 1, 1846)

Reigning as Pope from 1831 to 1846, Gregory XVI led the faithful during a time of severe political upheaval in Europe. He was born Bartolomeo Alberto Cappellari, in Belluno, Italy, the son of an aristocratic lawyer. Entering the Camaldolese monastery of San Michele at Murano, Venice, he was ordained in 1787. At Rome from 1795, he wrote in 1799 *Il Trionfo della Santa Sede contro gli assalti dei novatori* (*Triumph of the Holy See Against the Innovators*), upholding the idea of papal infallibility at a time when Pius VI was imprisoned by the

French Directory. Made abbot of San Gregorio in 1807, he was forced to flee Rome the following year because of Napoleon's oppression in Italy and the suppression of religious orders. Returning in 1814, he served as vicar general of the Camaldolese, was made a cardinal in 1825 by Pope Leo XII, and was appointed prefect of the Congregation for the Propaganda Fide in 1826. On February 2, 1831, he was elected pope and succeeded Pius VIII.

His pontificate was dominated by political strife in the Papal States. Austrian troops were needed to help suppress revolutions, and papal finances were in a chronic state of disarray because of the need to maintain sizable forces and the remarkably poor administrative skills of the clerics charged with overseeing the Papal States. Gregory's relations with the major powers were thus strained. He was

Pope Gregory XVI

responsible, however, for the promotion of missions, the restoration of the Dominicans and Franciscans in France, and the foundation of the Etruscan and Egyptian Museums at the Vatican and Christian Museums at the Lateran. His successor was Blessed Pius IX, who reigned from 1846 to 1878.

Pope Gregory promoted the missions in the United States and was responsible for establishing a number of dioceses, including Detroit in 1833, Vincennes (Indianapolis) in 1834, Dubuque, Nashville, and Natchez in 1837, Los Angeles in 1840, Chicago, Little Rock, Milwaukee, and Pittsburgh in 1843, and the Vicariate of Oregon in 1843.

Gruenther, Alfred Maximilian (May 23, 1899–May 30, 1983)

The youngest four-star general in the history of the U.S. Army, Alfred Maximilian Gruenther was also supreme commander of the NATO forces. He was born in Platte Center, Nebraska, the son of a newspaper editor. At the age of fifteen, Gruenther entered the United States Military Academy at West Point and was commissioned a second lieutenant in 1918. In 1922 he married Grace E. Crum and was assigned to Fort Knox and then as a teacher at West Point. Gruenther was assigned to the Command and General War College in 1937 and the Army War College in 1939.

Dwight Eisenhower was a personal friend, and Gruenther accompanied him to Europe in 1942 as part of his general staff. He headed the planning for the invasion of North Africa, the invasion of Sicily, the invasion of Salerno, and the landings at Anzio, Italy. General Mark Clark then appointed Gruenther Chief of Staff of the Fifth Army, and he was made a major general in 1942. At the war's close, he headed the occupation forces in Austria and then returned to the United States to serve as deputy commander of the War College. In 1951 Gruenther became the youngest four-star general in the Army and took command of NATO.

Retiring, he became the president of the American Red Cross. He received the Laetare Medal from the University of Notre Dame and numerous military awards. He died at Walter Reed Hospital in Washington, D.C.

Guérin, St. Theodore (October 2, 1798–March 17, 1856)

The canonized American founder of the Sisters of Providence, St. Theodore Guérin was a pioneer in education. She was born Anne-Therese Guérin in Etables, France. Entering the Sisters of Providence at Ruillé sur Loire in 1823, she served as superior in the congregation houses and then was sent to the United States in response to an invitation by Bishop Celestine René Lawrence Guynemer de la Hailandiere of the Diocese of Vincennes (now the Archdiocese of Indianapolis).

With six religious companions, St. Theodore, who had been appointed superior general of the Sisters of Providence in the United States, bought land and established St. Mary-of-the-Woods near Vincennes. She was a gifted woman, intellectually and spiritually. For a time, she was engaged in a series of conflicts with Bishop de la Hailandiere, who excommunicated her in 1847 on charges of disobedience and obstinacy. He retired soon after, and his successor lifted the excommunication and returned St. Theodore to her community. The congregation grew steadily under her leadership, opening the College of St. Mary-of-the-Woods and eighty elementary schools and academies. The Sis-

St. Theodore Guérin

ters of Providence also expanded their ministries to Baltimore, Boston, Chicago, and other cities, and in 1920 they sent missionaries to China.

She died at St. Mary-of-the-Woods and was buried there at the Church of the Immaculate Conception. The cause of canonization for St. Theodore was opened in 1909 and found subsequent support from the American bishops. She was declared venerable in 1992, and Pope Blessed John Paul II beatified her on October 25, 1998, in Rome. In April 2006 Pope Benedict XVI signed the formal recognition of a miracle that cleared the way for her canonization. She was canonized on October 15, 2006, in Rome by Pope Benedict XVI. Her feast day is September 3.

Gueslis, François Vaillant de (1646–September 24, 1718)

A Jesuit missionary to the Mohawks and a religious founder, François Vaillant de Gueslis was a defender of the Five Nation Confederacy of the Iroquois. He was born in Orléans, France, and entered the Society of Jesus in November 10, 1665, making his seminary studies in Canada. He was ordained on December 1, 1675, and began his mission assignments. From 1679 to 1684, Father de Gueslis served the Mohawk settlements, adapting to the harsh lifestyle and the changing tenor of the tribe. As the pastor of the Mohawks, he fought gallantly against the efforts of Colonel Peter Schuyler and other Protestant leaders to have the Five Nation Confederacy of the Iroquois driven out of Onondaga and other traditionally Mohawk sites.

In 1688 Father de Gueslis served as the ambassador of Canada to Governor Thomas Dongan of New York, who was a Catholic and suppressed the harsh penalties inflicted on the faithful by the former administrations. When Governor Dongan was overthrown by the Protestants of New York and was forced to flee, Father de Gueslis was assigned to missions in present-day Detroit and then in Québec and Montréal. He founded a religious congregation for men, Villemarie, and directed the community until 1715, when he was recalled to France. Father de Gueslis died in Moulins.

Guilday, Peter (1884–July 31, 1947)

Honored as the first professional American Catholic historian, Peter Guilday served as a professor of history at The Catholic University of America in Washington, D.C., and labored for many years to establish the study of American Catholic history. Born in Chester, Pennsylvania, and raised a devout Catholic, he entered the archdiocesan seminary of Philadelphia at Overbrook, Pennsylvania. Considered a promising seminarian, he was sent for studies at the American College in Louvain and was subsequently ordained to the priesthood. He then continued on at Louvain to earn a doctorate in history.

In 1914 Guilday began his life's work at The Catholic University of America. Named a member of the faculty, he took as his primary area of research the unique history of the faith in the United States, a previously underdeveloped area of academic concern. In 1915 Father Guilday supported the start of the *Catholic Historical Review* and the American Catholic Historical Association. He also published biographies and histories that provided rich accounts of the trials and victories of the Catholic Church in the nation. In an era also marked by its continuing anti-Catholicism, Guilday lent his support to defending the faith and intellectually developing a generation of Catholic leaders graduating from The Catholic University of America. Father Guilday died in Washington, D.C.

H

Haas, Francis (March 18, 1899–August 29, 1953)
A bishop and labor-management expert, Francis Haas served two presidents in labor concerns and in areas of social justice. He was born in Racine, Wisconsin, and was educated locally. He entered St. Francis Seminary in Milwaukee in 1904 and was ordained in 1913. His graduate studies were pursued at Johns Hopkins University and at The Catholic University of America. He received his doctorate in 1922.

Father Haas taught at St. Francis Seminary and at Marquette University from 1922 to 1931. In 1931 he became the director of the National Catholic School of Social Services in Washington, D.C., holding that position for four years. In 1933 Father Haas traveled to Europe to study labor practices in Germany and France, and upon his return began to advise American government agencies. In 1943 he became the dean of the School of Social Sciences at The Catholic University of America.

In that same year, he was appointed the bishop of the Diocese of Grand Rapids. Also, in 1943, President Franklin Delano Roosevelt asked him to head the Fair Employment Practices Commission. Bishop Haas served President Harry S. Truman on the same commission. He founded the Catholic Conference on Industrial Relations and the Catholic Conference on Industrial Problems. Bishop Haas also served as the president of the Catholic Association for International Peace. President Truman appointed him as well to the Commission on Civil Rights. Bishop Haas died in Grand Rapids, Michigan.

Haid, Leo Michael (July 15, 1849–July 24, 1924)
A Benedictine abbot and vicar apostolic of North Carolina, Leo Michael Haid was a monastic pioneer in the United States. He was born near Latrobe, Pennsylvania, and was educated at the Benedictine abbey there, entering the order's novitiate in 1868. He was ordained on December 21, 1872, after completing theological studies and served as a professor in the monastery college. In 1885 he became the abbot of Maryhelp Abbey, now Belmont, in North

Carolina, and was appointed vicar apostolic of North Carolina in 1888 and consecrated as the first abbot-bishop in the United States. In 1910 Bishop Haid was appointed abbot nullius by Pope St. Pius X, with canonical jurisdiction over eight counties in North Carolina. He died at Belmont Abbey.

Haig Jr., Alexander M. (December 2, 1924–February 20, 2010)
United States Secretary of State and four-star general, Alexander Haig was born in Bala Cynwyd, Pennsylvania. After studies at the United States Military Academy at West Point, he graduated in 1947 and served in the Korean and Vietnam wars. In Vietnam, he commanded a battalion of the 1st Infantry Division, and for his combat service he earned the Distinguished Service Cross, the Silver Star with oak-leaf cluster, and the Purple Heart.

Haig then earned a master's degree in international relations from Georgetown University in 1961. He rose through the ranks of the U.S. Army and was NATO commander from 1974 to 1979.

Notably, he was White House chief of staff from 1973 to 1974, during the Watergate scandal that ended with President Richard Nixon's resignation. Haig was recognized for the key role he played in the last days of Nixon's presidency and the transition to President Gerald Ford. As part of the new Republican administration, President Ronald Reagan named him secretary of state in 1981, making him the second Catholic to hold that post. He resigned in 1982 and made an unsuccessful run for president in 1988.

Hallinan, Paul J. (April 8, 1911–March 27, 1968)
The first archbishop of the Archdiocese of Atlanta, Paul J. Hallinan was a noted figure in the civil rights movement of the 1960s. He was born in Painesville, Ohio, near Cleveland, and attended the University of Notre Dame. After finishing his college studies, he entered St. Mary's Seminary in Cleveland and undertook studies for the priesthood. Ordained a priest for the Diocese of Cleveland on February 20, 1937, he served for several years in a parish and

then volunteered for the chaplain corps in 1942 during World War II.

Upon his return to the United States, Father Hallinan became involved with the Cardinal Newman Society in Cleveland and became director of the Newman Hall at Western Reserve University from 1947 to 1958. From 1952 to 1954, he was national chaplain of the National Newman Club Federation. In 1958 he hoped to begin studies in history at The Catholic University of America, but his appointment as the bishop of the Diocese of Charleston, South Carolina, on September 16, 1968, ended any thoughts of becoming a professor.

Bishop Hallinan was a shepherd over a small diocese, as Catholics were barely one and a half percent of the population, and he also encountered long-standing problems of bigotry and anti-Catholicism. The hostility only increased during the 1960 presidential campaign of the Catholic John F. Kennedy. In 1961 Bishop Hallinan began work with his fellow bishops in Savannah and Atlanta to desegregate Catholic schools and to issue a joint pastoral letter on the subject. The actual desegregation of the schools in Charleston was left to his successor, but Bishop Hallinan was able to achieve the desegregation of the Catholic hospitals in the diocese during his tenure.

On February 21, 1962, he was transferred to Atlanta and named at the same time the first archbishop. He wasted little time implementing the promise to desegregate Catholic schools in the archdiocese, followed by Catholic hospitals. He was then obligated to travel to Rome to take part in the Second Vatican Council. Archbishop Hallinan served on the Liturgical Commission and became a well-known leader in the United States in the liturgical reform movement during and after the council.

During the same period, he continued his support of the civil rights movement. In 1964 he congratulated Martin Luther King, Jr., when he won the Nobel Peace Prize. He also issued a pastoral letter on the Vietnam War in 1966, written with the close assistance of his auxiliary bishop, Bishop (later Cardinal) Joseph Louis Bernardin.

Archbishop Hallinan's health deteriorated from 1964 when he was stricken with hepatitis. His condition worsened in early 1968, and he died at the age of 57. He left behind a solid legacy of desegregation.

Hardey, Aloysia (1809–June 17, 1866)

A pioneering founder of the Society of the Sacred Heart, Mother Aloysia Hardey established the convents of her order in the eastern part of the United States, Canada, and Cuba. She was born at Piscataway, Maryland, and raised in an old Catholic family. When the Hardeys moved to Louisiana in 1822, she became one of the first pupils of the Academy of the Sacred Heart, Grand Coteau. She entered the order and in 1835 served as superior of St. Michael's, and then was asked by Bishop John Dubois to open a house of the order on Houston Street, in Manhattan, New York, now located on Aqueduct Avenue.

Mother Hardey made a visit to Rome, where she received the benediction of the pope. She then visited St. Madeleine Sophie Barat in France. The saintly founder prepared Mother Hardey for her future work, and she founded thirty convents, maintaining serenity and trust. Mother Hardey endured ten voyages to Europe, five to Cuba, and constant travel as the mother provincial of the order.

During the Civil War, Mother Hardey served both the North and South, providing food, money, hospital supplies, and provisions for the celebration of Mass. She also traveled freely between the battle lines to aid convents and the faithful. In 1866 Mother Hardey made her residence in Kenwood, Albany, New York, and she started a novitiate there in the same year. In 1871 she became assistant general of the order, an office that demanded her presence in the motherhouse in Paris. In 1884 she was appointed to the general council. However, a year later she became gravely ill and died in Paris. Mother Hardey was buried in Conflans crypt, but when the persecutions of the French government started, her remains were interred at Kenwood.

Harney, William Selby (August 27, 1800–May 9, 1889)

A military man and convert, William Selby Harney was a friend of the famed missionary Jesuit Father Pierre-Jean De Smet. Harney was born near Haysboro, Tennessee, and entered the U.S. Army in 1818. He saw action in the wars against the Black Hawks,

Seminoles, and then against the Sioux in 1855. He was also involved in the Mexican-American War. While on the campaigns against the Native Americans, Harney met and became a major supporter of Father De Smet, who had played a key role in negotiating a settlement with the Sioux.

At the start of the Civil War in 1861, Harney was serving as commander of the Department of the West at St. Louis, Missouri. On a journey to Washington, D.C., he was captured by Confederate forces but released after a brief imprisonment. Promoted to the rank of major general, he retired in 1863. His brother, John Milton, was a physician and also a convert.

Harris, Joel Chandler (1848–July 3, 1908)

A writer, folklorist, novelist, and convert, Joel Chandler Harris was best known for his famed Uncle Remus stories. He was born at Eatonton, Georgia, where he was first exposed to the rich African-American folklore. Apprenticed in 1862 to a plantation editor, Harris learned printing methods and began to read from the man's large library. Harris worked on newspapers in Louisiana and Georgia and from 1876 until his retirement in 1890 was on the staff of the Atlanta *Constitution*.

The Tar Baby, contributed by him in 1877, opened the door for him as a folklorist. His knowledge of nature and African-Americans prompted a series of volumes in which "Bre'r Rabbit," the hero, caught the fancy of Americans and became immensely popular. "Bre'r Fox," the villain in the series, and other animals, such as Mr. Sun, Sister Moon, Uncle Wind, and Brother Dust are the *dramatis personae*. "Uncle Remus," a wise old African-American, is the narrator. Harris's humor and wisdom, framed in each of the works in the unique dialect of his youth, charmed readers, although they are considered distinctly anachronistic today and offensive to many modern readers. Harris also published *Uncle Remus, His Songs and Sayings* (1881), *Nights with Uncle Remus* (1883), *Uncle Remus and His Friends* (1893), *Little Mr. Thimblefinger* (1894), and

Joel Chandler Harris

Mr. Rabbit at Home (1895). They were translated into twenty-seven languages. Harris also wrote novels, including *Mingo* (1884), *Free Joe* (1887), *Daddy Jake the Runaway* (1889), *Balaam and His Master* (1891), *Aaron in the Wildwoods* (1893), and *The Chronicle of Aunt Minervy Ann*. *Sister Jane* and *Gabriel Tolliver*, stories of his native Shady Dale, were written in his later years. *Uncle Remus's Magazine* was founded in 1906.

Harris was married to a cultured Canadian Catholic who encouraged him in his study of the faith. On June 20, 1908, a few weeks before his death, Harris received baptism in the Church. He died with the sole regret that he had so long deferred his entrance into the Catholic Church.

Harrisburg, Diocese of

Established on March 3, 1868, by Pope Blessed Pius IX, the Diocese of Harrisburg serves counties in southeastern Pennsylvania. The state capital, Harrisburg is a center for agriculture, milling, mining, and transportation. John Harris founded the city in 1705, establishing a trading post on the site and a ferry. The city was called Louisburg, in honor of King Louis XVI, in 1785, but was again called Harrisburg in 1791. The Diocese of Harrisburg is a suffragan see of the Archdiocese of Philadelphia.

William Penn founded the colony of Pennsylvania in 1681, having received a charter from the British monarch. Penn tolerated various religious groups, especially those fleeing from the harsh openly anti-Catholic laws of other colonies. The Jesuit missionaries from Canada had long been active in the area, serving the Native American communities.

In 1673 Father John Pierron was in Pennsylvania. A Test Oath, however, a public declaration of allegiance to the Protestant cause, was enacted in Pennsylvania and was effective from 1693 to 1775. This discrimination against Catholics did not halt the Jesuit missions, as the needs of the growing Catholic population had to be met with ministries and facilities.

In 1730 a mission chapel (now the Minor Basilica of the Sacred

Heart of Jesus) was established at Conawago, and eleven years later the Assumption of the Blessed Virgin Mary was open at Lancaster. St. Patrick's at Carlisle dates to 1779, and Corpus Christi started at Chambersburg in 1792.

Following the Revolutionary War, as recognition of their courage and loyal support of the American cause, Catholics in Pennsylvania were granted civil rights and religious liberty. The Trappists opened a monastery in the Harrisburg area, at Pigeon Hill, in 1803, and the Sulpicians began ministries in Hanover soon after. In 1808 the Diocese of Philadelphia was established as a suffragan see of the Archdiocese of Baltimore. The Catholic population continued to grow in Pennsylvania, and new parishes were opened to accommodate the faithful. The Immaculate Heart of Mary Church in Abbotsville dates to 1809. The dioceses of Pittsburgh and Erie were also erected in this period.

The Diocese of Harrisburg was established in 1869, and Bishop Jeremiah F. Shanahan was consecrated on July 12, 1868, and assumed the see. He had an estimated Catholic population of twenty-five thousand at the time. Bishop Shanahan served almost two decades, establishing offices and ministries and expanding facilities to meet the ever-growing needs of the diocese. Religious congregations responded to his urgent invitations and started educational institutions. Bishop Shanahan died on September 24, 1886.

His successor was Bishop Thomas McGovern, who was consecrated on March 11, 1888. Bishop McGovern opened national parishes to aid the immigrants arriving in the diocese and continued to strengthen parishes and social services. He died on July 25, 1898.

The third bishop of Harrisburg was John W. Shanahan, the brother of the diocese's founding bishop. He was consecrated on May 1, 1899, and began a massive construction program, opening charitable institutions, including an orphanage for girls. The Cathedral of St. Patrick was also dedicated. In 1907 Bishop Shanahan established the congregation of the Sisters of St. Casimir. He died on February 19, 1916.

His successor was Bishop Philip R. McDevitt, who was consecrated on September 21, 1916. Bishop McDevitt spearheaded educational programs and introduced the Society for the Propagation of the Faith to the diocese while supporting the military efforts of the nation in World War I. The diocese also celebrated a Golden Jubilee in 1918, at which Bishop Jeremiah F. Shanahan was memorialized. The apostolic delegate, Archbishop Giovanni Bonzano, was present for the festivities. Bishop McDevitt died on November 11, 1935, having led the faithful through World War I and the grim days of the Great Depression.

The fifth bishop of Harrisburg was George L. Leech, who had served as auxiliary bishop of the diocese and succeeded Bishop McDevitt. He took possession of the see on December 19, 1935. Bishop Leech recognized that increases in the Catholic population demanded new agencies and facilities. He also led the faithful of the diocese in the dark days of World War II. He served for decades in the diocese, attending the Second Vatican Council and implementing the reforms of that council. He also presided over the 100th anniversary of the diocese before retiring on October 19, 1971.

His successor was Bishop Joseph T. Daley, who had been appointed coadjutor bishop of the Diocese of Harrisburg in 1967. He acceded to the see when Bishop Leech retired. Bishop Daley instituted diocesan programs and facilities for adult education, youth ministries, and vocations. He also opened lay councils and started fundraising programs. Bishop Daley died of cancer on September 2, 1983.

Bishop William H. Keeler, who would become an American cardinal, was the seventh bishop of Harrisburg. He had served as auxiliary bishop of the diocese since 1979 and was installed on January 4, 1984. He presided over a diocesan synod and instituted lay ministries until May 23, 1989, when he was promoted to the Archdiocese of Baltimore. He was made a cardinal priest on November 26, 1994.

The eighth bishop of Harrisburg was Nicholas C. Dattilo, who was consecrated on January 26, 1990. He began a series of consultations and reorganizations to revitalize the diocesan priorities and responses to the needs of the faithful. Bishop Dattilo died on March 5, 2004.

The ninth bishop of Harrisburg, Kevin C. Rhoades, a priest of the diocese, was appointed on October 14, 2004, and ordained a bishop on December 9, 2004. As bishop, he was active in promoting Eucharistic adoration and presided over the 100th anniversary celebration of the Cathedral of St. Patrick in 2007. He also placed a strong emphasis on promoting vocations and enjoyed considerable success, despite the absence of any Catholic colleges in the diocese. In November 2009 Bishop Rhoades was appointed the bishop of the Diocese of Fort Wayne-South Bend. On June 22, 2010, Joseph P. McFadden was named the new bishop of Harrisburg. He had served since 2004 as an auxiliary bishop of Philadelphia, and was installed on August 18, 2010. In 2011 there were 235,000 Catholics served by 173 priests, 330 women religious, and 89 parishes in the diocese.

Hartford, Archdiocese of

Established as a diocese on November 28, 1843, by Pope Gregory XVI, Hartford was erected a metropolitan provincial see, an archdiocese, on August 6, 1953, by Pope Pius XII. A state capital, the city of Hartford was originally a Dutch fort in 1633 and then called New Town (Cambridge) in 1635. Congregationalists Thomas Hooker and Samuel Stone renamed the site Hartford after Stone's birthplace, Hartford, England, in 1637. The city grew and became an industrial center and the "Insurance Capital of the World." The Archdiocese of Hartford serves counties in Connecticut and has suffragan sees in Connecticut and Rhode Island.

The Catholic heritage of Hartford opens in 1633, when Catholic colonists settled on the Connecticut River. In 1651 Jesuit Father Gabriel Druillettes visited New Haven on a diplomatic mission and was well received, despite the anti-Catholic policies of the colonial government. A century later, some four hundred Acadians arrived in the area, devout Catholics who had been forced from their homes by British authorities and deposited in hostile colonies in order to destroy their faith.

In 1781 Father Claude Robin celebrated Mass for the French troops aiding the American revolutionaries under the command of the Comte de Rochambeau. Soon after, Connecticut entered the Union, but maintained anti-Catholic laws. Catholics would not gain their civil rights and religious freedoms for another decade.

In 1808 the Diocese (now the Archdiocese) of Boston was erected, and Bishop Jean-Louis Lefe-

bvre de Cheverus, who would become a cardinal in France, visited the area of Hartford. Religious freedom was given to Catholics, and missionary labors increased. Father Bernard O'Cavanaugh was the first resident priest of the city. The Church of the Holy Trinity was opened at Hartford and dedicated by Bishop Benedict Joseph Fenwick in 1834. Bishop Fenwick, recognizing the devotion of the Catholics there, recommended the establishment of a new ecclesiastical jurisdiction for Connecticut and Rhode Island, and the Holy See erected Hartford.

The first bishop of Hartford, William Tyler, was consecrated on March 17, 1844. He chose to reside in Providence, but the designation of the see was not changed. A convert to the faith, Bishop Tyler labored to establish the offices and agencies for diocesan administration and to reduce the large debt owed by the Church at the time. He died on June 18, 1849, exhausted by his labors.

His successor was Bishop Bernard O'Reilly, who established more than twenty parishes and schools. He was consecrated as the successor of Bishop Tyler on November 10, 1850, and faced an era of severe anti-Catholic campaigns in the nation. He also faced a severe shortage of priests and had to recruit ordained missionaries for the diocese. Bishop O'Reilly brought religious communities to Hartford, including the Sisters of Mercy, who established a hospital. In January 1856 Bishop O'Reilly was lost at sea, on board the steamer *Pacific*.

His successor was Bishop Francis Patrick McFarland, who was consecrated on March 14, 1858. Bishop McFarland attended the First Vatican Council and led the diocese through the grim period of the Civil War. The rapidly growing Catholic population in the area brought about the establishment of the Diocese of Providence in 1872. Bishop McFarland resided in Hartford. He brought other religious communities into the diocese and established national parishes for the needs of the immigrants. He died on October 12, 1874.

The fourth bishop of Hartford was the Augustinian Thomas Galberry, who was consecrated on March 19, 1876. He started the diocesan newspaper and visited every parish in the diocese to improve ministries. Bishop Galberry died of a heart attack on October 10, 1878.

His successor was Bishop Lawrence Stephen McMahon, who was consecrated on August 10, 1879. Bishop McMahon opened forty-eight new parishes to serve the burgeoning Catholic population. The Knights of Columbus was founded by Father Michael J. McGivney in Hartford in 1882 with the patronage of Bishop McMahon. He also sent seminarians to European and Canadian institutes and invited more religious communities into the diocese. He died on August 21, 1893.

The sixth bishop of Hartford was Michael A. Tierney, who was consecrated on February 22, 1894. The priests of Hartford had petitioned the Holy See to consecrate Bishop Tierney, as he had served as chancellor of the diocese and as rector of the cathedral. Bishop Tierney opened diocesan hospitals, a preparatory seminary, and parochial schools. He died on October 5, 1908.

His successor was Bishop John J. Nilan, who was consecrated on April 28, 1910, after a two-year vacancy of the see. He continued expanding diocesan facilities, including social service agencies and a new seminary building. Two colleges were also founded. Bishop Nilan led the faithful of Hartford through World War I, supporting the nation's military efforts, and through the dire early years of the Great Depression. He died on April 13, 1934.

Bishop Maurice F. McAuliffe became the eighth bishop of the Diocese of Hartford and was installed on May 29, 1934. He had served as auxiliary bishop of Hartford since 1925. Bishop McAuliffe introduced the CYO into the diocese and helped to found Fairfield College in 1942. He supported the nation's military efforts in World War II and aided the workers of the diocese, promoting interracial programs. Bishop McAuliffe presided over the celebration of the centenary of the diocese in 1943. He died on December 15, 1944.

The ninth bishop and the first archbishop of Hartford was Henry J. O'Brien, who had served as auxiliary bishop of Hartford since 1940. He assumed the see on April 7, 1945. On August 6, 1953, Pope Pius XII designated Hartford as a metropolitan provincial see, and Bishop O'Brien was promoted to the rank of archbishop. Archbishop O'Brien promoted social services and housing. On New Year's Eve in 1956 a fire completely destroyed St. Joseph's Cathedral. Archbishop O'Brien started a building program immediately. He attended the Second Vatican Council and was appointed Assistant at the Pontifical Throne on April 29, 1955. Archbishop O'Brien retired on November 20, 1968.

His successor was Archbishop John F. Whealon, who had served as the auxiliary bishop of Cleveland and then as the bishop of Erie since 1967. He was installed as the archbishop of the Archdiocese of Hartford on March 19, 1969. Archbishop Whealon implemented the reforms mandated by the Second Vatican Council and was a noted biblical scholar. He taught at a local seminary, trained permanent deacons for the archdiocese, and promoted charitable and social programs. Archbishop Whealon died on August 2, 1991.

Archbishop Daniel A. Cronin succeeded Archbishop Whealon. He had served as auxiliary bishop of Boston and then as the bishop of Fall River since 1970. His installation in Hartford took place on January 28, 1992. Archbishop Cronin instituted lay ministries and outreach programs in the archdiocese. He retired on October 20, 2003.

His successor was Henry J. Mansell, who had served as auxiliary bishop of New York and then as the bishop of Buffalo since 1995. He was promoted to the Archdiocese of Hartford on October 20, 2003, and installed on December 18, 2003. As archbishop of Hartford, Archbishop Mansell helped formulate a ten-year plan in the city of Hartford to end chronic homelessness in the capitol region. He also helped to start the Malta House of Care mobile clinic, with free medical care in the inner city, and the Institute for the Hispanic Family. The archdiocese is also the center for the cause of canonization of Father Michael J. McGivney, the one-time priest of Hartford and founder of the Knights of Columbus. In 2011 there were 610,000 Catholics served by 400 priests, 669 women religious, and 213 parishes in the archdiocese.

Hartke, Gilbert (January 16, 1907–February 21, 1986)

A Dominican priest and longtime head of the drama department at The Catholic University of America, Gilbert Hartke was honored in 1981 by *Washingtonian* magazine as "one of the five most powerful men in Washington, D.C." Born in Chicago, he became fascinated with the theater as a young boy and was introduced to acting by the Chicago film colony. His first work included appearances in several early films, including *The Mischief Makers.*

Called to the priesthood, he entered the Dominicans in 1925 and was immediately placed in charge of several productions while in the seminary. He subsequently studied English at The Catholic University in 1935 and was one of the founders of the Blackfriar Institute of Dramatic Arts. On the basis of the early work of the Blackfriar Institute, Hartke was asked to start a Department of Drama in 1937. He remained head of the department for thirty-seven years. During his long time at Catholic University, Father Hartke was dedicated to promoting racial equality in the theater and to training and educating several generations of performers.

Father Hartke also served as a presidential envoy to Germany, Israel, Romania, and Korea. In addition, he was a member of the first National Council on the Arts and, at one time or another, president of the USO, Ford's Theatre, the American Educational Theatre Association, and the National Catholic Theatre Conference. He was a friend and adviser to a host of political, theatrical, and film figures, including presidents, politicians, and athletes. For his labors, he was honored as the most important figure in Catholic theater in the United States. His funeral was attended by several thousand admirers and friends.

Hassard, John (September 4, 1836–April 18, 1888)
A convert to the Catholic Church, John Hassard served as an editor and a historian. He was born in New York City, and his parents were Episcopalians, his mother the granddaughter of Commodore Willliam Nicholson of Revolutionary War fame. Hassard became a Catholic at the age of fifteen and, after graduating from St. John's College (later Fordham University) in New York, entered the diocesan seminary, intending to study for the priesthood. His poor health, however, did not allow him to undertake such a program, and he became the secretary of Archbishop John Hughes of New York. He also wrote a biography of Archbishop Hughes in 1866.

Hassard served as the first editor of the *Catholic World* magazine and as assistant editor of the *Chicago Republican*. His lifelong career, however, was with the *New York Tribune*. He served on the staff as a literary and musical critic. Hassard was one of the first in the nation to openly show respect for the music of Richard Wagner. His letters describe the festivals at Bayreuth and were among the first to advance the highest musical art forms. Hassard's impartial mind aided him in his role as a journalist, but in addition to that work and to his contributions to the magazines, he published biographies and prepared a history of the United States in both extended and abridged forms for use in Catholic colleges and schools.

Haughery, Margaret Gaffney (c. 1814–February 9, 1882)
Called affectionately "Our Margaret" by the people of New Orleans, Margaret Gaffney Haughery was also known as "Mother of Orphans." She was born in Cavan, Ireland, and brought to Baltimore, Maryland, by her parents, who both died in 1822. Margaret was not educated, but a Welsh family sheltered her in their home. In 1835 Margaret married Charles Haughery and the couple started life together in New Orleans. Within a year, Margaret lost both her husband and her infant child.

Alone in the world, she became employed in the local orphan asylum; when the orphans were without food she bought it for them from her earnings. The Female Orphan Asylum of the Sisters of Charity built in 1840 was practically her work, for she cleared it of debt. During the yellow fever epidemic in New Orleans in the 1850s she went from house to house to nurse victims and to promise dying mothers that she would look after their little ones. Margaret established a dairy and drove around the city delivering the milk herself. She then opened a bakery and for years went on her rounds with the bread cart. Margaret's bakery (the first steam bakery in the South) became famous. Seated in the doorway of the bakery in the heart of the city, she became an integral part of its life, for besides the poor who came to her continually to tell her their problems, people of all walks of life went to her to hear her prudent and wise counsel.

The people of New Orleans proudly called her "Our Margaret," and when she died, her death was announced in the newspapers with blocked

Our Margaret statue

columns as a public calamity. The archbishop of New Orleans, the governor, and the mayor were at her funeral. Margaret was buried in the grave of Sister Francis Regis Barret, the Sister of Charity who died in 1862 and with whom Margaret had cooperated in all her early work for the poor. Following her death, the people decided to raise a monument in her honor. The memorial was unveiled on July 9, 1884, and the little park in which it is erected is officially named Margaret Place.

Hawaii

Called the Aloha State, Hawaii is located in the Pacific Ocean over 2,400 miles southwest of the mainland United States. Comprising more than twenty islands in a chain, the state entered the Union in 1959. The main islands of Hawaii are the "Big Island" of Hawaii, Kahoolawe, Kauai, Lanai, Maui, Molokai, and Oahu. The islands have active volcanoes. Pearl Harbor on Oahu is the headquarters of the U.S. Pacific Fleet and was the site of the Japanese attack on December 7, 1941, that brought America into World War II. The state capital is Honolulu, also on the island of Oahu.

A people who sailed from the far western parts of the Pacific Ocean centuries ago came to the islands

and established themselves on the major islands. Each island had a chieftain until Kamehameha invaded their domains and united all the islands under his supremacy. He ruled from the later 1700s until 1819.

The visit of the first European explorer, Captain James Cook, who arrived in Hawaii in 1778, changed Hawaii forever. The islanders killed Cook during a quarrel in 1779, but the chain of islands became known as the Sandwich Islands. Cook had named them after his patron, the Earl of Sandwich. These isles beckoned to other Europeans, and traders, adventurers, and explorers arrived on their shores.

In 1820 missionaries of the Congregationalist Church in America arrived in Honolulu and won the respect of Queen Kaahumanu, who was serving as regent for the throne. Prince Liholiho, the son of King Kamehameha I, assumed the throne, becoming Kamehameha II. In 1823 he sailed with his consort, Queen Kamamalu, to England. There the royal couple was feted and honored, but they contracted measles and died of complications.

In 1826 Pope Leo XIII designated Hawaii as a prefecture apostolic and entrusted it to the Fathers of the Sacred Hearts of Jesus and Mary (Picpus Fathers). Father Alexis Jean Bachelot, SS.CC., arrived in Honolulu with companions but faced prejudice and false accusations from the entrenched American Protestant advisers of the throne. The Sacred Hearts Fathers were exiled to California.

King Kamehameha III, however, discovered a French warship in the harbor of Honolulu on July 9, 1839. The captain, Cyril P. T. La Place, informed the Hawaiians that they were now officially at war with His Catholic Majesty of France because of the ill-treatment of French missionaries, the complete disregard for the diplomatic courtesies used throughout the world, and the bigotry demonstrated against the Catholic faith. Kamehameha III had issued "An Ordinance Rejecting the Catholic Religion" on December 18, 1837, at Lahaina, Maui. He was now forced to accept five French demands in order to save Honolulu, because Captain La Place intended to attack the city with his artillery pieces unless Kamehameha III complied with his demands. Catholics were given religious freedom and basic civil rights as a result, and

Catholic prisoners, all island converts, were freed. A site was made available for a Catholic church in Honolulu.

The Sacred Hearts Congregation returned to Hawaii, joined by Sacred Hearts Sisters, and parishes and educational institutions were opened. A line of apostolic prefects administered Catholic affairs on all the islands as the faith prospered.

One of the early priests serving the islands was ordained on May 21, 1864, in the Cathedral of Our Lady of Peace in Honolulu. He had arrived in Hawaii only two months before as a volunteer of the congregation to the missions. His name was Damien de Veuster, now St. Damien, the "Hero of Molokai." St. Marianne Cope led a group of Franciscan Sisters to Hawaii, landing in Honolulu in November 1883. The Marianists, Christian Brothers, Maryknoll, and other congregations came to serve also.

American influences were changing the islands during St. Damien's era, as industrial companies assumed island agricultural projects. In 1893 Queen Liliuokalani, the ruler of Hawaii, was overthrown by American businessmen, and in 1898, Hawaii became an American territory.

During World War I, Hawaii served as a military outpost and naval center. The faith continued to grow on all the islands, and the Sacred Hearts Fathers continued to serve as prefects. Pope Pius XII, on September 10, 1941, erected the Diocese of Honolulu in recognition of the history of devotion in the islands. Bishop James J. Sweeney was appointed to Honolulu, just as the Japanese attacked Pearl Harbor and brought America into World War II on December 7, 1941.

The buildup of necessary military commands on the islands along with the increased Catholic population in Hawaii brought about demands for chaplains. After the war, the Catholic population continued to grow, and Bishop John J. Scanlan, Bishop Sweeney's successor, built parishes and schools to meet the needs of the faithful. His successors maintained the levels of social and religious programs in the islands. Bishop Clarence Silva, appointed in 2005, became the first native-born islander to be installed as the bishop of Honolulu. In 2011 there were 221,000 Catholics served by 129 priests, 148 women religious, and 66 parishes in the state.

Hawthorne, Mother Alphonsa (Lathrop) (May 20, 1851–July 9, 1926)

The younger daughter of the American novelist Nathaniel Hawthorne, Mother Alphonsa was the founder of the Congregation of St. Rose of Lima, the Hawthorne Dominicans. She was born Rose Hawthorne in Lenox, Massachusetts, and at the age of two was taken to England, where her father served as the U.S. consul in Liverpool. After seven years, the family moved to Italy, and she had the opportunity to see Rome.

Mother Alphonsa had been raised as a Unitarian, but she had knowledge of the Catholic faith from her Italian experiences. When the family returned to the United States to reside at "The Wayside," a residence in Concord, she asked to return to Europe to continue her studies. Mother Alphonsa attended educational programs in Dresden, Germany, and then in London.

She married George Lathrop, an American writer, and they lived in the United States. He became an assistant editor of the *Atlantic Monthly* and wrote *A Study of Hawthorne.* A son, Francis, was born to the couple, who began writing together when George found himself unemployed. Mother Alphonsa published *Along the Shore* in 1888. In 1881 Francis died, and the couple sold the house and moved to New York and then to New London, Connecticut. Three years later they published *A Story of Courage,* a study of the Visitation order in America. The couple converted to Catholicism in 1891, receiving approval and disapproval from their friends and families. Because of marital difficulties, in part a result of George's drinking problem, she left him permanently in 1895. Alphonsa wrote *Memories of Hawthorne* in 1897, and she was able to purchase The Wayside, which had been sold earlier.

Mother Alphonsa began to perform charitable work in New York, having been advised by a priest friend of the horrors of terminal-cancer wards in existence at the time. She rented an apartment and cared for the poor ill, conducting a fundraising and information campaign. Young women became interested in her work, especially one named Alice Huber. On April 19, 1897, George died, freeing Mother Alphonsa to embrace a religious vocation. In 1899 St. Rose's Free House was in operation. Mother Alphonsa and Alice became Dominican

Tertiaries that same year. In 1900 the community formed by Mother Alphonsa accepted habits and became an official religious congregation. Mother Alphonsa moved to Rosary Hill, New York, and there established a motherhouse. She died peacefully in her sleep, knowing that young women would carry on her work with the ill and poor. Her cause for canonization was opened in 2003.

Hayes, Carlton (May 16, 1882–September 2, 1964)

A diplomat and historian, Carlton Hayes was the U.S. ambassador to Spain and the co-founder of the National Conference of Christians and Jews. He was born in Afton, New York, to Philetus Arthur Hayes and Permilia Mary Huntley Hayes. Hayes entered Columbia University in 1900 and received his doctorate eight years later, then joined the faculty. He became the Seth Low Professor of History from 1935 to 1950. In 1945 he was elected president of the American Historical Association. Hayes also wrote respected historical studies and a high school history text. Pioneering European theories, Hayes wrote about the destructive elements appearing in European nationalist views in the twentieth century.

In 1920 Hayes married Mary Evelyn Carroll, and four years later he converted to the Catholic Church. He became a co-founder of the National Conference of Christians and Jews, the president of the American Catholic Historical Association and a member of the original editorial council of *Commonweal*. In 1942 President Franklin Delano Roosevelt appointed him ambassador to Spain, an office he held until 1945. Hayes wrote a defense of his cordiality to the Francisco Franco regime upon his return to the United States. His book, *Wartime Mission in Spain*, detailed his influence in preventing Spain from joining the Axis during World War II. In 1950 Hayes retired to his farm in Afton, where he died.

Hayes, Helen (October 10, 1900–March 17, 1993)

A popular stage, screen, and television actress, Helen Hayes had a career spanning sixty years. She was the daughter of Francis van Arnum Brown and his wife, Catherine Estelle Hayes, and was educated at Sacred Heart Academy in Washington, D.C. In 1920 she appeared on Broadway in a short-lived play. Helen Hayes did not give up her desire for acting, however, and she starred in many Broadway productions, including *Mary of Scotland* (1933), *Victoria Regina* (1935), *The Glass Menagerie* (1948 and in subsequent revivals) and *Harvey* (1970). The winner of two Academy Awards for *The Sins of Madelon Claudet* and *Airport*, she also won Emmy and Tony Awards.

Married to Charles McArthur, Helen Hayes had a daughter, born in 1930, and an adopted son, James McArthur. When the daughter died in 1950, Charles McArthur was inconsolable, and he died seven years later. Helen Hayes continued to work and to contribute her time and energies to Catholic and charitable causes. She received the Laetare Medal from the University of Notre Dame in 1972. Helen Hayes wrote an autobiography, *My Life in Three Acts*, in 1990. She died in Nyack, New York, of congestive heart failure.

Hayes, Patrick Joseph (November 20, 1867–September 4, 1938)

A popular and influential Catholic cardinal, Patrick Joseph Hayes was the archbishop of New York, but also served as a prominent statesman. He was born in New York City, the son of Daniel and Mary Gleason Hayes. Educated at Manhattan College in New York City and at St. Joseph's Seminary in Troy, New York, he was ordained on September 8, 1892. He also completed graduate studies at The Catholic University of America, earning a licentiate in sacred theology in 1894.

After ordination, Father Hayes was assigned to pastoral work in St. Gabriel's Parish in Manhattan, serving under Monsignor John Murphy Farley. In 1902 he became the secretary to Bishop (later Archbishop) Farley, who had been made an auxiliary of the archdiocese. One year later, Father Hayes was appointed chancellor of the archdiocese and president of Catholic College in New York; Archbishop Farley made the appointments. He was made a domestic prelate on October 15, 1907, and on July 3, 1914, was appointed auxiliary of New York. He was also appointed Military Vicar of the United States Armed Forces on November 24, 1917.

Bishop Hayes was promoted to the metropolitan see of New York and installed in the archdiocese on

March 10, 1919, as the successor to Cardinal Farley. He began his leadership by unifying Catholic welfare activities under Catholic Charities, a concern he supported throughout his life. He was called the "Cardinal of Charities" because of his sustained aid to programs that benefited those in need. Archbishop Hayes also aided the founding of the National Catholic Welfare Conference, the National League of Decency, and the Cardinal Hayes Literature Commission. He established more than sixty new parishes in the archdiocese, despite the changing demographics of the era, as suburban communities grew.

Cardinal Patrick Hayes

On March 24, 1924, Pope Benedict XV created him a cardinal priest, with the titular church of Santa Maria in Via. On August 20, 1935, Cardinal Hayes served as the personal representative of Pope Pius XI at the National Eucharistic Congress in Cleveland. In 1932 he suffered a massive heart attack and restricted his activities thereafter. He died in his sleep at St. Joseph's Camp in Monticello, New York. He was buried under the altar of St. Patrick's Cathedral in New York.

Hazotte, Mary Agnes (May 7, 1847–March 5, 1905)

Co-foundress of the Congregation of Sisters of St. Agnes, with Father Caspar Rehrl, Mother Agnes was born in Buffalo, New York, to a family of French immigrants. She grew up in Detroit and endured a severe family tragedy that claimed the lives of her father, two sisters, and a brother. In 1860 Agnes's mother died. Two years later, she first encountered the recently established Congregation of Sisters of St. Agnes in Barton, Wisconsin. The community had been established by Father Rehrl with the purpose of educating children of immigrants, and he had encountered much difficulty in convincing religious women from Europe to help him in his work. He had thus secured approval from Pope Blessed Pius IX to establish at Barton a community of young pioneer women under the patronage of St. Agnes of Rome. The Congregation of the Sisters of St. Agnes began officially on

August 12, 1858, with the entry of three young women.

The early days of the community were a time of great struggle, but the arrival of Hazotte in 1863 marked the decisive turning point in the fortunes of the congregation. Received into the community as Sister Mary Agnes, she was elected its general superior the following year on her profession day, at the age of seventeen. Soon after, Sister Agnes and Father Rehrl disagreed on the best use of the resources of the community. Rehrl wanted to place sisters and candidates directly into ministry after a brief training period, while Sister Agnes believed that more time was needed to ensure their proper preparation. In June 1870 Father Rehrl resigned as director of the congregation, in large measure because of his exhaustion and advancing age.

In the months that followed, the community stood on the verge of extinction, but vital assistance was provided by Father Francis Haas, a Capuchin Franciscan, who revised Father Rehrl's earlier rule and gave spiritual direction to the sisters. Through the intervention of Father Haas the institute was not disbanded, and Sister Agnes led a small group of sisters to Fond du Lac, Wisconsin, in 1870. The members of the institute took up work in schools and overcame more hardships and challenges to grow over the next decades and take over direction of schools in Indiana, Illinois, Kansas, Michigan, New York, Ohio, Pennsylvania, and Texas. Mother Agnes also took over a hospital and dispatched sisters to New York to operate a home for the safety of newly arrived immigrants. Repeatedly reelected as head of the community, Mother Agnes died at the age of fifty-eight from exhaustion after years of ceaseless labor and dedication.

Healy, George Peter Alexander (July 15, 1813–June 24, 1894)

An American portrait and historical painter, George Peter Alexander Healy was internationally honored in his lifetime. He was born in Boston, the eldest of five children. The family was left fatherless early, and Healy helped to support his mother. When sixteen years of age he began drawing; at eighteen he began painting portraits and was soon very successful. In 1834 he went to Europe, leaving his mother well provided for, and remained abroad sixteen years, during which he studied with Baron Antoine Jean Gros and won in 1840 a third-class medal in the Salon. His *Franklin Urging the Claims of the Colonists Before Louis XVI* gained him a second-class gold medal at the Paris International Exhibition of 1855.

Healy returned to Chicago in 1855, where he remained until 1869, when he again visited the Continent, painting steadily, chiefly in Rome and Paris, for twenty-one years. He painted more portraits than any other American artist, and of more eminent men than any other artist in the world, including Pope Blessed Pius IX, Bismarck, Abraham Lincoln, Ulysses S. Grant, Cardinal John McCloskey, King Louis Philippe, Daniel Webster, Henry Wadsworth Longfellow, and eleven U.S. presidents. Healy was an honorary member of the National Academy of Design and wrote a delightful book, *Reminiscences of a Portrait Painter*. He died in Chicago.

Healy, James Augustine (April 6, 1830–August 5, 1900)

The first African-American bishop in the United States, James Augustine Healy was appointed as the second bishop of Portland and served from 1875 to 1890. He was the son of an Irish immigrant father and an African-American mother, and was born near Macon, Georgia. He had two brothers who also became prominent priests. Graduating from Holy Cross and the Grand Seminary of Saint-Sulpice in Montréal and in Paris, he was ordained in 1854. Father Healy was then assigned as the secretary of the bishop, becoming diocesan chancellor and vicar general in 1857. He founded St. James Church and promoted charitable institutions, including St. Anne's Foundling Home, the Catholic Laymen's Union, the House of the Good Shepherd, and the Home for Destitute Children.

Bishop James Healy

On June 2, 1875, he was consecrated as the second bishop of Portland, Maine. There he served for a quarter of a century and was known as the "Children's Bishop." Bishop Healy founded sixty parishes, sixty-eight mission stations, and eighteen schools and convents. He also served as a consultant to the U.S. Bureau of Indian Affairs. He died in Portland.

Hecker, Isaac Thomas (December 18, 1819–December 22, 1888)

The founder of the Congregation of Missionary Priests of St. Paul the Apostle, the Paulists, Isaac Thomas Hecker was a convert and a figure of international controversy. He was born in New York City, the son of German immigrants, John and Caroline Freund Hecker. A reverse in the family fortune made it necessary for Isaac, who was the youngest of three sons, to begin work at the age of eleven, helping his elder brothers in their business as bakers. While working in the bakery, he studied philosophical writers and social theses.

He was concerned about the social conditions of American workingmen and went out into the streets to make speeches. He was a friend and correspondent of Orestes A. Brownson and lived in a community in Brook Farm in Massachusetts with the family of Henry David Thoreau. His studies led him to the faith, and he converted to Catholicism in 1844.

A year later, he entered the Redemptorists and studied for the priesthood in Clapham, London, and he was ordained in 1849. Father Hecker was assigned to parishes in England but returned to the United States in 1851 and began evangelizing Catholics and non-Catholics. This apostolate led Father Hecker and his companions to consider establishing a congregation that would adapt to American culture and evangelize the young. He proposed such a congregation to the Holy See in 1857 and was subsequently dismissed from the Redemptorists with his companions.

Pope Blessed Pius IX supported the formation of the Paulists, the Congregation of Missionary Priests of St. Paul the Apostle.

Father Hecker served as superior of the Paulists and gave missions across the country. He also served as an adviser to Archbishop Martin J. Spalding at the Second Plenary Council of Baltimore in 1866 and at the First Vatican Council. Father Hecker developed an apologetic that stressed the benefits of American culture and political traditions and promoted the apostolate of the press among Catholics in America. He organized the Catholic Publication Society, founded and edited the *Catholic World* magazine, directed *The Young Catholic*, a paper for children, and created a new movement in Catholic literary activities. Father Hecker was the author of three books, *Questions of the Soul, The Aspirations of Nature*, and *The Church and the Age*. Following his death, the Americanist controversy raged across Europe and prompted Pope Leo XIII's encyclical *Testem Benevolentiae* in 1899. (*See also* Americanism.)

Isaac Hecker

Heckler, Margaret M. *See* Cabinets, Catholics in Presidential

Heeney, Cornelius (1754–May 3, 1848)

A successful businessman and philanthropist, Cornelius Heeney helped establish old St. Patrick's Cathedral in New York. He was born in King's County, Ireland, and migrated to New York in 1784. For a time, he was a partner of John Jacob Astor in fur trading and then established his own merchant business. He also served as a patron of John McCloskey, the future cardinal archbishop of New York, and gave time and money to Catholic charities. In possession of a considerable fortune and a bachelor, he devoted his income to Catholic programs. He was one of the first Catholics to hold public office in New York, and he served five terms in the State Assembly beginning in 1818. In 1837 Heeney retired from business and went to live in Brooklyn, New York, where he continued his charitable benefactions. He also secured his estate under a legislative act of incorporation, and over time the

society he founded for distribution of the money gave Catholic programs more than a million dollars. Heeney died in Brooklyn.

Heiss, Michael (April 12, 1818–March 26, 1890)

The first bishop of the Diocese of La Crosse, Michael Heiss also served as the second archbishop of the Archdiocese of Milwaukee. Born in Pfahldorf, Bavaria, he studied theology at the University of Munich and was ordained on October 18, 1840. After ordination, he served for two years in his home diocese of Eichstaett and then volunteered for service in the American missions. He first held a pastoral post in St. Mary's Church in Covington, Kentucky, and then was asked to take up the post of episcopal secretary in 1844 to Bishop John M. Henni of Milwaukee.

After several years of dedicated work as the bishop's secretary, Father Heiss was appointed pastor of St. Mary's Church in Milwaukee. In 1856 he was named the first rector of St. Francis Seminary. During his time as rector, he encouraged vocations among German-speaking Catholic men to serve the German Catholics of the archdiocese. He remained as rector until 1868, when he was appointed the first bishop of La Crosse on March 3, 1868, and was ordained a bishop on September 6, 1868. Bishop Heiss proved a dedicated shepherd. He traveled extensively throughout the region and worked to improve Church institutions in the fledgling diocese. He also attended the First Vatican Council.

In 1878 Archbishop Henni expressed his desire for a coadjutor archbishop and put forward Bishop Heiss's name as the most ideal candidate. Bishop Heiss was finally named coadjutor with right of succession on April 9, 1880. Upon the passing of Archbishop Henni in 1881, Bishop Heiss succeeded him as archbishop on September 7, 1881.

Archbishop Heiss served during a time of tension between English-speaking and German-speaking Catholics in the archdiocese. He was a supporter of the rights of German-speaking Catholics. He thus opposed the 1889 Bennett Law that required English-only instruction in Wisconsin schools, but he also allowed English to be taught in parish schools.

Elsewhere, Archbishop Heiss worked to stabilize the finances of the archdiocese, introduced a parish tax, established the first archdiocesan school board, and regularized the legal status of parishes. In 1883 he was invited to Rome to take part in the deliberations that would prepare for the Third Plenary Council of Baltimore; he also attended the council in 1884. In 1886 he convoked the First Provincial Council of Milwaukee and opened its sessions in St. John's Cathedral.

Archbishop Heiss was well known in the American Church for his theological knowledge. He was thus given a position on the Dogmatic Commission at the First Vatican Council, and his theological writings — such as *De Matrimonio* (1861) and *The Four Gospels Examined and Vindicated on Catholic Principles* (1863) — were highly esteemed. Archbishop Heiss died in La Crosse and was buried, according to his own wishes, beneath the chapel at St. Francis Seminary.

Helena, Diocese of

Established on March 7, 1884, by Pope Leo XIII, the Diocese of Helena serves counties in western Montana. Helena was founded in 1864, just a few months after gold was discovered at Last Chance Gulch, now part of the city's main street. Mining and refining industries, as well as farming, tourism, and sheep raising sustain the economy of Helena, which also serves as the state capital. The Diocese of Helena is a suffragan see of the Archdiocese of Portland in Oregon.

The Catholic heritage of Helena opened in 1743 when Jesuit Father Claude G. Coquart arrived in the area, accompanying the expedition of Pierre Gaultier de Varennes, Sieur de La Vérendrye, in the region. Catholic missionaries were established for the local Indian tribes near modern-day Helena soon after. John Jacob Astor erected fur-trading posts in the early 1800s, and by 1840 Jesuit Father Pierre-Jean De Smet, the revered missionary of the western United States, served these posts and extended his mission rounds into the territory. He and other Jesuits established St. Mary's in the Bitterroot Valley in 1841.

The eastern part of Montana was then included in the Vicariate Apostolic of Nebraska, and the western part of Montana was in the Vicariate Apostolic of Idaho. In 1877 the Montana Territory became an independent vicariate apostolic, headed by Bishop John Baptist Brondel, who had served as the bishop of Victoria. The Sisters of Charity of Leavenworth, Kansas, were teaching at various educational institutions in the area at the time.

When the Diocese of Helena was erected, Bishop Brondel was appointed as the ordinary on March 7, 1884. He established the offices and agencies for diocesan administration and then established forty-nine churches and ten schools, traveling to the remotest parts of the diocese, and convened diocesan synods. He also petitioned the Holy See to divide the diocese because of its vastness. This pioneering bishop died on November 3, 1903.

His successor was Bishop John Patrick Carroll, who was consecrated on December 21, 1904. The Diocese of Great Falls was established on May 18, 1904, and Helena assumed its present boundaries. Bishop Carroll founded Mount St. Charles College, now Carroll College, and invited religious congregations to Helena. He also built the Cathedral of St. Helena, which had been opened as a parish in 1866. Bishop Carroll led the diocese through the era of World War I while erecting thirty-two parishes and promoting Catholic education. He died on November 4, 1925.

Bishop George J. Finnigan was the third bishop and the first Holy Cross priest to be appointed as a bishop of a diocese in the United States. He was consecrated on August 1, 1927. Soon after, the Great Depression brought economic suffering to the nation. Bishop Finnigan introduced the Confraternity of Christian Doctrine to Helena and established charitable programs to aid the needy. He supported Carroll College, founded the diocesan newspaper, and took a great interest in the Blackfeet Indians, being adopted into the tribe in 1928. Bishop Finnigan died on August 14, 1932.

His successor was Bishop Ralph Leo Hayes, who was consecrated on September 21, 1933. Bishop Hayes was appointed rector of the North American College in Rome on September 11, 1935. Soon after, a series of severe earthquakes struck the area of Helena. Catholic institutions and facilities were damaged, and dioceses across the United States contributed to a fund to aid the stricken city.

Bishop Joseph M. Gilmore was consecrated on February 19, 1936, as Bishop Hayes's successor. He set about rebuilding the Catholic institutions in the diocese and established Catholic social services. Bishop Gilmore also aided the local Native Americans and promoted the lay apostolate in Helena. He led the faithful during World War II, and in 1941 celebrated the centennial of the arrival of the Catholic Church in Montana. The Diamond Jubilee of the diocese was celebrated in 1959. Bishop Gilmore died in San Francisco on April 2, 1962.

His successor was Bishop Raymond G. Hunthausen, who was consecrated on August 30, 1962. He attended the Second Vatican Council and implemented the reforms of that council. Bishop Hunthausen established a diocesan pastoral council, the Diocesan Ecumenical Commission, as well as the Montana Catholic Conference on Social Welfare. He also opened a mission in Guatemala. On February 25, 1975, he was promoted to the Archdiocese of Seattle.

Bishop Elden Francis Curtiss was appointed as the seventh bishop of Helena on March 4, 1976, and was consecrated on April 28. Bishop Curtiss faced a shortage of priests and religious and worked to revitalize the diocese. He started renewal programs, convened a diocesan synod, and established parish councils and the program of formation of lay ministries. Bishop Curtiss also focused on youth programs for the region. On May 4, 1993, Bishop Curtiss was promoted to the Archdiocese of Omaha.

His successor was Bishop Alexander J. Brunett, who was consecrated on July 6, 1994. He conducted diocesanwide visitations and promoted ecumenism. Educational programs were also part of Bishop Brunett's ministry. On October 28, 1997, he was promoted to the Archdiocese of Seattle.

The ninth bishop of Helena was Robert C. Morlino. He was appointed to Helena on July 6, 1999, and was consecrated and installed in the diocese on September 21. Bishop Morlino was transferred to the Diocese of Madison on May 23, 2003.

His successor, Bishop George L. Thomas, had served as auxiliary bishop of the Archdiocese of Seattle since 1999. He was promoted to the Diocese of Helena on March 23, 2004, and installed on June 4, 2004. In 2011 there were 45,000 Catholics served by 80 priests and 57 parishes in the diocese.

Hellriegel, Martin B. (November 9, 1980–April 10, 1981)

A protonotary apostolic, Martin B. Hellriegel was one of the leading figures of the twentieth-century liturgical movement inspired by Pope St. Pius X. A native of Heppenheim, Germany, he journeyed to the United States in 1906 and entered St. Meinrad's Seminary in Indiana in 1909. He remained there for a year and then completed his studies at Kenrick Seminary in St. Louis. Ordained a priest on December 20, 1914, he served as a parish priest in St. Charles, Missouri, and then was the long-time chaplain to the Sisters of the Most Precious Blood in O'Fallon, Missouri, from 1918 to 1940, and pastor and pastor emeritus of Holy Cross Parish in St. Louis from 1940 to 1981. He was named a monsignor in 1940 and protonotary apostolic in 1964.

At an early period in his life he became deeply committed to the liturgical movement launched by Pope St. Pius X in 1903, and he was soon known as a major liturgical innovator in the period before the Second Vatican Council, especially in light of the renewal promoted by Pope Pius XII in the 1947 encyclical *Mediator Dei*. He was especially in favor of the active participation of the faithful and the role of public and solemn prayer. In the period after the Second Vatican Council, his own parish became a model for liturgical renewal through the authentic implementation of the council's Constitution on the Sacred Liturgy, *Sacrosanctum Concilium*.

In 1925 Hellriegel founded with noted liturgists Virgil Michel, O.S.B., and Gerald Ellard, S.J., the liturgical journal *Orate Fratres* (later *Worship*). He also wrote extensively, lectured, and helped to found the Liturgical Conference, of which he served as president. In addition, he edited the monthly magazine *The Living Parish* from 1940 to 1956 and contributed to the *National Liturgical Week's Proceedings*.

Henderson, Isaac A. (1850–March 1909)

A writer, Isaac A. Henderson was a convert to the Church. He was born in Brooklyn, New York, to a Scottish-Irish family. He studied at Williams College and earned a doctorate in civil law before taking a position in 1872 with the *New York Evening Post*; his father was joint owner of the newspaper with William Cullen Bryant and John Bigelow. He became assistant publisher in 1875 and from 1877 served as publisher, stockholder, and member of the Board of Trustees.

Henderson sold his interest in the *Evening Post* in 1881 and went to live in London and Rome. He published his first novel, *The Prelate*, in 1886, followed by *Agatha Page* in 1888. The latter was turned into a stage play in 1892 (as *The Silent Battle* in London and *Agatha* in Boston). A second drama, *The Mummy and the Humming Bird*, opened in 1901 in Boston and moved to Broadway the following year.

Henderson converted to Catholicism in 1896 and took the name of Austin at his confirmation. In 1903 he was honored with an appointment as a private chamberlain to Pope St. Pius X. He devoted much of his time to charitable fundraising and supporting the needs of poor children in Rome, in particular those of the Trastevere quarter. He died in Rome.

Hennepin, Louis (May 12, 1626–after 1701)

A Recollect Franciscan missionary, Louis Hennepin was an explorer in America and a prisoner of the Sioux. He was born at Ath, Hainaut, Belgium. Entering the novitiate of the Recollect Franciscans Order at Béthune, province of Artois (now the department of Pas-de-Calais), France, he studied for the priesthood and was ordained. Shortly after his ordination, Father Hennepin made a journey to Italy and then was appointed as a preacher in Halles in Hainaut for a year. He went to Artois and Calais and journeyed as a missionary to most of the towns of Holland. At Maastricht he remained for eight consecutive months during the year 1673 and was in the midst of the war then in progress between the French and the Spanish. At the Battle of Seneffe in 1674, Father Hennepin ministered to the wounded. He then received orders from his superiors to go to Canada as a missionary, and he set sail on July 14, 1675, for the New World.

Father Hennepin was a member of an expedition under the leadership of René-Robert Chevalier, Sieur de la Salle, who had recently been endowed with a title and had been appointed to the governorship of Fort Frontenac in modern-day Canada. Father Hennepin served as a preacher in Québec. He was assigned to this duty by Blessed François de Montmorency Laval, newly appointed bishop of Québec, who had been a passenger on the ship that brought Hennepin to New France.

Father Hennepin then was sent with Father Luke Buisset to take care of a mission at Fort Frontenac on the north shore of Lake Ontario near the headwaters of the St. Lawrence River.

On September 18, 1678, La Salle started his expedition by sending forward a detachment to establish a post on the Niagara River near Lake Erie. On January 20, 1679, La Salle arrived at the place and took command. During the winter months, Father Hennepin went to Fort Frontenac but returned to the Niagara outpost shortly before July 30, 1679, accompanied by two other Recollect Fathers, Gabriel de la Ribourde and Zenobius Membré.

Father Hennepin was instructed by La Salle to proceed down the Illinois River and then up the Mississippi River as far as possible upon a voyage

Louis Hennepin Memorial

of discovery. He traveled with two Frenchmen and started out on February 29, 1680, soon after reaching the Mississippi River and turning northward. On April 12 the priest and his companions were captured by a band of Sioux, who took the three explorers on a nineteen-day journey to their home settlement.

Whenever the Sioux moved about from place to place in their territory, the Franciscan and the two other captives were forced to accompany them. During one of their excursions the wanderers stopped at the great cataract in the Mississippi that is now encircled by the city of Minneapolis and that still bears the name of St. Anthony Falls, given to it by Father Hennepin in honor of St. Anthony of Padua.

Soon after, the famous French explorer Daniel Greysolon, Sieur du Lhut, came into the area and managed to have Father Hennepin and his companions released. The Franciscan made his way gradually to Montréal, where he made a report to the Comte de Frontenac, the governor-general of New France, concerning his wanderings and experiences. At the request of the governor-general and his guest, Father Hennepin proceeded to Québec. He retired to a cloister to recuperate and then sailed for Europe.

Father Hennepin resided in a monastery of his order at St.-Germain-en-Laye, during which period he published his first book about his explorations and adventures. The book was printed at Paris and was issued in January 1683. In 1697 Father Hennepin published another book at Utrecht, in which he claimed for the first time that he had traversed not only the upper but the lower Mississippi, and had traced the course of the stream to its outlet in the Gulf of Mexico. Because the time involved in such a journey cannot be certified, many historians and historical critics denounced him as "an arrant falsifier." Father Hennepin lost the favor of the French monarch as a result and dedicated a book to William III of England. He spent his last years in Rome, where he died.

Henni, John M. (1805–September 7, 1881)

The first bishop and archbishop of Milwaukee, John M. Henni was a pioneering missionary in the United States. He was born in Misanenga, Swit-

zerland, and was educated at St. Gall and Lucerne and then at the Urban College of the Propaganda in Rome. There he met Father Frederick Résé, who would serve as the first bishop of the Diocese of Detroit, and volunteered for the American missions. In 1828 he arrived in the United States and completed his theological studies at Bardstown, Kentucky, and was ordained by Bishop Edward D. Fenwick on February 2, 1829.

Father Henni traveled throughout Ohio after his ordination, settling in Canton and then in Cincinnati, where he served the German Catholics of the area. He also founded a German Catholic newspaper in 1837. In 1843 the Diocese of Milwaukee was erected, and Father Henni was appointed the first bishop. This ecclesiastical jurisdiction included all of the territory of Wisconsin and part of eastern Minnesota. Bishop Henni traveled throughout the diocese, which reportedly had a Catholic population of about nine thousand, and he built a cathedral and a seminary. St. John's Cathedral was constructed in 1853, and St. Francis de Sales Seminary was in operation three years later.

Attracting vast numbers of German Catholics migrating to the United States, Bishop Henni invited German religious congregations to the diocese and opened a German Catholic press. He attended the First Vatican Council and supported the erection of the Dioceses of Green Bay and La Crosse. In 1875 Milwaukee was established as a metropolitan provincial see, and he was promoted to the rank of archbishop. Archbishop Henni continued consolidating diocesan facilities until his health deteriorated. He died in Milwaukee.

Herbermann, Charles George (December 8, 1840–August 24, 1916)

An author, editor, and educator, Charles George Herbermann was a co-founder of the United States Catholic Historical Society and editor of the *Catholic Encyclopedia*. He was born in Saerbeck, Westphalia, Germany, and was brought to New York by his parents in 1851. In 1858 he graduated from St. Francis Xavier College and then earned his doctorate while on the faculty of the college.

Herbermann joined the faculty of the College of New York City and with John Gilmary Shea founded the United States Catholic Historical Society in 1884, serving as president of the organization from 1898 until his death. In 1905 Herbermann became editor-in-chief of the *Catholic Encyclopedia*, despite gradually losing his vision. In recognition of his outstanding service to the American Catholic Church and his historical documentation of the Catholic experience, Herbermann received the Order of St. Gregory in 1909, the *Pro Ecclesia et Pontifice* medal from Pope St. Pius X and numerous other honors. He died in New York City.

Hesburgh, Theodore. *See* Notre Dame, University of

Hess, Bede (Frederick John) (November 16, 1885–August 8, 1953)

An American Franciscan Conventual, Bede (Frederick John) Hess saved the town of Assisi and the Basilica of St. Francis from the Nazis in World War II. He was born in Trenton, New Jersey, and was educated at St. Francis College. In November 1900 he entered the novitiate of the Friars Minor Conventual and was educated in the United States and at Innsbruck, Austria. On July 26, 1908, he was ordained and later that year was awarded a doctorate of theology.

Father Bede was assigned to Trenton for a time and then assumed leadership positions within the order, including minister general. He was in Assisi when the commanding Nazi general of the region was ordered to destroy the town and the basilica when the German forces withdrew. Father Bede was asked to intercede because of his fluency in German, and he petitioned the Nazi general to spare the holy sites and the city. The general, a Catholic, was willing to hear Father Bede's pleas and agreed that the destruction of the basilica was out of the question, even though it would cost him dearly for not obeying a command. The retreating German units did not damage Assisi, and the basilica remained safe. Father Bede lived the rest of his life in the city that he had protected and was elected minister general for a third term in 1948. He died there.

Heuser, Herman Joseph (October 23, 1851 or 1852–August 22, 1933)

A priest, professor, and editor, Herman Joseph Heuser was the founding editor of *American Ecclesiastical Review* from 1899 to 1914 and the founding editor of the *Dolphin* from 1900 to 1908. He was born in Potsdam, Prussia, and was educated at Breslau. Moving to Philadelphia in 1868, he entered the seminary at Glen Riddle, Pennsylvania, and then completed his priestly studies at St. Charles Seminary in Overbrook, Pennsylvania. He was ordained on February 2, 1876.

In January 1899 Father Heuser founded the *American Ecclesiastical Review* and labored to make Catholicism known and understood by the people of the United States in his era. He was particularly concerned about recruiting priestly intellectuals who could counter Americanism and modernism in the country. He also founded the short-lived *Dolphin*, directed at American lay Catholics. Father Heuser was profoundly interested in a variety of fields concerning the faith and was a close friend of St. Katharine Drexel. Pope St. Pius X honored him in 1905. He died in Philadelphia.

Hewit, Augustine F. (November 27, 1829–July 3, 1897)

One of the founders of the Paulists, Augustine F. Hewit served as the second superior general of the congregation. He was born at Fairfield, Connecticut, the son of the prominent Congregationalist minister Nathaniel Hewit and Rebecca Hillhouse Hewit, a daughter of James Hillhouse, United States senator from Connecticut. Augustine graduated from Amherst College in 1839 at which time he finally began to take part in the services of the Congregationalists, owing to his long-standing reluctance to embrace the teachings of the church. Having joined the community, he commenced theological studies at the Congregationalist seminary at East Windsor, Connecticut.

Almost immediately after his graduation, however, Hewit converted to the Episcopal Church and became one of the most dedicated members of the Oxford Movement in America. Ordained a deacon in 1844, he was soon influenced by the departure of John Henry Newman to the Catholic Church the following year and likewise entered the Church in March 1846. He proceeded to study theology with the help of Dr. Patrick N. Lynch (later bishop of Charleston) and Dr. James A. Corcoran and was ordained the following year by Bishop Ignatius A. Reynolds of Charleston.

After serving as a teacher, Father Hewit entered the Congregation of the Most Holy Redeemer (the Redemptorists) in 1849 and made his religious profession in November 1850. During his time as a Redemptorist, he worked with Fathers Isaac Thomas Hecker, Clarence A. Walworth, Francis A. Baker, and George Deshon until 1858, when he helped to establish the Paulists in New York. He was chosen to write the first constitution and laws of the Paulists and was instrumental in managing the publication *Catholic World* founded in 1865 by Father Hecker. A noted writer and apologist, Hewit was a regular contributor to *Catholic World* and the *American Catholic Quarterly Review*. His best known books were *The Life of Reverend Francis A. Baker* and *The King's Highway*.

With the death of Father Hecker in 1888, Father Hewit was elected superior general of the institute and remained in office until his own passing. As superior he gave his strong commitment to The Catholic University of America at Washington, D.C., and St. Thomas College — intended as a place of study for candidates of the institute — was opened on the grounds of the university in 1889. He died in New York City.

Hibernians, Ancient Order of

An American fraternal and social association whose members are Catholics of Irish descent, the Ancient Order of Hibernians claims its roots in Ireland, where Catholics banded together in various secret societies to preserve Irish faith and culture in the face of centuries of English oppression on the isle. When the Irish began their extensive migration to the United States, they found similar intolerance and anti-Catholicism in American cities. Again for security, self-preservation, and keeping the faith in the face of attacks and prejudice, many Irish formed similar bands and societies, such as the Hibernian Sick and Funeral Society, the St Patrick's Fraternal Society, the Charitable Irish Society, the Corkonians, and the O'Connell Guards.

By the 1830s the different Irish societies decided that there would be even greater strength in numbers. On St. Patrick's Day in 1836 members of the Hibernian Benevolent Society of Pennsylvania made their way to New York's annual parade and met with their counterparts in the St. Patrick's Fra-

ternal Society to discuss a national organization. Three months later, the Ancient Order of Hibernians was founded officially in Pennsylvania and New York. Members maintained guard over Irish and Church property against attacks from the Know-Nothings and other anti-Catholics. Assisting the growth of the new society was the support given by the Irish back home, where secret societies also adopted the title of the Ancient Order of Hibernians. For purposes of safety, the activities and membership of the Ancient Order of the Hibernians in America maintained strict secrecy, although it won great respect for its assistance to immigrants in finding jobs and for providing many social welfare programs at a time when little thought was given to the plight of the Irish in America.

The order continued to prosper, demonstrating loyalty to the country, aiding Irish immigrants, and standing armed and ready in front of Catholic properties during the terrible days of anti-Catholic riots and arsons. Archbishop John Hughes of New York used the Hibernians and others to deter threatened damages from Protestant mobs in 1844. The Hibernians faced the American Protective Association and other Protestant hate groups and halted their marches and attacks.

During the Civil War, vast numbers of Hibernians were killed in action on both sides of the conflict. The order also experienced some opposition because of the activities of the Molly McGuires, the Irish miners and railroad workers in Pennsylvania coalfields who fought for decent wages and working conditions. The Molly McGuires resorted to violence and murder as the industry's magnates held out against them. In order to distance itself from the Pennsylvania group, the Ancient Order of Hibernians denounced them at the national convention of 1877. (*See also* Civil War, American.)

Cardinal James F. McIntyre and Cardinal Francis Spellman were members of the order and aided the promotion of Irish culture and charitable programs. The Hibernians founded the Chair of Gaelic Language and Literature at The Catholic University of America. The Ladies Auxiliary was opened in 1894 and then became an independent organization in 1906.

The Hibernians are today the oldest Catholic lay

organization in America and the largest Irish ethnic society in the world. The society promotes Irish culture, is active in charity work, and supports the Church in many different ways.

Hickel, Walter J. *See* Cabinets, Catholics in Presidential

Hickey, James A. (October 11, 1920–October 24, 2004)

The archbishop of Washington from 1980 to 2000 and a cardinal from 1988, James A. Hickey was known for his commitment to education and the care of the poor. Born in Midland, Michigan, to James P. and Agnes Hickey, he entered the seminary at the age of thirteen and studied at St. Joseph's Seminary and Sacred Heart Seminary College in Detroit. He then studied at the Catholic University of America and was ordained as a priest for the Diocese of Saginaw on June 15, 1946.

Father Hickey served briefly as an associate pastor at St. Joseph in Saginaw and was sent to Rome for further studies; there he earned a doctorate in canon law from the Pontifical Lateran University in 1950 and a doctorate in moral theology at the Pontifical University of St. Thomas, the Angelicum, in 1951.

Father Hickey was then named priest-secretary to Bishop Stephen S. Woznicki and rector of St. Paul Seminary in Saginaw. He took part in the Second Vatican Council as a *peritus* (or theological expert). In 1967 Pope Paul VI appointed him auxiliary bishop of Saginaw, and two years later he was appointed rector of the North American College in Rome, where he directed the formation of seminarians from eighty U.S. dioceses.

Cardinal James Hickey

In 1974 he was appointed as the bishop of the Diocese of Cleveland. During his time in the diocese, he was active in the area of social justice and was concerned especially with conditions in El Salvador. He attended the funeral of the martyred Archbishop Oscar Romero and was grieved by the murder of two laywomen whom he had commissioned to serve as missionaries in El Salvador. He

kept their photographs on the wall of his private chapel for the rest of his life.

On June 17, 1980, Pope Blessed John Paul II appointed him archbishop of the Archdiocese of Washington. He was installed on August 5, 1980, at the Cathedral of St. Matthew. Eight years later, on June 28, 1988, Pope Blessed John Paul II elevated him to the College of Cardinals, with the titular church of St. Mary Mother of the Redeemer.

As archbishop, Cardinal Hickey was actively engaged in a host of initiatives, including the promotion of Catholic Charities, the Archdiocesan Health Care Network and Archdiocesan Legal Network, Birthing and Care (to provide prenatal, delivery, and postnatal medical care and other support to women in financial need), Faith in the City (an initiative to revitalize inner-city Catholic elementary schools), Victory Housing (a nonprofit agency that develops assisted and independent living for senior citizens and affordable family housing), and Gift of Peace Convent for the Missionaries of Charity.

He issued pastoral letters on nuclear weapons (1982), on the Sacrament of Penance (1984), on the Eucharist (1984), on substance abuse (1989), on evangelization in the schools (1993), on young Catholics (1993), on care of the sick and dying (1993, with the other bishops of Maryland) and on the *Catechism of the Catholic Church* (1994); he also published a major document on combating racism (1991). He established twelve parishes, four pastoral missions, and two schools, including the Cardinal Hickey Academy. At the time of his retirement, the Archdiocese of Washington boasted 140 parishes and 106 schools serving more than 510,000 Catholics.

He received the Pope Pius XI Award in 1993 and the Karski Award from the Anti-Defamation League in 2000 for his efforts to strengthen relationships between Catholics and Jews, and the *Gaudium et Spes* award, the highest honor given by the Knights of Columbus. Cardinal Hickey was interred in the Crypt Church of the Basilica of the National Shrine of the Immaculate Conception.

Higgins, George (January 21, 1916–May 1, 2002)
One of the most famous labor priests of the twentieth century, George Higgins devoted most of his life to the field of Catholic social thought and labor relations and to the welfare of workers and their families. Born in Chicago, he entered the seminary and was ordained for the Archdiocese of Chicago in 1940. He was then sent to study economics at The Catholic University of America in Washington, D.C.; he obtained a master's degree in economics in 1942 and a Ph.D. in 1944.

That year, Father Higgins began thirty-six years of assisting the National Catholic Welfare Conference and its efforts at social action. He served as director of the NCWC's Social Action Department from 1954 to 1967 and was the principal author of the bishops' annual Labor Day message for several decades. At the same time, from 1945 to 2001, he wrote "The Yardstick," a column syndicated by Catholic News Service that was concerned with labor issues and Church teachings on a variety of issues, including human rights, peace and justice, and racism and anti-Semitism.

He was a leading figure in the United States in writing about the plight of farm laborers, including their unjust working conditions, and in 1969 was instrumental in the decision of the U.S. bishops to establish a special committee to mediate the negotiations between grape growers and the United Farm Workers union. He traveled frequently from Washington, D.C., to California to advance negotiations. He was also a founding member of the United Auto Workers' Public Review Board and was its chairperson from 1962 until 2000. In addition, he served as a crucial liaison between American labor unions and the fledgling Polish labor union Solidarity during the early 1980s, at a time when the Polish workers were in danger of repression at the hands of the communist government of Poland. His efforts brought him into contact with Solidarity leader Lech Walesa, and the two became good friends.

In 1953 Father Higgins was appointed a papal chamberlain with the title of monsignor by Pope Pius XII and named a domestic prelate in 1959 by Pope Blessed John XXIII. In the subsequent period of the Second Vatican Council, Monsignor Higgins served as a *peritus* (or theological expert), and was a member of the U.S. bishops' staff for delivering the daily press briefing. He was a consultant to the Preparatory Commission on the Lay Apostolate, helped to draft the council's decree on the laity, *Apostolicam Actuositatem,* in 1965, and worked with his friend, the American Jesuit theologian Father John Courtney Murray, in drafting the council's Declaration on Religious Freedom, *Dignitatis Humanae,* in 1965.

Although he was not a member of the council's committee that created the declaration on relations with non-Christian religions, *Nostra Aetate,* also in 1965, Monsignor Higgins nevertheless was consulted on its development and acted as a behind-the-scenes liaison between the bishops and Jewish observers in attendance. He had long been an advocate of Catholic-Jewish relations and was a founding member of the official International Catholic-Jewish Liaison Committee that was launched after the council.

He taught at The Catholic University of America from 1974 to 1994 as a lecturer on labor and social ethics. He then served as professor emeritus until 2000. In 1984 he received the St. Francis de Sales Award, the highest honor of the Catholic Press Association. He received the Presidential Medal of Freedom from President Bill Clinton, the nation's highest civilian honor, in 2000. He also was honored with the University of Notre Dame's Laetare Medal in 2001.

Hildebrand, Dietrich von (October 12, 1889–January 26, 1977)
One of the most prominent and devoutly Catholic philosophers of the second half of the twentieth century, Dietrich von Hildebrand was called by Pope Pius XII "the twentieth century Doctor of the Church." Born in Florence, Italy, he was the son of the famous German sculptor Adolf von Hildebrand and Irene Schaueffelen. Although his parents were secular Protestants and did not make religion a major part of their lives, young Dietrich came to faith in Christ at the age of five, and his mother and father never tried to shake his beliefs. Raised with private tutors, he knew that he wished to pursue philosophy from the age of fifteen.

At seventeen, von Hildebrand began studies at the University of Munich, and from 1909 to 1911 he studied at Goettingen with the noted philosophers Edmund Husserl and Adolf Reinach. He completed his doctorate in philosophy in 1912 under the direction of Husserl, and in 1916 he published his first philosophical work, *Die Idee der Sittlichen Handlung*. In 1918 he was named *privat-dozent* at the University of Munich and in 1924 an associate professor. Meanwhile, in 1914 von Hildebrand underwent a conversion and entered the Church with his first wife, Margaret Denck (whom he had married in 1912).

Over the next years, he was active in writing, and his home in Munich was frequented by many of the leading figures of German and European thought and life, including the papal nuncio to Germany, Cardinal Eugenio Pacelli (the future Pope Pius XII), royalty and the aristocracy, diplomats, and professors. Many others attended his regular gatherings from 1924 to 1930 to discuss topics of importance or intellectual interest. Long concerned with the dangers of German nationalism, von Hildebrand condemned the invasion of Belgium in 1914 and was branded a traitor by some in the country. His opposition to nationalism and the Nazis forced him to flee Munich after the 1923 putsch by Adolf Hitler. The subsequent rise of the Nazis to power in Germany compelled von Hildebrand in 1933 to give up everything and leave the country. He went to Italy in March with fifteen dollars in his pocket.

Making his way to Austria, von Hildebrand established the anti-totalitarian Catholic weekly, *Der Christliche Staendestaat*, which became a powerful voice against Nazism but which also earned him even greater hatred of the Nazi Party. In 1935 he was named a professor of philosophy at the University of Vienna. Three years later, however, as the *Anschluss*, the Nazi seizure of Austria, began, he was warned to leave the country as the Gestapo (the German Secret Police) would be coming for him. On March 11, 1938, he and his wife escaped across the border into Czechoslovakia; that night the Gestapo arrived at his home. The couple had narrowly avoided arrest and certain death.

They traveled to Switzerland through Hungary and Italy, settling in France, where he took up a post as a professor at the Catholic University of Toulouse. France soon fell to the German Army

in 1940, and the von Hildebrand family found itself trapped in the country. With the assistance of friends, they were hidden in the slums of Toulouse and eventually were taken to Marseilles, where an exit visa was provided. They reached Lisbon, and there von Hildebrand learned that he had been chosen as one of a hundred European scholars invited by the Rockefeller Foundation to go to the United States.

They arrived in New York on December 23, 1940. Von Hildebrand was appointed to the faculty of the Graduate School of Fordham University in February 1941 and remained there until his retirement in 1960. He spent the rest of his life writing. His wife died in 1957. In July 1959, he wed the philosopher Dr. Alice M. Jourdain (von Hildebrand), an internationally renowned and respected philosopher and theologian.

Von Hildebrand was the author of dozens of books, both in German and English, including *Marriage: The Mystery of Faithful Love* (1929); *In Defense of Purity* (1931); *Metaphysics of Community* (1930); *Transformation in Christ* (1948); *Liturgy and Personality* (1943); *Actual Questions in the Light of Eternity* (1931); *The Essence of Philosophical Research and Knowledge* (1934); *Fundamental Moral Attitudes* (1950); *Christian Ethics* (1952); *The New Tower of Babel* (1953); *True Morality and Its Counterfeits* (1955) and *Graven Images*, both with Alice M. Jourdain (1957); *The Devastated Vineyard* (1973); and *Jaws of Death: Gate of Heaven* (1976).

Hilger, Marie Inez (October 16, 1891–May 18, 1977)

A noted anthropologist and sociologist, Marie Inez Hilger was a member of the Benedictine Sisters. Born to a family of German immigrants in Roscoe, Minnesota, she entered the order of the Sisters of St. Benedict in 1914 and became the first woman fully admitted to The Catholic University of America. She received a master's degree in sociology in 1925 and a doctorate in anthropology in 1939. In 1955 she was named a research associate at the Bureau of American Ethnology. Her doctoral dissertation focused on Ojibwa Indians in Minnesota, and she went on to do fieldwork that concentrated on the many social problems of Chippewa Indians of Minnesota. Eventually, under the influence of

Margaret Mead, she devoted her primary attentions to children. She studied the Chippewa (1932–66), Arapaho (1935–42), Araucanians (1946–47; 1951–52), and Ainu and Japanese (1962–63).

Sister Marie Inez Hilger prepared a field guide for the study of child life for the Human Relations Area File, and her final field study of the Ainu people of Japan was performed with the support of the Smithsonian Institution and the National Geographic Society in the early 1960s. Her research on the Ainu led to an article in *National Geographic* in 1967, a film on the subject in 1970, and a book, *Together with the Ainu: A Vanishing People,* in 1971. Her final years were spent among the Blackfeet, where she collected what she termed "grandmother tales." In all, she wrote eight books and over seventy articles and essays. Sister Inez died in St. Joseph, Minnesota.

Hillenbrand, Reynold H. (July 19, 1904–May 22, 1979)

A priest, Reynold Henry Hillenbrand served as a seminary rector, liturgist, and activist. He was born in Chicago to George and Eleanor Schmitt Hillenbrand, the second of nine children. He studied at Quigley Preparatory Seminary and St. Mary of the Lake Seminary and was ordained for the Archdiocese of Chicago in September 1929. He was then sent to Rome for additional studies at the Pontifical Gregorian University. The following year, he returned and took up a post teaching Latin and English literature at Quigley; at the same time he served as a priest of Holy Name Cathedral.

In 1936 Cardinal George Mundelein surprised the archdiocese by appointing the then thirty-one-year-old Father Hillenbrand to the post of rector of St. Mary of the Lake Seminary. Appointed because of his imagination and obvious energy, he embarked upon a revitalization of the seminary, including holding the first Chicago Summer School of Social Action for priests in 1938. During his eight years as rector, he helped shape a number of priests who shared his interest in liturgical renewal and social concerns. Of particular note was his effort to study and develop further the writings of liturgical reformers Prosper Guéranger, Odo Casel, and Lambert Beauduin.

After his time as rector ended, he was asked in 1940 by the Benedictine Liturgical Confer-

ence to serve as co-chairman of the first National Liturgical Week, convened at Holy Name Cathedral annually. The following year, he launched the first National Summer School of Liturgy. He went on to be a founding member of the Liturgical Conference as well as an active figure in Catholic Action. In 1945 he was named coordinator of Catholic Action in the archdiocese. Two years later, he became national chaplain of the Young Christian Workers, and in 1949 he was appointed national chaplain of the Young Christian Students and the Christian Family Movement.

In 1944 Father Hillenbrand was assigned to serve as pastor of Sacred Heart Parish in Hubbard Woods, Illinois. The parish became a noted site for the implementation of liturgical renewal, and Hillenbrand brought with him his dedication to social concerns. He remained as pastor until 1974, when he retired. He faced severe medical difficulties until his passing.

Hispanic Catholics. *See* Latino Catholics

Hitchcock, Alfred (August 13, 1899–April 29, 1980)

A world-renowned motion-picture director of suspense films, Alfred Hitchcock inspired new generations of directors with his unique cinematic style and innovative camera work. He was born in London, the son of a poultry dealer, and was educated at the Jesuit St. Ignatius College and at the University of London, where he studied engineering. In 1920, drawn to the emerging film industry, Hitchcock began his lifelong career. He directed his first film five years later and was recognized in 1926 for his hit film *The Lodger.* In 1929 his *Blackmail* was the first truly successful talking film in London. He followed that hit with *The Thirty-nine Steps* in 1935 and *The Lady Vanishes* in 1938.

Invited to Hollywood, Hitchcock directed *Rebecca* in 1940, which received the Academy Award for Best Picture. Other films included *Notorious* (1946), *Strangers on a Train* (1951), *Rear Window* (1954), and *Vertigo.* In 1960 Hitchcock stunned moviegoers around the world with *Psycho,* in which the beautiful heroine is brutally murdered early in the film. *The Birds* was a success in 1963, followed by *Torn Curtain* (1966), *Topaz* (1969), and *Frenzy* (1972).

A private man, Hitchcock preferred to spend

his evenings at home with his wife, Alma Reville, whom he had married in 1926. Nevertheless, he was famed for his practical jokes, his subtle sense of humor, and his tradition of appearing in every film in a cameo of some fashion. His profile became a hallmark when he produced and sometimes directed television shows.

During his long career in the United States he became a U.S. citizen and supposedly declined the honor of a British C.B.E. (Commander of the Order of the British Empire) in 1962. In the New Year's honor's list of 1980 (just before his death), he was named an Honorary (as he was a U.S. citizen) Knight Commander of the British Empire. Although he never won the Academy Award for Best Director, he was awarded the Irving Thalberg Memorial Award at the 1967 Oscars. He also received a host of other honors, including the Lifetime Achievement Award in 1979. He appeared on a 32-cent commemorative postage stamp in the Legends of Hollywood series.

Hoban, James (c. 1762–December 8, 1831)

The architect and builder of the presidential residence of the United States, the White House, James Hoban also designed the U.S. Capitol in Washington, D.C. He was born in County Kilkenny, Ireland, but moved to Dublin at an early age. He was a gifted architect and artist, winning a medal from the Dublin Society for his drawings. Hoban was also architecturally involved in the Royal Exchange and Dublin Customs House designs.

He arrived in the United States in 1785, first going to Philadelphia and then to Charleston. Henry Laurens of Charleston aided him in becoming known, and he designed and built public buildings and mansions in the area. In 1791 Hoban's reputation became known to George Washington when he visited South Carolina, and he provided the architect with a letter of recommendation to the commissioners of the District of Columbia, then known as the Federal City. In the following year, Hoban won the competition for best design of the "Presidential Palace" and was hired for about $1,500 a year. He planned a central building with wings and supervised the construction. He also built the U.S. Capitol, laboring on the project until 1803. Hoban restored the White House after it was

burned in the War of 1812, when British troops set fire to it on August 4, 1814. Repainted, the residence became known as the White House.

James Hoban was the most prominent Catholic layman in Washington, and was welcomed into social groups and gatherings. He married Susannah Sewell in 1799, and they had ten children.

Hodur, Francis. *See* **Polish National Catholic Church**

Hoecken, Christian (1808–1851)

Called "Father Kickapoo" in the wilds of Missouri and Kansas, Christian Hoecken was a Jesuit missionary and trail companion of the highly revered Father Pierre-Jean De Smet. He was born in the Netherlands and entered the Society of Jesus in 1832. Ordained to the priesthood, he was assigned to the American missions soon after.

Father Hoecken served the Kickapoo nation from 1836 to 1838, becoming particularly fluent in the language and receiving his lasting nickname. In 1838 he established a Potawatomi mission on the Osage River and then went to Sugar Creek, Kansas, where he compiled a tribal dictionary and grammar. St. Rose Philippine Duchesne served at Sugar Creek for a time.

He accompanied the Potawatomi to Kaw Valley, where he also served the Miami, Peoria, Piankashaw, and Sauk. Father Hoecken gathered medicine, food, and blankets, and was present when exiled tribes were brought from their homelands to Kansas by U.S. troops. His brother, Father Adrian Hoecken, was also in the missions.

In 1851 Father Christian Hoecken was asked by Father De Smet to accompany him to the Great Council of Indian tribes in the West. The two missionaries began their journey, but Father Hoecken contracted cholera while on the trail and died, mourned by the various Indian nations he had served faithfully.

Hofstee, Anthony Leo (July 30, 1903–April 26, 1986)

A Dominican priest, Anthony Leo Hofstee was a missionary to the lepers of the Philippines. He was born in Utrecht, Holland, and was taken as a child to Everett, Washington. In 1925 he entered the Dominican order in Benecia, California, and studied at the Dominican house of studies in Washington, D.C., where he was ordained. Father Hofstee was assigned then to parishes in California, and he labored there until America entered World War II, when he became a military chaplain and joined the marines in the Philippines.

At Tala, near Manila, Father Hofstee discovered a group of lepers who had been neglected because of the military actions in the region. He received permission from Archbishop Michael O'Doherty of Manila to serve these lepers, and in May 1947 took up residence in Tala. Father Hofstee had a parish of 600 lepers when he started his ministry, and he was able to raise funds to establish schools, a college, a hospital, and nursery. By 1955 he served 1,900 lepers and their children. In order to care for the extraordinary number of babies, Father Hofstee asked Franciscan Sisters to aid him, and they generously responded.

In 1953 the apostolic nuncio to the Philippines, Archbishop Egidio Vagnozzi, asked Father Hofstee to coordinate all the leper colonies in the Philippines into one organization, a task that he accomplished with success. Mother Teresa awarded him a medal personally for his labors before he died. Father Hofstee died at Tala and is buried beside the church that he built.

Hogan, William. *See* Hogan Schism

Hogan Schism

A scandal that took place in Philadelphia from 1820 to 1823, the Hogan Schism led also to a renewal of rampant anti-Catholicism all across the United States. At the center of the scandal was William Hogan, who had been born in Limerick, Ireland, in 1788. An ordained Catholic priest, Father Hogan arrived in the United States, having left Limerick without episcopal permission. Father Hogan served in Albany, New York, and then went to St. Mary's Church in Philadelphia in 1820.

Once in that parish, he won over the lay trustees of the property and publicly attacked Bishop Henry Conwell, the newly arrived ordinary of the Diocese of Philadelphia. Pope Pius VII intervened in the Hogan affair by sending a letter, *Non Sine Magno,* in which he rebuked the priest and requested the

archbishop of Baltimore to do what he could to curb the dangers of trusteeism. Father Hogan was suspended and then excommunicated for conspiring to lead a parish into schismatic separation from the bishop and the diocese.

The term "Hoganism" became popular as the code word for trusteeism and clerical obstinacy, following the democratic mood of the nation at the time. Bishop Conwell did not solve the problem, however, and his contemporaries commented upon his haste in the matter and his display of temper. Two court cases involving Father Hogan labeled him as immoral. In 1824 he married and left the Church; he subsequently became a lawyer and the U.S. consul to Cuba. He wrote numerous anti-Catholic pamphlets and attacked the Church across the nation. He died in 1848 in Nashua, New Hampshire. (*See also* Trusteeism.)

Holmes, John (1799–1852)

A priest, John Holmes was also an educator. He was born at Windsor, Vermont, and grew up a determined anti-Catholic, so much so that after studies at Dartmouth College he traveled to Canada to preach against the Church. While there, however, he was himself converted and entered the faith in 1817 through the influence of Abbé Lecuyer in Québec. He proceeded to study philosophy at Montréal Seminary and theology at Nicolet College and was ordained in 1823.

After service in a parish in Drummondville, Father Holmes was appointed to the post of professor at Québec Seminary. He was responsible for improving the quality of education at the seminary, and he earned many accolades for his 1832 work on geography, *Traité de Géographie.* He also initiated the idea of a Catholic university in Montréal, a vision that found realization in Laval University, whose foundation was begun soon after his death. Holmes was also credited with starting the first normal schools in Canada and with conceiving a commercial union of the British provinces in North America, an idea that was formalized in 1867. A brother and six sisters all became Catholics through his example.

Holy Cross College

A four-year undergraduate liberal arts institution, the College of the Holy Cross was founded in 1843 by the Society of Jesus in Worcester, Massachusetts. The impetus for its creation was given by the second bishop of Boston, the Jesuit Benedict Joseph Fenwick, who hoped to establish a Catholic college in his New England diocese. Recognizing the growing population of Catholics in the region, Bishop Fenwick wanted to offer them a place for a proper Catholic education that would also serve as fertile soil for vocations to the religious life and priesthood.

Possessing an academic background as a graduate of Georgetown, Bishop Fenwick was realistic in his planning and knew that his fellow Jesuits in the Maryland Province were prepared to lend their assistance and faculty. The location chosen for the new college was on the site where Father James Fitton had purchased fifty-two acres of land for an academy for boys in 1836. The academy flourished, but Father Fitton's other pastoral responsibilities in Massachusetts, Rhode Island, and Connecticut compelled him to transfer control to the bishop. To drive home the importance of the new institution and to express its diocesan relationship, the bishop named the college Holy Cross after his cathedral church, the Cathedral of the Holy Cross.

Father Thomas F. Mulledy, previously the provincial of the Maryland Province of the Jesuits, was appointed as the chief organizer of the new institution. The cornerstone of the college was laid on June 1, 1843, and the first six students began their classes in early November. The college held its first graduation ceremony in 1849; the valedictorian was James Healy, the son of a slave. Anti-Catholicism played a part in the inability of the college to receive a state charter in 1847, forcing it to confer degrees from Georgetown University until 1865, when a charter was at last granted with the support of Governor John A. Andrews.

Holy Cross developed slowly over the next years, overcoming chronic financial problems and the very real danger that the Jesuits might be forced by monetary exigencies to close the school. Vital progress was achieved during the time of Bishop Fenwick's successor, Bishop John B. Fitzpatrick, and the fourth president, Father Anthony F. Ciampi, S.J. Once placed on a surer footing, the college enjoyed a growth in enrollments. The program of studies followed the seven-year curriculum of the Ratio Studiorum for the first decades, but with the start of the twentieth century, a more contemporary curriculum was adopted to ensure greater conformity with prevailing academic norms in the United States. In addition, entrance was granted for the first time to non-Catholics.

The twentieth century brought considerable expansion and growth even as the college strove to remain faithful to its Jesuit tradition and character. There were 1,000 students in 1924, 2,000 in 1964, and there are currently about 2,700 men and women students from across the United States. Women were admitted for the first time in 1972, and in 1984 Holy Cross became active in intercollegiate sports by signing as a charter member of the Patriot League.

Holy Cross Congregation

The Congregation of the Holy Cross (C.S.C.) of men and women religious has been one of the most active religious communities in the United States; it is best known for educational and pastoral work, home missions and retreats, foreign missions, social services, and apostolate of the press. The congregation was established in 1837 by Reverend Basile Moreau and derives its name from Sainte-Croix, a suburb of Le Mans, France. Moreau established the community by uniting the Brothers of St. Joseph and the Auxiliary Priests of Le Mans. Papal approbation was received in 1857 from Pope Blessed Pius IX. Moreau also attached a branch for women, the Marianites of Holy Cross, in 1841; this was approved in 1860, with the requirement of separating the women as their own congregation.

The Congregation first arrived in the United States in 1841 when Bishop Celestine René Lawrence Guynemer de la Hailandiere of Vincennes, Indiana (later the Archdiocese of Indianapolis), invited members to undertake missionary work in Daviess County. Six brothers under the leadership of Father Edward Sorin responded, and by the following year the community moved to St. Joseph County, Indiana, and established the school that became the University of Notre Dame du Lac in 1842. The school became the center for the congregation's efforts in the United States until the middle of the twentieth century. The first member of the congregation for women arrived in 1843. Both communities, of men and women, were swiftly able to attract members from within the United States.

The North American province for the Congregation of priests and brothers was established in 1865, and Father Sorin was named the first superior. The following year, the province was limited in its jurisdiction to the United States, save for houses in Louisiana, which remained under the administration of the French house. Additional restructuring took place over the years.

A testament of this success is seen in the fact that by 1865 the Holy Cross community of women claimed more members in the United States than in France or Canada. This growth did not come without difficulties, for the question emerged inevitably as to whether the motherhouse should be moved from France to the United States. To solve the problem, the sisters in the United States separated officially from the motherhouse in France in 1869 and assumed the name Congregation of the Sisters of the Holy Cross, with their headquarters at St. Mary's at Notre Dame. The communities in Louisiana and New York City chose to remain affiliated with the motherhouse in France. Meanwhile, the sisters in Canada also separated in 1883 and became the Sisters of the Holy Cross and the Seven Dolors.

Having established themselves with great success at Notre Dame, the Congregation expanded its involvement in education by opening schools in other states, including orphanages, asylums, agricultural schools, and various parish schools and academies in Indiana, Louisiana, Maryland, Ohio, Texas, Washington, D.C., and Wisconsin.

The Congregation also became increasingly involved in parish ministry, starting in 1853 with their involvement in St. Joseph's Parish in South Bend. Over the next decade, Holy Cross priests and brothers became active in parishes in Wisconsin, Texas, and New Orleans. In subsequent decades, the Congregation was concerned especially with the pastoral care of minorities, especially Hispanic and African-American parishes in Indiana and Texas.

The Sisters of the Holy Cross focused attention on the education of women, and by the start of the twentieth century they had opened academies all around the country, including California, Utah,

Texas, and Virginia. The Marianites of Holy Cross also opened schools in Louisiana and New York. In addition, the Sisters of the Holy Cross were involved in nursing during the Civil War and in 1867 opened their first hospital in Cairo, Illinois. This first institution was followed by hospitals elsewhere in Illinois, as well as California, Idaho, Indiana, Maryland, Missouri, New Mexico, South Dakota, and Utah. This tradition of hospital work has continued since.

Currently, there are over 1,600 Holy Cross priests and brothers serving in fifteen countries on four continents. In the United States, they remain active in education, parish work, and social ministry. The members of the other branches of the Holy Cross are engaged in service in schools and hospitals, both in the United States and around the globe.

Holy Ghost Fathers

Called the Spiritans, the Holy Ghost Fathers are a religious congregation for men devoted to missionary and social work in Africa, South America, and the United States. The congregation was founded in 1703 in France by Claude Francis Poullart des Places, the son of a wealthy businessman and lawyer. He intended to follow in his father's footsteps, but underwent a conversion at the age of twenty-one. He became closely associated with the needs and the care of the poor and the common chimney sweeps of Paris, and from this foundation Poullart discerned a priestly vocation. At the age of twenty-four, when he was still a seminarian, he founded the new congregation to provide spiritual and material assistance to those in need, including some of his fellow but impoverished students. The seminary of the Holy Ghost Fathers was founded to provide training to students with limited financial means and send them into the world as missionaries. Poullart died in 1709, only two years after his ordination, but his foundation proved immensely successful in France and beyond.

The first members of the Spiritans in North America arrived in Québec in 1732. Three years later, Spiritan missionaries began preaching and working among the Indians and the French settlers of Acadia in Nova Scotia. The first Holy Ghost priest to arrive in the United States was Father

John Moranville, who reached Baltimore in 1794 or 1795 and served in St. Patrick's Church.

Major events in Europe posed severe problems for the congregation — namely, the French Revolution and the decades of war and political and social upheaval that followed. The Spiritans were all but extinct in France. To provide for the future, in 1848 the Spiritans merged with the Congregation of the Holy Heart of Mary, a missionary society founded by Venerable Francis Libermann. With this new beginning, the Holy Ghost Fathers soon flourished anew, and missionary activities started again in Africa and elsewhere.

In 1872, when the Spiritans were expelled from Germany as part of the *Kulturkampf,* the decision was made to establish a province in the United States. After two failed efforts to begin houses in Kentucky and Ohio, respectively, the Spiritans under Father Joseph Strub chose Pittsburgh for the headquarters of the new province. A college was started in 1878 that grew into Duquesne University. By Father Strub's death in 1890, the Spiritans were found in five states. Minor and major seminaries were established in Pennsylvania, Connecticut, and Michigan.

One of the most important developments in the ministry of the Holy Ghost Fathers was the service to minorities, in particular African-Americans. The members of the congregation braved racism, intolerance, and anti-Catholicism in their efforts to establish parishes for African-Americans. Their first small parish was begun in Pittsburgh in 1888, followed by a larger one in Philadelphia in 1889, begun with the help of Archbishop Patrick John Ryan and St. Katharine Drexel. From this courageous effort, the Spiritans were able to open new parishes for African-Americans in New York, Michigan, and throughout the South. Vocations from among black communities in the United States were first permitted in the 1880s, although the first ordination was celebrated in 1907. Problems of racism made new vocations problematic until World War II, even though they had been accepting blacks elsewhere in the world in 1843.

The growth of the Holy Ghost Fathers in the period after World War II led to a discussion on the need to divide the U.S. province for better administration. In 1963 the Generalate and the American Province agreed on a division into two provinces; all territory west of the Mississippi and all of Louisiana became the West Province, and areas to the east of the Mississippi became the East Province.

Holy Name Society

The Confraternity of the Most Holy Name of God and Jesus Christ, called the Holy Name Society in the United States, was founded in Europe. In 1274 the Holy See advocated devotion to the Holy Name, and Pope Blessed Gregory X commissioned St. John of Vercelli, the master general of the Order of Preachers, the Dominicans, to promote reverence for the Divine Name. Diego of Victoria wrote a constitution for the society in 1514, as the confraternity had grown rapidly.

On April 13, 1564, Pope Pius IV sanctioned the confraternity, again entrusting it to the Dominicans. In May 1896, Pope Leo XIII reorganized the confraternity, basing it in parishes and dioceses. The revered missionary Father Charles Nerinckx established the first Holy Name Society in the United States in 1808 at St. Charles Church in Marion County, Kentucky. Other parishes followed, including St. Vincent Ferrer in New York City and St. Patrick in Lowell, Massachusetts.

The American promoter of the society, however, was Dominican Father Charles Hyacinth McKenna, who was appointed spiritual director of the Holy Name Society in the eastern part of the United States in 1900. He received permission from Pope Leo XIII to establish more than one society in a city; originally only a Dominican parish could form a society. By 1917, because of Father McKenna's labors, some 1,734 such American parishes were part of the apostolate.

On July 25, 1975, the National Association of the Holy Name Society was incorporated. Still entrusted to the Dominicans, the society continues its mission all across the United States today, encouraging members to receive holy Communion and promoting prayer, reverence, and loyalty to the Holy See. U.S. bishops now serve as national spiritual directors.

Holy See–U.S. Relations

The Catholic Church in America has never lost the close ties to the Holy See that were so in evidence during the time of Bishop John Carroll in the late eighteenth century. Indeed, several popes had a profound influence on the development of the Church in America beyond the creation of dioceses and archdioceses, after close consultation with the bishops of America and the Congregation for the Propaganda Fide — which had control over much of ecclesiastical life as the United States was still considered mission territory until June 23, 1908.

One other important area of papal concern was the desire to establish a permanent diplomatic presence in the country in the form of an ambassador, either a nuncio or an apostolic delegate. This proved a difficult task, however, owing to the degree of anti-Catholicism in the young country and the stiff resistance in the U.S. Congress for many years to any formal diplomatic relations with the Holy See.

Nevertheless, the Holy See was able to forge diplomatic connections with the United States from a very early time. When, for example, Rome was considering appointing a Superior of the Missions for the growing Church in America, Vatican diplomats carefully studied the issue and consulted with French and American representatives. The papal nuncio to France went so far as to meet with Benjamin Franklin — then serving as a diplomat to the French court — to discuss suitable candidates. Franklin endorsed Bishop John Carroll, and in June 1784 Pope Pius VI appointed him.

From these informal discussions, consular relations between the United States and the Holy See developed in the wake of an announcement made by the papal nuncio in Paris to the American mission there on December 15, 1784, that the Papal States had agreed to open several Mediterranean ports to U.S. shipping. There were subsequent loose diplomatic contacts between the United States and the Holy See, but formal relations were simply impracticable given the widespread hostility of so many.

U.S. consular representation in the Papal States began with the appointment of John Baptist Sartori, a native of Rome, in June 1797. Sartori's successors as consuls were Felix Cicognani, also a Roman, and Americans George W. Greene, Nicholas Browne, William C. Sanders, Daniel LeRoy, Horatio V. Glentworth, W. J. Stillman, Edwin C. Cushman, and David M. Armstrong.

Consular officials of the Papal States who served in the United States were Count Ferdinand Lucchesi (1826–1829), who resided in Washington, D.C.; John Baptist Sartori (1829–1841), who resided in Trenton, New Jersey; Daniel J. Desmond (1841–1850), who resided in Philadelphia; and Louis B. Binsse (1850–1895), who resided in New York. Binsse held the title until his death on March 28, 1895. No one was appointed to succeed him.

Notably, the United States recognized the Holy See, and the recognition of the consul of the Papal States did not cease when the states were absorbed into the Kingdom of Italy in 1871, despite pressure from Baron Albert Blanc, the Italian minister.

The U.S. Senate approved a recommendation made by President James K. Polk in December 1847 for the establishment of a diplomatic post in the Papal States. Jacob L. Martin, the first chargé d'affaires, arrived in Rome on August 2, 1848, and presented his credentials to Pope Blessed Pius IX on August 19. Martin, who died within a month, was succeeded by Lewis Cass Jr. Cass became minister resident in 1854 and served in that capacity until his retirement in 1858.

John P. Stockton, who later became a U.S. senator from New Jersey, was minister resident from 1858 to 1861. Rufus King was named to succeed him, but instead accepted a commission as a brigadier general in the army. Alexander W. Randall of Wisconsin took the appointment. He was succeeded in August 1862 by Richard M. Blatchford, who served until the following year. King was again nominated minister resident and served until 1867, when the ministry was ended because of objections from some quarters in the United States and failure to appropriate funds for its continuation. J. C. Hooker, a secretary, remained in the Papal States until the end of March 1868, closing the ministry and performing functions of courtesy.

The hostility against Catholics was made abundantly clear to the Vatican in 1853 and with the visit of the papal nuncio to Brazil, Archbishop Gaetano Bedini, to the United States. Commissioned by Pope Pius IX to visit, Archbishop Bedini arrived in New York in June of that year. He made a courtesy call on President Franklin Pierce in Washington, D.C., and was cordially received. His arrival, however, sparked vicious anti-Catholic demonstrations that marred his tour of America. There were even plots to assassinate him. Undaunted, the archbishop visited Pittsburgh, Cincinnati, and Louisville, Kentucky. An assassination plot was foiled in Cincinnati, resulting in riots. Archbishop Bedini remained in the United States until February 3, 1854, when he had to be taken covertly to his ocean liner by a tugboat. The violence and intolerance did not mean that the popes had abandoned the possibility of diplomatic relations entirely.

As the Holy See and the Papal States did not have diplomatic relations with the United States in the traditional sense, it was not possible to name an ambassador. But Pope Leo XIII wished to have a permanent representative to the Church in America who might be able to make close reports on the country and above all provide the Holy See with names and dossiers on prospective American bishops and archbishops. And so, in 1893, he appointed Francesco Satolli, the archbishop of Lepanto, to the post of apostolic delegate in Washington, D.C.

It was not until 1984, however, that formal diplomatic relations were established with the United States. In 1939 Myron C. Taylor was appointed by President Franklin Delano Roosevelt to serve as his personal representative to Pope Pius XII and continued serving in that capacity during the presidency of Harry S. Truman until 1951. Henry Cabot Lodge was named to the post by President Richard M. Nixon in 1970, and served also during the presidency of Gerald Ford. He represented President Jimmy Carter at the canonization of St. John Neumann in 1977. Miami attorney David Walters served as the personal envoy of President Jimmy Carter to the pope from July 1977 until his resignation on August 16, 1978. He was succeeded by Robert F. Wagner, who served from October 1978 to the end of the Carter presidency in January 1981. William A. Wilson, appointed by President Ronald Reagan in February 1981, served as his personal envoy until 1984, when he was named ambassador to the Holy See. None of the personal envoys had diplomatic status.

President Harry S. Truman nominated General Mark Clark to be ambassador to the Holy See in 1951, but withdrew the nomination at Clark's request because of controversy over the appointment. None of Truman's three immediate successors — Dwight D. Eisenhower, John F. Kennedy, and Lyndon Baines Johnson — had a personal representative to the pope.

With the election of Ronald Reagan in 1980, there was finally a general agreement that the United States should normalize its relations with the Holy See. This stemmed in part from the close diplomatic relationship that developed quickly between President Reagan and Pope Blessed John Paul II in resisting the Soviet Union and its satellite regimes in Eastern Europe.

The United States and the Holy See announced the establishment of full diplomatic relations on January 10, 1984, thus ending a period of 117 years in which there was no formal diplomatic relationship. The announcement followed action by Congress in November 1983.

William A. Wilson, President Reagan's personal representative to the Holy See from 1981, was confirmed as the U.S. ambassador by the Senate on March 7, 1984. He presented his credentials to Pope Blessed John Paul II on April 9, 1984, and served until May 1986, when he resigned. He was succeeded by Frank Shakespeare, who served from 1986 to 1989, and Thomas P. Melady, who served from 1989 to 1993. Raymond L. Flynn, the mayor of Boston, was appointed to the post by Bill Clinton and confirmed by the Senate in July 1993. He served until 1997, when he was succeeded by Corinne Claiborne "Lindy" Boggs, who served until 2001. She was succeeded by James Nicholson, who served until 2005. He was succeeded by L. Francis Rooney III, an Oklahoma and Florida businessman. He served until 2007, when President George W. Bush nominated Mary Ann Glendon to become ambassador to the Holy See. She served until 2009 and was succeeded by Miguel Diaz, a theology professor.

Archbishop (later Cardinal) Pio Laghi, apostolic delegate to the United States since 1980, was

Myron C. Taylor

named first pro-nuncio by the pope on March 26, 1984. He served until 1990, when he was named prefect of the Congregation for Catholic Education. Archbishop Agostino Cacciavillan was appointed pro-nuncio on June 13, 1990. He served until he was named president of the Administration of the Patrimony of the Apostolic See and was succeeded on December 7, 1998, by Archbishop Gabriel Montalvo. Archbishop Montalvo served as nuncio from 1998 to 2005. He was succeeded by Archbishop Pietro Sambi, who died on July 27, 2011, at the age of seventy-three. On October 19, 2011, Pope Benedict XVI appointed Archbishop Carlo Maria Viganò as the new nuncio to the United States.

In 1984, when the United States and the Holy See announced the establishment of full diplomatic relations, the nature of relations between the two was described in nearly identical statements by John Hughes, a U.S. State Department spokesman, and the Holy See. Hughes said, "The United States of America and the Holy See, in the desire to further promote the existing mutual friendly relations, have decided by common agreement to establish diplomatic relations between them at the level of embassy on the part of the United States of America, and nunciature on the part of the Holy See, as of today, January 10, 1984."

The Holy See statement said, "The Holy See and the United States of America, desiring to develop the mutual friendly relations already existing, have decided by common accord to establish diplomatic relations at the level of apostolic nunciature on the side of the Holy See and of embassy on the side of the United States beginning today, January 10, 1984."

The establishment of relations was criticized as a violation of the separation of church and state by spokesmen for the National Council of Churches, the National Association of Evangelicals, the Baptist Joint Committee on Public Affairs, Seventh-Day Adventists, Americans United for Separation of Church and State, and the American Jewish Congress.

U.S. District Judge John P. Fullam, ruling on May 7, 1985, in Philadelphia, dismissed a legal challenge to Holy See–U.S. relations brought by Americans United for Separation of Church and State. He stated that Americans United and its allies in the challenge lacked legal standing to sue, and that the courts did not have jurisdiction to intervene in foreign policy decisions of the executive branch of the U.S. government. Parties to the suit were the National Association of Laity, the National Coalition of American Nuns, and several Protestant church organizations. Bishop James W. Malone, president of the United States Catholic Conference, said in a statement: "This matter has been discussed at length for many years. It is not a religious issue but a public policy question which, happily, has now been settled in this context." Russell Shaw, a conference spokesman, said the decision to send an ambassador to the Holy See was not a church-state issue and "confers no special privilege or status on the Church."

Holy Sepulchre of Jerusalem, Equestrian Order of the

One of the great orders of chivalry, the Knights of the Holy Sepulchre trace their origins to Godfrey de Bouillon, who instituted it in 1099. The order took its name from the Basilica of the Holy Sepulchre, where its members were knighted. After the fall of the Latin Kingdom of Jerusalem and the consequent departure of the knights from the Holy Land, national divisions were established in various countries.

The order was reorganized by Pope Blessed Pius IX in 1847, when he reestablished the Latin Patriarchate of Jerusalem and placed the order under the jurisdiction of its patriarch. In 1888 Pope Leo XIII confirmed permission to admit women — Ladies of the Holy Sepulchre — to all degrees of rank. Pope St. Pius X reserved the office of Grand Master to himself in 1907; Pope Pius XII gave the order a cardinal patron in 1940 and, in 1949, transferred the office of Grand Master to the cardinal patron. Pope John XXIII approved updated constitutions in 1962; the latest statutes were approved by Paul VI in 1977.

The purposes of the order are strictly religious and charitable, and the Knights provide immense assistance to the Holy Land through schools, hospitals, and clinics, and are instrumental in maintaining a Christian presence in the sacred places. Members are committed to sustain and aid the charitable, cultural, and social works of the Catholic

Church in the Holy Land, particularly in the Latin Patriarchate of Jerusalem. The order is grouped into three classes: Knights of the Collar and Ladies of the Collar; Class of Knights (in four grades); and Class of Ladies (in four grades). Members are appointed by the cardinal grand master according to procedures outlined in the constitution.

Presently, the order has some twenty-three thousand members (Knights and Dames) in fifty countries. Its governing body in Rome consists of a Cardinal Grand Master, a governor-general, and an international council, called the Grand Magisterium. Under the present constitution the order is divided into national lieutenancies. There are nine lieutenancies in the United States and one in Puerto Rico. Membership is by invitation only. Entrance is offered to Roman Catholic men and women, lay or clerical, twenty-five years or older, who have demonstrated an exemplary record of service to the Church and community. In 2007 Pope Benedict XVI appointed Archbishop John P. Foley, long-time president of the Pontifical Council for Social Communications, as Grand Master. He was named to the College of Cardinals that same year. In 2011 he retired and was succeeded by Archbishop Edwin F. O'Brien, archbishop of Baltimore since 2007. In 2012 Archbishop O'Brien was named to the College of Cardinals.

Homiletic and Pastoral Review

A magazine designed to serve the clergy and laity of the United States, the *Homiletic and Pastoral Review* was founded in 1900 by Joseph F. Wagner, a publisher. It was originally called the *Homiletic Monthly and Catechist*, but the name was changed in 1916. Father John Brady of St. Joseph's Seminary in Dunwoodie, New York, served as the pioneering editor of the magazine.

The Dominican priests Fathers John McHugh and Charles Callan served as editors following Father Brady. When Father McHugh died, Father Callan continued alone, assisted for a time by Father Aidan M. Carr, a Conventual Franciscan who became a Trappist monk in 1970. Monsignor John F. Yzermans then assumed the editorial post, followed by Father Kenneth Baker, S.J., who came on board in 1971. The periodical, which migrated to the Internet in 2012, remains one of the foremost publications in the Catholic Church on significant moral, theological, and liturgical matters.

Honolulu, Diocese of

Established on September 10, 1941, by Pope Pius XII, the Diocese of Honolulu serves all the Hawaiian Islands. Honolulu is the capital of the state of Hawaii, the base for the United States Pacific Fleet and other vital military units, and the site of the attack that led to the entry of America into World War II. Hawaii is situated some 2,400 miles west of California in the Pacific Ocean. The Diocese of Honolulu is a suffragan see of the Archdiocese of San Francisco.

A people from the western Pacific arrived in large sailing crafts and brought agricultural materials and techniques with them. This people spread to all the main islands of Hawaii (the Big Island), Kauai, Lanai, Maui, Molokai, and Oahu, and developed a unique culture. Hawaii came in contact with the first recorded European in the Hawaiian Islands, Captain James Cook, in 1778. He named the chain of islands after his patron, the Earl of Sandwich, the first lord of the British Admiralty. One year later, Captain Cook was slain in a confrontation with the Hawaiians, but the islands were open at that point to Europeans who arrived to make their fortunes.

King Kamehameha I had united the islands by conquering the various ruling chiefs and instituting a series of laws and traditions for social harmony. When he died in 1819, his son, Liholiho, became Kamehameha II. He went to England with his wife, Queen Kamamalu, and there they succumbed to measles.

In Hawaii, American Protestants arrived in 1820 and began to construct missions, winning the respect of Queen Kaahumanu, who served as regent for the throne. The first Catholic missionaries arrived seven years later. On July 7, 1827, Father Alexis Jean Bachelot, accompanied by two other Sacred Hearts Fathers (Picpus Fathers), landed at Honolulu to begin the mission given to them by the Holy See. Father Bachelot was a prefect apostolic, and Queen Kaahumanu and her Protestant advisers rejected his position and his right to be in the islands. The priests were exiled from Hawaii after a time, and converts to the faith were punished.

Father Bachelot returned to Hawaii on April 17,

1837, but was banished again, despite his ill health. Father Louis Désiré Maigret, another Sacred Hearts Father, carried Father Bachelot onboard a small vessel. Father Bachelot died at sea on December 5, 1837, and hope of establishing a mission in the islands was in doubt.

Two years later, however, King Kamehameha III watched a French warship under the command of Captain Cyril P. T. La Place enter the harbor of Honolulu. The French captain informed the king that Hawaii was officially at war with His Catholic Majesty of France because of the ill-treatment of French citizens and the Hawaiian disregard for diplomatic protocol and courtesy. Catholics would have to be given religious freedom, or the warship would open fire on Honolulu and the surrounding area. King Kamehameha agreed to all of the captain's demands, attending a Catholic Mass, granting religious freedom, and paying an indemnity to France to ensure his future behavior.

The successor as prefect apostolic to Father Bachelot was Bishop Stephen Rouchouze, who was vicar apostolic of Eastern Oceania. Hawaii would be given the status of vicariate apostolic in 1844. Assessing the needs of the island missions, Bishop Rouchouze sailed to France in 1841 and recruited Sacred Hearts priests and sisters for Hawaii. Late in 1842 seven priests, seven brothers, and ten sisters of the congregation set sail on the *Marie-Joseph,* a 128-ton brig. The ship never arrived in Honolulu. It was last seen off the waters of St. Catherine Island near Brazil.

Bishop Rouchouze's successor was Bishop Louis Désiré Maigret, after another Sacred Hearts priest refused the office. Bishop Maigret was consecrated on October 31, 1847. He established the faith solidly in Hawaii, aided by the Sisters of the Sacred Hearts. He also ordained St. Damien de Veuster, the "Hero of Molokai."

Bishop Herman Koeckemann, Bishop Maigret's successor, was consecrated on August 21, 1881. He invited the Franciscan Sisters of Syracuse to the islands, and St. Marianne Cope led a group of

Bishop Stephen Rouchouze

religious companions to being a ministry of health care and education.

Bishop Gulstan Ropert was the next vicar apostolic, and was consecrated on September 25, 1892. He kept the faithful steady when Queen Liliuokalani was overthrown by island Americans. Sanford B. Dole served as head of the new republic formed by the Americans. Bishop Ropert also led the faithful through the terrible fire and plague of 1900.

Bishop Libert Boeynaems succeeded as the next vicar apostolic in July 1903. He renovated the Cathedral of Our Lady of Peace and aided the military efforts of the nation in World War I. He died of influenza on May 13, 1926, and was succeeded by Bishop Stephen Alencastre, who had served as his coadjutor. He invited the Maryknoll priests and sisters to the islands and celebrated the Centennial Year of the Church in Hawaii in 1927. Bishop Alencastre was the last vicar apostolic of Hawaii, as the Diocese of Honolulu was erected on September 10, 1941.

Bishop James J. Sweeney was consecrated on July 25, in anticipation of the establishment of the diocese. The attack on Pearl Harbor on December 7, 1941, put the islands on a war footing, and Bishop Sweeney had to combine his diocesan duties with ministries for the armed services. Bishop Sweeney reportedly was not in the islands when the attack took place, but he arrived on the first military convoy as military vicar. A population increase followed the end of the war, and Bishop Sweeney had to expand diocesan facilities to meet growing needs. He also led the Catholic Church as Hawaii became the fiftieth state on August 21, 1959. Bishop Sweeney died on June 19, 1968.

The second bishop of Honolulu was John J. Scanlan, who had served as auxiliary bishop of the diocese since September 21, 1954. He succeeded to the see on March 13, 1968. He attended the ceremonies in Statuary Hall in Washington, D.C., as a statue of St. Damien de Veuster was erected as Hawaii's representative, beside King Kamehameha I. Bishop Scanlan invited many religious congregations and orders into the diocese, particularly from the Philippines, in order to promote education among the recent immigrants from that land. He conducted pro-life programs and marches and organized an ecumenical council that included the leaders of all faiths in the islands and influenced legislation and policies. Bishop Scanlan retired on June 30, 1981.

His successor was Bishop Joseph A. Ferrario, who had served as auxiliary bishop of Honolulu since 1978. Bishop Ferrario succeeded on June 25, 1982. He reformed liturgical practices in the islands, brought in religious groups, and consolidated diocesan offices at the seminary. Bishop Ferrario retired because of ill health on October 12, 1993.

The fourth bishop of Honolulu was Francis X. DiLorenzo, who had served as auxiliary bishop of the Diocese of Scranton. He was appointed apostolic administrator on October 12, 1993, and succeeded to the see on November 29, 1994. Bishop DiLorenzo labored to organize diocesan funds and to liquidate a severe debt. On March 31, 2004, he was transferred to the Diocese of Richmond.

The successor to Bishop DiLorenzo was Bishop Clarence Silva, who was appointed on May 17, 2005. Born in Honolulu, Bishop Silva was ordained in 1975 and had served in the Oakland diocese until his appointment to Honolulu; he was consecrated on July 21, 2005. In 2011 there were 221,000 Catholics served by 129 priests and 66 parishes in the diocese.

Hope, Bob (Leslie Townes) (May 29, 1903–July 27, 2003)

One of America's most beloved entertainers, Bob Hope was honored in 1999 as the top entertainment figure of the millennium in an ABC News poll. He was a convert to Catholicism at the age of ninety-three after retiring from show business, although he had long supported Catholic causes with his wife of nearly seventy years, Dolores. He was born Leslie Townes Hope in Eltham, England, and his family moved to Cleveland in 1907.

Bob Hope's career spanned radio, television, and movies, and he won the admiration of Americans for his continued appearances before military troops during World War II and other military engagements, including the Vietnam and Persian Gulf wars. His relationship with NBC began in 1936 on its radio network, and he performed on NBC television.

Hope starred in almost fifty films, becoming popular in the famous "Road" movies with Bing Crosby and Dorothy Lamour. He received an honorary degree from Georgetown University and countless other honors.

Horgan, Paul George Vincent O'Shaughnessy (1903–March 8, 1995)

One of America's most respected authors and historians, Paul George Vincent O'Shaughnessy Horgan depicted the giants of the Catholic mission era and provided insight into turbulent eras of the nation. He was born in Buffalo, New York, into a cultured Catholic family and moved in 1915 to New Mexico, when his father, Edward, developed tuberculosis. His experiences in New Mexico provided depth and passion to his later writings, and he learned the art of journalism there, joining the staff of the *Albuquerque Journal* after graduating from high school.

In 1923 Horgan went to the Eastman School of Music in Rochester, New York, having a genuine interest in the field of music. He published his first poems while at the school, and he turned as well to novels. He published *Men of Arms* in 1931 and won the Harper Prize for *The Fault of Angels* in 1933. The *Devil in the Desert,* published in 1952, was popular, and he won the Bancroft Prize for *The Saintmakers' Christmas Eve* in 1955. Horgan was writing a book every eighteen months at that time. They include *A Distant Trumpet, The Common Heart, Give Me Possession, The Habit of Empire, A Lamp on the Plains, Main Line West, Memories of the Future,* and *One Red Rose for Christmas.*

He was awarded two Pulitzer Prizes for his histories, and his *Lamy of Santa Fe* was well received across the country. Horgan became a Fellow of the Center for Advanced Studies at Wesleyan University in Middletown, Connecticut, in 1960. He was then appointed director, but resigned to serve as professor of English and Permanent Author in Residence at the university. He taught that the world could be grasped securely in Catholic terms, in redemptive graces and daily heroism. Horgan died in Connecticut.

Houma-Thibodaux, Diocese of

Established on June 5, 1977, by Pope Paul VI, the Diocese of Houma-Thibodaux serves parishes (counties) in southwestern Louisiana. Houma was founded in 1810 as a fishing, fur, and shrimp center and was named after the Houma Indians. Thibodaux, on the Bayou Lafourche, is an agricultural and industrial complex. The diocese is a suffragan see of the Archdiocese of New Orleans.

The Diocese of Houma-Thibodaux is located in an area of the United States that has a profound Catholic heritage. Louisiana was visited by Hernando de Soto in 1541 and then explored by René-Robert Chevalier, Sieur de La Salle, in 1679. Father Zenobius Membré, a Recollect Franciscan who was martyred later in Texas, was on the expedition. Twenty years later, Pierre Le Moyne, Sieur d'Iberville, built a fort in the area.

Jean-Baptiste Le Moyne, Sieur de Bienville, founded New Orleans in 1718, and the French had control of the area until 1763, when England took the region as a result of the Treaty of Paris. The Louisiana Purchase in 1803 ceded the area to the United States. Louisiana, including Houma and Thibodaux, received the Acadian exiles who had been driven from their homes in Acadia by the British, and they settled throughout the area.

The Diocese of Louisiana and the Two Floridas was established in 1793, and in 1826 Louisiana was divided between two ecclesiastical jurisdictions: Lower Louisiana, which became part of the Diocese (now Archdiocese) of New Orleans, and Upper Louisiana, which was part of the Diocese of Natchitoches (now the Diocese of Alexandria). Louisiana became a member of the Union in 1812, and the area prospered. When the Civil War started, Louisiana seceded from the Union in 1861 and was restored seven years later. Federal troops and carpetbaggers overran the area during the Reconstruction period.

The people of Houma-Thibodaux maintained the Catholic faith during these historical eras. The Cathedral of St. Francis de Sales in Houma dates to 1847, and the co-cathedral of St. Joseph in Thibodaux was started in 1817. Other early parishes in the diocese include Holy Savior in Lockport (1850), St. Mary's Nativity in Raceland (1850), St. Lawrence in Chacahoula (1858), Sacred Heart of Jesus in Morgan City (1859), Sacred Heart in Montegut (1864), Our Lady of the Rosary in Larose (1873), St. Eloi in Theriot (1875), and St. Anthony's in Bayou Black (1876).

Lafayette was erected as a diocese in 1918, as all of Louisiana was supporting the military efforts of the United States in World War I. The Great Depression brought economic hardships, followed by the grim period of World War II. Parishes within the modern-day diocesan boundaries were established, and the Catholic population continued to grow in the area. In 1961 the Diocese of Baton Rouge was established, and Houma-Thibodaux became a diocese in 1977.

The first bishop of the Diocese of Houma-Thibodaux was Warren L. Boudreaux, who had served as auxiliary bishop of Lafayette and as bishop of Beaumont. Bishop Boudreaux instituted the agencies and offices for diocesan administration and expanded diocesan facilities. He built parishes and schools, promoted lay ministries, and aided the Vietnamese Catholic refugees in the area. Bishop Boudreaux retired on December 29, 1992.

The second bishop of Houma-Thibodaux was Michael Jarrell, who was consecrated and installed on March 4, 1993. Bishop Jarrell continued the expansion programs and implemented the reforms of the Second Vatican Council, establishing lay ministries and social service programs. On November 8, 2002, Bishop Jarrell was transferred to the Diocese of Lafayette.

The third bishop, Samuel G. Jacobs, had served as the bishop of Alexandria since 1989. He was appointed to Houma-Thibodaux on August 1, 2003, and was installed on October 10, 2003. The most important event of his brief time as bishop was the staggering damage inflicted on the diocese by Hurricane Rita in 2005. Many thousands of homes were destroyed or damaged in the southern parts of the diocese. Also, in response to the devastation caused by Hurricane Katrina elsewhere in Louisiana, the bishop organized the diocese to provide financial, material, and above all spiritual relief and care to the thousands of Gulf people impacted by one of the greatest natural disasters in American history. In 2005 the Sisters of St. Joseph of Médaille celebrated their 150th anniversary of service in the diocese. In 2011 there were 111,000

Catholics served by 68 priests and 39 parishes in the diocese.

Houses of Mercy. *See* **Mercy, Sisters of**

Howard, Edward D. (November 5, 1877–January 2, 1983)

Archbishop of Portland in Oregon, from 1926 until 1966, Edward D. Howard was one of the longest-serving bishops in American history and, at the time of his passing at the age of 105, he was the oldest Catholic prelate in the world. He was born in Cresco, Iowa, to John R. and Marie Fleming Howard; his father was an Irish immigrant who had fought in the Civil War. Edward's twin brother, Emmett, died at the age of nine months.

After studies at St. Joseph (now Loras) College in Dubuque, Iowa, he transferred in 1900 to St. Paul Seminary in St. Paul, Minnesota, for seminary work. Ordained a priest by Archbishop John Ireland on June 12, 1906, in St. Paul, he returned to St. Joseph College to teach Greek and Latin in the high school. Named principal in 1908, he was moved to the post of dean of the college in 1916 and president in 1920. On December 23, 1923, Father Howard was appointed by Pope Pius XI to the titular see of Isaura and as auxiliary bishop of the Diocese of Davenport. Consecrated on April 6, 1924, in Dubuque by Archbishop Austin Dowling of St. Paul, Bishop Howard served as auxiliary bishop with great dedication and on April 30, 1926, was transferred to serve as archbishop of Oregon City on April 30, 1926. He was installed in the Cathedral of the Immaculate Conception in Portland on August 25, 1926. On September 26, 1928, the name of the see was changed by the Sacred Consistorial Congregation in Rome to the Archdiocese of Portland in Oregon.

As archbishop of Portland for four decades, Archbishop Howard was shepherd over the Catholic community there from the time of the Great Depression through the Second World War, the Vietnam War, and especially the Second Vatican Council and its immediate aftermath. Much of his early focus was on improving diocesan administration and centralization, starting with a chancery and the acquisition of the archdiocesan weekly newspaper (begun in 1870). The paper had previously been owned privately, but the archbishop was able to place it in the hands of Monsignor Charles T. Smith and the Catholic Truth Society of Oregon. In 1932 he also convened the Fourth Provincial Council of the Archdiocese of Portland in Oregon, and three years later organized a Synod for the priests of his archdiocese.

Significantly, Archbishop Howard fought and won a landmark court case that ended efforts to block church and parochial school construction through the use of local zoning ordinances. The case stemmed from the effort to build a parish school in 1931 for All Saints Church in Portland that was blocked by the claim that the building would conflict with a local zoning ordinance. His victory was an important precedent for the Church in the United States. (*See also* Education, Catholic.) He also fought long and hard for the construction of a high school for boys, although it took until 1939 for the objective to be realized.

Pope Pius XII named him Assistant at the Pontifical Throne in 1939, and despite his advancing years he remained in excellent health and was still archbishop at the start of the Second Vatican Council. A year after the end of the council, Archbishop Howard was transferred by Pope Paul VI to the titular archiepiscopal see of Albule on December 9, 1966, and appointed administrator of the archdiocese, *sede vacante,* until the naming of his successor early the next year. His health was still excellent enough for him to deliver a sermon at the Mass celebrating his 100th birthday. He died in Portland, and his funeral Mass was telecast live.

Hubert, Jean-François (February 23, 1739–October 17, 1799)

The bishop of Québec from 1788 to 1799, Jean-François Hubert was a pioneer in defending the rights of Catholics. A native of Québec, Canada, Jean-François was the son of a baker. After studies at the seminary of Québec, he was forced to wait for six years before he could be ordained as the diocese was vacant for years after the death of Bishop Henri-Marie du Breuil de Pontbriand in 1760. He served with distinction as a priest in the diocese and was conspicuous in his ministry among the Hurons at Detroit starting in 1781. Four years later, he received word that he had been named coadjutor bishop to Bishop Louis-Philippe Mariauchau d'Esgly in 1785. With the passing of Bishop Mariauchau d'Esgly in 1788, he acceded to the see.

Conscious of the unique nature of French Canadians, especially in the difficult period after the end of the American War of Independence, Bishop Hubert fought with great vigor against a plan for a university concocted in 1789 by a group of English loyalists who had emigrated from the United States. The new university was to place firm state control over education and had as its purpose the extermination of traditional French-Canadian culture. The plan also was designed to stamp out the Catholic faith. Bishop Hubert succeeded in blocking it, despite determined support from many official quarters.

Also preoccupied with vocations and acquiring priests for his diocese, Bishop Hubert recruited heavily from France and relied upon various exiled French priests from France to begin the difficult task of replacing the Jesuits and the Recollects in Canada. By 1794 Bishop Hubert could claim 160 priests and 160,000 Catholics, including Native Americans. His diocese extended across the whole of Canada, which meant he was shepherd over a territory larger than Europe.

Hughes, John J. (June 24, 1797–January 3, 1864)

The first archbishop of the Archdiocese of New York, John J. Hughes was a fearless and prominent prelate and a personal friend of American presidents. He was born in Annaloghan, County Tyrone, Ireland, the son of Patrick Hughes and Margaret McKenna. Patrick Hughes migrated to the United States in 1816, and settled in Chambersburg, Pennsylvania. The son followed his father to America in 1817, and aided his family for a year or more.

In 1819 he went to Mount St. Mary's College in Emmitsburg, Maryland, first as an employee and then as a student. He was ordained on October 15, 1826, in St. Joseph's Church, Philadelphia, and he was assigned to St. Augustine's in Philadelphia, and to Bedford, Pennsylvania, returning to Philadelphia to become pastor of St. Joseph's, and then of St. Mary's. The trustees of St. Mary's were in open revolt against the bishop, and were calmed and brought into submission by Father Hughes.

On the national scene, Father Hughes attracted attention when he confronted Reverend John A. Brekenridge, a distinguished Presbyterian clergyman, in a public religious debate. Brekenridge was leveling vicious attacks on Catholics, and Father Hughes was able to turn aside the attacks and defend the Church before the nation. His ability brought admiration from many quarters, and on January 7, 1838, he was consecrated titular bishop of Basileopolis and coadjutor of New York. One year later he became administrator apostolic of New York, and on the death of Bishop John Dubois acceded to the see on December 20, 1842.

Even when he served as the administrator apostolic of New York, Bishop Hughes was dedicated to the abolition of trusteeism, having witnessed personally the damage done by lay interference in Church administrative affairs. He consolidated ownership and control of the diocesan facilities and gained the right to maintain church property from a New York State law concerning religious incorporation. He also convoked the first diocesan synod of New York in 1841, which enacted timely legislation affecting spiritual matters and advised regulations for tenure and administration of church property.

He was the most visible Catholic in America, promoting Catholic education and founding St. Joseph's College at Fordham. Bishop Hughes confronted the Public School Society, a private corporation controlling the management of schools and the distribution of the school fund provided by the municipality. He based his objection to this society on the grounds that it violated a fundamental American principle — namely, freedom of conscience, and after two years halted the powers of the society. An anti-Catholic outbreak of the Nativist political party occurred in 1844 in Philadelphia, where churches and convents were destroyed.

The next assault on Catholic property was scheduled to take place in New York City. Bishop Hughes armed his Catholic men, mostly Irish, and stationed them on the grounds of parishes, schools, and convents. When the mayor of New York predicted violence if the Catholics defended their properties, Bishop Hughes told him to warn the anti-Catholics that there would be blood in the streets, adding the counsel that the Protestants should be careful not to rile the Irish of the diocese. Not one Catholic property was attacked, as the mobs faded away at the sight of the armed Catholics ready to do battle.

Two years later, President James K. Polk asked Bishop Hughes to serve as a counselor. In 1847 he also addressed Congress on the role of Christians in preserving American political institutions, having been invited by John Quincy Adams, Stephen A. Douglas, and John C. Calhoun. President Polk, through Secretary of State James Buchanan, in 1846 proffered him a diplomatic mission to Mexico, which he was unable to accept.

On July 19, 1850, New York was elevated to the status of a metropolitan provincial see, and he was raised to the dignity of an archbishop. Archbishop Hughes received the pallium personally from Pope Blessed Pius IX in Rome on April 3, 1851. He was in Rome again in 1854 for the promulgation of the dogma of the Immaculate Conception.

At the outbreak of the Civil War, Archbishop Hughes was asked by William H. Seward, the secretary of state, to go to France to visit Napoleon III, who received him most graciously and was convinced by him not to recognize the Confederacy. During the Draft Riots of 1863 in New York City, Governor Horatio Seymour invoked the aid of Archbishop Hughes to suppress disorder.

Aware of the future greatness of New York City, Archbishop Hughes laid the cornerstone of St. Patrick's Cathedral on August 15, 1858. When he died in New York City, he was interred in old St. Patrick's Cathedral, but was transferred on January 30, 1883, to his final resting place under the sanctuary of the new cathedral on Fifth Avenue. His death brought a great public expression of sympathy and respect, and his memory was honored by tributes from President Abraham Lincoln and other American leaders.

Hungarian Catholics

The immigration of Hungarians in general and Hungarian Catholics in particular is an often overlooked but highly significant aspect of the development of the country. It is estimated that between 1820 and the middle of the twentieth century, nearly two million Hungarians migrated to the United States. Influencing directly and significantly the expansion of the Hungarian population in the United States were the sometimes tragic political events that engulfed Hungary in the nineteenth and twentieth centuries. Chief among these were the Hungarian rebellion against the Habsburgs in 1848–49 and the savage oppression of the Hungarian people under the communists, especially after the 1956 uprising.

There was little migration from Hungarian regions during the colonial period in North America. One of the few notable Hungarians of the pre-1848 period was Agoston Haraszthy de Mokcsa, an immigrant in 1840 who founded Sauk City, near Madison, Wisconsin, and journeyed west in 1849 to California. He later became sheriff of San Diego. The general starting date for large-scale movement from Hungary to America is the turbulent year in Europe of 1848. In that year, the European order was shaken by revolutions, including one against the Habsburgs in Hungary. The vanguard of the migration was led by Lajos Kossuth, the Hungarian revolutionary leader who had been proclaimed, briefly, president of an independent Hungary. He arrived in the United States in December 1851 on the warship *Mississippi*, after the collapse of his revolution. He visited the country as a hero, but he later died in exile in Italy. With him, however, were comrades and supporters, some of whom remained in America.

Compelled to leave Hungary because of the turmoil and the subsequent war between Austria and Prussia, many Hungarians left Europe for the United States. They were initially considered Austrians since they had traveled from the Austrian Empire. Thousands fought in the Civil War, and there were some eight hundred officers of Hungarian descent in the Union Army.

Additional immigration took place in the decades after the war. As economic conditions remained stagnant in rural parts of Hungary, coupled with political unrest and social dissatisfaction,

Archbishop John Hughes

Hungarians left to find work and the promise of a better future in the Industrial Revolution underway in the United States. They worked as miners, as laborers in factories, and as artisans. One of the most famous Hungarian émigrés was Joseph Pulitzer, the publishing magnate and founder of the Columbia University School of Journalism. In the last decade of the nineteenth century, over two hundred thousand Hungarians settled in the country, a number eclipsed in the first decade of the twentieth century when over four hundred thousand Hungarians completed the long trip from Central Europe. Estimates have been made that approximately half of all Hungarian immigrants were Catholic. The rest were Protestant, Jewish, or unaffiliated. Hungarians settled initially on the East Coast, but then moved to New Jersey, Connecticut, and Pennsylvania, as well as the cities and mining centers of Ohio, Indiana, Illinois, and West Virginia.

Hungarian Catholics were not identified as such for some time after their arrival in large numbers. They tended to be grouped with the German and Slavic Catholic communities and often worshipped in the ethnic churches that cared for those groups. Slavic priests most regularly attended to their pastoral care as they were most apt to speak the languages needed for proper ministry. Around 1891, however, Bishop Ignatius Horstmann of Cleveland was successful in bringing the Hungarian priest, Father Károly Böhm, to provide direct ministry to the Hungarians of the diocese.

Father Böhm arrived in December 1892 in Cleveland and proved deeply dedicated to the Hungarian Catholics. He soon found his sphere of activity extended across the entire country. As the only Hungarian priest known to the Hungarian Catholic community, he was compelled to travel as far as California. He constructed the first Hungarian church, St. Elizabeth's, in Cleveland, and founded two Hungarian Catholic papers, *Szent Erzsébet Hirnöke* and *Magyarok Vasárnapja*. Many more Hungarian churches soon followed, in Connecticut, Pennsylvania, Indiana, Ohio, New York, New Jersey, Illinois, Virginia, and Michigan.

By the early twentieth century, there were over thirty Hungarian priests in the country caring for some half a million Hungarian Catholics. This number had increased to about two hundred priests by 1950. In addition, there were active communities of Hungarian Eastern Catholics. (*See also* Eastern Churches, Catholic.)

To assist the pastoral care of Hungarians, and in recognition of the long-standing difficulty of recruiting priests directly form Hungary for service in the United States, Bishop Michael A. Tierney sent eight seminarians to study in Hungary to improve their awareness of the Magyar language and of Hungarian culture.

As the Hungarian communities in the United States developed, so too did the need for newspapers and other publications in the Hungarian language. The first to be published was the *Magyar Számüzöttek Lapja* (*Hungarian Exiles' Journal*) in 1853, followed by the *Amerikai Nemzetör* (*American Guardsman*) in 1884. One of Father Böhm's publications began as a weekly in Cleveland, *Magyarországi Szent Erzsébet Hirnöke* (*St. Elizabeth's Hungarian Herald*); two years later it became an eight-page newspaper, the *Magyarok Vasárnapja* (*Hungarian Sunday News*). A number of other Hungarian Catholic periodicals followed, including *Hajnal* (*Dawn*) and *Magyar Zászló* (*Hungarian Standard*).

A second intense period of immigration began in the years immediately after World War II. Hungarians struggled to escape the harsh communist dictatorship imposed on the country by the Soviet Union. In 1946 Catholic organizations were disbanded, followed by the suppression of Catholic schools, colleges, and other institutions. A wave of terror in 1948 saw the arrest of Cardinal József Mindszenty and the murder of Bishop Vilmos Apor of Györ. In 1950 religious orders were suppressed; thousands of clergy were imprisoned and sent to labor camps, while others were exiled or murdered. The uprising of 1956 freed Cardinal Mindszenty, but the merciless Soviet response reinstalled the communists.

As a result of the descent of even more severe repression, Hungarians fled their homeland. Large numbers of religious made their way to the United States after the 1950 suppression of all religious orders and congregations. Among the religious men who arrived during the twentieth century were Benedictines, Cistercians, Franciscans, and Jesuits, as well as members of the Custody of St. Stephen, King, and

Custody of St. John Capistran. The women religious included members of the Daughters of Divine Redeemer, the Daughters of Divine Charity, the Social Mission Sisters, and the Sisters of Mercy.

Huntington, Jedediah Vincent (January 20, 1815–March 10, 1862)

A convert to the Catholic faith, Jedediah Vincent Huntington was a noted author. He was born in New York City and raised an Episcopalian. After studies at Yale College and the University of New York, he proceeded to study in the field of medicine at the University of Pennsylvania and earned his degree in 1838. He never practiced medicine, but worked as a professor of philosophy in St. Paul's Episcopal School near Flushing, New York. During this period he also studied to become a minister and received ordination in 1841. Soon after, he became rector of the Episcopal church at Middlebury, Vermont, but doubts soon began to enter his heart about his theology and he left America for Europe.

Huntington devoted himself to research in England and then in Rome. Initially convinced of the Anglican position on papal authority, he was persuaded swiftly of the truth of Catholic teaching after spending time in Rome. With his wife, he entered the Church in 1849. Sailing back to the United States, he lectured extensively and served as editor of the Catholic periodicals *Metropolitan Magazine* and *The Leader*. His true success, however, came in the field of fiction writing. His novels, such as the semiautobiographical *Alban, or the History of a Young Puritan* and *Rosemary, or Life and Death*, earned him praise from contemporaries. He died in Pau, France, where he spent his last years.

Hunton, George K. (March 24, 1888–November 11, 1967)

A Catholic lawyer, George K. Hunton was a prominent figure in interracial justice. He was born in New Hampshire and attended Holy Cross College and Fordham Law School. Soon after graduation, Hunton began work at the Harlem Legal Aid Society in 1910. He served in the U.S. military forces during World War I and then returned to New York City to begin a career as a practicing lawyer.

In 1931 Hunton was named executive director of the Cardinal Gibbons Institute, an organization that sought to provide educational opportunities to African-Americans. Three years later, he moved to the position of executive director of the Catholic Interracial Council of New York (CICNY) and editor of its magazine, *Interracial Justice*. His position brought him into close contact with Father John LaFarge, S.J., a dedicated promoter of civil rights, and Hunton became a key figure in the effectiveness of the CICNY in advancing race relations in the United States.

Hunton was a presence in virtually all the efforts at interracial dialogue and race relations over the succeeding three decades. He was aggressive in securing the passage of federal anti-lynching legislation and in advancing the role of African-Americans in labor during the Second World War. He also assisted the work of the National Association for the Advancement of Colored People (NAACP) in crafting an effective civil rights legislative agenda and was honored by that organization with election in 1955 to its board of directors. Over the years, he was honored with the *Pro Ecclesia et Pontifice* medal in 1950 and the St. Francis Peace medal in 1961. Hunton retired in 1962.

Hurley, Joseph Patrick (January 21, 1894–October 30, 1967)

A papal diplomat and the bishop of the Diocese of St. Augustine, Joseph Patrick Hurley was one of the most outspoken Catholic prelates of America and received the personal title of archbishop. He was born in Cleveland, educated in the priesthood, and ordained on May 29, 1919. After completing graduate studies at the University of Toulouse in France in 1927, Father Hurley became secretary to Archbishop (later Cardinal) Edward Mooney, who was the apostolic delegate to India. Father Hurley also accompanied Archbishop Mooney to Japan in 1931, and from 1933 to 1934 served as chargé d'affaires in Japan. In 1935 he was made an attaché in the Secretariat of State in the Vatican, serving in that office until 1940.

In August 1940 he was appointed bishop of the Diocese of St. Augustine, which had ecclesiastical jurisdiction over all of Florida east of the Apalachicola River in the Panhandle. He assumed the see and began building and buying land for future parish needs, but he also became a spokesman for anti-Nazi sentiments in America. His CBS Radio address in 1941 urged Americans to abandon all ideas of neutrality in the face of the Nazi advance across Europe. When the war ended, Bishop Hurley was outspoken about his anti-communist opinions also, having had the opportunity to assess the dangers of the Soviet Union.

In October 1945 he was made regent of the apostolic nunciature in Belgrade, in present-day Serbia, and there he attended the trial of Archbishop (later Cardinal) Alojzije Stepinac, with all its communist cruelty. Priests, religious, and Catholics all across Yugoslavia were being persecuted by the communists, and Bishop Hurley used his own money to aid them. He left Belgrade having made known his animosity to the communist cause. In 1949 Pope Pius XII gave him the personal title of archbishop.

Returning to his diocese, Archbishop Hurley moved quickly to meet the needs of the growing Catholic population of Florida. He built forty-eight new parishes and promoted charitable and social programs. In 1958 the Archdiocese of Miami was erected, and a large portion of the Diocese of St. Augustine was moved to the new jurisdiction. Archbishop Hurley continued aiding the faithful, building twenty-four more new parishes and thirty-three schools. He attended the Second Vatican Council and implemented the reforms mandated by that council with vigor. He died in St. Augustine.

I

Iberville, Pierre Le Moyne, Sieur d' (July 16, 1661–July 9, 1706)

A French military leader and explorer who founded forts and settlements in modern-day Alabama, Mississippi, and Louisiana, Pierre Le Moyne, Sieur d'Iberville, had brothers who were particularly noted for their exploits, especially Jean-Baptiste Le Moyne, Sieur de Bienville. Iberville was born at Villamarie, Montréal, to a prominent noble family. With his brother, Bienville, he co-founded Fort Louis de la Mobile on the Mobile River and extended French and Catholic influences throughout the area.

He entered the navy as a young boy and was often described by his contemporaries as being as "military as his sword." Iberville joined the forces of the Chevalier de Troyes in Hudson Bay and in 1686 took part in a raid against the English at Fort Rupert with another of his brothers, Maricourt. The brothers and nine men attacked an English vessel and captured it, taking the English governor of Hudson Bay as a prisoner. Iberville then captured Fort Nelson in Hudson Bay and Fort Pemaquid in Maine. In 1696 he took all the English settlements on Newfoundland, using a squadron of four warships and a brigantine.

In the following year, Iberville set sail for France, where he received a hero's welcome. There he was appointed as the leader of an expedition to explore and colonize Louisiana. His small fleet left France, and Iberville sailed to Santa Rosa Island at present-day Pensacola, Florida, and then to Mobile Bay. On February 27, 1699, he led a small group of men in two canoes and two rowboats to look for the mouth of the Mississippi, which he discovered on March 2. He also found two lakes, naming them the Maurepas and the Pontchartrain. In May of that year he founded a fort at Biloxi, called Old Biloxi, and on January 16, 1702, worked with Bienville at Mobile.

Iberville destroyed every English outpost he could find and planned a massive assault on the Carolinas. He sailed to Havana to obtain Spanish allies for the venture, and in 1706 captured 30 English ships and 1,750 prisoners. In Havana, however, he contracted yellow fever and died.

Idaho

Called the Gem of the Mountains, Idaho is located in the northwestern part of the United States. The state is bounded on the north by Canada, on the east by Montana and Wyoming, on the south by Utah and Nevada, and on the west by Oregon and Washington. Idaho entered the Union as the forty-third state on July 3, 1890. There are three natural land regions in Idaho: the Rocky Mountains in the north, the Columbia Plateau in the south, and the Great Basin in the southwest. The original American Indian tribes in Idaho were the Bannock, Coeur d'Alene, Flathead, Kutenai, Lemhi, Nez Pérce, Pend d'Oreille, Sheepeater, and Shoshone.

Circa 1743, Pierre Gaultier de Varennes, the Chevalier de La Vérandrye, the governor of Québec, visited the area of modern-day Idaho. Sixty-two years later, Meriwether Lewis and William Clark crossed Idaho on their famous expedition. French-Canadian fur trappers were regular visitors to the region over the decades, and in 1809 David Thompson opened a trading post on Lake Pend d'Oreille.

Three years later, Young Ignace La Mousse, an Iroquois warrior who had arrived among the Flatheads with a hunting party, explained the Catholic faith to the local Native Americans and urged them to seek a "Black Robe," a Catholic priest. Delegations of Flatheads traveled on several occasions to nearby Catholic authorities, asking for a missionary, but it was not until February 1840 that one was available. Jesuit Father Pierre-Jean De Smet was sent to the area and met the tribes at Pierre's Hole. On July 22, 1840, Father De Smet celebrated Mass at Henry's Lake in Yellowstone. He was appointed superior of the Jesuit Rocky Mountain Missions. Jesuit Father Nicholas Point founded a Coeur d'Alene mission on the St. Joe River in 1843, near present-day St. Marie's, but the mission was moved later to a tribal reservation. Sacred Heart, in time designated as the Cataldo Mission in honor of the pioneering Jesuit, was the oldest building in Idaho.

Gold was discovered at Orofino Creek in 1860, and a vast gold rush took place at Boise Basin. By act of Congress, the Territory of Idaho was established in 1863, and in March 1868 Pope Blessed Pius IX erected the Vicariate Apostolic of Idaho. Father Louis Aloysius Lootens was consecrated as a bishop on August 9, 1868, serving as vicar apostolic. Bishop Lootens resigned in 1875 and returned to Vancouver Island, his former mission territory. The people of Idaho were then caught up in the confrontation between U.S. troops and Chief Joseph of the Nez Pérce.

Idaho was placed under the jurisdiction of the bishops of Oregon City (now the Archdiocese of Portland in Oregon). Then the Diocese of Boise was established, and Bishop Alphonsus Joseph Glorieux was consecrated as the first ordinary of the see. He established parishes in Idaho and built eighty churches. In 1867 the Sisters of the Holy Names of Jesus and Mary opened the first Catholic school at Idaho City. The Church prospered, even during the mine disputes and the opening of public lands. When the railroads arrived in Idaho, the Catholic Church Extension Society provided railroad cars for missionary tours.

World War I involved the faithful of the diocese as Idaho supported the nation's military efforts. New schools were established and staffed by Benedictine Sisters. The Catholics of Idaho maintained their parishes and schools even in the harsh economic times of the Great Depression and then during the grim era of World War II. A diocesan newspaper was started in 1958, and charitable facilities were expanded.

In 1962 Bishop Sylvester William Treinen was consecrated as the fifth bishop of Boise. He attended the Second Vatican Council and implemented the reforms of that council. Lay aposto-

Sacred Heart Mission in Idaho

lates were also promoted, and religious education was stressed. The state Catholic facilities were also designed to aid Hispanic, Basque, Asian, and African-American missions, as well as the historic American Indian apostolate. Today Idaho's Catholics are involved in providing spiritual and charitable services to the people in the new high-tech and communications industries. In 2011 there were 170,000 Catholics served by 94 parishes and 52 parishes in the state.

Illig, Alvin Anthony (August 17, 1926–August 2, 1991)

The founding director of the Paulist National Catholic Evangelization Association, Alvin Anthony Illig was the first executive director of the National Conference of Catholic Bishops' Committee on Evangelization, from 1977 to 1982. He was born in Los Angeles to Joseph and Katherina Illig. After attending the Junior Seminary of the Archdiocese of Los Angeles in 1945, he entered the Paulists and was sent to continue his studies at St. Paul's College in Washington, D.C. Having completed his preparations for the priesthood, he was ordained in 1953 by then Bishop (later Archbishop) Fulton J. Sheen. His first assignment was to St. Paul the Apostle Parish, but he was also ordered to assist the Paulist Press.

Over the next years, Father Illig studied at New York University and Columbia University to develop his knowledge of publishing and social communications. In 1955 he was appointed the editor of *Information* magazine; he went on to launch the National Catholic Reading Distributors and the Unified Magazine Program. He was next instrumental in arranging the merger between Newman Press and Paulist Press. Following the Second Vatican Council, Father Illig helped start the American edition of the noted theological journal *Concilium*. He then provided crucial assistance to the Catholic Library Association in organizing the American Library and Education Service Company, a program that provided books to parochial schools in a variety of key areas of study.

In 1973 Father Illig entered into work in evangelization, starting with inactive Catholics. His efforts in Mississippi proved so successful that Cardinal William W. Baum, in 1975, invited Father Illig to establish new initiatives in evangelization in Washington, D.C. As a major part of that wider goal of evangelization, he established the Paulist National Catholic Evangelization Association in 1977 as an apostolate of the Paulist Fathers. That same year, he was named the first executive director of the National Conference of Catholic Bishops' Committee on Evangelization. In 1980 he started *Share the Word*, a magazine devoted to assisting Catholics seeking to deepen their faith through Bible study. In 1983 he received the *Pro Ecclesia et Pontifice* medal from Pope Blessed John Paul II.

Prior to his death, Father Illig urged the bishops of the United States to formulate a national plan for evangelization. He died before the plan, *Go and Make Disciples*, was published. In recognition of his contributions, the plan was dedicated to his memory. The bishops wrote in the dedication: "Father Alvin Illig, C.S.P., devoted his life to the task that Pope Paul VI called 'the essential mission of the Church.' Touched by the Holy Spirit, he labored to spread the Gospel of Jesus Christ and the truth of the Catholic faith before the duty to evangelize was widely accepted. He led the way for the rest of us."

Illinois

Called the Prairie State, Illinois is located in the north-central part of the country. It is bounded on the north by Wisconsin, on the east by Lake Michigan and Indiana, on the south by Kentucky, and on the west by Iowa and Missouri. The twenty-first state, Illinois entered the Union in 1818. Two principal land regions dominate: the Central Plains and the Ozark Plateau, which is in the southern portion. The original Native American inhabitants were the Mound Builders, Cahokia, Flathead, Fox, Kaskaskia, Kickapoo, Michigamea, Moingwena, Pend d'Oreille, Peoria, Potawatomi, Sauk, and Tamora.

Some of America's most revered missionaries labored in the area that would become Illinois. In 1673 Jesuit Father Jacques Marquette and Louis Joliet were in the area, and in 1675 Father Marquette founded the Mission of the Immaculate Conception near present-day Utica, later transferred to Kaskaskia. In 1680 René-Robert Chevalier, Sieur de La Salle, built a French fort near Kaskaskia. Fathers Louis Hennepin, Gabriel de la Ribourde, and Zenobius Membré were present. Father de la Ribourde was later martyred near modern-day Seneca. Father Membré would also lose his life in the missions.

The Jesuit mission leader Father Claude Allouez and Jesuit Father Jacques Gravier also served the local tribes, but then had to move south because of local unrest. Father Gravier was wounded by a party of Peorias and died. In 1680 Kaskaskia was moved and reopened at a new location on the banks of the Mississippi River across from St. Louis, and Fathers Allouez and Gravier compiled dictionaries for the local American Indians. Missions were opened at Peoria, Starved Rock, and Rockford. At Kaskaskia, priests of the Foreign Missions of Québec joined in the ministries, opening Cahokia Mission in 1699, dedicated to the Holy Family.

In 1692 the first permanent settlement was opened at Peoria Lake, as French trappers and fur traders established their headquarters. More French Canadians entered the region, starting other communities. These settlements were threatened by the French and Indian War, and in 1763, when the English controlled the region, many left the area to resettle in the vast French territory called Louisiana. Priests were banished by the English, but Jesuit Father Sebastian L. Meurin and Father Pierre Gibault worked with Sulpician Father Gabriel Richard to keep the missions active. In 1778 Father Gibault championed the American cause in the Revolution and aided greatly in securing the states of Ohio, Indiana, Illinois, Michigan, and Wisconsin for the Americans.

After the war, Illinois was American territory, and Catholics in the area were under the jurisdiction of Bishop John Carroll of the Diocese of Baltimore (now the Archdiocese of Baltimore), which was erected in 1789.

In 1808 the Diocese of Bardstown (now the Archdiocese of Louisville) assumed jurisdiction over the Catholics of Illinois. Chicago's Fort Dearborn had been in operation since 1803, and the area became part of the Territory of Illinois in 1809, by act of Congress, having been included originally in the Indian Territory established in 1800. Illinois entered the Union in 1818. Chicago was incorporated in 1833, and Father Jean Marie Irenaeus St. Cyr was serving Catholics in the new city. Ten years later, the Diocese of Chicago was established, with Bishop William J. Quarter as the first ordinary. The Diocese of Vincennes (now the Archdiocese of Indianapolis) had been erected in 1834. The Black Hawk War of 1832 had hampered settlements, but more Catholic communities developed, and the Diocese of Springfield was erected. When the Civil War raged across the nation, Illinois was part of the Union. The Great Chicago Fire ravaged that city in 1871, leaving some one hundred thousand people homeless.

The Archdiocese of Chicago was established in 1880, and Illinois prospered. The Dioceses of Peoria and Belleville were in operation as well. During World War I, the Catholics of Illinois supported the military efforts of the nation. The Great Depression that followed brought need and suffering, but the faith continued to expand in Illinois, as the Diocese of Rockford was erected. Educational institutions and parochial school systems became a hallmark of the Church in the area. The Diocese of Joliet was

erected after the war, and the Ukrainian Diocese of St. Nicholas in Chicago followed.

World War II involved the faithful of Illinois. The University of Chicago was the scene of the research and tests that ushered in the atomic age. At the war's close, St. Frances Xavier Cabrini was canonized as the first saint of the United States. The Second Vatican Council impacted on Illinois Catholics as the reforms mandated by that council were implemented throughout the dioceses. The Catholic community in Illinois at the start of the new century faces the major challenges of changing demographics and increasing cultural diversity. In 2011 there were 4 million Catholics, 2,654 priests, 379 men religious, 3,479 women religious, and 988 parishes in the state.

Immaculate Conception, National Shrine of the. *See* National Shrine of the Immaculate Conception

Indian Catholics. *See* Native American Catholics

Indiana

Called the Hoosier State, Indiana is located in the north-central part of the nation in the Great Lakes region. The state is bounded on the north by Lake Michigan and the state of Michigan, on the east by Ohio, on the south by Kentucky, and on the west by Illinois. Indiana has three natural land regions: the Great Lakes Plain in the north, the Central Lowlands, and the Southern Hills. Indiana entered the Union on December 11, 1816, as the nineteenth state. The original American Indian inhabitants of Indiana were the Delaware, Kickapoo, Miami, Piankashaw, Potawatomi, Shawnee, and Wea.

The Catholic heritage of the state dates to 1675, when Jesuit Father Jacques Marquette entered the region. Four years later, René-Robert Chevalier, Sieur de La Salle, was in Indiana with Recollect Franciscan Father Louis Hennepin and Father Gabriel de la Ribourde, followed by the famed Jesuit missionaries Fathers Claude Allouez and James Gravier. Jesuits were active in South Bend as early as 1686, as the French claimed the territory after La Salle's expedition.

Fur trappers settled in the areas of modern-day Lafayette at Fort Quiatenon in 1717 and at Fort

Wayne, and in 1730 François Marie Bissot, Sieur de Vincennes, established a settlement and fort on the Wabash River. St. Francis Xavier Church was erected on the site for the state's oldest Christian congregation. Father Stephen Doutreleau served at Fort Vincennes, as did Father Sebastian L. Meurin. The nearly uninterrupted records of St. Francis Xavier at Vincennes date to 1749. Jesuit Father Pierre de Jounay was with the Miami at Lafayette, and other missions prospered.

By 1763 the English gained control of Indiana as a result of the Seven Years' War with France. When the Revolutionary War began, English troops occupied Vincennes, but George Rogers Clark arrived to take possession of the area, aided by Father Pierre Gibault, who sided with the American cause and was called the "Patriot Priest" because he ensured an American victory in Indiana and Illinois. In 1792 Sulpician Father Benedict Joseph Flaget, who would pioneer the largest diocese in American history, and Father John Rivet were in Vincennes, opening the first school in Indiana. Fathers Stephen T. Badin and Charles Nerinckx also arrived in the region.

By an act of Congress the Indiana Territory was established, an event that brought about hostilities with the local American Indian tribes. General "Mad Anthony" Wayne had fought against the Indians in 1794, and William Henry Harrison defeated Tecumseh at the Battle of Tippecanoe in 1811. The War of 1812 cost the Native Americans many of their holdings, and white settlers moved into the area. In 1816 Indiana entered the Union.

In 1824 the Sisters of Charity of Nazareth, Kentucky, opened St. Clare's Academy in Vincennes. The next year the cornerstone was laid for the third church of St. Francis Xavier, which later became the cathedral of the Vincennes diocese. The church was designated a minor basilica in 1970 and is still in use as a parish church. In 1834 the Holy See erected the Diocese of Vincennes, and Simon William Gabriel Bruté de Rémur was appointed as the first bishop. Six years later, the Sisters of Providence founded St. Mary-of-the-Woods Academy for women.

The University of Notre Dame was founded in 1842 by Holy Cross Father Edward Sorin, on land given to the Diocese of Vincennes by Father Badin. In 1854 the first Benedictine community was established in Indiana at St. Meinrad, designated as an abbey in 1870 and an archabbey in 1954.

The Diocese of Fort Wayne (now the Diocese of Fort Wayne-South Bend) was established in 1842. Soon after, the state was impacted by the Civil War, as raids and guerilla skirmishes took place within its borders. In the southern part of the state in 1863, Morgan's Raiders, a Confederate cavalry unit, fought against Union forces. At the close of the Civil War, new settlements appeared in Indiana. The state legislature enacted progressive laws, and the economy prospered. The people of Indiana also supported the military efforts of the nation in World War I. *Our Sunday Visitor* was founded in 1912 by Father John F. Noll, who became the bishop of the Diocese of Fort Wayne in 1925 and was given the personal title of archbishop.

The Great Depression brought severe hardships to Indiana as it caused extreme suffering across the nation. The beginning of World War II brought other sacrifices, but Indiana's industrial expansion was prompted by the need for military weapons and logistical supplies.

In 1944 Indianapolis was designated a metropolitan provincial see, an archdiocese, and the new Dioceses of Lafayette in Indiana, Evansville, and Gary were established. Religious orders and congregations were thriving. the University of Notre Dame had been established in 1842 by the Congregation of the Holy Cross, and other colleges were providing educational opportunities for returning veterans of the war.

The Church experienced rapid growth, even as religious congregations and priests declined following the Second Vatican Council. Catholics, however, supported local and universal causes and parishes promoted lay activities that provided outreach and social services. In 2011 there were 747,000 Catholics served by 800 priests, 191 men religious, 1,429 women religious, and 419 parishes in the state.

Indianapolis, Archdiocese of

Established as the Diocese of Vincennes on May 6, 1834, by Pope Gregory XVI, and designated as the Diocese of Indianapolis on March 28, 1898, by Pope Leo XIII, Indianapolis was elevated to the status of an archdiocese on December 14, 1944, by Pope Pius XII. Originally the diocese had jurisdiction over the entire state of Indiana and eastern Illinois. The archdiocese now serves counties in central and southern Indiana.

The capital of the state, Indianapolis was founded in 1821 and benefited by the opening of the National Road in 1827. In 1911 the Indianapolis Motor Speedway was opened. The city is now an industrial and manufacturing center. The Archdiocese of Indianapolis has suffragan sees.

The Catholic heritage of Indianapolis opened in 1675, when Jesuit Father Jacques Marquette entered the area, followed by René-Robert Chevalier, Sieur de La Salle, who was accompanied by Recollect Franciscan Father Louis Hennepin. Father Gabriel de la Ribourde was also in the expedition. The famed Jesuit missionaries Father Claude Allouez and Father Jacques Gravier arrived shortly after, and Father Allouez founded St. Joseph's Mission.

In 1732 or 1736 François Marie Bissot, Sieur de Vincennes, established a fort on the Wabash River, and St. Francis Xavier Church was opened. Jesuit Father Sebastian L. Meurin served there with other missionaries until France ceded the territory to England as part of the Treaty of Paris in 1763. Father Pierre Gibault was assigned to Vincennes and aided George Rogers Clark and the American cause during the Revolutionary War. After the British were defeated and forced to surrender control of the American colonies, Sulpician Fathers Benedict Joseph Flaget, who would become the head of the largest diocese in America, and Father John Rivet were sent to Vincennes, and in 1793 they opened the first school in Indiana.

In 1808, when the vast Diocese of Bardstown (now the Archdiocese of Louisville) was erected, Bishop Flaget was installed as the pioneering prelate. Indiana was part of the Diocese of Bardstown, and Fathers Stephen T. Badin and Charles Nerinckx, famed missionaries, were sent to Vincennes to aid the growing community. Father Louis Champomier served as resident pastor of Vincennes from 1822 to 1830.

Four years later, the Diocese of Vincennes was erected, the result of a petition from the American bishops at the Second Provincial Council of Baltimore. Sulpician Father Simon William Gabriel Bruté de Rémur was appointed the first bishop of Vincennes and was consecrated in 1834. Bishop Bruté de Rémur brought eighteen missionary priests from Europe and opened a college and a seminary. A zealous, pioneering prelate, Bishop Bruté de Rémur died from his labors in 1839.

His successor as the bishop of the Diocese of Vincennes was Celestine René Lawrence Guynemer de la Hailandiere, who had served as coadjutor bishop to Bishop Bruté de Rémur from 1836. He was in Europe, recruiting priests and religious, when Bishop Bruté de Rémur died. Bishop de la Hailandiere started the cathedral, convened a diocesan synod, and maintained facilities and ministries while facing financial problems and the loss of some clergy. He resigned in 1847 and returned to France, where he died.

The succeeding bishop of Vincennes was John Stephen Bezin, who was consecrated on October 24, 1847. He died suddenly on April 23, 1848. The fourth bishop of Vincennes was Maurice de St. Palais. He was consecrated on January 14, 1849. He increased the number of parishes and schools and tried to save St. Charles Seminary, which ultimately closed. He also led the faithful through the Civil War, a traumatic time in Indiana because of the military skirmishes in the southern areas of the state. Bishop de St. Palais brought priests and religious from Europe, including Swiss Benedictines, who founded St. Meinrad's Seminary. Franciscans and others accepted his invitation and served the Catholics of the area. Bishop de St. Palais died on June 28, 1877.

The fifth bishop of Vincennes was Bishop Francis Silas Chatard, who had served as the rector of the North American College in Rome. He was consecrated on May 12, 1878. Bishop Chatard transferred his episcopal residence to Indianapolis and set about reorganizing the diocese. He convened four diocesan synods, developed a union for clergy relief, formed a diocesan school system, and constructed the Cathedral of Sts. Peter and Paul. Bishop Chatard witnessed the transfer of the diocese to Indianapolis, decreed by the Holy See on March 18, 1898. He died on September 7, 1918.

Bishop Joseph Chartrand acceded to the Diocese of Indianapolis on September 7, 1918, having served as coadjutor bishop of the diocese since 1910. America was involved in World War I at the time, and the diocese supported the military efforts of the nation. Bishop Chartrand promoted the spiritual development of the faithful throughout the diocese. Devoted to the Eucharist, he fostered frequent reception of holy Communion and vocations to the priesthood and religious life. Many high schools were added to the diocesan facilities and homes for children and a hospital were established. Bishop Chartrand died on December 8, 1933, having led the faithful through the difficult days of the Great Depression.

His successor was Bishop Joseph E. Ritter, who would become an American cardinal in 1961. Bishop Ritter was promoted to the rank of archbishop on December 19, 1944, as Pope Pius XII created Indianapolis a metropolitan provincial see, an archdiocese. The Dioceses of Evansville and Lafayette in Indiana were established by the same decree. Archbishop Ritter revised the archdiocesan administration, convened synods, erected parishes, and promoted education and the National Council of Catholic Women. He also supported the military efforts of the nation in World War II. On July 20, 1946, Archbishop Ritter was transferred to St. Louis and was created a cardinal priest on June 16, 1961.

Archbishop Paul C. Schulte was appointed as the second archbishop of the Archdiocese of Indianapolis, having served as the bishop of Leavenworth (now the Archdiocese of Kansas City in Kansas) since 1937. He was installed in Indianapolis on October 10, 1946. Archbishop Schulte established new parishes and schools and promoted education and charitable works. He took part in the Second Vatican Council and implemented the reforms mandated by that council. He retired on January 14, 1970.

His successor was Archbishop George J. Biskup, who had served as the auxiliary bishop of Dubuque and then as bishop of Des Moines before being appointed coadjutor archbishop of Indianapolis with right of succession in 1967. He acceded to the see upon Archbishop Schulte's retirement. Archbishop Biskup continued expanding the archdiocesan facilities while maintaining the educational standards in the Catholic schools, despite a shortage of priests and religious. He retired on March 26, 1979.

The fourth archbishop of Indianapolis was Edward T. O'Meara, who had served as auxiliary bishop of St. Louis since 1972. He was installed in Indianapolis on January 10, 1980. Archbishop O'Meara consolidated and maintained diocesan facilities and ministries and promoted lay activities. He died on January 10, 1992.

The fifth archbishop of Indianapolis was Daniel Mark Buechlein, O.S.B. He had served as the bishop of Memphis from 1987. Archbishop Buechlein was promoted to Indianapolis on July 13, 1992, and was installed on September 9, 1992. During his long tenure, the archdiocese faced the growing pastoral issues of an increasing population and the influx of Spanish-speaking Catholics. He resigned owing to health concerns on September 21, 2011, at the age of seventy-three. In 2011 there were 225,000 Catholics, 238 priests, 579 women religious, and 139 parishes in the archdiocese.

Iowa

Called the Hawkeye State, Iowa is located in the north-central part of the United States. It is bounded on the north by Minnesota, on the east by Wisconsin and Illinois, on the south by Missouri, and on the west by Nebraska and South Dakota. There are three natural land regions in the state: the Driftless Area in the northeast, the Young Drift Plain in the north, and the Dissected Till Plain in the south. The original inhabitants of the Iowa region were the Mound Builders, Fox, Illinois, Iowa, Miami, Missouri, Omaha, Oto, Ottawa, Peoria, Sac, and Sioux. Iowa entered the Union as the twenty-ninth state in 1846.

The Catholic heritage of Iowa dates to 1673, when Jesuit Father Jacques Marquette and his companion, Louis Joliet, visited the region. René-Robert Chevalier, Sieur de La Salle, led an expedition into the area several years later, accompanied by the Franciscan Recollect Father Louis Hennepin and other priests. Father Gabriel de la Ribourde was also visiting tribal communities on the Mississippi River. Few missions were conducted in the area after Father de la Ribourde's ministry, and the Revolutionary War and the defeat of the English opened Iowa to new settlers.

In 1788 Julien Dubuque, a French-Canadian, started a lead mine near modern-day Dubuque, and he obtained a grant of land from the local tribes and expanded his holdings. In 1804 Meriwether Lewis and William Clark passed through the region on their historic expedition. A year later, Zebulon Pike led another exploratory party into parts of present-day Iowa. In 1832 the Black Hawk War took place, and the Fox and Sac warriors were defeated and forced to remove themselves from their homelands to make room for white settlers. Six years later, the U.S. Congress established the Territory of Iowa, prompting increases in settlements.

There were outstanding Catholic missionaries in Iowa at the time. Jesuit Father Charles Van Quickenborne was serving as an itinerant priest, and the famous Jesuit Father Pierre-Jean De Smet was with the various Indian communities. In 1836 Venerable Samuel Mazzuchelli, a Dominican, opened the first Catholic Church in Iowa, dedicated to St. Raphael.

Pope Gregory XVI erected the Diocese of Dubuque on July 28, 1837, and Bishop Mathias Loras was appointed to the diocese. A year later, Father De Smet founded St. Joseph's Mission at Council Bluffs. In 1843 the Sisters of Charity of the Blessed Virgin Mary became the first sisterhood in the state, founding Clarke College in Dubuque. In 1850 the Trappist monks opened a monastery in the state, Our Lady of New Melleray. Iowa entered the Union in 1846.

The Civil War impacted upon Iowa, a state that supported the Union cause. New settlements were created, and the Diocese of Davenport was erected. The American Protective Association and the Ku Klux Klan, extreme anti-Catholic groups, targeted Iowa, and they preached hatred for the "foreign" Catholics. The anti-Catholic bigotry was protested and halted by Americans across the land, who believed in freedom of religion. The state also served as the home base of the Populist Party in 1891.

Dubuque was elevated to the rank of an archdiocese in 1893, and the Dioceses of Sioux City and Des Moines were erected in 1902 and 1911. World War I brought sacrifices to the state, and Iowans supported the military efforts of the nation. The Great Depression brought more suf-

fering, and the Catholic dioceses instituted social service and charitable programs to alleviate the economic tragedy. In the Archdiocese of Dubuque, Archbishop Francis J. L. Beckman led the faithful through the grim days of World War II. Iowa's Catholics were involved in interracial programs and the National Catholic Rural Life Conference. They also responded to the reforms of the Second Vatican Council, and liturgical changes and lay ministries were adopted. Vietnamese Catholics and other new arrivals were welcomed. The state was also honored in October 1979 when Pope Blessed John Paul II visited Iowa and celebrated an outdoor Mass near Des Moines. In 2011 there were 494,000 Catholics served by 561 priests, 995 women religious, and 450 parishes in the state.

Ireland, John (September 11, 1838–September 25, 1918)

The first archbishop of the Archdiocese of St. Paul (now the Archdiocese of St. Paul and Minneapolis), John Ireland served the Catholic faithful in an era of controversy. He was born in Burnchurch, County Kilkenny, Ireland, the son of Richard Ireland and Judith Naughton Ireland, who came to the United States in 1850 when the Irish famine was desolating his homeland. The family went to Chicago and then St. Paul. He studied for the priesthood in France but returned to St. Paul for his ordination in 1861. During the Civil War, Father Ireland served as a chaplain for the Minnesota Infantry Regiment.

At the war's end, he resumed pastoral ministries and became a well-known advocate of building Catholic enclaves in the Midwest region. Father Ireland represented his bishop at the First Vatican Council in 1869 and 1870. He was appointed coadjutor bishop of the Diocese of St. Paul in 1875, acceding to the see in 1884. In 1888 he was promoted to the rank of archbishop, as the diocese was made a metropolitan provincial see. Archbishop Ireland promoted The Catholic University of America and was an ardent support of Americanizing the

Archbishop John Ireland

Church to adapt to the changing times in the United States He gave his backing to the eventually controversial Knights of Labor and to the equally contentious Faribault-Stillwater Plan. His views on inculturation subsequently involved him in the Americanist controversy. When, therefore, the papal condemnation of Americanism was issued in 1899 through Pope Leo XIII's encyclical *Testem Benevolentiae*, Archbishop Ireland focused on his own diocesan affairs.

He directed the building of St. Thomas College, St. Thomas Seminary, St. Catherine's College, the Cathedral of St. Paul, and the Basilica of St. Mary. Archbishop Ireland focused on educational institutions in order to prepare American Catholics for their role in the pluralistic arenas of America. An eloquent orator, Archbishop Ireland reflected the buoyant era in which he lived. He was called the "Consecrated Blizzard of the Northwest." He died in St. Paul.

Ireland, Mother Seraphine (July 1, 1842–June 20, 1930)

Mother superior of the Sisters of St. Joseph of Carondelet, province of St. Paul, from 1882 to 1921, Mother Seraphine Ireland was the sister of Archbishop John Ireland. Mother Seraphine helped to promote the congregation in the Midwest of the United States. Born in Burnchurch, Kilkenny, Ireland, she was the daughter of Richard Ireland and Judith Naughton Ireland. At the age of ten, she traveled to the United States with her family and settled in St. Paul, Minnesota. Drawn to the religious life, she entered the Sisters of St. Joseph of Carondelet in 1858 and took the name Seraphine.

From the start of her religious life, she became engaged very heavily in the area of education, and she was a strong advocate of providing the sisters of the congregation with as fine an education as possible to ensure a high quality of teaching in the schools the congregation was operating. After election as superior in 1882, she thus promoted sending the sisters to colleges in the United States and Germany. Her time as superior was marked also by the steady expansion of the congregation in the Midwest; between 1882 and 1921, when she retired, Mother Seraphine was able to guide the increase of the sisters from 162 to 913 and to over-

see the founding of the College of St. Catherine in 1911, as well as dozens of parochial schools and five hospitals.

Irish Catholics

The history of the Catholic Church in the United States has been shaped by the immense contributions of immigrants from abroad, ranging from Latin America to Eastern Europe. Perhaps the most influential group of immigrants has been the Irish. From the early eighteenth century to the middle of the twentieth century approximately five million Irish migrated to North America and the United States. Of these immigrants, the majority in the earliest period of the eighteenth century were Protestant Scots-Irish, while during the second long period of Irish migration from the early nineteenth century into the twentieth century the vast majority of arrivals in the country were Catholic.

The Irish Catholic presence in American ecclesiastical life can scarcely be overemphasized. As will be seen, the Irish (and to a lesser degree the Italians and Germans) dominated Catholic culture in the United States, provided sizable numbers of priests, and enjoyed massive influence in the American Catholic hierarchy.

The earliest Irish immigration began in the first days of the English colonies in North America. Catholic migration was limited, but one of the earliest causes was the brutal repression instigated by Oliver Cromwell during the Protectorate. Cromwell commanded that Irish who opposed English rule be deported to the West Indies and to America, so that from 1651 to 1654 over six thousand Irish were forcibly removed and sent to Barbados and various English colonies in America. They were followed by thousands more over the next decade.

The few Catholic Irish who made their way willingly to America found themselves in a thoroughly Protestant environment that was hostile to Catholics and often placed severe religious disabilities upon them. Many Catholics from Ireland lost their faith in this setting, and others simply stopped practicing the faith owing to the shortage of priests. Irish Catholics settling in America were given welcome in only a small number of places, such as Pennsylvania and Maryland. Even there, however, the Irish Catholics were not numerous;

in 1757 there were a mere 400 Irish Catholics in Pennsylvania out of over 1,300 total Catholics (the population of the time was around 200,000). Ships bearing Irish immigrants also arrived in Boston from the early eighteenth century. This was an unwelcome development to the authorities in Massachusetts who, in 1720, issued an ordinance directing that those recently arriving from Ireland be warned off. Three years later, a second ordinance was enacted that required all Irish to be registered.

The Irish also settled in some numbers in New York. Thomas Dongan, who was appointed the first colonial governor of New York in 1683 and provided the colony its first charter of liberties, was an Irish Catholic from County Kildare. Ships also reached Philadelphia.

An increase in Irish travelers began around 1765 when the city of Waterford, a port on Ireland's east coast, was first developed as an embarkation point for sea travel to Canada. As the Canadian ports were easily reached by ships setting sail from Ireland, Canada became a significant arrival spot for immigrants who then made their way south to the colonies. In fact, the Canadian ports were the primary entryway for the Irish into North America until the 1830s.

The Irish in America at the start of the American Revolution were divided in their sympathies. Like their Catholic counterparts in America, the Irish had long endured anti-Catholicism at the hands of the very same leaders who were assuming important posts in the Continental Army and the American government. There was, as a consequence, little inducement to fight for the cause of independence when it seemed likely that the legal and social disabilities would continue after the war under a new government. Equally, the Irish had no love for the English crown, as King George III reigned over an empire that had long oppressed the Irish people.

The Scots-Irish, the most populous among the Irish in America, split in various colonies; in Pennsylvania they mostly supported the Revolution, while in the South there were many Tories among them. Catholic Irish were likewise divided but most sided with the forces of the Revolution; a contingent of Irish Catholics did join the British side, and the English army used them to form several Catholic regiments, such as the Volunteers of Ireland.

Irish Catholics made important contributions to the American cause during the war. Charles Carroll of Carrollton, like his distinguished brother John Carroll (the first bishop and archbishop of Baltimore) was of Irish descent and was one of the foremost leaders in the war as a signer of the Declaration of Independence. Among a few of the many Irish who served with great distinction in the war were General Henry Knox, master of ordnance and later first secretary of war; General John Stark, who fought at the Battle of Bennington; General "Mad Anthony" Wayne, who fought in Georgia and the Carolinas and at the Battle of Monmouth; General Stephen Moylan, first Quartermaster General of the Continental Army; and Commodore John Barry, who was offered £2000 by the British General Howe if he would join the English side and who received the first commission in the United States Navy. There were also the many simple Irish farmers and laborers who joined the American cause in the hopes that a new country would offer them a better future.

In the immediate aftermath of the war, the Irish became active in the new political climate. Scots-Irish tended to favor the Republican Party of Thomas Jefferson while the Irish Catholics belonged especially to the more conservative Federalist Party. Among the most notable of the Irish Federalist supporters was Thomas FitzSimons of Pennsylvania, who helped draft the United States Constitution and was a member of the first Congress.

The first decades of the nineteenth century witnessed the slow growth of Irish immigration, in particular among the Catholics. The Irish in America demonstrated a process of assimilation epitomized by the great success story of Mathew Carey, a Dublin-born printer who arrived in Philadelphia in 1784 and went on to become one of America's most prominent publishers. Other Irish reached the United States to escape the ongoing political and religious persecution in Ireland.

The great tide of Irish immigration began in the 1820s and 1830s, when Ireland suffered through the first horrors of the potato famine. Compounding the crisis in Ireland was the English land-reform program that forced many Irish farmers from their lands. The lower costs of passage across the Atlantic at the time made fleeing Ireland cost effective, and many Irish jumped at the opportunity. There followed the great potato famine of 1845–49, which resulted in the deaths of between half a million and one million men, women, and children. Facing starvation if they stayed, over two million Irish fled the island, and in the years between 1847 and 1854 over one million Irish set sail for America.

The conditions under which the Irish left their native land were horrific. The ships were often barely seaworthy, provisions were minimal, and during the weeks at sea many died in the cramped and unsanitary conditions on board. Those who died at sea were thrown overboard, and many arrived in New York or elsewhere sick and malnourished. They found little welcome and were preyed upon by unscrupulous travel agents, ticket-sellers, and moneylenders. The immigrants were swindled out of the little money they had brought with them and forced to remain in the squalid conditions of New York with little hope of escaping a hard life in the city.

The sudden flood of Irish that was felt in the cities of the eastern United States caused a severe Nativist and anti-Catholic response. Irish Catholics endured discrimination, social stigmas, and religious persecution, and anti-Irish sentiments helped spur the formation of the Know-Nothing Party in the 1850s. (See also Know-Nothing Movement.)

The hostility toward Irish Catholics in the cities stemmed in part from the financial burden they created for city and state governments, as well as the perception that they were stealing jobs from Americans and undermined wages by accepting low-paying jobs and appalling working conditions. Anti-Catholicism was also a common element in the anger and discrimination, but so too was the industriousness of the Irish workers, who were able to climb swiftly up the economic ladder and to secure election to public office. Shut out of traditional means of reaching prosperity, Irish Catholics worked as laborers, but they also found advancement in politics and later in the labor unions.

The Church welcomed the arrival of thousands of Irish Catholics with open arms but with recognition of the difficult task of pastoral care for the new arrivals and the need to assist them in acclimating to the new country. One of the first and most dedicated American prelates to plead for the cause of the

Irish was Archbishop John Hughes of New York. He was assisted by Irish Americans, who formed the Irish Emigrant Society, which offered assistance to Irish immigrants arriving in New York.

Irish Catholics took part in very large numbers in the Civil War on both the Confederate and the Union sides. Over 150,000 Irish Catholics served in the Union army, and the Irish soldiers earned a well-deserved reputation for their courage in battle by serving with distinction in such famed units as the Irish Brigade, the 20th Maine, and the 69th New York Irish Volunteers.

The Union made an effort to recruit and draft the Irish into army service, and the draft efforts in 1863 after the Battle of Gettysburg instigated Irish Catholics to riot in protest, as poor Irish immigrants were most often targeted for the draft. Over 120 people were killed before the riots were suppressed by the New York police. Still, some eight hundred thousand made their way to the United States to fight for the Union, thanks in large part to the Homestead Act of 1862 and the promise of a better future as American citizens.

Irish immigration continued in large numbers in the decades after the war. Over six hundred thousand Irish arrived in the years between 1880 and 1890. It then declined after the start of the twentieth century. The chief pattern of Irish-American life was by then well established. Irish Catholics were slowly making their way into the American middle class, but they retained as well a great devotion to the Church and an equally fierce commitment to Irish nationalism. Most lived in the largest cities of the east, New York and Boston, for it was there that the Irish found work in greatest abundance. A century later, those cities were still centers of Irish life and population, although Irish Catholics also moved west to cities such as Chicago and San Francisco when those new areas were established as places of economic growth and opportunity.

Irish-American newspapers promoted the cause of Irish independence and national pride, but they also helped promote the ideals of civic duty and were thus valuable instruments of assimilation. Irish-American organizations also provided material and financial assistance to Irish immigrants as well as remarkable charitable work. The most celebrated organization is the Ancient Order of Hibernians, started in America in 1836.

The Irish nationalist sentiment in the United States forged close ties between Irish Americans and their countrymen struggling to secure Irish independence and social reforms from Great Britain. Irish Americans joined the Fenian Society, a revolutionary organization that raised money and arms to support the violent overthrow of British rule. Similar organizations, such as the Clan na Gael, provided financing to the Easter Uprising of 1916, and the Friends of Irish Freedom was instrumental in galvanizing American support for the Irish cause in the Anglo-Irish War of 1919–21.

The Irish succeeded especially in gaining a strong political presence in various cities, including New York and Boston. They became a powerful urban voting bloc and by the 1880s were dominant in the Democratic Party, a close association that continued throughout the twentieth century. In 1880 William Russell Grace was elected the first Irish Catholic mayor of New York. Political prominence continued within the Democratic Party in the first decades of the new century and culminated in the nomination in 1928 of Alfred E. Smith, governor of New York, as the Democratic presidential candidate. (*See also* Smith, Alfred E.)

The emergence of Irish Catholic political power provoked a new wave of anti-Catholic hysteria in some parts of the country. The American Protective Association in the 1890s and the Ku Klux Klan in the 1920s both promoted anti-Catholic and anti-Irish hostility, but neither enjoyed the widespread following of the years before the American Civil War, nor did they succeed in becoming national political movements. Nevertheless, anti-Catholic sentiment contributed directly to Smith's defeat by Herbert Hoover in the 1928 presidential election.

Irish Catholics were a mainstay of the Democratic Party's dominance in many cities, and the Irish Catholic vote was essential in the victory of Franklin Delano Roosevelt as president in 1932 and his reelections in 1936, 1940, and 1944. The assimilation of the Irish into American culture continued in the period after World War II. The acceptance of the Irish into American life reached its climax with the election in 1960 of President John F. Kennedy. (*See also* Kennedy, John F.)

The election also heralded the final stage in the assimilation of Irish Catholics into the American mainstream. Stung by the anti-Catholic reaction to the nomination of Al Smith, many Irish Catholics retreated back into the insular Irish cultural setting of the cities. Kennedy's successful campaign, which overcome anti-Catholic and anti-Irish sentiments in various parts of the country, permitted Irish Americans to leave their neighborhoods and aggressively enter the American social milieu. The change brought with it a gradual decline in the long-standing Irish cultural strength and ardent Catholicity.

The impact of Irish Catholicism on the development of the Catholic Church in America can scarcely be overestimated. The strong faith of the Irish immigrants provided a deep well from which the Church was able to draw. The Irish also brought about the massive growth of the Catholic population; the rise of Catholic social, economic, and political influence; and a steady source of clergy and men and women religious. Equally, Irish Catholic laypeople have been boundlessly generous in their financial and material assistance to the Church's institutions and have long given voice to the Church's abiding concerns for the dignity of workers, the poor, and the defenseless.

For their part, Irish Catholics found the Church a place of welcome in a routinely cruel new country where they suffered legal and social discrimination, anti-Catholic hostility, violence at the hands of Nativists and bigots, and conditions of squalor and economic hardship. Catholic clergy and religious offered hope and pastoral care to the Irish immigrants, and assisted them in the process of becoming assimilated to the United States. Parishes were havens of education and active communities of faith that established networks of support. Irish Catholic families in turn were active in parish life and regularly contributed sons to the seminary and daughters to the convents.

Catholic priests were honored by the Irish Catholic communities, and Irish families were honored to claim that a son or a brother had entered the priesthood. Women religious also helped shape generations of Irish Catholic youth in the parochial school system and cared for the sick and the elderly in hospitals and homes for the poor and orphaned.

The steady flow of talented young Irish men into the priesthood paved the way for the domination of the Irish in the American hierarchy. The increase in Irish-American or Irish-born prelates in American dioceses can be traced across the length of the nineteenth century. In 1829, at the First Provincial Council of Baltimore, two of the nine prelates in attendance were of Irish descent. By 1852 fifteen of the twenty-seven sees in the country were headed by Irish bishops. By 1876 there were four Irish archbishops and twenty-eight Irish bishops in the United States. This only increased by the start of the twentieth century to nine archbishops and forty-eight bishops of Irish descent in charge of the fourteen provinces and seventy-eight dioceses. The two most powerful Church leaders in the United States in the nineteenth century were the Irishmen John McCloskey, archbishop of New York and the first American cardinal, and Cardinal James Gibbons of Baltimore. The ascendancy of Irish Catholics over the American hierarchy remained a reality of American ecclesiastical life throughout the twentieth century.

Italian Catholics

The Church in the United States has benefited immeasurably from the contributions of Italian Catholics, even though extensive Italian immigration to the country began only in the late nineteenth century. What started as a stream of immigrants in the 1880s grew over the next decades into a tidal wave, so that by 1920 over four million Italians had arrived on the shores of America. The vast majority of those who settled in the country were Catholic. The result was a sudden, at times overwhelming, influx of new members in the Catholic communities in the east, especially the urban parishes and dioceses. Meeting the pastoral and spiritual needs of the Italians was one of the great projects of American Catholicism in the early twentieth century.

The earliest contributions of Italians to the history of North America were made by the great explorers of Italian birth, at a time when Italy did not exist as a nation. Chief among them were the Genoese Christopher Columbus and the Genoese John Cabot and his son, Sebastian. Also notable were Amerigo Vespucci and Giovanni da Verrazano. In recognition of Vespucci's vivid descriptions of the new continent, the name "America" was bestowed upon the New World in the 1507 book published by the mapmaker Martin Waldseemüller. In 1524 Verrazano explored much of the Atlantic Coast and was the discoverer of New York Bay and the Hudson River; the suspension bridge over the Narrows in New York that was completed in 1964 was named in his honor.

Few Italians migrated to North America during the colonial period. The Florentine physician and agriculturist Philip Mazzei settled in Virginia in the eighteenth century. He became a friend of Thomas Jefferson and was engaged in the political life of the colonies; his writings influenced the Declaration of Independence. Charles Constantine Pise was named the first Catholic Italian-American chaplain of the United States Senate and served from 1832 to 1833.

A larger Italian presence was felt in the missionary field and also in the Dioceses of New Orleans and St. Louis. Further, there were Italian Vincentian priests and members of the Society of Jesus in New Orleans and St. Louis, and the first bishop of St. Louis, Joseph Rosati, was originally from Naples. Bishop Ignatius Persico, O.F.M. Cap., bishop of Savannah from 1870 to 1872, was also from Naples. Several of the greatest missionaries in the history of the country were Italians by descent: Jesuit Father Eusebius Kino, Jesuit Father Juan Maria Salvatierra, Venerable Dominican Father Samuel Mazzuchelli, the Jesuit Antonio Ravalli, Sister Blandina Segale, S.C., and Jesuit Joseph M. Cataldo.

An increase in immigration was felt following the bloody and unsuccessful Revolution of 1848 in Italy. Italian leaders of the movement fled to the United States, including the famed revolutionary figure Giuseppe Garibaldi, who spent two years living on Staten Island and working in a candle factory. In addition, Jesuits who fled Italy during the 1848 Revolution also settled in the United States; many took up positions at St. Louis University. Nevertheless, prior to 1860, there were barely 15,000 immigrants from Italy in the United States; by 1880 there were only around 44,000 Italians in America.

The great change began in 1860 with the *Risorgimento*, Italian for "resurgence" or "revival," a movement that brought about Italian unification. Victor Emmanuel II was crowned king of Italy in 1861, an event that made the demise of the Papal States virtually inevitable. In 1870 Italy took control of the Papal States, ending the temporal holdings of the papacy save for Vatican City and other minor possessions. The unification of Italy brought with it severe financial and economic problems that were felt with particular acuteness in the agricultural southern regions of the country. Farmers faced great difficulties from taxation and lost their land to confiscation; they chose to leave the country for a better future.

Other factors contributed to the mass departures from Italy. The Italian population increased by six million from 1880 to 1910 and brought with it challenges to find employment. Compounding the problem was the slow growth of Italian industry, which failed to produce the needed jobs in the cities after the countryside began to face its own difficulties. There was, as well, the positive aspect to immigration. Italians saw the United States, with its booming industries and cities of apparent opportunity, as a land where dreams could be realized.

Whereas the great influx of Irish brought men and women to America, the wave of Italian immigration was overwhelmingly male. Most were young men, but many were married men who left their families behind. Once they arrived in the United States and found work, they regularly summoned their relatives to join them. The majority were Southern Italians and Sicilians.

The minority of Northern Italians tended to settle out of the cities, in rural areas, including California, Texas, and Louisiana. There they were often engaged in raising grapes and vegetables. By far, most Italian immigrants settled in the major American cities of New York, Philadelphia, Boston, Chicago, and Detroit. Those in the cities were chiefly employed as unskilled workers. The typical Italian immigrant worked in construction, ditch digging, dock work, and on the railroads. Italians with skills worked as carpenters, tailors, masons, and other skilled professions. Industrious and frugal, they patiently acquired funds to bring their families to America, but they also prepared to return home.

One of the unique characteristics of the Italian immigrants to the United States was the high propensity they had of returning to Italy. Termed *Americani*, they generally came to America with the goal of raising sufficient capital to pay off their debts in Italy, to secure land, and to resume their lives in their homeland with greater financial security and new job skills. The number of *Americani* were large. Although nearly four million Italians arrived in the United States in the first decades of the twentieth century, over two million returned to Italy.

For those who chose to stay in America, their industriousness made possible the pursuit of the dream of their own property and personal happiness with their families who had joined them. As their aspirations of finding work were often realized quickly, Italian immigrants sent letters home to friends encouraging them to make the same journey. Adding to the appeal of emigration was the return of the *Americani* with what seemed large fortunes gained in a short amount of time.

While life in America offered many inducements to Italian immigrants, there were also many obstacles and hardships. Most arrived unable to speak English, and as they tended to remain in their own established neighborhoods, there were few opportunities to learn the English language. The legal system in place did little to assist this process of assimilation. Until the Naturalization Act of 1906, immigrants needed only residence of three or four years to gain citizenship, and knowledge of English was not required. In addition, the process of citizenship was hastened by local politicians who saw the Italians as potential voters.

Italians found also economic hardships because of discrimination and intolerance. The rise of anti-immigrant sentiment in the late nineteenth century and early twentieth century found the Italian ghettos teeming with Catholic foreigners a useful target for intolerance. As Italians were often excluded from many forms of advancement, some grew embittered. Others adapted to the limitations and pursued careers in civil service, politics, and industry. The degree of injustice, unfair labor practices, and intolerance of Americans to those recently arrived workers prompted Pope Leo XIII in 1888 to issue a plea to the bishops to the United States to work with vigor to assist the Italian immigrants who were now under their pastoral care.

Two of the great hallmarks of Italian immigrants were their willingness to work hard and make their way into the middle class and to sacrifice everything for their families. The first generation of Italians in the United States made possible the success of their children, who flourished thanks to the social progress in the country in the years after World War II. Second generation Italian Americans found more opportunity for material wealth and social mobility.

The massive immigration wave that had begun in the late nineteenth century declined in the period after World War I, when Congress placed curbs on immigration. Quotas were established in the Immigration Restriction Act of 1921, and the number of Italians was limited to 42,000 out of a total permitted number of immigrants of 356,000. Further limits were applied over the next years until loosened in the aftermath of World War II. By 1950 there were approximately 4.5 million Italian Americans in the United States.

The challenge created by the arrival of so many new Catholics who did not speak English and who quickly crowded into American dioceses along the East Coast was soon termed the "Italian problem." On the one hand, there was the need to care for their spiritual needs as best as possible with limited resources. On the other, there was the need to help them to adjust to the new environment and to become productive Americans.

The immediate solution was to try to care for the new arrivals in existing parochial structures and then to work as quickly as possible to bring in Italian-speaking priests for Italian congregations, that would permit Italian parishes to be founded. Few priests migrated from Italian dioceses to the United States, so it was necessary to develop a clergy base within the United States. Religious communities and orders were instrumental in first meeting the needs of the immigrants. Among the most influential were the Italian Franciscans, Augustinians, and Servites. There were also the great contributions made by such communities such as the Pallottines, the Scalabrinians, and the Cabrini nuns. The Scalabrinians were founded in 1887 by Blessed Giovanni Scalabrini with the express purpose of assisting Italian immigrants in the United States. The Cabrini nuns (the Missionary Sisters of the Sacred Heart) were founded by St. Frances Xavier Cabrini, the first American citizen to be canonized a saint and who is honored as the "Patroness of the Immigrants."

The cultural traditions of the Italian immigrants were a source of tension and also misunderstanding on the part of some bishops and parish priests. Deeply committed to devotional practices, Italians in American cities soon founded benevolent societies named in honor of the patron saints of various Italian towns and held festivals on their feast days. The parades were at times misinterpreted as excessive and were discouraged in some places. Still, they were manifestations of the devotion of Italian immigrants to their faith and became cherished annual events.

Bishops in the east also found help from those American priests who had studied in Rome during their seminary days and hence spoke Italian and had a familiarity with Italian culture. Bishops likewise used every means to bring into service qualified priests who were able and willing to assist the difficult situation. One of the most important of these was Reverend Gherardo Ferrante, who was named by Archbishop Michael A. Corrigan of New York to the post of Italian Secretary. Ferrante remained in his post under Corrigan's successors, Cardinal John Murphy Farley and Cardinal Patrick Joseph Hayes. He provided a vital voice in organizing pastoral programs, served as liaison between the prelates and the Italian Catholic communities, and gave sage advice on maintaining cultural sensitivity.

By the middle of the twentieth century, Italian parishes that had been founded during the height of the migration period were producing large numbers of priests and religious of Italian descent. Such second-generation Italians marked the progress of the Italian Americans both in society and in ecclesiastical affairs. In 1954 Father Joseph M. Pernicone was consecrated titular bishop of Hadrianopolis in Honoriade and auxiliary bishop of New York. He was the first Sicilian-born auxiliary bishop for the archdiocese. Two Italian Americans have since been named members of the College of Cardinals. In 1982 Archbishop Joseph Louis Bernardin was named archbishop of Chicago; he was appointed a cardinal in 1983. Bishop Anthony J. Bevilacqua of

Pittsburgh was named archbishop of Philadelphia in 1988 and appointed to the College of Cardinals in 1991; he retired in 2003.

Ives, Levi Silliman (September 16, 1797–October 13, 1867)

A convert to Catholicism, Levi Silliman Ives was a patron of the poor and homeless of New York City. He was born into a Presbyterian family in Connecticut and dedicated his life to his faith. In his early twenties, he became an Episcopalian priest and served in Batavia, New York, and in Philadelphia and Lancaster, Pennsylvania. In 1827 he became assistant rector of Christ Church and the rector of St. Luke's Church in New York. In 1831 he became the second Episcopal bishop of North Carolina.

In that office he labored tirelessly for the slaves of the state's plantations. In 1845 Bishop Ives established Valle Crucis, a religious community known as the Brotherhood of the Holy Cross. The Tractarian Movement in the Episcopal Church had led him to this founding, but he was attacked within the church because of the Roman Catholic influences evident in his group.

He left Valle Crucis and the Episcopal Church, seeking continuity with historical Christianity and true apostolic authority. Touring Europe, he became a Catholic and returned to New York to teach at St. Joseph's Seminary. He also organized the New York Catholic Protectory to aid the poor and homeless youngsters of the city. He was honored at his death for his courageous loyalty to the faith and for his endless labors for others.

J

Jackson, Diocese of

Established on July 28, 1837, as the Diocese of Natchez by Pope Gregory XVI, and designated as the Diocese of Natchez-Jackson on March 7, 1957, by Pope Pius XII, this ecclesiastical jurisdiction was designated as the Diocese of Jackson on June 6, 1977, by Pope Blessed John XXIII. The diocese serves counties in the state of Mississippi and is a suffragan see of the Archdiocese of Mobile. The state capital, Jackson is the financial and industrial center of Mississippi. Louis Le Fleur established the city as a trading post on the Pearl River in 1792. After the Treaty of Doak's Stand, the city became the capital and was named Jackson.

The area was explored as early as 1541 by Hernando de Soto, but no Spanish claims were made. The French began their dominance in the region in 1682, when René-Robert Chevalier, Sieur de La Salle, declared the area part of Louisiana. Father Zenobius Membré, who was later martyred, was part of La Salle's expedition and celebrated Mass near modern-day Fort Adams. In 1699 Pierre Le Moyne, Sieur d'Iberville, established a settlement at Old Biloxi, near modern-day Ocean Springs, but the site was abandoned around 1718. Fort Rosalie, which had been started in 1716 and was served by Jesuit and Capuchin missionaries, was attacked in 1729, resulting in a massacre of the white settlers and then, in retaliation, the near obliteration of the Natchez Indians.

In 1788 the Spanish, who had gained a foothold in the region again, opened the parish of San Salvador del Mundo at Natchez. Bishop Luis Ignacio Peñalver y Cárdenas came to the area to confirm the faithful in 1796. Natchez and the surrounding lands became part of the United States two years later, and the Spanish withdrew. Local Catholics, having no episcopal authority present for four decades, safeguarded Church properties,

Bishop Joseph Chanche

visited from time to time by missionaries or served by changing resident priests. In 1817 Mississippi entered the Union as the twentieth state. Five years later the Vicariate Apostolic of Mississippi and Alabama was erected. Alabama separated from Mississippi in 1825 and was placed under the jurisdiction of the Diocese of New Orleans.

In 1837 the Diocese of Natchez was established, and Bishop John Mary Joseph Chanche, S.S., was consecrated on March 14, 1841. Bishop Chanche started the offices and agencies for diocesan administration and in 1842 started constructing Our Lady of Sorrows Cathedral, now St. Mary's Basilica. There were large Catholic communities at Natchez and Vicksburg, and other smaller settlements prospered throughout the state, but there was only one priest available. Bishop Chanche invited the Sisters of Charity into the diocese and recruited the necessary clergy. At the time of his death on July 22, 1852, there were eleven priests serving the faithful in parishes.

His successor was Bishop James Oliver Van de Velde, a Jesuit, who was serving as the bishop of Chicago and was transferred to Natchez on July 29, 1853. Bishop Van de Velde died on November 13, 1855.

Bishop William Henry Elder succeeded Bishop Van de Velde and was consecrated on May 3, 1857. He would later become an archbishop. Bishop Elder led the diocese during the harsh era of the Civil War and the Reconstruction period. In July 1864 Bishop Elder was sent out of Mississippi and imprisoned in a military compound because he refused to obey the orders of General Y. M. Tuttle to schedule prayers in all Catholic churches for President Abraham Lincoln and for the success of the Union army. The imprisonment ended in August 1864, in response to Bishop Elder's letters to President Lincoln and to Secretary of War

Edward Stanton. The federal authorities apologized to Bishop Elder and restored him to his diocese. He attended the First Vatican Council and aided the people of Mississippi in restoring ruined cities and towns. He also worked with freed slaves and nursed victims during the 1878 yellow fever epidemic. On January 30, 1880, he was promoted to the office of coadjutor archbishop of Cincinnati.

The fourth bishop of Natchez was Francis Anthony Janssens, who was from the Netherlands. Bishop Janssens promoted an apostolate to the African-Americans in the area, opening a parish for their needs in 1890 and providing a parish for the Catholic Choctaw community. He erected parishes, missions, schools, and orphanages. On August 7, 1888, he was promoted to the Archdiocese of New Orleans.

His successor was Bishop Thomas Heslin, who was consecrated on June 18, 1889. He expanded diocesan facilities and parishes and faced anti-Catholic movements. Bishop Heslin died on February 22, 1911.

The sixth bishop of Natchez was John Edward Gunn, S.M., who was consecrated on August 29, 1911. Bishop Gunn led the diocese through the tense days of World War I, supporting the military efforts of the nation. He also erected new parishes and established mission chapels throughout Mississippi, aided by the Catholic Church Extension Society and the Society for the Propagation of the Faith. The Society of the Divine Word also accepted his invitation and established a seminary to train African-American priests in 1920 at Greenville and then at Bay St. Louis in 1921. Bishop Gunn died on February 19, 1924.

His successor was Bishop Richard Oliver Gerow, who was consecrated on October 15, 1924. The Great Depression impacted severely on Mississippi, as other regions of the nation suffered. During his years of service, however, Bishop Gerow blessed more than eighty churches and led the faithful through the turmoil of World War II. He also aided the faithful as the postwar population expanded greatly. In 1948 he moved the diocesan offices to Jackson in order

to serve the large Catholic population there. He also founded a diocesan newspaper and took part in the Second Vatican Council. On December 18, 1956, the Holy See designated the diocese as Natchez-Jackson. Bishop Gerow ordered the integration of Mississippi's Catholic schools. He retired on December 2, 1967. Bishop Gerow's successor was Joseph B. Brunini, who served until retiring on Jan. 24, 1984.

William R. Houck, who had served as auxiliary bishop of the diocese since 1979, was installed on June 5, 1984. Spiritual renewal was the theme of his leadership programs in the diocese, and lay ministries were supported in the spirit of the Second Vatican Council. Bishop Houck retired on January 3, 2003.

The tenth bishop of Jackson, Joseph Latino, succeeded Bishop Houck on January 2, 2003, and was ordained a bishop on March 7, 2003. The diocese remains committed to the needs of the small but active Catholic community in the region. Catholics, of course, remain a very small minority in this overwhelmingly Protestant part of the country. In 2011 there were 49,000 Catholics, 85 priests, 163 women religious, and 75 parishes in the diocese.

Jadot, Jean (November 23, 1909–January 21, 2009)

The ninth apostolic delegate to the United States, Archbishop Jean Jadot was later appointed by Pope Blessed John Paul II to the office of pro-president of the Secretariat for Non-Christians. Born in Brussels and the son of Lambert and Gabrielle Jadot, he studied at the American College of Louvain and went on for graduate studies in Louvain at the Institut Supérieur de Philosophie and at the Institut Catholique de Paris. Returning to Brussels, he completed a doctorate in philosophy at Louvain and then entered the seminary of the Archdiocese of Mechelen-Brussels. He was ordained on February 11, 1934.

Father Jadot performed pastoral labors in the Archdiocese of Malines and then served as a military chaplain to the Congolese forces in the Belgian Congo in the

Archbishop Jean Jadot

1960s. When he returned to Belgium, he assumed the office of National Director of the Society for the Propagation of the Faith. He was also made an Honorary Prelate of His Holiness on August 16, 1955.

As his work had brought him into close contact with Vatican officials, including the influential Cardinal Sergio Pignedoli, he was invited to enter the papal diplomatic corps. Although he was not a graduate of the Pontifical Ecclesiastical Academy (the traditional training ground for papal diplomats), in 1968 he was appointed titular archbishop of Zuri and apostolic delegate to Laos, Malaysia, and Singapore; the following year he was named apostolic nuncio to Thailand. In 1971 he was moved from Asia to Africa when he was named apostolic delegate to Equatorial Guinea and apostolic pro-nuncio to Cameroon and Gabon. On May 22, 1973, he was appointed apostolic delegate to the United States.

Archbishop Jadot served as apostolic delegate to the United States during a tumultuous period in modern Catholic history, in the time after the Second Vatican Council. He attended diocesan events throughout the United States and assisted American Catholic reforms and ministries. His principal task was, as Pope Paul VI reportedly told him at the time of his appointment, to find "good bishops." His time as apostolic delegate was controversial, at times owing to his reputation as a progressive.

On June 28, 1980, Pope Blessed John Paul II appointed him pro-president of the Secretariat for Non-Christians in the Vatican, the forerunner of the modern Pontifical Council for Interreligious Dialogue. On April 8, 1984, he resigned from this office and retired to Belgium, where he died.

Jankiewicz, Mary Cajetan (Alexandra) (1839– December 9, 1907)

A Felician pioneer in the United States, Mary Cajetan (Alexandra) Jankiewicz was an educational leader in the Catholic school systems. She was born in Warsaw, Poland, and entered the Felician Congregation in 1867. In 1874 she was one of five Feli-

Mary Cajetan Jankiewicz

cian sisters sent to the United States by the congregation in response to an invitation from Father Joseph Dabrowski of Polonia, Wisconsin.

Sister Mary Cajetan taught in the parish school, and established and directed the Seminary of the Felician Sisters in Detroit, incorporating the institution in 1882. She also wrote and printed needed school texts and prepared teachers for certification tests in Catholic dioceses. From 1900 to 1907 she served as the provincial superior of the congregation. She was then assigned to Poland for the congregation's general chapter and was elected as a general councilor. Attending a retreat at Nowe Miasto, Sister Mary Cajetan suffered a heart attack and died.

Janssens, Francis Anthony (October 17, 1843– June 9, 1897)

A missionary bishop of Natchez (Jackson) from 1881 to 1888, Francis Anthony Janssens also served as the archbishop of New Orleans from 1888 to 1897. He was born in Tilbourg, North Brabant, Holland, to a devout Catholic family. Moved profoundly by a sermon given by Bishop John McGill of Richmond regarding the severe shortage of priests in the South after the devastation of the Civil War, Francis studied for the priesthood for service in the United States. His studies began at the American College at Louvain, Belgium, and he set sail for America in 1868 after ordination and a visit to Rome.

In Richmond, he began pastoral service that lasted for thirteen years. While posted at the cathedral, he also traveled extensively in ministry throughout Virginia and became a respected priest of the diocese. Hence, in 1877, when Bishop James Gibbons (who had succeeded Bishop McGill) was appointed coadjutor archbishop of Baltimore, Father Janssens served as diocesan administrator until Bishop John Joseph Keane arrived the following year as the new bishop.

There was little surprise, then, when in 1881 Father Janssens was appointed the bishop of Natchez. He was consecrated on May 1, 1881, and set to work to serve one of the poorest regions in the country. Despite great financial hardships, he succeeded in building churches and parishes in Mississippi, paid off the debt of the cathedral, launched a minor seminary, and started a mission among the local Choctaw Indians. He received financial help from the Society for the Propagation of the Faith, and to stretch money even further he paid his own salary back into diocesan funds. At the same time, he was earning national recognition for his gifts as a missionary and also an administrator. In 1884 he attended the Third Plenary Council of Baltimore and served as a junior promoter and a member of the Committee on the Catechism.

On August 7, 1888, Bishop Janssens was promoted to the Archdiocese of New Orleans and took possession of his see on September 16, 1888. The initial reception of the Dutch-born archbishop was a mixed one as the population, especially among the clergy, was largely French. Undeterred, the new archbishop traveled across the archdiocese and served as shepherd with tremendous energy. He established schools, improved the parishes and churches, and used his travels to forge a bond with his people. St. Louis Cathedral was restored under his leadership, and priests were secured for Italian immigrants through the help of Bishop Giovanni Scalabrini. Through his initiative, a leper home was founded at Carville and a home for deaf children was begun at Chinchuba.

Archbishop Janssens was also a determined supporter of the often-forgotten black Catholics. He favored the ordination of black priests and also launched a parish for black Catholics to foster their own Catholic identity and to ensure the best pastoral service for them. He gave his backing to the Sisters of the Holy Family, a community for black women religious, and likewise found encouragement in his efforts from St. Katharine Drexel, who sent him financial assistance. Archbishop Janssens died suddenly on a sea voyage to New York. His remains were brought back to New Orleans, where they were interred under the sanctuary of the cathedral.

Jeanmard, Jules Benjamin (September 26, 1879–February 23, 1957)

The first bishop of the Diocese of Lafayette, Jules Benjamin Jeanmard laid the foundation for the present diocese. He was born in Breaux Bridge, Louisiana, the seventh of nine children, and was educated at St. Joseph's Seminary in Gessen, Holy Cross College in Massachusetts, Kenrick Seminary in St. Louis, and St. Louis Seminary in New Orleans. He was ordained on June 10, 1903.

Serving as an assistant at St. Louis Cathedral, Father Jeanmard was appointed in 1906 as the secretary to Archbishop James H. Blenk, who appointed him as chancellor of the archdiocese in 1914. When Archbishop Blenk died in 1917, he served as apostolic administrator of New Orleans and took part in the plans to erect the Diocese of Lafayette. On December 8, 1918, he was consecrated as the first bishop of Lafayette and was installed on December 12.

Bishop Jeanmard was beloved in the region, having led the faithful through World War I, the Great Depression, and World War II. He built the parishes and schools needed by the expanding Catholic population and promoted a large African-American ministry. On December 8, 1943, he was appointed an Assistant at the Pontifical Throne. He retired on March 13, 1956, and died in Lake Charles, Louisiana.

Jefferson City, Diocese of

Established on July 2, 1956, by Pope Pius XII, the Diocese of Jefferson City serves counties in the north-central part of the state of Missouri. The capital of the state, Jefferson City is an agricultural trading center named originally for President Thomas Jefferson. The site was selected as the capital in 1821 and laid out by Daniel M. Boone, son of the famous frontiersman. The Diocese of Jefferson City is a suffragan see of the Archdiocese of St. Louis.

The Catholic heritage of the diocesan area dates to 1673, when Jesuit Father Jacques Marquette was in Perry County with Louis Joliet. In 1682 René-Robert Chevalier, Sieur de La Salle, scouted the region and claimed it for France. Trappers and missionaries followed, and in 1735 Ste. Genevieve, the first white permanent settlement, was started. St. Louis was founded as a result of the Treaty of Paris of 1763, which divided the area between France and England. The British took French possessions east of the Mississippi River and north of the Ohio River, including Canada.

St. Louis attracted French settlers caught on the east side of the Mississippi, and they moved to the new site. Catholics in the region were under the jurisdiction of the Catholic bishop of Havana, Cuba, at the time. The American Revolution, of course, forced the English to cede their claims to the lands of the United States. The Louisiana Purchase, in which Napoleon Bonaparte sold all the lands that had been ceded to France by Spain, placed the entire Missouri region into the hands of Americans.

Catholics were raising communities throughout the area, including the Barrens Colony, which later was named Perrysville. In 1790 Father James Maxwell began his remarkable ministries. The Vincentians also established a seminary at Barrens Colony. Missouri entered the Union in 1821, as part of a compromise over slavery issues, and five years later, the Diocese (later Archdiocese) of St. Louis was established. Bishop Louis DuBourg was transferred to the Archdiocese of Montauban and then Besançon, France.

Bishop Joseph Rosati became the first bishop of the Diocese of St. Louis and the administrator of the Diocese of New Orleans. He died in Rome in 1843 and was succeeded by Bishop Peter Richard Kenrick. Four years later, St. Louis was designated as a metropolitan provincial see, and he was promoted to the rank of archbishop.

The Civil War impacted upon Missouri, but the state continued to prosper. A new state constitution, drawn up in 1865, included a Test Oath that discriminated against Catholics. Archbishop Kenrick took the matter to court, where the Test Oath provision was declared unconstitutional. He also promoted the erection of the Diocese of St. Joseph in 1868 and Kansas City in 1880.

Cardinal John Joseph Glennon became the archbishop of St. Louis in 1905, as the first signs of European turmoil appeared. General John J. Pershing, a native of Missouri, led America's fighting forces when the nation was drawn into World War I. The Great Depression followed and then another Missourian, Harry S. Truman, led the nation as president in the last stages of World War II. The industrial expansion demanded by the war brought more Catholics into the state, and in 1956 Jefferson City was designated as a diocese. The Diocese of

Springfield-Cape Giradeau was erected at the same time.

Bishop Joseph M. Marling was the first bishop of Jefferson City, appointed on August 24, 1956. He had served as auxiliary bishop of the Diocese of Kansas City since 1947. Bishop Marling attended the Second Vatican Council and implemented the reforms mandated by that council. He also established St. Joseph's Cathedral and started charitable and spiritual ministries as well as programs for the Catholic schools. In 1962 Bishop Marling responded to a plea from Pope Blessed John XXIII and sent diocesan priests to Peru to aid in evangelization efforts. He retired on July 2, 1969.

His successor was Bishop Michael F. McAuliffe, who was consecrated on August 18, 1969. Bishop McAuliffe instituted lay ministries and opened parishes in the newly developed areas of the diocese. He also maintained diocesan properties that date to early eras in the region. He retired on August 27, 1997.

The third bishop of Jefferson City, John Raymond Gaydos, was appointed on June 25, 1997, and consecrated on August 27. He worked to implement the norms established to create a safe environment in the wake of the clergy sex abuse scandal, strove to solidify Catholic education, and reached out to meet the pastoral needs of the growing Hispanic population in Missouri. In 2011 there were 80,600 Catholics, 105 priests and 95 parishes in the diocese.

Jesuit Missions. *See* Society of Jesus

Jesuit North American Martyrs. *See* North American Martyrs

Jesuit Order. *See* Society of Jesus

Jesuit Relations

Jesuit Relations is a remarkable record of the earliest eras of American history, compiled from transcripts of letters written by the first Jesuit missionaries laboring in the present-day United States. These records are intimate, firsthand accounts of mission efforts among the Abenaki, Algonquin, Huron, Illinois, and Iroquois nations. The Jesuit missionaries sent their letters to Québec and then to France, where they were published in 1581 as letters and then annually in book form from 1632 to 1672. The Holy See halted the publishing in that year, and the letters and maps produced by Jesuit Father Jacques Marquette were not included because they did not arrive in France until 1673.

Jesuit Relations serves as a primary source of historical information about the lives of Native Americans before white settlers invaded their lands. The letters are detailed accounts of dress, traditions, ceremonies, tribal practices, and religious beliefs, gathered by the Jesuit missionaries at personal risk. The accounts of the martyrdom and tortures of Jesuit priests were recorded by their companions, who also died for the faith.

The maps and exploratory records of Jesuit Father Jacques Marquette are treasured as vital accounts of American geographical and geological data. His explorations with Louis Joliet were so extensive and prolonged that Father Marquette was able to render accurate and detailed records of vast regions. He traced the Missouri and Ohio Rivers as well as the Mississippi River. St. John de Brébeuf mapped Lake Erie from Niagara to Detroit before he died a martyr's death. Other Jesuits documented the geographic factors of Lake Superior and Lake St. John, as well as the midwestern and northwestern regions of America. Jesuit Father Eusebius Kino, the revered missionary, also provided maps and charts of Baja, California, proving that it was a peninsula.

Some of the most important historical documents are the dictionaries and grammars of Native American languages all across the continent. Jesuit Father Sebastian Râle and countless other linguistically capable Jesuit missionaries compiled such texts for the use of their own Native American congregations, but surviving in *Jesuit Relations*, these records of the original languages of the tribes are historical treasures.

The first forty volumes of *Jesuit Relations* were widely distributed throughout Europe. Some seventy-two volumes were also published by Barrows Brothers of Cleveland, in French and in English. Additional information was also made available by the archivist of St. Mary's College in Montréal, Father Arthur E. Jones, who made notes on the matters recorded and provided historical explanations throughout.

Jogues, Isaac, St. (1607–October 19, 1646)

A Jesuit martyr of North America, St. Isaac Jogues was a missionary of the Society of Jesus who suffered terrible tortures at the hands of the Mohawks. He was born in Orleans, France, and entered the Jesuits in 1624. Ordained to the priesthood, St. Isaac volunteered for the Québec missions. He served the Hurons until 1642, when he and St. René Goupil, a lay missionary, were taken captive with a Frenchman named William Coutre. The martyrs were marched to Ossernenon (Caughnawaga), near present-day Auriesville, New York. St. René was slain, but after a year of torture, St. Isaac was ransomed from the Mohawks by passing Dutch traders.

He returned to France, where everyone wanted to touch his hands. St. Isaac's fingernails had been torn out, his thumb had been sawed off, and two fingers had been crushed by the bites of Mohawk women. Such mutilations made St. Isaac canonically dis-

St. Isaac Joques

qualified to celebrate Mass. A petition was sent to Pope Innocent X asking for a dispensation, and the Holy Father reportedly exclaimed, *"Indignum esse Christi martyrem, Christi non bebere sanguinam"* ("It would be unjust if a martyr for Christ could not drink the blood of Christ.")

In 1646 St. Isaac returned to the Québec missions with St. Jean de Lalande, and in May the two returned to the Mohawk territory willingly. They had been commissioned to complete a treaty made between the tribal leaders and Québec. Unfortunately, the missionaries were not informed in time that the Mohawks were at that point angry about some event and unwilling to negotiate. The Jesuits were taken prisoner instead of being welcomed as representatives and again marched to Ossernenon. Both priests were tortured hideously for two days, and then St. Isaac was beheaded. His head was displayed in the Mohawk enclave and his body was dumped into a river. St. Jean de Lalande was slain the next day. Pope Pius XI canonized the two Jesuit martyrs in 1930.

John XXIII, Pope Blessed (November 25, 1881– June 3, 1963)

The pope from 1958 to 1963, Blessed John XXIII was one of the most popular of all pontiffs. He was best known for launching the Second Vatican Council. Angelo Roncalli, the future Blessed John XXIII, was born at Sotto il Monte, near Bergamo, Italy, to a family of peasant farmers. He studied at the seminary of Bergamo and then from 1901 at the Pontifical Athenaeum S. Apollinare in Rome, and was ordained in 1904. Appointed secretary the next year to Bishop Radini-Tedeschi of Bergamo, he also taught Church history at the seminary. At the start of World War I in 1914, he was conscripted, eventually serving as a chaplain. After the war, he was named by Pope Benedict XV as the national director of the Congregation for the Propagation of the Faith. Devoting much of his spare time to historical research, most notably on his own diocese and on St. Charles

Borromeo, he studied documents in the Ambrosian Library, coming into contact with its greatest director, Achille Ratti, the future Pope Pius XI. In 1925 Pope Pius XI made him the titular archbishop of Areopolis and apostolic delegate to Bulgaria, and he served in the same post from 1934 in Turkey and Greece.

Having acquired an excellent reputation for his dealings with the Orthodox Church, Archbishop Roncalli was transferred in 1944 to the very difficult post of nuncio to France. He was quickly confronted with the demands of the recently reconstituted French government that thirty-three bishops be removed for collaboration during the German occupation. Archbishop Roncalli investigated and suggested to the accused bishops that they resign. He negotiated concessions from the French over the financing of schools and called for the humane treatment of German prisoners in the tense period of repatriation.

In 1952 he became a permanent observer for the Holy See at UNESCO, the United Nations Educational, Scientific, and Cultural Organization. The next year, Pope Pius XII made him a cardinal and patriarch of Venice. While there, he was a very popular figure known for his wit, cordiality, and approachable pastoral style. After the death of Pius XII on October 9, 1958, Cardinal Roncalli was not considered a strong contender to succeed to the throne of Peter, but on October 28, 1958, he was elected on the twelfth ballot. Largely thought by observers to have been a compromise candidate (he was seventy-seven at the time), Blessed John XXIII proved full of surprises.

One of his first acts was to rescind the regulation in force since the time of Sixtus V that fixed the number of cardinals at seventy. His subsequent appointments internationalized the College of Cardinals and brought the number to eighty-seven. On January 25, 1959, he declared his desire for three main goals to be achieved: a diocesan synod, a revision of canon law, and an ecumenical council. The synod

Blessed John XXIII

was held in January 1960 and was a foreshadowing of the greater council to come in its effort to revitalize the life of the Roman diocese. Canon law revisions were to be the task of a pontifical commission begun in March 1962. The ecumenical council, which he called the Second Vatican Council (answering suggestions that he simply reconvene the First Vatican Council, which had never adjourned), was to prove the most important event in the history of the Church since the time of the Council of Trent. Said by Blessed John XXIII to be an inspiration of the Holy Spirit, the council was the fullest expression of the pope's vision of *aggiornamento* (renewal), a new vibrant presentation of the faith.

Beyond the council, Pope John XXIII made numerous other efforts to bring reform and revitalization. He issued several notable encyclicals, including *Ad Cathedram Petri* in 1959, *Mater et Magistra* in 1961, and *Pacem in Terris* in 1963, which preached "universal peace in truth, justice, charity, and liberty." He thereby took the first steps toward a dialogue with the Soviet bloc that would become the Ostpolitik. In ecumenical affairs, he established the Secretariat for Christian Unity in 1960 under Cardinal Augustin Bea with the aim of reaching out to other Christian denominations. He also sent observers to the World Council of Churches and was highly sensitive to Jewish concerns. In liturgical matters, he approved new rubrics for the breviary and missal in 1960, inserted the name of St. Joseph in the Canon of the Mass in 1962, and permitted the use of the vernacular in the liturgy of the Melkites.

His pontificate lasted only five years, but in that time he established eight dioceses in the United States: Allentown, Baton Rouge, and San Angelo in 1961; and Atlanta, Fairbanks, Oakland, Santa Rosa, and Stockton in 1962. He presided over the 1963 beatification of St. Elizabeth Ann Seton, who was canonized in 1975. He also appointed five members of the American hierarchy to the College of Cardinals: Cardinal Richard James Cushing and Cardinal John Francis O'Hara in 1958, Cardinal Albert G. Meyer and Cardinal Aloisius Joseph Muench in 1961, and Cardinal Joseph E. Ritter in 1962. The pope also received in audience at the Vatican President Dwight D. Eisenhower in 1959 and Vice President Lyndon Baines Johnson in 1962.

Known throughout the world as a simple, kind, and genuinely earnest pastor, Pope Blessed John XXIII became almost legendary for his humor and peasant's common sense. He cultivated the goodwill of all nations through his honest acts of goodness, be it meeting with pilgrims to St. Peter's or visiting prisoners in the Regina Coeli prison. Long in poor health, he fell ill after the closing of the first session of the Second Vatican Council in December 1962 and died months later from stomach cancer. He had made Archbishop Giovanni Battista Montini of Milan a cardinal and had given him a prominent role in organizing the council; Archbishop Montini succeeded him as Pope Paul VI. Pope Blessed John XXIII was beatified by Pope Blessed John Paul II on September 3, 2000, along with Pope Blessed Pius IX.

John Paul II, Pope Blessed (May 18, 1920–April 2, 2005)

Pope from 1978 to 2005, Karol Wojtyla was the first Polish pope and the first non-Italian pontiff since the reign of Adrian VI in 1522–23. His pontificate, the third longest in the history of the papacy, was marked by his global travels, his unprecedented theological and philosophical writings, and his labors on behalf of human dignity and global peace. Pope Blessed John Paul II also left a lasting influence on the history of American Catholicism by his visits to the country and by his appointment of a large number of bishops over the course of his time as pope. He was beatified by Pope Benedict XVI on May 1, 2011.

Karol Wojtyla was born in the town of Wadowice, Poland, the son of a retired army lieutenant. His mother died while he was still young, and the family was a poor one. He attended the local primary school and then high school, entering Jagiellonian University in Kraków, Poland, in 1938. His field of study was literature and Polish language, but he also distinguished himself as a gifted sportsman, a poet, and a fine performer in amateur theater. Owing to the seizure of Poland in 1939 by the Nazis, the university was closed, and Wojtyla ended up working in a limestone quarry and a chemical factory. Throughout, he continued his studies through an underground association and took part in a secret theater club.

After his father's death in 1942, and having survived two near-fatal accidents, Karol Wojtyla chose to enter the priesthood. He studied theology in the clandestine program adopted by the Church in Poland to circumvent the Nazis. In August 1946 he graduated and was ordained on November 1 by Cardinal Adam Sapieha, archbishop of Kraków. He was then sent to the Pontifical University of St. Thomas, the Angelicum, in Rome, earning a doctorate in theology in 1948. His dissertation was on St. John of the Cross.

Returning to Poland, he worked as a parish priest from 1948 to 1951 and then studied philosophy at Jagiellonian University. A lecturer at the Kraków seminary, he was also appointed in 1956 a professor of ethics at Lublin. Two years later, Pope Pius XII appointed him auxiliary bishop of the Diocese of Kraków and titular bishop of Ombi. On December 30, 1963, Paul VI named him archbishop of Kraków. Four years later, on June 26, 1967, he was created a cardinal. As a bishop, he had written a treatise on sexuality, *Love and Responsibility*, and had been an active member of the preparatory commission for the Second Vatican Council. He attended all four sessions of the council and took part in the post-conciliar commissions. A firm adherent of the decrees of the council, he implemented the reforms and in 1971 was elected a permanent member of the council of the Roman Synod of Bishops. A well-known figure in Europe, he traveled extensively to North America (including to the Eucharistic Congress in Philadelphia in 1976), the Middle East, Asia, and Africa. Meanwhile, back in Poland, he worked with the Polish primate, Cardinal Stefan Wyszynski, to promote political liberty and to give inspiration to Catholics against the communist regime.

On October 16, 1978, Wojtyla was elected pope by the conclave convened to choose a successor to the briefly reigning John Paul I. He was elected most likely on the eighth ballot and took the name John Paul II in deference to his predecessor.

Pope John Paul I

Like John Paul I, he was not crowned pope but was installed in a simple ceremony on October 21, proclaiming his devotion to the continued promotion and authentic interpretation of the Second Vatican Council.

From the very start of his pontificate, he demonstrated his desire to be "a witness for universal love," spending much of the next few years in extensive travels to Mexico, Poland, Ireland, the United States, Turkey, Zaire, Congo, Ghana, the Ivory Coast, Kenya, Upper Volta, France, Brazil, Germany, the Philippines, and Japan. Tensions were quite high in Poland, however, owing to the Solidarity movement under Lech Walesa, the declaration of martial law by the Polish government, and the chronic threat posed by the Soviet Union. In the midst of these crises, an assassination attempt was made upon Blessed John Paul II on May 13, 1981, by Mehmet Ali Agca, while the pope was being driven through St. Peter's Square. A long recovery period followed, but in 1982 the pope resumed his globe-trotting, traveling to Britain, becoming the first pontiff ever to visit the isle. That same year, he went to Fátima to give thanks to the Blessed Mother for his survival.

His unceasing trips from the time of his recovery made him the most traveled pope in history and the most recognized leader in the entire world. Some of his most significant visits were to South Korea (1984), Oceania (1986), the United States (1987, 1993), Scandinavia (1989), Mexico and Czechoslovakia (1990), Poland, Hungary, and Brazil (1991), Latvia, Lithuania, and Estonia (1993), Lebanon (1997), Cuba (1998), Egypt and Mount Sinai, and the Holy Land (2000), Greece, Syria, and Malta (2001), and Toronto (for World Youth Day, 2002). By the end of his pontificate, he had covered over 750,000 miles during 104 pastoral visits outside Italy, over 146 within Italy, and 301 to the parishes of Rome.

Deeply concerned with doctrinal orthodoxy and the genuine interpretation of the Second Vatican Council in the post-conciliar Church, Pope Blessed John Paul II was extremely active in voicing his concerns over troubling issues. In 1979 he spoke at the Puebla Conference in Mexico about liberation theology and approved instructions on that movement that were prepared by the Congregation for the Doctrine of the Faith in 1984 and 1986. He moved against such radical priests as Leonardo Boff, Hans Küng, Charles Curran, and Edward Schillebeeckx, O.P. At the same time, in the face of the intransigence of Archbishop Marcel Lefebvre, he decreed the prelate's excommunication in 1988 even as he promoted reunion with the Society of St. Pius X through the Pontifical Commission Ecclesia Dei. To promote the sacramental life of the Church, the pope issued the letter *Misericordia Dei* in 2002 to foster the Sacrament of Penance, and the encyclical *Ecclesia de Eucharistia* in 2003 to reiterate the Church's teachings on the Eucharist.

Blessed John Paul II

On a more positive note, the pope presided over the *Catechism of the Catholic Church* in 1994, the first since the Roman Catechism of the sixteenth century, and issued the encyclical *Veritatis Splendor* in 1993, on pressing concerns in moral theology. These measures, coupled with Pope Blessed John Paul II's forceful personality and his determination to provide a steady course for the direction of the faith, restored much of the Church's vitality and organization that had been lost in the turbulent years following the close of the Second Vatican Council.

Highly experienced in the areas of marriage, sexual ethics, issues of human rights, and economic justice, Pope Blessed John Paul II was unequivocal in reaffirming the Church's teaching on matters of reproduction while providing new insights into the nature of the family, the relationship between husband and wife, and the vital sacredness of all life. This position was most seen in his opposition to the 1994 Cairo Conference on Population Growth sponsored by the United Nations and in his 1995 encyclical, *Evangelium Vitae*.

Concerning the internal administration of the Church, he codified the new Code of Canon Law for the Western Church in 1983 and the new Code for the Eastern Churches in 1990. In 1988 he issued the apostolic constitution *Pastor Bonus*, by which the Curia was reorganized. He continued to increase the international nature of the College of Cardinals and the Curia, and had made a point to foster collegiality and to convoke synods for the good of the Church.

In the field of ecumenism, Pope Blessed John Paul II carried on the work of Paul VI in reaching out to all faiths and promoting Christian unity, declaring in 1984 that the commitment to religious unity was irreversible. Under his leadership, ecumenism has taken many strides in the last decade, and the pontiff pointed to the commonality of baptism, prayer, and Scripture, while remaining firm in refusing to permit the sharing of the Eucharist. His vision for ecumenism was expressed eloquently in the encyclical *Ut Unum Sint* in 1995.

One of the happiest and most fruitful achievements of his ecumenism efforts was his relationship with Judaism. In 1986 he visited a synagogue in Rome and in 1994 normalized relations with Israel. He also encouraged the work of the Pontifical Commission for Religious Relations with the Jews, especially under former president Cardinal Edward Idris Cassidy.

In 2000 Pope Blessed John Paul II's pontificate witnessed one of the most tumultuous periods in history. The pope had the once unthinkable opportunity to reestablish the Church in the one-time lands of communist Eastern Europe, including Hungary, Poland, the Baltic States, and even Russia. Deeply committed to religious freedom, human rights, and economic and social justice, and to alleviating the suffering of the poor and the afflicted, the pope regularly used his travels as a platform to address these issues. His social concerns were the subject of several encyclicals: *Laborem Exercens* in 1981, *Sollicitudo Rei Socialis* in 1987, and *Centesimus Annus* in 1991. He negotiated also a new concordat with Italy in 1984 and formalized relations with the United States (1984).

The Holy Father looked with considerable anticipation to the new millennium, the occasion of the Great Jubilee. Leading up to the event, the pontiff issued the apostolic letter *Tertio Millennio Adveniente* in 1994 and followed the Jubilee with the letter *Tertio Millennio Ineunte*.

One other aspect of his pontificate was his determination to demonstrate the universality of holiness. The pope has thus canonized and beatified more men and women than his predecessors combined. By the time of his passing, he had proclaimed 1,338 blesseds in 147 ceremonies and had proclaimed 482 saints in 51 liturgical celebrations; his 17 predecessors from Pope Clement VIII to Pope Paul VI canonized a total of 302 people. The Holy Father used his many apostolic journeys to proclaim that sanctity and heroic virtue are found in every setting and every culture. The beatifications and canonizations helped to make that point manifest to the world.

Karol Wojtyla was one of the most accomplished and superbly educated cardinals ever to be elected to the throne of St. Peter and was the youngest pontiff, fifty-eight at his election, since Blessed Pius IX in 1846. The holder of multiple degrees and a brilliant philosopher and theologian, he was also a poet, playwright, and avid skier, whose enjoyment of the slopes was curtailed only in 1994 after a hip injury from a fall in the apostolic apartments.

His pontificate in its later years became marked by two important events. The first was his own declining health, in particular the advance of a Parkinson's-like syndrome that left him clearly in pain. He made his advancing years and suffering one more means of conforming himself to Christ, and he proclaimed himself in solidarity with the elderly. Second, the pope and the world were confronted with war and instability. In the aftermath of the Cold War, the pontiff called upon the world to avoid the traps of secular humanism, excessive capitalism, and religious and nationalistic intolerance. He labored to end the violence that took place in Rwanda in the 1990s, the former Yugoslavia in 1998, and the ongoing conflict in the Middle East. He was also grieved by the terrorist attack upon

the United States in 2001 and the subsequent war in Iraq in 2003.

The pope had already visited the United States in the years prior to his election in 1978 as archbishop of Kraków and also as one of the world's leading ethicists and moral theologians. He was thus familiar with America and its many blessings, as well as its many challenges and problems.

The pontiff wasted little time in visiting the United States within the first year after his election. He made a triumphant journey from September 29 to October 7, 1979, including a visit to the United Nations. He went on to make major visits to the United States again in 1987, from September 10 to 19; in 1993, from August 9 to 15 for World Youth Day in Denver; in 1995, from October 4 to 8, including visits to New York, Baltimore, and the United Nations; and in 1999, from January 26 to 27 to St. Louis.

Each of the papal visits was used by the Holy Father to impart important lessons to Catholics and to make vital outreach to the American people regarding the most important issues of our time. In 1979, as he said Mass for crowds stretching into the tens of thousands and then the hundreds of thousands, the pope spoke poignantly of the dignity of the human person and called on people everywhere to defend life in all its forms, especially when it is threatened by abortion, exploitation, indifference, economic injustice, and neglect. This, he contended, was not alien to the American tradition of honoring and promoting human rights. In 1995 he stressed again the need for America to reclaim the moral foundations on which it was built and to understand fully the true meaning of human freedom.

The visits of Pope Blessed John Paul II to America were filled with surprises, from his ability to capture the imaginations of millions with simple gestures, to his humor, to the way he could demolish the media's frequently slanted coverage of his trips from positions of dissent (on abortion, contraception, the ordination of women). Perhaps the biggest surprise, however, was the vibrant Catholicism to be found in the United States, above all among Catholic youths. The pontiff's apostolic journeys to the United States were occasions for enormous gatherings of youth, starting with the thousands of overjoyed and hollering kids who greeted him at Madison Square Garden on October 3, 1979, to the triumphant gatherings in Denver in 1993 for World Youth Day and in St. Louis in 1999.

The Church in the United States faced a number of severe challenges during his pontificate. Chief among these were the problems of dissent and the sex abuse scandal that struck in the pope's last years. American Catholicism was buffeted by chronic expressions of dissent from authentic Catholic teaching throughout Blessed John Paul II's reign. During his first visit to the United States in 1979, the pope heard the public demand for the ordination of women from the then-head of the Leadership Conference of Women Religious. A few years later, dissent in Catholic academic circles endured a crisis when long-simmering controversy over Father Charles Curran (an advocate of the position that it was possible for Catholics to dissent from such noninfallible teachings as contraception) came to a climax in 1986 with the withdrawal of Father Curran's *missio canonica* by Cardinal James A. Hickey of Washington, D.C. (*See also* Catholic University of America, The.)

The Curran Affair raised critical questions regarding the identity and mission of Catholic colleges and universities. The central element in subsequent discussions was on Pope John Paul II's 1990 apostolic constitution *Ex Corde Ecclesiae*, on the pope's vision of what a Catholic university should be. On November 17, 1999, the Catholic bishops of the United States approved *The Application of Ex Corde Ecclesiae for the United States*, implementing the apostolic constitution. This action received the *recognitio* from the Congregation for Bishops on May 3, 2000. The implementation, including the requirement of the *mandatum*, sparked opposition in some circles to what was perceived as a discouragement of academic freedom, but it also served to remind theologians of their role in the Church.

A key to understanding the relationship between the theologian and the Church was published by the Congregation for the Doctrine of the Faith under then-Cardinal Joseph Ratzinger (now Pope Benedict XVI) in 1990 with the full approval of Pope Blessed John Paul II. The title of the instruction was "On the Ecclesial Function of the Theologian" and had as its stated purpose "to shed light on the mission of theology in the Church." The instruction details the relationship between the theologian and the Magisterium, stating positively that, "The living Magisterium of the Church and theology, while having different gifts and functions, ultimately have the same goal: preserving the People of God in the truth which sets free and thereby making them 'a light to the nations.'" Nevertheless, for the theologian, when the Magisterium of the Church makes an infallible pronouncement and solemnly declares that a teaching is found in revelation, "the assent called for is that of theological faith."

Compounding the question of dissent on the part of some theologians were the related issues of Americans deviating from Church teaching and Catholic politicians who chose to support such morally unacceptable actions as abortion in their role as public officials. Catholics in the United States exhibited a dichotomy in expressing love and admiration for the pope while deviating in large numbers from Church teachings on contraception and even abortion.

Dissent from Catholic teachings was especially controversial in the area of American political life. A number of Catholic politicians in the United States took public stances in favor of abortion and so brought about discussions among the Catholic bishops and American Catholics over the degree to which politicians's public life and policy positions should be informed and guided by their faith. The issue came to the fore especially in the 2004 presidential campaign when Senator John Kerry, a Catholic and a Democrat from Massachusetts, ran for president as the Democratic nominee. On June 18, 2004, the United States Conference of Catholic Bishops issued a statement, "Catholics in Political Life," that called upon Catholics in public life to protect the rights of the unborn and to oppose legal abortion.

The last years of John Paul II's pontificate were also deeply troubled by the sex abuse scandal that rocked the Church in the United States and in a few other countries, such as Ireland, starting in 2002. In April 2002 Pope Blessed John Paul II convened in Rome a gathering of the American cardinals, along with the heads of the USCCB and Vatican officials. At the time, he declared forcefully that there was "no place in the priesthood and religious life for those who would harm the young," although he added that it was important to remember "the power of Christian conversion." (*See also* Sex Abuse Crisis.)

More positively, in the nearly three decades during which he was pope, Pope Blessed John Paul II presided over the one of the greatest periods of Catholic expansion across the world. This growth was seen in the United States as well. In 1978, at the time of his election, the number of American Catholics was 49.8 million out of an overall population of 217.7 million. In 2005 there were 67.8 million Catholics out of an overall population of 295.8 million. Sadly, sharp declines were seen in the numbers of priests, from 58,485 in 1978 to 43,422 in 2005, and women religious, from 129,391 in 1978 to 69,963 in 2005.

Pope Blessed John Paul II also left an indelible mark on American Church life by appointing bishops and establishing new dioceses and ecclesiastical territories. By the time of his passing, all but a few dioceses were headed by bishops named by him. Further, he created a large number of new dioceses and elevated several others to the status of archdioceses. The primary area of activity was in the South and West, but he also established several new jurisdictions for the care of Eastern-rite Catholic communities in the country. The new dioceses were Lake Charles, Louisiana (1980); Metuchen, New Jersey (1981); San Jose, California (1981); Las Cruces, New Mexico (1982); Victoria, Texas (1982); Colorado Springs, Colorado (1983); Lubbock, Texas (1983); Palm Beach, Florida (1984); Venice, Florida (1984); Shreveport, Louisiana (1986); Tyler, Texas (1986); Knoxville, Tennessee (1988); Lexington, Kentucky (1988); Las Vegas (1995); and Laredo, Texas (2000).

The new Eastern Catholic jurisdictions were Apostolic Eparchy for Armenian Catholics in the United States and Canada (1981, elevated to an eparchy in 2005); Van Nuys, California (Byzantine, Ruthenian, 1981), St. George's in Canton, Ohio (Byzantine, Romanian, 1982; elevated to an eparchy in 1987); St. Thomas the Apostle of Detroit (Chaldean, 1982; elevated to an eparchy in 1985); St. Josaphat in Parma, Ohio (Byzantine, Ukrainians, 1983); Our Lady of Lebanon of Los Angeles, California (Maronite, 1994); Our Lady of Deliverance of Newark (for Syrian-rite Catholics of the United States and Canada, 1995); St. Thomas of the Syro-Malabars of Chicago (Syro-Malabars, 2001); and St. Peter the Apostle of San Diego (Chaldean, 2002). In addition, the pope elevated the Dioceses of Mobile (founded in 1829) and Galveston-Houston (founded in 1847) to the rank of archdioceses in 1980 and 2004, respectively; he also restructured the Archdiocese for the Military Services (founded in 1957) in 1985.

After a slow decline in health, Pope Blessed John Paul II died in the papal apartments on April 2, 2005. Soon after his passing, the cause for his canonization was opened. After formal approval of a miracle, he was beatified on May 1, 2011, in Rome by Pope Benedict XVI. His feast day is October 22.

Joliet, Diocese of

Established on December 11, 1948, and canonically erected on March 24, 1949, by Pope Pius XII, the Diocese of Joliet serves counties in the northeastern part of the state of Illinois. The city is situated in the plains region of the state on the Des Plaines River and is an agricultural, industrial, and commercial center. Originally the city was named Juliet, in honor of the daughter of a settler. It was renamed Joliet in 1845, after the explorer Louis Joliet, the companion of Jesuit Father Jacques Marquette, and was known as "Stone City" for the limestone available there. The Diocese of Joliet is a suffragan see of the Archdiocese of Chicago.

In 1673 Father Marquette and Joliet were in the area of modern Illinois, and the great Kaskaskia Mission was founded, dedicated to the Immaculate Conception. Seven years later, René-Robert Chevalier, Sieur de La Salle, built a French fort near the mission, and some of America's most revered missionaries labored in the region. Fathers Louis Hennepin, Gabriel de la Ribourde, and others were present. Father de la Ribourde was slain near modern-day Seneca. The Jesuit mission leader, Father Claude Allouez, and Jesuit Father Jacques Gravier also served the local tribes but were forced to move south because of hostile groups entering the area. Father Gravier was wounded by a party of Peoria Indians and died.

Kaskaskia Mission was moved in 1680, and

other Catholic outposts were established at Peoria, Starved Rock, and Rockford. Cahokia Mission was also opened. French traders were at Peoria Lake, erecting the first permanent settlement. New groups entered the region and prospered until the French and Indian War, and in 1763 France ceded the lands to the English, who banished Catholic priests and services. The Revolutionary War halted the English control, and the newly established Diocese of Baltimore (now the Archdiocese of Baltimore) administered Illinois Catholic affairs after 1789. In 1808 the Diocese of Bardstown had ecclesiastical jurisdiction.

Joliet was founded in 1831, and Father Jean Marie Irenaeus St. Cyr, who served as the pastor of a log-cabin chapel in Chicago, visited the settlement, which became part of the Diocese of Vincennes (now the Archdiocese of Indianapolis). Bishop Simon William Gabriel Bruté de Rémur, the brilliant, tireless missionary, visited Joliet in 1835 and 1838. In 1843 the Diocese of Chicago was erected, followed by other state dioceses.

The completion of the Illinois and Michigan Canal continued to open the area to ever-increasing settlements, and Joliet had a sizable Catholic population. Two Chicago priests, Fathers Bernard Schaffer and James O'Meara, served Joliet by visiting Catholics living along the canal route. Father John F. Plunkett had established St. Patrick's as well as other parishes. When Father Plunkett died in 1840, Father Hippolyte du Pontavice took up his ministry.

America expanded its settlements, and new states entered the Union, responding to world affairs by joining with allies in World War I. The Great Depression followed the military intervention in Europe, impacting on Illinois Catholics and other Americans. When World War II challenged the resources and courage of America yet another time, the faithful of Joliet supported the military efforts of the nation. After the close of the war, the Diocese of Joliet was established on December 11, 1948, and St. Raymond's, begun in 1917, was designated as the diocesan cathedral.

The first bishop of Joliet was Martin D. McNamara, who was appointed on December 17, 1948, and consecrated on March 7, 1949. He opened the offices and agencies necessary for diocesan administration and began building parishes and schools.

Bishop McNamara established a diocesan newspaper and social services and charitable programs. He took part in the Second Vatican Council and died on May 23, 1966.

The second bishop of Joliet was Romeo Blanchette, who had served as auxiliary bishop of the diocese since 1965. He was installed on August 31, 1968, and implemented the reforms of the Second Vatican Council in the diocese. Bishop Blanchette also promoted religious education and lay ministries. He retired on January 30, 1979,

He was succeeded by Joseph J. Imesch, who had served as an auxiliary bishop of the Archdiocese of Detroit since 1973. He was appointed to the Diocese of Joliet on June 30, 1979, and was installed on August 28, 1979. Aside from strong and steady administration of the diocese during his lengthy tenure, Bishop Imesch was responsible for bringing a constant spirit of renewal. This was accomplished in part through the use of RENEW (1983–86) and RENEW 2000 (1998–2001), as well as through the convening of a diocesan synod in 1989 and the formation of a diocesan pastoral council. Bishop Imesch also launched a variety of initiatives for the promotion of evangelization and formation for ministry. He retired on May 16, 2006.

He was succeeded on the same day by Bishop James Peter Sartain, who had been bishop of Little Rock since 2000. Bishop Sartain was appointed archbishop of Seattle on September 16, 2010. He was succeeded on May 17, 2011, by Bishop R. Daniel Conlon, who had been bishop of Steubenville since 2002. In 2011 there were 659,000 Catholics, 300 priests, almost 500 women religious, and 120 parishes in the diocese.

Joliet, Louis (1645–c. 1700)

The companion of Jesuit Father Jacques Marquette, Louis Joliet was an explorer and cartographer of the American wilds. He was born in Beaupré, near Québec, Canada, and received a Jesuit education. Joliet did not continue his studies for ordination to the priesthood but turned to exploration and hunting in the untamed lands. With Father Marquette, Joliet traversed the Mississippi River from its confluence with the Fox River in Wisconsin to the mouth of the Arkansas River. Prior to his journey with Father Marquette, Joliet had led a party from Lake Huron to Lake Erie and had explored Lake Superior for copper deposits.

In 1672 he was commissioned to begin an expedition with Father Marquette, and the two set out on May 17, 1673, in two canoes with Indian guides. The expedition traveled from present-day St. Ignace, Michigan, to Green Bay, coming upon the Fox River. Traveling down the Wisconsin and the Mississippi Rivers, they arrived at the Quapaw Indian settlement, where they were welcomed. They returned north in July. Louis Joliet also explored Hudson Bay and the Labrador coast, as he continued his expeditions after parting with Father Marquette. In 1697 he was named a royal cartographer of New France (Canada). He died in Québec province.

Louis Joliet

Jones, Mary (May 1, 1830–November 30, 1930)

Labor activist best known by the name "Mother Jones," she was born in Cork, Ireland, and journeyed to the United States as a young girl with her family in 1835. Her grandfather had been an Irish freedom fighter and died by hanging for participation in the Irish Republican movement, and her father had been forced to flee to America with his family. They moved to Toronto, where her father worked in railroad construction. Mary attended high school in Toronto and went on to teach briefly in Michigan before opening a dressmaking shop in Chicago. Moving to Memphis, Tennessee, she married George Jones, an iron molder. They had four children, but she lost them all in 1867 when a yellow fever epidemic claimed their lives. Four years later, having moved to Chicago, she lost everything she owned in the Great Chicago Fire.

Mary had learned a great deal of labor and labor practices from her husband, and she soon became involved in the early labor movement and active in the Knights of Labor. This start marked a decisive turning point in her life, for she devoted the rest of her days to the cause of workers' rights and organized labor. She took part in some of the most pitched struggles of the first decades of the labor movement, including the American Railway Union

Strike of 1894, the coal strikes of 1900 and 1902, and the garment and streetcar workers' strikes of 1915–16. In 1903 she organized children working in mills and mines in a march from Kensington, Pennsylvania, to Oyster Bay, New York, to demand the help of President Theodore Roosevelt.

In 1898 Mother Jones (as she was called by the workers) helped found the Social Democratic Party, and in 1905 she took part in the establishment of the Industrial Workers of the World. She was active in the labor efforts of the United Mine Workers and the Socialist Party of America. Arrested in 1913 during the Paint Creek-Cabin Creek strike in West Virginia, she was convicted with other union organizers of conspiring to commit murder, after organizing another children's march. Her arrest, however, caused a major stir, and she was soon released from prison. The U.S. Senate then ordered an investigation into the conditions in the local coal mines. A short time later she was arrested again, in Colorado, served some time in prison, and was deported from the state. Further court troubles plagued her in the shape of charges for libel, slander, and sedition in 1924. The next year she lost a suit to Charles A. Albert, publisher of the fledgling *Chicago Times*, and an award of $350,000 judgment was made against her.

A fixture in the labor movement, she was widely recognized by her tiny stature and fierce oratorical style. Her efforts on behalf of workers continued into her later years, as she was present at the side of coal miners on strike in West Virginia in 1923, despite being ninety-three years old. Although raised a Catholic, she departed the Church during the time of her involvement with the radical aspects of labor rights. In her final years, however, she returned to the faith. She wrote of her experiences in the labor movement as *The Autobiography of Mother Jones* (1925).

Jordan, Mary Dorothy (unknown–September 1759)

Born in New England, Mary Dorothy Jordan was raised as a Protestant and was captured at a very young age by the Abenaki Indians of the area. She was raised as a maiden of the tribe and favored by many. She was also instructed in the Catholic faith and attended Abenaki services until she reached the age of fifteen. A Jesuit missionary discovered her in the Abenaki settlement and received permission to take her to Québec, where she was warmly received. Mary Dorothy was also introduced to the Ursuline nuns in Québec, and she received the grace of a religious vocation. She entered the Ursuline Convent in 1722 and became a superior of the order. She died in the convent in Québec.

Josephites (S.S.J.)

The Josephites (St. Joseph's Society of the Sacred Heart, S.S.J.) were founded by the Mill Hill Fathers in 1871 and are a pontifical clerical society engaged in evangelization in the African-American community. The Josephites began through the efforts of the Foreign Missionary Society of England (founded in 1866 by Herbert Vaughan) in answer to an appeal from Archbishop Martin J. Spalding of Baltimore to provide for evangelization and pastoral outreach among the recently emancipated African-American slaves following the Civil War. The first four Mill Hill priests arrived in Baltimore in 1871 and took over pastoral care of St. Francis Xavier Church in Baltimore in early December.

From this beginning, the Mill Hill priests expanded their commitment to Kentucky, South Carolina, Maryland, Washington, D.C., Virginia, and Delaware. To assist these growing initiatives, Father John Slattery, provincial from 1878 to 1883, proposed establishing a seminary in America. The new institution, St. Joseph's Seminary, was dedicated in 1888 and claimed the distinction of being integrated. On December 19, 1891, Charles Randolph Uncles was ordained as the first black priest to have been prepared for the priesthood and to receive ordination in the United States. In 1889 a minor seminary was also established in Baltimore.

By 1892 Father Slattery requested and received permission to make the American foundation in the United States independent of the Mill Hill Fathers. The Josephites established their headquarters in Baltimore in 1893 as a diocesan institute under the authority of Cardinal James Gibbons. In 1932 it was elevated to the rank of pontifical insti-

tute and was given a new constitution. Additional changes and a new constitution were approved in 1984 by the Holy See. Missions in African-American communities have continued and remain one of the greatest achievements of the congregation across some forty dioceses in the United States. It can be said that the Josephites have been one of the most crucial instruments of evangelization and pastoral care of black Catholics in the United States.

Joset, Pierre Joseph (1810–June 19, 1900)

Revered as the "Apostle to the Coeur d'Alene," Pierre Joseph Joset was a Jesuit missionary. He was born in Canton Berne, Switzerland, the youngest of five children. All his brothers became priests, and he attended the Jesuit College in Fribourg. He entered the Society of Jesus, was trained, and was ordained on September 19, 1840. After ordination, Father Joset was assigned to the American missions and arrived in the United States with three other priests and a lay brother. Father Joset volunteered for the Rocky Mountain missions and was supposed to meet the famous missionary Father Pierre-Jean De Smet, but Father De Smet was not at the meeting place.

Father Joset and his companions began looking for St. Mary's Mission in Montana but became lost in the wilderness. They then met an Iroquois Indian, Young Ignace La Mousse, who led them to the mission. Young Ignace had been part of an Iroquois hunting party that stayed with the Flatheads of the region and taught them the advantages of having a "Black Robe" in the tribal settlements.

Father Joset then made his way to Sacred Heart Mission for the Coeur d'Alene, eventually moving the mission to Cataldo, Idaho. He served as superior general of the Rocky Mountain Missions, serving until he died at age ninety.

Jouin, Louis (June 14, 1818–June 10, 1899)

A priest, Louis Jouin was respected as a writer and philosopher. He was born in Berlin, Germany, to a French Huguenot family living in Prussia as descendants of exiles from France. Raised a Protestant, he spent time in Poland and was converted to the Church. After a brief period of service in the Prussian military, he traveled to Rome and entered the Society of Jesus in August 1841. After studies at the Roman College and additional preparation, he was ordained on April 30, 1848.

Owing to the severe political upheaval in Italy, he was forced to flee the country and made his way to the United States. He arrived in New York City in October 1848, and progressed to additional studies at Fordham College from 1852 to 1856. He taught at Fordham until 1859; after a year in Canada, he went back to Fordham and resumed teaching from 1860 to 1863 and again from 1866 to 1872. Further travels brought him to England and again to Canada, but in 1879 he took up once again a position at Fordham, where he served for the rest of his life.

Father Jouin was a noted instructor in the field of philosophy and was the author of a number of works on the subject, including *Evidences of Religion* in 1877, *Elementa Logicae et Metaphysicae* in 1884, and *Elementa Philosophiae Moralis* in 1886. He was also a brilliant linguist and was fluent in German, French, Italian, Spanish, English, Polish, and Latin, as well as Greek, Hebrew, and Gaelic.

Judge, Thomas Augustine (August 23, 1868– November 23, 1933)

Vincentian priest and noted missionary, Thomas Augustine Judge was the founder of the Missionary Cenacle Apostolate. He was born in Boston and grew up in a solid environment of the faith. While hoping to enter the seminary, he was compelled instead to help the family by going to work in the post office after the death of his father in 1887. In 1889, however, he entered the novitiate of the Congregation of the Missions (the Vincentians), largely in response to the mission given by several Vincentian priests in his local parish. After studies, he was ordained on May 27, 1899, and sent to pastoral assignments in Maryland.

In 1903 Father Judge joined the Vincentian Mission Band and so preached extensively throughout Maryland, Pennsylvania, New Jersey, and New York. In 1909 he was transferred to Brooklyn, New York, and there made an appeal for a greater participation of the laity in the mission and ministry of the Church. The six women who accepted the call began work in such pastoral areas as catechetical instruction, home visitations, and dedication to the most vulnerable in society. From this first group of women was born Cenacle Lay Apostolate. Father Judge carried his zeal for the activity of the laity to New England when he was moved in 1910 to Springfield, Massachusetts, and preached from Maine to West Virginia. He established lay bands everywhere he went, and in 1912, under the authority of Cardinal James Gibbons, the women associates opened a Missionary Cenacle in Baltimore for the homeless and unemployed women, and to meet the needs of Italian immigrants.

In 1915 Father Judge was sent to the rural Vincentian mission in Opelika, Alabama. He found there a mission territory of several thousand square miles dotted with only a few Catholics across its hostile and anti-Catholic social terrain. He thus sent out an appeal for lay assistance, and many women and men of the Missionary Cenacle traveled to the South. In the face of prejudice, the missionaries persevered and finally won admiration and acceptance through their tireless efforts to care for the sick and dying during the terrible influenza epidemic of 1917–18.

Deepening their commitment to the life of service, members of the Missionary Cenacle Apostolate went on to form two new missionary religious congregations, the Missionary Servants of the Most Blessed Trinity for women in 1919 and the Missionary Servants of the Most Holy Trinity for men in 1921. The Missionary Cenacle Apostolate continues to serve in a variety of ways throughout the United States, Puerto Rico, Mexico, and Costa Rica. The indefatigable Father Judge remained the inspiration and spiritual director for the foundations until his death.

Juneau, Diocese of

Established on June 23, 1951, by Pope Pius XII, the Diocese of Juneau serves the entire southeastern part of the state of Alaska, including the Alexander Archipelago and other islands. The capital of Alaska, Juneau is a center for lumber, mining and national defense programs. Joseph Juneau and Richard Harris founded the city in 1880 after discovering gold there. It is also a major American seaport. The Diocese of Juneau is a suffragan see of the Archdiocese of Anchorage.

Anchorage was originally claimed by Russia in 1741. The first Catholics in the area were the

Spanish missionaries Franciscan Fathers Juan Riobo and Matias de Santa Catarina y Noriega, accompanying an expedition in 1779. An Oblate, Father Jean Seguin was at Fort Yukon in 1862–63. Others serving there were Oblate Bishop Isidore Clut and Fathers Auguste Lecorre and Emile Petitot.

Alaska was purchased by the United States from Russia in 1867, and the Diocese of Vancouver Island (now Victoria) administered Catholic affairs in the territory. Bishop Charles J. Seghers, called the "Apostle of Alaska," labored and died there. In 1878 Father John Althoff was at Wrangell, where he founded a parish. In 1886 the Sisters of St. Anne from Victoria, British Columbia, arrived in the area and founded a hospital and a school.

Pope Leo XIII established a prefecture apostolic in Alaska on July 27, 1894, appointing Jesuit Father Paschal Tosi as the first prefect. Other Jesuits succeeded Father Tosi in this office until 1916. In that year, Pope Benedict XV raised the prefecture to a vicariate apostolic. Jesuit Father Joseph R. Crimont was appointed vicar apostolic. He was consecrated a bishop on July 25, 1917. Other vicars apostolic served until 1951, when the Diocese of Juneau was established on June 23.

The first bishop of Juneau was Dermot O'Flanagan, who was appointed on July 9, 1951. Northern Alaska was still a vicariate, with Bishop Francis Gleeson, a Jesuit, as vicar until 1962, when he was appointed to the Diocese of Fairbanks. Bishop O'Flanagan was consecrated for Juneau on October 3, 1951, and instituted the offices and agencies for diocesan administration. He also put in place ministries and services for the Haida, Tlingit, and other tribes inhabiting the region. A veteran missionary, Bishop O'Flanagan visited the far-flung missions and parishes until he retired on June 19, 1968.

His successor was Bishop Francis T. Hurley, who had served as auxiliary bishop of Juneau since 1970. He succeeded on July 20, 1971. He continued programs and ministries for the vast territory of the diocese until May 4, 1976, when he was promoted to the Archdiocese of Anchorage. He remained administrator of Juneau until his successor was installed.

The third bishop of Juneau was Michael H. Kenny, who was consecrated on May 27, 1979, and installed in the diocese on June 15. Bishop Kenny served the local Alaskan tribes and expanded the diocesan facilities until his sudden death in Jordan on February 19, 1995.

The fourth bishop of Juneau, Michael W. Warfel, was appointed to Juneau on November 19, 1996, and consecrated a bishop on December 17, 1996. He devoted more than a decade to the diocese and on November 20, 2007, was appointed bishop of Great Falls-Billings, Montana. He was succeeded on January 19, 2009, by Edward J. Burns, a priest of the Diocese of Pittsburgh. He was ordained a bishop in Pittsburgh on March 3, 2009, and installed as the fifth bishop of Juneau on April 2, 2009. In 2011 there were some 10,000 Catholics, 12 priests, and 9 parishes in the diocese.

K

Kalamazoo, Diocese of

Established on July 21, 1971, by Pope Paul VI, the Diocese of Kalamazoo serves nine counties in the southwestern part of the state of Michigan. The city started as a fur-trading post, and in 1829 Titus Bronson built a log cabin there. Kalamazoo was originally called Bronson, but was renamed *Kee-Kalamazoo*, the local Indian term for "boiling water," in 1836. This term is a reference to the local hot springs and spas. The city of Kalamazoo is an agricultural and manufacturing center. The Diocese of Kalamazoo is a suffragan see of the Archdiocese of Detroit.

The diocese shares in the rich Catholic heritage of Michigan, as countless missionaries entered the Great Lakes wilderness to establish Catholic enclaves over the decades. As early as 1640, the Jesuit martyr St. Isaac Jogues and Father Charles Raymbaut were at Sault Ste. Marie. Other Jesuits, including Fathers Claude Allouez, René Menard, and Jacques Marquette were also in the area. In 1660 Father Menard was on Keweenaw Bay, but he disappeared on a mission tour the next year. In 1689 Father Claude Allouez founded St. Joseph's Mission, which became St. Joseph's Parish in 1720. The famed superior of the Jesuit missions, Father Allouez, died in the area just after founding the mission.

Detroit had been founded as Fort Ponchartrain in 1701 by Antoine Cadillac, and Franciscan Recollect Father Nicholas Constantin Delhalle opened the chapel of St. Anne de Detroit there. Detroit and the Michigan region were claimed by the English in 1763 as victors of the Seven Years' War. Chief Pontiac of the Ottawa attacked settlements of whites in that same year, but was defeated by General "Mad Anthony" Wayne in a later battle. Detroit was ceded to the United States by the English in 1796, and Father Gabriel Richard, who had aided the American cause, served there.

In the War of 1812, the English again took Detroit but were defeated in the Battle of Lake Erie by U.S. Admiral Oliver Hazard Perry. In 1833 Detroit became a diocese, and four years later Michigan entered the Union as the twenty-sixth state. In the Kalamazoo area, Sacred Heart of Mary Parish was erected in 1838 as a result of a treaty with Chief Leopold Pohagan at Silver Creek. Other Michigan dioceses were established as new settlers added to the Catholic population. Parishes were founded within the limits of Kalamazoo diocese to meet the growing demands of the faithful. St. Charles Borromeo at Coldwater dates to 1849, followed by St. Mary's Parish at Marshal, which dates to 1852. St. Augustine Cathedral in Kalamazoo dates to 1856, St. Mary of the Lake in New Buffalo to 1857, St. Mary's Visitation at Byron Center to 1866, St. Mary's at Bronson to 1867, and St. Philip's in Battle Creek to 1869. Other parishes were established in the next decades as the Catholic population expanded.

World War I, the Great Depression, and World War II impacted on the Catholics in the region, and they supported the nation's military efforts and struggled to overcome the economic disaster of the Depression era. After World War II, the region experienced new growth, and small towns flourished. On July 21, 1971, the apostolic delegate, Archbishop Luigi Raimondi, announced the establishment of the Diocese of Kalamazoo, and the first bishop of the diocese was Paul V. Donovan. Bishop Donovan instituted the agencies and offices for diocesan administration and began his ministry to some eighty-three thousands Catholics, including a large number of Native Americans in fifteen tribal enclaves. Expansion of facilities, including parishes and schools, was the focus of Bishop Donovan's labors. He retired on November 22, 1994, having provided a firm foundation for the diocese.

His successor was Bishop Alfred J. Markiewicz, who had served as the auxiliary bishop of Rockville Centre since 1986. Bishop Markiewicz was appointed to Kalamazoo on November 22, 1994, and was installed on January 31, 1995. He had served for less than two years when he died suddenly on January 9, 1997.

The third bishop of Kalamazoo, James A. Murray, was appointed on November 18, 1997. He was installed in the diocese on January 27, 1998, and retired on April 6, 2009. Bishop Murray was succeeded on April 6, 2009, by Bishop Paul J. Bradley, who had been an auxiliary bishop in Pittsburgh since 2004. In 2011 there were 102,000 Catholics, 70 priests, 217 women religious, and 46 parishes in the diocese.

Kaminski, Stephen. *See* Polish Catholics

Kansas

Called the Sunflower State, Kansas entered the Union as the thirty-fourth state in 1861. It is located in the west-central part of the United States, bounded on the north by Nebraska, on the east by Missouri, on the south by Oklahoma, and on the west by Colorado. The state has three major land regions: the Dissected Till Plains and the Osage Plains in the eastern part of Kansas, and the Great Plains in the west. The original inhabitants of the state were the Arapaho, Cheyenne, Comanche, Kansas, Kickapoo, Kiowa, Osage, Pawnee, Potawatomi, and Wichita.

The Catholic history of Kansas opened in 1541 with the expedition of Francisco Vázquez de Coronado. Coronado was seeking the fabled cities of gold, and he did not remain in the area for long. The Franciscan Father Juan de Padilla, however, had come into the region with Coronado and stayed behind with the Wichita Indians. He was slain soon after by members of another tribe and became the protomartyr of the United States.

No other recorded mission efforts in Kansas have survived, but there were fur traders in the area in 1700, and in 1763 Kansas became a Spanish holding as part of the Treaty of Paris. France, which had ceded the land in 1763, regained Kansas in 1800 and three years later sold it to the United States as part of the Louisiana Purchase. Kansas was also explored by Zebulon Pike and Stephen Long.

By 1812 Kansas was part of the Missouri Territory, later designated as the Indian Territory. Ten years later, Jesuit Father Charles de la Croix was on the Neosho River serving the Osage. Chief Sans-Nerf, the Osage leader, had requested missionaries. In 1827 Colonel Henry Leavenworth established the state's first permanent settlement.

Jesuit priests followed Father de la Croix into the area. Jesuit Charles Van Quickenborne was near

Leavenworth with the Kickapoo, and in 1839 St. Rose Philippine Duchesne was with the Potawatomi. The Jesuit Father Christian Hoecken, a companion of the revered Father Pierre-Jean De Smet, also served at Sugar Creek. In 1847 the Osage Mission of St. Paul was opened by Jesuit Fathers John Schoenmakers and John Bax and served as a base for Jesuit Father Paul Mary Ponziglione, who traveled across the southeastern part of Kansas.

The Vicariate Apostolic of the Indian Territory (from east of the Rocky Mountains to Missouri) was established by Pope Blessed Pius IX, and in 1851 Bishop Jean Baptiste Miège, also a Jesuit, was made vicar apostolic. The Catholics of Kansas took part in the Civil War, as the area became a battleground for both sides, including John Brown. Kansas prohibited slavery in 1859 and entered the Union in 1861. In Catholic affairs, religious communities entered the area to serve the growing Catholic population. The Homestead Act of 1863 opened the land to families and brought about dramatic changes in the region, as Kansas developed into a major cattle-shipping center. The Farmers' Alliance, the Populist Party, and Carry Nation, who waged a campaign against alcohol, added to the turmoil of the era. The Diocese of Leavenworth (now the Archdiocese of Kansas City in Kansas) was erected on May 22, 1877. In 1887 the Diocese of Leavenworth was divided into three separate ecclesiastical jurisdictions with the establishment of the Diocese of Wichita and Concordia (now the Diocese of Salina).

World War I and the Great Depression brought sacrifices and suffering to Kansas, and in World War II the state provided needed military equipment for America's war effort. The Diocese of Leavenworth was transferred to Kansas City in Kansas on May 10, 1947, which, on August 9, 1952, was elevated to the rank of a metropolitan provincial see. The state now has a thriving Catholic community, including the Diocese of Dodge City, which was erected in 1951. In 2011 there were 409,000 Catholics, 156 priests, 489 women religious, and 110 parishes in the diocese.

Kansas City in Kansas, Archdiocese of

Established as the Diocese of Leavenworth on May 22, 1877, by Pope Blessed Pius IX and as the

Diocese of Kansas City in Kansas by Pope Pius XII on May 10, 1947, Kansas City in Kansas was given the ecclesiastical rank of an archdiocese on August 9, 1952, by Pope Pius XII. The archdiocese originally served Kansas and the vicariate apostolic erected on July 19, 1850, by Pope Blessed Pius IX.

Kansas City in Kansas is located at the confluence of the Kansas and Missouri rivers, opposite Kansas City in Missouri. The city serves as an agricultural, refinery, railroad, and manufacturing center. With its suffragan sees, the Archdiocese of Kansas City in Kansas has a rich Catholic heritage, having been served in the past by the protomartyr of the United States, Franciscan Father Juan de Padilla, and by some of America's most dedicated missionaries.

In 1541 the expedition of Francisco Vázquez de Coronado entered the area of present-day Kansas, seeking legendary cities of gold. Father de Padilla was part of the expedition, and he stayed among the Wichita when Coronado left the area. He was later murdered by members of another tribe. Records of visits by later missionaries have not survived.

Kansas became a Spanish territory through the Treaty of Paris but was returned to France in 1800. In 1803 the region was sold to the United States as part of the Louisiana Purchase. In 1818 present-day Kansas City in Kansas was made part of the Wyandotte Indian domain, called Wyandotte City. Five years later, the Osage Chief Sans-Nerf went to St. Louis to ask Bishop Louis Dubourg for a missionary, and in 1822 Father Charles de la Croix arrived in the area of the Neosho River and served the Osage. Jesuit priests followed Father de la Croix into the region, and Colonel Henry Leavenworth established the state's first permanent settlement in 1827.

Jesuit Father Charles Van Quickenborne opened a Kickapoo Mission in 1836, serving as well the Osage, Peoria, Pienkishaws, and Weas. Other missions followed in the region, and a series of military forts were erected. In 1847 Jesuit Fathers John Schoenmakers and John Bax opened a school, and in the next year Jesuit Father Christian Hoecken, a

Bishop Jean Baptiste Miège

revered companion of the renowned Father Pierre-Jean De Smet, opened a mission at Sugar Creek. Jesuit Father Paul Mary Ponziglione and others labored throughout the territory. Also present was St. Rose Philippine Duschesne, who worked among the Potawatomi and was called "the Woman Who Always Prays."

On July 19, 1850, Pope Blessed Pius IX established the Vicariate Apostolic of the Indian Territory, serving the area from east of the Rocky Mountains to Missouri. Bishop Jean Baptiste Miège, also a Jesuit, was appointed vicar apostolic and was consecrated on March 25, 1851. St. Mary's Mission became his headquarters until 1855, when he moved the see to Leavenworth. Traveling constantly to visit the faithful, Bishop Miège invited religious communities into the area and labored increasingly until his retirement on November 8, 1874.

His successor was the Benedictine Louis M. Fink, who became the first bishop of Leavenworth when the diocese was established on May 22, 1877. Kansas, having survived the grim era of the Civil War and the population explosion brought about by the Homestead Act of 1863, was a member of the Union, having become the thirty-fourth state in 1861. Bishop Fink, faced with the task of serving all of Kansas, petitioned the Holy See for the erection of two additional dioceses. In 1887 the Diocese of Leavenworth was divided into three separate ecclesiastical jurisdictions with the establishment of the Diocese of Wichita and Concordia (now the Diocese of Salina). Bishop Fink died on March 17, 1904.

The diocese's second bishop was Thomas F. Lillis, who was consecrated on December 27, 1904. He faced urban growth in the diocese and instituted a ministry for African-American Catholics, as many had migrated to the city from Tennessee. On March 14, 1910, Bishop Lillis was appointed coadjutor bishop of the Diocese of Kansas City (now the Diocese of Kansas City-St. Joseph), with right of succession.

His successor was Bishop John Ward, who was

consecrated on February 22, 1911. He expanded diocesan facilities and led the faithful through World War I, supporting the military efforts of the nation. He also invited the Augustinian Recollects into the diocese to care for Mexican day laborers who were employed by the Santa Fe Railroad. Bishop Ward started educational and charitable institutions as well. He died on April 20, 1929.

Bishop Francis Johannes succeeded Bishop Ward, having served as coadjutor bishop of the diocese since May 1, 1928. He acceded to the see and was installed on April 20, 1929. He began a special apostolate for the poor and needy, as the Great Depression took a terrible toll in Kansas. Bishop Johannes founded charitable and social services programs and continued to build parishes for the expanding demands of the Catholic population. He died on March 13, 1937.

The fifth bishop was Paul C. Schulte, who was consecrated on September 21, 1937. Bishop Schulte continued the charitable programs of the diocese and led the faithful through the turmoil and the sacrifices of World War II. The war efforts brought a new prosperity to the people of Kansas as military weapons and provisions were needed by the U.S. armed forces. Bishop Schulte was promoted to the Archdiocese of Indianapolis on July 20, 1946.

The sixth bishop and the first bishop of the Diocese of Kansas City in Kansas was George J. Donnelly. He had served as auxiliary bishop of St. Louis since 1940. Bishop Donnelly was appointed to the diocese on November 9, 1946. He labored to provide diocesan facilities and programs to meet the demands of the rapidly growing Catholic population. The diocese was designated as the Diocese of Kansas City in Kansas on May 10, 1947, and Bishop Donnelly supervised the changes in offices and agencies. He died on December 13, 1950.

His successor was Bishop Edward J. Hunkeler, who had served as the bishop of Grand Island since 1945. Bishop Hunkeler was transferred to the Diocese of Kansas City in Kansas on March 28, 1951. He was promoted to archiepiscopal dignity on August 9, 1952, when the diocese was erected as a metropolitan provincial see. Attending the Second Vatican Council, Archbishop Hunkeler implemented the reforms mandated by that council, introducing lay ministries and organizations. He

also aided school programs and charitable agencies. Archbishop Hunkleler retired on September 10, 1969.

The second archbishop of the Archdiocese of Kansas City in Kansas was Ignatius J. Strecker. He had served as the bishop of Springfield-Cape Girardeau since 1962 and was promoted to the archdiocese on September 10, 1969. Archbishop Strecker dealt with the loss of clerical and religious personnel and with the social unrest in the nation. He maintained diocesan facilities and charitable programs while further implementing the reforms of the Second Vatican Council. He also promoted parishes and lay ministries. Archbishop Strecker retired on September 8, 1993.

The third archbishop of Kansas City in Kansas was James P. Keleher. He had served as the bishop of Belleville since 1984 and was installed in the archdiocese on September 8, 1993. Archbishop Keleher continued the lay ministries and social service programs throughout the archdiocese. In 2004 Coadjutor Archbishop Joseph F. Naumann was installed in the archdiocese with right of succession. Archbishop Keleher retired on January 15, 2005.

The fourth archbishop of Kansas City in Kansas, Joseph F. Naumann, had served as auxiliary bishop of St. Louis since 1997 and was appointed coadjutor archbishop of Kansas City in Kansas on January 7, 2004. He acceded to the see on January 15, 2005. In 2011 there were 206,000 Catholics, 156 priests, 489 women religious, and 110 parishes in the archdiocese.

Kansas City-St. Joseph, Diocese of

The Diocese of St. Joseph was established by Pope Blessed Pius IX on March 3, 1868, and the Diocese of Kansas City was erected on September 10, 1880, by Pope Leo XIII. The dioceses were designated as Kansas City-St. Joseph on August 29, 1956, by Pope Pius XII. A suffragan see of the Archdiocese of St. Louis, the diocese serves counties in northwestern Missouri. Kansas City and St. Joseph are industrial cities and transportation centers serving Missouri's livestock industry and the grain market. Manufacturing, wheat marketing, and petroleum production are also vital to these urban areas. Both have historical Catholic roots, dating to the missionary eras before the Revolutionary War.

Hernando de Soto was in the area with his expedition in the 1540s, and René-Robert Chevalier, Sieur de La Salle, claimed the region for France in the following century. In 1673 Jesuit Father Jacques Marquette and Louis Joliet were in the vicinity of present-day Missouri. Church affairs were administered by Québec at the time, and missionaries entered the area to begin their ministries. Jesuit Father Sebastian L. Meurin was joined by Father Pierre Gibault in St. Louis, and Capuchin Franciscans also served the local Catholic trappers and traders and then the settlers.

Missouri entered the Union in 1821 as part of a political compromise, and five years later St. Louis was erected as a diocese, now an archdiocese. François Chouteau, a fur trader, established a trading post in 1821 in the vicinity of modern-day Kansas City. St. Joseph was founded in 1826 by another fur trader, Joseph Robidoux. The first Mass was celebrated in St. Joseph in 1838, and Father Thomas Scanlon was appointed pastor and resident priest in the city.

The Diocese of St. Joseph was erected in 1868 because of the number of Catholics residing in the area, an estimated three thousand. Bishop John J. Hogan was appointed to the new diocese and consecrated on September 13, 1868. He instituted the offices and agencies for diocesan administration and aided rural communities with spiritual and charitable programs. Bishop Hogan had founded the Irish Wilderness settlements and was energetic in his labors. On September 10, 1880, he was transferred to the newly erected Diocese of Kansas City and remained the administrator of the Diocese of St. Joseph until 1893. The Diocese of Kansas City had a reported population of fifty-five thousand Catholics in 1910. Bishop Hogan died on February 21, 1913, having served the faithful of Missouri for decades.

His successor was Bishop Thomas F. Lillis, who had been the bishop of Leavenworth (now the Archdiocese of Kansas City in Kansas) since 1904. He was appointed coadjutor bishop of Kansas City with right of succession on March 14, 1910. He acceded upon the death of Bishop Hogan. Bishop Lillis led the Catholics of Missouri through World War I and the Great Depression. He was appointed an Assistant at the Pontifical Throne on August 19, 1935. Bishop Lillis died on December 29, 1938.

His successor was Bishop Edwin Vincent O'Hara, who had served as the bishop of Great Falls since 1930. He was transferred to Kansas City on April 15, 1939. An outstanding scholar, Bishop O'Hara expanded parishes and diocesan facilities, promoting education throughout the area. On June 29, 1954, the Holy See awarded him with the personal title of archbishop. Bishop O'Hara died on September 11, 1956, while in Milan. In that same year, on August 29, 1956, the Dioceses of St. Joseph and Kansas City were united.

The former bishops of the Diocese of St. Joseph had continued the traditions of Bishop Hogan. His successor in the diocese was Bishop Maurice Francis Burke, who had served as the bishop of Cheyenne since 1887. He was transferred to the Diocese of St. Joseph on June 19, 1893. In 1911 the diocese received additional counties as part of the ecclesiastical jurisdiction. New schools and parishes were erected for the growing Catholic population. Bishop Burke led the faithful through World War I, and died on March 17, 1923.

His successor was Bishop Francis Gilfillan, who had served as his coadjutor with right of succession from July 8, 1922. Bishop Gilfillan led the Catholics of St. Joseph into the grim opening days of the Great Depression, starting charitable programs to alleviate the local economic suffering. He died on January 13, 1933.

The last bishop of St. Joseph was Charles H. LeBlond. He succeeded Bishop Gilfillan, and was consecrated on September 21, 1933. He continued the charitable organizations and programs and promoted parishes and schools. Bishop LeBlond guided the diocese through the difficult days of World War II, supporting the military efforts of the nation. He retired on August 24, 1956, five days before Kansas City and St. Joseph were designated as one diocese.

Bishop John Patrick Cody, who would become an American cardinal in 1967, was appointed the first bishop of Kansas City-St. Joseph on August 24, 1956. He had served as auxiliary bishop of St. Louis since 1947 and as coadjutor bishop with right of succession in St. Joseph since 1954. He was installed in Kansas City-St. Joseph and started uniting diocesan offices and agencies, providing expanded facilities for the growing number of the faithful. On August

10, 1961, he was promoted to the rank of coadjutor archbishop of the Archdiocese of New Orleans with right of succession and acceded to the see on November 8, 1964. One year later, Archbishop Cody was transferred to the Archdiocese of Chicago and was created a cardinal in 1967.

The second bishop of Kansas City-St. Joseph was Bishop Charles H. Helmsing, who had served as auxiliary bishop of St. Louis since 1949 and as bishop of Springfield-Cape Giradeau since 1956. He was transferred to Kansas City-St. Joseph on January 27, 1962. The Second Vatican Council was in session during his episcopacy, and Bishop Helmsing implemented the reforms mandated by that council. He also promoted the Catholic Interracial Council and invited religious orders and congregations into the diocese. He retired on August 17, 1977.

The third bishop of Kansas City-St. Joseph was John J. Sullivan, who had served as the bishop of Grand Island since 1972. Bishop Sullivan was appointed to the diocese on June 27, 1977, and installed on August 17. He continued implementing the reforms of the Second Vatican Council and promoted lay ministries. Bishop Sullivan retired on September 9, 1993.

The fourth bishop of Kansas City-St. Joseph was Raymond J. Boland. He had served as the bishop of Birmingham since 1988 and was appointed to the diocese on June 22, 1993. He was installed in the diocese on September 9, 1993. Bishop Boland had served as episcopal moderator of the National Catholic Risk Retention Group and thus helped to shape the development of an adult education program about child sexual abuse. The program, "Protecting God's Children," was subsequently adopted by seventy-seven dioceses in the United States. He also maintained diocesan programs despite the shortages of priests and religious and supported lay programs. On March 9, 2004, Bishop Robert W. Finn was appointed coadjutor bishop. Bishop Boland retired on May 24, 2005, and Bishop Finn acceded to the see. In 2011 there were 133,000 Catholics, 180 priests, 236 women religious, and 87 parishes in the diocese.

Kapaun, Emil (April 20, 1916–May 23, 1951)

A military chaplain, Emil Kapaun died in a Chinese prisoner of war camp during the Korean War after bringing immense spiritual comfort to his fellow prisoners. He was born in Pilsen, Kansas, to Enos and Elizabeth Kapaun, and was described by friends as having been born to a priestly vocation. He studied classical languages and philosophy at Conception College in Conception, Missouri, and, after graduation in 1936, was able to enter Kenrick Theological Seminary in St. Louis with the help of his pastor and the bishop. After studies for the priesthood, he was ordained in June 1940.

The next few years were spent in pastoral work in his old parish in Pilsen, where he served as pastoral associate to his great friend and mentor, a Father Sklenar. When, however, in late 1943, Father Kapaun was named to succeed Father Sklenar as pastor, he requested to be relieved of the position because he felt in conscience and humility that he should not serve as pastor of a parish in which he had grown up and in which there were so many Catholics possessed, in his mind, of greater wisdom and education.

The bishop agreed and permitted him to enter the U.S. Army Chaplain Corps in 1944–45. He was sent to China and Burma. After the war, he was separated from the army and was sent by the bishop to study education; in 1948 he graduated from The Catholic University of America in Washington, D.C., with a master's degree in education. That same year, he secured permission from the bishop to return to the army.

In January 1950 Father Kapaun was sent to Japan and was then sent to Korea as part the 35th Brigade of the 8th regiment of the 1st Cavalry Division when North Korean communist forces invaded the South. He was awarded the Bronze Star in September 1950, shortly before his capture. On November 2, 1950, Father Kapaun was captured as he gave the last rites to a dying soldier and was sent to a Chinese prisoner of war camp. Over the next months, Father Kapaun devoted his energies to the spiritual needs of his brother captives and helped to nurse the sick and the dying with no concern for their color or creed. He soon fell ill himself from dysentery, pneumonia, and a blood clot in his leg. Taken to the primitive shack that served as the camp hospital, he died on May 23, 1951. Father Kapaun's memory was honored by the soldiers of the camp, and he was awarded the Distinguished

Service Cross. The cause for his canonization was opened in 2003.

Kappa Gamma Pi

A national Catholic college honor society for graduates, Kappa Gamma Pi has more than thirty-seven thousand members in 139 colleges and alumnae chapters in metropolitan areas across the United States. This honor society requires that its members demonstrate not only academic excellence but also leadership in extracurricular activities.

Kaskaskia

A famous Catholic mission near modern-day Utica, Illinois, Kaskaskia was destroyed by a change of course of the Mississippi River. Jesuit Father Jacques Marquette founded Kaskaskia as the Mission of the Immaculate Conception circa 1675. The mission served the Kaskaskia Indians, as well as the Peorias and others. Famous Jesuit missionaries, including the martyr Father Sebastian Râle, Father Claude Allouez, Father Zenobius Membré, also martyred, and Father Gabriel de la Ribourde, served Kaskaskia and the local tribes. Five years after its opening, the mission had to be moved because of hostile neighboring tribes. Cahokia, another vast mission program, was also opened.

Fort Kaskaskia, established by the French in 1733, was destroyed by the British thirty years later. Colonel George Rogers Clark, representing the American cause in 1778, captured Kaskaskia with the aid of Father Pierre Gibault, who sided with the American revolutionaries and roused the locals. Kaskaskia became the capital of the Illinois territory in 1809 and remained the capital when Illinois entered the Union in 1818. The Mississippi, which had flooded the Kaskaskia area time and again, erased all trace of the mission and the town when it changed course and flooded the entire region in 1881.

Katrina, Hurricane

In late August 2005 Hurricane Katrina, the most destructive storm in American history, struck the Gulf Coast of the United States. The sixth strongest Atlantic hurricane ever recorded and the third strongest to make landfall, Katrina brought severe devastation to the coastlines of Alabama, Mis-

sissippi, and Louisiana, in particular the cities of Mobile, Biloxi, and Gulfport.

The most well-known area of damage occurred in New Orleans, where the images of massive flooding and the suffering of tens of thousands of inhabitants of the city were broadcast around the world. For the Catholic Church along the Gulf Coast, Katrina brought colossal damage to churches, schools, convents, and hospitals, and an enormous financial loss that will take many years from which to recover fully. At the same time, Hurricane Katrina revealed the boundless charity of Americans, the goodwill of people all over the world, and the tireless labors of Catholic aid workers and volunteers in assisting the needs of those whose lives were destroyed along with their homes.

The hurricane formed in the Caribbean and then crossed Florida as a Category 1 hurricane. It then grew in strength over the Gulf of Mexico; fortunately, it weakened to a Category 3 storm on August 29 as it made landfall in southeast Louisiana. The severity of Katrina was such that the levees separating Lake Pontchartrain and Lake Borgne from New Orleans collapsed beneath the surge. The resulting flood inundated approximately 80 percent of the city and some of the surrounding parishes. The cost of the damage across the Gulf was measured in the billions, but far more tragic was the loss of life. Katrina caused the deaths of 1,836 people. It was the deadliest U.S. hurricane since the 1928 Okeechobee Hurricane.

The staggering damage caused by Katrina was estimated at $75 billion, but this did not include the long-term economic effects, the money needed for reconstruction, the severe displacement of victims across the country, and the painful process of renewal by the city of Biloxi and especially the famed and beloved city of New Orleans. Almost the entire city was uninhabitable for two months. Even by early November, when most of the city's wards were reopened to residents, many areas still lacked basic services, especially electricity.

Hurricane Katrina brought unparalleled devastation to the dioceses of Louisiana and Mississippi. Bishop Thomas J. Rodi of Biloxi, Mississippi, estimated immediately after the storm that 20 percent of the diocese's churches and a third of its schools had been destroyed. He added that every rectory, school, convent, and diocesan building sustained damage to some degree. Archbishop Alfred C. Hughes of New Orleans reported that his archdiocese faced even greater levels of destruction as the floods and subsequent problems in the evacuated city took their toll.

A preliminary report on Church-owned properties in the archdiocese that had suffered wind or flood damage placed the destruction at an estimated $84 million, about $70 million more than the insurance carried by the archdiocese. Of the approximately 1,200 buildings in the 142 parishes and nine missions of the Archdiocese of New Orleans, 387 were flooded by storm surge or the result of levee breaches and more than 864 received major wind damage.

Reflective of the severity of the problems in the Archdiocese of New Orleans, Archbishop Alfred C. Hughes was able to celebrate Mass in St. Louis Cathedral in the famed French Quarter only on October 2. Less destruction was reported by the Dioceses of Shreveport and Baton Rouge, which were far enough north to have escaped the more extreme components of the storm.

The response of the Church around the country and the world was immediate. Church facilities in the Gulf area and nationwide launched into assisting both emergency and long-term needs through shelters, food, medicine, and schools for the thousands displaced by the hurricane. Millions of Catholics responded with assistance, food, money, and even their own homes. Notable work was undertaken by Catholic Charities, St. Vincent de Paul Societies, Catholic schools, Catholic hospitals, parishes, retreat centers, and even average families. Supplementing the charitable work were collections and special fundraisers.

The U.S. bishops subsequently appointed a task force under Archbishop Joseph A. Fiorenza, then archbishop of Galveston-Houston, to address the needs in the aftermath of the hurricane. In announcing the task force on September 14, 2005, Bishop William S. Skylstad of Spokane, Washington, president of the United States Conference of Catholic Bishops, stated:

"Our hearts and prayers go out once again to all those whose lives, homes and families have been damaged or destroyed by Katrina. Within the Catholic community, many of our people have lost everything and our Church has lost parishes and schools, hospitals and charitable ministries, and many of the structures which help us preach the Gospel, educate the young, and serve the vulnerable. The loss of these institutions affects not only our Church, but is a significant loss for the entire community. As powerful as the winds and water of Katrina have been, our ongoing care and help, our practice of charity and search for justice must become more powerful. The hurricane and the flood came and went in a matter of hours and days. Our support, compassion, and commitment to help make things right must last far longer — not days, but months and years."

Over the next months, the tireless efforts of Catholics and Catholic organizations continued, often without any credit or publicity. In a letter of December 6, 2005, Archbishop Hughes expressed his thanks to American Catholics for their "outpouring of love and concern" for the Church in New Orleans and neighboring dioceses. He noted that dioceses, parishes, lay organizations, corporations, individuals, and even young schoolchildren contributed thousands of hours of volunteer time and funds in excess of $12 million to rebuild parishes and schools. On February 6, 2006, the Archdiocese of New Orleans issued a pastoral plan to implement the enormous task of rebuilding in the wake of Katrina. The plan called for the closing of seven parishes and delays in reopening twenty-three others until enough parishioners had returned to the area. In addition, the plan called for establishing six centralized elementary schools, in place of the prestorm pattern of individual parish elementary schools.

The plan sought to create fourteen "cluster" parishes in the affected areas. These would facilitate pastoral care to parishes that had yet to reopen, a process that would be particularly attentive to the many communities of African-American, Asian, and Hispanic Catholics.

Archbishop Hughes estimated that the archdiocese had projected a $40 million deficit in operations by the end of December 2005. However, insurance reimbursements, employee layoffs, and the return to relatively normal operations in outlying parishes had reduced that deficit to $4.5 million.

Kaupas, Mother Maria (January 6, 1880–April 17, 1940)

A Lithuanian-born naturalized American who founded the Sisters of St. Casimir in Chicago in 1907, an order dedicated to education and care for the sick, Mother Maria was known especially for her Eucharistic devotion. She was born Casimira Kaupas in Ramygala, Lithuania, and raised in the faith. As conditions in Lithuania at the time were harsh, and as she was determined to assist the education of Lithuanians who had migrated to America, Casimira decided to enter a teaching order of women religious. She thus accepted the invitation of Father Anthony Milukas to travel to Ingenbohl, Switzerland, for studies with the Sisters of Mercy of the Holy Cross. Casimira spent three years in Ingenbohl, during which she succeeded in having Father Staniukynas, a friend of her brother, secure the sponsorship of Bishop John W. Shanahan of Harrisburg, Pennsylvania, for the congregation in the United States.

At the request of the bishop, Mother M. Cyril, I.H.M., accepted Casimira and her two companions into the novitiate of the Sisters, Servants of the Immaculate Heart of Mary in Scranton, Pennsylvania. In August 1907 Sister Casimira and her companions entered the novitiate. From this beginning was born the new congregation of the Sisters of St. Casimir, and on August 28, 1907, Casimira received the new name of Sister Maria; her two companions, Sister Judith and Sister Antanina, took the names Sister Concepta and Sister Immaculata, respectively.

The newly professed sisters took as their primary task the care of Lithuanian immigrants. To assist their preparations, they studied at Mount Carmel, Pennsylvania, and then established their new motherhouse in Chicago in order to be able to serve the large population of Lithuanian immigrants. The response to the call for vocations was stunning, as many young women proved eager to enter the religious life, and in 1911 St. Casimir Academy was opened in the motherhouse.

Mother Maria was elected the first superior general in 1913, an office she held by reelection for the rest of her life. In 1928 she founded Holy Cross Hospital in Chicago and went on to assume direction over hospitals in Chicago and Nebraska. Sisters were also sent to serve in New Mexico in 1937, and although she desired to send members to South America, this became a reality only in 1941, after her death.

In 1933 the Lithuanian government bestowed its highest decoration, the Order of the Grand Duke Gediminas, on Mother Maria in recognition of her work for the Lithuanians in America. She continued to serve with all her energies even as she suffered immensely from cancer. She died surrounded by the members of the community at the motherhouse in Chicago. Her cause for canonization was opened in 1986 and the cause of her beatification was introduced in Rome in 1996. In October 2001 Cardinal Francis George, archbishop of Chicago, presented the position of the cause to Pope Blessed John Paul II.

Kavanagh, Edward (April 27, 1795–January 21, 1844)

The governor of Maine, Edward Kavanagh was a noted diplomat and statesman. He was born in Newcastle, Maine; his father, James Kavanagh, was an immigrant from Ireland and a wealthy merchant and shipowner, and his mother, Sarah Jackson, was a Catholic convert from Boston. The family was devoutly Catholic, and the house in which Edward grew up was a place of frequent visits by priests, including the famed Father (later Cardinal) Jean-Louis Lefebvre de Cheverus.

Edward studied at the Jesuit Colleges in Montréal and Georgetown and graduated from St. Mary's College in Baltimore in 1813. He subsequently undertook classical studies in Europe and then returned to Maine to work briefly with his father in shipping. As he had little taste for commerce, he studied the law and tried to enter the diplomatic service. Failing in this, he won election to the Maine legislature in 1826, served as secretary of the Senate in 1830, and then earned election to Congress in 1831. After two terms in Congress, he was named chargé d'affaires at Lisbon, Portugal, in 1835 and became the chief American representative in that country. In that position, he negotiated a commercial and navigation treaty.

Returning to Maine in 1841, Kavanagh was elected to the state senate and played a role in the negotiations leading to the Webster-Ashburton

Treaty of 1842 that settled the long-disputed boundary between Maine and the British Provinces of Canada. On the resignation of Governor Fairfield in March 1843, Kavanagh succeeded him, as he was president of the state senate. His last years were marked by severe suffering from poor health. He was buried in St. Patrick's churchyard in Newcastle.

Kavanaugh, John P. (July 11, 1871–November 12, 1940)

An attorney best known for his skillful opposition to the Oregon referendum that tried to force all children of the state into public schools, John P. Kavanaugh was born in St. Louis, Oregon. He studied at Mount Angel College and the University of Oregon and went on to distinguish himself as an attorney. In 1902 he was named chief deputy city attorney of Portland and won election as city attorney; with the nomination of both political parties, he won reelection in 1909. The next year, he was elected a County Circuit Court judge.

In 1922, the year of his retirement from the bench, he was appointed by Archbishop Alexander Christie of Portland to serve as one of the attorneys representing the archdiocese in its effort to challenge the constitutionality of the referendum passed in the state that would have compelled children to attend public schools. He argued the case all the way to the U.S. Supreme Court and helped win a favorable decision. In 1931 he received the De Smet Medal from Gonzaga University.

Keane, John Joseph (September 12, 1839–June 22, 1918)

The bishop of the Diocese of Richmond from 1878 to 1888, John Joseph Keane also served as the titular archbishop of Damascus from 1897 to 1900 and archbishop of Dubuque from 1900 to 1911. He was also the first rector of The Catholic University of America. He was born in Ballyshannon, County Donegal, Ireland, and traveled to the United States with his family as a boy owing to the Great Famine. The family arrived in St. John, New Brunswick, in 1846 and in 1848 moved on to Baltimore, where Keane grew up. He studied for the priesthood at St. Charles College in Ellicott City, Maryland, and then at St. Mary's Seminary

in Baltimore. He was ordained in 1866. Named an assistant at St. Patrick's Cathedral in Washington, D.C., he distinguished himself as a supporter of the temperance movement and Catholic education and helped found the Catholic Total Abstinence Union of America in 1872. That same year, he requested permission to join Father Isaac Thomas Hecker and the Missionary Society of St. Paul, but his bishop refused his request; nevertheless, Hecker exercised a considerable influence on Father Keane.

In 1878 he was appointed as the first bishop of Richmond and was consecrated on August 25, 1878, by Archbishop James Gibbons, his predecessor. Over the next ten years, Bishop Keane promoted evangelization within the African-American community and fought prejudice and intolerance in Virginia. In addition to his duties as bishop, he served as apostolic administrator for North Carolina and volunteered to resign as bishop of Richmond and to become bishop there owing to the difficulty the Holy See was encountering in finding a candidate to take up such a challenging see.

Appointed a member of the committee to organize a Catholic university for the United States in 1885, Bishop Keane was one of four bishops charged with fundraising for the initiative. An ardent supporter of the university, he succeeded in 1887 along with Bishop John Ireland in winning papal approval of the new school's statutes. He was appointed first rector of the university in September 1887 and resigned his see in order to devote himself fully to the arduous task of launching the university. The university formally opened on November 13, 1889. Under his leadership, the first buildings were constructed, faculty and students were drawn to the campus, fundraising was highly successful, and the reputation of the university was well established. In 1893 he was part of the Catholic delegation to the World's Parliament of Religions held at the Columbian Exposition and in 1890 was Dudleian lecturer at Harvard University.

Bishop Keane departed the university in September 1896, owing in part to his sympathies for the so-called Americanist position among the U.S. hierarchy. Offered a choice between an American diocese and Rome, Bishop Keane chose Rome and was named titular archbishop of Damascus and a canon of the Basilica of St. John Lateran. In Rome, he also served as a consultor to the Congregations for the Propagation of the Faith and of Sacred Studies.

In 1899 Archbishop Keane returned to the United States and began fundraising for the university once more. The following year, he was named archbishop of Dubuque, remaining there until 1911. His health had been declining since 1909, and he requested that an auxiliary bishop or coadjutor be named. Finally, on January 10, 1911, he resigned as archbishop and was appointed titular bishop of Ciana. He died in Dubuque.

Keely, Patrick Charles (August 9, 1816–1896)

An architect, Patrick Charles Keely is best known for his many contributions to nineteenth-century neo-Gothic church architecture. He was born in Thurles, County Kilkenny, Ireland, and received his early training in Ireland through his father, who was a draftsman and builder. In 1842 he migrated to the United States and settled in Brooklyn, New York, where he worked as a carpenter until 1847. That year, he was asked to design the new Church of Sts. Peter and Paul in the Williamsburgh section of Brooklyn, and his resulting work was so impressive that he was soon hired as an architect for other church building projects. Assisting his rapidly growing professional reputation was his renown for being honest and scrupulous.

Over the next decades, Keely designed churches throughout the eastern United States and Canada, in particular in New York and New England; he was commissioned by a number of bishops and archbishops to design new cathedrals across New England. Although he worked extensively with Catholic diocesan leaders, he also accepted several commissions for Protestant churches. The most notable project for Protestants was the Asylum Hill Congregational Church in Hartford, Connecticut, which included Mark Twain and Harriet Beecher Stowe in its congregation and is on the National Register of Historic Places. In Massachusetts alone, Keely designed and oversaw the construction of dozens of churches, schools, and monasteries, including the Cathedral of the Holy Cross in Boston, St. Mary's Cathedral in Fall River, and St. Michael's Cathedral in Springfield. In all, he designed over six hundred churches and sixteen cathedrals throughout the United States between 1846 and 1896. His other notable cathedrals included those in Chicago; Cleveland; Buffalo, New York; Hartford, Connecticut; and Newark, New Jersey. His designs appeared in places as far south as Charleston, South Carolina, as far north as Halifax, Nova Scotia, and as far west as Iowa.

As one of the United States' most respected architects, he was also responsible for training other experts in the field, including family members such as his sons Charles Keely, John J. Keely, and son-in-law Thomas F. Houghton. He received the second Laetare Medal from the University of Notre Dame in 1884. He also continued to work right up until his death, despite deteriorating health. The Keely Society in Connecticut was established to promote and protect his work.

Keeler, William Henry (March 4, 1931–)

The fourteenth archbishop of Baltimore, from 1989 to 2007, William Henry Keeler served as a cardinal from 1994. He was born in San Antonio, Texas, the son of Thomas L. Keeler and Margaret T. (Conway) Keeler. Raised in Lebanon, Pennsylvania, he attended St. Charles Seminary in Overbrook, Pennsylvania, and graduated in 1952. Sent to Rome for additional studies and preparation for the priesthood, he was ordained on July 17, 1955, in the Church of the Holy Apostles by Archbishop (later Cardinal) Luigi Traglia. The following year, he earned a licentiate in sacred theology from the Pontifical Gregorian University in Rome.

Returning to the United States, the young priest served in several pastoral assignments in the Diocese of Harrisburg and was also appointed secretary of the diocesan tribunal from 1956 to 1958. He was then sent back to Rome for further studies, this time in canon law at the Pontifical Gregorian University. In 1961 he received his doctorate.

Returning to the diocese, he was again given pastoral assignments, but in addition he was named Defender of the Bond of the diocesan tribunal and secretary to Bishop George L. Leech during the Second Vatican Council's gatherings in Rome. He served as a *peritus* (or theological expert) to the council by appointment of Pope Blessed John XXIII. During the council, he also was a member of the staff of the *Council Digest*, a daily communication service organized by the United States bishops.

In 1965 he was appointed vice chancellor of the Harrisburg diocese and then chancellor and vicar general. On July 24, 1979, he was appointed auxiliary bishop of Harrisburg and titular bishop of Ulcinium (Dulcigno) by Pope Blessed John Paul II. He received episcopal ordination on September 21, 1979, at St Patrick Cathedral in Harrisburg. Four years later, Bishop Keeler was elected administrator of the Diocese of Harrisburg by the College of Consultors following the death of Bishop Joseph T. Daley. That same year, on November 10, 1983, Pope Blessed John Paul II appointed him bishop of Harrisburg; he was installed on January 4, 1984.

After five years of service as shepherd of the Harrisburg diocese, Bishop Keeler was appointed archbishop of Baltimore by Pope Blessed John Paul II on April 11, 1989; he was installed on May 23, 1989. On November 28, 1994, Archbishop Keeler was appointed a cardinal priest by Pope Blessed John Paul II, with the titular church of Saint Mary of the Angels.

As part of his duties as a cardinal, he served as a member of the Pontifical Council for Promoting Christian Unity and the Congregation for the Oriental Churches. As a cardinal elector, he was a voting member of the conclave of 2005 that elected Cardinal Joseph Ratzinger as Pope Benedict XVI.

As archbishop, Cardinal Keeler worked to improve Catholic education in the archdiocese and across the United States. In 1992 he launched the Lenten Appeal, a campaign to raise money for Catholic schools in Baltimore and to assist those most in need. The campaign raised over $44 million. The cardinal was also a national leader in the pro-life movement. From 1998 to 2001 and again from November 2003 he served as Chair for the Committee on Pro-Life Activities. Active in the field of effective interreligious dialogue, especially the promotion of Catholic-Jewish dialogue, the cardinal later served as moderator of Catholic-Jewish relations for the United States Conference of Catho-

Cardinal William Henry Keeler

lic Bishops and was a member of the International Catholic Orthodox Commission for Theological Dialogue since 1986. As Chair of the Bishops' Committee for Ecumenical and Interreligious Affairs from 1984 to November 1987, he was instrumental in arranging Pope Blessed John Paul II's meetings with Jewish leaders in Miami and with Protestant leaders in Columbia, South Carolina, during the 1987 papal visit.

Archbishop Keeler was elected president of the National Conference of Catholic Bishops and the United States Catholic Conference in November 1992 after serving as vice president of the NCCB from 1989. Cardinal Keeler was also Chairman of the Maryland Catholic Conference, and chair of the board and chancellor of St. Mary's Seminary and University in Baltimore as well as of Mount St. Mary's Seminary in Emmitsburg, Maryland. Cardinal Keeler retired on July 12, 2007.

Kelley, Francis Clement (1870–February 1, 1948)
The founder of the Catholic Church Extension Society, Francis Clement Kelley also served as the bishop of the Diocese (now Archdiocese) of Oklahoma City. He was born on Prince Edward Island, Canada, and received the grace of a priestly vocation. He studied for the Diocese (now Archdiocese) of Detroit and was ordained in 1893. Father Kelley served as a military chaplain during the Spanish-American War and then as a rural pastor. His experiences led him to understand the great need for a program that would provide white Americans with spiritual advantages and inspirations, as various service organizations were already in place for Native Americans and African-Americans. Father Kelley explained his program to Archbishop James Edward Quigley of Chicago, who shared his vision. With Archbishop Quigley as his patron, Father Kelley established the Extension Society in Chicago in 1905. He also opened and edited *Extension* magazine in that same year.

The Catholic Church Extension Society, as it is known today, served rural parishes with innovative equipment and evangelization techniques.

The society was active in many newly erected dioceses, building chapels in distant parts of the jurisdictions and providing railroad cars that were turned into chapels and sent to remote regions.

In 1924 Father Kelley was appointed as the bishop of Oklahoma City (now the Archdiocese of Oklahoma City) and was active in developing the American Board of Catholic Missions, which provided funds for home missionary programs. Bishop Kelley understood the spiritual yearnings of the Americans of his time and sought ways to bring them to a realization of the faith.

He was also a friend of the noted author H. L. Mencken, who considered him a gifted literary figure in America. Bishop Kelley wrote books concerning issues of faith and spirituality. He continued to serve the needs of Oklahoma Catholics as his health worsened. In 1944 he received a coadjutor and four years later, as Mencken had predicted, fell into a coma and died in Oklahoma City.

Kelly, Princess Grace (November 10, 1929–September 14, 1982)

A popular American actress, Grace Kelly became the Princess Consort of Monaco. She was born in Philadelphia, the daughter of John B. Kelly and Margaret Majer. Educated in local schools, including the Stevens School, she went to the American Academy of Dramatic Arts in New York, desiring to dedicate her life to the theater. After a series of roles on television and stage, she launched a major film career in *High Noon* in 1951 and appeared in *Dial M for Murder, Rear Window,* and *High Society.* In 1954 she won the Academy Award for Best Actress for *The Country Girl.*

At the Cannes Film Festival, she met Prince Rainier III of Monaco and married him in 1956, becoming the Princess Consort. Princess Grace had three children: Albert, Stephanie, and Caroline. Like her family, Princess Grace was a devout Catholic who organized many charitable works and programs. She served Monaco faithfully until September 14, 1982, when she was driving with Princess Stephanie and died in a violent accident.

Kenkel, Frederick P. (October 16, 1863–1952)

The longtime head of the Central Bureau of the German Catholic Central Verein, Frederick P.

Kenkel was a social reformer. He was born in Chicago, the son of German immigrants. Having gone to Germany to begin his college education, he left school and traveled across Europe instead. He married in 1885 and returned to the United States, where he took up a position in Chicago in bookselling. After the death of his first wife, he underwent a profound spiritual conversion and returned to active participation in the Catholic faith.

In 1892 he remarried and soon became influential as managing editor of the German Catholic newspaper *Amerika*, a prominent daily newspaper in St. Louis. He remained as editor until 1920, and his work brought him into close contact with the Central Verein, the highly influential German Catholic organization. From 1908 he directed its social-reform program.

In the aftermath of World War I, Kenkel bitterly opposed America's entry into the war in 1917. However, he encountered a changed atmosphere and many of his views regarding social reform encountered a sharp decline in enthusiasm. Nevertheless, he remained committed to many worthy causes, including assistance to refugees and liturgical renewal. (*See also* German Catholics.)

Kenna, John Edward (April 10, 1848–January 11, 1893)

A member of the United States House of Representatives, John Edward Kenna also served as a U.S. senator from West Virginia. He was born near St. Albans, Kanawha County, Virginia (now West Virginia), and was the son of an immigrant from Ireland, Edward Kenna, and the daughter of a prominent family of Virginia, Margery Lewis. His father died in 1856, and he and his two siblings were raised by their mother in Missouri.

Although never given a formal education, Kenna enlisted in the Confederate Army in 1864 and was severely wounded in battle. After the surrender of his regiment, he returned to West Virginia and began studies at St. Vincent's College in Wheeling. He went on to study law and was admitted to the bar in 1870. He practiced law in Charleston, West Virginia, and served as prosecuting attorney for Kanawha County from 1872 to 1877.

In 1877 Kenna was elected as a Democrat to

Congress. Reelected several times, he resigned from the House on March 4, 1883, after his election to the United States Senate. Reelected in 1889, he served until his death in Washington, D.C. His funeral services were held in the Chamber of the United States Senate, and he was interred in Mount Olivet Cemetery in Charleston. As senator, Kenna promoted tariff reform and the regulation of railroads. Actively involved in the Church, he was responsible for the design of St. Joseph's Church in Charleston.

Kennedy, Anthony M. (July 23, 1936–)

An associate justice of the United States Supreme Court, Anthony M. Kennedy was born in Sacramento, California, studied at Stanford University and the London School of Economics, and earned his law degree from Harvard Law School. He was admitted to the California bar in 1962 and began private practice in San Francisco in 1961 as an associate of Thelen, Marrin, John & Bridges, next in Sacramento as a sole practitioner from 1963 to 1967, and then as a partner of Evans, Francis & Kennedy from 1967 to 1975.

From 1965 to 1988, he served as a professor of constitutional law at the McGeorge School of Law, University of the Pacific. In addition, he served as a member of the California Army National Guard in 1961, the board of the Federal Judicial Center from 1987 to 1988, and two committees of the Judicial Conference of the United States, the Advisory Panel on Financial Disclosure Reports and Judicial Activities (subsequently renamed the Advisory Committee on Codes of Conduct) from 1979 to 1987, and the Committee on Pacific Territories from 1979 to 1990 (which he chaired from 1982 to 1990).

Kennedy was appointed to the United States Court of Appeals for the Ninth Circuit in 1975 by President Gerald Ford and took the oath of office on May 30, 1975. Following the defeat of the Supreme Court nomination of Robert Bork, President Ronald Reagan nominated him as an associate justice of the Supreme Court. He took his seat on February 18, 1988. Judge Kennedy has long been held to be a moderate voice on the court. For many years, he was ranked with Justice Sandra Day O'Connor as a swing vote on many crucial issues, including abortion. With the retirement of Justice O'Connor in 2006, Justice Kennedy became the primary swing vote between the liberal- and conservative-leaning justices.

Kennedy, John Fitzgerald (May 20, 1917–November 22, 1963)

The thirty-fifth president of the United States, John Fitzgerald Kennedy was the first and only Catholic in the history of the nation to hold that office. He was born in Brookline, Massachusetts, the son of Joseph Patrick and Rose Fitzgerald Kennedy, and was educated at Canterbury School, Choate, and Harvard, earning his degree in 1940. The year before, he toured Europe.

In May 1940 Kennedy entered the U.S. Navy and as a lieutenant junior grade took part in combat on PT-109. He was awarded service medals for heroism during combat. Prior to his enlistment in the navy, he had written a book, *Why England Slept.* Upon returning to civilian life at the close of the war, Kennedy's first elected office was in the U.S. House of Representatives in 1946. In 1952 he defeated Henry Cabot Lodge and became the junior U.S. senator from Massachusetts. While a senator, Kennedy married Jacqueline Lee Bouvier, and they had two children, Caroline and John. Kennedy also wrote *Profiles in Courage* in 1957 and was awarded the Pulitzer Prize.

In 1960 Kennedy entered the presidential primary in West Virginia and proved himself a popular candidate. He became an official candidate for the presidency at the Democratic National Convention on July 12, 1960, in Los Angeles. Lyndon Baines Johnson was nominated as his vice presidential running mate. Kennedy began a series of campaigns among the Protestants of America, assuring them of his loyalty, qualifications, and abilities. The old charge made by Protestants of the past — that Catholics could not be qualified to serve in the highest office of the land because they swore allegiance to a foreign head of state, the pope — faded as Kennedy spoke to vast crowds across the nation. A series of televised debates followed in which he faced Richard Nixon, the Republican candidate. On November 8, 1960, Kennedy won 49.7 percent of the vote. Nixon won 48.5 percent.

At his inauguration, President Kennedy uttered

the famous challenge to the nation: "And so, my fellow Americans, ask not what your country can do for you — ask what you can do for your country." The inauguration and subsequent events set a new tone for the White House, as Mrs. Kennedy became a dazzling figure on the world stage and presidential celebrations were stylish.

In October 1962 President Kennedy faced a missile crisis in Cuba, as the premier of the Soviet Union, Nikita Krushchev, engaged in the Cold War, sent missiles to the island nation off the American coast. President Kennedy's stand against such missiles proved successful, and the Russians withdrew the weapons and their personnel.

In November the president and Mrs. Kennedy traveled in the Southwest, and Kennedy was assassinated in Dallas. Lee Harvey Oswald was arrested soon after. Monsignor Oscar L. Huber, C.M., of Holy Trinity Parish, performed the last rites for the slain president at Parkland Memorial Hospital in Dallas. Vice President Lyndon Baines Johnson was then given the oath of office on the plane carrying Kennedy's remains to Washington, D.C. Lee Harvey Oswald was slain a few days later by Jack Ruby, an event televised live. The state funeral for President Kennedy was seen by people around the world. He was buried in Arlington National Cemetery.

President John Kennedy

The brief presidency of John F. Kennedy lasted a little under three years, but it was known as Camelot because of its atmosphere of promise, notoriety, and also its tragic ending. The presidential campaign of Kennedy overcame deep-seated anti-Catholic sentiment in parts of the country and demonstrated the progress Catholics had made in finding acceptance in American public life.

His success paved the way for the eventual but equally tragic candidacy of his brother, Senator Robert Kennedy, in 1968, and the failed presidential bids of another brother, Senator Edward Kennedy. For this reason alone, the Kennedy presidency was a landmark moment in American Catholic history.

Kennedy, Joseph Patrick, Sr. (September 6, 1888– November 18, 1969)

The patriarch of the Kennedy family, Joseph Patrick Kennedy Sr., was a diplomat, self-made millionaire, and scion of one of America's foremost political families. He was born into the family of a ward boss in Boston and quickly learned political and business skills. Renowned for his ambitions, he attended Harvard and, after graduation in 1912, took his first job as a state-employed bank examiner. Learning that a particular bank was planning on taking over the smaller Columbia Trust Bank, in which his father was a minority shareholder, Joseph borrowed $45,000 and bought control. At the age of twenty-five, he became the youngest bank president in the country. By the age of thirty he was a millionaire, and his shrewd skills for business permitted him to retire from business before the Great Depression, thereby assuring the survival of the family fortune. He made money from investment banking, movie theaters, film production, and liquor; it was alleged that he participated in the liquor trade during Prohibition.

He married Rose Fitzgerald in 1913, the daughter of Boston mayor John "Honey Fitz" Fitzgerald. She gave him nine children, including Joseph Kennedy Jr., who was killed in World War II; John Fitzgerald Kennedy, who was elected to Congress in 1946 and became president in 1961; and two other sons, Robert and Edward, who both became United States senators. John and Robert were both assassinated, in 1963 and 1968, respectively. Edward Kennedy was elected a senator from Massachusetts and was viewed for a time as a front-runner to become the Democratic Party's presidential candidate. One daughter, Kathleen ("Kick"), was killed in a plane crash in France after the war while another, Rosemary, was given a lobotomy in 1941 and spent the rest of her life in an institution.

After giving his strong support to the presidential candidacy of Franklin Delano Roosevelt in 1932, Joseph was named in 1933 to the post of chairman of the Securities and Exchange Commission. From 1938 to 1940, he was the U.S. ambassador to the Court of St. James in Great Britain, the first Irish Catholic to hold that position. His time as ambassador was marked by his own personal prominence in England and his strong opposition to Winston Churchill's warnings about Nazi Germany. Instead, Kennedy favored the policy of appeasement that was a hallmark of Prime Minister Neville Chamberlain's foreign policy. He subsequently resigned in September 1940 because of his disagreement with President Roosevelt's tough anti-Nazi position. Nevertheless, Kennedy remained a political supporter of the president and worked to turn out the Irish vote for his reelection campaigns. Kennedy also supported fellow Irishman Senator Joseph McCarthy.

When he retired from the diplomatic service, Joseph Kennedy devoted his main efforts to the political fortunes of his sons. While he had always been aware that he could not be president, he worked for many years to bring about the election of a member of the family. He played a key role in the campaigns of John Kennedy, especially in the 1960 presidential campaign. The following year, he suffered a stroke from which he never fully recovered.

Kennedy, Robert Francis (November 20, 1925–June 6, 1968)

A United States senator and attorney general, Robert Francis Kennedy was the third son of Joseph Patrick and Rose Fitzgerald Kennedy and the brother of President John F. Kennedy. He was born in Brookline, Massachusetts, and educated at Portsmouth Priory, Milton Academy, and Harvard. He graduated from the University of Virginia Law School in 1951. The year before, he had married Ethel Skakel, and they had eleven children.

Called Bobby, Robert Kennedy managed his brother's successful senatorial bid in 1952 and worked for Senator Joseph McCarthy's Committee on Government Operations. Robert Kennedy wrote *The Enemy Within* in 1960 and also worked against Jimmy Hoffa and the unions. In 1960 Kennedy managed his brother's presidential bid and was subsequently named Attorney General of the United States. Robert Kennedy served as his brother's chief adviser and had a significant role in the passing of the Civil Rights Act in 1964 and

in the Cuban Missile Crisis of 1962. He used the National Guard to integrate the University of Mississippi in that same year.

The assassination of President John F. Kennedy ended Robert Kennedy's White House influence. He was elected U.S. senator from New York in 1964 and launched a campaign for president in 1968. While in Los Angeles, Kennedy was assassinated by Sirhan Bishara Sirhan. He was buried in Arlington National Cemetery.

Kennedy, Edward M. ("Ted") (February 22, 1932–August 25, 2009)

A Democrat and United States senator for almost forty-seven years, Ted Kennedy was the youngest son of Joseph Patrick and Rose Fitzgerald Kennedy and brother of President John F. Kennedy and Senator Robert Kennedy.

He was born in Brookline, Massachuetts, into the powerful political Kennedy family. As his father, the patriarch of the Kennedy clan, was named in 1937 by President Franklin D. Roosevelt to the post of ambassador to Great Britain, Ted Kennedy lived in London. In 1950 he was sent to begin studies at Harvard University. There he proved a poor student and was embroiled in a scandal when he paid a fellow student to take an exam for him; he was expelled. After a two-year stint in the army, he returned to Harvard in 1953 and completed a bachelor's degree in government in 1956. He was unable to secure admission to Harvard Law School.

He married the former model Joan Bennett in 1958 and that same year began his long political career when he became campaign manager for his brother John's senate run in Massachusetts. In 1959 he earned a law degree from the University of Virginia School of Law and was admitted to the Massachusetts bar. In 1960 he worked with his brother Robert to manage John's successful presidential campaign against Richard Nixon.

Two years later, Kennedy was elected to the Senate for the first time as a representative of Massachusetts. Over the next years, he established himself as one of the most committed liberals in the Senate and was a determined opponent of the Vietnam War. He devoted himself to Robert's presidential campaign in 1968 and was devastated by his assassination after winning the California Democratic primary.

In January 1969 Kennedy was elected Senate Majority Whip, the youngest senator ever to hold that position. That same year, in July, he became embroiled in the most severe scandal of his life: the death of Mary Jo Kopechne when the car he was driving went off a bridge at Chappaquiddick Island, near Martha's Vineyard. The scandal ended his anticipated presidential run in 1972. He remained in the Senate and ran an unsuccessful primary challenge to President Jimmy Carter in 1979. Edward Kennedy and Joan Bennett Kennedy were divorced in 1982. In 1992 he remarried, to Victoria Reggie.

Over the next years, Kennedy remained one of the most outspoken proponents of liberalism in American politics in general and the Senate in particular. In May 2008 he was diagnosed with a malignant brain tumor. His last months were spent pushing for passage of the massive healthcare plan of President Barack Obama.

Kennedy was credited by liberal Catholics for his efforts on behalf of the poor with government programs, arms control, and immigrant rights. He was very heavily criticized for his many other positions that were diametrically opposed to the teachings of the Church, including his enthusiastic advocacy of abortion, embryonic stem-cell research, and homosexual marriage.

Kenrick, Francis Patrick (December 3, 1796–July 8, 1863)

The archbishop of Baltimore from 1851 to 1863, Francis Patrick Kenrick served during a turbulent era in American history and had a profound influence on the American Catholic Church. He was born in Dublin, Ireland, to Thomas and Jane Foy Kenrick and at the age of eighteen was sent to Rome for studies for the priesthood at the College of the Propaganda. He distinguished himself as a student and, after receiving ordination on April 7, 1821, was asked to volunteer for the missions in the vast Diocese of Bardstown in Kentucky.

After arriving in the United States, Father Kenrick was named to the faculty of St. Thomas Seminary. He taught theology there for nine years while also teaching Greek and history in the College of St. Joseph, also in Kentucky, and serving as a missionary and apologist at a time when there was great animosity toward the Church. In 1829 he served as a secretary and theological consultor for the First Provincial Council of Baltimore.

A year later, he was consecrated as the coadjutor bishop of Philadelphia with right of succession, having jurisdiction over Catholic affairs in Pennsylvania, Delaware, and part of New Jersey, owing to the health problems of Bishop Henry Conwell. Consecrated in Bardstown by Bishop Flaget on June 6, 1830, as titular bishop of Arath, he was only thirty-four years old but assumed his many difficult duties with swift vigor. To clarify the correct delineation of his authority in the diocese, Bishop Kenrick received from Rome a certification of his right to episcopal jurisdiction. This was published in the diocese in 1831 and was a necessary first step in bringing the troubled diocese into some order. He acceded formally to the see in 1842.

As the diocese was then facing the problems of trusteeism, Bishop Kenrick moved to end the dispute with the trustees of St. Mary's by placing an interdict upon the church. This soon won the day, and the bishop remained firm in his opposition to the pernicious practice; in 1850 he was compelled to excommunicate the leaders of a new effort at trusteeism at Holy Trinity Church.

Bishop Kenrick next took up the issue of a seminary, and in 1832 established St. Charles Borromeo Seminary at Overbrook, Pennsylvania. He also made parochial schools and building churches a priority for the diocese; in all he constructed more than sixty churches, including the Cathedral of St. John the Evangelist, which replaced the notorious St. Mary's. The progress of the seminary was assisted by the arrival of his brother, Peter Richard Kenrick, who took over as rector and later became bishop and first archbishop of St. Louis.

Bishop Kenrick's diocese, for most of his time as bishop, extended the length of Pennsylvania and included Pittsburgh, as well as Delaware and part of New Jersey. He was tireless in traveling across the far-flung diocese on visitations, and he braved primitive conditions and difficult travel to serve as shepherd. As this was proving to be a massive pastoral task, the bishop was delighted when the Diocese of Pittsburgh was established in 1843 and Reverend

Michael O'Connor was consecrated bishop of Pittsburgh. Two years later, Bishop Kenrick traveled to Rome and was received by Pope Gregory XVI.

The year before, the diocese was rocked by virulent anti-Catholic riots that resulted in loss of life as mobs attacked Catholic churches, schools, and convents, and killed both defenseless Catholics and non-Catholic citizens caught up in the violence. Troops were called in to end the chaos, and Bishop Kenrick worked to bring an end to the riots by taking such measures as ordering his priests not to wear distinctive clerical dress.

On August 19, 1851, Bishop Kenrick was promoted to the Archdiocese of Baltimore. In his time as bishop of Philadelphia, he had presided over a remarkable expansion in the number of priests, churches, and parishes, and Catholics; his tenure saw the Catholic population grow from 35,000 to 170,000. In addition to his title as archbishop of Baltimore, he received the great favor of being named apostolic delegate by Pope Blessed Pius IX. As such, he convened and then presided over the First Plenary Council of Baltimore in 1852. Additional councils were held in 1855 and 1858, and diocesan synods were held in 1853, 1857, and 1863.

He introduced the devotion of the Forty Hours to the United States in 1853, and the next year went back to Rome to deliver the opinions of the American bishops on the doctrine of the Immaculate Conception. That same year, he was in Rome for the official proclamation of the dogma by the Holy Father. Pope Pius declared in 1858 that the Archdiocese of Baltimore be given the status of "Preeminence of Place" as the primal see of the United States.

Archbishop Kenrick was a supporter of the North American College in Rome, which opened in late 1859, and continued expanding diocesan facilities. He built St. Vincent's Infant Asylum and St. Agnes's Hospital, as well as parishes and schools. He also faced new anti-Catholicism owing to the arrival of Archbishop Gaetano Bedini as papal nuncio. Churches and convents were burned and people were killed in parts of New England and in Kentucky and Ohio. As archbishop at the outbreak of the Civil War, Bishop Kenrick sided with the Union and stressed the patriotic duty of citizens. The stress of the Civil War years took its toll, and

Bishop Kenrick died soon after the Battle of Gettysburg in a state of severe distress over the carnage of the terrible engagement.

A respected theologian and biblical scholar, he wrote a number of works, including a new translation of the Bible, with a commentary; a four-volume *Dogmatic Theology* in 1840; a three-volume *Moral Theology* in 1843; and apologetic writings in defense of papal primacy and the authority of the general councils.

Kenrick, Peter Richard (August 18, 1806–March 4, 1896)

Bishop and first archbishop of St. Louis, Peter Richard Kenrick served as shepherd over his diocese from 1843 to 1895. His brother, Francis, was archbishop of Baltimore. Born in Dublin, Ireland, to Thomas and Jane Foy Kenrick, he was given an education by a private tutor and also developed a taste for literature in part from the poet James Clarence Mangan, with whom he had worked in the scriveners' office of his father. Seeking to enter the seminary in his brother's footsteps (Francis P. Kenrick was sent to Rome for studies), Peter was accepted into Maynooth at the age of twenty-one with the help of his uncle, a priest.

Ordained to the priesthood by Archbishop Daniel Murray of Dublin on March 6, 1832, Father Kenrick was initially assigned to the cathedral but soon received a request from his brother, by now the coadjutor bishop of Philadelphia, to come assist him in America. Arriving in Philadelphia in 1833, he was given the post of president of the recently established St. Charles Borromeo Seminary at Overbrook, Pennsylvania, as well as rector of the cathedral and vicar general of the diocese. He subsequently earned a reputation for his theological writings, including such works as *Validity of Anglican Ordinations Examined*, *New Month of Mary*, and *History of the Holy House of Loretto*.

In 1840 he left for Rome with the intention of entering the Society of Jesus, but his hopes were unfulfilled at the urging of the superior. Instead, he met Bishop Joseph Rosati of St. Louis. The bishop was impressed with the young man and petitioned the Holy See to name him the coadjutor of St. Louis on November 30, 1841. Father Kenrick returned to the United States with Bishop Rosati and received consecration as a bishop in Philadelphia. Bishop Rosati then left to assume the post of apostolic delegate to Haiti and subsequently died on September 25, 1843. With his passing, Bishop Kenrick acceded to the see of St. Louis. On January 30, 1847, Pope Blessed Pius IX named Bishop Kenrick the first archbishop of St. Louis with the elevation of the see as the third metropolitan see in the country.

At the time of accession as bishop, he assumed a diocesan territory that extended from the lower Mississippi to Canada and encompassed Missouri, Arkansas, the western half of Illinois, and a huge territory between the Missouri River and the Rocky Mountains; from this region eventually were formed forty-five new dioceses. The city of St. Louis was also in a state of rapid growth and by 1850 there were some eighty thousand inhabitants. The population included large numbers of German Catholics as well as many French-speaking Catholics. That rapid growth led to the elevation of the diocese to the status of metropolitan see.

Noted for his administrative abilities, he was put to the test immediately by the severe financial problems facing the diocese when he became archbishop. The cathedral faced severe problems of debt, and he found a long-term solution in real estate. To improve the equally grim situation of a lack priests, the bishop appealed for assistance from the Lazarists and the Jesuits and promoted vocations among the German Catholics. He also invited into the diocese the Visitation nuns, the Sisters of St. Joseph, and the Sisters of Charity.

Confronted by the challenge of the Civil War, Archbishop Kenrick struck a determined neutral position and refrained from preaching on the subject or commenting on the controversies of the conflict. Instead, he prayed ardently for peace and encouraged his priests to follow his model. As he wrote to his brother, "I have decided to stay out of these troubles as much as possible . . . so that with God's help, I shall be useful to the end."

His position placed him in the middle of a state bitterly divided over the war. When, however, the Missouri State Legislature adopted the Drake Amendment requiring all clergy to take an oath of allegiance before they could preach or preside at marriages, the archbishop issued a pastoral letter ordering his priests not to follow the law. A priest was soon arrested, and Archbishop Kenrick fought it all the way to the U.S. Supreme Court, where he won the case. In 1869 he journeyed to Rome to take part in the First Vatican Council. In December 1869 he opposed the dogma of papal infallibility, but with its promulgation he publicly submitted to the majority and never again spoke on the subject. To avoid voting on the matter, he departed Rome ahead of time and went to Naples.

Archbishop Kenrick celebrated his golden jubilee in 1891, although his later years were troubled by poor health. Most archdiocesan affairs were conducted under his coadjutor, Archbishop Patrick John Ryan, and, after he was moved to Philadelphia in 1884, by Archbishop John J. Kain, who succeeded him. He died in St. Louis.

Kentucky

Called the Bluegrass State, Kentucky is located in the east-central part of the United States. It is bounded on the north by the states of Illinois, Indiana, and Ohio, on the east by West Virginia and Virginia, on the south by Tennessee, and on the west by Missouri. There are five major land regions in Kentucky: the Appalachian Plateau and the Bluegrass region in the east; the Pennyroyal region; the Western Coal Field and the East Gulf Coastal Plain in the west. The original Native American inhabitants of Kentucky were the Mound Builders, Catawba, Cherokee, Chickasaw, Delaware, Shawnee, and Wyandot.

The Catholic history of Kentucky opens in the late 1660s when René-Robert Chevalier, Sieur de La Salle, entered the region and claimed it for France. No missions or settlements were recorded, however, until 1750, when Daniel Boone, Thomas Walker, and Benjamin Cutbird explored the area thoroughly. In 1774 James Harrod opened the first settlement, Harrodsburg. A year later, Dr. George Hart and William Coomes and his wife, all Catholics, moved into the region. Mrs. Coomes opened a school in the settlement, called the "Holy Land," an area composed of three counties along the Ohio River. In that same year, Daniel Boone led an expedition through the Cumberland Gap, later called the Wilderness Road and serving as a major passage for settlers seeking religious freedom and new beginnings. In 1776 Virginia assumed Kentucky, but that union did not last. Kentucky entered the Union as the fifteenth state. The Kentucky Resolutions, drafted by Thomas Jefferson, were passed a year later.

Father Charles Whelan served as the first resident priest in Kentucky; he arrived in the area in 1787 and labored there until 1789. Father William de Rohan was in the area by 1791, and he built Holy Cross, the first Catholic Church, at Pottinger's Creek. Father Stephen T. Badin, the famous missionary, was in the area by 1793, becoming the vicar general of Kentucky in 1806. Father Badin was accompanied by Father Michael Barrieres in his early labors and then by the revered Father Charles Nerinckx. In 1812 Father Nerinckx founded the Sisters of Loretto, the first religious community in the United States without foreign affiliation. The second native community of women in the west, the Sisters of Charity of Nazareth, was founded soon after.

Father Michael Fournier also worked in the region until his death in 1803. Fathers John Thayer and Anthony Salmon labored unceasingly. Father Badin founded St. Stephen's, which became the motherhouse of the Sisters of Loretto. Also on hand was the Dominican priest Father Edward D. Fenwick, who started a foundation at Springfield. This became St. Rose Priory.

On April 8, 1808, new dioceses were established in the United States as suffragan sees of the Archdiocese of Baltimore. The Diocese of Bardstown, Kentucky (now the Archdiocese of Louisville), was the largest ecclesiastical jurisdiction ever erected in the nation. Bishop Benedict Joseph Flaget was appointed as the first bishop of Bardstown, and he was responsible for Catholic affairs in Kentucky, Tennessee, Indiana, Missouri, Ohio, Illinois, Michigan, and Wisconsin. Bishop Flaget was installed in Bardstown on June 9, 1811.

He traveled endlessly throughout the diocese to administer Church matters and founded parishes, schools, and colleges. He also established a seminary and St. Joseph's Cathedral in 1816, now a national monument. In 1832 Bishop Flaget retired, but the uproar caused by his absence in Bardstown caused the Holy See to reinstate him. In 1841 the Diocese of Bardstown was transferred to Louisville. The Trappists founded Gethsemani Abbey near New Haven seven years later. The Diocese of Covington was erected in 1853.

Kentucky Catholics found themselves enduring an era of severe persecution. On August 6, 1855, called Bloody Monday, Protestant rioters killed more than a hundred Catholics in vicious assaults, and the Church suffered arson attacks and other outrages. The Civil War brought Catholics relief, as Kentucky, a border state, remained neutral. There were high emotions involved, as both President Abraham Lincoln and Jefferson Davis, the president of the Confederacy, were from Kentucky.

Industries such as coal mining flourished after the war, and Kentucky became a leader in the production of hemp, tobacco, and whiskey. From 1906 to 1909, the Black Patch War was conducted over a tobacco monopoly. The state, however, progressed and supported the military efforts of the nation in World War I. The Great Depression, however, gripped Kentucky, and the people suffered from the economic collapse.

In 1937 Fort Knox became the depository for American gold reserves. In that same year, the Diocese of Owensboro was erected, and the Diocese of Louisville was raised to the rank of a metropolitan provincial see. With the entrance of the United States into World War II, Kentucky's industrial facilities became part of the munitions and defense programs.

After the war, Kentucky bishops served expanding Catholic populations and attended the Second Vatican Council. Catholics took part in ecumenical and interreligious programs and formed the Cathedral Heritage Foundation. Catholics reside throughout the state, and great enclaves of the faithful still inhabit the "Holy Land" founded in the early eras. In 2011 there were 380,000 Catholics, 456 priests, around 1,200 women religious, and 277 parishes in the state.

Kerby, William J. (February 20, 1870–July 27, 1936) A priest, William Joseph Kerby was a noted sociologist. He was born in Lawler, Iowa, the son of Daniel Kerby and Ellen Rochford; his father was a merchant banker. After studies at St. Joseph's College (now Loras College), he entered St. Francis Seminary in Milwaukee in 1899. Ordained a priest for the Archdiocese of Dubuque on December 21, 1892, he was soon sent to The Catholic University of America in Washington, D.C., for additional studies. He earned a licentiate in sacred theology in 1894 and the following year was appointed head of the newly established Department of Sociology at Catholic University. To prepare him, he was sent in 1895 to study at the Universities of Bonn and Berlin and then completed his doctorate in social and political science from the Catholic University of Louvain in 1897. He then returned to the United States and assumed his duties as head of the department. He remained in his position from 1897 to 1932 and also taught sociology at Trinity College from 1902 to 1932.

In his many years as a sociologist, Monsignor Kerby was responsible for playing a truly significant role in promoting the field in American Catholic academic circles. He was a strong advocate of the use of Catholic teachings in theology and philosophy in the field of sociology that integrated both the scientific aspects of human nature and the supernatural reality of the created person. Flowing from his work, Kerby became a strong advocate of social reform in the United States, especially as a means of staving off the dangers of socialism. He urged a social program that was aimed at the poor but that was rooted firmly in the wider mission of the Church and the call of the Gospel. He called upon those engaged in charitable work to be grounded thoroughly in the social sciences to ensure the correct organizational and methodological structure of the charitable outreach.

He was a founder in 1910 of the National Conference of Catholic Charities, founded the *Catholic Charities Review* in 1917, and was editor of the *St. Vincent de Paul Quarterly* from 1910 until 1916 and the *American Ecclesiastical Review* from 1927 until 1936. He was given the rank of monsignor in 1934 and died in Washington, D.C.

Kernan, Francis P. (January 14, 1816–September 7, 1892)

A congressman, Francis P. Kernan became a United States senator. He was born in Wayne, Steuben County, New York, and was the son of General William Kernan, an Irish immigrant, and Rose Anna Stubbs. He attended Georgetown College

(later Georgetown University) from 1833 to 1836 and then proceeded to study law in Utica, New York, in the office of Joshua A. Spencer; Kernan was admitted to the bar in July 1840 and later became Spencer's partner. In 1843 he married Hannah A. Devereux, with whom he had ten children.

Kernan acquired a sparkling reputation as one of the best lawyers in the country that led inevitably to encouragement that he should enter politics. After serving in various capacities — including school commissioner of Utica, manager of the New York State Hospital, official reporter of the Court of Appeals from 1854 to 1857, and member of the New York State Assembly from 1860 to 1862 — he was elected to the U.S. House of Representatives in 1862. Defeated in his reelection bid in 1864, he ran for governor of New York in 1872 but again lost. Nevertheless, he was considered one of the most powerful figures in New York politics; with Roscoe Conkling and Horatio Seymour, he belonged to what was called the Utica Trio.

In 1874 Kernan was elected a United States senator from New York. He was the first Catholic senator from the state, and the first Democratic senator in twenty-four years. He served from 1875 to 1881. At the Democratic convention in 1876 in St. Louis, Senator Kernan nominated Samuel J. Tilden for president. A popular and respected political leader, Kernan claimed among his friends President Abraham Lincoln, Tilden, and President Grover Cleveland. He died in Utica.

Keyes, Erasmus (May 29, 1810–October 14, 1895)

A soldier and Civil War veteran, Erasmus Keyes was a Catholic convert. He was born in Brimfield, Massachusetts, and grew up in Kennebec County in Maine. His father, Justus Keyes, was a noted surgeon. Receiving an appointment to the the United States Military Academy at West Point, he graduated in 1832 and was commissioned a lieutenant in the Third Artillery. He served in the nullification troubles of 1832–33 in the South and then was an aide to General Winfield Scott from 1837 to 1841. Promoted to the rank of captain in 1841, he served as an instructor of artillery and cavalry at West Point until 1848, when he was sent for service on the frontier and in garrisons until 1860. He served with distinction in the Northwest and was promoted to the rank of major in 1858.

Military secretary to General Scott from 1860 to April 1861, Keyes was named colonel of the Eleventh Infantry and then brigadier general of volunteers in May of that year. He subsequently fought at the Battle of Bull Run in 1861 and in the Peninsula Campaign in 1862. Commander of IV Corps of the Army of the Potomac from March 1862, he was brevetted brigadier general in the regular army in May 1862 for his actions at the Battle of Fair Oaks. After several other engagements, he resigned on May 6, 1864, and departed for California. Kernan was then president of a Mexican gold-mining company from 1867 to 1879 and vice president of the California vine-culture society from 1868 to 1872. He entered the Church in 1866 and died in Nice, France.

Kilmer, Alfred Joyce (December 6, 1886–c. July 30, 1918)

An American poet, Alfred Joyce Kilmer was a convert and a casualty of World War I action. He was born in Brunswick, New Jersey, and educated at Rutgers College from 1904 to 1906 and at Columbia University, where he earned his degree. Following graduation, Kilmer held various editorial posts, including one at the *New York Times Sunday Magazine* and at the *New York Times Review of Books*.

In 1908 Kilmer married Aline Murray, and five years later converted to Catholicism in New York. He gave literary lectures and became a poet of considerable note. His first book of poems, *Summer of Love,* appeared in 1911, and in 1915 his poem *Trees,* which was immensely popular, was included in *Trees and Other Poems.* Subsequent volumes include *The Circus and Other Essays* (1916), *Main Street and Other Poems* (1917), *Literature in the Making* (1917), and *Dreams and Images: An Anthology of Catholic Poets* (1917).

Kilmer enlisted in the famous Sixty-Ninth Regiment of New York City during World War I and was killed in the Battle of the Marne near the village of Seringes, France. He was posthumously awarded the *Croix de Guerre.*

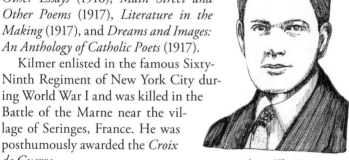
Joyce Kilmer

Kino, Eusebius Francisco (August 10, 1645– March 15, 1711)

One of the foremost Jesuit missionaries of America, Eusebius Francisco Kino was also a noted cartographer and explorer who proved that Lower California, the Baja, was a peninsula. He served mainly in Pimería Alta, the area presently part of modern-day Arizona and Sonora, Mexico, and even the Apaches, who shunned whites, respected his faith and his sense of honor. Born in Segna, Tirol, Italy, he was the son of lesser nobles and entered the Society of Jesus on November 20, 1665. He had been seriously ill and attributed his restored health to the intercession of St. Francis Xavier, becoming a Jesuit in gratitude and volunteering for the missions. Prior to his ordination, the Duke of Bavaria offered him a professorial chair because of his noted brilliance in science and mathematics. Father Kino, however, held to his decision to enter the American missions and after ordination to the priesthood left Cadiz, Spain, for Mexico in January 1681. An earlier attempt to depart for mission service had ended in a shipwreck.

Father Kino joined an expedition from Mexico to Lower California in 1683, keeping diaries, drawing maps and charts, and providing documentation that established the fact that Lower California was a peninsula. Returning from the expedition and realizing that he could not maintain missions in the Baja, Father Kino accepted an assignment to Pimería Alta, where he would spend the rest of his life as the "Priest on Horseback." He arrived in the Pimería Alta in March 1687, starting a quarter of a century of ministerial service there. He made his headquarters at Cosari on the San Miguel River and founded Our Lady of Sorrows Mission.

Father Kino made more than fifty mission journeys on horseback, traveling from a hundred to a thousand miles on each circuit. He also founded missions, including the famed San Xavier del Bac in Tucson, Arizona, and had to defend these establishments before the political and military authorities of Spain in the region. Father Kino had a rapport and a sense of justice in his dealings with Native Americans, and other Spaniards resented his knowledge and determined defense of the rights of converts. He also wanted to reopen the California missions but was thwarted in this by the Spanish authorities.

It is estimated that Father Kino served some four thousand Indians, and he is revered as the founder of Christianity in the Southwest. He also aided local tribes by teaching them advanced agricultural and irrigation techniques, as well as ranching practices that are still used today. The Apaches, normally distrusting of whites, asked Father Kino to visit their camp. Before he could travel to the Apaches, however, he was stricken with his last illness, brought on by decades of constant labor and travel.

Eusebius Kino

After celebrating Mass, Father Kino asked Father Agustin de Campos and his other companions to place him on two sheepskins that he had used as a bed while on missions. His head resting on his packsaddle, he held a crucifix as he calmly died. Father Kino was buried at Magdalen Mission, beside the chapel of St. Francis Xavier. In 1970 a memorial plaza was built at the site, and the name of the town was changed to Magdalena de Kino. Statues of Father Kino on horseback have also been erected in Magdalena and Hermosilla, and in Phoenix and Tucson. Father Kino's statue was also erected in Segno, Tirol, Italy. He represents the state of Arizona in Statuary Hall in the U.S. Capitol in Washington, D.C. In 2006 his cause for canonization was introduced, and he was given the title Servant of God.

Knights of Columbus

The world's largest Catholic family fraternal service organization, the Knights of Columbus was instituted to provide financial assistance to members and families and to promote education and charitable, social, and religious welfare. The Knights began on October 2, 1881, when several men gathered in the basement of St. Mary's Church on Hillhouse Avenue in New Haven, Connecticut, at the urging of their parish priest, Father Michael J. McGivney. The priest hoped that the men might

form a fraternal society for the purposes of assisting their Church, their country, and their families through their Catholic faith, by following the ideal of Christopher Columbus, who first brought Christianity to the New World.

The Knights of Columbus were incorporated on March 29, 1882, with membership open to Roman Catholic men age eighteen or older. The first governing body of the Knights of Columbus established local units called councils, and the organization was chartered at the same time. From this humble beginning, the Knights of Columbus became one of the foremost fraternal organizations in the world. Early on, the Knights were able to develop a powerful and attractive American Catholic identity that stressed fidelity to the Church as well as a patriotic love for the United States. Central to their imagery was the prominent place of the Christian knight, Christopher Columbus, and a stress upon the Church that helped arm members against the often pervasive anti-Catholicism that was still found in the country. The Knights were thus successful in finding members from all Catholic ethnic groups, including Irish, German, and Italian Catholics.

One of Father McGivney's greatest concerns was for the Knights to establish a life insurance program to provide for the widows and orphans of deceased members. As with the start of the fraternal organization, the insurance program that began in the earliest days of the Knights is today considered one of the soundest insurance, annuity, and long-term care opportunities in the country.

To combat anti-Catholic sentiment, the Knights launched the Commission on Religious Prejudices in 1914. The organization also established hospital beds and services for the destitute and provided other healthcare programs. Scholarships were started in local councils, and a Chair of American History was formed at The Catholic University of America.

When the United States entered World War I in 1917, the Knights of Columbus were asked to sponsor recreational facilities and programs for Catholic servicemen and for American Indians in the armed forces. These facilities and programs were the forerunners of the modern USO. The Knights spent a recorded $44 million on the services and an additional $9 million on veterans' educational projects. The Knights also sponsored programs that promoted the sale of U.S. Savings Bonds and opened forums and started radio programs that served as anti-communist elements after the Russian Revolution.

In 1921 the Knights of Columbus responded to a plea from Pope Benedict XV to aid him in maintaining programs for the young people of Rome, who were being influenced by a growing Protestant presence in the city. The Knights raised $1 million for the Italian Welfare Fund and sponsored successful youth programs, including St. Peter's Oratory. During the Great Depression, the Knights aided the needy and revived their anti-communist programs.

In 1944, after supporting the military efforts of the nation in World War II, the organization raised millions of dollars to provide scholarships for children of killed or disabled veterans. A youth program, the Columbian Squires, was introduced, and Catholic promotional advertising was introduced across America. In 1952 the Knights supported adding the phrase "under God" to the Pledge of Allegiance and saw an amendment signed by President Dwight D. Eisenhower in June 1954.

Under the leadership of Supreme Knight Virgil C. Dechant, who served from 1977 to 2000, the Knights of Columbus streamlined operations and promoted social services programs. The hallmark of the Knights, loyalty to the Holy See, was evident when the Knights microfilmed the manuscripts and documents of the Vatican Library, establishing a Vatican Film Library at St. Louis University. The magazine *Columbia* continued its informative and instructive mission.

The present Supreme Knight, Carl Anderson (since 2000), has continued the expansion of the Knights of Columbus. Currently, there are over 1.6 million Knights, more than ever in the organization's history. Together with their families, the Knights are nearly six million strong. From the first local council in New Haven, the organi-

zation has grown to more than twelve thousand councils in the United States, Canada, Mexico, the Philippines, Puerto Rico, Cuba, the Dominican Republic, Panama, the Virgin Islands, Guatemala, Guam, and Saipan. *Columbia* has long been the most widely read Catholic magazine in the United States.

In keeping with their general purpose to be of service to the Church, the Knights and their families are active in many apostolic works and community programs. The Knights cooperate with the U.S. bishops in pro-life activities and are engaged in other apostolic endeavors as well. In the decade of the 2000s, the Knights donated nearly $1 billion to numerous charitable causes and nearly four hundred million hours of volunteer service.

The Knights funded the restoration of the Maderno Atrium of St. Peter's Basilica in Rome, named for the architect Carlo Maderno. The atrium is the big "front porch" through which every visitor to St. Peter's passes. This is one of a series of projects for the restoration of St. Peter's funded by the Knights over the years, including renovation of the roof of the Blessed Sacrament Chapel in 1993, renovation of the Room of the Architects and Room of the Window Panes in 1987–88, restoration of the facade in 1985–86, and construction of chapels in the grottoes in 1981–82.

Knights of the Holy Sepulchre. *See* Holy Sepulchre of Jerusalem, Equestrian Order of the

Knights of Labor

The first widely successful national labor union in the United States, the Noble and Holy Order of the Knights of Labor was founded in 1869 and opened a Catholic chapter in the saga of labor movements in America. Uriah Stevens, a garment worker in Philadelphia, founded the organization with nine other workers, with the aim of promoting the interests and welfare of working people. By 1873 the union claimed eighty local assemblies in the area around Philadelphia, and in 1878 district delegates gathered in Reading, Pennsylvania, for the first general assembly. In 1879 Terence Powderly became the Grand Master Workman of the Knights. He introduced democratic principles to the membership and opened the organization to both men and women regardless of race. Powderly sought to reform the labor field in the nation through education and conducted lectures, study clubs, and seminars.

As was true with other union organizations in the earliest days of the labor movement, the Knights of Labor relied upon secrecy for the protection of its members; the organization also used assorted secret ceremonies, passwords, and handshakes. While supporting the ideals of the Knights of Labor, the Catholic hierarchy had some reservations about the element of secrecy, as well as its public association with the violent Molly McGuires. Responding to the difficulties created by the secret ceremonies, Powderly had such trappings dropped in 1881. Nevertheless, in 1884 the Knights were condemned by Archbishop Eleazar Taschereau of Québec, and the Holy Office twice prohibited Catholic membership in Canada.

In 1884 the Third Plenary Council of Baltimore established a committee to review the status of fraternal societies while Cardinal James Gibbons urged moderation on the question. In 1886 most of the committee members were opposed to the condemnation of the Knights, and the final question was referred to Rome. Cardinal Gibbons publicly supported the Knights, knowing that Catholic members would feel alienated from the Church if he did not. Moreover, while in Rome in 1887 to receive his red hat as cardinal, the powerful American prelate spoke to officials of the Roman Curia on behalf of the movement. His gesture was deeply appreciated by union members and did much to foster a close relationship between the Church and organized labor that endured throughout the twentieth century.

By 1886 the Knights of Labor claimed over seven hundred thousand members, but decline set in almost immediately thereafter. Crippled by internal organizational problems and connections with the 1888 railroad strike and, unfairly, with the Haymarket Square bombing in Chicago, the Knights started to decline in influence and members. Also impacting the Knights was the development of other union organizations, such as the American Federation of Labor. Powderly, meanwhile, left the Church and joined the Masonic Lodge in 1901. The Knights ceased to exist in 1917 under John W. Hayes, the final grand master and workman.

Knights of Malta (K.M.)

The name used from 1530 for the military order that was established in the late eleventh century to care for pilgrims to the Holy Land, the Knights of Malta is still in existence and is one of the most respected honorary bodies in the Church. Originally known as the Knights Hospitallers, the Order of the Hospital of St. John, or the Knights of Jerusalem, the first organization was born around 1070 out of the hospital that was begun to care for travelers to the Holy Land. With the onset of the First Crusade (1095–99), it adopted a military function in the struggle against the Muslims, receiving papal approval in 1113 from Pope Paschal II. Along with the Knights Templar, the Knights Hospitallers were participants in all the major military campaigns of the Crusades, helping to defend Acre until its fall in 1291 to the Mamelukes. They then retreated to Cyprus. In 1310 they conquered Rhodes, making it their headquarters.

Over the next years, the Knights of Rhodes (as they were then known) benefited handsomely from the uprooting of the Templars in 1312, and became politically, financially, and militarily powerful throughout the Mediterranean. Their ships were one of the main defenses against the Ottoman Turks. In 1480 Rhodes itself was besieged by a huge armada under Sultan Muhammad II, or Mehmet II the Conqueror, who captured Constantinople. The Knights, led by Pierre d'Aubusson, though outnumbered, repulsed the Turks. This proved only a respite, for Sultan Suleiman the Magnificent took the island in 1522. Ejected from Rhodes, the Knights were granted Malta by Emperor Charles V in 1530. They remained in control of the island until 1798, when Malta was seized by Napoleon as part of his Egyptian campaign.

The order managed to survive in relative obscurity throughout the first part of the nineteenth century. Its headquarters were opened in Rome in 1834, and in 1879 Pope Leo XIII restored the office of grand master. The Knights of Malta henceforth were a religious body fully approved by the Holy See. Today, the Knights continue to provide assistance to the poor and promote hospital and charitable endeavors. The 12,000 Knights and Dames of Malta, along with the 80,000 trained volunteers and 11,000 employees, are active in over 120 countries. They run hospitals and centers for the disabled and elderly, manage disaster relief, and care for those afflicted with HIV/AIDS, leprosy, and drug addictions. Recent efforts have included relief work in the troubled regions of Darfur and Southern Sudan.

There are three classes of members. Members of the First Class are called Knights of Justice, or Professed Knights, and Professed Conventual Chaplains. They have made vows of "poverty, chastity and obedience aspiring to perfection according to the Gospel" and are religious by the terms of canon law, although they are not obligated to live in community. Members of the Second Class give a Promise of Obedience and are committed to dedicate their lives according to Christian principles and the principles of the order. They are subdivided into three categories: Knights and Dames of Honour and Devotion in Obedience, Knights and Dames of Grace and Devotion in Obedience, and Knights and Dames of Magistral Grace in Obedience. Members of the Third Class are laymen and women who do not profess religious vows or the Promise; rather, they live according to the principles of the Church and the order. They are divided into six categories: Knights and Dames of Honour and Devotion, Conventual Chaplains *ad honorem*, Knights and Dames of Grace and Devotion, Magistral Chaplains, Knights and Dames of Magistral Grace, and Donats (male and female) of Devotion.

The order is unique in its relationship to the papacy, for even while it depends on the pope as a religious order, it is an independent sovereign state and maintains full diplomatic relations with the Holy See, as well as over ninety-four countries throughout the world. The grand master is the only person other than a cardinal accorded the title "Eminent" by the Holy See.

In the United States, the Knights are organized into three associations, established by decree of the grand master and vote of the Sovereign Council of the order in Rome. The three associations are the American Association, based in New York City and founded in 1927; the Western Association, based in San Francisco and founded in 1953; and the

Federal Association, U.S.A., based in Washington, D.C., and founded in 1974 as the Southern Association (it became the Federal Association in 1985).

Knights of Peter Claver

A national Catholic fraternal organization of men, women, young men, and young ladies, the Knights of Peter Claver was founded on November 7, 1909, in Mobile, Alabama, by four priests of the St. Joseph's Society of the Sacred Heart (Josephites) from Baltimore and three laymen. The formal incorporation was made on July 12, 1911, followed by other branches of the organization, including the Ladies' Auxiliary and the Junior Daughters and Junior Knights.

The organization takes as its objectives supporting the work of the Church, promoting the activities of Catholic Action, and assisting the sick and disabled. Currently, the order operates in over fifty-six archdioceses and dioceses.

Know-Nothing Movement

A violently nativist and anti-Catholic movement that flourished in the United States during the 1850s, the Know-Nothing Movement was so called because of the strict secrecy that was maintained regarding its members and the standard answer, "I know nothing," that was given by its adherents when talking to outsiders. The Know-Nothings were essentially composed of various nativist organizations and political factions, starting with the Order of the Star Spangled Banner, began in 1849. They were soon joined by other similarly minded societies that were united in their hatred of the Catholic Church and in opposing the arrival of new immigrants to the United States. In 1855 they joined together to establish the American Party, a harsh nativist political movement that made anti-Catholicism one of its key tenets. (*See also* American Protective Association.)

The Know-Nothings found fertile recruitment ground from Americans in both the North and the South. Anti-immigrant hysteria went hand-in-hand with anti-Catholicism; in the North, workers feared the presence of immigrants as a drain on jobs and the cause of disease and squalor in the large cities of the East. As the majority of immigrants were Catholics, the Church was a convenient target for Know-

Nothing propaganda. In the South, the waves of immigrants were seen as a threat to the assumed economic stability of the institution of slavery.

The Know-Nothings preached a platform of hate against the Church, condemnation of the power and influence of the papacy over American life, exclusion of most immigrants from entry into the United States on the grounds of poverty and disease, and tough standards for citizenship that would have rendered it impossible for most immigrants to apply. The agenda was lobbied in Congress, but various proposed measures all failed on the basis that they violated the Bill of Rights. Some success was found in various state legislatures, especially in New England, but for the most part the efforts were easily defeated politically.

The Know-Nothing Party nominated Millard Fillmore for president and Andrew Donelson for vice president in 1856, and the ticket gained 25 percent of the popular vote. The distribution of votes, however, was such that they could acquire only eight electoral votes. The election proved a fleeting moment of political strength, as the Know-Nothings soon fell apart under the weight of internal disagreements, public opposition, and especially the bitterly divisive issues of secession that shattered the wider political unity of the country. By the start of the Civil War in 1861, the Know-Nothings were all but extinct, although their philosophy was felt in subsequent years in such organizations as the Ku Klux Klan.

Knoxville, Diocese of

Established on September 8, 1988, by Pope Blessed John Paul II, the Diocese of Knoxville serves counties in the eastern part of Tennessee. The city of Knoxville was founded in 1785 as a frontier outpost called White's Fort. The present name dates to 1791, honoring Henry Knox, a hero of the Revolutionary War and the first Secretary of War. Knoxville is an agricultural, manufacturing, mining, and quarrying center. The Diocese of Knoxville is a suffragan see of the Archdiocese of Louisville.

The diocese shares in the Catholic heritage of Tennessee. Its Catholic history opens in 1540, when the expedition of Hernando de Soto entered the area. The Spaniard Juan Pardo led another expedition in the region later, and he tried to establish a

fort at Chattanooga. The Spanish named the Mississippi River *El Rio del Santo Espiritu*, the River of the Holy Spirit.

In 1673 Jesuit Father Jacques Marquette and Louis Joliet visited Chickasaw Bluffs in the modern-day Memphis area. A French fort, Prud'homme, was established at Memphis in 1682. In that same year, René-Robert Chevalier, Sieur de La Salle, was in Tennessee. Missions were conducted throughout the region, and Catholics such as Daniel Boone were exploring Tennessee, which entered the Union on June 1, 1796, as the sixteenth state.

Catholics were under the jurisdiction of Bishop John Carroll of Baltimore, to whom Father Stephen T. Badin reported that he was serving Catholic families in Hawkins County. Father Badin also served families in Knoxville in 1808, the year that the Diocese of Bardstown was established. Bishop Benedict Joseph Flaget of Bardstown sent Father Robert Abell to Nashville, and there he built the first Catholic Church in Tennessee, Holy Rosary.

During the period of anti-Catholic rhetoric and assaults, the faithful of Tennessee were defended by Congressman Andrew Johnson. Tennessee joined the Confederacy during the Civil War, and major battles were conducted within the state. The Catholic Church prospered after the war's end, as Bishop Thomas Sebastian Byrne of Nashville invited religious congregations into Tennessee and was given aid by St. Katharine Drexel.

The Great Depression caused suffering in Tennessee and was followed by World War II. The Tennessee Valley Authority was in operation in 1930, bringing flood control and power to the region. Also, the Oak Ridge Atomic Program was opened in 1942. In 1971 the Diocese of Memphis was established, and in 1988 the Diocese of Nashville was erected.

Bishop Anthony J. O'Connell was the first bishop of the Diocese of Knoxville. He was appointed on May 27, 1988, and installed on the day the diocese was formally decreed. Bishop O'Connell established the offices and agencies for diocesan administration and instilled a sense of unity and purpose in the region. New parishes and schools were opened and lay ministries promoted. Bishop O'Connell was transferred to the Diocese of Palm Beach on November 11, 1998.

The second bishop of Knoxville, Joseph E. Kurtz, was appointed on October 26, 1999. He was installed in the diocese on December 8, 1999. Bishop Kurtz expanded social, charitable, and lay ministries. He also introduced a Vietnamese apostolate into the area, ordained the diocese's first class of permanent deacons, and initiated a four-year Renew program to assist pastoral life in the growing diocese.

Bishop Kurtz retired on January 12, 2009, and was succeeded by Father Richard Stika, a priest of the Archdiocese of St. Louis. Bishop Stika was ordained a bishop on March 19, 2009. In 2011 there were 63,000 Catholics, 74 priests, and 47 parishes in the diocese.

Kohlmann, Anthony (July 13, 1771–April 11, 1836)

A French Jesuit, Anthony Kohlmann was a noted educator and missionary. He was born in Kaiserberg, Alsace, but he spent his youth in Switzerland owing to the political upheaval in France. He studied at the College of Fribourg and received ordination as a priest in 1796. That same year, he joined the Congregation of the Fathers of the Sacred Heart, a French community that based itself on the recently suppressed Society of Jesus. As a member of the Fathers of the Sacred Heart, he ministered for two years in Austria, including distinguishing himself during a plague in Hagenbrunn, Austria, and in Italy as a military chaplain. Sent to Dillingen in Bavaria, he was named rector of a seminary for a time before serving in Berlin and Amsterdam, where he headed a college run by the Fathers of the Faith of Jesus, with whom the Congregation of the Fathers of the Sacred Heart had merged in 1799.

As the rumor was spreading that Pope Pius VII would soon reconstitute the Jesuits, Father Kohlmann expressed his desire to join and applied to the Jesuit novitiate at Dunébourg in June 1803. In March 1805 he set out for White Russia to join the community of Jesuits that was planning to work in Russia. A year later, answering a plea for additional priests to serve in the United States, Father Kohlmann was sent to Georgetown, where he was appointed assistant to the master of novices. Among his many duties were frequent missionary visits to the German Catholic communities in Pennsylvania and Maryland.

Owing to the severe delays in travel caused by the Napoleonic Wars (1796–1815), the newly appointed bishop of New York, Richard Luke Concanen, O.P., was trapped in Italy and was unable to assume his see. To solve the pastoral dilemma, Archbishop John Carroll named Father Kohlmann to the post of vicar general and administrator of the Diocese of New York. He assumed his duties in 1808 and took up residence at St. Peter's Church on Barclay Street. He proved remarkably vigorous as administrator. The cornerstone of old St. Patrick's Cathedral, the second church in the city, was laid; he began a school, the New York Literary Institution; and he invited the Ursuline nuns, recently arrived from Ireland, to start a girls' school.

In 1813 he refused to break the seal of confession to local authorities, and the resulting legal case led to his refusal being sustained by the courts. The event marked a crucial precedent, for New York enacted a law fifteen years later that exempted ministers from being compelled to disclose confessions made under ministerial conditions. The act that made confessions privileged communications (Revised Statute of 1828, Part 3, Chapter 7, Title 3, Section 72) declared, "No minister of the gospel, or priest of any denomination whatever, shall be allowed to disclose any confessions made to him in his professional character, in the course of discipline enjoined by the rules or practice of such denomination."

With the appointment of Bishop John Connolly in New York in 1815, Father Kohlmann returned to Maryland, where he became master of novices and then superior of the Jesuits in America. In 1824 he was summoned to Rome, where he took up a position as chair of theology at the Pontifical Gregorian University, one of the most prestigious theological posts in the Church. He included among his students the future Pope Leo XIII. Father Kohlmann served also as consultor to Vatican congregations in Rome from 1824 to 1836. He died suddenly in Rome from pneumonia.

Konings, Anthony (August 24, 1821–June 30, 1884)

A Redemptorist priest, Anthony Konings was a moral theologian. He was born at Helmond, Holland, and entered studies for the priesthood, distinguishing himself as a dedicated and holy seminarian. In 1842 he felt compelled to pursue a more rigorous spiritual life than offered by diocesan service and entered the Redemptorist novitiate at St. Trond in Belgium. He made his profession in November 1845 and was sent immediately for additional studies. Ordained a priest in December 1884, he was assigned to be a teacher of the humanities in the preparatory college of the Redemptorists and then taught moral theology and canon law before receiving appointment as prefect of students and master of novices.

In 1860 Father Konings was appointed rector of Amsterdam and the house of studies at Wittem. He held several other posts, including Provincial of Holland, but in 1870 he was sent to Baltimore to assume new duties as a professor of moral theology and canon law at the Redemptorist house of studies at Ilchester, Maryland. To assist the instruction of moral theology, he wrote what he hoped would be a useful handbook on the subject, subsequently published in two volumes in 1874. The work stressed the teachings on moral theology of St. Alphonsus Liguori and was much respected for its comprehensive but useful approaches.

Noted for his piety and the depth of his learning, Father Konings was often consulted by the American hierarchy as an expert, especially involving canon law and theology; he was involved in the trial resulting from the financial problems of Archbishop John Baptist Purcell of Cincinnati. The *Freeman's Journal* of July 12, 1884, wrote of his passing: "Those who studied him found him a profound theologian, and a true exponent of St. Alphonsus. The beacon light of theologians in America has gone down, but his fame will linger in the heart of the Catholic Church in America. As a scholar he was known to the world."

Kosciuszko, Thaddeus Andrzej Bonaventure
(October 12, 1746–October 15, 1817)

A hero of the American Revolution, Thaddeus Andrzej Bonaventure Kosciuszko was a Polish army officer who arrived in America in 1776 to support the American cause. He was born in Mereczowszyno, Lithuania, which had been merged with Poland in 1569, was educated in Poland and France, and was a member of the minor Polish aris-

tocracy. Kosciuszko was commissioned as a colonel when he arrived in Philadelphia in August 1776 and appointed to the Corps of Engineers of the American Army. He erected the defense fortifications on the Delaware River and then was stationed at Fort Ticonderoga in New York, where General Horatio Gates ignored Kosciuszko's advice and lost the position to the enemy.

At Saratoga, his engineering designs played a large part in the British defeat and the surrender of General John Burgoyne's forces. He then visited the United States Military Academy at West Point and traveled with the cavalry unit of General Nathanael Greene. After General Charles Cornwallis's surrender of all British forces at Yorktown, he stayed for a time in Cincinnati.

Kosciuszko returned to Poland in 1784 and was appointed a major general, fighting for Poland's freedom from Russia. Captured by the Russians, he was treated well but held for two years. He visited Philadelphia in 1796, welcomed by the Americans and proclaimed a hero. His homeland, Poland, was divided between Russia, Prussia, and Austria, and Kosciuszko retired to Solothurn, Switzerland, where he died. Many American institutions and monuments were named in his honor, including Kosciuszko in Mississippi and Mount Kosciuszko in Australia.

Koudelka, Joseph Maria (December 8, 1852–June 24, 1921)

The bishop of the Diocese of Superior from 1913 to 1921, Joseph Maria Koudelka was a gifted linguist. He was born in Chlistova, Bohemia. His parents, Markus and Anna Koudelka, migrated to the United States with their children and settled in Wisconsin. There he completed his studies for the priesthood and received ordination on October 8, 1875, for service in Cleveland. Appointed pastor of St. Procop, a Bohemian parish, while still a deacon, he proved energetic in founding a parochial school and launching several Bohemian-language textbooks.

In 1882 Father Koudelka was sent to St. Louis to work as editor of *Hlas,* a Bohemian journal. Soon after, however, he returned to Cleveland and began the German parish there. The bishops of Cleveland also used his considerable language skills to attract

European clergy and seminarians for service in the United States and to mediate the sometimes difficult discussions and disagreements among the various ethnic groups in the diocese. When, therefore, Bishop Ignatius Horstmann petitioned Rome for an auxiliary bishop, he asked for Father Koudelka, as he would be invaluable in dealing with the sizable Slavic communities in the diocese. Named auxiliary bishop on November 29, 1907, he was consecrated the titular bishop of Germanicopolis on February 25, 1908, with the unique distinction of being appointed to serve Slavic Catholics exclusively.

Bishop Horstmann's successor, Bishop John Patrick Farrelly, informed Rome that he did not need an auxiliary bishop, and Bishop Koudelka was transferred to Milwaukee. Appointed the first auxiliary bishop of Milwaukee on September 4, 1911, he had served for only two years when he became bishop of Superior on August 1, 1913. Bishop Koudelka dedicated himself to his new diocese and once again applied his language skills, this time learning several Native American dialects to better serve his flock. During his time as bishop, he remained a prominent national figure among Slavic Catholics. He requested that his funeral take place in St. Michael's Parish in Cleveland, and he was buried in St. Mary Cemetery.

Kozlowski, Anthony. *See* Polish Catholics

Kreisler, Fritz (February 2, 1875–January 29, 1962)

A composer and violinist, Fritz Kreisler came to America as a refugee from Nazi tyranny. He was born in Vienna, Austria, and displayed masterful talent as a violinist as a young child. In 1885 he attended the Paris Conservatory, earning honors, and three years later, at age thirteen, debuted in New York as a virtuoso violinist, touring the country from 1888 to 1889. At sixteen, Kreisler was awarded the Vienna Conservatory medal.

In 1898 Kreisler appeared with the Vienna Philharmonic, having studied in Paris and served a term in the Austrian Army. He opposed the Nazis and was banned from appearing in concerts in 1933. He went to France in 1938, knowing that he would be arrested if he remained in his homeland, and in 1939 he sailed to the United States. Fritz Kreisler became an American citizen in 1943.

Kreisler had married Harriet Lies Woerz, a divorcee, and Archbishop Fulton J. Sheen brought her back to the Church in 1944. America honored Kreisler and applauded his music. He died in New York City.

Krol, John Joseph (October 26, 1910–March 3, 1996)

The archbishop of Philadelphia from 1961 to 1988 and a cardinal from 1967, John Joseph Krol was also a promoter of the cause of Bishop St. John Nepomucene Neumann. He was born in Cleveland, the son of John and Ann Krol, and was educated in local schools. He started working as a meat cutter while young and was a store manager at age eighteen. In 1929 he entered St. Mary's College in Orchard Lake, Michigan, and then St. Mary's Seminary in Cleveland, studying for the priesthood. He was ordained on February 20, 1937, and served briefly in a Cleveland parish. His bishop then sent him to Rome, where he earned a licentiate in canon law; he returned to the United States at the start of World War II. He went on to earn a doctorate in canon law at The Catholic University of America.

Father Krol served the Diocese of Cleveland as a professor of canon law at St. Mary's Seminary in 1942, served on the marriage tribunal and as a chaplain, and was on the faculty of St. John College in Cleveland from 1943 to 1953. In 1943 he became vice chancellor of the diocese, and in 1949, as a monsignor, served as chancellor and vicar general. On July 11, 1953, he was appointed auxiliary bishop of the diocese and titular bishop of Cadi. He was consecrated on September 2, 1953. From 1953 to 1961, he was vicar general of the Diocese of Cleveland.

On February 11, 1961, Bishop Krol was promoted by Pope Paul VI to the Archdiocese of Philadelphia and was installed in the Cathedral of Sts. Peter and Paul. He also held chairmanships in the National Catholic Welfare Conference and served as first president of the National Conference of Catholic Bishops and the United States Catholic Conference. He represented the United States bishops at synods in Rome and celebrated Mass at

St. Peter's Basilica for the beatification of St. John Nepomucene Neumann. During the Second Vatican Council, he was undersecretary of the general secretariat of the council.

On June 26, 1967, Pope Paul VI announced that he had elevated Archbishop Krol to the College of Cardinals as a cardinal priest with the titular church of Santa Maria della Mercede e San Adriano, Martyr. Installed in the College on June 28, 1967, he took possession of his titular church on June 30, 1967.

In October 1972 Cardinal Krol celebrated Mass at Auschwitz, the site of the infamous death camp of the Nazis, joined by half a million of the faithful in honoring then Blessed Maximilian Kolbe, who was later canonized. This was the first visit of an American cardinal to Poland since World War II. He became a close friend of then Cardinal Karol Wojtyla, archbishop of Kraków, and was subsequently one of his most dedicated supporters in the conclave of 1978 that saw the Polish cardinal elected pope as John Paul II. He became one of the pope's closest advisers.

As archbishop, Cardinal Krol served as a shepherd of the faithful throughout the long and often turbulent period following the Second Vatican Council and when the Catholic community was moving steadily from the city to the suburbs. The demographic changes posed a considerable challenge to the archdiocese. He also implemented the reforms of the council at a deliberate and careful pace and was respected especially for his abiding concern for the elderly and Catholic social services, his dedication to the pro-life cause in the country, and his reorganization of Catholic schools. He was also active in the ecumenical movement and was a leading supporter of the cause for the canonization of St. Katharine Drexel.

Owing to poor health, Cardinal Krol had his resignation accepted on December 8, 1987, by Pope Blessed John Paul II. He retired as archbishop on February 11, 1988, exactly twenty-seven years after his appointment. His tenure made him the longest-serving shepherd of the archdiocese. Cardinal Krol

Cardinal John J. Krol

was buried in the crypt of the Cathedral of Sts. Peter and Paul in Philadelphia.

Kuhn, Bowie (October 28, 1926–March 15, 2007)

The Commissioner of Major League Baseball from 1969 to 1984, Bowie Kuhn served during a period of considerable upheaval in the sport. Born Bowie Kent Kuhn in Takoma Park, Maryland, he grew up in Washington, D.C., and studied at Princeton University. He earned a law degree from the University of Virginia and secured his first job with a law firm that represented the National League. He then served for twenty years as a legal counsel to the league, and in 1968 he was considered the obvious person to succeed William Eckert as commissioner.

His time as commissioner was marked by severe problems in the league, including five work stoppages, two season-shortening strikes, and the emergence of free agency for players.

More happily, Kuhn also presided over the expansion of the league to twenty-six teams, the start of night games for the World Series, which expanded considerably the viewing audience around the country, and increases in the presence of baseball on television. These changes, in turn, helped the sport capture new fans and guaranteed a larger television contract.

After leaving the post of commissioner, Kuhn supported many Catholic causes, including the founding of the Catholic Campaign for America, and took part in a Catholic Task Force launched by the Republican National Committee that helped defeat a plan to deprive the Holy See of permanent observer status at the United Nations.

Ku Klux Klan

A racist and virulently anti-Catholic secret society that has existed in two forms; the first emerged in the immediate aftermath of the Civil War and the second around 1915.

The first incarnation of the KKK began in 1865 when six Confederate veterans in Pulaski, Tennessee, founded a club for purposes of association and opposition to the Union occupation of the South and Reconstruction. Taking its name from the Greek *kyklos,* "circle," the Ku Klux Klan soon grew into a secret society and a movement against all who favored equality for blacks and who were the products of the imposed political system in the wake of the war. Costumes were adopted to hide the faces of members, and the society grew swiftly. It found little trouble in recruiting members willing to commit acts of violence against emancipated blacks, Northern sympathizers, carpetbaggers, and any who supported Reconstruction.

At a convention in 1867 in Nashville, a constitution was adopted, and the society used stringent entrance requirements to prevent any whites from joining who were in favor of racial equality, had fought against the Confederacy, or wavered in their adherence to white supremacy. A one-time Confederate cavalry officer, General Nathan Bedford Forrest, served as head of the secret empire. Its activities included intimidation, murder, arson, and mayhem against its enemies and any deemed traitors to the cause. Suppressed in various states, the Klan was disbanded in 1869 by order of General Forrest, although elements continued their activities for some years. Congress also sought to curb its activities through the Ku Klux Act of April 20, 1871.

The second era of the Klan began in 1915 in Georgia and soon spread across the country. Within a short time, it claimed over one million members, who adopted most of the rituals of the old Klan, including its uniforms. Where, however, the original Klan worked against blacks and Northerners, the new Klan focused its hatred and animosity on Catholics, Jews, immigrants, and blacks. Much attention was paid to Catholics both because of the growth of the immigrant Catholic populations (the Klan opposed immigration in most if its forms) and the vast expansion of Catholic education through the parochial school system. Klansmen entered politics and used political pressure to oppose parochial schools and weaken Catholic influence in society.

The Klan came to wield political power in regions as diverse as Maine and Indiana to Texas, Oklahoma, Louisiana, and Kansas. At the Democratic Convention in 1924, the Klan was denounced, but the weak effort caused a near split in the party as Klansmen labored to secure the defeat of Alfred E. Smith, a Catholic, who had won the Democratic nomination in 1928.

The Klan remained active and bitterly anti-Catholic throughout the Great Depression. In 1960 the Klan opposed the election of the Catholic John F. Kennedy. The violence of the Klan against the civil rights movement spurred federal action against it, and the Federal Bureau of Investigation, local leaders, and journalists all helped to reduce much of its power and influence, mostly in the South and Midwest. (*See also* Anti-Catholicism.)

L

Labor and the Church

The Catholic Church has long upheld the rights of workers to organize themselves into labor unions, starting with Pope Leo XIII's seminal encyclical on Catholic social teaching, *Rerum Novarum,* in 1891. The relationship between labor and the Church has thus been a long-standing one.

The closing decades of the nineteenth century marked the difficult beginnings of the American labor movement, and the Church was deeply involved. The Industrial Revolution had brought with it massive difficulties for workers. Masses of poorly educated workers concentrated in cities and were forced to work and to live with their families in inhuman conditions. Men, women, and children labored without contracts for fourteen or more hours a day, and for paltry wages. The Church strove initially to deal with the new circumstances through a combination of direct assistance and the formulation of ethical norms for the changed economic reality. Direct assistance was provided through hospitals and schools, and bishops around the world additionally provided important leadership.

In his monumental 1893 encyclical, Pope Leo XIII provided a key first step for the Church in addressing the dominant social question of the time: the exploitation and suffering of workers that was the byproduct of the Industrial Revolution. He defended the rights of the worker against socialism and capitalism, insisted on a just wage, defended private property as a natural right, and proclaimed the integrity of the family against the dangers of modern industrialization. For his achievement, Pope Leo XIII was hailed as the "Pope of the Worker," and *Rerum Novarum* became a key document in Catholic social teaching. It was hailed immediately for its candid recognition of the existence of the social crisis. For the first time, a document by a pope examined the social problems of the era in a comprehensive manner and sought to formulate a solution, with a particular eye on the plight of the worker and the needs of their families. In unprecedented fashion, it gave the average worker clear guidance from the Church.

For Catholics in the United States, *Rerum Novarum* was seen as key direction for how to deal with labor and the question of unions. Labor unions had been forming ever since the end of the Civil War, often in the face of considerable opposition. Catholics, as part of the vast ocean of poor laborers in the cities, joined the unions with much enthusiasm. The Molly Maguires, a group of radical terrorists in the coal mines of Pennsylvania, brought discredit to the labor movement for a time, but some bishops gave their support to the workers. This support was not without controversy because of the semi-secret association of workers, the Knights of Labor, and the question of whether Catholics could be members.

The Knights had been founded in 1869, boasted many Catholic members, and was later headed by Terence Powderly, at the time a Catholic. Because of the Knights' tendency toward secrecy and the understandable fear that they might be promoting socialism and Freemasonry, in 1884, at the request of the archbishop of Québec, the Holy See included the Knights among those secret societies prohibited to Catholics. Most American bishops adopted the position that the decision applied to Canada and not the United States, as they were not convinced yet of the danger. Grasping the potential alienation of Catholic workers, the archbishops of the United States, at their meeting in October 1886, decided to prevent a broader condemnation. Cardinal James Gibbons and Archbishop John Ireland were leaders in this effort. As it was, the Knights went into sharp decline with the rise of the American Federation of Labor, but the Church had established a relationship with labor that was never lost.

Various papal writings assisted Catholic thought in the area of labor, and these writings found a rich application in the field of American labor. Among the most significant were Pope Pius XII's encyclical *Quadragesimo Anno,* written on the fiftieth anniversary of *Rerum Novarum,* and Pope Blessed John XXIII's encyclical *Mater et Magistra* in 1961. The basis for much of Catholic support was the philosophical foundation of neutral and Christian unions (as compared with communist and socialist unions) in natural law. Unions traditionally supported such issues as freedom of conscience and religion, the basic dignity of the human person, a strong family, and a cooperative relationship between workers and management.

These views were consistent with Catholic social teachings and promoted the close relationship, and this was evident in the response of the bishops and Catholic leaders to the question of labor legislation. In February 1919 the Administrative Committee of the National Catholic War Council (precursor to the National Conference of Catholic Bishops) issued an eleven-point plan for labor reform that anticipated many of the key elements of the modern rights of workers. These included a minimum wage, unemployment insurance, the right to organize, extension of the National War Labor Board to assist the right to organize, a national employment service, public housing, a long-term program for assisting wages, appropriate regulation of public utilities, a progressive income tax, the participation of labor in management, and control of monopolies. In 1940 the U.S. bishops issued the statement "Church and Social Order," which reiterated many of the teachings of *Quadragesimo Anno*.

During the Great Depression in the 1930s, Catholic dioceses and archdioceses all across the country helped Americans with soup kitchens and shelters, but there also occurred a stunning burst of Catholic activity in the areas of social justice and labor. Catholics were important players in the formation of the Committee for Industrial Organization, the CIO, in 1935 (it became the Congress of Industrial Organizations in 1938); Catholics were more than 30 percent of the membership and 40 percent of the leadership. Catholics also founded the Association of Catholic Trade Unionists in 1937.

In addition, Catholic priests were actively assisting unions and defending the rights of workers to join and organize. Among the most notable Catholic experts in the area of labor during these years were Monsignor George Ryan and Father George Higgins.

The bishops continued to issue various statements on the issue of labor in the next decades. Notable was the 1986 statement "Economic Jus-

tice for All: Social Teaching and the U.S. Economy," which reflected the social teachings that were advanced by Pope Blessed John Paul II in the encyclical letter *Centesimus Annus* in 1991, on the hundredth anniversary of *Rerum Novarum*. In the 1993 statement "The Harvest of Justice Is Sown in Peace," the bishops offered "A Catholic Framework for Economic Life" and asserted: "All people have the right to economic initiative, to productive work, to just wages and benefits, to decent working conditions as well as to organize and join unions or other associations. . . . All people, to the extent they are able, have a corresponding duty to work, a responsibility to provide for the needs of their families and an obligation to contribute to the broader society." (*See also* Catholic Worker Movement; Chavez, Cesar; Day, Dorothy; Maurin, Aristode Pierre.)

Lacombe, Albert (1848–1890)

An Oblate missionary, Albert Lacombe was called the "Man of the Good Heart" by the Native Americans he served for decades. He was born in Canada and entered the Oblates of Mary Immaculate. Ordained to the priesthood, Father Lacombe was sent to Buffalo, New York, Dubuque, Iowa, and St. Paul, Minnesota, on missionary assignments.

He was fluent in many Indian languages and compiled dictionaries and grammars for the tribes. He lived as a member of the tribes he served, hunting buffalo, moving to seasonal campsites, and exploring the Hudson Bay region. Father Lacombe ministered to the Blackfeet, Blood, Piegan, Strongwood, and Plains Cree. He labored as well in Montana and the Dakotas.

During a Cree attack on the Blackfeet, Father Lacombe was struck by a stray bullet that grazed his head. The Blackfeet shouted to the Cree, "You have wounded your Black Robe!" Horrified, the tribes halted the battle while Father Lacombe's wound was bandaged. He returned to Calgary when he retired and died there.

La Crosse, Diocese of

Established on March 3, 1868, by Pope Blessed Pius IX, the Diocese of La Crosse serves counties in central and western Wisconsin. La Crosse was developed around a trading post in 1841 and was named Prairie La Crosse after the game played by the local Indian tribes. A natural port, the city became important in transportation quickly and was reached by rail in 1858. The area is involved in the agricultural, dairy, and farming industries, as well as in manufacturing. The Diocese of La Crosse originally encompassed all the territory north and west of the Wisconsin River but was subdivided in 1905 and 1946. It shares in the profound Catholic heritage of the region and has been served by some of America's greatest missionaries. The diocese is a suffragan see of the Archdiocese of Milwaukee.

Jean Nicolet and other French fur trappers visited the area of Redbanks, near Green Bay, as early as 1634, and the trappers were established on Lake Superior by 1656. Jesuit Father René Menard was laboring among the Ottawa and Huron at Keweenaw Bay and Chequamagon Bay around 1660, then disappeared while on a mission near Lac Courte Oreilles. He is considered the victim of a hostile attack.

Five years later, the revered Jesuit Father Claude Allouez, a pioneering mission superior, founded the Mission of the Holy Spirit across from La Pointe and then went to Sault Ste. Marie and Green Bay. He also founded St. Francis Xavier Mission near De Pere. Jesuit Fathers Jacques Marquette and Claude Dablon were with him for a time. Father Marquette and Louis Joliet were on the Wisconsin River and then on the Mississippi River in 1673.

Six years later, Recollect Franciscan Father Louis Hennepin was in the expedition of René-Robert Chevalier, Sieur de La Salle. La Salle claimed Green Bay and the surrounding area for France. The Fox War, which started in 1682, kept whites out of the region for a time, but settlements were starting nearby. Antoine Cadillac opened a post and fort at Detroit in 1701.

Jesuit Father Jean Baptiste Chardon and others were beginning missions as well, and by 1728 Father Chardon was at Green Bay, serving as the only priest in the territory. In 1763, as the result of the Treaty of Paris that ended the French and Indian War, France ceded the area of present-day Wisconsin to the British. The American Revolution brought about a withdrawal of British troops from Wisconsin, which became a United States territory in 1783. Four years later, the region was

part of the lands governed by the Northwest Ordinance. Catholics in Wisconsin had been under the jurisdiction of the Diocese of Baltimore and then became part of the Diocese of Bardstown in 1808. Forts were opened in the Wisconsin region, and Trappist Father Marie Joseph Dunand served at Prairie du Chien in 1816. Five years later, the faithful of Wisconsin were under the jurisdiction of the Diocese of Cincinnati, and Bishop Benedict Joseph Fenwick visited the area in 1829.

The Erie Canal prompted the migration of settlers to Wisconsin, which entered the Union in 1848. The Venerable Samuel Mazzuchelli, a Dominican, and other devout missionaries continued their labors as the Catholic population increased rapidly. In 1843 the Diocese of Milwaukee assumed jurisdiction over the area. Milwaukee was elevated to the status of an archdiocesan metropolitan see in 1875.

The Diocese of La Crosse was established in 1868, and Bishop Michael Heiss was appointed as first bishop and was consecrated on September 6, 1868. Tall, dignified, and a veteran missionary, he introduced the Sisters of the Third Order of St. Francis to the diocese. This congregation became the Franciscan Sisters of Perpetual Adoration. Bishop Heiss recruited priests, dedicated St. Joseph the Workman Church as the diocesan cathedral and built schools for the growing Catholic population. He also convened a diocesan synod and aided the Indian missions in his jurisdiction. On March 14, 1880, Bishop Heiss was promoted to the office of coadjutor archbishop of Milwaukee.

His successor was Bishop Kilian Caspar Flasch, who was consecrated on August 24, 1881. Bishop Flasch continued expanding diocesan facilities and joined with other Wisconsin bishops in opposing the Bennett Law of 1889, which regulated the use of languages, districting, and other aspects of Catholic schools. The law was repealed. Bishop Flasch also served at the Third Plenary Council of Baltimore. He promoted education until his death on August 3, 1891.

The third bishop of the diocese was James Schwebach, who was consecrated on February 25, 1892. He promoted education and built parishes and charitable programs for the diocese. He led the Catholics of the area in the opening days of World

War I and supported the nation's military efforts, which brought prosperity to La Crosse industries. Bishop Schwebach died on June 6, 1921.

His successor was Bishop Alexander J. McGavick, who had served as auxiliary bishop of Chicago since 1899. He was promoted to the Diocese of La Crosse on November 21, 1921. Bishop McGavick started a diocesan newspaper and a college during the grim years of the Great Depression. He also aided farmers in the region and supported the military efforts of the nation during World War II. Bishop McGavick died on August 25, 1948.

The fifth bishop of La Crosse was John P. Treacy, who had served as coadjutor bishop with right of succession since 1945. He acceded to the see upon the death of Bishop McGavick and began expanding diocesan facilities and programs. Bishop Treacy erected a new St. Joseph the Workman Cathedral and opened a diocesan seminary. He also raised funds for programs to aid local groups and established the Brothers of Pius X for diocesan ministries. Bishop Treacy died on October 11, 1964.

His successor was Bishop Frederick W. Freking, who had served as bishop of Salina since 1957. He was transferred to La Crosse on December 30, 1964, and installed on February 24, 1965. Bishop Freking implemented the reforms of the Second Vatican Council and inaugurated a Priests' Senate in the diocese. He retired on May 10, 1983.

The seventh bishop was John J. Paul, who had served as auxiliary bishop of the diocese since 1977. Bishop Paul was installed on December 5, 1983. He promoted the reforms of the Second Vatican Council and aided social and charitable programs in the region. Bishop Paul retired on December 10, 1994.

His successor was Bishop Raymond L. Burke, who was appointed to the see on December 10, 1994, consecrated on January 6, 1995, and installed on February 22. Bishop Burke maintained diocesan facilities and promoted lay ministries. He also introduced consultative programs. On December 2, 2003, he was promoted to the Archdiocese of St. Louis and was eventually named prefect of the Apostolic Signatura in Rome and appointed to the College of Cardinals in 2010.

The ninth bishop of the Diocese of La Crosse was Jerome E. Listecki, who had served as auxiliary bishop of Chicago since 2000. Bishop Listecki was promoted to the Diocese of La Crosse on December 29, 2004, and was installed on March 1, 2005. He was appointed archbishop of Milwaukee on November 14, 2009.

His successor was Bishop William P. Callahan, O.F.M. Conv., who had served as an auxiliary bishop of Milwaukee since 2007 and was appointed on January 11, 2010. He was installed on August 11, 2010. In 2011 there were 186,000 Catholics, 179 priests, 384 women religious, and 165 parishes in the diocese.

Laetare Medal

Considered the most prestigious award given to American Catholics, the Laetare Medal is bestowed by the University of Notre Dame. The medal was introduced in 1883 and awarded to John Gilmary Shea, the noted Catholic historian. The Laetare Medal is a gold disc inscribed with the name of the recipient and the motto: *Magna est veritas et praevalebit*, "Truth is mighty and will prevail."

The list of honorees reflects all eras of the American Catholic experience, and includes General William Rosecrans, Monsignor John Tracy Ellis, Cardinal John F. Dearden, Cardinal Joseph Louis Bernardin, Alfred E. Smith, Clare Boothe Luce, Irene Dunne, President John F. Kennedy, and Helen Hayes. The names of honorees are also inscribed on plaques in Notre Dame's Basilica of the Sacred Heart.

LaFarge, John (March 31, 1835–November 14, 1910)

An American artist, critic and lecturer, John LaFarge was a specialist in murals and stained-glass windows. He was born in New York City to a prominent Catholic family and was educated at St. John's College (later Fordham University) and Mount St. Mary's College in Emmitsburg, Maryland, graduating in 1853. After completing his formal education, LaFarge toured Europe and studied art in Paris and London. He was a friend of Winslow Homer. Returning to New York, LaFarge was commissioned by Father Isaac Thomas Hecker, the founder of the Paulists, to design murals and windows for the Paulist church. He also painted the "The Ascension of Our Lord" at the Episcopal Church of the Ascension in New York.

In 1860 LaFarge married Margaret Mary Perry, who was the granddaughter of Commodore Matthew Perry and the great-granddaughter of Benjamin Franklin. They had a son, the Jesuit Father John LaFarge Jr. LaFarge wrote about art, having studied the Chartres techniques and Japanese and Pacific Island styles. He also aided programs at the Metropolitan Museum of Art in New York. He died in Providence, Rhode Island.

LaFarge, John, Jr. (February 13, 1880–November 24, 1963)

An American author and editor, John LaFarge Jr., was a member of the Society of Jesus. He was the son of the muralist John LaFarge and was born in Newport, Rhode Island. He was educated at Harvard and at the University of Innsbruck, Austria, earning a licentiate in theology. On November 12, 1905, he became a Jesuit and after ordination taught at Canisius College and Loyola College. Father LaFarge earned a master's degree at Woodstock College in 1910, serving then as a chaplain. In 1926 he joined the editorial staff of *America*, the Jesuit weekly. He had also founded the Cardinal Gibbons Institute in 1924, to educate African-Americans in Maryland. Father LaFarge became the executive editor of *America* in 1942 and editor-in-chief in 1944. He founded the Laymen's Union to promote spiritual formation among African-Americans and helped to found the National Catholic Rural Life Conference and the New York Catholic Interracial Committee. A prolific writer, Father LaFarge wrote *Interracial Justice* in 1937, *The Catholic Viewpoint on Race Relations* in 1958, and *Reflections on Growing Old* in 1963.

Lafayette, Marie Joseph Paul Yves Roche Gilbert du Motier, Marquis de (September 6, 1757–May 20, 1834)

A French nobleman revered by Americans because of his valor in their cause in the Revolutionary War, the Marquis de Lafayette is called the "Hero of Two Worlds." He was born in Chavaniac, Auvergne, France, and inherited vast estates and wealth. He married Adrienne, the daughter of the Duc d'Ayen,

in 1744 and took part in the court of King Louis XVI. The marquis volunteered to aid the American military forces when France agreed to support the cause and arrived in Philadelphia in July 1777.

Lafayette joined the Continental Army and was commissioned a major general, becoming a close ally of George Washington. He distinguished himself at the Battle of Brandywine in Pennsylvania on September 11, 1777, and then led a division of American troops to safety from Barren Hill in May 1778. Returning to France, Lafayette persuaded King Louis XVI to send six thousand more French troops and, upon arriving back in America, was given command of the Army of Virginia. Lafayette cornered the British forces led by General Charles Cornwallis at Yorktown, bringing about the surrender of the enemy. He spent days with George Washington and his family, a close friend and wise counselor. When Washington talked about retiring, Lafayette told him to stay active because the young nation would need him.

Lafayette was commissioned a brigadier general when he returned to France at the end of the war. He was horrified to discover that Adrienne and their children had been in hiding in a secluded chateau and had been taken prisoner by the forces of the French Revolution; she was released because she was the wife of the great Lafayette. Adrienne's mother and sister had died at the guillotine.

Lafayette led an aristocratic group that sought dialogue with the masses, the end of slavery, and a limit to the powers of the king. He was a representative at the Estates General in May 1789. On July 11, he presented his "Declaration of the Rights of Man and of the Citizen." Lafayette's document was revised several times and was adopted by the Assembly on August 27.

Lafayette also had command of the National Guard of Paris. He saved Louis XVI and Queen Marie Antoinette from an assault at Versailles and brought them to Paris. On July 17, 1791, however, Lafayette's guard units had to fire upon an unruly mob on the Champs de Mars, and he resigned his command. Appointed com-

Marquis de Lafayette

mander of the army at Metz in December 1791, Lafayette saw Louis XVI overthrown. He defected to Austria on August 19, 1792. The Austrians kept him a prisoner for the next five years, and he returned to France, which was then ruled by Napoleon. Lafayette sat in the chamber of deputies during the 1814–24 reign of Louis XVIII.

In 1824 Lafayette returned to the United States, bringing his son, named George Washington Lafayette, to be raised at Mount Vernon. His daughters, Anastasie and Virginie, had married. In America, Lafayette was hailed as a hero throughout his stay. In July 1830 Lafayette helped overthrow Charles X and put Louis Philippe on the throne. He then retired in Paris, where he died.

Lafayette, Diocese of

Established on January 11, 1918, by Pope Benedict XV, the Diocese of Lafayette serves parishes (counties) in southwestern Louisiana. Lafayette, originally called Vermilionville, was established in 1824 and renamed in 1884. The city is a center for agricultural and industrial enterprises of the region and is uniquely related to the enforced migration of the Acadians, conducted by the British before the Revolutionary War. The diocese is a suffragan see of the Archdiocese of New Orleans.

The Catholic history of Lafayette as part of the vast Louisiana missions dates to 1541, when Hernando de Soto entered the area. Priests accompanied this expedition, including Franciscan Juan de Padilla, who was slain in Kansas in 1542, and became the protomartyr of the United States. In April 1682, René-Robert Chevalier, Sieur de La Salle, claimed Louisiana for France, naming it after King Louis XIV, the Sun King. La Salle was accompanied by Recollect Franciscan Zenobius Membré, who would be martyred on a later mission. In 1699 Pierre Le Moyne, Sieur d'Iberville, built a series of forts in the area, and in 1718 Jean-Baptiste Le Moyne, Sieur de Bienville, was at New Orleans, which became the capital in 1722.

Despite political upheavals caused by European rivalries, missionaries continued to labor in the region. In 1722 the Jesuits had spiritual jurisdiction in Louisiana, serving there until their expulsion in 1763. The Acadians of Nova Scotia, devoted Catholics, began to settle in Louisiana in

the 1750s, coming to the area in large groups after having been forcibly dispersed by the British into the American colonies. The Acadians and other settlers also arrived in Lafayette.

The French had ceded Louisiana to Spain in a treaty in 1769, and the Spanish occupied New Orleans. In 1793 the Diocese of Louisiana and the Two Floridas was headed by Bishop Luis Ignacio Peñalver y Cárdenas, who took up residence in New Orleans in 1795. Louisiana was ceded back to France by Spain and then sold to the United States as part of the Louisiana Purchase in 1803. The Catholic affairs of the area were then placed under the jurisdiction of Bishop John Carroll of Baltimore, the first bishop of the United States. New Orleans became a diocese in 1793, and in 1812 Louisiana became a state of the Union.

Louisiana seceded from the Union prior to the Civil War, and Union troops occupied New Orleans. The state rejoined the Union in 1868, but federal troops and carpetbaggers caused suffering for a long time, particularly in Lafayette. New Orleans had been raised by the Holy See to the status of a metropolitan province, an archdiocese, before the Civil War, in 1850, and had jurisdiction over all of Louisiana, Alabama, Mississippi, Oklahoma (the Indian Territory), and Texas. Religious orders and congregations entered the archdiocese, and economic progress was made following the discovery of gold in Caddo Lake. One of the outstanding figures of the era was St. Frances Xavier Cabrini, who served in New Orleans in 1892, establishing educational and charitable facilities.

In 1918 the Diocese of Lafayette was erected as World War I raged in Europe. Bishop Jules Benjamin Jeanmard was installed as the first bishop of the diocese on December 12, 1918. He would lead the faithful through World War I, the Great Depression, and World War II. Bishop Jeanmard instituted the offices and agencies for diocesan administration and opened Immaculata Minor Seminary and St. Mary's Children's Home. A diocesan newspaper and communications facilities were also promoted. St. Katharine Drexel aided Bishop Jeanmard in his African-American ministries, and Divine Word Missionaries were invited into the diocese for this apostolate. Bishop Jeanmard was appointed Assistant at the Pontifical

Throne on December 8, 1943. He retired on March 13, 1956.

His successor was Bishop Maurice Schexnayder, who had served as auxiliary bishop of Lafayette since 1951. Bishop Schexnayder was installed on May 24, 1956. He conducted vast building and expansion programs, including parishes and schools. He also promoted Catholic Charities and the Confraternity of Christian Doctrine. Bishop Schexnayder implemented the reforms mandated by the Second Vatican Council, instituting parish councils, lay ministries, and school boards. He retired on November 7, 1972.

The third bishop of Lafayette was Gerard L. Frey, who had served as the bishop of Savannah since 1967. He was transferred and installed in Lafayette on January 7, 1973. Bishop Frey dedicated the renovated Cathedral of St. John the Evangelist, convened a diocesan synod, and instituted lay ministries. The Diocese of Lafayette lost almost half of its jurisdiction when the Diocese of Lake Charles was erected in 1980. Bishop Frey retired on May 13, 1989.

The fourth bishop of Lafayette was Bishop Harry J. Flynn, who had served as coadjutor with right of succession to Bishop Frey since 1986. He acceded to the see upon Bishop Frey's retirement and instituted educational programs, vocations, outreach programs, and religious training. He visited parishes and schools and worked with other bishops of Louisiana to defend the unborn. On February 22, 1994, Bishop Flynn was promoted to the Archdiocese of St. Paul and Minneapolis as coadjutor archbishop.

Bishop Edward Joseph O'Connell was Bishop Flynn's successor, having served as auxiliary bishop of St. Louis from 1984. He was installed in Lafayette on December 16, 1994. Bishop O'Donnell promoted an apostolate to black Catholics in the diocese and expanded diocesan facilities and programs. He retired on November 8, 2002.

The sixth bishop of Lafayette, Michael Jarrell, had served as the bishop of Houma-Thibodaux since 1993. He was appointed to Lafayette on November 8, 2002, and was installed on December 18, 2002. The years of his episcopal ministry were marked by the two great concerns of implementing the program "A Safe Environment for the Protection of Children and Young People" and providing assistance to the recovery in the Archdiocese of New Orleans and the Diocese of Biloxi from the severe destruction brought about by Hurricanes Katrina and Rita. Through the charity of Catholics in the Lafayette diocese, nearly $500,000 was sent by May 2006 to Catholic Charities, USA, to aid the victims of the hurricanes. In 2011 there were 308,000 Catholics, 206 priests, 152 women religious, and 121 parishes in the diocese.

Lafayette in Indiana, Diocese of

Erected on October 21, 1944, by Pope Pius XII, the Diocese of Lafayette in Indiana serves counties in north-central Indiana. Founded in 1805 on the Wabash River, the city was named after the Marquis de Lafayette. The nearby Fort Ouiatenon was an early landmark in the region. The Battle of Tippecanoe was fought near Lafayette in 1811. An industrial and agricultural center, the Lafayette area is the seat of Purdue University, founded in 1869. The diocese is a suffragan see of the Archdiocese of Indianapolis.

The Catholic history of the state and diocese dates to 1675, when the Jesuit priest-explorer Father Jacques Marquette was in the area. Four years later, René-Robert Chevalier, Sieur de La Salle, was also in the region with Recollect Franciscan Fathers Louis Hennepin and Gabriel de la Ribourde. Jesuits were also active in present-day South Bend as early as 1686, and the great Jesuit missionary superior, Father Claude Allouez, was at St. Joseph Mission in 1687.

The first white settlement, at Ouiatenon, near Lafayette, was started circa 1717. François Marie Bissot, Sieur de Vincennes, opened a fort on the Wabash in 1702, and St. Francis Xavier Mission was opened. Father Stephen Doutreleau was at Vincennes with Father Sebastian L. Meurin, and Jesuit Father Pierre de Jounay served the Miami in present-day Lafayette. By 1763 the British had control of Indiana, and British troops were at Vincennes, which had become a major center. Father Pierre Gibault, hailed as the "Patriot Priest" by Americans, was also serving in Vincennes. He welcomed the American George Rogers Clark to the area when the Revolutionary War started. Siding with the American cause, Father Gibault, at considerable risk from the British, brought about the surrender of the entire area to the American forces.

Other noted missionaries were also serving Catholics in the region by 1792, including Fathers Benedict Joseph Flaget (who would become a pioneering bishop), John Rivet, who opened the first local school, Stephen T. Badin, and Charles Nerinckx, all revered as mission leaders. By an act of Congress, Indiana became a territory, an event that brought about hostilities among the Native American tribes who believed correctly that they would lose their lands. General "Mad Anthony" Wayne fought the local tribes in 1794 and more battles ensued in 1811. After the War of 1812, the Indian lands were confiscated and white settlers opened new areas. In 1816 Indiana entered the Union as the nineteenth state.

The Diocese of Vincennes was created in 1834, becoming the Diocese (now the Archdiocese) of Indianapolis in 1898. Bishop Simon William Gabriel Bruté de Rémur was appointed to Vincennes, and he performed heroic services for the growing Catholic population. The Sisters of Providence opened St. Mary-of-the-Woods Academy, and St. Theodore Guérin was there. The University of Notre Dame was founded in 1842, and St. Meinrad Abbey was established in 1870.

The Diocese of Fort Wayne (now the Diocese of Fort Wayne-South Bend) had been erected in 1857. Indiana was impacted by the Civil War, as Morgan's Raiders, a Confederate cavalry group, fought in the southern regions of the state. After the Civil War, the population of Indiana grew steadily and the faithful of Lafayette prospered. They supported the military efforts of the nation in World War I, and all suffered economic losses in the Great Depression. The beginning of World War II brought other sacrifices, but the entire state of Indiana expanded industrially to meet the need for military weapons and supplies. The Diocese of Lafayette in Indiana was established during World War II, and over fifty parishes were serving some 31,700 Catholics at the time.

The first bishop of Lafayette in Indiana was John George Bennett. He was consecrated on January 10, 1945, and started the agencies and offices for diocesan administration. Bishop Bennett expanded the diocesan facilities and programs and labored to welcome new Catholics entering the area. In 1956 Bishop Bennett received a coadjutor, John Joseph Carberry, who would become an American cardinal. Bishop Bennett died on November 20, 1957.

Bishop Carberry, having the right of succession, acceded to the see upon the death of Bishop Bennett. He attended the Second Vatican Council and labored tirelessly to erect parishes and schools in the diocese until January 20, 1965, when he was transferred to the Diocese of Columbus. In 1969 he was promoted to the Archdiocese of St. Louis and created a cardinal.

The third bishop of Lafayette in Indiana was Raymond J. Gallagher, who was appointed on June 23, 1965, and consecrated on August 11. Bishop Gallagher implemented the reforms mandated by the Second Vatican Council and instituted lay programs while expanding diocesan facilities. He retired on October 26, 1982.

His successor was Bishop George A. Fulcher, who had served as auxiliary bishop of the Diocese of Columbus since 1976. He was installed in the diocesan Cathedral of St. Mary on April 14, 1983, and continued the lay ministries and other Second Vatican Council programs. He died on January 25, 1984.

The fifth bishop of Lafayette in Indiana, William L. Higi, was from Anderson in the diocese. He was consecrated and installed in the see on June 8, 1984. He retired on May 12, 2010.

His successor, Timothy L. Doherty, was a priest of the Diocese of Rockford and was appointed on May 12, 2010. He was ordained a bishop on July 15, 2010. In 2011 there were 96,000 Catholics, 130 priests, and 62 parishes in the diocese.

Lafitau, Joseph-François (January 1, 1681–1746)

A Jesuit missionary to the Iroquois, Joseph-François Lafitau discovered the prized ginseng root near Sault Saint-Louis, the mission in which St. Kateri Tekakwitha spent her last years on earth. He was born in Bordeaux, France, and in 1696 entered the Society of Jesus. After ordination to the priesthood, Father Lafitau pleaded to be sent to the missions in New France (present-day Canada). He was assigned to Sault Saint-Louis, an outpost erected in honor of St. Francis Xavier, and there he worked endlessly on a detailed record of Iroquois customs, traditions, and character traits. His record was published in 1724.

Father Lafitau also announced his discovery of the ginseng root growing in the mission area, which at the time was a rare and costly commodity in Europe. Plans to grow and market the root collapsed after amateur agricultural methods, inadequate delivery processes, and destruction of the root by rot brought about delays, despite the enthusiasm of European traders. Father Lafitau returned to France in 1717 to get permission to move Sault Saint-Louis to its present position. His colorful renditions of Iroquois events and practices made him popular in the court. He wanted to return to the American mission, and the Jesuits serving in those missions needed his expertise in dealing with the Iroquois Confederacy, but Father Lafitau was kept in France. He spent the rest of his life writing about the Iroquois and earning the respect of many as a historian and naturalist. He died in Bordeaux.

Lafortune, Bellarmine (December 11, 1869–October 22, 1947)

A Jesuit missionary priest, Bellarmine Lafortune was revered as the "Little Father" by the Inupiat Inuit of Alaska. He was born in Saint-Roch-de-l'Achigan, Canada, and entered the Society of Jesus in 1890. Father Lafortune was assigned to the Inuit missions on Seward Peninsula and erected a chapel for the Nome Inuit in 1905. He also founded other missions in the Inuit region and was a favorite of the local Catholics. In 1916 Father Lafortune was assigned to King Island, and there he converted the local populace. He became an American citizen in 1918. In 1929 he erected a mission on the island. Father Lafortune died there after a stroke.

Laghi, Pio (May 21, 1922–January 11, 2009)

Cardinal, papal representative to Jerusalem, Argentina, and the United States, and prefect of the Congregation for Catholic Education, Pio Laghi was born in Castiglione (Forlí), Italy. He studied at the Salesian Institute in Faenza before entering the diocesan seminary. Sent to Rome for theological studies at the Pontifical Lateran University while continuing his priestly formation at the Pontifical Roman Seminary, he was ordained on April 20, 1946, for the Diocese of Faenza. After a brief parish assignment, he was sent back to Rome for additional education at the Pontifical Lateran University. He earned doctorates in theology in 1947 and canon law in 1950 and then was assigned to the Pontifical Ecclesiastical Academy (the training center for future Vatican diplomats) in the fall of 1950.

In 1952 Father Laghi was appointed secretary to the apostolic nunciature in Managua, Nicaragua. While there he mastered Spanish. Three years later he was posted to the apostolic delegation in Washington, D.C., where he learned English and grew interested in American culture. After six years in Washington, in 1961 he was transferred to the nunciature in India. Three years later, he was recalled to Rome and worked for five years in the Council for Public Affairs of the Secretariat of State. In 1969 he was ordained titular archbishop of Mauriana and named apostolic delegate to Jerusalem and Palestine; he went on to serve as nuncio to Argentina from 1974 to 1980. In 1980 he was named apostolic delegate to the United States as successor to Archbishop Jean Jadot.

Archbishop Laghi's time as apostolic delegate and then nuncio were marked by several significant controversies in the American Church, but far more positively by the development of relations between the Holy See and the United States. Archbishop Laghi was nuncio during the conclusion of the Curran controversy at The Catholic University of America as well as during the difficult period in the Archdiocese of Seattle involving its archbishop, Raymond G. Hunthausen. Archbishop Laghi also was involved in several important appointments in the U.S. Church, including those of Joseph Louis Bernardin as archbishop of Chicago, John J. O'Connor as archbishop of New York, Bernard F. Law as archbishop of Boston, and James A. Hickey as archbishop of Washington; all of them were subsequently named to the College of Cardinals.

The United States and the Holy See announced on January 10, 1984, the establishment of full diplomatic relations, thus ending a period of 117 years in which there was no formal diplomatic relationship. The announcement followed action by the U.S. Congress in November 1983 to end a prohibition on diplomatic relations enacted in 1867. William A. Wilson, President Reagan's personal representative to the Holy See from 1981, was confirmed as the U.S. ambassador by the Senate on March 7, 1984. He presented his credentials to Pope Blessed John Paul II on April 9, 1984. Archbishop Laghi was appointed on April 13, 1984, the first pro-nuncio to the United States; he was pro-nuncio, for although he was a full ambassador, he was not dean of the diplomatic corps, and hence a nuncio (under the then-established protocol).

He remained nuncio until 1990, when he was appointed pro-prefect of the Congregation for Catholic Education. On June 28, 1991, he was appointed by Pope Blessed John Paul II to the College of Cardinals as a cardinal deacon, with the deaconry of St. Mary Auxiliatrix in Via Tuscolana. He served as prefect of the Congregation for Catholic Education from 1991 to 1999. In addition, he served as grand chancellor of the Pontifical Gregorian University, was named Patron of the Sovereign Military Order of Malta in 1993, and was protodeacon from 1999 to 2002.

Cardinal Pio Laghi

Lake Charles, Diocese of

Established on April 25, 1980, by Pope Blessed John Paul II, the Diocese of Lake Charles serves parishes (counties) in southwestern Louisiana. Lake Charles was laid out in 1852 and was named after an early settler who was promoting the timberlands of the region. Local mineral deposits led to the rise of the city as a vast petrochemical center. The Diocese of Lake Charles is a suffragan see of the Archdiocese of New Orleans.

The Catholic heritage of the diocese as part of the Louisiana missions opens in 1541, when the Spanish explorer Hernando de Soto entered the area. Franciscan priests were in the expedition of de Soto, including Father Juan de Padilla, the protomartyr of the United States. He was slain in Kansas in 1542. René-Robert Chevalier, Sieur de La Salle, claimed Louisiana for France in 1682, naming it after King Louis XIV. The La Salle expedition included the revered Recollect Franciscan martyr Zenobius Membré. In 1699 Pierre Le Moyne, Sieur d'Iberville, built a series of forts in the region, and in 1718 Jean-Baptiste Le Moyne, Sieur de Bienville, was in New Orleans. That city became capital of the area four years later.

European rivalries and wars and the establishment of British colonies on the northeastern and mideastern coasts of America caused upheavals, but the Louisiana missions continued. In 1722 the Society of Jesus had jurisdiction in Louisiana, and the Jesuits were laboring there until their expulsion in 1763. In the 1750s the Acadians began to settle in Louisiana after having been forcibly removed from Acadia and scattered throughout the colonies by the British.

In 1769 the French ceded Louisiana to Spain, and in 1793 the Diocese of Louisiana and the Two Floridas was established. Bishop Luis Ignacio Peñalver y Cárdenas resided in New Orleans. Louisiana was returned to France as the result of another treaty between Spain and the French monarchy and was sold to the United States in 1803 as part of the Louisiana Purchase. The area came under the ecclesiastical jurisdiction of Bishop John Carroll of Baltimore, America's first bishop, and in 1812 Louisiana became a state. Louisiana was occupied in part by Union troops during the Civil War and rejoined the Union in 1868. The area around Vermilionville, present-day Lafayette, suffered for a long period after the war from federal troops and carpetbaggers.

Lafayette was established as a diocese in 1918, and Bishop Jules Benjamin Jeanmard was installed there. He lead the faithful of the area through World War I, the Great Depression, and World War II. Bishop Maurice Schexnayder succeeded Bishop Jeanmard. Bishop Gerard L. Frey was in Lafayette when the Diocese of Lake Charles was erected in 1980. This new ecclesiastical jurisdiction was made up of almost half of the Diocese of Lafayette.

Lake Charles had always been predominately Catholic, and priests and religious congregations had served the faithful for decades. The Cathedral of the Immaculate Conception in Lake Charles dates to 1869. Other parishes, including Sacred Heart of Jesus in Creole, Cameron Parish, dating to 1890, and Our Lady Help of Christians in Jennings, Jefferson Parish, dating to 1891, attest to the historical legacy of Catholicism in the diocese.

The first bishop of the Diocese of Lake Charles was Jude Speyrer, who was appointed on January 29, 1980, and installed on April 25. He served the diocese for two decades, establishing the agencies and offices for diocesan administration. He also expanded facilities and initiated renewal programs for historical sites. Bishop Speyrer retired on December 12, 2000, having provided a firm foundation for the diocese.

The second bishop of the Diocese of Lake Charles was Edward K. Braxton, who had served as auxiliary bishop of St. Louis since 1995. He was appointed to Lake Charles on December 12, 2000. Bishop Braxton was installed in the diocese on February 22, 2001. He continued the expansion and renewal programs until March 15, 2005, when he was appointed the bishop of Belleville.

On March 6, 2007, Father Glen Provost, a priest of the Diocese of Lafayette, was appointed the new bishop of Lake Charles. He was ordained a bishop on April 23, 2007. In 2011 there were 75,000 Catholics, 60 priests, and 38 parishes in the diocese.

Lalande, St. Jean de (unknown–October 18 or 19, 1646)

The lay missionary companion of St. Isaac Jogues, St. Jean de Lalande suffered martyrdom in the Mohawk encampment of Ossernenon, modern-day Auriesville, New York. He was born in Dieppe, Normandy, France, and was devout. When he volunteered as a layman for the Canadian missions, St. Jean was sent to the Three Rivers district and labored there. In 1646 St. Isaac Jogues, who had been brutally tortured and disfigured by the Mohawks years before, was returning to Ossernenon to negotiate a peace treaty, and St. Jean was assigned as St. Isaac's companion.

The two missionaries did not know that the Mohawks had been offended by an event and no longer wanted to see white men near their enclaves. When they arrived at the settlement, they were taken captive and brutally tortured, dying after hours of pain at the hands of their tormentors.

Lalor, Teresa (unknown–September 9, 1846)

The co-founder of the Visitation Convent in America, Teresa Lalor was a spiritual daughter of Archbishop Leonard Neale of Baltimore. She was born in Ireland and was about to enter an Irish convent when her family migrated to America, taking her with them. She arrived in Philadelphia in 1797 and met Father Neale, who was then pastor of St. Joseph's Church. Teresa Lalor started a group of companions in charitable works with the intention of forming a congregation under the leadership of Father Neale. However, a yellow fever epidemic brought the group into daily contact with victims, and all but Teresa died as a result.

Then, in 1799, Father Neale was transferred to Georgetown, where he became president of the college. Teresa followed him there and opened a school with two companions. Father Neale appealed to the Holy See for authorization and received from Pope Pius VII permission to make the convent part of the Visitation order in 1816.

Mother Teresa and her community prospered, and three more convents were opened in Mobile, Alabama, Kaskaskia, Illinois (transferred in time to St. Louis), and Baltimore. Father Neale succeeded Archbishop John Carroll in Baltimore. Both Mother Teresa Lalor and Archbishop Neale were interred in crypts in the Visitation Convent chapel.

Lalemant, Gabriel, St. (October 10, 1610–March 17, 1649)

Martyr, saint, and Jesuit missionary honored as the patron saint of Canada, Gabriel Lalemant was born in Paris and was the nephew of Charles and Jérôme Lalemant. He entered the Jesuits in Paris in March 1630 and taught at Moulins for three years before going to Bourges for further studies. Ordained in 1638, he continued on as a teacher until 1646, when he requested to serve in the demanding field of the North American missions.

He arrived in Canada on September 20, 1646, and remained at Québec for two years in preparation for his mission work. In 1648 he was sent to serve as an assistant to St. John de Brébeuf. Not long after his arrival at the Wendake Mission, he was captured by the Iroquois along with St. John de Brébeuf. He was taken away and slowly and cruelly tortured to death. Once the Iroquois withdrew, the bodies of the two priests were carried to St. Mary's, where they were interred. Some of the relics of Lalemant were then taken to Québec.

St. Gabriel Lalemant is counted among the Jesuit North American Martyrs, along with Sts. Isaac Jogues, Anthony Daniel, John de Brébeuf, Charles Garnier, Noel Chabanel, René Goupil, and Jean de Lalande. They were all martyred between 1642 and 1649 and were canonized on June 29, 1930, by Pope Pius XI. Their feast day is October 19.

Lambert, Louis Aloysius (April 13, 1835– September 25, 1910)

A pioneering priest in American journalism, Louis Aloysius Lambert debated well-known atheists and agnostics of his era. He was born in Charleroi, Pennsylvania, and studied at St. Vincent's College in Latrobe, Pennsylvania, and at Kenrick Seminary in St. Louis. After ordination, Father Lambert served in the Diocese of Alton (now the Diocese of Springfield in Illinois). He served also as a chaplain during the Civil War.

In 1868 Father Lambert taught at the Paulist house of studies in New York and then was appointed pastor of St. Mary's Church in Waterloo, New York. He founded the *Times* paper in Waterloo and combined it with the *Buffalo Union*, which became the *Catholic Union and Times*. During this period, Father Lambert debated the famous agnostic Robert G. Ingersoll, and demonstrated that Ingersoll was unfounded in his beliefs.

A quarrel with Bishop Bernard J. McQuaid of Rochester resulted in the bishop sending a condemnation of Father Lambert to Rome, a condemnation that was not backed by the Holy See. Nevertheless, Father Lambert was appointed to Ascension Parish in Scotsville, New York. He labored there for twenty years, but he also served as editor of the *Freeman's Journal* for a time. Father Lambert was buried in Scotsville.

Lamberville, Jacques de (1641–1710)

A Jesuit missionary, Jacques de Lamberville instructed and baptized St. Kateri Tekakwitha. He was born in Rouen, France, and entered the Society of Jesus in 1661. Ordained to the priesthood, Father de Lamberville was sent to the Jesuit

missions in Canada and began his labors with the Iroquois. He was called the "Divine Man" by the Mohawks, whom he served at Ossernenon, now Auriesville, New York. His brother, Jean, labored among the Onondaga Iroquois.

Meeting St. Kateri Tekakwitha, a Mohawk maiden, Father de Lamberville was cautious about her conversion, recognizing a spiritual maturity in her but also realizing that her conversion would cause difficulties in the tribe. After her reception into the Church and her baptism, he arranged for her to journey north to a Christian Indian community to ensure her safety, describing her in a letter as a treasure that must be safeguarded. The Mohawks did not retaliate against Father de Lamberville, and he served them until he was recalled to Québec. Considered by the Iroquois as one of the holiest priests in the region, Father de Lamberville died in Québec.

Lamy, Jean Baptiste (October 11, 1814–February 13, 1888)

The first archbishop of the Archdiocese of Santa Fe, Jean Baptiste Lamy was a pioneering missionary and an esteemed leader of New Mexico. He was born in Lempes, Puy de Dome, France, and educated at the seminary of Clermont-Ferrand and ordained on December 22, 1838. Bishop John Baptist Purcell of the Diocese of Cincinnati called for volunteer missionaries, and Father Lamy and a companion, Father Joseph P. Machebeuf, who would become the "Apostle of Colorado," responded to the invitation. They arrived in Cincinnati the following year, and Father Lamy started his ministry in Danville, Ohio, then called Sapp's Settlement. In 1847 Father Lamy was assigned to Covington, Kentucky, and demonstrated pastoral leadership.

On November 24, 1850, he was consecrated the titular bishop of Agathonica and installed as the vicar apostolic of New Mexico, having jurisdiction over that state, as well as Arizona, Colorado, and part of Utah. The New Mexico region had been gained recently by the United States in the Treaty of Guadalupe-Hidalgo and there was reluctance among the local Catholics to adjust to the new political realities. Bishop Lamy endured a shipwreck and a severe illness while traveling to

New Mexico, and Father Machebeuf joined him there for the mission. The native clergy did not accept Bishop Lamy's jurisdiction as vicar apostolic with good grace. He countered their enmity by bringing priests from France and by welcoming the Sisters of Loretto and the Christian Brothers, as well as the Sisters of Charity, to the vicariate. The Jesuits arrived in 1867 and opened a newspaper and a college. Bishop Lamy also had 135 churches and chapels in operation.

Archbishop John B. Lamy

In recognition of the growth and vitality of the vicariate, Pope Blessed P i u s IX established the Diocese of Santa Fe on July 29, 1853. Father Machebeuf, who had served alongside Bishop Lamy, was sent to Colorado to pioneer the faith, and another priest, Father John Baptist Salpointe, was assigned to Arizona, becoming vicars apostolic of their assigned regions. Father Salpointe would also become coadjutor in Santa Fe.

Bishop Lamy started the Cathedral of St. Francis of Assisi, reportedly using his personal funds for the construction. He traveled constantly, attending the First Vatican Council and the Plenary Councils of Baltimore while administering his vast see. He was trusted as a faithful friend of New Mexico and aided all faiths, and he was memorialized by the state legislature. On February 12, 1875, Santa Fe was elevated to the rank of archdiocese, and Bishop Lamy was promoted to archbishop. He continued his labors but requested a coadjutor archbishop. Archbishop Lamy retired on July 18, 1885.

The celebrated writer Willa Cather honored Archbishop Lamy in *Death Comes for the Archbishop*, a novel published in 1927. The work was based on his life and was heralded and popular in the United States and Europe.

Lange, Mary Elizabeth (c. 1784–February 3, 1882)

The founding superior of the first religious congregation for African-American women in the United States, Mary Elizabeth Lange started the Oblate Sisters of Providence in Baltimore. She was born in Saint Dominque, Haiti, to a free family of color

and was educated in France. Her family, faced with unrest in their island home, migrated to Cuba and then to the United States.

With the aid of Sulpician Father James Hector Nicholas Joubert, also a refugee from Saint Dominique, Mary Elizabeth started teaching children in Baltimore. She and three companions started the Oblate Sisters of Providence, and on June 17, 1828, Archbishop James Whitfield of Baltimore provided formal ecclesiastical approval. She dedicated her life to showing "the face of Providence to the world," educating African-American children, and serving the poor, the sick, and the dying, especially during the cholera epidemic in Baltimore in 1832. Mother Mary faced anti-Catholic attacks and the uneasy state of free women of color, but St. John Nepomucene Neumann aided her in her mission endeavors. She died in the community's motherhouse. Her cause for canonization was opened in 1995.

Langford, Joseph (June 25, 1951–October 14, 2010)

Joseph Langford was the co-founder, with Blessed Mother Teresa of Calcutta, of the Missionaries of Charity Fathers, the community of men associated with the Missionaries of Charity.

Born in Toledo, Ohio, Langford grew up in San Diego and graduated from the University of San Diego High School in 1969. Called to the religious life, he entered the congregation of the Oblates of the Virgin Mary and studied for the priesthood at the Pontifical University of St. Thomas, the Angelicum. He was ordained on March 25, 1978, in Rome for the congregation.

While studying in Rome, he encountered a book about Mother Teresa, Malcolm Muggeridge's *Something Beautiful for God*, and was moved to commit his life to her work. He met with her, and in 1981 she and Langford founded a community of priests within Mother Teresa's Missionaries of Charity. The new community was called the Corpus Christi Movement and was intended for diocesan priests who hoped to share in the remarkable apostolate of Mother Teresa. In 1984 the community became the Missionaries of Charity Fathers. It was based at first in the Bronx, New York, but moved to Tijuana, Mexico, in 1988, where its permanent motherhouse was established. With the support of Bishop Emilio Carlos Berlie in Tijuana, the community was approved as a congregation of diocesan right on March 25, 1992.

Father Langford served as superior general for fifteen years. In 1986 he wrote *I Thirst for You*, a spiritual meditation that subsequently was widely translated and led to Father Langford traveling to give retreats and conferences. He also wrote *Secret Fire*, an account of Mother Teresa's spirituality.

Lansing, Diocese of

Established on May 22, 1937, by Pope Pius XI, the Diocese of Lansing serves counties in south-central and southwestern Michigan. Lansing became the capital of the state in 1847, replacing Detroit, and was originally called Michigan. The present name was taken from Lansing Township, in which it is located. Automotive firms were formed there, including the Olds Motor Works and the Reo Motor Car Company. The city of Lansing is located on the Grand River. The Diocese of Lansing is a suffragan see of the Archdiocese of Detroit.

The diocese shares in the Catholic legacy that dates to 1641, when Jesuit Fathers Jacques Marquette and Charles Raymbaut entered present-day Michigan and conducted their ministry around Sault Ste. Marie. The Mission of Sault Ste. Marie was founded circa 1668. Other famous Jesuit missionaries working in the area include Father René Menard, Father Claude Allouez, and Recollect Franciscan Louis Hennepin. The revered Bishop Irenaeus Frederick Baraga was also a pioneer in early Michigan.

In 1701 Fort Ponchartrain, the original site of present-day Detroit, was founded by Antoine Cadillac. A series of frontier wars and Indian attacks took place in the area, however, delaying settlements. At the close of the Revolutionary War, the British were forced to cede Detroit and the entire Michigan area, opening the way for American settlers. Having been part of the ecclesiastical jurisdiction of Québec, Michigan became part of the Diocese of Baltimore, the primal see of the United States.

In 1833 the Diocese (now Archdiocese) of Detroit was erected and given jurisdiction over the entire state. The Diocese of Grand Rapids was established in 1882.

In the region that would become the Diocese of Lansing, communities of Catholics were well settled. In Lansing itself, St. Mary's Cathedral dates to 1866. St. Patrick's in Brighton was founded in 1832, and St. Patrick's in Adrian opened the year before. In Westphalia, St. Mary's was operating in 1836, and St. Joseph's in Dexter was serving the faithful in 1840.

The Catholics in Michigan faced changing times as the United States opened new territories and strengthened the Union. The Civil War brought challenges and new political realities, and the faithful made their presence known. With their fellow citizens, Catholics endured the sacrifices of World War I and the Great Depression. As storm clouds of war gathered over Europe, Pope Pius XI recognized the vitality of the faithful in Lansing and erected the state capital as a diocese in 1937.

The first bishop of Lansing was Joseph H. Albers, who had served with distinction as a chaplain in World War I and then as auxiliary bishop of the Archdiocese of Cincinnati from 1929. He was appointed to the Diocese of Lansing on August 4, 1937. He instituted the offices and agencies for diocesan administration and erected over 250 diocesan facilities. He also led the Catholics of the area through the turmoil of World War II. Bishop Albers, who laid the foundation of the diocese, received the office of Assistant at the Pontifical Throne on the occasion of the twenty-fifth anniversary of his episcopal consecration in 1954. He died on December 1, 1965.

His successor was Bishop Alexander M. Zaleski, who had served as auxiliary bishop of Detroit from 1950 and had been transferred to Lansing on October 7, 1964. Bishop Zaleski also served on a committee of the National Conference of Catholic Bishops and implemented the reforms mandated by the Second Vatican Council. He died on May 16, 1975.

The third bishop of Lansing was Kenneth J. Povish, who had served as the bishop of Crookston since 1970. Bishop Povish was transferred to Lansing on October 8, 1975, and installed on December 11.

He continued the expansion programs in the diocese while chairing two committees and serving on the executive committee of the National Conference of Catholic Bishops. Bishop Povish retired on November 7, 1995.

The fourth bishop of Lansing, Carl F. Mengeling, was appointed to the diocese on November 7, 1995, and consecrated and installed on January 25, 1996. Bishop Mengeling presided over the Great Jubilee of 2000, started a ministry for Vietnamese Catholics, and established lay community and social programs for diocesan parishes. He retired on February 27, 2008, and was succeeded on the same day by Bishop Earl A. Boyea, who had been an auxiliary bishop of Detroit since 2002. Bishop Boyea was installed on April 29, 2008. In 2011 there were 207,000 Catholics, 194 priests, 350 women religious, and 84 parishes in the diocese.

Laredo, Diocese of

Established on August 9, 2000, by Pope Blessed John Paul II, the Diocese of Laredo serves counties in southern Texas. Located on the Rio Grande River, Laredo was established in 1755 and was named after Laredo in Santander, Spain. A major port of entry for the United States, the city conducts import-export trade and is the center for agricultural goods, ranching, and the gas and oil industries of the region. The Diocese of Laredo is a suffragan see of the Archdiocese of San Antonio.

The diocese shares in the profoundly Catholic heritage of the state of Texas, begun by Franciscan missionaries circa 1682. Among the most revered was Venerable Antonio Margil de Jesús, who was among the pioneering mission bands. Father Damian Massanet and Father Antonio de San Buenaventura y Olivares labored throughout the area, creating missions. Mexican authorities secularized the missions and Catholic properties were given to local tribes when Spain's dominance was overthrown, a process completed in 1820.

Five years later, Stephen F. Austin and countless settlers arrived in Texas, embracing the Catholic faith. Texas at the time was under the episcopal jurisdiction of the bishop of Monterey, Mexico. In 1842 Vincentian Father John M. Odin was made prefect apostolic of Texas and five years later became the first bishop of the Diocese of Galves-

ton. In 1874 the Vicariate Apostolic of Brownsville was established, and Bishop Pedro Verdaquer was appointed as vicar. He selected Laredo as his residential city, which already had a devout population and parishes. The Cathedral of San Agustin in Laredo dates to 1762.

The Catholics of Laredo experienced the birth of the Republic of Texas and statehood, followed by the Civil War and new periods of growth during World War I. Corpus Christi became a diocese in 1912, and in the 1920s the people of the area opened their homes to ranking Mexican prelates who fled from Mexico or were expelled by the anti-Catholic authorities. In 1936 Bishop Mariano S. Garriga, the coadjutor bishop of the Diocese of Corpus Christi, resided in St. Peter's in Laredo.

The Great Depression brought suffering to the area, and the Catholics of Laredo joined their fellow Americans in supporting military defense during World War II. Economic recovery followed the war, and Texas was provided with new dioceses. The Second Vatican Council also impacted on the area, as the reforms mandated by that council were implemented with the introduction of lay ministries.

In 1990 the Western Vicariate of the Diocese of Corpus Christi was established, and this jurisdiction included Laredo. Bishop James A. Tamayo was appointed the first episcopal vicar. He established offices and agencies for evangelization and charitable outreach. On January 26, 1993, he was appointed auxiliary bishop of Galveston. Other Texas prelates worked to have Laredo erected as a diocese, and on August 9, 2000, Bishop Tamayo, who had been transferred to Laredo as the founding ordinary, was installed in the diocesan cathedral. In 2011 there were 290,000 Catholics, 52 priests, and 32 parishes in the diocese.

La Richardie, Armand de (1686–1758)

A Jesuit missionary who spent his priestly life with the Huron nation, Armand de La Richardie served the Native Americans even though plagued by paralysis and pain. He was born in Periqueux, France, and entered the Society of Jesus on October 4, 1703. Ordained to the priesthood and serving at various Jesuit posts, Father de La Richardie was assigned to the Canadian missions in 1725.

He spent his first weeks in Canada studying the Huron language and then went to Detroit to begin his ministry.

The Petun-Hurons were the first Native Americans that Father de La Richardie served. Some had left the faith, but by 1741 all were brought back to the Church. Father de La Richardie continued his labors until 1746, when he became seriously ill on March 24 and was paralyzed. The Hurons transported him to Québec in a canoe. In 1747, however, the Hurons demanded that Father de La Richardie return to them, and he went to "Little Lake," near modern-day Sandusky, Ohio. Father de La Richardie remained with the Hurons until 1751, when he was taken again to Québec and allowed to live in retirement until he died.

La Salle, René-Robert Chevalier, Sieur de (November 22, 1643– March 19, 1687)

The French explorer who established France's claims to the Great Lakes, the Mississippi Valley, and Louisiana, René-Robert Chevalier, Sieur de La Salle, entered the Society of Jesus but then left to take up a life of adventure in the New World. He was born in Rouen, France, to a noble family and was well educated. In 1667, lured by the opportunities in New France, modern-day Canada, La Salle joined his brother, Abbé Jean Chevalier, a Sulpician, in Montréal, and he was granted an estate at Lachine.

René-Robert Chevalier de La Salle

He set about learning the various languages of the Native Americans of the region in order to become a fur trapper. La Salle then joined two Sulpicians, Fathers Francis Dollier de Casson and René de Galinés on an expedition to the Ohio River. The Sulpicians joined up with Louis Joliet, the famous explorer, but La Salle tried to reach the Ohio River unsuccessfully.

In 1672 the Comte de Frontenac became the governor of France and two years later erected Fort Frontenac on Lake Ontario. La Salle was sent to France to explain the presence of the fort as a defense position to King Louis XIV. The king took a liking to La Salle and gave him a letter of royal permission to explore the Mississippi River all the way to the delta. Jesuit Father Jacques Marquette and Louis Joliet had mapped the waterway only as far south as present-day Arkansas.

Henri de Tonti accompanied La Salle back to Montréal when he returned from France, and the two planned an expedition, which was joined by the Franciscan Recollect Father Louis Hennepin. The expedition headed to Niagara, where they erected a fort and then built the first sailing ship, the *Griffon*, designed to navigate the Great Lakes. In time, the vessel entered Green Bay, and there La Salle loaded the ship with furs traded from local Indian tribes and sent it back to Niagara. The *Griffon* disappeared on this voyage. On the Illinois River, La Salle and his companions traveled by canoe on the rest of their journey and erected Fort Crevecoeur and then went back to Montréal to raise additional financing. Restocked, the explorers entered the Mississippi Valley and upon reaching the delta claimed the entire region for France, calling it Louisiana. La Salle also gave Henri de Tonti a land grant in Arkansas, which was the first European settlement in the area, called Arkansas Point and Arkansas Post. La Salle sailed to France to present his claims to the king. At the royal court he received permission to establish a colony in the Mississippi delta. In 1684 he set out for the proposed site but unexpectedly landed with his crew at Matagorda Bay in Texas. He led the men northward, but the crew mutinied and murdered La Salle near the Brazos River in present-day Texas.

Las Cruces, Diocese of

Established on October 18, 1982, by Pope Blessed John Paul II, the Diocese of Las Cruces serves counties in southern New Mexico. Las Cruces was founded in 1848. According to historical accounts, a caravan of settlers moving through the area was attacked by hostile Indians. The bodies of the slain settlers were left unburied on the site of the future Las Cruces. A second caravan discovered the remains and buried them, marking the graves with crosses. These crosses, *las cruces* in Spanish, gave the city its name. Las Cruces is famous for cotton and pecan crops. The White Sands Missile Range and the White Sands National Monument are also in the area. The Diocese of Las Cruces is a suffragan see of the Archdiocese of Santa Fe.

The Catholics of Las Cruces are heirs to a profound legacy of faith dating to 1539. Franciscan Father Marcos de Niza and a Moorish companion entered the area of present-day New Mexico in that year. They were seeking Cibola, the legendary Seven Cities of Gold, but were forced to retreat under an attack that claimed the Moor's life. A year later, Francisco Vázquez de Coronado came into the area, having heard of the Franciscan's account of his adventures. Some Franciscans traveling with Coronado chose to remain in the area and established a mission. Father Juan de Padilla, the protomartyr of the United States, and Father Juan de la Cruz, the first martyr of New Mexico, were with the expedition at the time.

In 1598 Juan de Oñate began a colony in the area, starting San Juan de los Caballeros on the eastern bank of the Rio Grande River. A new settlement was opened two years later, called San Gabriel. In 1608 Pedro de Peralta was given command of the colony, and he established a new capital, La Villa Real de la Santa Fe de San Francisco de Asis, in 1610. The Franciscans assumed the ministry of the colony, which did not produce the wealth expected in Spain.

One Franciscan visitor, Father Francisco de Ayeta, viewed the New Mexico missions and settlements as imminent disasters and returned to his superiors with warnings about coming Indian uprisings. Father de Ayeta packed up medicines and other supplies and went to the area that is now El Paso, Texas, knowing that any survivors of the expected uprising would make their way there. On August 10, 1680, the long-suffering Pueblo Indians rose up and slaughtered twenty-one Franciscans and some four hundred Spanish colonists. Survivors did reach El Paso, walking all the way from Santa Fe, and Father de Ayeta was waiting for them.

Thirteen years later, Diego de Vargas led a small military unit to subdue the area, and Franciscans and colonists took up residence again, reclaiming and maintaining the former missions and villages. When the Revolutionary War took place, the Catholics of Santa Fe were not involved, as the area was under the ecclesiastical jurisdiction of the Diocese of Durango, Mexico. When Mexico won independence from Spain in 1821, however, the entire region was severely impacted. The bishop of Durango had started replacing the Franciscans with native clergy, and the independent Mexican government ordered all Spaniards out of the area. The Franciscans were gone by 1848.

In that same year, the Treaty of Guadalupe-Hidalgo brought New Mexico into the possession of the United States. The American bishops, meeting in the Seventh Provincial Council of Baltimore in 1849, recognized the new territory and instituted a request to the Holy See that a new vicariate be established to serve the territory.

The Vicariate Apostolic of New Mexico was erected on July 19, 1850, by Pope Blessed Pius IX. The seat was located at Santa Fe, and a pioneering missionary, Bishop Jean Baptiste Lamy, became the vicar apostolic. He brought another revered missionary into the region when he arrived in Santa Fe on August 10, 1851, Father Joseph P. Machebeuf, honored today as the "Apostle of Colorado." In 1853 Santa Fe was erected as a diocese and in 1875 was elevated to the rank of a metropolitan archdiocese. The Franciscans were invited to return to their missions and labored to solidify the faith.

In Las Cruces, Catholics were building their own parishes and emerging as a true presence. St. Genevieve Parish in Las Cruces dates to 1859. St. Edward's in Carlsbad opened in 1893, and St. Anthony's Church in Anthony, Dona Ana County, was serving the faithful in 1899. Las Cruces Catholics sacrificed with their fellow Americans during World War I and suffered in the Great Depression. During World War II, they supported the military defense programs that were a vital part of the final victory of the Axis forces. Catholics in the area also took part in the reforms mandated by the Second Vatican Council and aided expansion programs as new parishes were erected to meet the needs of the growing population of the faithful. In 1982 these Catholics were recognized by the Holy See, and the Diocese of Las Cruces was established.

The first bishop of the Diocese of Las Cruces, Ricardo Ramirez, C.S.B., was appointed on August 31, 1982. He had served as auxiliary bishop of the Archdiocese of San Antonio from 1981. Bishop Ramirez instituted the agencies and offices for diocesan administration and conducted programs to expand facilities and services. In 2011 there were 133,000 Catholics, 78 priests, and 45 parishes in the diocese.

Las Vegas, Diocese of

Established as the Diocese of Reno by Pope Pius XI on March 27, 1931, and designated as the Diocese of Reno-Las Vegas by Pope Paul VI on December 13, 1976, the Diocese of Las Vegas was erected by Pope Blessed John Paul II on March 21, 1995. Las Vegas was settled in 1855 by Mormons, who valued the valley's artesian springs. Las Vegas is Spanish for "the meadows." The Mormons left the area in 1857, and an army fort was erected on the site. The area grew slowly as the railroads brought new people from the east, and the erection of Hoover Dam brought workers and visitors. Resorts followed, and the city became famous for "the Strip," the avenue of casinos and hotels. Las Vegas is one of the fastest-growing cities in America. The Diocese of Las Vegas is a suffragan see of the Archdiocese of San Francisco.

The area is steeped in Catholic history, dating to 1775, when a Mass was celebrated on the Colorado River near present-day Laughlin by Franciscan Father Francisco Garcés, who was exploring the region with his Franciscan companion, Father Pedro Font. In the next year, Franciscan Fathers Francisco Atanasio Domínguez and Silvestre Velez de Escalante journeyed through Nevada on their way to the Great Salt Lake of Utah. The area remained a remote wilderness after these expeditions until 1825, when Peter Ogden led fur trappers into Nevada, followed by Jedediah Smith the next year. In the 1830s, Nevada became part of the Old Spanish Trail between Los Angeles and Santa Fe, New Mexico, and John C. Fremont and Kit Carson mapped the region in the 1840s. At that time, the area was under the jurisdiction of the Diocese of Sonora, Mexico, and was administered by Bishop Francisco Garcia Diego y Moreno, O.F.M., of the Two Californias. The Treaty of Guadalupe-Hidalgo in 1848 resulted in Mexico surrendering Nevada to the United States. The Diocese of Monterey was given jurisdiction over the northern part of the region.

Mormon Station (Genoa) and Gold Canyon (Dayton) were developing, and Nevada became part of the Archdiocese of San Francisco and the Vicariate Apostolic of Marysville. In 1861 the Nevada Territory was established by an act of Congress, and in 1864 Nevada entered the Union as a state. Two years later, the Vicariate Apostolic of Salt Lake City was erected, and soon afterward Father Patrick Manogue arrived in Nevada and established parishes and schools. In 1886 Nevada was included in part in the Diocese of Sacramento. Basque Catholics arrived in the area, and a large group of Italian immigrants also became part of the Catholic population.

The vicar apostolic of the Vicariate of Salt Lake City was Bishop Lawrence Scanlan, who established parishes throughout Nevada, including present-day Clark County. Parishes were already serving the faithful in the area that would become the diocese. Sacred Heart Church at Ely dates to 1869, and Holy Child Parish was opened in Caliente. St. Patrick's in Tonopah was established in 1902, and St. Joan of Arc was serving Las Vegas at that time. In 1931 St. Andrew's opened in Boulder City.

The Diocese of Reno was erected in 1931, and Bishop Thomas K. Gorman was installed in the diocese on August 19 of that year. Gambling was legalized in Nevada in 1931 as well, an event that would impact heavily on Las Vegas. The city was developing quickly, as the construction of Hoover Dam brought workers and their families, and Nellis Air Force Base aided the economy. Las Vegas Catholics struggled through the Great Depression and then World War II.

Bishop Gorman was succeeded by Bishop Robert J. Dwyer, who instituted a diocesan synod in 1957. Bishop Joseph Green, his successor, implemented the reforms of the Second Vatican Council and faced financial difficulties. He retired in 1974. Bishop Norman F. McFarland was appointed apostolic administrator in 1974, and he labored to regulate the financial affairs of the diocese. Bishop McFarland also petitioned the Holy See to designate the diocese as Reno-Las Vegas.

The Diocese of Reno-Las Vegas was erected on October 13, 1976, and Bishop Daniel F. Walsh was appointed as the ordinary. He had served as auxiliary bishop of San Francisco since 1981. Guardian Angel Shrine in Las Vegas was dedicated as the co-cathedral. Nevada Catholics also celebrated the golden anniversary of the establishment of the diocese in 1981. Bishop Walsh instituted the offices and agencies necessary to administer the expanded diocese and erected parishes for the rapidly growing population. He established the chancery and his residence in Las Vegas.

In 1995 the Diocese of Las Vegas was established, and Bishop Walsh was installed on July 28. After a series of clergy and laity meetings, the Las Vegas Genesis Project was instituted, and a Youth Council and liturgical commission were established, along with a vocations office and a catechetical ministry. Bishop Walsh was transferred to the Diocese of Santa Rosa on April 22, 2000.

The second bishop of La Vegas, Joseph A. Pepe, was appointed on April 6, 2001. He was consecrated and installed in the diocese on May 31, 2001. As ordinary of the diocese, Bishop Pepe confronted the immense challenges of a growing Catholic community. He started several new parishes to meet the demands of an increasing population and also a population shifting toward the sprawling Las Vegas suburbs. In 2011 there were 574,000 Catholics, 56 priests, and 28 parishes in the diocese.

Lathrop, Rose Hawthorne. *See* **Hawthorne, Mother Alphonsa**

Latino Catholics

According to the recent official census estimates, there is a population of 48.4 million Hispanics in the United States, or about 16 percent of the total population. They are the fastest-growing minority group in the United States, and the Hispanic population in the country is the second largest one in the world, after only Mexico. The nation's Hispanic Catholic population (not including Puerto Rico) has increased by 71 percent since 1960, and the total Hispanic Catholic population as a percentage of the U.S. Catholic population is 39 percent. Of these Hispanic Catholics, 64 percent attend church services regularly.

The numbers represent a massive sea change in American Catholicism and demonstrate the significant place of Hispanics in the present and future life of the Church in the United States. The mistake is often made, however, in thinking that the development of the Hispanic Catholic community is a new or recent phenomenon. The reality is that Hispanics have been a part of American Catholicism since the first days of the Church in the New World.

Spanish exploration and colonial conquest were colored intensely by the zeal that accompanied the journey across the western seas. The voyages of Columbus were followed by other expeditions and then the thunderous campaigns of the conquistadors. Spanish missionaries were involved every step of the way. There was no shortage of volunteers to serve in the New World from among clergy of Spain, including Franciscans and Augustinians, as well as the Jesuits after their founding in the middle of the sixteenth century. The missionaries were often among the best-educated and dedicated priests and friars in Spain (an identical phenomenon was found among the French missionaries), and many willingly gave their lives for the faith through years of toil in the wilds or as martyrs at the hands of hostile tribes. The Black Legend — the maligning of the Spanish Empire in the New World, including the Church's role — and modern anti-Catholicism have sullied the reputation of these remarkable missionaries.

In 1511 Pope Julius II decreed the creation of the first diocese in what became the United States with the Diocese of Puerto Rico (later renamed the Diocese of San Juan and today an archdiocese), and Alonso Manso became the first resident bishop in the New World. Two years later, Juan Ponce de León departed the Spanish-held Caribbean and entered Florida. Missionaries then made Florida the first region for serious evangelization in what became the United States. For the first half of the sixteenth century, however, Spanish expeditions failed to establish a lasting presence, and missionaries traveling with them encountered determinedly hostile native tribes. In 1558 a more concerted effort was made when the Dominicans assumed direction of the missions, starting with the expedition of Tristán de Luna in 1559. This proved a failure, and the Dominicans were succeeded by the Jesuits. They in turn left Florida in 1572 as the general of the Jesuits, St. Francis Borgia, concluded that the conditions there and the hostility of the Indians offered little prospect for a permanent settlement.

As the French were by then making their presence felt in North America, the Spanish government decided to make another try. Under Pedro Menéndez de Avilés, an expedition founded St. Augustine in 1565, the first permanent city in Spanish Florida. De Avilés was accompanied by two priests, who began the first parish in the United States at St. Augustine. Real progress followed after 1577 with the Franciscans, who forged a chain of missions across Florida and then into Georgia. They converted more than thirty thousand Indians by 1634.

The toil and sacrifice of the missionaries and converted Indians ultimately proved fleeting. As the English colonies expanded to the north, the missions fell under attack as part of the wider conflict between Spain and England. During Queen Anne's War from 1702 to 1713 (known in Europe as the War of the Spanish Succession), English troops and colonists, with their Indian allies, launched brutal attacks on the Florida missions from their bases in the Carolinas. Already suffering decline because of the weakened Spanish government in Florida, the missions received further blows during the French and Indian Wars (in Europe, the Seven Years' War). St. Augustine was sacked in 1763. That same year, Spain lost Florida to England in the Treaty of Paris. There was supposed religious freedom in Florida under the English, but the lingering Spanish elements soon left the area.

Twenty years later, Florida was reclaimed by Spain following the American Revolution. The Franciscans asked permission to return to Florida, but by then the Spanish crown had little interest in assisting the Church. The request was refused, with the result that by 1819, when Florida became a possession of the United States, the pale Catholic presence was soon completely overshadowed by Protestant American immigrants. Effectively, Catholicism would have to start over again.

Spanish missionaries had hoped to set out for the lands north of Mexico soon after the capture of the Aztec Empire. Franciscans thus regularly ventured out with the first explorers. One of the greatest of these was the Franciscan Juan de Padilla, who set out with Francisco Vázquez de Coronado on his expedition of 1540. Padilla was martyred by an Indian band two years later in what is now Kansas; by his death he became the protomartyr of the United States, the first of literally hundreds of martyrs among the early missionaries.

The lasting missions in New Mexico were begun in 1598 by nine Franciscans under Alonso Martínez, following the work of the explorer Juan de Oñate, who then introduced Spanish settlers into the region. Santa Fe was founded in 1609 and served as the center for considerable missionary labors, so that by 1630 there were over eighty thousand Indian converts living in pueblos under the Franciscans. The dislike for the Spaniards, unfortunately, stirred up such ill feeling among some of the Indians that the Pueblos revolted in 1680. Most of the missions were destroyed in the uprising, and Franciscans could not resume their efforts until 1692. One final rebellion occurred in 1696, after which the Church in New Mexico enjoyed quiet for centuries under the Franciscans and the overall ecclesiastical jurisdiction of the bishop of Durango. The 1927 novel by Willa Cather, *Death Comes for the Archbishop*, presents a remarkable literary portrait of the Church in the later New Mexico Territory; the work is ranked as one of the greatest novels of the twentieth century. The Hispanic community that grew out of these early years is still present in New Mexico, and its members journeyed to other parts of the Southwest, including Texas, Arizona, Colorado, and Nevada.

In nearby Texas, Spanish explorers made a survey as early as 1629, but it was not until 1657 that the Franciscan Juan Larios opened a mission along the Nueves River in southeastern Texas. Little progress was made until 1685, when word arrived in Mexico that the great French explorer René-Robert Chevalier, Sieur de La Salle, had made his way into the Lower Mississippi Valley. Fearing further French incursions, the Spanish built a fort on Matagorda Bay. Franciscans provided pastoral care for the soldiers and the growing community and served as missionaries to the surrounding tribes.

Expansion of the Texas missions was accomplished following the founding of the beloved

Mission San Antonio de Valero, near San Antonio (the Alamo), in 1718, by the remarkable Franciscan missionary Venerable Antonio Margil de Jesús. Margil was particularly famed for his missions among the Nacogdoches Indians; according to popular legend, he ended a drought among the Nacogdoches by striking a rock with a cane and drawing out water. Among the other missions he founded were Mission Dolores and Mission San Miguel. In 1720 he founded Mission San Jose, which was soon declared "the Glory of New Spain."

Life for the Franciscans was incredibly arduous as there were few colonists, the Indians were nomadic by culture, and many of the tribes, such as the Apaches, were bitterly opposed to the Spanish. By the end of the eighteenth century, the Franciscans were replaced by regular diocesan priests and evangelization among the Native Americans effectively ended. In the early nineteenth century, with the end of Spanish rule, Texas had a European population of barely four thousand, and a quarter of them were soldiers. Already by that time, Americans were on the move into Texas in the wake of the Louisiana Purchase, and the future of the region was destined to be an American one.

The missions of Alta California (the name given to California above Baja) begin officially on July 16, 1769, with the start of the Franciscan mission at San Diego, the first of twenty-one missions founded between 1769 and 1823. The Franciscans were responsible for forging *El Camino Real* (the "Royal Road"), a chain of missions that extended from San Diego to San Francisco. The California missions served as the principle centers of evangelization in California, and "life under the bells" was the chief way of living for thousands of Indians who were taught trades and assisted in finding a place in the Spanish society that had suddenly been thrust upon them.

The central figure in the California missions was the Franciscan friar Blessed Junípero Serra. With the Mexican Revolution against Spain in 1821, the California missions came to an end as they became the property of a hostile Mexican government. In 1834 the secularization of the missions was declared, but the promises to the Indians of land and livestock never materialized, and the death rate of the Native Americans was worse than that of the slaves in the American South. Chaos ensued as the Mexican government slid into anarchy, and by 1850 there were barely thirteen priests in the whole of California. The circumstances were already changing quickly, however, with the discovery of gold at Sutter's Mill in 1848 and the massive invasion of prospectors into the territory. Spanish California was soon replaced by an American California, and from 1850 Catholicism looked east rather than south. The legacy of the Spanish missions in North America must not be overlooked. This tradition has become most apparent as the Hispanic Catholic population has increased extensively in the last decades.

The drive to the West became one of the major social and political forces in American history during the nineteenth century. The great push was given great impetus through the Louisiana Purchase of 1803 during the presidency of Thomas Jefferson, which literally doubled the size of the United States. In 1819 the United States acquired Florida from Spain, but the central preoccupation was toward the West. Texas entered the Union in 1845, and the achievement of reaching the Pacific Coast was accomplished through the Mexican-American War (1846–48). The United States acquired New Mexico, California, and the Texas boundary as far south as the Rio Grande through the Treaty of Guadalupe-Hidalgo and the so-called Mexican Cession. At the same time, Great Britain agreed to establish the Oregon border at the 49°N latitude. By the agreement, the United States received the important Columbia River Valley. Gold was discovered in California during the brief presidency of Zachary Taylor, and the territory was soon brought into the United States as a state. The future states of Idaho, Washington, and Oregon were also firmly in American hands.

The takeover of the Southwest and West by the expanding United States thus brought a direct collision between the American settlers pushing ever westward and southward and the inhabitants who had been living there for centuries and who were suddenly without power and often viewed as second-class citizens by the Americans. Claims to land dating back to the time of Emperor Charles V were ignored or set aside, and indigenous peoples were expected to assimilate to the new demands of American culture.

Most of the Hispanics were devout Catholics and were determined to maintain their cultural traditions despite the pressures of assimilation. Across the Southwest, their numbers held steady throughout the second half of the nineteenth century, but this changed with the collapse of political and social stability in Mexico, which forced Mexicans to flee the violence and settle in the United States. The pace of immigration increased with the Mexican Revolution of 1910 and especially with the horrific Cristero War in the 1920s.

After a brief decline because of the Great Depression, Mexican and then Hispanic immigrants continued to move into the United States in search of a new life and also work. They settled initially in the Southwest, but many then set out for opportunities in the Northwest and the Midwest, especially Chicago. They brought with them their language and culture, but they also faced pressures to assimilate and of continuing second-class status in many places. There was hostility on the part of many Americans that Hispanics were taking jobs away and were not real Americans. This was a serious charge in the aftermath of World War II, in which many Hispanics had fought and died for their country.

The Church had undergone a transformation in the West and Southwest in the nineteenth century that mirrored the wider political and social changes in the regions. There were few Hispanic priests left in many of the areas, and the clergy and leadership of the multiplying dioceses tended to come from the Eastern dioceses. They focused especially on providing facilities and pastoral care for the American settlers who were arriving in the area, mirroring in some ways the pastoral concerns in the East, in archdioceses such as New York, Chicago, Philadelphia, and Boston, where the influx of immigrants from Europe were swamping the resources at hand. Hispanic Catholics were a sometimes forgotten part of the Catholic community.

This began to change in the middle of the twentieth century. First, Hispanic Catholics themselves fostered a deeper awareness of their traditions and cultural heritage. Second, the Church recognized the importance of pastoral care and outreach to Hispanic Catholics. Crucial in this was the promotion of vocations among Hispanics and the appointment of the first Hispanic bishops across the United States. An important figure in this was Father Patricio Fernández Flores, a priest of the Galveston diocese who was appointed an auxiliary bishop of San Antonio in 1970, and was then bishop of El Paso and the first Latino archbishop of San Antonio from 1979 to 2004.

From this beginning, there were by 2011 forty-two bishops of Hispanic origin in the United States, twenty-nine of them active. Notable especially was Archbishop José H. Gomez, the first archbishop of Los Angeles, the largest archdiocese in the United States. There were also 1,600 Hispanic priests and 2,900 Hispanic nuns in the United States

Pastoral ministry to Hispanics has varied depending on cultural differences and the availability of personnel to carry it out. The pattern in cities with large numbers of Spanish-speaking people was built around special and bilingual churches, centers, or other agencies where pastoral and additional forms of service are provided in a manner suited to the needs, language, and culture of the people. Many Spanish-speaking communities remain in need of special ministries. An itinerant form of ministry best meets the needs of the thousands of Hispanic migrant workers who follow the crops.

Meeting the needs of the growing Hispanic community became a priority for the U.S. bishops in the 1970s and 1980s and was the central concern of three national meetings, Encuentros, held in 1972, 1977, and 1985. A national secretariat for Hispanics was established by the United States Catholic Conference in 1971, to promote and coordinate pastoral ministry to the Spanish-speaking. At their annual meeting in November 1983, the U.S. bishops approved and subsequently published a pastoral letter on Hispanic ministry under the title "The Hispanic Presence: Challenge and Commitment."

The third National Encuentro in 1985 produced a pastoral plan for ministry that the National Conference of Catholic Bishops approved in 1987. Its four keys are collaborative ministry; evangelization; a missionary option regarding the poor, the marginalized, the family, women and youth; and the formation of lay leadership. A National Encuentro was held in 2000. In 2002 the secretariat published

Encuentro and Mission: A New Pastoral Framework for Hispanic Ministry.

According to statistics based on the 2010 Census, there are 4,000 U.S. parishes with Hispanic ministry, and 20.6 percent of U.S. parishes have a majority Hispanic presence. There are approximately 2,900 Hispanic priests and 25 active Hispanic bishops. Over the past few years, 15 percent of all new priests ordained in the United States have been of Hispanic descent. Hispanics constitute 25 percent of all laypeople engaged in diocesan ministry programs.

The ten metropolitan areas with the largest Hispanic populations are Los Angeles, New York, Chicago, Miami, Houston, Phoenix, San Antonio, and Dallas, and Riverside-San Bernardino and Orange County, both in California. Seven states in 2000 had more than one million Hispanic residents: Arizona, California, Florida, Illinois, New Jersey, New York, and Texas. Approximately half of the Hispanic population lived in just two states, California and Texas. In New Mexico, Hispanics made up 42 percent of the state's total population, the highest for any state.

Current U.S. Census figures reveal that the Hispanic population increased by 13 million between 1990 and 2000. Hispanics also accounted for 40 percent of the nation's increase in population over the decade. The Hispanic population more than tripled between 1990 and 2000 in Alabama, Arkansas, Georgia, Nevada, North Carolina, South Carolina, and Tennessee.

Data demonstrate that the Hispanic population in the United States is young. The median age in 2009 was 27.4 years, compared with 36.8 years for the general population. The Hispanic population comprises 26 percent of the children under the age of five; Hispanics comprise 22 percent of children younger than eighteen. Only 5.3 percent of Hispanics are older than sixty-five. More than 50 percent of all Catholics in the United States under age twenty-five are of Hispanic descent. The poverty rate in the general population in 1999 was 7.7 percent among non-Hispanic whites; the poverty rate among Hispanics was 21.2 percent or 7.2 million people. It is projected that Hispanics will surpass the 132.8 million mark by the year 2050 and will comprise 30 percent of the total population.

Laval, François de Montmorency, Blessed (April 30, 1623–May 6, 1708)

The first bishop of the Diocese of Québec, Blessed François de Montmorency Laval, was the Catholic administrator for all of North America, including the present-day United States, except for Spanish-held lands and a few English colonies in modern New England. He was also revered as "a bishop according to God's heart."

Blessed François was born in Montigny-sur-Aure, France, a member of a distinguished family whose ancestor baptized St. Clovis. He studied with the Jesuits and became a canon at age twelve. Blessed François received the titles and estates of his family in 1645, following the deaths of two older brothers. He was ordained to the priesthood in 1647 and became archdeacon of Evreux and the vicar apostolic of Tongkin, in present-day Vietnam.

Blessed François did not take up residence in Tongkin because of the political upheavals in that area. He resigned the position and spent four years as a hermit in Caen, called away from his seclusion in 1658. Pope Alexander VII appointed him vicar apostolic of New France, modern-day Canada. He was consecrated a bishop and arrived in Québec on June 16, 1659.

Blessed François instituted administrative offices and began serving one and all. His contemporaries, Indians and whites alike, reported, "His heart is always with us." He could be stern in dealing with whites, who controlled the liquor trade with the local tribes, but his devotion benefited all the faithful. Blessed François erected the Immaculate Conception Cathedral and restored the shrine of St. Anne de Beaupré. He also instituted a vast school system. All the while, he was sending trained missionaries into the American wilderness, sowing the seeds of the faith in what would become the United States.

Gathering the Iroquois and other Indian chiefs in Québec, Blessed François asked for their opinions on conducting missions in their lands. One chief, the greatly respected Garaconthié of the Oneida Iroquois, converted during the meeting and was baptized by Blessed François, and was followed by other chiefs. Returning to the Iroquois Confederacy lands, Chief Garaconthié reopened the Catholic missions among the Iroquois. By doing this, he paved the way for the baptism of the "Lily of the Mohawks," St. Kateri Tekakwitha.

Blessed François retired in 1684 to the seminary he had founded, then came out of retirement in 1701 to aid the diocese. He died in Québec. Pope Blessed John Paul II beatified Blessed François de Montmorency Laval on June 22, 1980.

Law, Bernard F. (November 4, 1931–)

Archbishop of Boston from 1984 to 2002, Cardinal Bernard F. Law resigned in the midst of the sexual abuse scandal that rocked the Boston archdiocese. The future cardinal was born in Torreon, Mexico, the son of a U.S. Air Force colonel. He studied at Harvard University and earned a bachelor's degree in 1953, just prior to entering studies for the priesthood at St. Joseph Seminary in St. Benedict, Louisiana, and then at the Pontifical College Josephinum in Ohio. Ordained a priest for the Jackson diocese on May 21, 1961, he served in several pastoral assignments and was editor of the Natchez-Jackson diocesan paper from 1963 to 1968, and then director of the National Conference of Catholic Bishops Committee on Ecumenical and Interreligious Affairs from 1968 to 1971.

On October 22, 1973, Pope Paul VI appointed him the fourth bishop of Springfield-Cape Girardeau; he was consecrated a bishop on December 5, 1973. On January 11, 1984, he was appointed by Pope Blessed John Paul II the eighth bishop and fifth archbishop of Boston, as successor to Cardinal Humberto S. Medeiros; he was installed on March 23, 1984. The following year, on May 25, 1985, he was created a cardinal priest with the titular church of Santa Susanna.

As archbishop, he became one of the most influential of the American members of the College of Cardinals and a determined reformer of the archdiocesan administration. Most innovative was his establishment of a cabinet structure for administrative affairs, to provide greater bureaucratic cohesion. He also took the unusual step of appointing a layman to the post of archdiocesan

Cardinal Bernard Law

chancellor and a woman religious as a judge on the archdiocesan marriage tribunal. Cardinal Law confronted the need to close older churches, but he established new ones in the suburbs as well to meet the changing demographics facing the archdiocese. He also erected new churches in the Boston-area urban districts to provide better pastoral care for Catholics of Asian, Haitian, and Latin American backgrounds.

Cardinal Law's final years as archbishop were tragically marked by the eruption of the sex abuse scandal that afflicted the archdiocese and created the greatest crisis in its history. Facing accusations of having moved pedophile priests from one assignment to another, he resigned on December 13, 2002. He was appointed Archpriest of the Patriarchal Basilica of Santa Maria Maggiore in Rome in May 2004. He resigned his post in November 2011, upon reaching his eightieth birthday.

Lawler, Ronald (July 29, 1926–November 5, 2003)

Capuchin Franciscan, moral theologian, and religious educator, Ronald Lawler was born in Cumberland, Maryland. He entered the Capuchins on July 14, 1946, and was ordained on August 28, 1951. He went on to earn a doctorate in 1959, with a dissertation on "The Moral Judgment in Contemporary Analytic Philosophy," and then held a wide variety of teaching posts. From 1960 to 1969, he taught at then Fidelis College, which included as one of his students the future archbishop of Boston, Cardinal Seán O'Malley, O.F.M. Cap. Father Lawler was also a spiritual director to then Bishop (now archbishop of Washington) Donald W. Wuerl and taught a number of other future bishops, including Archbishop Charles J. Chaput, O.F.M. Cap., of Philadelphia.

His career in teaching stretched more than fifty years, and he taught at universities all over the world, including Oxford University, The Catholic University of America, St. John's University, and Franciscan University of Steubenville. He served as Dean of Theology for the Pontifical College Josephinum.

Father Lawler was a prolific author, writing such notable books as *Philosophical Analysis and Ethics* (1968), *Philosophy in Priestly Formation* (1978), *The Christian Personalism of John Paul II* (1981), *Perspectives in Bioethics* (1983), *Catholic Sexual Ethics* (1985), *The Catholic Catechism* (1986), and *Excellence in Seminary Education* (1988). He also wrote hundreds of articles for scholarly and popular journals. By far his most popular work, *The Teaching of Christ*, was cowritten with his brother Thomas Lawler and the future Bishop Wuerl. Originally published in 1976, the work was the first authoritative adult catechism in the English-speaking world in the period after the Second Vatican Council, and was written at the request of Cardinal John J. Wright, then prefect of the Vatican's Sacred Congregation for Clergy and Pastoral Work. The book was a major success and was praised by Pope Paul VI.

Father Lawler was also the only American on the Pontifical Roman Theological Academy, a board of papal advisers on theological matters. He was inducted into the academy in 1982; two other new members that year were Cardinal Henri de Lubac, S.J., and Father (later Cardinal) Hans Urs von Balthasar. In 1977 he was the founding president of the Fellowship of Catholic Scholars, an organization that was intended to foster official Church teachings during the difficult postconciliar period.

Lawrence, David Leo (June 18, 1889–November 21, 1966)

The first Catholic governor of Pennsylvania, serving from 1959 to 1963, David Leo Lawrence was born to the working-class Irish Catholic family of Charles B. Lawrence and Catherine Conwell Lawrence in the Golden Triangle neighborhood of Pittsburgh. His family did not have the money to send him to college, so he worked instead as a clerk for the chairman of the local Democratic Party and labor leader William Brennan. He entered the insurance business in 1916 and then enlisted in the United States Army in 1918. During the final days of World War I, he was an officer in the adjutant general's office in Washington, D.C.

Returning home in 1919, he was elected chairman of the Allegheny County Democratic Party and helped improve the long-term prospects of the party in Pittsburgh and the state. In 1931 Lawrence ran unsuccessfully for Allegheny County Commissioner. In 1933 he was named U.S. Collector of Internal Revenue for western Pennsylvania and worked to assist other Democrats. The following year he became Secretary of the Commonwealth and state chairman of the Democratic Party.

In 1945 Lawrence was elected mayor of Pittsburgh. He took as his chief task to improve the terrible conditions of pollution in the city, including a seven-point program and a political partnership with Richard K. Mellon, chairman of one of the largest banks in America and a Republican. The two were instrumental in achieving what came to be called a renaissance in Pittsburgh. After an unprecedented four terms as mayor, Lawrence ran for governor in 1958 and was elected by a close margin. Despite his age — he was seventy at the time of his election — he proved an active governor and was responsible for a wide range of legislative acts. He proved important also in the election of John F. Kennedy in 1960 and so earned the title "Maker of Presidents."

Lead, Diocese of. *See* Rapid City, Diocese of

Leadership Conference of Women Religious

A national organization, the Leadership Conference of Women Religious was founded in 1956 as the Conference of Major Superiors of Women. The group was canonically established in 1959 and approved by the Vatican's Congregation for Religious in 1962. The original concerns of the conference were centered on aspects of religious life and women's communities.

After the Second Vatican Council, however, the organization widened its area of focus. The National Sisters' Survey, conducted in 1968, demonstrated a desire among women religious for updating and change within congregations and orders. Three years later, the organization changed its name to the Leadership Conference of Women Religious and instituted collaborative structures to adapt to perceived modern needs. In 1976 the conference adopted the priorities of education, women's issues, justice, and further collaboration.

The LCWR publishes a newsletter and a journal

and promotes selected programs. In 1990 the organization began aiding religious women in Central and Eastern Europe, and in 1991 it began working with the Conference of Major Superiors of Men. Currently, the conference has approximately 1,000 members, leaders of their respective communities in the United States and who represent approximately 95 percent of the 73,000 women religious in the United States.

In February 2009 the Congregation for the Doctrine of the Faith appointed Bishop Leonard Blair of Toledo to oversee an assessment of the LCWR and its programs from a doctrinal perspective. Bishop Blair issued his reports to the congregation in December 2009 and June 2010. In 2012 the congregation issued a "Doctrinal Assessment of the Leadership Conference of Women Religious."

The assessment noted the remarkable work of the women religious of the LCWR communities, but it also listed a number of serious issues with the activities of the conference, in particular the absence of clear teachings on the right to life from conception to natural death, deviations in some areas from Church teachings in human sexuality and the ordination of women, and concerns with the materials being used for the formation of new religious. The Congregation for the Doctrine of the Faith named Archbishop J. Peter Sartain of Seattle to proceed with a process of discussion with the LCWR, including revising the LCWR statutes to provide greater clarity about its mission and responsibilities; reviewing LCWR plans and programs, including speakers invited to the annual assembly; creating new materials for initial and ongoing formation that provide deeper understanding of the Catholic faith; reviewing and offering guidance on liturgical texts and practices, putting the Eucharist and the Liturgy of the Hours at the center of LCWR events and programs; and reviewing affiliated organizations — namely, Network and the Resource Center for Religious Institutes. On June 1, 2012, the LCWR issued a statement largely rejecting the assessment. Nevertheless, the assessment would be subject to ongoing meetings and discussions.

Leavenworth, Diocese of. *See* **Kansas City in Kansas, Archdiocese of**

Legion of Decency

An organization founded in April 1933 by the American Catholic bishops to aid the faithful in their choices of motion pictures for their families, the Legion of Decency was initially called the Catholic Legion of Decency. The rationale for its existence was stated by the apostolic delegate to the United States, Archbishop (later Cardinal) Amleto Cicognani, when he described the legion as being designed and instituted "for the purification of the cinema, which has become a deadly menace to morals."

Although established by the bishops, the Legion attracted Protestant clerics and even Jewish rabbis, so that the following year it was renamed the National Legion of Decency. The organization provided a biweekly critique of films and led to the establishment of Catholic film centers around the world. Pope Pius XII clearly defined the cinematic ideals being sought in his encyclical *Miranda Prorsus*, issued on September 8, 1957. A pledge was also distributed to participating Catholics to clarify their views and cooperation. The Legion also produced a list of ratings for films in order to provide "a moral estimate of current entertainment feature motion pictures."

The national structure gradually became more focused as a Catholic initiative, and in 1966 the Legion was renamed the National Catholic Office for Motion Pictures. In time, it was attached to the United States Catholic Conference. The Legion of Decency's influence on the content and themes of films was considerable for a number of decades. Its waning influence, however, signaled a decline in the ability of the Church to shape the content and quality of modern film.

Legion of Mary

The largest apostolic organization of Catholic laypeople in the Church, the Legion of Mary is dedicated to promoting the glory of God through the sanctification of its members under the banner of Our Lady. The Legion boasts a long list of martyred members in China and in other communist countries, killed by the authorities in those countries because of their zeal and effectiveness.

The Legion of Mary was founded on September 7, 1921, in Ireland by Frank Duff. Members seek to work with their pastors and bishops to conduct evangelization and ministerial apostolates. Dedicated to the Blessed Virgin Mary, the Legion is aware of the ongoing war between the Church and secular humanism, as well as political or ideological positions that refute religion. The Legion of Mary was introduced into the United States on November 27, 1931, by Father Nicholas Schaal in Raton, New Mexico. Since then, it has grown throughout the country. The work of members includes gatherings once a week for prayer and extensive programs of service, including door-to-door evangelization, parishioner visitation, prison ministry, visits to the sick and the aged, and spiritual support for the parish community. Currently, there are over three million members around the world.

Lemcke, Henry (July 27, 1796–November 29, 1882)

A convert and a missionary priest, Henry Lemcke served as an aide to Father Demetrius Augustine Gallitzin. He was born in Rhena, Mecklenburg, Germany. Ordained as a Protestant minister, he converted to Catholicism on April 21, 1824, and studied for the priesthood. Ordained on April 11, 1826, Father Lemcke arrived in the United States in 1834. He was assigned to Holy Trinity Church in Philadelphia and then was sent to Loretto, Pennsylvania, to assist Father Gallitzin, who had founded the Catholic community.

Father Lemcke resided at Ebensburg near Loretto and assumed the pastoral duties of a portion of Father Gallitzin's parish area. In 1836 he established another settlement in a region called Carrollton. When Father Gallitzin died, Father Lemcke became the pastor of Loretto. He also induced the Benedictine abbot Boniface Wimmer to come to the United States to found an abbey, St. Vincent's, in 1802. Father Lemcke joined that community and three years later went to Kansas to prepare for the founding of the Abbey of Atchison. After serving in New Jersey for a time, Father Lemcke went back to Carrollton, where he died. He wrote a respected biography of Father Gallitzin.

Le Mercier, François (October 4, 1604–June 12, 1690)

A French missionary in New France, François Le Mercier was born in Paris and entered the Society of Jesus there in 1620. He was subsequently assigned to serve as a teacher before receiving his orders to go to Canada for duties as a missionary. He arrived in Québec in July 1635 and set out with Father Pierre Pijart for the territory of the Hurons. He spent the next fifteen years laboring among them and received the Huron name of Chaüosé. He abandoned his mission among them only in 1650, when the Iroquois brought extensive destruction to the region.

Going back to Québec, he served in pastoral ministry until 1653 when he was named rector of a college and superior of the whole Canadian mission. He remained in his post until 1656, when he named himself the head of a dangerous mission to the Onondagas. His labors continued over the next years, and he again served as superior of the Canada missions from 1665 to 1671. In 1671 he became an official at the Jesuit College at Québec. Two years later, he was sent to be a visitor of the French missions in South America and in the Antilles. He remained in this post for ten years and died on Martinique. He is also known for his work in compiling the *Jesuit Relations* for 1653, 1654, 1655, and 1665 to 1670.

Le Moyne, Charles (1626–1683)

A French colonial leader in Canada, Charles Le Moyne was also the founder of a prominent Canadian family. Born in Dieppe, France, Le Moyne migrated to Canada in 1641 and worked for the Jesuits among the Hurons in a variety of roles, including as a trader and interpreter, owing to his proficiency in Native American languages. He also earned a well-deserved reputation for his martial prowess against the Iroquois.

In 1654 Le Moyne married Catherine Primot, and their union resulted in fourteen children. Seven of his sons were renowned for their bravery and several became governors of cities or provinces, and were awarded the title of "Maccabees of New France." The two most prominent were Pierre Le Moyne, Sieur d'Iberville, and Jean-Baptiste Le Moyne, Sieur de Bienville. In recognition of his services to France in the New World, Le Moyne was made a noble in 1668 and received the title of Sieur de Longueuil.

Le Moyne, Simon (1604–1665)

A Jesuit missionary to the Iroquois nation, Simon Le Moyne was an expert in Native American languages and thoroughly aware of Indian traditions and lifestyles. He was born in Beauvais, France, and entered the Society of Jesus in 1622. Completing his seminary training, he was ordained and assigned to various positions in the Society and then sent to the missions. Father Le Moyne arrived in Canada in 1638.

He went immediately to the Iroquois villages and to the Mohawks, traveling to present-day Manhattan, where Peter Stuyvesant welcomed him courteously. Sent on five separate missions to Mohawk enclaves, Father Le Moyne earned their respect, although on more than one occasion he was threatened with death. The esteemed Chief Garaconthié trusted Father Le Moyne and kept him alive in one incident after the priest had been tortured. Father Le Moyne was able to counsel other prisoners and to secure their release, leading them to safety. When peace came to the area, Father Le Moyne asked to return to the Mohawks, but died at Cap de la Madeleine. Chief Garaconthié eulogized him at the funeral, as the Iroquois openly mourned their loss.

L'Enfant, Pierre Charles (August 2, 1754–June 14, 1825)

An architect and engineer, Pierre Charles L'Enfant designed the city of Washington, D.C. The plan of the city is based on principles employed by André Le Nôtre in the palace and garden of Versailles, where L'Enfant's father had worked as a court painter, and on Domenico Fontana's scheme for the replanning of Rome under Pope Sixtus V in 1585. He was born in France and arrived in America in 1777. L'Enfant, who stood six feet tall and had an aristocratic bearing, had received a commission from Americans in France. During the War of Independence, he spent time at Valley Forge, was wounded in action, and in 1783 attained the rank of major of engineers. Following the war, L'Enfant painted portraits of George Washington and designed pavilions and stages for patriotic events. When Congress decided in 1791 to build a capital city on the Potomac, George Washington asked L'Enfant to prepare a design,

which was accepted, but dismissed him in the following year because of his insistence on complete control of the project. Virtually penniless because he was not paid for his work, L'Enfant haunted the halls of Congress for some kind of payment for his designs. He received two small grants — most of which went to his creditors — and ended up as the guest of Thomas and William Digges. He was buried at the base of a tree on a Digges estate. L'Enfant also designed the old City Hall in New York circa 1787 and the townhouse of the financier Robert Morris in Philadelphia, which was begun in 1793. In 1889 L'Enfant's plans were recovered from the archives, and the capital was developed in 1901 along the lines of his vision. In 1901 he was reinterred in Arlington National Cemetery, after his immortal contribution to the capital of America was fully recognized.

Leo XII, Pope (August 22, 1760–February 10, 1829)

Pope from 1823 to 1829, the successor to Pope Pius VII, Annibale Sermattei della Genga was born near Spoleto to a noble family. Ordained in 1783, he was appointed private secretary to Pius VI, subsequently serving as the papal representative to Lucerne, Cologne, and a number of royal courts in Germany. Made a cardinal in 1816 and vicar general of Rome in 1820, he was elected pope on September 28, 1823, in opposition to the Austrians by the so-called Zelanti, conservatives who were against the moderate reforms of Cardinal Ercole Consalvi, the secretary of state. Pope Leo XII proved a generally stern pontiff, resisting the spread of liberal ideas, especially in matters of doctrine. He condemned Freemasonry and strengthened the papacy's political control over the Papal States. His measures reduced taxation within the States, but their precarious financial situation remained. Although the European powers feared a sharp reversal of Pius VII's conciliatory foreign policy, Pope Leo XII actually came to an understanding of the value of sound relations, going so far as to seek the advice of Cardinal Consalvi. Concordats were negotiated with Hanover in 1824 and the Netherlands in 1827. He also promoted the emancipation of Catholics in England.

During Pope Leo XII's pontificate, the Catholic

Church in the United States continued to grow apace. He was responsible for the creation in 1825 of the Vicariate Apostolic of Alabama and in 1826 of the creation of the Diocese (later Archdiocese) of St. Louis.

Leo XIII, Pope (March 2, 1810–July 20, 1903)

Pope from 1878 to 1903, the successor to the long-reigning Pope Blessed Pius IX and predecessor to Pope St. Pius X, Gioacchino Vincenzo Pecci was born in Carpineto, near Rome, a son of a family of Italian minor nobility. Before his ordination in 1837, he studied at Viterbo from 1818 to 1824, the Roman College from 1824 to 1832, and the Academy of Noble Ecclesiastics from 1832 to 1837. The next year, he was named governor of Benevento and served from 1838 to 1841, and then governor of Perugia from 1841 to 1843. In

Pope Leo XII monument

1843 he was sent by Pope Gregory XVI as nuncio to Belgium and was made a titular archbishop. Appointed bishop of Perugia in 1846, he was elevated to the cardinalate in 1853 by Pope Blessed Pius IX. In Perugia, he was outspoken in his promotion of Thomism, founding in 1859 the Academy of St. Thomas Aquinas, and in his resistance to the anticlerical tendencies of the Sardinian government after its seizure of Perugia in 1860. Pope Blessed Pius IX named him camerlengo in 1877, and the next year, on February 20, 1878, he was elected pope on the third ballot.

Pope Leo XIII was probably chosen as a compromise temporary candidate, especially given his age (he was sixty-eight) and his supposed poor health. He thus surprised many observers by his energetic pontificate, his cautious, careful, and conciliatory policies, and his excellent health. His reign lasted twenty-five years and had two main concerns: turning the Church toward recognition of the social problems created by the Industrial Revolution and attempting to resolve the lingering crises in relations between the Church and various secular powers.

Clearly desirous of reestablishing the temporal power of the papacy that had been irrevocably lost in 1870, Pope Leo XIII commanded that no Catholics should participate in Italian elections. In Germany, he was able to reverse Pope Blessed Pius IX's intransigence toward Otto von Bismarck, thereby allowing the minister to ease the *Kulturkampf* without loss of political face. His hope of winning German support against Italy was a failure, however, and papal foreign policy received setbacks in England (where diplomatic efforts were rebuffed) and in France (where anticlerical legislation and anti-Catholic measures deeply troubled the French Church).

Pope Leo XIII had long been concerned with social issues, coming into contact with the implications of the industrial age while visiting London, Paris, and elsewhere when serving as a Vatican diplomat; he was also much impressed with the labors of St. John Bosco. He utterly rejected socialism, communism, and anarchy as leading inevitably to oppression and as inconsistent with Christian charity. Socialism was denounced in *Quod Apostolici Muneris* on December 28, 1878, but the pope recognized that more than denunciatory proclamations were needed.

A clear social policy for the Church was thus enunciated on May 15, 1891, in the encyclical *Rerum Novarum*, which has been called the Charter of Catholic Social Doctrine by Pope Blessed John

XXIII and earned Leo the title of the "Workers' Pope." He also maintained the heart of the policies of Pope Blessed Pius IX, condemning Freemasonry in *Humanum Genus* in 1884 and keeping tight control over the central administration of the Church.

With his doctrinal efforts, Pope Leo XIII promoted Thomism and learning, and missionary activities throughout the world. In the encyclical *Aeterni Patris* in 1879, he gave a profound affirmation of the greatness and value of St. Thomas Aquinas. Advancing Catholic scholarship, he gave impetus to scientific and astronomic studies and, in a significant gesture, opened the Vatican Archives in 1883 to all scholars, not just Catholic ones. He established a guide for biblical research in the encyclical *Providentissimus Deus* in 1893. Hierarchies were created in various countries, including North Africa, India, and Japan; his pontificate brought forth 248 new sees, 28 of them in the United States.

The long pontificate of Pope Leo XIII had a significant impact on the development of the Church in the United States. The pontiff was responsible for creating the metropolitan sees of Chicago (1880), St. Paul (1888), and Dubuque (1893); the dioceses of Kansas City (1880), Davenport and Trenton (1881), Grand Rapids (1882), Helena and Manchester (1884), Omaha (1885), Sacramento and Syracuse (1886), Belleville, Cheyenne, Denver, Salina, Lincoln, and Wichita (1887), Duluth, Jamestown (now Fargo), St. Cloud, Sioux Falls, and Winona (1889), Dallas (1890), Salt Lake (1891), Boise (1893), Tucson (1897), Altoona (1901), Lead (now Rapid City) and Sioux City (1902), Baker (1903); and the Vicariates Apostolic of Utah (1886) and the Indian Territory (1891).

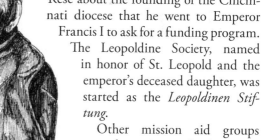

Pope Leo XIII

In 1884 Pope Leo XIII confirmed the decrees of the Third Plenary Council of Baltimore and issued three documents of note to the American Church: *Longinqua* ("To the bishops of the United States, on Catholicism in the United States") in 1885; a message to the American bishops in response to their congratulations on the papal jubilee in 1902; and the famous letter *Testem Benevolentiae* in 1898 on the issue of the Americanist controversy. (*See also* Americanism.)

He also named one American, Cardinal James Gibbons of Baltimore, to the College of Cardinals in 1886. In 1889 the pope sent then Monsignor (later Cardinal) Francesco Satolli as his representative to the founding of The Catholic University of America. He then sent Monsignor Satolli back to the United States in 1892 as the first apostolic delegate to the United States.

Leopoldine Society

A major benefactor of the young American Catholic Church, the Leopoldine Society, formed by Austrians in 1828 to aid missions, contributed vastly to the faithful in the United States. The society ended its sponsorship in 1921.

The program came about as a result of a visit by Father Frederick Résé, then the vicar general of the Diocese of Cincinnati, to Bavaria and Austria. He was seeking priests and funds. The archbishop of Vienna was so impressed with the account provided by Father Résé about the founding of the Cincinnati diocese that he went to Emperor Francis I to ask for a funding program. The Leopoldine Society, named in honor of St. Leopold and the emperor's deceased daughter, was started as the *Leopoldinen Stiftung*.

Other mission aid groups were also assisting the American Church at the time. The Society for the Propagation of the Faith, founded in Lyons, France, in 1822, and the Ludwig-Missionsverein served American mission needs. By 1861 the Leopoldine Society had given $430,000 to American missions. Many of the earliest dioceses in the nation benefited.

Some of the leading missionaries in America, including St. John Nepomucene Neumann and Bishop Irenaeus Frederick Baraga, were able to come to the United States because of Leopoldine support.

Lernoux, Penny (January 6, 1940–October 9, 1989)

A Catholic journalist and writer, Penny Lernoux was born in Los Angeles. She studied at the University of Southern California and became a journalist for the United States Information Agency, a government agency with the task of promoting U.S. policy overseas. Lernoux worked in Rio de Janeiro, Brazil, and Bogotá, Colombia, for the USIA until 1964, when she transferred to Caracas, Venezuela, to write for Copley News Service. She continued writing for Copley until 1976 and reported from Venezuela, Argentina, and Colombia. In 1976 she was given the Alicia Patterson Foundation grant for her work on South America and subsequently became a freelance writer.

Deeply concerned with the sociopolitical conditions in Latin America, Lernoux began writing extensively on social issues and became an outspoken supporter of liberation theology. Her first book, *Cry of the People: The Struggle for Human Rights in Latin America,* published in 1977, won a Sidney Hillman Foundation Book Award in 1981. Lernoux later won the Maria Moors Cabot Award from Columbia University in 1986 and several honorary doctorates. Around that time, she also began writing for the *National Catholic Reporter* as a Latin American correspondent and wrote additionally for *The Nation.* In 1989 she published *People of God: The Struggle for World Catholicism,* a sympathetic examination of dissent in the Church. At the time of her diagnosis with lung cancer, she was working on a history of the Maryknoll Sisters. She died in Mount Kisco, New York.

Her book on the Maryknoll Sisters was completed by Arthur Jones and Robert Ellsberg and published in 1993 as *Hearts on Fire: The Story of the Maryknoll Sisters.* The Penny Lernoux Memorial Library in Minneapolis was established in her honor.

Levada, William J. (June 15, 1936–)

Prefect for the Congregation of the Faith from 2005, former archbishop of Portland and San Francisco, and a cardinal, William Joseph Levada was born in Long Beach, California. He was the son of Joseph Levada Jr. and Lorraine Nunez Levada. He spent three years in Texas, but most of his youth was in Long Beach. Called to the priesthood, he studied at the seminary college in the Archdiocese of Los Angeles and was then sent in 1958 for seminary formation in Rome at the North American College. Ordained in Rome on December 20, 1961, he completed his graduate theological studies at the Pontifical Gregorian University, where he earned a doctorate in sacred theology magna cum laude.

Returning to the United States, he was assigned to pastoral service for five years in the Archdiocese of Los Angeles, including part-time high school instruction and college campus ministry. He went on to teach theology at St. John's Seminary School of Theology in Camarillo, California, and was the first director of Continuing Education for the Clergy in the archdiocese.

In 1976 Father Levada was named an official of the Congregation for the Doctrine of the Faith in Rome. He served there for six years and also taught theology at the Pontifical Gregorian University. In 1982 he was appointed executive director of the California Catholic Conference of Bishops in Sacramento. The following year, on March 24, 1983, he was named titular bishop of Capri and auxiliary bishop of Los Angeles. Consecrated on May 12, 1983, he was appointed in 1984 by Cardinal Timothy Manning of Los Angeles episcopal vicar for Santa Barbara County. Two years later, he was named chancellor and moderator of the curia. That same year, on July 1, 1986, he was promoted to the metropolitan see of Portland in Oregon.

While serving as archbishop of Portland, from 1986 to 1993, Archbishop Levada was also the only American bishop on the editorial committee of the Vatican Commission for the *Catechism of the Catholic Church.* He wrote the *Catechism*'s glossary, which was published in the English-language second edition.

On August 17, 1995, Archbishop Levada was appointed coadjutor archbishop of San Francisco and assumed direction of the archdiocese on December 27, 1995. As archbishop, he took part in the Special Assembly for America of the World Synod of Bishops, held in Vatican City from November 16 to December 12, 1997; he was also named to its post-synodal council.

On May 13, 2005, he was named prefect of the

Congregation for the Doctrine of the Faith, as successor to Cardinal Joseph Ratzinger, who had been elected only weeks before as Pope Benedict XVI. The new prefect was charged with defending the integrity of Catholic teachings. He attended the XI General Ordinary Assembly of the World Synod of Bishops in Vatican City October 2–23, 2005. On March 24, 2006, he was created cardinal deacon in the consistory of March 24, 2006, and received the deaconry of Santa Maria in Domnica. He retired as prefect on July 2, 2012.

Levadoux, Michael (April 1, 1746–January 13, 1815)

A member of the first Sulpicians to come to the United States and a founder of St. Mary's Seminary in Baltimore, Michael Levadoux was born in Clermont-Ferrand, in Auvergne, France. He joined the Sulpicians at Clermont in 1769, where he studied theology. In 1774 he was named director of the seminary at Limoges. He served there until 1791. Owing to the deteriorating conditions in France because of the Revolution, the superior-general of the Sulpicians considered it a sensible precaution to evacuate to a new country, where more could be accomplished for the faith. At the urging of Cardinal Antonio Dugnani, then nuncio to Paris, the Sulpicians chose the United States.

On July 10, 1791, the four Sulpicians sent to the United States — Charles Nagot, Anthony Gamier, John Tessier, and Michael Levadoux — purchased land and founded St. Mary's Seminary in Baltimore and opened the doors to the school in October of that year. Father Levadoux served as treasurer for a year and was then assigned to the Illinois Mission. He worked chiefly in the area around Cahokia and Kaskaskia.

Considered as a strong candidate to succeed Father Nagot as superior of the Sulpicians in the United States, Father Levadoux was asked by Bishop John Carroll instead to assist in the ministry around Detroit. His work took him as far as Fort Wayne, Indiana. In 1801 he was recalled to Baltimore by Father Nagot. Two years later, he was ordered back to France, where he became superior of the Seminary of St. Flour in Auvergne. After the end of the Napoleonic Wars in 1815, he was named head of the Seminary of Le-Puy-en-Velay.

Lewis, Edmonia (c. 1845–d. after 1909)

The first African-American sculptress, Edmonia Lewis was the daughter of an African-American father and an Ojibwe mother. Probably born in upstate New York, she was orphaned early in life, and it is likely that she grew up with a nomadic lifestyle in her mother's tribe. Her brother is generally credited with securing her entry into Oberlin College, the first to admit women and African-Americans.

While at Oberlin, she discovered a talent for drawing, and in 1863 she moved to Boston to study under the neoclassical sculptor Edward Brackett. Her early works focused on various abolitionists and heroes of the Civil War, including a noted bust of Colonel Robert Shaw, leader of an all-Negro regiment during the war. Copies were sold to raise money for the sadly underpaid black Union soldiers.

After the Civil War, she emigrated to Rome, where she remained for the rest of her life. She cut her own marble in her early years in Italy, and she soon became part of the crowd of artists and writers residing in Rome at the time, including Nathaniel Hawthorne, Henry Wadsworth Longfellow, and Harriet Beecher Stowe. Her reputation soon spread across Italy, and she was paid considerable sums for her work. Pope Pius XI visited her studio. Her works, at times forgotten in the years after her death, have been displayed across Europe and the United States, including the National Museum of American Art (now the Smithsonian American Art Museum). She is honored as a true pioneer for African-American women. Her last years and even her date of death are uncertain.

Lexington, Diocese of

Established on March 2, 1988, by Pope Blessed John Paul II, the Diocese of Lexington serves counties in the central and eastern sections of the state of Kentucky. Lexington was founded in 1775 in the Bluegrass area of the state and soon became known as the "Athens of the West" because of its college, public library, and musical society. The American Thoroughbred Breeders Association established its headquarters in Lexington, and the city also became a trading center for manufactured goods. The Diocese of Lexington is a suffragan see of the Archdiocese of Louisville.

The diocese has a profound Catholic heritage, as Kentucky was an early hub of the Church's development in the United States. René-Robert Chevalier, Sieur de La Salle, was in Kentucky in the late 1660s, but no permanent settlement appeared there for almost a century. Then, in 1750, Daniel Boone, Benjamin Cutbird, and Thomas Walker conducted a major exploration of the region. In 1774 James Harrod started Harrodsburg, and others came into the area, which they called "the Holy Land" because it offered Catholics freedom to worship according to the Church's rites. Daniel Boone, a Catholic, led another expedition through the Cumberland Gap, later called the Wilderness Road.

In 1787 Father Charles Whelan became the first resident priest in the area, and five years later Father William de Rohan began his ministry at Pottinger's Creek. Other pioneering missionaries were in Kentucky as well. Father Stephen T. Badin and Father Charles Nerinckx labored in the area of present-day Lexington in the late 1790s, joined by Dominican Father Edward D. Fenwick, who would become one of America's leading bishops. In 1805 Father Fenwick opened the Priory of St. Rose.

In 1808 the Diocese of Bardstown (now the Archdiocese of Louisville), was serving the Catholics of Kentucky, Indiana, Missouri, Ohio, Illinois, Wisconsin, and Michigan. One year before the diocese was erected, Sts. Peter and Paul Church was opened in Danville in Boyle County, within the modern boundaries of the Diocese of Lexington. The Diocese of Bardstown, under the leadership of Bishop Benedict Joseph Flaget, was transferred to Louisville on February 13, 1841. Twelve years later the Diocese of Covington was established amid turbulent times. The Bloody Monday riots on August 6, 1855, brought about the deaths of more than one hundred Catholics at the hands of Protestants.

The Civil War impacted on Kentucky, but the faith continued to prosper. St. Peter's (1812), St. Paul's (1865), and St. Peter Claver (1887) were opened in Lexington. Other parishes pioneering the faith were Good Shepherd at Frankfort (1845), Annunciation of the Blessed Virgin Mary at Paris 1856), St. Andrew at Harrisburg (1858), and Holy Family (1860) at Ashland.

The Black Patch War and coal mining brought new tensions to the area as Americans watched European clashes and then entered World War I. The Great Depression followed, and Louisville was elevated to the status of a metropolitan provincial see. Fort Knox was also designated as a federal gold reserve. The faithful of Kentucky joined their fellow citizens in supporting the nation's military effort in World War II.

Following the war, Lexington experienced an influx of the faithful and new parishes were opened throughout the area. The Holy See recognized the ever-increasing devotion of the Catholics of the area and erected the city as a diocese in 1988. The first bishop of Lexington was James Kendrick Williams. Bishop Williams had served as the auxiliary bishop of Covington since 1984 and was promoted to Lexington on January 14, 1988. He was installed in the Cathedral of Christ the King on March 2. Bishop Williams began his ministry by instituting the agencies and offices for diocesan administration and by consolidating and expanding diocesan resources. He retired on June 11, 2002, and was succeeded by Ronald W. Gainer, a priest of the Allentown Diocese. Bishop Gainer was appointed on December 13, 2002, and ordained a bishop on February 22, 2003. In 2011 there were 45,000 Catholics, 74 priests, and 49 parishes in the diocese.

Ligutti, Luigi (March 21, 1895–December 28, 1983)

Director of the National Catholic Rural Life Conference and an advocate of rural ministry, Luigi Ligutti was born near Udine, Italy. He migrated to the United States with his family in 1912, and they settled in Iowa. Called to the priesthood, he entered St. Ambrose College in Davenport and then completed his training at St. Mary's Seminary in Baltimore. Ordained a priest on September 22, 1917, for the Diocese of Des Moines, he subsequently studied at The Catholic University of America in Washington, D.C., and then held a variety of pastoral assignments.

The experience of performing his ministry in the rural environment of Iowa left a considerable mark on him, and Father Ligutti developed a commitment to the cause of rural life. In 1937 he was appointed the executive secretary of the National Catholic Rural Life Conference. With Father John Rawe, S.J., he wrote *Rural Roads to Security*. Owing to his many duties, in 1940 he resigned as pastor in Iowa and devoted himself full-time to the work of the NCRLC. He remained its executive secretary until 1958, when he was appointed director of international affairs.

Respected throughout the Church for his work, Father Ligutti was named in 1948 the Vatican Observer to the Food and Agricultural Organization of the United Nations. In this capacity, he was consulted by Pope Blessed John XXIII on pertinent sections of his famous encyclical *Pacem in Terris* (1958) and influenced the pope's subsequent encyclical, *Mater et Magistra* (1961). Father Ligutti took part in the Second Vatican Council and directly helped shape conciliar statements on migration, rural life, and land issues, particularly in the pastoral constitution *Gaudium et Spes*. In 1971 he founded Agrimissio, an international organization based in Rome and dedicated to agrarian life in the developing world. His last years were spent in Rome, where he served as a canon of Santa Maria Maggiore.

Lincoln, Diocese of

Established on August 2, 1887, by Pope Leo XIII, the Diocese of Lincoln serves counties in the southern part of the state of Nebraska, below the Platte River. Lincoln is the capital city of Nebraska, originally called Lancaster and renamed for President Abraham Lincoln when it was chosen as the state seat. By 1870 the city was a railroad junction and maintained its connection with transportation while developing as a grain and manufacturing center. The Diocese of Lincoln is a suffragan see of the Archdiocese of Omaha.

The Catholic legacy of Lincoln dates to about 1720, when the expedition of Pedro de Villasur, accompanied by a large military force and by Franciscan Father Juan Mingues, entered the area. Villasur and Father Mingues were slain by the Pawnees in a bloody confrontation. The Mallet brothers, Paul and Pierre, were in the region in 1739, and French Catholic fur trappers followed. The territory was included in the Louisiana Purchase in 1803 and became part of the United States.

One of America's most revered missionaries, Jesuit Father Pierre-Jean De Smet, established a mission at Council Bluffs, Iowa, in 1827, and he entered Nebraska to baptize babies of the Oto Indian nation. He also celebrated Mass during the Great Plains Council on September 14, 1851, which was held just inside the present-day state border.

The Holy See had established a Vicariate Apostolic of the Territory East of the Rocky Mountains in 1850, and the Jesuit missionary, Father Jean Baptiste Miège served as vicar apostolic. Seven years later, Congress established the Nebraska Territory, which included all the lands between the Missouri River and the Rocky Mountains, from Texas to Canada. In 1857 the Holy See erected the Vicariate Apostolic of Nebraska, appointing Bishop James Miles O'Gorman, a Trappist, as vicar apostolic. He established Omaha as his see city, invited religious communities to labor for the faithful, and provided a firm diocesan foundation.

Bishop O'Gorman was succeeded in 1876 in Omaha by Bishop James O'Connor, the former spiritual director of St. Katharine Drexel. In 1885 Omaha was erected as a diocese, and two years later, Lincoln was established canonically as well. The Lincoln area of Nebraska was highly Catholic, and parishes were serving the faithful. St. Benedict's Church in Nebraska City was erected in 1856, St. Mary's in Lincoln dates to 1867, and Immaculate Conception in Rulo to 1863. St. Andrew's was opened in 1866, and St. Joseph's in Beatrice opened in 1869. Sts. Peter and Paul in Falls City and St. Stephen in Exeter were operating in 1871. Other parishes were founded in the area that would become the diocese.

Bishop Thomas A. Bonacum was the first bishop of Lincoln, consecrated on November 20, 1887. Attending the Third Plenary Council in Baltimore as a theologian, he had been nominated as the first bishop of the Diocese of Belleville. That diocese was not erected immediately, so he was appointed to Lincoln. He found twenty-nine parishes operating and seventy-four missions in the diocesan territory, and he expanded other facilities and instituted the agencies and offices for diocesan administration. Bishop Bonacum also established schools, hospitals, and more parishes. The area suffered a severe drought and economic depression, but the diocese continued to maintain older institutions and to provide new parishes for the growing Catholic population. Bishop Bonacum died on February 6,

1911, and was buried on the grounds of St. Thomas Orphanage after decades of faithful service.

The second bishop of Lincoln was J. Henry Tihen, who was consecrated on July 6, 1911. Bishop Tihen continued the expansion programs of the diocese and built new facilities until September 21, 1917, when he was transferred to the Diocese of Denver.

His successor was Bishop Charles J. O'Reilly, who had served as the bishop of Baker City since 1903. Bishop O'Reilly was transferred to Lincoln on March 20, 1918, as America was supporting the military defenses for World War I. He supported the war efforts and continued to build diocesan facilities until he died on February 4, 1923.

The fourth bishop of the Diocese of Lincoln was Francis J. L. Beckman, who was consecrated on May 1, 1924. He led the diocese in the era following World War I, a turbulent time in which Nebraska experienced growth and manufacturing expansion, and then economic collapse. Bishop Beckman was promoted on January 17, 1930, to the Archdiocese of Dubuque.

His successor was Louis B. Kucera, who was consecrated as the bishop of Lincoln on October 28, 1930. Bishop Kucera was installed in the diocese in an era of economic suffering, as the nation was in the grip of the Great Depression. He maintained diocesan services, founded the Congregation of the Marian Sisters of the Diocese of Lincoln, and established a diocesan newspaper. Bishop Kucera also initiated charitable organizations to alleviate the needs of the faithful and led the diocese through the grim years of World War II. He died on May 9, 1957.

The sixth bishop of Lincoln was James V. Casey, who had served as auxiliary bishop of the diocese and succeeded to the see on June 14, 1957. Bishop Casey built the new Cathedral of the Risen Christ, which was dedicated on August 18, 1965. He also erected a new chancery, a Marian Center, and high schools. Bishop Casey served the diocese for a decade, being promoted to the Archdiocese of Denver on February 22, 1967.

His successor was Bishop Glennon P. Flavis, who had served as auxiliary bishop of the Archdiocese of St. Louis since 1957. He was promoted to the Diocese of Lincoln on May 29, 1967. He

implemented the reforms mandated by the Second Vatican Council and maintained diocesan facilities in the face of changing populations from rural to urban areas. Bishop Flavin also instituted ministries for Hispanic Catholics in the area. He retired on March 24, 1992.

The eighth bishop of Lincoln, Fabian W. Bruskewitz, was consecrated on March 24, 1992. Bishop Bruskewitz inaugurated the Diocesan Eucharistic Congress, a diocesan synod, and charitable programs. He also opened St. Gregory the Great Seminary in 1998 and Our Lady of Guadalupe Seminary in 2000. Bishop Bruskewitz attracted religious orders and congregations to the diocese, welcoming Carmelite Cloistered nuns from Las Vegas. In 2011 there were 96,000 Catholics, 158 priests, 141 women religious, and 133 parishes in the diocese.

Little Rock, Diocese of

Established on November 28, 1843, by Pope Gregory XVI, the Diocese of Little Rock serves all of the state of Arkansas. The capital of the state, the site was named by Bernard de la Harpe in 1722, who called two rocks on the banks of the Arkansas River *la petite roche* and *la grande roche*. La Harpe started a trading post beside the little rock. In 1812 William Lewis, a trapper, built a home at Little Rock, and in 1821 the site became the territorial capital. A river port with railroad connections, the city is also a manufacturing center. The Diocese of Little Rock is a suffragan see of the Archdiocese of Oklahoma City.

The Catholic heritage of the region opened in 1541 when Hernando de Soto led an expedition into present-day Arkansas. His chaplains conducted a *Te Deum* ceremony in the area on June 25 of that year. In July 1673 Jesuit Father Jacques Marquette and Louis Joliet spent two weeks at the mouth of the Arkansas River. René-Robert Chevalier, Sieur de La Salle, was in the region in 1682. He gave a land grant to Henri de Tonti, who founded a settlement, listed as "Arkansas Post" or "Arkansas Point," at the junction of the Arkansas and Mississippi rivers, but abandoned the site eventually.

In 1700 Jesuit Father Jacques Gravier celebrated a Mass on November 1 in Arkansas. De Tonti's settlement of Arkansas Post was reopened two decades after Father Gravier visited there. Another Jesuit, Father Paul du Poisson, who was later slain in Mississippi, served Arkansas Post for two years. He was followed by the Jesuit Father Louis Carette, who labored there from 1750 to 1758. Father Pierre Janin, sent to the area by the bishop of New Orleans in 1796, left after three years.

By 1826 Arkansas was under the ecclesiastical jurisdiction of the Diocese of St. Louis and Bishop Joseph Rosati. The area of Little Rock already had a Catholic presence. The Vincentians were in the area, serving the Indian tribes and white settlers from 1824 to 1830. In 1838 the Sisters of Loretto opened an academy near Pine Bluff and a school in Little Rock, but these institutions did not survive long.

The faithful of Little Rock were recognized by the Holy See in 1843, when the city was erected as a diocese. The first bishop of the Diocese of Little Rock was Andrew Byrne, who was consecrated on March 10, 1844. Bishop Byrne built churches, schools, and academies, laboring for almost two decades. He erected a wooden cathedral and welcomed the Sisters of Mercy and other congregations into the diocese.

Bishop Edward Fitzgerald

In the 1850s, Catholics of the area faced vicious attacks by Protestants, especially members of the Know-Nothing Movement, and Bishop Byrne had to defend the faith and safeguard Catholic properties. He died in Helena on June 10, 1862, and his remains were transferred to the Cathedral of St. Andrew in 1881.

The second bishop of Little Rock was Edward M. Fitzgerald. His appointment was delayed because of the Civil War, a period in which the Sisters of Mercy of Little Rock tended the wounded on both sides. Bishop Fitzgerald was consecrated on February 3, 1867, at age thirty-three. He attended the First Vatican Council, opposing papal infallibility when it was discussed but defending the doctrine when it passed the council vote. Bishop Fitzgerald started parishes, schools, and charitable programs. He was offered the sees of Cincinnati and New Orleans and declined them. Bishop Fitzgerald also introduced an outreach program for African-Americans and welcomed a large influx of immigrants into the diocese. He died of a stroke in Hot Springs on February 21, 1907.

His successor was Bishop John B. Morris, who had served as coadjutor bishop of the diocese with right of succession since 1906. Bishop Morris acceded to the see upon the death of Bishop Fitzgerald and faced a need for diocesan expansion and defense of the faith. He founded a college, a seminary, an orphanage, and a diocesan newspaper. He also had to contend with the Convent Inspection Act, passed by the Arkansas General Assembly in 1915. Government agents were mandated to inspect Catholic convents and rectories in response to attacks made on religious women by Protestants. The act was later repealed. Bishop Morris led the Diocese of Little Rock through the grim eras of World War I, the Great Depression, and World War II. He died on October 22, 1946.

The fourth bishop of Little Rock was Albert L. Fletcher, who had served as auxiliary bishop of the diocese since 1940. He succeeded Bishop Morris on December 7, 1946. Bishop Fletcher led the diocese through the era of racial integration, a turbulent time in which he defended the changes being made. He attended sessions of the Second Vatican Council and implemented the reforms mandated by that council. Bishop Fletcher retired on July 3, 1972.

His successor was Bishop Andrew J. McDonald, who was appointed to the diocese on July 4, 1972, and consecrated on September 5, 1972. Bishop McDonald led the diocese through a difficult period. Schools had to be consolidated or closed, and religious personnel declined. He ministered to the Hispanic Catholics who had entered the area and provided for immigrants from Southeast Asia. The Catholic population continued to grow, and Bishop McDonald provided for the faithful. He retired on January 4, 2000.

The sixth bishop of the Diocese of Little Rock, Bishop James Peter Sartain, was consecrated and installed on March 6, 2000. He was transferred after six years to the Diocese of Joliet and in 2011 was appointed archbishop of Seattle.

On April 10, 2008, Father Anthony B. Taylor, a priest of the Diocese of Oklahoma City, was appointed in succession to Bishop Sartain. He was ordained a bishop on June 5, 2008. In 2011 there were 132,000 Catholics served by 111 priests, 178 women religious, and 89 parishes in the diocese.

Lombardi, Vince (June 11, 1913–September 3, 1970)

A legendary football coach and devout Catholic, Vince Lombardi won five National Football League championships durin\g his ten years as head coach of the Green Bay Packers from 1959 to 1968. He was born in Brooklyn, New York, to an Italian immigrant, Enrico Lombardi, a butcher, and Brooklyn-born Matilda Izzo, the daughter of Italian immigrants. Lombardi entered the seminary in 1928, but after four years he decided against the priesthood and entered St. Francis Preparatory High School.

In 1933 he accepted a football scholarship to Fordham University in the Bronx and played on an impressive defensive line that became known as the Seven Blocks of Granite. It held Fordham's opponents scoreless several times during a string of twenty-five consecutive victories. Lombardi graduated with a bachelor's degree in June 1937. Two years later, after various jobs, he earned an assistant coaching job at St. Cecilia, a Catholic high school in Englewood, New Jersey. Lombardi also taught Latin, chemistry, and physics. He wed Marie Planitz in 1940 and in 1942 became the head coach at St. Cecilia.

The next years were spent in several increasingly prominent posts: assistant coach at Fordham from 1947 to 1948; assistant coach at the United States Military Academy at West Point from 1948 to 1953; assistant coach with the New York Giants from 1954 to 1959; and then head coach of the Green Bay Packers. He went on to lead the Packers to five world championships as well as victories in the first two Super Bowls. His Packer teams became legends in professional sports and included a host of future Hall of Fame athletes. Lombardi stepped down as head coach following the 1967 NFL season owing to illness.

In 1969 he took over as head coach of the Washington Redskins. He enjoyed immediate success, but in June 1970 he was diagnosed with intestinal cancer and died weeks later. His funeral at St. Patrick's Cathedral in New York City was attended by thousands, and President Richard M. Nixon sent a telegram of condolence signed "The People." The following year, he was enshrined in the Pro Football Hall of Fame, and a week after his death the NFL's Super Bowl trophy was renamed the Vince Lombardi Trophy. One of the fiercest competitors in sports history, Lombardi embodied many of the ideals of the Christian athlete and was one of the greatest motivational coaches of all time.

Longinqua Oceani

An encyclical letter issued on January 6, 1895, by Pope Leo XIII and addressed to the archbishops and bishops of the United States. The encyclical letter expressed the pontiff's good wishes and praises for the remarkable growth and development of the Church in America as well as the praiseworthy customs of the American people. The letter also warned against the dangers of the separation of church and state.

Pope Leo XIII noted that the success of the American republic was important to all, and he praised the immense progress of the Church. The pontiff noted, "Now if, on the one hand, the increased riches and resources of your cities are justly attributed to the talents and active industry of the American people, on the other hand, the prosperous condition of Catholicity must be ascribed, first indeed, to the virtue, the ability, and the prudence of the bishops and clergy; but in so slight measure also, to the faith and generosity of the Catholic laity."

Pope Leo XIII noted, as well, the condition of the Church in America: "The Church amongst you, unopposed by the Constitution and government of your nation, fettered by no hostile legislation, protected against violence by the common laws and the impartiality of the tribunals, is free to live and act without hindrance." Nevertheless, the pope warned that one should not draw the conclusion that America was the ideal situation in which the Church should exist. He stressed that the Church "would bring forth more abundant fruits if, in addition to liberty, she enjoyed the favor of the laws and the patronage of the public authority."

Pope Leo XIII proceeded to discuss two topics of importance to him that related to the American Church: the advancement of learning, and the perfecting methods in the management of Church affairs. He observed that progress in the first area was manifested in the foundation of The Catholic University of America in Washington, D.C., and also in the establishment of the North American College in Rome under his predecessor Pope Blessed Pius IX. The students, he felt, benefited from studies in the Eternal City, because, "they will carry back to their homes and utilize for the general good the wealth of intellectual attainments and moral excellence which they shall have acquired in the city of Rome." Progress on the second front, ecclesiastical administration, included the establishment by the Apostolic See of an American Legation and the progress of the bishops in their leadership and the care of souls.

The pope was also concerned for the welfare of those who have dissented from the faith, writing that, "Surely we ought not to desert them nor leave them to their fancies; but with mildness and charity draw them to us, using every means of persuasion to induce them to examine closely every part of the Catholic doctrine, and to free themselves from preconceived notions." Finally, he turned his attention to Native Americans and African-Americans.

General James Longstreet

Longstreet, James (January 8, 1821–January 2, 1904)

Noted Confederate general during the Civil War, James Longstreet was a convert to the faith. He was born in Edgefield, South Carolina, but moved with his family to Alabama in 1836. He graduated from the United States Military Academy at West Point in 1842 and served with distinction in the Mexican War and eventually became a major. With the start of the Civil War, he resigned from the U.S. Army in June 1861 and joined the Confederate cause.

Prized for his military abilities, Longstreet was named a brigadier general in the Confederate Army and fought with great skill at the First Battle of Bull Run. Promoted to major general, he began earning his reputation as a commander in the summer of 1862, when he campaigned with General Robert E. Lee and the Army of Northern Virginia. He fought during the Seven Days Battles, at the Second Battle of Bull Run, and at Antietam, where he held the Confederate line against a vastly superior Union attack.

Promoted to lieutenant general, Longstreet fought again at Chancellorsville and then at Gettysburg in 1863. During the course of the latter battle, Longstreet disagreed with Lee about strategy. He was sent next to Tennessee, where he played a key role in the Battle of Chickamauga. In 1864 he returned to the east and took part in the Battle of the Wilderness, where he was accidentally shot by his own men. He recovered and served during the Siege of Petersburg, where he commanded the defenses of the capital of Richmond. He surrendered with Lee at Appomattox Court House on April 9, 1865.

When the war ended, Longstreet went to New Orleans, where President Grant made him a surveyor of customs. On March 7, 1877, he converted to the Catholic faith. He then served as head of the Internal Revenue Department and as postmaster of Gainesville, Georgia. In 1880 Longstreet became the U.S. Ambassador to Turkey and was later U.S. Commissioner of Railroads under Presidents William McKinley and Theodore Roosevelt. His memoirs, *From Manassas to Appomattox*, was a defense of his military career. He died in Gainesville.

Lootens, Louis Aloysius (March 17, 1827–January 12, 1898)

The vicar apostolic of Idaho, Louis Aloysius Lootens pioneered the spread of the faith in the young United States. He was born in Bruges, Belgium, and studied for the priesthood at St. Nicholas Seminary in Paris. Ordained on June 14, 1851, he was assigned to the mission on Vancouver Island, but his poor health made it necessary for him to be appointed instead to San Francisco in 1860.

On March 3, 1868, he was made vicar apostolic of Idaho, and consecrated a bishop. He took up residence in Granite. In 1869 he approved the establishment of the first Catholic Church in Idaho, erected in Boise. Bishop Lootens attended the First Vatican Council and returned to Idaho to continue his ministry. Traveling across vast territories on horseback to visit every Catholic settlement in the region, he watched the mines close in southern Idaho and the exodus of Catholic families. He also faced staggering debts in the vicariate.

On October 25, 1875, Bishop Lootens retired from his vicariate because of exhaustion and ill health. He went to Vancouver Island, and there he served the local Native American communities and wrote books and articles. When he died, Bishop Lootens was buried in the cemetery of the Indians.

Lopez de Mendoza Grajales, Francisco (d. after 1569)

The first founder of a Catholic parish in the present-day United States, Francisco Lopez de Mendoza Grajales was a missionary to Florida. He accompanied the expedition of Pedro Menéndez de Avilés to Florida, landing in 1565 at modern St. Augustine. Father Lopez celebrated the first Mass in Florida on the feast of the Nativity of the Blessed Virgin Mary.

He tried to found a mission at Santa Lucia but was attacked by local hostile tribes. Starting a return voyage to Cuba, he was caught in a storm and blown back to the Florida coast. Believing that he was meant to labor in Florida, in June 1565 he founded St. Augustine Church (now a basilica) and started a parish. In time he was joined by five other priests. The last recorded documents concerning his pastorate date to 1569.

Loras, Mathias (August 30, 1792– February 19, 1858)

First bishop of the Diocese of Dubuque, Mathias Loras was a schoolmate and lifelong friend of St. John Vianney, the Curé of Ars. He was born in Lyons, France, and his family members, including his father, were victims of the French Revolution. He was trained for the priesthood by Father Ambrose Maréchal, who would become the archbishop of Baltimore. He was ordained on November 12, 1815, and had a distinguished career in France, serving as the head of two seminaries.

In 1827 Father Loras volunteered for the mission in America, accepting the invitation of Bishop Michael Portier of Mobile. Father Loras served as vicar general of the diocese and aided the foundation of Spring Hill College. On December 10, 1837, he was consecrated as the first bishop of the Diocese of Dubuque. After his consecration he returned to Europe to gather priests and funds. He arrived in Dubuque on April 18, 1839, with priests and seminarians, including Father Joseph Cretín, who would become the first bishop of St. Paul. Venerable Samuel Mazzuchelli, the Dominican missionary pioneer, was also on hand.

Bishop Loras erected a cathedral and seminary and took steamboats and canoes to travel up and down the Mississippi River to visit his scattered flocks. He purchased tracts of land for future parishes and welcomed the Sisters of Charity of the Blessed Virgin Mary, who had been the victims of arson attacks by Protestants in Philadelphia. The Trappist monks of Mount Melleray, Ireland, founded New Melleray Abbey near Dubuque, and in 1857 Bishop Loras returned to Europe to find even more priests and financial support. On Christmas morning in 1857, he celebrated Mass in the new Cathedral of St. Raphael, which was originally erected in 1833. Bishop Loras died in Dubuque, revered as a pioneer in the faith and a courteous, ascetic prelate.

Lord, Daniel A. (April 23, 1888– January 15, 1955)

One of America's most popular Catholic authors, Daniel A. Lord was a Jesuit priest. He was born in Chicago and educated at Loyola and St. Louis Universities. He entered the Society of Jesus in 1909 and was ordained in 1923. In 1925 Father Lord became the editor of *Queen's Work*, a magazine of Marian devotion, and he organized the Sodality of Our

Daniel A. Lord

Lady and the Handmaids of the Blessed Sacrament. He served as the director of the Sodality of the Blessed Virgin from 1948 to 1955, the largest Catholic youth organization in the United States. The author of thirty books, fifty plays, twelve musicals, and six pageants, Father Lord became a popular figure in the American Church. He served as a consultant to Cecil B. DeMille on the film *King of Kings* and helped draft the Motion Picture Production Code. Father Lord died in St. Louis.

Los Angeles, Archdiocese of

Established as the Diocese of the Two Californias on April 27, 1840, by Pope Gregory XVI, as the Diocese of Monterey-Los Angeles in 1859 by Pope Blessed Pius IX, and as the Diocese of Los Angeles and San Diego in 1922, the Archdiocese of Los Angeles was established on July 11, 1936, by Pope Pius XI. Los Angeles has diverse industries and manufacturing, and the area is the center of the nation's cinematic production studios. The archdiocese serves counties in a vastly populated area in Southern California and has suffragan sees in the region.

When the Diocese of the Two Californias (designating the Baja and the northern regions of the state) was erected, Catholic affairs were administered by Bishop Francisco Garcia Diego y Moreno, a Franciscan. He selected San Diego as his episcopal city but moved to Santa Barbara in 1842. He died on April 30, 1846.

The war between Mexico and the United States led to the ceding of California and other territories to the United States by Mexico as terms of the Treaty of Guadalupe-Hidalgo. California entered the Union in September 1850, and on June 30 of that year Dominican Father Joseph Sadoc Alemany, a revered pioneer of the faith, was consecrated for the Diocese of Monterey. Three years later, because of the population explosion resulting from the Gold Rush, the diocese was divided on July 29, and the Archdiocese of San Francisco was established. Bishop Alemany was promoted to that see, and the Vincentian Thaddeus Amat was consecrated as his successor in Monterey on March 12, 1854.

Bishop Amat was alert to the rapidly developing Los Angeles area and invited the Sisters of Charity of St. Vincent de Paul to establish a hospital, as well as a school and orphanage. By 1859 he recognized the pivotal position of Los Angeles and requested the Holy See to change the name of the Diocese to Monterey-Los Angeles. He moved to Los Angeles, and the Old Plaza Church of Our Lady of the Angels was designated as the co-cathedral. In 1865 Bishop Amat aided the opening of St. Vincent's College in Los Angeles. He also built the Cathedral of St. Vibiana, which was dedicated by Archbishop Alemany on April 30, 1876. Bishop Amat died on May 12, 1878, and was buried in the cathedral.

His successor was Bishop Francis Mora, who had served as coadjutor bishop of the diocese since 1873. Bishop Mora acceded to the see upon the death of Bishop Amat and began a series of expansion programs to meet the demands of the growing Catholic population. The Cathedral School was opened, and academies and homes for the aged and working girls were started as well. Bishop Mora suffered from poor health and requested a coadjutor. He retired on May 6, 1896, and returned to his native Spain.

Bishop George Montgomery, who had served as coadjutor bishop with right of succession in the diocese since 1894, acceded to the see upon the retirement of Bishop Mora. He continued expanding diocesan facilities until January 1, 1903, when he was promoted to coadjutor archbishop of the Archdiocese of San Francisco.

Bishop Thomas James Conaty was the fourth bishop of the Diocese of Monterey-Los Angeles, appointed on March 27, 1903. He had served as rector of The Catholic University of America since 1901. Bishop Conaty restored the diocesan missions and began ministries for the Native Americans on local reservations. He also instituted settlement relief programs in the poor districts and invited the Society of Jesus into the diocese. Bishop Conaty died at Coronado, California, on September 18, 1915.

His successor was Bishop John J. Cantwell, who was consecrated on December 5, 1917, while the United States was involved in World War I. Bishop Cantwell supported the military efforts of the nation while organizing charitable programs. He introduced the Confraternity of Christian Doctrine to the diocese and established an African-American apostolate. He was made the bishop of the Diocese of Los Angeles-San Diego in 1922, and was appointed an Assistant at the Pontifical Throne on September 30, 1929. Bishop Cantwell then led the faithful of the diocese through the Great Depression and World War II. On July 11, 1936, he was promoted to the rank of archbishop, as the diocese was created a metropolitan see. California became the first state to have two archdioceses. Archbishop Cantwell continued expanding facilities and aided the Legion of Decency, which he had founded in 1934. He opened seminaries, hospitals, and charitable agencies, and promoted other lay organizations and programs. His pastoral care of Mexican migrants earned him the Golden Rose of Tepeyac. Archbishop Cantwell died on October 30, 1947.

The second archbishop of the Archdiocese of Los Angeles was James F. McIntyre, who would become an American cardinal. He had served as an auxiliary bishop of the Archdiocese of New York since 1940 and as coadjutor archbishop of Los Angeles since 1946. Archbishop McIntyre was installed in Los Angeles on March 19, 1948. He started an expansion program, erecting almost one hundred parishes, thirty high schools, and five hospitals. He also established a seminary, a chancery office, a diocesan paper, and an office of Catholic welfare. On January 12, 1953, Pope Pius XII created him a cardinal priest. Continuing to serve the archdiocese, Cardinal McIntyre introduced a black apostolate and supported the founding of the Lay Mission Helpers. He retired on January 20, 1970, to St. Basil's Parish.

His successor was Archbishop Timothy Manning, who had served as an auxiliary bishop of Los Angeles in 1946 and then had been promoted as the first bishop of the Diocese of Fresno in 1967. On May 26, 1969, he was appointed as the coadjutor archbishop of the Archdiocese of Los Angeles and acceded to the see upon the retirement of Cardinal McIntyre. Pope Paul VI created him a cardinal priest on March 5, 1978. Cardinal Manning expanded the diocesan facilities and promoted pastoral outreach to the growing Latino population. He retired on September 4, 1985.

His successor was Bishop Roger M. Mahony, who was appointed archbishop of Los Angeles by Pope Blessed John Paul II on July 16, 1985. He was installed as the fourth archbishop of Los Angeles on

September 5, 1985. He had been auxiliary bishop of Fresno from 1975 to 1980 and then bishop of Stockton from 1980. Pope Blessed John Paul II created him a cardinal on June 28, 1991. Born in Hollywood, Cardinal Mahony was the first native Angeleno and the third archbishop of Los Angeles to be created a cardinal.

As archbishop, Mahony was long engaged both in the pastoral care of the sprawling Archdiocese of Los Angeles and in crucial social issues in California and in the United States. To assist the pastoral care of his flock of five million, in 1986 he created five pastoral regions (Our Lady of the Angels, San Pedro, Santa Barbara, San Fernando, and San Gabriel). In 1995 he announced plans to build the Cathedral of Our Lady of the Angels to replace the earthquake-damaged Cathedral of St. Vibiana. The new cathedral was dedicated on September 2, 2002, and was built at a cost of $190 million.

He likewise sought to increase lay involvement in archdiocesan affairs and administration, and he used a pastoral letter on the liturgy, "Gather Faithfully Together," to promote renewal in the parishes. Other vital documents and statements promoting pastoral and liturgical life included "As One Who Serves: Pastoral Statement on Parish Leadership" and "The Centrality of the Eucharist as the Source and Summit of the Life and Mission of the Church."

Cardinal Mahony was long engaged in issues of social justice and culture. To influence and provide direction to the film industry based in Los Ange-

St. Vibiana Cathedral in Los Angeles

les, he issued the statement "Film Makers, Film Viewers: Their Challenges and Opportunities" and established Catholics in Media to have Catholic concerns heard in the film and television industry. He has worked to promote ecumenical and interreligious dialogue, including issuing a document on the fortieth anniversary of *Nostra Aetate* (the Second Vatican Council's Declaration on the Relationship of the Church to Non-Christian Religions). He has also been one of the country's most outspoken advocates of immigration reform.

The archdiocese was also deeply troubled by the sexual abuse crisis. More than a thousand victims had filed claims against the archdiocese involving cases dating back to the 1930s. Since 2000 the archdiocese has reached a series of settlements that culminated in a 2007 agreement to pay $660 million in a global settlement. This was by far the most extensive settlement for any diocese or archdiocese in the long and terrible crisis. The costs of the settlement required the archdiocese to sell the Archdiocesan Catholic Center for $31 million.

On April 6, 2010, Archbishop José H. Gomez, the archbishop of San Antonio, was named coadjutor archbishop of Los Angeles. He acceded to the see on March 1, 2011. In 2011 there were 4.2 million Catholics in the archdiocese, served by 1,065 priests, nearly 2,000 women religious, and 287 parishes. There are also four Catholic colleges and universities, 51 high schools, and 230 elementary schools.

Louisiana

Known as the Pelican State, Louisiana is located in the south-central part of the United States. Louisiana is bounded on the north by Arkansas, on the east by Mississippi and the Gulf of Mexico, on the south by the Gulf of Mexico, and on the west by Texas. There are three natural land formations in the state: the East Gulf Coastal Plains in the east, the Mississippi Alluvial Plain in the central region, and the West Gulf Coastal Plain in the west. Louisiana entered the Union in 1812. The original inhabitants of the state were the Atakapa, Caddo, Mushogee, Natchez, and Tunica.

The faith was present in Louisiana from the earliest eras. Alvar Nuñez Cabeza de Vaca led an expedition into present-day Louisiana in 1526.

Hernando de Soto is believed to have been in the region as well in 1541. René-Robert Chevalier, Sieur de La Salle, claimed the entire area for King Louis XIV of France in 1682, and he gave Louisiana its name, honoring the French monarch. La Salle brought Franciscan Recollect missionaries with him, and they served the local Native American tribes. Fathers Anastase Douay, Maxime Le Clerq, and Zenobius Membré, who was martyred, began a series of missionary efforts.

In 1699 Pierre Le Moyne, Sieur d'Iberville, and Jean-Baptiste Le Moyne, Sieur de Bienville, erected a fort in Louisiana, and Franciscans served there until 1705. They were joined by members of the Québec Seminary mission program. Fathers François Jolliet de Montigny, Antoine Davion, and Jean-François Buisson de Saint-Cosmé all labored in the region. On March 3 of that year, Father Douay reportedly celebrated the first Mass in Louisiana. Father Buisson de Saint-Cosmé was slain in 1706 near present-day Donaldson.

Franciscans were also in western Louisiana, including Venerable Antonio Margil de Jesús, the revered pioneer of Louisiana and Texas. Antoine Crozat started a trading post in Natchitoches around 1700, and eight years later Father Jacques Gravier was slain by the Tunica. In 1718 Sieur de Bienville started the city of New Orleans, and in time a chapel was established at Kellona, Les Allemande. Capuchin Fathers Bruno de Langres and Philibert de Viandes arrived to serve in New Orleans, and Recollect Father Prothais Boyer became the resident priest of the city. Jesuit missionaries were also in the area, and the Acadians, who had been exiled from their homeland in the northeast by the British, found their way to Louisiana in great numbers. The Ursuline nuns started a convent in New Orleans in this era, the oldest convent in what is now the United States. They conducted a school, a hospital, and an orphan asylum.

European rivalries impacted upon Louisiana and other parts of the evolving colonies. In 1763 the Jesuits were expelled from the area, and the possession of New Orleans and Louisiana was determined by the Treaty of Paris, which provided that the British were the present owners of the region. In 1796 Spain was once again in control as the Treaty of Fontainebleau ceded the area to that country. St. Louis Cathedral in New Orleans was devastated by fire in 1788, at which time the Catholic ecclesiastical authority was Bishop Cirillo de Barcelona. In 1783 the Diocese of Louisiana and the Two Floridas was created by the Holy See, and Bishop Louis Ignacio Peñalver y Cárdenas arrived in New Orleans on July 17, 1795, to assume the see. He celebrated Mass in the restored cathedral. Bishop Peñalver y Cárdenas was transferred to Guatemala in 1801, and two years later Louisiana became part of the United States under the conditions of the Louisiana Purchase. Bishop John Carroll of Baltimore, America's first bishop, had jurisdiction over Louisiana as of that transfer.

Bishop Carroll appointed Bishop Louis Dubourg as administrator apostolic of the area, and Bishop Dubourg recruited priests and religious for missions. He resigned his see in 1826 and went to France, where he served as the archbishop of Besançon. Bishops Joseph Rosati, C.M., Leo-Raymond de Neckere, C.M., and Antoine Blanc labored in New Orleans following Bishop Dubourg. A seminary on Bayou Lafourche, colleges, academies, and hospitals were built. In 1842 the Sisters of the Holy Family, a black congregation, was founded at New Orleans by Henriette DeLille and Juliette Gaudin. Blessed Francis X. Seelos also served in New Orleans, which became an archdiocese in 1850. Three years later, the Diocese of Alexandria was erected as the Diocese of Natchitoches.

The Civil War impacted on Louisiana, and Archbishop John M. Odin led the faithful during the ordeal. Federal troops occupied New Orleans on May 1, 1862, and many establishments were damaged in the occupation. Louisiana was readmitted to the Union in 1868, but the Reconstruction lasted in the state until 1877. Cities and towns were occupied by carpetbaggers and adventurers from the north.

Dedicated archbishops served the faithful, and St. Frances Xavier Cabrini founded a school and orphanage in 1892. The archdiocese celebrated a centennial anniversary in 1893, attended by Cardinal James Gibbons and other prelates. In that same year, a hurricane devastated Louisiana, and Archbishop Francis Anthony Janssens used rafts and boats to visit and aid the suffering. Louisiana

also endured a yellow fever epidemic in 1905. Ten years later, St. Katharine Drexel opened educational institutions in the city of New Orleans. The Diocese of Lafayette was established in 1918.

The Catholics of Louisiana joined their fellow citizens in supporting the U.S. military efforts of World War I and suffered during the Great Depression that followed. Oil was discovered at Caddo Lake and elsewhere in the state, and Governor Huey P. Long was assassinated in 1935. Three years later, New Orleans held a National Eucharistic Congress, hosted by Archbishop Joseph Francis Rummel.

Louisiana was a vital port during World War II and prospered in the postwar era. In 1984 the New Orleans World Exposition was held, and the Vatican Pavilion was a starring display. Other dioceses were also erected in the state: Baton Rouge, Houma-Thibodaux, Lake Charles, and Shreveport. The state welcomed Vietnamese refugees following the military actions in Vietnam, and lay ministries were opened in conformity with the Second Vatican Council.

In August 2005 the state was again devastated by hurricanes. The most serious of these was the calamitous Hurricane Katrina that brought massive devastation to Louisiana and the Gulf Coast. Much of the city of New Orleans was flooded when the levees protecting the city collapsed. The long-term financial, pastoral, and administrative effects of Katrina will be felt for many years to come as the state and the dioceses and archdiocese in the Gulf Coast region struggle to rebuild. (*See also* New Orleans, Archdiocese of.) In 2011 there were 1.2 million Catholics, 900 priests, 789 women religious, and 451 parishes in the state.

Louisiana and the Two Floridas, Diocese of

An ecclesiastical jurisdiction established by Pope Pius VI in 1793 and lasting only a brief period of time, the Diocese of Louisiana and the Two Floridas served the region of the United States extending from the Gulf of Mexico to the Canadian border and west from the Missouri River to the Rocky Mountains. The term the Two Floridas denotes an artificial delineation between the eastern and western parts of the present-day state.

The first bishop of the diocese was Luis Ignacio Peñalver y Cárdenas. He chose the city of New Orleans as his seat, thus establishing the precedence of that city as a diocese. In 1801 Bishop Peñalver y Cárdenas was transferred to Guatemala, and in 1803 Louisiana became part of the United States. The area was divided into Upper and Lower Louisiana, and the Diocese of Natchitoches (now the Diocese of Alexandria) was erected. The Diocese of New Orleans was created as a metropolitan provincial archdiocese in 1850. The Two Floridas progressed on their own, and the Diocese of Louisiana and the Two Floridas was no longer needed and ceased to exist in America.

Bishop Luis J. Peñalver y Cárdenas

Louisiana Missions

A remarkably vast system of outposts of the faith during the French colonial period in America, the Louisiana missions served an area comprising the present-day states of Alabama, Arkansas, Louisiana, Mississippi, and Missouri, as well as the Tamaroa Mission at Cahokia, Illinois, and the Caddo Missions in Texas.

The first recorded missionaries in Louisiana were Recollect Franciscans, who arrived in 1682 with the expedition of René-Robert Chevalier, Sieur de La Salle. Fathers Anastase Douay, Maxime Le Clerq, Paul Du Ru, and Zenobius Membré came with the famed explorer but served the local tribes. Father Membré would later be martyred.

As early as 1560, Dominican missionaries were in Alabama and opened a mission at Santa Cruz de Nanipacua in present-day Wilcox County. La Salle was also in Alabama in 1682, and a Catholic colony was started by Pierre Le Moyne, Sieur d'Iberville, and Father Douay in 1699. In 1702 Fort Louis de Mobile was founded by La Salle at 27-Mile Bluff. Joining Father Douay at Mobile were priests from the Foreign Mission Seminary of Québec, and in 1721 the Carmelite Father Charles of St. Alexis served the Apallachee north of Mobile. Capuchin Franciscans were also present in Alabama. In 1724 Jesuit Michael Baudouin was with the Chickasaw and Choctaw. Missions were also established

at Fort Toulouse, Fort Tombeckbé, and Chickasaw. The missions in Alabama continued to prosper, and more Capuchins and Jesuits entered the area, serving the Chapitoula, Natchitoches, and Natchez. The British closed Alabama's Catholic missions in 1763.

In Arkansas, René-Robert Chevalier, Sieur de La Salle, visited Quapaw villages with Father Membré in 1682. In 1700 Jesuit Father Jacques Gravier celebrated Mass in Arkansas, and Father Nicholas Foucault labored with the Quapaw. Fort Toulouse opened for the Choctaw and remained a vital mission until the British outlawed the Catholic faith in that colony. Some of America's most renowned missionaries served in Arkansas, including Jesuit Fathers Paul du Poisson, Louis Carette, and Sebastian L. Meurin.

Priests from the Foreign Mission Seminary of Québec entered present-day Mississippi in 1699. Fathers Jean-François Buisson de Saint-Cosmé, Antoine Davion, François Jolliet de Montigny, and Thaumer de la Source began missions there. The Mississippi missions remained active, but many priests died in the Natchez War and others were martyred in Indian enclaves.

By 1659 Jesuit priests were at Ste. Genevieve on the western bank of the Mississippi River in present-day Missouri. In 1700 Jesuit Father Gabriel Marest founded a mission near St. Louis. The Old Mines area was also being served by priests from Cahokia, and the faith prospered with missions at St. Charles, the Carondelet, and Florissant. (*See also* Louisiana.)

Louisville, Archdiocese of

Established on April 8, 1808, by Pope Pius VII as the Diocese of Bardstown, transferred to Louisville on February 13, 1841, by Pope Gregory XVI, and created a metropolitan provincial archdiocese on December 10, 1937, by Pope Pius XII, the Archdiocese of Louisville serves counties in central Kentucky and has suffragan sees.

Louisville was organized in 1779, when George Rogers Clark and other settlers established Fort-on-Shore and Fort Nelson, within the limits of the present-day city. Louisville, located opposite the Falls of the Ohio, instantly assumed a strategic military and commercial importance. It was incorporated in 1780 and named after King Louis XVI of France, who had aided the American cause in the War for Independence.

The Archdiocese of Louisville shares in the Catholic legacy of Kentucky, which was called the "Holy Land" by the faithful because it offered freedom from Protestant persecutions. René-Robert Chevalier, Sieur de La Salle, was in the area in the 1660s, accompanied by priests. Almost one hundred years later, Daniel Boone, a Catholic, entered present-day Kentucky with Thomas Walker and Benjamin Cutbird. In 1774 James Harrod established the first permanent settlement, Harrodsburg, and in 1775 Dr. George Hart and William Coomes and his wife arrived. Mrs. Coomes established a school. In that same year, Daniel Boone led an expedition through the Cumberland Gap, later called the Wilderness Road. In 1776 Kentucky was made part of Virginia but then separated. Kentucky entered the Union in 1792 as the fifteenth state.

The Diocese of Bardstown was erected in Kentucky in 1808, and St. Joseph's Proto-Cathedral was established by Bishop Benedict Joseph Flaget. Many outstanding missionary priests were laboring in the diocese, which served as the ecclesiastical jurisdiction for Kentucky, Illinois, Indiana, Michigan, Missouri, Ohio, Tennessee, and Wisconsin. Fathers Stephen T. Badin, Charles Nerinckx, Edward D. Fenwick, O.P. (who would later become a pioneering bishop), Guy Chabrat, John Thayer, Anthony Salmon, Michael Fournier, Michael Barrieres, and Martin J. Spalding (who would become an archbishop) all served the faithful in the diocese. In Louisville, Father Philip Hosten was serving as pastor. He cared for victims of a typhoid fever outbreak and died of the disease.

In 1832 Bishop Flaget retired, and another Sulpician, John B. David, who had come to Kentucky with him, was appointed his successor. He delayed his consecration because he felt unworthy of the office and was made coadjutor bishop of the Diocese of Bardstown on August 15, 1819. The public outcry about the retirement of Bishop Flaget was so great that the Holy See reinstated him in 1833. Bishop David happily submitted his resignation and returned to his post at the diocesan seminary. He trained priests and administered the Sisters of Charity of Nazareth, which he had co-founded in 1812.

Bishop Flaget, recognizing the geographical challenges of the diocese in 1834, requested a coadjutor, and Guy Chabrat, a Sulpician who had been the first priest ordained west of the Alleghenies, was appointed to that position. He was consecrated on July 20, 1834, and assumed the administrative duties of the diocese. Parishes were being established throughout the sprawling episcopal jurisdiction, and religious communities were increasing.

In 1841 Bishop Flaget considered the strategic advantages of Louisville and petitioned the Holy See to relocate the diocese in that city. In 1848 the Trappists founded Gethsemani Abbey near New Haven, and five years later the Diocese of Covington was established. Catholics in Kentucky were being harassed, and arson was a constant threat. On February 11, 1850, the august Bishop Benedict Joseph Flaget died. The year before, the Cathedral of the Assumption in Louisville had been started. When it was completed in 1852, the remains of Bishop Flaget were placed in the cathedral crypt.

Bishop Chabrat, suffering from approaching blindness, had resigned in 1847 and had been given a pension and taken to his home in France. Bishop Martin J. Spalding had replaced him as coadjutor with right of succession on September 10, 1848. He became the fourth bishop of the Diocese of Louisville upon the death of Bishop Flaget.

Bishop Spalding consecrated the cathedral and welcomed new religious congregations into the diocese. On August 6, 1855, the Catholics of the diocese faced Bloody Monday, a day of Protestant rioting that caused deaths among the faithful. In the next decade, Kentucky remained neutral in the Civil War. The brother of Bishop Spalding, Father Benedict Joseph Spalding, administered the diocese throughout the tense era, and together they built parishes and served a rapidly growing Catholic population. On May 6, 1864, Bishop Spalding was promoted to the Archdiocese of Baltimore.

His successor was Bishop Peter Joseph Lavialle, who was consecrated on September 24, 1865. He had come to Kentucky with Bishop Chabrat and had been serving at St. Thomas Seminary.

He invited the Dominicans into the diocese and attended the Second Council of Baltimore. Bishop Lavialle visited every parish in the diocese. Becoming ill, he retired to Joseph's Infirmary and died on May 11, 1867.

Bishop William George McCloskey was the successor to Bishop Lavialle. He had served as the first rector of the newly opened North American College in Rome since 1859. Bishop McCloskey served the diocese for over four decades. He was consecrated on May 24, 1868, and started expanding diocesan facilities. Bishop McCloskey established parishes and invited religious communities into the diocese. The Carmelite Fathers, the Sisters of Mercy, the Little Sisters of the Poor, and the Congregation of the Resurrection entered the archdiocese, and Franciscan Sisters also arrived to serve the faithful. Bishop McCloskey's leadership provided steady growth, although he did experience some difficulties in his relationships with priests and religious. Bishop McCloskey died at Preston Park Seminary on September 17, 1909.

His successor was Bishop Denis O'Donaghue, who had served as auxiliary bishop of the Diocese (now Archdiocese) of Indianapolis since 1900. Bishop O'Donaghue was promoted to Louisville on February 7, 1910. He invited the Xaverian Brothers into the diocese, established a college, and supported the military efforts of the nation during World War I. Bishop O'Donaghue became very ill, and the diocese was assigned to an apostolic administrator. On November 7, 1925, he died.

Bishop John Floersh succeeded Bishop O'Donaghue, having served as coadjutor bishop with right of succession since 1923. He acceded to the see on July 26, 1924. In 1930 the Discalced Carmelite Nuns arrived in Louisville, and eight years later Bishop Floersh directed the opening of Ursuline College. In 1937 the Diocese of Owensboro was established, and Louisville was designated a metropolitan provincial see, an archdiocese. Archbishop Floersh continued establishing parishes and schools, as well as homes for children, a preparatory seminary, and Bellarmine College. He aided the people of Louisville during the Great Depression and World War II. Archbishop Floersh retired on March 1, 1967.

The second archbishop of Louisville was Thomas J. McDonough, who had served as the bishop of the Diocese of Savannah since 1960. He was promoted to Louisville on May 2, 1967. Archbishop McDonough continued maintaining archdiocesan facilities and implemented the reforms mandated by the Second Vatican Council. He retired on September 29, 1981.

The third archbishop of the Archdiocese of Louisville, Thomas C. Kelly, a Dominican, served as general secretary of the National Conference of Catholic Bishops and the United States Catholic Conference from 1977 and as auxiliary bishop of the Archdiocese of Washington. He was promoted to the archdiocese on December 29, 1981, and was installed in the Cathedral of the Assumption on February 18, 1982.

Archbishop Kelly embarked quickly upon a number of pastoral activities, including the restoration of the downtown Cathedral of the Assumption as a source of wider renewal in the city. His time as archbishop also included the creation of the see of Lexington in 1988, established with territory taken from the archdiocese. He retired on June 12, 2007, and was succeeded on the same day by Bishop Joseph E. Kurtz, who had been bishop of Knoxville since 1999. Archbishop Kurtz was installed on August 15, 2007. In 2011 there were 193,000 Catholics, 185 priests, 620 women religious, and 102 parishes in the archdiocese.

Louvain, American College of

A seminary for U.S. students in Louvain, Belgium, that also served as a community for English-speaking graduate-student priests and religious priests pursuing studies at the Catholic University of Louvain, founded in 1425. The college was administered by an American rector and faculty, and operated under the auspices of a committee of the National Conference of Catholic Bishops. The American College of Louvain was founded in 1857 through the efforts of Bishop Martin J. Spalding, bishop of Louisville, Kentucky, and Bishop Peter Paul Lefevere, bishop of Detroit, at the encouragement and blessing of Pope Blessed Pius IX.

The Catholic University of Louvain had been founded in Belgium by Pope Martin V on December 9, 1425, and the faculty of this prestigious institution had been established in 1432. The American

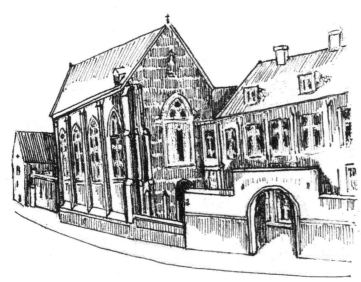

The American College of Louvain

bishops wanted to offer worthy American seminarians opportunities for classical European studies. Father Peter Kindekens had been sent in 1856 by Archbishop Francis P. Kenrick of Baltimore to establish a Roman school but had been forced to give up the project. A Belgian, Father Kindekens visited the Catholic University of Louvain and found that the administrators there supported the concept of an American establishment within their academic domain. The American bishops approved, and Father Kindekens returned to Belgium in 1857 as rector of the American College of the Immaculate Conception, using a property originally occupied by Cistercians in 1629.

The college was amalgamated formally with the Catholic University of Louvain in 1897. The initial plans for the college were for students to follow a course of theology and priestly formation, with the understanding that their preparations in philosophy would be undertaken in the United States. In 1906, however, a faculty of philosophy was established to provide a two-year course for students.

During World War I, the college served as an emergency hospital and dispensary, providing assistance to as many as fifteen hundred people a day. In the years after the war, the college underwent swift growth and accompanying financial and practical difficulties. In December 1939, as World War II began, the administration and faculty made the difficult decision to shut their doors and send students home for the duration of the conflict. In the next terrible years, the college survived the fighting, but the long-term fate of the seminary remained in doubt. Throughout the war, the American flag flew over the college, and the American seminarians who had remained on the campus served as ambulance drivers. The administrators were harassed by local German authorities, and one college official was taken prisoner but then released. The college remained intact when the war ended.

In 1949 the American bishops were uncertain whether the seminary should be reopened. In the end, the decision was made to reopen, thanks especially to the support of Bishop Russell J. McVinney, the bishop of Providence. In 1952 the college reopened its doors to the first new American seminarians. Father Thomas F. Maloney of Providence, Rhode Island, was named rector. Three years later, because of national support, the college had 114 students, representing 26 United States dioceses. The college also received encouragement from the Second Vatican Council, which provided guidelines and spiritual impetus in 1965.

Over the many years, the college educated a number of American bishops and almost 1,000 priests for the American Church. Owing to declining numbers of students, the college closed its doors in June 2011.

Lubachivsky, Myroslav John (June 24, 1914– December 14, 2000)

Major archbishop of Lviv and a cardinal, Myroslav Lubachivsky was born and raised in western Ukraine, in Dolyna, Eparchy of Ivano-Frankisvk of the Ukrainians. Called to the priesthood, he studied for three years in Lviv at the Greek-Catholic Theological Academy and went on to study at Innsbruck University in Austria, the theological faculty at Sion, Switzerland, the Pontifical Gregorian University and the Pontifical Biblical Institute in Rome, where he earned a doctorate in theology. Ordained a priest on September 28, 1938, at Lviv, he did pastoral work in Lviv from 1938 to 1942 and then did further studies from 1942 to 1947 that culminated in his doctorate.

Owing to the oppressive Soviet occupation of the Ukraine, Father Lubachivsky was sent to serve the Church abroad, specifically the Ukrainians who had migrated to the United States. From 1947 to 1980, he served in active ministry among Ukrainians in Michigan, Pennsylvania, Ohio, and Wisconsin. He was also secretary to the archbishop of Philadelphia of the Ukraines, secretary of Ukrainian section of National Catholic Welfare Conference, and a faculty member of the Ukrainian Seminary of Stamford. From 1967 to 1968, he was a faculty member of the Pontifical Ukrainian College of St. Josafat, Rome, and from 1969 to 1979 he was a faculty member for several schools and colleges.

On September 13, 1979, Father Lubachivsky was elected archbishop of Philadelphia of the Ukraines. He was consecrated on November 12, 1979, in Vatican City by Pope John Paul II, and on March 27, 1980, he was named archbishop coadjutor with right of succession of the major archbishopric of Lviv of the Ukraine. He acceded to the see of Lviv of the Ukraines on September 7, 1984. The following year, he was named to the College of Cardinals as a cardinal priest on May 25, 1985; he received the title of Santa Sofia a Via Boccea.

As major archbishop, Cardinal Lubachivsky was a major figure in the renewal of the Ukrainian Greek Catholic Church in the Ukraine, especially in the tumultuous period after the collapse of the Soviet Union. He had the enormous task of revitalizing a Catholic community that had long suffered true horrors under Soviet occupation, working to ease tensions with the Orthodox Church, and reestablishing Church institutions and relations with government officials. The task was an arduous one, and in 1995 Lubachivsky suffered a bout of pneumonia.

After Cardinal Lubachivky's death five years later, thousands of faithful stood in freezing temperatures to pay their last respects. He was buried in the crypt of St. George's Cathedral in Lviv. His successor was Bishop (now Cardinal) Lubomyr Husar.

Lubbock, Diocese of

Established on June 17, 1983, by Pope John Paul II, the Diocese of Lubbock serves the faithful in counties in northwestern Texas. The city, formed in 1890 from the settlements of Old Lubbock and Monterey, is the commercial center of the South Plains. It is named after Tom S. Lubbock, a signer of the Texas Declaration of Independence. Originally a ranching area, Lubbock markets cotton and grains as well as cattle, and promotes diversified agricultural and industrial products. The Diocese of Lubbock is a suffragan see of the Archdiocese of San Antonio.

The diocese shares in the Catholic history of Texas, begun by Franciscan missionaries circa 1682. Between 1690 and 1794, these priests and lay brothers opened three chains of missions in the area. Among the most revered was Venerable Antonio Margil de Jesús, who pioneered in evangelizing several regions of the present-day state, as well as Louisiana. Franciscan Friars Damian Massanet and Antonio de San Buenaventura y Olivares labored among many Native American tribes. In this era, Mission San Antonio de Valero was erected, honored today as the Alamo.

Mexican authorities secularized the missions, and Catholic properties were taken from the Church in a process that was completed by 1794. Spanish missionaries were expelled in 1820. Five years later, Stephen F. Austin and countless other settlers came into present-day Texas, embracing the Catholic faith. Texas at the time was under the ecclesiastical jurisdiction of the bishop of Monterey, Mexico. In 1842 the Vincentian John M. Odin was made prefect apostolic of Texas, and five years later became the first bishop of the Diocese of Galveston. San Antonio was erected as a diocese (now an archdiocese) in 1874, and Dallas became a diocese in 1890.

The Catholics of Lubbock had experienced the birth of the Republic of Texas and then statehood, followed by the Civil War and new eras of growth. Significant numbers of Catholics had moved into the area to work on the railroads and to start ranches and farms. Father David H. Dunn and other itinerant missionary priests were laboring in the region by 1900. Father Dunn served the burgeoning Catholic communities. Churches were established throughout the present diocese in the early 1900s.

The Catholics of the area supported the military efforts of the nation in World War I and endured suffering during the Great Depression. Circuit-rider priests, following the pioneering evangelical efforts of early American missionaries, visited communities, and the Diocese of Amarillo was erected in 1926. Agricultural industries flourished, oil fields were discovered during the 1930s, and the war effort during World War II aided the economy. In 1961 the Diocese of San Angelo was erected and the Cursillo Movement was active in the region. Lubbock's Catholics displayed a vibrant faith, and in 1983 the Holy See gave official recognition of that vitality by erecting the diocese.

The first bishop of Lubbock was Michael J. Sheehan. He was installed on June 17, 1963, in Lubbock and designated Christ the King as the diocesan cathedral. Bishop Sheehan also instituted the agencies and offices for diocesan administration and opened Catholic family services. A Diocesan Catholic Appeal was started to raise funds for diocesan facilities. Bishop Sheehan also instituted a diocesan newspaper. He headed a committee that produced a pastoral letter on evangelization by the Texas bishops. Lay movements and a deacon formation program were introduced into the diocese as well. Bishop Sheehan was appointed apostolic administrator of the Archdiocese of Santa Fe in 1993 and was installed as the archbishop of Santa Fe on September 21.

The second bishop of the Diocese of Lubbock, Plácido Rodriguez, C.M.F., had served as auxiliary bishop of the Archdiocese of Chicago since 1983. He was installed in the Diocese of Lubbock on June 1, 1994. Bishop Rodriguez took active steps to halt drugs and gang violence in the area and celebrated the Great Jubilee of 2000. In 2011 there were 81,000 Catholics, 58 priests, and 62 parishes in the diocese.

Lucas, Fielding, Jr. (1781–1854)

A noted cartographer, artist, and publisher, Fielding Lucas Jr., helped make Baltimore a publishing center in the early nineteenth century. Little is known about his early life, but in 1804 he founded Lucas Bros., Inc. in Baltimore and so established the first stationers in the United States. Two years later, he served as the Baltimore manager of the Philadelphia publishing firm Conrad, Lucas, and Co. when it opened its Baltimore offices. Lucas went on to become the earliest successful commercial map publisher in Baltimore. His first atlas was published in 1815–17.

In 1834 Lucas published *The Metropolitan Catholic Calendar and Laity's Directory,* a work that was given the new name of *Metropolitan Catholic Almanac* in 1838. In the 1845 edition, he included a map of the United States that was intended to provide a "glance" at the current situation of the dioceses in the United States. The almanac included as well a useful table of statistics from 1835 to 1845. Through his efforts and those of the Irish-born John Murphy, Baltimore emerged as a major center of publishing, and especially of Catholic publishing, until it was supplanted by New York.

Luce, Clare Boothe (April 10, 1903–October 9, 1987)

Author, playwright, ambassador, and politician, the wife of Henry C. Luce (publisher of *Time, Fortune,* and *Sports Illustrated*), and a convert to Catholicism, Clare Boothe Luce was born in New York City. Her father was a businessman and violinist, and her mother was a dancer. She grew up in Chicago and Memphis, Tennessee, and, after her parents separated, in France, where she lived with her mother. She studied at St. Mary's School in Garden City, New York, and Miss Mason's School in Tarrytown, New York, and early on wanted to be an actress. She understudied Mary Pickford before enrolling in Clare Tree Major's School of Theatre, but she soon lost interest in the theater. She journeyed to Europe with her parents, and in August 1923 she married George Tuttle Brokaw, a New York clothing manufacturer who was twenty-four years her senior. On August 25, 1924, Clare gave birth to a daughter, Ann Clare Brokaw, but her marriage ended in divorce in 1929 because of her husband's alcoholism.

In 1930 Clare joined the staff of the fashion magazine *Vogue* as an editorial assistant. The next year, she became associate editor of *Vanity Fair* and soon gained a wide reputation for her writing, especially her satires of New York society. In 1933 she became managing editor of *Vanity Fair*. The next year, however, she resigned.

On November 23, 1935, Clare Boothe, now thirty-two years old, married Henry "Harry" Luce, publisher and founder of *Time* magazine and the business periodical *Fortune;* he later founded *Life* magazine and *Sports Illustrated*. At the same time, Clare's play *Abide with Me* opened on Broadway, starting her career as a playwright. Her plays included *The Women* in 1936, *Kiss the Boys Goodbye* in 1938, and *Margin of Error* in 1939.

During World War II, she was active as a writer and a world traveler with her husband, and in 1942 she ran for a seat in the United States House of Representatives from Connecticut. She won easily and was reelected to a second term in 1944. The same year, her daughter was killed in an accident, and she suffered a nervous breakdown. Through the help of then Monsignor Fulton J. Sheen, she recovered her health and entered the Church in 1946.

Choosing to depart the House, she wrote about her conversion to Catholicism and in 1949 wrote the screenplay for the film *Come to the Stable*, a drama about two nuns. She then returned to writing plays, including *Child of the Morning* in 1952. That year, she returned to politics to campaign for Republican candidate Dwight D. Eisenhower, who named her ambassador to Italy. She resigned because of poor health in 1956 after being poisoned with arsenic from paint chips falling from the stucco on her bedroom ceiling. In 1959 President Eisenhower appointed her ambassador to Brazil, but she resigned only after a few days owing to an intemperate remark regarding a senator.

Clare Boothe Luce retired in 1964, the same year her husband retired. After Harry's death in 1967, she lived in Hawaii for many years. In 1981 President Ronald Reagan appointed her to the Foreign Intelligence Advisory Board. She died in Washington, D.C., at the Watergate Apartments. She is honored as one of the great women of the twentieth century.

Lucey, Robert E. (March 16, 1891–August 2, 1977)

Archbishop of San Antonio from 1941 to 1969 and one of the leading figures in the early efforts in the twentieth century in the promotion of Catho-

lic social teachings, Robert E. Lucey was born in Los Angeles, California, to John and Mary Nettle Lucey, the fourth of nine children.

Called to the priesthood, Lucey undertook his preparatory studies at St. Vincent's College in Los Angeles and St. Patrick's Seminary in Menlo Park, California. He was then sent to Rome for further studies at the North American College. He subsequently earned a doctorate in theology and was ordained on May 14, 1916, in the Church of St. Apollinaris in Rome.

Returning to the United States, Father Lucey devoted the next eighteen years to pastoral service in the Archdiocese of Los Angeles. He also worked as director of Catholic Charities, was a director of hospitals, acted as president of the California Conference of Social Work, and was a member of the executive board of the California State Department of Social Welfare. In addition, he launched the Confraternity of Christian Doctrine for the archdiocese and started a radio program called *The St. Anthony Hour*.

On May 1, 1934, Father Lucey was consecrated the bishop of the Diocese of Amarillo in the Cathedral of St. Vibiana in Los Angeles. His long pastoral experience in California proved enormously helpful in Texas. He promoted the apostolate of the Confraternity of Christian Doctrine and founded the *Texas Panhandle Register*, a diocesan newspaper. His reputation for social concerns and his ability made him the obvious choice to become archbishop of San Antonio when Archbishop Arthur J. Drossaerts passed away in 1940.

He was appointed to San Antonio on January 21, 1941, and set to work immediately. He started the Catholic Welfare Bureau, the Catholic Action Office, and the Archdiocesan Council of Catholic Men. Archbishop Lucey later began the Archdiocesan School Office, the Archdiocesan Council of Catholic Women, and the Archdiocesan Council of Catholic Youth.

He also asked the Vincentian Fathers to staff St. John's Seminary in San Antonio and was responsible for a massive program of construction that included churches, schools, convents, and seminaries. His concern for the welfare of Mexican-Americans in the archdiocese was remarkable for its time and was not without its critics. He served as the executive chairman of the bishops' Committee for the Spanish Speaking.

In 1950 President Harry S. Truman appointed him to the Commission on Migratory Labor. Three years later, Archbishop Lucey integrated the Catholic schools in the archdiocese. In 1965 he was asked by President Lyndon Baines Johnson to give the invocation at his inauguration. He went on to be an active supporter of the Vietnam War. His last years as archbishop were marked by poor relations with his presbyterate. He retired on June 4, 1969. His term as archbishop was one of immense growth in the Texas archdiocese, and he earned lasting notoriety for his abiding concern for the poor and the Mexican-Americans under his care.

Ludwig-Missionsverein

An organization established in Bavaria in 1838 by King Ludwig I of Bavaria to give aid to missionary activities in North America, the idea for the society had been the work of the German-born priest Frederick Résé, who became the first bishop of Detroit. He had begun the Leopoldine Society Association and was an active servant of the North American missions. His initial requests of the king were declined, but the monarch did permit a collection to take place in Bavaria. Finally, after years of pleas, Bishop Résé was heard successfully, and King Leopold I granted his permission for an association to assist the young Church in America, as well as in Asia and Palestine.

The early years of the Ludwig-Missionsverein were spent in close association with the Society for the Propagation of the Faith in Lyons, France (which had been founded in 1922). By 1844, however, the money being raised was sent to the Congregation for the Propagation of the Faith in Rome and then distributed to worthy causes. Although he abdicated in 1848, King Leopold I remained an ardent supporter of the association until his death in 1868.

Through financial grants, enormous help was provided to the religious orders, such as the Redemptorists and the Benedictines, working in the growing American Church; money was also sent to the Franciscans caring for shrines in the Holy Land. By 1921 over a million dollars had been given to the Church in the United States. (*See also* German Catholics.)

Lusk, Hall S. (September 21, 1883–May 15, 1983)

A United States senator from Oregon, Hall S. Lusk was born in Washington, D.C., and attended Georgetown Preparatory School from 1897 to 1900. He graduated from Georgetown University in 1904 and from Georgetown Law School in 1907 and was secretary to a chief justice of the United States Court of Appeals for the District of Columbia Circuit from 1906 to 1909. In 1907 he was admitted to the District of Columbia bar and then to the Oregon bar in 1910. Soon after, he opened a practice in Portland. From 1918 to 1920, he was an assistant United States Attorney of Oregon. In 1922 he ran unsuccessfully for election to the Oregon Legislature.

In 1922 Lusk assisted the Archdiocese of Portland and its archbishop, Alexander Christie, by serving as one of four attorneys fighting against the constitutionality of Oregon's 1922 law that would have required all children to attend public schools. Lusk was instrumental in writing the appeal to the United States Supreme Court that subsequently found the law to be unconstitutional.

From 1930 to 1937 Lusk was circuit judge of Multnomah County. In 1937 he was elected and then reelected to the Oregon Supreme Court. He served until 1960, when he was appointed as a Democrat to the U.S. Senate to fill the vacancy caused by the death of Richard L. Neuberger. He served from March to November 1960 and chose not to run for election to a full term. He went back to the Oregon Supreme Court as a justice pro tempore in 1961 and served until 1968. He was buried at Mount Calvary Cemetery in Portland.

Lynch, Dominick (1754–1825)

Irish-born philanthropist and merchant, Dominick Lynch was born in Galway, Ireland, the son of James and Anastasia Joyce Lynch. In 1780 Lynch made his way to Bruges, Flanders, to establish a commercial trading house for his father, who was an eminent merchant. Young Dominick made a fortune trading flaxseed and soon sought to expand his interests by partnering in 1783 with Thomas Stoughton to begin a trading house in the United States. Lynch moved with his family to America in 1785 and settled in New York. The partnership with Stoughton lasted until 1795, when the two had a falling out over the way the business was being run. The partnership was officially dissolved, but Lynch continued to expand his extensive business interests through a variety of ventures, including land speculation.

Lynch was an active layman in the Catholic community of New York. He was instrumental in raising funds, and also in contributing his own, needed for the building of St. Peter's Church, the first Catholic church in New York. Lynch was also one of the five signers in 1790 of the "Address of the Roman Catholics to George Washington," which was sent when he became president. In addition, Lynch is credited with being the man who introduced opera to America.

Lynch, Patrick N. (March 10, 1817–February 26, 1882)

Bishop of Charleston from 1857 to 1882 and a leading Catholic in the South during the Civil War, Patrick Neison Lynch was born in County Monaghan, Ireland, the son of Conlaw Lynch and Eleanor MacMahon Neison. He migrated to America with his family in 1819 and grew up in South Carolina. Called to the priesthood, he studied at St. John the Baptist Seminary in Charleston, South Carolina, but owing to his obvious intellectual abilities, he was sent by Bishop John England of Charleston to complete his priestly formation in Rome with James A. Corcoran. Lynch attended the Urban College of the Propaganda and excelled as a student. He was ordained on April 4, 1840, by the cardinal prefect of the Propaganda; that same year, he earned a doctorate in sacred theology.

Returning home, Father Lynch was assigned a variety of posts: secretary to the bishop, editor of the *United States Catholic Miscellany*, rector of St.

Mary's Church in Charleston, and professor at St. John the Baptist Seminary. In 1855, upon the death of Bishop Ignatius A. Reynolds, he was named administrator of the diocese and was considered a likely candidate to become bishop.

On December 11, 1857, he was appointed bishop of Charleston. As a dedicated Southerner, Lynch's sympathies were with the South in the growing crisis in the country over issues of slavery, states' rights, and federalism. He did not approve of slavery and expressed a desire to free the slaves, but he supported the rights of the states with regard to the slave trade and antebellum Southern culture.

Thus, when the Civil War started, Bishop Lynch sided with the Confederacy, and he was sent twice to Europe to plead the Southern cause. He tried but failed to have Pope Blessed Pius IX recognize the Confederacy. In 1863 he issued a pastoral letter pleading for an end to the war and a just peace.

When the war ended in 1865 while he was still in Europe, Bishop Lynch made arrangements to return home. This proved difficult as American officials in Paris refused him the proper documents. Only after the intervention of Archbishops John McCloskey and Martin J. Spalding was the bishop permitted to return to the United States and then only following a presidential pardon and the taking of an oath of allegiance to the United States. In the period after the war, he launched several programs for the education of former slaves.

Most of Bishop Lynch's remaining years were taken up with the difficult task of rebuilding the devastated Diocese of Charleston. One of the most challenging tasks was repairing diocesan finances. He also took part in the First Vatican Council and was in favor of papal infallibility. He died in Charleston.

M

Machebeuf, Joseph P. (August 11, 1812–July 10, 1889)

The first bishop of Denver, called the "Apostle of Colorado," Joseph Projectus Machebeuf was born in Riom, France, and was educated for the priesthood. In 1860, at the request of Archbishop Jean Baptiste Lamy of Santa Fe, New Mexico, Father Machebeuf entered the American missions. He served briefly in Tucson, Arizona, celebrating Masses in Catholic homes in 1859 until a chapel was created.

Father Machebeuf had adapted to the itinerant mission life and had constructed a wagon with a square canvas top that served both as his nomadic residence and as a chapel on wheels. Assigned to Denver by Archbishop Lamy, Father Machebeuf arrived there on October 29, 1860. Local Catholics had already purchased tracts of land, and Father Machebeuf had a church, the first Catholic house of worship in Denver, open in time for Christmas. Father Jean Raverdy assisted Father Machebeuf in the Colorado missions, and they opened outposts of the faith in Arapahoe City, Golden, and Central City. Father Machebeuf also trained Colorado farmers in the latest European agricultural techniques.

Appointed the vicar apostolic of Colorado and Utah in 1868, he was consecrated a bishop on August 16, 1868. Bishop Machebeuf brought priests from Europe and promoted education. In 1871 his labors were eased by the transfer of Utah to the Archdiocese of San Francisco. Bishop Machebeuf had been involved in the Catholic affairs and missions of Utah since becoming vicar apostolic.

Two years later, he opened the Carmelite Institute and, a decade later, Regis College. In 1878 he instituted the St. Vincent de Paul Society in Denver and in 1882 began St. Vincent Orphanage to care for hundreds of children.

On August 16, 1887, the Diocese of Denver was established by

Bishop Machebeuf

Pope Leo XIII, and Bishop Machebeuf assumed the see. Bishop Nicholas C. Matz (bishop from 1889 to 1917) was appointed coadjutor bishop of Denver with right of succession to aid Bishop Machebeuf, who was by then exhausted by his long labors. The "Apostle of Colorado" died having brought sixty-four priests to Denver. In all, he also established 102 churches and chapels, ten hospitals, nine academies, and a college.

Mack, Connie (December 22, 1862–February 8, 1956)

Baseball player and manager of the Philadelphia Athletics from 1901 to 1951, Connie Mack took part in nine American League pennants and five World Series Championships between 1902 and 1930 and is considered one of the greatest managers in the history of the sport. Born in East Brookfield, Massachusetts, to Irish immigrants, Mack began his baseball career on September 11, 1886, and played for eleven seasons in the National League. The last three years he served as a player-manager with the Pittsburgh Pirates. In 1901 he was named manager, general manager, and part owner of the newly founded Philadelphia Athletics. New York Giants manager John McGraw derisively termed the Athletics "a white elephant nobody wanted." Mack embraced the symbol of the white elephant as the team's logo, and the Athletics have used it generally ever since.

Mack was termed "the Tall Tactician" for his style of management, and he cut a memorable figure by wearing suits in the dugout and dealing with his players with stern dignity. Although overshadowed by the famed dynasty of the New York Yankees, Mack built several legendary Athletics teams. He won four pennants in five years from 1910 to 1914 and three in a row from 1929 to 1931 and won five World Series. He holds the record for the most wins by a manager (3,776). He died in Philadelphia. Connie Mack was a lifelong Catholic.

Madison, Diocese of

Established on January 9, 1946, by Pope Pius XII, the Diocese of Madison serves counties in the south-central part of the state of Wisconsin. The capital of the state, Madison was founded in 1836 and was named after President James Madison. The city has federal agencies, the University of Wisconsin, and other educational institutions within its limits. Madison also serves as a center for agricultural, industrial, and manufacturing industries.

The Catholic history of the diocese and the state opens in 1634 when the French explorer Jean Nicolet landed at Green Bay and claimed the area of present-day Wisconsin and the Great Lakes for France. Traders and missionaries followed, halted for a time by Iroquois hostilities, but returning when peace was restored in the region. A Jesuit headquarters was established at Chequamegan Bay, and the Jesuit missionary Father René Menard was serving there. He was slain on the Menominee River in 1661. Jesuit Father Claude Allouez, the revered superior of the Society of Jesus missions, was also in the area, having accompanied a band of Potawatomi from Sault Ste. Marie Mission. He founded a mission at De Pere and Holy Spirit across from La Pointe.

Jesuit Jacques Marquette also served in this mission area, followed by Father Irenaeus Frederick Baraga, the pioneer missionary who became a bishop. Father Baraga labored for eight years near Madison and converted some seven hundred Native Americans. In 1679 René-Robert Chevalier, Sieur de La Salle, led an expedition to Green Bay, claiming lands for France. The Fox War began in 1688, a perilous disruption that led to the withdrawal of missionaries from the region for a time. Soon after, the British took possession of the territory and forbade Catholic missionaries to continue their ministries. Priests came from Detroit on mission circuits despite the dangers, but no permanent parish was maintained until after the Revolutionary War. A church was erected in Green Bay in 1823, and Catholics at Prairie du Chien were being served by the Trappist Father Marie Joseph Dunand. The cornerstone of St. Raphael, now the diocesan cathedral, was reportedly laid in 1804.

The Diocese of Baltimore had jurisdiction over Wisconsin until 1808, when the Diocese of Bardstown (now the Archdiocese of Louisville) was erected. In 1821 the Diocese (now Archidiocese) of Cincinnati assumed jurisdiction, and Bishop Edward D. Fenwick, a Dominican, visited the area. Venerable Samuel Mazzuchelli, another Dominican, opened a school at Green Bay and then began founding parishes (eleven of which are still active in the diocese), a religious community of women, and St. Thomas College. In 1843 the Diocese of Milwaukee, now an archdiocese, was established. The Dioceses of Green Bay and La Crosse were erected in 1868.

Catholics, however, were already building a community in Madison.

The faithful supported the military activities of the nation in World War I and endured the grim economic conditions of the Great Depression. World War II brought economic recovery and sacrifices, and Wisconsin's bishops promoted charitable works and the expansion of schools.

By 1946 Madison was a major city as well as the capital, and Catholics were recognized for their loyalty and fervor with the establishment of the diocese. William P. O'Connor was the first bishop of the Diocese of Madison. He had served as the bishop of Saginaw since 1941. The transfer took place on February 22, 1946, the day the new diocese was formally erected. Bishop O'Connor opened Queen of Apostles Seminary and St. Joseph's College. While instituting the offices and agencies for diocesan administration, he promoted educational and charitable facilities. Hispanic ministries were started also, and St. Raphael Cathedral was renovated. He attended the Second Vatican Council and implemented the reforms mandated by that council. Bishop O'Connor retired on February 22, 1967.

His successor was Bishop Cletus F. O'Donnell, who had served as auxiliary bishop of the Archdiocese of Chicago since 1960. He was promoted to the Diocese of Madison on February 22, 1967, and continued expanding educational programs. Bishop O'Donnell further implemented the reforms of the Second Vatican Council and instituted family values studies and programs. He retired on April 18, 1992.

The third bishop of the Diocese of Madison was William H. Bullock, who had served as auxiliary bishop of the Archdiocese of St. Paul and Minneapolis since 1980. He was promoted to the Diocese of Des Moines in 1987 and transferred to Madison, and was installed on June 14, 1993. Bishop Bullock promoted pro-life issues and instituted a study of the seminary, turning it into a diocesan center. He retired on May 23, 2003.

The fourth bishop of the Diocese of Madison, Robert C. Morlino, had served as the bishop of the Diocese of Helena since 1999. He was transferred to Madison and installed on August 1, 2003. In 2011 there were 280,000 Catholics, 156 priests, nearly 400 women religious, and 127 parishes in the diocese.

Magnien, Alphonse (June 9, 1837–December 21, 1902)

A Sulpician educator of the clergy, Alphonse Magnien was famous among the priests of the United States. He was born at Bleymard, in the Diocese of Mende in France. After studies at Chirac and Orléans, he was affiliated with the Diocese of Orléans. In the seminary he had developed a Sulpician vocation, but the bishop assigned him for two years after his ordination in 1862 as professor in the preparatory seminary of La Chapelle St.-Mesmin. Entering the Sulpicians finally, Father Magnien served as professor of sciences at Nantes in 1864–65 and professor of theology and Holy Scripture at Rodez in 1866–69. In 1869 he was sent to the United States and began teaching at St. Mary's in Baltimore. In 1878 he was made superior of the seminary, a post that he would hold for a quarter of a century. Under his administration, St. Austin's College was founded at The Catholic University of America in Washington, D.C., for the recruiting of American vocations to Saint-Sulpice. His abilities as a churchman and a theologian were conspicuously revealed at the Third Plenary Council of Baltimore. He frequently preached retreats to the clergy, and during a retreat in St. Louis in 1897 he was seized with an attack of the disease from which he had suffered for years. Some months later he went to Paris for special treatment and was operated on. Returning to his post at Baltimore, Father Magnien never fully regained his health, and in the summer of 1902 he resigned from the seminary and died shortly thereafter.

Maguire, Charles Bonaventure (December 16, 1768–July 17, 1833)

An Irish Franciscan, Charles Bonaventure Maguire was a pioneer in the Diocese of Pittsburgh. He was born in County Tyrone, Ireland, and entered the Franciscans. Educated at the Catholic University of Louvain, Father Maguire was appointed as a theology professor after his ordination. He taught at the College of St. Isidore, the Franciscan institution in Rome, and also spent time in missions in the Netherlands. In 1817 Father Maguire was appointed as a missionary apostolic by the Congregation for the Propagation of the Faith and sent to the United States. Reporting to Archbishop Ambrose Maréchal of Baltimore, Father Maguire was assigned to the western Pennsylvania missions. Three years later, he became pastor of St. Patrick's Church in Pittsburgh. He was an outstanding apologist for the Catholic faith in a period of persecution and nativism in the United States. An apologetic document that he published in 1825 aided the Church in a hostile environment. He also laid the cornerstone for St. Paul the Apostle Church, which became the cathedral of Pittsburgh. At his death, people of all faiths mourned his passing.

Mahony, Roger M. (February 27, 1936–)

Archbishop of Los Angeles from 1985 and a cardinal from 1991, Roger Michael Mahony was born in Hollywood, California, to Victor James and Loretta Marie Baron Mahony. Young Roger Mahony attended St. Charles School in North Hollywood and Los Angeles College, then Mission Hill's Queen of Angels Seminary. He proceeded to study for the priesthood at St. John's Seminary in Camarillo, California, and was ordained on May 1, 1962, for the Fresno diocese.

Father Mahony served from 1962 to 1973 in various areas of pastoral ministry in the Diocese of Monterey-Fresno and was also sent for studies in social work at The Catholic University of America in Washington, D.C. From 1964 to 1970 he was the diocesan director of Catholic Charities and Social Services, then served as diocesan chancellor from 1970 to 1980. In addition, he was a diocesan consultor and pastor of St. John's Cathedral from 1973 to 1975.

On January 2, 1975, he was named titular bishop of Tamascani and appointed auxiliary of the Diocese of Fresno by Pope Paul VI. Consecrated on March 19, 1975, Bishop Mahony continued to serve as chancellor until 1980. On February 15, 1980, he was transferred to the see of Stockton. Five years later, on July 12, 1985, Pope Blessed John Paul II named him to the metropolitan see of Los Angeles as successor to Cardinal Timothy Manning. He became the first head of the Los Angeles archdiocese to have been born in Los Angeles.

Archbishop Mahony attended the Seventh Ordinary Assembly of the World Synod of Bishops in Vatican City October 1–30, 1987. Created cardinal priest in the consistory of June 28, 1991, by Pope Blessed John Paul II, he received the red biretta and title of Santi Quattro Coronati on June 28, 1991. He was the third archbishop of Los Angeles to be created a cardinal.

Soon after assuming pastoral care of the massive Archdiocese of Los Angeles, in 1986 he instituted five pastoral regions to improve administration and ministry (Our Lady of the Angels, San Pedro, Santa Barbara, San Fernando, and San Gabriel), each with an episcopal vicar. Following the 1994 Northridge earthquake that damaged the former Cathedral of St. Vibiana, Cardinal Mahony began plans to build the Cathedral of Our Lady of the Angels. The new cathedral was dedicated on September 2, 2002, and was built at a cost of $190 million.

He issued several pastoral letters and statements, including "Gather Faithfully Together," to promote renewal in the parishes; "As One Who Serves: Pastoral Statement on Parish Leadership"; and "The Centrality of the Eucharist as the Source and Summit of the Life and Mission of the Church."

Deeply committed to the issues of social justice and culture, Cardinal Mahony has been an outspoken advocate of immigration reform. He publicly opposed the immigration bills debated by Congress in 2005 and 2006 and took the controversial step of declaring that he would instruct his priests in the parishes of the Los Angeles archdiocese to defy provisions of the Sensenbrenner-King immigration bill should they become law.

In other areas, the cardinal sought to influence and provide direction to the film industry based in Los Angeles in his statement "Film Makers, Film Viewers: Their Challenges and Opportunities," and established Catholics in Media to have Catholic concerns heard in the film and television industry. He worked to promote ecumenical and interreligious dialogue, including issuing a document on the 40th anniversary of *Nostra Aetate* (the Second Vatican Council's Declaration on the Relationship of the Church to Non-Christian Religions). Recent years were marked by ongoing challenges brought by allegations of priestly sexual abuse by some clergy of the archdiocese. In July 2007 the archdiocese settled over 500 lawsuits for $600 million.

Cardinal Mahony was one of the cardinal electors who participated in the 2005 papal conclave that selected Pope Benedict XVI. He has also been a member of the Council of Cardinals for the Study of Organizational and Economic Problems of the Holy See, and attended the Special Assembly for America of the World Synod of Bishops in 1997. He retired on March 1, 2011.

Maida, Adam Joseph (March 18, 1930–)

Archbishop of Detroit from 1990 and a cardinal from 1994, Adam Joseph Maida was born in East Vandergrift, Pennsylvania, the first of three sons born to Adam Maida and Sophie Cieslak Maida. His father was an immigrant from Poland and his mother was born in the United States. One brother, Thaddeus, is a priest serving in the Diocese of Pittsburgh.

Answering a call to the priesthood, Maida entered St. Mary's College in Orchard Lake and in 1950 transferred to St. Vincent's College in Latrobe, Pennsylvania, where he graduated in 1952 with a bachelor's degree in philosophy. He then studied at St. Mary's University in Baltimore and graduated with a licentiate in sacred theology in 1956.

Ordained a priest on May 26, 1956, for the Diocese of Pittsburgh, he was sent to Rome for additional studies. In 1960 he received a licentiate in canon law from the Pontifical Lateran University in Rome. In 1964 he was granted a doctorate in civil law from Duquesne Law School in Pittsburgh. He was admitted to the bar in Pennsylvania, the

Federal Bar in Western Pennsylvania, and the United States Supreme Court.

Father Maida served in the Diocese of Pittsburgh in a variety of posts, including associate pastor, vice chancellor, and general counsel of the diocese, in the diocesan tribunal, and as assistant professor of theology at La Roche College and adjunct professor of law at Duquesne University Law School.

On January 25, 1984, he was ordained and installed as the ninth bishop of the Diocese of Green Bay. On May 7, 1990, Pope Blessed John Paul II appointed him archbishop of Detroit as successor to Cardinal Edmund C. Szoka. He was installed as archbishop of Detroit on June 12, 1990.

Created a cardinal priest in the consistory of November 26, 1994, he received the title of SS. Vitale, Valeria, Gervasio, e Protasio. He was also papal legate to the 19th International Marian Congress in Czestochowa, Poland, in 1996, and attended the Special Assembly for America of the World Synod of Bishops in Vatican City in 1997 and the Second Special Assembly for Europe of the World Synod of Bishops in Vatican City in 1999.

As archbishop of Detroit, Cardinal Maida undertook a reorganization of archdiocesan administration, developed the Hispanic Pastoral Plan for the archdiocese in 1992, opened the St. John Center for Youth and Family in 1995, celebrated the 300th anniversary of the city and the Roman Catholic Church of Detroit in 2001, and played a key role in the establishment of the Pope Blessed John Paul II Cultural Center in Washington, D.C. In addition, he issued a number of pastoral letters, including ones focusing on youths and assisted suicide. He also participated in the conclave of 2005 that elected Cardinal Joseph Ratzinger as Pope Benedict XVI. He retired on January 5, 2009.

Maigret, Louis Désiré (September 14, 1804–June 11, 1892)

Called *Lui Ka Epikopa*, "Louis, the Bishop," Louis Désiré Maigret was the spiritual guide of St. Damien de Veuster and played an important role in the establishment of the Catholic Church in the Hawaiian Islands (then called the Sandwich Islands) by the Sacred Hearts missionaries. He was born in Mailee, Poitou, France, entered the Sacred Hearts Seminary in Poitiers, and was ordained in 1829. Father Maigret was assigned to the Paris seminary and was revered as a brilliant professor of theology.

When Bishop Stephen Rouchouze was appointed the Sacred Hearts vicar apostolic for Eastern Oceania, Father Maigret accompanied him to Managareve in the Gambier (Tuamatu) Islands. In time, Father Maigret sailed to Hawaii to aid Father Alexis Jean Bachelot, who had been exiled from the islands by Queen Kaahumanu, the acting regent. Father Bachelot had returned to Hawaii, and Father Maigret found him there, desperately ill and once again under the penalty of exile. On November 23, 1837, Father Maigret took him on board a schooner, the *Notre Dame de Paris,* and set sail. Father Bachelot died while they were at sea, and Father Maigret continued on to other Sacred Hearts missions.

Bishop Louis Maigret

The Sacred Hearts missionaries then heard news of the arrival of a French warship, *L'Artemise*, captained by Cyril P. T. La Place, in Honolulu harbor. Captain La Place conveyed to King Kamehameha III the fact that the Hawaiian Islands were officially at war with His Catholic Majesty of France because of the outrageous treatment of French priests and Catholics and the violation of international diplomatic traditions. La Place also informed the monarch that he had to issue a proclamation declaring religious freedom for Catholics in the islands or the French warship would fire on Honolulu and full-scale war would commence. The Protestant Americans who had instigated the anti-Catholic policies in Hawaii gathered the funds demanded by the French as guarantee and Kamehameha III attended a Catholic Mass.

Bishop Rouchouze, elated by the news, sailed to Honolulu to begin the mission in earnest and then returned to France to recruit priests and Sacred Hearts Sisters. When the ship that the missionaries boarded for the return voyage to Hawaii was listed as lost at sea, another member of the congregation was chosen as Bishop Rouchouze's successor, but he declined. Father Louis Maigret was consecrated on July 11, 1847. He began his apostolate in earnest immediately, bringing priests and nuns to the islands, installing a printing press, and ordaining St. Damien de Veuster on May 21, 1864. Bishop Maigret also took St. Damien to Molokai, where a settlement had been erected for victims of Hansen's disease, the dreaded leprosy. They landed at the settlement on May 10, 1873. Bishop Maigret continued the expansion and strengthening of the vicariate until 1881, when he became ill and a recluse. He died in Honolulu.

Maine

Called the Pine Tree State, and also the Star in the East, Maine entered the Union as the twenty-third state. Maine is bounded on the north and east by Canada, on the south by the Atlantic Ocean, and on the west by New Hampshire and Canada. There are three natural land regions in Maine: the Seaboard Lowlands in the southeast, the New England Uplands in the central part of the state, and the White Mountains in the west. The original inhabitants of Maine were the Abenaki, Passamaquoddy, and the Penobscots. Missions to these Indian nations opened Catholic activities in the region, and explorers were there as well.

In 1498 John Cabot visited the coast of modern-day Maine, and his son, Sebastian, made charts of the area. In 1603 Pierre du Guast, Sieur de Monts, received a grant from King Henry IV of France to begin a colony, originally called St. Croix. Starting an expedition with Samuel de Champlain and a group of settlers, de Monts selected the island that now bears his name for a colony site. The Jesuit Father Nicholas Aubry was also a member of the expedition and celebrated the first Mass in the area for the Abenaki. De Monts was abandoned within months as the group

moved to Port Royal on Annapolis Bay. Ten years later, Jesuits started a mission on Mount Desert Island. Fathers Pierre Biard, Enemond Masse, and two other Jesuits founded Saint-Sauveur for the Abenaki. Father Biard had been a professor of scholastic theology and Hebrew and had some mission experience. Reportedly, he cured a severely ill infant.

In 1614 Samuel Argall of Virginia destroyed the mission, slaying Brother Gilbert du Thet, S.J. The priests were arrested, and Father Biard was taken to England, and he eventually returned to France. In 1619 French Franciscans began work among settlers and Indians, but they were driven out by the English in 1628. In 1622 Sir Ferdinando Gorges received a patent from the British crown to hold the "Province of Maine." He and Captain John Mason landed in the area between the Merrimac and the Kennebec River. A Pilgrim trading post opened at Castine (Penobscot Bay) seven years later. The Capuchin Franciscans were in the area, however, and Jesuits served at Assumption Mission on the Kennebec. In 1646 Jesuit Father Gabriel Druillettes arrived on a diplomatic mission at Augusta and was treated with courtesy because of his elegance and obvious intellect. Three years later, Maine's residents received religious freedom, except for Catholics. Jesuit Father Sebastian Râle was at Old Town with the Abenaki, but the mission was attacked by the British forces and was destroyed and rebuilt in 1705 and 1722. In 1724 Father Râle was slain by Mohawks, who collected the price that the British had put on the missionary's head.

Point Pleasant Abenaki Mission in Maine

When the American colonies started the Revolutionary War, Maine, which had been attached to Massachusetts, supported the American cause. The Abenaki were asked to aid the cause as well, and they agreed on the basis that a priest would be made available to them. At the war's end, Father Jean-Louis Lefebvre de Cheverus, who would become the first bishop of the Diocese of Boston and a cardinal and Peer of France, served at Pleasant Point, followed by Father James Romagné. Bishop de Cheverus of Boston was given ecclesiastical jurisdiction over Maine in 1808. Catholic settlements were already prospering in the state at Eastport, Augusta, and Portland. The Diocese of Portland (now the Diocese of Portland in Maine) was erected in 1853, and Bishop David Bacon assumed the see after a prior bishop-elect declined. The Civil War impacted upon Maine in the decade that followed, and at its close French immigrants from Canada entered Maine, relying on the diocese to provide parishes and schools. Religious orders and congregations also answered the bishop's invitation and arrived to provide charitable, parochial, and educational facilities.

Bishop Louis Walsh established thirty-six new parishes and defended the Church from the Ku Klux Klan and other anti-Catholic groups. He also led the faithful through World War I, supporting the nation's military efforts. During the Great Depression and World War II, Bishop Joseph E. McCarthy issued bonds to defray diocesan expenses. Maine prospered in World War II, providing materials for the war efforts. The state remained steady, although a decline in priests and religious caused problems, and recent population declines have affected the state's economic bases. Currently, the Catholic population comprises nearly 19 percent of the total population of the state, with nearly 200,000 members of the Catholic community centered in the Diocese of Portland. There are also some 200 priests, over 350 men and women religious, and 133 parishes.

Mallinckrodt, Blessed Pauline (June 3, 1817–April 30, 1881)

Founder of the Sisters of Christian Charity and sister of the German political figure Hermann Mallinckrodt, Blessed Pauline Mallinckrodt was born in Minden, Westphalia (in modern-day Germany). Her father, Detmar, was a Lutheran government official, and her mother, Bernardine, was a Catholic. From an early age, she demonstrated an abiding love for the poor and those in need. At the age of seventeen, she lost her mother and so took on the responsibility of helping to raise her sister and brothers and run the household for her father. She did not lose her love for the poor, however, and with several other women she decided to focus on those in need in Aix-la-Chapelle. These labors she continued when the family moved to Paderborn, but she also dedicated herself to children ages two to six who were without proper care. She thus started a kindergarten in 1840 and two years later began caring for the blind. This last apostolate became one of the cornerstones of her congregation.

On August 21, 1849, Blessed Pauline and three other women entered as the first members of the Sisters of Christian Charity. They took their vows on November 4, 1850, in Paderborn. Their new establishment flourished swiftly across Germany, and by 1871 the congregation included nearly 250 members in 19 houses.

Sadly, this progress was cruelly curtailed by the Prussian government during the harsh anti-Catholic program under Otto von Bismarck, the *Kulturkampf*. Blessed Pauline and the sisters moved to Belgium, and soon afterward she received pleas for some of her sisters to journey to the United States and provide their valuable services as teachers to German immigrant children. In 1873 a small group of sisters traveled to New Orleans. They were followed by other members of the community, and soon a provincial motherhouse and novitiate were established in Wilkes Barre, Pennsylvania.

Blessed Mother Pauline was able to return home to Germany with the easing of the *Kulturkampf* in the late 1870s, and the number of sisters in the United States continued to grow. She remained active in the life of the congregation until her death from pneumonia on April 30, 1881.

The Sisters in the United States in 1915 moved the motherhouse from Wilkes Barre to Wilmette, Illinois. In 1927 a second province was established, with a motherhouse and novitiate in Mendham, New Jersey, with the primary goal of promoting Catholic education. The sisters also established hospitals in Pennsylvania. Currently, they serve across North and South America, Europe, and Asia. Blessed Pauline was beatified by Pope Blessed John Paul II in Rome on April 14, 1985.

Mallory, Stephen Russell (1813–November 9, 1873)

An American statesman, Stephen Russell Mallory served as the Secretary of the Navy of the Confederacy. He was born on the island of Trinidad and was educated at Springhill College in Mobile, Alabama, and then studied law. In 1839 he was admitted to the bar in Florida. Mallory served as a volunteer in the Seminole War of 1835–42 and took part in many campaigns. In 1851 he was elected to the United States Senate from Florida, and reelected in 1857. At the start of the Civil War, Mallory resigned his seat in the Senate in 1861, and President Jefferson Davis appointed him Secretary of the Navy. Mallory had to create the Confederate Navy, as the South had no vessels or fleets. When the war ended in 1865, Mallory accompanied Jefferson Davis out of Richmond. Going to La Grange, Georgia, Mallory was arrested and kept a prisoner for ten months in Fort Lafayette, on a small island in New York harbor. He was released on parole in 1866 and returned to Pensacola, Florida, where he practiced law until his death.

Malone, Sister Stanislaus (1863–June 8, 1949)

The superior of the Daughters of Charity at Charity Hospital in New Orleans, Sister Stanislaus Malone aided the United States Army during the 1918 influenza epidemic. She arrived in New Orleans in 1884 and remained a vital force in the hospital for decades. In 1895 she received her diploma in nursing, having been sent to study operating-room techniques. In 1914 Sister Stanislaus was promoted to the position of superior of Charity Hospital. Four years later, during the influenza epidemic, the army asked Sister Stanislaus for sisters to nurse the soldiers at Jackson Barracks. She promptly assigned nineteen teaching sisters to Charity Hospital and sent twelve nursing sisters to care for the soldiers.

In the 1930s, during a trip to New Orleans, President Franklin D. Roosevelt requested that his motorcade route be changed so he could visit Charity Hospital and meet Sister Stanislaus. When the new $12 million hospital building was completed in 1937, Sister Stanislaus gave it her highest praise with the words, "This is a hospital fit for the poor." She retired in 1944 and died four years later.

Manchester, Diocese of

Established on May 4, 1884, by Pope Leo XIII, the Diocese of Manchester serves the entire state of New Hampshire. Settled in 1722–23, Manchester was originally called Namoskeag, an Indian word for "Place of Much Fish." It was then called Old Harry's Town, Tyngstown, and Derryfield, receiving its present name in 1810. One of America's first textile mills was opened in Manchester in 1805. The largest city in the state, Manchester is a center for manufacturing, agriculture, and the lumber industry. The Diocese of Manchester is a suffragan see of the Archdiocese of Boston.

The Catholic history of Manchester and New Hampshire opens in 1694 when Jesuit priests visited the Abenaki near Durham. The priests had to withdraw because of the Puritan anti-Catholic policies, and it was not until the late 1770s that missionaries once again toured the state, seeking communities of the faithful. One of the thirteen colonies, New Hampshire took part in the Revolutionary War and entered the Union in 1788 as the ninth state. The revised state constitution of New Hampshire imposed a religious test that excluded Catholics from holding major offices in the state government. That test oath was later rescinded.

Father Jean-Louis Lefebvre de Cheverus, who would become the first bishop of the Diocese of Boston in 1808 and then a cardinal and Peer of France, and Father Francis A. Matignon served scattered Catholic settlements, stopping at Portsmouth on their travels through the state. When Father de Cheverus was appointed the bishop of Boston, he was given ecclesiastical jurisdiction over New Hampshire. In 1816 Virgil Barber, a member of a remarkable family of converts from the Episcopalian Church, entered the faith. He was ordained a Jesuit in 1822 and founded a church and an academy at Claremont. The first parish in Dover was founded by Father Charles Ffrench in 1828. Father Michael Healy succeeded him. Father William McDonald, the first permanent priest in Manchester, started St. Joseph's, the present cathedral, and Franciscan

Father John B. Daly served almost two decades in the parish. In 1853 the Diocese of Portland was erected, and New Hampshire was part of this new episcopal jurisdiction. The Church was under attack by the Ku Klux Klan and other Protestant groups, but the faithful stayed loyal and active during the Civil War and the period of growth throughout the nation. The new 1877 state constitution provided Catholics with the civil liberties long denied them. French Catholics had arrived in the area, and St. Augustine Parish opened in Manchester.

The Diocese of Manchester was erected in 1884, and the first bishop of the Diocese was Denis M. Bradley, who was consecrated on June 11 of that year. Bishop Bradley brought energetic leadership to the region and established churches, missions, and schools. He reportedly opened thirty-four new parishes and a vast number of schools while providing the offices and agencies for diocesan administration. The Benedictines were in Manchester in 1893, and the Sisters Adorers of the Precious Blood arrived in 1898. Bishop Bradley died on December 13, 1903.

The second bishop of Manchester was John B. Delany, who was consecrated on September 8, 1904. Bishop Delany continued to build in the diocese to accommodate the increased Catholic population. He died suddenly, however, on June 11, 1906, from appendicitis.

His successor was Bishop George Albert Guertin, who was consecrated on March 19, 1907. He was destined to lead the faithful during critical historic periods. Bishop Guertin opened new parishes and defended the Church against the anti-Catholic propaganda of national groups who claimed that Catholics had allegiance to a foreign power, the pope. He also faced raging debates and attacks and then the grim period of World War I and the influenza epidemic of 1918. Bishop Guertin faced the demands of the Great Depression as well, and he died on August 6, 1931.

The fourth bishop of Manchester was Bishop John Bertram Peterson, who had served as auxiliary bishop of the Archdiocese of Boston. He was promoted to Manchester on May 10, 1930. Bishop Peterson was able to provide charitable assistance to those in need while reducing the diocesan debt. He led the diocese during the stressful era of World War II. Bishop Peterson died on March 15, 1944.

His successor was Bishop Matthew F. Brady, who had served as the bishop of the Diocese of Burlington since 1938. He was transferred to Manchester on November 11, 1944. Bishop Brady established a large number of new parishes and schools and invited religious congregations into the diocese. He also instituted programs for the elderly and the ill. He died of heart disease on September 20, 1959.

The sixth bishop of Manchester was Ernest J. Primeau, who was appointed to the see on November 27, 1959, and was consecrated on February 25, 1960. Bishop Primeau was active in the Second Vatican Council and implemented the reforms mandated by that council. He convened a diocesan synod and consolidated diocesan offices into one chancery. He also promoted lay ministries and programs. Bishop Primeau retired on January 30, 1974.

Bishop Odore J. Gendron was his successor and was consecrated on February 3, 1975. Bishop Gendron faced a critical decline in the number of priests and religious as well as population shifts that caused the abandonment of ethnic parishes. He consolidated the parishes and schools of the diocese and closed those facilities that could not be sustained. He also promoted the Emmaus Program and the permanent diaconate, as well as Hispanic ministries. Bishop Gendron retired on June 12, 1990.

The eighth bishop of Manchester was Leo E. O'Neil, who had served as coadjutor bishop to Bishop Gendron since 1989. He acceded to the see on June 12, 1990. Bishop O'Neil instituted ministries for Hispanics, Sudanese, Vietnamese, and Eastern Europeans who had settled in the area. He also joined parishes and promoted lay ministries and programs. Bishop O'Neil died on November 30, 1997.

The ninth bishop of Manchester, John B. McCormack, had served as auxiliary bishop of the Archdiocese of Boston since 1995. He was installed in the diocese on September 22, 1998. Bishop McCormack maintained ministries for immigrants and focused on establishing parishes in the newly developed suburban regions of the diocese to ensure pastoral care in a changing diocesan environment. He developed an unprecedented strategic plan for the diocese's schools. As with many dioceses, Manchester was deeply troubled by cases and lawsuits stemming from the sex abuse crisis. In 2011 there were 288,000 Catholics, 229 priests, 428 women religious, and 92 parishes in the diocese.

Manning, Timothy (November 15, 1909–June 23, 1989)

Archbishop of Los Angeles from 1970 to 1985 and a cardinal from 1973, Timothy Manning was born in Ballingeary, Ireland, the son of Cornelius Manning and Margaret Cronin. Called to the priesthood, he studied at Mungret College in Limerick and then sailed for America and further preparation for the priesthood at St. Patrick's Seminary in Menlo Park, California. Ordained a priest for the Diocese (later the Archdiocese) of Los Angeles-San Diego on June 16, 1934, he was sent soon after for additional studies at the Pontifical Gregorian University in Rome. There he earned a doctorate in canon law from 1934 to 1936.

Returning to California, he served in pastoral ministry in the archdiocese from 1936 to 1938 and held the post of secretary to John J. Cantwell, archbishop of Los Angeles, from 1938 to 1946. In 1943 he was appointed privy chamberlain of Pope Pius XII on April 15, 1943, and then domestic prelate of the pope on November 17, 1945. After a further period of parish ministry, he was named chancellor of the Archdiocese of Los Angeles on March 19, 1946; that same year, on August 3, 1946, he was elected titular bishop of Lesvi and appointed auxiliary of Los Angeles. Consecrated on October 15, 1946, he subsequently served as vicar general from 1955.

As a bishop, Manning attended the Second Vatican Council. After the council, on October 16, 1967, he was transferred to the Diocese of Fresno. A mere two years later, he was promoted to titular archbishop of Carpi and appointed coadjutor of Los Angeles with right of succession on May 26, 1969. He acceded to the see of Los Angeles on January 21, 1970.

On March 5, 1973, Archbishop Manning was created cardinal priest in the consistory convoked

Cardinal Timothy Manning

by Pope Paul VI and received the title of Santa Lucia a Piazza d'Armi. Over the next years, he took part in the Fourth Ordinary Assembly of the World Synod of Bishops in 1977 and also in the two conclaves of 1978 that elected first Pope John Paul I and then Pope Blessed John Paul II. In addition, he attended the First Plenary Assembly of the Sacred College of Cardinals in Vatican City in November 1979, was a special papal envoy to the celebration of the third centennial of St. Oliver Plunkett's martyrdom, in Drogheda, Ireland, in 1981, and took part in the Sixth Ordinary Assembly of the World Synod of Bishops in 1983.

As archbishop of Los Angeles, Cardinal Manning served as shepherd over a rapidly expanding community in the years after the Second Vatican Council. This was a tumultuous time, and the cardinal displayed remarkable patience and forbearance in dealing with the many liturgical and structural changes that were implemented in the 1970s.

Cardinal Manning was also a gentle and humble caretaker of an archdiocese whose rapid growth necessitated the creation in 1976 of the Diocese of Orange and the separation of Orange County from the archdiocese. Even with this development, the Catholic population of the archdiocese rose steadily, so that by the time of Cardinal Manning's retirement, it numbered some 2.5 million Catholics. To assist pastoral care in the large archdiocese, Cardinal Manning ordained the first permanent deacons for the archdiocese in 1975. He also confirmed more than 650,000 young people.

The second cardinal in the history of Los Angeles, Cardinal Manning retired on July 12, 1985, and was succeeded by Bishop (later Cardinal) Roger M. Mahony. Cardinal Manning died in Los Angeles and was buried in Calvary Cemetery in East Los Angeles.

Manogue, Patrick (March 15, 1831–February 27, 1895)

The first bishop of the Diocese of Sacramento, Patrick Manogue was a pioneering missionary in

California. He was born in County Kildare, Ireland, but was orphaned while in his teens. He migrated to the United States in 1856, after studying classics and mathematics in a college in Callan, County Kilkenny.

Interested in dedicating his life to the priesthood, he entered the University of St. Mary of the Lake in Chicago, where he followed a course of theology and philosophy. The Gold Rush, however, lured him to Nevada in 1853, where he worked in the mines and then became part owner of a mine in Moore's Flat. Still bent on the priesthood, however, he sold his shares in the mine and went to Paris to enroll in Saint-Sulpice Seminary, and was ordained by Archbishop Joseph Sadoc Alemany. Father Manogue was appointed the pastor of Virginia City in 1862, with jurisdiction over almost the entire area that now forms the state of Nevada, and served there for two decades.

Standing well over six feet, he was a builder and organizer who brooked no nonsense in the performance of his ministry, and his exploits became legends in the area. As a result, he maintained a great influence among the miners and won the affection of the Piute Indians, large numbers of whom became converts.

The most popular story about Father Manogue tells of the occasion when he was called out into the desert to give the sacraments to a dying woman in an isolated cabin. When he arrived at the homestead, however, Father Manogue found the woman's husband standing on the porch, barring the way with a rifle and shouting that no papist was ever going to enter his house. Father Manogue got off his horse, walked up to the man, and knocked him unconscious. Taking the rifle inside, he went to the dying woman and gave her the sacraments. When he had completed his visit, he returned the gun to the husband, got on his horse, and rode back to town.

Father Manogue was for several years vicar general of the Diocese of Grass Valley, part of the Vicariate Apostolic of Marysville in Nevada. He built one of the finest churches in the West in Virginia City. In 1880 he was appointed coadjutor bishop of the diocese and was consecrated a bishop on January 16, 1881. On March 17, 1884, he acceded to the see, but then was part of the reorganization of the region and became the founding bishop of the Diocese of Sacramento. Bishop Manogue brought the same energies to serving Sacramento that had characterized his missionary days in the Nevada desert. When he died, Bishop Manogue was buried, as he requested, in the cemetery with his people, not in the cathedral.

Mansfield, Michael "Mike" (March 16, 1903– October 5, 2001)

A member of the U.S. House of Representatives from 1943 until 1953 and the U.S. Senate from 1953 until 1977, Michael Joseph Mansfield was the longest serving majority leader in the history of the Senate. Born in New York City to an Irish Catholic family of immigrants, he grew up in Great Falls, Montana, but left home in 1917 and entered the United States Navy at the age of fourteen. He subsequently served for a year in the army and then, in 1920, enlisted in the Marine Corps. His service in the Marines took him around the world, including the Philippines and China.

Discharged in 1922 and awarded the Good Conduct Medal for his excellent character, he returned to Montana and worked for a time as a miner and mining engineer. As he had not attended high school, he was required to take various entrance exams to be accepted into any college. He studied at the Montana School of Mines from 1927 to 1928 and the University of Montana (then known as Montana State University) from 1930 to 1934. He graduated with both bachelor's and master's degrees and taught for ten years as a professor of Latin American and Far Eastern History at the University of Montana. He was also a member of the American Federation of Teachers.

Elected as a Democrat in 1942 to the U.S. House of Representatives, he served from 1943 until 1953, when he won election to the U.S. Senate. In 1961 he was chosen majority leader, a post he held until 1977, the longest tenure as majority leader in the history of the Senate.

Mansfield was one of the very first American political leaders to oppose the U.S. involvement in Vietnam, but gave his initial support to Richard Nixon's Vietnam policy. Mansfield then urged Congress to reduce the American presence in the Asian country. He later introduced the Mansfield

Amendment of 1973 that limited appropriations for defense research to those projects that had direct military application.

Retiring from the Senate in 1976, he was appointed by President Jimmy Carter in 1977 to the post of Ambassador to Japan. He was kept in the post by President Ronald Reagan until 1988. He became famous for the maxim that United States-Japan relations are "the most important bilateral relationship in the world, bar none." After retirement as ambassador, he continued to be involved in Asian affairs as an adviser to Goldman Sachs.

Mansfield retired from public life in 1989 and received the United States Military Academy's Sylvanus Thayer Award and the Presidential Medal of Freedom from President Ronald Reagan in 1989. Buried at Arlington Cemetery, he was honored with the Mike and Maureen Mansfield Memorial Library at the University of Montana, Missoula, and the annual Mansfield-Metcalf Dinner held by the Montana Democratic Party.

Maréchal, Ambrose (August 28, 1764 or 1766– January 29, 1828)

Archbishop of Baltimore from 1817 to 1828, Ambrose Maréchal, a Sulpician, was revered by King Louis XVIII of France. He was born at Ingres, near Orléans, France, and initially studied the law at the urging of his family. Called to the priesthood, he entered the Sulpician seminary at Orléans.

Political conditions during the French Revolution compelled him to flee Orléans and go to Bordeaux to be ordained in 1792. On the very day of his ordination, he set sail for the United States. They arrived in Baltimore in June 1792 and Father Maréchal celebrated his first Mass. He then presented himself to Bishop John Carroll and offered his services to the Church in the New World. Sent initially to the mission in St. Mary's County, Maryland, he served later in Bohemia along the eastern shore of Maryland. In 1799 he was appointed a professor of theology at St. Mary's College in Baltimore. By 1801 he was on the staff of Georgetown College.

With the rise of Napoleon Bonaparte in France and the initially positive restoration of civil government, the conditions for the Church seemed to improve, and Father Maréchal was recalled to France. He taught at Saint-Flour, Lyons, Aix, and Marseilles, and earned the respect and affection of his students, the people, and even Emperor Napoleon. As a gift of thanks to him, his pupils at Marseilles presented him with a marble altar that was later placed in the Baltimore Cathedral.

In 1812 Father Maréchal returned to Baltimore and was serving again as a professor in 1816 when he was informed of his nomination as bishop of Philadelphia. He replied with the request that the nomination be withdrawn. The following year, however, on July 24, 1817, he was appointed coadjutor to Archbishop Leonard Neale of Baltimore. Archbishop Neale then died before Father Maréchal could be consecrated, so he was consecrated by Bishop de Cheverus of Boston on December 14, 1817.

As the new archbishop, Maréchal was forced to confront immediately the vexing issue of trusteeism, as elements of the laity demanded the right to appoint priests for their own parishes and churches. In the face of the trustees, Archbishop Maréchal stood firm in defending the legitimate rights of the bishop to make appointments and also to hold property.

Owing to a dispute with the Jesuits over his claim to the diocesan property of White Marsh plantation, he journeyed to Rome in 1821 and secured a bull for the land. His trip to Rome marked the first *ad limina* visit undertaken by a Baltimore archbishop.

The chief accomplishment of his time of service as archbishop was the completion of the Baltimore Cathedral that had been started under Archbishop John Carroll in 1806. Archbishop Maréchal took great pleasure in dedicating it on May 31, 1821. The marble altar for the new church was the one presented from the priests and students of Marseilles. In addition, there were various other paintings and objects of art sent to him from France. (*See also* Baltimore, Archdiocese of.)

Archbishop Maréchal traveled to Canada in 1826 and soon after suffered a severe decline in health. As had been his own case, his coadjutor, James Whitfield, had not yet been consecrated when Archbishop Maréchal died.

Margil de Jesús, Venerable Antonio (August 18, 1657–August 6, 1726)

One of America's outstanding missionaries, Venerable Antonio Margil de Jesús was a Franciscan priest honored as the "Apostle of Guatemala." He was born at Valencia, Spain, the son of Juan Margil and Esperanza Ros, and had two sisters. He entered the Franciscan order at La Corona de Cristo in Valencia in 1673. Immediately after he was ordained, he was sent at his own request for service in the Indian missions. He arrived at Vera Cruz, Mexico, in June 1683.

Named to the faculty of the Missionary College of Santa Cruz, Querétaro, he nevertheless devoted his primary labors to the missions through Mexico and Central America. It was noted by his contemporaries, for example, that he walked barefoot everywhere, including on the arduous trek from Texas to Guatemala. He preached everywhere he stopped, founded missions, and became renowned among the indigenous peoples for his austerities, penance, and prayerful disposition. A profoundly humble person, he referred to himself by the nickname *La Misma Nada* ("Nothingness Itself").

In June 1706 Venerable Father Margil was named the first guardian, or superior, of the recently established missionary college of Guadalupe, in Zacatecas. Ten years later, he was appointed head of a group of Franciscans that headed into Texas and established the missions of Guadalupe among the Nacogdoches Indians. According to popular legend, he ended a drought among the Nacogdoches by striking a rock with a cane and drawing out water.

Among the missions he founded were Mission Dolores and Mission San Miguel. Owing to the hostility of the French, however, he was forced to return to the Rio San Antonio area around modern-day San Antonio. In 1720 he founded Mission San Jose, which was soon declared the "Glory of New Spain." Two years later, he was reelected guardian of the college, a post that required him to return to Mexico.

He eagerly departed his post at the end of his tenure and went back to the missions in Mexico. Exhausted by his years of toil, he succumbed to pneumonia in the Convento Grande de San Francisco in Mexico City. He was eventually buried in Zacatecas. Pope Gregory XVI declared Father Antonio Margil de Jesús to be venerable in 1836.

An interesting record indicates that Venerable Father Margil was walking in arid wilderness and looked up in astonishment as a large cross was raised on a hill in front of him. He went to the Native Americans who had raised the cross, and they identified themselves as the Tejas Indians. They were waiting for him, because a "woman in blue" had lived among them for a time, teaching them abut Christ and the Church. Venerable Margil asked if the Blessed Virgin Mary had been the visitor, but they said no. The "woman in blue" had explained Mary's role as Christ's mother and had taught them the Hail Mary. Years later, a Vatican archivist reading Venerable Father Margil's account recognized certain details. The archivist studied the accounts of Venerable Maria de Agreda, a mystic of Spain who had recounted her visions while in prayer. Her details about the Tejas Indians matched the descriptions provided by Venerable Antonio Margil de Jesús's accounts. Venerable Maria de Agreda always wore a blue gown.

Statue of Venerable Antonio Margil de Jesús

Marianists (S.M.)

The Society of Mary, the Marianists, or Marianist Brothers and Priests, is a congregation of brothers and priests that was founded in 1817 by Blessed William Joseph Chaminade in Bordeaux, France. Chaminade also founded the Marianist Sisters, the Daughters of Mary.

The Marianists were first established in the United States in 1849 when Father Francis Xavier Weninger, S.J., wrote to the congregation from Cincinnati to request that members be sent to teach in the local parish schools. Marianist Father Leo Meyer reached Cincinnati the next year, and he was soon joined by several Marianist brothers. The congregation thus embarked on significant work among the many immigrant groups who had settled in the United States and who had specific pastoral needs. In the meantime, Father Meyer had acquired land in the Dayton area to establish a permanent presence in the country. This foundation became St. Mary's Institute (later the University of Dayton), and facilities were also begun for a novitiate, Nazareth, which was the basis for the motherhouse for the first Marianist province in 1855.

As the Marianists became more established in the Midwest, bishops from the region and then across the country began to recruit them for the staffing of schools. The congregation soon found its members teaching in Cincinnati, Cleveland, Pittsburgh, New York, Baltimore, Chicago, and New Orleans. By 1880 they were in Canada, running a school in Winnipeg, and by 1882 they had reached Hawaii and started several schools across the islands. The Marianists in Hawaii went on to start a junior college in Honolulu, which became Chaminade College in 1957 and Chaminade University in 1977. In 1884 the congregation started a school in the Archdiocese of San Francisco.

By the middle of the 1880s, the Marianist presence in the United States and Hawaii boasted over 40 houses and 350 priests and brothers. This number increased continually over the next decades, and by the early twentieth century there were 50 schools and 500 members. The growth encouraged the creation in 1908 of a second province for the western part of the country, based in St. Louis. In 1949 the Marianist Sisters opened their first house in the United States, and their success and rapid development led to the founding of a province in 1969.

In a sign of the maturity of the Marianist community in the United States, in 1946 Father Sylvester Jurgens, an American and former provincial of the western province, was elected superior general of the congregation during its general chapter. Under his leadership, a Pacific province was founded with a focus on California and Hawaii. By 1961 there were approximately 1,500 Marianists in the United States, and that same year a New York province was begun.

Today there are more than 1,500 Marianists — about five hundred priests, including three bishops, and a thousand brothers — laboring in thirty countries. There are two provinces in the United States, the Province of the United States and the Province of Meribah.

The Province of the United States has jurisdiction over activities in Hawaii, Missouri, Ohio, and Texas. Members run three universities (including the University of Dayton), eighteen high schools, six elementary/middle schools, and eleven parishes. The Meribah Province was founded in 1976 and operates only in the Diocese of Rockville Centre on Long Island, New York.

Marie of the Incarnation, Blessed (October 28, 1599–April 30, 1672)

The founder of the Ursulines in Canada, Blessed Marie of the Incarnation Guyart became the patroness of the Algonquin and Iroquois nations. She was born in Tours, France. Married and widowed, she joined the Ursuline convent in Tours and then sailed for Canada with Madame de la Peltrie, a rich widow of Alençon. They arrived in Québec on August 1, 1639, to found the oldest institution of learning for women in North America. Marie of the Incarnation's son, Dom Claude Martin, became a Benedictine priest and her biographer.

Blessed Marie of the Incarnation spent three years in the lower town of Québec, taking over a convent in 1642 that was given to the Ursulines by the company of New France. Their first pupils were Native Americans, and Blessed Marie of the Incarnation mastered Algonquin and Iroquois in order to provide her students with a catechism and a sacred history. Eventually she would compose dictionaries in both languages. When the convent was destroyed by fire in 1650, Blessed Marie saw a new one built upon the ashes of the old. When her friend Madame de la Peltrie died in 1671, Blessed Marie of the Incarnation continued her labors and her particular devotion to the Sacred Heart of Jesus alone. Bishop Blessed François de Montmorency Laval approved the rule of her congregation in 1681.

A devout, brilliant woman who guided the Ursulines through perilous times by combining a contemplative spirituality with acute administrative skills, Blessed Marie of the Incarnation was greatly mourned when she died in Québec. Her correspondence, some twelve thousand letters, provides a valuable look at life in Québec in the seventeenth century.

Pope Blessed John Paul II beatified Marie of the Incarnation Guyart on June 22, 1980, declaring that she had come to the New World from France but had completed her life in Québec, attaining holiness and a record of service that elevated her to the honor roll of Canada's founding settlers. The Holy Father also praised Blessed Marie's contemplative gifts, treasures that she put at the service of her fellow Canadians.

Mariological Society of America

The Mariological Society of America was founded in Washington, D.C., in 1949 by Father Juniper B. Carol, O.F.M. The inspiration for the Society was the desire of young priests of the Antonianum, the Franciscan College in Rome, to do what they could for the glory of Mary. World War II delayed the activities first expressed by the Franciscans in 1939, although Father Gabriel Roschini, O.S.M., remained at Rome and founded the Marianum, which is the name of both the Pontifical Faculty of Theology and the journal of Marian theology. Father Narciso García Garcés, C.M.F., founded the Spanish Mariological Society in 1941 and the journal *Ephemerides Mariologicae* in 1951. Father Paul Strater returned to Germany and edited a three-volume work on the Blessed Virgin. Father Carol called a preparatory meeting on October 11, 1949, the feast of the Maternity of the Blessed Virgin Mary, in the library of Holy Name College in Washington, D.C. Those present favored the formation of a society to be devoted to "the furtherance of that section of sacred theology which deals with Our Lady." The archbishop of Washington approved of the Society and a constitution was drawn up in 1950, and charter members were designated. In 1969 the Society's Mariological Award was renamed the Cardinal Wright Mariological Award.

The Society conducts conferences on doctrine, Scripture, Mary, and ecumenism. Also under consideration is the tension between the traditional Mariology and the theology of the Second Vatican Council. Archbishop Jean Jadot, the apostolic delegate to the United States, sent a letter to the Society in 1974, congratulating the members for their contributions to the pastoral letter "Behold Your Mother." The topics covered in the fifty volumes of *Marian Studies* include the relation of Marian devotion and spirituality to Scripture, ecumenism, liturgy, catechesis, ecclesiology, popular devotion, interreligious dialogue, and religious art. Since 1979 the Mariological Society of America has been based at the Marian Library of the University of Dayton.

Maris, Roger (September 10, 1934–December 14, 1985)

One of the most famous American professional baseball players, best known for breaking Babe Ruth's single-season home run record in 1961, Roger Maris was born in Hibbing, Minnesota. His father, a Croatian immigrant, worked for the Great Northern Railroad and moved the family to North Dakota in 1942, and Roger and his brother, Rudy, grew up in Grand Forks and Fargo. Roger excelled in sports and played baseball in the American Legion program during the summers; he led his American Legion team to the state championship.

Recruited by the legendary coach Bud Wilkinson to play for the University of Oklahoma, Maris decided against accepting a scholarship to sign a $15,000 contract to play for the Cleveland Indians. Roger spent his first four years in the minor leagues playing for Fargo-Moorhead, Keokuk, Tulsa, Reading, and Indianapolis. Brought up from the minors, he played for a season and a half for the Indians and then was traded to the Kansas City Athletics. For his play, he was chosen to the 1959 All-Star team.

Traded to the New York Yankees, then the foremost team in baseball, in 1959, Maris flourished.

He won the Gold Glove Award in 1960, was named the American League's Most Valuable Player, and hit two World Series home runs. The following year he and teammate Mickey Mantle competed in a friendly rivalry in the pursuit of the single-season home run record of 60 set by Babe Ruth in 1927. The chase was followed eagerly by the entire sports world and ended on the last day of the season, October 1, 1961, when Maris hit his 61st home run, against the Boston Red Sox. He went on to win the Most Valuable Player award in the American League for the second straight year.

In 1962 Maris was again named to the All Star team and was the league's Most Valuable Player, and the Yankees repeated as World Series Champions. The Yankees traded Roger Maris to the St. Louis Cardinals after the 1966 season. He played his last two years there and was immensely popular with fans. He was also instrumental in leading the Cardinals to the World Series in 1967 and 1968. Maris retired after the 1968 season. In his career, he played in seven World Series in the sixties (1960, 1961, 1962, 1963, 1964, 1967, 1968), hit six World Series home runs, and drove in eighteen World Series tuns. He finished his career with 275 home runs.

On July 21, 1984, the Yankees retired his number, 9, in a ceremony in Yankee Stadium and erected a plaque in his honor in Monument Park. A life-long Catholic. Maris died of lymphoma at the age of fifty-one. He was buried in Holy Cross Cemetery in Fargo.

Marists (S.M.)

The Society of Mary, or Marists, is a Roman Catholic religious congregation founded in 1816 in France. The origins of the congregation are traced to a French seminarian, Jean-Claude Courveille, who spoke to his fellow seminarians of a desire inspired by the Blessed Virgin Mary to establish a religious community that might bring back to the faith the many souls who had been lost as a result of the French Revolution. He based his model on the Society of Jesus and its founder, St. Ignatius Loyola. On July 23, 1816, Father Courveille and seven other recently ordained priests, including Jean-Claude Colin, made an act of consecration at the Marian shrine of Fourvière, just outside of Lyons, France. The priests were technically diocesan priests, although Father Courveille eventually joined the Benedictines and died at Solesmes in 1866.

Father Colin proved the chief impetus for the establishment of the Society of Mary. He drafted the early rule, encouraged St. Marcellin Champagnat to found the Marist Brothers, and encouraged the start of the Marist Sisters.

On April 29, 1836, Pope Gregory XVI gave his formal approval to the Society of Mary. The Marists were intended by the pope to work as missionaries in the South Pacific, and the first group sailed from France toward the end of 1836. Included in their number was St. Peter Chanel, the first martyr of Oceania.

The Little Brothers of Mary and the Sisters of the Holy Name of Mary, commonly called Marist Brothers and Marist Sisters, were designated as separate institutes, and Father Colin was elected superior general on September 24, 1836. In the Pacific, the Marists worked in the Vicariate Apostolic of Western Oceania, comprising New Zealand, Tonga, Samoa, the Gilbert (now known as Kiribati) and Marshall Islands, Fiji, New Caledonia, New Guinea, and the Solomon and the Caroline islands. In France and then elsewhere, the Marists labored in home missions and then also in the wide field of education.

The first Marists arrived in the United States in 1863 at the invitation of Archbishop John M. Odin of New Orleans. Two Marists were assigned to a parish in Convent, Louisiana. The next year, more Marists arrived to take up the direction of Jefferson College. The congregation soon established itself elsewhere in the New Orleans archdiocese, and then in Massachusetts, Maine, Minnesota, and San Francisco, California.

There are over 1,100 Marists in service around the world. There are two American provinces, based in Atlanta and Boston. There are approximately 200 Marist priests and brothers in the United States engaged in educational work, foreign missions, and pastoral labors. Marists are also found in Australia, Canada, Ireland, France, Germany, Italy, Mexico, the Netherlands, New Zealand, Senegal, Cameroon, parts of South America, as well as across Oceania.

Markoe, William (May 11, 1892–December 6, 1969)

Jesuit priest and advocate of interracial justice, William Markoe was born in St. Paul, Minnesota, to Dr. James Cox and Mary Prince Markoe, one of seven children. He studied at St. Thomas College in Minnesota and then entered St. Louis University in 1912. Called to the priesthood and to the Society of Jesus, he entered the order in 1913 at Florissant, Missouri, and took his final vows in 1915.

Father Markoe took serving poor blacks as his chief task and was granted permission by the Jesuits to labor on behalf of the salvation of the African-Americans. Toward this end, he wrote extensively in *America* magazine throughout the 1920s and early 1930s, calling for a wider program of evangelization of African-Americans. He likewise saw the vital necessity of interracial cooperation and dialogue and tried to advance this cause through *St. Elizabeth's Chronicle,* later renamed the *Interracial Review,* and established with the help of famed Jesuit priest John LaFarge. He allowed control of the journal to pass to LaFarge in 1934.

To promote evangelization, Father Markoe also founded the Peter Claver Association to help educate black children, and the Knights of Peter Claver (along with a Ladies' Auxiliary), a fraternal organization that allowed black membership.

Father Markoe spent most of his later ministry in the Midwest. He served in parish ministry and was a missionary in the Jesuit mission band in Missouri province from 1948 to 1951. In 1951 he was sent by his Jesuit superiors to teach at Marquette University. He remained there until his retirement in 1966. He died in Milwaukee.

Marquette, Diocese of

Established as the Diocese of Sault Ste. Marie by Pope Blessed Pius IX in 1857, designated as the Diocese of Sault Ste. Marie and Marquette on October 23, 1869, and as the Diocese of Marquette in 1937 by Pope Pius XI, this episcopal jurisdiction serves the Northern Peninsula of the state of Michigan. Marquette was founded in 1849 as Worcester and then renamed for the famed missionary Jesuit Father Jacques Marquette. The city became an important port, bordered by Lakes Huron, Michigan, and Superior. There are also agricultural and dairy industries in the region. The Diocese of Marquette is a suffragan see of the Archdiocese of Detroit.

The Catholic history of the region opens in 1622 when Recollect Franciscans were serving in Nipissing. Jesuit Father Claude Pijart labored among the Algonquins at Nipissing and Georgia Bay from 1641 to 1650. In 1641 Jesuit Fathers St. Isaac Jogues (who would be martyred by the Mohawks) and Charles Raymbaut planted a cross at Sault Ste. Marie for the Chippewas. Jesuit Father René Menard spent a winter at L'Anse in 1660. He left the area the following year and lost his life in Wisconsin. St. Ignatius Mission was founded, and in 1670 René-Robert Chevalier, Sieur de La Salle, led an expedition into the area. The famed Jesuit superior Father Claude Allouez and Father Claude Dablon visited Sault Ste. Marie. Jesuit Father Marquette, popular with the Native Americans, died in May 1675, and the Kickapoo Indians brought his remains to St. Ignatius Mission. Fathers Henri Nouvel, Philip Pierson, and Etienne de Carheil were also in the region. Father Carheil served at Detroit, where Antoine Cadillac had erected a fort.

The Treaty of Paris of 1783 gave the young United States control of the region. Michigan was under the ecclesiastical jurisdiction of the Diocese of Baltimore in 1789 and then part of the Diocese of Bardstown in 1808. The Diocese of Cincinnati was given jurisdiction over the faithful of the area in 1821. Three remarkable priests served Michigan in that era: Father Stephen T. Badin, Venerable Samuel Mazzuchelli, O.P., and Father Irenaeus Frederick Baraga. Bishop Baraga, who had been consecrated a bishop and appointed vicar apostolic of Sault Ste. Marie on July 29, 1853, was one of the nation's most distinguished missionaries. A Slovenian noble, he had volunteered for the American missions and had dedicated his life to the faithful in Michigan. He is revered as the "Apostle to the Chippewa" and is ranked as one of the leading experts on American Indian literature.

Bishop Baraga was appointed the first bishop of Sault Ste. Marie and received permission from the Holy See to move his episcopal seat to Marquette on October 23, 1865; the diocese was given the ecclesiastical jurisdiction of the Diocese of Sault Ste. Marie and Marquette, a designation that was changed to Marquette at a much later date.

Bishop Baraga served not only the entire Northern Peninsula of Michigan but northern Wisconsin and the northern shore of Lake Superior as well. He provided the offices and agencies for diocesan administration and traveled continuously in order to visit the far-flung parts of the diocese. He was cherished by the Chippewa nation and was mourned by people of all faiths in the region when he died on January 19, 1868.

His successor was Bishop Ignatius Mrak, another Slovenian, who had aided Bishop Baraga over the years in the missions. Bishop Mrak was consecrated on February 7, 1869. He carried on the labors of Bishop Baraga and attended the First Vatican Council in Rome. Having served for many years in the American missions, and suffering from poor health, Bishop Mrak retired in 1878.

Bishop Mrak was succeeded by another Slovenian, John Vertin, who was consecrated on September 14, 1879. He was an energetic builder and administrator, expanding diocesan facilities and centralizing authority. Bishop Vertin died on February 26, 1899, at which time the diocese had over fifty churches, schools, charitable programs, and hospitals. He also rebuilt St. Peter's Cathedral after a disastrous fire demolished the structure.

The fourth bishop of Marquette was Frederick Eis, who was consecrated on August 24, 1899. Bishop Eis convened a diocesan synod in 1905 and expanded parishes and schools. He retired on July 8, 1922, having led the faithful of Michigan through the grim era of World War I. On July 13, 1922, Bishop Eis was made an Assistant at the Pontifical Throne.

Bishop Paul Joseph Nussbaum was the successor of Bishop Eis, having served as the bishop of the Diocese of Corpus Christi. He was appointed to the Diocese of Marquette on November 14, 1922. He opposed anti-Catholic school legislation and dealt with the financial problems brought about by the Great Depression and a regional economic decline. Facing a shortage of priests, Bishop Nussbaum still managed to open charitable and social programs. He died on June 24, 1935.

The sixth bishop of Marquette was Joseph Casimir Plagens, who had served as the auxiliary bishop of Detroit. He was promoted to the Diocese of Marquette on November 16, 1935. Bishop Plagens continued expanding the diocesan charitable programs and aided the needy until he was transferred to the Diocese of Grand Rapids on December 16, 1940.

Bishop Francis J. Magner succeeded Bishop Plagens and was consecrated on February 24, 1941. World War II brought sacrifices to the faithful of the diocese as well as economic relief because of the military buildup of the nation's armed forces. Bishop Magner founded a diocesan newspaper and promoted charitable causes. He died on June 13, 1947.

The eighth bishop of Marquette was Thomas L. Noa, who had served as coadjutor bishop of the Diocese of Sioux City. He was appointed to the diocese on August 20, 1947. The postwar era was a time of economic recovery, and new diocesan institutions and some one hundred new buildings were opened. Bishop Noa convened a synod in 1950 and attended the Second Vatican Council. Having served for two decades, Bishop Noa retired on March 25, 1968.

Bishop Charles A. Salatka was Bishop Noa's successor, having served as auxiliary bishop of the Diocese of Grand Rapids since 1961. He was installed in Marquette on March 25, 1968. Bishop Salatka implemented the reforms of the Second Vatican Council and aided lay ministries. On October 11, 1977, he was promoted to the Archdiocese of Oklahoma City.

The tenth bishop of Marquette was Mark F. Schmitt, who had served as auxiliary bishop of the Diocese of Green Bay since 1970. He was appointed to Marquette on March 21, 1978, and installed in the diocese on May 8. Bishop Schmitt maintained diocesan programs and services despite the decline in the number of priests and religious. He promoted professional training of the laity and sponsored pastoral ministries. Bishop Schmitt retired on November 11, 1992.

The eleventh bishop of Marquette, James H. Garland, had served as auxiliary bishop of the Archdiocese of Cincinnati since 1984. He was appointed to Marquette on October 6, 1992, and installed on November 11, 1992. He added facilities and programs to meet the growing needs of the people and retired on December 12, 2005.

His successor, Bishop Alexander King Sample, was appointed bishop of Marquette on December

13, 2005, by Pope Benedict XVI. He was ordained and installed on January 25, 2006. He established a strategic plan for faith formation, education, and catechesis. In 2011 there were 50,000 Catholics, 86 priests, and 72 parishes in the diocese.

Marquette, Jacques (1636–May 18 or 19, 1675)

A tireless Jesuit missionary and explorer, Jacques Marquette was the discoverer of the Mississippi River. He was born in Laon, France, the son of an ancient family distinguished for its civic and military services to the nation. Entering the Society of Jesus at age seventeen, he was ordained and then taught for twelve years in the Jesuit colleges of France. In 1666 Father Marquette was sent by his superiors to the Indian missions in Canada. His first assignment was at Three Rivers on the St. Lawrence, where he labored with Jesuit Father Gabriel Druillettes, studying the Huron language. He would become fluent in six Indian languages.

In 1668 Father Marquette was recalled to Québec and assigned to the mission at Sault Ste. Marie and then to Holy Ghost Mission at La Pointe, near the present-day city of Ashland. He heard about the Mississippi River from the Illinois Indians, who described the great waterway in detail. The Illinois villages numbered eight thousand souls, and they wanted Father Marquette to come to instruct them in the faith. Father Marquette responded enthusiastically, and he received encouragement from the Hurons, who offered him a sturdy canoe. His plans, however, had to be postponed because the Hurons were forced from La Pointe because the Dakotas were bent on attacking them. Father Marquette evacuated the area with the tribe and accompanied them to the northwest shore of the Straits of Mackinac. He erected a chapel there and aided Father Druillettes.

The Jesuits, encouraged by Father Marquette's descriptions of the great river, gave him permission to set out from Mackinac for the exploration he had so long desired. Louis Joliet came to join him, and on May 17, 1673, the expedition, which included five Frenchmen in two canoes, set out on the voyage. The group followed the northern shore of Lake Michigan, entered Green Bay and the Fox River, and crossed a short portage into the Wisconsin River, which emptied into the Mississippi. Father

Marquette drew maps of the areas and kept a diary of the voyage; it is one of the most important documents of early American history. He was precise in keeping records of the villages and customs of the different tribes, the topography of the country, the possible value of navigable streams, and the nature and variety of the flowers and trees, birds and animals of the regions he explored. At the mouth of the Arkansas River, Father Marquette and his party learned that the great river upon which they were navigating flowed into the Gulf of Mexico, with Spanish forts and settlements along its banks. The group turned north to the Illinois River. Near present-day Utica, Father Marquette entered an Illinois village and then moved on to the site of the modern-day city of Chicago on Lake Michigan. They continued to the mission of St. Francis Xavier at the head of Green Bay. Here Father Marquette remained while Louis Joliet continued on to Québec to report on the explorations.

A year later, in 1675, Father Marquette started a journey to the village of the Illinois Indians he had met on his return voyage, but the cold forced him to spend the winter at present-day Chicago. He did not reach the village until the following spring, celebrating Mass beside Starved Rock. Knowing he was ill, Father Marquette stayed only three weeks with the Illinois and started out for

Jacques Marquette's grave

Mackinac. At the mouth of a small stream near the present city of Ludington, he told his two companions, who had been with him throughout his entire trip, to carry him ashore. There he died at the age of thirty-nine. Two years later the Kickapoo Indians carried his bones to the mission at Mackinac. In 1887 a statue of Father Marquette was placed in Statuary Hall in the Capitol, representing the state of Wisconsin. Bronze replicas of this statue have been erected at Marquette, Michigan, and at Mackinac Island.

Marquette League

A society of laypeople dedicated to promoting the Catholic faith among the Native Americans, the Marquette League was founded in May 1904 in New York by Father H. G. Ganss of Lancaster, Pennsylvania. Twenty-five laymen formed a directorate to cooperate with ecclesiastical authorities in helping to preserve the faith in tribal communities. The Marquette League was founded to support mission schools, build chapels, train catechists, and improve the lives of Native Americans. The League established chapels at Holy Rosary and St. Francis Missions in South Dakota, and aided the Maquis Indians of Arizona, the Winnebagos of Nebraska, and the Fort Berthold Reservation in North Dakota. Material goods, including liturgical vestments and sacramental vessels, were also provided, and for a number of years the society published *The Calumet* quarterly. The League disbanded in 1992, and its archives from 1904 to 1992 are stored at Marquette University.

Marquette University

An independent institution of higher learning founded by members of the Society of Jesus in 1881 in Milwaukee, Marquette University was named in honor of the famed explorer Jacques Marquette. The founding of the university is credited to the efforts of Bishop John M. Henni, the first bishop and archbishop of Milwaukee, who was eager to establish a Catholic college but encountered many obstacles in bringing it about. To advance his plans, he journeyed to Europe to raise funds and found financial backing from a Belgian businessman, Guillaume Joseph DeBuey. DeBuey promised $16,000 for the proposed "academy of learning."

The funds proved a key first step, and within a number of years Bishop Henni purchased land in Milwaukee for the future site of the school. Nevertheless, thirty years were needed to bring all his plans to fruition. On August 28, 1881, Marquette College was opened, a tiny liberal-arts school for men. Archbishop Henni lived long enough to see his dream a reality and died only a few days after the opening.

The small school developed slowly and attained its status as a university in 1907. That same year, Marquette University High School, previously the preparatory department of the university, was established as a separate institution. Over the next few years, the school launched new departments, including law, medicine, nursing, music, dentistry, and journalism. In 1912 Marquette University became the first Jesuit university to admit women as students. Within five years there were over 375 female students.

The university grew rapidly in the years after World War II and began graduate and professional programs, as well as doctoral programs in history, religious studies, biology, and chemistry. In 1969 an extensive reorganization of the Board of Trustees created a lay majority to oversee the direction of the university. In the 1990s the university promoted a $50 million Campus Circle Project to encourage investment in the local community, and Marquette was acknowledged as a leading U.S. university for community service by students. Today, Marquette University has a student body of 11,000 students and claims the distinction of ranking among the top 100 schools in the United States.

Martin, Augustus M. (February 1, 1803– September 29, 1875)

The first bishop of Natchitoches, Louisiana, from 1853 to 1875, Augustus M. Martin was born in Saint-Malo, France, the son of Pierre-François Martin and Marie-Françoise Gautier. Called to the priesthood, he studied at the College of Rennes and was ordained on May 31, 1828. He served over the next years in a variety of pastoral positions in the Diocese of Rennes and also in diocesan administration. In 1841 he journeyed to the United States.

Father Martin held several early posts in Louisiana, including being a member of the household of Bishop Antoine Blanc of New Orleans and chaplain to the Ursuline convent. From 1843 to 1853 he was a pastor of several churches in Louisiana.

On July 18, 1853, Pope Blessed Pius IX established the Diocese of Natchitoches, with territory taken from New Orleans and stretching across north Louisiana. Father Martin was named the diocese's first bishop and received consecration on November 30, 1853. His new diocese enjoyed a Roman Catholic population of over twenty-five thousand, but there were only a handful of priests, six churches, and a convent school.

Bishop Martin took as his primary concern the expansion of the diocese in order to be able to provide the proper care for his flock. The region was also plagued by chronic poverty, frequent droughts, and other hardships that placed further obstacles in front of the bishop. He remained remarkably determined to establish the new diocese on a firm footing. He established convents and schools under the direction of the Sisters of Mercy and the Daughters of the Cross, recruited priests from across Europe, and increased the number of churches and chapels to over sixty. Bishop Martin also opened the first school for free black children in 1857.

Bishop Martin supported the Confederacy during the Civil War and issued a pastoral letter at its start defending secession and the institution of slavery. In December 1864 the Congregation of the Index in Rome demanded that he correct the errors in the pastoral letter. He nevertheless provided considerable pastoral concern for the severe plight of the people of northern Louisiana during the years of bloody conflict, especially as a result of the Red River Campaign of 1864. He later attended the First Vatican Council and kept a personal journal of his experience. He was buried in the cathedral of Natchitoches.

Martinelli, Sebastiano (August 20, 1848–July 4, 1918)

The second apostolic delegate to the United States, Sebastiano Martinelli, was created a cardinal in 1902. He was born in Borgo Sant'Anna, Italy, the son of Cosma Martinelli and Maddalena Pardini, and was the brother of Cardinal Tommaso Martinelli. He was educated in the Seminary of San Michele in Lucca. He also attended the San Agos-

tino College in Rome, where he was ordained on March 4, 1874. An Augustinian, Father Martinelli had been professed in the Order of the Hermits of St. Augustine on January 6, 1865. He served on the faculty of the Irish Augustinian house of studies in Rome from 1874 to 1881, and then became the Regent of Studies. In 1881 he served at the Augustinian San Carlo al Corso in Rome and from 1881 to 1888 served as the postulator of Augustinian Causes. The following year he became the prior general of the order and in 1982 was appointed a consultor of the Holy Office.

On April 18, 1896, Pope Leo XIII appointed him the apostolic delegate to the United States, giving him the rank of titular archbishop of Ephesus on August 30. Archbishop Martinelli arrived in the United States on October 4, 1896. He served American Catholics until April 15, 1901, when he was created a cardinal priest. He received a red biretta in Baltimore on May 8. On June 9, 1902, he received the red hat in Rome. Cardinal Martinelli participated in the papal conclave of 1903 and then served as apostolic visitor to the Catechumenal Hospice in 1904. He also was appointed to the commission for the codification of canon law in 1906–17, as Camerlengo of the Sacred College of Cardinals from 1907 to 1909, and as prefect of the Sacred Congregation of Rites on February 8, 1909. Cardinal Martinelli did not participate in the conclave of 1914 because of illness. He died in Rome and was buried in the Augustinian mausoleum in Campo Verano Cemetery in Rome.

Martínez, Antonio José (January 17, 1793–July 27, 1867)

A priest, publisher, writer, and politician in New Mexico, Antonio José Martínez was born in Abiquiu, New Mexico, at a time when the area was still under the control of Spain. When he was five, he moved with his family to Taos, then a flourishing town. He learned ranching from his father as well as farming at the Hacienda Martínez. In 1811 Martínez married María de la Luz, but she died in childbirth. Her death caused a great spiritual crisis for Martínez, and after much reflection and consultation with the bishop of Durango, in 1817 he entered the seminary of the Diocese of Durango. He left his daughter in the care of his mother. His mother died around 1824 or 1825. Martínez found the seminary a profound experience and did well both in his studies and in developing a love and respect for the ideals of the Mexican leaders of the age who were laboring to free Mexico from Spain, especially Miguel Hidalgo, the executed independence figure.

Ordained in 1822, Father Martínez returned to Taos and took up his ministry. He served in several pastoral assignments at Tomé and Abiquiu and then went back to Taos, where he spent the rest of his life.

In Taos, he founded a school for boys and girls and then a minor seminary to prepare young men for the seminary. He also purchased the first printing press in New Mexico, a device that was used for his school and for the needs of the Church, but also for the various political causes in which Martínez became involved over the next tumultuous years.

An advocate of social change, Father Martínez held the post of deputy in the Departmental Assembly of the Territory of New Mexico in 1831, 1833, and 1836, and in 1834 he used the printing press to launch the first newspaper in the area, *El Crepusculo de la Libertad* (the *Dawn of Liberty*). He was especially concerned with such pressing issues as the inconsistency in the issue of land grants, the treatment of native peoples, and genuine freedom for the people.

In the wake of the United States' seizure of New Mexico in 1846, Father Martínez did not approve or help to incite the Taos Revolt of 1847 that led to the death of Charles Bent, the newly appointed American governor. Kit Carson, who had played an instrumental role in the American takeover of New Mexico, was convinced that Martínez had been aware of the uprising, but no evidence was ever found proving the suspicion. In the years that followed the uprising, Father Martínez was a key voice in the political process, most so in the conventions and activities of the state legislature.

Father Martínez initially welcomed the arrival of the new American bishops to New Mexico and gave his support to Bishop Jean Baptiste Lamy, the first vicar apostolic, bishop, and then archbishop of Santa Fe. Relations deteriorated, however, from 1854, when Bishop Lamy issued a letter barring Catholics from the sacraments if they failed to tithe. Two years later, Father Martínez resigned as pastor on the grounds of poor health. His open criticism of Bishop Lamy in the Santa Fe newspapers culminated in his suspension and then, in 1858, his excommunication. He chose to ignore the excommunication and in his final years conducted an unauthorized ministry with a group of supporters. His followers were eventually reconciled to the Church.

Martinez, Pedro (unknown–October 6, 1567)

The Jesuit protomartyr of America, Pedro Martinez received personal blessings from Pope St. Pius V and St. Francis Borgia before sailing to the missions in the New World. He was born in Aragon, Spain, and raised as a noble. Entering the Society of Jesus, he served as rector of colleges and as a chaplain to the Spanish military forces on an expedition against the Moors.

Father Martinez volunteered for the American missions despite the fact that he knew of the perils of such service. He accompanied the expedition of Pedro Menéndez de Avilés to an area on the coast of present-day Georgia, called Guale by the Spaniards. Father Martinez established a mission on Cumberland Island, then called Tacatucuru, with other Jesuits, but the local Indian tribe remained hostile and killed the priests.

Marty, Martin (January 13, 1834–September 19, 1896)

A brilliant Benedictine missionary and the first bishop of the Diocese of St. Cloud, Martin Marty was called the "Black Robe Lean Chief" by the American Indians. He was born in Schwyz, Switzerland, and educated by the Jesuits and then by the Benedictines at Maria Einsiedeln. He was ordained on September 14, 1856. After coming to America, Father Marty served as the abbot of St. Meinrad's Benedictine Abbey in Indiana in 1870. In 1876 he was asked by Father Jean Baptiste Abraham Brouillet of the Bureau of Catholic Indian Missions to send a priest to the Dakota Sioux Indians. Father Marty assumed the mission personally, going to Yankton in the Dakotas. There he endured the travails of missionaries in the area. He visited the Dakota Sioux and established missions and catechetical centers.

Pope Leo XIII appointed Father Marty the titular bishop of Tiberias and the vicar apostolic of the Dakotas in 1880. Consecrated, Bishop Marty toured all the settlements in the vast vicariate and added missions wherever possible. He mastered the Indian languages and translated prayers and hymns for his people. In February 1889 the Dakota Territory was divided by the U.S. Congress, and on November 2 of that year, North and South Dakota entered the Union as the thirty-ninth and fortieth states. The Diocese of Sioux Falls was also established by the Holy See, and Bishop Marty was installed there. In 1894 he was transferred to the newly erected Diocese of St. Cloud. Missionaries in the area depended

Bishop Martin Marty

upon Bishop Marty for counsel and aid, as he was considered a veteran of the mission field and a practical, innovative evangelizer. The Sioux held him in high esteem, calling him the "Black Robe Lean Chief." After the Battle of Little Bighorn, when Chief Sitting Bull went north to Canada, Bishop Marty traveled to the area and distributed blankets, medicine, and food to the exiled Sioux. He died in St. Cloud.

Mary, Blessed Virgin

The Blessed Virgin Mary is honored as the Patroness of the Americas and has been honored as the Patroness of the United States of America since 1846. The history of devotion to the Blessed Virgin Mary in America, however, dates to a far earlier period, and the special place of Our Lady has remained a great constant since the very arrival of Christopher Columbus in 1492. Indeed, the lead ship of Columbus was the Santa María, and the first gold brought back from the New World to Queen Isabella of Spain was sent to assist the gilding of the west apse of the Basilica of Santa Maria Maggiore.

Devotion to Mary became profoundly intertwined with the conversion of the New World, and a decisive turning point in that process occurred in 1531, when Mary appeared four times to an Indian, Juan Diego (who was beatified in 1990 and canon-

ized in 2002), on Tepeyac hill outside of Mexico City. The Blessed Mother instructed him to tell Bishop Zumarraga of her wish that a church be built there. The bishop complied with the request about two years later, after being convinced of the genuineness of the apparition by the evidence of a miraculously painted life-size figure of the Virgin on the mantle of the Indian. The mantle bearing the picture has been preserved and is enshrined in the Basilica of Our Lady of Guadalupe. The shrine church, originally dedicated in 1709, was subsequently enlarged.

Pope Benedict XIV, in a 1754 decree, authorized a Mass and Office under the title of Our Lady of Guadalupe for celebration on December 12 and named Mary the patroness of New Spain. Our Lady of Guadalupe was designated patroness of Latin America by St. Pius X in 1910 and of the Americas by Pius XII in 1945.

In recognition of the special place of the Virgin Mary in the New World, several decrees were issued by Spanish kings. The first was by King Philip IV in an edict addressed to his viceroys in America on May 10, 1643, that dedicated Spanish territory in the Americas to Mary the Mother of God. The second was by King Charles III in 1760, extending the dedication to "the Spanish borderlands," a reference to those areas that eventually became the United States.

Meanwhile, French missionaries, who were such a key part of the colonial enterprise of France in North America, brought with them their own devotions. As missionaries made their way along the Mississippi Valley, as well as through Maine, along the St. Lawrence River, and across the Great Lakes, they founded many chapels and missions, and devotion to Mary was part of their daily ministry and evangelization. They recited the Angelus and the Rosary in French forts, the camps of hunters and trappers, and among the Hurons, Mohawks, and Iroquois. Devotion to the Blessed Virgin was especially significant among French Canadians, as seen in the national shrine to Our Lady in Three Rivers, Canada.

The first Catholics to arrive in the English colonies brought with them their devotion to Our Lady. Catholics reached the colony of Maryland on board the ships *Ark* and *Dove* on the feast of the Annunciation, March 25, 1634. The first Mass was celebrated in what were later the thirteen colonies by Jesuit Father Andrew White, and while Maryland was named after Queen Henrietta Marie (wife of King Charles I of England), the first capital of the colony, St. Mary's City, was named in the Blessed Virgin's honor.

From this tradition came perhaps the key figure for the special place of the Virgin Mary in American history, Archbishop John Carroll, the first bishop and then first archbishop of Baltimore. Deeply devoted to Mary, Carroll had recourse frequently to her intercession during the long years in which he toiled to establish an ecclesiastical structure for the Church in America. He chose August 15, 1790, as the date for his consecration as bishop of Baltimore, the feast of the Assumption. Bishop Carroll then used his first pastoral letter, on May 28, 1792, to dedicate his diocese and the country to the Mother of God. The cathedral of Baltimore was dedicated to the Assumption.

Over the next decades, as Archbishop Carroll worked to increase the size and prosperity of the Church in the United States, his devotion to Mary remained one of his greatest weapons in confronting new challenges, above all the long-standing anti-Catholicism and bigotry in the nation.

At the Sixth Provincial Council of the Church in America in May 1846, under the presidency of Archbishop Samuel Eccleston of Baltimore, the decree requesting that the Blessed Virgin Mary under the title of the Immaculate Conception be named as the Patroness of the United States was passed by twenty-one bishops and one archbishop. Pope Pius IX ratified this action of the American hierarchy in February 1847. The dogma of the Immaculate Conception was not defined until 1854.

The Seventh Provincial Council, in 1849, petitioned the Holy See for the definition of the dogma and asked the faithful to offer daily prayer that the pronouncement be made. When Pope Blessed Pius IX defined *ex cathedra* the dogma of the Immaculate Conception on December 8, 1854, every church in the country held services of thanksgiv-ing. The Eighth Provincial Council, in 1855, gave official expression to the delight of the American Church, and the Second Plenary Council in 1866 decreed that December 8 be observed in every diocese as a holy day of obligation.

Devotion to the Blessed Virgin Mary was fostered even further in the next years by the continued arrival of new religious orders and congregations and especially by the waves of immigrants from Europe. The Irish, Italian, Polish, and other groups brought with them their own ancient devotional practices, such as Our Lady of Knock from Ireland, Our Lady of Czestochowa and Our Lady of Ostrobrama from Poland and Lithuania, and Our Lady of Good Voyage from Portugal. Great enthusiasm accompanied devotion to the Miraculous Medal and then to Our Lady of Fátima.

Catholic devotion to Our Lady became a common sight in American cities and in American Catholic culture. Outdoor May processions, pilgrimages to local and diocesan shrines, the saying of the Rosary on radio stations across the country were a staple of American Catholicism, and these activities were also a reflection of the great many private devotions by American Catholics. Other significant movements of devotion included the Sodality Movement and the Family Rosary Crusade. (*See also* Peyton, Patrick.)

A powerful reflection of the honor paid to the Immaculate Conception as Patroness of the United States was the call for the building of a national shrine. In 1913 the idea for a national shrine in honor of the Immaculate Conception was submitted to the Holy See by Cardinal John Gibbons and Bishop Thomas J. Shahan and was given approval by Pope St. Pius X. Funds were collected from Catholics all over the country, and the cornerstone of the National Shrine of the Immaculate Conception in Washington, D.C., was blessed by Cardinal Gibbons on September 23, 1920. The dedication of the Great Upper Church was held on November 20, 1959; the shrine was designated a minor basilica by Pope Blessed John Paul II on October 12, 1990.

In the era after the Second Vatican Council, there was an erroneous sense that Marian devotion had declined and an equally erroneous interpretation that somehow the council had called for a reduced place for Our Lady in the life of the

Church. In truth, the council had devoted the last chapter of the Dogmatic Constitution on the Church, *Lumen Gentium*, to her, and noted her role in salvation history and her place in the Church. The council likewise urged that the cult, "especially the liturgical cult, of the Blessed Virgin, be generously fostered." Pope Paul VI stressed her vital role in the Church. Particularly important direction was provided by Pope Blessed John Paul II throughout his long pontificate, both through his personal love of the Virgin and through his official teachings, such as the 1987 encyclical *Redemptoris Mater*.

Mary Immaculate, Oblates of (O.M.I.). *See* Oblates of Mary Immaculate

Maryknoll

The Catholic Foreign Mission Society of America, known as the Maryknoll Fathers and Brothers, is a community of priests and lay brothers dedicated to mission work outside the United States and to the apostolate of educating Catholics about missions. A mission pontifical institute, Maryknoll was founded in 1911 by two diocesan priests, Father James A. Walsh and Thomas F. Price. The origins of the institute are traced to the Eucharistic Congress in Montréal in 1910, when Fathers Walsh and Price met and decided at once to found a missionary society and seminary. Father Price secured the help of Cardinal James Gibbons of Baltimore, who also suggested that they seek the advice of the apostolic delegate, Archbishop Diomede Falconio. He recommended that the planned seminary should be independent from a diocese.

On March 25, 1911, Cardinal Gibbons addressed a letter to the archbishops of the United States suggesting that the Society and mission seminary be endorsed. On April 27, 1911, the archbishops passed two resolutions: the establishment of an American Seminary for the Foreign Missions and a visit to Rome to request immediate approval from Rome. The priests brought the proposal to the Congregation of the Propa-

ganda, and the cardinal prefect, Girolamo Gotti, granted them formal papal authorization for the founding of the Catholic Foreign Mission Society of America. The two priests were also received by Pope St. Pius X.

Beginning the Society, Fathers Walsh and Price initially used the Hawthorne Dominican house in Hawthorne, New York, and then acquired in 1912 a tract of hilltop land above the Hudson River near Ossining, New York. The site was dedicated to the Virgin Mary, Queen of Apostles, and they named it "Maryknoll." Six seminarians were enrolled in the first year. By 1917 there were twenty-five studying at Maryknoll, thirty-five in the Scranton seminary, and eleven priests enrolled as Society members.

In that same year, Father James A. Walsh received an invitation from Archbishop Jean-Baptiste Budes de Guebriant of Canton, China, to serve in that mission. On September 7, 1918, the first departure of priests from Maryknoll took place. Fathers James E. Walsh, Francis X. Ford, and Bernard F. Meyer, under the leadership of Father Price, began the apostolate in territory granted to Maryknoll by the Paris Foreign Mission Society. Working in Yeungkong, China, the priests served people in an area of twenty thousand square miles. They learned the language and made a thousand adult converts in the first six years.

Father Price died in Hong Kong on September 12, 1919, and was succeeded as superior of the mission by Father James E. Walsh. Maryknoll expanded its ministry over the next years, establishing missions in Korea, South China, Japan, and the Philippines. In 1925 Maryknoll also assumed the territories of Wuzhou, Guilin, and Jiaying. In 1927 Father James E. Walsh was ordained bishop of the Jiangmen vicariate. Father Ford became bishop of Jiaying in 1935.

On December 8, 1941, there were 200 Maryknoll missionaries in the Orient. Many Maryknollers in Japan, Hong Kong, and the Philippines were interned when the Japanese forces overran their missions. Others moved with refugees, and others gave their lives

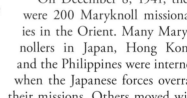

Bishop James A. Walsh

in different forms of sacrifice. In 1942 the Holy See assigned Maryknoll to Latin America, opening a new field of missionary endeavors. Maryknoll priests went to Bolivia, which was followed by missions in Chile, Peru, Ecuador, Guatemala, and Mexico. By 1945 there were 105 Maryknoll priests and brothers working in Latin America.

With the end of World War II in 1945, the institute returned to its mission activities in Asia. In a memorable moment, Maryknoll Monsignor Patrick J. Byrne was asked by General Douglas MacArthur to speak on the radio in Tokyo to prepare the Japanese for the U.S. occupation. In 1949 Monsignor Byrne was appointed apostolic delegate to Korea and consecrated an archbishop. He was subsequently captured in Seoul by the communist forces from the north in June 1950. He died of pneumonia as a result of a forced winter march.

Bishop Francis X. Ford

In China, Maryknoll faced an even greater threat when the communist regime that came to power ordered the expulsion of all foreign Church officials. Nearly one hundred Maryknoll priests and brothers were expelled, while Bishop Francis X. Ford was placed on public trial and brutally tortured. He died in prison in 1952. Bishop James E. Walsh was also sentenced to twenty years' imprisonment and then was granted release in 1970, just before President Richard Nixon's visit to the People's Republic of China.

Maryknoll continued to expand its missionary horizons across the globe over the next decades. New fields were established in the Philippines and Africa (including Tanzania and Kenya). In 1966 the Society accepted diocesan and religious priests and brothers as limited term associates, and in 1972 lay associates were incorporated to the Society's work. By 1995 the Maryknoll Mission Association of the Faithful became a self-governing branch of Maryknoll. Missions were also given into the responsibility of Maryknoll brothers in Western Samoa, Venezuela, Brazil, Indonesia, Sudan, Bangladesh, Nepal, Yemen, Costa Rica, Honduras, Egypt, Palestine, Thailand, Cambodia, Vietnam, and Mozambique. Currently, there are 534 members of Maryknoll, with 439 priests in service around the world.

Maryknoll also published *Maryknoll* magazine and operates Orbis Books, a publishing house that focuses on theology and other topics relevant to the needs of the modern Catholic Church.

The Maryknoll Sisters of St. Dominic (M.M.) were founded in 1912 by Mother Mary Joseph Rogers, under the direction of Father James A. Walsh. She and six other women gathered in a farmhouse near Ossining, New York, and began their ministry, associating in time with the Dominican order. The Holy See granted approval to the group as a religious congregation in February 1920, and the first members spent a year in novitiate training and made their vows in 1921. They were already involved in mission work among the Japanese in the United States. Some of the sisters made their way to Hong Kong, and Maryknoll sisters went on to serve in South China, Japan, Korea, Hawaii, Manchuria, and the Philippines. In 1932 the Maryknoll Sisters founded a cloister to give spiritual support to those engaged in the mission fields. Other contemplative communities were established in Guatemala, Sudan, and Thailand.

During World War II, members of the Maryknoll Sisters faced imprisonment and even death across Asia from the fighting and the hardship of war and persecution. Like the religious men of Maryknoll, the Maryknoll Sisters began during the war to labor in Latin America, with members active in Bolivia, Nicaragua, and the Panama Canal Zone. Later expansions took them to Formosa, Ceylon, the Caroline Islands, and Tanganyika.

After the Second Vatican Council, the Maryknoll Sisters became actively involved in the issue of global justice and the needs of the poor. Two members of Maryknoll, Sisters Maura Clarke and Ita Ford, were among four churchwomen (the others were fellow missionaries Jean Donovan and Dorothy Kazel) killed by the military in El Salvador in December 1980 because of their ministry to the poor.

Currently, there are over seven hundred members engaged in a wide variety of ministries, with sisters in El Salvador, Guatemala, Somalia, Sudan, Thailand, Mozambique, and Hong Kong. Some members also returned to mainland China to teach English in institutes of higher learning. In 2005–06 the Maryknoll Sisters celebrated the fiftieth anniversary of Mother Mary Joseph's death on October 9, 1955.

Maryland

Called the Old Line State, Maryland is located on the Middle Atlantic seaboard of the United States. It is bounded on the north by Pennsylvania and Delaware, on the east by Delaware and the Atlantic Ocean, on the south by Chesapeake Bay, the Potomac River, the District of Columbia, Virginia, and West Virginia, and on the west by West Virginia. There are two main land regions in Maryland: the Atlantic Coastal Plain in the east and the Appalachian Highlands in the west. The original inhabitants of Maryland were the Nanticoke, Yaocomoco, and Piscataway. One of the original thirteen colonies, Maryland entered the Union in April 1788 as the seventh state.

Maryland was colonized as a Catholic haven by George Calvert, Lord Baltimore of England, but Catholic explorers were in the area as early as the 1500s. William Claiborne led a group from the colony of Virginia to Kent Island in 1631 to establish a trading post. In 1632 George Calvert, Lord Baltimore, received a grant of Maryland land from King Charles I. Calvert, a convert to Catholicism, envisioned the colony as a haven for Catholics. He died soon after, and the grant was inherited by his son, Cecilius, who made his brother, Leonard, the proprietary governor when the first settlers landed on St. Clement's Island on March 25, 1634. The colony was named Maryland in honor of Henrietta Marie, the consort of Charles I.

Among the first settlers were Jesuit Fathers Andrew White, John Altham, and Thomas Gervase. The priests had boarded the ship at a special stop in order to avoid the English regulations concerning Catholics of the realm. Father White celebrated the first Mass in Maryland upon landing on the island and was welcomed by the Yaocomoco Indians of the area. He immediately started a ministry with the populous Piscataway tribe. In 1637 Jesuit Fathers Thomas Copley and John Knoller joined the mission band in Maryland. Two years later, Father White opened the Kittamaquindi mission for the Piscataway, with stations at Mettapony, Anacosta, and Potopaco. On July 5, 1640, Chilomachou, the "Emperor of the Piscataway," was baptized with other members of the tribe. Father White gave the chief the baptismal name of Charles, and Governor Calvert attended the ceremony.

Seeing the influx of Puritans into Maryland, many of whom came from England or from nearby colonies, Governor Calvert managed to have the colonial legislature pass the Act of Toleration in 1649. This act provided religious freedom to all who believed in Christ. In 1654 the Puritans seized control of the colony and repealed the law. In 1658 Lord Calvert regained authority in Maryland, and Catholics once again had religious liberty. The Jesuits and then the Franciscans, led by Father Massius Massey, served the faithful.

The Glorious Revolution in England in 1688 brought the forced abdication of King James II and an end to Catholic liberties in Maryland. The Protestant Association, under John Coode, seized control, and under William and Mary, the new Protestant monarchs, Maryland was governed as a royal colony. That meant that Catholic public worship was forbidden. In 1694 the capital of the colony was moved from the predominantly Catholic St. Mary's to Annapolis. The three thousand Catholics and the missionaries acted discreetly during this period, and the faith remained solid through the private celebration of Mass and the sacraments. The fifth Lord Baltimore, however, became a Protestant and instituted new restrictions against Catholics in 1715. Franciscans had been arrested and deported, but Jesuit Father Thomas Mansell had managed to found St. Xavier's in Cecil County.

Soon after, Maryland was involved in the growing quest for freedom, which sparked various responses to British laws and policies by the colonists. Taxes and neglect on the part of Britain fueled a rebellion, and in 1774 Maryland colonials set fire to the British ship *Peggy Stewart* and destroyed the vessel and its prized cargo of taxed tea in Annapolis harbor. Maryland declared independence from England on November 8, 1776, and the Second

because no Massachusetts citizen could vow allegiance to a foreign power. The Vatican was deemed such a power, and that restriction was maintained in the state until 1821. When the French military allies left the United States in 1782, a Catholic ceremony had been held, attended by all officials and leaders of the young nation. In 1788 Massachusetts became the sixth former colony to ratify the United States Constitution.

In Massachusetts, Father Jean-Louis Lefebvre de Cheverus, who would become a Peer of France and a cardinal, was winning the respect and admiration of local Protestants. He was consecrated as the first bishop of the Diocese of Boston in 1808, also serving all of New England. When the king of France recalled Bishop de Cheverus, a petition, signed by Catholics and Protestants, including Daniel Webster, was sent to the French monarch, protesting such a loss to America.

In 1825 Bishop Benedict Joseph Fenwick succeeded Bishop de Cheverus and discovered only eight parishes. He soon was faced by a great influx of Irish Catholics during the 1830s and 1840s. The Protestants viewed the Irish with anxiety, and the Broad Street Riots erupted, with Catholics and Protestants clashing openly. The Church survived the onslaughts, and Bishop Fenwick expanded parishes and diocesan facilities, including those in Vermont, Connecticut, and Rhode Island, as well as those for the Abenaki Indians in Maine. In 1843 he opened Holy Cross College.

The successor to Bishop Fenwick, John Bernard Fitzpatrick, was installed in 1846 and welcomed more Irish Catholics, immigrants forced to flee Ireland because of the Great Famine. His time was also marked by the arrival of Italian and French Canadian Catholics, and Bishop Fitzpatrick faced the attacks of the Know-Nothings, anti-Catholics, and then the sacrifices of the Civil War. He continued to administer Catholic affairs with such grace and zeal and displayed such courtesy to all people of good will that he received an honorary doctorate from Harvard University. He was responsible for founding Boston College in 1863.

In 1875 Pope Blessed Pius IX elevated the Diocese of Boston to the status of an archdiocese, and Bishop John J. Williams became the first archbishop. Bishop Williams pioneered a parochial school system and took part in the erection of the Dioceses of Springfield, Providence, and Fall River. For his accomplishments, his time as bishop became known as "the brick and mortar age of the Catholic Church in New England." Nevertheless, the rise of the Irish as a major population in the state and the fact that there were such large numbers of Catholic Eastern Europeans only encouraged anti-Catholic fervor in some quarters.

Archbishop William H. O'Connell marked the next stage in the growth of the Church in Massachusetts. He became a cardinal in 1911 and led the Church in Massachusetts during the period of World War I and the Great Depression. The Church under Cardinal O'Connell underwent a rigorous process of centralization, strict financial vigilance, and equal vigor in expanding the parishes in Massachusetts to ensure pastoral care. During O'Connell's time in Boston, the number of parishes increased by over a hundred.

His successor, Cardinal Richard James Cushing, became one of the best-known, most beloved prelates in the United States. He led the faithful of the archdiocese during the last period of World War II and then into the economic postwar expansion. Cardinal Cushing presided over a time of immense influence for the Church in Massachusetts as Catholics comprised half the entire state's population. The greatest moment for Catholics in the era was the 1960 election of President John F. Kennedy. The exuberance was short-lived, as Cardinal Cushing had the sad duty of celebrating the funeral Mass for the assassinated president in 1963 in St. Matthew's Cathedral in Washington, D.C.

The colossal building projects required to keep pace with the expansion of the Catholic population left the Archdiocese of Boston with an enormous debt, and Cardinal Cushing's successor, Cardinal Humberto S. Medeiros, dealt with financial rebuilding. Named a cardinal in 1973, Cardinal Medeiros also carried the weight of trying to implement the reforms of the Second Vatican Council in the midst of the turbulent 1970s. Massachusetts underwent enormous social upheaval, including the legalization of abortion, and the bishops of the state were confronted with a radically changing environment.

The Church recovered much of its élan in the

1980s, mostly so under Cardinal Bernard F. Law, who became a cardinal in 1985. In 2002, however, the state was rocked by the onset of the sex abuse scandal and the resulting trials and massive legal troubles for the Archdiocese of Boston. Cardinal Law resigned in 2002 in the wake of the ecclesiastical disaster.

Cardinal Law's successor was Archbishop Seán O'Malley, O.F.M. Cap. He was appointed in 2003 and created a cardinal in 2006, and has worked since to rebuild Catholic morale and unity as well as to overcome the severe financial problems resulting from the lawsuits and scandals. This has proven an immensely difficult task. The 2004 U.S. presidential campaign also raised serious questions regarding the fidelity of political leaders to the teachings of the Church. Democratic nominee Massachusetts Senator John Kerry, a Catholic, was also a supporter of abortion and homosexual rights, sparking a debate over whether political figures holding positions contrary to the Church should be permitted to receive the Eucharist.

Despite the scandals and significant loss of prestige in the first decade of the new century, the Church in Massachusetts remains almost 43 percent of the total population, with a membership of nearly five million. There are also over 2,200 priests, nearly 3,000 men and women religious, and 644 parishes in the state.

Masse, Enemond (d. May 12, 1646)

A Jesuit missionary, Enemond Masse was taken prisoner by British forces while serving the Abenaki Indians in Maine. He was born in Lyons, France, and entered the Society of Jesus. In 1574 he arrived in the American colonies and opened a mission at present-day Bar Harbor, Maine. British authorities, alert to his presence, swiftly destroyed the mission and took Father Masse prisoner. He was insulted and abused in captivity and then put into a small open boat and towed far out on the Atlantic Ocean. There he was abandoned without food or water. Father Masse, however, was rescued by a passing French ship and returned to France, where he made known his treatment by the British. In 1625 Father Masse returned to the missions, working among the Hurons and other Indian nations in Canada until his death at Sillery.

Mathevon, Lucille (1793–March 11, 1876)

A member of the Religious of the Sacred Heart and a superior who performed remarkable labors among the Potawatomi tribes in Kansas, Lucille Mathevon was born near Lyons, France. She entered the Society of the Sacred Heart in 1813 and took her final profession in 1818. Her early years in community were spent in the company of St. Rose Philippine Duchesne, and Sister Lucille also knew St. Madeleine Sophie Barat as the convent was paid visits by the future saint.

Sister Lucille was called to serve in the Native American missions in North America, and in 1822 she received permission to make the arduous journey to America. She was assigned to the congregation's houses in Missouri, at Florissant, St. Charles, and St. Louis, and devoted the next decades to faithful service. In 1841 she was chosen to lead as superior a group of sisters to be sent to Sugar Creek, Kansas, as Father Pierre-Jean De Smet had asked the Religious of the Sacred Heart to open a school for Potawatomi girls.

Mother Lucille spent the next three decades among the Potawatomi. She moved the school to Kansas, in 1847, and in 1852 she could write to St. Rose that she had more than sixty pupils in her boarding school, with four lay teachers who assisted the nuns.

Such was the love and esteem of the Potawatomi for Mother Lucille that when she was transferred in 1868 to St. Charles because of her declining health the tribe made an official request that she be permitted to return. In 1871 she was allowed to go back to Kansas, where she died. While overshadowed by the famed labors of St. Rose, Mother Lucille is honored as an important figure in the immense work of the Religious of the Sacred Heart.

Matignon, Francis A. (1753–September 18, 1818)

A missionary in the young United States, Francis A. Matignon was a companion of Father Jean-Louis Lefebvre de Cheverus, who would become the first bishop of the Diocese of Boston and then a Peer and cardinal of France. Both he and Father de Cheverus were exiles from France because of the terrors of the French Revolution, and Father Matignon is recorded as having brought Father de Cheverus to America. He was ordained in

France in 1773 and arrived in Boston on August 20, 1792. The two priests established parishes and other Catholic facilities, including a library, and served the Catholics of the region. Both of them won the respect and admiration of non-Catholics because of their education, simplicity of lifestyle, and intelligence. Many outstanding leaders of the young United States donated to the fund-raising campaign conducted by the priests to erect a parish. During the yellow fever epidemic of April 1798, Father Matignon distinguished himself especially in caring for countless victims. Father Matignon was offered a see but declined consecration and continued to serve in Boston. He died there, beloved by people of all faiths.

Maurin, Aristode Pierre ("Peter") (May 9, 1877– May 15, 1949)

A lay activist, Aristode "Peter" Maurin was co-founder with Dorothy Day of the Catholic Worker Movement. Born in Oultet, Lanquedoc, France, he embraced a Franciscan spirit of poverty. At sixteen Peter Maurin entered the Christian Brothers, but during 1898–99 his community life was interrupted by obligatory military service. In 1902, when the French government closed many religious schools, Maurin left the order and became active in a Catholic lay movement that advocated Christian democracy and supported cooperatives and unions. He left the group, however, in 1908. The following year Maurin emigrated to Canada, and for two years he homesteaded in Saskatchewan and then went to the United States. Through years of economic difficulties and hard labor, he came to embrace poverty more fully. As often as possible, Maurin visited New York City, and there George Shuster, editor of *Commonweal* magazine, gave him the address of Dorothy Day, a Catholic convert supporting herself as a freelance journalist. Maurin introduced himself to her in December 1932.

Maurin believed that Dorothy Day could "move mountains, and have influence on governments, temporal and spiritual." He began, therefore, to educate her in the Catholic faith and spirituality. He proposed that Day start a newspaper to publicize Catholic social teaching and promote steps to bring about the peaceful transformation of society. *The Catholic Worker* was started as a result. In the paper, Maurin advocated ancient Christian practices, including a "Christ Room" in every home. Catholic Workers also took up his call to start farming communes, which Maurin preferred to call "agronomic universities." In 1938 Maurin moved to Mary Farm, a ten-acre property the Catholic Worker community bought in Easton, Pennsylvania. The farm was sold in 1944, the year in which Maurin suffered a minor stroke and slowly began losing his memory.

His last five years were lived quietly and humbly at the Catholic Worker's Maryfarm Retreat Center near Newburgh. His death in 1949 was reported by the *New York Times* and the Vatican newspaper, *L'Osservatore Romano. Time* magazine noted that Maurin was buried in a "castoff suit and consigned to a donated grave," appropriate arrangements for a man who "had slept in no bed of his own and worn no suit that someone had not given away."

Maynard, Theodore (November 3, 1890–October 18, 1956)

Historian, poet, and literary critic, Theodore Maynard was a convert and an influential chronicler of American Catholic history. Born in Madras, India, to English missionary parents of the Plymouth Brethren, he was sent to England for his schooling with the expectation that he would become a missionary. He was not suited for the Brethren, however, and joined the Baptists in what became a long journey to the Catholic Church. Particularly influential in his spiritual development was G. K. Chesterton's *Orthodoxy* (1908), especially the importance of the relationship between faith and reason.

Maynard traveled to the United States and worked in various jobs between 1909 and 1911. He went back to England, joined the Unitarians, and in 1912 met the famed writer Hilaire Belloc. The next year, Maynard entered the Church. He devoted the next years to writing and published poetry, various reviews, and essays in numerous publications, including *New Witness* (where he worked with G. K. Chesterton and his brother, Cecil Chesterton), the *London Poetry Review,* and the *London Times.* His first collection of poems, *Laughs and Whifts of Song,* was published in 1915.

Maynard married Sara Casey, a novelist and

playwright, in 1918. In 1920 he set sail for America and a series of lectures. Offered a teaching post at the Dominican College in San Rafael, California, he moved the family to the San Francisco Bay area in 1921. He taught there until 1925, and over the next years he published a number of books and began a keen interest in Church history, especially Catholicism in the United States. In all, he went on to write twenty-seven books of Catholic history and biography among his forty books, including an autobiography, *The World I Saw,* in 1938.

Maynard also taught at Fordham University, Georgetown University, and Mount St. Mary's College. At the same time, he worked on several degrees and earned a master's degree from Georgetown University and a doctorate from The Catholic University of America. He served as president of the Catholic Poetry of America Society in 1948. He died at Port Washington, New York.

Mazzella, Camillo (February 10, 1833–March 26, 1900)

A Jesuit theologian, Camillo Mazzella was created a cardinal by Pope Leo XIII. He was born in Vitulano, Italy, and entered the ecclesiastical seminary of Benevento at about eleven years of age. He was ordained in September 1855, a dispensation for defect of canonical age having been granted by Pope Blessed Pius IX. For two years after his ordination he remained at Vitulano, attending to the duties of a canon in the parish church, a position he held from his family. Resigning this office, he entered the Society of Jesus on September 4, 1857. When the Jesuits were expelled from Italy in 1860, he was sent to Fourvières. In 1867 Father Mazzella came to America and taught theology for two years at Georgetown University. On the opening of Woodstock College in Maryland, he was appointed prefect of studies and professor of dogmatic theology. While there he published four volumes: *De Religione et Ecclesia*, *De Deo Creante*, *De Gratia Christi*, and *De virtutibus infusis*, which went through several editions.

In October 1878 Father Mazzella was called to Rome by Pope Leo XIII to fill the chair of theology at the Pontifical Gregorian University. On June 7, 1886, the pope created him a cardinal deacon, and ten years later he became a cardinal priest. On April 18, 1897, he was appointed the cardinal bishop of Palestrina. Cardinal Mazzella took an active part in the deliberations of a number of Vatican congregations and was for several years the president of the Academy of St. Thomas, and, at various times, prefect of the Congregations of the Index, of Studies, and of Rites.

Mazzuchelli, Venerable Samuel C. (November 4, 1806–February 23, 1864)

Declared venerable by Pope Blessed John Paul II, Samuel C. Mazzuchelli was a pioneering Dominican missionary in America. He was born in Milan, Italy, to Luigi Mazzuchelli and Rachele Merlini Mazzuchelli and was educated there and in Switzerland. In 1823 he entered the Order of Preachers, the Dominicans, in Faenza, Italy. After initial studies, he was sent to Rome. While there, he learned of the plea from the Dominican Bishop Edward D. Fenwick of Cincinnati for priests to serve in the missions in the wilds of the United States. With great zeal and eagerness, Mazzuchelli volunteered for the missions, and his superiors gave their permission.

He set out for the United States in June 1828 in the company of the vicar general of Cincinnati, Father Frederick Résé. After saying farewell to his family in Milan, Mazzuchelli journeyed to Paris and then made the trip to the United States alone, as Résé departed suddenly for Germany. He reached Cincinnati in November 1828 and was received with great enthusiasm by Bishop Fenwick. The next year, as a deacon, he was sent to St. Joseph's Parish in Somerset, Ohio, and there learned about mission service from several Dominicans.

Ordained a priest on September 5, 1831, in Cincinnati, he was sent into the northern regions of the vast diocese, stretching south from the Canadian border across northern Illinois and into Upper Michigan and Wisconsin. He reached Mackinac Island in November 1830 at the age of twenty-four and was the only priest in the area. The following year, he was joined by the holy Irenaeus Frederick Baraga, a Slovenian priest who became a legendary missionary in his own right. The two became good friends and shared the immense burden of evangelization in the wilderness.

Father Mazzuchelli devoted the years 1830 to

1835 to the pastoral care of French Canadian fur traders and gave special concern to the Native Americans, the Ojibwa, Ottawa, Winnebago, and Menominee. He learned their customs and used catechists to preach in their languages. A prayer book was published in Winnebago, a liturgical calendar was developed for the Menominee, and schools were opened, although money was always scarce for the cause.

In 1835 Father Mazzuchelli was assigned to be the only priest in the Mississippi valley and proved instrumental in laying the foundations for parishes

Venerable Samuel Mazzucheli

throughout the extensive territory. He became a trusted pastoral leader whose contributions were valued by the bishops in Michigan, Missouri, Wisconsin, Illinois, and Iowa, and the degree of public esteem for him was made manifest in the request in 1836 that he serve as chaplain of the first legislature of the territory of Wisconsin.

As the towns and parishes developed, he focused next on promoting education. He established a Dominican center at Sinsinawa Mound, Wisconsin (later a college) and in 1847 started the Sinsinawa Dominican Sisters, who founded the St. Clara Academy in 1853. Father Mazzuchelli continued to develop parishes, and in 1849–50 he won great praise for his fearless care of poor souls during a cholera epidemic. He died from pneumonia after traveling in harsh winter weather to bring the sacraments to several dying parishioners. His passing was the cause for mourning among both Catholics and Protestants. He was buried at St. Patrick's in Benton, Wisconsin. In 1993 he was declared venerable by Pope Blessed John Paul II.

McAvoy, Thomas Timothy (September 12, 1903–July 7, 1969)

Historian and teacher, Thomas McAvoy was born in Tipton, Indiana, and grew up heavily influenced by the remarkable members of the Sisters of St. Joseph, who oversaw his education. At the age of fourteen, he became the reporter for the Tipton *Times* and by 1920 was employed as full-time city editor and reporter. That same year, he began stud-

ies for the priesthood and entered the Congregation of the Holy Cross. College studies began at the University of Notre Dame, where in his senior year he won the Dockweiler Medal in Philosophy and the O'Brien Medal in History. His theological studies were undertaken at Holy Cross College at The Catholic University in Washington, and on June 24, 1929, he was ordained.

Father McAvoy went on to earn a master's degree from Notre Dame and completed his doctoral studies at Columbia University. His dissertation was a study of the history of the Church in Indiana during the transition period between the decline of the French missions and the reestablishment of the Church under the American hierarchy. It was published as *The Catholic Church in Indiana, 1784–1834* in 1940. Even before completing his doctorate, he was named head of the Department of History at Notre Dame and went on to serve as one of the more significant scholars of American Catholic history in the twentieth century. His chief interests lay in the study of the American Catholic minority and its encounter with the mainstream of American culture. He studied in particular the crisis of Americanism. His work in the fields led to *The Great Crisis in American Catholic History, 1895–1900,* published in 1957. He also wrote *Roman Catholicism and the American Way of Life* in 1960 and *A History of the Catholic Church in the United States* in 1969.

McCarran, Patrick (August 8, 1876–September 28, 1954)

A powerful United States Senator from Nevada, Patrick McCarran was born in Reno, Nevada, the son of Irish Catholic immigrants. He attended public schools and the University of Nevada at Reno and worked as a janitor to pay his way through college. In 1903 he married Martha Weeks. That same year, he was elected to the Nevada Legislature, but he supported his family by farming and raising sheep. He also studied law and was admitted to the bar in 1905. He practiced in Tonopah and Goldfield, Nevada, and served as district attorney of Nye County from 1907 to 1909.

McCarran resumed the practice of law in Reno in 1909. In 1913 he was elected an associate justice of the Supreme Court of Nevada and chief justice in 1917–18; he was also a member of the Nevada Board of Pardons from 1913 to 1919, the Nevada State Board of Parole Commissioners from 1913 to 1918, chairman of the Nevada State Board of Bar Examiners from 1919 to 1932, and an unsuccessful candidate for the U.S. Senate in 1916 and 1926. Finally, in 1932, he was elected as a Democrat to the United States Senate, and reelected in 1938, 1944, and 1950. He was chairman of the Committee on the District of Columbia, the Committee on the Judiciary, and co-chairman of the Joint Committee on Foreign Economic Cooperation.

Although a Democrat, McCarran proved to have an independent mind. He opposed President Franklin D. Roosevelt and President Harry S. Truman on a variety of issues. In the period after World War II, he was a staunch opponent of communism. He was sponsor of the Internal Security Act of 1950, which sought to root out alleged communists in the government, and the Immigration and Nationality Act of 1952, which sought to eliminate people deemed to be "security risks" to national security. His opinions made him a natural supporter of Senator Joseph McCarthy. Interred in Mountain View Cemetery in Reno, McCarran was honored in 1960 with his statue in Statuary Hall in the Capitol, representing Nevada.

McCarrick, Theodore (July 7, 1930–)

Archbishop of Washington from 2001 to 2006 and a cardinal from 2001, Theodore Edgar McCarrick was born in New York City to Theodore Egan McCarrick and Margaret McLaughlin. He studied at Fordham Preparatory School and then Fordham University before entering the seminary. In preparation for the priesthood, he studied at St. Joseph's Seminary in Yonkers, New York, where he earned a bachelor's degree in 1954 and a master's degree in history in 1958. New York Cardinal Francis Spellman ordained him to the priesthood on May 31, 1958. He subsequently earned a second master's degree in social sciences and then a doctorate in sociology from The Catholic University of America.

Father McCarrick was assigned as assistant chaplain of Catholic University and then dean of students and director of development. Appointed president of the Catholic University of Puerto Rico in Ponce in 1965, he marked his tenure there by focusing on the extensive development of the school and received the title of monsignor from Pope Paul VI that same year. In 1969 Monsignor McCarrick was recalled to New York, where he was named by Cardinal Terence J. Cooke as associate secretary for education and an assistant priest at Blessed Sacrament Parish from 1969 to 1971, and then as the cardinal's secretary from 1971 to 1977.

In 1977 Monsignor McCarrick was appointed by Pope Paul VI titular bishop of Rusubisir and auxiliary bishop of New York. He was consecrated a bishop on June 29, 1977, and served as vicar of East Manhattan and the Harlems. Four years later, on November 19, 1981, he was appointed by Pope Blessed John Paul II to be the first bishop of Metuchen, when the diocese was established. Installed on January 31, 1982, he remained in Metuchen for only four years as on June 3, 1986, he was named archbishop of Newark, and was installed on July 25, 1986. That same year, and again in 1992, the National Conference of Catholic Bishops elected him chair of the Committee on Migration. In 1992 he was also named to head the Committee for Aid to the Church in Central and Eastern Europe; in 1996 he was elected chair of the Committee on International Policy. He has served on or headed a variety of other bishops' committees, including the Domestic Policy Committee, and committees on administration, doctrine, laity, Latin America, and the missions.

In 1997 he was elected one of fifteen U.S. bishops to serve as a member of the Synod for America. Following the synod, he was chosen to serve on the post-synodal council. Further, he has been chancellor of The Catholic University of America and president of the Board of Trustees of the Basilica of the National Shrine of the Immaculate Conception, as well as a founding member of the Papal Foundation and a member of the board of Catholic Relief Services.

Following the passing of Cardinal James A. Hickey, on November 21, 2000, Archbishop McCarrick was appointed by Pope Blessed John

Paul II to serve as archbishop of Washington, D.C. Installed on January 3, 2001, he was elevated to the College of Cardinals as a cardinal priest on February 21, 2001, with the titular church of SS. Nereus and Achilleus. As archbishop, Cardinal McCarrick was renowned for his charm, sense of humor, and great concern for the faithful of the diocese and for the residents of the District of Columbia. He was also active in a whole range of Catholic social justice issues, including war and peace, the death penalty, and the promotion of the culture of life. Known around the world for his diplomatic skills and deep concern for human rights and the needs of the poor, Cardinal McCarrick was named by the Vatican to the Pontifical Council for Justice and Peace, the Pontifical Council for the Pastoral Care of Migrants and Itinerant Peoples, and the Pontifical Commission for Latin America. He served also on the Secretary of State's Advisory Committee on Religious Freedom Abroad and from 1999 to 2001 was a member of the United States Commission for International Religious Freedom. In January 2000 the president of Lebanon named him an Officer of the Order of the Cedars of Lebanon, and in December 2000 President Clinton presented him with the Eleanor Roosevelt Award for Human Rights. Cardinal McCarrick retired on May 16, 2006.

McCarthy, Joseph R. (November 14, 1908–May 2, 1957)

A Republican U.S. Senator from the state of Wisconsin between 1947 and 1957, Joseph Raymond McCarthy rose to national prominence through the Permanent Subcommittee on Investigations, which looked into the threat of communists in the country. His tactics and style of investigation became known as McCarthyism and defined an era of the Cold War between the United States and the Soviet Union. He was born in the township of Grand Chute, Wisconsin, near Appleton, the son of Tim and Bridget McCarthy. Having dropped out of high school to help his parents run the family farm, he returned to high school at the age of twenty, swiftly graduated, and then went to college. He earned a law degree from Marquette University in Milwaukee and was admitted to the bar in 1935. After a brief run for political office, he was elected as the nonpartisan 10th District circuit judge.

Soon after the entry of the United States into World War II, McCarthy enlisted in the United States Marine Corps and served as an intelligence briefing officer for a dive bomber squadron in the Solomon Islands and Bougainville. Using his military career as a springboard for elected office, he ran for the Republican Senate nomination in Wisconsin while still on active duty in 1944. Defeated for the nomination by Alexander Wiley, he resigned his commission in April 1945 and was reelected unopposed to his circuit court position. He then campaigned for the 1946 Republican Senate primary nomination, defeated the famed Robert M. La Follette Jr., and easily won election to the United States Senate.

Senator McCarthy first attained national prominence as a result of a speech he delivered on February 9, 1950, to the Republican Women's Club of Wheeling, West Virginia. In his address, he claimed to have a list of known communists who were working for the State Department and who were directly shaping American foreign policy. The exact number of communists whom he claimed were active has long been a matter of dispute, but McCarthy is usually quoted to have said: "I have here in my hand a list of 205 people that were known to the Secretary of State as being members of the Communist Party, and who, nevertheless, are still working and shaping the policy of the State Department."

The Tydings Committee was a subcommittee of the Senate Foreign Relations Committee that was set up in February 1950 to conduct "a full and complete study and investigation as to whether persons who are disloyal to the United States are, or have been, employed by the Department of State."

In 1953 McCarthy married Jean Kerr, a researcher in his office (they adopted a baby girl in January 1957), the same year that he won a second term to the Senate. He was then named chairman of the Senate Committee on Government Operations, a position that placed him in charge of the Senate Permanent Subcommittee on Investigations. This proved a suitable instrument to investigate the presence of communists in the U.S. government, and McCarthy was assisted by Roy Cohn as chief counsel and Robert F. Kennedy as an assistant counsel to the subcommittee. The next years witnessed the controversial Army-McCarthy hearings that culminated in his condemnation by the United States Senate on December 2, 1954, by a vote of 67 to 22.

McCarthy died in Bethesda Naval Hospital and received a state funeral attended by seventy senators. The requiem Mass was held at St. Matthew's Cathedral, and he was buried in St. Mary's Parish Cemetery in Appleton, Wisconsin. One of the most controversial and incendiary figures in American history, McCarthy became so vilified in American culture that his name was adopted to denote witch-hunting and heavy-handed tactics. He remains the source of debate and disagreement among scholars and writers, even as he represented a national concern regarding the Soviet Union and communism in the country, a fear that was a palpable part of the Cold War and that he used to some effect in establishing himself on the national scene. McCarthy also represented a genuine concern among many Catholic leaders regarding the evils and the dangers of communism for the Church throughout the world and in American institutions.

McCloskey, John (March 10, 1810–October 10, 1885)

The second archbishop of New York, from 1864 to 1885, and the first American cardinal, from 1875, John McCloskey was an important symbol of Catholicism's progress in the city and the prosperity of its members. He was elevated to the College of Cardinals in recognition of his work and the prominence of the New York archdiocese. Born in Brooklyn, New York, he was the son of Irish Catholic immigrants, Patrick and Elizabeth McCloskey. His parents had emigrated from Dungiven, County Derry, Ireland, in 1808, and his father worked as a clerk. Young John was educated in a school for boys, run by Mrs. Charlotte Milmoth, and then in a Latin school after the family moved to New York City in 1817.

In 1820 Cardinal McCloskey's father died, but the family was assisted by the wealthy businessman Cornelius Heeney, who served as his guardian and made possible his entrance into Mount St. Mary's College in Emmitsburg, Maryland, in September 1821. Over the next years, McCloskey studied under a number of instructors who became promi-

nent figures in American Catholic history, including Simon William Gabriel Bruté de Rémur and John Hughes. Completing his program of studies in Maryland in 1827, he returned to New York and went on to receive ordination to the priesthood in old St. Patrick's Cathedral on January 12, 1834. He was the first native of New York state to become a diocesan priest.

Father McCloskey was assigned to serve as professor of philosophy in the new seminary at Nyack, New York, but his period of service ended abruptly in 1834 with a fire. That same year, he was sent for additional studies at the Pontifical Gregorian University in Rome, and he availed himself of the opportunity to travel extensively elsewhere in Europe when he had the time.

Returning to New York in 1837, McCloskey was named rector of St. Joseph's Church. He dealt there with assorted difficulties with the parish trustees and members of the congregation, and as pastor he proved a gifted voice of reconciliation and patience. In 1841 he was appointed by Bishop John Hughes as the first president of St. John's College (later Fordham University). He devoted himself to organizing the new school, but resigned the next year to commit himself to his other duties. He was responsible for the conversions of James Roosevelt Bayley, who went on to become archbishop of Baltimore, in 1842 and Isaac Thomas Hecker, the founder of the Paulists, in 1844. Having impressed Bishop Hughes, McCloskey was named by Pope Gregory XVI titular bishop of Axiere and coadjutor bishop of New York with right of succession to Bishop Hughes. He was consecrated on March 10, 1844.

As coadjutor, Bishop McCloskey proved an invaluable assistant to Bishop Hughes, but when the sees of Albany and Buffalo were created in 1847, he was named the first bishop of Albany and installed on September 19, 1847. Bishop McCloskey proved an energetic shepherd for the expansive diocese and presided over the swift growth of the Church, including construction of the Cathedral of the Immaculate Conception. The Catholic population increased from some 60,000 to over 290,000 and the number of churches expanded from 47 to 120. Archbishop McCloskey's time was also marked by his stern but unsuccessful opposition to New York's Putnam's Bill of 1855, which prohibited Catholic bishops from handing on church property to their successors; the bill thus essentially enforced trusteeism. Although it passed, the bill was repealed after seven years, but was nevertheless an example of the pervasive anti-Catholic atmosphere of the times. Still, McCloskey proved an adroit political figure and won the respect of a number of powerful New York political leaders.

Meanwhile, on July 19, 1850, New York was elevated to the status of a metropolitan provincial see, and Bishop Hughes was raised to the dignity of an archbishop. He died in January 1864, and Bishop McCloskey was considered the leading candidate to succeed him. He tried unsuccessfully to avoid being named, but on May 6, 1864, he was appointed archbishop of New York by Pope Blessed Pius IX and was installed in old St. Patrick's Cathedral on August 21, 1864.

Archbishop McCloskey took as his immediate task the completion of the new St. Patrick's Cathedral, which had been begun in 1858; work, however, had been suspended while the Civil War raged. McCloskey traveled to Europe to solicit funds for the undertaking and was able to dedicate the finished church on May 25, 1879. At the time, it was the largest Gothic building in the United States. The old St. Patrick's Cathedral was destroyed by a fire in 1866 and rebuilt.

Archbishop McCloskey also dedicated himself to the continued growth and nurturing of the archdiocese. By 1885 there

Cardinal John McCloskey

were over a million Catholics in the archdiocese and McCloskey doubled the number of churches, clergy, and schools. He welcomed sixteen religious communities to New York and encouraged the Sisters of Charity, the Paulists, and the Belgian Fathers and Brothers, who assumed direction of the new provincial seminary at Troy, New York, in 1864.

He gave his support to the Sisters of Charity in opening the New York Foundling Asylum (later the New York Foundling Hospital), to Dr. Levi Silliman Ives in opening the New York Catholic Protectory, and to Father John Drumgoole in establishing the Mission of the Immaculate Virgin. In 1866 Archbishop McCloskey issued a pastoral letter discouraging Irish Catholics from taking part in the violent schemes against English rule of Canada and Ireland.

Archbishop McCloskey attended the First Vatican Council and served as a member of the commission on discipline. Although he opposed the definition of papal infallibility, he voted *placet* at the final session. He had impressed Pope Pius IX during the proceedings, and five years later, on March 15, 1875, he was elevated to the College of Cardinals, the first American to receive the honor. He received the red biretta from Archbishop James Roosevelt Bayley of Baltimore in old St. Patrick's Cathedral on April 27. In September of that year, he returned to Rome to take possession of his titular church, Santa Maria sopra Minerva.

In 1878 he was summoned to Rome for the conclave to choose a successor to Pius IX; he arrived too late to take part in the election of Pope Leo XIII, but he did assist at the coronation. His position as a cardinal was a great honor to the American Church and to Cardinal McCloskey and enhanced the status of the American Catholic community in Europe and especially in Rome.

Owing to advancing years and declining health, Cardinal McCloskey received Bishop Michael A. Corrigan of Newark in 1880 as his coadjutor with right of succession. Health problems forced him to surrender most of his responsibilities, although he presided over the Fourth Provincial Council of New York in September 1883. His last public act was to make a successful appeal, largely through his coadjutor, to President Chester A. Arthur and Secretary of State Frederick T. Frelinghuysen to spare the North American College in Rome from seizure by the Italian government in 1884. He spent his last year in retirement at Mount St. Vincent-on-Hudson, where he died. He was buried in the crypt beneath the high altar of the new St. Patrick's Cathedral.

McCloskey, William George (November 10, 1823–September 17, 1909)

Bishop of Louisville from 1868 to 1909, William George McCloskey was born in Brooklyn, New York, and was the youngest of five brothers, two of whom became priests. Ordained a priest in October 1852 by Bishop John Hughes in old St. Patrick's Cathedral in New York, he served as a pastoral assistant to his brother George at the Church of the Nativity. Appointed to the faculty of Mount St. Mary's College in Emmitsburg, Maryland, he taught moral theology, Scripture, and Latin for six years and was then appointed in December 1859 to serve as the first American rector of the American College at Rome.

Having received a Doctor of Divinity degree from Georgetown University, he was the unanimous choice of the American bishops for the post. Father McCloskey arrived in Rome in March 1860 and served as rector until May 1868, when he was appointed bishop of Louisville. As rector, Father McCloskey guided the college during the long and difficult years of the American Civil War. Internal tensions and disagreements over the war combined with the shortage of funds and mounting political crises in Italy caused severe hardships. Many bishops declined to send students or financial support, often because they had neither seminarians nor disposable funds during the war, but Bishop McCloskey patiently and steadfastly overcame the doubts of some bishops about whether the college should continue.

Consecrated in Rome, Bishop McCloskey reached Louisville in late summer 1868. Although often stern and willful, and enduring poor relations with the priests and women religious of the diocese, he presided over the expansion of the Catholic community of Louisville. He expanded the number of churches from 64 to 164 and the number of priests from 80 to 200. In 1869 he founded the diocesan Preston Park Seminary. He also encouraged religious orders to come into the diocese, including the Passionists, Benedictines, Fathers of the Resurrection, Sisters of Mercy, Little Sisters of the Poor, Franciscan Sisters, and Brothers of Mary.

McCloskey took part in the First Vatican Council, and in the Second and Third Plenary Councils of Baltimore in 1866 and 1884, respectively. He remained a strong advocate for the North American College at Rome.

McCormick, Anne O'Hare (May 16, 1882–May 29, 1954)

A journalist and correspondent for *The New York Times* who became the first woman member of its editorial board, Anne McCormick was born in Wakefield, Yorkshire, England, to Irish Catholic parents. Her family emigrated to the United States while she was an infant. She attended the academy and college of St. Mary of the Springs in Columbus, Ohio. She secured journalistic experience by serving as associate editor of the *Catholic Universe Weekly*, the diocesan newspaper of the Cleveland diocese. She also worked as a freelance writer and wrote articles for *Smart Set*, *The New Republic*, *Collier's*, *Atlantic Monthly*, and other magazines. In 1920 she traveled to Europe and took the then remarkable step of offering articles to *The New York Times*. Her first, "The New Italy of the Italians," was accepted and began her career with the newspaper; in 1922 she became a regular correspondent.

McCormick soon became the most respected and famous woman in journalism. She interviewed a host of European leaders, including Benito Mussolini, Adolf Hitler, Neville Chamberlain, Joseph Stalin, Winston Churchill, and Eamon de Valera. Her writing style, combining solid journalism with an eye for the concerns and perspective of average people, earned her great respect and a wide readership that included President Franklin D. Roosevelt. In 1936 she was named to the editorial board of *The New York Times,* the first woman to hold that position. The next year, she became the first woman to win a Pulitzer Prize for journalism. She worked for *The New York Times* for thirty-two years. Her book, *The Hammer and the Scythe: Communist Russia Enters the Second Decade,* was published in 1928 and was widely read and respected.

McCormick served as a U.S. delegate to UNESCO (the United Nations Educational, Scientific, and Cultural Organization) in 1946 and 1948 and was elected to the National Institute of Arts and Letters in 1947. She also received a host of other awards, such as the Laetare Medal from the University of Notre Dame and sixteen honorary doctorates. In 1939 she was voted Woman of the Year by the New York World's Fair by members of various women's groups. She met with Popes St. Pius X, Benedict XV, Pius XI, and Pius XII. In her time, she was also praised as one of the model Catholic women in the United States. She died in New York.

McCrory, Angeline Teresa (January 21, 1893– January 21, 1984)

Foundress of the Carmelite Sisters of the Aged and Infirm, Mother Angeline Teresa was born Bridget Teresa McCrory in Mountjoy, County Tyrone, Ireland. She and her family migrated to Scotland, but she left her family at nineteen to enter the Little Sisters of the Poor. She made her novitiate in La Tour, France, and was sent to the United States in 1915. In 1926 she was named superior of the Home of the Little Sisters of the Poor in the Bronx, New York. She was determined to provide care for the aged and the sick.

As she was limited in what she could do within her community, she asked the advice of Cardinal Patrick Joseph Hayes of New York. He encouraged her in her new apostolate, and Mother Angeline and six other sisters received permission from Rome to launch a new community devoted to the care of the aged. By 1931 the new community was officially affiliated with the great Order of Carmel.

The motherhouse of the Carmelite Sisters was at St. Patrick's Home in the Bronx, and from there Mother Angeline established fifty-nine homes for the aged throughout the United States, Ireland, and Scotland. Currently, the Sisters have twenty-four residences for the aged and care for over five thousand elderly men and women each day.

On July 15, 1989, Bishop Howard J. Hubbard of Albany received official approval from the Congregation for the Causes of Saints that the cause for canonization of Mother Angeline had been approved. She was granted the title Servant of God.

McGee, Thomas D'Arcy (April 13, 1825–April 7, 1868)

Editor, politician, and poet, Thomas D'Arcy McGee was born at Carlingford, County Louth, Ireland, and grew up attending the so-called hedge schools of Ireland. He migrated to the United States in 1842 and secured a job as a writer for *The Pilot*.

His eloquent writing earned him the job of editor, and he used his position to advocate for Irish independence. In 1845 he sailed back to Ireland and in Dublin assumed a post on the editorial staff of the *Freeman's Journal*; soon after, he joined *The Nation*, for which he wrote a variety of patriotic poems and essays.

McGee was a leader in the Irish rebellion, serving as secretary of the Irish Confederation. He was arrested and imprisoned for a short time and then fled back to the United States in the disguise of a priest. Back in New York, he launched a newspaper called *The Nation*, but his advocacy of violent rebellion for Ireland earned the disfavor of Bishop John Hughes. He changed the name of the publication to *The American Celt*.

In 1857 McGee settled in Montréal, where he started another newspaper, *The New Era*. He was elected to the Canadian Parliament and soon acquired a reputation for his oratorical skills. He also displayed a considerable change in his political outlook by favoring British rule and played a role in crafting the confederation of the British colonies of North America as the Dominion of Canada. His shift brought the ire of former fellow political radicals and helped bring about his assassination in Ottawa by a member of the Fenians.

Aside from his many speeches, McGee was the author of a wide variety of works. His books include *Irish Writers of the Seventeenth Century* (1846); *History of the Irish Settlers in North America* (1854); *History of the Attempt to Establish the Protestant Reformation in Ireland* (1853); *Catholic History of North America* (1854); and *History of Ireland* (1862). Although a controversial figure in his life, McGee is honored in the United States, Canada, and Ireland for his many contributions to Irish culture.

McGinley, Phyllis (March 21, 1905–February 22, 1978)

Pulitzer Prize–winning writer and poet Phyllis McGinley was born in Ontario, Oregon, but spent her youth in Colorado and Utah. She studied at the University of Southern California and at the University of Utah in Salt Lake City and then taught for a year in Ogden and in New Rochelle, New York. Embarking on a writing career, McGinley moved to New York City, where she worked at various jobs, including as a copywriter at an advertising agency and poetry editor for *Town and Country*. She married Charles Hayden in 1937 and moved to Larchmont, New York.

McGinley's early writings appeared in the *New York Herald Tribune,* and her poems began to appear in the *New Yorker* and other periodicals. Her first book of poems, *On the Contrary* (1934), was followed by *One More Manhattan* (1937), *A Pocketful of Wry* (1940), *Husbands Are Difficult* (1941), *Stones from a Glass House* (1946), *Merry Christmas, Happy New Year* (1958), and *Confessions of a Reluctant Optimist* (1973), among others. McGinley was also the author of a number of essays and children's books, and wrote the lyrics for the 1948 musical revue *Small Wonder.* Her essays were first published in magazines, including *Ladies' Home Journal* and *Reader's Digest,* and were collected in *Province of the Heart* (1959). *Sixpence in Her Shoe* (1964) was a series of autobiographical essays about the suburbs.

Elected to the National Academy of Arts and Letters in 1955, McGinley was the first writer to win the Pulitzer Prize for a light verse collection, *Times Three: Selected Verse from Three Decades* (1960). She died in New York City.

McGivney, Venerable Michael J. (August 12, 1852–August 14, 1890)

Founder of the Knights of Columbus, Michael J. McGivney was born in Waterbury, Connecticut, to Patrick and Mary Lynch McGivney, Irish immigrants. His father worked as a molder in the Waterbury brass mill, and Mary McGivney gave birth to thirteen children, six of whom died in infancy or childhood; Michael was their first child. He was raised in a working-class environment and went to work at the age of thirteen as a spoon maker in a brass factory. At sixteen he went to Québec, Canada, and began studies at the College of St. Hyacinthe in anticipation of the seminary. He went on to study at Our Lady of Angels Seminary, then part of Niagara University, and then St. Mary's College in Montréal.

His father died in June 1873, and Michael returned home to his family. The bishop of Hartford, Bishop Francis Patrick McFarland, asked him to complete his studies at St. Mary's Seminary in Baltimore. After four years of study, he was ordained in Baltimore on December 22, 1877, by Archbishop (later Cardinal) James Gibbons. He said his first Mass in Waterbury a few days later, with his widowed mother in attendance.

Father McGivney served initially as curate at St. Mary's Church in New Haven. His pastoral duties included the care of inmates at the city jail, the young people of the parish, and the hardworking Catholic laymen of the area. Convinced of the need for a benefit society for laymen, Father McGivney discussed the situation with Bishop Lawrence Stephen McMahon of Hartford and received his approval to proceed.

On October 2, 1881, several men gathered with Father McGivney in the basement of St. Mary's to start the new society. The name Knights of Columbus was adopted, and the first public reference to the order appeared on February 8, 1882, in the New Haven *Morning Journal and Courier.* A charter for the Knights was granted on March 29 by the Connecticut Legislature.

To support the growth of the order, Father McGivney traveled extensively across Connecticut, even as he remained a dedicated priest in the parish. In November 1884 he was named pastor of St. Thomas Church in Thomaston, Connecticut, a factory parish. He was a zealous pastor, and he overcame problems of debt and the economic hardships of his parishioners, even while serving as supreme chaplain of the Knights. His younger brothers, Monsignors Patrick and John J. McGivney, both served as supreme chaplains from 1901 to 1939.

Father McGivney contracted a sudden case of pneumonia in January 1890. Always plagued by poor health, he had difficulty recovering, and slowly his energy declined. He died at the age of thirty-eight after thirteen years as a priest. The organization he founded continued to grow in the decades after his death. Today the Knights claim over 1.6 million members with more than 12,000 councils in the United States, Canada, Mexico, the Philippines, Puerto Rico, Cuba, the Dominican Republic, Panama, the Virgin Islands, Guatemala, Guam, and Saipan.

In 1997 Archbishop Daniel A. Cronin of Hartford opened Father McGivney's cause for canonization. In 2000 the diocesan phase was closed and presented to Rome. Father McGivney's heroic virtue was recognized and he was granted the title of Venerable.

McGlynn, Edward (September 27, 1837–January 7, 1900)

Priest and controversial social activist, Edward McGlynn was born in New York City and was sent to Rome for his priestly studies in 1851 at the age of thirteen. From 1851 to 1860 he studied theology at the Urban College of the Propaganda in Rome, where he earned a doctorate. Ordained a priest in 1860, he returned to New York and was assigned to be an assistant pastor and hospital chaplain. In late 1865 he was assigned as assistant pastor and then pastor of St. Stephen's Church in Manhattan, then the largest parish in New York City.

Father McGlynn proved immensely popular as pastor. He started a home for children, but he also spoke publicly in favor of the public schools, a stand that caused some friction with authorities in the archdiocese. He went on to argue against government money for parochial schools and was roundly criticized by the priests of the archdiocese. He was, in addition, a supporter of Irish and also American land reform. His public advocacy of the issue and his speeches on behalf of the reformer Michael Davitt caused Rome to instruct the archbishop of New York, Cardinal John McCloskey, to demand that McGlynn cease his political involvement. Nevertheless, Father McGlynn became friends with the reformer Henry George and embraced his socialist theories of a single tax. He supported George's run for mayor of New York and spoke at the candidate's formal nomination in 1886.

Censured by the archbishop, Father McGlynn was suspended for several weeks. When, however, the new archbishop, Michael A. Corrigan, issued a pastoral letter condemning socialism and advocating private property, Father McGlynn gave an interview to a local newspaper in which he proposed the abolition of private property. Suspended by Archbishop Corrigan, he was soon summoned to Rome to be questioned by the Congregation for the Propaganda Fide (which then had overall authority over the American Church, as it was still considered mission territory). Father McGlynn tried to delay his appearance, but in January 1887 he was removed as pastor. That same year, he became presi-

dent of the Anti-Poverty Society and delivered a fiery speech on the single tax and workers' rights.

On May 4, 1887, Father McGlynn was informed that he was to present himself at Rome or be excommunicated. As he failed to respond, he was excommunicated on July 3. The excommunication was upheld by Pope Leo XIII. McGlynn publicly attacked the leaders of the Church in reply and the next year set out on a speaking tour across the country.

Events took a significant turn with the involvement of Archbishop Francesco Satolli, the papal representative. On December 23, 1892, he met with Satolli at The Catholic University of America, and the censures were removed. Finally, in June 1893, McGlynn went to Rome and met with Pope Leo XIII. He met in December 1894 with Archbishop Michael A. Corrigan and was assigned to a parish at Newburgh, New York, where he died.

McGranery, James Patrick (July 8, 1895–April 1, 1963)

Member of the U.S. House of Representatives, federal judge, and attorney general of the United States, James P. McGranery was born in Philadelphia to Irish Catholic parents. Growing up in a hardworking Catholic family, at a young age he took up his first job in a Philadelphia printing plant before volunteering for the army in 1917, when the United States entered World War I. Returning from the war, he was determined to become educated and entered Philadelphia's Maher Preparatory School in 1919 to prepare for entry into Temple University. He studied at Temple and also the Temple Law School and passed the bar in 1928.

McGranery was immediately involved in Democratic politics and prepared for a political career by launching the legal firm of Masterson and McGranery. After several failed bids for elected office, he was elected in 1936 as a Democrat to represent Pennsylvania's 2nd Congressional District. He was reelected in 1938, 1940, and 1942, and served on the House Banking and Currency, Interstate, Foreign Commerce, and Ways and Means Committees.

He resigned his seat in the fall of 1943 when his congressional district was eliminated by reapportionment. President Franklin Delano Roosevelt then found him a place in the Justice Department as assistant to Attorney General Francis Biddle, in which capacity he served as chief administrative officer and chief liaison with Congress and various federal departments and agencies throughout World War II.

After the war, McGranery continued to serve in the Justice Department until 1946, when he was appointed by President Harry S. Truman as a federal judge in the Eastern District of Pennsylvania. Considered a conservative jurist, he was proposed for a variety of other posts and offices, but only in 1952 was he offered the position of attorney general. He resigned in early 1953 owing to his resistance to an investigation into possible corruption inside the Department of Justice and the Bureau of Internal Revenue. He died in Palm Beach, Florida.

McHugh, Antonia (May 17, 1873–October 11, 1944)

Member of the Sisters of St. Joseph and a noted educator, Antonia McHugh was born in Omaha, Nebraska, to Irish parents and a large family. Her youth was filled with wanderings as the family worked to develop land and towns along the path of the railroad. She spent time in Deadwood, South Dakota, Chicago, and Langdon, North Dakota. As her family desired her to receive a Catholic education, she was sent to St. Paul, Minnesota, in 1885 to the St. Joseph Academy and completed her high school at St. Mary's Academy with the Grey Nuns (the Sisters of the Holy Name) in Winnipeg, Manitoba, Canada.

In 1890 Antonia joined the Sisters of St. Joseph and made her permanent vows in 1898. As she had already been teaching elementary school and displayed considerable talent, she was chosen by Mother Seraphine Ireland as one of the sisters sent to complete college degrees through the University of Minnesota and the University of Chicago. She received her bachelor's degree in 1908 and a master's degree the following year.

In 1905 Sister Antonia was one of the founding sisters of a preparatory school, Derham Hall, and the College of St. Catherine in St. Paul. Through her tireless efforts, the school became widely recognized for its academic excellence and in 1936 received the honor of being the first Catholic college or university to establish a chapter of the famed national honor society, Phi Beta Kappa. Sister Antonia was also invited to take part in the White House Conference on Child Health and Protection in 1930 and served as chair of the National Catholic Educational Association. She was granted the *Pro Ecclesia et Pontifice* decoration in 1931 from Pope Pius XI.

McHugh, John Ambrose (1880–April 9, 1950)

A Dominican priest and theologian, John Ambrose McHugh was best known as a writer, especially with his friend and colleague, the Dominican priest Charles Callan. McHugh was born in Louisville, Kentucky, and entered the Dominican novitiate in 1897. During his preparatory studies, he first met and became friends with Callan, and the two were subsequently ordained together in 1905. Father McHugh was then sent for additional studies in Rome, at the Minerva, from which he earned an advanced degree in sacred theology. Sent back to the United States in 1908, he was assigned to the faculty of the Dominican house of studies in Washington, D.C. He was joined there by Father Callan.

Both priests were assigned to Holy Rosary Parish in Hawthorne, New York, in 1915, exchanging the title of pastor over the next years. They then began teaching at the recently established Maryknoll seminary and assumed the post of joint editors of the *Homiletic and Pastoral Review.*

Fathers McHugh and Callan became very well known in ecclesiastical circles for their prolific writings. Both received the prestigious titles of master of sacred theology, and their collaboration was made possible in large measure by the way that both complemented the academic and literary strengths and weaknesses of the other. Among their foremost works were the four-volume *A Parochial Course of Doctrinal Instruction* (1920), the two-volume *Moral Theology* (1930), a new translation of *The Catholic Missal* (1936), and a host of devotional and liturgical works.

The duo also served as noted biblical scholars. They completed the editing of Father Francis Spencer's translation of the New Testament from Greek and took part in the translation of the Vulgate into English that had been authorized by the American bishops in 1935. They then served on the first board of the Catholic Biblical Association of America; McHugh served as president in 1938. He died largely from overwork and was buried at his request on the grounds of the Maryknoll seminary.

McIntyre, James F. (June 25, 1886–July 16, 1979)

Archbishop of Los Angeles from 1948 to 1970 and a cardinal from 1953, James Francis McIntyre was born in New York, the son of James Francis McIntyre and Mary Pelley. After leaving school, he worked for a number of years on the New York Stock Exchange but then declined the offer of a junior partnership in a brokerage firm in order to answer the call to the priesthood. At the age of twenty-nine, he entered Cathedral College, the preparatory seminary for the Archdiocese of New York. He then entered St. Joseph's Seminary in Dunwoodie, New York, where he completed his priestly formation.

Ordained to the priesthood on May 21, 1921, he spent his first two years as a pastoral associate in St. Gabriel's Parish in New York City. In 1923 he was named vice chancellor of the Archdiocese of New York, a post he held until 1934, when he became chancellor. Appointed a Privy Chamberlain of His Holiness in 1934 and a Domestic Prelate of His Holiness in 1936, Monsignor McIntyre was then named an archdiocesan consultor in 1939 and then auxiliary bishop of New York and titular bishop of Cirene on November 16, 1940; he was consecrated on January 8, 1941. In 1945 he was appointed vicar general of the archdiocese. The following year, on July 20, 1946, he was promoted to titular archbishop of Palto and appointed coadjutor archbishop of New York, shortly after Cardinal Francis Spellman was elevated to the College of Cardinals.

On February 7, 1948, Pope Pius XII transferred him to the Archdiocese of Los Angeles, after nearly three decades of ministry in the Archdiocese of New York. On January 12, 1953, he was created cardinal priest in the consistory of January 12, 1953; he received the title of Santa Anastasia on January 15, 1953, and became the twelfth American cardinal. He was also the first cardinal in the western United States.

Cardinal James McIntyre

Cardinal McIntyre served as archbishop of Los Angeles during a period of phenomenal growth for the Church in California and oversaw the most unprecedented expansion of a diocesan church in the history of the American Church. Between 1948 and 1963, 82 parishes were constructed and the number of Catholic schools tripled from 147 to 347. By 1970 there were 318 parishes and 350 schools. In addition, he supported Confraternity of Christian Doctrine programs and seminary education through the building of a new preparatory seminary in 1954 and various new facilities at St. John's Major Seminary. Under his leadership, the number of seminary students increased from 312 to 536 between 1948 and 1962. The number of women religious increased in the same period from 1,965 to 3,735. He also expanded Catholic medical care by expanding the number of hospitals from 12 to 17, treating nearly 450,000 people a year. Through his efforts, the campaign to reduce taxation on Catholic schools in 1952–53 proved successful.

His years as archbishop witnessed, additionally, the considerable diversification of Los Angeles through the arrival of Chinese, Japanese, Korean, and other Asian ethnic groups, as well as increases in the populations of Hispanics and African-Americans. To provide pastoral care and social services for the immigrants and new arrivals in the archdiocese, he started a Job Finding Bureau in 1965 and in 1967 the Department of Special Services. In 1955 he began the Lay Mission Helpers, an organization that soon spread its services internationally.

Cardinal McIntyre was one of the two American cardinals (with Cardinal Spellman) to take part in the 1958 conclave that elected Pope Blessed John XXIII. He then took part in the Second Vatican Council and served as a member of the Central Preparatory Commission. In 1963 he voted in the conclave that elected Pope Paul VI. While he opposed the liturgical changes brought about by the council, he was nevertheless faithful, if not cautious, in the implementation of the conciliar and post-conciliar decrees. He resigned the pastoral government of the archdiocese on January 21, 1970, and was succeeded by Archbishop (later Cardinal) Timothy Manning. Cardinal McIntyre was buried in the bishops' mausoleum in Calvary Cemetery in East Los Angeles. His remains were transferred to a mausoleum in the crypt of the new metropolitan cathedral of Our Lady of the Angels in Los Angeles in 2003.

McKenna, Charles Hyacinth (1835–February 21, 1917)

A Dominican priest, Charles Hyacinth McKenna is best known for his instrumental role in building up the Holy Name Society in the United States. For his efforts, he is honored as the "Apostle of the Holy Name." Born near Maghera, in County Derry, Ireland, he made his way to the United States at the age of seventeen and worked for some time as a stonecutter. He then studied at the Dominican College in Sinsinawa, Wisconsin, and joined the Order of Preachers. Ordained in 1867, he was swiftly appointed master of novices and earned a considerable reputation for his preaching. In 1870 his homiletic skills were put to use when his superiors transferred him to the parish of St. Vincent Ferrer in New York City to establish him as a member of the mission band of preachers. In 1880 he became provincial of the Eastern Mission Band and in 1881 was honored with the title of preacher general.

In 1892 Father McKenna requested to be relieved of his duties with the band in order to devote himself full-time to the cause of promoting the Holy Name Society. One of his first tasks to achieve the expansion of the society was to secure from Rome a papal dispensation to permit more than one branch of the society in any city (a ban that dated to Pope Clement VIII in 1604). Pope Leo XIII, in 1896, granted the dispensation and so paved the way for the Holy Name Society to become a fixture in every parish.

Father McKenna wrote a variety of books and manuals for the society and also to promote rosary confraternities in the United States. His writings include *The Crown of Mary* (1900), the *Pocket Manual of the Holy Name Society* (1909), and *The Treasures of the Rosary* (1913). He founded *The Holy Name Journal* in 1907. Through his ceaseless labors, he built the Holy Name Society into one of the most influential lay organizations in the Church, and his rallies regularly attracted tens of thousands of men. (*See also* Holy Name Society.)

McKenna, Joseph (August 10, 1843–November 21, 1926)

An American jurist, Joseph McKenna served as an associate justice of the U.S. Supreme Court from 1898 to 1925. Born in Philadelphia, he was the son of Irish Catholic immigrants and attended St. Joseph's College and the Collegiate Institute at Benicia, California. Admitted to the bar in 1865, he served as district attorney for Solano County and then served in the California State Assembly for two years. In 1885 he was elected to the United States House of Representatives and went on to serve four terms.

In 1892 he was appointed to the Ninth Circuit Court of Appeals by President Benjamin Harrison. Five years later, he was appointed attorney general of the United States by President William McKinley. He remained in this post until 1898, when he was appointed an associate ustice of the Supreme Court, to succeed Justice Stephen J. Field. McKenna's nomination was opposed by some elements in the Senate, but his confirmation was achieved in January 1898. Owing to his lack of legal experience, McKenna undertook additional studies at the Columbia Law School prior to assuming his seat on the high court.

As a justice, McKenna was noted for never crafting a specific legal philosophy, but he did author important decisions, including *United States v. U.S. Steel Corporation* in 1920, in which the application of the "rule of reason" found fertile ground in an antitrust case. Other significant opinions included *Hipolite Egg Co. v. United States* and *Hoke v. United States*. In 1915 McKenna suffered a stroke that left him increasingly impaired. He resigned from the Supreme Court in January 1925 at the urging of Chief Justice William Howard Taft.

McKenna, Mary Paul (September 21, 1888–January 11, 1984)

A Maryknoll missionary and sister, Mary Paul McKenna was the leader of the first Maryknoll Sisters to go China, in 1921. Born in Reading, Pennsylvania, to an Irish family, she joined the

Maryknoll women auxiliaries in 1917 and soon impressed her superiors with her intelligence and missionary zeal. She was thus chosen to head the first group of nuns to China, despite the fact that she had virtually no knowledge of the Chinese language or Chinese culture.

Arriving in Hong Kong, Sister Mary secured a collection of books on the Chinese language and culture to begin preparing herself and her sisters for the tasks that lay ahead. Having established the community, she then began taking the steps necessary to ensure the long-term viability of the Maryknoll enterprise. This included opening a kindergarten, the first foundation of what became the famed Maryknoll Convent School. She then oversaw the swift expansion of houses throughout China. She braved the harsh conditions of rural China and also the dangers of bandits, xenophobia, and diseases to visit her sisters and to assist the evangelization of China. In 1934 she accepted Bishop Francis X. Ford's invitation to work among the Hakka people of China.

In 1941, with the fall of Hong Kong to the Japanese, the Convent School was taken over by the Japanese military as their headquarters. The sisters were limited to a small part of the academy, but Mother Mary proved successful in establishing good relations with the Japanese officers. The next year, all American citizens were interned in Stanley Prison in Hong Kong, and Mother Mary worked to arrange the repatriation of her sisters. She was released in 1942 on the basis of her Irish roots. In 1946 she returned to the United States and was elected twice to the office of vicar general for Maryknoll. She went back to Hong Kong in 1968 and retired in 1978.

McKenzie, John L. (October 9, 1910–March 2, 1991)

A Jesuit priest and biblical scholar, and the first Catholic president of the Society of Biblical Literature, John L. McKenzie was born in Brazil, Indiana, and entered the Society of Jesus in 1939. He had been chosen to pursue doctoral studies in Rome, but the onset of World War II prevented his travel. Instead, he was sent to Weston College and the Jesuit house of studies, but his doctoral work was interrupted by the decision of his superiors to send him to teach at the Jesuit seminary in West Baden, Indiana. He taught there from 1942 to 1960.

In 1960 he transferred to Loyola University, where he became a faculty member of the history department. He served subsequently as a visiting professor at the University of Chicago Divinity School from 1965 to 1966 and taught at the University of Notre Dame from 1966 to 1970. He later taught for eight years, from 1970 to 1978, at DePaul University. Owing to disagreements with his superiors, he departed the Society of Jesus and was incardinated into the Diocese of Madison.

Father McKenzie is chiefly remembered for being one of the foremost American Catholic adherents of biblical criticism at a time when the field was first finding wide support in Catholic academic biblical scholarship. He worked as a book reviewer for the *Catholic Biblical Quarterly* and published his first book, *The Two-Edged Sword: An Interpretation of the Old Testament,* in 1956. The work received wide acclaim in both Catholic and Protestant academic circles and found a broad international readership. Father McKenzie went on to write a number of influential works, including *The Bible in Current Catholic Thought* (1962), *Myths and Realities: Studies in Biblical Theology* (1963), *The Power and the Wisdom: An Interpretation of the New Testament* (1965), *Authority in the Church* (1966), *Mastering the Meaning of the Bible* (1966), *New Testament for Spiritual Reading: The Revelation of St. John* (1971), *A Theology of the Old Testament* (1974), and *The Dictionary of the Bible* (1965), which he took eight years to complete and considered his magnum opus. He died in Madison, Wisconsin.

McKniff, John Joseph (September 5, 1905–March 24, 1994)

An Augustinian priest and missionary, Father John Joseph McKniff is best known for his missionary and pastoral labors in Cuba and Peru. He was born in Media, Pennsylvania, and entered the Augustinian order, for which he took professed religious vows in 1924. Ordained a priest in 1930, he was sent by the order to work as a teacher in the Philippines, then returned to the United States to teach at Villanova College and then the Augustinian Seminary on Staten Island, New York. After four years, he volunteered to go back to the Philippines and, while there in 1938, suffered damage to his lungs and resulting in pneumonia. To recover his health, he was sent back to the United States.

The next year he was sent to Cuba, where he taught and then was named pastor of Cristo del Buen Viaje Parish in Havana. Pastor from 1941 to 1968, he became a beloved fixture in the city's old sections and was responsible for launching Catholic Action groups, including Young Catholic Workers and the Legion of Mary. He was also known for his preaching and his prayerful ministry. To promote local education, Father McKniff opened a free school for the poor children of the parish. From this outreach began a free medical and dental clinic, and he supervised clothing drives for poor children.

In the wake of the Cuban Revolution and the rise of Fidel Castro, the Church entered a period of severe tension and the risk of oppression. After the unsuccessful 1961 Bay of Pigs invasion, Castro expelled all foreign priests from Cuba. There was, however, one exception: Father McKniff. Over the next years, he endured imprisonment, danger to his health, and the loss of his own community. In 1968 he traveled to the United States and the Cuban government prohibited his return.

After serving in several New York parishes, Father McKniff was sent to northern Peru in 1972 to provide pastoral ministry and to organize the Augustinian Seculars and Legionaries of Mary. He helped the Diocese of Chulucanas launch a new pastoral plan, *New Image of the Parish*, and he was active especially in evangelization in the most remote parts of the area. He died in Miami in 1994 after suffering from typhoid and declining health from years of ministerial labor. The cause for his canonization was launched in 1999, and in 2002, at the close of the diocesan phase, all documentation had been sent for review by the Congregation for the Causes of Saints in Rome.

McLoughlin, John (October 19, 1784–September 3, 1857)

A hero of the pioneering Oregon era, John McLoughlin was a physician called the "Father of Oregon." He was born in the parish of La Riviere du Loup, Canada. McLoughlin's father died when

he was very young, and he was raised in the home of his maternal grandfather. He was educated in Canada and Scotland. McLoughlin earned a medical degree, but he did not practice for long. He became a partner of North West Company, a trade organization, and when that company combined with the Hudson Bay Company in 1821, he was put in charge of Fort William on Lake Superior. In 1824 McLoughlin was sent to Fort George (Astoria) near the mouth of the Columbia River, but soon moved the headquarters of the company to Fort Vancouver. For twenty-two years he was in control of the Oregon Country. He had no military force, but maintained order and kept the local Indian population at peace. Missionaries of all faiths were protected by McLoughlin.

In 1842 he joined the Catholic Church and became a devoted Catholic, created a Knight of St. Gregory in 1846. When settlers arrived in Oregon in 1843, McLoughlin fed and clothed them and cared for the sick. He also supplied them with necessary farming implements and even seeds, and loaned the settlers domestic animals. He gave similar assistance to the immigrants of 1844 and 1845. His policy of extending credit for such materials brought about his forced resignation from the Hudson Bay Company in 1846. For the rest of his life he resided at Oregon City. There he developed water power, and erected flour and sawmills that he personally operated. Some of the Methodist missionaries and their followers, all of whom had been befriended by McLoughlin, started legal action against him, and in the Donation Land Law a section was inserted that deprived him of his land claim and gave it to the Territory of Oregon for the establishment and endowment of a university. The land was restored to his heirs by the legislature of Oregon five years after his death. He died in profound sorrow over the treatment given him and was buried in the churchyard of St. John's Catholic Church in Oregon City.

McMahon, Brien (October 6, 1903–July 28, 1952)

A United States Senator from Connecticut, Brien McMahon served from 1945 to 1952. He was born James O'Brien McMahon in Norwalk, Connecticut, and studied at Fordham University in New York and graduated in 1924. Three years later, he graduated from the Yale Law School and was admitted to the bar the same year. He then changed his name to Brien McMahon and started to practice law in Norwalk.

Named a city judge of Norwalk in 1933, he resigned the office that same year to become special assistant to the attorney general of the United States from 1933 to 1935, when he became assistant attorney general of the United States in charge of the Department of Justice, Criminal Division. In 1939 he resumed his law practice, in Washington, D.C., and Norwalk. In 1944 he was elected as a Democrat to the United States Senate and won reelection in 1950.

As senator, McMahon served as co-chairman of the Joint Committee on Atomic Energy and played a major role in the establishment of the Atomic Energy Commission through the Atomic Energy Act of 1946, the so-called McMahon Act. McMahon was a crucial figure in the first days of nuclear energy and nuclear weapons and was a strong advocate for the civilian control of nuclear development.

In 1952 he was proposed as a possible vice presidential candidate, but he was forced to withdraw from any such consideration as his health was declining. He did not recover from his illness and died in Washington, D.C. He was buried in Norwalk. A 4-cent commemorative postage stamp in honor of his role in promoting peaceful uses of atomic energy was issued by the United States on July 28, 1962, at Norwalk.

McMahon, Martin (March 21, 1838–April 21, 1906)

A soldier during the Civil War, Martin McMahon was also a lawyer of some note in the late nineteenth century. Born in Laprairie, Canada, he moved with his family to the United States when he was three years old. He went on to study at St. John's College, Fordham, and graduated in 1855. He then went to Buffalo to study law. After completing his studies, he journeyed west and became a special agent for the post office on the Pacific Coast. He was admitted to the bar in Sacramento, California, in 1861.

With the start of the Civil War, he raised a company of cavalry, the first to be formed on the Pacific Coast. He resigned his commission, however, when he was informed that the troops would not be used in the east, where the fighting was taking place. McMahon then traveled east and secured a position as an aide-de-camp to General George B. McClellan. He remained active with the Army of the Potomac throughout the war, won a medal for bravery, and reached by war's end the rank of brevet Major General of Volunteers.

McMahon resigned from the army in 1866 and was appointed counsel for New York City. He was then sent as an ambassador to Paraguay from 1868 to 1869. After his overseas mission, he practiced law until 1881, when he became receiver of taxes for the United States. He was subsequently a state assemblyman and state senator. In 1896 he was elected a judge.

McMaster, James (April 1, 1820–December 29, 1886)

A journalist and convert best known as editor of *Freeman's Journal,* which became a powerful voice in American Catholicism, James McMaster was born in Duanesburg, New York, to a Presbyterian family. His father was a Presbyterian minister. James studied at Union College prior to working as a private tutor. He then studied law at Columbia College and worked for a time as a lawyer. Entering the Union Theological Seminary for studies in ministry, he was soon influenced by the Oxford Movement and Tractarianism and was asked to leave the seminary. He entered the Church in 1845. Over the next years, he discerned a possible vocation to the priesthood and entered the novitiate for the Redemptorists. His studies in Belgium, however, convinced him that he was not meant for the religious life, so he returned to the United States. In 1846 he began a career in journalism.

In 1848 McMaster considered starting a magazine and then a semiweekly independent Catholic paper. As these ideas proved impractical, he used some money loaned to him by George V. Hecker and purchased *Freeman's Journal* from Bishop John Hughes. He assumed control over its editorial direction and remained in the post for the rest of his life. In 1850 he married Gertrude Fetterman; three of their daughters entered the religious life.

Under McMaster, the journal became a major voice for Catholicism in the United States. McMaster himself was fiercely independent and did not hesitate to criticize and disagree with others, including members of the American hierarchy. While he agreed with Bishop Hughes regarding Catholic schools, he entered into a disagreement with him over the Irish question. Politically he was a strong advocate of states' rights and so opposed the abolitionist movement. During the Civil War he was a vocal critic of President Abraham Lincoln and his administration. The result was that McMaster was arrested in 1861 and confined for eleven months. The journal was also suppressed and could not begin publication again until April 19, 1862.

Over the next years, McMaster was a spokesperson for decentralizing tendencies in the Church, including the idea of the clergy enjoying the right of participation in the selection of bishops. In the last years of the nineteenth century, the influence of the paper waned as other newspapers increased in number and circulation. Notably, McMaster inaugurated the first American pilgrimage to Rome. He died in Brooklyn, New York.

McNicholas, John T. (December 15, 1877–April 22, 1950)

A Dominican priest and archbishop of Cincinnati from 1925 to 1950, John T. McNicholas was born in Kiltimagh, County Mayo, Ireland. He migrated with his family to the United States in 1881 and grew up in Chester, Pennsylvania. Called to the priesthood, he entered St. Joseph's Preparatory College and then joined the Dominican novitiate at the age of seventeen at St. Rose Priory in Springfield, Kentucky. He made his simple profession in October 1895 and was ordained on October 10, 1901.

After ordination, Father McNicholas was sent to Rome for additional studies. He earned an advanced degree in sacred theology from the Minerva in 1904 and then returned to the United States for active ministry in New York and then a teaching post at the Dominican house of studies in Washington, D.C. In 1909 he was named the national director of the Holy Name Society and was sent back to Rome in 1916 to serve in the generalate of the Order of Preachers in Rome.

On July 18, 1918, he was appointed bishop of Duluth, was consecrated on September 8, 1918, and installed on November 15, 1918. His years in Duluth were noted chiefly for his commitment to education, in particular seminary formation. In May 1925 he was named the bishop of Indianapolis by Pope Pius XI. He never had the chance to occupy the diocese, however, as on July 8, 1925, he was transferred to the see of Cincinnati and installed in August.

As archbishop of Cincinnati, McNicholas was committed to all levels of Catholic education in the diocese and nationally. His educational efforts included the founding of the Athenaeum of Ohio in Cincinnati and the Institutum Divi Thomae in 1935. He supported the Holy Name Society and gave his encouragement to programs of evangelization among African-Americans. He presided over the construction of fifty new parishes. Archbishop McNicholas was also a noted figure on the national Church scene, in particular as president of the National Catholic Educational Association from 1946 to 1950, chairman of the Department of Catholic Education of the National Catholic Welfare Conference from 1930 to 1935 and again from 1942 to 1945, and chairman of the NCWC administrative board from 1945 to 1950. In addition, he enjoyed wide influence among his fellow bishops. He died in Cincinnati from a heart attack.

McQuaid, Bernard (December 15, 1823–January 18, 1909)

The first bishop of the Diocese of Rochester, from 1868 to 1909, Bernard J. McQuaid promoted Americanization and education. He was born in New York City, a member of a devout family. His father, Bernard J. McQuaid, was from Tyrone, Ireland, and migrated to Powel's Hook (now Jersey City), New Jersey. It was in the McQuaid home that Mass was first celebrated there, by Father John Conron in November 1829. Father McQuaid entered St. John's Seminary at Fordham and was ordained in old St. Patrick's Cathedral in New York on January 16, 1848. When the Diocese of Newark was created in 1853, Bishop James Roosevelt Bayley, who would become an archbishop, appointed Father McQuaid rector of the cathedral church and later, in 1866, his vicar general. With the bishop, Father McQuaid founded Seton Hall College and served as its president for ten years. When the Civil War started, Father McQuaid supported the Union cause and volunteered as a chaplain. He accompanied the New Jersey Brigade to battle and was captured by the Confederates.

When the Diocese of Rochester was erected in 1868, Father McQuaid was appointed its first bishop, and he was consecrated in St. Patrick's Cathedral in New York on July 12, 1868. He was installed in Rochester on July 16. He especially devoted himself to the cause of Catholic education, organizing a diocesan parochial school system, taught by nuns, and affiliating it with the state university. He opened St. Andrew's Preparatory Seminary and extended parishes throughout the diocese. In 1893 Bishop McQuaid opened St. Bernard's Seminary, which became regarded by the country as a model. Bishop McQuaid attended the First Vatican Council in 1870. In 1905 he asked for a coadjutor, and Bishop Thomas F. Hickey was consecrated on May 24, 1905.

McSherry, Richard (November 21, 1817–October 7, 1885)

A noted physician, Richard McSherry was born in Martinsburg, Virginia (modern-day West Virginia), and was the son of a doctor. Deciding to follow in his father's footsteps, he studied at Georgetown College and at the University of Maryland, and completed his medical training at the University of Pennsylvania, graduating in 1841. He had already served as an assistant surgeon in the U.S. Army Medical Corps from 1838 to 1840. His time of service included a stint in the Seminole War. He resigned his commission in April 1840 and then completed his medical training.

After graduation, McSherry married in 1842 and entered the U.S. Navy, where he served as assistant surgeon. He left the navy after several years and set up a practice in Baltimore. He remained an active physician until his retirement in 1883. One of the most respected physicians in the city, he helped found the Baltimore Academy of Medicine and was its first president. He also wrote several books and contributed a number of articles to the medical journals of the time. He died in Baltimore.

McSorley, Joseph (December 9, 1874–July 3, 1963)

A writer and superior general of the Paulists from 1924 to 1929, Joseph McSorley was born in Brooklyn, New York, and studied initially at St. John's University in Brooklyn, where he received a bachelor's degree at the age of sixteen. He went on to St. Thomas College in 1891 and the novitiate of the Paulist Fathers on the campus of The Catholic University of America in Washington, D.C. He earned a bachelor's degree and then a licentiate in sacred theology in 1895 and 1897, respectively, and was ordained in October 1897.

After ordination, he was assigned to St. Paul's Parish in New York. After two years of parish ministry, in September 1899 he was transferred to Washington to teach dogmatic theology. He also gave retreats and continued one of his great passions, writing. He subsequently was engaged in parish work among the Italians in the Paulist's New York parish. To assist his pastoral care of his parishioners, he was sent to Italy to improve his language skills. From his experience, Father McSorley prepared the book *Italian Confessions and How to Hear Them* in 1916. In addition, he gave retreats and wrote two books on the subject, *Primer of Prayer* in 1934 and *Think and Pray* in 1936.

After service as a chaplain during World War I, Father McSorley returned to the United States and was elected superior of the Paulists in 1924. Under his leadership, the Paulists launched St. Peter's College in Baltimore and the radio station WLWL to promote Catholic evangelization. He served briefly in St. Paul's in Toronto, then was transferred back to St. Paul's parish in 1932, where he remained for the rest of his life. His other writings include *Outline History of the Church by Centuries* in 1943, *Father Hecker and His Friends* in 1952, and numerous articles for the *Catholic Encyclopedia* in 1963. He died in New York.

Meagher, Thomas Francis (August 3, 1823–July 1, 1867)

A soldier during the Civil War, Thomas Francis Meagher was born in Waterford, Ireland, and studied under the Jesuits in their schools at Clongowes and Stonyhurst. Graduating in 1843, he became actively engaged in the cause of Irish independence, an effort that put to use his considerable skill as a speaker. His fiery oratory led to his arrest in 1848 for agitating rebellion among the Irish, but the jury could not agree on a verdict. In 1849, however, he took part in the abortive uprising for which he was arrested and sentenced in July to be hanged for high treason. The sentence was commuted to penal servitude for life and, with several other leaders of the rebellion, Meagher was sent to Tasmania.

Meagher escaped from the penal colony in 1852 and arrived in New York to a joyous welcome by the Irish of America. He spent the next years on the lecture and speech circuit, started the *Irish News* newspaper in 1856, and earned a law degree. In 1858 he went on a journey of exploration into Central America, and *Harper's* magazine printed an account of his exploits.

Thomas Meagher

At the start of the Civil War, he raised a company of Zouaves and took part in some of the heaviest fighting in the war with the famed 69th New York Volunteers at the First Battle of Bull Run and the Seven Days in 1861, Antietam and Fredericksburg in 1862, and Chancellorsville in 1863. The losses that his company faced became so acute that Meagher resigned his command. He was then transferred to command a military district in Tennessee. After the war, he was named Territorial Secretary of Montana. He drowned in the Missouri River after falling from a steamer; his body was never found.

Meany, William George (August 16, 1894– January 10, 1980)

A famed labor leader and president of the American Federation of Labor and Congress of Industrial Organizations from 1955 to 1979, George Meany was one of the most influential figures in organized labor in the twentieth century. Born in New York City to an Irish Catholic family, he grew up chiefly in the Bronx. His father, Michael Meany, served as president of the Bronx local of the United Association of Plumbers and Pipefitters, and in 1910 Meany joined the union as an apprentice. He spent the next years working as a plumber in New York. In 1920 he was elected as the youngest member of the local union's executive board. Two years later he became a full-time business agent and remained

active in the New York City Central Labor Council and the New York State Federation of Labor. He was elected president of the New York State Federation of Labor in 1934. As president, he was largely responsible for galvanizing the political power of the federation that was then used to help reelect President Franklin Delano Roosevelt in 1936 and to secure the passage of one of the country's first unemployment insurance laws.

In 1939 Meany was elected secretary-treasurer of the national American Federation of Labor (AFL) and proved a key figure in overseeing the expansion of membership, especially during World War II. He also supported the creation of the International Confederation of Free Trade Unions following the war. When, in 1947, Congress passed the Taft-Hartley Act, Meany launched the League for Political Education, the first massive effort to register and mobilize union members in the arena of American politics. Labor proved crucial to the election of Harry S. Truman in 1948, the first demonstration of the growing political power of the unions. Meany was elected president of the AFL in 1952 and proceeded swiftly to unite the largest union organizations in the country, the AFL and the Congress of Industrial Organizations (CIO). He succeeded in 1955 with the birth of the AFL-CIO, and Meany was elected unanimously as the first president of the merged labor federation.

Meany led the AFL-CIO to a position of enormous influence both politically and in the arena of legislation. He supported the civil rights movement and the 1964 Civil Rights Act and was a leading voice in the passage of various social programs as well as for worker rights all over the world, including in Eastern Europe. He spoke out against apartheid in South Africa and the military dictatorships in Spain and Chile and denounced the economic policies of President Jimmy Carter for their negative impact on the American worker. He resigned as president in 1979 in favor of his second in command, Lane Kirkland. Meany was married for over sixty years to Eugenia McMahon and had three daughters, Regina, Eileen, and Genevieve. He died in Bethesda, Maryland.

Medeiros, Humberto S. (October 6, 1915–September 17, 1983)

Archbishop of Boston from 1970 to 1983 and cardinal from 1973, Humberto Sousa Medeiros was shepherd of the Boston faithful during a turbulent period in modern U.S. Catholic history. Born in the village of Arrifes in the Azores to a Portuguese family, he migrated to the United States with his family in 1930, settled in Fall River, Massachusetts, and became a U.S. citizen in 1940. Called to the priesthood, he studied at The Catholic University of America in Washington, D.C., and received ordination to the priesthood for the Fall River diocese on June 15, 1946. He served for several years in pastoral assignments in the diocese and in 1952 was sent to Catholic University and the Pontifical Gregorian University in Rome to complete his doctorate in sacred theology.

Returning to the diocese in 1953, he was named vice chancellor and then chancellor. In 1958 he was designated a domestic prelate, then pastor in 1960. He remained pastor of St. Michael's Parish in Fall River until April 14, 1966, when he was appointed bishop of Brownsville, Texas, by Pope Paul VI. Consecrated on June 9, 1966, he soon established a reputation for his passionate support of workers' rights, his pastoral care of migrant workers, and his concern for the needs of the Church in Latin America. He was a well-known figure, addressing human and civil rights and visiting prisons regularly, and he became renowned for his ability to touch the lives of the poor and the working class, especially Mexican-Americans. Bishop Medeiros also served as chairman of the United States Catholic Conference Subcommittee on Allocations for Latin America and the Ad Hoc Committee on Farm Labor.

Following the retirement of Cardinal Richard James Cushing in 1970, Bishop Medeiros was appointed archbishop of Boston by Pope Paul VI on September 8, 1970. Three years later he was cre-

Cardinal Humberto Medeiros

ated a cardinal priest in the consistory of March 5, 1973, and received the title of Santa Susanna. As archbishop, he brought with him to Boston the same abiding concern for the poor, the workers, and the forgotten, and for the Church in Latin America. He was also a powerful voice in the country for the unborn. He stressed racial equality and "the worth and dignity of every human being, however obscured it may have become through circumstances, weakness, or even deliberate malice."

Fluent in several languages, Cardinal Medeiros was honored as much for his pastoral care of the archdiocese as he was for his personal goodness and humility.

He served as special papal envoy to the celebration of the sixtieth anniversary of the apparition of Our Lady in Fátima, Portugal, in 1977. The next year he took part in the conclave that elected Pope John Paul I in August and then the conclave that elected Pope Blessed John Paul II in October. Cardinal Medeiros died from complications of open heart surgery in Boston. He was buried in St. Patrick's Cemetery in Fall River.

Meehan, Thomas F. (September 19, 1854–July 7, 1942)

A historian and journalist, Thomas Francis Meehan was best known for his labors on behalf of *America* magazine and with the American Catholic Historical Society and United States Catholic Historical Society. Born in Brooklyn, New York, to Irish immigrant parents, Meehan studied at St. Francis Xavier College and earned both a bachelor's and a master's degree in 1874. After graduation, he went to work for his father, Patrick Meehan, the owner and editor of the *Irish American* from 1857 to 1906. Thomas was named managing editor and remained there until 1904. He also worked as a reporter for several newspapers and was a member briefly of the editorial board of the *New York Herald*.

Over the next decade, Meehan became a fixture in Catholic publishing, especially in the area of American Catholic history. He contributed numerous articles to the *Catholic Encyclopedia,* served on the editorial board of *America* from 1909 until his death, and was president of the Catholic Writers' Guild in 1919–20. A keen interest in American Catholic history led to his involvement with the American Catholic Historical Society from 1928 and the United States Catholic Historical Society, for which he served as president from 1939 to 1942. He was also editor of the society's publications and was largely responsible for its massive thirty-two-volume *Historical Records and Studies*. In addition, he contributed articles to the *Encyclopedia Britannica*, the *Catholic Historical Review*, *Catholic World*, *Commonweal*, and many other publications.

Mégret, Antoine (May 23, 1797–December 5, 1853)

A priest and missionary, Antoine Désiré Mégret is honored as the founder of Abbeville, Louisiana. Born in the Diocese of Coutances, France, he was called to the priesthood and received ordination on September 22, 1822. His first years as a priest were spent in pastoral service and also in establishing a close association with the controversial French religious and political writer and priest Félicité-Robert de Lamennais. Father Mégret contributed articles to de Lamennais's newspaper, *L'Avenir,* a publication that was compelled to cease publication by Pope Gregory XII for its liberal ideas.

Deciding to cease his involvement with de Lamennais, Father Mégret set sail for the United States to offer himself for service to the Church in Louisiana. He arrived in New Orleans on board the ship *Talma*, and by February 1842 he had been sent by Bishop (later Archbishop) Antoine Blanc to St. John's Church in Vermilionville (now Lafayette). As elsewhere in the diocese, the parish was troubled by the tendencies toward trusteeism displayed by the wardens. Father Mégret's personality did little to ease the situation, and the wardens soon entrenched themselves further. The priest was also attacked in the press and was physically attacked by a thug hired by the wardens. Undaunted, he withdrew from the church, ceased saying Mass, and started a new church in Vermilionville even as he dedicated himself to the surrounding missions, thereby depriving the wardens of the sacraments. In 1846 the wardens surrendered and signed over the control of the church to Father Mégret.

Meanwhile, after failing to secure suitable land for a church in Perry's Bridge (Pont Perry), south of Vermilionville, Father Mégret found an ideal spot to the north and purchased it for $900 in July 1843. The residents in the area asked him to name what was considered to be the start of a new town. He called it Abbeville and established there the chapel of St. Mary Magdalene. Land was sold all around it, and the name of the town became fixed as the city of the Abbé Mégret. He was a key figure in establishing the town and in having a courthouse built, thereby ensuring that Abbeville would be the permanent seat of justice after a long legal battle that was resolved only in 1854.

The priest then provided pastoral care to both Abbeville and Vermilionville until late in 1853, when an epidemic of yellow fever struck the region. Father Mégret cared for the sick and the dying until he also contracted the disease and succumbed to it at the age of fifty-six. He is honored in Abbeville by a statue in Magdalen Square.

Membré, Zenobius (1645–1687)

One of the dedicated Recollect Franciscan missionaries, Zenobius Membré was an American martyr. He was born in Mapaune (Bapaume), Pas-de-Calais, France, and entered the Franciscans. Volunteering for the missions, he arrived in Canada in 1675. Four years later, he was a member of the expedition of René-Robert Chevalier, Sieur de La Salle, to Illinois and wrote a description of the journey. In 1681 he again served as chaplain for the famed explorer, this time descending the Mississippi to an Arkansas village, where Father Membré planted a cross. In 1682 he was with La Salle at present-day Fort Adams, celebrating Mass there on March 29. He then returned with La Salle to Europe to serve as superior of a Franciscan monastery in his native city.

In 1684 Father Membré, with two other Franciscans and three Sulpicians, accompanied La Salle into Texas. They erected Fort St. Louis at Espiritu Santo Bay in 1685, but Father Membré wanted to open a mission there with Father Maxime Le Clerq. After about two years of toil among the native population, he was killed, along with Father Le Clerq and Father Chefdeville. The small garrison that La Salle left at the settlement also perished.

Memphis, Diocese of

Established on January 6, 1971, by Pope Paul VI, the Diocese of Memphis serves counties in western Tennessee. The city of Memphis was founded in 1819 on the site of a former Chickasaw Indian village. It was named after the ancient Egyptian capital because the Mississippi River flows past the city in a Nile-like manner. One of the founders of Memphis was Andrew Jackson, who would later become U.S. president.

Cotton plantations bolstered the local economy in the city's early days, but the yellow fever epidemic of 1878 killed some eight thousand residents, including twenty priests and twenty-three women religious. The city was forced to surrender its charter in 1879, but sanitary reforms and economic recovery led to a renewal of the charter in 1893. Memphis became a major market for cotton, lumber, pharmaceuticals, and chemicals. The Diocese of Memphis is a suffragan see of the Archdiocese of Louisville.

Having a colorful history, Memphis also has a Catholic history that dates to 1540 when Hernando de Soto entered the area with an expeditionary force. De Soto named the present-day Mississippi River El Rio del Santo Espiritu, the Holy Spirit River. In 1673 Jesuit Father Jacques Marquette and Louis Joliet were on the Mississippi River, followed in 1682 by René-Robert Chevalier, Sieur de La Salle, who built Fort Prud'homme on Chickasaw Bluffs. La Salle was accompanied by the Recollect Franciscan martyr Zenobius Membré and Father Anastase Douay. Less than a century later, Daniel Boone, a Catholic, mapped the Wilderness Road. Fort Assumption was opened in 1739, and in 1757 the area became part of North Carolina. The land comprising present-day Tennessee was designated as the State of Franklin. It joined the Union as Tennessee in 1796, after being part of the Southwest Territory enacted by an act of Congress in 1790.

The revered missionary Father Stephen T. Badin was in the area in 1808, remaining there about two years. The first diocese in the state was Nashville, erected in 1837. Tennessee was the last Confederate state to leave the Union in the Civil War and the first to be readmitted. An estimated three hundred battles took place in the area during the Civil War. The city of Memphis experienced tumult and suffering during the era following the war, including the yellow fever epidemic and the activities of the Ku Klux Klan, but there were Catholic gains. The Christian Brothers, the Sisters of the Good Shepherd, and the Poor Clares entered the area to labor among the faithful.

During World War I, the Catholics of Memphis supported the nation's military defenses and sent more than a hundred thousand men into battle. Sergeant Alvin C. York, a hero of the war, was from Tennessee. In 1925 Tennessee was the site of the Scopes Monkey Trial. The Great Depression followed, and in 1933 the Tennessee Valley Authority was instituted.

During World War II, the Catholics of Memphis once again supported the nation's military efforts. Introducing the atomic age, the Oak Ridge complex, activated in 1942, aided atomic defenses and energy sources. Memphis flourished in the years following the war, and the implementation of lay ministries aided the growth of the faith.

On June 20, 1970, Pope Paul VI issued the bull instituting the division of the Diocese of Nashville. The Diocese of Memphis was erected the following January. Bishop Carroll T. Dozier was appointed on November 17, 1970, as the first bishop of Memphis and was consecrated and installed on January 6, 1971. Bishop Dozier instituted the offices and agencies for diocesan administration, while opposing racism and promoting charitable programs. He was faced with huge debts upon assuming the see and responded to the Vietnam War and the issue of disarmament. His labors took a toll on his health, and Bishop Dozier retired on July 27, 1982.

The second bishop of Memphis was James Francis Stafford, who would become an American cardinal. He had served as auxiliary bishop of the Archdiocese of Baltimore since 1976 and was promoted to Memphis on November 16, 1982. Bishop Stafford settled the financial problems of the diocese and supported evangelization programs. He was promoted to the Archdiocese of Denver on June 3, 1986, and later was given a post in the Roman Curia and became a cardinal.

His successor was Bishop Daniel Mark Buechlein, O.S.B., who was appointed to the diocese on January 20, 1987. He instituted expansion programs and the Bishop's Annual Appeal. On July

14, 1992, Bishop Buechlein was promoted to the Archdiocese of Indianapolis.

The fourth bishop of Memphis, J. Terry Steib, S.V.D., had served as auxiliary bishop of St. Louis since 1983 and was promoted to Memphis on March 23, 1993. He was installed in the Cathedral of the Immaculate Conception on May 5, 1993. Bishop Steib has focused especially on improving and developing the Catholic schools of the diocese and the construction of several key facilities, including a retired priests' home and a retreat center. In 2011 there were 79,000 Catholics, 84 priests, and 42 parishes in the diocese.

Menard, René (1604–August 10, 1661)

A revered missionary, René Menard is considered a martyr of America. He was born in Paris and as a priest volunteered for the Canadian missions. He arrived in Québec in 1640 and was assigned to the Huron territories and to the Nippiserians until his mission was destroyed. Father Menard then went to the Three Rivers area, and there the Iroquois and Cayugas abused him at first but then accepted him.

In 1659, when Father Menard was fifty-five years old, he started out with three hundred members of the Ottawa tribe, moving to the west to escape the increasing conflicts in their original homelands. They arrived safely at Keweenaw, to the west of Sault Ste. Marie. Seeing the tribe settled, Father Menard set out for the Dakotas. He also visited Chequanegas Bay on Lake Superior. Becoming separated from his guide, Father Menard was reportedly slain by hostiles at the first rapid of the Menominee River.

Menéndez de Avilés, Pedro (February 15, 1519–September 17, 1574)

A Spanish naval officer and colonizer, Pedro Menéndez de Avilés was the founder of St. Augustine in Florida, the oldest city in the United States. Going to sea as a youth, he held the rank of captain generalcy of the Indies fleet at age thirty-five. The Indies fleet convoyed treasure ships from the New World to Spain. In 1556 he was appointed by the Spanish House of Trade, but he resigned in protest over the dishonesty he witnessed in the organization. King Philip II of Spain then gave him a patent to establish a Spanish colony in Florida. On March 20, 1565, he was given proprietory rights to the area and the title of provincial governor.

Menéndez de Avilés commanded an expedition of eleven ships and five hundred colonists and sailed from Spain, reaching the harbor he named for St. Augustine on August 28. At the mouth of the St. John's River on September 4 he encountered a French fleet, but the forces did not engage in combat. Menéndez de Avilés then returned to St. Augustine, where he began to build a fort. The French, however, hoping to take the Spanish by surprise, sailed to attack them, but their fleet was wrecked in a storm. With San Mateo (Fort Caroline) virtually defenseless, Menéndez de Avilés marched overland and on September 21 killed most of the French there and in another battle near St. Augustine.

Having completed a good part of his mission, Menéndez de Avilés sailed to Cuba for supplies and then explored the Gulf Coast, where he made friendly contacts with the local Indians. Before he returned to Spain in 1567, he had established Spanish posts on St. Helena Island in South Carolina and on Chesapeake Bay, in addition to St. Augustine and San Mateo. Although he remained governor of Florida until his death, Menéndez de Avilés returned only for a brief stay in 1571. He died in Santander, Spain, and later his remains were transferred to St. Nicholas Church in Avilés.

Mengarini, Gregorio (July 21, 1811–September 23, 1886)

A Jesuit missionary in the young United States, Gregorio Mengarini was gifted in languages and sang so beautifully that he had to give concerts for assembled American Indian communities. He was born in Rome and there entered the Society of Jesus in 1828. In 1839 he answered the call made by the Vincentian Bishop Joseph Rosati of St. Louis and sailed to America immediately following his ordination to the priesthood. Traveling with the famous Jesuit Father Pierre-Jean De Smet and Jesuit Father Nicholas Point, Father Mengarini went to Fort Hall, Idaho, meeting the Flatheads there on August 15, 1841. He then went to St. Mary's River in Montana, where he erected a log mission, St. Ignatius. Father Mengarini composed a grammar in Salish, as well as songs for children. He also organized a band. In 1849 the mission was closed because of intertribal warfare.

Father Mengarini went to the Jesuit mission in Oregon and then to Santa Clara. When the Flatheads sent for him again, he returned to St. Ignatius and wrote a Flathead grammar. His concerts became a favorite rendezvous for the various tribes in the region, and the Indians would gather eagerly to hear him sing. For thirty years he also served as treasurer for the Jesuit missions. After a severe stroke, Father Mengarini started going blind. He was taken to Santa Clara, and there he died.

Meouchi, Pierre Paul (April 1, 1894–January 11, 1975)

The patriarch of Antioch from 1955 to 1975 and a cardinal from 1965, Pierre Paul Meouchi was one of the great Maronite leaders of the twentieth century. Born in Jezzine, Lebanon, he was educated under the Maronite Sisters at Deir el Kamar and the College of la Sagesse in Beirut, Lebanon. Called to the priesthood, he was sent to Rome to undertake his studies before the beginning of World War I and attended the Pontifical Urbanian Athenaeum de Propaganda Fide and the Pontifical Gregorian University.

Ordained a priest on December 7, 1917, in Rome, he was appointed secretary to the bishop of Saïda of the Maronites and served from 1917 to 1920. He was then secretary to the titular bishop of Tiro of Maronites for his visitation to Maronites in the United States from 1920 to 1921. As a result of this trip, Father Meouchi undertook pastoral work among Maronites in the United States from 1922 to 1934.

On April 29, 1934, he was elected bishop of Tyr of the Maronites, in Lebanon, and was consecrated on December 8, 1934, at Bkerké, Lebanon, by Antoine-Pierre Arida, the Maronite patriarch of Antioch. Meouchi was himself elected Maronite patriarch of Antioch on May 25, 1955. As patriarch he attended the Second Vatican Council and spoke memorably about the rights and difficulties being faced by Catholics in the Middle East.

On February 22, 1965, he was created cardinal patriarch by Pope Paul VI and received his red biretta on February 25, 1965. He was the first Maronite cardinal. Over the next years, he attended the first assemblies of the world Synod of Bishops (in 1967, 1969, and 1971) and had the pleasure of serving at a time when Father Sharbel Makhlouf was declared blessed (Sharbel was canonized a saint in 1977). Cardinal Meouchi died in Beirut and was buried in Bkerke.

Merrick, Mary Virginia (November 2, 1866–January 10, 1955)

The foundress of the National Christ Child Society, Mary Virginia Merrick devoted her entire life to assisting poor and suffering children regardless of race or creed. She was born to prominent parents in Washington, D.C.; her father was a Catholic lawyer, and her mother was a convert to Catholicism. Mary was raised in a devoutly Catholic environment, and she developed a deep commitment to the faith and a concern for the poor that were unusual for her age. Mary's desire to assist those in need led her to accompany her mother on visits to the homes of the disadvantaged. There she learned that to serve the poor was to serve God.

In her teen years, Mary fell from the window of a playhouse and was eventually confined to her bed or to a wheelchair for the rest of her life. In spite of her pain, she began sewing clothes for needy children and encouraged family and friends to join her. From this beginning, in 1887 she founded a society to serve impoverished children. These early members made clothes for infants and children, and gifts were distributed in the name of the Christ Child to children in need.

By 1898 the society claimed over three hundred members, and Mary arranged for a house to be rented, the first "Christ Child House." In 1903 the society was officially incorporated, and that same year additional Christ Child Centers were opened throughout the city. By 1908 the society had expanded to Baltimore, New York, Chicago, and elsewhere. When financial resources became scarce, Mary was never deterred, saying simply, "The Christ Child will provide." By 1912 there were twenty-four chapters, and in 1916 the National Christ Child Society was organized officially as a federation of chapters.

In 1915 Mary was awarded the Laetare Medal from the University of Notre Dame in recognition of her service to others, one of many honors she received, including the *Pro Ecclesia et Pontifice* medal from Pope Pius XI for her service to the Church, as well as an honorary degree from Georgetown University.

Merrick died in Washington, D.C. At her funeral, Bishop John M. McNamara proclaimed, "She took her cross and out of it fashioned a bridge over which she and others would walk on their way to God." She was buried at Oak Hill Cemetery in Georgetown. At the time of her death, the National Christ Child Society had thirty-eight chapters stretching from New York to California. All of them had been founded and directed through her labors, her prayers, and her determination to serve God by serving the poor. In 2003 the cause for her canonization was approved by the Congregation for the Causes of Saints.

Merton, Thomas (January 31, 1915–December 10, 1968)

An immensely popular American writer and poet, as well as a theologian and mystic, Thomas Merton was a longtime member of the Trappists. He was born in France to an Anglican family and was orphaned at the age of sixteen, prompting a period of wandering in France and England that cultivated a wild lifestyle and a lack of discipline. This wanton tendency cost his scholarship to Cambridge University. Moving to America to live with his maternal grandparents, he attended Columbia University and received a bachelor's degree in literature and poetry in 1937 and then a master's degree in 1939. During this period he underwent a spiritual journey and a profound conversion that culminated in 1938 with his entry into the Church, partly through the influence of the Thomistic writer Etienne Gilson.

After completing his studies at Columbia, he taught literature at St. Bonaventure's College and was attracted to Catholic social justice, which included a visit to the Friendship House of Catherine de Hueck Doherty in Harlem. Ultimately, he was drawn to the contemplative life and in 1941 entered the Trappist Abbey of Our Lady of Gethsemani, near Bardstown, Kentucky. Ordained in 1949, he served also as a master of novices. The year before, he published his spiritual autobiography, *The Seven Storey Mountain*, a profoundly honest record of his early life that became an international bestseller and remains an immensely popular book. Merton, however, found the book so successful that he later renounced much of it because he found it unequal to his developed skills as a writer and his heightened mysticism.

In 1965 Merton was allowed by the community to adopt a solitary lifestyle away from the abbey itself. He lived in a small house in the adjoining hills where he focused on the mystical life and studied the mysticism of Eastern philosophers. His increased interest in the East led to a tour of Asia, where he met with numerous Eastern religious leaders, including the Dalai Lama. While in Bangkok, he died by accidental electrocution while bathing.

Merton was one of the most widely read Catholic authors of the twentieth century. After first achieving fame for *The Seven Storey Mountain* in 1948, he wrote numerous books, including poetry, and hundreds of articles. Among his most important works were *Ascent to Truth* in 1951, *No Man Is an Island* in 1955, *Faith and Contemplation* in 1962, and *Mystics and Zen Masters* in 1967. His broad interests have raised questions among critics who consider his later intellectual pursuits to have strayed far from the domain of authentic Catholic spirituality; he is also considered a controversial figure because of his concerns with militarism, nuclear weapons, Eastern mysticism, and ecumenism.

Mesplié, Toussaint (1824–November 20, 1895)

A missionary best known for his labors among Native Americans in Oregon and Idaho, Toussaint Mesplié was born in France and made the journey to the United States to offer his services to the Church. He made his way west and found himself in the rugged area of Idaho in the early 1860s. He found there military camps and forts, large numbers of miners, and struggling tribes of Native Americans, and without hesitation he began providing pastoral care to all of them.

The miners were chiefly new arrivals to the area in the wake of the end of the California Gold Rush, and many were Irish Catholics. Father Mesplié communicated with Church officials and priests in the territory to begin building churches for them. From 1863 to 1864, four churches were constructed. Having earned the trust of Bishop Louis Aloysius Lootens, the first vicar apostolic of

Idaho, Father Mesplié was named administrator of the vicariate in 1869–70, while the bishop was in Rome attending the First Vatican Council.

Around the same time, Father Mesplié volunteered his services, without pay, to the U.S. Army as a chaplain. Appointed in 1872, he performed his duties as a chaplain for the next two decades and was a beloved figure in the forts of Idaho, especially Fort Boise. He also evangelized among the Native Americans, in particular in Oregon, once baptizing two hundred in one day, and was a tireless defender of their rights. Father Mesplié died in Grass Valley, California, while visiting a nephew. Bishop Edward D. Kelly erected a statue in his honor in 1950.

Messmer, Sebastian Gebhard (August 29, 1847– August 4, 1930)

Archbishop of Milwaukee from 1903 to 1930, Sebastian Gebhard Messmer was born in Goldach, Switzerland, and was the last European-born archbishop of Milwaukee. Called to the priesthood, he studied at the University of Innsbruck, Austria, and was ordained on July 23, 1871, in Innsbruck. That same year, in reply to the request of Bishop James Roosevelt Bayley of Newark, New Jersey, he made the journey to the United States to serve on the faculty of Seton Hall College in South Orange, New Jersey, in the Newark diocese. Father Messmer taught theology and canon law for the next eighteen years, but he was also actively engaged in pastoral ministry as an associate at St. Mary's Orphanage in Newark.

Respected for his knowledge and theological skill, Father Messmer was appointed a consulting theologian to the Third Plenary Council of Baltimore in 1884. Such was the distinction he demonstrated at the council that Pope Leo XIII bestowed upon him an honorary doctorate in divinity. In 1889 he was named to the new faculty of the recently established Catholic University of America in Washington, D.C. To prepare himself for the new duties, he was sent to Rome to the Pontifical Athenaeum S. Apolinnaire, where he earned a doctorate in canon law.

His time at Catholic University was cut short in 1891 when he was chosen by Leo XIII to succeed Bishop Frederick Xavier Katzer as the bishop of Green Bay. Consecrated on March 27, 1892,

Bishop Messmer spent his years in Green Bay promoting Catholic education and as a dedicated voice for German Catholics, in particular for German-speaking schools and parishes. His time in Green Bay ended on November 28, 1903, when he was appointed to succeed Bishop Katzer again, this time as archbishop of Milwaukee.

As archbishop, Messmer remained very much in favor of Catholic ethnicity, but he also softened his position in order to ensure good relations with the other Catholic groups in Milwaukee, especially the Polish Catholics. He was assisted in his episcopal ministry by an auxiliary bishop from Bohemia, Bishop Joseph Maria Koudelka, and from Poland, Bishop Edward Kozlowski, and he resolved many problems lingering from ethnic identity by his determined centralization of archdiocesan administration. To promote centralization, the archbishop wrote the first *Handbook for Catholic Parishioners* in 1907 to establish needed guidelines for ethnic groups in the diocese. He nevertheless encountered considerable resistance from some quarters, including elements in the Polish community, and his heated disagreements with Polish priest Father Wenceslaus Kruszka nearly ended in a schism in the Milwaukee church.

Archbishop Messmer was also renowned for his commitment to Christian charity and to Catholic education. Known as the "Archbishop of Christian Charity," he personally contributed large amounts of money to help subsidize a charitable bureau he founded in 1916 that cared for the sick, the poor, the elderly, and orphans. He oversaw the increase in Catholic schools in the archdiocese and assisted the start of Mount Mary College and the development of Marquette College to Marquette University. In addition, Archbishop Messmer helped start the first ministry to African-Americans through his approval of St. Benedict the Moor church and school in 1908. He also permitted the founding of Our Lady of Guadalupe Mission for Mexican Catholics in 1929.

Although opposed to women's suffrage, he approved of Catholic women's organizations, such as the Marquette Women's League and the Milwaukee Archdiocesan Council of Catholic Women. He likewise backed numerous lay organizations, including the Archdiocesan Union of the Holy

Name Society, the Federation of American Catholic Societies, the Western Catholic Summer School, the Knights of Columbus, and a revived St. Vincent de Paul Society. He also supported the brief emergence of the American Federation of Catholic Societies that strove to offer a cohesive Catholic response to the pressing issues of the day in American culture. In 1922 he founded the *Catholic Herald*, the official Catholic English-language paper of the Archdiocese of Milwaukee.

Archbishop Messmer's health deteriorated steadily in the 1920s. He died while visiting his native Switzerland and was buried in Goldach.

Meštrović, Ivan (August 15, 1883– January 16, 1962)

One of the greatest sculptors of the twentieth century, Ivan Meštrović was born in Vrpolje in Slavonia, then part of the Austro-Hungarian Empire, and he spent most of his youth in the village of Otavice in Dalmatia. The son of Croatian peasants, he was raised in an atmosphere of faith that left him with a great familiarity with the Bible. At the age of thirteen he was apprenticed to a marble cutter from Split, Pavle Bilinić, and Meštrović developed his artistic skills in sculpture. At the age of sixteen and with the help of Bilinić, he was granted admission to the Art Academy of Vienna. He married Ruža Klein in 1904.

In 1905 Meštrović exhibited at the Vienna Secession exhibitions. As his work became immediately popular, he was able to move to Paris in 1908 and earn a truly international reputation. In 1911 he moved to Belgrade (in modern-day Serbia) and then to Rome, where he won the grand prix for the Serbian Pavilion at the 1911 International Exhibition in Rome. Over the next years, he continued to travel to present his sculptures in Paris, London, and other cities.

Prevented from going home because of World War I, he was able at last to move back to the newly founded Yugoslavia. There he met and married his

Ivan Meštrović

second wife, Olga Kesterčanek, with whom he had four children. Named a professor and later the director of the Art Institute in Zagreb, he also continued to travel, including for exhibits at the Brooklyn Museum in New York in 1924, to Chicago in 1925, and to Egypt and Palestine in 1927.

Owing to his determined opposition to the Nazis in Germany and the Fascists in Italy, he was arrested and imprisoned by the Ustaše during World War II. His release was negotiated through the help of the Vatican, and he went first to Venice, Italy, and then Rome, and later to Switzerland.

After the war, he was invited back to Yugoslavia by Marshal Tito, but he refused as he did not wish to live under the communists, particularly after they arrested and imprisoned his own brother, Petar.

In 1946 Syracuse University offered him a professorship. Meštrović accepted, and President Dwight D. Eisenhower later presided over the ceremony granting him American citizenship in 1954. He subsequently became a professor at the University of Notre Dame in 1955. Prior to his death, Meštrović made a final journey to Yugoslavia to visit the imprisoned Cardinal Alojzije Stepinac. He died in South Bend, Indiana, and his remains were transferred to a mausoleum in his childhood home of Otavice. A truly renowned sculptor, Meštrović was influenced by Auguste Rodin and also by classical Greek sculpture and profound biblical themes. He customarily carved in marble and wood and cast his sculptures in plaster and bronze. He was the first sculptor to be honored with a one-man show at the Metropolitan Museum of Art in New York. In addition, he was a noted architect, and the home he designed for himself in Split, Yugoslavia (now in Croatia), is now a museum for his work.

Metuchen, Diocese of

Established on November 19, 1981, by Pope Blessed John Paul II, the Diocese of Metuchen serves four counties in the state of New Jersey. Metuchen was settled early on by New Englanders, Scots, and French Huguenots. The name is derived possibly from the Lenni-Lenape Indian word for "firewood" or a derivation of the name of the local subchief of the tribe, Metochahegan. The Diocese of Metuchen is a suffragan see of the Archdiocese of Newark.

The Dutch established colonies in New Jersey in the early 1600s, although an Italian, Giovanni da Verrazano, who was in the area in 1524, and an Englishman, Henry Hudson, who visited in 1609, were the first to explore the region. Present-day Jersey City was the site of the first settlement by the Dutch, called Bergen. A Swedish colony was started there in the 1630s but had to be abandoned within a few years. Peter Stuyvesant, who was the governor of the Dutch holdings, surrendered to the British in 1664, and the area became an English colony.

Catholics arrived in the region, where their freedom of religion had been guaranteed. The overthrow of the Catholic English King James II in 1688, however, altered the policies of tolerance in New Jersey. Around 1672 the first Mass in Middlesex County was celebrated near present-day Woodbridge, but the Catholic presence was harassed. In 1702 Queen Anne established New Jersey a royal colony, outlawing "papists," the term used for Catholics. The Catholic enclave became invisible in order to survive the mounting laws against the faith.

During the 1740s, Jesuit Father Theodore Schneider served the isolated Catholics in the area of Salem. He had medical skills and passed inspection by pretending to be a physician. Father John Ury and fourteen others were executed in New Jersey in 1741, charged with taking part in the alleged "Negro Plot." Fathers Ferdinand Steinmeyer and Robert Harding managed to serve Catholics of the area, however. Father Steinmeyer, known as "Father Farmer," was remarkably skilled in eluding the British authorities.

When the Revolutionary War began, the heroic activities of Catholics won the respect of their fellow citizens. Patrick Colvin furnished the boats that carried General Washington and American troops across the Delaware. "Molly Pitcher," Mary McCauley, carried buckets of water to the Americans fighting at the Battle of Monmouth. By the close of the war, there was little enthusiasm for continuing to persecute Catholics.

The Church in America was led by Bishop John Carroll of Baltimore until 1808, when his see became an archdiocese. Some New Jersey Catholics were under the jurisdiction of the recently established Diocese of Philadelphia. In 1853 the Diocese of Newark was erected by Pope Blessed Pius IX to serve all of New Jersey. Bishop James Roosevelt Bayley, a convert and nephew of St. Elizabeth Ann Seton, was the first bishop of the Diocese of Newark. The Diocese of Trenton was established in 1881, and the Dioceses of Camden and Paterson in 1937.

The Catholics of Metuchen took part in the Civil War and continued to experience economic progress as New Jersey–based railroads and corporations flourished. John D. Rockefeller and other magnates established their firms in the state. By 1900 New Jersey was one of the nation's leading producers of manufacturing and agricultural products. The people of the state also boasted of Thomas A. Edison and Menlo Park.

Metuchen's Catholics supported the nation's military efforts in World War I and suffered through the grim era of the Great Depression. World War II brought renewed demands for military supplies and port facilities. The Catholic faith had grown steadily in Metuchen. The Cathedral of St. Francis has been serving the faithful since 1871,

Molly Pitcher

and other parishes, such as St. Bernard's in Bridge-water, Somerset County, date to 1843 or soon after. Given the degree of zeal in the region, the Holy See established the Diocese of Metuchen.

The first bishop of Metuchen was Theodore E. McCarrick (later the archbishop of Newark, then archbishop of Washington, D.C., and a cardinal). He had served as auxiliary bishop of the Archdiocese of New York since 1977. He was promoted to the Diocese of Metuchen on November 19, 1981. Bishop McCarrick established the offices and agencies for diocesan administration and maintained diocesan facilities while expanding the Church's presence. On June 3, 1986, Bishop McCarrick was promoted to the Archdiocese of Newark. In 2000 he was transferred to the Archdiocese of Washington.

The second bishop of Metuchen was Edward T. Hughes. Bishop Hughes had served as auxiliary bishop of Philadelphia since 1976. He was appointed to Metuchen on December 16, 1986, and installed on February 5, 1987. Bishop Hughes opened facilities and services for the increasing number of Catholics in the diocese and promoted charitable and lay programs. He retired on September 8, 1997.

The third bishop of Metuchen was Vincent DePaul Breen, who was appointed to the diocese on July 8, 1997, and installed on September 8, 1997. Bishop Breen aided the Donna Santa Marie case, a class-action suit concerning abortion. Becoming critically ill, Bishop Breen retired on January 4, 2002, and died the next year.

On January 4, 2002, Bishop Paul Gregory Bootkoski, an auxiliary bishop of the Archdiocese of Newark, was appointed the fourth bishop of Metuchen. He was installed on March 19, 2002. Currently, the diocese has a Catholic population of over 560,000, 42 percent of the population of the area, 224 priests, and 100 parishes.

Meyer, Albert G. (March 9, 1903–April 9, 1965) Archbishop of Chicago from 1958 to 1965 and a cardinal from 1959, Albert G. Meyer was archbishop during the Second Vatican Council and its immediate aftermath. Born in Milwaukee, he was called to the priesthood and entered St. Francis Seminary in Milwaukee for his initial studies.

He was then sent to the North American College in Rome where he was ordained on July 11, 1926, in the Church of Santa Maria sopra Minerva by Cardinal Basilio Pompilj, the vicar of Rome. After ordination, he was permitted to continue his graduate studies and earned a doctorate in Scripture in 1930 from the Pontifical Biblical Institute.

Returning to the Archdiocese of Milwaukee, Father Meyer was assigned to pastoral work in St. Joseph Parish in Waukesha from 1930 to 1931. In 1931 he was assigned to the faculty of St. Francis Seminary, where he taught religion, Greek, Latin, Christian archaeology, dogmatic theology, and Sacred Scripture. In 1937 he was named rector even as he performed pastoral work among Italian immigrants and was chaplain of the Serra Club. On February 14, 1938, he was named a Domestic Prelate of His Holiness by Pope Pius XI.

On February 18, 1946, Father Meyer was elected bishop of Superior by Pope Pius XII and was consecrated on April 11, 1946. On July 21, 1953, he was promoted to the metropolitan see of Milwaukee. As bishop of Superior and then as archbishop, he oversaw the rapid expansion of Catholic schools and also of churches and parishes to keep pace with the growth of the Catholic population. In Milwaukee, he built over seventy new schools and fifty new churches, and expanded the seminary from 190 to 400 students.

On September 19, 1958, Archbishop Meyer was transferred to the metropolitan see of Chicago as successor to Cardinal Samuel Alphonsus Stritch. The next year, on December 14, 1959, he was created a cardinal priest by Pope Blessed John XXIII and received the title of Santa Cecilia on December 17, 1959. As archbishop of Chicago, the shy and scholarly Cardinal Meyer became shepherd over one of the largest archdioceses in the world and the largest in the United States. Only sixteen days after assuming his see, he was faced with the staggering disaster of the fire at Our Lady of the Angels School that claimed over ninety lives. In response, the archbishop launched a massive program of improvements and modernization in archdiocesan education, including the construction of new schools and facilities.

Cardinal Meyer attended the first three sessions of the Second Vatican Council, from 1962 to 1964, and was a member of the board of presidency for the council during that time. He also participated in the conclave of 1963 that elected Pope Paul VI. He praised the council's Constitution on the Liturgy (*Sacrosanctum Concilium*) and stressed the need for greater participation of laypeople in the life of the Church. In keeping with the council, he also promoted the ecumenical movement and addressed the 33rd Annual Ministers' Week at the Chicago Theological Seminary. In addition, he was a strong advocate for the civil rights movement. He condemned seg-

Cardinal Albert Meyer

regation and urged Catholics to welcome African-Americans into the Church. In 1963 he served as cohost of the First National Conference on Religion and Race with its theme of "Interracial Justice and Love."

Cardinal Meyer died very unexpectedly on April 9, 1965, at Mercy Hospital, Chicago, of a heart attack after an operation to remove a malignant brain tumor. He was buried in the cemetery of St. Mary of the Lake Seminary in Mundelein.

Miami, Archdiocese of

Established as the Diocese of Miami on August 18, 1958, by Pope Pius XII, the see was elevated to the rank of an archdiocese on May 8, 1968, by Pope Paul VI. The Archdiocese of Miami serves sixteen counties in southern Florida. Located on Biscayne Bay, Miami was founded on the site of a Tequesta Indian village at the mouth of the Miami River. Growing steadily, the city was incorporated in 1896, the year that the Royal Palm Hotel was opened. Miami is a transportation and business hub, a major port, and a resort area.

The Catholic heritage of Miami is profound and dates to 1513, when Juan Ponce de León led an expedition to its shores. He named the site Pascua Florida, or Easter Flowers. In 1549, landing at Tampa Bay, Luis Cáncer de Barbastro and his companions were slain. In 1566 three Jesuit missionaries were sent by St. Francis Borgia to Florida: Fathers Pedro Martinez, the Jesuit protomartyr of

the United States, Juan Rogel, and Francisco Villareal.

In 1573 Franciscans arrived and served in the vast Florida missions, which included the coast of Georgia and South Carolina. By 1605 these Franciscans had founded a monastery at St. Augustine. Bishop Juan de las Cabezas de Altamirano visited the missions in 1606, confirming colonists and the local Native Americans. The missions continued to expand, and by 1675 there were some seventy-five Franciscans laboring in the region. The year before, Bishop José Gabriel Calderón visited the missions and ordained priest candidates. Slaves fleeing from English colonies to the north were given their freedom by the Spanish authorities and allowed to flourish as part of the community.

The English retaliated against this slave policy in 1702, when Governor James Moore of Carolina attacked and destroyed Catholic missions. As a result, an estimated ten thousand to twelve thousand Christian Indians were taken to Carolina by the governor and sold into slavery. Some three thousand were slain by their attackers.

The missions were rebuilt wherever possible and maintained until 1763, when Spain ceded Florida to England. Twenty years later, Spain was once again in control of the "Two Floridas," an east and west designation. Bishop Louis Dubourg was the administrator of the Two Floridas and Louisiana, appointed by Bishop John Carroll of Baltimore. In 1820 Bishop John England of Charleston received ecclesiastical jurisdiction over Florida and the Diocese of Mobile.

In 1845 Florida entered the Union, and fifteen years later a vicar apostolic, Bishop Jean-Pierre Augustin Verot, a Sulpician, was appointed for the state. The Civil War brought considerable devastation to the area, and Catholic leaders tried to rebuild and to alleviate the suffering of the innocent victims of the fighting.

In 1958 the Holy See recognized the vitality of the faith in Miami and erected the city as a Catholic diocese. A major factor in the elevation was the remarkable influx into the diocese of new Catholics, most notably from the northern states of the country, but also from throughout the Caribbean, making Miami a truly diverse Catholic community.

The first bishop was Coleman F. Carroll. He had served as auxiliary bishop of the Diocese of Pittsburgh since 1953. He was installed on October 7, 1958, and immediately began a vast building program. Forty-five new parishes were established, and fifty-eight churches were founded, as well as schools. Some thirty-five religious communities arrived in Miami to serve the faithful, all invited into the diocese by Bishop Carroll. He also built two seminaries and attended the Second Vatican Council.

In September 1961 the first large assembly of Cuban exiles occurred in Miami in honor of Cuba's patroness, Our Lady of Charity of Cobre. The Mass proved so successful that it became an annual tradition and continues even today. In 1966, at the suggestion of Bishop Carroll, the Cubans began work on building a shrine to Our Lady. The shrine was dedicated in December 1973. On March 2, 1968, Pope Paul VI promoted the diocese to the rank of metropolitan archdiocese. Archbishop Carroll died on July 26, 1977.

The second archbishop of Miami was Edward A. McCarthy. He had been appointed coadjutor archbishop of Miami with right of succession in 1976, having served as the bishop of Phoenix since 1969. He acceded to the see upon the death of Archbishop Carroll and continued the building program, while promoting the reforms mandated by the Second Vatican Council. Among the changes that he introduced were a reorganization of the chancery staff into seven ministries and the building of a permanent chancery.

Notably, in 1985 Archbishop McCarthy held the first Archdiocesan Synod, what was described at the time as "a dramatic moment when the future is fashioned and a mark is left on history that will catch the attention of generations yet unborn." Enormous care was taken to listen to the needs and opinions of the laypeople in the archdiocese, and the result was the publication of 165 decrees, or policy recommendations, and their promulgation

by the archbishop at the synod's closing ceremony in May 1988.

The other significant event of the era was the arrival in 1980 of more than 125,000 Cubans from the port of Mariel. The archdiocese gave them welcome and care. The next year, Catholics of Miami demonstrated the same concern for several thousand Haitians who were detained in federal camps and denied asylum. In 1981 the archbishop opened the Pierre Toussaint Haitian Catholic Center, situated in Miami's "Little Haiti" section.

In 1984 the archdiocese lost some of its territory with the creation of the Dioceses of Venice and Palm Beach. Three years later, Miami celebrated the great distinction of a papal visit, when Pope Blessed John Paul II included the city as part of his six-city American tour. Archbishop McCarthy retired on November 3, 1994.

The third archbishop of Miami, John C. Favalora, was installed in St. Mary's Cathedral on December 20, 1994. Archbishop Favalora had served as bishop of Alexandria from 1986 to 1989 and as the bishop of St. Petersburg from 1989. He was shepherd over an archdiocese that continued to grow in population, and by the end of his tenure it had reached more than 750,000 Catholics, with some 350 diocesan and religious priests, over 300 women religious, and over 100 parishes. With the phenomenal growth of Florida both in population and economic importance, it is likely that the archdiocese will be an increasingly significant voice for the diverse Catholic presence in the state and beyond during the twenty-first century.

Archbishop Favalora retired on April 20, 2010, and was succeeded on the same day by Bishop Thomas G. Wenski, who had been bishop of Orlando since 2004. Archbishop Wenski has continued to provide for the pastoral needs of Miami's remarkably diverse Catholic population. He also was active in assisting the people of Haiti in the aftermath of the devastating earthquake that struck the island in 2010. In 2011 there were 732,000 Catholics, 283 priests, 290 women religious, and 100 parishes in the archdiocese.

Michel, Virgil (June 26, 1890–1938)

A famed pioneer in the field of the liturgy and a Benedictine, Virgil Michel is considered the founder of the American Catholic liturgical movement. Born George Francis Michel in St. Paul, Minnesota, he entered the Order of St. Benedict at the age of nineteen at St. John's Abbey in Minnesota. Ordained a priest in 1916, he was sent for additional studies at The Catholic University of America, where he earned a doctorate in English in 1918.

Over the next few years, Michel filled several assignments for the order and in 1924 was sent to Rome for additional studies in scholastic philosophy. His time in Europe, however, proved exceedingly crucial to his development as he encountered the great early figures in the Catholic liturgical reform movement, including the Benedictine Lambert Beauduin, and visited the centers of renewal such as Solesmes, Maria Laach, and Mont-César. His encounter with liturgical renewal had a powerful impact on him, and he requested permission to abandon doctoral work in philosophy in favor of liturgical studies.

Returning to the United States in 1925, Father Michel began working with the recently founded Liturgical Press to publish English translations of texts on the liturgy that were then becoming influential in European Catholic circles. While teaching at St. John's College in Minnesota, he founded in 1926 the liturgical periodical *Orate Fratres* (later *Worship*). The first issue appeared on the First Sunday of Advent in 1926, and Michel served as editor, with the collaboration of several other well-known pioneers of the liturgical movement, including Gerald Ellard, S.J., Martin Hellriegel, William Busch, Justine Ward, Donald Attwater, and James O'Mahony, O.F.M. The chief objective of the periodical was to improve knowledge regarding the liturgy and to encourage a greater and more active participation on the part of laypeople in the Church's liturgical life.

Between 1925 and 1930 Father Michel was remarkably active as an editor, writer, lecturer, and instructor at St. John's. By 1930 his health had begun to deteriorate, and he spent some time in the hospital. After his recovery, he was sent to work among the Chippewa Indians from 1930 to 1933. Returning to St. John's in 1933, he dedicated the next years to continuing to develop his deep awareness of the liturgy and its potential for build-ing up the faithful, bringing spiritual renewal, and promoting social justice at a time when the country was grappling with the most severe aspects of the Great Depression. In 1935 he became director of the St. John's Institute for Social Studies. By November 1938 his health had deteriorated significantly and he died suddenly at the age of forty-eight. His death was met with shock and grief in many countries, especially among the leaders of the Church's growing liturgical movement.

Michigan

Called the Wolverine State, Michigan is located in the Great Lakes region of the north-central United States. The state is bounded on the north by Lake Superior, on the east by Canada, Lake St. Clair, and Lake Huron, on the west by Lake Michigan and Wisconsin, and on the south by Indiana and Ohio. The area is divided into two major areas, the Upper and Lower Peninsula, which are separated by the Straits of Mackinac and link Lakes Michigan and Huron. Geologically, Michigan has two natural land regions: the Central Lowlands, comprising all of the Lower Peninsula and the eastern part of the Upper Peninsula, and the Superior Uplands, comprising the western part of the Upper Peninsula. The original Native Americans residing in present-day Michigan were the Chippewa, Ottawa, and Potawatomi.

The state has a Catholic legacy that dates to 1620, when Etienne Brulé, a French-Canadian explorer, visited the area seeking the fabled "Northwest Passage," a route to the Orient. Two decades later, Jesuit Father St. Isaac Jogues and Charles Raymbaut were at Sault Ste. Marie. In 1660 the Jesuit superior Father Claude Allouez and Jesuit Father René Menard, revered as a martyr, were also in Michigan, joined by Father Jacques Marquette, who was at Sault Ste. Marie. Jesuit Claude Dablon was at St. Ignatius Mission. An Ottawa mission was also opened. Other explorers in the region were René-Robert Chevalier, Sieur de La Salle, and Louis Joliet.

In 1701 Fort Ponchartrain, which became Detroit, was founded by Antoine Cadillac. The Recollect Franciscan Nicholas Constantin Delhalle was at the Chapel of Ste. Anne de Detroit, and he was slain by Indians in 1706.

Ojibevo Tabernacle in Michigan

The British were involved in the Seven Years' War in Europe, and in 1763 they annexed Detroit. In that same year, Ottawa Chief Pontiac attacked the settlement. He would be defeated in 1794 by American General "Mad Anthony" Wayne at Fallen Timbers. The American Revolution forced the British to cede Detroit, but they did not evacuate the city until 1798. Missionaries were still in the area in 1812, when the British once again occupied Detroit, but they had to cede the city again after the Battle of Lake Erie.

In 1805, by an act of congress, Michigan became a territory, and public lands were made available to settlers in 1818. Father Gabriel Richard served as territorial delegate to the U.S. Congress in 1823. In 1825 the Erie Canal opened the West to settlers, and eight years later Detroit was erected as a diocese, headed by Bishop Frederick Résé.

Michigan entered the Union on January 26, 1837, as the twenty-sixth state. Some of America's outstanding missionaries continued evangelizing in the state. Bishop Irenaeus Frederick Baraga, a revered missionary and friend of the Native Americans, was at Marquette, and assumed the see in 1857. The Diocese of Grand Rapids was erected in 1882.

Michigan continued to prosper, and the new auto industry pioneered there by Henry Ford benefited the nation, especially during World War I. The rise of the automotive industry through Henry Ford's first plant in the Highland Park area of Detroit marked a significant change in the life of the state. Michigan became the automotive center of the country, a position that was not lost until the 1970s when the state's industrial base eroded as part of the wider change in the industry and globalization.

In recognition of the phenomenal growth of Detroit, in 1937 Pope Pius XI promoted the Diocese of Detroit to the rank of a metropolitan archdiocese. At the same time, the Dioceses of Lansing and Saginaw were founded. Archbishop Edward Mooney, the first archbishop of Detroit, was created a cardinal in 1946. All his successors have also received appointment to the College of Cardinals.

Today, Michigan's Catholic population numbers over two million, out of a population of over ten million. Detroit remains the largest population center, although the last decades have witnessed a major decline in the city's economic condition. The fastest-growing areas are in the western parts of the state, around Grand Rapids, Holland, and Muskegon. The Church has devoted many resources to providing pastoral care to those new centers of population, but the Archdiocese of Detroit remains deeply committed to the needs of the people of Detroit. In 2011 there were 2.1 million Catholics, 1,220 priests, 2,300 women religious, and 749 parishes in the diocese.

Miège, Jean Baptiste (September 18, 1815–July 21, 1884)

A Jesuit priest, vicar apostolic of Leavenworth, and missionary, Jean Baptiste Miège is honored as the "Bishop East of the Rockies." He was born in Albertville, France, in what was then Savoy and studied at the College of Conflans and then the minor seminary of Moûtiers, where his older brother, Urban Miège, was an instructor. After considering a career in the military, he discerned a vocation and entered the Society of Jesus in their novitiate in Milan. After preparatory studies and teaching briefly at Chambéry and Milan, he was sent to complete his theological studies at the Roman College.

Ordained a priest on September 7, 1847, he faced with other Jesuits the closure of the Society's schools in Rome as a result of the Revolution of 1848. Father Miège then asked permission to make the journey to the United States to labor among Native Americans. His superiors acquiesced, and Miège arrived in Missouri in late 1849 and taught briefly in local Jesuit schools. The next year, on July 23, 1850, he was named the first Vicar Apostolic of the Indian Territory East of the Rocky Mountains and titular bishop of Messene by Pope Blessed Pius IX. He initially declined the office on the basis of his personal humility, but he accepted when the formal command arrived from Rome for him to assume his duties. He was consecrated on March 25, 1851, by Archbishop Peter R. Kenrick.

To establish his cathedral, Bishop Miège chose a site at St. Mary's College, which had been founded in 1848 as an Indian mission among the Potawatomi in Kansas. The log cathedral was the first west of the Missouri River and east of the Rockies and was consecrated in 1851.

Over the next years, Bishop Miège concentrated on the needs of the Native Americans and earned their respect and love for his pastoral care. As the Kansas-Nebraska Act of 1854 marked a massive influx of settlers to the area, he recognized the need to provide for their pastoral needs as well. He thus moved to Leavenworth, Kansas, and there established on August 15, 1855, the cathedral parish of the Immaculate Conception for what was the first and fastest-growing city in the Kansas Territory. He also hoped to reopen the Sacred Heart Mission in Kickapoo, but the church had been taken over by the town company. Bishop Miège spent the next two decades serving as shepherd over his far-flung territory, traveling in a wagon.

He attended the First Vatican Council in Rome and then went to South America to raise funds for the local churches. He resigned on November 18, 1874, and departed Kansas to take up a post at Woodstock College in Maryland. He later served from 1877 until 1881 as the president of a new

Jesuit college in Detroit, Michigan. His last years were spent at Woodstock as a spiritual adviser to Jesuits in training. He died there.

Miles, Richard Pius (May 17, 1791–February 21, 1860)

A Dominican priest and the first bishop of Nashville, from 1838 to 1860, Richard Pius Miles was born in Prince George's County, in Maryland. He grew up in the area around Bardstown, Kentucky, where his family moved when he was four. Raised in a devout Catholic family, he entered the school run by several Dominican friars, St. Thomas College at St. Rose, Kentucky, at the age of fifteen. He subsequently entered the Order of Friars Preachers and made his profession in May 1810. He took the name Pius, after Pope St. Pius V. After completing his studies, he was ordained on September 21, 1816, and took up a post as a teacher at the college.

Father Miles was then given a variety of assignments, including serving as a missionary in Ohio and as a respected preacher with particular skills in apologetics. When the first Dominican Sisters arrived at St. Magdalen's (now St. Catharine's), Kentucky, Father Miles served as their chaplain and spiritual director. In 1828 he took up a post as a pastor in Zanesville, Ohio, and in 1833 he was elevated to superior of St. Rose's. Four years later, in April 1837, he was elected provincial for the Dominican Province of St. Joseph.

On July 28, 1837, Father Miles was appointed the first bishop of Nashville. The new bishop was consecrated in Bardstown on September 16, 1838. He assumed the role of shepherd over a region in which Catholics were a tiny population, with very limited resources, and where those Catholics who were to be found spent large periods of time without the benefit of a priest or the sacraments. There was only one church, the Most Holy Rosary, and this new "cathedral" was in a severely deteriorated condition. In all, there were barely three hundred Catholics.

Bishop Miles took as one of his most important tasks finding priests to care for the far-flung Catholics of the diocese. This proved a permanent challenge, although he found greater success in bringing women religious to the diocese. The Sisters of Charity of Nazareth, Kentucky, arrived in

1842 to open St. Mary's Academy. They were followed by Dominican Sisters. In 1847 Bishop Miles was able to consecrate a new cathedral, The Seven Sorrows of Mary, one of many new churches completed during his tenure. When he died at the age of sixty-eight from exhaustion and overwork, he left behind thirteen priests, fourteen churches, six chapels, a seminary, three communities of sisters, an academy for girls, nine parochial schools, an orphanage, and a population of twelve thousand Catholics. He was buried beneath the altar of St. Mary's.

Military Services, Archdiocese for the

Previously called the Military Ordinariate, the Archdiocese for the Military Services provides the pastoral and sacramental needs of the members of the armed forces of the United States and their families. The archdiocese serves specifically military personnel and families, patients in Veterans Administration hospitals, and federal employees serving overseas.

The origins of the Military Ordinariate can be traced to the first days of the Continental Army and the American Revolution. The Continental Congress embraced the standing custom of the British Army that military forces should have chaplains to assist soldiers. There was precedent for it in American armed forces as colonial governors had already been appointing chaplains to serve in their colonial militia. On July 29, 1775, the Continental Congress authorized American clergymen to serve as chaplains in the army with the pay of captains. The role of the chaplains was to conduct services on Sundays and to lead the soldiers in prayer during the rest of the week, as well as to provide comfort and help to the wounded and the dying.

On April 30, 1779, John Paul Jones requested that a Catholic priest be permitted to serve aboard the famed warship Bonhomme Richard as there were many French sailors in service at the time. The request was not filled, however, and Catholic chaplains were not permitted in large numbers. There were a mere twenty priests in all of the thirteen colonies at the time (all former Jesuits, owing to the suppression of the order in 1773–74). They cared for some twenty thousand Catholics out of a total population of over two million. Moreover,

the anti-Catholic atmosphere of the times made the appointment of Catholic chaplains a challenge.

Catholic troops were ministered to by local civilian clergy and sometimes by the chaplains of the French forces (about a hundred priests accompanied the French Army and Navy to America), but on an informal basis.

The first Roman Catholic priest to serve as a chaplain of the Continental Army was Father François-Louis Chartier de Lotbinière. He was, however, a French Canadian appointed by General Benedict Arnold for a regiment of Canadian volunteers, and so his official canonical status was in question.

The numbers of chaplains in subsequent years remained small, in keeping with the relatively few Catholics in the United States. There were at least twelve chaplains who served in the War of 1812, but details are not known because the records of the War Department were destroyed when the British burned Washington. Notably, all twelve were not Catholic, and so the indications are that pastoral care of Catholic soldiers was undertaken by civilian priests from the communities in which the army units were stationed.

The first Catholic priest to serve as a navy officer was Jesuit Father Adam Marshall, who sailed on the North Carolina from 1824 until his death onboard the ship in September 1825. He technically had the position of "schoolmaster," but he was also a chaplain to the Catholic sailors. He is generally recognized as the first priest commissioned to serve in the armed forces of the United States.

The Mexican-American War waged between 1846 and 1848 brought many Catholic soldiers into battle in the American army, and the lack of chaplains was felt keenly by the soldiers. Devout Catholic soldiers were forced to cross enemy lines to receive the sacraments from Mexican priests, and the hostility that existed toward Catholics compelled President James A. Polk to improve the increasingly tarnished image of the conflict as bitterly anti-Catholic. Polk requested that Catholic priests be commissioned as army chaplains. Bishop John Hughes of New York responded by coordinating with the superior of the Jesuits to send two Jesuits, Father John McElroy and Father Anthony Rey, to the forces under the command of General

Zachary Taylor. They were not considered regular army chaplains but civilian government employees. Father Rey was killed in Mexico during the fighting, and Father McElroy served one year and returned to the east, where he later founded Boston College.

The conditions for Catholic soldiers did not improve appreciably in the next years. As the First Plenary Council of Baltimore of 1852 noted in its Nineteenth Decree, Catholic soldiers were regularly forced to attend Protestant services. The numbers of chaplains also remained very low. In the year leading up to the Civil War, several Catholic priests were appointed to forts on the western frontier. They included Father Ignacio Ramirez at Fort Montgomery, California, from 1850 to 1852, Father Michael Sheehan at Fort Belknap, Texas, from 1855 to 1859, and Father Pierre-Jean De Smet, S.J., in Utah in 1858.

The Civil War proved a turning point as the example of Catholic soldiers and chaplains as competent, loyal, and courageous put to rest much of the anti-Catholic sentiment that remained in the armed forces. Priests served as chaplains in both armies, and their zeal was noted by generals and soldiers in the Confederate and Union armies. There were approximately forty Catholic chaplains in the Union Army and twenty-eight in the Confederate forces. These were supplemented by some fifty priests who provided pastoral assistance without rank as auxiliary chaplains. The numbers remained pitifully small, of course, and at the Battle of Gettysburg in 1863 there was only one Catholic chaplain for the entire Union Army, Father William Corby of the Holy Cross Fathers. (*See also* Civil War, American.)

The reality was that the scarce number of chaplains meant that thousands of Catholic soldiers only rarely, if ever, saw a priest and received the sacraments. At the same time, chaplains had to request faculties from the local bishops in the areas in which they traveled, and navy chaplains needed faculties at each port. This posed severe limitations on the chaplains and great hardships on the soldiers and sailors for whom they cared.

In 1888 the first Catholic priest was commissioned as a chaplain in the U.S. Navy, Father Charles Henry Parks of New York, who served from 1888 to 1900. He was soon joined by several other chaplains, including the famous Father William Reaney of Baltimore, who had actually been born on the frigate *Constitution* and was given the middle name Ironsides. Twelve priests served as chaplains during the Spanish-American War, as well as nine more priests who served with various state regiments.

On July 4, 1888, a letter from the Apostolic See granted exclusive competency to the archbishop of New York in the appointment of navy chaplains and the right of granting special faculties to the new chaplains; the faculties were still to be exercised with the approval of the local diocese where the priest functioned. Two years later, a commission of the U.S. archbishops under Cardinal James Gibbons was established to recruit priests for the military chaplaincy, and the commission named Paulist Father Alexander Doyle in 1905 to act as their representative with the federal government in all matters related to Catholic chaplains. These two events helped lay the groundwork for the later Military Ordinariate.

With the entry of the United States into World War I in 1917, the need for additional chaplains was most acute. There were initially only sixteen priests in the regular army and eight in the navy (the number that was allowed by the War Department); ten more were in the National Guard. To answer the call, the bishops of the United States, who had formed the National Catholic War Council, urged dioceses and the religious communities to do their part. By Armistice Day and the end of the war in 1918, there were 1,026 priests (762 diocesan and 264 religious) serving with the armed forces; 740 were commissioned in the army and 44 in the navy. There were also 165 priests who served without commission as civilians who received pay from the Knights of Columbus; they were under the jurisdiction of their own ecclesiastical authorities. Seventeen priests died during the war.

In the wake of the experience of the war, a decisive step was taken to improve the obvious and mounting obstacles to effective administration and pastoral ministry being faced by the chaplains in the armed forces. As the problem was not unique to the United States, the Holy See decided to appoint a bishop for each impacted country to be the Ordinarius Castrensis, or Bishop for the Military. On November 24, 1917, Pope Benedict XV named Bishop Patrick Joseph Hayes, auxiliary of New York, to be "Ordinary of all Catholics who fight in the army and the navy during the present war." Henceforth, while chaplains were incardinated, Bishop Hayes was considered their proper ordinary for the time they served in the military. Bishop Hayes was recognized by the United States government in his capacity as head of the chaplains. In the years after World War I, the ordinariate was directed by Monsignor George Waring.

Bishop Hayes provided organization to the military diocese, called the Military Vicariate, and headquartered in New York, assisted by five regional vicariates. The offices of the diocese were termed the Military Ordinariate.

In the years leading up to the war, Pope Pius XII recognized that the United States would likely be involved in a major conflict, and in 1939 he appointed Archbishop (later Cardinal) Francis Spellman of New York as his military vicar. The Military Vicariate and Ordinariate were severely tested from December 7, 1941, the date of the Japanese attack on Pearl Harbor that thrust America into World War II. At the start of America's entry into the war, there were five hundred chaplains on duty (there were 1,670 total chaplains). Over the next four years, over 2,400 priests served as army chaplains and 817 as navy chaplains. Over 9 percent of all Catholic clergy in the United States served as commissioned chaplains, and seventy-six priests died in the war. There were also some two thousand civilian auxiliary chaplains.

Owing to America's transformed presence in world affairs in the postwar world, additional changes were needed to ensure that the military received the best possible pastoral care. On June 13, 1946, Pope Pius XII extended the vicariate's jurisdiction to include civilians serving the U.S. government overseas; a further expansion was permitted in November 1954. At the same time in 1946, the Veterans Administration program was placed under the canonical jurisdiction of the Military Vicariate.

During the conflict in Korea, from June 1950 to July 1953, a special circumstance developed because the operations against the communists in North Korea were under the auspices of the United

Nations' police action. To deal effectively with the reality that various countries were contributing troops and that there were chaplains from around the world, Pope Pius XII, in September 1950, ordered all Catholic chaplains in Korea, regardless of country, to have the same faculties and to be placed under the American military vicar. There were 932 priests commissioned as American chaplains, assisted by 427 auxiliary chaplains in Korea, and six priests died in service. One of them, Father Emil Kapaun, died in 1951 in a Korean prisoner of war camp; his cause for canonization was opened in 2003.

In 1957 Pope Pius XII canonically established the Military Vicariate as the U.S. Military Vicariate. It was placed under the jurisdiction of the New York archbishop. At the time, the archbishop was Cardinal Spellman, who had enjoyed a very long relationship with the U.S. military. Succeeding vicars were Cardinal Terence J. Cooke and Cardinal John J. O'Connor.

Catholic chaplains served with distinction throughout the Vietnam War. In 1970 there were over two million service people in the conflict, and they received care from 435 priests in the army (68 regular, 367 active reserve), 298 in the navy (122 regular, 176 active reserve), and 385 air force chaplains (114 regular, 271 active reserve). There were also 615 reserve chaplains and 288 priests working in the Veterans Administration. Seven priests died in the war, including Father Vincent Capodanno, M.M., a navy chaplain who was killed in action. On May 21, 2006, the cause for his canonization was opened with the permission of the Congregation for the Causes of Saints in Rome.

The Military Ordinariate continued to provide pastoral ministry across the world for all branches of the armed forces. Catholic chaplains ministered to U.S. troops in all modern conflicts, such as in Bosnia, in Operation Desert Shield and Operation Desert Storm during the Gulf War, and most especially in the post–September 11, 2001, operations in Afghanistan and Iraq.

In 1985 the ordinariate was restructured into the present Archdiocese for the Military Services as an independent jurisdiction. Archbishop Joseph T. Ryan was named the first archbishop of the archdiocese. He was succeeded on May 14, 1991, by

Archbishop Joseph Thomas Dimino, who served until his retirement on August 12, 1997. He was followed by Archbishop Edwin F. O'Brien, who served until July 12, 2007, when he was appointed archbishop of Baltimore, Maryland. On November 10, 2007, Archbishop Timothy P. Broglio was named archbishop. He had served previously as a Vatican nuncio.

Currently, there are over 1.4 million Catholic men and women in the archdiocese, including 375,000 in uniform and over 900,000 family members, as well as 300,000 Catholics in the reserves and coast guard, in government service overseas, or in Veterans Administration hospitals. There are approximately 1,000 priests serving as chaplains supported by members of the Catholic laity.

Millet, Pierre (November 19, 1635–December 31, 1708)

A Jesuit missionary in New York, Pierre Millet labored for many years among the Native Americans and was known to the Onondaga nation as the "Looker-up to Heaven." Born at Bourges, France, he entered the Society of Jesus at Paris in October 1655 and studied philosophy at La Fléche and Compiégne. He completed his theology studies at the Collège Louis-le-Grand in Paris from 1664 to 1668 and was then sent to Canada, where he was expected to assist the remarkable labors of Father Claude Allouez. His actual duties, however, took him to the Onondaga with Father Etienne de Carheil, where he enjoyed great success.

In 1671 Millet made his solemn profession as a Jesuit, and the following year he was appointed the Jesuit missionary to the Oneidas. For the next sixteen years, he evangelized with great success and then was sent in 1688 to be chaplain at Fort Niagara. The following year, Father Millet was taken captive by a band of Iroquois. Severely mistreated, he was given finally into the hands of the Oneida, who placed him on trial for his life. With the assistance of Christian Oneida families, he was spared death and granted entry into the Iroquois nation by Chief Gannassatiron.

Father Millet remained with the Iroquois for several years. He preached among them, provided pastoral care, and also assisted the French prisoners captured during the wilderness fighting of the period. He returned at last to Québec around 1694 and reached Montréal in October. He spent 1695 at Québec College and was then sent the following year to Lorette to work among the Hurons. From 1697 to 1703, he served in the mission at Sault-St.-Louis. Soon after, however, his health declined from years of work, but he remained hopeful to the end of his life of returning to the Iroquois to continue his work among them. He died at Montréal.

Milwaukee, Archdiocese of

Established as a diocese on November 28, 1843, by Pope Gregory XVI, and raised to the rank of a metropolitan provincial see on February 12, 1875, by Pope Blessed Pius IX, the Archdiocese of Milwaukee serves counties in southeastern Wisconsin. The city is a port of entry on Lake Michigan, founded in 1835 by Solomon Juneau. The name is either from the Algonquin for "good land" or from *Mahn-a-waukeem Seepe*, a local Indian term for "gathering place on the river." Two villages were erected and joined in 1839 to form Milwaukee, with Walker's Point added in 1845. German immigrants prompted rapid growth and industrialization, and the Civil War added economic impetus. The city now thrives on manufacturing and beer, and serves as a gateway to the Great Lakes-St. Lawrence Seaway.

The Catholic history of Milwaukee dates to 1634, when Jean Nicolet and other French explorers visited the Menominee Indians in present-day Wisconsin. In 1681 Jesuit Father René Menard, who was later martyred in the Dakota region, opened the missions of Wisconsin. Jesuit Fathers Jacques Marquette, Claude Allouez, and Claude Dablon were in the area of Prairie du Chien and Green Bay in 1674, the years in which Wisconsin was attached to the Diocese of Québec.

The missions continued in the area until 1763, when Wisconsin was ceded to the British at the close of the Seven Years' War. In 1764 the British declared Wisconsin an Indian Territory, closed to Caucasians. French Jesuits still served the tribes. In 1783 Wisconsin became part of the new United States. Congress created the Wisconsin Territory in 1836, and immigrants flooded into the region to begin settlements.

In 1837 Father Florimond Bonduel celebrated

Mass in the home of Solomon Juneau, the founder of Milwaukee. Two years later, St. Peter's was started and then moved. Some of America's most revered missionaries were in the region, including Dominican Venerable Samuel Mazzuchelli and his companion, Dominican Theodore van den Broek, and Father (later Bishop) Irenaeus Frederick Baraga. The Catholics of the region were initially under the jurisdiction of the vast Diocese of Bardstown and then part of the Diocese of Detroit from 1833.

The Diocese of Milwaukee was established in 1843, and the first bishop of the diocese was John M. Henni. A German-speaking Swiss, Bishop Henni had long served German Catholics in the Ohio Valley region. He was consecrated bishop on March 19, 1844, in Cincinnati. His primary task was to establish the new diocese on a firm footing. He founded many new parishes, the first parochial schools, hospitals, and orphanages, as well as St. Francis Seminary, which was started out of his own residence in 1845 before finding a permanent home in Milwaukee in 1856. Bishop Henni likewise encouraged religious orders to come to the diocese, including the Daughters (Sisters) of Charity, the School Sisters of Notre Dame, the School Sisters of St. Francis, the Franciscan Sisters of Penance and Charity, the Jesuits, and the Capuchin Franciscans. To assist the Catholic community, he launched the first German-language newspaper in Milwaukee and gave his support to the English-language Catholic newspapers.

Owing to the swift development of the Church in the diocese, in 1868 Bishop Henni requested Pope Blessed Pius IX to create two new dioceses, Green Bay and LaCrosse, out of the Milwaukee diocese. Pope Pius agreed and decreed as well the Province of Milwaukee and raised the Milwaukee diocese to the rank of archdiocese in 1875. Bishop Henni was appointed the first archbishop of Milwaukee on February 12, 1875. He died on September 7, 1881, in Milwaukee, exhausted from thirty-seven years of toil. For

Bishop John M. Henni

his labors, he was given the title of "Patriarch of the Northwest."

Archbishop Henni's successor was Archbishop Michael Heiss, a German-born priest who had served as Archbishop Henni's secretary and then later as the first bishop of the Diocese of La Crosse in 1868. Bishop Heiss was named coadjutor of Milwaukee on April 9, 1880, and succeeded Archbishop Henni on September 7, 1881. Although a truly learned theologian, his appointment was contested for a time by English-speaking Catholics.

His time as archbishop was preoccupied with placing the finances of the archdiocese on a firm footing. At the same time, he improved the ethnic situation by encouraging American-born women in the archdiocese to enter religious communities and gave his permission for English to be taught in parish schools with greater regularity. In addition, he took part in the preparations for the Third Plenary Council of Baltimore, held in 1884. Archbishop Heiss died on March 26, 1890, after nine years in office.

Archbishop Heiss was succeeded by Archbishop Frederick Xavier Katzer as the third archbishop of Milwaukee, an Austrian who arrived in America in 1864 and became a priest in 1866. He served on the faculty of St. Francis Seminary, where he taught mathematics, philosophy, and theology until 1875. In 1886 he was named bishop of Green Bay. He became the third archbishop of Milwaukee on January 30, 1891.

Archbishop Katzer was described by Cardinal James Gibbons of Baltimore as "thoroughly German and thoroughly unfit to be an archbishop," and he did prove to be dedicated to the sympathies of the ethnic German clergy and laity. Nevertheless, he proved to be an able shepherd of the diocese, supported the growth of Catholic schools, and successfully fought against the Bennett Law in 1898, an act that would have mandated English instruction in all public schools and so was seen as an attack on parochial schools. Archbishop Katzer also encouraged ethnic parishes, particularly the Polish. Connected to that support, he was firmly against the ideas of Americanism and thanked Pope Leo XIII for his famous letter *Testem Benevolentiae* in 1899. He also helped to bring the Sisters of the Divine Savior to Milwaukee.

Archbishop Katzer died in Fond du Lac on July 23, 1903, the same day as Pope Leo XIII.

He was succeeded by Sebastian Gebhard Messmer, a Swiss-born priest and the last European-born archbishop of Milwaukee. Messmer succeed Bishop Katzer as the bishop of Green Bay in 1892 and was then named to the Milwaukee archdiocese, now as Archbishop Katzer's successor, on November 28, 1903.

Archbishop Messmer faced the ongoing question of ethnicity by working to ease tensions in the city and by advancing a program of centralization for the archdiocese. As part of that program, he wrote the first *Handbook for Catholic Parishioners* in 1907 to establish guidelines for diverse ethnic groups in the diocese and was a strong supporter of the American Federation of Catholic Societies, an organization that worked to present a united Catholic voice in American social concerns.

Archbishop Messmer encountered controversy with the Polish community in the archdiocese, specifically with the Polish priest Father Wenceslaus Kruszka, a disagreement that nearly caused a schism in the Milwaukee church. Archbishop Messmer's time witnessed the appointment of the first auxiliary bishops, Bishops Joseph Maria Koudelka and Edward Kozlowski.

Known as the "Archbishop of Christian Charity," Messmer was famous for his charitable efforts, many from his own funds; he founded a charitable bureau in 1916. Through his leadership, the archdiocese significantly developed the Church's care of the sick, orphaned, poor, and aged. He also actively promoted education; he built Messmer High School and forty other schools, and welcomed the establishment of Mount Mary College and Marquette College's growth into Marquette University. He approved the first ministry to African-Americans when a Catholic couple, Lincoln C. and Julia Valle, organized St. Benedict the Moor church and school in 1908; supported the establishment of Our Lady of Guadalupe Mission for Mexican Catholics in 1929; and encouraged the formation of Catholic women's organizations, such as the Marquette Women's League and the Milwaukee Archdiocesan Council of Catholic Women, even though he was opposed to women's suffrage. Twenty-nine orders of religious men and women settled in the archdiocese during his time as archbishop. In 1922 he started the *Catholic Herald*, the official Catholic English-language paper of the Archdiocese of Milwaukee.

Archbishop Messmer died on August 4, 1930, and was succeeded by Samuel Alphonsus Stritch as the fifth archbishop of Milwaukee.

Archbishop Stritch was born in Nashville, Tennessee, and had served as bishop of Toledo from 1921 until his installation as archbishop of Milwaukee on August 26, 1930. Archbishop Stritch devoted most of his energies to assisting the faithful with the hardships of the Great Depression. In 1935 a fire destroyed the interior of the Cathedral of St. John the Evangelist. Aware of the economic problems facing his people, Archbishop Stritch delayed all restoration and did the same with St. Francis Seminary.

He supported the first National Catholic Social Action Conference, held in Milwaukee in 1938, and then he helped galvanize support for the Catholic Action movement in answer to the call by Pope Pius XI. He went on to found the Catholic Youth Organization in the archdiocese to assist the development of youth. Archbishop Stritch was transferred to the Archdiocese of Chicago on December 27, 1939, and was made cardinal on February 18, 1946.

The sixth archbishop of Milwaukee, Moses E. Kiley, was born in Margaree, Cape Breton, Nova Scotia, and had been spiritual director of the North American College in Rome and then bishop of Trenton from 1934 to 1940. He was transferred to the Milwaukee archdiocese on January 1, 1940, and was installed on March 28, 1940.

Archbishop Kiley embarked upon the restoration of the Cathedral of St. John the Evangelist, especially as part of the diocesan centennial in 1943. He also devoted financial resources to rebuilding St. Aemillian's Orphanage after a fire, and the restoration of St. Francis Seminary, and converted Pio Nono High School into St. Francis Minor Seminary.

Much of his time as archbishop was taken up with World War II, and he sent thirty priests from the archdiocese to the war as chaplains. At the same time, he started a Catholic Family Life Bureau in 1948 and supported the Legion of Mary. Because of declining health, his last years were spent with his auxiliary bishop, Roman Atkielski, assuming more of his duties. Archbishop Kiley died on April 15, 1953, in Milwaukee, and was succeeded by Albert G. Meyer.

A Milwaukee native, Archbishop Meyer was the first archbishop of Milwaukee who was born, raised, and educated in his own archdiocese. After teaching at St. Francis Seminary, he had served as bishop of the Diocese of Superior and was consecrated bishop in 1946. Appointed archbishop of Milwaukee on July 21, 1953, he assumed his duties as shepherd, determined to continue the vast postwar expansion of the archdiocese that had begun under Archbishop Kiley. He undertook a $3.2 million building program, which included improvements to the facilities of St. Francis Seminary, seventeen new parishes, and the upgrading of five missions to parish status. He also began a religious information program that brought about an increase in converts and was attentive especially to the needs of African-Americans in the city as well as lay participation in the work of the Church. In 1958 he established a Council of Catholic Men to join the Archdiocesan Council of Catholic Women. In 1956 he issued a pastoral letter, "Decency and Modesty," that stressed the need for proper dress.

Archbishop Meyer was transferred to Chicago as successor to Cardinal Stritch and departed Milwaukee on September 24, 1958. He was installed as archbishop of Chicago on November 16, 1958, and became a cardinal on December 14, 1959. He died in Chicago on April 9, 1965, from a brain tumor.

Cardinal Meyer's successor as the eighth archbishop of Milwaukee was Archbishop William E. Cousins. A native of Chicago, he had served as an auxiliary bishop to then Archbishop Stritch and then was bishop of Peoria from 1952 to 1958, when, on December 18, he was appointed the eighth archbishop of Milwaukee.

Archbishop Cousins spent his first years as Milwaukee's shepherd participating in the Second Vatican Council. During the council, he was a member of the Commissions on Communications Media and the Lay Apostolate. He then devoted the years after returning from Rome to an attempted implementation of the reforms decreed by the council. He succeeded to a large degree in preventing many of the problems and uncertainties that emerged in other dioceses and archdioceses, and tried with patience and humility to steer the faithful and clergy in Milwaukee through one of the most tumultuous periods in American history.

Archbishop Cousins retired in 1977 and died on September 14, 1988, in Milwaukee. He was succeeded by Archbishop Rembert G. Weakland, O.S.B. A native of Patton, Pennsylvania, he had entered the Benedictines and had served as an arch-abbot, and then was elected abbot primate of the International Benedictine Confederation on September 29, 1967. He was appointed archbishop of Milwaukee by Pope Paul VI on September 20, 1977, and was ordained a bishop on November 8, 1977.

Archbishop Weakland closed the preparatory seminary and opened an urban parish for Native Americans. He also welcomed Asian refugees into the archdiocese and was active in the National Conference of Catholic Bishops and its subsequent incarnation as the United States Conference of Catholic Bishops. His time as archbishop ended under the shadow of several controversies, including the effort to remodel the Cathedral of St. John the Evangelist and the revelation that he had used diocesan funds to pay a settlement for an alleged inappropriate relationship. Having reached the mandatory retirement age of seventy-five on April 2, 2002, Archbishop Weakland stepped down on May 24, 2002.

Archbishop Weakland was succeeded on August 28, 2002, by the tenth archbishop of Milwaukee, Archbishop Timothy M. Dolan. He was born in St. Louis and had served as secretary to the apostolic nunciature in Washington, D.C., vice rector of the Kenrick-Glennon Seminary in St. Louis, where he also taught Church history, and then rector of the North American College in Rome from 1994. On June 19, 2001, he was named the auxiliary bishop of St. Louis, and on June 25, 2002, he was appointed archbishop of Milwaukee. He was installed on August 28, 2002. Archbishop Dolan focused on archdiocesan unity, providing the seminary with a firm foundation for the future, and a successful Catholic Stewardship Appeal to fund archdiocesan ministries and education. He was appointed archbishop of New York on February 23, 2009.

Bishop Jerome E. Listecki, who had been bishop of La Crosse since 2004, was installed as archbishop on January 4, 2010. Archbishop Listecki was confronted from the start by the massive problems created by the sex abuse crisis and nearly two dozen lawsuits facing the archdiocese. The Church in Milwaukee had already paid out more than $29 million, and as attempts to reach a negotiated settlement with the victims failed, the archdiocese was forced to file for Chapter 11 bankruptcy protection on January 4, 2011. In 2011 there were 634,000 Catholics, 664 priests, 1,366 women religious, and 208 parishes in the archdiocese.

Minnesota

Called the Gopher State, Minnesota is located in the north-central part of the United States. Minnesota is bounded on the north by Canada, on the east by Lake Superior and Wisconsin, on the south by Iowa, and on the west by North Dakota and South Dakota. The name of the state comes from a Dakota word, *minisotah*, meaning "sky-colored water." Minnesota comprises three main land regions: the Superior Uplands in the northeast, the Young Drift Plains in the west, and the Dissected Till Plains in the southwest. The original inhabitants of the area were the Chippewa and the Sioux. Minnesota, depicted by Henry Wadsworth Longfellow in the poem *Hiawatha*, entered the Union in 1858.

The Catholic history of the state opens in 1655 with the first mission chapel for the Dakota Sioux near Hastings. Another mission was established at Fond du Lac two decades later. One of the most revered explorers of the era, Daniel Greysolon, Sieur du Lhut, was in the region in 1680 with Franciscan Recollect Father Louis Hennepin and visited Mille Lacs. Father Hennepin discovered St. Anthony's Falls, the site of modern-day Minneapolis. Nine years later, Nicholas Perrot claimed the area for France, and other explorers were active in the region.

Jesuit Father Michael Guignas and Nicholas de Gonnor erected St. Michael the Archangel Mission

in 1727, and other Jesuits served in the various forts erected by trappers and explorers. In 1736 Father Jean-Pierre Aulneau was slain by Sioux, becoming Minnesota's first martyr.

In the early 1800s missions were operating near Lac Qui Perle, Fond du Lac, Grand Portage, and Crow Wing. Minnesota's territories were included in the Louisiana Purchase of 1803 and became the possession of the United States. A treaty made in 1819 opened some of these territories to white settlers. Fort Snelling had been erected in the region the year before.

By 1840 there was a chapel at Mandata, and in the following year Father Lucien Galtier founded a log chapel at St. Paul's on Pig's Eye Landing, marking the start of St. Paul. Eight years later, Minnesota, now open to settlement, became a territory by act of Congress. It entered the Union in 1858 as the thirty-second state.

On July 19, 1850, the Diocese of St. Paul (now the Archdiocese of St. Paul and Minneapolis) was established by the Holy See. Bishop Joseph Crétin was given ecclesiastical jurisdiction over the area from Lake Superior to the Missouri River, and from Iowa to the Canadian border. The railroads brought new settlers to St. Paul and to the region destined to become Minneapolis. In 1858 the Benedictines erected a monastery near St. Cloud, in time called Collegeville.

The rich natural resources of Minnesota formed the economic base for rising populations and progress. After the Civil War, more settlers arrived, and St. Paul was elevated to the rank of an archdiocese in 1888. In the following year, Dr. William Mayo and his sons opened the now internationally famed clinic in Rochester. The following year, Pope Leo XIII decreed the founding of the Dioceses of Duluth, St. Cloud, and Winona. The Diocese of Crookston was founded in 1909 by Pope St. Pius X.

The revered Archbishop John Ireland headed the Archdiocese of St. Paul from 1884 to 1918. He expanded Catholic facilities and spearheaded education programs throughout the archdiocese. He died just as Americans became deeply involved in World War I. The faithful of Minnesota supported the military efforts of the nation in the war.

The Great Depression brought renewed economic suffering to the faithful in the state. Minnesotans also supported the war effort in World War II both by contributing thousands of American soldiers and workers and by bringing mining and manufacturing to peak conditions during the global conflict.

In 1957 the Diocese of New Ulm was established by Pope Pius XII. In 2011 there were over one million Catholics in the state, comprising approximately 22 percent of the total population in Minnesota. There are also 950 priests, 1,770 women religious, and 689 parishes.

Minton, Sherman (October 20, 1890–April 9, 1965)

Associate Justice of the United States Supreme Court from 1949 to 1956, Sherman Minton was also a Democratic United States Senator from Indiana and a convert to Catholicism. Born in New Albany, Indiana, Minton studied at Indiana University and Yale Law School and began the practice of law in his hometown in 1916. The following year he married Gertrude Gertz, a Catholic, and then served overseas in World War I as a captain in the Motor Transport Corps from 1917 to 1919; he was also a captain in the Infantry section, Officers' Reserve Corps, from 1919 to 1943. Returning home, he resumed his law practice in Indiana and also in Florida. After a brief time as public counselor for the Public Service Commission of Indiana in 1933–34, he ran for the U.S. Senate from Indiana and won as part of the massive Democratic landslide in 1934.

Minton served in the Senate from 1935 until 1940. He proved a strong supporter of President Franklin Delano Roosevelt and the New Deal, going so far as to give his backing to Roosevelt's ill-fated "court-packing" plan (by which the president sought to bring the Supreme Court into a position to advance the New Deal). Minton's position cost him reelection in Indiana in 1940. Nevertheless, he was a popular figure in the Democratic Party, and in 1940 Roosevelt appointed him an administrative assistant in the Executive Office of the President. In 1941 Roosevelt named him to the Seventh Circuit Court of Appeals.

In 1949 President Harry S. Truman, who had served with Minton in the Senate, chose him to join the Supreme Court. Approved by the Senate,

he took the oath of office on October 12, 1949. As a justice, Minton was generally in favor of government authority, but he was also a determined anti-communist and upheld the 1951 conviction of the leader of the U.S. Communist Party. He also voted to strike down school segregation in 1954's *Brown v. Board of Education.*

Minton retired on October 15, 1956, because of declining health. He beaome a Catholic in 1961. He died at New Albany and was buried in Holy Trinity Catholic Cemetery.

Mississippi

Called the Magnolia State, Mississippi is located in the southeastern part of the United States. Mississippi is bounded on the north by Tennessee, on the east by Alabama, on the south by the Gulf of Mexico and Louisiana, and on the west by Louisiana and Arkansas. The state has two principal land regions: the Gulf Coastal Plain, which comprises the major portion, and the Mississippi Alluvial Plain in the west. The original inhabitants of Mississippi were the Biloxi, Chickasaw, Choctaw, Natchez, Pascagoula, and Yazoo.

The Catholic history of the state began in 1540 when Hernando de Soto led an expedition into the region. In 1673 Jesuit Father Jacques Marquette and Louis Joliet were in present-day Mississippi, and in 1682 René-Robert Chevalier, Sieur de La Salle, led another expedition into the area, claiming it for France. The Franciscan martyr Father Zenobius Membré was in the La Salle expedition and celebrated Mass on March 29 at present-day Fort Adams.

In 1699 Seminary of Québec missionaries were at Natchez and Ocean Springs. Fathers Jean-François Buisson de Saint-Cosmé, who was martyred, and others such as François Jolliet de Montigny and Thomas de la Source all served in the area. Father Jacques Gravier was with the Tunicas, and Father Nicholas Foucault was martyred in Koros. Also present was Carmelite Father John Matthia, who labored in Biloxi. The city of Natchez, Fort Rosalie, was founded in 1717, and three years later Biloxi achieved the status of city also. The Natchez War claimed the life of Jesuit Father Paul du Poisson at Fort Rosalie. In 1768 Recollect Franciscan Father Luke Collet also died in the mission.

The Spanish, who had also created missions in Mississippi, departed from the area in 1798. They had opened Coles Creek parish ten years before, and San Salvador del Mundo at Natchez, as well as a mission chapel at Nogales. In 1776 Bishop Luis Ignacio Peñalver y Cárdenas arrived in the region to confirm the faithful. The Capuchin Franciscans came from New Orleans to continue the evangelization programs.

When the area was ceded to the United States, Congress organized the Mississipi Territory on April 7, 1798; the land was taken from territory ceded by Georgia and South Carolina. The territory was enlarged in 1804 and again in 1813, and land was purchased or acquired through various treaties (generally considered to be inequitable) from Native Americans over the next decades. Mississippi entered the Union as the twentieth state on December 10, 1817.

The Diocese of Natchez (now the Diocese of Jackson) was established by Pope Gregory XVI on July 28, 1837. The first bishop of the diocese was Bishop John Mary Joseph Chanche, S.S., who served from 1841 to 1852. He arrived to find no churches or priests and no money. He laid the cornerstone of the diocesan cathedral in 1842. When his time ended, Bishop Chanche had established ten parishes with resident pastors and had an orphanage and a school in operation.

Mississippi was the second state to secede from the Union in the lead-up to the Civil War and was occupied in the aftermath by federal troops. During the war, Bishop William Henry Elder (bishop from 1857 to 1880) was ordered to have Catholics pray for President Abraham Lincoln and the Union troops in the churches. When he refused to obey the order, he was sent into exile. When word of Bishop Elder's exile reached the authorities in Washington, the sentence was countermanded. Mississippi reentered the Union in 1870, but federal troops remained in the state for five more years as part of Reconstruction programs. Bishop Elder served in Natchez until 1880, building schools and inviting priests and religious orders into the diocese. Some of these priests and religious tended the wounded of both sides during the Civil War and during the yellow fever outbreaks that swept across Mississippi in the 1870s.

The Dioceses of Biloxi and Jackson were founded in 1977. Both were placed as suffragan sees of the Archdiocese of Mobile. The Diocese of Natchez subsequently became a titular see, a see in name only.

The Church in Mississippi today remains a small minority in a chiefly Baptist state. Catholics make up barely 4 percent of the overall population of nearly three million. There are over 150 priests in ministry, as well as nearly 300 men and women religious and 120 parishes in the state.

Missouri

Called the Show Me State, Missouri is located in the central part of the United States. It is bounded on the north by Iowa, on the east by Illinois, Kentucky, and Tennessee, on the south by Arkansas, and on the west by Oklahoma, Kansas, and Nebraska. Four principal land regions form Missouri: the Mississippi Alluvial Plain in the northeast, the Ozark Plateau in the south, the Osage Plain in the southwest, and the Dissected Till Plain in the north. The original inhabitants of present-day Missouri were the Fox, Missouri, Osage, and Sauk.

The Catholic heritage of Missouri opened with the expedition of Hernando de Soto, around 1542, accompanied by priests. Jesuit Father Jacques Marquette and Louis Joliet were in Missouri in 1673. Jesuits had already established Ste. Genevieve in the southeast. The discovery of lead deposits there prompted mining expeditions. In 1700 Jesuit Gabriel Marest founded a mission at present-day St. Louis. Thirty-four years later missionaries from Cahokia arrived in the Old Mines area.

Father Pierre Gibault began the first Catholic church in St. Louis, which had been founded in 1764. Recollect Franciscan Luke Collet, who died in Mississippi, and Jesuit Sebastian L. Meurin were serving the area in the 1760s. A mission was also opened at St. Charles, followed by the Carondelet mission.

In 1763 France ceded the area to Spain but assumed control again in 1800. Three years later, Missouri became part of the United States in the Louisiana Purchase. The U.S. Congress declared Missouri part of the Louisiana Territory, making it a separate territory in 1812, with William Clark as governor. White settlers came in large numbers, and they brought slaves with them. The Jesuits started an Indian mission at Florissant in 1811, and St. Rose Philippine Duchesne was there for a time and at St. Charles. Seven years later, Bishop Louis Dubourg arrived in St. Louis with Vincentians Joseph Rosati and Felix de Andreis. Missouri asked to enter the Union in 1817, and a political uproar ensued over the question of slavery. The Missouri Compromise allowed Missouri to become the twenty-fourth state on August 10, 1821.

Immigrants continued to arrive in the state, which was under the ecclesiastical jurisdiction of the Diocese of Louisiana, and Bishop Dubourg made St. Louis his see. He founded the parent institution of St. Louis University, began a seminary, and eventually moved to New Orleans. In November 1826 he retired, believing that an American could better serve the New Orleans diocese.

During this period, Father Charles de la Croix was serving the Osage, while Jesuit Charles Van Quickenborne was in St. Louis. In 1826 the Diocese of St. Louis was officially founded by Pope Leo XII. Rosati was named the first bishop, and he served from 1827 to 1843. St. Louis was elevated to the rank of an archdiocese in 1847 under his successor, the long-serving and memorable Archbishop Peter R. Kenrick (bishop and then archbishop from 1843 to 1895).

The Indian missions continued, and Jesuit Fathers John Schoenmaker and Paul Mary Ponziglione labored there in the 1840s and 1850s. A mission was opened later for the Arapaho on the Wind River Reservation.

During the Civil War, most Missourians remained loyal to the federal cause, but men from the state enlisted in both the Confederate and Union armies. Guerrilla fighting and bloody clashes took place in the state, and violence persisted even after the war and was characterized by the activities of outlaws such as Jesse James. In 1865 a new constitution was drawn up that included a Test Oath that discriminated against Catholics. Archbishop Kenrick took the matter to the United States Supreme Court, which declared the Test Oath unconstitutional and released the priest imprisoned for refusing to take the discriminatory oath.

Archbishop Kenrick presided over the rapid development of the Church in Missouri at a time when the state embarked upon a new era in history. The older ways of life, based chiefly on the river, began to fade. In their place Missouri emerged as a much more urban and industrialized region. In keeping with the growth of the Catholic community in Missouri, Pope Blessed Pius IX established the see of St. Joseph in 1868, and Pope Leo XIII decreed the see of Kansas City in 1880. The two dioceses were united in 1956.

In 1903 Archbishop John Joseph Glennon, who later became a cardinal, assumed the see of St. Louis. He became known as the "Cathedral Builder" for his tireless work to expand the pastoral labors of the Church in Missouri. He built churches, schools, hospitals, and a seminary, while earning fame as a gifted orator and speaking at gatherings across the country. In 1908 he began the Cathedral of St. Louis, now a basilica. In addition, he led the faithful through the hardship of the Great Depression and throughout World War II before his death in 1946.

The postwar industrial boom continued Missouri's growth as a major economic center in the United States and brought a phenomenal growth in population. Missouri emerged as the second largest producer (behind Michigan) of automobiles in the country. To keep pace with the population increase, two dioceses were created in 1956, Jefferson City and Springfield-Cape Girardeau.

Currently, there are over 850,000 Catholics in Missouri, with the largest concentrations found in the Archdiocese of St. Louis. Catholics comprise over a quarter of the population in St. Louis, while the population is considerably smaller elsewhere in the state. The state has also witnessed major demographic changes, as the suburbs increased steadily in population, so much so that St. Louis lost half its population between 1950 and 1990. The Church has kept pace with these changes and has continued to focus pastoral programs accordingly, without losing sight of the needs of the people still in the city.

In 2011 there were over 1,200 priests in the state, around 2,500 men and women religious, and over 430 parishes. The Church also enjoys an impressive educational presence with four universities and colleges and over 270 high schools and elementary schools.

Mitty, John J. (January 20, 1884–October 15, 1961)

Archbishop of San Francisco from 1935 to 1961, John Joseph Mitty was considered one of the most financially and administratively capable prelates in the United States in the period immediately before the Second Vatican Council. Born in New York City, Mitty was orphaned by the age of fourteen after the deaths first of his mother in 1894 and then his father in 1898. He subsequently studied at Manhattan College and then St. Joseph's Seminary, in Dunwoodie, New York, in preparation for the priesthood. Ordained a priest on December 22, 1906, he was sent for additional studies in theology at The Catholic University of America and then went to Rome, where he earned a doctorate in sacred theology from the Pontifical Lateran University in 1908. He then completed further study in psychology at the University of Munich in 1908.

Returning to the United States in 1909, Father Mitty was given a pastoral assignment and then was appointed to the faculty of St. Joseph's Seminary from 1909 to 1917. He served as a chaplain in the 49th and 101st Regiments of the U.S. Army during America's participation in World War I. Coming back to New York in 1919, he was named a pastor in Highland Falls, New York, and then an associate pastor in the Bronx until 1926.

On June 21, 1926, Father Mitty was appointed by Pope Pius XI the bishop of Salt Lake City, Utah. Consecrated on September 8, 1926, he was installed as bishop on October 7. His primary focus as bishop was to promote the Catholic faith in the heart of Mormon country, and he used all means of social communications, including radio and print. Particularly important was his promotion of the diocesan newspaper.

On January 29, 1932, he was appointed by Pope Pius as the titular archbishop of Aegina and the coadjutor archbishop of San Francisco to Archbishop Edward J. Hanna. He acceded to the see on March 2, 1935, with the retirement of Archbishop Hanna. He assumed the duties of archbishop at a time when the country was in the grip of the Great Depression and was a dedicated shepherd over the remarkable decades that followed, including World War II and the postwar boom in California.

Archbishop Mitty turned his immediate attention to archdiocesan finances and placed them on a firm footing that proved essential preparation for the growth in the Catholic population after the war. He also gave great attention to priestly formation and to ongoing education for priests. The archdiocese was thus soon well known for the quality of its pastoral services, and Archbishop Mitty was also a noted innovator in reaching out to the pastoral needs of migrant workers and the swiftly growing Latino population in the Bay Area. He began, for example, the Spanish Mission Band that helped lead to the United Farmworkers Movement.

In his time as archbishop, the Catholic population increased from around 400,000 to over 1.1 million, and through his careful financial planning he was able to meet the challenge by constructing over 80 new parishes and well over 500 other building projects, as well as new schools and a host of other initiatives. At the time of his death, there were some 243 parishes, 1,100 priests, and nearly 3,000 women religious, as well as 174 elementary schools and 42 high schools in the archdiocese, all significant increases from 1935.

Mobile, Archdiocese of

Established as a diocese on May 15, 1829, by Pope Pius VIII, and designated as the Diocese of Birmingham on July 9, 1954, by Pope Pius XII, the diocese was designated as Mobile on June 29, 1969, by Pope Paul VI, and was then elevated to the rank of a metropolitan archdiocese on November 16, 1980, by Pope Blessed John Paul II. Mobile is a French adaptation of the name of the local Indian tribe, the Maubilians, meaning "canoe builder."

The city of Mobile lies on Mobile Bay and is a seaport and river port. Mobile is a center for shipbuilding and manufacturing of pulp, paper textiles, and chemical and petroleum products.

In 1579 the Catholic presence in the region started with Alonso Alvarez de Pineda sailing into Mobile Bay. Hernando de Soto arrived in the area with his expedition in 1540, accompanied by Dominicans, Capuchin Franciscans, and Jesuits. Dominican missionaries served at Santa Cruz de Nanipacna in present-day Wilcox County.

In 1682 René-Robert Chevalier, Sieur de la Salle, claimed Mobile and the surrounding area for France, leading to a colony founded by Pierre

Le Moyne, Sieur d'Iberville, with Father Anastase Douay around 1699. In 1700 Father Antoine Davion was serving the Tunica Indians, with a Father Dougé. Two years later he was followed by Father Jean-François de Saint-Cosmé, who was martyred in 1706. Fathers François Jolliet de Montigny and Dougé were from the Québec Seminary, and they labored with Fathers Alexis de Guyenne and Alexander Huvé. A parish dedicated to the Immaculate Conception was established in Mobile in 1704. Jesuit Fathers Michael Baudouin and Mathurin le Petit served in the Chickasaw and Choctaw missions. Father Constantine McKenna was also serving in the region.

In 1702 Jean-Baptiste Le Moyne, Sieur de Bienville, founded Fort St. Louis de la Mobile, which was moved to the present site in 1711, and served for a time as the capital of French Louisiana. Father Henry Roulleaux de la Vente served there as pastor.

In August 1825 Bishop Michael Portier was appointed the vicar apostolic of Louisiana and the Two Floridas. Mobile was erected as a diocese in 1829, and Bishop Portier traveled to Europe to recruit priests and funds. Spring Hill College was founded and then given to the Jesuits in 1846. Bishop Portier also created parishes throughout the diocese, inviting religious communities into Mobile. He died on May 14, 1859, having given the Church a solid foundation for the future.

Bishop John Quinlan was consecrated for Mobile on December 4, 1859, and began a time as bishop that lasted until his death on March 9, 1883. His arrival coincided with the intense debate over slavery that troubled and divided the nation. He brought seminarians from Ireland and refurbished the Cathedral of the Immaculate Conception. During the Civil War, Bishop Quinlan aided the wounded from both sides in the conflict and tried to safeguard properties and funds during the fighting. After the Battle of Shiloh in 1862, he traveled by a special train to the devastated battlefield to give spiritual and material assistance to fallen and wounded soldiers. He labored to assist the region after the war, especially during the difficult years of Reconstruction, despite the severe shortages of money. Bishop Quinlan rebuilt destroyed churches and in 1876 invited the Benedictines from St. Vincent's Abbey, Pennsylvania, to the diocese.

The third bishop of Mobile was Dominic Manucy, who had served as vicar apostolic of Brownville. He was transferred to Mobile on March 9, 1884, but retired on September 27, 1884, because of failing health. He died in Mobile on February 7, 1885.

His successor was Bishop Jeremiah O'Sullivan, who was consecrated on September 20, 1885. He resolved the severe financial problems facing the diocese and tried to find ways to stem the decline in the Catholic population in Mobile. Revered as a holy prelate, Bishop O'Sullivan added towers to the cathedral and was a popular administrator, known for his oratory. He died on August 10, 1896.

The fifth bishop of Mobile was Edward P. Allen, who served from 1897 to 1926. He was consecrated on May 16, 1897, and pioneered schools and parishes for African-American Catholics and promoted the labors of the Josephites, Trinitarians, and Edmundites, who accepted his invitation to the diocese. Bishop Allen brought about a rapid growth in the Catholic presence in Mobile.

In September 1906 the city of Mobile suffered a storm and tidal wave that brought about devastating destruction. Bishop Allen led the reconstruction of diocesan facilities and aided victims. He went on to serve as a shepherd for the Catholic community during World War I. He died on October 21, 1906.

The sixth bishop of Mobile was Thomas J. Toolen, who was bishop for four decades, from 1927 to 1969. Appointed on February 20, 1927, he was consecrated a bishop on May 4. He was shepherd throughout the Great Depression, World War II, the Korean War, the phenomenal postwar economic boom, and then through the era of the Second Vatican Council and its initial implementation.

His term of service as bishop began with his religious education program in diocesan parishes and the establishment of new parochial schools as well as health care facilities. During the Great Depression, he instituted Catholic Charities to assist those hardest hit by the economic collapse in the country. He gave his full support to the country during World War II and then had the pleasure of presiding over the economic recovery in the postwar period. The Diocese of Mobile was renamed the Diocese of Mobile-Birmingham on May 27, 1954, at which time Bishop Toolen was appointed by Pope Pius XII the Archbishop of Mobile-Birmingham *ad personam* (as a personal title). Bishop Toolen retired on September 29, 1969, when the diocese was split into the Diocese of Birmingham in Alabama and the Diocese of Mobile. Upon his retirement, he was named titular archbishop of Glastonia. He died on December 4, 1976.

The seventh bishop of Mobile was John L. May, who had served as an auxiliary bishop of the Archdiocese of Chicago since 1967. He was promoted to Mobile on October 8, 1969. A national leader in the area of ecumenism, Bishop May instituted adult formation programs in the diocese and started mission parishes. On January 29, 1980, he was named archbishop of St. Louis, succeeding Cardinal John Joseph Carberry. He served in that position until his retirement in 1992. He died in 1994.

On July 29, 1980, Oscar H. Lipscomb was appointed the first archbishop of Mobile. The diocese was promoted to the rank of an archdiocese on the day of Archbishop Lipscomb's appointment. He was consecrated on November 16, 1980, by his predecessor, Archbishop John L. May. He had served as a parish priest in Mobile, as a professor at McGill Institute and Spring Hill College, and as chancellor of the Mobile archdiocese. Archbishop Lipscomb labored to continue the development of the Catholic community in the Mobile area and helped to establish the archdiocese on a firm financial and administrative footing. He retired on May 2, 2008.

On the same day as Archbishop Lipscomb's retirement, Bishop Thomas J. Rodi, bishop of Biloxi since 2001, was appointed the new archbishop of Mobile. Currently, there are over 65,000 Catholics in Mobile, approximately 4 percent of the overall population of 1.6 million. The archdiocese is served by over 130 priests, some 200 men and women religious, and 76 parishes.

Modernism

A movement that developed within the Church in the late nineteenth century, modernism attempted to reconcile the teachings of the Church with modern advances in science, historical and biblical research, and philosophical trends by altering Catholic doctrine through innovation and reinterpretation. Because of the errors that were advanced by many of its differing proponents, the movement was called by Pope St. Pius X "the synthesis of all the heresies."

Modernism originated in the atmosphere of revived learning that was fostered by Pope Leo XIII, in which he gave encouragement to the study of science, current sociopolitical processes, and philosophy. Some intellectuals, however, attempted to adopt many of the trends in the thinking of the period to meet the criticisms of theology and Scripture. The most influential non-Catholic system then being advanced was Kantianism, from the works of Immanuel Kant (1724–1804), which advanced the ideas of the subjective nature of natural knowledge and the unknowableness of God by natural means. On the basis of much in Kantianism, the modernists came to consider religion a matter of personal and collective experience, claiming that faith comes naturally from within, a part of human nature that occurs naturally. It is a "religious feeling" or "a kind of motion of the heart," instinctual and inexpressible in any naturalistic definition of religion. Ultimately, many modernists denied revelation, Scripture, and Church authority, rejecting also the credibility of the Christian faith as supported by historical documentation and miracles. In its most extreme form, it questioned the very divinity of Christ, describing the Church as a sociological institution and Scripture a kind of literature.

While Modernism appeared in spontaneous fashion in various places, some scholars consider its foundation to rest with the professors at the Institut Catholique, the most famous being Louis Duchesne (1843–1922). It is a matter of debate whether the movement was ever organized, but it did have a large set of important contributors. Among them were Alfred Loisy (1857–1940), Maurice Blondel (1861–1949), Lucien Laberthonnière (1860–1932), Edouard le Roy (1870–1954), Romolo Murri (1870–1944), Antonio Fogazzaro (1842–1911), George Tyrrell (1861–1909), and Friederich von Hügel (1852–1925).

Pope St. Pius X opposed Modernism very strenuously, condemning it in the July 3, 1907, decree *Lamentabili* and the encyclical *Pascendi Dominici Gregis,* promulgated on September 8 of that year.

These were followed by the *motu proprio Sacrorum Antistitum* in 1910, requiring an anti-modernist oath from the clergy. The steps against the modernists were carried out so vigorously in the next years that a call for moderation was made by Pope Benedict XV.

In the United States, Modernism found only a limited number of advocates, many of whom were also supporters of the trend toward Americanism (the effort to conform Catholicism to American ideals of pluralism, religious liberty, and the separation of church and state). One of the earliest exponents in the country was Father John Zahm, who lectured extensively in Brussels, Belgium, and Fribourg, Switzerland, on the central theme that there should be no conflict between religion (in particular Catholic doctrine) and science. His 1896 book, *Evolution and Dogma*, was placed briefly on the Index of Prohibited Books in 1898.

In 1902 a group of priests teaching in St. Joseph's Seminary in Yonkers, New York, launched a far-reaching reform of the curriculum at Dunwoodie to introduce the new forms of biblical criticism and a number of courses for seminarians that dispensed with the traditional scholasticism in favor of the new learning. With the publication in 1907 of *Pascendi Dominici Gregis,* and the rebuke of Archbishop John Murphy Farley of New York by Pope Pius himself, the program was closed, the professors transferred, and the nascent journal the *New York Review* (which had served as a venue for articles and theory) ceased publication. Over the next years, other followers of modernist tenets were censured by their superiors and discouraged from writing and teaching. (*See also* Americanism.)

Moeller, Henry K. (December 11, 1849–January 5, 1925)

Archbishop of Cincinnati from 1904 to 1925, Archbishop Henry K. Moeller was a native of Cincinnati and grew up in a devout Catholic family; his sister became a member of the Sisters of Charity at Mount St. Joseph, Ohio, and two brothers also became priests. Called to the priesthood, he studied at St. Xavier College and was then sent for theological preparation at the North American College in Rome. Ordained a priest in Rome on June 10, 1876, at St. John Lateran, he returned to Cincinnati and

was given a pastoral assignment in Bellefontaine, Ohio. In October 1877 he was named a professor at Mount St. Mary's Seminary, where he remained until 1879. That same year, he was granted a brief leave of absence to serve as assistant to Bishop Francis Silas Chatard, bishop of Vincennes. He soon returned to Cincinnati to take up the post of secretary to Bishop William Henry Elder, at the time the coadjutor to Archbishop John Baptist Purcell of Cincinnati. In 1886 he was appointed chancellor of the archdiocese and thus had a role in the arduous task of rebuilding archdiocesan finances in the wake of the disaster of Archbishop Purcell's financial administration.

On April 6, 1900, Moeller was appointed bishop of Columbus and received consecration on August 25, 1900, in Cincinnati. His primary concern in the short time he spent in Columbus was to restore health to diocesan finances. On April 27, 1903, he was appointed coadjutor to Archbishop Elder and titular archbishop of Areopolis. With the passing of Archbishop Elder, he acceded as the fourth archbishop of Cincinnati on October 31, 1904, and was installed on February 15, 1905.

Archbishop Moeller was deeply concerned with Catholic education and so labored to expand the school system in the archdiocese. He also helped establish Cincinnati as the national headquarters of the Catholic Students' Mission Crusade. In addition, he increased the number of parishes and built a new archdiocesan seminary. He died at Cincinnati.

Molloy, Thomas E. (September 4, 1884–November 26, 1956)

Bishop of Brooklyn from 1921 to 1956, Thomas E. Molloy presided over his large diocese throughout the Great Depression, World War II, and the massive postwar period of American prosperity. He was born in Nashua, New Hampshire, and studied at St. Anselm College in Manchester, New Hampshire, and then St. Francis College in Brooklyn, New York. For his preparation for the priesthood, he attended St. John's Seminary and then was sent to the North American College in Rome. He was ordained on September 19, 1908, then completed additional studies in Rome before returning home for service in the Brooklyn diocese.

Assigned to pastoral duties, Father Molloy was

named secretary to Auxiliary Bishop (later Cardinal) George Mundelein. He continued to serve for some months as his secretary after Mundelein was appointed archbishop of Chicago in 1915. Father Molloy then came back to Brooklyn for further pastoral duties and to serve as chaplain to St. Joseph's College for Women and spiritual director of Cathedral College. On June 28, 1920, he was appointed titular bishop of Lorea and auxiliary bishop of Brooklyn. He was consecrated on October 3, 1920. The following year, he was named diocesan administrator upon the death of Bishop Charles E. McDonnell in August; on November 21, 1921, Pope Benedict XV appointed him bishop of Brooklyn. He was installed on February 15, 1922, at the age of thirty-seven. He remained bishop for over thirty years.

Determined to continue the development of the diocese, Bishop Molloy was aware of the growing needs of the Catholic population and invested heavily in building new parishes, schools, and facilities to meet the pastoral needs of his flock. He opened over 80 new parishes and over 100 parochial schools, and promoted Immaculate Conception Seminary. The number of priests in the diocese increased from over 600 to nearly 1,200 between 1921 and 1956. By 1956 there were over 5,500 women religious, 327 parishes, 257 elementary schools, and 52 high schools in the diocese. He also presided over the diocese's centennial celebration in 1953.

In recognition of his labors in one of the largest dioceses in the United States (the Catholic population of Brooklyn was larger than most archdioceses), Bishop Molloy was given the personal title of archbishop by Pope Pius XII on April 7, 1951. He died in Brooklyn and was buried in the crypt of the Immaculate Conception Seminary.

Monaghan, John P. (February 12, 1889–July 26, 1961)

A priest and social activist, John P. Monaghan was born in County Tyrone, Ireland, and made the journey to the United States as a young man. He grew up in New York and, called to the priesthood, studied at St. Francis College in Brooklyn and then St. Joseph's Seminary in Yonkers. Sent to Rome to finish his studies at the North American College,

he was ordained on June 2, 1917. Returning to the United States, he served in several pastoral assignments and was then permitted to earn a doctorate in English literature from Fordham University. He taught at Cathedral College in New York from 1922 to 1938 while also providing noted pastoral care at Corpus Christi Church in Morningside Heights in Manhattan. There he acquired a reputation for his homilies, in particular his abiding concern for social justice during the dark days of the Great Depression.

His interest in the needs of the common worker, his hope that there might be a Catholic voice in the union movement, and his desire to educate Catholic trade unionists in Catholic social teaching, led Father Monaghan in 1937 to become co-founder, with John C. Cort, of the Association of Catholic Trade Unionists. Father Monaghan helped to give ACTU a firm foundation through his preaching, radio appearances, and speeches at labor conventions. He also assisted its growth across the country and helped secure approval from many bishops. The movement was nevertheless not without controversy; its support of the 1947 Wall Street Strike cost donations to Catholic Charities, and its support of the 1949 Calvary Cemetery Strike earned the considerable displeasure of Cardinal Francis Spellman of New York.

In 1939, meanwhile, Father Monaghan was assigned to be pastor of St. Margaret Mary Parish in Midland Beach, Staten Island. He remained pastor from 1939 to 1954 and became a beloved figure. He was transferred in 1954 to St. Michael's Parish and again proved a popular pastor. He died while still serving as pastor.

Monasticism. See Benedictines; Carmelites; Carthusians, Order of; Trappists

Monk, Maria (1816–1839)

Maria Monk was a Canadian woman whose name became attached to the infamous book *Awful Disclosures of Maria Monk, or, The Hidden Secrets of a Nun's Life in a Convent Exposed*, which was published in January 1836. The book detailed in lurid fashion the supposed criminal and scandalous behavior of the Sisters of Charity in the Montréal convent of the Hôtel-Dieu. According to the account, Maria, a Protestant, had entered the convent and endured severe mental and physical abuse by the nuns, including being forced to have vile relations with the priests from the seminary next door. The priests supposedly reached the convent through a secret tunnel. Even worse, the book claimed that any children conceived in the convent were born, baptized, and then strangled.

The publication of the book came in the immediate aftermath of the 1835 book by Rebecca Reed, *Six Months in a Convent*, with its own slanderous accusations against the Ursuline nuns in a convent school in Charlestown, Massachusetts. The convent had been burned down by a mob the year before when wild rumors were spread that a woman was being held against her will.

Maria Monk's book caused an immediate sensation in the hands of anti-Catholics. The subsequent investigation by Church authorities found not a shred of evidence of the charges, but many American Protestants charged the bishop with a cover-up. In 1836 Colonel William Leet Stone, a Protestant newspaper editor from New York City, received permission to undertake his own investigation. He found with little trouble that the claims were completely false. No credible historian believes that there was ever any truth to the charges in the book or to the charges hurled against the Church related to the events and the alleged coverup.

Maria Monk became a lightning rod for American anti-Catholics, but there are reasons to believe that she was used throughout the controversy by publishers and Protestant friends and associates who sought to capitalize on her claims. Her own life proved a disastrous one, with rumors of prostitution, petty theft, illegitimate children, and mental instability. Abandoned by her supporters once she served no further use to their anti-Catholic campaign, she died in the summer of 1839 in an almshouse in New York, according to an obituary published in *The Pilot* in September of that year.

Monroe, James (September 10, 1799–September 7, 1870)

A United States Congressman from New York from 1839 to 1841, soldier, and convert, James Monroe was the nephew of President James Monroe. He was born in Albemarle County, Virginia, and was

admitted to the United States Military Academy at West Point, and graduated in 1815. Commissioned a lieutenant of artillery, he subsequently saw action and was wounded in the war with Algerian pirates in 1815 while aboard the frigate *La Guerrière* off the coast of Spain.

He went on to serve as an aide to General Winfield Scott from 1817 to 1822 and then did garrison duty as a first lieutenant until 1832, when he resigned from the army. He next began a period of public service with his election in New York to the Board of Aldermen in 1833 and then to the United States Congress in 1839. He was nominated to Congress again in 1846, but the election was contested and he chose not to run again. From 1850 to 1852 he was a member of the New York legislature, then retired from public life. He moved to Orange, New Jersey. He sought unsuccessfully to speak to the people of Virginia against impending secession in the period just before the start of the Civil War in 1861. He died in Orange and was buried in Trinity Cemetery in New York City.

Montalvo Higuera, Gabriel (January 27, 1930–August 2, 2006)

Papal nuncio to the United States from 1998 to 2006, Archbishop Gabriel Montalvo Higuera was an accomplished and deeply respected Vatican diplomat. He was born in Bogota, Colombia, and his father was a ranking government official and onetime Colombian ambassador to the Holy See. Called to the priesthood, he completed his theological studies and was ordained on January 18, 1953. He went on to earn a doctorate in canon law from the Pontifical Lateran University and was appointed to the Pontifical Ecclesiastical Academy, the training center for future papal diplomats. He entered the Vatican diplomatic corps in 1957 and served in Vatican embassies in Bolivia, Argentina, and El Salvador before being summoned to Rome in 1964 to work in the Vatican's Secretariat of State. Over the next years, he focused on the Catholic Church in Eastern Europe.

On June 30, 1974, he was ordained titular archbishop of Celene and was sent by Pope Paul VI as nuncio to Honduras and Nicaragua. In 1980 he was named pro-nuncio to Algeria and Tunisia and apostolic delegate in Libya. In 1982 he was appointed by

Pope Blessed John Paul II as an assistant mediator in Argentina and Chile's dispute over the Beagle Channel, and through the Vatican's efforts a possible war was averted. In 1986 he was transferred to serve as pro-nuncio to Yugoslavia. To these duties were added those of nuncio to Belarus in 1993. A mere two weeks later, the archbishop received a third post as president of the Pontifical Ecclesiastical Academy. In 1994 a new nuncio was named to Belarus, but Archbishop Montalvo continued to serve as nuncio to Yugoslavia until 1996.

On December 7, 1998, Archbishop Montalvo was appointed nuncio to the United States and permanent observer to the Organization of American States and assumed his duties in Washington in January 1999. He served as the Holy See's representative to the United States during one of the most tumultuous periods in American Catholic history, including the crisis caused by the sex abuse scandal and the aftermath of the attacks on the World Trade Center on September 11, 2001, and America's war on terror. By virtue of his role as papal representative, he was also a key voice in the appointment of bishops who will shape the American Church for many years into the future. On December 17, 2005, Archbishop Pietro Sambi was named nuncio to the United States and Archbishop Montalvo retired to Rome. Archbishop Montalvo was diagnosed with cancer and died in Rome in a hospice run by the Sisters of Mercy of Alma, Michigan.

Archbishop Gabriel Montalvo Higuera

Montana

Called the Treasure State, Montana is located in the northwestern part of the United States. Montana is bounded on the north by Canada, on the east by North Dakota and South Dakota, on the south by Wyoming and Idaho, and on the west by Idaho. The state has two natural land regions, the Great Plains in the east and the Rocky Mountains in the west. The original inhabitants of the region were the Arapaho, Assiniboines, Blackfeet, Cheyenne, Crows, Flatheads, and Shoshones. Thousands of American Indians still reside on reservations in Montana. The state entered the Union on November 8, 1889.

In the 1680s René-Robert Chevalier, Sieur de La Salle, was in the area, claiming the land for France. In 1742 Francis and Louis Joseph, the sons of Pierre Gaultier de Verennes, Sieur de La Vérendrye, explored Montana, reaching the "Gate of the Mountains," present-day Helena. Jesuit Father Claude G. Coquart accompanied their expedition.

No further exploration was recorded in the region until after the Louisiana Purchase, which gave present-day Montana to the United States. William Clark and Meriwether Lewis conducted an expedition into the area soon after, and fur traders such as John Jacob Astor followed them into Montana. Manuel Lisa set up a trading post on the Yellowstone River in 1807, and John Colter worked to open up trails for more fur traders. The steamboat the *Yellowstone* sailed down the Missouri River to Fort Union in 1832.

A year later, the Second Provincial Council of Baltimore entrusted the area's missions to the Jesuits. At the time, the Flathead Indians in Montana were hosting Young Ignace and Old Ignace La Mousse, Iroquois warriors who had ventured into the region. The Iroquois spoke about the need for "Black Robes," the priests who served their people in the east. They sent a delegation to St. Louis on several occasions asking for Black Robes, and in 1840 Jesuit Father Pierre-Jean De Smet was sent into the area.

Father De Smet became the outstanding missionary of the era, respected by Native Americans and whites, and was a trusted friend of Chief Sitting Bull of the Sioux. He immediately established St. Mary's in the Bitterroot Valley, near modern-day Stevensville. In the next decade, missions were opened at St. Peter's, near Great Falls, and at a site in Missoula County. St. Ignatius Mission was also serving the local tribes. Father Nicholas Point and Antonio Ravalli served the Blackfeet at St. Peter's. Father Christian Hoecken, a Jesuit, was also in the area.

In the 1860s the discovery of gold at Grasshopper Creek near the Beaverhead River spurred white settlements. Gold was also found at Last Chance Gulch, now part of present-day Helena, and at Alder Gulch, now Virginia City. Silver was mimed at Butte and Philipsburg. In 1869 the Sisters of Charity of Leavenworth, Kansas, entered what became a violent and lawless area and established a hospital, school, and orphanage in Helena. The first white parish had opened in Hellgate in 1863. At the same time, Montana was part of both the Washington and Idaho Territories, as well as the Louisiana Territory.

The Territory of Montana was established by the U.S. Congress in 1864, and settlers streamed into the region. The Vicariate Apostolic of Montana had been established the year before. The Sioux, under the leadership of Sitting Bull and Crazy Horse, alarmed at the influx of gold seekers and the harsh treatment received from the federal officer George Armstrong Custer and his forces, confronted Custer in 1876 at the Battle of the Little Bighorn. In the engagement, Lieutenant Colonel Custer was killed along with almost his entire command. The next year, Nez Perce Chief Joseph and his people tried to flee to Canada for safety from relocation, but they were caught and forcibly sent to eastern Kansas and then the Indian Territory in Oklahoma, where many died on the reservation from diseases.

The Utah and Mountain Railroad merged with the United Pacific system in 1880. Four years later, the Diocese of Helena was established by the Holy See. Bishop John Baptist Brondel, who had served as vicar apostolic, became the first bishop of the diocese. When he ended his service in 1903, he had started forty-two churches and ten schools.

A year later, the Diocese of Great Falls was established by Pope St. Pius X, and the first bishop was Mathias Clement Lenihan, who served from 1904 to 1930. He built St. Ann's Cathedral and led the diocese through the era of World War I. Bishop Edwin Vincent O'Hara founded the College of Great Falls and served the diocese until 1939.

Bishop John Patrick Carroll of Helena was called "the Builder," as he was responsible for a cathedral, the state's first seminary, and over thirty parishes. The faithful of Montana participated in World War II, and mills, meat-packing, and manufacturing proved the long-term industries for the state. The Church in Montana, through the suffragan Dioceses of Great Falls-Billings and Helena, remains part of the ecclesiastical province of Portland. Currently, there are approximately 110,000 Catholics out of a population of nearly one million. There are more than 160 priests, more than 100 men and women religious, and 125 parishes in the state.

Monterey in California, Diocese of

Established as the Diocese of the Two Californias on April 27, 1840, by Pope Gregory XVI, Monterey was designated as the Diocese of Monterey on June 30, 1850, by Pope Blessed Pius IX and then designated as the Diocese of Monterey-Los Angeles in 1859. On December 13, 1922, Pope Pius XI designated it the Diocese of Monterey-Fresno. It was then established as the Diocese of Monterey on December 14, 1967, by Pope Paul VI. The diocese serves the four counties of Monterey, Santa Cruz, San Benito, and San Luis Obispo in central California and is a suffragan see of the Archdiocese of Los Angeles.

A central California seaport, Monterey was founded on June 3, 1770, when Blessed Junípero Serra, the Franciscan pioneer, opened the Mission of San Carlos Borromeo at Monterey Bay. The mission served as the capital of Alta California, founded by Gaspar de Portolá.

Franciscan Bishop Francisco Garcia Diego y Morena was the first prelate to assume the see of the Diocese of the Two Californias, and was consecrated on October 4, 1840. The episcopal residence was at San Diego in 1841, but in the following year Bishop Morena moved it to Santa Barbara. He founded a seminary near Santa Inez and served until his death on April 30, 1846.

Bishop Joseph Sadoc Alemany, a Dominican pioneer, was consecrated on June 30, 1850, and assumed the see, establishing his residence at Monterey. Baja California, originally part of the diocese, was not accepted as part of Bishop Alemany's jurisdiction by Mexico and was removed by the Holy See in 1852.

The Gold Rush resulted in the steady influx of miners and settlers into California, and on July 29, 1853, the Archdiocese of San Francisco was established by Pope Blessed Pius IX. Bishop Alemany assumed that see, and Bishop Thaddeus Amat, a Vincentian, succeeded him. Bishop Amat resided at Santa Barbara, bringing the Daughters of Charity of St. Vincent de Paul into the diocese. In 1859 he moved to Los Angeles, and the Diocese of Monterey-Los Angeles was designated by the Holy See. Bishop Amat built the Cathedral of St. Vibiana in 1871. He died on May 12, 1878, and was buried in the cathedral.

His successor was Bishop Francis Mora, who had been coadjutor bishop with right of succession since 1873. The diocese was well established, and the railroad brought ever-increasing numbers of settlers. Bishop Mora expanded diocesan facilities until his retirement, caused by ill health, on May 6, 1896.

His coadjutor bishop, Bishop George Montgomery, had been consecrated on April 8, 1894, and acceded to the diocese. He continued the expansion programs until he was promoted to the Archdiocese of San Francisco on January 1, 1903.

The next bishop was Thomas James Conaty. He promoted the care of the Native Americans in the diocese and aided the restoration of the missions. He instituted programs for the poor and invited the Jesuits into the diocese, as well as other religious communities. Bishop Conaty died on September 18, 1915, at Coronado.

His successor was Bishop John J. Cantwell, who was appointed on September 21, 1917, and consecrated a bishop on December 5, 1917. In 1920 he was named an Assistant at the Pontifical Throne by Pope Benedict XV and transferred to the newly established Diocese of Los Angeles-San Diego in 1922. In 1936 he became archbishop of Los Angeles.

On December 3, 1922, Pope Pius XI established the Diocese of Monterey-Fresno as a suffragan see of the Archdiocese of Los Angeles. Bishop Cantwell served as administrator until March 24, 1924, when John B. MacGinley was appointed the first bishop. The former Bishop of Nueva Caceres in the Philippines, he became noted in the diocese for his dedication to education. He founded schools and catechetical centers. He also instituted chapel car services for migrant workers. Bishop MacGinley retired on September 30, 1932, because of declining health.

At the time of Bishop MacGinley's retirement, the country was engulfed in the Great Depression. His successor, Bishop Philip G. Scher, was appointed on April 28, 1933, and consecrated a bishop on June 29, 1933. He faced immediately the severe economic conditions created by the Great Depression. When diocesan bonds went into default, he instituted a new contract with creditors and redeemed the bonds in 1944. He also opened a center for African-Americans and Asians in the diocese and built eleven new parishes. After leading the diocese through the equally difficult years of World War II, in July 1946 he suffered a stroke. He died on January 3, 1953.

Bishop Aloysius J. Willinger, C.SS.R., Bishop Scher's successor, was originally a Redemptorist priest and had served as coadjutor bishop since 1946 and acceded to the see upon Bishop Scher's passing. Because of the booming postwar economy, he was able to rebuild or refurbish diocesan facilities. Catholic schools were tripled, and a seminary, hospitals, and a home for the aged were established. Bishop Willinger also led the diocese through the era of the Second Vatican Council. He retired on October 6, 1967, and was succeeded by Bishop Harry Anselm Clinch, who was named by Pope Paul VI on October 16, 1967.

On the day of Bishop Willinger's retirement, the Holy See split the Diocese of Monterey-Fresno through the creation of the Diocese of Fresno. Henceforth, the diocese was that of Monterey in California. Bishop Clinch presided over the diocese during the tumultuous period after the Second Vatican Council. He was succeeded by Bishop Thaddeus A. Shubsda, who had been an auxiliary bishop of Los Angeles since 1976. Appointed bishop of Monterey on May 26, 1982, Bishop Shubsda was shepherd over a period of considerable growth for the diocese as the Catholic population doubled during his tenure. He died on April 26, 1991, at the age of sixty-six.

Pope Blessed John Paul II appointed Bishop Sylvester D. Ryan as Bishop Shubsda's successor on January 28, 1992. Bishop Ryan had been an auxiliary bishop of Los Angeles since 1990. Installed on March 19, 1992, he was, like his predecessor, confronted with the remarkable growth in the Catholic population in the region and worked over the next years to ensure pastoral care for his people. In 1992 there were approximately 160,000 Catholics in the diocese; by 2003 there were over 300,000. Many of these were of Latino descent, and great care was taken to meet their spiritual and educational needs.

Bishop Ryan retired on December 19, 2006. His successor was Bishop Richard J. Garcia, who was appointed on the same day and consecrated a bishop on January 30, 2007. Aside from the large Catholic population, there are 120 priests, over 200 men and women religious, and 46 parishes in the diocese.

Mooney, Edward (May 9, 1882–October 25, 1958)

The first archbishop of Detroit, from 1937 to 1958 and a cardinal from 1946, Edward Mooney was also a brilliant papal diplomat and one of the first Americans to serve in the Vatican's diplomatic service. Born in Mount Savage, Maryland, to Irish immigrants, he moved with his family to Youngstown, Ohio, when he was young and grew up there. Called to the priesthood, he entered the Sulpician Seminary at St. Charles College in Ellicott City, Maryland, and then went to St. Mary's Seminary in Baltimore. Considered a seminarian of considerable promise, he was sent to complete his studies at the North American College in Rome and earned a doctorate in sacred theology from the Propaganda College.

Ordained a priest on April 10, 1909, he returned to the United States and entered into pastoral ministry for the Cleveland diocese before receiving appointment to the faculty of St. Mary's Seminary in Cleveland, where he taught dogmatic theology. After six years, he was assigned the task of establishing the Cathedral Latin School in 1916 and held the post of principal until 1922. In August 1922 he became pastor of a parish in Youngstown, but after six months he was ordered to return to Rome to serve as spiritual director at the North American College. In 1925 he was given the title of domestic prelate by Pope Pius XI.

On January 31, 1926, Mooney was consecrated titular arch-

bishop of Irenopolis and appointed apostolic delegate to India. His time as delegate was marked by his activity to develop the Church in India, including the establishment of eleven new mission territories, the appointment of native clergy, and the settlement of a dispute between Indian and Portuguese bishops over jurisdictional questions, the so-called Goan Schism, through an agreement between the Holy See and the colonial government of Portugal. In 1931 Bishop Mooney was named apostolic delegate to Japan, a post he held for two years.

On August 28, 1933, Archbishop Mooney was named bishop of Rochester, even as he retained the personal title of archbishop. He returned to the United States, took up his duties, and in 1934 was elected to the administrative board of the National Catholic Welfare Conference; in November 1935 he became the board's chairman. On May 30, 1937, he was appointed by Pope Pius XII the first archbishop of Detroit. He was installed on August 3, 1937. On February 18, 1946, he was appointed the cardinal priest of Santa Susanna, the home of the American Catholic Church in Rome, by Pope Pius XII.

As archbishop of Detroit, Cardinal Mooney was from the start deeply concerned with the needs and rights of workers, especially in a region that was so heavily dependent upon industrial labor. He defended the rights of workers to form unions, sponsored the Archdiocesan Labor Institute to promote Catholic social teaching, and encouraged the work of the Association of Catholic Trade Unionists to assist education. In 1942 he also curtailed the activities of Father Charles Coughlin, the controversial radio priest. (*See also* Coughlin, Charles Edward.)

One of his other primary concerns was restoring the finances of the Church in Detroit as he inherited a colossal debt of some $20 million. He launched an annual Archdiocesan Development Fund and slowly brought the debt under control. In the years after World War II and with finances rehabilitated, he was able to

Cardinal Edward Mooney

expand the archdiocese's pastoral programs and initiatives, especially social services, a home for the aged, catechetical centers, and St. John's Provincial Seminary in Plymouth, Michigan.

In October 1958 Cardinal Mooney traveled to Rome with the expectation that he would take part in the conclave to elect a successor to Pope Pius XII. Literally hours before he was to enter the conclave, he became ill and died. The conclave elected Cardinal Angelo Roncalli, who took the name John XXIII, now Blessed.

Moore, Thomas Verner (October 22, 1877–June 5, 1969)

A Paulist, Benedictine, and Carthusian priest, Thomas Verner Moore was a noted psychologist and one of the first advocates of modern psychology among Catholics in the United States. Born in Louisville, Kentucky, he entered the Paulists at St. Paul's College in Washington, D.C., and after completing his theological training he was ordained in 1901. He then was granted permission to undertake studies in psychology at The Catholic University of America. Two years later, he earned a doctorate in psychology and took up a teaching post at Catholic University. The following year, he was sent for further studies at the Psychological Institute of Wilhelm Wundt in Leipzig, Germany, followed by additional study at Georgetown Medical School in 1910 and then at the University of Munich. He earned a doctor of medicine degree from Johns Hopkins University in 1915. After service in World War I as an officer in the Medical Corps and a chaplain, Father Moore returned to the United States and began teaching again at Catholic University.

Father Moore was committed to establishing a religious community for men that might be affiliated with Catholic University. After securing the cooperation of the English Benedictine Congregation of St. Benedict's Abbey in Fort Augustus, Scotland, Moore was able to found St. Anselm's Priory (later Abbey) in Washington, D.C., in 1924. He then resumed his post as teacher at Catholic University and remained there for the next five decades. He later served as head of the Department of Psychiatry and Psychology and became an advocate for the care of developmentally disabled children. He was also a prolific writer; he wrote over twenty books and one hundred articles on psychology and psychiatry, and many were used as textbooks.

In 1947 Father Moore resigned from Catholic University in order to be able to fulfill his desire to enter a more contemplative environment. He taught briefly at the University of Salamanca, Spain, and then entered the Carthusian monastery at Mira Flores, also in Spain. He returned to the United States in 1950 to help start the first Carthusian house in the country before going back to Spain, where he spent the remainder of his life. He was buried at Mira Flores.

Moran, Mary Concilia (August 7, 1930–January 7, 1990)

A member of the Scranton Sisters of Mercy who is honored today for her contributions to Catholic health care, Sister Mary Concilia Moran was born in Altoona, Pennsylvania, into an Irish family. Called to the religious life, she entered the Sisters of Mercy of the Scranton province in 1948 and took her final vows in 1954. Her service to the congregation over the next decades was remarkably varied as she worked as an elementary school teacher, a director of nurses, and a hospital administrator. She was elected in 1970 as provincial and served until 1977 during the difficult period immediately after the Second Vatican Council.

Sister Moran was also a noted pioneer in the area of Catholic health care. She was a determined voice for the development of well-organized health provider systems who never lost sight of the most important Catholic obligation, to proclaim and live the Gospel in all aspects of service, especially medicine. Her subsequent leadership in the Sisters of Mercy Health Corporation in Michigan became a model for other such systems in the country. She died after a difficult struggle with cancer.

For her many contributions to Catholic health care, the Catholic Health Association established the annual Sister Mary Concilia Moran, R.S.M., Award recognizing visionary leaders and drawing attention to their innovative ideas, unique projects, or outstanding achievements in Catholic health care.

Moranvillé, Jean-François (July 19, 1760–May 17, 1824)

A French priest and missionary, Jean-François Moranvillé is best known for his labors in the city of Baltimore. He was born in Cagny, France, and entered the seminary of Saint-Esprit in 1778. Ordained a priest in 1784, he was sent soon after to Cayenne, French Guiana, where he dedicated himself to the instruction of the slaves, much to the consternation of French colonial officials. Such was his influence on the African slaves that in 1792 he was summoned by officials and duped into signing the oath that was demanded in the Civil Constitution of the Clergy in revolutionary France. When the priest learned the true nature of the oath and that it had been condemned by the Church, he issued a formal retraction and fled Cayenne, narrowly escaping capture by the French Navy.

Father Moranvillé arrived in Baltimore in early 1795 and was granted a teaching position before assuming direction of St. Peter's Church at the behest of Bishop John Carroll. As he was skilled especially in liturgical music, he gave valuable assistance to improving the choirs and liturgies in the city's churches and is honored as the creator of the religious chant in the Church of the United States. As Napoleon Bonaparte had come to power in 1799, he was able to return home in 1801, but he chose to go back to Baltimore and became pastor of St. Patrick's Church.

A brilliant preacher, he was able to draw enormous crowds to the church and was thus assisted in his desire to build a new church in 1807 and to launch, in 1815, the charitable society of St. Patrick and a free school for girls, the first such institution in Baltimore. Owing to declining health, he retired to St. Mary's College in Emmitsburg, Maryland, but he returned several times to provide pastoral assistance, especially during the yellow fever epidemics of 1819 to 1821. He was himself stricken with the disease, and such was the state of his health that he was forced to leave for France in October 1823. The voyage, however, hastened his death, and he died soon after reaching his native city.

Moriarty, Patrick Eugene (July 4, 1805–July 10, 1875)

A priest and Augustinian superior, Patrick Eugene Moriarty was famous as a preacher and temperance reformer. He was born in Dublin, Ireland, and grew up attending a private academy that his father had started for the education of Catholic youths. In 1820 he entered the novitiate of the Order of St. Augustine (the Augustinians) at Callan and so began preparations for the priesthood. He went on to study at Lucca and Rome and was ordained in Rome in January 1828. After his ordination, he served in Dublin, and in 1835 was sent as a missionary to India, where he was secretary of the vicar apostolic of Goa and also a chaplain to the British troops at Madras; in this post, he was the first Catholic chaplain to be so recognized by the English crown since the Reformation. Father Moriarty returned to Rome from India and brought with him a message to Pope Gregory XVI from the Catholics of Madras.

In 1839 he was named to the Augustinian mission in the United States and soon took up a post at St. Augustine Church in Philadelphia. Almost immediately, he earned fame for being one of the greatest homilists and speakers in the United States, and his oratory was much in demand in all social circles.

Chosen superior of the Augustinians in the United States, he presided over the expansion of the order until 1847, when he was brought back to Rome and appointed assistant general. He returned to the United States in 1850 and served as president of Villanova College from 1851 to 1855. He was later the first pastor of St. Augustine's Parish in Lansingburg (now Troy), New York. He died at Villanova. Moriarty Hall, a residence building on the campus of Villanova University, is named in his honor.

Morris, Martin (December 3, 1834–September 12, 1909)

A lawyer and noted jurist, Martin Morris is known especially for his work on behalf of Georgetown University. He was born in Washington, D.C., to an Irish Catholic family and studied at Georgetown. He graduated in 1854, but his connection to the university became a lifelong one. After graduation, he entered the Jesuit novitiate in Frederick, Maryland, in order to begin studies for the priesthood. His hopes, however, were brought to an end with the death of his father a short time later, necessitating his departure from the seminary to support his mother and sisters. He thus entered the law and in 1863 launched a practice in Baltimore. Four years later, he moved to Washington and became the partner of Richard T. Merrick. His association continued until Merrick's death in 1885, whereupon Morris began a partnership with George E. Hamilton. President Grover Cleveland appointed Morris an associate justice of the Court of Appeals of the District of Columbia upon the establishment of that court in 1893.

Morris was a deeply respected lawyer and judge in Washington. He also was known for his enthusiastic support of his alma mater, Georgetown. He helped to start the Georgetown Law School in 1871, and in 1877 was honored by the university with the honorary title of Doctor of Letters. Morris was also concerned with other areas of Catholic education and promoted the development of Catholic schools.

Mount St. Mary's College and Seminary

The second oldest Catholic college and seminary in the United States (after Georgetown University), Mount St. Mary's College and Seminary was founded in Emmitsburg, Maryland, in 1808 by Sulpician Father John Dubois, later the third bishop of New York, from 1826 to 1842. Dubois had fled his native France because of the dangers of the French Revolution and arrived at Norfolk, Virginia, in August 1791. He was given a warm welcome and later entered the Society of Saint-Sulpice in 1808.

Dubois established the foundation for the new college in 1806 when he purchased land in Frederick County, Maryland, on part of a mountain that had been christened Mount St. Mary's by the people in the area. He first built a church there in 1806 and then started a small school for local children. With the encouragement of the Sulpicians in Baltimore, he began a *petit séminaire* with eight students when the preparatory seminary run by the Sulpicians at Pigeon Hill, Pennsylvania, was transferred to Emmitsburg. He was soon joined by St. Elizabeth Ann Seton in 1809 with her own Sisters of Charity to begin St. Joseph's Academy.

Father Dubois faced from the start severe financial challenges, and progress was slow in the early

years. He sought to prepare young men for entry into the Sulpician seminary in Baltimore, and therefore Mount St. Mary's was a seminary, but he also was obligated by financial need to accept all paying students, including those who were not planning for the priesthood.

From 1812 Father Dubois was assisted by Father Simon William Gabriel Bruté de Rémur (the future bishop of Vincennes). Father Bruté de Rémur served with great zeal from 1812 until 1834, when he was named a bishop, with only a brief interruption between 1814 and 1818. He served also as a chaplain to the Sisters of Charity, a spiritual adviser to St. Elizabeth Ann Seton, and a professor in the seminary.

Father Dubois himself was named bishop of New York in 1826. He was succeeded as head of the college by Father Michael de Burgo Egan (1826–28), and then Father J. F. McGerry (1828–29), and Father John Baptist Purcell (1830–33), later archbishop of Cincinnati. In January 1830 Father Purcell secured from the General Assembly of Maryland a charter of incorporation for the college. Further development came under Father Thomas R. Butler (1834–38), who won a new charter in 1836 by which the college was empowered to confer all degrees save for doctor of medicine.

Father Butler was followed by the lengthy presidency of Father John J. McCaffrey (1838–72). His time brought continuing growth to the seminary, including new halls and a celebration of the fiftieth anniversary in 1858. In 1861, however, the college faced the start of the Civil War, and the next years witnessed a steady stream of departures from the student body, even as the college and seminary maintained a position of formal neutrality. By 1864 there were only two students left in the college's graduating class, although the seminary maintained its numbers. By war's end, the college was burdened with severe debt.

Father McCaffrey's immediate successors were Fathers John McCloskey (1872–77) and John A. Watterson (1877–80), bishop of Columbus in 1880, introduced a variety of financial reforms. These two presidencies proved only partially successful, and in 1881 the new president, Father William J. Hill, asked that the college be placed in receivership. Under the guidance of Monsignor William

M. Byrne of Boston, the college was given a new financial lease on life. By 1908 and its hundredth anniversary, the college was once more financially healthy and enjoying a period of expansion.

The college and seminary continued to prosper throughout the twentieth century, surviving both World Wars and the Great Depression to embark on new building programs in the 1950s. In 1972 the college welcomed women students after the closing of St. Joseph's College. Currently, Mount St. Mary's University boasts a total enrollment of over 2,100 students, with over 1,600 undergraduates.

The seminary of Mount St. Mary's early in its history began calling itself the "Cradle of Bishops" because of the number of alumni who went on to become bishops (and cardinals). By 1908 the seminary claimed twenty-eight bishops among its alumni, including John Hughes, first archbishop of New York, and Cardinal John McCloskey, also archbishop of New York and the first American cardinal. By 2005 forty-eight alumni had gone on to become bishops, archbishops, or cardinals.

Mount St. Mary's also celebrates the presence of the Grotto of Lourdes, a mountain shrine devoted to Mary that attracts hundreds of thousands of pilgrims each year from all over the world. The grotto traces its origins to the first Catholics in the area, who arrived around 1740 and found shelter from anti-Catholics in "St. Mary's Mount." The first grotto was established under Father Dubois, who placed a cross in a natural site on the mountain. It was visited frequently by St. Elizabeth Ann Seton, and the site was blessed by Father Bruté de Rémur, who led seminarians in treasuring the natural beauty and meditative qualities of the grotto. The grotto was proclaimed a public oratory by Cardinal Lawrence J. Shehan, archbishop of Baltimore in 1965, and a chaplain was assigned on a permanent basis.

Moylan, Stephen (1737–April 11, 1811)

A famed general during the American Revolution, Stephen Moylan served as quartermaster

general of the Continental Army and was later a distinguished businessman. He was born in Cork, Ireland, in 1737 to a wealthy family. He received an excellent education in Paris, prior to embarking on a career in the shipping business. His work brought him to Lisbon, Portugal, and then to Philadelphia. He settled in Philadelphia in 1768 and became both immensely wealthy and a prominent figure in Pennsylvania society. Thus, in 1771, when the Friendly Sons of St. Patrick was established and boasted membership from among many merchants of note, Moylan was elected the first president.

Moylan was long a supporter of American independence, so much so that John Dickinson, the prominent Philadelphia lawyer and member of the Continental Congress, recommended him to General George Washington. Moylan then joined the army at Cambridge, Massachusetts, and Washington gave him the post of muster-master general in August 1775. While initially hopeful of being appointed ambassador to Spain for the newly declared American government, Moylan embraced his opportunity in the Continental Army. He was first secretary to General Washington and then, on June 7, 1776, Congress named him quartermaster general.

Moylan took part in the disastrous New York campaign in the summer of 1776. By its conclusion, the crushing defeat of the American forces had been compounded by the loss of most of the Continental Army's wagons and supplies, and Moylan was largely, but unfairly, held responsible. He resigned in order to assist the rebuilding of morale and logistical support for the American troops, but he immediately volunteered for combat. He fought with distinction at the Battle of Princeton, and in late 1776 he received orders from General Washington to muster a regiment of dragoons, the First Pennsylvania regiment of cavalry. He served as its colonel and took part at Valley Forge, the horrendous winter of 1777–78, and the Battle of Germantown. The regiment joined the cavalry force commanded by Count Casimir Pulaski, and Moylan soon was engaged in a

Colonel Stephen Moylan

quarrel with the Polish officer. Moylan was court-martialed for the disagreement, but acquitted; he then succeeded Pulaski as general when the latter resigned. Moylan served with great skill and success over the next years, including participation in the Yorktown campaign that brought an end to the war in 1781. In recognition of his skill and bravery in the war, in 1782 he was brevetted a brigadier general.

Declining health forced Moylan to leave the army after Yorktown and to return home to Philadelphia to resume his business life. His remaining years were generally quiet. In 1792 he was named register and recorder of Chester County, Pennsylvania, and then served as commissioner of loans of Pennsylvania for a few years before his death. He was buried on the grounds of St. Mary's Church in Philadelphia.

Moynihan, Daniel Patrick (March 16, 1927–March 26, 2003)

A United States Senator from New York for twenty-four years, an ambassador, and an eminent sociologist, Daniel Patrick Moynihan was also the recipient of the Presidential Medal of Freedom from President Bill Clinton in 2000. Born in Tulsa, Oklahoma, he moved with his family to New York City when he was six. He was raised in a poor neighborhood, made money by shining shoes, and attended various schools until graduating from Harlem High School. He attended the City College of New York for one year before joining the U.S. Navy. After serving on active duty from 1944 to 1947, he went on to graduate studies at Tufts University; he subsequently earned three graduate degrees from the Fletcher School of Law and Diplomacy (a Tufts University graduate school) and then studied as a Fulbright Fellow at the London School of Economics. Years later he was given an honorary Doctorate of Law from Tufts and was celebrated for being the only person to hold five degrees from that university.

Embarking on a career in politics, Moynihan became a member of Averell Harriman's New York gubernatorial campaign in 1954 and was on the governor's staff for four years. In 1960 he was a John F. Kennedy delegate at the Democratic National Convention. He was then an assistant secretary of labor for policy in the Kennedy administration and in the early part of President Lyndon Johnson's administration. He left the Johnson administration in 1965 and ran unsuccessfully for the presidency of the New York City Council. Over the next years, he was director of the Joint Center for Urban Studies at Harvard University and the Massachusetts Institute of Technology, and focused especially in his writings on the plight of the poor in American cities.

As he agreed with President Richard Nixon's social policies, Moynihan joined the Nixon administration as an urban affairs adviser and was later ambassador to India from 1973 to 1975 and as the United States Permanent Representative to the United Nations, including a time as president of the United Nations Security Council in 1976. That same year, he ran and was elected to the U.S. Senate from New York. He remained in the Senate for four terms and proved an independent voice within the Democratic Party. For example, he was one of very few liberal Democrats to support the partial-birth abortion ban. He declined to run for reelection in 2000.

A popular speaker and writer, Moynihan wrote nineteen books, including *Beyond the Melting Pot* (1963), *The Negro Family: The Case for National Action* (1965), *The Politics of a Guaranteed Income* (1973), *Family and Nation* (1986), *Came the Revolution* (1988), *On the Law of Nations* (1990), and *Secrecy* (1998). Aware of the lingering aspects of anti-Catholicism in America, he made a famous remark that anti-Catholicism is "the only bigotry that intellectuals tolerate."

Mrak, Ignatius (October 16, 1818–January 2, 1901)

The second bishop of Marquette, Ignatius Mrak was also a great missionary among the Native Americans. Born in Carinthia, Austria, he studied in a school in Laibach and then undertook studies for the priesthood at the local diocesan seminary. Ordained a priest on August 13, 1837, he was sent by his bishop for additional studies and then spent two years in Legnago, near Verona, Italy. He went back to the diocese and served in several academic and pastoral positions until 1845, when he volunteered for service in the United States missions.

Father Mrak arrived in Detroit and was greeted warmly by Bishop Peter Paul Lefevere, who sent him to Arbre Croche to assist the famed missionary Father Francis Pierz in his work among the Native

Americans. For two years the missionaries worked fruitfully together, and when Father Pierz moved to Minnesota in 1851, Father Mrak retained charge of the Indian mission. In 1855 he was transferred to Eagle Town on Grand Traverse Bay, while at the same time providing care to ten other Indian mission stations.

Father Mrak impressed Bishop Irenaeus Frederick Baraga with his zeal and love of the Native Americans as well as his skill, and in 1860 he was appointed vicar general of the Diocese of Sault Ste. Marie. On September 25, 1868, he was named the second bishop of Sault Ste. Marie-Marquette. Father Mrak at first declined the office, but he was finally persuaded, and on February 7, 1869, he was consecrated a bishop in Cincinnati. He served for ten years, and his duties required him to travel extensively, so much so that his health at last began to deteriorate. Unable to bear the demands of being bishop over such a rugged region, he resigned on April 28, 1879, and became titular bishop of Antinoë and bishop emeritus of Sault Ste. Marie-Marquette.

In the years after his retirement, Father Mrak remained in the diocese and served as a dedicated parish priest. As his health recovered, he requested and received permission from his successor, Bishop John Vertin, to serve again in the Indian missions at Eagle Town. He finally retired to Marquette and died there. He is buried in the vault beneath the cathedral.

Mudd, Samuel (December 20, 1833–January 10, 1883)

A Maryland doctor who was imprisoned for aiding John Wilkes Booth in the assassination of President Abraham Lincoln, Samuel Mudd remains a controversial figure owing to the question of his supposed membership in the conspiracy against the president in 1865. Born in Charles County, Maryland, he was the son of a plantation owner. His education included studies at St. John's College in Frederick City, Maryland, Georgetown College in Washington, D.C., and then the University of Maryland, from which he graduated in 1856 as a doctor. After graduation, he went home to Charles County to practice medicine. The next year, he wed Sarah Frances Dyer. Aside from his practice,

he grew tobacco, and his work as a farmer included the ownership of several slaves.

During the Civil War, the Mudd family struggled to maintain their farm, and their financial position became untenable when Maryland abolished slavery in 1864. As he could not find field hands, he considered selling his farm. Events took an unexpected turn when he was introduced to the actor John Wilkes Booth sometime in November 1864. Booth was supposedly looking for property, but his true intention was to scout escape routes for his plan to kidnap Lincoln and ransom him for Confederate prisoners of war. Mudd met Booth again in Washington, D.C., in December, and it is a matter of debate whether the encounter was arranged.

The Lincoln assassination took place on April 14, 1865, and Booth broke his left leg while fleeing Ford's Theatre. Booth fled to Maryland with David Herold, and the pair stopped at Mudd's house early in the morning of April 15 for medical treatment. Mudd set and bandaged Booth's leg and asked a local carpenter to make a pair of crutches for the injured actor and assassin.

The next day, news of the assassination had spread, and the actions of Booth became well known. Mudd, who had left the house on errands, returned home, and accounts differ as to whether he met Booth and Herold. He did not, however, inform authorities until the next day, when he asked his second cousin, Dr. George Mudd, to alert the 13th New York Cavalry.

Samuel Mudd was soon considered a suspect in the conspiracy, and was arrested almost immediately after the death of Booth on April 26, 1865. He was tried by a nine-member military commission along with Mary Surratt, Lewis Powell, George Atzerodt, David Herold, Michael O'Laughlen, Edmund Spangler, and Samuel Arnold with conspiracy to murder Lincoln. On June 29, 1865, Mudd was found guilty, as were the others, and he avoided the death penalty by one vote. Instead, he was given a sentence of life imprisonment.

Sent to Fort Jefferson, in the Dry Tortugas off the coast of Key West, Florida, Mudd tried to escape in September 1865 in fear of his life. As he had tried to escape, he was forbidden from practicing medicine, but during an outbreak of yellow fever in the fall of 1867 Mudd provided great assistance.

On February 8, 1869, Mudd was granted a pardon by President Andrew Johnson. He was released from prison on March 8, 1869, and returned home to Maryland, where he slowly returned to the practice of medicine and was later involved in local politics. He died of pneumonia and was buried in the cemetery at St. Mary's Church in Bryantown, Maryland. It was the same church where he first met John Wilkes Booth. Historians are divided over the guilt of Mudd, but unquestionably his Catholicism did play a role in his conviction, and the supposed involvement of Catholics in the plot was hailed as proof by anti-Catholics that the Lincoln assassination was orchestrated by the Church. The "theory" was given publicity through the 1886 book *Fifty Years in the Church of Rome*, by Charles Chiniquy.

Muench, Aloisius Joseph (February 18, 1889– February 15, 1962)

A cardinal from 1959 and the first American to hold office in the Roman Curia, Aloisius Joseph Muench was also the bishop of the Diocese of Fargo from 1935 to 1959 and nuncio to Germany from 1951 to 1959. Born in Milwaukee to a German immigrant family, he was the son of Joseph Muench and Theresa Kraus. Called to the priesthood, he attended St. Francis Seminary in Milwaukee and was ordained on June 8, 1913, by Archbishop Sebastian Gebhard Messmer of Milwaukee. He was given pastoral assignments in the archdiocese until 1919, when he was permitted to study for a master's degree at the State University of Wisconsin in Madison. He was then sent for advanced work in theology at the University of Fribourg in Switzerland, where he earned a doctorate in theology summa cum laude.

After taking additional courses at the University of Louvain in Belgium, the University of Oxford and the University of Cambridge in England, and the Sorbonne University in France, he returned to the United States and became a faculty member of

St. Francis Seminary in Milwaukee from 1922 to 1929. From 1929 to 1935 he was the rector of St. Francis Seminary and became a monsignor in 1934.

On August 10, 1935, Pope Pius XI named him bishop of Fargo. He was consecrated on October 15, 1935, in Milwaukee. He remained bishop during the turbulent years of the Great Depression and World War II and proved a very able administrator. He established the Catholic Church Expansion Fund and the Priests Mutual Aid Fund and also the diocesan newspaper, the *Catholic Action News*. He earned, in addition, considerable notoriety for his 1946 pastoral letter "One World in Charity," in which he called for mercy on the part of the victors of the war toward their defeated enemies. That same year, Bishop Muench was appointed by Pope Pius XII the military vicar delegate of the U.S. Armed Forces in Germany and apostolic visitor in Germany. He was also regent of the nunciature in Germany from 1949 to 1951.

On October 28, 1950, he was given the personal title of archbishop, and the next year, on March 9, 1951, he was appointed nuncio to Germany. As he was the first foreign diplomat to present his credentials to the German Federal Republic in 1951, he held the post of dean of the diplomatic corps in Bonn. On December 9, 1959, he was promoted to titular archbishop of Selimbria by Pope Blessed John XXIII. A mere five days later, on December 14, 1959, he was named to the College of Cardinals as a cardinal priest and received the title of San Bernardo alle Terme on December 17, 1959. He thus became the first American to hold office in the Curia. He died in Rome and was buried in Holy Cross Cemetery in Fargo, North Dakota.

Mulholland, Clair Augustine, St. (April 1, 1839–February 17, 1910)

An Irish-born soldier and a noted criminologist, St. Clair Augustine Mulholland was also one of the most respected laymen in the city of Philadelphia. He was born in Lisburn, County Antrim, Ireland, but migrated to Philadelphia with his parents while a young man and grew

Cardinal Aloisius Muench

up in the city. Drawn toward the military life, he served in militia, and at the start of the Civil War he received a commission as lieutenant colonel of the 116th Pennsylvania Volunteers. The unit was attached to the famed Irish Brigade. Mulholland subsequently saw action in some of the war's most terrible fighting and became the colonel of the regiment. As its head, he took part in the disastrous charge of the Irish Brigade up Marye's Heights at the Battle of Fredericksburg on December 13, 1862. He then fought with such distinction at the Battle of Chancellorsville in May 1863 that he was awarded the Medal of Honor. Two months later, at the Battle of Gettysburg, he watched his regiment suffer such severe losses in the first day's fighting that he transferred to the 140th Pennsylvania Volunteers as he no longer had enough men to muster. The next year, he was wounded at the Battle of the Wilderness and was soon promoted to the rank of brigadier general. For his successful leadership in the war, he was made a major general in October 1864.

After the war, Mulholland went back to Philadelphia and in 1868 was named chief of police. President Grover Cleveland appointed him United States Pension Agent, an office he also held under Presidents William McKinley and Theodore Roosevelt. Respected for his knowledge of the justice system, he was much in demand as a lecturer, but he was also a popular speaker and writer on the Civil War. He was a strong Catholic voice in the city of Philadelphia.

Mulry, Thomas Maurice (February 13, 1855–March 10, 1916)

A philanthropist who helped to professionalize social work and to reform charitable institutions, Thomas Maurice Mulry was also one of the early leaders of the St. Vincent de Paul Society in the United States. Born in New York City, he was educated at the De La Salle Academy and Cooper Union and then began a career in business as a building contractor working with his father. Immediately successful, by 1906 he was the president of the Emigrant Industrial Savings Bank. He had married Mary Gallagher in 1880, and the couple had thirteen children, several of whom entered the religious life.

Deeply concerned with the need for Catholic charity efforts, Mulry became one of the United States's leading laymen in promoting charitable activities. He joined the Society of St. Vincent at the age of seventeen and was the first Catholic member of the Charity Organization Society, which began in 1882 and brought together over 130 charitable organizations for a comprehensive approach to charity. From 1907 to 1916 he was a member of New York State Board of Charities and in 1915 was elected president of the Superior Council of the St. Vincent de Paul Society. Under his leadership, the society expanded swiftly in the United States. He went on to help found a host of social service organizations, charities, and homes. His funeral was attended by many of the most prominent Catholic leaders in the country, and he was honored especially by Archbishop Patrick Joseph Hayes.

Mundelein, George (July 2, 1872–October 2, 1939)

Archbishop of Chicago from 1915 to 1939 and a cardinal from 1924, George Mundelein was the first cardinal in the Midwest. He was born in New York City to Francis Mundelein and Mary Goetz, both of German ancestry, grew up in a solid Catholic environment, and went on to study at the La Salle Academy and Manhattan College in New York. Called to the priesthood, he entered St. Vincent Seminary at Latrobe, Pennsylvania, and was then sent to Rome to complete his studies at the Pontifical Urbanian Athenaeum De Propaganda Fide.

Ordained a priest on June 8, 1895, in Rome, he returned to the United States and began pastoral ministry in the Diocese of Brooklyn and served as secretary to the bishop from 1895 to 1897. He then held the post of chancellor from 1897 to 1909. Proving himself immensely capable despite his young age, he was named a monsignor when he was thirty-four, and on June 30, 1909, he was appointed by Pope St. Pius X the titular bishop of Loryma and auxiliary bishop of Brooklyn. He was consecrated a bishop on September 21, 1909, and assumed a host of different duties in the diocese.

On December 9, 1915, Pope Benedict XV appointed him archbishop of Chicago. At the time of his installation on February 9, 1916, he was the youngest archbishop in the country and faced the enormous task of inheriting an archdiocese that had the largest Catholic population in the United States. At the same time, however, unity in the Catholic community was sorely lacking, and the recent history of the archdiocese was marked by severe problems with the clergy, financial instability, and a weak central administration. Archbishop Mundelein proved himself a brilliant administrator and extremely capable in the area of finance.

Archbishop Mundelein founded Quigley Preparatory Seminary, named in honor of the late Archbishop James E. Quigley. Four years later, he started development of St. Mary of the Lake Seminary, which quickly became one of the largest seminaries in the United States. In addition, the town around St. Mary later changed its name to Mundelein in his honor. The archbishop also focused on expanding the archdiocesan parochial school system, including high schools, grammar schools, and two colleges, Rosary and Mundelein. To improve the unity of the archdiocese, he sought to bring together the many different ethnic groups. He also presided over a significant growth in the charitable activities of the archdiocese, most so during the Great Depression, and he looked with some pride on the establishment of a wide network of St. Vincent de Paul Societies and in 1930 the start of the Catholic Youth Organization. Archbishop Mundelein was additionally instrumental in promoting Catholic pride and self-confidence in the years of the Great Depression and during the presidency of Franklin Delano Roosevelt.

Cardinal George Mundelein

On March 24, 1924, he was appointed by Pope Pius XI to the College of Cardinals as a cardinal priest with the title of Santa Maria del Popolo. The consistory in which he took part was called the "American consistory" because only two new cardinals were named, Mundelein and Archbishop Patrick Joseph Hayes of New York. When Cardinal Mundelein returned to the United States he was given an enormous reception in Chicago by civic leaders, including a check for $1 million to help pay for St. Mary Seminary.

In 1926 Cardinal Mundelein had the great pleasure of hosting the 28th International Eucharistic Congress, the first to be held in the United States. The event was celebrated in unprecedented fashion as more than a million people took part. One event at Soldier Field in Chicago attracted some four hundred thousand people, and the closing ceremonies at St. Mary Seminary drew over eight hundred thousand. The cardinal additionally promoted the Eucharist through the creation of three chapels of perpetual adoration.

Although never engaged actively in politics, Cardinal Mundelein nevertheless gained national attention in 1937 with a speech he delivered on Adolf Hitler, whom he condemned. President Roosevelt invited him to the White House the next year, and the two became friends. It is considered likely that Cardinal Mundelein assisted in convincing President Roosevelt to appoint Myron C. Taylor as his personal representative to the Vatican, an appointment that began the process of Holy See–U.S. relations, ultimately culminating in the establishment of full diplomatic relations in 1984.

In 1938 he was named by Pope Pius XI a papal legate to the 8th National Eucharistic Congress in New Orleans and journeyed to Rome that same year to deliver a report on the event to the Vatican. The next year, he took part in the conclave following the death of Pope Pius XI on February 10, 1939. The cardinals elected Cardinal Eugenio Pacelli on March 2, 1939, who became Pope Pius XII. The cardinal died unexpectedly in his sleep, in Mundelein. Over a million people paid their respects as he lay in state in the cathedral. He was buried in St. Mary of the Lake Seminary Cemetery.

Mundelein Seminary

The University of St. Mary of the Lake and Mundelein Seminary is the major seminary and school of theology for the Archdiocese of Chicago. It was founded as a seminary for the archdiocese in 1921 and currently provides training for seminarians from around the country and the world. The seminary and university trace their origins to 1844 and St. Mary's College, the first institution of higher learning in the state of Illinois, started by the first bishop of Chicago, Bishop William J. Quarter. The bishop received a charter from the state of Illinois to grant degrees, and the university, originally staffed by Holy Cross priests from Notre Dame, Indiana, flourished at first, but then encountered financial problems and closed in 1866; by 1868 it had ceased also to serve as a seminary, although the charter remained, as did the board of directors.

In 1902 Archbishop James Edward Quigley made an effort to start the seminary again by sending several priests to Rome for studies with the intention of using them as his faculty. His hopes did not come to fruition, however, chiefly because of the challenge of raising funds for the project. In 1916 Quigley's successor, Archbishop George Mundelein, took the first steps toward a new seminary by announcing plans for Quigley Preparatory Seminary. This was followed in 1918 by the start of a new seminary on a large tract of land located to the north of Chicago.

St. Mary of the Lake Seminary opened officially on October 4, 1921, under the same charter originally granted to the University of St. Mary of the Lake; as a result it has the longest continuous academic charter in the state of Illinois. The grand seminary soon became such a presence that the nearby town changed its name to Mundelein. The seminary gained national attention in 1926 when it was the host site of the 28th International Eucharistic Congress, the first to be held in the United States. The closing celebration at the seminary attracted over eight hundred thousand people.

In 1929 the seminary was granted a second charter, from the Sacred Congregation for Seminaries and Universities, to bestow the academic degrees of the Holy See for five years. In 1934 the Ecclesiastical Faculty of Theology at the seminary received permanent status. As such, the seminary was the first American institution to be honored as a pontifical theological faculty.

In 1961, under Cardinal Albert G. Meyer, the seminary opened a second campus in Niles, Illinois. The campus offered a two-year liberal-arts program as preparation for the last two years of study at Mundelein Seminary in philosophy. This undergraduate program was eventually affiliated with Loyola University of Chicago and became Niles College of Loyola University under Cardinal John Patrick Cody. Henceforth, St. Mary of the Lake Seminary was exclusively a graduate school of theology. In 1971 the seminary became affiliated with the Association of Theological Schools of the United States and Canada.

In 1976, through the cooperation of the Archdiocese's Center for Pastoral Ministry, the seminary launched a program of studies culminating in a doctor of ministry degree. That same year, the seminary celebrated the fiftieth anniversary of the first ordinations held in the Chapel of the Immaculate Conception.

Under Cardinal Joseph Bernardin, St. Mary of the Lake Seminary once more embraced the name on the original 1844 charter, the University of St. Mary of the Lake. In honor of its second founder, the graduate school was renamed Mundelein Seminary. Further developments followed under Cardinal Francis George. In 2000 he transferred the Archdiocese of Chicago's programs of ministry formation to the seminary, and the board of advisers adopted the name the University of St. Mary of the Lake and Mundelein Seminary. That same year, Cardinal George established the Liturgical Institute, with its own faculty dedicated to training, research, and publication in the fields of sacramental theology and liturgy.

Murphy, Frank (April 13, 1890–July 19, 1949)

Attorney general of the United States from 1939 to 1940 and associate justice of the United States Supreme Court from 1940 to 1949, Frank Murphy served as mayor of Detroit, governor of Michigan, the last governor-general of the Philippines, and the first high commissioner of the Philippines. He was born in Harbor Beach, Michigan, the son of a lawyer. He pursued a career in law and studied at the University of Michigan, followed by graduate work in law at Lincoln's Inn in London and Trinity College in Dublin.

During World War I, he served in the U.S. Army and reached the rank of captain. After leaving the service in 1919, he began the practice of law in Detroit and went on shortly after to serve as the Chief Assistant U.S. Attorney for the Eastern

District of Michigan. He was then a judge in the Detroit Recorder's Court from 1923 to 1930. In 1930 he was elected mayor of Detroit and was a supporter of President Franklin Roosevelt and the New Deal. His backing led to his appointment in 1933 to the post of governor-general of the Philippines; subsequently, he was the U.S. high commissioner there until 1936.

Returning home, he was elected governor of Michigan in 1937. Two years later, President Roosevelt appointed him attorney general of the United States. The very next year, however, President Roosevelt nominated him to be an associate justice of the Supreme Court. As a justice, Murphy proved a frequent supporter of individual rights and was especially opposed to the forced relocation of Japanese-Americans during World War II. He dissented in the 1944 case of *Korematsu v. United States* and lamented that, by upholding internment of the Japanese, the Supreme Court was falling into "the ugly abyss of racism." He died in his sleep in Detroit and was buried at Our Lady of Lake Huron Cemetery in Harbor Beach.

Murray, Jane Marie (March 18, 1896–July 22, 1987)

A Dominican sister, writer, and educator, Sister Jane Marie Murray made significant contributions to Catholic education and also to liturgical renewal. She was born Mary Winifred Murray in Freeport, Michigan, and studied initially at St. Andrew's School. In 1907, however, she lost both of her parents and was raised by her uncle and his family. In 1908 she and her sister Marion entered Holy Rosary Academy, from which she graduated in 1913. She then went to Sacred Heart Academy in Grand Rapids, Michigan, and entered the novitiate of the Dominican Sisters at St. John's Home in Grand Rapids on September 12, 1914. She received the habit and the name Sister Jane Marie of the Holy Rosary on April 6, 1915, and made her final profession on August 24, 1923.

Sister Jane was appointed by her superiors to several teaching posts, including college courses at Sacred Heart Academy in Grand Rapids, and she also wrote for her community. In 1928 she attended a meeting of the International Federation of Catholic Alumnae and became fascinated with

the liturgy. She and her friend and colleague Sister Estelle Hackett subsequently approached Father Virgil Michel, O.S.B., the founder of the recently established liturgical journal *Orate Fratres* (later *Worship*), and, with his help, they began to write textbooks on religion, starting with the five-book series *With Mother Church,* which was intended to serve as a supplement to the *Baltimore Catechism.*

They soon progressed to the famed *Christ Life* series and then to a textbook series for high school and college students. The first volume was *The Life of Our Lord* (1942), followed by *Living in Christ* (1946). Sister Estelle Hackett died in 1948, and Sister Jane finished the project with the assistance of consultants. The *Christ Life* series left a major mark on Catholic education. As Berard Marthaler wrote in "The Modern Catechetical Movement in Roman Catholicism: Issues and Personalities" (in *Source Book for Modern Catechists,* 1983), the series was "distinctive in that it represented a first attempt in this country to design textbooks with an avowed purpose of bringing children to take an active part in the liturgical life of the Church."

Meanwhile, Sister Jane undertook a program in medieval studies at the Institute of Medieval Studies in Toronto and became the first woman to receive a licentiate in theology from the institute. Based on her work there, she organized a course of studies for high school students based on a simplified text of the *Summa Theologiae* of St. Thomas Aquinas.

Sister Jane continued to write extensively over the next years, including articles for a host of liturgical and catechetical periodicals. She also lectured at Notre Dame and Marquette Universities, and was a guest professor at The Catholic University of America. In addition, she was a member of the board of the National Liturgical Conference, a charter member of the Society of College Teachers of Sacred Doctrine, and an associate member of the Catholic Biblical Association.

Sister Jane later assisted in the development of a pastoral ministry program at Aquinas College and then became involved with prison ministry. She retired in 1975 and was awarded the Thomas Aquinas Medal in Catechetics from the Dominican Fathers' Pontifical Institute in Washington, D.C. She died in Grand Rapids.

Murray, John Courtney (September 12, 1904–August 16, 1967)

A Jesuit priest and influential theologian, John Courtney Murray is best known for his studies on the Church's relationship to society and state and on religious pluralism and for his contributions to the declaration of the Second Vatican Council *Dignitatis Humanae*.

He was born in New York City and entered the Society of Jesus in 1920. He studied at Boston College and earned a master's degree in 1927. Sent by his superiors to the Philippines, he taught Latin and English literature at the Ateneo de Manila and then returned to the United States in 1930. Ordained to the priesthood on June 25, 1933, he was sent for further studies at the Pontifical Gregorian University in Rome. He earned a licentiate in sacred theology in 1934 and then a doctorate in 1937.

Upon his return to the United States, Father Murray began teaching theology at the Jesuit theologate at Woodstock, Maryland, a post he held until his death. Likewise, in 1941 he was named editor of the Jesuit journal *Theological Studies* and remained its head until his passing. He was also a visiting professor of philosophy at Yale from 1951 to 1952 and then worked with Robert Morrison MacIver of Columbia University on a study of academic freedom and religious education in American public universities. From 1958 to 1962 he served at the Center for the Study of Democratic Institutions.

By the 1950s Father Murray was a prominent national figure, and his research into the question of church and state led to several articles on the relationship between Catholic theology and the American pluralistic society. To Father Murray, the United States offered a wholly different model with regard to Church-state relations than that found in Europe, in which unity between the two was enunciated vigorously by popes in the nineteenth and twentieth centuries in the face of continental liberalism.

In the United States, Father Murray argued, the state brings no interest to the question of religion but is concerned with matters of the temporal order. Likewise, the Church makes no claim to direct power over the state even as it exercises its mission within the temporal order and influences citizens through teachings and ministry. This issue, he suggested, could be supported by a reading of papal teachings within a historical context.

Father Murray's views found considerable opposition in the United States and also in Rome. In March 1953 Cardinal Alfredo Ottaviani of the Holy Office (now the Congregation for the Doctrine of the Faith) spoke out against the liberalizing tendencies in the United States with respect to state and Church. The following year, the Holy Office instructed Father Murray that he was to cease writing on religious freedom and that the publication of an essay on the subject in a book by the University of Notre Dame Press should be halted. As the book was published, Father Murray was instructed to append an explanatory note in subsequent editions. Further censorship was placed upon him in succeeding years.

Father Murray continued writing on a variety of topics. His best-known book, *We Hold These Truths: Catholic Reflections on the American Proposition*, was a collection of essays published in 1960 that contended that the Catholic theory of the state and American constitutional principles had a common foundation. He received considerable publicity for the book, including a cover story in *Time* magazine.

Nevertheless, the suspicion regarding his views meant that he was not invited to take part in the preparatory work of the Second Vatican Council, nor was he invited to the first session of the council. He was then invited to the second session in 1963, and Cardinal Francis Spellman secured his appointment as a *peritus* (or theological expert). In this capacity, he played a significant role in the drafting of the third and fourth versions of the council's 1965 document on religious freedom, *Dignitatis Humanae*.

In the years immediately after the council, he wrote extensively on the document. In 1966 he was named the head of the John LaFarge Institute in New York. Father Murray died of a heart attack in New York City. Since his death, his writings and thought have been the source of considerable discussion and examination by theologians and philosophers. His ideas remain controversial, but he is also acknowledged as one of the foremost theologians to emerge out of modern American Catholicism.

Muskie, Edmund S. (March 28, 1914–March 26, 1996)

A Democratic politician, United States Senator from Maine, and candidate for vice president of the United States, Edmund Sixtus Muskie was born in Rumford, Maine. His father, Stephen Marciszewski, was a Polish Catholic immigrant who changed his name to Muskie, and his mother was Josephine Muskie, also a Catholic and a child of Polish immigrants. Muskie studied at Bates College in Lewiston, Maine, and Cornell University Law School, in Ithaca, New York, from which he graduated in 1939.

During World War II, Muskie served in the United States Navy and after the war entered into private practice in Waterville, Maine. At the same time, he became active in local Democratic politics and was elected to the Maine House of Representatives and then governor in 1954. In 1958 he won election to the United States Senate and then won reelection in 1964, 1970, and 1976.

In 1968 Muskie was nominated for vice president on the ticket with then Vice President Hubert H. Humphrey. The Humphrey-Muskie campaign lost the 1968 election to Richard M. Nixon and Spiro Agnew. Muskie was then a leading candidate for the 1972 Democratic nomination, but he was unable to overcome the surprise antiwar candidacy of South Dakota Senator George McGovern. His cause was damaged further by his emotional defense of his wife (who had been attacked for her supposed drinking and foul language) in a snowstorm in New Hampshire.

Muskie was named by President Jimmy Carter to serve as secretary of state in 1980 following the resignation of Cyrus Vance in the wake of the failure of U.S. diplomacy to secure the release of American hostages in Iran and the disastrous effort to rescue them through military operations. Muskie continued the unsuccessful diplomatic attempts and left office after the defeat of Carter in the 1980 presidential election. For his long and distinguished career in public service, Muskie was awarded the Presidential Medal of Freedom by Carter on January 16, 1981. He retired in 1981 but continued to serve as a lawyer in Washington, D.C. In 1987 he was named to the Tower Commission, the Special Review Board that was assembled to investigate the Iran-Contra scandal. He died in Washington, D.C., and was buried in Arlington National Cemetery.

N

Nagle, Urban (September 10, 1905–March 11, 1965)

A Dominican friar and co-founder of the Blackfriars Guild, Urban Nagle was born Edward John Nagle in Providence, Rhode Island. He attended Providence College and then joined the Dominicans in 1924, taking the name Urban. After studies at the Dominican houses of studies in Illinois and Washington, D.C., he received ordination in 1931. The following year, he founded with Thomas Carey the Blackfriars Guild, an organization that sought to promote plays and drama in the Catholic tradition.

After completing his doctorate at The Catholic University of America, Nagle took up a post teaching drama and English at Providence College. While there, he established a Providence chapter of the Blackfriars Guild in 1935 and co-founded the Catholic Theatre Conference in 1937. Three years later, he assumed a position on the *Holy Name Journal* in New York City, eventually serving as editor until 1946. He also promoted the Blackfriars Guild in the city and was a playwright for the Blackfriars Theater. Among his plays were *Lady of Fátima* (1948) and *City of Kings* (1951). His autobiography was published in 1951.

Narváez, Pánfilo de (1470–1528)

A Spanish conquistador and explorer, Pánfilo de Narváez was the leader of several notable expeditions to the New World. Born in Castile, Spain, he joined in the campaigns in the Americas and fought in Jamaica in 1509. Three years later, he took part in the conquest of Cuba and was named commander of a force that captured the eastern part of the island. He was joined by the famed Bartolomé de Las Casas and Juan de Grijalva.

Taking up residence in Hispaniola and Cuba, de Narváez was appointed to a mission to Mexico, and had ambitions, but his position became a precarious one when most of his troops deserted to Hernando Cortés immediately after Narváez arrived in Mexico. Cortés subsequently defeated him in 1520 and made him a prisoner for over two years. After his release, de Narváez returned to Spain. Within a short time, however, he was named governor of Florida by Emperor Charles V.

De Narváez had reached the Florida coast with three hundred men in April 1528. He had lost over half of his command to storms, disease, and desertions, and he soon encountered extremely hostile Indians. After an unsuccessful effort to find gold and to explore the regions around modern Tampa Bay, de Narváez attempted to return to his ships. He found the vessels destroyed, however, and so began a severe ordeal by land in the desperate hope of reaching Mexico on foot. Only four members of the expedition survived: Alvar Nuñez Cabeza de Vaca, Alonso del Castillo Maldonado, Andrés Dorantes de Carranza, and a Berber slave named Estevanico. Notably, Estevanico was the first African-born person to set foot in what became the United States.

Nashville, Diocese of

The Diocese of Nashville was established on July 28, 1837, by Pope Gregory XVI and given jurisdiction over the entire state of Tennessee. Nashville is the capital of the state and is situated on the banks of the Cumberland River. The center of agricultural marketing, Nashville is also the national center for country music and specializes in printing and publishing religious and traditional books. Founded in 1779, the city was originally called Fort Nashborough. The Diocese of Nashville is a suffragan see of the Archdiocese of Louisville.

The Catholic history of the area dates to 1540, when the Spanish explorer Hernando de Soto arrived on June 1 with an expedition. The Spanish were in present-day Tennessee soon after, calling the Mississippi River the El Rio del Santo Espiritu, the "River of the Holy Spirit."

More than a century later, Jesuit Father Jacques Marquette and Louis Joliet were in the region. A decade after that, René-Robert Chevalier, Sieur de La Salle, founded Fort Prud'homme on the Chickasaw Bluffs, claiming the area for France. In 1714 Charles Charleville erected a trading post at French

Lick near modern-day Nashville. The entire territory was ceded by the French in the Treaty of Paris in 1763, giving control to the British.

In 1770 Daniel Boone, a Catholic, mapped the Wilderness Road in the area, and in 1779 James Robertson, considered the "Father of Tennessee," was in Nashville. Soon after, it was proposed that the region be called "Frankland, the Land of the Free," and reorganized as a state. In 1796 Tennessee entered the Union.

In 1808, when the vast Diocese of Bardstown was established by Pope Pius VII, Tennessee became part of that ecclesiastical jurisdiction, and the noted missionary Father Stephen T. Badin labored in the territory. In 1822 the first Catholic church was built in Nashville, by Father Robert Abell. Six years later, Father James Congrove became the first resident priest.

The Diocese of Nashville was erected in 1837 at the urging of the Third Council of Baltimore, which saw as desirable a diocese for Tennessee. Father Richard Pius Miles, a member of the Dominicans, was appointed the first bishop. A native of Maryland, he had been ordained in 1816 and served with great distinction as a missionary in Ohio and Kentucky. He also founded a community of women, the Sisters of the Third Order of St. Dominic. Consecrated in the Cathedral of Bardstown on September 16, 1838, he went to work as bishop with the same zeal evident in his labors in the mission field. He laid the cornerstone of the cathedral, established a seminary, schools, and a hospital, and ordained the first priest in Tennessee. In 1843 Nashville became the state capital, a position that aided Catholics, although the diocese was also troubled in 1854 by a severe outbreak of violence at the hands of the Know-Nothings. Exhausted by his years of toil, Bishop Miles requested the appointment of a coadjutor in 1859. He died on February 21, 1860, with the threat of the Civil War looming on the near horizon.

The second bishop of Nashville was James Whelan, another Dominican who had been appointed coadjutor bishop to Bishop Miles on April 15, 1859. Born in Kilkenny, Ireland, he had been ordained in 1846. Consecrated a bishop on May 8, 1859, he acceded to the see on February 21, 1860, with the death of Bishop Miles. Bishop

Whelan inherited a diocese that would soon be caught up in the bloody Civil War. Tennessee seceded from the Union on June 24, 1861, and was the site of several of the costliest and most destructive campaigns of the war (some three hundred battles were fought in the state). The state was left devastated by the struggle, and Bishop Whelan labored to provide pastoral care to his people and to provide material and spiritual assistance to the soldiers on both sides, and to the large numbers of civilians caught up in the fighting and carnage. Exhausted by the strain of the war, Bishop Whelan resigned his see on February 12, 1864, and returned to the Dominicans. His remaining years were spent at work writing theological and historical works and undertaking studies in chemistry. He died on February 18, 1878.

The third bishop of Nashville was Patrick Augustine Feehan, who had been a priest of the St. Louis diocese at the time of his appointment on July 7, 1865. A native of Killenaule, Ireland, he was ordained in 1852. As a priest, he was known for his gifts as a homilist. Consecrated on November 1, 1865, he inherited a diocese in severe economic condition in a state devastated as a result of the war and suffering from social upheaval, including the subsequent rise of the Ku Klux Klan. Bishop Feehan proved up to the immense task. He promoted a large rebuilding program, vocations, and the arrival of religious congregations to assist the needs of the faithful. In 1878 the diocese was also stricken by a terrible outbreak of yellow fever that claimed two-thirds of the population, including over twenty priests and forty sisters, as well as his vicar general. On September 10, 1880, Bishop Feehan was promoted to become the first archbishop of Chicago. He died on July 12, 1902.

The fourth bishop of Nashville was Joseph Rademacher, who had been a priest of the Diocese of Fort Wayne, Indiana. Born in Westphalia, Michigan, he had been ordained on August 2, 1863. He served with distinction as a priest in the Fort Wayne diocese until his appointment to Nashville on April 21, 1883; he was consecrated on June 24. Bishop Rademacher labored for ten years to build on the legacy of Bishop Feehan. He encouraged parishes and consolidated diocesan resources to meet the needs of a growing Catholic population. On July 13, 1893, however, he was transferred to the Diocese of Fort Wayne, where he served until his death on June 12, 1900.

The fifth bishop of Nashville was Thomas Sebastian Byrne. A native of Hamilton, Ohio, he was ordained on May 22, 1869, and appointed bishop of Nashville on May 10, 1894. Consecrated on July 25, 1894, he worked especially to improve diocesan finances, to pay off debts, and to promote the faith. He was aided in the latter effort by St. Katharine Drexel, who was instrumental in opening missions throughout the state. Bishop Byrne also promoted vocations to the priesthood and the religious life and led an ambitious building program that included a new cathedral, new parishes, and numerous charitable and educational institutions. As bishop, he led the diocese during World War I, a conflict in which over one hundred thousand men from Tennessee fought, among them the famed hero Sergeant Alvin C. York. Bishop Byrne was likewise a respected writer. He died on September 4, 1923.

The sixth bishop of Nashville was Alphonse John Smith, who had been a priest of the Diocese of Indianapolis prior to his appointment as bishop on December 23, 1923. A native of Madison, Indiana, he was ordained on April 18, 1908, and consecrated bishop of Nashville in the cathedral of Indianapolis on March 25, 1924. Bishop for twelve years, he presided over the diocese during a time of great social and economic unrest. Despite his chronic poor health, he was bishop during the famous Scopes Monkey Trial in 1925. Four years later, the country was hit by the Great Depression, and Bishop Smith managed even in the midst of the hardship to build schools and a hospital to educate young people and care for the sick. He gave his support to the Tennessee Valley Authority in 1933 as a means of improving conditions in the state. He also promoted vocations; twenty-six priests were ordained for the diocese during his tenure. He died on December 16, 1935, at the age of fifty-two.

The seventh bishop of Nashville was William Lawrence Adrian, who had been a priest of the Davenport diocese until his appointment as bishop on February 2, 1936. Born in Sigourney, Iowa, he studied for the priesthood at the North American College in Rome and was ordained in Rome on April 15, 1911. He was consecrated bishop on April

16, 1936, and became known swiftly as "a man who gets things done." His thirty-three years as bishop extended from the depths of the Great Depression through World War II, the first decades of the Cold War, and the period of the Second Vatican Council. He opened parishes in Chattanooga, Nashville, and Memphis, built new churches, remodeled and renovated many others, including the cathedral, held a diocesan synod, founded the diocesan newspaper, and worked to implement the first reforms of Vatican II. He retired on September 4, 1969, and died on February 13, 1972.

The eighth bishop of Nashville was Joseph Aloysius Durick, who was the first native-born Tennessean to serve as bishop of Nashville. Born in Dayton, Tennessee, he was ordained on May 23, 1940, and served as a priest in Alabama prior to his appointment as titular bishop of Cerbali and auxiliary bishop of Mobile-Birmingham in 1954. Named coadjutor bishop of Nashville on December 11, 1963, he was installed on March 3, 1964, and acceded to the see on September 10, 1969. Bishop Durick was best known as a leader in the civil rights movement. He served as chairman of the board of Project Equality of Tennessee and was a member of the Tennessee State Advisory Committee to the United States Commission on Civil Rights. He also began the first Priests' Convention, promoted a Priests' Senate, a Priests' Personnel Board, and a Priests' Association for the diocese. On April 2, 1975, Bishop Durick resigned for reasons of health at the age of sixty. He died on June 26, 1994.

The ninth bishop of Nashville was James D. Niedergeses, the second bishop of Nashville to be from Tennessee. Born in Lawrenceburg, Tennessee, he was ordained on May 20, 1944, and was appointed bishop of Nashville on April 8, 1975. Consecrated on May 20, 1975, Bishop Niedergeses was active in promoting the reforms of the Second Vatican Council and was also a noted leader in the area of ecumenism. He served on the National Conference of Catholic Bishops' Committee for Ecumenical and Interreligious Affairs as the bishops' liaison with the Southern Baptists, and received a number of awards for his work to promote ecumenical and interreligious dialogue. He retired on October 13, 1992, but served as administrator of the diocese until December 1992.

The tenth bishop of Nashville, Edward U. Kmiec, was appointed to the see on October 13, 1992. Born in Trenton, New Jersey, to Polish immigrant parents, he studied for the priesthood in Rome and was ordained at St. Peter's Basilica on December 20, 1961. On November 3, 1982, he was consecrated titular bishop of Simidicca and auxiliary bishop of the Diocese of Trenton. Ten years later he was named to Nashville and installed on December 3, 1992. In the twelve years he spent as bishop, he was devoted especially to promoting vocations, Catholic education, and the permanent diaconate program. On August 12, 2004, Bishop Kmiec was installed as the bishop of Buffalo.

The eleventh bishop of Nashville, David R. Choby, a native of Nashville, was named bishop on December 20, 2005. After studies at The Catholic University of America in Washington, D.C., he was ordained on September 6, 1974, by Bishop Durick at St. Henry Church in Nashville. He had been elected diocesan administrator for the Diocese of Nashville by the diocesan College of Consultors in 2004 after Bishop Kmiec was installed as the bishop of Buffalo. Bishop Choby was consecrated on February 27, 2006. Currently, the diocese has over 69,000 Catholics, served by 74 priests, over 175 men and women religious, and 51 parishes.

Natchez, Diocese of. *See* Jackson, Diocese of

National Catholic Conference for Interracial Justice

The National Catholic Conference for Interracial Justice was established formally in 1960 as a means of promoting for the Church in the United States the vital issue of civil rights advocacy. The conference began as a result of the creation in the 1950s of various diocesan Catholic Interracial Councils to promote interracial justice at a time when the issues of civil rights and justice for minorities were becoming increasingly important in the sphere of political and social policy. The impetus for a national conference was provided by the first national meeting of the Catholic Interracial Council in Chicago in 1958. The official organization inaugurated in December 1959, and the inaugural meeting was held in August 1960 in St. Louis.

Today, the NCCIJ is active in the promotion of interracial dialogue, in particular in the areas of social and economic justice. It is also actively involved in the areas of equal employment and purchasing opportunities for minority- and women-owned small businesses.

National Catholic Educational Association

The largest private professional education organization in the world, the National Catholic Educational Association assists and currently represents two hundred thousand Catholic educators and serves over seven million students in Catholic elementary and secondary schools, as well as in religious education programs, seminaries, and colleges and universities.

The NCEA traces its official history to a meeting held in St. Louis on July 12–14, 1904. At that meeting several important but separate Catholic education organizations (chiefly the Education Conference of Catholic Seminary Faculties, the Association of Catholic Colleges, and the Parish School Conference) decided to unite their organizations to form the Catholic Educational Association. The first secretary general was Father Francis William Howard, who later became bishop of Covington, and the first headquarters were established in Columbus, Ohio.

In 1919 the creation of the National Catholic War Council (later the National Catholic Welfare Conference) led to the decision of the bishops to become actively engaged in the area of Catholic education, a desire that naturally marked the development of a close relationship between the CEA and the newly formed Department of Education of the NCWC.

In 1929 the word "national" was added to the group's name by a decision made at the annual meeting in Toledo, Ohio, and the association headquarters were moved to Washington, D.C. The move facilitated the association's efforts to foster a rapport with the various federal agencies involved in education. Currently, the NCEA is a voluntary association of educators and institutions whose organization utilizes various departments, including the Association of Catholic Colleges and Universities, the National Association of Boards of Catholic Education, and the Chief Administrators of Catholic Education.

National Catholic Register

A national Catholic newspaper first founded in 1927 by Monsignor Matthew Smith as the national edition of the *Denver Catholic Register*, noted for its faithful adherence to Catholic teaching on such subjects such as abortion, homosexual marriage, embryonic stem-cell research, cloning, and in vitro fertilization. The newspaper is one of the largest national Catholic newspapers in the United States. The *National Catholic Register* reached its largest circulation in the 1950s, with more than seven hundred thousand readers nationwide, including thirty-five diocesan editions.

In 1970 Patrick Frawley purchased the paper and eventually moved its headquarters to Los Angeles. Among its new contributors were future leaders in the Catholic press, including George Weigel, Phil Lawler, and Greg Erlandson. Unable to maintain itself financially in the difficult period of the 1990s the *Register* was taken over by the Legion of Christ in 1995. The headquarters were transferred to New Haven, Connecticut. They were again moved in November 2010 to Thornwood, New York. In January 2011, the newspaper was acquired by EWTN.

National Catholic Reporter

An independent weekly newspaper, the *National Catholic Reporter* was founded in 1964 in Kansas City, Missouri, by Robert Hoyt, Michael J. Greene, and Father Vincent J. Lovett. The newspaper was first published on October 28, 1964, with the intention of providing a platform for laypeople in the wake of the Second Vatican Council. From its inception, the *National Catholic Reporter* was aggressive in serving as a voice for progressive Catholicism, and by October 1968 Bishop Charles H. Helmsing of Kansas City-St. Joseph demanded unsuccessfully that the editors remove "Catholic" from the paper's title.

The newspaper has a national distribution in the United States and also is read in nearly one hundred countries. It offers a variety of news and features, including a focus on spirituality, human rights, social justice, and Catholic culture, from a distinctly liberal Catholic perspective. The paper stresses specific editorial areas, including homosexual rights, peace activism, opposition to capital punishment, and support for an end to clerical celibacy and for the ordination of women. It was an outspoken opponent editorially to the Iraq War and most of the policies of the administration of President George W. Bush. Its notable columnists include the feminist Joan Chittister and Bishop Thomas J. Gumbleton. The paper's long-time Rome correspondent, John L. Allen Jr., is one of the Catholic press's leading authorities on the Holy See and global Catholicism.

National Catholic Welfare Conference (NCWC). *See* United States Conference of Catholic Bishops (USCCB)

National Conference of Catholic Bishops (NCCB). *See* United States Conference of Catholic Bishops (USCCB)

National Conference of Christians and Jews. *See* National Conference for Community and Justice

The National Conference for Community and Justice

A civic organization devoted to resisting all forms of racism, intolerance, and bigotry in the United States, the conference began in 1927 as the National Conference of Christians and Jews. It was originally a coalition of Catholics, Jews, Orthodox, and Protestants. The founders of the conference included former Chief Justice Charles Evans Hughes, former Secretary of War Newton D. Baker, former president of the National Council of Churches Dr. S. Parkes Cadman, professor Carlton J. H. Hayes, and industrialist Roger W. Straus.

The new organization was especially active in 1928 during the often bitter presidential campaign that included vicious anti-Catholic propaganda against the Catholic candidate Alfred E. Smith and the demonstrated bigotry of the Ku Klux Klan. The conference did not intend, from the start, to represent or speak for any religious organization or denomination, nor did it seek to alter the religious beliefs or doctrines of the member faiths. Rather, it sought to reduce tensions and misunderstandings among believers and to foster cooperation among participants, always with an effort to avoid any forms of indifferentism.

The organization eventually renamed itself the

National Conference for Community and Justice out of recognition of the growing religious diversity in the United States. Currently, its membership includes representatives of every race, ethnic group, and religious tradition in the country. Its current programs include human-relations training, educational partnerships, youth development, community dialogue, and promotion of interfaith understanding.

National Council of Catholic Women

A lay organization comprising over 5,000 affiliated Catholic women's groups, the National Council of Catholic Women represents several hundred thousand Catholic women. The council was founded in 1920 at the request of the bishops of the United States, who sought to galvanize the remarkable efforts of women throughout World War I into a national organization. At its height in the 1960s, the council claimed over ten million members, throughout 115 dioceses with over 14,000 affiliated organizations.

Closely connected with the work of Catholic Action, the NCCW was intended to offer Catholic women opportunities for prayer, study, and other spiritual support to become deeply imbued in Catholic doctrine, in particular the social teachings of the Church. Today, the council is composed of numerous affiliated parish or regional women's groups, as well as diocesan and national organizations and various supporting members. The present organization is a member of the World Union of Catholic Women's Organizations and Women in Community Services, as well as an affiliate organization of the United States Conference of Catholic Bishops.

National Shrine of the Immaculate Conception, Basilica of the

The eighth-largest religious building in the world and the largest Catholic church in the Western Hemisphere, the Basilica of the National Shrine is dedicated to the honor of the Blessed Virgin Mary, who was declared patroness of the United States under this title in 1847, eight years before the proclamation of the dogma of the Immaculate Conception.

The idea for a national shrine in honor of the Immaculate Conception was submitted to the Holy See by Cardinal John Gibbons and Bishop Thomas J. Shahan and given approval by Pope St. Pius X in 1913. Washington, D.C., was selected as the site for the shrine, and the architectural firm of Maginnis & Walsh was chosen to oversee the construction. Land for the building was donated by The Catholic University of America, on the southwest edge of its campus. Funds were collected from Catholics all over the country, and the cornerstone was blessed by Cardinal Gibbons on September 23, 1920.

Construction progressed sporadically, with delays caused by both the Great Depression and World War II, and a second major effort was necessary after the war to complete the mammoth task of the shrine. Chief among the Catholic leaders spearheading the efforts were Washington's Archbishop Patrick A. O'Boyle and Archbishop John F. Noll of Fort Wayne, Indiana. With the enthusiastic assistance of the American bishops, the funds were raised for the completion of the upper church. On November 20, 1959, the dedication of the great upper church was held in the presence of virtually the entire American hierarchy. The shrine was designated a minor basilica by Pope Blessed John Paul II on October 12, 1990, and visited by Pope Benedict XVI during his trip to the United States in 2008, who held a meeting with the bishops of the United States in the crypt chapel.

The shrine is in the form of a Latin cross in the neo-Byzantine-Romanesque architectural style; with normal seating and standing accommodations, the basilica holds six thousand people. Among its many remarkable architectural features are the Knights' Tower, the bell tower in honor of the Knights of Columbus, the second tallest structure in Washington, D.C., after the Washington Monument; the crypt church, completed in 1926, with a main altar of Algerian onyx; the ornate mosaics of the dome; the baldacchino; the statue of Mary Immaculate by George Snowden; and the colossal mosaic of "Christ in Majesty" designed by John de Rosen. There are also numerous special chapels.

Native American Party

A political party organized in the 1840s to promote and exploit feelings of intolerance and prejudice against immigrants the Native American Party was especially successful in promoting anti-Catholic fervor as immigrants were most often closely associated with the Catholic Church. The origins of the movement can be traced to the pervasive anti-Catholic and anti-immigrant sentiment in the colonial period, rising with the Nativist tendencies in the nineteenth century. By the 1840s the Nativist fervor had reached a level in which political activism became one response to the growing numbers of immigrants, specifically non-Protestants. The influx of European Catholics, such as German and Irish Catholics, had increased in large numbers throughout the two decades of the 1830s (to 600,000) and 1840s (to 1,500,000). The arrival of so many Catholics was viewed as an intolerable development by many Protestants, who denounced the rising influence of Irish and German Catholics and condemned what they proclaimed was Europe's willingness to dump its surplus population on the United States.

Compounding the resentment was the Panic of 1837 and the ensuing depression. Protestant leaders declared that Catholic immigrants were taking the jobs of Americans and lowering both the standard of living and wages. Partly in response, organizers launched the American Republican Party in New York City in June 1843. The first national convention was held in July 1845 under the name the Native American Party. In the elections of 1843, the new party received a mere five thousand votes. In the elections of spring 1844, however, they made massive gains in New York, surpassing the Whig Party. The movement then spread to nearby states, including Massachusetts, New Jersey, Pennsylvania, and South Carolina.

In April 1844 the *Native American* newspaper began its run in Philadelphia, using such inflammatory language that riots soon ensued. Two churches, a convent, and a seminary were set upon and burned by mobs; thirteen people were killed and fifty wounded in further violence in July 1844, requiring Bishop Francis P. Kenrick to close temporarily all Catholic churches in the city.

The Native American Party attempted to build on this early momentum. At its convention in Philadelphia in July 1845, delegates approved a Declaration of Principles addressed to the "Citizens of the United States." The manifesto restated the same rhetoric that had been voiced over the previous decades concerning the dangers of immigrants. It proposed bringing to an end all "sectarian" interference in politics; the promotion of public schools, without which the government of the people must degenerate into one of depravity and ignorance; the formal recognition of the Protestant Bible as the most potent weapon against the enemies of America (a thinly veiled reference to the Catholic Church and the papacy); and the proposition that immigrants should be required to wait for twenty-one years before being permitted to vote. The Church was also condemned for a variety of "crimes," including inciting murder and riots, taking part in elections as a separate political organization comprised of foreigners, organizing and arming foreigners into "banditti" in order to intimidate the electorate, and plotting to assassinate and murder "unarmed native citizens."

Seemingly poised to rise to genuine national prominence, the Native American Party proved politically fleeting. It failed to retain its vigor in the face of internal squabbles, the ineptitude of its elected representatives, and the larger issues of the westward expansion and especially slavery. Versions of the party, however, emerged in the 1850s with the Know-Nothings and later still with the Ku Klux Klan. (*See also* Nativism.)

Native American Catholics

According to the United States Conference of Catholic Bishops's report "Native American Catholics at the Millennium," there are nearly half a million Native American Catholics in the United States. They are a remarkable part of the contemporary tapestry of American Catholicism, but they are also the inheritors of a legacy of faith that stretches back to the end of the fifteenth century. The encounter between Catholic missionaries and the Native American peoples was not always a happy one, but unquestionably it was also marked by heroism, sacrifice, holiness, and dedication.

The native people of the New World had their first encounter with Europeans as the expedition of Christopher Columbus embarked from Spain on August 3, 1492, with three vessels, the *Niña*, *Pinta*, and *Santa Maria*. The small fleet reached the shore of Guanahani (as its inhabitants referred to it) — most likely Watlings Island in the Bahamas — on October 12. Columbus renamed the island San Salvador. After claiming the island in the name of Spain, Columbus sailed southwest and reached Hispaniola (modern-day Haiti and the Dominican Republic) and Cuba, which he designated Duina. Columbus chose Hispaniola to be his first settlement and constructed the fort of La Natividad (built out of the remains of the Santa Maria, which had run aground). After some further exploration, he returned to Spain. Columbus made three more voyages between 1493 and 1502. By the time of his death in 1506, the New World was known to Europe and explorations had begun in earnest.

The inhabitants of the islands and the New World encountered by Columbus were described as "Indians," as he was convinced they were a people of the East Indies. They were from Asia, but they had migrated to the Americas many thousands of years before. Scholars estimate that they

Native American, Short Bull

first reached North America between 12,000 and 35,000 years ago, when groups followed the migrating herds over the Bering Straits, at the time frozen over by an ice age. By the time of Columbus, it is estimated that there were 20 million Native Americans spread out across two continents. There were approximately 2 million inhabitants of North America, a rich tapestry of tribes with established cultures.

The impact of the arrival of the European powers upon the peoples of the New World cannot be overestimated. The presence and relentless movement of the Europeans dispersed the tribes even in the earliest stages and brought about massive destruction of their way of life. As the Indian nations were pushed westward, further disruptions resulted in tribal consolidations or the divisions of some nations.

Enormous controversy today surrounds the history and especially the legacy of the European colonial enterprise in the New World. Much has been written about the demolition of the Meso-Amer-

ican cultures such as the Aztecs and the South American Andean civilization of the Incas by the Spanish conquistadors, the severe oppression of the indigenous peoples, and the devastation delivered upon the Indian tribes across the Americas from displacement, disease, war, and slavery. Much like other aspects of Catholic history, the activities of the Spanish colonial age were the subject of the so-called *leyenda negra*, the Black Legend — absolutely hostile coverage by scholars who advanced the propaganda that had its start in the anti-Catholic schools and royal court of England.

The plight of the Native Americans in North America was the source of great concern to the Church, and missionaries distinguished themselves for their heroic defense of Indian rights. There is no question that European colonialism wrought vast troubles for the tribes and cultures of the New World. But it is unfair to blame the Church for the actions of the European powers, who regularly punished Jesuits, Franciscans, Augustinians, and countless priests, nuns, and laypeople for speaking out in defense of the suffering natives.

This view of the Church was first expressed by Pope Alexander VI in 1493, when he stressed to Spain and Portugal that the Native Americans were capable of deciding whether to embrace the faith and should not be mistreated or oppressed. Pope Paul III, in 1537, issued the bull *Sublimis Deus,* in which he declared:

> The said Indians and all other people who may later be discovered by Christians, are by no means to be deprived of their liberty or the possession of their property, even though they be outside the faith of Jesus Christ.

The authentic approach to the history of the encounter between the Native Americans and the Church was expressed eloquently by Pope Blessed John Paul II in 1987, when he addressed a gathering of Indians in Phoenix. The pope noted:

The early encounter between your traditional cultures and the European way of life was an event of such significance and change that it profoundly influences your collective life even today. That encounter was a harsh and painful reality for your peoples. The cultural oppression, the injustices, the disruption of your life and of your traditional societies must be acknowledged. At the same time, in order to be objective, history must record the deeply positive aspects of your people's encounter with the culture that came from Europe. Among these positive aspects I wish to recall the work of the many missionaries who strenuously defended the rights of the original inhabitants of this land. They established missions throughout this southwestern part of the United States. They worked to improve living conditions and set up educational systems, learning your languages in order to do so. Above all, they proclaimed the Good News of salvation in our Lord Jesus Christ, an essential part of which is that all men and women are equally children of God and must be respected and loved as such. This Gospel of Jesus Christ is today, and will remain forever, the greatest pride and possession of your people.

The voyages of Columbus were followed by other expeditions and then the thunderous campaigns of the conquistadors. The West Indies were firmly in Spanish hands by 1515; the Aztec Empire had fallen by 1521 to the troops of the conquistador Hernando Cortés; and by 1536 the Incan Empire had been toppled by Francisco Pizarro. The end of the Incan Empire marked the last of the major Spanish conquests, and Spain began the much longer process of consolidation, forging a permanent Spanish presence in Central America and South America, and then exploring into North America. Only Brazil was outside their sphere of control, as it was under the Portuguese by the terms of the Treaty of Tordesillas of 1496 negotiated by Pope Alexander VI.

Spanish missionaries were involved every step of the way. There was no shortage of volunteers to serve in the New World from among the clergy of Spain, including the Franciscans and Augustin-

ians, as well as the Jesuits after their founding in the middle of the sixteenth century. The missionaries were often among the best educated in Spain (an identical phenomenon was found among the French missionaries), and many willingly gave their lives for the faith through years of toil in the wilds or as martyrs at the hands of hostile tribes. The Black Legend and modern anti-Catholicism have sullied the reputation of these remarkable missionaries.

In 1511 Pope Julius II decreed the creation of the first diocese in what became the United States with the Diocese of Puerto Rico (later renamed the Diocese of San Juan and today an archdiocese), and Alonso Manso became the first resident bishop in the New World. Two years later, Juan Ponce de León departed the Spanish-held Caribbean and first entered Florida. Missionaries then made Florida the first region for serious evangelization in what became the United States. For the first half of the sixteenth century, however, Spanish expeditions failed to establish a lasting presence, and missionaries traveling with them encountered determinedly hostile native tribes. In 1558 a more concerted effort was made when the Dominicans assumed direction of the missions, starting with the expedition of Tristán de Luna in 1559. This proved a failure, and the Dominicans were succeeded by the Jesuits. They in turn left Florida in 1572 as the general of the Jesuits, St. Francis Borgia, concluded that the conditions there and the hostility of the Indians offered little prospect for a permanent settlement. Progress was made from 1577 with the Franciscans, who forged a chain of missions across Florida and then into Georgia. They converted more than thirty thousand Indians by 1634.

The toil and sacrifice of the missionaries and converted Indians proved ultimately fleeting. As the English colonies expanded to the north, the missions fell under attack as part of the wider conflict between Spain and England. During Queen Anne's War from 1702 to 1713 (known in Europe as the War of the Spanish Succession), English troops and colonists, with their Indian allies, launched brutal attacks on the Florida missions from their bases in the Carolinas. Churches were burned to the ground, friars were tortured and then killed, and Catholic Indians were slaughtered.

Spanish missionaries had hoped to set out for the lands north of Mexico soon after the capture of the Aztec Empire. Franciscans thus regularly went out with the first explorers. One of the greatest of these was the Franciscan Juan de Padilla, who set out with Francisco Vázquez de Coronado on his expedition of 1540. Padilla was martyred by an Indian band two years later in what is now Kansas; by his death he became the protomartyr of the United States, the first of more than a hundred martyrs among the early missionaries.

The lasting missions in New Mexico were begun in 1598 by nine Franciscans under Alonso Martínez, following the work of the explorer Juan de Oñate, who then introduced Spanish settlers into the region. Santa Fe was founded in 1609 and served as the center for considerable missionary labors, so that by 1630 there were over eighty thousand Indian converts living in pueblos under the Franciscans. The dislike for the Spaniards, unfortunately, stirred up such ill feeling among some of the Indians that the Pueblos revolted in 1680. Most of the missions were destroyed in the uprising, and Franciscans could not resume their efforts until 1692; one final rebellion occurred in 1696, after which the Church in New Mexico enjoyed peace for centuries under the Franciscans and the overall ecclesiastical jurisdiction of the bishop of Durango.

Native American, Wolf Robe

In nearby Texas, Spanish explorers made a survey as early as 1629, but it was not until 1657 that the Franciscan Juan Larios opened a mission along the Nueves River in southeastern Texas. Little progress was made until 1685, when word arrived in Mexico that the great French explorer René-Robert Chevalier, Sieur de La Salle, had made his way into the Lower Mississippi Valley. Fearing further French incursions, the Spanish built a fort on Matagorda Bay. Franciscans provided pastoral care for the soldiers and the growing community and served as missionaries to the surrounding tribes.

Expansion of the Texas missions was accomplished following the founding of the beloved mission of San Antonio de Valero, near San Antonio, in 1718. The mission is known in history as the Alamo.

In 1718 the remarkable Franciscan missionary Venerable Antonio Margil de Jesús was particularly famed for his missions among the Nacogdoches Indians. According to popular legend, he ended a drought among the Nacogdoches by striking a rock with a cane and drawing out water. Among the missions he founded were Mission Dolores and San Miguel. In 1720 he founded Mission San Jose, which was soon declared "the Glory of New Spain."

Life for the Franciscans was incredibly arduous as there were few colonists, the Indians were nomadic by culture, and many of the tribes, such as the Apaches, were bitterly opposed to the Spanish. By the end of the eighteenth century, the Franciscans were replaced by regular diocesan priests and evangelization among the Native Americans effectively ended. In the early nineteenth century and the end of Spanish rule, Texas had a European population of barely four thousand, and a quarter of them were soldiers. By that time, Americans were on the move into Texas in the wake of the Louisiana Purchase; the future of the region was destined to be an American one.

One final figure in the history of the Southwest missions is the saintly Jesuit priest Eusebius Kino. Father Kino spent his life on horseback and founded missions across the Southwest and Lower California. For his defense of the Native Americans, his long travels, and his holiness, he is revered as the founder of Christianity in the Southwest. Mission San Xavier del Bac stands today as a monument to Father Kino's labors. He represents the state of Arizona in Statuary Hall in the U.S. Capitol in Washington, D.C., and in 1995 his cause for canonization was introduced in Rome.

The missions of Alta California (the name given to California above Baja) begin officially on July 16, 1769, with the start of the Franciscan mission at San Diego, the first of twenty-one missions founded between 1769 and 1823. The Franciscans were responsible for forging *El Camino Real* (the "Royal Road"), a chain of missions that extended from San Diego to San Francisco. The California missions served as the principle centers of evangelization in California, and "life under the bells" was the chief way of living for thousands of Indians who were taught trades and assisted in finding a place in the Spanish society that had suddenly been thrust upon them. The central figure in the California missions was Franciscan Blessed Junípero Serra.

With the Mexican Revolution against Spain in 1821 the California missions came to an end as the property of a hostile Mexican government. In 1834 the secularization of the missions was declared, but the promises to the Indians of land and livestock never materialized, and the death rate of the Native Americans was worse than that of the slaves in the American South.

The missions of *El Camino Real*, much like the entire Spanish mission era, have been the subject of much controversy. Some have charged the Franciscans with abuse and repression; Father Serra was accused of perpetrating genocide against the California Indians. It is true that the Indian population declined severely, in the main from the diseases of the white settlers (a common tragedy across the whole of North America). Still, Serra loved the Indians under his care, and a balanced understanding is crucial to appreciating the true legacy of the California missions. Further, the legacy of the Spanish missions in North America must not be overlooked. This tradition has become most apparent as the Hispanic Catholic population has increased extensively in the last decades. The scope of the Spanish missionary effort in North America was unmatched by any other major European Catholic power and had lasting effects.

The efforts of evangelization undertaken by France in what is now America represents yet another remarkable legacy of religious zeal, bravery, and commitment to the Native Americans. Progress in understanding the extent of the lands before

Native American, Geronimo

them was made by the French explorer Jacques Cartier, whose expeditions on the North American coast and the St. Lawrence River served as the basis of France's claim to Canada. Like Columbus, Cartier received royal permission (in this case from Francis I of France) to set out on a voyage to discover a passage to the East. His trips, from 1534 to 1541, astounded France by introducing the court to two Native Americans and giving promise of lands and riches.

Amazingly, the French missions endured for barely a century. They were originated in Canada and extended from there to parts of Maine, New York, and areas around the Great Lakes and along the Mississippi River. One of the most significant successes was in the region that today is Louisiana.

From the French possessions in Canada, especially Québec, priests — the famed "Black Robes" — went out into the wilderness. They bore the immense responsibility of preaching the Gospel among the Native Americans. The result was that complaints and demands about the welfare of the Indians found greater reception among the representatives of the French crown than their counterparts ever enjoyed with the officials in charge of New Spain.

Like the Spanish friars and priests, the French were deeply dedicated to the pastoral care of the Indians and to saving their genuinely worthy souls. The Jesuits, Recollects (a reformed branch of the Franciscans), Capuchins, and other religious orders found many young men and women eager to sail to New France. As with the Spanish missions, the French happily sent out their brightest, best educated, and holiest priests as Black Robes. As far as they were concerned, the Native Americans deserved nothing but the best to bring them Christ.

The first missionaries to arrive were four Recollect Franciscans in 1615, followed ten years later by a group of Jesuits. Progress was slow, and by 1627 there were perhaps barely a hundred people living in Québec. The brief life of New France had appeared to have ended in 1629 when an English expedition marched into Canada and captured the city. Three years later, France was given back Canada, and new French explorers arrived, but this time with the awareness that the English to the south were going to be a permanent threat, and all too often the Native Americans were used as pawns in the struggle.

At the time there were approximately 220,000 Native Americans in what became Canada (the region stretching from the Gulf of St. Lawrence in the east to Lake Superior in the west). Samuel de Champlain had wasted no time in befriending the main tribe in the region, the Hurons (the Wendat) to guarantee a perpetuation of the fur trade and begin forging good relations with the locals. Over the next decades, many of the Hurons became Catholic converts. Still, Champlain's decision had considerable historical consequences, for the bitterest enemies of the Hurons were the powerful Iroquois, the so-called Five Nations, the Iroquois Confederacy, including the Mohawk, Oneida, Onondaga, Cayuga, and Seneca tribes, spread out across northern New York. Initially allied with the Dutch, they soon switched their allegiance to the English. As the French were allied to the Hurons, the Iroquois became their enemy and so, by consequence, did the French missionaries.

In an act of stunning heroism, Jesuit missionaries set out from Canada and made their way into New York to convert the Iroquois. These Jesuits were highly educated men who lived with the Indians and packed up portable altars and supplies to accompany them on seasonal migrations and buffalo hunts.

In 1642 the great Jesuit St. Isaac Jogues was captured with several companions, including fellow lay missionary St. René Goupil, by the Mohawks. St. René Goupil was martyred, and St. Isaac Jogues endured unspeakable tortures that left him terribly mutilated. He escaped captivity in 1643, returned to France, and then went back to the Iroquois as a peace ambassador. Captured once again by the Mohawks, he was martyred near the present site of Auriesville, New York, on October 18, 1646. Others followed in death, including the Jesuit priests Anthony Daniel, John de Brébeuf, Gabriel Lalemant, Charles Garnier, Noel Chabanel, and the lay missionary Jean de Lalande. With Goupil

and Jogues, the martyrs were canonized in 1930 by Pope Pius XI and are honored as the North American Martyrs.

St. Isaac Jogues's ostensibly pointless death actually served as the basis for future missions among the Mohawks, but the Hurons remained a target for annihilation by the Iroquois and the English. From 1648 to 1650, the Iroquois waged a staggeringly savage war upon the Hurons during which literally thousands of the Hurons were slaughtered, to the considerable satisfaction of the English. The remnants of the Hurons relocated near Québec City and finally settled at Wendake.

The Jesuit missions nevertheless continued among the Iroquois, including the Onondaga and finally even the Mohawks. Progress was made, and among the Mohawk converts was an extraordinary young woman, St. Kateri Tekakwitha, called the "Lily of the Mohawks," who was declared blessed by Pope Blessed John Paul II in 1980 and was canonized in October 2012 by Pope Benedict XVI. The Iroquois once more turned against the French, and by 1684 there were only two priests left among the Indians of New York.

In Maine, the Capuchins, in 1633, started a mission at the French military outpost of Pentagoët (modern Castine) on Penobscot Bay. It survived only until the early eighteenth century, when the English destroyed it. To the south, meanwhile, the Abenaki Indians in modern-day New England made the decision to ask that missionaries be sent to them, marking one of the great stories of Indian Catholicism. The Jesuit priest Gabriel Druillettes founded a mission at Norridgewock, Maine, on the Kennebec River in the 1630s, an outpost for the devoted Abenaki that was raided by the English in 1704, 1722, and 1724. During the last attack, the beloved missionary among the Abenaki, Father Sebastian Râle, S.J., was murdered after refusing to leave his people. The British had put a price on his head, and Mohawks beheaded him and took his head to the British for the reward.

The French colonial focus had been centered chiefly in Canada for much of the seventeenth century at the expense of ambitions in the Midwest. Alarmed by the expansion of the English colonies, the French crown widened its interests and a new area opened for missionaries. Jesuits St. Isaac

Jogues and Charles Raymbaut visited Sault Ste. Marie, Michigan, and the borders of Lake Superior in 1641, and Claude Allouez had opened several missions there. From these bases, Jesuit missionaries roamed south and then west into modern-day Michigan, Illinois, and Wisconsin.

The European discovery and exploration of the Mississippi Valley was spearheaded in 1673 by Louis Joliet, accompanied by the indefatigable Jesuit Jacques Marquette, who had earlier founded a mission at St. Ignace, on the north shore of the Straits of Mackinac. Marquette and Joliet followed the northern shore of Lake Michigan, entered Green Bay and the Fox River, and crossed a short portage into the Wisconsin River that emptied into the Mississippi. Father Marquette drew maps of the areas and kept a diary of the voyage, some of the most important documents of early American history. He returned the next year to live with the Illinois Indians at Kaskaskia, Illinois, but died a year later.

The missions in the Midwest soon became fertile soil for evangelization. Father Allouez worked for thirty-two years among the Indians and baptized an estimated ten thousand. The daily demands on the priests, of course, were enormous. They made their way through territory never before seen by a European and needed immense perseverance as they followed migratory tribes. The priests were much respected by Indians as they learned their languages, dealt with them honorably, and defended them against the sometimes corrupt fort commanders, fur traders, and soldiers.

Missions were opened in Detroit, Green Bay, and St. Joseph that endured until 1763 and the withdrawal of the Jesuits from the region. Other work was accomplished by the Recollects and also seminary priests sent from Québec. Altogether, French priests and missioners placed footholds of the faith all along the Mississippi. The defeat of France in the French and Indian War all but brought an end to the missions, as they had depended upon government assistance. By the terms of the Treaty of Paris in 1763, France lost Canada, and the English assumed the task of governing seventy-thousand French-speaking Catholic inhabitants. The task of evangelization fell to the Catholics who originated in the English colonies and then the United States.

As the people of the United States pushed ever westward, new Catholic communities slowly planted their roots, started new parishes, schools, hospitals, orphanages, and places of refuge for the sick and the forgotten. Courageous missionaries, priests and nuns, set out to preach the Gospel to Native Americans and often gave their lives on their behalf.

Among the greatest were Bishop Irenaeus Frederick Baraga and Father Pierre-Jean De Smet. The "Apostle to the Chippewas," Baraga was the first bishop of Marquette. Born in the Austrian dukedom of Carniola and the son of nobles, he was orphaned in 1812 and raised by a university professor at Laibach. He entered the University of Vienna in 1816, earned a law degree, and became fluent in English, French, Italian, and Spanish. Receiving the grace of a religious vocation, he entered the seminary and was ordained on September 21, 1823. Attracted to the missionary efforts in the United States, Father Baraga left his homeland and arrived in America, welcomed by Bishop Edward D. Fenwick of Cincinnati in 1831. He labored in the diocese until the following spring, when he started his ministry in Michigan.

The only priest in Upper Michigan for many years, Father Baraga cared for white congregations as well as Native Americans in the area. He founded churches and schools and went to Europe in 1836 and 1853 to gather funds and mission personnel. In his missions, Father Baraga denounced liquor traders and others who tried to exploit the Indians. On July 29, 1853, the Northern Peninsula of Michigan was detached from the Diocese of Detroit and made a vicariate apostolic. Father Baraga was appointed the first bishop, consecrated in the cathedral of Cincinnati. He issued two episcopal letters soon after, one in English and the second in Chippewa. His jurisdiction extended not only to the whole Northern Peninsula of Michigan but to a large part of the Lower Peninsula, northern Wisconsin, and the northern shore of Lake Superior. On October 23, 1864, by apostolic authority, he transferred his see from Sault Ste. Marie to Marquette, where he labored throughout the area for another fifteen years. When he was too exhausted by his ministries to ride his faithful horse, he used a sleigh that was pulled by a sturdy dog.

Bishop Baraga composed the first recorded Chippewa grammar and the first Chippewa dictionary. Both works took hours of research and study. He also compiled prayer books and catechisms, as well as *Dusna Tasa*, a Slovenian-language prayer book. He wrote many other literary and spiritual works as well, including an Ottawa prayer book, *Animie Misinasaigan*, and instructions and sermons. For his amazing achievements, he is honored as the "Father of Indian Literature" in America.

The most revered Catholic missionary of the Native Americans west of the Mississippi River in the mid-nineteenth century, Jesuit Father Pierre-Jean De Smet was a friend of Sitting Bull and a staunch defender of the Sioux and other Indian nations. He was born in Termonde, Belgium, and became interested in a missionary vocation. Coming to America in 1821, he entered the Jesuit novitiate, was ordained in 1827, and set out on his first mission labors. In 1833, however, he suffered a series of illnesses and went to Belgium to recover his health. In 1838 Father De Smet returned to St. Louis and began working with the Potawatomi near Council Bluffs, Iowa. When his mission, St. Joseph's, was endangered by the nearby Sioux, who threatened attacks, Father De Smet walked into the Sioux camp, introduced himself, and asked the Sioux to leave the Potawatomi and the mission in peace. The astonished Sioux heard his pleas and agreed to refrain from any such assaults.

In 1840 Father De Smet responded to a call for a "Black Robe" and went to the Rocky Mountains, where the Jesuits were establishing a missionary province. The Flatheads and Pen d'Oreilles welcomed him, and he went among the Crows, Gros Ventres, and others on a journey of 4,814 miles. In 1841 Father De Smet founded St. Mary's Mission on the Bitterroot River, thirty miles north of Missoula, Montana. Realizing the vast numbers of local tribes and their receptive acceptance of the faith, Father De Smet went to Europe to recruit six Sisters of Notre Dame de Namur and other workers, as well as funds. On his return to his mission area, he went by canoe to

Native American, Chief Sitting Bull

the residence of Bishop Francis Norbert Blanchet at Fort Vancouver. The two men spent time planning the missions in the region. Father De Smet, who attended the Rendezvous of the mountain men and fur trappers, came to this planning session with great experience. He even spent time with Brigham Young, advising him of the splendors of the Great Salt Lake. Young followed his advice because of his knowledge of the district and the tribes.

Father De Smet was a traveler who endured hardship without complaint. He respected the Native Americans's traditions and values and never took sides in debates. Because he spoke only the truth, he served as a mediator in tribal conflicts, such as the Blackfoot and Flathead confrontation in 1846. Father De Smet also served as a mediator at Fort Laramie in 1851, in the Mormon Wars in 1858, and in other regional disputes.

Founding the Kalispel St. Ignatius Mission as part of the overall mission strategy for the territory, he accompanied the Blackfoot Indians into the Yellowstone Valley in 1846. He and the tribe then went to Fort Lewis, and there the Blackfoot adopted peaceful relations with their neighbors. He addressed the ten thousand Indians holding council in Horse Creek Valley near Fort Laramie and urged peace.

Father De Smet's most unforgettable feat took place in 1868 as a result of the federal government's request for his assistance. Sitting Bull and the Sioux threatened war as a result of white treachery concerning their lands, and a federal peace commission was formed to avoid such a conflict. Father De Smet joined the commission on the way to the Sioux enclave but soon left the whites, whom he recognized as bureaucrats and politicians with their own agendas, and went his own way. He walked unarmed into a camp of five thousand Sioux warriors and asked to see Sitting Bull. Warmly received, Father De Smet and the great chief talked alone for a long period. The Jesuit missionary left the Sioux camp with a pledge of peace.

Another notable figure during this time was St. Rose Philippine Duchesne, the founder of the Society of the Sacred Heart in America who was later so revered by Native Americans. She was elderly and spoke only French, but the Indians became aware of her spirituality and they called her "The Woman Who Always Prays." St. Rose arrived in the United States in 1818 with four companions and headed west. In Missouri she aided Bishop Louis Dubourg by opening the first school in St. Charles, Missouri, and then founded Indian schools, orphanages, and an American novitiate for the congregation. She later spent time with the Potawatomi at Sugar Creek Mission but was recalled to St. Louis the following year, where she died on November 18, 1852, at the age of eighty-three. She is honored as a pioneer in the Hall of Fame of the state of Missouri. Pope Blessed John Paul II canonized her on July 3, 1988.

The plight of the Native Americans deteriorated steadily throughout the nineteenth century as they were subject to relocation from their traditional lands in the East to largely inhospitable reservations in the West, where the Indians were subjected to acculturation and various forms of abuse, and suffered from diseases (especially smallpox), alcoholism, and despair. In 1830, for example, President Andrew Jackson and the U.S. Congress passed the Indian Removal Act that drove large numbers of Native Americans east of the Mississippi River to the west through treaties that were then regularly violated. The most infamous of these relocations was the so-called Trail of Tears, in which Cherokees, Potawatomis, and other Indians died while on their way to a reservation carved out of arid wastelands.

The Office of Indian Affairs, which was attached to the Department of War, was the government agency charged with negotiating the treaties. In the aftermath of the Battle of the Little Bighorn in 1876 that brought the deaths of Lieutenant Colonel George Armstrong Custer and some 268 U.S. soldiers, the federal government was relentless in subjugating the last pockets of Native American resistance. The brutal methods used massacres of Indian men, women, and children, and climaxed with the Wounded Knee Massacre on December 29, 1890, near Wounded Knee Creek on the Lakota Pine Ridge Indian Reservation in South Dakota. As many as 300 Indians were slaughtered, and the event was seared into the historical memory of Native Americans.

Under President Ulysses Grant's administration, Protestant missionaries were regularly used as Indian agents in a system that was scandalously corrupt, robbed and mistreated the Indians, and was also anti-Catholic in its approaches to schools and evangelization. The massacres and relocation were exacerbated further by the Code of Indian Offenses of 1883 that prohibited traditional Indian customs, and the Dawes Allotment Act of 1887 that divided up the reservations for individual ownership, which obliterated tribal life and left Indian lands subject to unscrupulous acquisition by white settlers.

To reduce further the survival of Native American culture, the federal government adopted Native American boarding schools under the assumption that the children of Indians needed to be taught the ways of the white man, which prohibited them from speaking their own language and compelled them to dress like whites and forget their own customs. Many of the boarding schools were placed in the hands of missionaries, and there were Catholics involved in the schools. Their intentions were good, but the result was all too often to add to the decline of Native American culture.

Nevertheless, the Church did fight on behalf of Native American peoples. The most active of the Catholic organizations in this regard was the Bureau of Catholic Indian Missions, which was established in 1874 as the representative of the missions before the federal government and the public. The bureau was made a permanent organization in 1884 by the Third Plenary Council of Baltimore. It remains the major representative of the Catholic Church in the United States in assisting and caring for Native Americans.

In the early twentieth century, the Indian schools were gradually placed into the hands of religious communities of women. By the 1970s and the passage of the Indian Education Act in 1972, the Indians themselves were empowered to direct their own schools. This development was also part of the wider revitalization movements of the era.

Today, in addition to the important work of the Bureau of Catholic Indian Missions, the Church serves Native Americans through the Subcommittee on Native American Affairs, part of the United States Conference of Catholic Bishops's Committee on Cultural Diversity, which works directly with the standing committee and other USCCB committees to address the pastoral needs of Native American Catholics. The key mission priorities are to continue to support and collaborate with key national organizations, including the Bureau of Catholic Indian Missions and the Tekakwitha Conference; identify and develop culturally and ethnically specific resources in the areas of catechesis, lay ministry formation, liturgy, evangelization, and the diaconate; and collaborate with other USCCB offices, including Laity, Marriage, Family Life, and Youth; Education; Evangelization and Catechesis; Vocations; Liturgy; and Pastoral Practices.

The Tekakwitha Conference, so named in honor of St. Kateri Tekakwitha, was established in 1939 as a missionary-priest advisory group in the Diocese of Fargo. It was a missionary-priest support group from 1946 to 1977, but since 1977 it has been a gathering of Catholic Native peoples and the men and women — priests, religious, and laypersons — who minister to their communities. The primary focus of conference concern and activity is evangelization, with specific emphasis on the development of Native American ministry and leadership. Other priorities include catechesis, liturgy, family life, social justice ministry, chemical dependency, youth ministry, spirituality, and Native Catholic dialogue. Conferences and local Kateri Circles serve as occasions for the exchange of ideas, prayer, and mutual support. Since 1980 the national center has promoted and registered 130 Kateri Circles in the United States and Canada.

On June 19, 2003, the United States Conference of Catholic Bishops issued a report, "Native American Catholics at the Millennium," on the current state of Native American Catholics in the United States. There are 2.9 million people who identify themselves as Native American. Of these, 580,000 Native Americans, or 20 percent of the total population, are considered Catholic. Native Americans comprise 3.5 percent of all Catholics in the United States. More than 340 parishes in the United States serve predominantly Native American congregations, and 30 percent of all dioceses and archdioceses have an office that serves Native American Catholics. There is presently one Native American bishop in the United States: Archbishop Charles J. Chaput, O.F.M. Cap., of Philadelphia. The first Native American prelate was Bishop Donald E. Pelotte, S.S.S., who served the Diocese of Gallup from 1990 to 2008.

Nativism

The social and political policy of favoring native inhabitants against immigrants and "foreigners," nativism was manifested throughout much of American history, with anti-Catholic bigotry one of the key components of its appeal. The movement included severe prejudice and hostility toward all immigrants, including Jews, but the chief targets of nativism remained the Catholic immigrants who arrived in the United States throughout the nineteenth century seeking a better life.

Nativist tendencies were visible from the earliest days of the English colonies, most notable among the Puritans in New England in the seventeenth century. They feared and were suspicious of any form of papist plot, scheming priest, or active Catholic missionary. In this view, chief among the immigrants who were likely agents or supporters of papism were Irish Catholics, as well as German Catholics. The Catholic population remained small in the colonies, numbering barely 35,000 in 1790 and concentrated chiefly in Pennsylvania and Maryland.

The rise in immigrant population proved steady over the next decades, however, with Catholics making up the majority of new arrivals. The appearance of so many immigrants came at a time when anti-Catholic fervor was also on the rise for a variety of reasons. Among these were the success of the Catholic Church in establishing an effective hierarchy; the defeat of Protestant-supported trusteeism, such as in Philadelphia; the hostile reaction to the Catholic Emancipation Act in England in 1829; the popular preaching of bigoted Protestants and Tractarian societies; the vocal efforts of Catholic newspapers to respond to anti-Catholicism; and the exaggerated criticism of the First Provincial Council of Baltimore in 1829. Finally, there was the simple reality of the vast wave of immigration

— 600,000 in the 1830s, 1.5 million in the 1840s, and 2.5 million in the 1850s.

Various journals promoted anti-immigrant and anti-Catholic sentiment. Jesuits were targets of supposed exposés revealing their conspiracies, and Catholics were condemned for being servants of foreign powers. The New York Protestant Association of William C. Brownlee helped to organize protests against immigrants, and the fierce rhetoric of the times led to riots and extended periods of violence. In 1830 the Protestant Association was established to fight against "Romish corruption," and in 1834 the Ursuline convent in Charlestown, Massachusetts, was burned to the ground. The publication in 1836 of the *Awful Disclosures of Maria Monk, or, The Hidden Secrets of a Nun's Life in a Convent Exposed*, by Maria Monk, was used as further inspiration against Catholics. (*See also* Monk, Maria.) Also, in 1834, there appeared the nativist "Brutus" letters in the *New York Observer* that led to the publication of Samuel F. B. Morse's *Imminent Dangers to the Free Institutions of the United States through Foreign Immigration* under the pseudonym "An American."

The popular social sentiment against immigrants led to the rise of a political movement to rid "native Americans" of the threat of unwanted (Catholic) immigrants who were flooding American shores and were the refuse of Europe. One of the earliest issues was that of the rumor that Catholics were planning to seize the Mississippi Valley through the arrival of so many foreigners, an unfounded claim that inspired Lyman Beecher's *A Plea for the West*. Most important was the formation in 1835 of the nativist American Democratic Association in New York. Similar groups were formed in various cities, including Cincinnati, Philadelphia, and New Orleans, and in 1843 organizers launched the American Republican Party in New York City. Renamed the Native American Party, the group displayed great strength in the elections of spring 1844 and spread their anti-immigrant and anti-Catholic platform to nearby states, including Massachusetts, New Jersey, Pennsylvania, and South Carolina. Further hostilities erupted when Bishop (later Archbishop) John Hughes of New York demanded in 1842 a fair share of public school funds. The result was action by the New York Leg-islature to create local school boards and to remove control of public education from the Public School Society (hence ending the presence of Protestant textbooks and Bibles in public schools).

The bloody riots and deaths in Philadelphia in 1844 caused a national backlash against the nativists, but decline did not set in until after 1850, when larger issues eclipsed temporarily the concerns of anti-immigrant voices. These included the move west and above all the issue of slavery. Continued immigration once more encouraged nativists, and in the 1850s the Know-Nothings gained a foothold in the political life of the country. (*See also* Know-Nothing Movement.)

Anti-immigrant and anti-foreign fervor were still prevalent in the 1850s, as demonstrated by the protests and angry marches against Archbishop Gaetano Bedini, the papal nuncio to Brazil and extraordinary envoy to the United States. Throughout his visit, he was burned in effigy and given a hostile reception. The following year, the Know-Nothings began a series of political successes, capturing several statehouses and sending members to Congress. The movement then suffered a severe setback in 1856 when the American Party candidate, Millard Fillmore, was crushed in the presidential election. American political life was then dominated by the issue of slavery and the move to civil war.

Nativism reappeared in the late nineteenth century with the next great wave of immigration, taking shape in the Ku Klux Klan, anti-immigrant legislation, and the obstacles to Catholic education that had emerged during the administration of President Ulysses Grant. Similarly, anti-foreign sentiment was present during the 1928 and 1960 presidential campaigns.

Neale, Leonard (October 15, 1746–June 18, 1817)

The second archbishop of Baltimore ,from 1815 to 1817, Leonard Neale was born near Port Tobacco, Charles County, Maryland, and was a descendant of Captain James Neale, who had settled in Maryland around 1642. Leonard was sent to the Jesuit College at St. Omer in French Flanders, and studied in Bruges and Liège, where he was ordained a Jesuit priest. Following the suppression of the Jesuits in 1774, Father Neale, with the English Jesuits, sailed to England, where he served for four years in pastoral work. Eventually, however, his request to serve in the missions was accepted, and he received assignment to Demarara in British Guiana, South America, and served there from 1779 to 1783.

Returning to America in January 1783, he was welcomed back among the former Jesuits, including then Father John Carroll. That same year, he replaced several priests who died from a yellow fever epidemic in Philadelphia, and received appointment as vicar general by Bishop Carroll after the latter was named bishop of Baltimore. In 1798 Bishop Carroll asked Father Neale to assume the presidency of Georgetown College. In the meantime, Bishop Carroll requested Rome to have Father Neale appointed as his coadjutor. Carroll subsequently consecrated him a bishop in 1800, although Bishop Neale remained president of Georgetown until 1806, when he was succeeded by Father Robert Molyneux.

Upon the death of Archbishop Carroll on December 3, 1815, Bishop Neale acceded to the see of Baltimore and received the pallium from Pope Pius VII the following year. By the time of his accession, Neale was already nearly seventy years old and had survived a bout of yellow fever in Philadelphia. He preferred to live, for reasons of health, at Georgetown, traveling to Baltimore for the fulfillment of his episcopal duties. Owing to his poor health, his time as archbishop proved a brief one. He petitioned Rome to name Bishop Jean-Louis Lefebvre de Cheverus of Boston his assistant in diocesan administration. This plan was not supported by Bishop de Cheverus, who suggested instead that a coadjutor be appointed. Archbishop Neale then proposed Father Ambrose Maréchal, a priest accepted by the Holy See. Archbishop Neale, however, died at Georgetown before the formal brief of Pope Pius VII arrived in the United States.

Nebraska

Called the Cornhusker State, Nebraska is located in the north-central part of the United States. It is bounded on the north by South Dakota, on the east by Iowa and Missouri, on the south by Kansas and Colorado, and on the west by Wyoming. Nebraska has two natural land regions: the Missouri Lowlands in the east and the Great Plains,

which comprise over 75 percent of the state, in the west. The original inhabitants of Nebraska included the Apache, Cheyenne, Dakota, Missouri, Omaha, Pawnee, Ponca, and Sioux. Nebraska entered the Union in 1867.

The Catholic heritage of Nebraska dates to the early 1540s when Francisco Vázquez de Coronado led a gold-hunting expedition into the area. His expedition was accompanied by Franciscans, two of whom remained in present-day Nebraska when Coronado withdrew. Franciscan Father Juan de Padilla was slain in the region, becoming the protomartyr of the United States.

In 1682 René-Robert Chevalier, Sieur de La Salle, entered present-day Nebraska, claiming all lands drained by the Mississippi River for France. In 1720 Lieutenant Colonel Pedro de Villasur and Franciscan Father Juan Mingues were in the region and were slain in a Pawnee attack. Soon after, Pierre and Paul Mallet opened a fur-trading business and explored the plains.

From 1754 to 1763 the French and Indian War raged across several territories, halting explorations and settlements. France ceded Nebraska and other lands to Spain for a brief period, but then reclaimed them and sold them to the United States as part of the Louisiana Purchase of 1803.

The Lewis and Clark expedition soon after the Louisiana Purchase opened the region of the future Nebraska, and fur trappers began their own explorations. In 1808 Manuel Lisa established trading posts along the Missouri River, and the Oregon Trail was opened by Robert Stuart in 1812. Others, including John C. Fremont, were also exploring the region.

In 1857 Nebraska became part of the vicariate apostolic administered by Jesuit Bishop Jean Baptiste Miège. Four years later, the Nebraska Territory established by the U.S. Congress was opened to white settlements. The first Catholic Mass in Nebraska was celebrated by the revered Jesuit Father Pierre-Jean De Smet.

In 1856 Father Jeremiah Tracy led a wagon train into the territory and founded St. Patrick's Colony in northeast Nebraska. In 1858 German settlers founded Argo in the southern part of the present-day state, and three years later Benedictine Emmanuel Hartig was on the scene. St. John's

Fountain Bluff settlement was abandoned by many, but some farmers remained. The discovery of gold in Colorado in 1859 brought vast numbers into the territory. By 1870 Holt County was thriving, founded by the towns of Connor and Spalding. The Union Pacific Railway also delivered new settlers every month.

The Trappist Bishop James Miles O'Gorman served as vicar apostolic from 1859 to 1874, facing a lack of priests and funds. Bishop James O'Connor assumed the role of vicar apostolic in 1876. On October 2, 1885, the Diocese of Omaha was erected, and two years later the Diocese of Lincoln was established, followed by the Diocese of Kearney, which became the Diocese of Grand Island in 1917. The slavery question delayed Nebraska's entry into the Union, but in 1867 it became the thirty-seventh state. The grasshopper plague of the 1870s was followed by a drought and economic depression.

The Church labored to provide pastoral care to Nebraskans during these difficult times. In 1917 Father Edward Flanagan founded Boys Town, and a year later the Chinese Mission Society was started to train priests for the evangelization of China. During the 1930s, when the nation was gripped in the Great Depression, Nebraska suffered another period of severe drought. Many left the state, hoping to rebuild their lives elsewhere. Bishop Joseph Francis Rummel led the Diocese of Omaha and established the Catholic Board of Child Welfare in 1933.

On August 10, 1945, Omaha was elevated to the rank of an archdiocese, and Bishop James Hugh Ryan was promoted as the ordinary. Over the next years, the Church in Nebraska continued to serve the declining rural populations and parishes and instituted programs for ethnic newcomers. The reforms and programs of the Second Vatican Council were also introduced throughout the state. The Pope Paul VI Institute was started in 1985. The Diocese of Nebraska pioneered programs for the promotion of the faith, and Lincoln opened St.

Gregory the Great Seminary in 1997. Three bishops of Nebraska joined together in 2000 to support a proposed "Defense of Marriage," a referendum concerning a state law on marriage. In 2011 there were 373,000 Catholics, 493 priests, 575 women religious, and 301 parishes in the state.

Nerinckx, Charles (October 2, 1761–August 12, 1824)

A missionary priest best known for his labors in Kentucky, Charles Nerinckx also founded the Sisters of Loretto at the Foot of the Cross. A native of Herffelingen, Belgium, he was the eldest of fourteen children; two of his six brothers were priests, and three of his seven sisters became nuns. Nerinckx studied at the American College of Louvain and entered the seminary of Mechlin in 1781. Ordained on November 1, 1785, he became vicar at the cathedral of Mechlin and then a pastor at Everberg-Meerbeke.

In 1793 the forces of the French Revolution forced him to go into hiding, and he remained in danger of his life for many years. In 1804 Father Nerinckx sailed to the United States after becoming committed to serving in the missions. Bishop (later Archbishop) John Carroll assigned him to Kentucky in 1805 to assist the famed missionary priest Stephen T. Badin; the area of his ministry covered nearly half the state.

Charles Nerinckx

Over the next years, Father Nerinckx earned the title of "Apostle of Kentucky." He was well known for his powerful stamina as well as his pastoral zeal, and such was his reputation that Bishop Carroll encouraged the Vatican to appoint him bishop of New Orleans; Father Nerinckx, however, refused the honor. Convinced of the need for education, he founded the Congregation of the Sisters of Loretto at the Foot of the Cross in 1812. He also attempted, unsuccessfully, to launch two other religious communities.

After disagreements with his bishop, Father Nerinckx went to Missouri in 1824 with the intention of working among the Native Americans. He died that same year at Ste. Genevieve, Missouri. His remains were later brought back to the motherhouse at Loretto in Kentucky, where the Sisters erected a marble statue in his honor in 1910.

Neuhaus, Richard John (March 14, 1936–January 8, 2009)

A convert and a one-time Lutheran minister, Father Richard John Neuhaus was one of the great American Catholic minds of the twentieth century. The son of a Lutheran pastor, he was born March 14, 1936, in Pembroke, Ontario, Canada, and became a Lutheran minister in 1960, after studies at Concordia Theological Seminary in St. Louis. He ministered in Brooklyn, New York, and became a leading voice in the fields of civil rights, social justice, and opposition to the Vietnam War. He was adamantly opposed to the 1973 U.S. Supreme Court decision on abortion in *Roe v. Wade*. He founded the Center on Religion and Society at the Rockford Institute in 1984 and in 1989 started the Institute on Religion and Public Life and then its influential journal, *First Things*.

On September 8, 1990, he entered the Church and was ordained the next year by Cardinal John J. O'Connor as a priest of the Archdiocese of New York. An influential voice in the areas of bioethics, religion in society, and outreach between Catholics and evangelicals, he was deeply respected by Catholics and Protestants alike. A prolific writer, his work was widely read, and he earned considerable notoriety for stressing that the current pro-life struggle should be compared to the 1960s civil rights movement.

Neumann, John Nepomucene, St. (March 28, 1811–January 5, 1860)

The fourth bishop of Philadelphia and the first canonized American bishop, St. John Nepomucene Neumann was born in Bohemia, then part of the Austrian Empire. He studied at the school of Budweis and in 1831 entered the Budweis Seminary. He transferred to the University of Prague in 1833 and was a distinguished scholar, completing

St. John Neumann

his education there in 1835. While preparing for ordination, he was inspired to journey to America by the remarkable letters sent by Father Irenaeus Frederick Baraga (later bishop of Marquette) to the Leopoldine Society. While preparing to travel to the United States, he desired to master both French and English. Discovering that such courses were not available, he taught himself and became fluent in both.

Arriving in America in 1836, he was ordained in New York on June 25 by Bishop John Dubois. His first priestly assignment was to Buffalo, where he served at North Bush (now Kenmore), Williamsville, Lancaster, and other parishes. In 1840 he joined the Redemptorists and became the first of their number to be professed in America in 1842. He served in Baltimore and in 1844 became Redemptorist superior of St. Philomena's Church in Pittsburgh. In 1847 he became the Redemptorist superior in America; the next year he was made vice provincial, and he labored to stabilize the congregation's school system and finances. He also published two catechisms and a German history of the Bible.

In 1849 St. John was replaced by a new vice provincial and served as pastor at St. Alphonsus Church in Baltimore in 1851. Pope Blessed Pius IX, at the suggestion of Archbishop Francis P. Kenrick of Baltimore, appointed St. John as bishop of Philadelphia; he was consecrated a bishop on March 28, 1852.

St. John was a profound theologian and was fluent in eight modern languages, as well as Latin, Hebrew, and Greek. As bishop, he worked strenuously to improve education; at the time of his consecration there were two parochial schools in the diocese, but by the time of his death they numbered nearly a hundred, making him an important figure in the organization of the American Catholic school system. He erected some fifty churches and advanced the work on the city's cathedral. He was the first American bishop to introduce the Forty Hours devotion, in 1853.

St. Charles Borromeo Seminary, which had been founded in 1852, benefited from St. John's interest, as he raised the academics and discipline at the institution. He also established the preparatory college seminary at Glen Riddle.

Having had a major role in the First Plenary Council of Baltimore in 1852, he was invited to Rome by Pope Pius IX in 1854 to take part in the formal definition of the dogma on the Immaculate Conception.

St. John died in Philadelphia and was buried in a vault before the altar in the lower chapel of St. Peter's Church. He left few published works: two catechisms of Christian doctrine, a Bible history, confraternity manuals, a Latin Forty Hours pamphlet, and acts of the diocesan synods. On December 15, 1896, he received the title of venerable and was beatified by Pope Paul VI on October 13, 1963. He was canonized on June 19, 1977. His feast day is January 5.

Nevada

Called the Silver State, Nevada is located in the western part of the United States. It is bounded on the north by Oregon and Idaho, on the east by Utah and Arizona, and on the south and west by California. Nevada is part of the Great Basin and has mesas, buttes, and deserts. The Sierra Nevada Mountains rise in the southwestern region of the state. The original inhabitants of Nevada were the Bannock, Paiute, Shoshone, and Washoe Indians.

The Catholic heritage of Nevada began in 1775, when Franciscan Fathers Pedro Font and Francisco Garcés crossed the southern part of the state with the expedition of Juan Bautista de Anza. Going from Santa Fe to Los Angeles, the Franciscans opened the Old Spanish Trail. Father Garcés celebrated a Mass in present-day Laughlin. A year later, Father Francisco Atanasio Domínguez and fur trappers began to enter the area, and, with Father Silvestre Velez de Escalante, he journeyed from New Mexico across the Virgin River and into Utah. In 1825 Peter Ogden and a group of trappers explored the northeastern part of Nevada, followed by Jedediah Smith, who traced the earlier Franciscan route. The Old Spanish Trail became popular, and in the 1840s John C. Fremont and Kit Carson charted the region around present-day Las Vegas.

The region was under the ecclesiastical jurisdiction of Mexico and remained part of the Diocese of Sonora until 1840, when it was placed under the jurisdiction of Bishop Francisco Garcia Diego y Moreno, O.F.M., the first bishop of California. Soon after, it became part of the Diocese of Monterey in California, until the Archdiocese of San Francisco was established in 1853 under its first archbishop, Joseph Sadoc Alemany.

In 1848 the Treaty of Guadalupe-Hidalgo made the area part of the United States, and the discovery of gold in California made the Old Spanish Trail even more popular with miners moving toward the newly opened fields of gold. In 1849 the Mormons were in present-day Genoa, called Mormon Station, but moved north. A decade later, gold was discovered in Virginia City, which brought about a tremendous influx of miners, adventurers, and settlers.

In 1860 the territory north of the 39th parallel and west of the boundary of Utah was placed under the Vicariate Apostolic of Marysville with the remaining territory still under the Archdiocese of San Francisco. In 1886 the Vicariate Apostolic of Salt Lake City was launched, later becoming the Diocese of Las Vegas. The first vicar was Father Lawrence Scanlan. He founded the parish of Pioche and was the pioneer priest and bishop for most of southern and eastern Nevada, including White Pine, Nye, Lincoln, and later Clark Counties in the Diocese of Salt Lake City.

On March 2, 1861, the Nevada Territory was separated from the Utah Territory and adopted its current name, shortened from Sierra Nevada. Nevada was established on October 31, 1864, and entered the Union as the thirty-sixth state. The silver and gold found in Nevada aided the Union in the Civil War, but in 1873 Congress placed the nation on the gold standard. Nevadans called the coinage act the "Crime of '73," as silver-mining cities collapsed and disappeared.

The silver rush, however, had attracted Catholic settlers, and in 1880 Father Joseph Gallagher established a parish in Virginia City, and in the following year built the first Catholic church at Genoa. Father Patrick Manogue, who would become a bishop, pioneered in Virginia City in 1881, becoming legendary for his tenacity, energetic Catholicism, and administrative skills. Parts of Nevada were eventually attached in the Dioceses of Sacramento and Salt Lake City.

In the early 1900s, new silver deposits were found at Tonopah and gold was being mined at Goldfield. Ely also had copper deposits. Father James Dermody built a parish at Goldfield and served the area. Nevada's mines were important assets as America entered World War I, but the demand declined at the war's end and the faithful of the area suffered during the Great Depression.

Unregulated gambling was permitted in the early mining camps, but this was banned in 1909. In order to improve the economy, Nevada legalized gambling in 1931. Although considered a temporary measure, legalized gambling became a fixture in the state and eventually became Nevada's primary source of revenue.

In 1931 Pope Pius XI established the Diocese of Reno, and the first bishop was Thomas K. Gorman. During this period, Hoover Dam was constructed near Las Vegas, and Nellis Air Force Base was opened. The state responded to the demands of World War II, and mines and industries flourished. After the war, tourism and cattle raising prospered as well. The population base shifted significantly in the second half of the twentieth century toward southern Nevada.

In 1951 Bishop Gorman was transferred to Dallas-Fort Worth and was succeeded by Bishop Robert J. Dwyer in August 1952. Bishop Dwyer presided over the expansion of schools and churches and the renovation of St. Thomas Aquinas Cathedral in Reno. In 1966 he was appointed archbishop of Portland in Oregon and was succeeded by Bishop Joseph Green from Lansing, Michigan. Bishop Green had the difficult task of implementing the reforms of the Second Vatican Council and ultimately retired in 1974.

Bishop Norman F. McFarland, auxiliary bishop of San Francisco, became the next bishop in April 1974 and was faced with an immediate financial crisis. Having resolved the diocesan finances, he subsequently petitioned Pope Paul VI to redesignate the Diocese of Reno as the Diocese of Reno-Las Vegas, with Guardian Angel Shrine in Las Vegas as the cathedral. The petition was accepted in October 1976. Five years later, the Church in Nevada celebrated its Jubilee.

On December 29, 1986, Bishop McFarland was appointed to the Diocese of Orange, and on June 9, 1987, Pope Blessed John Paul II named Bishop Daniel F. Walsh, then auxiliary bishop of San Francisco, as the fifth bishop of the Diocese of Reno-Las Vegas. Bishop Walsh labored to develop the Church in Nevada to keep pace with the phenomenal growth in population, and within the decade ten new churches were built. Bishop Walsh also launched Hispanic ministry to provide for the pastoral care of Spanish-speaking Catholics. On March 31, 1995, Pope Blessed John Paul II split the state of Nevada into two dioceses, establishing the Dioceses of Reno and Las Vegas. Bishop Phillip F. Straling was named the first bishop or Reno. He retired in 2005 and was succeeded by Bishop Randolph R. Calvo. Bishop Daniel F. Walsh was named the first bishop of Las Vegas. He was succeeded by Bishop Joseph A. Pepe in 2001.

The Church in Nevada has worked to assist the pastoral needs of the many thousands of Nevadans hard hit by the economic downturn since 2008 and the large number of foreclosed houses resulting from the collapse of the housing bubble. In 2011 there were 700,000 Catholics, 95 priests, and 56 parishes in the diocese.

Newark, Archdiocese of

Established as a diocese on July 29, 1853, by Pope Blessed Pius IX, Newark was designated as a metropolitan provincial see by Pope Pius XI on December 10, 1937. It serves counties in central New Jersey and has suffragan sees.

Puritans from Connecticut founded Newark in 1666 on land leased from the local Native American tribe and was originally named Pesayak Towne, then Milford. Becoming Newark, the city was chartered in 1693. After the Revolutionary War, Newark developed slowly, becoming a center for leather goods. The city emerged as a transportation hub and as a major port and distribution center.

New Jersey had become a royal colony in 1702 and was never a haven for Catholics, but priest pioneers made their way to Newark, including Father Ferdinand Steinmeyer, known as "Father Farmer." Jesuit Father Theodore Schneider was also serving in the area. Jesuits had been in the region earlier but had been outlawed by the government. In 1780

Catholic officers and nobles from France settled in New Jersey despite the discriminatory laws enacted by the state.

In 1826 St. John's Parish was opened in Newark and developed an active Catholic populace. The Catholics of northern New Jersey were initially placed under the jurisdiction of the Archdiocese of New York, while the Catholics in southern New Jersey were under the direction of the Diocese of Philadelphia. Catholics, however, did not enjoy full legal rights as citizens in New Jersey until 1844.

The Diocese of Newark was first established in 1853 through a papal brief of Pope Blessed Pius IX to include all of New Jersey. Bishop James Roosevelt Bayley, a convert and nephew of St. Elizabeth Ann Seton, was named the first bishop. Bishop Bayley had been an Episcopalian minister prior to his conversion in 1842; he was ordained on March 2, 1844, in New York. On October 30, 1853, Bishop Bayley was consecrated and then set to work to give the new diocese a firm foundation. He focused especially on Catholic education, and in 1857 he invited a group of Benedictine Sisters from Pennsylvania. They were the first of many communities of religious men and women who settled in the diocese. Bishop Bayley also opened a Catholic college on August 31, 1856, Chegary Academy (Old Seton Hall) in Madison; in 1860 the school moved to its present location in South Orange and was incorporated into a college by the state of New Jersey in 1861. Bishop Bayley was also instrumental in the establishment of the North American College in Rome. The first student he sent to Rome was Michael A. Corrigan. When Bishop Bayley was appointed archbishop of Baltimore on July 30, 1872, Corrigan, who was now a bishop, succeeded him.

Bishop Corrigan was consecrated the second bishop of Newark on May 4, 1873. At the age of thirty-four, Corrigan was the youngest bishop in the United States. The new bishop faced a variety of challenges, including the Panic of 1873. He founded the Catholic Protectory for the care of orphan boys and girls. He also presided over the start of St. Peter's College in Jersey City in September 1878, before his appointment in 1880 as coadjutor to Cardinal John McCloskey in New York.

He was succeeded by Bishop Winand M. Wig-

ger, who was consecrated the third bishop of Newark on October 18, 1881. He served at a time of phenomenal growth in the diocese and faced difficulties from German Catholics, who resented the Americanization of their parishes in the diocese. In January 1898 Bishop Wigger broke ground for a new cathedral on land purchased decades before by Bishop Bayley. He also convened three diocesan synods and was a dedicated opponent of the Americanist trends in late nineteenth-century American Catholicism. During his time, too, the state was divided into two dioceses. Bishop Wigger died on January 5, 1901.

Bishop John J. O'Connor was consecrated the fourth bishop of Newark on July 25, 1901, by Archbishop Corrigan. Like Bishop Wigger, Bishop O'Connor's term was marked by the massive increase in population in the period before World War I and its aftermath. Indeed, the Catholic population of the diocese more than doubled during his tenure. He campaigned for funds in order to complete the cathedral and to revitalize the seminary. He also built many parishes and schools and introduced the Holy Name Society in the diocese, as well as the Confraternity of Christian Doctrine. He died on the campus of Seton Hall on May 20, 1927.

Bishop Thomas J. Walsh, the bishop of Trenton, was appointed the fifth bishop of Newark on March 2, 1928. Bishop Walsh inaugurated the new cathedral and was installed on May 1, 1928. During his time, the diocese was divided again in 1937 to form the Paterson diocese, and in the same year the Newark diocese was elevated to the rank of archdiocese and Bishop Walsh was appointed archbishop on December 10, 1937. He was installed on April 27, 1938, in the cathedral. Deeply committed to Catholic education, he raised $2 million in twenty-five days to build the Immaculate Conception Seminary in 1936, and promoted Seton Hall College. In addition, he revitalized the sacred liturgy in the diocese and introduced the Mount Carmel Guild and its publications; he also launched the diocesan newspaper, *The Advocate*, which first appeared on December 30, 1951. Archbishop Walsh died on June 6, 1952, and was buried in the cathedral crypt.

Archbishop Thomas A. Boland was installed as

the second archbishop of Newark on January 14, 1953. He had served from 1940 to 1947 as auxiliary bishop of Newark and bishop of Paterson from 1947. Archbishop Boland took part in the Second Vatican Council in Rome. He was elected to head the Bishops' Study Committee and was reelected for the next three years. He served also as a member of the Catholic Mission Board of the United States, chair of the Episcopal Committee, and liaison between women religious and the hierarchy of the United States. Over the years after the council, Archbishop Boland was active in the civil rights movement and urged compliance with the 1958 "Bishops' Letter on Social Justice." He also dedicated the Cathedral of the Sacred Heart on October 19, 1954. Archbishop Boland retired on April 2, 1974, and died on March 16, 1979. He was buried in Sacred Heart Cathedral's crypt.

Bishop Peter L. Gerety of Portland, Maine, was appointed the third archbishop of Newark on April 2, 1974, and installed on June 28, 1974. Gerety had been bishop of Portland since 1969. His first task was to alleviate the debt of the archdiocese, and in 1975 he began the Archbishop's Annual Appeal, which raised sufficient funds. He also promoted ecumenism and charismatic programs, and to assist parish renewal he created the Office of Pastoral Renewal. In 1976 he sent a letter protesting the Democratic Party platform's position on abortion at the Democratic National Convention. Archbishop Gerety retired on June 1, 1986.

Bishop Theodore E. McCarrick was appointed the fourth archbishop of Newark on May 30, 1986, and was installed on July 25, 1986. He had served as auxiliary bishop of New York from 1977 to 1981 and first bishop of Metuchen, from 1981 to 1986. As archbishop, McCarrick focused on ministries to provide for the pastoral care of Hispanics. He also established an office for the care of people infected with HIV, a comprehensive drug prevention program, and an Office of Evangelization. At the same time, he served as chairman of the United States Conference of Catholic Bishops' Committee on Aid to the Church in Central and Eastern Europe from 1992 to 1997, was twice elected to head the USCCB's Committee on Migration, and was named by Pope Blessed John Paul II to the Pontifical Commission for the Pastoral Care of Migrants and Itinerant Peoples. In 1994 he summoned the Tenth Archdiocesan Synod and issued the "Pastoral Letter in Response to the Synod." The following year he hosted Mother Teresa and then Pope Blessed John Paul II during his visit in October. Following the papal visit, the cathedral was declared the Cathedral Basilica of the Sacred Heart. On November 21, 2000, Archbishop McCarrick was named to head the Archdiocese of Washington, D.C. He was installed as the fourth archbishop of Washington on January 4, 2001, and was elected to the College of Cardinals on February 21, 2001.

Bishop John J. Myers was appointed the fifth archbishop to the Archdiocese of Newark on July 24, 2001, and installed on October 9 in the Cathedral Basilica of the Sacred Heart. He had served previously as coadjutor bishop of Peoria from 1987 to 1990 and bishop of Peoria from 1990. His installation was held only weeks after the terrible events of September 11, an event that had impacted many in the archdiocese. He issued a pastoral letter on the one-month anniversary of the tragedy, "If God Is for Us, Who Can Be Against Us? Reflections on Faith and Terrorism." Archbishop Myers subsequently released additional pastoral letters, including "A Reason for the Hope That Lies Within Us," which addressed the role of the Church of Newark within the context of the greater Church in the United States and the universal Church; it was followed by "And the Word Became Flesh: A Theological Reflection on the Human Body," reflecting the Church's teaching on the human body and human sexuality. Archbishop Myers was also heavily involved in crafting the USCCB's response to the sex abuse crisis in the United States. In 2011 there were 1.3 million Catholics, 900 priests, 874 women religious, and 220 parishes in the archdiocese.

New Hampshire

Called the Granite State, New Hampshire is located in the northeastern part of the United States. It is bounded on the north by Canada, on the east by Maine and the Atlantic Ocean, on the south by Massachusetts, and on the west by Vermont. New Hampshire has three natural land regions: the White Mountains in the north, the New England Uplands in the south, and the Seaboard Lowlands in the southeast. The original inhabitants of New Hampshire were the Abenaki, the Piscataqua, and the Bannock confederacy.

The Catholic history of New Hampshire dates to 1605 when the French explorers Samuel de Champlain explored the coast. Martin Pring, an Englishman, had sailed to the mouth of the Piscataqua River two years earlier. The British took possession of New Hampshire during the reign of King James I, and Ferdinando Gorges and John Mason received a land grant for the region in 1622. Present-day Rye was a settlement by 1623, founded by David Thomson, and other communities were formed soon after. New Hampshire became a royal colony in 1679.

In 1694 the first Mass was celebrated by Jesuits at Durham. These Jesuits were part of a French military expedition in the area during King William's War. The colony of New Hampshire was involved in continuing battles between the French and English. The Indian allies of the French were dangerous perils to settlements. In New Hampshire, there was a ban on all Catholic priests, and the penalty for such priests could be death. Catholics in the colony faced the Toleration Act, which decreed that members of the Roman Catholic Church had to swear disloyalty to the pope and to doctrines of the faith. In time Catholics were banned "from Command and Places of Trust," which meant that they could not hold any government or military office.

One of the thirteen colonies, New Hampshire took part in the Revolutionary War and entered the Union on June 21, 1788. The revised state constitution eased some restrictions against Catholics. Father Jean-Louis Lefebvre de Cheverus, who would become the bishop of the Diocese of Boston and a cardinal and Peer of France, worked with Father Francis A. Matignon in scattered New Hampshire settlements. They were at Portsmouth on their tour of the state. In 1808 the Diocese of Boston (now an archdiocese) was erected, and Bishop de Cheverus had ecclesiastical jurisdiction over the Catholics of New Hampshire.

In 1816 Virgil Barber, a member of a family that converted from the Episcopalian Church, entered the faith. Ordained a Jesuit, he founded a church and an academy at Claremont, the first such facilities in the state. In Dover, Father Charles Ffrench founded a parish in 1828, and Father William McDonald was the first permanent priest in Manchester. He opened St. Joseph's, the present cathedral, in 1869. Franciscan Father John B. Daly served there for almost two decades.

In 1853 the Diocese of Portland in Maine was founded, and Catholic matters in New Hampshire were administered from that diocese. Catholics were under attack by the Know-Nothing Movement and then by the American Protective Association and the Ku Klux Klan. The 1877 state constitution provided Catholics with true civil rights and offered some protection against Protestant nativism. In Manchester, St. Augustine's Parish was serving the Catholic populace, and New Hampshire received a large influx of French Catholics.

The Diocese of Manchester was established on May 4, 1884, by Pope Leo XIII, and the appointed bishop was Denis M. Bradley, who brought energy and leadership to the area. He is reported to have opened thirty-four new parishes and a large number of schools. The Benedictines and the Sister Adorers of the Precious Blood arrived soon after the diocese was erected. The third bishop of Manchester, Bishop George Albert Guertin, faced a coalition of Protestants who wanted the faithful to leave New Hampshire. Bishop Guertin also dealt with national churches within the diocese while leading the faithful through World War I. The influenza epidemic of 1918 brought suffering to the people of New Hampshire, and the Catholic Church mobilized to care for the stricken. Bishop Guertin also faced the calamitous Great Depression that crippled the nation.

Portsmouth had become a vital military site during World War I, and the Treaty of Portsmouth in 1905 had settled the Russo-Japanese War. During the Great Depression, Portsmouth and other areas of the state faced economic struggle. The state subsequently enjoyed a revival of the leather and textile industries. These collapsed in the postwar years, but the state enjoyed a considerable revival through high technology and service industries.

In 1959 Bishop Ernest J. Primeau of Manchester began his episcopal ministry and was thus leader of the Catholics in New Hampshire throughout the period of the Second Vatican Council and its difficult years after. He took part in the council and then returned to implement the mandated reforms. The era was a challenging one, and Bishop Primeau tried to weather the storms of difficulty as best he could. His successor was Bishop Odore J. Gendron, who led the diocese from 1975 to 1990 and hence much of the pontificate of Pope John Paul II. Under Bishop Leo E. O'Neil, bishop since 1990, and John B. McCormack, bishop since 1998, the Church in New Hampshire welcomed Eastern Europeans and Vietnamese into the area. Currently, Catholic comprise some 24 percent of the population, with some 313,000 Catholics, served by over 250 priests, over 500 men and women religious, and 108 parishes in the state.

New Jersey

Called the Garden State, New Jersey is located in the Middle Atlantic region of the United States. It is bounded on the north by New York, on the east by New York and the Atlantic Ocean, on the south by the Atlantic Ocean and Delaware Bay, and on the west by Delaware and Pennsylvania. There are four principal land regions in New Jersey: the Appalachian Valley in the north, the Atlantic Coastal Plain in the south, the New England Highlands, and the Piedmont Lowlands. The original inhabitants of New Jersey were members of the Delaware who called themselves the Lenni-Lenape.

The first European to explore present-day New Jersey was Giovanni da Verrazano, an Italian Catholic, who arrived in 1524. The Dutch, however, began settlements in the area soon after the exploration by Henry Hudson in 1609. Bergen, now Jersey City, was established in 1618. Peter Stuyvesant, the governor of the region, used an armed force to put an end to Swedish settlements nearby. Stuyvesant governed New Netherlands, so named by the Dutch. In 1664 he had to surrender to a British commander.

New Jersey was then divided into East Jersey and West Jersey, and Lord John Berkeley and Sir George Carteret were named proprietors and were mandated to begin English settlements. Lord Berkeley sold his share, and John Fenwick used the land to establish a Quaker settlement. Catholics arrived in the early 1670s, establishing a community at present-day Salem. In 1691, however, the regional legislature passed acts penalizing Catho-

lics, and Queen Anne, in 1702, made New Jersey a royal colony with religious freedom granted to all but "papists."

Father Theodore Schneider, who was also a physician, was able to serve Catholics of the Salem area because he was known as a medical man and not suspected of being a priest. Father John Ury was not as fortunate. He and fourteen others were executed for the "Negro Plot," a supposed plan to burn New York City. The revered Father Ferdinand Steinmeyer, "Father Farmer," labored with Father Robert Herding in New Jersey in the 1760s.

New Jersey declared its independence from Britain in 1776, and during the Revolutionary War battles were fought in the state at Trenton, Princeton, and Monmouth. Catholics were active and courageous in this period. The famous "Molly Pitcher," Mary McCauley, supplied American soldiers with water at the Battle of Monmouth.

In December 1787 New Jersey entered the Union as the third state. The region had been industrialized, and German Catholics had arrived on the scene to work in the new factories. Trenton experienced a vast rise of Catholics, and in 1814 the first Catholic Church in New Jersey was established in the growing city. In 1828 another church was opened in Newark. In the late 1840s Father Bernard J. McQuaid built the first Catholic school in Madison.

The Diocese of Newark was erected by the Holy See in 1853, and James Roosevelt Bayley, a convert and a nephew of St. Elizabeth Ann Seton, became the first bishop. He founded Seton Hall College and invited religious communities into the diocese. The Diocese of Trenton was established in 1881, and the first Catholic college for women, St. Elizabeth's, opened at Convent Station in 1899.

Various corporations were adding to New Jersey's economy, including John D. Rockefeller's Standard Oil Company, the Camden & Amboy Railroad, and the Pennsylvania Railroad. In 1910 Woodrow Wilson was elected governor, then president of the United States in 1912.

The Catholic Church had suffered indignities and even attacks, including the riot of September 1854, but the faithful prospered. Catholics served in World War I. New Jersey played a vital role in military defense programs, establishing not only the manufacturing of armaments but also serving as a training center and as a port of embarkation for U.S. troops. Catholics and their neighbors suffered during the Great Depression, but the Diocese of Newark became a metropolitan provincial see, and the Dioceses of Camden and Paterson were established. The Diocese of Metuchen was erected in 1981.

World War II once again mobilized the industries of New Jersey, and Catholics served in the vast military units in combat zone around the globe. Following the war, the state continued expanding industrially, and the Eparchy of Passaic for Byzantine Ruthenian Catholics was erected in 1963. The Eparchy of Our Lady of Deliverance for Syrian Catholics was established in 1995. The reforms of the Second Vatican Council were instituted throughout the state, and despite a loss in the number of priests and religious, the Catholics dioceses of New Jersey continue to flourish in the modern world. Currently, there are more than 3.5 million Catholics in New Jersey, over 52 percent of the total population in the state. They are served by over 2,100 priests, nearly 3,000 men and women religious, and 687 parishes.

New Mexico

Called the Land of Enchantment, New Mexico is located in the southwestern part of the United States. It is bounded on the north by Colorado, on the east by Oklahoma and Texas, on the south by Texas and Mexico, and on the west by Arizona. There are four natural land regions in New Mexico: the Great Plains in the east, the Rocky Mountains in the north-central area, the Colorado Plateau in the northwest, and the Basin and Range in the southwest. The original inhabitants of the New Mexico area were the Navajo, Pueblo, Hopi, Acoma, Apache, and numerous other tribes.

The Catholic history of New Mexico dates to 1530, when the Viceroy of Mexico sent Franciscan Father Marcos de Niza into modern-day New Mexico in search of Cibola, the legendary Seven Cities of Gold. Tales of such a site were brought to Mexico by survivors of the ill-fated expedition of Pánfilo de Narváez in Florida. Father de Niza was accompanied by one of the survivors, a Moor named Estebán, who was slain by the Zuñi. The

Franciscan is credited with the discovery of New Mexico and Arizona. He reportedly planted a cross in the area before moving southward, and claimed the region for Spain as the "New Kingdom of St. Francis."

A year later, Francisco Vázquez de Coronado led another expedition into New Mexico, accompanied by Franciscans. Father Juan de la Cruz was slain, becoming the first martyr of New Mexico, and Brother Luis de Escalona also died. The protomartyr of the United States, Juan de Padilla, was slain in Kansas in 1544, having traveled in the expedition.

In 1563 Francisco de Ibarra was in the area with another expedition, and he named the region New Mexico. In 1581 the Spanish explorer Antonio de Espejo renamed it Nueva Andalusia. The Franciscans, however, did not give up on the potential of the area and returned to begin missions. Fathers Francisco López, Agustin Rodriguez, and Juan de Santa Maria served the local tribes but were also martyred. In 1598 Juan de Oñate established a settlement called San Juan de los Caballeros on the east bank of the Rio Grande, but then moved to another site on the Rio Chama, called San Gabriel.

In 1610 the new governor, Pedro de Peralta, established a new Spanish capital in present-day New Mexico, La Villa Real de la Santa Fe de San Francisco de Asis. Missions were opened and more Franciscans sent to promote evangelization. In 1625 Franciscan Father Alonso de Benavides arrived in Santa Fe with a sacred image of the Blessed Virgin Mary, which is still venerated in the cathedral in Santa Fe.

On August 10, 1680, the Pueblo people of the region launched the Pueblo Indian Revolt of 1680 that drove the Spanish settlers out of New Mexico and resulted in the deaths of many Franciscan missionaries. The revolt also destroyed many churches and convents that had been built by the Franciscans during their missionary work. The Spanish subsequently retreated to the area of El Paso del Norte (present day El Paso-Juarez), where a mission had been established several years before.

In 1692 newly appointed Governor Diego de Vargas restored Spanish authority in New Mexico. This permitted a return of ecclesiastical structures, and missionaries reentered New Mexico in 1693.

The new Franciscan friars rebuilt the destroyed churches and established new ones throughout New Mexico. Santa Cruz was opened in 1695 and Albuquerque in 1706.

The region continued to prosper in comparative isolation for decades, as the rest of the nation experienced the Revolutionary War and the opening of new lands as a result of the Louisiana Purchase. New Mexico was in the ecclesiastical jurisdiction of the Diocese of Durango, but the local Franciscans regulated their affairs without interference. Episcopal jurisdiction was granted in 1797, and all the churches in New Mexico were secularized and made responsible to the bishop of Durango. When Mexico declared independence from Spain in 1821, the Franciscans lost their support and departed from New Mexico. The area remained part of the Diocese of Durango until 1850.

That year, the U.S. Congress established the New Mexico Territory, which included parts of Colorado and Arizona. The southern border with Mexico was settled in 1853. On July 19, 1850, Pope Pius IX created the Vicariate Apostolic of New Mexico and appointed Father Jean Baptiste Lamy as its first bishop. Bishop Lamy arrived in New Mexico in the summer of 1851. His early efforts were directed to the building of more churches, the creation of new parishes, and the establishment of educational and medical facilities.

During the Civil War, Confederate troops took Santa Fe and Albuquerque, and in 1862 the Union won a decisive battle at Glorietta. Kit Carson, a colonel, forced the Apache and Navajo Indians from their lands and onto reservations. In the 1870s the Lincoln County Cattle War was waged. In 1886 Geronimo was captured, bringing an end to the Apache Wars. The next years brought a concerted effort on the part of the federal government to take control of Native American populations and also to curb the unsettled social environment in the region among the white settlers and transients.

The development of the railways hastened the cattle boom of the 1880s and the rise of the cattle barons. The efforts to maintain control over the state for cattle created considerable conflict with the sheepherders, homesteaders, and squatters, although ranching remains today one of the pillars of the New Mexican economy.

By 1853 the vicariate apostolic had become a see in its own right, the Diocese of Santa Fe, and on February 12, 1875, the diocese was elevated to an archdiocese, with Jean Baptiste Lamy as its first archbishop. The size of the Archdiocese of Santa Fe required the establishment in 1868 of the Vicariate of Arizona and Colorado; they later became dioceses in their own right. In 1869 Bishop Lamy began building a stone cathedral to replace the old adobe church, parts of which had served the parishioners of Santa Fe since 1717 (the Conquistadora Chapel is all that remains). The new cathedral was

Isleta Pueblo in New Mexico

built around and over the old church, in the style of the Romanesque churches of France familiar to Bishop Lamy. By 1884 the main part of the cathedral was finished and the old church was torn down from under it.

The Sisters of Loretto and the Christian Brothers responded to Archbishop Lamy's call and began their apostolates in education. The Sisters of Charity and Jesuits also entered the diocese. Santa Fe became an archdiocese in 1875. The Franciscans also returned to New Mexico in 1900.

Archbishop Lamy died on February 14, 1888, and was buried under the sanctuary floor of his beloved cathedral. A bronze statue of him was placed in front of the cathedral on May 23, 1915. He was succeeded as archbishop of Santa Fe by John Baptist Salpointe.

World War I brought changes to New Mexico. Archbishop Jean Baptiste Pitaval, Archbishop Salpointe's successor, resigned, and in 1919 the Holy See appointed a Franciscan, Albert T. Daeger, as archbishop, and native young men were ordained to the priesthood. Following the war, New Mexico prospered until the Great Depression, which brought economic hardship everywhere.

On October 7, 1945, the Archdiocese of Santa Fe was solemnly consecrated to the Immaculate Heart of Mary, and in 1954, a Marian Year, Pope Blessed John XXIII formally crowned New Mexico's own image of the Blessed Virgin Mary, *La Conquistadora*, as queen of the archdiocese. In 1992 the title of "Our Lady of Peace" was added by Archbishop Robert F. Sanchez. The Catholic Church in New Mexico is deeply committed to the pastoral care of the large Hispanic and Native American populations within the state. Currently, the state of New Mexico has a population of nearly two million, of whom nearly 42 percent are Hispanic and approximately 11 percent are Native American. The Native American community is the third largest in the United States, behind Oklahoma and Alaska. Bishop Donald E. Pelotte, S.S.S., became the first priest of Native American ancestry to be named a bishop in the United States when he was appointed bishop of Gallup on March 20, 1990. In 2011 there were nearly half a million Catholics, 300 priests, 250 permanent deacons, over 400 men and women religious, and 191 parishes in the state.

New Orleans, Archdiocese of

Established as the Diocese of Louisiana and the Two Floridas by Pope Pius VI on April 25, 1793, and designated as the Diocese of New Orleans by Pope Leo XII on July 18, 1826, the diocese was erected as an archdiocese on July 19, 1850, by Pope Blessed Pius IX. Louisiana traces its origins to April 9, 1682, when René-Robert Chevalier, Sieur de La Salle, planted a cross on the soil of the future Louisiana and claimed the lower Mississippi Valley in the name of God and France. A Catholic colony soon started in what became New Orleans after 1718, established by Jean-Baptiste Le Moyne, Sieur de Bienville. Colorful and dynamic, New Orleans has always been blessed by its cultural and ethnic diversity and has survived natural disasters, climaxing historically with the devastation of Hurricane Katrina in 2005.

As early as 1526, explorers from Europe were in Louisiana. In that year, Alvar Nuñez Cabeza de Vaca led an expedition to the region. In 1541 Hernando de Soto was also conducting explorations there, but no settlements were established. In 1682 La Salle accompanied the Franciscan Recollect priests Zenobius Membré and Anastase Douay and claimed the region for France.

Pierre Le Moyne, Sieur d'Iberville, and his brother, Bienville, began developing the region and eventually founded New Orleans. Priests from the Québec Seminary began missions in the area, including Fathers François Jolliet de Montigny, Antoine Davion, and Jean-François Buisson de Saint-Cosmé, who were martyred near Donaldson in 1706. In 1700 Jesuit Father Paul Du Ru was at Bayou Gaule in Iberville Parish.

New Orleans was reportedly laid out by Adrien de Pauger, who designated the site for the Cathedral of St. Louis, which was completed in 1720. Other missions were founded in the region, and Recollect Franciscan Father Prothais Boyer became the first resident priest of New Orleans. In 1727 Ursuline nuns from France arrived in New Orleans to assume the direction of the Royal Hospital and also to provide education to the colony's girls and young women. Notable for the era was the fact that the Ursulines provided educational opportunities to African and Native American girls as well as the daughters of European settlers.

In 1758 the Acadians, who had been forced from their lands in the northeast by the British and taken to the colonies, found their way to New Orleans in large numbers. Five years later, the Jesuits were expelled from the territory. In 1771 the city became part of the Diocese of Santiago de Cuba, and in 1787, with the formation of the Diocese of San Cristobal of Havana, the region of Louisiana and the Two Floridas become part of the new diocese. In 1796 Spain was given possession of Louisiana in the Treaty of Fontainebleau.

The Cathedral of St. Louis was destroyed by fire in 1788 and rebuilt. The ecclesiastical authority of New Orleans at the time was Bishop Cirillo de Barcelona. In 1793 the Diocese of Louisiana and the Two Floridas was established by Pope Pius VI. Bishop Luis Ignacio Peñalver y Cardenas arrived in New Orleans on July 17, 1795, to assume the see. He celebrated Mass in the cathedral, which by then had been restored, and he built new parishes. Bishop Peñalver y Cardenas was transferred to Guatemala in 1801.

The 1803 Louisiana Purchase incorporated most of the Diocese of Louisiana and the Two Floridas into the United States. The boundaries were further delineated when Louisiana was admitted to the Union as a state in 1812. As a result of these developments, Bishop (later Archbishop) John Carroll received jurisdiction of Louisiana. Bishop Carroll appointed Bishop Louis Dubourg as apos-

Cathedral of St. Louis, New Orleans

tolic administrator, and he in turn recruited priests and religious for New Orleans. St. Rose Philippine Duchesne visited the city during that period. In 1821 a diocesan synod was also convened. Five years later, Bishop Dubourg resigned his office and went to France, where he became the archbishop of Besançon. On July 18, 1826, the Diocese of Louisiana and the Two Floridas was redesignated the Diocese of New Orleans.

The decades that followed the Louisiana Purchase marked a time of immense difficulty for the Church in Louisiana, owing to the absence of clear direction, an acute shortage of priests and religious, and the severe social problems in Louisiana. Reflecting the state of affairs, only one new parish was established in New Orleans in the thirty years following the Louisiana Purchase, St. Patrick in 1833, and only four rural parishes were established.

This situation began slowly to change. On March 25, 1824, Joseph Rosati, a Vincentian, was consecrated as the coadjutor bishop of New Orleans, but he was transferred to St. Louis on March 20, 1827. Another Vincentian, Leo-Raymond de Neckere, was consecrated as bishop of New Orleans on June 24, 1830, at the age of thirty, and began building parishes and facilities. Bishop de Neckere embraced his episcopal duties with immense vigor, but he died on September 4, 1833, from yellow fever.

Bishop (later Archbishop) Antoine Blanc was consecrated on November 22, 1835, as bishop of New Orleans. His long tenure marked the swift expansion of the Church in Louisiana and the elevation of the see to the rank of an archdiocese and metropolitan provincial see on July 19, 1850, with the province's suffragan sees including Natchez, Mobile, Galveston, and Little Rock. The Catholic population struggled against rampant anti-Catholicism in the northern parts of the state and the rise of the Know-Nothings and nativist anti-immigrant campaigns, as well as internal challenges from vexatious churchwardens who seized control of the Cathedral of St. Louis. There were also the chronic difficulties of yellow fever outbreaks that claimed the lives of clergy, religious, and laity, and had already taken Bishop de Neckere.

Archbishop Blanc also promoted Catholic education, promoted greater influxes of religious and clergy, and supervised the development of the Church in Texas. He likewise convened two diocesan synods and two provincial councils and presided over the expansion of parishes, schools, orphanages, and hospitals.

With the improvement in the ecclesiastical situation, the far-flung archdiocese was divided to permit the creation of other dioceses for the better pastoral care of the Catholics and people of Louisiana and Mississippi. In 1837 the Diocese of Natchez, comprising the state of Mississippi, was established. In 1853 the Diocese of Natchitoches was formed to serve northern Louisiana.

In 1838 Bishop Blanc opened the first diocesan seminary under the direction of Vincentian Fathers. The Jesuits came back to Louisiana in 1837 and started a college at Grand Coteau. They were followed by the Redemptorists, who started their first parish in New Orleans in 1843. Meanwhile, the Ursulines, Religious of the Sacred Heart, Sisters of Mount Carmel, and Daughters of Charity all increased their important work in the city and area, and they were joined over the next years by the Marianites of Holy Cross, Christian Brothers, School Sisters of Notre Dame, Sisters of St. Joseph, Sisters of the Good Shepherd, and Dominican Sisters from Cabra, Ireland. The Sisters of the Holy Family, a community of African-American women, also began in 1836, and the archdiocese began the cause for canonization of their foundress, Henriette DeLille, in 1988.

Archbishop Blanc died suddenly on June 2, 1860. He was succeeded by the French-born Archbishop John M. Odin, a Vincentian who had served as vicar apostolic of Texas from 1842 to 1847 and as bishop of Galveston since 1847. Archbishop Odin was appointed on February 15, 1861, and took possession of his new see immediately after the start of the Civil War. He thus served as archbishop during an immensely difficult period. He was an outspoken advocate of peace and an end to hostilities. He permitted several priests of the archdiocese to serve as Confederate Army chaplains, and the Daughters of Charity volunteered for city and battlefield hospitals in Alabama, Louisiana, Florida, Mississippi, and Virginia, even as they continued their remarkable work caring for the sick of the city.

New Orleans was occupied by Union forces on May 1, 1862, under General Benjamin Butler, and there was much devastation caused in the state from the fighting. Parish churches, convents, and schools were destroyed, damaged, or sequestered for use by the two armies. Union forces forbade the publication of *Le Propagateur Catholique*, the archdiocesan newspaper, and its editor, Father Napoléon Perché (the future archbishop), was placed under house arrest.

The war nevertheless brought progress in the growth of new parishes outside of New Orleans and the arrival of many new priests into the archdiocese. It served as well as a foundation for progress in the challenging period of Reconstruction after the war. For twelve years after the end of hostilities, Louisiana was governed by federal military officials, and the immediate task for the Church was providing pastoral care to the large numbers of newly emancipated African-Americans. This enterprise proved immensely successful, and southern Louisiana claimed the largest concentration of African-American Catholics at the end of the war.

Archbishop Odin attended the First Vatican Council and then died in France on May 25, 1870. He was succeeded on the same day by Napoléon Perché, the third archbishop of New Orleans, who had been named coadjutor archbishop earlier that year. Archbishop Perché attended the last sessions of the First Vatican Council and then took as his primary task the continued growth and development of the parishes and schools. A determined opponent of the public school system, he proved very successful in providing a Catholic alternative to what he saw was the poor and atheistic environment of public education. During this time, too, a number of religious communities established themselves in the archdiocese, including the Sisters of Mercy, Marist Brothers, Brothers of the Sacred Heart, Benedictine Sisters, Sisters of Christian Charity, Discalced Carmelite Sisters, Poor Clares, and Sisters of the Perpetual Adoration. In 1871 Father Cyprien Venissat began a second indigenous community, the Institute of the Immaculate Conception.

The colossal growth proved financially problematic, and by 1875 the archdiocese had amassed an enormous debt. To assist with this financial crisis, Pope Leo XIII appointed Bishop Francis Xavier Leray of Natchitoches as Archbishop Perché's coadjutor with the right of succession and Administrator of Temporal Affairs on October 23, 1879. Archbishop Leray struggled to find solutions to the debt issue; even after he acceded to the see with the passing of Archbishop Perché on December 27, 1883, finances remained a major issue. Archbishop Leray died on September 23, 1887, and was succeeded by Archbishop Francis Anthony Janssens, who had served as the bishop of Natchez since 1881.

Archbishop Janssens, the fifth archbishop of New Orleans, was installed on September 16, 1888, and his time as shepherd was noted for progress in the pastoral care of African-Americans. In 1895 St. Katharine's on Tulane Avenue was established as the first parish for Catholic African-Americans, although attendance was optional. Further progress was made in succeeding years when the Josephites and the Holy Ghost Fathers established parishes in New Orleans. New religious communities also arrived, including Benedictine monks, Dominicans, Josephites, Holy Ghost Fathers, Scalabrini Fathers, Missionary Sisters of the Sacred Heart, Sisters of the Blessed Sacrament, Sisters of the Most Holy Sacrament, and Teresian Sisters.

In 1893 the Catholic community in New Orleans celebrated its centennial, and Cardinal James Gibbons of Baltimore arrived to participate in the festivities. That event was soon overshadowed by a hurricane that struck the region that year. Archbishop Janssens used boats and rafts to distribute aid. He also founded the leprosarium at Carville.

Archbishop Janssens died on June 9, 1897, and was succeeded by the French Archbishop Placide Louis Chapelle, who had served as coadjutor archbishop of Santa Fe from 1893 and then archbishop of Santa Fe from 1894. He continued to develop the parishes of the archdiocese and worked especially to complete the long-term task of stabilizing finances. On Christmas Eve, he announced that the archdiocese was debt free. The new year began with great promise, but on August 9, 1905, Archbishop Chapelle died in one of the last outbreaks of yellow fever.

The seventh archbishop of New Orleans was James H. Blenk, a German member of the Society of Mary who had also served as bishop of Puerto Rico since 1899. Like his predecessors, Archbishop Blenk was concerned deeply with the state of Catholic education. To improve administration, he founded an archdiocesan school board and also encouraged the founding of a college by the Jesuits, now modern-day Loyola University. In 1914 he hosted the National Catholic Educational Association Convention in New Orleans. He also aided the start of the Knights of St. Peter Claver and proposed that Lafayette be established as a diocese. Archbishop Blenk died on April 20, 1917.

His successor was John William Shaw, who had been bishop of San Antonio since 1911 and had been honored by Pope Benedict XV with the rank of Assistant at the Pontifical Throne. He was appointed to the archdiocese on January 25, 1918, and was immediately confronted with guiding the faithful during the last days of World War I and then into the so-called Roaring Twenties. He opened Notre Dame Seminary and started thirty-three new parishes. Catholic schools continued to grow, assisted greatly by the presence of such institutions of higher learning as Loyola University and Xavier University.

Archbishop Shaw fought resurgent anti-Catholicism and used the considerable social prominence of the Church to defeat the influence of the Ku Klux Klan and others to impose mandatory public schools on Catholic families. Through the efforts of Governor Huey P. Long, the state provided school books directly to all Louisiana children regardless of their specific school, an act that survived several challenges to its constitutionality.

During Archbishop Shaw's tenure, the Church continued to develop. The Diocese of Lafayette was begun in 1918, and in 1926 the Province of San Antonio was established, so that Texas and Oklahoma were no longer part of the Province of New Orleans. Archbishop Shaw died on November 2, 1934, as the country found itself in the grip of the Great Depression.

The ninth archbishop of New Orleans was Joseph Francis Rummel, who had been bishop of Omaha since 1928. Promoted to New Orleans on March 9, 1935, Archbishop Rummel served as shepherd of New Orleans for the next thirty years. He provided desperately needed pastoral care to those hit by the Depression, and despite the economic conditions he forged ahead with an expansion of archdiocesan services. He sponsored the memorable National Eucharistic Congress of 1938 and promoted the Confraternity of Christian Doctrine, the Cana Conference, and other lay apostolates. In the years after World War II, Archbishop Rummel proved a determined supporter of social justice and worked to end the segregation of Catholic schools. He was the first bishop in the South to accept African-American students into the seminary, and in March 1953 he issued the pastoral letter "Blessed Are the Peacemakers," which called for an end to all parish segregation. He gave his support to the 1954 Supreme Court decision that ended segregation in public schools, and on February 11, 1956, he declared compulsory racial segregation morally wrong and sinful. In 1953 he celebrated the Golden Jubilee of his ordination to the priesthood.

Archbishop Rummel's last years were troubled by deteriorating vision problems and poor health, so much so that in 1961 John Patrick Cody was named coadjutor archbishop of New Orleans. Cody had been an auxiliary bishop in St. Louis and bishop of Kansas City-St. Joseph from 1956. In 1962 he was placed in charge of archdiocesan administration.

Soon after assuming his duties as administrator, Archbishop Cody pushed for the declaration calling for the desegregation of all Catholic schools, elementary and secondary, parochial and private, for the 1962–63 school year. The decree, issued on March 27, 1962, caused an immense storm of controversy, but the desegregation order was accepted by the Catholic community and enrollment increased over the following years.

Archbishop Rummel died on November 8, 1964, and Archbishop Cody became shepherd of New Orleans. He had already been in attendance at the first sessions of the Second Vatican Council. On June 16, 1965, he was transferred to Chicago to serve as archbishop there; two years later he was created a cardinal by Pope Paul VI. He died on April 25, 1982.

Bishop Philip M. Hannan was named the eleventh archbishop of New Orleans on September 29, 1965. He had been an auxiliary bishop of Washington, D.C., and a press spokesman at Vatican II. He arrived as archbishop just as New Orleans began a painful recovery from Hurricane Betsy. He launched an ambitious program of pastoral ministry to the poor and the elderly, including such major initiatives as Christopher Homes, Inc., to provide safe and affordable housing for those who would otherwise be unable to afford a home of their own; the Social Apostolate, with its ten-week Summer Witness Program for underprivileged children; and Catholic Charities. By 1989 the archdiocese was recognized as the largest single private provider of social services in the entire state.

At the same time, Archbishop Hannan presided over the continued expansion of parishes and schools. Between 1966 and 1988, thirty-one new parishes were established, and by 1989, 55,000 students were attending 27 high schools and 88 elementary schools. Loyola University, Xavier University, and Our Lady of the Holy Cross College were all flourishing. Archbishop Hannan also presided over the Eighth Archdiocesan Synod in 1987, with its commitment to "renew the life of the People of God by setting forth regulations accommodated to the needs of the times." Reflecting those needs, the Holy See created three new dioceses in Louisiana: Houma-Thibodaux in 1977, Lake Charles in 1980, and Shreveport in 1986.

On September 12, 1987, Pope Blessed John Paul II visited New Orleans as part of his United States visit. The pontiff celebrated Mass at the University of New Orleans' lakefront campus and then took part at a Louisiana Superdome rally attended by more than sixty thousand young people.

The next year, on December 6, 1988, Archbishop Hannan retired and was succeeded on that same day by Francis B. Schulte, who had served as an auxiliary bishop of Philadelphia and then bishop of Wheeling-Charleston. On February 14, 1989, he was installed as the twelfth archbishop of New Orleans.

Archbishop Schulte concentrated extensively on archdiocesan administration. He reorganized the various offices and ministries in 1991 and also undertook a comprehensive study of archdiocesan schools. In 1992 the archdiocese issued a new mission statement that stressed the multicultural nature of the archdiocese and the pledge to proclaim the Gospel and serve all in need. Through his efforts, the sizable debt of the archdiocese was eliminated by 1989, and from 1990 the archdiocese was assisted by the presence of a finance council of local business leaders.

In 1993 the Archdiocese of New Orleans celebrated the bicentennial of the creation of the Diocese of Louisiana and the Two Floridas. To mark the occasion, a series of celebrations took place, including a bicentennial Mass at the University of New Orleans Lakefront Arena and the publication of a volume of original historical articles, *Cross, Crozier, and Crucible: A Volume Celebrating the Bicentennial of a Diocese in Louisiana*.

During the Great Jubilee of 2000, New Orleans rejoiced in the beatification of Father Francis Xavier Seelos by Pope Blessed John Paul II. This was followed on October 1 with the canonization of St. Katharine Drexel, foundress of the Sisters of the Blessed Sacrament and Xavier University in New Orleans.

On May 2, 2001, Archbishop Alfred C. Hughes was installed as coadjutor archbishop of New Orleans and successor to Archbishop Schulte. Archbishop Hughes had served as an auxiliary bishop of Boston and as bishop of Baton Rouge since 1993. He acceded to the see on January 3, 2002.

The history of the archdiocese was changed forever in late August 2005 when Hurricane Katrina, the most destructive storm in American history, struck the Gulf Coast of the United States. The sixth-strongest Atlantic hurricane ever recorded and the third strongest to make landfall, Katrina brought severe devastation to the coastlines of Alabama, Mississippi, and Louisiana, in particular the cities of Mobile, Biloxi, and Gulfport. The most well-known area of damage was New Orleans, where the images of massive flooding and the suffering of tens of thousands of inhabitants of the city were broadcast around the world.

In a letter published on December 6, 2005, Archbishop Hughes expressed his thanks to American Catholics for their "outpouring of love and concern" for the Church in New Orleans and neighboring dioceses. He noted that dioceses, parishes, lay organizations, corporations, individuals, and even young schoolchildren contributed thousands of hours of volunteer time and funds in excess of $12 million to rebuild parishes and schools. The bishop projected that by year's end the archdiocese would face a multimillion-dollar deficit due to tge

enormous damage to property. The recovery of the archdiocese from the destruction is a long-term process for the entire Catholic community in the Gulf Coast.

On February 6, 2006, the Archdiocese of New Orleans issued a pastoral plan to implement the enormous task of rebuilding in the wake of Katrina. Archbishop Hughes estimated that the archdiocese might benefit from a return of upward of 60 percent of its pre-Katrina population over the next two years. Before the storm, there were approximately a half-million Catholics in 142 parishes in the archdiocese. Katrina remains the most decisive event to take place in the long life of the archdiocese, even as the Catholic faithful have demonstrated consistent resiliency and commitment to the faith in the face of natural disasters over the centuries. (*See also* Katrina, Hurricane.)

Archbishop Hughes retired on June 12, 2009, and was succeeded by Bishop Gregory M. Aymond, bishop of Austin since 2001. Archbishop Aymond was installed on August 20, 2009. Currently, there are about 500,000 Catholics, served by 357 priests, nearly 500 men and women religious, and 108 parishes in the archdiocese.

Newman Movement

The name used for Catholic centers established on non-Catholic college and university campuses in the United States to provide important aspects of ministry to meet the needs of Catholic students. The movement took its name from the famed nineteenth-century writer, apologist, educator, and convert Cardinal John Henry Newman. Especially influential was Newman's work *The Idea of a University*, which provided a vision for what a true university should be.

In 1883 a group of Catholic students gathered together at the University of Wisconsin in Madison and took the name the "Melvin Club" in honor of the fact that they met in the house of a woman named Mrs. Melvin. In 1890, the year of Cardinal Newman's death, one of the students from the Melvin Club began graduate studies at the University of Pennsylvania and established the first "Newman Club" in the United States. Over the next years, Newman Clubs began to appear on other campuses, and the Newman Movement was embraced for Catholic ministry on non-Catholic campuses. Currently, there are over two thousand Catholics Campus Ministry programs throughout the United States.

Newman Society, Cardinal

The Cardinal Newman Society is a national organization established in 1993 and dedicated to the renewal of Catholic identity in Catholic higher education in the United States. The society has more than eighteen thousand members nationwide who share a common concern for the future of Catholic higher education and who urge fidelity to the magisterium. The society seeks to promote discussion and understanding of the message of the Catholic Church concerning the nature and value of Catholic higher education; assist college leaders, educators, students, and alumni in their efforts to preserve the religious identity of Catholic institutions of higher learning; and advocate the faithful implementation of *Ex Corde Ecclesiae* by facilitating an active dialogue among members of the Catholic university community. The society also publishes a widely read *Guide to Choosing a Catholic College*.

Newton, John (August 24, 1823–May 1, 1895)

A general and engineer who was active in the Union Army throughout the Civil War, John Newton was born at Norfolk, Virginia. He graduated in 1842 from the United States Military Academy at West Point; he was second in the class that included future generals William Rosecrans and James Longstreet. He rose rapidly as an engineer, holding a variety of posts, including assistant professor of engineering at West Point, chief engineer of the Utah Expedition in 1858, chief engineer of the Department of Pennsylvania, and commander of the defenses for Washington, D.C., after the start of the Civil War. He subsequently served with distinction in the chief campaigns of the East, including participation at the battles of Antietam in 1862, Chancellorsville in 1863, and Gettysburg in 1863.

Following the war, he became one of the most respected engineers in the country. Among his most notable projects were the improvements of the Hudson River and the removal of the dangerous rocks in Hell Gate, the chief waterway between the Long Island Sound and the East River. In 1886

he was appointed commissioner of public works for New York City and in 1888 president of the Panama Railroad Company. A convert to Catholicism while a young man, he remained active in the Church until his death.

New Ulm, Diocese of

Established as a diocese by Pope Blessed John XXIII on November 18, 1957, New Ulm serves counties in Minnesota. The city was founded in 1854 and was destroyed on August 23, 1862, by a Sioux war party. A monument commemorates the defenders of the site. The diocese is a suffragan see of the Archdiocese of St. Paul and Minneapolis.

The Catholic history of New Ulm opens in 1655 when a Sioux mission was opened in Hastings. Another mission opened two decades later, and Daniel Greysolon, Sieur du Lhut, was in the area with Franciscan Recollect Father Louis Hennepin in 1680. Father Hennepin discovered St. Anthony's Falls (now modern-day Minneapolis). Nine years later, the entire region was claimed for France by Nicholas Perrot.

In 1727 Jesuits were at St. Michael the Archangel Mission, and forts were established by trappers and traders, also staffed by priest-chaplains. In 1736 Father Jean-Pierre Aulneau was slain by the Sioux, becoming Minnesota's first martyr. By the early 1800s missions were flourishing near Fond du Lac, Grand Portage, Crow Wing, and elsewhere. Minnesota was included in the Louisiana Purchase and became a possession of the United States in 1803. It was opened to settlement by 1840 and entered the Union in 1858 as the thirty-second state.

On July 19, 1850, the Diocese of St. Paul (now the Archdiocese of St. Paul and Minneapolis) was established by Pope Pius IX. Bishop Joseph Crétin had ecclesiastical jurisdiction of the area from Lake Superior to the Missouri River and from Iowa to the Canadian border. Four years later, New Ulm was founded. The New Ulm Cathedral of the Holy Trinity was opened as a parish in 1856, and two parishes, St. Brendan in Green Isle and St. Thomas (Mission) in Jessenland opened in 1854 and 1855, respectively. St. Gabriel in Forest City was operating in 1857, and St. Joseph in Henderson and St. Philip in Litchfield were serving the faithful in 1859.

After the Civil War, more settlers arrived in the region, and the Diocese of St. Paul was elevated to the status of a metropolitan provincial see. The revered Archbishop John Ireland headed the archdiocese from 1884 to 1918.

During the early 1900s, farmers and laborers aided the small farms and workers, and during the Great Depression, charitable agencies and programs instituted relief efforts. World War II aided the economic development of the region. New Ulm was growing at a steady pace and was given the status of a diocese by Pope Pius XII on November 18, 1957.

The first bishop of New Ulm was Alphonse J. Schladweiler, who was appointed on November 28, 1957. He was ordained a bishop on January 29, 1958, and installed as bishop of the Diocese of New Ulm on January 30, 1958. Bishop Schladweiler had the difficult task of providing a firm footing for the new diocese even as he was shepherd during the tumultuous period of the Second Vatican Council and the difficult postconciliar period. He founded the diocesan chancery and encouraged the various ministries needed for the new diocese. He participated in all the sessions of the Second Vatican Council in Rome and then labored to implement its decrees. Bishop Schladweiler was also one of the first bishops in the United States to foster the development of missions in South America. The diocese agreed to commit its resources to a parish in the highlands of Guatemala. He retired on December 23, 1975, and died on April 3, 1996.

Bishop Schladweiler was succeeded by Bishop Raymond A. Lucker, who had been an auxiliary bishop of St. Paul and Minneapolis since 1971. Appointed on December 23, 1975, he was installed on February 19, 1976. His primary undertaking as bishop was to continue the implementation of the Second Vatican Council and the renewal that the council had mandated. Toward that end, he encouraged renewal in a variety of areas in the diocese, including religious education, catechesis, and evangelization. He was especially committed to catechetical renewal and was a national leader in the development of the Confraternity of Christian Doctrine and the National Conference of Diocesan Directors of Religious Education, and was one of the founders of the Catechetical Forum,

an association of catechetical writers, professors of catechetics, CCD directors, and other catechetical leaders. Bishop Lucker was also the first bishop in the United States to appoint pastoral administrators as heads of parishes, starting in 1981.

Bishop Lucker retired on November 17, 2000, and was succeeded by Bishop John C. Nienstedt, who since 1996 had been an auxiliary bishop of the Archdiocese of Detroit. Bishop Nienstedt had also served in Rome as an official of the Vatican Secretariat of State in Rome from 1980 to 1985. On June 12, 2001, Pope Blessed John Paul II named Bishop Nienstedt the third bishop of the Diocese of New Ulm; he was installed on August 6, 2001. On April 24, 2007, Pope Benedict XVI named Bishop Nienstedt the coadjutor archbishop of the Archdiocese of St. Paul and Minneapolis. On July 14, 2008, Father John M. LeVoir, a priest of the Archdiocese of St. Paul and Minneapolis, was appointed as Bishop Nienstedt's successor. In 2011 there were 63,000 Catholics, 66 priests, and 76 parishes in the diocese.

New York

Called the Empire State, New York is located in the Middle Atlantic region of the United States. It is bounded on the north by Canada, on the east by Connecticut, Massachusetts, and Vermont, on the south by the Atlantic Ocean, New Jersey, and Pennsylvania, and on the west by Pennsylvania and Canada. Eight natural land regions are in New York: the St. Lawrence Lowlands, the Adirondack Highlands and the Mohawk Valley, the New England Uplands, the Hudson Valley, the Atlantic Coastal Plain in the southeast, the Lake Plains in the northwest, and the Appalachian Plateau in the south. The original inhabitants of New York included the Mohawk, Oneida, Onondaga, Cayuga, and Seneca of the Iroquois Five Nations, joined in 1715 by the Tuscarora.

The Catholic heritage of the state dates to 1524 when Giovanni da Verrazano explored the area for France. In 1609 the French had missions on Lake Champlain, and Henry Hudson explored New York harbor for the English. The Dutch settled in New York in 1624, purchasing Manhattan from the local tribes two years later and naming it New Amsterdam.

Father Joseph de la Roche d'Aillon was near Niagara Falls by 1627, followed by Jesuits, including Sts. René Goupil and Isaac Jogues, both of whom were subsequently martyred. (*See also* North American Martyrs.) Syracuse was the site of the first important Catholic mission in New York, established in 1655. Three years later, many missions were destroyed by Indian raids but rebuilt by Onondaga Chief Garaconthié.

In 1664 Peter Stuyvesant, the Dutch governor, was forced to surrender his lands to the British. They renamed the area after James, the Duke of York. The French, however, contested rights to the region, citing the claim made by René-Robert Chevalier, Sieur de La Salle. The Catholics in the area fared poorly throughout the colony until the arrival of Governor Thomas Dongan, who brought Father Thomas Harvey and other Jesuits to the territory. Dongan secured the passage of legislation insuring tolerance of Catholics, but the Glorious Revolution of 1688 brought with it the reign of William and Mary in England and a sharp anti-Catholic reaction in all English lands. A year later, Calvinist Jacob Leisler led an armed rebellion against Governor Dongan, who was forced to flee the colony. The priests were ordered out of New York on pain of death, and Father John Ury was executed for a supposed plot against New York.

The growing animosity against the British took hold in New York, and in 1775 the colony declared independence. Despite their legal status and disabilities, Catholics rallied to the cause and gave their support to a state constitution in 1777. In the Revolutionary War that followed, several key campaigns and battles took place in New York, including the capture of Fort Ticonderoga and the Battles of Long Island and Saratoga. In 1788 New York became the eleventh state to ratify the United States Constitution. New York City served as the first capital of the nation from 1785 to 1790.

In 1784 Father Charles Whelan became the first resident priest of New York, and a year later the cornerstone of St. Peter's Church in New York City was laid. The region was prospering with canals opening and factories and industries developing.

The Diocese of New York was erected on April 8, 1808, as part of the extensive reorganization of the Church in America that brought the eleva-

Old St. Peter's Church in New York City

tion of Baltimore to the rank of an archdiocese and the creation of the new dioceses of New York, Philadelphia, Boston, and Bardstown (modern-day Louisville) as suffragan sees. Father Richard Luke Concanen, an Irish Dominican priest who was then in Rome, was appointed the first bishop of New York. He was unable to make the journey to the United States, however, as the upheaval of the Napoleonic Wars prevented travel. He died at Naples in 1810. During the subsequent vacancy of the see, diocesan affairs were administered by Father Anthony Kohlmann, who rebuilt St. Peter's Church in Barclay Street and in 1809 purchased the site of old St. Patrick's Cathedral in Mott Street, a project that was finished in 1815 and dedicated on May 4, 1815, by Bishop Jean-Louis Lefebvre de Cheverus. In 1809 he also secured the land that became part of the site of the present St. Patrick's Cathedral.

At last, in November 1815, after a delay of six years, Bishop John Connolly, a Dominican, like Concanen, arrived at New York and took up his duties as shepherd of the seventeen thousand Catholics in the archdiocese. He was assisted initially by a mere four priests and worked for the next decade to increase parishes and recruit priests and religious from Europe. By 1822 there were two churches in New York City, one in Albany, one in Utica, one in Auburn, and one in Carthage on the Black River, served by one bishop and eight priests. Bishop Connolly died on February 5, 1825, and was buried under the altar of the new St. Patrick's Cathedral.

Bishop Connolly was succeeded on October 29, 1826, by John Dubois, P.S.S., a French Sulpician priest who had fled France in the wake of the French Revolution. One of the founders of Mount St. Mary's College in Emmitsburg, Maryland, Dubois served during the period of massive expansion in the population of the state and diocese.

The rise of the inland waterways, such as the Erie and the Champlain-Hudson Canals, brought with them a massive influx of workers, most of whom were Irish, part of the first great wave of Irish immigration that so shaped American Catholicism in the nineteenth century. The population of the state increased from 340,120 in 1790 to 1.9 million in 1830, while the population in New York City rose from 33,131 in 1790 to 202,589 in 1830. Meanwhile, by 1830, the Catholic population grew to 35,000 in New York City and 150,000 in the state, including northern New Jersey. Most Catholics were immigrants, and the majority were poor Irish who had sailed to America in the hope of finding work and a new life. Making conditions worse was the poor welcome they received, as anti-Catholicism was common in the city and the state, and nativist tendencies compounded the hostility.

Bishop John Loughlin

Bishop Dubois worked with great zeal to expand the Church's presence in the city and state, to bring new priests and religious, and to offer pastoral care to the newly arrived immigrants. He was especially praised for his leadership during the cholera epidemic of 1832 that claimed three thousand people in New York City. Bishop Dubois also ordained in June 1836 the future saint John Nepomucene Neumann, who later became bishop of Philadelphia

and was canonized in 1977. Bishop Dubois's health declined from overwork, and in 1837 he received a coadjutor, Father John Hughes, an Irish-born priest from Philadelphia.

On December 20, 1842, Bishop Hughes acceded to the see and oversaw the continued expansion of the Church in New York. In April 1847 the sees of Albany and Buffalo were created, and in October 1850 the Diocese of New York was elevated to the rank of an archdiocese with the sees of Boston, Hartford, Albany, and Buffalo as its suffragans. Archbishop Hughes then sailed for Rome and received the pallium from the hands of Pope Blessed Pius IX.

In 1853 the Dioceses of Brooklyn in New York and of Newark in New Jersey were established, with Reverend John Loughlin named the first bishop of Brooklyn and the famed Reverend James Roosevelt Bayley named the first bishop of Newark (he later became archbishop of Baltimore). In 1868 the Diocese of Rochester was separated from Albany, under Bishop Bernard J. McQuaid as its first bishop. In 1872 the Diocese of Ogdensburg was created, followed by Syracuse in November 1886.

During the second half of the nineteenth century, the Church continued to grow rapidly in size and influence owing chiefly to the burgeoning influx of immigrants who arrived in four great waves throughout the nineteenth century, comprised respectively of the Irish, Germans, Italians, and Eastern Europeans. By 1906 there were over 2.2 million Catholics in New York, out of a population of nearly 3.5 million.

The pastoral care of the new arrivals became one of the primary concerns of the Archdiocese of New York and its suffragans. Accomplishing this proved an immense challenge to the resources, manpower, and money of the dioceses and parishes in the eastern United States, and the Church constructed parishes, missions, schools, orphanages, hospitals, and homes for the aged.

The importance of the Catholic community in New York was made manifest in 1875 when Pope

Pius IX named Archbishop John McCloskey the first American cardinal. His successors, from the time of John Murphy Farley onward, were all subsequently named to the College of Cardinals.

By the end of the nineteenth century, Catholic influence in the state was undeniable. Irish Catholics were firmly entrenched in Tammany Hall and thus came to dominate the vast Democratic political machine in the state. By 1880 the strength of the Catholic vote was demonstrated in the election of William Russell Grace as the first Catholic mayor of New York City. There followed a close association between the leaders of New York state and other major cities and the Irish Catholic voters and the leaders of the Church, in particular the archbishop of New York.

The degree to which Catholic prominence had grown in New York was visible especially during the service of Cardinal Farley, from 1902 to 1918, the last Irish-born archbishop of New York, and Cardinal Patrick Joseph Hayes, from 1919 to 1938, as archbishops of New York. In 1908 Cardinal Farley led the celebrations for the 100th anniversary of the founding of the Diocese of New York, which included a grand procession of nearly fifty thousand Catholics up Fifth Avenue to St. Patrick's Cathedral.

The demographics of the Catholic community by 1908 had already begun to change, however, driven by the massive influx of hundreds of thousands of Italian immigrants. This made the face of Catholicism much less Irish and offered a foretaste of the diverse Catholic Church that developed in the state throughout the rest of the twentieth century.

Nevertheless, Catholicism was increasingly acceptable to voters of all religious origins. In 1922 Alfred E. Smith was elected governor of New York, a watershed moment and a political achievement that catapulted Smith into national politics. The popular governor ran for president in 1928, secured the nomination of the Democratic Party, and lost the general election to Herbert Hoover. Crucial to his defeat was the explosion of anti-Catholicism that erupted in many states.

With the start of the Great Depression, the Church in New York under Cardinal Hayes and then Archbishop (later Cardinal) Francis Spellman provided immense assistance to the poor and the unemployed, especially in New York City. Spellman was one of the most prominent and powerful Catholic leaders in the United States, both during the Depression and throughout World War II. He also presided over a large program of expansion and construction that marked the last major period of growth in Catholic parishes and schools, working to keep pace with the high number of ordinations, entries into the religious life, and the growth of the Catholic population in the state in the years after the war and throughout the postwar economic expansion.

The era after the Second Vatican Council was marked by considerable upheaval in American Catholicism, and the challenges were not avoided in New York. The chief figure dealing with the challenge was Cardinal Spellman's successor, Cardinal Terence J. Cooke, who presided over the introduction of the reforms of the council, in particular liturgical renewal. The problems facing the Church in the state were exacerbated by the financial turmoil of the 1970s, the *Roe v. Wade* decision by the U.S. Supreme Court in 1973, and the deterioration of vocations, which was accompanied by the growing diversity of the Catholic population. In 1979 the recently elected Pope Blessed John Paul II visited New York City and was hosted by Cardinal Cooke. Cardinal Cooke died in 1983 after a heroic battle with cancer, and his cause for canonization was approved in 1992.

He was succeeded by John O'Connor, who would become a cardinal. He was an outspoken advocate for the pro-life cause and had several controversial episodes with New York political leaders, including Geraldine Ferraro, a Catholic Democrat who ran as the vice-presidential candidate in 1984 and was criticized by Cardinal O'Connor and many other pro-life Catholics for her position on abortion.

Cardinal O'Connor died of cancer in 2000 and was succeeded by Edward M. Egan, who was named a cardinal in February 2001. On September 11, 2001, the World Trade Center was destroyed in a terrorist attack on America. The loss of the Twin Towers caused the deaths of more than three thousand people and touched the lives of every citizen of New York and the entire Catholic community. Cardinal Egan retired on February 23, 2009, and was succeeded by Timothy M. Dolan as archbishop.

Dolan and the other bishops of New York worked to prevent the legalization of same-sex marriage in June 2011. The Marriage Equality Act passed by the New York State Legislature was signed by Governor Andrew Cuomo, a Catholic.

One of the chief challenges for the Church in New York in the last decades has been the financial challenge of maintaining vibrant Catholic schools, finding a balance between keeping parishes open and closing those that are no longer viable financially, fostering vocations to the priesthood, and caring for the Catholics who have come to New York from all over the globe. Another challenge is the widespread increase in secular thought and the effort to reduce the influence of Catholic teaching in the public square. In 2011 the Catholic population of New York was more than seven million, out of a total population of 38 million. There are also more than 1,300 parishes, nearly 4,000 priests, and 8,000 men and women religious in the state.

New York, Archdiocese of

Established as a diocese on August 8, 1808, by Pope Pius VII and designated as an archdiocese on July 19, 1850, by Pope Blessed Pius IX, the Archdiocese of New York serves New York, the Bronx, and Richmond Counties in New York City, as well as Duchess, Orange, Putnam, Rockland, Sullivan, Ulster, and Westchester counties in New York state. The archdiocese also has suffragan dioceses across the state of New York. It is one of the largest archdioceses in the United States with more than 2.6 million members making up its remarkably diverse community.

Catholic explorers were in the area of New York as early as 1524, when Giovanni da Verrazano explored the region for France. In 1609 the French had missions on Lake Champlain, while the explorer Henry Hudson scouted New York harbor for the British, thus setting up a lasting rivalry between those nations. The first settlers of New York, however, were the Dutch, who arrived in 1624, purchasing present-day Manhattan from a local Indian tribe and naming the site New Amsterdam. In 1627 Father Joseph de la Roche d'Aillon was at Niagara Falls, followed by Jesuit missionaries, including the famed martyrs René Goupil, Isaac Jogues, and Jean de Lalande. They were canonized

with the other North American Martyrs in 1930. Isaac Jogues was the first priest to set foot in New York City, in 1643, when the site was called New Amsterdam. At the time of his arrival, there were only two Catholics, an Irishman and a Portuguese woman, out of a population of about five hundred.

The Dutch under Peter Stuyvesant surrendered New York to the British in 1664. The English imposed severe anti-Catholic regulations until 1674, when the colony passed to the authority of James, the Duke of York, the future King James II. Under Thomas Dongan, an Irish Catholic and governor from 1683 to 1688, toleration was decreed for Catholics, and Jesuits were invited to New York. The first, Father Thomas Harvey, celebrated the first Mass in New York City in 1683. Sadly, the brief era of toleration ended with the Glorious Revolution in 1688 that toppled James II from the throne and brought the ardent Protestants William and Mary to the throne. A Calvinist rebellion led by Jacob Leisler ended Dongan's time, and Catholicism was once more forbidden. Priests were banned from returning on pain of death or life in prison. By 1696 there were only ten Catholics in the city.

The tiny Catholic community took part in the American Revolution on the side of the rebels, and independence from England marked a new era of freedom for Catholics. Free at last to worship publicly, Catholics in New York City established St. Peter's Church on Barclay Street in 1785; the small brick building was the first Catholic church in New York. Dedicated on November 4, 1786, the church's first pastors were the Irish Capuchins Charles Whelan and Andrew Nugent.

Owing to the growth of the Catholic population in New York, on April 8, 1808, Pope Pius VII established the Diocese of Baltimore as a metropolitan see and created new dioceses in Boston, Philadelphia, Bardstown, Kentucky, and New York. The first bishop of New York was an Irish Dominican, Richard Luke Concanen, who was prevented from even reaching his see owing to the Napoleonic Wars, which made sea travel a major problem. He died in Naples on June 19, 1810, without ever seeing his new diocese.

As Bishop Concanen was stranded in Europe, Archbishop John Carroll appointed an administrator, Jesuit Father Anthony Kohlmann, who is honored as the key figure in giving the diocese a firm administrative foundation.

On October 4, 1814, Pope Pius VII appointed another Dominican, John Connolly, the second bishop of New York, who was consecrated on November 6 that same year. He took control of the diocese on November 24, 1815, a Catholic community that at that point numbered seventeen thousand scattered across New York City and the rest of the state. Most of the Catholics were Irish, but there were soon French, Germans, Spanish, Portuguese, Italians, English, and African-Americans.

Connolly had at his disposal only four priests. The cathedral of the diocese, old St. Patrick's Cathedral on Mott Street, had been finished in 1815 and dedicated by Bishop Jean-Louis Lefebvre de Cheverus of Boston. With some foresight, Bishop Connolly purchased land in 1809 on Fifth Avenue at Fiftieth Street to start a boys' school. The land became especially significant as it provided the diocese with a central location for the new St. Patrick's Cathedral.

In 1817, meanwhile, the first Sisters of Charity arrived in the diocese to establish the first charitable institution in the diocese, the Catholic Orphan Asylum. During this period, too, the city was blessed by the presence of Venerable Pierre Toussaint, a Haitian-born slave who became a beloved figure for his holiness, wisdom, and care of the poor. He was declared venerable in 1997.

Bishop Connolly died on February 6, 1825, and was succeeded on October 29, 1826, by John Dubois, a French priest who had fled his homeland at the onset of the French Revolution. His years were marked by the troubles of trusteeism and rising anti-Catholicism in the city and state, and by a severe epidemic of cholera in 1832 that killed more than three thousand people in the city. Notably, in 1836, he ordained at St. Patrick's John Nepomucene Neumann, the future bishop of Philadelphia and saint. In 1837, owing to poor health, Bishop Dubois requested a coadjutor bishop. That bishop was his successor, John Hughes.

Consecrated on February 9, 1838, Hughes, the fourth bishop of New York, succeeded to the see upon Bishop Dubois's passing on December 20, 1842. In recognition of the immense progress in the diocese and the growth of Catholicism in the state, in October 1850 the Diocese of New York was promoted to the rank of an archiepiscopal see with the dioceses of Boston, Hartford, Albany, and Buffalo as its suffragans.

Describing himself as "bishop and chief," Hughes presided over the archdiocese during a tumultuous period of growth and social unrest. He established sixty-one new churches, invited religious communities to staff schools and hospitals, and labored to provide pastoral care to the booming population that included large numbers of Irish and German immigrants. Bishop Hughes also laid the cornerstone of St. Patrick's Cathedral on August 15, 1858.

St. Patrick's Cathedral in New York City

At the same time, he fought against the evils of trusteeism in Catholic parishes and resisted the anti-Catholic and nativist hatred in the city. In 1844 the same fervor that had caused anti-Catholic riots in Philadelphia threatened churches in New York City, and Bishop Hughes allowed the Irish to be armed and positioned in front of churches and convents. He then warned the mayor that "New York would become a second Moscow" if the mobs were allowed to continue, a reference to the burning of Moscow during Napoleon's invasion in 1812. The result was that New York was spared from the violence and bloodshed. Archbishop Hughes died on January 3, 1864.

Bishop Hughes was succeeded by John McCloskey, the second archbishop of New York, on May 6, 1864. He had been named coadjutor archbishop of New York in 1844 but had been assigned to the Diocese of Albany in 1847. Returning to New York, he assumed a diocese that had been provided a strong foundation by Bishop Hughes and was continuing to grow steadily. In recognition of the progress of American Catholicism and also the importance of New York, in 1875 McCloskey became the first American cardinal.

The Catholic presence in New York City by Cardinal McCloskey's death on October 10, 1885, was undeniable. There were now more than six hundred thousand Catholics, and the flexing of potential political power was at last realized in 1880 when the Irish-born businessman William Russell Grace was elected the first Catholic mayor of New York. Several more Catholic mayors were elected in the next years.

The next archbishop of New York, Michael A. Corrigan, had been bishop of Newark and then coadjutor archbishop of New York since 1880. Acceding to the see on Cardinal McCloskey's death, Archbishop Corrigan was confronted by the next great wave of immigrants to the United States, as New York City stood at the very front of the

Archbishop Corrigan, New York

onrushing human deluge from Europe, especially Italy. To keep pace, he established ninety-nine new parishes as well as schools, convent, and hospitals. He also continued the growth of religious communities so that by 1900 there were some fifty communities of men and women religious.

Archbishop Corrigan was succeeded by John Murphy Farley, the last Irish-born archbishop of New York. Farley had been an auxiliary bishop of New York since 1895 and was appointed as archbishop on September 15, 1902. The highlight of his time in the see was in 1908, when the New York archdiocese celebrated its centenary. In a display of the influence of the Catholics in the city, tens of thousands Catholic men marched in procession up Fifth Avenue to St. Patrick's Cathedral. Like his predecessors, Archbishop Farley coped with the arrival of new immigrants, especially from Italy, and started the needed ethnic or national parishes to provide pastoral care in various languages. The care of these new immigrants was assisted greatly by St. Frances Xavier Cabrini, who landed in New York City in 1889 with her Missionary Sisters of the Sacred Heart and set to work. She was canonized in 1946, the first American citizen to be declared a saint, and was declared Patroness of Immigrants in 1950. Archbishop Farley was named a cardinal in 1911 and died on September 17, 1918, shortly before the end of World War I. His successor, Patrick Joseph Hayes, had been an auxiliary bishop of New York since 1914.

A native of New York City's Lower East Side, Hayes was appointed archbishop on March 10, 1919, and served as shepherd between the wars and throughout the first decade of the Great Depression. Throughout the Depression, the archdiocese provided pastoral care for those thousands left in dire straits by the economic collapse. In 1928, meanwhile, Catholic New Yorkers took pride in the presidential run of their Catholic governor, Alfred E. Smith, who had also been born on the Lower

East Side. The presidential campaign, sadly, was marked by vicious anti-Catholicism, and Smith lost in a landslide. Hayes was appointed a cardinal in 1924 and died on September 4, 1938.

Cardinal Hayes was succeeded on April 15, 1939, by Francis J. Spellman, who had been an auxiliary bishop of Boston since 1932. Archbishop Spellman arrived as one of the most influential Church leaders in the United States. He was a friend of Pope Pius XII and came to enjoy the trust and friendship of President Franklin Delano Roosevelt throughout the war. Under Archbishop Spellman, the Church in New York and across the United States enjoyed immense influence and was squarely in support of the American effort during World War II. This was aided further by Archbishop Spellman's appointment as the Military Vicar for the Armed Forces.

Spellman's time as archbishop also witnessed the last major period of expansion, with new parishes, churches, and schools. By the time of his retirement in 1967, he presided over the largest Catholic school system in the country. Named a cardinal in 1946, he attended the Second Vatican Council and was a determined voice for caution in its reforms. In October 1965 he welcomed Pope Paul VI as part of the papal trip to the United Nations and New York City. He died on December 2, 1967.

His successor was Terence J. Cooke, an auxiliary bishop of New York since 1965. He was appointed as tenth archbishop of New York on March 2, 1968, in an era in which great upheaval — social, political, and economic — struck the city, the state, and the archdiocese. He was named a cardinal on April 28, 1969, with the title of SS. Giovanni e Paolo. There were problems in implementing the authentic reforms of the Second Vatican Council, the reaction in some Catholic quarters against the Vietnam War and the assault on traditional morality and the culture of life by the 1973 *Roe v. Wade* decision of the U.S. Supreme Court that legalized abortion. Archbishop Cooke was a prophetic voice in this difficult era and was noted especially for his goodness. He died on October 6, 1983, after a valiant struggle with cancer.

Cardinal Cooke was succeeded by John J. O'Connor, who had been a rear admiral, chief chaplain at the United States Naval Academy, an auxiliary bishop of the Military Ordinariate, and

bishop of Scranton since 1983. On January 25, 1984, within months of his appointment to Scranton, he was named to New York and elevated to the rank of cardinal in the consistory of May 25, 1985, with the title of SS. Giovanni e Paolo.

As archbishop, Cardinal O'Connor launched programs in the archdiocese for the sick and disabled, including the victims of AIDS in New York City. He was an outspoken advocate of the pro-life cause, and publicly disagreed with Geraldine Ferraro, the vice presidential candidate in 1984, and Catholic politicians over abortion. He was also a leader in promoting ecumenism and interreligious dialogue, labored for peace in the Middle East, helped draft the 1989 statement calling for a Palestinian homeland, and from 1984 was head of the Catholic Near East Welfare Association. In the archdiocese, he worked to maintain the Catholic school system in the face of mounting financial challenges, and founded the Sisters of Life in 1991. Diagnosed with a brain tumor, he heroically fought the disease but eventually succumbed and died on May 3, 2000, in New York.

St. James Pro Cathedral in Brooklyn, New York

The twelfth archbishop of New York, Edward M. Egan had been a priest in service in Rome with the Sacred Roman Rota and had been bishop of Bridgeport since 1988. Appointed archbishop of New York on May 11, 2000, he was elevated to the rank of cardinal in the consistory of 2001, with the title of SS. John and Paul. He inherited an archdiocese with growing financial problems and the challenge of declining vocations to the priesthood. He moved to improve finances and also worked to provide pastoral care to Catholics outside the city, where the population was shifting to places such as Dutchess County and Orange County.

The archdiocese was struck grievously by terrorist attacks on September 11, 2001, and Cardinal Egan preached a memorable homily at the memorial service in the days that followed. The Church in New York worked to provide pastoral care to the victims' families and to the grieving. Egan also later welcomed Pope Benedict XVI to New York City during his papal visit to the city and to the United Nations, and celebrated the 200th anniversary of the founding of the Diocese of New York.

Cardinal Egan retired on February 23, 2009, on the same day that Archbishop Timothy M. Dolan was appointed his successor. Dolan had been the rector of the North American College in Rome, an auxiliary bishop of St. Louis, and then archbishop of Milwaukee from 2002. He was installed in New York on April 15, 2009. He worked immediately to strengthen Catholic education in the diocese, to stabilize diocesan finances, and to promote vocations to the priesthood and the religious life. He also worked with the bishops of New York state to oppose passage of the 2011 Marriage Equality Act in the New York State Legislature; the bill was eventually approved and signed by Governor Andrew Cuomo, a Catholic.

The Archdiocese of New York is one of the most diverse particular churches in the United States. There are hundreds of languages spoken within its boundaries, and it stands today in the great tradition of the first archdiocese's days of welcoming Catholics and non-Catholics from all walks of life into the arms of the Catholic community. In 2011 there were more than 2.6 million Catholics, served by 1,400 priests, nearly 3,000 men and women religious, and 370 parishes in the archdiocese.

Nogar, Raymond Jude (1916–1967)

A Dominican friar and philosopher, Raymond Jude Nogar was born in Monroe, Michigan. He studied at the University of Michigan but left the school of graduate studies after his conversion in 1939 to the Catholic faith. In 1940 he entered the Dominican novitiate and studied at the Aquinas Institute of Philosophy and Theology in Illinois, eventually earning a doctorate in the philosophy of science. After ordination, he served on the faculty of the institute and was later co-founder of the Albertus Magnus Lyceum.

Nogar was a noted writer on the subject of the relationship and dialogue between religion and science. He differed sharply from the position of Teilhard de Chardin regarding convergence between science and religion. He offered his views in such works as *The Wisdom of Evolution* in 1963, in which he proposed what was termed a "theistic evolution." In *The Lord of the Absurd*, in 1966, he presented his thoughts on the numerous lectures he had offered across the country and his affirmation of the radical autonomy of God. He was thus opposed to the current notion of an orderly universe as the foundation of dialogue between religion and science.

Noll, John F. (January 25, 1875–July 31, 1956)

Bishop of Fort Wayne from 1925 to 1956 and personal titular archbishop from 1953, John F. Noll is best known as the founder and publisher of *Our Sunday Visitor* in 1912. He was born in Fort Wayne, Indiana, and studied for the priesthood at Mount St. Mary's Seminary in Cincinnati, Ohio. Ordained to the priesthood for the Fort Wayne diocese in 1898, he served in parishes until 1925, but he was also engaged actively in evangelization. In 1904 he authored the booklet *Kind Words from Your Pastor*, intended for non-Catholics interested in the faith. Four years later, he was responsible for the start of *The Family Digest*.

To resist anti-Catholicism in Indiana (especially the activities of the Ku Klux Klan in the area), he launched the newspaper *Our Sunday Visitor* in 1912, benefiting immensely from the offer of a printing press in Huntington, Indiana (which became the headquarters of the paper). Father Noll continued his duties as pastor, but he was also *Our Sunday Visitor*'s director for many years. It was his intention to produce a newspaper that might eventually reach Catholics all over the country. His hopes were fulfilled rapidly, as *Our Sunday Visitor* was soon distributed throughout many parishes and boasted hundreds of thousands of subscribers from virtually every state. As the venture proved immensely successful, Noll established a fund in 1915 to support charitable, spiritual, and educational programs that became the Our Sunday Visitor Institute, which continues his legacy today.

The next year, Noll began to develop an idea that had been started by Protestants. Members of the congregation were provided with offering envelopes (in lieu of charging pew rent) that could be handed in each week at Mass. This soon proved a very effective means of improving collections, and offering envelopes became a mainstay in parishes across the country, with most provided by Our Sunday Visitor.

Bishop Noll launched a magazine for priests called *The Acolyte* in 1925. It is still published under the title *The Priest* and was the first of a host of periodicals over the next decades that were to be published by Our Sunday Visitor.

In 1912 Noll had started a series called "Father Smith Instructs Jackson," a useful means of introducing non-Catholics to the teachings of the Church. The next year, Our Sunday Visitor offered a reward that became

Archbishop John Noll

a recurring challenge, namely to pay $10,000 to anyone who could prove the anti-Catholic accusations then being spread by the Klan and others. The reward was never claimed.

Noll was named bishop of Fort Wayne by Pope Pius XI and consecrated on May 12, 1925, and on September 12, 1953, he was granted the personal title of archbishop by Pope Pius XII. (*See also Our Sunday Visitor.*) He remained involved with *Our Sunday Visitor* throughout his time as bishop. On January 3, 1926, Noll began a diocesan newspaper (a local edition of *Our Sunday Visitor*); he put the printing presses of *Our Sunday Visitor* at the service of dioceses across the United States for their diocesan papers as well.

In 1933 Bishop Noll was appointed one of the four bishops charged with starting the Legion of Decency. He remained a dedicated opponent of indecent magazines and publications. He was also instrumental in guiding the fundraising campaign needed to bring about the completion of the Basilica of the Immaculate Conception in Washington, D.C.

Noll proved an effective shepherd of the diocese and was diligent in meeting the needs of the local Catholic community. He was especially dedicated to charitable initiatives during the Great Depression, and oversaw an extensive building program across the diocese. Notably, he declined proposed appointments to larger dioceses. In his tenure as bishop, he confirmed 133,000 people and ordained 500 priests.

Norris, James Joseph (August 10, 1907– November 17, 1976)

Lay activist and longtime executive director of Catholic Relief Services, James Joseph Norris was born in Roselle Park, New Jersey. He joined the Missionary Servants of the Most Holy Trinity (the Trinitarians) in 1924, but left in 1934. Two years later, he was named an assistant at the Mission of the Immaculate Virgin, a welfare center on Staten Island, New York, and then in 1941 became involved with National Catholic Community Services, the Church's participation in the U.S.O. organization. During World War II, he was a commander in the U.S. Navy.

Following the war, he was appointed by his longtime friend Father (later Cardinal) Patrick A. O'Boyle to the new post of European Director of War Relief Services for the National Catholic Welfare Conference, which was assisting in the massive humanitarian endeavor in postwar Europe and which later became Catholic Relief Services. He helped to establish the Conference of Voluntary Agencies Working for Refugees and the International Conference of Non-Governmental Agencies Interested in Migration; he also served as president of the International Catholic Migration

Commission from 1951 to 1974, a position that brought him into close contact with then Monsignor Giovanni Battista Montini, the future Pope Paul VI. In 1959 he was asked to become executive assistant to the executive director of Catholic Relief Services, then Bishop Edward Swanstrom, a post Norris held until his death. Pope Paul named him a founding member of the Pontifical Commission (later Council) for Justice and Peace in 1967 and of the Pontifical Council Cor Unum in 1971. Norris also served as the papal representative at the funeral of Martin Luther King Jr. in 1968. Shortly before his death, he received the Nansen Medal from the United Nations High Commissioner for Refugees.

North American College

The residence in Rome for seminarians from dioceses in the United States, the seminary was founded by Pope Pius IX in 1859. Hundreds of men have been trained for the priesthood for service in dioceses located around the United States, Canada, Mexico, and Puerto Rico, as well as the United States Military Archdiocese.

Bishops had been sending seminarians to study in Rome from as early as 1790, but there was for many decades no formal house of studies for Americans in the Eternal City. In 1855 Pius IX requested that the bishops of the United States open a formal seminary in Rome. On December 8, 1859, the feast of the Immaculate Conception, twelve seminarians from the United States entered what was soon termed the North American College. Facilities for the students were located in a renovated 250-year-old former Dominican convent on the Via dell'Umiltà, down the hill from the papal residence on the Quirinale. The students at first attended the Urban College of the Propaganda until 1932, when they transferred to the Pontifical Gregorian University.

From the start, the college faced challenges owing to financial difficulties, a situation exacerbated in 1884 when the property was confiscated by Italian authorities of the severely anticlerical government. A crisis was averted when President Chester A. Arthur intervened on behalf of the college at the behest of Cardinal John McCloskey, the archbishop of New York. On October 25, 1884, Pope Leo XIII issued the brief *Ubi Primum,* which

raised the status of the college and bestowed the honorary title of "Pontifical."

In 1931 Pope Pius XI issued the apostolic constitution *Deus Scientiarum Dominus,* reforming the program of studies at pontifical universities for advanced theological degrees. As a result of the reform, the North American College established a house for graduate students, initially acquiring a villa on the Janiculum Hill for the purpose of providing housing.

The college was closed from 1940 to 1948 owing to World War II. Following the war, the eleventh rector, Bishop Martin J. O'Connor, supervised the construction of a new college on the Janiculum Hill, overlooking St. Peter's Basilica, from 1946 to 1953. The spacious facility for three hundred students was dedicated by Pope Pius XII on October 14, 1953. Once the new college was completed, the graduate house was moved to the original college building, which was renamed the Casa Santa Maria dell'Umiltà.

By 1959 the centennial of the college, over 2,500 seminarians had enrolled and studied in Rome (most of them graduated), and the college had produced over one hundred bishops, including seven cardinals. By 2000 the college had enrolled over 4,500 students.

Currently, the North American College comprises several programs: the seminary on the Janiculum Hill; the Casa Santa Maria for American priests doing graduate work in theology and other fields of ecclesiastical study; and the Institute for Continuing Theological Education, a three-month sabbatical program for priests offered twice a year and located as well on the Janiculum Hill. The college also administers the Bishops' Office for U.S. Visitors to the Vatican, located at the Casa Santa Maria, to assist pilgrims to make their journey to Rome truly rewarding spiritually, especially by seeing the Holy Father.

North American Martyrs

The North American Martyrs are the eight remarkable Jesuits martyred between the years 1642 and 1649 during their efforts at bringing the Gospel to the Native Americans in modern-day upstate New York and southeastern Canada. The North American martyrs are: René Goupil, a lay medic (d.

1642); Isaac Jogues (d. 1647); Jean de Lalande (d. 1647); John de Brébeuf (d. 1649); Anthony Daniel (d. 1649); Gabriel Lalemant (d. 1649); Charles Garnier (d. 1649); and Noel Chabanel (d. 1649). (*See also* individual entries for details on their lives.)

The martyrs are venerated at two shrines, one in Auriesville, New York, and one in Canada. They were canonized on June 29, 1930, by Pope Pius XI. St. Kateri Tekakwitha, the "Lily of the Mohawks," was brought into the faith by the Jesuits and is also honored at the shrine in Auriesville. The feast day of the North American Martyrs is October 19.

North Carolina

One of the original thirteen colonies, North Carolina is one of the traditional states of the South and has the motto *"Essere quam videri"* ("To be, rather than to seem to be"). The capital of the state is Raleigh, with other major cities in Charlotte, Asheville, Greensboro, and Winston. The original inhabitants of what became North Carolina were the Catawbas, Cherokee, and Tuscaroras. The first Europeans arrived following the granting in 1584 of a royal charter by Queen Elizabeth I of England to explore the New World. Efforts to establish a permanent colony failed until 1663, when King Charles II granted land to Sir George Carteret and others that made them "absolute lords proprietors" of the province of Carolina. This was expanded in 1665, and in 1669 the lords proprietors promulgated the "Fundamental Constitutions of Carolina," although the development of the colony proved slow and painful. In 1729 Carolina was declared a royal province after the crown purchased seven-eighths of the colony from the lords proprietors.

The Catholic faith entered what became North Carolina in 1526 through the Spanish Lucas Vázquez de Ayllón expedition, which attempted to establish a settlement on the Carolina coast. This did not endure, however. In 1540 an expedition headed by Hernando de Soto and accompanied by chaplains entered the region. Anti-Catholic sentiment was strong in the royal colony, reflecting the number of Puritans and Protestants who had settled there and the general antipathy toward the Catholic faith on the part of the royal government in the seventeenth and eighteenth centuries. In 1776 the state constitution denied office to "those who denied the truths of the Protestant religion."

By the start of the nineteenth century, there were few Catholics in the state, and they were served by visiting missionaries. In 1821 Bishop John England of Charleston celebrated Mass in the ballroom of the home of William Gaston at New Bern, marking the start of the organization of the first parish in the state, St. Paul's.

The onerous disqualification of Catholics from public office remained in force until the Constitutional Convention of 1835. The repeal was spearheaded by Gaston, who was elected associate justice of the state supreme court in 1833 and then took part as an influential member in the state's convention. In a famous speech, he secured the repeal of the clause, thereby bringing an end to many long years of discrimination against Catholics.

Despite this progress, Catholics continued to face local legal and social disabilities. As a result, the first Catholic church was built in Charlotte only in 1852, and Catholics did not finally obtain full civil liberty and rights until 1868. That year, Pope Blessed Pius IX officially established the Vicariate Apostolic of North Carolina, with counties separated from the Diocese of Charleston. Its first apostolic vicar was James (later Cardinal) Gibbons, and it comprised the entire state until 1910, when eight counties were attached to Belmont Abbey. The vicariate was established as the Diocese of Raleigh on December 12, 1924.

In 1874 vital support arrived for the Catholic community through the Sisters of Mercy, who opened an academy, several schools, hospitals, and an orphanage. Two years later, a Benedictine priory and school was founded at Belmont (later Belmont Abbey College). The priory was designated an abbey in 1884, and by a papal bull of Pope St. Pius X on June 8, 1910, the counties of Gaston, Lincoln, Cleveland, Rutherford, Polk, Burke, McDowell, and Catawba were used to form the the Diocese of the Cathedral Abbey at Belmont. Territory was lost over the next decades as the Church developed in North Carolina, including the Diocese of Raleigh in 1944 and 1960. The Belmont Diocese was suppressed in 1977. Meanwhile, the Diocese of Charlotte was created by Pope Paul VI on November 12, 1971.

The Church in North Carolina has grown considerably in the last half century, although it remains a small percentage of the overall population. Catholics have settled in the area as part of the growth of Charlotte and especially the Raleigh-Durham corridor. In 2011 there were nearly 390,000 Catholics, 299 priests, 173 women religious, and 150 parishes in the state.

Abbot Haid, Vicar Apostolic of North Carolina

North Dakota

A state in the northwestern part of the United States, North Dakota was admitted to the Union on November 2, 1889, at the same time as South Dakota. Its state motto is "Liberty and Union Now and Forever, One and Inseparable." North Dakota is one of the least populated states in the country. The territory that became North Dakota was the domain of at least ten tribes of Native Americans, including the Mandan, Hidatsa, Arikara, and Sioux.

The first European exploration of note was that of Pierre Gaultier de Varennes, Sieur de La Vérendrye, in 1736. He was looking for a passage to the Pacific, but he was also accompanied by the Jesuit priest Jean-Pierre Aulneau, who hoped to preach and evangelize among the Native Americans. His labors were ended tragically on June 8, 1736, when he and twenty other members of Gaultier's expedition were killed by a band of Sioux near Warroad, Minnesota.

The Louisiana Purchase in 1803 sparked a great interest in the exploration of the area, and the parts of the Dakotas that were not acquired by the United States in the Louisiana Purchase were acquired in 1818 from the British. Notable was the expedition of Lewis and Clark during the winter of 1804–05, which included a journey up the Missouri River on their way to the Pacific. The demanding geography initially attracted chiefly hunters and trappers, but in 1812 the first white settlers arrived, Scottish and Irish families at Pembina. By 1849 the mineral and coal value of the territory and the furs found there caused the area east of the Missouri and White Earth Rivers to be attached to the Territory of

Minnesota; the rest of the area was added to the Territory of Nebraska in 1854. In 1861 Congress created the Territory of North Dakota.

After the Gaultier expedition, there was virtually no major Catholic presence again until 1818, when Canadian priests began to minister to Catholics who had begun settling there. The priests included Father Joseph Norbert Provencher and Father Sévére Dumoulin, and they provided pastoral care to Catholic settlers and endeavored to evangelize among the Native Americans. The first baptism of Indians took place in 1840 at Fort Clark by Father Christian Hoecken.

The most remarkable of the missionaries and frontier priests was the Jesuit Father Pierre-Jean De Smet, who made the first of several trips among the Mandan and Gros Ventre Indians in 1840. His labors were carried forward by Abbot Martin Marty, O.S.B., who reached Fort Yates in 1876. Meanwhile, in 1848, Father George Belcourt became the first American resident priest in the territory and reestablished the abandoned Pembina Mission, while Father Jean Baptiste Marie Genin started a mission at St. Michael's, Fort Totten, in 1865.

Further outreach to the Sioux was made possible from 1874 with the arrival of Grey Nuns under Sister Mary Clapin at Fort Totten, who started a school and worked with the Catholic Indian agent, Major Forbes. Important assistance was provided by the Catholic Indian Bureau. Various priests served as chaplain to the school and worked for the care of the Sioux, going so far as to write a Bible history, prayer book, and hymns in the Sioux language.

The Apostolic Vicariate of Dakota was established by Pope Leo XIII on August 12, 1879. This reflected the growth of the population in the territory, in large measure because of the advent of the railroad and the sad decimation of the Indian tribes. A decade later, on November 10, 1889, the Diocese of Jamestown was erected, with John Shanley appointed on November 15 as its first bishop. The name of the diocese was changed in 1897 to Fargo (Jamestown was reestablished as a titular see in 1995).

The diocese was challenged from the start by a shortage of priests, as well as an even greater shortage of German-speaking priests for the largely German population. To assist in th is area, in 1893 the Benedictines founded St. Gall Monastery at Devil's Lake. The community was moved to Richardton in 1899 and became an abbey in 1903. On December 21, 1909, Pope St. Pius X created the Diocese of Bismarck as the second diocese of the state, with Abbot Vincent Wehrle as its first bishop.

In 2011 there were 143,000 Catholics out of a general population of 650,000, with some 233 priests, more than 200 men and women religious, and 230 parishes in the state.

Norwich, Diocese of

The Diocese of Norwich was established on August 6, 1953, by Pope Pius XII. It is a suffragan diocese of the Archdiocese of Hartford and encompasses the Connecticut counties of Middlesex, New London, Windham, and Tolland; it also includes Fishers Island, New York, in Suffolk County. It stretches for nearly two thousand square miles.

The first Mass in what became the Diocese of Norwich took place in 1781 at Lebanon, Connecticut. The environment of the colony was, like most of New England, decidedly hostile to Catholicism, as the colony itself was first settled in 1633 by a group of Puritans. The population was long ardently Protestant, and Catholics were unwelcome until the large influx of Irish, Italian, Polish, and French-Canadian Catholics began in the second half of the nineteenth century.

The tiny Catholic population was long administered by the vicar apostolic of London, but in 1789 jurisdiction was transferred to the see of Baltimore and its first bishop, John Carroll. In 1808, with the expansion of the ecclesiastical jurisdictions, Connecticut was placed under the authority of the new bishop of Boston. Infrequent visits were made by the bishops, but in 1828 the first resident priest was established, Reverend Bernard O'Cavanaugh. The first Catholic church was started in 1829.

The territory of what became the Diocese of Norwich was included in the original jurisdiction of the Diocese of Hartford when it was founded in 1843. Owing to the growth of the Catholic community, the decision was made to elevate the Diocese of Hartford to the rank of a metropolitan archdiocese on August 6, 1953, and the Diocese of Norwich was created on the same day, along with the other new suffragan Diocese of Bridgeport.

The first bishop of Norwich was Bernard J. Flanagan, who had been a priest in the Burlington diocese and had served as its chancellor. Named bishop on September 1, 1953, he was ordained a bishop on December 3, 1953, and assumed the task of providing a foundation for the diocesan institutions. He was transferred to the Diocese of Worcester on August 8, 1959.

Flanagan was succeeded by Vincent Joseph Hines. Father Hines had been a chaplain in the U.S. Army and had taken part in the D-Day invasion in Normandy, France, in 1944 and was awarded a Bronze Star. Appointed the second bishop of Norwich on November 27, 1959, he was ordained a bishop on March 17, 1960. He took part in the sessions of the Second Vatican Council and devoted his efforts to the expansion of Catholic education, including a million-dollar fundraising campaign for diocesan high schools. As part of the renewal program after the council, he appointed the first nun to head a diocesan school system in Connecticut. Bishop Hines retired on June 5, 1975.

Bishop Hines was succeeded on that same day by Bishop Daniel P. Reilly, who had been a priest of the Diocese of Providence. Ordained a bishop on August 6, 1975, Bishop Reilly was noted for his efforts to provide stability to diocesan finances, launching a $50 million Forward in Faith campaign. On October 27, 1994, he was transferred to the Diocese of Worcester.

Bishop Reilly was followed by Bishop Daniel Hart, who had been an auxiliary bishop of Boston since 1976. Bishop Hart was appointed the fourth bishop of Norwich on September 12, 1995, and installed on November 1. He provided further help to diocesan services through a $15 million Response of Faith campaign in 1998 and was active in promoting Catholic Charities. He retired on March 11, 2003, and was succeeded by Bishop Michael Richard Cote, an auxiliary bishop of the Diocese of Portland, Maine. In 2011 there were

239,000 Catholics, 173 priests, 185 women religious, and 76 parishes in the diocese.

Notre Dame of Maryland, College of

Established in 1895 on North Charles Street in Baltimore, the College of Notre Dame of Maryland is a liberal arts college for women. Conducted by the School Sisters of Notre Dame, the college holds the distinction of being the first Catholic college for women in the United States. The chief figure in the development of the school was Sister Mary Meletia Foley, S.S.N.D., who recognized the need for a college for women, especially after the founding of The Catholic University of America in 1889.

Notre Dame, University of

One of the most prestigious Catholic universities in the United States, the University of Notre Dame is located in South Bend, Indiana, and owned and directed by the Congregation of the Holy Cross. The university was founded in 1842 by Father Edward Sorin, C.S.C., with six other priests of the congregation, on land that was given to the Diocese of Vincennes by Father Stephen T. Badin.

The college opened in September 1843 with a temporary brick building serving as the central campus until another building was finished in 1844. Larger facilities were opened in 1853. Assisting the development of the school was a charter enacted in 1844 by the legislature of Indiana granting it the right to grant degrees in the liberal arts and sciences and in law and medicine. Enrollment was low, with only sixty-nine students studying in 1850, though the student body increased to two hundred by 1861.

Father Sorin was president throughout this early period, serving until 1865. That year, a department of science was inaugurated, followed by the College of Law in 1869 and the College of Engineering in 1872, the first program on the subject anywhere in the country. A fire in April 1879, however, destroyed virtually all the university buildings save for the church and the theater. The rebuilding established much of the university that is still visible today.

As the university continued to develop in the early twentieth century, public focus was on Notre Dame athletics, in particular the enormously successful football team of the Fighting Irish under the legendary coach Knute Rockne, head of the football team from 1918 to 1931. Through Rockne and the excellence of the faculty and graduates, Notre Dame soon emerged as one of the best-known schools in the United States. Additional esteem was achieved during the long presidency of Reverend Theodore Hesburgh, during whose tenure from 1952 to 1987 enrollment increased to ten thousand, women were admitted as undergraduates beginning in 1972, and important doctoral programs were introduced in the fields of liturgical studies and theology. Notre Dame subsequently became one of the largest centers for theology and philosophy in the United States, including the establishment of the Jacques Maritain Philosophical Center.

Nuncios. *See* **Holy See-U.S. Relations**

O

Oakland, Diocese of

Established on February 21, 1962, by Pope Blessed John XXIII, the Diocese of Oakland serves northern counties in California. The diocese is situated on the eastern side of San Francisco Bay and was once part of Rancho San Antonio. In 1851 Horace W. Carpentier founded Oakland as part of his ferry service. The towns of Oakland and Brooklyn were amalgamated in 1872. Oakland received refugees from the 1906 San Francisco earthquake, and the vast San Francisco-Oakland Bay Bridge opened in 1936. Military installations were also established in the city, and industrial and maritime activities developed rapidly. The Diocese of Oakland is a suffragan see of the Archdiocese of San Francisco.

The Catholic heritage of Oakland dates to the opening of Mission San Jose in 1797. Juan Rodriguez Cabrillo had discovered California as early as 1542, and Sebastian Vizcaino visited the area in 1602. The region was colonized in 1769, as the Spanish secured California against Russian adventurers. The first Catholic church in Oakland was St. Mary's, serving as a mission in 1853 and as a parish in 1858. The Holy Name Sisters started their education apostolate in the region in 1868.

The Catholics of Oakland had been under the jurisdiction of the Diocese of Sonora, which included the Two Californias. The Franciscans had pioneered in California after the Jesuits were expelled, and they remained in the missions founded by Blessed Junípero Serra and others. Bishop Francisco Garcia Diego y Moreno, also a Franciscan, served the faithful in the region. Then, in 1848, the Treaty of Guadalupe-Hidalgo gave California to the United States. The Gold Rush brought countless settlers to the area, and California entered the Union in 1850.

Pope Blessed Pius IX appointed the Dominican Joseph Sadoc Alemany to the Diocese of Monterey, and the new bishop also served the San Francisco area. On July 29, 1853, he became the first archbishop of San Francisco. The faithful of Oakland were served by this pioneering prelate and his successors as the population of the state increased

steadily over the succeeding decades. The military, notably the naval needs of the country, brought workers to California, especially in the years after World War I.

In the face of the Great Depression, the Church responded with Catholic Charities programs and welcomed Hispanics into the area. African-American apostolates also became part of the Church's mission in the 1920s and 1930s. World War II accelerated the growth of Oakland, as naval operations were centered in the Bay area, as well as in San Diego to the south.

In 1962 Oakland became a diocese, and Bishop Floyd L. Begin was named the first bishop on January 27, 1962. He had served since 1947 as an auxiliary bishop for Cleveland. Installed on April 28, 1962, Bishop Begin had the task of establishing the diocese on a firm footing and providing it with needed administrative offices and a diocesan curia. He also had the immense task of attending the Second Vatican Council and then implementing the many reforms of the council in the diocese. To assist Catholic social communications, he founded a diocesan newspaper.

Bishop Begin served faithfully until his death on April 26, 1977. He was succeeded by Bishop John S. Cummins, who had been an auxiliary bishop of Sacramento since 1974. Bishop Cummins was appointed the second bishop of Oakland on May 3, 1977, and was installed on June 30, 1977. He expanded diocesan facilities, meeting the needs of the movement away from the city of Oakland to the surrounding suburban communities. He also promoted ministries for the Asian communities developing in the area. He retired on October 1, 2003, and was succeeded on the same day by Bishop Allen H. Vigneron, who had been named the coadjutor bishop of Oakland on January 10, 2003, and installed on February 26.

Bishop Vigneron, who had served previously as an auxiliary bishop of Detroit from 1996 to 2003, acceded to the see and began his labors as shepherd over the faithful of the Northern California counties of Alameda and Contra Costa. One of the main tasks facing the bishop was the immense project of building the Cathedral of Christ the Light for the diocese. Work began on the massive cathedral in December 2006.

On January 5, 2009, Bishop Vigneron was appointed archbishop of Detroit. He was succeeded on March 23, 2009, by Bishop Salvatore Cordileone, who had been an auxiliary bishop of San Diego. He was installed on May 5, 2009.

In 2011 the Catholic population of Oakland was over 468,000, served by 270 priests, more than 400 men and women religious, and 86 parishes. The diocese also boasts three Catholic colleges and universities, including the Graduate School of Theology, part of the Graduate Theological Union, as well as 9 high schools and 47 elementary schools.

Oblates of Mary Immaculate (O.M.I.)

A religious community of priests and brothers, the Oblates of Mary Immaculate was founded in France in 1816 by Father St. Charles Joseph Eugene de Mazenod, who died in 1861 and was canonized in 1995. Its mission was to preach the Gospel to the poor working people in southern France and later to advance the missions and assist in priestly formation. The congregation received episcopal approval in 1818 and papal approval from Pope Leo XII in 1826. From the start of their labors, the Oblates proved invaluable in promoting the life of rural parishes, and in 1824 the members took up the task of seminary training, assuming control of various seminaries in France, including the major seminary of Marseilles. By 1831 the Oblates had also begun assisting the vast missionary efforts that were to become a hallmark of the Church in the nineteenth century.

Members of the community first arrived in Canada in 1841 at the request of Bishop Ignace Bourget of Montréal to assist the pastoral needs of Catholics in eastern Canada. The evangelizing zeal of the Oblates took them to the wildest regions of Canada, from Labrador to, ultimately, Alaska and the Arctic. At the same time, the Oblates opened missions and parishes among the new dioceses of Canada. They also became invaluable in teaching; in 1848 they established the University of Ottawa.

The Oblates arrived in the United States in 1843 when they preached missions to Canadian immigrants in northern New York state and Vermont. Their ministry centered in missionary work and parish service, and members soon traveled into Oregon and as far south as Texas. They then entered into missionary and parish service in Mexico. The Oblates were soon distinguished in the United States as gifted preachers and dedicated priests and brothers among the Native Americans and the poor. They were especially known for their willingness to accept the most difficult mission assignments in isolated regions and under severe climatic and geographic conditions, from Texas to Alaska.

Over the years, members have been named bishops in the United States, including several serving over the last decade, such as Bishop Michael D. Pfeifer of San Angelo, Archbishop Roger Lawrence Schwietz of Anchorage, and Cardinal Francis George of Chicago. There are also several Oblate bishops serving as shepherds of Canadian dioceses and archdioceses.

In 2011 there were over four thousand Oblates serving in sixty-eight countries. In the United States, over six hundred Oblates serve in the U.S province in a host of ministries, including prison and hospital chaplaincies, education, shrines, and parishes. Members from the United States also serve in missions in Central America, South America, Asia, Africa, Europe, and Oceania.

Oblate Sisters of Providence

A religious congregation of women founded in 1829 in Baltimore, the community has the remarkable distinction of being the first successful Catholic religious order composed entirely of African-American women. The start of the community is traced to the work of the French-born Sulpician priest James Hector Nicholas Joubert and four African-American women: Mary Elizabeth Lange, Maria Balas, Rosine Boegue, and the American-born Theresa Duchemin. In 1828 Joubert became associated with Lange and Balas when he learned of their work among poor black children in Baltimore. He asked them to help him start a community with the primary mission of teaching and caring for African-American children. Joined by Boegue and Duchemin, they began preparation for the religious life and then opened a Catholic school for girls in their convent in Baltimore. The school became St. Frances Academy, now the oldest continuously operating school for black Catholic children in the United States.

The new congregation began officially on July 2, 1829, when the four sisters took their vows. The community developed rapidly in the next years, so that a new school and chapel were built in 1836. The chapel was also used by the African-Americans of Baltimore. This was another first, as it represented for the first time a separate chapel for use by black Catholics.

Father Joubert died in 1843, and his death marked a period of decline for the congregation. By 1846 enrollment had fallen to a mere eight students paying tuition. At the same time, Mother Theresa Duchemin left the order to help establish the Sisters, Servants of the Immaculate Heart of Mary (I.H.M.). In 1847 the Redemptorist Father Thaddeus Anwander became the congregation's ecclesiastical director, inaugurating a new period of growth. Soon another school was opened, for boys, and the sisters launched other schools in the city as well as evening classes for adult women and a home for widows. In 1860 the Redemptorists ceased their role with the community, but for his contributions Father Anwander is honored as the second founder of the Oblates.

With the departure of the Oblates began the association with the Society of Jesus. With their encouragement, the Oblates expanded outside of Baltimore by opening a mission in Philadelphia in 1863 and another one in New Orleans in 1867. The sisters maintained their connection with the Jesuits until 1871, when directors were appointed from the Josephite Fathers and Brothers. The Oblates, meanwhile, continued to prosper and gradually established schools in eighteen states. By the 1950s there were over three hundred Oblate Sisters of Providence in ministry in the United States.

Cardinal Patrick O'Boyle

Foreign missions were also started in 1900, with the opening of a mission in Havana. The Oblates were a beloved presence in Cuba until 1961, when they were forced to leave in the wake of the Cuban Revolution and the rise of Fidel Castro's totalitarian regime. The congregation also started houses in the western Caribbean, as well as in the Dominican Republic and Costa Rica.

Today, there are over a hundred Oblate Sisters of Providence active in twenty-five United States cities. They are also engaged in ministry in the Caribbean, Costa Rica, and also, most recently, in Africa. Their motherhouse is in Baltimore.

O'Boyle, Patrick A. (July 18, 1896–August 10, 1987)

Archbishop of Washington, D.C., from 1948 to 1973 and a cardinal from 1967, Patrick A. O'Boyle was born to a working-class family in Scranton, Pennsylvania, and worked as a young man in a variety of odd jobs until convinced to complete his college education by his widowed mother. He graduated from St. Thomas College, the future University of Scranton, in 1916 and entered the seminary, receiving ordination for the Archdiocese of New York in 1921. He served as a parish priest ministering to the working poor in Manhattan's infamous Hell's Kitchen, where he saw firsthand the struggle of the lower classes in the 1920s. In 1926 he entered the graduate school of the New York School of Social Work and later taught at Fordham University.

As his talent was recognized by archdiocesan officials, Father O'Boyle was named to several posts, including assistant director of the children's division of Catholic Charities. In 1941, however, he was appointed director of the War Relief Services and in 1942 director of War Relief Services of the National Catholic Welfare Conference. In this capacity he played a key role in assisting the countless victims of World War II, helping to distribute food, clothing, medicine, and supplies across the globe. In May 1947 Cardinal Francis Spellman of New York named him head of Catholic Charities, but he was soon appointed instead archbishop of Washington by Pope Pius XII.

Consecrated archbishop on January 21, 1948, O'Boyle began a time as shepherd of Washington that lasted for a quarter of a century. He soon distinguished himself by his determination to be a champion of civil rights. In 1949 he launched a program of integration for the Catholic schools in the District of Columbia and became one of the most committed and active members of the U.S. hierarchy in the civil rights movement of the 1950s and 1960s. He served as chairman of the Interracial Committee on Race Relations, took part in the 1963 March on Washington, and helped to organize the Urban Rehabilitation Corporation in 1967. That same year, he was named to the College of Cardinals by Pope Paul VI as a cardinal priest in the consistory of June 26, 1967. He received the title of Santa Nicola in Carcere.

The next year, Cardinal O'Boyle entered into a period of controversy over the papal encyclical *Humanae Vitae*. A staunch defender of the encyclical and the Church's teachings on contraception, he found himself at odds with some of his own priests and with theologians in the Washington area, in particular at The Catholic University of America. Reiterating that the encyclical was binding in conscience, he took the dramatic step of depriving thirty-nine priests of faculties to various degrees. The Congregation for the Clergy in Rome eventually upheld the archbishop's right to impose disciplinary action while seeking to end the controversy with an appropriate reinstatement of those dissenters who accepted the decision of the congregation. Cardinal O'Boyle retired in 1973 and died in Washington, D.C.

O'Brien, Edwin F. (April 8, 1939–)

Grand Master of the Equestrian Order of the Holy Sepulchre of Jerusalem since 2011, archbishop of Baltimore from 2007 to 2010, archbishop of the Military Ordinariate of the United States from 1997 to 2007, and a cardinal from 2012, Edwin F. O'Brien was born in the Bronx, New York, the eldest of the three children of Edwin Frederick Sr. and Mary Winifred O'Brien. Called to the priesthood, he entered St. Joseph's Seminary in Yonkers and obtained a bachelor's degree in 1961, followed by a master of divinity degree in 1964 and a master of arts in 1965. Ordained a priest on May 29, 1965, by Cardinal Francis Spellman, archbishop of New York, he served as a priest for the Arch-

diocese of New York and received as his assignment a posting as a civilian chaplain at the United States Military Academy at West Point, New York. He subsequently joined the military chaplain corps, and served with the 82nd Airborne Division, including a tour of duty during the Vietnam War with the 173rd Airborne Brigade and the 1st Cavalry Brigade. In 1973 he ended his military service and was sent to Rome for doctoral studies in moral theology at the Pontifical University of St. Thomas, the Angelicum. He earned a doctorate in 1976 and returned to New York, where he became vice chancellor for the archdiocese and associate pastor at St. Patrick's Cathedral. In 1979 he was responsible for planning the visit of Pope Blessed John Paul II to New York. He then served as rector of St. Joseph's Seminary from 1985 to 1989 and again from 1994 to 1997. From 1990 to 1994, he served as rector of the North American College in Rome.

On February 6, 1996, O'Brien was named titular bishop of Tizica and appointed auxiliary bishop of New York. Consecrated a bishop on March 25, 1996, he was appointed the next year as coadjutor archbishop of the Military Ordinariate of the United States. He acceded to the ordinariate on August 12, 1997, and worked to promote the Chaplain Corps and to provide for the needs of Catholics in the U.S. military in the wake of the attacks of September 11, 2001, and the wars in Iraq and Afghanistan that followed. In 2006 he was named by the Holy See to coordinate the papal visitation of Seminaries and Houses of Priestly Formation in the wake of the sex abuse crisis.

On July 12, 2007, Archbishop O'Brien was appointed to the metropolitan see of Baltimore. On August 29, 2011, he was named Pro-Grand Master of the Equestrian Order of the Holy Sepulchre of Jerusalem. He was appointed by Pope Benedict XVI to the College of Cardinals on February 18, 2012, and received the title of Grand Master of the Knights.

O'Brien, William Vincent (1740–May 14, 1816)

An Irish Dominican priest and noted preacher, William Vincent O'Brien was born in Dublin. He left Ireland and journeyed to Rome, where he entered the Dominicans in 1760. After ordination, he returned to Ireland and devoted the next years to preaching; in honor of his labors, he was named preacher general of the order in 1785. Two years later, he sailed to the United States to assist the missions in the young country. Then-Father John Carroll sent him first to Philadelphia and then to New York. There, O'Brien marched into the midst of the controversy at St. Peter's Parish, a community that had been divided between two priests, Charles Whelan and Andrew Nugent, and had been additionally troubled by the presence of trusteeism. Father O'Brien proved able to win the support of the parishioners once Fathers Whelan and Nugent had departed, although the parish was troubled for several more years by Father Nugent and his supporters.

Once established as pastor, Father O'Brien launched plans to pay for the completion of St. Peter's Church, journeying to Mexico to solicit funds from the archbishop of Mexico. He also was responsible for the founding of St. Peter's Free School, the first Catholic school in New York. He became famous in the city for his selfless devotion to the victims of yellow fever. He retired in 1806 but received a pension (unusual in its time) from his grateful parishioners.

O'Callaghan, Edmund Bailey (February 27, 1797– May 29, 1880)

An Irish-born physician and historian, Edmund Bailey O'Callaghan was born at Mallow, Cork, Ireland. After studies in Ireland, he went to Paris in 1820 to study medicine and then migrated to Montréal in 1830. There he became involved in Canadian independence and served in the Provincial Parliament in 1836. The following year, however, he fled to the United States after treason charges were made against him. He settled in Albany, New York, where he resumed his medical practice and founded the industrial journal *Northern Light*.

Always interested in history, O'Callaghan wrote a number of significant historical works, including *History of New Netherland* (1846–49), *Documents Relating to the Colonial History of New York Albany*, a collection of historical documents on New York colonial history in eleven volumes (1855–61), *Journal of the Legislation Council of the State of New York, 1691–1775* (1860), and a valuable study on the *Jesuit Relations* (1847). He died in New York.

O'Connell, Denis (January 28, 1849–January 1, 1927)

Bishop of Richmond from 1912 to 1926 and a vigorous opponent of anti-Catholicism in Virginia, Denis J. O'Connell is best known for his tenure as rector of the North American College and his support of Americanist ideas. He was born in Donoughmore, Ireland, although his family emigrated to Columbia, South Carolina, when he was a boy and then to Charlotte, North Carolina, after the Civil War. Three of his uncles were already serving in the Carolinas as priests. At the encouragement of his uncles, he started at a seminary at St. Charles College in Ellicott, Maryland. There he met and became a friend of James Gibbons, the vicar apostolic of North Carolina. Gibbons became bishop of Richmond in 1872, and he sent O'Connell to Rome to study at the North American College. O'Connell was ordained there in 1877, the same year that Bishop Gibbons became coadjutor archbishop of Baltimore. He remained in service in Richmond in pastoral work, but in 1883 Archbishop Gibbons appointed him a key assistant in the preparations for the Third Plenary Council of Baltimore. Father O'Connell served as secretary to the council and went to Rome afterward to secure formal approval for its decrees.

In 1885 he was appointed rector of the North American College. His tenure was marked by the considerable Americanist controversy, and Father O'Connell was a supporter of the general positions of Bishop John Ireland and Archbishop Gibbons. In 1895 he was compelled to resign at the request of Pope Leo XIII owing to the complaints of a number of American bishops, in particular Archbishop Michael A. Corrigan of New York, concerning his earlier sympathies. He continued to advance the intellectual position of Americanism in Europe, however, delivering a noted address in 1897 in Fribourg, Switzerland, entitled "A New Idea in the Life of Father Hecker," which supported the general principles of a separation of church and state as beneficial to the Church.

Despite the condemnation of Americanism by Pope Leo XIII in 1899, Father O'Connell regained the support of Roman officials, thanks in part to Cardinal Gibbons, and was named rector of The Catholic University of America in 1903. He proved an able rector, doing much to improve the academic and financial health of the then relatively obscure school. In 1908 he was appointed auxiliary bishop of San Francisco. Four years later, he was named bishop of Richmond, where he spoke out with considerable effort against the anti-Catholic tendencies of the area, in particular the activities of the Ku Klux Klan. He resigned in 1926 and became titular archbishop of Mariamne, andhe died the following year in Richmond.

O'Connell, William H. (December 8, 1859–April 22, 1944)

Archbishop of Boston from 1907 to 1944 and cardinal from 1911, William Henry O'Connell was born in Lowell, Massachusetts, the youngest of eleven children in a poor Irish immigrant family. After a brief time of seminary studies in Maryland, he entered Boston College, graduated in 1881, and then was sent to the North American College in Rome, where he was ordained in 1884. Returning home, he served in several pastoral assignments, so distinguishing himself as a priest that he was named in 1895 to replace the controversial Father Denis J. O'Connell as rector of the North American College. Taking up his duties in the midst of the Americanist crisis, he proved committed to the position of those opposed to Americanist tendencies, also becoming friends with Cardinal Francesco Satolli and then Archbishop (later Cardinal) Rafael Merry del Val.

Cardinal William O'Connell

As rector, he increased both enrollment and a sense of stability during a troubled time, and by 1901 he was named bishop of Portland, Maine. While active as bishop — he visited every parish and promoted Catholic youth — he served as envoy for the Holy See in 1905 to the Imperial Court of Japan. His suggestion that a Catholic university be established was brought to fruition in 1907. On February 8, 1906, while returning home from Japan, he was informed that he had been named coadjutor archbishop of Boston. The following year, in August 1907, he succeeded Archbishop John J. Williams. In 1911 he was named a cardinal priest in the consistory of November 27, 1911; at the age of fifty-one, he was one of the youngest cardinals in the world. As he arrived late to the conclaves of 1914 and 1922, he made the request of Pope Pius XI that the time between the death of the pope and the opening of the conclave be extended. He later participated in the conclave of 1939 that elected Pope Pius XII.

As archbishop, O'Connell devoted considerable effort to reforming the administrative life of the archdiocese, introducing bureaucratic techniques that were then considered quite innovative. The chief thrust of the reform was to increase diocesan centralization, especially the chancery and Catholic charities. Through his financial reforms, he was able to institute a number of notable programs, including the Guild of St. Apollonia in 1920 to provide free dental care to children in the parochial schools, Catholic Guilds for the Blind, and the St. Paul's Rehabilitation Center for the Blind.

Cardinal O'Connell also presided over the steady growth of the archdiocesan population. Between 1910 and 1940, the Catholic population in Boston increased by more than 300,000; parishes increased from 194 in 1907 to 302 in 1944. Similar increases were seen in priests and men and women religious. (*See also* Boston, Archdiocese of.) Cardinal O'Connell wielded considerable political and social influence as archbishop, establishing the sway of Catholics in the city for decades. In 1937 he was awarded an honorary degree by Harvard University, the first native Catholic prelate to be so honored.

O'Connor, Carroll (August 2, 1924–June 21, 2001)

A film and television actor best known for his longtime roles as Archie Bunker on *All in the Family* and police chief Bill Gillespie on *In the Heat of the Night*, Carroll O'Connor was born in Manhattan, New York, and raised in Forest Hills, a community in Queens, New York. In 1942 he joined the Merchant Marines and served on ships in the Atlantic. In 1946 he enrolled at the University of Montana to study English and there became interested in theater. While there, he met his future wife, Nancy Fields, whom he married in 1951. He then moved to Ireland, where he continued his acting studies at the National University of Ireland.

He returned to New York in 1954 but was unable to land a Broadway role. He took a position in a high school until 1958, when he finally landed a role in an Off-Broadway production, *Ulysses in Downtown*. Around the same time, he earned roles on television. After a variety of film and televisions appearances, he was signed in 1971 as the star of *All in the Family*. He subsequently earned numerous Emmy awards.

Cardinal John O'Connor

A devout Catholic, he was involved in extensive charitable activities, including serving with his wife as a founder of the John Wayne Cancer Clinic, funding numerous scholarships for American Indians at the University of Montana, and promoting anti-drug legislation after the drug-related suicide of his adopted son, Hugh, in 1995. He was given numerous honors, such as a Life Achievement Award from the Christophers and a Lifetime Special Achievement Award from Catholics in Media in 1996.

O'Connor, Edwin (July 29, 1918–March 23, 1968)
Author, columnist, and novelist Edwin O'Connor was born in Providence, Rhode Island, and studied at the University of Notre Dame, graduating in 1939. After serving from 1942 to 1945 in the Coast Guard during the Second World War, he became a freelance writer and wrote a weekly column for the *Boston Herald* under the pseudonym "Roger Swift." He became chiefly known, however, for his novels, including *The Oracle* (1951), *The Last Hurrah* (1958), *The Edge of Sadness* (1961), *I Was Dancing* (1964), and *All in the Family* (1966). He died in Boston.

O'Connor, John J. (January 20, 1920–May 3, 2000)
Archbishop of New York from 1984 to 2000 and a cardinal, John Joseph O'Connor was one of the

Catholic Church's most eloquent and determined spokespersons for the culture of life in America. He was born in Philadelphia, the fourth of five children of Thomas O'Connor and Dorothy Gomple. Called to the priesthood, he studied at St. Charles Borromeo Seminary and was ordained on December 15, 1945, and subsequently taught for seven years at St. James High School in Philadelphia. He also earned a master's degree from Villanova University, worked as an assistant pastor, conducted two weekly radio programs, developed programs to teach mentally handicapped children, and worked on psychiatric wards.

In 1952 he entered the armed forces during the Korean War as a chaplain. What began as a two-year stint in the navy ended twenty-seven years later with O'Connor's retirement as a rear admiral. In 1972 he was appointed Chief Chaplain at the United States Naval Academy, Annapolis, Maryland. During this time, he also earned a master's degree in clinical psychology from The Catholic University of America and a doctorate in political science from Georgetown University. Among his professors was Jeane Kirkpatrick, former ambassador to the United Nations.

Soon after his retirement in 1979, O'Connor was named an auxiliary bishop of the Military Ordinariate and titular bishop of Curzola on April 18, 1979. He was consecrated a bishop on May 27, 1979, by Pope Blessed John Paul II in St. Peter's Basilica. On May 6, 1983, he was appointed the bishop of Scranton, but within months, on January 25, 1984, he was named the archbishop of New York. The following year, Pope Blessed John Paul II elevated him to the rank of cardinal priest in the consistory of May 25, 1985, with the title of SS. John and Paul.

From the start of his time as archbishop of New York, O'Connor displayed a powerful personality, genuine humor, and an unwavering commitment to the pro-life cause. Cardinal O'Connor also launched numerous programs in the archdiocese for the sick and disabled, including the victims of AIDS in New York City. He was also a leader in promoting ecumenism and interreligious dialogue, labored for peace in the Middle East, helped draft the 1989 statement calling for a Palestinian homeland, and from 1984 was head of the Catholic Near East Welfare Association. In 1984 he had a famous public disagreement with Geraldine Ferraro, the vice-presidential running mate of Walter Mondale, over her stand on abortion as a Catholic politician. In 1991 he founded the Sisters of Life to promote the sanctity of life in all its dimensions. In recognition of his work, he was awarded the Congressional Gold Medal on March 7, 2000. Diagnosed with a brain tumor, he heroically fought the disease but eventually succumbed and died in New York. He was buried in the crypt of St. Patrick's Cathedral in New York.

O'Connor, Mary Flannery (March 25, 1925– August 3, 1964)

A novelist and short-story writer best known for her deeply insightful writings set in the South, Flannery O'Connor was born in Savannah, Georgia, and grew up and studied at Georgia State College for Women in Milledgeville. After graduation she went on to study creative writing at the University of Iowa, earning a Master of Fine Arts degree. From there she went eventually to New York City and then to Connecticut, where she lived with fellow writers Sally and Robert Fitzgerald. Her first published work was a short story that appeared in *Accent* magazine in 1946. This was followed by the novels *Wise Blood* in 1952, *The Violent Bear It Away* in 1960, and other short stories, collected in such works as *A Good Man Is Hard to Find* in 1955.

In 1951 she returned home to Georgia and settled in with her mother on a farm near Milledgeville. By the time of the publication of her first novel, she had already endured the onset of lupus, the disease that had shortened the life of her father. The chronic illness eventually caused her death at the age of thirty-nine.

She had written only two novels and thirty-two short stories, as well as commentaries and reviews. Nevertheless, O'Connor is honored as one of America's greatest writers. In 1963 she received the O. Henry Award for her story "Everything That Rises Must Converge," and she received several honorary degrees. Her importance, literary skills, and above all her deeply imbued catholicity came to be appreciated even more after her death. O'Connor's faith was made manifest in her writings, deliberately so, in particular her abiding embrace of the Church's teachings on redemption and the Incarnation. Her style was never overly pious and was unflinching in its presentation of fallen humanity, set within the culture she understood best, the Deep South. Interwoven profoundly, however, was the redemption from that state by Christ.

O'Connor, Michael (September 27, 1810–October 18, 1872)

The first bishop of Pittsburgh, from 1843 to 1853, Michael O'Connor was born in Queenstown, Ireland. Discerning a vocation, he was sent to Rome to study, receiving ordination in June 1833. He subsequently served at the Irish College in Rome and then in Ireland before receiving an invitation from Bishop Francis P. Kenrick of Philadelphia to come to the United States to take up a professorship at St. Charles Borromeo's Seminary in 1838. Three years later, he was named vicar general of the western part of Pennsylvania. In 1843 the Holy See established the Diocese of Pittsburgh to serve the growing Catholic population in western Pennsylvania, and while in Rome O'Connor was appointed bishop on August 7, 1843. He was consecrated in Rome on August 15, 1843.

The seventeen years of Bishop O'Connor's episcopate were marked by the steady increase in the Catholic population of Pittsburgh and western Pennsylvania. Launching immediately into the development of his diocese, he convoked the first diocesan synod in 1844 and established key diocesan offices. He also opened a chapel for the use by black Catholics of the city and launched the publication *The Pittsburgh Catholic*. That same year, St. Michael's ecclesiastical seminary was established to train candidates for the priesthood.

In order to assist the local Church, O'Connor encouraged the arrival of religious orders. His invitation was accepted by the Sisters of Mercy (1843), the Benedictine monks (1846), the Brothers of the Third Order of St. Francis (1847), the Sisters of Notre Dame (1848), and the Passionists (1852).

Owing to poor health, O'Connor resigned in 1860, but then petitioned Rome to permit him to enter the Jesuits, thereby fulfilling a lifelong aspiration. By the time of his departure, there were over fifty thousand Catholics in the diocese, served by seventy-seven parishes, eighty-six priests, and two religious orders of women. After serving his novitiate in Germany, he returned to the United States and became an accomplished preacher and lecturer. He was buried by the Jesuits at Woodstock, Maryland.

O'Conor, Charles (January 22, 1804–May 12, 1884)

A noted lawyer, Charles O'Conor was born in New York City to Irish immigrant parents and became a lawyer in New York in 1824. He first rose to prominence for his participation in the legal case against the election for trustees of St. Peter's Church in New York (*see also* Trusteeism), and thereafter enjoyed a swift climb to the top of the legal profession in the city, including appearances before the state supreme court.

By 1846 O'Conor was ranked among the chief legal minds in the United States. He became especially famed for his participation in the divorce trial of the actor Edwin Forrest and for his decision in 1865 to serve as counsel for the former president of the Confederacy, Jefferson Davis, on charges of treason. In 1871 he was counsel for the State of New York in its historic case against the infamous Boss Tweed, William M. Tweed, and his cohorts on charges of fraud; he refused all compensation. In 1875, however, he fell ill during the proceedings, dramatically leaving his sickbed to appear in the courtroom to complete the trial. He died in Nantucket, Massachusetts, and was declared by Samuel J. Tilden to be "the greatest jurist among all the English-speaking race."

O'Daniel, Victor Francis (February 15, 1868–June 12, 1960)

A Benedictine friar and historian, Victor Francis O'Daniel was born Washington County, Kentucky, and entered the Dominicans at the age of eighteen, receiving ordination to the priesthood on June 16, 1891. He then studied at the American College of Louvain in Belgium and subsequently held teaching posts at Dominican houses of study in California and Washington, D.C. In 1907 he was appointed the first archivist of the St. Joseph

Province, devoting most of his remaining life to a variety of historical writings and research. In 1915 he became a participant in the effort to launch the *Catholic Historical Review,* serving as associate editor. In addition to his articles for the review, he wrote a biography of Edward D. Fenwick, O.P., the first bishop of Cincinnati; a biography of Charles Hyacinth McKenna, founder of the Holy Name Society in the United States; and a history of the Dominican Province of St. Joseph. He is especially honored as an archivist for his efforts to preserve the remarkable record of the Dominicans in the United States.

Odermatt, Adelhelm (December 10, 1844–November 6, 1920)

Karl Odermatt was born in Nidwalden, Switzerland, and entered the Benedictines at Engelberg in 1866, taking the name Adelhelm; he was ordained in 1869. In 1873 he was assigned to the United States, establishing the first foundation of the Engelberg House in Missouri. After a brief period of service in the Portland area, in 1882 he was named head of the new Benedictine community in Oregon. He served in a variety of offices, including prior and administrator, distinguishing himself especially for his gift at fundraising to assist the rebuilding of Mount Angel Monastery and Seminary after a fire in 1892. He was named a titular abbot in 1916.

Odin, John M. (February 25, 1800–May 25, 1870)

French-born missionary and the second archbishop of New Orleans, John M. Odin was born in Hauteville, France, and entered the seminary in 1814 at Lyons. After further studies, he embarked upon a voyage to the United States to serve in the missions. Arriving in the Diocese of Louisiana and the Two Floridas, he was assigned by Bishop Louis William Dubourg to the Vincentian seminary of St. Mary's of the Barrens in Missouri. Ordained in 1823, he was also by then a member of the Vincentians, taking his final vows in 1825.

Father Odin served for the next years as a professor of theology, vice rector, and finally rector of the seminary in Missouri. In 1840, however, he set out for service in the Texas missions with the title of vice prefect apostolic. In 1841 he was appointed vicar apostolic and bishop; in 1847 he became the first bishop of Galveston after the founding of the diocese on May 4, 1847. One of his first notable acts was to secure from the Republic of Texas legal recognition of the Church's claim to those possessions dated to the time of Mexican ownership of Texas. His labors over the twenty years in Texas also did much to strengthen the Church in the region. Bishop Odin started numerous churches, a college, and a seminary, ordained and recruited priests, and provided a firm ecclesiastical structure for a rapidly developing state.

Archbishop John M. Odin

Such was Bishop Odin's success that in 1861 he was appointed archbishop of New Orleans, serving with distinction throughout the terrible period of the Civil War. He received encouragement from Pope Pius IX to promote peace and was especially beloved by the many soldiers of both armies who marched through the city at different times in the struggle. In the terrible aftermath of the war, he devoted his efforts and resources to assisting the victims of the fighting. Despite poor health, he traveled to Rome to attend the First Vatican Council. He grew so ill while in Rome that he went home to Hauteville, where he died. (*See also* Texas.)

O'Dwyer, Joseph (1841–January 7, 1898)

A physician and inventor of intubation, Joseph O'Dwyer was born in Cleveland. He studied medicine in New York and earned notoriety for his service in the City Hospital of New York City, twice contracting cholera during his care of the many victims of the disease. In 1872 he was named to the staff of the New York Foundling Asylum (later the New York Foundling Hospital). While treating victims of diphtheria, he successfully invented the procedure of intubation — placing a tube in the larynx to ensure his young patients would be able to breathe. He died in New York.

Oertel, John James (April 27, 1811–August 21, 1882)

A journalist, John James Oertel was born in Ansbach, Bavaria, into a Lutheran family who sent him

to the Lutheran University of Erlangen to study theology. Ordained a minister, he migrated to the United States, arriving in New York in October 1837. By 1840 he had grown so disillusioned with the Lutherans in the United States that he converted to Catholicism. The published account of his conversion in 1850 was the source of considerable controversy in Protestant circles. After teaching German at St. John's College (later Fordham University), he edited the *Wahrheitsfreund*, a German Catholic weekly in Cincinnati, and in 1846 founded the Baltimore weekly paper *Kirchenzeitung*, which became the most widely read German Catholic publication in the United States. In 1875 he was declared a Knight of St. Gregory in recognition of his service to the Church by Pope Blessed Pius IX.

O'Farrell, John Andrew (February 13, 1823–May 22, 1900)

A business leader in Idaho, John Andrew O'Farrell was born in County Tyrone, Ireland. He left his native country to become a sailor at the age of fifteen and saw much of the world on his voyages. He was in California on the day it became a state and so was immediately an American citizen. After further voyages at sea and after participating in the Crimean War, he returned to California in 1853, where he prospected for gold. In 1860 he struck gold in Colorado and the next year married Mary Ann Chapman in Louisville, Kentucky. The two eventually settled in Boise, Idaho, where they were active in assisting the Church. They offered their simple home as the local Catholic center until the first church could be built on land they donated. O'Farrell became one of the key figures in the development of Boise and was one of the most respected philanthropists in Idaho. (*See also* Idaho.)

O'Gara, Cuthbert (April 1, 1886–May 13, 1968)

A Passionist missionary and bishop in China, Cuthbert O'Gara was born in Ottawa, Canada. He entered the Passionists and made his profession in 1914; he was ordained in 1915. After teaching for several years in the Passionist seminary, Father

O'Gara requested in 1921 to be sent to the missions in China. He went three years later and quickly distinguished himself as director of the minor seminary in Shenchow, Hunan, and as a missionary elsewhere in the Hunan province from 1925 to 1930. In 1930 he was appointed prefect apostolic of Shenchow; four years later, he was named vicar apostolic of Yuanling and titular bishop.

O'Gara served as bishop during one of the most tumultuous periods in Chinese history, a time marked by the collapse of the Chinese government, the predations of warlords, the Japanese invasion of China, and the terrible civil war that ended with the rise of the communist state. He was arrested by the Japanese in 1941, and upon his return to Yuanling in 1947 his efforts to reestablish the Church were soon overshadowed by the civil war and the arrival of the communists. Arrested by communist officials in 1951, he escaped death through the intervention of the Canadian government. Exiled from China in 1953, he returned to the United States and was honored for his courage and zeal in preaching the Gospel. Over the next years, he supported the anti-communist movement in the United States.

Ogdensburg, Diocese of

Established on February 15, 1872, by Pope Blessed Pius IX, the Diocese of Ogdensburg serves counties in the northern part of the state of New York. The city was first known as Oswegatchie but was renamed in 1792 when Colonel Samuel Ogden settled in the area. Ogdensburg is a port of entry on the Oswegatchie River and is a shipping and transportation center. The region was originally inhabited by the Five Nations of the Iroquois Confederacy. The diocese is a suffragan see of the Archdiocese of New York.

The Catholic heritage of Ogdensburg dates to the expedition of Samuel de Champlain in 1609. Records indicate that the martyr St. Isaac Jogues spent time at Lake Saranac in the area, and other Jesuits, including Sts. René Goupil and Jean de Lalande, were also involved in missionary labors and were also martyred. It is presumed that St. Kateri Tekakwitha, the "Lily of the Mohawks," also traveled through the area of Ogdensburg on her way to sanctuary near Montréal.

The city of Ogdensburg was originally a mission founded by Sulpician Father François Picquet. He arrived on the site on October 30, 1749, with French trappers and Indian guides and established La Presentation Mission. Bishop Henri-Marie du Breuil de Pontbriand of Québec was at the mission in 1753 to baptize and confirm Native American converts. The British took control of the territory seven years later and halted missionary efforts. They relinquished it only in 1796.

Ogdensburg was under the ecclesiastical jurisdiction of the bishop of Québec and then the Diocese of New York when it was established in 1808. In 1847 it was placed under the jurisdiction of the newly established Diocese of Albany. With the decree of Pope Blessed Pius IX, the new Diocese of Ogdensburg was formed in 1872 with territory taken from the Diocese of Albany.

The first bishop of the diocese was Bishop Edgar P. Wadhams, who was appointed on February 15, 1872, and consecrated on May 5, 1872. He served until his death on December 5, 1891. The son of General Luman Wadhams of the War of 1812, Bishop Wadhams was a convert to the Catholic faith and took upon himself the immense task of providing a sound foundation for the new diocese. He worked to ensure a proper financial basis for his successors as well as an effective administration and diocesan curia.

The second bishop of Ogdensburg was Henry Gabriels, who was appointed on December 20, 1891, and consecrated on May 5, 1892. The former rector of St. Joseph's Seminary in Troy, New York, Bishop Gabriels had been born in Wannegem-Lede, Belgium. He served as shepherd over a Catholic population of over three hundred thousand, with sixty-five parishes and eighty-six priests. He developed diocesan facilities to meet the growing needs of the Catholic population and welcomed religious orders and congregations to assist pastoral care, especially for the sick and the orphaned. He died on April 23, 1921.

The third bishop of Ogdensburg was Joseph Henry Conroy, who had been auxiliary bishop of Ogdensburg since 1912. Appointed bishop on November 21, 1921, he led the faithful during the immense hardship caused by the Great Depression. He also welcomed Father Paul Francis of Graymoor and his companions when they converted and began the future Friars of the Atonement. Bishop Conroy continued the expansion of the diocesan programs and facilities before his death on March 20, 1939.

The fourth bishop was Bishop Francis Joseph Monaghan, who had been named coadjutor of the Diocese of Ogdensburg on April 17, 1936, and acceded to the see at the time of Bishop Conroy's death. He led the diocese during the first dark days of World War II, but he died unexpectedly on November 13, 1942.

The fifth bishop was Bryan Joseph McEntegart, who had been as a priest a key figure in organizing Catholic Charities. He was named bishop on June 5, 1943, and was consecrated on August 3. Bishop McEntegart assumed the role of shepherd in the middle of World War II. He also had the task of rebuilding the cathedral when it was destroyed by fire. On June 26, 1953, he was named rector of The Catholic University of America and went on to serve as bishop of Brooklyn from 1957 to 1968; he received the personal title of archbishop in 1966 and died on September 30, 1968.

The sixth bishop was Walter Philip Kellenberg, who had been an auxiliary bishop of New York since 1953. Appointed bishop of Ogdensburg on January 19, 1954, he was installed on March 25, 1954. He continued to build schools and parishes and to consolidate the charitable programs of the diocese until April 16, 1957, when he was appointed bishop of Rockville Centre. He retired on May 3, 1976, and died on January 11, 1986.

The seventh bishop was James Johnston Navagh, who had been an auxiliary bishop of Raleigh since 1952. Appointed on May 8, 1957, he was the founder of the Missionary Apostolate and was bishop at the start of the Second Vatican Council in 1962. The next year, on February 12, 1963, he was transferred to the Diocese of Paterson. He served there until his unexpected death on October 2, 1965.

The eighth bishop was Leo Richard Smith, who had been an auxiliary bishop of Buffalo since 1952. A noted canon lawyer, he was appointed bishop of Ogdensburg on May 13, 1963, and so assumed the see in the midst of the era of the Second Vatican Council. Traveling to Rome to take part in the council, he died unexpectedly in the Eternal City on October 9, 1963. His successor was Bishop

Thomas Andrew Donnellan, another well-trained canon lawyer who had also been rector of the Major Seminary of New York. Appointed bishop of Ogdensburg on February 28, 1964, he was consecrated a bishop on April 9, 1964. He attended the closing sessions of the Second Vatican Council and subsequently concentrated on implementing the reforms of the council. On May 24, 1968, he was appointed the archbishop of Atlanta and served until his death on October 15, 1987.

The tenth bishop was Stanislaus Joseph Brzana, who had been an auxiliary bishop of Buffalo since 1964. Appointed on October 22, 1968, Bishop Brzana provided long and steady leadership to a diocese that had experienced the loss of five bishops since 1953. He carried forward the effort to implement the reforms of the council and promoted lay ministries and ethnic programs to meet the needs of the growing Catholic population. He retired on November 11, 1993.

The eleventh bishop was Paul S. Loverde, an auxiliary bishop of Hartford since 1988. Appointed on November 11, 1993, he continued to promote the modernization of the diocesan administration and to meet the changing pastoral needs of his diocese. He was transferred on January 25, 1999, to the Diocese of Arlington.

The twelfth bishop was Gerald M. Barbarito, who had been an auxiliary bishop of Brooklyn since 1994. Appointed on October 26, 1999, he spent four years as shepherd of the Ogdensburg faithful and was transferred to the Diocese of Palm Beach on July 1, 2003. His successor was Bishop Robert J. Cunningham, who had been the diocesan administrator of the Diocese of Buffalo and was appointed on March 9, 2004, and consecrated a bishop on May 18, 2004. Bishop Cunningham was appointed the bishop of Syracuse on April 21, 2009. On February 23, 2010, Father Terry LaValley was appointed the fourteenth bishop of Ogdensburg. A priest of the diocese, he was ordained a bishop on April 30, 2010. In 2011 there were 104,000 Catholics, 130 priests, 112 women religious, and 102 parishes in the diocese.

O'Gorman, Thomas (May 1, 1843–September 13, 1921)

The second bishop of Sioux Falls, from 1896 to 1921, Thomas O'Gorman was a noted Church historian and preacher. Born in Boston, he entered the seminary in France and was ordained in St. Paul, Minnesota, in 1865. As a young priest, he earned a wide reputation as a preacher and made a memorable appearance in St. Patrick's Cathedral in New York City. In 1894 he provided assistance to Pope Leo XIII in the drafting of the encyclical *Longinqua Oceani* ("To the Bishops of the United States: On Catholicism in the United States"), which was published in 1895.

That same year, he assumed a position at The Catholic University of America in Washington, D.C., but within a year he had been appointed the successor of the famed Bishop Matin Marty as bishop of Sioux Falls. Bishop O'Gorman built on the work of Bishop Marty and oversaw the expansion of the diocese, most notably the construction of St. Joseph Cathedral in Sioux Falls. Upon his death, condolences were sent by former President William Howard Taft. Bishop O'Gorman was also a longtime friend of Archbishop John Ireland of St. Paul.

O'Grady, John (March 31, 1886–January 2, 1966)

A priest and important figure in Catholic Charities and Catholic social work, John O'Grady was born in County Clare, Ireland, and attended All Hallows College in Dublin. Picked for service in the United States, he was ordained in 1909 and sent to the Diocese of Omaha, where he served for several years. In 1912 he was sent to study at The Catholic University of America, where he earned a doctorate in 1915 and became a professor of economics. From 1934 to 1938, he served as dean of the School of Social Work at Catholic University.

Father O'Grady was one of the best-known Catholic social reformers in the United States. He served as editor of *Catholic Charities Review* from 1920 until his retirement in 1961, had a role in the development of the 1919 document "The Bishops' Program for Social Reconstruction," and in 1920 was named the secretary of the National Conference of Catholic Charities, a post he held also until his retirement. In his later years, he was influential in the development of the International Conference of Catholic Charities and assisted the Holy See in its programs to assist refugees following World War II and in African countries.

O'Hara, Edwin Vincent (September 6, 1881– September 11, 1956)

Bishop of Great Falls from 1930 to 1939 and bishop of Kansas City from 1939 to 1956, Edwin Vincent O'Hara was a leading promoter of social justice and a key figure in the development in the United States of the Confraternity of Christian Doctrine (CCD). Born in Lanesboro, Minnesota, O'Hara studied at the College of St. Thomas in St. Paul, Minnesota, before entering St. Paul Seminary in 1900. While in the seminary, he earned renown for his literary efforts, including a translation in 1904 from the original German of Eberhard Dennert's *At the Deathbed of Darwinism*, which was reviewed in *The New York Times*. He transferred to the Archdiocese of Oregon City (his brother John was editor of the diocesan newspaper there) and was ordained in 1905.

From 1906 to 1920, Father O'Hara served as superintendent of schools for the archdiocese and was an outspoken opponent of the then pervasive anti-Catholic sentiment in Oregon. Starting in 1912, he also became nationally recognized for his efforts on behalf of social justice as chairman of the Oregon Consumers' League's committee studying the working conditions of women in Oregon. The bill that resulted, calling for a minimum wage for women, was eventually passed by the Oregon Legislature and upheld by the U.S. Supreme Court. Father O'Hara next played a major role in defeating the infamous Oregon bill that would have required all children in the state to attend public schools.

After serving as a chaplain in World War I, Father O'Hara returned to the United States and in 1920 proposed the creation of a Rural Life Bureau to assist dioceses in their pastoral outreach and care of those living in rural communities. In 1922 he published *A Program of Catholic Rural Action* and in 1927 *The Church and the Country Community*. Three years later, he was appointed the second bishop of Great Fall and was consecrated on October 28, 1930. As bishop, he proved an able shepherd, but he also distinguished himself nationally for his leadership in promoting the CCD. In 1939 he helped establish the Catholic Biblical Association and the *Catholic Biblical Quarterly*.

In 1939 he was named the bishop of Kansas City, presiding over the rapid expansion of the diocese. He also chaired the bishops' committee on the revision of the *Baltimore Catechism* in 1941. For his many contributions to the Church he was named a personal archbishop by Pope Pius XII in 1954. Shortly before his death, O'Hara opened the first integrated Catholic health care center in the city of Kansas City in 1955. He died in Milan, Italy, while traveling to a liturgical congress.

O'Hara, John F. (May 1, 1888–August 28, 1960)

Archbishop of Philadelphia from 1951 to 1960, John Francis O'Hara was also a cardinal from 1958. Born in Ann Arbor, Michigan, he grew up in Peru, Indiana, where his family had relocated. At the age of seventeen his family went to Uruguay, where his father was the American consul. There he entered the Colegio de Sagrado Corazon (College of the Sacred Heart), a Jesuit school at Montevideo. He studied there until 1907, then went to Brazil in 1908 and on to the University of Notre Dame, where he earned a degree in 1911. That same year, he entered the Holy Cross Seminary and was ordained on September 9, 1916, as a member of the Congregation of the Holy Cross.

After graduate studies at The Catholic University of America, Father O'Hara returned to Notre Dame, where he devoted the next twenty years of his life to a variety of positions, including dean of the department of commerce, vice president of the university in 1933, and president from 1934 to 1939. Under his direction, Notre Dame expanded its graduate programs and established several new departments. During his term, he also served as a member of the United States delegation to the 1938 Lima Conference of American Republics in Peru.

On December 11, 1939, O'Hara was named by Pope Pius XII a bishop and delegate of the U.S. military vicar, then Archbishop (later Cardinal) Francis Spellman. As delegate, he traveled extensively to assist Catholics in the military throughout the world. In March 1945 he was appointed bishop of Buffalo. As bishop, he was a powerful voice against discrimina-

Cardinal John O'Hara

tion in the diocese, abolishing segregated parishes and schools.

In November 1951 O'Hara was named archbishop of Philadelphia as successor to Cardinal Dennis J. Dougherty. He took as one of his chief endeavors the improvement of archdiocesan education, building sixty-nine new schools and improving three hundred standing ones. He also modernized the seminary and opened its doors to dioceses other than his own and Harrisburg, started four schools for the mentally handicapped and one school for the blind, and opposed public funding for schools on the basis that it only added to the burdens of Catholics, who were helping the Catholic school system. The diocese was also expanded by over fifty parishes. On November 15, 1958, O'Hara was named a cardinal by Pope Blessed John XXIII. His health was already failing, however, and he died less than two years later. He was buried at the University of Notre Dame.

Ohio

Called the Buckeye State, Ohio is located in the Great Lakes region of the United States. It is bounded on the north by Michigan and Lake Erie, on the east by Pennsylvania and West Virginia, on the south by West Virginia and Kentucky, and on the west by Indiana. Ohio has three natural land regions: the Allegheny Plateau in the east, the Lakes Plains region on the northern border, and the Central Plains in the west. The original inhabitants of Ohio were the Adena and Hopewell, who built mounds, and the Delaware, Miami, Maumee, Shawnee, Seneca, and Wyandotte.

René-Robert Chevalier, Sieur de La Salle, visited the area in the 1670s, laying claim for France. Ohio was part of the Northwest Territory; the dispute between Great Britain and France over it brought about the French and Indian War from 1754 to 1763. In 1749 France sent Pierre-Joseph Céloron de Blainville into the Upper Ohio Valley. He was accompanied by Jesuit Father Joseph-Pierre de Bonnecamps, who celebrated Mass on the Little Miami River.

Jesuit Father Pierre Potier was also in the region. He labored among the Indian communities with Father Bonnecamps. In 1751 Jesuit Father Armand de La Richardie was at Sandusky, coming into the area with the Hurons, having accompanied the tribe from Lake Erie. In 1795 Father Edmund Burke was at Fort Miège, modern-day Toledo, serving the Maumee.

The British had tried to keep white settlers out of the Ohio Valley, declaring the area banned in 1763. The Revolutionary War ended British control, however, and land grants given to military veterans promoted further settlements. The Northwest Ordinance of 1787 also provided freedom of worship for settlers under a territorial government. Marietta was the first permanent white settlement, opening in 1788, and the local Indian tribes retaliated. In 1794 General "Mad Anthony" Wayne defeated the Indians, and Ohio subsequently entered the Union as the seventeenth state in 1803.

Ohio was under the ecclesiastical jurisdiction of the Diocese of Baltimore until 1808, when the Diocese of Bardstown (now the Archdiocese of Louisville) was established. In 1802 a group of settlers led by Jacob Dittoe had arrived in Somerset and had petitioned Bishop John Carroll of Baltimore for a priest. The Dominican Father Edward D. Fenwick arrived and founded St. Joseph, the first permanent chapel in the region. His nephew, Father Nicholas Young, another Dominican, also served at Somerset.

On June 19, 1821, the Diocese of Cincinnati was established by Pope Pius VII, and Father Fenwick was consecrated as the first bishop. He faced serious problems, as lay trustees were prevalent in some parishes. Bishop Fenwick secured these as diocesan properties and willed them to his successors. He traveled throughout Ohio and went to Europe, seeking financial aid and priests for his far-flung see. Exhausted by his labors, he died on September 26, 1832.

His successor was Bishop John Baptist Purcell, who was consecrated on October 13, 1833, and proved a popular prelate. He aided the transition of the Catholic population at a time when Irish Catholics were soon outnumbered by German Catholics. The change in population reflected the flood of settlers as a result of the opening of the Erie Canal, and in 1835 the Territory of Michigan disputed the border between it and Ohio, claiming parts of the Ohio Valley. The "Toledo War" almost led to a military confrontation between Ohio and Michigan, but President Andrew Jackson intervened, and in 1836 the U.S. Congress awarded the disputed land to Ohio.

Bishop Purcell had to steady the faithful during this turbulent period. He was also forced to debate Protestants in public forums and thus did much to defend the faith against active anti-Catholicism. In 1853 Protestants attempted to assassinate Archbishop Gaetano Bedini, the papal legate, during a visit to Cincinnati.

In June 1850 Purcell was promoted to the rank of archbishop as Cincinnati was designated a metropolitan archdiocese. The Diocese of Cleveland had been erected in 1847 and served as a suffragan see. Archbishop Purcell resigned and moved with his brother, Father Edward Purcell, to an Ursuline convent because of the disastrous economic crisis brought upon the archdiocese by his brother's banking system during the Panic of 1878.

Ohio contributed large numbers of soldiers to the Union Army during the Civil War, and the industries of the state helped the Union to maintain its overwhelming industrial edge in the conflict. There were, nevertheless, many in Ohio who had sympathies with the Confederate cause, and they were given the name Copperheads. Many of the more than three hundred thousand Ohio soldiers who fought in the war were Catholic.

Bishop William Henry Elder of Natchez was appointed coadjutor archbishop to Purcell and succeeded him on July 14, 1883. Archbishop Elder handled the difficulties with great care and tact and served Ohio for almost a quarter of a century. Reflecting the growth of the Catholic population in Ohio, the Diocese of Columbus was established on March 3, 1868, and the Diocese of Toledo on April 15, 1910.

Outstanding prelates also served in these dioceses, and religious congregations and orders provided facilities and leadership in education, charitable programs, and evangelization. The dioceses were expanding their parishes and schools as the country entered World War I, but there followed the severe hardship brought by the Great

Depression, and the Church provided massive social assistance.

The Church continued to grow during the period of World War II and the long era of postwar prosperity, and two new dioceses were founded, Youngstown in 1943 and Steubenville in 1944. Two major figures in this time were Archbishop John T. McNicholas, O.P., archbishop of Cincinnati from 1925 to 1950, and his successor, Archbishop Karl J. Alter, archbishop from 1950 to 1969. Archbishop Alter was responsible for a colossal building program, including the extensive renovations of the Cathedral of St. Peter in Chains. He also struggled to have the education system keep pace with the population growth. Through his efforts, by the early 1960s an amazing 77 percent of all Catholic school-age children were in parochial or diocesan schools.

With the decline of industries and the emergence of Ohio as one of the so-called Rust Belt states, the state's Catholic communities have in recent decades been compelled to provide pastoral care to large numbers of unemployed and their children, as well as to care for the changing populations as they gradually have departed the large cities for suburban areas and parishes. These changes have been felt most acutely in the Dioceses of Youngstown and Steubenville. In 2011 there were more than two million Catholics in Ohio, nearly 19 percent of the total population. They were served by more than 1,800 priests, more than 3,600 men and women religious, and more than 875 parishes. There are also thirteen Catholic colleges and universities, 77 high schools, and more than 400 parochial schools educating over 150,000 young people every year in the state.

Oklahoma

Called the Sooner State, Oklahoma is located in the south-central part of the United States. The state is bounded on the north by Colorado and Kansas, on the east by Arkansas and Missouri, on the south by the Red River and Texas, and on the west by Texas and Mexico. There are four natural land formations in Oklahoma: the Central Lowlands in the east-central part of the state, the Great Plains in the northwest, the Ozark Plateau in the east, and the Ouachita Mountains. The original inhabitants of

Oklahoma were the Arapaho, Cheyenne, Comanche, Kiowa, and Osage. The name Oklahoma is taken from two Native American words for "red people."

The Catholic history of Oklahoma opened in April 1541 when the Spaniard Francisco Vázquez de Coronado entered the region in search of Cibola, the legendary Seven Cities of Gold. The protomartyr of the United States, the Franciscan Juan de Padilla, who was later slain in Kansas, was with the expedition. Captain Francisco Leyva de Bonilla reportedly was in the present-day Oklahoma Panhandle in the 1590s, exploring the region. Four decades later, Franciscan Father Juan de Sales and other missionaries were serving the Indian tribes along the old Santa Fe Trail.

In 1682 René-Robert Chevalier, Sieur de La Salle, claimed Oklahoma as part of the French possessions of Louisiana. France had to cede the lands to Spain, however, in 1763. Louisiana was returned to France in the Treaty of San Ildefonso in 1800. The Revolutionary War and the Louisiana Purchase of 1803 made Oklahoma part of the United States. Oklahoma, however, did not join the Union until November 16, 1907, when it became the forty-sixth state.

In the 1820s Jean Pierre Chouteau settled at Salina in the northeast and opened a fur trading post. Jesuit missionaries started visiting the Indians of the region. Initially placed under the jurisdiction of the Diocese of St. Louis, Oklahoma was redesignated as part of the Diocese of Little Rock in 1843. Throughout this period, Native Americans were walking on the "Trail of Tears," enforced marches from their homelands to the barren outposts and reservations that had been set up by the federal government to house the displaced Indian tribes. In 1834 the U.S. Congress established the Oklahoma Territory, which was supposed to be an Indian possession forever and free of white settlers. The Cherokee, Chickasaw, Choctaw, Creeks, and Seminoles were brought to Oklahoma to survive as best they could.

These tribes took sides in the Civil War, and because some fought for the Confederacy, the entire Oklahoma Indian population was penalized severely. Lands were taken from them to be given to other tribes forced to live in Oklahoma, and white settlers began to claim territory as squatters. The railroad and cattlemen put an end to independence.

In 1876 Benedictine Father Isidore Robot was appointed prefect apostolic of the territory. He served until 1887 and established missions throughout the region. He was aided by Benedictine Father M. Bernard Murphy. The Sisters of Mercy, in 1887, opened the first Catholic day school of the territory at Krebs in the southeast.

A group called the Boomers campaigned for white settlements, and at noon on April 22, 1889, thousands of settlers lined up in carts, in wagons, on horseback, and on foot to race into Oklahoma to claim land. It was later discovered that more sophisticated entrepreneurs had moved onto properties "sooner than expected," hence the nickname of the state. Other races were held as the federal government took more lands from the Indians over the years.

On May 29, 1891, the Vicariate Apostolic of Oklahoma and the Indian Territory was established by the Holy See, and Benedictine Father Theophile Meerschaert was appointed the first vicar apostolic. He resided in Guthrie. St. Katharine Drexel aided the vicariate, as Bishop Meerschaert labored to serve the large population of the faithful that was spread out across the state and to assist the suffering Indian tribes.

Five years later oil was discovered on the Osage Reservation, and by 1900 there were oil fields at Tulsa. The Diocese of Oklahoma was established on August 17, 1905, as a suffragan of the Archdiocese of San Antonio. Bishop Meerschaert established the offices and diocesan administration for the diocese. Two years later, Oklahoma entered the Union, and Bishop Meerschaert went on to lead the faithful during World War I and during Prohibition negotiated with legislators during the Sacramental Wine Case to secure an exemption for the Church in the use of sacramental wine.

On November 14, 1930, the diocese was redesignated as Oklahoma City and Tulsa by Pope Pius XI. Bishop Francis Clement Kelley succeeded Bishop Meerschaert, who died in 1924. He also provided charitable programs during the economic hardships of the Great Depression and then supported the military efforts of the nation in World War II. He also served the Holy See on several diplomatic missions. He died in 1948. Bishop Eugene Joseph McGuinness (1948–57), who had been a coadjutor bishop of the diocese, acceded to the see upon Bishop Kelley's death. He built over a hundred churches and instituted programs to meet the needs of a growing Catholic population. His successor, Bishop Victor J. Reed (1958–71), took part in the Second Vatican Council and the worked to implement the reforms mandated by the council.

Bishop John R. Quinn, acceded to the see on November 30, 1971. On December 13, 1972, he was appointed the first archbishop of Oklahoma City. At the same time, Tulsa was erected as a diocese and Bishop Bernard J. Ganter was named the first bishop. Over the next years, the Catholic population continued to grow, and Archbishop Charles A. Salatka, who succeeded Archbishop Quinn when he was moved to San Francisco in 1977, continued promoting lay ministries and programs for evangelization until his retirement in 1992.

The Church in Oklahoma has also been consistently active in assisting the pastoral needs of the Native Americans in the state. In 2011 there were more than 160,000 Catholics, approximately 5 percent of the total population of 3.4 million, as well as about 230 priests, 250 men and women religious, and nearly 150 parishes in the state.

Oklahoma City, Archdiocese of

Established as the Diocese of Oklahoma on August 17, 1905, by Pope St. Pius X, the see was redesignated as the Diocese of Oklahoma City and Tulsa on November 14, 1930, by Pope Pius XI, and was elevated to the status of a metropolitan archdiocese by Pope Paul VI on February 6, 1973. Tulsa became a diocese at the same time in 1973. The archdiocese has several suffragan dioceses.

Oklahoma City was the gathering place for the "Run of '89," when thousands of homesteaders raced to stake out land claims in the region. Called Oklahoma Station, the site was a stop established by the Santa Fe Railroad two years before. A meeting in May 1889 organized a provisional town government. In May 1890 the name became official with the establishment of the Oklahoma Territory. Oklahoma City was designated as the state capital in 1910.

The Catholic history of the archdiocese opens

in 1541 when the Spaniard Francisco Vázquez de Coronado led an expedition into modern-day Oklahoma in search of Cibola, the legendary Seven Cities of Gold. The protomartyr of the United States, Juan de Padilla (who was later slain in Kansas) was a member of the expedition. In 1590 Captain Francisco Leyva de Bonilla led another expedition into the area of the Oklahoma Panhandle, and four decades later Franciscan Father Juan de Sales and other missionaries evangelized among the tribes along the old Santa Fe Trail.

In 1682 René-Robert Chevalier, Sieur de La Salle, exploring the Mississippi River, also laid claim to present-day Oklahoma for France. Part of the territory of Louisiana, Oklahoma was sold to the United States in 1803. Two decades later, Jean Pierre Chouteau opened a trading post at Salina, and Jesuit missionaries started visiting the Native American tribes in the area. When the Diocese of Little Rock was established in Arkansas in 1843, the faithful of Oklahoma were included under the ecclesiastical jurisdiction of the diocese.

In 1834 the United States Congress founded the Oklahoma Territory and promised the various Indian tribes forced to march on the infamous "Trail of Tears" to Oklahoma that the lands given them would be their possessions forever. The tribes, however, came to discover that such promises carried little value. In the Civil War (1861–65), some tribes sided with the Confederacy and were punished at the end of the war. All of the tribes, however, were included in the punitive actions of the federal government. New tribes were brought in to share the lands, and the railroads began to encroach on Indian Territory, as did cattle ranchers and other white settlers.

In 1876 a new era in Catholic history in Oklahoma began with the arrival of the Benedictine Father Isidore Robot. Robot acquired a square mile of land to use for a mission and a school for the Potawatomi. The location was Young's Crossing on the Southern Canadian River, and on the site were eventually established an abbey and school, what became known as Sacred Heart Mission, the first Catholic center in the Indian Territory. On May 14, 1876, Father Robot was named prefect apostolic of the territory, and he worked to expand the Catholic presence. He was aided by Benedictine Father

M. Bernard Murphy and the Sisters of Mercy who opened the first Catholic day school in the territory in Krebs in 1887.

On April 22, 1889, Oklahoma was opened officially to white homesteaders who took part in the "Run of '89," racing to get land in the region. On May 29, 1891, the Vicariate Apostolic of Indian Territory was started by Pope Leo XIII, and Benedictine Father Theophile Meerschaert was chosen to be the first vicar apostolic. He was consecrated a bishop on September 8, 1891, in Natchez, Mississippi, and arrived on September 18, 1891, to discover the massive size of his new vicariate and the fact that he had three diocesan priests at his disposal. There were, in addition, twenty-three Benedictine priests, twenty-one churches, seven day schools, five Indian boarding schools, one college, one monastery, six convents, and about five thousand Catholics.

The Belgian-born Bishop Meerschaert devoted the rest of his life to Oklahoma. He struggled to give the Church in the region a firm footing in administration and pastoral service. Recruiting priests was a major challenge, travel conditions were harsh, and there were lingering problems of anti-Catholicism. He nevertheless persevered, and he enjoyed the satisfaction of being appointed the first bishop of Oklahoma on August 23, 1905. For his long labors, he was also appointed on November 30, 1916, as Assistant at the Pontifical Throne by Pope Benedict XV. He died at the age of seventy-six on February 21, 1924.

Bishop Meerschaert's successor was the fifty-three-year old Monsignor Francis Clement Kelley, who was appointed on June 25, 1924, and consecrated a bishop on October 2, 1924. He had served as a chaplain in the United States Volunteer Army during the Spanish-American War and was a noted lecturer, writer, and diplomat for the Holy See. He arrived with the firm intent of expanding the Catholic presence in Oklahoma and implemented a sweeping plan of evangelization that included the use of a chapel railroad car, door-to-door efforts, regional mission houses, and the radio to reach out to Catholics and interested non-Catholics. Bishop Kelley also confronted the immense problems created by the Great Depression. The stress of the Depression, combined with the challenges of America's entry into World War II in December 1941, contributed to a heart attack in October 1942. His health never recovered fully, and he died on February 1, 1948. During his time, the diocese was renamed the Diocese of Oklahoma City-Tulsa on November 14, 1930, by Pope Pius XI.

Oklahoma's third bishop, Eugene Joseph McGuinness, was appointed coadjutor bishop of Oklahoma City-Tulsa on November 11, 1944. He had served previously as bishop of Raleigh from 1937 until his appointment, and he succeeded Bishop Kelley on the latter's passing. He took as his primary task the development of vocations to the priesthood and religious life and the continuation of Bishop Kelley's efforts at evangelization. His efforts in recruiting priests proved immensely successful. At the time of his arrival, there were eleven seminarians for the state, but within a decade there were more than 120 seminarians for the diocese in various years of study. At the same time, religious vocations flourished, and Oklahoma was blessed by the arrival of new postulants for the communities of women religious (Benedictines, Third Order Carmelites, Discalced Carmelites, and Felicians). His efforts at evangelization likewise succeeded, so that the Catholic population grew by over 40 percent during his time, to more than ninety-three thousand in 1957. He died suddenly on the morning of December 27, 1957.

The fourth bishop of Oklahoma was Bishop Victor Joseph Reed, who was appointed on January 21, 1958. He had been an auxiliary bishop to Bishop McGuinness since early December 1957, then received swift appointment as his successor. He was consecrated a bishop on March 5, 1958, and began a long tenure that ended with his death on September 7, 1971, at the age of sixty-seven. He took part in the Second Vatican Council and was a determined supporter of its many liturgical and ecclesiastical reforms. The years after the council were hard ones, as the diocese faced a considerable exodus of priests from active ministry, and the stress of the turmoil took its toll on him. He died suddenly of a heart attack.

The fifth bishop of Oklahoma was John R. Quinn, who was an auxiliary bishop of San Diego at the time of his appointment on November 30, 1971. Only forty-two years old at the time, Bishop Quinn had been named an auxiliary bishop at the age of thirty-eight. A pastoral shepherd, he met frequently with his presbyterate and made visits to his parishes a priority. On December 13, 1972, he was promoted to the rank of archbishop as the diocese was declared by Pope Paul VI the Archdiocese of Oklahoma City. On the same day, the Diocese of Tulsa was erected. Archbishop Quinn relaunched the archdiocesan newspaper and was named personally by Pope Paul VI to participate in the 1974 world Synod of Bishops. On February 16, 1977, he was transferred to the Archdiocese of San Francisco; he resigned that see on December 27, 1995.

Archbishop Quinn's successor was Archbishop Charles A. Salatka, who was appointed on October 11, 1977. He had served as auxiliary bishop of Grand Rapids from 1961 to 1968 and then as bishop of Marquette from 1968. Installed on December 15, 1977, he was keenly pastoral in his service and was concerned especially with spiritual renewal for the archdiocese and with providing for the needs of the growing ethnic and minority groups in Oklahoma. He founded the Office of Hispanic Ministry in the late 1970s, began in 1992 the first Catholic Multi-Cultural Festival, and embarked on outreach programs to African-Americans, Hispanics, and Vietnamese immigrants. He also learned Spanish to be able to serve the Spanish-speaking Catholics in the archdiocese and, above all, to be able say Mass in their native language. In addition, he approved a wide variety of charitable efforts, including a Migration and Resettlement for Refugees program, a Parish Social Ministry, the St. Vincent de Paul Society, and an Immigration Assistance Program. He retired on January 22, 1993, and died in Oklahoma City on March 17, 2003.

Archbishop Salatka was succeeded by Archbishop Eusebius J. Beltran, who had been bishop of Tulsa from 1978 and was appointed archbishop on November 24, 1992, as the third archbishop of Oklahoma City. Installed on January 22, 1993, Archbishop Beltran began his time as shepherd by leading opposition to a proposed state law that would have removed all state and local regulations concerning abortion. He also dedicated himself to expanding the archdiocese's charitable programs, working to develop archdiocesan financial stability, and continuing to ensure Catholic education.

Archbishop Beltran retired on December 16, 2010. He was succeeded on the same day by Bishop Paul S. Coakley, who had been bishop of Salina since 2004. He was installed on February 11, 2010. In 2011 the Catholic population in the diocese numbered 105,000, with 123 priests, 140 men and women religious, and 70 parishes.

Omaha, Archdiocese of

Established as the Diocese of Omaha on October 2, 1885, by Pope Leo XIII, the see was elevated to the status of an archdiocese on August 7, 1945, by Pope Pius XII. The archdiocese serves counties in northeastern Nebraska.

Founded in 1812 by Manuel Lisa, a pioneering American fur trader, as a trading post, the site was given the name of the local Native American tribe. Omaha was made the state capital, and Council Bluffs, Iowa, across the Missouri River, was made the eastern terminus of the new transcontinental railway by President Abraham Lincoln. The capital of Nebraska was moved to Lincoln in 1867, but Omaha continued to thrive in agricultural marketing, cattle, meatpacking, insurance, and manufacturing.

The Catholic heritage of Omaha dates to the expedition of Francisco Vázquez de Coronado in the 1530s. The protomartyr of the United States, Franciscan Father Juan de Padilla, was with the expedition and remained in the area when Coronado withdrew. In 1862 René-Robert Chevalier, Sieur de la Salle, claimed Nebraska for France as part of the lands in Louisiana, the massive French holdings in North America. On August 13, 1720, Pedro de Villasur and Franciscan Father Juan Mingues were slain in the area in a Pawnee attack. Soon after, Paul and Pierre Mallet opened a fur-trading business and explored the region. Nebraska became a part of the United States in the Louisiana Purchase of 1803, and the Lewis and Clark expedition soon after sparked wider interest in Nebraska.

The faithful of the newly founded Omaha and

Bishop O'Gorman

their neighbors were under the ecclesiastical jurisdiction of the Diocese of St. Louis in 1826. The revered Jesuit missionary Pierre-Jean De Smet is known to have visited the region as part of his labors, and by 1850 the region was under the jurisdiction of the Vicariate Apostolic of the Indian Territories. The first church in the Nebraska Territory was St. Mary's Church in Omaha, which was dedicated in August 1856.

Soon after, Father Jeremiah Tracy led a wagon train into the area and founded St. Patrick's Colony in the northeastern part of the present-day state. German settlers founded Argo in the southern area, and Benedictine Father Emmanuel Hartig was active in the territory.

On January 6, 1857, Pope Blessed Pius IX established the Vicariate Apostolic of the Nebraska Territory, although no one was appointed to administer it until 1859, when James Miles O'Gorman, a Trappist monk, was named the first bishop of the area. His enormous see was 367,265 square miles and claimed 5,000 Catholics and three priests; the territory included what is now the state of Nebraska, as well as modern-day northeastern Colorado, Wyoming, and parts of Utah, Montana, and the Dakotas.

Bishop O'Gorman wasted little time after his consecration on May 5, 1859, in adding to his clergy. On June 25, 1859, he ordained Father William Kelly, the first priest ordained on Nebraska soil. Badly needed help arrived also in the form of the Sisters of Mercy, who came to the area in 1864, followed by the Benedictine Sisters in 1865. Meanwhile, Bishop O'Gorman was able to build a new cathedral to replace St. Mary's Church (which had been renamed St. Philomena and used as a cathedral) with a new cathedral in 1868.

By the time of his death at fifty-nine on July 4, 1874, Bishop O'Gorman was shepherd of nineteen priests and twelve thousand Catholics in twenty parishes and fifty-six missions. Nebraska, meanwhile, had become the thirty-seventh state on March 1, 1867.

On February 12, 1875, Father John Ireland was

named vicar apostolic of Nebraska, but on July 28 of that same year, he was transferred to become coadjutor bishop of St. Paul. On June 26, 1876, Father James O'Connor, a priest of the Pittsburgh diocese, was named vicar apostolic of Nebraska. Consecrated on August 20, 1876, he focused on continuing to increase the number of parishes and improving the pastoral care of the Catholic faithful. Early in his time, he was given the college that the Creighton family had endowed, and Father O'Connor entrusted its development to the Jesuits in 1878. The school became Creighton University. He also helped the people of the state cope with a grasshopper plague and drought, and with the assistance of St. Katharine Drexel, Indian schools and other facilities had their beginning.

On October 2, 1885, the vicariate apostolic was elevated to the rank of a diocese and O'Connor was named the first bishop. His diocese included Nebraska and Wyoming, and it was a suffragan see under the Archdiocese of Dubuque. Further changes came in 1887 when the diocese was reduced in size to permit the creation of the Dioceses of Lincoln and Cheyenne. Bishop O'Connor died on May 27, 1890.

The second bishop of Omaha was Richard Scannell, who had been bishop of Concordia (now Salina), in Kansas, since 1887. Appointed on January 30, 1891, he oversaw the continued growth of the diocese, so that under his leadership the Catholic population grew to over eighty thousand in ninety-five parishes. In 1907 he also laid the cornerstone for St. Cecilia's Cathedral. In 1912 the western part of the diocese became the Diocese of Kearney; in 1917, the name of that see was changed to Grand Island. Bishop Scannell died on January 8, 1916.

The third bishop of Omaha was Jeremiah J. Harty, who had been archbishop of Manila since 1903 and was transferred from the Philippines to Nebraska. Appointed on May 16, 1916, he retained the personal title of archbishop. He had overseen the care of over one million Catholics in Manila, but the hardships of missionary life and administration had taken their toll on his health. He served for eleven years as bishop, but then became seriously ill in 1927. To receive proper care, he went to Tucson, Arizona, where he was cared for by the

Sisters of St. Joseph. He never recovered his health, and he died on October 29, 1927.

Owing to Archbishop Harty's health, Bishop Francis J. L. Beckman of Lincoln had been appointed apostolic administrator of the Omaha diocese; he served in that capacity after Harty's death until March 30, 1928, when Father Joseph Francis Rummel, a German-born New York City priest, was appointed bishop of the Diocese of Omaha. During his seven years in Omaha, Bishop Rummel hosted the Sixth National Eucharistic Congress in 1930, during which tens of thousands of faithful gathered at Creighton University. Bishop Rummel led the diocese during the first dark days of the Great Depression, but he was transferred in 1935 to become the archbishop of New Orleans. He died at the age of eighty-eight on November 8, 1964.

Rummel's successor was Bishop James Hugh Ryan, a priest of Indianapolis, who was appointed bishop of Omaha on August 3, 1935. He had been rector of The Catholic University of America and had been named titular bishop of Modra in 1933. A noted scholar, he had written several important books, including *An Introduction to Philosophy* and *A Catechism of Catholic Education*. As bishop, he presided over the continued expansion of the Catholic population during the last days of the Great Depression and into World War II, and on August 4, 1945, he was appointed by Pope Pius XII as the first archbishop of Omaha. He died only two years later at the age of sixty, on November 23, 1947.

On February 7, 1948, Bishop Gerald T. Bergan was named the second archbishop of Omaha. He had been bishop of Des Moines since 1934. He served as shepherd over the diocese through the postwar economic boom and then through the period of the Second Vatican Council. To him fell the initial implementation of the decrees of the council. In 1964 he received an auxiliary bishop with the appointment of Monsignor Daniel E. Sheehan. With the retirement of Archbishop Bergan on June 11, 1969, Sheehan was named his successor.

Installed on August 8, 1969, as the third archbishop of Omaha, Archbishop Sheehan was the first native son of the archdiocese to hold the office of archbishop. He soon earned national fame for his support of Catholic education, which included a campaign that raised more than $26 million to improve Catholic education in the Omaha metropolitan area. In addition, the archdiocese became a leader in the country for its development methods to assist Catholic education and its tuition-support program. In 1992 the National Catholic Educational Association presented him with the Elizabeth Ann Seton Award. Archbishop Sheehan also established the archdiocesan pastoral council and promoted lay involvement in the life of the archdiocese. He retired on May 4, 1993, and died on October 24, 2000.

Archbishop Sheehan's successor was Bishop Elden Francis Curtiss, who had been bishop of Helena since 1976. Installed as archbishop of Omaha on June 25, 1993, he undertook a major fundraising campaign to provide a retirement home for priests, tuition relief for students at Catholic high schools, support for archdiocesan centers for adult and youth activities, needed repairs to St. Cecilia Cathedral, and financial assistance to seminarians.

Archbishop Curtiss retired on June 3, 2009, and was succeeded on the same day by Bishop George J. Lucas, who had been bishop of Springfield since 1999. Archbishop Lucas was installed on July 22, 2009. In 2011 there were more than 225,000 Catholics in the archdiocese, with nearly 300 priests, 350 men and women religious, and 139 parishes. There are also two Catholic college, 17 high schools, and 58 elementary schools.

O'Malley, Seán P. (June 29, 1944–)

Archbishop of Boston from 2003 and a cardinal from 2006, Seán Patrick O'Malley was born in Lakewood, Ohio, the son of Theodore O'Malley and Mary Louise Reidy. Called to the religious life, he entered the Order of the Friars Minor Capuchins and was professed on July 14, 1965. He took the name Seán in honor of St. John. His studies were taken at St. Fidelis Seminary in Butler, Pennsylvania, and at Capuchin College and The Catholic University of America in Washington, D.C., where he earned a master's degree in religious

Cardinal O'Malley

education and a doctorate in Spanish and Portuguese literature.

Ordained a priest on August 29, 1970, Father O'Malley served as a faculty member of Catholic University from 1969 to 1973 and was then executive director of *Centro Católico Hispano* for the Archdiocese of Washington; episcopal vicar for the Hispanic, Portuguese, and Haitian communities; and executive director of the Office of Social Ministry from 1978. In 1974 he was named a Knight Commander of the Order of Prince Henry the Navigator, an honor conferred by the Portuguese government for outstanding service to the Portuguese people.

Appointed coadjutor bishop of St. Thomas, Virgin Islands, on June 2, 1984, Bishop O'Malley was consecrated on August 2, 1984, and succeeded to the see on October 16, 1985. In 1991 he was appointed a chaplain ad honorem of the Sovereign Military Order of Malta. Transferred to the see of Fall River on June 16, 1992, he took part by papal appointment in the Special Assembly for Oceania of the world Synod of Bishops in the Vatican City from November 22 to December 12, 1998. On September 3, 2002, he was transferred to the see of Palm Beach. The new assignment was to a diocese recently troubled by the resignation of its bishop and required intense pastoral care and a capacity to bring authentic healing to a troubled Catholic community.

On July 1, 2003, he was promoted to the metropolitan see of Boston as successor to Cardinal Bernard F. Law, who had resigned in the midst of the serious sex abuse crisis that had brought immense turmoil to the archdiocese and had become a national scandal for the Church. (*See also* Boston, Archdiocese of.) On March 24, 2006, he was created a cardinal priest and received the title of Santa Maria della Vittoria.

O'Neill Jr., Thomas P. (Tip)
(December 9, 1912–January 5, 1994)

Speaker of the House of Representatives from 1977 to 1987, Thomas P. O'Neill was born in Cambridge, Massachusetts, and grew up in a working-class family. He was always aware of his humble beginnings. After graduating from Boston College, he was elected in 1936 to the Massachusetts General Court and became its speaker, the first Catholic to hold the office, in 1949. In 1952 he ran and won the congressional seat left vacant by the decision of John F. Kennedy to seek a seat in the Senate. Over the next decades, he became a fixture in the House, representing one of the politically safest districts in the Democratic Party. In 1971 he became majority whip of the House Democrats, and in 1973 majority leader. Four years later, he was elected speaker and served from 1973 to 1977.

O'Neill's long career spanned the presidencies of Dwight D. Eisenhower through Ronald Reagan. He opposed Lyndon Johnson's Vietnam War policy, worked assiduously against Richard Nixon, and was an active opponent of Reagan's military buildup and policies in Central America against Marxist expansion in the 1980s. He thus advanced a liberal agenda throughout his career, but he also stressed the dictum that "all politics is local."

Opus Dei

Latin for "Work of God," the Prelature of the Holy Cross and Opus Dei is a worldwide association of Catholics that was founded in Madrid in 1928 by St. Monsignor Josemaría Escrivá de Balaguer y Allia. Opus Dei has as its aims the attainment of Christian perfection that is the universal call for all people, the giving of theological and ascetical formation for its members so as to lead to personal sanctity in their daily lives, and the enabling of them to carry on a personal apostolate in their conduct of work. Opus Dei is composed of two main sections, one for men and another for women. Both contain single and married members under the direction of a president general. Priests for the association are chosen from among the laymen of the organization, although diocesan priests are permitted to be members through the Priestly Society of the Holy Cross while remaining under the authority of their bishops and continuing their regular diocesan assignments.

Opus Dei was given first formal approval in 1947 by Pope Pius XII, who declared it universal, thereby permitting it to function internationally. By 1964 members were found in over fifty countries. On November 28, 1982, Pope Blessed John Paul II declared it to be a personal prelature, a clear statement of papal favor. It is customarily inserted into dioceses with the local ordinary having jurisdiction over the chapter within his diocese. Members are thus directed in their religious activities while retaining full freedom in their secular affairs.

According to the *Annuario Pontificio*, Opus Dei claims over 82,000 laypeople of every class and social condition as well as more than 1,800 priests. The Prelature is found in eighty countries, supported by nearly 1,700 churches and pastoral centers. The prelature also operates the Pontifical University of the Holy Cross in Rome, established in 1985 and granted approval as a pontifical institution in 1995.

Opus Dei was first established in the United States in 1949 in Chicago when Sal Ferigle, a graduate student, and Father Joseph Muzquiz, one of the first priests ordained for Opus Dei, opened the first center near the University of Chicago. Additional centers were opened over the next decades, and by 1975 there were eight centers across the country. Currently, there are over 3,000 members in the United States, with sixty centers in nineteen cities.

The prelature also helps to operate one college and five secondary schools in the United States. The college is Lexington College in Chicago, the only all-women's college offering hospitality management in the United States. The secondary schools are Heights and Oakcrest in Washington, D.C., Northridge Prep and The Willows in Chicago, and the Montrose School in Boston. Members are also active in a host of different activities in their respective dioceses. The most prominent member of Opus Dei in the American hierarchy is Archbishop José H. Gomez, archbishop of Los Angeles since 2011.

Orange in California, Diocese of

Established on June 18, 1976, by Pope Paul VI, the Diocese of Orange serves counties along the southern California coastline. Orange dates to 1776, when famed Franciscan Blessed Junípero Serra founded the seventh of the California missions at San Juan Capistrano. The city of Orange on the Santa Ana River was founded as Richland in 1868 and received its present name in 1875. The Diocese of Orange in California is a suffragan see of the Archdiocese of Los Angeles.

Los Angeles and the surrounding areas, including Orange, were part of Jesuit and then Franciscan mission efforts. In 1842 the region became part of the Diocese of the Two Californias, administered by Bishop Francisco Garcia Diego y Moreno, a Franciscan. The war between Mexico and the United States led to the ceding of California by Mexico, and the region entered the Union in September 1850. Dominican Joseph Sadoc Alemany was consecrated for the Diocese of Monterey in 1850 and went on to become the archbishop of San Francisco in 1853. Bishop Thaddeus Amat was consecrated for Monterey on March 12, 1854, residing in Santa Barbara but moving to Los Angeles in 1859. The Holy See honored his request and established the Diocese of Monterey-Los Angeles. Bishop Francis Mora, Bishop George Montgomery, Bishop Thomas James Conaty, and Bishop John J. Cantwell were the successors of Bishop Mora and expanded Catholic holdings and services to aid the growing populations. From 1936 the Catholics of Orange were part of the Archdiocese of Los Angeles. Particularly notable were Cardinal James F. McIntyre, archbishop from 1948 to 1970, and his successor, Cardinal Timothy Manning, whose time as archbishop witnessed the official founding of the Orange diocese.

Cardinal Manning installed the first bishop of Orange, William R. Johnson, on June 16, 1976, in Holy Family Cathedral. Bishop Johnson had served as auxiliary bishop of Los Angeles since 1971. He assumed the task of establishing the first diocesan administration, diocesan curia, and pastoral services. In November 1976 he celebrated with Cardinal Manning the bicentennial of Mission San Juan Capistrano. He founded a number of new parishes and a new diocesan paper, *The Diocese of Orange Bulletin*; inaugurated important outreach programs for Hispanics, Vietnamese, and other ethnic groups; and oversaw the financial development of the diocese through a successful development campaign. His labors continued until his death on July 28, 1986.

With the passing of Bishop Johnson, Auxiliary Bishop John T. Steinbock served as apostolic administrator until February 24, 1987, when Bishop Norman F. McFarland was installed second bishop of Orange. Bishop McFarland had been an auxiliary bishop of San Francisco from 1970 to 1974, apostolic administrator of the Diocese of Reno-Las Vegas from 1974 to 1976, and bishop of Reno-Las Vegas from 1976 to 1986. He was appointed bishop of Orange on December 26, 1986. He continued the extensive expansion program started by his predecessor, and he also convened a clergy conference to plan for the pastoral needs of the rapidly changing population of the diocese. In the previous years, Orange County had grown by 25 percent, and the Hispanic population had increased by 75 percent. The bishop also established the first annual Bishop McFarland Open to benefit Catholic Charities. He retired on June 30, 1998.

On September 3, 1998, Bishop Tod David Brown was installed as third bishop of Orange. He had served since 1988 as the bishop of Boise. Bishop Brown continued the diocesan outreach to the growing number of Latino and Asian Catholics, especially ensuring that they received needed pastoral care. He has been an active figure in the national ecumenical movement, especially in his capacity as the former chairman of the bishop's Committee on Ecumenism and Interreligious Affairs. Bishop Brown also launched a new diocesan newspaper, the *Orange County Catholic*. The Catholic population, nearly one-half of the total population of Orange County, is one of the largest Catholic communities in the United States. In 2011 the diocese had a Catholic population of over one million, served by 58 parishes, 289 priests, and over 340 men and women religious.

Oregon

Called the Beaver State, Oregon is located in the northeastern part of the United States. It is bounded on the north by Washington, on the east by Idaho, on the south by California and Nevada, and on the west by the Pacific Ocean. There are five natural land regions in Oregon: the Columbia Plateau in the northeast, the Great Basin in the southeast, the Cascade Mountains in the west, the Klamath Mountains in the southwest, and the Coast Range on the Pacific. The original inhabitants of Oregon were the Bannock, Cayuse, Chinook, Klamath, Modoc, Nez Perce, Paiute, Tillamook, and Umatilla.

As early as the 1540s explorers were in the region, including an expedition led by Bartolomé Ferrelo, who sailed along the coast of Oregon. Sir Francis Drake's ships were also in the area in 1579, but no recorded settlements were established. In 1720 Vitus Bering, in the service of Russia, was on the Oregon coast. Juan Perez followed in 1714, and in 1775 Bruno de Heceta (Hezeta) y Dudagoitia, another Spaniard, landed in Oregon with Franciscan missionaries. The British explorer James Cook and George Vancouver also explored the Oregon coastal waters.

In 1792 the Columbia River was discovered by Robert Gray on behalf of the United States. The Lewis and Clark expedition of 1804–06 also sailed on the Columbia River. Oregon was a rich source for trappers, and by 1811 John Jacob Astor had established the Pacific Fur Company in the northwestern part of the present state, taken by the British in 1812. Spain and Russia, which had historic claims on the region, ceded all control in 1819 and 1824, respectively. The British remained, and John McLoughlin acted as governor of the area. Called the "Father of Oregon," he became an American and converted to Catholicism.

A group of American Methodists founded the first permanent settlement in Oregon's Willamette Valley in 1835, and Canadian trappers were also establishing residences in the Northwest. Three years later, Catholic missionaries Father (later archbishop) Francis Norbert Blanchet and Father (later Bishop) Modeste Demers arrived in Oregon. The first Catholic church was dedicated in Champoeg soon after.

The revered Jesuit missionary Pierre-Jean De Smet was in Oregon by the early 1840s, consulting with Bishop Blanchet, the vicar apostolic. The two veteran missionaries recognized the need for funds, religious personnel, and priests and made efforts to bring such necessary elements from Europe. The Sisters of Notre Dame de Namur were among the volunteers in the diocese, operating a school for girls.

The famed Oregon Trail was opening the way for countless settlers, who took part in the Great Migration. The Archdiocese of Oregon was established in 1846 by Pope Blessed Pius IX, with suffragan sees of Walla Walla and Vancouver Island. This population increase led to boundary disputes with Britain and

a final designation of Oregon's borders. The Church faced many difficulties in Oregon, however. The Whitman Massacre of 1847, in which Protestants were killed by Cayuse Indians near Walla Walla, brought about grave problems. A Protestant survivor accused Catholics of having instigated the massacre. His charges were discredited, but they had a lasting influence in fostering anti-Catholic sentiment.

Archbishop Blanchet toured South American dioceses and raised funds for his work in the Northwest, and he sent Father Jean Baptiste Abraham Brouillet to Washington, where Archbishop James Roosevelt Bayley of Baltimore founded the Bureau of Catholic Indian Missions and appointed Father Brouillet its first head, with the task of halting government interference in the Church's programs of evangelization among Native Americans. Archbishop Blanchet retired in 1880 after more than six decades of priestly service, and his coadjutor, Charles J. Seghers, acceded to the see.

Oregon had been designated a territory by the U.S. Congress and became the thirty-third state of the Union in 1859. The Catholic population grew steadily again over the next years. The University of Portland was opened and the Diocese of Baker was established just after the turn of the century.

Catholics, however, aided by people of all faiths, had to fight for their rights as a truly remarkably intolerant piece of legislation was passed in the state in 1922. The Oregon School Law had the sole intent of eliminating parochial schools in Oregon. Joined by countless leaders and civil rights organizations, Catholics, led by Archbishop Alexander Christie, sued, and in 1925 the U.S. Supreme Court declared the Oregon School Law unconstitutional.

In 1928 Archbishop Edward D. Howard received permission from the Holy See to move the see to Portland. The people of Oregon had endured the sacrifices of World War I and faced the economic hardships of the Great Depression.

The state experienced enormous development in economic diversity and in population in the years after World War II. Timber harvesting was long a mainstay of the economy, although the 1990s witnessed a sharp decline in the industry. The result has been the emergence of other sectors, including the high-tech industry, vineyards, and hazelnut production. The population of the state has increased steadily over the last decades, with significant growth in Latino and Asian American populations. As a result, the Church has developed extensive outreach and pastoral care programs for the minority groups, especially the Latino communities. In 2011 the Catholic population was nearly 450,000, comprising some 13 percent of the total population. Catholics are the largest Christian denomination in the state, served by nearly 350 priests, over 500 men and women religious, and 160 parishes.

Oregon School Law

The Oregon Compulsory Education Act of 1922, known as the Oregon School Law, stipulated that as of September 1, 1926, every child in the state of Oregon between the ages of eight and sixteen was obligated to attend public school. The act represented a deliberate effort to cripple Catholic schools and was one of the most blatant efforts to limit freedom of education in American history.

The Oregon School Law originated in the anti-Catholic and anti-immigrant sentiment then prevalent in parts of the United States, including Oregon, despite its traditionally opened-minded culture. Encouraged by groups such as the Masons and especially the Ku Klux Klan, a petition drive was launched to secure enough signatures to place the petition on the ballot in November 1922. On November 7, 1922, the measure was approved by voters by a plurality of only 10,000 votes, out of approximately 204,000 ballots cast.

The law was initially opposed by the Catholic Church in Oregon, but once passed by the legislature the threat that similar laws might be approved in states all across the country attracted the concern and the action of the National Catholic Welfare Conference in Washington, D.C., the forerunner of the modern-day United States Conference of Catholic Bishops. The administrative committee of the NCWC authorized the raising of $100,000 to launch a legal campaign that might go all the way to the U.S. Supreme Court. The two key officials in the effort were Father John J. Burke, C.S.P., general secretary of the NCWC, and Father James H. Ryan, chairman of the Education Department of the NCWC. They organized the legal support team and the nationwide publicity campaign that sought to galvanize public opinion beyond the support of

American Catholics. In December 1923 legal arguments began in Portland, and the attorney for the NCWC succeeded in convincing the three-judge federal panel to impose an injunction on March 31, 1924. The state responded by filing an appeal against the injunction, thereby ensuring that the case would go to the U.S. Supreme Court.

Representing the NCWC was the prominent New York attorney William D. Guthrie, assisted by Oregon Judge John P. Kavanaugh. *Amici curiae* briefs were filed by the North Pacific Union Conference of the Seventh-Day Adventists, the Domestic and Foreign Missionary Society of the Protestant Episcopal Church, and the American Jewish Committee; the ACLU also supported the NCWC case. The case, *Pierce v. Society of Sisters,* was heard by the Supreme Court on March 16–17, 1925. The justices heard a three-pronged argument by Guthrie and Kavanaugh — namely, that the law violated the contract that existed between the sisters in charge of the Catholic parochial schools; that the law was a violation of the Fourteenth Amendment as it deprived the sisters of their property rights; and that the law violated the rights of parents to direct the education of their own children. The high court agreed unanimously on June 1, 1925, declaring the law unconstitutional. In expressing the unanimous decision, Justice James Clark McReynolds declared, "The child is not the mere creature of the state."

The decision of the Supreme Court proved one of the most significant in the history of American education. It prevented an egregious interference on the part of the state in Catholic education, guaranteed the rights of private and parochial schools, and ensured the flowering of the Catholic parochial school system throughout the United States. (*See also* Education, Catholic; Oregon.)

O'Reilly, Bernard (September 20, 1820–April 26, 1907)

Priest and historian Bernard O'Reilly was born in County Mayo, Ireland, and moved to Canada at an early age. There he studied at Laval University in Québec and was ordained on September 12, 1843. His early years as a priest were marked by his heroic care of Irish immigrants during a typhus epidemic. He later entered the Jesuits and was a chaplain to the famed Irish Brigade during the Civil War. After leaving the Jesuits, he devoted his energies to writing, serving on the staff of the *New American Cyclopedia* and writing for the *New York Sun* newspaper, including riveting accounts of his travels in Europe. Settling in Rome, he was appointed a protonotary apostolic in 1887 by Pope Leo XIII, who provided him with key information for his biography, *Life of Leo XIII*, which was published in 1887. Father O'Reilly also published *Life of Pius IX* (1877), *Key of Heaven* (1878), and *The Two Brides* (1879). He later returned to the United States and died in New York.

O'Reilly, John Boyle (June 24, 1844–August 10, 1890)

A poet, author, and editor, John Boyle O'Reilly was born at Douth Castle, Drogheda, Ireland, and studied at the National School (which was administered by his father) before working as a printer on the *Drogheda Argus* and on the staff of *The Guardian*, in England. He next enlisted in the Tenth Hussars and belonged at the same time to the Fenian movement, a pro-Irish organization that was opposed to English domination of Ireland. Discovered by his superiors, he was court-martialed and given a life sentence. Owing to his youth the sentence was commuted to twenty years' penal servitude in Australia. O'Reilly escaped from Australia in 1869, with the assistance of the captain of a whaling ship from New Bedford, Massachusetts. His journey to the United States became much celebrated, and upon his arrival in the United States in 1869 he asked to become an American citizen.

In 1870 O'Reilly became editor of *The Pilot*, and was soon well known as a writer and poet. His chief works included several books of poems, *Songs of the Southern Seas* (1873), *Songs, Legends, and Ballads* (1878), and *In Bohemia* (1886), and the novel *Moondyne* (1875), based on his experiences in Australia.

In 1876 O'Reilly worked with Boston Archbishop John J. Williams to save *The Pilot* from bankruptcy, contributing thousands of dollars of his own money. As the paper's chief editorial voice, he crafted it into one of the most influential voices of Irish-American Catholicism. He was also a much sought-after lecturer. His daughter, Mary Boyle O'Reilly, became a noted journalist in her own right.

O'Reilly, Mary Boyle (May 18, 1873–October 21, 1939)

A journalist and daughter of Irish-born novelist and poet John Boyle O'Reilly, Mary Boyle O'Reilly was born in Charlestown, Massachusetts. She grew up in the household of her famed father and became well known for her many adventures. After studies, she was named to the Prison Commission of Massachusetts from 1907 to 1911, embarking at the same time on a flamboyant journalistic career. In 1910 she disguised herself and exposed a ring of "baby farms" in New Hampshire that were trading in unwanted children; her efforts led to legislation against the industry.

In 1914, at the start of World War I, she sailed to Europe and began sending home reports on the fighting. That same year, she managed to sneak into Belgium and was arrested by the Germans on suspicion of being a spy. After the war, she promoted the cause of women, helping to establish the St. Elizabeth's Settlement House in Boston for women and lecturing on the plight of women workers.

O'Reilly, Thomas (1831–September 10, 1872)

A priest best known for his labors during the Civil War, Thomas O'Reilly was born in County Cavan, Ireland. He studied at All Hallows College in Dublin and received ordination in 1857. That same year, he was assigned to the United States, arriving in Savannah, Georgia. After a brief period of service in Savannah, he was moved and named pastor of Immaculate Conception parish in Atlanta in 1861. Throughout the Civil War he provided pastoral care for the garrison and also the prisoners at the infamous Andersonville Prison, using his official posting as chaplain to the Confederate troops there as a means of assisting the long and terrible conditions faced by the Union prisoners. In 1864, as Atlanta fell to advancing Union forces, Father O'Reilly successfully petitioned General Henry Slocum to prevent the burning of Immaculate Conception Church, as well as the nearby churches of several Protestant denominations. As the area also included several important local public buildings, including City Hall, Father O'Reilly helped to save part of the city from the fires of General William T. Sherman's relentless "March to the Sea." His death was greeted with great mourning in the city of Atlanta. In 1945 Father O'Reilly was honored with a statue.

Orlando, Diocese of

Established on June 8, 1968, by Pope Paul VI, the Diocese of Orlando serves counties in the central part of the state of Florida. The area was settled around 1844, with Fort Gatlin, an army post, defending new arrivals. The town was originally called Janigen but was renamed in 1857 to honor Orlando Reeves, who died in the Seminole War. Orlando benefited from the arrival of the South Florida Railroad in 1880 and prospered as the citrus-growing industry developed, along with tourism, military bases, and electronics. The Strategic Air Command has long been headquartered in the area, along with other military and defense posts. The Diocese of Orlando is a suffragan see of the Archdiocese of Miami.

Juan Ponce de León named Florida in 1513, when he celebrated the feast of Easter there, calling it *Pascua florida*, "Easter of Flowers." On April 3, 1513, he erected a cross in the area. Other Spanish explorers followed him, including Francisco Fernandez de Cordova, Alonso Alvarez de Pineda, Lucas Vázquez de Ayllón, and Tristán de Luna. Hernando de Soto marched through Florida in 1539 and passed present-day Ocala. The native Indians around Cape Canaveral proved quite hostile to the invading Spaniards, and mission centers could not be established immediately. In 1548 the revered missionary Dominican Luis Cáncer de Barbastro and companions were slain at Tampa Bay.

Rival colonies of France and Spain were opened and then suppressed, but in September 1565 St. Augustine was founded, the oldest city in the nation. Jesuit and Franciscan missionaries subsequently labored in Florida, and some endured martyrdom for the faith. Despite attacks by British forces, these missionaries endured, and the bishop of Havana (the Church in Florida was then under that jurisdiction) traveled to Florida to administer confirmation and to ordain priests.

Queen Anne's War from 1702 to 1713 brought massive devastation to the mission structure in Florida, mostly in the early part of the struggle, when an English force from the colony of Carolina marched south and captured and burned St. Augustine. In 1763 the Spanish ceded Florida to Britain, but in 1783 the region was returned to Spain, and Cuban bishops resumed their jurisdiction.

The area was designated as part of the Diocese of Louisiana and the Two Floridas in 1793. In 1819, by terms of the Adams-Onís Treaty, Spain ceded Florida to the United States in exchange for the renunciation of any American claims on Texas. In 1825 the Vicariate Apostolic of Alabama and the Floridas was established. Florida entered the Union in 1845 as the twenty-seventh state.

In 1858 Bishop Jean-Pierre Augustin Verot was named vicar apostolic of part of Georgia and Florida; he then became bishop of Savannah in 1861, but he also remained vicar apostolic of Florida. In 1870 the Diocese of St. Augustine was erected with Bishop Verot as the first bishop of what was the only diocese in Florida.

In 1958 the southern half of the state was established as the Diocese of Miami, and ten years later, the diocese was elevated to the rank of an archdiocese. To assist the needs of Catholics in Florida, two new suffragans were created, St. Petersburg and Orlando. At the time of its founding, the Diocese of Orlando consisted of fifty parishes and served 128,000 Catholics.

Orlando's first bishop was William D. Borders, who was installed on June 14, 1968. A one-time army chaplain and priest of New Orleans, Bishop Borders set himself the immediate task of providing the new diocese with a solid footing, both spiritual and administrative. He established parish councils and parish education boards, launched a migrant ministry and an acclaimed campus ministry program, and promoted the laity as extraordinary ministers of the Eucharist. On March 24, 1974, he was named the archbishop of Baltimore. He remained archbishop until his retirement in 1989.

Bishop Borders was succeeded by Bishop Thomas J. Grady, who had been director of the National Shrine of the Immaculate Conception in Washington, D.C., and an auxiliary bishop of Chicago since 1967. Installed on December 16, 1974, he presided over the diocese during a period of immense growth. To provide for the pastoral care of the rapidly growing Catholic population, he established eighteen new parishes, a tourism ministry, and the San Pedro Center (a spiritual life center), and promoted the greater participation of women in the work of the Church. Bishop Grady also was forced to change cathedrals following the destruction by a fire of St. Charles Borromeo in 1976 and the designation of St. James Church as the new cathedral on March 25, 1977. He also secured the designation of Mary, the Mother of God, as the patroness of the diocese. By the time of his retirement in 1989, the diocese's population had grown by a staggering 76 percent. Bishop Grady died on April 21, 2002.

The third bishop of Orlando was Norbert M. Dorsey, who was installed on May 25, 1990. A priest of the Congregation of the Passion, he had served since 1986 as an auxiliary bishop of Miami and had also been assistant general of the Passionist order. Bishop Dorsey continued the work of guiding the diocese during an era of swift expansion and population growth. He built new parishes and schools and made a particular effort to expand the ministry to the burgeoning Hispanic community, including the founding of Radio Paz and health clinics for migrants and farmworkers.

Bishop Dorsey worked with Bishop Grady to found the Mary, Queen of the Universe Shrine, for ministry to tourists, and Bishop Grady Villas, a residential community for adults whose primary diagnosis is mental retardation. Bishop Dorsey also began a Catholic cemetery for priests of the diocese at the San Pedro Retreat Center. He retired on November 13, 2004.

The fourth bishop of Orlando, Bishop Thomas G. Wenski, had been named on July 1, 2003, as the first coadjutor bishop of the Diocese of Orlando. He acceded to the see on November 13, 2004. Bishop Wenski had been an auxiliary bishop of Miami since 1997 and is the first Florida-born bishop of the diocese. He assumed the still-growing diocese and continued his long personal commitment to immigrants and the poor. He was appointed the archbishop of Miami on April 20, 2010.

His successor, Bishop John G. Noonan, was appointed on October 23, 2010. He had served as an auxiliary bishop of Miami since 2005 and was installed in Orlando on December 16, 2010. In 2011 the diocese had a Catholic population of 369,151, nearly 10 percent of the total population in the area. There were over 175 priests, 100 men and women religious, and 77 parishes.

O'Rourke, Patrick (March 25, 1837–July 2, 1863)

A soldier in the Union Army during the Civil War, Patrick O'Rourke was born in County Cavan, Ireland. He grew up Rochester, New York, after his family migrated to the United States. He graduated from the United States Military Academy at West Point with highest honors in 1861 and was commissioned a lieutenant.

In the war that followed, he was eventually named colonel of the 140th Regiment of New York Volunteers, taking part in the bloody Battles of Fredericksburg and Chancellorsville in 1863. At the Battle of Gettysburg, he took his regiment into combat on Little Round Top. In the furious fighting, he was shot dead while mounting a countercharge against advancing Confederate troops. His widow entered the Religious of the Sacred Heart in New York.

Ortynsky, Stephen Soter (January 29, 1866– March 24, 1916)

The first Eastern-rite Catholic bishop of the Western Hemisphere and the first Ukrainian Catholic bishop of the United States, Stephen Soter Ortynsky was born in Ortynstki, Galicia, in old Russia. He entered the Basilian order in 1884 and was sent for studies at the University of Graz. After completing his education, he was ordained on July 18, 1891, and served over the next years as a teacher, preacher, and missionary. On the basis of his skills, homiletic ability, and reputation for hard work, he was appointed in 1907 to the post of ordinary for American Byzantine Catholics and titular bishop of Daulia. The task was to prove a difficult and often painful one owing to the conditions facing Byzantine Catholics in the United States and the opposition of some in the American hierarchy to his appointment.

After episcopal consecration in Lviv in May 1907, he traveled to the United States and arrived in August ready to assume his duties. Immediately he discovered problems. Foremost was the apostolic letter that delineated his authority, *Ea Semper*, issued by the Holy See. While confirming his position, the letter also circumscribed his authority, withholding ordinary jurisdiction and placing him as an auxiliary bishop to the Latin-rite bishops in the various dioceses where Byzantine Catholic populations were to be served. Further, the letter abrogated the practice of confirmation at baptism and married clergy among Eastern-rite Catholics. Bishop Ortynsky also found serious divisions among the Byzantine Catholics, specifically between the Galician and Transcarpathian Catholics, and chronic efforts by the Orthodox Church to proselytize.

Bishop Ortynsky proceeded aggressively in the face of these challenges. He convoked a gathering of clergy and parish representatives in October 1907 to establish the administrative and pastoral structure for the far-flung Byzantine Catholic community. He also launched a newspaper, *Ameryka,* and a mutual assistance society, *Provydinia.* By 1913 his achievements made possible the declaration by Pope St. Pius X that henceforth he should have ordinary jurisdiction, thereby creating the first exarchate for Byzantine Catholics in the United States; the exarchate eventually grew into the current metropolitan archdiocese of Philadelphia. By the time of his death, the exarchate claimed over 500,000 members and over 220 priests. For his part, Bishop Ortynsky continued to face severe trials of division within the Byzantine Catholic community. He died from overwork and pneumonia on March 24, 1916.

O'Sullivan, Mary Kenney (January 8, 1864– January 18, 1943)

A labor organizer and founder of the National Women's Trade Union League, Mary Kenney O'Sullivan was born in Hannibal, Missouri, and worked from an early age in a bindery, eventually moving to Chicago to find work. There she found conditions for female workers to be so appalling that she founded, with Jane Addams, the Chicago Women's Bindery Workers' Union, part of the American Federation of Labor (AFL). In 1892 she was named by Samuel Gompers to serve as the national organizer for the women of the AFL; her position was eliminated by the AFL a mere five months later, despite her work in New York and Massachusetts. While traveling to Boston, she met John F. O'Sullivan, the labor editor of the *Boston Globe* and a fellow member of the AFL. They were married in 1894, but O'Sullivan was killed in an accident in 1902. The next year, Mary founded the National Women's Trade Union League. From 1914 to 1934 she supported her fam-

ily by working as a Massachusetts factory inspector while promoting a variety of women's issues, including women's suffrage and labor rights. She died in West Bedford, Massachusetts.

Our Lady of Deliverance of Newark. *See* Eastern Churches, Catholic

Our Lady of Lebanon of Los Angeles. *See* Eastern Churches, Catholic

Our Sunday Visitor

One of the largest national Catholic newspapers in the United States, *Our Sunday Visitor* was founded in 1912 by the Indiana priest Father (later Archbishop) John F. Noll, chiefly in response to the anti-Catholic literature that was being distributed throughout the state, in particular the widely circulated anti-Catholic newspaper *The Menace.*

The first thirty-five thousand copies of *Our Sunday Visitor* rolled off the press with an issue dated May 5, 1912. The first offices and plant were located on the Jefferson Street Roche Building in downtown Huntington, Indiana. Within a year the paper's circulation had reached 160,000. In that same year, the paper offered a $10,000 reward to anyone who could prove the charges then being distributed by anti-Catholic publications, including the scurrilous accusations made against bishops, priests, and nuns, and the charges of papal interference and machinations for world domination by the papacy. The reward was never claimed. By 1914 circulation had reached 400,000, and shortly after World War I weekly readership exceeded 500,000. Copies were sold at church doors for one cent; pastors were granted discounts by ordering one hundred copies for sixty cents.

Father Noll served as pastor of St. Mary's Church in Huntington, but he also held the post of chief executive for many years, even after his appointment in 1925 as bishop of Fort Wayne. Throughout this period, he remained determined to answer the critics of the Church. Aside from defending the faith, *Our Sunday Visitor* featured in its early years conversion stories, including the 1918 coverage of the deathbed conversion of Buffalo Bill Cody.

Owing to the paper's phenomenal success, in 1924 new offices were established according to

Father Noll's exacting specifications at the corner of East Park Drive and Warren Street; the building was dedicated in April 1925.

In the period between the World Wars and throughout the Great Depression, *Our Sunday Visitor* was at the forefront of Catholic social communications, proclaiming Catholic positions in a host of social areas, including workers' rights, fair-wage issues, education for black children, and above all the right to Catholic parochial schools. The paper was thus ideally positioned to challenge the anti-Catholicism of the 1920s and 1930s, particularly the manifestations of intolerance and bigotry on the part of the Ku Klux Klan and during the 1928 presidential campaign of Al Smith, the popular Catholic governor of New York, who ran as the Democratic Party nominee against Herbert Hoover. The anti-Catholicism throughout the campaign provoked sharp rebuttals by the paper, but Bishop Noll maintained strict neutrality in the race and did not endorse Smith.

Throughout the Great Depression, the paper encouraged American Catholics to embrace a spiritual renewal that would lift the country out of its economic malaise and that would assist in cultivating an authentic Catholic identity. The effort was given considerable assistance by then Father Fulton J. Sheen, who began writing for *Our Sunday Visitor* in 1938. As the world drifted toward world war, Bishop Noll steered an isolationist course, but after Pearl Harbor, *Our Sunday Visitor* was a strong supporter of the war and also of a just and lasting peace, even as the paper called for a moral renewal at home. By the end of the global conflict, Bishop Noll was predicting accurately that the Soviet Union and communism would be the next threat to peace and to freedom. *Our Sunday Visitor* editorialized against communism and stressed patriotism throughout the late 1940s and early 1950s. Other concerns were not forgotten, such as that expressed in the 40th anniversary issue (published on May 4, 1952): "They Do Not Want God in Our Schools: Secular Trend Is Certain to Bring Disaster."

Bishop Noll stepped down as editor in 1953 and died in July 1956. The paper continued in his tradition of serving the Church through coverage of the important events of the time, including the ongoing communist scare, the Korean War, the Cold War, and the growing civil rights debate in the country. Of particular note were the paper's coverage of the election of Pope John XXIII in 1958 and the election of the first Catholic president, John F. Kennedy, in 1960. The paper reflected the excitement of Catholics at the time and the sense of anticipation for the future, especially when Pope Blessed John XXIII announced the convoking of the Second Vatican Council.

In 1961 circulation reached one million readers, and the expansion arrived in time for the paper to cover the upheaval of the decade, as President Kennedy was assassinated in 1963, the Vietnam War began, and the civil rights movement became marked by riots and social tension. *Our Sunday Visitor*'s pages reflected the somber mood of the country and also of many in the Church. In the post-conciliar period, disenchantment and even division were discussed in the pages, as editors and articles asked questions about the direction the changes were making in the life of the Church. The deep problems that confronted the Church in the next years were discussed openly by the paper, and readership declined in the polarized atmosphere. Nevertheless, in 1978 the expansion of the company had reached the point at which a split was effected between the not-for-profit Our Sunday Visitor, Inc., and Noll Printing, a wholly owned subsidiary.

In 1968 *Our Sunday Visitor* supported the encyclical *Humanae Vitae* by Pope Paul VI and was one of the most vocal voices in America against the 1973 *Roe v. Wade* decision legalizing abortion. Its coverage was prophetic in anticipating the disastrous consequences that would emerge as a result of the decision and the promotion of the secularization of American society and religious indifference.

Currently, Our Sunday Visitor publishes not only one of the largest Catholic newspapers but has a publishing division that offers religious periodicals, religious books, and religious-education materials. Periodicals include *The Priest* magazine, *My Daily Visitor*, *The Pope Speaks*, and *The Catholic Answer*. More than five hundred books are available on a wide range of subjects, including apologetics and catechetics reference, prayer, heritage and saints, and family and parish materials. Since 1973, Our Sunday Visitor has also published the *Catho-*

lic Almanac, and in 2000, Our Sunday Visitor was chosen by the U.S. bishops to be the primary distributor of the *Catechism of the Catholic Church*. The Our Sunday Visitor Offertory Solutions Division serves more than 6,000 parishes in this country and in Canada and prints approximately 300 million offering envelopes every year. In 2009 Our Sunday Visitor acquired Harcourt Religion Publishers, expanding significantly its presence in the area of Catholic curriculum publishing. Our Sunday Visitor celebrated its hundredth anniversary in 2012.

Owensboro, Diocese of

The Diocese of Owensboro was established on December 9, 1937, by Pope Pius XI and serves the western regions of the state of Kentucky. It includes thirty-two counties and covers approximately 12,500 square miles. Owensboro is an industrial and commercial center in an area of resources rich in coal fields and natural petroleum and gas. The city also serves as an important tobacco market and has meatpacking plants. Originally settled in the 1790s by frontiersman William "Bill" Smeathers, the first town was given the name of Yellow Banks (owing to the color of the banks of the Ohio River). In 1817 the name was changed to Owensborough, after Colonel Abraham Owen (also the namesake of Owen County, Kentucky), and in 1893 the name was shortened to Owensboro. The diocese is presently a suffragan see of the Archdiocese of Louisville.

Called the "Holy Land," Kentucky was settled by families of the faithful, having been explored in the late 1660s by René-Robert Chevalier, Sieur de la Salle. A century later, in 1750, Daniel Boone, Thomas Walker, and Benjamin Cutbird entered the region. In 1774 James Harrod opened the first settlement, Harrodsburg. A year later, Dr. George Hart, and William Coomes and his wife, Catholics, settled at Harrodsburg, where Mrs. Coomes opened a school. In 1775 Boone led an expedition through the Cumberland Gap, later called the Wilderness Road. This trail opened Kentucky to Catholics seeking religious freedom and new beginnings. In 1776 Virginia claimed the region, but Kentucky was soon independent again and in 1792 entered the Union as the fifteenth state.

Father Charles Whelan served as the area's resident priest, having arrived in the region in 1787. Father William de Rohan was serving the faithful in Kentucky by 1791, and he and his Catholic flock built Holy Cross at Pottinger's Creek. Two years later, Father Stephen T. Badin, the famous missionary, was serving in Kentucky, accompanied by Father Michael Barrieres and then by the revered Father Charles Nerinckx. Father Michael Fournier worked in the region until his death in 1803. Fathers John Thayer and Anthony Salmon also labored unceasingly among the faithful. Also on hand was Dominican Father Edward D. Fenwick, who opened a religious house at Springfield, which became St. Rose Priory.

On April 8, 1808, new dioceses in the United States were established as suffragan sees of the Archdiocese of Baltimore. The Diocese of Bardstown (now the Archdiocese of Louisville), the largest episcopal jurisdiction ever established in the nation, was given into the care of Bishop Benedict Joseph Flaget, who was responsible for Catholics in Kentucky, Tennessee, Indiana, Missouri, Ohio, Illinois, Michigan, and Wisconsin. Bishop Flaget was installed in Bardstown on June 9, 1811.

He traveled endlessly to other regions to administer Church affairs, and he founded parishes, schools, and colleges. He also founded a seminary and St. Joseph's Cathedral, now a national monument. In 1832 Bishop Flaget retired, but the uproar caused by his absence in Bardstown convinced the Holy See to reinstate him. In 1841 the Diocese of Bardstown was transferred to Louisville. The Trappists founded Gethsemani Abbey near New Haven seven years later.

On August 6, 1855, called Bloody Monday, more than a hundred Catholics were killed by Protestants, and the Church suffered arson attacks and other outrages. The Civil War brought Catholics relief, as Kentucky, a border state, remained neutral. Emotions ran high on both sides in the conflict, however, as both Abraham Lincoln and Jefferson Davis, the presidents of the United States and of the Confederacy, respectively, were from Kentucky.

Industries such as coal mining flourished after the war, and Kentucky became a leader in hemp tobacco and whiskey. From 1906 to 1909, the Black Patch War was conducted over the tobacco monopoly. The state, however, progressed and supported the military efforts of the nation during World War I. The Great Depression gripped Kentucky, and the people suffered severely.

Partly to meet the mounting pastoral needs of the population in Kentucky, in 1937 Pope Pius XI elevated Louisville to the rank of an archdiocese, and the Diocese of Owensboro was erected on December 9 of that year. On December 16, 1937, Father Francis Ridgley Cotton, a priest of Louisville, was named the first bishop. Consecrated on February 24, 1938, he focused resources on providing the new diocese with a solid administrative footing, but he was also greatly concerned with mission projects, aided by the Catholic Students' Mission Council. His time as bishop witnessed the end of the Great Depression, World War II, and the postwar economic boom that accompanied Kentucky's efforts in the war.

Bishop Cotton also introduced charitable programs and built missions, schools, hospitals, and nursing homes. In 1946 Brescia College was reorganized as a senior liberal-arts college, having been operated by the Ursuline Sisters of Mount St. Joseph. The Benedictines founded St. Maur Priory and Seminary in South Union. Desegregation within the diocese was introduced and accomplished successfully. Bishop Cotton died unexpectedly on September 25, 1960, at the age of sixty-five.

The second bishop of Owensboro was Father Henry J. Soenneker. Consecrated a bishop on April 26, 1961, he took up many of the projects launched by Bishop Cotton and was eager to continue the development of Catholic schools and other diocesan educational initiatives. He also instituted Catholic chaplaincy programs in secular colleges. Bishop Soenneker was shepherd of the diocese during the Second Vatican Council and in the long and tumultuous period after the council. He worked to implement the decrees and reforms of the council in the diocese and to steer a course of authentic renewal in an era of uncertainty and social upheaval.

Bishop Soenneker retired on June 17, 1982, and died on September 24, 1987. He was succeeded as bishop on October 23, 1982, by John J. McRaith, a priest of the Diocese of New Ulm. Consecrated on December 15, 1982, he inherited a diocese known for the devotion of its Catholic population. Indeed, the diocese enjoys one of the highest church attendance rates in the country, with almost 60 percent of registered Catholics attending Mass every Sunday. Bishop McRaith was also deeply committed to the pastoral needs of the Catholic population, especially in the rural communities that comprise 59 percent of the diocese. He retired on January 5, 2009, and was succeeded on December 15, 2009, by Father William F. Medley, a priest of the Diocese of Louisville. Medley was ordained a bishop on February 10, 2010. In 2011 there were over 52,000 Catholics in the diocese, 90 priests, over 200 men and women religious, and 79 parishes.

P

Pace, Edward (July 3, 1861–April 26, 1938)

A priest and scholar, Edward Pace was the founder and dean of the philosophy department of The Catholic University of America. He was born in Starke, Florida, and entered the seminary at St. Charles College in Maryland and was then sent to the North American College in Rome, where he was ordained on May 30, 1885. After earning a doctorate in theology, he returned to the United States and was then sent back to Europe, where he earned a second doctorate, this time in psychology from the University of Leipzig in 1891.

Named to the faculty of the recently established Catholic University of America in Washington, D.C., Father Pace held a variety of posts and was distinguished for establishing the School of Philosophy in 1894 and what became the School of Education in 1899. Pace was also the founding editor of the *Catholic Encyclopedia* and the founder and first president of the American Catholic Philosophical Association. He was a respected figure in American education and was appointed in 1929 to the National Advisory Committee on Education by President Herbert Hoover.

Padilla, Juan de (c. 1500–c. February 1544)

A member of the Franciscans (the Order of Friars Minor), Juan de Padilla is the protomartyr (or first martyr) of the United States. Little is known about de Padilla's early life, but he was born in Andalusia, Spain, and joined the Franciscans. He was sent to Mexico around 1528. From 1529 to 1531 he served with an unnamed friar as a chaplain to the advancing Spanish forces in Mexico, working to prevent the cruel treatment of the indigenous tribes. He then served as a missionary from 1531 to 1540 among a variety of local communities, including the natives of Tzacoalco, Tuchpán, Tzapotitlán, Totlamán, Amula, Atoyac, and Colima. He also established the convent of Tzapotlán, served as its first superior, and then launched another community at Tuchpán. Tuchpán then served as the headquarters for the friars.

In 1540 he set off as a chaplain with the Spanish forces of Francisco Vázquez de Coronado on his famous trek in search of Cibola, the legendary Seven Cities of Gold. (*See also* Coronado, Francisco Vázquez de.) After reaching as far as Kansas, Coronado abandoned his search in October 1541 and left New Mexico. Father de Padilla, along with Father Juan de la Cruz and Brother Luis de Ubeda, chose to remain in the region to preach the Gospel. After meeting with some success among indigenous tribes on the Rio Grande, de Padilla headed north with his small band, including several native converts. Once on the plains, perhaps in modern-day Colorado or Kansas, they were attacked by local tribes, and Father de Padilla was killed while kneeling in prayer. The exact location or date of his death is uncertain, although Father Vetancurt in his *Menologio* fixed the date at November 30, 1544. A statue was raised in his honor in Herington, Kansas. Father Juan de Padilla is honored as the first martyr of the United States. Over one hundred priests and bishops followed in his remarkable footsteps, all slain while laboring for the faith.

Palladino, Laurence, S.J. (August 15, 1837–August 19, 1927)

A Jesuit missionary, Laurence Palladino is honored as the last pioneer missionary of the Northwest. Born in Italy, Palladino entered the Jesuits and was ordained and then sent to the United States to labor as a missionary. His Jesuit superiors sent him to the Montana Territory in 1867, and he is credited with building the first church in the Helena Mission (later the first cathedral) in 1873. He was then used in various offices by Bishop John Baptist Brondel of Helena, including director of schools, chancellor, and vicar general. In 1894 he was appointed president of Gonzaga College. Although successful in his many administrative posts, Palladino's first love was serving as a missionary among the many Native American tribes of the Northwest.

Pallottines

Officially the Society of the Catholic Apostolate (S.C.A.), the Pallottines are a Society of Apostolic

Life, founded in 1835 as the *Societas Apostolatus Catholici* by St. Vincent Pallotti, a Roman priest. He was canonized by Pope Paul VI in 1963. The Pallottines are part of the Union of Catholic Apostolate; they serve in 45 countries and include 2,300 members in 300 communities. The society is in charge of schools, missions, parishes, clinics, and other expressions of Catholic charity. The Pallottines arrived in the United States in the early 1880s and established the Midwest Province in Milwaukee in 1923. Today there are two provinces in the United States: the Mother of God Province in Milwaukee and the Immaculate Conception Province in Hyattsville, Maryland.

Palm Beach, Diocese of

Established on June 16, 1984, by Pope Blessed John Paul II, the Diocese of Palm Beach encompasses the five Florida counties of Indian River, Okeechobee, St. Lucie, Martin, and Palm Beach. It is a suffragan see of the Archdiocese of Miami.

Little is known about the Catholic presence in the area under Spanish rule, but among the first non-Native American inhabitants were former slaves and runaway slaves who had settled in eastern Florida and often found safety among the Seminoles. Considerable development in what became Palm Beach was undertaken by Henry Flagler, the tycoon and partner of John D. Rockefeller in Standard Oil. He established his home in Palm Beach, brought the railroad service to it, and established the surrounding area as a resort. This brought a population of workers and service staff that became a permanent community. Palm Beach was incorporated as a town in 1911.

The Catholic heritage of the diocese opened with the arrival of the Spanish and the labors of the gallant missionaries who labored in the region. The Two Floridas operated a vast mission program, which was crushed by the British and the military forces of the colony of Georgia.

The area remained a wilderness for decades and then attracted settlers who recognized the agricultural resources of the region.

The first Catholic Chutrch in the Palm Beach area was dedicated in 1896 in West Palm Beach on land donated by Henry Flagler to provide for the needs of his Catholic workers. These Catholic workers and their families supported the military efforts of the nation during World War I and endured the sufferings of the Great Depression. Additional parishes followed, and by 1930 there were five in the region. The Catholics of the area also supported the military efforts of the United States during World War II and worked to rebuild the nation's economy when peace was restored.

The parishes of the Paterson area were attached to the Diocese of Miami when it was established in 1958, and the counties of Indian River, Okeechobee, and St. Lucie were attached to the Diocese of Orlando when it was established in 1968.

Owing to the continuing growth of the Catholic community in Florida, Pope Blessed John Paul II erected the Diocese of Palm Beach. On October 24, 1984, Bishop Thomas V. Daily, an auxiliary bishop of Boston since 1974, became the first bishop of the diocese, with thirty-eight parishes and around one hundred thousand Catholics. Bishop Daily immediately proceeded to establish the new diocese on a firm footing. After six years of work, he was transferred to the Diocese of Brooklyn on February 20, 1990.

On June 12, 1990, Pope Blessed John Paul II appointed Bishop J. Keith Symons as the second bishop of Palm Beach. He had been bishop of Pensacola-Tallahassee since 1983. On June 6, 1998, Bishop Symons resigned in the face of allegations of sexual abuse of minors when he was a priest.

On November 12, 1998, Bishop Anthony J. O'Connell, who had been bishop of Knoxville since 1988, was appointed the third bishop of Palm Beach. On March 13, 2002, he resigned owing to allegations of sexual abuse years before.

With the diocese in a state of understandable shock from the resignations of two bishops in a row under the cloud of the sexual abuse scandal, the primary task of the next bishop was to heal the demoralized Catholic community. On September 3, 2002, Bishop Seán Patrick O'Malley, who had been bishop of Fall River since 1992, was appointed as the fourth bishop of the Palm Beach. In less than a year, the Capuchin Franciscan bishop was appointed the archbishop of Boston, an archdiocese what was itself suffering beneath the weight of the sexual abuse scandal. On the same day, July 1,

2003, Bishop Gerald M. Barbarito, who had been bishop of Ogdensburg since 1999, was named the fifth bishop of Palm Beach.

In 2011 the diocese had a Catholic population of more than 260,000, with more than 130 priests and 49 parishes.

Palou, Francisco (January, 1722–April 6, 1789)

A Franciscan missionary in California, New Mexico, and Texas, Francisco Palou was the author of the *Noticias de la Nueva California*. Palou was born at Palma, on the island of Majorca, and entered the Franciscan order around 1739. He subsequently studied under Blessed Father Junípero Serra. Ordained in 1747, he volunteered for service in the missions of the Americas and was sent to the missionary College of San Fernando de Mexico for further studies. Around 1750, Palou was assigned to the Indian missions of the Sierra Gorda, north of Querétaro, and in the San Sabás region of Texas. In 1767, with Blessed Junípero Serra and fourteen other Franciscan friars, he was sent to Lower California to assume the missions following the expulsion of the Jesuits. In April 1768 he was named head of Mission San Francisco Javier and then succeeded Father Serra as superior of the lower missions. When in 1773 the Franciscans handed control of the missions to the Dominican Fathers, Father Palou went to Upper California.

In 1774 he accompanied Captain Fernando D. Rivera's expedition to the Bay of San Francisco, and in December of that year planted the cross on Point Lobos on the Pacific Ocean. In June 1776 he traveled with José Joaquín de la Santísima Trinidad Moraga to the same bay; there he celebrated the first Mass on the site that became Mission Dolores (or San Francisco), which was founded a few weeks later. He remained in the mission until July 1784, when he was summoned to Mission San Carlos to offer the last sacraments to Father Serra. Upon the latter's death on August 28, 1784, Palou became acting superior of the missions. The next year, however, he retired to Mexico City owing to poor health. While in charge of Mission Dolores, Palou compiled his four-volume *Noticias de la Nueva California*, a history of the Spanish colonization in early California and the most reliable history of the California missions from 1767 to 1784. He also wrote the *Life and Apostolic Labors of the Venerable Father Junípero Serra* in 1787.

Pandosy, Charles (November 21, 1824–February 6, 1891)

A member of the Oblates of Mary Immaculate (O.M.I.), Charles Pandosy served as a missionary among the Native Americans of the Northwest. Born in Margerides, France, he entered the Oblates and volunteered for service in the United States. He reached New York in 1847 and undertook the arduous journey to the Northwest along the Oregon Trail, reaching Fort Walla Walla in October 1847. In January 1848 Father Pandosy was ordained with a Father Chirouse, the first priests ordained in what became Washington state. He served in Yakima and witnessed the destruction of the mission there during the Yakima Indian War, which raged from 1855 to 1858. In 1859 he went to British Columbia, where he founded the mission in Okanogan Valley and directed its missionary labors among the native population for the next four decades. He applied the vast knowledge he acquired of the Native Americans by writing a native-language dictionary and grammar that was published by the Smithsonian Institution.

Papal Representatives to the United States. *See* Holy See–U.S. Relations

Parater, Frank (October 10, 1897–February 7, 1920)

Born to a devout Catholic family in Richmond, Frank Parater was educated at the Xaverian Brother's School and Benedictine High School in Richmond. He graduated with honors in 1917 and was active in the Boy Scouts of America. Called to the priesthood, he began his studies in 1917 at Belmont Abbey College in North Carolina with the intention of joining the Benedictines. After prayer and reflection, he felt called to be a diocesan priest in Richmond and in 1919 was sent by Bishop Denis J. O'Connell of Richmond to study at the North American College in Rome. He was a popular and deeply prayerful student. In December 1919 he composed an Act of Oblation to the Sacred Heart of Jesus; this was then placed in an envelope and marked to be read only after his death.

In January 1920 he contracted rheumatism, which became rheumatic fever. After immense suffering, he received his final Communion and the last rites and died soon after. He was buried in the College Mausoleum at Campo Verano. His Act of Oblation was later found in his room by a fellow seminarian and eventually was shown to Pope Benedict XV. The pontiff had it published in the Vatican newspaper *L'Osservatore Romano*.

The seminarian was not forgotten, and in the decades after his death the Diocese of Richmond continued to commemorate his life and to hold him up as a role model for seminarians. In 2002 Bishop Walter F. Sullivan of Richmond officially opened his cause for canonization, and Frank Parater was approved for the title of Servant of God.

Pareja, Francisco (d. January 25, 1628)

A Franciscan missionary in Mexico, Francisco Pareja was born at Auñon, Spain, and entered the Franciscans, who sent him with eleven other Franciscans to St. Augustine, Florida, in late 1593. He dedicated himself to the missions among the local tribes for many years and then, after 1613, was sent to Mexico. He is best known for publishing the first books in the language of a Native American tribe within the United States, the Timuquanan, from 1612 to 1627, including a catechism, grammar, and treatise on Catholic teachings.

Pariseau, Mother Mary Joseph (April 16, 1823– January 19, 1902)

A Canadian religious, the first superior of the Sisters of Charity of Providence in the Northwest, Mother Mary Joseph Pariseau served as a missionary in the state of Washington. Born Esther Pariseau in Montréal, she entered the Sisters of Charity of Providence in 1843 and made her profession in 1845. When Bishop Augustin Magliore Blanchet made the request of Bishop Ignace Bourget of Montréal that the Sisters of Charity of Providence send several members to assist the Diocese of Nesqually, Mother Mary Joseph was chosen to lead a group of four sisters. They reached Fort Vancouver in December 1856 and immediately set to work assisting the needs of the diocese in the education and care of the many Native Americans in the Northwest.

From the start, Mother Mary Joseph applied her talents as carpenter and woodworker, as well as architect, first to provide facilities for the sisters and then to build schools, orphanages, and especially hospitals. In 1857 St. Joseph Hospital in Vancouver, the first permanent hospital in the Northwest, was opened, almost entirely through her efforts as architect and supervisor. She designed and oversaw the construction of St. Vincent Hospital in Portland in 1875 and Sacred Heart Hospital in Spokane in 1886. To assist the funding of these and many other projects, she traveled by horseback and stagecoach to mining camps, where she implored the workers to contribute money.

By the time of her death in 1902, the order had opened schools, hospitals, and orphanages throughout the Northwest, including Washington, Oregon, Idaho, and Montana. She represents Washington State in Statuary Hall in the U.S. Capitol.

Parma, Ohio, Byzantine Ruthenian Eparchy of. *See* Eastern Churches, Catholics

Passaic, New Jersey, Byzantine Ruthenian Eparchy of. *See* Eastern Churches, Catholics

Passionists (C.P.)

The Congregation of the Discalced Clerks of the Most Holy Cross and Passion of Our Lord Jesus Christ is a religious order founded by St. Paul of the Cross, who lived from 1694 to 1775. The Passionists were born as a result of a vision by St. Paul in 1720. In 1725 he was granted permission to start a congregation by Pope Benedict XIII; two years later, the pope ordained St. Paul and his brother John Baptist. The rule was approved on May 15, 1741, by Pope Benedict XIV. The congregation spread rapidly, and in 1771 St. Paul also founded the Sisters of the Cross and Passion (C.P.), known as the Passionist Nuns.

The first Passionist community in the United States was established in 1852 in Pittsburgh at the invitation of Bishop Michael O'Connor. Despite not being proficient in English, the Passionists founded houses across the country, including in Cincinnati, Baltimore, Louisville, Kentucky, and Hoboken, New Jersey.

A second American province was founded in 1906 under the title of Holy Cross. It covered the communities of Cincinnati, Louisville, St. Louis, Chicago, and St. Paul, Kansas. In 1913 the Passionist priest Paul Joseph Nussbaum was named the first bishop of Corpus Christi. The Passionists in the United States continued to expand over the next decades, including evangelization among African-Americans and Spanish-speaking immigrants, and using of new means of social communications, such as television and radio.

In keeping with the call of the Second Vatican Council, the Passionists held a Chapter of Renewal from 1968 to 1970 that resulted in the Chapter Document of 1970 for the reform of the congregation's life and labors. In 1982 the congregation also issued a revised Rule. Currently, there are two provinces of Passionists in the United States: St. Paul of the Cross, the Eastern Province, and Holy Cross, the Western Province. The congregation has 2,400 members worldwide, with nearly 1,700 priests.

Passionist Nuns (C.P.)

The Religious of the Most Holy Cross and Passion of Jesus Christ, the Passionist Nuns were founded in 1771 in Corneto (modern-day Tarquinia), Italy, by St. Paul of the Cross. The Passionists bind themselves to the passion of Our Lord. Crucial to the founding and development of the Passionists was Mother Mary of Jesus Crucified, who was born Faustina Gertrude Constantini in Corneto, Italy. With ten postulants, she received the Passionist habit in 1771 and served as the first mother superior of the order until her death in 1787. Pope Blessed Pius IX permitted a new house to be established at Mamers in Le Mans, France, in 1872, and the order spread swiftly.

Five Passionist nuns from Italy arrived in Pittsburgh in 1910 and began the first community in the United States. A second house was started in Scranton, Pennsylvania, in 1926, and from this foundation was begun a new community in Owensboro, Kentucky, in 1946. It was relocated to Whitesville, Kentucky, in 1995. The Pittsburgh community also established a monastery in Erlanger, Kentucky, in 1947 and in the Archdiocese of St. Louis at Ellisville. Additional houses were founded in Asia, England, and Latin America.

Passionist Sisters of the Cross and Passion (C.P.)

The second congregation of Passionist religious women was established in 1850 in England through the leadership of Elizabeth Prout, with the help of Passionist Fathers Gaudentius Rossi and Ignatius Spencer. The Sisters of the Cross and Passion were established as a means of providing badly needed pastoral care, education, hope, and charity to the rapidly growing population of young female laborers in the factories and tenements of industrial Lancashire, England. The community's rule was approved by Pope Blessed Pius IX in 1876 and given final approval by Pope Leo XIII in 1887.

The Passionist Sisters arrived in the United States in 1924. The present community belongs to the Our Lady of Dolors Province, with members serving in Connecticut, New York, New Jersey, Rhode Island, and Tennessee. The Sisters internationally serve in Argentina, Bosnia, Botswana, Chile, England, Ireland, Jamaica, Peru, Papua New Guinea, Scotland, and Wales.

Paterson, Diocese of

Established on December 9, 1937, by Pope Pius XI, the Diocese of Paterson comprises the three counties of Passaic, Morris, and Sussex in northern New Jersey. It is a suffragan of the Archdiocese of Newark and covers an area of 1,214 miles.

The Catholic population in northern New Jersey dates to a time before the American Revolution, and members of the Catholic community took part in the war. Priests traveling through the area celebrated Mass as early as 1762, in Macopin. A church was built there in 1819. In 1780 Morristown, New Jersey, witnessed the first official celebration of St. Patrick's Day in what became the United States when it was authorized by George Washington for the Irish and Catholic soldiers encamped at the site.

The continued growth of parishes and the Catholic population in northern New Jersey was a contributing factor to the creation in 1853 by Pope Blessed Pius IX of the Diocese of Newark, which encompassed the whole of New Jersey and was created out of territory from the Dioceses of Philadelphia and New York.

The Catholics of Paterson took part in the Civil War, and the presence of the faith became more prominent in the decades following that conflict.

Paterson Catholics also supported the military efforts of the nation during World War I and suffered with other Americans during the Great Depression.

By 1937 the size of the Catholic population warranted the elevation of Newark to the rank of a metropolitan provincial see, an archdiocese, with several new suffragans, including Camden and Paterson.

The first bishop of Paterson was Thomas H. McLaughlin, who had been an auxiliary bishop of Newark since 1935. He understood immediately the keys to the demography and geography of the new diocese, which has remained largely unchanged: Passaic County is more industrial, while Morris and Sussex are more agricultural. He thus launched rural missions and provided a foundation for the diocesan institutions. He also supported the military efforts of the nation during the long years of World War II.

With Bishop McLaughlin's passing in 1947, Bishop Thomas A. Boland, an auxiliary bishop of Newark, was appointed as his successor. In the five years of his service as bishop, he continued the expansion of diocesan facilities, including schools, hospitals, and convents. On November 15, 1952, he was appointed the archbishop of Newark.

On April 9, 1953, Bishop James A. McNulty, an auxiliary bishop of Newark since 1947, was named the third bishop of the diocese. His ten years as bishop saw the continuing growth of the diocese, and to keep pace he established eight dioceses and several new high schools. His tenure ended with his appointment as bishop of Buffalo on February 12, 1963.

Bishop McNulty was followed by James Johnston Navagh, who had been an auxiliary bishop of Raleigh since 1952. He died after only two years, on October 2, 1965, and was followed by Bishop Lawrence B. Casey, who had been an auxiliary bishop of Rochester since 1953. Appointed on March 4, 1966, as the fifth bishop of Paterson, he was presented with the immediate task of implementing the decrees of the Second Vatican Council, which had concluded the previous year. Bishop Casey retired on June 13, 1977.

On December 5, 1977, Bishop Frank J. Rodimer, a priest of the Paterson diocese, succeeded Bishop Casey. His long tenure included the many economic challenges faced by northern New Jersey, including the decline in industry and population and the gradual aging of the population. This necessitated pastoral care and outreach for the unemployed. Bishop Rodimer retired on June 1, 2004.

He was succeeded by Bishop Arthur J. Serratelli, an auxiliary bishop of Newark since 2000. Installed on July 6, 2004, as the seventh bishop of Paterson, Serratelli has focused on encouraging vocations to the priesthood and promoting evangelization. The diocese has also worked to alleviate the suffering caused by severe flooding in the aftermath of Hurricane Irene in 2011. In 2011 there were 425,000 Catholics, 380 priests, 760 women religious, and 111 parishes in the diocese.

Patronato Real

Patronato real, meaning "royal right," described the special privilege granted to the Spanish and Portuguese kings by the Holy See to appoint individuals to ecclesiastical posts in the colonial territories and to have claim over all ecclesiastical benefices (Church property or revenue attached to spiritual offices for the support of the clergy). The *patronato real,* called originally the *Real Patronato de las Indias* ("Royal Patronage of the Indies"), was demanded by the Spanish and Portuguese rulers in recognition of the fact that the Church would be a key agent in establishing Spanish and Portuguese culture in the New World. The kings thus sought to exercise as much control as possible over the organizational structure of the Church and to re-create to the highest degree possible the close association that already existed between church and state in Spain and Portugal.

The *patronato real* was confirmed in 1508 by Pope Julius II through his bull *Universalis ecclesiae* ("The Universal Church"), which confirmed the legal rights bestowed by the Holy See on the kings of Spain to exercise jurisdiction over the Catholic Church in the Americas or granted them for the first time. By the terms of the bull, appointments of clergy and bishops were required first to receive the approval of civil authorities. The crown also enjoyed the same power of appointment over governors, *audiencias,* and viceroys. The control over Church appointments extended from the archbishops down to the parish level. Recognizing the influence of the Church to resist the harsh intentions of the colonial government toward the native populations, the crowns made certain that the authority of the bishops and local royal officials were often at odds, using a principle of divide and conquer to maintain a position of advantage over both. Construction of churches was also forbidden in any part of the Spanish territories in America without the consent of the king of Spain. The practical effect of the *patronato real* was that permission was necessary for the construction of buildings or the filling of vacant offices and sees. Such permission meant long delays as the requests were sent to the royal courts in the Iberian Peninsula. In this way, progress was to some degree impeded in cultivating the missions in South American, Central America, Mexico, the Carribbean, and the southwestern United States, especially Florida.

Paul VI, Pope (September 26, 1897–August 6, 1978)

Pope from 1963 to 1978, Giovanni Battista Montini was born at Concesio, near Brescia, Italy, the son of a lawyer and political editor of the Catholic paper *Il Cittadina di Brescia*. Despite poor health in his youth, he entered the seminary and studied mostly from home and received ordination on May 29, 1920. He then attended the Pontifical Gregorian University in Rome and worked in the Secretariat of State before holding a variety of posts, including assistant to Cardinal Eugenio Pacelli (the future Pope Pius XII) from 1937, accompanying him to the Eucharistic Congress at Budapest in 1938. Pacelli was elected pope the next year, and in 1944, following the death of Cardinal and Secretary of State Luigi Maglione, Pope Pius XII did not appoint a new one. Father Montini was named pro-secretary for the internal affairs of the Church, distinguishing himself for leading relief efforts in the closing phases of World War II. In 1952 he was named pro-secretary of state, but declined elevation to cardinal in December 1952. Almost two years later, in November 1954, Pope Pius XII sent him to Milan as its archbishop. The pope died in 1958 without creating Montini a cardinal.

As archbishop of Milan, Montini demonstrated an intense pastoral zeal and a commitment to rebuilding the city after the war. After the election of Cardinal Angelo Roncalli as Pope John XXIII, Archbishop Montini was named one of the first new cardinals of the pontificate. He then played a key role in the preparations for the Second Vatican Council. During the first session of the council in 1962, he spoke only twice. Nevertheless, having made many positive statements about the process of reform, he was a leading candidate to succeed Pope John XXIII, who died on June 3, 1963.

In the conclave that convened at the Vatican on June 19, 1963, Archbishop Montini entered a definite favorite and was elected pope on June 21, 1963. The new pope convened the second session of the Second Vatican Council on September 29, 1963, and guided its remaining sessions to a conclusion on December 8, 1965. He devoted the next years to the colossal task of implementing the reforms of the council, eventually exhausting himself in the endeavor. He also published seven encyclicals: *Ecclesiam Suam* (1964), *Mense Maio* (1964), *Mysterium Fidei* (1965), *Christi Matri Rosarii* (1966), *Populorum Progressio* (1967), *Sacerdotalis Caelibatus* (1967), and *Humanae Vitae* (1968). *Humanae Vitae* proved his last encyclical and his most controversial, owing to the open dissent that erupted over its reaffirmation of the Church's teaching on contraception.

Pope Paul VI

He had taken the name Paul to embody his desire to be a pilgrim to all nations, and his pontificate was noted for its then unprecedented travels. In January 1964 he made a pilgrimage to the Holy Land, the first pope since St. Peter the Apostle to visit Palestine. After visiting the many holy sites, he met the Ecumenical Patriarch Athenagoras I of Constantinople, marking the first meeting between a pope and a patriarch in five centuries. His apostolic journeys over the next years included India (1964), Fátima, Portugal (1967), Turkey (1967), Bogota, Colombia (1968), Geneva, Switzerland (1969), Africa (1969), and an extensive trip to the Philippines, Australia, Iran, Samoan Islands, Indonesia, Hong Kong, Ceylon, and East Pakistan (1970).

Pope Paul VI became the first pope to visit the United States on October 5, 1965, an official visit of only fourteen hours, to plead for the cause of peace at the United Nations General Assembly in New York. He visited St. Patrick's Cathedral, where he was greeted by Francis Cardinal Spellman, archbishop of New York, and celebrated a Mass for peace at Yankee Stadium.

During his pontificate, Pope Paul VI appointed 194 American bishops. He also established twenty archdioceses and dioceses: Archdioceses of Washington and Anchorage (1966); Oklahoma City (1972); Dioceses of Fresno (1967); Phoenix (1969); Gaylord, Kalamazoo, and Memphis (1970); Charlotte (1971); Tulsa (1972); Arlington (1974); Pensacola-Tallahassee (1975); Orange (1976); Houma-Thibodeau, Biloxi, and St. Thomas (1977); San Bernadino (1978); Eparchy of Passaic (1963); and Exarchies for the Melchites and for the Maronites (1966). From 1965 to 1976, he named ten American prelates to the College of Cardinals: Cardinal Lawrence J. Shehan, archbishop of Baltimore (1965); Cardinal Patrick A. O'Boyle, archbishop of Washington, Cardinal John Joseph Krol, archbishop of Philadelphia, Cardinal John Patrick Cody, archbishop of Chicago, and Cardinal Francis Brennan, Dean of the Sacred Roman Rota (1967); Cardinal John Joseph Carberry, archbishop of St. Louis, and Cardinal Terence J. Cooke, archbishop of New York (1969); Cardinal Timothy Manning, archbishop of Los Angeles, and Cardinal Humberto S. Medeiros, archbishop of Boston (1973);

and Cardinal William W. Baum, archbishop of Washington (1976). Pope Paul died at Castel Gandolfo on August 6, 1978.

Paul of St. Peter (June 21, 1746–October 15, 1826)

A Carmelite missionary, Michael Joseph Plattner was born in Dettelbach, Germany, and entered the Discalced Carmelites in 1767. After ordination in 1769, he served in various Carmelite houses until 1780, when he was sent to North America to serve as a chaplain with French forces serving under General George Washington at the Battle of Yorktown. After a brief period in Europe, he returned to the United States and requested permission from Father John Carroll in Baltimore to minister to the sizable population of French-speaking Catholics settling along the Mississippi River in the Illinois Territory. He devoted the rest of his life to the missions in Illinois and Louisiana, earning the trust and love of the Catholics of those regions. He died at Iberville, Louisiana, in the church of St. Gabriel, where he had established himself in 1803.

Paulists (C.S.P.)

The first religious congregation of men founded in the United States, the Paulists were started in New York City in 1858 by Father Isaac Thomas Hecker, along with Augustine F. Hewit, George Deshon, Francis A. Baker, and Clarence A. Walworth. They were all converts to Catholicism and had belonged to the Redemptorists but had left for various reasons, chiefly to pursue missionary work in the United States under the direction of the American bishops. Father Hecker expressed his specific vocation by declaring that he was "set apart to undertake in some leading and conspicuous way the conversion of this country."

During the summer of 1858, the four priests made a practical start to their community in New York, where they received a generous welcome from Archbishop John Hughes. He gave them a parish in what was then a suburb and is now the heart of the city — the parish of St. Paul the Apostle. As they had given missions as Redemptorists in all parts of the country, they were well known to the bishops and clergy and were very popular with the people. Father Hecker especially was known as a gifted preacher. The first program for members was drawn up in 1858 and approved by Archbishop Hughes. From the start, the Paulist vocation was chiefly to work for the conversion of non-Catholics, utilizing lecturing and preaching, parish missions, and printing and distributing missionary literature.

To assist their missions, in 1925 the Paulists established the radio station WLWL in New York City. A decade later they converted three motor trailers as chapels, with lights and public address systems, and drove into parts of the South and into Utah to preach. In the late 1940s, they embraced the new medium of television. They remain known as active innovators in the area of Catholic social outreach and use of media through their highly successful Paulist Media Works (PMW), Paulist Productions, and Paulist Press, one of the largest Catholic publishing houses in North America. The Paulists are also engaged in campus ministry, including centers atthe Massachusetts Institute of Technology, the University of California, Los Angeles, and Ohio State. Never a large religious community, they number today about 177 priests and 189 total religious.

Peck, Gregory (April 5, 1916–June 12, 2003)

An Academy Award–winning actor, Gregory Peck was born in La Jolla, California, the son of a druggist. His parents divorced when he was five, and he was sent to live with his grandmother. Originally planning to become a doctor, he studied pre-med at Berkeley but, while there, he became involved with acting and changed majors, graduating in 1939. He enrolled in the Neighborhood Playhouse in New York and appeared on Broadway after graduation. He debuted in Emlyn Williams's stage play *The Morning Star* in 1942, and in 1944 he debuted in his first film, *Days of Glory.*

His next role, as a Roman Catholic priest in *Keys of the Kingdom,* also in 1944, earned him his first Academy Award nomination and launched his stellar career. Over the next years he made a number of hit films, including Alfred Hitchcock's *Spellbound* (1945), *The Yearling* (1946), for which he was again nominated for an Oscar, and David O. Selznick's *Duel in the Sun* (also in 1946). He was nominated again for the Academy Award for his roles in *Gentleman's Agreement* (1947) and *Twelve*

O'Clock High (1949). Having established himself as a major star, he chose to appear in roles that interested him, such as the classics *Captain Horatio Hornblower* (1951), *Roman Holiday* (1953), and *Moby Dick* (1956). After four nominations, Peck finally won the Oscar for Best Actor for his performance as lawyer Atticus Finch in *To Kill a Mockingbird* (1962). In 1967 he received the Academy's Jean Hersholt Humanitarian Award. He was also awarded the Presidential Medal of Freedom from Richard M. Nixon in 1969.

As a Catholic, Peck promoted the *Family Theater* radio drama anthology in the 1940s and 1950s started by Father Patrick Peyton, the Holy Cross priest and advocate of the program, who also advocated the Rosary for families. Peck was also involved in various Catholic causes and forms of social and political activism.

Pegis, Anton (August 24, 1905–May 13, 1978)

A Thomistic philosopher who played a major role in reviving Thomistic studies in modern philosophy in the United States, Anton Pegis was born in Milwaukee. He studied at Marquette University and earned a doctorate in philosophy from the University of Toronto. In 1930 he converted to Catholicism from the Greek Orthodox Church. Pegis devoted the rest of his life to teaching and writing, holding a variety of posts at Marquette, Fordham University, and the Pontifical Institute of Medieval Studies at the University of Toronto.

Pegis focused chiefly on the thought and writings of St. Thomas Aquinas and Thomistic philosophy. He wrote an important translation of St. Thomas's *On the Truth of the Catholic Faith* and edited the two-volume *Writings of St. Thomas* in 1945 and *Introduction to St. Thomas* in 1948. His own works included *St. Thomas and the Greeks* in 1939 and *The Middle Ages and Philosophy* in 1963.

Peña, Federico F. *See* Cabinets, Catholics in Presidential

Peñalver y Cárdenas, Luigi Ignacio (April 3, 1749–July 17, 1810)

Bishop of New Orleans from 1794 to 1801 and archbishop of Guatemala from 1801 to 1805, Luigi Ignacio Peñalver y Cárdenas was the son of a noble family. He was born in Havana and received a superb colonial education, eventually graduating with a doctorate in theology from the Universidad de San Jerónimo in 1771. After further studies, he was ordained on April 4, 1772. In 1793 Pope Pius VI created the Diocese of Louisiana and the Two Floridas, and Peñalver y Cárdenas was named its first bishop by King Carlos IV of Spain, in keeping with the *patronato real*. Soon after his installation, he published *Instrucción para el govierno de los párrocos de la diócesis de la Luisiana* and embarked upon a thorough effort to launch the new diocese on a firm spiritual and ecclesiastical footing. Although he lamented the sad state of religious affairs in much of the vast Louisiana Territory, he worked to instill firm discipline among the faithful and expanded parishes. He also cooperated with Bishop John Carroll to ensure the spiritual welfare of Catholics living on both sides of the Mississippi River.

In July 1801 Bishop Peñalver y Cárdenas was promoted to the Archdiocese of Guatemala, where he once more demonstrated a zeal and commitment to strengthening the Church, focusing especially on education. With his own money, he built a hospital and several schools. Owing to poor health, he resigned his see in March 1806 and returned to Havana, where he died. In his will, he bequeathed the equivalent of $200,000 to the poor and schools.

Pennings, Bernard Henry (June 9, 1861–March 17, 1955)

Premonstratensian abbot and founder of St. Norbert Priory and St. Norbert College, Bernard Henry Pennings was born in Gemert, Holland, and entered the canons regular of Prémontré in 1879; his final profession was made in 1881, and he was ordained in 1886. After holding several posts, including master of novices in the abbey of Berne in Heeswijk, he was chosen as part of a group of Premonstratensians being sent to Green Bay, Wisconsin, at the invitation of Bishop Sebastian Gebhard Messmer, who desired priests for pastoral service among the Belgians of his diocese. Arriving in November 1893, Pennings and his companions served in several parishes for Belgians. They were soon joined by other members of the Berne community. In 1898 Abbot Pennings established St.

Norbert Priory and St. Norbert College. In 1902 he received papal permission to separate formally from the Berne mother abbey, and St. Norbert Priory became the basis for missionary activities in Canada and the United States. In 1947 a coadjutor abbot was appointed, Sylvester Killeen. Before his death, Abbot Pennings received numerous honors for his labors on behalf of the Church.

Pennsylvania

One of the thirteen original states, Pennsylvania is called the Keystone State and is located in the northeastern United States. It is bounded on the north by New York, on the east by New York and New Jersey, on the south by Delaware, Maryland, and West Virginia, and on the west by West Virginia and Ohio. There are three land regions in the state: the Appalachian Mountains, the Piedmont Plateau in the east, and the Appalachian Plateau in the west. The original inhabitants of the region were the Erie, Huron, and Susquehannah Indian nations.

The European history of Pennsylvania began with Etienne Brulé, from Canada, who had been part of the expedition of Samuel de Champlain and explored the Susquehanna Valley in the winter of 1615–16. St. Isaac Jogues, the Jesuit martyr, was among the Susquehannah in 1643, and other Jesuits as well as Recollect Franciscans and Sulpicians were there in 1670. In 1687 Jesuit Father Henry Harrison also served Indian tribes in the area. The Hurons especially were receptive to the faith and steadfastly devout.

The area of present-day Pennsylvania had been colonized originally by the Swedes and was occupied by the Dutch in 1655. Nine years later, the British took "New Netherlands" from Peter Stuyvesant. In 1683 William Penn, whose father had lent money to King Charles II in England, received land from the crown as repayment of the debts. The colony of Pennsylvania, which was the second colony of the original thirteen states to ratify the Constitution in 1787, was formed and governed by Penn, who was respectful of Native Americans and considerably tolerant of the Catholic faith. The constitution of Pennsylvania declared religious liberty, although Catholics were barred from public office but otherwise comparatively free to practice their religion.

By 1720 Jesuits visited Catholic families regularly in Pennsylvania. Jesuit Father Joseph Wheaton went to Philadelphia, where he bought land, erected a chapel, and started what became St. Joseph's Parish in 1733. From a small group of Irish and Germans Catholics, the parish grew to some three thousand by 1787, making it perhaps the largest parish in the United States at the time.

Around 1740, Jesuit Father William Wappeler was in Lancaster and Conewago. Jesuit Father Richard Molyneux was also in Lancaster. Jesuit Father Joseph-Pierre de Bonnecamps was at the chapel of the Assumption of the Blessed Virgin Mary of the Beautiful River at Fort Duquesne with Father Denis Baron. The famed "Father Farmer," Father Ferdinand Steinmeyer, was at St. Mary's in Philadelphia. In 1755 Jesuit Father Claude François Virot was on the Delaware River with local tribes. Meantime, from around 1768, German Catholics in Philadelphia built Holy Trinity Church and then St. Mary's. The French and Indian War caused suffering in Pennsylvania settlements and prompted riots and anti-Catholic sentiments. When a final peace treaty was signed in the late 1760s, the Pennsylvanians began to work for independence.

As the Revolutionary War neared, the city of Philadelphia played an important role. The city was chosen as the site for First Continental Congress, and it was there that the Declaration of Independence was drafted and signed in 1776. The small Catholic population supported the American side during the Revolution, and several Pennsylvania Catholics played significant roles in the American victory, including Commodore John Barry, Thomas Fitzsimmons, and Stephen Moylan. Philadelphia was also the capital of the United States until 1800 and the capital of the state until 1812, when it was replaced by Harrisburg.

In the improved atmosphere for Catholics, the Church moved forward rapidly. In western Pennsylvania, the earliest Catholic school was started at Sportsman's Hall in Westmoreland County around 1787, on the site that was chosen by the Benedictines for St. Vincent's Abbey and College. In the same area, Father Demetrius Augustine Gallitzin, a Russian-Lithuanian prince who became a priest in the United States, helped establish and guide the Catholic community in Cambria County from 1799 until his death in 1840. Farther west, the first Catholic Church was built in Pittsburgh in 1811, and in 1828 members of the Order of St. Clare from Belgium founded a convent and academy. They opened more schools across western and central Pennsylvania.

It came as no surprise that when the Archdiocese of Baltimore was created in 1808, Philadelphia was one of the new dioceses erected by Pope Pius VII, along with the Dioceses of New York, Boston, and Bardstown.

The first bishop of Philadelphia, Michael F. Egan, served as shepherd over a diocese that encompassed the entire state of Pennsylvania and the western and southern parts of New Jersey. It was reduced in size with the creation in 1843 of the Diocese of Pittsburgh; this was followed in 1853 by the Diocese of Erie and then the Diocese of Newark that same year. In 1868 the Dioceses of Scranton and Harrisburg were founded, followed by the briefly existing Diocese of Allegheny in 1876, which formed the basis of the Diocese of Altoona. In 1875 Philadelphia was declared a metropolitan see by Pope Blessed Pius IX, with Bishop James F. Wood appointed the first archbishop.

In the period after the Civil War, tens of thousands of immigrants arrived in Pennsylvania, drawn by the search for work in the mines, mills, and factories. The Diocese of Philadelphia worked to keep pace with the influx of new Catholics, building new parishes and schools and striving to provide pastoral care to the immigrants in their native tongues, including German, Italian, Polish, Slovak, Lithuanian, and Spanish. Among those arriving were Easter-rite Catholics, who brought about the establishment of the Apostolic Exarchate of Philadelphia in 1913. The influx of new Catholics met with challenges at times, as witnessed by the break from the Church of Polish Catholics in Scranton in 1897 over a dispute regarding control of Sacred Heart Church. A Polish priest, Father Francis Hodur, and more than two hundred Polish families were eventually excommunicated; in 1904 they elected Father Hodur their head and formed the Polish National Catholic Church.

Similar challenges attended the participation of Catholic workers in labor organizations, most notably the Knights of Labor, America's first national labor union, which was headed from 1879 to 1893 by a Catholic from Scranton, Terence Powderly. While some bishops were opposed to Catholic membership in unions, the movement had the support of Cardinal James Gibbons of Baltimore, who used his visit to Rome in 1887 to receive his red hat as cardinal to give his voice in support of the Knights to officials of the Roman Curia.

The expansion of the Catholic community in Pennsylvania was exemplified in the early twentieth century by Cardinal Dennis J. Dougherty's time as archbishop, from 1918 to 1951. Known as "God's Builder," he established 112 parishes, as well as schools, hospitals, and colleges. Elsewhere in the state, dioceses continued their own development, especially in the area of Catholic education.

The Great Depression brought economic disasters and suffering to Pennsylvania and the nation. The state subsequently took part in major defense programs as America entered World War II. After the war, dioceses coped with rising populations and the movement of Catholics out of the cities. In 1951 the Diocese of Greensburg was created, and a decade later the Diocese of Allentown was established. By 1965 there were more than 3.6 million Catholics in the state, with some 5,000 priests, more than 18,000 men and women religious, and 1,500 parishes and missions.

In the decades that followed, the state's dioceses coped with massive changes in the economy that came with the decline of the steel and coal industries. The Church in the state provided pastoral outreach to the populations in the cities and also to those who were migrating to the suburbs. Likewise, ministry was needed for the pastoral care of the new immigrants from around the world, especially Asia. In 2011 there were 3.2 million Catholics, 2,773 priests, 5,800 men and women religious, and 1,070 parishes in the state.

Pensacola-Tallahassee, Diocese of

Established on October 1, 1975, by Pope Paul VI, the Diocese of Pensacola-Tallahassee comprises twenty counties in the panhandle of Florida. It is a suffragan diocese of the Archdiocese of Miami. The diocese was established as a result of the growing population of Catholics in northern Florida and was created out of territory taken from the thirty-

five counties that formed the Diocese of St. Augustine. The bulk of the population has traditionally resided in the western region of the diocese, around Pensacola.

While historically possessed of a small population and an even smaller Catholic population, the region that eventually became the present-day Diocese of Pensacola-Tallahassee has a long Catholic history. The first Mass was celebrated in 1559, when a Spanish colonial expedition led by Tristán de Luna, including five Dominican priests and a lay brother, reached what became Pensacola and began a settlement. The small community was abandoned a mere two years later, after a hurricane. There were small settlements served by Franciscans, but a formal resettlement was not attempted until 1693. From the late eighteenth century, Pensacola was placed under the jurisdiction of the Diocese of San Cristobal of Havana, which encompassed Cuba and the territories of Louisiana and the Two Floridas. In 1791 the Catholic population in the area was numbered only about 250. Four years later, the region was placed under the jurisdiction of the newly established Diocese of New Orleans. The first bishop, Luis Ignacio Peñalver y Cárdenas, visited Pensacola in 1798.

The jurisdiction again changed in 1829 with the creation of the Diocese of Mobile, extending across Alabama and Florida. Its first bishop, Michael Portier, visited Pensacola and started the first parish school, at St. Michael's in 1837, which had been incorporated in 1823.

In 1850 Florida was transferred to the jurisdiction of the new Diocese of Savannah; this jurisdiction was offset by the Diocese of St. Augustine in 1870, which covered Florida east of the Apalachicola River. By 1968 the growth of the Catholic population in Florida warranted the creation of an archdiocese in Florida. The diocese chosen was Miami, and two new dioceses were created in St. Petersburg and Orlando. The counties of northwest Florida were then transferred from Mobile to the Diocese of St. Augustine.

On October 1, 1975, Pope Paul VI created the Diocese of Pensacola-Tallahassee, and on November 6 he appointed Bishop René Gracida, an auxiliary bishop of Miami since 1971, to serve as first bishop. The cathedral for the diocese was decreed by elevating Sacred Heart Church in Pensacola, with a co-cathedral, St. Thomas More Church in Tallahassee. Bishop Gracida established the diocesan offices and ministries for diocesan administration and began the diocesan programs. He was transferred to the Diocese of Corpus Christi in 1983.

His successor was appointed on November 8, 1983. Bishop J. Keith Symons, who had been an auxiliary bishop of St. Petersburg since 1981, was named to the see. He built parishes and diocesan programs until he was transferred to the Diocese of Palm Beach in 1990.

After a vacancy of a year, Bishop John M. Smith, auxiliary bishop of the Archdiocese of Newark since 1987, was appointed on June 25, 1991, to be the third bishop of Pensacola-Tallahassee.

Bishop Smith was transferred to the Diocese of Trenton as its coadjutor in 1995. He acceded to the see in 1997. He was followed as bishop of Pensacola-Tallahassee by Bishop John H. Ricard, S.S.J., who was installed as the fourth bishop on March 13, 1997. Bishop Ricard celebrated the twenty-fifth anniversary of the diocese in 2000, implemented the various reforms to create a safe environment in the wake of the sex abuse crisis, and coped with the remarkable growth in the size of the Catholic population. He retired on March 11, 2011, for reasons of health. In 1975 the diocese had a Catholic population of 37,000, out of nearly 700,000. In 2011 that population had doubled, both in the Catholic community and the wider population, with 86 priests, and 49 parishes.

Peoria, Diocese of

The Diocese of Peoria was created on February 12, 1875, by Pope Blessed Pius IX and encompasses twenty-six counties in central Illinois. The diocese is centered in a largely agricultural area but has a long industrial and business history; the city of Peoria is the home of the large Caterpillar corporation. There are approximately two hundred thousand Catholics, comprising some 12.5 percent of the total population. The diocese is a suffragan of the Archdiocese of Chicago.

The earliest history of the Church in the region is traced to the remarkable journey of the French explorer Louis Joliet and the French Jesuit missionary Jacques Marquette. They reached the Native American village in what became Peoria in 1673, and Father Marquette performed the first baptism there; two years later, he founded the Mission of the Immaculate Conception at Starved Rock.

After Marquette's death in 1675, other French Jesuit missionaries continued his labors, including Father Claude Allouez, the Jesuit superior, and Father Jacques Gravier. Fort St. Louis was established in 1682 and served as a trading post and center for missionary work until its abandonment in 1702. The missions declined in the aftermath of the French withdrawal, culminating in English domination after the end of the French and Indian War in 1763. Priests, however, were active in central Illinois, even more so after 1789 and the creation of the Diocese of Baltimore under Bishop John Carroll.

With the expansion of the Catholic population westward, the area of central Illinois fell under varying jurisdictions, including the Dioceses of Bardstown, St. Louis, and Vincennes.

In 1836 construction of the Illinois-Michigan Canal brought hundreds of Irish laborers into the area. Three years later, the cornerstone was laid for St. Patrick's Church in Kickapoo. More Catholic workers arrived in the next years to work on the railroads, increasing the Irish and German Catholic populations and creating a need for new churches and missions. In 1843 the Diocese of Chicago was erected, with jurisdiction over the entire state of Illinois. The presence of these immigrant workers also caused incidents of anti-Catholic violence and bigotry. Nevertheless, the steady increase in the Catholic population warranted the decision in 1875 to create a new diocese in Illinois out of twenty-one counties detached from the Diocese of Chicago.

On May 1, 1877, Reverend John Lancaster Spalding, a priest of the Louisville Diocese, was consecrated the first bishop of Peoria. Spalding began what became a remarkable ecclesiastical career by giving the diocese a firm footing. He began with fifty-one priests and forty-five thousand Catholics; by the time of his retirement in 1908, the population had tripled, as had the number of priests, and the number of parishes rose from forty to two hundred. Bishop Spalding became a nationally known figure in the area of education and played a crucial role in the founding of The Catholic University of America. He retired and died in 1916.

On September 1, 1909, Bishop Edmund M. Dunne, a priest and the chancellor of the Archdiocese of Chicago, was installed as the second bishop of Peoria. Bishop Dunne continued the expansion of diocesan facilities and focused especially on Catholic schools and school enrollment. He is also remembered for an ordination he performed in 1919, that of Fulton J. Sheen, the future archbishop and one of the greatest Catholic communicators in the twentieth century.

Bishop Dunne died on October 17, 1929, at the age of sixty-five, and was succeeded by Father Joseph H. Schlarman, a priest of the Diocese of Belleville, who was ordained a bishop on June 17, 1930, and was confronted immediately with the great challenges of the Great Depression. His time as bishop was marked by the pastoral care of those hit hard by the economy and then the demands of the Second World War. Bishop Schlarman also renovated the cathedral and started a diocesan newspaper. In June 1951 he was granted the personal title of archbishop in recognition of his achievements. The archbishop died suddenly of a heart attack on November 10, 1951.

He was followed by Bishop William E. Cousins, who had been an auxiliary bishop of Chicago since 1948. Bishop Cousins was installed as the fourth bishop of Peoria on July 2, 1952, and presided over an era of large-scale diocesan expansion in churches and schools as well as increases in vocations. He was appointed archbishop of Milwaukee on December 18, 1958.

On November 4, 1959, Bishop John Baptist Franz, bishop of Dodge City since 1951, was installed as the fifth bishop of Peoria. Bishop Franz continued the expansion of diocesan facilities. He also attended the Second Vatican Council and then had the arduous task of implementing the decrees of the council in the tumultuous period of the 1960s.

He retired on May 24, 1971, and was succeeded on the same day by Father Edward W. O'Rourke, a priest of the Peoria diocese. Bishop O'Rourke was consecrated on July 15, 1971. He dealt with the unsettled social and economic situation in the 1970s and is remembered especially for reinstituting the permanent diaconate program. He retired on January 22, 1990, and died on September 29, 1999.

Father John J. Myers, a priest of the Peoria diocese, was appointed coadjutor bishop of Peoria in 1987, and acceded to the see as the seventh bishop on January 23, 1990. Bishop Myers focused on promoting vocations and was noted for his numerous pastoral letters on the liturgy and in support of religious education and the culture of life. On July 24, 2001, he was promoted to the rank of archbishop of Newark.

Archbishop Myers was succeeded on February 12, 2002, by Bishop Daniel R. Jenky, C.S.C., who had been an auxiliary bishop of Fort Wayne-South Bend since 1997. He was installed on April 10, 2002. Bishop Jenky has dealt with the implementation of the norms for protecting children and is also well known for his efforts to promote the cause of canonization of Archbishop Fulton J. Sheen. In 2011 there were 128,000 Catholics, 228 priests, 193 women religious, and 156 parishes in the diocese.

Percy, Walker (May 28, 1916–May 10, 1990)

Noted Southern writer and philosopher Walker Percy's novels reflect his love for and insights about the South, his abiding Catholic faith, and the shattering and dislocating impact of the modern world on man. He was born in Birmingham, Alabama, to a wealthy family. The suicide of his lawyer father when he was thirteen left a great mark on him and was followed only two years later by the death of his mother in an automobile accident. Walker and his brothers grew up in the care of their father's cousin, who cultivated a love of the arts and literature in the boys.

He studied at the University of North Carolina at Chapel Hill and graduated in 1937 with a degree in chemistry. He then studied at the College of Physicians and Surgeons at Columbia University and earned a degree in medicine in 1941. His life soon changed, however, after contracting tuberculosis, as the long recovery was accompanied by a period of deep introspection.

He returned to the South in 1946, married Mary Bernice Townsend, settled in New Orleans, and embarked on a career as a writer. In 1947 he and his wife entered the Church. Over the next years, he wrote for the *Journal of Philosophy, Commonweal,* and *America,* but he settled on fiction as his writing of choice. His first novel, *The Moviegoer,* was published in 1961 and won the 1962 National Book Award for Fiction. He wrote five more, including *Love in the Ruins* in 1971 and *The Second Coming* in 1980; his last novel was *The Thanatos Syndrome* in 1987. He remains one of the most respected Catholic novelists of the second half of the twentieth century.

Persico, Ignatius (January 30, 1823–December 7, 1895)

An Italian cardinal, Capuchin Franciscan, and diplomat, Ignatius Persico was born in Naples, Italy. He entered the Capuchin Franciscans in April 1839 and was ordained in November 1846. He was then sent to Patna, India, where he proved valuable to the vicar apostolic there, Anastasius Hartmann. Father Persico assisted the bishop in founding a seminary and establishing the *Bombay Catholic Examiner.* In March 1854 he was consecrated a bishop and named auxiliary to Bishop Hartmann. The next year, however, he was appointed visitor of the Vicariate of Agra, and afterward vicar apostolic. Not long after, there occurred in India the bloody Sepoy Rebellion, the Indian mutiny against British rule. Bishop Persico faced threats to his life several times during the political and social upheaval, and the events of the time shattered his health. In 1860 he returned to Italy. In 1866, his health improving, he was sent by the Holy See on a mission to the United States, during which he took part in the Council of Baltimore. From 1869 to 1870 he was in Rome, where he attended the First Vatican Council. On March 20, 1870, he was named bishop of Savannah. Owing to poor health, he resigned after only two years and was succeeded in 1873 by Bishop William Hickley Gross, C.SS.R. In 1874 Bishop Persico was named apostolic delegate to Canada. Five years later, he

Cardinal Ignatius Persico

was appointed bishop of Aquino in Italy, and in March 1887 he was appointed titular archbishop of Tamiatha and apostolic delegate to Ireland. After examining the political and social situation there, he went back to Rome, where Pope Leo XIII named him a cardinal priest in January 1893.

Peter, Carl J. (April 4, 1932–August 20, 1991)

Priest, theologian, member of the International Theological Commission, and one of the foremost theologians in the United States, Carl J. Peter was born in Omaha, Nebraska, and ordained in July 1957. Completing his studies in Rome, he earned a doctorate in sacred theology from the Pontifical Gregorian University in 1962 and a doctor of philosophy degree from the University of St. Thomas Aquinas in 1964. During this period in Rome, he served as vice rector of the North American College. In 1964 he joined the faculty of The Catholic University of America.

Father Peter's longtime service on behalf of Catholic University earned him a reputation as one of the school's greatest scholars. He served as chairman of the theology department from 1975 to 1977, dean of the School of Religious Studies from 1978 to 1985, and later Shakespeare Caldwell-Duvall Professor of Theology. Beyond his duties at Catholic University, he held the post of adviser to the bishops of the United States at the bishops' synods in 1971, 1983, and 1985. In 1975 he was honored with the John Courtney Murray Award from the Catholic Theological Society of America, and in 1980 he was named to the International Theological Commission by Pope John Paul II. After his death, the university established the Carl J. Peter Chair in theology.

Peyton, Patrick (January 9, 1909–June 3, 1992)

Holy Cross priest and evangelist, Patrick Peyton established the Family Rosary Crusade in 1947 to promote the Rosary among families. Father Peyton was born in Carracastle, County Mayo, Ireland, the sixth of nine children of John Peyton and

Mary Gillard. After migrating to the United States in 1928, he and his brother both entered the Holy Cross Seminary at Notre Dame, Indiana, in 1929. They professed vows in 1933 and were ordained together on June 15, 1941. According to his own accounts, Father Peyton contracted tuberculosis while in the seminary and made a promise to the Blessed Virgin Mary that should he be cured, he would promote the Rosary among families.

After serving as a high school chaplain in the Vincentian Institute in Albany, New York, Father Peyton began his famed preaching of the Rosary. He started a radio program in Albany to say the Rosary over the air, and soon received the support of the the Mutual Radio Network, which aired him nationwide starting on May 13, 1945, Mothers' Day, with the Family Rosary. Two years later, he founded the Family Theater in Hollywood, California, and the *Family Theater* radio series. From there, he directed the expansion of the Family Theater into the forefront of producing religious dramas for radio and television. Father Peyton also received support from Hollywood, including such stars as Bing Crosby, Gregory Peck, and Grace Kelly, as well as major producers and directors.

In 1947 he also launched the Family Rosary Crusade in London, Ontario, and coined the famed motto "The family that prays together, stays together." He devoted the rest of his life to the cause, traveling ceaselessly to over forty countries on six continents. The Crusade drew half a million people in San Francisco in 1961, two million people in Sao Paulo in 1964, and over two million people in Manila, the Philippines, in 1985. Father Peyton is buried at Stonehill College in North Easton, Massachusetts. His cause for canonization was opened in the Fall River diocese in 2001, and the documentation was submitted to Rome in 2010.

Philadelphia, Archdiocese of

Established on April 8, 1808, by Pope Pius VII and promoted to the rank of a metropolitan provincial see, an archdiocese, on February 12, 1875, by Pope Blessed Pius IX, the Archdiocese of Philadelphia serves counties in southeastern Pennsylvania, including the city and county of Philadelphia, as well as Bucks, Chester, Delaware, and Montgomery counties. It has suffragan sees in Allentown,

Altoona-Johnstown, Erie, Greensburg, Harrisburg, Pittsburgh, and Scranton.

Philadelphia, the City of Brotherly Love, was founded on October 27, 1682, by William Penn and was a haven for colonists seeking religious and social freedom. One of the largest freshwater ports in the world, Philadelphia was intended to serve both as a port for commerce and as the political center for the colony of Pennsylvania. By the middle of the eighteenth century, the city was the largest port in the American colonies.

Philadelphia also served as a gathering place for the growing colonial resistance to British rule. The Declaration of Independence was signed on July 4, 1776, in Philadelphia, as was the Constitution in 1787. The city also served as a capital for the American cause during the Revolutionary War and was the national capital from 1790 to 1800. In the nineteenth century Philadelphia remained a vital port, but it also became a major industrial center and railroad hub, and nearly half of the country's textiles were produced there.

The Catholic history of Philadelphia dates to a time before William Penn, when Catholic missionaries were in the region visiting local Indian tribes. The Huron especially were receptive to the faith and sacrificed over the decades to remain in the Church and to protect the priests. St. Isaac Jogues, the revered Jesuit martyr, was with the Susquehanna Indians in 1643, and Jesuits, Recollect Franciscans, and Sulpicians served the area as well. Father John Pierron, from Canada, journeyed across Pennsylvania as part of his travels in 1673–74.

The colony of Pennsylvania was formed and governed by Penn, who was respectful in his dealings with the local Native American tribes and tolerant about the practice of the Catholic faith. A Test Oath, taken by individuals seeking public office, did deter Catholics from colonial offices. Such individuals had to swear that they did not bear the taint of Catholicism. However, Penn did not conduct the usual colonial assault upon the Church or priests. Relations were generally good, so that in 1771 the inauguration of Richard Penn as successor to John Penn as governor of Pennsylvania was the occasion for congratulations from the Catholics of Philadelphia. The message, delivered by Father Robert Harding, was cordially received.

The first-known Catholic resident of Philadelphia was a German, Francis Daniel Pastorius, the founder of Germantown, who lived there by 1683. The first chapel in Philadelphia and Pennsylvania was established in 1720 through the work of the Jesuit Father Joseph Greaton. By 1733 St. Joseph's Church had been started, with a congregation made up of Irish and Germans. Father Greaton's labors were continued by Father Robert Harding. By 1787 it reportedly had a congregation of three thousand. Meanwhile, Father Ferdinand Steinmayer, known to the colonists as "Father Farmer," was serving the faithful at St. Mary's in 1783. The parish school was opened around the same time, while in 1801 St. Augustine Parish was opened. Father Harding's successor, Father Robert Molyneux, worked with Father Farmer to assist Catholics in Philadelphia during the American Revolution. He was also a key figure in the start of Catholic publishing in America, which was also given a crucial boost by the prominent Philadelphia publisher Mathew Carey, who printed the first American Catholic version of the Bible, the so-called Carey Bible.

When the French and Indian War ended in the late 1760s, Pennsylvania moved toward the coming American Revolution. Although small, the Catholic population generally supported the cause of the Revolution, and several Philadelphia Catholics made immense contributions to the war, including Commodore John Barry, Thomas Fitzsimmons, and Stephen Moylan.

On July 4, 1779, a *Te Deum* was celebrated at St. Mary's Church in Philadelphia for the victory of the American and French forces at Yorktown. Members of Congress and French military leaders attended the ceremony. After the war, French priests arrived and assisted the growing Catholic population. These numbers increased further with the arrival of French immigrants fleeing the French Revolution, which started in 1789. By 1808 American Catholicism had progressed to the point that new dioceses were needed. In 1808 Bishop John Carroll was promoted to the rank of archbishop as a result of the elevation of Baltimore to an archdiocese. At the same time, new dioceses were created for New York, Boston, Bardstown, and Philadelphia.

The first bishop of Philadelphia was a Franciscan from Ireland, Michael F. Egan. The diocese encompassed the whole of Pennsylvania and the western and southern parts of New Jersey. Over the succeeding decades, the territory of the diocese was reduced with the creation of new dioceses in Pennsylvania, including Pittsburgh in 1843, Erie in 1853, Newark in New Jersey that same year, and Scranton, Harrisburg, and Wilmington in Delaware in 1868.

Egan was consecrated a bishop on October 28, 1810, by Archbishop Carroll. His consecration had been delayed because the needed papal bulls had been delayed by the arrest and imprisonment of Pope Pius VII by Napoleon Bonaparte. Bishop Egan worked to give the new diocese a firm footing in its early years, but his brief time was marked chiefly by struggles with the lay trustees of St. Mary's Church, which had been designated to serve as the cathedral for the diocese. Bishop Egan died on July 22, 1814, and was buried at St. Mary's Church. His remains were transferred in 1869 to the Cathedral of Sts. Peter and Paul.

The see was left vacant for several years, with Father Louis de Barth serving as administrator. As the trustees remained a severe problem, several priests declined appointment to the see, including Father de Barth.

The second bishop of Philadelphia, Henry Conwell, had served as a priest in Ireland for most of his years. Conwell was appointed bishop of Philadelphia on November 26, 1819, by Pope Pius VII, when he was almost seventy-two. He received consecration as a bishop in England on September 24, 1820, and reached his new see in December of that year. Like his predecessor, Bishop Conwell was faced with the major problem of trusteeism. The crisis grew worse with the arrival of Father William Hogan at St. Mary's. Father Hogan's support of the trustees and intransigence sparked what became known as the Hogan Schism. He was excommunicated and left the Church in 1824.

Bishop Conwell tried to deal with the trustees and proved so lenient that he was summoned to Rome in 1829 to explain his approach to the Congregation for the Propagation of the Faith, which had grown increasingly alarmed that the trustee issue was endangering the rights of the Church in the young country. In the end, Rome decided to leave him in place as archbishop, but he was given a coadjutor bishop, Francis P. Kenrick, on February 25, 1830. Kenrick was given administrative authority, while Conwell was permitted to retain his title of bishop of Philadelphia and to perform episcopal functions. He died of pneumonia at the age of ninety-four on April 22, 1842.

As coadjutor, Bishop Kenrick brought an end to the bitter struggle with the trustees of St. Mary's and in 1832 founded St. Charles Borromeo Seminary. That same year, he demonstrated immense heroism in leading the Catholic community through a severe cholera outbreak. Once bishop, Kenrick continued to develop the diocese. He founded seventy new parishes, including the foundation of the Cathedral of Sts. Peter and Paul, increased the number of priests from thirty-five to more than one hundred, and presided over an increase in the Catholic population from 35,000 to 170,000.

In 1844 the diocese was troubled by an outbreak of nativism that led to anti-Catholic and anti-immigrant sentiment; St. Augustine's Church and Catholic homes were burned, and Irish Catholics were attacked. On August 19, 1851, Kenrick was appointed archbishop of Baltimore.

The fourth bishop of Philadelphia, St. John Nepomucene Neumann, was canonized in 1977. A native of Bohemia and a member of the Redemptorists, he was appointed bishop of Philadelphia on February 5, 1852, and consecrated on March 28 in Baltimore. Determined to meet the needs of his growing diocese, he made it a priority to establish new parishes, develop the first diocesan school system in the country (by the time of his passing, there were more than a hundred Catholic schools), and invite religious orders into the diocese, including the School Sisters of Notre Dame. He founded the Sisters of the Third Order of St. Francis of Philadelphia. In 1854 he attended Pope Blessed Pius IX's solemn definition of the dogma of the Immaculate Conception in Rome.

During his time as bishop, several new dioceses were established in Pennsylvania (Pittsburgh in 1843 and Erie in 1853) and New Jersey (Newark in 1853). St. Bishop Neumann died on January 5, 1860, at the age of forty-eight. Beloved for his holiness, he was mourned across the whole of the American Church. He was beatified by Pope Paul VI in 1963 and canonized on June 19, 1977. His feast day is January 5.

The fifth bishop of Philadelphia and the first archbishop of Philadelphia, James F. Wood, acceded to the see upon St. John Nepomucene Neumann's passing. A convert from the Unitarians in Cincinnati, Wood was brought into the Church through the influence of Archbishop John Baptist Purcell, archbishop of Cincinnati. Appointed coadjutor bishop of Philadelphia on February 17, 1857, he was an indispensable figure in the diocese in its admin-

Cathedral of Sts. Peter and Paul in Philadelphia

istration. At the time of his accession, the diocese still encompassed the eastern half of Pennsylvania and all of Delaware. He was soon confronted by the outbreak of the Civil War, and Pennsylvanian Catholics died on the battlefield and in military encampments. On November 20, 1864, Wood dedicated the Cathedral of Saints Peter and Paul. The next year, he purchased land in Overbrook, Pennsylvania, to be home to the new St. Charles Borromeo Seminary; it opened in September 1871. He also started an orphanage and welcomed to the diocese several religious communities, including Little Sisters of the Poor, Sisters of the Third Order of St. Francis, Sisters of the Holy Child Jesus, and Sisters, Servants of the Immaculate Heart of Mary,

In 1869 the diocese lost territory from the formation of the Dioceses of Wilmington, Scranton, and Harrisburg. Six years later, Philadelphia was elevated by Pope Blessed Pius IX to the rank of a metropolitan provincial see, an archdiocese. Archbishop Wood died on June 20, 1883. By the time of his death, there were more than 300,000 Catholics in the archdiocese, 260 priests, and 127 churches serving the faithful.

The second archbishop of Philadelphia, Patrick John Ryan, was a native of Ireland and was a priest of St. Louis, serving as coadjutor archbishop there since 1872. Ryan was appointed archbishop of Philadelphia on June 8, 1884, and began a period of dedicated service that stretched across the end of the nineteenth century. He served at the same time as the next great wave of immigration, especially from Italy and Eastern Europe, and in response he established national churches for Italians, Poles, Lithuanians, Greeks, and Slovaks. He also tried to keep pace with the other national elements of the Catholic population, which had nearly doubled to more than five hundred thousand. He also founded 170 churches and more than 80 schools. Archbishop Ryan died at the age of seventy-nine, on February 11, 1911.

The third archbishop of Philadelphia, Edmond F. Prendergast, a native of Ireland, had been an auxiliary bishop of Philadelphia since 1897. He was active in assisting the ailing Archbishop Ryan and served as administrator until his own appointment on May 27, 1911. His term as archbishop was taken up with the events of World War I and the contin-

ued expansion of the diocese, including an increase in the number of parishes and facilities for the sick and the elderly. He died on February 27, 1918.

The fourth archbishop of Philadelphia, Dennis J. Dougherty, was a native of Ireland and a priest of Philadelphia. He had served as bishop of Nueva Segovia and then Jaro in the Philippines, and was then bishop of the Diocese of Buffalo from 1915. Appointed archbishop of Philadelphia on May 1, 1918, he would become the first archbishop of the see to be created a cardinal with his appointment to the College of Cardinals on March 7, 1921.

The first major event of his term as archbishop was the outbreak of the Spanish influenza that forced him to galvanize all available Catholic resources to care for the stricken. In the next decades, he dealt with the crisis of the Great Depression and then World War II and its aftermath. He was likewise a supporter of Irish independence and helped raise money for that cause.

As archbishop, Cardinal Dougherty became known as the "Great Builder" for his immense labors in expanding the archdiocese. In his time, the archdiocese saw the creation of more than 100 parishes and 75 churches, 146 schools, and orphanages, hospitals, and homes for the elderly. He marked in this the last era of "brick and mortar" Catholicism that had characterized the advance and institutional progress of American Catholics. Cardinal Dougherty died suddenly at the age of eighty-five on May 31, 1951.

The fifth archbishop of Philadelphia, John Francis O'Hara, was a member of the Congregation of the Holy Cross and had been bishop of Buffalo since 1945. Appointed to Philadelphia on November 23, 1951, he continued the work of expanding diocesan life and built new parishes, schools, colleges, and facilities for those with disabilities. He also restored the Cathedral of Sts. Peter and Paul. On December 15, 1958, he was appointed to the College of Cardinals with the titular church of of SS. Andrea e Gregorio al Monte Celio, the first member of the Congregation of the Holy Cross to be so honored. His health declined in the late 1950s, and he died at the age of seventy-two on August 28, 1960.

The sixth archbishop of Philadelphia was John Joseph Krol, who had been a priest of the Cleveland diocese and had served as an auxiliary bishop of Cleveland since 1953. Appointed to Philadelphia on February 11, 1961, he was named to the College of Cardinals on June 26, 1967, with the title of Santa Maria della Mercede e Sant'Adriano a Villa Albani. He was the first Polish American to become an archbishop, and it was generally believed that he had played a role in the election of Cardinal Karol Wojtyla of Kraków, Poland, as Pope Blessed John Paul II in 1978. His term as archbishop witnessed the era of the Second Vatican Council and the difficult period of trying to implement its reforms. He took part in its sessions and was an active member as one of six permanent undersecretaries for the council's proceedings. Cardinal Krol was considered a conservative interpreter of the council and strove to implement the conciliar decrees in a manner that was faithful to the documents.

During the same period, he was confronted by the shift in the Catholic population out of the city and into the suburbs. This meant providing new parishes and ministries to developing areas while still preserving pastoral care for those in the city. He served as president of the National Conference of Catholic Bishops from 1971 to 1974, and in 1977 he had the pleasure of attending the canonization of Bishop John Nepomucene Neumann by Pope Blessed John Paul II. He retired on February 11, 1988.

The seventh archbishop of Philadelphia, Anthony J. Bevilacqua, had been an auxiliary bishop of Brooklyn and had served as bishop of Pittsburgh since 1983. Appointed archbishop of Philadelphia on December 8, 1987, he was named to the College of Cardinals under the title of S. Redentore e S. Alfonso in Via Merluana on June 28, 1991. His term as archbishop was marked by the continued demographic changes in the archdiocese that necessitated consolidation of schools and parishes. The archdiocese was also struck by the first problems that would trouble it for the next decade, the clergy sexual abuse crisis. Cardinal Bevilacqua retired on July 15, 2003.

The eighth archbishop of Philadelphia, Justin F. Rigali, had enjoyed a distinguished ecclesiastical career prior to his appointment to Philadelphia. He had served as president of the Pontifical Ecclesiastical Academy (the training school for Vatican diplomats), was secretary to the Congregation of Bishops in the Roman Curia, and had been archbishop of St. Louis since 1994. Named to Philadelphia on July 15, 2003, and installed on October 7, 2003, Rigali was also appointed to the College of Cardinals with the titular church of Santa Prisca on October 21, 2003. Cardinal Rigali was a concelebrant at the 2005 funeral Mass for Pope Blessed John Paul II and took part in the conclave that elected Pope Benedict XVI. Ranked as one of the most influential American Church leaders, he was also a dedicated spokesman for the Committee on Pro-Life Activities for the United States Conference of Catholic Bishops. In his last year as archbishop, the archdiocese was rocked on February 10, 2011, by a grand-jury accusation that archdiocesan officials had failed to provide proper protection of children from the dangers of clergy sexual abuse; there were also charges against one priest official of Philadelphia for endangering the welfare of children and against two other priests for rape and indecent assault of a minor. The news caused a firestorm of controversy.

On July 19, 2011, the archbishop of Denver, Charles J. Chaput, O.F.M. Cap., was appointed as Cardinal Rigali's successor; he was installed on September 8, 2011. A member of the Prairie Band Potawatomi and a Capuchin Franciscan, Archbishop Chaput was noted in Denver for his pastoral leadership and his promotion of Catholic culture and education. In 2011 there were more than 1.3 million Catholics in the archdiocese, served by nearly 950 priests, 2,800 men and women religious, and 267 parishes.

Philadelphia, Byzantine Ukrainian Archdiocese of. *See* Eastern Churches, Catholic

Phoenix, Diocese of

Established on December 2, 1969, by Pope Paul VI, the Diocese of Phoenix serves the counties of Maricopa, Mohave, Yavapai, and Coconino (excluding the territorial boundaries of the Navajo Indian Reservation), and also includes the Gila River Indian Reservation in Pinal County. It is located in one of the fastest-growing parts of the country. The Diocese of Phoenix is a suffragan see of the Archdiocese of Sante Fe.

The history of the diocese technically begins in 1969, but realistically it is tied closely to the development of the Catholic community in Arizona and the Southwest. The first significant date is 1539, when the Franciscan friar Marcos de Niza journeyed into what became Arizona from the Gulf of California and named the area he found the "New Kingdom of St. Francis." He is honored as the discoverer of Arizona and New Mexico.

The territory was placed under various jurisdictions, starting in 1548 with the creation of the Diocese of Guadalajara, in Mexico, by Pope Paul III. In 1620 the newly established Diocese of Durango in north-central Mexico was established by Pope Paul V, with jurisdiction over the Arizona and New Mexico Territories. In 1689 the revered Jesuit priest Father Eusebius Kino began to forge a permanent Catholic presence in southern Arizona. A more local jurisdiction was created in 1779 with the Diocese of Sonora, with its boundaries encompassing Sonora, Sinalda, and Upper and Lower California (New Mexico and northern Arizona remained attached to the Diocese of Durango).

With the increasing Catholic population in Arizona and New Mexico, vicariates apostolic were formed in New Mexico in 1850 and Arizona in 1869. The Diocese of Santa Fe (the New Mexico vicariate apostolic) was erected by Pope Blessed Pius IX in 1853, with the famed Jean Baptiste Lamy named the first bishop. The Vicariate Apostolic of Arizona, founded on September 25, 1869, also by Pope Blessed Pius IX, was placed under the care of Father John Baptist Salpointe, who was named vicar apostolic of Arizona and consecrated a bishop. In 1875 New Mexico became the Archdiocese of Sante Fe, with Arizona designated as a suffragan see.

The area of present-day Phoenix was visited in 1867 by Jack Swelling, a developer who recognized the agricultural potential of the region. Swelling organized an irrigation project that brought water from the Salt River in canals, guaranteeing seasonal harvests on previously parched lands. From that beginning, the site became Phoenix. Expanded agriculture, timber, and other local products were then bolstered by military installations. After World War II, Phoenix experienced a vast population increase.

Meantime, the local Catholic community in Arizona was developing, including the founding of Sacred Heart Church, the oldest parish in the Diocese of Phoenix, in Prescott in 1877, and St. Mary's Church in Phoenix in 1881 (it was made a minor basilica by Pope Blessed John Paul II in 1985). On May 8, 1897, Pope Leo XIII established the Diocese of Tucson, encompassing the entire Arizona territory and the southern counties of Dona Ana, Grant, and Sierra in New Mexico. Arizona became the forty-eighth state in 1912.

By the 1960s the growth of the Catholic population in the Phoenix area necessitated another diocese. This was decreed by Pope Paul VI. Our Lady of Guadalupe was named the patroness of the diocese, and Bishop Edward A. McCarthy, who had been an auxiliary bishop of Cincinnati since 1965, was appointed the first bishop of Phoenix on August 25, 1969. He established various diocesan offices and ministries. At the time of the start of the diocese, there was a Catholic population of about 180,000, with 51 parishes, 61 missions, and 182 diocesan and religious priests. On September 17, 1976, Bishop McCarthy was appointed the coadjutor archbishop of Miami.

On March 22, 1977, Bishop James S. Rausch, a former general secretary of the National Conference of Catholic Bishops and an auxiliary bishop of St. Cloud, was installed as the second bishop of Phoenix. He died unexpectedly on May 18, 1981.

He was succeeded on November 24, 1981, by Monsignor Thomas J. O'Brien, a pastor and vicar general of the Phoenix diocese. O'Brien was consecrated the third bishop of Phoenix in Rome by Pope Blessed John Paul II on January 6, 1982, and installed on January 18, 1982. The chief highlight of Bishop O'Brien's term as bishop was the 1987 visit to Phoenix by Pope Blessed John Paul II. Blessed Mother Teresa also visited the diocese in 1989 and established a home for the poor. Bishop O'Brien promoted the return of inactive Catholics to the Church, and in 1999 three thousand lapsed Catholics returned to the sacraments in a special diocesan event. Bishop O'Brien retired on June 18, 2003, owing to poor health.

On November 25, 2003, Bishop Thomas J. Olmsted, bishop of Wichita since 2001, was transferred to Phoenix. Bishop Olmsted has promoted the spiritual life of the diocese and other programs to assist the pastoral needs of the rapidly growing diocese. In 1969 there were approximately 200,000 Catholics; this grew to more than 821,000 in 2011, with 222 priests, 185 women religious, and 92 parishes.

Picquet, François (December 4, 1708–1781)

A French Sulpician missionary in Canada, François Picquet was born at Bourg, Bresse, France. He entered the seminary of Lyons in 1727 and earned a doctorate from the Sorbonne in Paris prior to his ordination at the Seminary of Saint-Sulpice in Paris. He asked to be sent to the Canadian missions and arrived in Montréal in July 1734. For five years he was engaged in ministry among the local Indian tribes through the Indian mission of the Lac-des-Deux-Montagnes. During this time, he mastered the Algonquin and Iroquois languages and acquired such esteem among the tribal elders that numerous converts were won to the faith. During the French and Indian War between France and England, Father Picquet used his influence to keep members of the Five Nations neutral in the terrible conflict, although both sides in the war profited from the involvement of Indians as scouts and soldiers. After the war, Father Picquet established a post on Presentation River. It was used to preach the Gospel among the Iroquois, and eventually became the Fort of the Presentation that formed the basis of the later town of Ogdensburg, New York.

In 1751 Father Picquet set out for the Lake Ontario region for further missionary work among the Iroquois. The following year, Bishop Henri-Marie du Breuil de Pontbriand, the last French bishop of Québec, baptized 132 converts who had been brought into the faith by Father Picquet. The following year, he sailed to France for consultation with the French government on the needs of the Canadian colony and the best way to maintain its existence in the face of British colonial ambitions. By 1754 war had started again, and Father Picquet proved so determined to resist the British seizure of Canada that English authorities placed a price on his head. When the war turned against France, Picquet was ordered home to France to avoid his capture and execution by the advancing British forces.

Pierron, Jean (September 28, 1631–after 1677)

A French Jesuit missionary, Jean Pierron was born at Dun-sur-Meuse, France. He entered the Jesuit novitiate at Nancy in 1650 and taught for a time at Reims, Verdun, and Metz. He then volunteered for the missions in 1667 and was sent to Canada, where he took up a position in the missions among the Iroquois of Sainte-Marie. His methods of evangelization included mastering the Iroquois language, painting pictures to illustrate his catechetical lessons, and inventing a game to provide memorable lessons in Church teachings. Pierron was also concerned with the possibility of reopening the missions in Acadia (the Acadians had been expelled in 1655). His hopes proved fruitless. He labored among the Iroquois until 1677 when he returned to France.

Pilot, The

The official newspaper of the Archdiocese of Boston and America's oldest Catholic newspaper, *The Pilot* was founded in September 1829 by Bishop Benedict Joseph Fenwick. In the first edition of the paper, he wrote that he had started the publication so that it could present and defend the teachings of the Church and refute the "crying calumnies and gross misrepresentations which in this section of the country have been so long, so unsparingly, so cruelly heaped upon the Church."

The Pilot was first introduced under the title of *The Jesuit or Catholic Sentinel*, the first of several names used in the early years of the paper, including the *United States Catholic Intelligencer* and the *Literary and Catholic Sentinel*. As the publication was struggling, Bishop Fenwick sold it in 1834 to Henry Devereux and Patrick Donahoe, both laymen who became the publisher and editor, respectively. The name was changed to *The Pilot* in 1836, partly in honor of the *Dublin Pilot* newspaper. Devereux and Donahoe made the enterprise a great success, so much so that by 1854 it had more than one million readers. It was a powerful expression of Irish Catholicism in the United States, enjoyed strong ties to Ireland, and actively supported the cause of Irish independence.

The offices of *The Pilot* were destroyed in the Great Fire of 1872, but the newspaper suffered several more fires within the next week. The damage and the sheer costs involved forced Donahoe to sell the newspaper, although in 1876 Archbishop John J. Williams, the first archbishop of Boston, was able to secure a three-fourths interest. In 1890 Donahoe once again acquired the paper and was its head until his passing in 1891. Cardinal William H. O'Connell purchased it from the Donahoe family in 1908 and declared it the official newspaper of the archdiocese. In 2006 the newspaper began an online edition.

Pious Fund of the Californias

El Fondo Piadoso de las Californias, the Pious Fund of the Californias, was the name for the voluntary donations made by individuals and various religious bodies in Mexico to the Society of Jesus to fund their missionary labors in the territory of California. The Pious Fund began in 1697 with the first donations going directly to the missionaries, in particular Juan Maria Salvatierra and Eusebius Kino. As the Pious Fund developed, contributions became formal agreements involving both money and property, with the capital resting in the hands of the Jesuits until 1768, when the Society of Jesus was expelled from Mexico by the Spanish government through the Pragmatic Sanction of King Carlos III of Spain. After the expulsion, the Spanish crown assumed control of the former Jesuit holdings. These remained under the control of the government until 1821 and Mexican independence. (*See also* California.) In 1821 the Mexican government assumed administration of the fund.

In 1836 the Mexican government authorized the petition by the Holy See requesting a diocese for California. By the terms of the agreement, the property that had belonged to the Pious Fund of the Californias was placed at the disposal of the new bishop and his successors. In 1840 Pope Gregory XVI created a diocese out of the two Californias and named Francisco Garcia Diego y Moreno (then president of the missions of the Californias) as the first bishop. Keeping its part of the agreement, the Mexican government handed over the properties of the Pious Fund to the bishop. The decree remained in effect for only two years, however, as in 1842 General Antonio López de Santa Anna, president of Mexico, repealed the act and seized control of the fund. Santa Anna then commanded that the

properties be sold and the resulting profits be added to the national treasury; he added the provision that the sale should be for a sum representing the annual income of the properties capitalized at 6 percent per annum.

A new situation emerged in 1848 when, by the Treaty of Guadalupe-Hildago, Upper Mexico was ceded to the United States by Mexico. The bishops of California used their new position as American citizens to sue the Mexican government for the funds that had been denied for the benefit of the missions in California and that had not been paid by the Mexican government, despite its promise to do so. In 1869 a Mexican and American Mixed Claims Commission was established to decide the issue. As no agreement could be reached, the decision was placed with Sir Edward Thornton, then British ambassador in Washington, D.C. He decided in favor of the bishops in November 1875, ordering that the agreed-upon sum (the annual interest on the sum at 6 percent, per the rate fixed in 1842) should be paid. By 1875 it totaled over $2 million. The ambassador decided further that half of the amount should be held for the missions of Upper California, the portion located in American territory. The amount thus given to the archbishop and bishops of California was over $904,000, an amount paid in gold in thirteen annual installments by Mexico. The Mexican government, however, refused to pay any further interest after the period covered by the award. The matter was finally sent to the Permanent Court of Arbitration at The Hague. Only in October 1902 was a decision reached in favor of the Church.

Pise, Charles C. (November 22, 1801–May 26, 1866)

A Jesuit priest, writer, and chaplain to the United States Senate, Charles C. Pise was born in Annapolis, Maryland, and studied at Georgetown College before teaching at Mount St. Mary's College in Emmitsburg, Maryland. Among his students was John Hughes, later the archbishop of New York. He was ordained in 1825 and served at the cathedral in Baltimore and St. Patrick's Church in Washington, D.C. In December 1832 he was elected to serve as chaplain to the United States Senate, the first Catholic priest to hold that position. Over the next years, he was pastor of St. Peter's Church in New York and St. Charles Borromeo in Brooklyn. Father Pise was an accomplished writer and scholar, the author of *A History of the Catholic Church* (five volumes, 1829), *Alethia, or Letters on the Truth of Catholic Doctrines* (1845), and *Christianity and the Church* (1850). He was also a personal friend of President James Tyler.

Pitass, John (1844–December 11, 1913)

A priest and a leader of Polish Catholics in the United States, John Pitass was born in Piękary, Poland. He studied in Rome, then migrated to the United States in 1873. That same year, he was ordained in Buffalo, New York, and assigned to start the parish of St. Stanislaus. Over the next years, he emerged as a gifted voice and promoter for Polish Catholics, starting the first Polish school in Buffalo and founding the Polish newspaper *Polak w Ameryce* in 1887. Named vicar forane of the Polish clergy in Buffalo in 1894, he also encouraged and helped organize the first national conventions for Polish immigrants in 1896 and 1901. He was elected to serve as one of two delegates to represent the will of the conventions in Rome, but ill health prevented his travel.

Pittsburgh, Byzantine Ruthenian Archdiocese of. *See* Eastern Churches, Catholic

Pittsburgh, Diocese of

Established on August 11, 1843, by Pope Gregory XVI, the Diocese of Pittsburgh serves counties in western Pennsylvania. The diocese is a suffragan see of the Archdiocese of Philadelphia. The city stands on the confluence of the Allegheny, Ohio, and Monongahela Rivers at what is called the "Golden Triangle."

The Catholic history of Pittsburgh dates to 1643 when St. Isaac Jogues, the Jesuit martyr, was serving the Susquehanna. Other Jesuit missionaries, Recollect Franciscans, and Sulpicians labored in Pennsylvania, following the ministry of Jesuit Father Henry Harrison.

The colony of Pennsylvania was founded by William Penn in 1680 and was comparatively tolerant of Catholic activities. The Test Oath, demanding Catholics to denounce the Church in order to hold public office, was in effect. The Jesuits, however, were not driven from the colony, which was the practice elsewhere.

Fort Duquesne was erected on the site in 1754 and attacked by the French and British who claimed the area. Jesuit chaplains labored at the fort, which was then called "Assumption of the Blessed Virgin of the Beautiful River." In 1758 the British gained control, and it was renamed Fort Pitt after William Pitt the Elder. The city of Pittsburgh was laid out in 1784 by John Campbell, and it became a center for outfitting settlers moving down the Ohio River. In 1792 George Anschutz built a blast furnace in Pittsburgh, starting the iron and steel industry there. The railroad and the Pennsylvania Canal of 1834 aided the prosperity of the area. The presence of the vast inland port and the rapidly developing industries drew countless workers and their families to the city.

By 1874 Catholics were residing in Pittsburgh, served by the Carmelite Father Paul in the following year. Capuchin Franciscan Charles Whelan and others soon joined him, visiting families. In 1808 Father William F. X. O'Brien founded Old St. Patrick's Church, and in 1811 Bishop Michael F. Egan of the Diocese of Philadelphia dedicated the church and confirmed the faithful.

The constitution of the state of Pennsylvania honored the valiant sacrifices of Catholics during the American Revolution, and more and more of the faithful arrived to work in the developing industries. By 1820 Father Charles B. Maguire was known fondly across the city as the "Priest Maguire." He founded St. Paul's Church, which when dedicated was the largest church in the young United States. In 1829 a Poor Clare convent opened in Pittsburgh. Father Maguire died of cholera in 1833, and Father John O'Brien took over his vast ministry.

Owing to the rapid growth of the Catholic population in the Pittsburgh area, the Fifth Provincial Council of Baltimore, which was held in May 1843, recommended to the Holy See the creation of the Diocese of Pittsburgh and nominated Michael O'Connor as its first bishop. The Holy See agreed to both requests. O'Connor, however, made a journey to Rome to petition Pope Gregory XVI to revoke his appointment and allow him to enter the Society of Jesus. The pope declined, and O'Connor was appointed on August 11, 1843. He was consecrated a bishop on August 15 in Rome. To assist the needs of his diocese, Bishop O'Connor traveled through Ireland recruiting priests and women religious, including members of the Sisters of Mercy from Dublin.

Upon his arrival in Pittsburgh, he found his new diocese composed of 14 priests, 33 churches, and some 25,000 Catholics. He went to work immediately and convened a diocesan synod in 1844. Over the next few years, he started a seminary and a diocesan newspaper, the *Pittsburgh Catholic,* and secured the help of several communities of religious, including the Benedictines under the famed leader Boniface Wimmer, who founded St. Vincent's Abbey at Latrobe, and started an orphanage and girl's academy. A mere three years after his arrival, however, Bishop O'Connor was transferred to the newly established Diocese of Erie. Father Joshua Maria Young was named his successor in Pittsburgh by Pope Blessed Pius IX, but the Catholics of Pittsburgh petitioned the Holy See to reverse its decision; this, combined with Father Young's reluctance to be the bishop, won the day. Bishop O'Connor was brought back to Pittsburgh after five months and reappointed on December 20, 1853. The next year, he journeyed to Rome to participate in the definition of the dogma of the Immaculate Conception. His health soon deteriorated, and he resigned on May 23, 1860, at the age of forty-nine. He left behind him a diocese with 86 priests, 77 churches, a seminary, a hospital, and a Catholic population of more than 50,000.

The successor to Bishop O'Connor was Father Michael Domenec, a priest of the Congregation of the Missions, the Vincentians. Consecrated a bishop on December 9, 1860, Bishop Domenec presided over the diocese during the Civil War and proved unequal to the task of maintaining sound diocesan finances during the Panic of 1873. He continued spending on diocesan facilities during a time when fiscal austerity was needed and plunged the diocese into debt.

The timing of this proved more problematic in 1876 when the decision was made by the Holy See to establish the Diocese of Allegheny out of the Pittsburgh diocese on January 11, 1876. Bishop Domenec was named the new bishop of Allegheny, and Father John Tuigg of Altoona was appointed the third bishop of Pittsburgh.

From the start, the division of the diocese created massive problems as the poorest and most financially stressed areas remained with Pittsburgh. Negotiations failed to resolve the situation, and Bishop Domenec traveled to Rome in 1877 to find a settlement. In the end, the Holy See reunited Pittsburgh with the Allegheny diocese, and Bishop Domenec resigned. Bishop Tuigg served as bishop

Pittsburgh Cathedral

of Pittsburgh and as apostolic administrator of the Diocese of Allegheny. The see of Allegheny was formally suppressed in 1889. Bishop Domenec died in Spain in 1878.

Bishop Tuigg, consecrated a bishop on March 19, 1876, confronted a host of troubles as shepherd of Pittsburgh, including the financial worries caused by the financial panic and debt issues. He devoted years to fixing the fiscal problems and ruined his health from his labors. Owing to his poor health, a coadjutor bishop, Father Richard Phelan, was appointed in 1885. Bishop Tuigg died at the age of sixty-eight on December 7, 1889, and was succeeded by Bishop Phelan, the fourth bishop of Pittsburgh, who led the diocese during a period of phenomenal growth. Vast numbers of Europeans were arriving for work in the mines, mills, and foundries. Bishop Phelan erected national churches to ease the plight of immigrants and provided priests fluent in the various European languages. When the Diocese of Allegheny was suppressed in 1889, Bishop Phelan began restoring diocesan facilities and services in the reincorporated counties. Some territory was lost, however, when the Diocese of Altoona was formed on May 30, 1901. Bishop Phelan died on December 20, 1904.

His successor was Bishop J. F. Regis Canevin, who had served as coadjutor bishop since 1902. He was the first Pittsburgh native to become bishop. Canevin continued the expansion of the diocese, including 140 new parishes, further development of the school system, and the introduction of the Confraternity of Christian Doctrine and Catholic Charities. He was also shepherd during the challenging years of World War I. He retired on November 26, 1920, and was given the personal title of archbishop.

The sixth bishop of Pittsburgh was Hugh C. Boyle, a priest of the diocese. He was born in Johnstown and suffered the loss of his father and most of his siblings in the terrible Johnstown Flood in 1889. Appointed on June 16, 1921, Boyle was consecrated a bishop on June 29. Bishop Boyle was a well-known educator and promoted Catholic education. His long tenure meant that he was bishop through the Great Depression and World War II. He served as chairman of the National Catholic Welfare Conference's Committee for Polish Relief

during the war. He was also active with the Legion of Decency. He died on December 22, 1950.

Bishop John F. Dearden was his successor, having been appointed coadjutor bishop of the diocese on March 13, 1948. Nicknamed "Iron John" for his administrative style, he presided over the postwar growth of the diocese. He was named an Assistant at the Pontifical Throne in 1957. On December 18, 1958, he was appointed the archbishop of Detroit and was created a cardinal priest in 1969, with the titular church of San Pio X alla Balduina.

The eighth bishop of Pittsburgh was John J. Wright, who had served as the bishop of Worcester since 1950; he was appointed on January 23, 1959. His term as bishop in Pittsburgh was dominated by the Second Vatican Council, during which he participated in the drafting of several conciliar documents. On April 23, 1969, he was appointed Prefect of the Congregation for the Clergy in Rome and was created a cardinal with the titular church of Jesus the Divine Teacher that same year.

Bishop Vincent M. Leonard, who had been an auxiliary bishop of Pittsburgh since 1964, was appointed the ninth bishop of Pittsburgh on June 1, 1969, and had as his primary task implementing the decrees of the Second Vatican Council. He was a supporter of diocesan transparency and worked to maintain stability in the liturgy at a time of great confusion. He resigned on June 30, 1983, owing to poor health.

On October 7, 1983, Bishop Anthony J. Bevilacqua, an auxiliary bishop of Brooklyn since 1980, succeeded him. Installed on December 12, 1983, he served for only four years before he was appointed archbishop of Philadelphia on December 8, 1987. He was created a cardinal on June 28, 1991.

The eleventh bishop of Pittsburgh was Donald W. Wuerl, who had been an auxiliary bishop in Seattle. Appointed on February 12, 1988, and installed on March 25, 1988, Bishop Wuerl served as shepherd until 2006 and presided over a diocese in flux as a result of the changing economy and demographics of the city. He provided stability to the schools by merging two high schools and launched a diocesan restructuring plan that closed 117 parishes in a way that worked so well that the Parish Reorganization and Revitalization Project is considered a model for other dioceses. Bishop

Wuerl also hosted a highly regarded television program, *The Teaching of Christ,* in 1990 and wrote a best-selling adult catechism with the same name. On June 22, 2006, Bishop Wuerl was installed as the archbishop of Washington. He was created a cardinal priest with the titular church of San Pietro in Vincoli in November 2010.

On July 18, 2007, Bishop David A. Zubik was appointed the twelfth bishop of Pittsburgh. He was installed on September 28, 2007. Bishop Zubik had served previously as an auxiliary bishop of Pittsburgh and had been serving as bishop of Green Bay since 2003. In 2009 he held a remarkable Service of Apology at St. Paul Cathedral, during which he asked for forgiveness from anyone who had been hurt by the Church. He was also confronted with the pastoral challenges of an aging population and a city and community hard hit by the economic downturn in previous years. In 2011 there were 656,000 Catholics served by 480 priests, more than 1,100 women and men religious, and 212 parishes in the diocese.

Pope Pius VI

Pius VI, Pope (December 27, 1717–August 29, 1799)

Pius VI's pontificate (1775–1799) was troubled by the French Revolution, which began in 1789. Born Giovanni Angelo Braschi at Cesena, Emilia, Italy, he belonged to a noble but poor family. After studying with the Jesuits and earning a doctorate in law, he became secretary in 1740 to Cardinal Antonio Ruffo, then legate of Ferrara. Named a papal secretary in 1755, he was ordained in 1758 and appointed by Pope Clement XIII treasurer of the Apostolic Chamber, or Camera, in 1766; Clement XIV appointed him a cardinal in 1771. Four years later, after a conclave lasting 134 days, he was elected Clement's successor on February 15, 1775. His early days as pope were distinguished by his patronage of the arts; he spentlavishly on the Museum of Pio-Clementine in the Vatican and on the sacristy of St. Peter's. He also made an expensive attempt to drain the Pontine Marshes of Rome.

The reign of Pope Pius VI, however, was overshadowed by the coming to fruition of the various philosophical strands of the Enlightenment throughout the eighteenth century, including Febronianism and Josephism, which challenged the authority of the pope and secularized numerous monarchies, with the local Church under state control. The pope traveled to Vienna in 1782 and received an enthusiastic welcome from the faithful, but his effort did little to sway Austrian Emperor Joseph II from granting concessions. Febronianism spread to Germany and in Tuscany, where Joseph's brother, Grand Duke Leopold II (later emperor from 1790 to 1792), used the ideas to curb papal influence. In September 1786 the Synod of Pistoia under Bishop Scipione de' Ricci gave its support to Leopold and adopted the Four Articles of 1682. Bishop Ricci was soon compelled to resign, and Febronianism was condemned in the bull *Auctorem Fidei* in 1794.

Far worse for the Church was the Revolution in France. Pope Pius VI at first declined action against the revolutionary regime when it issued the Civil Constitution of the Clergy in 1790, but when an oath was demanded, the pope condemned the constitution as heretical. Relations soon deteriorated. France seized the papal holdings of Avignon and Venaissin in 1790, and in 1797 the young general Napoleon Bonaparte annexed the Papal States. In the arbitrary peace that followed (the Peace of Tolentino in 1797), Pope Pius VI had to accept the loss of the papal territories of Romagna, Bologna, and Ferrara, as well as treasures and manuscripts. That same year the French general Mathieu Léonard Duphot was killed while stirring up a riot in Rome, a disaster that allowed the French to enter the Eternal City under General Louis-Alexandre Berthier (later Napoleon's chief of staff) on February 10, 1798. Pope Pius VI was deposed as head of state and a Roman Republic was established. The pope was forced to leave Rome and was incarcerated in Florence from where, on March

28, 1799, he was moved by troops of the French Directory over the Alps to Briançon and then to Valence in July, where he died. His successor was Pius VII.

In the midst of these difficulties, Pope Pius VI created two dioceses in the United States, Baltimore in 1789 and Louisiana and the Two Floridas in 1793. The founding of Baltimore had momentous consequences for the Church in the United States, as his successor elevated the see to the first archdiocese in 1808, setting the American Church on a path to rapid development.

Pius VII, Pope (August 14, 1742–August 20, 1823) Pius VII's pontificate (1800–1823) was dominated by the events of the Napoleonic Wars, which raged from 1800 to 1815. Luigi Barnaba Chiaramonte was born to noble parents in Cesena, in Emilia, Italy, and entered the Benedictine order at the age of fourteen, taking the name Gregorio. After studies at Padua and Rome, he served as a professor of theology at Parma and from 1766 to 1781 was a professor in various abbeys and schools. In 1782 he was named bishop of Tivoli, from where he was transferred three years later to Imola in 1785. That same year he was made a cardinal. He was elected pope on March 14, 1800, by the conclave convened in Venice, as successor to Pope Pius VI, who had died the previous year a prisoner of the French. The new pope was thus aware that the central crisis facing him was France, under the control of Napoleon Bonaparte.

Relying upon his brilliant cardinal secretary of state, Ercole Consalvi, Pope Pius VII negotiated with Napoleon the Concordat of 1801, which the French leader promptly violated by adding to it the Organic Articles in 1802, tightening his hold over the French Church. Hoping to win concessions from Napoleon, the pope accepted his invitation in 1804 to travel to Paris to crown him emperor, despite the opposition of the members of the Curia. Pope Pius VII said the Mass at the coronation of Napoleon on December 1, but the emperor crowned himself and gave no concessions to the Church.

The following year war erupted again, and the pope adopted strict neutrality. Relations with the French Empire soon deteriorated, climaxing with

Pope Pius VII

Napoleon's arrest of Pope Pius VII after the pontiff issued the condemnatory bull *Quum Memoranda*. The pope was moved from Rome to Grenoble, then Savona, and finally, in 1812, to Fontainebleau. He was subjected to ill-treatment, finally accepting under coercion the so-called Concordat of Fontainebleau on January 25, 1813, making numerous concessions to the emperor. Two months later he retracted his signature.

Released on March 10, 1814, coinciding with the fall of Napoleon, Pope Pius VII returned to Rome on March 24. After a brief flight to Genoa in 1815 with the escape of Napoleon from Elba, he came back on June 7. Renowned in Europe for his brave resistance to the emperor, the pope enjoyed heightened prestige and international favor.

Pope Pius VII reappointed Cardinal Consalvi on May 7, 1814, sending him to the Congress of Vienna in 1814–15, where he won the nearly complete restoration of the Papal States. Concordats were arranged with a number of states, including Prussia in 1821, Bavaria in 1817, and Russia in 1818. In rebuilding the Papal States, he and Cardinal Consalvi introduced various governmental, judicial, and financial reforms. The pope devoted his final years to promoting a renewed Church in Europe. On July 31, 1814, he reinstituted the Society of Jesus. He died on August 20, 1823, and was succeeded by Pope Leo XII.

The reign of Pope Pius VII saw the rapid development of the Church in the United States. The pope assisted the process by creating a number of new dioceses. In 1808 he elevated the see of Baltimore to the rank of archdiocese, creating Bishop John Carroll as the first archbishop of Baltimore. At the same time, he created the Dioceses of Boston, Bardstown, New York, and Philadelphia as suffragans. These dioceses were followed in 1820 by Charleston and Richmond and in 1821 by Cincinnati.

Pius VIII, Pope (November 20, 1760–November 30, 1830)

The pope from 1829 to 1830, Francesco Saverio Castiglione was born to a noble family in Cingoli, near Ancona, Italy. After studies at Orsimo, Bologna, and Rome, he became a respected expert on canon law and was appointed by Pope Pius VII in 1800 to be bishop of Montalto.

From 1808 to 1814 he shared the imprisonment of the leaders of the Church at the hands of Napoleon. After being freed, he was named a cardinal in 1816. Pope Pius VII made it clear that he hoped that Castiglione would succeed him, once, according to Cardinal Nicholas Wiseman, telling Castiglione during some business, "Your Holiness Pius VIII may one day settle this affair."

Although a leading candidate in 1823, Cardinal Castiglione did not get elected to succeed Pius VII; instead, the cardinals elected Cardinal Annibale della Genga as Pope Leo XII.

On March 31, 1829, however, he succeeded Leo, and to no one's surprise, took the name Pius VIII. His brief pontificate saw the recognition of the new regime in France under King Louis Philippe after the Revolution of 1830 and the acceptance of the Roman Catholic Relief Acts in England, which passed in April 1829. Pope Pius VIII also gave his approval to the decrees of the First Council of Baltimore in October 1829, and in that same year decreed the creation of the Diocese of Mobile.

Pope Pius VIII

Pius IX, Pope Blessed (May 13, 1792–February 7, 1878)

The pope from 1846 to 1878, Pope Blessed Pius IX was the longest reigning pontiff in the history of the Church, after Peter. His pontificate of 31 years, 7 months, and 22 days witnessed the demise of the Papal States and the convening of the First Vatican Council in 1869–70. His time as pope also included one of the greatest periods of expansion of the Catholic Church in the United States. Born in Sinigaglia, Marche, Italy, Giovanni Maria Mastai-Ferretti was the seventh child of Hieronimo Count Mastai-Ferretti and Countess Caterina Solazzi. After studies in Volterra, Italy, and in Rome, he was ordained on April 10, 1819.

In 1823 he was appointed apostolic delegate to Chile, and in 1827 he was named by Pope Leo XII to the Archdiocese of Spoleto. Although named a cardinal in pectore in 1839, he was formally proclaimed a cardinal priest by Pope Gregory XVI in December 1840. On June 16, 1846, he was elected pope.

The reign of Pope Blessed Pius IX witnessed one of the most tumultuous periods in Church history, including the Italian Revolution of 1848, which forced him to flee and return to Rome in 1850 only with the help of the Austrian army. From then on the pontiff struggled against the relentless process of the Risorgimento, the movement of Italian Unification that led in 1860 to the seizure of the Papal States by the troops of the Piedmontese ruler King Victor Emmanuel II and finally the loss of Rome itself on September 20, 1870. Although the pope was given assurances of the inviolable nature of the Vatican and his person by the Law of Guarantees of May 13, 1871, Pope Blessed Pius IX protested vehemently and declared himself a prisoner of the Vatican, which he never left. He issued the decree *Non Expedit* in 1868, forbidding Catholics from participating in Italian political affairs, thus beginning the conflict that was not to be resolved until 1929 with the Lateran Treaty.

Blessed Pope Pius IX

While filled with disasters, the pontificate also saw immense achievements for the Church. On December 8, 1854, he proclaimed the Immaculate Conception of the Blessed Virgin as a dogma of the Church. He convened the First Vatican Council on December 8, 1869, during which, on July 18, 1870, papal infallibility was made a dogma of the Church. He adjourned the council in the summer of 1870, owing to the outbreak of the Franco-Prussian War.

Pope Blessed Pius IX restored the hierarchy in England in 1850 and in the Netherlands in 1853, negotiated a number of concordats with various states in Europe and beyond, and worked with bishops to respond to the loss in political power by devoting even greater emphasis to spiritual concerns. Also, in 1864 he denounced several errors that had sprung up in Church teaching with the encyclical *Quanta Cura,* to which he attached the *Syllabus Errorum.*

He was also concerned for the expansion of foreign missions and for the development of the Church in the United States. He founded the Latin American College in Rome in 1853, and marked a

new era for seminary studies in Rome for American seminarians when he approved the founding of the North American College in 1859. Given the length of Pope Blessed Pius IX's reign, it was not surprising that he made numerous appointments to sees in the United States and created new ones. What was extraordinary was the period of growth over which the pontiff presided in his almost thirty-two years as pope. He created nine metropolitan sees in the United States: Oregon City in 1846, St. Louis in 1847, Cincinnati, New Orleans, and New York in 1850, San Francisco in 1853, and Boston, Milwaukee, and Philadelphia in 1875. He also created thirty-four dioceses: Albany, Buffalo, Cleveland, and Galveston in 1847, Nesqually (Seattle), St. Paul, Santa Fe, Savannah, and Wheeling in 1850, Brooklyn, Burlington, Covington, Erie, Natchitoches (Alexandria), Newark, Portland, and Qunicy (Alton) in 1853, Fort Wayne and Sault Ste. Marie (Marquette) in 1857, Columbus, Green Bay, Grass Valley (Sacramento), Harrisburg, La Crosse, Rochester, St. Joseph, Scranton, and Wilmington in 1868, St. Augustine and Springfield in 1870, Ogdensburg and Providence in 1872, San Antonio in 1874, and Peoria in 1877. Pope Blessed Pius IX also established eleven vicariates apostolic: Indian Territory and Nebraska in 1851, Northern Michigan in 1853, Florida in 1857, North Carolina, Idaho, Colorado, and Utah in 1868, Arizona in 1869, and Minnesota in 1874. Finally, he named the first American cardinal, John McCloskey, archbishop of New York, in 1875.

Known for his charm, kindness, and forbearance, Pope Blessed Pius IX was genuinely respected throughout the world for standing firm in his principles. Such was the anticlerical sentiment in Rome, however, that a mob tried unsuccessfully to hurl his body into the Tiber after his death on February 7, 1878. In 1985 his cause for canonization was opened. Pope Blessed John Paul II beatified him on September 5, 2000. His feast day is February 7.

Pius X, Pope St. (June 2, 1835–August 20, 1914)
The pope from 1903 to 1914, Pope St. Pius X was the last pontiff to be canonized and the first since Pius V in 1712. Giuseppe Melchiore Sarto was born in Riese, Upper Venetia, the son of a post-

man and a seamstress. After studies at Riese and Castelfranco, he entered the seminary in Padua in 1850 and was ordained in 1858. He then spent the next years in various pastoral and diocesan assignments, culminating in his appointment in 1884 as bishop of Mantua. His time as bishop was marked by a complete spiritual revitalization of the diocese that earned him elevation to the cardinalate in June 1893 by Pope Leo XIII. He was then chosen to serve as patriarch of Venice, a post he held for ten years with genuine distinction, winning the respect and love of the populace through hard work and cooperation with both local and central government. In the conclave of 1903 to choose a successor to Leo, Cardinal Sarto was elected pope on August 4, 1903, taking the name Pius in honor of other popes who had fought against oppression.

Pope St. Pius X chose as his motto *"Instaurare omnia in Christo"* ("To restore all things in Christ"). The choice signaled his intention to be a pastoral and spiritual pontiff, but he was forced by circumstances to confront a host of challenges facing the Church. He protested the anti-Catholic measures by the French government, causing a break in relations in 1904, and denounced the Law of Separation of 1906, creating considerable difficulties for the French Church, but his position made it possible for the Church to be free of secular interference in France and much stronger in the long term. Similar protests were made to the Portuguese government in 1911 when it too separated church and state.

Concerned with the effects of modernism and other heresies, the pope condemned modernism in the decree *Lamentabili* on July 3, 1907, the encyclical *Pascendi Dominici Gregis* on September 8, 1907, and the *motu proprio Sacrorum Antistitum* on September 1, 1910, by which all clergy were required to take an oath against modernism, called by Pope St. Pius X the "synthesis of all the heresies." A stern program was then launched to expunge the contemporary Church of all modernist tendencies. He also condemned the Le Sillon movement in France in 1910, the group begun by Marc Sangier, which worked for a synthesis or adaptation of Catholic teaching with the ideals of the French Revolution. The pontiff's main achievements were constructive, for he brought extensive reforms to the life of the Church. The Curia was reorganized through the decree *Sapienti Consilio* in 1908, the Code of Canon Law was codified (then promulgated in 1917 under Benedict XV), and Church music was reformed, including the restoration of Gregorian chant to the liturgy in 1903, a major impetus to the liturgical movement. Catholic Action was established on a sure footing through the encyclical *Il Fermo Proposito* in 1905, and the breviary was revised by *Divino Afflatu* in 1911. Of all his reforms, he is best known for his wholehearted encouragement of daily Communion.

The pontificate of Pope St. Pius X was also noted for the decision in 1908 to issue the apostolic constitution *Sapienti Consilio* by which the pontiff removed the dioceses of the United States from the authority of the Sacred Congregation of the Propaganda. Henceforth, the dioceses were under the common law of the Church, subject to the other congregations and offices of the Holy See. The act marked the recognition by Rome of the maturing of the American Church.

The pontiff created eleven dioceses in the United States: Fall River and Great Falls in 1904, Oklahoma City and Superior in 1905, Rockford in

St. Pope Pius X

1908, Bismarck and Crookston in 1909, Toledo in 1910, Des Moines in 1911, Corpus Christi in 1912, and El Paso in 1914. He also created two American cardinals: Cardinal William H. O'Connell, archbishop of Boston, and Cardinal John Murphy Farley, archbishop of New York, in 1911.

Having predicted the outbreak of World War I, he was powerless to stop it and died of a broken heart on August 20, 1914, only a few weeks after its commencement. Revered in his lifetime, he was beatified on June 3, 1951, and canonized on May 29, 1954, by Pope Pius XII. His feast day is August 21.

Pius XI, Pope (May 31, 1857–February 10, 1939)

The pope from 1922 to 1939, Ambrogio Damiano Achille Ratti was born at Desio, near Milan, Italy, the son of a manager of a silk factory. Ordained at the Lateran on December 27, 1879, he received three doctorates from the Pontifical Gregorian University and from 1883 to 1888 taught dogmatic theology at the seminary of Milan. In 1888, owing to his remarkable scholarship and paleographic ability, he was elected to the staff of the Ambrosian Library of Milan, where he became prefect in 1907. From 1911 to 1918 he worked at the Vatican Library, first as pro-prefect, then prefect. As prefect, Ratti was responsible for the systematic cataloging of its many collections. At the command of Pope Benedict XV, he was sent in 1918 as an apostolic visitor to Warsaw, Poland, receiving the post of nuncio at the request of the Polish government. He was bestowed the Order of the White Eagle by the Poles for remaining in Warsaw in 1920 during the invasion in August of that year by the Bolsheviks. Recalled in 1921, he was made archbishop of Milan and on June 13, 1921, was elevated to the cardinalate. Although a cardinal for only some seven

Pope Pius XI

months, he was elected pope on February 6, 1922, to succeed Benedict XV.

Pope Pius XI took as his motto "To seek the peace of Christ through the reign of Christ," and devoted much energy to promoting peace in a world drifting toward war. He also strove to preach the Gospel across the globe; he thus encouraged the missions and promoted the work of the Pontifical Academy of Sciences and the Vatican Observatory. He issued the encyclicals *Ubi Arcano* in 1922 to launch Catholic Action, *Divini Illius Magistri* in 1929 on education, and *Quadragesimo Anno* in 1931 on a variety of social issues. Particularly significant to him was the institution of the feast of Christ the King. His notable canonizations included Thérèse of Lisieux, John Fisher, Thomas More, Bernadette Soubirous, and John Bosco. Robert Bellarmine, John of the Cross, Albertus Magnus, and Peter Canisius were named Doctors of the Church. Pope Pius XI canonized thirty-four new saints and beatified sixty-six new beati.

Much of his pontificate was occupied with foreign matters. Chief among his many achievements was the Lateran Treaty of 1929, ending the Roman Question and creating Vatican City as an independent state. His early secretary of state, Cardinal Pietro Gasparri, was succeeded in 1930 by Cardinal Eugenio Pacelli, who traveled extensively on his behalf, dealing with international issues and crises. Pope Pius XI condemned communism sharply in the encyclical *Divini Redemptoris* in 1937, and his opposition to communism prompted him to negotiate a concordat with Adolf Hitler in 1933. The agreement, entered into with ultimately meaningless promises from Hitler, earned criticism for the pope and gave Nazi Germany considerable prestige in some circles. Nazi persecution, however, only intensified, and Pope Pius XI released the condemnatory encyclical *Mit Brennender Sorge* in 1937, denouncing Nazi Germany for its treatment of the Church, its anti-Christian policies, and its repeated violations of the concordat. His relations with the Fascist regime in Italy likewise suffered toward the end of the late 1930s as Benito Mussolini drew closer to Hitler's program and introduced Nazi racist policies in 1938. In 1929 the pope also reached an agreement with Mexico, ending the disagreement between church and state that had existed since 1926 and at last reopening churches, although Church-state tensions continued.

Dedicated to building up the Church around the world, he created a total of 148 prefectures apostolic, 190 vicariates apostolic, 120 new dioceses, 35 archdioceses, 10 apostolic delegations, and 15 apostolic nunciatures. He established five metropolitan sees in the United States: San Antonio in 1926, Los Angeles in 1936, and Detroit, Louisville, and Newark in 1937. He also created twelve dioceses in the United States: Monterey-Fresno in 1922, Raleigh in 1924, Amarillo in 1926, Oklahoma City and Tulsa in 1930, Reno in 1931, San Diego in 1936, Camden, Lansing, Owensboro, and Paterson in 1937, and Saginaw in 1938. He also created two American cardinals: Cardinal Patrick Joseph Hayes, archbishop of New York, and Cardinal George Mundelein, archbishop of Chicago, in 1924.

Pope Pius XI's lengthy reign was overshadowed by the terrible events that occurred under his successor, Eugenio Pacelli, Pius XII. World War II had been building throughout his reign and erupted only months after his death.

Pius XII, Pope (March 2, 1876–October 9, 1958)

Pope Pius XII's reign (1939–1958) witnessed World War II and anticipated many of the reforms launched by the Second Vatican Council. Eugenio Maria Giuseppe Giovanni Pacelli was born to the highly respected Pacelli family of Rome. After studies at the Pontifical Gregorian University, the Capranica College, and the Pontifical Athenaeum S. Apollinaire in Rome, he was ordained in April 1899. Two years later, he entered papal service and rose swiftly through the Secretariat of State. In 1917 he was made titular archbishop of Sardes by Pope Benedict XV and was sent as apostolic nuncio to Bavaria, representing Benedict in working for peace. He was then appointed in 1920 as nuncio to the German Republic, and negotiated a concordat with Bavaria in 1924 and Prussia in 1929. On December 16, 1929, he was elevated to the cardinalate by Pope Pius XI, who then named him secretary of state on February 7, 1930.

As secretary of state, Pacelli traveled extensively, making visits to France in 1935 and 1937, Argentina in 1934, and elsewhere. In October 1936 he visited the United States and conferred with President Franklin Delano Roosevelt. His arrival marked the first time a Vatican secretary of state had visited the United States. In 1933 he negotiated the concordat with Nazi Germany. As Europe moved toward war, Pacelli was thus considered the most ideally suited papal candidate to deal with what was anticipated to be a deteriorating global situation. He was elected successor to Pius XI on the third ballot (the first secretary of state to be chosen since Clement IX in 1667) on March 2, 1939.

Pope Pius XII led the Church through the terrible days of World War II and its aftermath. His first encyclical, *Summi Pontificatus,* on October 20, 1939, extolled humanity to restore God to his rightful place, and as war raged he used his Christmas allocution of 1939 to declare five principles of peace, the Five Peace Points: a true Christian Spirit among nations; recognition of the rights of every nation; true disarmament; recognition of the rights of minorities; and the creation of an international court to guarantee peace.

For the rest of the war, Pope Pius XII maintained a position of neutrality, but he devoted all available resources to easing the suffering of refugees through the Pontifical Aid Commission. He also opened the Vatican to refugees, including Jews, in 1943. In perhaps the most memorable moment of his pontificate, he greeted the Allied army that liberated Rome in the summer of 1944.

Pope Pius XII has been criticized for failing to speak out against the treatment of the Jews by Nazi Germany. While much discussed in recent years, the charge is unsupported by the record. In 1943 he ordered sacred vessels to be melted to help pay a ransom to the Germans to keep the Jews of Rome safe; the Jews had been ordered to pay one million lire and one hundred pounds of gold. The

Vatican churches, basilica, and Church properties were opened to give shelter; there were fifteen thousand Jews at Castel Gandolfo alone, and thousands more at nearly two hundred different sites. The pope also denounced Nazi policies and atrocities. He believed that more explicit and provocative moves would be dangerous, especially as Hitler had made certain threats about removing the pontiff from the Vatican. The Church in Nazi lands was also being severely persecuted — millions of Catholics, including nuns and priests, died in the Holocaust — and the pope was gravely concerned about the loss of even more innocent life. After Rome's liberation, the chief rabbi of the city, Dr. Israel Zolli, expressed his gratitude to Pope Pius XII for his bravery and for having saved so many Jews in the difficult circumstances. Dr. Zolli entered the Church soon after, dying a Catholic in 1956.

Pope Pius XII

Having weathered the terrible storm of the war, the pontiff turned his attention to the postwar world. He recognized both the heightened prestige of the papacy coming out of the struggle and the incalculable degree of devastation and ruin throughout Europe. He continued to use the Church's resources to aid those in need and also spoke out against communism, which was making much unfortunate progress in European states, most notably in Eastern and Central Europe.

Pope Pius XII was also pleased to preside over the continued expansion of the faith all over the world. He was responsible for thirty-three canonizations, excavations beneath St. Peter's Basilica, and the issuing of forty-one encyclicals, including *Mystici Corporis Christi* in 1943, *Divino Afflante Spiritu* in 1943, *Mediator Dei* in 1947, *Humani Generis* in 1950, and *Ad Caeli Reginam* in 1954. He also issued the apostolic constitution *Christus Dominus* in 1953, relaxing the Eucharistic fast, and used the *motu proprio Sacram Communionem* in 1957 to promote attendance at evening Masses; these reforms anticipated many of the changes brought by the Second Vatican Council.

Wildly popular in the United States throughout his pontificate, Pope Pius XII established five metropolitan sees for the American Church: Washington in 1939, Denver and Indianapolis in 1944, Seattle in 1951, and Hartford in 1953. He also created twenty-three dioceses: Gallup in 1939, Honolulu and Pueblo in 1941, Youngstown in 1943, Evansville, Lafayette (Indiana), and Steubenville in 1944, Madison in 1946, Austin and Joliet in 1948, Worcester in 1950, Dodge City, Greensburg, Juneau, and Yakima in 1951, Bridgeport and Norwich in 1953, Atlanta, Jefferson City, and Springfield-Cape Girardeau in 1956, Gary and Rockville Centre in 1957, and New Ulm in 1958. Pius also created five American cardinals: Cardinal Samuel Alphonsus Stritch, archbishop of Chicago, Cardinal Edward Mooney, archbishop of Detroit, Cardinal John Joseph Glennon, archbishop of St. Louis, and Cardinal Francis Spellman, archbishop of New York, at the consistory of February 18, 1946, and Cardinal James F. McIntyre, archbishop of Los Angeles, in 1953.

Pope Pius XII died at Castel Gandolfo on October 9, 1958. His passing signaled the end of an era in the Church. His successor, John XXIII, launched *aggiornamento* and the Second Vatican Council.

Plassman, Thomas Bernard (March 19, 1879– February 13, 1959)

A Franciscan priest and biblical scholar, Thomas Bernard Plassmann was born at Avenwedde bei Gueterlch, Westphalia, Germany, and arrived in America at the age of fifteen. After studies at Quincy College in Illinois, he entered the Franciscan order in 1898 and was sent to The Catholic University of America to complete his studies. By the time of his ordination in 1906, he had already finished his doctorate at Catholic University, with a dissertation on "The Signification of Beraka (The Jewish Benediction)." Plassmann also earned a doctorate in theology from the Pontifical Athenaeum

S. Apollinare in Rome and did further studies in the Holy Land, at Louvain, Belgium, and at the University of Bonn. In 1910 he was assigned to St. Bonaventure College and Seminary in Allegany, New York, remaining there for most of his life, although his reputation and influence extended far beyond the confines of the school and seminary. In 1919 he founded the Franciscan Educational Conference and served as its president until 1947, and from 1920 to 1949 he served as president of St. Bonaventure College. In 1952 he became rector of Christ the King Seminary. In addition to these posts, he was named visitor general for the order to Canada, Mexico, and postwar Germany, prefect of studies of Holy Name Province, and provincial of Holy Name Province. He was also responsible for founding Siena College in Albany, New York. In 1931 the Franciscans honored him with the title Lector Generalis of Sacred Scripture, and Plassmann received three honorary degrees. He was a deeply respected professor of Scripture, as well as oriental languages, dogmatic theology, and patrology. He was also ranked as one of the foremost speakers and preachers in the American Church during the 1940s and 1950s. Among his published works were books on spirituality, including *The Priest's Way to God, From Sunday to Sunday, The Upper Room,* and *The Radiant Crown of Glory.*

Poels Controversy

The name given to the controversy that erupted at The Catholic University of America and continued from 1906 to 1910, the Poels Controversy concerned the opinions of the Dutch scholar Father Henry Poels. Poels began teaching at Catholic University in 1904, focusing on Old Testament studies. On June 27, 1906, the Pontifical Biblical Commission promulgated a decree in which it affirmed the "substantive Mosaic authenticity and integrity of the Pentateuch." Such a decree was unacceptable in Father Poels's opinion, and in the summer of 1907 the priest met with Pope St. Pius X. Subsequent versions of the meeting were disputed, but Father Poels labored under what he believed to be permission to remain at the university. The following year, the rector, Father Denis J. O'Connell, prohibited Father Poels from teaching until a decision had been reached about his case by the chancellor of

the university, Cardinal James Gibbons. The cardinal ruled in favor of Poels, and in early 1909 the university trustees kept him on the faculty.

Later that year, the new rector, Father Thomas J. Shahan, met with the pope, who expressed his unhappiness that Poels was still teaching at Catholic University. The secretary of state, Cardinal Rafael Merry del Val, next involved himself, sending to Cardinal Gibbons an oath that would have to be taken by Poels to remain in his teaching post. Father Poels journeyed to Rome, where he declared the condition on which he was willing to accept the oath. In November 1909 the trustees of the university demanded that Poels accept the oath, and Poels again declared his own conditions. Additional communications followed between Cardinal Gibbons and Rome, and in June 1910 Father Poels was officially dismissed. The Poels Controversy was a byproduct of the charged atmosphere that had emerged as the Church came to grips with modernism in general and Americanism in particular. (*See also* Americanism.)

Point, Nicholas (April 10, 1799–July 4, 1868)

A Jesuit missionary serving in the United States, in particular among the Native Americans in Montana, Nicholas Point was born in the Ardennes region of France to a poor family. He entered the Society of Jesus in 1822, his vocation influenced both by reading the life of St. Francis Xavier and by the stories of the Jesuit Reductions in South America. He left the novitiate that same year but returned in 1826 and received ordination in 1831 in Switzerland (as the Jesuits had been expelled from France the previous year). After a number of years teaching at Fribourg, he went to Spain and then back to France. In 1836 his request to serve in the United States was accepted, although his specific request to serve among Native Americans was not at first approved. Instead, Point was assigned to educational posts. He served as principal of St. Mary's College in Kentucky and in 1837 founded St. Charles College in Grand Coteau, Louisiana. Finally, in 1841, he was given the opportunity to travel with the famed Jesuit missionary Pierre-Jean De Smet and established a Jesuit base among the Flatheads in Montana. Point next built the first church in Idaho in 1842 and became the first missionary among the Blackfeet and the Coeur d'Alenes, devoting the next years to missionary labors. In 1847 he was transferred to Canada to work with the Jesuits there. He died at Québec.

Point was especially well known for his paintings and sketches of trappers and Native American tribes. He was also a gifted naturalist, architect, and writer. In his youth, the French Marshal Michel Ney, a noted soldier in the army of Napoleon, had offered to pay for his education at the Paris School of Fine Art. Point's mother, however, refused the offer.

Polish Catholics

The country of Poland has traditionally been one of the most devoutly Catholic in all of Europe and, tragically, a nation much oppressed and partitioned by its neighbors, including Germany, Russia, and Austria. The history of Poland colored the quality and the commitment of Polish immigrants to the Catholic faith, in particular those who made their way to America for a new life.

The earliest Polish immigrants arrived in North America in the seventeenth century and settled in small numbers in Virginia, New York, Pennsylvania, and later in the Ohio Valley. Notably, the Poles in Virginia, craftsmen by profession, were initially excluded from legal rights by the House of Burgesses in the colony, chiefly because they were Catholics. The craftsmen went on strike in 1619 (the first known strike in the New World) and were granted full rights.

The pace of arrivals increased in the second half of the nineteenth century owing to the partitions of Poland in 1772, 1793, and 1795. Poles, feeling oppressed by the severe treatment of the country by Prussians, Austrians, and Russians, fled Europe in search of political freedom. Poles fought for the American cause during the Revolutionary War, and the Continental Army was aided in training and battlefield leadership by Thaddeus Kosciuszko and Count Casimir Pulaski.

The vast majority of Polish immigrants were Catholics, a pattern that never changed. More Polish refugees arrived from Europe after several unsuccessful rebellions against Russia in 1830, 1831, 1863, and 1864, and against Austria in 1846. The new Polish immigrants were often members of the Polish aristocracy and the middle class. They

brought with them education and learning, and in 1834 some of them founded the first Polish-American organization in New York City and the first Polish-language newspaper in the United States, *Echo z Polski* ("Echo from Poland") in 1863. Poles also fought in the American Civil War on both the Union and Confederate side.

The political, economic, and social crises in Eastern Europe in the late nineteenth century created a much larger pattern of migration, and Poles arrived in America in increasing numbers. By the middle of the nineteenth century there were fewer than fifty thousand Poles in the United States. This changed in the 1870s, when large numbers of Poles began departing their homeland. Over the next half century, over two million Poles settled in America. Like the Italian immigrants of the same period, most Poles who reached American shores were from the lower classes and were young men in search of work.

Many of the newly arrived Poles settled in rural areas, in keeping with their desire to emulate their farming lives back in Europe. They reached Texas in the 1850s and soon made their way to Michigan, Illinois, Wisconsin, and Indiana. Others settled in the major industrial cities, including Chicago, Detroit, Milwaukee, Pittsburgh, New York City, and Philadelphia. By 1930 there were more than three million Poles in America. Most were Catholics, and the Church worked to provide their pastoral and spiritual needs. By 1942 there were 831 Polish Catholic parishes, more than sixty elementary and high schools, and four seminaries. There were also fifteen communities of Polish women religious, including the Sisters of the Holy Family of Nazareth and the Felician Sisters.

Problems arose starting in 1894 over the treatment of Polish Catholic clergy and also the disposition of Church property. The dispute culminated in a schism, during which some Polish Catholics left the Church in 1904 and formed the Polish National Catholic Church. The leader of the Polish National Catholic Church from 1904 until his death in 1953 was Father Francis Hodur. Dialogue between the Catholic Church and the Polish Nationals was started in 1984 and continues today.

The first Polish American bishop was Paul Peter Rhode, who was named an auxiliary bishop of

Chicago in 1908. Since that first appointment, there have been numerous priests of Polish descent named to the hierarchy, including Cardinal John Joseph Krol, who served as archbishop of Philadelphia.

Polish American Catholics developed support organizations in the nineteenth century, including the Polish Roman Catholic Union, founded in 1873. In 1886 it began providing life insurance to its members. These organizations assisted members and also proved determined to assist both the United States and their homeland. In World War I, more than two hundred thousand Poles fought for the United States, while another twenty-eight thousand formed the Polish Army of America to fight in France. During World War II, Poles fought in great numbers for the United States. At the same time, Polish Americans contributed financial and material resources to assist the millions of victims of the Nazi and Soviet occupations of Poland. Polish Americans also promoted an independent Poland and were horrified that the Nazi oppression was replaced in 1945 by a brutal Soviet-based dictatorship, which endured until 1989. Immense joy accompanied the election of Cardinal Karol Wojtyla as Pope Blessed John Paul II in 1978.

According to the 2000 census, there are more than nine million Polish Americans, the vast majority of whom are Catholic. They reside in the largest numbers around New York City and Chicago.

Polish National Catholic Church. *See* Polish Catholics

Ponce de León, Juan (1460–1521)

The Spanish explorer best known for his discovery of Florida, which he claimed for Spain, and his search for the fabled Fountain of Youth, Juan Ponce de León was born in the province of Campos to a Spanish noble family. He grew up among the aristocracy, serving as a page to Pedro Nuñez de Guzmán, the tutor of Infante Don Fernando, brother of Emperor Charles V.

In 1493 de León sailed to Hispaniola (Santo Domingo) with Columbus on his second voyage. When, in 1502, Nicolás de Ovando was named governor of Hispaniola, the island was in a state of chaos owing to an uprising of the local population.

De León proved especially useful in the restoration of order. As a reward, Ovando named him his lieutenant. After hearing stories from the locals that the neighboring island, which became Puerto Rico, had wealth, Ponce received permission to mount an expedition in 1508. On the basis of the various treasures he found there, he was named governor of the island. He was later removed for his harsh treatment of the natives.

While serving as governor, de León likely first heard rumors of what became his most famous obsession — the Fountain of Youth. Tales of a spring that provided both youth and vitality reminded de León of the common European legend of the *fons juventutis,* and after further investigation, he determined the possible source of the stories were to be found in Bimini, north of Hispaniola. In 1513, with permission from Charles V, de León set sail with three ships. On March 27 he reached a coast that he named Florida after its lush vegetation. He landed on April 2 at what became St. Augustine and formally claimed the region for Spain; he then set sail for Hispaniola as he lacked sufficient troops to make a permanent settlement, but the native tribes were very aggressive. In 1521 he set sail again to settle the newly discovered regions. Landing on the Florida coast, he set out to explore and was attacked by natives while attempting to erect a permanent settlement. Wounded in battle, de León was forced to abandon his explorations and set sail back to Hispaniola. He died soon after from his wounds.

Poncet, Joseph Anthony de la Rivière (May 17, 1610–June 18, 1675)

A Jesuit missionary among the Algonquin Indians, Joseph Anthony de la Rivière Poncet was born in Paris and entered the Society of Jesus in 1629. After studies at Clermont, Rome, and Rouen, he taught at Orléans from 1631 to 1634. In 1638 he sailed for Canada and service in the Canadian missions. Upon arrival, he was sent immediately to the Huron mission. In 1645 Poncet founded an Algonquin mission on the Island of St. Mary. Soon after, while journeying to Québec, he was taken captive by an Iroquois party. As was often the case, Poncet was tortured by his captors and was saved from death only by a rescue party of French soldiers. His companion, Mathurin Franchelot, was burned at the stake. In 1657 Poncet was sent back to France after a disagreement with his superiors. He later served on the island of Martinique, where he died.

Pontifical College Josephinum

A seminary and college in Columbus, Ohio, founded in 1888 by the German immigrant priest Monsignor Joseph Jessing, the Pontifical College Josephinum was granted pontifical status in 1892 by Pope Leo XIII; it remains the only pontifical seminary in the Western Hemisphere. Joseph Jessing was born in in Münster, Westphalia, in 1836. After a distinguished but obligatory service in the Prussian Army, he left Germany in 1867 and emigrated to the United States in order to remove all possible obstacles to his vocation to the priesthood. The next year, he began studies at Mount St. Mary's Seminary in Cincinnati and was ordained by the first bishop of Columbus, Sylvester Harden Rosecrans, on July 16, 1870.

Assigned to Sacred Heart Church in Pomeroy, Ohio, Father Jessing soon discovered the considerable problems faced by the large number of orphan boys in his parish. In 1873, with the assistance of the Brothers of St. Francis, he opened St. Joseph Orphanage, a shelter and home funded chiefly through the German-language newspaper *Ohio* (later, *Ohio Waisenfreund*, "Ohio Orphan's Friend"), which Father Jessing edited and published. In August 1877 Jessing moved the orphanage to downtown Columbus, Ohio, as it provided easier access to the railroad.

In 1888 Father Jessing received a request from four older boys to study for the priesthood, a request that coincided with the desire expressed among readers of the *Ohio* for an increase in German-speaking priests. He placed an advertisement in the paper that he was willing to sponsor some boys for seminary studies. Father Jessing received more than forty applicants, and twenty-three were accepted. As he lacked the financial means to sponsor all of them, he decided instead to start his own seminary. The first classes began on September 1, 1888, and the school offered programs for a minor seminary (high school and college pre-theology) and a major seminary (college pretheology and

theology). The first six seminarians were ordained in June 1899.

By the time of the first seminarians' ordinations, the college had already been placed under the protection of the Holy See through the promulgation of pontifical status in 1892. The unique status of the college meant that it was under the direction of the Congregation for Seminaries and Institutes of Study, with the apostolic nuncio to the United States as its chancellor. At the same time, the Josephinum was incorporated under the laws of the state of Ohio in 1894. Its constitution was first approved by Pope Pius XI in 1938 and was revised and approved by the Congregation for Catholic Education in 1996.

As its origins through Jessing made logical, the Josephinum devoted much of its early energy to providing priests for the many German immigrants in the United States. In the years after World War I, it became an important center for training priests from dioceses that lacked their own seminaries. In 1931 the Josephinum moved to its present location north of downtown Columbus. The orphanage closed in 1932, and changes in curriculum reflected the more formal development of distinct but interrelated college and seminary programs. The first college graduation took place in June 1953, and in 1958 the college dedicated improved facilities for that department. The high school closed in 1967 owing to a decline in students.

In recent decades, the Josephinum has accepted seminarians from around the world, including Eastern Europe, Asia, and Africa. In all, over 1,500 priests have been educated at the Josephinum. The College of Liberal Arts has also graduated over 350 students.

Poor Clares (P.C., O.S.C., P.C.C., P.C.P.A.)

The so-called Second Order of Franciscans, founded by St. Clare in 1214, the Poor Clares spread swiftly and became one of the greatest orders of the Middle Ages. In the wake of the suppression of the order in Italy by the anti-Catholic government, two Poor Clares, Maria Maddelena and Maria Costanza Bentivoglio, traveled to the United States at the urging of Pope Blessed Pius IX in response to a request from the Third Order Regulars of St. Francis. After starting a community in Cleveland, they were joined by a community of German Poor Clares; these sisters eventually assumed control of the convent and became members of the Colettine reform. The two nuns went to Omaha, Nebraska, and founded a new community, approved in 1882, through the generous donation of John Creighton. From this community developed a Poor Clare presence in the United States that is found in twenty-six states.

Poor Handmaids of Jesus Christ

A community of women religious founded by Catherine Kasper in 1851, the Poor Handmaids of Jesus Christ are also called the Ancilla Domini Sisters. Formal approval was granted by Pope Leo XIII. By the time of Catherine Kasper's death in 1898 the congregation had houses in Germany, Austria, England, Holland, and North America. The first community in the United States was begun in the Diocese of Fort Wayne, at Hesse Cassel in 1863, through the appeal of Bishop Joseph Henry Luers. From this house was founded a community in Chicago. Meanwhile, by 1869, the Fort Wayne sisters had expanded to include a hospital, a parochial school, and soon the motherhouse of the congregation in the United States. The sisters eventually established houses in several cities, including Chicago, Philadelphia, and St. Louis. The chief house in the United States is in Donaldson, Indiana.

Popes and America. *See* Holy See–U.S. Relations

Portier, Michael (September 7, 1795–May 14, 1859)

A missionary in Alabama and the first bishop of Mobile from 1829 to 1859, Michael Portier was born in Montbrison, France, and entered the seminary in Lyons. While still studying, he encountered the appeal for missionaries in America that was then being made by Bishop Louis Dubourg, S.S., of New Orleans.

Accepting the challenge, Portier traveled to the United States with Bishop Dubourg and completed his seminary studies at Mount St. Mary's College in Emmitsburg, Maryland. He was ordained in September 1818 and set out for New Orleans. There, Portier served in a number of posts, including missionary along the Gulf Coast. On November 5,

1826, he was consecrated the first vicar apostolic of Alabama and the Floridas by Bishop Joseph Rosati, C.M.

Portier proved a vigorous vicar apostolic, establishing parishes in Mobile and Pensacola, but he proved unable for various reasons to keep priests and found himself serving alone. A fire in 1827 destroyed much of Mobile, including the parish church. Portier sailed for Europe to appeal for help and found a warm reception from the Society for the Propagation of the Faith.

By 1830 and his return home, he had four priests and several seminarians at his disposal. His efforts at reconstituting the ecclesiastical presence were assisted further by the founding of Spring Hill College (which was staffed by the Jesuits after 1847) and the arrival of the Visitandine Sisters, the Daughters of Charity, and the Brothers of the Sacred Heart. The Daughters also established Providence Hospital after being forced out of the City Hospital in 1852 by anti-Catholic protests.

Portier continued to stabilize and then expand the Catholic presence in Alabama throughout his remaining years. By the time of his death, the population had grown from two thousand to ten thousand. Portier also attended all but the First Provincial Council of Baltimore and the First Plenary Council in 1852. He is credited with establishing the innovation of diocesan consultors; over the next years, dioceses all over the world adopted the consultors for their diocesan structures.

Portland in Maine, Diocese of

Established on July 29, 1853, by Pope Blessed Pius IX, the Diocese of Portland in Maine encompasses the entire state. It is a suffragan see of the Archdiocese of Boston.

The origins of the diocese are traced to the efforts of French missionaries and settlers to establish a colony in the early seventeenth century. A settlement was started on the island of Sainte-Croix (modern-day De Monts Island) where, in July 1604, the first Mass was offered in New England by Father Nicholas Aubray of Paris.

In 1613 French Jesuits established a mission on Mount Desert Island to evangelize among the Abenaki. The settlements struggled to survive, but they were also a base for the important expedition of Samuel de Champlain and the missionary labors of several priests, including the Jesuit Fathers Pierre Biard and Enemond Masse, who labored among the Abenaki. They were followed by Capuchins who in 1633 founded missions along the Penobscot River. In 1646 Father Gabriel Druillettes founded the Assumption Mission among the Abenaki. His work was advanced by Franciscan Father Laurent Molin and a Father Morain among the Penobscots and Passamaquoddy Indians. The chapels and missions founded by these and other heroic priests were systematically eradicated by the English in the early eighteenth century. Among the dead was Father Sebastian Râle, who had founded a chapel at Norridgewock and served for thirty years among the Indians. He was brutally murdered in 1724, and his remarkable dictionary in Abenaki was carried off and eventually put on display at Harvard University.

The Abenaki remained faithful to the Catholic faith and requested a priest from Bishop John Carroll in 1784. The Sulpician Father François Ciquard served among them for nearly a decade. They later received the support of Bishop Jean-Louis Lefebvre de Cheverus of Boston.

In 1825 Bishop Benedict Joseph Fenwick, the Jesuit successor to Bishop de Cheverus in Boston, visited Maine and in 1833 raised a monument to Father Râle at Norridgewock. Priests were serving in the region again, as Father Charles Ffrench was at St. Joseph's in Eastport and Father Denis Ryan was at Augusta.

The white Catholic population, meanwhile, continued to grow as immigrants from Ireland had been arriving in larger numbers. By the 1850s it was deemed time for a bishop to be appointed to oversee the Catholic community in Maine.

The creation of the Diocese of Portland in Maine was met with a harsh anti-Catholic reaction from the Know-Nothings. The church in Manchester, New Hampshire, was destroyed by a mob, and Jesuit Father John Bapst was assaulted by Protestants at Old Town in 1854, tarred and feathered, and almost killed. The event horrified the nation and brought recriminations against the attackers and their anti-Catholicism.

The first bishop of Portland was Henry B. Coskery, the vicar general of the Archdiocese of Baltimore, but he declined the appointment. Pope Blessed Pius IX then named Father David W. Bacon. He was consecrated on April 22, 1855, and was installed in the diocese on May 31, 1855. Bishop Bacon purchased land for the building of the Cathedral of the Immaculate Conception and led the Catholics during a difficult time of anti-Catholicism. In July 1866 the city of Portland was ravaged by a great fire that left more than ten thousand people homeless, and Church property was devastated, including the cathedral, the bishop's residence, a convent, and a chapel. The cathedral was rebuilt, and Bishop Bacon also opened new parochial schools and academies.

In 1874 he traveled to Rome with his friend Archbishop John McCloskey of New York. He fell ill at Brest and was taken back to New York, where he died on November 5, 1874.

Bishop Bacon was followed by Bishop James Augustine Healy, a priest of Boston. He was consecrated on June 2, 1875. The first African-American priest, Bishop Healy was also the first African-American bishop. He assumed direction over a diocese with considerable debts and established a strict financial regime. He also welcomed a large number of French Canadians, who migrated to Maine and established residences and businesses. Some ten congregations of women religious accepted Bishop Healy's invitation to come to the diocese, as did Dominicans and Marist priests. He used the new priests and nuns to evangelize the rural areas of the state, also establishing orphanages and homes for the disabled and needy. Bishop Healy died on August 5, 1900, having faithfully served the diocese for a quarter of a century.

The third bishop of Portland, William H. O'Connell, later became a cardinal. A priest of Boston and the rector of the North American College in Rome, he was consecrated on May 19, 1901. His brief tenure as bishop included being sent in 1905 by Pope St. Pius X as a special envoy to Japan. He earned the respect of the pope, who named him on January 26, 1906, the titular archbishop of Tomi and coadjutor of Boston. He succeeded to the see the next year and became a cardinal in 1911.

Bishop O'Connell was succeeded by Father Louis Walsh, a priest of Boston. Consecrated a bishop on October 18, 1906, he was a noted scholar and restored monuments and in 1908 founded the Maine Catholic Historical Society. He commemorated the lives and times of the early missionaries in Maine. Bishop Walsh also promoted the National Catholic Educational Association and revitalized the school system. He led the faithful as well through World War I, supporting the nation's military efforts. Bishop Walsh died on May 12, 1924.

The fifth bishop of Portland, John G. Murray, had served as an auxiliary bishop of Hartford since 1919. Installed on October 12, 1925, he was bishop at the start of the Great Depression and helped Catholics survive the severe financial and economic hardships of the time. He was appointed archbishop of St. Paul on October 29, 1931.

His successor was Joseph E. McCarthy, a priest of the Archdiocese of Hartford. Bishop McCarthy was consecrated on August 24, 1932, an event that held the distinction of being the first to be broadcast on radio. His lengthy tenure extended throughout the Great Depression and World War II. He brought contemplative orders into the diocese and the return of the Jesuits, and also oversaw an extensive period of expansion. Owing to poor health, he received a coadjutor bishop, Bishop Daniel J. Feeney, in 1952. Bishop McCarthy died in 1955 and was succeeded by Bishop Feeney on September 9, 1955.

Bishop Feeney had been named an auxiliary bishop in 1946 and became the first priest of Portland to be named bishop of Portland. As the seventh bishop of Portland, he took part in the Second Vatican Council and began the work of implementing its decrees. He died on September 15, 1969, after a long illness.

Bishop Peter L. Gerety became the next bishop of Portland after serving as auxiliary bishop since 1966. Consecrated a bishop on June 1, 1966, Gerety acceded to the see on the day of Bishop Feeney's passing. He continued implementing the reforms of the council until April 2, 1974, when he was appointed the archbishop of Newark.

On December 18, 1974, Bishop Edward C. O'Leary, auxiliary bishop of Portland since 1970, was installed as the ninth bishop of Portland. His time was marked by the upheaval in the time after the Second Vatican Council, and he struggled with the departure of many priests and religious from

active ministry. He promoted lay ministries in the diocese and sought to stabilize diocesan facilities. He retired on September 27, 1988.

His successor was Bishop Joseph J. Gerry, O.S.B., a Benedictine abbot and an auxiliary bishop of Manchester since 1986. He was installed as bishop on February 21, 1989. Bishop Gerry faced a dramatic shift in the Catholic population from the city to the suburbs. He inaugurated new parishes and ministries to cope with the changes and gained considerable notoriety with his book, *Ever Present Lord*. He retired on February 10, 2004.

Bishop Gerry was succeeded by Bishop Richard J. Malone, who had been an auxiliary bishop of Boston since 2000. Installed on March 31, 2004, Bishop Malone continued to implement programs for the protection of young people and to provide for the changing needs of the Catholic community at the start of the twenty-first century. In 2011 there were 185,000 Catholics, 181 priests, 300 women religious, and 64 parishes in the diocese.

Portland in Oregon, Archdiocese of

Established as the Diocese of Oregon City on July 24, 1846, by Pope Blessed Pius IX, the see was elevated to the rank of an archdiocese on July 29, 1850, and redesignated the Archdiocese of Portland in Oregon on September 26, 1928, by Pope Pius XI. The archdiocese covers counties in Oregon and has the suffragan sees of Baker, Boise City, Great Falls-Billing, and Helena. The city was settled in 1829 on the Willamette River, on the site of a former Indian compound. In 1844, the city was formally laid out and named for Portland, Maine. The choice was the result of a penny-toss ceremony. Portland was on the Oregon Trail and a crossroad during the Gold Rush era. A commercial hub, Portland marketed agriculture from the Cascade Range and Willamette Valley and began industries based on food processing and the area's natural resources. In time the city became a source of hydraulic power. The original settlement area of Portland is connected to the developing outlying districts by a series of bridges.

The Catholic history of the archdiocese opened with the arrival of the expedition of Bartolomé Ferrelo in the area. Other Europeans sailed into the region soon after, and in 1774 the Spaniard Juan

Perez, accompanied by Franciscans, was traveling in the region. In 1775 Bruno de Heceta (Hezeta) y Dudagoitia claimed present-day Oregon for Spain.

Robert Gray discovered the Columbia River in 1792, and the Lewis and Clark expedition visited the area soon after. In 1811 John Jacob Astor was trading there, and outposts of the Pacific Fur Company brought trappers into Oregon. In 1812 England claimed Oregon, but in 1818 it was considered a joint holding of the United States and England. Spain and Russia dropped their claims to Oregon in 1819 and 1824, respectively.

In 1830 the Willamette Valley (French Prairie) was settled by French Catholics from Canada. On February 28, 1836, Oregon was administered by the Vicariate Apostolic of Red River County. In April 1838 Father Modeste Demers and Father Francis Norbert Blanchet arrived in Oregon. Father Blanchet celebrated Mass and blessed Fort Prairie's church, dedicated to St. Paul the Apostle, on January 6, 1839. He also established missions at Fort Vancouver, Cowlitz, Oregon City, and Fort Nesqually.

By 1842 several other priests were serving in Oregon, including Fathers Anthony Langlois and John Bolduc. The famed Jesuit Father Pierre-Jean De Smet was also at Fort Vancouver, and he worked with Father Blanchet on mission plans and then went to Europe to find priests, religious, and funding. He recruited five Jesuits and the Sisters of Notre Dame de Namur. The mission of St. Francis Xavier opened soon after.

On December 1, 1843, the Vicariate Apostolic of the Oregon Territory was established by Pope Gregory XVI, and Father Blanchet was appointed vicar apostolic and spent two years in Europe, seeking funds and religious volunteers. On July 24, 1846, the Diocese of Oregon City was created, at the same time as the start of the Dioceses of Walla Walla and Vancouver Island. A year later, the Whitman Massacre and the false charges made against the Church by Protestants threatened all mission efforts. The charges were publicly refuted, and evangelization continued. Oregon entered the Union in 1859 as the thirty-third state. The next year, on July 29, 1850, the diocese was elevated to the rank of an archdiocese and Bishop Blanchet became an archbishop.

Archbishop Blanchet and the archdiocese faced anti-Catholic groups and interference by the U.S. government in the Indian missions. He sent Father Jean Baptiste Abraham Brouillet to Archbishop James Roosevelt Bayley of Baltimore to find a way to protect the missions. Archbishop Bayley, a convert and nephew of St. Elizabeth Ann Seton, established the Bureau of Catholic Indian Missions as a result.

In Oregon, the Gold Rush and growing settlements made the shortage of mission personnel critical. Archbishop Blanchet toured dioceses in South America and brought back funds. Parishes were established throughout the region. St. John Church opened in Oregon City in 1846, followed by St. Paul Church in St. Paul. In late 1851 Father James Croke served Portland at Immaculate Conception.

In 1862 Archbishop Blanchet moved his episcopal residence to Portland, making Immaculate Conception Church his co-cathedral. He founded a diocesan newspaper, a hospital, and other diocesan agencies. He likewise convoked a provincial council in St. Paul in 1848, attended the First and Second Councils of Baltimore in 1852 and 1866, and journeyed to Rome for the First Vatican Council in 1869–70. Exhausted by his labors, Archbishop Blanchet was given a coadjutor archbishop, Charles J. Seghers, in 1878. Archbishop Blanchet retired on December 12, 1880. At the time of his retirement, the archdiocese had twenty-three churches, twenty-three priests, almost seventy nuns, schools for boys and girls, and various mission schools for Native Americans.

Prior to his appointment as coadjutor bishop of Portland, Archbishop Seghers had served as bishop of Vancouver Island. He acceded to the see on December 20, 1880, and began visiting every community in the archdiocese, promoting educational programs, including bringing in the Benedictines to direct Mount Angel Abbey. He brought some thirty priests to serve the archdiocese and reduced its debt. In 1884, however, Archbishop Seghers resigned from the archdiocese and was transferred to Vancouver Island. He returned also to Alaska, where he had pioneered missionary efforts. Archbishop Seghers was killed by a deranged trail guide on November 28, 1886.

Archbishop Seghers was succeeded by Bishop

William Hickley Gross, who had served as bishop of Savannah since 1873. Installed in the Archdiocese of Portland on March 31, 1885, he dedicated the new cathedral and visited parishes, missions, and religious communities throughout the archdiocese. He also established the first archdiocesan community of religious women, the future Sisters of St. Mary of Oregon. He likewise invited the Christian Brothers from San Francisco to run St. Michael's College in Portland, as well as Dominican Sisters, the Sisters Adorers of the Precious Blood, and the Sisters of Mercy. During a retreat at Annapolis, Maryland, Archbishop Gross became ill and died soon after on November 14, 1898.

The fourth archbishop of Portland was Bishop Alexander Christie, who had served as the bishop of Vancouver Island since 1898. Promoted to the archdiocese on March 4, 1899, he was installed on June 15, 1899, and, like his predecessors, made a visit to parishes, missions, and religious communities. In September 1901 he founded the University of Portland, and in 1903 he played a major role in the formation of the Diocese of Baker. Innovative and energetic about evangelization, Archbishop Christie used a railroad chapel car to bring the faith to outposts of the diocese. He likewise led the Church in Oregon during World War I.

When the infamous Oregon School Bill passed in November 1922, he started a campaign to keep parochial schools from being outlawed by the state. He was aided by religious and civil rights groups across the country, and although he did not live to see the U.S. Supreme Court reject the law as unconstitutional, he was honored as the main defender of Catholic civil rights. Archbishop Christie was named an Assistant at the Papal Throne during the defensive campaign and died on April 6, 1925.

The fifth archbishop of Portland, Edward D. Howard, had served as an auxiliary bishop of Davenport since 1924. He was installed in Portland on August 25, 1926, and embarked on a tenure that stretched many decades. Two years after his arrival, the archdiocese was renamed the Archdiocese of Portland in Oregon on September 26, 1928. The archbishops reorganized the offices and agencies for diocesan administration and introduced new organizations, such as the Holy Name Society and the St. Vincent de Paul Society.

The archdiocese was beset by the problems of the Great Depression, and Archbishop Howard launched pastoral and charitable efforts for those in need. He then led the Catholics of Portland through World War II. He was named an Assistant at the Papal Throne in 1939 and presided over the rapid expansion of the archdiocese in the postwar era, including the construction of schools, a chancery and rectory for the cathedral, and the acquisition of the *Catholic Sentinel* to serve as the archdiocesan newspaper. His last years were taken up with the Second Vatican Council. He retired on December 6, 1966. At the time of his death on January 2, 1983, at the age of 105, he was the oldest bishop in the world.

The sixth archbishop of Portland, Robert J. Dwyer, had been bishop of Reno since 1952. Installed on February 6, 1967, he immediately launched a fundraising program to pay off a large archdiocesan debt. He was also a noted author and columnist. Owing to long-standing health issues, including a weak cardiac condition, he resigned on January 22, 1974, and died two years later.

Archbishop Dwyer's successor, Bishop Cornelius M. Power, had been the bishop of Yakima since 1969. Installed on April 17, 1974, Archbishop Power began a series of reorganizational programs to ensure financial stability. He began vicariates in the diocese, including one for the growing Hispanic and Asian populations. He likewise organized the Oregon Catholic Conference and reorganized Catholic Charities and Catholic media outreach in the archdiocese.

Archbishop Power retired on July 3, 1986, and was succeeded by Bishop William J. Levada, the eighth archbishop of Portland, who would eventually become a cardinal. Bishop Levada had served as an official of the Congregation for the Doctrine of the Faith in Rome and as an auxiliary bishop of Los Angeles since 1983.

Installed on September 21, 1986, Archbishop Levada commissioned a $5 million fund drive for a retirement fund and celebrated the 150th anniversary celebration of the archdiocese in 1996. He served as the sole American bishop on the editorial committee of the Holy See's Commission for the *Catechism of the Catholic Church*. On August 17, 1995, he was appointed coadjutor archbishop of

San Francisco and acceded to the see on December 27, 1995. On May 13, 2005, Pope Benedict XVI appointed him prefect of the Congregation for the Doctrine of the Faith. He became a cardinal on March 24, 2006.

Archbishop Levada was followed in Oregon by Bishop Francis George, O.M.I., who, like his predecessor, went on to become a cardinal. Bishop George had served as the bishop of Yakima since 1990. Appointed the ninth archbishop of Portland in Oregon on April 30, 1996, he was installed on May 27, 1996. He visited parishes and began programs for those with disabilities. He also fought an effort to use a tape recording of a sacramental confession made at the Lane County jail in a criminal case. In 1997 the Ninth Circuit Court of Appeals ruled that the tape recording was unconstitutional and illegal. Less than a year after his arrival in Portland, Archbishop George was transferred by Pope Blessed John Paul II to Chicago on April 8, 1997. He was subsequently made a cardinal on February 21, 1998.

On October 28, 1997, Bishop John G. Vlazny, bishop of Winona since 1987, was appointed the tenth archbishop of Portland. During his time as archbishop, the archdiocese has continued to develop ministries to meet the changing demographics of the region, including the significant growth of the Catholic population over the last decade.

The archdiocese was also troubled by the sex abuse scandal, including some 150 cases that led to the difficult decision to file for bankruptcy in 2004. The action made Portland the first Catholic archdiocese or diocese in the nation to file for bankruptcy. The archdiocese has a population of 412,000 Catholics, out of a population of more than 3.2 million, served by 300 priests, about 500 men and women religious, and 124 parishes.

Powderly, Terence (January 22, 1849–June 24, 1924)

Labor leader and director of the Knights of Labor, Terence Powderly dominated American labor throughout the 1880s. Born in northeastern Pennsylvania, he began his labor career in 1871 when he joined the Machinists' Union and Blacksmiths' Union. Three years later, he helped to launch the Industrial Brotherhood, an early but unsuccessful effort at a national labor movement. That same year, he joined the Knights of Labor, a secret society that used the traditional symbols of a secret movement (oaths, rituals, and pledges) to disguise its true purpose — promoting organized labor and attracting members without drawing the attention of the extensive antilabor forces then in the country.

While advancing through the ranks of the Knights, Powderly was elected mayor of Scranton, Pennsylvania, in 1878, holding the post until 1884. In 1879 he assumed the leadership of the Knights of Labor, succeeding Uriah Stevens, the founder. Under Powderly's leadership, the Knights enjoyed a period of swift expansion, eventually claiming membership in excess of seven hundred thousand by 1886; membership in 1879 had been a mere nine thousand.

The prosperity of the 1880s was soon recognized as the high-water mark of the Knights owing to two different challenges. First, the recently established trade unions in the American Federation of Labor began draining away members and influence, in particular the badly needed skilled workers who comprised the most important element of membership. Equally, in 1886 the Canadian province of Québec imposed with Vatican approval a strict prohibition on Catholic membership in the Knights. The prevailing view at the time was that the organization was a secret one, with rituals and possibly an anti-Catholic agenda.

Two years later, the ban was lifted through the efforts of Cardinal James Gibbons of Baltimore, but the organization was already in irreversible decline. By 1890 the Knights had lost most of its sway in the American labor movement.

Powderly, however, had played a key role in establishing an atmosphere of reconciliation between the Church and labor, giving many assurances to Cardinal Gibbons of the solid faith of the members and thereby winning his decisive support in the controversy. The rapprochement also signaled Catholic support for labor movements, backing that was further encouraged in 1893 by the promulgation of Pope Leo XIII's famed encyclical *Rerum Novarum*.

Powderly could not prevent his own ouster as president of the Knights in 1893. In 1896, he enthusiastically supported the Republican candidate for president, William McKinley. After his election, McKinley appointed Powderly commissioner general of immigration, a post he held from 1897 to 1902. By that time, he had joined the Masons and was soon married outside the Church. Although he remained friends with such Catholic leaders as Archbishop John Ireland, he nevertheless felt embittered by the Church's long-standing mistrust of organized labor. He later served as director of information for the Bureau of Immigration from 1907 to 1921 and as commissioner of conciliation in the Department of Labor. His autobiography, *The Path I Trod,* was published posthumously. He died in Washington, D.C. (*See also* Knights of Labor.)

Powers, J. F. (July 8, 1917–June 12, 1999)

Author and novelist, James Farl Powers is ranked as one of the foremost American Catholic writers of the twentieth century. Born in Jacksonville, Illinois, he studied at Northwestern University and worked in a variety of jobs in Chicago as he embarked on his career in writing. During World War II, he declared himself a conscientious objector and spent more than a year in prison. He later lived in Ireland and in the United States and taught at Marquette University, the University of Michigan, and St. John's University in Collegeville, Minnesota.

Although Powers's literary output was not large, he gained a wide following for his three collections of short stories and two novels and garnered membership in the American Academy and Institute of Arts and Letters. His 1962 novel *Morte d'Urban* won the National Book Award and Thormod Monsen Award, and his 1988 novel *Wheat That Springeth Green* won the National Book Award and was a National Book Critics Circle finalist.

Powers was noted for his brilliant skills in affectionate satire and was especially influenced by the Church. He wrote in a gentle but brilliant fashion about postwar American Catholicism, gave sharp pictures of priests (five of the eleven short stories in his 1947 collection *Prince of Darkness and Other Stories* deal with priests), and also examined the forgotten and the suffering. His writing was praised by Flannery O'Connor and Walker Percy.

Prendergast, Edmond F. (May 3, 1843–February 26, 1918)

Archbishop of Philadelphia from 1911 to 1918, Edmond F. Prendergast was born in County Tipperary, Ireland. He migrated to the United States at the age of sixteen and entered St. Charles Borromeo Seminary to study for the priesthood. Ordained in 1865, he served for several years in different pastoral assignments until 1874, when he was named pastor of St. Malachy Parish in Philadelphia, where he served for some thirty-seven years. In 1896 he was named vicar general, and the following year received appointment by Pope Leo XIII as auxiliary bishop of Philadelphia. On July 16, 1911, he succeeded Archbishop Patrick John Ryan as archbishop.

As archbishop for seven years, Prendergast focused his efforts chiefly on expanding the parishes of the archdiocese and improving the schools. Parishes were opened wherever the need was greatest, including for the Italian, Lithuanian, Slovak, Hungarian, German, and Spanish Catholic populations. He also established the Archbishop Ryan Memorial Institute for the Deaf, St. Edmond's Home for Crippled Children, and West Philadelphia Catholic High School for Boys, as well as various charitable institutions, including Misericordia Hospital and the Archbishop Ryan Memorial Library at the seminary. From 1914 to 1915, he undertook the renovation of the Cathedral of Sts. Peter and Paul.

Presentation Sisters (P.B.V.M.)

An order of women religious founded in Cork, Ireland, by Nano (Honoria) Nagle in 1775, the community initially took the name Sisters of the Sacred Heart. The name was changed in 1791 to the Presentation Sisters. The rule was approved in 1791 by Pope Pius VI. In 1800 Pope Pius VII approved them as a religious order focused on teaching. The houses spread across Ireland and arrived in England in 1833, founding a house in Manchester. They soon were established in India in 1841 and Australia in 1873.

Presentation Sisters reached San Francisco in November 1854 from Ireland under Mother M. Teresa Comerford. After overcoming many initial hardships, the sisters, with the help of Archbishop

Joseph Sadoc Alemany of San Francisco, founded two convents in the area, in Sonoma and Berkeley. Both were destroyed by the earthquake of 1906. Another convent was started in New York City in 1874. They then established houses in Iowa, Massachusetts, Rhode Island, and Nebraska. Currently, they have houses in California and South Dakota.

Preston, Thomas Scott (July 23, 1824–November 4, 1891)

Convert, preacher, and vicar general of the Archdiocese of New York, Thomas Scott Preston was born in Hartford, Connecticut. He was raised in the Episcopalian Church and eventually entered the general seminary in New York. In 1847 he received ordination as a priest and held various posts in the New York Episcopalian Church. His ordination had been delayed owing to the objections of his own bishop. Instead, he was ordained by Bishop William Heathcote DeLancey of western New York. He then undertook studies in Church history and underwent a gradual conversion toward Catholicism. He was received into the Church in November 1849 and ordained in 1850.

In 1853 Preston was named secretary to Archbishop John Hughes, and chancellor of the diocese. He subsequently served as pastor, vicar general, and diocesan administrator. Preston enjoyed the confidence of several archbishops and was especially noted for his support of papal infallibility and ultramontanism. He also was an early opponent of the tendencies toward American democracy and liberalism, marking him as one of the leading conservative clerics in the archdiocese and the Church in the eastern United States.

Preston founded (with Mother Mary Veronica Starr) and provided direction for the Sisters of the Divine Compassion. A famed preacher in the New York area, he was also a popular writer. Among his works were *Reason and Revelation* (1868), *The Divine Paraclete* (1879), *Ark of the Covenant* (1860), *Vicar of Christ* (1878), *The Protestant Reformation* (1879), *Protestantism and the Church* (1882), and *Protestantism and the Bible* (1888).

Preuss, Arthur (1871–1934)

Journalist and editor, Arthur Preuss was the son of Edward F. Preuss. Born in St. Louis, Missouri, he was baptized into the Church in January 1872 at the same time as his father, a convert from Lutheranism. He studied at St. Francis Solanus College (modern-day Quincy College), in Quincy, Illinois. After completing a master's degree, he started working for his father and wrote for the German-language Catholic daily *Die Amerika* as well as the Catholic weekly *Church Progress*. He later served as editor of *Katholisches Sontagsblatt* and *Die Glocke* before launching his own journal in 1894, the *Review* (later renamed the *Forthnightly Review*). The journal emerged as a major voice for German Catholics in the United States over the next four decades.

In his capacity as editor Preuss was engaged in some of the leading issues facing German Catholics in the United States, including the foundation of American Federation of Catholic Societies, the impact of World War I, the formation of the National Catholic Welfare Conference, and the start of the Great Depression.

Preuss also served as editor of *Die Amerika,* the *Echo* of Buffalo, and the B. Herder Publishing Company. For that company, Preuss edited the famed *Lehrbook der Dogmatik,* a ten-volume series on dogmatic theology by Joseph Pohle published between 1910 and 1918. The series became a standard text for seminaries throughout the United States in the years before the Second Vatican Council.

Preuss, Edward F. (1834–1904)

Convert and journalist Edward F. Preuss was born in Königsberg, Prussia. He was raised as a Lutheran and earned a doctorate in philosophy from the University of Königsberg in 1853 and a doctorate in theology from the University of Berlin in 1857. Over the next years, he served as a tutor, including service to the royal house of Prussia, a position that brought him into contact with the highest ranked members of the Prussian government, including the powerful Prime Minister Otto von Bismarck, as well as the Church historian Theodor Mommsen. In 1865 he wrote an anti-Catholic book attacking the dogma of the Immaculate Conception, a work that nevertheless brought him into conflict with more conservative Lutheran elements. The debates and disagreements prompted him to resign from the University of Berlin in 1868 and migrate to the

United States, where he assumed a post at the Concordia Lutheran Seminary in St. Louis.

While teaching in St. Louis, Preuss reached the decision after intense personal struggles to convert to the Catholic faith, receiving baptism in January 1872. Soon after his conversion, he was welcomed warmly by the Lutherans in St. Louis and was offered the position of assistant editor of the German Catholic newspaper *Die Amerika*. He did not assume the post until 1878. Nevertheless, under his direction, the paper expanded its circulation and became the chief publishing voice for German Catholics in the United States. For his efforts, Preuss received the Laetare Medal from the University of Notre Dame in 1887. He declined the honor in humble recognition of his conversion. His son, Arthur, followed him into prominence in German Catholic publishing.

Price, Thomas F. (August 19, 1860–September 12, 1919)

Priest and co-founder with Father James A. Walsh of Maryknoll, the Catholic Foreign Missions Society of America, Thomas F. Price was born in Wilmington, North Carolina. His parents were Alfred Lanier Price and Clarissa Bond Price, both converts. He attended a school headed by his two sisters (who both later became Sisters of Mercy) and started studies for the priesthood at the age of fifteen in Baltimore. On his way to the seminary, he barely survived a shipwreck, crediting his survival to the intervention of the Blessed Virgin Mary.

Ordained in 1886, he was the first North Carolinian to be ordained. His first assignment took him to a district in the state of some three hundred square miles. In 1894 he became chiefly engaged in missionary work throughout the state. To assist this effort, he launched a magazine called *Truth* and founded an orphanage and school to provide a training environment for future priests.

In 1904 Father Price attended the Washington conference of the Catholic Missionary Union and there met Father Walsh, then director for Boston of the Congregation for the Propagation of the Faith, who appealed for priests for the foreign mission seminary. Six years later, Father Price met Father Walsh again at the Eucharistic Congress in Montréal, and the two agreed to pool their resources to establish a seminary to train American youths for service in the foreign missions. Father Price worked subsequently to gather support from American prelates, and the topic of a seminary was placed on the agenda for the bishops' meeting at The Catholic University of America in April 1911. The bishops approved the plan, and Fathers Price and Walsh went to Rome to secure approval from the Holy See. On June 29, 1911, the Congregation for the Propagation of the Faith endorsed the foundation, and the next day the two priests were received by Pope St. Pius X, who gave them his apostolic blessing.

After handing over administration of *Truth* magazine and the orphanage, Father Price devoted his efforts to the foreign missions. He traveled extensively to promote vocations and to raise funds. Official headquarters were established at Maryknoll, near Ossining, New York, where Father Price also started the Bureau of the Immaculate Conception to foster devotion to the Blessed Virgin Mary. Only in 1918 were the first missionaries ready to embark for China. Among them was Father Price, who insisted on setting out for China despite his advancing years. Soon after arriving in Hong Kong, he fell ill and died. He was buried in Happy Valley Cemetery in Hong Kong; his heart was buried in Nevers, France, near the body of his favorite saint, Bernadette Soubirous. His remains were transferred in 1936 to Maryknoll, where he was placed beside his friend Father Walsh. (*See also* Maryknoll.)

Prohibition

The name given to the national ban on the sale, manufacture, and transportation of alcohol in the United States. Prohibition was the law of the land from 1920 to 1933, and was declared through the Eighteenth Amendment to the Constitution. It was finally repealed on December 5, 1933, through the ratification of the Twenty-first Amendment. Prohibition was generally supported by Catholics and raised important legal questions regarding the Church's use of sacramental wine.

The idea of a ban on alcohol had been proposed throughout the nineteenth century by various anti-liquor movements. The formal proposal was advanced in the Senate in 1917. Promoted with intense pressure by the temperance movement, it was subsequently approved by thirty-six states and ratified on January 16, 1919. Known popularly as the Volstead Act, the National Prohibition Act was passed through Congress over President Woodrow Wilson's veto on October 28, 1919, as the means of enforcing the Eighteenth Amendment.

The sale of alcohol was prohibited, but the mechanism for enforcement was never a comprehensive one, and from the start Americans took the law lightly. Bootlegging, criminal operations to smuggle alcohol, and speak-easy clubs serving liquor were all commonplace, especially in the cities. Organized crime, including the Mafia, profited handsomely from Prohibition, and the ban caused bloody violence as different criminal groups vied for control of illegal alcohol sales. Thousands of speak-easies were found in every city, and average Americans, from political leaders to average citizens, became willing lawbreakers by buying illegal alcohol smuggled into the country from Canada, Mexico, and elsewhere.

Many Catholics had long supported the cause of temperance, including Archbishop John Ireland of Minneapolis, who had been a key figure in the formation of the Catholic Total Abstinence Union of America (CTAU). As the campaign to ban alcohol progressed in the first decades of the twentieth century and grew sharper and more severe in tone, Catholic support declined. Cardinal John Gibbons addressed the CTAU in 1891 and spoke bluntly about the dangers of hypocrisy and the simply impractical realities of enforcing such a prohibition.

The Volstead Act included a provision by which liquor intended for medical and sacramental use was exempt. Thus the Catholic Church received a dispensation from the law when it came to the use of wine. However, some states, such as Oklahoma, passed "bone dry laws" that outlawed every form of alcohol, including sacramental wine. The State Supreme Court ruled in favor of the Church, and by 1926 priests were able to use a federal form (Form 1412) to ensure they could say Mass.

Nevertheless, Catholics generally came to oppose Prohibition for several reasons. First, as predicted by Catholic opponents, the law placed citizens in the position of disobeying a ridiculous law that could not be enforced and was broken on a regular basis by much of the population. Second, the law shut down many traditional social clubs for the Irish and Italians. Third, the law exposed Catholics

to new accusations of unpatriotic behavior because so many members of organized crime were Italians and Irish and hence deemed Catholics.

The unpopularity of Prohibition among Catholics was soon shared by most Americans, and the Great Depression only added to its unpopularity. On March 23, 1933, President Franklin Delano Roosevelt signed the Cullen-Harrison Act, an amendment to the Volstead Act, which permitted the manufacture and sale of certain kinds of alcoholic beverages. On December 5, 1933, the formal ratification of the Twenty-first Amendment repealed the Eighteenth Amendment.

Pro-Life Movement. *See* Abortion

Providence, Diocese of

Established on April 16, 1872, by Pope Blessed Pius IX, the Diocese of Providence serves the state of Rhode Island. The diocese is a suffragan of the Archdiocese of Hartford. The city was founded as a colony in 1636 by Roger Williams, who had been banished for his religious beliefs by Plymouth Colony. Williams received the land from the Narragansett Indian chiefs Canonicus and Miantonomi. He had treated the local tribes with courtesy and respect and had won their confidence. King Philip's War, which was European in origin but played out in the American colonies from 1675 to 1676, halted development for a time. In 1680, however, Pardon Tillinghast built a wharf at Providence and started the lucrative trade of molasses and rum for slaves. Providence and Rhode Island prospered as an active seaport. The colony joined the American cause in the Revolutionary War. The city remains an active seaport and a commercial, financial, and industrial center.

The Catholic history of Providence began during the American Revolution, although it is probable that Native American tribes were visited by Catholic missionaries before then. During the Revolution, a French naval fleet was stationed at Newport; among the French officials was the famed leader Comte de Rochambeau. After the war, French sailors and soldiers remained in Rhode Island and established a growing Catholic community. The first-known Mass in the area was celebrated around 1780 as part of the funeral of a French naval officer.

In 1783 long-standing restrictions on Catholics were lifted by the Rhode Island Assembly. The Catholic community continued to grow in Rhode Island, and the first Mass was celebrated in Providence in 1789. In 1808 the Diocese of Boston was erected by Pope Pius VII, and the first bishop of Boston, Bishop Jean-Louis Lefebvre de Cheverus, visited Rhode Island in 1812 and celebrated Mass and confirmation. In 1837 the parish of Sts. Peter and Paul was opened in Providence. On March 17, 1844, Father William Tyler was consecrated first bishop of Hartford and took up residence at Saints Peter and Paul. The church itself was declared a cathedral in April 1847.

The Church in Rhode Island continued to develop, including the arrival of the Sisters of Mercy and the rapid growth of the Catholic population after the Civil War. The Catholic population consisted chiefly of Irish and French Canadians, but there were also Germans, Italians, Lithuanians, Poles, and Portuguese immigrants.

This progress led to the creation of the Diocese of Providence, encompassing the whole state of Rhode Island and the Massachusetts counties of Bristol, Barnstable, Dukes, and Nantucket. The first bishop of Providence was Thomas F. Hendricken, who was consecrated on April 28, 1872, and took up residence in the house traditionally used by the bishops of Hartford. In 1878 Bishop Hendricken laid the cornerstone for the present Cathedral of Saints Peter and Paul. He died on June 11, 1886, and his funeral was the first Mass celebrated in the unfinished cathedral.

The second bishop of Providence was Matthew Harkins, who was consecrated on April 14, 1887. A noted scholar, Bishop Harkins faced anti-Catholic and anti-Irish demonstrations and led a protest against the Bourn Amendment, designed to restrict the civil liberties of residents who were not landowners. Bishop Harkins built parishes and schools, and established hospitals, a home for working girls, and an infant asylum. He also supported the founding of Providence College and welcomed Dominicans and other religious communities into the diocese. In 1904 the Diocese of Fall River was created, with Providence losing the Massachusetts counties that had originally been part of the diocese. By the time of his passing on May 25, 1921, Bishop Harkins was honored as "the ideal Catholic bishop."

The third bishop of Providence was William A. Hickey, who had been the coadjutor bishop of Providence since 1919. He acceded to the see on the passing of Bishop Harkins and headed the diocese throughout the so-called Roaring Twenties and into the Great Depression. He was also confronted by a rebellion among the French Canadian Catholics of the diocese who wanted Canadian traditions to be established for their parish. After their efforts to remove Bishop Hickey by writing to the Holy See failed, the French Canadians sued the diocese in civil court and lost. Bishop Hickey excommunicated sixty-five men. The French Canadians returned to the Church two years later. Bishop Hickey died of a heart attack on October 4, 1933.

The fourth bishop of Providence was Francis P. Keough, a priest of the Hartford diocese. Consecrated on May 22, 1934, he assumed direction of the diocese in the midst of the Great Depression. He continued the projects that were started by Bishop Hickey and expanded the number of parishes and schools and started a minor seminary. He led the diocese through the demands of World War II, and promoted Catholic Charities and instituted

Cathedral of Sts. Peter and Paul in Providence

the Catholic Youth Organization in the diocese. On November 29, 1947, he was promoted to the Archdiocese of Baltimore.

Archbishop Keough was succeeded by Russell J. McVinney, who was consecrated the fifth bishop of Providence on July 14, 1948. He built Our Lady of Fátima Hospital and in 1955 established the Sisters of Our Lady of Providence. Bishop McVinney supported the Fair Housing Laws of 1965 and took part in the Second Vatican Council. The dioceses experienced substantial growth during his episcopate. In 1953 Providence became a suffragan of the newly established Hartford province, including the Archdiocese of Hartford and the Dioceses of Norwich and Bridgeport. Bishop McVinney resigned on June 12, 1971, and died on August 10, 1971.

The sixth bishop of Providence was Louis E. Gelineau, a priest of the Diocese of Burlington. He was consecrated on January 26, 1972, and confronted the difficult task of implementing the decrees of the Second Vatican Council. He was also faced with declines in the priestly and religious population, school closures, and changes in the demographics of the diocese as new immigrants arrived from Southeast Asia, Latin America, and the Caribbean. These changes required new ministry initiatives in pastoral care. He retired on June 11, 1997, the same year the diocese celebrated its 125th anniversary.

Bishop Gelineau was succeeded by Bishop Robert E. Mulvee, who had served as bishop of Wilmington from 1985 and then as coadjutor bishop of Providence with right of succession since 1995. Bishop Mulvee continued to expand the diocesan ministry, outreach to immigrants, and lay participation. He retired on March 31, 2005.

He was succeeded by Bishop Thomas J. Tobin, who had served as bishop of Youngstown since 1996. Installed as the eighth bishop of Providence on May 31, 2005, Bishop Tobin earned considerable notoriety for his writings, including a popular column, "Without a Doubt," for the diocesan newspaper and articles in a wide number of Catholic publications. Notably, in 2011 the diocese claimed more than 620,000 Catholics, comprising nearly 60 percent of the population of Rhode Island. There were also some 420 priests, 605 women religious, and 74 brothers, serving some 144 parishes.

Provincial and Plenary Councils of Baltimore. *See* Baltimore, Councils of

Pueblo, Diocese of

Established on November 15, 1941, by Pope Pius XII, the Diocese of Pueblo serves counties in southern Colorado. It is a suffragan see of the Archdiocese of Denver. Pueblo was established by James Beckwourth, a former war chief of the Crow nation, who established a trading post on the site in 1842. In 1858 a community called Fountain City developed but became part of Pueblo. The community of Pueblo grew rapidly when General W. J. Palmer started the Central Colorado Improvement Company, and the city was incorporated in 1885.

The Catholic history of Pueblo dates to the sixteenth century when Spanish Franciscans entered the region on mission tours. No permanent missions were recorded, but it is known that the Franciscans conducted an outpost of the faith on the northern route of the Santa Fe Trail from 1822 to 1872. In 1853 the region was included in the Diocese (now Archdiocese) of Santa Fe.

On June 10, 1858, the parish of Our Lady of Guadalupe in Conejos was blessed by Bishop Jean Baptiste Lamy of Santa Fe. The revered mission pioneer, Father Joseph P. Machebeuf, who would become a bishop, served the mining settlement in the area in 1860. Eight years later, the Pueblo region was included in a vicariate apostolic and then became part of the Diocese of Denver with Father Machebeuf named as the first bishop. In 1876 Denver became a state, and the population increased steadily through the expansion of the railroad and the growth of mining camps as men and women settled in the region in search of silver and gold. The new arrivals included Irish, Germans, and Lithuanians.

The faithful built parishes throughout the present diocese, and Sacred Heart Cathedral in Pueblo dates to 1872. Other historic Pueblo parishes include Christ the King, which dates from 1857, St. Joseph, from 1860, and St. Patrick's, from 1882.

Taking part in the sacrifice of World War I and the Great Depression, the Catholics of Pueblo were recognized by the Holy See. The Diocese of Denver was created a metropolitan see, and Pueblo was erected as a diocese in 1941. At its founding, the diocese contained thirty counties and had a population of some seventy-eight thousand faithful Catholics.

The first bishop of Pueblo was Joseph C. Willging, a priest of the Diocese of Helena. Consecrated on March 12, 1942, he devoted his efforts to organizing the foundational offices and ministries of the diocese. He expanded the number of parishes, started the Confraternity of Christian Doctrine, and promoted Catholic schools. To assist the process of education, he invited communities of women religious into the diocese. Bishop Willging died suddenly on March 3, 1959, of a heart attack.

The second bishop of Pueblo was Charles A. Buswell, a priest of the Oklahoma City-Tulsa diocese. Consecrated on September 30, 1959, he served as bishop during the period of the Second Vatican Council and the difficult years after it. He attended all the sessions of the council and then worked to promote its decrees, including the liturgical changes and a greater degree of lay participation in diocesan programs. He retired on September 18, 1979.

The third bishop of Pueblo, Arthur N. Tafoya, was a priest of the Archdiocese of Santa Fe. Appointed on July 1, 1980, he was consecrated a bishop on September 10, 1980, and embarked on an episcopal tenure of some twenty-nine years. He was faced immediately with the declines in priestly and religious vocations and continuing challenges in diocesan life from the post-conciliar period. Bishop Tafoya launched a diocesan process called "Our Journey Together, 1985–90" to establish guidelines for the future of the diocese. He then initiated further diocesan pastoral plans for the twenty-first century. He also established a program for the permanent diaconate and a Catholic Diocese Foundation. He retired on October 15, 2009.

On October 15, 2009, Fernando Isern, a priest of the Archdiocese of Miami, was appointed the fourth bishop of the Diocese of Pueblo. Bishop Isern was consecrated on December 10, 2009. In 2011 the diocese celebrated its 70th anniversary. There were 100,000 Catholics, 74 priests, and 53 parishes.

Pugh, George Ellis (November 28, 1822–July 19, 1876)

A jurist and the first native Ohioan to be elected to the United States Senate, George Ellis Pugh was born in Cincinnati to Lot Pugh and Rachel Anthony. He studied at Miami University in Ohio, completing a law degree and earning admission to the bar of the Supreme Court of Ohio in 1844. After serving in the Mexican-American War from 1847 to 1848, he was elected to the Ohio House of Representatives, held the post of state attorney general, and was elected to the U.S. Senate in 1855. He served until 1861, when he was defeated for reelection owing to his support of popular sovereignty. Throughout the Civil War, he pushed for the exercise of all forms of constitutional power by the federal government to ensure the survival of the Union. He was defeated, however, in his bids for lieutenant governor of Ohio in 1863 and for a return to the House of Representatives in 1864. Although elected a delegate to the constitutional convention of Ohio in 1872, he declined to serve. Pugh was a convert to the Church in 1855, with his wife, Thérèse Chalfant.

Pulaski, Casimir (March 4, 1748–October 11, 1779)

A Polish patriot and soldier who assisted the American cause during the American Revolution and served on the staff of General George Washington, Count Casimir Pulaski was born at Winiary, Poland, the eldest son of Count Joseph Pulaski and Maria Zislinska. His father intended his son to follow him into the law and provided him also with comprehensive training as a soldier. In 1768, however, Pulaski became one of the leaders, under his father's direction, of the movement to free Poland from Russian domination. The confederation was expelled from Poland to Moldavia, where they seized the monastery of Berdichev and withstood a siege by Russian forces for several weeks.

The following year, the elder Pulaski was arrested and died in the custody of the Russians. Casimir Pulaski embarked on another revolt, this time sparking a rebellion that soon encompassed much of Poland and Lithuania. Defeated by the Russians at Lomazy, near Wladowa, he spent the winter of 1769–70 in the Carpathian Mountains. In August 1770 he seized the monastery of Czestochowa and grimly survived a siege until January 1771, when the Russians withdrew. The subsequent campaign against the Russians proved a failure, and Pulaski fled in 1772 to Turkey and then France after the interventions of Prussia and Austria caused the partition of Poland. His family's holdings had been confiscated.

In October 1776 Pulaski offered his services to Benjamin Franklin, then serving as American agent in France. He landed at Boston in July 1777 and entered into the service of General George Washington. He demonstrated skill and bravery at the Battle of Brandywine in 1777 and was commissioned in September 1777 by the Continental Congress with the rank of brigadier. He distinguished himself at the Battle of Germantown in October 1777 and in the New Jersey campaign during that winter. In March 1778 he resigned his command to organize an independent corps

Count Casimir Pulaski

called the Pulaski Legion, with headquarters in Baltimore.

The unit under his flamboyant command took part in several battles and entered Charleston, South Carolina, in May 1779, holding the city for several days against British efforts to recapture the strategically important site. In the siege of Savannah, Georgia, he commanded American and French cavalry and was wounded in the leg. Taken on board the brig *Wasp*, he died from his wounds and was buried at sea off St. Helena's Island, South Carolina.

Purcell, John Baptist (February 26, 1800–July 4, 1883)

Bishop of Cincinnati from 1833 to 1850 and the first archbishop from 1850 to 1883, John Baptist Purcell was born in Mallow, Ireland, but was forced to leave his native country in order to receive an education, owing to the harsh penal laws under the British at that time. After reaching Baltimore, Purcell earned a teacher's certificate at Asbury College and worked as a private tutor for the children of the most prominent families of Baltimore. In June 1820 he fulfilled a longtime hope and entered Mount St. Mary's Seminary in Emmitsburg, Maryland, to study for the priesthood. Given his

background, he served both as a student preparing for ordination and as a teacher of the classics. After receiving minor orders from Archbishop Ambrose Maréchal of Baltimore in 1823, he was sent to complete his studies in the Sulpician Seminaries of Issy and Paris. On May 26, 1826, he was ordained in the cathedral of Paris. After further studies, he returned to the United States to serve as a professor at Mount St. Mary's Seminary, where he later became president.

In August 1833 Purcell was appointed bishop of Cincinnati, succeeding the beloved Bishop Edward D. Fenwick, O.P. He attended the sessions of the Third Provincial Council of Baltimore, which opened on the day of his consecration, and then set out for Cincinnati, where he was met by Bishops Benedict Joseph Flaget, John B. David of Bardstown, Frederick Résé of Detroit, and a few priests. At the age of thirty-three, he inherited a diocese that had only one church and encompassed the entire state of Ohio.

The first and most pressing problem facing the new bishop was providing pastoral care for the many German and Irish immigrants who had been settling in large numbers in the city and throughout Ohio. The influx had also increased as a result of the opening of the Miami Canal in 1828 and the expansion of Cincinnati as a railroad center in Ohio. In 1834 Bishop Purcell opened the city's first German parish; in 1839 he established an orphanage for German boys and four years later founded an orphanage for German girls.

Marking the period of expansion for the Church in the city was the consecration in 1846 of the new cathedral of St. Peter's, built of Dayton limestone. In 1851 Bishop Purcell was also pleased to establish Mount St. Mary's of the West, a seminary. Needing priests to provide ministry for the diocese, he made several trips to European seminaries to encourage seminarians and priests eager to serve in the Ohio missions. He found support from a pool of talented young priests, including Fathers Joseph P. Machebeuf (later first bishop of Denver) and Jean

Baptiste Lamy (later first archbishop of Santa Fe). By 1847 the numbers spoke for themselves: ninety thousand Catholics, eighty churches and chapels, and seventy-seven priests. The rapid growth of the diocese and the success of Bishop Purcell led to the decision in 1850 by Pope Blessed Pius IX to elevate Cincinnati to an archdiocese. The pallium was conferred on Archbishop Purcell by the pope, who also declared him an Assistant at the Pontifical Throne in appreciation of his personal labors. The new ecclesiastical province of Cincinnati had for suffragans the Dioceses of Cleveland, Detroit, Indianapolis, and Louisville.

Archbishop Purcell continued to meet the needs of the Catholics in Cincinnati, finding much needed support from the religious orders and communities he invited into the archdiocese. The communities included the Sisters of Charity, who took the name of the Sisters of Charity of Cincinnati; Jesuit Fathers, who assumed direction over St. Mary's College in 1840; the Sisters of Notre Dame de Namur in 1840; the Precious Blood Fathers in 1840; the Franciscan Fathers in 1844; the Ursulines in 1845; the Sisters of St. Dominic in 1851; the Sisters of Charity in 1852; the Good Shepherd Sisters in 1857; the Sisters of Mercy in 1858; the Sisters of the Poor of St. Francis in 1858; the Ladies of the Sacred Heart in 1869; and the Passionist Fathers in 1870. In 1852 the Sisters of Charity established St. John's Hospital, and in 1858 the Sisters of St. Francis founded St. Mary's Hospital.

The remarkable progress of the Church in Cincinnati caused a severe anti-Catholic reaction in Ohio that was expressed by the Know-Nothings, increasing nativist tendencies, and blatant anti-Catholicism. Then Archbishop Purcell engaged in a series of public debates in 1837 against anti-Catholics. In the 1840s, the Catholic paper the *Catholic Telegraph* refuted anti-Catholic propaganda and nativist charges against the German Catholics and immigrants. Even more severe were the eruptions of public violence in the 1850s. In 1853 Archbishop Purcell hosted the papal nuncio to Brazil, Archbishop Gaetano Bedini. A mob attacked the cathedral and attempted to lynch the papal representative. His life was saved only by the police. Similar troubles occurred again in 1855 when nativists stirred up a riot against German Catholics. Militia were needed to disperse the mob, including the use of artillery.

Archbishop Purcell attended the First Vatican Council in 1869–70. Although he did not support the proclamation of papal infallibility by the council, he gave his unstinting acceptance once it had been approved, declaring in a sermon he preached in the cathedral, "I am here to proclaim my belief in the infallibility of the pope in the words of the Holy Father defining the doctrine." He celebrated his Golden Jubilee of ordination in May 1876. By the time of the anniversary, the archdiocese boasted over 150,000 Catholics (out of a population of over 300,000) served by 150 diocesan and 50 religious priests.

By 1876, however, Purcell and the archdiocese were confronted by the financial scandal that clouded his final years. The finances of the archdiocese had been left in the hands of his brother, Father Edward Purcell, and the priest had acted as an informal bank for Catholics who were fearful of putting their funds in banks owing to the instability that had characterized the Civil War period. The financial Panic of 1873 caused an initial run on Father Purcell's financial arrangement, and by 1878 the bank's resources had been exhausted. Inevitably, legal action followed, and the archdiocese was forced to assume some $200,000 of the debt, but the impact of the scandal brought bankruptcies, lost savings, and financial problems for Catholics throughout Ohio. The archdiocese was also forced to close the seminary, and the progress of the Church in the region was damaged for decades to come.

In January 1880 William Henry Elder, bishop of Natchez, was appointed coadjutor archbishop; he assumed administrative control in April 1880. Archbishop Purcell's health, already strained by the financial crisis, continued to deteriorate. He died three years later with his reputation severely damaged by what came to be called the Purcell Failure. The end of his time as archbishop overshadowed the immense achievement of his years as shepherd of the archdiocese. By 1880 the Church in Ohio boasted over 450,000 Catholics, 400 churches and chapels, 450 priests, 3 seminaries, 250 parochial schools, and 20 orphanages; in the archdiocese itself, there were 180,000 Catholics.

Putzer, Joseph (March 4, 1836–May 15, 1904)
Theologian, canonist, and writer, Joseph Putzer was born at Rodaneck, in Tyrol, Austria. He entered the Congregation of the Most Holy Redeemer in 1856, studied at Mautern, Austria, and was ordained in August 1859. Migrating to the United States, he arrived in New York in August 1876 and was assigned to parish work in Baltimore. In 1887 he was named to head the chair of moral theology and canon law at Ilchester College in Maryland. One of the most respected canonists of his time, he also wrote extensively for periodicals and journals, his work often appearing under the initials "J. P." Among his writings were *Civiltà Cattolica* in 1893, *Il Monitore* in 1897, and the *Jubilæum anni 1901 — Commentarium*. He died at Ilchester.

Quarter, William J. (1806–48)

The first bishop of the Diocese of Chicago, serving from 1844 to 1848, William J. Quarter was born in Ireland. He began his studies at St. Patrick's Seminary in Maynooth, Ireland, and in 1822 traveled to the United States, where he completed preparation for the priesthood at Mount St. Mary's College in Emmitsburg, Maryland. Ordained on September 29, 1829, he spent the next years in ministry in New York, earning for himself a sound reputation as a pastor. When, therefore, on November 23, 1843, Pope Gregory XVI established the Diocese of Chicago, Quarter was named its first bishop.

Bishop Quarter arrived in Chicago on May 5, 1844, following his consecration by Bishop John Hughes. His diocese encompassed the entire state of Illinois and contained eighteen churches and eight priests. He thus took as his first task increasing the number of clergy, and by the end of the first year he had recruited fifteen additional priests. He also founded a school for boys, the College of St. Mary, and received permission to establish the University of St. Mary of the Lake to train future priests. To raise funds for the seminary, Bishop Quarter petitioned Catholics across the country and the missionary societies of Europe. On July 4, 1846, he dedicated the main building of the new institution. That same year, the Sisters of Mercy sent sisters to open a house in the city.

Bishop Quarter avoided the problems of trusteeism in 1845 by obtaining authority from the state legislature to hold all church property in trust for the members of the congregation.

Over the next two years, he worked actively to advance the progress made in diocesan expansion. He began eight missions in 1846 and convoked a diocesan synod in 1847. The synod was attended by thirty-two priests, and Bishop Quarter promised semiannual clergy gatherings. Already, however, his health was deteriorating, and he died at the age of forty-two. He left a diocese with a Catholic population of eighty thousand, served by forty-eight churches, including the Cathedral of St. Mary, and forty priests.

Quasten, Johannes (May 3, 1900–March 10, 1987)

A priest and expert in patristics and liturgy, Johannes Quasten was born in Homberg, Germany. He studied at the University of Münster and was ordained in February 1926. After completing two doctoral dissertations, he began teaching at the University of Münster in 1931, although within a few years he faced the growing oppression of the Nazi regime that came to power in 1933. By 1937 he had been forbidden to teach, prompting his departure from Germany.

In 1938 Father Quasten journeyed to the United States, where he assumed a post on the theology faculty of The Catholic University of America.

During the Second Vatican Council, Quasten served as a member of the council's Preparatory Commission on the Liturgy, whose work directly influenced the drafting of the conciliar document *Sacrosanctum Concilium*. He remained on the faculty until his retirement in 1970; he returned to Germany in 1977 and died in Freiburg.

One of the most deeply respected patristic scholars, Father Quasten was the author of numerous works, including translations of patristic writings, with Joseph C. Plumpe, published in the 1940s under the title *Ancient Christian Writings*. His most famous work, however, was *Patrology* (published in three volumes), a massive compendium on patristics that became the standard text in the study of the Fathers of the Church.

Québec Act of 1774

Passed by the British Parliament, the Québec Act was intended to assist the governance of the province of Québec following the ceding of French Canada to Britain in 1763, according to the terms of the Treaty of Paris.

The Québec Act was a reflection in part of the considerable problems that had emerged from the acquisition of Canada by England, most notably the issues of race, language, and especially religion. It was the hope of the British authorities to transform Canada into a fourteenth American colony, working toward stable relations with the inhabitants under Governor James Murray until British traders arrived and insisted upon favorable legislation.

By the time of the administration of Governor Guy Carleton, who replaced Murray in 1766, it was clear that resentments had been growing among the French Canadians, mostly owing to the efforts to Anglicize them, and propaganda against the region spread from New England. Carleton was thus disposed toward supporting legislation that might solve the social, religious, and political problems in Canada. Aside from solving the issues of French Canadians and delineating the rights of the English-speaking minority, the intended Québec Act would promote public acceptance of the British crown and solidify the strategic value of Canada for possible future military operations.

The provisions of the act, called the Magna Carta of the French Canadian people, extended the territory of French Canada, encompassing the lands between the Ohio River and the Great Lakes to the Mississippi. The act also established a central administrative system that was based more on the French model than the English, utilizing seigneural dues and perpetuating the French code of civil laws, with modifications of the English code of justice. A representative assembly was also promised. Significantly, the act decreed that the Catholic faith was guaranteed freedom from interference by the state. The clergy continued to receive their appropriate rights and dues, and the standing British oaths were modified to permit Catholics to hold citizenship and public office.

The Québec Act provoked a favorable reaction among the Catholic clergy and the Catholic population in Québec. Positively, it also solidified the French institutions in Canada, strengthening British administration. Far less positive was the response from the American colonies. As the Québec Act had been promulgated with the four infamous acts by the British government following the Boston Tea Party in 1773, it was ranked among the so-called Intolerable Acts of 1774, and propagandists cast the act as confirmation of British oppression and arbitrary government. Anti-Catholic polemics described the act as an attack on the Protestant religion and was the occasion for a wave of anti-Catholic displays not seen since the Seven

Years' War in 1756–63. Fears of an imminent attack on the colonies by Catholics from Québec and the Native American allies were spread with enthusiasm. Catholics in the American colonies suffered from the anti-Catholic sentiment, with assorted incidents of violence and attacks in several colonies. The act remained a source of propaganda and vitriol for decades.

Quigley, James Edward (October 15, 1855–July 10, 1915)

Bishop of Buffalo from 1897 to 1903 and the second archbishop of Chicago, from 1903 to 1915, James Edward Quigley was born in Oshawa, Ontario, Canada, but lived from the age of ten in Buffalo, New York, where his family had settled. After initial preparation for the priesthood in the seminary in Buffalo, he studied at the University of Innsbruck and then at the Urban College of the Propaganda in Rome, where he earned a doctorate in theology and received ordination in 1879.

Returning home after ordination, he spent the next years in ministry in the Buffalo diocese, succeeding to the see in 1897 as successor to the recently deceased Bishop Stephen Vincent Ryan; he was consecrated on February 24, 1897.

As bishop of the Diocese of Buffalo from 1897 to 1903, Quigley proved a strong advocate of labor in the diocese. He sought to improve working conditions and defend trade unions. In 1899 he mediated the Buffalo dock strike. At the same time, he was clear in his opposition to socialism, writing a pastoral letter in 1901 against the labor unions in the city that were promoting socialism.

In 1902, however, Archbishop Patrick Augustine Feehan of Chicago died, and Quigley emerged as his successor, a surprising appointment given his few years of experience as bishop. The new archbishop assessed the needs of the Church in Chicago and determined that among its most pressing needs were a better sense of unity and an increase in the clergy. Divisions had troubled the archdiocese in the years before his arrival, particularly among the ethnic communities, and Quigley tried to heal some of the bitter feelings by improving relations with the Polish Catholic community. Even more pressing was the need for clergy to serve the rapidly growing Catholic population. To promote vocations, he founded the Cathedral College in 1905 (it later became Quigley Memorial Seminary). He also gave his support to the foundation of Loyola University in 1912 and established the Working Boys' Home and St. Joseph's Home for the Friendless. By the time of his death, the archdiocese was served by over 790 priests and members of 45 religious orders.

Archbishop Quigley also encouraged Father Francis Clement Kelley in the establishment in 1905 of the Catholic Church Extension Society to support the Church in American and foreign missions. In 1908 he sponsored the first American Missionary Congress and lent his support to the Extension Society as it pursued papal approval and overcame some opposition from bishops. (*See also* Catholic Church Extension Society.)

In 1915 Archbishop Quigley suffered a stroke and died in Rochester, New York. His period as archbishop was comparatively brief, but he proved an important figure in promoting the full maturity of the archdiocese.

Quigley, Martin (May 6, 1890–May 4, 1964)

An editor and publisher, Martin Quigley was the founder of the Motion Picture Production Code. He was born in Cleveland and studied at Niagara University and The Catholic University of America. After graduating, he went to work in journalism in Cleveland, Detroit, and Chicago, and then founded in 1915 the *Exhibitor's Herald,* a trade paper for the motion-picture industry. Over the next years, he acquired several other publications, including *Motion Picture News* in 1931, which he renamed the *Motion Picture Herald.*

In 1930 Quigley founded, with Father Daniel A. Lord, S.J., the first Motion Picture Production Code. He soon convinced Will Hays and the various heads of the Hollywood studios to adopt the code for their productions, although it became apparent that there was no instrument for enforcing the measure. Quigley subsequently took part in the discussions between the Hays Office and the Catholic bishops that led to the Production Code Administration in 1934. Quigley was active in the foundation of the Legion of Decency. He died in New York City.

Quincy, Diocese of. *See* Springfield in Illinois, Diocese of

Quiroga, Vasco de (1470–March 14, 1565)

A Spanish missionary in Mexico and the bishop of Michoacán, Mexico, Vasco de Quiroga was born at Madrigal de las Altas Torres, Spain, and proved a gifted student in law at the University of Valladolid, Spain.

Little else is know about him until around 1530, when he entered into the service of the Royal Chancellory in Valladolid, including a position in the governing body of New Spain. He reached Mexico City in January 1531 and soon distinguished himself as an administrator and a leading patron and protector of the local native tribes. In assisting them, he founded hospitals, orphanages, and schools, most often at his own expense.

Quiroga focused his efforts on the province of Michoacán, demonstrating such success that he was named its first bishop, despite being a layman. Ordained to the priesthood, he was consecrated by Archbishop Juan de Zumarraga in Mexico City in December 1538. He assumed his position as bishop in early 1539 with his residence at Pátzcuaro. He then built a cathedral and established schools for the native peoples as well as the Royal College of San Nicolás Obispo around 1540. He also edited a history of the Church in Michoacán, a manual for baptism, and various sermons.

R

Raffeiner, John (December 26, 1785–July 16, 1861)

A German missionary honored as the "Apostle to the German Immigrants," John Raffeiner was born in the Austrian Tyrol and studied under the Benedictines, preparing for the priesthood. His studies were interrupted by the events of the Napoleonic Wars, so he opted for a career in medicine, receiving his degree in 1813 and serving as a surgeon in the Austrian army during the last campaigns against Napoleon in 1813–15, then working in private practice in Switzerland.

The call of a vocation, however, remained, and Raffeiner returned to seminary studies, receiving ordination in 1825. In 1830, despite being forty-five years old, he set sail for service in America. While he had intended originally to serve in Cincinnati, Father Raffeiner chose to remain in New York to assist Bishop John Dubois. The chief focus of his pastoral care was the population of German Catholics in the city. To assist the German faithful under his care, he founded a school, an orphanage, a hospital, and Most Holy Trinity Parish in Brooklyn.

In 1853 Father Raffeiner first established a ministerial relationship with Dominican nuns from Germany who had recently arrived and spoke virtually no English. With his often stern assistance, the nuns eventually founded the congregation of the Dominican Sisters of Amityville, New York, later establishing their ministry on Long Island.

Father Raffeiner died soon after the start of the Civil War in 1861, ordering at the beginning of hostilities that a Union flag be raised patriotically over Holy Trinity Parish.

Raimondi, Luigi (October 25, 1912–July 24, 1975)

Apostolic delegate to the United States from 1967 to 1973, Luigi Raimondi was born in Acqui Lus-

Cardinal Luigi Raimondi

sito, Piedmont, Italy. He studied in the diocesan seminary of Acqui, Italy, and then at the Lateran Seminary and Pontifical Athenaeum S. Apollinaire, where he earned a doctorate in canon law. He later undertook further studies in the Pontifical Ecclesiastical Academy, the training school for Vatican diplomats. Ordained on June 6, 1936, he was named subsequently to various posts in the apostolic nunciatures of Guatemala (1936–42), the United States (1942–49), and India (1949–53).

In 1953 he became a member of the staff of the Secretariat of State. That same year, he was elevated to the rank of archbishop and was named apostolic nuncio to Haiti and apostolic delegate to the British and French Indies. In 1956 he was moved to the post of nuncio to Mexico, where he served until 1967.

On June 30, 1967, Archbishop Raimondi was named apostolic delegate to the United States, assuming his duties on September 26, 1967, serving the Holy See as its representative during the tumultuous period following the Second Vatican Council. During his five and a half years, he ordained twenty-two bishops and announced the creation of a dozen new dioceses and three archdioceses.

On March 5, 1973, Raimondi was elevated by Pope Paul VI to the rank of cardinal deacon and received an appointment as prefect of the Congregation for the Causes of Saints. He held this post for only two years, dying suddenly of a heart attack.

Râle, Sebastian (January 20, 1652–August 23, 1724)

A beloved missionary and martyr, Sebastian Râle was a faithful shepherd to the Abenaki Nation. Born in Pontarlier, France, Râle entered the Jesuit novitiate at Dole, in the province of Lyons, in 1675, and studied also at Carpentras and Lyons.

In 1688 Father Râle volunteered for the missions

in America and reached Québec in the following year. His first assignment as a missionary was in an Abenaki village near Québec, starting a long period of service to that nation and to the Illinois Indians.

During this period, Father Râle found himself in the middle of the struggle between the French and English, recognizing that the Native Americans were often pawns in the colonial ambitions of the two powers. Father Râle, however, was also viewed suspiciously by the colonists of New England, who considered him a possible agent against English interests and a champion of the Catholic faith among the Abenaki.

Father Râle traveled with the Abenaki and hunted with them in the forests. He had a distinct respect for them, some of the first Catholics in America. Because of him, they continually refused the bribes offered by the British if they would accept an Episcopalian minister and the Protestant Bible.

Thus, during King William's War from 1689 to 1697 and Queen Anne's War from 1702 to 1713, Father Râle resisted the efforts of the English among the Abenaki. He established his center of missionary effort at Norridgewock, Maine, building a church in 1698. In 1705 English forces burned the church to the ground, and Father Râle and his Indian converts fled for their lives. The conflict was ended briefly by the Treaty of Utrecht in 1713.

English ambitions toward Canada shattered the short-lived peace with the eruption of new hostilities in September 1721. As Father Râle remained a chief obstacle to their plans, the English placed a bounty on the head of the priest. Several expeditions were launched to capture him, in 1722 and again in 1724. In August 1724 English forces attacked Norridgewock, crushing the Indians who resisted. Father Râle was shot during the assault and died of his wounds, along with many Abenaki under his care. His head was also taken by the Mohawk participants of the raid to claim the bounty offered. Word of his murder was the cause of celebration among Protestants in New England, especially in Boston.

As he was fluent in the Abenaki language, Father Râle compiled a dictionary of the Abenaki language; copies of the manuscript are preserved in the library of Harvard University and by the Maine Historical Society.

Raleigh, Diocese of

Erected on December 12, 1924, by Pope Pius XI, the Diocese of Raleigh originally served the entire state of North Carolina with the exception of the Abbey Nullius of Belmont. The diocese is a suffragan of the Archdiocese of Atlanta. At its founding, it covered some forty-six thousand square miles and had a Catholic population of approximately eight thousand. The future city of Raleigh was settled in 1788, and was laid out beside a tract of trees in 1792. Named for the English explorer Sir Walter Raleigh, it was eventually made the capital of North Carolina. The first capital building was destroyed by a fire in 1831 and replaced with the present structure in 1840.

During the Civil War, Raleigh was occupied by Union troops under the command of General William Tecumseh Sherman. The city is now an educational center of note, as it is part of North Carolina's Research Triangle.

The Catholic history of Raleigh dates to 1540 when Hernando de Soto led an expedition into the area. Father Juan de Padilla, the protomartyr of the United States, was with this Spanish group. Father Padilla would be slain years later in the area of modern-day Kansas. Lucas Vázquez de Ayllón, another Spanish explorer, had visited the region about two decades earlier. In 1663 North Carolina became a colony of Lord Proprietors and was given the rank of a royal colony in 1729. The Catholic presence, if there was one, was very limited prior to the American Revolution because of restrictions against those of the Catholic faith.

In 1784 an Irish priest, Father Pierre Cleary, was in New Bern for a short period. In 1781 Dr. Thomas Burke, a well-known Catholic, was elected governor of the state, and he labored with others to give Catholics civil rights under the new state constitution. At the time, Catholics in North Carolina were part of the ecclesiastical territory of the Diocese (later Archdiocese) of Baltimore. In 1820 the territory of North Carolina was transferred to the newly established Diocese of Charleston.

The revered Bishop John England served as shepherd over the region, building parishes and introducing the popular "circuit priests," roving missionaries who went great distances to serve the scattered settlements of the faithful.

On March 3, 1868, the Holy See erected the Vicariate Apostolic of North Carolina, appointing Father James Gibbons, the future archbishop of Baltimore, as the first vicar apostolic. The Benedictines at Belmont Abbey served the Catholics in the state with immense dedication, and they were joined in the late nineteenth century by the Sisters of Mercy. Father Thomas F. Price, co-founder of Maryknoll, served the faithful of North Carolina for two years.

The Catholics in North Carolina joined their fellow citizens in the sacrifices demanded by World War I, supporting the nation's military programs. In 1824 the loyalty and faith of the Catholics in the state were recognized and honored by the establishment of the Diocese of Raleigh.

The first bishop of Raleigh was William J. Hafey, who was consecrated at the age of thirty-seven on June 24, 1925. Bishop Hafey invited religious communities into the diocese as he established diocesan offices and ministries. He was especially active in giving the new diocese a firm financial footing and aiding the needs of those suffering during the grim Great Depression. On the basis of his achievements, he was appointed the coadjutor bishop of Scranton on October 2, 1937.

The second bishop of Raleigh was Eugene Joseph McGuinness, a priest of the Archdiocese of Philadelphia who had worked for the Catholic Church Extension Society. Consecrated on December 21, 1937, Bishop McGuinness expanded diocesan facilities and guided the diocese during the early years of World War II. On November 11, 1944, he was appointed as the coadjutor archbishop of Oklahoma City–Tulsa.

Bishop McGuinness was succeeded by Vincent S. Waters, a priest from Richmond, Virginia. Bishop Waters was consecrated on May 15, 1945, and installed on June 6. He established many new parishes to serve the faithful and conducted a rigorous campaign to improve diocesan finances. He instituted the North Carolina Layman Association and a missionary apostolate to evangelize across the state, and took the brave decision to desegregate all diocesan educational institutions as a result of the civil rights movement in the 1950s. Bishop Waters also attended the the Second Vatican Council and took on the task of implementing the decrees of the council during a difficult period that saw declines in vocations, the numbers of priests, and schools. In 1960 the diocese received jurisdiction over virtually all of North Carolina by assuming control over the territory of the Abbey Nullius of Belmont. Such was the growth of the diocese, however, that by 1971 Bishop Waters was obliged to petition for the creation of another diocese in the state. Pope Paul VI responded by creating the Diocese of Charlotte. After a tenure of some twenty-nine years, Bishop Waters died of a heart attack at the age of seventy on December 3, 1974.

The fourth bishop of Raleigh was Francis Joseph Gossman, who had served as an auxiliary bishop of Baltimore since 1968. Installed on May 19, 1974, Bishop Gossman carried forward the development of diocesan facilities and ministries to keep pace with the growing Catholic population. Noted for his collegiality, he labored to provide a steady hand for the diocese, and his episcopal tenure nearly coincided with the pontificate of Pope Blessed John Paul II, who reigned from 1978 to 2005. By the time Bishop Gossman retired on June 8, 2006, the Catholic population had grown from 46,000 to more than 180,000.

The fifth bishop of Raleigh, Michael F. Burbidge, had served as an auxiliary bishop of Philadelphia since 2002. He was appointed bishop of Raleigh on June 8, 2006, and installed on August 4. Like his predecessors, Bishop Burbidge was challenged by the steady increase of the Catholic population. By 2011 there were more than 220,000 Catholics in the diocese, with 139 priests and 96 parishes.

Randall, James R. (January 1, 1839–January 15, 1908)

Journalist and poet James R. Randall was considered the "Poet Laureate of the Lost Cause" for his literary labors on behalf of the Confederacy. Born at Baltimore, he studied at Georgetown University, leaving before his graduation. He then traveled through South America and the West Indies. After returning to the United States, he taught at Poydras College in Louisiana. In 1861, with the start of the Civil War, Randall composed the martial poem "Maryland, My Maryland," which was first published in the New Orleans *Sunday Delta* in April

1861. It was subsequently set to music. In the years after the war, Randall worked in journalism, holding a post as Washington correspondent for the *Augusta Chronicle*. He died in Augusta, Georgia.

Rapid City, Diocese of

Established on August 4, 1902, as the Diocese of Lead by Pope Leo XIII, and renamed the Diocese of Rapid City by the Holy See on August 1, 1930, the diocese serves counties in the western part of the state of South Dakota as well as the Black Hills, Rosebud, and other Indian Reservations. The diocese is a suffragan of the Archdiocese of St. Paul and Minneapolis.

Rapid City was founded by settlers in 1876 and is located on Rapid Creek. Situated in the Black Hills, the site was part of the gold rush of the era. The city became a tourist and gold center, with industries developing in the manufacturing of natural resources products, including precious metals, gems, lumber, and agriculture. Mount Rushmore and other national monuments are in the vicinity. Catholics were present in Rapid City in its earliest stages, and the Cathedral of Our Lady Perpetual Help dates to 1890.

The Catholic heritage of the region began in 1848 when missionaries started their labors there. No earlier missions are recorded before the arrival of Father Augustin Ravoux, who visited Fort Pierre on the Missouri River. Settlers came into the Black Hills in 1856, but the Sioux defended the sites, which they considered sacred. In 1861 the U.S. Congress created the Dakota Territory, comprising present-day North Dakota and South Dakota.

The revered Jesuit missionary Father Pierre-Jean De Smet baptized the local tribes and served the Sioux as he was trusted by them and could walk freely into Sioux camps. He warned the Sioux that the rich gold and mineral deposits in the Black Hills would inevitably lead to the seizure of the territory by the white man.

A parish church was created in 1867 at Jefferson by Father Pierre Boucher, followed by the work of Father George Belcourt. Father Martin Marty, a pioneering Benedictine who became a bishop, also served in the region, and on August 12, 1879, when the Vicariate Apostolic of the Dakotas was erected, he was consecrated and appointed vicar apostolic.

When Sitting Bull and his followers went into Canada to find new lands and a new beginning, Bishop Marty journeyed north to care for them. He used Yankton as his base of operations for the vicariate, an area covering 149,000 square miles.

In 1889 the Diocese of Sioux Falls was created by Pope Leo XIII, and Bishop Marty was named the first bishop. He built churches and brought the Benedictine Sisters into the area. In 1894 Bishop Marty was transferred to the Diocese of St. Cloud. In 1902 all of South Dakota west of the Missouri River was separated from the Diocese of Sioux Falls by the Holy See and established as the Diocese of Lead. At its founding, the diocese had a Catholic population of around six thousand, including the Catholic Indians of the Sioux reservations. The first bishop was John N. Stariha, the vicar general of the Archdiocese of St. Paul. He was consecrated on October 28, 1902.

The new bishop worked over the next years to establish diocesan institutions and to keep pace with the growth of settlers who were arriving on the railroads, which were reaching new territories in the West. He opened new parishes and churches in the burgeoning towns and also promoted education and care of Native Americans. Owing to poor health and exhaustion, Bishop Stariha retired on March 29, 1909, and returned to his native Austria.

The second bishop of Lead was Father Joseph F. Busch, a priest from Minnesota, who was consecrated on May 19, 1910. He continued the growth of diocesan facilities and promoted missions for the local Native Americans. On February 21, 1915, he was transferred to the Diocese of St. Cloud.

The third bishop of Lead was John J. Lawler, who had been an auxiliary bishop of the Archdiocese of St. Paul since 1910. Appointed by Pope Benedict XV on January 29, 1916, he served as bishop through the years of World War I, the booming 1920s, the Great Depression, and World War II. In 1930 the diocese was transferred from Lead to Rapid City, where he established new offices and agencies for administration. He then began charitable programs and services to aid those suffering from the economic collapse of the Great Depression. After serving with distinction for three decades, he grew ill and asked for a coadjutor bishop. A priest of the Fargo diocese,

Leo F. Dworschak, was named coadjutor on June 22, 1946, but he was transferred to the Diocese of Fargo on April 10, 1947. A new coadjutor bishop was named on the same day, Bishop William T. McCarty, who had been an auxiliary bishop of the Military Vicariate since 1943. When Bishop Lawler died on March 11, 1948, Bishop McCarty acceded to the see.

A Redemptorist, Bishop McCarty served during the postwar era and throughout the period of the Second Vatican Council. He worked to meet the needs of the large numbers of Native Americans on the reservations and then took up the task of implementing the decrees of the council. He retired on September 11, 1969.

Bishop McCarty was succeeded by Harold J. Dimmerling, a priest of the Diocese of St. Cloud. Consecrated a bishop on October 30, 1969, he labored to implement the reforms of the Second Vatican Council during the turbulent 1970s. He also created relief services during the Black Hills Flood of 1972, when 225 people lost their lives and the whole region was distressed economically. He died on December 13, 1987, at the age of seventy-three.

The seventh bishop of Rapid City was the Capuchin Franciscan priest Charles J. Chaput, a member of the Plains Band Potawatomi and the second Native American consecrated as a bishop. Appointed to the diocese on April 11, 1988, he was consecrated a bishop on July 26, 1988, and continued ministries on the Indian reservations in the diocese and supported lay programs. On February 18, 1997, he was promoted to the Archdiocese of Denver. In 2011 he was named archbishop of Philadelphia.

Bishop Chaput was followed by Father Blase J. Cupich, a priest of the Diocese of Omaha. Named on July 7, 1998, and consecrated a bishop on September 21, 1998, he guided the diocese through the Great Jubilee of 2000 and worked to implement the new norms and protections for the prevention of clergy sexual abuse. On June 30, 2010, he was named bishop of Spokane.

On May 26, 2011, Robert D. Gruss, a priest of the Diocese of Davenport, was named the ninth bishop of Rapid City. He was consecrated a bishop on July 28, 2011. In 2011 there were 26,000 Catholics, served by 53 priests and 88 parishes, in the diocese.

Rappe, Louis Amadeus (February 2, 1801– September 8, 1877)

The first bishop of Cleveland, from 1847 to 1870, Louis Amadeus Rappe was born in Audrehem, France. He studied for the priesthood at Boulogne-sur-Mer and Arras and received ordination in March 1829. While serving in a parish and as chaplain to the Ursuline Sisters in Boulogne-sur-Mer, he met Bishop John Baptist Purcell of Cincinnati, who was recruiting priests for service in the United States. Convinced that he should serve in America, Father Rappe arrived in October 1840 and became a pastor in Toledo, Ohio. As pastor, Rappe distinguished himself for his zeal and his strong advocacy of the temperance movement, in particular among the Irish workers laboring on the canal projects in Ohio.

On April 23, 1847, Pope Blessed Pius IX established the new Diocese of Cleveland and named Rappe its first bishop. At the time of his consecration on October 10, 1847, he assumed pastoral care of a diocese that claimed fifteen diocesan priests and six religious to staff fourteen parishes, thirty missions, and over thirty stations. As he was confronted with the need to establish parishes to meet the needs of the various ethnic groups in the diocese, Bishop Rappe was at first opposed to the establishment of national parishes. As the call was incessant, especially from among German Catholics, he relented, despite his personal opposition to them. Relations with the Germans were consequently strained, but more difficulties emerged in the 1850s with the Irish Catholics. A group of Irish priests under the leadership of Fathers E. M. O'Callaghan, Robert Sidley, and James Monahan eventually brought false charges against the bishop in Rome, causing Bishop Rappe's resignation. He left the diocese in September 1870 and immediately resumed missionary work in Vermont. He was finally fully exonerated of all charges by Rome, but he refused appointment to another diocese. Instead, he remained in the Vermont missions until his death.

In his over two decades as bishop of Cleveland, he had overseen the steady growth of parishes. By 1870 the original 44 parishes had increased to 158; of these, 75 had parochial schools. Bishop Rappe also founded other schools, a cathedral, a hospital, and a seminary. He attracted eight religious orders of women to the diocese and made several journeys to Europe to promote further vocations and new priests for service in the diocese.

Raskob, John Jakob (March 19, 1879–October 15, 1950)

A philanthropist and financier best known for his role in the growth of General Motors and as chairman of the Democratic National Committee from 1928 to 1932, John Jakob Raskob was born in Lockport, New York. He grew up in a devoutly Catholic home and studied at Clark's Business College. After working in Nova Scotia, Canada, he was hired as private secretary to Pierre du Pont, who was then a manager of a railroad company in Ohio. Raskob proved invaluable to du Pont and his cousin after they assumed control of E. I. du Pont de Nemours and Company in Wilmington, Delaware. Within a short time, Raskob had assisted them in making the company one of the most successful dynamite manufacturers in the country. Over the next years, Raskob held a variety of posts, rising in the company as he assisted in its expansion. In 1906 he married Helena Springer Green. They had thirteen children, but eventually separated without ever divorcing.

By 1915 du Pont and Raskob had acquired enough stock in the General Motors Corporation to ensure that du Pont was appointed chairman of the board; Raskob received the post of one of the directors. In 1918 he became head of the company's finance committee, introducing various modern accounting procedures. In 1928 he was appointed chairman of the Democratic National Committee by his friend Alfred E. Smith, then a candidate for president. After the failed bid by Smith, Raskob could not deliver his renomination and was replaced as chairman by the nominee, Franklin Delano Roosevelt. Raskob then opposed President Roosevelt's New Deal legislation and worked unsuccessfully to prevent his renomination in 1936.

Raskob served as a director of General Motors until 1946 and as a vice president and a direc-

tor of the company in charge of the Empire State Building. He was made a Knight of the Order of St. Gregory and was a member of the Knights of Malta.

Ravalli, Antonio (1811–October 2, 1884)

An Italian Jesuit and missionary in the far-western regions of the United States, Father Antonio Ravalli labored especially in Montana. He was born in Ferrara, Italy, entered the Society of Jesus around 1833, and was ordained in 1837. In 1843 he received the appeal then being made by Father Pierre-Jean De Smet, the revered Jesuit pioneer in America, for priests to assist with the western missions. With Fathers Vercruyesse, Accolti, and Nobili, Brother Huybrechts, and six sisters of the Congregation of Notre Dame de Namur, Father Ravalli sailed to North America and reached Fort Vancouver in early August 1844.

He studied English at the Mission of St. Paul on the Willamette River in Oregon before joining Father Christian Hoecken in early 1845 at the St. Ignatius Mission on the upper Columbia in Washington.

After a period of service, Father Ravalli was sent to oversee the Flathead Mission of St. Mary's on the Bitterroot River in western Montana. He remained there until 1850 when the threat posed by the Blackfeet necessitated the temporary abandonment of the mission. In 1854 he was placed in charge of the Sacred Heart Mission for the Coeur d'Alene tribes of northern Idaho. While in service there, he constructed a church for the region and continued to foster excellent relations with the tribes.

Father Ravalli was thus positioned well to convince many of them not to participate in the unrest led by Yakima in 1856–67. During that troubled period, he held a variety of posts, including a brief stint as an instructor at the Santa Clara Mission. Recalled to the missions in 1863, he was instrumental in building the first church for whites, St. Michael's, at Hellgate. In 1866 he was able to return to the Mission of St. Mary's, among the Flatheads on the Bitterroot. He remained among them, beloved, until his death.

Antonio Ravalli

Ravoux, Augustin (January 11, 1815–January 17, 1906)

A French missionary in the Midwestern and Western regions of present-day America, Augustin Ravoux was born in Langeac, Auvergne, France. He entered the seminary in 1834 and was still a seminarian when he was recruited by Bishop Mathias Loras of Dubuque for service in the missions. Completing his studies at Mount St. Mary's College in Emmitsburg, Maryland, and then at Dubuque, Iowa, he was ordained in 1840. His first assignment was at Prairie du Chien, Wisconsin.

In 1841 he was named to the missions among the Dakota in northern Iowa (modern-day Minnesota). Once among the Native Americans, he translated a catechism and hymnal into the Dakota language. He was also the only missionary for an area that extended across most of Minnesota from 1844 to 1851, when the Diocese of St. Paul was created. He then labored in close cooperation with the first bishop of St. Paul, Joseph Crétin, serving as his vicar general.

In 1868 he was appointed the first vicar apostolic of the newly created Vicariate of Montana, although his failing health compelled him to decline the appointment. He continued, however, to serve as vicar general and was named a domestic prelate by Pope Leo XIII in 1887. His long years of missionary work were documented in his memoirs, *Reminiscences, Memoirs and Lectures* in 1890 and *Labors of Monsignor A. Ravoux at Mendota, St. Paul and Other Localities* in 1899.

Raymbaut, Charles (1602–1643)

A French Jesuit and missionary among the Indians of Canada and the northern United States, Charles Raymbaut was born in France. He entered the Society of Jesus at Rouen in 1621 and after studies and ordination volunteered for the American missions.

Appointed procurator of the Canadian missions, he was sent to Québec in 1637 and used the city as his base of operations for missionary work among the Huron, Nipissing, and Algonquin, who were then residing near Lake Huron and the islands of the Ottawa.

Raymbaut proved a gifted evangelist, earning such a reputation that his presence was requested by the Saulteaux Indians in 1641 as their "Black Robe." Raymbault journeyed as far as Sault Ste. Marie with the future Jesuit martyr St. Isaac Jogues, using the trip as a means of exploring the vast wilderness. Planning to continue his mission work, he returned to minister among the Nipissing but fell ill and died from fever at Québec. He was the first Jesuit to die in Canada and was buried next to Samuel de Champlain.

Redemptorists (C.SS.R.)

The Congregation of the Most Holy Redeemer is a society of priests founded by St. Alphonsus Liguori in Italy in 1732. It was the intention of St. Alphonsus that the Redemptorists should be devoted to evangelization and preaching as missionaries among the poor. The congregation was approved in 1749 by Pope Benedict XIV. In the next year, the Redemptorist nuns were granted approval.

The congregation grew rapidly in Italy and the Papal States, and then across Europe, starting in Austria under St. Clement Maria Hofbauer in 1785 and then Poland, Bavaria, and Switzerland. In the next decades, they opened houses in France, Portugal, Belgium, Bulgaria, Holland, Germany, and England. They arrived in the United States in 1832.

After a slow start, the Redemptorists by 1850 had established a province with nine houses, including New York City and New Orleans. Preachers were active in many other cities and preached in a number of languages, such as English, German, French, Italian, Polish, Spanish, and Portuguese. They were active among the recently arrived immigrants and started schools for orphans in a host of cities.

There are currently more than five thousand Redemptorists worldwide, with more than four thousand priests in nearly eighty countries. There are two Redemptorist provinces in the United States. The most famous Redemptorist in American Catholic history is St. John Nepomucene Neumann, a missionary and the fourth bishop of Philadelphia. He is the first American bishop to be canonized a saint.

Reedy, John L. (October 16, 1925–December 2, 1983)

A priest and editor, John L. Reedy is best known for his work for *Ave Maria* and as a columnist for *Our Sunday Visitor*. Born in Newport, Kentucky, he entered the Congregation of Holy Cross at Notre Dame, Indiana, in 1944, and received ordination in 1952. After graduate studies in journalism at Marquette University and the University of Notre Dame, he received the post of assistant editor of *Ave Maria*, published by the congregation. He worked at Notre Dame, where the family-oriented weekly was published. In 1955 he became editor of the magazine as well as the head of Ave Maria Press.

In 1970 circulation problems resulted in the closing of *Ave Maria*, and Reedy launched *A.D. Correspondence* to discuss the climate and issues facing the Church in the post-conciliar period. That same year, he began work as a columnist for *Our Sunday Visitor* and was a syndicated columnist for various Catholic newspapers and magazines. He died at Notre Dame.

Reid, Richard (January 21, 1896–January 24, 1961)

Editor, lawyer, and respected lay leader, Richard Reid was born in Winchester, Massachusetts, and studied at Holy Cross College, Fordham University, and Columbia University. In 1921 he was admitted to the Georgia bar and served from 1930 to 1940 as a partner in the firm of Mulherin and Reid. In 1921 he was named executive secretary of the Georgia Catholic Laymen's Association and also editor of the *Bulletin,* a Catholic newspaper for the region. Over the next years, he held a variety of prominent positions, including general counsel of the National Council of Catholic Men and president of the Catholic Association. In 1940 he became editor of the *New York Catholic News,* the unofficial newspaper of the Archdiocese of New York. He received a number of awards, including the Laetare Medal from the University of Notre Dame in 1936.

Reinhold, Hans (September 9, 1897–January 26, 1968)

Priest and noted liturgist Hans Reinhold was born in Hamburg, Germany. He served in the German Army in World War I, receiving a wound but surviving to hold a position in army intelligence, where his language skills proved useful. Following the war, he studied at the University of Freiburg, the Jesuit seminary in Innsbruck, Austria, and the

monastery of Maria Laach. Ordained in 1925 for the Diocese of Osnabruck, he went to Rome for additional graduate studies at the Pontifical Institute of Archaeology. In 1929 he became chaplain of the German Seaman's Apostolate, and the following year he helped establish the International Council of the Apostolate of the Sea.

Owing to the emergence of the Nazi Party to supremacy in Germany, Reinhold fled his homeland in 1935, especially as he was a vocal critic of the Hitler regime. After stays in the Netherlands and England, he migrated to the United States, where he held several posts, including teaching at Portsmouth Priory in Rhode Island.

In 1938 he became chaplain for a port in Seattle and then pastor of a parish in Yakima, Washington. In 1944 he became an American citizen. Already Reinhold was writing on liturgical reform and renewal, including a column for *Orate Fratres* (later *Worship*). He subsequently wrote a number of books on liturgy, including: *The Soul Afire: Revelation of the Mystics* (1944), *The American Parish and the Roman Liturgy* (1958), *Bringing the Mass to the People* (1960), *The Dynamics of the Liturgy* (1961), and *Liturgy and Art* (1966). In his writings, he was a leading advocate for liturgical renewal in the years before the Second Vatican Council and the Constitution on the Liturgy, *Sacrosanctum Concilium*.

In 1956, owing to poor health, Reinhold received permission to take a leave of absence from Bishop Joseph P. Dougherty of Yakima. He had disagreements with the bishop that led to his request to transfer to the Diocese of Pittsburgh. Bishop (later Cardinal) John J. Wright accepted him into the Pittsburgh diocese, and Reinhold was soon diagnosed with Parkinson's disease. He died in Pittsburgh.

Reno, Diocese of

Established on March 27, 1931, by Pope Pius XI, the Diocese of Reno comprises counties in northern Nevada. At its founding, this episcopal jurisdiction stretched across an area of 110,540 square miles. It was renamed the Diocese of Reno-Las Vegas by Pope Paul VI on October 13, 1976. On March 21, 1995, Pope Blessed John Paul II designated the jurisdiction as the Diocese of Reno. The Diocese of Las Vegas became a separate jurisdiction. The diocese is a suffragan see of the Archdiocese of San Francisco.

The city of Reno was first settled in 1860, when C. W. Fuller erected a toll bridge across the Truckee River. Three years later, M. C. Lake acquired the property and named it Lake's Crossing. Soon after, the Central Pacific Railroad used the site as a depot and brought an endless stream of settlers into the region. A true city took form, named after General Jesse Lee Reno of Virginia. Around 1900, Reno started attracting individuals interested in contracting simple divorces, as the city offered uncomplicated procedures for dissolving marriages and provided scenic interests as well. Gambling was legalized in the region in 1931, and Reno emerged as a popular tourist destination. The city is known today especially for its status as a gambling resort town.

The Catholic heritage of Reno and Nevada opened in 1775 when the Franciscan priest-explorer Father Francisco Garcés arrived on the banks of the Colorado River and celebrated a Mass there. His expedition was near present-day Laughlin. A year later, two other Franciscans, Fathers Francisco Atanasio Domínguez and Silvestre Velez de Escalante were in the area. No missions were developed, however, and only the occasional trapper or hunter ventured into the region. In 1825 Peter Ogden and other trappers made their way across the territory; Jedediah Smith, one of America's famous "mountain men," also scouted the region.

Around 1830, present-day Las Vegas was part of the Old Spanish Trail, a route followed by migrating settlers and others involved in long-range hunting and trapping adventures. In 1848, as a result of the Mexican-American War and the Treaty of Guadalupe-Hidalgo, Mexico ceded Nevada to the United States.

At that time, Nevada's Catholic population was under the ecclesiastical jurisdiction of Bishop Francisco Garcia Diego y Moreno of California. In 1848 northern Nevada became part of the newly erected Diocese of Monterey. Three years later, Father Joseph Gallagher celebrated Mass at Mormon Station, present-day Genoa.

In 1853 the region became part of the newly established Archdiocese of San Francisco, under the jurisdiction of the revered pioneering missionary Archbishop Joseph Sadoc Alemany. He brought a vigor and spirit of dedication to the see and began long-term mission programs. The discovery of silver in Nevada prompted Archbishop Alemany to send more priests into the region, particularly to the mining towns springing up alongside claim areas.

In 1861 the U.S. Congress created the Nevada Territory, and three years later Nevada entered the Union as the thirty-sixth state. Irish priests from the famous All Hallows Seminary in Dublin entered northern Nevada as part of the evangelization program of the Vicariate Apostolic of Marysville.

Bishop Lawrence Scanlan was vicar apostolic, having served as a missionary in Nevada since 1862. Father Patrick Manogue, a legendary figure who would become a bishop, served Reno and other communities with vigor and enthusiasm. A large number of Basque immigrants arrived in the area at that time, joining many other settlers who wanted to be part of the mining and manufacturing opportunities.

During World War I, Catholics joined their fellow citizens in supporting the military programs of the nation. The faithful also endured the economic sufferings brought by the Great Depression. Owing to the growth of the Catholic population, the Holy See established the Diocese of Reno in 1931. The first bishop of Reno was Father Thomas K. Gorman, a priest of the Diocese of Moneterey-Los Angeles. Consecrated a bishop on July 22, 1931, Bishop Gorman gave the diocese its foundation and built schools, parishes, and missions across the whole of Nevada. He set up charitable programs to assist those hit hard by the Great Depression and then provided leadership during World War II. He started a diocesan newspaper and promoted vocations to the priesthood and religious life. On February 8, 1952, he was transferred to the Diocese of Dallas as coadjutor bishop.

The second bishop of Reno was Robert J. Dwyer, a priest of Salt Lake City. He was consecrated a bishop on August 5, 1952, and began work on the renovaton of the Cathedral of St. Thomas Aquinas and invited religious communities into the Reno diocese. He also continued establishing parishes and schools to accommodate the needs of the steadily increasing Catholic population. In 1957 he convened a diocesan synod. Bishop Dwyer also took part in the Second Vatican Council. Not long after his return from the council, he was named, on December 9, 1966, the archbishop of Portland.

The third bishop of Reno was Joseph Green, who had served as auxiliary bishop of the Diocese of Lansing since 1962. He was installed in Reno on May 25, 1967. Bishop Green instituted the reforms of the Second Vatican Council and conducted ecumenical programs. He brought priests into the diocese and began the Catholic Services Appeal. Because of ill health and severe problems in diocesan finances, Bishop Green retired on December 6, 1974.

He was succeeded by Bishop Norman F. McFarland, who had served as auxiliary bishop of San Francisco since 1970. He was appointed apostolic administrator on December 6, 1974, and moved to stabilize the finances of the diocese. Visiting every parish and implementing new monetary regulations, Bishop McFarland managed to rid the diocese of its financial crisis. He was appointed the bishop of Reno on February 10, 1976, and petitioned the Holy See to designate the diocese Reno-Las Vegas because of the spectacular demographic changes in Nevada. The renaming was approved on October 13, 1976, and Guardian Angel Shrine in Las Vegas was named co-cathedral. On December 29, 1986, Bishop McFarland was transferred to the Diocese of Orange.

The fifth bishop of Reno was Daniel F. Walsh, who had served as an auxiliary bishop of San Francisco since 1981. Bishop Walsh moved his residence and chancery to Las Vegas and opened new parishes throughout that city. He also promoted a ministry for the Hispanic community. In 1995 the Holy See split the diocese, creating the Diocese of Reno and redesignating the Diocese of Reno-Las Vegas the Diocese of Las Vegas. Bishop Walsh remained the bishop of Las Vegas.

The sixth bishop of Reno was Bishop Phillip F. Straling, who had been bishop of San Bernardino since 1978. Bishop Straling was installed on June 29, 1995. He reopened the chancery office and launched the offices needed for the new diocese. He retired on June 21, 2005.

The seventh bishop of Reno, Randolph R. Calvo, was appointed on December 23, 2005. A native of Guam, Bishop Calvo was consecrated on February 17, 2006. Presently, the diocese encompasses some 70,000 square miles, with about 100,000 Catholics, 28 parishes, and 37 active priests.

Repplier, Agnes (April 1, 1855–December 15, 1950)

The author of essays and biographies who wrote for *Atlantic Monthly,* Agnes Repplier was a native of Philadelphia. She displayed a talent for writing even in her youth; her first stories were published by *Catholic World* and *Young Catholic* when she was a teenager. She later wrote for *Atlantic Monthly,* as well as various essays and histories. Her historical works focused often on the examples of such notable figures as Blessed Junípero Serra and Jesuit Father Jacques Marquette.

She was also a social conservative advocating equality of the sexes, although she was opposed to the suffrage movement, as she held the view that equality could be achieved without the right to vote.

Résé, Frederick (February 6, 1791–December 31, 1871)

The first bishop of Detroit, from 1833 to 1871, Frederick Résé was born in Hanover, Germany. He served in the forces of Hanover in the War of 1815 against Napoleon Bonaparte and fought at the Battle of Waterloo on June 18, 1815. In the aftermath of the fighting, Résé entered the seminary and studied at the Urban College of the Propaganda in Rome; he was ordained in 1822. After a brief time as a missionary in Africa, he returned to Rome and in 1824 was encouraged by Bishop Edward Fenwick of Cincinnati to enlist for service in the United States.

His journey to America was funded by the branch of the Society for the Propagation of the Faith in Lyons and the Leopoldine Society, which Résé had helped to establish. After several years of service in Cincinnati, Father Résé was named on March 8, 1833, to be the first bishop of the newly established Diocese of Detroit by Pope Gregory XVI.

Bishop Résé arrived in Detroit in January 1834 and chose St. Anne's as his cathedral. The Diocese of Detroit extended across Michigan, Wisconsin, and Minnesota. Bishop Résé had at his disposal only fourteen priests, although their number included the revered missionary Bishop Irenaeus Frederick Baraga and the tireless missionary pioneer Stephen T. Badin.

As bishop, Résé focused his attention on the new diocesan organization, including the opening of new parishes, the St. Anne Classical Academy for boys, and the St. Clare Institute for young women. He fell into disagreement, however, with his fellow bishops over fundraising in Europe for the missions and resigned in 1837 at the Third Provincial Council of Baltimore. He then changed his mind and went to Rome to reverse his resignation.

Bishop Résé, meanwhile, continued to raise money, and his effort caused the concern of officials in Rome. He went to the Vatican in 1839 and in the following year, citing poor health, accepted the appointment of a coadjutor. While he continued to hold the title of bishop, he ceded all episcopal authority to his coadjutor, Bishop Peter Paul Lefevere, who served for thirty years. Bishop Résé remained in Europe, although anti-Catholic propagandists claimed that he had been imprisoned in Rome. In his later years, he was placed under the care of the Sisters of Charity in Hildesheim in 1859.

Rhode Island

The smallest state in the Union, Rhode Island was one of the original thirteen colonies and is located in the northeastern part of the country. It is bounded on the north and east by Massachusetts, on the west by Connecticut, and on the south by the Atlantic Ocean, with a land mass of some 1,054 square miles. There are two chief traditional land regions in Rhode Island: the Seaboard Lowlands in the east and the New England Uplands in the north. The original inhabitants of the state's area were the Narragansett, Niantic, Nipmuck, Pequat, and Wampanoag.

The earliest European exploration of what became Rhode Island was likely performed by Giovanni da Verrazano, who operated under the French flag, around 1524. He was followed by the Dutch around 1614 under Adriaen Block, who explored Narragansett Bay.

Roger Williams is honored as the "Father of Rhode Island," having purchased land from the Narragansett Indians to found the city of Providence. Williams had been exiled from Plymouth Colony in 1635 because of his religious beliefs and his protests against the chronic interference of civil authorities in religious affairs. Williams was joined by other exiles from Plymouth Colony, including William Coddington, Anne Hutchinson, John Clarke, and Samuel Gorton, who established other free communities.

In 1644 Roger Williams was granted the first charter for "Providence Plantation" by the English Parliament, and King Charles II granted another charter for "Rhode Island and Providence Plantation" in 1663. In 1675, however, the colony was threatened when the local tribes united in a rebellion. The Native Americans were defeated in the so-called Great Swamp Fight in the area near South Kingston. The charter granted by King Charles II was one of the most tolerant and open in the English colonies with its provision of religious toleration and freedom of conscience.

The colony of Rhode Island prospered under a plantation system that included trade in sugar, rum, and slaves. Heavy taxation and interference in colonial affairs by the British, however, alienated the colonists. In May 1776 Rhode Islanders announced their independence, the first colony to make such a proclamation.

During the Revolutionary War, British troops occupied Newport. As the French naval forces, allies of the Americans, advanced, the British were forced to withdraw. In 1780 a Mass, the first recorded in Rhode Island, was celebrated at the Newport State House by a French chaplain. A decade later, Rhode Island entered the Union.

The Catholic presence in Rhode Island was long virtually nonexistent as Catholics were most unwelcome in New England. The numbers increased as a result of the Revolutionary War and the arrival of Irish Catholics. By 1828 there were approximately a thousand Catholics in the state, under the jurisdiction of the Diocese (later Archdiocese) of Boston. In 1828 Bishop Benedict Joseph Fenwick of Boston assigned Father Robert Woodley to care for the pastoral needs of the Catholics, and he built the first Catholic church in the state, St. Mary's, at Pawtucket in 1829. Other priests arrived over the next few years, including Father John Corry, who built a church in Taunton in 1830. In 1837 the first

Catholic church in Providence was built; in that same year, the first parochial school was opened.

In 1843 the Diocese of Hartford was created and included Rhode Island and Connecticut. At the time, there were only six priests in the two states. This changed quickly, assisted by the arrival of the Sisters of Mercy in 1851. Notably, the first bishops of Hartford resided in Providence because Rhode Island was the center of the Catholic population. This reality was confirmed in 1872 when the Diocese of Providence was established by Pope Blessed Pius IX.

The new diocese encompassed all of Rhode Island and a part of southeastern Massachusetts. Bishop Thomas F. Hendricken was the first bishop, and he not only had the task of establishing the diocese, but also of assisting Catholics as they endured prejudice and anger from Protestants and violent anti-Catholics.

The arrival of French Canadians between 1860 and 1910 added to the Catholic population, altering demographics. There were also Italians, Portuguese, Poles, Armenians, and Syrians. National churches were established, and priests fluent in the native tongues of the immigrants had to be brought into the diocese.

In 1878 Bishop Hendricken started construction of Sts. Peter and Paul Cathedral, and the first Mass celebrated in the new cathedral was Bishop Hendricken's funeral in 1886. The burgeoning Catholic population in Providence proved an important discouragement to anti-Catholic sentiment and also hastened the expansion of Catholics in political life. The first Catholic governor of Rhode Island, the Democrat James H. Higgins, was elected in 1907.

The turn of the century saw the continued growth of the Catholic population, but the Peck Act and others placed limitations on immigration. This development was combined with the rise of the Ku Klux Klan to create a new anti-Catholic atmosphere in parts of the state. This subsided over the decades, as Catholics supported the cause of their country in World War I and

Gabriel Richard Monument

suffered during the Great Depression. They supported the nation's military efforts in World War II and then took part in the immense postwar prosperity of the 1950s. In 2011 Rhode Island had a Catholic population of more than 620,000, with 400 priests, more than 500 religious, and 144 parishes. Catholics comprise nearly 60 percent of the total population.

Richard, Gabriel (October 15, 1767–September 13, 1832)

A missionary, a member of the Society of Saint-Sulpice, and the central figure in the birth of the Diocese of Detroit, Gabriel Richard was born in Saintes, France, and, after entering the Society of Saint-Sulpice, was ordained in October 1791 at Issy, near Paris. After teaching briefly at the Sulpician institute in Issy, he was compelled to leave France with three fellow priests (including Ambrose Maréchal), owing to the hostile anti-Catholic atmosphere in France during the French revolutionary period.

Father Richard and his fellow priests arrived in Baltimore in late June 1792, and he was immediately assigned by Bishop John Carroll to the missions. He served for six years at Prairie du Rocher and Kaskaskia, Illinois. Transferred to Detroit in 1798, he became the immensely successful head of the missions in Wisconsin and Michigan.

In 1804 Richard founded a seminary and an academy for girls in Detroit, but a fire soon destroyed both institutions as well as the local church. Undaunted by the setback, he went back to work, building over the next years a new church, two academies for girls, and six primary schools.

In 1807 Richard presented a series of lectures on pressing topics of the day and purchased a printing press the following year to launch the first paper in Michigan, the *Michigan Essay or Impartial Observer*. Over the next several years, he published a number of books dealing with religion and education. During the War of 1812, Richard was imprisoned in Canada, although his captors treated him with respect and courtesy. When freed, he went back to Detroit and in 1817 proved instrumental in the founding of the University of Michigan in Ann Arbor. He served as vice president and professor.

In 1823 Father Richard was elected as a representative to the U.S. Congress, running at the behest of his parishioners to represent the territory of Michigan. He remained pastor during his time of public service, and while in Washington, he became a friend of Henry Clay, who assisted Richard with his English. The priest was defeated in his reelection effort in 1826, in part because of deteriorating relations with his parishioners, the opposition of local trustees, and the controversy over Richard's excommunication of a parishioner for securing a civil divorce. He was considered the likely candidate to become the first bishop of Detroit, but he died during a cholera outbreak six months before Pope Gregory XVI officially created the Diocese of Detroit in 1833.

Richmond, Diocese of

Established on July 11, 1820, by Pope Pius VII, the Diocese of Richmond serves most of the counties of central and southern Virginia. It is a suffragan see of the Archdiocese of Baltimore. Richmond is the capital of the state.

The area of what became Richmond was visited in 1607 by Christopher Newport and John Smith. In 1637 Thomas Stegg built a trading post there, which was guarded in 1644 by Fort Charles. Major William Mayo laid out the town on modern-day Church Hill in 1737. The newly developed settlement was named for Richmond-on-Thames in England.

The city embraced the growing spirit of rebellion in the American colonies and in 1774 hosted the Virginia Convention, which formed the crucial component of the American cause. When the American Revolution erupted, Richmond was pillaged by the British. In 1785 Thomas Jefferson designed the capital building in Richmond, as the city expanded its trade in tobacco, textiles, and paper products. In time, the economic base became more and more diverse, including chemicals, pharmaceuticals, metals, and wood. The University of

Richmond, founded in 1830, began the educational programs and facilities available in the area.

The Catholic history of the diocese opens in 1526 when Lucas Vázquez de Ayllón arrived in the area with 600 settlers. Dominican Fathers Antonio de Montesinos, Antonio de Cervantes, and Brother Pedro de Estrada were in the group and began mission labors. Guadalupe Mission was founded, dedicated to St. Michael the Archangel, and the Spanish worked to make the settlement secure. On October 18, 1526, however, Ayllón died of fever. Severe weather and virulent diseases decimated entire families, reducing the settlement to only 150. They abandoned the site and boarded two vessels to return to their homeland, but one vessel was lost at sea.

In 1570 the Spanish attempted once again to open a mission in present-day Virginia, and on September 10 of that year two Jesuit priests and six Jesuit lay brothers, sent by Governor Pedro Menendez de Avilés of Florida, entered the area. They arrived at the Rappahannock River at a site they named Axacan. Three of the Jesuit missionaries were slain by a hostile tribe near present-day Williamsburg.

The charter for Jamestown started the Colony of Virginia and the open persecution of Catholics. All priests were banned from the colony in 1642, on pain of death. Fort Charles was established two years later. Some Catholics did settle in present-day Virginia, notably Giles Brent and Captain George Brent, both related by marriage to the family of John Carroll, America's first bishop. By 1737, when Richmond was laid out as a city, Catholics resided in several enclaves in Stafford County. Priests had defied the ban over the years, and two had been arrested and removed. Others followed, going to Catholic households in Richmond and throughout the colony.

The American Revolution put an end to most of the anti-Catholic sentiment and measures, as Richmond served as a host city to conventions of patriots. Catholics in Virginia were relatively free of persecution by 1776, and priests began to establish the Church in the area without interference. Father John Dubois came in 1791 with letters from the Marquis de Lafayette, and he served the faithful in Norfolk and then Richmond, where he won the respect of leading Protestants. Father Dubois would become the third bishop of the Diocese of New York.

In Alexandria, a brick church was erected by Father John Thayer. Father Benedict Joseph Fenwick, who was later a pioneering bishop, served in the region with Father Leonard Neale, who would be the second archbishop of Baltimore, and others. During that early period, Father James Burke opened a parish in Norfolk.

By 1820 the Catholic population warranted the creation of a diocese for the area, and Pope Pius VII established the Diocese of Richmond. Father Patrick Kelly, who was consecrated on August 24, 1820, as the first bishop of Richmond, did not establish his residence in Richmond as he faced open hostility from the lay trustees of the city's parishes. He also had severe financial problems. Bishop Kelly was transferred to a diocese in Ireland in 1822, and Archbishop Ambrose Maréchal of Baltimore served as apostolic administrator of Richmond. During this period, Father Timothy O'Brien became a pastor in the diocese in 1822, establishing St. Peter's in Richmond and laboring in the city for some eighteen years. He also founded an orphanage and trained priests to serve as circuit riders to the rural Catholic communities.

Succeeding archbishops in Baltimore continued on as administrators. Finally, on December 19, 1840, Pope Gregory XVI appointed a second bishop of Richmond, Father Richard V. Whelan. Consecrated a bishop on March 21, 1841, Bishop Whelan took as his immediate priority recruiting new priests for the diocese, as he had only six priests on hand. He sent appeals to Societies for the Propagation of the Faith across Europe and founded a seminary to provide training for new vocations. Notably, he recruited from All Hallows Seminary in Ireland.

Five years of assessing the state of the Catholic community in the region prompted Bishop Whelan to move his residence to Wheeling. On his recommendation, the Holy See accepted his recommendation that a second diocese be created in Virginia, at Wheeling, and he was appointed the first bishop there in 1850.

Father John McGill was appointed by Pope Blessed Pius IX to be the third bishop of Richmond on July 23, 1850. Consecrated a bishop on November 10, 1850, he arrived and faced immediate problems with Father O'Brien, who subsequently left the diocese, and an eruption of anti-Catholic violence by the Know-Nothings and other bigoted Protestant organizations. He defended the faith and led the diocese during the yellow fever epidemic of 1855. Father Matthew O'Keefe of Norfolk and the Daughters of Charity displayed genuine heroism while caring for the victims. On December 7, 1856, St. Patrick's Church was burned to the ground during a Protestant riot. Father O'Keefe rebuilt the church, dedicating it to the Immaculate Conception, a structure designated by the Holy See as a major basilica in 1991. To promote and defend the Catholic faith, McGill wrote *The True Church Indicated to the Inquirer* and *Our Faith, the Victory*, republished as *The Creed of Catholics*.

Two years earlier, Bishop McGill journeyed to Rome to take part in the definition of the dogma of the Immaculate Conception by Pope Blessed Pius IX. Returning home, he convoked the first diocesan synod the next year. He went back to Rome to attend the First Vatican Council in 1869–70.

During the Civil War, Richmond was the capital of the Confederacy. Captured by Union General Ulysses S. Grant in 1865, the city suffered immensely from the conflict. Bishop McGill led the faithful during this terrible era. To rebuild the diocese materially and spiritually, he recruited from the American College of Louvain in Belgium and brought religious communities into the diocese. He died from exhaustion on January 14, 1872.

The fourth bishop of Richmond, James Gibbons, went on to become one of America's most prominent prelates and a cardinal. Having served as vicar apostolic of North Carolina since 1868, he was appointed bishop of Richmond on July 30, 1872, and installed on October 20. As bishop, Gibbons began ministry programs for African-Americans and visited Catholic and non-Catholics in the area, blunting the anti-Catholic sentiments with his courtesy, charm, and eloquence. Bishop Gibbons built parishes and schools and revitalized the faithful in the wake of Reconstruction. On October 3, 1877, he was promoted to the rank of coadjutor archbishop of Baltimore and in 1886 was created a cardinal.

His successor was the thirty-eight-year-old John Joseph Keane, a priest of the Baltimore Diocese. Appointed on March 28, 1878, by Pope Leo XIII, he was consecrated a bishop on August 25, 1878, and was an eloquent defender of the rights and place of the Church. He also courageously promoted evangelization and pastoral care for African-Americans and established the Confraternity of the Holy Ghost in the diocese. An ardent supporter of The Catholic University of America, he was appointed its first rector in 1886; two years later, he was given the post permanently. In 1900 he was named archbishop of Dubuque.

The sixth bishop of Richmond was Augustine Van de Vyver, a priest of the diocese. His appointment was petitioned by the priests of the diocese, and he was named on July 16, 1889, and received consecration on October 20. On June 4, 1903, he had the great pleasure of welcoming to Richmond papal representative Archbishop Diomede Falconio, who laid the cornerstone of the new Sacred Heart Cathedral, the building of which was made possible by Thomas Fortune Ryan of New York, at the cost of nearly a half million dollars. The cathedral was consecrated on November 29, 1906. Bishop Van de Vyver also continued the expansion of the diocesan facilities and schools and invited religious congregations into the diocese. He made several efforts to resign owing to health problems and died on October 16, 1911, at the age of sixty-six.

Bishop Augustine Van de Vyver

The seventh bishop of Richmond, Bishop Denis J. O'Connell, had served as rector of the North American College in Rome and was an auxiliary bishop of San Francisco since 1908. During his term of service as bishop, he witnessed the hardships of World War I and then the severe eruption of anti-Catholic fervor, led by some Protestant groups and the Ku Klux Klan. He also continued to develop the schools and parishes of the diocese until his retirement on January 15, 1926.

The eighth bishop of Richmond, Andrew J. Brennan, had served as an auxiliary bishop of Scranton since 1923. Named bishop of Richmond,

Bishop Brennan was appointed on May 28, 1926. He reorganized the diocesan offices and created St. Joseph's Villa, an orphanage. He likewise instituted charitable efforts in the wake of the Great Depression. In 1934, however, he suffered a stroke that rendered him unable to communicate. He asked for and received an apostolic administrator and was given the services of Bishop Peter L. Ireton. Brennan retired on April 14, 1945.

Bishop Ireton acceded to the see on the day of Bishop Brennan's retirement. He had served as coadjutor bishop of Richmond since 1935. His time as bishop stretched across the postwar boom in the aftermath of World War II, during which the diocese increased significantly in size; the Catholic population grew from 37,000 to 147,000, and Ireton built schools and parishes to keep pace, including parishes for African-Americans. He also promoted civic and ecumenical programs. He died on April 27, 1958.

The tenth bishop of Richmond, John J. Russell, had served as bishop of Charleston since 1950. Appointed to Richmond on July 3, 1958, and installed on September 30, he attended the Second Vatican Council and then worked to implement the decrees of the council. In the diocese, he opened St. John Vianney Seminary in 1961 and had to close some parishes owing to demographic changes. He was also a respected leader in promoting the civil rights movement in Virginia and beyond. He retired on April 28, 1973.

The eleventh bishop of Richmond, Walter F. Sullivan, had served as an auxiliary bishop of Richmond since 1970 and was appointed bishop on June 6, 1974. Installed on July 19, 1974, he had the arduous task of guiding the diocese in the difficult period after the Second Vatican Council, with challenges from declining vocations. During his time, the Diocese of Arlington was established in 1974, and Bishop Sullivan helped in the planning for the changes. He retired on September 16, 2003.

On March 31, 2004, Bishop Francis X. DiLorenzo was named the twelfth bishop of Richmond and installed on May 24, 2004. He had

Cathedral of the Sacred Heart in Richmond

served as an auxiliary bishop of Scranton and had been bishop of Honolulu since 1994. In assuming direction of the diocese, Bishop DiLorenzo made immediate changes to the diocesan liturgical life and sought to bring the diocesan women's commission into closer line with the official teachings of the Church. He likewise worked to streamline the diocese's parish structure. In 2011 there were 235,000 Catholics served by 179 priests and 146 parishes in the diocese.

Riepp, Benedicta (June 28, 1825–March 15, 1862)

A Benedictine nun who established the first monastery of women Benedictines in North America, Benedicta Riepp was born Maria Sybilla Riepp in Waal, Bavaria. She entered the Benedictine convent in Eichstätt, Bavaria, in 1844. After making her final vows in 1849, she was named novice mistress, a post she held until 1852. That year, she was given the task of traveling to the United States to establish schools for the education of the children of German immigrants. Mother Benedicta reached St. Mary, Pennsylvania, in July 1852 and founded the first community of Benedictine nuns in the United States. Although she encountered some difficulties

over jurisdiction with the Benedictine community of men at St. Vincent Abbey in Latrobe, Pennsylvania, under Archabbot Boniface Wimmer, nevertheless, over the next few years Mother Benedicta was responsible for the founding of houses in Erie, Pennsylvania, in 1856, Newark, New Jersey, in 1857, and St. Cloud, Minnesota, in 1857.

In 1857 Mother Benedicta journeyed to Europe to settle the issues of jurisdiction, but she failed in her hopes of presenting the case directly to officials in Rome. She returned home to the United States in 1858 and was given welcome by Willibalda Scherbauer, prioress in St. Cloud, as she had been removed by Wimmer. There Mother Benedicta resided until her death from tuberculosis. In 1859 Roman officials ruled that Benedictine convents should be placed under the jurisdiction of local bishops. (*See also* Benedictines.)

Rigali, Justin F. (April 19, 1935–)

Cardinal, archbishop of St. Louis from 1994 to 2003, and archbishop of Philadelphia from 2003, Justin F. Rigali was born in Los Angeles, one of seven children born to Henry A. Rigali and Frances Irene White. He studied at the archdiocesan seminaries of Los Angeles College, Our Lady Queen of Angels Seminary in San Fernando, and St. John's College and St. John's Seminary in Camarillo, California, and was ordained on April 25, 1961. In October 1961 he began graduate studies in canon law at the Pontifical Gregorian University, obtained a doctorate in 1964, and then studied at the Pontifical Ecclesiastical Academy while serving in the English-language section of the Secretariat of State of the Vatican. After service in various Vatican diplomatic posts, in 1970 then-Monsignor Rigali was named director of the English-language section of the Secretariat of State and the English-language translator for Pope Paul VI. He later accompanied Pope Blessed John Paul II on several international pastoral visits, including the pope's trips to the United States in 1979 and 1987. Monsignor Rigali also served as a professor at the Pontifical Ecclesiastical Academy in Rome from 1972 to 1973.

On June 8, 1985, he was named president of the Pontifical Ecclesiastical Academy and titular archbishop of Bolsena. From 1985 to 1990 he also held various positions in the Roman Curia and in 1989 was appointed secretary of the Congregation for Bishops; in January 1990 he became the secretary of the College of Cardinals.

On January 25, 1994, Pope Blessed John Paul II appointed Rigali the seventh archbishop of St. Louis. As archbishop, Rigali focused on improving diocesan finances, vocations, and authentic diocesan renewal. Through his financial management of the archdiocese, a deficit was ended and a highly successful capital campaign was launched.

At the same time, Archbishop Rigali launched the archdiocese's first strategic pastoral plan to promote renewal in every parish, especially through the sacraments and Catholic education. Hand in hand with the effort was a focus on vocations and evangelization and ministry to young people. In 1995, for example, the archdiocese assumed administrative control of Kenrick-Glennon Seminary.

His term as archbishop was noted as well by several events. In 1997 Rigali was elected by his fellow bishops to serve as a delegate to the Special Assembly for America of the Synod of Bishops. In 1999 the archdiocese was given the distinct privilege of a visit by Pope Blessed John Paul II, the only pastoral visit to a single diocese in the United States during the pontificate. In 2001 the pontiff appointed him to serve on the Tenth Ordinary General Assembly of the Synod of Bishops, the theme of which was "The Bishop, Servant of the Gospel of Jesus Christ for the Hope of the World."

On July 15, 2003, Pope Blessed John Paul II named Rigali the eighth archbishop of Philadelphia. He was installed on October 7, 2003, and assumed the pastoral care of 1.4 million Catholics. Two weeks after his installation as archbishop, Rigali was elevated to the College of Cardinals in a public consistory in St. Peter's Square on October 21, 2003. He was created a cardinal priest with the titular church of Santa Prisca.

Cardinal Rigali devoted himself to visiting the five counties of the Archdiocese of Philadelphia. He also held a variety of positions in the United States Conference of Catholic Bishops, was a member of the board of directors of the Black and Indian Mission Office, and held a number of membership positions in the Roman Curia, including the Vatican Congregation for Divine Worship and the Dis-

cipline of the Sacraments, and the Administration of the Patrimony of the Apostolic See. He retired on July 19, 2011.

Riobó, Juan Garcia (1740–c. 1805)

A Franciscan missionary and explorer, Juan Garcia Riobó was a native of Malpica, Spain, and entered the Franciscans in 1760. In 1769 he was sent to the Franciscan missions of Mexico and was then named to the Lower California missions in 1771. In 1779 he joined the third Spanish expedition in search of the Northwest Passage. He left Mexican waters on board *La Princesa* and *La Favorita* and sailed north, reaching perhaps as far as Alaska. In 1783 he returned to California and had a long career among the various missions of San Carlos in Monterey, San Diego, and San Gabriel in the 1780s. A contemporary of Blessed Junípero Serra, he traveled with the famed missionary before returning to Mexico, where he devoted the rest of his life. His diary was translated and published in 1918 in *Historical Records and Studies*.

Riordan, Patrick William (August 27, 1841– December 27, 1914)

The second archbishop of San Francisco, from 1884 to 1914, Patrick William Riordan was born in Chatham, New Brunswick, Canada. He grew up in Chicago after the family moved there in 1848 and subsequently studied at St. Mary of the Lake Academy in Chicago and the University of Notre Dame. Entering the seminary in 1858, he was sent to Rome to complete his studies at the Urban College of the Propaganda. He was also chosen to be one of the first students sent to reside at the North American College in Rome, although bouts of poor health forced his withdrawal from his studies there. He devoted some time to study in Paris and then entered the American College of the Louvain in 1861. Ordained in Belgium in June 1865, he continued studies and earned a licentiate in theology at the Louvain the following year.

Riordan returned to Chicago in 1866, where he taught at the seminary of St. Mary's of the Lake. From 1871 to 1883 he held a variety of pastoral assignments, so distinguishing himself that in 1883 he was appointed the coadjutor archbishop of San Francisco, with the right of succession to the famed Archbishop Joseph Sadoc Alemany. Riordan acceded to the archdiocese on December 28, 1884.

At the time of his accession as archbishop, there were 120,000 Catholics served by 156 priests in 133 churches and chapels. He took as his chief tasks the strengthening of the archdiocese, both materially and spiritually. His ambitious building program included new parish schools (as ordered by the Third Plenary Council of Baltimore and assisted by a board of diocesan education), the new St. Mary's Cathedral, which was dedicated on January 11, 1891, and above all, St. Patrick's Seminary in Menlo Park, which was begun in September 1898. In 1890 the Dominican College of San Rafael was started for women, and Catholic students in Bay area colleges were assisted by Newman Centers.

The archbishop also encouraged the arrival of different communities of men and women religious, assumed control of the official diocesan paper, *The Monitor*, in 1892, and commissioned Father Peter C. Yorke to fight against the activities of the American Protective Association in the 1890s.

In 1902 he represented the California bishops in the appeal before the International Court of the Hague for the Pious Fund of the Calfornias, thus securing for the Church those funds that had been donated to the California missions but had been confiscated by the Mexican government (*see also* Pious Fund of the Californias) in the nineteenth century. By 1903 and the 50th anniversary of the founding of the diocese, there were 250,000 Catholics, 271 priests, and 148 missions and churches.

The chief event of his long episcopate, however, was the terrible earthquake of 1906. Archbishop Riordan was away at the time, but he wasted no time upon his immediate return in rallying the people of the city. He gave impassioned speeches for unity in the face of the disaster and was a leading voice in organizing a rebuilding program, including the restoration of churches, parishes, and religious institutions. His last years were troubled by declining

Cardinal Joseph Ritter

health and the need for an auxiliary bishop. His first auxiliary, Bishop George Montgomery, died in 1907 after serving only four years, and his second choice, Bishop Edward J. Hanna, was delayed until 1912 owing to Hanna's reputation for modernist sympathies. By the time of his passing, the archdiocese was superbly organized and had been provided with a sound financial footing.

Ritter, Joseph E. (July 20, 1892–June 10, 1967)

Archbishop of St. Louis from 1946 to 1967 and cardinal from 1961, Joseph E. Ritter was born in New Albany, Indiana. He studied for the priesthood at St. Meinrad's Seminary in southern Indiana, and received ordination on May 30, 1917, for the Archdiocese of Indianapolis. Immediately after ordination, he was assigned to the cathedral of Indianapolis and later became rector there. In 1930 he was appointed a diocesan consultor and member of the commission charged with reorganizing diocesan finances. He later held the posts of vicar general and vice president of the diocesan paper (the modern-day *Criterion*).

On February 3, 1933, Ritter was consecrated titular bishop of Hippos and auxiliary bishop of the Diocese of Indianapolis. He was forty-one at the time, thus one of the youngest bishops in the United States. A little over a year later, on March 24, 1934, Ritter succeeded to the see upon the passing of Bishop Joseph Chartrand. In 1944 the diocese was elevated to the rank of archdiocese and on November 11, 1944, Ritter became its first archbishop.

During his years as bishop and archbishop of Indianapolis, Ritter embarked upon an ambitious program of renewal and revitalization of the Church in Indianapolis. He improved finances to the point that a $500,000 reduction in debt was achieved and a lay advisory board for diocesan finances was launched, an innovation that anticipated the developments of the Second Vatican Council. A home mission fund was begun, by which wealthier parishes agreed to share their income with poorer parishes, and reforms were made in diocesan administration. He also urged close cooperation between clergy and laity, organizing units of the National Council of Catholic Men and National Council of Women and the Catholic Youth Organization.

Above all, Ritter took on the forces of racism and intolerance in Indiana. The Ku Klux Klan had its headquarters in Indianapolis and was actively engaged in racist and anti-Catholic activities. He spoke out against all forms of injustice and was concerned especially for the plight of poor African-American Catholics. He built a church for them, established a cultural and recreational center for black youths, and quietly but deliberately integrated parochial schools in his jurisdiction.

Although little known outside of Indiana, Ritter became far more prominent after his appointment on July 20, 1946, his fifty-fourth birthday, as archbishop of St. Louis a few months after the death of Cardinal John Joseph Glennon. Once installed on October 6, 1946, Ritter declared his determination to complete the work begun by Cardinal Glennon in the area of integration. At the beginning of the school term for 1947, Archbishop Ritter decreed the integration of all Catholic schools in the archdiocese, an act that predated the Supreme Court decision on desegregation of public schools by six years.

The decree met with resistance by some in the archdiocese, including unsuccessful appeals to the apostolic delegate. When, however, the committees against segregation threatened civil action, the archbishop ordered a letter read in every parish on September 21, 1947, reminding Catholics that canon law forbade civil suits against lawful superiors in the Church and that those attempting such suits would be subject to excommunication. The letter ended the public resentment of some Catholics and made Archbishop Ritter well known across the country for his determined stand on equal rights.

He also promoted social programs, including the Alverne Hotel for elderly laypeople and Regina Cleri for older priests. His concerns for global justice prompted him to support the Bishop's War Emergency and Relief Fund (*see also* Catholic Relief Services), and in 1953 he hosted a successful World Missions Exhibition. He also worked to support relief efforts for the Church in Latin America, and in 1955 he sent three volunteer priests for service in the missions of La Paz, Bolivia, the first such mission funded by a diocese in the United States.

In 1958 he applied enthusiastically the Instruction on Sacred Music and the Sacred Liturgy from the Congregation of Rites, which took early key steps in promoting greater lay participation in the liturgy. The following year, he issued a pastoral letter implementing the decree for all parishes. As a result of his long-standing interest in authentic liturgical reform, he was named in 1958 head of the bishops' Commission on the Liturgical Apostolate. On December 16, 1960, he was created a cardinal priest with the titular church of SS. Redentore e Alfonso in Via Merulana by Pope Blessed John XXIII, receiving his red hat at a consistory held in Rome on January 16, 1961.

Cardinal Ritter subsequently was an active supporter of the Second Vatican Council and was a member of the Central Commission charged with planning the agenda for the council. Among his chief concerns were the liturgy, ecumenism, and religious freedom, topics that placed him in the forefront of discussions on key documents, in particular *Sacrosanctum Concilium*, on the liturgy. In the aftermath of the council, Cardinal Ritter was named by Pope Paul VI on March 4, 1964, to the commission for the supervision and coordination of the liturgical reforms called for by the council. He died from a heart attack.

Roberts, John G. (January 27, 1955–)

Seventeenth chief justice of the United States Supreme Court, the third Catholic chief justice, and the tenth Catholic justice, John G. Roberts was born in Buffalo, New York. His family moved to Long Beach, Indiana, when he was two years old, and he was raised in a devout Catholic environment. He graduated from Harvard University summa cum laude in 1976 and then attended Harvard Law School, where he served as managing editor of the *Harvard Law Review* and graduated magna cum laude in 1979.

After graduating from law school, Roberts served as a law clerk for Judge Henry Friendly on the Second Circuit Court of Appeals. He then served from 1980 to 1981 as a law clerk to then

Associate Justice William H. Rehnquist on the United States Supreme Court. He held several positions in the Reagan White House, including special assistant to U.S. Attorney General William French Smith and associate counsel to the president in the office of White House Counsel Fred F. Fielding.

Roberts entered private law practice in 1986 but returned to the government to serve in the administration of President George H. W. Bush as Principal deputy solicitor general from 1989 to 1993. In 1992 President Bush nominated him to the U.S. Court of Appeals for the District of Columbia Circuit; no Senate vote was held, however, and Roberts's nomination expired after the 1992 election of Bill Clinton. Roberts returned to private practice and was also an adjunct faculty member at the Georgetown University Law Center.

President George W. Bush nominated Roberts to the Court of Appeals for the District of Columbia Circuit on May 9, 2001; his nomination, like twenty-nine others, failed to make it out of the Democratic-controlled U.S. Senate Judiciary Committee. He was renominated on January 7, 2003, and was approved by the Senate under unanimous consent. President Bush then nominated John Roberts as associate justice of the Supreme Court on July 19, 2005, after the announcement of Justice Sandra Day O'Connor's retirement. The nomination was subsequently changed following the death of Chief Justice Rehnquist, so that Roberts could replace Rehnquist as head of the court.

His nomination first as associate justice and then as chief justice was approved on September 22, 2005, by the Senate Judiciary Committee. Roberts was confirmed by the full Senate on September 29, by a vote of 78–22. Appointed at the age of fifty, he is the third-youngest man to become chief justice (John Jay was appointed at age forty-four in 1789 and John Marshall was appointed at age forty-five in 1801). Roberts is the third Catholic to hold the post of chief justice. The first Catholic on the Supreme Court was also the first Catholic chief justice, Justice Roger B. Taney, who served from 1836 to 1864. The second Catholic chief justice was Edward Douglass White (associate justice from 1894 to 1910 and chief justice from 1910 to 1921).

Robinson, Paschal (April 26, 1870–August 26, 1948)

A Franciscan priest, writer, and apostolic nuncio to Ireland from 1929, Paschal Robinson was born in Dublin, Ireland. Charles (his baptismal name) migrated to the United States with his family while he was still a a boy and grew up in New York.

In 1896 he entered the novitiate of the Order of Friars Minor and received the name Paschal. He took his solemn vows in Rome in 1900 and was ordained in December 1901. Over the next years, the Franciscans posted Robinson to studies and writing, and the priest wrote a variety of books and articles, including *The Real St. Francis* (1903), *Some Pages of Franciscan History* (1905), *The Writings of St. Francis* (1906), and *The Life of St. Clare* (1910); he also contributed articles to the monumental *Catholic Encyclopedia* and served as associate editor of the international Franciscan Review, the *Archivum Franciscanum Historicum*.

In 1913 Robinson assumed a teaching post in medieval history at The Catholic University of America, serving until 1919. The next year, he became a fellow of the Royal Historical Society of England. Following World War I, he became a consultant to the U.S. government at the various meetings of the Versailles Conference.

He subsequently was named by the Holy See to several posts in the Near East, including Custodian of the Holy Land and Latin Patriarch in Jerusalem. He also served as consultor to several congregations of the Roman Curia. In 1927 he was created titular archbishop of Tyana. Father Robinson soon distinguished himself as chief mediator between religious and state leaders on Malta. For his many efforts on behalf of the Holy See, he was appointed papal nuncio to Ireland in 1929.

Robinson, William Callyhan (July 26, 1834–November 6, 1911)

A lawyer and professor, William Callyhan Robinson was born at Norwich, Connecticut, and studied at Dartmouth College. After graduation in 1854, he entered the Episcopal Theological Seminary and was ordained in 1857. After ministry in Pittston, Pennsylvania, from 1857 to 1858, and Scranton, Pennsylvani, from 1859 to 1862, he left the Episcopalian Church and was received into the Catholic

Church in 1863. In 1864 he was admitted to the bar and served as a law professor at Yale University from 1869 to 1895. He also held the posts of city court judge and appeals court judge, and was a member of the state legislature. In 1895 he was named to the faculty of The Catholic University of America, where he was instrumental in establishing the School of Social Sciences, and was dean of the School of Law until his death.

Rochambeau, Comte de (July 1, 1725–May 10, 1807)

A French marshal, diplomat, and soldier who took part in the American Revolution, the Comte de Rochambeau was born at Vendôme, France, to a noble French family. He embarked upon a military career in 1745 and was named as an aide-de-camp to Louis Philippe, Duc d'Orleans. Demonstrating his skills, he was named the colonel of a regiment and took part in a number of campaigns with considerable distinction. When the American Revolution began, Rochambeau's name emerged at the royal court as a likely commanding general for French forces that were to be dispatched to assist the Americans in their struggle against England. Although Rochambeau was offered the rank of lieutenant general, King Louis XVI was willing to commit only six thousand men to the endeavor, a force considered by Rochambeau to be far too small to be effective. Nevertheless, he was impressed by the determination of the American leaders and had great sympathy for the cause of freedom.

Rochambeau arrived at Newport, Rhode Island, in July 1780. He joined the American army under General George Washington where it was encamped on the Hudson to the north of New York. Following his first meeting with Washington, Rochambeau marched south to Virginia and took part with great distinction in the Yorktown campaign that brought an end to the war in 1781. At the surrender of General Charles Cornwallis on

Compte de Rochambeau

October 19, 1781, Rochambeau was presented one of the captured cannons. At the time of his departure from America, Rochambeau was immensely popular and greatly respected by his American counterparts. For his labors, he was awarded honors by the French crown.

Owing to his service in the American Revolution, Rochambeau was accepted by the new French revolutionary regime and was given the rank and baton of Marshal of France in 1791. In 1792 he was given command of French forces facing the Austrians, but the darkening political circumstances in France compelled his resignation. He was soon arrested and barely avoided the guillotine when the radical Jacobins seized power over the revolutionary government in Paris. Once the Reign of Terror of Robespierre passed, Rochambeau was rehabilitated and was granted a pension by Napoleon Bonaparte in 1804; Napoleon also granted him the Cross of Grand Officer of the Legion of Honor. He died an honored figure in the eyes of his country.

Rockne, Knute Kenneth (March 4, 1888– March 31, 1931)

The head coach of the the University of Notre Dame football team from 1918 to 1931, Knute Kenneth Rockne was born in Voss, Norway, and migrated to the United States as a young man. After working as a chemist, assistant track coach, and assistant football coach, he was named the head coach of the Fighting Irish of Notre Dame in 1918. Over the next thirteen years, Rockne assembled an astonishing record of 105 victories, 12 losses, 5 ties, and 6 national championships, the greatest all-time winning percentage of any college coach. Rockne also coached Notre Dame to five undefeated seasons without a tie.

Rockne was famed for his innovative approach to coaching and football strategy, creating "The Four Horsemen," a backfield composed of Harry Stuhldreher, Don Miller, Jim Crowley, and Elmer Layden, that led Notre Dame to a 28–2 record. Rockne also coached one of the most famous players of modern sports, George "Gipper" Gipp, Notre Dame's first All-American and the subject of Rockne's legendary motivational pregame speech, "Win one for the Gipper."

Rockne's career ended when the airplane carrying him from Kansas City to Los Angeles crashed into a field in Bazaar, Kansas. Will Rogers said of Rockne: "It takes a big calamity to shock a country all at once, but Knute, you did it. You died one of our national heroes. Notre Dame was your address, but every gridiron in America was your home."

Knute Rockne

Rochester, Diocese of

Established on March 3, 1868, by Pope Blessed Pius IX, the Diocese of Rochester serves counties in northwestern New York. It is a suffragan of the Archdiocese of New York. The city is a port of entry on Lake Ontario, and the first settlement on the site was made in 1789. Ebenezer Allen operated a great mill on the site, providing an economic base and encouraging development. He laid out the city in 1811, calling it Rochesterville. The name was shortened in 1822. The city was part of a chain of stops on the Erie Canal and welcomed new settlers every year. It became a major industrial and port center.

The Catholic history of Rochester opened in 1756 when Jesuit missionaries from Québec labored among the Iroquois and opened missions. The New York Assembly banned such Catholic priests from the colony on pain of death; a few Catholics chose to stay in the area but they had severely limited rights. The bravery and commitment of these Catholics during the American Revolution led to their gaining the same rights as other citizens when New York became a state and a new constitution was approved. An influx of Catholic immigrants arrived in Rochester in the years after the war, when the penal laws were lifted.

In 1808 the Diocese of New York was erected by the Holy See and the faithful of Rochester were part of that ecclesiastical jurisdiction. In 1832 the bishop of New York, John Connolly, founded St. Patrick's Church in Rochester. A parish for Ger-man-American Catholics, St. Joseph's, was opened in 1836, and other parishes were erected soon after.

In 1847 Rochester was part of the ecclesiastical jurisdiction of the Diocese of Buffalo. The revered Vincentian Bishop John Timon, served as the bishop of Buffalo, and faced trusteeism in some Rochester parishes, as well as anti-Catholic activities in the region. The Know-Nothings tried to burn down a church in Palmyra, St. Anne's.

Rochester continued to prosper and promote the Catholic presence despite the attacks, and St. Mary's Hospital opened in 1857. The Diocese of Rochester, which was a visible recognition by the Holy See of the vibrant faithful of the area, was established in 1868.

The first bishop of Rochester was Bernard J. McQuaid, who was consecrated a bishop in St. Patrick's Cathedral in New York on July 12, 1868. He was installed in Rochester on July 16. He arrived in a diocese with more than sixty parishes and thirty-eight priests serving the Catholics of the area. He doubled the number of parishes and was a pioneer in Catholic education. In 1870 he opened St. Andrew's Preparatory Seminary and in 1893 started St. Bernard's Seminary. He was also noted for his programs to care for children, the aged, and the ill. He attended the First Vatican Council in 1870 and later attended the Fourth Plenary Council of Baltimore in 1883. In 1905 he requested a coadjutor bishop, and Bishop Thomas F. Hickey was consecrated on May 24, 1905. A native of Rochester, he succeeded to the see on January 19, 1909, upon the passing of Bishop McQuaid.

Thomas F. Hickey was the second Catholic bishop of Rochester. He continued the expansion of schools and parishes and was famed for his devotion to Catholic education. He assisted the opening of Nazareth College, promoted catechetical instruction for Catholic children in public schools, supported an apostolate for the deaf, and was an ardent backer of Catholic Charities. He also led the faithful during World War I and then during the boom years of the 1920s. He retired on October

30, 1928, and was appointed a titular archbishop by the Holy See.

The third bishop of Rochester, John Francis O'Hern, was a priest of Rochester. Consecrated on March 9, 1929, he became bishop at the same time that the country entered into the Great Depression, and he mobilized Catholics to survive the terrible economic ordeal. He died suddenly on May 22, 1933, at the age 58.

The fourth bishop of Rochester was Archbishop Edward Mooney, a brilliant diplomat who was serving as an apostolic delegate to Japan at the time of his appointment as bishop of Rochester, with the personal title of archbishop, on August 28, 1933. He was installed on October 12, as America was in the grip of the Great Depression, and he organized relief programs and maintained diocesan services in the midst of the crisis. To provide for the needs of African-Americans, he supported Catholic Action and the Knights of Peter Claver. In 1935 he was elected chairman of the National Catholic Welfare Conference, a post he held until 1945. On May 26, 1937, he was appointed the archbishop of Detroit and was created a cardinal in 1946.

Archbishop Mooney was succeeded by Bishop James E. Kearney, who had been bishop of Salt Lake City since 1932. Named as fifth bishop of Rochester on July 31, 1937, he served throughout World War II and the postwar boom, and then through the Second Vatican Council. He presided over a large expansion of the diocese, seeing increases in the number of parishes, schools, and ordinations. He supported the Basilians in opening St. John Fisher College, as well as foundations by the Benedictines and Trappists. Concerned with the declining morality of American culture, he condemned the 1947 film *Forever Amber* and called for a Catholic boycott. He retired on October 26, 1966.

The successor to Bishop Kearney was one of the towering figures in American Catholicism, Bishop Fulton J. Sheen, who had been an auxiliary bishop of New York since 1951 and a famed radio and

Bishop Bernard McQuaid

media figure. Appointed to Rochester on October 21, 1966, he served the diocese for three years until October 6, 1969, when he retired and was named a titular archbishop. (*See also* Sheen, Fulton J.)

The seventh bishop of Rochester was Father Joseph L. Hogan, a priest of the Rochester diocese. Consecrated on November 28, 1969, Bishop Hogan implemented the reforms mandated by the Second Vatican Council and instituted lay ministries and programs in the diocese. At the same time, he grappled with declines in vocations to the priesthood and religious life. He retired on November 22, 1978.

The eighth bishop of Rochester, Father Matthew H. Clark, was appointed on April 23, 1979, at the age of forty-one. Consecrated on May 27, 1979, by Pope Blessed John Paul II, he was installed in Rochester on June 26, 1979. Second only to Bishop McQuaid in the length of his episcopal tenure, Bishop Clark served during a time of immense social upheaval, with the need to undertake parish and school closings because of changing demographics. He also presided during a variety of controversies, most notably the sex abuse crisis, and he worked to implement the norms for the protection of youth. In 2011 there were 310,000 Catholics, served by 227 priests, almost 500 women religious, and 106 parishes in the diocese.

Rockford, Diocese of

Established on September 23, 1908, by Pope St. Pius X, the Diocese of Rockford serves counties in north-central Illinois. It is a suffragan see of the Archdiocese of Chicago. The site of present-day Rockford was settled in 1834 by migrants from New England and was called Midway, as the settlement served as a coach stop between Chicago and Galena. The name was changed in honor of a local ford across the river. A dam completed in 1844 provided water power for the start of local manufacturing. In the 1850s, John Murray started a farm-machinery firm and invented a reaper and a type of mower, which became popular.

The Swedish carpenters who came to Rockford as immigrants started furniture manufacturing as well. In 1852 Rockford was incorporated as a city and prospered. The city also became a terminal for the Galena and Chicago Union Railroad. During World Wars I and II, Camp Grant served the nation's military.

The Catholic history of Rockford opened in 1673 when the region was visited by the Jesuit explorer Father Jacques Marquette and his companion, Louis Joliet. During their stay in present-day Illinois, Father Marquette founded the famous Kaskaskia Mission. In 1680 René-Robert Chevalier, Sieur de la Salle, the revered French explorer, built a fort in the area, and some of the most renowned Catholic missionaries of the era labored in Illinois. Father Louis Hennepin was there for a time, as were Father Gabriel de la Ribourde and Zenobius Membré. Jesuit superior Father Claude Allouez and Father Jacques Gravier served the local Indian villages until unrest forced them to move south.

Kaskaskia Mission, dedicated to the Immaculate Conception, was moved to a new location on the Mississippi River, across from St. Louis, and there Fathers Allouez and Gravier completed dictionaries of local Indian languages. Missions were founded at Rockford, Starved Rock, and Peoria, and priests from the Foreign Mission of Québec began serving in the region, opening another famous outpost of the faith, Cahokia Mission, which was dedicated to the Holy Family.

The French and Indian War, which raged from 1754 to 1763, brought tribulation to the missions, and the British took control of Illinois, attempting to banish the Catholic priests in 1763. As Americans resolved to be free of British rule, priests returned to the area. Jesuit Father Pierre Gibault served in the region, aiding the American cause during the American Revolution. He became a popular hero of the young nation at war's end.

Catholic trappers and hunters in the region of present-day Rockford were in the ecclesiastical jurisdiction of Bishop John Carroll, America's first bishop, who resided in Baltimore. In 1808 the Diocese of Bardstown (now the Archdiocese of Louisville) assumed jurisdiction over Illinois. In the following year, the U.S. Congress established the

Illinois Territory, and in 1827 Illinois entered the Union. Rockford was settled in 1834, and the city was impacted by the Civil War, with many soldiers from the state dying on the battlefield or from disease in Union forts and encampments. The Catholic population continued to grow after the war, and by 1908 a diocese was deemed needed.

The first bishop of Rockford, Peter James Muldoon, had served as an auxiliary bishop of Chicago since 1901. He was appointed on September 28, 1908, and established the offices and agencies for diocesan administration. The next year, he was named the bishop of Monterey-Los Angeles, but the priests of the diocese protested and Bishop Muldoon declined the appointment. Over the next years, the bishop became a promoter of the cause of labor in the diocese. With the entry of the United States into World War I, he served as chairman of the National Catholic War Council and became nationally prominent. After the war, he proposed that the council continue in a peacetime capacity, and the council became the National Catholic Welfare Conference in 1919. Bishop Muldoon died on October 8, 1927, after an illness.

The second bishop of Rockford was Edward F. Hoban, who had served as auxiliary bishop of Chicago since 1921. Appointed on February 21, 1928, he led the faithful during the Great Depression and the first grim years of World War II. He also promoted Catholic education and launched a diocesan newspaper. In honor of his leadership, Pope Pius XI named him an Assistant at the Pontifical Throne on November 25, 1937. On November 14, 1942, he was appointed the coadjutor bishop of Cleveland.

Bishop Hoban was followed by John J. Boylan, a priest of the Des Moines diocese. Appointed to Rockford on November 21, 1942, Boylan was consecrated on February 17, 1943. He led the diocese through the last years of World War II and the postwar economic boom. A builder bishop, Boylan labored until his death on July 19, 1953, at Narragansett, Rhode Island, at the age of sixty-three.

The fourth bishop of Rockford, Father Raymond P. Hillinger, a priest of the Archdiocese of Chicago, was appointed on November 3, 1953. Consecrated on December 29, 1953, he served as bishop for two years until he was named an auxiliary bishop of Chicago on June 27, 1956.

On June 27, 1956, Donald M. Carroll, a priest from Chicago, was named bishop of Rockford. Owing to poor health, he resigned on September 25, 1956.

The next bishop of Rockford was Loras T. Lane, who had served as auxiliary bishop of Dubuque since 1951. Appointed to Rockford on October 11, 1956, he spearheaded education efforts and reorganized the diocesan offices and agencies. In 1961 he was named a member of the preparatory commission for the Second Vatican Council and a permanent member of the Commission for Seminaries, Studies, and Catholic Education. He took part in all of the sessions of the council and died on July 22, 1968, at the age of fifty-seven.

Bishop Lane was followed as bishop of Rockford on August 19, 1968, by Arthur J. O'Neill, a priest of the Diocese of Rockford. Consecrated on October 11, 1968, he began his long tenure as bishop by implementing the Second Vatican Council and its reforms. He was faced by a variety of challenges, including changing demographics, declines in vocations, and financial demands on the diocese. He retired on April 19, 1994.

On the same day as Bishop O'Neill's retirement, Thomas G. Doran, a priest of the diocese, was appointed the seventh bishop of Rockford. Consecrated on June 24, 1994, Bishop Doran presided over the diocese throughout the upheaval of the sex abuse crisis, the economic crises of the 2000s, and the changing face of the Catholic community. A noted expert in canon law, Bishop Doran was named on September 2, 2000, a member of the Supreme Tribunal of the Apostolic Signatura, and on March 2, 2001, a bishop member of the Congregation for the Clergy. In 2011 there were 457,000 Catholics served by 235 priests and 104 parishes in the diocese.

Rockville Centre, Diocese of

Established on April 6, 1957, by Pope Pius XII, the Diocese of Rockville Centre serves eastern counties on Long Island, New York, and was created out of territory taken from the Diocese of Brooklyn. It is a suffragan see of the Archdiocese of New York.

Rockville Centre traces its origins to 1524 when Giovanni da Verrazano, an Italian in service to King Francis I of France, became the first European in the New York area. By 1609 the French were in the Lake Champlain region, establishing missions and facing the threats of the local Native Americans. In that same year, Henry Hudson explored New York Harbor for the Dutch East India Company. The Dutch founded New Netherlands and occupied Manhattan Island, where Fort Amsterdam was built. The Dutch formally prohibited Catholicism but were courteous in their dealings with the missionaries. St. Isaac Jogues, the courageous Jesuit martyr, was released from his captivity by the Iroquois and was received courteously by Dutch Governor William Kieft.

In 1664 New Netherlands was ceded by the Dutch authorities, and King Charles II of England gave it to his brother, James, Duke of York. James became a Catholic in 1672 and sent Colonel Thomas Dongan, also a Catholic, as governor. He brought Jesuit Father Thomas Harvey to New York, and two other Jesuit priests and two Jesuit brothers soon joined them. Governor Dongan planned to erect a series of missions, but in 1689 an armed rebellion of Calvinists in the colony forced him to flee. The Church of England was made the established church, and the Calvinists were punished. Priests were outlawed, and anyone harboring them was severely fined. Penal laws were in place until the American Revolution, and few Catholics resided in New York Colony.

The dedication and courage of the Catholics in New York and throughout the colonies put an end to much of the persecution against the faithful. The presence of the French allies, who won the respect and admiration of the Americans, added to the modification of legislation. However, the state constitution passed in New York in 1777 excluded foreign-born Catholics from citizenship. The Catholic faithful, however, began to gather openly, and the Church became a presence in New York affairs.

The industrious projects of the region, such as the Erie Canal, demanded laborers, and the Irish and other Catholic groups responded to the call. These laborers started their own settlements, as the population of the area soared and the presence of Catholics became commonplace. In 1808 New York City was established as a diocese by the Holy See, followed by Albany and other sees. Old St. Patrick's Cathedral was started in New York City, and diocesan offices and agencies were initiated. By 1817 Catholic parishes were being opened throughout the region.

Nativism and other forms of bigotry and anti-Catholicism were rampant in the 1840s, but Catholic bishops such as John Hughes provided protection for Church properties in New York. The vandalism and arson experienced in other cities did not take place in New York.

The Civil War brought unrest and violence to the area, and New York was elevated to the status of a metropolitan see. The Diocese of Rochester was established in 1868 and the Diocese of Ogdensburg in 1872. In 1886 the Diocese of Syracuse was also established.

The faithful on Long Island were being served by parishes such as St. Boniface in Elmont, opened in 1852, St. Patrick's in Bayshore, started in 1883, and St. Joseph's in Babylon, dating to 1877. The Cathedral of St. Agnes in Rockville Centre was established as a parish in 1894.

By 1957 the size of the Catholic population warranted the development of a new diocese for Long Island. Rockville Centre was chosen by the Holy See.

The first bishop was Walter Philip Kellenberg, who had served as an auxiliary bishop of New York and then bishop of Ogdensburg since 1954. Appointed on April 16, 1957, Bishop Kellenberg began the offices for the diocese, designated St. Agnes as his cathedral, and founded the Seminary of the Immaculate Conception and St. Pius X Preparatory Seminary. He also established Mercy Hospital, Good Samaritan Hospital, and a diocesan newspaper. He attended the Second Vatican Council and in May 1964 celebrated Mass at the Vatican Pavilion at the World's Fair. He retired on May 3, 1976.

The second bishop of Rockville Centre was Bishop John R. McGann, who had served as an auxiliary bishop of the diocese since 1970. Installed on June 24, 1976, Bishop McGann promoted the reforms of the Second Vatican Council during a period of considerable social upheaval. He also launched the permanent diaconate, presided over the diocese's twenty-fifth anniversary, and continued meeting the pastoral needs of the diocese in the midst of declining vocations and changing demographics. He retired on January 4, 2000.

Bishop McGann was succeeded by Bishop James T. McHugh, who had served as auxiliary bishop of Brooklyn, bishop of Camden, and then coadjutor bishop of Rockville Centre since 1998. Bishop McHugh acceded to the see upon Bishop McGann's retirement.

Bishop McHugh died on December 10, 2000 and was followed by Bishop William F. Murphy, who had been an auxiliary bishop of Boston since 1995. Installed as the third bishop of Rockville Centre on September 5, 2001, he arrived in the diocese only a few days before the terrorist attack on New York and Washington, D.C., on September 11. The diocese shared in the mourning and grief as many members of the community lost their lives. In 2011 there were 1.5 million Catholics served by 426 priests, more than 1,000 women religious, and 133 parishes in the diocese.

Rogers, Mary Joseph (October 27, 1882–October 9, 1955)

The foundress of the Maryknoll Sisters of St. Dominic, Mary Rogers was born in Boston to a large Catholic family. After graduating from Smith College in Northampton, Massachusetts, in 1905, she returned on a teaching fellowship in biology and established a Mission Study Class to promote Catholic zeal in students. To provide adequate reading materials to her students, she contacted Father James A. Walsh at the Society for the Propagation of the Faith in Boston, starting a longtime collaboration with the famed missionary priest. In 1908 she took a post teaching in the public schools while she assisted Father Walsh with a new mission publication, *The Field Afar*.

Father Walsh and Father Thomas F. Price began the Catholic Foreign Mission Society of America, or Maryknoll, in 1911, and Rogers gathered together a group of women to provide assistance to the new evangelizing effort. The group grew so rapidly that by 1920 the women were granted formal ecclesiastical recognition as the Foreign Mission Sisters of St. Dominic. Rogers became the first mother general of the new congregation, under the name Mother Mary Joseph, and remained in her post until 1946. In 1921 the first members set out for China.

To assist the new congregation's efforts, Mother Mary began a teachers' college in Maryknoll, New

York, promoted the contemplative life, and worked to assist Maryknoll in developing the missions in China. On the basis of these efforts, the congregation soon spread around the world. By the time of her death, the congregation was flourishing in the United States, Africa, Asia, Latin America, and the Pacific Islands.

Rosati, Joseph (January 12, 1789–September 25, 1843)

An Italian Vincentian missionary and the first bishop of St. Louis, from 1826 to 1843, Joseph Rosati was the first American bishop of Italian descent. Born in Sora, in the Kingdom of Naples, Italy, Rosati entered the seminary while still a boy and studied in the Roman Seminary of the Vincentian Fathers. Ordained in 1811, he spent the next several years in parish ministry in Rome and Naples. In 1815 he received an invitation from Father Felix de Andreis, one of his professors of theology, to journey to the United States and assist in the missions there, specifically to aid Bishop Louis Dubourg, the apostolic administrator of Upper and Lower Louisiana.

Bishop Joseph Rosati

Fathers Rosati, de Andreis, and several other priests and brothers arrived in Baltimore in July 1816 and set out for Bardstown, Kentucky, to improve their English and to serve as instructors of theology in the local seminary. In 1818 they were sent by Bishop Dubourg to found St. Mary's Seminary in Perryville, Missouri. Rosati soon was serving as a pastor, seminary rector, and superior of the Vincentian Community after Father de Andreis died in October 1820. Recognizing Father Rosati's many talents, Bishop Dubourg requested in 1822 that the trusted priest be appointed the vicar apostolic over what the bishop hoped to be the new territory of Mississippi and Alabama, split from his own extensive administrative jurisdiction. Father Rosati was reluctant to accept, both out of humility and in recognition of the paltry resources available. Undeterred, Bishop Dubourg suggested in 1823 that Rosati be named coadjutor bishop of Louisiana and the Two Floridas with responsibility over the vast stretches of the northern parts of the

Louisiana Territory. He was consecrated on March 25, 1824.

On July 18, 1826, Rosati was appointed the first apostolic administrator of St. Louis and at the same time the apostolic administrator of New Orleans as well, a post he held until 1829, as Bishop Dubourg had departed for France to serve as bishop of Montauban.

On March 20, 1827, Rosati was named the first bishop of the Diocese of St. Louis. He was best remembered for establishing the cathedral church of in St. Louis. The cornerstone was solemnly blessed by Bishop Rosati on August 1, 1831, and the solemn consecration of the cathedral took place on October 26, 1834. The bishop was also concerned with supporting the missions that extended along the Mississippi Valley and were as far-flung as Oregon. He also encouraged various religious communities to assist the missionary labors, including the Jesuits, who founded St. Louis University, the Sisters of St. Joseph, the Sisters of the Visitation, and the Daughters of Charity.

Bishop Rosati took part in the first four Provincial Councils of Baltimore, and he played an instrumental role in drafting several of the conciliar documents. After the completion of the Fourth Provincial Council in 1840, he journeyed to Rome to confer with the Holy See about the progress in the diocese. While there, he was asked by Pope Gregory XVI to serve as apostolic delegate to the Republic of Haiti, with the task of negotiating a settlement between the Church and the local government. His work was completed in 1842 with the signing of an effective concordat. Bishop Rosati then returned to Rome for additional consultation. While there, he fell ill and died. As bishop, Rosati was known for his intensely pastoral manner of governance, in particular his devotion to the confessional and his wide accessibility to the faithful of the diocese.

Rosecrans, William (September 6, 1819–March 11, 1898)

A Union general during the Civil War, William Rosecrans was born at Kingston, Ohio, the grandson

General William Rosecrans

on his mother's side of Samuel Hopkins, one of the signers of the Declaration of Independence.

After graduating from the United States Military Academy at West Point in 1842, he served briefly with the engineer corps and then returned to West Point as a professor. During his time there, he converted to the Catholic faith, around 1845. In 1854 he resigned from the army, but with the start of the Civil War he was appointed a colonel of volunteers and returned to active service. In June 1861 he became a brigadier general and served in campaigns and posts in West Virginia, Mississippi, and Tennessee. His military career was all but finished by his defeat by the Confederate army under General Bragg in September 1863 at the Battle of Chickamauga. Soon after, he was relieved of command and finally resigned from the army at the end of the war. In 1868 he served as the United States minister to Mexico; in 1880 he was elected to Congress, winning reelection in 1882. From 1885 to 1893 he held the post of registrar of the U.S. Treasury, and in 1889 Congress restored his rank (as well as his pay) of retired brigadier general of the regular army.

Rosecrans's brother, Sylvester Harden Rosecrans, was dis-

tinguished as the first bishop of the Diocese of Columbus. Like his brother, Sylvester was a convert. William's conversion left a great impression upon him. Ordained a priest in 1852, he ministered in Cincinnati for several years and was named titular bishop of Pompeiopolis and auxiliary bishop of Cincinnati. After the founding of the Diocese of Columbus in 1868, Sylvester Rosecrans was transferred as its first bishop. He remained in his office until his death on October 21, 1878.

Rouquette, Adrien Emmanuel (February 13, 1813–July 15, 1887)

A missionary among the Choctaw Indians, Adrien Emmanuel Rouquette was a native of New Orleans of French descent. From an early time, he developed a fascination with the Choctaw Indians and desired greatly to serve as a missionary among them. Such was his fascination that his parents sent him to France in 1829 for his education in order to take his mind off the subject of the Native Americans.

He completed his collegiate studies in Paris, Nantes, and Rennes, earning a bachelor's degree in 1833 before returning to New Orleans. He went back to Paris to study law but soon ceased studies and returned to Louisiana. There he dabbled in poetry, sailed again to France, and published his first poetic essay, "*Les Savannes.*" He then returned to New Orleans as editor of *Le Propagateur Catholique.*

Rouquette then entered the seminary, received ordination on July 2, 1845, and served until 1859 as a parish priest. He acquired a reputation for his homiletic skill, and Catholics gathered at the Cathedral of St. Louis in New Orleans to hear him speak. In 1859, however, he requested permission to serve among the Choctaw as he had always desired. Father Rouquette devoted the rest of his life to the tribe along the Bayou Lacombe. He died among his beloved Choctaw converts as one of the most respected experts in Choctaw heritage and language.

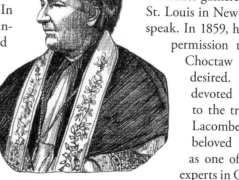

Bishop Sylvester Rosecrans

Rudd, Daniel (August 7, 1854–December 3, 1933)

A journalist, lecturer, civil rights leader, and leading African-American Catholic, Daniel Rudd was born in Bardstown, Kentucky, one of twelve children born of Catholic slaves, and was raised in the Catholic faith. Following the Civil War, he moved to Springfield, Ohio, to join his brother. There he completed his basic education and soon after launched a newspaper in Springfield, the *Ohio Star Tribune*. In 1886 the paper was changed to the *American Catholic Tribune*, the first black Catholic weekly newspaper in the country. Rudd's editorial direction represented his conviction that the Catholic Church was uniquely qualified to preach and inculcate genuine racial equality. He also supported Pope Leo XIII's encyclical *Rerum Novarum* and its promotion of Catholic social doctrine. Rudd moved the newspaper to Cincinnati and then to Detroit, continuing as its editor until 1894. The following year, the paper ceased publication.

Rudd was a popular lecturer on the pressing issues of African-Americans and slavery. He was an honored guest-lecturer throughout the United States and made a famed 1899 trip to Europe

Archbishop Joseph Rummel

that included meeting Cardinal Charles Lavigerie, attending a congress on international slavery, and delivering a lecture in Westminster Cathedral in England. Inspired by the success of the various Catholic congresses of the period, he organized five National Black Catholic Congresses between 1889 and 1894 in Washington, D.C., Cincinnati, Philadelphia, Chicago, and Baltimore. The congresses proved immensely successful and went far in galvanizing African-American Catholic activities and self-identification.

Rummel, Joseph Francis (October 14, 1876–November 8, 1964)

The ninth archbishop of the Archdiocese of New Orleans, from 1935 to 1962, Joseph Francis Rummel was born in Steinmauern, Baden, Germany. His family migrated to the United States when Joseph was six, and he became a naturalized American with his parents on February 2, 1888.

He studied at St. Anselm's College in Manchester, New Hampshire, St. Joseph's Seminary in Dunwoodie, New York, and then completed his seminary studies at the North American College in Rome. He was ordained for the Archdiocese of New York in the Basilica of St. John Lateran by Cardinal Pietro Respighi on May 24, 1902. The following year, he finished a doctorate in sacred theology and returned home to begin his priestly ministry.

After holding several pastoral assignments from 1903 to 1924, he was named an official of the archdiocese's marriage tribunal and the executive secretary of a committee charged with assisting the poor in ravaged postwar Germany. In April 1924 he was appointed a papal chamberlain, and four years later, on March 20, 1928, Pope Pius XI appointed him bishop of the Diocese of Omaha. He was consecrated a bishop by Cardinal Patrick Joseph Hayes on May 29, 1928, and assumed his duties in Omaha on July 4, 1928.

As bishop of Omaha, Rummel distinguished himself by convoking a diocesan synod in 1934 to assist the spiritual and administrative life of the diocese. He also hosted the Sixth National Eucharistic Congress in September 1930 and founded and encouraged the Confraternity of the Laity Campaign to provide a mechanism for diocesan fundraising. His time in Omaha ended on March 9, 1935, when he was appointed by Pope Pius XI the new archbishop of New Orleans.

Installed in New Orleans on May 14, 1935, he wasted little time embarking on his duties. He promoted the Confraternity of Christian Doctrine, organized the Eighth National Eucharistic Congress in October 1938 in New Orleans, and labored to assist the archdiocese throughout the Depression and World War II. Following the war, he inaugurated a vigorous building campaign, opening forty parishes between 1946 and 1961. To pay for these developments, Archbishop Rummel supported extensive fundraising. He also convened a diocesan synod in 1949 to reform the archdiocesan administration.

Archbishop Rummel emerged in his later years as a leader in the desegregation movement. In March 1953 he issued a pastoral letter entitled "Blessed Are the Peacemakers," in which he declared that segregation was unsupportable in the Catholic Church. This was followed in February 1956 by another pastoral letter, "The Morality of Racial Segregation," directly refuting segregation. In March 1962 he declared that at the start of the next term all archdiocesan schools would open their doors to any qualified student. In the face of opposition from a small group of local Catholics, Archbishop Rummel reluctantly excommunicated three of it members.

As archbishop, Rummel was renowned for his pastoral approach and his gifts as a homilist and speaker; he was in constant demand as a speaker across the country. He served on a host of boards and committees and received awards and honors from the Netherlands, France, Italy, and Haiti. Although suffering from partial blindness from glaucoma, he remained active until his death. His successor was his coadjutor, Archbishop John Patrick Cody, the future cardinal and archbishop of Chicago.

Russell, Mother Mary (April 18, 1829–August 6, 1898)

The foundress and superior of the Order of Sisters of Mercy in California, Mary Russell was a native of Killowen, Ireland. She entered the Order of the Sisters of Mercy in Kinsale, Ireland, and made her profession in August 1851. After caring for the poor and the victims of famine and cholera, she was named by her superiors to head a group of eight volunteer sisters sent by the Sisters of Mercy to San Francisco at the invitation of Archbishop Joseph Sadoc Alemany, O.P. Mother Mary and her sisters arrived in San Francisco in December 1854 and set out immediately to care for the poor and sick in the city. The sisters brought critically needed care to the community, and such was the gratitude of city officials that they provided the small group of religious with oversight of the county hospital during an outbreak of cholera in 1855.

After refurbishing the facilities, Mother Mary reopened the hospital as St. Mary's Hospital in 1857, the first Catholic hospital on the West Coast. Over the next years, Mother Mary organized a home for delinquent girls in 1855 and an old-age home in 1872. Services for the sick and destitute were also opened in the California cities of Sacramento and Grass Valley. In 1871 Mother Mary was at last able to embark on Catholic education, devoting her next years to establishing five schools.

Ruth, George Herman "Babe" (February 6, 1895–August 16, 1948)

The baseball player known as "The Sultan of Swat," George Herman Ruth was born in Baltimore, Maryland, one of eight children born to Kate Schamberger-Ruth and George Herman Ruth Sr.

When he was seven, young George was taken to St. Mary's Industrial School for Boys, a reformatory and orphanage. He was thus placed in the custody of the Xaverian Brothers, who found the youth difficult to discipline and labeled him "incorrigible." Young George, however, was deeply influenced by Brother Matthias, the Prefect of Discipline, who shaped both Ruth's love of sports and his lifelong commitment to helping other disadvantaged children. After developing a genuine talent on the St. Mary's baseball team, Ruth was discovered at the age of nineteen by Jack Dunn, the owner of the Baltimore Orioles (then a minor-league team for the Boston Red Sox). Signed to a contract, Ruth was nicknamed "Jack's newest babe," owing to his youthful appearance and so acquired the name "Babe" that stayed with him ever after.

Signed by the Boston Red Sox in 1915, Ruth made an immediate impact on the field and became famed for his off-the-field antics in the bars of Boston. Nevertheless, he was instrumental in leading the Red Sox to their World Series championship in 1918. In December 1919 he was sold to the New York Yankees by Red Sox owner Harry Frazee for $125,000 and a $350,000 loan for Frazee's Broadway interests. The move became one the most significant in the history of sports as the New York Yankees went on to numerous World Series titles (twenty-seven at last count). As an outfielder for the New York Yankees from 1920 to 1935, Ruth hit 714 home runs, played in 10 World Series, and held 54 major-league records.

In October 1914, Ruth married the seventeen-year-old waitress Helen Woodford, and in 1921 they adopted a baby girl named Dorothy. Helen died in a house fire in 1929, and Ruth married the actress and model Claire Hodgson in April 1929. On the following day, at the Yankees' opening game against the Boston Red Sox, the "Babe" hit a home run out of Yankee Stadium for his new bride on his first at-bat.

Ruth retired in 1935 and devoted his time to promoting orphanages and hospitals and serving as a spokesperson for United States War Bonds during World War II. In 1936 he became one of the first five inductees into the Baseball Hall of Fame, along with Ty Cobb, Walter Johnson, Christy Mathewson, and Honus Wagner. He died from complications of throat cancer. His body lay in state at the main entrance of Yankee Stadium for two days, and over a hundred thousand people came to pay their final respects. Thousands attended his funeral at St. Patrick's Cathedral in New York and lined the route to Gate of Heaven Cemetery in Hawthorne, New York.

Ryan, James Hugh (December 15, 1886–November 23, 1947)

The first archbishop of Omaha, from 1945 to 1947, rector of The Catholic University of America from 1928 to 1935, and a promoter of education, James Hugh Ryan was born in Indianapolis. He was the son of John Marshall Ryan and Brigid Rogers Ryan. He attended Holy Ghost College (later Duquesne University) in Pittsburgh and then studied at Mount St. Mary's Theological Seminary in Cincinnati. Sent to Rome to complete his seminary studies at the North American College, he earned doctorates from the Pontifical Athenaeum S. Apollinaire in 1908 and the Pontifical University of the Propaganda in 1909. After receiving a special dispensation due to his youth, Ryan was ordained on June 5, 1909, at the Basilica of St. John Lateran in Rome.

Sent home, he served briefly in a parish and then became a professor of psychology at St. Mary-of-the-Woods in Terra Haute, Indiana, from 1911 to 1921. In 1920 he became president of the college. Soon after, he became executive secretary of the Department of Education of the National Catholic Welfare Conference in Washington, D.C. In 1928 he was named rector of Catholic University. Five years later, on October 25, 1933, he was consecrated titular bishop of Modra. His time as rector was noted for his determined effort to improve the quality of the academic programs, in particular in the areas of theology, philosophy, and biblical studies, as well as the university's finances and facilities. He was also a prolific speaker and writer in the areas of philosophy and education. He wrote *A Directory of Catholic Colleges and Schools* (1921), *A Catechism of Catholic Education* (1922), *An Introduction to Philosophy* (1924), and *The Encyclicals of Pius XI* (1927). He was also the recipient of a host of honors, including Knight Commander of the Crown of Italy in 1930, Chevalier of the Legion of Honor of France in 1934, Cavaliere Magistrale of the Order of Malta in 1935, and various honorary degrees.

On August 3, 1935, he was appointed bishop of the Diocese of Omaha and was installed on November 1, 1935. On October 10, 1945, he was elevated to the rank of archbishop and installed as the first metropolitan archbishop of Omaha. He died in Omaha.

Ryan, John (May 25, 1869–September 16, 1945)

A priest, social philosopher, and one of the most prominent social reformers of the twentieth century, John Ryan was born in Vermillion, Minnesota. He was the eldest son of eleven children born to Irish immigrants William and Mary Luby Ryan. After early schooling under the Christian Brothers, he began preparations for the priesthood at St. Thomas College and St. Paul Seminary in 1887. He was ordained by Archbishop John Ireland on June 4, 1898. Sent by Archbishop Ireland for advanced studies in theology at The Catholic University of America in Washington, D.C., young Father Ryan earned a licentiate in moral theology in 1900 and later returned to complete his doctorate in 1906. His dissertation, "A Living Wage: Its Ethical and Economic Aspects," anticipated his future concerns for social justice and was noticed throughout the Church. In 1902, meanwhile, he had been appointed a professor in moral theology at St. Paul Seminary. He remained there for thirteen years.

Already well known for his commitment to

social justice and social reforms, Father Ryan was named to the faculty of Catholic University as a teacher of political science and then moral theology, a post he held until 1939. He wrote his second most influential work, *Distributive Justice*, in 1916, focusing on the ethical demands placed on industrial societies. At the same time, he was active in supporting labor unions and other groups, and in organizing and working toward genuine social reform. He was an outspoken advocate of minimum-wage legislation, federal legislation for workers' rights, and the moral foundation of organized

Msgr. John Ryan

labor. In 1919 he was chosen to serve as dean of the School of Sacred Theology at Catholic University for the first time; he held the post several more times. He also taught courses at Trinity College in Washington, D.C. In 1917 he founded the *Catholic Charities Review*, and in 1919 he became director of the Department of Social Action for the National Catholic Welfare Council (later Conference), a post he held until his death. In this capacity, he wrote the draft of the "Bishops' Program of Social Reconstruction," a comprehensive legislative outline that advocated proposals for the minimum wage, unemployment, and other concerns for workers. While most eventually became law, at the time the ideas were considered quite radical.

In the 1920s Ryan lectured extensively across the country on issues of social justice, served as a lecturer in social ethics at the National Catholic School of Social Service, helped to organize the Catholic Association for International Peace, and became associated with the Federal Council of Churches of Christ in America and the Central Conference of American Rabbis. Father Ryan also joined the American Civil Liberties Union.

In the wake of the Great Depression, Father Ryan was a major supporter of President Franklin Delano Roosevelt and the New Deal legislation, in particular the National Labor Relations Act and the Fair Labor Standards Act. He also became a member of the Industrial Appeals Board of the National Recovery Administration. Father Ryan

subsequently was an ardent supporter of Roosevelt's reelection campaigns, giving the benediction at two inaugurations. For his support of the New Deal, Ryan was given the nickname "Right Reverend New Dealer." In 1933 Pope Pius XI named him a domestic prelate.

Ryan, Mary (April 10, 1912– October 13, 1993)

A writer and educator, Mary Ryan was born in Boston. She married John Julian Ryan in 1942 and the couple raised five sons. After graduating from Manhattanville College in 1933, she was hired on to the United States staff of the noted Catholic publisher Sheed & Ward. Over the next years, she became an expert in the liturgy and the liturgical movement. In 1954 she accepted a post at the Liturgical Institute founded at the University of Notre Dame and subsequently served as co-editor of *The Art of Teaching Christian Doctrine* in 1957 with Johannes Hofinger, S.J. She also wrote, edited, or translated twenty-seven books, including *Are Parochial Schools the Answer?* in 1964 and translations of the writings of Louis Bouyer and Jean Daniélou.

Ryan, Patrick John (February 20, 1831–February 11, 1911)

The sixth bishop and second archbishop of Philadelphia from 1884 to 1911, Patrick John Ryan was born in Thurles, County Tipperary, Ireland. He studied under the Christian Brothers in his native Ireland and then embarked on classical studies in Dublin and once gave a speech in honor of the imprisoned Irish patriotic leader Daniel O'Connell. O'Connell complimented the young Ryan and supposedly predicted a bright future for the lad.

In 1847 Ryan entered St. Patrick's College in Carlow with the expectation of service in the St. Louis Diocese in the United States under Archbishop Peter R. Kenrick. In 1852 Ryan completed his studies, but as he was still too young canonically for ordination to the priesthood, he was sent to St. Louis ahead of time. Once in the United States, he so impressed Archbishop Kenrick with his homilies that he was permitted to preach in the cathedral while still a deacon. On September 8, 1853, after receiving a special dispensation, he was ordained priest and was given several pastoral assignments.

In 1866 Father Ryan attended the Second Plenary Council of Baltimore as one of Archbishop Kenrick's theologians. During the council, Ryan was one of only three priests chosen to preach, with Archbishop John Lancaster Spalding and Father Isaac Thomas Hecker, C.S.P. In 1868 Father Ryan then traveled to Europe with Archbishop Kenrick, where he was received with great enthusiasm and was given the great honor of delivering the English Lenten sermon in Rome at the request of Pope Blessed Pius IX. While Archbishop Kenrick attended the First Vatican Council from 1869 to 1870, Ryan served as vicar general and administrator of the diocese.

On February 14, 1872, Ryan was consecrated titular bishop of Tricomia and coadjutor bishop of St. Louis with right of succession. On January 6, 1884, he was made titular archbishop of Salamis. That same year, on June 8, 1884, Archbishop Ryan was appointed to the vacant see of Philadelphia. As archbishop of the second largest diocese in the United States, Ryan oversaw the rapid expansion of the archdiocese, including increases of the Catholic population from 300,000 to 525,000 in 1911, the clergy population from 260 to 582, and nuns from 1,020 to 2,565. Archbishop Ryan also supported a host of educational initiatives, founding a new high school for girls, the St. Francis' Industrial School, St. Joseph's Home, and Philadelphia Protectory for Boys; he also established a foundling asylum and maternity hospital, and the St. Vincent's Home for younger orphan children, a project paid for through the archbishop's Golden Jubilee Fund of $200,000. The archbishop also opened an old-age home.

Deeply concerned with the needs of immigrants and minorities, he built a number of churches for Italian, Polish, Greek, Slovak, and Lithuanian Catholics, and established two congregations for African-Americans in Philadelphia. He was also instrumental in encouraging St. Katharine Drexel in the foundation of the Sisters of the Blessed Sacrament to serve Native Americans and African-Americans. The Holy Ghost Fathers, dedicated to ministering to black Catholics, were invited to establish themselves at Cornwells Heights in suburban Philadelphia. The archbishop also attended the Lake Mohonk conferences and the meetings of the U.S. Indian Commission, to which he had been appointed by President Theodore Roosevelt.

Archbishop Ryan was renowned as one of the country's great orators, and he was in frequent demand as a speaker at both ecclesiastical and secular functions. He was the honored speaker at the dedication of St. Patrick's Cathedral in New York, at the funeral of Archbishop Kenrick, and at President William McKinley's memorial service in Philadelphia, after the president's assassination in 1901. He also addressed the Committee of the United States Senate on Indian Affairs and opened the Republican National Convention in Philadelphia in 1900.

His speeches and homilies provided a powerful forum for the presentation of Catholic perspectives on the pressing issues of the day and a chance for apologetics in a frequently hostile anti-Catholic social and political atmosphere. His lecture topics included "What Catholics Do Not Believe" in 1877 and "Agnosticism" in 1894. The celebrations of the Silver Jubilee of his episcopal consecration in 1897 and the Golden Jubilee of his priesthood in 1903 were enthusiastically received and offered a testament to the degree of respect and fondness he had earned both from Catholics and non-Catholics in many walks of American life.

Ryan, Thomas Fortune (October 17, 1851– November 23, 1928)

A financier and founder of the American Tobacco Company and the National Bank of Commerce, Thomas Fortune Ryan donated more than $20 million to Catholic charities.

He was born near Lovingston, Virginia, the son of a tailor and hotel manager; his mother died when Ryan was five years old. He converted to the Church at the age of seventeen while traveling to Baltimore, where he worked as a merchant and then as a stockbroker. He soon established his own brokerage firm with two partners. In 1873 he wed Ida Mary Barry, the daughter of a former boss. Among his seven children was John Barry Ryan, who became a writer and financier in his own right. A mere year later, his firm purchased him a seat on the New York Stock Exchange, making him the youngest member in the history of the stock exchange. Over the next years, Ryan founded the New York Cable Railroad and swiftly expanded his holdings in public transport in New York. He made even more money in the tobacco industry and formed the Union Tobacco Company in 1898, which was then merged with the Consolidated Tobacco Company to form the American Tobacco Company. He later owned interests in dozens of companies and industries, although he had a reputation as a smart and ruthless business magnate.

Nevertheless, at the encouragement of his wife, he proved immensely generous to the Church, including donations to fund churches, hospitals, convents, and a host of charitable initiatives. Among his most significant donations were to fund St. Jean Baptiste Catholic Church on the Upper East Side of Manhattan and the Cathedral of the Sacred Heart in Richmond, Virginia, which was dedicated in 1906. Ida died on October 17, 1917. By the time of his own death, his vast fortune was estimated to be $200 million.

Sacramento, Diocese of

Established on May 28, 1886, by Pope Leo XIII, the Diocese of Sacramento serves counties in the central valley of California. It is a suffragan of the Archdiocese of San Francisco. Sacramento is a port situated at the confluence of the American and Sacramento Rivers. In 1839 John Sutter founded the colony of New Helvetia on the present site of Sacramento. He established a trading post there, and the settlement was developed by Sutter's Swiss countrymen. In time, the colony served as a vibrant agricultural center and as a haven for American pioneers who had trekked across the land in search of new beginnings. On January 28, 1848, however, gold was discovered there, and armies of prospectors, miners, and adventurers arrived and pillaged the area, starting claim sites. A new town, called Sacramento, was established, becoming the state capital in 1854. Enduring fires and floods, Sacramento survived and prospered as a center of river transport and as a depot of the Pony Express and the railroad.

The Catholic history of Sacramento began with its discovery by Juan Rodriguez Cabrillo in 1542. Sebastian Vizcaino visited the area in 1602, but there were no reported colonies there until 1769. José de Galvez, the Spanish vicar general of Mexico, fearing Russian interest in California, ordered the conquest of the region. Jesuit missionaries had served in California under the leadership of such priests as Juan Maria Salvatierra, who started the Pious Fund of the Californias. These priests, including Father Eusebius Kino, had explored Lower California and had founded Our Lady of Loreto at Concepcíon Bay in 1697. Jesuit Father Juan Ugarte had also lived in the area. The Jesuits also taught local Native American tribes European agricultural techniques and cattle raising. The Jesuits were expelled from California in 1767, and José de Galvez, the Spanish vicar general of Mexico, turned to the Franciscans of the Apostolic College of San Fernando in Mexico City, asking them to assume the California missions. Blessed Junípero Serra and his companion Franciscans began their labors as a result, founding twenty-one missions between 1769 and 1823.

Sacramento was settled around 1839 and the first Mass was said on August 10, 1850, by Father Peter Augustine Anderson, a Dominican, in a private home on Fifth and L streets in Sacramento. Anderson had accompanied a group of miners, and he died in November of that year during a typhoid outbreak while caring for the sick.

Four years later, Sacramento was designated as the capital of California. In 1861 the city became part of the Vicariate Apostolic of Marysville, which encompassed all of Northern California and most of the state of Nevada. The first vicar apostolic was Bishop Eugene O'Connell, who was appointed the first bishop of Grass Valley in 1868 when the vicariate was elevated to a diocese. Father Patrick Manogue, the pioneering priest of Virginia City, Nevada, was appointed coadjutor bishop in 1881 and acceded to the see on March 17, 1884, when Bishop O'Connell retired.

The Diocese of Grass Valley struggled financially, and the decision was made to establish a new diocese in Northern California. The result was the Diocese of Sacramento, and Father Manogue was named its first bishop. Already an almost legendary figure in California and Nevada, Manogue was a no-nonsense priest who rode on horseback to visit the faithful far and wide. A large and imposing man who was not alarmed by anti-Catholic displays, Bishop Manogue kept order in the mining camps and inspired other Catholics to stand up for their rights. In Sacramento, he established parishes, missions, schools, and charitable programs, and with the help of John Mackay, a longtime friend and the discoverer of the Comstock Silver Lode in Virginia City, Bishop Manogue established the Cathedral of the Blessed Sacrament in 1889. Bishop Manogue died on February 27, 1895.

The second bishop of Sacramento, Thomas Grace, a priest of the diocese, was consecrated on June 16, 1896, and began a time as bishop that stretched into the new century. The Catholic population was growing rapidly, and the gentle-natured

Bishop Grace expanded diocesan facilities, founded parishes and schools, and managed to promote peace in mining camps. He also served as a leader in the burgeoning and increasingly cosmopolitan city of Sacramento. In his time, the population more than doubled with the arrival of Irish, Italian, German, and Portuguese immigrants. Owing to poor health, Bishop Grace asked for an auxiliary bishop, Father Patrick J. Keane, who succeeded Grace as the third bishop of Sacramento upon the latter's death on December 27, 1921.

Bishop Keane succeeded to the see of Sacramento on March 17, 1922, and continued to expand diocesan facilities, promoted vocations in the diocese, and established new parishes. He died on September 1, 1928, at the age of fifty-six.

The fourth bishop of Sacramento, Robert Armstrong, a priest from Seattle, was consecrated a bishop on March 12, 1929. He led the diocese during the tumultuous periods of the Great Depression, World War II, and the postwar boom. During his time, Sacramento's population more than doubled, and he labored to keep pace with the need for new schools, parishes, and vocations. Exhausted by his years of work, he died on January 14, 1957, at the age of seventy-two.

The fifth bishop of Sacramento, Bishop Joseph T. McGucken, had been named an auxiliary bishop of the Archdiocese of Los Angeles in 1941 and had been appointed coadjutor bishop of Sacramento in 1955. He acceded to the see at Bishop Armstrong's death. Bishop McGucken continued the expansion programs of his predecessor and was especially active in promoting the Confraternity of Christian Doctrine. On February 21, 1962, he was promoted to archbishop of San Francisco.

Bishop McGucken was succeeded by Bishop Alden J. Bell, a native of Canada who had been an auxiliary bishop of Los Angeles since 1956. Bishop Bell promoted the growth of Catholic high schools, assisted Hispanic ministries, built a home for the aged, and took part in the Second Vatican Council. He then faced the task of implementing the decrees of the council in a difficult time, until his retirement on March 15, 1979.

The seventh bishop of Sacramento, Bishop Francis A. Quinn, had been an auxiliary bishop of San Francisco since 1978. Named to Sacramento on December 18, 1979, Bishop Quinn focused many of his efforts on the pastoral needs of the growing Asian, Filipino, and Hispanic populations in the diocese. He also promoted a diocesan program of spiritual renewal, called Renew, and launched a diocesan pastoral council. He retired on November 30, 1993.

The eighth bishop of Sacramento, Bishop William K. Weigand, had been bishop of Salt Lake City since 1980. Installed on January 27, 1994, he celebrated the Great Jubilee of 2000, promoted a diocesan capital campaign, and provided leadership during the difficult time of the sex abuse scandal. He retired on November 29, 2008, owing to health problems.

The ninth bishop of Sacramento, Bishop Jaime Soto, had been an auxiliary bishop of Orange since 2000 and was named coadjutor bishop on October 11, 2007. Bishop Soto stressed Catholic education and identity from the start of his time in Sacramento. In 2011 there were nearly one million Catholics, served by 260 priests, nearly 200 men and women religious, and 105 parishes.

Sacred Hearts, Congregation of the

The Congregation of the Sacred Hearts of Jesus and Mary (SS.CC.) is a religious order of brothers, priests, and nuns that was responsible for remarkable missionary labors in the Pacific and is largely credited with the establishment of the Church in Hawaii. The Sacred Hearts Congregation is also famed for one of its greatest priests, St. Damien de Veuster of Molokai.

Known also as the Picpus Fathers, in honor of Picpus Street in Paris, where the order was founded, the congregation began in 1800, although its origins are traced to the dark period of the French Revolution. In March 1792 Pierre Coudrin was ordained in secret owing to the intense hostility of the French government to the Church. He was forced subsequently to go into hiding owing to the persecution of the clergy. While hiding in the attic of a granary in the Chateau d'Usseau, Father Coudrin beheld a vision of priests, brothers, and sisters dressed in white robes. Called to begin a new religious community, he left the safety of the granary and started an underground ministry in Poitiers. He was assisted from 1794 by Henriette Aymer de

Chevalerie, and the two were committed to creating a religious order to assist the Church in revolutionary France.

On Christmas Eve 1800, Father Coudrin and Henriette Aymer de Chevalerie officially founded the Congregation of the Sacred Hearts of Jesus and Mary. The chief purpose of the new community was to promote adoration of the Blessed Sacrament and the Hearts of Jesus and Mary. From this beginning, the first members of the congregation opened schools for poor children, started seminaries, and conducted parish missions, first in France and then throughout Europe. By the time of Father Coudrin's death in 1837, the congregation had some 275 priests and brothers and over 1,100 sisters.

In 1826 the congregation began a new era when the decision was made to embark upon missionary labors in the Pacific. Sacred Heart priests, brothers, and sisters soon became one of the great mainstays of evangelization in Oceania, above all in what was then the Kingdom of Hawaii. Pope Leo XIII designated Hawaii as a prefecture apostolic and entrusted it to the Fathers of the Sacred Hearts. Father Alexis Jean Bachelot arrived in Honolulu with companions, and he and his successors in the congregation overcame difficult conditions, exile, and frequent persecutions and hostility by Protestants in the Hawaiian Islands. Through their labors, the Sacred Hearts congregation essentially established the Diocese of Honolulu, and built the Cathedral of Our Lady of Peace, the oldest Roman Catholic cathedral in continuous use in the United States. The first six bishops in Hawaii, from 1833 to 1940, were members of the congregation.

The most famous of their priests, St. Damien de Veuster, gave his life on behalf of the lepers of Molokai and was beatified in 1995. On June 15, 2006, Father Eustaquio van Lieshout, a beloved missionary in Brazil, was beatified in Belo Horizonte, Brazil. In 2011 there were some 760 priests and over 2,000 religious brothers and sisters in 37 countries worldwide.

Sacred Heart, Society of the (R.S.C.J.)

The Society of the Sacred Heart is a congregation of Catholic women serving in forty-five countries and dedicated to a truly wide variety of ministries, including work in schools, parishes, and retreat centers, and as nurses, doctors, pastoral counselors, spiritual directors, and social workers. Two figures are most connected to the life of the congregation in the United States: The first is the founder, St. Madeleine Sophie Barat, who devoted sixty-five years of her life to the development of the community, and the second is St. Rose Philippine Duchesne, who established the congregation in the United States.

The Society of the Sacred Heart of Jesus began on November 21, 1800, when twenty-year-old Madeleine Sophie Barat and her companions made their first vows in Paris. From that beginning, the community grew rapidly. On December 22, 1826, the Society received acceptance of its constitution from Pope Leo XII. Thereafter, the congregation expanded swiftly throughout Europe. Credit goes to St. Madeleine Sophie Barat; by the time of her death in 1865 the Society had grown to more than 3,500 religious in nearly 90 houses in 17 countries. St. Madeleine was canonized on May 24, 1925.

St. Rose Philippine Duchesne is honored as the founder of the Society of the Sacred Heart in America and was revered by Native Americans, who called her "The Woman Who Always Prays." She entered the Society and took her vows on December 31, 1804. St. Rose served with absolute dedication in America for thirty-three years, until her death. She opened the first house of the Society in St. Charles, Missouri, in 1818 and oversaw the expansion of the community throughout Missouri, Louisiana, and Canada, and before her death she realized her dream of working among the Potawatomi. She died on November 18, 1852, and was canonized on July 3, 1988.

The first century of the congregation was dedicated chiefly to the area of education, and in the decades following St. Madeleine's death the sisters continued to increase in numbers and also in the number of the institutions that they ran. The great tumult caused by World War I brought with it challenges to the Society. By 1958 there were nearly 7,000 religious in 183 houses around the world.

In the next years, the Society underwent the same period of reform that shaped the institutes of religious life in the wake of the Second Vatican Council. In 1964 the Society defined itself as an "apostolic community" and removed the rule of cloister at the general chapter of that year. Careful study followed to determine the best way to remain faithful to the charism of St. Madeleine Sophie Barat and the needs of the modern faithful.

In 1982 new constitutions were written that called on the members to "be women of communion, to live lives rooted in prayer, and to work for justice in all its dimensions." The modern era of the order, especially in the United States, also entailed the movement away from the older systems of education to a network of Sacred Heart Schools that could reflect more completely the specific regional needs of education without sacrificing the rigorous demands of quality and fidelity to the vision of St. Madeleine. In 2011 the Society of the Sacred Heart had nearly 3,500 women in over 500 communities in 45 countries.

Sadlier, Mary (December 30, 1820–April 5, 1903)

Novelist, philanthropist, and the author of over thirty novels and books, Mary Sadlier was born in Cootehill, Ireland. She settled in Montréal in 1844 after the death of her father. In 1846 she married James Sadlier, the manager of the Montréal branch of the American publisher D. & J. Sadlier & Co., devoting much of the next fourteen years to her own literary pursuits.

In 1860 Mary moved to New York, where she and her family owned a weekly paper, the *New York Tablet*, to which she regularly contributed stories and columns that found a large and welcome audience among Irish Americans. After her husband's death she remained several years in New York and then returned to Canada, where she spent the remainder of her days.

She was the author of some sixty books and a large number of essays that were published in the *Pilot*, the *New York Tablet*, and various other prominent publications. In her time, she was one of the most widely read Catholic authors in the country. Her writings were infused with Catholic apologetics, and she stressed the merits of the good home and the role of women in wider society. She also opposed the idea of Americanization of Catholic immigrants toward a Protestant Yankee lifestyle.

Saginaw, Diocese of

Established on February 26, 1938, by Pope Pius XI, the Diocese of Saginaw serves counties in the northwestern part of the Lower Peninsula in Michigan. The diocese is a suffragan of the Archdiocese of Detroit.

The city is located on the Saginaw River. The names of both the city and the river are derived from the Chippewa language and mean "the land of the Sauks." A fur-trading post was erected on the site of present-day Saginaw in 1816. A settlement opened around the post and prospered, becoming chartered in 1857. South Saginaw and East Saginaw, originally separate settlements, became part of the modern-day city in 1873 and 1889, respectively.

The Catholic heritage of Saginaw opened early during the exploration of the New World in the seventeenth century. Etienne Brulé, the explorer, was in the region by 1620. By around 1640, the Jesuits St. Isaac Jogues and Charles Raymbaut labored together at Sault Ste. Marie, followed by their Jesuit companions. The Jesuit superior Father Claude Allouez, and Father René Menard, who later disappeared while traveling on an inland trail, also served the local Indian villages. The famed French leader René-Robert Chevalier, Sieur de La Salle, and other expeditions were in the region, and St. Ignace Mission was established. The illustrious Jesuit pioneer Father Jacques Marquette, along with Jesuit Fathers Francis Dollier de Casson and Gabriel Druillettes, and the Franciscan Recollect Father Louis Hennepin, were also laboring nearby. Jesuit Father Henri Nouvel was on the site of present-day Saginaw and then at Thunder Bay with Father Hennepin in 1677.

The struggle between the French and Indians in 1687 created havoc for the missionaries, and the Jesuits had to withdraw for about a year, and at least one mission was burned to the ground. The missionaries returned, however, joined by Jesuit Father Sebastian Râle, who translated Indian languages and wrote a detailed history of the Ottawa. The original Fort Ponchartrain at Detroit was open, and Franciscan Recollect Father Nicholas Constantin Delhalle was slain there. Missions were also opened at Burt Lake and Harbor Springs, originally called L'Arbre Croche, or "Crooked Tree."

Fort Ponchatrain at present-day Detroit had been established by Antoine Cadillac. The fort and other Michigan regions were threatened by the English during the Seven Years' War from 1745 to

1763, and the English took control of the area as a result of that European conflict. In 1763 Ottawa Chief Pontiac attacked Detroit.

Soon after, the American Revolution broke the English hold on the colonies and the territories beyond. English forces remained in Detroit, however, until 1798. During the War of 1812, the British again occupied parts of Michigan but had to withdraw after the Battle of Lake Erie proved that the American forces were capable of inflicting damage on an enemy. The Sulpician Father Gabriel Richard labored in Michigan, as the Catholic population increased annually. Detroit was established as a diocese in 1833, and Michigan entered the Union in 1837 as the twenty-sixth state. Twenty years later, a remarkable European nobleman, Bishop Irenaeus Frederick Baraga, was at Sault Ste. Marie. He served as the founding bishop of the Diocese of Marquette and won the respect of Americans for his skill in languages, his cultural elegance, and his personal holiness.

By 1938 the great progress of Catholicism in Michigan warranted the creation of a new diocese in the area of Saginaw. The first bishop of the new diocese was a priest of the Archdiocese of Detroit, William F. Murphy, who was consecrated on March 17, 1938. He designated St. Mary's Church as the diocesan cathedral and instituted the offices and agencies needed for the diocese. He supported the League of Catholic Women and established Catholic Charities. After World War II, he instituted an apostolate for the Mexican workers who were starting to make their way to the area for work. An immensely popular bishop, Murphy died on February 7, 1950.

The second bishop of Saginaw, Stephen S. Woznicki, had been an auxiliary bishop of Detroit since 1938 and was named bishop in Saginaw on March 28, 1950. Called the "Great Builder," Bishop Woznicki presided over the expansion of the diocese in the era after the war and founded more than twenty parishes and missions, thirty schools, and St. Paul Seminary in Saginaw. He also attended the Second Vatican Council and began the process of implementing the reforms of the council. He retired on October 30, 1968.

The third bishop of Saginaw, Francis F. Reh, had served as vice chancellor for the Archdiocese of New York, vice rector of the North American College in Rome, rector of St. Joseph's Seminary in New York, and then bishop of Charleston in 1962. In 1964 he had been appointed as rector of the North American College in Rome and was serving in that post at the time he was named bishop of Saginaw in December 1968. Installed on February 26, 1969, he worked to implement the reforms of the council during a difficult period, promoted greater lay participation in the diocese, and renovated the Cathedral of Mary of the Assumption. Bishop Reh retired on April 29, 1980.

The fourth bishop of Saginaw, Kenneth E. Untener, was rector of St. John Provincial Seminary in Plymouth at the time of his appointment on October 4, 1980. He was consecrated a bishop on November 24, 1980. Bishop Untener became famous for his decision to sell the bishop's residence and then adopt a migratory existence by going from parish to parish and taking up temporary residence with his priests. He also wrote several devotional books on Lent and Advent that sold more than three million copies. He died from leukemia on March 27, 2004.

The fifth bishop of Saginaw, Robert J. Carlson, had served as an auxiliary bishop of St. Paul and Minneapolis and then bishop of Sioux Falls from 1994. Installed in Saginaw on February 24, 2005, he served for four years until his appointment as archbishop of St. Louis on April 21, 2009.

The sixth bishop of Saginaw, Joseph R. Cistone had served as an auxiliary bishop of Philadelphia since 2004 and was installed in Saginaw on July 28, 2009. In 2011 the diocese had a Catholic population of nearly 109,000, served by 97 priests and 105 parishes.

St. Agnes, Congregation of (C.S.A.)

The Congregation of Sisters of St. Agnes was established under the patronage of St. Agnes of Rome by the Austrian missionary Father Caspar Rehrl, in Barton, Wisconsin, on August 12, 1858. Father Rehrl had journeyed to Milwaukee to labor in the young diocese then headed by Bishop John M. Henni. The priest served with zeal among the German-speaking immigrants in the Wisconsin region and tried, albeit unsuccessfully, to bring religious women from Europe to assist the missions. Determined to start a new community of women, he received approval from Pope Blessed Pius IX to establish at Barton the Congregation of St. Agnes of Rome, to whom he had a special devotion. The new community began with three women.

The early history of the community was a difficult one, and by 1861 its membership consisted of one blind sister. With the arrival of Mary Hazotte in 1863, however, a new era began for the congregation. The brilliant woman religious provided crucial leadership and was elected in 1864 at the age of seventeen to serve as general superior. Mother Agnes Hazotte moved the sisters from Barton to Fond du Lac, Wisconsin, in 1870 and served as the community's leader until her death in 1905. In 1870 Father Francis Haas, O.F.M. Cap., became the spiritual director of the community and assisted in revising the original rule.

Today, the Sisters of St. Agnes are dedicated to education, health care, and social services in the United States and Latin America. They have approximately 330 members in 129 houses.

St. Augustine, Diocese of

Established on March 11, 1870, the Diocese of St. Augustine serves counties in northern and central Florida. It is a suffragan diocese of the Archdiocese of Miami. St. Augustine is the oldest city in the continental United States and was the site of the earliest known Mass in the continental United States.

The city of St. Augustine dates to 1565 when, after destroying the French Fort Carolina on the present-day site of St. Augustine, the Spanish Admiral Pedro Menéndez de Avilés founded the city and named it in honor of St. Augustine of Hippo.

For the next 250 years, St. Augustine served as the Spanish outpost in the present-day United States. Since 1821 the city has been part of the United States, and the preserved fort, the Castillo de San Marcos, is also the oldest in the country and a major tourist destination.

The Catholic heritage of the region dates to April 3, 1513, when Juan Ponce de León landed in Florida and set up a stone cross to signify his visit. He returned in 1521, planning to start a colony, but he died of wounds he received in a battle with local Indian tribes. Other Spanish explorers followed, including Francisco Fernandez de Cordova, Alonso Alvarez de Pineda, and Lucas Vázquez de Ayllón, who arrived in the area in 1517, 1519, and 1520, respectively. Pánfilo de Narváez, Hernando de Soto, and Tristán de Luna also explored the region.

The French were active in Florida also, but the Spanish were able to destroy their colonies. On September 8, 1565, Admiral Menéndez de Avilés officially founded St. Augustine, and Father Martin Francisco Lopez de Mendoza Grajales said the first Mass. The Nombre de Dios Mission was opened soon after. Jesuit missionaries arrived in 1566, many martyred by local tribes. In 1573 Franciscans missions were operating in the area.

Toward the end of the sixteenth century, the Spanish missions began facing a new threat, one that remained constant over the next centuries: the English. In 1586 Sir Francis Drake attacked the city, the first of many more assaults upon Spanish missions and holdings in Florida. Undeterred, the Franciscans opened more missions in the region and along the Georgia coast, despite severe losses. St. Augustine, meanwhile, was in the ecclesiastical jurisdiction of the Diocese of Havana, and in 1606 Bishop Juan de las Cabezas Altamirano, a Dominican, arrived to confirm some 1,500 Native Americans in the faith. The Franciscans extended their missions in the following years to Gainesville and Tallahassee; the mission region was designated the Province of Santa Elena de la Florida in 1612. Bishop José Gabriel Calderón visited the area in 1674 to ordain priests, and slaves fleeing from the English colonies to the north were given their freedom by the Spanish authorities of the missions and were allowed to be part of the general population.

The English retaliated in 1702–04 as Florida became a battleground in the global imperial struggle between England and Spain. In 1704 the infamous Moore's Raid was launched that destroyed the Mission San Luis Apalachee and enslaved the Native American converts living there. In 1763 Spain ceded Florida to England, and the result was the near extinction of the Catholic faith in northern Florida, as there were only four missions left on the peninsula.

Catholics returned to St. Augustine in 1768 and were allowed to remain by the English, and in 1784 Florida was returned to Spain through the treaty that ended the American Revolution. Designated the Two Floridas (an east-west designation), the area was placed under the jurisdiction of the Diocese of Louisiana by 1819; by that time, Spain had sold the territory to the United States. Florida entered the Union in 1845.

Ecclesiastical control changed hands repeatedly during the next decades: the Diocese of Louisiana and the Two Floridas from 1793 to 1825, the Vicariate of Alabama and the Floridas from 1825 to 1829, the Diocese of Mobile from 1829 to 1850, and the Diocese of Savannah from 1850 to 1857. In 1857 the decision was made to establish Florida as a vicariate apostolic. The first vicar apostolic was named in December 1857, Father Jean-Pierre Augustin Verot, a Sulpician priest who in 1861 was also appointed the third bishop of Savannah. Finally, in 1870 Pope Pius IX created the Diocese of St. Augustine and appointed Bishop Verot its first bishop. The diocese encompassed nearly all of Florida and extended some 58,000 square miles.

Bishop Verot had earned a reputation during the Civil War for his support of the Confederacy and his sermon in defense of slavery while urging that the abuses of slavery be ended. He attended the First Vatican Council and spoke forcefully on behalf of the freed slaves in the United States. In St. Augustine, he invited the Sisters of St. Joseph from Le Puy, France, to start Catholic schools for the children of freed slaves. He also traveled extensively across the diocese, started churches and schools, and recruited priests and nuns for service in the diocese. A man of great vigor, he labored to give the diocese a firm footing and died on June 10, 1876.

The second bishop of St. Augustine, Father John Moore, had served in the Diocese of Charleston and was consecrated on May 13, 1877. He welcomed the Society of Jesus into the diocese and supported the founding of St. Leo College. In 1884 he attended the Third Plenary Council of Baltimore. He also promoted vocations from within the diocese and pastoral programs for African-Americans. In 1887 he organized repairs to the cathedral in St. Augustine and secured donations for it, including from the famed Henry Flagler. Bishop Moore died on July 30, 1901.

The third bishop of St. Augustine, William

John Kenny, a priest of the diocese, was also the first bishop of St. Augustine born in the United States. Consecrated on May 18, 1902, he proved a vigorous shepherd in expanding the services of the diocese, promoting the arrival of Irish priests and nuns, and encouraged evangelization and care of African-Americans. He founded the first African-American parish in the state, St. Benedict the Moor, in St. Augustine in 1911, and gave his backing to ecumenical programs. He died on October 23, 1913.

The fourth bishop of St. Augustine was Father Michael J. Curley, a priest from Florida who was consecrated on June 30, 1914. Only thirty-four years old at the time, he led the diocese through the years of World War I and used the conflict as a means of demonstrating the patriotism of American Catholics. This was important given the growing atmosphere of anti-Catholicism in Florida through the efforts of the Ku Klux Klan. He promoted programs to inform the people of Florida about the truths of the Church and was a valiant defender of several Sisters of St. Joseph when they were arrested for teaching African-American chil-

Cathedral of St. Augustine

dren in their convent school. At the age of forty-two, he was appointed the archbishop of Baltimore on August 10, 1921, as successor to the legendary Archbishop Gibbons.

Bishop Curley was succeeded as fifth bishop of St. Augustine by Father Patrick Joseph Barry, a priest from Florida who was originally from Ireland. Consecrated on May 3, 1922, he dealt with the crisis of the Great Depression and the severe financial difficulties of the diocese. To promote the spiritual welfare of the Catholic community, in 1931 he instituted an annual pilgrimage to the shrine of Nuestra Señora de la Leche at the Mission Nombre de Dios. He also invited Dominican Sisters and Franciscans to serve in the diocese. The sisters founded Barry College (now Barry University) in Miami Shores. He died on August 13, 1940.

Bishop Barry's successor was Father Joseph Patrick Hurley, a priest who had served for a time as a member of the papal diplomatic corps. He was consecrated on October 6, 1940, and led the diocese through the difficult time of World War II and then the postwar boom. In 1949 Pope Pius XII asked him to resume his work as a papal diplomat by appointing him the regent *ad interim* to Belgrade, Yugoslavia. This appointment made Bishop Hurley the first American to hold the post of papal nuncio. He defended the rights of the Church and Catholic clergy against the violations by Marshal Tito; for his efforts, he was given in 1950 the personal title of archbishop. During his tenure in papal service, the diocese was administered by Auxiliary Bishop Thomas J. McDonough. Archbishop Hurley later attended the Second Vatican Council and anticipated brilliantly the development of Florida in years to come, and so made a series of adroit real estate purchases that were much appreciated by future bishops. In a sign of things to come, in 1958 territory was taken from St. Augustine to facilitate the creation of the Diocese (later Archdiocese) of Miami. Bishop Hurley died on October 30, 1967.

The seventh bishop of St. Augustine, Bishop Paul F. Tanner, had served as the assistant general secretary of the National Conference of Catholic Bishops and was general secretary from 1958 to 1968. Consecrated a bishop in 1965, he was appointed to St. Augustine on February 21, 1968. He worked to implement the reforms of the Sec-

ond Vatican Council and was especially noted for his criticism both of the 1973 U.S. Supreme Court decision *Roe v. Wade*, which legalized abortion, and of capital punishment. He was a leader in the U.S. bishops' call for Congress to adopt a Human Life Amendment to the Constitution and was a signer of the 1972 Florida Bishops' Statement on Capital Punishment. In 1968 a major change was made to the Church's life in Florida with the creation of the Dioceses of Orlando and St. Petersburg, both of which received territory taken from St. Augustine. Bishop Tanner retired on April 21, 1979.

The eighth bishop of St. Augustine was John J. Snyder, who had served as the auxiliary bishop of Brooklyn since 1972. Appointed to St. Augustine on October 2, 1979, Bishop Snyder maintained diocesan facilities and ministries during a time of enormous population growth in Florida as well as large changes in the diversity of the state. He promoted education, lay ministry, and programs to ensure the pastoral care of the diverse and vibrant Catholic community. Bishop Snyder retired on December 12, 2000.

The ninth bishop of St. Augustine, Victor Galeone, was appointed to the diocese on June 26, 2001. Having served as a priest of the Archdiocese of Baltimore, he was consecrated a bishop on June 26, 2001. His arrival was followed by the attacks of September 11, 2001, and the immense challenge of the sex abuse crisis in the United States. He also presided over the continued growth of Florida and the growing pastoral needs of the developing Catholic community. He retired on April 27, 2011. On the same day, Pope Benedict XVI named Auxiliary Bishop Felipe J. Estévez of the Archdiocese of Miami as the tenth bishop of St. Augustine. As of 2011, the Catholic population of the diocese was 181,000, served by 118 priests, 100 women religious, and 52 parishes.

St. Claire, Mother (September 8, 1829–October 11, 1898)

Frances Valentine, called Mother St. Claire, founder of the Sisters of the Incarnate Word and Blessed Sacrament in Texas. She was born in Coeurs, France, entered a convent at the age of seventeen, and took the name St. Claire. Health problems caused her community to send her to Belmont, France, where she made her religious profession on September 8, 1848. Four years later, she volunteered for the Texas missions and arrived with several companions that same year.

In March 1853 Bishop John M. Odin sent Sister St. Claire to assist in the Brownsville area, a challenging assignment as there were few Catholics there at the time and considerable anti-Catholic sentiment. Within a few days of their arrival, Sister St. Claire and her companions opened the Villa Marie of the Incarnate Word, a school for girls. A convent soon followed, and Sister St. Claire became the first superior.

In 1866 Mother St. Claire was sent to Victoria, Texas, to establish another house, Nazareth Convent and Academy, to provide an education for girls. Initially attended by Catholics exclusively, such was the quality of education and upbringing that within a short time non-Catholics were sending their daughters. Mother St. Claire was also responsible for having sisters found other houses in Texas, including Houston, Hallettsville, and Shiner. Sisters likewise took charge of parochial schools in the rapidly developing Texas dioceses. She died at Corpus Christi, Texas, not long after celebrating her Golden Jubilee and was buried in Victoria.

St. Cloud, Diocese of

Established on September 22, 1889, the Diocese of St. Cloud serves counties in central Minnesota. It is a suffragan of the Archdiocese of St. Paul and Minneapolis. The site was originally a wilderness fur-trading post that was laid out as a town in 1854 and named after a French city. In 1862 St. Cloud became a haven for settlers fleeing from the dangers of the Sioux uprising. The site was also called the "Granite City" because of the rich quarries in the area, in use since 1870.

The Catholic heritage of the diocese dates to 1655 when the first mission chapel for the Dakota Sioux was founded near Hastings. Another Sioux mission was created at Fond du Lac two decades later. Also on hand was one of the most respected explorers of early America, Daniel Greysolon, Sieur du Lhut, who aided missionaries and promoted the outposts of the faith in the region. He was quite active in the late 1600s and much honored by the local Indian tribes. Franciscan Recollect Father Louis Hennepin visited Mille Lacs, the present-day site of Minneapolis, with du Lhut in 1680. Du Lhut saved Father Hennepin when the missionary was held captive in an area Indian village.

Nine years later, Nicholas Perrot claimed the entire region for France, and he was followed by other French explorers, eager to chart the territory. Jesuit missionaries were on hand by the early 1700s, and Jesuits established the Mission of St. Michael the Archangel in 1727. From there, Jesuits traveled to the scattered trapper enclaves. In 1736 Jean-Pierre Aulneau was slain by the Sioux, becoming the protomartyr of Minnesota.

The American Revolution did not halt Catholic ministries in Minnesota, and in the early 1800s, as Americans were starting the trek to the West, missions were open in Lac Qui Perle, Fond du Lac, Grand Portage, and Crow Wing. Minnesota became part of the United States in 1803, considered part of the lands of the Louisiana Purchase. Fort Snelling was operating in the area as more and more settlers came west.

By 1840 there was a chapel at Mandata, and a year later Father Lucian Galtier, a respected missionary, opened a log chapel at "Pig's Eye's Landing," the start of present-day St. Paul. Minnesota became a territory by an act of Congress and entered the Union as the thirty-second state in 1858. In that same year, the Benedictines were in St. Cloud.

On February 12, 1875, the Holy See created the Vicariate Apostolic of Northern Minnesota. The first vicar apostolic, Rupert Seidenbusch, was also the first abbot of the Benedictine community. He served until 1888, when he retired owing to poor health. The next year, the Diocese of St. Cloud was created, and Father Otto Zardetti was named its first bishop. Consecrated on October 20, 1889, Bishop Zardetti proved a brilliant organizer and gave a firm foundation to the Catholic community of some thirty thousand. One of his greatest achievements was to provide a parochial school for every parish. On February 23, 1894, Bishop Zardetti was named archbishop of Bucharest in Romania and later served in the Roman Curia until his death in Rome in 1902.

His successor was the legendary Benedictine

missionary Martin Marty. In 1879 he had served as vicar apostolic of Dakota and had been the first bishop of Sioux Falls since 1889. Appointed to St. Cloud on January 21, 1895, Marty brought decades of experience with him, but he died unexpectedly on September 19, 1896, and was mourned by Catholics across the country.

The third bishop of St. Cloud, Father James Trobec, was a priest of the Archdiocese of St. Paul and was consecrated on September 21, 1897. He brought the diocese into the new century and helped establish the College of St. Benedict at St. Joseph. He retired on April 15, 1914.

The fourth bishop of St. Cloud was Bishop Joseph F. Busch, who had been bishop of Lead (now the Diocese of Rapid City) since 1910. He served as bishop for thirty-eight years, and his tenure extended through World War I, the Great Depression, and World War II, and provided a steady hand throughout. In 1941 he received a coadjutor bishop, Peter W. Bartholome, but Busch stayed on until his death on May 31, 1953, at the age of eighty-seven.

Bishop Bartholome acceded to the see on Bishop Busch's passing. He promoted the Christian Family Movement and established catechetical programs. Taking part in the Second Vatican Council, he returned from Rome and began the implementation of the conciliar reforms. He retired on January 31, 1968.

The sixth bishop of St. Cloud, Bishop George Henry Speltz, had been appointed coadjutor bishop in 1966 and acceded to the see upon the retirement of Bishop Bartholome. Bishop Speltz faced the challenge of implementing the Second Vatican Council's decrees in a difficult era and meeting the pastoral needs of a demographically shifting Catholic population that was moving into the suburbs. He retired on January 13, 1987.

The seventh bishop of St. Cloud, Jerome George Hanus, O.S.B., a Benedictine priest, was appointed on July 6, 1987; he was consecrated on August 24. He served as bishop for seven years before being named coadjutor archbishop of Dubuque on August 23, 1994.

Bishop Hanus was succeeded by Bishop John Francis Kinney, who had been an auxiliary bishop of St. Paul and Minneapolis and had been bishop of Bismarck since 1982. Appointed on May 9, 1995, Bishop Kinney led the diocese into the new century and coped with the challenges of continuing demographic shifts, shortages in priestly vocations, and the demands of implementing the norms for protection of minors in the wake of the sex abuse crisis. He also issued pastoral letters on social justice and marriage. In 2011 there were 139,000 Catholics served by 214 priests, more than 500 men and women religious, and 134 parishes.

Saint-Cosmé, Jean-François Buisson de (February 1667–1707)

French missionary to the areas of Illinois and Mississippi, Jean-François Buisson de Saint-Cosmé was born in Québec, Canada. He entered the Séminaire des Missions Etrangères of Québec and was ordained in 1690 and sent to Nova Scotia before heading west to labor in the Cahokia Mission in Illinois. He then set out to the lower Mississippi River region and preached among the Natchez in Mississippi. Through his efforts, he established the first mission among the tribes in late 1699. The mission, however, proved unsuccessful, and by 1704 missionary efforts were all but abandoned. Father Saint-Cosmé was thus alone in the region, and he continued to persevere in the missionary enterprise. In 1707 he was martyred, along with three French companions, by a group of Indians while journeying along the Mississippi.

St. George's in Canton. *See* Eastern Churches, Catholic

St. Josaphat in Parma. *See* Eastern Churches, Catholic

St. Louis, Archdiocese of

Established as a diocese on July 18, 1826, by Pope Leo XII, the Archdiocese of St. Louis was elevated to the status of a metropolitan provincial see by Pope Blessed Pius IX on July 20, 1847. The archdiocese has suffragan sees and serves counties in the east-central part of the state of Missouri.

In 1764 Pierre Laclede Liquest of New Orleans opened a fur-trading post on the site of the present-day city. Soon after, René Auguste Chouteau started a village on the site, dedicated to King Louis IX of France. St. Louis became a Spanish holding in 1770 but was then returned to France and sold to the United States as part of the Louisiana Purchase. The Lewis and Clark expedition of 1804–06 visited St. Louis, and the city prospered and served as the seats of government for the District of Louisiana, the Territory of Louisiana, and then the Territory of Missouri in 1812. When Missouri entered the Union, St. Louis was not designated as the capital. The city served as the crossroads for all of the pioneering trails into the west. During the Civil War, the city was totally divided in loyalty to the warring causes. St. Louis was held as a federal base under martial law.

The profound Catholic heritage of St. Louis began around 1520 when Hernando de Soto and his expedition arrived in the area, accompanied by priests. In 1673 Jesuit Jacques Marquette and Louis Joliet were exploring in the region, although they did not remain there long. They were followed, however, by René-Robert Chevalier, Sieur de La Salle, who claimed the lands for France.

In 1764 the Recollect Franciscan Father Luke Collet and the Jesuit Father Sebastian L. Meurin were at St. Genevieve, which had been founded earlier, and when Father Collet died, Father Meurin continued on alone. He wrote to the bishop of Québec, and in 1768 Father Pierre Gibault arrived at St. Louis. He built a log-cabin church, the first in Missouri. In 1772 Father Valentine, a Franciscan Capuchin, served as the first pastor of St. Louis. Father Bernard de Limpach, another Capuchin, became pastor and remained at St. Louis for thirteen years.

St. Louis had been under the ecclesiastical jurisdiction of the Diocese (now Archdiocese) of Baltimore but was transferred to the Diocese of Louisiana and the Two Floridas in 1793. Barrows Colony, later called Perryville, was thriving, and a Vincentian Seminary was open there. In 1803 St. Louis became part of the United States as France sold it as part of the Louisiana Purchase. In 1808 St. Louis was part of the Diocese of Bardstown.

Pierre Laclede Liquest, a founder of St. Louis

Bishop Benedict Joseph Flaget of Bardstown visited St. Louis as part of his ceaseless journeys across his ecclesiastical domain.

The Benedictine Father Joseph Didier had served in St. Louis until 1779, and then Father Thomas Flynn served in the city. In 1815 Bishop Louis Dubourg was appointed to the Diocese of Upper and Lower Louisiana, and he took up residence in St. Louis. He founded St. Louis Academy, now St. Louis University. The Vincentians were laboring vigorously in Missouri, including the revered Fathers John M. Odin, John Timon, and Joseph Rosati. All of these pioneering missionaries went on to become prelates of America.

When Missouri entered the Union in 1821, Bishop Dubourg secured a government loan to educate the local Indian peoples. Jesuit missionaries also came into the region, and St. Rose Philippine Duchesne was at St. Charles pioneering the educational programs of the Society of the Sacred Heart. The Indians who came into contact with the saint called her "The Woman Who Always Prays." In 1824 Father Joseph Rosati was appointed coadjutor bishop to Bishop Dubourg, who had chosen St. Louis as his episcopal residence. In 1829 the Diocese of St. Louis was established by the Holy See. Bishop Dubourg resigned and was transferred to the Diocese of Montauban in France on August 13, 1826, and was later the archbishop of Besançon. In 1827 Father Rosati was named the first bishop of the new St. Louis diocese, and assumed direction over a diocese that encompassed the state of Missouri but that also included parts of Illinois and all American territory west of the Mississippi and north of Louisiana. At its start, it was the largest American diocese and had a population of some forty thousand Catholics.

Bishop Rosati provided a foundation for the new diocese and dedicated the stunning new Cathedral of St. Louis on October 26, 1834. He also promoted the work of Mother Duchesne in opening schools and a convent and encouraged the Sisters of Charity to open a hospital. The Sisters made immense contributions to the diocese, heroically cared for victims of cholera during the epidemic of 1832, and opened the first Catholic orphanage for boys in the West. During this era, the Jesuits also arrived to assume direction over St. Louis University, and the Vincentians started a seminary. Bishop Rosati was also a supporter of the missions among the Native Americans. In 1840 he sent the revered Jesuit priest Pierre-Jean De Smet to the Flatheads in response to an appeal from them for pastoral care.

From the start, Bishop Rosati was challenged to place the diocese on a firm financial footing. To help this, and also to increase the priestly population to care for the polyglot Catholic community, he journeyed to Europe. While on one of the trips, he was assigned by Pope Pius IX to the post of apostolic delegate to Haiti. He died, however, in Rome, at the age of fifty-four, on September 25, 1843.

The second bishop of St. Louis was Bishop Peter R. Kenrick, who had served as coadjutor bishop of St. Louis since 1841. He acceded to the see on the death of Bishop Rosati but had already been administering the diocese during the bishop's long absence in Europe. Bishop Kenrick continued the development of the diocese by introducing the St. Vincent de Paul Society to the diocese and to the United States. He confronted the ongoing problems of debt, but he also became a banker of sorts as he assisted recently arrived immigrants with loans. This enterprise proved so successful that during the financial crisis of 1857 Kenrick was able to assist the city.

The rapid growth of the diocese in such a short time led on July 20, 1847, to the designation of the Diocese of St. Louis as the first ecclesiastical province in the region, and Kenrick was promoted to the rank of archbishop. The very next year, in December, the city was stricken by a cholera epidemic that killed more than five hundred people and left thousands sick. Conspicuous work was done by the Sisters of St. Joseph in caring for the sick. Around the same time, the city was devastated by a fire.

Upheavals of another kind came in the 1850s with new forms of anti-Catholicism and bigotry, especially in the form of the Know-Nothings. The hostility erupted into violence when Irish Catholics were denied the vote during an election. Riots followed, and Catholic churches and even St. Louis University were threatened by mobs. During the Civil War, Kenrick fought against a Test Oath law that discriminated against Catholics. He took the issue to the Supreme Court, where such practices were declared unconstitutional.

Bishop Kenrick took part in the First Vatican Council in 1869–70 and returned home to continue the development of the diocese. He invited a number of religious communities to serve in the archdiocese, including the Visitation Sisters, the Sisters of St. Joseph, the Ursuline Sisters, the Order of the Good Shepherd, the Christian Brothers, who were instrumental in developing the parochial schools of the archdiocese, the Sisters of Mercy from New York, the School Sisters of Notre Dame, the Redemptorist Fathers, the Franciscan Friars and Sisters, the Carmelites, the Alexian Brothers, the Little Sisters of the Poor, the Sisters of St. Mary of the Third Order of St. Francis, the Oblate Sisters of Providence, and the Sisters of the Most Precious Blood.

Bishop Kenrick served the faithful as bishop and archbishop for some five decades. He led the archdiocese during the transitional era in which the United States was pushing west, had fought a terrible Civil War, and was growing rapidly in population and industrialization. He retired on May 21, 1895, at the age of eighty-eight. His death the next year was marked by great mourning in St. Louis and across the country. He was known as "the Lion."

The second archbishop of St. Louis, John J. Kain, had served as coadjutor archbishop of St. Louis since 1893 and was active in working with Archbishop Kenrick on the needs of the archdiocese. His tenure began with a severe tornado that struck the city and destroyed several churches. More positively, he reopened the archdiocesan seminary and renamed it in honor of the late Archbishop Kenrick. He also regularized parish boundaries and promoted increases in the parochial school system. He started the development of a new cathedral, but his health deteriorated steadily over these years, and he requested a coadjutor archbishop in 1903. He died in Baltimore on October 3, 1903.

The third archbishop of St. Louis, John Joseph

Glennon, had served as coadjutor archbishop since 1903, and he acceded to the see upon the passing of Archbishop Kain. Glennon served as shepherd of the St. Louis archdiocese for forty-three years, guiding the Catholic community through the years of World War I, the Great Depression, and World War II.

Called the "Eloquent Builder," Archbishop Glennon succeeded to the see at the age of forty-one and brought immense vigor to his labors. He made one of his greatest projects the completion of the new cathedral. The cornerstone was installed on October 18, 1908, and on June 29, 1926, he had the great joy of dedicating the completed St. Louis Cathedral.

To build up the Church in St. Louis and Missouri, Archbishop Glennon promoted parishes both in the city and in the rural parts of the archdiocese. He also supported outreach programs for rural life, including the first meeting of the organization that became the National Catholic Rural Life Conference in St. Louis.

In the area of education, he started parochial schools and high schools. He also welcomed the start of Webster College, under the Loretto Sisters; Fontbonne, started by the Sisters of St. Joseph of Carondelet, and Maryville, begun by the Religious of the Sacred Heart, as well as the formation of the National Catholic Educational Association in St. Louis in 1904. He was happy to bring into the diocese new religious orders and congregations, such as the Religious of the Sacred Heart and the Marianists.

On February 18, 1946, Archbishop Glennon received the great honor of being named a cardinal by Pope Pius XII, with the title of San Clemente. Sadly, he died while in Dublin, Ireland, on his way home to St. Louis from Rome. He was eighty-three years old.

The fourth archbishop of St. Louis, Archbishop Joseph E. Ritter, had served as the archbishop of Indianapolis since 1944 and was transferred to St. Louis on July 20, 1946. Ritter arrived at a time of postwar growth and optimism, when the city reached its peak in population, at more than 850,000.

Archbishop Ritter arrived determined to be a leader for the Church in the area of civl rights. He wasted no time in ordering an end to all racial segregation in the archdiocesan parochial schools, anticipating the wider movement across the country that culminated in the U.S. Supreme Court's decision to desegregate public schools in 1954. When some local Catholics tried to oppose the decision of the archbishop, Ritter responded in September 1947 with the threat of excommunication. He later established the Archdiocesan Commission on Human Rights in 1963 and was a supporter of the 1964 Civil Rights Act.

Even as he worked to promote authentic justice for African-Americans, Archbishop Ritter expanded the Catholic schools in the archdiocese and founded new parishes to meet the growing needs of the Catholic community that was also moving into the suburbs. To pay for the development, he launched the Archdiocesan Expansion Fund in 1954.

Cathedral of St. Louis

Also committed to the missions around the globe, he sent three priests to Bolivia in 1956 and was a major figure in galvanizing American Catholics to help fund world missions.

In recognition of his accomplishments, Pope John XXIII appointed Ritter a cardinal on January 16, 1961, with the title of SS. Redentore e Alfonso in Via Merulana. The next year, Cardinal Ritter traveled to Rome to take part in the Second Vatican Council and participated in the conclave of 1963 that elected Pope Paul VI. He then worked to implement the decrees and reforms of the council, but died suddenly of a heart attack on June 10, 1967.

The fifth archbishop of St. Louis wasArchbishop John Joseph Carberry, who had been bishop of Lafayette in Indiana since 1956 and had been bishop of Columbus since 1965. Installed archbishop of St. Louis on March 25, 1968, Carberry arrived just as American Catholicism entered a period of great upheaval. He was appointed to the College of Cardinals by Pope Paul VI on April 28, 1969, with the title of San Giovanni Battista de' Rossi.

Carberry adopted a deliberate and cautious path for the implementation of the council and worked to prevent much of the revolutionary atmosphere that plagued other dioceses in the years after the council. He supported Marriage Encounter and the Charismatic Renewal and was a vocal opponent of the 1973 legalization of abortion by the United States Supreme Court, founding an Archdiocesan Pro-Life Committee, the first in the country. He took part in the conclaves of 1978 that elected Pope John Paul I and then Pope John Paul II. The following year, he retired, on July 31, 1979.

John L. May, the sixth archbishop of St. Louis, had served as bishop of Mobile since 1969. Installed on March 26, 1980, he guided the archdiocese through the first years of the pontificate of Blessed John Paul II and was best known for his renovation of the Cathedral of St. Louis. He also worked to assist the poor and homeless in the archdiocese and labored to find solutions to declining vocations. He resigned on December 9, 1992.

The seventh archbishop of St. Louis, Archbishop Justin F. Rigali, had served as Secretary of the Congregation for Bishops in the Roman Curia since 1989. Installed on March 16, 1994, he developed an archdiocesan pastoral plan, promoted Eucharistic renewal for the archdiocese by hosting an Archdiocesan Eucharistic Congress in 2001, and had the pleasure of welcoming Pope John Paul II to St. Louis in 1999. On July 15, 2003, Archbishop Rigali was transferred to the Archdiocese of Philadelphia; he was later named a cardinal.

The eighth archbishop of St. Louis, Raymond L. Burke, had served as bishop of La Crosse since 1995. Installed on January 26, 2004, he arrived as one of the foremost experts in canon law in the modern Church and proved a fearless defender of the culture of life in the United States. Archbishop Burke also promoted vocations to the priesthood and supported the Tridentine Mass, including the ordination of several members of the Institute of Christ the King Sovereign Priest, which marked the celebration of the Tridentine rite of ordination in the Cathedral of St. Louis for the first time in four decades. On June 27, 2008, he was appointed by Pope Benedict XVI to the post of prefect of the Apostolic Signatura in Rome. He was appointed to the College of Cardinals in 2010.

The ninth archbishop of St. Louis, Robert J. Carlson, had served as bishop of Saginaw since 2005. Appointed on April 21, 2009, he was installed on June 10, 2009. The Catholic population of the archdiocese in 2011 was more than 520,000, served by 700 priests, more than 1,500 men and women religious, and 188 parishes.

St. Louis University

A Jesuit-run university currently boasting more than 11,800 students, St. Louis University was founded in 1818. It is the oldest university west of the Mississippi and the second-oldest Jesuit university in the United States. The origins of the school are found in the opening of St. Louis College in November 1818, the idea of Bishop Louis Dubourg, then bishop of Louisiana. He had served as president of Georgetown College from 1796 to 1798 and was desirous of starting a Catholic school in the St. Louis area.

By 1826 the college was struggling, however, and Bishop Dubourg invited the Society of Jesus to assume its operation. The Jesuits had been in Missouri since 1823 and were already running a seminary and a school for Native American boys in Florissant, Missouri, only a few miles away from the college. They assumed control in November 1829, under the leadership of Father Peter J. Verhaegen, S.J., who was only twenty-nine years old at the time. With the Jesuits taking control of the school, the college moved from its original location near the riverfront to a new site at Washington Avenue and Ninth Street.

St. Louis University, as it was henceforth called, received a formal charter from the state of Missouri in 1832, making it the oldest university west of the Mississippi River. Rapid growth and development followed, so that within twenty-five years it boasted both law and medical programs, and in 1842 a medical department was launched. By 1867 the growth of the school was such that a move to larger facilities was desirable. Construction on the new university began in 1886, with the formal opening celebrated on July 31, 1888, the feast of St. Ignatius Loyola.

In 1908 the university began admitting women students, and five women enrolled in the newly reorganized School of Law. Over the next several years, women enrolled in other departments, including the graduate school when it was established in 1924. As there were still limitations on women being enrolled with men in the Arts and Sciences, in 1925 the university opened the School of Education, which included the same requirements as the College of Arts and Sciences, but registered the women students in a different program. The School of Education was later renamed the University College, and in 1949 women were officially permitted to register and attend classes with the men in St. Louis University's College of Arts and Sciences.

In 1944 the university also set out on the groundbreaking mission of racial integration. That year, the school admitted five African-American students, two undergraduates and three graduate students, making St. Louis University the first school in St. Louis to admit black students and the first university in any of the fourteen former slave states to admit nonwhite students.

St. Maron, Brooklyn, New York *See* Eastern Churches, Catholic

St. Nicholas in Chicago. *See* Eastern Churches, Catholic

St. Paul and Minneapolis, Archdiocese of

Established as the Diocese of St. Paul by Pope Blessed Pius IX on July 19, 1850, and raised to the status of metropolitan provincial see on May 4, 1888, by Pope Leo XIII, the archdiocese was designated as St. Paul and Minneapolis on June 11, 1966, by Pope Paul VI. The archdiocese currently comprises twelve counties in Minnsesota.

St. Paul and Minneapolis are called the "Twin Cities," and St. Paul is the capital of Minnesota. Recollect Franciscan Father Louis Hennepin was in the area in 1680, followed by the explorer Jonathan Carver, who was seeking the Northwest Passage in 1706. Hennepin was soon a captive of the Sioux. He later discovered and named St. Anthony's Falls, which would later serve as a power source for Fort Snelling. The village of St. Anthony was incorporated in 1855, and Minneapolis was incorporated in 1885.

Almost a century after Hennepin's discovery, Zebulon Pike led an expedition into the region, exploring the headwaters of the Mississipi River. Pike made an unofficial treaty with the Dakota Sioux and established a post, which became Fort Snelling. In 1838 Pierre "Pig's Eye" Parrant established a settlement on the site, called "Pig's Eye's Landing" until 1941. Then Father Lucien Galtier built a log-cabin chapel, St. Paul's. The Northern Pacific Railroad, under the leadership of James J. Hill, was completed. As the settlement flourished, it was named after Father Galtier's log chapel.

The first recorded French expedition to the Minnesota region opened the Catholic influence of the area in 1654. The expedition of Pierre Radisson and Medard Chouart de Groseilliers took place at Knife Lake. The great French explorer, Daniel Greysolon, Sieur du Lhut, arranged the release of Father Hennepin from the Sioux and traveled with him through the area. Another French trader had established a fort earlier. Nicholas Perrot was near Wabash setting up trade operations, and the Jesuit Father Joseph-Jean Marest served at Perrot's fort for a time. Trade was also being conducted on Prairie Island in 1693, and the Dakota Sioux Mission near present-day Hastings was in operation.

In 1700 Fort L'Huillier was opened by the French on Blue Earth. Fort Beauharnais was also erected on Lake Pepin, as well as Fort St. Charles at Lake of the Woods. Jesuit Father Jean-Pierre Aulneau and twenty companions were slain in the region in 1736.

In the early 1800s, Swiss Catholics from Canada settled at Mandata, and in 1839 Bishop Mathias Loras of Dubuque visited the area. A year later, Bishop Loras sent Father Lucien Galtier to present-day St. Paul, where he built the Chapel of St. Paul. In 1844 the revered missionary Augustin Ravoux served at St. Paul's, having labored among the Sioux. Father Ravoux would serve the faithful for six decades, at times the only priest in Minnesota. Other Catholic missions opened at Lac Qui Parle, Fond du Lac, Grand Portage, Mandata, and Crow Wing.

In 1849 Minnesota was declared a territory by the U.S. Congress, becoming a state in 1858. Formerly part of a vicariate apostolic, St. Paul was erected as a diocese on July 19, 1850. The first bishop of St. Paul was Joseph Crétin, a French-born priest who had long served the Native Americans in the area of Dubuque. Consecrated a bishop on January 26, 1851, he proved a pioneering missionary and traveled throughout the diocese to serve the faithful. His jurisdiction at the time extended from Lake Superior to the Missouri River and from Iowa to the Canadian border. When first established, the diocese also included parts of North and South Dakota. In his first year, Bishop Crétin started a stone Cathedral of St. Paul to replace the log chapel. The Sisters of St. Joseph of Carondolet came to St. Paul to start a girls' school, and the Brothers of the Holy Family started a boys' school. The Benedictines started a monastery at St. Cloud. All of the building and expansion of diocesan facilities was aided by the Society for the Propagation of the Faith. Bishop Crétin died of exhaustion on February 22, 1857, leaving the diocese with ninety-nine churches, thirty-five missions, a hospital, and an orphanage.

Bishop Crétin was succeeded by Father Thomas L. Grace, a Dominican. Consecrated a bishop on July 29, 1859, he faced an increased Catholic population and used seven synods and various deaneries in order to promote diocesan unity. He also

presided over the diocese during the violent Sioux uprising of 1862 and throughout the Civil War. He started a diocesan newspaper and opened a preparatory seminary, while opposing school-tax legislation. Bishop Grace established schools, protective and charitable institutions, and hospitals, inviting religious orders into the diocese. He was too ill to attend the First Vatican Council and retired on July 31, 1884, receiving the personal title of archbishop from the Holy See.

The third bishop of St. Paul was the famed John Ireland, who was also the first archbishop of St. Paul when the diocese was raised to a metropolitan see in May 1888. Ireland had served as coadjutor bishop of St. Paul since 1875. His time as bishop witnessed a remarkable era of growth that included the creation in 1889 of the Dioceses of Fargo, St. Cloud, Duluth, and Winona, and then of Crookston in 1909. Ireland became known as the "Consecrated Blizzard of the Northwest" for his energy and zeal and his belief in the need for Catholics to participate fully in American life. He represented Bishop Grace at the First Vatican Council in Rome and then became one of the great leaders in Catholic education. He founded the College (now University) of St. Thomas in 1885, helped launch the College of St. Catherine, and started St. Paul Seminary. He likewise supported the foundation of The Catholic University of America in Washington, D.C. He also started parishes and schools and was responsible for the creation of the Cathedral of St. Paul and the Church (later Basilica) of St. Mary in Minneapolis. Archbishop Ireland died on September 25, 1918.

The second archbishop of St. Paul, Archbishop Daniel Austin Dowling, had served as the bishop of Des Moines since 1912. Installed in St. Paul on March 25, 1919, Dowling established the Archbishop Ireland Education Fund and raised millions to bolster Catholic education. To assist the needs of rural Catholics, he started the National Catholic Rural Life Conference. Archbishop Dowling died on November 29, 1930, from heart problems.

The third archbishop of St. Paul, John G. Murray, had been bishop of Portland in Maine since 1925. Appointed to St. Paul on October 29, 1931, he arrived in the dark days of the Great Depression and worked to provide pastoral care to the many suffering souls. Archbishop Murray also promoted evangelization, including the use of a radio show, the Confraternity of Christian Doctrine, and the Family Guild. He served as shepherd in the era of World War II and its aftermath. He died on October 11, 1956.

The fourth archbishop of St. Paul, William O. Brady, had been bishop of Sioux Falls since 1939. Named coadjutor archbishop of St. Paul in 1956, he acceded to the see upon Archbishop Murray's death. In 1958 he consecrated the cathedral that had long been delayed because of the Depression and the war. He also launched a diocesan newspaper, promoted vocations to the priesthood, and developed programs for the pastoral care of Catholics who were departing the cities for the suburbs. He died unexpectedly in Rome on October 1, 1961.

The fifth archbishop of St. Paul, Leo Binz, had been archbishop of Dubuque since 1954. Installed on April 28, 1962, Archbishop Binz's tenure was taken up with the Second Vatican Council and its implementation. In 1966 the archdiocese was renamed the Archdiocese of St. Paul and Minneapolis, and the Basilica of St. Mary was designated the co-cathedral for the archdiocese. As his health began to decline, he received a coadjutor, Leo

St. Paul Cathedral

Christopher Byrne, who died in 1971. Archbishop Binz retired on May 28, 1975.

The sixth archbishop of St. Paul and Minneapolis, John R. Roach, had been an auxiliary bishop since 1971. Appointed on May 28, 1975, Archbishop Roach encouraged a variety of ministries in the archdiocese, including outreach to the increasingly diverse Catholic population, including Latinos and Southeast Asians. He also established the nation's first written policy on sexual abuse by priests. In addition, he served as president of the National Conference of Catholic Bishops from 1983 to 1985. He retired on September 8, 1995.

The seventh archbishop of St. Paul and Minneapolis, Harry J. Flynn, had been bishop of Lafayette in Louisiana since 1989 until his appointment as coadjutor archbishop of St. Paul and Minneapolis in 1994; he acceded to the see on September 8, 1995. As archbishop, he proved remarkably successful in nurturing vocations and proved a strong leader in addressing the crisis of clergy sexual abuse. He also launched a $100 million capital campaign for the archdiocese. He retired on May 2, 2008.

The eighth archbishop of St. Paul and Minneapolis, John C. Nienstedt, had served as bishop of New Ulm and had been appointed coadjutor archbishop of the diocese in 2007. He acceded to the see on May 2, 2008, and continued to be a powerful voice for the culture of life and Catholic family life as one of the foremost moral theologians among the U.S. bishops. In 2011 the archdiocese had a Catholic population of more than 800,000, served by some 400 priests, 700 men and women religious, and 200 parishes.

St. Petersburg, Diocese of

Established on June 17, 1968, out of the Diocese of St. Augustine and the Diocese (later Archdiocese) of Miami, the Diocese of St. Petersburg serves counties on the west-central coast of the state of Florida. It is a suffragan see of the Archdiocese of Miami.

The city is located on the Pinellas Peninsula, adjacent to Tampa Bay. St. Petersburg was founded by John C. Williams and Peter A. Demens, and it was named after Demen's birthplace in Russia. The two men brought a railroad to the site. St. Petersburg pioneered the idea of Florida as a retirement locale, and the city is a popular tourist destination, also having some industry.

The Catholic heritage of St. Petersburg opens on April 3, 1513, and the mission of exploration of Juan Ponce de León, whose discovery of Florida and Tampa Bay was marked with a stone cross. De León returned in 1521 with plans to establish a colony, but he died of wounds received in an attack by local Indians. Other Spanish explorers followed, including Pánfilo de Narváez, Hernando de Soto, and Tristán de Luna. In 1549 the revered Dominican missionary Luis Cáncer de Barbastro and companions were martyred at Tampa Bay in 1549. Spain, however, was able to establish a permanent colony in 1565 with the founding of St. Augustine. Two years later, Jesuits launched a colony, but it was abandoned because of the hostility of the local peoples.

The area around Tampa Bay remained largely unoccupied, and the few missionary efforts did not survive. Lasting progress was not possible until 1821, when Florida became a territory of the United States. Three years earlier, General Andrew Jackson had fought the Seminoles and had seized Pensacola and other parts of Florida. Spain had then sold the area to the United States for $5 million. In 1825 the Holy See erected the Vicariate Apostolic of Alabama and the Floridas. Florida entered the Union in 1845 as the twenty-seventh state.

The establishment of Fort Brooke in what is now Tampa permitted the start of a Catholic presence. In 1860 St. Louis Church was founded in Tampa. Only four priests were in the area, and three died in 1888 during a yellow fever epidemic. The Jesuits assumed the Tampa ministry and built parishes and schools, including Sacred Heart Church, which opened in 1905. Benedictine monks and nuns also arrived in the region, founding and staffing parishes. Other religious orders followed, including the Redemptorists and Salesians.

The Catholic population increased steadily in the years after World War II, and the Catholic community was a great concern of Archbishop Joseph Patrick Hurley, the bishop of St. Augustine. He presided over a massive buildup of Catholic schools and churches, which provided the basis for the creation of the diocese in 1969.

The diocese was established on June 17, 1968, and the first bishop was Charles B. McLaughlin, who had served as an auxiliary bishop of Raleigh since 1964. Bishop McLaughlin instituted diocesan offices and ministries. A licensed pilot, he flew to the most distant parts of the diocese and won the affection and respect of his flock. He also took as one of his tasks the implementation of the reforms of the Second Vatican Council until his sudden death on December 14, 1978, at the age of sixty-five.

The second bishop of St. Petersburg, Monsignor W. Thomas Larkin, had served as vicar general of the diocese and diocesan administrator until his appointment on April 17, 1979. Consecrated a bishop on May 27, 1979, he assumed direction of a swiftly growing diocese and founded new parishes and schools. Owing to the wider growth of Catholicism in the state of Florida, in 1984 territory was taken from the diocese to help form the Diocese of Venice. Bishop Larkin retired on November 28, 1988, owing to poor health.

The third bishop of St. Petersburg, John C. Favalora, had been bishop of Alexandria since 1986. Installed on May 16, 1989, he continued to preside over the rapid expansion of the diocese and placed particular emphasis on Catholic education. He also celebrated the twenty-fifth anniversary of the founding of the diocese. On December 20, 1994, he was installed as the archbishop of Miami.

The fourth bishop of St. Petersburg, Robert N. Lynch, had been rector of the St. John Vianney College Seminary in Miami and general secretary to the National Conference of Catholic Bishops. He was consecrated on January 26, 1996, and devoted his efforts to improving diocesan administration, built a new pastoral center, continued a focus on Catholic education, and celebrated the Great Jubilee of 2000 with a Renew 2000 program. He also launched the first capital campaign for the diocese. IN 2011 the Catholic population numbered more than 425,000, served by 265 priests and 74 parishes.

St. Raphael Society

The St. Raphael Society was an immigrant aid society founded in New York in 1891 by Bishop Giovanni Scalabrini of Piacenza, Italy with the purpose of providing for the spiritual, the pastoral, and to a degree the temporal needs of Italian immigrants to America. The Society of St. Raphael was started specifically to assist Italian immigrants in New York. Its primary service was a home operated by the Sisters of Charity (the Pallottines) that offered shelter to women and children; men were permitted to eat there, but they were required to sleep elsewhere. A branch of the society was founded in Boston in 1902. Today, the Scalabrinian Congregation cares for migrants and refugees in twenty-four nations throughout Asia, Australia, Africa, Europe, North America, and South America.

St. Thomas the Apostle of Detroit. *See* Eastern Churches, Catholic

St. Vincent de Paul, Society of

An international association of Catholic laymen dedicated to the service of the poor, the Society of St. Vincent de Paul was founded in 1833 in Paris, when eight young men studying at the Sorbonne gathered in the office of the newspaper *Tribune Catholique* to establish a society whose purpose would be to assist the poor of the city. The chief figure in the new society was Blessed Antoine Frédéric Ozanam, a young French lawyer, writer, and professor in the Sorbonne. He worked closely with the editor of the *Tribune Catholique*, Emmanuel Bailly — who would be the first president of the society — in the first days of what they soon called the Society of St. Vincent de Paul, in honor of the great saint who was their patron.

The society soon spread across France and arrived in the United States at least as early as 1845, when it was established in St. Louis at the Cathedral of St. Louis. The main figure responsible for the establishment of the society in St. Louis was Father John Timon, C.M., an American Vincentian priest from Pennsylvania (he was later bishop of Buffalo), who returned from Ireland with copies of the Rule of the Society of St. Vincent de Paul. Support for the society was given by Bishop Peter R. Kenrick of St. Louis, who requested that Father Ambrose Heim establish the Society. The first meeting of the group in the United States was held on November 20, 1845, in St. Louis. Dr. Moses Linton was elected the first American president, and the following year the St. Louis chapter or conference was formally

recognized by the Society's International Council in Paris.

In 1846 a conference was organized in New York City, and by 1856 the sheer growth of the Society's labors made it necessary to establish local councils so that a relationship could be established with all of the dioceses in the United States. By the early twentieth century, there were four superior councils, four central councils, 34 particular councils, 730 conferences, and 12,062 members nationally. In 1911 an extensive reorganization was undertaken through a national conference held in Boston. The decision was made to establish a council in every archdiocese of the United States and for each diocese to have its own council as well. There was to be one superior council for the entire United States.

The Society of St. Vincent de Paul includes 875,000 members in 47,000 conferences in 131 countries on five continents. In the United States it performs a vast number of services for the poor and those in need, and was especially active in bringing relief and comfort in the wake of Hurricane Katrina in 2005.

Salesian Society

Known as the Salesians of Don Bosco (S.D.B.), and originally known as the Society of St. Francis de Sales, the Salesians are a religious congregation founded by St. John Bosco in 1859 to care for poor and abandoned children, especially those who were victims of the Industrial Revolution. The society was named after St. Francis de Sales, whose holiness and gentleness were to be emulated by all members of the society. Don Bosco also chose Mary, Help of Christians, as the patroness of the society.

Since its founding, the Salesian Society has become a worldwide organization that is also the second largest religious order in the Church behind only the Jesuits. Today, there are over 40,000 Salesian priests, brothers, sisters, and laypeople working in 120 countries. The Salesian family also encompasses the Daughters of Mary Help of Christians (Salesian Sisters), Salesian Cooperators, Past Pupils of Don Bosco (Don Bosco Alumni), and Don Bosco Volunteers.

The Salesians first arrived in the United States in March 1897 at the request of Archbishop Patrick

William Riordan of San Francisco when Father Raphael Piperni, with several other Salesians, reached San Francisco. The priests were given charge of a parish to assist Italian immigrants. In 1902 the Salesians established the St. Philip the Apostle Province in New Rochelle, New York. This was followed by the creation of the province of St. Andrew in San Francisco in 1926. Like their brethren in San Francisco, the early labors of the Salesians in the United States focused on pastoral care of immigrants. From this ministry the Salesians soon branched out to schools and the congregation's fabled care of children and youth. In July 1908 the first four missionary Salesian Sisters arrived in New York City and settled in Paterson, New Jersey, to begin their work with the children of Italian immigrants.

Salesian communities operate shelters for homeless or at-risk youths, schools, technical, vocational, and language instruction centers for youths and adults, and boys' clubs and community centers. In the 1990s the Salesians also began working in the area of higher education. Worldwide, there are almost 16,000 members, with nearly 11,000 priests.

Salina, Diocese of

Established on August 2, 1887, as the Diocese of Concordia by Pope Leo XIII, the diocese was redesignated the Diocese of Salina by Pope Pius XII on December 23, 1944. The diocese serves counties in northeastern Kansas. It is a suffragan of the Archdiocese of Kansas City in Kansas.

The city of Salina, named after the Salina River, was founded in 1858 on the Smoky Hill River. Colonel William A. Phillips and his antislavery companions settled on the site. Growth was slow until the Kansas-Pacific Railroad arrived in 1867.

The Catholic history of Kansas opens in 1541 when the expedition of Francisco Vázquez de Coronado arrived in the region seeking Cibola, the legendary Seven Cities of Gold. He did not remain in present-day Kansas. The protomartyr of the United States, the Franciscan priest Juan de Padilla had already started a mission in the region and stayed behind with the Wichita Indians. He was slain by a member of another tribe.

No other mission was recorded following the Franciscan effort, but fur traders were in present-day Kansas in 1700, and in 1763 the area became a Spanish territory as a result of the Treaty of Paris. France regained Kansas in 1800 and three years later sold it to the United States as part of the Louisiana Purchase. Zebulon Pike and Stephen Long then explored the territory.

By 1812 Kansas was included in the Missouri Territory, which was later designated as the Indian Territory. Ten years after that, Father Charles de la Croix served the Osage after Chief Sans-Nerf had requested missionaries. Colonel Henry Leavenworth was also in the area, founding a permanent settlement in 1827.

Jesuit missionaries came into present-day Kansas after Father de la Croix, and Father Charles Van Quickenborne was at Leavenworth with the Kickapoo, and St. Rose Philippine Duchesne was with the Potawatomi. Father Christian Hoecken, a companion of the famous Jesuit Pierre-Jean De Smet, served at Sugar Creek. In 1847 the Osage Mission of St. Paul was started by Jesuit Fathers John Schoenmaker and John Bax. Father Paul Mary Ponziglione also traveled through the area.

The Vicariate Apostolic of the Indian Territory was established by Pope Blessed Pius IX, and in 1851 Bishop Jean Baptiste Miège, also a Jesuit, led the vicariate. The Diocese of Leavenworth (now the Archdiocese of Kansas City in Kansas) was established in 1877, including the territory of what became the Diocese of Concordia.

The first bishop of Concordia, Richard Scannell, had been a priest from Nashville, Tennessee. Consecrated on November 30, 1887, he instituted diocesan offices and established the Church of Our Lady of Perpetual Help as the cathedral of the diocese. He also invited the Sisters of St. Joseph to assist in Catholic schools, recruited priests for the diocese, and provided pastoral care to the community in the face of natural disasters, including an invasion of grasshoppers. He was transferred to the Diocese of Omaha on January 30, 1891.

Scannell's successor, Thaddeus Butler, was appointed to the see, but died before his consecration on July 17, 1897. For the next seven years, Bishop John Joseph Hennessy of Wichita served as the apostolic administrator of the Diocese of Concordia. He was finally relieved of his duties on September 21, 1898, when Father John F. Cunningham was consecrated bishop of Concordia. A native of Ireland, Cunningham was a priest of long experience in Kansas. As bishop, he earned the nickname "Diocesan Builder," and he devoted the next three decades to developing the institutional needs of the diocese, including churches and schools. The Catholic population doubled during his time, as did the number of churches and priests. He also witnessed the start of the Knights of Columbus in the diocese in 1901. Bishop Cunningham died on June 23, 1919.

Bishop Francis J. Tief, who had been a priest of Hartford, Connecticut, was consecrated the next bishop of Concordia on March 30, 1921. He continued the development of the diocese, including a home for the aged, a hospital, and several colleges. He also promoted vocations, opened a new chancery for the diocese, and started the *Northwestern Kansas Register* as the diocesan newspaper in 1937. He was also forced to assist the faithful during the Great Depression and throughout the terrible Dust Bowl period, in which erosion and windstorms brought agricultural disaster. Bishop Tief retired after many ordeals on June 11, 1938.

His successor was Frank A. Thill, who had been chancellor of the Archdiocese of Cincinnati. Appointed bishop of Concordia on August 26, 1938, he was consecrated on October 28, 1938. The new bishop arrived at the start of World War II and inherited various financial problems. He provided pastoral care to the community during the war and was able to restore the financial health of the diocese. In 1944 he secured the transfer of the diocese from Concordia to the larger city of Salina. He then presided over the large postwar expansion across the diocese. Bishop Thill died on May 21, 1957.

The next bishop of Salina, Frederick W. Freking, had been a priest of the Winona diocese. Consecrated a bishop in Rome at the North American College on November 30, 1957, he was installed as bishop of Salina on January 7, 1958. He attended the sessions of the Second Vatican Council, presided over the 75th anniversary of the establishment of the diocese, and in 1963 secured permission from Rome to designate Our Lady of Perpetual Help as the patroness of the diocese, with St. Francis of

Assisi as secondary patron. On December 27, 1964, Bishop Freking was transferred to the Diocese of La Crosse.

On April 20, 1965, Cyril J. Vogel, vicar general of the Greensburg diocese, was appointed the next bishop of Salina. Consecrated a bishop on June 17, 1965, he attended the final session of the Second Vatican Council and then worked to implement the reforms of the council. He established diocesan and parish councils, a Priests' Senate, and a Clergy Personnel Board. He also promoted education and opened a number of new parishes. Even as these developments were proceeding, the diocese was faced with severe economic problems in the region, social upheaval, and declines in priestly vocations and in the general population. Bishop Vogel died unexpectedly on October 4, 1979.

The Benedictine Bishop Daniel W. Kucera, who had been auxiliary bishop of Joliet since 1977, was appointed bishop of Salina on March 11, 1980, and installed on May 7, 1980. In his four years as bishop, he promoted the work of the Priests' Council and the establishment of a Diocesan Office of Planning and the Bishop's Council for Catholic Education. He was appointed archbishop of Dubuque on December 20, 1983.

Bishop Kucera was succeeded by Bishop George K. Fitzsimons on April 3, 1984. An auxiliary bishop of Kansas City-St. Joseph since 1975, Bishop Fitzsimons was installed on May 29, 1984. He made among the priorities of his time as bishop the promotion of lay ministry, the Renew parish program of spirituality, and the Diocesan Rural Life Commission. He also faced parish closings and mergers because of declining vocations and demographic changes in the diocese. New churches were then opened in areas where the Catholic population was shifting. He retired on October 21, 2004.

The tenth bishop of Salina, Paul S. Coakley, was appointed on October 21, 2004, and consecrated a bishop on December 28, 2004. A priest of the Diocese of Wichita, Bishop Coakley was systematic in his analysis of the diocese and in 2008 began work on a pastoral plan to provide for the future needs of the Catholic community. The plan, "Stewards of Hope: A Pastoral Plan for the Diocese of Salina," was promulgated in December 2010. He also promoted the permanent diaconate and vocations to the priesthood, and established an office of the New Evangelization in 2010. On December 16, 2010, he was appointed the archbishop of Oklahoma City. In 2011 there were about 45,000 Catholics served by 72 priests and 86 parishes in the diocese.

Salpointe, John Baptist (February 22, 1825–July 15, 1898)

The first bishop of Arizona and the second archbishop of Santa Fe, John Baptist Salpointe was born in Saint-Maurice, Puy-de-Dôme, France. He studied in Agen and the College of Clermont and subsequently prepared for the priesthood in the theological seminary of Montferrand. He was ordained on December 20, 1851, and in 1859 he volunteered to journey to the New Mexico territory as a missionary.

In 1860 Salpointe was given his assignment in a parish in Mora, New Mexico. He served there for six years, ministering to the needs of his flock across a vast two-hundred-mile area. Aside from his daily labors, he also succeeded in bringing the Sisters of Loretto and the Christian Brothers to establish schools.

In 1864 Salpointe was named vicar general of the Arizona missions by Bishop Jean Baptiste Lamy of Santa Fe after the bishop was told that the Jesuits in Arizona had been recalled by their superior, thus leaving the Arizona Territory without priests. Salpointe arrived in Tucson, Arizona, in 1866, with two priests from Santa Fe. He immediately went to work building churches, founding schools and hospitals, and providing for the pastoral needs of the residents. Owing to his tireless work, in 1868 Arizona was granted by Pope Blessed Pius IX the status of a vicariate apostolic and Salpointe was appointed its first bishop.

On February 19, 1885, Bishop Salpointe was appointed coadjutor to Archbishop Lamy of Santa Fe. He remained as administrator of the Vicariate Apostolic of Arizona until the appointment of his successor, Bishop Peter Bourgade, in early 1885. He then succeeded Lamy as archbishop of Santa Fe on July 18, 1885. Archbishop Salpointe retired on January 7, 1894. He settled in Tucson, where he wrote a history of the Catholic Church in the southwestern United States. Salpointe died in Tucson and is buried under the altar of St. Augustine Cathedral.

Salt Lake City, Diocese of

Established on January 27, 1891, by Pope Leo XIII, the Diocese of Salt Lake City serves the entire state of Utah. It is a suffragan see of the Archdiocese of San Francisco. Salt Lake City, the capital of Utah, was founded in 1847 by Brigham Young and the Mormons, the Church of Jesus Christ of Latter-Day Saints. Originally called the Great Salt Lake City, the site was planned as the world capital of the Mormons, according to the plans of Joseph Smith for the "City of Zion." Brigham Young had met with the revered missionary Father Pierre-Jean De Smet and asked for possible havens for the Mormons, and the priest described the area of the Great Salt Lake in present-day Utah.

The first year of the Mormon settlement was harsh, but converts to Mormonism from northern Europe arrived to reinforce the community's resources. These converts were experienced farmers who instituted irrigation projects. The Mormons used the natural resources of the area as well and started manufacturing and mining operations.

The Catholic history of Salt Lake City opened with the sixteenth-century expedition of García López de Cárdenas, led by Francisco Vázquez de Coronado. In 1776 Franciscan Fathers Silvestre Velez de Escalante and Francisco Atanasio Domínguez entered the region and camped at Lake Utah. They were seeking an overland route from the New Mexico Franciscan missions to California. Their records proved invaluable to later explorers, and the Old Spanish Trail, a major pathway to the West, was used as part of the Franciscan expeditionary route. By 1800 fur traders were in the area, including Kit Carson and the famous Jim Bridger. A small group of settlers led by Miles Goodyear entered Utah in the early 1840s. The Mormons, however, established the permanent communities there. Other immigrants followed, including Catholics, and the U.S. government established a military post in the area. In 1848 Utah became part of the United States as the result of the Treaty of Guadalupe-Hildago.

Archbishop Joseph Sadoc Alemany of San Francisco administered Catholic affairs in Utah in 1853, but there were few priests to send to the widely scattered Catholic communities of the territory or to the Native American enclaves. The

Mormons named Utah "Deseret" and applied for statehood, but they were refused admission to the Union. The U.S. Congress established Utah as a territory, and in 1869 the Transcontinental Railroad celebrated the linking of the east and west. Utah entered the Union on January 4, 1896, as the thirty-second state.

In 1866 Father Edward Kelly celebrated a Mass in Assembly Hall, courtesy of Brigham Young. The first Catholic church in Utah was built in 1871 by Father Patrick Walsh; he dedicated it to St. Mary Magdalene. The present Cathedral of the Madeleine evolved from this first parish. In 1873 Father (later Bishop) Lawrence Scanlan arrived to serve as pastor and also as vicar forane for San Francisco. He was a key figure in developing the Catholic community over the next years; he established churches, schools, an orphanage, and a hospital, and he recruited the Sisters of the Holy Cross. When it became clear that the growth of the Church locally was outstripping the resources available, a vicariate apostolic was founded in 1887; four years later, the Diocese of Salt Lake City was erected and Scanlan was named the first bishop. Scanlan traveled across Utah and negotiated with Mormons to establish parishes, such that Catholic enclaves developed in Salt Lake City, Ogden, and elsewhere. Religious congregations of women responded to his urgent invitations and founded schools and convents as well as a hospital. Brigham Young and other Mormons enrolled their own children in the Catholic academy. Priests and religious men also responded, including the Trappists.

The Society for the Propagation of the Faith supported Bishop Scanlan's heroic efforts, and the Catholic Church Extension Society later donated a railroad car to serve as a traveling chapel that visited far-flung communities. Bishop Scanlan also began work on the new Cathedral of the Madeleine that was completed after nearly a decade in 1909 at a staggering cost for the time of some $340,000. Bishop Scanlan died on May 10, 1915, and was mourned by Catholics and Mormons alike.

On June 1, 1915, the second bishop of Salt Lake City was appointed, a Vincentian priest, Joseph S. Glass, who was consecrated a bishop on August 24, 1915. At the time of his arrival, he had seven priests in service for the entire state of Utah and for some of the mining camps in Nevada. Glass refurbished the cathedral and recruited over twenty priests for the diocese. The Catholic laity responded to the needs of the diocese and supported the military efforts of the nation at war. Bishop Glass opened schools and parishes and promoted the Catholic Women's League. He died on January 26, 1926, at the age of fifty-one.

The third bishop of Salt Lake City, John J. Mitty, was appointed on June 21, 1926, and received episcopal consecration on September 6 of that year. Bishop Mitty was faced with a diocese in a difficult financial condition as Bishop Glass had been forced to take out loans to provide for the needs of the diocese. He worked to solve the financial problems and was then confronted with the onset of the Great Depression. He instituted charitable programs and sought to assist those badly hit by the economic collapse, but he also launched a diocesan newspaper and a Catholic radio apostolate. On February 4, 1932, he was appointed the coadjutor archbishop of San Francisco and became in coming years one of the best-known Catholic prelates in the country.

On July 1, 1932, the fourth bishop of Salt Lake City was named, James E. Kearney, who was consecrated a bishop on October 28, 1932. In his five

Salt Lake City Cathedral

years as bishop, Kearney dealt with the problems of the Great Depression. He was also a noted opponent of communism and gave a memorable address to the Knights of Columbus in 1936. On July 31, 1937, Kearney was appointed the bishop of Rochester.

The fifth bishop of Salt Lake City, Duane G. Hunt, was named on August 6, 1937. A priest of the diocese and the first Methodist convert to become a bishop in the United States, he was consecrated on October 28, 1937. His time as bishop coincided with the Second World War and the postwar optimism, and he expanded the number of parishes and schools and encouraged religious orders to serve in the diocese. These included the Carmelites and the Sisters of Charity of the Incarnate Word. Bishop Hunt died on March 31, 1960.

The sixth bishop of Salt Lake City, John Lennox Federal, had served as auxiliary bishop of Salt Lake City and coadjutor bishop of Salt Lake City since May 1, 1958. He acceded to the see upon Bishop Hunt's passing and went on to attend the Second Vatican Council. Bishop Federal renovated the cathedral and worked to implement the reforms of the council, including new lay ministries and outreach to the increasingly diverse Catholic community. Bishop Federal retired on April 22, 1980.

The seventh bishop of Salt Lake City, William K. Weigand, was appointed on September 9, 1980, and was consecrated a bishop on November 17, 1980. Bishop Weigand focused on the need to refurbish the Cathedral of the Madeleine, and to apply the liturgical reforms of the Second Vatican Council. He also promoted sound relations with the Mormons in the city. On January 27, 1994, he was installed as bishop of Sacramento.

The eighth bishop of Salt Lake City, George H. Niederauer, was appointed on November 3, 1994, and consecrated a bishop on January 25, 1995. He continued the expansion of programs of evangelization and education. On December 15, 2005, he was named archbishop of San Francisco.

The ninth bishop of Salt Lake City, John C. Wester, had been auxiliary bishop of San Francisco since 1998. He was appointed to Salt Lake City on January 8, 2007, and installed on March 14, 2007. In 2012 there were about 265,000 Catholics, served by 76 priests and 48 parishes in the diocese.

Salvatierra, Juan Maria (November 15, 1648–July 17, 1717)

Spanish Jesuit missionary and founder of the first of the California missions, Juan Maria Salvatierra was born in Milan, Italy. He studied under the Jesuits in their college in Parma and, by chance, one day found a book on the Indian missions. He was so moved by the account of the evangelization in the New World that he committed himself to assisting the cause. He joined the Jesuits in Genoa and set out for Mexico in 1675. After further theological studies, he was assigned to work as a professor in the college of Puebla. As he was determined to labor in the missions, he was sent in June 1680 to the tribes of southwestern Chihuahua.

Father Salvatierra spent the next ten years among the tribes. He founded several missions and won both the respect and affection of the local people. In 1690 he was named *visitador* (or inspector) of the Jesuit missions in the district. Not long after, he expressed a desire to work in Lower California, especially after fruitful conversations with the great missionary Eusebius Kino. He set out in 1697 and worked with Father Juan Ugarte. As the cost of the mission was to be entirely at the expense of the missionaries, contributions were sought to assist the undertaking. The donations that were made became the basis for the *Fondo Piadoso*, or the Pious Fund of the Californias. (*See also* Pious Fund of the Californias.)

Father Salvatierra landed with six soldiers at Concepcion Bay in Lower California in October 1697. From humble beginnings of mastering the local dialects by direct interaction, Father Salvatierra established six missions. In 1704 he was called back to Mexico to serve as provincial, but three years later he was back in the mission field. He spent the next decade at work in evangelization and died while on his way to Mexico to meet with the new viceroy. His writings included *Cartas sobre la Conquista espiritual de California* (1698) and his *Relaciones* (1697–1709) in *Documentos para la Historia de Mexico*.

San Angelo, Diocese of

Established by Pope Blessed John XXIII on October 16, 1961, the Diocese of San Angelo serves counties in west-central Texas. It is a suffragan see of the Archdiocese of San Antonio. The city was founded in 1869 and was called, locally, "Over the River." The name San Angelo was adopted later. The area of San Angelo is a farming and sheep-raising community, with oil deposits in certain locations.

The Catholic heritage of San Angelo was instituted by Franciscan missionaries who evangelized portions of present-day Texas in the seventeenth century. San Clemente Mission was opened in 1632 but closed soon after. Santa Cruz de San Sabá Mission was begun in 1757 but was destroyed by the Comanches; Franciscan Fathers Alonzo Ferrares and José San Esteban were slain in the mission in 1783.

During the historical period of domination by independent Mexico, the Catholic missions of the area were suppressed. In 1836, however, Texas became a republic, and the Vicariate Apostolic of Texas was established by the Holy See soon after. The revered Vincentian missionary John Timon was consecrated as the vicar apostolic. In 1842 Bishop John M. Odin became the vicar and then the bishop of Galveston.

San Angelo was visited by French missionaries, and in 1874 the Diocese (now Archdiocese) of San Antonio was erected, and San Angelo was included in that new ecclesiastical jurisdiction. In 1880 the parish of the Immaculate Conception was established in San Angelo by Father Maturin Perier, and Oblates and Franciscans labored in the area. Six years later, Carmelites from Kansas established a German Catholic community in present-day Stanton, and the Sisters of Divine Providence were operating a school in the region. In 1887 Sisters of Charity of the Incarnate Word opened an academy in San Angelo. St. John's Hospital opened in 1910.

Owing to the development of the Catholic community, the Holy See established the Diocese of San Angelo in 1961, with Thomas J. Drury appointed as the diocese's first bishop. Consecrated on January 24, 1962, Drury established the offices and agencies for diocesan administration and dedicated Sacred Heart Cathedral out of a parish church that had been founded in 1884. He also promulgated the reforms of the Second Vatican Council and was aided by the Catholic Church Extension Society and the continued presence of the Franciscans and Oblates. Bishop Drury was transferred to the Diocese of Corpus Christi on July 19, 1966.

The second bishop of San Angelo was Thomas Tschoepe, who was consecrated on March 9, 1966. Bishop Tschoepe promoted lay ministries and programs for the Hispanic laborers in the region. He also supported the Catholic schools during a period of financial challenge. On August 27, 1969, Bishop Tschoepe was transferred to the Diocese of Dallas.

The third bishop of San Angelo, Stephen Aloysius Leven, had been an auxiliary bishop of San Antonio since 1956. A noted orator and a former vice rector of the Amerian College of the Louvain, Leven promoted lay ministries and the reforms of the Second Vatican Council, including the permanent diaconate. He served during a difficult period after the council and retired on April 16, 1979.

The fourth bishop of San Angelo, Joseph A. Fiorenza, was a priest of Galveston. Consecrated on October 25, 1979, Bishop Fiorenza launched a large fundraiser for the construction of a retreat center in San Angelo, which was completed in 1983. He also promoted the diocesan newspaper. He was transferred to the Diocese of Galveston-Houston on December 18, 1994.

The fifth bishop of San Angelo, Michael D. Pfeifer, O.M.I., was a priest of the Oblates of Mary Immaculate. Consecrated a bishop on July 26, 1985, he presided over the diocese during a time of increasing diversity. In 2011 the diocese celebrated its fiftieth anniversary. There are some 85,000 Catholics in the diocese, served by 62 priests and 47 parishes.

San Antonio, Archdiocese of

Established on September 3, 1874, as a diocese by Pope Blessed Pius IX, San Antonio was raised to the rank of a metropolitan provincial see on August 3, 1936, by Pope Pius XI. The archdiocese serves counties in south-central Texas and has suffragan sees. The city of San Antonio was founded on the San Antonio River on May 1, 1718, by Spaniards on the site of an Indian village.

The entire history of San Antonio is steeped in Catholic traditions, as Spanish Franciscans began mission programs in present-day Texas as early as 1682. Earlier French priests had been in the area, including the revered Father Zenobius Membré, as well as Franciscans and Sulpicians. The expedition of Alonzo de León entered Texas in 1689. The Mission of San Francisco de las Tejas was established in 1691, followed by other missions. In 1718 the missions were transferred to San Antonio.

Mission San Antonio de Valero, now known as the Alamo, was opened in 1718 under the direction of Franciscan Father Antonio de San Buenaventura y Olivares. Venerable Antonio Margil de Jesús, an ascetic and missionary, was establishing missions in northern Texas at the time and at Natchitoches. The Mission La Purisima Conception, Mission San Jose y San Miguel de Aguayo, San Francisco de la Espada, and San Juan Capistrano rose in San Antonio as a result of Franciscan endeavors. San Fernando Church, now the cathedral, opened in 1731. Two years before, some four hundred families were moved by the King of Spain from the Canary Islands. The new San Fernando Church was built and dedicated on November 6, 1749.

The area remained under the jurisdiction of Guadalajara until 1777, when it was attached to the newly created Diocese of Nuevo León, or Linares. In 1813 the missions were suppressed by the government, but in 1839 Pope Gregory XVI established a prefecture apostolic in Texas. The revered Bishops John Timon and John Odin served as prefect and vice prefect. Texas was a republic at the time, having gained independence from Mexico. The affairs of the Church in the area were governed by the vicar apostolic until 1847, when San Antonio was placed under the episcopal jurisdiction of the Diocese of Galveston.

San Antonio and south-central Texas were expanding, and Father Leopold Moczygemba, O.F.M., was serving in the diocese. Immigrants arrived and started churches and schools. These developments led in 1874 to the creation of the Diocese of San Antonio.

The first bishop of San Antonio, Anthony Dominic Pellicer, was consecrated a bishop on December 8, 1874. He found a vibrant Catholic community that boasted parishes and the presence of many remarkable communities of religious, including the Ursuline Sisters, the Sisters of the Incarnate Word and Blessed Sacrament, the Sisters of Charity of the Incarnate Word (who founded Incarnate Word College of San Antonio in 1881), the Sisters of Divine Providence (who founded Our Lady of the Lake College in 1896), the Sisters of the Holy Spirit and Mary Immaculate, the Society of Mary (who founded St. Louis College in 1893, presently St. Mary's University), and the Oblates of Mary Immaculate. Bishop Pellicer died on April 14, 1880.

The second bishop of San Antonio, John Claudius Neraz, was consecrated a bishop on May 8, 1881. Bishop Neraz had served for decades as a missionary priest in Texas and applied that zeal to expanding the ministries and offices of the diocese to meet the pastoral needs of the Catholic community. Oblates and Marianists became active during this time and did much to nurture the growing reputation of the diocese for the quality of its education. Bishop Neraz died on November 15, 1894.

The third bishop of San Antonio, John Anthony Forest, had also been a dedicated missionary in southern Texas. Consecrated a bishop on October 28, 1895, he welcomed the opening of Our Lady of

Bishop Pellicer of San Antonio

Mission Espada, San Antonio

the Lake College and Incarnate Word College and promoted parochial education in the diocese. He died on March 11, 1911, at the age of seventy-two.

The fourth bishop of San Antonio, John William Shaw, was a convert and had served as a priest in Alabama before becoming coadjutor bishop of San Antonio in 1910. He acceded to the see upon the passing of Bishop Neraz. He encouraged the arrival of Irish priests into the diocese and established St. John's Seminary. He also gave haven to several Mexican bishops when they were forced to flee Mexico during the oppression of the Church. On January 25, 1918, Shaw was appointed the archbishop of New Orleans.

The fifth bishop of San Antonio and the first archbishop, Arthur J. Drossaerts was consecrated a bishop on December 18, 1918. He proved a vigorous bishop and opened the new St. John's Seminary in 1920, and sued over a taxation issue regarding Catholic hospitals in the diocese. He also reorganized the chancery and surrendered the Alamo to the state of Texas so that it might be protected as an important landmark in Texas history. In 1926 he was promoted to the rank of archbishop with the elevation of the diocese to an archdiocese. He then led the Catholic community through the dark era of the Great Depression and died on September 8, 1940, as America was heading into the Second World War.

The second archbishop of San Antonio, Robert E. Lucey, had served as the bishop of Amarillo since 1934. Appointed archbishop on January 23, 1941, by Pope Pius XII, Lucey swiftly earned the title "The Great Laborer" for his work on behalf of the Catholic community, including the promotion of the Catholic Welfare Bureau, the Catholic Action Office, and Council of Catholic Men. He also was noted for his work on behalf of social justice issues, established the Catholic newspaper the *Alamo Register*, and worked to improve and expand Catholic education and establish hospitals and clinics. He was notable also for starting the Patrician Movement to provide care for juveniles with drug-addiction issues and for advancing the cause of civil rights, including Project Equality, which worked toward equality in pay. He retired on July 4, 1969.

The third archbishop of San Antonio, Francis J. Furey, had been an auxiliary bishop of Philadelphia and then bishop of San Diego since 1966. He was promoted to the Archdiocese of San Antonio on June 4, 1969, during a tumultuous period. Archbishop Furey had encountered problems with a rebellious presbyterate and faced assorted financial challenges. In 1973 Archbishop Furey began the Mexican American Cultural Center and lay programs were encouraged according to the mandates of the Second Vatican Council. He died on April 23, 1979.

Patricio Fernández Flores had been named an auxiliary bishop of San Antonio in 1970 and was serving as bishop of El Paso when he was appointed the fourth archbishop of San Antonio on August 23, 1979. The first Mexican-American bishop or archbishop of San Antonio, he presided over the archdiocese during a time of considerable challenges of increasing diversity.

Archbishop Flores built a new chancery, founded the San Antonio Missions National Historical Park, and coordinated fundraising for archdiocesan programs. In June 2000 he was held hostage for nine hours by a native of El Salvador and legal U.S. resident who was worried he might be deported after being

The Alamo, San Antonio

arrested for driving with a suspended license. Archbishop Flores retired on December 29, 2004.

The fifth archbishop of San Antonio, José H. Gomez, was a priest of the Prelature of Opus Dei and had been an auxiliary bishop of Denver since 2001. He was appointed coadjutor archbishop of Los Angeles on April 6, 2010, and acceded to the see on March 1, 2011.

The sixth archbishop of San Antonio, Gustavo García-Siller, a priest of the Missionaries of the Holy Spirit, had been serving as an auxiliary bishop of Chicago since 2003 at the time of his appointment to San Antonio on October 14, 2010. He was installed on November 23, 2010. In 2011 the Catholic population in the diocese was more than 700,000, served by 327 priests, more than 1,000 men and women religious, and 139 parishes.

San Bernardino, Diocese of

Established on July 14, 1978, by Pope Paul VI, the Diocese of San Bernardino serves the San Bernardino and Riverside counties in Southern California. It is a suffragan diocese of the Archdiocese of Los Angeles.

The diocese was named for St. Bernard of Siena and emerged from a series of Jesuit and Franciscan missions that were opened in the early days of the Spanish missions of California. Catholic settlers traveling from New Mexico came into the region in 1842. These settlers named their encampment in the San Bernardino Valley Agua Mansa and established San Salvador Mission as their parish. The flood of 1862 prompted many of these pioneers to leave the area for Colton. In 1852 there were also a number of Mormons in present-day San Bernardino, and they laid out a town but abandoned it soon after.

A continuing stream of settlers arrived in San Bernardino in the following decades, and the site assumed the municipal structures and offices of a developing city. San Bernardino evolved into an aerospace hub, aided by the presence of Norton Air Force Base and industrial centers.

Jesuit missionaries were laboring in the area of Southern California until they were expelled from the region in 1767 and cruelly treated by the Spanish authorities. In order to provide new priests for the region, José de Galvez, the Spanish visitor general of Mexico, representing the Crown, ordered the formal occupation of California and enlisted the aid of Blessed Junípero Serra in opening outposts of the faith. As a result of Blessed Junípero Serra's leadership, some twenty-one missions were founded in the California region between 1769 and 1823.

In San Bernardino, the settlements flourished until the disastrous flood of 1862. The damage inflicted by the raging waters forced some settlers to abandon their homesites. Others remained and started parishes. St. Bernardino Parish was opened in 1862, followed by St. Francis de Sales in Riverside in 1886, St. Frances of Rome in Lake Elsinore in 1887, and others. As part of the Diocese (later Archdiocese) of Los Angeles, San Bernardino welcomed the growing number of new settlers and witnessed the signs of progress everywhere into the twentieth century.

The growth of Catholicism in California led to the creation of numerous dioceses across the state, and San Bernardino became one of those new territories in 1978. At the time of its foundation, San Bernardino was under the jurisdiction of the Diocese of San Diego, and a priest of the San Diego diocese, Philip F. Straling, was appointed the first bishop of San Bernardino. The new cathedral was designated at Holy Rosary Parish, where Father Straling had been pastor. Appointed on July 18, 1978, and consecrated a bishop on November 16, 1978, Straling devoted his first years to establishing diocesan offices and agencies for the more than 235,000 Catholics of the local community. Bishop Straling was also dedicated to providing pastoral care to the increasingly diverse Catholic population, in particular the growing number of Hispanics. On March 25, 1995, he was appointed the bishop of Reno.

The second bishop of San Bernardino, Bishop Gerald R. Barnes, had served as auxiliary bishop of the diocese since 1992. Appointed bishop on December 28, 1995. and installed on March 12, 1996, Bishop Barnes was shepherd over a growing diocese—the Catholic population increased from 235,000 in 1978 to more than one million by the end of the century. As of 2011, there were more than one million Catholics served by 228 priests and 92 parishes.

Sánchez, Jose Bernardo (September 7, 1778– January 15, 1833)

A Franciscan missionary in California, Jose Bernardo Sánchez was born at Robledillo, Old Castile, Spain. He entered the Franciscans in 1794 and began his missionary labors in North American in 1803 when he arrived in Mexico. He joined the missionary college of San Fernando in Mexico in 1803. He went to California the next year and served at the Mission San Diego for the next sixteen years, followed by Mission Purisima from 1820 to 1821 and then Mission San Gabriel for his remaining years.

Ever vigorous, he set out on a missionary expedition with Father Mariano Payeras in 1821. In 1827 he was named head of the missions and vicar forane to the bishop. This post he tried repeatedly to escape. While head of the missions he opposed a secularization plan by the local governor. In 1831 he managed to return to the missions but lived for only another two years. He died at the San Gabriel Mission and was buried under the altar.

San Diego, Diocese of

Established on July 11, 1936 by Pope Pius XI, the Diocese of San Diego serves San Diego and Imperial counties in Southern California and is the southernmost diocese in the state of California. It is a suffragan of the Archdiocese of Los Angeles.

San Diego was first sighted by Juan Rodriguez Cabrillo in 1542, and he named it San Miguel. The expedition of Hernando Cortés had visited the area in 1535. Franciscan Father Martin de la Coruña was with that expedition. In 1602 the site was renamed San Diego de Alcala de Henares by Sebastian Vizcaino. Carmelite Father Antonio de Ascensión celebrated Mass in San Diego as part of Vizcaino's expedition. Two other Carmelites, Father Andrew of the Assumption and Thomas of Aquinas, were also on the site. The Spanish vicar general of Mexico, José de Galvez, started the official colonization of San Diego in 1769, asking Blessed Junípero Serra and the Franciscans to aid him. Gaspar de Portolà founded a presidio there in July 1769, and a mission was opened.

In 1846 Americans started an urban settlement on the site, called Old Town by 1850. The Santa Fe Railroad arrived in 1884, and the city also became home to the U.S. Navy's 11th District and remained one of the most important bases for the navy anywhere.

The remarkable missions established by the Carmelites and Franciscans endured a terrible ordeal from 1821 when Mexico, having secured its independence from Spain, sought to exterminate Spanish influence in California. In 1832 the missions were secularized by the Mexican government. At the same time, Americans began entering the region in growing numbers. In 1846 these Americans joined the rebellion against Mexican rule that led to the Mexican-American War and the Treaty of Guadalupe-Hidalgo in 1848, which forced Mexico to cede California to the United States. California entered the United States in 1850.

Over the next century, the Catholic population continued to increase, and the Church responded with the creation of ecclesiastical jurisdictions, starting with the Diocese of California in 1840 and then San Francisco in 1853. At the start of the twentieth century, the area of San Diego was part of the Diocese of Monterey-Los Angeles and from 1922 the Diocese of Los Angeles-San Diego. By 1936, with the creation of the Archdiocese of Los Angeles, a separate diocese for San Diego was deemed desirable.

The first bishop of San Diego, Charles F. Buddy, was a priest from St. Joseph, Missouri. Consecrated on December 21, 1936, he launched the needed diocesan offices and ministries for the new diocese, started a diocesan newspaper, built more than one hundred parishes, and co-founded the University of San Diego in 1949. Bishop Buddy also served as shepherd during World War II and attended the Second Vatican Council. He died at the age of seventy-eight on March 6, 1966.

The second bishop of San Diego, Francis J. Furey, had been an auxiliary bishop of Philadelphia since 1960. Named coadjutor bishop of San Diego in 1963, he acceded to the see upon the passing of Bishop Buddy. Bishop Furey began the implementation of the reforms of the Second Vatican Council but was appointed on May 23, 1969, as archbishop of San Antonio.

The third bishop of San Diego, Leo T. Maher, had been bishop of Santa Rosa since 1962. Appointed on August 22, 1969, he inherited a diocese with considerable financial problems, which he was able to repair by 1980. He launched parish development, encouraged the promotion of the reforms of the council, and created the first diocesan pastoral council. He was also a supporter of the culture of life and prohibited Catholics who belonged to pro-abortion organizations from receiving Communion or serving as lectors. He likewise prohibited a Catholic state assemblywoman from receiving Communion because of her support for abortion. Bishop Maher retired on July 10, 1990.

The fourth bishop of San Diego, Robert H. Brom, had been Bishop of Duluth from 1983 and coadjutor bishop of San Diego since 1989; he was installed on July 10, 1990, upon the retirement of Bishop Maher.

Bishop Brom focused on Catholic education and started two Catholic high schools. He also established a more efficient pastoral center for the diocese and sold the old chancery office to the University of San Diego. Sadly, the dominant event in the recent life of the diocese was the fallout from the clergy sexual abuse scandal. On February 28, 2007, the diocese filed for bankruptcy protection after failure to reach a settlement agreement with various plaintiffs suing the diocese over cases of abuse. In September 2007, the diocese agreed to pay $198.1 million to settle 144 claims. In 2011 the Catholic population of the diocese numbered about one million, served by some 250 priests and 99 parishes.

Sands, Benjamin F. (February 11, 1812–June 30, 1883)

A rear admiral in the United States Navy, Benjamin Sands was born in Baltimore to non-Catholics. He converted in 1850 and married a Catholic, Henrietta M. French, sister of a prominent major general, William H. French. Appointed a midshipman in the navy in 1828, Sands enjoyed a long and distinguished career that culminated in his appointment as rear admiral in April 1871.

He took part in the Civil War and in 1867 was named superintendent of the Naval Observatory in Washington, D.C. His time there marked its emergence as an internationally respected institution. Sands was also a member of the Catholic Indian Bureau in Washington. He retired in 1874 and died

in Washington, D.C. His son, James H. Sands, also became a rear admiral.

Sands, James Hoban (July 12, 1845–October 26, 1911)

A rear admiral in the United States Navy, James Sands was the son of Rear Admiral Benjamin Sands and was born in Washington, D.C. Like his father, Sands chose the navy as his career. Appointed to the Naval Academy in Maryland in 1859, he took part in the Civil War and distinguished himself in the North Atlantic Blockading Squadron that interdicted Confederate shipping. Twice during the war he was recommended by boards of admirals to receive promotion, despite his rank as ensign, in recognition of his gallantry.

After the war, Sands took a command in the West India Squadron and was later placed in charge of the Brooklyn, Boston, Philadelphia, and Washington navy yards. He received promotion to rear admiral in 1902 and served as head of the Naval Academy at Annapolis from 1906 to 1907. He retired in 1907.

Admiral Sands worked hard during his career to promote the cause of Catholics in the armed forces. In particular, he helped ease the anti-Catholic sentiment that was still found in the navy and the other branches. Two of his daughters became Religious of the Sacred Heart.

San Francisco, Archdiocese of

Established on July 29, 1853, by Pope Pius IX, the Archdiocese of San Francisco serves counties in west-central California and is centered in the city of San Francisco.

In March 1776 Captain Juan Bautista de Anza and Franciscan Father Pedro Font designated San Francisco as a foundation site for a later mission and a presidio. The settlement was started by José Joaquín de la Santísima Trinidad Moraga. On November 1, 1769, Blessed Junípero Serra and Gaspar de Portolá, a representative of the military administration, had also visited the site. Colonists who made the long trek from Sonora, Mexico, followed Captain de Anza and Father Font into the region. They were led by Father Francisco Palou, a missionary of distinction, and Moraga. The colonists reached the Arroyo de los Dolores on

June 27, 1776, and two days later Mission Dolores was founded. The great port city of San Francisco grew steadily from this first settlement, impacted by the Gold Rush and the devastating earthquake of 1906.

As is clear from its foundation, San Francisco has a deep Catholic heritage. Part of the great chain of missions throughout California, San Francisco was served not only by Franciscans but by Jesuits and other religious orders. In 1542 Juan Rodriguez Cabrillo, the Spanish explorer, was in San Francisco Bay, followed by Sebastian Vizcaino, who arrived in the coastal waters in 1602 and then again in 1603. The first foundation of missions in San Francisco brought about Spanish and Mexican aid and concern as the population in the area was growing dramatically. Americans were also arriving in the area, many becoming Catholic, and they began to unite against Mexican rule, leading to the Mexican-American War and Treaty of Guadalupe-Hidalgo in 1848 that ceded California to the United States.

In 1840, having watched the growth of Catholic populations in the region, the Vatican established the Diocese of Upper and Lower California. Bishop Francisco Garcia Diego y Moreno, a Franciscan, administered the diocese, including San Francisco, from Santa Barbara.

The Archdiocese of San Francisco, at its foundation, extended to Oregon and south to Monterey. The first archbishop of San Francisco, the Spanish-born Dominican priest Joseph Sadoc Alemany, had been a missionary in Kentucky, Ohio, and Tennessee, and had served as bishop of Monterey since 1850.

The three decades of Alemany's tenure as archbishop saw the rapid development of the Catholic community. He promoted the Catholic school system, built orphanages, hospitals, and homes for the elderly, and encouraged the arrival of congregations and orders of women religious, in particular the Dominican Sisters, Notre Dame de Namur Sisters, Sisters of Charity, Presentation Sisters, Mercy Sisters, and Sisters of the Holy Family. He likewise recruited the services of the Jesuits, Dominicans, Salesians, Paulists, and Franciscans. He also provided pastoral care for the mining camps during the Gold Rush and worked in the legal system to compel the government of Mexico to repay the monies due from the Pious Fund of the Californias. Exhausted by his labors, Archbishop Alemany requested and received in 1883 a coadjutor archbishop, Patrick William Riordan. Alemany retired on December 28, 1884, and returned to Valencia, Spain. His departure was the source of immense sorrow for the people of San Francisco.

Archbishop Riordan acceded to the see upon Alemany's retirement. He built on Alemany's work and continued to develop parishes and schools, started a new St. Mary's Cathedral, and in 1898 opened St. Patrick's Seminary in Menlo Park. He also appointed Father Peter C. Yorke, the editor of the archdiocesan newspaper, *The Monitor*, to lead the charge against the anti-Catholic American Protective Association, which was causing upheaval in the area. Archbishop Riordan also continued the legal effort against Mexico regarding the Pious Fund and went to the Hague in 1902 to witness the final settlement.

The chief event of the period occurred on April 18, 1906, when the City of San Francisco and the area were hit by an earthquake estimated by scientists to be 8.4 on the Richter scale. The city was absolutely devastated, and a quarter of a million people were left homeless. Archbishop Riordan visited the injured and the homeless, and promised to work to rebuild the damaged and destroyed churches and homes. He died at his post on December 27, 1914.

The third archbishop of San Francisco, Edward J. Hanna, had served as an auxiliary bishop of San Francisco since 1912. He was appointed on June 1, 1915, and presided over the continued growth of the school system and worked to modernize diocesan administration. He appointed the former archbishop of Los Angeles, John J. Cantwell, as his vicar general, instituted a marriage court, and promoted summer educational programs for teachers. He led the Catholic community through World War I and the Great Depression, and retired on March 2, 1935, having served the faithful locally and nationally.

The fourth archbishop of San Francisco, John J. Mitty, had served as bishop of Salt Lake City since 1926. He was promoted to San Francisco as coadjutor archbishop on January 29, 1932, and acceded to the see upon Archbishop Hanna's retirement. Archbishop Mitty served for thirty years, a time that included the Second World War and the postwar era of rapid growth. He built parishes and schools to keep pace with the growing Catholic population and promoted vocations. He died on October 15, 1961. The next year, the Dioceses of Oakland, Santa Rosa, and Stockton were established from territory in the archdiocese.

The fifth archbishop of San Francisco, Joseph T. McGucken, had served as bishop of Sacramento since 1957 and was installed in San Francisco on April 3, 1962. Archbishop McGucken arrived on the eve of the Second Vatican Council, and he attended the sessions of the council and then worked to implement its reforms in a time when San Francisco was undergoing immense social upheaval and swift diversification through the arrival of Catholics from Asia and Africa. He also worked to build a new St. Mary's Cathedral after the old cathedral suffered a fire. Archbishop McGucken retired on February 16, 1977.

The sixth archbishop of San Francisco, John R. Quinn, had been the first archbishop of Oklahoma City since 1972. Appointed on February 16, 1977, he placed much of his pastoral focus on the poor and forgotten of the city, including a wider pastoral plan for the archdiocese that was marked by parish closings to deal with population movement. In 1987 the archdiocese welcomed Pope Blessed John Paul II, who celebrated a Mass at Candlestick Park that was attended by seventy thousand Catholics. Archbishop Quinn also worked to assist the rebuilding effort after the 1989 Loma Prieta earthquake. He resigned on December 27, 1995, at the age of sixty-six.

On August 17, 1995, Archbishop William J. Levada, archbishop of Portland since 1986, was named coadjutor archbishop of San Francisco. He acceded to the see upon the resignation of Archbishop Quinn. Faced with closed churches in the city, Archbishop Levada cleverly converted them into other forms of ministry, including a National Shrine of St. Francis, a homeless center, and missions. He also presided over successful Great Jubilee celebrations in 2000. In 2005, with the election of Cardinal Joseph Ratzinger as Pope Benedict XVI, Archbishop Levada was named prefect of the Congregation for the Doctrine of the Faith on May 13, 2005; he was appointed to the College of Cardinals in 2006.

On February 15, 2006, the eighth archbishop of San Francisco was appointed, George H. Niederauer, who had been bishop of Salt Lake City since 1994. He focused on the pressing social issues facing the archdiocese, including immigration. There are more than 220,000 Catholics in the archdiocese served by more than 400 priests, nearly 700 men and women religious, and 91 parishes.

San Jose, Diocese of

Established on January 27, 1981, by Pope Blessed John Paul II, the Diocese of San Jose in California serves fifteen counties in northern California. It is a suffragan see of the archdiocese of San Francisco. In 1776 Juan Bautista de Anza chose the site as a colony in the Santa Clara Valley. On November 29, 1977, José Joaquín de la Santísima Trinidad founded San José de Guadalupe in 1797, a settlement unique because it was not part of a mission or a presidio.

San José served as part of the vast chain of missions developed by Blessed Junípero Serra and his fellow Franciscans. Spanish expeditions were in the area as early as 1542, including those of Juan Rodriguez Cabrillo and Sebastian Vizcaino. Mexican colonists, led by priests and military officers, began moving into the area as the United States became independent on the East Coast and then expanded westward. Land grants were also made to some individuals by the Spanish crown.

The people of San José also welcomed the first Americans who came to live in the area, many converting to Catholicism. On July 14, 1846, the American flag flew over San Jose as California joined the Union. The mercury mines, such as those south of the city, were part of the Gold Rush and added to the population and prosperity of the city. As a result, San José was incorporated on March 27, 1850. St. Patrick's Cathedral dates to this era, and the city served as the capital of California for a brief period.

The city was included as part of Upper California and the Diocese of Sonora, Mexico, during the early days, but it was placed from 1850 under the care of the great Spanish Dominican Joseph Sadoc

Alemany, bishop of Monterey and then from 1853 the first archbishop of San Francisco.

The area remained under the Archdiocese of San Francisco throughout the twentieth century, but it became clear that the city and Santa Clara County needed their own diocesan church to meet the needs of the growing Catholic community.

The first bishop of San Jose, Pierre DuMaine, had served as an auxiliary bishop of San Francisco since 1978. Installed on March 18, 1981, he assumed direction over the new diocese. St. Patrick Church in San Jose was designated the cathedral, but in 1987 St. Joseph Church was designated to replace it as the cathedral and was designated a minor basilica in 1995 and renamed the Cathedral Basilica of St. Joseph. Meantime, Bishop DuMaine founded the needed diocesan offices for ministry and governance and strengthened the parishes and schools of the diocese. He also worked to assist in reconstruction in the aftermath of the 1989 Loma Prieta earthquake.

On June 30, 1998, Bishop Patrick J. McGrath, auxiliary bishop of San Francisco, was appointed the coadjutor to the bishop of San Jose. He acceded to the see when Bishop DuMaine retired on November 27, 1999. In 2011 the Catholic population of the diocese was about 580,000, served by 350 priests, more than 350 men and women religious, and 49 parishes.

Sansbury, Angela (1794–1839)

The first woman to become a Dominican Sister in the United States and honored as the foundress of the Dominican Sisters in the country, Mariah Hamilton Sansbury was born in Prince George County, Maryland, in 1794. She grew up in Kentucky after her father died. Her family was active in the parish near their home in Springfield, Kentucky, and Mariah responded to the call of the Dominican Father Samuel Wilson for young women to help establish a community of Dominican Sisters dedicated to education.

Mariah entered the Dominican community in 1822 in St. Rose Parish in Springfield and took the name of Sister Angela. She joined several other postulants to begin the Congregation of St. Catherine of Siena. The first motherhouse was a small cabin, but after her mother died, Sister Angela was able to move the sisters to her family home. They then started a small school on the property.

As Sister Angela was clearly respected as the leader of the community, Father Wilson secured for her permission to make her profession early. Her status as prioress was confirmed in June 1823. She went on to serve two terms as prioress and in 1830 moved to Ohio at the request of Bishop Edward D. Fenwick. Sister Angela and four sisters from Kentucky established a new community and an academy of St. Mary's in the settlement at Somerset. Mother Angela was elected twice as prioress but died during her second term

Santa Fe, Archdiocese of

Established as a diocese on July 29, 1853, by Pope Blessed Pius IX, and elevated to the rank of a metropolitan provincial see on February 12, 1875, the Archdiocese of Santa Fe serves counties in the north-central part of the state of New Mexico. It has suffragan sees.

Santa Fe was reportedly founded by the governor of New Mexico, Pedro de Peralta, in 1610, and he named the site Villa Real de la Santa Fe de San Francisco ("The Royal City of the Holy Faith of St. Francis of Assisi"). Spanish settlers established the city, and the local Pueblo Indians were served by the Franciscans until 1680, when the Pueblos rose up against the monks and settlers. Under siege, the city was evacuated and was not occupied again by the Spanish until 1693, when it was renamed Santa Fe. Prospering from the production of metals and agriculture, the city welcomed the growing number of Americans on the westward migration after the Revolutionary War. When New Mexico became part of the United States after the Treaty of Guadalupe-Hidalgo in 1848, Santa Fe became the capital, and it developed into a commercial center for the state.

The Catholic history of Santa Fe dates to 1536 and the expedition of Alvar Nuñez Cabeza de Vaca. In his expedition were Fathers Andrés Dorantes de Carranza and Alonzo de Cabrillo. Three years later, Franciscan Father Marcos de Niza explored the territory that became New Mexico. He returned again in 1540 as part of the expedition of Francisco Vázquez de Coronado. The protomartyr, Father Juan de Padilla, was also in the expedition, going into Kansas, where he was slain. The region was named New Mexico by Francisco de Ibarra while leading another expedition. In 1581 Franciscan Father Agustin Rodriguez was in New Mexico with the expedition of the Spanish explorer Antonio de Espejo. This group called the region Nueva Andalusia.

The first permanent settlement in New Mexico, San Gabriel, was established in 1598 by Juan de Oñate, near modern-day San Juan Pueblo. The oldest church, still in use, is Mission San Miguel. Pedro de Peralta, the city's founder, had replaced de Oñate as governor of the territory in 1608. In 1620 Santa Fe was under the ecclesiastical jurisdiction of Durango. The settlement prospered, but there were signs of tension. The settlers conducted their affairs with the assumption that they were superior to the native populace. Other intolerant practices developed, and the Pueblos began to hold councils about the situation. The seriousness of the situation was apparent to Franciscan Father Francis de Ayeta who studied the mission situation and predicted disaster to his superiors. He could not prevent what followed: The Pueblo Indian Revolt of 1680 led to the deaths of twenty-one Franciscan missionaries and four hundred Spanish settlers. The rest were driven out of New Mexico.

The new governor, Diego de Vargas, was able to restore Spanish control over New Mexico, and Santa Fe was reopened in 1693, and the Franciscans restored churches and planned their renewed efforts across the region. From 1797 ecclesiastical jurisdiction was under Durango, and in 1821 the Franciscan friars departed after Mexico gained its independence. The area was under Durango until 1850, when Pope Blessed Pius IX created the Vicariate Apostolic of New Mexico and appointed Father Jean Baptiste Lamy as vicar apostolic. In 1853 the vicariate apostolic was designated a see, with its territory stretching between California and the Rocky Mountains, with its seat at Santa Fe.

The first bishop of Santa Fe, and from February 12, 1875, the first archbishop of Santa Fe, was Bishop Lamy. An extraordinary missionary, the French-born Lamy had been consecrated in Cincinnati on November 4, 1850, and arrived in Santa Fe on August 10, 1851, accompanied by another pioneering priest, Father Joseph P. Machebeuf. His

arrival, however, was met with hostility by the local priests, who resented the transfer of the territory into American hands after the Mexican-American War, and they refused to accept his credentials. Bishop Lamy was forced to travel seven hundred miles to Durango and returned with documentation of his authority from the bishop of Durango.

Bishop Lamy established the new diocesan offices and proved so talented and dedicated a shepherd over the diocese that Willa Cather, the noted American author, celebrated his life and labors in the 1927 novel *Death Comes for the Archbishop*. He built the Cathedral of St. Francis of Assisi, now a basilica, and invited priests and religious communities into the diocese and then archdiocese, including the Sisters of Loretto and the Christian Brothers. Exhausted by decades of work, he retired on July 18, 1885, and after his death on February 14, 1888, was buried in the cathedral.

The second archbishop of Santa Fe, John Baptist Salpointe, had served as vicar apostolic of Arizona since 1869. On April 22, 1884, he was promoted to coadjutor archbishop of Sante Fe. He acceded to the see of his friend and mentor upon Bishop Lamy's retirement. He was already famous for his devotion to the various Native American nations in the region, and he received support from St. Katharine Drexel, who founded St. Catherine's Indian School in the archdiocese. Bishop Salpointe expanded Catholic facilities and ministries until his retirement on July 7, 1894. After retirement, he wrote the widely read book *Soldiers of Christ*.

The third archbishop of Santa Fe was Placide Louis Chapelle, who had been appointed coadjutor archbishop and was consecrated on November 1, 1891. A gifted linguist and diplomat, he acceded to the see upon Bishop Salpointe's retirement. He was instrumental in the renovation and adornments made in the sanctuary of the cathedral, and he labored to improve facilities and ministries. On December 1, 1897, however, he was transferred to the Archdiocese of New Orleans.

The fourth bishop of Santa Fe, Peter Bourgade, had served as vicar apostolic of Arizona and had been the first bishop of Tucson since 1897. Appointed archbishop of Santa Fe on January 7, 1899, he notably invited the Franciscans back to the archdiocese and was a key figure in the start of the Catholic Church Extension Society. He died on May 17, 1908, in Chicago.

The fifth archbishop of Sante Fe, John B. Pitaval, had been an auxiliary bishop of Santa Fe since 1902. Promoted to archbishop on January 3, 1909, he served Sante Fe throughout World War I. He strove to improve the spiritual life of the community and recognized the need for greater outreach to the Native Americans in New Mexico. He resigned in February 1918 because of poor health and urged the Holy See to appoint a Franciscan as his successor.

Archbishop Pitaval's request was honored by Pope Benedict XV, who named the Franciscan Albert T. Daeger, who was consecrated archbishop of Santa Fe on May 7, 1919. He promoted vocations to the archdiocese, opened a seminary, and fostered programs for his priests. He died from an accident on December 2, 1932, in Santa Fe.

The seventh archbishop of Santa Fe, Rudolph A. Gerken, had been the first bishop of Amarillo since 1927. Appointed archbishop of Santa Fe on June 2, 1933, and installed on August 23, 1933, he arrived at the dark time of the Great Depression and worked to assist those in economic distress. He also opened a minor seminary and helped introduce the Legion of Mary to the Church in the United States. He died on March 2, 1943, in the midst of the Second World War.

The eighth archbishop of Santa Fe, Edwin V. Byrne, had been the first bishop of Ponce, in Puerto Rico, and bishop of San Juan since 1929. Appointed archbishop of Santa Fe on June 15, 1943, Archbishop Byrne was noted for his devotion to the Blessed Virgin Mary and the Eucharist. On October 7, 1945, the archdiocese was solemnly consecrated to the Immaculate Heart of Mary, and in 1954, a Marian Year, the Blessed Virgin Mary under the title of "La Conquistadora," was proclaimed queen of the archdiocese. In the period after the war, the archdiocese underwent a major growth time, and the Church there established parishes and schools to keep pace. Exhausted by his labors, Archbishop Byrne died on July 25, 1963.

He was succeeded by James P. Davis, who had been bishop of San Juan, and the first archbishop of San Juan, since 1960. Appointed archbishop of Santa Fe on January 3, 1964, he was installed on February 25, 1964. He was named in the midst of the Second Vatican Council and worked to implement the reforms of the council. In 1967 he moved the archdiocesan offices and the episcopal residence to Albuquerque. He resigned on June 1, 1974.

The tenth archbishop of Santa Fe, Robert F. Sanchez, was a native son of New Mexico. Appointed archbishop of Santa Fe on June 1, 1974, he was consecrated and installed on July 25, 1974. He promoted recognition of the local cultures and maintained archdiocesan facilities while aiding lay ministry programs. In 1992 the title of "Our Lady of Peace" was added to the titles of the archdiocese. Archbishop Sanchez resigned on April 6, 1993, in the wake of a scandal.

The eleventh archbishop of Santa Fe, Michael J. Sheehan, had been the first bishop of Lubbock since 1983. Appointed apostolic administrator of Santa Fe on April 6, 1993, he was named archbishop of Santa Fe on August 17, 1993, and installed on September 21, 1993. Archbishop Sanchez inherited a difficult pastoral situation in the diocese. He also remedied diocesan finances, promoted family life, spoke out for the needs of immigrants, and worked to preserve Santa Fe's rich historical legacy, including the small adobe churches so familiar on the New Mexican landscape. In 2011 there were more than 317,000 Catholics in the diocese, served by more than 220 priests, 200 men and women religious, and 92 parishes.

Santa Rosa in California, Diocese of

Established on February 21, 1962, the Diocese of Santa Rosa in California, commonly known as the Diocese of Santa Rosa, serves counties in northern California. It is a suffragan of the Archdiocese of San Francisco.

Santa Rosa is the county seat of Sonoma County and is well known for the surrounding wine country, and the diocese later encompassed the famed wine centers of Napa and Sonoma.

The earliest European settlement in the area was established by the Carrillo family, relatives of Mariano Guadalupe Vallejo, who was best known for settling the Sonoma pueblo and Petaluma region. Further development came under Dona Maria Carrillo, whose family founded the Rancho Cabeza de Santa Rosa. In the 1830s the settlers raised livestock and slaughtered animals along the Santa Rosa and Matanzas Creeks.

A Wells Fargo post and general store were established in the 1850s in what is now downtown Santa Rosa. Julio Carrillo, son of Maria Carrillo, was responsible for laying out the grid street pattern for Santa Rosa, which was incorporated as a city in 1867. Immense damage was done to the city during the 1906 San Francisco earthquake. It took many years for Santa Rosa to recover fully, but the city and area grew rapidly after World War II.

The Catholic history of the region dates to the expedition of Juan Rodriguez Cabrillo, the Spanish explorer, who was in the Bay area around 1542, followed by Sebastian Vizcaino, who arrived around 1602. Three Discalced Carmelite friars were members of the expedition. The priests and friars who followed attached northern California to the remarkable string of missions across California through the last one, Mission San Francisco Solano, which was founded at Sonoma in 1823 by Father José Altamira.

In 1828 Father Juan Amoros celebrated Mass in what became the city and baptized a Native American woman with the name of Rosa, and that name was used for the city that emerged there. Priests continued to come in to say Mass for the settlers, especially the Vallejo family.

The Catholic population kept pace with settlers, and parishes and missions were started at St. Vincent in Petaluma in 1857, St. Bernard in Eureka in 1858, St. John the Baptist in Napa in 1859, St. Teresa of Avila in Bodega in 1861, St. Anthony in Mendocino in 1864, and others. The Catholics of Santa Rosa were part of the San Francisco archdiocese from 1853 and later part of the Diocese of Sacramento, which was established in 1886. By 1962 the number of Catholics warranted the foundation of a new diocese by Pope Blessed John XXIII. At its start, the diocese included some 58,000 Catholics, 42 parishes, and 22 mission churches.

The first bishop of Santa Rosa, Leo T. Maher, had served in San Francisco and was consecrated a bishop on April 5, 1962. He focused on developing diocesan offices and ministries, promoted schools and new parishes, and worked to bring priests into the diocese. He also attended the Second Vatican Council and began the process of implementing the reforms of the council. On August 22, 1969, Bishop Maher was transferred to the Diocese of San Diego.

The second bishop of Santa Rosa, Mark J. Hurley, had served as auxiliary bishop of San Francisco since 1967. Installed on January 14, 1970, he took as one of his chief goals the implementation of the reforms of the Second Vatican Council, including pastoral and financial councils for parishes. He also worked to stabilize diocesan finances and founded the Priests' Retirement Fund, Vigil Light (a low-income senior residence), and the Centro Pastoral Hispano, to assist pastoral care for the growing number of Latino Catholics in the area. On April 15, 1986, Bishop Hurley resigned as bishop of Santa Rosa and took up a post in the Vatican Congregation on Education and the Secretariat for Non-Believers.

The third bishop of Santa Rosa, John T. Steinbock, an auxiliary bishop of the Diocese of Orange since 1984, was appointed on January 27, 1987, and installed on March 31, 1987. The installation also marked the Silver Anniversary of the diocese. Bishop Steinbock focused on the welfare of his priests, encouraged the program for the permanent diaconate and pastoral outreach to Latinos, and undertook a diocesan pastoral plan for the future of the Catholic community in Santa Rosa. He was appointed bishop of Fresno on October 15, 1991.

Bishop Steinbock was succeeded as bishop of Santa Rosa by G. Patrick Ziemann, who had been an auxiliary bishop of Los Angeles since 1986. Appointed on July 14, 1992, he resigned on July 22, 1999, at the age of sixty-eight, owing to a scandal.

Bishop Ziemann was succeeded by Daniel F. Walsh, who had been an auxiliary bishop of San Francisco and had been bishop of Las Vegas-Reno from 1987 and then bishop of Las Vegas from 1995. Installed on May 22, 2000, he took over as shepherd of a diocese deeply wounded by the resignation of its previous bishop under a cloud of scandal. The diocese continued to have problems related to the clergy sexual abuse scandal.

Bishop Walsh resigned on June 30, 2011, and was succeeded on that same day by the recently appointed coadjutor bishop, Bishop Robert Francis Vasa, who had served previously as bishop of Baker from 2000. In 2011 the diocese had approximately

150,000 Catholics served by some 100 priests and 42 parishes.

Sapienti Consilio

An apostolic constitution issued on June 29, 1908, by Pope St. Pius X, *Sapienti Consilio* ended the status of the Catholic Church in the United States as a "missionary church" and hence no longer under the control of the Congregation for the Propaganda Fide. By custom, young churches around the world were placed under the jurisdictions of several offices of the Roman Curia to assist their gradual development and careful progress. The Church in the United States was thus placed under the care of this as part of that long-term process. It existed in that state throughout the nineteenth century, along with several other younger churches, such as Canada. The Catholic Church in England (after the restoration of the hierarchy in 1850), Holland, and Luxembourg, were also under that jurisdiction.

By the terms of *Sapienti Consilio*, Pope Pius removed all these countries from the jurisdiction of the Propaganda. At the same time, the vicariates and prefectures apostolic of America and the Philippines, under the Congregation of Extraordinary Ecclesiastical Affairs, were promoted to be under the care of the Propaganda. The constitution also stipulated that all matters related to faith, the sacraments, rites, and religious communities (involving their work in the missions) was henceforth to be under the care of the germane congregations of the Roman Curia, such as the Holy Office, and the Congregations of the Sacraments, Rites, and Regulars.

The historical significance of *Sapienti Consilio* was to mark the palpable and manifest progress and success of the Catholic Church in the United States. In 1785 Bishop John Carroll had informed Rome that there were some 25,000 Catholics in the United States. By 1908 there were over 14 million Catholics, 93 dioceses, 1,200 parishes, 15,000 priests, and over 50,000 women religious. The Church in the United States was truly no longer a mission territory.

Satolli, Francesco (July 21, 1839–January 8, 1910)

Cardinal and the first apostolic delegate to the United States. Francesco Satolli was born in Marsciano, near Perugia, Italy. He entered studies for the priesthood and was ordained in June 1862 by then Cardinal Gioacchino Pecci, the future Pope Leo XIII. He went on to receive a doctorate at the Sapienza University in Rome and then to teach in the seminary at Perugia. In 1870 he was named a pastor in his native town and served on the faculty of the Benedictines at Monte Cassino from 1872 to 1874. After further pastoral work from 1875 to 1880, he became a professor of theology in Rome at the College of Propaganda from 1880 to 1892, and also at the Roman Seminary from 1882 to 1886. During this time, in 1884, he became rector of the Greek College in Rome. In 1886 he was appointed by Pope Leo XIII the president of the Pontifical Academy of Noble Ecclesiastics, the training ground for Vatican diplomats, where he served from 1886 to 1892, and also lectured on canon law. In addition, he was one of the leading proponents in academic and ecclesiastical circles of Neo-scholasticism and Thomism, especially as they were promoted by Pope Leo XIII.

Archbishop Francesco Satolli

On June 1, 1888, he was named titular archbishop of Lepante and was consecrated on July 10, 1888. The archbishop was appointed to several congregations of the Roman Curia, and in 1889 was sent to the United States as a papal legate to the centenary celebration in Baltimore of the establishment of the American hierarchy and to the inauguration of The Catholic University of America, in Washington, D.C. He returned to the United States in 1892, when he represented the pope at the anniversary of Christopher Columbus, the Columbian Exposition, in Chicago. He was established at The Catholic University of America, where he lectured on philosophy.

The following year, on January 24, 1893, Pope Leo XIII established the permanent apostolic delegation to the United States in Washington, D.C., and named Archbishop Satolli as the first delegate. On November 29, 1895, he was created cardinal priest, with the title of Santa Maria in Ara Coeli. Called back to Rome in October 1896, he was appointed prefect of the Congregation of Studies and archpriest of the Basilica of St. John Lateran. He was named the cardinal bishop of Frascati in June 1903 and made his last visit to the United States in 1904, when he attended the St. Louis Exposition.

Savannah, Diocese of

Established on July 3, 1850, by Pope Blessed Pius IX, the Diocese of Savannah serves counties in the southern part of Georgia. Formed out of territory taken from the Diocese of Charleston, the diocese was redesignated by Pope Pius XI the Diocese of Savannah-Atlanta on January 5, 1937. It was renamed by Pope Pius XII the Diocese of Savannah on July 2, 1956. The diocese is a suffragan see of the Archdiocese of Atlanta.

The city of Savannah was founded in 1733 by the British under the command of James Edward Oglethorpe and emerged as a vital port and industrial center. Savannah served as the capital of colonial Georgia.

The Catholic heritage of the area dates to the early dominance of the Spanish, who established the vast Florida missions for the Native American tribes. In 1539 Hernando de Soto led an expedition into present-day Georgia, accompanied by priests. In 1566 Jesuit missionaries arrived in Cumberland to start an outpost of the faith. Jesuit Father Pedro Martinez was slain at the site of his labors there. In 1599 Jesuit missionaries were on St. Catherine's Island but withdrew. Georgia became part of the Florida missions, and dedicated Franciscans established missions on the coast. Bishop Juan de las Cabezas de las Altamirano of Cuba arrived in the area in 1666 to confirm and visit the local populace.

In the early 1700s, however, the British assumed control of Georgia, driving out the Spanish holdings in Florida. Catholic Native Americans were taken captive and sold as slaves by the British. In 1754 Georgia became a Crown Colony, and Catholicism was banned. A year later, some four hundred Acadians, forced from their homeland by British troops, arrived in Georgia but were eventually sent out of the region.

There was, however, a Catholic presence in Savannah. Peter Tondee, the owner of a tavern, was part of the charitable Union Society, a religious group dedicated to the care of orphans and the needy in 1760. The Sons of Liberty, an early colonial organization that fostered the spirit of the American Revolution, met in Tondee's tavern regularly. The few Catholics in the area demonstrated considerable valor in the fight for America's freedom. As a result, civil liberties for Catholics were permitted.

In 1798 these Catholics received a parcel of land upon which to erect a church. The Catholics of Savannah were joined by French survivors of the slave insurrection of Santo Domingo. Father Jean le Moyne ministered to these immigrants in Savannah. Irish and German immigrants soon joined the Catholic population in the city. In 1776 Father Oliver le Mercier was authorized by Bishop John Carroll to administer the region, and by 1798 he was serving from St. John the Baptist Parish in Savannah. In time, Father Antoine Carles led the faithful.

In 1820 the Catholics of Savannah belonged to the Diocese of Charleston, under the brilliant administration of Bishop John England. Irish lumber magnates aided the Church with financial backing during the early decades of the 1800s.

The Diocese of Savannah was established on July 19, 1850, and the first bishop was Francis X. Gartland, who had served as vicar general of the Diocese of Philadelphia. At its start, the diocese encompassed the whole of Georgia and much of Florida. There were some 5,500 Catholics. Bishop Gartland built three churches, rededicated the cathedral in 1853, and was blessed with funds for the diocese from Ireland. He died on September 20, 1854, during a yellow fever epidemic at the age of forty-nine.

The second bishop of Savannah, John Barry, served as diocesan administrator for three years after Bishop Gartland's death. He was appointed bishop of Savannah on January 9, 1857. Consecrated on August 2, 1857, he struggled to replace the priests who had died from the yellow fever epidemic. He journeyed to Europe to search for new priests and money, and died in Paris in November 1859 at the age of sixty-nine.

The third bishop of Savannah, the Sulpician Jean-Pierre Augustin Verot, had served as vicar apostolic of Florida since 1858. Appointed to Savannah on July 14, 1861, he arrived at the start of the Civil War and earned the nickname of the "Rebel Bishop" for his support of the rights of the Southern states. He also worked to moderate the plight of slaves in his diocese and after the war was prophetic in calling for the Church to evangelize among the recently emancipated slaves. During the war, he helped to relieve as best he could the suffering of the people of Savannah during the Union blockade. He was transferred in March 1870 to the Diocese of St. Augustine.

The fourth bishop of Savannah, the Capuchin Franciscan Ignatius Persico, had served as a remarkable missionary in Asia, including vicar apostolic of Bombay and Agra in British India and a missionary bishop in China. Named to Savannah on March 11, 1870, he assumed direction of a diocese that had grown significantly since its founding and began working on plans for the future. In 1872, however, he resigned for health reasons and returned to Italy. On January 16, 1893, he was made a cardinal by Pope Leo XIII and served as a papal nuncio.

Bishop Persico's successor, William Hickley Gross, C.SS.R., was consecrated a bishop on April 27, 1873. He took pleasure in placing the cornerstone of the new cathedral on November 19, 1873, and worked to open a new hospital and a school of nursing. He also led the faithful during an outbreak of yellow fever. On February 1, 1885, he was appointed archbishop of Oregon City (later Portland in Oregon).

The sixth bishop of Savannah, Thomas A. Becker, had served as bishop of Wilmington since 1868 and was a well-known figure across the country for his writings on Catholic education and his support of the temperance movement. Appointed to Savannah on March 26, 1886, he finished work on the cathedral in 1896 and then faced catastrophe in 1898 when it was severely damaged in a fire. He requested during his time to move the see to Atlanta, but this was refused by the Holy See. He also assisted on a regular basis in pastoral service in the parishes and at the diocesan orphanage. Owing to the stress of rebuilding the cathedral, his health collapsed, and he died on July 29, 1899.

The seventh bishop of Savannah, Benjamin J. Keiley, had served locally and was rector of the restored cathedral. Consecrated on June 3, 1900, he faced a new era of anti-Catholic furor from the Ku Klux Klan and others. He promoted the Catholic Laymen's Association of Georgia, finished repairs on the cathedral (which was consecrated in 1920), and founded a diocesan newspaper. He also invited into the diocese the Society of African Missions to provide pastoral care to African-Americans of the area. He retired on February 13, 1922.

The eighth bishop of Savannah, Michael J. Keyes, S.M., was appointed on July 8, 1922, and consecrated a bishop on October 18, 1922. He served throughout the dark days of the Great Depression and was able to ensure the financial survival of the diocese through prudent guidance, even as he provided pastoral care for those hit hard by the economy. He resigned on September 23, 1935, because of declining health.

The successor to Bishop Keyes, Gerald P. O'Hara, had been an auxiliary bishop of Philadelphia since 1929. At the time of his consecration he was thirty-four years old and was the youngest bishop in the world. Appointed to Savannah on November 16, 1935, he served as bishop throughout the remaining years of the Depression, through World War II, and into the postwar boom. In 1946 he was appointed an archbishop by Pope Pius XII and named a papal representative to Romania, Ireland, England, and Wales; he remained bishop of Savannah, but administration was placed in the hands of the auxiliary, Bishop Francis E. Hyland. In 1950 Bishop O'Hara was arrested by the communist authorities in Romania and expelled.

In a demonstration of the increasing complexity of the diocese, in 1937 the diocese was renamed the Diocese of Savannah-Atlanta, then was changed back to Savannah in 1956. Archbishop O'Hara resigned on November 11, 1959. Bishop Hyland, meanwhile, was appointed the first bishop of Atlanta with its creation in 1956.

The tenth bishop of Savannah, Thomas J. McDonough, had been auxiliary bishop of St. Augustine from 1947 to 1957, when he was transferred to Savannah to assist Archbishop O'Hara. He was appointed bishop of Savannah on March 2, 1960, and served throughout the Second Vatican Council. He focused on promoting vocations and founded St. John Vianney Minor Seminary. On March 1, 1967, he was named archbishop of Louisville.

The eleventh bishop of Savannah, Gerard L. Frey, was appointed on May 31, 1967, and consecrated a bishop on August 8, 1967. He promoted the implementation of the Second Vatican Council and pushed for the Civil Rights Act of 1964. He was transferred to the Diocese of Lafayette on November 7, 1972.

The twelfth bishop of Savannah, Raymond W. Lessard, was a superbly educated priest who had served in Rome in the Congregation for Bishops and was director of Villa Stritch, a residence in Rome for American priests and bishops working at the Vatican. Appointed to Savannah on March 5, 1973, he was consecrated a bishop on April 27, 1973. He presided over the steady growth of the diocese that witnessed the doubling of the Catholic population from 35,000 to more than 68,000 by the time of his retirement. He established the permanent diaconate in the diocese and was successful in finding vocations during a period of great upheaval. He likewise believed strongly in evangelization within the diocese and used *A Heart Renewed*, a three-year program of spiritual and pastoral renewal, as a key component in the Catholic community he served. He resigned on February 7, 1995, because of health problems.

The thirteenth bishop of Savannah, John Kevin Boland, was a priest of Savannah at the time of his appointment. Consecrated on April 18, 1995, he worked to meet the continuing pastoral needs of a growing diocese and was active in the United States Conference of Catholic Bishops.

The fourteenth bishop of Savannah, the Conventual Franciscan Gregory J. Hartmayer, was appointed on July 19, 2011, and consecrated a bishop on October 18, 2011, overseeing some 78,000 Catholics in the diocese, served by 101 priests and 55 parishes.

Scalia, Antonin (March 11, 1936–)

Associate justice of the United States Supreme Court since 1986, Antonin Scalia was born in Trenton, New Jersey, and is the son of S. Eugene and Catherine Scalia. His father emigrated from Sicily and became a professor of Romance languages. When Scalia was five years old, his family moved to the Elmhurst section of Queens, New York City, and his father taught at Brooklyn College in Flatbush. Scalia studied at Georgetown University, graduated first in his class, and earned a bachelor's degree summa cum laude in 1957. While at Georgetown, he spent time at the University of Fribourg in Switzerland. After graduation, he proceeded to the Harvard Law School, where he was a note editor for the *Harvard Law Review*, graduated magna cum laude in 1960 and was a Sheldon Fellow of Harvard University in 1961. On September 10, 1960, Scalia married Maureen McCarthy, an English major at Radcliffe College. They have nine children.

Scalia worked in private practice in Cleveland from 1961 to 1967. From 1967 to 1971, he was a professor of law at the University of Virginia. In addition, he served as general counsel of the Office of Telecommunications Policy from 1971 to 1972, chairman of the Administrative Conference of the United States from 1972 to 1974, and assistant attorney General for the Office of Legal Counsel from 1974 to 1977 under President Gerald Ford. With Ford's defeat in 1976 to Jimmy Carter, he became a professor of law at the University of Chicago from 1977 to 1982 and a visiting professor of law at Georgetown University and Stanford University. He was chairman of the American Bar Association's Section of Administrative Law from 1981 to 1982 and its Conference of Section Chairmen from 1982 to 1983.

In 1982 President Ronald Reagan appointed him judge of the United States Court of Appeals for the District of Columbia Circuit. Four years later, Reagan nominated him an associate justice of the Supreme Court to fill the vacancy left by Reagan's nomination of Associate Justice William H. Rehnquist to be chief justice of the United States. Scalia's nomination was supported by liberals such as Mario Cuomo, and he was approved by the United States Senate in a vote of 98–0. He took his seat on September 26, 1986, and was the first Italian-American justice on the Supreme Court.

Justice Scalia is considered one of the most articulate adherents of textualism on the court and is also ranked as one of the foremost conservative minds in modern American history. He is known especially for his wit, his far-reaching grasp of legal history, and his firm belief that (as in such cases as *Webster v. Reproductive Health Services* and *Planned*

Parenthood v. Casey) the Constitution does not protect the right to have an abortion.

Scammon, Ellakim Parker (December 27, 1816–December 7, 1894)

A soldier and teacher, Ellakim Parker Scammon was born at Whitefield, Maine, and studied at the United States Military Academy at West Point. After graduation in 1837, he was invited to remain at the academy as a tutor in mathematics. He gave assistance to such future generals as Ulysses S. Grant and William Rosecrans. Scammon took part in the Second Seminole War from 1835 to 1842 and in the Mexican War from 1846 to 1847, during which he served as an aide-de-camp to General Winfield Scott. Prior to his service in the Mexican War, Scammon made the decision to enter the Church.

From 1847 to 1854 he was a member of the topographical corps and was sent as part of a team surveying the Upper Lakes. He left the army in 1856 and subsequently took up a post as a teacher of mathematics at St. Mary's College and at the Polytechnic College in Cincinnati. With the start of the Civil War in 1861, he volunteered for service and received a commission as a brigadier general in October 1862. After the war, he served as U.S. Consul at Prince Edward Island from 1866 to 1871. He resumed his work as a professor of mathematics at Seton Hall College in South Orange, New Jersey, from 1875 until his retirement in 1882.

Scanlan, Patrick Francis (October 7, 1894–March 27, 1983)

The longtime editor of *The Tablet*, Patrick Francis Scanlan was born in New York City, one of seven children born to Michael and Maria O'Keefe Scanlan. Three of his brothers became priests. The family moved to Philadelphia in 1901, where Scanlan grew up and attended St. Joseph's College, from which he earned a bachelor's degree in 1914. He then entered St. Joseph's Seminary in Dunwoodie, but his preparations for the priesthood were ended by illness. He left the seminary and worked as a high school teacher in Staten Island until 1917, when he took a temporary position as managing editor of *The Tablet*, the diocesan newspaper for the Diocese of Brooklyn. The job became permanent

in 1918, and Scanlan went on to serve as editor for fifty-one years.

As editor, Scanlan became one of American Catholicism's most determined voices in opposing anti-Catholicism and communism. He supported the election of Franklin Delano Roosevelt in 1932, although his enthusiasm cooled over the next years as President Roosevelt's massive New Deal lapsed into what Scanlan considered dangerous tendencies toward socialism or communism. Scanlan ardently backed the famed but controversial "radio priest" Father Charles Coughlin, even in the face of accusations of anti-Semitism against Coughlin. Although an isolationist in the prewar period, Scanlan urged his fellow Catholics to serve their country in the wake of Pearl Harbor in 1941.

Always an ardent anti-communist, Scanlan was even more determined after World War II and the onset of the Cold War. He endorsed Senator Joseph McCarthy's program against communists in the U.S. government. He supported the candidacy of John F. Kennedy in 1960, but he was also disappointed that Kennedy was not public enough in demonstrating his Catholicism. Likewise, he gave his public backing to the Second Vatican Council but expressed grave reservations about some of its expressions in the areas of liturgy and ecumenism. Scanlan retired in 1968.

Schisms. *See* Hogan Schism; Polish Catholics

Schmitz, Carl (October 10, 1917–April 7, 1988)

A Passionist missionary murdered in the Philippines, Carl Schmitz was born and baptized William Schmitz in Chicago. As a youth, he had been inspired by the heroic martyrdoms of Fathers Walter Coveyou, Clement Seybold, and Godfrey Holbein at the hands of bandits in Hunan, China, on April 24, 1929. Moved by their example, he left his family and entered the Passionist Preparatory Seminary in St. Louis. Taking the name Carl in the religious life, he subsequently studied in Detroit, Chicago, and Louisville, Kentucky, and was ordained on April 26, 1944.

Sent to labor in the missions of China in 1946, Father Schmitz began studies in Beijing in the fall of 1946, but the adventure was cut short by the Chinese civil war and the takeover of China by the communists. Forced to return to the United States, he conducted retreats for laymen in Cincinnati and in 1950 was sent to Ensley, Alabama, to minister in the South. There he strove to assist impoverished African-Americans in the Birmingham area. In 1953 he was informed that he and Father Matthew Vetter were being sent to Japan to open a Passionist Mission.

In 1974 Father Schmitz volunteered for missionary duties in the Philippines. After work in a parish in Mindanao, he requested to be sent to minister among the pagan Bila'ans in the mountains. The Bila'ans had been displaced from their lowland homes and driven to a hard existence in the mountains. Father Schmitz's duty was thus a demanding and rugged one, and required immense hardships. Among the dangers were bandits in the region and the communist New Peoples Army. Resisting their violent actions, Father Schmitz placed his own life in danger, and he was assassinated. On April 26, 2004, the cause for his canonization was opened officially by the Passionists in the Philippines and by the local bishop.

School Sisters of Notre Dame (S.S.N.D.)

A congregation of women religious, the School Sisters of Notre Dame was founded in Bavaria, in modern-day Germany, in 1833 by Blessed Mother Mary Theresa of Jesus Gerhardinger with the assistance of Bishop Michael Wittman. The purpose of the new community was to improve the grim social conditions of the period through education and by assisting young women and children, in keeping with the vision that true social renewal had to begin with the Christian family and the proper education of young women.

The official start of the congregation is dated to October 24, 1833, when Mother Mary Theresa and two other women entered into the religious life. Caroline took the religious name Mary Theresa of Jesus and gave her entire life to the needs and development of the congregation. The constitution of the School Sisters of Notre Dame was approved by Pope Blessed Pius IX in 1865.

The first members of the congregation arrived in Baltimore in 1847, when Blessed Mother Mary Theresa decided to assist the Germans in America. She sailed with five companion sisters only to be informed that as they lacked an invitation it would be best for them to sail home. Undaunted, she found the help of Father John Nepomucene Neumann, now St. John Neumann, then provincial superior of the Redemptorists. He helped them win permission to teach in Baltimore, and Blessed Mother Mary Theresa left two years later after giving direction to the community to Sister Caroline Friess. By the time of her death in 1879, there were more than 2,500 School Sisters of Notre Dame.

Mother Caroline Friess was the key figure in the early history of the School Sisters. She led the community as it developed rapidly and established schools throughout the United States and Canada. The motherhouse was transferred to Milwaukee in December 1850. In July 1876, owing to the growth of the congregation, two provinces were established in the United States, the Western, with its motherhouse at Milwaukee, and the Eastern, with its motherhouse at Baltimore. In 1895 another province was begun in the South, with its motherhouse in St. Louis. Mother Caroline Friess died on July 22, 1892, after serving as superior of the congregation for forty-two years. Today, there are over 4,000 Schools Sisters of Notre Dame in 581 houses worldwide.

Schools, Catholic. *See* Education, Catholic

Schrembs, Joseph (March 12, 1866–November 2, 1945)

The first bishop of Toledo, Ohio, and an archbishop, Joseph Schrembs was born in Wurzelhofen, Regensburg, Bavaria. A member of a large family, he made the journey to the United States at the age of eleven to enter St. Vincent Archabbey in Latrobe, Pennsylvania; his older brother Ignatius was already a priest there. A prodigious youth, Joseph became a teacher at St. Martin's Parish school in Louisville, Kentucky, at the age of sixteen and entered the seminary for the Diocese of Grand Rapids two years later.

His preparation for the priesthood included studies at Laval University in Québec and the Grand Séminaire in Montréal. He was ordained on June 29, 1889, and began active ministry in Saginaw, Michigan. On January 8, 1911, he was named titular bishop of Sophene and auxiliary bishop for the diocese; he was consecrated on February 22, 1911. On August 11 of that same year he was appointed the first bishop of Toledo.

Bishop Schrembs spent the next decade establishing the new diocese on a firm administrative, financial, and spiritual footing. On June 16, 1921, he was appointed the fifth bishop of Cleveland and installed on September 8. As bishop of Cleveland, Schrembs proved dedicated to education and improved administration. He encouraged the work of the Ursuline nuns and Sisters of Notre Dame in establishing colleges, started parochial schools, and he launched a new diocesan seminary. He also was a key figure in the early days of the National Catholic War Council of the bishops during World War I and was instrumental in securing approval from Rome for the National Catholic Welfare Conference. He served as chairman of the NCWC Department of Lay Organizations and was a key figure in the start of the National Council of Catholic Men and the National Council of Catholic Women in 1920. In 1939 he received the personal title of archbishop from Pope Pius XII.

Schrieck, Louise Van der (November 14, 1813–December 3, 1886)

A noted educator and member of the Sisters of Notre Dame de Namur, Louise Van der Schrieck was born in Bergenop-Zoom, Holland. Educated in Belgium, she entered the Sisters of Notre Dame de Namur and in 1840 came to the Diocese (now Archdiocese) of Cincinnati to assist the work of the sisters in America. In 1848 she was named superior of all houses of the Sisters of Notre Dame east of the Rockies. Over the next years, she was responsible for the extensive development of the congregation in the United States, with houses begun in Boston, Philadelphia, Washington, D.C., and elsewhere, as well as assuming control over some fifty parochial schools. Through her ceaseless labors, the congregation became one of the great bulwarks of Catholic education in the United States. She died in Cincinnati.

Scranton, Diocese of

Established on March 3, 1868, by Pope Blessed Pius IX, the Diocese of Scranton serves counties in northeastern Pennsylvania. It is a suffragan see of the Archdiocese of Philadelphia. The city of Scranton emerged as part of the coal mining communities in Pennsylvania and was established in the Lackawanna River valley. Scranton was incorporated as a borough on February 14, 1856, and incorporated as a city on April 23, 1866.

Settlers started entering the area as early as 1615, and in 1681 King Charles II of England gave William Penn, a Quaker pioneer, land grants in the various river valleys, and settlements opened. Penn did not forbid the start of Catholic enclaves, and many of the faithful arrived to start new lives in peace. He opened several settlements and welcomed a party of Dutch merchants and farmers into Pennsylvania. The first community in the area was started in 1788 and was originally called Slocum Hollow, then Unionville, Harrison, and Scrantonia. The name Scranton was adopted in 1851 in honor of a local family that pioneered the development of the coal-mining industry. As coal mining developed, the city became prosperous.

The Catholic history of Scranton dates to 1615 and to the exploration of Etienne Brulé, who was the first European in the region and a Catholic. Penn did not encourage Catholic communities, but he did not display prejudice against them. Catholics maintained their residences unobtrusively so that Penn did not face complaints from his Protestant allies.

In 1787 Bishop John Carroll, aware of the Catholic presence in Pennsylvania, sent Father James Pellentz to the Susquehanna Valley to minister to the scattered families of the faithful. In 1793 the French founded a settlement at present-day Standing Stone. The site was a proposed haven for Queen Marie Antoinette. The queen was to flee France and take up residence in a mansion that had been built there. A number of nobles did reside there for a decade but returned to their homeland in 1804.

Catholic missions were opened at Friendsville and at Silver Lake in the county of Susquehanna. In 1825 Father Jeremiah Flynn, also listed in some records as John O'Flynn, was appointed in 1825 as the resident pastor for ten counties in Pennsylvania and five counties in New York. Catholic churches were erected at Silver Lake and elsewhere. By 1842 St. Joseph's College was operating in the region. As the coal industry picked up speed, more settlers began arriving in larger numbers, including Irish, Germans, Slavs, and Italians.

On March 3, 1868, the Holy See publicly recognized the vitality of the Catholic community and created the Diocese of Scranton. The first bishop of Scranton, William G. O'Hara, had served as a priest in Philadelphia. Consecrated as bishop of Scranton on July 12, 1868, he assumed direction over a new diocese that included fifty churches and twenty-five priests. Over the next years, he added seventy parishes and recruited priests to serve in the region. He founded a diocesan newspaper and was instrumental in opening the University of Scranton. His time was also marked by the start of troubles with some local Polish Catholics and what became the Polish National Catholic Church. Bishop O'Hara died on February 3, 1899.

The second bishop of Scranton, Michael J. Hoban, had been coadjutor bishop of Scranton since 1896. He was confronted with the ongoing problems with the Polish National Catholics and worked to establish an orphanage and a home for the elderly. He also established three religious congregations for the diocese and opened Marywood College and Misericordia College. He led the faithful during the years of World War I and the Spanish influenza epidemic. Bishop Hoban hosted President Theodore Roosevelt and John Mitchell, the head of the United Mine Workers' Union, as houseguests. He died on November 13, 1926.

The third bishop of Scranton, Thomas C. O'Reilly, was consecrated a bishop on February 16, 1928. He built new parishes despite the problems of the Great Depression and stressed educational initiatives. He died on March 25, 1938.

Bishop O'Reilly's successor, William J. Hafey, had been bishop of Raleigh and was coadjutor bishop of Scranton since 1937. He succeeded to the see upon Bishop O'Reilly's death, and served as bishop throughout World War II and into the postwar economic boom. To provide for a stable financial future for the diocese, he launched the "House of Charity" campaign, which raised more than $4 million. He promoted Catholic education and established several new parishes. He died on May 12, 1954.

The fifth bishop of Scranton, Jerome D. Hannan, was a noted scholar and expert in canon law at

The Catholic University of America. Consecrated a bishop on September 21, 1954, he founded a diocesan seminary and promoted vocations to the priesthood. He also invited religious communities into the diocese, sponsored catechetical programs, and built a new chancery office in Scranton. Bishop Hannan attended the sessions of the Second Vatican Council and died in Rome on December 15, 1965, while taking part in its final work.

The sixth bishop of Scranton, J. Carroll McCormick, had been bishop of Altoona since 1960. Transferred to Scranton on March 4, 1966, he worked to implement the reforms of the Second Vatican Council and strove to provide stability during a challenging era. He also expanded diocesan facilities and celebrated the diocese's centenary year in 1968, which was also used to launch a long-term diocesan fundraising platform called "Project Expansion." He retired on February 15, 1983.

The seventh bishop of Scranton, John J. O'Connor, was a retired admiral in the U.S. Navy and had served as an auxiliary bishop in the Military Vicariate. Appointed to Scranton on June 29, 1983, he served the diocese for only nine months before he was named archbishop of New York on January 31, 1984. He later became a cardinal and one of the foremost leaders in American Catholicism.

Archbishop O'Connor's successor, Bishop James C. Timlin, had been an auxiliary bishop of Scranton since 1976. The only Scranton native to become bishop, he was a dedicated shepherd of the diocese and was active in the National Conference of Catholic Bishops and was named by Pope Blessed John Paul II to the Synod of Bishops on Consecrated Life in 1994. He maintained diocesan facilities and lay ministries and solved the diocese's financial problems through careful administration and a "Bishop's Annual Appeal." Bishop Timlin retired on July 25, 2003.

The ninth bishop of Scranton, Joseph F. Martino, had been an auxiliary bishop of Philadelphia since 1996. A brilliant scholar, he earned a doctorate in Church history in Rome and also compiled the *positio* (or official documentation and biography) for the cause of canonization of St. Katharine Drexel, foundress of the Sisters of the Blessed Sacrament. Installed on October 1, 2003, he faced a variety of challenges, including a priest shortage and economic problems with parishes and Catholic schools. To solidify the needs of the diocese, he consolidated schools and parishes, although the decision caused some upheaval. Bishop Martino was also firm in upholding what he considered the need for pro-abortion candidates and political leaders not to be given platforms to speak at Catholic events. Owing to health concerns, Bishop Martino resigned his office on August 31, 2009.

Bishop Martino's successor, Joseph C. Bambera, had been a priest of the Scranton diocese and had served as diocesan administrator following Martino's resignation. He was appointed bishop of Scranton on February 23, 2010, and was consecrated on April 26, 2010. In 2011 there were some 310,000 Catholics served by more than 345 priests, 500 men and women religious, and 108 parishes. The diocese is also blessed by the presence of a large number of religious communities, including the Sisters of Mercy of the Americas, Congregation of Sisters, Servants of the Immaculate Heart of Mary, Congregation of Notre Dame, Sisters of Sts. Cyril and Methodius, Little Sisters of the Poor, Sisters of Christian Charity, Bernardine Sisters of St. Francis, Jesuits, Passionists, Oblates of St. Joseph, Congregation of Holy Cross, the Priestly Fraternity of St. Peter, and Religious Teachers Fillippini.

Seattle, Archdiocese of

Established on May 31, 1850, by Pope Blessed Pius IX as the Diocese of Nesqually, the diocese was renamed Seattle on September 11, 1907, and was elevated to the rank of a metropolitan provincial see on June 23, 1951. The archdiocese has several suffragan sees and serves much of the state of Washington.

Seattle is the largest city in the Pacific Northwest and a site of great natural beauty. Explorers were in the area early on, but the first settlement dates to Alki Point. The town of Seattle was laid out in 1853 and was named after the Suquamish Indian chief. A port of entry, Seattle started a sawmill and faced an Indian attack in 1856 and then riots and a fire. Part of the passage to Alaska, however, the town survived all disasters and became diversified in its economic base.

The Catholic heritage of Seattle and the Washington area opened on July 14, 1775, when a Franciscan priest accompanied the expedition of Bruno de Heceta (Hezeta) y Dudagoitia and Juan Francisco de la Bodega y Quadra into the region. The Franciscans erected a cross at Point Grenville. The French-Canadian Metis, a group of Native American and French-Canadian heritage, opened trade in Washington, which was then part of the Oregon Territory. They also opened a Catholic cemetery at Fort Vancouver. Father Francis Norbert Blanchet and Father Modeste Demers arrived on the scene in November 1838 and began intense missionary labors. They were joined by Father Jean-Baptiste Bolduc and Jesuit fathers, including the revered Pierre-Jean De Smet. In 1843 Pope Gregory XVI established an apostolic vicariate serving the region from the Pacific to the Rockies and from Alaska to California. In 1846 the vicariate became the Province of Oregon City. Archbishop Blanchet assumed the see, and Father Demers became the bishop of Vancouver Island.

This original mission team had expanded the Catholic presence dramatically, opening a mission in 1839 at Cowlitz, a log structure named after St. Francis Xavier. They had also introduced the "Ladders," a unique catechetical method used effectively with the Native Americans. In 1840 Oblates were at Puget Sound, and Father De Smet had brought mission priests from Europe to serve the local Catholic communities.

On September 27, 1846, Father Augustin Magliore Blanchet, the brother of Archbishop Francis Blanchet, was consecrated as the bishop of Walla Walla. He arrived in the area accompanied by Father Jean Baptiste Abraham Brouillet and the Oblate Father Pascal Ricard. Five seminarians also arrived with the bishop.

The following year, the Cayuse Indians massacred Dr. Marcus Whitman and other Protestant missionaries. Protestants falsely accused Father Brouillet of promoting the massacre, and Catholic interests were severely threatened. Bishop Blanchet had to abandon his labors in Walla Walla and, with the support of the First Provincial Council of Oregon, he was appointed to the Diocese of Nesqually and took up residence at Fort Vancouver on October 27, 1850. He labored to establish missions, parishes, and schools, also recruiting priests and religious to serve the growing American Catholic population. He retired in 1879, exhausted by his labors, at the age of eighty-one.

The second bishop of Nesqually, Egidius Junger, was appointed to the see on August 6, 1879, and was consecrated a bishop on October 28, 1879. He continued the expansion of the diocese to meet the needs of the growing Catholic population. In 1885 he established a stone cathedral and recruited Jesuits, Benedictines, and Redemptorists to serve in new parishes. He died on December 26, 1895, at the age of sixty-two.

The third bishop of Nesqually and the first bishop of Seattle, Edward John O'Dea, was consecrated on June 13, 1896. He served during the first decades of the new century, including World War I and the start of the Great Depression. The diocese was continuing to grow, however, and the center of population had shifted significantly to Seattle by the early twentieth century. For this reason, in 1907 the diocese was transferred to Seattle and renamed. Bishop O'Dea fought to prevent the Ku Klux Klan from becoming a genuine threat to Catholics and opposed the Oregon School Law that declared parochial schools to be illegal. He died on December 25, 1932, at the age of seventy-six.

The next bishop of Seattle, Gerald Shaughnessy, was appointed on July 1, 1933, and consecrated on September 19, 1933. He assumed direction of the diocese in the time of the Great Depression and led the diocese through the Second World War. He was an important figure in the start of Serra International and served as its first chaplain. He also was an advocate for the rights of Japanese-Americans during the war. After suffering a cerebral hemorrhage in late 1945, he endured a long recovery period, and in 1948 he received a coadjutor bishop, Thomas Arthur Connolly, an auxiliary bishop of San Francisco since 1939. Bishop Shaughnessy died on May 18, 1950, one day before his sixty-third birthday.

Bishop Shaughnessy's successor, Thomas A. Connolly, was also the first archbishop of Seattle. Becoming bishop upon his predecessor's death, Connolly welcomed the elevation of the diocese to an archdiocese the next year. His term was noted for the continued expansion of the archdiocese, and Archbishop Connolly was called the "brick and mortar bishop." He renovated St. James Cathedral and established forty-three new parishes, and built churches, schools, and convents. He attended the Second Vatican Council and worked to implement the reforms of the council in a stable fashion. Archbishop Connolly retired on February 13, 1975.

The second archbishop of Seattle, Raymond G. Hunthausen, had been bishop of Helena since 1962 and was appointed to Seattle on February 25, 1975. His time as archbishop proved a controversial one owing to his outspoken opposition to the policies of the Reagan administration (he famously withheld half of his income tax to protest nuclear weapons). The archdiocese was also subject to a Vatican visitation and an investigation by Cardinal Joseph Ratzinger and the Congregation for the Doctrine of the Faith regarding various aspects of teaching, liturgy, and ministry. In 1986 Father Donald W. Wuerl was named an auxiliary bishop of Seattle with authority over certain aspects of diocesan life; this situation ended with Bishop Wuerl's departure the next year (he was appointed bishop of Pittsburgh in 1988) and the appointment of Thomas J. Murphy as coadjutor archbishop of Seattle that same year. Arch-

Seattle Cathedral

bishop Hunthausen retired on August 21, 1991, and was succeeded by Archbishop Murphy.

Archbishop Murphy inherited an archdiocese troubled by controversies and division. He worked to restore a sense of unity and visited parishes across the Seattle archdiocese. He also renovated the Cathedral of St. James and promoted ministries to the poor and minorities. He died on June 26, 1997 at the age of sixty-four.

The fourth archbishop of Seattle, Alexander J. Brunett, had been bishop of Helena since 1994. Appointed on October 28, 1997, he was active in the Church's ecumenical outreach to Anglicans, took part in the 1998 Lambeth Conference, and served as co-chair of the Anglican-Roman Catholic International Commission in 1999. Sadly, the archdiocese was troubled by cases involving clergy sexual abuse, and the archdiocese paid out $31 million in settlements and other costs, although bankruptcy was avoided. Archbishop Brunett retired on September 16, 2010.

The fifth archbishop of Seattle, James Peter Sartain, had been bishop of Little Rock and then bishop of Joliet since 2006. He was appointed on September 16, 2010. In 2011 there were 580,000 Catholics in the diocese, served by 279 priests, around 400 men and women religious, and 147 parishes.

Seattle, Chief (c. 1786–June 7, 1866)

The leader of the Suquamish and Duwamish Native American tribes in what is present-day Washington state, Chief Seattle was a convert to the Church. The city of Seattle is named in his honor.

Chief Seattle was born on Blake Island, Washington, the son of a Suquamish tribe leader. He grew up as a respected warrior among his people and was renowned for his skill in battle, his powerful voice, and also for his height, as he was six feet tall, unusual for a member of his tribe. He married several wives and counted among the most famous of his children Princess Angeline. Owing to his leadership skills, he was elected chief of the Coast Indians.

Around 1848 he chose to enter the Church, near modern Olympia, Washington, and his children entered the Catholic faith with him. His baptismal name was Noah. His conversion was followed sev-eral years later by the arrival of white settlers into the region, and Chief Seattle gave them welcome. In the succeeding years, he proved a good friend to the whites. In January 1854 he attended the famed Port Elliott Treaty Conference headed by Territorial Governor Isaac I. Stevens. Stevens gave a speech, and Chief Seattle supposedly delivered a reply that was reported by Dr. Henry A. Smith in the *Seattle Sunday Star* in 1887. Termed *Seattle's Reply*, the speech is considered almost certainly apocryphal. Seattle's acceptance of the treaty, however, was in recognition that it was the only way to save his people from a catastrophic war with the white man. He was vilified by some among the Native Americans as a traitor. In the war of 1855–56 between white settlers and other tribes, Seattle prevented his own people from becoming involved, an action that brought him great personal suffering as he longed for peace between the two worlds.

Chief Seattle died on the Suquamish reservation at Port Madison, Washington. He was laid to rest with two ceremonies, one in the traditions of his tribe and one Catholic. Both ceremonies were attended by large crowds. He was buried in the Suquamish churchyard; a monument was erected over the grave twenty-three years later by the whites who had known and loved him. His daughter, Princess Angeline, remained a devout Catholic for her entire life and was buried in a coffin in the shape of a canoe.

Sedella, Antonio de (November 17, 1748–January 22, 1829)

A Capuchin Franciscan, Antonio de Sedella was born Antonio Ildefonso Moreno y Arce in Granada, Spain, and entered the Franciscans. Around 1774 he volunteered for the Louisiana missions and so was sent to New Orleans. There he became known and loved as Père Antoine, the pastor of St. Louis Church. He assisted those in prison, cared for the slave population in New Orleans, and dedicated himself to the free African-Americans and their children. He earned the enmity of the governor, who secured his deportation in 1790, but he was able to win his appeal to the Spanish crown and was reinstated as pastor of St. Louis Church. When the Diocese of New Orleans was established in 1793, the church became St. Louis Cathedral.

When Louisiana passed to the United States as part of the Louisiana Purchase in 1803, Père Antoine remained at his post as pastor. Nevertheless, American officials demanded that he take an oath of loyalty to the United States owing to his close connections to the Spanish crown. He also encountered a variety of controversies during his tenure and had poor relations with Bishop Louis Dubourg. Père Antoine served as pastor until his death and was loved especially among the poor. His funeral was attended by vast crowds.

Seelos, Blessed Francis X. (January 11, 1819–October 4, 1867)

A Redemptorist missionary in Pittsburgh and New Orleans, Francis X. Seelos was born at Füssen, Bavaria. Determined from his childhood to be a missionary, he studied at Augsburg and Munich and entered the Congregation of the Most Holy Redeemer, with the hope of preaching the Gospel in America. He arrived in America in April 1843, and the next year he made his religious profession at the Redemptorist novitiate in Baltimore and was ordained by Archbishop Samuel Eccleston of Baltimore.

After a brief period of service in Baltimore, he was sent in May 1845 to Pittsburgh, where he had as his mentor St. John Nepomucene Neumann. In 1851 Father Blessed Francis Seelos was appointed superior of the Pittsburgh Redemptorist community. He became a beloved figure

Blessed Francis X. Seelos

in the city and was consulted by people of every social class for his spiritual advice.

In 1860 he suffered a brief but severe illness while serving in Baltimore again. Upon his recovery he was suggested as a candidate to become bishop of Pittsburgh by Bishop Michael O'Connor of Pittsburgh, who had retired and entered the Jesuits. Father Seelos, however, wrote to Pope Blessed Pius IX to remove his name from consideration.

In 1863 the priest was named head of the Redemptorist band of missionaries, a task that delighted him as it meant he would be engaged actively in evangelization. For three years he gave retreats and preached parish missions across the East and Midwest, as far as the Mississippi and Missouri rivers.

In 1866 Father Seelos was sent to New Orleans, where his facility in languages proved immediately helpful in ministering to the diverse population of the Crescent City. His zeal and love for all those in his care were revealed to New Orleans when a severe epidemic of yellow fever struck the region. Father Seelos and several other Redemptorists were stricken with the disease while they cared for the sick. Seelos died after several weeks of intense suffering.

The cause for his canonization was launched by the Redemptorists in 1903. On April 9, 2000, Pope Blessed John Paul II beatified him. The pontiff declared of him: "In the various places where he worked, Father Francis Xavier brought his enthusiasm, spirit of sacrifice and apostolic zeal. To the abandoned and the lost he preached the message of Jesus Christ, 'the source of eternal salvation' (Heb 5:9), and in the hours spent in the confessional he convinced many to return to God."

Segale, Blandina (May 23, 1850–February 23, 1941)

A Sister of Charity who served with distinction in the Southwest, Blandina Segale was born Rosa Maria Segale in Cicagna, Italy. With her family, she immigrated to the United States and settled in Cincinnati. Called to the religious life, she entered the Sisters of Charity in Cincinnati in 1866 and received the name of Sister Blandina in religious life.

At the age of twenty-two, she was sent by her superiors to the territory of Colorado, and arrived on December 9, 1872, in Trinidad, a rough Western town known as a haven for outlaws and renegades. Sister Blandina was not welcomed with overwhelming enthusiasm, but she was determined to live the life of the Gospel in the town, and she had a remarkable patron.

Sister Blandina visited the jail regularly, cared for the homeless wanderers in Trinidad and made sure they received decent burials, settled various disputes among miners, and managed to end the long practice of lynching. She also built a school and won the respect and friendship of the people of the area after facing an angry group of Apaches and saving the town.

Her patron had watched her reception in the first days and had warned the townspeople that if they did not act courteously and aid the nun, he would kill them. The townspeople listened and took his words to heart because the patron's name was William Bonney, now known as Billy the Kid. Sister Blandina had given nursing care to one of Billy's companions when he was shot and left for dead. The famous outlaw was repaying her for her merciful care of his friend and had even agreed not to scalp the four physicians of Trinidad.

Sister Blandina Segale

In December 1876 Sister Blandina was sent to Santa Fe and there built a three-story school, singlehandedly buried the dead, and worked to build a hospital. She also spoke forcefully about the treatment of Native Americans and for the rights of women religious to wear their habits after an ordinance was passed in Trinidad in 1889 prohibiting sisters from wearing habits while teaching in the school. She was unable to reverse the ordinance, however.

She then went to Albuquerque to oversee the building of St. Joseph Hospital in 1901. She later was sent to Cincinnati to work among Italian immigrant children. She died there.

Seghers, Charles J. (December 26, 1839–November 28, 1886)

A Belgian missionary bishop in North America, the "Apostle of Alaska," and archbishop of Oregon City, Charles J. Seghers was born at Ghent, Belgium, but lost his parents at a young age. Raised by his uncles, he was called to the priesthood and studied in various local seminaries and the American College at Louvain. Ordained a priest in 1863, he departed that same year for Canada for service in the missions. In September 1863 he began ten years of service on Vancouver Island, where he worked among the white and Native American population.

In 1871 he was made administrator of the Diocese of Vancouver Island, and on March 23, 1873, he was appointed successor to Bishop Modeste Demers, "Apostle of the Pacific Coast of North America." On June 29, 1873, he was consecrated bishop of the diocese. Eager to evangelize throughout the Northwest, Bishop Seghers was committed especially to the Native Americans and strove to establish the Church across parts of the Yukon and elsewhere. His labors took him to the wilds of Alaska, and he journeyed on snowshoes, dogsleds, and canoes to reach the tribes.

In September 1878 Bishop Seghers was named coadjutor to the archbishop of Oregon City. He succeeded to the see on December 12, 1880, and reached Portland on July 1, 1879. He devoted the next year to exploring the Washington Territory, Idaho, and Montana. His wanderings were the source of a series of letters that were published in various Catholic periodicals in the East.

Although devoted to the see, Bishops Seghers desired to resign and devote himself to missionary work in Alaska. He went to Europe and in 1883 requested permission from Pope Leo XIII to step down. His resignation was accepted, and he was reappointed bishop of Vancouver Island, retaining his title of archbishop. He returned to Vancouver on April 2, 1885. He then set out from Victoria for Alaska and established missions at Sitka and Juneau. He spent several weeks among the Native Americans and then pushed on down the Yukon river. He was murdered by a traveling companion who became deranged. His remains were taken to Victoria.

Seltice, Andrew (c. 1865–1902)

Chief of the Coeur d'Alene tribe of Salish in Idaho, Andrew Seltice became head of his tribe around 1858. He went on to serve as chief until his death. The tribe had converted to Christianity soon after meeting the great missionary Pierre-Jean De Smet,

S.J., in 1842 and soon built a mission church that is still the oldest standing structure in Idaho.

Andrew's leadership, coming after a bitter struggle against the United States, helped to guide the tribe during the trying period of the second half of the nineteenth century, when white immigrants were arriving in increasing numbers in the region. In 1878 he led his people to the area southeast of Lake Coeur d'Alene. The resulting settlement included active missionary labors, a mission church, and schools.

Andrew negotiated a final agreement with the federal government in 1889 and devoted his remaining years to organizing the tribe as a community looking toward the future. He was assisted in many of his educational ventures by the missionaries.

Semmes, Raphael (September 27, 1809–August 27, 1877)

Confederate naval commander and writer Raphael Semmes was born in Charles County, Maryland, to a family descended from the original Catholic colonists of Maryland. Appointed a midshipman in the U.S. Navy in 1826, he was granted a leave of absence to study law. Returning to the navy in 1835, he served with distinction and earned the rank of commander. When, however, the Civil War started, Semmes joined the Confederacy, having been a resident of Alabama in 1841.

Semmes was appointed commander in 1861 and rapidly rose through the ranks to captain in 1862 and rear admiral in 1865. His career in the Confederate Navy was an active one, and he proved a major thorn in the side of the Union Navy. In command of the Confederate privateer *Sumter* in 1861, he destroyed eighteen Union ships, and as captain of the *Alabama*, he captured sixty-nine vessels and damaged American trade. After the *Alabama* was sunk off the French coast in 1864, Semmes made his way to England. From there he returned to Virginia and took part in the defense of Richmond.

After the war, he went back to Alabama and started a law practice. His career in the Confederate navy, however, was a political disability, despite receiving a pardon and amnesty. He was the author of *Service Afloat and Ashore During the Mexican War* (1851), *The Campaign of General Scott in the Valley of Mexico* (1852), *The Cruise of the Alabama and Sumter* (1864), and *Memoirs of Services Afloat during the War Between the States* (1869).

Separation of Church and State

The principle expressed but not specifically enunciated in the United States Constitution, separation of church and state stipulates there should be a separation between organized religion and the state and that there should not be some kind of state church. The First Amendment of the Constitution declares, "Congress shall make no law respecting an establishment of religion, or prohibiting the free exercise thereof." The term was first expressed by Thomas Jefferson in 1802 when he wrote: "I contemplate with sovereign reverence that act of the whole American people which declared that their legislature should 'make no law respecting an establishment of religion, or prohibiting the free exercise thereof,' thus building a wall of separation between Church & State."

The origins of the principle are traced to the very founding of the country. Having won their independence, the thirteen colonies now faced the task of building a lasting government and political order. One of the major issues faced by the new republic was the nature of the relationship between church and state, especially in a country with a variety of denominations and clearly intending to codify the principles of religious toleration and pluralism. The First Amendment in the Bill of Rights, enacted in 1791 and amended to the Constitution, institutes two key principles. The first was the Establishment Clause, which prohibited an established (or tax-supported) national religion or the preference of one religion over another. The second was the Free Exercise Clause, which safeguarded the right of all citizens to worship freely.

This separation of church and state became the hallmark of the new republic, but it was a genuine departure from the long traditions of Europe. The history of the Christian West from the third century onward had been characterized by a common polity of Christendom between the church and the state for the common good. This arrangement was certainly marked by tensions, crises, and conflict, but it remained in effect even after the tragic shattering of Christendom's unity through the Protestant

Reformation. In Europe, church and state remained united in some fashion, from Catholic Spain, France, and the Holy Roman Empire, to Anglican England, Lutheran Germany, and Calvinist Switzerland.

In the United States, however, the nation made the decision to separate church and state as its official policy. It was adduced to be the only reasonable solution to the perpetuation of domestic religious tranquility and toleration in a society that claimed a multitude of denominations and religions. This separation, of course, was not intended to be a hostile one. God's name was invoked on the currency, churches were given tax-exempt status, chaplains were assigned to the legislatures and especially the armed forces, and religious holidays were recognized by the government. As for Catholic leaders, the development was a welcome one as it guaranteed to Catholics what had been for so long denied them in the English colonies — the freedom to worship freely and without penalty or proscription.

A key reason for this support was expressed by Pope Benedict XVI during his visit to the United States in April 2008. The pontiff declared at the White House:

"From the dawn of the Republic, America's quest for freedom has been guided by the conviction that the principles governing political and social life are intimately linked to a moral order based on the dominion of God the Creator. The framers of this nation's founding documents drew upon this conviction when they proclaimed the 'self-evident truth' that all men are created equal and endowed with inalienable rights grounded in the laws of nature and of nature's God. The course of American history demonstrates the difficulties, the struggles, and the great intellectual and moral resolve which were demanded to shape a society which faithfully embodied these noble principles. In that process, which forged the soul of the nation, religious beliefs were a constant inspiration and driving force, as for example in the struggle against slavery and in the civil rights movement. In our time too, particularly in moments of crisis, Americans continue to find their strength in a commitment to this patrimony of shared ideals and aspirations."

Church-State Decisions of the Supreme Court

The nature and ramifications of the separation of church and state has been the subject of considerable legal discussion over the last two centuries. The following are the major church-state decisions by the U.S. Supreme Court:

Watson v. Jones, 13 Wallace 679 (1872): The court declared that a member of a religious organization may not appeal to secular courts against a decision made by a church tribunal within the area of its competence.

Reynolds v. United States, 98 US 145 (1879), ***Davis v. Beason, 133 US 333*** (1890), ***Church of Latter-Day Saints v. United States, 136 US 1*** (1890): The Mormon practice of polygamy was at issue in three decisions and was declared unconstitutional.

Bradfield v. Roberts, 175 US 291 (1899): The court denied that an appropriation of government funds for an institution (Providence Hospital in Washington, D.C.) run by Roman Catholic sisters violated the Establishment Clause.

Pierce v. Society of Sisters, 268 US 510 (1925): The court denied that a state can require children to attend only public schools. The court held that the liberty of the Constitution forbids standardization by such compulsion, and that the parochial schools involved had claims to protection under the Equal Protection Clause of the Fourteenth Amendment.

Cochran v. Board of Education, 281 US 370 (1930): The court upheld a Louisiana statute providing textbooks at public expense for children attending public or parochial schools. The court held that the children and state were beneficiaries of the appropriations, with incidental secondary benefit going to the schools.

United States v. MacIntosh, 283 US 605 (1931): The court denied that anyone can place allegiance to the will of God above his allegiance to the government since such a person could make his own interpretation of God's will the decisive test as to whether he would or would not obey the nation's law. The court stated that the nation, which has a duty to survive, can require citizens to bear arms in its defense.

Everson v. Board of Education, 330 US 1 (1947): The court upheld the constitutionality of a New Jersey statute authorizing free school bus transportation for parochial as well as public school students. The court expressed the opinion that the benefits of public welfare legislation, included under such bus transportation, do not run contrary to the concept of separation of church and state.

McCollum v. Board of Education, 333 US 203 (1948): The court declared unconstitutional a program for releasing children, with parental consent, from public school classes so they could receive religious instruction on public school premises from representatives of their own faiths.

Zorach v. Clauson, 343 US 306 (1952): The court upheld the constitutionality of a New York statute permitting, on a voluntary basis, the release during school time of students from public school classes for religious instruction given off public school premises.

Torcaso v. Watkins, 367 US 488 (1961): The court declared unconstitutional a Maryland requirement that one must make a declaration of belief in the existence of God as part of the oath of office for notaries public.

McGowan v. Maryland, 81 Sp Ct 1101, Two Guys from Harrison v. McGinley, 81 Sp Ct 1135, Gallagher v. Crown Kosher Super Market, 81 Sp Ct 1128, Braunfeld v. Brown, 81 Sp Ct 1144 (1961): The court ruled that Sunday closing laws do not violate the Establishment Clause, even though the laws were religious in their inception and still have some religious overtones. The court held that, "as presently written and administered, most of them, at least, are of a secular rather than of a religious character, and that presently they bear no relationship to establishment of religion as those words are used in the Constitution of the United States."

Engel v. Vitale, 370 US 42 (1962): The court declared that the voluntary recitation in public schools of a prayer composed by the New York State Board of Regents is unconstitutional on the ground that it violates the Establishment Clause.

Abington Township School District v. Schempp and Murray v. Curlett, 83 Sp Ct 1560 (1963): The court ruled that Bible reading and recitation of the Lord's Prayer in public schools, with voluntary participation by students, are unconstitutional on the ground that they violate the Establishment Clause.

Chamberlin v. Dade County, 83 Sp Ct 1864 (1964): The court reversed a decision of the Florida Supreme Court concerning the constitutionality of prayer and devotional Bible reading in public schools during the school day, as sanctioned by a state statute that specifically related the practices to a sound public purpose.

Board of Education v. Allen, No. 660 (1968): The court declared constitutional the New York schoolbook loan law that requires local school boards to purchase books with state funds and lend them to parochial and private school students.

Walz v. Tax Commission of New York (1970): The court upheld the constitutionality of a New York statute exempting church-owned property from taxation.

Earle v. DiCenso, Robinson v. DiCenso, Lemon v. Kurtzman, Tilton v. Richardson (1971): In *Earle v. DiCenso* and *Robinson v. DiCenso,* the court ruled unconstitutional a 1969 Rhode Island statute that provided salary supplements to teachers of secular subjects in parochial schools; in *Lemon v. Kurtzman,* the court ruled unconstitutional a 1968 Pennsylvania statute that authorized the state to purchase services for the teaching of secular subjects in nonpublic schools. The principal argument against constitutionality in these cases was that the statutes and programs at issue entailed excessive entanglement of government with religion. In *Tilton v. Richardson,* the court held that this argument did not apply to a prohibitive degree with respect to federal grants, under the Higher Education Facilities Act of 1963, for the construction of facilities for nonreligious purposes by four church-related institutions of higher learning, three of which were Catholic, in Connecticut.

Yoder, Miller and Yutzy (1972): In a case appealed on behalf of Yoder, Miller and Yutzy, the court ruled that Amish parents were exempt from a Wisconsin statute requiring them to send their children to school until the age of sixteen. The court said in its decision that secondary schooling exposed Amish children to attitudes, goals, and values contrary to their beliefs, and substantially hindered "the religious development of the Amish child and his integration into the way of life of the Amish faith-community at the crucial adolescent state of development."

Committee for Public Education and Religious Liberty, et al. v. Nyquist, et al., No. 72-694 (1973): The court ruled that provisions of a 1972 New York statute were unconstitutional on the grounds that they were violative of the Establishment Clause and had the "impermissible effect" of advancing the sectarian activities of church-affiliated schools. The programs ruled unconstitutional concerned: (1) maintenance and repair grants, for facilities and equipment, to ensure the health, welfare, and safety of students in nonpublic, nonprofit elementary and secondary schools serving a high concentration of students from low-income families; (2) tuition reimbursement ($50 per grade-school child, $100 per high school student) for parents (with income less than $5,000) of children attending nonpublic elementary or secondary schools; tax deduction from adjusted gross income for parents failing to qualify under the above reimbursement plan, for each child attending a nonpublic school.

***Sloan, Treasurer of Pennsylvania, et al. v. Lemon, et al.,* No. 72-459** (1973): The court ruled unconstitutional a Pennsylvania Parent Reimbursement Act for Nonpublic Education, which provided funds to reimburse parents (to a maximum of $150) for a portion of tuition expenses incurred in sending their children to nonpublic schools. The court held that there was no significant difference between this and the New York tuition reimbursement program (above), and declared that the Equal Protection Clause of the Fourteenth Amendment cannot be relied upon to sustain a program held to be violative of the Establishment Clause.

***Levitt, et al. v. Committee for Public Education and Religious Liberty, et al.* No. 72-269** (1973): The court ruled unconstitutional the Mandated Services Act of 1970 under which New York provided $28 million ($27 per pupil from first to seventh grade, $45 per pupil from seventh to twelfth grade) to reimburse nonpublic schools for testing, recording, and reporting services required by the state. The court declared that the act provided "impermissible aid" to religion in contravention of the Establishment Clause.

In related decisions handed down on June 25, 1973, the court: (1) affirmed a lower-court decision against the constitutionality of an Ohio tax credit law benefiting parents with children in nonpublic schools; (2) reinstated an injunction against a parent reimbursement program in New Jersey; (3) affirmed South Carolina's right to grant construction loans to church-affiliated colleges; and (4) dismissed an appeal contesting its right to provide loans to students attending church-affiliated colleges (*Hunt v. McNair, Durham v. McLeod*).

Wheeler v. Barrera (1974): The court ruled that nonpublic school students in Missouri must share in federal funds for educationally deprived students on a comparable basis with public school students under Title I of the Elementary and Secondary Education Act of 1965.

***Norwood v. Harrison,* 93 S. Ct. 2804** (1974): The court ruled that public assistance that avoids the prohibitions of the "effect" and "entanglement" tests (and therefore does not substantially promote the religious mission of sectarian schools) may be confined to the secular functions of such schools.

Wiest v. Mount Lebanon School District (1974): The court upheld a lower-court ruling that invocation and benediction prayers at public high school commencement ceremonies do not violate the principle of separation of church and state.

Meek v. Pittenger (1975): The court ruled portions of a Pennsylvania law providing auxiliary services for students of nonpublic schools unconstitutional; at the same time, it ruled in favor of provisions of the law permitting textbook loans to students of such schools. In denying the constitutionality of auxiliary services, the court held that they had the "primary effect of establishing religion" and involved "excessive entanglement" of church and state officials with respect to supervision; objection was also made against providing such services only on the premises of nonpublic schools and only at the request of such schools.

***TWA, Inc. v. Hardison,* 75-1126, *International Association of Machinists and Aerospace Workers v. Hardison,* 75-1385** (1977): The court ruled that federal civil rights legislation does not require employers to make more than minimal efforts to accommodate employees who want a particular working day off as their religion's Sabbath Day, and that an employer cannot accommodate such an employee by violating seniority systems determined by a union collective bargaining agreement. The court noted that its ruling was not a constitutional judgment but an interpretation of existing law.

Wolman v. Walter (1977): The court ruled constitutional portions of an Ohio statute providing tax-paid textbook loans and some auxiliary services (standardized and diagnostic testing, therapeutic and remedial services off school premises) for nonpublic school students. It decided that other portions of the law, providing state funds for nonpublic school field trips and instructional materials (audiovisual equipment, maps, tape recorders), were unconstitutional.

Byrne v. Public Funds for Public Schools (1979): The court decided against the constitutionality of a 1976 New Jersey law providing state income-tax deductions for tuition paid by parents of students attending parochial and other private schools.

Student Bus Transportation (1979): The court upheld a Pennsylvania law providing bus transportation at public expense for students to nonpublic schools up to ten miles away from the boundaries of the public school districts in which they lived.

Reimbursement (1980): The court upheld the constitutionality of a 1974 New York law providing direct cash payment to nonpublic schools for the costs of state-mandated testing and recordkeeping.

Ten Commandments (1980): The court struck down a 1978 Kentucky law requiring the posting of the Ten Commandments in public school classrooms in the state.

Widmar v. Vincent (1981): The court ruled that the University of Missouri at Kansas City could not deny student religious groups the use of campus facilities for worship services. The court also, in *Brandon v. Board of Education of Guilderland Schools,* declined without comment to hear an appeal for reversal of lower-court decisions denying a group of New York high school students the right to meet for prayer on public school property before the beginning of the school day.

Lubbock v. Lubbock Civil Liberties Union (1983): By refusing to hear an appeal in this case, the court upheld a lower-court ruling against a public policy of permitting student religious groups to meet on public school property before and after school hours.

Mueller v. Allen (1983): The court upheld a Minnesota law allowing parents of students in public and nonpublic (including parochial) schools to take a tax deduction for the expenses of tuition, textbooks, and transportation. Maximum allowable deductions were $500 per child in elementary school and $700 per child in grades seven through twelve.

Lynch v. Donnelly (1984): The court ruled 5–4 that the First Amendment does not mandate "complete separation of church and state" and that, therefore, the sponsorship of a Christmas Nativity scene by the City of Pawtucket, Rhode Island, was not unconstitutional. The case involved a scene included in a display of Christmas symbols sponsored by the city in a park owned by a nonprofit group. The majority opinion said "the Constitution (does not) require complete separation of church and state; it affirmatively mandates accommodation, not merely tolerance, of all religions and forbids hostility toward any. Anything less" would entail callous indifference not intended by the Constitution. Moreover, "such hostility would bring us into 'war with our national tradition as embodied in the First Amendment's guaranty of the free exercise of religion.' " (The additional quotation was from the 1948 decision in *McCollum v. Board of Education.*)

Christmas Nativity Scene (1985): The court upheld a lower-court ruling that the Village of Scarsdale, New York, must make public space available for the display of privately sponsored Nativity scenes.

Wallace v. Jaffree, **No. 83-812** (1985): The court ruled against the constitutionality of a 1981 Alabama law calling for a public school moment of silence that specifically included optional prayer.

Grand Rapids v. Ball, **No. 83-990**, *Aguilar v. Felton,* **No. 84-237** (1985): The court ruled against the constitutionality of programs in Grand Rapids and New York City allowing public school teachers to teach remedial entitlement subjects (under the Elementary and Secondary Education Act of 1965) in private schools, many of which were Catholic.

Bender v. Williamsport Area School District (1986): The court let stand a lower federal-court decision allowing a public high school Bible study group the same "equal access" to school facilities as that enjoyed by other extracurricular clubs. A similar decision was handed down in 1990 in *Board of Education v. Mergens,* involving Westside High School in Omaha.

County of Allegheny v. American Civil Liberties Union (1989): The court ruled (1) that the display of a Christmas Nativity scene in the Allegheny County Courthouse in Pittsburgh violated the principle of separation of church and state because it appeared to be a government-sponsored endorsement of Christian belief; and (2) that the display of a Hanukkah menorah outside the Pittsburgh-Allegheny city-county building was constitutional because of its "particular physical setting" with secular symbols.

Unemployment Division v. Smith (1990): The court ruled that religious use of the hallucinogenic cactus peyote is not covered by the First Amendment protection of religious freedom.

Lee v. Weisman (1992): The court banned officially organized prayer at public school graduation ceremonies.

Lamb's Chapel v. Center Moriches Union School District (1993): The court reversed a ruling by the 3rd U.S. Circuit Court of Appeals, declaring that the school district was wrong in prohibiting the congregation of Lamb's Chapel from using public school meeting space after hours to show a film series addressing family problems from a religious perspective. In view of the variety of organizations permitted to use school property after school hours, said the court's opinion, "There would have been no realistic danger that the community would think that the district was endorsing religion or any particular creed, and any benefit to religion or to the church would have been no more than incidental."

5th U.S. Circuit Court of Appeals (1993): The court let stand a ruling by the 5th U.S. Circuit Court of Appeals permitting students in Texas, Mississippi, and Louisiana to include student-organized and student-led prayers in graduation exercises.

Church of Lukumi Babalu Aye v. City of Hialeah (1993): The court ruled that municipal laws that effectively prohibit a single church from performing its religious rituals are unconstitutional. The ordinances at issue singled out one religion, Santeria, for the purpose of restricting its members from the practice of ritual animal sacrifices.

Zobrest v. Catalina Foothills School District (1993): The court ruled that a public school district may provide a sign-language interpreter for a deaf student attending a Catholic school without violating constitutional separation of church and state. The majority opinion said, "Handicapped children, not sectarian schools are the primary beneficiaries of the Disabilities Education Act; to the extent sectarian schools benefit at all from [the act], they are only incidental beneficiaries."

Fairfax County, Virginia, School District (1994): The court upheld lower-court rulings against a Fairfax County, Virginia, school district's practice of charging churches more rent than other entities for the use of school buildings.

Board of Education of Kiryas Joel Village School District v. Grumet (1994): The court ruled in 1994 that a school district created to meet the special education needs of a Hasidic Jewish community violated the Establishment Clause of the Constitution. The court said the New York legislature effectively endorsed a particular religion when it established a public school district for the Satmar Hasidic Village of Kiryas Joel.

Agostino v. Felton (1997): The court reversed, 5–4, its 1985 *Aguilar v. Felton* ruling, which had declared it unconstitutional for teachers employed by public school districts to hold Title I remedial programs for low-income students on the property of church-related schools.

Boerne v. Flores (1997): The court ruled, 6–3, that the Religious Freedom Restoration Act (1993) was unconstitutional because Congress overstepped its constitutional authority in enacting the law. Congress "has been given the power to 'enforce,' not the power to determine what constitutes a constitutional violation," said the majority opinion.

Mitchell v. Helms (2000): The court ruled, 6–3, that a Louisiana parish can distribute money for instructional equipment — including computers, books, maps, and filmstrip projectors — to private schools as long as it is done in a "secular, neutral and nonideological" way. The court's decision overturned two previous Supreme Court bans on giving public materials to parochial schools.

Santa Fe Independent School District v. Doe (2000): The court affirmed a lower court ruling that said prayer in public schools must be private and that such prayers at high school football games violate the constitutionally required separation of church and state. At issue in the Santa Fe case was a Texas school policy which permitted students selected by their peers to deliver an inspirational message of their own design at football games and the graduation ceremony. In 1999 the Santa Fe policy was struck down by the 5th U.S. Circuit Court of Appeals. The Court of Appeals held that the policy violated the Establishment Clause of the First Amendment, even though the government played no role in creating the message or selecting the messenger.

Chandler v. Siegelman (2001): The court let stand a lower-court ruling that students may participate in group prayers at school functions such as football games or graduations.

The Good News Club v. Milford Central Schools (2001): The court ruled that if the Boy Scouts and 4-H can use a public school as a meeting hall, a children's Bible-study class can also.

Brown v. Gilmore (2001): The court declined to hear a challenge to Virginia's mandatory minute of silence in schools.

Children's Health Care Is a Legal Duty Inc. v. McMullan (2001): The court turned down an appeal that claimed that Medicare and Medicaid payments to church-run health centers violate the constitutional separation of church and state.

Gentala v. Tucson (2001): The court ordered a federal appeals court to take another look at a case that asked whether taxpayers must cover $340 in expenses from a prayer rally in a city park, saying it should be reconsidered in light of the high court's earlier ruling that a Bible club cannot be excluded from meeting at a public school so long as other groups with a moral viewpoint are allowed to gather there.

Cleveland Voucher Program (2002): By a 5–4 ruling, the court upheld the Cleveland voucher program that had been implemented in 1995 to assist the improvement of one of the worst public school systems in the country.

Ten Commandments (2005): By a 5–4 vote, the court prohibited the posting of the Ten Commandments in courthouses; at the same time, the court permitted their posting in state houses.

Gonzales v. Carhart, Gonzales v. Planned Parenthood (2007): By a 5–4 vote, the court upheld the Partial Birth Abortion Ban Act that Congress passed and President George W. Bush signed into law in 2003, saying that the prohibi-

tion does not violate the constitutional right to an abortion.

Serra, Blessed Junípero (November 24, 1713– August 28, 1784)

One of the greatest of the Spanish Franciscan missionaries, who labored for twenty years and established nine of the twenty-one Franciscan missions along the Pacific Coast, Blessed Junípero was born at Petra, on the island of Majorca. He entered the Franciscans in September 1730, made his profession the following year, and chose the name Junípero in honor of a companion of St. Francis. As he demonstrated great proficiency in philosophy, he was appointed a lecturer in philosophy prior to his ordination. He went on to receive a doctorate in theology from the Lullian University at Palma, Spain, where he also was named the Duns Scotus chair of philosophy. The date of his ordination is uncertain, although it is possible that it was around 1738.

While respected as a great professor of philosophy, Blessed Junípero desired above all to serve in the missions. He received permission from his superiors to set out for Mexico and sailed from Palma. He reached Veracruz in December 1749 and then walked the several hundred miles to Mexico City despite a leg injury he sustained on the journey. In January 1750 Blessed Junípero joined the missionary college of San Fernando in Mexico.

That same year, Blessed Junípero volunteered for the missions among the Sierra Gorda Indians, north of Queretaro. He served there for nine years and mastered the language of the Pame Indians and translated the catechism into their tongue. During his time among the Indians, Blessed Junípero oversaw a rapid expansion of the missions and proved a defender of the rights of the native peoples against the abuses of Spanish colonial officials.

Summoned back to San Fernando College in 1758, Blessed Junípero expected to be sent to Texas and the San Sabá Mission, but the journey never took place. Instead, he remained at the college until 1767. He was also actively engaged as a preacher of missions and earned a sparkling reputation.

In 1767 he was appointed superior of a band of fifteen Franciscans for the Indian missions of Lower California, as the Jesuits had been expelled from Spanish territories. Blessed Junípero assumed his post in April 1768, but he soon volunteered to accompany the expedition to Upper California headed by Captain Gaspar de Portolá, a decision that opened up new territories for the Franciscans. In May 1769 Blessed Junípero established the Mission San Fernando de Velicatá in Lower California and arrived at San Diego on July 1.

Blessed Junípero devoted the next fifteen years to the evangelization of Upper California and founded several missions: San Carlos at Monterey (June 3, 1770), San Antonio (July 14, 1771), San Gabriel (September 8, 1771), San Luis Obispo (September 1, 1772), San Francisco de Asis (October 8, 1776), San Juan Capistrano (November 1, 1776), Santa Clara (January 12, 1777), and San Buenaventura (March 31, 1782). He was also in attendance at the founding of the Presidio of Santa Barbara in April 1782; he was unable to establish a mission there owing to the hostility of Governor Felipe de Neve.

He was one of the greatest travelers in the history of California and was devoted especially to the Native Americans. Through his efforts, he baptized some six thousand Indians and confirmed almost five thousand. He also spoke out on their behalf and journeyed to Mexico City to speak about their rights.

Blessed Junípero was compelled in 1773 to plead his case on their behalf before Viceroy Antonio María de Bucareli. The viceroy drafted documents to oversee the proper governance of the province. Blessed Junípero was given his wishes on all but two points. He devoted his remaining years to fostering the missions and the faith among the Native Americans. Despite severe health problems, he traveled repeatedly throughout the missions from San Diego to San Francisco.

Revered for his zeal, dedication to the missions, and his concern and love for the Indians in his charge, in 1884 the California Legislature passed a resolution declaring August 29, the centennial of Blessed Junípero's burial, a legal holiday. Blessed Junípero also represents California in Statuary Hall in the Capitol in Washington, D.C. He was declared venerable on May 9, 1985, and was beatified on September 25, 1988, by Pope Blessed John Paul II. The pope declared at the time of the beatification that this Franciscan "sowed the seeds of Christian faith amid the mountainous changes wrought by the arrival of European settlers in the New World. . . . In fulfilling this ministry, Father Serra showed himself to be a true son of St. Francis. Today his example inspires in a particular way the many Serra Clubs around the world, the members of which do so much praiseworthy work in fostering vocations." Blessed Junípero's feast day is July l.

Sestini, Benedict (March 20, 1816–January 17, 1890)

Jesuit priest, astronomer, and mathematician Benedict Sestini was born in Florence, Italy, and entered the Society of Jesus at Rome in 1836. After studies at the Roman College, he worked as an assistant to Father Francesco de Vico, director of the Roman Observatory. Ordained a priest in 1844, he was named to the chair of higher mathematics at the Roman College. His academic labors were ended abruptly, however, with the Revolution of 1848 in Italy, which brought about his departure from the country. Father Sestini sailed for the United States and settled in the Washington, D.C, area and took up a post at Georgetown College until 1869. Sent to Woodstock, Maryland, he served there until 1884, when poor health ended his long career. Aside from scientific writings, he wrote *Memoirs of the Roman College* in 1845 and 1847. His scientific writings included treatises on natural science, *Theoretical Mechanics* (1873), *Animal Physics* (1874), and *Principles of Cosmography* (1878).

Seton, Elizabeth Ann, St. (August 28, 1774–January 4, 1821)

The first American-born saint and the founder and first superior of the Sisters of Charity, St. Elizabeth Ann Seton was born in New York and was the daughter of non-Catholics. Her father, Richard Bayley, was professor of anatomy at Columbia College and a well-known official of the health authorities of the Port of New York, and her mother, Catherine Charlton Bayley, was the daughter of an Anglican minister. Her mother died in 1777, and St. Elizabeth, with her sisters, was educated by her father. When he married Charlotte Amelia Barclay, Elizabeth came to be very fond of her stepmother.

On January 25, 1794, she wed William Magee

Seton, one of the founders of the Bank of New York and a founder of a highly successful shipping company. St. Elizabeth worked with her sister-in-law, Cecilia Seton, to perform various missions of mercy. St. Elizabeth also gave birth to five children between 1795 and 1802. The death of her father in 1801 was the source of great grief, adding to the considerable financial strain that had begun in 1798 with the passing of her father-in-law after his business failed. Her husband's health soon deteriorated, necessitating a journey in 1803 to recover his strength. He died in Pisa, Italy, on December 27, 1803, and St. Elizabeth lived with business friends of her husband,

St. Elizabeth Ann Seton

the Filicchi brothers, and their families.

During this difficult time, St. Elizabeth became attracted to the Catholic faith, so that by the time she returned home in May 1804 she was convinced that she should enter the Church. The prospect of her conversion was most distressing to her Anglican friends, but, aided by her friend Antonio Filicchi, and advised by Jean-Louis Lefebvre de Cheverus (first bishop of Boston), she entered the Church on March 14, 1805.

To be able to care for her children, St. Elizabeth opened a boardinghouse for some boys at a nearby Protestant school, the necessity for money being especially acute because of the hostility of her relatives and the dwindling funds left by her husband. Early in 1806, meanwhile, her sister-in-law expressed a desire to become a Catholic. Her powerful family and friends were so outraged that moves were made to have St. Elizabeth expelled from New York. Perceiving the volatile conditions in the city, she proposed to travel to Canada and there enter a convent, a plan rejected by Bishop John Carroll of Baltimore. Instead, she went to Baltimore in 1808, opening a school next to the chapel of St. Mary's Seminary. St. Elizabeth was soon joined by other women, and in June 1809 the little community was transferred to Emmitsburg, Maryland, to take over a house that had been established to care for poor children.

Having become the head of a nascent religious community, St. Elizabeth asked the local bishop to request from the Sisters of Charity of St. Vincent de Paul rules by which the members could live. This rule was approved by Archbishop Carroll in January 1812. Against her will, St. Elizabeth was elected superior. All the sisters took their vows on July 19, 1813, and soon spread to other cities. St. Elizabeth continued to work until the time of her death in Emmitsburg after a long period of suffering. Her congregation continued to grow in the years after her death. She was beatified in 1963 and was canonized by Pope Paul VI on September 14, 1975. Her feast day is January 4.

Seton, William (January 28, 1835–March 15, 1905)

Author and grandson of St. Elizabeth Ann Seton, William was the son of William Seton and Emily Prime. After studies at St. John's College (later Fordham University), at Mount St. Mary's in Emmitsburg, Maryland, and at the University of Bonn, he began practicing law in New York. Soon after his admission to the bar he answered President Abraham Lincoln's first call for troops in 1861. With the start of the Civil War that year, Seton volunteered for service in the Union Army. He fought as a captain in the 41st New York Volunteers and was wounded at the Battle of Antietam. He recovered from his wounds and the next year fought as captain of the 16th Artillery.

After the war, he became a writer. His works included the novels *Romance of the Charter Oak* in 1870 and *Pride of Lexington* in 1871, and the poem "The Pioneer" in 1874. Around 1886 he journeyed to Europe, where he devoted himself to the study of paleontology and psychology. He subsequently wrote on matters of science for *Catholic World*.

Seton Hall University

The first Catholic college in New Jersey and the first diocesan university, Seton Hall was founded in 1856 as Seton Hall College by Bishop James Roosevelt Bayley, the first bishop of Newark, at Madison, New Jersey. Bishop Bayley, a nephew of St. Elizabeth Ann Seton, would become the archbishop of Baltimore.

The school moved to its present location in South Orange, New Jersey, in 1860, and received a charter in 1861. The first degrees were granted in 1862. That same year, Immaculate Conception Seminary was founded to provide suitable preparation for young men entering the priesthood.

The college endured long periods of difficulty during the Civil War, but it was still able to expand throughout the remaining years of the nineteenth century and into the twentieth. In 1930 graduate programs were introduced in English, modern languages, history, and education. By 1937 Seton Hall had established a university college and so marked the first matriculation of women at Seton Hall. The university became coeducational in 1968.

Owing to an extensive reorganization, the college was granted status as a university in 1950. The School of Law was opened in 1951, with Miriam T. Rooney as the first woman dean of law in the United States. Over the next decades, the university continued to grow, with new programs introduced and new extensive construction, including business and nursing classroom buildings and an art center. The university is home to eight schools, over sixty majors, and about ten thousand students.

Sex Abuse Crisis

In the long history of Catholicism in North America, there have been several major crises, including trusteeism, the waves of immigrants in the nineteenth century, Americanism, the upheaval following the Second Vatican Council, and theological dissent in the American Church, but arguably the most shattering crisis has been the sexual abuse crisis. The crisis exploded into the public consciousness in 2002, and by the end of the decade Catholic dioceses had paid out more than $1 billion in settlements and court cases.

The Church has always faced cases of priests and members of the clergy who have violated their vows and committed sexual improprieties and crimes. Nevertheless, the scale of the sex abuse crisis that emerged in the modern Church was unprecedented.

The Early Crisis

The first public disclosures of the coming crisis are dated to 1985, when a priest in Louisiana, Gilbert Gauthe, pleaded guilty to eleven counts of molesting boys and was sentenced to prison. The details of the case were described in Jason Berry's book *Lead Us Not into Temptation: Catholic Priests and the Sexual Abuse of Children*. That was followed by the 1992–93 trial of Father James Porter of the Fall River diocese in Massachusetts, who was accused and later pled guilty to forty-one counts of abuse of children in five states in the 1960s and 1970s.

A slow rise in reports of clergy abuse of children continued after the initial shock of the Gauthe case, and financial penalties mounted as plaintiffs began to seek both compensatory damages to cover the cost of counseling as well as punitive damages.

Partly as a result of the Porter case, the U.S. bishops first tried to deal with the problem of clergy sexual abuse collectively in 1992. Members of what was then the National Conference of Catholic Bishops gathered that year as a body in South Bend, Indiana, and during their deliberations they looked at the growing problem of cases and accusations. The bishops approved five principles for handling abuse accusations. The principles demanded:

Church officials were to respond immediately to abuse allegations.

Priests were to be removed and referred for medical help if evidence supported the allegations.

All incidents were to be reported as required by law.

The victims of abuse should receive all forms of pastoral, spiritual, and emotional assistance.

Transparency in dealing with the situation should be embraced, with all due respect to the privacy of all involved.

While a clear opportunity existed for many bishops to implement or update policies in their dioceses and to educate clergy and people as to the growing awareness of these issues, the moment in many dioceses sadly passed. Some bishops chose to add the new principles to the list of unheeded laws and norms or chose not to implement them as was their right under Church law. What was learned in hindsight, however, is that in those dioceses where the principles were followed, and where the laws and norms of the Church were followed, cases of abuse were limited and the toxic effects of priestly sexual abuse were largely contained. Two such examples of the early and effective enforcement were the Archdiocese of Washington and the Diocese of Fort Wayne-South Bend.

The next years brought new cases and trials, including the five-year legal odyssey in Dallas over the activities of Father Rudolph Kos, which culminated in 1998 with the Dallas diocese ordered to pay more than $31 million to Kos's victims. In 1999 the one-time Massachusetts priest John Geoghan was indicted on child rape charges. Later dismissed from the clerical state, he was convicted of child abuse and subsequently murdered in prison.

The Crisis in Boston

The Geoghan trial was just the start of the storm of controversy in the Boston archdiocese, with the scandal coverage driven by the *Boston Globe* newspaper. The names of accused priests became known across the country: John Birmingham, Paul R. Shanley, and Robert V. Gale. In 2002 the *Boston Globe* won a lawsuit that allowed them access to court records, and therefore documents, of lawsuits settled between the Archdiocese of Boston and victims of Geoghan. The documentation from archdiocesan files painted a picture of repeated complaints and warnings about Geoghan, and at the same time his movement from parish to parish, where he inevitably molested more children. The archdiocese pointed to psychiatric evaluations that said the chances that he would abuse more children after treatment were low, yet he continued to abuse and complaints continued to be filed. For its reporting on the sex abuse scandals in Boston, the *Boston Globe* won a Pulitzer Prize. The publication of these documents was a watershed moment for the Church in America.

The archdiocese struggled to pay the legal costs of the cases, and on December 13, 2002, Boston Cardinal Bernard F. Law, until then one of the most powerful prelates in the United States, resigned. At the time he stepped down, Cardinal Law apologized, saying, "To all those who have suffered from my shortcomings and mistakes I both apologize and from them beg forgiveness." He remains the highest-ranking American to resign as a result of

the scandal, and even his departure was not without controversy. Law was named the archpriest of the Basilica of Santa Maria Maggiore in Rome, and the media uproar followed him to the Eternal City, as critics of the appointment charged that this was far from a punishment. In 2005 critics complained again that he should have not been permitted to vote in the conclave following the passing of John Paul II that elected Pope Benedict XVI. Law retired from his post in November 2011.

News that priest abusers were being brought to justice encouraged other victims in the archdiocese, across the country, and, eventually, around the world to come forward and launched a torrent of other accusations, charges, and hundreds of millions of dollars in lawsuits.

Compounding the scandal was the discovery that bishops, religious orders, and communities had reassigned accused priests to other parishes or schools, thereby permitting the abuse to continue for years. Many bishops had followed the recommendations of psychiatrists at the time that such troubled priests could be treated and then reassigned, but the media impression was one of conspiracies and criminal negligence.

Statistics

The actual numbers of priests and victims involved was documented in the John Jay Report commissioned by the United States Conference of Catholic Bishops to assess the dimensions of the problem. The report stated: Between 1950 and 2002, a total of 10,667 individuals had made allegations of child sexual abuse 4,392 priests. The number represented 4 percent of the 109,694 priests who had served during those five decades; of the 4,392 priests who were accused, police were contacted regarding 1,021 individuals and of these 384 were charged, resulting in 252 convictions and 100 prison sentences. In total, as of 2009, 6 percent of all priests against whom allegations were made were convicted and about 2 percent received prison sentences.

Around 17 percent of accusers had brothers or sisters who were also allegedly abused, and nearly 47 percent of victims claimed to have been abused numerous times.

According to the John Jay study, 81 percent

of the victims were males. The vast majority (78 percent) of the victims were between the ages of 11 and 17; 15 percent of the victims were 16 to 17 years of age; 51 percent were between the ages of 11 and 14. Contrary to the general media image of the abusing priests, only 6 percent of victims were 7 years of age or younger. Sixteen percent of the victims were between age 8 and age 10. The statistics indicate that most abusers were not technically designated pedophiles (adults or older adolescents who evidence a sexual preference for prepubescent children), but were either hebephiles (a sexual preference for pubescent children, approximately between the ages of 10 and 14) or ephebophiles (sexual preference of adults for adolescents, approximately between the ages 15 and 19).

Further details revealed that the majority of incidents of abuse took place in the 1970s and then declined slowly throughout the 1980s and 1990s. The John Jay Report found that the problem was "widespread and affected more than 95 percent of the dioceses and approximately 60 percent of religious communities."

This number is consistent with the same statistics for other religious denominations and in society as a whole. According to the Crimes Against Children Research Center at the University of New Hampshire in 2004, approximately 200,000 children a year are sexually abused in the United States. A national report on child sex abuse by educators in public schools prepared for the U.S. Department of Education found that in 2000, 9.6 percent of public school students from kindergarten through eleventh grade reported unwanted sexual harassment or abuse by public school employees; most of the abusers were teachers.

Meanwhile, according to *Insurance Journal*, the insurance companies that insure the majority of Protestant churches in America receive an average of 260 reports each year of young people under 18 being sexually abused by clergy, church staff, volunteers, or congregation members. That number is actually higher than the average of 228 reports each year of "credible accusations" made against Catholic clergy.

The Response of the Church

The bishops gathered in Dallas in June 2002 and chartered the future for dealing with the sex abuse problem. They began with a recognition of the shortcomings of previous statements and initiatives. The principles had lacked any enforcement mechanisms, individual bishops had failed to meet the requirements and norms of Church law, and the bishops had not pursued an investigation into the root causes of the crisis.

The archbishops and bishops on the front line of the crisis in those dioceses beset by lawsuits and new revelations had the immediate task of repairing the breach of trust that had occurred with Catholics in the pews, even as they struggled with the canonical, legal, and financial implications of the many cases now inundating them. Several bishops would retire or step down in the year following the scandal. The financial toll was also beginning to mount and would soon impact severely the functioning of many dioceses.

The bishops instituted what became known as the Dallas Charter ("Charter for the Protection of Children and Young People"). The charter made clear that the bishops themselves saw this as primarily a problem involving priests, and the focus of the charter provided guidelines for priests and Church employees. Key provisions of the charter include:

The establishment of the National Review Board and the Office of Child and Youth Protection.

The "Essential Norms for Diocesan/Eparchial Policies Dealing with Allegations of Sexual Abuse of Minors by Priests or Deacons," which established legal procedures under Church law for applying charter policies. The norms were approved by the Vatican.

Encouraging bishops or their representatives to meet with victims.

Establishing offices to receive accusations and to provide professional counseling to victims.

Setting up diocesan review boards to examine accusations and advise the bishop on policies.

Permanently removing a priest or deacon from ministry after he admits committing abuse or after his guilt is established after an appropriate church process, commonly referred to as "zero tolerance."

Prohibiting confidentiality clauses in settlements with victims, unless requested by the victim.

Improving seminary training and providing

ongoing priestly formation programs to strengthen the commitment to celibacy.

The new National Review Board commissioned the John Jay Report, which was was officially titled "The Nature and Scope of the Problem of Sexual Abuse of Minors by Catholic Priests and Deacons in the United States" and was undertaken by the John Jay College of Criminal Justice. The report covered the period from 1950 to 2002 and was completed in 2004. It remains the single most significant effort to document all of the relevant details of the sex abuse problem and has since served as the template for other national churches in their own investigations. It is also one of the few comprehensive studies of its type undertaken by any organization, and perhaps the most thorough. The "causes and contexts" study was released in early 2011.

At the conclusion of discussions, the U.S. bishops approved the Charter for the Protection of Children and Young People by a vote of 239 to 13. Several bishops did not support the charter and did not comply with some of the mandates, as they deemed them unnecessary for their particular dioceses. For example, Bishop Fabian W. Bruskewitz of the Diocese of Lincoln refused to sign the charter, stating that the diocese was already in full compliance with the laws of the Church and all civil laws. He has subsequently not participated in the audits by the National Review Board. That is his right as a bishop under Church law.

The charter and its related documents were controversial because of their mandates upon bishops, which some considered an infringement on episcopal authority in the Church. Still, they were approved by the bishops because all the bishops recognized the need for a more effective response than had been given to that point.

The primary focus of the charter was to create clear and enforceable parameters for every diocese and Catholic institution that would guarantee a "safe environment" for all children and young people who might have any kind of contact with the Church or take part in any activities sponsored by the Church. This entailed strict enforcement of a "zero tolerance" policy for sexual abuse and sexual abusers, along with uniform national procedures for the investigation of sex abuse allegations against all personnel working for and serving the Church,

including lay teachers in Catholic schools, parish staff, coaches, and all other volunteers assisting the Church in the care of young people. Oversight entailed background checks for Church employees and training in creating and sustaining a safe environment for youth, as well as in recognizing and reporting potential abuse. To guarantee that every diocese in the country would follow the same procedures and regulations in handling abuse allegations, the bishops approved on June 14, 2002, the Essential Norms, which were then sent for approval, or *recognitio*, by the Holy See.

This procedure was required because a national bishops' conference does not possesses the authority to enact legislation except where granted it by the Church's universal law. This was not one of those situations. The Essential Norms represented the imposition of regulations and laws on the dioceses of the United States and so needed to be examined for any possible conflicts with wider Church law governing the universal Church. Law governing part of the universal Church is called particular law and must be approved by the Holy See. To assist this process, a delegation of bishops met in Rome with officials of the relevant offices of the Roman Curia in October 2002, including the Congregation for the Doctrine of the Faith. Minor changes were made and the *recognitio* from the Holy See was given on December 8, 2002. The norms were accepted as particular law for all the dioceses of the United States effective March 1, 2003, and were accepted as complementary to the universal law of the Church, which had already stipulated the penalties for the grave sins and acts of sexual abuse against minors. The bishops reapproved the set of norms in 2006.

The Vatican monitored closely the events in Dallas in 2002 and met with the American bishops to clarify and assist their work. In April 2002 Pope Blessed John Paul convened in Rome a gathering of the American cardinals, along with the heads of the United States Conference of Catholic Bishops, Cardinal Joseph Ratzinger, and other Vatican officials. At the time, he declared forcefully that there was "no place in the priesthood and religious life for those who would harm the young," although he added that it was important to remember "the power of Christian conversion."

Progress and Challenges

For the Church in the United States, the Dallas Charter and the Essential Norms were a vital starting point toward reconciliation and renewal. A shield had been installed for dioceses, and there was at last an enforceable set of norms particularly aimed at the laws and needs of the Catholic community in the United States. This was, as many bishops readily acknowledged, only a start.

As a result of these provisions, progress was made in three key areas that were considered vital in the charter: creating a safe environment and preventing further abuse, improving seminaries and priestly formation, and promoting genuine healing for victims.

In March 2010 the results of the 2009 annual report on compliance with the U.S. bishops' Charter for the Protection of Children and Young People was a striking testimony to the success of the Essential Norms, the work of the bishops, and the achievement of Pope Benedict XVI in bringing genuine hope for the future after the tragedy of sex abuse by the clergy. The numbers revealed the fewest number of victims, allegations, and offenders in dioceses since 2004, and most of the cases reported to dioceses were from decades ago.

In 2009 there were 398 allegations and 286 offenders reported to dioceses. Of the allegations reported, a total of six allegations (or a mere 2 percent) involving children under the age of 18 took place in 2009 out of a Catholic population of nearly 70 million. Approximately one-eighth of the allegations in 2009 (48 in all) were unsubstantiated or determined to be false. Similar results were reported for members of religious orders of men. The majority of new allegations (71 percent) involved cases in which the abuse took place between 1960 and 1984, with most occurring between 1975 and 1979. As a result of these declines, there was a one-year decline of 83 percent in the amounts paid out for settlements from the previous year. Dioceses also paid more than $21 million to continue their efforts in child protection, such as training programs, background checks, and salaries for staff. Nearly six million, or 96 percent of, children in Catholic schools or religious education programs, had received "safe environment" training. Background evaluations were also performed on over two million priests, deacons, seminarians, educators, employees, and volunteers.

In a memo to all bishops, Cardinal Francis George, president of the USCCB, wrote: "The number of children now equipped with the skills to protect themselves more effectively continues to grow. The *Charter* is causing a cultural change in the U.S. Catholic Church, one I hope will permeate all areas of society. Of course, as bishops, we take the responsibility to reach out to victims/survivors and create safe environments seriously. The life and dignity of the victims/survivors and of little ones lie at the core of our responsibilities as shepherds."

Pope Benedict XVI expressed the Church's response to the crisis when he visited the United States in 2008:

"We will absolutely exclude pedophiles from the sacred ministry; it is absolutely incompatible, and whoever is really guilty of being a pedophile cannot be a priest. So at this first level we can do justice and help the victims, because they are deeply affected; these are the two sides of justice: one, that pedophiles cannot be priests and the other, to help in any possible way the victims. Then there is a pastoral level. The victims will need healing and help and assistance and reconciliation: this is a big pastoral engagement and I know that the bishops and the priests and all Catholic people in the United States will do whatever possible to help, to assist, to heal. We have made a visitation of the seminaries, and we will do all that is possible in the education of seminarians for a deep spiritual, human and intellectual formation for the students. Only sound persons can be admitted to the priesthood and only persons with a deep personal life in Christ and who have a deep sacramental life. So, I know that the bishops and directors of seminarians will do all possible to have a strong, strong discernment, because it is more important to have good priests than to have many priests. This is also our third level, and we hope that we can do, and have done and will do in the future, all that is possible to heal these wounds."

The Price of the Crisis

The fallout from the scandal in the United States has been monumental. Several bishops were forced to resign, including Cardinal Law of Boston, and the lawsuits stemming from the scandal have cost the Catholic Church in the United States well in excess of $2 billion, with many suits still to be settled or tried. The Boston archdiocese in 2003 agreed to pay $85 million to settle more than 500 civil suits, and the archdiocese avoided bankruptcy by agreeing to sell land and buildings for more than $100 million to help fund the legal settlements. The California Dioceses of Orange, Sacramento, Oakland, and San Diego each settled cases by paying tens of millions of dollars, with Orange paying out a sum of $100 million and San Diego paying $198 million. The largest settlement was made by the Archdiocese of Los Angeles. In 2007 Cardinal Roger M. Mahony agreed to have the archdiocese pay more than $660 million to victims and their lawyers. This was in addition to the $60 million paid out the year before. The deal brought to an end the scheduled trials for a host of abuse claims that dated all the way back to the 1940s.

Several dioceses have been forced into bankruptcy because of the cases, including the Archdiocese of Portland and the Dioceses of Spokane, Tucson, and Wilmington. The Church's reputation has also been deeply stained, with relentless media attention severely damaging the public esteem of priests and crippling the moral authority of bishops, even though most had inherited the disaster and were never personally responsible for the mistakes of their predecessors.

Shahan, Thomas Joseph (September 11, 1837– March 9, 1932)

Bishop and rector of The Catholic University of America, Thomas Joseph Shahan was born in Manchester, New Hampshire, of Irish immigrant parents. Called to the priesthood, he studied at the Sulpician College in Montréal from 1872 to 1878 and then from 1878 to 1882 at the North American College in Rome, where he was ordained on June 3, 1882. He began his priestly life with a doctorate in theology. In 1883 he was appointed chancellor of the Diocese of Hartford and secretary to Bishop Lawrence Stephen McMahon. He remained in this post until 1888, when he was invited to teach at Catholic University in Washington, D.C.

Prior to assuming his post, Father Shahan studied at the University of Berlin from 1889 to 1891

under the famed scholar Adolf Harnack, and then at the Sorbonne and Institut Catholique in Paris in 1891, under Louis Duchesne. He returned to the United States in 1891 and began teaching Church history and patrology. In 1909 he was named a domestic prelate and rector of Catholic University. In 1914 he was named titular bishop of Germanicopolis and was consecrated by Cardinal James Gibbons. As rector, he sought to expand the faculty and bring significant improvements to it, especially in the fields of theology and canon law. He also oversaw a significant building program. He was especially devoted to the Blessed Virgin Mary and was thus a key figure in securing the construction of a national shrine to the Mother of God.

In addition to his duties as rector, Bishop Shahan was one of the founders of the National Catholic Educational Association (he was president from 1909 to 1928), the National Conference of Charities, the American Catholic Historical Association in 1917, the International Federation of Catholic Historical Associations in 1917, and the National Shrine of the Immaculate Conception. He retired in 1928 and spent his remaining years at Holy Cross Academy in Washington, D.C.

As a prolific scholar, Bishop Shahan wrote extensively for the *Catholic University Bulletin*, was associate editor of the old *Catholic Encyclopedia*, and was the author of such notable works as *The Blessed Virgin in the Catacombs* (1892), *Giovanni Baptista de Rossi* (1900), *The Beginnings of Christianity* (1903), *The Middle Ages: Sketches and Fragments* (1904), and *St. Patrick in History* (1904). In 1923 he received the very rare honor of a doctorate of theology from the University of Louvain, Belgium. In 1926 he was elected a fellow of the Medieval Academy of America.

Shakespeare, Frank. *See* Holy See-U.S. Relations

Shanley, John (January 4, 1852–July 16, 1909)

The first bishop of the Diocese of Fargo, John Shanley was born in Albion, New York, and was ordained on May 30, 1874, for the Archdiocese of St. Paul. The Diocese of Fargo was established on November 12, 1889, as the Diocese of Jamestown (the see city was changed to Fargo on April 6, 1897). At its inception, the diocese extended across the whole of North Dakota and included approximately nineteen thousand Catholics, many of them Native American. There were thirty priests, forty churches, one hospital, three parochial schools, and an academy for girls. Father Shanley was consecrated its first bishop on December 27, 1889, by Archbishop John Ireland.

Bishop Shanley found his new diocese a challenge from the very start as he lacked any significant local financial support. Such were his financial difficulties that he toured the Eastern states to find money. His second major crisis was finding vocations for the rapidly growing population in North Dakota. He also was a strong supporter of the rights of Native Americans and the temperance movement. He established and edited the *Bulletin of the Diocese of Fargo* and was active in defending the Church in the face of frequent anti-Catholic attacks by Protestant ministers. By the time of his death from pneumonia and overwork, the diocese claimed 110 priests, 215 churches, 15 parochial schools, four Native American schools, 6 academies for girls, 5 hospitals, and an orphanage.

Shea, John Gilmary (July 22, 1824–February 22, 1892)

The "Father of American Catholic historians," and editor and author of over two hundred publications, John Gilmary Shea was born in New York and studied as a youth under the Sisters of Charity. His father, James Shea, was an Irish immigrant and later principal of Columbia College Grammar School; his mother, Mary Ann Flannigan, was a native of Boston. Shea attended the Columbia College Grammar School and also mastered Spanish through his work as a clerk in a Spanish merchant's office. In 1838, at the age of fourteen, he contributed an article to the *Young People's Catholic Magazine* on Cardinal Gil de Albornoz. While interested especially in Church history, he completed his studies in law and was admitted to the bar in 1846.

The following year he entered the novitiate of the Society of Jesus. His studies were conducted at St. John's College (later Fordham University) and

John Gilmary Shea

at St. Mary's College in Montréal, where he was under the academic direction of the noted scholar Father Felix Martin, S.J., who was then rector of the college. In 1852, however, Shea departed the novitiate and returned to New York, where he began life as a writer and editor. In 1854 he wed Sophie Savage, and the couple had two daughters.

Shea's first major publication was *Discovery and Exploration of the Mississippi Valley* in 1852. An impressive work that was highly praised, it was followed two years later by *History of the Catholic Missions among the Indian Tribes of the United States, 1529–1859*. Once again Shea received wide reknown for his research and was praised by Catholic and non-Catholic critics. A wide variety of writings appeared over the next years, including *A Bibliographical Account of Catholic Bibles, Testaments and Other Portions of Scripture* (1859), his fifteen-volume *Library of American Linguistics*, devoted to the grammars and dictionaries of Indian languages, *The Life of Pius IX* (1877), and *The Hierarchy of the Catholic Church in the United States* (1886). Shea also contributed historical articles to *History of America, Catholic World*, and the *U.S. Catholic Historical Magazine*, of which he was the founder and first editor. He also served as editor for some years of D. & J. Sadlier's *Catholic Directory and Almanac* and was editor from 1889 to 1892 of the *Catholic News*. In 1884 he was the first president of the United States Catholic Historical Society. Shea's greatest literary and scholarly achievement was the *History of the Catholic Church in the United States*, published from 1886 to 1892, which took up the main part of his final years.

In honor of his immense achievements as a Catholic historian, Shea was awarded honorary degrees by St. Francis Xavier's College, Fordham University, and Georgetown University. The University of Notre Dame awarded him the first Laetare Medal in 1883. Ranked as the greatest Catholic historian in the United States in the nineteenth century, Shea demonstrated a remarkable ability to gather documents and to labor as a pioneer in scientific historical research. He was also a noted defender of the

Church, the American hierarchy, and the contributions of Catholics to American life and history. For his labors and legacy, he has been called justifiably the "Father of American Catholic Historians." He died in Elizabeth, New Jersey.

Sheed, Francis "Frank" (March 20, 1897– November 20, 1981)

Author, famed apologist, and co-founder of the publisher Sheed & Ward, Frank Sheed was born in Sydney, Australia. His father was John Sheed, a dedicated Marxist, and his mother was Mary Maloney, a Roman Catholic from County Cork, Ireland. His mother was able to influence him in the faith and managed to send him to a parish school run by Sacred Heart nuns. His father, however, soon sent him to public school and insisted on his participation in the Methodist Church.

Sheed later studied law at Sydney University and also visited London. After graduation, he settled in London and joined the Catholic Evidence Guild, an organization started in 1918 to provide public speakers in defense of the Church, especially in the open areas such as Hyde Park and the streetcorners of London. Sheed was soon one of the Guild's best and most popular speakers, displaying a great fearlessness in going out into the most hostile environments, where he matched wits and won the day against anti-Catholics, Protestant preachers, and communists.

In 1926 he married Maisie Ward, a fellow Guild member. The two subsequently founded the publishing house of Sheed & Ward, with the aim of publishing works that might promote Catholic intellectual revival in England. Their pantheon of famous writers included G. K. Chesterton, Hilaire Belloc, Ronald Knox, and Christopher Dawson. They then added translations of such writers as Jacques Maritain, Sigrid Undset, Paul Claudel, Romano Guardini, and Léon Bloy.

In 1933 Sheed & Ward established an office in New York and soon began publishing American authors, including Dorothy Day and Catherine de Hueck. In 1940 Sheed made the decision to settle in New Jersey, although he spent his remaining years traveling extensively in the United States, England, and Australia on behalf of the publishing house's interests. In 1973 Sheed & Ward was sold to the Universal Press Syndicate, and the firm's name was changed to Andrews McNeel. The name Sheed & Ward was adopted for an imprint that published many of the classic works published in earlier years. Sheed, meanwhile, continued speaking and traveling. He wrote several books, the best known being *Theology and Sanity* (1947), *A Map of Life, Theology for Beginners*, and *To Know Christ Jesus* (1962). His other works included the translation of Etienne Gilson's *The Philosophy of St. Bonaventure* (1938), *Society and Sanity* (1953), *God and the Human Condition* (1966), and *Genesis Regained* (1969). Following the Second Vatican Council, he wrote *Is It the Same Church?* (1968). Maisie died in 1975, and Frank passed away from complications following a stroke. He and Maisie were both buried in the Jersey City Cemetery.

Sheehan, Luke (February 28, 1873–February 11, 1937)

A Capuchin missionary in Oregon, Luke Sheehan was born in Cork City, Ireland, and entered the Capuchins at the age of fifteen in Cork. He was ordained in 1896 and taught philosophy at the Capuchin house of formation in Kilkenny before volunteering for missionary work in Aden, on the Arabian Peninsula. Compelled to return to Ireland because of poor health, he volunteered for service in the United States and arrived in 1910 at Hermiston, Oregon, in response to Bishop Charles J. O'Reilly's request that the Irish Capuchins send members of the order to the Diocese of Baker City.

Father Sheehan departed Hermiston to conduct a study of Crook County, Oregon, for the purposes of possible evangelization. He found in eastern Oregon a tiny Catholic population spread out over a vast territory. His journeys took him by foot and horseback, and slowly he built up the Church's presence in the region.

The railroad arrived at Bend, Oregon, in 1916, and Father Sheehan welcomed Irish Catholics and built a new church and later a clinic that became the modern St. Charles Medical Center. In subsequent years, he opened a parish school and invited the Sisters of the Holy Names to staff it. He also fought against the vicious anti-Catholicism found among many of Crook County's residents, as well as members of the Ku Klux Klan. Through Father

Sheehan's labors, the Klan's influence was greatly reduced.

Sheen, Fulton J. (May 8, 1895–December 9, 1979)

Archbishop, radio and television personality, and educator who was internationally famous as a preacher, Fulton J. Sheen was perhaps the most popular and socially influential American Catholic of the twentieth century.

Born in El Paso, Illinois, he was baptized Peter but chose to use his mother's maiden name. After studying at St. Victor's College and Seminary in Bourbonnais, Illinois, he entered St. Paul's Seminary in Minnesota, where he was ordained on September 20, 1919. He then attended The Catholic University of America and earned his doctorate from the University of Louvain in 1923. Still more studies followed at the Sorbonne and the Pontifical University of St. Thomas, the Angelicum, and Father Sheen then taught at St. Edmund's College in Ware, England.

In 1925 his doctoral thesis, "God and Intelligence in Modern Philosophy," was published, winning him the Cardinal Mercier Prize for International Philosophy and the renowned *Agrégé en philosophie*, the first American to receive this distinction. He went on to further studies at the Sorbonne in Paris and the Collegio Angelico, where he earned a doctorate in sacred theology.

Returning to the United States, he served as a curate at St. Patrick's in Peoria, Illinois, before being appointed to teach at The Catholic University of America.

He held this post from 1926 to 1950, during which time he rose to national prominence as one of the most eloquent Catholic preachers. A regular on ABC's *Catholic News Broadcast,* he attracted millions with his theological depth, spoken with consummate skill and in terms that were comprehensible to the average person, Catholic and non-Catholic.

Named in 1950 as the director for the Society for the Propagation of the Faith, he spent the next years raising millions of dollars for Catholic missions. In 1951 he was made an auxiliary bishop of New York, under Cardinal Francis Spellman. That same year, he launched the amazingly successful television program *Life Is Worth Living* for ABC;

the show, which ran in the early 1950s, became the number-one program in the ratings. Father Sheen appeared on the cover of *Time* magazine and won an Emmy. His work attracted untold numbers to the Church, and he was personally responsible for the conversion of a large number of men and women, including his housekeeper, Fanny Washington, Heywood Hale Broun, and Clare Boothe Luce.

In 1966 Pope Paul VI appointed him bishop of the Diocese of Rochester, but he remained there only three years, resigning in 1969. He then traveled constantly throughout the world. Before his death, he was made a titular archbishop. The author of over seventy books, he was especially known for his best-selling *Life of Christ,* which was published in 1958. His cause for canonization was opened in 2002 by the Diocese of Peoria, and he was granted the title of Servant of God. In 2012 Sheen was declared Venerable by Pope Benedict XVI.

Sheerin, John Basil (October 12, 1906–January 13, 1992)

Priest and editor of *Catholic World* from 1948 to 1974, John Basil Sheerin was born in Brooklyn, New York, the son of Frank and Margaret Sheerin. He studied at Fordham University and then Fordham Law School and, after graduation, was admitted to the bar of New York in 1932; in 1938, he was licensed to appear before the United States Supreme Court. In 1933 Sheerin entered the novitiate for the Paulists and was ordained in 1937. After earning a master's degree from The Catholic University of America, he taught English at St. Paul's College in Washington, D.C. In 1945 he founded the Paulist Information Center in Boston.

In 1948 Father Sheerin was appointed senior editor of *Catholic World*, the premiere publication of the Paulists. He remained at the helm for nearly four decades and was awarded the St. Francis de Sales Award by the Catholic Press Association in 1975. As editor, he demonstrated a farsighted commitment to ecumenical dialogue and also to Catholic-Jewish dialogue. In 1957 he was named, with the Jesuit Gustave Weigel, to be the first Catholic observers for the Vatican at the World Council of Churches meeting in North America. He went on to serve as a *peritus* (or theological expert) at the

Second Vatican Council and was later an adviser to the United States Conference of Catholic Bishops' Secretariat for Catholic-Jewish Relations. He also was a vocal opponent of the Vietnam War.

Father Sheerin's writings were published in *America, Commonweal, Lumen Vitae,* the *American Ecclesiastical Review,* and many other periodicals. He also wrote a number of books. His last years were marked by a decline caused by Alzheimer's.

Shehan, Lawrence J. (March 18, 1898–August 26, 1984)

Archbishop of Baltimore from 1961 to 1974 and cardinal from 1965, Lawrence J. Shehan was born in Baltimore, the son of Irish immigrants Thomas P. and Anastasia Shehan. He studied for the priesthood at St. Charles College in Catonsville, Maryland, St. Mary's Seminary in Baltimore, and the North American College in Rome. Ordained a priest in Rome on December 23, 1922, he earned a doctorate in theology from the Pontifical Urban University in Rome the following year. Returning home, he served in pastoral work in the Archdiocese of Baltimore and Washington, D.C., from 1923 to 1947 and was named to several offices in the curia of the Archdiocese of Baltimore and Washington from 1938 to 1945.

Appointed a papal chamberlain in 1939 and a domestic prelate of the papal household in 1945, he was named that same year titular bishop of Lydda and auxiliary bishop of Baltimore and Washington. Following the creation in 1947 of the Archdiocese of Washington, Bishop Shehan was named vicar general of the Archdiocese of Baltimore. He served in this post until 1953, when Pope Pius XII appointed him first bishop of Bridgeport. Bishop Shehan devoted his next years to providing the new diocese with a firm footing and a sound organizational structure.

Cardinal Lawrence Shehan

He oversaw the creation of eighteen new parishes, many new schools, and a host of diocesan offices. In 1960 he celebrated the first diocesan synod. During this period, he was also president of the National Catholic Educational Association, vice president of the International Eucharistic Congresses, and chairman of various episcopal committees.

On July 10, 1961, Pope Blessed John XXIII elevated him to the titular archepiscopal see of Nicopolis ad Nestum, and he was appointed coadjutor archbishop of Baltimore and installed on September 27, 1961. On December 8, 1961, upon the death of Archbishop Francis P. Keough, he acceded to the see and was installed as the twelfth archbishop of Baltimore.

On February 22, 1965, Pope Paul VI named Archbishop Shehan to the College of Cardinals, with the rank of cardinal priest with the titular church of San Clemente in Rome. He took part in the Second Vatican Council and was named by Pope Paul VI to the Body of Presidents of the council on July 9, 1965.

Deeply committed to the cause of ecumenism, Cardinal Shehan emerged as one of the leaders of the movement in the American Church. In 1962 he established America's first Commission for Christian Unity, and in 1964 was chosen head of the United States Conference of Catholic Bishops' Committee for Ecumenical Affairs. A year before he had been named to the Vatican Secretariat for Christian Unity. In 1965 he was awarded the National Brotherhood Award by the National Conference of Christians and Jews. He was also chosen by Pope Paul VI as his representative to Istanbul to deliver to Patriarch Athenagoras I of Constantinople the historic lifting of the act of excommunication that had been imposed in 1054 and that sparked the schism between the Catholic Church and the Orthodox Church.

Cardinal Shehan was also concerned with racial equality. In March 1963 he issued his famous pastoral letter, "Racial Justice," which ended all forms of discrimination based on color in Catholic hospitals, schools, and all other institutions of the archdiocese. He wrote in the pastoral letter, "Our Christian faith imposes upon us all a special duty of both justice and charity toward all men, no matter what may be their racial and social origin." His determination to promote racial equality remained unswerving, and he spoke out on behalf of priests and nuns when they marched in civil rights demonstrations and took part in the funeral ceremonies for Dr. Martin Luther King Jr. in 1968. Cardinal Shehan died in Baltimore and was interred beneath the sanctuary of the cathedral.

Sheil, Bernard (February 18, 1886–September 13, 1969)

Archbishop and founder of the Catholic Youth Organization in 1931, Bernard Sheil was honored with the titles of "Apostle of Youth" and "Apostle of the Poor." Born in Chicago, he passed up a potentially great baseball career to enter the seminary, and after studies he was ordained on May 21, 1910, for the Chicago archdiocese. After pastoral service for several years and then service as a chaplain, Father Sheil was appointed assistant chancellor in 1924 and chancellor in 1928. That same year, he was named auxiliary bishop of Chicago and vicar general. He was also appointed pastor of St. Andrew Parish, a post he held until 1966.

In 1931 Cardinal George Mundelein appointed Bishop Sheil to establish the Catholic Youth Organization. He remained in charge of the CYO until 1954 and left it a national organization. He also was instrumental in 1949 in starting the radio station WFJL with the purpose of airing Catholic news. It soon became one of the most important Catholic media outlets in the United States. At the same time, Bishop Sheil became a powerful voice for the labor movement.

Bishop Sheil publicly opposed the activities of the outspoken radio priest Charles Coughlin. In 1954 he also spoke out against the methods of Senator Joseph McCarthy of Wisconsin in his campaign against communism. In 1961 he was given the title of titular archbishop by Pope Blessed John XXIII. He retired in 1967 and died in Tucson, Arizona.

Sheridan, Philip (March 6, 1831–August 5, 1888)

A Union general best known for his exploits during the Civil War, Philip Sheridan was born in Albany,

General Philip Sheridan

New York, to a Catholic family that moved to Ohio in his youth. In 1848 Sheridan entered the United States Military Academy at West Point and graduated in 1853. He received the rank of brevet second lieutenant in the infantry and served in Texas and Oregon. At the start of the Civil War, he was appointed chief quartermaster and in 1862 was commissioned colonel of the Second Michigan Volunteer Cavalry. Within a short time he was promoted to brigadier general and given command of a Union division in the Army of the Ohio.

In April 1864 Sheridan was named commander of the cavalry of the Army of the Potomac. He proved one of General Ulysses S. Grant's most reliable generals in the final stages of the war. He defeated Confederate forces in the Shenandoah Valley and brought such massive destruction to the valley that the campaign was termed "the Burning" by the people there. In October 1864 Sheridan won a significant victory over Confederate forces at Cedar Creek and was quickly rewarded with the rank of major general in the regular army. His cavalry raids proved a major factor in slowly wearing down the Army of Northern Virginia and so hastening the surrender of the Confederate Army at Appomattox in April under General Robert E. Lee.

After the war, Sheridan was named commander of the military department in Louisiana, Texas, and Missouri. Returning to the West, he waged a pitiless war on the tribes of the Great Plains in 1868–69, with attacks upon the Cheyenne, Kiowa, and Comanche. One of the officers infamously active under his command was Colonel George Armstrong Custer. According to legend, Sheridan once observed, "The only good Indians I ever saw were dead," a quote that soon became in popular telling, "The only good Indian is a dead Indian."

While noted for his merciless campaigns against Native Americans, General Sheridan also was more positively a leader in the establishment of Yellowstone National Park. In 1870–71 he visited Europe and observed the Franco-Prussian War. He was promoted to the rank of lieutenant general in 1869 and became commander of the army in 1883. Just before his death, he was given the rank of general of the army.

Shields, James (December 12, 1806–June 1, 1879)

Union general during the Civil War, U.S. Senator, and member of the Illinois Supreme Court from 1843 to 1845, James Shields was the only person to represent three states in the U.S. Senate (Illinois, Minnesota, Missouri). He was born in Dungannon County, Tyrone, Ireland, and migrated to the United States in 1826. He entered studies in law and started practicing at Kaskaskia, Illinois, in 1832. Elected to the state legislature in 1836, he was named judge of the state supreme court in 1843. While serving in the legislature and as state auditor, he challenged Abraham Lincoln to a duel over criticisms that Lincoln had made about him publicly. The two, however, made peace and became friends.

When, in 1846, the Mexican-American War began, Shields was commissioned a brigadier general by President James K. Polk and subsequently fought with distinction. He was wounded at Cerro Gordo and again at Chapultepec. In 1848 he was appointed governor of the Territory of Oregon, but he resigned in order to represent Illinois in the United States Senate as a Democrat. Following his term, he moved to Minnesota, where he again served in the Senate, from 1858 to 1860. He then moved to California.

At the start of the Civil War, Shields was appointed brigadier general of volunteers and took part in the Shenandoah Valley campaign. Again wounded in battle, he inflicted an unprecedented defeat on Confederate General Thomas "Stonewall" Jackson at Kernstown in March 1862, but was then beaten badly at Stonewall's hands at Port Republic in May 1862. He resigned his commission in March 1863 and returned to California. He then moved to Missouri, where he again practiced law and was elected to the state legislature in 1874, and once more served in the United States Senate. He died while giving a lecture tour at Ottumwa, Iowa, and was buried at Carrolltown, Missouri. Archbishop John Joseph Glennon unveiled a statue in his honor in 1910 at St. Mary's Cemetery at Carrollton.

Shields, Thomas (May 9, 1862–February 5, 1921)

A priest, psychologist, and professor at The Catholic University of America, Thomas Shields was born in Mendota, Minnesota, to an immigrant family from Ireland. He studied for the priesthood at St. Francis Seminary in Milwaukee, and St. Thomas Seminary in St. Paul, Minnesota. During his studies, he published his first book, *Index Omnium*, in 1888. Ordained on March 4, 1891, he embarked on doctoral studies at Johns Hopkins University in Baltimore and completed his dissertation in 1895. He subsequently took up a teaching post in psychology at Catholic University in 1902.

Father Shields was a key figure in the development of Catholic University's program in education. He helped establish the Department of Education in 1909 and was its first chair. He also concentrated on providing education to women religious who were to serve in the growing parochial school system in the United States. In 1911 he started a Summer Institute for Catholic Sisters at Catholic University.

A supporter of the use of modern science, psychology, and philosophy in Catholic education, Shields wrote *The Philosophy of Education* in 1917, which expressed his wide-ranging outlook on the subject. He was ahead of his time in the promotion of educational opportunities for women and encountered opposition to his ideas in various quarters.

Shreveport in Louisiana, Diocese of

Established on June 16, 1986, by Pope Blessed John Paul II, the Diocese of Shreveport serves counties in northwestern Louisiana. It is a suffragan see of the Archdiocese of New Orleans. The city of Shreveport was founded in 1836 by the Shreve Town Company along the Red River and to provide access for commercial interests on the Texas Trail that led to the recently founded Republic of Texas. The city was named in honor of Captain Henry Miller Shreve of the United States Army Corps of Engineers, who oversaw making the river navigable. The city of Shreveport was incorporated on March 20, 1839, and rapidly developed as a commercial center, especially for steamboats. Shreveport was the capital of Louisiana during the latter part of the Civil War, after the fall of Baton Rouge to the Union forces. The region was the last to surrender in the war owing to its isolated position. The place of the city as a commercial center remained, and Shreveport is the third largest city in Louisiana.

The history of the Catholic community in Shreveport is tied closely to the development of the Diocese of Natchitoches, which was created by Pope Blessed Pius IX on July 29, 1853. Later, the city came under the ecclesial jurisdiction of the Diocese of Alexandria, which was created on August 6, 1910. The diocese was designated as the Diocese of Alexandria-Shreveport in 1977 and redesignated as the Diocese of Alexandria in 1986, when Shreveport was made a diocese.

The more distant history of the diocese can be traced to the expedition of Hernando de Soto in 1541 and then the French expedition of René-Robert Chevalier, Sieur de La Salle, in 1682. The Franciscan Recollect Father Zenobius Membré, later martyred, started missionary work in the area, and in 1699 Pierre Le Moyne, Sieur d'Iberville, and Jean-Baptiste Le Moyne, Sieur de Bienville, opened French settlements in the region.

French priests from the Québec Seminary of the Foreign Missions entered the region also. Father François Jolliet de Montigny, founded a chapel as he labored in the area and visited the Native Americans. The missionary priest Father Jean-François Buisson de Saint-Cosmé served in the region and was killed in 1706 by hostile Native Americans in the area.

The Venerable Antonio Margil de Jesús, a Spanish Franciscan pioneer in Louisiana and Texas, served in Sabine Parish in 1717 and founded San Miguel de Aguayo Mission, the first such site in northern Louisiana. Another chapel was erected at Presidio Nuestra Senora del Pilar on the site of modern Rabeline. Venerable Antonio also founded St. Jean Baptiste in Natchitoches in 1714.

The Jesuits who had served faithfully in the Louisiana missions were expelled in 1763. The next year, the Capuchin Franciscan Father Stanislaus established the chapel of St. Louis de Appalaches in Pineville, Louisiana. New Orleans, meanwhile, was established as a diocese in 1793, followed by the opening of Our Lady of Mount Carmel in Avoyelles. In 1800 Father Luis de Quintanilla, another Spanish Capuchin Franciscan, founded a chapel in Miro (Monroe).

The First Council of Baltimore, meeting in 1852, took note of the growing numbers of devout Catholics in Louisiana and recommended that another diocese be established in the area. Pope Blessed Pius IX thus erected the Diocese of Natchitoches, naming Augustus M. Martin as the first bishop. When he arrived in the new diocese he found that he had jurisdiction over three-fifths of the state with only five priests, six parish churches, one school, and twenty thousand Catholics. Bishop Martin recruited priests and invited religious into the diocese and led the faithful during the terrible period of the Civil War and in the outbreaks of yellow fever. One such epidemic claimed five of his priests in 1873. He also attended the First Vatican Council with Archbishop John M. Odin. Bishop Martin died on September 29, 1875.

Bishop Cornelius Van de Ven, who was consecrated for Natchitoches on November 30, 1904, requested that Pope St. Pius X transfer the see to Alexandria.

On January 12, 1977, the title of the see was changed to the Diocese of Alexandria-Shreveport, and St. John Berchmans became the co-cathedral. Bishop William B. Friend was installed as bishop on January 11, 1983. In 1986 Pope Blessed John Paul II established the Diocese of Shreveport from portions of the Diocese of Alexandria-Shreveport, and Bishop Friend became the bishop of this new diocese. He was installed on July 30, 1986, and founded the needed diocesan offices and provided a long and stable direction for the new diocese. He retired on December 20, 2006.

On April 1, 2008, Michael Duca, a priest of the Diocese of Dallas, was appointed the second bishop of Shreveport. Consecrated a bishop on May 19, 2008, he celebrated the 25th anniversary of the diocese on June 11, 2011. In 2011 there were some 41,000 Catholics, served by 50 priests and 27 parishes in the diocese.

Shrines

There are literally hundreds of shrines across the United States. Listed below, according to state, are shrines, other centers of devotion, and some places of historical interest with special significance for Catholics. The list is as of 2012.

Alabama

- Our Lady of the Angels, Hanceville; Birmingham diocese.
- St. Jude Church of the City of St. Jude, Montgomery (1934; dedicated, 1938); Mobile archdiocese.
- Shrine of the Most Blessed Trinity, Holy Trinity (1924); Missionary Servants of the Most Blessed Trinity.

Arizona

- Chapel of the Holy Cross, Sedona (1956); Phoenix diocese.
- Mission San Xavier del Bac, near Tucson (1692); national historic landmark; Franciscan Friars and Tucson Diocese.
- Shrine of St. Joseph of the Mountains, Yarnell (1939); erected by Catholic Action League, currently maintained by the board of directors.

California

- Mission San Diego de Alcala (July 16, 1769); first of the twenty-one Franciscan missions of Upper California; minor basilica; national historic landmark; San Diego diocese.
- Carmel Mission Basilica (Mission San Carlos Borromeo del Rio Carmelo), Carmel by the Sea (June 3, 1770); Monterey diocese.
- Old Mission San Luis Obispo de Tolosa, San Luis Obispo (September 1, 1772); Monterey diocese; parish church.
- San Gabriel Mission, San Gabriel (September 8, 1771); Los Angeles archdiocese; parish church, staffed by Claretians.
- Mission San Francisco de Asis (October 9, 1776) and Mission Dolores Basilica (1860s); San Francisco archdiocese.
- Old Mission San Juan Capistrano, San Juan Capistrano (November 1, 1776); Orange diocese.
- Old Mission Santa Barbara, Santa Barbara (December 4, 1786); national historic landmark; parish church, staffed by Franciscan Friars.
- Old Mission San Juan Bautista, San Juan Bau-

tista (June 24, 1797); national historic landmark; Monterey diocese; parish church.
- Mission San Miguel, San Miguel (July 25, 1797); Monterey diocese; Franciscan Friars; parish church.
- Old Mission Santa Inés, Solvang (1804); national historic landmark; Los Angeles archdiocese; parish church, staffed by Capuchin Franciscan Friars.
- Shrine of Our Lady of Sorrows, Sycamore (1883); Sacramento diocese.

Colorado

- Mother Cabrini Shrine, Golden; Missionary Sisters of the Sacred Heart.

Connecticut

- Shrine of Our Lady of Lourdes, Litchfield (1958); Montfort Missionaries.
- Shrine of the Infant of Prague, New Haven (1945); Dominican Friars.

District of Columbia

- Mount St. Sepulchre, Franciscan Monastery of the Holy Land (1897; church dedicated, 1899); Order of Friars Minor.
- Basilica of the National Shrine of the Immaculate Conception. The basilica is dedicated to the honor of the Blessed Virgin Mary, declared Patroness of the United States under this title in 1846, eight years before the proclamation of the dogma of the Immaculate Conception. The church was designated a minor basilica by Pope Blessed John Paul II on October 12, 1990. The church is the eighth-largest religious building in the world and the largest Catholic church in the Western Hemisphere, with numerous special chapels and with normal seating and standing accommodations for six thousand people.

Florida

- Mary, Queen of the Universe Shrine, Orlando (1986, temporary facilities; new shrine dedicated, 1993); Orlando diocese.
- Our Lady of La Leche Shrine (Patroness of Mothers and Mothers-to-be) and Mission of Nombre de Dios, St. Augustine (1565); Angelus Crusade Headquarters; St. Augustine diocese.

Illinois

- Holy Family Log Church, Cahokia (1799; original log church erected 1699); Belleville diocese; parish church.
- Marytown/Shrine of St. Maximilian Kolbe and Retreat Center, Libertyville; Our Lady of the Blessed Sacrament Sanctuary of Perpetual Eucharistic Adoration (1930); and Archdiocesan Shrine to St. Maximilian Kolbe (1989); conducted by Conventual Franciscan Friars.
- National Shrine of Our Lady of the Snows, Belleville (1958); Missionary Oblates of Mary Immaculate.
- National Shrine of St. Jude, Chicago (1929), located in Our Lady of Guadalupe Church; founded and staffed by Claretians.
- National Shrine of St. Therese and Museum, Darien (1930), at St. Clara's Church, Chicago; new shrine, 1987, after original was destroyed by fire; Carmelites of the Most Pure Heart of Mary Province.
- Shrine of St. Jude Thaddeus, Chicago (1929), located in St. Pius V Church; staffed by Dominicans, Central Province.

Indiana

- Our Lady of Monte Cassino Shrine, St. Meinrad (1870); Benedictines.
- Old Cathedral (Basilica of St. Francis Xavier), Vincennes (1826, parish records go back to 1749); Evansville diocese; minor basilica, 1970.

Iowa

- Grotto of the Redemption, West Bend (1912); Sioux City diocese; life of Christ in stone.

Louisiana

- National Votive Shrine of Our Lady of Prompt Succor, New Orleans (1810), located in the Chapel of the Ursuline Convent; national historic landmark.
- Shrine of St. Ann, Metairie.
- Shrine of St. Roch, New Orleans (1876), located in St. Roch's Campo Santo (Cemetery); New Orleans archdiocese.

Maryland

- Basilica of the National Shrine of the Assumption of the Blessed Virgin Mary, Baltimore (1806). Mother Church of Roman Catholicism in the United States and the first metropolitan cathedral. Designed by Benjamin Henry Latrobe (architect of the Capitol), it is considered one of the finest examples of neoclassical architecture in the world.
- National Shrine Grotto of Our Lady of Lourdes, Emmitsburg (1809, Grotto of Our Lady; 1875, National Shrine Grotto of Lourdes); public oratory, Archdiocese of Baltimore.
- National Shrine of St. Elizabeth Ann Seton, Emmitsburg; foundation of Sisters of Charity (1809); first parochial school in America (1810); dedicated as minor basilica (1991).
- St. Francis Xavier Shrine, "Old Bohemia," near Warwick (1704); Wilmington diocese; restoration under auspices of Old Bohemia Historical Society, Inc.
- St. Jude Shrine (1873), Archdiocese of Baltimore.

Massachusetts

- National Shrine of Our Lady of La Salette, Ipswich (1945); Missionaries of Our Lady of La Salette.
- Our Lady of Fátima Shrine, Holliston (1950); Xaverian Missionaries.
- St. Anthony Shrine, Boston (1947); downtown service church with shrine; Boston archdiocese and Franciscans of Holy Name Province.
- St. Clement's Eucharistic Shrine, Boston (1945); Boston archdiocese; staffed by Oblates of the Virgin Mary.
- National Shrine of the Divine Mercy, Stockbridge (1960); Congregation of Marians.

Michigan

- Cross in the Woods Parish, Indian River (1947); Gaylord diocese; staffed by Franciscan Friars of Sacred Heart Province, St. Louis.
- Shrine of the Little Flower, Royal Oak (c. 1929, by Father Charles Coughlin); Detroit archdiocese.

Minnesota

- National Shrine of St. Odilia; St. Cloud diocese.

Missouri

- Memorial Shrine of St. Rose Philippine

Duchesne, St. Charles; Religious of the Sacred Heart of Jesus.

- National Shrine of Our Lady of the Miraculous Medal, Perryville; located in St. Mary of the Barrens Church (1837); Vincentians.
- Old St. Ferdinand's Shrine, Florissant (1819, Sacred Heart Convent; 1821, St. Ferdinand's Church); Friends of Old St. Ferdinand's, Inc.
- Shrine of Our Lady of Sorrows, Starkenburg (1888; shrine building, 1910); Jefferson City diocese.

Nebraska

- The Eucharistic Shrine of Christ the King (1973); Lincoln diocese and Holy Spirit Adoration Sisters.

New Hampshire

- Shrine of Our Lady of Grace, Colebrook (1948); Missionary Oblates of Mary Immaculate.
- Shrine of Our Lady of La Salette, Enfield (1951); Missionaries of Our Lady of La Salette.

New Jersey

- Blue Army Shrine of the Immaculate Heart of Mary (1978); National Center of the Blue Army of Our Lady of Fátima, USA, Inc.
- Shrine of St. Joseph, Stirling (1924); Missionary Servants of the Most Holy Trinity.

New Mexico

- St. Augustine Mission, Isleta (1613); Santa Fe archdiocese.
- Santuario de Nuestro Senor de Esquipulas, Chimayo (1816); Santa Fe archdiocese; Sons of the Holy Family; national historic landmark, 1970.
- Shrine of St. Bernadette (2003); Santa Fe archdiocese, St. Bernadette Parish.

New York

- National Shrine of Blessed Kateri Tekakwitha, Fonda (1938); Order of Friars Minor Conventual.
- Marian Shrine (National Shrine of Mary Help of Christians), West Haverstraw (1953); Salesians of St. John Bosco.
- National Shrine Basilica of Our Lady of Fátima, Youngstown (1954); national shrine (1994); Barnabite Fathers.
- Original Shrine of St. Ann in New York City (1892), located in St. Jean Baptiste Church; Blessed Sacrament Fathers.
- Our Lady of Victory National Shrine, Lackawanna (1926); minor basilica.
- Shrine Church of Our Lady of Mount Carmel, Brooklyn (1887); Brooklyn diocese; parish church.
- Shrine of Our Lady of Martyrs, Auriesville (1885); Society of Jesus.
- Shrine of Our Lady of the Island, Eastport (1975); Montfort Missionaries.
- Shrine of St. Elizabeth Ann Seton, New York City (1975), located in Our Lady of the Rosary Church.
- Shrine of St. Frances Xavier Cabrini, New York (1938; new shrine dedicated 1960); Missionary Sisters of the Sacred Heart.

Ohio

- Basilica and National Shrine of Our Lady of Consolation, Carey (1867); minor basilica; Toledo diocese; staffed by Conventual Franciscan Friars.
- National Shrine of Our Lady of Lebanon, North Jackson (1965); Eparchy of Our Lady of Lebanon of Los Angeles.
- National Shrine and Grotto of Our Lady of Lourdes, Euclid (1926); Sisters of the Most Holy Trinity.
- National Shrine of St. Dymphna, Massillon (1938), Youngstown diocese.
- Our Lady of Czestochowa Shrine, Garfield Heights (1939); Sisters of St. Joseph, Third Order of St. Francis.
- Our Lady of Fátima, Ironton (1954).
- St. Anthony Shrine, Cincinnati (1888); Franciscan Friars, St. John Baptist Province.
- Shrine and Oratory of the Weeping Madonna of Mariapoch, Burton (1956); Social Mission Sisters; Parma diocese (Byzantine).
- Shrine of the Holy Relics (1892); Sisters of the Precious Blood.
- Sorrowful Mother Shrine, Bellevue (1850); Society of the Precious Blood.

Oklahoma

- National Shrine of the Infant Jesus of Prague, Prague (1949); Oklahoma City archdiocese.

Oregon

- The Grotto (National Sanctuary of Our Sorrowful Mother), Portland (1924); Servite Friars.

Pennsylvania

- Basilica of the Sacred Heart of Jesus, Conewago Township (1741; present church, 1787); minor basilica; Harrisburg diocese.
- National Shrine Center of Our Lady of Guadalupe, Allentown (1974); located in Immaculate Conception Church; Allentown diocese.
- National Shrine of Our Lady of Czestochowa (1955); Order of St. Paul the Hermit (Pauline Fathers).
- National Shrine of St. John Neumann, Philadelphia (1860); Redemptorist Fathers; St. Peter's Church.
- National Shrine of the Sacred Heart, Harleigh (1975); Scranton diocese.
- Old St. Joseph's National Shrine, Philadelphia (1733); Philadelphia archdiocese; parish church.
- St. Ann's Basilica Shrine, Scranton (1902); Passionist Community; designated a minor basilica (August 29, 1996).
- Shrine of St. Walburga, Greensburg (1974); Sisters of St. Benedict.

South Dakota

- Fátima Family Shrine, Alexandria; St. Cloud diocese.

Texas

- Mission Espiritu Santo de Zuniga, Goliad (1749); Victoria diocese.
- Mission Nuestra Senora de la Purisma Concepcion, San Antonio; San Antonio archdiocese.
- Mission San Francisco de la Espada, San Antonio (1731); San Antonio archdiocese.
- Mission San Jose y San Miguel de Aguayo, San Antonio (1720); San Antonio archdiocese.
- Mission San Juan Capistrano, San Antonio (1731); San Antonio archdiocese.
- National Shrine of Our Lady of San Juan del Valle, San Juan (1949); Brownsville diocese; staffed by Oblates of Mary Immaculate.
- Nuestra Senora de la Concepcion del Socorro, Socorro, El Paso (1692).

- Oblate Lourdes Grotto Shrine of the Southwest, Tepeyac de San Antonio; San Antonio archdiocese.
- Old Mission San Francisco de los Tejas, Weches (1690); San Antonio archdiocese.
- Presidio La Bahia, Goliad (1749); Victoria diocese.
- San Elizario Presidio Chapel, El Paso (1789); El Paso diocese.

Vermont

- St. Anne's Shrine, Isle La Motte (1666); Burlington diocese; conducted by Edmundites.

Wisconsin

- Holy Hill — National Shrine of Mary, Help of Christians (1857); Discalced Carmelite Friars.
- National Shrine of St. Joseph, De Pere (1889); Norbertine Fathers.
- Shrine of Mary, Mother Thrice Admirable Queen and Victress of Schoenstatt (1965).

Shriver, Eunice Kennedy (July 10, 1921–August 11, 2009)

The founder of the Special Olympics, a member of the Kennedy family, and one of America's most dedicated voices for the culture of life, Eunice Kennedy Shriver was born in Brookline, Massachusetts. She was the daughter of Joseph Kennedy, and the sister of President John F. Kennedy and Senators Robert and Edward "Ted" Kennedy. In 1953 she married R. Sargent Shriver, and in 1968 she organized the first Special Olympics and was dedicated to helping the developmentally disabled.

Eunice Shriver was also dedicated to the pro-life cause, and her efforts earned her numerous awards, including the James Cardinal Gibbons Award from The Catholic University of America, the James Keller Award from the Christophers, the Presidential Medal of Freedom from President Ronald Reagan, and the title of Dame of the Papal Order of St. Gregory the Great by Pope Benedict XVI.

Shuster, George (August 27, 1894–January 25, 1977)

Author, editor, educator, and president of Hunter College from 1940 to 1969, George Shuster is considered one of the foremost Catholic educators of the twentieth century. He was born in Lancaster, Wisconsin, to Anton and Elizabeth Schuster (he later changed the spelling of his name). His family spoke German in the home, and he studied at the University of Notre Dame from which he graduated in 1915.

Enlisting for service in World War I, Shuster was posted as a sergeant in army intelligence and had the task for a time of translating German intercepts. After the war he remained in France and earned a certificate in French culture from the University of Poitiers. He then returned to the United States and earned a master's degree in English from Notre Dame. He then taught there and was head of the English department from 1920 to 1924.

In 1924 Shuster married Doris Parks Cunningham and moved to New York, where he started a doctoral program at Columbia University. He also taught at Brooklyn Polytechnic Institute and St. Joseph's College for Women from 1924 to 1934 and took a position with the recently founded magazine *Commonweal*. He served as managing editor for eight years and resigned in 1937 over the periodical's support of General Francisco Franco.

In 1940 Shuster began a twenty-year legacy as president of Hunter College. He then went back to Notre Dame to serve as assistant to the president from 1961 to 1971 and then also professor emeritus of English. During these years he was a United States delegate to the United Nations Conference on International Education in 1945 and played a part in the establishment of UNESCO.

Shuster was the author of a large body of writings that covered a wide number of issues and concerns. His books include *Catholic Spirit in Modern English Literature* (1922); *English Literature: A Textbook* (1926); *Catholic Church in America* (1927); *Catholic Church in Current Literature* (1930); *The World's Great Catholic Literature* (editor, 1942); several books on Nazi Germany, including *Germans: An Inquiry and an Estimate* (1932), *Strong Man Rules* (1934), *Like a Mighty Army: Hitler versus Established Religion* (1935), and *Germany: A Short History* (1944), with Arnold Bergstraesser; *Religion Behind the Iron Curtain* (1954); *In Silence I Speak* (1956), an account with Tibor Horanyi of the sufferings of Cardinal Joseph Mindszenty; *Education and Moral Wisdom* (1960); *The Ground I Walked On; Reflec-*tions of a College President (1961); and the controversial *Catholic Education in a Changing World* (1967).

Siegman, Edward (June 4, 1908–February 2, 1967)

A priest of the Missionaries of the Precious Blood and biblical scholar who taught at The Catholic University of America and the University of Notre Dame, Edward Siegman was born in Cleveland and entered the Missionaries of the Precious Blood in 1922. He received ordination to the priesthood in 1934 and went on to study at The Catholic University of America in Washington, where he earned a doctorate in sacred theology in Scripture and Semitic languages in 1937. From 1937 to 1951, he taught Scripture at the Precious Blood Seminary in Carthagena, Ohio, and was then invited back to Catholic University as an assistant professor. He was named associate professor in 1954 and then went to Rome for additional biblical studies at the Pontifical Biblical Institute. He earned a licentiate in Sacred Scripture in 1959.

Father Siegman was a leading contributor to the *Catholic Biblical Quarterly* and was a charter member of the Catholic Biblical Association. He became editor of the *Catholic Biblical Quarterly* in 1951 and served until 1958, when he went to Rome. Aside from serving as editor, he contributed a variety of articles and was considered one of the leading voices in the new approaches to biblical scholarship during the pre-conciliar period. He was opposed vigorously by other scholars, and in 1962, following a heart attack, his contract was not renewed by the university.

Father Siegman left Washington and took up a post at Yale University in 1963, where he engaged in campus ministry. He then taught at the congregation's seminary in Ohio until 1966, when he received a post at the University of Notre Dame. He died unexpectedly of a heart attack. Prior to his death, he had been elected president of the Catholic Biblical Association. He was also the New Testament editor for the *New Catholic Encyclopedia* and assisted with the translations of the Old Testament for the *New American Bible*.

Sieni, Cyril (d. after 1799)

A missionary bishop also known as Cyril of Barcelona, he was born in Catalonia, Spain. Little is known about his early life save that he joined the Capuchin Franciscans and was sent to New Orleans in 1772 to serve as vicar general by the bishop of Santiago, José de Echeverria. Father Sieni discovered the region of Louisiana to be deeply troubled by corruption among both government officials and the local religious. To assist his process of needed reform, Father Sieni was appointed titular bishop of Tricali and auxiliary of Santiago (under whose jurisdiction the Louisiana Territory was then placed).

Bishop Sieni was granted authority over a vast territory that extended across what is modern-day Louisiana, Alabama, Florida, and parts of the Mississippi River to Missouri. He was responsible for improving the pastoral care of Catholics in the region. He sent priests to care for the Catholics in Pensacola and St. Augustine in Florida, and in 1786 he issued a pastoral letter concerning the proper observance of Sunday.

Despite these efforts, Bishop Sieni encountered deeply entrenched local problems. He tried to rebuild the church of New Orleans after a fire in 1788, but he also faced resistance to his program of reform and made little progress. On the one hand he failed to restore ecclesiastical discipline and on the other found himself beset by the displeasure of King Charles III of Spain. Hence, in 1793, he was removed and sent back to Spain.

Sign, The

A national Catholic monthly magazine published from 1921 to 1982 by the Passionists, *The Sign* was a dedicated voice in the United States against anti-Catholicism throughout the twentieth century. The publication was founded to serve as a means of educating Catholics in the area of apologetics and to answer the many errors that were then being perpetuated in the press and popular imagination. The first editor was Father Harold Purcell, who served until 1934.

The Sign started with a small subscription base and grew rapidly into one of the most popular Catholic publications in the United States. Its content, although oriented toward apologetics, was noted for its diversity, encompassing all aspects of American Catholic culture. One of the most eagerly read sections of the magazine was "With the Passionists in China," a chronicle of the missionary labors of the Passionists in Hunan from the 1920s until the grim period of the 1950s and the communist oppression of the Church in China. The magazine also boasted such eminent contributors as Archbishop Fulton J. Sheen, G. K. Chesterton, Daniel A. Lord, Hilaire Belloc, and Dorothy Day. The magazine also included a long-running sports column.

The Sign was noted for its patriotic tendencies during World War II and its staunch anti-communist stand in the early years of the Cold War. Its editorial position was very supportive of the Second Vatican Council. The magazine ceased publication in 1982 owing to financial demands and changes in the ministerial priorities of the Passionists.

Sioux City, Diocese of

Established on January 15, 1902, by Pope Leo XIII, the Diocese of Sioux City serves counties in northwestern Iowa. The diocese is a suffragan see of the Archdiocese of Dubuque.

The Lewis and Clark expedition visited the area in 1804. A member of the expedition, Sergeant Charles Floyd, died of acute appendicitis on August 20, 1804, and was buried at what became known as Floyd's Bluff in modern-day Sioux City. From there, the expedition pushed on to the Great Plains.

The city was founded in 1849 as Thompsonville and then renamed for the Sioux Indian nation. The first settlements in the region attracted Germans and Irish farmers. Located on the Missouri River, the site benefited from steamboat trade and was then part of the expansion brought about by the railroads. As more and more families moved to Sioux City, Catholic enclaves were opened and parishes established. Early on, Sioux City emerged as a major population center and then as a commercial hub.

The Diocese of Sioux City was established out of twenty-four counties that had been part of the Archdiocese of Dubuque. At its foundation, the new diocese had a Catholic population of fifty thousand, with ninety-five priests, eighty-four parishes, and thirty-two missions. The first bishop of Sioux City, Philip J. Garrigan, had served as vice rector of The Catholic University of America in Washington, D.C. He was consecrated a bishop on May 25, 1902, and was installed on June 18, 1902. St. Mary's Church in Sioux City was designated the new cathedral of the diocese and was renamed Cathedral of the Epiphany. Bishop Garrigan proved an active founding bishop, establishing diocesan offices and also visiting all the parishes of the new diocese. He died on October 14, 1919, at the age of seventy-nine.

Bishop Garrigan was succeeded upon his passing by his auxiliary bishop since 1918, Edmond Heelan. He arrived at the end of World War I and served as shepherd throughout the years of the Great Depression and the collapse of the farm economy. This was a very difficult time for Iowans. Bishop Heelan was a steady and caring bishop who convened three diocesan synods to provide for the spiritual needs of the Catholics in the area. He also provided leadership throughout World War II. He died on September 20, 1948.

The third bishop of Sioux City, Joseph M. Mueller, had been coadjutor bishop since 1947. He acceded to the see upon Bishop Heelan's death. His long time as bishop encompassed the postwar boom and the era of the Second Vatican Council. He established new parishes and schools and worked to provide a long-term structure for Catholic education in the diocese. He retired on December 8, 1970.

The fourth bishop of Sioux City, Frank H. Greteman, had served since 1965 as an auxiliary bishop of the diocese. The first native Iowan to become bishop, he was appointed on October 15, 1970, and took as his primary task implementation of the reforms of the Second Vatican Council. He also continued the work of his predecessor in consolidating and maintaining diocesan Catholic schools. He retired on January 25, 1983.

The fifth bishop of Sioux City, Lawrence D. Soens, had been pastor of St. Mary's Church in Clinton, Iowa. Consecrated a bishop on August 17, 1983, he provided for a priests' retirement fund and promoted youth ministry. He retired on November 28, 1998.

The sixth bishop of Sioux City, Daniel N. DiNardo, had been coadjutor bishop of Sioux City since 1997. He acceded to the see on the same day that Bishop Soens retired. On January 16, 2004, Bishop DiNardo was named coadjutor bishop of

the Diocese of Galveston-Houston. He became archbishop of Galveston-Houston in 2006 and was appointed a cardinal the next year.

On November 10, 2005, Walker Nickless, a priest of the Archdiocese of Denver, was named the seventh bishop of Sioux City. He was consecrated as bishop on January 20, 2006. In 2011 there were some 98,000 Catholics, served by 138 priests and 113 parishes in the diocese.

Sioux Falls, Diocese of

Established on November 12, 1889, by Pope Leo XIII, the Diocese of Sioux Falls serves counties in South Dakota east of the Missouri River. Located beside a confluence of rivers, the site attracted settlers because of the waterways and was named after the Sioux nation. The diocese was established as a suffragan of the Archdiocese of St. Paul; today, it is a suffragan of the Archdiocese of St. Paul and Minneapolis.

The European farmers who entered the region in the 1850s were forced to withdraw from their proposed settlements when the Sioux understandably refused to surrender ground they considered sacred. In 1861, however, Congress established the Dakota Territory, which served as an invitation to settlers across the nation to enter the region and to possess the land. Fort Dakota was founded in 1865, providing federal troops as protection for families entering the territory. With water power and fertile lands available, Sioux Falls emerged as a center for the distribution of agricultural and other products.

The Catholic heritage of the diocese can be traced to the travels of Father George Belcourt and Monsignor Augustin Ravoux. The first parish church in the region dates to 1867 and was established by Father Pierre Boucher in Jefferson. On August 12, 1879, the Vicariate of Dakota was established by Pope Leo XIII.

A Benedictine from St. Meinrad, Indiana, the legendary pioneering priest Father Martin Marty, was consecrated a bishop and took up his vicariate duties at Yankton. Bishop Marty moved to Sioux Falls to continue his labors and was named the first bishop of Sioux Falls on November 12, 1889. He was transferred to the Diocese of St. Cloud in 1894 and died two years later.

Bishop Marty was succeeded in Sioux Falls on

January 24, 1896, by Thomas O'Gorman, who had served as a brilliant scholar of Church history at The Catholic University of America. He was also the author of *A History of the Roman Catholic Church in the United States*. Consecrated on April 19, 1896, he was installed in Sioux Falls on May 1, 1896. He worked to continue the expansion of diocesan ministries, built schools and parishes, dedicated St. Joseph's Cathedral in 1919, and started Columbus College in 1921. He died on September 18, 1921.

The third bishop of Sioux Falls, Bernard J. Mahoney, had served as spiritual director of the North American College in Rome and was named to Sioux Falls on May 24, 1922. Consecrated a bishop on June 29, 1922, he served as shepherd throughout the Great Depression and died on March 20, 1939, as the world moved toward a new war.

The fourth bishop of Sioux Falls, William O. Brady, was appointed on June 10, 1939, and consecrated a bishop on August 24, 1939. He served throughout the Second World War and the post-war period of rapid growth. On June 21, 1956, he was appointed coadjutor archbishop of the Diocese of St. Paul and Minneapolis.

The fifth bishop of Sioux Falls, Lambert A. Hoch, had been bishop of Bismarck since 1952. Appointed to Sioux Falls on November 2, 1956, he was the first priest of South Dakota to become a bishop. His time as bishop included attendance at all four sessions of the Second Vatican Council and efforts to implement the reforms of the council. He retired on June 13, 1978.

The sixth bishop of Sioux Falls, Paul V. Dudley, had been an auxiliary bishop of St. Paul and Minneapolis since 1976. He was named bishop of Sioux Falls on September 26, 1978; his was the first U.S. episcopal appointment made by the recently elected Pope Blessed John Paul II. He worked to continue the implementation of the council, promoted ecumenical dialogue, and was especially active in promoting the pro-life cause. An immensely popular bishop, he retired on March 21, 1995.

The seventh bishop of Sioux Falls, Robert J. Carlson, had been an auxiliary bishop of St. Paul and Minneapolis since 1983 and was named coadjutor bishop of Sioux Falls on January 13, 1994. He acceded to the see on March 21, 1995. He was transferred to the Diocese of Saginaw on Febru-

ary 24, 2005, and was appointed archbishop of St. Louis on April 21, 2009.

The eighth bishop of Sioux Falls, Paul J. Swain, was serving in the Diocese of Madison at the time of his appointment as bishop of Sioux Falls on August 30, 2006. He was consecrated a bishop on October 26, 2006. In 2011 there were more than 123,000 Catholics in the diocese, served by 153 priests, 260 men and women religious, and 150 parishes.

Sisters of the Blessed Sacrament (S.B.S.)

A congregation of women religious founded on February 12, 1891, in Torresdale, Pennsylvania, by St. Katharine Drexel, the Sisters of the Blessed Sacrament were established specifically to provide pastoral care for Native Americans and African-Americans. St. Katharine Drexel was the first member to pronounce her vows as a member, and she went on to establish schools around the country for Native Americans and African-Americans, including Xavier University, until her death in 1955. In all, she opened and sustained nearly sixty-five schools and missions. (*See also* Drexel, St. Katharine Marie.) Today, the sisters continue to serve in a variety of ministries, including religious education programs, schools, and social service centers in fourteen states, as well as Haiti and Guatemala. The Sisters of the Blessed Sacrament continue in the footsteps of their foundress.

Sisters of Charity of Our Lady of Mercy (O.L.M.)

A community of women religious founded in 1829 by Bishop John England in Charleston, South Carolina, the origins of the Sisters of Charity of Our Lady of Mercy are traced to Baltimore, where Bishop England was attending the First Provincial Council. There he met a group of young women who expressed an interest in entering the religious life through his assistance. Three of the first four members were from Ireland and a fourth, Mary Elizabeth Burke, was American-born.

The new community was based in part on the structure of the Sisters of Charity, which had been founded by St. Elizabeth Ann Seton, and Bishop England gave the sisters simple vows based on the Rule of St. Vincent de Paul. He also hoped to write a constitution for the sisters, but its completion was left instead to his successor, Bishop Ignatius

A. Reynolds, the second bishop of Charleston. By the time of Bishop England's death, however, there were nineteen members running an orphanage, schools, and an academy.

During the Civil War, the Sisters of Charity served as nurses to both the Confederate and Union armies. Such was their level of service and distinction that a memorial was placed in Washington, D.C., in their honor. In the years after the war, the Sisters became involved in hospital work with the start of St. Francis Xavier Hospital in Charleston in 1882 and a subsequent school for nursing. Members of the community labored in the Dioceses of Trenton and Camden during the 1940s and 1950s. Today, they are engaged in education, campus ministry, and social services.

Sisters of Charity of the Blessed Virgin Mary (B.V.M.)

A congregation of women religious, the Sisters of Charity of the Blessed Virgin Mary were established in 1833 in Philadelphia by Mary Frances Clarke, with the assistance of Reverend Terence James Donaghoe. Mary Frances Clarke arrived in the United States from Dublin in 1833 with four companions in the hope of teaching children of immigrants. Within the year, and with the help of Father Donaghoe, the small group was formed into a new religious community. They made their act of consecration on November 1, 1833.

Ten years later, the growing community of nineteen sisters migrated to Dubuque, Iowa, at the invitation of Bishop Mathias Loras. The BVMs, as they are known, embarked on the education of children, including Native Americans, the children of pioneers and miners, and especially young girls. They established St. Mary's Academy, a log-cabin school, close to the cathedral, and soon staffed elementary and high schools along the Upper Mississippi Valley and farther west. In 1867 they launched a new educational ministry in Chicago and from there went on to start communities across the United States as far as Hawaii. Formal approval of the rule was confirmed by Pope Leo XIII in 1885, and by the early twentieth century there were over one thousand members tasked with educating some twenty-five thousand children. Since the 1960s, the order has been serving also in South America.

Sisters of the Good Shepherd (R.G.S.)

A congregation of women religious founded in 1829, in Angers, France, by St. Mary Euphrasia Pelletier, who was canonized in 1940 by Pope Pius XII, the Sisters of the Good Shepherd were established in the United States in 1843. St. Mary was originally a member of the congregation of Our Lady of Charity of the Refuge, founded in 1641 by St. John Eudes. Convinced that the congregation should care for those suffering in society, St. Mary began her own community. It took as its inspiration the idea that God is like a compassionate shepherd of boundless love, and the congregation functioned from the recognition of the unique value of each person living in the world. Initially a diocesan community, St. Mary secured formal approval in 1835 from Pope Gregory XVI.

The Sisters of the Good Shepherd first arrived in the United States in 1842 in Louisville, Kentucky, at the invitation of Bishop Benedict Joseph Flaget, who was concerned about the welfare of young women in the rough and often seedy environment of the ports in Louisville of the time. From this foundation, Good Shepherd Sisters soon went to St. Louis in 1849, Philadelphia in 1850, Baltimore in 1864, and St. Paul, Minnesota, in 1868. In 1852 Louisville also received a group of contemplative sisters, part of the contemplative community established in 1831 by St. Mary.

The expansion of the Good Shepherd Sisters in the United States matched the wider growth of the congregation. By the time of her passing, St. Mary had presided over the establishment of over one hundred houses. Today, the Sisters of the Good Shepherd are found in 71 countries on five continents; they number over 4,500 worldwide. In the United States, the Sisters serve in 23 states and in Canada and number over 600. They are assisted by the Associates of the Good Shepherd, the Companions of the Good Shepherd, and the Good Shepherd Volunteers, including both men and women laypeople.

Sisters of the Holy Cross (C.S.C.)

A congregation of women religious founded in Le Mans, France, in 1841 by Father Basil Moreau, C.S.C., under the title of Marianites of the Holy Cross, the Sisters of the Holy Cross apostolate was to support the ministry of the Holy Cross priests and brothers. They first came to the United States in 1843 to assist the Holy Cross community that had just established the University of Notre Dame in South Bend, Indiana.

Within a short time, the sisters were engaged in activities beyond their original purpose in South Bend, for they began to direct schools and orphanages and in 1844 opened an academy in Bertrand, Michigan, which became St. Mary's College in Notre Dame, Indiana.

A group of sisters established a province in Montréal in 1847, with their residence at St. Laurent, a suburb of Montréal. In 1859 the sisters began St. Patrick's School in Baltimore, followed by additional schools, including one in Salt Lake City in 1875. They went on to staff and operate Notre Dame College in Manchester, New Hampshire. There are approximately 780 members of the congregation in the United States.

Sisters of the Holy Family

A community of African-American women religious founded in 1842 by Mother Henriette DeLille, a free black woman, in New Orleans, the Sisters of the Holy Family was started to provide care and education for the children of slaves. DeLille and her friend Juliette Gaudin, the Cuban-born child of Haitian parents, felt called to give their lives to the education of these children, as well as caring for the sick, the poor, and the elderly. Owing to the social and legal issues surrounding the activities of blacks during this era, the Sisters of the Holy Family were not officially recognized until 1842. They were joined the next year by Josephine Charles, a free woman.

By 1847 the Society of the Holy Family was formed by a group of free men and free women to provide material and financial support. In 1852 Sisters Henriette, Juliette, and Josephine pronounced first vows in St. Augustine Church. The following year, the small community took care of the large number of orphans caused by the yellow fever epidemic of 1853. They provided similar heroic care again in 1897. In 1892 the St. John Berchmans' Orphanage was opened.

The congregation continued to develop in the first years of the new century, and in 1906 Mother Austin Jones purchased 123 acres of land in the Gentilly area. This provided the means to establish St. Mary's Academy, St. Paul the Apostle Church and School, the House of the Holy Family, the DeLille Inn, the Lafon Day Care Center, the Lafon Nursing Facility of the Holy Family, and the present motherhouse.

The Congregation of the Sisters of the Holy Family continues its original ministries of educating youth and caring for the aged, the poor, and the sick. They also operate the oldest continuously running Catholic home for the aged in the United States as well as a large number of schools in the United States, Nigeria, and Belize. In 1988 the cause for canonization of Henriette DeLille's was opened.

Sisters of the Holy Family of Nazareth (C.S.F.N.)

A pontifical congregation of women religious, the Sisters of the Holy Family of Nazareth was founded in Rome in 1875 by Blessed Mary of Jesus the Good Shepherd, Frances Siedliska. Blessed Frances and several companions arrived in Chicago in 1885 to provide pastoral care for the large numbers of immigrants who had settled in America. The sisters began by establishing an orphanage and a parochial school, and by the time of Blessed Frances's death in 1902 the congregation had launched twenty-nine foundations throughout Europe and the United States. The members of the congregation labored as teachers in colleges and universities, as well as in secondary and elementary schools and in social work.

The congregation has four provinces in the United States. Three were founded in 1918: Sacred Heart Province, based in Des Plaines, Illinois; Immaculate Conception Province, based in Philadelphia; and St. Joseph Province, based in Pittsburgh. The fourth province, the Blessed Frances Siedliska Province, headquartered in Grand Prairie, Texas, was begun in 1993.

The motherhouse is in Rome, and the congregation has houses across Europe and in Belarus, Lithuania, Russia, Ukraine, Israel, Australia, and the Philippines. Pope Blessed John Paul II beatified Blessed Frances Siedliska on April 23, 1989. On March 5, 2000, the pontiff also beatified eleven sisters of the congregation, the Martyrs of Nowogródek, who were executed by the Nazis in 1943.

Sisters of Loretto (S.L.)

The Sisters of Loretto at the Foot of the Cross is a congregation of women religious founded in 1812 by Father Charles Nerinckx in Kentucky under the name Friends of Mary and with the purpose of teaching the children of the frontier settlers. The founding member was Mary Rhodes, a young woman from Maryland who visited family in Kentucky and decided to give herself to the education of young children and their catechesis. Once word spread of her work with the local children, other parents asked her assistance, and she was soon joined by other young women. From this small beginning, the young women asked for the help of the pastor, Father Nerinckx, to establish themselves as a religious community. He gave them a simple rule and suggested that the log cabin that served as their headquarters should be called Little Loretto.

In 1823 the sisters established a house in Missouri, the first outside of Kentucky. The new establishment began the expansion of the congregation. In 1847 the sisters went to Kansas and started a school for Osage Indians, and five years later, at the invitation of Bishop Jean Baptiste Lamy, members traveled to Santa Fe, New Mexico, to teach among the Spanish-speaking children of the area. Soon new houses were opened in Colorado, Texas, California, Illinois, Ohio, Arizona, and Alabama. The primary focus of the sisters was education.

In the early 1920s, the Sisters of Loretto began working in the missions in China. Their fruitful labors were brought to a tragic end with the communist takeover of China, but the congregation's efforts in international ministry were established. Today, the Loretto Community, based in the rural community of Nerinx, Kentucky, maintains chapters in sixteen states and the countries of Bolivia, Chile, China, Ghana, and Peru. The community also enjoys nongovernmental organization (NGO) status with the United Nations. The Loretto Community is currently actively engaged in pastoral ministry and issues of social justice and peace. They publish *Loretto Magazine*, *In Brief*, *Loretto Earth News*, and the *Justice and Peace Newsletter*.

Sisters of Mercy of the Americas (R.S.M.)

A religious congregation of women first founded in Dublin by Catherine McAuley in 1831, the Sisters of Mercy today comprise a number of religious congregations of women. They adopted the rule of the Presentation Sisters, itself based on the Rule of St. Augustine as adapted by St. Thomas of Villanova. The modified rule was approved by Pope Gregory XVI in 1835 and given final confirmation in 1841. The Sisters of Mercy first arrived in the United States in 1843.

The houses in Ireland and England founded by Mother McAuley were placed under general observance, but following her death they all became independent. The first house outside of the British Isles was founded in Newfoundland in 1842. The next year, Mother M. Francis Xavier Warde and six companions from Carlow, Ireland, arrived in the United States and made the first American foundation at Pittsburgh. Over the next years, new houses were begun in New York in 1846, Little Rock, Arkansas, in 1851, San Francisco in 1854, Cincinnati in 1858, and Middletown, Connecticut, in 1872. Until 1929, the houses were all independent.

Their primary ministry was education on the elementary, secondary, and college levels, but the sisters have also been active in nursing. Sisters served as nurses to both Union and Confederate soldiers during the Civil War and also provided care to the victims of the Chicago fire of 1871.

Members of the different houses were also engaged in missionary efforts around the globe in the twentieth century. The Sisters of Mercy from Pittsburgh entered the missions in Puerto Rico in 1941, and sisters from Belmont, North Carolina, launched missions in Guam in 1946. Other sisters went to India, the Philippines, Honduras, and Peru.

The independent nature of the houses of the Sisters of Mercy became a significant issue in the early twentieth century, and efforts were made to encourage the congregation to adopt some form of general government. Finally, in 1929, thirty-nine of the sixty independent motherhouses in the United States amalgamated to form the Institute of the Religious Sisters of Mercy of the Union in the United States of America, which brought together more than five thousand sisters into six provinces. The new structure was implemented at the invitation of the Holy See and was arranged through the assistance of Archbishop Pietro Fumasoni-Biondi, then apostolic delegate to the United States. Mother

Carmelita Hartman was the first mother general. Revised constitutions were given approval by Pope Pius XI in 1931 and were then confirmed by Pope Pius XII in 1940.

The Union claimed some seven thousand members by the time of the Second Vatican Council; a like number belonged to those houses that remained independent. At the time of the council, the Sisters of Mercy claimed a global membership of over twenty-seven thousand. In the years after the council, the sisters embarked upon a diversification of their ministries beyond their traditional focus on education and health care. The members became active in issues of social justice and the care for the poor.

In 1991 the Sisters of Mercy of the Union was dissolved with the decision by seventeen congregations to form the Institute of the Sisters of Mercy of the Americas. Further reorganization is expected over the next years. There are over 4,600 members of the congregation, located in the United States and throughout Central and South America, as well as the Caribbean, Guam, and the Philippines.

Sisters of Notre Dame de Namur (S.N.D.deN.)

A congregation of pontifical right of women religious, the Sisters of Notre Dame de Namur was founded by St. Marie Rose Julie Billiart in Amiens, France, in 1804. The congregation was begun to provide for the education of poor children, and St. Julie, with the help of the Countess Françoise Blin de Bourdon, developed a comprehensive program of education for poor girls and oversaw the expansion of the new community. By the time of her death in 1816, she had established nineteen schools in five dioceses across northwestern France and Belgium. Important leadership was provided by Countess Françoise in the years after St. Julie's death.

The first members of the congregation to be established in the United States arrived at the invitation of Bishop John Baptist Purcell of Cincinnati. Eight sisters under the direction of Sister Louise Van der Schrieck started a house that soon served as the impetus for new houses in Massachusetts, Rhode Island, Pennsylvania, and Washington, D.C. In 1844 several sisters made their way to Oregon, where they served with distinction until moving to California in 1852. The members were engaged principally in education on all levels, and their schools included Trinity College, which was chartered in 1897, Notre Dame de Namur University in Belmont, California, which was chartered in 1868, and Emmanuel College, which was founded in 1919. Continued expansion took the sisters to Africa and East Asia in the early twentieth century. Missionary activities increased in the period after World War II in Africa and South America, and the U.S. communities contributed many sisters to the growing endeavors around the globe.

In the years after the Second Vatican Council, the congregation held a Special General Chapter from 1968 to 1969 that laid the groundwork for the approval of the new constitutions of 1989. The new era of service brought with it a diversification of the ministries for the congregation, including religious education, hospital ministry, and a commitment to social justice and work with immigrants, refugees, and the homeless. In 2011 there were over 2,400 members worldwide.

Sisters of St. Joseph (S.S.J.)

The Sisters of St. Joseph are congregations of women religious who trace their origins back to the community founded at Le Puy, in Velay, France, by the Jesuit priest Jean-Pierre Médaille. Father Médaille encouraged young women under his pastoral care to enter into the religious life and dedicate themselves to God. To secure official favor for the new community, he turned to the bishop of Le Puy, Bishop Henri de Maupas,. With the bishop's approval, Father Médaille founded the new community on October 15, 1650, and placed it under the protection of St. Joseph with the name Congregation of the Sisters of St. Joseph. Formal episcopal recognition was granted in 1651 by the bishop.

The primary task of the sisters was to teach young children, and the spiritual model for the community was the Visitation Order (founded in 1610) and the Daughters of Charity (begun in 1633). The constitutions adopted by Father Médaille were based heavily on the rule of St. Ignatius, with vows of chastity, poverty, and obedience. Each community was to consider the local bishop the superior of the community. The postulant was to have a probation period of three months, and then four years as a novitiate. The successor of Bishop de Maupas, Bishop Armand de Béthune, gave his approval to the congregation on September 23, 1655.

From this beginning, the Sisters of St. Joseph grew rapidly. By the time of Father Médaille's death there were over thirty houses in six dioceses. By the start of the French Revolution in 1789 there were some 150 houses. The Revolution brought immense suffering to the sisters as the radical French government considered them hostile to the revolutionary cause and in 1793 confiscated most of their convents and chapels. Several sisters also died as martyrs during this dark period of French history.

In the years after the Revolution, the Sisters of St. Joseph were reconstituted, with diocesan congregations and a centralized government, first at Clermont in 1811 and then at Lyons. Renewed growth followed in swift order, and the Sisters of St. Joseph established houses across Europe and then around the world, including the United States in 1836, India in 1849, Brazil in 1858, and Algeria in 1884. The congregation at Lyons was responsible for the first foundation in the United States, when six members arrived at St. Louis on March 25, 1836. This was followed by the arrival of Mother St. John Fournier in Philadelphia in 1847 from the congregation at Carondelet, France. Subsequent houses established in the United States were either of diocesan or pontifical status and claimed descent from one of the congregations in France — Carondelet, Le Puy, Chámbery, or Bourg.

The Sisters of St. Joseph were engaged throughout the nineteenth century in a variety of ministries, chiefly education. They ran schools of all levels, but they also were involved in the education of Native Americans and African-Americans. They also ran orphanages and hospitals and were especially active among the working poor.

In the first half of the twentieth century, the Sisters of St. Joseph continued to increase in membership and activities, so that the American congregations could make significant contributions to missionary activities, including the Chinese missions, Central and South America, Africa, the Middle East, and Asia. In the aftermath of the Second Vatican Council, the Sisters in the United States formed the Federation of Sisters of St. Joseph in 1966, a voluntary association of congregations.

Today, there are approximately nine thousand members of the Sisters of St. Joseph.

Sisters, Servants of the Immaculate Heart of Mary (I.H.M.)

A congregation of women religious founded in 1845 in Monroe, Michigan, by the Redemptorist missionary and priest Louis Florent Gillet, the Sisters, Servants of the Immaculate Heart of Mary are involved in a variety of ministries, including education, hospital care, and prison ministry.

On November 10, 1845, Father Gillet began the new community with Mary Theresa Maxis (later Mother M. Theresa), Charlotte Ann Schaaf, and Therese Renauld. Based on the spirituality of St. Alphonsus Liguori, it was intended to be an educational apostolate. In 1858, at the invitation of St. John Nepomucene Neumann, bishop of Philadelphia, the sisters took control of St. Joseph School in Susquehanna, Pennsylvania. They went on to open a second house in Reading, also in Pennsylvania, in 1859, where they established a motherhouse. In 1871 Bishop William G. O'Hara of Scranton asked the sisters to form a new community and motherhouse in the diocese.

These three branches of the congregation continued to flourish. The motherhouse in Reading was moved to a larger location in West Chester, Pennsylvania, in 1872; it was moved in 1966 to the Villa Maria House of Studies, in Immaculata, Pennsylvania. Today, the Sisters staff schools in Connecticut, Georgia, Florida, New Jersey, Pennsylvania, and Virginia, and in Peru and Chile.

Siuwheem, Louise (c. 1800–1853)

A Native American member of the Couer d'Alene tribe in Idaho, Louise Siuwheem was known for her zeal and care for the sick. She was also a friend of the revered Jesuit Father Pierre-Jean De Smet.

The granddaughter of the Coeur d'Alene Chief Circling Raven, Siuwheem was born at Hayden Lake, Idaho, and was baptized in 1842 by Father De Smet during one of his visits to the Coeur d'Alenes. It was the remarkable priest who gave her the baptismal name of Louise, and she was ardent in her faith.

When Father De Smet sent Father Nicholas Point to begin a permanent mission among the bands of the Coeur d'Alenes, Louise and her husband, Adolph Polotkin, moved to the new settlement, and then went on to a new site on the Coeur d'Alene River three years later, then again to be near the church that had been built. Through her labors, large numbers of the Coeur d'Alenes were brought into the Catholic faith. She was much honored by Father De Smet, who left a biographical sketch of her, the only one he penned in all his writings.

Slavery

The social and economic institution by which a segment of a population or an entire race is held in various types of servitude has been viewed by the Church as an inherently inhuman system.

After centuries of decline in Europe, slavery erupted once more as the result of the extensive discoveries made by Spain and Portugal in the New World. When it became a matter of commerce to seize native peoples and carry them off to work on plantations, in mines, or elsewhere, the slave trade became a worldwide industry, with sources for the brutal business found in Africa and the Americas. Contrary to long-held misconceptions, the Church was an outspoken enemy of slavery over the centuries, from popes and cardinals to missionaries and theologians.

In 1537 Pope Paul III, in response to the common enslavement of the Indians and the ruthless seizing of their territory, excommunicated those persons who took part in the slave trade among the Native Americans. The Jesuits in the Americas were much feared and hated by Spanish government officials because of their efforts to protect the rights of the native peoples.

The nineteenth century was a particularly active period for the Church in its fight against the slave trade. Pope Gregory XVI in 1838 wrote the apostolic letter *In Supremo Apostolatus* to the bishops of Brazil to commend Brazil on having at long last outlawed slavery. Of lasting importance was the founding of the Anti-Slavery League in France by Cardinal Charles Lavigerie in 1890, whose Congregation of the White Fathers (Missionaries of Africa) had long labored to end slavery in Africa, often at great personal risk. The Church continues to fight slavery of all kinds, be it through the chains of iron or the chains of spiritual, intellectual, or economic repression and oppression.

Slavery had been present in the American colonies long before the birth of the Republic. It existed as an institution in the colonies and the United States from early in the seventeenth century, starting in the colony of Virginia, until President Abraham Lincoln's Emancipation Proclamation in 1862 and then the passage of the Thirteenth Amendment to the United States Constitution at the end of the Civil War in 1865.

Many Catholics were slaveholders. The Jesuits in Maryland owned slaves in the Maryland colony, as did members of the Carroll family. Just before his death in 1815, Archbishop John Carroll of Baltimore ordered that his "black servant Charles" should receive manumission within a year of Carroll's passing. John's cousin, Charles Carroll of Carrollton, owned slaves but was also a supporter of gradual manumission and the American Colonization Society, founded in 1817, with the aim of settling freed slaves in Liberia. In *In Supremo Apostolatus,* Pope Gregory XVI condemned slavery in 1838 and declared:

> We warn and adjure earnestly in the Lord faithful Christians of every condition that no one in the future dare to vex anyone, despoil him of his possessions, reduce to servitude, or lend aid and favour to those who give themselves up to these practices, or exercise that inhuman traffic by which the blacks, as if they were not men but rather animals, having been brought into servitude, in no matter what way, are, without any distinction, in contempt of the rights of justice and humanity, bought, sold, and devoted sometimes to the hardest labor.

The letter received an unenthusiastic reception in many Catholic quarters, although it was received warmly in England and among abolitionists. Anti-abolitionist Catholics argued that the pope had not focused on slavery in the United States, and that the letter was merely an attack on the slave trade rather than a direct condemnation of slavery. This sentiment was expressed by Bishop John England of Charleston. He published the apostolic letter in English and Latin in the newspaper *United States Catholic Miscellany,* but noted that *In Supremo* "is far from censuring those who, without their own choice, have been placed under the necessity of managing their property with a delicacy, a responsibility and a perplexity, to which they who vilify us [are] strangers."

Nevertheless, Catholics worked to provide care to slaves and freed slaves. Bishop England operated a school for free blacks in Charleston until 1835, and Bishop Peter R. Kenrick in St. Louis started a school for slave and freed children. These and other efforts were the source of controversy and fierce hate-filled opposition by Protestants and also some Catholics. In 1846, for example, sisters running the school in St. Louis were threatened with violence by an anti-Catholic mob.

In the decades before the start of the Civil War, the controversy over slavery tore apart the country, and the religious communities of America were not spared. The main Protestant churches split into southern and northern jurisdictions. Catholics, possessed of a greater sense of unity because of severe social hindrances and biases, were not as sharply opposed to each other. Catholics were at times reluctant to join the abolition movement because so many of its adherents were also anti-Catholics and nativists opposed to the arrival of Irish and other foreigners.

There were other issues involved as well, such as the ideas of federal versus states' rights, the concept of individual rights versus the corporate rights of the government, and the idea of distinctive cultures in the same country — that is, between the largely industrial North and the agrarian South. Some saw this as emblematic of American Protestant culture. Chief among these was the fiery James McMaster, editor of the Catholic newspaper in New York, *Freeman's Journal*. He argued that the division in the country was a direct reflection on Protestants, writing, "Protestant sects . . . in working the ruin of the country . . . have exposed . . . the hollowness of Protestantism and its destructive and separating tendencies."

Not surprisingly, there were many in the Church in the North who saw little incentive in supporting the Union cause, in giving their lives for a system that had for so long treated them as second-class citizens and denigrated the Catholic faith. Many Northern Catholic periodicals were vehemently opposed to the war, such as the *Freeman's Journal*.

McMaster was jailed for his opposition to government policy, and the newspaper was denied the use of the mails. Against this position was that of the *Katholiche Kirchenzeitung*, edited by Father Edward Purcell, which was ardent in its support of the Union cause.

With the end of the war in 1865, the Church recognized the immense pastoral needs of the emancipated slaves, who numbered some four million, as well as an opportunity for evangelization. Central in the planning was the Second Plenary Council of Baltimore, which was held October 7–21, 1866. In the face of postwar issues, Archbishop Martin J. Spalding, in close consultation with the Congregation of the Propaganda in Rome, sought to have the council reiterate Catholic teaching, issue warnings about the religious errors then being propagated, and express in clear fashion important aspects of Church discipline and law.

Further, to assist pastoral care, the council, in a pastoral letter, urged the creation of new dioceses and suggested a special ministry among the recently emancipated slaves. It was a heartfelt concern, but, ultimately, with resources limited after the war and so many other concerns pressing in upon the bishops, the freed slaves proved a tragically missed opportunity.

Heeding the call of the council in 1866, Archbishop Spalding tried to propose a national Catholic apostolate to blacks, but the idea met with opposition and was dropped. A partial solution to the lack of such an apostolate came in 1871, when the Mill Hill Fathers of England arrived in Baltimore. The American branch of the Mill Hill Congregation separated from the English foundation and became the Society of St. Joseph of the Sacred Heart. These religious priests conducted missions and ministries among African-Americans.

In 1906 the Society of the Divine Word also arrived in the United States from Germany, and the congregation began a black apostolate that was also successful. St. Katharine Drexel used part of her vast fortune to build educational and religious facilities for African-Americans, founding the Sisters of the Blessed Sacrament.

Mary Elizabeth Lange, a former Haitian, and Henriette DeLille, the daughter of a former slave, both started religious communities for African-

American Catholic women. The Oblate Sisters of Providence, founded by Lange and Sulpician Father James Hector Nicholas Joubert, served Baltimore. One of the original members of this community, Theresa Duchemin, was part of the founding of the Sisters, Servants of the Immaculate Heart of Mary in Monroe, Michigan.

The Sisters of the Holy Family was started by DeLille, whose cause for canonization has been opened. This congregation served in New Orleans. In Savannah, Georgia, Mother Theodore Williams started a third black religious community of women, which moved to Harlem, in New York City, where the congregation still serves as the Franciscan Handmaids of Mary.

All these steps were well and good, but the population of African-American Catholics remained small. The Church was challenged by opposition to outreach in the South by both Protestants and Catholics, and dioceses and religious communities were reluctant to embark on active initiatives out of fear of alienating white Catholics. The result was a missed opportunity for the Church in the country. Indeed, there were fewer than a million black Catholics in the late 1960s out of a total African-American population of 22 million.

Smith, Alfred E. (December 30, 1873–October 4, 1944)

Four-time governor of New York (from 1919 to 1920 and from 1923 to 1928) and presidential candidate in 1928, Al Smith was the first Roman Catholic candidate for president. Born on Manhattan's Lower East Side, he was a member of an Irish family and left school after the death of his father and worked briefly at the Fulton Fish Market. His political career began in 1894, and by 1903 he was elected to the New York Assembly, then was picked to be Democratic leader in 1913 and speaker of the assembly in 1915.

That same year, he was elected New York County sheriff, and then president of the New York City board of aldermen in 1917. In 1920 he was elected for the first time as governor but failed in his reelection bid. Reelected in 1922, 1924, and 1926, he was an immensely popular figure in the state and worked hard to improve working conditions, including passing child labor laws, improving factory safety, and developing social welfare programs.

With the support of Franklin Delano Roosevelt, Smith was proposed as the Democratic Party's presidential nominee in 1924, but at a deadlocked at convention the nomination went to a compromise candidate, John W. Davis. The party went on to a crushing defeat in the general election. In 1928 Smith was again nominated by Roosevelt at the Democratic convention. This time he won the nomination easily. The achievement was remarkable, for Smith was the first Catholic to be nominated for president.

In the general election, however, Smith was confronted with virulent anti-Catholicism. Protestants and bigots, including the Ku Klux Klan, and ardent Prohibitionists staged protests against Smith as he campaigned, and stories were spread that he was planning to install the pope in the White House and would force all Protestant children to attend Catholic schools.

The result of one of the most vicious campaigns in American history was that Smith lost the traditional Democratic stronghold of the Southern states; half the South voted for a Republican, Herbert Hoover, for the first time since the Civil War. Smith's hopes were also not helped by his New York accent, the still favorable economic conditions that assisted a continuation of Republican control of the White House, and his opposition to Prohibition. In the end, Smith lost forty states and by six million votes.

Roosevelt won the nomination in 1932 as the country was in the grips of the Great Depression. Smith went on to found the American Liberty League, a group of conservative Democrats who opposed many of the New Deal programs and in 1936 and 1940 actually supported the Republican presidential candidates. He also served as the president of the company that operated the Empire State Building in New York City.

Smith remains one of the most significant Catholic political leaders in the twentieth century, and his experience in 1928 proved a valuable lesson to John F. Kennedy during his presidential run in 1960. The Al Smith Dinner, an annual charity event in New York, was started in his honor in 1945 and is still held every year.

Smith, William B. (August 4, 1939–January 24, 2009)

A professor of moral theology at St. Joseph's Seminary in Yonkers, New York, from 1971, Monsignor William B. Smith was one of the leading Catholic moral theologians in the United States. Born and raised in Yonkers, he was ordained on May 28, 1966, completed a doctorate in moral theology at The Catholic University of America, and then taught at St. Joseph's Seminary for thirty years. He was a respected adviser on questions of moral theology and ethics to the archbishops of New York, including Cardinals Terrence Cooke, John O'Connor, and Edward Egan, and a much sought-after speaker on the whole range of issues related to moral theology, including sexual ethics. He appeared regularly on EWTN and was one of the greatest defenders of the culture of life, of *Humanae Vitae*, and of the Church's authentic teachings on life. Smith was also a charter member and a former president of the Fellowship of Catholic Scholars.

Society of Jesus (S.J.)

The largest of the religious orders of men in the Church, the Society of Jesus, commonly called the Jesuits, is an order of clerks regular founded in Paris in 1534 by St. Ignatius Loyola with six companions: St. Francis Xavier, Blessed Peter Faber, Alphonso Salmeron, Simon Rodrigues, Nicholas Bobadilla, and Diego Laynez. Loyola and the six cemented their union in 1534 by gathering in a Benedictine chapel on Montmartre and taking vows of chastity and poverty, and a promise to embark, if possible, on a pilgrimage to the Holy Land. As the latter was to be impractical, the group journeyed to Rome to offer itself to the service of the papacy. Formal approbation for the new religious order was given by Pope Paul III on September 27, 1540, in the papal bull *Regimini Militantis Ecclesiae*. They were given the name Society of Jesus, and St. Ignatius Loyola was elected the first general.

In 1550 St. Ignatius submitted the constitution for the Society. The motto of the order, *Ad majorem Dei gloriam* (abbreviated AMDG; "To the Greater Glory of God"), reflected Ignatius's aspiration that its members would work for the honor of God and to save men. Toward this end, the members would aid the reform of the Church and offer themselves to missionary efforts around the globe. Beyond the vows of chastity, obedience, and poverty, the Jesuits took a special oath of obedience to the Holy See, placing themselves entirely at the disposal of the popes, going forth immediately and without question wherever they might command. For the fulfillment of these tasks, Ignatius desired priests who were superbly educated and trained, highly disciplined but exceedingly rational, and cultivated in the faith. Jesuits were not to accept any preferment or office unless specifically pressed upon them by the pope, and their habit was to be simple and without any distinction. For the education of the priests, the order launched a system of studies called the *Ratio Studiorum* in 1599. Jesuits soon spearheaded the Catholic Reformation, became important pioneers in Catholic education, and spread across the globe as some of the greatest of the Church's missionaries.

Jesuits were crucial to the very foundation of the Catholic faith in the New World. Members of the order were involved in the great efforts at evangelization in North America and also helped cement the Catholic presence in the English colonies. Jesuit Father Andrew White and four other Jesuits from the English missions were part of the expedition under Cecil Calvert that arrived in the newly established colony of Maryland on March 25, 1634, on board two small ships, the *Ark* and the *Dove*, which landed at St. Clement's Island in southern Maryland. The first Catholic Mass in the colonies was then said by Father White; other Jesuits were Father John Altham and Brother Thomas Gervase. The Jesuits existed in the colony much like the gentlemen, meaning that they assumed the position of landowners. They began the first formal Catholic religious base in the colonies at the newly founded town of St. Mary's and then devoted themselves to the conversion of the Native Americans along the Chesapeake Bay and the Potomac River. In 1644 Maryland was invaded by Puritans from Virginia, and Father White was seized and sent in chains to England. When he was released, he made his way to the safety of Belgium.

The Jesuits also founded one of the earliest permanent Catholic establishments in the English colonies, St. Francis Xavier Mission, Old Bohemia, in northern Maryland, founded in 1704 to serve

Catholics in Delaware, Maryland, and southeastern Pennsylvania. Its Bohemia Manor, established in the 1740s, was attended by sons of prominent Catholic families in the area.

Catholics in the colonies were served by a shockingly small group of priests; for most of the eighteenth century there were about one hundred Jesuits priests based chiefly in Maryland and providing pastoral care to the communities in St. Mary's and Charles County, Maryland. The Jesuits also assisted with the needs of Catholics in Pennsylvania belonging to St. Joseph Parish in Philadelphia, with its diverse congregation of Irish, Germans, and English. The German Jesuit Ferdinand Steinmeyer, knows as "Father Farmer," said Mass in secret to the Catholics in New York City as late as 1776.

Until 1773, colonial Catholicism was squarely in the hands of the Society of Jesus. Some 186 Jesuit priests and 30 Jesuit brothers served in Maryland and Pennsylvania between 1634 and the start of the American Revolution. Over that time, 41 Americans entered the Jesuits. Not surprisingly, the suppression of the Jesuits in 1773 came as a terrible blow to colonial Catholics, and the priests affected (including the American Jesuit priest John Carroll) were shocked and left largely to fend for themselves. Most of the Jesuits at the time chose to remain in service in the colonies, but they were forced to devote resources, time, and energy to reorganize.

The work of the Jesuits in their missions was complicated after the suppression by the lamentable lack of any formal ecclesiastical structure in the colonies. The ancient hierarchy in England had died out in 1585 and over a hundred years passed until any attempt was made to restore some semblance of oversight by bishops for the Catholics in the kingdom. In the colonies, priests received their faculties to administer the sacraments directly from Rome, but there were still no bishops available to visit the colonies and administer confirmation. All seminarians were sent abroad to study.

In 1688 four vicars apostolic were appointed to govern English Catholics. The vicar apostolic for London became by necessity the bishop with jurisdiction over the colonies, but the distances involved and the continuing anti-Catholicism made utterly impractical serious hands-on governance over the

Catholic community in America. This situation was the subject of several letters to Rome by Bishop Richard Challoner in 1756 and 1763. In reality, the most direct way by which priests received their faculties and direction for their ministry was through the general of the Jesuits in Rome who worked with the Congregation for the Propaganda Fide (the department in the Vatican with authority over the missions). Thus, when the Jesuits were suppressed in 1774, the situation became more complicated, made all the more so as the American colonies were moving fast toward war with their native country. This situation was ultimately remedied with the appointment of Father John Carroll as superior of the missions in 1784.

Meantime, the French missions were established out of the French colonies in Canada, and the Jesuits, Recollects (a reformed branch of the Franciscans), Capuchins, and other religious orders found many young men and women eager to sail to New France. As with the Spanish missions, the French happily sent out their brightest, best educated, and holiest priests as "Black Robes" to bring the Gospel to the Native Americans.

The Jesuits were active in the French missions from the very start, and the subsequent history of the missions was a treasury of heroism, sacrifice, and martyrdom. The members of the Society arrived in Québec in 1625, were driven out by the English in 1629, then returned in 1632 to began their missionary labors in earnest.

In an act of stunning heroism, Jesuit missionaries set out from Canada and made their way into New York to convert the Iroquois. In 1642 the great Jesuit St. Isaac Jogues was captured with several companions, including fellow lay missionary René Goupil, by the Mohawk. Father Goupil was martyred, and Father Jogues endured unspeakable tortures that left him terribly mutilated. He escaped captivity in 1643, returned to France, and then went back to the Iroquois as a peace ambassador. Captured once again by the Mohawks, he was martyred near the present-day site of Auriesville, New York, by Mohawks on October 18, 1646. Others followed in death, including the Jesuit priests Anthony Daniel, John de Brébeuf, Gabriel Lalemant, Charles Garnier, Noel Chabanel, and the lay missionary Jean de Lalande. With Fathers

Goupil and Jogues, the martyrs were canonized in 1930 by Pope Pius XI and are honored as the North American Martyrs.

St. Isaac Jogues's seemingly pointless death actually served as the basis for future missions among the Mohawks, but the Huron remained a target for annihilation by the Iroquois and the English. From 1648 to 1650, the Iroquois waged a savage war upon the Huron, during which literally thousands of the Huron were slaughtered, to the considerable satisfaction of the English. The remnant of the Huron relocated near Québec City and finally settled at Wendake.

The Jesuit missions nevertheless continued among the Iroquois, including the Onondaga and finally even the Mohawks. Progress was made between 1668 and 1686, and among the Mohawk converts was an extraordinary young woman, St. Kateri Tekakwitha, called the "Lily of the Mohawks," who was declared blessed by Pope Blessed John Paul II in 1980 and was canonized on October 21, 2012. Sadly, at the instigation of the English, the Iroquois once more turned against the French, and by 1684, there were only two priests left among the Indians of New York.

The Jesuit priest Gabriel Druillettes founded a mission at Norridgewock, Maine, on the Kennebec River in the 1630s, an outpost for the devoted Abenaki that was raided by the English in 1704, 1722, and 1724. During the last attack, the beloved missionary among the Abenaki, Jesuit Father Sebastian Râle, was murdered after refusing to leave his people.

The French colonial focus had been centered chiefly in Canada for much of the seventeenth century at the expense of its ambitions in the Midwest. Alarmed by the expansion of the English colonies, the French crown widened its interests, and a new area opened for missionaries. Isaac Jogues and Charles Raymbaut had visited Sault Ste. Marie, Michigan, and the borders of Lake Superior in 1641, and Claude Allouez had opened several missions there. From these bases, Jesuit missionaries roamed south and then west into modern-day Michigan, Illinois, and Wisconsin.

The European discovery and exploration of the Mississippi Valley was spearheaded in 1673 by Louis Joliet, accompanied by the indefatigable Jesuit Jacques Marquette, who had earlier founded a mission at St. Ignace on the north shore of the Straits of Mackinac. Fathers Marquette and Joliet followed the northern shore of Lake Michigan, entered Green Bay and the Fox River, and crossed a short portage into the Wisconsin River, which emptied into the Mississippi. Father Marquette drew maps of the area and kept a diary of the voyage, some of the most important documents of early American history. He returned the next year to live with the Illinois Indians at Kaskaskia, Illinois, but died a year later. Missions were opened in Detroit, Green Bay, and St. Joseph that endured until 1763 and the withdrawal of the Jesuits from the region.

In order to facilitate the missions across the massive territory of French Louisiana, the bishop of Québec in 1722 divided it into three territories among the Capuchins, the Carmelites, and the Jesuits. As the Carmelites withdrew in short order, the territory was redivided so that the Capuchins were given control over all areas to around the Ohio River and the Jesuits retained their jurisdiction over everything north. In 1726 the Jesuits were given control of the Indian missions in Louisiana, which brought some conflict with the Capuchins.

With the end of French Canada in 1763, Canada became a British possession, the missions were placed in an impossible situation, and the Jesuit college at Québec, started in 1635, was closed five years later.

The Jesuits were also active in the Southwest missions. One of the most important in the history of the Southwest Missions is the saintly Jesuit priest Eusebius Kino. Father Kino spent his life on horseback and founded missions across the Southwest and Lower California. For his defense of the Native Americans, his long travels, and his holiness, he is revered as the founder of Christianity in the Southwest. He represents the state of Arizona in Statuary Hall in the Capitol in Washington, D.C., and in 1995 his cause for canonization was introduced in Rome.

In 1814 Pope Pius VII was able to reestablish the Society of Jesus after decades of suppression. In the United States, there were nineteen priests who were able to form the reconstituted Jesuit presence. In 1833 the Jesuits in the United States became a province.

The missionary efforts of the Jesuits continued throughout the nineteenth century, and the Society was especially noted for its pioneering priests in the West and among the Native Americans. Of the Jesuits in the West, the most revered missionary of the Native Americans was Father Pierre-Jean De Smet, who traveled nearly 261,000 miles through the wilderness to serve the tribes.

Throughout the nineteenth century, even as they continued to work in the missions, the Jesuits were important in the growing field of Catholic education. Jesuit high schools were welcomed eagerly by bishops and were found in most dioceses. These led to the rise of the Jesuit universities, which became a hallmark of Catholic higher education. Jesuits helped establish Georgetown College (1789), and a host of colleges followed across the country: St. Louis University (1818), Spring Hill College (1830), St. Xavier's (1840), Fordham (1841), Holy Cross in Worcester (1843), St. Joseph's College in Philadelphia (1851), Santa Clara University (1851), Loyola College in Baltimore (1852), the University of San Francisco (1855), Boston College (1863), Canisius College (1870), Loyola in Chicago (1870), Detroit Mercy (1870), St. Peter's College (1872), Regis (1877), Creighton (1878), Gonzaga (1887), John Carroll (1887), the University of Scranton (1888), Marquette (1881), Seattle University (1891), and Brooklyn College (1908).

Jesuits likewise contributed significantly to Catholic intellectual life in the United States. Their publications included *America* magazine from 1909, the scholarly journal *Thought* from 1926, and the noted journal in theology, *Theological Studies,* that was started in 1940.

Jesuits also provided important figures in academics and theological studies. Among the most highly reputed American Jesuits of the twentieth century were John Courtney Murray, Timothy Healy, John Hardon, and Cardinal Avery Dulles. Other prominent modern American Jesuits are Joseph Fessio, James Martin, and Earl Weis. There are around three thousand Jesuits in the United States in ten provinces.

Society of the Divine Word

Known in Latin as *Societas Verbi Divini,* the Society of the Divine Word is the largest missionary congregation in the Church. Founded in 1875 in Steyl in the Netherlands by St. Arnold Janssen, the community was formed largely of German priests and religious who were living in exile in the Netherlands because of the anti-Catholic atmosphere in Germany as a result of the *Kulturkampf.*

By 1882 the Society was able to initiate the process of sending missionaries to Asia, starting with Shandong Province in China. A decade later, the congregation sent missionaries to Africa, and in 1898 they were laboring in South America.

The Society arrived in the United States in 1897 and formed the Divine Word North American Province in Illinois. The province subsequently opened a seminary for African-Americans, and in 1923 St. Augustine Seminary was moved to Bay St. Louis, Mississippi, to promote vocations to the priesthood and religious life among African-American men. In 2011 there were more than six thousand members of the congregation in sixty-two countries around the world.

Sorin, Edward F. (February 6, 1814–October 31, 1893)

A priest member of the Congregation of the Holy Cross, Father Edward Sorin is revered as the founder of the University of Notre Dame. Born in Ahuillé, France, he was called to the priesthood and was ordained a diocesan priest in 1838. Drawn to the missionary field, he entered the recently established Congregation of the Holy Cross and was chosen to lead the congregation's efforts to plant roots in the United States.

With six brothers, Father Sorin sailed for the United States in 1841 and arrived at New York in the fall. As expected, he set out immediately for Indiana, at a time when the Midwest was considered a distant territory. He reached the Diocese of Vincennes and set to work in 1842 establishing a school at Notre Dame. What began as a school in a farmhouse grew into one of the foremost Catholic universities in the United States, and Father Sorin was the primary reason for this immense achievement.

In 1855 he was responsible for the relocation of the Sisters of the Holy Cross college from Michigan to South Bend, Indiana, where the sisters opened St. Mary's College for women. The community flourished and provided vitally needed nurses for the care of soldiers during the Civil War. In 1865 Father Sorin founded Ave Maria Press, and in 1873 he founded St. Edward's University in Austin, Texas.

Father Sorin was elected superior general of his order in 1868. He remained in this post for the rest of his life. He is still revered as one of the great pioneers in the history of American Catholic education.

Sotomayor, Sonia (June 25, 1954–)

An associate justice of the Supreme Court of the United States since 2009, Sonia Sotomayor is the first Hispanic justice, the third female justice, and the thirteenth (at least nominal) Catholic to serve on the highest court. Born in the Bronx, New York City, to a Puerto Rican family, she was raised by her mother after the death of her father when she was nine. She attended Catholic school, then Princeton University, where she earned a bachelor's degree summa cum laude in 1976. She then went to Yale Law School in 1979, where she was an editor of the *Yale Law Journal*.

Sotomayor worked as an assistant district attorney in New York for five years and then went into private practice in 1984. She was an activist with the Puerto Rican Legal Defense and Education Fund, the State of New York Mortgage Agency, and the New York City Campaign Finance Board. Nominated to the U.S. District Court for the Southern District of New York by President George H. W. Bush in 1991 and confirmed in 1992, she came to the public's attention in 1995, when she issued a preliminary injunction against Major League Baseball as part of the 1994 baseball strike.

In 1997 Sotomayor was nominated by President Bill Clinton to the U.S. Court of Appeals for the Second Circuit. Despite opposition by Republicans, she was confirmed in 1998. She also taught at the New York University School of Law and Columbia Law School.

In May 2009 President Barack Obama nominated her for the U.S. Supreme Court to replace retiring Justice David Souter. Her nomination was confirmed by the Senate in August 2009 by a vote of 68–31. She belongs to what is generally termed the liberal or progressive wing of the high court.

South Carolina

Called the Palmetto State, South Carolina was one of the original states, joining the Union on May 23, 1788, as the eighth state of the new nation. Located on the southern seaboard, South Carolina is bordered by North Carolina on the north, by the Atlantic Ocean on the east and southeast, and by Georgia on the south and west. Three land regions compose the state: the Atlantic Central Plain in the east, the Piedmont Plateau in the west, and the Blue Ridge in the west. The original inhabitants of South Carolina were the Catawba, Yamassee, Cherokee, Casabo, Kusoe, Yuchi, and Shawnee.

The Catholic history of the state opened in 1511 when Lucas Vazquez de Ayllón's expedition, led by Francisco de Gordilla and Pedro de Guexas, entered the region. Ayllón settled at Winyah Bay, north of modern-day Charleston, with Dominicans Antonio de Cervantes and Antonio de Montesinos. The settlement was not permanent, but they reportedly celebrated Mass.

In 1564 French Huguenots who had arrived in the area were driven out of their lands by Pedro Menéndez de Avilés. The French had hoped to establish Charles Fort at Port Royal, and five years later, Jesuits arrived at Port Royal and started mission activities. Franciscan missionaries joined the mission efforts in 1586 but had to abandon the site when the Spanish withdrew to Florida. In 1663 British military units claimed the land, and grants for colonial settlement were provided by the English crown. South Carolina was designated as a royal province, a status that existed until the defeat of the British in the American Revolution. Catholics did not have civil rights in such a province, and priests were under constant threat of severe punishment for entering the region.

When South Carolina entered the Union in 1788, Father Matthew Ryan was serving Catholics in Charleston. The congregation that he served reportedly numbered about two hundred. They held liturgical services in a Methodist Church but then raised funds and in 1789 purchased a structure on Hasell Street that became St. Mary's. Father Ryan, who had been assigned to Charleston by Bishop John Carroll, welcomed new immigrants who had fled from slave revolts in Haiti and Santo Domingo.

In 1793 another priest served at St. Mary's and remained in that post for three decades. Father Simon Felix Gallagher, who had been educated in a Paris university, had a great impact on the parish and the city. He taught at Charleston College, founded a Catholic school, and helped institute the Hibernian Society.

When the Diocese of Charleston was established in June 1820, Bishop John England arrived to establish the agencies needed for the effective pastoral care of the still small Catholic community. The Diocese of Charleston at the time included both North Carolina and South Carolina. Bishop England proved capable and influential in advancing the Catholic cause within American culture. He erected St. Finbar's Cathedral, the Seminary of St. John the Baptist, and a Catholic newspaper that reported general as well as Catholic news. He also invited religious congregations into Charleston. In 1868 South Carolina was administered by a vicariate apostolic.

The Catholic presence, threatened in some eras by anti-Catholic groups and by trusteeism in St. Mary's Church, maintained steady growth, even during the Civil War. The bishop of Charleston at the time, Patrick N. Lynch, was an advocate of the Confederacy and traveled to Rome and Paris as an advocate for the Southern cause. When he was unsuccessful, he found himself stranded in Paris, as the United States government would not sanction his return to America. Bishop Lynch appeared before the U.S. ambassador in Paris and took a public oath of loyalty to the Union and was able to sail home.

During the Reconstruction period that followed the defeat of the Confederacy, Bishop Lynch labored to aid freed slaves. The era was one of turmoil, and Catholics were targeted by the Ku Klux Klan. Meanwhile, waves of immigrants to America added to the Catholic presence in the decades that followed the war, although the Catholic population remained relatively tiny, numbering around nine thousand in 1900.

In 1949 the rich spiritual tradition of the Trappists was established in South Carolina with the foundation of Mepkin Abbey on three thousand acres of land donated by Clare Boothe Luce and her husband, Henry Luce. Currently, the state has just the one diocese, Charleston. There are some 195,000 Catholics, served by 130 priests and 91 parishes.

South Dakota

Called the Sunshine State, South Dakota is located in the north-central part of the nation. It is bordered on the north by North Dakota, on the east by Minnesota and Iowa, on the south by Nebraska, and on the west by Wyoming and Montana. South Dakota joined the Union in 1889.

Three land regions compose the state: the Young Drift Plain in the east, the Great Plains in the central and western areas, and the Black Hills in the northwest. The original Native American inhabitants were the Arikara, Dakota Sioux, Lakota and other Sioux-related groups, as well as the Cheyenne, Kiowa, and the Plains people.

The Catholic history of South Dakota opened with the expedition of René-Robert Chevalier, Sieur de La Salle, who claimed all the lands that he visited for France. He was in the area of modern South Dakota in 1736, followed by Louis Joseph de La Verendrye around 1745, whose expedition was accompanied by a priest. Verendrye left a metal plate on the banks of the Missouri River. The plate was not discovered until 1913.

Between 1762 and 1800, France and Spain fought for territories on the American continent. France had the final control of a vast territory, which was sold to the United States in 1803 as part of the Louisiana Purchase. Fur traders and mountain men were in South Dakota at the time, and the Lewis and Clark expedition passed through the area in 1804. A steamboat, *The Yellowstone*, was on the Missouri River by 1831, carrying passengers and cargo. Fort Pierre was established in the next years by the famed fur trader Pierre Chouteau Jr., near modern-day Pierre, South Dakota; the fort was visited in 1842 by Father Augustin Ravoux, who baptized the children of the French Catholics in the fort. He made subsequent pastoral trips to other locations in South Dakota, including Vermillion and Yankton after permanent settlements were established in the 1850s.

In 1848 the legendary Jesuit Father Pierre-Jean De Smet began his labors among the Native Americans in the Dakotas. He established excellent relations with the Sioux and became an adviser and friend to the famed Sitting Bull. He counseled the Sioux to hide from the white man the presence of the region's minerals and natural resources, as the discovery of these resources would only hasten the arrival of more settlers and threaten the obliteration of Native American life and culture. De Smet served the Indians until his death in 1873, and was especially trusted as a mediator between the Indians and the federal government. Other priests in service in the Dakotas included the revered Father Christian Hoecken.

In 1861, with the arrival of large numbers of white settlers, Congress established the Dakota Territory, including North Dakota and South Dakota as well as parts of Wyoming and Montana. Fort Dakota and other military outposts were built to protect the vast number of settlers and establish firmer control over the natural resources of the region, largely at the expense of the Native Americans. In 1867, meanwhile, a mission was established at Jefferson to serve the needs of the growing white population, including French Catholics who were assisted by Father Pierre Boucher. He founded St. Peter's Church at Jefferson, the first Catholic Church in South Dakota.

Swifter development came after 1874 and the start of the so-called Great Dakota Boom with the discovery of gold in the Black Hills. Deadwood Gulch yielded the famous Homestake Lode that guaranteed the extension of the railroad to Yankton to assist surveyors. The stripping of the Black Hills sparked an uprising by the Sioux and the expulsion of the tribes from gold country, an event that accelerated the arrival of settlers.

In 1876 the Swiss Benedictine Martin Marty arrived to assist the pastoral care of Native Americans and settlers. Three years later, the Holy See established the Vicariate Apostolic for the Dakota Territory, and Bishop Marty administered Catholic affairs from Yankton. The see was transferred to Sioux Falls with the establishment of the Diocese of Sioux Falls in 1889, with Bishop Marty as the first bishop. In 1902 the Diocese of Lead was created (renamed Rapid City in 1930).

The Church in South Dakota in the early decades of the twentieth century focused on the pastoral care of settlers and also displaced and suf-

fering Native Americans. The 1930s brought economic hardships through the Great Depression, coupled with drought and the dust storms termed "black blizzards." Prosperity returned in the 1940s, and the state became one of the most productive in agriculture. The population increased steadily in the period after the war, partly through the benefits of agriculture, as did tourism, especially to Mount Rushmore, near Keystone, South Dakota.

The Catholic community by the 1960s had grown considerably. At its start in 1889, the Diocese of Sioux Falls claimed 15,000 members, served by 12 priests and 20 churches. By the early 1960s, there were 85,000 Catholics served by 200 priests and 200 churches. That growth continued in the succeeding decades. In 2011 there were 150,000 Catholics, served by 188 priests and 238 parishes. There are also important Native American reservations, and the state boasts the third-largest Indian population in the United States, especially the Lakota and Dakota Sioux. The Church has focused efforts on providing educational, medical, and pastoral care to these populations.

Spalding, Catherine (December 23, 1793–March 20, 1858)

Co-foundress of the Sisters of Charity of Nazareth, Kentucky, Catherine Spalding helped found a community that cared for orphans, educated the poor, and eventually expanded into health care. Born in Charles County, Maryland, she was moved when she was young to Nelson County, Kentucky; she soon lost her mother, and her father abandoned the family. Raised by her aunt and uncle, she spent time with her cousins before joining the Sisters of Charity of Nazareth, which had been founded in 1812 in Bardstown, Kentucky. Elected the first superior of the community at the age of nineteen, she became an important figure in the Catholic community in Kentucky and worked to establish a school. By 1822 the community moved to a larger property at modern-day Nazareth, Kentucky, near Bardstown. This academy emerged into one of the most prominent schools for young women in the South.

Credit was given to Mother Catherine, and she was reelected mother superior; in 1831 she directed the founding of Presentation Academy in Louisville. In 1832, when the city was stricken by cholera, the sisters cared for the sick and took direction of the orphans. From this beginning was born St. Vincent Orphanage.

Mother Catherine remained the guiding force for the congregation for the rest of her life and presided over the continued expansion of the community. The congregation grew in the century after her death and is now found in North America, Central America, Asia, and Africa.

Spalding, John Lancaster (June 2, 1840–August 25, 1916)

The first bishop of Peoria, from 1877 to 1908, John Lancaster Spalding was a nephew of Archbishop Martin J. Spalding and a crucial figure in the founding of The Catholic University of America. Born in Lebanon, Kentucky, he was ordained on December 19, 1863, for the Diocese of Louisville. On November 11, 1876, he was named bishop of the new Diocese of Peoria, and he was installed on May 23, 1877.

Bishop Martin Spalding

As bishop, Spalding established the needed administration for a new diocese and was soon noted for his promotion of education, including Catholic schools in the diocese and The Catholic University of America. He also wrote a biography of his uncle and published poetry under the pseudonym Henry Hamilton. In 1905 he suffered a stroke that limited his ability to govern the diocese, and that prompted his retirement on September 11, 1908, at the age of sixty-eight.

Spalding, Martin John (May 23, 1810–February 7, 1872)

The seventh archbishop of Baltimore, from 1864 to 1872, and one of the most influential Catholic apologists of the nineteenth century, Martin J. Spalding also promoted evangelization among former slaves and worked to shape and direct the immigrant influx in the nineteenth century.

Born in Bardstown, Kentucky, he studied at St. Mary's College in Lebanon, Kentucky, in 1821 and was teaching mathematics there by the age of four-

teen. He graduated at sixteen and entered studies for the priesthood. He spent four years in the seminary at Bardstown and in 1830 was sent to Rome to study at the Propaganda College, a tremendous honor in that period. Ordained a priest on August 13, 1834, he earned a doctorate in theology in Rome and returned home to Bardstown.

Father Spalding was assigned to be pastor of the cathedral as well as editor of the *Catholic Advocate.* He was named vicar general in 1844 and in 1848 was appointed coadjutor bishop of Louisville (the see had been moved from Bardstown to Louisville). He succeeded Bishop Benedict Joseph Flaget in 1850 and moved quickly to improve Catholic education, dedicated the cathedral in 1852, and journeyed to Europe to bolster his population of religious.

Inspired to open a college for American seminarians in Europe, Bishop Spalding pushed for a college in Louvain, which began in 1857 and remained in existence until 2011.

Back home, Bishop Spalding became one of the foremost Catholic apologists in the country. He wrote a variety of works against the Know-Nothing movement and won a wide readership for such works as *Evidences of Catholicity* and *History of the Protestant Reformation.* He was also a noted lecturer across the country, including at the Smithsonian Institution in Washington, D.C.

In 1864 Spalding succeeded Archbishop Francis Kenrick as archbishop of Baltimore. His eight years as shepherd of the archdiocese were filled with considerable activity. In 1867 he went to Rome to take part in the celebration of the martyrdom of St. Peter and then took part in the First Vatican Council, where he voted for the definition of infallibility. Upon reaching Baltimore from Rome, he spoke out in defense of the definition and published a pastoral letter to refute the egregious misrepresentations of the actions of the council.

In October 1866 he helped organize the Second Plenary Council of Baltimore. He pushed for the call for greater evangelization among former slaves and also for the bishops' endorsement of a Catholic university. He likewise organized the St. Vincent de Paul Society and finished the cathedral in Baltimore. He died at age sixty-one from bronchitis and was buried in the cathedral crypt in Baltimore. Bishop John Lancaster Spalding was his nephew.

Spanish Civil War

A bloody political and military struggle for control of Spain from 1936 to 1939, the Civil War was waged between the Nationalists under General Francisco Franco and the communist-supported Republicans. The Spanish Civil War became a testing ground for the wider conflict between fascism and communism, but it was also marked by staggering bloodshed and a savage persecution of the Church in Spain by the leftist Second Republic. Anti-Catholic and anticlerical forces slaughtered over seven thousand priests, hundreds of nuns, and thousands of Catholic laypeople.

Political strife in Spain that had been building for decades exploded into violence in 1936. From the start, both sides received material and financial support from other countries; the Nationalists were given aid by Italy and Germany, while the Republicans received help from the Soviet Union. The press in the United States generally sided with the Republicans, as did many writers, including Ernest Hemingway and George Orwell. More than forty thousand foreigners took part in the International Brigades on the Republican side, including the so-called Abraham Lincoln Brigade made up of Americans. Most of the foreigners were idealistic leftists who were soon disenchanted with the fighting and the inhuman actions of the supposed freedom fighters serving in the ranks of the Republican forces.

Murder, assassination, and torture were commonplace from the start on both sides, but the Republicans were marked by two characteristics. The first was a tendency toward disunity. The movement was made up of socialists and hard-line communists, but they disagreed on their leadership and ultimate ends. There were those who followed the Soviet agents sent by Joseph Stalin while others preferred his hated rival, Leon Trotsky. The Republican cause unraveled over time, undone by internal squabbling and assassinations of rivals. Second, the Republicans waged a terrible campaign against the

Church, massacring priests, nuns, and laypeople with great venom.

Often overlooked or ignored by historians of the Civil War (who focus instead on the reprisals by the Nationalists) were the murders of priests and bishops in the first months of the war. It is estimated that 6,832 priests were killed, including thirteen bishops. The slaughter depended almost entirely on geographical fortunes. Priests and nuns who found themselves in territories controlled by the Nationalists were generally safe, while those in places controlled by the Republicans were in enormous danger. The area in and around Madrid, for example, witnessed the murder of more than 1,100 priests.

Many writers and apologists for the Republicans have tried to explain away the atrocities, but there are few defenses for the murder of innocent priests and nuns, or the torture and abuse of elderly Catholic women who died simply because their sons and daughters had vocations. By 1939 the position of the Republican armies deteriorated, and on March 28, 1939, Madrid passed into the control of the Nationalists.

Estimates of the casualties in the war have been placed at between half a million and a million. The war had literally destroyed the unity of Spain, and it had served as the backdrop of the wider struggle between fascist Germany and Italy, and communist Russia, while the wider world saw yet another terrible war that the League of Nations was powerless to stop. Soon, an even bigger war began with Nazi Germany's invasion of Poland.

Americans were bitterly divided over the war. Many considered it fashionable to support the Republican cause, but Catholic sentiment was strongly on the side of Franco (a Gallup poll in 1938 found a solid 58 percent of Catholics supported the Nationalists, compared with a mere 17 percent among Protestants).

The Catholic position reflected both the recognition by Catholics of what would befall the Church in Spain should the Republicans win, and the fact that the Church stood in firm opposition to communism in all its forms. American Catholics were especially committed to resisting the Soviet Union, a dedication that continued throughout the Cold War.

Spanish Missions

The voyages of Christopher Columbus were followed by other expeditions and then the thunderous campaigns of the conquistadors. The West Indies were firmly in Spanish hands by 1515; the Aztec Empire had fallen by 1521 to the troops of the conquistador Hernando Cortés; and by 1536 the Incan Empire had been toppled by Francisco Pizarro. The end of the Incan Empire marked the last of the major Spanish conquests, and Spain began the much longer process of consolidation, forging a permanent Spanish presence in Central and South America, and then exploring into North America. Only Brazil was outside of their sphere of control as that was under the Portuguese by the terms of the Treaty of Tordesillas of 1496 negotiated by Pope Alexander VI.

Spanish missionaries were involved every step of the way. There was no shortage of volunteers to serve in the New World from among the clergy of Spain, including Franciscans and Augustinians, as well as the Jesuits after their founding in the middle of the sixteenth century. The missionaries were often among the best educated and dedicated priests and friars in Spain (an identical phenomenon was found among the French missionaries), and many willingly gave their lives for the faith through years of toil in the wilds or as martyrs at the hands of hostile tribes. The Black Legend and modern anti-Catholicism have sullied the reputation of these remarkable missionaries.

In 1511 Pope Julius II decreed the creation of the first diocese in what became the United States with the Diocese of Puerto Rico (later renamed the Diocese of San Juan and today an archdiocese), and Alonso Manso became the first resident bishop in the New World. Two years later, Juan Ponce de León departed the Spanish-held Caribbean and entered Florida. Missionaries then made Florida the first region for serious evangelization in what became the United States.

For the first half of the sixteenth century, however, Spanish expeditions failed to establish a lasting presence, and missionaries traveling with them encountered determinedly hostile native tribes. In 1558 a more concerted effort was made when the Dominicans assumed direction of the missions, starting with the expedition of Tristán de Luna in 1559. This proved a failure, and the Dominicans were succeeded by the Jesuits. They in turn left Florida in 1572 as the general of the Jesuits, St. Francis Borgia, concluded that the conditions there and the hostility of the Indians offered little prospect for a permanent settlement.

As the French were by then making their presence felt in North America, the Spanish government decided to make another try. Under Pedro Menéndez de Avilés, an expedition founded St. Augustine in 1565, the first permanent city in Spanish Florida. He was accompanied by two priests who began the first parish in the United States at St. Augustine. Real progress followed after 1577 with the Franciscans, who forged a chain of missions across Florida and then into Georgia. They converted more than thirty thousand Indians by 1634.

The toil and sacrifice of the missionaries and converted Indians proved ultimately fleeting. As the English colonies expanded to the north, the missions fell under attack as part of the wider conflict between Spain and England. During Queen Anne's War from 1702 to 1713 (known in Europe as the War of the Spanish Succession), English troops and colonists, with their Indian allies, launched brutal attacks on the Florida missions from their bases in the Carolinas. Churches were burned to the ground, friars were tortured and then killed, and Catholic Indians were slaughtered. Already suffering decline because of the weakened Spanish government in Florida, the missions received further blows during the French and Indian Wars (in Europe, the Seven Years' War); St. Augustine was sacked in 1763. That same year, Spain lost Florida to England in the Treaty of Paris. There was supposed religious freedom in Florida under the English, but the lingering Spanish elements soon left the area.

Twenty years later, Florida was reclaimed by Spain following the American Revolution. The Franciscans asked permission to return to Florida, but by then the Spanish crown had little interest in assisting the Church. The request was refused, with the result that by 1819, when Florida became a possession of the United States, the pale Catholic presence was soon completely overshadowed by Protestant American immigrants. Effectively, Catholicism had to start over again.

Spanish missionaries had hoped to set out for the lands north of Mexico soon after the capture of the Aztec Empire. Franciscans thus regularly went out with the first explorers. One of the greatest of these was the Franciscan Juan de Padilla, who set out with Francisco Vázquez de Coronado on his expedition of 1540. Father Padilla was martyred by an Indian band two years later in what is now Kansas; by his death he became the protomartyr of the United States, the first of the literally hundreds of martyrs among the early missionaries.

The lasting missions in New Mexico were begun in 1598 by nine Franciscans under Alonso Martínez, following the work of the explorer Juan de Oñate, who then introduced Spanish settlers into the region. Santa Fe was founded in 1609 and served as the center for considerable missionary labors, so that by 1630 there were over eighty thousand Indian converts living in pueblos under the Franciscans.

The local natives' dislike for the Spaniards, unfortunately, stirred up such ill feeling among some of the Indians that the Pueblos revolted in 1680. Most of the missions were destroyed in the uprising, and Franciscans could not resume their efforts until 1692; one final rebellion occurred in 1696, after which the Church in New Mexico enjoyed relative calm for centuries under the Franciscans and the overall ecclesiastical jurisdiction of the bishop of Durango.

The 1927 novel *Death Comes for the Archbishop*, by Willa Cather presents a remarkable literary portrait of the Church in the later New Mexico Territory; the work is ranked as one of the greatest novels of the twentieth century.

In nearby Texas, Spanish explorers made a survey as early as 1629, but it was not until 1657 that the Franciscan Juan Larios opened a mission along the Nueves River in southeastern Texas. Little progress was made until 1685, when word arrived in Mexico that the great French explorer René-Robert Chevalier, Sieur de La Salle, had made his way into the Lower Mississippi Valley. Fearing further French incursions, the Spanish built a fort on Matagorda Bay. Franciscans provided pastoral care for the soldiers and growing community and served as missionaries to the surrounding tribes.

Expansion of the Texas missions was accomplished following the founding of the beloved mission of San Antonio de Valero, near San Antonio (known today as the Alamo), in 1718 by the remarkable Franciscan missionary Venerable Antonio Margil de Jesús. Father Margil was particularly famed for his missions among the Nacogdoches Indians; according to popular legend, he ended a drought among the Nacogdoches by striking a rock with a cane and drawing out water. Among the other missions he founded were Mission Dolores and San Miguel. In 1720 he founded Mission San Jose, which was soon declared "the Glory of New Spain."

Life for the Franciscans was incredibly arduous as there were few colonists, the Indians were nomadic by culture, and many of the tribes, such as the Apaches, were bitterly opposed to the Spanish. By the end of the eighteenth century, the Franciscans were replaced by regular diocesan priests, and evangelization among the Native Americans effectively ended. In the early nineteenth century and the end of Spanish rule, Texas had a European population of barely four thousand, and a quarter of them were soldiers. Already Americans were on the move into Texas in the wake of the Louisiana Purchase, and the future of the region was destined to be an American one.

One final figure in the history of the Southwest missions is the saintly Jesuit priest Eusebius Kino. Father Kino spent his life on horseback and founded missions, such as the magnificent San Xavier del Bac, across the Southwest and Lower California. For his defense of the Native Americans, his long travels, and his holiness, he is revered as the founder of Christianity in the Southwest. He represents the state of Arizona in Statuary Hall in the U.S. Capitol in Washington, D.C., and in 1995 his cause for canonization was introduced in Rome.

The missions of Alta California (the name given to California above Baja) begin officially on July 16, 1769, with the start of the Franciscan mission at San Diego, the first of twenty-one missions founded between 1769 and 1823. The Franciscans were responsible for forging *El Camino Real* (the "Royal Road"), a chain of missions that extended from San Diego to San Francisco. The California missions served as the principle centers of evangelization in California, and "life under the bells" was the chief way of living for thousands of Indians, who were taught trades and assisted in finding a place in the Spanish society that had suddenly been thrust upon them.

The central figure in the California missions was the Franciscan friar Blessed Junípero Serra. Despite a severe limp as a result of an infected mosquito bite to his leg that made every step painful, Father Serra walked literally thousands of miles, personally founded nine of the missions on the *Camino Real*, converted and cared for thousands of Indians, and guided the California missions until his death from tuberculosis at Mission San Carlos. Junípero Serra was beatified by Pope Blessed John Paul II in 1988.

With the Mexican Revolution against Spain in 1821, the California missions came to an end as they became the property of a hostile Mexican government. In 1834 the secularization of the missions was declared, but the promises to the Indians of land and livestock never materialized, and the death rate of the Native Americans was worse than that of slaves in the American South. Chaos ensued as the Mexican government slid into anarchy, and by 1850 there were barely thirteen priests in the whole of California. The circumstances were already changing quickly, however, with the discovery of gold at Sutter's Mill in 1848 and the massive invasion of prospectors into the territory. Spanish California was soon replaced by an American California, and from 1850 Catholicism looked east rather than south.

The missions of *El Camino Real*, much like the entire Spanish mission era, have been the subject of much controversy. Some have charged the Franciscans with abuse and repression; Blessed Junípero Serra was accused of perpetrating genocide against the California Indians. It is true that the Indian population declined severely, in the main from the diseases of the white settlers (a common tragedy across the whole of North America). Still, Junípero Serra loved the Indians under his care, and a balanced understanding is crucial to appreciate the true legacy of the California missions. Further, the legacy of the Spanish missions in North America must not be overlooked. This tradition has become most apparent as the Hispanic Catholic population has increased extensively in the last decades.

Spellman, Francis J. (May 4, 1889–December 2, 1967)

Archbishop of New York from 1939 to 1967 and a cardinal from 1946, Francis J. Spellman was one of the most influential American Catholic leaders in the middle of the twentieth century. Born in Whitman, Massachusetts, the son of William Spellman and Ellen Conway Spellman, he was called to the priesthood and studied at Fordham University and then the North American College in Rome. While in Rome, he attended the Propaganda Fide, where he earned a doctorate despite bouts of poor health, including pneumonia. He also made a number of important contacts in Rome, including the future Cardinals Francesco Borgongini Duca and Domenico Tardini.

Ordained on May 14, 1916, in Rome, he returned to Boston and served in pastoral ministry from 1916 to 1918. From 1918 to 1922 he was vice chancellor of the archdiocese, and in 1925 he became the first American to be appointed an attaché in the Vatican Secretariat of State; in this post, he was named by Pope Pius XI a privy chamberlain of His Holiness.

While in Rome, Spellman became a friend of then Archbishop Eugenio Pacelli (the future Pope Pius XII). He also was given the delicate task in 1931 of smuggling Pius XI's encyclical *Non Abbiamo Bisogno* — which condemned national socialism in general and Benito Mussolini in particular — from Rome to Paris, where it was given global distribution.

On July 30, 1932, he was appointed titular bishop of Sila and auxiliary bishop of Boston; he was consecrated on September 8, 1932, in Rome by Cardinal Pacelli. It came as little surprise to observers of the Church in the United States when Spellman was named archbishop of New York on April 15, 1939; a few months later, he was named military vicar of the United States Armed Forces. He was created a cardinal priest in the consistory of February 18, 1946, and received the title of SS. Giovanni e Paolo on February 22, 1946.

As archbishop in New York, Spellman was the most powerful Catholic leader in the country, was given the nickname of "the Powerhouse," and presided over the continued expansion of diocesan facilities and schools. His skills in the area of finances were famous, and he became known in New York as "Cardinal Moneybags" because of his ability to provide for the financial well-being of the archdiocese.

He proved a friend and supporter of President Franklin Delano Roosevelt. Once America was in World War II, he was a close confidant to the president and was used by him as a reliable emissary around the world; he was a valuable figure in securing the declaration of Rome as an "open city" in the war, thereby saving it from possible destruction.

After the war, Cardinal Spellman was an ardent anti-communist and backed the investigations of Senator Joseph McCarthy. He opposed

Cardinal Francis Spellman

vehemently a strike by the gravediggers at Calvary Cemetery in Queens and recruited seminarians to serve as strikebreakers. He likewise had a public disagreement with Eleanor Roosevelt over federal funding for parochial schools. When in 1960 the Catholic Senator John F. Kennedy also came out against federal aid (and opposed the appointment of an American ambassador to the Holy See), Cardinal Spellman ended his longtime backing of the Kennedy family. In the 1960 presidential campaign, he threw his endorsement to Richard M. Nixon.

In 1958 Cardinal Spellman took part in the conclave that elected Cardinal Angelo Roncalli as Pope Blessed John XXIII, and in 1963 he also voted in the conclave that resulted in the election of Cardinal Giuseppe Montini as Pope Paul VI. He took part in the Second Vatican Council from 1962 to 1965 and represented the conservative element of American Catholicism in its proceedings. He took part in the debates and gave his backing to the Declaration on Religious Freedom, *Dignitatis Humanae*. He was opposed to the reform of the liturgy that included the adoption of the vernacular.

Back home in the United States, he threw his weight behind Lyndon Baines Johnson in 1964 and became a strong advocate for the Vietnam War as he saw it as a worthy cause to oppose the spread of communism. Similarly, he promoted U.S. policy

in Asia and Latin America. He spoke out against racial discrimination and provided funds for nuns and priests to take part in the Selma marches. Nevertheless, he opposed most of the trends of the era and found himself at odds with many of his flock who marched against the war.

Cardinal Spellman submitted his resignation to Pope Paul VI in 1966 upon turning seventy-five, but the pontiff asked him to stay on in his post. He died in New York, and his funeral was attended by President Johnson, Vice President Hubert Humphrey, Senators Robert Kennedy and Jacob Javits, Governor Nelson Rockefeller and Mayor John Lindsay of New York, and more than one hundred Catholic bishops. He was buried in the crypt of St. Patrick's Cathedral. A poet and novelist, he also made translations of a number of works on theology from the original Italian.

Spokane, Diocese of

Established on December 17, 1913, by Pope St. Pius X, the Diocese of Spokane serves counties in eastern Washington State. The site served as a trading post for trappers, located on the falls of the Spokane River. The waterway and the city were named after the Spokane Indians, the original residents. The diocese is a suffragan of the Archdiocese of Seattle.

The center of the activities of the North West Fur Company in 1810, Spokane welcomed the Northern Pacific Railroad and served as a shipping post. Rich in forests, agricultural lands, and mineral fields, the city grew steadily, allowing Spokane to become incorporated in 1881. A disastrous fire in 1889 destroyed much of the city, but it was rebuilt and reincorporated. The people of Spokane also made use of the metal fields in nearby Couer d'Alene.

The Catholic heritage of Spokane opened with the arrival in 1838 of the famous mission pioneers Fathers Francis Norbert Blanchet and Modeste Demers. At the time, the area was called the "Oregon Country." Coming to the region, these priests faced anti-Catholic sentiment from the local residents but persevered in their labors, forging the great Catholic presence in the northwestern part of the nation.

Also on hand was the Jesuit Father Pierre-Jean De Smet, who had served both the local Indian tribes and the fur trappers. He celebrated Mass at the annual Rendezvous of the area's mountain men and established St. Ignatius Mission. The revered Jesuit Father Joseph M. Cataldo also aided the growth of the faith, as he was beloved by the regional Indian nations.

In 1843 the territory was made a vicariate apostolic by the Holy See, and Blanchet was consecrated as a bishop. Serving as vicar apostolic, Bishop Blanchet had the aid of his brother, Augustin Magliore Blanchet, who became the bishop of Walla Walla. He moved to Nesqually in 1850 and then, in 1907, to Seattle. The Whitman massacre in 1847 and the Cayuse War that followed led to the departure of the Diocese of Walla Walla in 1850 to Nesqually and the subsequent movement of the see to Seattle in 1907.

Owing to the extensive growth of the Catholic population in eastern Washington, the Diocese of Spokane was erected in 1913, and the first bishop of the new diocese was Bishop Augustine Francis Schinner, who had been bishop of Superior from 1905 to 1913. He was installed as the first bishop of Spokane on April 18, 1914. He forged the first diocesan administration and offices for the new diocese and served throughout World War I. He retired on December 17, 1925, and began serving as a missionary in Bolivia from 1925 to 1928.

The second bishop of Spokane, Charles D. White, had been a priest of the Diocese of Grand Rapids. Appointed on December 20, 1926, he was consecrated a bishop on February 24, 1927. His time as bishop extended across the decades of the Great Depression, the Second World War, and the postwar era of growth. He built a variety of schools, hospitals, and convents, and encouraged the Confraternity of Christian Doctrine and the National Catholic Rural Life Conference. He died on September 25, 1955.

Bishop White's successor, Bernard Topel, who had been appointed coadjutor bishop of Spokane on August 9, 1955, was consecrated a bishop on September 21, and acceded to the see with Bishop White's passing only four days later. As bishop, Tobel attended the Second Vatican Council and was active in implementing the reforms of the council and in promoting new parishes, hospitals, and schools, and the spiritual life of the diocese. This effort included promoting the Maryknoll missions in Guatemala. He retired on April 11, 1978.

The fourth bishop of Spokane, Lawrence H. Welsh, had been a priest of Rapid City and was appointed on November 6, 1978, and consecrated a bishop on December 14, 1978. He resigned as bishop on April 17, 1989, after he was arrested for drunk driving. He subsequently served as an auxiliary bishop of St. Paul and Minneapolis.

The fifth bishop of Spokane, William S. Skylstad, was a priest of the Diocese of Spokane and had served as bishop of Yakima since February 22, 1977. Appointed on April 17, 1990, and installed on April 27, 1990, Bishop Skylstad sought to provide stability in leadership after the resignation of Bishop Welsh. He went on to become vice president of the United States Conference of Catholic Bishops from 2001 to 2004 and then president of the USCCB from 2004 to 2007. His time was also marked by the problems created by the sexual abuse crisis within the diocese, and in December 2004 the diocese was forced to declare bankruptcy in the face of cases being filed by victims. The Diocese of Spokane paid about $48 million as part of settlement agreements. Bishop Skylstad retired on June 30, 2010.

He was succeeded by Blase J. Cupich, who had been a priest of the Archdiocese of Omaha and then bishop of Rapid City since 1998. He was appointed bishop of Spokane on June 30, 2010. In 2011 there were 103,000 Catholics in the diocese, served by 160 priests and 58 parishes.

Springfield in Illinois, Diocese of

Established on July 29, 1853, as the Diocese of Quincy by Pope Blessed Pius IX, the ecclesiastical jurisdiction was transferred to Alton in 1857 and then transferred again to Springfield in Illinois on October 26, 1923, by Pope Blessed Pius XI. The diocese serves counties in the central part of Illinois. Springfield in Illinois is a suffragan of the Archdiocese of Chicago.

The city of Springfield was founded by John Kelly, who had arrived in the area from the Carolina region and built a cabin for hunting in 1818. Others joined his settlement, mainly fur trappers, and the site was named Springfield, after the nearby Spring Creek. Soon stagecoaches arrived on a biweekly basis, linking the area to the city of St. Louis. More and more families arrived to be part of the growing community. Young Abraham Lincoln was one of the new settlers in 1831, and he played an important role in the future of the growing town, especially the call for it to become the new capital of Illinois. Springfield became the capital in 1839, a position it retains today. The association with Lincoln continued with his burial there with his wife, Mary Todd Lincoln, and three of his four sons, in Oak Ridge Cemetery, as well as the Abraham Lincoln Presidential Library and Museum.

The city was a major hub for the Union Army during the Civil War and then for the railroads that promoted the local coal-mining industry. The city was also much troubled by the tragic violence of race riots in 1908 that led to the lynching of two African-Americans and the deaths of four whites. Today, the city has a population of about 116,000.

The Catholic history of Springfield traces itself back to the slow but steady arrival of immigrants in the area through the railroads and the search for work in Illinois on the part of Germans, Irish, and others. The ecclesiastical jurisdiction changed hands several times in the nineteenth century, including the Diocese of Bardstown in 1808, St. Louis in 1826, and Vincennes in 1834. In 1843 the entire state of Illinois was placed under the see of Chicago. In the face of the continuing development of the Catholic population, the decision was made by the First Plenary Council of Baltimore in 1852 to increase the number of dioceses. On July 29, 1853, Pope Blessed Pius IX founded the Diocese of Quincy, comprising the fifty-six counties of southern Illinois and encompassing what are now the Dioceses of Springfield in Illinois and Belleville.

The first bishop of Quincy was initially to be Joseph Melcher, who was serving as the vicar general of St. Louis, but he declined the position. As Catholics in the area pushed for the transfer of the see away from Quincy, on January 9, 1857, Pope Pius IX transferred it to Alton, with its first

bishop, Henry Damian Juncker, a priest from Ohio. Consecrated a bishop on April 26, 1857, in Cincinnati, Juncker focused his efforts on giving the new diocese a firm footing. He visited the parishes of the diocese, issued a pastoral letter to encourage the return of lapsed Catholics, and made a trip to Europe to recruit new priests. He invited the Recollect Franciscans of Paderborn, Germany, to establish a community in the diocese and used their skills to start St. Francis Solanus College in Quincy and St. Joseph's Seminary in Teutopolis. He also encouraged the arrival of communities of women religious to assist the diocese in various ways, including education. Bishop Juncker died on October 2, 1868.

The second bishop of Alton, Peter J. Baltes, had served as a priest of the Diocese of Chicago and was appointed to Alton on September 24, 1869, and consecrated a bishop in Belleville on January 23, 1870. He promoted Catholic education and invited additional communities of women religious, including the Springfield Dominicans, the Hospital Sisters of St. Francis, and the Sisters Adorers of the Precious Blood. By the time of his passing on February 5, 1888, the diocese was blessed with schools, orphanages, and hospitals. Meanwhile, in 1887, Pope Leo XIII established the Diocese of Belleville, taking territory from the Diocese of Alton.

The third bishop of Alton, James Ryan, had been a priest of the Diocese of Louisville and served in Bardstown and Peoria. Consecrated a bishop on May 1, 1888, he enjoyed the longest term of any bishop of the diocese, thirty-five years, and presided over a remarkable period of expansion as the next waves of immigration arrived in the diocese. He continued the development of Catholic education, improved the diocesan orphanage, and convoked a diocesan synod in 1889. Bishop Ryan died on July 2, 1923.

The fourth bishop of Alton, James A. Griffin, was appointed on November 10, 1923, only days after the October 26, 1923, announcement by Pope Pius XI that the diocese was being transferred from Alton to Springfield. Griffin was consecrated a bishop on February 25, 1924, and took as his main task reestablishing the diocese in Springfield. He raised money for a new cathedral and dedicated it on October 14, 1928, as part of the anniversary celebrations of the diocese. He was noted also for his efficient administration of the diocese and was active during the Great Depression, assisting the poor people impacted by the economic downturn, and World War II. He likewise encouraged a vibrant lay apostolate and supported a host of lay groups, including Catholic Action, the Holy Name Society, the Confraternity of Christian Doctrine, the Legion of Mary, and the Legion of Decency. Bishop Griffin died on August 5, 1948.

The second bishop of Springfield, William A. O'Connor, was a priest of the Archdiocese of Chicago. Appointed to Springfield on December 28, 1948, he was consecrated a bishop on March 7, 1949. He focused on promoting vocations and improving the education of seminarians. In 1961 the Latin School was declared the Diocesan Seminary of the Immaculate Conception, and it remained in operation until 1986. He attended all four sessions of the Second Vatican Council and was active in its deliberations. He then worked to implement the reforms of the council. Bishop O'Connor resigned on July 22, 1975, at the age of seventy-one, owing to health issues.

The third bishop of Springfield, Joseph A. McNicholas, was a priest of the St. Louis archdiocese and an auxiliary bishop for that archdiocese since 1969. Installed on September 3, 1975, he promoted civil rights and the desegregation of schools in the diocese. He also was a leader in the early pro-life effort after the Supreme Court's *Roe v. Wade* decision legalizing abortion in 1973. He died unexpectedly on April 17, 1983.

The fourth bishop of Springfield, Daniel L. Ryan, had been an auxiliary bishop for Joliet since 1981. Installed in Springfield on January 18, 1984, he was active in lay participation in the life of the diocese, including an Office for Lay Ministry and a Lay Ministry Formation Program. He also opened the Office for Campus Ministry. Bishop Ryan retired on October 19, 1999.

Bishop Ryan's successor, Bishop George J. Lucas, was appointed on the same day as Ryan's retirement. Consecrated a bishop on December 14, 1999, he made one of his priorities a capital campaign for the diocese, Harvest of Thanks, Springtime of Hope, which raised more than $22 million. He also established a program for the permanent diaconate,

celebrated the 150th anniversary of the founding of the diocese in 2002–03, and raised more than $11 million to restore the Cathedral of the Immaculate Conception. On June 3, 2009, he was appointed archbishop of Omaha.

On April 20, 2010, Bishop Thomas John J. Paprocki was appointed the sixth bishop of Springfield. He had served as an auxiliary bishop of Chicago since 2003. In 2011 there were more than 141,000 Catholics in the diocese, served by 160 priests, more than 550 men and women religious, and 132 parishes.

Springfield in Massachusetts, Diocese of

Established on June 14, 1870, by Pope Blessed Pius IX, the Diocese of Springfield in Massachusetts serves counties in central and western Massachusetts. The diocese is a suffragan of the Archdiocese of Boston. The original settlement, reportedly called Pynchon for a time, was on the west bank of the Connecticut River. Fear of attacks by local Indian tribes, however, led to a transfer of the site to the east bank in 1641. No Catholics were allowed to take part in public life, and priests were forbidden to enter the area. By 1700 the penalty for priests serving Catholics in the region was execution.

In 1755 and 1756 Acadians, deprived of their lands in the north because of their Catholicism and French customs, were brought by boat to Massachusetts and other states and given the status of indentured servants. The Acadians and other Catholics served in the American Revolution and earned the respect of their fellow inhabitants in Massachusetts. When the constitution of Massachusetts was enacted, Catholics received their civil rights. The Catholics in some parts, however, had to take an oath denying allegiance to any foreign power, particularly the Holy See in Rome. Catholics in New England were placed under the jurisdiction of Boston with the creation of that see in 1808.

Irish Catholic settlers began arriving in the area over the next decades, and they settled especially in western and central Massachusetts. In 1834 Father James Fitton constructed a church in Worcester, the first in what later became the Diocese of Springfield. He likewise worked to establish the College of the Holy Cross in Worcester in 1843, founded especially through the support of Bishop Benedict

Joseph Fenwick of Boston, the first Catholic college in New England. Famed local priests included John D. Brady, the first resident pastor in western Massachusetts, Jeremiah O'Callaghan, and Bernard O'Cavanaugh, who founded parishes and gave welcome to the growing Catholic community.

By 1870 the size of the Catholic population warranted the establishment of a new diocese in Massachusetts. Five counties of central and cestern Massachusetts — Worcester, Hampden, Hampshire, Franklin, and Berkshire — were separated from the Archdiocese of Boston.

The first bishop of Springfield was Patrick T. O'Reilly, an Irish-born priest of Boston, who was consecrated a bishop on September 25, 1870. He worked to establish the offices and structures needed for the diocese, all the while trying to keep pace with the growing population. In his time as bishop, the Catholic population increased from ninety thousand to two hundred thousand, and he founded forty-five churches and presided over the construction of more than one hundred other buildings. He died on May 28, 1892.

The second bishop of Springfield, Thomas D. Beaven, was a Springfield native and was appointed on July 31, 1892, and consecrated a bishop on October 18, 1892. Bishop Beaven continued the expansion of diocesan facilities, including various charitable institutions for the aged and orphans, and hospitals in Worcester, Springfield, Montague City, and Adams.

By 1900 there were many different religious communities of men and women in the diocese, including Sisters of Providence, Sisters of Mercy, Grey Nuns, Little Franciscan Sisters of Mary, Sisters of the Good Shepherd, Sisters of St. Joseph, Sisters of Notre Dame, Sisters of the Holy Cross and of the Seven Dolors, Sisters of St. Ann, Sisters of the Assumption, Sisters of Providence, Faithful Companions of Jesus, Sisters of St. Joseph from Hartford, Presentation Nuns, Felician Sisters, Franciscan Sisters from Buffalo, and Daughters of the Holy Ghost. There were also Jesuits, La Salette Fathers, Franciscans, Vincentians, Fathers of the Assumption, and Xaverian Brothers. The growth of the diocese was hastened by the steady influx of immigrants, including Irish, Canadians, Poles, and Lithuanians.

Bishop Beaven died on October 5, 1920. The third bishop of Springfield, Thomas M. O'Leary, had been a priest of the Manchester diocese. Appointed on June 16, 1921, he was consecrated a bishop on September 8, 1921, and continued the development of the diocese. He helped found the College of Our Lady of the Elms, a college for women, in Chicopee in 1928, promoted the Society for the Propagation of the Faith in each parish, started a monthly diocesan newspaper, the *Catholic Mirror,* and reorganized the diocesan school system. He also led the diocese through the Great Depression and World War II. He died on October 10, 1949.

The fourth bishop of Springfield, Christopher J. Weldon, was a priest of the Archdiocese of New York and had been a chaplain during World War II. Appointed on January 28, 1950, he was consecrated a bishop on March 24, 1950. His twenty-seven years as bishop marked the ongoing growth of the diocese, including the construction of new schools and the expansion of hospitals, as well as new parishes, the start of a weekly diocesan newspaper, and a center for the Hispanic community in Springfield. He also attended the Second Vatican Council and worked to implement the reforms of the council. Bishop Weldon retired on October 15, 1977.

The fifth bishop of Springfield, Joseph F. Maguire, had been an auxiliary bishop of Boston since 1971. Appointed coadjutor bishop of Springfield on April 13, 1976, he acceded to the see on October 15, 1977. He presided over the diocese during a time of considerable economic and social upheaval. He retired on December 27, 1991.

The sixth bishop of Springfield, John A. Marshall, had been bishop of Burlington since 1971. He was appointed to Springfield on February 18, 1992, but died after only three years, on July 3, 1994, at the age of sixty-six.

Bishop Marshall was succeeded by Bishop Thomas L. Dupré, who had been an auxiliary bishop of Springfield since 1990. Appointed bishop of Springfield on March 14, 1995, he was installed on May 8, 1995. He resigned for health reasons on February 11, 2004, and was subsequently indicted by a grand jury in September 2004 for sexual abuse of minors, although the charges were dropped owing to the expiration of the statute of limitations.

Bishop Dupré was followed by Timothy A.

McDonnell, who had been an auxiliary bishop of New York since 2001. Appointed to Springfield on March 9, 2004, and installed on April 1, 2004, he was faced with the challenge of repairing the spiritual damage caused by the ongoing sexual abuse crisis and the demographic changes in the diocese, including the controversial closing of various parishes. In 2011 there were 216,000 Catholics in the diocese, served by 185 priests, more than 400 men and women religious, and 82 parishes.

Springfield-Cape Girardeau, Diocese of

Established on July 2, 1956, by Pope Pius XII, the Diocese of Springfield-Cape Girardeau serves counties in southern Missouri. Springfield, founded in 1829, developed a solid economy based on dairy products and manufacturing. Cape Girardeau, on the Mississippi River, became an industrial center, with agriculture and livestock in the early years. The diocese is a suffragan see of the Archdiocese of St. Louis.

The Catholic legacy of the diocese began with French trappers, who founded St. Genevieve in 1735 and moved throughout the region. In 1770 the pioneering and revered missionary Father Pierre Gibault established the first Catholic parish in St. Louis, and soon after the Capuchin Franciscan missionaries came north from the Florida missions and established outposts of the faith. By 1780 Catholic families within the boundaries of the modern-day diocese were building enclaves served by visiting priests. The oldest parish in what became the diocese was in New Madrid, dedicated in 1789. The town was devastated in 1811 by an earthquake, and it took some ten years for the parish to be reorganized.

With the Louisiana Purchase of 1803, the population increased steadily, including Catholics. In 1818 Bishop Louis Dubourg, bishop of the Diocese of Louisiana and the Two Floridas (today the Archdiocese of New Orleans), established his episcopal residence in St. Louis. To assist the needs of Catholics he set up a series of Mass stations, and in 1826 Missouri was established as a separate ecclesiastical territory through the foundation of the Diocese of St. Louis, with its boundaries extending along the western Mississippi Valley.

The Congregation of the Missions, the Vincentians, opened a parish in Cape Girardeau in 1836. The Sisters of Loretto also established a convent in the area. In the 1870s, Springfield became a hub of Catholic presence, and St. Louis served as the heart of Catholic expansion.

In 1868 and 1880 the Dioceses of St. Joseph and Kansas City, respectively, were created out of territory taken from St. Louis. The Catholic population continued to increase in the area, and by 1956 a restructuring of the jurisdictions was needed. The two dioceses of St. Joseph and Kansas City were combined, and territory was taken from these dioceses and the Archdiocese of St. Louis to form the new Diocese of Springfield-Cape Girardeau. At its founding, there were some 36,000 Catholics in the diocese, served by 120 priests, some 400 men and women religious, and 90 parishes.

The first bishop of Springfield-Cape Girardeau, Charles H. Helmsing, had been an auxiliary bishop of St. Louis since 1949. Appointed on August 24, 1956, he established the foundational offices and administration for the diocese but was transferred to the Diocese of Kansas City-St. Joseph in 1962.

The second bishop of Springfield-Cape Girardeau, Ignatius J. Strecker, was a priest of the Diocese of Wichita. Appointed on April 11, 1962, he was consecrated a bishop on June 20, 1962. His arrival coincided with the Second Vatican Council, and throughout the council he had the distinction of sitting next to Bishop Karol Wojtyla, who went on to become Pope John Paul II. Bishop Strecker worked to implement the decrees of the council until his appointment as archbishop of Kansas City in Kansas in 1969.

On February 18, 1970, William W. Baum was appointed the third bishop of Springfield-Cape Girardeau. A priest of Kansas City, he was consecrated a bishop on April 6, 1970. Bishop Baum served for three years, until March 5, 1973, when he was appointed the archbishop of Washington. He was named a cardinal in 1976 by Pope Paul VI and was later the prefect of the Congregation for Education in Rome and then the Apostolic Penitentiary. He retired in 2001.

The fourth bishop of Springfield-Cape Girardeau, Bernard F. Law, was a priest of the Diocese of Natchez-Jackson, the editor of the diocesan newspaper, and a well-known figure in the civil rights movement. Appointed on October 22, 1973, he was consecrated a bishop on December 5, 1973. His decade was marked by efforts to implement the reforms of the Second Vatican Council and a significant role in ecumenical dialogue and interreligious dialogue. He started the Missouri Christian Leadership Conference, served as a member of the Secretariat for Promoting Christian Unity for the Holy See, and from 1976 to 1981 was a consultor to the Vatican's Commission for Religious Relations with the Jews; he also chaired the Committee on Ecumenical and Interreligious Affairs for the National Conference of Catholic Bishops. On January 11, 1984, he was appointed archbishop of Boston and was installed on March 23, 1984. The next year he was named to the College of Cardinals.

The fifth bishop of Springfield-Cape Girardeau, John J. Leibrecht, had been a priest of the Archdiocese of St. Louis. Appointed on October 20, 1984, Leibrecht was consecrated a bishop on December 12, 1984, and began a tenure that lasted for twenty-three years. He presided over the steady growth of the diocese and succeeded in maintaining the number of priests during a period of general decline. Bishop Leibrecht retired on January 24, 2008.

The sixth bishop of Springfield-Cape Girardeau, James Vann Johnston Jr., had been a priest of the Diocese of Knoxville. He was appointed bishop on January 24, 2008, and was consecrated a bishop on March 31, 2008. As of 2011, there were 68,000 Catholics in the diocese, served by 120 priests, and 66 parishes.

Stafford, James Francis (July 26, 1932–)

Archbishop of Denver from 1986 to 1996, president of the Pontifical Council for the Laity from 1996 to 2003, and Major Penitentiary of the Church from 2005 to 2009, James Francis Stafford served as a cardinal from 1998. Born in Baltimore, the only child of Francis Emmett and Mary Dorothy Stanton, Stafford initially considered a career in medicine. He answered the call to the priesthood, however, and entered St. Mary's Seminary in Baltimore. After two years of studies, he was sent to Rome to complete his formation at the Pontifical North American College. While in Rome, he earned a licentiate in sacred theology from the Pontifical Gregorian University. He later earned a

master's degree in social welfare from The Catholic University of America, in Washington, D.C.

Ordained a priest on December 15, 1957, at the North American College, Stafford spent several years in pastoral ministry in the Archdiocese of Baltimore and was also director of Archdiocesan Catholic Charities from 1966 to 1976. Appointed titular bishop of Respetta and auxiliary bishop of Baltimore on January 19, 1976, he was consecrated on February 29, 1976, and served as vicar general of Baltimore from 1976 to 1982. On November 17, 1982, he was appointed bishop of Memphis. During his time as bishop, he focused on diocesan finances and pastoral outreach to African-Americans. During this time, he also served as chairman of the United States Conference of Catholic Bishops Commission for Ecumenical and Interreligious Affairs from 1984 to 1991 and co-president of the Dialogue between Roman Catholics and Lutherans from 1984 to 1997.

Named archbishop of Denver on May 30, 1986, he launched a major fundraising drive for the archdiocese and celebrated the highlight of his tenure in 1993 when Denver hosted World Youth Day and a visit by Pope Blessed John Paul II. It is generally believed that the pontiff was so impressed with the archdiocese and with Archbishop Stafford that he appointed him president of the Pontifical Council for the Laity in Rome on August 20, 1996. Stafford was created a cardinal deacon on February 21, 1998, with the deaconry of Gesù Buon Pastore alla Montagnola. Named the Major Penitentiary for the Church on October 4, 2003, he took part in the 2005 conclave that elected Pope Benedict XVI and served as a special envoy for the Holy Father on numerous occasions. He retired on June 2, 2009.

Stamford, Eparchy of. See Eastern Churches, Catholic

Stans, Maurice H. See Cabinets, Catholics in Presidential

Starr, Ellen Gates (March 19, 1859–February 10, 1940)

A social reformer, Ellen Gates Starr converted to Catholicism in 1920. Born in Atlanta, Starr studied at the Rockford Female Seminary and there met Jane Addams, the future leader in the women's suffrage movement. The two became close friends and embarked on a tour of Europe in 1888, during which they were inspired by the progressive movements in England, including the idealistic Settlement Movement that sought to promote greater harmony between the classes. Returning to the United States, they tried to launch a similar movement in Chicago. The two went on to found Hull House in 1897, a socially progressive settlement house. Starr was a member of the Socialist Labor Party and worked as a reformer for child labor laws and conditions for workers in Chicago. In 1894 she founded and served as first president of the Chicago Public School Art Society. She subsequently helped organize strikes by garment workers and belonged to the National Women's Trade Union League. Impressed with Catholic social doctrine, she converted to the Catholic faith in 1920 and spent her last years in the care of the Sisters of the Holy Child Jesus.

Steinmeyer, Ferdinand (October 13, 1720– August 17, 1786)

A pioneering German Jesuit and missionary in Pennsylvania, New York, and New Jersey, "Ferdinand Farmer" was the name used by Ferdinand Steinmeyer as he ministered to Catholics under threat of the penal laws prohibiting entry of Catholic priests into various colonies. He was born in Weissenstein, Württemberg, Germany, and decided against a career as a doctor to enter the Society of Jesus at Landsberg in 1743. Ordained a priest around 1750, he was assigned initially to China but was then sent to North America for service in the Pennsylvania colony. He reached the colonies in 1752 and settled in Lancaster, Pennsylvania, adopting the name Father Ferdinand Farmer, or "Father Farmer."

From his base at Lancaster, Father Farmer embarked on a wide-ranging ministry among the Catholics of eastern Pennsylvania. In 1758 he moved to Philadelphia but continued to travel throughout surrounding colonies, including Delaware and New Jersey. With the start of the Revolutionary War, Father Farmer added to his ministry the pastoral care of soldiers and combatants, including the Hessian mercenaries then in the service of the British Army when they occupied

Philadelphia in 1777. When, however, the British sought to raise a regiment of Catholics to assist the Tory cause, Father Farmer declined to assist them. Following the British withdrawal the next year, he added New York to his mission area and organized the first Catholic congregation in New York City. In 1779 he was elected a trustee of the University of Pennsylvania.

Steubenville, Diocese of

Established on October 21, 1944, by Pope Pius XII, the Diocese of Steubenville serves counties in south-central Ohio. The diocese is a suffragan of the Archdiocese of Cincinnati.

The original settlement was on the Ohio River, across from West Virginia, in 1765. A pioneer named Jacob Walker reportedly built a cabin there. In 1786 Fort Steuben was established on the site, but the military garrison was destroyed by a fire in 1790. Settlers, however, started a community on the ruins of the fortress. They named their settlement Steubenville. Both the fort and settlement honored the memory of Friedrich Wilhelm, Baron von Steuben, a Prussian soldier and a Catholic who helped train American forces during the Revolutionary War.

The Catholic legacy of the diocese can be traced back to 1670, when René-Robert Chevalier, Sieur de La Salle, led an expedition into what is now Ohio. In 1749 Jesuit missionaries served the occasional trappers and families. In 1751 Father Armand de La Richardie, a revered missionary, was on Lake Erie. Ohio entered the Union in 1803, and Dominican priests visited Somerset and other areas.

Steubenville and other settlements in that part of Ohio were initially under the administration of the Diocese of Bardstown (now the Archdiocese of Louisville), founded in 1808. In 1821 the first Ohio diocese was established at Cincinnati, with jurisdiction over the entire state. Over the next decades, immigrants arrived in large numbers, especially German and Irish Catholics, and the increase in population led to the creation of other dioceses, including Cleveland in 1847, Columbus in 1868, Toledo in 1910, and Youngstown in 1943. Cincinnati, meanwhile, was elevated to an archdiocese in 1850.

Owing to the scale of the steel and coal industries, the population of Steubenville grew significantly, and the decision was made to separate the eastern counties of the Diocese of Columbus to form the Diocese of Steubenville in 1944.

The first bishop of Steubenville, John K. Mussio, was a priest of the Archdiocese of Cincinnati. He was appointed on March 10, 1945, and was consecrated a bishop on May 1. He served as bishop for thirty-two years, with his time extending beyond the end of World War II through the era of the Second Vatican Council and the difficult period after the council. In his time, he founded seventy-three parishes and twenty missions, the diocesan newspaper, the *Steubenville Register*, hospitals, high schools and elementary schools, and St. John Vianney Seminary and welcomed the College of Steubenville, staffed by the Third Order Regular of St. Francis. The college went on to become Franciscan University of Steubenville, a solid Catholic university and a center for the Charismatic Renewal. Bishop Mussio also started the Steubenville Ecumenical Institute to promote ecumenism and interreligious dialogue. He retired on September 27, 1977.

The second bishop of Steubenville, Albert H. Ottenweller, had been an auxiliary bishop of the Diocese of Toledo since 1974. Appointed to Steubenville on October 11, 1977, and installed on November 22, 1977, he provided stable leadership to the diocese during a period in which the traditional industries of coal and steel began to decline. This was marked by a decline in the general population and also in the Catholic population as the demographics of the city began to change. Bishop Ottenweller convoked a diocesan synod in 1983 and promoted a variety of pastoral programs and initiatives, including a diocesan finance board and lay deanery councils, as well as a Department of Religious Education (later the Office of Christian Formation). Bishop Ottenweller retired on January 28, 1992.

The third bishop of Steubenville, Gilbert I. Sheldon, had been an auxiliary bishop of Cleveland since 1976. Appointed to Steubenville on January 28, 1992, Bishop Sheldon led the diocese during a continued period of declining population and economic hardship. Franciscan University continued to flourish and became a leading center for orthodox theological studies. Bishop Sheldon was active as a teacher and encouraged the use of the *Catechism of the Catholic Church*. He also promoted the permanent diaconate in the Diocese of Steubenville and reorganized the diocesan deaneries. He retired on May 31, 2002.

On the same day as Bishop Sheldon's retirement, Father R. Daniel Conlon, a priest of the Archdiocese of Cincinnati, was appointed to succeed him. Consecrated as a bishop on August 6, 2002, Conlon immediately set about improving the quality of catechetics within the new diocese and developed a close working relationship with Franciscan University. He was also active in implementing programs for the protection of youths in the wake of the sexual abuse scandal; he issued the Decree on Child Protection in March 2002 and established a review board for the diocese. On May 17, 2011, he was appointed bishop of Joliet. In 2011 the diocese had a Catholic population of 37,700, served by 104 priests and 58 parishes.

Stevens, Georgia Lydia (d. March 28, 1946)

A member of the Society of the Sacred Heart and a noted figure in music education, Georgia Lydia Stevens was born in Boston. She displayed a talent for music at an early age and played the violin and cello. She studied at the Hoch Conservatory in Frankfurt and elsewhere. She converted to the Church in 1894 and twelve years later entered the Society of St. Joseph, completing studies in England and Belgium.

Returning to the United States, in 1916 she co-founded with Justine Ward the Pius X Institute of Liturgical Music that was connected to Manhattanville College in New York. The guiding influence for the school was the *motu proprio* issued in 1903 by Pope Pius X, *Tre le Sollicitudini*, which called for a renascence in the use of Gregorian chant and plainchant in the Church.

Stockton, Diocese of

Established on January 13, 1962, by Pope Blessed John XXIII, the Diocese of Stockton serves the counties of San Joaquin, Stanislaus, Calaveras, Tuolumne, Alpine, and Mono in the Central Valley and Mother Lode region of California. The diocese is a suffragan of the Archdiocese of San Francisco.

Located on the San Joaquin River, the town became a hub for a variety of agricultural products and manufacturing. The first structures were built by a combined force of the French and French Canadian hunters and trappers in 1830. The site was the terminus of the famed Oregon Trail and received wagon trains from the east. In 1847 Captain Charles M. Weber received a land grant from the Mexican government and started the community that would serve as a supply center for migrants and transportation. The site was initially named Tuleberg and was situated in the San Joaquin delta; it was renamed in honor of Weber's friend, Commodore Robert Field Stockton, in 1850. The primary business of the area in this early period was cattle raising, but it was soon joined by supplying goods and services for the gold prospectors flooding into the area from 1849, and that hastened the incorporation of the town in 1850.

For most of the twentieth century, the area was placed under the jurisdiction of the Diocese (later the Archdiocese) of San Francisco. The population continued to grow, with the chief economic activity in the San Joaquin Valley centering on agriculture. The community grew increasingly diverse as well, with both whites and Hispanics settling in the region.

By 1962 the Catholic population warranted the creation of a separate diocese, and the Diocese of Stockton was formed from territory taken from the Archdiocese of San Francisco and the Diocese of Sacramento.

The first bishop of Stockton, Hugh A. Donohoe, had been an auxiliary bishop of San Francisco since 1947. He was installed on April 24, 1962. He arrived as the Second Vatican Council was about to commence and took part in all its sessions between 1962 and 1965. He also gave the diocese a firm administrative footing, established a diocesan council, and promoted outreach to Hispanic Catholics in the diocese, including the Cursillo Movement. He was especially active in providing pastoral care to farmworkers and defended their rights. On August 22, 1969, he was transferred to the Diocese of Fresno.

The second bishop of Stockton was Merlin Guilfoyle, who had been an auxiliary bishop of San Francisco since 1950. Installed on January 13, 1970, he focused on providing the diocese with a sound financial footing in the wake of economic problems and struggled to stabilize Catholic schools. He retired on September 4, 1979, at the age of seventy-one, owing to poor health.

The third bishop of Stockton, Roger M. Mahony, had been an auxiliary bishop of Fresno since 1975. Installed as bishop of Stockton on April 17, 1980, he concentrated on pastoral outreach to the increasingly diverse Catholic population in the diocese, including whites, Latinos, and Southeast Asians, who were arriving in growing numbers in the aftermath of the Vietnam War, including Vietnamese, Laotians, Cambodians, and Hmong. On July 16, 1985, Bishop Mahony was appointed the archbishop of Los Angeles and became a cardinal in 1991.

The fourth bishop of Stockton, Donald Montrose, had been an auxiliary bishop of Los Angeles since 1983. He promoted the RENEW program in the diocese, invited the contemplative community of religious women, the Religious of the Cross of the Sacred Heart of Jesus, into the diocese, and furthered outreach to Hispanics. He retired on January 18, 1999.

Bishop Montrose was succeeded on March 16, 1999, by Stephen E. Blaire, who had been an auxiliary bishop of Los Angeles since 1990. Bishop Blaire continued the diocesan focus on pastoral care for the diverse Catholic population, including Asians and Pacific Islanders, most notably Filipinos, who have settled in the diocese. In 2006 he also held a diocesan synod. The Stockton diocese is today one of the fastest-growing in the United States, increasing from around 85,000 Catholics to more than 224,000 in 2011. It is served by nearly 70 priests and 34 parishes.

Stoddard, Charles Warren (August 7, 1843–April 23, 1909)

A poet and author, Charles Stoddard was also a convert and helped to make the world aware of the work of St. Damien de Veuster. Born in Rochester, New York, he moved with his family when he was young to New York City; in 1855, the family moved to San Francisco. He returned to New York in 1857 and lived with his grandparents for two years; in 1859, he went back to San Francisco and there began composing poetry that was first published anonymously in a local newspaper.

After failed efforts to start an acting career on the stage, he set sail for a tour of the Pacific Ocean, and his first major work, *South Sea Idyls* (a collection of letters), was published in 1864. He visited Molokai on several occasions and came to know St. Damien. Stoddard's book *The Lepers of Molokai* helped make the future saint well known around the world. Stoddard entered the Church in 1867 and wrote *A Troubled Heart and How It Was Comforted* to detail his conversion. In 1873 he began writing for the *San Francisco Chronicle*, and he went on to travel across Europe, Palestine, and Egypt. He later served as a professor of English literature at the University of Notre Dame and then at The Catholic University of America in Washington, D.C. Poor health plagued his later years, but he continued to write, including his only novel, *For the Pleasure of His Company*.

Stritch, Samuel Alphonsus (August 17, 1887– May 27, 1958)

Archbishop of Chicago from 1939 to 1958 and cardinal from 1946, Samuel Stritch was the first American named to one of the major offices in the Roman Curia when he was appointed in 1958 to the post of pro-prefect of the Congregation for the Propagation of the Faith.

Born on August 17, 1887, in Nashville, Tennessee, he was called to the priesthood and studied at St. Gregory's Preparatory Seminary in Cincinnati and then at the Propaganda Fide and the North American College in Rome. He was ordained on May 21, 1910, at the Basilica of St. John Lateran, Rome, but he needed a special dispensation because he was technically below the canonical age. Returning to Nashville, he served in pastoral ministry and was secretary to the bishop of Nashville and diocesan chancellor.

On August 10, 1921, he was appointed bishop of Toledo, Ohio. He was thirty-four years old and the youngest bishop in the diocese. Consecrated on November 30, 1921, he was bishop of a diocese barely a decade

Cardinal Samuel Stritch

old and devoted his time to opening schools and building the Cathedral of Our Lady Queen of the Most Holy Rosary. On August 26, 1930, he was promoted to become the archbishop of Milwaukee. There he served as shepherd throughout the darkest years of the Great Depression, and to assist those hardest hit he launched an annual charity drive. On December 27, 1939, he was appointed archbishop of Chicago; Pope Pius XII created him a cardinal priest on February 22, 1946, with the titular church of Santa Agnese fuori le mura.

As archbishop in Chicago, he provided quiet and steady leadership over a growing Catholic population during the years of World War II and into the postwar economic boom. One of his greatest postwar concerns was the sizable shift in Catholic population out of the city and the need to establish suburban parishes and ministries while still providing for the needs of the churches in the city itself. Concerned with home missions and evangelization in the United States, he promoted the Catholic Church Extension Society and also the Home Mission Society. Similarly, he was a leader of the National Catholic Welfare Conference, helped draft many of its statements, and was a public face for the conference during the war.

In a surprise, he was appointed in 1958 pro-prefect of the Sacred Congregation for the Propagation of Faith. Soon after his arrival in Rome, he suffered an occlusion of the main artery in his right arm. The arm was amputated above the elbow, but he suffered a stroke and died eight days later. He was buried in the bishops' chapel at Mount Carmel Cemetery, Hillside, just outside of Chicago.

Sullivan, John L. (October 15, 1858–February 2, 1918)

A professional boxer, Sullivan was called the "Boston Strong Boy" and the "Great John L." and was the first heavyweight champion boxing with gloves whose dominance lasted for a decade, from 1881 to 1892. Born in Roxbury, Massachusetts, to an Irish family, he had a fondness for fighting and boxing from an early age; he began boxing for money and fought literally hundreds of opponents. In 1883 he went on a national tour with other boxers and gained immense notoriety with his offer to box anyone under the Marquess of Queensberry Rules for $250.

In what was an evolving sport, in 1882 Sullivan won the bare-knuckles heavyweight championship over Paddy Ryan and in 1889 won the last bare-knuckles title bout ever over Jake Kilrain. His phenomenal streak of victories came to an end in 1892 when he was defeated, using gloves, by James J. "Gentleman Jim" Corbett. Sullivan by that point had earned more than $1 million. He died at the age of fifty-nine in considerable poverty and from the effects of his long years of fights in and out of the ring.

Sullivan, Peter J. (March 15, 1821–March 2, 1883)

An Irish-born soldier and lawyer, Sullivan was also an opponent of anti-Catholic bigotry in the country. Born in Cork, Ireland, he arrived in Philadelphia when he was two years old. He later studied at the University of Pennsylvania and entered the U.S. Army and fought in the Mexican-American War. He left the army with the rank of major and worked for a time for the U.S. Senate before settling in Cincinnati. Becoming a lawyer, he fought against the Know-Nothings and then fought in the Civil War as commander of the 48th Ohio regiment. From 1865 to 1869, he served as minister to Colombia.

Sulpicians (S.S.)

The Society of the Priests of St. Sulpice, the Sulpicians, was founded in Paris in 1641 by Father Jean-Jacques Olier with the intention of supplying priests to teach in seminaries and guide the formation of seminarians. The Sulpicians played a significant role in the formation of priests in America and provided some of the foremost bishops in the early years of American dioceses.

The Sulpicians arrived in the United States after Bishop John Carroll made the request in 1790 that the French Sulpicians help to establish a seminary for the Diocese of Baltimore. There was a genuine sense of urgency to the enterprise as the bishop had few native priests and a growing Catholic commu-

nity in the young United States. The timing was also ideal for the French Sulpicians as conditions in France were deteriorating. The French Revolution, which commenced in 1789, had turned its hatred on the Church. On July 10, 1791, four Sulpicians arrived in Baltimore, including Francis Charles Nagot, the superior, Anthony Gamier, Michael Levadoux, and John Tessier. The priests purchased the One Mile Tavern in Baltimore, dedicated the building to the Blessed Virgin, and then started classes for five students, all of them from France. From this beginning grew St. Mary's Seminary, the first seminary in the United States. By 1795 there were about a dozen Sulpicians working in the Diocese of Baltimore, which encompassed at that point the entire country.

The Sulpicians who arrived for service in the diocese included a stellar cast of great bishops in American Catholic history, including Benedict Joseph Flaget, the first bishop of Bardstown, in 1810, and Ambrose Maréchal, who became the third archbishop of Baltimore in 1817. Other notable Sulpicians were Father Gabriel Richard, who was in the U.S. House of Representatives from 1823 to 1825; Bishop Louis Dubourg, bishop of the Louisiana and the Two Floridas in 1815; Father Demetrius Augustine Gallitzin, a prince of Russia who helped plant the Church in western Pennsylvania; John B. David, bishop of Bardstown in 1832; Simon William Gabriel Bruté de Rémur, first bishop of Vincennes in 1832; and John Dubois, bishop of New York in 1825.

The growth and development of Catholic education in the United States was assisted greatly by the Sulpicians, who started schools across the country, including St. Mary's College in Baltimore in 1800, St. Charles' College in Ellicott City in 1831, St. John's Seminary in Brighton, Massachusetts, in 1884, St. Joseph's Seminary in Yonkers, New York, in 1896, St. Patrick's Seminary in Menlo Park, California, in 1898, and St. Austin's College in Washington, D.C., in 1901. By 1900 they were in charge of six American seminaries; this increased to twelve by the 1960s.

In 2011 the Sulpicians numbered nearly three hundred in the United States and operated several seminaries, including St. Mary's, St. Patrick's, and Theological College in Washington, D.C.

Superior, Diocese of

Established on May 3, 1905, by Pope St. Pius X, the Diocese of Superior serves counties in the northwestern part of Wisconsin. The diocese is a suffragan see of the Archdiocese of Milwaukee.

The city is located on the western end of Lake Superior and has extensive harbor facilities. The first European to visit the area was likely Etienne Brulé in 1622. Further exploration was made by Daniel Greysolon, Sieur du Lhut.

The first permanent site was established at Superior in 1853. A combination of three separate communities, the settlements were consolidated and incorporated in 1889. Immediate growth and prosperity were possible because of the local resources, including agricultural lands, limestone, iron ore, copper, and coal.

Jesuit missionaries arrived in the region as early as 1655, and fur trappers and hunters maintained trading posts there on a seasonal basis. Three great names are associated with the early history of the Church in Superior: Jesuit Fathers René Menard, Claude Allouez, and Jacques Marquette.

In 1661 Father René Menard arrived in the region and served the Ottawa, near Sault Ste. Marie. He was slain by the Sioux while visiting a tribe on the Black River, in Wisconsin, near the present city of Merrill. Father Allouez arrived at Chequamegon Bay, La Pointe, in 1665 and established the mission of the Holy Spirit. He was followed in 1669 by Father Jacques Marquette, who served at La Pointe for the next four years and then journeyed in 1673 with Louis Joliet on the expedition to explore the Mississippi River.

Another remarkable missionary and bishop took up the labors of the missions, Irenaeus Frederick Baraga, who arrived in La Pointe in 1835 and was the first missionary priest the Indians in the region had seen for more than a century. He devoted more than two decades to serving the Indians and the Catholic community. He expanded the mission of the Holy Spirit and relocated it to Madeline Island. The mission was christened St. Joseph.

On November 1, 1853, Baraga was consecrated bishop of the Vicariate Apostolic of Sault Ste. Marie and Marquette in Upper Michigan, from which emerged the Diocese of Marquette. With his departure, important work was carried on by Father John Chebul. In 1878 the Franciscan Fathers of the Sacred Heart Province of St. Louis, Missouri, arrived and began their own vital work among the Indians of northwestern Wisconsin. The first Franciscans, Fathers Casimir Vogt and John Gafron, joined by two Franciscan brothers, arrived in Bayfield in October 1878.

The growth of the Catholic population continued throughout the end of the nineteenth century, and the ecclesiastical jurisdiction for the area passed from the Diocese of Milwaukee to the Diocese of St. Paul in 1850 and then to the Diocese of La Crosse in 1868. By the start of the twentieth century, the desirability of a separate diocese led Pope Pius X in 1905 to create the Diocese of Superior out of sixteen counties in Wisconsin.

The first bishop of Superior, Augustine Francis Schinner, had served as a priest of the Archdiocese of Milwaukee. Appointed on May 13, 1905, and consecrated a bishop on July 25, 1905, he worked to provide the diocese with a firm footing and expanded diocesan facilities. He opened sixteen parishes, some fifty parochial schools and a high school, and built forty-three churches and a hospital. He resigned on January 15, 1913, and was appointed the first bishop of Spokane on March 18, 1914.

The second bishop of Superior, Joseph Maria Koudelka, had been an auxiliary bishop of Cleveland since 1907. He continued to expand the number of parishes and worked until his death on June 24, 1921.

The third bishop of Superior, Joseph G. Pinten, was a priest of the Diocese of Sault Ste. Marie (now the Diocese of Marquette). He was consecrated a bishop on May 3, 1922, but was transferred to the Diocese of Grand Rapids on June 25, 1926. His successor, Theodore H. Reverman, had been a priest of the Diocese of Louisville. Consecrated a bishop on November 30, 1926, he guided the diocese through the difficult years of the Great Depression and the onset of World War II. He died on July 18, 1941.

The fifth bishop of Superior, William P. O'Connor, was a priest of the Archdiocese of Milwaukee. Consecrated a bishop on March 7, 1942, he served as shepherd through the years of World War II and was transferred to the Diocese of Madison on January 15, 1946.

He was followed by Albert G. Meyer, a priest of the Milwaukee archdiocese. Appointed bishop of Superior on February 18, 1946, he was consecrated a bishop on April 11. He presided over the expansion of the diocese in the years after the war, and was promoted to the rank of archbishop of Milwaukee on July 21, 1953. He later served as archbishop of Chicago and was created a cardinal on December 14, 1959.

Joseph John Annabring, a priest of the Superior diocese, was appointed seventh bishop of Superior on January 27, 1954, and ordained a bishop on March 25, 1954. He served for five years and died on August 27, 1959.

His successor was George Albert Hammes, a priest of the Diocese of La Crosse. Appointed on March 28, 1960, he was ordained a bishop on May 24, 1960. After many years of bishops whose tenures proved brief for various reasons, Bishop Hammes served for some twenty-five years and was responsible for leading the diocese through the era of the Second Vatican Council, the difficult postconciliar period, and into the pontificate of Pope Blessed John Paul II. He retired on June 27, 1985.

The ninth bishop of Superior was Raphael Michael Fliss, a priest of the Archdiocese of Milwaukee who was appointed coadjutor bishop with right of succession on November 26, 1979. Ordained a bishop on December 20, 1979, he acceded to the see on June 27, 1985.

Bishop Fliss's time as bishop was marked by the challenges of meeting the changing financial and demographic situation in the diocese as the general population continued to increase while the Catholic population held steady, even as the number of priests began to decline. In 2005 the diocese celebrated the 100th anniversary of its founding and the 340th anniversary of the establishment of Christianity in the Upper Midwest. Bishop Fliss retired on June 28, 2007.

The tenth bishop of Superior, Peter F. Christensen, a priest of the Archdiocese of St. Paul and Minneapolis, was appointed on June 28, 2007, ordained a bishop on September 14, 2007, and installed on September 23, 2007.

In 2011 the Diocese of Superior had a Catholic population of 76,000, served by 71 priests and 105 parishes.

Supreme Court of the United States, Catholic Justices of the

The first Catholic appointed to the United States Supreme Court was also the first Catholic chief justice, Roger Brooke Taney. Taney was nominated for the high court in January 1835 in the immediate aftermath of his rejection by the Senate as treasury secretary.

President Andrew Jackson nominated Taney as an associate justice of the Supreme Court to replace the retiring Gabriel Duvall, but a vote was put off by the anti-Jackson Whigs, who controlled the Senate. The seat was left vacant for more than a year until Philip Pendleton Barbour was confirmed to it in 1836. In the intervening period, however, the political tide turned toward the Jacksonian Democrats, and with the death of Chief Justice John Marshall during the 1835 recess, President Jackson was able to nominate his close friend and adviser on December 28, 1835. Despite bitter opposition, Taney was confirmed on March 15, 1836.

As chief justice, Taney was best known for the 1857 Dred Scott decision regarding slavery, which helped set the stage for the Civil War. From the time of Taney's death in 1864, there were no Catholics on the high court until Edward Douglass White was appointed an associate justice in 1894 by President Grover Cleveland.

In 1910 White was appointed chief justice by William H. Taft, the first associate justice ever appointed chief justice. White made a significant impact on American law as he wrote several hundred opinions and was noted especially for his "rule of reason" in decisions in 1911 in the antitrust cases against Standard Oil and American Tobacco Company. The "rule of reason" distinguished between legal and illegal business combinations.

In 1898 another Catholic was appointed, Joseph McKenna, by President William McKinley. In 1923 Warren G. Harding appointed Pierce Butler, who served until 1939. Justice Butler was notable as the only Catholic on the court in 1923, when the court upheld a lower court's decision rejecting the infamous Oregon School Law that all but outlawed Catholic schools.

In 1940, Frank Murphy was appointed an associate justice by President Franklin Delano Roosevelt. Sherman Minton, meanwhile, served as an associate justice from 1949 to 1956; he became a Catholic several years before his death in 1965.

President Dwight D. Eisenhower appointed William Brennan an associate justice in 1956. Brennan proved a major disappointment to Catholics for his acceptance of the majority decision in the 1973 *Roe v. Wade* decision that legalized abortion under the specious argument of a constitutional right to privacy. Throughout his term, which ended in 1990, he consistently voted with the liberal wing of the high court.

President Ronald Reagan appointed two Catholic justices to the court, Antonin Scalia in 1986 and Anthony M. Kennedy in 1988. President George H. W. Bush appointed Clarence Thomas, the first Catholic African-American justice, in 1991. The three formed part of what became the conservative wing of the court (with non-Catholics Sandra O'Connor and Chief Justice William Rehnquist). Two more conservative Catholics were appointed by President George W. Bush: John G. Roberts, who was confirmed in 2005 as the tenth Roman Catholic to serve on the high court and the third to rank as chief justice, and Samuel Alito, who was also appointed in 2005. Sonya Sotomayor was appointed by President Barack Obama in 2010. She became the sixth Catholic justice on the court, the largest majority that Catholics have ever commanded. (*See also* Separation of Church and State.)

Catholics on the Supreme Court

Roger B. Taney, chief justice 1836–64, appointed by Andrew Jackson.

Edward Douglass White, associate justice 1894–1910, appointed by Grover Cleveland; chief justice 1910–21, appointed by William H. Taft.

Joseph McKenna, associate justice 1898–1925, appointed by William McKinley.

Pierce Butler, associate justice 1923–39, appointed by Warren G. Harding.

Frank Murphy, associate justice 1940–49, appointed by Franklin Delano Roosevelt.

William Brennan, associate justice 1956–90, appointed by Dwight D. Eisenhower.

Antonin Scalia, associate justice 1986–, appointed by Ronald Reagan.

Anthony M. Kennedy, associate justice 1988–, appointed by Ronald Reagan.

Clarence Thomas, associate justice 1991–, appointed by George H. W. Bush.

John G. Roberts, chief justice 2005–, appointed by George W. Bush.

Samuel Alito, associate justice 2005–, appointed by George W. Bush.

Sonya Sotomayor, associate justice 2010–, appointed by Barack Obama.

Sybilska, Mary Monica (December 6, 1824– September 15, 1911)

The first provincial-superior of the Felician Sisters in the United States, from 1874 to 1896, Mother Monica Sybilska was born in Warsaw, Poland. She entered the Felicians in 1854 after the passing of her husband, but left briefly to ensure that her son would receive a proper upbringing.

In 1874 Sybilska was sent with four sisters to the United States at the request of Father Joseph Dabrowski, pastor of the Sacred Heart Church, in Polonia, Wisconsin, to assume direction over the parish school. The school was opened on December 3, 1874, followed by a boarding school for girls, an orphanage, and a novitiate. A motherhouse was built in 1882 in Detroit, and Mother Monica devoted the next years to the rapid expansion of the congregation across the Midwest. She died in Detroit.

Syracuse, Diocese of

Established on November 20, 1886, by Pope Leo XIII, the Diocese of Syracuse serves seven counties in central and south-central New York State: Broome, Chenango, Cortland, Madison, Oneida, Onondaga, and Oswego. The diocese is a suffragan of the Archdiocese of New York.

The city of Syracuse is the fifth largest in the state of New York. The area was the home of the Five Nations of the Iroquois Confederacy — the Mohawks, Senecas, Onondagas, Oneidas, and Cayugas — from the middle of the seventeenth century. The Onondagas controlled the territory around Onondaga Lake in central New York. The first Europeans to visit the region came from Canada, including Samuel de Champlain in 1615, who attacked the Oneidas with the help of the Huron and Algonquian Indians.

The central part of New York remained a battleground between the English and French, and many of the great Jesuit priests and missionaries, the "Black Robes," were killed as a result. After the American Revolution, the Indians and a young American government negotiated the Treaty of Fort Stanwix in 1784, which marked the ascendancy of the white settlers, who were especially eager to secure control of the local sources of salt around Onondaga Lake.

What became the city of Syracuse was originally found in the Onondaga Salt Springs Reservation, and the first white settlement had a variety of early names: Salt Point (1780), then Webster's Landing (1786), Bogardus Corners (1796), Milan (1809), South Salina (1812), Cossits' Corners (1814), and Corinth (1817). The name Syracuse was chosen by John Wilkinson, the first postmaster, after Syracusa, Sicily. Syracuse was officially incorporated in 1825 and grew rapidly, especially with the start of the Erie Canal, which opened new economic opportunities.

The Catholic history of Syracuse dates, like the city itself, to the arrival of Europeans from Canada. The first priest to visit, Father Simon Le Moyne, a Jesuit missionary, reached the Onondaga at Indian Hill, in modern-day Manlius, New York, in 1654. He was the first European to discover salt deposits in Onondaga Lake.

On November 14, 1655, Jesuit Fathers Pierre-Joseph Chaumonot and Claude Dablon celebrated Mass on Indian Hill and started construction of the first mission, Fort Sainte Marie de Gannentaha; this was soon abandoned owing to the threats posed by the Iroquois, but new mission opportunities were created with the white settlements of Ephraim Webster's trading post in 1786 and James Geddes's salt center in 1794.

Swifter development was permitted in New York state after the declaration of religious freedom in the state constitution of 1777 and the subsequent declaration of religious equality in 1784. St. Mary's Church was built in Albany in 1797, serving as a springboard for the growth of Catholicism in central New York. In 1808 the Diocese of New York was founded and the growing community of Syracuse was placed under its jurisdiction; this was followed by the foundation of the Diocese of Albany in 1847. By 1886 the Catholic community

of Syracuse, growing extensively because of immigrants from Ireland and Germany, was established as a separate diocese.

The first bishop of the Diocese of Syracuse, Patrick A. Ludden, was a priest of the Diocese of Albany and had been rector of Albany's cathedral. Appointed bishop on December 14, 1886, he was consecrated on May 1, 1887, and originally chose St. John the Evangelist as his cathedral. In 1903 he designated St. Mary's as the cathedral of the diocese. He provided the diocese with a firm footing and guided it into the new century. He died on August 12, 1912, after decades of service, at the age of seventy-four.

The second bishop of Syracuse, John Grimes, was an Irish-born priest of the Diocese of Albany. Consecrated the coadjutor bishop of Syracuse on May 16, 1909, he acceded to the see on August 6, 1912, with Bishop Ludden's passing. He continued to develop the diocesan facilities until his death on July 26, 1922.

He was succeeded by Daniel J. Curley, a priest of the Archdiocese of New York. Appointed bishop of Syracuse on February 19, 1923, he was consecrated a bishop on May 1, 1923, and installed on May 15, 1923. His time as bishop included the onset of the Great Depression and the hardship that the economic downturn brought to the area. He launched the Society for the Propagation of Faith in the diocese, started twenty-eight parishes and eighteen schools, and invited the Dominican Sisters of the Perpetual Rosary into the diocese. He died on August 3, 1932.

The fourth bishop of Syracuse, John Aloysius Duffy, was a priest of the Diocese of Newark. Consecrated bishop of Syracuse on April 21, 1933, he was installed as bishop in the Cathedral of the Immaculate Conception on July 11, 1933. He continued to guide the Catholic community during the Depression until he was appointed bishop of Buffalo in 1937.

The fifth bishop of Syracuse, Walter Andrew Foery, was a priest of the Diocese of Rochester. He was consecrated a bishop on August 18, 1937, and served for the next three decades. His time as bishop extended through the Second World War, the era of the Second Vatican Council, and into the challenging post-conciliar period. His record was impressive. He started forty-two new parishes, dedicated eighty-four new church buildings, opened three hospitals, helped found Le Moyne and Maria Regina Colleges, started ten high schools and thirty-eight elementary schools, and established a new chancery building. He retired on August 4, 1970.

The sixth bishop of Syracuse, David F. Cunningham, was a priest of the Syracuse diocese. In 1950 he had been named auxiliary bishop of Syracuse, and on June 21, 1967, he was appointed coadjutor bishop of Syracuse with right of succession. He acceded to the see on August 4, 1970, and retired on December 3, 1975.

The seventh bishop of Syracuse, Frank J. Harrison, was a priest of the Diocese of Syracuse. Appointed an auxiliary bishop of Syracuse on March 1, 1971, he was appointed bishop of Syracuse on November 16, 1977. He was active in promoting the reforms of the Second Vatican Council and encouraged lay participation in the diocese and outreach to minorities. He retired on June 16, 1987.

Bishop Harrison was followed by Joseph T. O'Keefe, a priest of the Archdiocese of New York. Appointed an auxiliary bishop of the Archdiocese of New York in 1982, he was appointed bishop of Syracuse on June 16, 1987, and installed on August 3, 1987. He retired on May 29, 1995.

He was succeeded as the ninth bishop of Syrcause by James M. Moynihan, a priest of the Diocese of Rochester. He was appointed bishop of Syracuse on April 4, 1995, and was consecrated a bishop on May 29, 1995. He provided stability to the diocese and released a pastoral letter, "Equipping the Saints for the Work of Ministry," in 2001. He retired on April 21, 2009.

The tenth bishop of Syracuse, Robert J. Cunningham, had been bishop of Ogdensburg since 2004. Appointed to Syracuse on April 21, 2009, he was installed on May 26, 2009.

As of 2011, the Catholic population of the Diocese of Syracuse was 283,000, served by 281 priests, more than 300 men and women religious, and 133 parishes.

Szoka, Edmund C. (September 14, 1927–)

Archbishop of Detroit from 1981 to 1990, president of the Prefecture for Economic Affairs of the Holy See from 1990 to 1997, and president of the governatorate for the State of Vatican City from 2001 to 2006, Edmund C. Szoka was also a cardinal from 1988. Born in Grand Rapids, Michigan, the son of Polish immigrants Casimir Szoka and Mary Wolgat, he studied for the priesthood at St. Paul's Seminary in Grand Rapids, at St. John's Interdiocesan Seminary, at Sacred Heart Seminary in Detroit, and the Pontifical Urbanian University in Rome, where he earned a licentiate in canon law. Ordained a priest on June 5, 1954, he served in pastoral ministry in the Diocese of Marquette and was also secretary to the bishops of the diocese from 1954 to 1962. He accompanied Bishop Thomas L. Noa of Marquette to the first session of the Second Vatican Council in 1962.

On June 11, 1971, he was appointed bishop of Gaylord and consecrated on July 20, 1971. Ten years later, on March 21, 1981, he was named archbishop of Detroit. Pope Blessed John Paul II created him a cardinal priest in the consistory of June 28, 1988, with the title of SS. Andrea e Gregorio al Monte Celio. As archbishop, he dealt with the ongoing challenges of the flight from the city of Detroit to the suburbs, a demographic shift that entailed finding a balance between providing pastoral care to the growing suburbs while maintaining the ministerial needs of the city. One highlight of his tenure was the visit of Pope Blessed John Paul II to the archdiocese in 1987.

Cardinal Edmund Szoka

Appointed a member of the Council of Cardinals for the Study of the Organizational and Economic Problems of the Holy See in 1989, Szoka was chosen by Pope Blessed John Paul II a year later to become president of the Prefecture for Economic Affairs of the Holy See on April 28, 1990. On October 14, 1997, he was named president of the Pontifical Commission for the State of Vatican City, a position that placed him in charge of the day-to-day affairs of Vatican City.

Cardinal Szoka was a popular figure in the Vatican during his time there, and he was used extensively as a special papal envoy. He took part in the conclave of 2005 that elected Pope Benedict XVI. He resigned on April 21, 2005, because of the age limit, but he stayed on in his post until September 15, 2006.

T

Tabb, John Bannister (March 22, 1845–November 19, 1909)

Poet, priest, and educator, John Bannister Tabb was born near Richmond, Virginia, the son of a plantation owner. At the start of the Civil War in 1861, Tabb volunteered for the Confederate Army. In 1864 he was captured by Union forces and sent to Point Lookout prison camp. While there, he met and became a good friend of the poet and musician Sidney Lanier. Released at the end of the war, he settled in Baltimore with the ambition of becoming a concert pianist. He became friends with Episcopalian minister Alfred A. Curtis, who later converted to Catholicism and eventually became bishop of Wilmington.

Tabb took up a post teaching English at Racine College in 1870, but he was soon summoned back to Virginia owing to the poor health of his sister. Already drawn to the Church through the efforts of Curtis, Tabb was baptized by then Bishop (later Cardinal) James Gibbons in Richmond on September 8, 1872. That same year, he entered St. Charles College in Catonsville, Maryland. He received a post at St. Peter's School in Richmond in 1875; he later taught, from 1877 to 1881, at St. Charles College, where he studied philosophy in preparation for entering St. Mary's Seminary in Baltimore in 1881. On December 20, 1884, he was ordained, then spent the next years teaching at St. Charles until his retirement in 1907. Long plagued by poor and deteriorating eyesight, Tabb was almost completely blind by the time of his retirement.

A talented poet, Tabb published privately his first book of poetry, *Poems,* in 1882. After overcoming the hesitation of editors owing to his ornate Victorian style, Tabb went on to publish a number of books and collection, including *An Octave to Mary* (1893), *Poems* (1894), *Lyrics* (1897), *Child Verse* (1899), *Two Lyrics* (1900), *Later Lyrics* (1902), *The Rosary in Rhyme* (1904), *Quips and Quiddities* (1907), and *Later Poems* (1910). His poems reflected his classical education as well as his own priestly life and familiarity with Scripture. By the end of his life, he was admired for his lyrical gifts and poetic imagery.

Takach, Basil (October 27, 1879–May 13, 1948)

The first bishop of the Greek Catholic Exarchate of Pittsburgh, serving from 1925 until his death, Basil Takach was one of the great pioneering figures of Eastern-rite Catholics in the United States. Born in Maramoroš County in what was then Austria-Hungary, he entered the Užhorod Seminary and was ordained on December 14, 1902. The next years were spent in pastoral ministry in various capacities until his appointment as a bishop for the newly established Greek Catholic exarchate in the United States.

Consecrated a bishop in Rome on June 15, 1924, he arrived in New York on August 13, 1924, to a joyous welcome from throngs of Eastern Catholics. Initially, it was assumed that the exarchate for Greek Catholics would be New York City. This proved impractical, however, as the population of Carpatho-Russian Catholics was too small. The site eventually chosen for his episcopal seat was near Pittsburgh, at St. John the Baptist Greek Catholic Church in Homestead-Munhall, Pennsylvania. St. John's Church was designated his cathedral.

As the first bishop of a Catholic community of some 300,000 and 155 parishes, he founded the crucial diocesan offices and ministries and undertook a visitation program that took him to New Jersey, New York, Pennsylvania, and Illinois. He also promoted vocations and worked to find priests to serve the faithful. To support social communications in the exarchate, he raised funds for a monthly magazine, *Queen of Heaven* (*Nebesnaja Carica*), and the newspapers the *Chrysostom* and the *Eastern Observer.*

His time as bishop was troubled by a schism among some Eastern Catholics, who split from the Church over the requirement that the Greek Catholic clergy in America be celibate. Bishop Takach opposed the decision but accepted the determination of the Holy See. The American bishops of the Latin rite were crucial in this development. He sought to resolve the schism without success, and the breakaway parishes eventually formed the Independent Greek Catholic Church. Nevertheless, he was a pivotal figure in giving Greek Catholics a solid foundation in the United States.

Talbot, Francis X. (January 25, 1889–December 3, 1953)

Jesuit priest, editor and author, and editor in chief of *America* magazine from 1936 to 1944, Francis X. Talbot was also the founder of the Catholic Poetry Society of America. Born in Philadelphia, he was the youngest of seven children. After graduating from St. Joseph's High School in Philadelphia, he entered the Society of Jesus at St. Andrew-on-Hudson in Poughkeepsie, New York, in 1906. The next years were spent in theological and philosophical studies at Woodstock College in Woodstock, Maryland, followed by teaching assignments at Loyola School in New York City from 1913 to 1916 and at Boston College from 1917 to 1918. Ordained a priest at Woodstock on June 29, 1921, he held various posts until 1923 when he was named literary editor of *America*; he became editor in chief in 1936.

In 1928 Talbot helped establish the Catholic Book Club, followed by the Catholic Poetry Society in 1930 and the Spiritual Book Associates in 1932. He also launched the journal *Theological Studies* and played a role in the founding the Catholic Theatre Conference and the Catholic Library Association; he was also the chaplain of the National Motion Picture Bureau of the International Federation of Catholic Alumnae from 1924 to 1936. From 1947 to 1950 he served as president of Loyola College in Baltimore. His books included *Jesuit Education in Philadelphia* (1927), *Richard Henry Tierney* (1930), *Shining in Darkness* (1932), *Saint Among Savages* (1935), and *Saint Among the Hurons* (1949); he also contributed to the *Encyclopedia Britannica* and the *Britannica Yearbook*.

Talon, Jean (1625–November 23, 1691)

Intendant of New France, Jean Talon labored for many years to promote the presence of France in the New World. Born in Châlons-sur-Marne, France, he studied at the Jesuit College of Clermont in Paris, and embarked upon a military career. He served as war commissar in Flanders in 1654 and intendant to the army of French General Turenne.

Thanks to the skill he displayed in his duties, he secured the patronage of Cardinal Jules Mazarin and received rapid promotion. Hence, in 1665 King Louis XIV appointed Talon intendant of New France under the new governor, Daniel de Rémy de Courcelles. Talon wasted little time upon his arrival in Québec in organizing the colony, including taking the first census in 1666. He recommended with considerable passion that immigration be encouraged, but his plans were never adopted. He also proved instrumental in organizing the successful campaign of Courcelles against the Iroquois in 1666, and provided a solid foundation for the agricultural, administrative, and economic growth of the French colony.

Returning to France in 1668, he continued to promote the Canadian colony's interests. Reappointed in 1670, he returned to Québec with plans for extending French influence and exploration through a series of forts and outposts. In this way, France was able to lay claim, albeit fleetingly, to much of North America.

Talon returned home in 1672, having fulfilled most of the plans he had launched in 1665 and leaving behind him a French colony that endured for another century and that left deep cultural roots upon the region that became eastern Canada. In recognition of his accomplishments, Louis XIV created him Comte d'Orsainville in 1675. Talon later assisted the exiled English monarch, James II, in his failed efforts to regain his throne.

Taney, Roger Brooke (March 17, 1777–October 12, 1864)

Chief justice of the U.S. Supreme Court from 1836 to 1864, Roger Brooke Taney was best remembered for the Dred Scott decision of 1857, in which he ruled that slaves and their descendants had no rights as citizens. Born in Calvert County, Maryland, Taney was the son of Michael Taney, a member of the Irish Catholic gentry, and Monica Brooke, a devout Catholic. He studied in private schools and with tutors until the age of fifteen, when he entered Dickinson College in Carlisle, Pennsylvania. After graduating in 1795, he went to Annapolis, Maryland, and studied law in the offices of Jeremiah Townley Chase, one of the chief justices of the General Court of Maryland. In 1799 he was admitted to the bar and then returned to Calvert County to practice law. Soon after, Taney was elected to the House of Delegates at the age of twenty-three.

In March 1801, after being defeated in his bid for reelection, Taney settled in Frederick, Maryland, to start his own legal practice. In 1803 he was again defeated in a bid for election to the House of Delegates from Frederick County. On a happier note, three years later, he married Anne Phoebe Charlton Key, the only daughter of John Ross Key and the sister of Francis Scott Key, who later wrote "The Star Spangled Banner."

Taney gained considerable notoriety for his participation with John Hanson Thomas in the acquittal of General James Wilkinson, then commander in chief of the U.S. Army, during his court martial in 1811 on charges of being an accomplice of Aaron Burr. Both Taney and Thomas declined any fee for their services. In 1816 Taney was elected to the state senate of Maryland.

In 1823 he moved to Baltimore, where he added to his reputation as a leading lawyer and earned appointment in 1827 by Governor Joseph Kent as attorney general of Maryland. Four years later, President Andrew Jackson named him attorney general of the United States. Two years later, President Jackson appointed him secretary of the treasury upon the removal of William J. Duane from that post. His nomination, however, was rejected by the Senate, the first time such a nomination was rejected. Recovering from the setback, President Jackson nominated Taney to succeed Judge Gabriel Duvall of Maryland on the U.S. Supreme Court. Once again, Taney's appointment was opposed and postponed owing to severe opposition to Jackson's policies in the Senate. Once more undeterred, Jackson named Taney to the Supreme Court, this time as chief justice, to succeed John Marshall. Overcoming the opposition of such powerful figures as Senators Daniel Webster and Henry Clay, Jackson secured Taney's confirmation on March 15, 1836.

Roger Taney

Taney served as the first Catholic chief justice for twenty-eight years and guided the high court during the tumultuous period before the Civil War. His most famous decision was in the Dred Scott case in 1857, in which the court ruled that no African-American slave or descendant of a slave could be a citizen of the United States, that Congress did not have the right to prohibit slavery in the territories, and that the Missouri Compromise of 1820 was void. Taney himself early on manumitted the slaves he had inherited from his father and provided pensions for the older ones as long as they lived. (*See also* Slavery.)

Taney's wife died in an outbreak of yellow fever in 1855, followed by their youngest child within a few days. Taney was respected by his contemporaries, and despite the opposition to his appointment he was troubled by few personal enemies.

Taylor, Myron C. (January 18, 1874–May 6, 1959)

A lawyer and diplomat, Myron C. Taylor was best known as the personal representative of Presidents Franklin Delano Roosevelt and Harry S. Truman to Pope Pius XII in the years before and after World War II. Born in Lyons, New York, he studied at Cornell University in New York, and then embarked on a career in business and industry. For several years in the 1930s he served aas chairman of the board of directors and chief executive officer of the U.S. Steel Corporation. Taylor subsequently enjoyed a close relationship with different administrations of different parties, including Presidents Herbert Hoover, Roosevelt, and Truman. Under Hoover, he served on the executive committee of the President's National Business Survey Conference, and under Roosevelt he was a member of the President's Organization on Unemployment Relief and the industrial board of the National Recovery Administration.

In 1939, as the world embarked on global war, Roosevelt appointed Taylor, an Episcopalian, as his personal representative to Pope Pius XII; a formal ambassadorial post was then legally impossible.

Taylor's primary duty was to convey messages between the pontiff and president throughout the years leading up to the involvement of the United States in the world war, at the end of 1941. Following the war, Taylor returned to his envoy duties, and he remained at his post under Roosevelt's successor, Truman, until 1950. Taylor was thus a key figure in maintaining lines of communication and cooperation between two of the most key figures during World War II. Taylor received a variety of honors for his years of service from the United States (the Medal of Merit), Italy (Commander, Order of the Crown, Star of Solidarity), and France (Cross Commander, Legion of Honor). He was honored by the Church with several medals, including a Knight of the Order of Pius, first degree, Knight Grand Cross of Saints Mauritius and Lazarus, and Knight of the Order of Malta.

Tekakwitha, St. Kateri (c. 1656–April 17, 1680)

The "Lily of the Mohawks," St. Kateri Tekakwitha was a Mohawk maiden and mystic who was canonized in 2012. She was born at Ossernenon, in Auriesville, New York, the daughter of a Mohawk war chief and an Algonquin Christian woman named Kahenta. Orphaned at the age of four when her parents died in an epidemic of smallpox, she also was stricken by the disease, which left her with a disfigured face and damaged eyesight. An uncle assumed her care, and powerful older women of the tribe treated her kindly and raised her as a high-ranking Mohawk maiden. Her persistent refusal of marriage offers, however, caused distress to her family, as Indian maidens were normally married at a young age.

In 1667 missionaries arrived in her village. She was moved by their deep faith, but St. Kateri was unable to study the Christian faith owing to the opposition of her uncle. In 1675, however, she met Father Jacques de Lamberville, who was amazed by her direct request to be given instruction and to receive baptism. Father Lamberville gave her preparation and baptized her on Easter, April 5, 1676; she received the name of Kateri, or Katharine.

St. Kateri's open Catholic faith and contemplative nature added to the strain with her people, and she was subjected to abuse. To save her life, she fled to the Christian community of Sault Ste. Marie near Montréal, four hundred miles away, walking there under the protection of Christian Mohawk and Iroquois warriors.

In the safety of the Christian missions, St. Kateri flowered in prayer and in holiness. She endured many trials, including a false accusation by a jealous woman, but she remained steadfast in her devotion. She received her first Communion on Christmas Day in 1677. Two years later, she took a private vow of chastity, dedicating herself to Christ. However, when she asked to become a nun, her request was answered with gentle derision, as the concept of Native American vocations seemed totally alien to Europeans.

St. Kateri died at Caughnawaga, Canada, and as she was placed to lie in state, her face glowed and all blemishes from her smallpox disappeared. Two French trappers made her coffin, and the word of her passing quickly spread as people reported, "The saint is dead."

Pope Pius XII declared Kateri venerable. Pope Blessed John Paul II beatified her on June 22, 1980, and at the ceremony she was recognized as a unique American who symbolized the flowering of the faith in the New World. She was the first North American Indian to be declared blessed. She was canonized on October 21, 2012, by Pope Benedict XVI. Her feast day is April 17 in Canada and July 14 in the United States.

Temperance Movement. *See* Prohibition

Tennessee

Called the Volunteer State, Tennessee is located in the southeastern region of the United States. It is bordered on the north by Kentucky, on the east by North Carolina, on the south by Georgia and Mississippi, and on the west by Arkansas and Missouri. There are three major land divisions: in the east are wooded areas and rugged stone formations, middle Tennessee is a lush bluegrass region, and west Tennessee is a low-lying plain. The original inhabitants of Tennessee were the Mound Builders, and the succeeding Native American tribes of the Cherokee, Chickamauga, and Chickasaw.

The first Europeans to make their way into what became Tennessee were part of the expedition of Hernando de Soto. His group included twelve priests. The Spaniard Juan Pardo followed the path of de Soto and established a fort at the future site of Chattanooga. In 1673 Jesuit Jacques Marquette and Louis Joliet explored the Mississippi Valley. In 1682 René-Robert Chevalier, Sieur de la Salle, built Fort Prud'homme on Chickasaw Bluffs in western Tennessee, opening the door for future French advances under Charles Charleville, who established a trading post at French Lick in 1714. French claims were ended in 1763 by the ascendancy of the English under the terms of the Treaty of Paris that ended the Seven Years' War (the French and Indian War in North America).

In 1768 William Bean founded the first permanent white settlement in Tennessee on the Watauga River, starting what became known as the Watauga Association. The settlement of the Cumberland Valley region was assisted by the work of Richard Henderson and the Transylvania Land Company, while the journeys of Daniel Boone in the 1770s along the Wilderness Road became legendary.

With the surrender of the British in the Revolutionary War, Tennessee and other colonies set about forging the Union. Tennessee, having been part of North Carolina, was formally ceded to the United States. Dissatisfaction with governance under North Carolina prompted the colonists of Tennessee to form a convention to petition Congress to accept an independent government and to be admitted into the Union as a state. In November 1785 a provisional constitution was approved, and the new state was called "Frankland, the Land of the Free." This was soon changed to "Franklin." In 1788 the region was again placed under the authority of North Carolina, but in 1790 Tennessee was included in the Southwest Territory created by Congress and then entered the Union in 1796. The initial population was around sixty thousand, but settlers soon arrived from neighboring states. The white settlers soon spurred the hostility of the Indian tribes, and a long and severe series of wars followed. In 1813 the tribes were decisively routed by an army of Tennessee volunteers under the leadership of the future president, Andrew Jackson; the birth of this army gave Tennessee the nickname the "Volunteer State."

Such was the promise of the region for the Church in the new century after independence that in 1808 the Diocese of Bardstown was established, with the famed Bishop Benedict Joseph Flaget

named the first bishop. The Diocese of Bardstown was responsible for all the territories from the Great Lakes in the north to the 35th parallel in the south, and from the Allegheny Mountains in the east to the Mississippi River in the west. The diocese was transferred to Louisville on February 13, 1841, and eventually the territories served by the Diocese of Bardstown required the establishment of thirty-five new dioceses located in eleven states.

The first missionary priest and pastor in Tennessee was the famed Stephen T. Badin, the first priest ordained in the United States, who lamented the tiny number of Catholics in the state. He was active in the area from 1808 to 1810, visiting Catholic settlements, but a Catholic church was not opened until 1822, in Nashville, under the direction of Father Robert Abell.

In 1828 Father James Cosgrove was named the first resident priest in Nashville. In 1837 the Diocese of Nashville was created by Pope Gregory XVI. Its jurisdiction covered the entire state, and historically the Catholic population was a tiny one.

Tennessee became a bloody battleground during the Civil War, although the state was the last to enter the Confederacy and the first to reenter the Union. Nevertheless, it was the site of some of the bloodiest battles of the war, including Shiloh, Chickamauga, and Chattanooga.

Tennessee endured the period of Reconstruction better than surrounding states, but economic and social problems persisted and the Ku Klux Klan emerged in the southern part of the state. The Klan was especially virulent in its anti-Catholicism in the 1920s and was strongly opposed in the state by the editor of the *Commercial Appeal* of Memphis, C. P. J. Mooney. In 1878 the city of Memphis lost almost two-thirds of its population to a yellow fever epidemic. Throughout the epidemic, nuns and priests in the city served heroically, taking care of the stricken without concern for their own exposure to the disease.

The state was renowned in World War I for producing more than one hundred thousand volunteers for the armed forces, and the most famous American soldier of the war, Sergeant Alvin C. York, was from Fentress County. In the Great Depression, the Tennessee Valley Authority (TVA) was created by the federal government to develop the region economically by managing the Tennessee River, and the ambitious project encompassed parts of the surrounding states as well. Further economic development followed the boom of World War II and its aftermath as companies and industries moved into the state.

The Church remained a small part of the state, although the Catholic faith was handed on courageously by strong families that treasured both Southern traditions and their Catholicity. Progress in the size of the Catholic population was made after World War II, assisted by people moving into the state from elsewhere. The Catholic population more than doubled between 1950 and 1970, at which time the Diocese of Memphis was created by Pope Paul VI. Further increases led to the creation to the Diocese of Knoxville in 1988 by Pope Blessed John Paul II. As of 2011, the 217,000 Catholics in the state made up 4 percent of the population, served by 226 priests, nearly 400 men and women religious, and 142 parishes.

Tenney, William Jewett (1814–September 20, 1883)

An author and editor, William Jewett Tenney was married to Sarah Brownson. Born in Newport, Rhode Island, he graduated from Yale in 1832 and went on to study medicine. He gave up medicine for the law, however, and subsequently practiced in New York. Aside from his law practice, he also worked in journalism. He took a position on the editorial staff of the *Journal of Commerce*, contributed to the *Evening Post*, and later was an editor for the publisher D. Appleton and Co. He became a contributor from 1861 to *Annual Cyclopædia*, edited *The Queens of England* (1852), and wrote *Military and Naval History of the Rebellion in the U.S.* (1865) and *Grammatical Analysis* (1866). During a long residence at Elizabeth, New Jersey, he held several local public offices, including that of collector of the port during President James Buchanan's administration. A convert to Catholicism, he was married twice; his second wife was Sarah Brownson, the daughter of Orestes A. Brownson.

Testem Benevolentiae

An apostolic letter promulgated by Pope Leo XIII on January 22, 1899, and addressed to Cardinal James Gibbons, archbishop of Baltimore from 1877 to 1921, *Testem Benevolentiae* was intended to express the concern of the Holy See regarding the controversy of Americanism.

It opens with the assurance of the pontiff of his affection for the American people and for the Church in the United States. He praises their spirit and their progress, and his regard compels him to point out certain issues that should be corrected in order to settle controversies. Pope Leo XIII refers specifically to the preface of Abbé Felix Klein's French translation of Walter Elliott's *The Life of Father Hecker* as the occasion of these controversies. The pope cites the preface's propositions that in order to achieve converts the Church should adapt itself to modern advanced civilization and at the same time place reduced emphasis on, or minimize, certain points of doctrine.

Pope Leo XIII then cites the teachings of the First Vatican Council on the doctrine of faith, stating that the teachings of the Church are not proposed as a mere theory of philosophy. Rather, these teachings are a divine deposit that is to be guarded faithfully and declared infallibly.

The Church has the obligation to hold fast to its doctrine at all times, but the rule of Christian life does permit modifications to meet the needs of time, place, and national custom; such changes, however, are to reflect the judgment of the Church and do not depend upon the opinions of private individuals or some false notion of civil liberty.

The letter goes on to speak of the infallibility of the pope, noting that the First Vatican Council did not intend to allow the argument that, while acknowledging the papal prerogative, there is a wider field of action for the faithful in matters of religion; the council defined infallibility in order to defend against the special evils of modern times, including the mistaking of license for liberty. There was no intention to curb genuine research to enter into conflict with the truth; instead, it was intended to apply the authority of the Church more effectively in protecting against error.

Pope Leo XIII concludes with a brief call for unity against any spirit that might lead to the development of a national Church. Hence, the pope suggests that the term Americanism is appropriate when applied to those qualities that reflect favorably on the American people. When understood in ecclesial terms, the term was applied to the rejected opinions discussed in the letter. Pope Leo wrote: "If by that name be designated the characteristic qualities which reflect honor on the people of America, just as other nations have what is special to them; or, if it implies the condition of your commonwealths, or the laws and customs prevailing in them, there is no reason why we should deem that it ought to be discarded. But if it is to be used not only to signify, but even to commend the above doctrines, there can be no doubt that our venerable brethren, the bishops of America, would be the first to repudiate and condemn it, as being especially unjust to them and to the entire nation as well. For it raises the suspicion that there are some among you who conceive and desire a Church in America different from that which is in the rest of the world."

Testem Benevolentiae sought to end the controversy that had raged for a number of years at the end of the nineteenth century. In reply, the bishops of the United States reiterated their fidelity to the Holy See and their unqualified embrace of the statements in the letter. The bishops added that any enumerated abuses in the United States were not widespread, despite the apparent claims to the contrary in the preface to *The Life of Father Hecker.* (*See also* Americanism.)

Texas

Called the Lone Star State, Texas is located in the southwestern part of the United States. It is bordered on the north by Oklahoma, on the east by Arkansas and Louisiana, on the south by Mexico and the Gulf of Mexico, and on the west by Mexico and New Mexico. There are four major land divisions in Texas: the Coastal Plain in the east, the Central Plains in the east, the Great Plains in the west, and the Trans Plains in the west. The Rio Grande River forms a natural boundary between Texas and Mexico.

At the time of the arrival of the first European explorers and missionaries, Texas was inhabited by a variety of Native American peoples, including the Caddo, Comanche, and Querecho Apache.

The Catholic legacy of Texas is a very old one and dates to the first explorations of the region, and the origins were distinctly Spanish. Around 1500,

Alonso Alvarez de Pineda made his way along the coast to the mouth of the Rio Grande, and in 1528 Alvar Nuñez Cabeza de Vaca was shipwrecked on the coast and spent some six years wandering across the area. As more explorers arrived, they returned to the Spanish holdings in Mexico with wild stories about immense wealth and cities of gold. Others followed in search of Cibola, the legendary Seven Cities of Gold, and the most famous of these explorers was Francisco Vázquez de Coronado, who traveled across western Texas in 1540. One of his band was Father Juan de Padilla, who became the first priest to evangelize among the Texas Indians and later became the protomartyr of the United States when he was killed in Kansas. By 1682 the Franciscans had missions in modern-day El Paso.

In 1685 the great French explorer René-Robert Chevalier, Sieur de la Salle, arrived in Texas at Matagorda Bay and built Fort St. Louis. The fort was attacked by the Spanish in 1689, but upon their arrival it was found deserted, as the soldiers had died from disease or Indian attacks. Notably, the priest who accompanied the expedition, Father Damian Massanet, started two missions among the Indians in eastern Texas in the next years.

From the end of the seventeenth century, Franciscans launched a massive program of mission building, founding some sixty missions across Texas, including Mission Antonio de Valera in 1718, which became better known as the Alamo. A key figure in the birth of the Texas missions was the beloved Franciscan Venerable Antonio Margil de Jesús. The city of San Antonio became the seat of Spanish colonial government. Texas remained a challenge to develop given its sheer size, the hostility of the Indians, and the decline of the Spanish Empire, and there were by the time of the Louisiana Purchase in 1803 barely ten thousand white or European settlers in Texas.

From 1803 onward, Texas began receiving increasing numbers of white settlers from the United States. In the 1820s, with Mexican independence, Texas became part of the Republic of Mexico. Nevertheless, Americans were drawn to the territory by the promise of opportunity and new beginnings. Word, for example, spread about Texas after Philip Nolan's travels at the end of the eighteenth century during his search for horses for the United States Army. Similar excitement was generated by the report of Zebulon Pike early in the nineteenth century.

White settlers, such as Stephen F. Austin, John McMullen, and James McGloin, and other entrepreneurs, called *empresarios,* started permanent settlements. McMullen and McGloin founded Irish settlements, such as San Patricio in 1831, dedicated to St. Patrick, on the Nueces River. The Irish were served by various priests, including Father Henry Doyle and the very popular Father Michael Muldoon. Settlers were permitted to enter Texas, but they were also required to make some nominal profession of the Catholic faith. The scale of the migration soon alarmed Mexico, and prohibitions on further settlement were installed in 1830, sparking a decline in relations between the settlers and the Mexican government. The tension exploded into violence in 1835 when General Antonio López de Santa Anna seized power in Mexico and declared himself dictator. The Texas settlers used the political upheaval as a pretext to declare independence. There followed the famous siege of the Alamo and the final victory of the Texans over Santa Anna at the Battle of San Jacinto. Texas was declared a republic in 1836.

Texas entered the Union in 1845. The next year, a boundary dispute with Mexico led to the Mexican-American War, settled by the Treaty of Guadalupe-Hidalgo, by which Mexico surrendered all claims to Texas.

The Church during this long time of upheaval had straddled two cultural worlds — the long-standing ties to Mexico and the needs of the growing white Catholic community. There were few priests in Texas at the time, but two of the most notable were Fathers John M. Odin and John Timon, members of the Congregation of the Missions.

In 1839 a prefecture apostolic was established at Galveston, followed by a vicariate apostolic in 1841. Father Timon was named prefect of Texas (he later became bishop of Buffalo), and the first bishop of the vicariate was Father Odin, who was consecrated a bishop in 1842. Five years later, he was named the first bishop of Galveston. He had thirteen priests at his disposal for the entire state. They were soon joined by members of the Oblates

of Mary Immaculate, who began what became a permanent presence in the state. They were joined by the Ursulines, who founded academies in Galveston and San Antonio.

The Civil War brought little actual fighting but the state belonged to the Confederacy. In the aftermath of the war, Texas suffered from violence, rampant lawlessness, and a state government that imposed a severe program of Reconstruction. Texas rejoined the Union in 1870, and a period of swift population growth followed. By the end of the decade, there were more than one million inhabitants, and the growth of the Catholic population led to the decision to create new dioceses. In 1874 Pope Blessed Pius IX created the Diocese of San Antonio and the Vicariate Apostolic of Brownsville, which became the Diocese of Corpus Christi in 1912. The Diocese of Dallas was founded in 1890.

With the start of the twentieth century, oil was discovered in eastern parts of the state, starting the foremost of the industries for Texas. The population exploded in the next decades, reaching three million. To keep pace with the changes, the Diocese of San Antonio was promoted to the rank of an archdiocese in 1926; that same year, the Diocese of Amarillo was established by Pope Pius XI. The state endured the Great Depression well because of the oil industry and the sensible economic and financial policies of the state, and the Catholic population continued to rise. In the aftermath of World War II, the Diocese of Austin was founded in 1947, followed by the Dioceses of San Angelo in 1961, Brownsville in 1965, Beaumont in 1966, and Fort Worth in 1969. In 1959 Galveston was renamed the Diocese of Galveston-Houston. The new dioceses reflected not only the growth in the general population but also the increasing diversification of that population.

In 1963 President John F. Kennedy was assassinated in Dallas. The murder was the source of immense grief to Catholics and Americans, and it left a lasting sense of sadness on Texas Catholics.

Latino Catholics became an increasingly important voice in Texas Catholicism, and they were joined by new immigrants from around the world, including Southeast Asia. New dioceses were started in the 1980s: Victoria in 1982, Lubbock in 1983, and Tyler in 1986. The Diocese of Laredo was established in 2000. Finally, in 2004, the sheer needs of the Church in Texas prompted Pope Blessed John Paul II to promote the Diocese of Galveston-Houston to the rank of a metropolitan provincial see. In 2007 the archbishop of Galveston-Houston, Daniel N. DiNardo, was appointed to the College of Cardinals. As of 2011, there were approximately 7 million Catholics in the state, served by 2,000 priests, 2,400 men and women religious, and 1,055 parishes. There are also nine Catholic colleges and universities, 52 Catholic high schools and 224 elementary schools.

Thayer, John (1757–February 5, 1815)

A missionary and convert, John Thayer was the first New Englander to be ordained. Born in Boston, he belonged to a family of Puritan settlers and studied at Yale before becoming a Congregationalist minister. During the American Revolution, he served as a chaplain in a unit under the command of John Hancock.

After the war, Thayer made a trip across Europe and found himself in Rome in 1783 at the time that the so-called beggar-saint Benedict Joseph Labre died. He disputed the miracles that had been accomplished through Labre's intercession, and in the process he converted to the Catholic Church. He went on to write an account of his conversion that was published in 1787 and reissued in the United States, England, and Ireland, and translated into several languages.

To deepen his knowledge of the Catholic faith, he studied in Paris in 1789 under the Sulpicians and was ordained the same year. He was not only the first prominent New Englander to convert but was also the first to be ordained. He returned to the United States in 1790 and served briefly as the founding priest for a parish in Boston. His temperament proved poorly matched, however, to the community, and he was sent to Alexandria, Virginia, and then to Kentucky, where he labored as a missionary. He finally settled in Limerick, Ireland, where he served until his death.

Thébaud, Augustus (November 20, 1807– December 17, 1885)

A member of the Jesuits, Augustus Thébaud was also a noted writer and teacher. Born in Nantes, France, he grew up in the troubled time of Napo-leon Bonaparte. Called to the priesthood, he studied at the preparatory seminary at Nantes, then entered the *grand séminaire* and was ordained before entering the Society of Jesus in Italy in 1835. He returned to France in 1837 and studied science at the Sorbonne before setting sail for the United States the next year. He took up the post of chair of chemistry at St. Mary's College in Kentucky and was appointed rector in 1846. That same year, however, he was appointed by the Jesuits the first president of St. John's College (later Fordham University) in New York. He was president from 1846 to 1851 and again from 1860 to 1863, taught sciences at the school, and was rector from 1863 to 1869 and again from 1873 to 1874. A noted writer, he wrote articles for the *Catholic World* and the *Catholic Quarterly Review*, two novels, and numerous historical works.

Thomas, Clarence (June 23, 1948–)

Associate justice of the Supreme Court of the United States from 1991, Clarence Thomas is also the second African-American to serve on the court and was the tenth Catholic to be appointed to the high court. Born in Pinpoint, Georgia, he was raised by his mother after his father abandoned the family when Thomas was two years old. At the age of seven, he was sent with his brother to live with their grandfather in Savannah, Georgia, and attended an all African-American Roman Catholic primary school. He went to high school at a boarding-school seminary, where he graduated with honors and was the only African-American in his class.

A Catholic, he briefly considered the priesthood and attended Conception Seminary College in Missouri, the first member of his family to go to college. He left the seminary, however, after hearing a white seminarian make a slur about Martin Luther King Jr. on the very day that the famed civil rights leader was assassinated. On the encouragement of a nun, Thomas went to the College of the Holy Cross in Worcester, Massachusetts. He graduated with a bachelor's degree in 1971 and then earned a law degree from Yale University in 1974.

Thomas served as assistant attorney general in Missouri from 1974 to 1977, was a lawyer in private practice from 1977 to 1979, and was a legislative assistant to Republican Senator John C. Danforth of Missouri from 1979 to 1981. He then worked as assistant secretary in the U.S. Department of Education from 1981 to 1982, chairman of the Equal Employment Opportunity Commission (EEOC) from 1982 to 1990, and judge on the U.S. Court of Appeals for the Federal District in Washington, D.C., from 1990 to 1991.

That same year, the retirement of Thurgood Marshall created a vacancy on the Supreme Court, and President George H. W. Bush nominated Thomas. The nomination sparked a firestorm of protest by the American left and a controversial effort to derail his appointment through the claims of sexual harassment by an African-American former employee at the EEOC, Anita Hill, by then a law professor at the University of Oklahoma. Thomas was eventually confirmed by a vote of 52 to 48, but he has remained a target for liberal groups in the years since. He is considered one of the firmest members of the court's conservative wing and is closely allied with Justice Antonin Scalia.

Tierney, Richard H. (September 2, 1870–February 10, 1928)

A Jesuit priest, Richard H. Tierney was also editor of *America* magazine from 1914 to 1925. Born in New York City, he studied at St. Francis Xavier College in New York City and entered the Jesuit novitiate at Frederick, Maryland, in 1892. After further studies at Woodstock College in Woodstock, Maryland, he was ordained on June 27, 1907, and taught philosophy there from 1909 to 1914. That same year, he was appointed editor in chief of *America* magazine. He proved a capable editor and acquired for the magazine considerable public attention through his efforts to expose the anti-Catholic activities of the Mexican government and earned special thanks from Pope Benedict XV in 1915 in a letter to Cardinal James Gibbons. His editorship remained a successful one until his retirement in 1925.

Timon, John (February 12, 1797–April 16, 1867)

The first bishop of Buffalo, from 1847 to 1867, John Timon was also the superior of the Vincentian province in the United States. He served as prefect apostolic for the Republic of Texas from 1839 to 1847 as well. Born in Conewago Township, Pennsylvania, in a log cabin, he moved with his fam-

ily when he was three to Baltimore, and entered Mount St. Mary's College in Emmitsburg, Maryland, at the age of fifteen. In 1818 he went with his family to Louisville, Kentucky, and made his way to St. Louis, where he began studies for the priesthood. In July 1822 he transferred to the Vincentian seminary, St. Mary's of the Barrens in Perryville, Missouri. He took his vows for the Vincentians in June 1825 and was ordained on September 23, 1826, by Bishop Joseph Rosati.

Active for the Vincentians for the next years, in 1835 he was appointed the first superior or visitor of the American Vincentians and served in that post from 1835 to 1847. He was then prefect apostolic of Texas from 1839 to 1841 and worked to establish the Church on a firm footing across Texas after many years of little activity. He was honored with the title "Apostle of Texas."

Timon was a candidate for several sees, including Louisville, Kentucky, and St. Louis, but he was reluctant to accept them, owing to his desire to serve in a state without slavery. On April 23, 1847, Pope Blessed Pius IX appointed him the first bishop of Buffalo. Consecrated by Bishop John Hughes on October 17, 1847, he took up his post in Buffalo and discovered immediate problems with trusteeism. They ejected him from St. Louis Church in Buffalo, where he had taken up residence. A long struggle ensued, including the placement of the parish under interdict and legal battles that ended when the 1863 Church Trustee Law, which upheld episcopal rights and served as a model for other states, was enacted. He went on to take part in the First and Second Plenary Councils of Baltimore and provided for the start of St. Joseph's Cathedral. He died in Buffalo.

Tobin, Mary Luke (May 16, 1908–August 24, 2007)

A member of the Loretto congregation, Sister Mary Luke Tobin was one of the fifteen female observers at the Second Vatican Council. Born Ruth Marie Tobin in Denver, she entered the Loretto Sisters, took the religious name Mary Luke, and professed her vows in 1927.

Tobin held a variety of teaching roles in the congregation in Missouri, Colorado, and Illinois, and in 1952 she was elected general council. In 1958 she was elected mother general of the congregation, followed by her election in 1964 as the chairwoman of the Conference of Major Superiors of Women. In that role, she was named one of the women observers to the Second Vatican Council in 1964 and 1965.

She was subsequently a leader in the renewal of religious life in the aftermath of the council and was a founding member of the International Union of Superiors General. She was later involved in various issues of women's rights, peace, and social justice, and was active in ecumenical affairs.

Tobin, Maurice Joseph. *See* **Cabinets, Catholics in Presidential**

Toledo, Diocese of

Established on April 15, 1910, by Pope St. Pius X, the Diocese of Toledo serves counties in northwestern Ohio and is a suffragan of the Archdiocese of Cincinnati. Located on the Maumee River, the city is a Great Lakes port. The area was opened to white settlement after the Battle of Fallen Timbers in 1794, in which an army led by General "Mad Anthony" Wayne concluded the Northwest Indian War with a crushing defeat of the western confederacy of the Native Americans. The resulting Treaty of Greenville in 1795 essentially ceded Ohio to the United States and paved the way for rapid white expansion into the Midwest. Fort Industry, a military garrison, was established to protect the arriving settlers. The fort stood at the mouth of Swan Creek.

The first permanent settlements in the area, however, were not established until after the War of 1812. Two communities were started, Fort Lawrence and Vistula. These villages consolidated in 1833, and the result was named Toledo; the city was incorporated in 1837. There followed the so-called Toledo War of 1837 between Ohio and Michigan over the state lines; the war was essentially without fighting, and the only casualty was said to have been a Michigan deputy sheriff stabbed in the leg over a dispute regarding some farm animals. Ohio won the dispute, and the U.S. Congress compensated Michigan for the loss of territory.

Crucial in the disagreement and also in the future expansion of Toledo and Ohio were the Erie

and Miami Canals, intended to foster economic growth and development. Growth in the nineteenth century was nevertheless slow, picking up pace with the arrival of the railroads. Toledo became a major hub for the railroad industry as it penetrated into the Midwest. The city became a major industrial center and port for the Great Lakes.

The Catholic history of the diocese dates to the Jesuit missions among the Hurons on Lake Erie. In 1751 the first Catholic chapel was founded at Sandusky in the northeastern part of what became the diocese. French settlements remained until 1763 and the defeat of France in the French and Indian War. German Catholic arrived in increasing numbers from the start of the nineteenth century. They were joined by Irish immigrants, who arrived to work for the canals and the railroads.

In 1821 the Diocese of Cincinnati was founded by Pope Pius VII, and Toledo's small Catholic presence was placed under its jurisdiction. A more organized Catholic presence in the Toledo area was achieved from around 1830. A permanent pastor was named at St. Mary's, in Tiffin, in 1831. Ten years later, Father Louis Amadeus Rappe began St. Francis De Sales Parish in Toledo and served as pastor until his appointment as the first bishop of Cleveland in 1847. He was followed as pastor by Father Louis de Goesbriand, who later became the first bishop of Burlington. Other priests in the area were notable for their devotion, including Ignatius Mullon, Edward T. Collins, Joseph P. Machebeuf, the first bishop of Denver, and Henry Damian Juncker, later the bishop of Alton.

Jurisdiction passed to the Diocese of Cleveland in 1847, and the growth in the second half of the century was marked by the arrival of the next wave of Catholic immigrants from 1870, including Poles and Hungarians looking for work in the burgeoning factories. By 1910 the decision was made that a separate diocese was desirable for the region.

The first bishop of Toledo, Joseph Schrembs, had been an auxiliary bishop of Grand Rapids since January 1911. He was named to Toledo on August 11, 1911. He spent his years in Ohio providing a firm footing to the diocese and on June 16, 1921, was transferred to the Diocese of Cleveland.

The second bishop of Toledo, Samuel Alphonsus Stritch, had been a priest of the Diocese of Nashville and was appointed to Toledo on August 10, 1921; at the time of his consecration on November 30, 1921, he was, at the age of thirty-four, the youngest bishop in the United States. His ten years in Toledo saw the start of the Holy Rosary Cathedral and the founding of Mary Manse College in 1922. On August 26, 1930, he was named archbishop of Milwaukee and went on to serve as archbishop of Chicago and then pro-prefect of the Congregation for the Propagation of the Faith in Rome. He was named a cardinal priest with the title of Santa Agnese fuori le mura in 1946 by Pope Pius XII.

The third bishop of Toledo, Karl J. Alter, had been a priest of Toledo. Appointed on April 17, 1931, he was consecrated a bishop on June 17, 1931. His years as bishop in Toledo encompassed the Great Depression and World War II and its aftermath. He became a nationally known prelate for his call for peace in 1944 (signed with other religious leaders) and his ten-point program for economic revitalization after the war that included cost-of-living adjustments for wages and profit sharing. He also finished the work on Holy Rosary Cathedral and started DeSales College in 1942. On June 14, 1950, he was appointed archbishop of Cincinnati.

The fourth bishop of Toledo, George J. Rehring, had been an auxiliary bishop of Cincinnati since 1937. Appointed to Toledo on July 16, 1950, he presided over the postwar boom in construction and growth and then attended all four sessions of the Second Vatican Council between 1962 and 1965. He retired on February 25, 1967.

Bishop Rehring was followed as bishop of Toledo by John A. Donovan, who had been an auxiliary bishop of Detroit since 1954. Appointed bishop of Toledo on February 25, 1967, and installed on April 18, 1967, he took as his main course as bishop the implementation of the decrees of the recently completed Second Vatican Council. He was known for his outreach to minorities in the diocese, including African-Americans and Latinos, and his commitment to the elderly. He retired on July 29, 1980, at the age of sixty-nine, owing to poor health.

The sixth bishop of Toledo, James R. Hoffman, was at the time of his appointment an auxiliary bishop of Toledo, having been consecrated a bishop in 1978. Named bishop of Toledo on December 16, 1980, and installed on February 17, 1981, he was the longest-serving bishop of the diocese. He faced demographic changes in the diocese, which saw declines in the number of priests, and also the general economic downturn across the so-called Rust Belt. The diocese was also troubled by the sexual abuse crisis. Bishop Hoffman died of cancer at the age of seventy on February 8, 2003.

The seventh bishop of Toledo, Leonard P. Blair, had been an auxiliary bishop of Detroit since 1999. Appointed bishop of Toledo on October 7, 2003, he was installed on December 4, 2003. Bishop Blair focused on implementing the statutes approved by the bishops for the protection of children in the wake of the sex abuse crisis, strengthening Catholic identity and family life, and promoting Catholic social communications, partly through the apostolate of Catholic radio. In 2011 there were 322,000 Catholics in the diocese, served by 209 priests, more than 500 women religious, 127 parishes, and six Catholic hospitals.

Tolton, Augustus (April 1, 1854–July 9, 1897)

The first American diocesan priest of African descent, Augustus Tolton was the son of slaves. Born into slavery in Brush Creek, Missouri, to Peter and Martha Tolton, he was baptized at St. Peter's Church, a few miles from Hannibal, Missouri.

At the start of the Civil War, his father escaped

Toledo Cathedral

and joined the Union Army, and his mother fled Missouri with her three children in 1863 to the free state of Illinois. Once safely in Quincy, Illinois, Martha found work with her sons in a local cigar factory and took them to Mass in the local German parish of St. Boniface.

The family learned soon afterward of the death of Augustus's father from dysentery in St. Louis and endured great prejudice as his mother tried to secure a decent education for her children. An Irish priest, Father Peter McGirr, issued an unexpected invitation for Augustus to attend the local parochial school.

Tolton completed high school and then graduated from Quincy College. Called to the priesthood, he proved unable to gain entry into an American seminary and was finally admitted into the College of the Propaganda Fide in Rome to become a missionary in Africa, with the help of Father McGirr. In February 1880 Tolton set sail for Rome, and the next six years of intense studies in languages, theology, and missiology were the happiest of his life. Finally, on April 24, 1886, he was ordained in the Basilica of St. John Lateran in Rome.

Assigned not to Africa but to Illinois, he served as pastor to the African-American parish of St. Joseph Church in Quincy, but found such intolerance that he accepted an invitation from Archbishop Patrick Augustine Feehan of Chicago. On December 19, 1889, Tolton went to Chicago and became a leader of the African-American Catholics of Chicago. His parish of St. Monica's, on the corner of Thirty-fifth and Dearborn, attracted a congregation of more than six hundred and served as the spiritual center for black Catholic life in the city for decades to come.

As his fame spread he was also invited to speak at national gatherings. In 1889 he gave an address at the First Catholic Colored Congress in Washington, D.C., and he was asked to speak to Catholics in Boston, New York, and even as far away as Galveston, Texas. At the same time, he pressed ahead with future plans for St. Monica's. He died suddenly, however, during a heat wave in Chicago. His remains were taken to St. Peter's Cemetery in Quincy. His cause for canonization was opened in 2010.

Toscanini, Arturo (March 25, 1867–January 16, 1957)

An Italian conductor, Arturo Toscanini was one of the most respected figures in music throughout the first half of the twentieth century. Born in Parma, Italy, the son of a tailor, he studied cello and graduated with honors from the Parma Conservatory in 1885. In 1897 he married Carla dei Martini and was working as a cellist when he was unexpectedly asked to conduct Guiseppe Verdi's *Aïda*. After establishing his reputation as conductor of the Rio de Janeiro opera, he returned to Italy and conducted the premieres of Ruggero Leoncavallo's *Pagliacci* in 1892 and Giacomo Puccini's *La Bohème* in 1896. He was later musical director at La Scala in Milan.

Going to the United States, he conducted at the Metropolitan Opera from 1908 to 1914, the New York Philharmonic from 1926 to 1936, and the NBC Symphony, which was formed for him, from 1937 to 1954. His funeral Mass was held in St. Patrick's Cathedral in New York, in the presence of Cardinal Francis Spellman.

Touissant, Pierre (June 27, 1766–June 30, 1853)

A former slave and businessman, Pierre Touissant was a beloved figure in New York City and was declared venerable in 1997 by Pope John Paul II. Born into slavery in Haiti on the plantation of Jean Bérard, Pierre learned how to read and write, thanks to his grandmother, who was also a slave. As Monsieur Bérard observed the obvious intelligence of the boy, he gave him free run of his library, encouraged him to learn, and ordered that the boy should never work in the fields.

In 1787 Bérard journeyed to New York City and took Pierre as part of his entourage. Bérard's wife, Marie, suggested that Pierre be apprenticed to a professional hairdresser she had just employed. While they stayed there, however, Haiti suffered a slave uprising that destroyed Bérard's estates. Bérard died soon after returning home, leaving his wife to deal with the collapse of her entire life. Pierre remained faithful to his mistress and used his profession as a hairdresser to care for her, as well as his sister. His skills soon led to a flourishing business among the wealthiest ladies of New York. In time, Pierre purchased his sister's freedom but remained technically a slave to care for Marie and assumed direction over her affairs. At her death in 1807, Pierre was granted his freedom.

By this time, he had become much loved and respected for his professional skills and also for his wisdom as a counselor. Called "Our Saint Pierre," he attended Mass every day at St. Peter's on Barclay Street and later married Juliette Noel, a Haitian girl. The pair established a home for orphaned black children and worked to secure freedom for dozens of slaves. Pierre also helped raise money for Old St. Patrick's Cathedral, found employment for French widows, gave gifts of money to French aristocrats who had fled their homeland in the wake of the French Revolution, and was an honored philanthropist who cared for the poor and sick of the city. Juliette died in 1851, followed by Pierre two years later. A vast crowd of blacks and whites gathered in and around St. Peter's for the funeral.

In 1990 Cardinal John J. O'Connor of New York introduced the cause of canonization for Pierre, and on December 18, 1996, Pope Blessed John Paul II declared him venerable. His body was interred in the crypt of St. Patrick's Cathedral, in a place usually reserved for the archbishops of New York.

Tracy, Spencer (April 5, 1900–June 10, 1967)

A renowned film actor, Spencer Tracy won Academy Awards as Best Actor for *Captains Courageous* in 1937 and for *Boys Town* in 1938. Born Spencer Bonaventure Tracy in Milwaukee, he joined the navy in 1917 with the entry of the United States into World War I, but spent the war in the Norfolk Navy Yard in Virginia.

Discharged from the navy, he enrolled at Ripon College as a premed student and while there began acting. He auditioned at the Sargent School in New York, and by 1923 he belonged to an acting company from White Plains, New York. While there, he met the actress Louise Treadwell, and the two were married that year. In June 1924 Louise gave birth to a boy. When it was discovered that their son, John, was deaf, Louise began developing plans for what was later called the John Tracy Clinic, which was founded in 1942. In 1932 Louis gave birth to a daughter, Susie.

Tracy's career took its major turn with the 1930 play *The Last Mile*. Based on his performance, he was signed by Fox Films and moved to Hollywood in 1931. In 1935 he signed a contract with MGM and remained with that studio for the next two decades. His Oscars in 1937 and 1938 made him the first male actor to win the Academy Award for Best Actor for two consecutive years, matched only by Tom Hanks five decades later.

Tracy first worked with Katharine Hepburn in 1942, starting a longtime professional and personal relationship as his marriage had ended unhappily and the couple had separated. His career, meanwhile, continued with several notable roles, including *Judgment at Nuremburg* and *Guess Who's Coming to Dinner*, his last role. Tracy died of heart failure in Hollywood Hills, California.

Trappists

The Order of Cistercians of the Strict Observance, commonly known as the Trappists (O.C.S.O.), are a monastic order that was born out of the Cistercian Order, the monastic order founded by St. Robert of Molesme in 1098 and named after its motherhouse at Cîteaux, in Burgundy. The Order of Cistercians (O.Cist.) was born out of St. Robert's unhappiness with the lax attitude that pervaded his own monastery at Molesme. He departed the community with a group of fellow monks and established himself at Cîteaux, where he instituted a far more austere program of life, in keeping with traditional Benedictine ideals. St. Robert was succeeded as abbot by St. Alberic and then the truly remarkable St. Stephen Harding, who was abbot from 1109 to 1133. Called the second founder of the Cistercians, in 1119 St. Stephen wrote the Charter of Love, the constitution of the order. It was approved by Pope Callistus II, and called for manual labor, a simplified liturgy, and strict asceticism. During St. Stephen's time as abbot, there arrived in 1112 the foremost member of the Cistercians, St. Bernard of Clairvaux. He founded the Abbey of Clairvaux, and through the fame and brilliance of his work the order spread across Europe.

The Cistercians enjoyed wide prominence during the 1100s and 1200s, deeply influencing the monasticism of the times. The White Monks, as they were called, had over five hundred abbeys at the start of the thirteenth century, including houses in Scotland and Scandinavia, and the famed house of Rievaulx. The order gradually lost its preeminence from that time and subsequently suffered from the vicissitudes of the late Middle Ages, the Renaissance, and the Reformation.

The origins of the Trappists are traced to a reform movement that began in the 1600s and that called for the return to a more precise adherence to the rule. The members, known as the Strict Observance, found support among many in the French houses, so that a division grew in France between those of the Strict Observance and those of the Common Observance. The French Revolution had a terrible impact upon the Common Observance, but the order recovered.

Meanwhile, the Cistercians of the Strict Observance became centered in the monastery of La Trappe in France whose members were expelled by the Revolution but returned in 1817. Under their abbot, Augustine Lestrange, their austere rule was revitalized and found appeal among the houses that were reestablished throughout the country. They took their work into other countries. When, in 1898, Cîteaux was restored to the order, its community chose to join the Strict Observance. Its abbot is the general of the Cistercians of the Strict Observance, which is today a separate body from the Order of Cistercians. The name Trappists is still used for the monks of the Strict Observance. Trappists wear a white habit with a black scapular. There are currently over 2,500 Trappists worldwide and nearly 1,500 Cistercians.

The first Trappists arrived in the United States in the early nineteenth century. Several efforts to plant a community failed until 1848, when Irish Trappists were able to establish the famed community of Gethsemani, in Kentucky, and Irish Trapists launched a community at New Melleray, Iowa, the next year. By the end of World War II, there were a dozen Trappist monasteries that were later joined by two communities of Cistercian nuns under Trappist direction.

There are some eleven Trappist communities, including the Abbey of Gethsemani, Our Lady of New Melleray Abbey, and other houses established in the 1940s and 1950s that have continued as centers of prayer. In this century, the best-known Trappist was Thomas Merton. There are also Cistercian Nuns (O.Cist.) and the Order of Cistercian Nuns of the Strict Observance (O.C.S.O.).

Trenton, Diocese of

Established on August 11, 1881, by Pope Leo XIII, the Diocese of Trenton serves counties in southern New Jersey. It is a suffragan see of the Archdiocese of Newark.

Located on the Delaware River, Trenton is the state capital of New Jersey and is a major manufacturing center. It is considered to be located in the very center of the state. The city of Trenton was born out of the first settlements started by the Quakers in the late seventeenth century, and by 1719 was called "Trent-Towne." It was named after William Trent, a prominent landowner; the name Trenton was coined over time. After the Revolutionary War, the city was considered as a possible location for the new capital for the United States and served as the national capital in late 1784.

The Catholic history of Trenton and central New Jersey begins with the celebration of a Mass in Woodbridge, New Jersey, in 1672. Catholics were in the area at the time, but their numbers in the period before the American Revolution were small. Catholics suffered from a variety of legal disabilities and were not allowed to hold office or to vote. Catholic priests were also banned from the colony. The needs of the Catholics in New Jersey were nevertheless met by Jesuit Father Joseph Greaton, who was best known for his service in Philadelphia and for building Old St. Joseph's Church in Philadelphia in 1732. His labors were continued by the Jesuit Father Theodore Schneider, whose missions carried him to New Jersey and parts of Pennsylvania and Delaware. There was also the work of the famous Father Ferdinand Steinmeyer, another Jesuit, known as "Father Farmer," who ministered to Catholic families until his death in 1786.

Catholics received an improvement in their rights after the Revolution, and the Catholic population increased slowly. With the establishment of the Diocese of Philadelphia in 1808, the region around Trenton came under its ecclesiastical jurisdiction. Early in the 1800s, Masses for local Catholics were celebrated in homes and offices, such as the printing office of Isaac Collins in Trenton or the home of John Baptist Sartori, a representative of the commercial interests of the Papal States in the United States. As numbers increased, it became desirable to start a parish. This was accomplished in 1814, with a church financed partly by Sartori at Lamberton and Market Streets in Trenton and dedicated to St. John. It was the first parish in the state.

New parishes followed slowly, so that by 1842 there were churches in Middlesex, Burlington, and Hunterdon Counties. In 1853 the Diocese of Newark was created with ecclesiastical jurisdiction over the entire state of New Jersey. The Catholic population soon increased rapidly in the face of immigrant waves to the United States, mostly Irish and Germans. The Catholic community in New Jersey thus increased from 25,000 in 1860 to more than 130,000 in 1880. This growth prompted the Holy See to establish the Diocese of Trenton in 1881. At its birth, the new diocese covered 14 counties and served some 35,000 Catholics; there were 51 priests, 68 churches, and 23 parochial schools.

The first bishop of Trenton, Michael J. O'Farrell, was a priest of the Archdiocese of New York. Consecrated a bishop on November 1, 1881, he devoted his time to giving the diocese a firm footing, including establishing new parishes and institutions. By the time of his death at the age of sixty-one on April 2, 1894, he had increased the number of priests to 92, the number of churches to 101, and the number of parochial schools to 82.

The second bishop of Trenton, James A. McFaul, had been the vicar general of Trenton and diocesan administrator after Bishop O'Farrell's passing. Appointed bishop of Trenton on July 20, 1894, he was consecrated a bishop on October 18. He continued the expansion of the diocese, including new parishes, churches, and schools, as well as an orphanage and a home for the elderly. He also helped to found Mount St. Mary's College at Plainfield. These projects were essential because of the steady growth of the Catholic population, especially as a result of the next wave of immigration, from Italy and Eastern Europe. By 1910 the Catholic community numbered more than four hundred thousand. Bishop McFaul died on June 16, 1917, at the age of sixty-seven.

The third bishop of Trenton, Thomas J. Walsh, had been a priest of the Diocese of Buffalo. Appointed bishop of Trenton on May 10, 1918, Walsh was consecrated a bishop on July 25, 1918, as World War I was reaching its conclusion. In his ten years in Trenton, he continued to meet the needs of the growing Catholic population. On March 2, 1928, Walsh was appointed bishop of Newark and named its first archbishop on December 10, 1937.

Bishop Walsh was succeeded on March 2, 1928, by John J. McMahon, a priest of New York. Consecrated a bishop on April 26, 1928, he served for four years and died unexpectedly on December 31, 1932, at the age of fifty-seven.

The fifth bishop of Trenton, Moses E. Kiley, had been a priest of Chicago. Appointed on February 10, 1934, he was consecrated a bishop on March 17, 1934. He inherited a diocese that had grown to more than a million members, and he was faced with the difficult task of stabilizing diocesan finances and solving a debt issue of millions at a time when the country was struggling with the Great Depression. During his time in Trenton, in 1937 Pope Pius XI created the Diocese of Camden, with territory taken from Trenton. With the founding of Camden, the Diocese of Trenton had a Catholic population of 210,000 in eight counties with 212 priests and 121 parishes. On January 1, 1940, he was appointed archbishop of Milwaukee.

The sixth bishop of Trenton, William A. Griffin, had been an auxiliary bishop of Newark since 1938. Appointed to Trenton on May 21, 1940, he served as bishop throughout the Second World War and its aftermath. With the diocese poised to expand in the 1950s, Bishop Griffin suffered a stroke and died on January 1, 1950.

Bishop Griffin was succeeded by George W. Ahr, who had been a priest of the Archdiocese of Newark. Appointed on January 28, 1950, Ahr was consecrated a bishop on March 20, 1950, and embarked on a tenure as bishop that lasted for 29 years. He began his time with a massive building program to keep pace with the burgeoning Catholic population, which increased from 300,000 to 850,000. He established some fifty parishes and ninety schools. He also started *The Monitor*, the official weekly newspaper of the diocese. Bishop Ahr attended the Second Vatican Council and then worked to implement its decrees in a difficult time. He retired on June 23, 1979.

The eighth bishop of Trenton, John C. Reiss, had been an auxiliary bishop of the diocese since 1967. Named to succeed Bishop Ahr on April 22, 1980, he had the pleasure of presiding over the hundredth anniversary celebrations for the diocese in August 1981. Soon after, the Diocese of Metuchen was established with territory taken from the Trenton Diocese. After the start of Metuchen, Trenton had a Catholic population of some 447,000 with 193 priests and 119 parishes. Bishop Reiss also focused on the spiritual renewal and strengthening of the diocese through the Renew process for lay spirituality, a diocesan synod in 1991, and a diocesan capital and endowment-fund campaign that raised more than $38 million. He retired on July 1, 1997.

Bishop Reiss was succeeded on the same day by Bishop John M. Smith, who had been an auxiliary bishop of Newark and bishop of Pensacola-Tallahassee before his appointment on November 21, 1995, as coadjutor bishop of Trenton. Bishop Smith focused on promoting the activities of the laity, strengthening diocesan communications, and finding solutions to the changing demographic situation in the area, which necessitated a parish restructuring program starting in 2000 and education reforms. In 2009 he launched a diocesan pastoral plan. Bishop Smith retired on June 23, 2010.

On June 4, 2010, Vincentian Father David M. O'Connell, president of The Catholic University of America in Washington, D.C., was appointed coadjutor bishop of Trenton. He acceded to the see upon Bishop Smith's retirement. As of 2011, there were 858,000 Catholics in the diocese, served by 300 priests, 400 men and women religious, and 111 parishes.

Trusteeism

Trusteeism was the erroneous claim by lay leaders in a parish that they had the right to appoint, elect, and fire their pastors without the say of the bishop; equally, adherents of trusteeism went so far as to demand a say in matters of Church teaching. The problem of trusteeism was arguably one of the greatest faced by the early American Church. It stemmed from a variety of causes, but one of the most notable was the unavoidable fact that Catholicism existed in a predominately Protestant country. Put simply, trusteeism was a movement in which some laymen sought to take control over the administration of their parish beyond the traditions and the terms of ecclesiastical law. The claim was based on certain state laws that, in keeping with the Protestant custom, officially recognized the parishioners as the official administrators.

The causes are traced in part to the Protestant American culture of the era with its preference for congregationalism, a decentralized ecclesial structure that was adopted readily by Protestant groups in the country. Local Protestant congregations formed or elected a board of trustees responsible for maintaining church properties and the hiring and firing of pastors. For Catholics, parishes tended to be widely dispersed, and priests were still few in number, meaning that lay Catholics often had to play major roles in their own churches if the faith was to be preserved and handed on to their children.

Bishop Carroll accepted this system as necessary because of the shortage of priests and also in recognition of the need for collaboration with the laypeople of his diocese. He was absolutely determined, however, to reject what became lay trusteeism.

Under the influence of local Protestants, some Catholics in far-flung parishes were convinced that they were entitled to have the final say in who should own and lead their parish, and not the bishop in distant Baltimore. A legal basis was established for Protestants on April 6, 1784, when the New York Legislature passed a law providing for the general incorporation of parishes and the election of three to nine male parishioners as trustees with broad administrative powers; other states soon followed. Catholic parishes in New York and subsequent states had to accept the trustee form of corporation. Although the New York Act of 1784 declared that it did not intend to interfere with "the doctrine, discipline, or worship" of any parish being incorporated, the legislation omitted clergy as members of the trustee boards and left as an obvious option the so-called right of patronage (hiring and firing of clergy) in Catholic parishes. Many trustee boards took the opportunity and made the most of it. Matters were made worse at times by unscrupulous priests who would convince lay parish boards to oust the legitimate pastor and install them, against all Church law.

One of the earliest battles over trusteeism took place in Philadelphia at Holy Trinity Church, a largely German parish. The parishioners refused to accept the pastor appointed by the bishop and elected their own. This and other abuses led to a formal schism in 1796, a condition that existed until 1802, when they returned to canonical jurisdiction. Philadelphia was later the scene of the Hogan Schism in the 1820s, when Reverend William Hogan, with the aid of lay trustees, seized control of St. Mary's Cathedral. A native of Limerick, Ireland, Hogan had been ordained in his native country and had left for America without episcopal permission. He served in Albany, New York, and then went to St. Mary's Church in Philadelphia in 1820.

Once in that parish, he won over the lay trustees of the property and publicly attacked Bishop Henry Conwell, the newly arrived ordinary of the Diocese of Philadelphia. Father Hogan was suspended and then excommunicated for conspiring to lead a parish into schismatic separation from the bishop and the diocese. The term "Hoganism" became popular as the code word for trusteeism and clerical obstinacy, following the democratic mood of the nation at the time. Two court cases involving Father Hogan labeled him as immoral, and his movement was nullified finally by a decision of the Pennsylvania Supreme Court in 1822. In 1824 Hogan married and left the Church; he subsequently became a lawyer and the U.S. consul to Cuba and wrote numerous anti-Catholic pamphlets and attacked the Church across the nation. He died in 1848 in Nashua, New Hampshire.

Aware of the crisis, two popes issued letters: Pope Pius VII sent the letter *Non Sine Magno* to the U.S. bishops in 1822; and Pope Leo XII sent the letter *Quo Longius* in 1828 to Bishop Joseph Rosati of St. Louis. Similar troubles still seriously disturbed the peace of the Church in other places for many years, principally in the dioceses of New York, Baltimore, Buffalo, Charleston, and New Orleans. In the end, the dangers arising from the exploitation of lay control were gradually diminished with the extension and enforcement of canonical procedures and with changes in civil law about the middle of the nineteenth century.

Bishop John England, the first bishop of Charles-ton, worked toward a solution by creating a diocesan constitution that delineated the rights of laypeople in parishes. More important, he convinced Archbishop James Whitfield of Baltimore to convoke the First Provincial Council in 1829, the first such gathering of bishops in the country. In attendance were six bishops and the apostolic administrator of Philadelphia. The council took up a variety of matters, including the call for proper and universal Catholic education and the use of a uniform catechism. But the council was concerned especially with trusteeism. It instructed bishops to demand the deed for a new church before its dedication, denied the canonical right of patronage to trustees in the Archdiocese of Baltimore, and imposed canonical penalties on any clerics or laypeople who were disobedient. Anti-trustee legislation was advanced by subsequent Councils of Baltimore (including those in 1837, 1840, 1843, and 1849).

The efforts by the bishops to secure the Church's rights were assisted by various wins in state courts and legislatures. Bishop Antoine Blanc of New Orleans, for example, in 1844 won an appeal against the trustees to the Louisiana Supreme Court. More significant was the New York state act of March 25, 1863, which accepted the principle that Catholic parishes should have a type of "corporation aggregate" that was acceptable to Catholic canon law. As codified, the board of trustees comprised the bishop, his vicar general, the pastor, and two lay trustees chosen by the three clerical trustees. This solution was promoted by the Third Plenary Council of Baltimore in 1884, and in 1911 the Vatican Sacred Congregation of the Council in Rome issued a decree declaring its preference for this form of incorporation.

Tucson, Diocese of

Established on May 8, 1897, by Pope Leo XIII, the Diocese of Tucson serves counties in southern Arizona. It is a suffragan of the Archdiocese of Santa Fe. Located on the Santa Cruz River, Tucson is in a broad valley surrounded by mountains, including the Tucson Mountains, the Rincon Mountains, and the Santa Catalina Mountains. The site was originally called Syukeshon, a Native American term for a "village of the dark spring at the foot of the mountains."

In 1539 a Franciscan missionary, Marcos de Niza, explored the Arizona territory, and the next year he and several Franciscans journeyed with the Spanish explorer Francisco Vázquez de Coronado in his quest to find Cibola, the legendary Seven Cities of Gold, which were reputed to be in the Southwest. When, of course, the expedition proved fruitless, the Franciscans chose to remain in Arizona to evangelize and to establish missions. These did not last, but more permanent missions were founded from 1629 by the Franciscans, who sought the conversion of the Hopi Indians. The four missions that were built, however, were destroyed in 1680 during the tragic Pueblo revolt.

In the next years, the leading missionary of the time, the Jesuit Eusebius Kino, began to work in southern Arizona from around 1691, and in 1700 established a series of churches, in particular Mission San Xavier del Bac. The Spanish were able to reestablish control over the region and built a fortress, Presidio San Agustín del Tucsón, in 1775. These holdings were attacked by Native Americans, especially the Apaches, but the town survived and was eventually called Tucson, which became part of the territory of the United States in 1854 as part of the Gadsden Purchase and was included with the rest of Arizona in the New Mexico Territory until 1863 and the creation of the Arizona Territory. It served as the capital of the territory from 1867 to 1877. Further development was achieved from 1880 with the arrival of the Pacific Railroad and the finding of silver and other natural resources near the city.

From the early time of the missions in southern Arizona, the region was under the jurisdiction of Mexico, including the Diocese of Durango. In 1821 Mexican independence was achieved, and the Spanish priests were expelled from Arizona. This effectively ended evangelization in the area as the missions were closed.

In 1858 the Diocese of Santa Fe was founded, and Arizona was placed under its jurisdiction. Bishop Jean Baptiste Lamy of Santa Fe sent the revered priest Joseph P. Machebeuf to make a study of the needs of southern Arizona. He was the first American priest in Arizona and stayed there for four months. Progress was interrupted by the Civil War and the hostility of the Apaches, but in 1866

a semblance of order was restored in southern Arizona, and Bishop Lamy sent Father John Baptist Salpointe to Tucson with two other priests as his vicar general for the Arizona missions. Under difficult conditions and a small population of settlers, miners, and Native Americans, Father Salpointe began building churches and schools.

In 1868 the Holy See created the Vicariate Apostolic of Arizona, and Salpointe was named its vicar apostolic and consecrated a bishop on June 20, 1869. He spent the next years laboring to continue the development of the vicariate. On February 19, 1885, however, he was appointed coadjutor to Archbishop Lamy and was succeeded by Father Peter Bourgade. He was consecrated a bishop on May 1, 1885.

On May 8, 1897, soon after the dedication of the cathedral in Tucson, the Diocese of Tucson was created with Bourgade named its first bishop. He was named archbishop of Santa Fe two years later.

On April 19, 1900, Henry R. Granjon was appointed the bishop of Tucson and was consecrated on June 17, 1900. He worked to develop the diocese's parishes and schools. Territory was lost in 1914 with the creation of the El Paso diocese. Bishop Granjon died on November 9, 1922, while on his way to Rome.

The next bishop of Tucson, Daniel J. Gercke, was a priest of Philadelphia who had also worked as a missionary, including service in the Philippines. Appointed on June 21, 1923, he was consecrated a bishop on November 6, 1923, and was the first American-born bishop of the diocese. His time as bishop stretched some thirty-seven years and encompassed the Great Depression and the Second World War as well as the postwar boom. He built new parishes and founded the Regina Cleri Seminary in Tucson. He retired on September 28, 1960, and was named titular archbishop of Cotyaeum by Pope John XXIII in recognition of his achievements.

Archbishop Gercke was succeeded by Francis J. Green, who had been named auxiliary bishop of Tucson in 1953 and coadjutor bishop of Tucson since May 11, 1960. He acceded to the see upon the resignation of Bishop Gercke. He attended the Second Vatican Council and then worked to implement the decrees and reforms of the council. He restored St. Augustine Cathedral and was a strong advocate for the pastoral care of the minorities in the diocese. He retired on July 28, 1981.

Bishop Green was succeeded by Manuel D. Moreno, who had been an auxiliary bishop of Los Angeles since 1977. He became the bishop of Tucson on January 12, 1982, and was installed in Mission San Xavier del Bac. As bishop, he advocated outreach to Hispanics and focused on issues of migration. He was instrumental in organizing the first joint pastoral letter issued by the U.S. and Mexican Bishops' Conferences, "Strangers No Longer: Together on the Journey of Hope," in 2002. He resigned on March 7, 2003, and was succeeded on the same day by Bishop Gerald F. Kicanas, who had been the coadjutor bishop of Tucson since 2001.

Bishop Kicanas began his time as bishop confronting the sex abuse crisis, owing to a number of cases that predated his arrival. He was praised for his handling of the situation, and the diocese emerged from bankruptcy in 2005, a year after filing for protection in the face of the sex abuse cases. A $22.2 million settlement with sex abuse victims was approved by the bankruptcy court in July 2005. As of 2011, there were 194,000 Catholics in the diocese served by 175 priests, nearly 200 men and women religious, and 76 parishes.

Tulsa, Diocese of

Established on February 7, 1973, by Pope Paul VI, the Diocese of Tulsa serves thirty-one counties in the eastern part of Oklahoma. The diocese was originally part of the Diocese of Oklahoma City and Tulsa. It is a suffragan see of the Archdiocese of Oklahoma City. The city is located on the Arkansas River. Its origins are traced to around 1836, when the site was occupied by the Creek tribe of Native Americans who had been evicted from their lands in Alabama. The name Tulsa was given to the new settlement in honor of their former holdings, from the Creek word "Tallasi," which became Tulsa.

White settlers slowly penetrated into the territory toward the end of the nineteenth century, a process accelerated by the arrival in Tulsa in 1898 of the St. Louis–San Francisco Railroad. That same year, Tulsa was officially incorporated and had its first mayoral election. Three years later, the first of Tulsa's oil wells was discovered, and by 1905

new deposits were being developed in Glenn Pool (modern-day Glenpool) and Red Fork. Oklahoma entered the Union in 1907.

Thousands soon flocked to the area and contributed to Tulsa becoming known as the "Oil Capital of the World." The city was also the site of the bloody Tulsa Race Riot in 1921 that destroyed whole parts of the city and caused the deaths of dozens, perhaps even hundreds, of blacks and more than a dozen whites.

The Catholic history of the region opened in 1541, when Francisco Vázquez de Coronado headed an expedition into the area, seeking Cibola, the legendary Seven Cities of Gold. The protomartyr of the United States, Franciscan Father Juan de Padilla, was part of Coronado's expedition. He was slain in Kansas soon after. Francisco Leyva de Bonilla led another expedition into the area in 1590. Four decades later, Franciscan Juan de Sales arrived with priest companions following the Santa Fe Trail. In 1682 René-Robert Chevalier, Sieur de La Salle, explored the area.

The Tulsa settlement established by the Creek Indians became a flourishing site as the United States evolved and established territories. The Catholic affairs of the region were administered by the Diocese (later the Archdiocese) of St. Louis and then by the Diocese of Little Rock in 1843. In 1834 the U.S. Congress had established the Oklahoma Territory, placing Indian nations on the land. The Cherokee, Chickasaw, Choctaw, and Seminoles joined the Creek in Oklahoma.

Benedictine monks entered the area around 1875 to establish a permanent Catholic presence. The next year, the Holy See established the Prefecture Apostolic of the Indian Territory and appointed the Benedictine Isidore Robot. He died in 1887 and was succeeded by another Benedictine, Ignatius Jean. In 1891 the Holy See established the Vicariate Apostolic for the Oklahoma and Indian Territory, and its first vicar was Theophile Meerschaert, who was appointed the first bishop of Oklahoma in 1905. He died in 1924 at the age of seventy-six. Six years later, during the time of Bishop Francis Clement Kelley, the diocese was renamed Oklahoma City-Tulsa by Pope Pius XI. Oklahoma City was elevated to the rank of a metropolitan provincial see in December 1972 by Pope Paul VI.

At the same time, the Diocese of Tulsa was established out of territory taken from the new archdiocese. The first bishop of Tulsa, Bernard J. Ganter, had been a priest of the Diocese of Galveston-Houston. Appointed to Tulsa on December 13, 1972, he was consecrated a bishop on February 2, 1973, and set to work immediately to establish the diocese on a firm footing. On December 13, 1977, he was appointed the bishop of Beaumont.

The second bishop of Tulsa, Eusebius J. Beltran, had been a priest of the Archdiocese of Atlanta. In the 1960s he took part in the civil rights movement and participated in the 1965 Selma March. Named to Tulsa on February 28, 1978, he was consecrated a bishop on April 20, 1978. As bishop of Tulsa, he continued the work of developing the administrative and pastoral needs of the diocese, including the care of AIDS victims, the homeless, and the unborn. On November 24, 1992, Bishop Beltran was appointed archbishop of Oklahoma City.

The third bishop of Tulsa, Edward J. Slattery, had been a priest of the Archdiocese of Chicago. Named bishop of Tulsa on November 3, 1993, and consecrated a bishop on January 6, 1994, he led the diocese through the Great Jubilee of 2000 and into the new century. Concerned deeply with the immigration issues facing the Church in the region, he published a pastoral letter in 2007 on the subject, "The Suffering Faces of the Poor are the Suffering Face of Christ." As of 2011, there were nearly 62,000 Catholics in the diocese, served by 101 priests and 76 parishes.

Tumulty, Joseph (May 5, 1870–April 19, 1954)

A politician and attorney from New Jersey, Joseph Tumulty served as private secretary to Woodrow Wilson. Born in Jersey City, New Jersey, he studied at St. Peter's College in New Jersey, and became a figure in the Democratic Party in New Jersey and served in the New Jersey General Assembly from 1907 to 1910. Although initially not a supporter of Wilson, as he was concerned that Wilson would not be a supporter of the Progressive cause and would not resist the corrupt political bosses, Tumulty soon changed his mind. He became a trusted adviser to Wilson and was appointed private secretary in 1911. He encouraged Wilson to run for president and, when Wilson moved to Washington,

D.C., after the election, he was named presidential private secretary, a role that would later be called White House Chief of Staff. The appointment was opposed by some in Congress because of Tumulty's Catholic faith. Prejudice troubled his service, and in 1916 he was briefly fired because of the anti-Catholic bigotry and the opposition of Wilson's new wife, Edith Galt, whom Wilson had married in 1915, and another adviser, Colonel Edward M. House. Although he was reinstated, Tumulty never again had the increasingly frail Wilson's support. After leaving White House service in 1921, Tumulty returned to private practice in New Jersey.

Tunney, Gene (May 25, 1897–July 11, 1978)

One of the greatest boxers in the history of the sport, "The Fighting Marine" Gene Tunney suffered only one defeat in his career and retired as champion in 1928.

Born in New York City to Irish parents, he was drawn to a career in boxing at an early age. He went undefeated between 1915 and 1918 before enlisting in the Marines during World War I; he became the U.S. Expeditionary Forces champion in boxing. After fighting for years at middleweight, Tunney became a heavyweight fighter in 1922. He went on to fight with the greatest boxers of his era, culminating with a series of bouts with the legendary Jack Dempsey. On September 23, 1926, he defeated Dempsey in Sesquicentennial Stadium in Philadelphia, the so-called "Upset of the Decade." He retired in 1928 and was declared the first-ever *Ring* magazine Fighter of the Year for 1928. That same year, he married a wealthy socialite, Mary "Polly" Lauder.

Turner, Thomas (March 16, 1877–April 21, 1978)

An educator and civil rights leader, Thomas Turner was a professor of biology at Howard University and an important lay leader among African-American Catholics in the twentieth century. He worked against discrimination, especially in the Church, through the Federated Colored Catholics.

Born in a sharecropper's cabin in Charles County, Maryland, he was baptized a Catholic as an infant and grew up at a time when African-Americans were free but still faced discrimination, both in society and also in the Church. Offered a scholarship to an Episcopalian school in Maryland if he left the Church for the Episcopalians, he declined and instead attended Howard University in Washington, D.C. He worked his way through school and graduated with a bachelor's degree in 1901; he then went to The Catholic University of America in Washington, D.C., to study science, but his financial situation proved untenable. He accepted an invitation from Booker T. Washington to teach at the Tuskegee Institute.

The next year, Turner returned to Maryland to teach at the Baltimore High and Training School; he was one of the first African-Americans to teach in an African-American school in Maryland. He earned a master's degree from Howard in 1905 and then a doctorate in botany from Cornell University in 1921. Meantime, in 1913 he became a professor of biology at Howard University and became active in the recently established National Association for the Advancement of Colored People (NAACP). From 1914 to 1920 he was acting dean of the School of Education at Howard and in 1924 became the first chairman of the biology department at the Hampton Institute in Virginia.

To promote better conditions for African-Americans in the Church, he organized the Committee Against the Extension of Race Prejudice in the Church, which in 1924 became the Federated Colored Catholics. He served as its first president.

Tyler, Diocese of

Established on December 12, 1986, the Diocese of Tyler serves thirty-three counties in northeast Texas. It is a suffragan diocese of the Archdiocese of Galveston-Houston. The city was laid out as early as 1846 and was named for President John Tyler. The area was a prosperous farming center until the 1930s when the East Texas Oil Fields were developed. Tyler then became the administrative headquarters for petroleum interests. The city was also involved in transportation and other vital industries. Flowers, especially the Texas rose, are part of the economic base of the region.

The Catholic history of the diocese dates to 1500 when Spanish explorers were moving through the region. Such famous explorers as Alonso Alvarez de Pineda, Alvar Nuñez Cabeza de Vaca, and Hernando de Soto were on the scene. By 1682 Francis-

can missionaries had started outposts of the faith in the south. Around 1685, René-Robert Chevalier, Sieur de La Salle, claimed Texas for France.

By 1690 the great missions of San Antonio were being established, including San Antonio de Valero, known more commonly as the Alamo. Texas was evolving as the American Revolution freed the colonies and established the United States. The Louisiana Purchase of 1803 opened new lands, and Americans began moving west. By 1820 many Americans were in Texas, including Stephen F. Austin. When the Mexicans fought and won their freedom from Spain in 1821, the Mexican government exiled the Spanish missionaries. The recognition of the increased number of Americans residing in Texas alarmed the Mexican authorities, who tried to halt the immigration. This sparked the revolt of the Americans in Texas that ended with Texan independence from Mexico in 1836. Texas entered the Union in 1845.

In 1839 the Holy See created a prefecture apostolic at Galveston, followed by a vicariate apostolic in 1841. In 1847 the Diocese of Galveston was founded. San Antonio was created a diocese in 1874 and later became an archdiocese in 1926.

Throughout the twentieth century, the territory that became the Diocese of Tyler was under the jurisdiction of several dioceses, including the Diocese of Galveston-Houston, Dallas (created in 1890), and Beaumont (created in 1966). By 1986 the progress of the Catholic community warranted the creation of a diocese for Tyler. This was approved by Pope Blessed John Paul II, and Charles E. Herzig, a priest of the Archdiocese of San Antonio, was appointed the first bishop on December 12, 1986. Consecrated a bishop on February 24, 1987, he spent the next years giving the diocese its foundation in pastoral care and administration. He died on September 7, 1991, at the age of sixty-two.

The second bishop of Tyler, Edmond Carmody, was a native of Ireland and a priest of the Archdiocese of San Antonio. He served for a time as a missionary in Ecuador and was an auxiliary bishop of San Antonio from 1988. Appointed bishop of Tyler on March 24, 1992, and installed on May 25, 1992, he assumed direction over a diocese that had around 30,000 Catholics. In the next decade, the population increased to more than 53,000, and the diocese worked to keep pace with the pastoral needs. On March 17, 2000, Bishop Carmody was transferred to the Diocese of Corpus Christi in Texas.

The third bishop of Tyler, Alvaro Corrada del Rio, was a native of Puerto Rico and joined the Society of Jesus in 1960. He had also served as an auxiliary bishop of Washington, D.C., since 1985. Appointed bishop of Tyler on December 5, 2000, he was installed on January 31, 2001. During his time in Tyler, Bishop Corrado del Rio was concerned with conscience and the role of faith in the areas of health care, including sterilization. He also wrote a pastoral letter to the diocese on discipleship and promoted the implementation and expansion of the Safe Environment Program in the diocese in response to the sex abuse crisis. On July 6, 2011, he was appointed bishop of Mayaguez, Puerto Rico. As of 2011, there were more than 61,000 Catholics in the diocese, served by 100 priests and 44 parishes.

U

Ukrainian Catholics. *See* **Eastern Churches, Catholic**

Unger, Dominic (March 30, 1907–July 11, 1982)
A Capuchin Franciscan and scholar, Dominic Unger was born Joseph Unger in Herndon, Kansas. He studied at Hays Catholic College before entering the Capuchin novitiate in 1928, taking the name Dominic, and professed his final vows in 1932. Father Unger was ordained in 1934. After ordination, he studied at the Pontifical Gregorian University in Rome and then at the Pontifical Biblical Institute, where he earned a licentiate in Sacred Scripture under the direction of the famed biblical scholar (and later Cardinal) Augustin Bea. His doctoral studies were cut short by the start of World War II in 1939.

Returning to the United States, Father Unger received a teaching post at St. Fidelis Seminary in Victoria, Kansas, the first of many professorships over the next decades; he taught at St. Conrad Friary in Annapolis, Maryland, at the Franciscan Historical Institute in Rome, and in Capuchin houses in Washington, D.C., St. Louis, and Ellis, Kansas. In addition to his teaching, Father Unger was named by Pope John XXIII as a consultor to the theological commission charged with assisting the preparations for the Second Vatican Council, and served on the Pontifical International Marian Academy and the Mariological Society of America. He was also a prolific author and translator, particularly of an edition of Irenaeus's *Adversus Haereses*, and his scholarly writings appeared in the *American Ecclesiastical Review*, the *Catholic Biblical Quarterly*, *Franciscan Studies*, and *The Priest*.

United States Catholic Conference (USCC). See **United States Conference of Catholic Bishops**

United States Conference of Catholic Bishops (USCCB)
The United States Conference of Catholic Bishops is an assembly of the bishops of the United States and the U.S. Virgin Islands intended to assist them in the joint exercise of various pastoral functions as leaders of the Catholic Church in the United States. The USCCB states that its purpose is "to promote the greater good which the Church offers humankind, especially through forms and programs of the apostolate fittingly adapted to the circumstances of time and place. This purpose is drawn from the universal law of the Church and applies to the episcopal conferences which are established all over the world for the same purpose."

The effort of the bishops to work together to assist the Catholic community in the United States as a body dates back to 1917, when the U.S. bishops formed the National Catholic War Council as a means for U.S. Catholics to contribute funds and material support to servicemen during World War I.

In 1919, in their first national gathering since 1884, they agreed to meet annually and to form the National Catholic Welfare Council to serve as their organized voice on the national scene. They also organized themselves in response to the request of Pope Benedict XV for bishops to work with him to promote peace and justice in the aftermath of the world war. The bishops established the first Administrative Committee of seven members to handle the council's business between plenary meetings, and headquarters were established in Washington, D.C., with a general secretary of staff appointed. The word "Council" was replaced by the word "Conference" in 1922.

In 1966, following the Second Vatican Council, the NCWC was reorganized into two parallel conferences. The National Conference of Catholic Bishops — sometimes referred to as the canonical arm — would deal with matters connected to the internal life of the Church, such as liturgy and priestly life and ministry. The U.S. Catholic Conference — in effect the civil arm — would represent the bishops as they related to the secular world, in areas such as social concerns, education, communications, and public affairs.

During the period from 1992 to 1996, a conference committee on mission and structure, headed by the late Cardinal Joseph Louis Bernardin of Chicago, led the bishops in extensive consultation on restructuring. A primary purpose of this undertaking was to provide more of the nation's approximately three hundred bishops with an opportunity to be directly involved in the work of the conference, which operated primarily through a committee structure.

In 1997 the bishops voted to combine NCCB-USCC into one conference, to be called the United States Conference of Catholic Bishops. They decided that in the future only bishops would be voting members of committees, but nonbishops could serve on some committees as consultants or advisers. A new committee on statutes and bylaws was formed to lead the rest of the reorganization process, headed by Archbishop Daniel E. Pilarczyk of Cincinnati. The new statutes and bylaws were subsequently approved by the Holy See.

The bishops merged their two national organizations on July 1, 2001.

The conference, one of many similar territorial conferences envisioned in the conciliar Decree on the Pastoral Office of Bishops in the Church (*Christus Dominus*) is "a council in which the bishops of a given nation or territory [in this case, the United States] jointly exercise their pastoral office to promote the greater good which the Church offers mankind, especially through the forms and methods of the apostolate fittingly adapted to the circumstances of the age."

Its decisions, "provided they have been approved legitimately and by the votes of at least two-thirds of the prelates who have a deliberative vote in the conference, and have been recognized by the Apostolic See, are to have juridically binding force only in those cases prescribed by the common law or determined by a special mandate of the Apostolic See, given either spontaneously or in response to a petition of the conference itself."

All bishops who serve the Church in the United States, its territories and possessions, have membership and voting rights in the USCCB. Retired bishops cannot be elected to conference offices nor can they vote on matters that by law are binding by two-thirds of the membership. Only diocesan bishops can vote on diocesan quotas, assessments, or special collections.

The conference operates through a number of bishops' committees with functions in specific areas of work and concern. Their basic assignments are to prepare materials on the basis of which the bishops, assembled as a conference, make decisions and put suitable action plans into effect. The officers, with several other bishops, hold positions on executive-level committees, including administrative, executive, budget and finance, personnel, and priorities and plans. They also, with other bishops, serve on the USCCB Administrative Committee.

United States Catholic Historical Society

An organization established in 1884 by the respected Catholic historian John Gilmary Shea for "the appreciation and preservation of American Catholic heritage." The society has focused throughout its history on promoting historical studies through scholarly work, seminars, and research projects, as well as through several notable publications, including the quarterly journal *Catholic Historical Review*.

United States Catholic Mission Association

A nonprofit religious, educational, and charitable organization that exists to promote global missions, the U.S. Catholic Missions Association is a voluntary association of individuals and organizations for whom the missionary presence of the universal Church is of central importance. Its primary emphasis is on cross-cultural evangelization and the promotion of international justice and peace. The association is also responsible for gathering and publishing annual statistical data on U.S. missionary personnel overseas.

United States Supreme Court. *See* Supreme Court of the United States, Catholic Justices of

Ursulines (O.S.U.)

A religious order of women founded by St. Angela Merici in 1535 at Brescia, Italy. It is remarkable for being the first such institute devoted exclusively to education. The Ursulines took their name from and placed themselves under the care of St. Ursula. The society of virgins began as a loose organization, since members lived with their families. They were engaged in numerous programs of charitable work, but their main endeavor was to promote Christian education. Initially approved by Pope Paul III in 1544, the Ursulines quickly spread from Italy to

France. In 1572, at the urging of St. Charles Borromeo, Pope Gregory XIII imposed a simple rule and the beginning of a community life. The Ursulines of Paris in 1612 were allowed by Pope Paul V to adopt solemn vows and to reside in strict cloister. Convents following this pattern increased, with new communities in France and Canada.

The Ursuline house in Québec was founded in 1634 by Marie Gruyard (Marie of the Incarnation), making the Ursulines the first congregation of women to be formally organized in North America. Although receiving a setback in their numbers during the French Revolution, the Ursulines prospered once more in the 1800s. In 1900 Pope Leo XIII proposed at a congress in Rome that all the Ursuline convents around the world should be united. Similar unions were made in Belgium in 1832, Canada in 1953, Germany in 1957, and Ireland in 1973.

The Ursulines established their first school in the United States in 1727, when ten nuns arrived in New Orleans from France. The following year, a novice in this group became the first Ursuline to make her profession in the United States. The Ursuline Academy that was founded in New Orleans is the oldest girls school and the oldest continuously operating Catholic school in the United States. Through this remarkable institution, the Ursulines made a vital contribution not only to Catholic education in the country but also to the progress of educating women. They were noted for their outreach to what were called free women of color, Native Americans, and Hispanic girls and women. They also opened a hospital and an orphanage.

Subsequent Ursuline communities were established across the United States by nuns from France and Germany, including Boston in 1820, Cleveland in 1850, and New York in 1855. They were subsequently very active in Catholic higher and secondary education and founded colleges and academies all over the country, including Ursuline College in Ohio in 1871, the College of New Rochelle in 1904, and Great Falls Junior College for Women in 1932, now the University of Great Falls.

Utah

Known as the Beehive State, Utah is located in the western United States. It is bordered on the north by Idaho and Wyoming, on the east by Colorado, on the south by Arizona, and on the west by Nevada. Utah has three major land areas: the Middle Rocky Mountains, the Colorado Plateau, and the Great Basin. It entered the Union in 1896. The original inhabitants of Utah were Native Americans, including the Paiute, Shoshone, Gosiute, and Ute.

The first European to explore the area was perhaps García López de Cárdenas, who was part of Francisco Vázquez de Coronado's expedition, although the first certain explorers were two Franciscan priests, Silvestre Velez de Escalante and

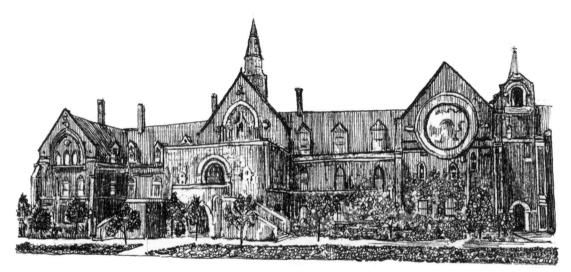

Ursuline Convent

Francisco Atanasio Domínguez. They were seeking an overland route from the New Mexico Franciscan missions to California and encountered Native Americans in the area that became Utah. They were followed by fur traders. Around 1824, the famous explorer and mountain man Jim Bridger reached the Great Salt Lake. The first settlement was started in 1840 by Miles Goodyear and other pioneers at Ogden.

Around this time, the brilliant and revered Jesuit missionary priest Pierre-Jean De Smet traveled across the entire region as part of his historic evangelization among the Native Americans. As he headed east in 1846, he encountered the advance parties of the Mormons, who were migrating west under Brigham Young to escape persecution. Father De Smet met with Young in Omaha, Nebraska, and was likely the key source of information for the Mormons. He advised them to explore the region of the Great Salt Lake as a haven. The Mormons reached Salt Lake Valley the next year and chose it as the site of their new community.

At the time of the arrival of the Mormons, Utah was still part of the territory of Mexico.

This changed, however, in 1848 with the Treaty of Guadalupe-Hidalgo after the Mexican-American War. The first attempts by the Mormons to enter the Union as the State of Deseret — from the Book of Mormon — were rejected owing to their acceptance of polygamy, and over the next years relations were poor between the Mormon community and the federal government. The situation climaxed in the Utah Mormon War of 1857–58, which ended with the arrival of a non-Mormon governor and the resignation of Young as head of both church and state. Polygamy was finally abolished in 1890, with further prohibitions issued over the next years. The U.S. Congress established Utah as a territory, and in 1869 the Transcontinental Railroad celebrated the linking of the east and west. Utah entered the Union on January 4, 1896, as the thirty-second state.

The Catholic history in Utah began with Fathers Velez and Atanasio Domínguez in the late eighteenth century. By the middle of the nineteenth century, ecclesiastical jurisdiction was directed from San Francisco, although there were few priests

available for service in Utah. With the permission of Brigham Young, in 1866 Father Edward Kelly celebrated a Mass in Assembly Hall in Salt Lake City.

The first Catholic church in Utah was built in 1871 by Father Patrick Walsh and was dedicated to St. Mary Magdalene. In 1873 Father (later Bishop) Lawrence Scanlan arrived in Utah as pastor and also as vicar forane for San Francisco. He played a vital role in starting churches, schools, an orphanage, and a hospital, and also invited Sisters of the Holy Cross into the area.

A vicariate apostolic for Utah was founded in 1887, and four years later, the Diocese of Salt Lake City was created with Scanlan named the first bishop. He was an active first bishop for the diocese and founded parishes and invited additional congregations of religious women to provide greater structure to the Catholic community. They were joined by religious men, including the Trappists.

The state developed economically through the steel industry and mining, although the state was hard hit by the Great Depression and had one of the highest unemployment rates in the entire country. Bishop John J. Mitty, then bishop of the Diocese of Salt Lake, started charitable programs and sought to assist those badly hit by the economic collapse. He was named in 1932 the coadjutor archbishop of San Francisco. His work was carried forward by Bishop James E. Kearney.

With the start of World War II, Utah once again enjoyed economic growth owing to its natural resources, which were needed for the war effort. As the industries regained their strength, Catholics seeking work arrived in greater numbers. The task fell to the fifth bishop of Salt Lake City, Duane G. Hunt, bishop from 1937 to 1960, to build the needed parishes and schools and to invite more religious orders into the diocese, including the Carmelites and the Sisters of Charity of the Incarnate Word.

In 1950 there were some 23,000 Catholics in the state. This increased to more than 51,000 by 1966. By 2000 there were 100,000 Catholics in Utah. Catholics remain a small minority in the largely Mormon state, and make up barely 6 percent of the total population. In 2011 there were around 265,000 Catholics, served by 76 priests and 48 parishes.

V

Vagnozzi, Egidio (February 2, 1906–December 26, 1986)

A papal diplomat and apostolic delegate to the United States from 1958 to 1967, Egidio Vagnozzi was born in Rome. He studied at the Lateran Pontifical Seminary in Rome and earned three doctorates, in philosophy, theology, and canon law. Ordained to the priesthood at an earlier-than-normal age (and hence with a dispensation) on December 22, 1928, by Cardinal Rafael Merry del Val, he was soon appointed to Vatican Secretariate of State and then to the staff of the apostolic delegate in Washington, D.C., as secretary from 1932 to 1935 and auditor from 1935 to 1942.

Named a counselor, he served on the staff of the apostolic nunciatures in Lisbon, Portugal, from 1942 to 1945 and in Paris from 1945 to 1947; during his period in Paris, then Archbishop Angelo Roncalli (later Pope John XXIII) was papal nuncio to France. In 1946 he was sent as an extraordinary papal envoy to the independence celebration in Ceylon, India, and then held the post of chargé d'affaires in the apostolic delegation to India from 1948 to 1949.

Cardinal Egidio Vagnozzi

On March 14, 1949, Vagnozzi was appointed titular archbishop of Myra and consecrated on May 22. He was named apostolic delegate to Manila from 1949 to 1951 and then the first papal nuncio to the Philippines from 1951 to 1958. On December 29, 1958, Pope Blessed John XXIII transferred Archbishop Vagnozzi to the United States, where he remained until June 1967. In May 1967 Pope Paul VI created him cardinal deacon with the titular church of San Giuseppe al Trionfale and brought him back to Rome. As cardinal, Vagnozzi served as a member of the Congregation for the Bishops and for Extraordinary Ecclesiastical Affairs and was named Prefect of Economic Affairs of the Vatican in January 1968. He held the office until his death.

Vaillant de Gueslis, François (July 20, 1646–September 24, 1718)

A revered Jesuit missionary, François Vaillant de Gueslis was born at Orleans, France. He entered the Society of Jesus in November 1665 and was sent to the Canadian missions in 1670. Ordained a priest at Québec in December 1675, he spent several years preparing for the rough demands of the wilderness and missions and was finally sent to preach among the Mohawks in 1679. He remained with them until 1684, and was the first missionary to labor among the Indians at Detroit.

His efforts took place at a time when war and conflict were commonplace in the colonies, but after peace was settled between the French and the Iroquois he evangelized among the tribes of the Seneca from 1702 to 1707.

Through his efforts, the English strategy of convincing the Iroquois to force out the Catholic French missionaries was aborted. Father Vaillant centered his subsequent energies on the area around Montréal and Québec. He held several key posts in the Jesuit community in Canada, including procurator of the missions, preacher, and the first superior of the residence founded in 1692. He returned to France in 1715, where he died.

Van Nuys, Eparchy. See Eastern Churches, Catholic

Varela, Félix (November 20, 1788–February 27, 1853)

A Cuban patriot, priest, and scholar, Father Félix Varela was also a promoter of Thomistic philosophy, the abolition of slavery in Cuba, and education. A native of Havana, Varela was ordained at the age of twenty-threee and became a professor at San Carlos and San Ambrosio Seminary in Havana. He was renowned as one of the foremost teachers on the island and an expert in theology, music, philosophy, and chemistry. A supporter of Cuban independence, he was sentenced to death by the Spanish government and fled the island. He reached the United States in 1823 and spent the rest of his life working for the Church in America.

In 1825 Father Varela founded in Philadelphia the newspaper *El Habanero*, the first Spanish Catholic magazine in the United States; he went on to establish *The Protestant's Abridger and Annotator* in 1830, and *Catholic Expositor and Literary Magazine* in 1841–43, the first pastoral magazine and the first literary magazine for Catholics in the United States. He served as vicar general of the Diocese of New York from 1829, at a time when immigration was first becoming an issue for American Catholicism, especially as the Irish had begun to arrive in larger numbers. To assist his work, he learned Gaelic.

Beloved during his lifetime, he was also honored posthumously, especially in Cuba and by Cuban-Americans. In 1912 his body was exhumed from Tolomato Cemetery in St. Augustine, Florida, and returned to Cuba, where he was laid with honor in the University of Havana's Aula Magna. In 1988 the United States Postal Service honored Father Varela with a 32-cent commemorative stamp. The Diocese of St. Augustine also dedicated the east courtyard of the St. Augustine Cathedral as a place for pilgrimage in his honor. His cause for canonization was opened in 1985 by the bishops of Cuba, and he received the title Servant of God. In 1998, during his visit to Cuba, Pope Blessed John Paul II, in the Aula Magna, said that Varela "is in his person the best synthesis we can find between Christian faith and Cuban culture."

Vatican Council, First

The twentieth ecumenical (or general) council in the history of the Church, the First Vatican Council was convened by Pope Blessed Pius IX. The council was held between December 8, 1869, and September 1, 1870. Owing to the seizure of Rome by the troops of King Victor Emmanuel II, the council was adjourned by Pope Pius indefinitely; it was never officially ended and never reconvened.

The council was best known for two achievements: the dogmatic constitutions *Dei Filius* and *Pastor Aeternus*, the latter giving definition to papal infallibility. Pope Blessed Pius IX recognized the desirability of holding a council as there had not been one since Trent in 1545–63, and the world had changed immeasurably in the intervening years. The Church was being confronted with the rise of liberalism, rationalism, and wide regard for the sciences, which many felt were dangers to the faith by their promotion of rationalist criticism of Catholic doctrine and Scripture, religious indifference, hostility to many Christian tenets, and the questioning of the place of the Church in the modern world. A council was also desired to strengthen the authority and prestige of the papacy in the wake of the demise of the Papal States in 1860 by the Italians under Victor Emmanuel and the virtual extirpation of the centuries-old temporal power of the Holy See.

The announcement of his intentions to summon a council was made by the Holy Father to the cardinals of the Curia on December 4, 1864, two days before the publication of the *Syllabus Errorum* (*Syllabus of Errors*). In March 1865 Blessed Pius IX appointed a preparatory commission. The formal announcement of a council was made on June 29, 1867, and exactly one year later the pope issued the bull *Aeterni Patris*, which convoked the council.

The opening at St. Peter's Basilica had about seven hundred prelates, assorted officials, and dignitaries; interestingly, this was the first council that did not send invitations to ambassadors and princes. The first of the council's assemblies (called general congregations) was convened on December 10, 1869. Later that month, deliberations commenced on the dogmatic constitution on the faith. After spirited discussions and revisions, it was approved by final vote on April 24, 1870. *Dei Filius* was a profound reaffirmation of the teachings of the Church. Its chapters were concerned with God as Creator, revelation, faith, and faith and reason — with attached canons to clarify important points and to condemn those who denied certain aspects of the faith (fideists, rationalists, naturalists, and others). It vindicated human reason as sufficient to know God without revelation, stressed the reasonableness of faith, and elucidated the presence of the two kinds of knowledge: faith and reason.

While the question of infallibility was not specifically on Blessed Pius IX's planned list of topics to be discussed, it was uppermost in the minds of many council fathers, owing to the aspirations of the Ultramontanists to have it advanced and the concern of liberal Catholics that it should not be defined. In the period prior to the council, the matter had been the source of often bitter debate. The question was formally raised in January 1870 with a series of petitions supported by some five hundred council fathers in favor of giving papal infallibility definition. The debate continued for several months, ending on July 4. Finally, on July 18, the fourth session gave solemn definition of the primacy and infallible authority of the Roman pontiff in the *Constitutio Dogmatica Prima de Ecclesia Christi* (First Dogmatic Constitution on the Church of Christ).

The majority of the council fathers departed the hot city of Rome for the summer, reassembling in late August. The last (eighty-ninth) general congregation was convened on September 1. One week later, Italian troops pushed across the papal frontier and moved against Rome, which fell on September 20. The papal lands had been left virtually defenseless when French troops protecting Rome departed the Eternal City with the start of the Franco-Prussian War. Blessed Pius IX suspended the council, and it did not reassemble. When Pope Blessed John XXIII considered calling his own council, it was suggested to him that he simply reconvene the First Vatican Council; he chose to start a new one.

Pope Blessed Pius IX summoned fifty-six American bishops to attend the council, and there were forty-six in attendance at the council's opening. The American bishops worked chiefly on the special commissions that crafted the conciliar documents, and a few spoke publicly. In the deliberations over *Dei Filius,* four Americans spoke out: Archbishop Peter R. Kenrick of St. Louis, Bishop Jean-Pierre Augustin Verot of Savannah, Bishop Richard V. Whelan of Wheeling, and Bishop Thaddeus Amat of Monterey-Los Angeles. Bishop Verot spoke on the issue of Church discipline. On the matter of papal infallibility, the American delegation of bishops was divided. Several had signed a petition asking that the issue not be raised, and some asked for permission to return to the United States once deliberations began. The remaining bishops voted variously *placet* (in favor), *placet iuxta modum* (in

favor but with reservations), or *non placet* (against) at the general congregation on July 13, 1870. Those bishops in the general congregation who had voted *non placet* were Archbishop Kenrick, Bishops Michael Domenec of Pittsburgh, Edward M. Fitzgerald of Little Rock, William George McCloskey of Louisville, Bernard J. McQuaid of Rochester, Ignatius Mrak of Sault Ste. Marie-Marquette, and Jean-Pierre Augustin Verot of Savannah. At the public vote on July 18, Bishop McCloskey voted *placet*; Bishop Fitzgerald voted *non placet*, but he made his profession of faith before Pope Blessed Pius IX in person after the session. The others were absent for the vote but made their professions of adherence to the doctrine in writing after the council. Bishop Stephen Vincent Ryan of Buffalo was absent from both the general congregation and the public session owing to poor health, but confirmed his acceptance in a letter to the pope.

Vatican Council, Second

The twenty-first ecumenical (or general) council, held in Rome between 1962 and 1965, was one of the most important councils in the history of the Church. The Second Vatican Council was only the second such assembly since the Council of Trent in 1545–63, after the First Vatican Council in 1869–70. Although a council had been considered by Pope Pius XII, it had not come to fruition beyond the recognition of many in the Church that a council might be desirable to address the challenges confronting the faith in the radically changed world following the global conflict of World War II. (*See also* Pius XII, Pope.)

Blessed John XXIII, Pope Pius's successor, was given singular credit for deciding to summon another ecumenical gathering. Pope John claimed the idea was an inspiration of the Holy Spirit. At first discouraged by members of the Curia, he persisted and, despite probably knowing that his health might not permit him to see its end, Blessed John XXIII gave the order for preparations for the undertaking to go ahead.

On May 16, 1959, Cardinal Domenico Tardini was appointed the head of the first preparatory commission, with the task of consulting with the prelates of the Church around the globe and the esteemed theologians of the Catholic universities.

On June 29, Pope Blessed John XXIII issued the encyclical *Ad Petri Cathedram,* in which he gave formal explanation of the purpose of the council. The next year, he wrote the *motu proprio Superno Dei Nutu* on June 5, 1960, by which he announced the appointment of the preparatory commission and other ancillary and subordinate commissions and secretariats. Blessed John himself headed the central commission and appointed curial cardinals to preside over the others; the one exception was the Secretariat on Communications Media, under Archbishop Martin J. O'Connor, rector of the North American College (1946–64), and later nuncio to Malta and head of the Pontifical Commission for Social Communication.

These commissions initiated their work in November 1960 and were finished in June 1962. The previous year, on Christmas Day, Pope Blessed John XXIII published the apostolic constitution *Humanae Salutis*, instructing the council to begin in 1962. By the *motu proprio Concilium* of February 2, 1962, he designated the opening of the proceedings as October 1962. After commending the assembly to the protection of St. Joseph, on July 1, 1962, he asked all Catholics to do penance in anticipation of the work of the council fathers through the encyclical *Paenitentiam Agere.*

Pope John had as his stated goals the renewal and modernization of the Church, to facilitate the accomplishment of its mission in the modern world, and to foster the unity of all Christians. He used the term *aggiornamento* (updating) to describe his program and hopes. The council was given its organization by the *motu proprio Appropinquante Concilio* on August 2, 1962. There were to be three types of meetings: commissions of twenty-four members, general congregations where first votes and discussions would be held, and public sessions, headed by the pope, at which final votes on the assorted documents would be taken. The commissions focused on theology, bishops and the government of dioceses, discipline of clergy and laity, religious, discipline of sacraments, sacred litrgy, studies and seminaries, Eastern churches, missions, and apostolate of the laity. The two secretariats focused on (1) press, radio, and television and (2) Christian unity.

The work of the council was carried out in four sessions: Session I from October 11 to December 8, 1962; Session II from September 29 to December 4, 1963; Session III from September 14 to November 21, 1964; and Session IV from September 14 to December 8, 1965. At the first congregation of December 13, 1962, in Session I, two cardinals, Joseph Frings of Cologne and Achille Liénart of Lille, requested that the council fathers should adjourn until December 16 so as to familiarize themselves with possible candidates for the commissions and be granted the right to choose their own commission members instead of the ones picked by the Curia. This move, approved by Pope Blessed John XXIII, significantly altered the atmosphere, proceedings, and direction of the commissions and the council itself.

After the close of the first session, the remaining deliberations would be presided over by a new pontiff. Increasingly ill, Blessed John had attended the last meeting of the session with difficulty. His health deteriorated during the early part of 1963, and he died on June 3.

In the resulting conclave, the cardinals chose Cardinal Giovanni Montini, archbishop of Milan, on June 21, 1963, Pope Paul VI. Cardinal Montini had been a clear favorite on entering the conclave and had been used extensively by John in the preparation for the council. Besides being considered the chosen successor of Blessed John, Cardinal Montini also clearly desired to continue the council in the Johannine tradition (although he later confessed that he would not have summoned a council on his own). His eulogy of Blessed Pope John XXIII, in which he declared that the council must continue on the path chosen by John, and his own statements of approval of the work of the council were said by many observers to have been critical to his election.

Work resumed on September 29, 1963, and the sessions went on for two years. The results were embodied in the sixteen documents promulgated by the council, two dogmatic and two pastoral constitutions (the heart of the reforms), nine decrees, and three declarations. Pope Paul solemnly closed the council on December 8, 1965.

Unlike at the First Vatican Council, American bishops were actively involved in the preparations and deliberations of the new council. At the Second Vatican Council, forty-three Americans were appointed to commissions and preparatory committees. In addition, more than sixty Americans were invited to work as *periti*, or theological experts.

American bishops and the *periti* all played a significant role throughout the sessions of the council. American bishops made some 341 oral and written interventions, helping to shape some of the key documents that were produced by the council. Cardinal Francis Spellman issued 131 of the 341 interventions, and he and two other Americans, Cardinals Albert G. Meyer of Chicago and Lawrence J. Shehan of Baltimore, served among the council presidents.

The participation of Americans was especially evident in several documents, including the decrees on Ecumenism, *Unitatis Redintegratio*, and the Declaration on the Relationship of the Church to Non-Christian Religions, *Nostra Aetate*. But the bishops were most active in the deliberations over religious liberty, which became the decree *Dignitatis Humanae* (Declaration on Religious Freedom), promulgated on December 7, 1965. Interestingly, American bishops had proposed the idea at the First Vatican Council, and they brought to the new council nearly two hundred years of practical experience and the collective wisdom of Archbishop John Carroll, Archbishop John Hughes, Cardinal James Gibbons, and countless other American Catholics who contributed to the ideals of religious freedom in the country.

The key figure in drafting *Dignitatis Humanae* was Father John Courtney Murray, a Jesuit priest and influential theologian best known for his studies on the Church's relationship to society and state and on religious pluralism. As his views were viewed with some skepticism by some in Rome (the issue was still a relatively new one in many circles in Europe, where traditionally there was claim toward a unity between church and state, as enunciated vigorously by popes in the nineteenth and twentieth centuries in the face of continental liberalism), Father Murray was not initially invited to the council. Cardinal Spellman, however, intervened and secured his appointment as a *peritus* and his vital role in creating the document.

For American Catholics, the council was a time of immense curiosity and genuine interest. From the start, it was examined and covered by the world's collective media, which brought frequently shallow reporting and a search for conflict and drama. There was, as a result, a constant telling of struggles between progressives and conservatives for the heart and soul of the council's deliberations. This was given additional reinforcement by some Catholic commentators, particularly the Redemptorist priest and professor of theology in Rome, Francis X. Murphy.

Murphy wrote a number of articles on the inner workings of the council under the pseudonym Xavier Rynne for the *New Yorker* magazine from the very start of the council. His musings caused an international storm of interest and helped prompt the American bishops to open a press office in Rome to try to deal with the press clamoring to confirm the stories appearing in the *New Yorker*. Rynne helped to nurture in the media the whole idea of the "progressives" fighting to overcome the "reactionaries" of the Curia, and intransigent conservatives unwilling to allow hope and new life to be breathed into the Church. This, of course, became one of the most enduring memes of the entire council and was carried forward into the modern age of the Church. Nevertheless, while the murder of President John F. Kennedy was a time of grief, the overall conciliar period was one of optimism and expectation.

As the council years progressed, Catholics were able to read newspaper and television accounts of the sessions and the documents that were promulgated by the council fathers. The deliberations of the First Vatican Council (1869–70) had been little followed by Americans as newspaper accounts were scarce and the bishops in attendance did not make publicity any kind of a priority. At the Second Vatican Council, bishops held regular press sessions and discussed the progress of the council for the international press.

American Catholics next were introduced to the liturgical reforms that were ushered in by the council's 1964 Constitution on the Sacred Liturgy, *Sacrosanctum Concilium*, and the subsequent papal decrees that enacted the specific changes. The Mass was now in English for Americans, with the priest facing the congregation. There were soon other changes, including lay lectors, extraordinary ministers of the Eucharist, and Communion in the hand. Catholics also saw changes to the celebration of penance and wider efforts at ecumenism. Restoration of the permanent diaconate in the Roman rite — making it possible for men to become deacons permanently, without going on to the priesthood — was promulgated by Pope Paul VI on June 18, 1967, and approved for the United States in 1968.

When the council was brought to an end in December 1965, the task then became implementing the host of reforms that were mandated as well as entering into the dialogue with the modern world that had been the hope of Pope Blessed John XXIII when he first called for a new ecumenical council.

The decade after the council's climax in 1965 brought many reforms and changes to virtually every aspect of Catholic life in the United States, from liturgy and sacraments, to active ecumenism and interfaith dialogue, to significantly wider degrees of lay participation and wholesale changes to religious life. The implementation of the changes and the reforms proved one of the great challenges in modern Catholic history.

Documents of the Second Vatican Council

The following are the sixteen documents promulgated by the council. They comprise two dogmatic constitutions, two pastoral constitutions, nine decrees, and three declarations.

Lumen Gentium (Dogmatic Constitution on the Church), November 21, 1964.

Dei Verbum (Dogmatic Constitution on Divine Revelation), November 18, 1965.

Sacrosanctum Concilium (Constitution on the Sacred Liturgy), December 4, 1963.

Gaudium et Spes (Pastoral Constitution on the Church in the Modern World), December 7, 1965.

Inter Mirifica (Decree on the Instruments of Social Communication), December 4, 1963.

Unitatis Redintegratio (Decree on Ecumenism), November 21, 1964.

Orientalium Ecclesiarum (Decree on Eastern Catholic Churches), November 21, 1964.

Christus Dominus (Decree on the Bishops' Pastoral Office in the Church), October 28, 1965.

Optatam Totius (Decree on Priestly Formation), October 28, 1965.

Perfectae Caritatis (Decree on the Appropriate Renewal of the Religious Life), October 28, 1965.

Apostolicam Actuositatem (Decree on the Apostolate of the Laity), November 18, 1965.

Presbyterorum Ordinis (Decree on the Ministry and Life of Priests), December 7, 1965.

Ad Gentes (Decree on the Church's Missionary Activity), December 7, 1965.

Gravissimum Educationis (Declaration on Christian Education), October 28, 1965.

Nostra Aetate (Declaration on the Relationship of the Church to Non-Christian Religions), October 28, 1965.

Dignitatis Humanae (Declaration on Religious Freedom), December 7, 1965.

Venice, Diocese of

Established on October 25, 1984, by Pope Blessed John Paul II, the Diocese of Venice serves counties in southwestern Florida. It is a suffragan of the Archdiocese of Miami. The city is surrounded by parks and ocean beaches. Venice was a community planned as a retirement enclave for the Brotherhood of Locomotive Engineers in 1924–25. The stock market crash of 1929, however, brought development to a halt as the Great Depression gripped the nation.

Venice survived as a resort area known for fishing. During World War II, Venice was involved in military defense and manufacturing. It prospered after the war, becoming in time the winter headquarters of the Ringling Brothers and Barnum & Bailey Circus.

The Catholic history of Venice opens centuries before, as the missions of Florida were vast and influential. On April 3, 1573, the Spanish explorer Juan Ponce de León landed on the shore of modern-day Florida and erected a cross. The revered Dominican Luis Cáncer de Barbastro and companions were slain in Florida in 1549. The oldest city in the United States, St. Augustine was founded in Florida on September 8, 1565. Missions were erected throughout the region as a result, with Franciscans operating even in the northeastern part of the state by 1573.

The British led a series of attacks on these missions, and there were instances in which Native Americans murdered the missionaries. There was a resident bishop in Florida by 1709, but the attacks by the British colony of Georgia decimated the missions and cost the lives of devoted priests and Indian converts. Florida was ceded by Spain to England in 1763. The area became the Diocese of Louisiana and the Two Floridas in 1793. The remaining sections of the state, still held by Spain, were sold to the United States in 1821, and the U.S. Congress established the Florida Territory.

The faithful were among the settlers of Florida, and the Catholic presence was visible when Florida entered the Union in 1845. The Diocese of St. Augustine was established in 1870 by Pope Blessed Pius IX. Miami and St. Petersburg became dioceses following the Second World War. Miami was raised to the rank of metropolitan provincial see in 1968.

The growth of the Catholic community in southwestern Florida was sufficient by the early 1980s that in 1984 ten counties were taken from the Archdiocese of Miami and the Dioceses of Orlando and St. Petersburg to form the Diocese of Venice. The first bishop of Venice was John J. Nevins, who had served as an auxiliary bishop of Miami since 1979. Bishop Nevins was appointed to Venice on July 17, 1984, and was installed at Epiphany Cathedral in Venice on October 25, 1984.

Bishop Nevins presided over the rapid growth of the Catholic population, which expanded from 115,000 to more than 200,000. To keep pace with the growth, Bishop Nevins established fifteen parishes, an elementary school, and two retreat centers, and promoted vocations to the priesthood. He also focused on ministries to migrant farmworkers, unwed mothers, and those suffering with HIV/AIDS. He retired on January 19, 2007.

The second bishop of Venice, Frank J. Dewane, was a priest of the Diocese of Green Bay and had served as an official of the Vatican's Permanent Observer Mission to the United Nations, then as a member of the staff of the Pontifical Council Cor Unum in Rome and as undersecretary of the Pontifical Council for Justice and Peace. On April 25, 2006, he was appointed coadjutor bishop of Venice and was consecrated a bishop on July 25, 2006. He acceded to the see on January 19, 2007. In 2011 there were more than 225,000 Catholics in the diocese served by 164 priests and 58 parishes.

Vermont

Called the Green Mountain State, Vermont is located in the northeastern part of the United States. It is bordered on the north by Canada, on the east by New Hampshire, on the south by Massachusetts, and on the west by New York. The three major land regions of the state are: the White Mountains in the east, the Green Mountains in the central area, and the Taconic Mountains in the west. The original inhabitants of Vermont were the Indian nations of the Algonquin, Iroquois, Mohawk, and Mohicans.

The French aided the Algonquins in forcing the Iroquois to withdraw from the area in the early eighteenth century. This had ramifications for the French later as the Iroquois became allies of the British in revenge. French trappers were welcomed by the Algonquin when they arrived in the area of modern-day Vermont. On July 1, 1609, Samuel de Champlain had explored the region and claimed it for France. Other French representatives followed Champlain's expedition, and in a short time, Jacobus de Warm tried to settle a Dutch group at Chimney Point, but the settlement was attacked by the local Indian populations.

No further settlements of whites were attempted until 1724, when groups arrived from Massachusetts and established Fort Dummer, near Brattleboro. In 1763 British military units from New York claimed the territory and demanded payment from the settlers. Ethan Allen, the Vermont patriot, formed the Green Mountain Boys and fought the British with Indian-style attacks. The Green Mountain Boys became a rallying symbol for the American Revolution.

In 1777 Vermont established itself as a republic, but in 1791 it entered the Union as the first state that had not been part of the original thirteen colonies. Rapid development of the vast Lake Champlain as a link to the St. Lawrence and Hudson Rivers provided economic impetus.

Samuel de Champlain opened the Catholic presence in Vermont. In 1615 Recollect Franciscans were in the area, followed by Jesuit missionaries. A fort and shrine to St. Anne were established at Isle Le Monte in Lake Champlain in 1666, and outposts of the faith were visited by Bishop Blessed François de Montmorency Laval, vicar apostolic of New France in Québec.

The missions were closed with the coming of British control of Canada in 1760 in the wake of the French and Indian War. Severe anti-Catholic laws were put in to place, remaining until Catholics proved themselves during the Revolutionary War. The penal laws against Catholics were repealed in 1793.

Vermont was placed under the jurisdiction of the Diocese of Boston (now the Archdiocese of Boston) in 1808, and in 1830 the "Apostle of Vermont," Father Jeremiah O'Callaghan, became the first resident priest. He built a church that was burned to the ground by local Protestants. Father O'Callaghan immediately rebuilt the church and added a school. The Cathedral of the Immaculate Conception dates to this era, as the Catholic population of Burlington continued to increase and stood firm in the faith. In 1840 a large Irish immigration added to the Catholic strength.

In 1853 the Diocese of Burlington was created by Pope Blessed Pius IX. The revered Bishop Louis de Goesbriand led the Catholics of the state and established the ministries and offices needed for the growing Catholic population. Bishop de Goesbriand served for thirty-nine years in Burlington, providing a secure foundation for the coming years. He reportedly paid for the establishment of churches and charitable programs with his own personal fortune, estimated at approximately $1 million.

When the Civil War began in 1861, Vermont supported the Union. The people of the state were firmly opposed to slavery, and after the war the industrial base of the state grew significantly. Bishop John Stephen Michaud of Burlington opened the Fanny Allen Hospital, named after the daughter of Ethan Allen, who had become a Catholic and an Ursuline nun.

Vermont continued to prosper and entered the twentieth century with continued growth, including new Catholic colleges and other schools. The third bishop of Burlington, Joseph J. Rice, led the Catholics of the state through the turmoil of World War I and the Great Depression, but he also contended with Protestant bigotry and violence and the attacks of the Ku Klux Klan. Bishop Rice died in 1938.

Continued growth and development followed under Bishop Edward F. Ryan, bishop of Burling-ton from 1945 to 1956, and Bishop Robert F. Joyce, who served as shepherd of Burlington from 1957 to 1972. As of 2011, the Catholic population of Vermont was 118,000, served by 137 priests, 120 men and women religious, and 77 parishes.

Verot, Jean-Pierre Augustin, S.S. (May 23, 1805–June 10, 1876)

The third bishop of Savannah, the first bishop of St. Augustine, and a vocal participant at the First Vatican Council in 1869–70, Jean-Pierre Augustin Verot was born at Le Puy, France. He studied at Saint-Sulpice in Paris and was ordained on September 20, 1828. He subsequently joined the Society of St. Sulpice at Paris and in 1830 was sent to Baltimore to teach at St. Mary's College. He taught science, philosophy, and theology until 1853, when he was appointed pastor at Ellicott's Mills, and undertook pastoral work elsewhere in Maryland.

On April 25, 1858, Verot was consecrated titular bishop of Danabe and vicar apostolic of Florida by Archbishop Francis P. Kenrick in the cathedral of Baltimore. He took part in the Ninth Provincial Council of Baltimore in 1858 and then set out for his vicariate. He found there only three priests and two churches. He thus made an appeal to his friends in France and to his fellow bishops for financial assistance. The next year, Sisters of Mercy arrived from Hartford, Connecticut, joined by a number of priests and Christian Brothers, as well as other religious from Europe. Churches in St. Augustine, Jacksonville, and Key West were repaired, and new ones were opened at Tampa, Fernandina, Palatka, Mandarin, and Tallahassee; at the same time, schools were begun with the help of the women religious.

In July 1861 Bishop Verot was transferred to Savannah while retaining vicarial powers over Florida. His appointment came at the start of the Civil War, and Verot devoted his energies to the care of the diocese during a bloody and difficult time. The fighting brought immense suffering and destruction to the churches and people in both the Savannah diocese and the Florida vicariate. To bring needed relief, Verot traveled to the North to make a plea for more priests and wrote to Europe for personnel and money. Although a Southern sympathizer, he condemned the slave trade in

1861 in a famous sermon, "A Tract for the Times: Slavery and Abolitionism." He also sent priests and went himself to minister among the captured Union soldiers in the infamous Andersonville prison in Georgia. After the war, on August 1, 1866, he issued a pastoral letter that celebrated the eradication of slavery and invited African-Americans to benefit from Catholic education. He also spoke out against all forms of prejudice against African-Americans and asked the Sisters of St. Joseph from Le Puy, France, to settle in the diocese and provide care for African-Americans in Florida and Georgia.

In 1869 Verot journeyed to Rome and took part in the deliberations of the First Vatican Council. He was an outspoken participant at the council, calling for recognition of those of African descent, the vindication of Galileo, and ecumenical dialogue. He was opposed to the definition of papal infallibility and chose with fifty-four other bishops to be absent from the final public vote in order to avoid casting a *non placet*. Once the decision of the council was reached, he signed the conciliar document on papal infallibility. (*See* Vatican Council, First).

In March 1870 the Florida vicariate was constituted a diocese, and Verot became first bishop of St. Augustine. He surrendered his administration of the Savannah diocese, and as bishop in St. Augustine he remained determined to labor on behalf of African-Americans and the Seminole Indians.

Verrazano, Giovanni da (c. 1484–November 1527)

An explorer and navigator who searched for a westward route to Cathay, Giovanni da Verrazano reached the coast of North America. Born in Val di Greve, near Florence, Italy, he entered into the service of King Francis I of France as a sailor and earned considerable notoriety as a corsair, attacking the ships of Spain and Portugal. His greatest achievement during this period came in 1522, when he seized the treasure ship of Emperor Charles V that was being sent back to Spain by Hernando Cortés loaded with Mexican gold and treasure.

In January 1524 Verrazano set out at the behest of Francis I upon a voyage of discovery to the New World. His account of the trip was published in 1556 by Giovanni Ramusio, including a description of the expedition along the coast of North America. The account marked the first record of exploration of the North Atlantic in the years immediately after the famed voyage of Christopher Columbus. In 1529 Verrazano's brother, Hieronimo, drew a map of the North Atlantic coast. It is preserved in the Vatican.

Verrazano's later expeditions are uncertain, but it is believed that he set out for the Rio de la Plata and was killed in a skirmish with the native inhabitants on an island in the Caribbean. There was also a report that he was captured in 1527 by Spanish naval ships while sailing off the coast of Cadiz and was executed at the command of Emperor Charles V. Nevertheless, on the basis of his voyage for Francis I, France was provided with a useful claim to large arts of North America. Building on Verrazano's expedition, Jacques Cartier was able to make his own voyages between 1534 and 1542, which laid the foundation for French colonial possessions in the New World.

Vertin, John (July 17, 1844–February 26, 1899)

The third bishop of the Diocese of Marquette, from 1879 to 1899, John Vertin was born at Dobliče, in Carniolia, Austria. He received an early education in Austria and then migrated to the United States with his family in 1863, at the age of nineteen. After the family settled in Michigan, Vertin was presented to Bishop Irenaeus Frederick Baraga, the remarkable missionary and first bishop of Marquette. Bishop Baraga accepted Vertin as a seminarian and sent him to St. Francis in Wisconsin, where he completed his formation for the priesthood. Ordained on August 31, 1866, he spent the next years in various pastoral assignments.

On September 14, 1879, Vertin was consecrated the third bishop of Marquette, in succession to Bishop Ignatius Mrak. Bishop Vertin devoted his chief energies to the pastoral needs of the rapidly growing diocese. Using his own family's funds, he helped secure the construction of the second Cathedral of St. Peter at Marquette. To improve the spiritual condition of the diocese, he summoned the first diocesan synod in 1899, with the aim of implementing the decrees of the Third Plenary Council of Baltimore.

Vespucci, Amerigo (March 9, 1451–February 22, 1512)

The name of the explorer who first designated the American continent as the "New World," Amerigo Vespucci, was adopted by the German cartographer Martin Waldseemüller in a 1507 map to designate the region of "South America." A native of Florence, Italy, he was the third son of a Florentine notary. He received his first education in philosophy under his uncle, Giorgio Antonio, an instructor of the nobility of Florence. He then progressed to the study of literature and Latin, physics, geometry, astronomy, and cosmography. The family fortunes, however, declined suddenly upon the death of his father, and Vespucci was forced to enter into the service of the Medici family as a steward. After earning the confidence of his employers, he was named to the Florentine embassy in Paris from 1478 to 1480 and then served as a trusted agent of the Medicis in Spain.

In the wake of the successful voyages of Christopher Columbus, Vespucci sought and received permission from Ferdinand, King of Castile, to set out on an expedition to find the western passage to the Indies. Vespucci set sail with three ships on May 10, 1497, from Cadiz. He reached South America, perhaps Brazil, in early April, and sailed along the coast to the Gulf of St. Lawrence. He then sailed back to Spain. Vespucci took part in several more expeditions in 1499, 1501, 1503, and 1504.

Vespucci sailed both for Spain and Portugal, and he enjoyed a high reputation at both courts. In 1505 he was granted Spanish citizenship; in 1508 he was named by the Spanish crown *piloto mayor de España*, a title he was honored to hold until his death. Although an active voyager and explorer, he never earned the same notoriety as his far more famous contemporaries, Columbus and John Cabot. Vespucci used the term "New World" in a letter written to describe one of his voyages. He believed that the territory he was exploring was actually Asia. The use of his name by Martin Waldseemüller became attached both to South America and North America, even though Vespucci had only a peripheral role in the exploration of both continents.

Victoria in Texas, Diocese of

Established on May 29, 1982, by Pope John Paul II, the Diocese of Victoria in Texas serves counties in southern Texas. The diocese is a suffragan of the Archdiocese of Galveston-Houston. Located on the Guadalupe River, Victoria was founded in 1824 by Martin de Leon as Nuestra Señora de Guadalupe de Jesus Victoria. The area was Catholic, and other churches in the area were also established early. The people of Victoria, as it became known, took an active part in the revolution that led to Texas independence. The city was incorporated as part of the Texas Republic in 1859. Victoria in the late nineteenth century and early twentieth century was a center for cattle and served as a hub for the trail drivers moving north with their herds. In 1940 the city became part of the developing oil and gas industries on the Texas Gulf Coast.

The Catholic history of Texas was started in the sixteenth century with the Spanish explorers who arrived early in the century, including Alonso Alvarez de Pineda. Alvar Nuñez Cabeza de Vaca was shipwrecked off the Galveston coast in 1528 during his famous but calamitous search for the Seven Cities of Gold. He spent six years in the region that became Texas. In the next decades, other Spanish explorers arrived, including Hernando de Soto.

By 1682 Franciscans were operating missions in modern-day El Paso. Three years later, René-Robert Chevalier, Sieur de La Salle, was claiming the lands for France. La Salle built Fort Louis on Matagorda Bay, but it was abandoned several years later. By 1690 various missions were established by Father Damian Massanet and his Franciscan companions, including Mission San Antonio de Valera, known today as the Alamo. The city of San Antonio served as the administrative seat by 1700. Remarkable work was undertaken in the next years by Franciscan missionaries, most notably Venerable Antonio Margil de Jesús. He served in Texas and Louisiana and pioneered in mission labors among the Tejas Indians.

Mexico secured its independence from Spain in 1821, and Texas became part of the Mexican Republic. In the next decades, a wave of American immigrants arrived in Texas and eventually sparked a revolt that climaxed with the Battle of San Jacinto in 1836, by which Texas won its independence from Mexico and was established as a republic. Texas was admitted into the Union in 1845.

In 1839 a prefecture apostolic was established at

Galveston, followed by a vicariate apostolic in 1841. Six years later, the Diocese of Galveston was established, although there were only thirteen priests for the entire state. This state of affairs changed as the century progressed with the arrival of more immigrants and also priests, including the Oblates of Mary Immaculate. After the Civil War, the state suffered from violence, rampant lawlessness, and a state government that imposed a severe program of Reconstruction. Texas rejoined the Union in 1870, and a period of swift population growth followed. By the end of the decade, there were more than one million inhabitants, and the growth of the Catholic population led to the decision to create new dioceses.

In 1874 Pope Blessed Pius IX created the Diocese of San Antonio and the Vicariate Apostolic of Brownsville, which became the Diocese of Corpus Christi in 1912. The Diocese of Dallas was founded in 1890. Meantime, the Church in Victoria continued to develop with the start of several parishes, including Our Lady of Lourdes Church in Victoria and St. Michael's Church in Cuero, dating to 1875, and St. Agnes Church in Edna, which was established in 1880.

Early in the twentieth century, oil was discovered in the eastern parts of the state, starting the foremost of the industries for Texas. The population increased in the next decades, reaching three million, and the Diocese of San Antonio was promoted to the rank of an archdiocese in 1926; that same year, the Diocese of Amarillo was established by Pope Pius XI. In the aftermath of World War II, the Diocese of Austin was founded in 1947, followed by the Dioceses of San Angelo in 1961, Brownsville in 1965, Beaumont in 1966, and Fort Worth in 1969. In 1959 Galveston was renamed the Diocese of Galveston-Houston.

By the start of the 1980s, the Catholic population in Texas warranted the creation of other new dioceses, and one of them was Victoria in 1982. The diocese was created with territory from the Archdiocese of San Antonio and the Dioceses of Galveston-Houston and Corpus Christi. Some territory was added in 1989 from the Diocese of Austin. Initially a suffragan of San Antonio, Victoria was named a suffragan of the newly designated Archdiocese of Galveston-Houston in 2004.

The first bishop of Victoria in Texas was Charles V. Grahmann, who had been an auxiliary bishop of San Antonio for a year. He was installed in Victoria on May 29, 1982, and set to work establishing the needed diocesan offices and ministries. Bishop Grahmann was appointed coadjutor bishop of the Diocese of Dallas on December 18, 1989.

The second bishop of Victoria, David E. Fellhauer, was a priest of the Diocese of Dallas-Fort Worth. Appointed on April 7, 1990, he was consecrated a bishop on May 28, 1990. As shepherd of the diocese, Bishop Fellhauer concerned himself with the needs of the Catholic population, which makes up nearly half of the total population. He also faced the need to implement the norms for the protection of youth in the wake of the sex abuse crisis. In 2011 there were 102,860 Catholics in the diocese, served by 67 priests and 50 parishes.

Vieira, Antonio (February 6, 1608–July 18, 1697)

A Portuguese missionary, diplomat, and theologian, Antonio Vieira was born at Lisbon, Portugal. He moved as a child to Bahia, Brazil, with his family, where he studied under the Jesuits. Under their influence, he entered the Society of Jesus in 1623, pronounced his first vows in 1625, and was ordained in 1635. At the age of eighteen he was already serving as a teacher of rhetoric and soon after wrote a number of notable works, including commentaries on the Canticle of Canticles, Seneca, and Ovid. In 1641 he returned to Portugal and so impressed King John IV with his eloquence that the king named him preacher of the royal chapel in 1644, a member of the Royal Council, and a valuable diplomat to various courts in Europe. In his position as trusted royal adviser, Father Vieira worked to create a national bank and the Brazilian Trade Company and represented the crown in Paris, the Hague, London, and Rome.

In 1652 Vieira returned to Maranhâo, Brazil, and wasted no time in denouncing the slave trade. To advance the effort against slavery, he went back to Lisbon in 1654 and then returned to Brazil to minister among the native peoples of Maranhâo and along the Amazon. Over the six years of his ministry, he translated the catechism into tribal languages, traveled along the Amazon, and continued speaking out against slaveholders. His position earned the great enmity of slave owners, and the death of King John provided them with a means to attack the feared Jesuit. The local government exiled Father Vieira to Lisbon, and the new king, Alphonso VI, permitted his persecution on various charges by the Inquisition. He was forbidden to preach and remained a prisoner from 1665 to 1667.

Released under King Pedro II, Father Vieira settled in Rome from 1669 to 1675, where he was given a great welcome by Pope Clement X and the entire Roman Curia. In Rome, he added to his already great reputation with his oratory and homilies. He returned to Portugal armed with a papal brief signed in April 1675 that gave him complete immunity from the Portuguese Inquisition. Vieira, however, preferred to return to Brazil. He set sail in 1681 but found only hardship and heartache in his final years, owing to the continued and obdurate opposition of the slave owners and local government officials. He continued to write while in Bahia and produced his foremost work, *Clavis Prophetarum,* on the fulfillment of Christ's kingdom on earth. He died mourned by the poor and the slaves he loved and served. History judged him one of the greatest figures of the seventeenth century in Brazil.

Vietnam War

A conflict fought by the United States in Southeast Asia between 1959 and 1975, the Vietnam War not only caused deep political and social divisions in the United States but within the Church in the country as well.

Catholic leadership had taken an initially cautious approach to the war in Southeast Asia, generally supporting the expansion of American military involvement and taking their lead from Cardinal Francis Spellman, who remained a strong advocate of the war right up to his death in 1967, as he saw it in the stark terms of resisting the spread of communism. Related to the support by most Catholics in the early years was the fact that the South Vietnamese government was headed by the devout Catholic Ngo Dinh Diem, who was assassinated in 1963.

In 1966 the bishops issued a statement, "Peace in Vietnam: A Statement by the Catholic Bishops." The bishops, meanwhile, spoke about the war with an affirmation that it fulfilled the requirements of the Church's teachings on just war, but they also moderated their support by acknowledging the rights of conscientious objectors. They declared, "While we do not claim to be able to resolve these issues authoritatively, in the light of the facts as they are known to us, it is reasonable to argue that our presence in Vietnam is justified." They added, "On the basis of our knowledge and understanding of the current situation, we are also bound always to make sure that our government does, in fact, pursue every possibility which offers even the slightest hope of a peaceful settlement."

Pope Paul VI took a public position of neutrality on the war in 1967 and spoke several times in favor of a negotiated settlement. As the war dragged on and more and more Americans were turned away from supporting the effort, the bishops issued a much more critical statement, "Resolution on Southeast Asia." The bishops stated, "Whatever good we hope to achieve through continued involvement in this war is now outweighed by the destruction of human life and of the moral values which it entails."

Much as with the civil rights movement, Catholic priests, nuns, and laypeople took part in protests against the war. This was seen by some Catholics as a reflection on Catholic social doctrine, especially as enunciated by Pope Blessed John XXIII in his 1963 encyclical *Mater et Magistra.* One of the most surprising critics of the war was then Bishop (later Archbishop) Fulton J. Sheen in 1967, while he was bishop of Rochester. As the conflict dragged on, many Catholics grew as frustrated as the general American public with the war, and elements in American Catholicism were polarized.

Some Catholics, including priests and nuns, grew seriously radicalized in their opposition to the war and went beyond even civil disobedience. For example, in 1968 the priests Daniel and Philip Berrigan along with the so-called Catonsville Nine broke into the offices of a draft board and burned the files. Such behavior, while glamorized by the antiwar media, pointed to wider trends in some quarters of American Catholicism — namely, the rejection of legitimate authority and dissent from the teachings of the Church in the period after the Second Vatican Council. Nevertheless, the image of priests and nuns engaging in violence to end a war brought immense anguish to many Catholics and epitomized a period of great turmoil and dissent in the Church and in wider American culture.

Many Catholics continued to support the war effort to the very end, seeing it in the wider terms of patriotism and fighting against the threat of communism. Their position was seemingly vindicated by the takeover of South Vietnam and the imposition of a communist regime in Vietnam, with the persecution of the Church that continues today and the deaths of millions in neighboring Cambodia.

Viganò, Carlo Maria (January 16, 1941–)

The fourteenth papal representative to the United States since 1893 and the fifth to serve as apostolic nuncio since the establishment of diplomatic relations in 1984, Archbishop Carlo Maria Viganò was named papal ambassador to the United States on October 19, 2011.

A native of Varese, Italy, Viganò was ordained on March 24, 1968, and earned a doctorate in both canon and civil law. He entered the diplomatic service of the Holy See in 1973 and worked at the papal diplomatic mission in Iraq and Great Britain, and from 1978 to 1989 he was an official of the Secretariat of State in Rome. He was named Special Envoy and Permanent Observer of the Holy See to the Council of Europe in Strasbourg in 1989. In 1992 he was appointed titular archbishop of Ulpiana and apostolic nuncio to Nigeria and was consecrated a bishop on April 26, 1992. During his time as nuncio to Nigeria, Pope Blessed John Paul II visited the country. Viganò returned to the Secretariat of State in 1998 and served there until 2009, when he was appointed secretary general of the governatorate of Vatican City State. He ended his duty there in anticipation of his new assignment as nuncio to the United States as successor to the late Archbishop Pietro Sambi.

Vincentians (C.M.)

The Congregation of the Missions (*Congregatio Missionis*), a pontifical society of priests and brothers founded in Paris in 1625 by St. Vincent de Paul, the Vincentians are also known as the Lazarites or Lazarists. The Vincentians were founded by St. Vincent to assist his labors and to serve as a society of priests with the express task of missionary labor and the training of clergy. They were particularly charged with preaching among the people in the countryside. In 1633, with the remarkable St. Louise de Marillac, St. Vincent also established the Sisters (or Daughters) of Charity, the first congregation of women caring for the sick and the poor outside the confines of the convent.

The Vincentians spread quickly during St. Vincent's lifetime, eventually opening seminaries throughout France, and in Italy, Spain, and Poland. They arrived in the United States in 1818, and today number some 3,500 worldwide. The Daughters of Charity of St. Vincent de Paul (D.C.) also moved throughout the world. St. Elizabeth Ann Seton opened a house at Emmitsburg, Maryland, in 1809. There are several other congregations, including the Sisters of Charity of St. Vincent de Paul (S.V.Z.; founded in 1845 in Croatia), the Sisters of Charity of St. Vincent de Paul (S.C.H.; founded in 1856 in Halifax, Nova Scotia), and the Sisters of Charity of St. Vincent de Paul of New York (S.C.; founded in 1817). The Society of St. Vincent de Paul, a lay organization devoted to the care of the poor, was begun in 1833 by Blessed Antoine-Frédéric Ozanam in Paris.

Today, the society is involved in a wide variety of programs, including food centers, shelters, workshops, rehabilitation centers, and distribution programs for food and money.

The first Vincentians arrived in the United States in 1816 at the invitation of Bishop Louis Dubourg of New Orleans. They were under the direction of the revered Father Felix de Andreis. Their first permanent settlement was in Perryville, Missouri, and in 1835 the foundation became an independent province. The Vincentians went on to play an important role in the development of the Church in several states, including Illinois, Mississippi, Arkansas, and Texas, and directed three universities: DePaul University in Chicago, Niagara University in Niagara, and St. John's University in New York City. The Eastern Province was started in 1867, followed by the Midwest Province in 1888; in 1975, the Vincentians began the New England, Western, and Southern Provinces.

Virginia

Called the Old Dominion, the state of Virginia is located in the southeastern part of the United

States. One of the original thirteen colonies and original states, it is bounded on the north by West Virginia and Maryland, on the east by Maryland and the Atlantic Ocean, on the south by North Carolina and Tennessee, and on the west by Kentucky and West Virginia. Virginia has four main geographical areas: the Tidewater on the eastern coast, the Piedmont in the center, the Blue Ridge, and the Valley. Virginia is also dominated by several rivers, including the Potomac, Rappahannock, York, James, Roanoke, and Shenandoah. The original inhabitants of the modern-day Virginia region were the Algonquins, Iroquois, Conostoga, Nottaway, Powhatten, Sioux, Susquehanna, and Yuchi.

The Catholic history of Virginia opened in 1526, when Lucas Vazquez de Ayllón founded the settlement of San Miguel within the borders of the present-day state. Dominican Father Antonio de Montesinos celebrated Mass in a log chapel. The settlement soon suffered from attacks by hostile Indians, a savage winter, and problems internally, and only 150 survivors of the original 600 reached New Spain.

A second expedition reached the Rappahannock River in 1570. Among its members were several Jesuits. This effort ended tragically with the deaths of most of the expedition by treacherous Indian guides. Between 1584 and 1587, Sir Walter Raleigh made several expeditions in the name of England, but no permanent settlements were achieved. However, the name "Virginia" was given to the large stretch of land between the colonial possessions of the French in the north and those of Spain in the south. In 1607 Captain John Smith set sail from England, made his way up a river he dubbed the James, and started the first permanent English settlement in America at Jamestown for the Virginia Company of London. The settlers faced their struggles, including the so-called Starving Time, and further settlements were founded on Chesapeake Bay and the James, York, and Potomac Rivers. In 1613 John Rolfe married Pocahontas, the daughter of the great chieftain Powhatan, an event that proved helpful for peace between the Europeans and the Native Americans.

In 1619 a General Assembly was called to provide long-term stability, and in 1624 the London Company was dissolved as Virginia became a royal colony. William and Mary College, the oldest college in the United States after Harvard, was founded in 1693.

In contrast to Puritan New England, Virginia was largely established with Anglican sensibilities. In 1611 religious practice was codified by the short-lived Dale's Law that made any inhabitants who failed to worship every day subject to fines, flogging, and even death. Catholics were not welcome, this distaste exemplified by the resistance to a small colony of Catholics from Maryland in 1629–30; the law of 1641 against them brought a penalty of 1,000 pounds of tobacco for any Catholic attempting to hold office.

The following year, priests were ordered out of the colony, and in 1661 the colonial governor commanded the arrest of any priests who might be found in Virginia. In 1699 Catholics were stripped of voting rights and given a fine of 500 pounds of tobacco should they attempt to vote.

As late as 1753, priests were forbidden from testifying as competent witnesses in court cases. Virginia's anti-Catholicism was extended southward with the start of South Carolina in 1670, North Carolina in 1690, and Georgia in 1733. Nevertheless, Catholics had settled in the area as early as 1647, establishing the start of St. Mary's Church. These Catholics were barely tolerated, but kept the faith and remained cautious in the public observation of their faith.

Catholics in Virginia shared in the growing frustration of the American colonists with the governance of the colonies, even as prominent non-Catholic Virginians such as Thomas Paine, Richard Henry Lee, and Thomas Jefferson were key figures in the drive toward American independence. Recognizing the need for Catholics in the coming revolution, in 1776 Virginia declared religious freedom; in 1786, further guarantees were given.

With the American victory at Yorktown in 1781, the American Revolution was brought to an end. On November 6, 1789, the Diocese of Baltimore was established by Pope Pius VI, and John Carroll was named the first bishop. His diocese extended across the entire United States and included Virginia. In 1791 Father Jean Dubois arrived in Richmond with a letter of introduction from the Marquis de Lafayette and said Mass in the state capitol.

In 1796 Jesuits founded a parish in Alexandria, and the following year Father Francis Neale built a church. This was followed by a church in Norfolk, while in Richmond Father Xavier Michel was active in expanding the Church. He said Mass in private homes until 1815, when he was able to lease a church. The growth of the Catholic community by 1820 warranted the creation of a diocese for Virginia. The Diocese of Richmond was established on July 11, 1820, with Patrick Kelly named the first bishop. The diocese extended across the whole of Virginia, including what became West Virginia. Bishop Kelly resigned in 1822, and the administration of the diocese fell to the archbishops of Baltimore until 1840, when Richard V. Whelan was named bishop of Richmond. In the meantime, new churches were being built in Richmond and elsewhere in Virginia.

Virginia seceded from the Union in 1861, although Virginians were divided on the question of slavery. In the Civil War that followed, Richmond served as the capital of the Confederacy, and the state was the site of numerous bloody and terrible battles. The war came to an end on April 9, 1865, with Robert E. Lee's surrender to Ulysses S. Grant at Appomattox, Virginia. Much of the state had been left in ruins, and the Reconstruction period brought additional hardships. Virginia was readmitted into the Union in 1870, and crucial direction for the Catholic community in the state was provided by Bishop James Gibbons, who served in Richmond from 1872 to 1877, when he was named coadjutor archbishop of Baltimore. Gibbons managed to raise money, rebuild churches, and start schools. In the decades that followed the war, Catholics continued to increase across the state, including in the Norfolk area, where the U.S. Navy established a major presence.

In the early twentieth century, Catholics continued to arrive to find work in Virginia's gradually changing economy, with the traditional agricultural base slowly superseded by industry. This was especially the case during World War II, when Virginia's industries provided important war materials and also ships for the struggle with Germany and Japan.

In the period after the war, Catholics in the state participated in the economic boom and also in the civil rights movement of the 1960s, focusing especially on the end of various forms of discrimination and legal segregation. The Catholic population grew steadily during this period, increasing from 80,000 in 1950 to more than 217,000 in 1965.

By 1974 the Holy See determined that the Catholic Church in Virginia needed to be reorganized, and Pope Paul VI created the Dioceses of Arlington (out of territory from the Diocese of Richmond and the Archdiocese of Washington) and Wheeling-Charleston, in West Virginia (from territory taken from Richmond). As of 2011, there were some 690,000 Catholics in the state, served by 400 priests, more than 300 men and women religious, and 214 parishes. There are also five colleges or universities, and 45 elementary and high schools.

Visitation Nuns (V.H.M.)

Also called the Visitandines or the Salesian Sisters, Visitation Nuns are a contemplative order founded by St. Francis de Sales and St. Jane Frances de Chantal at Annecy in the duchy of Savoy in 1610. The purpose of the order was to offer the religious life for those women who, for reasons including physical or mental weakness, were unable to endure the severe austerity demanded by contemporary religious orders. St. Francis placed as his objective the attainment of God through interior modification and the performing of every act in accordance with the divine will. Initially, the Visitandines were intended to be a congregation with simple vows, and only novices were to reside in a cloister. After their profession, the nuns were permitted to leave the convent and go out among the sick, thereby gaining their name as visitors of the ill and performers of mercy. This effort was begun on June 6, 1610, but in 1615 the nuns encountered opposition from Archbishop Denis-Simon de Marquemont of Lyons, who disagreed with their work and refused to permit the nuns into the diocese unless they adopted more common practices for religious life. After initially resisting, St. Francis acquiesced and in 1616 compiled the *Constitutions pour les religieuses de la Visitation de Sainte-Marie*.

On April 23, 1618, Pope Paul V formally constituted the *Ordo Visitationis*, which received official approval in 1626 from Pope Urban VIII. The constitutions were a version of the Rule of St. Augustine. St. Francis insisted that the severe demands of the cloister not be placed upon the members but that private mortifications to foster the interior life be followed, especially chastity, poverty, and obedience. Of these, the most difficult was said to be the common life, for the nuns were said to be permitted to have absolutely no property and even their crosses and holy pictures were to be changed every year so as to discourage any sense of ownership. By the 1700s, the order had spread throughout Europe.

The first American house was established at Georgetown in Washington, D.C., in 1799. Two federations of Visitation Nuns were founded in the United States. The first is under major pontifical enclosure and the second under minor pontifical enclosure.

Vives y Tuto, Joseph Calasanto (February 15, 1854–September 7, 1913)

A Capuchin Franciscan and cardinal, Joseph Calasanto Vives y Tuto was born in San Andres de Llevaneras, near Barcelona, Spain, the son of a carpenter. Educated by the Scalopian (or Piarist) Fathers, he became a ward of the priests after both his parents died. In 1868 a Capuchin priest asked for volunteers from among the young men of the school to serve in Central America. Joseph volunteered and, along with sixteen other boys, arrived at Antigua, Guatemala, in June 1869. A month later, he was admitted to the Capuchin order and took his vows in 1870. His studies for the priesthood were soon interrupted by the revolution in Guatemala that resulted in the expulsion of the Capuchins from the country. The friars settled in California at the invitation of the Jesuits, and Joseph continued his studies at Santa Clara College. There, on July 14, 1872, he and his fellow seminarians made their solemn vows.

In September 1872, at the behest of Archbishop Joseph Sadoc Alemany of San Francisco, the Capuchins in California moved to Wisconsin, where they became affiliated with the community of Capuchins in Milwaukee. Although a number of Capuchins chose to return to Europe, Joseph was among those who decided to remain in Milwaukee. Unfortunately, the winters proved too severe for the friars, and five months later Joseph and his fellow Capuchins went back to Europe.

Joseph joined the Capuchins in Toulouse, France, and in 1875 was sent to the missions in Ecuador. Once again, his ministry was cut short, this time by poor health. Returning to France, he was ordained at last on May 26, 1877.

Owing to the severe anticlerical situation in France during the period, Father Joseph entered into exile in 1880 and became a member of the Capuchins in Spain. His labors there as rector of the Seraphic College in Igualadia, Spain, from 1880 to 1887, proved so remarkable that he was ordered to Rome in 1887 and given the post of secretary to the procurator general of the Capuchins. Named a consultor to the Holy Office in 1887 and definitor general of the Capuchin order in 1896, he was elevated to the rank of cardinal by Pope Leo XIII on June 19, 1899.

Cardinal Vives y Tuto earned considerable notoriety for his contributions to the Plenary Council of Latin America, held in Rome in 1899. He served as a member of the Biblical Commission in 1907 and prefect of the Congregation of Religious in 1908. He also was a leading opponent of modernism and was confessor to Pope St. Pius X.

Volpe, John A. *See* Cabinets, Catholics in Presidential

W

Wachter, Bernardine (August 25, 1846–June 3, 1901)

Benedictine nun and educator, Bernardine Wachter was born Josepha Wachter in Isny, Germany. She entered the Benedictine order in Switzerland in 1865 and took her vows in 1867. After spending the next nine years teaching in a convent school, she volunteered to take part in the missionary endeavor being launched in Missouri. Sister Bernardine then held a variety of teaching posts in Missouri and the Dakota Territory. She played a key role in establishing a Benedictine community in Portland, Oregon, in 1882, and in founding the St. Scholastica Academy. In 1887 Sister Bernardine was elected prioress of the community and subsequently supervised the construction of the new home for the sisters at Mount Angel. For her labors, she was honored as the foundress of the Queen of Angels Monastery, in Mount Angel, Oregon.

Wadhams, Edgar P. (May 17, 1817–December 5, 1891)

The first bishop of Ogdensburg, from 1872 to 1891, Edgar P. Wadhams was born in Essex County, New York. He grew up a Presbyterian and then became an Episcopalian while studying at Middlebury College in Vermont. In 1838 he entered the General Theological Seminary in New York and was ordained as a deacon. Over the next years, however, he became interested in the Oxford Movement and the writings of Cardinal John Henry Newman. In 1846 he entered the Church and St. Mary's Seminary in Baltimore, Maryland, and received ordination for the Diocese of Albany in 1850, by Bishop (later Cardinal) John McCloskey.

Father Wadhams served as rector of the cathedral and vicar general of Albany, and was named in 1872 the first bishop of the newly established Diocese of Ogdensburg. He was consecrated by Archbishop McCloskey on May 5, 1872. As bishop, Wadhams was noted for his energy in expanding the number of parishes and priests and in inviting various religious communities into the diocese. He also opened an orphanage, a hospital, and a

home for the elderly, as well as schools and various churches and chapels. By the time of his death the priest population had increased from 42 to 81, women religious from 23 to 129, and Catholic schools from 7 to 20. Bishop Wadhams also held three diocesan synods and attended the New York Provincial Council in 1883 and the Plenary Council of Baltimore in 1884.

Wagner, Robert (June 8, 1877–May 4, 1953)

United States Senator for New York from 1926 to 1949, Robert Wagner was born in Nastatten, Germany, and migrated with his family to the United States when he was nine, settling in New York City among the other German immigrants who had settled in the city. His father worked as the custodian of the building in which the family lived, and his mother made money doing laundry. Young Robert earned money as well by selling newspapers on the streets and in Central Park. Through his family's efforts and his own work, he was able to attend City College of New York and eventually graduated from the New York Law School.

In 1898 Wagner went to work for the Democratic bosses at Tammany Hall, even though he was a Methodist and not a Catholic. In 1904 Wagner was elected to the New York State Assembly, and in 1911 to the State Senate. While in this office, he was a leading voice in promoting reform of the conditions faced by workers and was a member of the commission that investigated the infamous Triangle Shirtwaist Factory fire that led to the deaths of 147 women.

Partly on the basis of his notoriety as a reformer and his friendship with Alfred E. Smith, a fellow state senator and future presidential candidate, Wagner was elected to the United States Senate in 1926. His election placed him in a position to support aggressively President Franklin Delano Roosevelt's New Deal program throughout the 1930s, and his influence was crucial in the passage of the Wagner Act in 1935 that created the National Labor Relations Board. He left the Senate in 1949 owing to declining health. Wagner married Margaret McTague, a Catholic, in 1908. He entered the Church in 1946.

Walker, Frank Comerford. *See* Cabinets, Catholic in Presidential

Walker, James ("Jimmy") (May 1, 1881– November 14, 1946)

The flamboyant New York City mayor from 1926 to 1932, James "Jimmy" Walker was born in Greenwich Village in New York City, the son of Ellen Roon and William Walker, a local Irish politician and city alderman. Walker thus grew up in the midst of New York's rough-and-tumble political environment and learned at an early age the power and value of oratory and political theater. He was also interested in entertainment and worked as a comic and actor on the stage.

In 1910 he followed in his father's footsteps in politics and was elected to the New York State Assembly. In 1914 he entered the state senate. He became immensely popular in his home district for his opposition to the Volstead Act and the implementation of Prohibition, as well as his support of calling for professional baseball to be played on Sunday. In 1926 he became mayor of New York with the help of the Tammany Hall machine and with the wide support of New Yorkers. He was a political celebrity and made a famous European tour in 1927.

In 1928 his administration was rocked by a series of scandals, climaxing in 1932 with his resignation owing to the pressure caused by the Seabury Commission. He also suffered deteriorated relations with the Church in New York because of his open relationship with the English-born actress Betty Compton. Divorced in 1933, Walker moved to England in 1935. He was reconciled to the Church before his death.

Walsh, James A. (February 24, 1867–April 14, 1936)

Co-founder, with Thomas F. Price, of Maryknoll, the first foreign mission society established in the United States and the first sponsor of a U.S. foreign mission seminary, Father James A. Walsh served as superior of Maryknoll from 1911 to 1936. Born in Cambridge, Massachusetts, he was the son of

Irish immigrant parents. After studying at Boston College and for a year at Harvard University, he entered St. John's Seminary in Brighton, Massachusetts, and was ordained for the Archdiocese of Boston on May 20, 1892. He devoted the next ten years as a parish priest at St. Mary's in Roxbury, Massachusetts. In 1903 he was named director of the archdiocese's office for the Society for the Propagation of the Faith.

In 1904 Walsh attended a conference of priests to promote the foreign missions. In a speech, he said that there should be a greater sense of zeal in the United States for the missions. In 1906 Walsh and three other priests founded the Catholic Foreign Mission Society in Boston to publish a magazine focusing on the vast efforts at evangelization being undertaken by the Church. To assist efforts at establishing a foreign mission seminary for the United States, the magazine *The Field Afar* was launched the following year, and Father Walsh was assisted by Mary Rogers, who went on to found the Maryknoll Sisters.

In 1911 Father Thomas F. Price, a priest working to expand a group of missionaries in Raleigh, North Carolina, joined Walsh in starting the Catholic Foreign Mission Society of America. With the support of Cardinal James Gibbons and the apostolic delegate Archbishop (later Cardinal) Diomede Falconio, Walsh and Price received formal approval by the U.S. hierarchy on April 27, 1911, and the two priests traveled immediately to Rome to secure permission from the Congregation for the Propagation of the Faith. On June 30, 1911, Pope Pius X gave his blessing to the missionary enterprise.

Once back in the United States, Father Walsh became superior of the new society at the behest of Father Price, an arrangement that permitted Walsh to oversee the daily operations of the society while Price devoted his energies to promoting vocations and fundraising. A crucial development was begun in 1912 when the society acquired property at the top of a hill near Ossining, New York, to serve as its official headquarters. The property was henceforth named Maryknoll. The remainder of Walsh's life was devoted to expanding the society, including trips to Asia to encourage the work of the members and to assist the Maryknoll Sisters under Mother Mary Joseph Rogers.

In 1933 Pope Pius XI honored the enormous success of Father Walsh by naming him titular bishop of Siene. He was ordained a bishop in Rome by Cardinal Fumasoni-Biondi, prefect of the Congregation for the Propagation of the Faith, and adopted as his episcopal motto that used by the mission, "Seek first the kingdom of God." Father Walsh died at Maryknoll.

Walsh, James E. (April 30, 1891–July 29, 1981)

Bishop, religious superior, and famed missionary who spent twelve years in a communist Chinese prison, James E. Walsh was born in Cumberland, Maryland, to Irish parents. He studied at Mount St. Mary's College in Emmitsburg, Maryland, and worked for the U.S. Rail steel mill in Cumberland. In 1912 he entered the Maryknoll Seminary near Ossining, New York, and received ordination as a priest on December 7, 1915. In 1917 he was sent to southern China to serve in the Maryknoll missions. In 1919 he was named Maryknoll superior of the Jiangmen (Kongmoon) mission following the death of its former superior, Father Thomas F. Price, the co-founder of Maryknoll. In 1927 Walsh was appointed vicar apostolic of Jiangmen, receiving ordination at the shrine of St. Francis Xavier on Shangchuan Island on May 22, 1927. Walsh wasted little time in developing the local Catholic community, founding the Little Flower minor seminary in 1926 and the Congregation of Sisters of the Immaculate Heart of Mary in 1927.

In 1936, after the death of Bishop James A. Walsh, the founder of Maryknoll, Bishop James E. Walsh succeeded him as superior of all Maryknoll. His ten years as head of Maryknoll encompassed the Second World War. In 1940–41 Walsh assisted the U.S. State Department in its negotiations with Japan. These efforts proved unsuccessful, but Walsh demonstrated his place as a respected figure in the Church in Asia. Bishop Walsh also expanded Maryknoll's efforts in Latin America in 1942 and Africa in 1946.

At the end of his ten years as head of Maryknoll, Bishop Walsh returned to China in 1947 to assume direction of the Catholic Central Bureau in Shanghai. This development coincided with the triumph of the communist Chinese under Mao Zedong and the institution of a severe anti-Catholic program.

In 1951 the communists closed the bureau. Bishop Walsh and his staff were then subjected to intense pressure by the government to leave. He refused to leave China, however, writing an article, "Why the Missionaries Remain," that was published in Hong Kong in 1951.

In 1958 Walsh was arrested on charges of being a spy for the United States and committing currency violations. The bishop suffered daily humiliations and interrogations for over a year, and in 1960 he was sentenced to twenty years' imprisonment. Sent to Ward Road Prison in Shanghai, he was seen only by his brother, William, in 1960. In 1970 he was released unexpectedly and deported to Hong Kong. Bishop Walsh returned to the United States and devoted his final years to assisting the Society at Maryknoll. He never lost his love for China and the Chinese people.

Among his numerous writings was the article "Shine On Farmer Boy," published in *Maryknoll* (July–August 1942), and the books *Mission Manual of the Vicariate of Kongmoon* (1937), *The Church's World Wide Mission* (1948), *Blueprint of the Missionary Vocation* (1953), and *Zeal for Your House* (1976).

Walsh, James Joseph (April 12, 1865–February 28, 1942)

Author, historian, and physician, James Joseph Walsh was born in Archbald, Pennsylvania. He studied at St. John's College (later Fordham University) and then spent a period in the Jesuit novitiate before departing for medical studies at the University of Pennsylvania. He then spent time in Europe and, upon his return home, established a practice in New York City. Over the next years, he became a noted neurologist and taught at the New York Polyclinic School of Medicine, the College of New Rochelle, and Mount St. Joseph's College in Philadelphia. In 1920 he was named head of the Fordham School of Sociology; he was also a fellow of the American Academy for the Advancement of Science.

As a devout Catholic, Walsh was concerned deeply with the anti-Catholic sentiment of the times and so devoted most of his spare time to writing Catholic apologetics. Of particular importance to him was the charge often made that Catholics in general and the popes in particular were enemies of progress. In all, he wrote forty-five books and more than five hundred articles.

Walsh, Robert (1784–February 7, 1859)

Journalist, diplomat, and literary founder Robert Walsh was born in Baltimore and studied at Georgetown College. In 1801 he became one of the first students at Georgetown to study law. After graduation, he traveled across Europe and wrote articles for journals and newspapers in Paris and London on the institutions and laws of the United States. Returning to the United States in 1808, he was admitted to the bar, and in 1811 founded the *American Review of History and Politics*, the first American quarterly review.

With the founding of the *American Review*, Walsh turned his chief energies to literary enterprises. In 1819 he wrote "Appeal from the Judgment of Great Britain Respecting the United States," which won great praise from the Pennsylvania legislature for its contribution to political discourse. In 1821 he founded with William Frye the *National Gazette and Literary Register*, devoted to politics, arts, letters, and science. The paper was highly respected under his editorship, so much so that when Walsh stepped down as editor in 1836, he was soon sent to Paris as consul general, where he served from 1837 to 1844. He remained in Paris, where he died. His son, Robert Moylan Walsh, followed in his father's footsteps and held several diplomatic posts in London, Naples, Italy, and Florence, Italy.

Walsh, William Thomas (September 11, 1891–February 22, 1949)

Born in Waterbury, Connecticut, William Thomas Walsh studied at Yale and then worked as a journalist for various newspapers, including the *Hartford Times* and the *Philadelphia Public Ledger*. He later became a teacher at Hartford High School and the Roxbury School of Cheshire, Connecticut, from 1917 to 1933. In 1933 he was named a professor of English at Manhattanville College of the Sacred Heart in New York City; he remained in this post until 1947. In 1930 he had begun writing extensively on various Catholic subjects, including *Isabella of Spain* (1930), *Our Lady of Fátima* (1947),

and *St. Peter the Apostle* (1948). In 1944 he received the Laetare Medal from the University of Notre Dame for his labors on behalf of the Church.

Walworth, Clarence (May 30, 1820–September 19, 1900)

Priest, convert, missionary, and member of the Redemptorists, Clarence Walworth was born in Plattsburgh, New York, the son of Mary K. Walworth and Reuben H. Walworth, a prominent Presbyterian, judge, congressman, and the last chancellor of New York state. Clarence studied at Union College in Schenectady, New York; after graduation in 1838 he studied law and was admitted to the bar in 1841. He practiced law for only a year in Rochester, New York, and then entered the General Theological Seminary in New York City. While a seminarian, he became interested in the Oxford Movement that was then a major topic of debate in Protestant intellectual circles. On the basis of his own studies, he entered the Church in 1845 and joined the Congregation of the Most Holy Redeemer, the Redemptorists. He was ordained in Wittem, Holland, on August 27, 1848.

Returning to the United States in 1851, Walworth worked with Isaac Thomas Hecker, serving briefly as a Paulist. He departed the community in 1858 over a dispute with Father Hecker over the plans for the Paulists to have community life without formal vows. Incardinated into the Albany, diocese, he served in Troy, New York, until 1861. After another brief period with the Paulists, in 1865 he left once more because of a severe bout of malaria and exhaustion. Named pastor of St. Mary's Church in Albany, he became known for his work on behalf of workers and the Native Americans of St. Regis Indian reservation. A well-known speaker and writer, he was justifiably famed for composing the verse paraphrase of the *Te Deum,* "Holy God, We Praise Thy Name."

Wanderer, The

A national Catholic weekly journal founded in 1867 and known for its unequivocal commitment to the teachings of the Church, *The Wanderer* began in St. Paul, Minnesota, under the name of *Der Wanderer*. It was published in German and was intended to assist the needs of German immigrants in Minnesota and the Dakotas at a time when there was pervasive anti-Catholic propaganda being spread in German by such organizations as the Masons.

From this beginning, *Der Wanderer* found a wide readership among German Catholic immigrants and soon gained a reputation for its commitment to authentic Church doctrine. It thus opposed the propagation of Americanism, supported Pope Leo XIII's 1899 apostolic letter, *Testem Benevolentiae*, and advocated to its readers Pope Leo's encyclical *Rerum Novarum,* which enunciated the Church's social teachings.

In 1931 an English-language edition was launched under the title of *The Wanderer*. Both journals continued to be published until 1957, when *Der Wanderer* ended its ninety-year run. Over the next years, *The Wanderer* became a leading voice in warning against the dangers of Adolf Hitler and the rise of Nazism in Germany. In September 1933 the newspaper was banned from Germany. While supporting the war, the editors also expressed concerns about the alliance between the Allies and the Soviet Union. Such were *The Wanderer*'s candid warnings about the threat of Soviet expansion that in 1945 the official Soviet newspaper, *Pravda*, demanded that *The Wanderer* be shut down for its anti-Soviet position.

In the years after the Second Vatican Council, *The Wanderer*'s editor, Walter Matt, resigned over disagreements about the direction of the council and its implementation.

Matt's brother, Alphonse J. Matt Sr., assumed the editorship and stressed the stated purposes of the council to its many readers. In the face of the turbulent post-conciliar period, *The Wanderer* adopted a steady position against the widespread dissent and ecclesial division in the U.S. Church. The journal was thus one of the most outspoken supporters of Pope Paul VI's encyclical *Humanae Vitae,* which reaffirmed the Church's teachings on birth control.

War of Independence

For much of the eighteenth century, resentment grew in the colonies toward the royal administration of England's possessions in America. Colonists struggled against the centralizing tendencies of the crown. This trend gathered speed in the second half of the century as a result of England's victory over France in the French and Indian War, which left the English in control, politically and economically, of American lands east of the Mississippi and north all the way to Hudson Bay. These acquisitions brought an extensive reorganization of the colonial system. entailing a new wave of mercantile regulations, stricter economic controls, and higher taxes. The spirit of rugged independence and freedoms that American colonists cultivated finally collided with the centralized controls of the crown's governors and agents. The tension was exacerbated by the Intolerable Acts and the push toward rebellion by many colonists. The Boston Massacre, the Boston Tea Party, and other incendiary events galvanized opposition to England. What started as a call for reform of colonial government and oversight ended in the War of Independence that raged from 1775 to 1781. American independence was recognized by England in the Treaty of Paris in 1783.

As noted, Catholics were a miniscule part of the population at the start of the American Revolution. There were around 25,000 Catholics out of a total population of 2.5 million. There were no priests in New England, none in New York, and none south of the Potomac River. Every colony included laws that restricted the religious, civil, and property rights of Catholics, and waves of anti-Catholicism were felt during the French and Indian War when Catholics were accused of being traitors to England, secretly working for Catholic France, and hoping to force popery upon the Protestant majority.

Given this background of intolerance, many American Catholics were understandably reluctant to believe that the growing independence movement would promise any substantive improvement in their situation. Some of the most ardent anti-Catholics in the colonies were also prominent leaders in organizing resistance to England, and Catholics feared that these men would continue anti-Catholic laws in an independent America. This concern seemed to have been confirmed in 1774 in the colonial reaction to the Québec Act. In a move to stabilize English rule over Canada, the crown granted Canadian Catholics the right to practice their own religion. For anti-Catholics in the colonies, the Québec Act was the establishment of popery in a neighboring colony. Frenzied protests and propaganda followed. Samuel Adams, a key figure in the revolutionary movement, declared that popery was more dangerous than the Stamp Act.

There were, nevertheless, important signs of hope and promise. In 1775 General George Washington, the head of the recently established Continental Army, forbade his troops from burning the pope in effigy and celebrating the traditional anti-Catholic festival of Guy Fawkes Day. The next year, the Continental Congress sent a delegation to Canada in the hope of winning its support in the Revolution. The delegation included Benjamin Franklin and Samuel Chase, but it also boasted prominent Catholics Charles Carroll of Carrollton and his distant cousin, Father John Carroll. The envoys failed in their mission to Québec as the Catholics there were unwilling to risk their newly won toleration, but the public service rendered by the Carrolls showed Catholics in the colonies that they could speak out and take part in shaping the future of the continent. Encouragement was given over the next year as Virginia, Maryland, and Pennsylvania passed laws of religious toleration.

Once the actual fighting began, Catholics were forced to choose sides. Some Catholics chose to stay loyal to England, but the majority eventually threw themselves into the American cause. There were several reasons. First, they followed the examples of their most prominent leaders, who were deeply committed to the Revolution. There was also the unprecedented achievement of the Declaration of Independence in 1776 with its remarkable principles of political freedom and the rights and dignity of man. Finally, Catholics saw the American cause receiving aid from the two Catholic powers of France and Spain, and they witnessed as well the warm reception that French troops and officials received in America.

There are no reliable numbers as to how many Catholics fought in the war, but it is assumed that there were not many Catholics in the Continental Army; still, 38 to 50 percent of the soldiers in Washington's army had Irish surnames. Catholics fought and died, serving with distinction in regiments that had no Catholic chaplains. About 650 Catholics served in British units as loyalists in Philadelphia, and several small regiments of loyal-ist Catholics were formed. After the war, most of them sailed back to England.

Maryland's Catholics generally fought in revolutionary militias, while those in Pennsylvania joined the Continental Navy. A large number of Marylanders from St. Mary's County joined the Old Line Company. Three of the most important leaders were Charles Carroll of Carrollton, Thomas FitzSimons, and Commodore John Barry.

Charles Carroll was a signer of the Declaration of Independence and, in fact, the last surviving signer of that historic document. A member of the wealthy and respected Carroll family of Maryland, he was educated at Bohemia Manor and then set sail for Europe with his cousin, John. They attended St. Omer College at Reims, and then Charles went to the Collège Louis-le-Grand in Paris. He completed his law degree in London and returned to America in 1768.

In 1773 Carroll accepted a public debate with a Protestant named Daniel Dulaney in the *Maryland Gazette*. The debate concerned taxes and a state-supported church, and Charles, who called himself "First Citizen," became renowned for his intelligence, wit, and good humor in the face of bigotry. Welcomed as a representative from Maryland to the Continental Congress, he helped to ratify the Declaration of Independence in 1776 and quieted Protestant irritation in that body by reminding them that his wealth, estimated at about $2 million, was being put at risk in order to see America free. Charles went on to serve as a congressman and as a U.S. senator in 1789. He retired in 1800, and his last public act was the laying of the cornerstone of the Baltimore and Ohio Railroad on July 4, 1828.

Thomas FitzSimons, a native of Philadelphia and a prominent merchant, became an early supporter of the movement that led to the American Revolution. He served as a deputy at the conference in Carpenters' Hall, Philadelphia, a gathering that led to the Continental Congress of 1774. His election as one of the provincial deputies in July 1774 marked the first time that a Catholic was chosen for public office in Pennsylvania. Once the Revolution began, he signed up with the militia and fought in the Trenton campaign in New Jersey and later assisted the Continental Army by raising funds and organizing supplies through his fellow merchants.

After the war, FitzSimons was elected in November 1782 as a member of the Congress of the old Confederacy and served as a member of the Continental Convention that gathered in Philadelphia in May 1787. He was, with Daniel Carroll of Maryland, one of two Catholics to hold the distinction of being a framer of the U.S. Constitution. He was then elected a member of the first House of Representatives.

Commodore John Barry is honored as the "Father of the American Navy." Born in Ireland, he landed in Philadelphia at the age of fifteen and was captain of his own ship, the *Black Prince*, at the age of twenty-one. When the war began, Barry volunteered, and throughout the war he commanded several ships, including the *Lexington*, the first ship commissioned by Congress. On February 22, 1797, Barry received the rank of commodore from George Washington, the first person to hold that position in the United States Navy.

The success of the American Revolution caught the imagination of Catholics outside the colonies as well, and the cause was aided by foreign Catholics who readily served in America. Among them were Count Casimir Pulaski and Thaddeus Kosciusko of Poland; Baron von Steuben of Prussia; and the Marquis de Lafayette, the Comte de Rochambeau, and the the Comte de Grasse of France. To the west, the French priest Pierre Gibault was working as a missionary along the Mississippi at the time of the Revolution. Despite the urging of the bishop of Québec that all priests under his jurisdiction should avoid any involvement in the conflict, Father Gibault spoke out to the rugged settlers of Kaskaskia, Vincennes, and elsewhere on behalf of the American General George Rogers Clark. This support was crucial and helped lay the groundwork for the expansion of the United States into the West. In California, meanwhile, Father Junípero Serra and the Franciscans offered prayers for the success of the American colonists on the other side of the continent.

By the end of the war, Catholics had earned the respect of Protestants in the Continental Army, the colonial militia, and the American Navy for their bravery and loyalty to the American cause. Acknowledgment of Catholic aid in the war and the founding of the Republic was made by General Washington. In 1789 prominent Catholic leaders and clergy sent him a letter congratulating him on his election as the first president. The four lay signers were FitzSimons, Charles and Daniel Carroll, and Dominic Lynch of New York. In reply, Washington wrote on March 12, 1790, "I presume your fellow citizens of all denominations will not forget the patriotic part which you took in the accomplishment of our Revolution and the establishment of our government or the important assistance which they received from a nation [France] in which the Roman Catholic faith is professed."

In the midst of the war in 1779, John Carroll observed that Catholics were holding offices in the Continental Congress, assemblies, and civil and military posts. In colonies where Catholics had been viewed with animosity and intolerance, grudging acknowledgment was made of their rightful place in the new order. In New York, for example, religious toleration was enacted in 1784 in the wake of the war and the new spirit of religious liberty. For Catholics, the task was now to embrace the changes in North America. The mentality of being a small oppressed minority gradually gave way to a sense of belonging that extended to the institutions of government, and social and intellectual life. They were no longer Catholics in the English colonies; they were Americans. What that meant was to be sorted out over the next decades as the Church in the United States became organized under the leadership of John Carroll.

Ward, James Harmon (1806–June 27, 1861)

The first Union naval officer to die in the Civil War, James Harmon Ward was born in Hartford, Connecticut, and studied at the Vermont Military Academy and at Trinity College in Hartford. In 1823 he was appointed a midshipman in the navy; in 1831, he was promoted to the rank of lieutenant. He subsequently served with distinction in Africa and earned considerable notoriety for his lectures on gunnery in Philadelphia in 1842. At that time, he promoted the establishment of a school for naval instruction. The resulting institution became the United States Naval Academy, and Ward served as one of its first instructors, from 1845 to 1847. He earned further reknown for his lectures, "Elementary Instruction on Naval Ordinance and Gunnery," and his book *Steam for the Million*. In 1853 he was promoted to the rank of commander. In 1858, he published the *Manual of Naval Tactics*.

At the start of the Civil War, Ward was called to Washington, D.C., to assist the Navy Department. He took command of the Potomac flotilla and was killed during an operation against Confederate forces on Matthias Point in Virginia. A convert to Catholicism, he was given a funeral in St. Patrick's Church in Hartford, which became the occasion of a large demonstration in favor of the war.

Ward, Maisie (January 4, 1889–January 28, 1975) Publisher, street preacher, and activist Maisie Ward was the wife of Francis Sheed, with whom she co-founded the publishing firm Sheed & Ward. The granddaughter of William George Ward and the daughter of Wilfred Ward, both noted English intellectuals, Maisie was born on the Isle of Wight. Her father converted to Catholicism in the 1840s, and Maisie grew up among some of the leading Catholic thinkers of the nineteenth century. During World War I, she worked as a nursing assistant. In her own right, she became an important leader in the English Catholic revival. In 1919 she became a charter member of the Catholic Evidence Guild, lecturing in the streets to defend Catholic teaching.

While in the Guild, Maisie met Frank Sheed, an Australian-born lawyer who joined the Guild in 1922. They were wed in 1926 and the next year founded Sheed & Ward. The publisher became an important element in advancing the Catholic revival in England. In 1933 a branch of the firm opened in New York City. Maisie Ward was the author of twenty-seven books as well as essays and biographies. She also supported numerous social reform organizations and programs, including the Catholic Worker and Friendship House.

Warde, Mary Frances Xavier (1810–September 17, 1884) Foundress of the Sisters of Mercy in the United States, Mary Frances Xavier Warde was born in Mountrath, Queen's County, Ireland, and lost her mother when she was still an infant. Largely raised by a greataunt, she met Mother Catherine McAuley and joined her newly founded Congregation of the Sisters of Mercy, the first of the congregation's

postulants. She took the name Sister Frances Xavier and assisted the community's labors on behalf of the poor and sick, working in the house for homeless children. In 1837 she was sent to Carlow, Ireland, to establish the first house of the congregation outside of Dublin. This house was followed in 1839 by a convent in Naas and in 1840 by one in Wexford.

In 1843 Bishop Michael O'Connor of Pittsburgh issued an invitation to the Carlow community to send six sisters to the Pennsylvania city. The group that arrived under Mother Warde's direction formed the first Sisters of Mercy in the United States. The sisters suffered severely from typhus and tuberculosis but still took over the cathedral Sunday school, several parochial schools and academies, a training center for young women, and the first hospital in Pittsburgh. Over the next years, Mother Warde opened convents in Chicago in 1846 and in Loretto, Pennsylvania, in 1848. In 1850 she accepted the invitation of Bishop Bernard O'Reilly of Hartford to open a convent in Providence, Rhode Island.

In the face of vicious anti-Catholic threats from the Know-Nothings, who had recently burned down the convent of the Ursulines near Boston, Mother Warde stood firm and then pushed ahead with houses in Hartford and New Haven, Connecticut, in 1852.

In 1858 Mother Warde and a group of sisters set out for Manchester, New Hampshire, at the invitation of Bishop David W. Bacon of Portland. There she established night schools for the children of factory workers. Three years later, she opened a convent at Philadelphia. Further Mercy convents were begun in Nebraska, Maine, California, New Jersey, and Vermont. Through Mother Warde's remarkable and ceaseless labors, the Sisters of Mercy in the United States numbered over two thousand and administered a large network of schools, convents, orphanages, soup kitchens, and hospitals.

Washington

Called the Evergreen State, Washington is located in the northwestern area of the United States. It is bordered on the north by Canada, on the east by Idaho, on the south by Oregon, and on the west by the Pacific Ocean. The state has five natural land regions: the Okanogan Highlands in the northeast, the Columbia Plateau in the southeast, the Cascade Mountains in the west-central section, Puget Sound, and the Olympic Peninsula. The original inhabitants of the region were the Cayuse, Nez Perce, Okinaga, Spokane, and Yakima Indians.

Explorers entered the boundaries of modern-day Washington as early as 1770, but no settlements were recorded. The Spaniard Bruno de Heceta (Hezeta) y Dudagoitia reached the northwestern coast in 1775, near modern-day Point Grenville. Three years later, the famed British explorer Captain James Cook sailed through the area, followed several years later by Captain George Vancouver. One of Vancouver's men, Peter Puget, is remembered for discovering Puget Sound in the 1790s.

The first Americans to reach what became Washington state were fur traders. They were joined in 1792 by Captain Robert Gray, who was on the Columbia River. The Lewis and Clark expedition reached the Washington area in 1805.

Five years later, the British North West Fur Company established Spokane House, a fur-trading post managed by David Thompson. John Jacob Astor's Pacific Fur Company established forts and trading posts in the region. The first United States settlement was Fort Okanogan in the northeast.

By 1818 the region was a valued source of furs for British and Americans. The British Hudson Bay Company had moved operations into the Pacific Northwest and assumed a dominant position. As a result, Americans were eager to expand their influence as well. A border dispute became a feature of the 1844 presidential campaign when Americans desiring the northern boundary for the United States to be 54°40' coined the phrase, "54–40 or Fight." In 1846 Great Britain signed a treaty with the United States establishing the 49th parallel as the border between Canada and the United States

The Catholic presence in the Northwest began in earnest in the early part of the nineteenth century. The first Mass in what became Washington state was celebrated on Thanksgiving Day 1838, by Fathers Francis Norbert Blanchet and Modeste Demers. The next year, they began a mission among the Native Americans at Cowlitz Landing, followed by a second mission the next year on Whitby Island in Puget Sound. Around this time,

the famed Jesuit missionary Father Pierre-Jean De Smet began working among the Native Americans in the Bitterroot Valley. He was joined by several Sisters of Notre Dame de Namur, who founded the Mission of St. Paul.

In 1843 the Holy See established a vicariate apostolic for the region, and in 1846 Pope Gregory XVI founded the Diocese of Walla Walla (now the Archdiocese of Seattle), with Bishop Augustin Magliore Blanchet named the first bishop. The episcopal residence was not there long; in 1848, a Protestant minister, Dr. Marcus Whitman, was killed by Indians in what came to be known as the Whitman Massacre. Whites were ordered out of the area and the Church was wrongly blamed for agitating the attack. The episcopal residence was then moved to Nesqually.

In the next decades, the general population continued to increase, and in 1853 the Washington Territory was created. It included all of Washington as well as parts of Idaho and Montana. The first permanent school was established in 1856 by the Sisters of Charity at Fort Vancouver.

With the discovery of gold in the region and the completion of the railroad in the 1880s, the population rose rapidly, as did the number of Catholics seeking work and their fortune. Washington became a state in 1889, and Bishop Blanchet's successors (especially Bishops Egidius Junger and Edward John O'Dea) worked to keep pace with schools, parishes, and churches. The see of Nesqualy was transferred to Seattle in 1907, and the Diocese of Spokane was founded in 1913 to provide for the needs of Catholics in the eastern portions of the state.

Catholics took part in the economic development of the state, including the burgeoning agricultural, fishing, and lumber industries, as well as the rise of the shipyards in Puget Sound in part because of the needs of the country in World War I.

After a decline in the 1920s, the economy rebounded slowly in the 1930s and throughout the years of World War II. The state witnessed a spike in population in the decades after the war, and in 1951 Pope Pius XII established the Diocese of Yakima and raised Seattle to the rank of an archdiocese. Washington was also blessed with a surge in diversity as Pacific Islanders, Asians, and

Hispanics arrived in large numbers. Seattle became one of the most vibrant cities in the country, and the Church focused resources on the pastoral care of the different communities. In 2011 there were more than 750,000 Catholics in the state, served by more than 500 priests, 600 women religious, and 246 parishes.

Washington, D.C., Archdiocese of

Established on July 22, 1939, by Pope Pius XII, the Archdiocese of Washington was administered initially by the archbishops of Baltimore. On November 15, 1947, the Archdiocese of Washington was separated from Baltimore to serve the District of Columbia and some counties in Maryland. It was established as a metropolitan see on October 12, 1965, and has the Diocese of St. Thomas in the Virgin Islands as a suffragan.

The history of Catholicism in the District of Columbia dates to 1634 and the arrival in Maryland of Jesuit Father Andrew White, who celebrated the first Mass in the original thirteen colonies in what was intended to be a colony where Catholics would enjoy religious toleration. He also evangelized among the local Native Americans, including the Anacosta.

The Colony of Maryland, founded by the Calvert family, enacted the Religious Act of 1649, but the freedoms granted to Catholics proved fleeting. The Puritan seizure of the colony brought great suffering to the Catholics of Maryland, and from the end of the seventeenth century to 1776 Catholics suffered legal and political disabilities. Catholic families, however, amassed holdings and discreetly practiced the faith. One of the most prominent of the Catholic families, the Carrolls, included John Carroll, who became the first American bishop and the first bishop (and then archbishop) of Baltimore. The Catholics of Maryland took part in the American Revolution and then helped craft the birth of the American republic and the creation of the national capital.

On July 16, 1790, Congress decreed a federal district to be designated the national capital, separate from any state in the Union. The designated location stretched along the Potomac River and included parts of Maryland and Virginia (the Virginia portion was later returned to Virginia). In 1791 the Catholic architect Pierre Charles L'Enfant designed the "Federal City" of Washington (his plans were not fully implemented until the early 1900s), and the next year James Hoban designed the White House. The first mayor of Washington, Judge Robert Brent, appointed by President Jefferson in 1802, was a Catholic.

Meantime, Catholic institutions were emerging in the new Federal City. In 1789 Georgetown, the first Catholic college in the United States, was established, and in 1794 Father Anthony Caffrey began St. Patrick's Church, the first parish church in the new Federal City. The Poor Clares opened a school for girls in Georgetown in 1801.

Over the ensuing years, the Catholic population of the District of Columbia remained under the jurisdiction of the Archdiocese of Baltimore, even as the Catholic population kept pace with the steady growth of the burgeoning national capital. One of the great achievements of the Catholic Church in the United States in the second half of the nineteenth century was the successful founding of The Catholic University of America in Washington, D.C., in 1887, to serve as a center for Catholic education. In 1893 an apostolic delegation was established by the Holy See; it became an apostolic nunciature in 1984 with the establishment of full diplomatic relations between the United States and the Holy See.

By 1939 the Catholic population in the District warranted a separate ecclesiastical territory, especially given the size and importance of the national capital. That year, Washington was named a separate archdiocese, under the direction of Archbishop Michael J. Curley of Baltimore. In 1947 Patrick A. O'Boyle, a priest of New York, was appointed the first resident archbishop, and Calvert, Charles, Montgomery, Prince George's, and St. Mary's Counties were attached to the archdiocese. Archbishop O'Boyle was consecrated a bishop on January 14, 1948, and set to work giving the new archdiocese a firm footing, including the start of schools, churches, and parishes. He took part in the Second Vatican Council, worked to implement the decrees of the council, and was elevated to the rank of cardinal in 1967 with the title of Santa Nicola in Carcere. He served until his retirement in 1973. During his time as archbishop, the Catholic population of the archdiocese had increased from around 150,000 in 1947 to nearly 400,000 in 1974.

The second archbishop of Washington, D.C., William W. Baum, had been the bishop of Springfield-Cape Girardeau since 1970. Appointed to Washington, D.C., on March 5, 1973, he was named a cardinal in 1976, with the title of Santa Croce in Via Flaminia. In 1979 he had the privilege of welcoming Pope Blessed John Paul II to Washington during the Holy Father's first visit to the United States. The next year, Cardinal Baum was named prefect for the Congregation for Catholic Education and in 1990 was named apostolic penitentiary. He retired in 2001.

The third archbishop of Washington, D.C., James A. Hickey, had been bishop of Cleveland since 1974. Named to Washington on June 17, 1980, he was elevated to the College of Cardinals in 1988 with the title of Santa Maria Madre del Redentore a Tor Bella Monaca. His time as archbishop was marked by progress in expanding diocesan ministries and services and outreach to the remarkably diverse Catholic population. Mass is said in nearly two dozen languages, including Vietnamese, Chinese, Korean, French, Polish, and Portuguese, and especially Spanish, as the archdiocese is home to some two hundred thousand Hispanic Catholics. There are also large numbers of Catholics from Africa and the Caribbean. Cardinal Hickey also worked to encourage orthodoxy in Catholic education and was a major figure in the Curran Controversy at The Catholic University of America in the mid-1980s. (*See also* Curran Controversy *under* Catholic University of America; Schools, Catholic.) Cardinal Hickey retired on November 21, 2000.

The fourth archbishop of Washington, D.C., Archbishop Theodore E. McCarrick, had been archbishop of Newark since 1986. Appointed to Washington, D.C., on November 21, 2000, and installed on January 3, 2001, he was elevated to the College of Cardinals on February 21, 2001, with the title of SS. Nereo e Achilleo. As archbishop, Cardinal McCarrick provided crucial leadership following the attacks on September 11, 2001, promoted vocations to the priesthood, and continued outreach to the growing Hispanic community. He retired on May 16, 2006.

On May 16, 2006, Pope Benedict XVI appointed Bishop Donald W. Wuerl of Pittsburgh as the fifth archbishop of Washington. Installed on June 22, 2006, he had the pleasure of welcoming Pope Benedict XVI during his apostolic visit to Washington, D.C., in April 2008. The trip was highlighted by a Mass at Nationals Park. On November 20, 2010, Archbishop Wuerl was elevated to the College of Cardinals, with the title of San Pietro in Vincoli. As archbishop, Cardinal Wuerl continued outreach to the diverse Catholic community of the nation's capital, worked to improve Catholic education, promoted the Sacrament of Reconciliation, and called on Catholic to assist refugees.

In 2011 there were more than 600,000 Catholics, 660 priests, nearly 700 men and women religious, and 140 parishes in the archdiocese. There were also 18 archdiocesan and private high schools and 87 archdiocesan elementary schools. In addition, the archdiocese is a leading center for Catholic higher education, with The Catholic University of America, Georgetown University, and Trinity Washington University, as well as theologates and houses of study for priestly formation.

Watkins, James D. *See* Cabinets, Catholic in Presidential

Wattson, Paul (January 16, 1863–February 8, 1940)

Founder of the Society of the Atonement and a Catholic convert, Paul Wattson was born in Millington, Maryland, and grew up an Episcopalian. After studies at St. Mary's Hall in Burlington, New Jersey, and St. Stephen's (modern-day Bard) College in Annandale, New York, he entered the General Theological Seminary in New York City in 1882. Following his ordination as an Episcopal priest in 1886, he took up as his chief labor improving relations with the Catholic Church, in particular achieving reunion with Rome.

Two year later, he joined with Mother Mary Lurana White, an Episcopal nun, to launch the Society of the Atonement at Graymoor, New York. Composed of Franciscan friars and Franciscan Sisters of the Atonement, the society was intended to pray for reunion. Wattson received the habit of the friars in 1900. In 1903 he began publication of *The*

Lamp, in which he advanced the work of the friars, promoted prayers for reunion, and defended such key Catholic teachings as papal infallibility as essential for Anglicans to embrace. To give further energy to the program of reunion, Wattson started the Church Unity Octave in 1909, a period of prayer and reflection lasting eight days. From this beginning, the Octave was celebrated by Catholics as the Chair of Unity Octave, held each year from January 18–25, and by non-Catholics as the Universal Week of Prayer for Christian Unity.

The same year, the decision was made by the members of the Graymoor community to enter the Catholic Church. Wattson himself studied for the priesthood at St. Joseph's Seminary in Dunwoodie, New York, and received ordination in 1910 by Archbishop John Murphy Farley. He remained head of the Graymoor Society and was later the founder of St. Christopher's Inn, a facility for the homeless, and the Graymoor Press. He also established with Richard Barry-Doyle the Catholic Near East Welfare Association.

Wehrle, Vincent (December 19, 1855–November 2, 1941)

A Benedictine monk, missionary, and bishop, Vincent Wehrle was born in Berg, Saint-Gallen, Switzerland, and entered the Benedictine order and in 1882 received ordination at the famed abbey of Einsiedeln. He was then sent to the United States and labored as a missionary in Arkansas, Indiana, and the Dakota Territory. In 1893 he founded St. Gall's Monastery at Devils Lake, but moved the community to Richardton in 1899 in order to provide better pastoral care for the large numbers of German-speaking Catholic immigrants settling in what became North Dakota. Wehrle served as abbot from 1904 to 1915, and in 1910 was named the first bishop of the Diocese of Bismarck. He resigned in 1939 owing to poor health. He has been honored as the "Apostle of the German-Russians and German-Hungarians."

Weigel, Gustave (January 15, 1906–January 3, 1964)

Jesuit priest, theologian, and ecumenist, Gustave Weigel was born in Buffalo, New York. He entered the Jesuit novitiate in 1922 and studied at Wood-

stock College in Maryland. Ordained in 1933, he was sent by the Jesuits to continue studies in Rome; in 1938 he earned a doctorate in theology from the Pontifical Gregorian University. From 1937 to 1948 he taught theology at the Universidad Católica de Chile and from 1948 to 1964 was a professor of ecclesiology at Woodstock College.

During his period at Woodstock, Father Weigel emerged as one of the most respected ecumenists in the United States. He considered himself a transitional figure in the area of ecumenism, between the pre-conciliar period of little ecumenical dialogue and what he hoped would be the post-conciliar effort at promoting Christian unity. In the year prior to the Second Vatican Council, he engaged in various forms of dialogue with Protestant theologians, including Paul Tillich, and was an observer at the Oberlin Conference of Faith and Order in 1957. In 1960 he was named a consulting member of the newly created Secretariat for Promoting Christian Unity, although he did not participate in the preparatory work of the council. During the Second Vatican Council he was attached to the secretariat as an official; during the first two sessions, he was a key liaison for journalists and provided English translations of the conciliar deliberations for the various non-Catholic observers in attendance.

Weigel was the author of eleven books: *Faustus of Riez* (1938), *El Cristianismo Oriental* (1945), *La Psicología de la Religión* (1945), *A Catholic Primer on the Ecumenical Movement* (1957), *Faith and Understanding in America* (1959), *American Dialogue* (with Robert McAfee Brown, 1960), *Churches in North America* (1961), *Catholic Theology in Dialogue* (1961), *Knowledge: Its Values and Limits* and *Religion and Knowledge of God* (with Arthur G. Madden, 1961), and *The Modern God* (1963). He also wrote numerous articles and was given numerous honorary degrees. He died in New York.

Weninger, Francis Xavier (October 31, 1805–June 19, 1888)

Jesuit missionary and theologian, Francis Xavier Weninger was born in Styria, Austria, where his family enjoyed the favor of the Austrian court and the young Francis Xavier was able to study at the University of Vienna through the sponsorship of Empress Carolina Augusta. In 1830 he earned a doctorate in divinity and was soon named to the theological faculty of the University of Graz. Two years later, however, he gave up his post to enter the Society of Jesus. He subsequently taught theology at Innsbruck from 1834 to 1848, but shared in the suppression of the Jesuits in Austria during the Revolution of 1848.

As his homeland had closed the door upon the Jesuit presence, Father Weninger volunteered for the missions in the United States. He served in Cincinnati and met with considerable success among the German-speaking Catholics in the region. He also proved instrumental in ending a longtime schism that had erupted in St. Louis Church in Buffalo, New York. Over the next years, he earned a sparkling reputation as a lecturer and mission preacher, speaking in German, French, and English, and remaining active until the age of eighty. He was also the author of over fifty books in German, English, and Latin.

West Virginia

Called the Mountain State, West Virginia is located in the east-central part of the United States. It is bordered on the north by Ohio, Pennsylvania, and Maryland, on the east and south by Virginia, and on the west by Kentucky and Ohio. The state has two natural land regions: the Appalachian Plateau and the Appalachian Valley. The original inhabitants of West Virginia were the Conoy, Delaware, Mohican, and Shawnee.

In 1607 John Lederer, a German, led an expedition into modern-day West Virginia near Harper's Ferry, but did not remain in the area. In the 1670s fur traders Thomas Batts and Robert Fallam surveyed the Allegheny Mountains. The first settlement was established at Bunker Hill in 1730 by Morgan Morgan, and a group of Germans began a settlement at New Mecklenburg. Welsh and Scots-Irish settlers also arrived but continued westward into the Ohio Valley. The first Mass celebrated within the future state's boundaries was offered by Jesuit Father Joseph-Pierre de Bonnecamps in 1749, in the expedition of Pierre-Joseph Céloron de Blainville. The expedition camped on August 18 at present-day Point Pleasant.

The French and Indian War halted settlements from 1754 to 1763, and the triumph of the English

in the war with France paved the way for their dominance in the Ohio Valley and opened the region for settlement. This was halted during the American Revolution and by the conflicts with the Native American tribes. During the Revolution, American colonists in the region took part and assisted General George Rogers Clark in his campaigns against the British in the Northwest Territory.

Catholics were not welcome in the early days of West Virginia. In 1642 priests were forbidden and Catholics were deprived of the vote and the right to hold public office. With the start of the American Revolution Catholics fought and died for the American cause. In recognition, officials in the region granted religious toleration with the 1786 Act for Establishing Religious Freedom. Wheeling then became a Catholic enclave, and a log cabin was built for Masses, followed by a church in 1821 constructed on land donated by Noah Zane and dedicated to St. James. The Sisters of Charity opened a school at Martinsburg in 1838.

The Catholic population increased over the next years as Irish laborers arrived to work on the National Road project and the Baltimore and Ohio Railroad. Catholic churches and parishes appeared at Harper's Ferry and Martinsburg. To give direction to the growth, Bishop Richard V. Whelan of Richmond arrived in 1846. In 1848 he established St. Vincent's School in Wheeling and invited the Visitation Nuns into the region; they founded a convent and an academy for girls at Mount de Chantal.

In 1850 the Diocese of Wheeling was established by Pope Blessed Pius IX, and Bishop Whelan was named the first bishop. St. James Parish in Wheeling was designated as the cathedral. Three years later, the Wheeling Hospital was opened by the Sisters of St. Joseph.

During this period, cultural and political differences between the people of western Virginia and Virginia became exacerbated by the vexing issue of slavery. Western Virginians were adamantly opposed to slavery and opposed the proslavery position of the eastern Virginians. The dispute climaxed in 1859 with John Brown's attack on Harper's Ferry. With the secession of Virginia from the Union in 1861, the people of western Virginia refused to join the Confederate cause and declared themselves for the Union. They drafted a constitution and entered the Union in 1863. In the terrible fighting that took place in the next few years, the Wheeling Hospital was used by the Union Army, and Catholic nuns provided care to the injured and wounded.

In the years after the war, Catholic immigration expanded rapidly, with Germans, Italians, Poles, and Lithuanians looking for work in the burgeoning lumber mills, coal mines, and other industries. Further economic development followed in the early twentieth century with the discovery of natural gas, and West Virginia's industries provided vital materials for the war effort in World War I. The miners and workers fought for better rights and conditions in the years after the war, and West Virginia again provided important materials for the American military in World War II.

The development of the Church in the decades after the war warranted changing the name of the diocese to Wheeling-Charleston in 1974. The Church has focused on providing pastoral care to a state that relies heavily on the severely challenged coal industry. Despite growth, the Catholic community remains small, making up about 5 percent of the wider population. In 2011 there were some 83,000 Catholics, served by 159 priests, 147 women religious, and 110 parishes in the state.

Weyrich, Paul (October 7, 1942–December 18, 2008)

A respected writer and a prominent leader in the modern conservative movement, Paul Weyrich was born in Racine, Wisconsin. He studied at the University of Wisconsin in Madison and became involved in politics when he joined the Racine County Young Republicans. He left the university before graduating and worked in journalism. In 1967 he started working as press secretary to Gordon L. Allott, the Republican senator from Colorado.

In 1973, with Edwin Feulner, he founded the Heritage Foundation and subsequently became one of America's most prominent and articulate conservative voices. He coined the term "Moral Majority." He was a deacon in the Melkite-rite Church.

Wheeling-Charleston, Diocese of

Established by Pope Blessed Pius IX on July 19, 1850, the Diocese of Wheeling served the entire state of West Virginia. It was redesignated the Diocese of Wheeling-Charleston on October 4, 1974, by Pope Paul VI, and is a suffragan of the Archdiocese of Baltimore.

The name Wheeling was derived from a Delaware Indian term meaning "place of the head." The earliest known Europeans to visit the area were the French, as part of the expedition of Pierre-Joseph Céloron de Blainville in 1749. The first Mass celebrated within the future state's boundaries was offered by Jesuit Father Joseph-Pierre de Bonnecamps, a member of the expedition. Two years later, Christopher Gist surveyed the area; another survey was done by George Washington in 1770. The year before, Ebenezer Zane explored what became Wheeling and established the first permanent settlement. Wheeling was officially established as a town in 1795 and was incorporated in 1805. It became a city in 1836.

Fort Fincastle was founded in 1774 and was later renamed Fort Henry in honor of Patrick Henry. The city developed with the arrival of the Cumberland Road and the railroads.

As was true elsewhere in the colony of Virginia, Catholics were viewed with hostility, and in 1642 priests were forbidden and Catholics were denied both the right to vote and to hold public office. This situation changed with the start of the American Revolution. Grateful for the help of Catholics in the war, West Virginians were granted religious freedom in 1786 through the Act for Establishing Religious Freedom.

With full civil and religious rights, Catholics began to migrate to western Virginia. To provide Masses for the local Catholics, traveling priests were able to have a log cabin built. Finally, a church was built in Wheeling in 1821, constructed on land donated by Noah Zane and dedicated to St. James. Other parishes followed at Harper's Ferry and Martinsburg to meet the needs of Irish laborers who had arrived to work on the National Road project and the Baltimore and Ohio Railroad.

In 1841 Bishop Richard V. Whelan was named bishop of Richmond and was concerned about the needs of the Catholic community in western Virginia. In 1848 he established St. Vincent's School in Wheeling and invited the Visitation Nuns into the region; they founded a convent and an academy for girls at Mount de Chantal.

In 1850 the Diocese of Wheeling was established by Pope Blessed Pius IX. Bishop Whelan was appointed the first bishop, and St. James Parish in Wheeling was designated as the cathedral. In 1853 the Wheeling Hospital was opened by the Sisters of St. Joseph.

By the end of the 1850s, the state of Virginia, like the rest of the country, was divided over the issue of slavery. Many in western Virginia were opposed to slavery and resented the proslavery position of the eastern Virginians. Virginia seceded from the Union in 1861, and the act spurred western Virginians to declare fidelity to the Union. They drafted a constitution and entered the Union in 1863. With the creation of West Virginia, ecclesiastical changes were needed as well, and eight counties in the eastern panhandle of West Virginia remained part of the Diocese of Richmond, while the Diocese of Wheeling included seventeen and a half counties in southwest Virginia.

In the years after the war, the Catholic population increased steadily through immigration, including Germans, Italians, Poles, and Lithuanians who were looking for work in the lumber mills, coal mines, and other growing industries. Bishop Whelan provided leadership throughout the war and in its aftermath, including a diocesan synod. He was succeeded on February 12, 1875, by John J. Kain, a priest of the Wheeling diocese who was thirty-three years old at the time. Consecrated a bishop on May 23, 1875, he continued to assist the needs of the diocese in a period of industrial progress. On May 21, 1893, he was appointed coadjutor archbishop of St. Louis.

The third bishop of Wheeling, Patrick J. Donahue, was a priest of the Archdiocese of Baltimore. Appointed on January 2, 1894, he was consecrated a bishop on April 8, 1894. His twenty-eight years as bishop witnessed the steady growth of the diocese. The number of priests increased from 35 to 115, and the diocese was given a solid foundation for the future. Bishop Donahue died on October 4, 1922, at the age of seventy-three.

The fourth bishop of Wheeling, John J. Swint, had been an auxiliary bishop of Wheeling since February 1922 and was appointed to succeed Bishop Donahue on May 11, 1922. He went on to be bishop of Wheeling for forty years, serving as shepherd throughout the events of the Great Depression, World War II, and the economic boom of the 1950s. He died at the age of eighty-two on November 23, 1962, at the start of the Second Vatican Council. In 1954 he had been given the honor by Pope Pius XII of being named the personal archbishop of Wheeling.

The fifth bishop of Wheeling, Joseph H. Hodges, had been an auxiliary bishop of Richmond and then coadjutor bishop of Wheeling since 1961. He acceded to the see on the passing of Bishop Swint. He attended the sessions of the Second Vatican Council and then worked to implement the reforms of the council. On October 4, 1974, Pope Paul VI recognized the development of the Catholic community across West Virginia by changing the name of the diocese to the Diocese of Wheeling-Charleston. Sacred Heart Church in Charleston was designated the co-cathedral. Bishop Hodges died on January 27, 1985, at the age of seventy-three.

Bishop Hodges was succeeded by Francis B. Schulte, who had been an auxiliary bishop of Philadelphia since 1981 and was named bishop of Wheeling-Charleston on June 4, 1985, and was installed on July 31. In November 1985, twenty-nine of West Virginia's fifty-five counties were struck by floods, and the Church committed resources to rebuilding and providing care to the victims. On December 6, 1988, Bishop Schulte was appointed archbishop of New Orleans.

Archbishop Schulte was followed by Bishop Bernard W. Schmitt, who had been an auxiliary bishop of Wheeling-Charleston since 1988. Installed on May 17, 1989, he launched several far-reaching diocesan programs to provide stewardship and financial stability for the diocese and wrote several pastoral letters, including one on family life. Bishop Schmitt retired on December 9, 2004.

On December 9, 2004, Michael J. Bransfield was named the eighth bishop of Wheeling-Charleston. Bransfield had been director and then rector of the National Shrine of the Basilica of the Immaculate Conception in Washington, D.C., since 1986. Consecrated a bishop on February 22, 2005, Bishop Bransfield has focused on providing pastoral care to a state that relies heavily on the coal industry and issued a pastoral letter, "On My Holy Mountain," noting the need for improved safety in

West Virginia's coal mines. He has also published pastoral letters on mental health issues and chemical dependency. The Catholic community remains vibrant but small, making up around 5 percent of the wider population. In 2011 there were some 83,000 Catholics, served by 159 priests, 147 women religious, and 110 parishes in the diocese.

Whipple, Amiel Weeks (1818–May 7, 1863)

Military engineer and Union soldier during the Civil War, Amiel Weeks Whipple was born in Greenwich, Massachusetts. He studied at Amherst College and then attended the United States Military Academy at West Point. After graduating in 1841, he proved himself an extremely capable military engineer and cartographer. Among his early achievements were his mapping surveys of the approaches to New Orleans and the Canadian and Mexican borders. In 1853 he supervised the survey to determine a railroad route to the Pacific Ocean near the 35th parallel. Four years later, he converted to the Catholic faith during the time he was supervisor of the lighthouse districts stretching from Lake Superior to the St. Lawrence.

At the start of the Civil War, Whipple was named chief topographical engineer under General George B. McClellan. In 1862 he was appointed brigadier general of volunteers and was given the task of organizing the defenses of Washington, D.C., along the Virginia side. He subsequently fought in the Battles of Antietam in 1862 and Fredericksburg in 1863. During the Battle of Chancellorsville, he was shot in the neck by a Confederate sniper. After receiving the last rites on the battlefield, he was taken to Washington. He died there from his wound, although immediately before his death was promoted to the rank of major general in recognition of his courage and service.

White, Andrew (1579–December 27, 1656)

English missionary and Jesuit, Andrew White was born in London. He belonged to a recusant Catholic family in Elizabethan England. As a Catholic, he faced considered legal disabilities and thus was forced to study in Europe, at St. Alban's College in Valladolid, Spain, then at the English College in Seville, Spain, and at Douai, where he was ordained in 1605. Sent back to England to assist the mis-

sions there, he was soon arrested, imprisoned, and banished in 1606 after possible complicity in the famous Gunpowder Plot to blow up Parliament. The following year, he joined the Society of Jesus at Louvain and returned to England in 1609. He also served as a professor in various Jesuit schools including Lisbon, Portugal, and Liège, Belgium, from 1610 to 1633.

In 1633, at the age of fifty-five, White volunteered for service in the Jesuit effort at evangelization in Maryland in response to the invitation from Lord Cecil Calvert to instill the Catholic faith there. Along with fellow Jesuits Father John Altham and Brother Thomas Gervase, White sailed from Isle of Wight to Maryland on the *Ark* in November 1633, reached St. Clement's Island on the feast of the Annunciation, March 25, 1634, and immediately said Mass. They then established the first English colonial Catholic church and made the mission a successful farming enterprise to ensure their self-sufficiency. Father White also proved himself a gifted missionary. He established sound relations with the local Native American tribes, as reported in his "Annual Letters," in particular among the Patuxent and Piscataways along the Potomac. In 1640 he performed a baptism of Indians in the presence of Lord Calvert and other Virginia leaders, and to assist his labors, he wrote a grammar, dictionary, and catechism in native languages.

Hopes of an enduring mission proved fleeting, however, for in 1645 Puritan raiders from Virginia invaded Maryland and laid waste to the Jesuit mission. Father White, with two companions, was seized and sent back to London in irons. There he was charged with treason for being a priest, which was a severe crime in Elizabethan England. He was soon acquitted as it was easily proven that he had been taken back to England against his will. Nevertheless, he was banished again. Once more, he returned in secret to England, where he expressed great hopes of going back to Maryland. This proved impossible, and he spent his remaining days providing pastoral care to the English Catholics in his care. He died near London.

White, Charles I. (February 1, 1807–April 1, 1878)

An editor and author, Charles I. White was born in Baltimore, studied at Mount St. Mary's College in Emmitsburg, Maryland, and was then sent to the seminary of Saint Sulpice in Paris to prepare for the priesthood. He received ordination at Notre Dame dathedral on June 5, 1830, and returned to Baltimore for service in the archdiocese. From 1833 to 1843 he was a member of the cathedral staff, and from 1843 to 1845 he taught moral theology at St. Mary's Seminary in Baltimore. During the next years, Father White attended several of the provincial and plenary councils of Baltimore and then served from 1857 as pastor of St. Matthew's Church (later Cathedral), in Washington, D.C. As pastor, he was responsible for founding a school and an old-age home for African-Americans. White also played an instrumental role in starting the St. Vincent de Paul Society in Washington.

Aside from his labors as a parish priest, Father White served as an editor of numerous periodicals, including the *Catholic Mirror* (1850–55) and the *Religious Cabinet* (co-founded in 1842, renamed the *United States Catholic Magazine* in 1843, and restarted in 1853 as the *Metropolitan Magazine* after ceasing publication in 1848). He was also the author of *Life of Mrs. Eliza A. Seton, Foundress and First Superior of the Sisters of Charity in the United States* (1853) and translations of *The Genius of Christianity*, by François-René de Chateaubriand (1856), and *Mission and Duties of Young Women*, by Charles Sainte-Foi (1858).

White, Edward Douglass (November 3, 1845– May 19, 1921)

Chief justice of the United States from 1910 to 1921 and associate justice from 1894 to 1910, Edward Douglass White was born near Thibodaux, in LaFourche Parish, Louisiana, the son of Edward Douglass White, a former governor of Louisiana. He studied at Mount St. Mary College in Emmittsburg, Maryland, Loyola College in New Orleans, and Georgetown College in Washington, D.C., but he left school at the age of fifteen to fight for the Confederacy in the Civil War. Assigned as an aide to General W. N. R. Beall, he accompanied him to Port Hudson. The port was forced to surrender to superior Union forces in 1863, and White was sent to a Mississippi prison camp. He was subsequently paroled. After the war, he studied law and was admitted to the Louisiana bar in 1868.

In 1874 White was elected a state senator. Four years later, he was appointed associate justice of the Louisiana Supreme Court. He served until 1881 and then returned to private law practice. Ten years later, he was appointed to the United States Senate, an office he held for a mere three years when President Grover Cleveland nominated him to the U.S. Supreme Court in 1894. In 1910 he was nominated chief justice by President William H. Taft. White was the first Southerner since Roger Taney to head the Supreme Court, and his appointment was noteworthy also for the facts that White was a Democrat even though Taft was a Republican. He was also the first associate justice ever appointed chief justice.

Considered a conservative member of the court, White wrote several hundred opinions and was noted especially for his "rule of reason" in decisions in 1911 concerning antitrust cases against Standard Oil and American Tobacco Company. The "rule of reason" distinguished between legal and illegal business combinations. In 1916 he wrote the decision upholding the constitutionality of the Adamson Act, establishing an eight-hour day for railroad workers. In 1914 he was given the Laetare Medal by the University of Notre Dame. He married Eleanor Kent, the widow of Linden Kent, on November 6, 1894, in New York City.

White, Stephen Mallory (January 19, 1853– February 21, 1901)

American statesman and United States Senator, Stephen Mallory White was born in San Francisco, the son of two Irish immigrants and noted pioneers in California of 1849, William F. White and Fannie J. Russell. White was also a cousin of Stephen Russell Mallory, secretary of the navy for the Confederacy during the Civil War. After studies at the Jesuit Colleges of St. Ignatius in San Francisco and Santa Clara in Santa Clara, California, he was admitted to the bar in 1874. In 1886 he was elected a state senator for the Democratic Party; he was soon elected lieutenant governor in 1888 and a United States senator in 1893. During his six years in the Senate, he devoted much of his attention to the settlement of the complicated questions related to the Spanish-American War and the annexations of Hawaii and the Philippines by the United States.

His extensive studies and examination of the questions were gathered together and published after his death in *Stephen M. White: His Life and Work* (1902). White was also one of the legal representatives of the Church in the difficult settlement of the lawsuits and negotiations surrounding the Pious Fund of the Californias. (*See also* Pious Fund of the Californias.) In 1896 he was asked to run for president by the state Democratic Party but declined.

Whitfield, James (November 3, 1770–October 19, 1834)

The fourth archbishop of Baltimore, from 1828 to 1834, best known for establishing the first of the provincial councils of Baltimore, James Whitfield was born in Liverpool, England, the son of a merchant. He assumed control of the business after his father died in 1787. He then moved to Italy with his mother as her health failed. Whitfield returned home in 1803, but the Napoleonic Wars began anew and the young man was trapped in Lyons, France. While there, he met Father (later Archbishop) Ambrose Maréchal, S.S., then rector of St. Irenaeus Seminary. The two became friends, and Whitfield entered St. Irenaeus to study for the priesthood; he was ordained on July 24, 1809. He entered the Jesuit novitiate at Stonyhurst, England, after his mother's death in 1811, and assumed the pastoral care of the small group of Catholics near Liverpool. Meanwhile, Maréchal had become coadjutor to Archbishop Leonard Neale of Baltimore and assumed administration of the see after Neale's death in June 1817. Whitfield accepted the archbishop's invitation to journey to Baltimore, receiving a post at St. Peter's pro-cathedral. He was named vicar general of the archdiocese in 1818, a position he held for ten years. In 1821 Whitfield was also appointed the first rector of the Cathedral of the Assumption. Three years later, he was awarded a doctorate in sacred theology from St. Mary's Seminary in Baltimore; he and two fellow priests were the first priest recipients of doctorates in theology in the United States.

On January 8, 1828, Whitfield was named coadjutor to Archbishop Maréchal and titular bishop of Apollonia. Maréchal died three weeks later, and on May 25, Whitfield was consecrated archbishop of Baltimore by Bishop Benedict Joseph Flaget of Bardstown, Kentucky. Archbishop Whitfield took a swift survey of the archdiocese and decided that it would be beneficial to convene the first of the famed provincial councils of Baltimore on October 4, 1829. He received his pallium on the same day as the opening of the council. Archbishop Whitfield also convened a synod for the priests in the archdiocese in 1831 and the Second Provincial Council in 1833. (*See also* Baltimore, Councils of.) Beyond the councils, Whitfield's brief episcopate was devoted chiefly to the spiritual and material growth of the diocese, including the construction of the towers of the cathedral and St. James Church in Baltimore. Both were paid for with Archbishop Whitfield's own funds. He was especially noted for his care of the African-Americans of the archdiocese.

Wichita, Diocese of

Established on August 2, 1887, by Pope Leo XIII, the Diocese of Wichita serves counties in southern Kansas. It is a suffragan of the Archdiocese of Kansas City in Kansas.

The city of Wichita was founded in 1864 in what had been declared Kansas Territory by act of Congress in 1826. It was erected as a vicariate apostolic by the Holy See in 1851. The Diocese of Leavenworth (now the Archdiocese of Kansas City in Kansas) was established in 1877.

Wichita was originally a trading post near the Wichita Indian settlement on the Arkansas River. The site was part of the Cumberland Trail, and its growth was aided by the arrival of the Atchison, Topeka, and Santa Fe Railway. An agricultural region, Wichita also developed mines and then a rich and diverse industrial base. In time, it would become an active center for the airline and refining industries.

The Catholic history of Wichita opens with the protomartyr of the United States, the Franciscan Juan de Padilla. He and a companion had entered the area in an early Spanish expedition and remained in the Kansas region when the expedition went south. He was slain in 1542. No major mission is recorded in Kansas following his martyrdom.

In the earlier periods of settlement, the faithful of Wichita were under the jurisdiction of the Diocese (now Archdiocese) of St. Louis from 1826. From 1851, Catholics arriving in the Wichita area were served by the Vicariate Apostolic of Territory East of the Rocky Mountains. In 1877 Pope Blessed Pius IX established the Diocese of Leavenworth, and all of Kansas fell under its jurisdiction. Meanwhile, the region had also been visited by the revered priest Charles de la Croix, who stayed with the Osage around 1822. In 1846 Jesuit missionaries were at Fort Scott, serving the military there. The Osage Mission of St. Paul was in operation by 1847, served by Jesuits. All Saints Parish in Wichita was founded in 1846, and St. Joseph's Parish was begun in 1886.

When the Diocese of Wichita was created in 1887 out of territory taken from the Diocese of Leavenworth, it had sixteen priests overseeing parishes, twenty-three missions, and nine parochial schools. The new diocese was also blessed by the presence of the Sisters of St. Joseph and the Sisters of Charity of the Blessed Virgin Mary from Dubuque.

The first bishop of Wichita, Father James O'Reilly, a priest from Topeka, Kansas, was appointed by the Holy See but died on July 26, 1887, before his consecration as bishop. The following year, Father John Joseph Hennessy, a priest from St. Louis, was named and consecrated a bishop on November 30, 1888. At the time of his arrival, there were eight thousand Catholics in the diocese. They were struggling, like the rest of the state, with chronic problems of drought and crop failures. He set to work providing pastoral care and giving the diocese a foundation for the future. In 1897, however, the Holy See detached seventeen counties from Leavenworth and attached them to Wichita; the diocese then encompassed the whole of southern Kansas. Bishop Hennessy worked to build new churches and schools to keep pace with the changes and a growing Catholic population. He died on July 13, 1920, at the age of seventy-three.

The second bishop of Wichita, Augustus J. Schwertner, a priest of the Diocese of Toledo, was appointed on March 10, 1921, and consecrated a bishop on June 8, 1921. His time as bishop stretched across the period of the Great Depression and the difficult period faced by the Great Plains during the collapse, as well as the droughts that made the economic crisis even worse. Bishop Schwertner died on October 2, 1939, at the age of sixty-eight.

The third bishop of Wichita, Christian H. Winkelmann, had been an auxiliary bishop of St. Louis since 1933. Appointed on December 27, 1939, he served as shepherd throughout World War II and died unexpectedly on November 19, 1946.

The fourth bishop of Wichita, Mark K. Carroll, had been a priest of the Archdiocese of St. Louis and was appointed to Wichita on February 15, 1947. Consecrated a bishop on April 23, 1947, he served in the period after the war and participated in the sessions of the Second Vatican Council. He resigned on September 27, 1967, at the age of seventy.

The fifth bishop of Wichita, David M. Maloney, had been an auxiliary bishop of Denver since 1960. Appointed to Wichita on December 2, 1967, he focused on implementing the reforms of the Second Vatican Council and guiding the Catholic community during the tumultuous period after the council. He retired on July 16, 1982.

The sixth bishop of Wichita, Eugene J. Gerber, had been bishop of Dodge City since 1976. Installed on February 9, 1983, he guided the diocese for nearly twenty years and worked to maintain the number of priests even as the Catholic population increased slowly during the same period. He retired on October 4, 2001.

The seventh bishop of Wichita, Thomas J. Olmsted, had been coadjutor bishop of Wichita in 1999 and acceded to the see upon Bishop Gerber's retirement. He served for only two years, as he was appointed bishop of Phoenix in 2003 and was succeeded as bishop of Wichita on January 28, 2005, by Father Michael O. Jackels, a priest of the Lincoln diocese. He promoted vocations to the priesthood and Catholic education, establishing the Drexel Fund to assist the financial needs of Catholic schools. In 2011 there were more than 114,000 Catholics in the diocese, served by 120 priests, 250 women religious, and 90 parishes.

Williams, Edward Bennett (May 31, 1920–August 13, 1988)

Celebrated trial lawyer and influential Washington attorney, Edward Bennett Williams was born in Hartford, Connecticut. He studied at the College of the Holy Cross and served in the Army Air Corps during World War II, then graduated from

Georgetown University Law School. Over the next decades, Williams became one of the most influential and respected legal minds in Washington, D.C. He founded the law firm of Williams & Connolly in 1944 and enjoyed a large client list owing to his reputation as the nation's foremost lawyer. His clients included William F. Buckley, Frank Sinatra, and the *Washington Post*, as well as notorious figures such as Teamster leader James R. Hoffa, mob boss Frank Costello, and Senator Joseph McCarthy.

Williams was the owner of the Baltimore Orioles professional baseball team and was president of the Washington Redskins professional football team for twenty years. He was also on personal terms with every president from Kennedy to Reagan and earned the particular dislike of President Richard M. Nixon, who once said on the Watergate tapes that Williams should be "fixed."

He held the post of national treasurer to the Democratic Party, and his most famous political act was his support of the effort to prevent then President Jimmy Carter from receiving the party's renomination in 1980. He was offered the post of CIA director by President Gerald Ford in 1975 and by President Ronald Reagan in 1987. Williams also donated large amounts of money to the College of the Holy Cross, Georgetown University, and the Archdiocese of Washington.

Williams, John J. (April 27, 1822–August 30, 1907)

The fourth bishop of Boston, from 1866 to 1875 and first archbishop of Boston, from 1875 to 1907, John J. Williams was a native of Boston and the son of Irish immigrants. He studied at the diocese's cathedral school before embarking upon preparations for the priesthood. He was sent to the Sulpician college in Montréal and then the Sulpician seminary in Paris. He was ordained on May 17, 1845, and was assigned to the Holy Cross Cathedral in Boston. In 1856 he was appointed cathedral rector, and the following year he became vicar general of the diocese. In 1866 Bishop John Bernard Fitzpatrick requested the appointment of an auxiliary bishop owing to his deteriorating health and urged that Father Williams be elected. On February 9, 1866, Williams was appointed, and Fitzpatrick died only

four days later. On March 11, 1866, Williams was consecrated the fourth bishop of Boston by Cardinal John McCloskey of New York.

As bishop and later first archbishop of Boston, he presided over the continuing expansion of the diocese, its elevation to the rank of archdiocese, and the creation and organization of several surrounding dioceses: Springfield in 1870, Providence in 1872, Manchester in 1884, and Fall River in 1905. From the start, the bishop was concerned with providing effective pastoral care for the host of different ethnic groups in the diocese. That entailed finding priests and men and women religious who spoke the many different languages of these congregations, including French, Italian, Portuguese, German, Polish, Lithuanian, and Syrian. Archbishop Williams also encouraged religious communities to settle in the diocese and archdiocese, including the Augustinians in 1861, the Sisters of St. Joseph in 1873, the Franciscan Sisters in 1884, the Religious of the Sacred Heart in 1880, the Carmelites from Baltimore in 1890, the Redemptorists in the late 1860s (they built a church in 1871), and the Marist Fathers in 1883.

Williams was also responsible for the construction of the new Cathedral of the Holy Cross, dedicated in December 1875, and St. John's Seminary in Brighton, dedicated in 1884, under the Sulpicians. In 1863 Boston College was opened by the Jesuits. There were also hospitals, orphanages, homes and asylums for poor children, and schools.

Archbishop Williams attended the Second Plenary Council of Baltimore in 1866 and the First Vatican Council in 1869–70. While in Rome, he proved an enthusiastic supporter of the North American College.

Pope Blessed Pius IX elevated Boston to a metropolitan see in February 1875. Bishop Williams was named its first archbishop and received the pallium on May 2, 1875. Despite his advancing years, Archbishop Williams requested an auxiliary bishop only in 1891, John Brady, and only in 1904, at the age of eighty-two, did Williams receive William Henry (later Cardinal) O'Connell as his coadjutor.

Williams, Mary Lou (May 8, 1910–May 28, 1981)

Jazz musician and composer who worked with many other famous jazz musicians, including Dizzy

Gillespie, Benny Goodman, and Duke Ellington, Mary Lou Williams was born in Atlanta. She was first exposed to music by her mother, who showed her how to play the traditional pump organ. When Mary Lou was four or five, her family moved to Pittsburgh. Displaying an aptitude muscially early in her life, she studied under the then-noted classical pianist Sturzio, and she earned money playing Irish songs for an uncle. Ultimately, she taught herself to play and became known as "the little piano girl" of Pittsburgh.

Before she was ten years old, Mary Lou played at private parties, including those of the powerful Mellons and the Olivers. At fifteen, she began traveling with the vaudeville act of Seymour and Jeanette, providing her an opportunity to learn another form of popular music. She then joined the dance band of John Williams, a saxophonist-clarinetist from Memphis, and was introduced to jazz. She later married Williams, and together they joined Andy Kirk's orchestra in 1928.

During the 1930s, the so-called swing era, Mary Lou was a key figure in the music style called Kansas City swing and was a sought-after composer and arranger for all the leading big bands and musicians, including Louis Armstrong, Tommy and Jimmy Dorsey, and Benny Goodman. Ultimately, she composed over 350 compositions and songs.

In 1941 Williams moved to New York City and took part in the explosion of jazz in that city through the 1940s. She based her activities in the Café Society Downtown in Manhattan. In 1945 she composed her most famous work, *Zodiac Suite,* a twelve-part interpretation of the zodiac scored for an eighteen-piece orchestra. She then journeyed to Europe, performing in nightclubs and on stage. In 1955, after Williams returned from Europe, she entered the Church and then devoted much of her creative effort to religious activities and charitable work.

Williams also composed religious music and was honored as the first jazz composer to write sacred music, including her *Hymn in Honor of Saint Martin de Porres* and three complete Masses; one of her Mass compositions was performed by her at St. Patrick's Cathedral in New York City in 1975 (and again in 1979). Williams also founded the Pittsburgh Jazz Festival.

Williams, Michael (February 5, 1877–October 12, 1950)

Author, founding editor of *Commonweal*, and a leading lay Catholic during and after World War I, Michael Williams was born in Halifax, Canada. He studied at St. Joseph's College in New Brunswick, Canada, but he left school and the Church after his father's death. He then led a wandering existence for several years, finally settling in Boston, where he became a writer of poetry and fiction. During this time, he met and became a friend of Philip Hale of the *Boston Journal*, who assisted in securing his employment as a reporter for the *Boston Post*; he then worked for the *New York World* and *Evening Telegram*. In 1906 he moved west and became city editor of the *San Francisco Examiner*. He was thus in the city when the 1906 earthquake struck.

Williams left San Francisco a short time later and traveled to Englewood, New Jersey, where he joined Upton Sinclair's utopian colony and was a coauthor with Sinclair of *Good Health* in 1909. As he found the colony to be incapable of providing what he was seeking, Williams reentered the Church in 1912 at Carmel, California. His experiences in returning to the Church were recorded in *The Book of the High Romance* in 1918. On the basis of the fame he achieved from that book, he was invited to become assistant director of the press department of the National Catholic War Council throughout World War I. After the war, at the request of the bishops, he wrote *American Catholics in the War* in 1921, a testament to Catholic patriotism during the war.

While living in New York in the early 1920s, Williams started a group of active laypeople, and in 1924 he and several close associates founded a journal, *Commonweal,* edited by lay Catholics and intended for lay Catholics. Williams served as editor until 1937, but thereafter continued to contribute a column, "Views and Reviews." *Commonweal* throughout his time as editor covered a host of major issues, including the presidential run of Al Smith, the persecution of the Church in Mexico, the Great Depression and the New Deal, the collapse of the Weimar Republic and rise of Nazism in Germany, and the Spanish Civil War. He left the post of editor chiefly because of his disagreement with his fellow editors over his support of Francisco

Franco in Spain (his colleagues were not supportive of the communists but were opposed to Franco). Among his other writings were *The Little Flower of Carmel* (1926), *Catholicism and the Modern Mind* (1928), *The Shadow of the Pope* (1932), and *The Catholic Church in Action* (1935).

Wilmington, Diocese of

Established on March 3, 1868, by Pope Blessed Pius IX, the Diocese of Wilmington served the state of Delaware and counties in Maryland and Virginia. In 1974 Pope Paul VI transferred the Virginia counties to the Diocese of Richmond. The territory of the diocese encompassed the Delmarva Peninsula.

By 1638 Swedish settlers were building beside the Christina and Delaware Rivers and out onto the banks of Brandywine Creek. The site was called Fort Christina, and the Dutch took control in 1655. In 1664 the English were in the area and claimed the lands. Wilmington, as it was named, had vast water-power resources and also developed a prosperous port in the 1730s when Quakers arrived on the scene. The city was large and powerful during the American Revolution. In 1802 a French merchant Eleuthère Irénée du Pont de Nemours established a gun powder mill in Wilmington. Industrialization followed, aiding the company that would become the Penn Central Railroad.

The Catholic presence in Delaware dates to around 1634, when families of the faithful arrived in the area. Jesuit missionaries served these families and maintained missions or small outposts of the faith on the Delmarva Peninsula for over 260 years. A Mass was celebrated, reportedly on Kent Island, as early as 1639. Coffee Run and other sites were used to establish missions from 1772; the mission at Coffee Run served as the basis in 1790 for the first church and the first resident pastor in what became the state of Delaware.

In 1789 Delaware and the Eastern Shore were placed under the ecclesiastical jurisdiction of the newly founded Diocese (later Archdiocese) of Baltimore. In 1808 jurisdiction was transferred to the newly founded Diocese (later Archdiocese) of Philadelphia, and in 1816, St. Peter's became the first church (and eventually the cathedral) in Wilmington. The population increased steadily as Irish, French, and German immigrants arrived to make

the Catholic presence permanent, and Franciscans, Benedictines, and Augustinians were active among the Catholic community.

A diocese for the Delmarva Peninsula was recommended to the Holy See by the bishops of the United States during the meetings of the Second Plenary Council of Baltimore in 1866. The bishops petitioned the Holy See, and in 1868 the Diocese of Wilmington was created. The first bishop of Wilmington, Thomas A. Becker, a priest of the Diocese of Richmond, was consecrated a bishop on August 16, 1868. He became shepherd of a diocese that had a Catholic population of some five thousand, served by eight priests, eighteen churches, a community of Sisters of Charity from Emmitsburg, Maryland, several parochial schools, and an orphanage and girls' school conducted by the sisters. Bishop Becker worked to give the diocese a firm footing, and he increased the number of priests and parishes. He was greatly assisted in this work by the communities of religious women, including the Franciscans of Glen Riddle, the Visitandines, Franciscans, Dominicans, and Benedictines. By 1886, when Bishop Becker was transferred to the Diocese of Savannah, the Catholic population had increased to eighteen thousand.

The second bishop of Wilmington, Alfred A. Curtis, a priest of the Archdiocese of Baltimore, was also a native of the Delmarva Peninsula. Consecrated a bishop on November 14, 1886, he worked to continue to develop the diocese's institutions. The Josephite Fathers arrived to provide pastoral care to the African-American community, and built St. Joseph Church in Wilmington with the help of St. Katherine Drexel. There were also Benedictine Fathers and Benedictine Sisters of the Pontifical Jurisdiction, the Ursulines, and the Visitation Sisters in the diocese. By the time of his retirement in 1896, Bishop Curtis had presided over the steady growth of the diocese: there were thirty priests, twenty-two churches, eighteen missions, three academies, and nine parochial schools.

The third bishop of Wilmington, John J. Monaghan, a priest of Charleston, South Carolina, was appointed to Wilmington on January 26, 1897, and consecrated a bishop on May 9, 1897. In the twenty-eight years he served as bishop, Monaghan established seven new parishes, seven new missions, and eight new schools. He invited the Little Sisters of the Poor into the diocese to start a home for the aged and the Oblates of St. Francis de Sales to open the Salesianum School for boys. Bishop Monaghan was instrumental in the start of St. Francis Hospital, operated by the Sisters of St. Francis of Glen Riddle. He resigned on July 10, 1925.

The fourth bishop of Wilmington, Edmond John FitzMaurice, had been a priest of Philadelphia and was appointed on July 24, 1925, and consecrated a bishop on November 30, 1925. He served as bishop for thirty-five years, a time that included World War I, the Great Depression, and World War II. He promoted new parishes and Catholic education to keep pace with the rise in population from the influx of workers into Delaware during World War II. He also gave his support to Catholic Charities and inaugurated the Catholic Welfare Guild, Catholic Youth Organization, Society for the Propagation of the Faith, Knights of Columbus, Catholic Interracial Council, Diocesan Book Forum, Catholic Education Guild, and Young Christian Workers in the diocese. He retired on March 2, 1960, with the Catholic population having grown to more than a hundred thousand.

The fifth bishop of Wilmington, Michael W. Hyle, was a priest of the Archdiocese of Baltimore and was appointed coadjutor bishop of Wilmington in 1958. He acceded to the see upon the retirement of Bishop FitzMaurice and was soon called to Rome to attend the Second Vatican Council. He then devoted his efforts to the implementation of the council's decrees. Bishop Hyle died on December 26, 1967, at the age of sixty-six.

The sixth bishop of Wilmington, Thomas J. Mardaga, had been the auxiliary bishop of Baltimore since 1968 and was appointed to Wilmington on March 9, 1968. He focused on the implementation of the decrees and reforms of the Second Vatican Council and promoted ecumenical dialogue and the role of the laity in the life of the diocese. He died on May 28, 1984, at the age of seventy-one.

Bishop Mardaga was succeeded by Robert E. Mulvee, who had been an auxiliary bishop of Manchester since 1977. Appointed to Wilmington on February 19, 1985, he worked to provide pastoral care to a growing Catholic population, which increased in his time from around 125,000 to more

that 165,000, as well as an increasingly diverse one. In February 1995 he was appointed coadjutor bishop of Providence.

On November 21, 1995, Michael A. Saltarelli, who had been an auxiliary bishop of the Archdiocese of Newark since 1990, was named eighth bishop of Wilmington. His time as bishop was marked by a period of growth, including a successful capital campaign, "Bringing the Vision to Life," the formation of new schools and parishes, and outreach to the diverse Catholic community that includes Hispanic, Filipino, Korean, and Vietnamese Catholics. Bishop Saltarelli also issued "For the Sake of God's Children," the diocesan safe environment and education program in the aftermath of the sexual abuse crisis in the United States. He retired on July 7, 2008.

On the same day as Bishop Saltarelli's retirement, W. Francis Malooly was appointed his successor. An auxiliary bishop of Baltimore since 2000, Bishop Malooly was installed on September 8, 2008. In 2011 the Catholic population of the diocese was more than 235,000, served by 197 priests, 224 women religious, and 57 parishes.

Wilson, Samuel, Jr. (August 6, 1911–October 21, 1993)

An architect, author, and native of New Orleans, Samuel Wilson Jr., demonstrated a love of architecture and so studied at Tulane University, where he received a degree in architecture in 1931. He then went to work for the architect Moise Goldstein and, in 1934, founded a partnership with Richard Koch that endured until the latter's death in 1971. Wilson was responsible for a number of memorable projects, especially his restoration of a host of buildings, including St. Patrick's Church, the French Market, and the Pitot House. He also wrote a number of books and articles.

Wimmer, Boniface (January 14, 1809–December 8, 1887)

Archabbot and founder of the first U.S. Benedictine community, Boniface Wimmer was born in Thalmassing, Bavaria. He was baptized Sebastian and grew up in the difficult years of the Napoleonic Wars, which ended in 1815. Wimmer studied the classics and theology at the University of Munich and the seminary in Regensburg, Germany. He was ordained on July 31, 1831, for the Diocese of Regensburg and served initially as a curate at Altötting, then a popular Marian shrine.

In 1832 Father Wimmer entered the recently restored Benedictine Abbey of Metten in Bavaria, where he was professed on December 27, 1833. During the next decade he held various posts in Bavaria. While stationed as prefect in a Munich boarding school, he became interested in the missions, particularly among German immigrants in the United States.

In 1845 he met the German priest Peter Lemke, who gave him encouragement to take his ministry to the United States. Father Lemke offered Wimmer land in western Pennsylvania if he promised to establish a monastery and so assist the pastoral care of German immigrants. Despite the reluctance of his Benedictine superiors, Wimmer was given permission to settle in America and arrived in New York in September 1846 with a group of Benedictine seminarians and postulants. The community moved west to the land in Carrolltown, Pennsylvania, promised by Lemke. This land, however, proved unsatisfactory, and the following year Wimmer moved the Benedictines to a plot near Latrobe that was given by Pittsburgh's Bishop Michael O'Connor.

After a period of adjustment, Wimmer and the Benedictines expanded their community. By 1855 there were 150 members, and Pope Pius IX in 1855 named Wimmer abbot and raised the house to a formal abbey. Over the next years, the abbey in Latrobe was declared St. Vincent Archabbey, and Wimmer aggressively pursued a policy of expansion into other states: Minnesota (1856), New Jersey (1857), Kansas (1857), Kentucky (1858), Texas (1859), Alabama (1875), and North Carolina (1876). He received much financial assistance from King Ludwig I of Bavaria, as well as the Ludwig Missionsverein and supporters throughout Bavaria. As an influential figure in the American Church, Wimmer attended the provincial and plenary councils of Baltimore and the First Vatican Council in 1869–70.

Winona, Diocese of

Established on November 26, 1889, by Pope Leo XIII, the Diocese of Winona serves counties in southern Minnesota. It is a suffragan of the Archdiocese of Minneapolis-St. Paul.

The city of Winona was founded on the Mississippi River in 1851 by a diverse group of settlers from New England. The site was originally called Montezuma but was renamed in 1852 for a legendary Indian princess. Located on high bluffs above the Mississippi River, Winona grew rapidly as a port for shipping wheat. The arrival of the railroads in 1860 aided the development of the area. The city then became home to various industries, in particular pharmaceuticals. The local timber reserves and a limestone quarry also assisted economic growth.

The Catholic history of Winona began in earnest in 1683, when Jesuit Father Joseph-Jean Marest opened a mission in Wabash for the Sioux. A trading post was operating there as well, as trappers entered the region from Canada. The French claimed the territory, and French explorers and missionaries were active in the seventeenth and eighteenth centuries. No permanent mission was recorded in the area, but Catholics gradually made their way into the area.

In 1826 the Minnesota territory was placed under the jurisdiction of the Diocese (later Archdiocese) of St. Louis; this was changed to the Diocese of Dubuque in 1837, and the bishop of Dubuque, Mathias Loras, sent Father Lucien Galtier to Minnesota. Father Galtier said the first Mass recorded in what became the Diocese of Winona in Wabasha.

The Diocese of St. Paul was created in 1850, and in 1856 its bishop, the remarkable missionary Bishop Joseph Crétin, made his way to Winona and helped establish the first parish there. Two years later, Minnesota entered the Union. There had already been a steady influx of Irish, German, and Polish Catholics in the 1860s, and in 1865 the School Sisters of Notre Dame arrived and eventually opened a provincial house in Mankato and started the first parochial school in Minnesota.

In 1877 coadjutor bishop John Ireland of St. Paul helped establish a colony in southwestern Minnesota and encouraged Irish and German farmers. Ireland was appointed the first archbishop of St. Paul in 1888, and the Holy See also created a province that included the new Diocese of Winona the next year. At its creation, the diocese had 49 priests, 45 parishes, 31 mission churches, and about 38,000 Catholics.

The first bishop of Winona, Father Joseph B. Cotter, had been a pastor of the Church of St. Thomas in Winona. Consecrated a bishop on December 27, 1889, Bishop Cotter worked to provide the diocese with a firm foundation. He promoted education and invited the Sisters of St. Francis of the Congregation of Our Lady of Lourdes to enter the diocese. The sisters helped launch the famed Mayo Clinic in 1889 and opened what became the College of St. Teresa in 1894. Bishop Cotter died on June 28, 1909, at the age of sixty-four.

The second bishop of Winona, Bishop Patrick Heffron, had been a priest of St. Paul. Appointed bishop of Winona on March 4, 1910, and consecrated a bishop on May 19, 1910, he welcomed the opening by the Brothers of the Christian Schools of Cotter High School, the diocese's first high school, in 1911, and the opening of St. Mary's College (now St. Mary's University) in 1913. He died on November 23, 1927, at the age of sixty-seven.

The third bishop of Winona, Francis M. Kelly, had been an auxiliary bishop of Winona since 1926. Appointed bishop of Winona on February 10, 1928, he served throughout the Great Depression and World War II and resigned on October 17, 1949, owing to health reasons, at the age of sixty-two. He died the next year.

Bishop Kelly was succeeded on October 20, 1949, by Bishop Edward A. Fitzgerald, who had been an auxiliary bishop of Dubuque since 1946. His time as bishop was marked by the Second Vatican Council, which he attended. He then worked to implement the council's decrees and reforms. He retired on January 8, 1969.

The fifth bishop of Winona, Bishop Loras J. Watters, had been an auxiliary bishop of Dubuque since 1965. Appointed on January 8, 1969, he served as bishop during the tumultuous periods after the Second Vatican Council and worked to provide pastoral care to the diocese in the face of declining vocations. He retired on October 14, 1986.

The sixth bishop of Winona, John G. Vlazny, had been an auxiliary bishop of Chicago since 1986. Appointed on May 19, 1987, he served for a decade in Winona and stressed the participation of the laity and promoted family life and youth ministry. He was also noted for the tradition of the "Harvest Mass," an annual outdoor Mass that was celebrated on a farm in the Winona diocese. On October 28, 1997, he was appointed the archbishop of Portland.

The seventh bishop of Winona, Bishop Bernard J. Harrington, had been an auxiliary bishop of Detroit since 1993. Named to Winona on November 4, 1998, he presided over the diocese throughout the crisis caused by clergy sex abuse and through the demographic changes that were taking place in the state. He retired on May 7, 2009.

The eighth bishop of Winona, John M. Quinn, had been an auxiliary bishop of Chicago since 2003 and on October 15, 2008, was appointed coadjutor bishop of Winona. He acceded to the see upon the resignation of Bishop Harrington on May 7, 2009. In 2011 there were 131,000 Catholics in the diocese, served by 121 priests, 365 women religious sisters, and 114 parishes and missions.

Wisconsin

Called the Badger State, Wisconsin is located in the north-central part of the United States. It is bordered on the north by Lake Superior and Michigan, on the east by Michigan, on the south by Illinois, and on the west by Iowa and Minnesota. Two land regions are in Wisconsin: the Superior Highlands in the north and the Central Lowlands in the south. There are more than eight thousand lakes in the state. Wisconsin entered the Union in 1848. The original inhabitants of Wisconsin were the Kickapoo, Ottawa, Potawatomi, Winnebago, and Sioux.

The Catholic legacy of the state began in 1634 when the French explorer, Jean Nicolet, led an expedition into the area of present-day Green Bay. In 1651 Medard Chouart de Groseilliers led another expedition into the region, accompanied by Pierre Radisson. They were surveying the land for possible trapping. Father Jacques Marquette and Louis Joliet followed the Groseilliers expedition into present-day Wisconsin. René-Robert Chevalier, Sieur de la Salle, was also in the region, claiming the lands for France. Jesuit Father René Menard was in the territory in 1660, and he was slain by a band of the Sioux.

In 1665 the revered Jesuit Claude Allouez started a mission at Bayfield. He founded a second mission at De Pere. There were some twenty Jesuit missions operating in present-day Wisconsin by 1670.

In 1712 a war broke out between the French and the local Indian nations over control of the Fox and Wisconsin Rivers. The Indians departed from the area as a result. The French and Indian War that took place from 1754 to 1763 ended with the victory of the British, and the British Hudson Bay Company began a fur trade and remained dominant in the region until 1812, when Wisconsin and other areas became the property of the United States. Settlers arrived in the present-day Wisconsin area soon after, and itinerant Catholic priests traveled among the settlements to serve the faithful.

Father Gabriel Richard built a parish and school in Green Bay in 1823. Meantime, the Diocese of Cincinnati was established in 1821, and its bishop, Edward D. Fenwick, visited Green Bay in 1829. In 1831 the famed Father Venerable Charles Mazzuchelli arrived in Green Bay and became its first permanent pastor. He established thirty parishes and served as a chaplain in the first state legislature.

The Black Hawk War started in 1832, and the Native Americans struggled to stem the tide of white settlers. They were defeated by a Union army, and in 1836 Wisconsin became a territory. The population at that time was some twelve thousand, but it increased significantly in the next years as new settlers, especially Europeans, arrived in the Midwest. The first Catholic church was established in the area in 1839 by Father Patrick O'Kelly in Milwaukee. The Diocese of Milwaukee was established by the Holy See in 1843.

Bishop John M. Henni was appointed as the first bishop of Milwaukee. In his long time in Milwaukee, he presided over the start of a new cathedral in 1853 and a seminary in 1856, and he helped found Marquette University in 1864. During his tenure, Wisconsin entered the Union in 1848. At its entry into statehood, the population was 150,000, which doubled within the next decade.

In 1854 the passage of the Kansas-Nebraska Act, with it ramifications for the spread of slavery, was the source of great unhappiness to the majority of people in Wisconsin, who opposed the institution of slavery, and led to the birth of the Republican Party. In the war that followed, Wisconsin provided soldiers for the Union effort, including the famed Iron Brigade, which had one of the highest casualty rates of any unit in the Union Army and fought in some of the bloodiest battles in the war.

In the aftermath of the Civil War, the Catholic population continued to expand, and to meet the needs of the swiftly increasing Catholic community, the Holy See founded the Dioceses of Green Bay and La Crosse in 1868. In 1875 the Diocese of Milwaukee was promoted to the rank of an archdiocese, and Bishop Henni became its first archbishop. By the time of his death in 1881, he had founded schools and other institutions, as well as some 460 churches. He also encouraged the arrival of religious communities in Wisconsin.

During this period of almost ceaseless expansion, ethnic tensions emerged in the state's Catholic community between German and Irish Catholics, especially at a time when the Irish enjoyed a position of dominance in the American hierarchy. In 1886 the Milwaukee priest Peter M. Abbelen sent Pope Leo XIII the so-called Abbelen Memorial, asking the Holy See to assist the rights of German Catholics. The ethnic situation was compounded in the last years of the nineteenth century by the arrival of Polish Catholics in large numbers, as well as Italians. By the end of the century, there were more than 450,000 Catholics in the state. In 1905 Pope St. Pius X created the Diocese of Superior, with Bishop Augustine Francis Schinner as its first bishop.

The early twentieth century was marked by the ascendancy in the state of the progressive movement. Wisconsin provided large amounts of material to the war effort during World War I. The state was hard hit in the Depression, and the bishops in Wisconsin, especially the archbishop of Milwaukee, Samuel Alphonsus Stritch (later a cardinal and archbishop of Chicago) worked to bring relief to those hit by the economic crisis.

In the period during and after World War II, Wisconsin returned to high levels of industrialization. In 1946 Pope Pius XII created the Diocese of Madison, with William P. O'Connor named the first bishop. To keep pace with the growth, the Church in Wisconsin established new schools; there were more than five hundred by 1960, by which time there were more than a million Catholics in the state.

The Catholics of Wisconsin generally welcomed the reforms of the Second Vatican Council. In the decades that followed, the state witnessed a significant change in demographics, including increases in the African-American population and also a shift away from the cities to the suburbs. Combined with the declines in the numbers of priests and men and women religious, the changes placed great pressure on Church leaders to provide effective pastoral care. In 2011 there were 1.5 million Catholics, served by 1,350 priests, more than 2,700 women religious, and 769 parishes in the state. There were also nine Catholic colleges and universities, 29 high schools, and 282 elementary schools.

Wolff, George Dering (August 25, 1822–January 29, 1894)

Editor and co-founder of the *American Catholic Quarterly Review*, George Dering Wolff was born at Martinsburg, West Virginia, the son of a Lutheran pastor. He grew up in Easton, Pennsylvania, and after graduating from Marshall College in Mercersburg, Pennsylvania, and then law studies, he chose not to pursue a career in law. Instead, he became a minister of the German Reformed Church, including membership in an ardently anti-Catholic sect headed by John Williamson Nevin. The inherent theological problems with Nevin's program convinced Wolff that Catholicism was indeed valid, and in 1871 he was received into the Church. The following year, he was named editor of the *Catholic Mirror* in Baltimore; he joined the staff of the *Catholic Standard* in Philadelphia in 1873, and remained its editor in chief until his death. In 1876 he launched, with James A. Corcoran and Father (later Bishop) James O'Connor, the *American Catholic Quarterly Review*. O'Connor departed that same year to become a bishop in Nebraska. Wolff and Corcoran remained editors until their death.

Wolff, Madeleva (May 24, 1877–July 25, 1964)

Educator, author, poet, and the first woman religious to receive a doctorate from the University of California at Berkeley, Madeleva Wolff was born Mary Evaline Wolff in Cumberland, Wisconsin. She studied at the University of Wisconsin for a year and then entered St. Mary's College at Notre Dame, Indiana, in 1906. After earning her bachelor's degree there in 1909, she joined the Congregation of the Holy Cross and was assigned to be a teacher. She was then sent to study at the University of Notre Dame and earned a master's degree in 1918. Sister Madeleva then taught at Sacred Heart Academy in Ogden, Utah, for several years before embarking upon doctoral studies at the University of California, Berkeley. She earned a doctorate in English in 1925. The following year, she became president of St. Mary of the Wasatch, in Salt Lake City and held the post until 1933. After a year of studies at Oxford University in England, she traveled across Europe and the Holy Land from 1933 to 1934. In 1934 she was appointed president of St. Mary's College, remaining at her post until 1961.

Sister Madeleva was a renowned educator, and during her tenure as president of St. Mary's College she was responsible for numerous innovations and the rise of the school to national prominence. Her 1949 work, *The Education of Sister Lucy,* represented a landmark in the development of higher education for women in the United States, and through her efforts the college established the first graduate program in theology for women and the first option to undertake a major in Christian culture. She was also a noted poet, composing twelve volumes and demonstrating a variety of interests in medieval customs and culture, Chaucer, and the English mystic Julian of Norwich. She contributed numerous essays and articles to the *New Republic, Commonweal, The New York Times*, and the *Saturday Review*. Her writings included *Chaucer's Nuns and Other Essays* (1925), *Pearl: A Study in Spiritual Dryness* (1925), *A Lost Language and Other Essays* (1951), *My First Seventy Years* (1959), *The Four Last Things: Collected Poems* (1959), and *Conversations with Cassandra* (1961).

Wood, James F. (April 27, 1813–June 20, 1883)

Bishop of Philadelphia from 1860 to 1875 and first archbishop, from 1875 to 1883, James F. Wood was a native of Philadelphia and grew up as a member of the Unitarians. While still a young man, he met and became a fried of Archbishop John Baptist Purcell; under Purcell's influence, he was received into the Church in 1838. The next year, Wood entered the seminary and was sent to Rome to study at the College of the Propaganda. He was ordained on March 25, 1844. Returning home, he served in various pastoral positions until 1857, when he was appointed coadjutor bishop of Philadelphia to Bishop John Nepomucene Neumann, C.SS.R. Upon Neumann's death three years later, Wood became the fifth bishop of Philadelphia.

At the time of Wood's accession as bishop, the diocese counted some 200,000 Catholics, 131 parishes, and 137 priests. He recognized immediately the need to expand the number of parishes and to bring construction of the cathedral to completion. The year after his installation, however, the Civil War began, and Wood devoted the next years to the pastoral care of the diocese throughout the dark period of the conflict. He proceeded nevertheless with the cathedral and inaugurated the finished church on November 20, 1864. The next year, he purchased a tract of land just outside the city, in Overbrook, for the establishment of a new seminary. St. Charles Borromeo Seminary opened in 1871 with 128 students. He took part in the Second Plenary Council of Baltimore, attended the First Vatican Council in 1869–70, and became a key supporter of the North American College. Bishop Wood's time also saw the creation of the suffragan Dioceses of Harrisburg, Scranton, and Wilmington.

In 1875 Wood was created archbishop, and Philadelphia was named a metropolitan see. In 1877 he journeyed to Rome to take part in the Golden Jubilee of Pope Pius IX's episcopate. Three years later, he presided over the First Provincial Council of Philadelphia, but his health, already troubled, continued to decline steadily. Upon his death, the city went into genuine mourning.

Worcester, Diocese of

Established on January 14, 1950, by Pope Pius XII, the Diocese of Worcester serves counties in central Massachusetts. The diocese is a suffragan of the Archdiocese of Boston.

Called the "Heart of the Commonwealth," Worcester is located on the Blackstone River and was settled by the English as early as 1673. The site was well populated by 1684, and Catholics were among the first settlers. Catholics, however, were

not allowed to vote or hold office, and Catholic priests were banned from the colony under threat of severe penalties.

When the Revolutionary War began in 1776, disenfranchised Catholics joined in large numbers in the rebellion and earned the respect of their Protestant neighbors. The town was noted for its strong revolutionary sentiment and served as a munitions depot during the war. With the end of the conflict, the colonies adopted state constitutions in which Catholics were gradually granted full civil rights. The Catholics of Massachusetts were under the jurisdiction of the Diocese of Baltimore from 1784 until 1808 and its remarkable shepherd, Bishop (later Archbishop) John Carroll. In 1808 Baltimore was elevated to the status of an archdiocese, and the Diocese of Boston was created by Pope Pius VII.

The town of Worcester, meanwhile, developed into an industrial and manufacturing center, a process assisted by the opening in 1828 of the Blackstone Canal, which permitted shipping and transportation; Worcester soon became a major hub in New England for textiles, clothing, metals, and paper.

In 1848, as the nation debated the slavery issue, the Free State Party was organized in Worcester. Massachusetts joined the Union's military response with the start of the Civil War in 1861, and soldiers from Massachusetts, including many Irish Catholics, fought with distinction.

By 1870 the development of the Catholic community in New England, aided significantly by the influx of Irish Catholics, was deemed ready for reorganization. The Diocese of Springfield was created in 1870, and five years later the Diocese of Boston was raised to the status of an archdiocese. Worcester became part of the ecclesiastical jurisdiction of Springfield, and the bishops there presided over the ongoing growth of parishes. The earliest church, Christ Church, was joined by St. John's Church in 1836, built by the revered Father John Fitton. Religious communities also established themselves, including the Jesuits and the Fathers of the Assumption.

Massachusetts Catholics took part in World War I and shared in the struggles of the Great Depression and World War II. As the Catholic population of Massachusetts had continued to grow, the decision was made by the Holy See to establish the Diocese of Worcester. At its founding, the new diocese claimed some 266,000 Catholics, 389 priests, 700 women religious, and 99 parishes. Its first bishop, John J. Wright, had been an auxiliary bishop of the Archdiocese of Boston since 1947. Installed on March 7, 1950, Bishop Wright established the first offices and institutions for the new diocese. He started thirty new parishes and invited eight different religious communities of men and women into the diocese. In 1951 he founded the diocesan newspaper, the *Catholic Free Press*. On January 23, 1959, Bishop Wright was appointed bishop of Pittsburgh and was later named a Vatican official and a cardinal.

The second bishop of Worcester, Bernard J. Flanagan, had been bishop of Norwich since 1953. Appointed to Worcester on August 8, 1959, Flanagan served as bishop until 1983, a tenure that covered the period of the Second Vatican Council and the tumultuous post-conciliar period. He also worked to deal with the decline in vocations to the priesthood. Bishop Flanagan retired on March 31, 1983.

The third bishop of Worcester, Timothy J. Harrington, had been an auxiliary bishop of Worcester since 1968. Installed on October 13, 1983, Bishop Harrington served for a decade that included changes in the city with movement to the suburbs and success in maintaining the numbers of priests in the diocese at a time of national declines in vocations. He retired on October 27, 1994.

The fourth bishop of Worcester, Daniel P. Reilly, had been bishop of Norwich, like Bishop Flanagan before him, since 1975. Appointed on the same day as Bishop Harrington's retirement, Bishop Reilly was able to keep the population of the diocese stable, including the number of priests and parishes, and conducted a successful capital campaign for the diocese. He was shepherd at a time when the Massachusetts Catholic community was convulsed by the sex abuse crisis that had as its epicenter the Archdiocese of Boston. He retired on March 9, 2004.

On May 14, 2004, Bishop Robert J. McManus, an auxiliary bishop of Providence since 1999, was installed as bishop of Worcester. He was faced with the ongoing problems created by the sex abuse cri-sis in Massachusetts, declines in vocations, and the need to streamline parishes in the face of demographic changes in New England. In 2011 there were 300,000 Catholics in the diocese, served by 284 priests, more than 370 men and women religious, and 108 parishes.

Workman, Mary Julia (1871–1964)

Social activist and Catholic leader in Los Angeles, Mary Julia Workman was born in Los Angeles, the daughter of William H. Workman, the Protestant mayor of Los Angeles, and Maria Elizabeth Boyle, a noted supporter of the Catholic Women's Club and the Women's Athletic Club. One of seven children, Mary was raised by her mother in the Catholic faith and received a thorough Catholic education at the Convent of the Sacred Heart of Mary and Jesus in Oakland. In 1902 she graduated from the State Normal School in Los Angeles with a focus on kindergarten instruction. She then taught in the city's public schools until 1923.

During this period, she became deeply imbued with the principles of the progressive movement. In 1901 she helped establish the Brownson House, dedicated to caring for inner-city people in need. In 1924 she began a diocesan branch of the National Council of Catholic Women, and in 1927 she became president of the Los Angeles City Civil Service Commission, where she served from 1927 to 1928. She also took part in the Municipal Light and Power Defense League and worked for the recall of corrupt Los Angeles Mayor Frank Shaw. An active Democrat, Workman participated in the Democratic National Committee, Southern California Division.

Dedicated to the principles of international peace, Workman promoted the participation of the United States in the League of Nations; she founded the Southern California chapter of the League of Nations Association. Likewise, she took part in the Catholic Association for International Peace, Southern California Committee. During Word War II, she protested the treatment of Japanese-Americans. Later, she helped bring about the short-lived Catholic Interracial Council of Los Angeles. In 1926 she was awarded the papal medal *Pro Ecclesia et Pontifice* by Pope Pius XI; she was the first woman in the Diocese of Los Angeles to receive the medal. Workman's sister-in-law, Margaret Kilgariff Workman, was also active in various philanthropic causes.

World War I

The so-called War to End All Wars, World War I was a European conflict that expanded swiftly into a truly global war that raged from 1914 to 1918. It cost the lives of more than 35 million soldiers and civilians, brought to an end much of the old European order, and made World War II inevitable because of the harsh terms of the Versailles Treaty imposed on Germany.

The war was caused by the shocking assassination of Archduke Franz Ferdinand of Austria at Sarajevo on June 28, 1914. Owing to a series of alliances made in the previous decades, Serbia was an ally of Russia, and when Germany and Austria placed severe demands on the Serbs, they were rebuffed. An ultimatum followed, and on July 28, 1914, Austria-Hungary declared war on Serbia. The trigger had been pulled: Germany declared war on Russia on August 1 and France on August 3. Once the war began, the two main combatants were the Central Powers of Germany, Austria, and Turkey, and the Allies of Great Britain, France, and Russia. Italy abandoned the Central Powers and soon joined the Allies. The United States entered the war in 1917.

Most American Catholics were initially little interested in the war, much like the rest of the country. With the entry of America into the war, German-Americans had to choose between their native land and their adoptive country. In the end, over one million Catholics fought in the war, enthusiastically displaying their patriotism and looking at the war as another chance to prove their worth to a still skeptical country.

In the first years of the war, the official position of the Church's leaders was to embrace both the declared neutrality of the Holy See and that of the United States. Pope Benedict XV was a voice for peace, and the result was that he was roundly criticized by the leaders of both sides. In truth, Pope Benedict XV offered a peaceful solution to the war, and had it been followed. the likely result might have been to prevent the disaster of the Treaty of Versailles and the catastrophe of World War II.

Irish Catholics had little sympathy for the Allies against the Central Powers, and some even expressed sympathy for Germany and its allies in the hope that a British defeat might hasten Irish independence. Not surprisingly, under the influence of Irish sentiment, a slight majority of Catholic publications expressed a greater degree of sympathy for the Central Powers than the Allies. German Catholics in America likewise shaped Catholic opinion.

The *Kulturkampf* in Germany (the campaign by Otto von Bismarck to dominate the Church and limit Catholic influence in the German Empire) had angered many German Catholics in America, but by 1914 Germans both Catholic and Protestant were proud of their native country and of the level of success they had achieved in their new land. German Catholics thus gave their backing to the Central Powers. The major German Catholic groups and publications, such as the *Deutsche Römisch-Katholische Central-Verein von Nord-America* (the German Roman Catholic Central Association of North America), called commonly the Central Verein, celebrated early German victories, but this enthusiasm faded as American opinion turned against Germany in the wake of the German sinking of the *Lusitania* in 1916 with men, women, and children aboard. The entry of America into the war in 1917 ended the robust enthusiasm of German Catholics for their homeland, at least in the sense it had been displayed in the previous decades.

Once in the war, American Catholics signed up in large numbers. More than one million Catholics served in the armed forces, over 20 percent of the entire force that fought in the conflict. Catholic chaplains in the armed forces increased from 28 to more than 1,500, and the Knights of Columbus opened some 250 recreation centers for soldiers in Europe and 360 in the United States, staffed by more than 27,000 volunteers.

American bishops also did their part by encouraging Catholics to support the war effort and buy war bonds. Cardinal James Gibbons was especially vocal in his backing of President Woodrow Wilson's grand plan "to make the world safe for democracy." He agreed to head the League of National Unity, an organization dedicated to galvanizing Americans of all creeds and nationalities to work toward victory.

He likewise dedicated sermons to reminding citizens of their duty to defend the country.

World War I not only gave Catholics a chance to show their patriotism, but it also provided vital impetus for Catholics to organize themselves nationally in new ways. The bishops, for example, had been meeting annually since the 1884 Third Plenary Council of Baltimore, but their gatherings were unofficial. Thus, when the country moved toward war, the bishops were forced to deal with a national emergency without any form of secretariat or other central body. Other Catholic groups and organizations similarly lacked national cohesion, save for the Knights of Columbus.

To remedy this, Cardinal Gibbons gave his blessing to the idea of creating the National Catholic War Council, a new national body made up of representatives of sixty-eight dioceses and twenty-seven organizations (especially the Knights of Columbus and the American Federation of Catholic Societies), to assist the Church's many different commitments during the war.

In 1919, after the armistice ended the fighting in November 1918, the bishops decided to keep the basic structure of the NCWC, which was renamed the National Catholic Welfare Council, with the planned purpose of bringing together the clergy and laity to work for genuine social and political progress in a way properly informed by Catholic teaching. The word "Council" was replaced by the word "Conference" in 1922. The first major document of the new council that year was the "Bishops' Program of Social Reconstruction." The statement was largely the work of the priest, social philosopher, and prominent social reformer Father John A. Ryan, who had been named director of the Department of Social Action for the NCWC, a post he held until his death. The bishops' program was a comprehensive legislative outline that advocated proposals for the minimum wage, unemployment, and other concerns for workers. Although the ideas were considered quite radical, many were eventually adopted as major components of the New Deal under President Franklin Delano Roosevelt. Still, the NCWC represented a new era for American Catholicism.

The Conference remained in existence until 1966, when, following the Second Vatican Council, it was reorganized into two parallel conferences. The National Conference of Catholic Bishops — sometimes referred to as the canonical arm — would deal with matters connected to the internal life of the Church, such as liturgy and priestly life and ministry. The U.S. Catholic Conference — in effect the civil arm — would represent the bishops as they related to the secular world, in areas such as social concerns, education, communications, and public affairs. Today, the body is known collectively as the United States Conference of Catholic Bishops.

World War II

The largest conflict in history, the Second World War, which was fought from 1939 to 1945, encompassed virtually the whole of the planet and cost the lives of more than 60 million people, including six million Jews who died during the Holocaust, 23 million soldiers and civilians of the Soviet Union, and perhaps 8 million Germans. There were more than four hundred thousand American lives lost.

The global war began in Europe in 1939 with the Nazi invasion of Poland and expanded in 1940 when Hitler launched Operation Barbarossa, the titanic invasion of the Soviet Union. The bishops of the United States expressed the alarm of Catholics well in their 1941 pastoral letter "The Crisis of Christianity," in which they lamented the genuine threat to world peace posed by both the Nazis and the communists; the bishops declared, "Christianity faces today its most serious crisis since the Church came out of the catacombs." There was a sense as well of inevitability that America would be dragged into the global conflict.

On December 7, 1941, the Japanese Navy attacked the United States at Pearl Harbor. The start of the war for America was yet another chance for Catholics to demonstrate their patriotism and willingness to fight for the country. Catholics of all ethnicities joined in very large numbers; in all, Catholics made up some 25 percent of American forces in the war.

Hundreds of Catholic priests served as chaplains in every major theater of operations, and seventy were killed in the line of duty. Particular support for the cause against Nazi Germany and Japan was also given by the bishops of the United States both as a body and also in individual enthusiasm for the war effort.

In November 1942 the bishops issued another joint statement, "Victory and Peace," which exhorted Americans to be united in the war against the Axis, who were "waging war to bring about a slave world—a world that would deprive man of his divinely conferred dignity, reject human freedom and permit no religious liberty." One of the most ardent leaders in the conflict was Archbishop (later Cardinal) Francis Spellman, who had been named archbishop of New York in 1939. Spellman was one of the most powerful Catholic figures in the country, a close friend of Pope Pius XII, and a dedicated military vicar, the head of all Catholic chaplains. He was also a close confidant of President Franklin Delano Roosevelt, and served as his liaison to the pope; in this capacity, the hardworking and at times imperious Spellman helped to spare Rome from Allied bombing and declared an open city in order to keep the wonders of Rome and the Vatican safe from destruction. In recognition of his role, Spellman was named a cardinal in 1946 and remained in his post until his death.

American Catholics were divided on the way the war ended. A slight majority of Catholics were in favor of the bombing of Hiroshima and Nagasaki, but a number of Catholic periodicals expressed either opposition or grave moral reservations concerning the use of nuclear weapons.

Europe was in a state of utter ruin after the war, and America came out of the global struggle as a true superpower poised to embark on an exciting time of economic growth and prosperity thought unthinkable a few decades before, especially in the dark days of the Depression. What was additionally manifest, however, was that while the war had been won, victory had ushered in a new era, a nuclear age that brought with it shattering change in the country.

Woywod, Stanislaus (August 10, 1880– September 19, 1941)

A noted canon lawyer, Stanislaus Woywod was born in Guttstadt, Germany, and studied for the priesthood in Holland before migrating to the United States in 1897. Once in the United States, he entered the Franciscan novitiate, in New Jersey,

and was ordained in June 1906. Sent to Rome for additional studies, he earned degrees in theology and canon law from the Atheneum Antonianum. Returning to the United States, he was named professor of canon law at St. Bonaventure Seminary in Allegany, New York, and in 1930 became first superior of Holy Name College in Washington, D.C. Woywod served also as editor of *St. Anthony's Almanac* (the earlier edition of the modern-day *Catholic Almanac*) and wrote various articles for the *American Ecclesiastical Review*. A respected canon lawyer, Woywod published in 1918 *The New Canon Law,* a explanation of the 1917 Code of Canon Law that helped immensely to explain the workings of the code to the average Catholic reader. He added further to his reputation with *A Practical Commentary on the Code of Canon Law* in 1925. He also wrote extensively on canon law from 1918 until 1941 for the *Homiletic and Pastoral Review.*

Wright, John J. (July 18, 1909–August 10, 1979)

Cardinal from 1969 and prefect of the Congregation of the Clergy from 1969 to 1979, the first American to head a congregation in Rome with global duties, and a theologian, John J. Wright was a native of Boston. The future cardinal attended Boston College and, entering preparations for the priesthood, he was sent to Rome for studies at the North American College and the Pontifical Gregorian University. He was ordained on December 8, 1935, and earned a doctorate in theology in 1939.

Upon his return to Boston in 1939, Wright taught at St. John's Seminary in Brighton, Massachusetts, until 1944, when he was appointed secretary to Cardinal William H. O'Connell, then archbishop of Boston. In 1944 he served as secretary to O'Connell's successor, Archbishop (later Cardinal) Richard James Cushing. On June 30, 1947, Wright was consecrated titular bishop of Aegea and auxiliary bishop of Boston. He remained as auxiliary until 1950, when he was installed as the first bishop of Worcester. In March 1959, Wright was installed as the eighth bishop of Pittsburgh.

Even as he assumed his duties as bishop in Pittsburgh, Wright was given an important position in the preparation for the Second Vatican Council. He was named a member of the theological Committee of the Preparatory Commission and so had a hand in the developments of several key documents, including *Lumen Gentium* and *Gaudium et Spes*. He also served as chairman of the subcommission for drafting the chapter on the laity in *Lumen Gentium*.

Back home from the council, Wright continued to serve as bishop of Pittsburgh and held various posts in the National Conference of Catholic Bishops. He was chairman of the committee charged with writing the draft of the first of the NCCB's post-conciliar pastoral letters, *The Church in Our Day*, in 1967, and *Human Life in Our Day*, in 1968. He was also chosen by his fellow bishops to attend the first two Synods of Bishops in 1967 and 1969.

On April 23, 1969, Bishop Wright was appointed by Pope Paul VI to the post of pro-prefect of the Congregation for the Clergy in Rome. Five days later, the pope named him a cardinal priest, with the titular church of Jesus the Divine Teacher. On May 3, 1969, he was named prefect of the congregation. In 1971 Pope Paul chose him to be one of three presidents of the Second General Assembly of the Synod of Bishops. His time as prefect saw the promulgation of several notable documents, including the *Circular Letter on Priest Councils* in 1969, which called for the creation of mandatory diocesan priest councils, the *General Catechetical Directory* in 1971, and the *Circular Letter on Pastoral Councils* in 1973. He also held many posts in the Roman Curia, including membership in the Congregations for Bishops and for the Evangelization of Peoples, the Council for the Public Affairs of the Church, the Commission for the Revision of the Code of Canon Law, and the Commission for Vatican City.

Cardinal John Wright

Owing to declining health, Cardinal Wright was unable to attend the conclave that elected Pope John Paul I in September 1978. He was able to take part, in a wheelchair, in the conclave that elected Pope John Paul II. Upon his return home, however, he continued to face health problems. A genuinely respected theologian, Cardinal Wright spoke out in his final years to express his deep concerns about the misinterpretations of the Second Vatican Council and the various abuses surrounding the implementation of its decrees.

Wuerl, Donald W. (November 12, 1940–)

Bishop of Pittsburgh from 1988 to 2006, archbishop of Washington from 2006, and a cardinal since 2010, Donald W. Wuerl was born in Pittsburgh. He studied at St. Gregory Seminary in Cincinnati and then at The Catholic University of America in Washington, D.C., as a Basselin Scholar in philosophy, earning a master's degree in philosophy. Sent to Rome for his priestly formation at the Pontifical North American College, he attended the Pontifical Gregorian University, where he obtained a master's degree in theology, and the Pontifical University of St. Thomas, the Angelicum, where he obtained a doctorate in theology in 1974.

Ordained a priest on December 17, 1966, in Rome, he served briefly in Pittsburgh as an associate pastor and then as secretary to Bishop John J. Wright of Pittsburgh from 1968 to 1969; he remained in this post when Bishop Wright was named prefect of the Sacred Congregation for the Clergy in 1969 and a cardinal in 1969. Owing to Cardinal Wright's health concerns, he was permitted into the conclave in 1978 that resulted in the election of Cardinal Karol Wojtyla as Pope John Paul II. He then served as vice rector of St. Paul's Seminary in Pittsburgh from 1980 to 1981 and then rector from 1981 to 1985.

On November 30, 1985, Wuerl was appointed titular bishop of Rosemarkie and auxiliary bishop of Seattle. Consecrated a bishop on January 6, 1985, he was given special authority in the Seattle archdiocese to assist Archbishop Raymond G. Hunthausen. On February 12, 1988, he was appointed bishop of Pittsburgh and installed on March 25, 1988.

As bishop of Pittsburgh, Wuerl promoted vocations and worked to establish a comprehensive program for the long-term viability of parishes and Catholic schools in the face of the changing demographics and economy of the Pittsburgh diocese. He closed some parishes and merged others through a plan titled "The Parish Reorganization and Revitalization Project." The plan became a model for other dioceses seeking similar reorganization. He also became a nationally best-selling author and television personality through his books, most notably *The Teaching of Christ*, a catechism of the Catholic Church.

On May 16, 2006, he was appointed to the metropolitan see of Washington, D.C., and was installed on June 22, 2006. In April 2008 he had the privilege of welcoming Pope Benedict XVI during his visit to the United States, including a Mass for more than fifty thousand in Nationals Stadium. He also served as the chair for the Committees for Education, Catechesis, Doctrine, Evangelization and Priestly Life and Ministry of the United States Conference of Catholic Bishops, and as director of the Commission for the Implementation of the Apostolic Constitution *Anglicanorum Coetibus* in the United States, by which Anglicans are able to enter the Church. On November 20, 2010, he was named a cardinal priest by Pope Benedict XVI with the title of San Pietro in Vincoli. On October 22, 2011, he was appointed relator general of the Thirteenth Ordinary General Assembly of the Synod of Bishops for October 2012, focusing on the New Evangelization. As archbishop of Washington, Cardinal Wuerl has focused heavily on Catholic identity, the promotion of vocations, and a renewal of Catholic sacramental life.

Wyatt, Jane (1910–October 20, 2006)

An actress who won three Emmy awards for her role as Margaret Anderson on the television comedy *Father Knows Best* in the 1950s, Jane Wyatt was born into a Catholic family. She was the daughter of Euphemia Van Rensselaer, a writer for *Commonweal* and *Catholic World* magazines and president of Catholic Big Sisters. Wyatt left college to embark on a Broadway career and then began working in film and television. She first came to prominence in 1937 in the movie *Lost Horizon,* and then appeared in *None But the Lonely Heart* in 1944 and *Gentlemen's Agreement* in 1948. In the 1960s she established a cult following that has long endured for her role as Amanda, the human mother of the half-human, half-Vulcan Mr. Spock on the television series *Star Trek,* reprising the role in the 1986 film *Star Trek*

IV: The Voyage Home. A lifelong Catholic, Wyatt won the College (now University) of Steubenville's Poverello Medal in 1962 and was active in Catholic radio, including Father Patrick Peyton's *Family Theater* radio series on the Mutual Broadcasting System.

Wynhoven, Peter (1884–September 14, 1944)

A priest and social activist, Peter Wynhoven was a native of the Netherlands who migrated to the United States in 1904 at the invitation of Father Arthur J. Drossaerts. At the time, he was a student in Holland, but spent the next years studying for the priesthood for the Archdiocese of New Orleans. Ordained a priest in 1909, he became an influential voice in the field of Catholic social action in New Orleans, especially at the encouragement of several archbishops of New Orleans, including Archbishops James H. Blenk and John William Shaw. Wynhoven founded St. Vincent's Hotel and Free Labor Bureau for homeless workers, the Catholic Women's Club for working girls, Hope Haven, a home for boys, and Madonna Manor, a home for girls. Wynhoven also founded a newspaper, *Catholic Action of the South,* to serve as the official paper for four dioceses in Louisiana. Despite these demands on his time, in addition to his service as a pastor and as vice chancellor, he also held a post on the National Labor Relations Board in 1933 at the behest of President Franklin Delano Roosevelt.

Under Archbishop Joseph Francis Rummel, Father Wynhoven served as pastor of Our Lady of Lourdes Parish in New Orleans, chairman of the Eighth National Eucharistic Congress in 1938, and head of the Youth Progress Program, formed to raise funds for an archdiocesan expansion of youth services. The wide variety of activities and duties eventually took their toll, and Wynhoven died soon after completing his work on the fundraising drive.

Wynne, John (September 30, 1859–November 30, 1948)

Jesuit priest, author, and founder of *America*, the foremost Jesuit journal of opinion in the United States, John Wynne was a native of New York. He studied at St. Francis Xavier College and entered the Jesuit novitiate at West Park, New York, in 1876. He then attended Woodstock College in Maryland and, after further studies, was ordained in 1890 by Cardinal James Gibbons. In 1891 Wynne was named to the staff of the *Messenger of the Sacred Heart* in New York and served as its editor for nearly two decades. He also was director of the Apostleship of Prayer, the Shrine of the Jesuit North American Martyrs at Auriesville, New York. He was later named vice postulator of the causes of the Jesuit Martyrs (who were beatified in 1925 and canonized in 1930) and St. Kateri Tekakwitha. Father Wynne also played a crucial part in organizing the Holy Hour movement.

In 1909 Father Wynne sought to publish a magazine that could reach out to average Catholics and so launched the weekly magazine *America.* He held the post of editor for one year and then stepped down to serve as associate editor of the *Catholic Encyclopedia,* a post he had held since 1905. From 1914 to 1917 he was editor of *Anno Domini,* the publication of the League of Daily Mass. He was also the editor of *The Great Encyclicals of Leo XIII* (1903), co-editor of *The New Catholic Dictionary* (1927), and editor of *The Jesuit Martyrs of North America* (1925).

Wyoming

Called the Equality State, Wyoming is located in the northwestern part of the United States. It is bordered on the north by Montana, on the east by South Dakota and Nebraska, on the south by Colorado and Utah, and on the west by Utah and Idaho. Three land regions are found in the state: the Great Plains in the east, the Wyoming Basin in the south-central area, and the Wyoming Rockies in the west. The original inhabitants of Wyoming were the Arapaho, Blackfeet, Cheyenne, Flatheads, Kiowa, Shoshone, and Sioux.

The Catholic heritage of Wyoming opened as early as 1682, when René-Robert Chevalier, Sieur de La Salle, entered the territory of modern-day Wyoming, claiming the lands for France. In the 1730s Pierre Gaultier de Varennes, Sieur de La Vérendrye, and his sons explored the region as well. Catholic priests normally served as members of such expeditions.

In 1803 the Louisiana Purchase gave the United States new lands in the West, and in 1807 John Colter explored Wyoming and was the first American explorer to discover the area of what is now Yellowstone Park. In 1812 Robert Stuart reached the Continental Divide and found South Pass, which would become an important component of the Oregon Trail. Twelve years later, trappers Thomas Fitzgerald and Jedediah Smith would survey South Pass. In 1834 two trappers, Robert Campbell and William Sublette, established Fort Laramie, paving the way for white settlers from the east. With the passage westward secured, Wyoming became the primary route to the West Coast, which caused immense unhappiness and resentment on the part of Native Americans, who perceived the threat posed by the whites.

The revered Jesuit missionary Father Pierre-Jean De Smet served in the area during his immense missionary labors in the middle of the nineteenth century and said the first Mass in Wyoming in 1840. He provided pastoral care to many mountain men (including Jim Bridger). His friendship with the Sioux leader Sitting Bull helped bring about the Treaty of Fort Laramie in 1868, which ended Red Cloud's War and provided guarantees of land to the Sioux.

The pace of settlement increased from 1867 with the discovery of gold in South Pass and the advance of the Union Pacific Railroad. That year, Father William Kelly became the first permanent pastor in Cheyenne; the next year, he founded the first permanent church. By 1870 Cheyenne was a center for outfitting the gold miners of the Black Hills and a shipping point for cattle. Wyoming remained a rugged place, however.

In 1850 Wyoming was included in part in the Vicariate Apostolic of the Indian Territory. The next year, the Vicariate Apostolic of the Rocky Mountains was erected, which also included some of the Wyoming territories. Bishop Jean Baptiste Miège, another Jesuit, was vicar apostolic and established his residence in Leavenworth, Kansas. Wyoming then became part of the Vicariate Apostolic of Nebraska in 1857.

Further support for the Catholic community arrived in 1884 when the Jesuits founded St. Stephen's Mission on the Wind River reservation of the Shoshone and Northern Arapahoes. The Sisters of Charity of Leavenworth arrived soon after to operate the mission school, replaced by the Sisters of St. Joseph and then by Franciscan Sisters.

On August 2, 1887, the Diocese of Cheyenne was established and included Yellowstone National Park, which had been so designated in 1872. Bishop Maurice Francis Burke was consecrated on October 28, 1887, as the first bishop of Cheyenne. He assumed the new see and instituted offices and agencies for diocesan administration. He had to defend the faithful from Protestant uprisings that included threats from the local Know-Nothings. At the start of the diocese, there were five Catholic parishes.

In the 1880s the territory was troubled by the immense growth of the cattle industry, which had led to the wealthy "cattle barons," struggles with cattle rustling, and homesteaders who fenced the once wide-open lands. The crisis culminated in the Johnson County Cattle War, which was ended with the intervention of federal troops. The next years also brought bloody conflict between the cattlemen and sheepherders who had arrived in large numbers in the last years of the nineteenth century. Meanwhile, in 1890, Wyoming became the forty-fourth state of the Union.

A major change in the state occurred in the early twentieth century with the start of the oil industry and the passage of the federal Homestead Act of 1909 to attract new farmers. Wyoming during this time proved ahead of the rest of the country in allowing women to vote, and in 1924 Nellie Ross was elected the first woman governor of a state.

The state faced many of the same hardships as the rest of the country during the Great Depression and provided important resources for the war effort during World War II, especially oil and wool. The key Catholic figure during this period was Bishop Patrick Aloysius McGovern, who served as bishop of Cheyenne from 1912 to 1950. During his time, the diocese was made a suffragan of the Archdiocese of Denver in 1941.

There was marked expansion in the economy after the war resulting from further oil productivity and the discovery of uranium. By 1960 the Catholic population in the state had reached 48,000. Bishop McGovern's successor, Bishop Hubert Newell, served in Cheyenne from 1951 to 1978, throughout the era of the Second Vatican Council and through the difficult post-conciliar period.

The Church continues to provide pastoral care to a state noted for its rural environment, its reliance on tourism (including Yellowstone), which accounts for millions of visitors each year, and the important mining and oil industries. In 2011 there were 52,000 Catholics, served by 63 priests and 34 parishes in the state.

X, Y, Z

Yakima, Diocese of

Established on June 23, 1951, by Pope Pius XII, the Diocese of Yakima serves counties in central Washington. It is a suffragan see of the Archdiocese of Seattle. The city is located on the Yakima River and is named after the Yakima Indian nation. In 1884 the Northern Pacific Railway selected a site, named Yakima City, as construction headquarters. Abandoned soon after, a new site some four miles to the north was chosen as a depot and called North Yakima. The site became a large cattle center, drawing settlers into the region.

Irrigation was introduced into the Yakima Valley in 1891, resulting in the creation of a rich agricultural resource. Food processing evolved rapidly as the industry attracted more families. The city of North Yakima was incorporated in 1886. The prefix "North" was removed from the name in 1918.

The Catholic history of Yakima dates officially to the 1830s when Fathers Francis Norbert Blanchet (later archbishop of Oregon City) and Modeste Demers (later bishop of Vancouver Island) were in the area.

In 1846 Bishop Augustin Magloire Blanchet arrived in the region of Walla Walla as the first bishop of the newly founded Diocese of Walla Walla. His extensive diocese included the territory of the Yakima tribes, and soon after his arrival Bishop Blanchet sent the Oblates of Mary Immaculate to establish a mission among them. The first two priests ordained for service in Washington state were intended to preach and provide care for the Indians, Fathers Eugene Casimir Chirouse and Charles Marie Pandosy, both Oblates. The famed Jesuit missionary Father Pierre-Jean De Smet was also laboring among the Indian settlements, joined by six Sisters of Notre Dame de Namur.

Bishop Blanchet established the first administrative programs in Walla Walla. A year after his arrival, however, the Whitman Massacre took place. This terrible slaughter of a Protestant missionary, his wife, and an assistant brought about anti-Catholic sentiment, with false charges being laid against the vicar general of the diocese, Father Jean Baptiste Abraham Brouillet, for instigating the uprising of Native Americans in the mission. The charges were proven false, but the Diocese of Walla Walla was suppressed in favor of Nesqually in 1850, which later became the Archdiocese of Seattle.

In 1855 the Yakima War began between federal forces and the Yakama Indians and ended with the defeat of the Native American people. The conflict brought the closing of the mission at Ahtanum in 1857. It was reestablished in 1867 and staffed for a time by the Jesuits.

The population increased steadily in the decades that followed, as more settlers arrived seeking work in the growing industries of the state. Washington entered the Union in 1889 as the forty-second state. The Catholic community kept pace, and in 1913 Pope St. Pius X established the Diocese of Spokane. The area of Yakima was placed under the jurisdiction of Spokane. The next decades were marked by the continuing increase in population, especially with the construction from 1933 to 1942 of the Grand Coulee Dam, which made possible the extensive expansion of agriculture in Yakima.

By 1951 the Catholics of Yakima were deemed ready for the erection of a new diocese. The Holy See detached counties from the Diocese of Spokane and the Archdiocese of Seattle to form the new Diocese of Yakima.

The first bishop of Yakima, Joseph P. Dougherty, was a priest of the Seattle archdiocese. Appointed on July 9, 1951, and consecrated on September 26, 1951, he worked to give the new diocese a firm footing. There were 31,000 Catholics at the time, but this grew by 10,000 over the next years, and Bishop Dougherty started parishes and promoted vocations to the priesthood and religious life. He also started schools and an outreach for the pastoral care of Hispanic Catholics, who were settling in the state or who arrived as migrant workers. In 1958 a parish was established on the Yakima Indian Reservation. Bishop Dougherty invited a number of communities of women religious, including the

Daughters of Charity of St. Vincent de Paul, the Sisters of Charity of Providence, the Dominican Sisters of the Congregation of St. Thomas Aquinas, the Sisters of St. Joseph of Newark, and the Sisters of the Holy Names of Jesus and Mary. They all did vital work in the diocese, especially in the area of education. Bishop Dougherty attended the sessions of the Second Vatican Council and later worked to implement the decrees of the council. He resigned on February 5, 1969, and was appointed an auxiliary bishop of Los Angeles.

The second bishop of Yakima, Cornelius M. Power, had been a priest of the Archdiocese of Seattle. Appointed on February 5, 1969, and consecrated a bishop on May 1, 1969, he worked to continue the implementation of the council. On January 15, 1974, he was named archbishop of Portland.

The third bishop of Yakima, Nicolas E. Walsh, had been a priest of the Archdiocese of Minneapolis. Appointed on January 15, 1974, and consecrated a bishop on October 28, 1974, he served for two years and was appointed an auxiliary bishop of Seattle on August 10, 1976.

The fourth bishop of Yakima, William S. Skylstad, had been a priest of Spokane. Appointed on February 16, 1977, and consecrated a bishop on May 12, he provided steady leadership for the growing diocese while working to prevent declines in vocations. On April 17, 1990, he was appointed bishop of Spokane.

The fifth bishop of Yakima, Francis George, was a priest of the Oblates of Mary Immaculate. Appointed on July 10, 1990, and consecrated a bishop on September 21, 1990, he served for six years as bishop and was then appointed on April 30, 1996, archbishop of Portland. He was later named archbishop of Chicago in 1997 and a cardinal in 1998.

The sixth bishop of Yakima, Carlos A. Sevilla, was a priest of the Society of Jesus and an auxiliary bishop of San Francisco since 1988. Appointed on December 31, 1996, he presided over the continued rise in the Catholic population, including growing numbers of Hispanics. Bishop Sevilla retired on April 12, 2011.

On the same day as Bishop Sevilla's retirement, Bishop Joseph J. Tyson, an auxiliary bishop of Seattle, was appointed bishop of Yakima. In 2011 there were 74,000 Catholics in the diocese, served by 80 priests and 41 parishes.

Yorke, Peter C. (August 15, 1864–April 5, 1925)

A priest, editor, and social activist, Peter C. Yorke was born in Galway, Ireland. He studied at St. Patrick's College in Maynooth and was granted permission to serve as a priest in the Archdiocese of San Francisco. He sailed to the United States, finished his training at St. Mary's Seminary in Baltimore and was ordained on December 17, 1887. He then went to The Catholic University of America, in Washington, D.C., earning a licentiate in sacred theology. He then entered into service in San Francisco.

In 1894 Father Yorke was named editor of *The Monitor,* the archdiocesan newspaper. He soon embarked upon an effort to defend the Church against the attacks of the American Protective Association in the San Francisco area. To advance the defense, he organized the American Women's Liberal League and the Catholic Truth Society of San Francisco. He also was a proponent of the principles of Catholic social doctrine established in Pope Leo XIII's encyclical *Rerum Novarum* in 1891. He thus supported the activities of the Teamsters union in their strike in 1901, and in 1902 founded the weekly newspaper *Leader* to give voice to those advocating labor rights.

A determined advocate of Irish nationalism, Father Yorke used the *Leader* to push for Irish independence, was vice president of the Sinn Fein in the United States, and was honored as the founder of Innesfael, a home for working girls. Likewise, a concern for education earned his appointment as a regent of the University of California and vice president of the National Catholic Educational Association.

Father Yorke wrote *Text Books of Religion* in 1901, which was subsequently used as the standard textbook for religious education in the parochial schools of various dioceses in the Western states. Father Yorke was also the author of *Lectures on Ghosts* (1897), *Roman Liturgy* (1903), *Altar and Priest* (1913), and *The Mass* (1921). In 1906 the Holy See bestowed upon him a doctorate in theology in recognition of his writings. Father Yorke was chancellor of the Archdiocese of San Francisco from 1894 to 1899 and a pastor in several parishes. In addition to his pastoral ministry, he was a popular and much sought after spiritual adviser.

Youngstown, Diocese of

Established on May 15, 1943, by Pope Pius XII, the Diocese of Youngstown serves counties in northeastern Ohio. The diocese is a suffragan see of the Archdiocese of Cincinnati. The city was settled on the Mahoning River near the Pennsylvania border, destined to become a steel and industrial center. Part of the Connecticut Western Reserve, the region was visited by John Young, a surveyor from New York, who bought land from the Reserve in 1797 and started Young's Town. A local trader, Colonel James Hillman, developed the site, which was organized as a town in 1802.

Three years later, James and Daniel Heaton bought a furnace and established an iron foundry in the area. This was soon joined by a steel industry that attracted workers and their families. The opening of the Sault Ste. Marie Canal linked Youngstown to the Upper Great Lakes, and the shipment of ore expanded. Other industries, including aluminum, aircraft, automobile parts, and paper products secured Youngstown's economic base.

The Catholic legacy of Youngstown began early in the nineteenth century when Catholics made their way into Ohio. The small Catholic community was placed under the jurisdiction of the Diocese of Bardstown after its establishment in 1808, as Ohio was part of the diocese's enormous territory. The chief figure in the early days of Catholicism in northeastern Ohio was the Dominican priest Edward D. Fenwick, the future first bishop of Cincinnati, who provided pastoral care to the Catholics in the area and was joined by other Dominicans and pioneering priests. It became apparent that Ohio needed its own ecclesiastical structure, and in 1821 the Diocese of Cincinnati was founded.

In 1847 northeastern Ohio was separated from Cincinnati to form the Diocese of Cleveland. The Catholics of Youngstown remained under the leadership of the bishops of Cleveland for the next century, a time in which the Catholic community underwent massive change. Waves of immigration brought Irish, German, and Slavic Catholics to the region in search of work and new lives.

By 1943 the Catholic community was large enough to prompt Pope Pius XII to establish the Youngstown diocese by removing six northeastern counties from the Diocese of Cleveland. At its founding, there were approximately 150,000 Catholics in 98 parishes, but the industrial strength of the city meant that those numbers would continue to rise.

The first bishop of Youngstown, James A. McFadden, had been auxiliary bishop of Cleveland since 1932. Appointed on June 2, 1943, he worked to establish the administrative needs of the new diocese and started a diocesan newspaper. He died at the age of seventy-one on November 16, 1952.

The second bishop of Youngstown, Emmet M. Walsh, had been bishop of Charleston and had been named coadjutor bishop of Youngstown in 1949. He acceded to the see upon Bishop McFadden's passing and guided the diocese in the period of the Second Vatican Council and its immediate aftermath. He worked to implement the council's reforms. He also built the new Cathedral of St. Columba after the destruction by fire of the old one and opened the first college in the diocese, Walsh College.

On March 24, 1960, James W. Malone, was named the first auxiliary bishop of the diocese and the successor to the see with the passing of Bishop Walsh on March 16, 1968. Appointed on May 2, 1968, Bishop Malone served as shepherd for the diocese for nearly three decades, through the tumultuous period after the Second Vatican Council and the decline of the steel industry in Youngstown. With the infamous September 19, 1977, "Black Monday" closure of a major part of Youngstown's steel industry, the Church provided pastoral resources to assist the hard-hit local workforce that soon lost more than forty thousand jobs. Bishop Malone retired on December 5, 1995.

The fourth bishop of Youngstown, Bishop Thomas J. Tobin, had been an auxiliary bishop of Pittsburgh since 1992. Appointed to Youngstown on February 2, 1996, he served as shepherd during the Great Jubilee of 2000 and also through the dark days of the sexual abuse crisis. He was appointed bishop of Providence on March 31, 2005.

The fifth bishop of Youngstown, Bishop George V. Murry, S.J., had been bishop of St. Thomas in the Virgin Islands since 1999. Appointed to Youngstown on January 30, 2007, he was installed on March 28, 2007. In 2011 there were 201,000 Catholics in the diocese, served by 167 priests, 222 women religious, and 106 parishes.

Zahm, John (June 14, 1851–November 11, 1921)

A Holy Cross priest, theologian, and scientist, John Zahm was born in New Lexington, Ohio. He was the son of a German immigrant, Jacob M. Zahm, and a Pennsylvania native, Mary Ellen Zahm, the grandniece of Major General Edward Braddock. He studied at the University of Notre Dame in Indiana, then entered the Congregation of Holy Cross. Ordained in 1875, he was named immediately to the post of professor of physics at Notre Dame. During his time on the faculty he pushed for improvements in the school's facilities and laboratories. His efforts led to Notre Dame becoming the first Catholic college to boast electrical lighting.

In 1892, after publication of his first book, *Sound and Music*, Father Zahm turned his chief academic focus to the issue of the relationship between religion and science. Over the next years, he lectured extensively on the topic, including a series of speeches in Brussels, Belgium, and Fribourg, Switzerland. Father Zahm's central theme was that there should be no conflict between religion (in particular Catholic doctrine) and science. These views were expounded in two of his most widely read books, *Bible, Science and Faith* in 1894 and *Evolution and Dogma* in 1896; the second book was placed briefly on the Index of Forbidden Books in 1898 during the Americanist controversy.

In 1898 Father Zahm became the provincial of the Congregation of the Holy Cross in the United States. During his term, he worked closely with Archbishop John Ireland and Bishops John Joseph Keane and Denis J. O'Connell to expand the Holy Cross community at Notre Dame and at Holy Cross College at The

Catholic University of America in Washington, D.C. Father Zahm traveled extensively after leaving his post as provincial in 1906, including a trip to South America with former President Theodore Roosevelt. His journey was the subject of a trilogy, *Following the Conquistadores* (1910, 1911, and 1916). He died in Munich, Germany, while finishing *From Berlin to Bagdad and Babylon* (1922).

Zumarraga, Juan de (1468–June 3, 1548)

A Spanish Franciscan, missionary, and the first bishop of Mexico, Juan de Zumarraga was a vigorous opponent of the exploitation of the native population by the Spanish colonial government. Born at Durango in the Basque provinces of Spain, he entered the Franciscan order as a young man. In 1527 Zumarraga was serving as custodian of the convent of Abrojo when Emperor Charles V came for a visit. As a result of this encounter, the emperor appointed him a judge in the courts that had been established to examine the supposed activities of witches. Zumarraga was noted for his sensible approach to the witchcraft hysteria. That same year, Charles nominated Zumarraga to the post of first bishop of Mexico.

He arrived in Mexico in December 1528 and found the Spanish occupation of the region to be a horrifying combination of incompetence and brutality. The native population, in particular the survivors of the fallen Aztec Empire, lived in abject slavery, were punished by severe taxes, and endured humiliations by Spanish colonials officials.

Archbishop Juan de Zumarraga

Zumarraga was determined to serve as the protector of the Indians, but his limited authority posed considerable problems for the achievement of his aims. Chief among his obstacles was the absence of any clearly enumerated powers from the Spanish Imperial Court and the fact that he had not yet received episcopal consecration. He was assisted by his fellow Franciscans but encountered opposition to change from among the secular clergy. While encountering some success in 1529–30, Zumarraga was still opposed sharply by Spanish colonial leaders, who conspired at the court for his removal. Summoned home in 1532 to answer charges, Zumarraga appeared at the Imperial Court and easily refuted the accusations made against him. On April 27, 1533, he was consecrated a bishop and reached Mexico in October 1534 with broad authority to deal with the auditors, those officials who had been in charge of the Indian population.

Bishop Zumarraga was assisted in the new period of leadership by the Franciscans and other religious orders that had sent missionaries to Mexico. Advancing the effort of evangelization was also the apparition of Our Lady of Guadalupe in 1531 to St. Juan Diego, to which Bishop Zumarraga gave his formal approval. The apparition proved of enormous help in converting the native people, so that by 1536 there had been five million baptisms.

Papal support for the Franciscan activities was given by Pope Adrian VI, who issued the bull *Exponi Nobis Fecisti,* handing authority over the missions to the Franciscans. At the same time, Father Bartolomé de las Casas secured from the Spanish government the Nuevas Leyes, the laws that forbade the enslavement of the Indians.

In his later years, Bishop Zumarraga established various schools for Indian girls and the famed Colegio Tlaltelolco. He introduced the first printing press in the New World, which published the first book in the Americas. Bishop Zumarraga also opened hospitals in Mexico City and Vera Cruz. Such was the success of his time as bishop that in 1546 Pope Paul III separated the See of Mexico from the metropolitan See of Seville and established the Archdiocese of Mexico. Zumarraga was named the first archbishop, with the suffragan sees of Oaxaca, Michoacan, Tlaxcala, Guatemala, and Ciudad Real de Chiapas. Sadly, Bishop Zumarraga died the month before the bull was officially promulgated.

APPENDICES

APPENDIX ONE

Missionaries to the Americas

Allouez, Claude Jean (1622–89): French Jesuit; missionary in Canada and Midwestern U.S.; preached to twenty different tribes of Indians and baptized over ten thousand; vicar general of Northwest.

Altham, John (1589–1640): English Jesuit; missionary among Indians in Maryland.

Amadeus of the Heart of Jesus (1846–1920): Provincial Superior of the Ursulines in the United States and missionary in Montana, Wyoming, and Alaska; founded twelve Ursuline missions for Native Americans.

Anchieta, José de, Bl. (1534–97): Portuguese Jesuit, born Canary Islands; missionary in Brazil; writer; beatified, 1980; feast, June 9.

Andreis, Felix de (1778–1820): Italian Vincentian; missionary and educator in Western U.S.

Aparicio, Sebastian, Bl. (1502–1600): Franciscan brother, born Spain; settled in Mexico, c. 1533; worked as road builder and farmer before becoming Franciscan at about the age of 70; beatified, 1787; feast, February 25.

Badin, Stephen T. (1768–1853): French missioner; came to U.S., 1792, when Sulpician seminary in Paris was closed; ordained, 1793, Baltimore, the first priest ordained in U.S.; missionary in Kentucky, Ohio, and Michigan; bought land on which the University of Notre Dame now stands; buried on its campus.

Baraga, Venerable Frederic (1797–1868): Slovenian missionary bishop in U.S.; studied at Ljubljana and Vienna, ordained, 1823; came to U.S., 1830; missionary to Indians of Upper Michigan; first bishop of Marquette, 1857–1868; wrote Chippewa grammar, dictionary, prayer book, and other works.

Bauer, Benedicta (1803–65): Missionary Dominican sister who helped establish convents and schools for German-speaking immigrants in New Jersey, California, Missouri, Washington, and Kansas.

Bertran, Louis, St. (1526–81): Spanish Dominican; missionary in Colombia and Caribbean, 1562-69; canonized, 1671; feast, October 9.

Betancur, Pedro de San José, Bl. (1626–67): Secular Franciscan, born Canary Islands; arrived in Guatemala, 1651; established hospital, school and homes for poor; beatified, 1980; feast, April 25.

Bourgeoys, Marguerite, St. (1620–1700): French foundress, missionary; settled in Canada, 1653; founded Congregation of Notre Dame, 1658; beatified, 1950; canonized, 1982; feast, January 12.

Brébeuf, John de, St. (1593–1649): French Jesuit; missionary among Huron Indians in Canada; martyred by Iroquois, March 16, 1649; canonized, 1930; one of Jesuit North American martyrs; feast, October 19 (U.S.).

Cancer de Barbastro, Louis (1500–49): Spanish Dominican; began missionary work in Middle America, 1533; killed at Tampa Bay, Florida.

Castillo, John de, St. (1596–1628): Spanish Jesuit; worked in Paraguay Indian mission settlements (reductions); martyred; beatified, 1934; canonized, 1988; feast, November 16.

Catala, Magin (1761–1830): Spanish Franciscan; worked in California mission of Santa Clara for thirty-six years.

Chabanel, Noel, St. (1613–49): French Jesuit; missionary among Huron Indians in Canada; murdered by renegade Huron, December 8, 1649; canonized, 1930; one of Jesuit North American martyrs; feast, Octtober 19 (U.S.).

Chaumonot, Pierre Joseph (1611–93): French Jesuit; missionary among Indians in Canada.

Clarke, Mary Frances (1803–87): Founder of the Sisters of Charity of the Blessed Virgin Mary; went to Iowa to start schools for children of white farmers and Native Americans; in Iowa Women's Hall of Fame.

Claver, Peter, St. (1581–1654): Spanish Jesuit; missionary among Negroes of South America and West Indies; canonized, 1888; patron of Catholic missions among black people; feast, September 9.

Cope, Marianne, St. (1838–1918): German-born immigrant; entered Sisters of St. Francis; led sisters to Hawaii to take over a hospital and then to Molokai to care for lepers, including Bl. Damien de Veuster; cared for women and young girls with the disease; beatified, 2005; canonized, 2012; feast, August 9.

Daniel, Anthony, St. (1601–48): French Jesuit; missionary among Huron Indians in Canada; martyred by Iroquois, July 4, 1648; canonized, 1930; one of Jesuit North American martyrs; feast, October 19 (U.S.).

De Smet, Pierre Jean (1801–73): Belgian-born Jesuit; missionary among Indians of Northwestern U.S.; served as intermediary between Indians and U.S. government; wrote on Indian culture.

Duchesne, Rose Philippine, St. (1769–1852): French nun; educator and missionary in the U.S.; established first convent of the Society of the Sacred Heart in the U.S., at St. Charles, Missouri; founded schools for girls; did missionary work among Indians; beatified, 1940; canonized, 1988; feast, November 18 (U.S.).

Farmer, Ferdinand (family name, Steinmeyer) (1720–86): German Jesuit; missionary in Philadelphia, where he died; one of the first missionaries in New Jersey.

Flaget, Benedict J. (1763–1850): French Sulpician bishop; came to U.S., 1792; missionary and educator in U.S.; first bishop of Bardstown (now Louisville), 1810–32; 1833–50.

Frances Xavier Cabrini, St. (1850–1917): The first American citizen to be canonized; honored as the patron saint of immigrants, she founded the Missionary Sisters of the Sacred Heart of Jesus (M.S.C.) in 1880 and brought the congregation to the U.S. in 1889; feast, December 22.

Friess, Caroline (1824–92): Mother superior of the School Sisters of Notre Dame in America, 1850–92; through her labors, the sisters opened 265 parochial schools in 29 dioceses and four institutes of higher education for women.

Gallitzin, Demetrius (1770–1840): Russian prince, born, The Hague; convert, 1787; ordained priest at Baltimore, 1795; frontier missionary, known as Father Smith; Gallitzin, Pennsylvania, named for him; cause for canonization opened in 2005.

Garnier, Charles, St. (c. 1606–49): French Jesuit; missionary among Hurons in Canada; martyred by Iroquois, December 7, 1649; canonized, 1930; one of Jesuit North American martyrs; feast, October 19 (U.S.).

Gibault, Pierre (1737–1804): Canadian missionary in Illinois and Indiana; aided in securing states of Ohio, Indiana, Illinois, Michigan, and Wisconsin for the Americans during Revolution.

Gonzalez, Roch, St. (1576–1628): Paraguayan Jesuit; worked in Paraguay Indian mission settlements (reductions); martyred; beatified, 1934; canonized, 1988; feast, November 16.

Goupil, René, St. (1607–42): French lay missionary; had studied surgery at Orleans, France; missionary companion of St. Isaac Jogues among the Hurons; martyred, September 29, 1642; canonized, 1930; one of Jesuit North American martyrs; feast, October 19 (U.S.).

Gravier, Jacques (1651–1708): French Jesuit; missionary among Indians of Canada and Midwestern U.S.

Guérin, St. Theodore (1798–1856): Pioneer educator and Sister of Providence; arrived in U.S. in 1830 and founded St. Mary-of-the-Woods in Vincennes, Indiana; canonized, 2006; feast, October 3.

Hennepin, Louis (d. c. 1701): Belgian-born Franciscan missionary and explorer of Great Lakes region and Upper Mississippi, 1675–81, when he returned to Europe.

Ireland, Seraphine (1842–1930): Mother superior of the Sisters of St. Joseph in the upper Midwest; opened thirty schools, five hospitals, and the College of St. Catherine, the second Catholic college for women in the U.S.

Jesuit North American Martyrs: Isaac Jogues, Anthony Daniel, John de Brébeuf, Gabriel Lalemant, Charles Garnier, Noel Chabanel (Jesuit priests), and René Goupil and John Lalande (lay missionaries) who were martyred between September 29, 1642, and December 9, 1649, in the missions of New France; canonized, 1930; feast, October 19 (U.S.).

Jogues, Isaac, St. (1607–46): French Jesuit; missionary among Indians in Canada; martyred near present-day site of Auriesville, New York, by Mohawks, October 18, 1646; canonized, 1930; one of Jesuit North American Martyrs; feast, October 19 (U.S.).

Kino, Eusebio (1645–1711): Italian Jesuit; missionary and explorer in U.S.; arrived Southwest, 1681;

established twenty-five Indian missions; took part in fourteen exploring expeditions in northern Mexico, Arizona, and Southern California; helped develop livestock raising and farming in the area; selected to represent Arizona in Statuary Hall, 1965.

Lalande, John, St. (d. 1646): French lay missionary, companion of Isaac Jogues; martyred by Mohawks at Auriesville, New York, October 19, 1646; canonized, 1930; one of Jesuit North American Martyrs; feast, October 19 (U.S.).

Lalemant, Gabriel, St. (1610–49): French Jesuit; missionary among the Hurons in Canada; martyred by the Iroquois, March 17, 1649; canonized, 1930; one of Jesuit North American Martyrs; feast, October 19 (U.S.).

Lalor, Teresa (d. 1846): Co-founder, with Bishop Neale of Baltimore, of the Visitation Order in the U.S.; helped establish houses in Mobile, Alabama, Kaskaskia, Illinois, and Baltimore.

Lamy, Jean Baptiste (1814–88): French prelate; came to U.S., 1839; missionary in Ohio and Kentucky; bishop in Southwest from 1850; first bishop (later Archbishop) of Santa Fe, 1850–85; nominated to represent New Mexico in Statuary Hall, 1951.

Las Casas, Bartolome (1474–1566): Spanish Dominican; missionary in Haiti, Jamaica, and Venezuela; reformer of abuses against Indians and black people; bishop of Chalapas, Mexico, 1544–47; historian.

Laval, Françoise de Montmorency, Bl. (1623–1708): French-born missionary bishop in Canada; named vicar apostolic of Canada, 1658; first bishop of Québec, 1674; jurisdiction extended over all French-claimed territory in New World; beatified, 1980; feast, May 6.

Manogue, Patrick (1831–95): Missionary bishop in U.S., born Ireland; miner in California; studied for priesthood at St. Mary's of the Lake, Chicago, and St. Sulpice, Paris; ordained, 1861; missionary among Indians of California and Nevada; coadjutor bishop, 1881–84, and bishop, 1884–86, of Grass Valley; first bishop of Sacramento, 1886–95, when see was transferred there.

Margil, Antonio, Ven. (1657–1726): Spanish Franciscan; missionary in Middle America; apostle of Guatemala; established missions in Texas.

Marie of the Incarnation, St. (Marie Guyard Martin) (1599–1672): French widow; joined Ursuline Nuns; arrived in Canada, 1639; first superior of Ursulines in Québec; missionary to Indians; writer; beatified, 1980; feast, April 30.

Marquette, Jacques (1637–75): French Jesuit; missionary and explorer in America; sent to New France, 1666; began missionary work among Ottawa Indians on Lake Superior, 1668; accompanied Louis Joliet down the Mississippi River to mouth of the Arkansas River, 1673, and returned to Lake Michigan by way of Illinois River; made a second trip over the same route; his diary and map are of historical significance; selected to represent Wisconsin in Statuary Hall, 1895.

Massias (Macias), John de, St. (1585–1645): Dominican brother; native of Spain; entered Dominican Friary at Lima, Peru, 1622; served as doorkeeper until his death; beatified, 1837; canonized, 1975; feast, September 16.

Mazzuchelli, Samuel C. (1806–64): Italian Dominican; missionary in Midwestern U.S.; called builder of the West; writer.; decree advancing beatification cause promulgated, 1993.

Membre, Zenobius (1645–87): French Franciscan; missionary among Indians of Illinois; accompanied LaSalle expedition down the Mississippi River (1681–82) in expedition that ended in Texas; murdered by Indians.

Mozcygemba, Leopold (1824–91): Polish Franciscan priest and missionary; patriarch of American Polonia; labored as a missionary in Texas and eleven other states for nearly forty years; co-founded the Polish seminary of Sts. Cyril and Methodius in Detroit, 1885; served as confessor at Vatican Council I.

Nerinckx, Charles (1761–1824): Belgian priest; missionary in Kentucky; founded Sisters of Loretto at the Foot of the Cross.

Nobrega, Manoel (1517–70): Portuguese Jesuit; leader of first Jesuit missionaries to Brazil, 1549.

Padilla, Juan de (d. 1542): Spanish Franciscan; missionary among Indians of Mexico and Southwestern U.S.; killed by Indians in Kansas; protomartyr of the U.S.

Palou, Francisco (c. 1722–89): Spanish Franciscan; accompanied Junípero Serra to Mexico, 1749; founded Mission Dolores in San Francisco; wrote history of the Franciscans in California.

Pariseau, Mary Joseph (1833–1902): Canadian Sister of Charity of Providence; missionary in state of

Washington from 1856; founded first hospitals in Northwest Territory; artisan and architect; represents Washington in National Statuary Hall.

Peter of Ghent (d. 1572): Belgian Franciscan brother; missionary in Mexico for 49 years.

Porres, Martin de, St. (1579–1639): Peruvian Dominican oblate; father was a Spanish soldier and mother a black freedwoman from Panama; called wonder worker of Peru; beatified, 1837; canonized, 1962; feast, November 3.

Quiroga, Vasco de (1470–1565): Spanish missionary in Mexico; founded hospitals; bishop of Michoacan, 1537.

Ravalli, Antonio (1811–84): Italian Jesuit; missionary in Western U.S., mostly Montana, for forty years.

Raymbaut, Charles (1602–43): French Jesuit; missionary among Indians of Canada and Northern U.S.

Richard, Gabriel (1767–1832): French Sulpician; missionary in Illinois and Michigan; a founder of University of Michigan; elected delegate to Congress from Michigan, 1823; first priest to hold seat in the House of Representatives.

Riepp, Benedicta (1825–62): Founder of the first Benedictine community of nuns in the U.S.; by the time of her death, the order had founded convents in Illinois, Kentucky, Minnesota, and New Jersey.

Rodriguez, Alfonso, St. (1598–1628): Spanish Jesuit; missionary in Paraguay; martyred; beatified, 1934; canonized, 1988; feast, November 16.

Rosati, Joseph (1789–1843): Italian Vincentian; missionary bishop in U.S. (vicar apostolic of Mississippi and Alabama, 1822; coadjutor bishop of Louisiana and the Two Floridas, 1823–26; administrator of New Orleans, 1826–29; first bishop of St. Louis, 1826–1843.

Russell, Mary Baptist (1829–98): Mother Superior of the Sisters of Mercy in San Francisco, 1854–98; founded St. Mary's Hospital in 1857, schools, and homes for the aged and former prostitutes.

Sahagun, Bernardino de (c. 1500–90): Spanish Franciscan; missionary in Mexico for over 60 years; expert on Aztec archaeology.

Seelos, Bl. Francis X. (1819–67): Redemptorist missionary; born, Bavaria; ordained, 1844, at Baltimore; missionary in Pittsburgh and New Orleans; beatified, 2000.

Seghers, Charles J. (1839–86): Belgian missionary bishop in North America; Apostle of Alaska; Archbishop of Oregon City (now Portland), 1880–84; murdered by berserk companion while on missionary journey.

Serra, Junípero, Bl. (1713-84): Spanish Franciscan; born, Majorca; missionary in America; arrived Mexico, 1749, where he did missionary work for twenty years; began work in Upper California in 1769 and established nine of the twenty-one Franciscan missions along the Pacific Coast; baptized some 6,000 Indians and confirmed almost 5,000; represents California in Statuary Hall; declared venerable 1985; beatified, 1988; feast, July 1 (U.S.).

Solanus, Francis, St. (1549–1610): Spanish Franciscan; missionary in Paraguay, Argentina, and Peru; wonderworker of the New World; canonized, 1726; feast, July 14.

Sorin, Edward F. (1814–93): French priest; member of Congregation of Holy Cross; sent to U.S. in 1841; founder and first president of the University of Notre Dame; missionary in Indiana and Michigan.

Todadilla, Anthony de (1704–46): Spanish Capuchin; missionary to Indians of Venezuela; killed by Motilones.

Turibius de Mogrovejo, St. (1538–1606): Spanish Archbishop of Lima, Peru, c. 1580–1606; canonized, 1726; feast, March 23.

Twelve Apostles of Mexico (early sixteenth century): Franciscan priests who arrived in Mexico, 1524: Fathers Martin de Valencia (leader), Francisco de Soto, Martin de la Coruna, Juan Suares, Antonio de Ciudad Rodrigo, Toribio de Benevente, Garcia de Cisneros, Luis de Fuensalida, Juan de Ribas, Francisco Ximenes; Brothers Andres de Coroboda, and Juan de Palos.

Valdivia, Luis de (1561–1641): Spanish Jesuit; defender of Indians in Peru and Chile.

Vasques de Espiñosa, Antonio (early seventeenth century): Spanish Carmelite; missionary and explorer in Mexico, Panama, and western coast of South America.

Vieira, Antonio (1608–87): Portuguese Jesuit; preacher; missionary in Peru and Chile; protector of Indians against exploitation by slave owners and traders; considered foremost prose writer of seventeenth-century Portugal.

Ward, Mary Francis Xavier (1810–84): Established the Sisters of Mercy in U.S.; arrived in Pittsburgh in 1843; founded convents in ten states to care for the sick and poor and provide education.

White, Andrew (1579–1656): English Jesuit; missionary among Indians in Maryland.

Wimmer, Boniface (1809–87): German Benedictine; missionary among German immigrants in the U.S.

Youville, Marie Marguerite d', St. (1701–71): Canadian widow; foundress of Sisters of Charity (Grey Nuns), 1737, at Montréal; beatified, 1959; canonized, 1990, first native Canadian saint; feast, December 23.

Zumarraga, Juan de (1468–1548): Spanish Franciscan; missionary; first bishop of Mexico; introduced first printing press in New World; published first book in America, a catechism for Aztec Indians; extended missions in Mexico and Central America; vigorous opponent of exploitation of Indians; approved of devotions at Guadalupe; leading figure in early Church history in Mexico.

APPENDIX TWO

Saints of the Americas

The following individuals have been canonized, beatified, or declared venerable. The date of their canonization is included in parentheses.

Saints

Three members of the eight North American Martyrs (1930): St. Isaac Jogues, S.J., St. René Goupil, S.J., and St. Jean de Lalande, S.J.

St. Frances Xavier Cabrini, M.S.C. (1946).
St. Elizabeth Ann Seton, S.C. (1975).
St. John Neumann, C.Ss.R. (1977).
St. Rose Philippine Duchesne, R.S.C.J. (1988).
St. Katharine Drexel, S.B.S. (2000).
St. Mother Théodore Guérin, S.P. (2006).
St. Damien de Veuster of Molokai, SS.CC. (2009).
St. Kateri Tekakwitha (2012).
St. Marianne Cope, O.S.F. (2012).
St. Pedro Calungsod (2012).

Blesseds

Blessed Carlos Manuel Rodriguez.
Blessed Diego Luis de San Vitores, S.J.
Blessed Francis Xavier Seelos, C.Ss.R.
Blessed Junípero Serra, O.F.M.

Venerables

Venerable Antonio of Jesus, O.F.M.
Venerable Nelson Baker.
Venerable Frederic Baraga.
Venerable Solanus Casey, O.F.M. Cap.
Venerable Cornelia Connelly, S.H.C.J.
Venerable Henriette DeLille, S.H.F.
Venerable Mother Mary Theresa Dudzik, O.S.F.
Venerable Mother Maria Kaupas, S.S.C.
Venerable Samuel Charles Mazzuchelli, O.P.
Venerable Mary Angeline Teresa McCrory.
Venerable Michael McGivney.
Venerable Miriam Teresa (Teresa Demjanovich).
Venerable Fulton J. Sheen.
Venerable Pierre Toussaint.
Venerable Félix Varela.

APPENDIX THREE

Catholics in Statuary Hall

Statues of thirteen Catholics deemed worthy of national commemoration are among those enshrined in National Statuary Hall and other places in the U.S. Capitol. The Hall, formerly the chamber of the House of Representatives, was erected by Act of Congress July 2, 1864.

Donating states, names, and years of placement are listed.

Arizona: Rev. Eusebio Kino, S.J., missionary, 1965.

California: Rev. Junípero Serra, O.F.M. missionary, 1931. (Beatified 1988.)

Hawaii: Fr. Damien, missionary, 1969. (Beatified, 1995; canonized, 2009.)

Illinois: Gen. James Shields, statesman, 1893.

Louisiana: Edward D. White, justice of the U.S. Supreme Court (1894–1921), 1955.

Maryland: Charles Carroll, statesman, 1901.

Nevada: Patrick A. McCarran, statesman, 1960.

New Mexico: Dennis Chavez, statesman, 1966. (Archbishop Jean B. Lamy, pioneer prelate of Santa Fe, was nominated for Statuary Hall honor in 1951.)

North Dakota: John Burke, U.S. treasurer, 1963.

Oregon: Dr. John McLoughlin, pioneer, 1953.

Washington: Mother Mary Joseph Pariseau, pioneer missionary and humanitarian.

West Virginia: John E. Kenna, statesman, 1901.

Wisconsin: Rev. Jacques Marquette, S.J., missionary, explorer, 1895.

Cathedrals, Basilicas, and Shrines in the U.S.

CATHEDRALS IN THE UNITED STATES
As of 2012. (Archdioceses are indicated by asterisk.)

Albany, NY: Immaculate Conception.

Alexandria, LA: St. Francis Xavier.

Allentown, PA: St. Catherine of Siena.

AltoonaJohnstown, PA: Blessed Sacrament (Altoona); St. John Gualbert (Johnstown).

Amarillo, TX: St. Laurence.

Anchorage,* AK: Holy Family.

Apostolic Exarchate for Armenian Catholics in the U.S. and Canada: St. Ann, New York, NY.

Arlington, VA: St. Thomas More.

Atlanta,* GA: Christ the King.

Austin, TX: St. Mary (Immaculate Conception).

Baker, OR: St. Francis de Sales.

Baltimore,* MD: Mary Our Queen; Basilica of the National Shrine of the Assumption of the Blessed Virgin Mary (co-cathedral).

Baton Rouge, LA: St. Joseph.

Beaumont, TX: St. Anthony (of Padua).

Belleville, IL: St. Peter.

Biloxi, MS: Nativity of the Blessed Virgin Mary.

Birmingham, AL: St. Paul.

Bismarck, N.D.: Holy Spirit.

Boise, ID: St. John the Evangelist.

Boston,* MA: Holy Cross.

Bridgeport, CT: St. Augustine.

Brooklyn, NY: St. James (minor basilica).

Brownsville, TX: Immaculate Conception.

Buffalo, NY: St. Joseph.

Burlington, VT: Immaculate Conception; St. Joseph (co-cathedral).

Camden, NJ: Immaculate Conception.

Charleston, SC: St. John the Baptist.

Charlotte, NC: St. Patrick.

Cheyenne, WY: St. Mary.

Chicago,* IL: Holy Name (of Jesus).

Cincinnati,* OH: St. Peter in Chains.

Cleveland, OH: St. John the Evangelist.

Colorado Springs, CO: St. Mary.

Columbus, OH: St. Joseph.

Corpus Christi, TX: Corpus Christi.

Covington, KY: Basilica of the Assumption.

Crookston, MN: Immaculate Conception.

Dallas, TX: Cathedral Santuario de Guadalupe.

Davenport, IA: Sacred Heart.

Denver,* CO: Immaculate Conception (Minor Basilica).

Des Moines, IA: St. Ambrose.

Detroit,* MI: Most Blessed Sacrament.

Dodge City, KS: Our Lady of Guadalupe.

Dubuque,* IA: St. Raphael.

Duluth, MN: Our Lady of the Rosary.

El Paso, TX: St. Patrick.

Erie, PA: St. Peter.

Evansville, IN: Most Holy Trinity (pro-cathedral).

Fairbanks, AK: Sacred Heart.

Fall River, MA: St. Mary of the Assumption.

Fargo, ND: St. Mary.

Fort Wayne-South Bend, IN: Immaculate Conception (Fort Wayne); St. Matthew (co-cathedral, South Bend).

Fort Worth, TX: St. Patrick.

Fresno, CA: St. John (the Baptist).

Gallup, NM: Sacred Heart.

Galveston-Houston, TX: St. Mary (minor basilica,

Galveston); Sacred Heart co-cathedral (Houston).

Gary, IN: Holy Angels.

Gaylord, MI: St. Mary, Our Lady of Mount Carmel.

Grand Island, NE: Nativity of Blessed Virgin Mary.

Grand Rapids, MI: St. Andrew.

Great Falls-Billings, MT: St. Ann (Great Falls); St. Patrick co-cathedral (Billings).

Green Bay, WI: St. Francis Xavier.

Greensburg, PA: Blessed Sacrament.

Harrisburg, PA: St. Patrick.

Hartford,* CT: St. Joseph.

Helena, MT: St. Helena.

Honolulu, HI: Our Lady of Peace; St. Theresa of the Child Jesus (co-cathedral).

Houma-Thibodaux, LA: St. Francis de Sales (Houma); St. Joseph (co-cathedral, Thibodaux).

Indianapolis,* IN: Sts. Peter and Paul.

Jackson, MS: St. Peter.

Jefferson City, MO: St. Joseph.

Joliet, IL: St. Raymond Nonnatus.

Juneau, AK: Nativity of the Blessed Virgin Mary.

Kalamazoo, MI: St. Augustine.

Kansas City,* KS: St. Peter the Apostle.

Kansas City-St. Joseph, MO: Immaculate Conception (Kansas City); St. Joseph (co-cathedral, St. Joseph).

Knoxville, TN: Sacred Heart of Jesus.

La Crosse, WI: St. Joseph the Workman.

Lafayette, IN: St. Mary.

Lafayette, LA: St. John the Evangelist.

Lake Charles, LA: Immaculate Conception.

Lansing, MI: St. Mary.

Laredo, TX: San Augustin.

Las Cruces, NM: Immaculate Heart of Mary.

Las Vegas, NV: Guardian Angel.

Lexington, KY: Christ the King.

Lincoln, NE: Cathedral of the Risen Christ.

Little Rock, AR: St. Andrew.

Los Angeles,* CA: Cathedral of Our Lady of the Angels of Los Angeles.

Louisville,* KY: Assumption.

Lubbock, TX: Christ the King.

Madison, WI: St. Raphael.

Manchester, NH: St. Joseph.

Marquette, MI: St. Peter.

Memphis, TN: Immaculate Conception.

Metuchen, NJ: St. Francis (of Assisi).

Miami,* FL: St. Mary (Immaculate Conception).

Milwaukee,* WI: St. John.

Mobile,* AL: Immaculate Conception (minor basilica).

Monterey, CA: San Carlos Borromeo.

Nashville, TN: Incarnation.

Newark,* NJ: Sacred Heart (minor basilica).

New Orleans,* LA: St. Louis. (minor basilica)

Newton, MA (Melkite): Our Lady of the Annunciation (Boston).

New Ulm, MN: Holy Trinity.

New York,* NY: St. Patrick.

Norwich, CT: St. Patrick.

Oakland, CA: St. Francis de Sales.

Ogdensburg, NY: St. Mary (Immaculate Conception).

Oklahoma City,* OK: Our Lady of Perpetual Help.

Omaha,* NE: St. Cecilia.

Orange, CA: Holy Family.

Orlando, FL: St. James.

Our Lady of Deliverance of Newark, New Jersey, for Syrian Rite Catholics in the U.S. and Canada: Our Lady of Deliverance.

Our Lady of Lebanon of Los Angeles, CA (Maronite): Our Lady of Mt. Lebanon-St. Peter.

Owensboro, KY: St. Stephen.

Palm Beach, FL: St. Ignatius Loyola, Palm Beach Gardens.

Parma, OH (Byzantine): St. John the Baptist.

Passaic, NJ (Byzantine): St. Michael.

Paterson, NJ: St. John the Baptist.

Pensacola-Tallahassee, FL: Sacred Heart (Pensacola); St. Thomas More (co-cathedral, Tallahassee).

Peoria, IL: St. Mary.

Philadelphia,* PA: Sts. Peter and Paul (minor basilica).

Philadelphia,* PA (Byzantine): Immaculate Conception of Blessed Virgin Mary.

Phoenix, AZ: Sts. Simon and Jude.

Pittsburgh,* PA (Byzantine): St. John the Baptist, Munhall.

Pittsburgh, PA: St. Paul.

Portland, ME: Immaculate Conception.

Portland,* OR: Immaculate Conception.

Providence, RI: Sts. Peter and Paul.

Pueblo, CO: Sacred Heart.

Raleigh, NC: Sacred Heart.

Rapid City, SD: Our Lady of Perpetual Help.

Reno, NV: St. Thomas Aquinas.

Richmond, VA: Sacred Heart.

Rochester, NY: Sacred Heart.

Rockford, IL: St. Peter.

Rockville Centre, NY: St. Agnes.

Sacramento, CA: Blessed Sacrament.

Saginaw, MI: St. Mary.

St. Augustine, FL: St. Augustine (Minor Basilica).

St. Cloud, MN: St. Mary.

St. George's in Canton, OH (Byzantine, Romanian): St. George.

St. Josaphat in Parma, OH (Byzantine): St. Josaphat.

St. Louis,* MO: St. Louis.

St. Maron, Brooklyn, NY (Maronite): Our Lady of Lebanon.

St. Nicholas in Chicago (Byzantine): St. Nicholas.

St. Paul and Minneapolis,* MN: St. Paul (St. Paul); Basilica of St. Mary (co-cathedral, Minneapolis).

St. Petersburg, FL: St. Jude the Apostle.

St. Thomas the Apostle of Detroit (Chaldean): Our Lady of Chaldeans Cathedral (Mother of God Church), Southfield, MI.

St. Thomas of Chicago (Syro-Malabar): Mar Thoma Shleeha Church.

Salina, KS: Sacred Heart.

Salt Lake City, UT: The Madeleine.

San Angelo, TX: Sacred Heart.

San Antonio,* TX: San Fernando.

San Bernardino, CA: Our Lady of the Rosary.

San Diego, CA: St. Joseph.

San Francisco,* CA: St. Mary (Assumption).

San Jose, CA: St. Joseph (minor basilica); St. Patrick (proto-cathedral.

Santa Fe,* NM: San Francisco de Asis (minor basilica.

Santa Rosa, CA: St. Eugene.

Savannah, GA: St. John the Baptist.

Scranton, PA: St. Peter.

Seattle,* WA: St. James.

Shreveport, LA: St. John Berchmans.

Sioux City, IA: Epiphany.

Sioux Falls, SD: St. Joseph.

Spokane, WA: Our Lady of Lourdes.

Springfield, IL: Immaculate Conception.

Springfield, MA: St. Michael.

Springfield-Cape Girardeau, MO: St. Agnes (Springfield): St. Mary (Cape Girardeau).

Stamford, CT (Byzantine): St. Vladimir.

Steubenville, OH: Holy Name.

Stockton, CA: Annunciation.

Superior, WI: Christ the King.

Syracuse, NY: Immaculate Conception.

Syro-Malankara Exarchate: St. John Chrysostom (pro-cathedral).

Toledo, OH: Queen of the Most Holy Rosary.

Trenton, NJ: St. Mary (Assumption).

Tucson, AZ: St. Augustine.

Tulsa, OK: Holy Family.

Tyler, TX: Immaculate Conception.

Van Nuys, CA (Byzantine): St. Mary (Patronage of the Mother of God), Van Nuys; St. Stephen's (pro-cathedral), Phoenix, AZ

Venice, Fla: Epiphany.

Victoria, TX: Our Lady of Victory.

Washington,* DC: St. Matthew.

Wheeling-Charleston, WV: St. Joseph (Wheeling); Sacred Heart (Charleston).

Wichita, KS: Immaculate Conception.

Wilmington, DE: St. Peter.

Winona, MN: Sacred Heart.

Worcester, MA: St. Paul.

Yakima, WA: St. Paul.

Youngstown, OH: St. Columba.

BASILICAS IN THE UNITED STATES

Basilica is a title assigned to certain churches because of their antiquity, dignity, historical importance, or significance as centers of worship. Major basilicas have the papal altar and holy door, which is opened at the beginning of a Jubilee Year; minor basilicas enjoy certain ceremonial privileges.

Among the major basilicas are the patriarchal basilicas of St. John Lateran, St. Peter, St. Paul Outside the Walls, and St. Mary Major in Rome; St. Francis and St. Mary of the Angels in Assisi, Italy. The patriarchal basilica of St. Lawrence, Rome, is a minor basilica. The dates in the listings below indicate when the churches were designated as basilicas (as of 2012).

Minor Basilicas in U.S., Puerto Rico, Guam

Alabama: Mobile, Cathedral of the Immaculate Conception (March 10, 1962).

Arizona: Phoenix, St. Mary's (Immaculate Conception) (September 2, 1985).

California: San Francisco, Mission Dolores (February 6, 1952); Carmel, Old Mission of San Carlos (February 5, 1960); Alameda, St. Joseph (January 21, 1972); San Diego, Mission San Diego de Alcala (November 17, 1975); San Jose, St. Joseph (Jan. 28, 1997); San Juan Capistrano, Mission Basilica of San Juan Capistrano (February 14, 2000).

Colorado: Denver, Cathedral of the Immaculate Conception (November 3, 1979).

Connecticut: Waterbury, Basilica of the Immaculate Conception (February 9, 2008); Bridgeport, Basilica of St. John the Evangelist (June 16, 2009).

District of Columbia: National Shrine of the Immaculate Conception (October 12, 1990).

Florida: St. Augustine, Cathedral of St. Augustine (December 4, 1976); Daytona Beach, Basilica of St. Paul (January 25, 2006); Orlando, Basilica of the National Shrine of Mary, Queen of the Universe (June 3, 2009).

Illinois: Chicago, Our Lady of Sorrows (May 4, 1956); Queen of All Saints (March 26, 1962); Basilica of St. Hyacinth (November 30, 2003).

Indiana: Vincennes, Old Cathedral (March 14, 1970); Notre Dame, Basilica of the Most Sacred Heart, University of Notre Dame (November 23, 1991).

Iowa: Dyersville, St. Francis Xavier (May 11, 1956); Des Moines, St. John the Apostle (August 10, 1989).

Kentucky: Trappist, Our Lady of Gethsemani (March 22, 1949); Covington, Cathedral of Assumption (October 19, 1953); Bardstown, St. Joseph Proto-Cathedral Basilica (2001).

Louisiana: Alexandria, Basilica of the Immaculate Conception (February 22, 2009); New Orleans, St. Louis King of France (December 9, 1964).

Maine: Lewiston, Basilica of Sts. Peter and Paul (May 22, 2005).

Maryland: Baltimore, Assumption of the Blessed Virgin Mary (July 14, 1937; designated national shrine, 1993); Emmitsburg, Shrine of St. Elizabeth Ann Seton (February 13, 1991).

Massachusetts: Boston, Perpetual Help ("Mission Church") (September 8, 1954); Chicopee, St. Stanislaus (June 25, 1991); Webster, St. Joseph (October 1998).

Michigan: Grand Rapids, St. Adalbert (August 22, 1979).

Minnesota: Minneapolis, St. Mary (January 18, 1926).

Mississippi: Natchez, St. Mary Basilica (September 8, 1998).

Missouri: Conception, Basilica of Immaculate Conception (August 8, 1940); St. Louis, St. Louis King of France (January 27, 1961).

New Jersey: Newark, Cathedral Basilica of the Sacred Heart (December 22, 1995).

New Mexico: Mesilla, Basilica of San Albino (June 2008); Santa Fe, Cathedral Basilica of St. Francis of Assisi (October 4, 2005).

New York: Brooklyn, Our Lady of Perpetual Help (September 5, 1969), Cathedral-Basilica of St. James (May 6, 1982); Buffalo, St. Adalbert Basilica (August 11, 1907); Lackawanna, Our Lady of Victory (July 14, 1926); Youngstown, Blessed Virgin Mary of the Rosary of Fatima (October 7, 1975); Syracuse, Sacred Heart of Jesus (August 27, 1998).

North Carolina: Asheville, St. Lawrence (April 6, 1993; Belmont, Our Lady Help of Christians (July 27, 1998).

North Dakota: Jamestown, St. James (October 26, 1988).

Ohio: Carey, Shrine of Our Lady of Consolation (October 21, 1971).

Pennsylvania: Latrobe, St. Vincent Basilica, Benedictine Archabbey (August 22, 1955); Conewago, Basilica of the Sacred Heart (June 30, 1962); Philadelphia, Sts. Peter and Paul (September 27, 1976); Danville, Sts. Cyril and Methodius (chapel at the motherhouse of the Sisters of Sts. Cyril and Methodius) (June 30, 1989); Loretto, St. Michael the Archangel (September 9, 1996); Scranton, National Shrine of St. Ann (October 18, 1997).

Texas: Galveston, St. Mary Cathedral (August 2, 1979); San Antonio, Basilica of the National Shrine of the Little Flower (September 27, 1931); Basilica of Our Lady of San Juan del Valle-National Shrine (May 2, 1954); Beaumont, St. Anthony Cathedral Basilica (August 2006).

Virginia: Norfolk, St. Mary of the Immaculate Conception (July 9, 1991).

West Virginia: Wheeling, Basilica of the Co-Cathedral of the Sacred Heart (November 9, 2009).

Wisconsin: Milwaukee, St. Josaphat (March 10, 1929); Hubertus, Holy Hill National Shrine of Mary, Help of Christians (November 19, 2006).

Puerto Rico: San Juan, Cathedral of San Juan (January 25, 1978).

Guam: Agana, Cathedral of Dulce Nombre de Maria (Sweet Name of Mary) (1985).

Basilica of the Shrine of the Immaculate Conception: Designated a minor basilica by Pope John Paul II October 12, 1990; eighth-largest religious building in the world and the largest Catholic church in the Western Hemisphere, with numerous special chapels and normal accommodations for 6,000 people.

SHRINES AND PLACES OF HISTORIC INTEREST IN THE U.S.
(Principal source: Catholic Almanac *survey.)*

Oranized by state are shrines, other centers of devotion, and some places of historical interest with special significance for Catholics. The list is necessarily incomplete because of space limitations.

Information includes, where possible: name and location of shrine or place of interest, date of foundation, sponsoring agency or group, and address for more information. All information as of 2012.

Alabama: Our Lady of the Angels, Hanceville.
- St. Jude Church of the City of St. Jude, Montgomery (1934; dedicated, 1938).
- Shrine of the Most Blessed Trinity, Holy Trinity (1924).

Arizona: Chapel of the Holy Cross, Sedona (1956).
- Mission San Xavier del Bac, near Tucson (1692).
- Shrine of St. Joseph of the Mountains, Yarnell (1939).

California: Mission San Diego de Alcala (July 16, 1769).
- Carmel Mission Basilica (Mission San Carlos Borromeo del Rio Carmelo), Carmel by the Sea (June 3, 1770).
- Old Mission San Luis Obispo de Tolosa, San Luis Obispo (Sept. 1, 1772).
- San Gabriel Mission, San Gabriel (Sept. 8, 1771).

- Mission San Francisco de Asis (Oct. 9, 1776) and Mission Dolores Basilica (1860s).
- Old Mission San Juan Capistrano, San Juan Capistrano (Nov. 1, 1776).
- Old Mission Santa Barbara, Santa Barbara (Dec. 4, 1786).
- Old Mission San Juan Bautista, San Juan Bautista (June 24, 1797).
- Mission San Miguel, San Miguel (July 25, 1797).
- Old Mission Santa Inés, Solvang (1804).
- Shrine of Our Lady of Sorrows, Sycamore (1883).

Colorado: Mother Cabrini Shrine, Golden.

Connecticut: Shrine of Our Lady of Lourdes, Litchfield (1958).

- Shrine of the Infant of Prague, New Haven (1945).

District of Columbia: Mount St. Sepulchre, Franciscan Monastery of the Holy Land (1897; church dedicated, 1899).
- Basilica of the National Shrine of the Immaculate Conception.

Florida: Mary, Queen of the Universe Shrine, Orlando (1986, temporary facilities; new shrine dedicated, 1993).
- Our Lady of La Leche Shrine (Patroness of Mothers and Mothers-to-be) and Mission of Nombre de Dios, Saint Augustine (1565).

Illinois: Holy Family Log Church, Cahokia (1799; original log church erected 1699).
- Marytown/Shrine of St. Maximilian Kolbe and Retreat Center, Libertyville; Our Lady of the Blessed Sacrament Sanctuary of Perpetual Eucharistic Adoration (1930) and Archdiocesan Shrine to St. Maximilian Kolbe (1989).
- National Shrine of Our Lady of the Snows, Belleville (1958).
- National Shrine of St. Jude, Chicago (1929).
- National Shrine of St. Therese and Museum, Darien (1930), at St. Clara's Church, Chicago (new shrine, 1987, after original destroyed by fire).
- Shrine of St. Jude Thaddeus, Chicago (1929) located in St. Pius V Church.

Indiana: Our Lady of Monte Cassino Shrine, St. Meinrad (1870).
- Old Cathedral (Basilica of St. Francis Xavier), Vincennes (1826, parish records go back to 1749).

Iowa: Grotto of the Redemption, West Bend (1912).

Louisiana: National Votive Shrine of Our Lady of Prompt Succor, New Orleans (1810).
- Shrine of St. Roch, New Orleans (1876).

Maryland: Basilica of the National Shrine of the Assumption of the Blessed Virgin Mary, Baltimore (1806). Mother Church of Roman Catholicism in the U.S. and the first metropolitan cathedral.
- National Shrine Grotto of Our Lady of Lourdes, Emmitsburg (1809, Grotto of Our Lady; 1875, National Shrine Grotto of Lourdes).

- National Shrine of St. Elizabeth Ann Seton, Emmitsburg. Foundation of Sisters of Charity (1809); first parochial school in America (1810).
- St. Francis Xavier Shrine, "Old Bohemia," near Warwick (1704).
- St. Jude Shrine (1873).

Massachusetts: National Shrine of Our Lady of La Salette, Ipswich (1945).
- Our Lady of Fatima Shrine, Holliston (1950).
- St. Anthony Shrine, Boston (1947).
- St. Clement's Eucharistic Shrine, Boston (1945).
- National Shrine of The Divine Mercy, Stockbridge (1960).

Michigan: Cross in the Woods Parish, Indian River (1947).
- Shrine of the Little Flower, Royal Oak (c. 1929, by Father Coughlin).

Minnesota: National Shrine of St. Odilia.

Missouri: Memorial Shrine of St. Rose Philippine Duchesne, St. Charles.
- National Shrine of Our Lady of the Miraculous Medal, Perryville.
- Old St. Ferdinand's Shrine, Florissant (1819, Sacred Heart Convent; 1821, St. Ferdinand's Church).
- Shrine of Our Lady of Sorrows, Starkenburg (1888; shrine building, 1910).

Nebraska: The Eucharistic Shrine of Christ the King (1973).

New Hampshire: Shrine of Our Lady of Grace, Colebrook (1948).
- Shrine of Our Lady of La Salette, Enfield (1951).

New Jersey: Blue Army Shrine of the Immaculate Heart of Mary (1978).
- Shrine of St. Joseph, Stirling (1924).

New Mexico: St. Augustine Mission, Isleta (1613).
- Santuario de Nuestro Senor de Esquipulas, Chimayo (1816).
- Shrine of St. Bernadette (2003).

New York: National Shrine of St. Kateri Tekakwitha, Fonda (1938).

- Marian Shrine (National Shrine of Mary Help of Christians), West Haverstraw (1953).
- National Shrine Basilica of Our Lady of Fatima, Youngstown (1954).
- Original Shrine of St. Ann in New York City (1892); located in St. Jean Baptiste Church.
- Our Lady of Victory National Shrine, Lackawanna (1926).
- Shrine Church of Our Lady of Mt. Carmel, Brooklyn (1887).
- Shrine of Our Lady of Martyrs, Auriesville (1885).
- Shrine of Our Lady of the Island, Eastport (1975).
- Shrine of St. Elizabeth Ann Seton, New York City (1975).
- Shrine of St. Frances Xavier Cabrini, New York (1938; new shrine dedicated 1960).

Ohio: Basilica and National Shrine of Our Lady of Consolation, Carey (1867).
- National Shrine of Our Lady of Lebanon, North Jackson (1965).
- National Shrine and Grotto of Our Lady of Lourdes, Euclid (1926).
- National Shrine of St. Dymphna, Massillon (1938).
- Our Lady of Czestochowa Shrine, Garfield Heights (1939).
- Our Lady of Fatima, Ironton (1954).
- St. Anthony Shrine, Cincinnati (1888).
- Shrine and Oratory of the Weeping Madonna of Mariapoch, Burton (1956).
- Shrine of the Holy Relics (1892).
- Sorrowful Mother Shrine, Bellevue (1850).

Oklahoma: National Shrine of the Infant Jesus of Prague, Prague (1949).

Oregon: The Grotto (National Sanctuary of Our Sorrowful Mother), Portland (1924).

Pennsylvania: Basilica of the Sacred Heart of Jesus, Conewago Township (1741; present church, 1787).
- National Shrine Center of Our Lady of Guadalupe, Allentown (1974).

- National Shrine of Our Lady of Czestochowa (1955).
- National Shrine of St. John Neumann, Philadelphia (1860).
- National Shrine of the Sacred Heart, Harleigh (1975).
- Old St. Joseph's National Shrine, Philadelphia (1733).
- St. Ann's Basilica Shrine, Scranton (1902).
- St. Anthony's Chapel, Pittsburgh (1883).
- Shrine of St. Walburga, Greensburg (1974).

South Dakota: Fatima Family Shrine, Alexandria (1987).

Texas: Mission Espiritu Santo de Zuniga, Goliad (1749).
- Mission Nuestra Senora de la Purisma Concepcion, San Antonio.
- Mission San Francisco de la Espada, San Antonio (1731).
- Mission San Jose y San Miguel de Aguayo, San Antonio (1720).
- Mission San Juan Capistrano, San Antonio (1731).
- National Shrine of Our Lady of San Juan Del Valle, San Juan (1949).
- Nuestra Senora de la Concepcion del Socorro, Socorro, El Paso (1692).
- Oblate Lourdes Grotto Shrine of the Southwest, Tepeyac de San Antonio.
- Old Mission San Francisco de los Tejas, Weches (1690).
- Presidio La Bahia, Goliad (1749).
- San Elizario Presidio Chapel, El Paso (1789).
- Ysleta Mission (Nuestra Senora del Carmen), Ysleta, El Paso (1744).

Vermont: St. Anne's Shrine, Isle La Motte (1666).

Wisconsin: Holy Hill — National Shrine of Mary, Help of Christians (1857).
- National Shrine of St. Joseph, De Pere (1889).
- Shrine of Mary, Mother Thrice Admirable Queen and Victress of Schoenstatt (1965).